CONGRESS AND THE NATION

VOLUME II

CONGRESS
AND THE
NATION

VOLUME II

1965 - 1968

A Review of Government and Politics

Published by

CONGRESSIONAL QUARTERLY SERVICE
1735 K Street, N.W.   Washington, D.C., 20006

Introduction

"...Most important of all...the United States has re-emerged into the fullness of its self-confidence and purpose. No longer are we called upon to get America moving. We are moving. No longer do we doubt our strength or resolution. We are strong and we have proven our resolve. No longer can anyone wonder whether we are in the grip of historical decay. We know that history is ours to make. And if there is great danger, there is now also the excitement of great expectations."

IN this spirit of euphoria, a confident President Lyndon B. Johnson addressed a joint session of the House and Senate, Jan. 4, 1965, in the traditional State of the Union Message. The year just ended—1964—had been a good one for the American President, a year of continuation and consolidation. On the domestic front, Johnson had taken firm hold of the Presidency, enlarging on the support engendered by President Kennedy's assassination and winning election in November 1964 by the largest popular vote margin in history. During the year, Mr. Johnson replaced the Kennedy phrase "New Frontier" with one of his own: "The Great Society."

Nothing visible foreshadowed the tragedy that awaited Lyndon B. Johnson little more than three years later when, immersed in an unpopular and costly war in Southeast Asia, he would announce his decision not to seek re-election in the interests of trying to reunite the country and bring peace through negotiation in Vietnam.

Vietnam did not figure heavily in the 1965 State of the Union Message, and why should it have? America's commitment at that time involved military aid and a modest-sized U.S. advisory force in South Vietnam. Yet a re-reading of the Johnson address uncovers certain pledges that later would be honored: "We are there (in Vietnam), first, because a friendly nation has asked us for help against Communist aggression. Ten years ago our President pledged our help. Three Presidents have supported that pledge. We will not break it now." Or, later in the speech: "What is at stake is the cause of freedom, and in that cause America will never be found wanting."

How was the public to know that this was not mere rhetoric and that a few months later President Johnson, buoyed by the feeling of success in Congress and in public opinion polls that showed nearly seven out of every ten Americans approving of his handling of his job, would send American boys to fight Asian boys in contradiction of his 1964 campaign promise.

On March 8, 1965, a Marine landing force came ashore at Da Nang to guard the city's giant airbase. Vietnamese maidens met the troops on the beach with floral wreaths. The Marines were the first organized units to supplement the U.S. advisory force in Vietnam and their arrival marked the beginning of the U.S. buildup. Such is the way the stage is set as our chronicle of the last four years of the Johnson Presidency begins.

IT was as a lawmaker that Johnson realized his genius and power. In one field after another—in civil rights, education, medical care, immigration, housing, poverty relief—programs frustrated during previous administrations were enacted. During the feverish activity of Johnson's first two years in the White House, 1964 and 1965, his mastery of Congressional politics—gained during 24 years in the House and Senate—served the President well. The legislative revolution over which he presided went beyond the fondest hopes of liberal advocates. Writing in 1964, Walter Lippmann praised Johnson for his success with Congress. "He's done," Lippmann said, (*New Republic*, April 25, 1964) "what President Kennedy could not have done had he lived."

The record will clearly show Johnson's contribution to legislative programs aimed at the nation's poor. For all the controversy about poverty programs—and all the disappointment—they nevertheless were launched in what is a probably irreversible course. Even if specific programs are ended, the federal government's commitment to the disadvantaged will have to be carried on in other forms.

The enactment of Medicare—an enlargement on the principle of Social Security—was of central importance in the list of LBJ's accomplishments. Persons who had reached a point in life where they had no defense, physically or financially, against the diseases and troubles of aging found new reason for hope. Of probably equal importance was the commitment of the Congress to a substantial program of federal aid to elementary and secondary education. The mark of President Johnson's domestic achievements was his recognition that there were people outside the mainstream of the nation's life that no longer should, or could, be ignored. When the climactic Congressional session of 1965 adjourned, the measures enacted that year and in the preceding year had brought the country closer to meeting the major social problems of the time.

YET these successes were to bring no lasting sense of fulfillment as the war in Vietnam and disorder at home mounted in the final years of the Johnson Administration. In the end, Johnson's grip on Congress became so feeble that he could not even win approval of his nominee for Supreme Court Justice. The intractable war in Southeast Asia cost President Johnson more than popular and Congressional support. It inhibited implementation of the vast legislative program his administration had launched.

In both achievements and frustrations the Johnson years unfolded on a grand scale, suffused with rays of irony. The lifelong legislator who revolutionized the laws guaranteeing minority rights saw defiance of law become the dominant expression of minority frustration. The old New Dealer who declared a "war" on poverty saw his poverty program vitiated by the competing costs of waging war in Asia. The statesman who sought and secured government by a broad "consensus" declined to seek re-election because his candidacy would prove "divisive." The onetime schoolteacher who ended years of Congressional stalemate to provide massive federal aid to education found his most bitter critics among students and professors. The first Southern President in a century left his party weaker and more divided in the South than at any time since before the Civil War. The man whose life was dominated by an abundant love of politics declined even to visit the 1968 Democratic National Convention that nominated Hubert Humphrey, who had served loyally as his Vice President for four years.

Riots in the ghettos and universities, and at the 1968 Democratic convention in Chicago, were symptoms of a malaise deeply penetrating the American conscience at the end of the Johnson years. Faith in political solutions to social problems was challenged precisely at the completion of the most sweeping social reforms ever enacted by the Federal Government. The initiative appeared to be shifting to other forces.

Less than a week after passage of the monumental Voting Rights Act of 1965, six days of rioting in the predominantly Negro Watts area of Los Angeles left 34 dead, 856 injured, and damage approaching $200 million. In succeeding summers the nation watched, in city after city, its Negro neighborhoods consumed by burning, looting and shooting. The nation's capital itself was darkened with columns of black smoke following the assassination in April 1968 of Martin Luther King, the apostle of nonviolent direct action.

Universities, where opposition to the Vietnam war and the draft combined with racial and educational protest, increasingly became the scene of direct action. Student unrest spread from the University of California at Berkeley, where in late 1964 student sit-ins brought mass arrests, and reached a new dimension at Columbia University in April 1968 when radical and Negro groups shut down the university by occupying university buildings. About 700 were arrested and 148 injured when police ejected the demonstrators a week after they had seized the buildings. In the following academic year student disruptions of universities reached epidemic proportions. Reaction to disorders in the ghettos and campuses made law and order a leading issue in the 1968 election and prompted anti-riot provisions in federal and state legislation.

WHILE extremists challenged traditional government processes, the great majority in the center felt uneasy at the apparent impotence of those processes. To some extent, growing concern stimulated participation in local decision making, a trend that might be viewed as a revival of an American tradition. Attempts to engage the energies of the Negroes and the young in the orderly processes of democratic government depended, however, on their renewed faith in the national leadership.

Excessive faith in the national government may have been the tragic flaw of a President determined to enact a "Great Society" at home and preserve the political status quo in Asia. The reins of authority that appeared to be slipping from Washington's hands may never have been held there. But while Congress after its heady legislative revolution slipped back to normalcy, the nation seemed to begin moving in the opposite direction. Volume II of *Congress and the Nation* seeks to describe those watershed years when the program of one generation was written into law and the aspirations of the next were emerging outside familiar centers of power.

About This Book

Congress and the Nation, Vol. II, is being issued in response to requests by librarians, historians, political scientists and others for a comprehensive summary of legislation and politics during the four-year period, 1965 through 1968, the last term of President Lyndon B. Johnson. Not only is the period involved a logical one for a summary, but it continues the practice of grouping coverage begun with the issuance of *Congress and the Nation, Vol. I*, in 1965. That book covered a 20-year period beginning in 1945 and ending in 1964.

With *Congress and the Nation, Vols. I and II*, researchers and scholars now have two handy volumes containing references for each field of legislation spanning 24 years. Greater detail on specific actions will, of course, be found in the appropriate CQ Almanacs published for each of the years. Many of the legislative actions and trends began well before the 1945-68 period; a ready understanding of them required tracing from the earlier years. Whenever necessary, that was done. A pertinent and often used source for these broad-brush approaches was the material found in the companion service to *Congressional Quarterly*, namely, *Editorial Research Reports*.

News Research

This book, *Congress and the Nation, Vol. II*, is news research in a refined form. Its purpose is to provide the essential details in the field of legislation and politics from 1965 through 1968, so that the reporter, the editorial writer, the political scientist, the politician and other students can work with greater ease and confidence.

News research is designed to make editorial and political comment more reliable and less burdensome. Without it, the writer, teacher or politician would be less informed or their time would be largely consumed with pursuit of basic facts, leaving less opportunity for creative reflection. Also, the deeper, harder-to-get data—full election returns, for example, or complete roll-call voting—might never even be sought except by those committed to a historical task.

News research lies somewhere between spot newspaper reporting and scholarly pursuit. It must produce lasting, useful and recognizable facts—originally organized if not original in themselves—without burying its reader in complexity and esoteric technique. These facts must be arranged so they are quickly found; careful indexing is therefore an important part of this technique.

News research, to be useful, must be pertinent. It must not only ride with the breaking news but, whenever possible, anticipate it. Nothing is more satisfying in this field than to watch a great news event unfold and know that there is available a report or assembled facts which make that event more meaningful, which help the harried reporter or editor cover the event with greater finesse and greater speed, accurately and completely.

As an exercise in news research, *Congress and the Nation, Vol. II,* attempts to meet these standards.

The Writers

The work of many dedicated people went into the writing, editing and production of this volume. Principal writers and the chapters for which they were responsible include:

Chapter I, Politics: Neal R. Peirce

Chapter II, Foreign Policy: David Tarr

Chapter III, Economic Policy: David Tarr (Budget, Tax, Banking); Mary Cohn (Transportation); James Phillips (Housing).

Chapter IV, Crime and Justice: Mary Cohn

Chapter V, Civil Rights: David Tarr

Chapter VI, Civil Liberties: Mary Cohn

Chapter VII, Election Law and Procedures: Charles Dennis McCamey

Chapter VIII, Veterans: Hoyt Gimlin

Chapter IX, Natural Resources and Power: Richard L. Worsnop (Conservation, Water and Power); Carolyn S. Mathiasen (Parks and Recreation).

Chapter X, Space Activities: Hoyt G. Gimlin

Chapter XI, Agriculture: Spencer A. Rich

Chapter XII, Labor: Robert A. Barnes

Chapter XIII, Presidency: Hoyt Gimlin

Chapter XIV, Health, Education and Welfare: Mary Cohn (Health); Georgiana Rathbun (Education); Carolyn S. Mathiasen (Welfare); David Tarr (Consumers).

Chapter XV, National Security: James Phillips

Chapter XVI, Government: Mary Cohn (Congress); Kenneth Shaffer (Postal); Robert A. Barnes (Federal Pay); Richard L. Worsnop (District of Columbia and Island Dependencies; Miscellaneous).

Appendix: Wayne Walker

Index: Mary Bourquin Korns

The following persons were responsible for the editing and production of Congress and the Nation, Vol. II:

Supervisory Editors: William B. Dickinson, Jr., and David Tarr

Chief Copy Editor: Buel W. Patch; Park Teter (assistant).

How to Use This Book

Briefly study the *Summary* of the *Table of Contents* which follows this introduction. It indicates the organization of *Congress and the Nation, Vol. II.*

A detailed Table of Contents follows the Summary, showing the outline and content of each chapter.

Note the organization of each legislative area—Foreign Aid, Agriculture, etc. Each usually contains a summary, a program discussion when necessary, and then a *chronology* of legislative action from 1965 through 1968. Often, related programs or legislative actions are discussed separately in a section.

The first chapter, Politics, constitutes a history of the kind of Congress each was and the resultant election issues that developed, Congress by Congress and election by election, from 1945 through 1968. This chapter forms a framework for the legislative chapters which follow.

The Appendix, which can be reached at the first thumb tab, contains material which will be used with all of the chapters of the book—biographical data on the Members; committee chairmen since 1947; Senate and House Key Votes 1965-1968, with each Member's vote given; the Presidents and their Cabinets; controversial nominations; Presidential Vetoes. Pages in the Appendix are numbered: 1a, 2a, 3a, etc.

The detailed *Index* to this book begins at the second thumb tab.

Production Supervisor: Richard C. Young (assisted by Anita Preston)

Proofing: Diane Huffman (chief).

Designer for Dust Jacket and Cover: Howard Eugene Chapman.

Production Clearance: Douglas Benkert

Editorial Assistance: Judy Aldock

Special mention must be made of the role played in the issuance of this book by Nelson Poynter, editor and president of Congressional Quarterly Inc., and Richard N. Billings, executive editor of Congressional Quarterly Inc. Without their constant support and encouragement the book would not have been possible.

WILLIAM B. DICKINSON, JR.
Supervisory Editor

Washington, D.C.
Oct. 1, 1969

HOW A BILL BECOMES LAW

Note: Parliamentary terms used below are defined in the Glossary, which follows.

Introduction of Bills

A House Member (including the Resident Commissioner of Puerto Rico) may introduce any one of several types of bills and resolutions by handing it to the Clerk of the House or placing it in a box called the hopper. A Senator first gains recognition of the presiding officer to announce the introduction of a bill. If objection is offered by any Senator the introduction of the bill is postponed until the following day.

As the next step in either the House or Senate, the bill is numbered, referred to the appropriate committee, labeled with the sponsor's name, and sent to the Government Printing Office so that copies can be made for subsequent study and action. Senate bills may be jointly sponsored and carry several Senators' names. In the House, until 1967, each bill carried the name of one sponsor only; however, the House April 25, 1967, voted to allow cosponsorship of bills, setting a limit of 25 cosponsors on any one bill. Bills written in the Executive Branch and proposed as Administration measures usually are introduced by the chairmen of the Congressional committees that have jurisdiction over the subjects involved.

Types of Congressional measures:

Bills—Prefixed with "HR" in the House, "S" in the Senate, followed by a number. Used as the form for most legislation, whether general or special, public or private.

Joint Resolutions—Designated H J Res or S J Res. Subject to the same procedure as bills, with the exception of joint resolutions proposing an amendment to the Constitution. These must be approved by two-thirds of both houses and are thereupon sent directly to the Administrator of General Services for submission to the states for ratification rather than being presented to the President for his approval.

Concurrent Resolutions—Designated H Con Res or S Con Res. Used for matters affecting the operations of both houses. These do not become law.

Resolutions—Designated H Res or S Res. Used for a matter concerning the operation of either house alone and adopted only by the chamber in which it originates.

Committee Action

A bill is referred to the appropriate committee by the House parliamentarian on the Speaker's order, or by the Senate President. Sponsors may indicate their preferences for referral, although custom and chamber rule generally govern this. An exception is the referral of private bills, which are sent to whatever group is designated by their sponsors. Bills are technically considered "read for the first time" when referred to House committees.

When a bill reaches a committee it is placed upon the group's calendar. At that time it comes under the sharpest Congressional focus. Its chances for passage are quickly determined—and the great majority of bills fall by the legislative roadside. Failure of a committee to act on a bill is equivalent to killing it; the measure can be withdrawn from the group's purview only by a discharge petition signed by a majority of the House membership on House bills, or by passage of a special resolution in the Senate. Discharge attempts rarely succeed.

The first committee action taken on a bill usually is a request for comment on it by interested agencies of the Government. The committee chairman may assign the bill to a subcommittee for study and hearings, or it may be considered by the full committee. Hearings may be public, closed (executive session), or both. A subcommittee, after considering a bill, reports to the full committee its recommendations for action and any proposed amendments.

The full committee then votes on its recommendation to the House or Senate. This is called "ordering a bill reported." Occasionally a committee may order a bill reported unfavorably; most of the time a report, submitted by the chairman of the committee to the House or Senate, calls for favorable action on the legislation since the committee can effectively "kill" legislation by simply failing to take any action.

When a committee sends a bill to the chamber floor, it explains its reasons in a written statement, called a report, which accompanies the bill. Often committee members opposing a measure issue a dissenting minority report.

Frequently, the committee proposes amendments to the bill. If they are substantial and the legislation is complicated, the committee may order a "clean bill" introduced, which will embody the proposed amendments. The original bill then is put aside and the "clean bill," with a new number, is reported to the floor.

The chamber must approve, alter, or reject the committee amendments before the bill itself can be put to a vote.

Floor Action

After a bill is reported back to the house where it originated, it is placed on the calendar.

There are five legislative calendars in the House, issued in one cumulative calendar titled Calendars of the United States House of Representatives and History of Legislation. The House Calendars are:

The Union Calendar to which are referred bills raising revenues, general appropriation bills and any measures directly or indirectly appropriating money or property. It is the Calendar of the Committee of the Whole House on the State of the Union.

The House Calendar to which are referred all bills, of a public character not raising revenue nor appropriating money or property.

The Consent Calendar to which are referred bills of a noncontroversial nature that are passed without debate when the Consent Calendar is called on the first and third Mondays of each month.

The Private Calendar to which are referred bills for relief in the nature of claims against the United States or private immigration bills that are passed without debate when the Private Calendar is called the first and third Tuesdays of each month.

The Discharge Calendar to which are referred motions to discharge committees when the necessary signatures are signed to a discharge petition.

There is only one legislative calendar in the Senate and one "executive calendar" for treaties and nominations presented to the Senate. When the Senate Calendar is called, each Senator is limited to five minutes' debate on each bill.

DEBATE

A bill is brought to debate by varying procedures. If a routine measure, it may await the call of the calendar. If it is urgent or important, it can be taken up in the Senate either by unanimous consent or by a majority vote. The Policy Committee of the majority party in the Senate schedules the bills that it wants taken up for debate.

In the House, precedence is granted if a special rule is obtained from the Rules Committee. A request for a special rule is usually made by the chairman of the committee that favorably reported the bill, supported by the bill's sponsor and other committee members. The request, considered by the Rules Committee in the same fashion that other committees consider legislative measures, is in the form of a resolution providing for immediate consideration of the bill. The Rules Committee reports the resolution to the House where it is debated and voted upon in the same fashion as regular bills. If the Rules Committee should fail to report a rule requested by a committee, there are several ways to bring the bill to the House floor—under suspension of the rules, on Calendar Wednesday or by a discharge motion.

The resolutions providing special rules are important because they specify how long the bill may be debated and whether it may be amended from the floor. If floor amendment is banned, the bill is considered under a "closed rule" which permits only members of the committee that first reported the measure to the House to alter its language, subject to chamber acceptance.

When a bill is debated under an "open rule," amendments may be offered from the floor. Committee amendments are always taken up first, but may be changed, as may all amendments up to the second degree, i.e., a changed amendment cannot be further altered.

Duration of debate in the House depends on whether the bill is under discussion by the House proper or before the House when it is sitting as the Committee of the Whole or the State of the Union. In the former, the amount of time for debate is determined either by special rule or is allocated with an hour for each Member if the measure is under consideration without a rule. In the Committee of the Whole the amount of time agreed on for general debate is equally divided between proponents and opponents. At the end of general discussion, the bill is read section by section for amendment. Debate on an amendment is limited to five minutes for supporters and five minutes for opponents.

Senate debate is usually unlimited. It can be halted only by unanimous consent or by "cloture," which requires a two-thirds vote.

The House sits as the Committee of the Whole on the State of the Union when it first considers any tax measure or legislation dealing with public appropriations. It can also resolve itself into the Committee of the Whole if a Member moves to do so and the motion is carried. The Speaker appoints a Member to serve as the chairman. The rules of the House permit the Committee of the Whole to meet with any 100 Members on the floor, and to amend and act on legislation with a quorum of the 100, within the time limitations mentioned previously. When the Committee of the Whole has acted, it "rises," the Speaker returns as the presiding officer of the House and the Member appointed chairman of the Committee of the Whole reports the action of the Committee and its recommendations.

VOTES

Voting on bills may occur repeatedly before they are finally approved or rejected. The House votes both on the rule for the bill, and various amendments to it. Voting on amendments often is a more illuminating test of a bill's support than is the final tally. Sometimes Congressmen approve final passage of bills after vigorously supporting amendments which, if adopted, would have scuttled the legislation.

The House and Senate vote both on untabulated voice votes and a recorded roll call of their names, to which they answer "yea" or "nay." The House also uses a standing vote, called a division, and a teller vote, when Members file up the center aisle past counters. The Senate also has a division, or standing vote. It does not employ the teller vote. House totals on division and teller votes are announced. Division vote totals in the Senate are not announced. Only a roll-call vote reveals the yea or nay vote of a Member.

After amendments to a bill have been voted upon, a vote may be taken on a motion to recommit the bill to committee. If carried, this vote removes the bill from the chamber's calendar. If the motion is unsuccessful, the bill then is "read for the third time." An actual reading usually is dispensed with. Until 1965, an opponent of a bill could delay this move by objecting and asking for a full reading of an engrossed (certified in final form) copy of the bill. After the "third reading," the vote on final passage is taken.

The final action vote may be followed by a motion to reconsider, and this motion itself may be followed by a move to lay the motion on the table. Usually, those voting for the bill's passage vote for the tabling motion, thus safeguarding the final passage action. With that, the bill has been formally passed by the chamber. While a motion to reconsider a Senate vote is pending on a bill, the measure cannot be sent to the House. Once a bill has been passed by either chamber, it becomes, officially, an "act," though it continues generally to be referred to as a bill.

ACTION IN SECOND HOUSE

After a bill is passed it is sent to the other chamber. This body may then take one of several steps. It may pass the bill as is—accepting the other chamber's language.

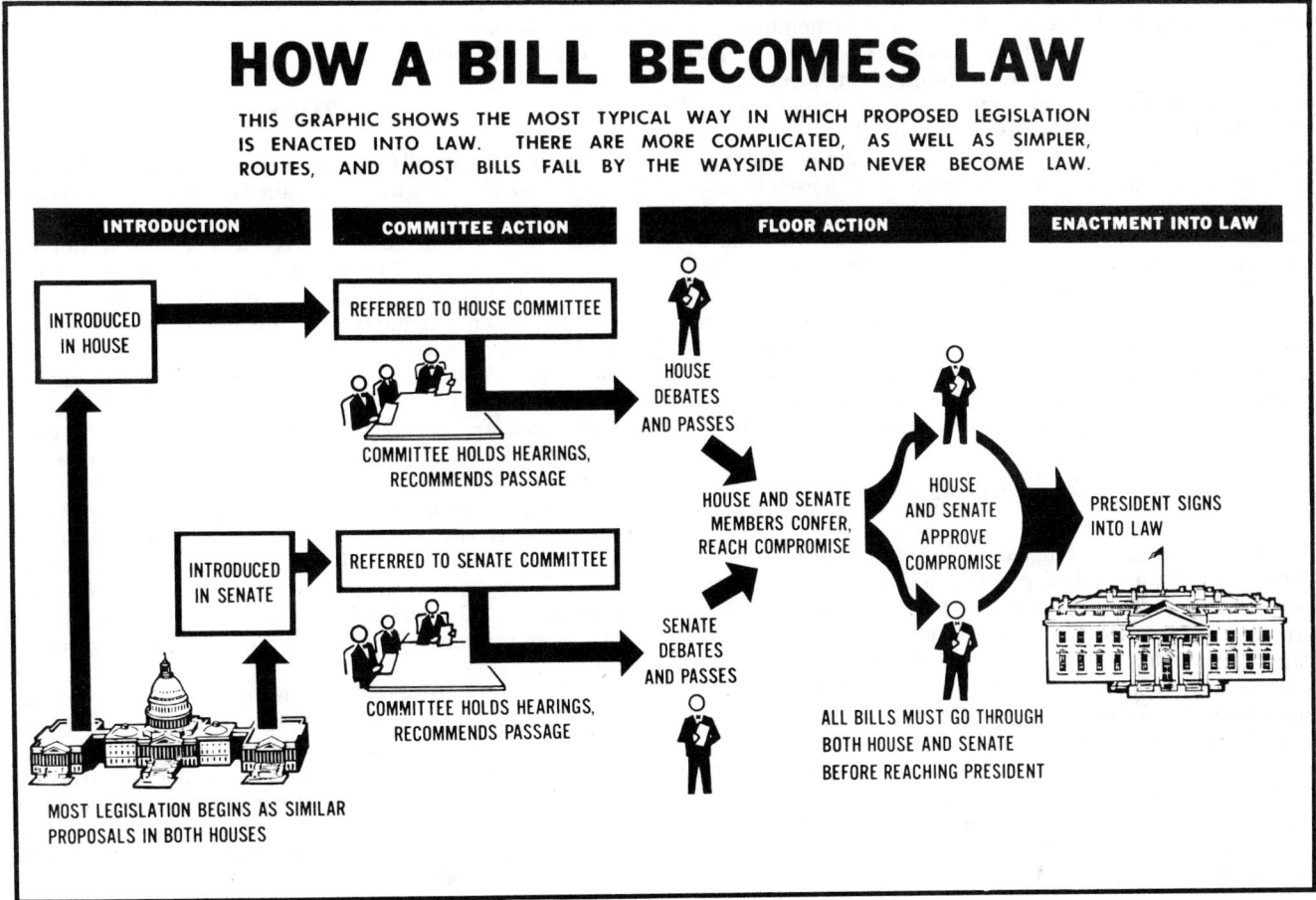

HOW A BILL BECOMES LAW

THIS GRAPHIC SHOWS THE MOST TYPICAL WAY IN WHICH PROPOSED LEGISLATION IS ENACTED INTO LAW. THERE ARE MORE COMPLICATED, AS WELL AS SIMPLER, ROUTES, AND MOST BILLS FALL BY THE WAYSIDE AND NEVER BECOME LAW.

INTRODUCTION   **COMMITTEE ACTION**   **FLOOR ACTION**   **ENACTMENT INTO LAW**

INTRODUCED IN HOUSE

REFERRED TO HOUSE COMMITTEE

COMMITTEE HOLDS HEARINGS, RECOMMENDS PASSAGE

HOUSE DEBATES AND PASSES

INTRODUCED IN SENATE

REFERRED TO SENATE COMMITTEE

COMMITTEE HOLDS HEARINGS, RECOMMENDS PASSAGE

SENATE DEBATES AND PASSES

HOUSE AND SENATE MEMBERS CONFER, REACH COMPROMISE

HOUSE AND SENATE APPROVE COMPROMISE

PRESIDENT SIGNS INTO LAW

ALL BILLS MUST GO THROUGH BOTH HOUSE AND SENATE BEFORE REACHING PRESIDENT

MOST LEGISLATION BEGINS AS SIMILAR PROPOSALS IN BOTH HOUSES

It may send the bill to committee for scrutiny or alteration, or reject the entire bill, advising the other house of its actions. Or it may simply ignore the bill submitted while it continues work on its own version of the legislation. Frequently, one chamber may approve a version of a bill that is greatly at variance with the version already passed by the other house, and then substitute its amendments for the language of the other, retaining only the latter's bill designation.

Often the chamber makes only minor changes. If these are readily agreed to by the other house, the bill then is routed to the White House for signing. However, if the opposite chamber basically alters the bill submitted to it, the measure usually is "sent to conference." The chamber that has possession of the "papers" (engrossed bill, engrossed amendments, messages of transmittal) requests a conference and the other chamber agrees to it.

Conference

A conference undertakes to harmonize conflicting House and Senate versions of a legislative bill. The conference is staffed by interested senior Members, appointed by the presiding officers of the two houses, from the committees which managed the bills. This charges the Members of one house who are most familiar with the bill with the duty of maintaining their chamber's position in the face of amending actions by the conferees (or "managers") of the other house.

The number of conferees from each chamber may vary, the range usually being from three to nine Members in each group, depending upon the length or complexity of the legislation involved. There may be five Representatives and three Senators on the conference committee, or the reverse. But a majority vote controls the action of each group so that a larger representation does not give one chamber a voting advantage over the other chamber's conferees.

Theoretically, conferees are not allowed to write new legislation in reconciling the two versions before them, but this curb sometimes is bypassed. Many bills have been put into acceptable compromise form only after new language was provided by the conferees.

Frequently the ironing out of difficulties takes days or even weeks. Conferences on involved appropriations bills sometimes are particularly drawn out.

As a conference proceeds, conferees reconcile their differences, but generally they grant concessions only insofar as they remain sure that the chamber they represent will accept the compromises. Once in a while uncertainty over this, or the positive refusal of a chamber to back down on a disputed amendment, results in an impasse, and the bills die in conference even though each was approved by its sponsoring chamber.

Conferees sometimes go back to their respective chambers for further instructions, when they report certain portions in disagreement. Then the chamber concerned can either "recede and concur" in the amendment of the other house, or "insist on its amendment."

When the conferees have reached agreement, they prepare a conference report, explaining why they did—or did not—retain some amendments, and cut out others. The reports are the justifications to their respective houses of the actions of the conferees, and the explanations, in document form, must be submitted to each house. Conference reports, with an explanation by the House conferees, are always printed in the House. In the Senate an explanation is often made orally by one of the conferees.

The conference report must be approved by each house. Consequently, approval of the report is approval of the compromise bill. In the order of voting on conference reports, the chamber which asked for a conference yields the other chamber the opportunity to vote first.

Final Steps

After a bill has been passed by both the House and Senate, all of the original papers are sent to the enrolling clerk of the chamber in which the bill originated. He then prepares an enrolled bill which is printed on parchment paper. When this bill has been certified as correct by the Secretary of the Senate and the Clerk of the House, depending on which chamber originated the bill, it is signed first (no matter whether it originated in the Senate or House) by the Speaker of the House and then by the President of the Senate. It is next sent to the White House to await Presidential action.

If the President approves the bill he signs it, dates it and usually writes the word "approved" on the document. If he does not sign it within 10 days (Sundays excepted) and Congress is in session, the bill becomes law without his signature.

VETOES

However, should Congress adjourn before the 10 days expire, and the President has failed to sign the measure, it does not become law. This procedure is called the pocket veto. Occasionally a President vetoes a bill by refusing to sign it and returning it to the Congress with a message stating his reasons. The message is sent to the chamber which originated the bill. If no action is taken there on the message, the bill affected dies. Sometimes, however, Congress attempts to override the President's veto and enact the bill, "the objections of the President to the contrary notwithstanding." This requires a two-thirds vote of those present, who must number a quorum and vote by roll call.

Debate can precede this vote, with motions permitted to lay the message on the table, postpone action on it, or refer it to committee. If the President's veto is overridden by a two-thirds vote in both houses, the bill becomes law. Otherwise it is dead, and can be revived only by reintroduction and routing through the process all bills undergo.

When bills are passed finally and signed, or passed over a veto, they are given law numbers in numerical order as they become law. There are two series of numbers, one for public and one for private laws, starting at the number "1" for each two-year term of Congress. They are then identified by law number and by Congress—i.e., Private Law 21, 90th Congress; Public Law 250, 90th Congress (or PL 90-250).

GLOSSARY OF CONGRESSIONAL TERMS

Act—The term for legislation which has passed both houses of Congress and has been signed by the President or passed over his veto, thus becoming law.

Also used technically for a bill that has been passed by one house and engrossed.

Adjournment sine die—Adjournment without definitely fixing a day for reconvening; literally "adjournment without a day." A session can continue until noon, Jan. 3, of the following year, when a new session usually begins.

Adjournment to a Day Certain—Adjournment under a motion or resolution which fixes the next time of meeting. Neither house can adjourn for more than three days without the concurrence of the other. A session of Congress is not ended by adjournment to a day certain.

Amendment—Proposal of a Congressman to alter the language or stipulations in a bill or act. It is usually printed, debated, and voted upon in the same manner as a bill.

Appeal—A Congressman's challenge of a ruling or decision made by the presiding officer of the Senate or House. The Congressman appeals to Members of the chamber to override the decision. If carried by a majority vote, the appeal nullifies the chair's ruling.

Appropriation Bill—Grants the actual monies approved by authorization bills, but not necessarily to the total permissible under the authorization bill. Normally an appropriation bill originates in the House, and is not acted on until its authorization measure is enacted. Regular appropriations are supposed to be passed before the start of the fiscal year to which they apply, but in recent years this has rarely happened. *(See Continuing Appropriations.)* In addition to general appropriation bills, there are two specialized types. *(See Deficiency and Supplemental.)*

Authorization Bill—Authorizes a program, specifies its general aim and conduct, and unless "openended," puts a ceiling on monies that can be used to finance it. Usually enacted before appropriation bill is passed. *(See Contract Authorization.)*

Bills—Most legislative proposals before Congress are in the form of bills, and are designated as HR (House of Representatives) or S (Senate) according to the house in which they originate and by a number assigned in the order in which they were introduced, from the beginning of each two-year Congressional term. "Public bills" deal with general questions, and become Public Laws if approved by Congress and signed by the President. "Private bills" deal with individual matters such as claims against the Government, immigration and naturalization cases, land titles, etc., and become Private Laws if approved and signed.

The introduction of a bill, and its referral to an appropriate committee for action, follows the process given in "How A Bill Is Passed." *(See also Concurrent Resolution, Joint Resolution, Resolution, in this Glossary.)*

Bills Introduced—In the Senate, any number of Senators may join in introducing a single bill. In the House, until 1967, only one Member's name could appear on a single bill. But the House April 25, 1967, voted to allow cosponsorship of bills, setting a limit of 25 cosponsors on any one bill.

Many bills in reality are committee bills and are introduced under the name of the chairman of the committee or subcommittee as a formality. All appropriation bills fall into this category, as do many other bills, particularly those dealing with complicated, technical subjects. A committee frequently holds hearings on a number of related bills, and may agree on one of them or on an entirely new bill. *(See Clean Bill and By Request.)*

Bills Referred—When introduced, a bill referred to the committee which has jurisdiction over the subject with which the bill is concerned. The appropriate reference for bills is spelled out in the Legislative Reorganization Act of 1946. Bills are referred by the Speaker in the House and the Presiding Officer in the Senate. Appeals may be made from their decisions.

Budget—The document sent to Congress by the President in January of each year estimating Government revenue and expenditures for the ensuing fiscal year and recommending appropriations to detail. The President's Budget Message forms the basis for Congressional hearings and legislation on the year's appropriations.

By Request—A phrase used when a Senator or Representative introduces a bill at the request of an executive agency or private organization but does not necessarily endorse the legislation.

Calendar—An agenda or list of pending business before committees or either chamber. The House uses five legislative calendars. *(See Consent, Discharge, House, Private and Union Calendar.)*

In the Senate, all legislative matters reported from committee go on a single calendar. They are listed there in order, but may be called up irregularly by the Majority Leader either by a motion to do so, or by obtaining the unanimous consent of the Senate. Frequently the Minority Leader is consulted to assure unanimous consent. Only cloture can limit debate on bills thus called up. *(See Call of the Calendar.)*

The Senate also uses one non-legislative calendar, for treaties, etc. *(See Executive Calendar.)*

Calendar Wednesday—In the House on Wednesdays, committees may be called in the order in which they appear in Rule X of the House Manual, for the purpose of bringing up any of their bills from the House or the Union Calendars, except bills which are privileged. General debate is limited to two hours. Bills called up from the Union Calendar are considered in Committee of the Whole. Calendar Wednesday is not observed during the last two weeks of a session, and may be dispensed with at other times -- by a two-thirds vote. It usually is dispensed with.

Call of the Calendar—Senate bills which are not brought up for debate by a motion or a unanimous consent agreement are brought before the Senate for action when the calendar listing them in order is "called." Bills considered in this fashion are usually noncontroversial, and debate is limited to five minutes for each Senator on a bill or on amendments to it.

Chamber—Meeting place for the total membership of either the House or the Senate, as distinguished from the respective committee rooms.

Clean Bill—Frequently after a committee has finished a major revision of a bill, one of the committee members, usually the chairman, will assemble the changes plus what is left of the original bill into a new measure and introduce it as a "clean bill." The new measure, which carries a new number, is then sent to the floor for consideration. This often is a timesaver, as committee-recommended changes do not have to be considered one at a time by the chamber.

Clerk of the House—Chief administrative officer of the House of Representatives with duties corresponding to those of the Secretary of the Senate. *(See Secretary of the Senate.)*

Cloture—The process by which debate can be limited in the Senate, other than by unanimous consent. A motion for cloture can apply to any measure before the Senate, including a proposal to change the chamber's rules. It requires 16 Senators' signatures for introduction and the votes of two-thirds of the Senators present and voting. It is put to a roll-call vote one hour after the Senate meets on the second day following introduction of the motion. If voted, cloture limits each Senator to one hour of debate.

Committee—A subdivision of the House or Senate which prepares legislation for action by the parent chamber, or makes investigations as directed by the parent chamber. There are several types of committees. *(See Standing, and Select or Special.)* Most standing committees are divided into subcommittees, which study legislation, hold hearings, and report their recommendations to the full committee. Only the full committee can report legislation for action by the House or Senate.

Committee of the Whole—The working title of what is formally "The Committee of the Whole House (of Representatives) on the State of the Union." Unlike other committees, it has no fixed membership. It is comprised of any 100 or more House Members who participate —on the floor of the chamber—in debating or altering legislation before the body. Such measures, however, must first have passed through the regular committees and be on the calendar.

Technically, the Committee of the Whole considers only bills directly or indirectly appropriating money, authorizing appropriations, or involving taxes or charges on the public. Actually, the Committee of the Whole often considers other types of legislation. Because the Committee of the Whole need number only 100 Representatives, a quorum is more readily attained, and business is expedited. None of the group's votes can be the time-consuming roll calls which require yeas and nays for the record.

When the full House resolves itself into the Committee of the Whole, it supplants the Speaker with a "chairman." The measure is debated or amended, with non-roll-call votes as needed. When the Committee completes its action on the measure, it dissolves itself by "rising." The Speaker returns, and the full House hears the erstwhile chairman of the Committee report that group's recommendations. The full House then acts upon them.

At this time Members may demand a roll-call vote on any amendment *adopted* in the Committee of the Whole.

Concurrent Resolution—A concurrent resolution, designated H Con Res or S Con Res, must be passed by both houses but does not require the signature of the President and does not have the force of law. Concurrent resolutions generally are used to make or amend rules applicable to both houses or to express the sentiment of the two houses. A concurrent resolution, for example, is used to fix the time for adjournment of a Congress. It might also be used to convey the congratulations of Congress to another country on the anniversary of its independence.

Conference—A meeting between the representatives of the House and Senate to reconcile differences between the two houses over provisions of a bill. Members of the conference committee are appointed by the Speaker and the President of the Senate and are called "managers" for their respective chambers. A majority of the managers for each house must reach agreement on the provisions of the bill (often a compromise between the versions of the two chambers) before it can be sent up for floor action in the form of a "conference report." There it cannot be amended, and if not approved by both chambers, the bill goes back to conference. Elaborate rules govern the conduct of the conferences. All bills which are passed by House and Senate in slightly different form need not be sent to conference; either chamber may "concur" in the other's amendments. *(See Custody of the Papers.)*

Congressional Record—The daily, printed account of proceedings in both House and Senate chambers, with debate, statements, and the like reported verbatim. Committee activities are not covered, excepting their reports to the parent body. Highlights of legislative and committee action are embodied in a Digest section of the Record, and Congressmen are entitled to have their extraneous remarks printed in an appendix. They may edit and revise remarks made on the floor, and frequently do, so that quotations reported by the press are not always found in the Record.

Congressional Terms of Office—Begin on Jan. 3 of the year following the general election.

Consent Calendar—Members of the House may place on this calendar any bill on the Union or House Calendar which is considered to be noncontroversial. Bills on the Consent Calendar are normally called on the first and third Mondays of each month. On the first occasion when a bill is called in this manner, consideration may be blocked by the objection of any Member. On the second time, if there are three objections, the bill is stricken from the Consent Calendar; if less than three Members object, the bill is given immediate consideration.

A bill on the Consent Calendar may be postponed in another way. A Member may ask that the measure be passed over "without prejudice." In that case, no objection is recorded against the bill, and its status on the Consent Calendar remains unchanged.

A bill stricken from the Consent Calendar remains on the Union or House Calendar.

Continuing Appropriations—When a fiscal year begins and Congress has not yet enacted all the regular appropriation bills for that year, it passes a joint resolution "continuing appropriations" for Government agencies at rates generally based on their previous year's appropriations.

Contract Authorizations—Found in both authorization and appropriation bills, these authorizations are stop-gap provisions which permit the Federal Government to let contracts or obligate itself for future payments from funds not yet appropriated. The assumption is that funds will be available for payment when contracted debts come due.

Correcting the Record—Rules prohibit Members from changing their votes after the result has been announced. But frequently, hours, days, or months after a vote has been taken, a Member announces that he was "incorrectly recorded" and requests -- and almost always receives -- unanimous consent to have the vote corrected in the permanent edition of the Congressional Record. This occurs more frequently in the House than in the Senate. Errors in the text of the Record may be corrected in the same manner.

Custody of the Papers—To reconcile differences on a bill between the House and Senate, a conference may be arranged. The chamber with "custody of the papers" -- the engrossed bill, engrossed amendments, messages of transmittal -- is the only body empowered to request the conference. That body then has the advantage of acting last on the conference report when it is submitted.

Deficiency Appropriation—An appropriation to cover the difference between an agency's regular appropriation and the amount deemed necessary for it to operate for the full fiscal year. In recent years deficiency bills have usually been called supplemental appropriations.

Dilatory Motion—A motion, usually made upon a technical point, for the purpose of killing time and preventing action on a bill. The rules outlaw dilatory motions, but enforcement is largely within the discretion of the presiding officer.

Discharge a Committee—Relieve a committee from jurisdiction over a measure before it. This is rarely a successful procedure, attempted more often in the House than in the Senate.

In the House, if a committee does not report a bill within 30 days after the bill was referred to it, any Member may file a discharge motion. This motion, treated as a petition, needs the signatures of 218 Members (a majority of the House). After the required signatures have been obtained, there is a delay of seven days. Then, on the second and fourth Monday of each month, except during the last six days of a session, any Member who has signed the petition may be recognized to move that the committee be discharged. Debate on the motion to discharge is limited to 20 minutes, and, if the motion is carried, consideration of the bill becomes a matter of high privilege.

If a resolution to consider a bill (*See Rule*) is held up in the Rules Committee for more than seven legislative days, any Member may enter a motion to discharge the Committee. The motion is handled like any other discharge petition in the House.

Occasionally, to expedite noncontroversial legislative business, a committee is discharged upon unanimous consent of the House, and a petition is not required. *(For Senate procedure, see Discharge Resolution.)*

Discharge Calendar—The House calendar to which motions to discharge committees are referred when they have the necessary 218 signatures and are awaiting action.

Discharge Petition—In the House, a motion to discharge a committee from considering a bill. The motion or petition, requires signatures of 218 House Members.

Discharge Resolution—In the Senate, a special motion any Senator may introduce to relieve a committee from consideration of a bill before it. The resolution can be called up on motion for approval or disapproval, in the same manner as other matters of Senate business. *(For House procedure, see Discharge a Committee.)*

Division Vote—Same as Standing Vote. *(See below.)*

Enacting Clause—Key phrase in bills saying, "Be if enacted by the Senate and House of Representatives...." A successful motion to strike it from legislation kills the measure.

Engrossed Bill—The final copy of a bill as passed by one chamber, with the text as amended by floor action and certified to by the Clerk of the House or the Secretary of the Senate.

Enrolled Bill—The final copy of a bill which has been passed in identical form by both chambers. It is certified to by an officer of the house of origin (House Clerk or Senate Secretary) and then sent on for signatures of the House Speaker, the Senate President, and the U.S. President. An enrolled bill is printed on parchment.

Executive Calendar—This is an additional, non-legislative calendar, in the Senate, on which Presidential documents such as treaties and nominations are listed.

Executive Document—A document, usually a treaty, sent to the Senate by the President for consideration or ratification. These are identified for each session of Congress as Executive A, 90th Congress, 1st Session; Executive B, etc. They are referred to committee in the same manner as other measures. Unlike legislative documents, however, treaties do not die at the end of a Congress, but remain "live" proposals until acted on by the Senate or withdrawn by the President.

Executive Session—Meeting of a Senate or a House committee (or, very rarely, of the entire chamber) which only the group's members are privileged to attend. Frequently witnesses appear before committees meeting in executive session, and other Congressmen may be invited, but the public and press are not allowed.

Expenditures—The actual spending of money as distinguished from the appropriation of it. Expenditures are made by the disbursing officers of the Administration; appropriations are made only by Congress. The two are rarely identical in any fiscal year; expenditures may represent money appropriated one, two or more years previously.

Filibuster—A time-delaying tactic used by a minority in an effort to prevent a vote on a bill which probably would pass if brought to a vote. The most common method is to take advantage of the Senate's rules permitting unlimited debate, but other forms of parliamentary maneuvering may be used. The stricter rules in the House make filibusters more difficult, but they are attempted from time to time through devices such as repeated demands for quorum calls.

Fiscal Year—Financial operations of the Government are carried out in a 12-month fiscal year, beginning on July 1 and ending on June 30. The fiscal year carries the date of the calendar year in which it ends.

Floor Manager—A Member, usually representing sponsors of a bill, who attempts to steer it through debate and revision to a final vote in the chamber. Floor managers are frequently chairmen or ranking members of the committee that reported the bill. Managers are responsible for apportioning the time granted supporters of the bill for debating it. The Minority Leader or the ranking minority member of the committee often apportions time for the opposition.

Frank—A Congressman's facsimile signature on envelopes, used in lieu of stamps for his official outgoing mail, thus postage-free. Also the privilege of sending mail postage-free.

Germane—Pertaining to the subject matter of the measure at hand. All House amendments must be germane to the bill. The Senate requires that amendments be germane only when they are proposed to general appropriation bills, bills being considered under cloture, or often when proceeding under an agreement to limit debate.

Grants-in-Aid—Payments by the Federal Government which aid the recipient state, local government or individual in administering specified programs, services or activities.

Hearings—Committee sessions for hearing witnesses. At hearings on legislation, witnesses usually include specialists, government officials and spokesmen for persons affected by the bills under study. Hearings related to special investigations bring forth a variety of witnesses. Committees sometimes use their subpena power to summon reluctant witnesses. The public and press may attend "open" hearings, but are barred from "closed" or "executive" hearings.

The committee announces its hearings, from one day to many weeks in advance, and may invite certain persons to testify. Persons who request time to testify may be turned down by the committee but most requests are honored.

Hopper—Box on House Clerk's desk where bills are deposited on introduction.

House—The House of Representatives, as distinct from the Senate, although each body is a "house" of Congress.

House Calendar—Listing for action by the House of Representatives of public bills which do not directly or indirectly appropriate money or raise revenue.

Immunity—Constitutional privilege of Congressmen to make verbal statements on the floor and in committee for which they cannot be sued or arrested for slander or libel. Also, freedom from arrest while traveling to or from sessions of Congress or on official business. Congressmen in this status may be arrested only for treason, felonies or a breach of the peace, as defined by Congressional manuals.

Joint Committee—A committee composed of a specified number of Members of both House and Senate. Usually a joint committee is investigative in nature. There are a few standing joint committees, such as the Joint Committee on Atomic Energy and the Joint Economic Committee.

Joint Resolution—A joint resolution, designated H J Res or S J Res, requires the approval of both houses and the signature of the President, just as a bill does, and has the force of law if approved. There is no real difference between a bill and a joint resolution. The latter is generally used in dealing with limited matters, such as a single appropriation for a specific purpose.

Joint resolutions also are used to propose amendments to the Constitution. These do not require Presidential signature, but become a part of the Constitution when three-fourths of the states have ratified them.

Journal—The official record of the proceedings of the House and Senate. The Journal records the actions taken in each chamber, but unlike the Congressional Record, it does not include the verbatim report of speeches, debate, etc.

Law—An Act of Congress which has been signed by the President, or passed over his veto by the Congress. Laws are listed numerically by Congress; for example, the Civil Rights Act of 1964 (HR 7152) became Public Law 88-352 during the 88th Congress.

Legislative Day—The "day" extending from the time either house meets after an adjournment until the time it next adjourns. Because the House normally adjourns from day to day, legislative days and calendar days usually coincide. But in the Senate, a legislative day may, and frequently does, extend over several calendar days. *(See Recess.)*

Lobby—A group seeking to influence the passage or defeat of legislation. Originally the term referred to persons frequenting the lobbies or corridors of legislative chambers in order to speak to lawmakers.

The exact definition of a lobby and the activity of lobbying is a matter of opinion. By some definitions, lobbying is limited to attempts at direct influence by personal interview and persuasion. Under other definitions, lobbying includes attempts at indirect influence, such as stirring members of a group to write or visit Congressmen, or attempting to create a climate of opinion favorable to a desired legislative action.

The right to attempt to influence legislation is based on the 1st Amendment to the Constitution, which says Congress shall make no law abridging the right of the people "to petition the Government for a redress of grievances."

Majority Leader—Chief strategist and floor spokesman for the party in nominal control in either chamber. He is elected by his party colleagues and is virtually program director for his chamber, since he usually speaks for its majority.

Majority Whip—In effect, the assistant majority leader, in House or Senate. His job is to help marshal majority forces in support of party strategy.

Manual—The official handbook in each house prescribing its organization, procedures and operations in detail. The Senate Manual contains standing rules, orders, laws and resolutions affecting Senate business; the House Manual is the equivalent for that chamber. Both volumes contain previous codes under which Congress functioned and from which it continues to derive precedents. Committee powers are outlined. The rules set forth in the Manuals may be changed by elaborate chamber actions also specified by the Manuals.

Marking Up a Bill—Going through a measure, usually in committee, taking it section by section, revising language, penciling in new phrases, etc. If the bill is extensively revised, the new version may be introduced as a separate bill, with a new number. *(See Clean Bill.)*

Memorial—A request for Congressional opposition or an objection from an organization or citizens' group to particular legislation or government practice under the purview of Congress. All communications, both supporting and opposing legislation, from state legislatures are embodied in memorials. They are referred to appropriate committees unless the legislation dealt with in the memorial has been reported to the Senate, in which case the memorial is placed on the table. It can be called up for consideration at the time the bill is read for amendments. *(See Petition.)*

Minority Leader—Floor leader for the minority party. *(See Majority Leader.)*

Minority Whip—Performs duties of whip for the minority party. *(See Majority Whip.)*

Morning Hour—The time set aside at the beginning of each legislative day for the consideration of regular routine business. The "hour" is of indefinite duration in the House, where it is rarely used. In the Senate it is the first two hours of a session following an adjournment, as distinguished from a recess. The morning hour can be terminated earlier if the morning business has been completed. This business includes such matters as messages from the President, communications from the heads of departments, messages from the House, the presentation of petitions and memorials, reports of standing and select committees, and the introduction of bills and resolutions.

During the first hour of the morning hour in the Senate, no motion to proceed to the consideration of any bill on the calendar is in order except by unanimous consent. During the second hour, motions can be made but must be decided without debate. Senate committees may meet while the Senate is in the morning hour.

Motion—Request by a Congressman for any one of a wide array of parliamentary actions. He "moves" for a certain procedure, or the consideration of a measure or a vote, etc. The precedence of motions, and whether they are debatable, is set forth in the House and Senate Manuals.

Nominations—Appointments to office by the Executive Branch of the Government, subject to Senate confirmation. Although most nominations win quick Senate approval, some are controversial and become the topic of hearings and debate. Sometimes Senators object to appointees for patronage reasons—for example, when a nomination to a local federal job is made without consulting the Senators of the state concerned. Then a Senator may use the stock objection that the nominee is "personally obnoxious" to him. Usually other Senators join in blocking such an appointment out of courtesy to their colleague.

One Minute Speeches—Addresses by House Members at the beginning of a legislative day. The speeches may cover any subject, but are limited strictly to one minute's duration.

Override a Veto—If the President disapproves a bill and sends it back to Congress with his objections, Congress may override his veto by a two-thirds vote in each chamber. The Constitution requires a yea-and-nay roll call. The question put to each house is: "Shall the bill pass, the objections of the President to the contrary notwithstanding?" *(See also Pocket Veto and Veto.)*

Pair—A "gentlemen's agreement" between two lawmakers on opposite sides to withhold their votes on roll calls so their absence from Congress will not affect the outcome of record voting. If passage of the measure requires a two-thirds majority, a pair would require two Members favoring the action to one opposed to it.

Two kinds of pairs—special and general—are used; neither is counted in vote totals. The names of lawmakers pairing on a given vote and their stands, if known, are printed in the Congressional Record.

The special pair applies to one or a series of roll-call votes on the same subject. On special pairs, lawmakers usually specify how they would have voted.

A general pair in the Senate, now rarely used in the chamber, applies to all votes on which the Members pairing are on opposite sides, and it lasts for the length of time pairing Senators agree on. It usually does not specify a Senator's stand on a given vote.

The general pair in the House differs from the other pairs. No agreement is involved and the pair does not tie up votes. A Representative expecting to be absent may notify the House Clerk he wishes to make a "general" pair. His name then is paired arbitrarily with that of another Member desiring a general pair, and the list is printed in the Congressional Record. He may or may not be paired with a Member taking the opposite position. General pairs in the House give no indication of how a Congressman would have voted. *(See Record Vote and Stand.)*

Petition—A request or plea sent to one or both chambers from an organization or private-citizens group asking support of particular legislation or favorable consideration of a matter not yet receiving Congressional attention. They are referred to appropriate committees and considered or not, according to committee decision. *(See Memorial.)*

Pocket Veto—The act of the President in withholding his approval of a bill after Congress has adjourned—either for the year or for a specified period. When Congress is in session, a bill becomes law without the President's signature if he does not act upon it within 10 days, excluding Sundays, from the time he gets it. But if Congress adjourns within that 10-day period, the bill is killed without the President's formal veto.

Point of Order—An objection raised by a Congressman that the chamber is departing from rules governing its conduct of business. The objector cites the rule violated, the chair sustaining his objection if correctly made. Order is restored by the chair's suspending proceedings of the chamber until it conforms to the prescribed "order of business." Members sometimes raise a "point of no order"—when there is noise and disorderly conduct in the chamber.

President of the Senate—Presiding officer of the upper chamber, normally the Vice President of the United States. In his absence, a President pro tempore (President for the time being) presides.

President pro tempore—The chief officer of the Senate in the absence of the Vice President. He is elected by his fellow Senators. The recent practice has been to elect to the office the Senator of the majority party with longest continuous service.

Previous Question—In this sense, a "question" is an "issue" before the House for a vote and the issue is "previous" when some other topic has superseded it in the attention of the chamber. A motion for the previous question, when carried, has the effect of cutting off all debate and forcing a vote on the subject originally at hand. If, however, the previous question is moved and carried before there has been any debate on the subject at hand and the subject is debatable, then 40 minutes of debate is allowed before the vote. The previous question is sometimes moved in order to prevent amendments. The motion for the previous question is a debate-limiting device and is not in order in the Senate.

Private Calendar—Private House bills dealing with individual matters such as claims against the Government, immigration, land titles, etc., are put on this calendar. When it is before the chamber, two Members may block a private bill, which then is recommitted to committee.

Backers of a private bill thus recommitted have another recourse. The measure can be put into an "omnibus claims bill"—several private bills rolled into one. As with any bill, no part of an omnibus claims bill may be deleted without a vote. When a private bill goes back to the floor in this form, it can be defeated only by a majority of those present. The Private Calendar can be called on the first and third Tuesdays of each month.

Privilege—Privilege relates to the rights of Congressmen and to the relative priority of the motions and actions they may make in their respective chambers. The two are distinct. "Privileged questions" concern legislative business. "Questions of privilege" concern legislators themselves. *(See below.)*

Privileged Questions—The order in which bills, motions and other legislative measures may be considered by Congress is governed by strict priorities. A motion to table, for instance, is more privileged than a motion to recommit. Thus, a motion to recommit can be superseded by a motion to table, and a vote would be forced on the latter motion only. A motion to adjourn, however, would take precedence over this one, and is thus considered of the "highest privilege."

Pro Forma Amendment—See Strike Out the Last Word.

Questions of Privilege—These are matters affecting Members of Congress individually or collectively.

Questions affecting the rights, safety, dignity and integrity of proceedings of the House or Senate as a whole are questions of privilege of the House or Senate, as the case may be.

Congressmen singly involve questions of "personal privilege." A Member's rising to a question of personal privilege is given precedence over almost all other proceedings. An annotation in the House Rules points out that the privilege of the Member rests primarily on the Constitution, which gives him a conditional immunity from arrest and an unconditional freedom to speak in the House.

Quorum—The number of Members whose presence is necessary for the transaction of business. In the Senate and House, it is a majority of the membership (when there are no vacancies, this is 51 in the Senate and 218 in the House). A quorum is 100 in the Committee of the Whole House. If a point of order is made that a quorum is not present, the only business in order is either a motion to adjourn or a motion to direct the Sergeant-at-Arms to request the attendance of absentees.

Readings of Bills—Traditional parliamentary law required bills to be read three times before they were passed. This custom is of little modern significance except in rare instances. Normally the bill is considered to have its first reading when it is introduced and printed, by title, in the Congressional Record. Its second reading comes when floor consideration begins. (This is the most likely point at which there is an actual reading of the bill, if there is any.) The third reading (usually by title) takes place when action has been completed on amendments.

Recess—Distinguished from adjournment in that a recess does not end a legislative day and therefore does not interfere with unfinished business. The rules in each house set forth certain matters to be taken up and disposed of at the beginning of each legislative day. The House, which operates under much stricter rules than the Senate, usually adjourns from day to day. The Senate often recesses.

Recommit to Committee—A simple motion, made on the floor after deliberation on a bill, to return it to the committee which reported it. If approved, recommittal usually is considered a death blow to the bill. In the House a motion to recommit can be made only by a Member opposed to the bill, and in recognizing a Member to make the motion, the Speaker gives the minority party preference over the majority.

A motion to recommit may include instructions to the committee to report the bill again with specific amendments or by a certain date. Or the instructions may be to make a particular study, with no definite deadline for final action.

Reconsider a Vote—A motion to reconsider the vote by which an action was taken has, until it is disposed of, the effect of suspending the action. In the Senate the motion can be made only by a Member who voted on the prevailing side of the original question, or by a Member who did not vote at all. In the House it can be made only by a Member on the prevailing side.

A common practice after close votes in the Senate is a motion to reconsider, followed by a motion to table the motion to reconsider. On this motion to table, Senators vote as they voted on the original question, to enable the motion to table to prevail. The matter is then finally closed and further motions to reconsider are not entertained. In the House, as a routine precaution, a motion to reconsider usually is made every time a measure is passed. Such a motion almost always is tabled immediately, thus shutting off the possibility of future reconsideration except by unanimous consent.

Motions to reconsider must be entered in the Senate within the next two days of actual session after the original vote has been taken. In the House they must be entered either on the same day or on the next succeeding day the House is in session.

Record Vote—This is a roll call of the entire chamber membership, to which each Member on the floor must answer "yea," "nay," or, if he does not wish to vote, "present." The Constitution requires yea-and-nay votes on the question of overriding a veto. In other cases, they can be obtained by the demand of one-fifth of the Members present. In the House, the yeas and nays are required automatically whenever a Member objects to a non-record vote taken when a quorum was not present, if the question is one which requires a quorum. The yeas and nays are not taken in the Committee of the Whole.

Report—Both a verb and a noun, as a Congressional term. A committee which has been examining a bill referred to it by the parent chamber "reports" its finding and recommendations to the chamber when the committee returns the measure. The process is called "reporting" a bill.

A "report" is the document setting forth the committee's explanation of its action. House and Senate reports are numbered separately and are designated S Rept or H Rept. Conference reports are numbered and designated in the same way as regular House reports.

Most reports favor a bill's passage. Adverse reports are occasionally submitted, but more often, when a committee disapproves a bill, it simply fails to report it at all. When a committee report is not unanimous, the dissenting committeemen may file a statement of their views, called Minority Views and referred to as a Minority Report. Sometimes a bill is reported without recommendation.

Recision—An item in an appropriation bill rescinding, or cancelling, funds previously appropriated but not spent.

Resolution—A simple resolution, designated H Res or S Res, deals with matters entirely within the prerogatives of one house or the other. It requires neither passage by the other chamber nor approval by the President, and does not have the force of law. Most resolutions deal with the rules of one house. They also are used to express the sentiments of a single house, as condolences to the family of a deceased Member or to give "advice" on foreign policy or other executive business. *(Also see Concurrent and Joint Resolutions.)*

Rider—A provision, usually not germane, tacked on to a bill which its sponsor hopes to get through more easily by including in other legislation. Riders become law if the bills embodying them do. Riders providing for legislation in appropriations bills are outstanding examples, though technically they are banned.

Rule—The term has two specific Congressional meanings. A rule may be a standing order governing the conduct of House or Senate business and listed in the chamber's book of rules. The rules deal with duties of officers, order of business, admission to the floor, voting procedures, etc.

In the House, a rule also may be a decision made by its Rules Committee about the handling of a particular bill on the floor. The Committee may determine under which standing rule a bill shall be considered, or it may provide a "special rule" in the form of a resolution. If the resolution is adopted by the House, the temporary rule becomes as valid as any standing rule, and lapses only after action has been completed on the measure to which it pertains.

A special rule sets the time limit on general debate. It may also waive points of order against provisions of the bill in question or against specified amendments intended to be proposed to the bill. It may even forbid all amendments or all amendments except, in some cases, those proposed by the legislative committee which handled the bill. In this instance it is known as a "closed" or "gag" rule as opposed to an "open" rule which puts no limitation on floor action, thus leaving the bill open to alteration. *(See Suspend the Rules.)*

Secretary of the Senate—Chief administrative officer of the Senate, responsible for direction of duties of Senate employees, education of pages, administration of oaths, receipt of registration of lobbyists and other activities necessary for the continuing operation of the Senate.

Select or Special Committee—A committee set up for a special purpose and a limited time by resolution of either House or Senate. Most special committees are investigative in nature.

Senatorial Courtesy—Sometimes referred to as "the courtesy of the Senate," it is a general practice without written rule applied to consideration of executive nominations. In practice, generally it means nominations from a state are not to be confirmed unless they have been approved by the Senators of the President's party of that state, with other Senators following their lead in the attitude they take toward such nominations.

Sine Die—See Adjournment sine die.

Slip Laws—The first official publication of a bill that has been enacted into law. Each is published separately in unbound single-sheet or pamphlet form. It usually takes two to three days from the date of Presidential approval to the time when slip laws become available.

Speaker—The presiding officer of the House of Representatives, elected by its Members.

Special Session—A session of Congress after it has adjourned sine die, completing its regular session. Special sessions are convened by the President of the United States under his constitutional powers.

Stand—A lawmaker's position, for or against, on a given issue or vote. He can make known his stand on a roll-call vote by answering "yea" or "nay," by "pairing" for or against, or by "announcing" his position to the House or Senate. Members also may go on record by answering the Congressional Quarterly Poll of unrecorded Congressmen on roll calls. *(See Pair, and Record Vote, above.)*

Standing Committee—A group permanently provided for by House or Senate rules. The standing committees at present are specified by the Legislative Reorganization Act of 1946, which broadly defines their respective jurisdictions.

Standing Vote—A non-record vote used in both House and Senate. A standing vote, also called a division vote, is taken as follows: Members in favor of a proposal stand and are counted by the presiding officer; then Members opposed stand and are counted. There is no record of how individual Members voted. In the House, the presiding officer announces the number of and against. In the Senate, usually only the result is announced.

Statutes-at-Large—A chronological arrangement of the laws enacted in each session of Congress. Though indexed, the laws are not arranged by subject matter nor is there an indication of how they affect previous law. *(See U.S. Code.)*

Strike from the Record—Remarks made on the House floor may offend some Member, who moves that the offending words be "taken down" for the Speaker's cognizance, and then expunged from the verbatim report to be carried in the Congressional Record.

Strike Out the Last Word—A move whereby House Members are entitled to speak for a fixed time on a measure then being debated by the chamber. A Member gains recognition from the chair by moving to strike out the last word of the amendment or section of the bill then under consideration. The motion is pro forma, and customarily requires no vote.

Substitute—A motion, an amendment, or an entire bill introduced in place of pending business. Passage of a substitute measure kills the original measure by supplanting it. A substitute may be amended.

Supplemental Appropriations—Normally are passed after the regular appropriation, but supposedly before the fiscal year to which they apply. Deficiencies are passed in the same fiscal year to which they apply but in recent practice have been called supplementals.

Suspend the Rules—Often a time-saving procedure for passing bills in the House. The wording of the motion, which may be made by any Member recognized by the Speaker, is: "I move to suspend the rules and pass the bill...." A favorable vote by two-thirds of those present is required for passage. Debate is limited to 40 minutes and no amendments from the floor are permitted. If a two-thirds favorable vote is not attained, the bill may be considered later under regular procedures.

Table a Bill—The motion to "lay on the table" is not debatable in either house, and is usually a method of making a final, adverse disposition of a matter. In the Senate, however, different language is sometimes used. The motion is worded to let a bill "lie on the table," perhaps for subsequent "picking up." This motion is more flexible, merely keeping the bill pending for later action, if desired.

Teller Vote—In the House, Members file past tellers and are counted as for or against a measure, but they are not recorded individually. The teller vote is not used in the Senate. In the House, tellers are ordered upon demand of one-fifth of a quorum. This is 44 in the House, 20 in Committee of the Whole.

Treaties—Executive proposals which must be submitted to the Senate for approval by two-thirds of the Senators present. Before they act on such foreign policy matters, Senators usually send them to committee for scrutiny. Treaties are read three times and debated in the chamber much as are legislative proposals, but are rarely amended. After approval by the Senate, they are ratified by the President.

Twenty-One-Day Rule—Permits the Speaker to recognize a committee member to call up for House consideration any bill reported by the committee that has been before the Rules Committee for 21 days without having received a rule for floor debate. Repealed in 1967.

Unanimous Consent—Synonymous with Without Objection. *(See below.)*

Union Calendar—Bills which directly or indirectly appropriate money or raise revenue are placed on this House calendar according to the date reported from committee.

U.S. Code—A consolidation and codification of the general and permanent laws of the United States arranged by subject under 50 Titles, the first six dealing with general or political subjects, and the other 44 alphabetically arranged from Agriculture to War and National Defense. The Code is now revised every six years and a supplement is published after each session of Congress.

Veto—Disapproval by the President of a bill or joint resolution, other than one proposing an amendment to the Constitution. When Congress is in session, the President must veto a bill within 10 days, excluding Sundays, after he has received it; otherwise it becomes law with or without his signature. When the President vetoes a bill, he returns it to the house of its origin with a message stating his objections. The veto then becomes a question of high privilege. *(See Override a Veto.)*

When Congress has adjourned, the President may pocket veto a bill by failing to sign it. *(See Pocket Veto.)*

Voice Vote—In either House or Senate, Members answer "aye" or "no" in chorus and the presiding officer decides the result. The term also is used loosely to indicate action by unanimous consent or without objection.

Whip—See Majority Whip.

Without Objection—Used in lieu of a vote on non-controversial motions, amendments or bills, which may be passed in either the House or the Senate if no Member voices an objection.

Summary of Table of Contents

TABLE OF CONTENTS

Introduction

Chapter 1 — Politics and National Issues

Chapter 2 — Foreign Policy

Chapter 3 — Economic Policy

Chapter 4 — Crime and Justice

Chapter 5 — Civil Rights

Chapter 6 — Civil Liberties and Internal Security

Chapter 7 — Election Law and Procedures

Chapter 8 — Veterans Affairs

Chapter 9 — Natural Resources and Power

Chapter 10 — Space Activities

Chapter 11 — Agriculture

Chapter 12 — Labor

Chapter 13 — The Presidency
And the Executive Branch

Chapter 14 — Health, Education and Welfare

Chapter 15 — National Security

Chapter 16 — Congress and Government

Appendix

Chapter 1—Politics and National Issues

Special Charts

Politics and National Issues

THE people of the United States enjoyed in the quarter century which followed World War II a sustained period of economic prosperity scarcely paralleled in world history. This factor, combined with the absence of any major world war, laid the groundwork for a period of domestic stability and growth and a broad politics of consensus, reflected in almost every national election through that of 1964.

In the late 1960s, however, the nation experienced a series of cataclysmic changes which—while they did not appear to endanger the basic economic health of the nation—did jeopardize the politics of consensus and promise as yet unpredictable changes in the social and political climate of American life.

In the field of foreign affairs, the American people had decided by the end of World War II that the United States was indeed a global power which could not retreat into isolationism. As the first atomic power, and subsequently as the leader of a community of free nations, the United States found itself at the forefront of the struggle to contain world communism. It constructed a complex series of global alliances, acted as the chief sponsor of the economic revival of postwar Europe and entered the Korean war to maintain its position in Asia. Only when the nation found itself entangled in a seemingly endless and unwinnable war in Vietnam in the mid-1960s did the first major cracks appear in the general national consensus behind U.S. foreign policy. For the first time, serious doubts were raised about the role of the nation as a global policeman, and there were indications that a period of limited isolationism might come in the wake of any Vietnam settlement. On the home front, the dispute over Vietnam seemed to have become the cutting edge for a new generation of social and political protest.

BY the end of World War II, the American people also seemed to have reached a consensus that the social and economic reforms of the New Deal years ought to be preserved and that government had a legitimate role in protecting the individual against economic disaster. In 1964, when Republican Presidential nominee Barry Goldwater seemed to many voters to represent a voice that would return to an earlier era in social relations, he was defeated by the most resounding popular and electoral vote margin of the postwar era.

The nation's economic base was so strong that a politics of consensus in domestic affairs might well have endured at least into the mid-1970s. But the problem of race, and the related problem of poverty among both city and rural Negroes, complicated the picture. Through 1964 and 1965, with passage of the landmark 1964 Civil Rights Act and the 1965 Voting Rights Act, the majority of Americans believed the plight of the Negro could be relieved by legal and civil action. But as their legal rights expanded, Negroes began to recognize that in economic terms, they never had and still did not enjoy the same fruits as other Americans. In the previous century, when Negroes were largely isolated on the farms of the South, they had little opportunity to unite for political or social ends. But with their massive migration to the cities of the North, a new self-awareness and militancy developed. As Negro economic demands escalated in the mid-1960s, so did the potential and actual opposition by whites. A shattering series of urban riots and civil disturbances in 1967-68 made it clear that fundamental changes would have to be made in the economic and social structure of the great cities if domestic peace were to be restored and preserved.

THROUGH the 1964 election, the United States enjoyed remarkably stable two-party politics in the postwar era. No major ideological gulfs existed between the parties, and while the Democrats were more frequently victorious at the polls than the Republicans (an apparent legacy of Franklin Roosevelt's New Deal), few Americans were deeply concerned when the party in power changed in Washington or the state capitals. Indeed, two-party politics infused virtually every region of America for the first time in its history: Democrats won in once impregnable Republican strongholds of Northern New England and the Midwest; Republicans made historic advances in the once solidly-Democratic South. And as the parties became more competitive, personal allegiances shifted more frequently and ticket-splitting became a favorite American electoral pastime.

But in 1968, the first really serious third-party Presidential effort in a half century appeared with Alabama's fiery segregationist ex-Governor, George C. Wallace, at its helm. For a period during the 1968 campaign, some analysts thought that the traditional political alliances inherited from the 1930s might be shattered—that the Democrats might lose major elements of

---

Reference

Discussion of political developments in the United States from 1945-64 will be found in *Congress and the Nation, Vol. I, p. 1-87.*

their traditional low income-labor-minorities-Southern coalition, and that the Republicans would lose some of their more conservative followers to the Wallace cause. In the end, organized labor and the minorities (blacks, Jews, Mexican-Americans) stayed with the Democrats, albeit with heavily reduced margins, especially in the big cities. But Democratic Presidential candidate Hubert Humphrey won only one Southern state (Texas), as Nixon and Wallace divided the rest, suggesting at least a possibility of substantial party realignment in the South in the coming years. And even in winning the Presidency, Richard M. Nixon was faced by the fact that the Wallace movement had deprived him of millions of votes he might otherwise have received.

Thus, at the end of the 1960s, both parties were clearly in transition. The Democrats, in order to hold their solid base among the low income voters and the minorities, would be obliged to remain strong advocates of wide-ranging social reform. But that very course could possibly seal their eventual downfall in the South, even if an increased black vote in that region compensated for some of that loss. And while organized labor had turned out a strong Democratic vote in 1968, its leaders were having increasing difficulty in convincing workers —many of whom were earning handsome wages and living in comfortable homes, as they enjoyed the economic prosperity of the times—that they should remain unswervingly loyal to the Democratic party.

The Republicans, even in winning the Presidential election of 1968, received only 43 percent of the national vote and had to recognize that in their major base of support—the predominantly white, middle-class rural areas and small cities—they faced a diminishing asset in overall population terms. It was clear that the Republicans' growing strength in the burgeoning white suburban areas of America would hold solid only as long as the party maintained domestic prosperity and found a way to calm inner city tensions. The 1960s had shown increasingly liberal attitudes among college graduates, who now composed a greater and greater portion of the population. As increasing numbers of Americans grew up, were educated and went to work in a world where they never feared where their next meal might come from, the successful political party of the future would be required to invent new ways to bridge the social chasms in American society and ensure real domestic tranquility.

1965-66—The 89th Congress

	House	Senate
Democrats	295	68
Republicans	140	32

As of Jan. 3, 1965

Congress in 1965

BUOYED by the largest party majorities enjoyed by any President in three decades, Lyndon Johnson led the 89th Congress in an amazingly productive 1965 session. The scope of the legislation

Republican Conventions, 1856-1968

Year	City	Date	Presidential Nominee	No. of Ballots
1856	Philadelphia	June 17-19	John C. Fremont	2
1860	Chicago	May 16-19	Abraham Lincoln	3
1864	Baltimore	June 7-8	Abraham Lincoln	1
1868	Chicago	May 20-21	Ulysses S. Grant	1
1872	Philadelphia	June 5-6	Ulysses S. Grant	1
1876	Cincinnati	June 14-16	Rutherford B. Hayes	7
1880	Chicago	June 2-8	James A. Garfield	36
1884	Chicago	June 3-6	James G. Blaine	4
1888	Chicago	June 19-25	Benjamin Harrison	8
1892	Minneapolis	June 7-10	Benjamin Harrison	1
1896	St. Louis	June 16-18	William McKinley	1
1900	Philadelphia	June 19-21	William McKinley	1
1904	Chicago	June 21-23	Theodore Roosevelt	1
1908	Chicago	June 16-19	William H. Taft	1
1912	Chicago	June 18-22	William H. Taft	1
1916	Chicago	June 7-10	Charles E. Hughes	3
1920	Chicago	June 8-12	Warren G. Harding	10
1924	Cleveland	June 10-12	Calvin Coolidge	1
1928	Kansas City	June 12-15	Herbert Hoover	1
1932	Chicago	June 14-16	Herbert Hoover	1
1936	Cleveland	June 9-12	Alfred M. Landon	1
1940	Philadelphia	June 24-28	Wendell L. Willkie	6
1944	Chicago	June 24-28	Thomas E. Dewey	1
1948	Philadelphia	June 21-25	Thomas E. Dewey	3
1952	Chicago	July 7-11	Dwight D. Eisenhower	1
1956	San Francisco	Aug. 20-23	Dwight D. Eisenhower	1
1960	Chicago	July 25-28	Richard M. Nixon	1
1964	San Francisco	July 13-16	Barry Goldwater	1
1968	Miami Beach	Aug. 5-8	Richard M. Nixon	1

Democratic Conventions, 1832-1968

Year	City	Date	Presidential Nominee	No. of Ballots
1832	Baltimore	May 21	Andrew Jackson	1
1835	Baltimore	May 20	Martin Van Buren	1
1840	Baltimore	May 5	Martin Van Buren	1
1844	Baltimore	May 27-29	James K. Polk	9
1848	Baltimore	May 22-26	Lewis Cass	4
1852	Baltimore	June 1-6	Franklin Pierce	49
1856	Cincinnati	June 2-6	James Buchanan	17
1860	Baltimore	June 18-23	Stephen A. Douglas	2
1864	Chicago	August 29	George B. McClellan	1
1868	New York	July 4-11	Horatio Seymour	22
1872	Baltimore	July 9	Horace Greeley	1
1876	St. Louis	June 27-29	Samuel J. Tilden	2
1880	Cincinnati	June 22-24	Winfield S. Hancock	2
1884	Chicago	July 8-11	Grover Cleveland	2
1888	St. Louis	June 5	Grover Cleveland	1
1892	Chicago	June 21	Grover Cleveland	1
1896	Chicago	July 7	William J. Bryan	5
1900	Kansas City	July 4-6	William J. Bryan	1
1904	St. Louis	July 6-9	Alton S. Parker	1
1908	Denver	July 7-10	William J. Bryan	1
1912	Baltimore	June 25-July 2	Woodrow Wilson	46
1916	St. Louis	June 14-16	Woodrow Wilson	1
1920	San Francisco	June 28-July 6	James M. Cox	43
1924	New York	June 24-July 9	John W. Davis	103
1928	Houston	June 26-29	Alfred E. Smith	1
1932	Chicago	June 27-July 2	Franklin D. Roosevelt	4
1936	Philadelphia	June 23-27	Franklin D. Roosevelt	Acclamation
1940	Chicago	July 15-18	Franklin D. Roosevelt	1
1944	Chicago	July 19-21	Franklin D. Roosevelt	1
1948	Philadelphia	July 12-14	Harry S. Truman	1
1952	Chicago	July 21-26	Adlai E. Stevenson	3
1956	Chicago	Aug. 13-17	Adlai E. Stevenson	1
1960	Los Angeles	July 11-15	John F. Kennedy	1
1964	Atlantic City	Aug. 24-27	Lyndon B. Johnson	Acclamation
1968	Chicago	Aug. 26-29	Hubert H. Humphrey	Acclamation

was even more impressive than the number of major new laws. Measures which taken alone would have crowned the achievements of any Congress were enacted in a seemingly endless stream. In the course of the year, Congress approved programs which had long been on the agenda of the Democratic party—in the case of medical care for the aged under Social Security, for as long as 20 years. Other long-standing objectives were met by enactment of aid to primary and secondary schools, college scholarships and immigration reform.

The pace of the 1965 session was so breathless as to cause a major revision of the image, widely prevalent in preceding years, of Congress as structurally incapable of swift decision, prone to frustrate demands for progress. The change was due to three primary factors not always present in past years: the decisive Democratic majorities elected in 1964, the personal leadership of President Johnson and the shaping of legislation to obtain maximum political support in Congress. On a number of occasions (most notably in conjunction with the Elementary and Secondary Education Act) the word was passed to approve the bill and worry about perfecting details later.

The expanded Democratic pluralities were most significant in the House, where the Democrats had not only scored a 38-seat net gain over the Republicans in the 1964 elections but had also traded a number of conservative Democratic votes in the South for liberal Democratic votes in the North. The new liberal strength in the House showed itself more dramatically in passage of the aid to education and medical care ("medicare") bills. The Senate had passed similar measures in previous years only to see them blocked by the hitherto powerful coalition of Republicans and conservative Southern Democrats in the House. But the "conservative coalition," where it did appear in House roll-call votes, was victorious only 25 percent of the time in 1965, compared with 67 percent in 1963 and 1964 and 74 percent in 1961, the first year of President Kennedy's term. The liberal Democratic strength in the House was further enforced by approval, at the start of the Congress, of a three-part revision of House rules that gave the Speaker authority to bring legislation to the floor if blocked by the Rules Committee and also impeded dilatory tactics of the opposition. Democratic ratios also were increased on House committees.

LBJ 'Consensus' Tactics

The President gained maximum political effect from his efforts to build a broad consensus of support. His fiscal 1966 Budget was drafted with great care to present a total under $100 billion and convince the business community that he intended to keep his pledge of economy in government. An excise tax cut, designed to keep the economy growing steadily, appealed to businessmen and consumers alike. Lack of strong opposition from business circles made it easier for Democrats to mount the Great Society program of greatly increased civil benefits, and tended to smother the protests of Republicans that Congress was merely "rubber-stamping" ill-conceived Administration proposals.

An outstanding example of the President's consensus-building technique and legislative leadership was provided by the Elementary and Secondary Education Act of 1965. Previous bills providing general aid to edu-

cation had become mired in Congress over the issue of aid to church-supported schools. But before the Johnson school bill was sent to Congress, Administration officials held meetings with leaders of the two major education lobbies, the National Education Assn. and the National Catholic Welfare Conference. Both groups gave their approval to a new approach to end the impasse: to aim the aid to children, whether in public or private school, and particularly in poor areas, rather than aid the schools per se. The lobby groups supported the bill; the formula withstood all challenges on the floor; and Mr. Johnson's legislative leaders pushed the program through by April 9, without major amendment.

The $6.5 billion medical care bill reached the President's desk by July. Two health care programs for persons 65 or older were included. One, called the basic plan and commonly referred to as "medicare," would cover most hospital and nursing home costs, diagnostic studies and home health-care visits. It would be compulsory, financed mainly by a payroll tax and administered by the Social Security system. Republicans and the American Medical Assn. strongly opposed this plan. The second health-care program, called the supplementary plan, would be voluntary and would be financed by $3 monthly premiums from participants and by general revenue. This program covered a variety of health services, including doctor bills. The supplementary plan was based mainly on Republican proposals.

Congressional Output

Other major bills passed by Congress in 1965 included:

• An immigration measure amending the 1952 McCarran-Walter Act to eliminate the national origins quota system, which had been in effect since 1925, and to establish general priorities for admission of immigrants to the U.S.

• The Voting Rights Act of 1965, the most comprehensive legislation to assure the right to vote in 90 years. Prompted by the brutal suppression of demonstrations to secure Negro voting rights in Selma, Ala., and other parts of the South, the bill went beyond the milder courtroom remedies of earlier civil rights acts to suspend the use of literacy tests or similar voter qualification devices and authorize appointment of federal voting examiners who could order the registration of Negroes in voting districts where less than 50 percent of the voting age citizens had been registered for the 1964 election. Six Southern states and isolated counties elsewhere were affected. In the wake of the legislation, an additional 500,000 Southern Negroes were registered by the time of the 1966 elections, increasing the Negro registration in the 11-state area from 2.2 million to 2.7 million.

• A housing bill authorizing $7.8 billion to fund new and existing housing programs through 1969. The measure included a new Administration-backed program for rent supplements to low-income families which could not obtain standard housing within their own incomes.

• A bill establishing a Cabinet-level Department of Housing and Urban Development—the first addition to the President's Cabinet since the Department of Health, Education and Welfare was created in 1953.

• A wide-ranging program to aid higher education: federal scholarships for college students, federally guaranteed low-interest loans, aid to struggling small colleges and community service programs, grants for college libraries and training.

• Amendments to the 1964 poverty bill, more than doubling the first year's authorization.

• New legislation authorizing over $1 billion for the development of the economically depressed 11-state Appalachian region.

Other major bills approved by Congress eliminated many federal excise taxes, established a national foundation to encourage and subsidize the humanities, raised general Social Security benefits and taxes, established a program to clean up the appearance of federally aided highways by screening junkyards, controlling placement of billboards and landscaping roads, and set up programs to combat water pollution.

The Administration suffered only two major reverses in 1965, as Congress refused to approve "home rule" for the District of Columbia and to repeal section 14(b) of the Taft-Hartley Act, which permitted states to enact laws banning the union shop.

Foreign Developments of 1965-66

The year 1965 was punctuated by major crises in Vietnam and the Dominican Republic. Faced with the threat of success by the Viet Cong Communist insurgents in South Vietnam, President Johnson initiated large-scale bombing raids in North Vietnam, which was giving major aid to the Viet Cong. When this tactic failed to turn the unfavorable course of the war, he ordered a vast increase—from about 20,000 to eventually more than 140,000—in American troop strength in the south and an aggressive prosecution of the land war. Both steps required new outlays for men and materiel. Despite highly vocal criticism of his Vietnam policy by a small band of Senators, Congress overwhelmingly approved Mr. Johnson's special request for funds.

In April 1965, the President sent more than 30,000 troops to the Dominican Republic to end a civil war he said threatened to place the country under Communist control. Senate Foreign Relations Committee Chairman Fulbright was highly critical of the Administration's course of action, but peace was restored in the Dominican Republic with the aid of the Organization of American States.

Other major foreign developments of 1965 included the crushing by the Indonesian army of a Communist-inspired coup d'etat in that land, followed by mass arrests and executions of Communists and an apparent end to the pro-Communist foreign policy of President Sukarno. The move represented a major victory for the United States in the Pacific area, even though neither U.S. diplomacy nor military force played any part. Early in 1965, the Soviet Union orbited a two-man spaceship on a 26-hour flight, during which one of the cosmonauts stepped out of the capsule on a tether line—the first man to "walk" in space. The United States orbited several spacecraft during the year, duplicating the Soviet "space walk" feat and chalking up a record of 330 hours and 206 orbits for one spacecraft, the Gemini 6 in December 1965.

The North Atlantic Treaty Organization encountered difficult times. France announced in March 1966 that she was withdrawing her armed forces from the 15-nation integrated NATO military command and, in effect, ordered that all NATO commands and installations leave French soil. However, the other NATO powers chose to continue their alliance despite the animosity of France under President de Gaulle's leadership. NATO command headquarters were shifted to Brussels.

Chinese-Soviet relations continued to worsen, as the Chinese Communists in March 1966 refused the Russians' invitation to a Soviet Communist Party Congress. The spring and summer of 1966 saw the beginning of a major political purge in China, described by the Chinese press as part of a "great proletarian cultural revolution." Forces loyal to Communist leader Mao Tse-tung mobilized thousands of Chinese teenagers into "Red Guard" units which began a violent antitraditionalist campaign to stamp out all manifestations of revisionism in China.

Congress in 1966

Spiraling U.S. involvement in the Vietnam war and the inflationary trend in the nation's economy—itself caused in major part by the war—were the dominant themes of the second session of the 89th Congress. Between the end of 1965 and the end of 1966, the United States increased its troop commitment in Vietnam from 181,000 to 389,000 troops, with increases to the neighborhood of 500,000 contemplated for 1967.

The year 1966 began with a concerted U.S. "peace drive" as Vice President Humphrey, Ambassador to the United Nations Arthur Goldberg and other Administration officials visited world capitals to restate the country's policies and sound out the possibilities of achieving a negotiated settlement to the Vietnam conflict. But the North Vietnamese showed no interest in opening discussions, and the Johnson Administration—while keeping the door open to negotiations—engaged in a steady escalation of the war throughout 1966.

During the course of the year, through heavy bombing and increased participation in "search and destroy" missions against the Viet Cong and North Vietnamese regulars in the South, the United States was able to brunt the Communist advances of 1964-65 and turn the tide of the military conflict against the Communists. But final victory over the Communist insurgents and the tens of thousands of North Vietnam regular troops constantly infiltrating the South still seemed distant.

A new element of stability in South Vietnam politics emerged with the selection in June 1965 of Air Vice Marshal Nguyen Cao Ky, 34, as premier. In 1966, a large majority of the South Vietnam population turned out for elections of a constituent assembly to write a permanent constitution for a democratic plan of government that would replace the military regime. In the meantime, bolstered by the U.S. military presence, the Ky government remained in firm control in Saigon.

Though many Americans found the war perplexing, Congress voted overwhelmingly to support it and the U.S. people generally backed the nation's military effort —even though more than 5,000 Americans were killed in the conflict during 1966 (as opposed to only 1,369 in 1965). Opposition was confined to vocal but distinctly minority groups. Hearings conducted by Fulbright's Foreign Relations Committee early in the year focused on the opposition, but the "peace" movement against the war made little headway, either in Congress or in primary and general election campaigns where "peace" candidates ran in 1966. Generally, the Administration's policies were criticized about equally by those wanting to reduce the U.S. commitment (to the point of actual withdrawal from Vietnam) and by those on the other side who advocated a radical escalation of U.S. bombing in the hope it would bring a rapid victory in the conflict.

Early in the 1966 session, Congress approved a request of $13.1 million in supplemental 1966 appropriations for the Defense Department and the Agency for International Development (AID), primarily in support of Vietnam operations. On the eve of adjournment in the fall, it approved a near record $58.1 billion fiscal 1967 defense appropriations bill, including Vietnam-related funds estimated at more than $13 billion. Estimates near the end of the session set the cost of the war at $2 billion a month.

In the face of the rapidly rising defense costs, President Johnson argued that the country could afford both those expenses and the bill for an expanding variety of Great Society programs at home. The Republican opposition, however, made increasing headway with its argument that the country could not afford full budgets for both "guns and butter" at the same time. By mid-1966, it was apparent that the fiscal 1966 budget, originally estimated at below $100 billion, had ballooned to $107.0 billion. The fiscal 1967 budget was expected to reach $126.7 billion (with a $9.7 billion deficit for the year).

The Vietnam budget pressures soon had serious impact on the domestic economy. As 1966 began, the U.S. economy was already strained to its noninflationary limit. After 59 months of stable economic growth, it was near full employment. Plant capacity was in full use. Any sizeable increase in demand under these conditions would be bound to result in inflation. This is precisely what occurred as the defense budget shot upward, without any significant offsetting measures to cut back on other purchasing power. The cost-of-living index jumped from 111.0 percent in January to 113.8 percent in August. The President early in the year asked and received Congressional approval of a $5.9 billion bill to accelerate certain types of tax payments and reimpose 1965 excise tax levies, but the measure was hardly adequate to counter the Vietnam spending boom. Almost every leading economist in the nation called for a general tax increase, but President Johnson refused.

With the public increasingly concerned with inflation and the Vietnam war, Congressional Republicans found new Democratic allies in the effort to curb the Great Society—not only its spending programs but almost any measure providing social reform. Despite strong persuasive efforts by the President, the Administration was rebuffed on many major bills. Outright defeat came on Administration-backed legislation to secure "open occupancy" in the nation's housing supply, to repeal section 14(b) of the Taft-Hartley Act and to broaden picketing rights for construction unions, another major goal of organized labor. Enacted, but in diluted form, were "truth-in-packaging," a new federal Department of Transportation, funds for rent supplements and the new Teacher Corps, and the foreign aid program. A bill to overhaul the unemployment compensation system was left languishing in conference when the session ended,

and the Congress refused to act on the President's request to ease East-West trade curbs, extend House terms to four years and reform campaign spending laws.

A number of major bills did pass the 1966 Congressional session, however. They included strong auto and highway safety bills, a substantially higher minimum wage (up to $1.60 an hour), new educational incentives, continuation of the war on poverty, bail reform, civil commitment for narcotics addicts and far-reaching antipollution measures. Just before adjournment, Congress approved a $900 million "demonstration cities" plan for intensive attack on urban blight. Participating cities, to be selected under rigid federal standards, were to receive up to 80 percent of local costs for the entire array of federal grant programs in the realm of housing, welfare and urban transport. The bill contemplated aid to an estimated 60 to 70 cities.

A major reason for the defeat of the Administration's new civil rights proposals was a wave of summertime riots in Negro "ghetto" areas of the large cities. In August 1965, a six-day disturbance had erupted in Los Angeles' 95-percent Negro Watts area, with 6,000 to 7,000 young Negroes participating in rioting, looting of stores, arson, rock-throwing and sniping. The National Guard finally restored order, but only after 34 deaths. In summer 1966, other riots followed in the Negro areas of Cleveland, Brooklyn, Baltimore, Chicago, San Francisco and several other American cities. The 1966 riots were attributed not only to decades of frustration of urban Negroes in the education, housing and employment fields but to the growth of a new philosophy of "black power" expounded by extremist civil rights groups such as the Congress of Racial Equality (CORE) and the Student Nonviolent Coordinating Committee (SNCC). The "black power" movement was opposed by more old-line civil rights groups. Another factor working against new civil rights legislation, especially in the housing field, was that it would have a uniform effect throughout the country, while the thrust of previous legislation had been focused primarily in one region— the South. The pro-civil rights coalition which had operated so effectively in previous years—Republicans and Northern Democrats in Congress and civil rights, labor and church groups outside Congress—fell apart in 1966.

Another important civil rights development was the issuance by the U.S. Office of Education of broad new guidelines for desegregating schools, hospitals and other medical facilities under Title VI of the 1964 Civil Rights Act. The guidelines encountered bitter opposition in Congress, especially from Southern Members.

The conduct of two Members of Congress, Sen. Dodd (D Conn.) and Rep. Powell (D N.Y.), came under investigation during 1966. Senate hearings were begun on charges that Dodd had used his Senatorial position to do favors for Julius Klein, a public relations man and registered foreign agent, and that he had misused $200,000 or more in campaign funds raised through testimonial dinners. The House Education and Labor Committee voted to reduce Powell's powers as its chairman after criticizing him for supporting "black power" politics, delaying the antipoverty bill and misusing committee funds. (In early 1967, the charges against Powell would lead to his removal as Education and Labor Committee chairman and his exclusion from the 90th Congress.)

Leadership

Rep. McCormack (D Mass.) continued as Speaker of the House and Sen. Mansfield (D Mont.) as Majority Leader in the Senate, with Sen. Dirksen (R Ill.) his Republican counterpart. But in the House, Minority Leader Halleck (R Ind.), 64, was defeated for re-election to his leadership post by Rep. Gerald R. Ford (R Mich.), 51, by a 73-67 secret vote of House Republicans on Jan. 4, 1965, just before formal opening of the 89th Congress. Ford's election as Minority Leader was a continuation of the revolt of younger House Republicans that had begun with Ford's election as House GOP Conference chairman two years before. As in 1963, the leadership struggle seemed to be based less on ideological differences than the question of which man could give the most forceful leadership to the depleted Republican House ranks. Rep. Laird (R Wis.), who had helped engineer Ford's election to the leadership in 1963 and later emerged as a power as chairman of the platform committee at the 1964 Republican National Convention, was elected to replace Ford as GOP House Conference chairman.

House Democrats took a major step at the start of the 89th Congress, when they voted by a secret ballot of 157-115 to censure two Southern party members, Reps. Williams (Miss.) and Watson (S.C.), for publicly supporting GOP Presidential candidate Goldwater in the 1964 election. Both men were stripped of their seniority rights—an action that cost Williams the chairmanship of the House Interstate and Foreign Commerce Committee when that post became open in 1966. Watson resigned from the House, ran for re-election from his district as a Republican and was overwhelmingly re-elected in a special 1965 election.

Domestic Politics

The 1964 elections had left the Republicans at such a low point that some resurgence seemed inevitable. In 1965, it began in a spectacular way as Republican-Liberal John V. Lindsay won election as Mayor in heavily Democratic New York City, defeating the regular old-line Democratic nominee, City Controller Abraham D. Beame, by a plurality of 136,144 votes. Editor William F. Buckley, a Goldwater ally running on the Conservative party ticket, polled 13.4 percent of the vote but failed in his attempt to prevent Lindsay's election.

Lindsay's victory, combined with the victories of liberally inclined Republican candidates for district attorney in Philadelphia and mayor in Louisville, Ky., signaled a potential Republican resurgence on the left in the very areas where Goldwater had been weakest —in the major cities, and especially among Negroes and other minority groups.

In New Jersey, however, the Republican gubernatorial candidate took a conservative tack similar to that of the 1964 Goldwater campaign and found himself defeated by Democratic Gov. Richard J. Hughes by a record 363,572-vote margin. Democrats also held the Virginia Governorship and Legislature and easily maintained control of the mayors' offices in major cities like New Haven, St. Louis, Pittsburgh and Detroit. In Cleveland, a Negro state legislator running as an independent came within 2,143 votes of upsetting the incumbent Democratic mayor. In the smaller cities, some of the most interesting contests took place June 8 in Hattiesburgh and Columbus, Miss., where for the first time in the 20th century Republicans—all staunch conservatives—were elected mayors.

The 1966 Elections

From the start of the 1966 campaign, the Democrats realized they faced formidable odds if they hoped to maintain their overwhelming margins of control in the Congress, the state Governorships and legislatures. Yet at the end of 1965, it looked as if the minority Republicans might be held to minimal gains. The first session of the 89th Congress had passed laws with benefits for almost every segment of the population; President Johnson still enjoyed the wide "consensus" support he had enjoyed in 1964, from every group from organized labor to big business and the minorities; and the economy was booming on virtually every front.

By the start of the 1966 campaign, however, it was apparent that the odds had shifted significantly to the benefit of the Republicans. Behind the change was the escalation of the Vietnam war, with its heavy toll, both in American lives and dollars. The Republicans did not pretend to have an easy solution for the Vietnam war; indeed, most Republicans tended to support the Johnson Administration's Vietnam policies, and the Republicans were sharply critical of Democratic critics of the war for failing to give solid support to the American war effort. But like the Korean War, the conflict in Vietnam, because of its limited nature, increased frustrations across the country and began to undermine public support of the Administration in power.

The war effort, in turn, generated inflationary pressures that were being felt throughout the country by mid-1966. The Republicans were able to argue with some effectiveness that the Johnson Administration should be cutting down, rather than increasing, national expenditures for a wide variety of Great Society programs. Moreover, those very social welfare programs that had looked so politically attractive at the end of 1965 were beginning to encounter serious administrative difficulties, with wide gaps between the promises of the Johnson Administration to improve educational standards, end conditions of poverty and assure racial peace and the Administration's actual ability to deliver on those promises.

President Johnson's own personal popularity plummeted during the year; wide splits appeared in the Democratic party in many key states; and at the very same time, a number of attractive Republican candidates appeared to lead the GOP in critical states—in sharp contrast to the unpopularity of Goldwater, the party's 1964 standard bearer.

Early in 1965, the Democrats had launched an ambitious "Operation Support" from within the Democratic National Committee, designed to re-elect a large portion of the 71 freshman Democratic Representatives who came into office in the 1964 Democratic sweep—38 of them from formerly Republican districts. The program included constant liaison with aid-dispensing federal agencies to assist with projects for the Congressional Members' home districts, free transmission of "audio press releases" to freshman Democrats to radio stations in their home districts, an ambitious home district mailing program utilizing the computer sorting and addressing facilities of the National Committee and general research and speech-writing assistance. But while "Operation Support" functioned smoothly in 1965, it tended to fall off in 1966 as the National Committee obeyed Presidential orders to cut back on its activities in order to pay off a heavy debt left from the 1964 campaign.

The Republican Congressional effort, on the other hand, was bolstered by a massive fund-raising campaign that made it possible to funnel thousands of dollars into every doubtful Congressional district in the country. Reports just before the elections showed national-level gifts of $1.6 million to GOP Congressional candidates from their party headquarters, compared with only $250,000 from national-level Democratic committees.

The primary season indicated some significant shifts in the political landscape. In California, long a bastion of liberal Republicanism in the mode of former Gov. (later Chief Justice) Earl Warren, actor Ronald Reagan, an outspoken conservative, won a sweeping primary victory over more liberal opposition. In the Virginia primary, two aging representatives of traditional conservatism Southern Democracy—House Rules Committee Chairman Smith (D), 83, and Sen. Robertson (D), 79, were defeated by younger men of more moderate persuasion. In Florida, the mayor of Miami, Robert King High (D), won the Democratic gubernatorial primary with liberal support over the more conservative incumbent Governor, Haydon Burns (D). Staunch segregationist candidates, on the other hand, won Democratic gubernatorial primaries in the Deep South—Jim Johnson (D), in Arkansas, Lester Maddox (D) in Georgia, and Mrs. Lurleen Wallace (D), wife of outgoing Gov. George C. Wallace (D) (who was ineligible to succeed himself), in Alabama. In Massachusetts, former House Speaker Martin (R), 81, was defeated for renomination by a woman challenger, in part because of changes in his district wrought by equal population districting.

As the campaign gathered steam in the fall, the Republicans concentrated their fire increasingly on the issues of inflation, Vietnam, crime and the alleged "credibility gap" between what President Johnson and his Administration said they were doing and their actual performance. President Johnson himself fed the "credibility gap" at the height of the campaign when he arrived back in the United States from a mid-October conference of Asian government leaders in Manila on the Vietnam war to announce that he was going to undergo minor abdominal and throat surgery in about 15 days, and would rest prior to the operation. Asked at a Nov. 4 press conference about the resulting cancellation

of his widely reported concluding campaign tour, the President replied: "We don't have any (campaign) plans so when you don't have plans, you don't cancel plans." Yet it had been common knowledge that the President had planned a last-minute tour taking him to Massachusetts, Illinois, Nevada, Idaho, Washington, Oregon, California, Montana, Wyoming and Colorado.

Prior to the Manila trip, which kept him out of the country from Oct. 18 to Nov. 2, the President had visited 22 states since late spring on technically "nonpolitical" and avowedly "political" tours. His most partisan attacks on the Republicans had come Oct. 7 and 12 in Newark, N.J., and New York City, when he accused Republican candidates of running on a platform "made up of one word—fear." Johnson said the Republicans had no real programs to fight inflation, ease racial tensions or end the war in Vietnam. "Afraid, afraid, afraid. Republicans are afraid of their own shadows and afraid of the shadow of progress," Johnson alleged.

The brunt of campaigning for the Democrats was undertaken by Vice President Humphrey, who visited 26 states by election time. Sens. Robert and Edward Kennedy also campaigned extensively for Democratic candidates. On the Republican side, former Vice President Nixon undertook the most extensive campaigning and saw a large portion of the candidates in whose behalf he appeared elected.

Results of the 1966 Elections

The Republican party reasserted itself as a major force in American politics by capturing eight new Governorships, three new seats in the U.S. Senate and 47 additional U.S. House seats in the Nov. 8 elections. In a striking comeback from its devastating defeat of 1964, the GOP elected enough new Governors to give it control of 25 of the 50 states with a substantial majority of the nation's population. The Senate and House gains left the party still short of a majority but in a position of new power and relevance on the national scene.

A new vigor shown by Republican candidates across the country marked a return to more competitive two-party politics in the United States and the possibility that the 1968 Presidential election could be closely contested. The vast majority of successful Republican candidates, both for Congressional and state offices, appeared to have rejected the ultraconservative ideology which former Sen. Goldwater had symbolized. But the winning Republicans did represent a somewhat more conservative philosophy than that of the President and his Administration, reflecting a national movement to the right which many observers felt was reflected in the slowdown on major domestic reforms in the closing

Results of 1966 Elections

	HOUSE			SENATE			GOVERNORS		
	Old Lineup	Gains/ Losses	New Lineup	Old Lineup	Gains/ Losses	New Lineup	Old Lineup	Gains/ Losses	New Lineup
Democrats	295	—47	248	67	—3	64	33	—8	25
Republicans	140	+47	187	33	+3	36	17	+8	25

session of the 89th Congress. The 1966 elections appeared to lay the groundwork for a strong moderate Republican challenge to President Johnson in 1968. Moreover, the elections gave prominence to some of the candidates who might be chosen to make that race:

• Michigan's Gov. Romney, re-elected with an overwhelming 61.4 percent majority, who was also able to pull a Republican Senator and five new Republican House Members into office on his coattails.

• Former Vice President Nixon, who campaigned tirelessly for Republican candidates throughout the land and took the role in public Republican debate with the President in the closing days of the campaign.

• Reagan, elected to the California Governorship by a margin of nearly 1 million votes, who was able to shed his one-time ultraconservative image in the campaign and demonstrate a broad appeal across party lines.

• Charles H. Percy of Illinois, elected to the U.S. Senate over veteran Sen. Douglas (D) by a strong majority, including support from suburbanites, downstaters and even a significant portion of Chicago's Negro population.

Although less likely to figure in immediate Presidential speculation, another strong generation of Republican leaders emerged from the elections:

• Oregon's new Senator and two-term Governor, Mark Hatfield, who modified his "dove"-like position on Vietnam enough to overcome opposition from a strong Administration supporter.

• Ohio's Gov. Rhodes, who won re-election by the largest majority in his state's history.

• Pennsylvania's new Gov. Raymond P. Shafer, handpicked successor of outgoing Gov. Scranton (R).

• Massachusetts' Edward W. Brooke (R), the first Negro of the century to win election to the U.S. Senate.

• Texas' Sen. Tower (R), whose strong re-election victory illustrated his ability to buck the odds against the amassed efforts of the Texas Democratic establishment, even in a regular election. (Tower had first been elected in a special 1961 run-off.)

• New York's Sen. Javits (R), who managed the re-election campaign of Gov. Rockefeller (R). Counted a sure loser earlier in 1966, Rockefeller campaigned skillfully and benefitted from deep splits within the Democratic party to win a third four-year term. Although he counted himself out of future Presidential politics, Rockefeller's support and control of the New York delegation would be of major importance to the moderates at the 1968 Republican National Convention. There was some speculation he might back Javits, at least as a favorite son candidate.

Party Balances

The party control among the 50 state Governorships shifted from 33-17 in favor of the Democrats to 25-25—the greatest Republican strength since the early 1950s. The Republicans gained California and held New York, Pennsylvania, Ohio and Michigan to give them control of five of the nation's seven largest states. In addition to California, the Republicans added Alaska, Arizona, Arkansas, Florida, Maryland, Minnesota, Nebraska, Nevada and New Mexico to the list of Governorships under their control. Among the new Governors were Winthrop Rockefeller (R Ark.), brother of the New York Gov-

ernor; Claude R. Kirk Jr. (R), in traditionally Democratic Florida; and Spiro T. Agnew (R Md.), a political moderate who defeated George P. Mahoney (D), the narrow victor in a three-way Democratic primary who had pitched his campaign to the "white backlash" vote with the campaign slogan, "Your Home is Your Castle—Protect It." (In general, "backlash" candidates were unsuccessful in the elections.) Republican gubernatorial candidate Howard Callaway (R) actually won a plurality of the votes in the one-time impregnable Democratic stronghold of Georgia. But Callaway failed to poll an absolute majority, and under the Georgia constitution, the election was thrown into the state legislature, which chose the Democratic runner-up, Lester Maddox.

The Republicans' most spectacular gain was in the House of Representatives, where they picked up 52 seats and lost only five to the Democrats. The new party line-up in the House would be 248 Democrats, 187 Republicans. The Republican total in the 13 Southern states went up to 28 seats, compared with only 14 in 1962. In Senate elections, Republicans gained seats in Illinois, Oregon and Tennessee to give them 36 Senate seats to the Democrats' 64. Democrats failed to take any Senate seats from the Republicans.

On the state legislature level, the Republicans scored net gains of 156 senate seats and 401 seats in the lower houses—reflecting not only the strong party trend running in the Republicans' favor but the fact that reapportionment, by adding seats in suburban areas, was helping them as much as it helped the Democrats, if not more.

1967-68—The 90th Congress

	House	**Senate**
Democrats	248	64
Republicans	187	36

As of Jan. 10, 1967

THE United States in 1967-68 underwent two of the most trying years in its history as a rising wave of rioting and looting swept over its largely Negro central cities, the Vietnam war continued to build in human and dollar costs, inflationary pressures mounted and two major national leaders were assassinated. President Johnson, recognizing the inability of his Administration to command continued strong popular support, announced in March 1968 that he would not seek re-election to a second full term in the White House. A divided and confused nation finally selected Republican Richard M. Nixon as its next President in the 1968 general election; but Nixon's popular vote margin over Democrat Hubert H. Humphrey was a small one, and third-party contender George C. Wallace drew 13.5 percent of the national vote. The voters elected more Republicans to Governorships but registered a confused mandate by simultaneously maintaining strong Democratic majorities in both houses of Congress.

Congress in 1967

The year 1967 was largely one of stalemate in Congress—a result of frustrations over Vietnam and urban rioting and the substantial gain in U.S. House seats which the Republicans had registered in the 1966 elections. With the House Democratic margin down to 61 and many of the party's seats held by conservative Southerners, the House Democratic leadership appeared to be less effective than in previous years.

House Republicans, pointing to the enormous costs of the war and the "incongruity" of "rewarding" the ghetto rioters with new federal aid, set out to emasculate most aspects of the President's once widely hailed "Great Society" program. A substantial number of Southern Democrats aided the GOP in its House budget-paring.

The conservative coalition was less potent in the Senate, but that chamber too was immobilized for part of the session. It spent six weeks on leisurely debate on legislative reorganization and five weeks on see-saw arguments over repeal of Majority Whip Russell B. Long (La.) 1966 plan to finance Presidential election campaigns. In the end, the Long plan was suspended and never tried in an actual election campaign.

Although President Johnson's requests were modest in comparison to those of the previous three sessions, few Administration bills except Vietnam war appropriations moved through Congress unscathed. Mr. Johnson's major legislative proposal—an income tax surcharge to pay for the war and fight domestic inflation—never moved out of House committee in 1967. A civil rights package fared little better. In addition, funds for existing programs—such as foreign aid, model cities, rent supplements and the Teacher Corps—were scaled back drastically from the President's requests.

The President also suffered major setbacks in 1967 on draft reform, highway beautification, a new anti-crime package including a federal gun-control law, a truth-in-lending bill, pipeline safety, mutual funds regulation, rural development aid, East-West trade, authority to sell arms to underdeveloped countries and a number of other proposals. His only impressive victories came in Senate ratification of the outer space and U.S.-Soviet consular treaties, approval of a nongovernmental corporation to improve educational radio and television programming, legislation to strengthen meat inspection requirements and increase postal rates, and boosts of federal civilian and military pay.

More qualified Administration victories could be claimed for enactment of the Social Security and anti-poverty bills. The first carried welfare restrictions the Administration objected to, while poverty funds were cut below the requested level. Assessing the record of the 1967 session, President Johnson Nov. 9 blamed the "old coalition of stand-patters and nay-sayers" for his domestic defeats. The session, which began Jan. 10, did not adjourn until Dec. 15.

Outside of specific legislation, the most significant action of the first session of the 90th Congress was in disciplining two Members—Harlem's Rep. Adam C. Powell (D), chairman of the House Education and Labor Committee from 1961 to 1967, and Connecticut's Sen. Thomas J. Dodd (D). Both men, in the eyes of their colleagues, had stepped beyond the bounds of acceptable ethical conduct for Members of Congress.

By far the more harsh treatment was dealt Powell, who was excluded from membership in the 90th Congress. Powell was charged with misappropriation of Education and Labor Committee funds and other im-

Governor Party Control		
Following elections of	**Democrats**	**Republicans**
1946	23	25
1948	30	18
1950	23	25
1952	18	30
1954	27	21
1956	28	20
1958	35	14
1960	34	16
1962	34	16
1964	33	17
1966	25	25
1968 [1]	19	31

[1] *The Republican total includes Gov. Agnew of Maryland who was elected Vice President. Following his resignation, a Democrat was elected by the state legislature to succeed him, making the new lineup: Democrats 20; Republicans 30.*

proprieties. One of the seven Negroes elected to the 90th Congress, Powell had won respect as an effective legislator over his years in the House but was also a flamboyant, controversial figure. He was involved in court cases concerning income tax evasion and libel, was a vocal exponent of "black power", made numerous trips at Government expense, and employed his wife as a $20,578-a-year clerk while she lived in Puerto Rico. Powell's high-handed conduct of Education and Labor Committee business in the 89th Congress offended many of his colleagues, and a special House Administration subcommittee issued a report early in 1967 criticizing Powell for mishandling committee funds for travel and pay of his wife for no work. Meeting Jan. 9, the Democratic Caucus deposed Powell as committee chairman; then the House Jan. 10 denied Powell his seat pending investigation by a Select Committee. The Select Committee Feb. 23 recommended that Powell be seated but censured for "gross misconduct." It also recommended stripping him of his seniority and levying a $40,000 fine—punishments never before prescribed for a Member of Congress. The Committee held that because Powell met constitutional requirements of age, residence and citizenship, he could not be excluded from the House.

Approval of the Select Committee report was widely predicted, but the House was in an angry mood and March 1 voted 307-116 to exclude Powell from membership altogether. A new election was called in Powell's district, and he was re-elected with 86.1 percent of the vote. But he did not apply to the House to be seated, remaining instead at his vacation retreat on Bimini Island in the Bahamas while his lawyers pushed a law case challenging the legality of the exclusive action by the House. (The suit was dismissed by lower federal courts but accepted by the U.S. Supreme Court on appeal late in 1968.)

In the wake of its action on the Powell case, the House in April 1967 established a 12-man Committee on Standards of Official Conduct which wrote a limited code of ethics approved by the House the following year.

Dodd was censured by a 92-5 roll-call vote of the Senate June 23, 1967, on a charge of spending money he raised at political affairs to pay his personal bills.

The action made Dodd the seventh Member in the history of the Senate to suffer official censure. The censure resolution said Dodd was guilty of "conduct which is contrary to accepted morals, derogates from the public trust expected of a Senator, and tends to bring the Senate into dishonor and disrepute."

The nine-day Senate debate on the censure resolution probed deeply into ethical issues such as political spending, fund solicitation and the need for explicit guides to the conduct of Senators and Senate employees. Dodd's censure was recommended by the Senate Select Committee on Standards and Conduct following a 14-month investigation. The Committee recommended censure of Dodd on two counts—using for personal purposes $116,083 of $450,273 he raised at testimonial and campaign events, and billing both the Senate and private groups for numerous trips he had taken. The Senate agreed to censure Dodd on the improper use of campaign funds but struck the charge of double-billing from the censure resolution, apparently feeling the evidence was inconclusive. Charges against Dodd had first been undertaken on the basis of a wide series of allegations in syndicated newspaper columns by Drew Pearson and Jack Anderson.

Like the House, the Senate followed up its action with 1968 approval of rules of ethical conduct including private disclosure of Members' personal finances.

The Senate Ethics Committee also investigated charges by *Life* magazine against Sen. Edward V. Long (D Mo.) that he had misused his position as chairman of a Judiciary Committee investigating subcommittee and improperly accepted legal referral fees from an attorney representing Teamster Union President James R. Hoffa. The Committee reported late in 1967, however, that it found no evidence to support the charges. But *Life* maintained its criticism and Long was defeated for renomination in the 1968 Missouri Democratic primary.

In a related development in the ethics field, Robert G. (Bobby) Baker, former secretary to the Senate Majority, was convicted Jan. 29, 1967, in U.S. District Court in Washington on charges of income tax evasion, theft and conspiracy to defraud the Government.

Vietnam

The Vietnam war became an increasingly troublesome problem for the United States in 1967-68. It often overshadowed civil rights and city problems, distorted the U.S. economy and loomed over U.S. foreign policy. Its cost soared to more than $2 billion a month; reflecting the expense of the war, the federal budget by fiscal 1969 was at a record $186 billion, with $80 billion of that for defense.

During 1967, American leaders still spoke optimistically of a successful conclusion to the war in the foreseeable future. The appearance of growing stability in South Vietnam was reinforced by the country's ability to hold democratic elections in September 1967, elections in which Chief of State Nguyen Van Thieu was chosen President and Premier Nguyen Cao Ky was elected Vice President. But the U.S. troop commitment escalated steadily; by the end of 1967, almost 486,000 U.S. troops were involved in the struggle, fighting along side of 750,000 South Vietnamese and other allied troops.

The U.S. troop commitment rose to close to 535,500 late in 1968. The allied forces were opposed in South Vietnam by an estimated 240,000 enemy troops (North Vietnamese and the indigenous Vietcong), plus an equal number of political agents and active collaborators. Neither side seemed able to win a decisive military victory or to achieve a favorable position which would set apparent terms for negotiations.

The confidence of Americans in the U.S. military effort was shaken severely by the ability of the enemy, in the so-called Tet or February 1968 offensive, to stage spectacular attacks on the capitals of most of South Vietnam's 44 provinces, inflicting heavy damage on Saigon, Hue and other allied strongholds. And despite assertions of U.S. military leaders that the enemy was suffering heavy casualties, the U.S. casualty figures also mounted seriously. The total U.S. death figure since the start of the hostilities in 1961 was 6,664 in January 1967 but had risen to 30,614 by the end of 1968. The increasing human and financial costs of the war were brought home to the American people in a number of ways: regular television coverage of on-the-scene fighting in Vietnam; increasing waves of anti-war demonstrations by students and others at home; inflationary pressures and the 1968 tax surcharge; and the Presidential campaign bids of three Democrats strongly opposed to the U.S. role in Vietnam—Sens. Eugene J. McCarthy (Minn.), Robert F. Kennedy (N.Y.) and George S. McGovern (S.D.).

The first indication of U.S. readiness to de-escalate the conflict came March 31, 1968, when President Johnson—in the same speech in which he announced he would not run for re-election—said that he would order a limited bombing halt of North Vietnam. Formal talks between the United States and North Vietnam began May 13 in Paris, but were stalemated for several months by the demand of the North Vietnamese that the United States unconditionally halt the bombing of the North as a precondition to substantive peace discussions. The United States insisted that the North Vietnamese promise reciprocal restraint.

Hopes for a political settlement were bouyed Oct. 31 when President Johnson announced he was ordering a complete halt to all American bombing of the North. Though not officially confirmed, it was believed that the bombing halt was undertaken with tacit agreement that it would last only so long as the North Vietnamese did not use it to their military advantage. A new and complicated round of negotiations then began in Paris on the means and protocol for substantive peace negotiations with representatives of both the Saigon government and the National Liberation Front participating.

Civil Disorder

Racial discord in the nation's great cities, compounded by Negroes' dissatisfaction with poverty conditions in ghetto areas, led in 1967-68 to the worst urban rioting yet experienced by the nation in the 20th Century. In fact, violent actions by Negroes in the slums and ghettos of the great cities of the North eclipsed continuing civil rights efforts in the South and created reservoirs of white resentment which George Wallace would seek to exploit in the 1968 Presidential campaign.

Public concern over rioting in 1967 focused on two major riots, in Newark, N.J., and Detroit, Mich. The Newark riot, beginning July 12, 1967, when a Negro taxi driver was allegedly beaten by police, resulted in five days and six nights of disturbances which included sniper fire, arson and looting, and the death of 25 persons. Some 1,462 persons were arrested and the National Guard called in to help restore order. Underlying causes were seen in Newark's high unemployment rate and an acute shortage of housing for Negroes. Within a week of the subsidence of the Newark riot a more severe one broke out July 22 in Detroit; the riot in six days left 43 dead and at least 657 injured. There were over 7,000 arrests and property damage much greater than in any previous riot. More than 4,000 fires were set and there was extensive sniper fire. To bring the situation under control, federal troops were requested by Gov. George Romney (R) and ordered into the city by President Johnson—the first time regular troops had been requested by a Governor to restore civil order in 24 years—since 1943 race riots in Detroit.

While they were the most spectacular, Newark and Detroit were not the only cities hit by riots in the summer of 1967. Other disturbances occurred in such widely separated places as Atlanta, Birmingham, Chicago, San Francisco and scores of smaller cities across the country. Some 83 persons died; property damage exceeded $500 million. While Detroit still burned, President Johnson announced he was establishing a Special Advisory Commission on Civil Disorders to investigate the causes of urban riots and to recommend measures "to prevent or contain such disasters in the future." Illinois Gov. Otto Kerner (D) became the Commission chairman and New York Mayor John F. Lindsay (R) the vice chairman.

The Presidential Riot Commission, as it was popularly known, conducted intensive investigations in major cities across the nation and reported Feb. 29, 1968. The chief message of the report: that "white racism" had "long permeated much of American life" and could be identified as the deep, underlying cause of urban riots. The Commission said that discrimination and segregation and the lack of concern of "white America" with the problems of the Negro had created, over the years, an "explosive mixture" of poverty, unemployment, inadequate housing, poor education and ghetto life. "This is our basic conclusion," the Commission said. "Our nation is moving towards two societies, one black, one white—separate and unequal." The alternative to this polarization, the Commission indicated, was a "commitment to national action—compassionate, massive and sustained." It would be expensive, requiring "unprecedented levels of funding," but "the nation has substantial financial resources...in spite of a war and in spite of current budget requirements." The Commission avoided any specifics on how much its recommendations would cost, however, and there was little response in 1968 from a budget-minded Congress to Commission proposals for immense new federal efforts in the fields of employment, education, welfare and housing.

The Riot Commission stated unequivocally that the 1967 riots "were not caused by, nor were they the consequence of, any organized plan or conspiracy." But the Commission acknowledged that "militant organizations" and "individual agitators" created "an atmosphere that contributed to the outbreak of disorder."

Especially during 1967, there had been allegations that Stokely Carmichael, chairman and subsequently a field worker for the Student Non-Violent Coordinating Committee, and H. Rap Brown, his successor as SNCC chairman, had actually encouraged and abetted the rioting, and that Communist Party-USA or Chinese Communist influences had been present in the disorders. Carmichael spent the summer of 1967 abroad, traveling to England, Cuba and Hanoi. Brown toured Negro ghettoes, urging blacks to arm themselves, and, if necessary, to burn their ghettoes.

The patterns of violence in American life reasserted themselves soon after the report of the Riot Commission as two prominent Americans became victims of assassins' bullets. The first was the Rev. Dr. Martin Luther King Jr., 39, who was shot and killed April 4, 1968, in Memphis, Tenn., where he had gone to assist striking garbage workers. King was head of the Southern Christian Leadership Conference, an apostle of nonviolence in the civil rights revolution and the 1964 winner of the Nobel Peace Prize. Following his death, rioting, looting and burning broke out in Negro districts in more than 100 cities; 39 people died, arrests approached 20,000 and property damage exceeded $30 million. Among the worst-hit cities was the nation's capital, Washington, D.C. King was buried April 9 in Atlanta, Ga., his birthplace, after the largest funeral ever held for a private citizen in the United States. A white suspect, James Earl Ray, June 8 was arrested in London and charged with the crime, climaxing one of the largest manhunts in history. He was returned to Memphis for trial on murder charges.

On June 5, yet another apostle of social progress and reconciliation between the races was struck down. Leaving the Los Angeles hotel ballroom in which he had made his California Presidential primary victory statement, Sen. Robert F. Kennedy (D N.Y.), 42, was shot in the head; he died 25 hours later. The alleged assassin, Sirhan B. Sirhan, a native of Jordan, was apprehended at the scene.

Kennedy had been a leading liberal in the Senate. He was Attorney General (1961-64) during the Administration of his brother, President John F. Kennedy, who was assassinated in 1963. Kennedy was elected to the Senate in 1964. A third brother, Joseph P. Kennedy Jr., was killed in World War II. The last remaining brother was Sen. Edward M. Kennedy (D Mass.).

Robert Kennedy June 8 was buried in Arlington Cemetery next to the late President Kennedy.

The assassinations made the nation give new and serious thought to the violence which seemed to pervade its life—reflected not only in the killings of two national leaders and urban riots but in moves by student militants to seize buildings, imprison university officials and destroy property at dozens of campuses across the country and in August 1968 in repeated clashes between police and youths at the Democratic National Convention in Chicago.

Americans' reaction to violence in the nation varied sharply. Some elements of society expressed fear that the morality of the nation in general was breaking down. They condemned what they described as the "permissiveness" of American life, and traced that characteristic in part to the liberal decisions of the

Supreme Court. Another, and perhaps smaller, element of society traced the issue of crime and violence in part to the conditions of mass living which had developed in the nation's major cities. President Johnson was of this school of thought. While condemning crime and violence, he continued to urge broad programs to strike at what he considered the root of the problem—poverty, ghetto conditions, inadequate police protection and unsuccessful correctional systems.

In the wake of Kennedy's assassination, the President appointed a National Commission on the Causes and Prevention of Violence. In 1968 hearings, the Commission explored the history of violence in American life, the implications of congested living conditions, the tendencies of human beings toward violent behavior and the impact of the violence depicted on television and in other mass media.

The related problem of crime, highlighted by sharply increasing national crime rates, also received attention in 1967-68. In February 1967, the National Crime Commission (officially the President's Commission on Law Enforcement and Administration of Justice) submitted its historic report, the most exhaustive study of crime in over three decades. The Commission concluded that crime was a far more serious, far more prevalent and more complicated problem than generally had been thought. It recommended broad and concerted action at all levels of government and private endeavor, including a multi-million dollar federal aid program to update state and local police departments. (The Federal Bureau of Investigation Aug. 26, 1968, reported that more than 3.8 million serious crimes had been committed in 1967, 16 percent over the 1966 level. There was a marked increase in the use of firearms in crimes of violence.)

Perhaps the only hopeful sign of the 1967-68 period was an indication by late 1968 that the crest of urban rioting might have passed; after the outbreaks in the wake of Dr. King's assassination, relatively few serious outbreaks were reported in 1968 in the chief problem areas—the nation's inner cities where Negroes were coming to represent a constantly greater percentage of the population.

Congress in 1968

Congress was in a conservative mood in 1968, preoccupied chiefly with inflation and crime and disorders in the streets and on the campuses. Yet this same session of Congress enacted a landmark housing and urban development bill and approved a remarkably strong civil rights law, prohibiting discrimination in most of the nation's housing.

Economy was a key issue as the nation continued its heavy commitment in Vietnam, the fiscal 1968 federal Budget deficit reached $25 billion, and the cost of living rose more sharply than in previous years. The Johnson Administration continued to press for the 10 percent income tax surcharge which it had vainly sought in 1967, and in 1968 it finally won Congressional approval—but only after agreeing to a spending ceiling in fiscal 1969 which would require cuts of $6 billion in estimated 1969 expenditures. To get the tax surcharge, the President had to agree not only to the spending ceiling but to limitations in federal employment—both steps he had

earlier warned would "really bring chaos into the Government."

The 1968 Congressional session was the last under the Johnson Administration. It was marked by some legislative victories for the President, a number of compromises and a stinging personal defeat in the Senate's refusal to consider Mr. Johnson's nomination of Supreme Court Associate Justice Abe Fortas, a close friend of the President, to be Chief Justice of the United States. Opposition to the Fortas nomination, led by Sen. Robert P. Griffin (R Mich.), was based primarily on allegations of "cronyism" and charges that Fortas had, as Associate Justice, continued to play a role in White House affairs and helped draft legislation. Both in hearings and Senate floor debate, however, it was clear that liberal Supreme Court decisions, especially in the fields of criminal procedural law and obscenity, had roused the ire of many Senators and that Fortas was a convenient target for their frustrations. Chief Justice Earl Warren June 13 had informed President Johnson of his intention to retire, contingent upon qualification of a successor. The President nominated Fortas June 26, but it was not until Oct. 1 that the conclusive Senate vote—45-43 on a motion to invoke cloture, requiring two-thirds approval—was taken, indicating that the appointment was dead. President Johnson did not make a substitute appointment, and it was later revealed that Warren had agreed with President-elect Nixon to remain in office until the end of the 1968-69 Supreme Court winter term.

The major housing bill passed by Congress in 1968 was not only a victory for the Administration but for Republicans as well because of its new emphasis on involving the private sector in alleviating the cities' problems. The bill contained a number of provisions designed to encourage industry and non-profit groups to build or rehabilitate low- and moderate-income housing. The bill also included a new program to encourage home ownership among lower income families by providing federal subsidies of mortgage payments. Other provisions of the bill were designed to make property insurance available in ghetto areas and to provide Federal Housing Administration mortgage insurance in borderline neighborhoods.

Even the sponsors of open housing legislation were surprised by their success in 1968. The provisions of the 1968 civil rights bill forbade discrimination in the sale or rental of housing, with 80 percent of all sales or rentals in the United States to be covered by 1970. Some supporters said that the way had been opened for open housing by recognition of the clear relationship between housing and riots, the growing importance of the Negro in U.S. politics and the bipartisan nature of the open housing effort.

Other major successes for the Johnson Administration included a strong truth-in-lending law and a group of conservation measures. Several health and education programs, many of which originated during the Johnson Administration, were extended and expanded with little controversy. Congress also indicated its acceptance of several of the President's programs which initially had been controversial, moving in 1968 to vote increased appropriations. Among the programs benefitting from the new mood were the poverty program, the Teacher Corps, model cities and rent supplements.

The crime and gun control bills passed by Congress in 1968 were a mixed victory for the President. The gun legislation, which prohibited most interstate sales of firearms, was much stronger than it had appeared possible to get through Congress at the beginning of the year. But even in the wake of the King and Kennedy assassinations, Congress rejected stronger provisions for gun registration and owner licensing. The crime bill, which had been proposed by the President to strengthen local law enforcement, became the vehicle for other crime provisions attacking Supreme Court decisions and permitting the use of wiretapping, proposals opposed by the Administration. The crime bill provided a vehicle for one of the Republicans' first successful attempts to incorporate the block grant principle in federal aid. (The bill was rewritten, on the Republicans' suggestion, to provide block grants to the states to be distributed among local law enforcement agencies rather than direct federal grants to local agencies, thus limiting federal power over the program.)

Foreign aid was one of the major areas in which Congress cut back on previous spending levels; the $1.8 billion voted for aid was the lowest in the 20-year history of the program.

A nuclear nonproliferation treaty, considered by President Johnson to be one of the great foreign policy accomplishments of his Administration, was delayed in being considered by the Senate in spite of Presidential pressure for action. Opposition to early ratification was brought on by the Soviet invasion of Czechoslovakia in August 1968.

Other Foreign Developments

Important international developments in the 1967-68 period included:

• Lightning victory by Israel in war with Arab states, beginning June 5, 1967. Egyptian President Nasser had threatened extinction of Israel but instead saw his United Arab Republic suffer staggering losses, relinquishing all of the Sinai Peninsula and the Gaza strip and suffering major losses of aircraft. Israel also took the Old City of Jerusalem, occupied by Jordan since the 1948-49 Arab-Israeli war. After the 1967 hostilities, Israel declared she would hold her gains, and did so, though the Soviet Union quickly began rearming the defeated Arab powers.

• U.S.-U.S.S.R. Summit Conference. President Johnson and Soviet Premier Alexei N. Kosygin met for personal discussion of major world issues June 23-24, 1967, in Glassboro, N.J., concentrating on the then-heated Mideast crisis (which had brought Kosygin to United Nations debates in New York), on Vietnam and on nuclear weapons proliferation.

• Seizure of Pueblo. The U.S. Navy electronic surveillance ship Pueblo and its 83-man crew were captured Jan. 23, 1968, in the Sea of Japan by patrol boats of North Korea and taken prisoner. North Koreans claimed the vessel has violated the 12-mile limit of its territorial waters. Prolonged negotiations finally resulted in the freeing of the crew two days before Christmas 1968, but North Korea did not release the ship itself.

• Gold Crisis. Intermittent panic buying hit international gold markets during 1968 as fears mounted that the U.S. would be unable to maintain the $35-an-ounce price for gold.

• Chaos in France. A massive wave of civil and economic disobedience broke over France in May 1968, sparked by student protests against the government. At one point, the economic and transportation system of the country had come virtually to a standstill. But in special June elections, backers of President Charles de Gaulle emerged triumphant.

• Birth Control Ban. Pope Paul VI of the Roman Catholic Church July 25, 1968, issued an encyclical condemning all methods of birth control except rhythm as against the will of God. Storms of protest soon rose within and without the Church, with indications that millions of Catholics would disregard the Papal instructions.

• Czechoslovakia. The most wide-ranging move toward political and economic liberalization in Eastern Europe since World War II developed in Czechoslovakia, only to be choked off by physical invasion of the land by hundreds of thousands of Soviet troops in late August 1968. The unified and outraged Czech people staged massive nonviolent demonstrations in protest, and the Soviets were roundly attacked throughout the world for their repressive move. Eventually, Czech Communist Party First Secretary Alexander Dubcek, leader of his country's renaissance, was allowed to stay in power but his government had to agree to re-establishment of stiff controls over the press and radio to discontinuance of plans for a multi-party system.

Other Domestic Events

Other important domestic events included:

• 25th Amendment. Precise procedures to be followed in the event of a Presidential disability were spelled out in the Constitution for the first time in American history with final ratification Feb. 10, 1967, of the 25th Amendment. The amendment also stipulated that whenever the office of Vice President became vacant, the President could appoint a new Vice President, subject to approval by Congress.

• NSA-CIA controversy. The National Student Assn. early in 1967 acknowledged that it had received more than $3 million between 1952 and 1966 from foundations that acted as conduits for funds from the Central Intelligence Agency. The NSA used the money to send representatives to student congresses, to finance exchange students and provide counseling and technical help in educational seminars—in order to balance, defenders of the funds said, heavy governmental moneys invested by the Soviets in international student affairs. Critics accused the CIA of using taxpayers' money to influence policies of allegedly independent student groups.

• D.C. Reform Plan. Washington, D.C., made a step toward more efficient and responsive government if not home rule when President Johnson submitted a reorganization plan eliminating the archaic three-commissioner form of government in use since the late 19th Century, substituting a single chief executive for the city with a nine-member city council, all nominated by the President and subject to confirmation by the Senate. The reorganization plan went into effect Aug. 11,

1967, after a disapproval resolution had failed in the House, 160-244. As first commissioner—or mayor, as he quickly became known—Johnson named Walter E. Washington, former head of the city's public housing authority and a respected Negro leader. (Early in 1969, President Nixon named Washington to a full four-year term.)

● **Heart Transplants.** The first heart transplant in human history was performed Dec. 3, 1967, in South Africa, quickly followed by numerous heart transplants in the United States as well.

● **Student Protests and Violence.** Dissatisfaction among university students over administration of the nation's institutions of higher learning led to widespread campus demonstrations and disorders in the spring of 1968. The most spectacular unrest hit Columbia University in New York City, where a left-wing student protest burgeoned into a major upheaval marked by student takeovers of many university buildings, bloody clashes with the police and virtual paralysis of one of the nation's top educational institutions. Original cause of the student protest was opposition to Columbia's construction of a gymnasium in neighboring Morningside Park, a move strongly opposed by Negroes in nearby Harlem. The students also opposed Columbia's ties with the Institute of Defense Analyses and the entire national military-industrial complex. Eventually it became clear, however, that the goal of protesting groups like the Students for a Democratic Society was nothing less than total subversion of the existing institutions of society, both within the universities and without. Another issue in disorders on other campuses was the demand of Negro students that institutes to teach black history and culture be established within the universities. Most protesting student groups were vociferously opposed to U.S. participation in the Vietnam war.

● **Poor People's Campaign.** Before his assassination, the Rev. Martin Luther King had planned a massive springtime demonstration in Washington, D.C., to dramatize the plight of 29 million poor Negroes, Mexican-Americans, Indians and other whites. King's successor as leader of the Southern Christian Leadership Conference, the Rev. Ralph D. Abernathy, continued plans for the campaign and early in May 1968 thousands of demonstrators began to arrive in the capital and set up a temporary "Resurrection City" of wooden huts in West Potomac Park. Poor management, bad weather and irresponsible actions by some young blacks afflicted "Resurrection City" from its inception, however. The most solid commitment the demonstrators won from the Government was an agreement by Agriculture Secretary Orville L. Freeman to expand the Department's food distribution plan for the needy. Early in June, tens of thousands of sympathizers assembled in the city for a massive demonstration at the Lincoln Memorial to back the protesters, but the turnout failed to match that of the 1963 march on Washington by civil rights advocates. A few days after the mass demonstration, the Federal Government closed down the campsite and Abernathy was arrested with others for an illegal demonstration on the Capitol grounds. Congress appeared to react with more hostility than sympathy to the Poor People's Campaign.

Space Exploration

The 1967-68 period for the U.S. space program began in tragedy and ended in one of the great scientific triumphs of all time.

Tragedy struck in January 1967, when the three U.S. astronauts who were scheduled to fly the first Apollo spaceship into orbit were killed by a flash fire in the spaceship during a training session at Cape Kennedy. Killed in the fire, which took place 218 feet above Cape Kennedy's Launch Complex 34 in the Apollo capsule atop an unfueled two-stage Saturn-1 rocket, were: Air Force Lt. Col. Virgil I. (Gus) Grissom, 40; Air Force Lt. Col. Edward H. White 2nd, 36; and Lt. Commander Roger B. Chaffee, 31.

The Soviet Union's space program also encountered tragedy when 40-year old Cosmonaut Col. Vladimir Komarov died April 24 in a crash of a new Soviet spaceship he was testing. The vehicle, Soyuz I, apparently encountered control difficulties with dangerous tumbling during its 18 orbits of the earth; Komarov was able to return the ship to earth, but the ship's parachute lines became tangled on re-entry, followed by the fatal crash.

In October 1968, both the U.S. and U.S.S.R. scored vital breakthroughs with their advanced space programs. The first manned Apollo flight, number 7, began Oct. 11 with three astronauts aboard for a successful 163-orbit flight around the earth. Fifteen days later, the Soviets made their first manned flight since Komarov's death.

Finally, at Christmas 1968, the United States succeeded for the first time in human history in sending men away from the gravitational pull of the earth. In a six-day mission, three U.S. astronauts circled the moon 10 times at altitudes as low as 70 miles, photographing its surface and beaming live television images back to earth. The three U.S. space explorers—Air Force Col. Frank Borman, Navy Capt. James A. Lovell and Air Force Maj. William A. Anders—returned to earth for a successful splashdown Dec. 27, providing a happy ending to one of America's most difficult years at home.

The spectacular success of the moon orbiting mission gave the U.S. an apparent commanding lead in the race with the Soviet Union to put a man on the surface of the moon; it appeared at the end of 1968 that President Kennedy's 1961 challenge to put a man on the moon within the decade would be fulfilled in 1969.

Election Contests of 1967

A variety of political trends, some potentially significant for the future of U.S. politics, emerged from the 1967 off-year elections for state and municipal office throughout the United States:

● In Cleveland, Ohio, and in Gary, Ind., Negroes were elected mayors for the first time. The winner in Cleveland was state Rep. Carl B. Stokes (D), 40, who narrowly defeated Seth C. Taft (R) to become the first popularly elected Negro mayor of a major U.S. city. In Gary, the winner was City Councilman Richard Hatcher (D), 34, who also won by a narrow margin. Both Stokes and Hatcher expected and received an almost solid Negro vote but achieved victory through the additional support of a minority of whites. Both men bucked the regular Democratic organization to win nomination, but while Stokes received at least pro-forma organization support in the general election, Hatcher's victory climaxed a bitter campaign in which his candidacy was repudiated by the long-dominant local Democratic party, traditionally controlled by descendants of East European ethnic groups hostile to Negro advances.

• The widely heralded "white backlash" vote of the year also proved to have its limitations in Boston, where Mrs. Louise Day Hicks, who based her mayoral campaign on opposition to school busing, was defeated by Massachusetts Secretary of State Kevin H. White. (Boston elections are technically nonpartisan but both White and Mrs. Hicks were Democrats.)

• In Kentucky and New Jersey, the Republican party scored major victories. The GOP's Louie B. Nunn, 43, rode a strong tide of discontent with Democratic administrations in Washington and Frankfort to become Kentucky's first Republican Governor in a quarter century. His election over Henry Ward (D) gave the Republicans a majority of the 50 state Governorships (26 to 24) for the first time since 1954. In New Jersey, Democrats were dislodged from overwhelming control of the Legislature and discovered that Republicans would outnumber them 3-1 for the next two years. In both Kentucky and New Jersey, Republicans claimed that the vote for them represented a repudiation of the Johnson Administration and could be seen as a prelude to the 1968 Presidential election.

• In Mississippi, a Republican who appealed for a new spirit of reason in race relations was overwhelmed by an all-out segregationist Democrat in the contest for Governor. The loser was Rubel Phillips (R), the winner U.S. Rep. John Bell Williams (D), who had been stripped of his seniority in the House in 1965 because he openly supported Barry Goldwater for President the year before. In the Louisiana Democratic primary for Governor, however, U.S. Rep. John R. Rarick (D), a fiery segregationist, was swamped by incumbent Gov. John J. McKeithen (D), 49, who had steered a middle course on race relations in his first term in office. (McKeithen subsequently defeated a Republican opponent in the Feb. 6, 1968, general election.)

• Republicans scored some victories in scattered mayor contests, including Hartford, Conn., Indianapolis, Ind., and Akron, Ohio. But they were disappointed in two major efforts to oust entrenched Democratic administrations in Philadelphia (the nation's fourth largest city) and in San Francisco (a technically nonpartisan election). The GOP lost the mayor's office in Baltimore which it had won in 1963.

• An historic $2.5 billion transportation bond issue, the largest ever proposed on a state level, was approved in New York. On the other hand, a proposed new constitution opposed by most civic groups in the state but backed by the Roman Catholic hierarchy was rejected in New York because of provisions that would have freed state aid for religious schools.

• In a Dec. 12 special election in California's 11th Congressional District (San Mateo County), Paul N. McCloskey (R), 40, an attorney, scored an easy victory over Democratic opposition to win the seat of a deceased Republican. Major interest had centered on the preliminary election Nov. 14, in which McCloskey had run ahead of nine other candidates, including Mrs. Shirley Temple Black (R), 39, the former child movie star. McCloskey campaigned as a "dove" on Vietnam, Mrs. Black as a "hawk."

• Earlier in 1967, Democrats maintained their control in Rhode Island's 2nd District (West—Part of Providence, Cranston, Warwick), as Democratic state Sen. Robert O. Tiernan (D), 38, narrowly edged Cranston Mayor James DiPrete Jr. (R), 39, a close political ally of liberal Gov. John H. Chafee (R). The contest was for the seat of veteran Rep. John E. Fogarty (D 1941-67), who died on the opening day of the 90th Congress.

The 1968 Elections

Few Presidential election years in the history of the nation brought as many surprising developments as 1968. Just a year before the election, it appeared likely that the two candidates might be President Johnson for the Democrats and Michigan's Gov. George W. Romney for the Republicans. But by late winter 1968, both Johnson and Romney were out of the picture and each of the major parties were plunged into spirited fights for their Presidential nominations. During 1968, continued racial tensions in the nation led to fears that Alabama's former Gov. George C. Wallace, running as the candidate of his own American Independent Party, might win a major share of the national vote or at least cause deadlock in the electoral college. In the end, Wallace's vote fell below expectations and he failed to cause a deadlock. Finally, the general belief that the Republicans' eventual nominee, former Vice President Richard M. Nixon, would win a landslide victory in the general election, was proven incorrect as incumbent Vice President Hubert H. Humphrey came close to staging what would have been one of the most spectacular political upsets of the century.

Democratic Nomination Fight

For the Democrats, the year of surprises began Nov. 30, 1967, when Minnesota's Eugene McCarthy, a quiet intellectual deeply opposed to the Administration's course in the Vietnam war, announced that he would enter four 1968 Presidential primaries to demonstrate opposition to the Johnson policies. McCarthy's candidacy struck an immediate chord of response, especially among younger Americans who shared his fervent distaste for the war in Vietnam. Most political observers discounted the seriousness of McCarthy's candidacy, but in the March 12 Presidential primary in New Hampshire, McCarthy scored an amazing "moral" victory by gathering 42 percent of the vote against the President's 49 percent.

The McCarthy vote in New Hampshire then triggered another major surprise: the entry of Robert Kennedy into the Democratic Presidential race, announced March 16. And on March 31, President Johnson stunned the nation by announcing, at the end of a lengthy radio and television address on Vietnam policy, that he would not seek re-election in 1968.

After the Johnson withdrawal, the race for the Democratic nomination turned into a three-way affair— McCarthy, Kennedy, and Vice President Humphrey, who entered the fray April 27. Whether by accident or design, the Humphrey announcement came too late for him to enter any of the Presidential primaries.

McCarthy marched on to an April 2 victory in Wisconsin, where Kennedy did not oppose him and the President's candidacy was already discounted because of his withdrawal. In the first direct McCarthy-Kennedy contest, May 7 in Indiana, Kennedy emerged as the clear winner with favorite-son Gov. Roger D. Branigin, considered by many a stalking horse for Humphrey, running third. On May 14, Kennedy upset McCarthy in a two-way race in Nebraska, but on May 28 McCarthy bounced back to defeat Kennedy in Oregon—the first defeat for a Kennedy since John F. Kennedy's first entry into Massachusetts politics in 1946. Finally, in the conclusive California primary June 4, Kennedy emerged the narrow victor over McCarthy—only to be assassinated as he left the hotel ballroom where he had claimed victory.

The death of Robert Kennedy, who had shared McCarthy's Vietnam views while taking a far more aggressive stance on urban and minorities' problems, was followed by an eerie moratorium in Democratic politics as the shaken party factions sought to decide on their next move. But within a few weeks, Humphrey emerged as the odds-on favorite for the nomination. Despite the unpopularity of the national Administration of which he was a part, Humphrey was able to win almost solid support from organized labor, the ruling circles in the big state Democratic organizations, and the South. McCarthy retained the enthusiastic backing of his youthful supporters and some of the most liberal circles within the party, but he lacked the personal stature or the political skill to win over the bulk of Kennedy's supporters or to cut into Humphrey's base of support in the Democratic establishment of the nation.

Democratic Convention

While violence flared in the city streets and thousands of police and guards imposed security precautions unprecedented in the annals of American Presidential conventions, the 35th quadrennial Democratic National Convention met Aug. 26-29 in Chicago to nominate Hubert Horatio Humphrey of Minnesota for the Presidency and to endorse the controversial Vietnam policies of the Johnson-Humphrey Administration.

In Humphrey, the Democrats chose a 57-year-old man with 23 years' seasoning in municipal and national government, an ebullient, optimistic liberal on domestic policy who had given almost complete support to Administration foreign policy in his four years as Vice President. The only real potential threat to Humphrey's nomination at the convention had come in an abortive boomlet for Sen. Edward M. Kennedy (D Mass.), 36, brother of the slain brothers John and Robert. Three days before the Convention opened, California House Speaker Jesse Unruh began to move for Kennedy and it appeared possible that Chicago's Mayor Richard J. Daley might join him. But the balloon was pricked the morning of Aug. 28 when Kennedy asked his backers to "cease all activity on my behalf."

Humphrey's selection as a Vice Presidential running mate was Maine's Sen. Edmund S. Muskie, 54, the father of the modern Democratic revival in Maine, a respected Senator and former Governor, whose views on policy at home and abroad almost exactly paralleled Humphrey's. In the subsequent campaign, Muskie's

---

Nixon Advisers—1968

Nixon's key staff and aides in the 1968 campaign:

John N. Mitchell, N.Y.—National campaign manager.

H.R. (Bob) Haldeman, Calif.—Chief of staff for Nixon campaign.

Herbert G. Klein, Calif.—Manager of communications (including press).

Leonard Garment, N.Y.—Chief talent scout and organization "trouble shooter."

Peter M. Flanigan, N.Y.—Deputy campaign manager.

Robert F. Ellsworth, Kan.—National political director.

Maurice H. Stans, N.Y.—Chairman, Republican National Finance Committee.

Frank Shakespeare, N.Y.—In charge of television productions.

Charles S. Rhyne, D.C.—National chairman of United Citizens for Nixon-Agnew.

Ray C. Bliss, Ohio—Chairman, Republican National Committee.

Mrs. Patricia R. Hitt, Calif., national co-chairman of Nixon-Agnew Campaign Committee.

Richard G. Kleindienst, Ariz.—Liaison between Nixon campaign organization and Republican National Committee.

Robert H. Finch, Calif.—Key adviser; the Lieutenant Governor of California.

Raymond K. Price, Patrick J. Buchanan, William Safire, William F. Gavin—Principal speechwriters.

Charles K. McWhorter, N.Y., and Dwight Chapin, N.Y.—Campaign trip political specialists.

John Ehrlichman, N.Y.—Tour manager.

---

calm-voiced appeals for understanding between the groups in American society would prove a distinct asset for the Democratic ticket.

Twin themes—physical force to keep order and political force to overrule minority sentiment within the Democratic party—were apparent throughout the Convention.

The physical force, exerted by police under the direction of Chicago Mayor Richard J. Daley, miscellaneous local and federal agents and finally the National Guard, was exerted to keep vociferous Vietnam war critics ranging from collegians and clergymen to hippies and yippies away from the downtown headquarters hotels of the Convention and the International Amphitheatre where official sessions were held. A security ring several blocks wide guarded the Amphitheatre, itself surrounded by a barbed wire fence and multiple security checkpoints for entering delegates, newsmen and guests. No violence erupted in the Amphitheatre area, but there were days of bitter demonstrations in the area of the downtown hotels which ended with repeated police use of tear gas and indiscriminate police attacks on demonstrators and on innocent bystanders alike.

The political force was exerted by the Johnson Administration forces which rallied behind Humphrey;

the Vice President's supporters enjoyed clear control of Convention proceedings from start to end. In a distinct minority were the antiwar factions which rallied around the candidacies of Sens. McCarthy and George S. McGovern (S.D.). The McCarthy forces mounted a series of challenges to the Humphrey faction—on credentials, rules, the platform and finally the nomination itself. An unprecedented number of credentials—those of delegates from 17 states—were challenged, mostly by McCarthy supporters. In an historic move, endorsed by Humphrey and McCarthy, the Convention seated a new loyalist Democratic faction from Mississippi and unseated the delegation of the traditionally segregationist, ultra-conservative regular party. A compromise was forced between the old-line conservative Georgia Democrats and a liberal, fully integrated insurgent slate. On all other contests, regular delegations were seated.

McCarthy, McGovern and other liberal factions won their greatest breakthrough on Convention rules, obtaining abolition of a mandatory unit rule for the 1968 Convention and at every level of party activity leading up to and including the 1972 Convention. Many Humphrey-pledged delegates also backed the move. For the first time in recent party history, the functioning of party machinery at every level had been questioned.

Platform debate and negotiations were dominated by the deeply divisive issue of U.S. policy in Vietnam. At one point, it appeared Humphrey might assent to a plank calling for a halt in U.S. bombing of North Vietnam, but President Johnson reportedly sent personal instructions that the plank should back up Administration policy. Humphrey took a harder line leading to a three-hour Convention floor fight on the issue.

Minority Vietnam Plank Rejected. At issue was acceptance or rejection of a minority plank, drafted by a coalition of anti-war factions, which called for an immediate cessation of all bombing of North Vietnam and of the offensive search and destroy missions of American combat units, for a negotiated withdrawal of troops by opponents in the hostilities and for a negotiated coalition government that would include the Communists. The majority plank, written into the Platform, endorsed in clear terms the precepts of the Administration's Vietnam policy and supported a bombing halt only when it "would not endanger the lives of our troops in the field." On the crucial vote Aug. 28, the minority plank was rejected by a vote of 1,041-1/4 to 1,567-3/4. After the result was announced, members of the New York delegation and others slipped on black armbands and sang "We Shall Overcome." Some 350 people met at a downtown Chicago Hotel to plan the course of the "new party." John J. Gilligan, Democratic nominee for Senator in Ohio, said supporters of Administration Vietnam policy could no longer claim their opponents were a small minority of beatniks, hippies and draft-dodgers.

While the Vietnam platform vote marked the turning point of the Convention, an incident about 12 hours before, at 2:00 a.m., Wednesday morning, had shown the gulf between the factions within the party. The Convention managers had sought to force debate and vote on the Vietnam plank at that early morning hour, when most television viewers were already asleep. But in the maneuver, they almost lost control. Permanent Chairman Carl Albert (Okla.), in violation of Convention rules, refused to recognize a motion from a McCar-

thy backer to adjourn until later in the day. But a few minutes later, when the Convention could not be brought to order, Albert recognized a similar motion from Mayor Daley.

Wednesday evening, while nominations and balloting for President took place at the Amphitheatre, the worse violence of the Convention broke out downtown and television screens carried pictures of phalanxes of Chicago police advancing on demonstrators.

At the same time, hundreds of "Daley's people" from Chicago were brought into the galleries with apparently improper credentials. Some delegates, apparently refusing to show their credentials to the omnipresent security guards, were physically ejected from the Convention floor. The McCarthy-McGovern forces charged "atrocities" and tried to adjourn the Convention for two weeks. Chairman Albert refused to accept their motions.

In addition to Humphrey, McCarthy and McGovern, only two other candidates were placed in nomination— the Rev. Channing E. Phillips (D.C.), a black favorite-son candidate, and North Carolina Gov. Dan K. Moore. Moore, however, withdrew before the end of the first ballot, although he received some votes. At 11:47 p.m., Pennsylvania gave Humphrey 103-3/4 votes to put him over the required 1,312 for the nomination. At the conclusion of the first ballot roll call, the vote was:

Humphrey	1,761-3/4	Kennedy, E.	12-3/4
McCarthy	601	Wallace, G.	1/2
McGovern	146-1/2	Bryant, Paul	1/2
Phillips	67-1/2	Gray, James H.	1/2
Moore	17-1/2		

Then, in a tumultuous ending to one of the wildest nights in American political history, Albert gavelled through a motion to make the nomination unanimous (despite major opposition on the floor) and adjourned the session. Humphrey had won his party's nomination, but he would lead a deeply and bitterly divided party into the autumn campaign.

At 4:34 p.m. the following afternoon, Aug. 29, Humphrey at a news conference announced his choice of Muskie to be his Vice Presidential running mate. Muskie was nominated at that night's Convention session by Sen. Fred R. Harris (D Okla.), who himself had been a major possibility for the Vice Presidential nomination. On the first ballot for Vice President, Muskie received 1,922-1/2 of the 2,622 votes.

Competition for GOP Nomination

By his overwhelming re-election win in Michigan in 1966, Gov. George Romney established himself as the early leader in the race for the 1968 Republican nomination. But Romney's liberalism was distasteful to many orthodox Republicans, and in 1967 Romney made the mistake of touring around the country making often contradictory statements on national issues (especially Vietnam), climaxed by a celebrated remark Sept. 5, 1967, that he had been "brainwashed" by U.S. authorities on a 1965 trip to Vietnam. Thus when Romney formally announced his Presidential bid the following Nov. 18, his candidacy was already under a heavy cloud.

Romney was followed into the GOP race by Nixon, who made his long-anticipated candidacy formal Feb. 1. The two frontrunners entered the New Hampshire Presidential primary, but it soon became apparent to Romney that he faced a likely loss and on Feb. 28 he surprised the nation by formally withdrawing from the contest for the nomination. Nixon went on to win an overwhelming victory in the March 12 New Hampshire GOP primary. Moderate and liberal Republicans hoped that New York's Gov. Nelson A. Rockefeller would step into the void created by Romney's withdrawal, but Rockefeller astonished the party by declaring March 21 that he would not run because "the majority of (Republican) leaders want the candidacy of Richard Nixon."

Without significant opposition, Nixon proceeded to sweep the Wisconsin, Indiana, Nebraska, Oregon and South Dakota primaries—in the process shedding most of the "loser" image he had acquired from his 1960 defeat for President and 1962 defeat for Governor of California. Rockefeller reversed his ground once again by entering the race April 30, but even in the primaries where write-ins were permitted, the vote for him was low. The sole exception was Massachusetts, where Rockefeller as a write-in defeated favorite son Gov. John A. Volpe.

Despite an intensive late-spring and early-summer campaign which carried him from one end of the nation to the other, Rockefeller was unable to make significant inroads in the huge blocs of Southern, Midwestern and Mountain states support for Nixon. Rockefeller pointed to public opinion polls showing he had a better chance than Nixon to defeat the Democrats in November, but the argument cut little ice with party regulars. Only in his native Northeast did Rockefeller score major gains, adding Pennsylvania and substantial New England support to his own New York.

After declaring early in the year that he would be a California "favorite son" but not seek delegates elsewhere, conservative Gov. Ronald Reagan moved toward a posture of increasingly positive candidacy as the Miami Beach Convention approached. Finally, on the day the Convention opened, Reagan announced as an avowed candidate. But except for some Deep South backing, he was unable to pick up any substantial out-of-state backing.

Republican National Convention

The 29th quadrennial National Convention of the Republican party, meeting in Miami Beach, Fla., Aug. 5-8, wrote a moderately progressive party platform and then chose candidates for President and Vice President who, at the moment of their selection, seemed to be taking increasingly restrictive attitudes on the sensitive national issues of law, order and civil rights.

For President, the party turned to Richard Milhous Nixon, 54, former U.S. Representative and Senator from California, Vice President of the United States from 1953 to 1961, unsuccessful Republican candidate for the Presidency in 1960, losing candidate for Governor of California in 1962, a New York City attorney and faithful party wheelhorse over two decades.

For Vice President, at Nixon's suggestion, the Republicans selected Spiro Theodore Agnew, 49, Governor of Maryland since his election in 1966, former Baltimore County executive (1962-66), who won election as Gov-

ernor in a normally Democratic border state by opposing a candidate who rode the "white backlash" issue. Since early 1968, however, Agnew had moved sharply to the right on race issues, lecturing moderate Negro leaders for irresponsibility following racial outbreaks in Baltimore and condemning the Poor People's Campaign in Washington, D.C.

Nixon's first-ballot nomination for the Presidency bore out the predictions of his smoothly functioning campaign organization, whose leaders had claimed for weeks that more than 700 of the 1,333 delegates were ready to support Nixon's candidacy.

At the nominating session Aug. 7, 12 names were placed in nomination: Reagan, Alaska Gov. Walter J. Hickel, Arkansas Gov. Winthrop Rockefeller, Romney (as a favorite son), Kansas Sen. Frank Carlson, Hawaii Sen. Hiram L. Fong, Rockefeller, Nixon, perennial candidate Harold E. Stassen, New Jersey Sen. Clifford P. Case, Ohio Gov. James A. Rhodes and South Carolina Sen. Strom Thurmond. Only Hickel and Thurmond withdrew before the start of the first ballot.

Alabama at 1:19 a.m. was the first state to cast its votes, giving Nixon 14, Reagan 12. At 1:50 a.m., Wisconsin gave all 50 of its votes to Nixon, placing him over the required 667 needed for nomination. The results of the first ballot before switches:

Nixon	692	Carlson	20
Rockefeller	277	W. Rockefeller	18
Reagan	182	Fong	14
Rhodes	55	Stassen	2
Romney	50	John V. Lindsay	1
Case	22		

After switches the vote totals were:
Nixon 1,238   Rockefeller 93   Reagan 2

A major reason for Nixon's successful comeback was doubtless the hundreds of campaign appearances he had made from coast to coast for Republican candidates over the preceding several years, creating a basis of goodwill that helped him win delegates in primary and non-primary states alike.

Perhaps most importantly, Nixon seemed to represent the middle ground of the Republican party of 1968 —substantially to the right of Governor Rockefeller, a liberal, whose on-again, off-again approach to the race undoubtedly damaged his chances, and well to the center of the road compared to the conservative Reagan, who advocated a stiff crackdown on agitators and rioters at home and strong military measures to bring a quick end to the war in Vietnam. The gaping ideological gulf between Rockefeller and Reagan made it difficult for them to agree on a common strategy to stop Nixon, even when Reagan abandoned his favorite-son status for active candidacy two days before the balloting.

Choice for Vice President

While in 1960 Nixon had selected as his running mate a man known for his liberal domestic views and wide foreign experience, Ambassador Henry Cabot Lodge, he decided to turn in 1968 to a man known for the newly conservative hue of his attitudes and for his experience in local and state government. In 1960, Nixon had suggested he would place Lodge in charge of U.S. foreign policy problems; in 1968, he suggested he would do the same with Agnew on the domestic front.

The selection of Agnew, one of the major surprises of the year, was announced by Nixon the morning after his own nomination, and in the wake of almost-solid all-night conferences with Republican leaders, chiefly those of a conservative bent. Liberal Republicans were outraged at Agnew's designation and a spontaneous effort developed on the Convention floor to nominate Romney for Vice President instead. But Agnew won in the balloting, 1,119 to 186.

Nixon's own campaign seemed to take a sharp tack to the right Aug. 6, when he told Southern delegations that he would not run an Administration which would "ram anything down your throats," that he opposed school busing, that he would appoint "strict constitutionalists" to the Supreme Court and that he was critical of federal intervention in local school board affairs.

By contrast, the Republican platform of 1968, adopted by the Convention Aug. 6 without a floor fight or any amendments, was generally moderate in tone and contained a preamble calling for major national effort to rebuild urban and rural slums and attack the root causes of poverty, including racism.

The platform did warn that "lawlessness is crumbling the foundations of American Society" and that violence would not be tolerated. A major floor fight on the platform was averted when resolutions committee members, led by Senate Minority Leader Everett McKinley Dirksen (Ill.), substituted for the originally drawn hard-line plank new language stressing the need for de-Americanization of both the military and civilian efforts in Vietnam. Both "hawks" and "doves" decided to go along with revised version.

Nixon Campaign

To conduct his second campaign for the Presidency, Nixon assembled a massive—and doubtless the best financed—campaign organization in U.S. history. Nixon was intent on avoiding the mistakes of his 1960 campaign, when a frenetic campaign pace, necessitated in part by his promise to visit all 50 states, resulted in exhaustion and snap decisions. So he paced himself carefully, limiting his number of hours campaigning each day, taking frequent rests in Florida, and leaving most campaign decisions with his managers, who functioned much like the management of a modern U.S. corporation. As a part of this approach, Nixon sought to convey the impression of Presidential dignity and demeanor in his personal appearances, reminding the nation that in 1952, by electing Gen. Eisenhower, it had also restored dignity to government and peace and stability on both the foreign and domestic fronts. Nixon generally avoided taking specific stands on key issues, avoiding most discussion of Vietnam policy, for instance, because he said he did not want to jeopardize the peace negotiations underway at Paris. The result was a campaign of calmness, dignity, efficiency, but not much color or interest.

Initially, the 1968 Nixon approach was spectacularly successful, carrying him to easy nomination on the first ballot at Miami Beach. And in mid-September, the Gallup Poll was showing Nixon the leader by a massive 12-point margin over Humphrey among the nation's voters. The figures: Nixon 43 percent, Humphrey 31 percent, Wallace 19 percent, Undecided 7 percent.

Humphrey Advisers—1968

Humphrey's key staff and aides in the 1968 campaign:

Lawrence F. O'Brien, Mass.—Campaign manager for Humphrey and Democratic National Chairman.

Sens. Fred R. Harris (Okla.) and Walter F. Mondale (Minn.)—Key advisers; were co-chairmen of Humphrey's pre-nomination campaign.

James H. Rowe Jr., D.C.—Adviser.

Orville L. Freeman, Minn.—Secretary of Agriculture, during campaign in charge of issues and scheduling division of Democratic National Committee.

W. Willard Wirtz, III—Secretary of Labor; adviser.

Max Kampelman, D.C.—Washington attorney, adviser.

John A. Gronouski, Wis.—Executive secretary of preconvention United Democrats for Humphrey.

George W. Ball, D.C.—Foreign affairs adviser; former U.S. Ambassador to United Nations.

Mrs. Geri Joseph, Minn.—Vice chairman, Democratic National Committee.

William Connell, Md.—Humphrey's executive assistant.

William B. Welsh, Va.—Humphrey's administrative assistant.

John Reilly and John G. Stewart—"Idea" men on foreign and domestic affairs respectively.

Ted Van Dyke—Humphrey aide, "executive officer" of campaign tour.

Terry Sanford, N.C.—Chairman of Citizens for Humphrey-Muskie; former Governor of North Carolina.

Robert E. Short, Minn.—Treasurer, Democratic National Committee.

From that point to election day, Nixon's share of the national vote remained almost static around 43 percent. But Humphrey gained steadily, cutting both into the Wallace and the undecided vote. By the weekend before the election, Gallup was showing 42 percent for Nixon, 40 percent for Humphrey, 14 percent for Wallace and 4 percent undecided. The Harris survey even reported Nov. 4 that Humphrey had forged into a 3-percent lead over Nixon. In the end, Nixon would win by less than a percentage point lead in the popular vote over Humphrey. And the question raised throughout the country was, why did the man who was originally so far in the lead almost lose the election of 1968?

Part of the answer doubtless lay in Humphrey's energetic campaign *(see below)*, but Nixon's own personality and decisions appeared to play a role as well. Basic voter uneasiness about Nixon, especially among independents and Democrats thinking of voting Republican, re-emerged in the campaign, stopping Nixon from picking up the extra support he needed for a solid victory. Secondly, Nixon's choice of Agnew as a Vice Presidential running mate encountered major public ridicule; the national joke immediately after Agnew's selection was "Spiro Who?"; Agnew's less than adroit campaign statements suggested Nixon may have made a major mistake. Finally, Nixon's refusal to debate with Humphrey on television appeared to detract from his popular image.

A central theme of Nixon's campaign, first spelled out in his well-received acceptance speech at the Republican National Convention, was an appeal to a group he called the "forgotten Americans" whom Nixon defined as "the non-shouters, the non-demonstrators, that are not racists or sick, that are not guilty of the crime that plagues the land," those who "work in America's factories, run America's business, serve in Government, provide most of the soldiers who died to keep us free." By suggesting that his Administration would look chiefly to the interest of this group, Nixon was able to make a strong bid for the support of white suburban and small-town America, traditional heartland of GOP strength in the nation. To solve center city ills, Nixon laid stress on the need for business to involve itself as sponsor and employer and said he believed in helping blacks set up their own businesses. But Nixon showed little interest in aggressive broadening of school desegregation and appeared reluctant in his acceptance of the 1968 open housing legislation approved by Congress.

On the campaign trail, Nixon accused Humphrey of being "tragically naive...about the nature of the crime crisis that grips America," and said that the Johnson Administration's war on poverty was "no substitute for a war on crime." He promised to wage a strong attack against "prowlers and muggers and marauders" in Washington, D.C., which he called "one of the crime capitals of the world." Nixon said he favored establishing a National Law Enforcement Council to coordinate federal policy on the control and prevention of crime. (Humphrey also had a long list of proposals to stem crime, but differed from Nixon in stressing that the major job had to be done by local police forces.)

For the most part, Nixon avoided direct attacks on Wallace, hoping to chip away at the Alabaman's strength, especially in the Southern border states. Nixon said that frustrated voters would be casting a vain ballot of protest in supporting Wallace, simultaneously helping Humphrey win election. Nixon's running mate, Agnew, made the toughest "law and order" speeches of the Republican campaign, frequently condemning yippies, hippies, black militants and other agitators. Agnew Sept. 10 charged that Humphrey had been "soft on inflation, soft on Communism and soft on law and order over the years." Under pressure from GOP Congressional leaders and others, Agnew subsequently withdrew the remark but remained the chief GOP critic of the Democrats' approaches to urban problems.

On other domestic issues, Nixon called for automatic increases in Social Security benefits to keep peace with rises in the cost of living and stressed his differences with Humphrey on repeal of the 27½ percent oil depletion allowance (Humphrey had in earlier years backed repeal, Nixon opposed) and repeal of Section 14(b) ("right-to-work" provision) of the Taft-Hartley Act (Humphrey for repeal, Nixon against). The status of the nation's defense systems came under public scrutiny as Nixon charged that a "gravely serious security gap" existed. Nixon said he did not believe "that parity with the Soviet Union is enough" and insisted instead that the U.S. should have "clear-cut military superiority" as a basis for any negotiations.

Humphrey Campaign

For Hubert Humphrey, the "Happy Warrior" of the Democrats' 1964 campaign, his own bid for the Presidency got off to a depressing start in September 1968 with sparse crowds, disordered schedules and vicious heckling by left-wing, anti-war elements virtually everywhere he sought to speak. Humphrey's first task was to establish some measure of independence from the vastly unpopular Johnson Administration, a step he sought to take Aug. 30 when he told the newly formed Democratic National Committee that "I'm the captain of the team— I'm supposed to call the signals." But Humphrey's really significant step to win some of the anti-war Democrats to his side came in a Sept. 30 nationally televised address from Salt Lake City, when he said he would stop the bombing of North Vietnam "as an acceptable risk for peace." When President Johnson actually took that step Oct. 31, Humphrey could hardly restrain his glee; the combination of his own softened stand and the Presidential position won him, at least at the last moment, the support of many of the Democrats who had been most disaffected at Chicago.

The other element in Humphrey's comeback during the campaign was his own indomitable spirit, even in the face of gloomy poll results and heckling on the road. Gradually even Humphrey's antagonists developed a grudging respect for his ability to perform under adverse circumstances, and the Humphrey underdog status contrasted sharply with the cool, confident complexion of the Nixon campaign.

Humphrey endorsed virtually all the social advances of the Kennedy-Johnson years but called for a substantial broadening of domestic efforts to meet minorities and city problems. He charged that Nixon's economic policies would bring America "back to McKinley," with recessions and unemployment like the country experienced during the Eisenhower years. Humphrey was especially critical of Nixon for his close ties with Sen. Thurmond (R S.C.), who had been the Dixiecrat Presidential nominee in 1948 and was an influential Southern backer of Nixon's 1968 Presidential nomination. (Some said Thurmond was the key man in Agnew's selection for the Vice Presidential spot.) Humphrey accused Nixon of having made "an awfully strange alliance with the most radical, extremist elements in your own party."

As for Wallace, Humphrey said the former Alabama Governor's "strategy of organized hate, if left unanswered and unchecked, can lead America to disaster just as surely as the radical tactics of the shouters and disrupters." Humphrey accused Wallace of seeking "to deliberately inflame the fears, frustrations and prejudices of our people, to bring this nation to the brink of broad scale civil disorder."

Humphrey and Nixon tangled on the issue of Senate ratification of the nuclear nonproliferation treaty, with Humphrey calling for immediate ratification to stem the spread of nuclear weapons while Nixon said there should be a delay because of the Soviet invasion of Czechoslovakia.

A chief point of contention between Humphrey and Nixon was the latter's refusal to debate. In Congress, and apparently at Nixon's behest, Republicans moved to kill pending legislation to suspend the "equal time" provisions of Section 315 of the Federal Communications Act.

(Action of this type had made possible the "Great Debates" between Nixon and Kennedy in 1960.) Later, when Humphrey challenged Nixon and Wallace to debate with him on television anyway, with the candidates sharing the costs or even with Humphrey paying the total bill, Nixon still demurred. Humphrey hit hard at the debate theme, accompanying it with charges that Nixon was really unwilling to commit himself on the vital issues of the day.

The result for Humphrey was an amazing surge in the final weeks of the campaign. For a few hours election night, it even looked as if he might have a chance to win.

Wallace Campaign

George C. Wallace, 49, the former Governor of Alabama, formally announced on Feb. 8, 1968, that he would run for President as a third party candidate under the banner of his American Independent party.

In his announcement, in Washington, D.C., Wallace said: "There has been no response from either of the parties which would show the American people that they are heeding the growing disillusionment with what amounts to a one-party system in the United States. No prospective candidate of the two existing parties, nor anyone in party leadership position, has come forward with any indication that there will be any difference in their platforms. No one has suggested that the wishes of the American people will be heard. So today, I state to you that I am a candidate for President of the United States.... I am in the race irrevocably. I will run to win."

Regardless of where he campaigned, the ingredients of Wallace's speech, as well as his delivery, followed a basic pattern. He exhorted the "little man" to believe that "this is a people's movement." His campaign slogan was "Stand Up for America," and he said the average man has a wisdom better than that of the experts. "You are one man and one woman," he would say, "and your thoughts are just as good as theirs."

His speeches invariably made these points: the little man is "sick and tired" of the Federal Government telling him "when to get up in the morning and when to go to bed at night"; there is "not a dime's worth of difference" between the Republicans and Democrats—"It's just Tweedledum and Tweedledee"; he is "sick and tired of some politicians, some educators, some judges and professors looking down their noses at the little people."

He drew particularly loud ovations when he told an audience that, "I couldn't care less where your children go to school. Why you can put them on a bus and send them to Philadelphia if you want to. What I'm going to do is get the Federal Government out of local schools." He also drew thunderous applause when he referred to the "fifty anarchists" who lay down in front of President Johnson's car in California in 1967, and then declared, "When I get to be President of these United States, if an anarchist laid down in front of my car, that would be the last thing he would ever lay down in front of on this here earth."

Wallace denied in his speeches that he was a racist. "When we talk about law and order they call us racists," he said. "You can't talk about law and order or property rights, or local problems without some liberal leftist calling you a racist." He says that "what we propose now is in the interest of every citizen regardless of race or color."

Wallace drew frenzied throngs of supporters to his campaign rallies throughout the country, sometimes enjoying larger crowds than the major-party candidates. Many Wallace campaign rallies, however, were marked by bitter heckling from Negroes and left-wing youth, often making Wallace's own words virtually inaudible.

Starting early in 1968, Wallace's supporters achieved the amazing success of qualifying their man (or his electors) for the Presidential ballot in all 50 states of the Union. A major success was scored early in the year in California, where the sum of 107,000 new party registrations for the American Independent Party was achieved, the necessary first step to qualifying it for the ballot. In Ohio, where 433,000 signatures were required by early in the year, Wallace supporters challenged the provision in court and won with an Oct. 15 U.S. Supreme Court ruling. The only jurisdiction of the country where Wallace failed to qualify for the ballot was the District of Columbia, where his vote would doubtless have been miniscule in any event.

Wallace's party toyed with the idea of holding a national convention as the Republicans and Democrats did but eventually decided against the idea. On Oct. 13, Wallace issued a lengthy American Independent Party platform, taking harder-line approaches than either major party on both foreign and domestic issues.

The Vice Presidential slot was a problem for Wallace; early in 1968 he designated former Gov. S. Marvin Griffin (D Ga. 1955-59) as his "interim" running mate; but on Oct. 3 he announced that his real Vice Presidential candidate would be retired Air Force General Curtis LeMay, 61, former head of the Strategic Air Command (1948-57) and Air Force Chief of Staff (1961-65). LeMay, known as a tough militarist, was quickly placed on the defensive by critics who said he would have too loose a finger on the nuclear trigger. LeMay said he opposed using nuclear bombs in Vietnam but said the country had "a phobia" about using atomic weapons and that "the world won't come to an end if we use a nuclear weapon." In retrospect, most observers believed the LeMay candidacy did little to help Wallace and may have harmed his candidacy.

For the record, Wallace frequently repeated his hope that he could win an outright majority in the electoral college, adding key Midwestern and Mountain states onto his hoped-for base in the Deep South and border states. In reality, the Wallace campaign had a narrower goal: to win the balance of power in electoral college voting, thus depriving either major party of the clear electoral majority required for election. Wallace made it clear that he would then expect one of the major party candidates to make concessions in return for sufficient support from the Wallace supporters to win election. Wallace indicated he expected the election to be resolved in the electoral college and not go to the House of Representatives for solution. At the end of the campaign, it was revealed that Wallace had obtained written affidavits from all his electors in which they promised to vote for Wallace "or whomsoever he may direct" in the electoral college.

Results of the 1968 Elections

In one of the closest elections of the century, Richard Milhous Nixon Nov. 5 was elected the 37th President of the United States. Republicans also advanced to control of 31 of the nation's Governorships. But the Democrats retained control of both houses of the Congress.

With 270 electoral votes required for election, Nixon received 302 (later reduced to 301 by defection of one faithless Republican North Carolina elector, Dr. Lloyd W. Bailey, to the Wallace column). Humphrey won 191 electoral votes, Wallace 45 (later increased to 46 by the North Carolina elector). In the popular vote, however, Nixon led Humphrey by only 510,315. The total vote, 73,211,562, represented only 61 percent of the voting age public—less than in either 1960 or 1964. Observers interpreted the low turnout as indication of widespread voter distaste for all of the candidates.

In percentage terms, Nixon had 43.4 percent of the popular vote—the lowest winning percentage for a winning Presidential candidate since 1912, when Woodrow Wilson won by 41.9 percent. Humphrey's percentage was 42.7; Wallace's was 13.5.

Nixon fashioned his electoral college majority by taking four closely contested big industrial states—Ohio, Illinois, New Jersey and California—winning most of the Southern border states and then sweeping the prairie and mountain states. He led in 32 states. Humphrey's base of strength was in four big states: New York, Pennsylvania, Michigan and Texas. But he was the first Democratic Presidential candidate of this century to win only a single Southern state, and he won only Washington and Hawaii in the Western part of the nation. Wallace won five Deep South states—Arkansas, Louisiana, Mississippi, Alabama and Georgia—but failed to take a single border state or state outside the South.

For the Republican party, Nixon's victory had special significance. He was the first successful GOP Presidential contender since the 1920s who was closely identified with the party organization. The victories of Dwight D. Eisenhower in the 1950s, followed by Nixon's defeat in 1960, had raised the possibility that the Republicans might lack the broad appeal ever to win a Presidential victory unless their candidate possessed special non-party appeal. The other bright spot for the Republicans Nov. 5 was on the

Governorship level, where the GOP added five seats for a new total of 31.

But Nixon was the first President since Zachary Taylor in 1848 not to bring in at least one house of the new Congress of his own political persuasion in his initial election to the White House. The Republicans scored a net gain of five seats in the Senate, but in the House the GOP failed completely in its well-organized and heavily financed campaign to gain control, adding a net of only four new seats. Even in a year of unprecedented division and bitterness within the Democratic party, the GOP could only battle the Democrats to a virtual standoff in the popular vote for President.

The Democrats had feared that the election would bring a final dissolution of the grand Democratic coalition that had controlled the Federal Government in most elections since the 1930s—low to middle income voters, labor union members, the more recent immigrant groups, Negroes, Mexican-Americans, Jews and the South. The election returns did show the South deserting the Democratic party in Presidential voting—the Deep South to Wallace, the border South to Nixon. But the other elements of the Democratic coalition held together remarkably well, helping the party win the electoral votes of several major states and to return a high proportion of its Congressional incumbents.

Wallace failed to make a substantial showing in any state outside the South, winning less than 10 percent of the non-Southern popular vote. Wallace's success in qualifying for the ballot in all 50 states would assure him an organizational base from which he could, if he wished, make another try for the Presidency in 1972. But even among working-class groups in the North where he had hoped to make his heaviest inroads, Wallace ran poorly. His share of the national popular vote—about 13.5 percent—was below the 16.6 percent received by Progressive Robert M. LaFollette in 1924 and even further below Theodore Roosevelt's 27.4 percent of the vote when he was the Progressive ("Bull Moose") candidate in 1912. Even in the 1856 election, the "Know-Nothings," a nativist American party similar in some ways to the Wallace

---

Results of 1968 Elections

PRESIDENT

	Popular Vote	Electoral Vote†
Richard M. Nixon (R)	31,785,480	301
Hubert H. Humphrey (D)	31,275,165	191
George C. Wallace (AIP)	9,906,473	46

	HOUSE			SENATE			GOVERNORS		
	Old Lineup	Gains/ Losses	New Lineup	Old Lineup	Gains/ Losses	New Lineup	Old Lineup	Gains/ Losses	New Lineup
Democrats	248	—5	243	63	—5	58	24	—5	19*
Republicans	187	+5	192	37	+5	42	26	+5	31*

†*Figures include one Republican elector vote cast for Wallace.*

*The Republican total includes Gov. Spiro T. Agnew of Maryland who was elected Vice President. Following his resignation from the state post, the Maryland State legislature elected a Democrat to succeed him. This made the new lineup: Democrats 20; Republicans: 30.

movement, had been able to receive a more substantial 21.1 percent of the popular vote. Thus the 1968 election, despite its uncertain mandate, did represent a broad affirmation for the American two-party system.

Aside from his disappointing share of the popular vote, Wallace also failed to win the balance of power in electoral college voting which he had hoped to use to wring policy concessions from one of the major-party Presidential candidates. Had Wallace won a few border states or if a few thousand more Democratic popular votes had been cast in Northern states barely won by Nixon, thus reducing Nixon's electoral vote below 270, Wallace would have been in a position to bargain for his electors or to throw the election into the House of Representatives for final resolution.

Pre-election surveys of Wallace voters had indicated that if they had been obliged to choose between Nixon and Humphrey, about twice as many would have preferred Nixon as Humphrey. If Wallace had not been on the ballot, Nixon would very possibly have carried some of the five Deep South states that went for Wallace, possibly building up a stronger national vote lead in the process. But it was difficult to tell from the election returns whether Wallace had hurt Nixon or Humphrey the more in the non-Southern states.

Senate Results

Republicans gained five new seats in the U.S. Senate for a total of 42, the largest number they had held since 1956.

The gain was a major accomplishment for the GOP. It was the biggest gain since 1950, when the Republicans also won five new seats.

The breakdown for the new Senate was 58 Democrats and 42 Republicans. In the 90th Congress, it had been 63 Democrats and 37 Republicans.

There were 34 seats at stake in the 1968 elections, 23 Democratic and 11 Republican. Of those, Republicans won 16 and Democrats 18.

Republicans actually won seven seats previously held by Democrats, but Democrats won two seats previously held by Republicans; so the net gain for the Republicans was five. No incumbent Republican standing for re-election was defeated, while four incumbent Democrats lost their bids for additional terms.

The makeup of the new Senate was expected to result in a shift, although not a dramatic one, to the right. While liberal strength remained the same as in the 90th Congress, strength among moderate Senators dropped and strength among conservative Senators rose correspondingly.

The seven Republicans who captured Senate seats previously held by Democrats included Barry Goldwater, 59, former Senator (1953-65) from Arizona and the unsuccessful Republican candidate for President in 1964. Goldwater, whose previous service gave him seniority over the other Republican freshmen, replaced retiring Carl Hayden, 91, president pro tempore of the Senate, a Member of the House from Arizona starting in 1912, when Arizona won statehood, and a Senator since 1927.

Three Republican Representatives also won Senate seats previously held by Democrats. They were Edward J. Gurney (R Fla. 1963-68), 54, a strong conservative, who beat former Florida Gov. LeRoy Collins (D), 59, a

moderate, for the seat held by retiring George A. Smathers (D Fla. 1951-69), 54; Charles McC. Mathias Jr. (R Md. 1961-69), 46, a liberal, who beat his friend, Daniel B. Brewster (D Md. 1963-69), 44, in a head-on contest; and Richard S. Schweiker (R Pa. 1961-69), 42, a moderate, who defeated Joseph S. Clark (D Pa. 1957-69), 67.

Other Republicans winning seats previously held by Democrats were: Henry Bellmon (R Okla.), 47, a farmer and a conservative, who beat incumbent A.S. Mike Monroney (D Okla. 1951-69), 66; Robert W. Packwood (R Ore.), 36, a lawyer and a moderate, who defeated Wayne Morse, 68, a fiery liberal who had been a Senator from Oregon as a Republican (1945-52), as an Independent (1952-55) and as a Democrat (1955-69); and William B. Saxbe (R Ohio), 52, attorney general of his state and a moderate, who beat former Rep. John J. Gilligan (D Ohio 1965-67), 47, a liberal, for the seat held by Frank J. Lausche (D Ohio 1957-69), 72, a strong conservative who was defeated by Gilligan in the primary.

The other two freshman Republicans were Marlow W. Cook (R Ky.), 42, a lawyer and a conservative, who beat Katherine Peden (D), 42, a moderate and the only woman running for the Senate, for the seat held by retiring Thruston B. Morton (R Ky. 1957-69), 61; and Rep. Robert Dole (R Kan. 1961-69), 45, a conservative, who beat William I. Robinson (D), 59, a moderate, for the seat held by retiring Frank Carlson (R Kan. 1950-69), 75.

The two Democrats who won seats previously held by Republicans were: Alan Cranston (D Calif.), 54, former controller of his state and a liberal, who beat Max Rafferty (R), 51, a strong conservative, for the seat held by Thomas H. Kuchel (R Calif. 1953-69), 58, a liberal whom Rafferty had defeated in the primary; and Iowa Gov. Harold E. Hughes (D), 46, a liberal, who defeated David M. Stanley (R), 40, a moderate, for the seat held by retiring Bourke B. Hickenlooper (R Iowa 1945-69), 72, a conservative.

House Results

The party breakdown for the House when the 91st Congress convened: 243 Democrats, 192 Republicans.

In all, Republicans took nine seats from the Democrats and, in turn, lost five of their own for their four-seat net gain. Republicans had scored a net gain of 47 seats in the 1966 elections and had won a special election to fill a Democratic vacancy earlier in 1968. The Republicans had lost 38 seats in the 1964 elections.

Of the 435 Representatives elected Nov. 5, 396 were incumbents (223 Democrats and 173 Republicans) and only 39 (20 Democrats and 19 Republicans) were newcomers. The new winners include two former Representatives, one a Democrat and the other a Republican.

The new 91st Congress would have the smallest crop of freshman Members in years. Between 1940 and 1948, an average of 96 newcomers were elected to each new House. The average dropped to 68 between 1950 and 1958 but rose to 72 between 1960 and 1966. In 1964 there were 91 newcomers elected and in 1966, 73.

Based on a study by CQ arbitrarily classifying all House candidates as liberals, conservatives and moderates, it appeared that moderates scored a slight gain as a result of the election. In the 90th Congress, CQ classified 172 Members as liberals, 193 as conservatives and 70 as moderates. The 91st Congress including the 39 newcomers will have 170 liberals, a loss of two; 189 conservatives, a loss of 4; and 76 moderates, a gain of 6.

The so-called "conservative coalition" probably would remain as powerful as it was in the 90th Congress in blocking enactment or funding of liberal-sponsored legislation.

The new House party line-up for the nation's four geographical regions (91st Congress final line-up in parentheses with vacancies credited to party that last held the seat):

	East	South	Midwest	West
Democrats	73 (74)	88 (90)	46 (45)	36 (38)
Republicans	49 (48)	31 (29)	79 (80)	33 (31)

Governorships

The Republican party, winning 13 of the year's 21 races and capturing seven seats held by Democrats, increased its control of the nation's statehouses from 26 to 31. Even after the selection of a Democrat to succeed Vice President-elect Spiro T. Agnew, governor of Maryland, the GOP would boast 30 Governors, equalling its holdings after the Eisenhower sweep of 1952 when there were two fewer states.

In light of the extremely close Presidential race and the continuing, though narrowed, control of Congress by the Democrats, the 10-man Republican margin gave the party its most broad-based mandate for leadership.

The GOP scored a net gain of three seats each in the East and the Midwest and lost one in the West. There were no party changes in the South.

President-elect Nixon's coattails had a less decisive effect than did former President Eisenhower's four national elections earlier. Nixon did carry six of the seven states in which Republicans took Governorships formerly held by Democrats (including two incumbents). But it was far from clear who helped whom in several of those races. In Montana, an easy Nixon win failed to save Gov. Tim M. Babcock, an early Nixon for President backer, who got into trouble over his advocacy of a state sales tax. Babcock, a strong conservative, was defeated by state Attorney General Forrest H. Anderson (D). In Rhode Island, the only other race in which a Republican incumbent was beaten, Gov. John H. Chafee's advocacy of a state income tax appeared to be the major factor in his defeat. Chafee, a popular liberal Republican, was defeated in his bid for a fourth two-year term by Frank Licht, a former state judge who became the first Jew elected Governor in the traditionally Democratic and heavily Catholic state.

One of the most satisfying successes for the Republicans was the 100,000-vote victory by Richard B. Ogilvie over incumbent Democratic Gov. Samuel H. Shapiro in Illinois. The win gave the Republicans control of the Governor's chair in six of the seven most populous states in the union. Only in fifth-ranked Texas did the Democrats still have a Governor.

Over-all, the Republicans would govern in states with a population of approximately 132 million and the Democrats would be in charge in states, including Maryland, with a combined population of about 67 million.

The other Democratic incumbent to taste defeat was Gov. Charles L. Terry Jr. of Delaware. Russell W. Peterson, a DuPont executive, won the race in which a major

---

Historical Comparisons

Nixon became the fourth President since the Civil War who was elected with a House of Representatives controlled by the opposition party. The other three were: Rutherford B. Hayes in 1876, Woodrow Wilson in 1916 and Dwight D. Eisenhower in 1956.

When the Presidency changes from control of one party to another, the President-elect's party usually—but not always—gains seats in the House. Since the Civil War this has happened in 6 of the 10 elections where the opposition party won the Presidency. In 4 of the elections, however, the party winning the Presidency lost seats in the House. This was because the party had made large gains in the off-year election preceding the Presidential election year.

The six Presidents whose party gained House seats were:

Harrison (R), 1888—plus 22 seats
Wilson (D), 1912—plus 62 seats
Harding (R), 1920—plus 63 seats
Roosevelt (D), 1932—plus 97 seats
Eisenhower (R), 1952—plus 22 seats
Nixon (R), 1968—plus 4 seats

The Presidents whose party lost seats in the House, despite winning the White House from the opposite party, were:

Cleveland (D), 1884 and 1892—lost 18 and 11 seats
McKinley (R), 1896—lost 40 seats
Kennedy (D), 1960—lost 20

---

issue was "law and order." Peterson struck a more moderate stance than either Nixon or Terry, who had kept the National Guard on the streets of Wilmington to prevent what he predicted would be a "hot summer" in 1968. Terry also suffered a heart attack in October.

Battling for seats vacated by Democratic incumbents, Republicans won in Indiana, Iowa, West Virginia, New Hampshire and Vermont. State matters, primarily fiscal, were the main issues in all five. The Democrats suffered especially through the voluntary retirement of their popular Governors in normally Republican Iowa, New Hampshire and Vermont.

Except for Montana and Rhode Island, the Democrats picked up no seats formerly held by Republicans.

State Legislatures

Republicans scored minimal gains in the contests for state legislature seats around the country. As a result of the elections, they would control 20 legislatures—the same number controlled by the Democrats. (The other 10 were split in control or nonpartisan.) The GOP rose in strength from 41.8 percent to 43.4 percent of the seats in all senate chambers around the country, but held static at just over 42 percent of all the seats in lower houses.

A CENTURY OF PRESIDENTIAL ELECTIONS

YEAR	NO. OF STATES	CANDIDATES		ELECTORAL VOTE		POPULAR VOTE	
		DEM.	GOP	DEM.	GOP	DEM.	GOP
1856 (a)	31	James Buchanan John C. Breckinridge	John C. Fremont William L. Dayton	174 59%	114 39%	1,839,237 45.6%	1,341,028 33.3%
1860 (b)	33	Stephen A. Douglas Herschel V. Johnson	Abraham Lincoln Hannibal Hamlin	12 4%	180 59%	1,379,434 29.4%	1,867,198 39.8%
1864 (c)	36	George B. McClellan George H. Pendelton	Abraham Lincoln Andrew Johnson	21 9%	212 91%	1,805,063 44.9%	2,219,362 55.1%
1868 (d)	37	Horatio Seymour Francis P. Blair Jr.	Ulysses S. Grant Schuyler Colfax	80 27%	214 73%	2,703,933 47.3%	3,013,313 52.7%
1872 (e)	37	Horace Greeley Benjamin Gratz Brown	Ulysses S. Grant Henry Wilson	(e)	286 82%	2,833,711 43.8%	3,597,375 55.6%
1876	38	Samuel J. Tilden Thomas A. Hendricks	Rutherford B. Hayes William A. Wheeler	184 50%	185 50%	4,287,670 50.9%	4,035,924 47.9%
1880	38	Winfield S. Hancock William H. English	James A. Garfield Chester A. Arthur	155 42%	214 58%	4,444,976 48.2%	4,454,433 48.3%
1884	38	Grover Cleveland Thomas A. Hendricks	James G. Blaine John A. Logan	219 55%	182 45%	4,875,971 48.5%	4,852,234 48.3%
1888	38	Grover Cleveland Allen G. Thurman	Benjamin Harrison Levi P. Morton	168 42%	233 58%	5,540,365 48.6%	5,445,269 47.8%
1892 (f)	44	Grover Cleveland Adlai E. Stevenson	Benjamin Harrison Whitelaw Reid	277 62%	145 33%	5,556,982 46.0%	5,191,466 43.0%
1896	45	William J. Bryan Arthur Sewall	William McKinley Garret A. Hobart	176 39%	271 61%	6,516,722 46.7%	7,113,734 51.0%
1900	45	William J. Bryan Adlai E. Stevenson	William McKinley Theodore Roosevelt	155 35%	292 65%	6,358,160 45.5%	7,219,828 51.7%
1904	45	Alton B. Parker Henry G. Davis	Theodore Roosevelt Charles W. Fairbanks	140 29%	336 71%	5,084,533 37.6%	7,628,831 56.4%
1908	46	William J. Bryan John W. Kern	William H. Taft James S. Sherman	162 34%	321 66%	6,410,665 43.1%	7,679,114 51.6%
1912 (g)	48	Woodrow Wilson Thomas R. Marshall	William H. Taft James S. Sherman	435 82%	8 1%	6,301,254 41.9%	3,485,831 23.2%
1916	48	Woodrow Wilson Thomas R. Marshall	Charles E. Hughes Charles W. Fairbanks	277 52%	254 48%	9,131,511 49.3%	8,548,935 46.1%
1920	48	James M. Cox Franklin D. Roosevelt	Warren G. Harding Calvin Coolidge	127 24%	404 76%	9,133,092 34.1%	16,153,115 60.3%
1924 (h)	48	John W. Davis Charles W. Bryan	Calvin Coolidge Charles G. Dawes	136 26%	382 71%	8,386,704 28.8%	15,719,921 54.0%
1928	48	Alfred E. Smith Joseph T. Robinson	Herbert C. Hoover Charles Curtis	87 16%	444 84%	15,007,698 40.8%	21,437,277 58.2%
1932	48	Franklin D. Roosevelt John N. Garner	Herbert C. Hoover Charles Curtis	472 89%	59 11%	22,829,501 57.4%	15,760,684 39.6%
1936	48	Franklin D. Roosevelt John N. Garner	Alfred M. Landon Frank Knox	523 98%	8 2%	27,757,333 60.8%	16,684,231 36.5%
1940	48	Franklin D. Roosevelt Henry A. Wallace	Wendell L. Willkie Charles L. McNary	449 85%	82 15%	27,313,041 54.7%	22,348,480 44.8%
1944	48	Franklin D. Roosevelt Harry S. Truman	Thomas E. Dewey John W. Bricker	432 81%	99 19%	25,612,610 53.4%	22,017,617 45.9%
1948 (i)	48	Harry S. Truman Alben W. Barkley	Thomas E. Dewey Earl Warren	303 57%	189 36%	24,179,345 49.6%	21,991,291 45.1%
1952	48	Adlai E. Stevenson John J. Sparkman	Dwight D. Eisenhower Richard M. Nixon	89 16%	442 83%	27,314,992 44.4%	33,936,234 55.1%
1956	48	Adlai E. Stevenson Estes Kefauver	Dwight D. Eisenhower Richard M. Nixon	74 14%	457 86%	26,022,752 42.0%	35,590,472 57.4%
1960 (j)	50	John F. Kennedy Lyndon B. Johnson	Richard M. Nixon Henry Cabot Lodge	303 62%	219 36%	34,220,984 49.5%	34,108,157 49.3%
1964	50*	Lyndon B. Johnson Hubert H. Humphrey	Barry Goldwater William E. Miller	486 90%	52 10%	43,129,484 61.1%	27,178,188 38.5%
1968 (k)	50*	Hubert H. Humphrey Edmund S. Muskie	Richard M. Nixon Spiro T. Agnew	191 36%	301 56%	31,275,165 42.7%	31,785,480 43.4%

*50 states plus District of Columbia.
(a) 1856: Millard Fillmore, American Party, polled 8 electoral votes.
(b) 1860: John C. Breckinridge, southern Democratic nominee, polled 72 electoral votes. John Bell, Constitutional Union, polled 39 electoral votes.
(c) 1864: 81 electoral votes were not cast.
(d) 1868: 23 electoral votes were not cast.
(e) 1872: Horace Greeley died after election; 63 Democratic electoral votes were scattered. 17 were not voted.
(f) 1892: James B. Weaver, People's Party, polled 22 electoral votes.
(g) 1912: Theodore Roosevelt, Progressive, polled 88 electoral votes.
(h) 1924: Robert M. LaFollette, Progressive, polled 13 electoral votes.
(i) 1948: J. Strom Thurmond, States' Rights, polled 39 electoral votes.
(j) 1960: 15 electoral votes cast for Sen. Harry Flood Byrd (D Va.).
(k) 1968: 46 electoral votes cast for George C. Wallace.

Party Line-Up, Congress and Presidency, 1854-1968

Election Year	Congress Elected	HOUSE Members Elected Dem.	Rep.	Misc.	HOUSE Gains/Losses Dem.	Rep.	SENATE Members Elected Dem.	Rep.	Misc.	SENATE Gains/Losses Dem.	Rep.	PRESIDENCY Elected	Popular Vote Plurality
1854	34th	83	108	43			42	15	5			Pierce (D)	
1856	35th	131	92	14	+ 48	— 16	39	20	5	— 3	+ 5	Buchanan (D)	498,209
1858	36th	101	113	23	— 30	+ 21	38	26	2	— 1	+ 6		
1860	37th	42	106	28	— 59	— 7	11	31	7	—27	+ 5	Lincoln (R)	487,764
1862	38th	80	103		+ 38	— 3	12	39		+ 1	+ 8		
1864	39th	46	145		— 34	+ 42	10	42		— 2	+ 3	Lincoln (R)	414,299
1866	40th	49	143		+ 3	— 2	11	42		+ 1	0	Johnson (R)	
1868	41st	73	170		+ 24	+ 27	11	61		0	+ 19	Grant (R)	309,380
1870	42nd	104	139		+ 31	— 31	17	57		+ 6	— 4		
1872	43rd	88	203		— 16	+ 64	19	54		+ 2	— 3	Grant (R)	763,664
1874	44th	181	107	3	+ 93	— 96	29	46		+ 10	— 8		
1876	45th	156	137		— 25	+ 30	36	39	1	+ 7	— 7	Hayes (R)	—251,746
1878	46th	150	128	14	— 6	— 9	43	33		+ 7	— 6		
1880	47th	130	152	11	— 20	+ 24	37	37	2	— 6	+ 4	Garfield (R)	9,457
1882	48th	200	119	6	+ 70	— 33	36	40		— 1	+ 3	Arthur (R)	
1884	49th	182	140	2	— 18	+ 21	34	41		— 2	+ 1	Cleveland (D)	23,737
1886	50th	170	151	4	— 12	+ 11	37	39		+ 3	— 2		
1888	51st	156	173	1	— 14	+ 22	37	47		0	+ 8	Harrison (R)	—95,096
1890	52nd	231	88	14	+ 75	— 85	39	47	2	+ 2	0		
1892	53rd	220	126	8	— 11	+ 38	44	38	3	+ 5	— 9	Cleveland (D)	365,516
1894	54th	104	246	7	—116	+ 120	39	44	5	— 5	+ 6		
1896	55th	134	206	16	+ 30	— 40	34	46	10	— 5	+ 2	McKinley (R)	597,012
1898	56th	163	185	9	+ 29	— 21	26	53	11	— 8	+ 7		
1900	57th	153	198	5	— 10	+ 13	29	56	3	+ 3	+ 3	McKinley (R)	861,668
1902	58th	178	207		+ 25	+ 9	32	58		+ 3	+ 2	Roosevelt (R)	
1904	59th	136	250		— 42	+ 43	32	58		0	0	Roosevelt (R)	2,544,298
1906	60th	164	222		+ 28	— 28	29	61		— 3	— 3		
1908	61st	172	219		+ 8	— 3	32	59		+ 3	— 2	Taft (R)	1,268,449
1910	62nd	228	162		+ 56	— 57	42	49		+ 10	—10		
1912	63rd	290	127	18	+ 62	— 35	51	44	1	+ 9	— 5	Wilson (D)	2,173,466
1914	64th	231	193	8	— 59	+ 66	56	39	1	+ 5	— 5		
1916	65th	210	216	9	— 21	+ 23	53	42	1	— 3	+ 3	Wilson (D)	582,576
1918	66th	191	237	7	— 19	+ 21	47	48	1	— 6	+ 6		
1920	67th	132	300	1	— 59	+ 63	37	59		—10	+ 11	Harding (R)	7,020,023
1922	68th	207	225	3	+ 75	— 75	43	51	2	+ 6	— 8	Coolidge (R)	
1924	69th	183	247	5	— 24	+ 22	40	54	1	— 3	+ 3	Coolidge (R)	333,217
1926	70th	195	237	3	+ 12	— 10	47	48	1	+ 7	— 6		
1928	71st	163	267	1	— 32	+ 30	39	56	1	— 8	+ 8	Hoover (R)	6,429,579
1930	72nd	216	218	1	+ 53	— 49	47	48	1	+ 8	— 8		
1932	73rd	313	117	5	+ 97	—101	59	36	1	+ 12	—12	Roosevelt (D)	7,068,817
1934	74th	322	103	10	+ 9	— 14	69	25	2	+ 10	—11		
1936	75th	333	89	13	+ 11	— 14	75	17	4	+ 6	— 8	Roosevelt (D)	11,073,102
1938	76th	262	169	4	— 71	+ 80	69	23	4	— 6	+ 6		
1940	77th	267	162	6	+ 5	— 7	66	28	2	— 3	+ 5	Roosevelt (D)	4,964,561
1942	78th	222	209	4	— 45	+ 47	57	38	1	— 9	+ 10		
1944	79th	243	190	2	+ 21	— 19	57	38	1	0	0	Roosevelt (D)	3,594,993
1946	80th	188	246	1	— 55	+ 56	45	51		—12	+ 13	Truman	
1948	81st	263	171	1	+ 75	— 75	54	42		+ 9	— 9	Truman (D)	2,188,054
1950	82nd	234	199	2	— 29	+ 28	48	47	1	— 6	+ 6		
1952	83rd	213	221	1	— 21	+ 22	47	48	1	— 1	+ 1	Eisenhower (R)	6,621,242
1954	84th	232	203		+ 19	— 18	48	47	1	+ 1	— 1		
1956	85th	234	201		+ 2	— 2	49	47		+ 1	0	Eisenhower (R)	9,567,720
1958	86th	283	154		+ 49	— 47	66	34		+ 17	—13		
1960	87th	263	174		— 20	+ 20	64	36		— 2	+ 2	Kennedy (D)	112,827*
1962	88th	258	176	1**	— 4	+ 2	68	32		+ 4	— 4		
1964	89th	295	140		+ 38	— 38	67	33		+ 2	— 2	Johnson (D)	15,951,296
1966	90th	248	187		— 47	+ 47	64	36		— 3	+ 3		
1968	91st	243	192		— 4	+ 4	58	42		— 5	+ 5	Nixon (R)	510,315

*Includes divided Alabama elector slate votes.
**Vacancy.

State-by-State Presidential Election Returns, 1856-1968

State	|	Victorious Party in Presidential Election in Each State, 1856 to 1968																												|	No. of Times Parties Won		
		1856	1860	1864	1868	1872	1876	1880	1884	1888	1892	1896	1900	1904	1908	1912	1916	1920	1924	1928	1932	1936	1940	1944	1948	1952	1956	1960	1964	1968		Dem.	Rep.	Other
ALA.		D	SD	[2]	R	R	D	D	D	D	D	D	D	D	D	D	D	D	D	D	D	D	D	D	SR	D	D[18]	D[19]	R	W		22	3	3
ALASKA																												R	D	R		1	2	0
ARIZ.																D	D	R	R	R	D	D	D	D	D	R	R	R	R	R		7	8	0
ARK.		D	SD	[2]	R	[4]	D	D	D	D	D	D	D	D	D	D	D	D	D	D	D	D	D	D	D	D	D	D	D	W		24	1	2
CALIF.		D	R	R	R	R	R	D[6]	R	R	D[7]	R[12]	R	R	R	PR	D	R	R	R	D	D	D	D	D	R	R	R	D	R		10	18	1
COLO.							R	R	R	R	PP	D	D	R	D	D	D	R	R	R	D	D	D	D	D	R	R	R	D	R		11	12	1
CONN.		R	R	R	R	R	D	R	D	D	D	R	R	R	R	D	R	R	R	R	D	D	D	D	R	R	R	D	D	D		12	17	0
DEL.		D	SD	D	D	R	D	D	D	D	D	R	R	R	R	D	R	R	R	R	D	D	D	D	R	R	R	D	D	R		15	13	1
D.C.																													D	D		2	0	0
FLA.		D	SD	[2]	R	R	R	D	D	D	D	D	D	D	D	D	D	D	D	R	D	D	D	D	D	R	R	R	D	R		19	8	1
GA.		D	SD	[2]	D	D[5]	D	D	D	D	D	D	D	D	D	D	D	D	D	D	D	D	D	D	D	D	D	D	R	W		25	1	2
HAWAII																												D	D	D		3	0	0
IDAHO											PP	D	D	R	R	D	D	R	R	R	D	D	D	D	D	R	R	R	D	R		10	9	1
ILL.		D	R	R	R	R	R	R	R	R	D	R	R	R	R	D	R	R	R	R	D	D	D	D	D	R	R	D	D	R		10	19	0
IND.		D	R	R	R	R	D	R	D	R	D	R	R	R	R	D	R	R	R	R	D	D	R	R	R	R	R	R	D	R		8	21	0
IOWA		R	R	R	R	R	R	R	R	R	R	R	R	R	R	D	R	R	R	R	D	D	D	R	D	R	R	R	D	R		6	20	0
KAN.			R	R	R	R	R	R	R	R	PP	D	R	R	R	D	D	R	R	R	D	D	R	R	R	R	R	R	D	R		6	20	1
KY.		D	CU	D	D	D	D	D	D	D	D	R[13]	D	D	D	D	D	D	R	R	D	D	D	D	D	D	R	R	D	R		22	6	1
LA.		D	SD	[2]	D	[4]	R	D	D	D	D	D	D	D	D	D	D	D	D	D	D	D	D	D	SR	D	D	R	D	W		21	3	3
MAINE		R	R	R	R	R	R	R	R	R	R	R	R	R	R	D	R	R	R	R	R	R	R	R	R	R	R	R	D	D		3	26	0
MD.		A	SD	R	D	D	D	D	D	D	D	R	D[14]	D[15]	D	D	R	R	R	R	D	D	D	D	R	R	R	D	D	R		10	19	1
MASS.		R	R	R	R	R	R	R	R	R	R	R	R	R	R	PR	R	R	R	R	D	D	D	D	R	R	R	D	D	D		10	18	1
MICH.		R	R	R	R	R	R	R	R	R	R	R	R	R	R	PR	R	R	R	R	D	D	D	D	R	R	R	D	D	D		8	20	1
MINN.			R	R	R	R	R	R	R	R	R	R	R	R	R	PR	R	R	R	R	D	D	D	D	D	R	D	D	D	D		10	17	1
MISS.		D	SD	[2]	[3]	R	D	D	D	D	D	D	D	D	D	D	D	D	D	D	D	D	D	D	SR	D	D	[20]	R	W		21	2	3
MO.		D	D	R	R	D	D	D	D	D	D	R	D	R	R	D	D	R	R	R	D	D	D	D	D	R	D	D	D	R		20	9	0
MONT.								R	R	R	R	D	R	D	D	D	D	R	R	R	D	D	D	D	D	R	R	R	D	R		10	10	0
NEB.				R	R	R	R	R	R	R	R	D	R	D	R	D	D	R	R	R	D	D	R	R	R	R	R	R	D	R		7	19	0
NEV.			R	R	R	R	D	R	R	R	PP	D	D	R	D	D	D	R	R	R	D	D	D	D	D	R	R	D	D	R		13	13	1
N.H.		R	R	R	R	R	R	R	R	R	R	R	R	R	R	D	D	R	R	R	R	D	D	R	D	R	R	D	D	R		6	23	0
N.J.		D	R[1]	D	D	R	D	D	D	D	D	R	R	R	D	R	R	R	R	D	D	D	D	R	R	R	D	R	D	D		12	17	0
N.M.																D	D	R	R	R	D	D	D	D	D	R	R	D	D	R		9	6	0
N.Y.		R	R	R	D	R	D	D	R	D	D	R	R	R	D	R	R	R	R	D	D	D	D	D	R	R	D	D	D	D		12	17	0
N.C.		D	SD	[2]	R	R	D	D	D	D	D	D	D	D	D	D	D	D	D	R	D	D	D	D	D	R	R	D	D	R		23	4	1
N.D.											[9]	R	R	R	R	D	R	R	R	R	D	D	R	R	R	R	R	R	D	R		5	14	1
OHIO		R	R	R	R	R	R	R	R	R	R[10]	R	R	R	R	D	D	R	R	R	D	D	D	D	R	R	R	D	R		7	22	0
OKLA.															D	D	D	R	R	R	D	D	D	D	D	R	R	R	D	R		10	6	0
ORE.			R	R	D	R	D	R	R	R	R[11]	R	R	R	R	D	D	R	R	R	D	D	D	D	R	R	R	D	R		7	21	0
PA.		D	R	R	R	R	R	R	R	R	R	R	R	R	R	PR	R	R	R	R	D	D	D	D	D	R	R	D	D	R		10	19	0
R.I.		R	R	R	R	R	R	R	R	D	D	R	R	R	R	D	R	R	R	R	D	D	D	D	D	SR	D	D	D	R		21	5	2
S.C.		D	SD	[2]	R	R	R	D	D	D	D	D	D	D	D	D	D	D	D	D	D	D	D	D	SR	D[17]	R	R	D	R		4	15	1
S.D.											R	R	R	R	R	PR	R	R	R	R	D	D	R	R	R	R	R	R	D	R		20	7	1
TENN.		D	CU	[2]	R	D	D	D	D	D	D	D	D	D	D	D	D	R	D	R	D	D	D	D	D	R	R	D	D	R		23	3	1
TEXAS		D	SD	[2]	[3]	D	D	D	D	D	D	D	D	D	D	D	D	D	D	R	D	D	D	D	D	R	R	D	D	D		8	11	0
UTAH												D	D	R	R	D	D	R	R	R	D	D	D	D	D	R	R	R	D	R		10	9	0
VT.		R	R	R	R	R	R	R	R	R	R	R	R	R	R	R	R	R	R	R	R	R	R	R	R	R	R	R	D	R		1	28	0
VA.		D	CU	[2]	[3]	R	D	D	D	D	D	D	D	D	D	PR	D	D	D	R	D	D	D	D	D	R	R	R	D	R		20	6	1
WASH.											R	R	D	R	R	PR	D	R	R	R	D	D	D	D	D	R	R	R	D	D		9	10	1
W.VA.				R	R	R	D	D	D	R	D	R[16]	R	R	R	D	D	R	R	R	D	D	D	D	D	R	R	D	D	D		15	12	0
WIS.		R	R	R	R	R	R	R	D	R	R	R	R	R	R	D	R	PR	R	R	D	D	R	R	D	R	R	R	D	R		7	21	1
WYO.											R	D	R	R	R	D	D	R	R	R	D	D	D	R	D	R	R	R	D	R		8	12	0
Winning Party		D	R	R	R	R	R	R	D	R	D	R	R	R	R	D	D	R	R	R	D	D	D	D	D	R	R	D	D	R		13	16	0

1. Four electors voted Republican; 3 voted Democratic.
2. Confederate States, did not vote in 1864.
3. Did not vote in 1868.
4. Votes were not counted.
5. 3 votes for Greely not counted.
6. One elector voted Republican; 5 voted Democratic.
7. One elector voted Republican; 8 voted Democratic.
8. 9 electors voted Republican; 5 voted Democratic.
9. 1 vote each for Democratic, Republican and People's Party.
10. 22 electors voted Republican and 1 voted Democratic.
11. 3 electors voted Republican and 1 People's Party.
12. 8 electors voted Republican and 1 voted Democratic.
13. 12 electors voted Republican; 1 voted Democratic.
14. 7 electors voted Democratic; 1 Republican.
15. 2 electors voted Republican; 6 Democratic.
16. 7 electors voted Republican; 1 Democratic.
17. 11 electors voted Democratic; 1 voted States' Rights.

18. 1 elector voted for Walter Jones.
19. Six of 11 electors not pledged to support national ticket and voted for Sen. Harry F. Byrd (D Va.).
20. Eight independent electors voted for Byrd.
21. One elector voted for Byrd.
22. One elector voted for Wallace.

Blanks indicate states not yet admitted to the Union.

A—American Party
CU—Constitutional Union Party
D—Democratic Party
PP—People's Party
PR—Progressive (Bullmoose) Party
R—Republican Party
SD—Southern Democratic Party
SR—States' Rights Party
W—American Independent Party

Final 1964 Presidential Election Results

*(For 1948-60 results, see Congress and
the Nation, Vol. I, p. 64-65.)*

*Based on complete vote totals reported to Congressional Quarterly
by the Governmental Affairs Institute and state government sources.*

Total popular vote cast: 70,644,510

STATE	TOTAL POPULAR VOTE			PLURALITY		PERCENTAGES†		ELECTORAL VOTE	
	JOHNSON	GOLDWATER	OTHER PARTIES			JOHNSON	GOLDWATER	JOHNSON	GOLDWATER
ALABAMA	‡	479,085	210,733	R	268,353		69.5		10
ALASKA	44,329	22,930	None	D	21,399	65.9	34.1	3	
ARIZONA	237,753	242,535	482	R	4,782	49.5	50.4		5
ARKANSAS	314,197	243,264	2,965	D	70,933	56.1	43.4	6	
CALIFORNIA	4,171,877	2,879,108	6,601	D	1,292,769	59.1	40.8	40	
COLORADO	476,024	296,767	4,195	D	179,257	61.3	38.2	6	
CONNECTICUT	826,269	390,996	1,313	D	435,273	67.8	32.1	8	
DELAWARE	122,704	78,078	538	D	44,626	60.9	38.8	3	
FLORIDA	948,540	905,941	None	D	42,599	51.1	48.9	14	
GEORGIA	522,556	616,584	195	R	94,028	45.9	54.1		12
HAWAII	163,249	44,022	None	D	119,227	78.8	21.2	4	
IDAHO	148,920	143,557	None	D	5,363	50.9	49.1	4	
ILLINOIS	2,796,833	1,905,946	62	D	890,887	59.5	40.5	26	
INDIANA	1,170,848	911,118	9,640	D	259,730	56.0	43.6	13	
IOWA	733,030	449,148	2,361	D	283,882	61.9	37.9	9	
KANSAS	464,028	386,579	7,294	D	77,449	54.1	45.1	7	
KENTUCKY	669,659	372,977	3,469	D	296,682	64.0	35.7	9	
LOUISIANA	387,068	509,225	None	R	122,157	43.2	56.8		10
MAINE	262,264	118,701	None	D	143,563	68.8	31.2	4	
MARYLAND	730,912	385,495	50	D	345,417	65.5	34.5	10	
MASSACHUSETTS	1,786,422	549,727	8,649	D	1,236,695	76.2	23.4	14	
MICHIGAN	2,136,615	1,060,152	6,335	D	1,076,463	66.7	33.1	21	
MINNESOTA	991,117	559,624	3,721	D	431,493	63.8	36.0	10	
MISSISSIPPI	52,618	356,528	None	R	303,910	12.9	87.1		7
MISSOURI	1,164,344	653,535	None	D	510,809	64.0	36.0	12	
MONTANA	164,246	113,032	1,350	D	51,214	58.9	40.6	4	
NEBRASKA	307,307	276,847	None	D	30,460	52.6	47.4	5	
NEVADA	79,339	56,094	None	D	23,245	58.6	41.4	3	
NEW HAMPSHIRE	184,064	104,029	None	D	80,035	63.9	36.1	4	
NEW JERSEY	1,868,231	964,174	15,258	D	904,057	65.6	33.9	17	
NEW MEXICO	194,015	132,838	1,792	D	61,177	59.0	40.4	4	
NEW YORK	4,913,102	2,243,559	9,614	D	2,669,543	68.6	31.3	43	
NORTH CAROLINA	800,139	624,844	None	D	175,295	56.2	43.8	13	
NORTH DAKOTA	149,784	108,207	398	D	41,577	58.0	41.9	4	
OHIO	2,498,331	1,470,865	None	D	1,027,466	62.9	37.1	26	
OKLAHOMA	519,834	412,665	None	D	107,169	55.7	44.3	8	
OREGON	501,017	282,779	2,509	D	218,328	63.7	36.0	6	
PENNSYLVANIA	3,130,954	1,673,657	18,079	D	1,457,297	64.9	34.7	29	
RHODE ISLAND	315,463	74,615	13	D	240,848	80.9	19.1	4	
SOUTH CAROLINA	215,723	309,048	8	R	93,325	41.1	58.9		8
SOUTH DAKOTA	163,010	130,108	None	D	32,902	55.6	44.4	4	
TENNESSEE	635,047	508,965	34	D	126,082	55.5	44.5	11	
TEXAS	1,663,185	958,566	5,060	D	704,619	63.3	36.5	25	
UTAH	219,628	181,785	None	D	37,843	54.7	45.3	4	
VERMONT	108,127	54,942	20	D	53,185	66.3	33.7	3	
VIRGINIA	558,038	481,334	2,895	D	76,704	53.5	46.2	12	
WASHINGTON	779,699	470,366	8,309	D	309,333	62.0	37.4	9	
WEST VIRGINIA	538,087	253,953	None	D	284,134	67.9	32.1	7	
WISCONSIN	1,050,424	638,495	2,896	D	411,929	62.1	37.7	12	
WYOMING	80,718	61,998	None	D	18,720	56.6	43.4	3	
DIST. OF COLUMBIA	169,796	28,801	None	D	140,995	85.5	14.5	3	
TOTAL	43,129,484	27,178,188	336,838	D	15,951,296	61.1	38.5	486	52

Other Party Vote Breakdown: Independent Democratic Electors Alabama only 210,732; Socialist Labor (Hass and Blomen) 45,219; Prohibition (Munn and Shaw) 23,267; Socialist Worker (DeBerry and Shaw) 32,720; Constitution (Lightburn and Billings) 5,060; National States Rights (Kasper and Stoner) 6,953; Universal (Hensley and Hopkins) 19; Scattered 12,868.

‡ Democratic electors were not pledged to Johnson, thus their vote appears under Other Parties column.
† Percentages of total Presidential vote cast, including minor party vote.

Final 1968 Presidential Election Results

*Based on complete vote totals reported to Congressional Quarterly
by the Governmental Affairs Institute*

Total popular vote cast: 73,211,562

STATE	TOTAL POPULAR VOTE				ELECTORAL VOTE			PLURALITY	PERCENTAGES		
	NIXON (R)	HUMPHREY (D)	WALLACE (AIP)	ALL OTHERS	NIXON	HUMPHREY	WALLACE		NIXON	HUMPHREY	WALLACE
ALABAMA†	146,923	196,579	691,425	14,982			10	494,846 AIP	14.0	18.7	65.9
ALASKA	37,600	35,411	10,024	——	3			2,189 R	45.3	42.6	12.1
ARIZONA	266,721	170,514	46,573	3,128	5			96,207 R	54.8	35.0	9.6
ARKANSAS #	190,759	188,228	240,982	——			6	50,223 AIP	30.8	30.4	38.9
CALIFORNIA	3,467,664	3,244,318	487,270	52,335	40			223,346 R	47.8	44.7	6.7
COLORADO	409,345	335,174	60,813	5,867	6			74,171 R	50.5	41.3	7.5
CONNECTICUT	556,721	621,561	76,650	1,300		8		64,840 D	44.3	49.5	6.1
DELAWARE	96,714	89,194	28,459	——	3			7,520 R	45.1	41.6	13.3
FLORIDA	886,804	676,794	624,207	——	14			210,010 R	40.5	30.9	28.5
GEORGIA	380,111	334,439	535,550	——			12	155,439 AIP	30.4	26.8	42.8
HAWAII	91,425	141,324	3,469	——		4		49,899 D	38.7	59.8	1.5
IDAHO	165,369	89,273	36,541	——	4			76,096 R	56.8	30.7	12.5
ILLINOIS	2,174,774	2,039,814	390,958	14,203	26			134,960 R	47.1	44.2	8.5
INDIANA	1,067,885	806,659	243,108	5,945	13			261,226 R	50.3	38.0	11.4
IOWA	619,106	476,699	66,422	5,454	9			142,407 R	53.0	40.8	5.7
KANSAS	478,674	302,996	88,921	2,192	7			175,678 R	54.8	34.7	10.2
KENTUCKY	462,411	397,541	193,098	2,843	9			64,870 R	43.8	37.6	18.3
LOUISIANA	257,535	309,615	530,300	——			10	220,685 AIP	23.5	28.2	48.3
MAINE	169,254	217,312	6,370	——		4		48,058 D	43.1	55.3	1.6
MARYLAND	517,995	538,310	178,734	——		10		20,315 D	41.9	43.6	14.5
MASSACHUSETTS	766,844	1,469,218	87,088	8,602		14		702,374 D	32.9	63.0	3.7
MICHIGAN	1,370,665	1,593,082	331,968	10,535		21		222,417 D	41.5	48.2	10.0
MINNESOTA	658,643	857,738	68,931	3,198		10		199,095 D	41.5	54.0	4.3
MISSISSIPPI	88,516	150,644	415,349	——			7	264,705 AIP	13.5	23.0	63.5
MISSOURI	811,932	791,444	206,126	——	12			20,488 R	44.9	43.7	11.4
MONTANA	138,835	114,117	20,015	1,437	4			24,718 R	50.6	41.6	7.3
NEBRASKA	321,163	170,784	44,904	——	5			150,379 R	59.8	31.8	8.4
NEVADA	73,188	60,598	20,432	——	3			12,590 R	47.5	39.3	13.2
NEW HAMPSHIRE	154,903	130,589	11,173	633	4			24,314 R	52.1	43.9	3.8
NEW JERSEY	1,325,467	1,264,206	262,187	23,535	17			61,261 R	46.1	44.0	9.1
NEW MEXICO	169,692	130,081	25,737	1,828	4			39,611 R	51.8	39.7	7.9
NEW YORK *	3,007,932	3,378,470	358,864	46,421		43		370,538 D	44.3	49.7	5.3
NORTH CAROLINA	627,192	464,113	496,188	——	12		1•	131,004 R	39.5	29.2	31.3
NORTH DAKOTA	138,669	94,769	14,244	200	4			43,900 R	55.9	38.2	5.7
OHIO	1,791,014	1,700,586	467,495	603	26			90,428 R	45.2	42.9	11.8
OKLAHOMA	449,697	301,658	191,731	——	8			148,039 R	47.7	32.0	20.3
OREGON	408,433	358,866	49,683	2,640	6			49,567 R	49.8	43.8	6.1
PENNSYLVANIA	2,090,017	2,259,405	378,582	19,924		29		169,388 D	44.0	47.6	8.0
RHODE ISLAND	122,359	246,518	15,678	383		4		124,159 D	31.8	64.0	4.1
SOUTH CAROLINA	254,062	197,486	215,430	——	8			38,632 R	38.1	29.6	32.3
SOUTH DAKOTA	149,841	118,023	13,400	——	4			31,818 R	53.3	42.0	4.8
TENNESSEE	472,592	351,233	424,792	——	11			47,800 R	37.8	28.1	34.0
TEXAS	1,227,844	1,266,804	584,269	489		25		38,960 D	39.8	41.1	19.0
UTAH	238,728	156,665	26,906	269	4			82,063 R	56.5	37.1	6.3
VERMONT	85,142	70,255	5,104	902	3			14,887 R	52.8	43.5	3.2
VIRGINIA @	590,319	442,387	321,833	6,950	12			147,932 R	43.4	32.5	23.6
WASHINGTON	588,510	616,037	96,990	2,744		9		27,527 D	45.1	47.2	7.4
WEST VIRGINIA	307,555	374,091	72,560	——		7		66,536 D	40.8	49.6	9.6
WISCONSIN	809,997	748,804	127,835	4,902	12			61,193 R	47.9	44.3	7.6
WYOMING	70,927	45,173	11,105	——	3			25,754 R	55.8	35.5	8.7
DIST. OF COL.	31,012	139,566	——	——		3		108,554 D	18.2	81.8	—
TOTALS	31,785,480	31,275,165	9,906,473	244,444	301	191	46	510,315 R‡	43.4	42.7	13.5

#Arkansas—Nixon, Humphrey, and Wallace vote each increased by amendment to early canvass in Jefferson County.

@Virginia—Wallace vote increased by 1,561 over state canvass for vote in Shanandoah County omitted in original report.

•One North Carolina Republican elector cast his vote for Wallace.

†Alabama—Humphrey total is a combination of National Democratic (54,144) and Independent Democratic (142,435) votes; the AIP Wallace vote was cast as Democratic in this state.

*New York—Humphrey total includes 311,622 votes as Liberal candidate.

‡Because of Humphrey's third-place finish in the South, plurality column does not add up to national total.

Democratic Convention Voting, 1940-68

1940—Chicago

- For President: Franklin D. Roosevelt, N.Y., by acclamation on the first ballot.
- For Vice President: Henry A. Wallace, Iowa, by acclamation on the first ballot.

1944—Chicago

- For President:

Franklin D. Roosevelt	1,086
Harry Flood Byrd, Va.	87
James A. Farley, N.Y.	1

- For Vice President: Harry S. Truman, Mo. (ballots as follows):

	1st	2nd
Wallace, Iowa	429 ½	105
Truman, Mo.	319 ½	1,031
Bankhead, Ala.	98	—
Lucas, Ill.	61	—
Barkley, Ky.	49 ½	6
Broughton, N.C.	43	—
McNutt, Ind.	31	1
O'Mahoney, Wyo.	27	—
Cooper, Tenn.	26	26
Kerr, Okla.	23	—
O'Conor, Md.	18	—
Thomas, Utah	10	—
Pepper, Fla.	3	—
Murphy, Mich.	2	—
Rayburn, Texas	2	—
Timmons, Texas	1	—
Douglas, Wash.	—	4

1948—Philadelphia

- For President:

Harry S. Truman, Mo.	947 ½
Richard B. Russell, Ga.	263
Paul McNutt, Ind.	½

- For Vice President: Alben W. Barkley, Ky., nominated by acclamation on the first ballot.

1952—Chicago

- For President: Adlai E. Stevenson, Ill. (ballots as follows):

	1st*	2nd**	3rd***
Kefauver, Tenn.	300 ½	362 ½	279 ½
Russell, Ga.	267 ½	294	260
Stevenson, Ill.	248 ½	324 ½	613
Harriman, N.Y.	126	121	—
Kerr, Okla.	69	5 ½	67 ½
Barkley, Ky.	49 ½	78 ½	67 ½
Williams, Mich.	40 ½	—	—
Dever, Mass.	37 ½	30 ½	½
Humphrey, Minn.	26	—	—
Fulbright, Ark.	22	—	—
McMahon, Conn.	16	—	—
Murray, Mont.	12	—	—
Truman, Mo.	6	6	—
Ewing, N.Y.	4	1	3
Douglas, P., Ill.	3	3	3
Douglas, W.O., Wash.	½	—	—

- For Vice President: John J. Sparkman, Ala., by acclamation.

After several delegations switched their vote, the final result was: Stevenson 273, Kefauver 340, Russell 268, Harriman 123½, Barkley 48½, Kerr 65, with other candidates holding the same total.

**This is the final result of the ballot. Before the final result was announced, changes were as follows: Harriman, one additional vote; Barkley, 5 additional votes; Stevenson, 5 less votes.*

***The ballot ended as carried in this column, with Stevenson 2½ votes short of the nomination. Utah which had balloted 7½ of its 12 votes for Stevenson, gave him the remaining 4½. A motion by Minnesota to make the nomination unanimous then was agreed to by voice vote.*

1956—Chicago

- For President: Adlai E. Stevenson, Ill. (balloting as follows):

	1st*		1st*
Stevenson	905 ½	Chandler, Ky.	36 ½
Harriman, N.Y.	210	Davis, Ga.	33
Johnson, Texas	80	Battle, Va.	32 ½
Symington, Mo.	45 ½	Timmerman, S.C.	23 ½
		Lausche, Ohio	5 ½

- For Vice President: Estes Kefauver, Tenn. (balloting as follows):

	1st	2nd**
Kefauver, Tenn.	483 ½	551 ½
Kennedy, Mass.	304	618
Gore, Tenn.	178	110 ½
Wagner, N.Y.	162 ½	9 ½
Humphrey, Minn.	134 ½	74
Hodges, N.C.	40	½
Maner, Ala.	33	—
Anderson, N.M.	16	—
Clement, Tenn.	13 ½	½
Brown, Calif.	1	½
Collins, Fla.	1 ½	—
Symington, Mo.	1	—
Johnson, Texas	½	—

The nomination was made unanimous when the first ballot ended.

**After switches the totals were: Kefauver 750, Kennedy 593, Gore 11½, Wagner 6, Humphrey 5½, Clement ½. Following the roll call, the nomination was made unanimous.*

1960—Los Angeles

- For President: John F. Kennedy, Mass. (balloting as follows):

	1st*		1st*
Kennedy	801	Smathers, Fla.	30
Johnson, Texas	409	Barnett, Miss.	23
Symington, Mo.	86	Loveless, Iowa	1 ½
Stevenson, Ill.	79 ½	Faubus, Ark.	½
Meyner, N.J.	43	Brown, Calif.	½
Humphrey, Minn.	41 ½	Rosellini, Wash.	½

- For Vice President: Lyndon B. Johnson, Texas, nominated by acclamation on the first ballot.

The nomination was made unanimous when the first ballot ended.

1964—Atlantic City

- For President: Lyndon B. Johnson, Texas, by acclamation.
- For Vice President: Hubert H. Humphrey, Minn., by acclamation.

1968—Chicago

- For President: Hubert H. Humphrey, Minn. (balloting as follows):

	1st*		1st*
Humphrey	1,760-1/4	Kennedy, Mass.	12-3/4
McCarthy, Minn.	601	Bryant, Ala.	1 ½
McGovern, S.D.	146 ½	Wallace, Ala.	½
Phillips, D.C.	67 ½	Gray, Ga.	½
Moore, N.C.	17 ½		

The nomination was made unanimous when the first ballot ended.

- For Vice President: Edmund S. Muskie, Maine (balloting as follows):

	1st*		1st*
Muskie	1,944 ½	McNair, S.C.	1 ½
Bond, Ga.	48 ½	Tate, Pa.	1 ½
Hoeh, N.H.	4	Sanford, N.C.	1
Kennedy, Mass.	3	Shriver, Ill. and Md.	1
McCarthy, Minn.	3	Lowenstein, N.Y.	1
Ribicoff, Conn.	2	Reuss, Wis.	1
McGovern, S.D.	2	O'Dwyer, N.Y.	1
Edwards, Calif.	2	Ryan, N.Y.	3/4
Daley, Ill.	1 ½		

Muskie was later declared nominee by acclamation before conclusion of first ballot.

Republican Convention Voting, 1940-68

1940—Philadelphia

- For President: Wendell L. Willkie (ballots as follows):

	1st	2nd	3rd	4th	5th	6th
Dewey, N.Y.	360	338	315	250	57	11
Taft, Ohio	189	203	212	254	377	310
Willkie, Ind.	105	171	259	306	429	633
Vandenberg, Mich.	76	73	72	61	42	—
James, Pa.	74	66	59	56	59	1
Martin, Mass.	44	26	—	—	—	—
McNider, Iowa	34	34	28	26	4	1
Gannett, N.Y.	33	30	11	4	1	1
Bridges, N.H.	29	9	1	1	—	—
Hoover, Calif.	17	—	—	—	20	9
McNary, Ore.	13	10	10	8	9	—

- For Vice President: Charles L. McNary, Ore.   890
  Dewey Short, Mo.   108
  Styles Bridges, N.H.   2

1944—Chicago

- For President: Thomas E. Dewey, N.Y.   1,056
  Douglas MacArthur, Wis.   1

- For Vice President: John W. Bricker, Ohio, unanimously nominated on first ballot.

1948-Philadelphia

- For President: Thomas E. Dewey, N.Y. (ballots as follows):

	1st	2nd	3rd
Dewey, N.Y.	434	515	All
Taft, Ohio	224	274	——
Stassen, Minn.	157	149	——
Vandenberg, Mich.	62	62	——
Warren, Calif.	59	57	——
Martin, Mass.	18	10	——
MacArthur, Wis.	11	7	——

- For Vice President: Earl Warren, Calif., nominated by acclamation on the first ballot.

1952—Chicago

- For President: Dwight D. Eisenhower, Kan. (balloting as follows):

	1st*
Eisenhower, Kan.	595
Taft, Ohio	500
Warren, Calif.	81
Stassen, Minn.	20
MacArthur, N.Y.	10

- For Vice President: Richard M. Nixon, Calif., by acclamation.

*After switches the totals were: Eisenhower 841, MacArthur 4, Taft 284, Warren 77. A motion to make the nomination unanimous then was agreed to by voice vote.

1956—San Francisco

- For President: Dwight D. Eisenhower, Kan., unanimously nominated on first ballot.
- For Vice President: Richard M. Nixon, Calif., unanimously nominated on first ballot.

1960—Chicago

- For President: Richard M. Nixon, Calif. (balloting as follows):

	1st*
Nixon	1,321
Goldwater, Ariz.	10

- For Vice President: Henry Cabot Lodge Jr., Mass., unanimously nominated on the first ballot.

*The nomination was made unanimous when the first ballot ended.

1964—San Francisco

- For President: Barry Goldwater, Ariz. (balloting as follows):

	1st
Goldwater	883
Scranton	214
Rockefeller	114
Smith	27
Fong	5
Judd	22
Romney	41
Lodge	2

- For Vice President: William E. Miller, New York, nominated by acclamation on the first ballot.

1968—Miami Beach

- For President: Richard M. Nixon N.Y. (balloting as follows):

	1st*
Nixon	692
Rockefeller, N.Y.	277
Reagan, Calif.	182
Rhodes, Ohio	55
Romney, Mich.	50
Case, N.J.	22
Carlson, Kan.	20
Rockefeller, Ark.	18
Fong, Hawaii	14
Stassen, Pa.	2
Lindsay, N.Y.	1

*Before switches. Because of parliamentary confusion, Nixon never was declared the unanimous choice.

- For Vice President: Spiro T. Agnew, Md. (balloting as follows):

	1st*
Agnew	1,119
Romney, Mich.	186
Lindsay, N.Y.	10
Brooke, Mass.	1
Rhodes, Ohio	1

*The nomination was made unanimous when the first ballot ended.

DISTRIBUTION OF HOUSE SEATS AND ELECTORAL VOTES

Based on Censuses of 1940, 1950 and 1960

| | U.S. HOUSE SEATS | | | | | ELECTORAL VOTES Presidential Elections of | | |
	1943-1953	1950 Census Changes	1953-1963	1960 Census Changes	1963-1973	1944, 1948	1952, 1956, 1960	1964, 1968
ALABAMA	9	—	9	—1	8	11	11	10
ALASKA			1	—	1		3	3
ARIZONA	2	—	2	+1	3	4	4	5
ARKANSAS	7	—1	6	—2	4	9	8	6
CALIFORNIA	23	+7	30	+8	38	25	32	40
COLORADO	4	—	4	—	4	6	6	6
CONNECTICUT	6	—	6	—	6	8	8	8
DELAWARE	1	—	1	—	1	3	3	3
DISTRICT OF COLUMBIA						—	—	3
FLORIDA	6	+2	8	+4	12	8	10	14
GEORGIA	10	—	10	—	10	12	12	12
HAWAII			1	+1	2		3	4
IDAHO	2	—	2	—	2	4	4	4
ILLINOIS	26	—1	25	—1	24	28	27	26
INDIANA	11	—	11	—	11	13	13	13
IOWA	8	—	8	—1	7	10	10	9
KANSAS	6	—	6	—1	5	8	8	7
KENTUCKY	9	—1	8	—1	7	11	10	9
LOUISIANA	8	—	8	—	8	10	10	10
MAINE	3	—	3	—1	2	5	5	4
MARYLAND	6	+1	7	+1	8	8	9	10
MASSACHUSETTS	14	—	14	—2	12	16	16	14
MICHIGAN	17	+1	18	+1	19	19	20	21
MINNESOTA	9	—	9	—1	8	11	11	10
MISSISSIPPI	7	—1	6	—1	5	9	8	7
MISSOURI	13	—2	11	—1	10	15	13	12
MONTANA	2	—	2	—	2	4	4	4
NEBRASKA	4	—	4	—1	3	6	6	5
NEVADA	1	—	1	—	1	3	3	3
NEW HAMPSHIRE	2	—	2	—	2	4	4	4
NEW JERSEY	14	—	14	+1	15	16	16	17
NEW MEXICO	2	—	2	—	2	4	4	4
NEW YORK	45	—2	43	—2	41	47	45	43
NORTH CAROLINA	12	—	12	—1	11	14	14	13
NORTH DAKOTA	2	—	2	—	2	4	4	4
OHIO	23	—	23	+1	24	25	25	26
OKLAHOMA	8	—2	6	—	6	10	8	8
OREGON	4	—	4	—	4	6	6	6
PENNSYLVANIA	33	—3	30	—3	27	35	32	29
RHODE ISLAND	2	—	2	—	2	4	4	4
SOUTH CAROLINA	6	—	6	—	6	8	8	8
SOUTH DAKOTA	2	—	2	—	2	4	4	4
TENNESSEE	10	—1	9	—	9	12	11	11
TEXAS	21	+1	22	+1	23	23	24	25
UTAH	2	—	2	—	2	4	4	4
VERMONT	1	—	1	—	1	3	3	3
VIRGINIA	9	+1	10	—	10	11	12	12
WASHINGTON	6	+1	7	—	7	8	9	9
WEST VIRGINIA	6	—	6	—1	5	8	8	7
WISCONSIN	10	—	10	—	10	12	12	12
WYOMING	1	—	1	—	1	3	3	3

Results of Elections in House of Representatives, 1946-68

	46	48	50	52	54	56	58	60	62	64	66	68
NATIONAL TOTALS												
Democrats	188	263	235	213	232	234	283	262	259	295	248	243
Republicans	246	171	199	221	203	201	153	175	176	140	187	192
ALABAMA												
Democrats	9	9	9	9	9	9	9	9	8	3	5	5
Republicans	0	0	0	0	0	0	0	0	0	5	3	3
ALASKA												
Democrats	—	—	—	—	—	—	1	1	1	1	0	0
Republicans	—	—	—	—	—	—	0	0	0	0	1	1
ARIZONA												
Democrats	2	2	2	1	1	1	1	1	2	2	1	1
Republicans	0	0	0	1	1	1	1	1	1	1	2	2
ARKANSAS												
Democrats	7	7	7	6	6	6	6	6	4	4	3	3
Republicans	0	0	0	0	0	0	0	0	0	0	1	1
CALIFORNIA												
Democrats	9	10	10	11	11	13	16	16	25	23*	21	21
Republicans	14	13	13	19	19	17	14	14	13	15*	17	17
COLORADO												
Democrats	1	3	2	2	2	2	3	2	2	4	3	3
Republicans	3	1	2	2	2	2	1	2	2	0	1	1
CONNECTICUT												
Democrats	0	3	2	1	1	0	6	4	5	6	5	4
Republicans	6	3	4	5	5	6	0	2	1	0	1	2
DELAWARE												
Democrats	0	0	0	0	1	0	1	1	1	1	0	0
Republicans	1	1	1	1	0	1	0	0	0	0	1	1
FLORIDA												
Democrats	6	6	6	8	7	7	7	7	10	10	9	9
Republicans	0	0	0	0	1	1	1	1	2	2	3	3
GEORGIA												
Democrats	10	10	10	10	10	10	10	10	10	9	8	8
Republicans	0	0	0	0	0	0	0	0	0	1	2	2
HAWAII												
Democrats	—	—	—	—	—	—	1	2	2	2	2	2
Republicans	—	—	—	—	—	—	0	0	0	0	0	0
IDAHO												
Democrats	0	1	0	1	1	1	1	2	2	1	0	0
Republicans	2	1	2	1	1	1	1	0	0	1	2	2
ILLINOIS												
Democrats	6	12	8	9	12	11	14	14	12	13	12	12
Republicans	20	14	18	16	13	14	11	11	12	11	12	12
INDIANA												
Democrats	2	7	2	1	2	2	8	3	4	6	5	4
Republicans	9	4	9	10	9	9	3	8	7	5	6	7
IOWA												
Democrats	0	0	0	0	0	1	4	2	1	6	2	2
Republicans	8	8	8	8	8	7	4	6	6	1	5	5
KANSAS												
Democrats	0	0	0	1	0	1	3	1	0	0	0	0
Republicans	6	6	6	5	6	5	3	5	5	5	5	5
KENTUCKY												
Democrats	6	7	7	6	6	7	7	7	5	6	4	4
Republicans	3	2	2	2	2	2	1	1	2	1	3	3
LOUISIANA												
Democrats	8	8	8	8	8	8	8	8	8	8	8	8
Republicans	0	0	0	0	0	0	0	0	0	0	0	0
MAINE												
Democrats	0	0	0	0	0	1	2	0	0	1	2	2
Republicans	3	3	3	3	3	2	1	3	2	1	0	0
MARYLAND												
Democrats	4	4	3	3	4	4	7	6	6	6	5	4
Republicans	2	2	3	4	3	3	0	1	2	2	3	4
MASSACHUSETTS												
Democrats	5	6	6	6	7	7	8	8	7	7	7	7
Republicans	9	8	8	8	7	7	6	6	5	5	5	5
MICHIGAN												
Democrats	3	5	5	5	7	6	7	7	8	12	7	7
Republicans	14	12	12	13	11	12	11	11	11	7	12	12
MINNESOTA												
Democrats	1	4	4	4	5	5	4	3	4	4	3	3
Republicans	8	5	5	5	4	4	5	6	4	4	5	5
MISSISSIPPI												
Democrats	7	7	7	6	6	6	6	6	5	4	5	5
Republicans	0	0	0	0	0	0	0	0	0	1	0	0
MISSOURI												
Democrats	4	12	10	7	9	10	10	9	8	8	8	9
Republicans	9	1	3	4	2	1	1	2	2	2	2	1
MONTANA												
Democrats	1	1	1	1	1	2	2	1	1	1	1	1
Republicans	1	1	1	1	1	0	0	1	1	1	1	1
NEBRASKA												
Democrats	0	1	0	0	0	0	2	0	0	1	0	0
Republicans	4	3	4	4	4	4	2	4	3	2	3	3
NEVADA												
Democrats	0	1	1	0	0	1	1	1	1	1	1	1
Republicans	1	0	0	1	1	0	0	0	0	0	0	0
NEW HAMPSHIRE												
Democrats	0	0	0	0	0	0	0	0	0	1	0	0
Republicans	2	2	2	2	2	2	2	2	2	1	2	2
NEW JERSEY												
Democrats	2	5	5	5	6	4	5	6	7	11	9	9
Republicans	12	9	9	9	8	10	9	8	8	4	6	6
NEW MEXICO												
Democrats	2	2	2	2	2	2	2	2	2	2	2	0
Republicans	0	0	0	0	0	0	0	0	0	0	0	2
NEW YORK												
Democrats	16	24	23	16	17	17	19	22	20	27	26	26
Republicans	28	20	22	27	26	26	24	21	21	14	15	15
NORTH CAROLINA												
Democrats	12	12	12	11	11	11	11	11	9	9	8	7
Republicans	0	0	0	1	1	1	1	1	2	2	3	4
NORTH DAKOTA												
Democrats	0	0	0	0	0	0	1	0	0	1	0	0
Republicans	2	2	2	2	2	2	1	2	2	1	2	2
OHIO												
Democrats	4	12	7	6	6	6	9	7	6	10	5	6
Republicans	19	11	15	16	17	17	14	16	18	14	19	18
OKLAHOMA												
Democrats	6	8	6	5	5	5	5	5	5	5	4	4
Republicans	2	0	2	1	1	1	1	1	1	1	2	2
OREGON												
Democrats	0	0	0	0	1	3	3	2	3	3	2	2
Republicans	4	4	4	4	3	1	1	2	1	1	2	2
PENNSYLVANIA												
Democrats	5	16	13	11	14	13	16	14	13	15	14	14
Republicans	28	17	20	19	16	17	14	16	14	12	13	13
RHODE ISLAND												
Democrats	2	2	2	2	2	2	2	2	2	2	2	2
Republicans	0	0	0	0	0	0	0	0	0	0	0	0
SOUTH CAROLINA												
Democrats	6	6	6	6	6	6	6	6	6	6*	5	5
Republicans	0	0	0	0	0	0	0	0	0	0*	1	1
SOUTH DAKOTA												
Democrats	0	0	0	0	1	1	0	1	0	0	0	0
Republicans	2	2	2	2	1	1	2	2	2	2	2	5
TENNESSEE												
Democrats	8	8	8	7	7	7	7	7	6	6	5	5
Republicans	2	2	2	2	2	2	2	2	3	3	4	4
TEXAS												
Democrats	21	21	21	21	21	21	21	21	21	23	21†	20
Republicans	0	0	0	0	1	1	1	1	2	0	2†	3
UTAH												
Democrats	1	2	2	0	0	0	1	2	0	1	0	0
Republicans	1	0	0	2	2	2	1	0	2	1	2	2
VERMONT												
Democrats	0	0	0	0	0	0	1	0	0	0	0	0
Republicans	1	1	1	1	1	1	0	1	1	1	1	1
VIRGINIA												
Democrats	9	9	9	7	8	8	8	8	8	8	6	5
Republicans	0	0	0	2	2	2	2	2	2	2	4	5
WASHINGTON												
Democrats	1	2	2	1	1	1	1	2	1	5	5	5
Republicans	5	4	4	6	6	6	6	5	6	2	2	2
WEST VIRGINIA												
Democrats	2	6	5	6	4	5	5	4	4	4	4	5
Republicans	4	0	0	1	0	2	1	1	1	1	1	0
WISCONSIN												
Democrats	0	2	1	1	3	3	5	4	4	5	3	3•
Republicans	10	8	9	9	7	7	5	6	6	5	7	7•
WYOMING												
Democrats	0	0	0	0	0	0	0	0	0	1	0	0
Republicans	1	1	1	1	1	1	1	1	1	0	1	1

*Shifted since 1964 election. South Carolina became 5D, 1 R in 1965; California became 24D, 14R in June 1966.

†Shifted since 1966 election. Texas became 20D, 3R in August 1968.
•Shifted since 1968 election. Wisconsin became 4D, 6R in April 1969.

Senate Elections, 1964-68

*(For results of elections from 1946-62, see Congress
and the Nation, Vol. I, p. 72-80.)*

1964

State	Winner	Winners %	Winners Plurality	Loser
ARIZONA	Fannin (R)	51.4	13,377	Roy L. Elson (D)
CALIFORNIA	Murphy (R)	51.5	216,643	*Salinger (D)
CONNECTICUT	*Dodd (D)	64.7	354,069	John Lodge (R)
DELAWARE	*Williams (R)	51.7	6,932	Elbert N. Carvel (D)
FLORIDA	*Holland (D)	63.9	435,373	Claude R. Kirk (R)
HAWAII	*Fong (R)	53.0	13,958	Thomas P. Gill (D)
INDIANA	*Hartke (D)	54.3	186,986	D. Russell Bontrager (R)
MAINE	*Muskie (D)	66.6	126,471	Clifford G. McIntire (R)
MARYLAND	Tydings (D)	62.8	276,256	*Beall (R)
MASSACHUSETTS	*Kennedy (D)	74.3	1,129,244	Howard Whitmore (R)
MICHIGAN	Hart (D)	64.4	900,640	Elly M. Peterson (R)
MINNESOTA	*McCarthy (D)	60.3	325,420	Wheelock Whitney (R)
MISSISSIPPI	*Stennis (D)	X	343,364	
MISSOURI	*Symington (D)	66.5	590,289	Jean Paul Bradshaw (R)
MONTANA	*Mansfield (D)	64.5	81,276	Alex Blewett (R)
NEBRASKA	*Hruska (R)	66.7	218,167	Raymond W. Arndt (D)
NEVADA	*Cannon (D)	50.0	48	Paul Laxalt (R)
NEW JERSEY	*Williams (D)	61.9	666,235	Bernard M. Shanley (R)
NEW MEXICO	Montoya (D)	54.7	30,647	*Mechem (R)
NEW YORK	Kennedy (D)	53.5	719,693	*Keating (R)
NORTH DAKOTA	*Burdick (D)	57.6	39,583	Tom Kleppe (R)
OHIO	*Young (D)	50.2	16,827	Robert Taft Jr. (R)
PENNSYLVANIA	*Scott (R)	50.6	70,635	Genevieve Blatt (D)
RHODE ISLAND	*Pastore (D)	82.7	252,892	Ronald R. Lagueux (R)
TENNESSEE	*Gore (D)	53.6	77,067	Dan H. Kuykendall (R)
TEXAS	*Yarborough (D)	56.2	329,621	George Bush (R)
UTAH	*Moss (D)	57.3	58,260	Ernest L. Wilkinson (R)
VERMONT	*Prouty (R)	53.5	11,422	Frederick J. Fayette (D)
VIRGINIA	*Byrd (D)	63.8	415,646	Richard A. May (R)
WASHINGTON	*Jackson (D)	72.2	538,812	Lloyd J. Andrews (R)
WEST VIRGINIA	*Byrd (D)	67.7	268,943	Cooper P. Benedict (R)
WISCONSIN	*Proxmire (D)	53.3	111,897	Wilber N. Renk (R)
WYOMING	*McGee (D)	54.0	11,300	John S. Wold (R)

*Incumbent
X - Unopposed

1964 Special Election

State	Winner	Winners %	Winners Plurality	Loser
OKLAHOMA	Harris (D)	50.2	21,390	Bud Wilkinson (R)
TENNESSEE	Bass (D)	52.1	51,575	Howard Baker Jr. (R)

Incumbent Senator Defeated for Renomination

OKLAHOMA	J. Howard Edmondson (D) *1*

1. Appointed Jan. 6, 1963.

1966

State	Winner	Winners %	Winners Plurality	Loser
ALABAMA	*Sparkman (D)	60.1	169,120	John Grenier (R)
ALASKA	*Bartlett (D)	75.5	33,328	Lee L. McKinley (R)
ARKANSAS	*McClellan (D)	X		
COLORADO	*Allott (R)	58.0	102,048	Roy Romer (D)
DELAWARE	*Boggs (R)	59.1	30,005	James M. Tunnell Jr. (D)
GEORGIA	*Russell (D)	X	631,002	
IDAHO	*Jordan (R)	55.4	27,182	Ralph R. Harding (D)
ILLINOIS	Percy (R)	55.0	422,302	*Douglas (D)
IOWA	*Miller (R)	60.9	198,225	E.B. Smith (D)
KANSAS	*Pearson (R)	52.3	46,854	J. Floyd Breeding (D)
KENTUCKY	*Cooper (R)	64.5	217,726	John Young Brown (D)
LOUISIANA	*Ellender (D)	X	437,695	
MAINE	*Smith (R)	58.9	57,155	Elmer H. Violette (D)
MASSACHUSETTS	Brooke (R)	61.7	438,712	Endicott Peabody (D)
MICHIGAN	*Griffin (R)	55.9	294,146	G. Mennen Williams (D)
MINNESOTA	*Mondale (DFL)	53.9	110,972	Robert A. Forsythe (R)
MISSISSIPPI	*Eastland (D)	65.6	153,098	Prentiss Walker (R)
MONTANA	*Metcalf (D)	53.2	16,469	Tim M. Babcock (R)
NEBRASKA	*Curtis (R)	61.2	108,166	Frank B. Morrison (D)
NEW HAMPSHIRE	*McIntyre (D)	54.1	18,647	Harrison R. Thyng (R)
NEW JERSEY	*Case (R)	60.0	490,822	Warren W. Wilentz (D)
NEW MEXICO	*Anderson (D)	53.1	16,217	Anderson Carter (R)
NORTH CAROLINA	*Jordan (D)	55.6	100,938	John S. Shallcross (R)
OKLAHOMA	*Harris (D)	53.7	47,572	Pat J. Patterson (R)
OREGON	Hatfield (R)	51.8	24,017	Robert B. Duncan (D)
RHODE ISLAND	*Pell (D)	67.7	114,493	Ruth M. Briggs (R)
SOUTH CAROLINA	*Thurmond (R)	62.2	106,342	Bradley Morrah (D)
SOUTH DAKOTA	*Mundt (R)	66.3	73,954	Donn H. Wright (D)
TENNESSEE	Baker (R)	55.7	99,220	Frank G. Clement (D)
TEXAS	*Tower (R)	56.4	198,646	Waggoner Carr (D)
VIRGINIA	Spong (D)	58.6	184,174	James P. Ould (R)
WEST VIRGINIA	*Randolph (D)	59.5	93,434	Francis J. Love (R)
WYOMING	Hansen (R)	51.8	4,407	Teno Roncalio (D)

*Incumbent
X - Unopposed

─────────────────── 1966 Special Elections ───────────────────

State	Winner	Winners %	Winners Plurality	Loser
SOUTH CAROLINA	Hollings (D)	51.3	11,758	Marshall Parker (R)
VIRGINIA	*Byrd Jr. (D)1	53.3	116,224	Lawrence M. Traylor (R)

*Incumbent
1. Appointed Nov. 25, 1965.

─────────── Incumbent Senators Defeated for Renomination in 1966 ───────────

SOUTH CAROLINA	Donald S. Russell (D) 1
TENNESSEE	Ross Bass (D)
VIRGINIA	A. Willis Robertson (D)

1. Appointed April 22, 1965.

1968

State	Winner	Winners %	Winners Plurality	Loser
ALABAMA	Allen (D)	70.0	437,547	Perry O. Hooper (R)
ALASKA	Gravel (D)	45.1	6,241	Elmer E. Rasmuson (R)
ARIZONA	Goldwater (R)	57.2	69,269	Roy L. Elson (D)
ARKANSAS	*Fulbright (D)	59.1	108,226	Charles T. Bernard (R)
CALIFORNIA	Cranston (D)	51.8	351,204	Max Rafferty (R)
COLORADO	*Dominick (R)	58.6	134,368	Stephen L.R. McNichols (D)
CONNECTICUT	*Ribicoff (D)	54.3	103,588	Edwin H. May Jr. (R)
FLORIDA	Gurney (R)	55.9	238,862	LeRoy Collins (D)
GEORGIA	*Talmadge (D)	77.5	628,297	E. Earl Patton Jr. (R)
HAWAII	*Inouye (D)	83.4	155,240	Wayne C. Thiessen (R)
IDAHO	*Church (D)	60.3	59,088	George V. Hansen (R)
ILLINOIS	*Dirksen (R)	53.0	285,705	William G. Clark (D)
INDIANA	*Bayh (D)	51.7	71,885	William D. Ruckelshaus (R)
IOWA	Hughes (D)	50.2	6,415	David M. Stanley (R)
KANSAS	Dole (R)	60.1	175,000	William I. Robinson (D)
KENTUCKY	Cook (R)	51.4	35,300	Katherine Peden (D)
LOUISIANA	*Long (D)	X	518,586	
MARYLAND	Mathias (R)	47.8	98,526	*Daniel B. Brewster (D)
MISSOURI	Eagleton (D)	51.1	36,870	Thomas B. Curtis (R)
NEVADA	*Bible (D)	54.8	14,554	Ed Fike (R)
NEW HAMPSHIRE	*Cotton (R)	59.3	53,347	John W. King (D)
NEW YORK	*Javits (R)	49.7	1,119,077	Paul O'Dwyer (D)
NORTH CAROLINA	*Ervin (D)	60.6	303,472	Robert Vance Somers (R)
NORTH DAKOTA	*Young (R)	64.8	74,153	Herschel Lashkowitz (D)
OHIO	Saxbe (R)	51.5	114,812	John J. Gilligan (D)
OKLAHOMA	Bellmon (R)	51.7	50,462	*A.S. Mike Monroney (D)
OREGON	Packwood (R)	50.2	3,293	*Wayne Morse (D)
PENNSYLVANIA	Schweiker (R)	51.9	282,100	*Joseph S. Clark (D)
SOUTH CAROLINA	*Hollings (D)	61.9	155,280	Marshall Parker (R)
SOUTH DAKOTA	*McGovern (D)	56.8	38,010	Archie Gubbrud (R)
UTAH	*Bennett (R)	53.7	32,907	Milton L. Weilenmann (D)
VERMONT	*Aiken (R)	X	157,154	
WASHINGTON	*Magnuson (D)	64.4	360,289	Jack Metcalf (R)
WISCONSIN	*Nelson (D)	61.7	387,021	Jerris Leonard (R)

*Incumbent
X - Unopposed

──────── Incumbent Senators Defeated for Renomination in 1968 ────────

ALASKA	Ernest Gruening (D)
CALIFORNIA	Thomas H. Kuchel (R)
MISSOURI	Edward V. Long (D)
OHIO	Frank J. Lausche (D)

GOVERNORS OF THE STATES SINCE 1944

Alabama

Four-Year Term

1943-1947	Chauncey M. Sparks (D)
1947-1951	James Elisha Folsom (D)
1951-1955	Gordon Persons (D)
1955-1959	James Elisha Folsom (D)
1959-1963	John Patterson (D)
1963-1967	George C. Wallace (D)
1967-1971	Lurleen Wallace (D)*
1968-1971	Albert Brewer (D)

*Wallace died May 7, 1968 and was replaced by Lt. Gov. Brewer who was sworn in on May 7, 1968.

Alaska

Four-Year Term

1959-1963	William A. Egan (D)
1963-1967	Egan
1967-1971	Walter J. Hickel (R)*
1969-1971	Keith Miller (R)

*Hickel resigned Jan. 20, 1969 to become Secretary of Interior. He was replaced by Secretary of State Keith Miller.

Arizona

Two-Year Term

1941-1942	Sidney P. Osborn (D)
1943-1944	Osborn
1945-1946	Osborn
1947-1948	Osborn*
1948	Dan E. Garvey (D)**
1949-1950	Garvey
1951-1952	J. Howard Pyle (R)
1953-1954	Pyle
1955-1956	Ernest W. McFarland (D)
1957-1958	McFarland
1959-1960	Paul Fannin (R)
1961-1962	Fannin
1963-1964	Fannin
1965-1966	Sam Goddard (D)
1967-1968	Jack Williams (R)
1969-1970	Williams

*Osborn died in office, May 23, 1948.
**Garvey served as Acting Gov. from July 25, 1948 to Nov. 2, when elected Governor.

Arkansas

Two-Year Term

1941-1943	Homer M. Adkins (D)
1943-1945	Adkins
1945-1947	Benjamin T. Laney (D)
1947-1949	Laney
1949-1951	Sidney S. McMath (D)
1951-1953	McMath
1953-1955	Francis Cherry (D)

ARKANSAS—TWO-YEAR TERM (Cont.)

1955-1957	Orval E. Faubus (D)
1957-1959	Faubus
1959-1961	Faubus
1961-1963	Faubus
1963-1965	Faubus
1965-1967	Faubus
1967-1969	Winthrop Rockefeller (R)
1969-1971	Rockefeller

California

Four-Year Term

1943-1947	Earl Warren (R)
1947-1951	Warren
1951-1953	Warren*
1953-1955	Goodwin J. Knight (R)
1955-1959	Knight
1959-1963	Edmund G. Brown (D)
1963-1967	Brown
1967-1971	Ronald Reagan (R)

*Warren resigned office on Oct. 5, 1953 to become Chief Justice of the United States; Knight, as Lt. Governor, sworn in as Governor on Oct. 5, 1953.

Colorado

Two-Year Term

1943-1945	John C. Vivian (R)
1945-1947	Vivian
1947-1949	William Lee Knous (D)
1949-1950	Knous*
1950-1951	Walter Warren Johnson (D)
1951-1953	Dan Thornton (R)
1953-1955	Thornton
1955-1957	Edwin C. Johnson (D)
1957-1959	Stephen L.R. McNichols (D)

Four-Year Term

1959-1963	McNichols
1963-1967	John A. Love (R)
1967-1971	Love

*Knous resigned March 1, 1950; Johnson sworn in March 1, 1950 for the remainder of the term.

Connecticut

Two-Year Term

1943-1945	Raymond Earl Baldwin (R)
1945-1946	Baldwin*
1946-1947	Charles Wilbert Snow (D)
1947-1948	James Lukens McConaughy (R)**
1948-1949	James Coughlin Shannon (R)
1949-1951	Chester Bowles (D)

*Baldwin resigned Dec. 26, 1946 to enter the U.S. Senate; Snow sworn in Dec. 26th, 1946 and served until Jan. 8, 1947.
**McConaughy died March 7, 1948 and was replaced by Shannon who was sworn in on March 8, 1948.

CONNECTICUT (Cont.)

Four-Year Term

1951-1955	John Davis Lodge (R)
1955-1959	Abraham A. Ribicoff (D)
1959-1961	Ribicoff***
1961-1963	John N. Dempsey (D)
1963-1967	Dempsey
1967-1971	Dempsey

***Ribicoff resigned Jan. 21, 1961 to become Secretary of Health, Education and Welfare. He was replaced by Lt. Gov. Dempsey who was sworn in on Jan. 21, 1961.

Delaware

Four-Year Term

1941-1945	Walter W. Bacon (R)
1945-1949	Bacon
1949-1953	Elbert N. Carvel (D)
1953-1957	J. Caleb Boggs (R)
1957-1961	Boggs
1961-1965	Elbert N. Carvel (D)
1965-1969	Charles L. Terry Jr. (D)
1969-1972	Russell W. Peterson (R)

Florida

Four-Year Term

1941-1945	Spessard Lindsey Holland (D)
1945-1949	Millard Fillmore Caldwell (D)
1949-1953	Fuller Warren (D)
1953	Dan E. McCarty (D)*
1953-1955	Charley E. Johns (D)
1955-1957	LeRoy Collins (D)
1957-1961	Collins
1961-1965	C. Farris Bryant (D)
1965-1967	Haydon Burns (D)**
1967-1971	Claude R. Kirk Jr. (R)

*McCarty died Sept. 28, 1953; Charley E. Johns sworn in Sept. 29, 1953 to serve until the 1954 elections.
**Burns served a two-year term necessitated by a changeover from electing Governors in Presidential election years to electing them in non-Presidential election years.

Georgia

Two-Year Term

1943-1945	Ellis Gibbs Arnall (D)
1945-1947	Arnall

Four-Year Term

1947-1948	Melvin E. Thompson (D)*
1948-1951	Herman E. Talmadge (D)**
1951-1955	Talmadge
1955-1959	S. Marvin Griffin (D)
1959-1963	Ernest Vandiver (D)
1963-1967	Carl E. Sanders (D)
1967-1971	Lester G. Maddox (D)

*Melvin E. Thompson was sworn in as acting Governor on Jan. 20, 1947 and was declared legal Governor on March 19, 1947. Eugene Talmadge (D) had been elected in 1946 for a four-year term but died Dec. 21, 1946, prior to inauguration date.
**Herman E. Talmadge was elected Governor in a special election Sept. 8, 1948, and was sworn in as Governor on Nov. 17, 1948.

Hawaii

Four-Year Term

1959-1962	William F. Quinn (R)
1963-1966	John A. Burns (D)
1967-1970	Burns

Idaho

Two-Year Term

1943-1945	C.A. Bottolfsen (R)
1945	Charles C. Gossett (D)*
1945-1947	Arnold Williams (D)

Four-Year Term

1947-1951	Charles A. Robins (R)
1951-1955	Leonard B. Jordan (R)
1955-1959	Robert E. Smylie (R)
1959-1963	Smylie
1963-1967	Smylie
1967-1971	Don Samuelson (R)

*Gossett resigned Nov. 17, 1945 and was succeeded the same day by Lt. Gov. Williams who then appointed Gossett to the U.S. Senate to succeed John Thomas who died Nov. 10, 1945.

Illinois

Four-Year Term

1941-1945	Dwight H. Green (R)
1945-1949	Green
1949-1953	Adlai E. Stevenson (D)
1953-1957	William G. Stratton (R)
1957-1961	Stratton
1961-1965	Otto Kerner (D)
1965-1968	Kerner*
1968-1969	Samuel H. Shapiro (D)
1969-1972	Richard B. Ogilvie (R)

*Kerner resigned May 20, 1968 to become a judge of the United States Court of Appeals in Chicago. He was replaced by Lt. Gov. Shapiro who was sworn in on May 21, 1968.

Indiana

Four-Year Term

1941-1945	Henry F. Schricker (D)
1945-1949	Ralph F. Gates (R)
1949-1953	Henry F. Schricker (D)
1953-1957	George N. Craig (R)
1957-1961	Harold W. Handley (R)
1961-1965	Matthew E. Welsh (D)
1965-1969	Roger D. Branigin (D)
1969-1972	Edgar D. Whitcomb (R)

Iowa

Two-Year Term

1943-1945	Bourke B. Hickenlooper (R)
1945-1947	Robert D. Blue (R)

IOWA—TWO YEAR TERM (Cont.)

1947-1949	Blue
1949-1951	William S. Beardsley (R)*
1951-1953	Beardsley
1953-1954	Beardsley
1954-1955	Leo Elthon (R)
1955-1957	Leo A. Hoegh (R)
1957-1959	Herschel C. Loveless (D)
1959-1961	Loveless
1961-1963	Norman A. Erbe (R)
1963-1965	Harold E. Hughes (D)
1965-1967	Hughes
1967-1969	Hughes
1969-1971	Robert Ray (R)

Beardsley died Nov. 21, 1954; Leo Elthon was sworn in as acting Governor on Nov. 22, 1954 to serve the remainder of the term.

Kansas

Two-Year Term

1943-1945	Andrew F. Schoeppel (R)
1945-1947	Schoeppel
1947-1949	Frank Carlson (R)
1949-1951	Carlson
1951-1953	Edward F. Arn (R)
1953-1955	Arn
1955-1957	Fred Hall (R)
1957-1959	George Docking (D)
1959-1961	Docking
1961-1963	John Anderson Jr. (R)
1963-1965	Anderson
1965-1967	William H. Avery (R)
1967-1969	Robert Docking (D)
1969-1971	Docking

Kentucky

Four-Year Term

1943-1947	Simeon S. Willis (R)
1947-1950	Earle C. Clements (D)*
1950-1951	Lawrence W. Wetherby (D)
1951-1955	Wetherby
1955-1959	Albert B. Chandler (D)
1959-1963	Bert C. Combs (D)
1963-1967	Edward T. Breathitt (D)
1967-1971	Louie B. Nunn (R)

Clements resigned office to become Senator on Nov. 27, 1950; Wetherby sworn in as acting Governor Nov. 27, 1950 for the remainder of the term.

Louisiana

Four-Year Term

1944-1948	Jimmie H. Davis (D)
1948-1952	Earl Kemp Long (D)
1952-1956	Robert F. Kennon (D)
1956-1960	Earl Kemp Long (D)
1960-1964	Jimmie H. Davis (D)
1964-1968	John J. McKeithen (D)
1968-1972	McKeithen

Maine

Two-Year Term

1941-1943	Sumner Sewall (R)
1943-1945	Sewall
1945-1947	Horace A. Hildreth (R)
1947-1949	Hildreth
1949-1951	Frederick G. Payne (R)
1951-1952	Payne *
1952-1953	Burton M. Cross (R)*
1953-1955	Cross
1955-1957	Edmund S. Muskie (D)
1957-1959	Muskie
1959	Clinton A. Clauson (D)**
1960-1961	John H. Reed (R)**
1961-1963	Reed

Four-Year Term

1963-1967	Reed
1967-1971	Kenneth M. Curtis (D)

Payne resigned Dec. 16, 1952 effective Dec. 25, 1952; Cross became acting Governor on Dec. 26, 1952.
**Clauson died Dec. 31, 1959; Reed sworn in Jan. 1, 1960.*

Maryland

Four-Year Term

1939-1943	Herbert R. O'Conor (D)
1943-1947	O'Conor
1947-1951	William Preston Lane Jr. (D)
1951-1955	Theodore R. McKeldin (R)
1955-1959	McKeldin
1959-1963	J. Millard Tawes (D)
1963-1967	Tawes
1967-1971	Spiro T. Agnew (R)*
1969-1971	Marvin Mandel (D)

Agnew resigned Jan. 7, 1969 to become Vice President of the United States. Mandel was elected Governor Jan. 7, 1969 by the State Legislature.

Massachusetts

Two-Year Term

1939-1941	Leverett Saltonstall (R)
1941-1943	Saltonstall
1943-1945	Saltonstall
1945-1947	Maurice J. Tobin (D)
1947-1949	Robert F. Bradford (R)
1949-1951	Paul A. Dever (D)
1951-1953	Dever
1953-1955	Christian A. Herter (R)
1955-1957	Herter
1957-1959	Foster Furcolo (D)
1959-1961	Furcolo
1961-1963	John A. Volpe (R)
1963-1965	Endicott Peabody (D)
1965-1967	John A. Volpe (R)

Four-Year Term

1967-1971	Volpe*
1969-1971	Francis W. Sargent (R)

Volpe resigned Jan. 20, 1969, to become Secretary of Transportation. He was replaced by Lt. Gov. Sargent who was sworn in on Jan. 20, 1969.

Michigan

Two-Year Term

1943-1945	Harry F. Kelly (R)
1945-1947	Kelly
1947-1949	Kim Sigler (R)
1949-1951	G. Mennen Williams (D)
1951-1953	Williams
1953-1955	Williams
1955-1957	Williams
1957-1959	Williams
1959-1961	Williams
1961-1963	John B. Swainson (D)
1963-1965	George W. Romney (R)
1965-1967	Romney

Four-Year Term

1967-1971	Romney*
1969-1971	William G. Milliken (R)

*Romney resigned Jan. 20, 1969, to become Secretary of Housing and Urban Development. He was replaced by Lt. Gov. Milliken who was sworn in on Jan. 20, 1969.

Minnesota

Two-Year Term

1943-1945	Edward J. Thye (R)
1945-1947	Thye
1947-1949	Luther W. Youngdahl (R)*
1949-1951	Youngdahl
1951	C. Elmer Anderson (R)
1951-1953	Anderson
1953-1955	Anderson
1955-1957	Orville L. Freeman (D Farmer-Labor)
1957-1959	Freeman
1959-1961	Freeman
1961-1963	Elmer L. Andersen (R)

Four-Year Term

1963-1967	Karl F. Rolvaag (D)
1967-1971	Harold E. LeVander (R)

*Youngdahl resigned Sept. 27, 1951 to accept appointment as judge of the United States District Court for the District of Columbia. Anderson sworn in Sept. 27, 1951 for remainder of the term.

Mississippi

Four-Year Term

1944-1946	Thomas L. Bailey (D)*
1946-1948	Fielding L. Wright (D)**
1948-1952	Wright
1952-1956	Hugh L. White (D)
1956-1960	James Plemon Coleman (D)
1960-1964	Ross R. Barnett (D)
1964-1968	Paul B. Johnson (D)
1968-1972	John B. Williams (D)

*Bailey died Nov. 2, 1946.
**Wright sworn in as Governor Nov. 2, 1946.

Missouri

Four-Year Term

1941-1945	Forrest C. Donnell (R)
1945-1949	Phil M. Donnelly (D)
1949-1953	Forrest Smith (D)
1953-1957	Phil M. Donnelly (D)
1957-1961	James T. Blair Jr. (D)
1961-1965	John M. Dalton (D)
1965-1969	Warren E. Hearnes (D)
1969-1973	Hearnes

Montana

Four-Year Term

1941-1945	Sam C. Ford (R)
1945-1949	Ford
1949-1953	John W. Bonner (D)
1953-1957	J. Hugo Aronson (R)
1957-1961	Aronson
1961-1962	Donald G. Nutter (R)*
1962-1965	Tim M. Babcock (R)**
1965-1969	Babcock
1969-1973	Forrest H. Anderson (D)

*Nutter died Jan. 26, 1962.
**Babcock sworn in as Governor Jan. 26, 1962.

Nebraska

Two-Year Term

1941-1943	Dwight P. Griswold (R)
1943-1945	Griswold
1945-1947	Griswold
1947-1949	Val Peterson (R)
1949-1951	Peterson
1951-1953	Peterson
1953-1955	Robert B. Crosby (R)
1955-1957	Victor E. Anderson (R)
1957-1959	Anderson
1959-1961	Ralph G. Brooks (D)
1961-1963	Frank B. Morrison (D)
1963-1965	Morrison
1965-1967	Morrison

Four-Year Term

1967-1971	Norbert T. Tiemann (R)

Nevada

Four-Year Term

1939-1943	Edward P. Carville (D)*
1943-1945	Carville
1945-1947	Vail Pittman (D)**

*Carville resigned from office July 24, 1945.
**Pittman succeeded Carville on July 24, 1945 and then appointed Carville to the U.S. Senate the same day.

NEVADA—FOUR-YEAR TERM (Cont.)

1947-1951	Pittman
1951-1955	Charles H. Russell (R)
1955-1959	Russell
1959-1963	Grant Sawyer (D)
1963-1967	Sawyer
1967-1971	Paul Laxalt (R)

New Hampshire

Two-Year Term

1939-1941	Robert O. Blood (R)
1941-1943	Blood
1943-1945	Blood
1945-1947	Charles M. Dale (R)
1947-1949	Dale
1949-1951	Sherman Adams (R)
1951-1953	Adams
1953-1955	Hugh Gregg (R)
1955-1957	Lane Dwinell (R)
1957-1959	Dwinell
1959-1961	Wesley Powell (R)
1961-1963	Powell
1963-1965	John W. King (D)
1965-1967	King
1967-1969	King
1969-1971	Walter R. Peterson Jr. (R)

New Jersey

Three-Year Term

1941-1944	Charles Edison (D)
1944-1947	Walter E. Edge (R)
1947-1950	Alfred E. Driscoll (R)

Four-Year Term

1950-1954	Driscoll
1954-1958	Robert B. Meyner (D)
1958-1962	Meyner
1962-1966	Richard J. Hughes (D)
1966-1970	Hughes

New Mexico

Two-Year Term

1943-1945	John J. Dempsey (D)
1945-1947	Dempsey
1947-1949	Thomas J. Mabry (D)
1949-1951	Mabry
1951-1953	Edwin L. Mechem (R)
1953-1955	Mechem
1955-1957	John Field Simms (D)
1957-1959	Edwin L. Mechem (R)
1959-1961	John Burroughs (D)
1961-1963	Edwin L. Mechem (R)
1963-1965	Jack M. Campbell (D)
1965-1967	Campbell
1967-1969	David F. Cargo (R)
1969-1971	Cargo

New York

Four-Year Term

1943-1947	Thomas E. Dewey (R)
1947-1951	Dewey
1951-1955	Dewey
1955-1959	Averell Harriman (D)
1959-1963	Nelson A. Rockefeller (R)
1963-1967	Rockefeller
1967-1971	Rockefeller

North Carolina

Four-Year Term

1941-1945	Melville Broughton (D)
1945-1949	R. Gregg Cherry (D)
1949-1953	William Kerr Scott (D)
1953-1954	William B. Umstead (D)*
1954-1957	Luther H. Hodges (D)**
1957-1961	Hodges
1961-1965	Terry Sanford (D)
1965-1969	Dan K. Moore (D)
1969-1973	Robert W. Scott (D)

Umstead died November 7, 1954.
**Hodges sworn in Nov. 9, 1954, to fill remainder of term.*

North Dakota

Two-Year Term

1939-1941	John Moses (D)
1941-1943	Moses
1943-1945	Moses
1945-1947	Fred G. Aandahl (R)
1947-1949	Aandahl
1949-1951	Aandahl
1951-1953	C. Norman Brunsdale (R)
1953-1955	Brunsdale
1955-1957	Brunsdale
1957-1959	John E. Davis (R)
1959-1961	Davis
1961-1963	William L. Guy (D)
1963-1965	Guy

Four-Year Term

1965-1969	Guy
1969-1973	Guy

Ohio

Two-Year Term

1939-1941	John W. Bricker (R)
1941-1943	Bricker
1943-1945	Bricker
1945-1947	Frank J. Lausche (D)
1947-1949	Thomas J. Herbert (R)

OHIO—TWO-YEAR TERM (Cont.)

1949-1951	Frank J. Lausche (D)
1951-1953	Lausche
1953-1955	Lausche
1955-1957	Lausche
1957-1959	C. William O'Neill (R)

Four-Year Term

1959-1963	Michael V. DiSalle (D)
1963-1967	James A. Rhodes (R)
1967-1971	Rhodes

Oklahoma

Four-Year Term

1943-1947	Robert S. Kerr (D)
1947-1951	Roy J. Turner (D)
1951-1955	Johnston Murray (D)
1955-1959	Raymond Gary (D)
1959-1963	J. Howard Edmondson (D)
1963-1967	Henry Bellmon (R)
1967-1971	Dewey F. Bartlett (R)

Oregon

Four-Year Term

1943-1947	Earl Snell (R)*
1947	Snell
1947-1949	John H. Hall (R)**
1949-1951	Douglas McKay (R)***
1951-1952	McKay
1952-1955	Paul L. Patterson (R)****
1955-1956	Patterson
1956-1957	Elmo E. Smith (R)*****
1957-1959	Robert D. Holmes (D)
1959-1963	Mark O. Hatfield (R)
1963-1967	Hatfield
1967-1971	Tom McCall (R)

*Snell died in office beginning his second term Oct. 28, 1947.

**John H. Hall sworn in Oct. 28, 1947, but was defeated by Douglas McKay in 1948 primary.

***McKay elected for remainder of four-year term on Nov. 2, 1948, re-elected for four-year term Nov. 7, 1950, resigned to become Secretary of Interior, Dec. 11, 1952.

****Patterson sworn in as Governor Dec. 11, 1952, re-elected for a four-year term in 1954 but died in office Jan. 31, 1956.

*****Elmo Smith sworn in Jan. 31, but lost to Robert D. Holmes in 1956 election.

Pennsylvania

Four-Year Term

1943-1947	Edward Martin (R)
1947-1951	James H. Duff (R)
1951-1955	John S. Fine (R)
1955-1959	George M. Leader (D)
1959-1963	David L. Lawrence (D)
1963-1967	William W. Scranton (R)
1967-1971	Raymond P. Shafer (R)

Rhode Island

Two-Year Term

1941-1943	J. Howard McGrath (D)
1943-1945	McGrath*
1945-1947	John O. Pastore (D)
1947-1949	Pastore
1949-1951	Pastore
1951-1953	Dennis J. Roberts (D)
1953-1955	Roberts
1955-1957	Roberts
1957-1959	Roberts
1959-1961	Christopher Del Sesto (R)
1961-1963	John A. Notte Jr. (D)
1963-1965	John H. Chafee (R)
1965-1967	Chafee
1967-1969	Chafee
1969-1971	Frank Licht (D)

*McGrath resigned Oct. 4, 1945 to become Solicitor General of the U.S.; Pastore sworn in as Governor Oct. 6, 1945.

South Carolina

Four-Year Term

1943-1945	Olin Dewitt Talmadge Johnston (D)*
1945-1947	Ransome Judson Williams (D)
1947-1951	J. Strom Thurmond (D)
1951-1955	James F. Byrnes (D)
1955-1959	George Bell Timmerman Jr. (D)
1959-1963	Ernest F. Hollings (D)
1963-1965	Donald S. Russell (D)**
1965-1967	Robert E. McNair (D)
1967-1971	McNair

*Johnston, who was previously Governor from 1935-1939, resigned from office to enter the U.S. Senate on Jan. 2, 1945; Williams was sworn in on Jan. 2, 1945 for the remainder of the term.

**Russell resigned April 21, 1965, to accept appointment to U.S. Senate; McNair sworn in as Governor on April 22, 1965.

South Dakota

Two-Year Term

1943-1945	M.Q. Sharpe (R)
1945-1947	Sharpe
1947-1949	George T. Michelson (R)
1949-1951	Mickelson
1951-1953	Sigurd Anderson (R)
1953-1955	Anderson
1955-1957	Joe Foss (R)
1957-1959	Foss
1959-1961	Ralph Herseth (D)
1961-1963	Archie M. Gubbrud (R)
1963-1965	Gubbrud
1965-1967	Nils Boe (R)
1967-1969	Boe
1969-1971	Frank Farrar (R)

Tennessee

Two-Year Term

1939-1941	Prentice Cooper (D)
1941-1943	Cooper
1943-1945	Cooper
1945-1947	Jim Nance McCord (D)
1947-1949	McCord
1949-1951	Gordon Browning (D)
1951-1953	Browning
1953-1955	Frank G. Clement (D)

Four-Year Term

1955-1959	Clement
1959-1963	Buford Ellington (D)
1963-1967	Frank G. Clement (D)
1967-1971	Buford Ellington (D)

Texas

Two-Year Term

1941-1943	Coke R. Stevenson (D)
1943-1945	Stevenson
1945-1947	Stevenson
1947-1949	Beauford H. Jester (D)*
1949-1951	Allan Shivers (D)
1951-1953	Shivers
1953-1955	Shivers
1955-1957	Shivers
1957-1959	Price Daniel (D)
1959-1961	Daniel
1961-1963	Daniel
1963-1965	John B. Connally (D)
1965-1967	Connally
1967-1969	Connally
1969-1971	Preston Smith (D)

Jester died in office July 11, 1949; Shivers sworn in as Governor July 16, 1949.

Utah

Four-Year Term

1941-1945	Herbert B. Maw (D)
1945-1949	Maw
1949-1953	J. Bracken Lee (R)
1953-1957	Lee
1957-1961	George Dewey Clyde (R)
1961-1965	Clyde
1965-1969	Calvin L. Rampton (D)
1969-1973	Rampton

Vermont

Two-Year Term

1941-1943	William H. Wills (R)
1943-1945	Wills

VERMONT—TWO-YEAR TERM (Cont.)

1945-1947	Mortimer R. Proctor (R)
1947-1949	Ernest W. Gibson (R)
1949-1950	Gibson*
1950-1951	Harold J. Arthur (R)
1951-1953	Lee E. Emerson (R)
1953-1955	Emerson
1955-1957	Joseph Blaine Johnson (R)
1957-1959	Johnson
1959-1961	Robert T. Stafford (R)
1961-1963	F. Ray Keyser (R)
1963-1965	Philip H. Hoff (D)
1965-1967	Hoff
1967-1969	Hoff
1969-1971	Deane C. Davis (R)

Gibson resigned Jan. 3, 1950 effective Jan. 15, 1950; Arthur sworn in on Jan 15, 1950 for the remainder of the term.

Virginia

Four-Year Term

1942-1946	Colgate W. Darden Jr. (D)
1946-1950	William Munford Tuck (D)
1950-1954	John Stewart Battle (D)
1954-1958	Thomas B. Stanley (D)
1958-1962	J. Lindsay Almond Jr. (D)
1962-1966	Albertis S. Harrison (D)
1966-1970	Mills E. Godwin Jr. (D)

Washington

Four-Year Term

1941-1945	Arthur B. Langlie (R)
1945-1949	Monrad Charles Wallgren (D)
1949-1953	Arthur B. Langlie (R)
1953-1957	Langlie
1957-1961	Albert D. Rosellini (D)
1961-1965	Rosellini
1965-1969	Daniel J. Evans (R)
1969-1973	Evans

West Virginia

Four-Year Term

1941-1945	Matthew Mansfield Neely (D)
1945-1949	Clarence W. Meadows (D)
1949-1953	Okey L. Patteson (D)
1953-1957	William C. Marland (D)
1957-1961	Cecil H. Underwood (R)
1961-1965	W.W. Barron (D)
1965-1969	Hulett C. Smith (D)
1969-1973	Arch A. Moore (R)

Wisconsin

Two-Year Term

1943-1945	Walter S. Goodland (R)
1945-1947	Goodland
1947	Goodland*
1947-1949	Oscar A. Rennebohm (R)
1949-1951	Rennebohm
1951-1953	Walter J. Kohler Jr. (R)
1953-1955	Kohler
1955-1957	Kohler
1957-1959	Vernon W. Thomson (R)
1959-1961	Gaylord A. Nelson (D)
1961-1963	Nelson
1963-1965	John W. Reynolds (D)
1965-1967	Warren P. Knowles (R)
1967-1969	Knowles
1969-1971	Knowles

Goodland died in office March 12, 1947; Rennebohm was sworn in on March 13, 1947 for the remainder of the term.

Wyoming

Four-Year Term

1943-1947	Lester C. Hunt (D)
1947-1949	Hunt*
1949-1951	Arthur G. Crane (R)
1951-1953	Frank A. Barrett (R)**
1953-1955	Clifford J. Rogers (R)
1955-1959	Milward L. Simpson (R)
1959-1961	J.J. Hickey (D)***
1961-1963	Jack Gage (D)
1963-1967	Clifford P. Hansen (R)
1967-1971	Stanley K. Hathaway (R)

Hunt resigned as Governor to become U.S. Senator on Jan. 3, 1949; Arthur G. Crane became Acting Governor on Jan. 3, 1949.

**Barrett resigned as Governor to become U.S. Senator on Jan. 3, 1953; C.J. Rogers became Acting Governor on Jan. 3, 1953.*

***Hickey resigned as Governor to become U.S. Senator on Jan. 3, 1961; Gage became acting Governor on Jan. 3, 1961.*

1968 ELECTORAL VOTES BY STATES

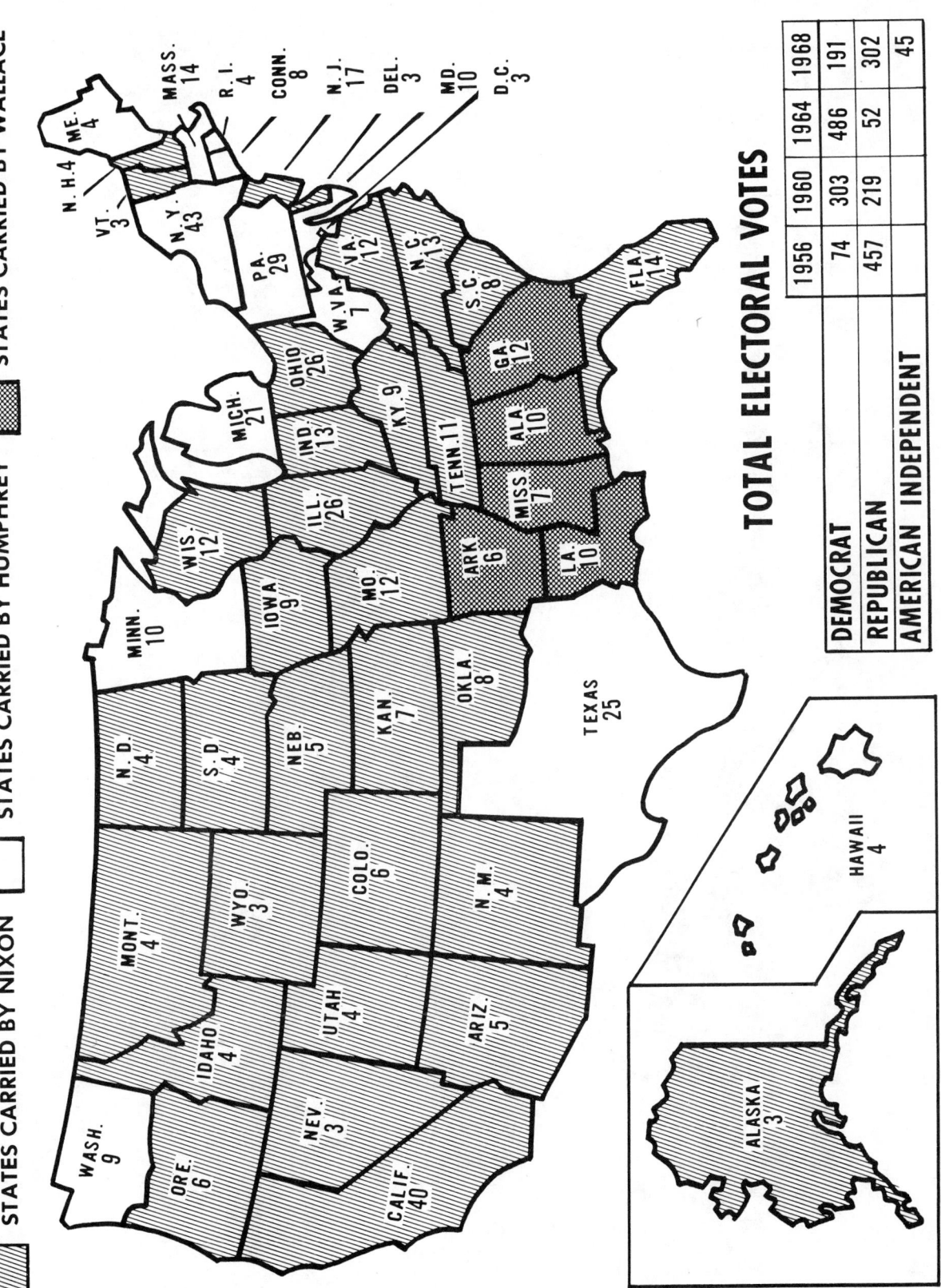

STATES CARRIED BY NIXON

STATES CARRIED BY HUMPHREY

STATES CARRIED BY WALLACE

TOTAL ELECTORAL VOTES

	1956	1960	1964	1968
DEMOCRAT	74	303	486	191
REPUBLICAN	457	219	52	302
AMERICAN INDEPENDENT				45

Chapter 2—Foreign Policy

Key Votes

In this chapter, key roll-call votes are shown in bold-face type. The party breakdown on each of these votes and the position taken by each Member of Congress may be found in the key vote charts which appear in the appendix to this book.

Foreign Policy

UNITED States foreign policy under President Johnson was dominated and directed by the agony of the Vietnam war. It was a war that deeply influenced all of Mr. Johnson's policies—not just foreign affairs but domestic programs as well. When the President left office in January 1969 the war was still being waged, although the thrust of the American effort in the conflict had shifted from a military to a political settlement. Dramatic events in 1968 had led Mr. Johnson to reappraise the country's war policy and to make a concentrated effort to begin negotiations which would result in an acceptable settlement of the conflict if not in a victory for the United States.

The foreign policy of the Johnson Administration was in many respects a continuation of the basic approach taken by the United States in foreign affairs during the 20 years since the end of World War II. A major difference, however, was the greatly expanded concern over the fate of Asia. It was a period during which American attention was turned to Asia and away from Europe. In Europe, the alliance of mutual interests, forged by the very real post-World War II threat of the Soviet Union, was threatened with disarray. In Asia, the policies of Communist containment, dating from the late 1940s and early 1950s in Europe, were put to a test in a bloody and protracted war. The justification for the Vietnam war was given in many ways by the Administration, but by 1968 increasing emphasis was placed on America's role in preventing the expansion of Communist China.

Although dominated by the war, the Johnson period in foreign policy reflected the continuation of other trends. The Administration continued to press for settlement of outstanding East-West issues such as the armaments race. The President also sought to continue the program of American economic aid to less developed parts of the world and American armaments for countries which the Administration believed were faced with external threats. These activities met increasing resistance by Members of Congress and other individuals who believed that they either had outlived their usefullness or had been diverted to serve unwise purposes. In addition, the policy of expanding international trade—which dated from before World War II—was pursued by the Johnson Administration, but with less success than it had hoped.

In spite of the Administration's efforts to pursue the policies that had guided U.S. foreign relations for more than two decades, there developed a fundamental challenge to both the wisdom and the efficacy of a continued American hegemony throughout the world. This challenge went directly counter to the traditional view of the United States as the pre-eminent global power—as well as the proper and legitimate force—to preserve Western interests in all parts of the world and to protect nations from the incursions of international Communism. By the end of the Johnson years, the position of America as the dominant force in the world was seriously questioned not only by other nations but by many Americans who were dismayed at the enormous costs and meager returns of a seemingly unending war over a remote piece of real estate in Asia. A basic question arose from this dismay: could the United States in fact accomplish all that had been thought during the 20 years since it emerged as the world's most powerful nation at the end of World War II.

The Vietnam war did not mark an end to American internationalism even though some persons believed a sharp turn toward isolationism was beginning. But the war left the nation fatigued and probably reluctant to undertake new adventures that would drain its energies further and divert its attention from the domestic problems that had grown to monumental proportions in the 1960s. By 1968, America was seeking an honorable way out of the Asia dilemma that would permit it to regain a more rational view of the entire world.

WAR Years. American support of the Vietnam war deteriorated measurably over the course of the Johnson years. From the beginning of expanded American involvement in the conflict, there was a substantial segment of the population that was vigorously and vocally opposed and which went to great lengths to let its opinions be known. But the opinion held by most Americans was, at best, vague until late in Mr. Johnson's term. It was a war that was frustrating and difficult to understand for most Americans; one of the most troubling aspects was the manner in which the nation appeared to have slid into the quicksand. It was equally troubling to many Americans that this happened almost without their knowledge and certainly without their consent—or at least the consent of their elected representatives. But there never was a massive upheaval of opposition to the war. Although the vocal opponents had their representatives in Congress who made plenty of noise, both houses continued to vote support of the war effort by large

---

Reference

Discussion of foreign policy developments from 1945-64 will be found in *Congress and the Nation, Vol. I, p. 91-232.*

margins. The 1966 elections proved nothing about the sentiments of the public on the war issue.

But by 1968, the war appeared no nearer a successful conclusion than it had in 1965 and discontent in the nation clearly was on the rise. Early in the year, a major Communist offensive took place in Vietnam which convinced many Americans that the United States and its Vietnamese allies were not winning the war and that no end to the conflict was in sight. This dramatic turning point helped lead to a cessation of American bombing of North Vietnam and to the start of negotiations in early 1969 to achieve a political settlement of the war. It also helped lead to the decision by President Johnson not to seek re-election in 1968 and to spend all of his time attempting to achieve peace in Vietnam. The President's

withdrawal went far to remove the Vietnam issue as a major domestic issue in the 1968 elections.

UNITED States-Soviet Relations. Although the two great world powers were supporting opposite sides in the Vietnam war, they managed—to the surprise of many—to work toward settlement of outstanding issues. This also was a continuation of a trend which had begun earlier in the postwar period after it became evident to both sides that a military confrontation between the two was no longer, in the nuclear world, a rational solution to problems. This understanding, however, did not rule out indirect use of force between their opposing views and this is what happened in Vietnam. The de-emphasis on American nuclear strength as the primary deterrent element to prevent aggression and the emphasis on stronger and more flexible conventional forces to fight limited wars was born in the early years of President Kennedy's Administration. The philosophy that exact amounts of conventional armed force could be applied to special situations was given a fair test in Vietnam and was found wanting by many persons. But the alternative of nuclear force was equally unappealing and this meant that the Soviet Union and the United States had little choice but to work for peaceful agreements wherever they could be achieved. In less than a decade, the world had experienced the terror of a nuclear confrontation over Cuba, the pain and cost of a destructive and perhaps pointless conventional war in Vietnam and the threat of a conflagration in the Middle East that could involve dozens of nations.

The U.S. and the Soviet Union came to no general resolve on all their disagreements, but step by step they worked toward understandings that would reduce the risk of wars between themselves or between nations in their circles of influence. The most significant of the steps taken during the Johnson years was the agreement in 1968 on a nuclear nonproliferation treaty under which all nuclear powers who signed agreed not to provide non-nuclear states with atomic weapons. It also pledged non-nuclear nations not to seek to acquire nuclear devices. The treaty was a major step toward halting a nuclear arms race by ever more nations. The treaty was not ratified by the United States by the end of Mr. Johnson's term but was endorsed by his successor, Richard M. Nixon, and was approved by the Senate on March 13, 1969.

The two nations went ahead on other fronts during these years. They signed a consular convention which was ratified by the Senate over the bitter opposition of conservatives, including many Republicans. The fact that the treaty was nevertheless ratified by the Senate was further sign that a majority opinion in the United States was prepared to accept accommodations with the Soviet Union that would forestall Armageddon. A decade earlier either of these treaties would have been unthinkable.

The most sour note that pervaded U.S.-Soviet relations came as a result of the Soviet's armed invasion in August 1968 of Czechoslovakia to halt a liberalization movement in that nation which threatened—from the Soviet viewpoint—to get out of hand. The Czechs were seeking greater independence and freedom of speech and press. The Soviet occupation was condemned by every important leader of the Western world and by virtually

History of Foreign Aid Cuts

Over the years Congress consistently reduced Administration requests for foreign aid in two steps, first by authorizing less money than the Administration sought, and then by appropriating less money than the two chambers had authorized. Presidents Truman, Eisenhower, Kennedy and Johnson each protested against the reductions made in their foreign aid programs.

Following are the cuts Congress inflicted on foreign aid requests from the fiscal 1948-49 bill to the fiscal 1969 bill. The table shows that the final fiscal 1969 appropriation of $1.8 billion constituted the largest percentage cut ever made. The next highest cuts were in funds for fiscal 1964, fiscal 1968, fiscal 1958 and fiscal 1953. President Johnson's fiscal 1965 and fiscal 1966 bills fared best.

(in billions)

Fiscal Year	Request	Authorization	Appropriation	Per Cent Cut [1]
1948-49	$7.37	$6.91	$6.45	12.5%
1950	5.68	5.59	4.94	13.0
1951	8.17	7.99	7.49	8.3
1952	8.50	7.58	7.28	14.4
1953	7.92	6.49	6.00	24.2
1954	5.83	5.16	4.53	22.3
1955	3.48	3.05	2.78	20.1
1956	3.53	3.42	2.70	23.5
1957	4.86	4.12	3.77	22.4
1958	3.86	3.39	2.77	28.2
1959	3.94	3.68	3.45	12.4
1960	3.93	3.58	3.23	17.8
1961	4.87	4.69	4.43	9.0
1962	4.77	4.26	3.91	18.0
1963	4.78	4.57	3.90	18.4
1964	4.53	3.60	3.00	33.8
1965	3.52	3.50	3.25	7.7
1966	3.46	3.36	3.22	6.9
1967	3.39	3.50	2.94	13.3
1968	3.23	2.68	2.30	28.8
1969	2.92	1.97	1.76	39.7

[1] *Appropriation below request.*

every politician in America. It had an immediate damp-ening effect on U.S.-Soviet relations and was the reason the Senate did not ratify the nuclear nonproliferation treaty in 1968. It also blocked the beginning of nego-tiations on arms limitations. But by the end of 1968, it did not appear that the Soviet action had produced a basic split between the United States and its allies and the Communist bloc. For all the rhetoric of condemna-tion, the desire to seek accommodations seemed still to be paramount.

One area in which the Soviet Union and the United States made less progress than they hoped was trade. President Johnson sought repeatedly to obtain Congres-sional approval for expanded East-West trade but—with a major war against a Communist foe in progress—this was more than the average Member of Congress could swallow.

INTERNATIONAL Trade. East-West trade was not substantially advanced by the John-son years, but the Kennedy Round trade negotiations were successfully concluded in 1967 just before the expi-ration date of the legislation which allowed the President to adjust tariffs. As had been expected, many American industries reacted with horror to the prospect of increased competition from foreign goods and, accordingly, began a vigorous campaign in Congress to enact protectionist bills. This drive in 1967 and 1968 was successfully blocked by the Administration through lobbying and through President Johnson's threat of a veto of any such bill that passed. On the other hand, the President did not win Congressional approval of a prime request he made—dealing with tariffs on chemicals—which grew out of the Kennedy Round agreements. He also failed to have his tariff cutting authority, granted under the 1962 Trade Act, extended in order to permit even further agreements with other nations on expanding trade.

FOREIGN Assistance. The Johnson Administra-tion sought to continue the policy of the previous 20 years of sharing America's abundance with poorer nations throughout the world. It was not only al-truism; it never had been just that. Foreign aid since the early 1950s had been a close ally of national security. Its advocates said it was not only humanistic to feed hungry people, but also was wise to economically bolster and to arm them against the incursions of unfriendly neighbors. This philosophy was not seriously challenged until the Vietnam war began to make some people in and out of Congress wonder whether the United States might not have committed itself, though foreign aid, to a policy of armed defense of any nation which had been receiving American assistance. Sen. J.W. Fulbright (D Ark.), in particular, argued that American economic aid had come to carry an implicit commitment of other forms of assis-tance in times of emergency.

Also involved in this chain of thought was the belief that the United States in the previous two decades had become overcommitted throughout the world. The argu-ment was that the United States was assisting too many nations, was promising too much to the recipient na-tions, and was attempting to accomplish things it could not achieve and probably should not attempt. In all of this there was a reflection of the bitter disenchantment over Vietnam. The Senate, in which the greatest unhap-piness centered, was particularly distressed because

the Administration had launched into a major war with no more Congressional authorization than a vague resolu-tion enacted in 1964 after two American ships were attacked off the coast of Vietnam. The disenchantment also showed concern about vast American expenditures abroad, primarily for a war that was difficult to under-stand when domestic social problems were more serious than ever and demanding greater expenditures than ever.

Foreign aid, consequently, came in for its worst battering in the 20-year history of the program. The Ad-ministration attempted to win reforms of the aid pro-gram from Congress but was rebuffed. Congress instead cut deeply into the authorizations and appropriations during the last two years of Mr. Johnson's term and in 1968 reduced the program's funding below $2 billion for the first time in history. In addition, restrictive riders were added each year in a continuing effort to direct American foreign policy from the halls of Congress. Deep reductions were made in the development loan program and in the Alliance for Progress.

OTHER Developments. In the years covered by the Johnson Administration, Congress acted on many matters relating to foreign affairs; some of the most controversial are discussed above. But there were other issues of substantial importance during the period which drew the attention of Congress.

One of the major ones was reform of the immigration laws to do away with the national origins quota system. After years of unsuccessful effort, advocates of reform achieved their goal in 1965 when Congress enacted a new system that did away with the discriminatory quotas system that favored Northern European nations at the expense of most other countries.

An issue that raged during the 90th Congress involved sale of American arms to less developed nations. It was an issue tied closely to America's role in supporting friendly nations against threats from the Communist bloc. Critics of arms sales argued that most poor nations should be working on economic development rather than building a military establishment. They also said that arms sales only encouraged the waging of war between states which long had been in disagreement on many subjects and contributed little to international peace.

I N addition to all of this, there was another event early in the Administration's history that was a prelude—on a small scale—to the controversy that was to envelop Mr. Johnson in the following years over his policies in Vietnam. That event included many of the same characters that were prominent in the following Vietnam drama. It revealed the divergent thinking that was to characterize later national debate about America's role in the world and demonstrated the problems the Administration was going to have in carrying the American public with it in support of the goals which had been set out for the nation, particularly in Asia.

In late April 1965 rebellion broke out in Santo Domingo, capital of the Dominican Republic, and four days later U.S. troops were sent in to help stem the fighting. U.S. troops continued to flow in, at first—President Johnson said—to protect American citizens but later in numbers far in excess of an adequate force for that purpose. Later it became clear from Administration statements that the primary purpose was to prevent a Communist takeover of that country. Whether such a threat ever existed, or was largely the imagination of the U.S. Ambassador there, became a hot issue in the United States. Some influential Members of Congress suggested that the President had acted on faulty evaluation of the problem while others suggested that the United States was doing precisely what was proper as guardian of the Western Hemisphere. The Administration received much criticism for what appeared to be heavy-handed, unilateral action reminiscent of the gunboat diplomacy of earlier years. The Administration also lost support among the public because of what appeared to be the changing multisided justification for the action and lack of candor by its officials throughout the episode.

Worst of all for President Johnson's future policies, the critics of the American intervention—many of whom became the outspoken opponents of the Vietnam adventure—saw it as a foolish and arrogant action by a nation that considered itself all but omnipotent in an age that no longer lent itself to omnipotency in international relations. Whether they were right or wrong was a question which Mr. Johnson trusted, with full confidence of vindication, to history; but it was clear that the critics' conviction that they were right, their eloquence in arguing their case and their position of influence as part of the intellectual leadership of the nation was to bode ill for the President as he carried his view of America's role in the world from the Caribbean to Asia.

Chronology

Of Developments

In Foreign Policy

1965

T HE United States' deep involvement in the Vietnam war was the major foreign policy development during 1965. It was an involvement that came about through the backdoor and was not fully appreciated by most Americans. President Johnson gradually committed substantial numbers of troops to the war that was eventually to cost more than $2 billion a month. But in 1965, no one acknowledged—it is unlikely anyone knew or expected—that the war would involve a half-million American men and cost billions of dollars annually.

Congress was preoccupied in 1965 with enacting a far-reaching domestic legislative program which made the first session of the 89th Congress one of the most productive in history. Those Members who watched the growing Vietnam conflict with a sense of foreboding could do little more than debate the issue (which some of them did continually) and vote funds to support the U.S. forces. Congress's power to influence American involvement in the war was sharply limited by the President's position as commander-in-chief and his authority to conduct foreign relations. But Members were entirely free to reflect on whether 20 years of foreign aid had led the nation to an expensive war of questionable merits. Few Members, however, went so far in public as to draw that conclusion; but there were signs, which became more evident in the following years, that many Members feared the United States had overreached itself in Asia and other parts of the world and had done so at least in part because of unwise commitments that came with the foreign economic and military assistance programs.

Signs of discontent with foreign aid were not new, but the war helped focus them. A Senate effort to require a new aid program met with failure because the House was opposed. In the end, Congress made no important changes in the program and only small funding cuts, but the debate over U.S. commitments abroad had just begun.

The major legislative action of the year was enactment of a bill reforming the immigration laws and ending the national origins quota system. In the area of trade, there was little progress except for legislation to implement the International Coffee Agreement. But the Kennedy Round trade talks produced little agreement; proposals to increase East-West trade remained only proposals.

Vietnam

The U.S. involvement in the Vietnam war, which had existed for a decade, increased dramatically in 1965 and led to a national debate that was to continue for the remainder of President Johnson's years in office.

America's deepening commitment to the war was to influence the course of national events in the following years more directly and with greater impact than any other single development. *(For background, see box p. 54.)*

Neither the course of the war nor the significance of individual events was clear. It was clear, though, that between January and December the American military involvement had mushroomed and the violence carried into North Vietnam; public pressure for a peaceful settlement of the war and Administration efforts to seek negotiations had increased; and the war had become an overriding issue in the United States.

American forces in Vietnam at the beginning of the year consisted of 23,300 military personnel who were described as advisors to South Vietnam forces. *(For summary, see box above.)* By the end of the year, American forces had increased to more than 184,000 troops which were engaged in combat as well as other duties. American efforts increased as indications multiplied that the South Vietnamese were in danger of losing the war and the country to the Viet Cong, the indigenous guerillas in the South, and their political arm, the National Liberation Front.

For the first half of the year, governmental chaos in Saigon threatened to undermine any efforts made by the United States to help South Vietnam. A succession of coups, counter-coups and short-lived governments continued until General Nguyen Cao Ky came to power in mid-June. Military events were going poorly also. A six-day battle at Binh Gia, which ended Jan. 2, was a major defeat for the South Vietnamese. The nature of the war changed markedly following a surprise attack Feb. 7 by Viet Cong guerillas on a U.S. military compound at Pleiku; the U.S. intention to remain in a limited advisory role was rapidly reassessed. U.S. and South Vietnamese bombers immediately retaliated against training and staging areas in North Vietnam, with the raids coming only a few hours after the arrival of Soviet Premier Alexei N. Kosygin in Hanoi, the capital of North Vietnam. The State Department conceded the failure to end the war by limiting fighting to the South and invited the North to choose between peace and an "increasingly destructive" conflict. By the end of February the air strikes against the North had been put on a continuing basis in hope of forcing negotiations.

One result of increased U.S. participation in the war was increased opposition to the war by many Americans. The United States was swept by a new phenomenon— "teach-ins" protesting the American presence in Vietnam. President Johnson and other Administration officials indicated a willingness to negotiate on a settlement to the war and made some well-publicized efforts to get talks started; nothing came of these efforts. As regular army units of the North Vietnamese began to appear in the South in the spring, the United States called a moratorium on bombing of the North between May 12 and May 18 in order to elicit peace feelers from Hanoi. There was no response. In the fall, demonstrations flared across the United States for three days, Oct. 15-17, as an estimated 70,000 people participated in marches and rallies in over 60 cities in opposition to the war. In addition, the Administration's interest in negotiations were greeted with increased skepticism when the State Department in the fall confirmed that in August 1964, the Johnson Administration had turned down

---

Escalation in Vietnam

U.S. Armed Forces in South Vietnam [1]

	Dec. 31, 1963	Dec. 31, 1964	Dec. 31, 1965	Dec. 31, 1966	Dec. 31, 1967	Dec. 28, 1968
Total	16,300	23,300	184,300	385,300	485,600	535,500

U.S. Military Casualties from Hostile Action

	1964	1965	1966	1967	1968	Jan. 1, 1961 through Dec. 28, 1968
Killed	147	1,369	5,008	9,378	14,592	30,614
Wounded [2]	1,039	6,114	30,093	62,025	92,820	192,582

South Vietnam Military Casualties from Hostile Action

	1964	1965	1966	1967	1968	Jan. 1, 1961 through Dec. 28, 1968
Killed	7,457	11,243	11,953	12,716	16,353	73,848
Wounded [3]	17,017	23,118	20,975	29,448	54,739	169,429

[1] *Figures are rounded and do not include armed forces stationed on seas around or on islands outside of Vietnam.*

[2] *U.S. figures include both the seriously wounded, who required hospital treatment, and the less seriously injured, who did not require hospital care. The totals of those requiring hospital care are: 1964, 522; 1965, 3,308; 1966, 16,526; 1967, 32,371; 1968, 46,799; 1961 through 1968, 99,786.*

[3] *These figures, compiled by the South Vietnamese government, include only persons seriously wounded who required hospital or extensive treatment.*

SOURCE: Department of Defense, Jan. 22, 1969

---

peace talks with North Vietnam that had been secretly arranged by UN Secretary General U Thant. (The Department said it was not convinced that the North was prepared for "serious talks.") Citizen protests reached a peak when an estimated 20,000 demonstrators Nov. 27 joined in a non-violent "March on Washington for Peace in Vietnam." Late in the year, it was increasingly apparent that the Administration had stepped up its diplomatic efforts for negotiations. As the year ended, a 30-hour Christmas truce which began Dec. 24 led into a second, and longer, moratorium on the bombing of North Vietnam which continued into the new year. At the same time—amid much publicity—numerous top U.S. diplomats were sent to capitals around the world in a massive drive to sell the American position, rally support, and communicate to Hanoi the sincerity of the U.S. desire to settle the war by negotiation. Again, nothing came of the effort.

The increased U.S. commitment required increased defense expenditures which Congress provided in appropriation bills. In May, Congress approved almost unanimously a special Presidential request for $700 million to fund the war, a move which some observers believed reflected more the President's desire for Congressional approval of his policies than an immediate need for the money. In the defense appropriations bill later in the year, Congress provided an additional $1.7 billion for Vietnam operations which the Administration had requested following a summer trip to Vietnam by Secretary of Defense Robert S. McNamara.

American Involvement in Vietnam Dated to Mid-1950s

American commitments to South Vietnam dated back to the Geneva conference of 1954 which met to negotiate armistice agreements between France and Cambodia, Laos and Vietnam—the three territories which had made up French Indo-China. Prior to these accords American involvement in the area had consisted of economic aid and military equipment to assist the French. Vietnamese nationalists, led by Ho Chi Minh, had been fighting a war of liberation against the French since the end of World War II. The U.S. Government did not formally subscribe to the Geneva agreements but agreed to support them.

As the French withdrew from Vietnam, the Americans moved in with large amounts of economic and military aid to support successive Saigon governments against Communist-directed guerillas. President Eisenhower in October 1954, in a letter to the president of South Vietnam, promised U.S. aid "in developing and maintaining a strong, viable state capable of resisting attempted subversion or aggression through military means." Also in 1954 the United States helped negotiate the Southeast Asia Collective Defense Treaty (SEATO), which pledged joint action against "armed attack" on any state or territory in the area (South Vietnam was included in a protocol to the treaty). The Senate approved ratification of the treaty by an 82-1 vote Feb. 1, 1955.

President Eisenhower sent U.S. military advisors to help train the South Vietnamese army in 1955. By 1961, after some 18 months of increasing activity by the Viet Cong, the number of U.S. military advisors had doubled, to more than 600. In May 1961, during a trip to South Vietnam, Vice President Johnson promised more U.S. military and economic aid, and May 13 President Kennedy ordered 100 specially trained jungle fighters (Special Forces) to South Vietnam. In October President Kennedy sent Gen. Maxwell D. Taylor, his military advisor, to South Vietnam to investigate the military situation there and make a personal report. Following Taylor's trip the President Nov. 16 announced the U.S. intention to step up its aid to the Saigon government. The announcement prefaced an influx of American military instructors, helicopter pilots and support personnel. Soon after, the number of "advisors" in Vietnam had risen to an estimated 1,650 and this number steadily increased until at the end of December 1964 there were approximately 23,300 U.S. troops in Vietnam.

Prior to 1965 the United States maintained that it was only an indirect participant in the conflict and that the U.S. military personnel in South Vietnam were there only in an "advise and support" capacity.

In spite of increased U.S. assistance, the political situation and the long-run war effort deteriorated markedly. American efforts to support a stable civilian government which could successfully combat the Viet Cong were continually frustrated. After the assassination of President Ngo Dinh Diem and his brother Ngo Dinh Nhu following a military coup in November 1963, one coup d'etat followed another, each one further weakening the nation's ability to successfully maintain its war effort. At the same time the Viet Cong steadily increased its control in both the rural areas and the cities.

A major turning point came on Aug. 2, 1964, when a U.S. destroyer cruising in international waters in the Gulf of Tonkin off North Vietnam was attacked by North Vietnamese torpedo boats. After strong U.S. protests, PT boats Aug. 4 again attacked U.S. destroyers in the area. President Johnson that night announced that retaliatory air action was being taken against military facilities in the North. This led to an inexorable policy of retaliation by both sides.

Immediately following the Tonkin incident, Congress Aug. 7 overwhelmingly adopted a joint resolution (H J Res 1145—PL 88-408), recommended by the President, affirming support of "all necessary measures to repel any armed attack against the forces of the United States...to prevent further aggression...(and) to assist any member or protocol state of the Southeast Asia Collective Defense Treaty requesting assistance...." *(See p. 70)* The resolution passed on roll-call votes of 414-0 in the House and 88-2 in the Senate, with only Sens. Wayne Morse (D Ore.) and Ernest Gruening (D Alaska) opposed. Although the voting on the resolution was not specific endorsement for enlargement of the war, bombing of North Vietnam and the commitment of large numbers of American ground troops, the Administration did cite it as evidence of support for its policies.

Following U.S. retaliation for the Tonkin attack, the Viet Cong concentrated their efforts against U.S. forces and installations in Vietnam and stepped up their terrorist activities in Saigon. On Nov. 1 the Communists carried out a devastating attack on U.S. installations at Bien Hoa, outside Saigon, and on Christmas Eve terrorists bombed a U.S. officers' billet in the heart of the capital city.

Foreign Aid

The nation's 20-year commitment to foreign aid was not disrupted in 1965, but an increasing disenchantment with the program was evident. The central issue during the 1965 Congressional consideration of the annual foreign aid authorization (HR 7750—PL 89-171) was not the size of the program but whether or not Congress should

take definite steps to force a major reworking of U.S. aid. In the end, the issue was postponed; no basic changes were made in the foreign aid program.

Action on the fiscal 1966 foreign aid legislation—both the authorization and the appropriations *(see p. 57)*—was unusual because, for the second consecutive year, Congress made only small reductions in the Administration's requests following years of substantial cuts in the President's proposals. As enacted, the authorization legislation permitted appropriations of $3,360,000,000 (including $1,170,000,000 in military aid) in fiscal 1966, just $99,470,000 less than the total appropriations requested by President Johnson.

The central dispute was basically between the Senate and the House: the Senate bill required major restructuring of foreign aid by 1968 while the House bill provided for continuation of the existing system. Enactment of the bill was delayed for two months in conference while House and Senate conferees debated their basic disagreement over the program's future. The Senate had authorized funds for two years and required an end to the aid program as currently constituted, while the House authorized a one-year extension without reference to possible changes. But both bills continued the basic existing program through fiscal 1966 (and fiscal 1967 in the case of the Senate bill). Although the House prevailed (through the adamant insistence of its conferees), Senate backers of reform obtained a vague concession from the House to consider revisions in the future and were hopeful that the Administration would recommend changes in 1966. President Johnson in 1965 sought only a traditional one-year extension of the program.

The foreign aid reform issue, although not newly born in 1965, focused sufficiently to find expression in a bill that passed one chamber of Congress. Debate on the issue did not indicate that Members of Congress urging reform had a clear idea of how the new aid program should be constructed after the old order was ended, although some ideas—such as multiyear authorizations—did emerge.

Sen. J.W. Fulbright (D Ark.), chairman of the Foreign Relations Committee, was a principal figure in the group urging aid reforms. He sought to separate economic and military aid into individual bills, to have multiyear authorizations and to channel more aid through international organizations. Fulbright at first said he would not manage the bill in 1965 unless the Administration revised the aid program, but later changed his mind, in part, he said, because no one else wanted the job either. Another outspoken critic was Sen. Wayne Morse (D Ore.), who had taken the aid program to task in previous years. Morse sponsored a section of the Senate bill terminating the program in two years, but he strongly disagreed with proposals on multiyear authorizations and increased use of multilateral aid. Morse argued that these proposals would abdicate Congressional responsibility over continuing review of the aid program. (In the following years, Morse's views won wider acceptance among Senators and others who were dismayed at U.S. involvement in the Vietnam war and considered excessive American commitments abroad as leading to the involvement; these individuals—including many favoring reform—then argued for closer Congressional review of foreign assistance.)

President Johnson's draft legislation which he submitted to Congress followed the pattern of the previous year by seeking what the Administration considered realistic sums rather than vastly inflated amounts which aid officials knew Congress would cut back. Mr. Johnson's request for specific programs were in most instances lower than those made the previous year. In the House, Foreign Affairs Committee Chairman Thomas E. Morgan

India-Pakistan Conflict

The outbreak of major hostilities between India and Pakistan in 1965 strained relations between those countries and the United States.

At the height of the warfare in September, the United States halted all shipments of military supplies to both countries and, beginning June 30, continued food shipments under PL 480 on a month-to-month basis. However, President Johnson Dec. 9 authorized a speed-up of grain shipments to India under the PL 480 program to help alleviate a threatened famine in that country. The allocation of 1.5 million tons was to cover the allocations of December, January and February. In addition, the President announced a $50 million loan to help India buy fertilizer in the United States.

The dispute between India and Pakistan over Kashmir had flared intermittently since the partition of the state in 1947, following India's and Pakistan's independence from Britain. Britain transferred power in a manner that permitted the rulers of the princely states that comprised British India to regain control of foreign and defense policies and to continue to exercise domestic powers. Most of these rulers quickly acceded to India or Pakistan as religious majorities, geographical contiguity or economic ties dictated. In Kashmir, with a Hindu ruler and a predominantly Moslem population, the ruler refused to accede to either. Late in 1947, Moslem tribesmen from Pakistan invaded Kashmir to avenge alleged mistreatment of Moslems, an invasion believed to have been encouraged and aided by Pakistan. The Kashmir ruler appealed to India for assistance and troops were sent but only after the ruler acceded to India. Fighting in Kashmir continued for more than a year before a cease-fire agreement was negotiated to go into effect on Jan. 1, 1949. Kashmir remained divided along the cease-fire line thereafter. India was left in control of about two-thirds of the area of Kashmir and Pakistan in control of the other one-third.

On Aug. 7, 1965, India charged that Pakistan had sent armed infiltrators into Indian-held Kashmir to start a guerrilla war. Pakistan replied that India was trying to cover up an internal revolt. Indian forces crossed the cease-fire line Aug. 16 to attack bases and staging areas of the infiltrators. Full-scale Indian-Pakistani hostilities followed.

As fighting continued, the United States and Britain halted all military aid shipments to both nations.

India Sept. 21 and Pakistan Sept. 22 accepted a UN Security Council resolution demanding a cease-fire. The fighting ended Sept. 22. Indian Prime Minister Lal Bahadur Shastri and Pakistan Mohammad Ayub Khan in early January met in Tashkent, in Soviet Central Asia, to discuss the Kashmir dispute. The U.S.S.R. arranged the meeting and Soviet Premier Alexei N. Kosygin helped achieve agreement. Although the Kashmir dispute was not resolved, the agreement signed Jan. 10 provided that both nations were to withdraw their armed personnel to positions held before Aug. 5. Shastri died early Jan. 11 of a heart attack after signing the agreement.

(D Pa.) said the bill was a revision prepared by the Administration at his request. He said the original draft bill separated economic and military assistance; that was wrong, Morgan argued, because the two programs had the same basic objective: "To prevent war and to maintain our security." Fulbright, looking at the same program, had a different analysis. He said it was "confusing" to mix military and economic assistance; he called the aid program "a hodgepodge" and "a conglomeration" of diverse activities, and asked, "How is a Senator or anybody else to know what he is voting for or...against?"

Congressional action on the authorization followed the general lines which had been established in the debate over reforms. The House accepted without change its Committee's recommendation for a regular one-year extension of the program. For the first time in the program's history, the House passed the authorization bill without substantive amendment. Debate was mild. Before passage, however, a key vote occurred when the House by a **178-219** roll call rejected a recommittal motion to cut the authorization for development loans by $130,958,000. The amendment, offered by a Republican, E. Ross Adair (Ind.), also included a number of policy amendments which had been rejected earlier by non-record votes. The bill, as passed by a 249-148 (R 44-86; D 205-62) roll call, authorized $2,004,195,000 which,

with carryover authority, permitted total appropriations of $3,367,670,000 in fiscal 1966.

In the Senate, the Foreign Relations Committee approved a bill with a two-year authorization (fiscal 1966 and 1967) and provisions to require a new program beginning in fiscal 1968. As passed by the Senate by a 68-20 (R 19-10; D 49-10) roll-call vote, the Senate bill authorized $3,243,000,000 in each of fiscal 1966 and 1967. Included in this was an additional $89 million requested by President Johnson two weeks earlier for economic and social development programs in Southeast Asia. The Senate voted on a number of amendments. One, a key vote, showed the reluctance—even in the Senate, where there was sentiment for aid reform—to reduce the military aid program even a relatively small amount. The amendment was offered by Frank Church (D Idaho) and would have cut the military aid authorization by $115 million, to $1,055,000,000; it was rejected by a **38-43** roll-call vote.

The conference action basically sustained the House's position against a multiyear authorization and a termination of the existing program. But House conferees said they were not "irrevocably" opposed to a multiyear authorization, and they noted that many shortcomings of the program which had drawn criticism "are basic and cannot be corrected merely by improvement in administrative procedures or in the quality of personnel."

Foreign Aid Funding, Fiscal 1966-1969

(in thousands of dollars)

ECONOMIC ASSISTANCE	FISCAL 1966		FISCAL 1967		FISCAL 1968		FISCAL 1969	
	Request	Appropriation	Request	Appropriation	Request	Appropriation	Request	Appropriation
Development Loan Fund	$780,250	$618,225	$665,388	$500,000	$774,000	$435,000	$765,000	$300,000
Technical Cooperation	210,000	202,355	231,310	200,000	242,815	180,000	235,000	167,000
American Schools Abroad	7,000	7,000	10,989	11,989	13,900	11,500	15,100	14,600
Investment-Surveys	——	——	——	——	2,000	1,250	3,000	——
Alliance for Progress	——	——	543,000	508,000	643,000	469,330	625,000	336,500
Loans	495,125	435,125	(455,300)	(420,300)	(543,000)	(389,000)	(515,000)	(255,000)
Grants	85,000	75,000	(87,700)	(87,700)	(100,000)	(80,000)	(110,000)	(81,500)
Partners of the Alliance	——	——	——	——	——	(330)	——	——
International Organizations	145,555	144,755	140,433	140,433	140,980	130,000	154,255	138,000
Supporting Assistance	——	——	——	——	720,000	600,000		
General	369,200	369,200	197,200	690,000	(170,000)	[2]	595,000	365,000
Vietnam	——	——	550,000	——	(550,000)	[2]	——	——
Contingency Fund	50,000	50,000	70,000	35,000	31,000	10,000	45,000	5,000
Special Southeast Asia Fund	89,000	89,000	——	——	——	——	——	——
Administrative Expenses								
AID	55,240	54,240	57,387	55,813.5	59,325	55,300	58,775	51,000
State Department	3,100	3,100	3,255	3,255	3,400	3,255	3,870	3,500
Total Economic Assistance	$2,289,470	$2,048	$2,468,962	$2,144,490.5	$2,630,420	$1,895,635	$2,500,000	$1,380,600
MILITARY ASSISTANCE	$1,170,000	$1,170,000	$ 917,000[1]	$ 792,000[1]	$ 596,000	$ 400,000	$ 420,000	$ 375,000
GRAND TOTAL	$3,459,470	$3,218,000	$3,385,962	$2,936,490.5	$3,226,420	$2,295,635	$2,920,000	$1,755,600

[1]*Does not include funds for South Vietnam military assistance program. Such funds were included in Department of Defense appropriations.*
[2]*Not separately identified.*

Foreign Aid Funds

Congress in 1965 appropriated $3,218,000,000 for foreign aid (including $1,170,000,000 in military assistance) in fiscal 1966, an amount $142 million below the authorization and just $241,470,000 or 6.9 percent below the Administration's Budget request. The appropriation was the smallest percentage reduction in the President's request in the program's history. The final figure compared with $3,285,000,000 appropriated by the House and $3,143,000,000 appropriated by the Senate.

The final bill (HR 10871—PL 89-273) also provided $714,188,000 for other programs, including $102 million for the Peace Corps and $455,880,000 for the Inter-American Development Bank.

Passage of the bill with the relatively small reductions marked the second consecutive year that the House had rejected attempts by Rep. Otto E. Passman (D La.), chairman of the House Appropriations Foreign Operations Subcommittee, to have the appropriations cut substantially below the amount authorized. In 1964, Passman had been stymied by the influence of Rep. George H. Mahon (D Texas), who had become chairman of the full Appropriations Committee following the death of Clarence Cannon (D Mo.). Cannon had supported Passman's previous efforts to cut foreign aid appropriations bills.

Mahon Jan. 28, 1965, announced a new membership list for the Foreign Operations Subcommittee, which had the effect of formalizing for the 89th Congress the loss of Passman's former power to bring about large cuts.

Consular Treaty

Opposition from conservatives prevented Congress from acting on a consular treaty (Exec. D, 88th Congress, 2nd Session) between the United States and the Soviet Union. The treaty was signed in Moscow in 1964 and sent by President Johnson to the Senate for ratification the same year. In 1965, the Administration, doubting that the treaty would receive the necessary two-thirds majority vote, postponed floor action on it even though it was approved by the Senate Foreign Relations Committee. The treaty provided procedures for the establishment and operation of consulates in each country and defined the functions and privileges of consular offices. The treaty met strong opposition from conservative Republicans and Democrats, right-wing groups (such as the Liberty Lobby, the American Legion and Young Americans for Freedom), and Federal Bureau of Investigation Director J. Edgar Hoover. The major charge was that provisions granting diplomatic immunity to all consular officers would encourage Soviet espionage in the United States.

Immigration Reform

A 40-year effort by minority groups to reform U.S. immigration laws succeeded in 1965 with enactment of legislation (HR 2580—PL 89-236) ending the national origins quota system. This system had been the basis of immigration to the United States by persons born outside the Western Hemisphere. It was started in rudi-

Reasons for 1965 Passage

Many of the immigration bill's most ardent supporters told Congressional Quarterly that they believed the public at large was not much interested in immigration reform or especially concerned about the national origins quota system. They attributed the success of the legislation in 1965, after many years of defeats for similar proposals in the past, to the following factors:

(1) The unusual parliamentary situation in Congress, where there were 2-1 Democratic majorities in each chamber that were generally responsive to President Johnson's wishes.

(2) Relatively strong support for the bill from the Johnson Administration—partly from general conviction that the national origins quota system was invidiously discriminatory, partly from a desire to ease U.S. relations with nations receiving unfavorable treatment under the national origins quota system and partly from a desire to win or retain political support of minority groups which believed they would benefit from repeal of the national origins quota system—particularly Italian-American groups.

(3) The presence as chairman of the House Judiciary Immigration and Nationality Subcommittee of Rep. Michael A. Feighan (D Ohio), who was more favorable to repeal of the national origins quota system than was the previous Subcommittee chairman, the late Francis E. Walter (D Pa. 1933-63). Walter had blocked all previous efforts at revision.

(4) The willingness of the Administration and many of the ethnic, labor and religious groups supporting immigration reform to compromise on the over-all quota, family reunification and other provisions, and thus help neutralize past opponents such as the American Legion and American Coalition of Patriotic Societies. Acceptance of the 120,000 limit for the Western Hemisphere was the most important Administration concession.

(5) Changing U.S. attitudes toward race and national origins. Several lobbyists told CQ that the fear of an "invasion" by "undesirable" immigrant ethnic and racial groups simply was not as great as in the past.

Opponents of the initial Administration bill said the sole explanations for passage, in their opinion, were the huge Democratic majorities in Congress and the desire of the Johnson Administration to win political support for the Democrats from minority groups.

mentary form in the 1921 Quota Act and was revised and continued in the 1924 Immigration Act and the 1952 Immigration and Nationality Act (the McCarran-Walter Act).

The system imposed country-by-country quotas to control immigration to the United States annually from all countries outside the Western Hemisphere. After the 1924 amendments, when the system received its basic long-term form, each country's quota was based on the number of persons of that national origin who were in the United States in 1920. Because the ethnic composition of the nation in 1920 was primarily British, Irish and German, use of the 1920 origins basis in assigning

Religious Organizations, Ethnic Groups and Labor Unions

Although public interest in the immigration bill was not as great as it was in measures such as medicare and civil rights, a number of minority ethnic groups, religious groups and labor unions lobbied in favor of the bill. Several groups, such as the American Legion and American Coalition of Patriotic Societies, supported a bill sponsored by Michael A. Feighan (D Ohio) rather than the original Administration proposals, while two groups, the Liberty Lobby and the American Committee on Immigration Policies, opposed all attempts to modify the existing law.

Major Groups for Bill. The major organizations actively working for passage of immigration reform legislation in 1965, according to a survey by Congressional Quarterly, were the American Immigration and Citizenship Conference; the National Committee for Immigration Reform; a number of minority ethnic groups, among the most active of which were the American Committee for Italian Migration, AHEPA (Greek-Americans), the National Council of Jewish Women and the Japanese American Citizens League; the United Steelworkers of America (AFL-CIO) and the AFL-CIO Industrial Union Department; the AFL-CIO; the National Council of Churches of Christ; the National Catholic Welfare Conference; and the Lutheran Immigration Service. All these groups favored the initial Johnson proposals outlined Jan. 13 by the President. Labor groups, however, wanted assurances that new immigrants would not provide too much job competition for U.S. workers. A large number of other groups testified for the immigration bill but did not work actively.

Major Groups Against Bill. According to reports obtained by Congressional Quarterly, there was relatively little strong, organized opposition to the immigration bill by large organizations. Among the chief active opponents were the conservative Liberty Lobby and the American Committee on Immigration Policies (formed in 1964 to support the principles of the 1952 Immigration and Nationality Act). The total membership of these groups, however, was comparatively small—far smaller than that of groups supporting the bill.

Major Opponents Neutralized. In past years, the American Legion, American Coalition of Patriotic Societies, and several similar organizations had provided the bone and muscle of organized opposition to proposals for repeal of the national origins quotas system. These groups whose past opposition was based in part on fears that a relaxation of existing restrictions would permit a massive influx of new immigrants, did not actively oppose the immigration bill in 1965—a fact cited by many as the major reason for the comparatively easy passage of the measure through Congress. The reason they ceased active opposition was that the Johnson Administration agreed to make substantial revisions in the initial Administration proposals, along lines proposed early in the year by Feighan, who was chairman of the House Judiciary Immigration and Nationality Subcommittee. One of the early concessions was the imposition of a 170,000-person over-all quota for the entire world outside the Western Hemisphere. Later in the year, when the Senate added to the bill the 120,000-person limit on annual immigration from the Western Hemisphere, spokesmen for these organizations said one of their major goals had been achieved—imposing what amounted to an over-all world immigration quota and thus guaranteeing against an excessive number of immigrants.

They pointed out that the net effect of the final bill was to limit immigration to about 320,000 persons a year—120,000 from the Western Hemisphere, 170,000 from the rest of the world and 30,000 immediate relatives who would enter quota-free. By comparison, the Johnson Administration's initial proposals would have permitted an estimated entry of 350,000 a year at first, and this eventually could have gone even higher because there was no limit on entries from the Western Hemisphere. (Total immigration in recent years had averaged about 300,000 annually.)

For the Bill

Immigration Conference. A major force for immigration reform, not only in 1965 but in previous years, was the American Immigration and Citizenship Conference, located in New York City. The Conference did not engage in lobbying of Congress as such; rather, it was a clearinghouse and coordinator of information and research on immigration and nationality problems. The AICC came into being in 1960, when two similar organizations merged—the National Council on Naturalization and Citizenship, which had been formed in 1930, and the American Immigration Conference, which had been formed in 1954. From 1960, the AICC was headed by Mrs. Ruth Z. Murphy, a nonpaid executive vice president, who previously had directed the National Council on Naturalization and Citizenship.

The AICC actually consisted of a large number of organizations (about 100 active or affiliated groups) interested in immigration reform. Most of them favored repeal or revision of the national origins quota system. Over the years, the AICC engaged primarily in educational and informational work on immigration—distributing pamphlets, a bimonthly newsletter, fact sheets, statements and research materials. Its general position was to work for a "mon-discriminatory" policy in immigration.

The president of the AICC in 1965 was former Sen. Kenneth B. Keating (R N.Y.) and the honorary president was former State Department Chief of Protocol Angier Biddle Duke.

National Committee. In the nation's capital, an important ad hoc lobbying group in favor of the original Administration bill was formed early in 1965—the National Committee for Immigration Reform. The

Lobbied To Help Passage of Immigration Reform Legislation

group actually consisted soley of individuals, not of organizations, but a large number of the members were affiliated with organizations which were strongly supporting the Johnson Administration bill.

The primary objective was to enlist the active support of various influential individuals who would write personal letters to their Representatives and Senators, and help urge others to do so, in favor of immigration changes. Former Presidents Truman and Eisenhower and a large number of other former public officials of both parties became members. Leading active figures or officers of the group included former Under Secretary of State Robert Murphy, RCA Chairman David Sarnoff, Detroit Edison Co. President Walter L. Cisler, AFL-CIO President George Meany, Inland Steel Co. Chairman Joseph Block and individuals connected with many of the unions and ethnic groups working most strongly for the bill.

Ethnic Groups. The chief ethnic lobbying for the bill was conducted by organizations representing Americans of Italian, Greek and Japanese stock. In general, minority ethnic groups took the position that a revision of the national origins quota system was needed to remove the stigma of racial or national inferiority (which, they said, was implied by sharp restrictions on immigration from Southern Europe and Asia) or to permit the entry of persons from countries with small quotas and long waiting lists.

The ardent support for the bill demonstrated by American-Italian and American-Greek organizations arose partly from the desire to open up the gates to the many thousands on the waiting lists from those two countries. By all accounts, the American Committee for Italian Migration, headed by Judge Juvenal Marchisio of New York, was the single most active ethnic group working for the bill outside the nation's capital. The group was a member of the American Immigration and Citizenship Conference and Marchisio was a member of the National Committee for Immigration Reform.

Other groups said to be highly active were AHEPA (American-Hellenic Educational Progressive Assn.), the Sons of Italy and the Japanese American Citizens League, the only one of these organizations maintaining a direct Washington, D.C., lobbying operation.

Religious Groups. The National Catholic Welfare Conference, the National Council of Churches of Christ, the Lutheran Immigration Service, the National Council of Jewish Women and a number of other Jewish organizations all gave strong and active support to the bill.

Unions. Major support came from the United Steelworkers of America (AFL-CIO), whose new president, I.W. Abel, was described as particularly interested in immigration reform; and from the Industrial Union Department of the AFL-CIO. The steel union and some of the other large unions in the IUD (Automobile Workers, Clothing Workers) were described as "little Leagues of Nations" containing many

first and second generation Americans seeking family reunification. These two union groups were active both in Washington, D.C., and in local lobbying elsewhere in the country. They helped put the muscle in a pressure campaign early in 1965 in Feighan's home district, designed to make clear to Feighan that there was strong support in his district for immigration reform and that he therefore should not delay in bringing a bill out of his subcommittee. The AFL-CIO national lobbying staff also testified for the bill and lobbied for it, particularly during late August and September. Although immigration was not at the very top of labor's legislative priority list, it was high up.

Against the Bill

The only organizations which actively worked against the bill from start to finish were the Liberty Lobby and the American Committee on Immigration Policies. The Liberty Lobby, a highly conservative group formed in 1955, claimed (through its executive secretary, W.B. Hicks, who testified in the Senate June 15), to speak for 137,000 persons of various national origins receiving its publications. Hicks testified against the immigration legislation; and Liberty Letter, the group's publication, in its September issue urged a letter-writing campaign against the bill, adding that if the bill were passed, at the very least it should include the Western Hemisphere limitation. Congressional offices said, for the most part, they had seen little or no mail directly traceable to Liberty Lobby. The group may have been responsible, however, for the heavy flow of mail received by Sen. Spessard L. Holland (D Fla.) in opposition to the bill. Holland's office said he had received about 2,000 letters, at a rate as high as 150 a day at one point, opposing the bill; and many of the letters also were against the U.S.-Russian consular treaty, strongly opposed by the Liberty Lobby.

The Liberty Lobby reported spending $37,448.84 to lobby Congress in 1964.

The American Committee on Immigration Policies was formed in June 1964 to send out educational material in support of the principles of the 1952 Immigration and Nationality Act. The group's director, Robert H. Goldsborough, said it was nonpartisan and that it did oppose the 1965 immigration bill but did not lobby against it directly or urge people to write letters in opposition. He said it was a small group, not a mass membership organization, had little money (he was working on an unpaid basis) and was neither a conservative nor a liberal organization, despite charges made by some liberal groups that it was extremely conservative. He said the group had no affiliation or connection with any other organization.

Goldsborough, a former staff member of the House Un-American Activities Committee (1959-61), said his group had placed advertisements involving immigration.

quotas heavily favored immigration of persons born in the British Isles, Ireland and Germany, while sharply limiting immigration from the rest of Europe, Africa and Asia. Supporters of the system said this was a desirable way of limiting immigration to persons most like Americans who would be easily assimilated. Opponents contended the system was based on false and grossly insulting notions of racial superiority of white Northern Europeans. Opponents also noted that much of each annual quota was wasted because of low immigration into the United States from the countries with the largest quotas. Elimination of the national origins quota system had been sought by every President since Harry Truman. *(Congress and the Nation, Vol. I, p. 218.)*

The end to the system came with the 1965 enactment of PL 89-236 abolishing the existing country-by-country quotas which fixed a legal maximum of about 158,000 persons who could enter annually on a quota basis from non-Western Hemisphere areas. In place of this system, PL 89-236 provided (with a few exceptions) that total immigration from non-Western Hemisphere areas should be limited to 170,000 persons a year—to be selected from all non-Western Hemisphere areas at random, on the basis of personal qualities such as possession of special labor skills, family relationship to U.S. citizens and residents, or the need for political or other asylum.

However, the legislation tightened restrictions on immigration from Western Hemisphere nations. It imposed for the first time a limit of 120,000 persons a year who could immigrate to the United States from the independent and self-governing nations of the Western Hemisphere. Previously, there were no numerical limits for such Western Hemisphere countries, except for Jamaica, Trinidad and Tobago. The Johnson Administration opposed this limit but finally accepted it as the price of getting the national origins quota system repealed. The limitation was backed by the American Legion, the American Coalition of Patriotic Societies and others fearing a further upsurge of Western Hemisphere immigration into the United States.

After the provisions of PL 89-236 went fully into effect in July 1968, there would be only three general categories of regular permissible immigrants: 120,000 persons a year from the Western Hemisphere; 170,000 annually from the rest of the world; and an estimated 30,000 to 40,000 immediate relatives of U.S. citizens (plus ministers and other small groups) who, under the law, could enter without regard to the above numerical limitations. In addition, under certain "parole" provisions of the basic Immigration and Nationality Act, the Attorney General could allow individuals temporarily into the United States and then adjust their status to that of immigrants.

Legislative Action. There was little opposition in Congress to passage of the legislation once the issue of an annual ceiling on Western Hemisphere immigration had been settled. The ceiling was the major concession to the groups opposing elimination of the national origins quota system and was the main point of controversy during Congressional action on the bill. In two key votes of the 1965 session, the House passed HR 2580 Aug. 25 by a **318-95** roll-call vote and the Senate passed it Sept. 22 by a **76-18** roll call. Both chambers

adopted the conference report Sept. 30 and President Johnson signed it into law Oct. 3.

Major Provisions of PL 89-236

In place of the immigration system in existence, PL 89-236—in its major sections—set up a new system to become fully effective in mid-1968 after a three-year transition period. The new system provided:

(1) For non-Western Hemisphere countries, previously governed by the national origins quota system, the latter was abolished. Instead of country-by-country quotas, an over-all quota of 170,000 annual immigrants from outside the Western Hemisphere was to be permitted. Applicants would be accepted on the basis of certain conditions applying to them as individuals, and regardless of which specific non-Western Hemisphere nation they had been born in. Under this system, first preference for immigration (20 percent of the 170,000 total) was to be given to adult, unmarried children of U.S. citizens, in order to unite families. The remaining preferences would go to other categories of relatives of U.S. citizens and residents; to persons possessing special skills, or needed to fill labor shortages in the United States; and to displaced persons and refugees from political, religious and racial persecution. The final bill specified that of the 170,000 immigrants from countries outside the Western Hemisphere, no more than 20,000 could come from any one country.

(2) For the Western Hemisphere, an over-all limit of 120,000 immigrants a year from all independent and self-governing countries combined was to be established, to be filled on a personal first-come, first-served basis, without country-by-country quotas, preferences or limits on how many persons could enter from any one country (subject to the over-all 120,000 hemispheric limitation).

(3) The provisions of previous law which had permitted non-quota entry of husbands, wives and minor unmarried children of U.S. citizens, plus ministers and certain other special groups, were to remain in effect, and were even broadened to include parents of U.S. citizens. However, a distinction was now made between the immediate relatives as a group, on the one hand, and the ministers and others. Immediate relatives were to be subject neither to 170,000 non-Western Hemisphere limitation nor the 120,000 Western Hemisphere limitation, while the ministers and other special groups, while not subject to the 170,000 non-Western Hemisphere limitation, would be subject to the 120,000 Western Hemisphere maximum. A total of 30,000-40,000 immigrants annually was anticipated under these non-quota provisions.

(4) The provisions of previous law which had permitted non-quota entry of certain groups of refugees were repealed, because it was felt that refugees could be handled adequately under various provisions of the new law, particularly the one making them a special preference group for admission under the 170,000 non-Western Hemisphere quota. Most of the special refugee admission laws had already lapsed, and PL 89-236 repealed the only remaining law specifically permitting further non-quota entry of refugees, the Fair Share Refugee Act of 1960, which had allowed refugees to enter under a "parole" system and then apply for an adjustment of their status to that of non-quota immigrants.

Under PL 89-236, persons already admitted under the 1960 law could still apply for adjustment of status, but no new entrants would be permitted under the 1960 provisions. (Note: While PL 89-236 repealed the parole provisions of the 1960 Fair Share law, it did not repeal the parole provisions of Section 212d5 of the basic immigration law, which, as indicated earlier, were not aimed specifically at refugees but rather, according to the Judiciary Committees, at permitting emergency entry of a few individuals for such things as emergency medical treatment.)

(5) The provisions of previous law which attributed an individual to his country of birth, rather than his place of residence or citizenship (if different), were retained for certain purposes—namely, to determine whether an individual was to be subject to the Western Hemisphere rules and regulations, or whether he was to be subject to the immigration provisos applying to the non-Western Hemisphere countries.

At the same time, the previous "Asia-Pacific triangle" provision under which non-white persons of Asian ancestry had been charged to the national quota of their racial ancestry rather than their country of birth, was repealed. Under this repealed provision, a person of Japanese ancestry, for example, even if he was born in England, was a citizen of England and had been resident there all his life, had been required to seek entry to the United States under the Japanese quota. Critics had called this an outright racial device, designed to exclude non-white persons of Asian ancestry by forcing them to seek entry under the tiny Asian quotas regardless of where they were born.

Henceforth, the birth rule was to be as follows: Persons born in independent and self-governing countries of the Western Hemisphere, such as Canada, Brazil, Chile, Jamaica, Trinidad and Tobago, etc., were to be considered applicants from the Western Hemisphere, subject to the rules and regulations applying to such applicants—even if they actually had moved to non-Western Hemisphere countries and taken citizenship there. Similarly, persons born in non-Western Hemisphere countries were to be considered applicants from outside the Western Hemisphere, subject to the rules and regulations applying to such applicants (and with racial ancestry now totally eliminated as a consideration)—even if they had actually moved to the Western Hemisphere and become a citizen of some country there. The 20,000 limitation on annual immigration from any one country outside the Western Hemisphere (*see provision 1, above*) also would be determined by country of birth.

A lesser but nevertheless notable provision of PL 89-236 strengthened safeguards in the existing immigration law designed to protect American workers against job competition from immigrants. The change was demanded by organized labor. The net effect of the changes in immigration law made by PL 89-236 was to eliminate race and national origin as the major basis of preference for admission to the United States from non-Western Hemisphere nations by eliminating country-by-country quotas as well as the Asian-ancestry provisions. One immediate result was expected to be sharply increased immigration from Italy, Greece, Poland and Portugal and some other countries which previously had low quotas and long waiting lists.

Coffee Agreement

Implementation of an important international agreement to stabilize the price of coffee, which Congress had blocked in 1964, was achieved early in 1965 by passage of an Administration-backed bill (S 701—PL 89-23) to enable the United States to carry out its obligations under the agreement. *(For 1968 action, see p. 113.)*

The United States Sept. 29, 1962, along with 32 coffee exporting nations and 21 other importing nations, signed the International Coffee Agreement, which was designed to prevent major fluctuations in the world coffee market by stabilizing minimum world prices at the 1962 level. The purpose was to end a long downtrend in coffee prices, stabilize production and so protect the foreign exchange and internal economies of coffee-producing nations, most of which were located in Latin America and all of which were "developing" nations. Over an eight-year period, the world price for Brazilian coffee (the most commonly used kind) had declined from an all-time high of 79 cents a pound in 1954 to a price of 34 cents in 1962. *(Congress and the Nation, Vol. I, p. 205.)*

The Senate in 1963 ratified the Agreement but the House the following year rejected the conference report on a bill to allow the United States to enforce the Agreement's provisions. Many House Members complained of the rise in coffee prices in 1963 and 1964, and attributed this in part to the quotas set under the Agreement (which the United States could participate in even without ratification). It was believed that a major factor in the defeat was the fortuitous chance that the bill came up immediately after the House, the same day, had passed a bill authorizing quotas on meat imports. The meat quota bill, although opposed by most Northern Democrats, had been worked out by cattle interests and Administration officials, and was expected to result in higher beef prices. Observers believed that many Northern Democrats broke with the Administration on the coffee bill because they were dissatisfied with the meat quota bill and did not want the responsibility for passing additional legislation that might raise consumer prices in an election year.

In 1965, the Administration made the passage of implementing legislation (S 701) one of its top priority requests. The United States had been in technical violation of the Agreement since Oct. 1, 1964, because it did not have authority to enforce the provisions concerning coffee imports. (On Oct. 1, 1964, the International Coffee Organization, which was established by the Agreement, required importing nations to begin enforcement of the Agreement's provisions barring imports which did not bear a certificate of origin.) The State Department said that if Congress failed in 1965 to reverse its 1964 action, the Coffee Agreement was likely to collapse, with serious consequences for the economies of Latin American and other developing nations.

However, Congress approved the implementing legislation with little controversy. The House passed S 701 by a 300-97 roll-call vote and the Senate by a 56-23 roll call. Absent in 1965 were two main factors contributing to the 1964 defeat: a rise in the price of coffee and election-year pressures. The new large Democratic majority elected in 1964 also helped because a majority of Republicans continued to oppose the bill.

Provisions. As signed by the President, S 701, the International Coffee Agreement Act of 1965:

Provided that the enabling legislation would remain in effect until Oct. 1, 1968, but would expire if Congress by concurrent resolution determined that there had been an "unwarranted increase" in coffee prices, or if the Coffee Agreement was terminated.

Authorized the President to limit entry into the United States of coffee imported from countries not participant to the Agreement; to prohibit entry of coffee shipments from participating members that were not accompanied by certificates of origin or re-export; to require certificates of origin for coffee shipments exported or re-exported from the United States; and to require record-keeping concerning coffee importation, distribution, prices and consumption.

Required the President to submit an annual report to Congress on the operation of the Agreement.

Authorized the appropriation of funds necessary to carry out the Agreement, but limited U.S. contributions for administration of the Agreement to 20 percent of total contributions and not more than $150,000 per fiscal year.

Monetary Fund

A bill passed by Congress with little controversy authorized an increase of $1,035,000,000 in the U.S. contribution to the International Monetary Fund (IMF). The sum represented the U.S. share of a general 25-percent increase in IMF quotas, and brought the total U.S. obligations to the Fund to $5,160,000,000. Only minor objections to the increase were raised in Congress but House Republicans used the bill (HR 6497—PL 89-31) as a vehicle for criticizing the Administration's balance-of-payments program. President Johnson requested enactment of HR 6497. The IMF was established by the Bretton Woods Conference of 1944 to deal with problems of foreign exchange. The Fund was designed to promote convertibility of currencies and stability of exchange markets by helping countries to finance temporary balance-of-payments deficits without resorting to measures restrictive to trade.

Provisions. As signed into law, HR 6497:

Authorized the U.S. Governor of the International Monetary Fund (the Secretary of the Treasury) to consent to an increase of $1,035,000,000 in the U.S. subscription to the Fund. (The bill also authorized appropriation of the funds. The fiscal 1966 Treasury-Post Office appropriations bill (HR 7060—PL 89-57) granted the full $1,035,000,000. Of this amount, $259 million (one-quarter of the total amount) would be paid in gold while the remaining $776 million would remain on call in the U.S. Treasury.)

Peace Corps

Congress authorized (S 2054—PL 89-134) $115 million for the Peace Corps in fiscal 1966, the amount requested by President Johnson. In the foreign aid appropriation bill (HR 10871—PL 89-273), Congress appropriated $102 million and continued the availability of $12.1 million in unspent funds from the previous appro-

priation. PL 89-134 also created a unified, non-career personnel system for the Peace Corps' foreign and domestic staffs, with appointments made under the new system limited to a maximum of five years' service.

Inter-American Development Bank

An Administration bill (HR 45—PL 89-6) was passed early in the session to authorize a $750 million increase in the U.S. contribution to the Fund for Special Operations (FSO) of the Inter-American Development Bank (IADB). The Bank, patterned after the International Bank for Reconstruction and Development (World Bank), was created by the members of the Organization of American States in 1959 to assist in the economic and social development of Latin American nations by providing capital and technical assistance, and promoting private investment in development projects. The Bank eventually became the chief banking instrument of the Alliance for Progress. (Another increase in the U.S. contribution to the FSO was enacted in 1967. *See p. 99.*)

The $750 million increase authorized in 1965 was to be paid out in three annual installments of $250 million beginning in fiscal 1965. (Congress later in the year appropriated $250 million for each of fiscal 1965 and 1966 to cover the first two installments.) The $750 million represented the U.S. share of a total increase in Fund resources of $900 million. The balance of $150 million was to be provided by 19 Latin American countries.

The Fund for Special Operations was one of two "windows" of the IADB which provided loans, on easy credit and repayment terms, for high-priority economic and social development projects in Latin America that could not be financed on regular commercial terms because of balance-of-payments or other economic considerations. The other "soft window" of the IADB was the Social Progress Trust Fund (SPTF). The FSO, jointly financed by the countries participating in the Inter-American Development Bank, provided loans for such projects as roads, dams, water facilities and industrial development. The SPTF, wholly financed by the United States, provided loans for four types of "social" projects only: water supply and sanitation; advanced education; housing; and land settlement and improved land use.

In authorizing U.S. participation in the increase in FSO resources, HR 45 also in effect gave U.S. consent to IADB plans to combine both of the "soft" loan operations into one operation under the FSO. This meant that funds for "social" projects of the sort financed by the SPTF, formerly provided entirely by the United States, would henceforth be provided in part by Latin American countries. Loans from the expanded FSO would be repayable in the currency of the borrower, with maturities of 20 to 30 years and interest between 3 percent and 4 percent, including a small insurance fee payable in dollars. (While the SPTF was not abolished, it became quiescent as practically all of its capital was committed in loans. It did not receive any more capital contributions.)

The final version of HR 45 differed from the bill requested by President Johnson only in requiring the

U.S. representative on the Bank's Board of Executive Directors to block loans, financed by the U.S. contribution, to any country where bilateral U.S. aid was suspended as a result of failure to make compensation for seized American property or businesses. The provision was a modified version of an amendment added on the Senate floor.

Provisions. As signed into law HR 45:

Authorized the U.S. Governor of the Bank (Secretary of the Treasury) to vote in favor of a resolution increasing the Fund for Special Operations of the Inter-American Development Bank by $900 million.

Authorized appropriations of $750 million as the U.S. share of the increased contribution.

Required the United States representative on the IADB Executive Board to disapprove any FSO loan to a country which expropriated property or business firms owned at least 50 percent by U.S. citizens, on or after Jan. 1, 1962, without taking steps to provide adequate compensation. Made the provision applicable only to loans made from U.S. contributions to the FSO and only during periods when U.S. bilateral aid to the country was suspended because property was expropriated without compensation.

Hague Protocol

The Senate in 1965 did not act on the Hague Protocol (Exec. H, 86th Congress, 1st Session) to the Warsaw Convention, which had been favorably reported by the Foreign Relations Committee. The Protocol amended the Convention to raise the limit of an international air carrier's liability to each passenger for death or injury from the existing $8,300 to $16,600.

Congress in 1965 also did not take action on separate but related legislation to provide additional compulsory insurance for passengers on international flights by American airlines.

Following the failure of the Senate to act on Exec. H, the United States Nov. 15 formally denounced the Warsaw Convention. The action was taken under Article 39 of the Convention, which permitted any member country to denounce and withdraw from the Convention upon six months notice. A Nov. 15 press release issued by the State Department said that if prior to the effective date of the denunciation—May 15, 1966—there were "reasonable prospect" of an international agreement raising the limits of liability (to approximately $100,000) in international air transportation, the United States would be prepared to withdraw its denunciation.

The Warsaw Convention was signed in 1929 and entered into force for the United States in 1934. Besides limiting the liability of air carriers to $8,300, it also established uniform rules governing the rights and obligations between international air carriers and passengers. Over 90 nations became party to the Convention.

The Hague Protocol was signed in behalf of the United States June 28, 1956, and submitted to the Senate June 24, 1959. The Protocol entered into force as a treaty (not with respect to the United States) Aug. 1, 1963.

The Senate Foreign Relations Committee recommended ratification of Exec. H, but said the United States should denounce the Convention if Congress did not enact pending legislation (S 2032, HR 8386) to provide automatic insurance for passengers on American airlines traveling internationally. The insurance legislation in combination with the Protocol would have provided maximum compensation of $66,600. Opponents of the treaty and the legislation said this figure would be inadequate for many persons, such as a young man with considerable earning potential who left a family, and would be a windfall for others, such as distant relatives, who suffered no financial hardship. They also said the treaty arrangements gave commercial airlines exemptions from liability enjoyed by no other commercial enterprises.

Arms Control Agency

The life of the U.S. Arms Control and Disarmament Agency was extended in 1965 for three years. The legislation (HR 2998—PL 89-27) authorized appropriations of $30 million over fiscal years 1966-68, thus continuing the program at the same authorization level as in fiscal 1964-65. The House wanted to provide a three-year, $40 million authorization while the Senate preferred a two-year, $20 million level. Although the agency had always been viewed with suspicion by many Republicans and conservative Democrats (particularly those favoring larger military expenditures), the major issue in 1965 was the length of the authorization and not the function of the ACDA. The Administration sought a four-year extension to permit "long-term planning" while supporters of a shorter period said Congress should have frequent review of the Agency's actions. *(For 1968 action on ACDA, see p. 106.)*

World Bank, IFC Charters

A bill (S 1742—PL 89-126) passed by Congress with limited debate authorized U.S. consent to certain changes in the charters of the International Bank for Reconstruction and Development (World Bank) and its affiliate, the International Finance Corporation (IFC). The major provision authorized the U.S. Governor of the Bank (the Secretary of the Treasury) to agree to World Bank proposals to permit the Bank to make loans to the IFC. A second provision allowed the United States to agree, without express Congressional approval, to an increase in the World Bank's capital stock if the increase did not entail additional U.S. subscriptions.

Export Control Act

Without opposition, Congress extended the Export Control Act of 1949 for four years—through June 30, 1969. The Administration proposed making the Act permanent. The Act contained the basic authority in law to control exports to Communist nations and to regulate exports in line with U.S. foreign policy aims.

The Act was administered by the Commerce Department by means of a licensing system. The Department, with the aid of other agencies, prepared a list of commodities validated for export: some items could go to any country, others only to certain nations. *(For a summary of U.S. policy on trade with Communist nations, see following item on East-West trade.)*

During action on the 1965 bill (HR 7105—PL 89-63), a controversy rose over a side issue involving an attempt by Arab nations to create an economic boycott of Israel. Some American companies doing business in Arab nations had told Congressional committees that they were required to reply to questionnaires as to whether they had branches in Israel, whether their goods were produced in Israel and similar questions. Companies refusing to cooperate or those doing business with Israel were prevented from operating in the 12 nations of the Arab League. A provision was added to HR 7105 which stated that U.S. policy was to oppose "restrictive trade practices and boycotts" and which required that requests for information be reported to the Commerce Department. An effort to add language flatly prohibiting U.S. businesses from furnishing information that would aid the boycott was rejected.

East-West Trade

In spite of considerable support for expanding U.S. trade with Communist nations in Eastern Europe, no substantive action occurred in this area during 1965. Various groups, in Government, business and farming, made studies and reports which, in general, argued that expanded trade—even with the Communist bloc—would be in the United States' interest. Organized labor, however, continued its hard anti-Communist position and denounced efforts to expand East-West trade. A State Department official late in the year summarized three key arguments favoring expanded trade: it would benefit the United States economically; it could help lessen world tensions; and it could encourage "external independence and internal liberalization in individual Communist countries." President Johnson in his State of the Union Message said the U.S. Government was exploring ways of increasing peaceful trade with the Soviet bloc. On Feb. 16 he established an advisory committee—the Special Presidential Committee on U.S. Trade Relations with Eastern European Countries and the USSR—to study means of expanding East-West trade. The group made a report in the spring with recommendations which it was thought would form the basis of any future legislation.

Background. The cold war between Eastern European countries and the Western Alliance in the Post-World War II era led to the imposition of barriers to trade, particularly in strategic and critical materials and arms. Under a variety of laws, the U.S. Government restricted exports from the United States to Communist countries and also limited imports from those nations, embargoing some countries altogether.

The major laws under which the Government limited U.S. trade with Communist nations were: the Export Control Act of 1949, administered by the Commerce Department, which allowed the Government to limit exports in the interests of national security and other considerations; the 1917 Trading with the Enemy Act, administered by the Treasury Department, which gave the Government power to restrict both imports and exports; the 1951 Battle Act (Mutual Defense Assistance Control Act), administered by the State Department, banning exports of arms and strategic goods to the Communist bloc; and Section 414 of the Mutual Security Act of 1954 (derived from the Neutrality Acts of the 1930s), administered by the State Department, permitting the Government to control both the import and the export of arms, ammunition and other instruments of war to and from any country—in the interests of national foreign policy objectives.

Although details of each of these laws differed, the general U.S. policy on trade with the Communist bloc as of 1965 was as follows:

(1) All U.S. trade (both imports and exports) was forbidden with Communist China, Manchuria, North Korea, Inner Mongolia, North Vietnam and Cuba, except that food and medicines could be sent to Cuba. This total embargo, imposed under the Trading with the Enemy Act and Export Control Act, went into effect in 1950 for the first four areas, in 1954 for North Vietnam and in 1960 for Cuba.

(2) The export of arms and strategic and critical materials from the United States to the Soviet Union, Outer Mongolia, and the Eastern European Communist countries was forbidden (with the restrictions somewhat less for exports to Poland and Romania). Trade in other types of items, like foods, was not forbidden, but exports receiving Government subsidies (such as wheat exports) had to get special Government permission.

(3) Generally, no restrictions were placed on trade with non-Communist nations and Yugoslavia.

In addition, various foreign-aid bills and amendments to the Agricultural Trade Development and Assistance Act of 1954 (PL 480) imposed restrictions on the granting by the U.S. Government of any foreign aid, credit guarantees, or PL 480 benefits to Communist countries. In general, the rule was that such assistance to Communist countries was forbidden, unless the President made some type of positive finding that giving benefits to the particular country in question would be in the interests of the United States.

As a result of all these restrictions, U.S. trade with Communist-bloc nations was substantially less in the post-World War II era than it was with the same nations before. In 1963, for example, U.S. exports to the Communist bloc amounted to only $166.7 million, which was only seven-tenths of 1 percent of total U.S. exports of $20.2 billion. By contrast, during the period 1926-30, U.S. exports to the countries which later made up the postwar Communist bloc averaged $214 million a year—or 4.7 percent of total exports, and this did not include exports to East Germany, for which separate figures were not then kept. The figure was 4.6 percent from 1936-40.

Kennedy Round Negotiations

The Kennedy Round tariff negotiations made little progress during 1965. By the end of the year, hopes had dimmed for making substantial progress toward lower tariffs and fewer nontariff barriers. The negotiations, which began May 4, 1964, at Geneva, Switzerland, under the auspices of GATT (General Agreement on Tariffs and Trade), had produced agreement on some industrial tariff cuts but made almost no progress on agricultural products. The Kennedy Round was authorized under the 1962 Trade Expansion Act. The Act gave the President a five-year authority—until July 1, 1967—to negotiate tariff reductions of up to 50 percent and to eliminate them in certain cases. The United States hoped to gain increased access for its agricultural and industrial products to foreign markets, particularly the European Economic Community. But internal problems of the EEC, particularly in formulating a common agricultural policy (without which the EEC could not negotiate meaningfully on questions of reducing agricultural tariffs), resulted in very limited progress in the talks.

U.S.-Canadian Auto Tariffs

In a move to improve U.S. and Canadian trade relations, Congress passed a bill (HR 9042—PL 89-283) authorizing the President to remove tariff duties at the manufacturer's level on Canadian automobiles and parts for original equipment. The U.S. tariffs, which had been 6.5 percent on autos and 8.5 percent on most parts, were abolished, retroactive to Jan. 18, 1965. The bill also established an Automotive Agreement Adjustment Board to aid U.S. workers "dislocated" by the tariff agreement.

PL 89-283 was designed to implement an agreement signed Jan. 16 by President Johnson and Canadian Prime Minister Lester B. Pearson to remove U.S. and Canadian tariff duties on cars and car parts. As a corollary to the U.S. Government's agreement, U.S. car manufacturers (whose subsidiaries produced most of the cars made in Canada) formally promised the Canadian government to increase their production in Canada through the 1968 model year, and in turn the Canadian government eliminated its tariffs on U.S. cars. In asking for Congressional approval of HR 9042, President Johnson said the agreement with Canada envisioned eventual "full integration of the North American automobile industry."

The bill won Congressional approval despite a heated floor debate in the Senate centering on the contention that the agreement would build up the Canadian automotive industry at the expense of the United States. Members of Congress also complained that the agreement favored Canada in violation of the General Agreement on Tariffs and Trade, but the majority accepted the Administration argument that it was needed to head off a U.S.-Canadian trade war. In 1963 Canada had taken steps to build up its automobile production by placing greater restriction on imports of U.S. automotive products.

The Senate passed HR 9042 by a 54-18 roll-call vote after rejecting by a 32-43 roll call a proposal by an opponent to delay action until 1966. Another proposal to delay the effective date of the agreement until 1966 and to require a Tariff Commission study of the provisions was rejected by a 34-40 roll call. The House passed the bill by a 280-113 roll call.

Provisions. As signed into law, Oct. 21, 1965, the Automotive Products Trade Act of 1965 contained the following major provisions:

Authorized the President to abolish retroactively to Jan. 18, 1965, the 6.5-percent U.S. tariff on Canadian automobiles and the 8.5-percent duty on Canadian parts, as applicable to those for use in original equipment.

Directed the President to report to Congress and, if necessary, to outline steps for legislative action if he should determine that the Canadian government after Aug. 31, 1968, had increased the percentage of local parts and labor that Canadian subsidiaries of U.S. auto companies had agreed to put into automobiles produced in Canada during model years 1965-68.

Established, until July 1, 1968, a special adjustment assistance program for U.S. auto firms and workers "dislocated" by the U.S.-Canadian agreement. Directed the Tariff Commission to investigate and report to the President on applications for assistance. Authorized the President, after consultation with the Departments of Commerce, Labor and the Treasury, and the Small Business Administration, to make final determination as to whether assistance should be granted.

UN Charter Amendments

The membership of the United Nations had increased during the years since its founding in 1945, but this growth was not reflected in the major councils of the organization. The UN membership had grown from its original 51 members to 114 members by June 1965. In 1963, the UN approved a resolution to enlarge the membership of the Security Council and the Economic and Social Council to reflect the increased membership in the UN as a whole. The amendments were the first revision of the UN Charter in the 20-year history of the organization.

The Senate in 1965 with little opposition and no negative votes consented to the ratification by the President of the amendments (Exec. A, 89th Congress, 1st Session). The roll-call vote was 71-0. Charter amendments must be approved by two-thirds of the General Assembly members and ratified by two-thirds of the member states including all five permanent members of the Security Council—the United States, the Soviet Union, Great Britain, France and Nationalist China. These requirements were met with the U.S. ratification, permitting the Charter revisions to go into effect Jan. 1, 1966.

President Johnson April 6, 1965, submitted the amendments to the Senate for consent to ratification. He said the proposed increases in the Councils were "clearly necessary to restore the balance which existed between the Councils and the General Assembly when the Charter came into force" but were "not such as to make the Councils unwieldy." The Senate voted on June 3. The only opposition was voiced by Sen. Strom Thurmond (R S.C.).

The amendments did not change the existing authority of the permanent members to veto nonprocedural matters in the Security Council.

Provisions. As consented to by the Senate, Exec. A, 89th Congress, 1st Session, authorized the President to ratify the United Nations resolution revising the UN Charter as follows:

Amended Article 23 of the Charter to increase the membership of the Security Council from 11 to 15 members and to increase the number of Council members to be elected by the General Assembly to two-year terms from 6 to 10; specified that in the first election following the increase in membership of the Security Council, two of the four additional members would be elected to terms of one year.

Amended Article 27 of the Charter to require nine, rather than seven, affirmative votes for decisions of the Security Council. (This did not change the veto privilege.)

Amended Article 61 of the Charter to increase membership of the Economic and Social Council from 18 to 27; specified that nine (rather than six) of the members would be chosen each year for a term of three years; specified that in the first election following the increase in membership in the Economic and Social Council, three of the nine additional members would be elected to one-year terms, three to two-year terms, and three to three-year terms.

Foreign Agents Act

The Senate, but not the House, passed a bill (S 693) to tighten and clarify provisions of the Foreign Agents Registration Act of 1938. The Senate in 1964 passed an identical bill (S 2136) which died in the House. The legislation was an outgrowth of hearings held in 1962-63 by the Senate Foreign Relations Committee on foreign lobbying activities. *(Congress and the Nation, Vol. I, p. 140, 1556, 1660, 1768.)*

S 693, which was supported by the Justice Department, imposed stricter disclosure requirements on lobbyists for foreign interests; redefined the activities of persons required to register under the Act; authorized the Attorney General to enjoin persons from activities not in compliance with the Act; outlawed contingency arrangements in which the agent's fee was based on his legislative success; and prohibited agents from making Congressional campaign contributions in behalf of a foreign principal. Senate Foreign Relations Committee Chairman J.W. Fulbright (D Ark.) said the Act was originally drawn to deal with subversive agents and propagandists. But in recent years, he said, such agents had been replaced by "the professional lobbyists and public opinion manipulators whose object is not to subvert the Government but to influence its policies to the satisfaction of their clients. The trench coat has been replaced by the grey flannel suit." *(For 1966 action, see p. 73.)*

Cuban Claims

Congress enacted a bill (HR 9336—PL 89-262) amending a 1964 law which authorized the Foreign Claims Settlement Commission to determine the amount of claims by U.S. citizens and corporations against the Cuban government. The claims resulted from expropriation of U.S. property in Cuba; the determination was intended for use in any eventual claims agreement with Cuba. The 1964 law specified that none of the claims would be paid from U.S. funds and that the administrative expenses of the bill would be paid by the proceeds from the sale of Cuban assets blocked by the United States. The latter provision conflicted with U.S. policy recognizing the sancity of property, and HR 9336 accordingly authorized appropriations to cover the Commission's administrative expenses.

International Wheat Pact

Congress in 1965 approved ratification of a one-year extension of the International Wheat Agreement (Exec. B, 89th Congress, 1st Session). However, action was not completed on a companion measure (S 2294) authorizing implementation of the extension. The Senate consented to the ratification of Exec. B by an 88-0 roll-call vote. It passed S 2294 soon after but the bill died in the House in the adjournment rush. The International Wheat Agreement was first concluded in 1949 and was extended in 1953, 1956 and 1959 and 1962. All these extensions were for a period of three years. Exec. B extended the 1962 Agreement without change except for the length of time involved. The Agreement specified the amount of wheat which importing countries agreed to take from exporting countries (as a percentage of their total needs), and the price range for the wheat. Exporting countries were bound to make the required amount of wheat available. *(For 1966, 1968 action, see p. 77, 113.)*

Dominican Republic Intervention

Rebellion broke out April 24, 1965, in Santo Domingo, capital of the Dominican Republic, and four days later U.S. troops were sent in to help stem the fighting. The Dominican rebels opposing the military-backed civilian junta of J. Donald Reid Cabral claimed to be fighting to restore the constitutional government under deposed President Juan Bosch. President Johnson April 27 announced that he had ordered the evacuation of U.S. citizens from Santo Domingo and the following day disclosed the landing of 400 U.S. Marines to protect and carry out the evacuation of Americans and other nationals caught in the revolution-torn capital.

U.S. troops continued to flow into the Republic, apparently well beyond the stated needs of protecting U.S. citizens. (U.S. troops involved in the operation eventually totaled more than 30,200 including men on ships and planes.) By May the Administration was suggesting that the danger of a Communist takeover in the Republic justified the increasingly large involvement of U.S. troops. Some sharp criticism of such a large military intervention in Latin America was voiced by influential U.S. newspapers and Members of Congress, but many others, with Castro's takeover of Cuba in mind, supported the President's actions. Criticism focused, in part, on the role played by U.S. Ambassador to the Dominican Republic W. Tapley Bennett Jr., for urging the intervention and sending exaggerated reports of Communist influence in the rebel camp. Critics felt that Bennett's policy was to support reactionary military elements and to oppose a "liberal" revolution.

The question of the exact number of Communists involved and their role in the revolution became for a while a "cause celebre" in the American press.

After the situation became more stable, with the fighting more or less halted and the capital under the

1966

supervision of an Organization of American States (OAS) Inter-American Peace Force, Congressional critics led by Sen. J.W. Fulbright (D Ark.) began to seriously question the Administration's actions in the Dominican Republic. Fulbright's Senate Foreign Relations Committee held nine days of closed-door hearings and, though no Committee report was issued, Fulbright Sept. 15 used information from the hearings as a basis for sharp criticism of the Administration in a Senate speech. Fulbright voiced the major complaints of the liberal critics: the change in emphasis from saving American lives to preventing a Communist takeover; the Administration's faulty evaluation of and overreaction to the threat of Communism; poor intelligence and advice from governmental officials on the scene; and, not least, the Administration's lack of candor with the American public. Fulbright questioned the legality of the intervention and over-all U.S. policy toward Latin America and asked for greater reliance on the OAS.

Strong reaction to Fulbright's speech was immediate in Congress.

The House Sept. 20, by a 312-52 roll-call vote, adopted under suspension of the rules a resolution (H Res 560) which in effect endorsed the unilateral use of force by any Western Hemisphere country to prevent a Communist takeover anywhere in the Hemisphere. The resolution mentioned no countries, but appeared tailored to give approval to situations such as the U.S. intervention. The resolution was opposed by 49 Northern Democrats and three Republicans.

The resolution, which expressed the "sense of the House," did not require Senate action or Presidential approval and did not have the force of law. The State Department, worried about repercussions from such a resolution, yet chary of offending the staunchest Congressional defenders of its Dominican policy, said it was "in accord with the objectives" of H Res 560. Numerous Latin American countries therefore looked on the resolution as a quasi-official U.S. endorsement of unilateral military intervention, a discouraging turnabout, in their eyes, in U.S. hemispheric policies. Many promptly voiced strong condemnation of the House action.

H Res 560 stated that "the intervention of international Communism, directly or indirectly, however disguised, in any American State, conflicts with the established policy of the American Republics for the protection of the sovereignty of the peoples of such states and the political independence of their governments...." It expressed the sense of the House that, "In any such situation any one or more of the high contracting parties to the Inter-American Treaty of Reciprocal Assistance may...take steps to forestall or combat intervention, domination, control and colonization, in whatever form, by the subversive forces known as international Communism and its agencies in the Western Hemisphere."

In support of H Res 560, of which he was sponsor, Rep. Armistead I. Selden Jr. (D Ala.), chairman of the House Foreign Affairs Inter-American Affairs Subcommittee, said the Rio Treaty had been designed "essentially to confront traditional forms of direct aggression. But in the two decades since the end of World War II, it has become increasingly apparent that the threat to the security of the Western Hemisphere lies in Communist subversion, rather than in armed intervention across frontiers."

The war in Vietnam again was the dominant issue in American foreign relations in 1966 as the conflict escalated, the United States became more deeply involved and no end appeared in sight. Public opposition to the war remained strong although it appeared that the most militant and vocal opponents did not represent the true sentiment of the majority of Americans. It was unclear what that true sentiment was: the Congressional elections in the fall gave few clues and Congress continued—with only a few dissenting votes—to approve funds for the war and to reject proposals to repudiate the American involvement. Not unexpectedly, debate on the U.S. foreign aid program was dominated by the war, with critics of the conflict continuing to argue that excessive American commitments abroad had unwisely led to the Johnson Administration's decision to send troops into the war. Administration proposals to reform the program, primarily through a multiyear authorization, were rejected by Congress. Congress then went on in its traditional manner and cut the aid appropriations 13.3 percent below the requests.

A major weakening of the 20-year post-World War II foreign policy in Europe began to take specific form when France announced its intention to withdraw from the integrated military command of the North Atlantic Treaty Organization. It later became clear that France also was expelling all foreign forces, including American, from French soil. Another disappointment to the Administration was the rejection by Congress of proposals to expand East-West trade. The Administration did not expect enactment of its major legislative proposal, but hoped for hearings—which were not held in either chamber—to prepare the groundwork for action in following years. One hopeful sign in foreign affairs was a detailed study in Congress of U.S. policy toward Communist China. Lengthy hearings were held in both houses. It was the first time in years that any substantial interest had been shown in learning more about the Asian nation, and was considered important in preparation for the day when the United States and China would have formal relations.

Vietnam

The Vietnam war and the United States' involvement in it continued to escalate during 1966, but by the end of the year neither side had persuaded the other to talk peace on any terms other than its own. The American Government generated substantial publicity about its desire to negotiate a settlement; President Johnson was very expansive at times: "We...have made it clear... that there are no arbitrary limits to our search for peace .... We will meet at any conference table, we will discuss any proposals...and we will consider the views of any groups." These remarks were made in his Jan. 12 State of the Union address. North Vietnam was less open, but this did not particularly matter because both sides appeared more intent on waging a military struggle than in settling differences at a conference table.

During the year, the United States vastly increased the scope of its military commitment in the war. The in-

'The Reality of Chaos'

President Johnson Aug. 30, 1966, in a speech to the American Legion National Convention outlined America's responsibilities to meet the root causes of chaos, aggression and war. Mr. Johnson said:

Each generation of Americans in turn has demonstrated that courage is deeply ingrained in the American character. But the years that lie ahead of us call for our imagination and compassion as well as they call for our courage.

Even the most narrowly self-interested must see that this is so. Unless we have the imagination to understand what is happening in the world, we may very well find ourselves—together with all of our friends among the highly developed nations—facing a series of explosive crises, in which our military involvement is urgently at issue.

Here are the raw data with which we must work:

By 1970 over one-half of the world's population will live in the southern half of the globe. Yet they will command only one-sixth of the world's total goods and services.

In 40 nations, the annual per capita income is rising by one percent a year, or less. By the end of the century, if this rate continues, their per capita income will have risen to $170 a year. Our per capita income here in America will then be approaching not $170 a year, but $5,000 per year.

Then let's ask ourselves this morning: What does this mean for peace in the world? What are the consequences when there is awakened in men the hungry desire for a better life, and there is really no way open to them to fulfill that desire?

One measure of what it means is the incidence of violence, the number of upheavals that stagger the civil order. Recently our very able Secretary of Defense, Robert Mc-Namara, gave us an accounting of these:

In eight years there have been more than 160 such outbreaks. Only 15 have involved military conflict between two nations. None have involved a formally declared war.

But as you must see, the tempo of violence in the world is increasing. In 1958 there were 34 significant conflicts. In 1965 there were not 34, but there were 58.

Where did they occur? Thirty-two took place among the very poorest nations where per capita incomes are now less than $100 per year.

So I submit the lesson could not be made clearer. The poor nations are on a road that is mined with potential turmoil. Poverty—and the hatred of poverty—can detonate those mines. The ranging search and quest for bread may bring on the reality of chaos.

We know that our adversaries see in this situation a very fertile field for exploitation. We know that it is not in the interest of freedom—our own freedom and that of the poorer nations—that our adversaries should succeed.

Indeed, we know now that so interwoven is our destiny with the world's destiny, so intricate are the bonds between us and every continent, that our responsibilities would be just as real in the absence of a Communist threat. For every school boy senses—what some statesmen may not yet comprehend—that responsibility is the price of power and influence....

Where we can help, we will. If our assistance is needed for development, for the work of teaching and healing and building, then that assistance will be forthcoming.

If our might is needed to help them defend themselves from aggression supported from without, it will be there: And it will remain there, and persevere, so long as it is required —and not a day longer.

For those thousands of you here today who have borne arms for our country know that an armistice can end the fighting without ending the war. Only when we root out the very causes of war—the poverty of man's body, the privation of his spirit, the imprisonment of his liberties—will there be a final surrender of violence itself....

creased effort probably denied a military victory to the Viet Cong and their North Vietnamese allies, but by year's end the Communists still controlled large land areas in South Vietnam. The number of U.S. forces almost doubled—to 385,300. At the close of the year, U.S. troops were in the process of taking over from the South Vietnamese the job of searching out the main Viet Cong and North Vietnamese battalions and were assisting in pacification work against local guerrillas. In another phase of the war, U.S. planes dropped bombs on targets within built-up sections of Hanoi and Haiphong in North Vietnam and were, in turn, faced with greatly increased antiaircraft fire from weapons and supporting equipment largely supplied by the Soviet Union. American officials said enemy forces in the South numbered about 275,000 by the end of the year: 45,000 North Vietnamese regulars; 62,000 main force Viet Cong troops; 110,000 Viet Cong irregulars (part-time soldiers); and 58,000 noncombat troops.

The year began with an extended holiday truce which included a halt in the U.S. bombing of the North. An intensive U.S. diplomatic effort to bring North Vietnam into peace talks, which came to be known as a "peace offensive," produced no results, and the President Jan. 31 announced that U.S. aircraft had resumed bombing targets in the North after a 37-day pause.

The war was, at best, perplexing to many Americans but Congress voted overwhelmingly to support it. Nevertheless, Administration policies came under increasing criticism from both "doves" who wanted to de-escalate the war and "hawks" who wanted an even larger military effort, particularly in bombing targets in the North. By late in the year, the bombing in the North probably had become the most controversial aspect of the war because of its impact on the civilian population.

To help finance the war, the Administration Jan. 19 submitted to Congress a $13.1-billion fiscal 1966 supplemental appropriations request. The funds were intended primarily for military operations in Southeast Asia. Although the money eventually was provided *(see below)*, the request presented an opportunity for Administration critics of all persuasions to vent their opinions and frustrations about the war. A major debate occurred in the Senate, but not in the House. In addition, the Senate Foreign Relations Committee held televised hearings on a portion of the request (for $415 million in economic aid). However, the hearings went far beyond that specific request to the essentials of U.S. policy in Vietnam, which is the way it was intended by Committee Chairman J.W. Fulbright (D Ark.), who was the principal Congressional critic of the Administration's involvement in the war. During the midst of the growing debate early in the year, the President Feb. 4 made the surprise announcement that he would fly to Hawaii to meet with leaders of the South Vietnam government. The trip helped divert the spotlight from the Senate hearings. A Feb. 8 communique issued at Honolulu affirmed U.S. commitments to South Vietnam and stressed a new plan combining civil reform and military progress.

The criticism from Fulbright and others sharing his views continued. In his most caustic reply, the President May 17 dismissed such critics as "nervous Nellies" and invited them either to submit alternative policies or remain quiet. Many alternatives were suggested by both Republicans and Democrats and doves and hawks, but nothing came of any of them and the war continued unabated. The Administration explained its position and goals throughout the year. Generally, the Government reiterated the goals which had been expressed during 1965: the maintenance of U.S. commitments, the halting of Communist aggression, the assurance of independence for South Vietnam and the containment of China. These goals were again emphasized when President Johnson Oct. 17-Nov. 2 visited seven Pacific and Asian nations and participated in a conference at Manila, the Philippines, with leaders of six other nations of the region. The purpose of the conference was "to consider the conflict in South Vietnam and to review (the allies') wider purposes in Asia and the Pacific." The other nations taking part (in addition to the United States) were Australia, South Korea, New Zealand, the Philippines, Thailand and South Vietnam.

A communique issued at the end of the Conference gave the "essential elements of peace." They were: (1) cessation of aggression, (2) preservation of the territorial integrity of South Vietnam, (3) reunification of Vietnam (but with respect for the partition set by the 1954 Geneva Agreements until reunification was achieved by free choice of all Vietnamese) and (4) removal of allied military forces "as the military and subversive forces of North Vietnam are withdrawn, infiltration ceases and the level of violence thus subsides." The participating nations declared that allied forces would be withdrawn from South Vietnam within six months of the time the "essential elements of peace" were met. (Hanoi's peace conditions, by contrast, called for U.S. withdrawal, settlement of South Vietnam's internal affairs in accordance with the program of the National Liberation Front, the political arm of the Viet Cong, and other requirements to be met. *See box.*)

The President's long trip was seen by some of his political opponents and others as an attempt to enhance the Administration's image prior to the U.S. Congressional elections. However, the results of the election were inconclusive as to the American public's attitude toward the war. Republican attempts to profit from voters' concern over the war were cautious and oblique. Most of the "peace" candidates who entered races were resoundingly defeated.

In South Vietnam, beginning in March and continuing through May, rioting and civil unrest almost brought to collapse the Saigon government led by Nguyen Cao Ky. Dismissal by Ky of a 10-man military directorate was the immediate cause but militant Buddhists attempted to exploit the unrest to enhance their own power. Conditions had quieted by summer. On Sept. 11, South Vietnam held elections to name a 117-member constituent assembly from among 582 candidates, a development which the United States considered encouraging.

The year closed with a new Christmas truce which had been preceded by increased military operations by the United States.

Congressional Action. Because the war was being waged by the President in his role as commander-in-chief under what he considered the Congressional authorization contained in the 1964 Tonkin Gulf resolution, Congress throughout the 1965-68 period was reduced to a relatively minor role. Members of Congress in 1966 again voted funds to support the American troops and

Hanoi Peace Conditions

North Vietnam Premier Pham Van Dong on April 8, 1966, gave the following "four points" as the basis for peace in Vietnam. He reiterated these points in an interview Jan. 2, 1967, with New York Times correspondent Harrison E. Salisbury, and added a fifth point, which is also given below:

1) Withdrawal of all U.S. military personnel, equipment, and bases from South Vietnam.

2) Pending reunification of the country, North and South Vietnam must refrain from entering into any foreign military alliances and there must be no foreign troops, or equipment or bases on the territory of either one.

3) The internal affairs of South Vietnam must be settled in accordance with the program of the National Liberation Front, the political arm of the Viet Cong.

4) The peaceful reunification of the country must be worked out by the people of both North and South without foreign interference.

5) The United States must put, unconditionally and for good, an end to bombing and all hostile activity against the North.

continued to debate the merits of the war. They could do no more.

The primary Congressional action on war legislation came early in the year after Mr. Johnson had sent up his supplemental appropriations request of $13,135,719,000 for war expenses. The first voting came on an authorization bill (HR 12889) for a portion of the military funds included in the request. In the Senate, Wayne Morse (D Ore.) offered an amendment to HR 12889 to repeal the Gulf of Tonkin resolution. *(For text of resolution, see p. 70.)* In a key vote on March 1, his amendment was tabled (killed) by a **92-5** roll call. Voting "no" were Morse, Ernest Gruening (D Alaska), Fulbright, Eugene J. McCarthy (D Minn.) and Stephen M. Young (D Ohio). Morse argued that the authorization bill was "a policy bill...that will lead to the escalation of the war in Vietnam" and "a blank check for expanding the war into Laos and Thailand." The President's supporters argued that the vote on tabling would be a test of endorsement of Administration policy. Both chambers then went on to pass HR 12889 (PL 89-367) authorizing $4,857,-450,000 in supplemental defense funds (the balance of the defense funds requested had existing authorization). The Senate acted by a 93-2 roll call and the House by a 393-4 roll call. Unlike the Senate, the House acted quickly and without heated debate. However, 78 Democratic House Members, including 27 freshmen, signed a statement declaring that their support of the bill should not be considered an endorsement of an enlarged war.

Both chambers at about the same time passed a separate bill (HR 12169—PL 89-371) authorizing $415 million in fiscal 1966 supplemental foreign aid funds to help finance the war and economic development in Southeast Asia. This amount also was part of the President's requests. The economic aid bill was the legislation that Fulbright used to conduct his televised hearings on the Government's Vietnam policy. The bill passed by wide margins in both chambers, although the Senate engaged in extensive debate on the war. Expected debate did not materialize in the House. Both authorization bills became law by March 18.

Once the authorization bills were enacted, Congress turned its attention to a bill (HR 13546—PL 89-374) appropriating the funds requested by the President. HR 13546 as it became law appropriated $13,135,719,000 in fiscal 1966 supplemental funds, primarily for U.S. operations in Southeast Asia. The amount, the same as Mr. Johnson requested, broke down as follows: $12,345,-719,000 for the Defense Department, $415 million for economic aid and $375 million to reimburse the military services for goods already delivered as military assistance.

The bill was passed overwhelmingly; the roll calls were among the few times in 1966 that Members could vote, in effect, on the Administration's policy in Vietnam. Two Senators and three Representatives voted against the bill in their chambers. They were Sens. Gruening and Morse, and Reps. Phillip Burton (D Calif.), John Conyers Jr. (D Mich.) and William F. Ryan (D N.Y.). In addition, Rep. George E. Brown Jr. (D Calif.) did not vote but later said he was opposed to HR 13546. The House vote on passage, a key vote, was by a **389-3** roll call. The Senate roll call was 87-2 (the Senate earlier had taken a key vote on repealing the Gulf of Tonkin resolution, which amounted to a vote on Administration policies—*see above*). HR 13546 became law on March 25.

Foreign Aid

As the U.S. involvement in Vietnam escalated in 1966, dissatisfaction over the nation's foreign assistance program also rose. The Administration proposed major changes in the authorization for the program, but the recommendations were rejected—for the most part—by Congress.

The regular foreign aid authorization bill, like the supplemental for Vietnam earlier in the year, was caught up in the escalating Congressional debate, particularly in the Senate, over Vietnam policy. The major issues of the length, amount and form of the authorization were debated against the backdrop of the war. The primary controversy again was in the Senate, although the relatively restrained criticism in the House was thought by many observers to mask a widespread concern among House Members about the increasing U.S. involvement in the war; it was said that this concern in the House was less evident on the surface than in the Senate partly because of uncertainty, during an election year, about the public's attitude toward the war.

The Senate action on the program again was led by Foreign Relations Committee Chairman J.W. Fulbright (D Ark.). Major changes in the Administration requests were first made in the Committee and later on the floor. Changes, which included cuts in authorization requests and addition of numerous restrictions, were encouraged by Fulbright's open dissatisfaction with the aid program and U.S. foreign policy. Fulbright did not lead the attack on the bill and, in fact, was the legislation's floor manager, but he did vote for some of the key cuts and restrictions.

Tonkin Gulf Resolution Text

Following is the text of the "Gulf of Tonkin" resolution (PL 88-408) enacted by Congress on Aug. 7, 1964, and signed into law Aug. 10 following North Vietnamese attacks on U.S. ships in the Gulf of Tonkin on Aug. 2 and 4. *(Congress and the Nation, Vol. I, p. 138.)* The Johnson Administration used the broad wording in this resolution as authority for expansion of the United States' involvement in the Vietnam war in 1965 and the following years. Whether the wording in fact gave the President authority to commit half a million American troops to a war without further Congressional approval was a highly controversial question during the 1965-68 period. It was, at the same time, a moot question because the President considered he had the authority and ordered the troops to Vietnam without seeking further direct Congressional authorization.

"Whereas naval units of the Communist regime in Vietnam, in violation of the principles of the Charter of the United Nations and of international law, have deliberately and repeatedly attacked United States naval vessels lawfully present in international waters, and have thereby created a serious threat to international peace;

"Whereas these attacks are part of a deliberate and systematic campaign of aggression that the Communist regime in North Vietnam has been waging against its neighbors and the nations joined with them in the collective defense of their freedom;

"Whereas the United States is assisting the peoples of southeast Asia to protect their freedom and has no territorial, military or political ambitions in that area, but desires only that these peoples should be left in peace to work out their own destinies in their own way: Now, therefore, be it

"Resolved by the Senate and House of Representatives of the United States of America in Congress assembled, That the Congress approves and supports the determination of the President, as Commander-in-Chief, to take all necessary measures to repel any armed attack against the forces of the United States and to prevent further aggression.

"SEC. 2. The United States regards as vital to its national interest and to world peace the maintenance of international peace and security in southeast Asia. Consonant with the Constitution of the United States and the Charter of the United Nations and in accordance with its obligations under the Southeast Asia Collective Defense Treaty, the United States is, therefore, prepared, as the President determines, to take all necessary steps, including the use of armed force, to assist any member or protocol state of the Southeast Asia Collective Defense Treaty requesting assistance in defense of its freedom.

"SEC. 3. This resolution shall expire when the President shall determine that the peace and security of the area is reasonably assured by international conditions created by action of the United Nations or otherwise, except that it may be terminated earlier by concurrent resolution of the Congress."

President Johnson in his foreign aid proposals requested a multiyear authorization and separation of economic and military aid into two bills. These proposals were in keeping with reforms proposed in the past by various Members of Congress, including Fulbright. When the fiscal 1967 aid authorization bill (HR 15750—PL 89-583) eventually became law late in the year (Sept. 19), it covered both economic and military aid and was basically for one year. Rejection of the President's reform proposals constituted the most important foreign aid setback encountered in Congress by Mr. Johnson since he became President.

The legislation was basically the same as enacted in previous years, but included numerous restrictive amendments added in both houses. It authorized fiscal 1967 appropriations of $3,500,735,500 which with some existing authorization permitted total appropriations of $3,503,990,500 (including $875 million for military aid). Because of Mr. Johnson's reform proposals, the total authorization turned out to be $118,028,500 above his appropriations request for the year. This was the first time in the program's history that Congress authorized more than the appropriations sought. (However, actual appropriations were—as usual—cut below the request. *See below.*) The unusual switch came about because Mr. Johnson proposed a five-year authorization at levels high enough to provide for anticipated expansion of the programs during the period. However, he requested fiscal 1967 appropriations at the approximate level of 1966. The increase in authorization above appropriations request did not appear to be an effort by Congress to enlarge the aid program; if anything, the sentiment in Congress was in the opposite direction. The only nod which Congress made in the direction of Mr. Johnson's reform requests was a three-year authorization for the Development Loan Fund and the Alliance for Progress. One-year authorizations were retained for the remainder of the aid programs. The Alliance authorization was $153.5 million more than the appropriation request, thus accounting for the excess of the total authorization above the Administration's requests. Most other authorizations were smaller.

The House, which up to 1965 had successfully insisted on annual control of the bulk of the aid legislation by Congress, in 1966 reversed its position and gave the President a modified multiyear program—five years for the Development Loan Fund and the Alliance for Progress, both of which had received similar longterm authorizations in the past, and two years for all other programs. The House also generally supported the President's funding requests based on the multiyear program, but insisted on retaining the entire legislation within a single bill. In spite of this action, there was evidence that many House Members were not convinced of the wisdom of a multiyear authorization. The primary evidence was during House floor action when a Republican motion to recommit the bill with instructions to cut the two-year authorizations to one year was defeated by a narrow 191-193 (R 121-4; D 70-189) roll-call vote. However, the motion also provided for a $250-million cut in the Development Loan authorization, a proposal attractive to many economizers which partly obscured House sentiment on the multiyear issue. It was thought that some members who might have been open to Administration overtures on a multiyear authorization probably favored the recommittal because of the opportunity to vote for a cut in foreign aid. The House passed the bill by a 237-146 (R 36-89; D 201-57) roll call.

The Senate also reversed its position of recent years and refused to give the Administration more than a one-year authorization for foreign aid, with the exception of a two-year authority for the Alliance for Progress. However, the Senate approved separate economic and military aid bills, as requested. The economic aid bill was passed by a 66-27 (R 18-12; D 48-15) roll-call vote. Passage came after seven days of sharp and often critical debate and the acceptance of an unusually large number of floor amendments—26—almost all restrictive. Seven other amendments were rejected.

Action on the military aid bill followed immediately. As passed by the Senate by an 82-7 (R 29-0; D 53-7) roll call, the bill authorized funds for foreign military aid and sales. In an unusual action which came on a key vote, the Senate by a **55-37** roll call accepted an amendment to reduce the authorization in the military bill by $100 million, from $892 million to $792 million. The Administration had requested $917 million which the House had approved. There was much criticism in debate of nations using U.S. arms to wage wars with neighbors; frequently cited examples included the India-Pakistan conflict, the Turkey-Greece dispute over Cyprus, and attempts in Latin America—particularly in Argentina—to overthrow constitutional governments. *(For stories on arms sales legislation, see p. 85, 107.)*

In conference, the chambers compromised on a one-year authorization for most programs and a three-year authorization for the Alliance and Development Loans. They also lumped economic and military aid in one bill. Participants in the conference said the most difficult items to settle were the authorization amounts, and Senate provisions seeking to limit aid to fewer nations and to increase aid for population control. The latter was dropped while the limit on the number of countries receiving help was retained but with modifications to allow the President flexibility in granting aid to additional nations if he decided it was in the national interest. The bill limited Development Loans to 10 nations, technical assistance to 40 nations, supporting assistance to 13 nations and military aid to 40 nations.

Both chambers accepted the conferees' actions, but there was much unhappiness about the compromises on both sides.

Foreign Aid Funds

Once Congress had disposed of the foreign aid reform controversy by prescribing a very small dose of revision, it quickly reverted to its traditional form on this legislation by cutting the aid appropriation 13.3 percent below the request. This was the largest percentage cut since a 33.8-percent reduction in fiscal 1964, but was only prologue to massive reductions Congress was to inflict on the program in the last two years of the Johnson Administration.

The 1966 bill (HR 17788—PL 89-691) appropriated $2,936,490,500 for foreign aid in fiscal 1967 including $792 million in military assistance. The 13.3-percent cut occurred even though the Administration's requests were the lowest in the history of the program. In addition, it was the first time since 1958 that less than $3 billion was appropriated for the aid program.

In addition to the $2.9 billion in economic and military aid, the bill appropriated $110 million for the Peace Corps, $250 million for the Inter-American Development

Bank, and $104 million for the International Development Assn. The final bill also contained a provision, long sought in similar form by Fulbright and others, allowing the President to transfer up to 10 percent of development loan funds to the World Bank and its affiliated institutions.

Congressional action was less bombastic than on the authorization bill, but there was evidence of strong and growing displeasure with the aid program.

In the House, a key vote developed on an effort by one of the most prominent Republican economizers, Frank T. Bow (Ohio), to limit total appropriations for economic aid to $2,222,065,800. The proposal was in the form of a recommittal motion which was accepted by a **186-183** roll-call vote. The motion did not specify where the cuts would be made, leaving that up to the Administration. Bow noted that the President had proposed a 10-percent cut in all Budget spending and said his motion would bring economic aid 10 percent under the President's requests. He also noted that the cut would affect only economic aid, not military assistance. His motion was designed to appeal to Congressional conservatives who approved of military aid but took a dim view of economic assistance. That the tactics paid off was seen in the voting when the conservative coalition formed on the 186-183 roll call; this occurs when a majority of Republicans and Southern Democrats vote against a majority of Northern Democrats. The breakdown: R 116-8; D 70-175 (ND 24-143; SD 46-32). The House then went on to pass the bill by a 234-141 (R 39-86; D 195-55) roll call. (Bow's appropriation limitation was dropped in conference.)

The Senate passed the bill soon after by a 52-22 (R 16-8; D 36-14) roll call after a surprisingly short debate. This resulted primarily because the floor manager, Sen. John O. Pastore (D R.I.), recognized that the Senate was in an economy mood and urged that amendments to cut aid programs not be debated at length. Consequently, the Senate accepted three amendments by Sen. Allen J. Ellender (D La.) cutting military aid, the contingency fund and development loans by a total of $110 million.

Conferees quickly reached agreement on the $2.9 billion figure. This compared to $3,047,065,800 actually appropriated by the House but with the ceiling of $2,222,065,800, and $2,936,490,500 voted by the Senate. Although the final amount was the same as the Senate's, certain balanced changes were made in individual items.

International Health, Education

President Johnson in a special message on World Health and Education urged Congress to enact a program to provide federal aid for international studies at American colleges and universities, and to build a core of U.S. medical personnel trained to deal with health problems in other countries. The international education program was enacted (PL 89-698) and authorized $131 million during fiscal 1967-69 for grants. *(See story in education chapter.)*

The health program, however, foundered on Republican opposition in the House on grounds that it would drain critically needed health personnel from the United States. A bill (HR 12453) was reported to the House,

but the Rules Committee denied a rule for floor consideration. No action was taken in the Senate. *(See story in health chapter.)*

Emergency Aid to India

In 1965, the annual monsoon rains did not come to India in sufficient quantities to permit that nation to produce even the minimal supply of food that it needed to feed its rapidly growing population. As a result, the Indian government in January 1966 estimated that 12 million Indians faced starvation unless outside assistance was provided. The U.S. Government estimated that India had to import at least 11 to 12 million tons of grain during 1966 to prevent widespread famine. In a March 30 news conference, President Johnson proposed that the United States provide 3.5 million tons of food grain, mostly wheat, (in addition to 6.5 million tons already scheduled for shipment) and that the remaining needs be supplied by other nations able to do so. Congress responded by quickly enacting a resolution (H J Res 997—PL 89-406) endorsing U.S. participation in an emergency food program for India. Mr. Johnson had signed the bill into law by April 19. The bill endorsed the U.S. effort to help relieve the crisis by making available U.S. agricultural commodities under PL 480 to meet India's normal import needs as well as its current emergency food shortage. In addition, the assistance was to help combat Indian malnutrition through a special program and to encourage and assist the expansion of India's own agricultural production. The Senate report on the bill estimated the cost of the assistance at about $500 million.

Asian Development Bank

Congress in 1966 passed an Administration bill (HR 12563—PL 89-369) providing for U.S. participation in the Asian Development Bank and authorizing $200 million for the full amount of the U.S. subscription. *(See p. 99.)*

The major purpose of the Bank was the economic development of the Southeast Asia area by Asians themselves. Roughly 65 percent of the Bank's total subscription of $1 billion was to come from Asian nations. The U.S. contribution was to come to 20 percent of the expected total, equal to the subscription from Japan, the other single largest contributor.

The Bank was first formally proposed by the United Nations Economic Commission for Asia and the Far East in 1963. President Johnson's pledge of U.S. aid for economic development in the Southeast Asia area in an April 7, 1965, speech, and his announcement April 20, 1965, that the United States would participate in the Bank if it was properly conceived, assured U.S. support for the proposal. The Bank was to be an international organization with charter members of 19 Asian countries and 12 developed countries, including the United States, outside the Asian region.

The authorized capital stock of the Bank was set at $1 billion. Half the capital subscribed by each member was to be paid in five equal annual installments. The other half, callable capital, was to be fully subscribed at the outset, but without cash payment. The callable capital in effect constituted a guarantee fund against which the Bank could sell securities in financial markets. Congress in 1966 appropriated $140 million for the U.S. subscription: $40 million for the first two installments ($20 million each) of the paid-in capital and $100 million (the full amount) of the subscription for callable capital.

The bill was passed by Congress with little opposition and debate. The House acted by a 293-80 roll-call vote and the Senate by voice vote.

Provisions. As signed into law, HR 12563:

Authorized the President to accept membership for the United States in the Asian Development Bank.

Authorized appropriation, without fiscal year limitation, of $200 million for purchase of 20,000 shares of capital stock in the Bank.

Provided that the President could not take the following actions without specific Congressional authorization: subscribe to an increase in the U.S. subscription to the Bank; vote for or agree to any amendment to the Bank agreement which would increase the U.S. obligations to the Bank, or change the purpose of functions of the Bank; and approve any U.S. loan or other U.S. financing to the Bank—except that funds, specifically limited to technical assistance in the amount of $1 million in any one year, could be provided to the Bank by a U.S. agency authorized by law to provide funds to international organizations.

Foreign Agents Act

After five years of deliberation, Congress completed action on a bill (S 693—PL 89-486) revising the Foreign Agents Registration Act of 1938. PL 89-486 tightened and clarified the Act. S 693 was passed by the Senate in 1965. The Senate had passed a virtually identical bill in 1964 after the Senate Foreign Relations Committee in 1962-63 held hearings on activities of lobbyists for foreign interests. Attention focused on tactics of lobbyists for countries seeking part of the U.S. sugar quota. One sugar lobbyist was shown to have contributed funds to the 1960 election campaigns of several Senators and Representatives. *(See 1965 action, p. 66.)*

The 1938 Act had been drawn up to protect the Government against foreign agents who sought to subvert it. Proponents of S 693 said amendments were needed to bring the Act up to date by placing stricter controls over the increasing number of public relations agents for foreign concerns who sought to influence, rather than subvert, the Government.

The bill imposed stricter disclosure requirements for foreign lobbyists and added to and redefined the scope of activities for which persons must register under the Act. It required foreign agents to disclose their status as agents when contacting Government officials and Members of Congress and to file copies of their latest registration statement with Congressional committees when testifying before the committees.

The bill also outlawed contingent fee contracts, where the fee is based on the success of political activities; prohibited campaign contributions on behalf of foreign interests; broadened certain commercial exemptions; and gave the Attorney General discretionary authority to allow exemptions from registration.

In addition, S 693 gave the Attorney General an injunctive remedy to bring about compliance with the Act without having to resort to long and cumbersome criminal proceedings. Sen. J.W. Fulbright (D Ark.), chairman of the Senate Foreign Relations Committee and a chief supporter of the bill, called this "the single most important provision in the bill."

The Senate version of S 693 was almost the same as a bill it had passed in 1964, in the 88th Congress. When the House acted on S 693 it made only two changes, and these appeared in the final bill in tightened form. These: (1) provided for exemption from registration of representatives of most foreign commercial and financial concerns with U.S. affiliates; and (2) provided for exemption of lawyers in formal Government proceedings.

Provisions. As signed into law, PL 89-486 amended the Foreign Agents Registration Act of 1938 as follows:

Redefined the phrase "agent of a foreign principal to specify a person who acted under request or control of a foreign principal, who was largely financed by a foreign principal and who:

● Engages in political activities in the United States on behalf of the foreign principal;

● Acts as a public relations counsel, publicity agent or political consultant on behalf of the principal;

● Collects or disburses contributions, loans, money or other things of value within the United States, in the interest of the foreign principal;

● Represents the foreign principal before any U.S. agency or official.

Required the agent within 10 days of assuming the position and every 60 days thereafter to file a detailed statement with the Department of Justice about his political activities and expenditures on behalf of his client. The statement was to include the interests or policies the agent sought to influence and the means to be employed in advancing this influence.

Exempted from registering under the Act all persons: engaged in private and nonpolitical activities furthering the commercial purpose of a foreign principal; or, in "other activities not serving predominantly a foreign interest." Provided that for the purposes of the above exemption domestic persons engaged in bona fide commercial, financial, or industrial interests shall not lose their exemption (i.e. be considered as engaging in other activities "serving predominantly a foreign interest") merely because the activities also assist a foreign subsidiary or a foreign parent of the U.S. company if: the foreign affiliate is not a foreign government or political party; the activities are not directed or substantially subsidized by a foreign government or political party; the identity of the foreign affiliate is disclosed; and the activities of a foreign affiliate owning or controlling a domestic company are substantially in furtherance of the bona fide commercial, industrial or financial interests of the U.S. company.

Exempted any person qualified to practice law insofar as he represents a "disclosed" foreign interest in legal matters before any court or agency of the U.S. Government.

Authorized the Attorney General, by regulation, to provide additional exemptions.

Required the agent to furnish a copy of his most recently filed registration statement to any Congressional committee before which he appeared and to disclose his foreign principal in all communications with agencies and officials of the U.S. Government. Required the filing with the Attorney General of political propaganda disseminated by the agent when it was "for or in the interests of" his foreign principal.

Required the agent to indicate on the label or cover of political propaganda disseminated by him the connection or relationship between himself and the propaganda.

Provided the Department of Justice with an injunctive remedy as a means of securing enforcement of the Act in addition to existing criminal sanctions if the agent's filings with the Department were found to be inadequate.

Prohibited contingent fee contracts between an agent and his foreign principal based on success in political activities undertaken by the agent.

Prohibited agents from making campaign contributions for their foreign principals in connection with any election including primaries, conventions or caucuses. Such contributions and the acceptance of them were made punishable by penalties of up to $5,000 or five years in prison, or both.

Prohibited officers and employees of the U.S. Government from acting as agents of foreign principals.

Failure of a person to disclose his identity as a foreign agent in the course of his political activities and the establishment of a contingent fee arrangement *(see above)* between the agent and his principal would be misdemeanors (punishable by a fine of up to $5,000 or imprisonment for not more than six months, or both) rather than felonies. Other violations of the Act would continue to be felonies (punishable by a fine of up to $10,000 or imprisonment for not more than five years, or both).

Future of NATO

French President Charles de Gaulle early in 1966 announced that France intended to withdraw from the integrated military command of the North Atlantic Treaty Organization (NATO). Subsequent detailed plans for the French pullout also made it clear that France was expelling all foreign forces, including Americans, from French soil. This military (but not political) withdrawal precipitated one of the most serious crises in the 17-year history of the Atlantic Alliance and constituted a major jolt to U.S. policy in Europe.

The French move not only threatened the viability and future of the Alliance, but, by placing in doubt the combat capability of NATO, posed serious problems for U.S. and Western strategies of defense and of allied troop deployment. France's decision also triggered a far-reaching review of the rationale behind the heavy commitment of American forces in Europe, and the 20-year-old policy of maintaining U.S. troops on the continent to counter the postwar Soviet threat came under increased Congressional attack.

Many in Congress called for a reappraisal of the Alliance. Senate Majority Leader Mike Mansfield (D Mont.) quickly suggested that the United States withdraw all but a token U.S. ground force from Europe. Other countries indicated they too might reduce their NATO force levels.

Late in the session, Mansfield and 12 other members of the Senate Democratic Policy Committee introduced a resolution (S Res 300) expressing the sense of

the Senate that U.S. forces in Europe be reduced. This proposal for a unilateral troop cut instantly met strong Administration opposition. President Johnson on two occasions said no steps should be taken without consultation with U.S. allies. The resolution was subsequently deferred indefinitely, and it never came to a vote in 1966.

At the root of the discussion of U.S. troop levels in Europe was the widely held belief—both in Europe and the United States—that there was little immediate likelihood of a Soviet attack on the West. It was argued that a reduction in troop levels would help both the U.S. manpower needs resulting from the Vietnam war and the adverse U.S. balance-of-payments situation, which was being intensified by the costs of maintaining such a large number of troops abroad.

West German Arms Purchases. The NATO crisis was also aggravated by frayed U.S.-German relations over the question of U.S. troop support in West Germany. The German government declared that it was finding some difficulty in meeting certain commitments to purchase arms in the United States in amounts sufficient to "offset" the U.S. costs, and resulting gold-drain, of keeping U.S. troops in Germany. At the end of September, West German Chancellor Ludwig Erhard met with President Johnson to discuss Germany's current difficulties and its inability and reluctance to enter into any new offset agreements after June 30, 1967. Differences between the two countries over the adequacy of Germany's purchases and Germany's unwillingness to make future commitments provided just that much more fuel to the debate on maintaining the current American troop levels in Europe.

In a related development, separate negotiations were held between France and West Germany to determine whether French forces stationed in Germany would remain there following the French withdrawal from the NATO military command. The two countries reached an agreement in December that they would remain, although the United States felt that the French forces should be withdrawn if they did not have a NATO mission. The agreement was therefore widely considered a French "victory" over the Americans in the complicated diplomatic maneuverings during the NATO crisis.

Hearings. Both the House and Senate held lengthy hearings on over-all U.S. policy in Europe and toward the Alliance—in addition to matters concerning U.S. troop levels. The Senate Government Operations Subcommittee on National Security and International Operations began hearings in April. The Senate Foreign Relations Committee began its own series of public hearings on NATO in June as part of the Committee's general examination of the Johnson Administration's foreign policy; and between March and June, the House Foreign Affairs Subcommittee on Europe also held hearings on the NATO crisis.

In October the United States, the United Kingdom and West Germany began trilateral talks to reappraise the Soviet threat, NATO force levels, burden sharing and financial problems of deploying U.S. and British forces in West Germany. By the time of the NATO ministerial meeting in Paris in December the confrontation between France and the United States and the other allies had for the most part subsided.

Background on North Atlantic Treaty Organization

REFERENCES—*Congress and the Nation, Vol. I, p. 103, 108, 110, 166-169, 264 and 301.*

The North Atlantic Treaty was signed April 4, 1949, by the United States, Canada and 10 European nations agreeing that "an armed attack against any one or more of them in Europe and North America shall be considered an attack against all." A direct reaction to Communist power moves, which included the 1948 takeover of Czechoslovakia, the NATO treaty laid down a policy of containment of Soviet expansionist ambitions which helped to preserve a territorial status quo on the European continent for many years. The original NATO members were: the United States, Belgium, Canada, Denmark, France, Great Britain, Iceland, Italy, Luxembourg, the Netherlands, Norway and Portugal. Greece and Turkey were admitted in 1952, and West Germany was included via the Western European Union in 1955.

From the outset, the United States, as the prime mover and most powerful member of the Alliance, assumed a dominant role in shaping NATO military policy. But American leadership met increasing resistance as NATO's European members regained their economic strength and the Soviets advanced toward nuclear parity with the United States, and by 1963 France was in open rebellion against the American view of NATO strategy.

Little progress was made initially in implementing the essentials of the NATO defense structure until the Communist attack on Korea in 1950 led to a quick activation of NATO: the United States decided to send four American divisions to Europe (two U.S. divisions were in Germany at the time) and to press for German rearmament while the allies agreed to "integrate" NATO forces under an American commander. NATO military preparations went forward in high gear in 1951 and 1952. Vast amounts of U.S. military supplies were moved to Europe where an elaborate "infrastructure" of air bases, communications facilities and supply lines began to take shape.

The summit conference of 1955, by raising hopes of East-West accord, marked the opening of an era of discord within the Alliance. Talk of "detente" or "disengagement" magnified differences between the United States and its European partners which were always somewhat less convinced of the Soviet threat.

Nuclear Force. French resentment of NATO's Anglo-American leadership and the special U.S.-British relationship in nuclear matters emerged clearly in 1958 when President Charles de Gaulle proposed in vain a three-nation directorate for NATO and rejected the stationing of U.S. intermediate range ballistic missiles on French soil, insisting on joint control over the warheads. France continued its efforts to build its own atomic weapons—testing three in 1960. By 1961, control over nuclear weapons had become a major strategic and political issue within NATO. De Gaulle continued to reject U.S. solutions to the problem which basically consisted of a plan to create a multilateral grouping for a nuclear force while still retaining effective U.S. control over the firing of nuclear weapons. At Nassau in 1962, Britain agreed to build a Polaris force —with U.S. missiles and its own nuclear warheads— and assign this to NATO, but De Gaulle rejected an offer of similar U.S. aid, continuing to insist that France would develop its own nuclear striking force.

France increasingly pointed out the need for, and insisted on, a revision of the Alliance and its policies. France felt that the Alliance was outdated and advocated such changes as increased overtures to the East, reduction of NATO's military role and a correction of the imbalance between Europe and the United States within the Alliance.

Unsuccessful in his attempts to change NATO, De Gaulle in a September 1965 news conference said that France would not accept an integrated Western defense system after 1969—the year the original North Atlantic Treaty expired. "At the end of our present commitments—that is, in 1969 at the latest," De Gaulle said, "we shall end the subordination which is described as integration and which puts our destiny into the hands of foreigners."

French forces were already to a large part withdrawn from NATO. The French Mediterranean fleet had been withdrawn in 1959; French army units had been retained under national command when they returned from Algeria in 1962 and 1963; and virtually all naval forces in the Atlantic for assignment to NATO were also withdrawn in the beginning of 1964.

China Policy

Congress in 1966, for the first time in many years, conducted a detailed study of U.S. policy toward Communist China. Lengthy hearings were held in both houses as Congress sought to educate itself and the public about Asia in general and China in particular. Interest stemmed primarily from increasing U.S. involvement in Vietnam and the mounting danger of direct military confrontation with China growing out of the war. President Johnson July 12 made a major speech on relations with China. *(See below.)*

On March 8, 1966, the Senate Foreign Relations Committee began hearings on U.S. policy toward Communist China, an outgrowth of its hearings on Vietnam policy. Describing the hearings as "educational," Committee Chairman J.W. Fulbright (D Ark.) said, "At this stage, perhaps the most effective contribution the Committee can make is to provide a forum for recognized experts and scholars in the field of China."

The main theme to emerge from the next three weeks of testimony was that U.S. policy had been aimed at not only containing China, but also isolating it.

A number of witnesses suggested that this policy had been both unwise and unsuccessful. They proposed three basic changes in U.S. policy: official diplomatic recognition of Communist China, an expansion of trade relations and admission of Communist China to the United

Nations. John K. Fairbank of Harvard's East Asian Research Center typified this theme when he concluded: "Containment alone is a blind alley unless we add policies of constructive competition and international contact.... Peking's rulers shout aggressively out of manifold frustrations.... Isolation intensifies their ailment and makes it self-perpetuating, and we need to encourage international contact with China on many fronts."

Other witnesses challenged these suggestions; one was former Rep. Walter H. Judd (R Minn. 1943-63). Judd said that "our choice—with Red China just as it was with Japan and Hitler—is not between checking and not checking, it is whether to check early, while we can, and with allies—or try to check the aggression later, when it is stronger, closer and we have fewer and weaker friends and allies."

In conclusion, Judd said: "This is the time to stand fast for the basic containment policies that have proved sound and more successful during the last 15 years than most people believed possible...."

More views on China were expressed at hearings held by the House Foreign Affairs Subcommittee on the Far East and the Pacific. The Subcommittee May 19 released a report which recommended that the United States continue to seek peaceful contacts with China while keeping up its efforts to contain China's aggressive expansion.

President's Comments. At his March 22 news conference President Johnson, referring to the Congressional hearings, said it was "good to have the opinion of these professors and experts and ambassadors...." He added, however: "It is not the position of this country that creates the problems with China. It is China's own position. We are very anxious to try to have more contact with her, and more exchanges with her, but as has been explained by all these people, she hangs up the phone. Until there is some change on China's part, I doubt that these academic discussions will do much more than satisfy people's yearning for information."

President Johnson July 12, in a speech by telephone (and broadcast by television) to a meeting in White Sulphur Springs, W.Va., made what was termed by White House officials his first major statement on Communist China. He said four essentials for a peace in Asia were: (1) "the determination of the United States to meet our obligation in Asia as a Pacific power;" (2) "to prove to aggressive nations that the use of force to conquer others is a losing game;" (3) "the building of political and economic strength among the nations of free Asia;" and (4) "reconciliation between nations that now call themselves enemies."

East-West Trade

Congress again rebuffed proposals to expand American trade with the Soviet Union and Eastern Europe. The House of Representatives, which was looking in the other direction, attempted but failed to block an action by President Johnson to expand trade with four Communist nations. This was one of several administrative actions taken by Mr. Johnson to increase trade in nonstrategic goods between the United States and the Soviet bloc. The action which provoked the House permitted exten-

sion of Export-Import Bank credit to Poland, Hungary, Bulgaria and Czechoslovakia.

The Administration's major legislative proposal, the East-West Trade Relations Act, gave the President authority to extend favorable tariff treatment to European Communist nations (except East Germany) if he thought it would be in the national interest. The proposal was virtually ignored in Congress; this came as no surprise to Administration officials who knew that few Members of Congress would vote in an election year to improve trade with Communist countries while the United States was fighting a Communist enemy in an Asian war. The Administration hoped only for a full discussion of the legislation by Congress, but even that was not forthcoming: no hearings were held in either chamber. In the House (where tariff legislation has to originate) Rep. Wilbur D. Mills (D Ark.) chairman of the tariff-writing Ways and Means Committee, even refused to introduce the Administration's draft bill. To be sure the point was not missed in the White House, Mills simply said: "I want to make my position clear, I am not for it." In the Senate, Majority Leader Mike Mansfield (D Mont.) introduced the draft bill (S 3363) which was referred to the Finance Committee, not to be heard from again. The draft bill gave the President authority to extend most-favored-nation (MFN) tariff treatment to any Communist nation (except Cuba, Communist China, North Korea, North Vietnam, East Germany and areas under their domination) if he thought such action would benefit the national interest. Under the most-favored-nation concept, tariff concessions granted to one trade partner are automatically granted to other partners. (The United States extended MFN treatment to Yugoslavia in 1948 and to Poland in 1960.)

Policy Speech. President Johnson Oct. 7 in New York City made a major foreign policy speech to the National Conference of Editorial Writers in which he announced several actions taken to ease East-West trading restrictions. "Our task," the President said, "is to achieve a reconciliation with the East—a shift from the narrow concept of coexistence to the broader vision of peaceful engagement....We seek healthy economic and cultural relations with the Communist states." He reiterated his intention to "press for" his MFN legislation.

Mr. Johnson announced that:

• The United States was negotiating a civil air agreement with the Soviet Union. (Representatives of the two countries Nov. 4 signed a pact to establish direct air service between Moscow and New York. Service was to begin in the spring of 1967, with Pan American World Airways the carrier for the United States and Aeroflot, the Soviet national airline, for the U.S.S.R.) However, the first flight did not occur until July 15, 1968.

• The Administration would reduce East-West trade controls on hundreds of items. (The Commerce Department Oct. 12 announced that it had relaxed export restrictions on about 400 nonstrategic commodities for shipment to the Soviet Union and East European bloc (by placing them in the category of goods that could be shipped under a "general license") in line with the Oct. 7 speech. The changes did not apply to the Soviet-controlled zone of East Germany.)

• The Export-Import Bank was prepared to guarantee Italian credit of U.S. machine tools for a joint Soviet-Italian FIAT automobile plant to be built in Russia.

• He had signed a determination that would allow the Eximbank to guarantee the credit of four additional Eastern European countries—Poland, Hungary, Bulgaria and Czechoslovakia—for purchases of U.S. goods and services.

Eximbank Controversy. Following the speech, House Republicans led a drive to curtail the Export-Import Bank's ability to carry out the President's credit plan for the four Eastern European countries. Since 1963, the Eximbank had been barred by statute from guaranteeing the credit of Communist nations unless the President made an express finding that it would be in the national interest. President Johnson had made two such findings in 1964, and as a result, the Eximbank was allowed to guarantee the credit of Yugoslavia and Romania for purchases of goods and services from U.S. businessmen and was also allowed to guarantee loans made by American commercial banks to those countries. The Soviet Union and four other bloc countries could receive credit guarantees only for purchases of agricultural goods. Upon President Johnson's Oct. 7 announcement, however, these four bloc countries—Poland, Hungary, Bulgaria and Czechoslovakia—became eligible also for the guarantees previously available only to Yugoslavia and Romania. It was this action which House Republicans—including the party leadership—concluded had to be reversed.

Their vehicle for attempting to do so was a fiscal 1967 supplemental appropriations bill (HR 18381) which contained provisions affecting the Eximbank. A conservative coalition of Republicans and Southern Democrats were successful in a key **167-121** roll-call vote Oct. 18 in attaching to the bill language which flatly prohibited the Eximbank from guaranteeing the credit of any Communist nation. The proposal was sponsored by Reps. Frank T. Bow (R Ohio) and Paul Findley (R Ill.). Only a handful of Republicans were opposed: R 85-8; D 82-113 (ND 29-97; SD 53-16). But the restriction was softened in the Senate and in conference to include a Presidential waiver clause; in other words, the ban was included but the President could waive it in the national interest. House Republicans criticized the waiver and sought to retain the original House language; rejection of the conference recommendation was urged by several House GOP leaders including Minority Leader Gerald R. Ford (Mich.), Whip Leslie C. Arends (Ill.), and GOP Policy Committee Chairman John J. Rhodes (Ariz.). However, the conference agreement was accepted by a 129-102 roll-call vote. The breakdown was: R 6-74; D 123-28 (ND 90-4; SD 33-24). A total of 32 Representatives—R 1; D 31 (ND 16; SD 15)—who voted Oct. 18 for the House version switched their position and voted to accept the Senate provision. They were: Cahill (R N.J.); Northern Democrats Gray (Ill.), Hamilton (Ind.), Fallon and Machen (Md.), Callan (Neb.), Minish and McGrath (N.J.), Addabbo, Dulski, Hanley, Murphy and Pike (N.Y.), Clark, Dent, Green and Vigorito (Pa.); Southern Democrats Sikes (Fla.), Landrum and Tuten (Ga.), Boggs and Morrison (La.), Rivers (S.C.), Grider (Tenn.), Burleson, Cabell, Casey, de la Garza, Teague and White (Texas), Downing and Hardy (Va.). If these 32 Members had voted against the House recommittal motion Oct. 18, it would have been rejected.

Dominican Republic

The Inter-American Peace Force (IAPF), which included U.S. troops, was withdrawn from the Dominican Republic on Sept. 22, 1966. The IAPF was established May 23, 1965, shortly after rebellion broke out in the Dominican Republic and U.S. forces intervened to settle the crisis. Secretary of Defense Robert S. McNamara in a "defense posture" statement released Feb. 23 said: "Our policy in the Dominican Republic has been to assist the provisional government which was installed last September in restoring more normal conditions prior to its holding free elections." The statement said that the peak strength of U.S. troops participating in the IAPF was 23,850, a total reached at the time the force was established, and that this had then dropped gradually to a current level of about 6,000 troops. *(See p. 66.)*

Elections were held in the Dominican Republic and Joaquin Balaguer June 1 won election to the Presidency with approximately 59 percent of the vote over his principal opponent, Juan Bosch. The official result was: Balaguer, Reformist Party, 766,137; Bosch, Dominican Revolution Party (PRD), 525,529.

Treaties

International Wheat Agreement. For the second year in a row, the Senate in 1966 approved a one-year extension of the International Wheat Agreement of 1962. In reporting the protocol (Exec. F, 89th Congress, 2nd Session), the Senate Foreign Relations Committee said a new Agreement was needed, but it must be "related to the outcome of the Kennedy Round of tariff negotiations and to the agricultural policies of the European Common Market." Negotiators in the Kennedy Round were in their third year of seeking tariff concessions on agricultural and industrial products. The Senate consented to ratification of Exec. F by an 89-0 roll-call vote. However, Congress did not complete action on a bill (S 2294) authorizing implementation of the extension. (An Agriculture Department spokesman Nov. 29, 1965, had said that the Secretary, under existing law, already had the discretionary authority necessary to implement the Agreement through export subsidy payments. He said the implementing legislation was desirable to show strong U.S. Government backing of the Agreement.)

Florence, Beirut Treaties. Congress in 1966 passed legislation (HR 8664—PL 89-651; H J Res 688—PL 89-634) authorizing the United States to implement the 1950 Florence Agreement and the 1948 Beirut Agreement permitting duty-free imports of certain educational and scientific materials. The Florence Agreement was ratified by the Senate in 1960. HR 8664 covered various books, publications and documents, art pieces and audiovisual materials of an educational, scientific or cultural nature. The Beirut Agreement on audiovisual materials also was ratified in 1960. H J Res 688 covered such materials as developed photographic film, photographic slides, transparencies, sound recordings, recorded video tape, models, charts, maps, globes and posters.

Investment Disputes Treaty. The Senate consented to ratification by the President of the International Convention for the Settlement of Investment Disputes (Exec. A, 89th Congress, 2nd Session). In August, Congress cleared a bill (S 3498—PL 89-532) enabling the President to carry out the United States' responsibilities under the treaty. The Convention was approved March 18, 1965, by the executive directors of the International Bank for Reconstruction and Development (the World Bank). It provided machinery for conciliation or arbitration of investment disputes between private foreign investors and governments of countries where the investments were made.

Other Bills

Peace Corps. Congress authorized $110 million for the Peace Corps in fiscal 1967. The amount was $5 million less than the sum authorized for fiscal 1966 and was $2,150,000 less than the President requested. The authorization was contained in S 3418, PL 89-572. Later, in the foreign aid appropriations bill (HR 17788), Congress appropriated $110 million for the Peace Corps. Most of the reduction from the Administration request resulted from disapproval by Congress of a proposal for an Exchange Peace Corps which would have offered young volunteers from other nations the opportunity to teach and serve in community projects in the United States. President Johnson proposed an Exchange Peace Corps in his Feb. 2 message to Congress on international health and education.

Shriver Resigns. President Johnson Jan. 17 announced that R. Sargent Shriver Jr., director of the Peace Corps since it was established, would resign to devote full time as director of the Office of Economic Opportunity. Mr. Johnson named Jack Hood Vaughn, Assistant Secretary of State for Inter-American Affairs, to succeed Shriver as Peace Corps director.

Cuban Refugees. Congress passed an Administration-backed bill (HR 15183—PL 89-732) allowing Cubans who entered the United States after Jan. 1, 1959 (the beginning of Fidel Castro's regime), and who remained physically present in the United States for at least two years to apply to the Attorney General for adjustment of their status to that of a permanent resident (immigrant) alien. The bill was designed to benefit Cuban refugees who entered the United States after Jan. 1, 1959, under visa waiver arrangements and remained in an indefinite nonresident status. Permanent resident status is necessary before an alien can apply for U.S. citizenship. In some states, it is a prerequisite to being licensed to practice a profession. Mr. Johnson estimated that about 123,000 Cuban refugees were eligible to apply for permanent resident status and about 4,000 would be eligible each month "as long as the stream of refugees continues at its current rate."

Nuclear Control. The Senate by an 84-0 roll-call vote adopted a resolution (S Res 179) commending the President's efforts to negotiate international agreements limiting the spread of nuclear weapons and urging further efforts to solve the problems of nuclear proliferation. Three days of hearings had been held on the resolution. The resolution's sponsors looked on the Senate's unanimous approval of the measure as evidence that any nonproliferation treaty agreed to at the 18-nation Disarmament Conference in Geneva would be ratified. The Administration hoped that the Senate's action, by reaffirming U.S. interest in a nonproliferation treaty, would hasten agreement at the Geneva Conference.

1967

Violence was a hallmark of international affairs in 1967. In the Far East, the United States continued to wage a costly and indecisive war on the Asian mainland against a tenacious foe that was willing to absorb staggering losses but would not quit. In the Middle East, the always bubbling pot boiled over into a short and decisive war which decimated the armed forces of one side—the Arabs—but which led to no permanent solution of the troubles in that part of the world.

The Vietnam war during 1967—as in the previous years—did not end. That is the most that could be said of what the United States and the North Vietnamese got for their efforts. There were truces, offensives, proposals for negotiations, increased bombing of the North, some signs of political stability in the South, many signs of rising political opposition to the war in the United States—but no end to the fighting. Both sides ended the year still trying to nail jelly to the wall.

In the Middle East, there was no such standoff. Israel in six days destroyed the bulk of the armed forces of surrounding Arab states after having been driven to use of force by various provocations—most notably, the blocking of access by Israel to a vital sea port. In the end, the Arabs saw their armies ruined and their air forces destroyed, while Israel had possession of much of what formerly was Arab territory.

Although these conflicts dominated the news, there were several instances of cooperation and agreement between the United States and the Soviet Union. Two formal understandings were put into treaties. One was a consular convention, dealing with the operation of consulates in each country if any were established, and the other was an outer space treaty, dealing with the peaceful exploration and use of outer space. In addition, President Johnson and Soviet Premier Alexei N. Kosygin met in Glassboro, N.J., to discuss major international problems. The meeting came about because Kosygin was at the United Nations to present Soviet views on the Arab-Israeli war. In Geneva, negotiations continued on a nuclear nonproliferation treaty. No agreement was reached but progress was reported.

In other areas, U.S. arms sales to less developed nations became a major issue in Congress when the amount of these sales became publicly known. A number of attempts were made to halt such sales and to prevent less developed nations from using their own resources or U.S. foreign aid to buy certain types of weapons. A major forward step in international trade occurred when the Kennedy Round of tariff negotiations was successfully completed. There was general agreement that the lower tariffs agreed upon would open new international trade opportunities for U.S. businesses, but some segments of the business community decided competition from abroad would be too costly and lobbied Congress for enactment of protectionist legislation. The protectionist effort was blocked—for 1967 at least—by threat of a Presidential veto of any such legislation which passed.

In the background of the actual events of 1967, the belief that the United States was overcommitted abroad continued to ferment. This belief, shared by many persons in and out of Congress, was not a central element in foreign affairs in 1967. But its influence was growing, fed by the seemingly endless war in Vietnam and the increasing disarray in the Atlantic alliance, and it contained the seeds of a basic reappraisal of future American foreign policy.

Vietnam

The Vietnam war remained the dominant issue facing the United States in 1967. As in the previous years, the violence of the war increased, the economic costs to the nation were substantial, opposition to the conflict was widespread and the Johnson Administration was adamant in pursuing its aims in Vietnam. By the end of the year, neither a negotiated nor a military settlement of the conflict was in sight.

But as 1967 drew to a close, there occurred an event that was to have far-reaching effects, although at the time it was considered more of a curiosity than anything. On Nov. 30, Sen. Eugene J. McCarthy (D Minn.) announced he would enter at least four Presidential primaries in 1968 to carry his dissent over the President's war policy "to the people of the United States." It was a generally accepted proposition at the time that President Johnson would seek re-election in 1968 if for no other reason than to win confirmation from the voters of his Administration's policies, particularly in regard to Vietnam. McCarthy's challenge was not considered serious. In 1968, however, McCarthy demonstrated—beginning with a strong showing in the March 12 New Hampshire Presidential primary—an unexpected appeal for many voters. His appeal was first to those most opposed to the Vietnam war, but later was widely thought to extend to other Americans who were dissatisfied with many trends in the nation and who were looking for new leadership and new approaches to problems. The possibility that the nation was ready for basic change in leadership drew others into the Presidential race, most prominently Sen. Robert F. Kennedy (D N.Y.). The challenge of McCarthy did not of itself force the Administration into new policies on Vietnam; but his appeal did indicate to many people that the American Government—regardless of who ran it—did not have an unlimited amount of time in which to resolve the conflict.

The domestic unrest over the war and the disagreement over its course continued and, if anything, increased during the year. The Government position, as expressed by men such as U.S. Vietnam commander Gen. William C. Westmoreland, was that the allied forces had made "tremendous progress." Secretary of State Dean Rusk said the enemy was "hurting very badly." But many Americans in Vietnam concluded that the war was going poorly, victory was far away and if any description of the situation applied it was stalemate.

American troops increased to 485,600 by the end of the year plus another 83,000 in Thailand and the off-shore fleet. In addition, there were some 750,000 allied troops committed to the struggle. There were an estimated 240,000 enemy troops and an equal number of political agents and active collaborators. But neither side could win a decisive military victory and neither wanted to negotiate on the other's terms. Thus, the United States pushed its military operations while also reorganizing the pacification program to achieve better results. In the North, the Johnson Administration's policy of limited, gradual increases in air operations brought a growing number of targets in and around Hanoi and Haiphong and along the China border under attack by U.S. planes. The bombing of the North became increasingly controversial and was a central sticking point in getting the adversaries in the war together to negotiate. On Feb. 2, President Johnson wrote North Vietnam President Ho Chi Minh proposing "direct talks" to end the war. He said he was prepared to end bombing of the North and halt "further augmentation" of American forces in Vietnam "as soon as I am assured that infiltration into South Vietnam by land and sea has stopped." The secret letter was received in North Vietnam on Feb. 10; five days later, Ho rejected the talks. The President continued to press for negotiations during the year. In a speech in San Antonio, Texas, on Sept. 29, the President said U.S. bombing of North Vietnam would be stopped "when this will lead promptly to productive discussions." In a key passage, he added, "We of course assume that while discussions proceed, North Vietnam would not take advantage of the bombing cessation or limitation." The "San Antonio formula," as it came to be known, was subsequently interpreted to mean that the United States would not insist on cessation of North Vietnamese support for the war in the South provided "good faith" negotiations began shortly after a bombing halt, and provided the Communist side did not launch a major offensive during the talks. None of the efforts by the United States or other nations or organizations to bring about negotiations met with success. There were five temporary truces during the year, but none was extended into a permanent ceasefire and negotiations.

President Johnson and other Administration officials spoke frequently on Vietnam, outlining U.S. objectives and commitments and U.S. policy on bombing and negotiations. American policy continued to be defended in terms of securing self-determination for South Vietnam. However, there was an increasing tendency for officials to emphasize the strategic importance of Southeast Asia. President Johnson, for instance, in his San Antonio speech said, "Is the aggression a threat—not only to the individual victim—but to the United States of America and to the peace and security of the entire world...? I cannot tell you tonight as your President—with certainty—that a Communist conquest of South Vietnam would be followed by a Communist conquest of Southeast Asia...(or)...that a Southeast Asia dominated by Communist power would bring a third world war much closer to terrible reality. One could hope that this would not be so. But all that we have learned in this tragic century strongly suggests to me that it would be so. As President of the United States, I am not prepared to gamble on the chance that it is not so. I am not prepared to risk the security—indeed, the survival—of this American nation on mere hope and wishful thinking. I am convinced that by seeing this struggle through now, we are greatly reducing the chances of a much larger war—perhaps a nuclear war." Soon after this speech, on Oct. 12, Secretary of State Rusk said, "Within the next decade or two, there will be a billion Chinese on the mainland, armed with nuclear weapons, with no certainty about what their attitude toward the rest of Asia will be .... From a strategic point of view, it is not very attractive to think of the world cut in two by Asian communism, reaching out through Southeast Asia."

Court Rejected Cases Challenging Legality of the War

The Supreme Court in 1967 and 1968 rejected a number of cases raising, in the eyes of two Justices, questions about the constitutionality of the war in Vietnam and of the draft law as applied in the absence of a declaration of war. The Court May 27, 1968, however, upheld the 1965 law making it a crime to destroy or mutilate a draft card. *(See civil liberties chapter.)*

Justice William O. Douglas consistently dissented. He was critical of the Court for refusing, in his view, to address itself to what he considered fundamental issues concerning the draft laws and the war in Vietnam. He set out his views at length in dissents to the draft card case and to Court orders refusing to review two cases, *Holmes v. U.S. and Hart v. U.S.*, which the Court rejected on May 27, 1968. Those two cases, Douglas said, raised the issue of whether Congress had the power, in the absence of a declaration of war, to compel conscription for a foreign war.

Justice Potter Stewart joined Douglas in saying that the Court should review cases raising legal issues about the war. He did not join Douglas in the *Hart* case, and in the *Holmes* case he said the issue was whether Congress had the power, without declaring war, to compel military service with the alternative of compulsory domestic civilian service under certain circumstances.

The Court refused to review two other draft cases in 1967. On Oct. 9, the Court rejected a case involving an irregularity in procedure by a local draft board in *Lipsitz v. Perez*, and on Nov. 13 it rejected a case, *Gearey v. U.S.*, involving the denial of a registrant's conscientious objector claim.

The Court Nov. 13 refused to hear an appeal in the case of Army Capt. Howard B. Levy, a doctor, who refused to instruct Special Forces ("Green Beret") medical aidmen in the treatment of skin diseases; the aidmen were bound for South Vietnam. Levy was convicted by a court martial of promoting disloyalty among the troops. His appeal in *Levy v. Corcoran* involved his efforts to convene a three-judge federal district court and to obtain an injunction against his prosecution.

Stewart and Douglas also dissented in the Court's refusal on Nov. 6, 1967, to review the war issue as raised in *Mora v. McNamara*. Stewart suggested there was no legal obligation to support the war, while Douglas argued in favor of hearing a challenge to the legality of the war.

This suit was brought by three Army privates to prevent the Secretary of Defense and the Secretary of the Army from carrying out orders transferring the men to duty in South Vietnam. They contended that the U.S. presence in South Vietnam was illegal. A federal district court dismissed the suit and the Court of Appeals for the District of Columbia affirmed the district court's action.

Dissent. Stewart said the case raised "questions of great magnitude," namely:

"I. Is the present United States military activity in Vietnam a 'war' within the meaning of Article I, Section 8, Clause 11 of the Constitution?*

"II. If so, may the Executive constitutionally order the petitioners to participate in that military activity, when no war has been declared by the Congress?

"III. Of what relevance to Question II are the present treaty obligations of the United States?

"IV. Of what relevance to Question II is the Joint Congressional ('Tonkin Bay') Resolution of Aug. 10, 1964?

"(a) Do present United States military operations fall within the terms of the Joint Resolution?

"(b) If the Joint Resolution purports to give the Chief Executive authority to commit United States forces to armed conflict limited in scope only by his own absolute discretion, is the Resolution a constitutionally impermissible delegation of all or part of Congress' power to declare war?

"These are large and deeply troubling questions. Whether the Court would ultimately reach them depends, of course, upon the resolution of serious preliminary issues of justiciability. We cannot make these problems go away simply by refusing to hear the case of three obscure Army privates. I intimate not even tentative views upon any of these matters, but I think the Court should squarely face them by granting certiorari and setting this case for oral argument."

Douglas said that ever since the *Prize Cases* (1863), two points of view had been put forward as to the meaning of the Constitution's war clause. One held that the President had strong powers regarding the prosecution of hostilities without a Congressional declaration of war; the other held that the Constitution should be read more strictly and that "war in actuality may not constitute war in the constitutional sense."

"A host of problems is raised," he continued. "Does the President's authority to repel invasions and quiet insurrections, his powers in foreign relations and his duty to execute faithfully the laws of the United States, including its treaties, justify what has been threatened of petitioners? What is the relevancy of the Gulf of Tonkin Resolution and the yearly appropriations in support of the Vietnam Effort?"

Douglas said the question of whether the Court could or should take the case on the merits was serious adding: "These petitioners should be told whether their case is beyond judicial cognizance. If it is not, we should then reach the merits of their claims, on which I intimate no views whatsoever."

Stewart and Douglas each concurred in the other's dissent.

* Article I, Section 8, Clause 11 states: "The Congress shall have power...to declare war, grant letters of marque and reprisal, and make rules concerning captures on land and water."

These arguments did not diminish the domestic opposition to the Administration's policies. In perhaps the most important development, the Rev. Dr. Martin Luther King Jr., president of the Southern Christian Leadership Conference, March 25 proposed a merger of the civil rights and peace movements. He said the war was an obstacle to civil rights progress.

President Johnson brought Gen. Westmoreland to the United States in late April for a pair of speeches. In one of them, Westmoreland suggested that the enemy was gaining support from U.S. antiwar protests. But the protests continued nonetheless, reaching a highpoint in an antiwar demonstration and march on the Pentagon in Washington on Oct. 21-22. Police estimated that more than 55,000 persons took part. Federal troops ringed the building and were held in reserve throughout Washington in case of widespread violence. There was a brief clash between troops and demonstrators at a door to the Pentagon.

In Vietnam, there was evidence of increasing political stability. A new constitution, prepared by a 117-member Constituent Assembly, went into effect April 1. The constitution provided for a popularly elected president and bicameral legislature (the National Assembly), a Supreme Court elected by the National Assembly from a list submitted by associations of judges, prosecutors and lawyers, and an "Inspectorate" whose members would be appointed equally by the president, the National Assembly, and the Supreme Court to serve as a sort of government watchdog agency. The constitution gave the president sweeping powers and made him both head of state and head of government. The National Assembly included an upper house of 60 senators and a lower house of 137 representatives. Elections were held under the constitution on Sept. 3. South Vietnam Chief of State Nguyen Van Thieu was elected president; Premier Nguyen Cao Ky was elected vice president. Both terms were for four years. The new government was inaugurated Oct. 31. In another development President Johnson named Ambassador at large Ellsworth Bunker to replace Vietnam Ambassador Henry Cabot Lodge; Bunker began work April 25.

Congressional Action. Congress remained deeply concerned about the war, but—as in previous years—had limited power to influence the course of the American involvement. In the only serious effort to do so, Congress approved a broad policy declaration that, in effect, gave support to the soldiers in the fields and urged statesmen to work harder for peace. In the absence of definitive action to directly influence policy, debate flourished, hearings were held, reports were issued and peace proposals multiplied.

The policy declaration which was enacted was the first Vietnam statement by Congress since the 1964 Tonkin Gulf resolution. It came when Congress early in the year was considering an authorization bill for supplemental Vietnam appropriations. President Johnson Jan. 24 requested $12.3 billion in extra funds to finance the war through June 30, the end of fiscal 1967. Most of the money could be appropriated under existing authorization, but a portion needed a new authorization. The Administration asked for $4,467,200,000 in new authorization. Legislation (S 665—PL 90-5) to accomplish this was enacted in mid-March. As passed, S 665 authorized $4,548,200,000; the extra $81 million above the request was for purchase of Marine Corps aircraft.

S 665 was the first opportunity the 90th Congress had to act on legislation directly related to the war. It thus became the vehicle by which a number of Members of Congress attempted to influence the Administration's conduct of the war. The declaration which was approved gave Congressional support for efforts to prevent expansion of the war and to bring about an honorable negotiated settlement; it also pledged support for U.S. armed forces in Vietnam. *(For text of declaration, see box.)* The mild language of the declaration was far less restrictive than that of several other proposals urged on Congress by war critics.

The declaration originated in the Senate under the sponsorship of Sen. Joseph S. Clark (D Pa.). Clark offered another amendment which stated the sense of Congress that appropriated funds should not be used "to carry out military operations in or over North Vietnam or to increase" U.S. forces in Vietnam beyond 500,000. This clearly was too strong a statement for the Senate to approve and Clark settled for acceptance of his milder proposal which (with minor modifications) became part of the final bill. The milder proposal was accepted by the Senate March 1 on a key **72-19** roll-call vote, the first key vote of the new Congress. Supporters of the Clark proposal said it was not developed in consultation with the Administration. Debate focused on the implications of the declaration, with opponents saying it would give comfort to the Communists and supporters contending it merely was an affirmation of current U.S. policies.

In the House, an effort was made to attach stronger language to S 665, but the proposal drew only a handful of supporters. The proposal would have stated the sense of Congress that no funds authorized by the bill could

---

Text of Vietnam Declaration

Following is the text of the Vietnam policy declaration added by Congress to S 665. It was the first Congressional policy declaration on Vietnam since enactment of the Gulf of Tonkin resolution in 1964. *(For text of 1964 resolution, see p. 70.)*

"The Congress hereby declares:

(1) its firm intentions to provide all necessary support for members of the armed forces of the United States fighting in Vietnam;

"(2) its support of efforts being made by the President of the United States and other men of good will throughout the world to prevent an expansion of the war in Vietnam and to bring that conflict to an end through a negotiated settlement which will preserve the honor of the United States, protect the vital interests of this country, and allow the people of South Vietnam to determine the affairs of that nation in their own way; and

"(3) its support for the convening of the nations that participated in the Geneva Conferences or any other meeting of nations similarly involved and interested as soon as possible for the purpose of pursuing the general principles of the Geneva accords of 1954 and 1962 and for formulating plans for bringing the conflict to an honorable conclusion."

Major Treaties Since 1945

In Congressional testimony in 1966 before the Senate Armed Services Preparedness Investigating Subcommittee, Secretary of State Dean Rusk said the United Nations Charter "explicitly provides for the existence of regional organizations, such as the Organization of American States, which would deal with problems of international peace and security in their respective areas. It also explicitly recognizes the inherent right of both individual and collective self-defense. Consistent with the UN Charter, we have entered into multilateral and bilateral treaty arrangements with more than 40 countries on five continents."

Following is Rusk's chronology of treaties signed by the United States since establishment of the United Nations in 1945:

• Inter-American Treaty of Reciprocal Assistance (the Rio Treaty of 1947), "the basic collective security instrument of the inter-American system... ratified by all 21 American republics."

• North Atlantic Treaty, 1949, signed by the United States and Canada and 10 nations of Western Europe; signed in 1952 by Greece and Turkey and in 1955 by the Federal Republic of Germany.

• Mutual Defense Treaty with the Philippines, 1951.

• Security Treaty with Japan, 1951.

• Security pact with Australia and New Zealand known as ANZUS, 1951.

• Mutual defense treaty with Korea, 1953.

• Mutual defense treaty with Republic of China, 1954.

• Southeast Asia Collective Defense Treaty with Australia, France, New Zealand, Pakistan, the Philippines, Thailand and the United Kingdom, 1954.

• Treaty of Mutual Cooperation and Security with Japan, 1960, replacing 1951 treaty.

The Senate late in the session unanimously approved a resolution (S Res 180) that urged the President to consider renewing U.S. efforts to have the UN Security Council consider the Vietnam issue. The resolution, which UN Ambassador Arthur J. Goldberg endorsed, did not require the President's signature and did not have the force of law.

Most other Congressional action on the war issue was confined to committee activities with much of the action centered in the Senate Foreign Relations Committee. The Committee early in the year held hearings on the "responsibilities of the United States as a great power" and later in the summer on a resolution (S Res 151) on national commitments *(see below)*. Throughout the year, however, the Committee was unsuccessful in persuading Secretary of State Rusk to testify before it on the war. He last testified publicly before the Committee on the war issue on Feb. 18, 1966. In 1967, three invitations from the Committee for additional public testimony were turned down, although Rusk made speeches across the country defending the Administrations's war policies. Rusk offered to testify in private; he argued it would be dangerous to discuss the war in public testimony while the conflict was under way. He said his refusal to testify publicly was consistent with the policy of all previous Administrations during a war.

In summary, Congress also acted on the following Vietnam related items:

Veterans Aid. (S 16—PL 90-77) Among other provisions, the Veterans' Pension and Readjustment Assistance Act of 1967 authorized wartime rates and compensation benefits for Vietnam veterans. The act also set Aug. 5, 1964, three days after the Gulf of Tonkin attack, as the start of the "Vietnam Era" for purposes of determining Vietnam veterans' qualifications. The act passed both houses without opposition. *(See story in chapter on veterans' affairs.)*

Sanctions. The Senate Oct. 10 by a 74-15 roll-call vote added an amendment to the State-Justice-Commerce appropriations bill for fiscal 1968 (HR 10345—PL 90-133) expressing the sense of Congress that the United States, having backed UN economic sanctions against Rhodesia, should initiate and support similar UN sanctions against North Vietnam. Voting against the amendment were six Republicans: Kuchel (Calif.), Cooper (Ky.), Brooke (Mass.), Case (N.J.), Scott (Pa.) and Pearson (Kan.); and nine Democrats: Gruening (Alaska), Inouye (Hawaii), McCarthy and Mondale (Minn.), Williams (N.J.), Young (Ohio), Morse (Ore.), McGee (Wyo.) and Hart (Mich.). The amendment later was dropped from the bill by House and Senate conferees.

Export Restrictions. The Senate Aug. 10 by a 56-26 roll-call vote adopted an amendment to a bill dealing with the Export-Import Bank (S 1155—HR 6649) that prohibited the Bank from financing exports to nations engaged in armed conflict with the United States, whether or not war had been declared, or to other countries engaged in trade with the belligerent nation. *(See story p. 90.)*

Aid to Viet Cong. The House Un-American Activities Committee May 31 reported a bill (HR 8) that prescribed a fine of $20,000 or up to 20 years in prison for persons soliciting or delivering money or a thing of value for use by any nation or group in armed conflict with the United States; and a fine of $10,000 or five years in

---

be used for military operations in or over North Vietnam. The language, which was very similar to the proposal favored in the Senate by Clark, was aimed directly at the controversial bombing of North Vietnam. But on a key vote, it was rejected by an **18-372** roll call. Although the proposal got only 18 votes, this was a record number for House doves"; all 18 were Northern Democrats.

S 665 later was sent to the President with the Senate's declaration of policy after conferees on the bill made minor revisions in the wording.

After the authorization bill was cleared, Congress went on quickly to vote the supplemental appropriations. The bill (HR 7123—PL 90-8) appropriated $12,196,520,000 which was $79,350,000 less than requested. It was the third consecutive year that Congress had provided supplemental appropriations specifically for the war effort in Southeast Asia. The bill passed both chambers by large margins on roll-call votes (House 385-11; Senate 77-3). There was some debate on the Administration's Vietnam policy but it was not as spirited as that on the authorization bill.

prison for obstructing the movement of personnel or supplies by U.S. armed forces. The House Nov. 17 adopted the rule for floor action on the bill, but the measure never reached the floor. *(See civil liberties chapter.)*

Foreign Aid Restriction. The House Aug. 24 by voice vote adopted an amendment to the fiscal 1969 foreign aid authorization bill (S 1872—PL 90-137) to eliminate the President's authority to engage in the sale or purchase of defense equipment or services with nations trading with or shipping to North Vietnam. House and Senate conferees dropped the amendment and a motion to recommit the bill to conference with instructions to restore the amendment was defeated Nov. 8 by a **196-200** roll-call vote. It was one of the key votes of the session. *(See story p. 84.)*

National Commitments

The Administration's continual escalation of U.S. involvement in the Vietnam war led various Members of Congress to conclude that the President had exceeded his constitutional powers. These Members were most concerned that the President had acted almost entirely on his own with only the vaguest of Congressional authorization in the Gulf of Tonkin resolution (the President, on the other hand, considered the resolution entirely adequate authority).

The result of this increasing Congressional concern was the introduction in the Senate of a resolution, which came to be known as the National Commitments Resolution, declaring the sense of the Senate that no future commitment of U.S. forces to hostilities abroad would be made without "affirmative action" by Congress. *(For text, see box)* The resolution (S Res 187) was reported Nov. 20 by the Foreign Relations Committee which was the focal point for Congressional dissent over Vietnam. Committee Chairman J.W. Fulbright (D Ark.) said he did not intend to press for action in 1967 but hoped the resolution "may provoke some very careful thought and analysis of the role of the Senate in the formulation of foreign policy in a democracy."

The issue was not just an academic debate about the U.S. involvement in the Vietnam war. It was at the center of a basic question of how American power in the 20th century—and particularly in the period since 1945 when the United States was world leader—should be exercised and controlled. It was at the heart of the role of the modern Presidency and the division of authority between the Presidency and Congress. It also had a very practical side beyond the immediate question of Vietnam: the State Department said the United States was definitely committed to the defense of 42 nations as a result of treaties and agreements given approval by the Senate. Defense agreements, agreements of cooperation, policy statements, and U.S. military installations in some 30 foreign nations added an unknown number of nations to the list of those that the United States might feel obligated to defend.

Vietnam was the moving force behind the Senate resolution, but there were other considerations too. An important factor was uneasiness in Congress over other foreign military involvements outside of Vietnam since 1945, and concern about U.S. ability to meet all its existing foreign obligations as well as pressing domestic needs. Another was the commitment by the Administration of three U.S. transport planes to aid the Congolese government against a July 1967 revolt by mercenaries. Still another was confusion during the 1967 Arab-Israeli war over the existence of U.S. commitments to Israel. Underlying most of these considerations, however, was traditional Congressional discontent with what Members considered Presidential disregard for their opinions in conducting foreign policy.

Past U.S. military involvement in such spots as Korea, the Dominican Republic, and the Bay of Pigs in Cuba, undertaken without specific Congressional backing, cast uncertainty over what authority was necessary to permit U.S. troops to be sent overseas. President Johnson in an Aug. 5, 1966, speech at Johns Hopkins University pledged U.S. support to any victim of aggression. Secretary of State Rusk told Congressional committees that the absence of a treaty with the United States did not mean the United States would leave a nation defenseless against attack.

Critics of U.S. policies also contended that Congressional resolutions, Government communiques, press conference statements, speeches and toasts to foreign dignitaries by U.S. officials, and foreign aid had been cited in the past as justification for U.S. foreign involvement.

The State Department itself seemed uncertain on the modern role of Congressional declarations of war. Rusk Aug. 30, 1966, told the Senate Preparedness Subcommittee that a Congressional war declaration was not "outmoded" by modern developments. Under Secretary of State Nicholas deB. Katzenbach told a hearing on the Fulbright resolution that such declarations were outmoded in wars like Vietnam.

The growing concern about U.S. commitments abroad also surfaced during Congressional consideration of the

---

National Commitments Resolution

Following is the text of S Res 187:

"Whereas the Executive and Legislative Branches of the United States Government have joint responsibility and authority to formulate the foreign policy of the United States; and

"Whereas the authority to initiate war is vested in Congress by the Constitution: Now, therefore, be it

"Resolved, That a commitment for purposes of this resolution means the use of, or promise to a foreign state or people to use, the armed forces of the United States either immediately or upon the happening of certain events, and

"That it is the sense of the Senate that, under any circumstances which may arise in the future pertaining to situations in which the United States is not already involved, the commitment of the armed forces of the United States to hostilities on foreign territory for any purpose other than to repel an attack on the United States or to protect United States citizens or property properly will result from a decision made in accordance with constitutional processes, which, in addition to appropriate Executive action, require affirmative action by Congress specifically intended to give rise to such commitment."

fiscal 1968 defense procurement bill (S 666). The Administration asked Congress for authorization to procure a fleet of fast deployment logistics ships (FDLs) to increase the nation's ability to respond quickly to brushfire wars. The concern of Senate Armed Services Committee Chairman Richard B. Russell (D Ga.) that the vessels would encourage U.S. intervention in more situations like Vietnam was a major factor in the refusal of Congress to grant the Administration's request.

U.S. Congo Aid

Foreign mercenaries in the Congo, joined by local forces loyal to former Congolese Premier Moise Tshombe, July 5 revolted against the regime of Congolese President Joseph D. Mobutu. After a week of sporadic fighting, Mobutu's forces, aided by a U.S. commitment of three C-130 transport aircraft, suppressed the rebellion and forced the mercenaries to begin withdrawal from the country.

President Johnson's decision to send the aircraft to the Congo, taken without the express approval of Congress, stirred considerable criticism on Capitol Hill. Opponents included a broad spectrum of Democrats and Republicans as well as supporters and opponents of U.S. involvement in the Vietnam war. The criticism by Vietnam "hawks" was widely interpreted as evidence of a growing reluctance in Congress for the United States to be cast in the role of the "world's policeman."

Leading the criticism against the Administration's move was Senate Armed Services Committee Chairman Richard B. Russell (D Ga.). Vietnam, Russell said, started out with a commitment "not much larger" than that made in the Congo. If any of the craft were lost or members of a small accompanying troop contingent killed, he said, the commitment could grow into a major intervention.

Administration Explanation. Following the sharp criticism from Congress, Secretary of State Dean Rusk July 11-12 appeared in closed session before the foreign affairs committees of both the House and Senate to set forth the Administration's explanation for its action. Following hearings before the Senate Foreign Relations Committee July 11, Rusk told the press that the planes had been dispatched because a mercenary victory would have unleashed a wave of antiwhite feeling which might have endangered the lives of some 3,000 Americans in the Congo as well as numerous Europeans.

Foreign Aid

The increasingly unpopular foreign aid program suffered a severe battering in 1967. Congress cut the annual authorization for the program to the lowest level in the 20-year history of foreign aid. As enacted, the fiscal 1968 foreign aid authorization bill (S 1872—PL 90-137) provided for appropriations of $2,674,614,000 for economic aid ($2,164,614,000) and military assistance ($510 million). The total was $787,691,000 below the Administration's authorization request and $28,727,750 less than the smallest amount ever appropriated—$2,703,341,750 in fiscal 1956.

In another defeat for the Administration, Congress refused to grant an advance authorization sought for the program for fiscal 1969; it even withdrew fiscal 1969 authorizations that had been approved the previous year for development loan funds and the Alliance for Progress. Moreover, the fiscal 1968 authorizations for these two programs, which also were enacted the previous year, were reduced by Congress in S 1872. The development loan fund reduction also was the largest cut made in any program—from the existing $750 million in fiscal 1968 to the new figure of $450 million for that year.

In addition to the reductions, Congress attached several restrictive amendments that curbed the President's authority to conduct foreign policy. After months of controversy, Congress agreed to a proviso terminating as of June 30, 1968, the Defense Department's authority to finance credit arms sales to underdeveloped nations. *(For summary of action on the controversial arms sales issue, see story and box p. 85-86.)*

Congress also required that aid be terminated to nations whose defense spending interfered "materially" with their economic growth and increased interest rates for the first ten years of development loans from 1 percent to 2 percent. It altered the ceilings on the number of countries that could receive most types of economic aid; the number eligible for development loans was doubled from 10 to 20, but the bill revoked the President's discretion to waive all such ceilings. The bill also required that the Administration furnish Congress greater detail about its projected aid commitments.

Most of the restrictions added in both houses remained in the final bill. However, the Administration was successful in deleting House-added riders which would have terminated the President's authority to engage in sales or purchases of defense supplies or equipment with countries that traded with North Vietnam and that would have suspended the most-favored-nation tariff privilege from Poland.

As the bill became law, it prohibited all forms of aid under the Foreign Assistance and other acts to countries which traded with North Vietnam "so long as the regime in North Vietnam gives support to hostilities in South Vietnam." Existing law barred aid under the Foreign Assistance Act to countries that permitted ships or aircraft under their registry to transport goods to North Vietnam; it did not affect countries that shipped goods to North Vietnam in the ships and aircraft of other nations. S 1872 broadened existing law to cover this latter situation. Existing law provided, and S 1872 did not change, authority for the President to waive the ban with respect to the sale of defense articles and services to countries trading with North Vietnam if the President determined that such assistance would strengthen U.S. security and promote world peace.

The issue of a Presidential waiver in such cases provoked a controversy and produced one of the key votes of the session. During House action on S 1872 in August, Rep. H.R. Gross (R Iowa) won acceptance of an amendment to terminate the President's waiver authority. However, when the bill went to conference, Senate-House conferees dropped Gross' amendment and another House amendment sponsored by Rep. Paul Findley (R Ill.) to suspend the most-favored-nation tariff privilege from Poland until it was determined that country was no longer supplying war material to North Vietnam. When the conference report came back to the House, Gross sponsored a motion to recommit the bill with instructions to restore both his and Findley's amendments. Gross' motion was rejected by a key **196-200** roll-call vote.

The Administration had strenuously objected to the Gross amendment on the grounds that it would injure U.S. relations with many nations. Administration officials said the provision barring the purchase of defense material or services from these nations might force the closing of U.S. bases in Britain because local procurement of goods and services would be banned. The outcome of the Gross motion was a narrow defeat for the "conservative coalition" of Republicans and Southern Democrats. Republicans voted for the motion 136-33, while Southern Democrats favored it by a margin of 51-30. The strong Administration lobbying effort kept the ranks of Northern Democrats nearly intact, however, and only nine of them voted for the motion; 137 were opposed.

During action earlier in the year, S 1872 was heavily cut by the Senate Foreign Relations Committee, and the Committee recommendations were generally accepted on the floor. The House Foreign Affairs Committee was much more willing to go along with the Administration requests, but the bill was then deeply cut on the floor. Many of the Administration defeats in the House came on the last day of debate, when the leadership was unable to keep sufficient Administration supporters on the floor. The final authorization was $140,794,000 less than the House sum and $46,131,500 above the Senate recommendation.

Even with the cuts and restrictions, S 1872 escaped defeat in the House by narrow margins. The House passed the original version of the bill by a 202-194 (R 52-124; D 150-70—ND 127-13, SD 23-57) roll-call vote and later adopted the final bill by a roll call of 205-188 (R 49-120; D 156-68—ND 129-14, SD 27-54). The Senate passed the bill by a large margin: 60-28 on passage and voice vote on the conference report.

Most of the opposition to the program appeared to be related to two major factors. One was a growing mood of discontent in Congress over the conduct of U.S. foreign policy, particularly with regard to the war in Vietnam. The other was an overwhelming Congressional concern, particularly in the House, over cost reductions in the face of a growing budget deficit, a continued high level of war spending, and the resulting threat of inflation in the domestic economy.

Foreign Aid Funds

After cutting the fiscal 1968 authorization to a record low, Congress proceeded to appropriate the smallest mount in the 20-year history of the aid program. The bill (HR 13893—PL 90-249) appropriated $2,295,635,000 for foreign economic aid ($1,895,635,000) and military assistance ($400 million) in fiscal 1968. The total was $930,785,000 less than Administration requests and $407,-706,750 below the previous all-time low appropriation in fiscal 1956. In addition to the above amounts for economic and military aid, the bill provided $107.5 million for the Peace Corps, $300 million for the Inter-American Development Bank, $104 million for the International Development Assn. and $49 million for Cuban refugee

relief. The most severe cut was a reduction of $339 million in the President's request for development loans. Like the authorization bill, HR 13893 carried numerous policy restrictions, many of which had been enacted in earlier years. The most notable new one sought to bar use of aid funds by underdeveloped nations for purchase of sophisticated weapons and ordered cuts in U.S. aid when such countries used their own resources for advance armaments. The provision included a Presidential waiver. *(For summary of action on arms sales restrictions, see story below and box p. 86.)*

The main controversy about the bill developed in the House when that chamber recommitted the conference report by a roll-call vote of 196-185 (R 147-17; D 49-168—ND 7-130; SD 42-38) with instructions to make additional cuts in the total appropriations. A second conference report was quickly filed which was $20 million less than the first figure. This was accepted by both chambers. Final action came the following day—Dec. 15—in one of the last actions of the first session of the 90th Congress.

Arms Sales

Widespread sale of U.S. arms to developing nations was one of the major foreign policy issues of the 1967 Congressional session. News of the sale of U.S. jet fighter planes and other sophisticated weaponry to poor countries circulated widely. Additional fuel for the arms debate was added in June when the Arab-Israeli war broke out. It was noted that the United States had helped to arm both sides in the conflict.

The scope of the U.S. arms sales program became known largely through a staff study for the Senate Foreign Relations Committee, whose results were released in January. Thereafter, critics claimed that a zealous U.S. arms sales program was keeping developing nations from using capital on badly needed economic development, and was contributing to tension or arms buildups in various parts of the world. The critics claimed that arms races were being fostered among countries that could not afford it, especially in Latin America.

The Administration and some Members of Congress —including prominent members of the Armed Services Committees—contended that developing countries needed the arms to block the threat of Communist insurgency.

Concern over arms races among developing nations was heightened by news in early October of an agreement by Peru to purchase 12 supersonic Mirage-V fighter bombers from France. Earlier in the year, the United States had turned down requests for the U.S. F-5 jet fighter from Peru, Argentina, Brazil, Chile and Venezuela, and Peru had turned down a U.S. counteroffer of old F-86 jet fighters. The Franco-Peruvian agreement tended to support arguments that nations desiring modern weaponry would seek it elsewhere if the United States refused to be the supplier. Concern also arose in the fall in reaction to reports that the United States was reconsidering its refusal to sell F-5s to Latin American nations. No F-5s were sold in 1967.

Disclosure of the scope of the U.S. arms sales program led to Congressional action on the issue during consideration in 1967 of three bills to which the program was related. (There was further action in 1968. *See box p. 86 for summary of 1967-68 arms sales legislation.)*

Congress Enacted Provisions To Restrict Arms Sales

The 90th Congress in both 1967 and 1968 enacted a number of provisions restricting credit sales of U.S. military equipment to foreign nations. The provisions were first enacted piecemeal in a number of bills, but in 1968 all were consolidated in a single arms sales measure. Although some of the provisions had a seemingly broad application, their thrust clearly demonstrated that Congress was most concerned with increasing militarization of small foreign nations and with the role of the United States in promoting that trend by providing credit for arms purchases. The provisions were not aimed at controlling direct sales of military equipment to the United States' large allies, such as Britain or France. The provisions limited the Administration's freedom to sell arms to underdeveloped nations in secret and were intended to give Congress the opportunity to keep a close watch over Pentagon sales activities. The provisions also sought to restrict U.S. economic aid to developing nations which spent large amounts on military equipment and sought to discourage developing nations from buying sophisticated weapons such as missile systems and jet aircraft. The provisions are summarized below. *(See accompanying story.)*

1967 Foreign Aid Authorization Bill

This legislation (S 1872—PL 90-137) was enacted Nov. 14, 1967, and provided the foreign aid authorization for fiscal 1968.

Country-X Revolving Fund. Terminated, as of June 30, 1968, the special Defense Department military assitance credit account used to guarantee loans by the Export-Import Bank for arms purchases by underdeveloped countries. Also placed a limitation of $190 million on the total amount of arms loans that the Department could guarantee during fiscal 1968.

Unnecessary Military Expenditures. Directed the President, in furnishing development loans or PL-480 food aid to foreign nations, to take into account what percentage of the recipient country's budget was spent for military purposes and the degree to which the country was using its foreign exchange resources to procure military equipment. Directed the President to terminate development loans and PL-480 assistance to nations that diverted such assistance to military expenditures or diverted their own resources to "unnecessary" military expenditures "to a degree which materially interferes" with their own development, until he was assured that such diversion no longer would take place. This provision became part of the permanent foreign aid law.

1967 Foreign Aid Appropriations Bill

This legislation (HR 13893—PL 90-249) was enacted Jan. 2, 1968 (it had been cleared the previous Dec. 15), and provided foreign aid funds for fiscal 1968. The arms sales provision:

Sophisticated Weapons. Prohibited use of the bill's military assistance funds and the Defense Department's credit sales revolving fund to finance the sale of "sophisticated weapons systems, such as mis-

sile systems and jet aircraft for military purposes." to "underdeveloped" countries (except for Greece, Turkey, Iran, Israel, Nationalist China, the Philippines and Korea) unless the President determined that such a transaction was "vital to the national security of the United States" and reported to Congress within 30 days of his determination.

Directed the President to withhold an equivalent amount of economic assistance from any underdeveloped country (except for those listed above) that used its own resources to purchase sophisticated weaponry from any country unless the President determined that such a transaction was vital to U.S. security and reported his determination to Congress within 30 days. As part of an appropriations bill, this provision continued only until the end of the fiscal year, June 30, 1968.

Export-Import Bank Extension

This legislation (S 1155—PL 90-267) was enacted March 13, 1968, although part of the action on it occurred during 1967.

Arms Sales. Prohibited Eximbank credits for military equipment sales to less developed countries unless the President determined such exports would be in the national interest and gave Congress 30 days notice.

Arms Sales Authorization

This legislation (HR 15681—PL 90-629) was enacted Oct. 22, 1968. After Congress sharply restricted the arms sales program in PL 90-137 and PL 90-267 *(see above)*, the Administration proposed legislation for a new program to be financed through direct annual appropriations.

Authorization. The bill authorized fiscal 1969 appropriations of $296 million to finance credit sales of defense articles to other nations. It made clear that credit sales to underdeveloped nations were to be made only from annual appropriations. (The full $296 million was appropriated later in a separate bill.)

Eximbank Role. Specifically prohibited the Eximbank from participating in any credit transaction for military sales to underdeveloped countries. This provision, which contained no Presidential waiver, superceded the less strict prohibition on Eximbank arms sale activities that was included in the Eximbank extension bill (PL 90-267).

1968 Foreign Aid Authorization Bill

This legislation (HR 15263—PL 90-554) was enacted Oct. 8, 1968, and authorized foreign aid funds for fiscal 1969.

Sophisticated Weapons. This bill contained in modified form the provisions in several other bills *(see above)* to prevent developing nations from using either U.S. military assistance funds or their own scarce resources to purchase sophisticated weapons.

Jets to Israel. The bill expressed the sense of Congress that the President should negotiate with Israel the sale of as many supersonic planes as necessary to prevent "future Arab aggression." The President began negotiations in October.

The following material details Congressional action in 1967 that related to the arms sales controversy.

Staff Study. In a report little noted at the time, a staff study for the Senate Foreign Relations Committee Jan. 25 said that U.S. military assistance in the past four years had undergone "a basic change" in which the sale of arms had replaced the "giving of arms as the predominant form" of aid. The volume of U.S. arms sales abroad had reached "something over the $2-billion-per-year level" by 1967, the study said. It concluded, "It is incumbent on the United States to reappraise the adequacy of the present machinery of policy control and legislative oversight governing the sale of arms."

U.S. arms sales abroad were made in a number of ways, the study said: private firms selling to a foreign government, private firms selling through a U.S. Government agency, the U.S. Government selling to a foreign government, or a U.S. firm licensing a foreign firm to produce its products. The study said that "almost two-thirds" of the sales were for cash but that credit had been offered on other sales, "mainly" to the underdeveloped nations. Credit sales were financed through private banking facilities, through direct loans from the Export-Import Bank, through so-called Country-X loans from the Eximbank, or through the military assistance credit account, a revolving fund administered by the Defense Department's International Logistics Negotiations (ILN) office.

Country-X Loans. Congressional attention in 1967 focused mainly on the link between the Eximbank and the Defense Department in making Country-X loans. Under existing law, the Defense Department was permitted to select recipients of arms loans by the Eximbank and was not required to identify the recipient either to the Bank or to Congress. The only requirement was that the military assistance credit account have sufficient funds to privide a cash guarantee of 25 percent of the face amount of the Eximbank loans; the Pentagon also assumed responsibility for the other 75 percent of the loan but did not have to maintain a cash revserve for it. The Pentagon revolving fund essentially was self-sustaining but was bolstered whenever necessary by funds from general military assistance appropriations. The program was known widely as the country-X loan program because the Eximbank provided the loan without knowing where the funds were going.

The Defense Department reported that more than $700 million in loans to underdeveloped countries for arms purchases were guaranteed by the Department's revolving fund during the period 1962-67.

Eximbank Bill. One of the first bills caught in the Congressional controversy on arms sales was a measure (HR 6649—S 1155) to grant a five-year extension for the Export-Import Bank and to increase its lending authority. The controversy delayed final action on the bill until 1968. (See p. 96.) The Senate and House Banking and Currency Committees approved the bill in May 1967 but then held it back from floor consideration as concern mounted over the Bank's role in financing arms sales. The Eximbank bill also became embroiled in an East-West trade controversy. (See p. 96.)

After holding more hearings July 25, the Senate Committee Aug. 4 reported S 1155 with an amendment expressing the sense of Congress that the Bank should not participate in Country-X loans. After debating the

U.S. Arms Sales, Grants — 1952-69

(in millions of dollars)

Fiscal 1952-61	Grants	Sales	Total
1952	$ 4,440	$ 532	$ 4,972
1953	1,965	230	2,195
1954	1,323	82	1,405
1955	2,556	98	2,654
1956	657	174	831
1957	1,283	663	1,946
1958	1,381	340	1,721
1959	1,318	853	2,171
1960	1,034	963	1,997
1961	1,450	630	2,080
Ten-year total	$17,407	$4,565	$21,972
Fiscal 1962-69			
1962	1,314	1,485	2,799
1963	958	1,483	2,441
1964	728	1,260	1,988
1965	721	1,766	2,487
1966	695	1,798	2,493
1967*	541	1,946	2,487
1968*	400	1,929	2,329
1969*	390	1,530	1,920
Eight-year total	$5,747	$13,197	$18,944

*1967 figure was preliminary; 1968 and 1969 figures were Committee estimates.

SOURCE: House Foreign Affairs Committee

issue for two days, the Senate Aug. 9 in a key vote rejected by a **40-49** roll call an attempt to end the Bank's participation in arms sales to less-developed countries. Allen J. Ellender (D La.) introduced the amendment to tighten the sense-of-Congress provision on arms sales. It was modified by Joseph S. Clark (D Pa.), with Ellender's approval, to flatly prohibit the Bank from financing arms purchases by underdeveloped countries. This was rejected by the **40-49** vote, leaving the Committee provision intact.

The House version (HR 6649) originally contained no provision on arms sales. But after the issue had become very controversial during the summer, the Committee Nov. 2 added an amendment to prohibit the participation by the Eximbank in extension of credit for purchase by underdeveloped nations of arms or defense services unless the President determined that such transactions would be in the national interest. However, floor action on the bill was postponed until 1968.

Foreign Aid Authorization. Arms sales were a major issue in action on this bill (S 1872—PL 90-137) and led to a deadlock of almost two months in the Senate-House conference on the measure. The bill as reported by the Senate Foreign Relations Committee included an amendment by Frank Church (D Idaho) to repeal, effective Dec. 31, 1967, the Pentagon's authority to maintain the revolving fund used in financing sales. The bill also included an amendment by Stuart Symington (D Mo.)

requiring the President to terminate all foreign assistance to any nation that diverted such assistance to military expenditures or diverted their own resources to "unnecessary military spending to a degree which materially interferes" with their own development. In floor action, the Senate rejected amendments by Henry M. Jackson (D Wash.) and John G. Tower (R Texas) to restore the revolving fund. They were rejected by roll-call votes of 43-50 (R 23-9; D 20-41—ND 11-30, SD 9-11) and 45-46 (R 22-8; D 23-38—ND 14-27, SD 9-11).

In the House, the bill approved by the Foreign Affairs Committee carried no restriction on the arms sales program. In fact, the Committee's bill broadened the program by including an Administration-requested provision to give the Defense Department authority to buy promissory notes given arms manufacturers by foreign governments and then to sell the notes to the Export-Import Bank or other financial institutions. However, during floor action, the House accepted an amendment by William B. Widnall (R N.J.) to eliminate the new authority. The roll call on Widnall's amendment was 236-157 (R 152-21; D 84-136—ND 45-95, SD 39-41).

The Senate-House conference on the bill lasted from Sept. 14 to Nov. 1 because of controversy over the arms sale provision. Finally, conferees agreed to terminate the Pentagon's Country-X revolving fund at the end of fiscal 1968 and to limit the amount of arms purchase loans that could be guaranteed during fiscal 1968 to $190 million. Conferees also accepted a modified version of the Symington amendment. It was restricted to cover only development loans and PL 480 food aid; the original version covered all forms of foreign aid.

Foreign Aid Appropriations. A further attempt to curb arms sales to underdeveloped nations was made in this bill (HR 13893—PL 90-249). The House bill prohibited the use of military assistance funds and the Pentagon's revolving fund to finance the sale of sophisticated weapons systems to underdeveloped countries— except for Greece, Turkey, Iran, Israel, Nationalist China, the Philippines and Korea. A corollary amendment directed the President to withhold an equivalent amount of economic assistance from an underdeveloped country (except those named above) that used its own resources to purchase such equipment. The Senate substituted similar but milder amendments permitting the President to bar military aid on revolving credit funds for nations spending heavily on advanced weapons, but included no comparable provision on withholding aid to nations using their own money. Conferees accepted the House provisions but added clauses allowing the President to waive them in the interest of national security.

U.S.-Soviet Consular Treaty

An important agreement between the United States and the Soviet Union was approved by the Senate in 1967. On March 16, by a narrow margin, the Senate consented to the ratification of a controversial Consular Convention between the two countries (Exec. D, 88th Congress, 2nd Session). The vote, one of the key roll calls of the session, was **66-28**, only three over the required two-thirds majority.

The treaty detailed the legal framework and procedures for the operation of consulates in each country, if and when any consulates were established.

President Johnson ratified the Convention March 31, without comment or ceremony.

The treaty contained two key provisions, added in a protocol to the treaty, that were novel to such conventions. One precedent-setting provision provided complete criminal immunities and extended diplomatic immunity to consular officials and employees. The other provided that each country would promptly notify the other of the detention or arrest of a citizen of the other country, and would permit quick access to the person. Notification was to occur within three days and access within four days and regularly thereafter.

The treaty, signed in 1964, had symbolic importance, beyond its specific purpose, as part of the Johnson Administration's effort to improve U.S.-Soviet relations. The treaty was the first of a bilateral nature ever made between the two countries. Its approval was the first legislative endorsement of the Administration's policy of "building bridges" to the Communist world of the U.S.S.R. and Eastern Europe despite the war in Vietnam. The Consular Convention was part of a legislative package that included a space treaty banning nuclear weapons in space and East-West trade legislation.

The 1964 treaty was reported by the Senate Foreign Relations Committee early in 1965. However, the treaty was delayed by the Administration in both 1965 and 1966 because of international tensions over Vietnam, heavy schedules of other major legislation and domestic political considerations. The Administration feared that the treaty would not receive the two-thirds Senate majority needed for treaty approval and that failure to pass the treaty would unnecessarily aggravate U.S.-Soviet relations.

The treaty was strongly opposed by conservative groups and Senators of both parties. Opponents frequently cited remarks by J. Edgar Hoover, director of the Federal Bureau of Investigation, who had said that the establishment of U.S.S.R. consulates in the United States would increase the possibilities of Soviet espionage and would correspondingly complicate the job of the FBI in controlling such activities.

President Johnson in 1967 began a determined effort to obtain Senate approval of the treaty, but for many weeks the outcome remained in doubt. As part of the effort, the State Department presented a series of letters between Hoover and Secretary of State Dean Rusk which showed that Hoover did not take a position on the treaty itself. The Department also promised not to permit any Soviet consulates without first consulting the Senate and other interested parties, such as local officials in an area in which a consulate would be located.

Efforts to obtain Senate approval of the treaty were given a crucial boost early in the year by Sen. Thruston B. Morton (R Ky.) who led a group of moderate Republicans in an independent campaign for ratification. Morton Jan. 31 also encouraged the Administration to give more active support to the pact and urged the President to speak out for it which Mr. Johnson did three days later at a Feb. 2 news conference.

These efforts by Morton and other moderate Republicans came in the face of strong initial opposition to the treaty by Senate Minority Leader Everett McKinley Dirksen (R Ill.). Although Dirksen vigorously opposed the treaty at first, he later said he was undecided about it and finally supported the measure before the ratification vote. Other important Republican support came from conservative Sen. Bourke B. Hickenlooper (Iowa), the ranking GOP member of the Senate Foreign Relations Committee. Like Dirksen, he initially opposed the treaty but changed his position to support before the vote.

Another move credited with gaining votes for the treaty was the withdrawal of Sen. J.W. Fulbright (D Ark.), chairman of the Foreign Relations Committee, as its floor manager during much of the debate. The treaty was handled in his stead by Senate Majority Leader Mike Mansfield (D Mont.). This was reportedly done because Morton indicated Mansfield would be more persuasive to Republicans in view of Fulbright's criticism of Administration Vietnam policy.

The 66-28 ratification vote was divided as follows: R 22-13; D 44-15 (ND 34-5; SD 10-10). Senate leaders of both parties, with three exceptions, supported ratification. The three opposed were Majority Whip Russell B. Long (D La.), Secretary of the Democratic Conference Robert C. Byrd (D W.Va.), and Secretary of the Republican Conference Milton R. Young (R N.D.).

Although there had been speculation prior to the vote that Southern Democrats and Midwestern Republicans would be overwhelmingly opposed to the treaty, this did not occur. Southern Democrats divided 10-10 and GOP Senators from the Midwest divided 6-5. Of the other eight Republicans opposed, two were from the South, four from the West and two from the East.

The five Northern Democrats voting against ratification were Dodd (Conn.), Gruening (Alaska), Bible (Nev.), Montoya (N.M.) and Lausche (Ohio).

Controversy over Ratification. The Administration contended that the treaty would improve East-West relations, would afford greater protection to American travelers in the Soviet Union, and would give the West another "window" to observe activity in the relatively closed society of the Soviet Union.

The Administration pointed out that the Convention did not provide for the specific opening of any consulates —a power already possessed by the Executive even if there were no treaty—but did provide for beneficial and necessary protections for U.S. tourists immediately upon ratification and for U.S. consular personnel later if and when consulates were actually established.

Debate focused on the desirability of easing relations with the Soviets in any manner while the Vietnam war continued and on the possibility of increased Soviet espionage in the United States if consulates were established. Sen. Karl E. Mundt (R S.D.), leading the fight against the treaty in the Senate, called it "the wrong treaty on the wrong subject at the wrong time and with the wrong approach to the basic problem of how best to end the fighting in Vietnam...."

Consideration of the treaty was accompanied by one of the largest pressure campaigns in recent years. Conservative groups, in particular the very conservative Liberty Lobby, flooded both Senators and Representatives with mail urging defeat of the treaty. *(See box.)*

Senate adoption of the resolution consenting to the treaty's ratification came after eight days of debate during which six attempts to alter or modify the effects of the treaty were defeated. Each attempt was met by Administration objections that the change would have the effect of killing the treaty. All but one of the proposed

Lobbying Against Treaty

Consideration of the U.S.-Soviet Consular Convention was marked by one of the largest mail and pressure campaigns in recent years.

The intense "grassroots lobbying" campaign against the treaty was led by the ultra-conservative, Washington-based Liberty Lobby, an organization set up in 1955 "for the purpose of reversing the dangerous trend towards socialization internally and to defeat the insidious effort to weaken our resistance to international Communism."

Other conservative groups also working against the treaty were the Manion Forum, the Dan Smoot Report, the United Republicans of America, the National Review and the Mothers of American Servicemen of South Pasadena, Calif.

Senators complained that they were swamped by mail which was, to a large extent, generated by these organizations. Opposition to the treaty far outweighed support for it.

The Liberty Lobby used its large mailing list, claimed to be over 170,000, for its campaign. Much of the Liberty Lobby support was attributed to a 16-panel comic strip entitled, "The Communist Next Door." The comic strip was described by Liberty Lobby as "a new technique to reach the voters...clear, direct, motivational." The strip included such statements as: "The most obvious danger from the treaty is provision for 'diplomatic immunity'.... To give Soviet personnel complete immunity is to invite an increase in Red espionage...even sabotage...since the treaty forbids any inspection of any baggage or equipment brought in as 'diplomatic pouch'." The strip showed a conspirator assembling a suitcase-size A-bomb and ended with the appeal: "How about it folks? Help your two Senators by letting them know how you feel about the Soviet Consular Treaty. There isn't much time left, so write today." The appeal was so successful that even House Members, who do not vote on treaties, received numerous letters.

The Liberty Lobby also purchased advertising space in 27 newspapers around the country to reproduce the comic strip. At least 17 other papers carried the ad placed by other individuals or groups. The Liberty Lobby ads were placed in newspapers in states where at least one Senator was already opposed to the treaty or where there was a good possibility to swing an uncommitted vote, according to a Lobby spokesman. The ads appeared for the most part in newspapers in the traditionally conservative Midwest and the South. They also appeared in states or cities with large populations that have close ties to the so-called "captive" nations of Eastern Europe.

restrictions were defeated by more than a two-thirds majority. The sixth, voicing the 'hope' that no consulates would be established until the war in Vietnam had come to a peaceful end, was rejected by a narrower margin.

Provisions. As agreed to by the Senate, the Consular Convention:

*Key State Department Officials**

Listed below are key officials of the State Department who served during President Johnson's years in office. A number of the officials began their terms during President Kennedy's Administration; the dates given reflect this. Key officials who served in earlier years are listed in the table on pages 100-101 of *Congress and the Nation, Vol. I.*

Secretary of State	Dean Rusk (1/21/61-1/20/69) Charles E. Bohlen (acting) (1/20/69-1/22/69)
Under Secretary	George W. Ball (12/3/61-9/30/66) Nicholas deB. Katzenbach (9/30/66-11/8/68)
Under Secretaries for Economic Affairs-E Political Affairs-P	W. Averell Harriman-P (4/4/63-3/17/65) Thomas C. Mann-E (3/11/65-6/1/66) Eugene V. Rostow-P (10/13/66-1/20/69)
Deputy Under Secretary for Political Affairs	U. Alexis Johnson (4/27/61-6/25/64) Llewellyn Thompson (interim) U. Alexis Johnson (9/27/65-10/13/66) Foy D. Kohler (10/13/66-12/15/67) Charles E. Bohlen (12/15/67-1/22/69)
Deputy Under Secretary for Administration	William J. Crockett (6/4/63-1/28/67) Idar Rimestad (1/26/67-)
Assistant Secretary for Inter-American Affairs	Thomas C. Mann (12/21/63-3/11/65) Jack H. Vaughn (3/11/65-2/25/66) Lincoln Gordon (2/25/66-6/30/67) Robert M. Sayre (acting) Covey T. Oliver (6/9/67-12/31/68)
Assistant Secretary for European Affairs	William R. Tyler (8/20/62-4/26/65) Richard H. Davis (acting) John M. Leddy (6/4/65-)

Assistant Secretary for Far Eastern Affairs	William P. Bundy (3/10/64-)
Assistant Secretary for Near East and South Asian Affairs	Phillips Talbot (4/21/61-9/11/65) Raymond A. Hare (9/11/65-11/30/66) William J. Handley (acting) Lucius D. Battle (4/5/67-9/30/68) Parker T. Hart (10/4/68-)
Assistant Secretary for African Affairs	G. Mennen Williams (2/1/61-3/23/66) Joseph Palmer II (4/1/66-)
Assistant Secretary for Economic Affairs	G. Griffith Johnson (5/12/62-4/12/65) Anthony M. Solomon (acting) (5/18/65-1/10/69)
Assistant Secretary for International Organi- zation Affairs	Harlan Cleveland (2/20/61-9/1/65) Joseph J. Sisco (9/1/65-)
Assistant Secretary for Administration	Dwight J. Porter (10/1/63-)
Assistant Secretary for Congressional Relations	Frederick G. Dutton (1/30/62-7/27/64) Robert E. Lee (interim) John P. White (interim) Douglas McArthur II (3/11/65-4/5/67) William B. Macomber Jr. (3/2/67-)
Assistant Secretary for Educational and Cultural Affairs	Lucius D. Battle (6/5/62-8/7/64) Harry C. McPherson Jr. (8/7/64-9/1/65) David L. Osborn (acting) Charles Frankel (9/11/65-12/31/67) Edward D. Re (2/2/68-1/9/69)
Assistant Secretary for Public Affairs	James L. Greenfield (8/7/64-3/12/66) Dixon Donnelley (3/17/66-1/31/69)

The dates are complete through Feb. 1, 1969. The date of appointment carried above is the date of commission, a formal enscrolling signed by the President following Senate confirmation of his nomination. The date of departure is the date of effective resignation, a date specified by the appointee or a date of acceptance of the resignation by the President.

Regulated the consular affairs of each country in the territory of the other and the treatment to be accorded consular officials and employees, including: the status of a consular establishment, the duties and functions of consular officers, and the rights, privileges, and immunities of the consular personnel stationed in the territory of the other country.

Provided for the establishment of consulates and consular districts, by separate agreement and with the consent of the receiving state.

Provided that the head of a consular establishment be approved by the receiving state prior to appointment and that the name and function of all consular officers and employees be submitted in advance to the receiving state.

Provided that the receiving state may at any time and without explanation notify the sending state that any consular official was *persona non grata* or that any consular employee was unacceptable and have them withdrawn from the country.

Provided that except for staff members of the diplomatic mission (embassy) of the sending state, no national of the sending state may be appointed as consular officer or employee if he is already present in or in transit to the receiving state.

Provided that consular officers, and all consular employees that are nationals of the sending state, be afforded full diplomatic immunity including immunity from the criminal jurisdiction of the receiving state; provided that the immunity from criminal jurisdiction may be expressly waived by the sending state.

Provided that the convention may be terminated on six-month notice by either country.

Provided that consular officers would be subject to laws and regulations of the receiving state concerning zones, entry into which was prohibited or regulated for reasons of national security.

Provided that the receiving state would: in no way restrict a national's access to his consulate, inform a consular officer about the arrest or detention of a national of his country, and give full rights to the sending state to visit and communicate with a national who was under arrest or detention. Specifically provided (in a protocol that was part of the Convention) that notification of arrest be within 1-3 days, depending on conditions of communication, and that the consular officer be allowed to visit and communicate with a national under arrest or detention within 2-4 days, depending on location, and on a continuing basis thereafter.

Nuclear Nonproliferation Treaty

Although the consular convention was ratified, agreement was not reached on another important international agreement sought by the Johnson Administration—a treaty on the non-proliferation of nuclear weapons. Representatives of 17 nations met in Geneva, Switzerland, throughout the year on the treaty. They reported making progress but were unable to reach a final agreement. On Dec. 2, President Johnson stated that the United States would accept international inspection of all U.S. nuclear facilities except those of direct defense signifi-

cance. The United States in late 1967 had 16 civilian nuclear power plants and about 70 more on order or being built. Two of the existing plants had been inspected by the International Atomic Energy Agency (IAEA), a United Nations affiliate, and the President's offer presumably would open up the other plants to the IAEA. The statement was seen as an attempt to meet the objections of several non-nuclear countries to the proposed nonproliferation treaty. More than a dozen such nations had objected to proposals that would have imposed inspection upon them but not on the major nuclear nations. Britain Dec. 4 also agreed to accept international inspection of its nondefense nuclear facilities. *(For 1968 action, see p. 104.)*

Glassboro Conference

President Johnson and Russian Premier Alexei N. Kosygin June 23 and 25 met in Glassboro, N.J., to discuss major international issues. Neither side claimed major gains as a result of the 10 hours of meetings, but the sessions produced a new, although short-lived, feeling of international goodwill—christened the *"spirit of Hollybush"* because of the site of the talks *(see below)*. The two men termed the meetings "useful," agreed to meet again sometime, and asked their foreign policy spokesmen to continue the talks.

Secretary of State Dean Rusk and Foreign Minister Andrei A. Gromyko June 27 met in New York. They concentrated on a treaty to limit the spread of nuclear weapons, the subject on which Mr. Johnson and Kosygin were reported to have made the most headway during the Glassboro meetings.

The impromptu summit conference came near the end of a nine-day visit by Premier Kosygin to the United States to present his country's views on a new crisis in the Middle East to the United Nations. Both the nature of the meeting and the meeting site had been in dispute. The talks were held without a fixed agenda. The meeting site, the "Hollybush" home of the president of Glassboro State College was selected because it allowed Mr. Johnson and Mr. Kosygin to meet about halfway between the United Nations and the White House.

The meeting between Mr. Johnson and Mr. Kosygin, the Soviet head of state as Chairman of the Council of Ministers, was the eighth meeting between leaders of the two countries since the United States recognized the Soviet Union in 1933. It was the fourth meeting since the end of World War II between the heads of the two governments. The last time the leaders of the two nations met was in 1961 when President Kennedy and Premier Nikita S. Khrushchev met June 3-4 in Vienna. *(Congress and the Nation, Vol. I, p. 130.)*

The first session at Glassboro lasted more than five hours and ranged over the Middle East, Vietnam and the nonproliferation of nuclear arms. The leaders agreed it was "very important" to reach an international accord against the spread of nuclear weapons. They agreed to meet again two days later and to let Rusk and Gromyko continue the talks after the summit meeting.

After the second meeting Sunday, the officials separated and announced progress on the nonproliferation pact but each acknowledged that vast differences still existed over Vietnam in the Middle East.

Outer Space Treaty

A second major agreement between the United States and the Soviet Union occurred a little more than a month after Senate approval of the consular treaty. On April 25, the Senate gave its unanimous consent to the ratification by the President of a treaty governing the peaceful exploration and use of outer space (Exec. D, 90th Congress, 1st Session). The resolution of ratification was adopted by an 88-0 roll-call vote.

The United States, the United Kingdom and the Soviet Union signed the treaty Jan. 27, 1967, with 57 other countries. Although 80 states had signed by April, France was not among them.

The treaty went into force Oct. 10 when 13 nations deposited notices of ratification in a White House ceremony.

The treaty, beside establishing general principles for the peaceful international exploration and use of outer space (including the moon and other celestial bodies), contained provisions for arms control in outer space, suspension of claims of national ownership or sovereignty, and the protection of astronauts.

A key provision of the treaty obliged signatory nations not to station in space or place into orbit any object carrying nuclear or other weapons of mass destruction (such as chemical or biological devices). The same provision also prohibited weapons testing and military bases, fortifications and maneuvers on celestial bodies.

To verify the peaceful use of space the treaty provided for the right to inspect installations and space vehicles on the moon and on other celestial bodies. Controversy focused on the fact that the inspection provisions did not apply to orbiting objects. This major objection was apparently overcome by statements by U.S. military leaders that they saw no danger to national security in the treaty and that they preferred to rely on military detection systems rather than grant other nations inspection rights and access to U.S. spacecraft.

Provisions. As agreed to by the Senate, the treaty on outer space, including the moon and celestial bodies:

Assured all nations a share in the benefits of space exploration without regard to their economic or scientific development, free access to all areas of celestial bodies, and freedom of scientific investigation in space.

Endorsed international cooperation in such investigations.

Outlawed claims of national sovereignty in outer space.

Delcared that activities in space must accord with international law and be in the interest of maintaining international peace and security.

Outlawed all vehicles carrying nuclear weapons or other kinds of weapons of mass destruction in outer space, and military bases, weapons testing or military maneuvers on celestial bodies.

Required that all stations, installations, equipment and space vehicles on celestial bodies—but not in orbit—be open to other states for inspection on a basis of reciprocity, given reasonable advance notice.

Permitted the use of military personnel for scientific research and other peaceful purposes, and the use of any equipment or facility necessary for peaceful exploration.

Assured prompt assistance to and safe return of astronauts who accidentally land in another state or on the high seas and prompt notification to the United Nations of the discovery of conditions in space hazardous to astronauts.

Made signatories internationally liable for damage that their space activities might cause.

Specified that nations retain ownership and jurisdiction of objects and personnel in space.

Outlined procedures to limit the possibility of space experiments that might cause harmful contamination and adverse changes in the earth's environment.

Permitted withdrawal from the treaty upon one-year's notice, provided the treaty had been in force for one year.

U.S. Troops in Europe

The increasingly serious problem of disunity in the Atlantic Alliance was reflected in a Senate examination in 1967 of the American commitment in Europe under the North Atlantic Treaty Organization (NATO). A primary source of difficulty was France's decision, announced in 1966, to withdraw from the integrated military structure of the alliance and to require removal of alliance forces and institutions from her soil. France's action coincided with growing economic difficulties in England and Germany, thereby straining their resources, and the rising costs of the Vietnam war to the United States. Considerable support for the Senate's 1967 review of European commitments came from Senators who believed that a reduction in U.S. troop strength there would ease the extra costs and manpower needs created by the Vietnam war.

Senate Majority Leader Mike Mansfield (D Mont.) March 1 was named chairman of a special Senate committee to study the commitment and possible adjustments in the size of the American forces in Europe. The special committee included six members of the Senate Foreign Relations Committee: Mansfield, Fulbright (D Ark.), Sparkman (D Ala.), Church (D Idaho), Hickenlooper (R Iowa), and Aiken (R Vt.). It also included five from the Armed Services Committee: Stennis (D Miss.), Symington (D Mo.), Jackson (D Wash.), Miller (R Iowa) and Pearson (R Kan.). The special committee considered two major proposals (S Res 49 and S Res 83), both of which would have amended S Res 99, adopted by the Senate in 1951, which approved a "fair share" American contribution to ground forces for the defense of NATO in Europe. S Res 49 declared the sense of the Senate that improved warfare techniques, including the United States' capacity to move forces quickly by air, permitted a "substantial reduction" of American troops in Europe. The resolution noted the increased European prosperity, the failure of other NATO members to contribute "men and materials on a fair and equitable basis," the relaxation of East-West tensions and the financial burdens on the United States in maintaining large numbers of troops in Europe. S Res 83 declared it the sense of the Senate that the United States continue to maintain "substantial and effective combat forces in Europe to meet any continuing military threat," and that European NATO members be urged to increase their contributions. It said any adjustments of U.S. forces in NATO should be left to allied consultation. The special committee April 26 and May 3 held closed hearings on the resolutions. Various Administration officials appeared, including Secretary of State Dean Rusk and Secretary of Defense Robert S. McNamara.

Middle East War

The perpetual Middle East tension developed into a major war June 5 between Israel and the Arab states. It was the third war in two decades involving Israel and her neighbors. Although the six-day war ended with a United Nations-sponsored cease fire June 10, periodic clashes continued throughout the remainder of the year. The Arab nations involved were Egypt, Jordan and Syria. Israel destroyed a substantial part of the armed forces of the other nations and captured large amounts of territory which she continued to occupy throughout 1967 and 1968. An emergency session of the UN General Assembly, called to consider the Middle East crisis, led to the U.S. visit of Soviet Premier Alexei N. Kosygin and his subsequent conferences with President Johnson in Glassboro, N.J., June 23-25. *(See p. 91.)*

Background To War. Arab-Israeli tensions increased in the first five months of the year from terrorist raids and retaliatory actions along common borders. The United Arab Republic and Syria massed troops on the borders of Israel May 14-20 and Saudi Arabian troops took up positions near the Jordanian port of Aqaba May 24. U.A.R. President Gamal Abdel Nasser May 18 demanded the withdrawal of the UN Emergency Force (UNEF) from the border of the U.A.R. and Israel, where it had been stationed as a peace-keeping force since March 1957. UN Secretary General U Thant complied immediately. He was criticized for doing so by numerous Members of Congress and others who considered the action unnecessarily precipitate. Thant declared, however, that UNEF was there only with the consent of the Egyptian Government. He also said that about half the force was comprised of Yugoslavs and Indians whose governments would have withdrawn them had he not acted at once.

Nasser May 22 declared the Gulf of Aqaba closed to Israeli ships and ships of other nations bound for Israel. President Johnson May 23 said the United States supported the maintenance of the Gulf as an international waterway, and Israel May 24 called the blockade an "armed attack." Egypt placed mines in the Strait of Tiran, a four-mile wide entrance to the Gulf of Aqaba in order to block Israeli shipping in the Gulf.

Nasser May 27 called for a "holy war" against Israel, and on May 30 Egypt and Jordan, in a surprise move, signed a five-year mutual defense pact against Israel. Iraq joined the treaty June 4. The war began on the following day.

Hostilities. Both sides charged that the other started the war. However, observers in Washington, D.C., believed the evidence indicated that Israel had launched the initial attack. Israeli planes in their first attack destroyed the bulk of the Egyptian air force while it was still on the ground. Israel late June 7 claimed complete defeat of the United Arab Republic. In the first 48 hours of combat, Israel destroyed 410 Arab planes and was believed to have destroyed the better part of the Arab armies. By June 11, Israel had:

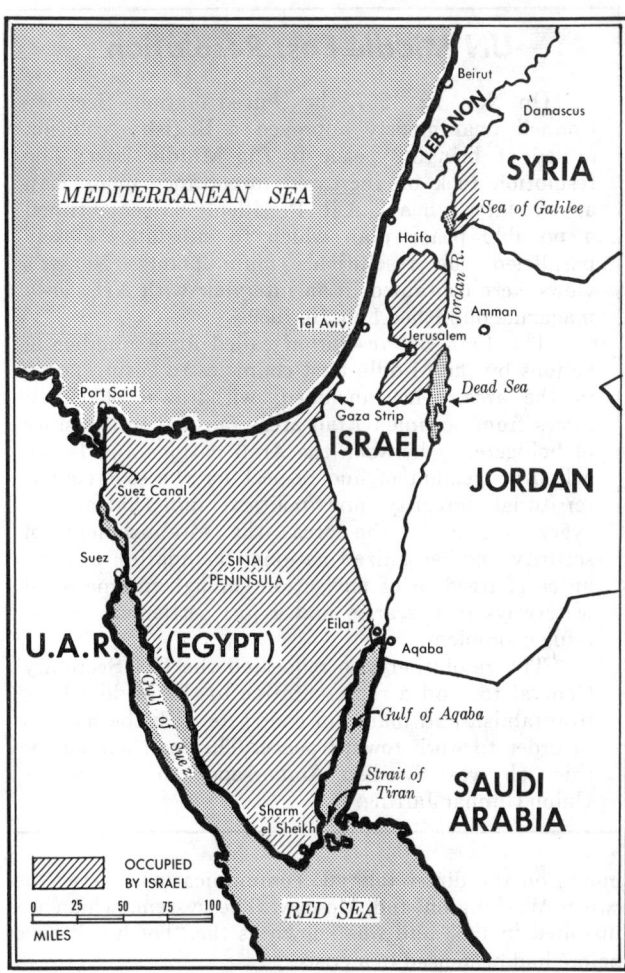

• Conquered all of Egypt's Sinai Peninsula and Gaza Strip, reaching the east bank of the Suez Canal (which Egypt later closed and did not reopen) and seizing Sharm El Sheikh to break the U.A.R. blockade of the Gulf of Aqaba.

• Captured the Old City of Jerusalem, occupied by Jordan since the 1948-49 Arab-Israeli war, and all Jordanian territory adjoining Israel west of the Jordan River.

• Driven 12 miles into Syria, seizing strategic heights from which Syrian guns for years had shelled Israeli settlements in northern Galilee.

Israeli casualties in the war totaled 679 killed and 2,563 wounded. Virtually all of the U.A.R.'s armor and air force was destroyed or captured and Egypt suffered thousands of casualties. (Nasser confirmed Nov. 23 that 80 percent of Egypt's military equipment had been destroyed, 10,000 soldiers and 1,500 officers had been killed and 5,000 soldiers and 500 officers had been captured). Jordanian casualties also numbered in the thousands; only Syria's losses were light.

Liberty Attacked, "Hot Line" Used. Israeli planes and naval vessels June 8 attacked the U.S. Navy communications ship Liberty about 15 miles off the Gaza Strip. American carrier-based aircraft went to the assistance of the Liberty. To prevent Soviet misunderstanding of the military moves in the Mediterranean, the White House immediately notified Moscow of the develop-

UN Middle East Resolution

On Nov. 22, 1967, the United Nations Security Council unanimously approved a British resolution aimed at bringing peace to the Middle East. The resolution took on increased importance more than a year later when U.A.R. President Nasser outlined a possible peace plan which in substance closely paralleled the resolution's main points. Nasser's views were contained in an interview with *Newsweek* magazine published Feb. 10, 1969.

The 1967 UN resolution called for a number of actions by the Middle East countries to ensure peace in the area. They included: withdrawal of Israeli forces from occupied Arab areas; an end to the state of belligerency between the Arab nations and Israel; acknowledgement of and respect for the sovereignty, territorial integrity and political independence of every nation in the area; the establishment of security and recognized national boundaries; a guarantee of freedom of navigation through international waterways in the area; and a just settlement of the refugee problem.

The resolution also requested the UN Secretary General to send a representative to the Middle East to establish and maintain contracts with the nations in order to work toward peace. The man named for this job was Swedish Ambassador to the Soviet Union Gunnar Jarring.

ments on the direct teletype communications system between Washington and Moscow. The system, which was installed in 1963 and was known as the "hot line," never before had been used in a crisis.

U.S. "Neutrality." A few hours after war broke out early June 5, Robert J. McCloskey, deputy assistant secretary of state for public affairs, declared that the U.S. position was "neutral in thought, word and deed." The McCloskey statement was criticized by Members of Congress and others who pointed to U.S. ties with Israel. Later June 5, George Christian, Presidential press secretary, said the McCloskey statement was "not a formal declaration of neutrality." And, at a late afternoon news conference at the White House Secretary of State Dean Rusk June 5 said the term "neutral" in international law expressed the fact that the United States was not a belligerent. He said it was not "an expression of indifference."

Cease-Fire. After 36 hours of behind-the-scenes negotiations, the UN Security Council June 6 unanimously adopted a resolution calling for a cease-fire.

On June 7, the Security Council adopted unanimously a Russian-proposed resolution that the time for the cease-fire be set at 4 p.m. that day, New York City time. Israel said it would accept the cease-fire if the Arab nations did. Jordan accepted the truce June 7, Egypt accepted it June 8 and Syria agreed early June 9. However, Israel and Syria continued to battle into June 10.

Johnson Formula. President Johnson June 19 laid down a five-point formula for peace in the Middle East. It was his first major statement of U.S. policy on the area since the Middle East war broke out June 5.

Speaking at a Foreign Policy Conference for Educators at the State Department, the President called for: (1) the right of every nation in the Middle East "to live and to have this right respected by its neighbors"; (2) justice for war refugees; (3) freedom of innocent maritime passage; (4) limitation of the arms race and military shipments to nations in the area; and (5) "respect for political independence and territorial integrity of all the states in the area."

Mr. Johnson said the the victorious Israeli troops "must be withdrawn." But he made it clear he would not press for a withdrawal to prewar lines in every respect.

Middle East Water Plan

A Republican-sponsored proposal to provide U.S. assistance in constructing three large nuclear-fueled water desalting plants in the Middle East was endorsed Nov. 17 by a State Department spokesman at a closed session of the Senate Foreign Relations Committee. The testimony was released Dec. 2 by the Committee. In favoring the proposal, which first was put forth in 1957 by former President Eisenhower, the State Department modified its previous position that the plan was "premature," pending the resolution of major disputes between Israel and the Arab nations.

Plan. The desalting plant proposal, reportedly drawn up for Mr. Eisenhower by former Atomic Energy Commission Chairman Lewis L. Strauss, was seen by its proponents as a method of easing political tensions in the Middle East by providing ample water supplies for the arid region through international cooperation. Under Eisenhower's proposal, an international corporation would be established to construct the desalting plants. Specific locations for the three plants were not suggested. The International Atomic Energy Agency would operate the facilities.

Action. The Senate Foreign Relations Committee Oct. 19-20 held public hearings on the proposal, which was contained in a "sense-of-the-Senate" resolution (S Res 155) introduced Aug. 14 by Sen. Howard H. Baker Jr. (R Tenn.) and 52 cosponsors. The State Department at these hearings indicated a lack of enthusiasm for the project because of the unsettled conditions in the Middle East. Despite the Nov. 17 policy shift by the State Department, the Committee did not report S Res 155 in 1967.

Trade Developments

International trade became a major issue in 1967 when, after three years of fruitless efforts, the United States and 52 other countries concluded the Kennedy Round of tariff-cutting negotiations. The successful negotiations were one of the most significant efforts in modern times toward international trade liberalization. The Administration hailed the agreements as opening broad new vistas for U.S. exports, but several major American industries took a different view of the matter. They saw the tariff cuts as a threat because of increased competition from low-cost imports from foreign countries. Consequently, they undertook a powerful drive to pressure Congress for protective legislation. Their drive, opposed by the Administration, was marked by intensive lobbying and succeeded in obtaining widespread legislative support. Largely because of the threat of a Presidential veto, however, none of their bills was approved in 1967.

The protectionist thrust, led by the steel, chemical, textile and oil industries, took varying approaches to counter the effects of the Kennedy Round. The chemical industry attempted to secure support against a Kennedy Round legislative proposal to repeal a special U.S. tariff-valuation procedure called the American Selling Price (ASP) which resulted in higher tariffs on certain chemical imports. Most other industries sought to meet the threat of increased imports through bills to impose quotas on imports of numerous products ranging from oil, steel and textiles to mink skins, meat, strawberries and baseball gloves.

The Kennedy Round, which precipitated the 1967 protectionist debate, resulted from the 1962 Trade Expansion Act and was named for President John F. Kennedy, who pushed the Trade Act through Congress. The 1962 Act authorized the President to cut U.S. tariffs by as much as 50 percent in return for appropriate foreign concessions on tariffs and other trade matters. The legislation required that the negotiations end before June 30, 1967, when the tariff-cutting authority granted the President was to expire.

After difficult bargaining, which often appeared headed for a complete stalemate, agreement finally was reached on May 15, 1967. The final accord reduced duties an average of about 35 percent on some 60,000 items representing an estimated $40 billion in world trade (based on 1964 figures—the base period for the Kennedy Round negotiations). Other terms included a U.S. agreement to seek Congressional repeal of the ASP and to grant additional tariff reductions on about $40 billion in world trade (based on 1964 figures—the base year for the negotiations.) In the industrial sector, the United States and the other participants agreed on cuts averaging about 35 percent, but in agriculture the reductions were less substantial. Other terms of the agreement included a U.S. commitment to seek repeal of the ASP and to grant additional tariff reductions on chemicals in return for further tariff cuts by the Common Market and other countries. In addition, other countries agreed to the U.S. requests for a new international grains arrangement guaranteeing a higher minimum price on wheat and the extension of the cotton textile import agreement which President Kennedy worked out in 1962 in order to help secure passage of the Trade Expansion Act.

Congressional Action. Two major parts of the U.S. agreement in the Kennedy Round required legislation—the new international grains agreement and the repeal of the ASP on chemicals. The grains agreement—which constituted a treaty—required ratification by the Senate. The ASP legislation, as a tariff measure, had to originate in the House Ways and Means Committee and win the approval of both chambers of Congress.

The Administration also said it would propose two other trade measures in 1967. One proposal envisioned new Presidential bargaining authority for "housekeeping" trade negotiations and to explore further liberalization of trade policy in such areas as nontariff barriers. The other would involve liberalization of the 1962 Act's terms under which U.S. firms and employees could obtain relief from economic injuries resulting from increased imports. Existing law required that an injured firm prove to the U.S. Tariff Commission that growing imports were the major cause of injury. This had been so difficult to substantiate that no awards were made from 1962 to 1967 although 20 applications had been made.

Largely because of the growing protectionist sentiment in Congress, however, the Administration did not submit its trade package during the 1967 session. It was widely believed that the protectionists might have the strength to defeat the measure altogether or use it as a vehicle to attach their quotas bills. (In 1968, the Senate approved a new grains treaty but legislation to repeal the ASP was not enacted. *See p. 112 and 113.*)

Congress in 1967 acted on several measures which the Johnson Administration viewed as protectionist. One was a bill dealing with low-wage imports and another was a bill revising cotton quotas. *See separate stories, below.*)

A protectionist effort early in the year occurred in the Senate April 19, during consideration of the investment tax bill (HR 6950). By a 55-19 roll-call vote, the Senate accepted an amendment by George S. McGovern (D.S.D.) to stiffen and broaden import quotas on beef, mutton, veal and lamb. The amendment later was dropped during complicated Senate maneuvering on the tax bill. The Senate Interior and Insular Affairs Committee May 4 reported a bill (S 289) providing quotas on lead and zinc imports, but no further action took place in 1967.

Another action came during consideration of the Defense Department appropriations bill (HR 10738) for fiscal 1968. The House June 13, by a 119-61 standing vote accepted an Administration-opposed amendment prohibiting construction in foreign shipyards of any Navy vessel funded under the bill. The amendment, deleted by the Senate, was reaffirmed by the House Sept. 12 on a 145-232 roll call rejecting a motion to concur in the Senate's action. The Senate Sept. 13 grudgingly accepted the amendment by a roll-call vote of 49-29. The amendment—aimed at preventing Britain from bidding on the construction of seven Navy minesweepers—was widely criticized as a protectionist measure which would endanger relations between the United States and Britain.

Low-Wage Imports

One of the protectionist bills considered by Congress in 1967 was HR 478, a measure which required investigation of charges that low-wage imports were detrimental to competing U.S. industries. The House passed the bill Sept. 28 by a 340-29 roll-call vote but the Senate did not act. (The Senate did not act in 1968 either and HR 478 died with the end of the 90th Congress.)

The Department of Labor opposed the legislation on the basis that it already had discretionary authority to conduct investigations on the effect of imports. A Department official, after House passage, said the agency opposed the provisions making investigation of all complaints mandatory. During hearings on the bill, chief U.S. Kennedy Round negotiator William M. Roth said the bill might bring retaliatory restrictions from other nations.

HR 478 amended the Fair Labor Standards (minimum wage) Act to allow various individuals or groups to ask the Secretary of Labor to investigate whether imports from areas of the world with low wages and long working hours were hurting American workers by capturing U.S. markets through lower prices. The Secretary was required to investigate and report his findings to the President. The President was authorized—but not required—to limit the imports through such customs actions as higher tariffs and quotas. The President already had these powers under existing law.

The bill was supported by many labor and business groups. It was opposed by the Committee for a National Trade Policy which included on its board of directors high officials from a number of the nation's largest corporations. The bill, introduced by John H. Dent (D Pa.), was the subject of lengthy hearings in previous years.

U.A.R. Cotton Quota

Another protectionist bill which Congress considered in 1967 resulted in part from the Middle East war and involved U.S. relations with Arab states. HR 10915, passed Oct. 30 by the House by a 276-63 roll-call vote, removed the extra-long staple cotton quota from Egypt and the Sudan and transferred it to American producers. The Senate did not act on the bill. The Senate did pass HR 10915 in 1968, but President Johnson vetoed it. *(See p. 113.)*

In its major provision, HR 10915 reduced the global quota on extra-long staple cotton by the amount of average annual imports during 1961-66 from nations which severed diplomatic relations with the United States during the year prior to enactment. This affected only the United Arab Republic (Egypt) and the Sudan, which broke relations at the time of the Middle East war. The reduction was to be permanent. The House rejected amendments to give the President discretionary authority to change the quota to meet future circumstances.

The thrust of the bill was to reduce the quota by about 56,500 bales (67 percent), thus permitting domestic producers (mainly in west Texas, New Mexico, Arizona, and California) to increase greatly their current output of 70,000 bales a year. Members of Congress from Southwestern states had pushed similar legislation in previous years to permit producers in their areas to increase production. The Administration strongly opposed HR 10915.

East-West Trade—Eximbank

A bill to provide a routine extension of the life of the Export-Import Bank (Eximbank) became embroiled in Congressional controversy over trade between Eastern European countries and the Western Alliance. (The same bill also was involved in controversy over sales of arms to less-developed nations. *See p. 85.*)

The two issues becames so controversial that final action on the bill (S 1155, HR 6649) was put over until the 1968 session. *(For 1968 action, see p. 111.)*

The Export-Import Bank was established in 1934 as a banking corporation and in 1945 was made an independent agency of the U.S. Government. Its purpose was to provide financial aid to promote U.S. exports. Its current authority ran until June 30, 1968.

The Senate acted on the legislation in August, and added several highly restrictive amendments to curtail the Eximbank's authority to continue arms sales credit programs and to finance exports to any country that traded with North Vietnam.

The House Banking and Currency Committee had reported the Eximbank extension bill in May, but then had delayed floor action after the arms sales issue had become highly controversial in the early summer. It reopened hearings for a day in July to hear the Administration's defense of its arms sales program. Then, after the Senate had acted on the Eximbank bill in mid-August, the Committee held one more day of hearings in September to hear Administration officials plead for deletion of the Senate East-West trade amendments.

In a closed session Nov. 2, the House Committee voted to adopt an arms sales amendment similar to the one added by the Senate, and an East-West trade rider that was substantially milder than the Senate version. Late in November, the House Rules Committee voted to grant a rule for floor action to the bill, thus clearing it for floor action early in 1968.

East-West Trade Issue. As reported to the Senate, S 1155 included the Administration-requested five-year extension of the Eximbank and an increase in the Bank's lending authority. It also contained Committee-added amendments restricting the Bank's involvement in arms sales to developing countries and stating Congressional policy that the Bank should not assist U.S. exports to Communist countries unless the President found such assistance in the national interest. The Communist bloc trade provision was at least in part a result of a 1966 announcement that the Eximbank was to loan about $50 million to Italy which would be used to buy U.S. machine tools for use in a plant which was to be built by the FIAT auto company in the Soviet Union. *(See box p. 97.)*

When S 1155 reached the Senate floor the Senate voted 56-26 to accept an amendment by Harry F. Byrd Jr. (D Va.) to prohibit the Bank from financing purchases by nations engaged in armed conflict with the U.S. or purchases by any other country that traded with such belligerent nations. It also adopted by voice vote an amendment specifically prohibiting the FIAT transaction.

Before the Senate acted on S 1155 the House Banking and Currency Committee had reported its companion (HR 6649) without major change. After the Senate passed its amended bill, Administration witnesses appeared before the House Banking and Currency Committee to testify against the Senate amendments. They said the amendments would neither block financing by other nations of the FIAT plant nor affect trading by other nations with North Vietnam, but would severely cut U.S. exports to European nations that had only minor contact with North Vietnam and further damage the shaky U.S. balance-of-payments position. The East-West trade amendment adopted by the Committee Nov. 2 was milder than the Senate's Byrd amendment. It prohibited

FIAT Deal Sparked East-West Trade Controversy

A key element in the controversy surrounding the proposal to extend the authority of the Export-Import Bank (Eximbank) was the plan for the Bank to participate in the financing of a joint Italian-Soviet FIAT automobile plant to be built in the Soviet Union. The issue arose Oct. 7, 1966, when President Johnson announced that the Eximbank was prepared to guarantee Italian credit for purchase of American machine tools to be used in the plant.

In what was the largest East-West trade deal ever undertaken, the FIAT motor company of Italy had agreed to build an $800-million automobile plant in the Soviet Union which would have an annual capacity of 600,000 automobiles. Of this sum, about $350 million was to be spent to buy machinery in the West. About $50 million was planned for direct purchases of automotive machine tools from the United States and a further sum was to be spent on purchases from European firms operating under license arrangements with U.S. companies.

The plans called for the Eximbank to make loans to the Instituto Mobiliare Italiano, an Italian financial institution, and for FIAT then to use the funds to buy the U.S. equipment.

Previous East-West Trade Proposals. The FIAT plan was one of the President's efforts to "build bridges" to Eastern Europe by increasing trade in nonstrategic goods between the United States and Communist countries. When it ran into trouble in Congress in 1967, it followed the route of most of Mr. Johnson's other East-West trade proposals. The major legislative part of the program, the East-West Trade Relations Act of 1966, had been so unpopular in Congress it did not get hearings.

Since 1963, Congress had annually barred the Eximbank from guaranteeing the credit of Communist nations for the purchase of U.S. goods and services unless the President made an express finding that it would be in the national interest. President Johnson made two such findings in 1964, affecting Yugoslavia and Romania. And in 1966, he allowed the Eximbank to guarantee the credit of Poland, Hungary, Bulgaria and Czechoslovakia.

House Republicans late in 1966 led a drive to curtail the Eximbank's ability to carry out the President's plan to guarantee credit to the four Eastern European countries named in 1966. In coalition with Southern Democrats, they succeeded in adding an amendment to the House version of the fiscal 1967 Supplemental Appropriations bill (HR 18381—Pl 89-697) flatly prohibiting the Bank from guaranteeing the credit of any Communist nation. Ultimately, the Senate insisted on its softer version, containing the traditional Presidential waiver. *(See p. 77.)*

FIAT Report. The question of the Eximbank financing of U.S. exports for the FIAT plant did not come under attack until 1967 when the extension bill came up. Prior to that, four 1966 members of the House Banking and Currency Committee March 1, 1967, issued a report for the Committee's International Trade Subcommittee on the proposed auto plant. They said they saw no reason to object to the Eximbank's participation in the plan. Three were members of the Subcommittee (composed of 12 members): Thomas L. Ashley (D Ohio), chairman, Chester L. Mize, (R Kan.) and Thomas M. Rees (D Calif). The fourth, James Harvey (R. Mich.), was a member of the full Committee at the time. Only the four participated in the study; they visited Italy, the Soviet Union and other countries during December 1966. The Banking and Currency Committee oversees the Export Control Act and Eximbank operations.

The report included a CIA study of present and future prospects for Soviet automotive capabilities and goals. Although the CIA report was cautious about concluding that there were signs of any abrupt change in Soviet economic goals, the House study said, "we would not underestimate the impact of installation of an auto assembly plant which by itself is capable of quadrupling current Soviet passenger automobile production."

The report said that the Italians, as early as 1962, had discussed the possiblity of U.S. participation with President Kennedy and said that they had been encouraged to pursue such a deal on the theory that increased automotive production might switch some Soviet economic resources toward consumer goods industries.

1967 Congressional Action. During floor action on the Eximbank extension bill, the Senate added an amendment specifically blocking the FIAT deal. The House Banking and Currency Committee in November adopted an amendment that would ban the deal, although the amendment gave "appropriate committees" discretionary authority to waive the ban. *(See accompanying story.)*

Late in 1967 the Instituto Mobiliare Italiano said that some credit and machine tools were being procured from non-U.S. sources. But plans still called for expenditure of about $30 million in the United States, whether or not Eximbank credit was made available, the organization said.

Eximbank credits only to North Vietnam and its active allies in the Communist bloc, and contained a clause allowing "appropriate committees of the House and Senate to waive the prohibition. However, the FIAT deal was blocked by a clause of the amendment which barred Eximbank credits for goods destined to be used by Communist countries.

Food For India

For the second time in two years, Congress enacted legislation (HJ Res 267—PL 90-7) to support emergency food assistance to famine-threatened India. A similar action was taken in 1966 after the poorest monsoon rains in a century caused a large reduction in India's food grain production. Widespread crop failure threatened famine in many areas. An emergency food program from the United States and other nations prevented this. *(See p. 72.)* However, in 1966-67 India suffered its second year of drought which again cut that nation's crop production and necessitated further outside help in 1967. Responding to this need, Congress enacted HJ Res 267 which had been requested by President Johnson to obtain special Congressional approval of authority he already had under existing law to give such aid. The resolution approved U.S. participation in efforts by multilateral organizations to supply India with food grains. The bill recommended that up to 3 million tons of food grain be provided by the United States to India in 1967 provided this amount was matched by contributions from other nations. The cost of the grain was estimated at $190 million. (Total U.S. contributions in 1967 were estimated at 6.6 million tons, but this figure included existing commitments for grain shipments. H J Res 267 also recommended an additional $25 million of emergency food relief for distribution through CARE and other American voluntary agencies. Both the food grain and relief program aid were to be provided under the PL 480 (Food for Peace) law. Nothing in the resolution changed or affected existing law in any way.

Sea Safety Treaty

The Senate by a unanimous vote (88-0) consented to the ratification by the President of a series of amendments (Exec. E, 90th Congress, 1st Session) to the 1960 International Convention for the Safety of Life at Sea (SOLAS). The amendments tightened the international safety standards for vessels on the high seas. The purpose of the amendments was to improve the fire protection of passenger ships. They eliminated from the SOLAS conventions the so-called grandfather clauses which permitted ships already in service to continue as they were with little or no safety improvements. They also eliminated from international passenger trade those vessels with considerable wood in them, required that all basic ship structure be of steel, and required fire barriers and steel bulkheads between passenger accommodations and dangerous areas of a ship. The President said the SOLAS amendments complemented U.S. legislation (PL 89-777) enacted in 1966 establishing higher standards for passenger ships sailing to and from U.S. ports. *(See transportation chapter.)*

Narcotics Treaty

The Senate consented by an 84-0 roll-call vote without debate to ratification by the President of a 1961 Convention on Narcotic Drugs (Exec. G, 90th Congress, 1st Session.) The Convention was designed to simplify international narcotic control machinery and to provide additional controls on such drugs. It terminated and replaced the provisions of eight multilateral treaties. Formulated at a United Nations Conference in 1961, it had been signed by 64 countries, not including the

United States. The main reason the U.S. had not signed was because the Convention permitted any country to produce and export up to five tons of opium and it was feared that this would encourage the illicit drug traffic. It was also feared that the Convention's provisions permitting reservations by countries participating could have crippled the narcotic control procedures it contained. However, the Department of State concluded that neither of these concerns had materialized and said the "national and international interest in drug control will be significantly advanced" by U.S. accession.

The 1961 Convention provided for the control of narcotic drugs ranging from production, sale and distribution to medical treatment, care and rehabilitation of addicts. It also limited production, manufacture and sales of such drugs to medical and scientific needs.

Latin American Summit Meeting

A summit meeting of American leaders, including President Johnson, was held at Punta del Este, Uruguay, April 12-14. It was the first such meeting since July 1956 and only the second in the history of the American Republics. But, it was a meeting which indirectly increased the already extensive enmity between the White House and the U.S. Senate Foreign Relations Committee. This occurred when the Committee refused to make an advance commitment, requested by President Johnson, to increase Latin American aid. *(See following story.)*

At the close of the Punta del Este conference, the American chiefs of state formally adopted the final Declaration of the Presidents of America outlining a plan of action for Latin American development.

The final Declaration was signed by all the heads of delegations except the interim-president of Ecuador, Otto Arosemena Gomez, who called U.S. promises of aid "inadequate" and said that the Declaration was "incomplete" and should have set "clearer and more practical procedures."

The principal result of the conference stated in the Declaration was an agreement to create, beginning in 1970, a Latin American Common Market with a target date for the market to be in "substantial operation" by 1985. The document also outlined plans for laying the physical foundations for Latin American integration with U.S. help through multinational projects, especially the building of "infrastructure" such as a land transportation network, a telecommunications system and interconnected power systems. Increased Latin American foreign trade and other social, economic and technological steps to help Latin American development were also spelled out as goals of the Latin American countries.

The main goals of the common market would be the lowering of tariffs among the member countries and, eventually, free labor and capital movement among the members and a common currency.

President Johnson, in a statement April 14 on the conference, said that "the first phase of the Alliance (for Progress) has been a success by any realistic standard" and that the "second phase is now under way." He said that the second phase would "cut to the heart of the problem—the modernization of over-protected Latin

American industry, under-financed Latin American agriculture and education." *(See p. 108-109.)*

Latin American Aid

The Latin American summit meeting *(see preceding story)* caused a sharp exchange between the White House and the U.S. Senate Foreign Relations Committee. It occurred when the Committee refused to make an advance commitment to increase Latin American aid. President Johnson had asked Congress to pass a resolution approving a commitment to a substantial aid increase prior to his departure for the summit meeting in Uruguay. The House passed a modified resolution which nevertheless provided the substance of what the President wanted. In the Senate, however, the Foreign Relations Committee balked at granting what it considered extremely broad authority without many specifics. Instead, it reported out a resolution with language so weak that it was considered useless by the Administration, whose strategists then decided not to press for a more favorable bill on the Senate floor. The Committee's attitude was not surprising. It had been waging a public battle with President Johnson ever since he used the broad and unspecific language of the Gulf of Tonkin resolution, enacted in 1964, to escalate the American involvement in the Vietnam conflict and commit the United States to fight a major war in Asia—and all without a specifi. grant of authority to wage war from Congress. The Committee and its supporters were no longer interested in general grants of authority to a President; they were, in fact, looking in the other direction by 1967 and seeking ways to contract the United States' commitments abroad and to prevent future Presidents from acting in what they considered the precipitous manner of Lyndon Johnson.

The President March 13, in a special message to Congress, had outlined the objectives and needs of the Alliance for Progress, which was established in 1961 as a broad cooperative program for economic and social development in Latin America. He estimated that about $1.5 billion above the existing level of U.S. support would be needed over five years to aid improvements in agriculture, health and education, to help create a Latin American Common Market and to increase the resources of the Fund for Special Operations (FSO) of the Inter-American Development Bank. The FSO provided "soft" loans for development projects. Mr. Johnson's request to Congress to "approve a commitment" to increase aid to Latin America was seen as a move to strengthen his hand at the Punta del Este conference. The Foreign Relations Committee said that there were "constitutional pitfalls" in the resolution requested by the President. It reported out a resolution of its own (SJ Res 60) welcoming the forthcoming meeting. The resolution said that as the Alliance for Progress reached agreement on how to achieve its objectives the United States should give "due consideration to co-operating" in the agreements and that funds should be authorized "in keeping with constitutional processes." A high White House official labeled the Committee's resolution "worse than useless" and that ended the matter: the President went to Uruguay without the desired Congressional endorsement.

Inter-American Development Bank

Congress passed an Administration bill (HR 9547—PL 90-88) authorizing a $900 million increase in the U.S. contribution to the Fund for Special Operations (FSO) of the Inter-American Development Bank. The contribution was to be made in annual payments of $300 million in fiscal years 1968-70. The sum represented the U.S. share of a $1.2-billion increase in the resources of the Fund for Special Operations; the remaining $300 million was to be paid by Latin American members of the Bank.

The Fund for Special Operations provided loans on "soft" terms where lending on regular commercial terms was not appropriate. Following the Inter-American summit conference at Punta del Este, Uruguay, in April 1967, the Bank's board of governors proposed to Bank members a resolution to increase over-all contributions to the FSO by $1.2 billion. HR 9547 authorized the U.S. Governor of the Bank (the Secretary of the Treasury) to vote in favor of the resolution and authorized contribution of the U.S. share.

From fiscal 1965-67, the United States had contributed $250 million a year to the FSO. (This was authorized under a 1965 bill. *See p. 62.)* HR 9547 authorized the United States to continue contributions to the fund for three additional years, while at the same time increasing the level of those contributions by $50 million a year.

Asian Development Bank

Congress did not act on a request by President Johnson Sept. 26 to authorize a U.S. contribution of up to $200 million to new special funds of the Asian Development Bank. The funds were to be used for long-term loans at low interest rates—"soft loans"—to finance foreign exchange costs of projects such as schools and roads which do not yield immediate financial returns. U.S. contributions were to be made over four years and were to constitute a minority share of total contributions to the special funds, the President said. The request for new authorization was in addition to a $200 million authorization (PL 89-426) for the Bank approved in 1966 by Congress. *(See p. 72.)* The 1966 authorization was for ordinary capital used largely to finance the foreign exchange costs of projects that have a relatively rapid and direct return on investment.

Peace Corps

Congress in 1967 passed a bill (S 1031—PL 90-175) authorizing appropriations of $115.7 million for the Peace Corps in fiscal 1968. The amount was $3 million below the Administration request.

The program was somewhat more controversial than in recent years. The primary issue involved drafting of Peace Corps volunteers. Several House Members attacked statements by Corps Director Jack Hood Vaughn criticizing Selective Service boards for drafting young men on duty with the Corps, thus interrupting their service and wasting the expensive training they had received. Vaughn said the Corps would actively aid its volunteers serving overseas in obtaining draft deferments. The Peace Corps previously had merely advised volunteers of their rights under the draft law.

In addition, some Members were critical of an intensive Peace Corps program in the U.S. Pacific Trust Territory islands in the South Pacific. It was charged that the program represented Corps entry into a domestic situation and that the ratio of Corpsmen to islands residents was too high. Other complaints were leveled at anti-Vietnam war statements by Corps members and the increase in high-salaried employees at the Corps headquarters. (Congress in the foreign aid bill appropriated $107.5 million for the Peace Corps.)

Informational Media

The Senate rejected an Administration bill (S 1030) designed to shift the financial base of a 20-year-old program of Government subsidies for the export of books and other publications. The bill also would have explicitly prohibited dissemination of U.S. Information Agency (USIA) material in the United States, but would have extended public access to USIA materials on request.

The Informational Media Guaranty Program (IMG) was started in 1948 in an effort to persuade U.S. publishers to sell books, magazines and other material to countries with inconvertible currencies. Under the program, an approved publisher sold his books and other publications through normal commercial channels for the foreign currency. He then traded in the currency to the USIA for dollars. The USIA sold the foreign currency to the Treasury, which, in turn, sold it to Government agencies which needed if for local expenses in the country concerned.

The program was financed by borrowing from the Treasury. In addition, Congress appropriated a total of $13 million through fiscal 1964. The Senate Appropriations Committee in 1963 ordered that the program be phased out. Congress appropriated no funds in fiscal years 1965-67, and the program operated on about $4 million remaining from Treasury borrowing.

Although at one time or another the program operated in 21 countries, by 1967 it was in effect in only seven—Afghanistan, Guinea, South Korea, Poland, Turkey, South Vietnam and Yugoslavia. The great majority of the materials exported were textbooks and technical and scientific works.

S 1030 was similar to bills requested by the Administration in the 88th and 89th Congresses which never were considered by the Senate Foreign Relations Committee.

S 1030 shifted the financial basis of IMG from Treasury borrowing to a revolving fund with a maximum appropriation of $10 million. But when the bill reached the Senate floor it was rejected by a 31-47 roll-call vote. Opponents said the bill would revive a publishing subsidy plan which Congress had sought to end. Others noted that opposition to the program was another reflection of Senate discontent with all types of foreign aid.

Panama Canal

The negotiation of new treaty agreements between the United States and Panama was announced in 1967. The agreements affected sovereignty over the Panama Canal and construction of a second canal. The announcement provoked much criticism in the United States from conservative Members of Congress and right-wing groups such as the John Birch Society and Liberty Lobby which contended that perpetual U.S. control of the canal was essential to American security. Maritime groups and unions also opposed a change in control of the canal. Many Members of Congress introduced resolutions expressing opposition to ratification of the treaties. No action, other than hearings, was taken on the resolutions, nor were the treaties submitted to Congress for ratification.

President Johnson and President Marco A. Robles of Panama proclaimed June 26 that three new treaties had been drafted. The contents were not disclosed officially, but subsequent press reports indicated that the treaties would (1) relinquish U.S. control over the Panama Canal in favor of administration by a binational authority; (2) provide for the defense of the Panama Canal; and (3) allow the United States to build a second canal across Panama if it chose to do so.

In the House, more than 130 Members swiftly introduced or cosponsored resolutions urging that the treaties be rejected. The House Foreign Affairs Committee's Subcommittee on Inter-American Affairs held hearings on the resolutions in July and August but took no final action in 1967. In the Senate, criticism was led by Strom Thurmond (R S.C.). Much of the criticism was based on fears that U.S. consent to end its control over the strategic Canal would open the way for Suez-like crises or Communist seizure. J.W. Fulbright (D Ark.), chairman of the Senate Foreign Relations Committee, and Senate Majority Leader Mike Mansfield (D Mont.) voiced approval of the pacts.

Background. The United States gained control over a 10-mile strip across Panama in the Hay-Bunau-Varilla Treaty, signed by President Theodore Roosevelt Nov. 18, 1903, and agreed to by the Senate Feb. 23, 1904. Immediately after the signing of the Treaty, the two countries began to disagree on the question of sovereignty over the Canal. The United States and Panama agreed to revisions of the 1903 Treaty in 1936 and 1955, changing certain provisions and raising the annuity paid by the United States to Panama from $250,000 to $1,930,000.

In 1959, Panama requested that her flag be flown alongside the American flag in the Canal Zone. Despite strong opposition in Congress, including a House resolution, passed by a vote of 381-12, protesting such action, President Eisenhower allowed the two flags to be flown together at certain sites. A later order banned the flying of flags in front of Canal Zone schools. In defiance of that order, U.S. students Jan. 7, 1964, raised the American flag at a high school, touching off a riot which left four Americans and 21 Panamanians dead.

As a result of the riot, Panama broke off diplomatic relations with the United States. The two countries resumed relations April 3, 1964. President Johnson Dec. 18, 1964, announced that the United States would negotiate a new treaty and would press for a new canal across the Isthmus of Panama. Presidents Johnson and Robles June 26, 1967, announced that the treaties had been drafted but did not disclose their contents.

Meanwhile, Congress in 1964 passed a bill creating a commission to determine the feasibility of and the best site for a new sea-level canal across the Isthmus. President Johnson signed the bill into law (PL 88-609) Sept. 24, 1964.

Sea-Level Canal Commission. On the last day of the session, Congress cleared for the President a bill (S 1566—PL 90-244) to extend the life of the Atlantic-Pacific Interoceanic Canal Study Commission for 17 months, from June 30, 1968, to Dec. 1, 1969. The Commission was authorized in 1964 (PL 88-609) and was to consist of five men appointed by the President to determine the feasibility of, and the most suitable site for, construction of a new sea-level canal connecting the Atlantic and Pacific Oceans. The program encountered delays, however. The Commission was not appointed until April 18, 1965, and agreements to conduct surveys through the territory were not signed with Panama until Feb. 15, 1966. The Atomic Energy Commission program to investigate nuclear excavation of the canal was two years behind schedule.

1968

The final year of President Johnson's term, 1968, was dominated by three key events in foreign affairs. They were: a savage Communist offensive in Vietnam that was launched during the Lunar New Year period called Tet in late January and early February; a two-stage cessation, in April and November, of the bombing of North Vietnam; and an invasion of Czechoslovakia in August by Soviet troops to reverse a liberalization move in that country.

The first two events constituted a turning point for American involvement in the Vietnam war. The Tet offensive was terribly costly for all participants in the war. But for Americans, both in Vietnam and at home, the developments swiftly increased the slowly growing realization that there could not be a satisfactory military settlement to the conflict. The destruction and carnage of the offensive reinforced the fears of many worried Americans that their Government's policy in Vietnam not only gave no hope for an early end to the fighting but threatened to produce years of costly and bloody struggle in Asia and bitter dissension at home. The despair at such a prospect was unexpectedly washed away on March 31 when President Johnson in a televised address to the nation, said he would not seek re-election and announced he had ordered a bombing halt over much of North Vietnam. He said he would spend the rest of his term working to bring peace to Vietnam. This was a turning point which gave Americans hope that a serious and sincere effort was being made to find a practical—and not just a military—solution to the war. The bombing decrease did, in fact, result in initial talks between the United States and North Vietnam which led in early 1969 to substantive negotiations at ending the war. In between March 31 and the 1969 talks, there was a seemingly

endless string of frustrating moves on both sides. The period was highlighted by President Johnson's Oct. 31 announcement that he was stopping all bombing over North Vietnam. This was the final breakthrough that enabled all participants in the war to get together for negotiations.

The Czechoslovakian invasion retarded Soviet-American relations at a time when it appeared they were improving in spite of the Vietnam war. The invasion presented an immediate obstacle to Senate approval of a nuclear nonproliferation treaty and prevented the initiation of negotiation on arms limitations which had been imminent. It also blocked any serious consideration in 1968 of withdrawal of some American troops from Europe. Nevertheless, by early 1969 there were signs that the worst effects of the invasion had receded and new efforts at improving East-West relations were in the works.

In other developments, Congress cut foreign aid to the lowest point in the program's 20-year history. Administration efforts to improve East-West trade and to advance American trade with other nations through lower tariffs met with resistance in Congress. However, protectionist moves by American industries were thwarted. In another area of controversy, Congress finished action on various arms sales bills. Taken together, the various bills sought to limit credit arms sales to less developed nations (without affecting sales to advanced nations) and to discourage nations from spending either American aid or their own scarce resources for advanced weapons they did not need.

Vietnam

The year 1968 was a turning point for the war in Vietnam and American involvement in the conflict. Early in the year, the Communists launched a major offensive which was to prove one of the central events in the war; at the end of the year, the adversaries were on the verge of substantive peace negotiations. In between much had happened: the bombing of the North was halted in two stages; President Johnson removed himself as a candidate for re-election; a Republican—Richard Nixon, who had said very little about how he would handle the war—was elected to succeed Mr. Johnson; unrest over the war continued in the United States, including a violent eruption in Chicago during the Democratic national convention; and a new U.S. commander took over in Vietnam.

Of the events during the year, two were crucial in bringing about peace negotiations: the Communist's Tet offensive in late January and February and the complete halt in bombing of North Vietnam. A week-long cease fire had been proclaimed for Tet, or the Lunar New Year period beginning in the last days of January. But on Jan. 30, Communist troops, ignoring the truce, invaded seven cities. From that point, the Tet offensive escalated into one of the major battles of the war and included attacks on the capitals of almost all of South Vietnam's 44 provinces. On Jan. 31, a Viet Cong squad briefly seized part of the American Embassy compound in Saigon. In early February, most of Hue was held by North Vietnamese forces which were not driven out until about Feb. 24.

The Tet offensive was a sobering affair for both Americans and South Vietnamese. If it did not achieve what many observers thought were its primary goals of inflicting unacceptable losses on the allied forces, capturing and holding major capitals and fomenting popular uprisings against the Saigon government, at least it demonstrated that the Communist forces could move at will into major population centers with devastating results and could disrupt much of the pacification program which the Americans and South Vietnamese were laboring to construct in rural areas. It also showed that the Communist forces were much stronger than was generally believed, particularly by the American public. But the Tet offensive and later battles produced staggering losses for the Communists. Military estimates at the end of 1968 put the number of "guaranteed" Communist deaths at 40,000, of which 30,000 were native Viet Cong. For the year, one expert Western reporter who had been in Vietnam for many years wrote that Communist losses were at least 100,000 and perhaps as many as 160,000 dead. There were other offensives in May and August, but they were only dim reflections of the Tet battles.

When the Tet offensive was over and Americans (and probably South and North Vietnamese also) began to reflect on its costs, belief in the efficacy of military force to end the war began to pall more than ever. Although never officially confirmed, there were many newspaper reports that U.S. military officials in Vietnam, and the U.S. Commander, Gen. William C. Westmoreland in particular, requested 206,000 additional troops above the existing levels. It was also reported that President Johnson decided to send only 35,000 to 50,000, a decision that was said to be a key turning point in achieving a political—rather than a military—settlement of the war. Later in the year, Westmoreland said that American military victory "in a classic sense" was not possible "because of our national policy of not expanding the war." (Westmoreland was named by President Johnson in March to succeed Gen. Harold K. Johnson as Army Chief of Staff, effective July 2. He in turn was replaced in Vietnam by Gen. Creighton W. Abrams.)

Bombing Restricted. A political settlement of the war became virtually a formal American policy when on March 31 President Johnson, in a nationwide television address, announced that he would not seek re-election and that he had ordered a halt in the bombing over about three-quarters of North Vietnam (including Hanoi) in which about 90 percent of the population lived. He said he was going to devote full time to seeking peace. He called upon North Vietnam to begin negotiations to end the war.

Mr. Johnson's speech reflected an appreciation of the bitter divisions that had grown up in America over the war. His removal of himself as a candidate for re-election and his partial halt in the bombing did not eliminate the war as an important domestic issue but it went far to mute it. From March 31 on, the war was in a new phase to the extent that it was a domestic political issue; the most vocal opponents continued to protest, even to the point of provoking police violence at the Democratic convention in Chicago in August which shocked the nation, but for the most part Americans waited and hopefully watched as the two sides in the conflict maneuvered for advantage before plunging into the negotiations to end the fighting.

The maneuvering was a tedious affair which frustrated many Americans, including the Secretary of Defense, by the end of the year. The first obstacle was finding a place to meet. After a deadlock, Paris was agreed upon. The first substantive meeting between the United States and North Vietnam occurred May 13 (a procedural meeting was held May 10). From then until Oct. 30, the two sides met 28 times in an effort to reach agreement on halting all bombing of the North and expanding the talks into full peace negotiations. Eventually, an agreement was reached and President Johnson Oct. 31 announced a complete halt to the bombing of the North effective Nov. 1. He said the United States would accept the participation in the talks of the National Liberation Front (NLF) and the North Vietnamese would accept the participation of the Saigon government. It was also widely believed that there was a tacit understanding that the bombing halt would continue only so long as the Communists did not use it to their military advantages, such as undertaking major attacks on cities. The NLF Nov. 3 accepted terms for the talks.

The first meeting of the expanded talks was to take place Nov. 6. However, South Vietnam balked at taking part in the talks, at least partly because of the presence of the NLF, which Saigon always contended had no legitimate status. Saigon continued to be reluctant to join in the talks; this provoked criticism of foot-dragging from Secretary of Defense Clark Clifford, who warned that the talks might have to go on without South Vietnam representatives. Many observers thought the Saigon government was moving slowly in order to postpone the substantive talks until after Richard M. Nixon was sworn in as President in hope that he would take a harder line on compromises; it was thought that Saigon officials feared that Mr. Johnson, soon to leave office, might be too willing to make concessions which would leave him with a record of having achieved peace in Vietnam or at least having made key steps in that direction. But in early December Saigon sent a large delegation to Paris headed by Vice President Nguyen Cao Ky.

The talks then were further delayed by a dispute over the conference table. The United States and South Vietnam wanted a table which in some way showed a division between them on the one side and North Vietnam and the NLF on the other; this was in keeping with Saigon's contention that the NLF was not a separate and legitimate entity but only an arm of North Vietnam. The Communists believed just the opposite and wanted an unmarked table at which each group would sit separately and would represent a separate, independent and equal entity. This dispute was resolved on Jan. 16, 1969, when the United States and North Vietnam agreed on a round unmarked table with two small rectangular tables at each side of the round table but about 18 inches away from it. The rectangular tables would accommodate secretarial and technical personnel. This agreement broke a 10-week deadlock. On Jan. 18, just two days before President Johnson left office, all four sides in the conflict met for the first time and reached an unexpectedly quick agreement on remaining procedural issues. This ended the preliminary maneuvering which dated back to the previous spring and opened the way the following week—with a new President in office in the United States—to begin substantive talks on concluding a war which had involved the United States since the mid-1950s and which had torn the countries of Indochina since the end of World War II.

Congressional Action. President Johnson's March 31 announcement limiting bombing of North Vietnam and removing himself as a candidate for re-election helped to make the war less of an issue in Congress as well as throughout the nation. There was not a single significant roll-call vote taken on the Vietnam issue during the year. But the issue did not vanish. Secretary of State Dean Rusk participated in public Senate hearings on the Administration's Vietnam policy for the first time in more than two years; his appearance again demonstrated the enormous gap between Administration officials and their critics in Congress. There was a review of the Gulf of Tonkin attack in 1964; a report by a Senate Government Operations subcommittee that "millions of dollars" in U.S. funds had been "squandered" in Vietnam "because of inefficiency, dishonesty, corruption and foolishness"; and the introduction of many resolutions in the House—generally in opposition to enlargement of U.S. involvement in the war (although none was brought to a vote).

Appropriations. Congress acted on several bills dealing with funds for U.S. activities in Southeast Asia. A supplemental appropriations bill for fiscal 1968, enacted in mid-year (PL 90-392), provided $3,750,950,000 in new appropriations and released $2,345,000,000 in funds appropriated in 1967 but later frozen by a Congressional spending restriction. A minor controversy developed in the Senate over a floor amendment to delete funds for a buildup in bomber operations in Vietnam. However, the proposal was swamped by a 10-79 roll call. The fiscal 1969 defense appropriations bill (PL 90-580) included an estimated $25.5 billion to support the Vietnam war. An antibombing amendment in the House was rejected by voice vote.

Rusk Testimony. In televised hearings March 11-12 before the Senate Foreign Relations Committee on the annual foreign aid bill, Secretary of State Rusk defended the Administration's Vietnam policy. It was his first public testimony on the war before a Congressional committee since Feb. 18, 1966, when he met with the Foreign Relations Committee. Rusk conceded that the Tet offensive produced "some severe setbacks" for both sides. The Committee's critics of the war fenced with Rusk much as they had for several years, but no minds were changed. Committee Chairman J.W. Fulbright (D Ark.) sought to extract a pledge from Rusk that he would consult with the Committee on further U.S. troop increases in Vietnam before any decision was made. Rusk would not make such a pledge. And so, once again, the Secretary of State and the Senate Foreign Relations Committee parted company with very different views of the world, and the United States' role in international affairs.

Tonkin Gulf Review. In February, the Senate Foreign Relations Committee held a hearing on the Aug. 2 and 4, 1964, attacks on the U.S. destroyers Maddox

and Turner Joy in the Gulf of Tonkin. The day of closed hearings, at which Secretary of Defense Robert S. McNamara and Chairman of the Joint Chiefs of Staff Gen. Earle G. Wheeler testified, came after a prolonged Committee staff investigation of the attacks. The hearing, however, settled nothing. The Administration stuck to its contention that the attacks on the U.S. vessels occurred and were unprovoked. Critics of the war said—as they had before—that the existence of the attacks or the reasons for any attacks that did occur still had not been established. No report on the hearings was filed by the Committee. Late in the year, the Committee published a number of documents relating to the attack which once again raised the question of whether the United States provoked the North Vietnamese torpedo boat raids on the destroyers.

Shoup Testimony. Former Marine Corps Commandant Gen. David M. Shoup testified in March before the Foreign Relations Committee that a military victory by the United States could not be achieved without an invasion of North Vietnam.

Pueblo Seizure

One of the most spectacular international developments of 1968 was seizure by North Korea on Jan. 23 of the 906-ton U.S. Navy intelligence collection ship Pueblo and its 83-man crew. The crew was released in December. The boat, according to U.S. officials, was in international waters 25 miles off North Korea. North Korean officials called the Pueblo "an armed spy boat" and contended that it had "intruded way into the territorial waters" of their country.

After initial U.S. diplomatic efforts to recover the ship and its crew failed, President Johnson Jan. 25 ordered the call-up of about 14,000 men in the Air Force and Navy Air Reserve and Air National Guard. The authority to order these men to active duty was contained in a 1966 amendment to the defense appropriations bill. During the year, U.S. and North Korean negotiators met numerous times at Panmunjom to secure release of the crew and ship. On Dec. 22, North Korea released the commander and crew of the ship but retained possession of the ship. Eighty-two men were released; the body of an 83rd crewman, who died of wounds received during the seizure, also was returned. The release of the crewmen was made possible when an American military officer at Panmunjom signed a North Korean draft statement assigning guilt in the incident to the United States. However, U.S. officials made it plain during and after the signing that the United States considered the document an expedient to free the crewmen and was not an official admission of guilt.

In January, 1969, a Navy court of inquiry began an official investigation of the incident.

Congressional Action. Congress in September passed a bill (HR 17780—PL 90-510) to authorize hostile-fire pay for the crew of the Pueblo. This amounted to $65 a month more than normal pay. The stipends were retroactive to Jan. 1. Before enactment of the bill, hostile-fire pay was authorized only for armed service personnel in Vietnam and surrounding waters and for those in a small enclave along the western end of the demilitarized zone of Korea.

U.S.-Soviet Relations

In spite of the Vietnam war, U.S.-Soviet relations showed signs of improving in the first half of 1968. But the optimism ended in August with a Soviet invasion of Czechoslovakia aimed at halting a liberalization move in that country. The invasion adversely affected a number of important problems of vital interest to the United States and the U.S.S.R.

One of the encouraging developments occurred Jan. 13 when the Consular Convention between the two nations was formally concluded in ceremonies at the White House. *(see p. 88 for story on treaty.)* On June 21, President Johnson formally approved the establishment of direct New York-Moscow air service by Pan American World Airways and the Soviet national airline Aeroflot. The initial flight was completed July 15 by a Soviet airplane which arrived at Kennedy International Airport in New York. In addition to these developments, President Johnson July 1 announced that the two nations had agreed to enter into talks on the limitation and reduction of nuclear arms sometime in the near future. Later in the year, U.S. Ambassador to the United Nations James Russell Wiggins said that an announcement on the start of talks had been imminent at the time of the Czechoslovakian invasion but had been postponed because of the Soviet action.

The Czechoslovakian invasion came as a shock to much of the world. On Aug. 20, Soviet forces invaded the country to put down a liberalizing movement by what the Soviet news agency Tass called "counter-revolutionary forces who had entered into a plot with external forces hostile to socialism." Soviet troops continued to occupy the country and to impose a limitations on freedoms, such as speech and press, which Czechoslovakians had begun to enjoy before the invasion. Although the government was not overthrown, the Russian occupation left it with no other choice but to acquiesce in Soviet demands to accept a list of "normalization" conditions including stricter control of the press and other news media.

The invasion quickly stalled efforts by the Johnson Administration to obtain approval of a nuclear nonproliferation treaty *(see below)* and to limit the spread of armaments, and blocked a move in the Senate to reduce the number of U. S. troops in Europe *(see p. 106)*.

Nuclear Nonproliferation Treaty

The Soviet occupation of Czechoslovakia in August *(see preceding item)* was a mortal blow to President Johnson's hope of ratifying a nuclear nonproliferation treaty before leaving office. Mr. Johnson continued to press vigorously for Senate action on the treaty, even to the point of considering recalling Congress after the elections, but to no avail.

On June 12, 1968, the United Nations General Assembly voted 95-4 with 21 abstentions, to approve a draft treaty banning the spread of nuclear weapons to states not already possessing them. The product of more than

four years of negotiations at the 18-Nation Disarmament Conference in Geneva, the treaty was signed July 1 by the United States, the Soviet Union and 60 other nations. Shortly thereafter, on July 9, it was submitted to the Senate for approval by President Johnson.

The President called it "the most important international agreement in the field of disarmament since the nuclear age began."

On Oct. 11, Senate Majority Leader Mike Mansfield (D Mont.) said he would not call up the treaty because "the leadership will not be a party to a partisan treatment of a matter which by its very nature is and must remain nonpartisan." The treaty had become involved in the Presidential election campaign. Vice President Hubert H. Humphrey, the Democratic candidate, urged quick ratification of the agreement. Richard M. Nixon, the Republican candidate, said that going ahead with the treaty might appear to be "condoning" the invasion. He said that could have "a tremendously bad moral effect, detrimental moral effect, all over the world." He said he supported the treaty but believed it desirable to delay ratification until a later date. After Mr. Nixon won the election, his views favoring delay took on increased importance. There was no further action in 1968, but on Feb. 5, 1969, President Nixon called for the Senate's "prompt consideration and positive action" on the treaty. Approval of the treaty at this time, he said, "would advance this Administration's policy of negotiation rather than confrontation with the U.S.S.R." On March 13, 1969 the Senate by an 83-15 roll-call vote consented to the ratification of the treaty.

Treaty Articles

The Nonproliferation Treaty consisted of a preamble and 11 articles, the most important of which were those banning the spread of nuclear weapons, providing for safeguards arrangements and ensuring non-discriminatory access to the peaceful uses of nuclear energy. The following is a brief description of each of the articles.

Articles I and II of the treaty contained the basic provisions prohibiting the spread of nuclear weapons. Under the terms of Article I, nuclear-weapons states adhering to the treaty were obliged not to transfer "to any recipient whatsoever" either nuclear weapons or any other nuclear explosive devices. Nor could they transfer control over such weapons or devices. In addition, they were prohibited from assisting, encouraging or inducing non-nuclear-weapon states from manufacturing or acquiring them or obtaining control over them.

Under the terms of Article II, signatory states not having nuclear weapons undertook not to receive such weapons or explosive devices (or control over them), either directly or indirectly, "from any transferor whatsoever." These states also agreed not to manufacture or acquire such weapons or devices, nor to seek or receive any assistance in the manufacture of them.

Article III, one of the more controversial in the treaty, dealt with the establishment of safeguards procedures to ensure that non-nuclear-weapon states were not diverting nuclear energy from peaceful uses to the manufacture of weapons. Under the terms of this article, each of these states undertook to accept safeguards, "as set forth in an agreement to be negotiated and concluded with the International Atomic Energy Agency (IAEA) in accordance with the Statute of the International Atomic Energy Agency and the Agency's safeguards system."

The IAEA, an international agency set up in 1957, was thus to have the chief responsibility for control and verification of the treaty's prohibitions. According to Article III, the safeguards were to apply to all nuclear materials, which were essential to the manufacture of nuclear weapons, but were not to hamper "international cooperation in the field of peaceful nuclear activities." The non-nuclear-weapon states were permitted to work out the safeguards agreements with the IAEA either individually or collectively. Negotiations on such agreements were to begin "within 180 days from the original entry into force of this treaty," with the agreements scheduled to take effect "not later than eighteen months after the date of initiation of negotiations." Nothing in the article made the nuclear-weapon states liable to safeguards arrangements.

Article IV protected "the inalienable right of all the Parties to the Treaty to develop research, production and use of nuclear energy for peaceful purposes without discrimination and in conformity with Articles I and II of this Treaty." It also obliged all signatories to facilitate "the fullest possible exchange of equipment, materials and scientific and technological information."

Article V was designed to compensate the signatory non-nuclear-weapon states for undertaking not to acquire nuclear explosive devices, even for peaceful purposes. Under the terms of the article "appropriate measures" were to be taken to ensure that the non-nuclear-weapon states had access to the benefits of the peaceful applications of nuclear explosions "on a nondiscriminatory basis." The cost of nuclear explosive devices was to be "as low as possible," with no charges being levied for research and development. The explosives were to be obtained either through "an appropriate international body" to be set up in the future, or through bilateral arrangements. In all cases where such explosives were provided, however, the actual ownership and control of them was to remain with the nuclear state involved.

Article VI placed the nuclear-weapon states themselves under certain disarmament obligations, stating in full: "Each of the Parties to the Treaty undertakes to pursue negotiations in good faith on effective measures relating to cessation of the nuclear arms race at an early date and to nuclear disarmament, and on a treaty on general and complete disarmament under strict and effective international control."

Article VII ensured that nothing in the treaty would affect "the right of any group of States to conclude regional treaties in order to assure the total absence of nuclear weapons in their respective territories."

Article VIII laid down the procedure for amending the treaty and also stated that five years after the treaty became effective a conference of all parties was to be held in Geneva, to review the treaty and ensure that its purposes and provisions were being realized. Thereafter, such review conferences were to be held at intervals of five years if a majority of the treaty's signatories favored them.

Nations Signing Treaty

The following is a complete list of treaty signatories, as of Feb. 12, 1969. Those countries which had also ratified the treaty are listed in italics.

United States, *Great Britain* and Northern Ireland, Soviet Union, Afghanistan, Austria, Barbados, Belgium, Bolivia, Botswana, Bulgaria, *Cameroon, Canada,* Ceylon, Chad, Republic of China, Colombia, Congo (Democratic Republic of), Costa Rica, Cyprus, Czechoslovakia.

Dahomey, *Denmark,* Dominican Republic, East Germany, Ecuador, El Salvador, Ethiopia, *Finland,* Gambia, Ghana, Greece, Guatemala, Haiti, Honduras, Hungary, Iceland, Iran, Iraq, *Ireland,* Italy, Ivory Coast, Jordan, Kenya, Republic of Korea, Kuwait, Laos, Lebanon, Lesotho, Liberia, Libya, Luxembourg.

Malagasy Republic, Malaysia, Maldive Islands, Mauritius, *Mexico,* Mongolia, Morocco, Nepal, Netherlands, New Zealand, Nicaragua, *Nigeria, Norway,* Panama, Paraguay, Peru, Philippines, Poland, Romania, San Marino, Senegal, Somali Republic, Southern Yemen, Sudan, Sweden, Syria, Togo, Trinidad & Tobago, Tunisia, Turkey, United Arab Republic, Upper Volta, Uruguay, Venezuela, Republic of Vietnam, Yemen Arab Republic, Yugoslavia.

Article IX declared that the treaty "shall be open to all States for signature" and would enter into force after instruments of ratification had been deposited by the United States, Great Britain, the Soviet Union and 40 other signatory states. It also defined a nuclear-weapon state as "one which has manufactured and exploded a nuclear weapon or other nuclear explosive device prior to January 1, 1967."

Article X reserved to each state the right, after giving three months' notice, of withdrawing from the treaty if it decided that "extraordinary events" were jeopardizing its "supreme interests." No attempt was made in the article, however, to define the terms "extraordinary events" and "supreme interests," which meant that a decision on withdrawal rested entirely with the individual state concerned. Article X also made provision for a conference to be called 25 years after the treaty had entered into force "to decide whether the Treaty shall continue in force indefinitely, or shall be extended for an additional period or periods." The decision on extension was to be taken by a majority of the parties to the treaty.

Article XI, the final article of the treaty, declared the English, Russian, French, Spanish and Chinese texts "equally authentic" and declared that the original treaty was to be deposited in the archives of the Depository Governments (the United States, Great Britain and the Soviet Union).

Congressional Action. President Johnson July 9 submitted the treaty (Exec. H, 90th Congress, 2nd Session) to the Senate for ratification. The Senate Foreign Relations Committee took the unprecedented step of beginning consideration of the treaty less than 24 hours after its submission by the President. Members of the Joint Committee on Atomic Energy joined with the Foreign Relations Committee to question top Administration witnesses about the treaty. A principal concern of the Senators, particularly those on the Foreign Relations Committee, was whether the treaty would impose any new obligation on the United States to defend any non-nuclear nation threatened with or actually experiencing a nuclear attack. While the testimony of Secretary of State Dean Rusk and U.S. Arms Control and Disarmament Director William C. Foster contained no direct reference to this point, Rusk said repeatedly under questioning that the treaty would in no way add to current U.S. military commitments abroad.

Committee Action. After three unsuccessful attempts to obtain a quorum, the Foreign Relations Committee Sept. 17 by a 13-3 vote (with three abstentions) ordered the treaty reported favorably and recommended ratification. Voting against it were Democrats Lausche (Ohio) and Dodd (Conn.) and Republican Mundt (S.D.) In its report, the Committee recommended that after the Senate acted, the President delay formal ratification (that is, depositing the actual instruments of ratification) until a majority of nations "nearest to a nuclear weapons capability" promised to honor the agreement.

U.S. Troops in Europe

Another casualty of the Soviet invasion of Czechoslovakia was the effort being made in Congress to reduce the number of American troops in Europe. Proponents of a troop reduction backed away from proposals they had been sponsoring to make token or substantial cuts in troop strength in NATO, although some of these individuals indicated they still wanted to see reductions later. One of the leaders of the troop-reduction advocates, Mike Mansfield (D Mont.), the Senate Majority Leader, said the invasion meant "we had no choice but to maintain our present position." But he added, "It remains desirable to undertake a gradual reduction in U.S. forces if and when the situation in Eastern Europe offers reasonable assurance that developments there are not going to spill over to Western Europe." The Senate Foreign Relations Committee had before it for consideration the resolutions (S Res 49, S Res 83) on troop reduction that were introduced in 1967, but took no action. *(See p. 92.)*

Arms Control Agency

After some controversy, Congress again extended (HR 14940—PL 90-314) the life of the Arms Control and Disarmament Agency (ACDA). The extension was for two years, through June 30, 1970, and included an appropriations authorization of $18.5 million during the period. President Johnson asked for a three-year extension, through 1971, and an appropriation of $10 million in fiscal 1969. Both Senate and House agreed that a two-year extension was preferable because it would allow each Congress to review the agency's activities. This argument was emphasized in particular by Republicans. In addition, a number of House Members who opposed the nuclear nonproliferation treaty *(see p. 104)* strongly criticized the ACDA for its role in the negotiations. In House floor action, a conservative coalition of

Republicans and Southern Democrats succeeded in reducing the authorization by $13 million and limiting the extension to two years. The vote was 241-162: R 171-7; D 70-155 (ND 7-134; SD 63-21). *(See p. 63.)*

A controversy arose in the Senate over expenditures by the ACDA for research projects outside the agency. Foreign Relations Committee Chairman J.W. Fulbright (D Ark.) said the agency had contracted for 180 studies in six years; he questioned their relevancy. Consequently, the Senate and final bill limited outlays for outside research, except for field testing activities, to $7 million.

The agency was established in 1961 as a permanent, independent agency to assume primary responsibility within the Government for directing and coordinating disarmament matters, including conduct of negotiations and sponsorship of research. Total authorizations for the agency from its founding through fiscal 1968 were $60 million; HR 14940 added $18.5 million to this total. Total appropriations from its founding through fiscal 1968 were $52.8 million. Congress in 1968 appropriated $9 million for the ACDA in fiscal 1969. (Congress appropriated the following amounts during the 1965-68 period: 1965, $9 million; 1966, $10 million; 1967 and 1968, $9 million each.)

Since its founding, the ACDA participated in more than 500 formal international meetings on arms control and disarmament. The 1963 treaty partially banning nuclear test explosions was based on an ACDA draft, and the 1963 agreement with the Soviet Union for the "hot-line" communications system between Washington and Moscow, as well as the mutual U.S.-Soviet pledge to ban nuclear bombs in orbit, were based on proposals developed by the ACDA.

Foreign Aid

The foreign aid program was cut to an all-time low by Congress in 1968, the last year of Mr. Johnson's Presidency. The bill (HR 15263—PL 90-554) authorized fiscal 1969 appropriations of $1,974,050,000. This was $987,425,000—about one-third—below the Administration's request and $700,564,000 less than the previous year's authorization. The total authorization was divided between $1,599,050,000 for economic aid and $375 million for military assistance. Disenchantment with the program was evident throughout Congressional consideration of the legislation. Both chambers sought to make reductions although the major cuts originated in the House and were sponsored by Republicans.

The deepest cut in the bill was in the development loan program, which was reduced by more than half from the Administration's $765 million request to a level of $350 million. Other substantial cuts were made in the Alliance for Progress (from $625 million to $420 million), supporting assistance (from $595 million to $410 million), the President's foreign aid contingency fund (from $100 million to $10 million) and military assistance (from $420 million to $375 million).

In addition to the cuts, Congress again approved a sizeable assortment of restrictions which attempted to influence the conduct of foreign policy. One provision directed the President to negotiate the sale of jet planes to Israel. Two other provisions were offshoots of the arms sales controversy which erupted in 1967 and carried over to 1968. One of these provisions directed that no military assistance funds could be used to furnish "sophisticated weapons systems" to any less developed nation unless the President determined that such action was important to national security. A second provision required withholding of economic aid in an amount equal to that spent by any less developed nation for the purchase of "sophisticated weapons systems"; again, the President was given a waiver authority. *(For summary of arms sales provisions enacted during 90th Congress, see box and accompanying story p. 85-86; see also other arms sales actions in 1968 chronology, below.)*

In another provision, the interest rate on development loans after an initial 10-year, lower-interest grace period was raised to 3 percent from 2½ percent.

The major cuts came in House action. The Foreign Affairs Committee cut $596,750,000 from the draft bill and the House removed an additional $370,875,000 on the floor, including $165 million as part of a Republican-sponsored recommittal motion. All but $3,775,000 of the total cut was made through proposals sponsored by Republicans.

Despite the big cuts, a conservative coalition of House Republicans and Southern Democrats fought passage of the bill. The measure passed the House by a 228-184 roll-call vote, with GOP Members voting 70-112 and Southern Democrats 25-58 against it. On the GOP recommittal motion, which was adopted by a 268-150 roll call, only 20 Republicans and 14 Southern Democrats were opposed to the cuts.

Senate approval of the bill was more bipartisan with only eight Republicans and 10 Southern Democrats in opposition. The Senate Foreign Relations Committee cut an additional $47,950,000 from the bill passed by the House, mainly in the military assistance and supporting assistance funds. No further cuts were made on the Senate floor. A number of proposed changes were rejected. One of the rejected amendments was a key foreign aid vote of the session. It was an amendment by Sen. Wayne Morse (D Ore.) to reduce the authorization for Alliance for Progress grants to $70 million from the House's figure of $90 million. It was rejected by a **31-43** roll call.

Foreign Aid Funds

When the foreign aid appropriations bill came before Congress late in the session, Members continued their efforts begun with the authorization bill to reduce the aid program to an all-time low level. As passed, the appropriations bill (HR 19908—PL 90-581) provided $1,755,600,000 for economic aid and military assistance in fiscal 1969, the smallest amount in the history of the program. Economic aid received $1,380,600,000 and military assistance, $375 million. The reduction was 39.7 percent below the Administration's request of $2,920,000,000. The bill also appropriated $102 million for the Peace Corps, $505,800,000 for the Inter-American Development Bank and $20 million for the Asian Development Bank. *(For story on Alliance for Progress, see p. 108-109.)*

The major cuts came in three primary aid programs: development loans, cut by $465 million to a total of $300 million; the Alliance for Progress, cut by $288.5 million to a level of $336.5 million; and supporting assistance (to aid countries facing an external Communist threat), cut by $230 million to a level of $365 million.

Although President Johnson had asked for the smallest aid appropriation in history, $2,920,000,000, it was clear from the outset that Congress would make substantial reductions. Members of Congress criticized the program for many reasons: reports of waste and mismanagement; the mounting costs of the Vietnam war; displeasure with the income tax surcharge which Mr. Johnson requested to help finance the war and fight inflation; and growing unpopularity of the aid program as such, particularly in light of continued criticism of U.S. policies by some recipient nations.

The fight against the bill was led by Republicans (who early in the year pledged to reduce the program's financing by $1 billion) and Southern Democrats. This was seen in House floor action after the Appropriations Committee cut the requested $2.9 billion to just over $1.6 billion. In spite of this enormous cut, a majority of Republicans and Southern Democrats—the conservative coalition—voted against passage of the bill. Northern Democrats provided the margin for passage on a key vote of **174-138** (R 54-83; SD 24-46; ND 96-9).

Arms Sales

The controversy about sales of American military weapons to less developed nations, which arose in 1967, continued into 1968 and again involved several pieces of legislation. Following is a summary of the major bills which included provisions on arms sales and which became law in 1968. *(For a summary of major arms sales provisions in 1967 and 1968, see box p. 86; for discussion of 1967 action in more detail, see story accompanying box.)*

Eximbank Bill. This piece of legislation (S 1155—PL 90-267) began its way through Congress in 1967 but was stalled in the House because of controversy over arms sales provisions. *(See p. 110 and 111 for other provisions of PL 90-267.)* S 1155 passed the Senate in 1967 and began 1968 awaiting House floor action. The Senate version stated the sense of Congress that the Bank should not provide arms sales financing for less developed nations unless the President determined it was in the national interest. The House Banking and Currency Committee flatly prohibited such financing but gave the President a waiver authority. When the bill reached the House floor in 1968 it produced a vigorous and partisan battle. Rep. William B. Widnall (R N.J.) sought to flatly prohibit Eximbank financing of arms sales to less developed nations; he proposed dropping the President's waiver authority. He said that an amendment which he had sponsored to drop the waiver would reaffirm the action taken by Congress in 1967 in terminating the Pentagon's Country-X revolving fund on June 30, 1968. His proposal was subjected to partisan attacks by Democrats, culminating in a vehement speech by John W. McCormack (D Mass.). McCormack, as Speaker, seldom participated in debate. But this time he felt compelled to express "amazement" at Widnall's proposal and linked it to the entire House Republican leadership. "If ever an amendment was against the national interests of our country, it is this amendment," McCormack argued. Other Democrats said the amendment would prohibit Eximbank credit to such friendly

(Continued on p. 110.)

Alliance for Progress in Its First Seven Years:

The record of the Alliance for Progress in its first seven years was a disappointing one, and by 1968 disillusionment with the program was growing.

The Alliance, established in 1961, was the first coordinated, multinational effort to bring about the social, political and economic development of Latin America. Its charter, signed by 20 member governments of the Organization of American States (OAS), set down 12 fundamental goals, all to be achieved by the end of the decade 1961-71. A total of $100 billion was earmarked for investment in the area.

According to the Inter-American Committee on the Alliance for Progress (CIAP), the projected investment total already had been surpassed by the end of 1967. In the period 1961-67, approximately $115 billion had been committed to Latin American development, 88 percent of which had come from the Latin Americans themselves, 6.7 percent from the United States and 5.3 percent from other external capital and resources.

Despite these investment figures, by 1968 it was clear that the Alliance was failing to meet its goals. Economic and social development in Latin America had proceeded far more slowly than was anticipated originally, and political development in the direction of democratic institutions was noted largely for its absence. Congress, disillusioned with the slow pace of the development effort, had made major cuts in Alliance funds in 1967 and 1968. And, during the 1968 Presidential election campaign, Republican candidate Richard M. Nixon called for a "sweeping re-evaluation" of the Alliance.

The U.S. Role

Although the major part of the financial burden of the Alliance for Progress was borne by Latin Americans, the United States commitment to the program was considered essential to its existence.

Furthermore, U.S. economic assistance was sizable and frequently was injected into key areas of development that otherwise might have been stifled by a shortage of funds.

The single major source of U.S. contributions to the Alliance for Progress was the U.S. foreign aid program. The figures below show amounts requested by the Kennedy-Johnson Administrations and amounts appropriated by Congress for the Alliance for Progress in annual foreign aid bills, in millions of dollars:

Fiscal Year	Appropriation Request	Final Appropriation
1963	$ 600	$ 525
1964	650	525
1965	550	510
1966	580	510
1967	543	508
1968	643	469
1969	625	336.5
Total	**$4,191**	**$3,383.5**

According to the Agency for International Development (AID), the State Department agency responsible for administering the U.S. share of the Alliance, the United States committed a total of $8.1 billion in economic assistance to Latin America from fiscal 1961 to fiscal 1967. Preliminary figures for fiscal 1968 showed an additional commitment of $1.4 billion, with fiscal 1969 commitments estimated at an additional $1.4 billion.

AID. A number of U.S. agencies were involved in the distribution of these funds, the most important of which was AID. Through fiscal 1968, AID had committed a total of $4.4 billion in economic assistance to Latin America. It was expected to commit a further $559.3 million in fiscal 1969. Most of these funds were committed in the form of repayable loans and distributed under three titles: program loans, which went principally to Brazil, Chile and Colombia and which were designed to enable these countries to import the U.S. goods necessary for the growth and expansion of their economies; sector loans, which dealt specifically with problems of agriculture, education and health; and project loans, which financed a wide range of activities from major road systems and agricultural research to the creation of intermediate credit institutions. AID also supported technical assistance activities through its grant-in-aid program.

Economic assistance distributed through AID during the period 1961-68 was concentrated largely on agricultural and transportation development (36 percent of total AID assistance), as well as the development of industry, mining and power (15 percent of the total)—all sectors in which Latin Americans found investment funds either unavailable or difficult to acquire. Beginning in 1967, greater emphasis was given to the problems of agriculture, education and health.

Other Assistance. The U.S. also assisted Latin American development through the Export-Import Bank, the Food for Freedom program (PL 480) and the Social Progress Trust Fund (SPTF), a special loan fund administered by the Inter-American Development Bank (IDB). More indirectly, the U.S. role in the Alliance was exercised through the International Bank for Reconstruction and Development (World Bank), the International Finance Corp., the International Development Assn. and the Inter-American Development Bank. These banks committed a total of $4.3 billion in loans to Latin America in the 1961-68 period.

Alliance Record

Following is a sector-by-sector review of the Progress of the Alliance.

Economic Development. During the first five years of the Alliance, the average increase in Latin America's Gross Domestic Product (GDP) was about 5 percent. This growth rate dropped, however, to 4.3 percent in 1966 and 1967. More importantly, the average increase in per capita GDP for the period

A Program Which Failed To Meet Many Major Goals

1961-67 was about 1.3 percent, compared to the 2.5-percent goal set down in the Charter.

Industry—According to the CIAP, the average industrial growth rate for the period 1961-67 was approximately 6.4 percent, with a high of 9.2 percent in 1964 and a low of 1.9 percent in 1963. (This compared with an industrial growth rate of 6.1 percent for the period 1950-55 and 6.4 percent for the period 1955-60.)

Agriculture—Agricultural production showed little region-wide improvement during the Alliance years 1961-67, growing at an average annual rate of approximately 3 percent and just keeping pace with the rate of population growth.

Land reform efforts, long viewed as fundamental to agricultural modernization in the region, met with some success, but resistance was strong and many programs were not being well implemented. By the end of 1968, major reform projects were well underway in Bolivia, Venezuela and Mexico and were in their initial stages in Chile, Colombia and Peru.

Public Sector Expenditures—Major tax reforms were instituted in many Latin American countries in the period 1961-67, which produced increased governmental revenues and, in most cases, a steady increase in government public sector investments. According to the 1968 CIAP report, central government savings increased in 1967 in ten countries which together accounted for 50 percent of the population of the region. In only four countries (Haiti, El Salvador, Nicaragua and Peru) was there no increase in public sector investments, according to the CIAP.

Income—Efforts to bring about a more equitable distribution of income were meager, achieving only modest results; and the 1968 CIAP report stated that "unless more far-reaching action is taken, additional deterioration of the distribution of income may be expected."

Economic Integration—The Latin American Free Trade Association (LAFTA) and the Central American Common Market (CACM), both set up in 1960, continued efforts to lower trade barriers, but progress on key agricultural and industrial products was slow.

Social Development. The Alliance made some progress during its first seven years in improving social conditions in Latin America, particularly in educational and health services, but failed either to alleviate the serious housing shortage or to supply much of the region with adequate water and sewage systems.

Education—Progress in education was perhaps the Alliance's most notable achievement. According to the CIAP, approximately 82 percent of the primary school age population was enrolled in school in 1967 (compared with 70 percent in 1960), with the projected enrollment for 1970 being 92 percent. Estimated enrollment in secondary and higher education institutions was 22 percent and 5 percent respectively, an increase of about 10 percent in both cases over 1960.

Housing—A five-year review of the Alliance, conducted by the Inter-American Economic and Social Council in March 1966, estimated that Latin America's housing shortage was between 15 and 19 million units and that yearly construction was averaging one-tenth of the units required. The 1968 CIAP report said that "generally speaking" the situation had deteriorated.

Health—The Charter goal of increasing life expectancy by five years during the decade 1961-71 was close to being on schedule at the half-way point of the Alliance. According to the Pan American Health Organization (PAHO), estimated life expectancy in Latin America increased from 60.2 years in 1960 to 62.5 years in 1966, a gain of 2.3 years.

Another Charter goal, that of providing sewage disposal and potable water for at least 70 percent of the urban population and 50 percent of the rural population of Latin America by 1971, met with varying results. According to the PAHO, 69 percent of the urban population had "easy access" to water supplies in 1967. Rural water supplies lagged behind, however, and only about 23 percent of the rural population was expected to have potable water by 1971. Little progress was made in providing sewage services to either rural or urban areas. In 1968, the PAHO estimated that less than two-thirds of the urban goal and less than 3 percent of the rural goal would be reached by 1971.

Significant progress was made in combating certain diseases, notably smallpox, malaria and diphtheria. The number of available hospital beds increased gradually during the seven-year period, but the ratio of beds to population remained at about the same level, 3.2 per 1,000 persons. The number of doctors in Latin America had by 1966 grown by 30 percent over the 1960 total, but, again, the ratio of doctors to population remained low, with only 6 doctors available for every 10,000 persons.

Political Development. Throughout the first seven years of the Alliance, the major portion of Latin America's territory and population remained outside the framework of democratic institutions. Progress was made in some countries, notably in Venezuela and Colombia, toward erecting and safeguarding democratic systems of government. But for the most part the area continued to abound in anti-democratic coups and the military continued to be the dominant force.

Of Latin America's major countries, only Chile, Mexico, Colombia and Venezuela managed to escape military takeovers during the 1960s, and they were the only large countries which continued to operate basically democratic political systems.

nations as Israel, South Korea and Nationalist China— a charge which Republicans denied on the grounds that other forms of arms financing were available. But after more Democratic talk about using America's "arsenal of democracy for democracy," as Ed Edmondson (D Okla.) put it, Widnall's amendment went down to defeat by a 63-93 standing vote. The bill then was passed with the Committee's provisions. In conference, the House version—rather than the Senate's sense-of-Congress approach—was adopted. As enacted, the bill prohibited Eximbank credits for military equipment sales to less developed countries unless the President determined such exports would be in the national interest and gave Congress 30 days notice. (An even more restrictive provision was contained in another bill HR 15681. *See below.*) The provision also contained a few guidelines—such as avoiding arms races and keeping weapons away from military dictators—to help the President.

Foreign Aid Authorization. This bill (HR 15263—PL 90-554) was the fiscal 1969 appropriations authorization for the foreign aid program. One of its provisions specified that no military assistance funds could be used to furnish "sophisticated weapons systems," such as jet warplanes and missile systems, to any less developed nation unless the President determined that such action was important to national security. A second provision required withholding of economic aid in an amount equal to that spent by any less developed nation for the purchase of "sophisticated weapons systems"; again, the President was given a waiver authority. Similar provisions were included in the fiscal 1969 foreign aid appropriations bill (HR 19908—PL 90-581) as had been done in the fiscal 1968 bill (HR 13893—PL 90-249).

Arms Sales Authorization. Having restricted the Administration's existing method of financing arms sales abroad, Congress enacted legislation (HR 15681—PL 90-629) to provide a new method of credit sales of weapons to foreign countries. The bill authorized sale of U.S. arms through credit financing under standards approved by the President. It also authorized the President to provide any company doing business in the United States with a guarantee against default on payment for military weapons sold by the company to a foreign nation. In addition, the bill authorized the President to sell promissory notes issued to the United States by purchasing countries and to guarantee payment on them. However, the bill specified that guarantees could not be issued to any Government agency (such as the Eximbank, as was done in the past) and that promissory notes could not be bought by any U.S. Government agency (again, such as the Eximbank had done in the past). As a result of these restrictions, the Eximbank was effectively prevented by the bill from entering into any new Country-X loans. Under that program the Bank, through the Defense Department, provided less developed nations with funds to buy weapons and the Department guaranteed the Bank that the loans would be repaid. In addition to these restrictions, the bill specifically prohibited the Eximbank from participation in military sales to less developed countries. (This provision, which contained no Presidential waiver, superceded the less strict prohibition on Eximbank arms sales activities that was included in the Eximbank extension bill—PL 90-267.) As a result of these provisions, credit sales to economically less developed nations were to be financed in the future solely from annual appropriations.

To finance the credit sales of arms and to provide guarantees for privately financed sales, the bill required annual appropriations; for the first year, fiscal 1969, $296 million was authorized for this purpose. The bill also provided a limit of $296 million on the aggregate total of credits and face amounts of guarantees issued during fiscal 1969. The sum covered all U.S. Government financing of credit sales to less developed nations, but did not cover Eximbank financing (without a guarantee, which was prohibited) of military credit sales to developed countries.

The bill also contained various other limitations in an attempt to control arms sales. It included provisions carried in other bills in the 90th Congress which prohibited credit for sales of sophisticated weapons to less developed countries and permitted the President to halt arms sales to such nations if they diverted their own resources to "unnecessary military expenditures." The bill also required a recipient of U.S. arms to agree not to transfer the articles to another nation or organization.

The legislation was requested by the Administration after Congress took action against the existing methods of credit arms sales. HR 15681 passed the House after a number of amendments were accepted to further restrict sales of arms to less developed nations. The bill passed the Senate without change. A number of Senators were opposed to the bill, but many of them were away from Washington campaigning for re-election when the measure came up for action.

East-West Trade

As in the case of arms sales, Congressional efforts to block Administration proposals to expand trade between Eastern European Communist nations and the Western Alliance carried over from the 1967 session. There was no enthusiasm for President Johnson's program to improve trade with Communist nations. Following is a summary of major action.

Eximbank Bill. This legislation (S 1155—PL 90-267) was held over from 1967 when enactment was blocked by controversy about East-West trade and arms sales *(see above).* As cleared early in 1968, S 1155 included a provision barring Eximbank credit for purchase of U.S. goods by nations at war with the United States or by nations that actively aided such belligerents. Conferees on the bill said that under then existing conditions, the provision would block aid to all Communist nations except Yugoslavia. The provision also blocked Eximbank credit to non-Communist nations for purchase of U.S. goods that would be passed on to a Communist nation that was at war—or was aiding a country at war—with the United States. This provision was intended to block a proposed $50-million Eximbank loan to an Italian financial institution. The loan was to be used to buy U.S. machine tools for use in a plant which was to be built by the FIAT auto company in the Soviet Union. *(See box p. 97.)*

A second trade provision prohibited the Eximbank from financing export purchases to Communist countries (including businesses or individuals in such countries)

U.S. East-West Trade Volume, 1964-68

(In thousands of dollars)

The table shows U.S. trade with Communist nations during the period of President Johnson's term in office, covering 1964 through 1968. (Figures for 1968 were preliminary and subject to revision.)

Country	1964		1965		1966		1967		1968	
	Exports	Imports	Exports	Imports	Exports	Imports	Exports	Imports	Exports	Imports
Albania	$ 19	$ 102	$ 8	$ 113	$ 166	$ 109	$ 56	$ 335	$ 8	$ 283
Bulgaria	5,020	1,177	3,613	1,666	3,631	2,529	4,219	2,814	4,036	3,731
Czechoslovakia	11,338	12,706	27,685	16,741	37,336	27,695	19,155	26,241	14,281	23,756
East Germany	20,211	6,686	12,413	6,537	25,152	8,194	26,329	5,647	29,236	5,934
Hungary	13,753	1,693	9,327	2,092	10,053	2,985	7,570	3,884	11,194	3,848
Poland	138,066	54,202	35,417	65,861	52,988	82,948	60,825	90,960	82,374	96,871
Romania	5,156	1,272	6,385	1,836	26,686	4,655	16,796	6,176	18,238	5,820
U.S.S.R	146,360	20,678	45,161	42,650	41,725	49,553	60,308	41,167	54,476	58,112
Yugoslavia	145,336	55,921	149,278	61,075	173,364	74,215	96,231	86,773	89,998	102,448
Cuba	73	11	5	10	82	0	18	44	2	11
China †	3	477	1	463	1	102	1	181	0	*
Outer Mongolia †	*	3,312	0	3,631	0	3,409	1	2,409	0	2,326
TOTAL	$485,335	$158,237	$289,293	$202,675	$371,184	$256,394	$291,509	$266,631	$303,843	$303,140

* Less than $500.

† China figures include Manchuria. Figures shown on each of last two lines include exports of printed matter under general license and shipments to diplomatic missions of friendly foreign countries. Also, imports are credited to country where goods originated, regardless of last country from which they were shipped.

SOURCE: U.S. Commerce Department, Foreign Trade Office, March 17, 1969

or to third parties in other countries who would pass on the goods to Communist nations, unless the President determined that such transactions were in the national interest and gave Congress 30 days notice.

The trade provisions in the final bill were a combination of Senate and House provisions. They were generally in line with the House committee provisions approved in 1967 *(see p. 96)* except that a committee waiver clause was dropped during House floor action. The final provisions—as drafted in the House—were less broad than the Senate's Byrd amendment *(p. 96)* in that they prevented Eximbank credit only for Communist nations that were active allies of North Vietnam. In addition, conferees incorporated the Senate language which barred Eximbank credit for exports to any Communist country unless the President found it to be in the national interest. This was done, conferees said, becaue if any Communist country stopped aiding North Vietnam, the bill's flat ban on Eximbank credit to that country would then become inoperative, and if the war ended the flat ban would become completely inoperative. In that case, the conferees said, Eximbank support of exports to Communist countries should be subject to a Presidential policy decision.

President's Program. Other than hearings in both houses, there was no action taken in 1968 to ease restrictions against trading with Communist nations. President Johnson repeated requests he made in earlier years to remove legal barriers to increased East-West trade, but Congress—worried by Communist adventures in Vietnam and Czechoslovakia—did not respond. The hearings, held by the House Foreign Affairs Subcommittee on Europe and the Senate Banking and Currency Subcommittee on International Finance, were designed to provide Congress with information on trade between the East and West blocs in preparation for action on the Export Control Act which was to expire in 1969.

Eximbank

Congress extended the life of the Export-Import Bank and broadened its lending authority. These actions were taken in separate pieces of legislation, one of which became involved with controversial riders on arms sales and East-West trade *(see previous stories)*.

Extension. Early in the year, Congress completed action on a bill (S 1155—PL 90-267) extending the life of the Eximbank for five years, through June 30, 1973. The bill also increased the limit on the amount of loans, guarantees and insurance permitted to be outstanding at any one time from $9 billion to $13.5 billion. A third provision increased the Bank's authority to issue export credit insurance and guarantees on loans by private institutions from $2 billion to $3.5 billion. (As under existing law, however, only 25 percent of the amount of such assistance outstanding was to be charged against the Bank's total lending authority.)

High-Risk Credit Fund. Congress passed with little controversy a proposal that was part of the Administration's balance-of-payments program to broaden the lending authority of the Eximbank. Mr. Johnson on Jan. 1 announced a number of steps to reduce the nation's chronic and worsening balance-of-payments deficit. Some of the remedies required enactment of legislation including one to enable the Eximbank to compete better with the export subsidy program of other nations. The result of this request was the bill (HR 16162—PL 90-390) permitting the Eximbank to provide relatively high-risk credit for export transactions that would be ineligible for credit under existing Eximbank standards. Supporters of the bill pointed out that Japan, Canada and some European countries had in recent years provided substantial government support to their exporters who were moving aggressively into markets in less developed nations.

The bill passed both chambers with little opposition after minor controversy about the amount of liability to be charged to the U.S. Treasury in case of defaults on Eximbank loans under the new program.

Provisions. Authorized the Eximbank to use up to $500 million of its $13.5-billion statutory lending authority to finance export transactions which, in the judgment of the Bank's directors, "offer sufficient likelihood of repayment to justify the Bank's support in order to actively foster the foreign trade and long-term commercial interest of the United States." (This permitted high-risk loans which were not possible under the existing test of "reasonable assurance of repayment" that the Bank applied to its normal lending transactions.)

Provided that the aggregate amount of direct loans plus 25 percent of the face value of credit guarantees and insurance were to be counted against the $500-million ceiling.

Provided that in the event the Eximbank suffered losses under the new high-risk program, the Bank would bear the first $100 million of the losses, the U.S. Treasury would bear the second $100 million, and the Bank would bear any further losses.

Authorized appropriations of $100 million to the Treasury Department to cover its share of losses.

Specified that credit extended under the new program was to be governed by normal Bank policies with respect to terms of repayment, interest rates, fees and premiums.

Prohibited use of the new program for the sale of defense equipment or services.

Trade Developments

Beyond the unsuccessful effort to expand East-West trade *(see above),* the Administration had only mixed success in other matters involving international trade. On the one hand, Congress did not pass the President's proposed Trade Expansion Act. But on the other hand, the Administration was able to defeat moves for increased import quotas. The protectionist drives began in 1967 to counter the effects of the Kennedy Round of tariff-cutting agreements, but were contained by Administration lobbying and by the threat of a Presidential

veto of protectionist legislation. President Johnson in 1968 vetoed a bill (HR 10915) to transfer a cotton quota from Egypt and the Sudan to American producers. In addition, Congress acted on a coffee agreement and a grains treaty. *(See separate stories about these actions on following pages.)*

There was intensive lobbying during the year by many American industries which sought to protect—or continue protection of—their products from foreign competition that might arise from the Kennedy Round tariff-cutting agreements. The most active groups included textiles, oil, steel and chemicals. An amendment to establish quotas on dairy imports was defeated by only one vote, 37-38, in the Senate during action on an income tax surcharge bill. An import quota amendment for textiles was added by the Senate to the same tax bill, but it was later dropped in conference.

U.S. participation in the International Antidumping Code, which was negotiated as part of the Kennedy Round, was challenged in Congress. Opponents of participation said that domestic industries would find it impossible to obtain relief against foreign dumping under provisions of a 1921 law. That law was designed to prevent injury to American industry from unfair pricing practices involving goods produced abroad and sold in the United States at prices lower than those charged in the producer's country—the practice known as "dumping." Relief under the 1921 law involved special tariffs on the imported goods. The Senate in 1968 adopted a rider to an unrelated bill (HR 17324—PL 90-634, dealing primarily with the Renegotiation Act) to block U.S. participation in the International Code. The Administration opposed this, noting that the Code was part of the Kennedy Round agreements it had negotiated. A compromise was agreed upon which provided that the 1921 law would have supremacy in any case where it and the Code were in conflict.

Trade Expansion Act. A major disappointment for the Administration was the failure of Congress to act on legislation to extend until June 1970 the President's authority to cut tariffs and to eliminate the American Selling Price (ASP) system. ASP provided special protection to the chemical industry. These proposals were contained in a proposed Trade Expansion Act (HR 17551). The bill also adjusted the terms of assistance to industries and workers injured as a result of U.S. trade policy to make it easier to obtain relief. The bill also extended to June 30, 1971, the Automotive Products Trade Act of 1965 (PL 89-283) which offered adjustment assistance to firms and workers in the automotive industry and permitted lower tariffs on autos and automotive equipment shipped between the United States and Canada. Mr. Johnson in a special message to Congress asked for enactment of HR 17551, but the only action was 19 days of hearings in June and July by the House Ways and Means Committee.

Coffee Agreement

Congress in separate actions ratified a treaty to stabilize coffee prices and enacted legislation to implement the treaty.

Ratification. By a 51-8 roll-call vote, the Senate consented to ratification by the President of the International Coffee Agreement of 1968 (Exec. D, 90th Congress, 2nd Session). The treaty extended the International Coffee Agreement of 1962, which was scheduled to expire Sept. 30, for five years with certain modifications. The Agreement was designed to keep coffee prices stable, avoiding the wild fluctuations that had hurt Latin American producers in the past.

The 1968 Agreement modified the 1962 treaty by providing more flexible provisions for adjusting export quotas so as to distinguish among the different types of coffee and avoid sharp price fluctuations within brief periods. It also improved the mechanism for enforcement of quotas and strengthened the penalties for non-compliance with quotas. President Johnson requested Senate approval of the treaty. *(See 1965 action, p. 61.)*

Implementation. Shortly before adjournment in October, Congress authorized the United States to continue to participate in the International Coffee Agreement. The authorization was included as a rider to an unrelated bill (HR 17324—PL 90-634) extending the life of the Renegotiation Board. Although the 1962 treaty had been extended for five years by Exec. D, HR 17324 authorized implementation for only two years to allow Congress to review operation of the Agreement sooner than would otherwise be possible. HR 17324 also permitted the President to suspend participation in the Agreement if he determined that U.S. ships were being discriminated against in transporting coffee and that the discrimination had not been ended by other methods.

Cotton Quota Veto

President Johnson in August vetoed a bill (HR 10915) to take away the extra-long staple cotton quota from Egypt and the Sudan and transfer it to American producers in the Southwestern states. The veto was the President's first of the year. No effort was made to override it. Mr. Johnson said the bill tied his hands and "deprives (me) of needed flexibility by forcing an automatic suspension of trade when diplomatic relations are severed." The bill transferred the cotton quota from nations which broke diplomatic ties with the United States; both Egypt and the Sudan had done this during the 1967 Middle East war between Israel and the Arab states. Mr. Johnson called the bill a protectionist measure that would "seriously inhibit the future resumption of both diplomatic relations and trade." He also said it would establish an undesirable precedent by connecting diplomatic and trade policy and would violate U.S. international obligations against nondiscrimination under the General Agreement on Tariffs and Trade.

HR 10915 was passed by the House in 1967. The Senate passed it in July 1968 after heated debate in which there were charges that the measure represented little more than special interest legislation to benefit Southwestern cotton producers. (Members of Congress from those states had been trying for years to obtain legislation that would permit larger production of the long-stable cotton produced in their areas.)

Other Treaties

Grains. The Senate in June by a 62-21 roll call consented to the ratification of the International Grains Arrangement (Exec. A, 90th Congress, 2nd Session). The treaty set prices for wheat traded in world markets and assured a steady supply of grains to be contributed to needy countries. President Johnson requested ratification. One section of the accord replaced the International Wheat Agreement which was first drawn up in 1949 and extended since then. Both treaties specified the amount of wheat which importing countries agreed to buy from exporting nations and set a price range for the wheat. Negotiated at the Kennedy Round of trade talks in 1967, the new treaty was to take effect July 1, 1968, and continue in effect for three years. It was supported by all major farm organizations except the American Farm Bureau Federation. *(See p. 66, 77.)*

Astronauts. The Senate in October consented to the ratification of a treaty (Exec. J, 90th Congress, 2nd Session) providing for the safe return of astronauts who landed in foreign countries. It provided that a country learning of an accident would inform the launching nation, would attempt to rescue the astronauts and would return them safely and promptly to the launching nation. It also provided for return of an object which came down in another nation.

Refugees. The Senate in October consented to the ratification of a protocol (Exec. K, 90th Congress, 2nd Session) on the status of refugees. The protocol updated the provisions of a 1951 treaty granting basic human rights to refugees. The 1951 treaty covered such matters as freedom of religion, access to courts of law and the right to hold gainful employment, to acquire property, to move freely and similar matters. It also prohibited the return of refugees to countries where their lives or freedom might be threatened.

International Fairs. The Senate in April consented to the ratification of the 1928 Convention Relating to International Exhibitions (Exec. P, 90th Congress, 1st Session) and two protocols. Under it the United States was to become a member of the bureau which administers the treaty and would be obligated not to participate in any international expositions which had not been sanctioned by it in accordance with its rules. The treaty was expected to protect the Government against repeated requests for endorsement of and participation in international fairs held in the United States which were primarily of regional and local interest.

Ship Safety. The Senate in May consented to the ratification of six amendments to the International Convention for the Safety of Life at Sea (SOLAS) which was intended to improve ship safety standards.

The amendments (Exec. C, 90th Congress, 2nd Session) were annexes to the 1960 SOLAS treaty which had been adopted by the Assembly of the Intergovernmental Maritime Consultative Organization. It was the third major effort by the Administration in as many years to improve safety on ships, particularly passenger ships. The loss of 90 lives aboard the Yarmouth Castle, which burned on a cruise from Florida in 1965, had focused attention on the problem of safety standards for foreign ships. U.S.-flag passenger ship construction had been regulated since 1936. *(See p. 98.)*

The annexes imposed new requirements on ships undergoing modification to prevent any reduction in safety standards, tightened safety standards for future passenger ships by requiring maximum use of noncombustible materials in ship construction and outfitting (as the United States had required since 1936) and established higher standards for fire safety and control plans and emergency procedures in both passenger and cargo vessels. Other minor provisions also were included.

Inter-American Development Bank

Congress enacted a bill (HR 15364—PL 90-325) to increase the United States' participation in the Inter-American Development Bank (IADB). HR 15364 authorized the U.S. representative to the IADB to vote in favor of a $1 billion increase in the IADB's callable capital stock. It also authorized a U.S. subscription of $411,760,000 to the IADB as its share of the increase, without fiscal year limitation. The IADB was established in 1959 and was generally modeled on the organization and procedures of the World Bank. It included 21 of 23 member nations of the Organization of American States (OAS). The two non-members were Barbados and Cuba; Cuba currently was suspended from the OAS and therefore not eligible for IADB membership. The bulk of ordinary IADB lending resources was derived from bond issues in private capital markets both in the United States and abroad. The "guaranteed" backing for the bonds was afforded by callable subscriptions to the capital stock by member nations. The callable amounts were not paid in cash when subscribed and appropriated. Rather, they remained as book entries unless needed by the IADB to pay off bonds because some loans were in default. The legislation was requested by President Johnson.

Congress in 1965 and 1967 enacted legislation to increase the U.S. contribution to the IADB's Fund for Special Operations, a "soft loan" operation. *(See p. 62 and 99.)*

IDA, Asian Development Bank

Disenchantment with the foreign aid program spilled over to related legislation in 1968. Bills to increase U.S. financial assistance to the Asian Development Bank and the International Development Assn. were not enacted even though both were part of the President's program.

International Development Assn. Legislation to assist the IDA was reported in both chambers but passed by neither. The bills (HR 16775, S 3378) provided a $480-million U.S. contribution to a $1.2-billion replenishment of the IDA's fund for "soft loans" to less developed counties. The refusal of Congress to pass the bill was expected to be a severe setback for the IDA even though up to $720 million of the increase still could come from other nations. It was expected that the IDA's fiscal 1968 lending rate of $107 million could be continued in 1969; however, that level of assistance was far below the 1967 level of $354 million. Congressional sources said a major reason for inaction on the IDA bills was a general dissatisfaction with the existing foreign assistance program. The House bill died in the House Rules Committee; the Senate bill was reported by the Foreign Relations Committee—after months of inaction—three days before Congress adjourned and too late for floor action.

The IDA, an affiliate of the International Bank for Reconstruction and Development (World Bank), was created in 1960 under U.S. leadership as a vehicle to channel non-Communist development financing into less developed nations under easier credit terms than were available from the World Bank. The loans were interest free, but carried a three-quarters of 1 percent service charge annually. They were repayable over 50 years in hard currencies.

Asian Development Bank. The Senate Foreign Relations Committee deferred action on an Administration bill (S 2479) to contribute $200 million to the Asian Development Bank. Mr. Johnson originally requested the funds in 1967 *(see p. 99)* and repeated the request in his 1968 foreign aid message. The funds were to be contributed over a four-year period for use in making long-term loans at low interest rates—"soft loans" as they were called. The Committee on May 27 by a 6-6 tie vote rejected a substitute bill which provided that no more than $25 million be appropriated for the Bank in any year until the Vietnam conflict ended. The effect of the Committee action was to leave the original bill pending and kill it for the session.

Special Drawing Rights

In an effort to improve international monetary procedures, Congress passed a bill (HR 16911—PL 90-349) to create a new monetary facility, called Special Drawing Rights (SDRs), and to provide for United States participation in it. The legislation, requested by President Johnson, accomplished the changes by amending the International Monetary Fund Agreement. The bill was passed with little controversy in either chamber. *(See box for a description of how the SDRs would work.)*

The creation of special drawing rights or "paper gold" had been under discussion by the major financial powers for more than four years. The purpose of the reform effort was to increase world monetary reserves to accommodate growing world trade. Between 1958 and 1965, economists said, the total value of world exports had increased by about 75 percent, while monetary reserves had grown by only about 22 percent. Continuation of this trend, they said, might result in restrictive policies which could sharply curtail world trade.

The President in 1965 directed the Secretary of the Treasury to initiate negotiations on the subject of SDRs.

The idea of using SDRs to supplement gold holdings and existing reserve currencies was agreed upon by the 10 major countries—the United States, Britain, Japan, Canada, Sweden and the Common Market countries of France, West Germany, Italy, Belgium and the Netherlands—at a meeting in London Aug. 27, 1967. The agreement was ratified by the IMF governors at a meeting of the 107-member body in Rio de Janeiro Sept. 28.

The finance ministers and state bank officials of nine of the 10 countries meeting in Stockholm, March 30, 1968, agreed to the draft of a plan creating a system of SDRs. Only France failed to support the plan. However, France left open the possibility of later participating in the plan. The Stockholm agreement had to be ratified by all 107 members of the IMF.

The agreement reached was actually a compromise, with the United States yielding greater voting influence in the IMF to the six Common Market countries (including Luxembourg, which was not represented at the Stockholm conference). The United States also yielded on arrangements that would make it easier for a country to refuse to participate in the SDR plan. At the same time, the United States and Britain retained the right to veto any effort aimed at changing the price of gold.

President Johnson in a special message April 30 asked Congress to approve legislation to provide for U.S. participation in the SDR plan.

Major Provisions. As signed into law, HR 16911 provided for U.S. participation in the creation of a new international reserve asset, SDRs, within the IMF.

SDRs, sometimes referred to as "paper gold," would be issued only to governments and would take the form of deposit entries on the books of the IMF. They would be used only in transactions among governments and central banks and would be backed by the obligations of IMF members to accept them and pay a convertible currency in return.

Participants would be required to accept SDRs in an amount equal to three times their allocations, although they would be free to accept more. The SDRs would be allocated to participating members in proportion to their quotas in the IMF, and would be issued in denomination units equivalent to the gold value of the dollar.

The actual creation of SDRs would require an 85 percent weighted majority vote among the 107 member nations of the IMF. (The United States had 21.8 percent of the total voting power in the IMF.) To make the facility operational, instruments of commitment would have to be deposited by members holding 75 percent of the total IMF quotas.

SDRs could be used to purchase foreign exchange in order to obtain resources for maintaining the value of a country's currency, in the same way that gold was used. In practice, the country using SDRs—probably one with balance-of-payments problems—would request the IMF to debit its SDR account and credit the account of the nation from which it was receiving foreign currency. While a country might use all its SDRs at once, over a five-year period it could not use more than 70 percent of its average allocations for that period.

Immigration

Congress enacted an Administration-backed bill (HR 15147—PL 90-633) easing naturalization requirements for alien servicemen stationed in the Vietnam combat area. HR 15147 extended provisions of the Immigration and Nationality Act, permitting immediate naturalization of an alien serving in the U.S. Armed Forces during a period of conflict. These provisions had been extended to alien servicemen who fought in World Wars I and II and in the Korean conflict. HR 15147 extended immediate naturalization to some 4,800 aliens who served in the Vietnam combat zone after Feb. 28, 1961, the date when the first American military advisers joined South Vietnamese forces in the field. Some 19,600 aliens serving outside the war zone were eligible for eased naturalization requirements that were less liberal than those incorporated in HR 15147. The bill also permitted the President, by executive order, to extend immediate naturalization at any time for a future combat area, without the need for action by Congress.

Operation of SDRs

During House hearings on HR 16911, the managing director of the International Monetary Fund gave the following example of how Special Drawing Rights transactions would operate:

"Let us suppose that, at some time in the future, drawing rights equivalent to a total of $1 billion a year are created by vote of the Board of Governors (of the IMF). If we assume that a given country A has a quota amounting to 1 percent of total Fund quotas, the Fund will accordingly credit to country A in the special drawing account an amount of SDRs equal to $10 million. Country A could add these to its reserves as it would be entitled to use them without question in case of need.

"Suppose, now, that country A does want to use them. In order to do so, it would have to convert them into a usable currency. It would therefore ask the Fund into what currencies it could convert an amount of SDRs, equivalent to, say, $5 million. The Fund would at any given time have a list of participating Fund members whose balance-of-payments and reserve positions were regarded as reasonably satisfactory. From this list the Fund would select appropriate countries to be designated. Since the amount involved in my illustration is small, we may reasonably assume that the Fund would select, say, two countries: Germany and Italy, for instance. In this event, the Fund would notify Germany and Italy that it was crediting their special drawing account with the equivalent of $2.5 million each in SDRs, and that they should place to the credit of country A in the books of their central banks a corresponding amount of deutsche marks and lire (or any other convertible currencies that Germany or Italy may own). At the same time the Fund would debit the special reserve account of country A an amount of SDRs equivalent to $5 million.

"As a result of these transactions, $5 million of SDRs in country A's reserves would be replaced by $5 million of currencies which it could then spend; and the reserves of Germany and Italy would increase, at least initially, by $2.5 million each owing to the receipt of additional SDRs.

"Country A would be charged a moderate rate of interest (perhaps 1½ percent) on the SDRs which it had used; and Germany and Italy would be paid interest at the same rate. The value of the additional SDRs held by Germany and Italy, like the value of those allocated to them by the Fund, would be guaranteed in terms of gold.

"As long as country A used less than 70 percent of the SDRs which had been allocated to it by the Fund (and in my illustration it would be using only 50 percent), no repayment (or reconstitution) would have to take place. In due time, as its payments position strengthened again, it would no doubt be called on itself to provide currency in return for SDRs and so would tend to restore its holdings of SDRs. But if over a period of time its average utilization of all the SDRs which had been allocated to it by the Fund did exceed 70 percent, the excess would have to be repaid.

"I might mention, to round off my illustration, that Germany and Italy would be obligated to receive additional SDRs—including the $2.5 million equivalent in my example—only up to a point where they were holding twice the amount allocated to them by the Fund."

Immigration Act. With the 1965 Immigration Act taking full effect July 1, 1968, a number of Members of Congress moved to make changes in the law. However, no action was taken on any proposals. One of the first results of the 1965 law was a reduction in immigration from the traditionally favored areas—Ireland, Britain, Germany and other Northern European countries—and an increase from Southern European nations and from Asia. The Select Commission on Western Hemisphere Immigration, created by the 1965 law to study its effects and recommend changes, reported Jan. 15 that it was unable to make a final, definitive recommendation on the proposed 120,000 ceiling on Western Hemisphere immigration. Commission members had asked Congress in 1967 to defer for one year the 120,000-ceiling and to extend the date for the Commission's report. A bill to do this passed the House but died in the Senate.

Other Bills

Sea-Level Canal. Congress passed a bill (HR 15190—PL 90-359) extending from Dec. 1, 1969, to Dec. 1, 1970, the deadline for completion of a study to determine a site for a new canal between the Atlantic and Pacific Oceans. The bill also increased the authorization for the study from $17.5 million to $24 million. Congress in 1967 had extended the original study deadline for 17 months. *(See p. 101.)*

Passports. Congress extended the period during which a U.S. passport remains valid to five years from the existing three years. The bill (S 1418—PL 90-428) also revised the fees charged to obtain a passport. The effect of the fee change was to slightly reduce the cost to a person who, in the past, kept his passport valid for the maximum five-year period (the initial three years plus the permissible two-year renewal), and to slightly increase the cost to a person who did not exercise the renewal option. Existing law provided a fee of $10 or $11 (depending on where a person obtained the passport) for

---

Peace Corps Funding, 1962-69

The figures below show the authorizations and appropriations for the Peace Corps since its inception.

(in thousands of dollars)

Fiscal Year	Original Appropriation Request	Authorization Enacted	Revised Appropriation Request	Appropriations Enacted
1962	$ 40,000	$ 40,000	——	$ 30,000
1963	63,750	63,750	——	59,000
1964	108,000	102,000	$102,000	95,964
1965	115,000	115,000	106,100	104,100
1966	125,200	115,000	——	114,100
1967	110,500	110,000	112,150	110,000
1968	124,400	115,700	118,700	107,500
1969	112,800	112,800	——	102,000

---

the three-year initial period and $5 for the two-year renewal. S 1418 provided a fee of $12 for five years. The State Department requested the changes.

Peace Corps. Congress passed a bill (S 2914—PL 90-362) to authorize appropriations of $112.8 million for the Peace Corps in fiscal 1969. It was the amount requested by the Administration. As in 1967, there was minor controversy surrounding the authorization. Republicans criticized salary levels higher than $12,000 a year, the ratio of administrative personnel to volunteers and the lack of progress in obtaining contributions for the Corps from host nations. The House by a 180-187 (R 116-51; D 64-136, ND 7-118, SD 57-18) rejected a GOP proposal to reduce the authorization by $15.8 million.

Chapter 3—Economic Policy

Key Votes

In this chapter, key roll-call votes are shown in bold-face type. The party breakdown on each of these votes and the position taken by each Member of Congress may be found in the key vote charts which appear in the appendix to this book.

Economic Policy

EXCEPT for American involvement in the Vietnam war, economic policy was the most controversial issue of the Johnson years. The two—the war and economic policy—were closely related. The U.S. war effort placed strains on the nation's productive capacity which led to imbalances in the economy and to controversy over the Government's management of economic policy. To the majority of Americans, the rapid inflation of the period—particularly during 1967 and 1968—was the most important consequence of the wartime economic pressures. There were many other consequences: the housing industry suffered troubled times, particularly in 1966; interest rates soared, limiting the availability of credit to businessmen and consumers; the nation's international trade surplus dwindled as imports rose; the balance-of-payments deficit reached crisis proportions and the U.S. gold stock declined.

In spite of these serious problems in the Johnson years, economic policy—when viewed over the 1961 to 1969 period of Democratic control of the White House—experienced many successes. The important measures of national economic activity improved substantially over the eight-year period. The gross national product rose from $482 billion in early calendar 1961 to just under $720 billion in the last quarter of 1968. More than 10.5 million jobs were created during the period, permitting a reduction in the unemployment rate to 3.3 percent (on a seasonally adjusted basis) in December 1968; in 1961, the rate was 6.7 percent. Disposable personal income per capita—after taxes and adjustment for price increases—increased by 33 percent from early 1961. Corporate profits doubled to just over $50 billion late in 1968.

There also were important developments in the formulation and implementation of economic policy during the period. Congress enacted several tax bills, two of which were of unusual importance in establishing new federal policies to influence the economy. In 1964, in Mr. Johnson's first major legislative success, Congress enacted a major reduction in personal and corporate income taxes which pumped billions of dollars of purchasing power into the private economy. This helped sustain and accelerate the economic expansion that had begun in 1961. At the end of Mr. Johnson's term, when the economy was operating in excess of its noninflationary potential and prices were rising rapidly, Congress enacted an income tax increase. The purpose was to draw purchasing power out of private hands and slow economic activity. The tax increase, however, came in mid-1968, almost a year after it was requested by the Administration. The delay allowed the economy to continue at a high level for many months before the restraint of the tax increase was felt. Nevertheless, the two tax bills—the reduction in 1964 and the increase in 1968—represented the implementation of the policy, which had been advocated by Mr. Kennedy's key economic advisers, that Government fiscal policy was a useful tool to help control the level of economic activity throughout the nation.

BOLD use of Government fiscal powers, involving both federal spending and taxes, was not a policy that had won many advocates during the eight years of President Eisenhower's term in office in the 1950s. Business fluctuations, with accompanying high unemployment and unused resources such as idle plants during the periods of economic contractions, had been a traditional pattern in the United States. The National Bureau of Economic Research had traced 27 business-cycle contractions between 1854 and 1961 on an average of once every four years. Attempting to reduce these fluctuations and to mitigate their seriousness had become an important goal of Government economic planners in the Kennedy-Johnson years.

The Council of Economic Advisers that served these Presidents established what they thought would be a "potential" output for the nation. A 4 percent unemployment rate was established as an "interim" goal for national policy early in the Kennedy Administration. Based on the 4 percent figure, the Council plotted the expected increase in the gross national product over the years and compared it with the actual GNP increase. The two were approximately together in 1955, but actual GNP fell below potential in the following years during recessions in 1957-58 and 1960-61 and even during the economic expansion between these two periods.

The Kennedy Administration came to power in 1961 as the nation was emerging from the 1960-61 recession. That recession reached a low point in February 1961 and the economy started on the expected expansion. From then until the end of President Johnson's term in 1969, the economy continued to advance; the expansion was in its 95th month in January 1969.

Reference

Discussion of economic policy from 1945-64 will be found in *Congress and the Nation, Vol. I, p. 337-562.*

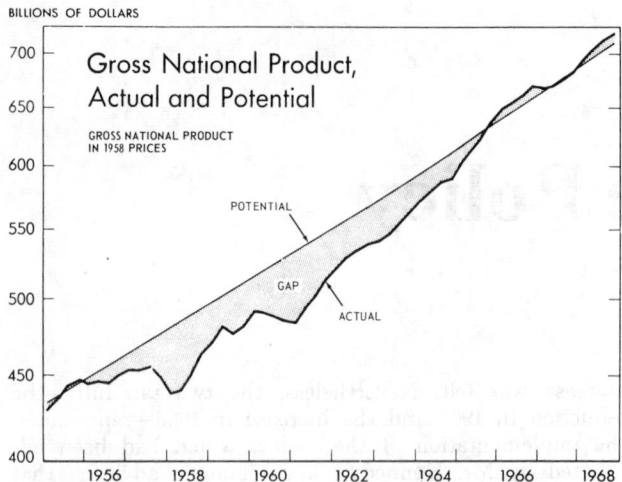

BILLIONS OF DOLLARS

Gross National Product,
Actual and Potential

GROSS NATIONAL PRODUCT
IN 1958 PRICES

POTENTIAL

GAP

ACTUAL

The gap between actual and potential output was slowly closed and eliminated in 1965. After that point, actual growth exceeded the calculated potential as unemployment dropped below 4 percent and inflation increased apace. The Council's calculations placed potential national economic growth at 4 percent a year during most of the Kennedy-Johnson years after adjustment for price increases. The actual growth generally was above this level as idle resources were brought into use; however, the high rate continued after the growth gap had been closed and the strains on the economy contributed to inflationary pressures. In the first half of 1968, for example, the GNP expanded at the torrid annual rate of 6.5 percent. This rate was far above the 4 percent noninflationary rate the President's economic advisers believed the economy capable of sustaining. During the second half of 1968, the GNP growth rate dropped back to 4.5 percent which still was more than economists thought wise in a time of rising prices.

THE first expansionary period extended from 1961 until about mid-1965. It was a time of steady economic growth as consumer and business demand expanded and Government fiscal and monetary policies helped to stimulate the economy. The unemployment rate dropped from 6.7 percent to 4.5 percent of the labor force. The Government provided substantial stimulus to the economy totaling about $37.5 billion through such measures as accelerated Social Security payments, liberalized public assistance payments, increased defense expenditures resulting from greater stress on conventional forces, the enactment of an investment tax credit for purchase of business equipment and liberalization of depreciation guidelines. A major stimulus was added in the 1964 income tax cut. Monetary policy provided a continuing source of funds for the expanding credit demands of the economy. Prices remained very stable as unused capacity was absorbed. Average hourly compensation increased, but so did productivity (output per man-hour) and consequently labor costs changed very little. *(See Table I.)*

This period of steady and noninflationary growth came to and end in 1965 when the U.S. involvement in Vietnam escalated. At the heart of the problem was increasing pressure on the economy caused by rapidly rising Government defense spending (which the Administration repeatedly underestimated), by continued high consumer demand and by substantial capital expenditures for plant and equipment. The combination of all of these forces pushing on the economy inevitably led to inflation. Between 1965 and 1967, on the average, consumer prices rose 2.5 percent annually. Between 1967 and 1968, they rose an average of 4.2 percent annually. The change from 1961-65 was only 1.3 percent annually. Average hourly compensation shot up dramatically as did unit labor costs. *(See Table I.)* The rate of growth in the real GNP was more than 8 percent between the second quarter of 1965 and the first quarter of 1966.

Efforts to restrain the economy during this period were inadequate at first and tardy when finally put into effect. When fiscal (tax and spending) policy was not used effectively until near the end of Mr. Johnson's term, monetary (interest rate, money supply) policy assumed a disproportionate share of the burden. The Johnson Administration from time-to-time prior to 1967 mentioned the possibility of a general income tax in-

Table I

Total Private Domestic Economy

(Nonfarm and Farm)

Average Annual Rate of Change

	Output per [1] Man-Hour	Compensation [2] Per Man-Hour	Labor Cost Per Unit of Output	Non-Labor [3] Cost Per Unit of Output	Consumer Price Index	Real Compensation Per Man-Hour
1947-67	3.2%	5.0%	1.7%	2.2%	1.7%	3.2%
1947-53	4.2	6.5	2.2	3.6	3.0	3.4
1953-61	2.6	4.6	1.9	2.2	1.6	3.0
1961-65	3.9	4.4	0.5	2.2	1.3	3.1
1965-67	2.7	6.5	3.8	1.0	2.5	3.6
1967-68 (Est.)	3.2	7.3	4.0	2.8	4.2	3.3

1. *Gross national product in constant (1958) dollars.*
2. *Wages, salaries, fringe benefits, labor compensation of self-employed.*
3. *Includes profits, non-corporate income, depreciation, indirect business taxes and other costs.*

SOURCE: Department of Labor, Bureau of Labor Statistics

Table II

Selected Economic Data, 1952-1968

The top portion of the chart shows the average annual rate of change (in percent) for selected economic indicators. The first two columns compare the average rate of change in each year of the eight years of the Eisenhower Administrations with the average rate of change each year of the Administrations of Presidents Kennedy and Johnson. Also shown are the average rates of change for each of the eight Democratic years. The bottom part of the chart shows average unemployment rates. In the first two columns, time periods are from the end of the first year shown through the end of the second year shown.

	1952-1960	1960-1968	1961	1962	1963	1964	1965	1966	1967	1968
Average annual percent changes in:										
Gross national product, 1958 dollars	2.7%	4.8%	1.9%	6.6%	4.0%	5.5%	6.3%	6.4%	2.4%	5.0%
Disposable personal income	4.9	6.7	4.1	5.7	5.0	8.3	8.0	8.1	6.8	7.8
Corporate profits after tax	3.9	8.4	1.9	14.7	6.1	16.0	21.1	9.7	—5.7	6.0
Industrial production index	3.2	5.4	.9	7.8	5.1	6.4	8.4	9.0	1.2	4.6
Housing starts	—2.0	2.3	4.4	12.0	10.0	—5.1	—3.4	—21.3	11.1	16.5
Money supply (demand deposits plus currency)	1.3	4.7	3.2	1.5	3.8	4.3	4.9	2.2	6.4	6.5
Consumer price index	1.4	2.0	1.1	1.2	1.2	1.3	1.7	2.9	2.8	4.2
Wholesale price index	.9	.9	—.4	.3	—.3	.2	2.0	3.3	.2	2.5
GNP deflator	2.1	2.1	1.3	1.1	1.3	1.5	1.9	2.6	3.1	3.8
Average unemployment rate	4.7	4.3	6.7	5.5	5.7	5.2	4.5	3.8	3.8	3.6
Nonwhite workers	8.7	8.1	12.4	10.9	10.8	9.6	8.1	7.3	7.4	6.7
White workers	4.2	3.8	6.0	4.9	5.0	4.6	4.1	3.3	3.4	3.2

SOURCE: Department of Commerce, Office of Business Economics

crease but did not propose it. Before leaving office, Mr. Johnson revealed that he had discussed such a rise privately with business and Congressional leaders early in 1966 and was convinced that it could not be enacted.

The Administration's public position in 1966 and 1967 was that the increasing costs of the Vietnam war could be financed by reducing nonessential expenditures and by speeding-up tax payments and instituting graduated tax withholding. The latter two proposals, which were mild forms of fiscal restraint, were enacted by Congress in 1966. Late in the year, Congress temporarily suspended the investment tax credit which was an incentive for business spending. (The credit was reinstated the following spring.) A reduction in federal expenditures, subject to many diverse influences, did not prove a very useful road to restraining the economy. Many observers doubted whether Mr. Johnson was serious about expanditure reduction in light of his Administration's commitment to a far-reaching social program to alleviate a multitude of domestic problems.

A major part of the effort to restrain the economy during this period fell to monetary policy, although it too was applied unevenly by the monetary officials. In 1966, monetary policy resulted in the highest interest rates and the tightest credit conditions since the early 1920s. Money markets dissolved into near crisis in August 1966. Conditions eased after that but tightened again as Mr. Johnson's term came to a close. In 1966, the resulting scarcity of lendable funds and the accompanying high interest rates affected many persons and businesses but was most seriously felt by the housing industry and prospective homebuyers. The situation

became so serious that Congress enacted legislation to control certain types of interest rates and to pump additional funds into the housing market.

THE rapid economic advance of 1965-66 continued into 1967 and 1968, but by this time the Johnson Administration had become convinced that increased restraint had to be placed on the economy. This view was shared by Members of Congress and by many economists, businessmen and other individuals outside the Government.

The first half of 1967 was sluggish as businesses consumed large inventory stocks accumulated previously. But the basic advance of the economy was still present, according to the Government economists, and a strong second half was anticipated. President Johnson, in his Budget Message of January 1967, proposed a 6 percent surcharge on individual and corporate income taxes. Because of the sluggish first half of the year, Mr. Johnson did not actually send a tax message to Congress until August, when the vigorous economic expansion resumed. Mr. Johnson then formally requested a tax surcharge, but at a higher rate of 10 percent.

Congress failed to react quickly and the surcharge did not become law until the following summer, many months after the time when Government economists believed it was essential. Congressional delay was due in part to lack of clear evidence that the economy was expanding at an excessive rate and in part to the preference of many Members to exercise economic restraint by cutting federal expenditures rather than by—or in addition to—raising taxes. The battle over a tax increase and spending reductions was one of the most important waged during Mr. Johnson's term in office. It was resolved by combining a tax hike (the 10 percent surcharge) with a mandatory reduction in federal expenditures, but only after an international financial crisis developed in March 1968 and accelerating credit demands pushed interest rates to record levels.

As the battle continued, inflation marched on with no sign of relenting. When the year was over, figures showed that the consumer price index had risen 4.7 percent from December 1967 to December 1968. The December to December increase for 1966-1967 was 3.1 percent. (These figures differ slightly from those in Table II because they represent a specific period; those in the table represent the average for the entire year.)

The tax increase and spending cut enacted in mid-1968 were widely thought to provide the major fiscal restraint which would slow and hopefully stop the inflationary spiral characteristic of 1965-68. However, many experts later concluded that the Federal Reserve Board had increased the nation's money supply so rapidly in 1968 (*see Table II*) that the restraining effect of the tax increase was neutralized. Delay in enactment also diluted the bill's effectiveness. Basic disagreements over economic policy caused the delay. This had been true throughout the post-war period leading up to the Kennedy-Johnson years. These two Administrations put the fiscal powers of the Government to use to influence the economy in a manner never before attempted. But the old differences about how the resources of the nation should be allocated—about how the resources of the nation should be allocated

—lower or higher taxes and for whom, more or less spending on this or that project—survived and lived on to plague the new economic policies of the Kennedy-Johnson economic teams. The idea of using fiscal policy to reduce economic fluctuations gained considerable acceptance during the Kennedy-Johnson period. However, execution of such a policy was hampered by political considerations and by the lack of adequate procedures in Congress and the Executive Branch to take action on spending and taxes at just the right moment to obtain the maximum results.

The remainder of this chapter is divided into subchapters on taxes, the federal Budget, housing, transportation, banking, and miscellaneous legislation. Immediately following is a summary of these subchapters.

Tax, Budget Policy

BUDGET policy and tax policy were considered together as complementary influences on economic developments during the Kennedy-Johnson years. Until 1965, the two were utilized successfully to stimulate the economy and bring lagging economic growth back to the potential that was inherent in the unused plant capacity and in the thousands of unemployed workers across the nation. From about mid-1965 until the end of President Johnson's term in 1969, the situation was reversed. Budget and tax policies were not used to their best advantage to slow the economic expansion which

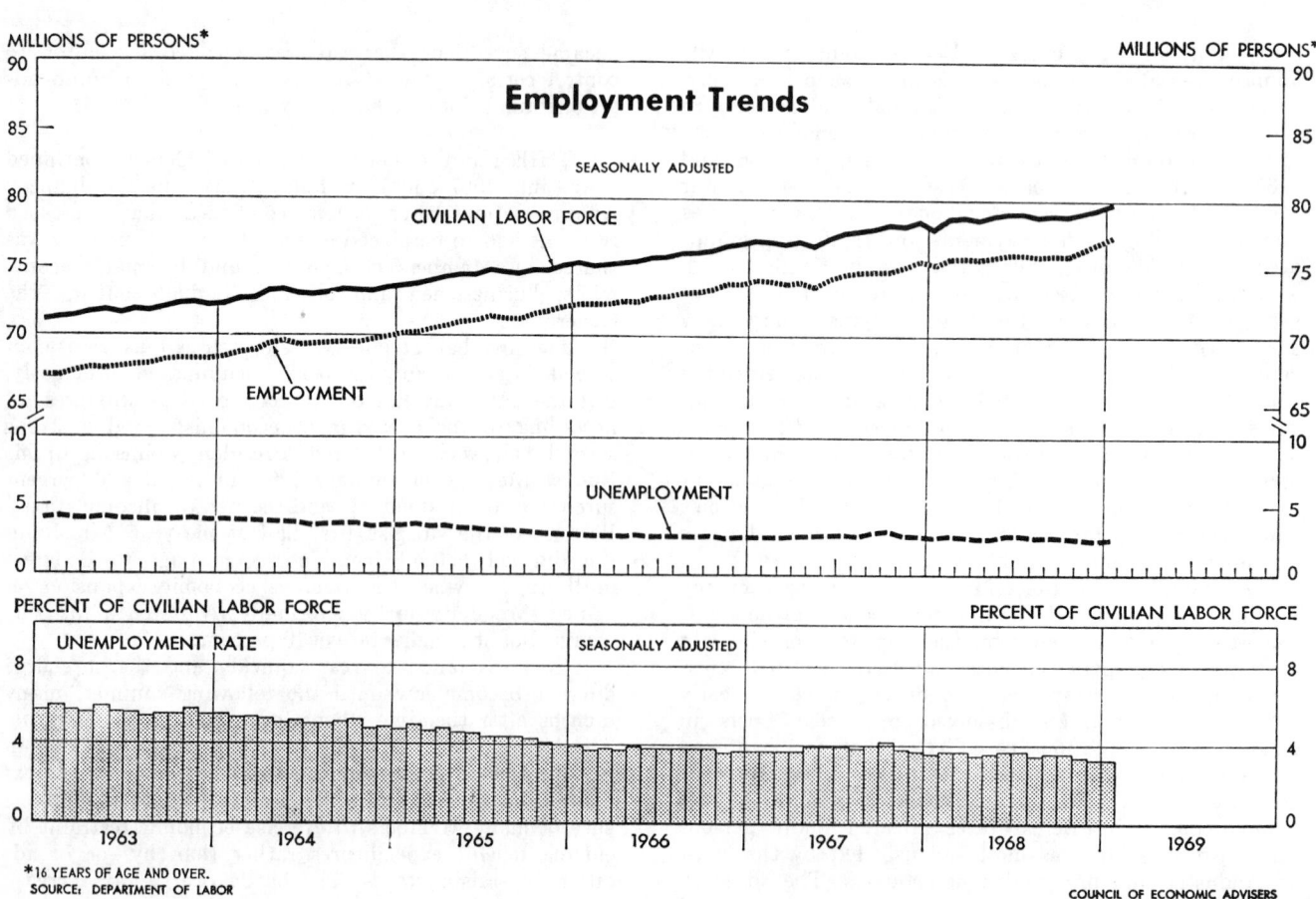

MILLIONS OF PERSONS*

Employment Trends

SEASONALLY ADJUSTED

CIVILIAN LABOR FORCE

EMPLOYMENT

UNEMPLOYMENT

PERCENT OF CIVILIAN LABOR FORCE

UNEMPLOYMENT RATE   SEASONALLY ADJUSTED

1963   1964   1965   1966   1967   1968   1969

*16 YEARS OF AGE AND OVER.
SOURCE: DEPARTMENT OF LABOR

COUNCIL OF ECONOMIC ADVISERS

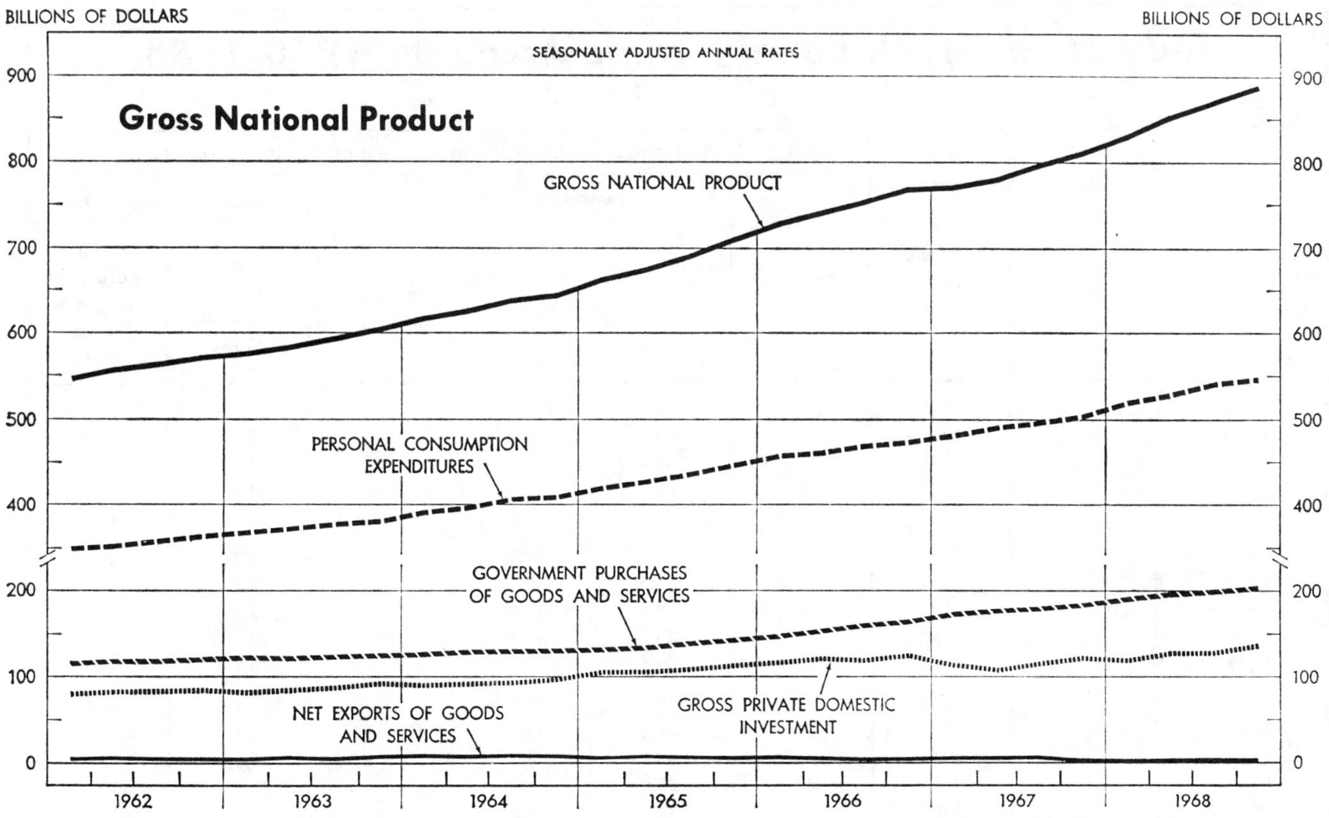

BILLIONS OF DOLLARS

BILLIONS OF DOLLARS

SEASONALLY ADJUSTED ANNUAL RATES

Gross National Product

GROSS NATIONAL PRODUCT

PERSONAL CONSUMPTION
EXPENDITURES

GOVERNMENT PURCHASES
OF GOODS AND SERVICES

NET EXPORTS OF GOODS
AND SERVICES

GROSS PRIVATE DOMESTIC
INVESTMENT

900
800
700
600
500
400
200
100
0

1962   1963   1964   1965   1966   1967   1968

SOURCE: DEPARTMENT OF COMMERCE

COUNCIL OF ECONOMIC ADVISERS

Index, 1957-59=100

Index, 1957-59=100

Consumer Prices

SERVICES

ALL ITEMS

FOOD

COMMODITIES
LESS FOOD

140
130
120
110
100

1962   1963   1964   1965   1966   1967   1968

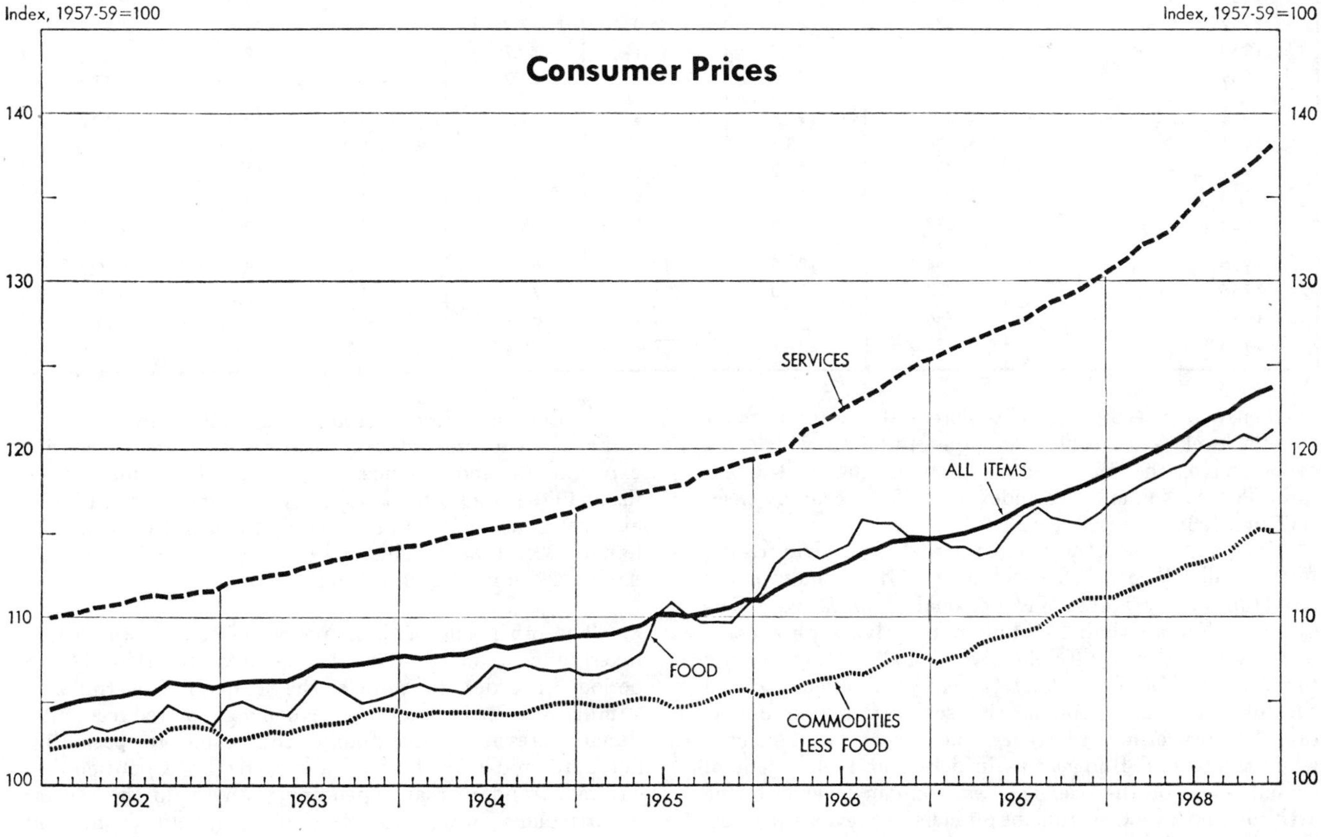

SOURCE: DEPARTMENT OF LABOR

COUNCIL OF ECONOMIC ADVISERS

Federal Sector, National Income Accounts, 1940-1968

(in billions of dollars)

Fiscal year	Gross national product	Federal sector of the national income and product accounts					
			Expenditure		Excess of receipts (+) or expenditures (—)	As a percent of GNP	
		Receipts	Total	of which purchases of goods and service		Total Federal expenditures	Federal purchases of goods and services
1940	$ 95.0	$ 7.6	$ 9.1	$ 5.3	$ —1.5	9.6%	5.5%
1941	109.4	12.1	13.4	9.6	—1.3	12.3	8.8
1942	139.2	19.6	33.6	29.9	—14.0	24.2	21.5
1943	177.5	28.9	76.8	72.3	—47.9	43.3	40.8
1944	201.9	43.1	91.3	85.6	—48.1	45.2	42.4
1945	216.8	43.0	98.2	89.7	—55.2	45.3	41.4
1946	201.6	38.4	55.5	40.1	—17.1	27.5	19.9
1947	219.8	42.7	29.5	13.0	+ 13.2	13.4	5.9
1948	243.5	43.6	30.9	13.2	+ 12.7	12.7	5.4
1949	260.0	40.0	39.6	19.3	+.4	15.2	7.4
1950	263.3	42.0	42.4	19.0	—.5	16.1	7.2
1951	310.5	60.8	44.6	25.1	+16.2	14.4	8.1
1952	337.2	65.1	66.1	46.6	—1.0	19.6	13.8
1953	358.9	69.3	75.8	56.1	—6.5	21.1	15.6
1954	362.1	65.8	74.2	53.2	—8.5	20.5	14.7
1955	378.6	67.2	67.3	43.9	—.1	17.8	11.6
1956	409.4	75.8	69.8	45.2	+6.0	17.0	11.0
1957	431.3	80.7	76.0	47.7	+4.7	17.6	11.1
1958	440.3	77.9	83.1	50.7	—5.1	18.9	11.5
1959	469.1	85.4	90.9	54.7	—5.5	19.4	11.7
1960	495.2	94.8	91.3	52.7	+3.5	18.4	10.6
1961	506.5	95.3	98.0	55.5	—2.7	19.3	11.0
1962	542.1	104.2	106.4	60.9	—2.1	19.6	11.2
1963	573.4	110.2	111.4	63.4	—1.2	19.4	11.1
1964	612.2	115.5	116.9	65.7	—1.4	19.1	10.7
1965	654.2	120.5	118.5	64.4	+2.0	18.1	9.8
1966	720.7	133.0	131.9	71.7	+1.0	18.3	9.9
1967	766.5	147.7	154.4	84.9	—6.7	20.1	11.1
1968	822.6	161.1	172.4	95.6	—11.3	21.0	11.6

by then was exceeding or at its potential non-inflationary growth level. The result was rapid inflation which became one of the most serious problems facing the nation. The consumer price index rose 12 percent between 1965 and 1968.

The stimulus of the 1961-65 period came significantly from a bill (PL 88-272), enacted in 1964, to make major reductions in corporate and personal income taxes. The bill added more than $11 billion to private purchasing power when it was fully effective in 1965. *(Congress and the Nation, Vol. I, p. 437.)* Government officials called the bill the largest stimulative fiscal action ever undertaken in peacetime. Moreover, the tax cut was enacted while the federal Budget was in deficit and while federal spending was on the rise. This was a major reversal of the attitude taken by Government officials in previous periods. The purpose, however, was to further stimulate the econ-

omy—supplementing similar action taken in 1961-63—rather than to provide additional revenues to cover rising expenditures and balance the Budget. The Budget from fiscal 1961 through fiscal 1964, as measured in the national income accounts, ran a deficit ranging from $1.2 billion to $2.7 billion. This indicated that the Budget was having a stimulative effect on the economy.

The other side of fiscal policy, of course, was higher taxes and reduced federal spending in the 1965-68 period in order to reduce the Federal Government's stimulative effect on the economy and reduce inflationary pressures. Eventually, this came to pass, but not until mid-1968. It is always easier for a politician to cut taxes and increase spending than to do the reverse —particularly when an election campaign is not far away as was the case when Mr. Johnson seriously pressed for higher taxes in 1967. The primary difficulty during this period was that Mr. Johnson and key Congressional leaders were slow to come to agreement on a proper course of fiscal action to slow the economy.

Mr. Johnson and his Administration were committed to a major social program covering dozens of activities ranging from helping the poor to building new parks. Many of these undertakings were opposed by Republicans and conservative Democrats in Congress who long had been leading the battle against rising federal spending for most causes (although, like most politicians, they tended to take a tolerant view of programs that benefitted their own constitutents.). The addition of greatly increased defense spending for the Vietnam war to the already substantial domestic outlays strained the Federal Budget and placed new demands on the economy. It took the White House and Congress upwards of a year (or a year and a half if Mr. Johnson's first request for a surcharge in January 1967 is used as a reference date) to reconcile their differences over spending and taxing.

Eventually a 10-percent surcharge and mandatory federal spending reductions were enacted. But the delay was evidence that Budget and tax procedures needed much refinement before they could be dependable devices to help regulate the economy in both good and bad times.

Transportation, Banking Policy

EFFORTS to develop one coordinated federal policy for the various modes of transportation continued in the 1965-68 period, but without notable success. Industry reluctance to give up special advantages under existing patchwork programs contributed to the difficulty of formulating a unified national policy.

President Johnson's proposal for a Cabinet-level Department of Transportation was intended to promote the development of a national transportation policy, but Congress so weakened the legislation that the Secretary of Transportation was effectively denied authority to coordinate or revise existing programs. Further, one major transportation agency—the Maritime Administration—was excluded from the new Department.

Attempts were made to revamp policies in two specific areas, maritime policy and airport policy, but the Administration and Congress failed to agree on the outlines of new programs and no effective action was taken.

In other transportation action, Congress authorized a program to explore the feasibility of high speed ground transportation, extended the urban mass transit program and postponed the completion date of the Interstate Highway System. Congress did not act on President Johnson's request for increased highway user taxes.

There was considerable banking legislation considered by Congress during President Johnson's years. Some of the most important bills related to the economic problems that had arisen because of the inflationary pressures on the nation. The U.S. gold stock had become an issue as the balance-of-payments crisis continued and more nations traded in their dollars for gold. Legislation to remove the gold backing from U.S. currency was enacted in 1968 in response to this situation. A somewhat similar problem arose over the supply of silver which was in considerable demand in industry.

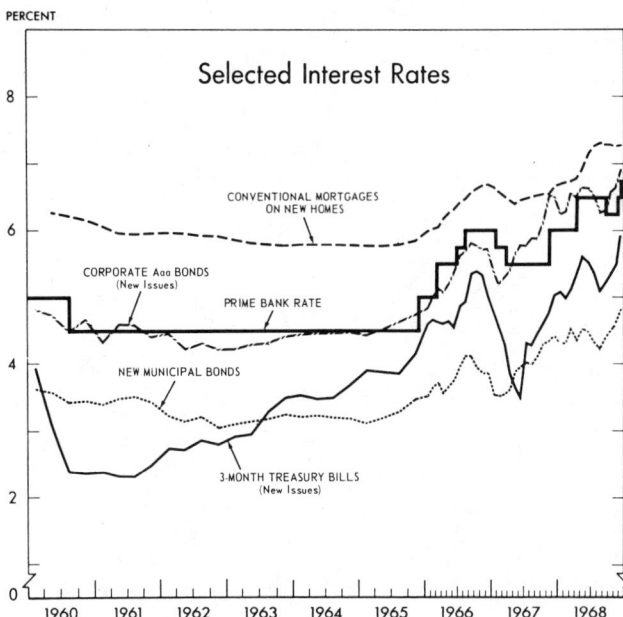

PERCENT

Selected Interest Rates

CONVENTIONAL MORTGAGES ON NEW HOMES

CORPORATE Aaa BONDS (New Issues)

PRIME BANK RATE

NEW MUNICIPAL BONDS

3-MONTH TREASURY BILLS (New Issues)

1960 1961 1962 1963 1964 1965 1966 1967 1968

Congress in response enacted a bill to lower the silver content of the nation's coins.

Congress also considered a number of bills dealing with banks. Included were measures on bank mergers, bank holding companies, and interest rates paid by banking institutions.

Housing Policy

MAJOR housing legislation was enacted in three of President Johnson's five years in office. The bills established a Department of Housing and Urban Development and created several innovative programs to help low-income families and individuals obtain adequate housing and to assist the nation's cities in rebuilding their deteriorating areas.

The most controversial of the bills, which became law in 1965, provided a program of rent supplements for low-income persons who could not afford standard housing on their own incomes. The bill was enacted over the outspoken opposition of Republicans and many conservative Democrats. In spite of the close battle on supplements in 1965, the Administration returned to Congress in 1966 with another major request—a model cities program to pump extra federal funds into carefully planned city projects that made a coordinate attack on blight through treatment of social as well as physical problems. After another major battle, the request was granted. In the case of both programs, however, the conservative coalition in Congress kept funding at levels considerably below the authorized amounts, thus in effect greatly hampering the programs whose enactment they were unable to prevent.

In 1968, Congress enacted a massive housing bill to promote home ownership by the poor. The bill provided a federal subsidy on mortgages for the purchase of homes and on apartment projects for the poor. The bill—in contrast to the 1965 and 1966 bills—had considerable Republican backing and was enacted with relatively little controversy. The bill also contained provisions on many other housing matters.

The Federal Budget

FEDERAL budget policy during the latter part of the Johnson years was dominated by the unexpectedly expensive Vietnam war, which was losing public support rapidly each year. The federal Budget also was subjected to increased demands from an ambitious social program sought by the Johnson Administration and from an even greater need—which was met in only the most rudimentary way—to rejuvenate the nations' decaying cities and to redress the grievances of the nation's poor people through education, housing and employment. Frequently, the Administration's social programs and the urban and antipoverty needs of the nation were one and the same thing in the federal Budget picture. In addition to these needs, the nation was both blessed and troubled by expanding business investment and consumer demand. Federal Budget and tax policies as formulated in the Johnson Administration were unable to accommodate all of these pressures—war costs, domestic needs and private spending—and still prevent inflation. *(See p. 141 for discussion of tax policy.)*

The demands made on the Budget led inevitably to conflict, both within Congress and between Congress and the Executive Branch. The Johnson Administration argued for a considerable period after the U.S. involvement in the Vietnam war escalated in 1965 that the nation could afford—in the phrase that was the symbol of the Budget crisis—both guns and butter. Budget priorities, if they were set at all, never were very clear except that the military needs of the Armed Forces in Vietnam had first call on the funds available; moreover, spending priorities that were put forth differed from one individual or group to another. This was nothing more than a reflection of the basic disagreement throughout the nation over the policies of the Johnson Administration: to one segment of the population, the war was a mistake and the money being spent on it, wasted; to another segment, the domestic needs of the nation simply had to wait until the United States successfully concluded a justified and necessary military action in support of a friendly country. This difference of opinion was never resolved and, accordingly, the Budget conflict was never entirely resolved.

However, by 1967 there was considerable agreement that the nation could not, as Mr. Johnson had hoped, afford both guns and butter and have both without inflation within the limits of the existing tax revenues.

The President's answer to the dilemma was to increase taxes and attempt to hold down expenditures, with the emphasis in that order. The men in positions of power in Congress, who would control the fate of tax and spending proposals, reversed the priorities. They preferred to force expenditure reductions on the Executive Branch and then, perhaps, to consider increased taxes. Mr. Johnson first proposed a tax increase in January 1967. He did not come forward with a detailed proposal to Congress until the following August when he requested enactment of a 10-percent surcharge on personal and corporate income taxes plus a few lesser measures to increase revenues. From August until the following summer when a surcharge was enacted, the two branches of Government fought, maneuvered and procrastinated over the combination of increased taxes and reduced spending that would be acceptable to both. In the meantime, the inexorable inflation that had been building throughout the economy rolled on to the detriment of everyone. In the end, Mr. Johnson obtained his 10-percent surcharge and Congress obtained its multibillion dollar mandatory reduction in Government spending, but the long delay, in combination with the record of budget policy for several years prior, suggested that much was to be learned about the use of federal spending to influence economic trends and to achieve national goals. *(See tax policy chapter, p. 141, for discussion of the surcharge proposal.)*

THE presentation of the federal Budget underwent important changes during Mr. Johnson's term in office. A study commission which he appointed recommended many revisions to clarify the information in the Budget and to make the document a more reliable, comprehensive and honest representation of the activities of the Federal Government. There had been criticism for decades that the Budget was too complex and too easily distorted by the party in power in order to hide information which the party did not want publicized. Although the Budget remained enormous and complex, many of the complaints were eliminated by the adoption of what became known as the unified budget, which incorporated the basic recommendations of the study commission. One result of the adoption of the new budget concept was to greatly enlarge the basic figures on Government spending which were presented to the public. (The enlarged amounts represented more comprehensive totals, not vast increases in public outlays.) By the end of Mr. Johnson's term, federal spending

---

Reference

For a discussion of federal Budget policy in the period 1945-64, see *Congress and the Nation, Vol. I, p. 387-395.*

was approaching $200 billion, as measured in the unified Budget; just a few years earlier, the Executive Branch had gone to great pains to keep the size of the then best known (but less comprehensive) budget under $100 billion. Mr. Johnson, who had something of a reputation for deviousness in dealing with Budget figures, was widely commended for political courage in implementing the budgetary changes which so dramatically increased the size of federal expenditures that were widely reported to the voting public.

Chronology

Of Action

On the Budget

1965

PRESIDENT Johnson, in the first federal Budget that was fully under his influence, stressed health, education and welfare spending and de-emphasized defense outlays. The Budget he sent to Congress was for fiscal 1966 and had been under preparation during Mr. Johnson's first full year in office in 1964. By the end of the year, however, the increasing U.S. commitment to the war in Vietnam required the Johnson Administration to substantially revise its estimates of spending for national defense. The war and other developments during 1965 pushed administrative-budget spending above $100 billion for the first time in history.

For the rest of Mr. Johnson's years in office, increased defense spending was the major factor in the intractable Budget problems that plagued the Administration. In his January 1965 presentation of the fiscal 1966 Budget, he estimated Defense Department outlays at $49 billion; the final total was more than $55 billion. This was to rise to almost $78 billion by the end of fiscal 1968, a half-year before Mr. Johnson left office, and related outlays pushed the total national defense figure to more than $80.5 billion.

In 1965, however, the Budget pinch that was to develop was only in its early stages and caused the Administration no more than the usual hardships in Congress as the conservative appropriations committees reduced spending allotments below requests. Congress during 1965 acted on 17 appropriations bills totaling $107,037,566,896. Requests totaled $109,448,074,896. It was the fourth consecutive year in which appropriations exceeded $100 billion.

Mr. Johnson's approach to the Budget was noticeably different than in his first Budget message in January 1964. In 1964, he emphasized the importance of controlling federal expenditures. He said that "an austere budget need not and should not be a standstill budget." In 1965, however, he stressed the importance of Government activity and hinted at future spending trends. He said the Budget he was sending to Congress "begins to

grasp the opportunities of the Great Society." He also said that unless defense requirements declined, total Government expenditures "will continue to rise over the long run. At the same time, we have good reason to expect that Government expenditures in the years ahead will grow more slowly than the gross national product, so that the ratio of federal spending to our total output will continue to decline." However, this did not happen during the remainder of Mr. Johnson's term. *(See table p. 129.)*

In other budget developments during the year, Mr. Johnson directed heads of federal agencies to introduce a system of budget preparation called planning-programming-budgeting (PPBS). This was described as an extension of the cost-effectiveness budgeting system used in the Defense Department and in a few other agencies. It was intended to permit agencies to better determine goals and alternate methods of achieving them, to measure the anticipated results of each dollar spent under each alternative and to do this throughout the year (rather than in just the few months in the fall when the Budget is being prepared) and for a period of five years at a time. Government agencies were instructed in March 1965 to begin establishing the system.

In another development, President Johnson appointed Charles L. Schultze as Director of the Bureau of the Budget. He was sworn in June 1, replacing Kermit Gordon who had held the post since Dec. 28, 1962.

Debt Limit

Congress in 1965 approved a $4 billion increase in the temporary national debt limit, to $328 billion. The increased limit was effective through fiscal 1966, ending June 30, 1966. If the legislation (HR 8464-PL 89-49) had not been enacted, the existing temporary debt ceiling of $324 billion would have declined to the permanent level of $285 billion on July 1, 1965. *(For background, see box, p. 139.)*

The permanent statutory debt limit was set at $285 billion in 1959. "Temporary" increases were approved by Congress in the following years as Government borrowing pushed up the national debt. In 1962 and 1963 Congress acted no less than five times on bills to increase the temporary debt limit. Republicans and Southern Democrats used the occasions for strong criticism of Administration fiscal policy. This was again true in 1965. The House passed the bill by a 229-165 roll-call vote: R 6-122; D 223-43. The Senate passed the bill by a 61-26 roll call: R 12-16; D 49-10.

1966

President Johnson in the fiscal 1967 federal Budget submitted to Congress in January 1966 proposed a substantial increase in spending for the Vietnam war and moderate increases in expenditures on Great Society programs. During the session, Congress appropriated the defense funds with little change. But it also threatened at various times to appropriate larger sums than requested for other programs and thereby require federal

Federal Finances and the Gross National Product

(in billions of dollars)

Fiscal year	Gross national product	Budget Receipts		Budget outlays (expenditures and net lending)			
				Total		Budget expenditures (excludes net lending)	
		Amount	Percent of GNP	Amount	Percent of GNP	Amount	Percent of GNP
1954	$362.1	$69.9	19.3%	$71.1	19.6%	( )	( )
1955	378.6	65.5	17.3	68.5	18.1	( )	( )
1956	409.4	74.6	18.2	70.5	17.2	(1)	(1)
1957	431.3	80.0	18.5	76.7	17.8	(1)	(1)
1958	440.3	79.6	18.1	82.6	18.8	$81.0	18.4%
1959	469.1	79.2	16.9	92.1	19.6	89.5	19.1
1960	495.2	92.5	18.7	92.2	18.6	90.3	18.2
1961	506.5	94.4	18.6	97.8	19.3	96.6	19.1
1962	542.1	99.7	18.4	106.8	19.7	104.5	19.3
1963	573.4	106.6	18.6	111.3	19.4	111.5	19.4
1964	612.2	112.7	18.4	118.6	19.4	118.0	19.3
1965	654.2	116.8	17.9	118.4	18.1	117.2	17.9
1966	720.7	130.9	18.2	134.7	18.7	130.8	18.2
1967	766.5	149.6	19.5	158.4	20.7	153.3	20.0
1968	822.6	153.7	18.7	178.9	21.7	172.8	21.0

[1] Not available.

SOURCE: BUREAU OF THE BUDGET

spending substantially in excess of the amount that Government officials and private economists believed the nation's economy—already under inflationary pressures—could absorb. Numerous public statements by the President criticizing the threatened additions resulted in Senate and House cutbacks which produced appropriation totals slightly under the Administration's final requests. However, Congress increased the amounts for new obligational authority beyond the President's requests. NOA, which generally includes appropriations but also includes other forms of authority for the Government to enter into obligations that will require expenditures sooner or later, are considered significant in estimating future federal spending plans.

The emphasis which Mr. Johnson placed on his fiscal 1967 Budget was basically different than that put on his fiscal 1966 Budget a year earlier. In the fiscal 1966 document, the President stressed health, education and welfare spending and de-emphasized defense expenditures. The expanded U.S. participation in Vietnam foreclosed this approach for fiscal 1967. The effect of rising defense costs was evident throughout the Budget. In numerous tables, figures were added to indicate what the Budget would have totaled in the absence of the Vietnam war costs. The Budget costs directly attributable to the war were estimated at $10.5 billion in 1967 (although Mr. Johnson's last Budget, sent to Congress in 1969, placed fiscal 1967 war costs at more than $20 billion).

Congress passed 15 appropriation bills providing $130,281,568,480 compared to requests of $131,164,926,586.

The increasing pinch on Government finances resulting from the war gave new impetus to Republicans and conservative Democrats to cut spending in other areas of the Budget. Attempting to reduce federal spending, particularly for domestic social programs, was nothing new for Congressional conservatives. But the financial pressures from the war were new and gave them an unexcelled opportunity to achieve their goals. Their efforts in 1966 were to lead in 1968 to enactment of a bill making a mandatory $6-billion cut in federal expenditures. The struggle in Congress over expenditures reductions was to dominate much of the last three years of Lyndon Johnson's Presidency and was to be the major Congressional controversy (save for the war itself) from mid-1967 until the following summer.

For 1966, however, Republicans were generally unsuccessful; they failed in their attempts to amend seven of the fiscal 1967 appropriation bills to limit spending in the agencies covered by each bill to 95 percent of the amounts estimated in the President's Budget. Six of these amendments were offered in the House by GOP Appropriation Committee members; the seventh was offered by a Republican who was not on that Committee. On the closest roll-call vote on the proposals, the GOP lost by 49 votes.

Participation Certificates

At President Johnson's request, Congress in 1966 authorized (S 3283—PL 89-429) the Federal Government to "pool" certain mortgages and other loan assets held by six federal agencies as a result of their having made direct loans to farmers, colleges and others under various federal programs, and then to sell shares in the pool to the public, in the form of interest-bearing "participation" certificates.

The new program was intended to convert $3.2 billion in paper assets held by the Government into ready cash in fiscal 1967 (and more later), and also, in effect, shift part of the burden of federal credit to private hands. The funds obtained by the six federal agencies through the sale of participation certificates based on their paper assets could be used by the agencies to finance further direct-loan operations under their existing program authorizations, in lieu of new appropriations from the Treasury that would otherwise be needed.

Mechanics of Program. The mechanics of the new program were as follows:

(1) Under various existing programs, a large number of federal agencies were authorized to make direct loans to individuals, colleges, local public agencies, etc. to help them build facilities and carry on activities which the Federal Government considered it desirable to encourage: home purchases by veterans and other special groups, construction of college dormitories and and academic facilities, farm housing and farm operat-

ing costs, and so forth. In many cases, these loans were made at very low interest rates in order to subsidize a particular type of activity. The total federal portfolio of mortgages and repayment commitments on all direct loans was about $33 billion as of mid-1966.

(2) In some cases, if the Government wished to obtain cash for the mortgages and loan repayment commitments, it simply sold them outright to private banks and other investors. However, loans which bore very low interest rates or were made to high-risk borrowers were extremely difficult to sell to banks and other private investors.

(3) Consequently, S 3283, the Participation Sales Act of 1966, authorized the Government, as an alternative to selling the mortgages and other loan assets held by six specificied agencies, simply to put them into a pool which was retained in the Government's hands and which was used as the backing for sale by the Government of participation certificates. The transaction was to be handled by the Federal National Mortgage Association (FNMA). The participation certificates were permitted to bear whatever interest rates were necessary to assure their sale, and could be either of short- or long-term maturities. The certificates were to be guaranteed both as to principal and interest by the FNMA. This guarantee together with the fact that the certificates were to be sold at an attractive rate of interest (estimated at 5 percent or more), made the certificates easy to sell to private investors.

(4) By selling the participation certificates, the federal agencies participating in the pool obtained cash—in

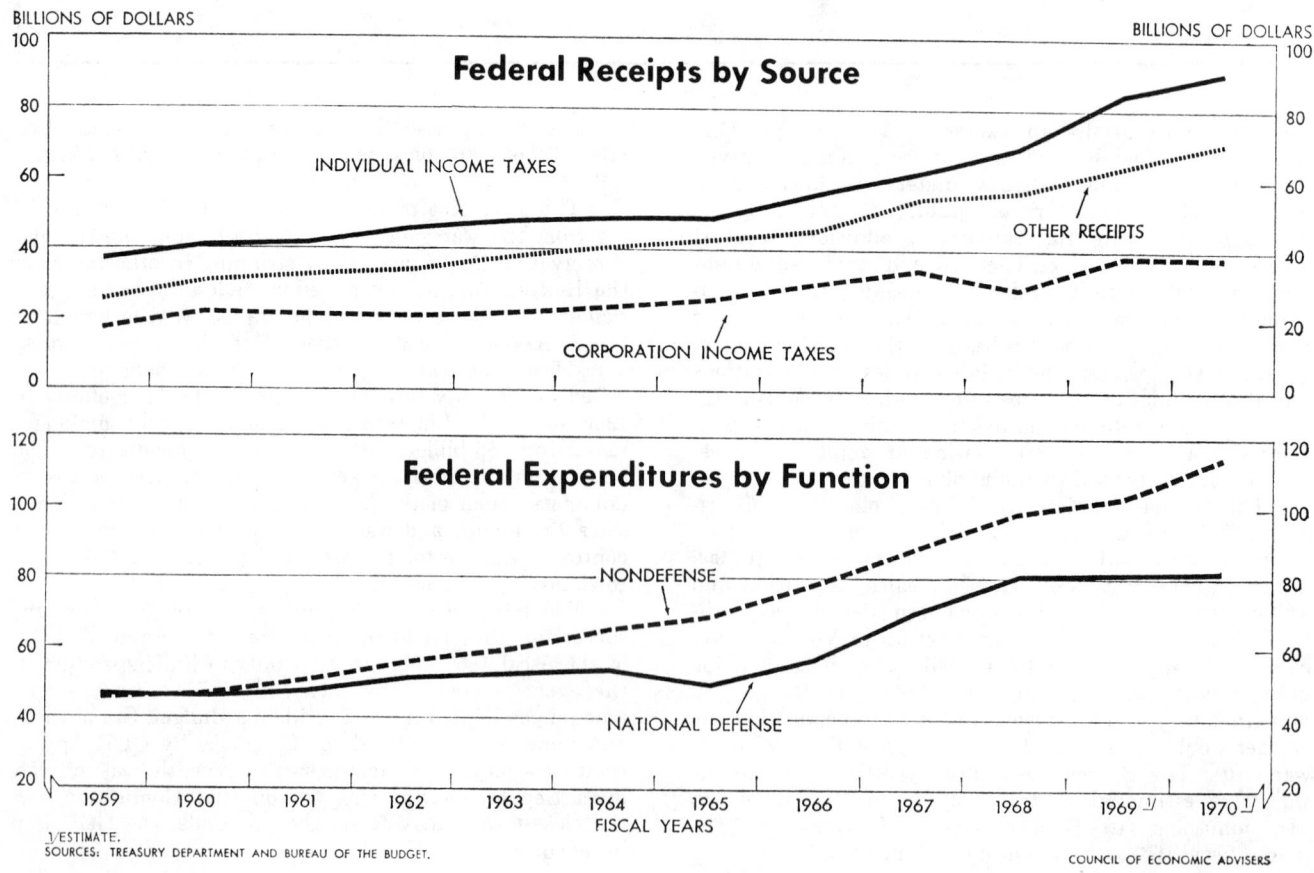

BILLIONS OF DOLLARS   BILLIONS OF DOLLARS

Federal Receipts by Source

INDIVIDUAL INCOME TAXES

OTHER RECEIPTS

CORPORATION INCOME TAXES

Federal Expenditures by Function

NONDEFENSE

NATIONAL DEFENSE

1959   1960   1961   1962   1963   1964   1965   1966   1967   1968   1969 [1]   1970 [1]

FISCAL YEARS

[1] ESTIMATE.
SOURCES: TREASURY DEPARTMENT AND BUREAU OF THE BUDGET.

COUNCIL OF ECONOMIC ADVISERS

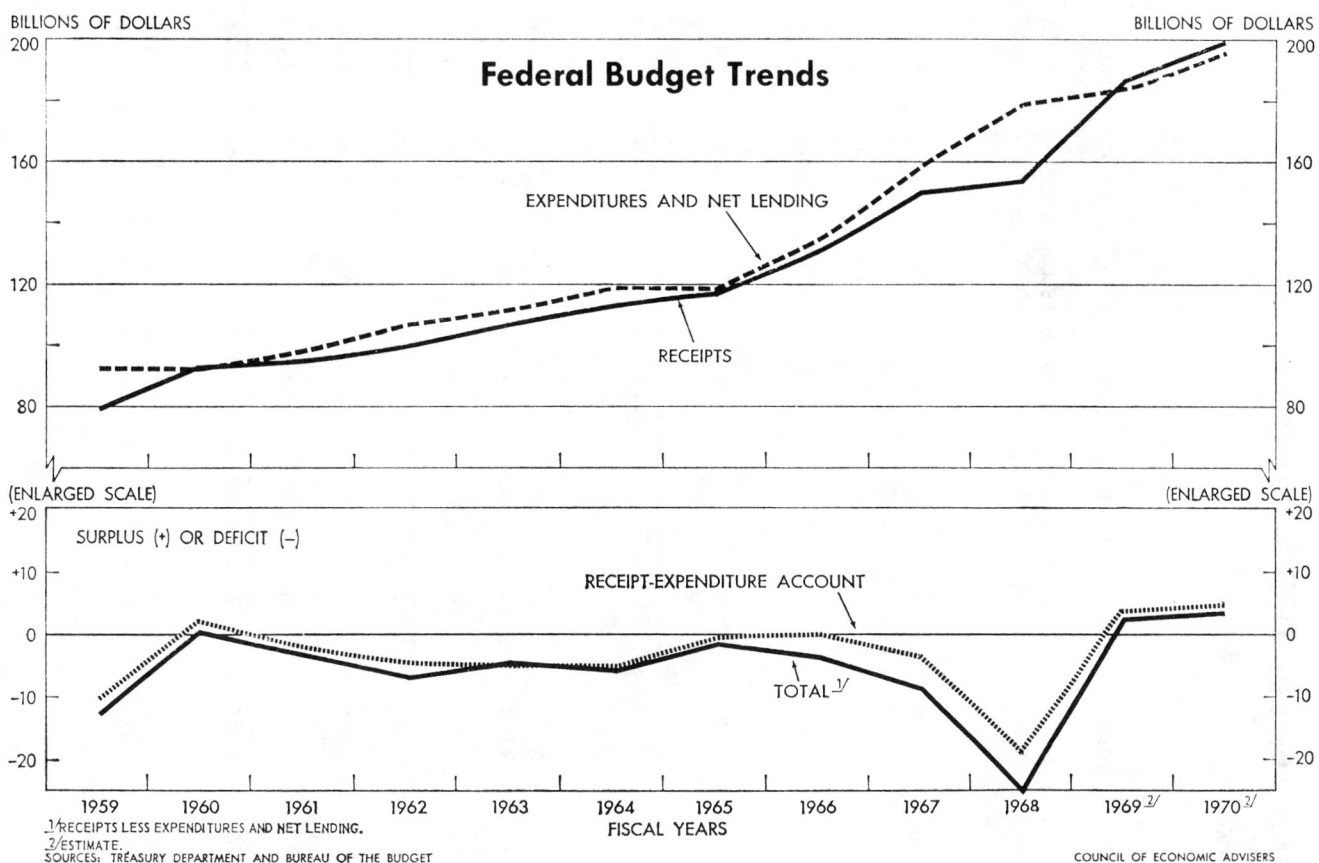

BILLIONS OF DOLLARS

Federal Budget Trends

EXPENDITURES AND NET LENDING

RECEIPTS

(ENLARGED SCALE)

SURPLUS (+) OR DEFICIT (−)

RECEIPT-EXPENDITURE ACCOUNT

TOTAL 1/

1/ RECEIPTS LESS EXPENDITURES AND NET LENDING.
2/ ESTIMATE.
SOURCES: TREASURY DEPARTMENT AND BUREAU OF THE BUDGET

FISCAL YEARS

COUNCIL OF ECONOMIC ADVISERS

effect—for their paper assets. Each agency would receive an amount of cash equal to the amount of paper assets it had put into the pool as backing for the participation certificates. These funds could be used to make additional direct loans under existing authorized lending programs, or to reduce Treasury advances to the agency.

(5) Both the principal and interest owed to purchasers of the participation certificates were to be paid off by the FNMA with the proceeds it obtained from repayments on those mortgages, loan repayment commitments and other paper assets which were in the pool. However, because of the low interest rates borne by many of the paper assets in the pool, such proceeds would not be large enough to fully service the participation certificates. Therefore, the Government would simply make up the deficit by appropriating enough funds to cover the difference. It was estimated that, on the amount of participation certificate sales which the Administration planned for fiscal 1967 ($3.2 billion,) the deficit would be about $10 to $14 million a year.

(6) Because the participation certificates were issued by the FNMA, rather than the Treasury directly, the certificates were not counted as part of the national debt. Their sale would not be subject to the debt limit. Moreover, the financing of new direct loans by federal agencies with funds obtained from the sale of participation certificates was not classified as spending in the federal Budget, whereas the use of new appropriations would have been. Use of participation certificates therefore had the effect of reducing the ostensible size of the federal budget deficit. These aspects of the certificates

were eliminated in a 1967 debt limit bill and in the fiscal 1969 Budget.

Changes in Request. Despite sharp Republican criticism of the program, Congress completed action on S 3283, the basic authorizing legislation, only one month and three days after Mr. Johnson's request. It made only two major changes in his proposals:

(1) It inserted language providing in effect, that except for one special sale of $530 million in participation certificates which the bill specifically authorized to take place in the remaining months of fiscal 1966, no sale of participation certificates by the FNMA could take place unless Congress in an appropriations bill had first granted permission and had spelled out the total amount to be sold. It was contemplated that at regular intervals, possibly annually, the Administration would submit to Congress information on how much in participations the FNMA wished to sell in the coming year, and Congress would then approve, disapprove or alter the amount.

(2) It limited the entire program to six agencies which, at that time, were holding about $11 billion in paper assets that might be eligible for inclusion in participation pools. The President's initial request would have applied the basic legislation to all federal agencies (eligible paper assets: $33 billion), although the President had made it clear that he actually planned the sale by the FNMA of only $3.2 billion in participation certificates during fiscal 1967.

Republican Criticism. Republicans charged that the whole idea of selling participation certificates was simply a gimmick to obtain funds for further broadening of

Budget Receipts by Source, Fiscal 1959-1968

(in millions of dollars)

Source	1959	1960	1961	1962	1963	1964	1965	1966	1967	1968
Individual income taxes	$ 36,719	$ 40,715	$ 41,338	$ 45,571	$ 47,588	$ 48,697	$ 48,792	$ 55,446	$ 61,526	$ 68,726
Corporation income taxes	17,309	21,494	20,954	20,523	21,579	23,493	25,461	30,073	33,971	28,665
Social insurance taxes and contributions (trust funds):										
Employment taxes and contributions:										
Old-age and survivors insurance	7,418	9,671	11,104	11,267	13,117	15,242	15,567	17,556	22,197	22,265
Disability insurance	878	970	1,005	1,004	1,058	1,124	1,156	1,530	2,204	2,651
Hospital insurance	—	—	—	—	—	—	—	893	2,645	3,493
Railroad retirement	525	607	571	564	572	593	636	683	776	814
Unemployment insurance [1]	2,131	2,667	2,902	3,337	4,112	4,045	3,819	3,777	3,659	3,346
Contributions for other insurance and retirement:										
Supplementary medical insurance	—	—	—	—	—	—	—	—	647	698
Employees' retirement—employee contribution	759	756	843	861	931	991	1,063	1,109	1,200	1,332
Other retirement contributions	10	10	12	12	13	15	16	18	19	20
Total social insurance taxes and contributions	$ 11,721	$ 14,682	$ 16,437	$ 17,045	$ 19,802	$ 22,010	$ 22,256	$ 25,565	$ 33,347	$ 34,620
Excise taxes:										
Federal funds:										
Alcohol	2,938	3,127	3,146	3,268	3,366	3,499	3,689	3,720	3,980	4,189
Tobacco	1,078	1,927	1,986	2,022	2,075	2,048	2,142	2,066	2,077	2,121
Other	4,487	4,084	3,931	4,295	4,474	4,664	5,081	3,358	3,221	3,390
Trust funds (highway)	2,074	2,539	2,798	2,949	3,279	3,519	3,659	3,917	4,441	4,379
Total excise taxes	$ 10,578	$ 11,676	$ 11,860	$ 12,534	$ 13,194	$ 13,731	$ 14,570	$ 13,062	$ 13,719	$ 14,079
Estate and gift taxes	1,333	1,606	1,896	2,016	2,167	2,394	2,716	3,066	2,978	3,051
Customs duties	925	1,105	982	1,142	1,205	1,252	1,442	1,767	1,901	2,038
Miscellaneous receipts [2]	594	1,193	910	826	1,036	1,093	1,576	1,885	2,120	2,498
Total budget receipts	$ 79,179	$ 92,470	$ 94,378	$ 99,657	$106,572	$112,669	$116,813	$130,864	$149,562	$153,676
MEMORANDUM										
Federal funds	$ 65,679	$ 75,563	$ 75,118	$ 79,635	$ 83,463	$ 87,111	$ 90,863	$101,344	$111,732	$114,627
Trust funds	$ 13,500	$ 16,907	$ 19,260	$ 20,022	$ 23,109	$ 25,558	$ 25,950	$ 29,520	$ 37,829	$ 39,049

[1] Includes Federal funds of $321 million in 1959 and $339 million in 1960.

[2] Includes both Federal funds and trust funds.

SOURCE: BUREAU OF THE BUDGET

Budget Outlays by Function, 1959-1968

(in millions of dollars)

FISCAL YEAR	1959	1960	1961	1962	1963	1964	1965	1966	1967	1968
National Defense	$ 46,617	$ 45,908	$ 47,383	$ 51,097	$ 52,257	$ 53,591	$ 49,578	$ 56,785	$ 70,081	$ 80,516
International Affairs & Finance	3,267	3,054	3,357	4,492	4,115	4,117	4,340	4,490	4,547	4,619
Space Research and Technology	145	401	744	1,257	2,552	4,170	5,091	5,933	5,423	4,721
Agriculture and Agricultural Resources	5,365	3,322	3,340	4,131	5,139	5,186	4,807	3,679	4,376	5,944
Natural Resources	1,209	1,019	1,568	1,686	1,505	1,972	2,063	2,035	1,860	1,702
Commerce and Transportation	4,451	4,774	5,048	5,410	5,745	6,482	7,364	7,135	7,652	8,076
Community Development and Housing	851	971	191	589	—880	—185	288	2,644	2,616	4,076
Education and Manpower	1,081	1,282	1,480	1,703	1,706	1,998	2,509	4,496	6,135	7,012
Health and Welfare	17,690	18,734	21,847	23,374	25,274	26,598	27,209	31,320	37,605	43,508
Veterans Benefits and Services	5,428	5,426	5,688	5,625	5,520	5,681	5,722	5,920	6,897	6,882
Interest	7,070	8,299	8,108	8,321	9,215	9,810	10,357	11,285	12,588	13,744
General Government	1,173	1,334	1,543	1,703	1,841	2,103	2,276	2,360	2,584	2,632
Undistributed Intragovernmental Transactions	—2,238	—2,296	—2,495	—2,558	—2,674	—2,939	—3,174	—3,431	—4,009	—4,570
TOTAL	$ 92,111	$ 92,230	$ 97,802	$106,830	$111,314	$118,585	$118,431	$134,654	$158,352	$178,862

SOURCE: BUREAU OF THE BUDGET

Background

Attempts to use participation certificates as a financial device began in 1962, when the Export-Import Bank, under existing powers in its charter, began selling participation certificates based on a pool of paper assets which it held. By 1966, the Bank had sold $1.7 billion in participation certificates.

In 1964, Congress in Title VII of the 1964 Housing Act authorized the FNMA to pool certain housing mortgages held by FNMA and the VA and sell participation certificates based on this pool. By March 16, 1966, the date of the latest FNMA offering under Title VII, the FNMA had sold $1.6 billion in participations including the March 16 issue.

The use of participations was justified on the grounds that it enabled the Government to shift part of its credit burden to private hands, and that it made it possible for the Government, in effect, to obtain cash for mortgages which, because of their poor risk or low return, could not actually be sold individually to private investors.

1965-66 Action on SBA Bill. President Johnson's fiscal 1966 Budget Document, submitted to Congress Jan. 25, 1965, proposed legislation to authorize the sale of participation certifcates based on a pool of Small Business Administration paper assets. Proceeds from the same were to be used to help finance further lending operations of the SBA. A bill (S 2499) to this effect was eventually introduced late in 1965 and reported March 4, 1966, by the Senate Banking and Currency Committee.

The Senate March 15, 1966, passed S 2499 by voice vote after rejecting, by a 26-51 (D 0-51; R 26-0) roll call, a motion by Leverett Saltonstall (R Mass.) to recommit (kill) the bill. Republicans made the same arguments against S 2499 as they subsequently did against S 3283. The House Banking and Currency Committee April 25, 1966, reported S 2499. However, after it became clear that S 3283 would be passed with provisions granting the same authority for sale of participations based on SBA assets in fiscal 1966 and thereafter as was included in S 2499, the House abandoned further action on S 2499 and it never reached the floor.

---

federal spending without substantial Congressional supervision, without having such spending show up as deficits in the federal Budget, and without having it subject to the national debt limit.

Democrats conceded that the use of proceeds from participation certificates to finance new federal loans would have the effect of "dressing up" the appearance of the federal Budget and federal debt position. But they said the real purpose of the new program was to find a way to continue to finance desirable federal social programs by the conversion of paper assets into cash, without having to raise taxes, without cutting back the programs, and without surpassing the debt limit. It

was not desirable to go to the Treasury for further appropriations, they said, when federal agencies were sitting on a tremendous pile of paper assets that could readily be converted into cash. Administration spokesmen also said that it was the Government's policy, wherever possible, to use private credit rather than federal credit to finance desirable loan programs: the sale of participation certificates would convert part of the credit burden now resting on the Federal Government into private credit.

Some Republicans charged that sale of the participation certificates would intensify the current credit squeeze and lead to higher interest rates on private borrowings throughout the economy. Guaranteed by the FNMA and expected to bear interest rates of over 5 percent (whereas direct Treasury bond issues of five years maturity or more were limited by law to paying 4-1/4 percent interest), the participation certificates would sop up funds from the private economy, it was charged, and drive up interest rates.

Some Republicans also charged that the participation certificates would ultimately cost the Government more, because of the high interest rates, than if it borrowed a similar amount of money by selling conventional Treasury bonds and notes. They said the Administration was willing to incur the greater costs in order to avoid running into the statutory national debt limit. The Administration responded that for various reasons, the ultimate cost of servicing the participation certificates would not be greater than direct borrowing by the Treasury.

Voting. Action on the bill was largely along partisan lines. The Senate passed it by a 39-22 (R 5-20; D 34-2) roll-call vote. A motion to kill the bill was defeated by a 23-45 (R 21-4; D 2-41) roll call. The house passed its own version of the bill by a 206-190 (R 0-126; D 206-64) roll-call vote.

PROVISIONS. As signed into law, S 3283, the Participation Sales Act of 1966:

Participation Sales. Authorized six specified federal agencies to place in pools a part or all of the notes or obligations made or acquired by them through the operation of their loan program.

Authorized the Federal National Mortgage Assn. (FNMA), acting as trustee of the pools, to sell to investors participation certificates based on the pools.

Specified that only the following agencies would be eligible to participate in the program: the Farmers Home Administration (only for operating loans, direct farm ownership loans, direct housing loans and direct soil and water loans; and, in addition, prohibited inclusion in the program of FHA loans for housing for the elderly and for nonfarm recreational development); the Office of Education (for academic facilities construction loans); the Department of Housing and Urban Development (except for secondary market operations of FNMA); the Veterans Administration; the Export-Import Bank; and the Small Business Administration.

Required that before participations could be issued, approval for the issuance had to be provided in an appropriations act. Specified that any such approval would remain in effect for only two fiscal years.

Provided that receipts from the sale of participations would be returned to the agencies to meet loan demands (within limits established by other laws) and to reduce the agencies' borrowings or advances from the U.S. Treasury.

Authorized Congress to appropriate funds to cover any deficit which might occur when the FNMA's servicing costs (principal and interest repayments) on participation certificates exceeded income from the pooled mortgages and other paper assets being used as backing for the participation certificates. (Such a deficit would normally occur whenever the paper assets in the pool bore interest rates lower than payable on the participation certificates, as would frequently be the case under the new program.)

Provided that the loans in the pools would be guaranteed by the lending agencies and provided that payments of principal and interest on the participation certificates would be guaranteed by FNMA.

Specified that purchase of participation certificates would be subject to state taxes, and that income received by holders of participation certificates would be taxed as dividend income.

Exempted participation certificates from regulation by the Securities and Exchange Commission.

Provided that after June 30, 1966, no agency listed in the bill could sell any obligation held by it except as authorized by the bill (through FNMA) or as approved by the Secretary of the Treasury.

Permitted the FNMA, during the remainder of fiscal 1966, to sell participations in a trust established by the Small Business Administration, plus participations in the Government Mortgage Liquidation Trust.

Other Provisions. Reduced by $450 million the aggregate authority of FNMA to purchase mortgages under its special assistance functions and repealed $300 million in fiscal 1967 borrowing authority granted by previous law to HUD's college housing loan program. Both reductions—affecting the 1965 omnibus housing law, PL 89-117—were made possible by anticipated sales of participation certificates under S 3283.

Amended the Higher Education Facilities Act of 1963 (PL 88-204) to establish a separate revolving fund for higher education academic facilities direct loans, available without fiscal year limitation. Specified that the fund would be financed by appropriations, by receipts from loan repayments and by receipts from the sale of participation certificates. Limited total loans from the fund in any fiscal year to amounts specified in appropriation bills.

Debt Limit

Congress in 1966 extended for another year the temporary national debt limit and raised it by $2 billion, to $300 billion. The higher limit was effective through the fiscal year ending June 30, 1967. The Administration had requested a $4-billion increase but the House Ways and Means Committee reduced it to $2 billion. Like previous debt limit bills, this one (HR 15202—PL 89-472) was passed along partisan lines. In the House, only one Republican voted for it. *(For background, see box p. 139.)*

TREASURY BORROWING. In a related development, Congress passed a bill (S 3368—PL 89-484) to extend for two years, through June 30, 1968, the section of the Federal Reserve Act which authorized the Federal Reserve Banks to purchase up to $5 billion in securities directly from the Treasury. The authority allowed the Government to obtain cash in time of need or national emergency. Normally, Federal Reserve banks purchase (or sell) securities in the open market. The authority, which was granted in 1942 and last used in 1958, in effect permitted Treasury borrowing.

1967

President Johnson's fiscal 1968 Budget provoked a year-long dispute between the Executive Branch and Congress which ended in something of a stalemate. It was a prelude to the 1968 conflict between the two branches of Government which ended in the imposition of strict mandatory expenditure controls. In 1967, Congress sought to impose spending restrictions but with mixed success. It refused to give President Johnson the tax increase he wanted and he in turn refused to cut back the spending total estimated in his Budget. He did, however, agree to help hold down increases over his January estimates.

In action on appropriation bills, Congress provided $141,872,346,664 which was almost $6 billion less than the President's requests of $147,806,557,929. In all, Congress acted on 17 appropriations bills. House Republicans continued their two-year effort to add mandatory expenditure-reduction provisions to the bills. Republicans tried to attach the 5-percent spending reduction provision to six regular appropriation bills. In a seventh bill, public works, a GOP proposal would have forced a 5-percent reduction in appropriations (as opposed to spending). The Republicans were successful with two appropriation bills, but both provisions were dropped in conference.

Spending Limit

In spite of the continual GOP efforts to amend appropriation bills, the most important and controversial action came on continuing resolutions for appropriations.

Continuing appropriations resolutions are normally routine bills, enacted as stopgap legislation after the beginning of a fiscal year to provide temporary funds for agencies until their regular appropriations bills are cleared by Congress. In 1967, however, these resolutions became in the House the vehicle for Republican-led attempts to force President Johnson to make over-all reductions in federal spending.

When the Senate refused to go along with large Budget cuts voted by the House, an impasse resulted, and there were lengthy periods of time between late October and mid-December when some agencies were completely without funds.

The Republican effort to add spending limitations to continuing appropriations bills was in large part a reaction to the President's request for a 10-percent surcharge on corporate and personal income taxes. In January, the President had asked for a 6-percent surcharge, but no detailed request was made and the proposal got no action from Congress. In a special message Aug. 3, Mr. Johnson raised his surcharge request to 10 percent and forecast a $29-billion deficit if Congress failed to approve it. The Republicans who led the House economy drive felt that holding back federal spending was preferable to raising taxes as a means of reducing the projected deficit and stemming inflationary pressures in the economy.

In the final continuing appropriations bill of 1967 (H J Res 888—PL 90-218), Congress included language mandating Executive Branch agencies to hold their obligations in fiscal 1968 to a figure about $9.1 billion below Budget requests. Spending related to the war in Vietnam and other "uncontrollable" expenditures were exempt from the cutback requirement.

The effect of the bill, in combination with Congressional cuts in regular appropriations bills, was to reduce 1968 spending for personnel expenses and "controllable" programs by an estimated $4.1 billion to $4.3 billion below Budget estimates. However, between January, when the Government submitted its original fiscal 1968 Budget, and November, estimated spending on programs that were considered "uncontrollable" had risen by about $5 billion. As a result, despite the cutbacks in "controllable" programs dictated by Congress, spending was estimated in December at $1 billion *more* than the $135 billion that had been estimated in January. A month later, when the President submitted his Budget for fiscal 1969, the estimate of spending in fiscal 1968 had risen another $1 billion—to $137.1 billion in the administrative budget.

The estimated spending reduction was far less than the reduction in obligations required by the bill because of the time lag between the obligation of federal funds—such as the awarding of Government contracts—and the actual cash payment.

The mandatory obligation-cutting formula contained in H J Res 888 had been proposed by the Johnson Administration Nov. 29 during House Ways and Means Committee hearings on the President's tax surcharge plan. Before this—especially during the controversy on the continuing appropriations bills—Administration forces had adamantly opposed attempts to place a ceiling on federal spending. The Administration contended that if Congress wanted to reduce spending it should cut appropriations.

Nevertheless, the Administration proposed the formula contained in H J Res 888 in the hopes that it would spur Congress to action on the surcharge. Since H J Res 888 had been tied up on conference for six weeks with no prospect of a compromise, conferees embraced the Administration plan, and it was quickly accepted on the floor of both chambers.

The formula required that each department and independent agency reduce its budgeted fiscal 1968 obligational authority for salaries and other personnel expenses by 2 percent and its funds for other "controllable" requests by 10 percent. It was incumbent upon each department and independent agency to make its own cutbacks.

In addition to the exemption of "any obligations for national defense which (the President) deems essential for the purposes of national defense," the bill excluded from the cutbacks such "uncontrollable" obligations as interest on the national debt, welfare and medicare payments and veterans pensions. Also exempted from the mandatory cuts were the Legislative and Judicial Branches of the Government.

The Budget Bureau estimated in December that the spending reductions forced by H J Res 888 amounted to

$2.4 billion. In addition, the effect of Congressional action on regular appropriation bills was to cut expenditures by an estimated $1.9 billion. The total cut of $4.3 billion reduced estimated expenditures, as calculated in December, from $140.3 billion to $136 billion.

H J Res 888 was one of six continuing appropriations bills considered by Congress in 1967, all of them controversial because of the spending issue. But the most controversial by far was H J Res 888; it produced two of the key roll-call votes of the session.

The first vote came in the House when that chamber considered the resolution as reported by the Appropriations Committee. As reported, the resolution extended the expiration date of an existing continuing resolution from Oct. 23 until Nov. 23. In addition, H J Res 888 imposed a 30-day "temporary restraining order" against obligation of federal funds for any new construction, research, demonstration, training, service or similar activity except for projects connected with national defense or welfare. It also imposed an across-the-board reduction of 5 percent below Budget estimates in fiscal 1968 funds available for federal civilian employment except for positions connected with the Vietnam war or the safety of human life and protection of property. When the bill reached the House floor Oct. 18, it was scuttled by a **238-164** key roll-call vote and replaced with a substitute offered by Jamie L. Whitten (D Miss.) which held the fiscal 1968 spending of all Government agencies, with a few exceptions, to the fiscal 1967 level. The vote breakdown was: R 171-9; ND 11-134; SD 56-21. Added to the Whitten amendment by a 192-131 teller vote was an amendment by Frank T. Bow (R Ohio), ranking Republican on the Appropriations Committee, which placed a ceiling of $131.5 billion on total fiscal 1968 spending except for needed increases for the Vietnam war. The House also added, without debate, amendments which cut deeply into the antipoverty and foreign aid programs.

The Senate would have none of this. Its Appropriations Committee Oct. 20 reported an amended version of H J Res 888 providing for a simple continuation of spending authority through Nov. 15. The Senate passed this version Oct. 25 after rejecting three Republican attempts to limit fiscal 1968 spending. One of them was rejected on a key vote. It was sponsored by Karl E. Mundt (R.S.D.) and required the President to reduce each line item in fiscal 1968 appropriation bills by 5 percent except for military funds and items found by the Budget Bureau to be beyond administrative control. It was defeated by a **43-46** key roll call. The vote breakdown was: R 26-5; ND 9-30; SD 8-11.

The bill was then passed by the Senate and sent to conference where it became deadlocked as the Oct. 23 expiration date of the existing continuing resolution approached and passed. This caused a number of agencies to lose their authority to spend. The two major agencies affected were the Office of Economic Opportunity and the Agency for International Development. Others were the Army Corps of Engineers, the Bureau of Reclamation, the Atomic Energy Commission, the Federal Water Pollution Control Administration and the District of Columbia government. The crisis continued through November as other limited and strictly emergency continuing resolutions were passed. The issue was resolved in early December when conferees accepted the Administration's proposal that was written into H J Res 888.

Provisions of H J Res 888

As signed into law (PL 90-218) Dec. 18, H J Res 888:

Extended from Dec. 2 to Dec. 20, 1967, the expiration date for temporary spending authority for federal agencies not yet covered by passage of fiscal 1968 appropriations bills. (This provision became inoperative Dec. 15 when Congress cleared the foreign aid appropriations bill (HR 13893), funding the AID, and the first fiscal 1968 supplemental appropriations bill (HR 14397), funding the OEO.)

Stated that federal obligations and expenditures for controllable programs in fiscal 1968 should be reduced by at least $9 billion and $4 billion, respectively.

Limited the funds available for fiscal 1968 obligation by each Executive Branch agency or department to the lesser of the two following amounts: (1) the amount available from appropriations bills which had become law; or (2) an amount determined by reducing budgeted fiscal 1968 obligational authority for each agency by 2 percent of the Budget estimates for salaries and other personnel costs, plus 10 percent of the Budget estimates for controllable programs other then salaries, subject to certain exceptions. *(For exceptions, see below.)*

Specifically exempted the following obligations from the percentage reduction formula: (1) permanent appropriations (such as interest on the national debt); (2) trust funds (such as Social Security, highway funds); (3) "relatively uncontrollable" obligations (such as veterans pensions, welfare payments, farm price supports, postal service costs and health insurance payments); and (4) up to $300 million in obligations for programs which the President decided were "vital to the national interest or security."

Specifically exempted Vietnam war costs from Defense Department obligation reductions.

Stipulated that other Defense Department obligations were not to be reduced by more than 10 percent of the obligational authority requested in the fiscal 1968 Budget, and authorized the President to exempt any defense obligations which he found "essential for...national defense" from the obligation-reduction formula.

Authorized agency heads to make any changes necessary in the amount of funds available for allocation for specific programs administered by their agencies.

Stipulated that obligations should be reduced "to the maximum extent practical" by not filling personnel vacancies that occurred in Executive Branch agencies and by stretching out federal construction timetables.

Stipulated that authorizations or appropriations not used in fiscal 1968 because of the mandatory obligation reductions could be available only for purposes and in amounts which would be prescribed by Congress in 1968.

Unified Budget

A special Presidential commission on the Federal Budget Oct. 17 released a 108-page report recommending the adoption of a single "unified summary (federal Budget statment...to replace the present three or more competing concepts" which were both "confusing to the public and Congress and deficient in certain essential characteristics." In the remaining years of his term, President Johnson adopted the Commission's key recom-

Budget Terminology

The federal Budget, like any budget, is a plan for expected receipts and expenditures. The document is prepared annually by the Administration and purports to show what it expects the Government to receive and to spend in the coming fiscal year. The 1967 Budget, for example, covered the period between July 1, 1966 and June 30, 1967. Congress must approve all spending at one time or another. However, some proposed spending for any given year was approved by Congress in previous years; other spending must be approved after the Administration submits the Budget to Congress. The following description applies to the federal Budget structure put into use by President Johnson in his last two years in office. The structure was based on recommendations of a study commission and differed in many respects from that used in previous years. *(See accompanying story.)*

What Congress acts upon, however, is not proposed expenditures—as such—but requests for new *budget authority.* Government agencies are permitted to enter into obligations, requiring immediate or future payments of money (expenditures), only when they have been granted budget authority by Congressional action.

Budget authority is divided into *new obligational authority* (NOA) and *loan authority* (LA) and it usually takes the form of *appropriations,* which permit obligations to be incurred and payments to be made. Some budget authority is in the form of *contract authorizations,* which permit obligations but require later appropriations. There are several other minor forms of budget authority.

Thus, in any given year the Administration in its Budget asks for specific amounts of budget authority, in the form of NOA or LA. Congress, through the appropriations process, grants all, part, or none of the authority requested.

Once NOA or LA is approved by Congress, agencies may enter into *obligations.* These may be immediate obligations, such as the purchase of military aircraft or payment of salaries to federal workers, and in fact most appropriations are granted for obligation within the year (one-year appropriations.) Some Congressional appropriations are for specified longer periods (multiple-year appropriations), while other appropriations for big projects—construction or research—are made available until expended (no-year appropriations).

As a result, a change in requested NOA or LA for a particular year does not necessarily change either the obligations incurred or the actual expenditures in that year by an equal amount. A change requested in NOA or LA in one year may be reflected in obligations in subsequent years and expenditures in even later years. Obligations are eliminated, or "liquidated" as Budget Bureau officials put it, by issuing checks, disbursement of cash or by several other methods. These are the Government's expenditures, a main part of the Budget.

Unified Budget Figures

Following is a table of unified Budget figures, prepared by the Budget Bureau, for fiscal 1954 through 1968.

(in millions)

Year	Receipts	Outlays	Surplus or Deficit
1954	$ 69,920	$ 71,138	— $1,218
1955	65,462	68,503	— 3,041
1956	74,581	70,461	+ 4,121
1957	79,958	76,748	+ 3,210
1958	79,621	82,575	— 2,954
1959	79,179	92,111	— 12,932
1960	92,470	92,230	+ 240
1961	94,378	97,802	— 3,424
1962	99,657	106,830	— 7,174
1963	106,572	111,314	— 4,742
1964	112,669	118,585	— 5,916
1965	116,813	118,431	— 1,618
1966	130,864	134,654	— 3,790
1967	149,562	158,352	— 8,790
1968	153,676	178,862	— 25,187

mendations in a revamping of the Budget format that was unprecedented in postwar years.

The 16-member President's Commission on Budget Concepts, which President Johnson appointed March 3, was headed by David M. Kennedy, board chairman of the Continental Illinois Bank and Trust Co. of Chicago. The bi-partisan group included the chairmen and ranking minority members of the Senate and House Appropriations Committees, Administration officials, university economists and spokesmen for the private financial community.

Major Recommendations. The Commission made 13 major recommendations which were intended, the report stated, to make the federal Budget "a more understandable and useful instrument of public policy and financial planning." Although the existing Budget document was "in many respects...the finest in the world, the Commission believed that "certain improvements in concepts and methods of presentation" were needed to "bring this document abreast of the times."

The adoption of a new summary budget statement, to be "the primary tabulation in the President's January Budget and in Treasury financial reports," was the "most important recommendation of the Commission," the report said. If approved the new concept would make "obsolete" the existing multiplicity of budgetary tabulations, which included administrative budget, consolidated cash budget and national income accounts budget figures.

The proposed budget statement was to include four major components: (1) appropriations; (2) receipts, expenditures and lending; (3) means of financing; and (4) federal securities and loans outstanding. Of these components, only the receipt-expenditure portion of the receipts, expenditures and lending statement was com-

parable to existing tabulations (administrative, consolidated cash and national income account budgets.)

In addition to the unified budget statement proposal, the Commission recommended that:

• The Budget should be considered as "a broad financial plan," including the four components described above, in contrast to an "historic tendency to view the Budget" as a "single number—the surplus or deficit."

• Greater importance should be given in the budget presentation to appropriations and other fiscal legislation requested of Congress. The term "appropriations" should be broadened to include all types of obligating authority and should replace the current term "new obligational authority" (NOA).

• All federal programs should be included in the budget statement.

• Expenditures and receipts should be reported as they become due (accrual basis) rather than when payments were actually made or received (cash basis).

• Distinction should be made between federal loans and federal expenditures in the calculation of the expenditure surplus or deficit.

• The subsidy portion of federal loan programs (which was the difference between market interest rates and the loan program interest rates) should be included in expenditures rather than in the loan account.

• Federal insurance or guarantees of private loans should be excluded from Budget totals (which was the current practice) because they represented "neither federal expenditures nor federal borrowing."

• Government sales of "participation certificates" in federally owned loans should be treated as a means of financing the deficit rather than as a deduction from gross expenditures, which was the current procedure.

• The Budget document should include a "means of financing section based on the Budget deficit or surplus." This section would detail the sources of funds which were used to bring the receipts, expenditures and lending account into balance.

• Government receipts (other than taxes) which were "enterprise or market-oriented," such as funds received from product sales, hunting and grazing fees, dividends and royalties and sales of federal property, should be consistently treated as offsets to expenditures to which they were related.

• Budget information provided for Congress and the public should provide: (1) more frequent revisions of January estimates; (2) more detailed figures by breaking down aggregate amounts into quarterly or semiannual units; and (3) more comprehensive coverage by extending estimates further into the future.

• The Commission "strongly" recommended against creation of a "capital budget" to provide separate financing of capital (investment) expenditures on the one hand and current (operating) expenditures on the other. Such a move, the report said, "would seriously distort the Budget as a decision making tool."

Four Accounts Compared. The proposed receipt-expenditure account of the recommended Budget differed in major ways from the three systems currently used to measure the Federal Budget surplus or deficit. The current systems included:

(1) The administrative budget, which excluded transactions of federally administered trust funds, such as Social Security and highway program funds. The Com-

mission proposed to include these receipts and payments in the new Budget.

(2) The consolidated cash budget, which included trust fund transactions on a cash basis, recording payments and receipts as they were made. The Commission urged adoption of an accrual accounting system, however, which entered receipts and payments as they became due.

(3) The national income accounts (NIA) budget, which excluded transactions in federal lending programs. The Commission recommended including loan operations as a distinct part of the total receipt-expenditure account.

Debt Limit

Congress in 1967 enacted two bills dealing with the national debt limit. One was (HR 4573—PL 90-3) to provide an increase in the temporary ceiling to meet immediate financing needs. The other (HR 10867—PL 90-93) was to increase the permanent national debt limit in order to provide a more orderly method for larger Government borrowing to finance federal programs. It was the first increase in the permanent debt ceiling since 1959, although Congress had enacted 14 temporary increases in the intervening period.

HR 10867 raised the permanent statutory debt limit to $358 billion from the existing $285 billion, beginning July 1, 1967. The new figure was to be effective for fiscal 1968. For later fiscal years, beginning with 1969, the bill provided a further but temporary increase of $7 billion, to a total of $365 billion. However, the extra $7 billion was to last only through June 29 of each year; on each June 30 it would drop back to $358 billion and then rise again on July 1 to $365 billion. This fluctuating temporary limit was provided, according to its Congressional supporters, because federal borrowing requirements were heavier in the late winter than at the end of a fiscal year in June. Moreover, they added, it would act as a restraint on Ad-

---

Background on National Debt Limit

The period 1789-1849 ended with a debt of $63 million. At the turn of the century, the debt was $1.4 billion; and up to World War I, it hovered around $1.2 billion. During the war, it jumped to $25.5 billion. In the 1920s, the debt receded a billion or a half-billion dollars a year; and at the end of fiscal 1930, it was at $16.2 billion, the lowest point since before the war.

During the "Great Depression," annual increases up to $5 billion carried the debt to $55.3 billion in fiscal 1941. Then came World War II. The debt passed the $100-billion mark ($140.8 billion) in fiscal 1943, the $200-billion mark ($202.6 billion) in 1944 and the $250-billion mark ($259.1 billion) in 1945. It reached a peak of $269.9 billion in 1946. The debt tapered off in subsequent years but never dipped below $250 billion again. From a low point of $252.4 billion in fiscal 1948, the debt began a climb, interrupted by three slight decreases in 1951, 1956 and 1957, which carried it over the $300-billion mark ($306.5 billion) in fiscal 1963.

Although the debt was rising sharply in dollar terms, it was decreasing as a percentage of gross national product. Economists consider this ratio a meaningful measure of the nation's capacity to carry a debt burden. (See table, below.)

The first over-all debt ceiling was established Sept. 24, 1917, in the Second Liberty Bond Act, when the limit was fixed at $11.5 billion. By 1945, the Act had been amended 16 times, and the ceiling had reached $300 billion. In June 1946, the high World War II limit was reduced to a "permanent" $275-billion ceiling.

But Congress in 1954, 1955 and 1956 voted "temporary" increases to bring the ceiling to $278 billion. With the debt at $270.6 billion in 1957, Congress let the "temporary" increases expire and the limit revert to its $275-billion level of 1946.

A "temporary" increase to $280 billion was approved in February 1958; and in September 1958, the "permanent" limit was raised to $283 billion, coupled with an additional "temporary" raise to make the ceiling $288 billion. In June 1959, Congress raised the "permanent" ceiling to $285 billion and granted a "temporary" increase to bring the ceiling to $295 billion. From 1960 through 1966, Congress approved 13 "temporary" increases on the "permanent" ceiling, carrying the ceiling for fiscal 1967 to $330 billion.

(in billions of dollars)

Fiscal year	Gross national product	Federal debt, end of year			
		Total		Held by the public	
		Amount[1]	Percent of GNP	Amount	Percent of GNP
1954	$362.1	$270.8	74.8%	$224.5	62.0%
1955	378.6	274.4	72.5	226.6	59.9
1956	409.4	272.7	66.6	222.2	54.3
1957	431.3	272.3	63.1	219.4	50.9
1958	440.3	279.6	63.5	226.3	51.4
1959	469.1	287.7	61.3	235.0	50.1
1960	495.2	290.8	58.7	237.1	47.9
1961	506.5	292.9	57.8	238.6	47.1
1962	542.1	303.2	55.9	248.3	45.8
1963	573.4	310.8	54.2	254.4	44.4
1964	612.2	316.7	51.7	257.5	42.1
1965	654.2	323.1	49.4	261.6	40.0
1966	720.7	329.4	45.7	264.6	36.7
1967	766.5	341.3	44.5	267.5	34.9
1968	822.6	369.7	44.9	290.6	35.3

[1] Not all subject to the statutory debt ceiling.

ministration borrowing plans because Treasury officials always would be faced with getting the debt back down to $358 billion.

Congress on March 1 completed action on another bill (HR 4573) to raise the temporary debt limit from $330 billion to $336 billion through June 30 to accommodate borrowing needs for the remainder of fiscal 1967.

The Administration on May 15 asked Congress to raise the permanent ceiling to $365 billion, effective July 1. It also asked that the Government be permitted to issue notes with maturities of up to 10 years rather than the existing limit of five years. Notes were not subject to the 4.25-percent interest rate ceiling applicable to Government bonds.

In addition, the Administration asked Congress to permit the sale of $2 billion in long-term bonds by exempting them from the interest-rate ceiling. Because of the ceiling, officials said, the Treasury had been unable to sell such securities since May 1965.

Congress provided a lower ceiling for fiscal 1968 than the Administration sought, but approved the substance of the request for a higher amount in later years by means of the unusual temporary limit.

Congress denied the Administration's request to free $2 billion in long-term bonds from the limit and allowed the sale of notes of up to seven years maturity, rather than the 10 requested. In addition, Congress added wording, which the Administration at first opposed but later acquiesced in, requiring that most participation certificate sales be included under the debt limit. This was a Republican proposal. The Administration in fiscal 1968 planned to sell $5 billion in certificates.

Enactment of the second debt limit bill was notable partly because it provided the first hike in the permanent limit since 1959 and partly because it produced a rare defeat for the powerful chairman of the House Ways and Means Committee, Wilbur D. Mills (D Ark.) The defeat occurred in early June when the House refused to accept a debt limit bill reported by the Committee. That bill (HR 10328) increased the permanent debt ceiling to $365 billion. The House, in an economy mood, rejected HR 10328 by a 197-211 roll-call vote.

The Committee then reported the new bill, HR 10867, providing the $358 billion permanent ceiling and the temporary $7 billion addition. It was enacted.

As in previous years, the debt limit bills provided a vehicle for the Congressional economy bloc to protest high Government spending.

Provisions. As signed into law (PL 90-39) June 30, HR 10867:

Raised the permanent national debt limit from $285 billion to $358 billion, effective July 1, 1967.

Increased the debt limit temporarily by $7 million, to $365 billion, effective July 1, 1968, and each July 1 thereafter, until June 29 of each succeeding year.

Provided that the limit would revert to $358 billion on each June 30.

Required that the face amount of participation certificates issued by the Federal National Mortgage Assn. for itself and other agencies during fiscal 1968 be included under the debt limit.

Permitted the Treasury to issue notes with a maturity of up to seven years, rather than the existing five

years. (Notes were not subject to the 4.25-percent interest rate ceiling applicable to Government bonds.)

1968

The confrontation between Congress and the White House over Government spending, which had been developing since the U.S. became deeply involved in the Vietnam war in 1965, reached its zenith in 1968.

The President in January submitted a Budget for fiscal 1969 which called for more than a $3-billion rise in national defense spending but a "hold-the-line" approach for most domestic programs. Considering the Administration's past inaccurate estimates of the Vietnam war costs, there was not too much hope placed in the defense-spending projection. At the same time, the economy was straining under severe inflationary pressures and there was deep domestic turmoil resulting from racial antagonisms, increasing crime and the plight of the cities. Against this background, the national Budget was the logical focus for the struggle over allocation of the nation's limited resources.

The President and his top officials had previously concluded that the nation could no longer meet from existing financial resources even the most basic responsibilities it had assumed—fighting a costly war, combating inflation and paying for vital domestic social programs. A tax increase was essential and the President had requested one in 1967, first at the beginning of the year without a detailed proposal and in August in a special message to Congress.

His basic proposal was for a 10-percent surcharge on personal and corporate income taxes. He believed that this was the best method of paying for the war and fighting inflation. On the other hand, many of the most powerful Members of Congress, who tended to be conservatives, believed that the best way to achieve these goals was to reduce federal spending. They were not necessarily unconvinced about the merits of a tax increase, but—at least initially—many were dubious. Thus, for almost a year, President Johnson's tax proposals were held hostage in Congress while an agreement was reached on mandatory limits on federal spending. It was the struggle over these limits which dominated Congressional budget action in 1968.

In the end, both sides obtained what they wanted, but Congress clearly obtained much more than the Administration had been prepared to give in the beginning. The Administration, for its part, obtained the 10-percent surcharge in a bill (HR 15414—PL 90-364) enacted June 28. In the same bill, however, Congress added provisions—which were its price for the tax increase—requiring a $6-billion reduction in federal spending in fiscal 1969. *(For a detailed discussion of Congressional action on HR 15414, see p. 167.)*

In other Budget developments, Congress approved appropriations of $133,339,833,734 which were carried in 18 separate bills. Requests totaled $147,908,802,996. In another development, Budget Director Charles L. Schultze, who had held the post since 1965, resigned in January. He was replaced by Charles J. Zwick, who had been Assistant Director of the Budget Bureau.

Tax Policy

CONGRESS enacted two major tax bills during President Johnson's years: one, in 1964, to lower taxes and the other, in 1968, to increase them. The 1964 tax cut was a carryover proposal from the Kennedy Administration and was designed to stimulate economic activity in the nation. The 1968 tax increase was Mr. Johnson's responsibility and was designed to help finance the Vietnam war and to dampen economic activity that was causing inflationary pressures.

Taken together, the two tax measures represented the first test of the economic philosophy popularized during the Kennedy Administration that the Federal Government's fiscal powers (taxing and spending) could be used to influence the nation's economy. By the time Mr. Johnson left office it was not yet clear whether the philosophy would work in application, but there were some signs by mid-1969 that economic activity was slowing. However, monetary policy also was at work to halt the inflation that had pushed up consumer prices 3 percent in 1967 and 4.7 percent in 1968.

The tax increase was in the form of a surcharge on personal and corporate income tax liabilities at the rate of 10 percent. It was proposed by Mr. Johnson reluctantly and enacted by Congress only after a long and at times bitter fight with the White House over Government spending. The President contended during the first two years of the expanded U.S. role in the Vietnam war, 1965 and 1966, that the nation could afford both the added military expenditures and increased outlays for domestic social programs without a general tax increase. A relatively minor effort to produce extra revenues was made in 1966. This involved speeding up the collection of certain taxes and delaying the reduction in automobile and telephone excise taxes that were scheduled to take effect. It also involved, in a separate bill, temporary suspension of both the investment tax credit that was originally intended to spur spending on plant and equipment and certain accelerated depreciation practices; however, both of these tax benefits were restored in early 1967 just one-half a year after they were suspended.

Mr. Johnson first mentioned a surcharge in his January 1967 messages to Congress. But because of uncertainty about economic trends, no detailed proposals were urged on Congress until August of that year, when the 10-percent surcharge was formally requested. From then until a bill was enacted the following summer, Congress and the Executive Branch were locked in a continuing struggle over the price that was to be extracted for the surcharge. The price, as it turned out, was a $6-billion cut in projected Government spending and even larger cuts in appropriation requests and existing spending

authority, and a substantial reduction in the number of federal employees. It was a price that the President and the agencies recoiled at but were forced to pay (although a number of departments managed to win special exemptions from the restrictions).

A SECOND major problem of the Johnson years, which was not unrelated to that of paying for the war and fighting inflation, was reducing the chronic balance-of-payments deficit. For most of the decade before President Johnson took office, the United States had run a deficit in its balance-of-payments accounts. The problem had been growing increasingly worse in the 1960s and had drawn special attention from President Kennedy. He proposed various methods, some involving legislation, to cure it. Little progress was made and the Johnson Administration was faced with a serious situation. It reacted with a gradually escalating program which led, in 1968, to mandatory controls on U.S. investment abroad.

The early effort by the Johnson Administration to control the deficit emphasized voluntary action by businesses and banks to reduce the amount of capital going abroad. The movement of capital for direct investment or lending had become a major element in the payments deficit. This approach was useful for a period and helped mitigate the problem, but eventually it proved to be inadequate and stronger measures were proposed. The strongest, which the President put into effect by administrative action, set strict limits on dollars that could be invested abroad annually and required repatriation of substantial amounts of earnings from abroad. These controls went into effect at the beginning of 1968 after the deficit had taken a very serious turn for the worse in late 1967. Mr. Johnson's 1968 program also called for a number of pieces of legislation including a highly controversial tax on Americans going abroad. Congress rejected most of these proposals.

Even though the Administration's far-reaching 1968 program was not entirely implemented because of Congress' rejection of the most important legislative proposals, the balance of payments improved substantially during the year. Preliminary end-of-the-year figures for

---

Reference

Discussion of tax policy from 1945-64 will be found in *Congress and the Nation, Vol. I, p. 397-442.*

1968 showed a surplus. It was not clear, however, if the improvement was due to basic changes in the U.S. payments position or to one-shot developments that would not be repeated in the future. There was evidence that the latter was the case.

ONE of the Administration's bills to improve the balance of payments became involved in 1966 in one of the best known Congressional controversies of the Johnson years. Interestingly, the controversy did not even involve the balance of payments. It centered, rather, on a proposal to establish a fund to finance Presidential campaigns. The proposal, which Congress approved in 1966, allowed taxpayers to check a box on their tax forms if they wished to allot $1 of taxes to Presidential campaigns. This plan was added as a rider along with many other riders to an obscure bill dealing basically with foreign investment in the United States. The campaign fund was so novel and its adoption so unexpected that immediate attention was drawn to the bill; in addition, the multitude of other riders that were added were so specialized in their effect that they were considered "gifts" for special interests and gave the basic legislation of foreign investors the reputation of a "Christmas Tree Bill." The controversy over the campaign fund had an unexpected echo in 1967, although by that time it no longer involved a balance of payments bill. The Christmas tree bill went through at the very end of the 1966 session; the campaign fund like the other riders was added by Congress with less than serious study. Over the winter, some Members had a change of heart. In the spring of 1967, after a bruising fight in the Senate, the plan was suspended until Congress adopted guidelines governing distribution of money from the fund. This proved to be an indefinite suspension which blocked the fund from being used in the 1968 Presidential elections.

ANOTHER major tax issue which began to receive public attention during the Johnson years was sharing. Proposals to share with states and communities some of the enormous revenues gathered through the federal tax structure were made in the 1950s. They did not receive much public discussion until put forth in the 1960s by Walter Heller, an economic adviser to President Kennedy.

The concept of tax sharing had merits that made it attractive to both conservatives and liberals. But there was enough controversy about the idea to block any substantive action in Congress by the end of 1968.

The Federal Government had for many years shared revenues with states and local governments but did so almost entirely through categorical grants intended for specific purposes. Tax sharing, on the other hand, involved returning sums of money to states and communities to use as they wished, or at least with very few strings attached. Republicans attempted to have their version of the concept written into several bills, with moderate success. The GOP approach, called block grants, sent money directly to state governments for use or redistribution. Democrats opposed this approach because they wanted the funds to go directly to cities where they believed the need was greatest.

Chronology Of Legislation On Tax Policy 1965

The continuing balance-of-payments crisis was again a major concern of Administration officials and Congress in 1965. The Administration announced a major program designed to reduce the worsening deficit which threatened the stability of the dollar. At the center of the program was a plea for voluntary action by businesses and banks to reduce the accelerating volume of American capital that was going abroad for loans and direct investment. Many observers were skeptical about the efficacy of a voluntary program, but as it turned out, cooperation was remarkably good and the balance-of-payment deficit improved during the year. Unfortunately, it did not improve enough and the improvement was not to last. The 1965 program to reduce the deficit was continued into 1966 and expanded and was to evolve into mandatory controls on overseas investments by 1968. Congress responded to the problem by enacting most of the proposals put forth by President Johnson to reduce the deficit.

In another major action, Congress reduced or eliminated federal excise taxes on a multitude of items. It was a victory for businessmen, consumers and tax collectors, all of whom had sought for years to rid themselves of the burden.

Balance of Payments

The U.S. balance of payments, in deficit since 1957, moved toward equilibrium in 1965. The deficit was down to $1.4 billion as measured on the liquidity basis, compared to $2.8 billion in 1964. By the end of the year, however, the problem remained serious enough to require increased efforts to reduce the dollar drain during 1966. *(For balance-of-payments figures, see table p. 175.)*

The 1965 improvement in the payments account was attributable, in considerable part, to Administration efforts to keep dollars at home, repatriate liquid funds held abroad and attract foreign capital to the United States. The program was announced by President Johnson Feb. 10 in a special message to Congress. The Administration's program was aimed at net capital outflows which had risen from $4.5 billion in 1963 to $6.6 billion in 1964 and to an annual rate of upwards of $9 billion in the fourth quarter of 1964. To stem the flow of dollars abroad, the President called on businessmen and bankers to exercise "voluntary restraint" in overseas lending and investment operations. Widespread compliance held 1964 net outflows of capital to about $3.8 billion.

In other key features of his program, the President proposed further reductions of U.S. Government expenditures abroad and outlined a legislative program which included proposals to extend and expand the 1964 Interest Equalization Tax, continue authority of U.S. banks to pay higher rates of interest on time deposits (short-term investments) of foreign governments than on domestic deposits, reduce the amount of duty-free purchases permitted tourists returning from abroad, and provide antitrust exemptions for bankers who cooperated to cut down on overseas dollar movements. All of these requests were enacted *(see below)*.

The payments deficit improved substantially in the first half of the year. Bank loans declined rapidly, large amounts of short-term capital were repatriated and a declining U.S. trade surplus improved with settlement of a major dock strike. During the second half of the year, however, the balance worsened as repatriations were completed and exports leveled off.

Balance of Payments Background

Simply stated, the U.S. balance of payments run a deficit because, in total, the United States spends more abroad for imports, travel, investments and Government outlays than the rest of the world spends here. The United States had a deficit in every year since 1949, except for 1957 and 1968 when small surpluses were achieved. The deficit means that, one way or another, the rest of the world has accumulated more claims against the United States than the U.S. has accumulated against the rest of the world. Eventually, central banks around the world (mostly in Europe) end up with an excess of dollars. The U.S. stands ready at any time to give them an ounce of gold for every $35 they have.

The balance-of-payments deficit first became a serious problem in 1958. Early in 1960 the first major attempt to deal with the deficit was outlined in a March 17 message to Congress by President Eisenhower. The message, however, was devoted largely to export expansion.

The first major balance-of-payments message was sent to Congress by President Kennedy on Feb. 6, 1961. The message proposed expanded efforts at increasing exports, improvement in Export-Import Bank facilities and a "Buy American" policy for foreign aid purchases by other nations. The message also proposed the reduction of the duty-free allowances from $500 to $100 and other measures.

In 1962, President Kennedy continued to push reductions in U.S. overseas spending, obtained enactment of the Trade Expansion Act and revised tax laws applying to American businesses and individuals overseas, and took other actions.

Mr. Kennedy July 18, 1963, sent Congress his second special payments message, in which he requested the Interest Equalization Tax. He indicated that the Administration hoped to achieve a near or complete balance in international transactions by 1965. He also outlined other efforts, including such familiar measures as export expansion and reduced Government outlays abroad. *(For additional background, see Congress and the Nation, Vol. I, p. 201, 202, 207, 381, 384.)*

Following are the major parts of the President's program to reduce the payments deficit.

CAPITAL. Major focus of the President's message centered on measures to reduce the increasing flow to other nations of private U.S. capital. The net outflow for direct investment increased by $350 million between 1963 and the end of 1964, for other long-term investment increased by $500 million, and for short-term investment increased by a staggering $1.4 billion. Mr. Johnson said he "reluctantly" proposed steps to "restrain" capital outflow, but contended that the deficit "leaves me no choice." He proposed and took the following actions:

Voluntary Cooperation. In the central part of the program, the President asked bankers and businessmen to "exercise voluntary restraint" in lending money or making investments in developed nations. He said the restraint should apply particularly to short-term loans and direct investments. He directed federal officials to devise a program to "sharply limit" bank loans abroad. In addition, he said he would ask "leading businessmen" to meet with Secretary of Commerce John T. Conner to discuss voluntary methods of controlling short-term corporate lending and direct investment abroad.

Direct investment abroad during 1965 rose dramatically to $3.5 billion from $2.3 billion in 1964 (thus making them a central target for later action). But the net outflow on other long-term investments declined to $1 billion from the 1964 level of $2.1 billion and short-term investment was completely reversed from a 1964 net outflow of $2.2 billion to a 1964 inflow of $753 million. (Some of this improvement was due, of course, to mandatory requirements imposed under the Interest Equalization Tax. *See below.*)

Bank Antitrust Exemption. To make substantial bank cooperation possible, the President requested Congress to exempt from the antitrust laws voluntary actions and agreements among bankers. In response, Congress enacted legislation (HR 5280—PL 89-175) to provide antitrust exemptions for agreements to curtail the flow of private dollars and credit to other nations. The law was to expire 20 months after enactment or upon certification by the President that its provisions were no longer necessary. The bill passed with little controversy.

Interest Equalization Tax. The President took and proposed several actions under a 1964 law known as the Interest Equalization Tax (PL 88-563). The purpose of the law was to stem the outflow of investment funds from the United States by making it equally as expensive for foreign borrowers to obtain capital in U.S. financial markets as it was to obtain capital from other industrial nations. *(Congress and the Nation, Vol. I, p. 384.)*

In actions regarding the tax, Mr. Johnson in his Feb. 10 message extended its coverage and requested its extension

Coverage—He issued an Executive Order broadening the IET to cover U.S. bank loans made abroad with maturities of one to three years. (Exemptions were to be available for borrowers in underdeveloped nations.) The President's action was taken under standby authority provided by an amendment to the 1964 law by Sen. Albert Gore (D Tenn.) and welcomed by the Administration. Bank lending of one to three years was not covered under existing law.

Extension—Mr. Johnson requested enactment of legislation to extend the tax for a two-year period, from

Interest Equalization Tax Background

The Interest Equalization Tax was enacted by Congress in 1964 (PL 88-563) as a temporary measure to reduce a heavy and continued outflow of dollars resulting from borrowing and stock issues of foreign governments and businesses in U.S. money markets. In order to prevent a large outflow of dollars during the period the measure was moving through the Congress, the law was made retroactive to the July 1963 date on which it was proposed by President Kennedy, and it remained in effect through Dec. 31, 1965.

The tax worked this way: Americans would pay the tax, at rates provided in the bill, when they acquired a foreign security (primarily stocks or bonds). The Americans then would pass on the extra cost of the tax to the foreign borrower, either through charging a higher interest rate on a loan or by demanding a discount on the purchase of the stock. With that increase, the cost of obtaining capital in the United States was expected to be at a level comparable with European markets.

For example, an American buying $100 worth of foreign stock would have to pay the Government a flat 15 percent, or $15, in tax. He presumably would insist that the foreign seller reduce the price of the stock to $85. If the American were buying debt obligations (primarily bonds), the tax would range from 1.05 percent on obligations of 1-year maturity to 15 percent on those of 28-½ years or longer maturity. The seller would be expected to increase the interest he would pay on the loan to compensate for the tax the American would pay.

Dec. 31, 1965 (the scheduled expiration date), to Dec. 31, 1967. He also proposed an amendment to the IET to broaden its scope to cover the purchase by Americans of foreign securities with a maturity period of one to three years. The IET did not impose a tax on securities maturing in less than three years. The amendment was necessary to make the act consistent following the extension of its provisions to one- to three-year bank loans.

Congress approved the Administration IET proposals in the fall (HR 4750—PL 89-243) with an amendment limiting extension of the levy to 19 months, through July 31, 1967. There was minor Republican opposition to the bill in the House. Republicans had strongly opposed enactment of the IET in 1964.

GOVERNMENT EXPENDITURES. Mr. Johnson said the Government would intensify efforts to reduce U.S. dollar outlays abroad. He said that foreign aid and defense officials had been directed to send dollar assistance abroad only if the aid could not be sent in the form of U.S. goods and services. All officials were instructed to cut overseas dollars expenses "to the bone."

FOREIGN TRAVEL. President Johnson requested legislation to discourage American travelers from spending as much abroad as they had in recent years. He proposed to lower the ceiling on the amount of purchases made abroad that returning U.S. residents could bring into the country duty-free. Historically, U.S. residents traveling abroad were allowed to bring back duty-free articles of $100 wholesale value. After World War II the amount was raised to $500 wholesale value to aid foreign countries with dollar shortages, but in 1961 the amount was reduced temporarily to $100 because of the balance-of-payments deficit. The 1961 reduction, extended in 1963, was to expire July 1, 1965. *(Congress and the Nation, Vol. I, p. 202, 207.)*

In his Feb. 10 message, President Johnson proposed to reduce the ceiling to $50, base it on retail—rather than wholesale—value and make it applicable only to goods which the traveler brought back with him. Government officials said the wholesale value of foreign goods was about 60 percent of their retail value, permitting a returning U.S. tourist to bring about $167 worth of retail merchandise into the United States under the $100 exemption.

Congress approved most of the requests in a bill (HR 8147—PL 89-62) enacted June 30 only hours before the temporary allowances were to expire. However, the bill set the ceiling at $100, rather than $50 as Mr. Johnson requested; it provided, as requested, that the duty exemption would be computed on the retail value of the goods. The bill also required the traveler to bring the goods back with him rather than ship or mail them. It also reduced the amount of duty-free alcoholic beverages which could be brought into the United States from one gallon to one quart (except from certain U.S. possessions) and changed the valuation under the existing $10 exemption on mailed gift packages from wholesale to retail.

FOREIGN INVESTMENT. In his message, Mr. Johnson said he would propose tax legislation to encourage foreign investment in U.S. corporate securities. A bill (HR 5916) providing tax reduction on foreign business income accumulated in the United States was introduced in Congress but did not receive action during 1965. *(See 1966 action, p. 149.)*

Foreign Bank Deposits. Congress enacted, with little debate, another request by Mr. Johnson to continue the authority of domestic banks to pay higher interest rates on time deposits (short-term investments) of foreign governments than on domestic deposits. The measure (HR 5306—PL 89-79) was designed to reduce the dollar drain by making U.S. capital markets more attractive to foreign investors. HR 5306 extended the exemption of foreign deposits from the existing 4-½ percent federal interest rate ceiling for a three-year period, from Oct. 15, 1965, to Oct. 15, 1968.

Other Developments

Alternate Accounting System. Administration officials in 1965 expressed interest in a second accounting system for balance-of-payments statistics which treated private dollars held in the United States by foreigners as a capital inflow. (The existing "over-all" or "liquidity" formula—the official Government method of measuring the nation's balance-of-payments performance—listed dollar investment abroad as payments but did not list as receipts reinvestment of these funds in short-term U.S. securities or their deposit in U.S. banks.) Officials said the proposed new accounting system would give a more realistic indication of the U.S. payments position.

Termed the "official settlements" balance, the new formula was recommended in an April 30 report issued by the Review Committee for Balance-of-Payments Statistics, a Government-sponsored panel headed by private economist Edward Bernstein. Under the Committee's recommendations the liquidity formula would be retained and the official settlements system adopted as an alternate accounting measure. (The Bernstein report indicated that the 1964 deficit on an official settlements basis would have been $1.5 billion, well below the $2.8-billion deficit recorded under the existing formula.) The Budget Bureau Aug. 27 announced that the Government would begin publishing U.S. balance-of-payments statistics under both formulas; however, the liquidity formula was to remain the only official measure pending further study of the new system.

Voluntary Restraints Broadened for 1966. President Johnson's Cabinet Committee on Balance-of-Payments, a group made up of the Secretaries of the Treasury, Defense, Commerce, Agriculture, and other high Administration officials, Dec. 6 announced an extension and tightening of the Administration's program for voluntary restraints on private capital outflows. The Committee said the objective of the program was to bring the U.S. balance-of-payments into equilibrium (a surplus or deficit no greater than $250 million) during 1966. (Treasury Secretary Fowler Feb. 14, 1966, expressed doubt that the goal could be reached, however, if foreign exchange costs of U.S. involvement in Vietnam increased over levels projected in Budget estimates for fiscal 1966 and fiscal 1967.)

In its major features, the new program:

• Requested bankers to limit new overseas lending to a level only slightly above the 1965 ceiling (5 percent over the amount of such loans outstanding at the end of 1964.) The program was to permit a 1-percent increase for each quarter of the year, culminating in a fourth quarter ceiling of 9 percent.

• Urged an additional 400 corporations to join the 500 corporate participants in the voluntary program in an effort to increase net business contributions to the balance-of-payments solvency by a total of $3.4 billion over 1965. The bulk of the total, some $2.4 billion, was to come from expanded exports, greater repatriations of foreign earnings, financing of foreign investment through borrowing abroad and the return of cash balances held overseas. The remaining $1 billion would come from cutbacks in direct investment outflows. To achieve these reductions, Commerce Secretary John T. Connor asked each of the corporations to limit its direct investment for the 1965-66 period to 90 percent of amounts invested during the period 1962-64.

Discount Rate Increase. The Federal Reserve Board Dec. 5 announced a one-half percent increase—to 4.5 percent from 4 percent—in its discount rate, the interest rate it charges for loans to commercial banks in the Reserve System. In a collateral move, the Board raised from 4.5 percent to 5.5 percent the ceiling on interest rates that member banks were permitted to pay on time deposits and deposit certificates. Although such adjustment of interest rates normally influence a nation's balance-of-payments performance, the Commerce Department early in 1966 forecast "comparatively minor" movements of capital in response to the higher U.S. rate structure. Officials said the higher U.S. rates were

still considerably lower than comparable rates in other developed countries and that the probable effect of the rate increase would be a "slight encouragement" to U.S. lenders to keep short-term funds at home and to foreign investors to diversity their portfolios by holding U.S. assets.

Excise Tax Cuts

After two decades of waiting, Congress in 1965 repealed a variety of federal excise taxes that had annoyed businessmen, consumers and tax collectors alike since they were first imposed as emergency measures in World War II and the Korean war. The bill (HR 8371—PL 89-44) completely eliminated many levies and reduced others to a low level. Some levies were left untouched; they were largely specialized items such as user taxes (primarily for highway construction), sumptuary taxes on alcoholic beverages and tobacco products, and regulatory taxes on marihuana, opium, gambling and similar items. *(See p. 147 for list of excise taxes.)*

In total, the bill provided a $4.7-billion cut in federal excise taxes between June 22, 1965, the effective date of the law, and Jan. 1, 1969, when the last stage of the reductions was to be effective. (As it turned out, however, not all of the stages actually took effect during the Johnson years. The rising cost of the Vietnam war forced the Administration in the years after 1965 to request Congress to postpone some of the excise reductions in order to prevent the revenue loss. Congress responded favorably and as a result some of the taxes—most importantly, the one on automobiles—still had not been dropped to the planned level when Mr. Johnson left office in 1969.)

The reductions provided in HR 8371 were essentially those requested by President Johnson early in 1965. The reductions were to take place over the same period, 1965-1969, but were to total $4.7 billion which was about $700 million more than Mr. Johnson requested. The additional revenue loss was due largely to a reduction in the automobile excise tax from 10 percent to 1 percent compared to the Administration's proposed reduction to 5 percent.

The only other significant difference from the Administration's request was the absence from the final bill of higher taxes on the users of highways, airways and waterways. As in other years of Mr. Johnson's Presidency, Congress in 1965 refused to consider the user taxes except to make permanent an existing temporary air travel tax.

Enactment of the legislation, from the time Mr. Johnson sent his requests to Congress in May, required only a few days more than one month. There was only one significant difference between the House and Senate bills. The House eliminated all of the 10 percent automobile tax while the Senate cut it to 1 percent and earmarked that amount for a special fund to aid in the disposal of old and wrecked cars and, in addition, made elimination of an additional 4 percent contingent upon manufacturers installing certain safety devices in cars. In conference, the House won by agreeing to retention of a 1-percent levy but refusing to accept the earmarking and the car-safety provisions.

Numerous U.S. business and trade organizations lobbied vigorously for enactment of legislation to lower

Background on Excise Taxes

HR 8371 was the third major reduction in federal tax liabilities since 1962. Congress in 1962 enacted legislation which provided a 7-percent investment tax credit for business and which also contained a few revenue-raising reforms. In early 1964, Congress enacted an $11.5 billion reduction in personal and corporate income taxes.

Most of the excises in force in 1965 were imposed originally during wartime as temporary sources of revenue which would be eliminated when conditions returned to normal. A number of World War I excises were reintroduced in 1932 to compensate for plummeting income tax collections. The Revenue Act of 1941 made the 1932 excises permanent and imposed numerous other excise levies. Other wartime excises were imposed during 1942 and 1944.

The Revenue Act of 1950 was conceived as a measure to cut the annual $7.5 billion excise tax intake by about $1 billion, but the outbreak of the Korean War in June 1950 forced an extension of the old taxes and imposition of new ones. Faced by expanding defense expenditures, Congress in 1951 increased excise taxes by $1.2 billion. In 1954, a number of the World War II excises were slashed; however, all of the 1951 rate increases were extended for one year. These included cigarettes (8 cents a pack), liquor ($10.50 a gallon), beer $9 a barrel), wines (varying rates), automobiles (10 percent of the manufacturer's price), auto parts and accessories (8 percent of the manufacturer's price.) All these rates were affected by the 1965 legislation. After 1954, the emergency rate increases of 1951 were re-extended for one-year periods in every session of Congress. Various taxes imposed in 1941 were made subject to annual extension in 1959. The major changes in the excise tax structure after 1954 were the 1956 levy on highway vehicles weighing more than 26,000 pounds and the 1962 reduction or repeal of various excises on passenger transportation.

Extension of excise taxes met strong opposition in Congress beginning about 1960. Early in 1964, White House intervention averted excise-cutting amendments to the 1964 income tax cut in the Senate Finance Committee and on the Senate floor. Legislation to erpeal numerous excises and to reduce others barely missed Congressional approval later in 1964. *(For action in earlier years, see chapter on tax policy in Congress and the Nation, Vol. I, p. 397.)*

or eliminate the federal levies. The excise tax reduction bill was cited by new lobby registrants in 1965 as one of their chief (and frequently their only) concern in lobbying.

Interstate Taxation

A special subcommittee of the House Judiciary Committee in 1965 concluded a study of state taxation of interstate commerce and made recommendations. The study was authorized by Congress in 1959.

Background. In 1959, in a series of cases dealing with the question of a state's right to tax a company which did business in that state but was located in another state, the Supreme Court ruled that states could tax that portion of a company's income which was earned through operations within their boundaries.

Later in 1959, Congress passed a law (PL 86-272) prohibiting a state from levying a tax on the net income of a business if its only activity within a state was (1) the solicitation of orders for tangible personal property, to be approved and filled from outside the state, or (2) the solicitation of orders for a client or customer if the orders were to be approved and filled from outside the state. PL 86-272 also called for a study of income taxes imposed on business in interstate commerce, the study to be submitted to Congress by July 1, 1962. In 1961 the scope of the study was broadened to cover "all matters pertaining to the taxation of interstate commerce by the states" and the deadline for the reports was extended. In 1964 Congress passed a law (PL 88-286) again extending the deadline, this time to June 30, 1965.

Committee Recommendations. The Special Subcommittee on State Taxation of Interstate Commerce, of the House Judiciary Committee, on Sept. 2 released a report summarizing its findings and making recommendations. A corporation's income would be divided among the states for tax purposes according to a two-factor formula based on the locations of its property and payroll. Sales would be taxable only by the state in which the buyer first received physical delivery of the goods. The state where goods were used (if other than the state of receipt) might also impose a tax but would have to give credit for prior taxes paid. A state could levy a sales or use tax if the business involved (1) owned or leased realty in the state, (2) had an employee whose services were performed entirely in the state or (3) regularly used its own vehicles or a private parcel service to make deliveries to private residences in the state. Prepaid mail order sales were exempted.

Bill Introduced. Subcommittee Chairman Edwin E. Willis (D La.) Oct. 22 introduced a bill (HR 11798) embodying the Subcommittee's recommendations, but by the end of 1968 interstate taxation legislation still had not been enacted. *(See p. 156, 163, 178.)*

Utility Tax Proposal

Action was postponed in the Senate on a controversial amendment to prevent federal regulatory agencies from requiring regulated utilities to pass on to consumers taxes saved by filing consolidated income tax returns. The amendment was sponsored in the Finance Committee by Sens. Everett McKinley Dirksen (R Ill.) and Russell B. Long (D La.) as a rider to a minor House-passed bill (HR 7502) to revise income tax treatment of property losses attributable to major disasters. (HR 7502—which was not enacted because of the controversy—benefitted tax payers who incurred losses on personal and certain types of business property because of storm, flood or other casualty which the President designated as a major disaster.) the controversial amendment was sought by the Tennessee Gas Transmission Co., one of the nation's largest pipeline companies. It was opposed by liberals on the Committee and by a majority of the Federal Power Commission (FPC), which had jurisdiction over pipelines, as well as by such other federal regulatory agencies as the Federal Communications Commission and the Interstate Commerce Commission. Also opposed were the nonprofit National Rural Electric Cooperative Assn., the Cooperative League of the U.S.A., and the Electric Consumers Information Committee, which conducted a publicity campaign against it.

Regulatory agencies allowed utilities and other rate-regulated industries (gas, electric and telephone companies, pipelines, airlines, bus lines, railroads, etc.) to charge rates which compensated them for their expenses of doing business, plus taxes, plus a reasonable rate of return on their investment in their regulated operations.

Following enactment of the 7-percent and 3-percent investment tax credits in 1962, the Federal Power Commission took the lead in demanding that these credits be "passed through" to consumers, on the grounds that rates charged by utilities should cover only taxes actually paid. (The credits reduced taxes of companies which invested in new plant and equipment.) However, Congress in the 1964 Revenue Act declared that regulatory agencies could not require companies receiving these tax credits to reduce their rates accordingly.

The Dirksen-Long amendment posed a somewhat similar issue, and arose from FPC efforts to require regulated companies which reduced their tax liabilities by filing consolidated returns (with affiliates which were entitled to tax credits) to "pass through" the savings to their consumers.

The amendment permitted a group of affiliated companies which gained a tax saving through a consolidated return to assign the saving to the companies which reduced the liability of the group. Regulatory agencies would be required in such cases to ignore the tax saving, and treat the regulated companies in the group as though each had paid its taxes separately.

In an example of how the amendment would work, used during the Finance Committee's hearings, a regulated utility, for instance a pipeline company that earns $100 million a year, forms an affiliation with a new company entitled to a sizable tax credit, for instance a company that is entitled to a $20-million tax credit because it is buying and installing a pipeline that is not yet producing revenue. The first company would ordinarily owe $50 million in taxes, but by filing a consolidated return with the second company, the total tax liability is reduced to $30 million. A regulatory agency could currently hold that the first company's tax costs had gone down by $20 million and seek to reduce its rates. The Dirksen amendment would permit the first company to transfer the $20 million dollars to the second company, and would require regulatory agencies to consider the transfer as the equivalent of tax paid. This would mean that the regulatory agencies could not require the first company to reduce its rates.

Opponents of the amendment said that it would permit a utility in one part of the country to subsidize an affiliate that was attempting to get started against competition in another part of the country, and to charge the costs of the subsidization to its own consumers while permitting the affiliate to charge lower, more competitive rates. Such was said to be true of a case currently before the FPC concerning Tennessee Gas Transmission Co. and El Paso Natural Gas Co., El Paso, which served the lucrative Southern California market, complained that Tennessee Gas wanted to use the book-

Federal Excise Tax Rates

	Existing Rates	New Rates
Liquor taxes:		
Distilled spirits, per gallon	$10.50	*(1)*
Beer, per barrel	$9	*(1)*
Still wines, by alcoholic content, per gallon	17¢ to $10.50	*(1)*
Special occupational taxes, per year	$24 to $255	*(2)*
Tobacco taxes:		
Cigarettes, small and large, per 1,000	$4 and $8.40	*(1)*
Cigars, by weight and retail price, per 1,000	$2.50 to $20	*(2)*
Snuff, smoking and chewing tobacco, per pound	10 ¢	0
Manufacturers' excises:	**Per cent of manufacturers' sales price**	
Air conditioners, self-contained	10%	0
Automobiles	10	1*
Automobile parts and accessories	8	0
Business machines	10	0
Cameras, lenses and film	10	
Electric, gas and oil appliances	5	0
Electric light bulbs and tubes	10	0
Firearms, shells and cartridges	11	*(2)*
Fountain and ballpoint pens, mechanical pencils	10	0
Musical instruments	10	0
Phonographs and phonograph records	10	0
Radio and television sets	10	0
Refrigerators and quick freeze units	5	0
Sporting goods and equipment	10	*(3)*
	Cents	
Matches, ordinary, per 1,000	2	0
Gasoline, per gallon	4	*(2)*
Tires, highway vehicle, per pound	10	*(2)*
Tires, other, per pound	5	*(2)*
Retailers' excises:	**Percent of retailers' sales price**	
Furs and fur articles	10%	0
Jewelry	10	0
Luggage, handbags and wallets	10	0
Toilet preparations	10	0
Miscellaneous excises:	**Per cent**	
Telegrams and telephone calls	10	0*
Safe-deposit box rental	10	0
Transportation of persons by air	5	*(2)*
Admissions, general, in excess of $1	10	0
Wagering, per amount of wager	10	*(2)*
Club dues and initiation fees	20	0
	Cents	
Playing cards, per pack	13	0

* When fully effective in 1969, however, a 1968 bill eliminated auto tax. See p. 173.
1 Extended rate on permanent basis.
2 No change.
3 Repealed except for tax on fishing equipment.

keeping device to start competing in Southern California.

Depreciation Allowances

The Treasury Department early in 1965 announced new rules liberalizing the manner in which income tax deductions for depreciation of plant and equipment could be taken, and at the same time limiting the ways in which such deductions could be calculated. The Department estimated that the regulations would increase depreciation tax benefits during 1965 by $600 million to $800 million.

The new measures liberalized depreciation rules that had been instituted July 12, 1962, by executive action of President Kennedy. The 1962 rules had consolidated the more than 5,000 separate items on which depreciation rates were set into about 75 general categories, and had reduced the average depreciable life allowed for manufacturing assets from 19 years to 12 years. Taxpayers were allowed to switch to the new depreciable lives and pay taxes on that basis. After three years, the Internal Revenue Service was to apply an arithmetical formula to determine whether a company's actual depreciation practices in replacing machinery were consistent with its depreciation deductions.

To provide taxpayers with a method of demonstrating that their depreciation deductions were justified, the 1962 regulations established a "reserve ratio" test. The "reserve ratio" was the ratio of the total depreciation deductions taken on assets still in use (called the "depreciation reserve") to the original cost of the assets. Failure of the taxpayer's reserve ratio to meet the Treasury standard could indicate that the taxpayer had been recovering the cost of equipment too quickly—that is, over a period substantially shorter than its actual useful life.

Tax Exempt Foundations

The Treasury Department recommended new restrictions on the activities of private tax-exempt charitable foundations. The proposals, aimed at preventing foundations from using their funds for private gains and reducing foundations' economic power exercised through their control of private commercial businesses, required legislation. Congress, however, did not act on a bill in 1965 or any of the following three years before President Johnson left office. (Serious consideration of legislation began in the House in early 1969.)

The Treasury report, requested by the Senate Finance Committee and the House Ways and Means Committee in 1963, was an outgrowth of more than a year of study by the Treasury. It was prompted in part by Rep. Wright Patman (D Texas) who had been studying the problem for several years. He had concluded that many "philanthropic" foundations had abused their tax-exempt privileges to gain control of industrial and commercial enterprises and had operated in competition with small businesses (which Patman had long championed) which did not enjoy similar tax advantages. Patman and the Select Small Business Subcommittee on Foundations: Their Impact on Small Business, which he chaired, had been investigating private foundations since 1961.

Treasury Recommendations. The Treasury Department's report noted that most private foundations did not abuse their tax-exempt privilege, but said enough "serious" problems existed to warrant action. It specified six major problem areas and proposed the following:

Self-Dealing—generally prohibit foundations from engaging in financial transactions with any "substantial" donor, officer, director or trustee, or any party related to them, except to pay "reasonable compensation" for services and to make purchases of supplies. This recommendation, an outgrowth of a provision passed by the House in 1950 but not agreed to by the Senate, would attempt to prevent a foundation's assets from being diverted from the foundation's charitable purpose to the private advantage of its donors. The existing law, according to the Treasury report, prohibited only donor-foundation transactions which "violate an arm's length standard," and had produced "unsatisfactory" results.

Deferred Charitable Benefits—require "non-operating" foundations (those which make gifts rather than operate active charitable institutions themselves) to disburse all of their net income (exclusive of long-term capital gains) within a period of approximately one year to "active charitable operations." This recommendation would alleviate the time lag between the loss of tax revenue from the immediate tax deduction and the public benefit derived from devoting an equivalent amount of funds to active charitable programs. Under existing law, such vague standards as "unreasonable" and "substantial" had proved "inadequate as well as difficult and expensive to administer," the report said, in attempting to prevent undue delay in use of tax-exempt funds.

Business Involvement—prohibit a foundation from owning, either directly or through stock holding, 20 percent or more of a business unrelated to the charitable activities of the foundation. The Treasury arrived at the 20-percent figure because it felt, according to the report, that "effective control of a corporation very frequently resides in a body of stock representing 20 percent of its voting power." The report said that "taxable businesses are often placed at a competitive disadvantage" because of tax loopholes and other advantages available to foundations. Among the examples cited of foundations involved in business was an unnamed organization which held controlling interests in 26 separate organizations, including a metropolitan newspaper worth approximately $10.5 million, the largest radio broadcasting station in the state, a life insurance business of book value exceeding $20 million, a lumber company, several banks, three large hotels, a garage and a variety of office buildings. "These properties," the report said, "constitute an economic empire of substantial power and influence." Newspaper reports identified the foundation as the Houston Endowment, Inc. of Texas.

Family Control—defer charitable deductions for gifts of family corporation stock to a foundation until the foundation sells or contributes the stock to a public charity or until the donor's control over the corporation or assets ceases. This recommendation would prevent families from using foundations "as convenient vehicles" for maintaining control of private corporations, the report said. Donors had accomplished this, it explained, by transferring voting stock in a family-controlled corporation to a foundation which the family also controlled in order to "substantially" reduce the family's income, gift and estate taxes.

Unrelated Financial Transaction—bar a foundation from engaging in all speculative practices and from borrowing for investment purposes; confine a foundation's loans to those which are "necessary, safe and appropriate for charitable fiduciaries." Although the report cited a 1963 Securities and Exchange Commission report which indicated that foundation speculating was not a severe problem (the average rates of turnover for foundations in 1963 were within a 1-2 percent range), the Treasury underscored the risks involved in trading and speculating with assets "which have been committed to charity." While the Treasury Department's statistics showed that borrowing accounted for less than 2.5 percent of total foundation assets in 1962, the report gave examples of the "limited" number of private foundations which had "borrowed heavily" to acquire productive assets. It also found evidence of certain foundations making loans without adequate security and with the "fundamental motivation" of creating "unwarranted" private advantage.

Broadening Management—prohibit foundation donors and related parties from constituting more than 25 percent of the organization's governing body after 25 years of existence; allow "substantial" donors of foundations which had currently been in existence for 25 years to continue their influence for five to ten years from tions from existing in "perpetuity." "Broadening the base of foundation management," the report said, would bring "fresh views" to the organization, "combat parochialism" and increase the "flexibility" of the institution in responding to social needs and changes." It would also provide a means for eliminating those foundations which have "doubtful or minimal utility."

1966

The Johnson Administration sought tax legislation in 1966 to moderate inflationary pressures in the economy and to finance the increasingly expensive Vietnam war. But the Administration did not come to grips with the basic question of whether or not to increase tax rates. Rather, it sought to reach its goals by lesser changes which prevented certain scheduled tax cuts from going into effect and which speeded up the collection of already existing taxes. The tax requests came early in the year and in the fall when it became apparent that the tax changes resulting from the first proposals were not going to do the job. (The sequence was to reach its natural conclusion in the following two years when President Johnson sought and finally obtained higher income taxes for individuals and corporations.)

The U.S. balance-of-payments deficit was not eliminated or reduced to a satisfactory level in 1966. The Administration continued its program of voluntary controls on foreign investment and lending to help solve the problem and Congress enacted a bill to induce foreign investment in the United States. That bill, however, became one of the best known of the year because it was loaded with extraneous amendments to give tax breaks to a multitude of individuals and organizations ranging from hearse owners to Presidential candidates. It was known, accordingly, as the Christmas tree bill.

Balance of Payments

The nation's balance of payments improved substantially under the Administration's 1965 program, but it did not improve enough to permit relaxation of efforts to slow the flow of dollars overseas. Mr. Johnson in late 1965 requested the extension of the program *(see p. 145)*. Administration officials predicted that another good performance would move the U.S. account into equilibrium (defined by the Administration as a deficit or surplus of no greater than $250 million). *(For balance-of-payments figures, see table p. 175.)*

It did not happen. When the final figures were tabulated, they showed a 1966 deficit of $1.4 billion on the liquidity basis, hardly changed from 1965. (On the newer official settlements basis, the 1965 deficit of $1.3 billion moved to a 1966 surplus of $266 million. Officials said this change was due to special circumstances, primarily high U.S. interest rates channeling foreign dollar holdings out of foreign official accounts and into private banks. They said this could not be relied upon as establishing a trend in the U.S. payments accounts.) Administration officials said the voluntary program which was carried over from 1965 again proved successful, but was more than offset for the rising foreign exchange costs of the Vietnam war and a decline in the U.S. trade surplus to $3.6 billion from $4.7 billion the year before. The adverse trade developments were attributed by officials to increased spending on defense-related imports and to near-capacity operation of many sectors of the U.S. economy.

Congress attempted to help relieve the deficit problem by enacting legislation requested by President Johnson in 1965 to encourage foreign investments in U.S. corporate securities. The 1965 bill (HR 5916) to accomplish this did not get out of committee. Revised legislation was considered in 1966 and a bill was reported. But in its route through Congress, the bill became the vehicle for so many unrelated, special interest, and pet-project amendments that it was christened the Christmas tree bill. Enactment of the bill was considered by many longtime Congressional observers to be a travesty of the legislative process. That this judgment was not unduly harsh was substantiated when Congress less than one year later enacted a bill to suspend one of the major provisions of the Christmas tree bill—a fund to finance Presidential election campaigns. *(See following story.)*

Foreign Investors-Christmas Tree Bill

One of the gems of legislative log-rolling and mutual Congressional accommodation of the Johnson years became law late in 1966. The bill (HR 13103—PL 89-809) ostensibly was intended to help the United States solve its balance-of-payments problems. But it also contained provisions to help Presidential candidates, self-employed individuals, persons in the mineral ore business, bigtime investors, an aluminum company, and even hearse owners.

These amendments, called riders because they were germane to the purpose of the legislation only in the broad sense that they amended the Internal Revenue Code, were added by the Senate to the House-passed version of HR 13103.

Lobbyists Trim 'Christmas Tree' Tax Bill

Alleged lobbying activities on the "Christmas Tree Bill" (HR 13103) were reported in a Dec. 25, 1966, article in the Washington Post by George Lardner Jr., a Post staff writer and columnist.

In the article, entitled "The Day Congress Played Santa: A Look at the Christmas Tree Bill," Lardner contended that the special interest riders added by the Senate "did not just happen" but were "planned that way." He said the measure was a "vivid example of how special interests influence the legislative process."

Because HR 13103 was the final bill of the session that applied to the Internal Revenue Code, Lardner said, the Senate viewed it as a last chance to tack on long-stalled tax legislation—"the last train out of the station," in Chairman Russell Long's phrase.

Lardner's 1,500 word article outlined the pressures allegedly brought to bear by each of the successful lobby groups and reported which Senators they approached. Following are the article's highlights:

Retirement Funds. Perhaps the most heavily lobbied of the bill's riders, Lardner said, was the successful effort to include the provisions of HR 10, amending the Self-Employed Individuals Tax Retirement Act. Treasury officials estimated the plan would mean a revenue loss of up to $60 million a year, with most of the benefits going to professionals who earn more than $25,000 a year.

The plan's chief Senate sponsor became Sen. Vance Hartke (D Ind.), who failed in an attempt to add HR 10 to the tax bill in committee but prevailed on the Senate floor. Groups supporting Hartke's move, the article said, included the American Medical Assn., the American Bar Assn., the American Dental Assn., the American Institute of Certified Public Accountants, the National Society of Professional Engineers, and "many more." The article quoted Hartke's administrative assistant, Mace Broide, as saying that "every damn one" of the groups dropped in at the Senator's office to press for enactment of HR 10.

Investment Credit Extension. Another major tax break for which lobbyists approached Hartke, the article said, was an amendment to extend the 7-percent investment tax credit to machinery purchased for use in U.S. possessions, an area not covered by the original 1962 law. Lardner said the purpose of the amendment, added in the Senate Finance Committee was to provide a $2-million tax cut for the Harvey Aluminum Co., which had recently opened a new $50-million plant in the Virgin Islands. He reported that Hartke was approached by Harvey's vice president, S. Keith Linden, a long-time political associate of Hartke.

Depletion Rates. Senators also encountered vigorous lobbying efforts by groups desiring higher percentage depletion allowances on mineral ores and other materials. With the aid of Sens. Herman E. Talmadge (D Ga.) and J.W. Fulbright (D Ark.), the article said, the Anaconda Co., the Aluminum Co. of America (Alcoa) and the Reynolds Metal Co. won higher depletion rates on alumina-bearing clay under their control in Georgia and Arkansas. As a result of other lobbying, Lardner said, Sen. Long sponsored and won higher rates for clam or oyster shells used for cement or lime; Sen. Frank Carlson (R Kan.) higher allowances for clay, shale and slate used as a lightweight aggregate; Talmadge an increased rate for clay and shale used in brick; and Hartke an increase for clay and shale used in sewer pipe.

"Swap Funds." Another major lobbying effort, Lardner said, centered on "swap funds"—investment funds designed primarily for large-scale investors who wanted to diversify their stock holdings without paying a tax on their capital gains. Appreciated securities "swapped" in this manner had long been exempted from the capital gains levy, but a Treasury regulation of July 14, 1966, had ruled them taxable. Pressures from promoters of the funds were channeled through Washington attorney Edward Merrigan, the article said, who sought to influence Sen. Eugene J. McCarthy (D Minn.), a former next-door neighbor. In the Senate, McCarthy won a permanent tax break for the funds, but conferees specified that the exemption would end June 30, 1967.

Other Amendments. Hearse manufacturers, represented by William A. Geoghegan, a former Assistant Attorney General, won Hartke's sponsorship of the excise tax cut for hearses; Sen. Thruston B. Morton (R Ky.), at the request of former Sen. Erle C. Clements (D Ky.), chief lobbyist for tobacco companies, sponsored an amendment easing the tax provisions on the import of J & B Scotch whisky by Liggett and Myers Tobacco Co., Lardner reported.

Tree Nearly Topples. As the "baubles" on the tree proliferated, the article said, Long and other Senate leaders cautioned that addition of too many extraneous amendments might result in refusal by House conferees to take the bill to conference. In the end, however, it was the popularity of HR 10 among House conferees that saved the bill, Long told Lardner.

Inclusion of many of the riders was the result of intensive lobbying efforts by special interest groups. Riders were first added in the Senate Finance Committee and later, with increased intensity, on the Senate floor. As the riders proliferated, the measure became widely known as the Christmas tree bill. President Johnson reportedly urged Congress to approve the final bill. He signed it into law, but his remarks on doing so indicated that except for a few important provisions (the foreign investors section and the "precedent setting" campaign finance plan) he would have vetoed it. (As it turned out, the "precedent setting" plan never got off the ground: Congress in early 1967—with second thoughts about its hasty action in 1966—suspended the provision. (See 1967 chronology.)

Following is a summary of the most controversial proposals and detailed provisions.

Foreign Investors Tax. The investors tax provisions of the bill, part of the Administration's long-range program to combat the U.S. balance-of-payments deficit, were designed originally to induce more foreign investment in U.S. stocks and bonds through favorable tax treatment. During the 19-month study accorded the measure, however, Congress rewrote the Administration bill to provide a comprehensive overhaul of relevant tax structures. Thus the bill in its final form tightened tax loopholes" that allegedly permitted foreigners to escape U.S. taxation, in addition to carrying out its original purpose of providing investment incentives.

Campaign Fund. Of the riders added to the bill, the most controversial and widely publicized was the Presidential Election Campaign Fund, which envisioned financing of future Presidential campaigns by voluntary contributions by individual taxpayers. The plan was sponsored by Senate Majority Whip Russell B. Long (D La.), chairman of the Finance Committee, who said its purpose was to diminish the influence of large political contributors and pressure groups.

As enacted in the final bill, the plan provided that taxpayers each year could choose to have $1 (or $2 for joint returns) allocated for expenses of the next Presidential campaign. Contributions would be evenly divided between the two major parties but could not exceed the parties' actual expenses or $1 times the number of votes cast for the two Presidential candidates in the previous election, minus $10 million. If any minor party won over 5 million votes for its Presidential candidate, it could receive, for the next election, $1 for each vote over 5 million. The plan was to be administered by the General Accounting Office (GAO). *(For additional details of the plan, see story in Election Law chapter.)*

Controversy over the campaign fund proposal arose when opponents contended the program would give rise to splinter parties and might leave itself open to mismanagement. Backers of the plan retorted that a third party would have to make a good showing before it could receive any funds at all, and that scrutiny of the fund by the General Accounting Office, Congress' "watchdog" over federal expenditures, ensured the proper use of payments.

An effort on the Senate floor to kill Long's proposal produced one of the key roll-call votes of the session. John J. Williams (R Del.) led a Republican-Southern Democratic attempt to delete the plan, but was defeated by a **33-39** roll call.

Retirement Funds. Controversy also focused on the inclusion of HR 10, a measure allowing self-employed individuals, effective in 1968, full, rather than the existing 50-percent tax deductibility on annual contributions to their own retirement funds (up to a maximum allowable contribution of $2,500) Doctors, lawyers and other self-employed individuals, represented by an organization called the American Thrift Assembly, lobbied vigorously for the plan, but it was opposed by the Administration on the basis of revenue loss (estimated at $60 million a year). Passed by the House June 6 on a 291-0 roll call, the plan then was pigeonholed by the Senate Finance Committee. It was added to HR 13103 on the Senate floor over the opposition of Long, who contended it discriminated against wage earners who were not allowed to deduct Social Security retirement taxes. Long later was reported as saying, however, that it was the popularity of HR 10 with House conferees that had apparently saved other Senate riders to the bill.

Provisions for the Elderly. Although the Senate fared well in conference with the House, it did not win approval of two major riders that provided broadened medical benefits for the elderly. Deleted by conferees were provisions to pay for drug costs of nonhospitalized elderly persons covered by the supplementary medicare program and to extend to elderly persons full tax deductibility for their medical expenses.

Provisions

As signed into law, HR 13103 contained the following major provisions:

Title I. Foreign Investors Tax Act. *Dividend Income.* Lowered the rate of taxation on a foreign investor's income derived from U.S. stocks and bonds from the regular graduated income tax rates (ranging up to 70 percent for individuals and 48 percent for corporations) to a flat rate of 30 percent, or if applicable, to a lower treaty rate.

Estate Taxes. Reduced taxation of U.S. estates held by nonresident foreigners to provide essentially the same tax treatment as accorded similar-sized estates of U.S. citizens.

Capital Gains Taxes. Provided for U.S. taxation of capital gains of nonresident foreigners not engaged in business in the United States only if the investor was in the United States for 183 days or more during the taxable year. (Existing law taxed such gains if the investor was physically present in the United States at the time the gain was realized or for periods totaling 90 days or more during the year.)

Bank Deposits. Provided for a six-year liberalization and then a tightening of U.S. tax rules regarding deposits in U.S. banks by nonresident foreigners. Stipulated that income tax on interest earned by deposits, and the estate tax on the deposit itself, would not be levied through Dec. 31, 1972, on deposits in U.S. banks, mutual savings banks, domestic building and loan associations, and on amounts deposited with insurance companies under interest-bearing agreements. (Existing law limited such exemptions to bank deposits.) Rescinded all such exemptions (including those on bank deposits) as of Jan. 1, 1973, and provided for income and estate taxation at regular U.S. rates.

Provided a permanent exemption from U.S. income taxes, however, on interest earned by nonresident aliens and foreign corporations on deposits with foreign branch banks of U.S. corporations or partnerships. Provided the same exemption from estate taxes on the deposit itself. (Existing law taxed such deposits if the depositor were engaged in a trade or business in the United States.)

"Effectively Connected" Rule. Provided for U.S. taxation of specified types of income from foreign sources at regular U.S. tax rates when it was determined that such income was "effectively connected" with U.S. business operations. Limited taxation generally to specified rents and royalties, income from banking, and certain sales income. Provided for exclusion, however, of transactions executed by certain agents and transactions in which the company's U.S. office was not a "material" factor or which were casual and nonrecurring. (The effect of the provision was to eliminate an existing procedure under which foreign companies were able to avoid U.S. taxation by acquiring U.S. merchandise through U.S. offices and reselling it in foreign countries.)

Expatriate Provisions. Retained regular tax rates for a period of 10 years for any American who abandoned his citizenship on or after March 8, 1965, if one of the principal purposes of expatriation was avoidance of U.S. income, estate or gift taxes.

Withholding. Authorized the Treasury to issue regulations requiring more current payment of taxes by non-resident foreigners and foreign corporations than was provided by existing law, which required only that such parties pay their full liabilities by March 15 of the following year. Also required nonresident foreigners and foreign corporations whose income was "effectively connected" with U.S. business operations to file declarations of estimated tax.

Tax Discrimination by Foreign Countries. Empowered the President, in the case of tax discrimination by a foreign government against U.S. citizens or corporations, to increase the U.S. tax on income received by nationals or corporations of the discriminating foreign nation to approximately the same discriminatory rates.

Title II. Other Amendments to Internal Revenue Code. *Investment Credit Extension.* Made the 7-percent investment tax credit authorized under the Revenue Act of 1962 (PL 87-834) applicable to machinery and equipment purchased by U.S. citizens or corporations for use primarily in a U.S. overseas possession and placed in service after 1965. (Investment credit was suspended for a 15-month period in legislation (HR 17607—PL 89-800) approved at the close of the 1966 session. The suspension was retroactive only to Oct. 10, however, allowing firms extended the new coverage to claim the credit for the first nine months of 1966.)

"Swap" Funds. Provided a specific exemption from the capital gains tax, through June 30, 1967, for appreciated securities "swapped" for shares in an investment fund. (A Treasury regulation issued July 14, 1966, ruled such transactions taxable under a new Treasury interpretation of existing capital gains tax statues.)

Provided specific regulations for eligibility for tax-free treatment of those particular swap funds which were required under other statutes to register with the Securities and Exchange Commission (SEC.) Required that such funds: (1) file registration applications with the SEC by Jan. 1, 1967; (2) complete their acquisition of stocks by May 1, 1967; and (3) complete the transfer of shares to shareholders by July 1, 1967.

Prohibited funds registering with the SEC from revising the maximum amount of the fund upward after Jan. 1, 1967.

Retirement Funds. Amended the Self-Employed Individuals Tax Retirement Act of 1962 to permit full, rather than the existing 50-percent, tax deductibility for a self-employed individuals' annual contribution to his retirement fund.

Retained the 1962 provision restricting an individuals' annual contribution to such funds to the lower of $2,500 or 10 percent of earned income, but liberalized the earned income formula to allow consideration of all net profits when income was earned from a business in which both the performance of personal services and capital were "material" income-producing factors (e.g., druggists, farmers, etc). (Existing law based the earned income computation on a maximum of 30 percent of such individual's net profits or $2,500, whichever was higher.)

Further amended the 1962 law by including in the earned income computation the gains (other than capital gains and net earnings resulting from the sale, transfer, or licensing of the use of property by an individual who created the property through his own personal efforts. (The provision was designed primarily to aid authors and investors.)

Made the full tax deductibility and the broadening of the earned income formula for druggists and farmers effective Jan. 1, 1968, and the liberalized formula for authors and inventors effective for the full taxable year 1966.

Depletion Rates. Increased the depletion allowance for clam or oyster shells used for cement or lime from 5 percent to 15 percent (the same rate allowed limestone used for cement), the allowance for alumina-bearing clay from 15 percent to 23 percent, the clay and shale used in sewer pipe and brick from 5 percent to 7-½ percent, and the clay, shale and slate used as a lightweight aggregate, from 5 percent to 7-½ percent. Made the new allowance effective Jan. 1, 1967.

"Straddle" Options. Provided for capital gains taxation of profits resulting from a "straddle"—an option by an investor to either sell or buy a specified number of securities at a stated price for a given period of time. Made the provision applicable to straddle transactions initiated after Jan. 25, 1965.

Hearse, Ambulance Excise. Revise the excise tax statutes to make hearses, like ambulances and combined ambulance-hearse vehicles, subject to the 7-percent excise on automobiles rather than the 10-percent levy on trucks. Made the lower rate effective upon enactment of the bill.

Interest Equalization Tax. Provided numerous exemptions from the interest equalization tax, including a major provision authorizing the President to exempt U.S. dollar loans made by foreign branches of U.S. banks, regardless of the maturities involved. (Existing law exempted all foreign currency loans of such banks and U.S. dollar loans with a maturity of less than one year.) Made the provision effective for loans written on or after the date of bill's enactment.

Title III. Presidential Election Campaign Fund Act. Established a Presidential Election Campaign Fund in the Treasury to provide federal revenues to subsidize costs of Presidential election campaigns.

Authorized taxpayers each year, beginning with the 1967 taxable year, to designate $1 of their income tax (or $2 for joint returns) for expenses of the next Presidential election campaign. Contributions would be evenly divided between major parties (those polling 15 million or more votes in the last Presidential election) but could not exceed the lower of actual expenses or $1 times the total number of votes above 10 million cast for major party candidates in the last election. A minority party (one polling more than 5 million but less than 15 million votes in the previous Presidential election) would receive $1 for each vote above 5 million.

Provided for supervision of the plan by the General Accounting Office (GAO), which would authorize payments beginning Sept. 1 of each election year, commencing in 1968. Stipulated that no payment could be made until the treasurer of an eligible party certified to the GAO the total amount of campaign funds spent or incurred by his party up to that time, together with any supporting records requested by GAO. Stipulated that payments could be made only for expenses already incurred. Authorized the GAO to prescribe such rules and regulations and to conduct such examinations and investigations as it determined necessary.

Title IV. Miscellaneous Provisions. Included in miscellaneous items a major provision directing the Secretary of the Treasury to submit to Congress, at the convening of each session, a report indicating the breakdown of the contingent and unfunded liabilities of the Federal Government as of the end of the preceding fiscal year. Required that the first report cover fiscal year 1967.

Tax Revenue Increase

The increasing costs of the war in Vietnam and accompanying signs of inflation in the domestic economy led President Johnson, in his first 1966 message to Congress, to ask for a quick $6 billion increase in tax revenues. He did not ask for higher income or corporate taxes, saying these were "not clearly required at this time." The President continued to hold back throughout the session in requesting tax increases, which Congress was bound to be reluctant to impose in an election year. In September Mr. Johnson asked for suspension of the investment tax credit in an effort to discourage what he called the "exaggerated boom in business investment" in plants, equipment and commercial construction. Congress complied with this request in October.

The President's September request was a clear admission that the revenue increases he recommended in January and the clamp-down he sought on federal spending were not sufficient to dampen the inflationary trend. The revenue increases enacted in March in the Tax Adjustment Act of 1966 (HR 12752—PL 89-368) were expected to raise $1.13 billion in fiscal 1966 (ending June 30, 1966) and $4.8 billion in fiscal 1967. Almost all the funds were to be raised from a speed-up in corporate income tax payments ($4.2 billion) and a two-year suspension of recently instituted cuts in telephone and automobile taxes ($790 million and $480 million, respectively). In addition, the bill increased tax withholding on most individuals' income taxes. These provisions were enacted largely as requested by the President.

In addition, the final version of HR 12752 contained several important sections which had not been requested by the Administration. The House Ways and Means Committee added to the new, graduated tax withholding system a provision designed to prevent overwithholding from persons with heavy deductions. The bill also contained a Senate provision prohibiting tax deductions for tickets to political dinners and advertising in political publications. Another Senate-added provision, modified in the final bill, temporarily extended Social Security benefits to persons over 72 who had no Social Security coverage. The fiscal 1967 cost was estimated at $95 million.

The modified Social Security amendment was reluctantly accepted by the Administration. Another Senate floor amendment was fought by the Administration and deleted in conference. The amendment, sponsored by Sen. Vance Hartke (D Ind.), would have excluded local residential telephone service from the provision restoring the 10 percent telephone excise tax. It would have cut fiscal 1967 revenue by $315 million. During both House and Senate debate on HR 12752, some Democrats who usually supported the Administration, and most Republicans, sharply criticized restoration of the excise tax cuts.

In general, Republican opposition to HR 12752 waned as Congressional consideration of the bill progressed.

After the President proposed the tax changes in his State of the Union message, House GOP Leader Gerald R. Ford (R Mich.) criticized new "tax burdens" and said, "With proper restraint on spending, we believe no new taxes are now needed." On House passage, GOP Members voted against the bill, 46-88. A month later they voted 68-59 in favor of the conference report. Senate GOP Members voted 24-4 for passage of the bill and 23-4 on the conference report.

Provisions

As signed into law, the Tax Adjustment Act of 1966 contained the following major provisions:

Excise Taxes. Suspended Jan. 1, 1966, reductions in automobile and telephone excise taxes and postponed other scheduled reductions in these levies until April 1, 1968. Effective for cars shipped by manufacturers beginning on March 16 (cars held by dealers or distributors on that date were not affected by the tax increase). Effective for telephone and communications services on bills sent on or after April 1. *(See box.)*

Graduated Withholding. Eliminated the existing flat 14-percent withholding rate for individual income taxes and established instead, effective May 1, 1966, a new system of six withholding rates, graduated from 14 to 30 percent, according to income.

Withholding Exemptions. Raised the value of personal exemptions for withholding purposes (but not for computation of actual tax liabilities) from $600 to $700; eliminated withholding from families or individuals whose incomes, after subtraction of $700 for each withholding exemption, were no greater than $200.

Withholding Allowance. Permitted a taxpayer with a large amount of itemized deductions to claim additional withholding exemptions (above those available for himself and dependents) in order to prevent overwithholding by the Government. Effective Jan. 1, 1967.

Provisions continued on next page.

Excise Rate Timetable

The Excise Tax Reduction Act of 1965 (PL 89-44) repealed a number of excise taxes and scheduled certain reductions to take effect Jan. 1, 1966, among them the excise taxes on automobiles and telephones. The Tax Adjustment Act of 1966 (PL 89-368) suspended the January automobile and telephone tax cuts and postponed further scheduled cuts until April 1, 1968.

Existing Law

	Telephone	Automobile
Jan. 1, 1966	3%	6%
Jan. 1, 1967	2	4
Jan. 1, 1968	1	2
Jan. 1, 1969	0	1

PL 89-368

	Telephone	Automobile
Enactment	10%	7%
April 1, 1968	1	2
Jan. 1, 1969	0	1

Tax Provisions for the Self-Employed. Required self-employed persons, beginning Jan. 1, 1967, to pay Social Security and hospital insurance taxes in quarterly installments during the year liabilities became due. (Existing law permitted payment of such taxes in a lump sum on April 15 of the following year.)

Underpayment of Estimated Tax. Required taxpayers to pay at least 80 percent (rather than the 70 percent required by existing law) of their estimated tax liability currently throughout the year, either through withholding, quarterly payments, or both. Effective Jan. 1, 1967.

Corporate Taxes. Accelerated corporate tax payment schedules established under the Revenue Act of 1964 (PL 88-272) to require corporations to pay all tax liabilities in excess of $100,000 in the calendar year in which income was earned instead of paying part in the following year. (Under the new schedule, current-year payment was to go into full effect in calendar 1967, rather than 1970, as provided under PL 88-272.)

Political Contributions. Barred income tax deductions for funds used to buy tickets to political dinners, inaugural balls or similar events or for advertisements in convention programs or other political publications, if any part of the proceeds accrued to a political party or candidate. Effective for taxable years after Dec. 31, 1965, but only for amounts paid or incurred after March 15, 1966.

Social Security Benefits. Provided monthly payments of $35 beginning Oct. 1, 1966, for all persons 72 or older who were not currently eligible for Social Security benefits. Provided a monthly $17.50 for a spouse when both husband and wife were entitled to benefits under the new provision.

Stipulated that the amount of any benefit accruing to a person under the provision would be reduced by the amount of payments received under Governmental pension systems or funds, such as veterans' or civil service pensions, public welfare payments, teacher retirement funds or other such programs. Provided funding of benefits from the Social Security trust fund (until fiscal 1969, when costs of such benefits would be reimbursed from general revenues).

Stipulated that new eligibility under the provision would be cut off on Jan. 1, 1968, except for persons who had contributed to the Social Security system for at least three quarters of each year between 1966 and the year in which they became 72.

Duty-Free Gifts. Amended U.S. tariff law to allow a $50 duty-free exemption (through Dec. 31, 1967) for gift packages shipped to the United States by members of the Armed Forces serving in combat zones. (Existing law provided a duty-free ceiling of $10 on all such gift packages. At the time of the bill's enactment, Vietnam and adjacent waters was the only area designated by the President as a combat zone.)

Investment Tax Credit

As part of the Administration's program to stem rising inflation in the United States, Congress enacted a bill (HR 17607—PL 89-800) suspending existing tax incentives for business investment.

HR 17607 was designed to reduce inflationary pressures in the capital goods industry by temporarily suspending both the 7-percent investment tax credit on the

purchase of machinery and equipment, and certain methods of accelerated depreciation of industrial and commercial buildings. The suspensions were for almost 15 months.

The final version of HR 17607 embodied essentially the same provisions sought by President Johnson when he proposed the measure Sept. 8 as a key part of his anti-inflation drive. Although House and Senate conferees agreed to certain minor exemptions from the suspensions, they delivered the President a major victory by deleting Senate-passed exemptions for railroad and other transportation interests. The President had sought an across-the-board suspension.

The suspension period provided by the final bill was the same as that approved by the Senate—Oct. 10, 1966 to Dec. 31, 1967. (The Administration sought an effective date of Sept. 1 and the House specified Sept. 9.) As provided under both the House and Senate versions continued use of both investment incentives was authorized when businessmen had committed themselves to substantial "binding orders" prior to the suspension date.

HR 17607 in its final form also included a nongermane Senate rider exempting the proposed merger of the National Football League (NFL) and the American Football League from prosecution under existing antitrust laws. The exemption plan, added on the Senate floor, had been previously approved by the Senate in separate legislation (S 3817), but died in the House when House Judiciary Committee Chairman Emanuel Celler (D N.Y.) blocked it in committee. The rider was accepted by House conferees and by the full House over the bitter opposition of Celler.

HR 17607 passed each chamber with considerable support from both parties. The House passed the bill by a key **221-118** roll-call vote. The Senate acted by a 38-19 roll call.

Throughout 1966, the President's Council of Economic Advisers (CEA) had urged suspension of the investment incentives, but this had been opposed by the Treasury Department. The CEA had contended that monetary policy alone was not sufficient to diminish inflationary pressures, while the Treasury asserted that permanent tax measures such as investment credit should not be altered to influence economic trends of a temporary nature.

President Johnson, who had accepted the Treasury's fiscal arguments until late summer, sought suspension after it became apparent that business was making record investments despite tight money and high interest rates. One survey, conducted jointly by the Securities and Exchange Commission and Commerce Department, estimated planned business investment in plant and equipment at $60.8 billion for the year—an increase of 17 percent over 1965. The projected increase compared with actual increases of 15.7 percent in 1965, 14.5 percent in 1964, and average annual increases of only 6.8 percent in each of the years 1962 and 1963.

Strong opposition to investment credit suspension came from business interests, whose general position was that a cutback in investment might more than offset inflationary trends. Some groups also criticized the suspension plan as a breach of faith because of the credit's intended and promised permanency as part of the U.S. tax structure. Organizations opposing the suspension plan included the U.S. Chamber of Commerce, the National Assn. of Manufacturers, the National Federation of Independent Business and numerous organizations representing specific industries.

Not all the business community was aligned against the measure, however. Qualified support came from three of the nation's largest corporations—the Campbell Soup Co., American Telephone and Telegraph Co., and the Pennsylvania Railroad. Spokesmen for the three corporations made their support contingent on a coupling of suspension with a substantial cutback in federal spending, as had been promised by the President in his anti-inflation plan. (A number of private economists and Congressional experts also supported suspension.)

Suspension of accelerated depreciation was opposed by homebuilders and real estate interests, who contended the plan would further depress the housing industry, already ailing from a lack of loan funds. After intensive lobbying, these interests won an exemption for buildings costing $50,000 or less.

The Commerce Department early in 1967 announced that business interests had cut back their investment plans by an estimated $300 million in the last three months of 1966 as a result of the investment credit suspension. For the full year 1967, the Department projected, suspension would induce a $2.3 billion cutback in investment plans. Even with the projected cutbacks, however, a survey by the McGraw-Hill Co. predicted that business investment in 1967 would increase by 7 percent over the level recorded in 1966.

Provisions

As signed into law, PL 89-800 contained the following major provisions:

Investment Tax Credit. Suspended, for a period beginning Oct. 10, 1966, and terminating Dec. 31, 1967, a provision of the Revenue Act of 1962 (PL 87-834) permitting a credit against tax liability of up to 7 percent of investments in new and used machinery and equipment.

Stipulated that the suspension would not apply to investment of less than $20,000 (allowing taxpayers to continue to claim a tax deduction of up to $1,400). (Existing law provided no ceiling on investments eligible for the tax credit.)

Made the suspension applicable to equipment *ordered* as well as received during the suspension period.

Allowed the full credit on costs of a machine, or piece of equipment when a firm, prior to Oct. 10, 1966, had placed a binding order for more than 50 percent of the machine's components.

Allowed the full credit for purchase of facilities to control air and water pollution.

1968 Broadening of Credit. Provided for a broadening of the investment credit upon its restoration Jan. 1, 1968, to increase the maximum amount of the tax credit to 50 percent of tax liabilities above $25,000, and to allow investors to carry unused balances forward for a period of up to seven years. (Existing law limited the maximum tax credit to $25,000, plus 25 percent of the taxpayer's liability over $25,000. Any unused portion of the credit could be used in any of the following five years.)

Accelerated Depreciation. Suspended, for the same period as the investment tax credit, a provision of the 1954 Internal Revenue Code authorizing two methods of accelerated tax write-off on industrial and commercial buildings—the "double declining balance" and "sum of

Credit, Depreciation Explained

As signed into law, HR 17607 provided a suspension for almost 15 months—from Oct. 10, 1966, through Dec. 31, 1967—of certain tax incentives for business investment. Following is a description of the tax laws affected by the bill.

Investment Tax Credit. The major program suspended under the bill was the "investment tax credit," enacted in 1962 as a measure to encourage taxpayers to modernize and expand their production facilities and capabilities by investing in new machinery and equipment. Under terms of the law, a taxpayer could subtract from his tax bill 7 percent of eligible investment (3 percent in the case of public utility property) up to a maximum subtraction of $25,000, plus 25 percent of tax liabilities above $25,000. Any unused portion of the credit could be used in any of the next five years. HR 17607 provided that upon restoration of the credit in 1968, a taxpayer could claim up to 50 percent of liabilities above $25,000, and carry over the unused portion for seven years.

Depreciation. Because buildings, like automobiles, depreciate rapidly in value, businessmen have been allowed to claim larger tax deductions (as business expense) for depreciation during the early years of a building's use than in its later years. Although the cumulative tax deduction will eventually be the same under any pace of depreciation, the accelerated method gives the businessman a more reasonable figure of his immediate costs of doing business. It also gives him higher initial profits.

Until the close of World War II, the only type of depreciation was the "straight line" method in which the cost of a building, less its salvage value, was depreciated evenly over the years of its useful life.

In 1945, the Internal Revenue Service (IRS) approved the first accelerated write-off technique—the "150-percent declining balance," which permitted the taxpayer to use a rate equal to one and one-half times the "straight line" method, applied the first year to the entire cost of the building and in subsequent years to the cost less depreciation to date. Congress in 1954 specifically provided for two even faster methods, which the taxpayer could use at his option. These were the "double declining balance," which provided for depreciation at twice the rate of the "straight line" plan, and the "sum of the years digits," which applied a steadily decreasing rate to a constant base, thus providing a sharply decreasing depreciation after the first year.

Under provisions of HR 17607, the accelerated methods enacted in 1954 were prohibited for any building constructed during the suspension period. A businessman would then have his choice of only the "straight line" or "150 percent declining balance" plans.

the years digits" techniques—both of which allowed larger tax deductions for depreciation during the earlier years of a building's use than in its later years. (*For explanation, see box above.*)

Allowed each taxpayer, however, to continue use of all accelerated depreciation techniques for buildings valued at $50,000 or less (up to a maximum total exemption of $50,000, regardless of the number of buildings purchased).

Stipulated that the two suspended methods would not be available after their 1968 restoration for any non-exempt building constructed or ordered during suspension. Provided, however, that either method could be used for a building whose construction was begun prior to suspension, or had been committed under terms of a binding contract in effect before Oct. 10, 1966.

Combined Exemption. Continued the investment credit and/or accelerated depreciation on the full cost of a building constructed or equipped during the suspension period when a firm, prior to Oct. 10, 1966, had placed a binding order or was otherwise committed for 50 percent or more of the project's total cost. Specifically stipulated that the exemption covered outdoor plants, such as drydocks and oil pipelines.

Football Merger, Other Provisions. Provided language exempting the merger of two or more professional football leagues from antitrust prosecution, providing such mergers increased, rather than decreased, the total number of teams participating. (The provision was designed specifically to permit the proposed merger of the National and American Football Leagues.)

Provided high school football games the same protection from telecasting of professional football games that was currently accorded to colleges. Prohibited the telecasting of a professional football game from a telecasting station located within 75 miles of the game site on Friday evenings, from the second Friday in September through the second Friday in December. (Similar restrictions on Saturday telecasts provided protection to colleges.)

Authorized the Treasury Department to issue a new type of "retirement savings bond" at interest rates above the current rate ceiling of 4.25 percent permitted for long-term Treasury bonds. Authorized a maximum interest rate of 5 percent on such issues and provided for their maturity over periods not less than 10, nor greater than 30 years.

Interstate Taxation

The controversial interstate taxation bill inched along in 1966 but remained far from enactment at the close of the year. The House Judiciary Committee in September reported a bill (HR 16491) but no further action was taken.

The bill was designed to establish uniform limitations on the power of states to tax small out-of-state firms doing business within their boundaries. It was the result of a five-year study by the Judiciary Special Subcommittee on State Taxation of Interstate Commerce, headed by Edwin E. Willis (D La.). The Subcommittee found an overwhelming disparity in the methods by which states taxed out-of-state companies and concluded that the disparity made it very difficult for the out-of-state firms to determine what laws applied, let alone to comply with them. The study also concluded that the states were missing about $6 billion a year in revenues because of loopholes in their methods of taxing very large corporations, the major source of state revenues.

The Subcommittee in 1965 approved a bill (HR 11798) designed to solve these problems. HR 11798 was strongly opposed by the National Assn. of Tax Administrators (NATA) and the Council of State Governments, who argued that it would invade states' rights and would result in substantial revenue losses to the states. Consequently, the Subcommittee in 1966 watered down HR 11798 and drafted a new bill (HR 16491) aimed at meeting their objections. It deleted powers HR 11798 gave the Internal Revenue Service.

Willis Sept. 30 said the "official position" of the NATA was "that any company which ships goods across state lines ought to be taxable in every state and locality into which its goods are sent. Close to half of all our state tax administrators are already asserting that any company, regardless of where located, which does no more than send advertising materials through the mails into a state, ought to be subjected to taxation by the state."

"They tell us that Congress ought not to intervene," he said, "yet it is the tax collectors themselves who are making the state tax problem into a national problem and who are therefore creating the pressures for federal legislation." Willis was "shocked" during hearings on the bill "to learn from the owners of small businesses that it is now easier for some of our small companies to market their products in Holland or in Germany or in Africa than it is for them to make shipments from one state to another within the United States itself."

Willis said HR 16491 had "widespread support from such diverse groups," as the National Assn. of Manufacturers; the U.S. Chamber of Commerce; the International Ladies' Garment Workers Union; the National Council of Salesmen's Organizations; "one of the foremost authorities on state taxation in the United States," Georgia Tax Administrator Fred Cox; John Dane, the former commissioner of revenue for Massachusetts; and "countless other tax experts representing every corner of the country."

Program Modified. After three months of hearings in early 1966 on a bill (HR 11798) embodying its proposed program, the Subcommittee rewrote the measure to eliminate Internal Revenue Service involvement and to limit the bill's taxation rules to smaller corporations. The changes were forced by state tax administrators, who strongly objected to any semblance of federal control and feared the bill's broad coverage would cut substantially into state revenues.

Mine Exploration

Congress in 1966 enacted legislation (HR 4665—PL 89-570) providing a new method of tax deductions for expenditures made in exploration for minerals in the United States. The bill was intended to provide incentives for exploration.

Existing law permitted taxpayers to deduct from taxable income up to $100,000 a year, or $400,000 overall for the costs of exploring for minerals other than oil and gas. (Oil and gas were covered by other regulations.) The purpose of HR 4665 was to establish an alternate method of tax deductions which would encourage domestic mineral exploration by large firms which had reached the $100,000 and/or $400,000 deduction limits. This was done by allowing unlimited deductions, but with a new proviso that deducted amounts had to be repaid to the Government once a mine became income-producing or was disposed of.

As first passed by the House, HR 4665 did not permit a choice between the two methods. It allowed unlimited deductions, with repayment to the Government once the mine became income-producing. At the insistence of small coal mine operators, coal mining was retained under the old deduction system. Large-scale coal operators prevailed upon the Senate to permit a choice between the two methods of deduction and this alternative system was accepted by House conferees and written into law.

Provisions. As signed into law, HR 4665 contained the following major provisions:

Authorized taxpayers to deduct expenditures for exploration of minerals other than gas or oil either (1) without limit or (2) under provisions of existing law which limited deductible amounts to $100,000 annually and a total of $400,000 for all taxable years.

Provided that if the taxpayer elected to take deductions without limitation, the Government would recover the amount saved by the deductions when the mine reached the producing stage or when the mining property was sold or otherwise disposed of. (If the existing-law method was elected, there was to be no recovery.)

Required that after a taxpayer had made an election (which he had not revoked within the time permitted) as to whether he would be covered by the existing system or the new system, he could not thereafter seek coverage under the other system.

Limited the taxpayer's right to elect which coverage he would come under (or to revoke a previous election) to a period ending three years after the filing of a return by the taxpayer in which exploration expenditures were deducted for the first time after the enactment of HR 4665.

Established rules for type of coverage where there were mergers or other similar combinations or divisions of corporations or partnerships which had chosen differing types of coverage.

1967

As inflationary pressures continued to mount throughout the economy and the cost of the Vietnam war rose, the Administration no longer could resist an increase in taxes. The President in January proposed a surcharge on personal and corporate incomes, but little more was heard of the proposal until August. The long delay resulted from a continuing debate in the Government and among economists about the course of the economy and the proper steps to take. Finally, the President decided that higher taxes were necessary and in August proposed a 10-percent surcharge.

The proposal brought directly before Congress a major controversy which had been simmering since the costs of the Vietnam war had begun to rise in 1965 and which was to carry into 1968 before a compromise was achieved. At the center of the issue was the long-standing effort by conservative Members of Congress, primarily Republicans and Southern Democrats, to sharply reduce Government spending. The surcharge proposal gave them a ready-made vehicle which they could ride to a major victory by tying the President's tax requests to a mandatory reduction in federal spending. This they did in 1968. But for the rest of 1967 Mr. Johnson's request received only hearings in the House Ways and Means Committee.

Another part of Mr. Johnson's economic program was enacted quickly. It was a bill to restore the investment tax credit and accelerated depreciation earlier than had been planned. The bill was delayed slightly by addition of a rider to suspend the Presidential election campaign financing law that was enacted in 1966.

The balance-of-payments deficit took a major turn for the worse late in the year and prompted a new program by the Administration in early 1968 to lower the dollar outflow. No major new efforts were made in 1967, but two existing laws dealing with the problem were extended.

Income Tax Surcharge

The stark fact of economic life which the Administration had been trying to avoid for two years could no longer be avoided in 1967. Inflation was in evidence throughout the economy as a result of rapidly rising Government defense spending for the war, continued high consumer demand and substantial capital expenditures for plant and equipment. The tightest monetary and credit conditions since the 1920s had not solved the problem. Neither had the half-hearted tax measures of 1966 which imposed no new taxes to restrain the galloping economy. Clearly something more needed to be done.

President Johnson's answer to the problem was to have Congress increase income taxes—a course he previously avoided—through the imposition of a surcharge on tax liabilities of individuals and corporations under existing rates. Congress, while not totally unreceptive to this approach to the problem, preferred to look in another direction. To the influential men in Congress (in both parties) who guided tax and spending policies the real problem was excessive expenditures by the United States Government and the solution was to cut spending. The two views—the President's on the one hand and Congress' on the other—were not easily reconciled. Consequently, the tax surcharge proposal, which was Mr. Johnson's most important legislative request of 1967, never got out of committee.

It was not entirely the fault of either side in the dispute. Uncertainty about the economic situation led the Administration to postpone submitting a detailed request until Aug. 3. After that late date, it fell victim to the 1967 Congressional economy drive, constituent pressure and conflicting readings of economic indicators. Even widespread concern about the safety of the dollar following Great Britain's Nov. 18 devaluation of the pound by 14 percent failed to give new life to the proposal.

Although the bill got no further than hearings in the Ways and Means Committee in 1967, pivotal Committee Chairman Wilbur D. Mills (D Ark.) promised Committee consideration in January 1968 if the Administration made satisfactory Budget reductions. He said he felt "very strongly that any appropriate action will be taken to assure the integrity of the dollar."

The Administration's proposal was for a temporary surcharge of 10 percent on personal income tax liability effective Oct. 1 and on corporate income tax liability retroactive to July 1. To arrive at the amount of the surcharge, the taxpayer would calculate his tax in the normal manner under existing rates. He would then figure 10 percent of the tax (prorated in 1966 from the October and July effective dates) and add it to the tax to obtain the total amount he owed the Government.

The surcharge was designed to increase fiscal 1968 revenues by $6.3 billion. Other parts of the Administration's tax package—a speedup in corporate tax payments and an extension of automobile and telephone excise taxes scheduled to expire under existing law—were to bring the total revenue increase to $7.4 billion. None of these proposals got out of committee. The proposals would have taken back about 40 percent of the tax decrease enacted in 1964.

Mr. Johnson originally proposed a 6-percent surcharge in his Jan. 10 State of the Union message. The tax was mentioned relatively briefly in the long message and was justified in terms of the Vietnam war. The request was met with almost no enthusiasm. Constituent mail against the proposal was said to be extraordinarily heavy. Among other factors, the surcharge plan, following on numerous state and local income tax increases in recent years, appeared to be the last straw for many voters. In addition, liberal economists questioned whether or not the economy might be heading into a recessionary phase rather than an inflationary situation in which a tax increase was needed to take money out of the economy and hold down prices. As the economic situation remained uncertain throughout the spring, the Administration postponed actually submitting a request to Congress.

Inflationary indicators were much stronger in the summer, and Administration economists re-estimated the possible Budget deficit at up to $29 billion ($8 billion, including surcharge revenues, had been predicted in January). President Johnson Aug. 3 sent a long and strongly worded message to Congress asking for the 10-percent surcharge. Although the President implied that a tax increase was needed because of the effect of the Vietnam war on the economy this was not emphasized. The message focused more generally on the dangers of inflation, which the President said would be inevitable without the increase.

At extensive Ways and Means Committee hearings in August and September, Administration witnesses and liberal economists made strongly worded cases for the economic necessity of a tax increase. They were joined by representatives of many (though by no means all) conservative and business groups, who called for an increase coupled with cuts in Government spending. Representatives of homebuilding groups, concerned about a repetition of a 1966 credit squeeze, were especially strong in support of the bill.

But generally favorable testimony and warnings of severe consequences of failure to vote the increase appeared to have little effect on the Ways and Means Committee. On Oct. 3, it voted 20-5 to set the bill aside until the Administration came up with an effective plan for reducing Government expenditures. In a strong Oct. 6 statement, Mills defended the Committee's action as being neither "irresponsible, bullheaded nor spiteful" but as a reflection of constituent concern. Mills said the constituent reaction was the result of concern about a recent sharp increase in federal activity, and that his Committee would take no further action until the President made basic, long-range changes in federal spending policies. Because tax legislation must originate with the Ways and Means Committee, the decision blocked further action on the bill in 1967. President Johnson responded that Mills and Minority Leader Gerald R. Ford (R Mich.)

would live to "rue the day" they decided to oppose the proposal.

The tax increase plan was revived briefly and unsuccessfully following concern about greater inflationary threats and speculative pressures against the dollar that were engendered by the Nov. 18 devaluation of the British pound. Mills reconvened the Committee Nov. 29-30 to hear the chief Administration economic experts present a new Administration spending plan which, if acceptable, would have led to reconsideration of the surcharge proposal in 1967. But he found the new plan—for a $4-billion decrease in federal expenditures coupled with the surcharge—unacceptable. He said the Administration was showing "increasing awareness" but "I feel that we still have some distance to go." (Congress did, however, write the new spending reduction plan into law in H J Res 888. (See p. 135.)

Economic Arguments for Tax Increase. During his questioning Nov. 29 and 30, Mills went to the center of the Administration's argument that the United States was being plagued by "demand pull" inflation because the level of incomes in the economy was too high. With incomes high, the Administration argued, demand was greater than the capacity of industry to meet it, and therefore prices were bound to go up. Mills did not dispute the existence of inflationary pressures, but he did dispute the Administration's analysis of their cause. In so doing he displayed a formidable grasp of economics.

Mills argued that such standard indicators of excessive demand as rapidly rising wholesale prices, utilization of plant capacity, retail sales and business plans for future investment simply did not support the argument for "demand pull" inflation. Rather, he suggested, inflationary pressures were of the "cost push" type. Thus, he argued, producers faced with higher costs (basically arising out of higher wage settlements) were passing these costs along by raising prices. Consumers were then reacting to the higher prices by demanding higher wage settlements.

The difference between these points of view was not merely academic. The Administration's tax increase was an appropriate economic remedy for demand pull inflation because it would work directly to slow down consumer spending. In a cost push inflationary situation, however, a tax increase could have the opposite effect. This is because consumers and businesses, faced with lower after-taxes earnings, might seek to maintain their earnings by demanding higher wages and higher prices. Mills was therefore arguing that inflationary pressures should be countered through Federal Government expenditure reductions. Reduced federal spending would help to cut down on demand, but would not squeeze directly personal and corporate incomes and therefore would not contribute to cost-push inflationary pressures.

Investment Credit—Campaign Fund

One of the first major laws enacted in the 90th Congress was an important part of the President's economic program for 1967. The bill (HR 6950—PL 90-26) provided for restoration of the 7-percent investment tax credit and certain accelerated depreciation practices.

Final action occurred just 12 weeks after President Johnson, in a message to Congress, asked that the busi-

Britain Devalues Pound; Gold Buying Heavy

Britain Nov. 18, 1967, devalued the pound, in relation to U.S. dollars (and other foreign currencies), from $2.80 to $2.40. It was thought that this action prompted the Ways and Means Committee to resume hearings on the Administration's surtax proposal. In other action, the British Labor Government Nov. 18 ordered severe deflationary measures, including an increase in the bank rate (comparable to the U.S. discount rate) from 6.5 percent to 8 percent. In a televised speech, Prime Minister Harold Wilson Nov. 19 said that the devaluation was made necessary by renewed speculative pressures against the pound and by continued adverse foreign trade figures.

The devaluation was the first for Britain since 1949, when the value of the pound was lowered from about $4.00 to $2.80. The effect of the action was to make British goods approximately 14.3 percent cheaper on world markets, and the British Government hoped that the action would stimulate exports and transform the current trade deficit into a surplus.

Administration spokesmen Nov. 20-21 made clear that the British devaluation strengthened the case for the proposed surcharge. In his Nov. 21 press conference, Treasury Secretary Fowler said the tax increase was "more important than ever."

The principal reason for the tax increase was to reduce inflation by taking money out of the economy. The British devaluation made inflation potentially more serious, because American goods in the export market were made relatively more expensive than (and hence less competitive with) comparable goods produced in Great Britain or in other countries which devalued their currencies. If inflation were not checked at home, economists feared that the United States might price itself out of important world markets, which in turn would increase the balance-of-payments deficit and result ultimately in a heavier drain on the nation's gold supplies.

Effect on the Dollar. Some observers feared that the British action would bring new pressure against the dollar, the only other national currency which doubled as an international reserve unit.

In a Nov. 18 White House statement, President Johnson had reaffirmed "unequivocally the commitment of the United States to buy and sell gold" freely at the existing rate of $35 per ounce. Mr. Johnson's assurance was welcomed abroad, experts felt, because foreign nations currently held far more dollars in their treasury reserves than the United States could actually redeem for gold. Therefore, any rush by foreign governments to convert their dollars would force the U.S. to devalue the dollar (i.e., raise the number of dollars which could be exchanged for one ounce of gold). It was the possibility of panic, Fowler Nov. 21 noted, that "we always fear." The role of the dollar as an international reserve unit, Fowler added, was "always filled with peril."

Heavy gold buying was triggered Nov. 22 by an announcement that the French Government in June had withdrawn its participation in the international gold pool. The pool had been formed in 1961 to support the gold price at $35 per ounce. Eight nations originally joined the pool, which stabilized the market by buying or selling gold according to market demands. Prompted by the French withdrawal and by rumors of other nations' leaving the pool, speculators hoped to make quick profits by holding gold and counting on eventual U.S. action to devalue the dollar (thus raising the price of gold).

Devaluation was possible, speculators believed, because without international cooperation the United States might be forced to rely solely on its own gold supply to satisfy the demand. Current U.S. gold supplies amounted to almost $13 billion, of which $10 billion was required by law to be held by the Treasury as backing for Federal Reserve notes (ordinary U.S. currency). Under emergency conditions, however, the $10 billion could be freed from this statutory requirement.

In contrast to the U.S. gold stock, an estimated $29 billion in short-term dollar claims on the gold supply was held by foreigners. Foreign governments and other official agencies held an estimated $16 billion, principally as reserves which backed their own currencies. The balance of $13 billion was estimated as the number of dollars owned by nonofficial foreign holders. Governments, if they wished, could exchange their dollars for gold directly through the U.S. Treasury, while nonofficial holders could purchase gold with their dollars at the supported price on European gold exchanges.

Experts believed that the "gold rush" had largely subsided by Nov. 29 because of the evident intention of the seven remaining international gold pool members to maintain the current price.

---

ness tax benefits be restored prematurely. They were suspended Oct. 10, 1966, (PL 89-800), in an effort to curb inflationary pressures by reducing new business investments. Restoration had not been scheduled to take place until Jan. 1, 1968.

Enactment of HR 6950's tax provisions could have occurred in much less time because there was general support for them in Congress. However, quick action was prevented when the Senate for more than five weeks debated a nongermane rider to repeal the 1966 Presidential Election Campaign Fund Act. After much confused voting, the Senate in the end agreed to make the 1966 law inoperative until Congress by law had adopted guidelines governing the distribution of money to candidates and their parties. The House had not considered the issue at all, but House conferees accepted the Senate provision without change and it was included in the final bill.

Tax Benefits Restoration

As President Johnson had requested, PL 90-26 ended the suspension of the 7-percent investment tax credit on the purchase of machinery and equipment and of certain methods of accelerated depreciation of industrial and commercial buildings after March 9, the day of the President's message. In requesting early restoration, the President told Congress the suspension had already "done the job" and that "excessive pressure" on machinery industries had "eased very dramatically." Administration officials denied that restoration was necessary to head off a recession; rather they simply argued that the suspension was no longer necessary.

The House and Senate agreed on the March 9 termination date for the suspension. However, there was a major difference between the House and Senate relating to treatment of property that was built or ordered during the Oct. 10-March 9 suspension period.

House-Senate conferees agreed on a bill that was essentially along the lines of the more liberal House measure. Conferees allowed the tax credit on property, which was ordered during the suspension period but delivered on or after May 24, the day they reached agreement. Fast depreciation and the tax credit were allowed on the portion of construction done after May 24 even though construction had begun during the suspension.

House Members argued that their more liberal provisions were fairer and administratively more workable. The Administration objected to the revenue loss and said the provision was unfair to those taxpayers who supported the Administration in holding off on projects or orders during the suspension period.

Voting on Campaign Fund Issue

The Senate between 1966 and during 1967 changed its position several times during the course of six roll-call votes on the campaign fund issue. This was due entirely to vote switches by Democratic Senators in combination with absentees on one side or the other; Republicans in 1967, as on the original 1966 vote, almost solidly opposed the campaign financing law. The one GOP exception was Thruston B. Morton (Ky.), former Republican National Committee chairman, who voted both for and against retaining the law. In addition, Clifford P. Case (R N.J.) announced in 1966 that he favored the Act (although he did not vote), but voted consistently against it in 1967.

A total of 15 Democratic and two Republican Senators changed their positions on one or more of the roll calls on the issue. Of these, eight were consistent in their changed views between 1966 and 1967. The following Senators switched from support of the Act in 1966 to consistent opposition in 1967: Democrats J. W. Fulbright (Ark.), Wayne Morse (Ore.), Joseph S. Clark (Pa.) and Harry F. Byrd Jr. (Va.) and Republican Case. The following Senators switched from opposition to the Act in 1966 to consistent support in 1967: Democrats E. L. Bartlett (Alaska), Birch Bayh (Ind.) and Fred R. Harris (Okla.).

The other nine Senators who switched on the issue in 1967 were: Democrats Lister Hill (Ala.), John J. Sparkman (Ala.), Edward M. Kennedy (Mass.), Stuart Symington (Mo.), B. Everett Jordan (N.C.), A.S. Mike Monroney (Okla.), Claiborne Pell (R.I.) and James O. Eastland (Miss.), and Republican Morton. In most cases, however, Senators switched on only one vote.

Campaign Fund Issue

Because the Constitution forbids the Senate from initiating legislation involving taxes, Senators must add riders to House-passed bills if they wish to authorize new programs related to the tax system. Thus the Senate in 1966 amended HR 13103, a House bill dealing with foreign investments in the United States, to contain the Presidential Election Campaign Fund Act, and in 1967 Senators sought to repeal that Act by adding such a rider to the Administration's investment tax credit bill.

The 1966 Presidential Election Campaign Fund Act was the most important legislation approved by Congress relating to campaign financing since the 1925 Corrupt Practices Act and 1940 Hatch Act. The 1966 Act permitted taxpayers to check a box on their tax forms if they wished to allot $1 of taxes to Presidential campaigns. The money from the resulting fund was to be divided evenly between the Democrats and Republicans by a formula determined from the number of votes cast in the preceding election. (Based on 1964 returns, each party would receive approximately $30 million.) If a minor party won more than 5 million votes—something no minor party had ever done—it would receive $1 for each vote over 5 million for the next election. The Act was the first plan for federal financing of U.S. election campaigns ever enacted.

In 1966, the Senate passed HR 13103, authorizing the fund, nine days before final adjournment. Before passing the bill, it approved the fund by a 33-39 roll-call vote. House conferees accepted the fund with an amendment raising from 1.5 to 5 million the minimum number of votes a minor party had to receive to qualify for funds under the Act. On the last day of the session Albert Gore (D Tenn.) led an attack on the campaign fund and called for defeat of the entire bill, which contained numerous special interest riders. Gore's motion to kill the conference report was defeated by a 15-37 roll call.

In 1967 Gore continued his fight, and on the opening day of Senate debate on the investment tax credit he offered, in conjunction with John J. Williams (R Del.), a motion to repeal the fund. The move was sturdily opposed by the author of the 1966 Act, Senate Majority Whip Russell B. Long (D La.). The Senate was unusually evenly divided on the issue and neither Gore nor Long was willing to accept defeat. The result was five weeks of repetitive and at times unusually vitriolic debate during which the Senate in effect voted three times to repeal the 1966 Act and three times to retain it in some form. Republicans were almost unanimous for repeal. The GOP traditionally had much larger available sources of private contributions than did the Democrats, and so many GOP Senators were not sympathetic to the concept of federal campaign financing. Most Senate Democrats fell into two categories—those who wanted to repeal the fund and write a new law, and those who wanted to keep the 1966 Act with amendments. The Administration was in the latter category and lobbied vigorously during the weeks of voting. Vice President Hubert H. Humphrey several times used his position as President of the Senate to aid Long.

The final compromise solution, suspending the tax check-off system until Congress adopted guidelines governing distribution of the money from the fund, was put forward by Senate Majority Leader Mike Mansfield (D Mont.). In the end, the chief actors disagreed on the effect of the provision. Williams claimed that it "got rid of the Act immediately" and Long predicted that the Act would be in operation by the 1968 elections. (Long's prediction was not fulfilled.)

Arguments for the Fund. The chief argument for retention of the 1966 Act was that it would free Presidential candidates from the necessity of having to accept private contributions which might prejudice their decisions. Another argument, often stated by Long, was that existence of a large public campaign fund would put a poor man on an equal level with a rich man in a Presidential race.

Supporters of the Act also contended that, although candidates for other offices would not qualify for funds under the Act and third party Presidential candidates probably would not qualify, existence of the campaign fund would have the effect of making more private money available to them.

Long and the other Senators who spoke in favor of retention agreed that the 1966 Act had serious flaws, and Long made a number of tentative proposals for alterations. However, they argued that to repeal rather than amend the Act—the first campaign spending legislation since 1940—would end chances for any campaign spending reform.

Arguments against the Fund. Those Members who spoke for repeal were agreed on the need for reform of the existing situation. However, they argued that the Long Act was so weak that it could make the existing situation worse. They also held that if reforms of campaign spending practices—such as reporting—were not tied to provisions for federal participation in campaign financing, reforms would never be made. Gore referred to that as the "carrot-and-the-stick approach." He said the 1966 Act "gave up the carrot without any reform at all. Without this carrot, reform will continue to elude us."

Among specific criticisms of the 1966 Act were the following: there were no safeguards against corrupt practices; there were no guidelines as to how the money should be spent; there was no limit on private contributions and these would be commingled with public money; the practical effect of the bill was to deny money to third parties; reform should include Congressional as well as Presidential campaigns; the Act was unclear as to who in a national party would receive and disburse money; the national parties would be made much freer from local controls, and would have great power to punish local candidates who strayed from the party line by setting up independent local organizations and by deciding how much money to spend in each state. In addition, Gore questioned the $1 tax checkoff system itself. He said it began an unwise new system of earmarking tax revenue which, in its logical extension, would see taxpayers deciding whether they wished to support the Vietnam war or the "war on poverty."

Provisions. As signed into law (PL 90-26) June 13, HR 6950:

Investment Credit, Accelerated Depreciation. Ended the suspension of the 7-percent investment tax credit and accelerated depreciation on March 9, 1967, instead of Dec. 31, 1967, as was provided in existing law. (Termination of the suspension automatically put into effect beginning March 10 provisions of the 1966 suspension law which broadened the credit by permitting the taxpayer a maxi-

Senate-House Procedures

The performance of the Senate during April was an interesting illustration of the manner in which that chamber sometimes legislates. It also provided a striking contrast between the operations of the two houses of Congress—the House of Representatives with its usually tidy and efficient floor procedures and the Senate with its virtually unlimited debate, its boundless Senatorial courtesy, and its indulgence of Senators with favorite projects.

Majority Leader Mike Mansfield (D Mont.) said that "misunderstandings" produced the confusion and delays. There were other reasons, also. Delays were caused in part by the absence of Senators who were out of town even though 1967 was not an election year. Undoubtedly most important, however, was the reluctance of Majority Whip Russell B. Long (D La.) to admit defeat on the principal issue at stake—repeal of the Presidential Election Campaign Fund Act—and the failure of Mansfield to even attempt to take control of the situation until after three weeks of confused voting.

In the House, by contrast, a bill is considered under tight restrictions which only rarely allow action to continue for more than two days and which prohibit any amendments not strictly germane to the legislation. Debate seldom is allowed for more than a few hours. Few roll-call votes occur because of the parliamentary procedures that are used.

The House procedures are even tighter for tax bills (including the one that tied up the Senate in April) and for Social Security, tariff and similar legislation. These types of bills almost always are considered under closed rules which prohibit any amendments from the floor; all that is allowed is one motion to recommit the bill to committee, either with or without instruction for changes. The purpose of this restriction, supporters say, is to prevent logrolling.

The Senate has no such qualms. Tax bills and other pieces of legislation sometimes are used as vehicles for a variety of related or unrelated amendments which a Senator considers important or useful and which, not infrequently, have not had a favorable reception in committee. In the case of tax legislation there is another reason that the Senate resorts to riders: the Constitution requires that revenue measures originate in the House, which means the Ways and Means Committee. The Senate Finance Committee is restricted to amending House tax bills. The Senate does not often load a bill with unrelated amendments. But when it does the event can be spectacular. An example was the 1966 Foreign Investors Tax Act which became known as the Christmas Tree Bill because of the multitude of unrelated amendments that were added in committee and on the floor—among them, the amendment authorizing the Presidential Election Campaign Fund Act.

Senate riders sometimes are the result of logrolling, sometimes are accepted simply out of courtesy to the sponsoring Senator who has a strong interest in the proposal, and sometimes are approved simply because they are popular but with the knowledge that they will be quietly dropped in conference later.

Chronology of Senate Floor Action

The Senate spent more than five weeks debating HR 6950 and the campaign fund issue. Following are the highlights of the action:

April 3—Senate begins debate. Albert Gore (D Tenn.) proposes an amendment to repeal the Presidential Election Campaign Fund Act of 1966. Debate on the issue continues until April 12.

April 12-13—Senate accepts various amendments to tighten operation of 1966 law.

April 13—Senate by 48-42 roll call accepts Gore-John J. Williams (R Del.) amendment to repeal the act July 1. Gore's April 3 amendment for immediate repeal, is withdrawn.

April 14-19—Senate votes on numerous unrelated amendments, including Social Security payments, education tax credits and excise taxes, accepting many of them.

April 20—Senate by 46-42 roll call accepts amendment by Russell B. Long (D La.), called the Honest Elections Act of 1967, which provided a Presidential election financing scheme similar to that under the 1966 Act.

April 25—Senate by 64-22 roll call adopts recommittal motion by Majority Leader Mike Mansfield (D Mont.) with instructions to drop all previously adopted floor amendments, to add wording repealing the 1966 Act on July 31, and to require the Finance Committee to report amendments to the 1966 law within six weeks. HR 6950 was immediately re-reported with the changes specified in the instructions.

April 25—Long offers amendment to delete July 31 repeal date added by Mansfield recommittal instructions. Senate rejects Williams motion to table Long amendment by 41-43 roll call.

May 2—Senate by 46-52 roll call rejects Long amendment to delete July 31 repeal date. Long continues fight.

May 9—Senate by 48-48 roll call rejects Gore-Williams amendment to make the Act inoperative after Sept. 15 unless Congress provides otherwise. Vice President Humphrey votes "nay" to break the tie although his vote was not necessary.

May 9—Senate by 93-4 roll call accepts Mansfield amendment to prohibit appropriations and disbursement of funds under the 1966 Act and to prohibit the $1 income tax checkoff system from going into operation until Congress adopted "guidelines" governing the distribution of funds.

May 9—Senate by 93-1 roll call passes HR 6950, as amended by Mansfield language *(above)*, and sends it to conference with the House.

mum credit of $25,000 plus 50 percent of the tax liability above $25,000 and allowing unused credits to be carried forward for seven years. The Revenue Act of 1962 had established a maximum credit of $25,000 plus 25 percent of tax liabilities above that amount, and allowed a five-year carry-forward.)

Permitted the investment tax credit to apply to equipment received on or after May 24, 1967, even though ordered during the suspension period ending March 9.

Provided that if a taxpayer either ordered property or began his own construction of property (such as on railway boxcars) during the suspension period ending March 9, then the portion of the construction which was completed before May 24 was to be ineligible for the investment credit or accelerated depreciation and the portion completed after May 24 was to be eligible. (For orders placed or work begun after March 9, the tax benefits were to be fully available for all work both before and after May 24.)

Provided that aircraft registered with the Administrator of the Federal Aviation Agency which were to be operated outside the United States pursuant to a contract with the Government would qualify for the investment credit. (Intended to assist certain airlines flying material to Vietnam from points outside the United States.)

Presidential Campaign Fund. Prohibited the appropriation and disbursement of funds under the Presidential Election Campaign Fund Act of 1966 until the adoption by law of guidelines governing their distribution.

Prohibited the $1 income tax checkoff system, established by the 1966 Act to provide funds for the campaign financing system, from going into effect until the distribution guidelines were adopted.

Balance of Payments

The nation's balance of payments took a serious turn for the worse in 1967. There was a major decline in the surplus from the sale of goods and services which coincided with a major increase in net capital outflows to other nations. These two important balances usually move in opposite directions and tend to offset each other; but in 1967 they moved in the same direction for the first time in eight years. The result was what the Commerce Department called "an extraordinary deterioration" in the balance of payments. As measured on the liquidity basis, the 1967 deficit was $3.6 billion compared to $1.4 billion the previous year. On the official settlements basis, the 1966 surplus of $266 million moved to a deficit of $3.4 billion. *(For balance-of-payments figures since 1946, see table p. 175.)*

Officials cited various individual factors that contributed to the problem. There was a sizable increase in the outflow of U.S. private capital, particularly in foreign and international securities exempt from the Interest Equalization Tax and through bank lending abroad, officials said. The net private capital outflow was more than $1 billion larger than the previous year. Officials said this development was a "normal reflection" of easier U.S. monetary conditions. The payments problem reached a new crisis in the last three months of the year and led the Administration at the beginning of 1968 to put strict mandatory investment controls into effect and to propose a major legislative program to control the deficit.

There was no major new program proposed to handle the deficit, but Congress acted on two pieces of legislation related to the problem.

INTEREST EQUALIZATION TAX. At President Johnson's request, Congress extended the Interest Equalization Tax for two years and gave the President the authority to eliminate the tax or to set it at any level up to 50 percent above the current amount of the levy.

The legislation (HR 6098—PL 90-59) continued a tax that was first imposed in 1963 and continued in 1965 *(see p. 143)* to help relieve the payments deficit by making it more expensive for foreigners to borrow from U.S. sources.

HR 6098 extended the tax from July 31, 1967, through July 31, 1969. It continued the existing tax rates which, in effect, provided the equivalent of an annual 1-percent increase in interest costs for foreign borrowers obtaining capital by selling securities to U.S. creditors. (These were a flat 15-percent tax on stocks and a variable levy on bonds according to their maturities.) In addition, the bill gave the President discretionary authority to drop the IET altogether or to establish it at any level up to an interest equivalent of 1.5 percent. This flexibility ensured that the President would be able to adjust the tax, as domestic or foreign interest rates fluctuated, so that it would cost foreigners as much to borrow from U.S. creditors as from foreign creditors.

However, fearing that U.S. creditors would quickly purchase large amounts of foreign securities in anticipation of an increase in the IET, Congress adopted an Administration-proposed provision making an effective rate of 1.5 percent mandatory over the period from Jan. 26, 1967, the day the President proposed the bill until 30 days after enactment. Unless the President ordered the 1.5-percent rate retained or established some other rate, the charge at the end of the 30-day period automatically would revert to the 1-percent rate of existing law. On Aug. 28, President Johnson signed an Executive Order reducing the effective rate of the IET from 1.5 percent to 1.25 percent. In addition to reducing the variable levy on bonds, the new rate, which went into effect Aug. 30, resulted in setting the flat tax on purchase of foreign stocks at 18.75 percent. (Under the 1.5-percent IET, the tax on stock purchases had been 22.5 percent.)

President Johnson, in requesting the bill Jan. 26, had asked for the two-year extension of the tax together with discretionary authority to vary the levy between the equivalent interest rates of zero and 2 percent. Both the House and the Senate provided the full two-year extension, but the House restricted the President's flexible rate-making authority to a range of only 1.0 to 1.5 percent. House and Senate conferees in agreeing on a final version of the bill accepted the House ceiling of 1.5 percent together with the Senate and Administration-proposed floor of zero.

In debate on the bill, Republicans in both chambers criticized the Administration for continuing to seek mere "palliatives" (as they called the IET) to solve the balance-of-payments problem and contended that the President should begin to seek a permanent solution. Some Republicans charged that the "real problem" was "excessive Government spending abroad" such as the foreign aid program.

Provisions. As signed into law (PL 90-59) July 31, HR 6098, the Interest Equalization Tax Extension Act of 1967:

Extension of Tax. Extended the Interest Equalization Tax for two years, from July 31, 1967, through July 31, 1969.

Continued the existing tax, which in effect provided the equivalent of a 1-percent increase in interest costs for foreign borrowers obtaining capital from U.S. sources

either from the sale of stocks or from the sale of bonds or other debt obligations with maturities of one year or more.

Provided discretionary authority for the President to eliminate the tax altogether or to set it at any level up to the equivalent of an interest charge of 1.5 percent.

Provided that during the period from Jan. 26, 1967, the day the President made his request to Congress, until 30 days after enactment of HR 6098, a tax equivalent to a 1.5 percent interest cost was to be in effect to forestall large purchases of foreign stocks and debt obligations in anticipation of an increase in the tax rate by Presidential order.

Anti-Evasion Provision. Authorized the continuation of tax-free sale of foreign securities from one American or American firm to another only when the seller obtained validation that the tax had been paid on the securities or that the securities were exempt from the tax. (Existing law required the sellers only to prove American ownership of the securities—a condition which presumed but did not ensure that the tax had been paid or that the securities were exempt.)

Stipulated that the validation requirement could be satisfied by the seller's receiving either a "validation certificate" issued by the Internal Revenue Service or an "IET clean confirmation" issued by an authorized private institution.

ANTITRUST EXEMPTIONS. A second bill which dealt with the balance-of-payments problem extended for two years, through June 30, 1969, the authority for the President to permit exemptions from the antitrust laws for banks and other institutions which participated in voluntary agreements that would have the effect of strengthening the U.S. payments position. The bill (S 1648—PL 90-62) provided only for a simple extension of the 1965 law and did not otherwise change the provisions of that statute. Opponents of the bill, mostly Republicans, argued that the measure should not be extended because the President had not yet found it necessary to use the authority, and that if he ever did Congress could act on the basis of the current merit of his proposals. Proponents argued that an emergency might arise which would require the President to act without delay to curtail capital outflows.

Interstate Taxation

Congress again failed to complete action on a bill which sought to establish uniform limitations on the power of states to tax small out-of-state firms doing business within their boundaries. The bill (HR 2158) was reported from the House Judiciary March 7, but no further action was taken.

Meanwhile, state tax administrators during 1967 pushed for approval of a "Multistate Tax Compact" as an alternative to HR 2158. While the Compact provided cooperative interstate machinery to apportion taxable income of interstate businesses, it did not include the restrictions of HR 2158 on taxation of small interstate businesses. Thirteen states had approved the Compact by Dec. 31. A spokesman for the Council of State Governments said the Council thought the "full Compact will get at the

Federal Tax Sharing, Block Grant Proposals Urged

One of the most important and potentially far-reaching debates that arose during the 1960s concerned proposals to share federal tax revenues with the states. There was enthusiastic and widespread support for the concept of sharing some of the enormous revenues produced by the federal tax system. However, there were many differences on details—particularly as to how sharing of federal revenues would influence existing federal financial-aid programs. In any event, the tax-sharing proposals had no chance of adoption so long as the Vietnam war and existing federal spending requirements left the Government without a surplus of money to share.

In the last years of the Johnson Administration, Congressional Republicans attempted to institute their approach to federal revenue sharing by attaching amendments to major bills. They sought to do this by eliminating the traditional mechanism of grants for specific projects and replacing it with block grants for states to disperse as they saw fit. They had some success in this effort *(see below)*.

Debate over the general concept of tax sharing went to the heart of the federal system of government. Supporters of the plan argued that the Federal Government, which had a growing base from which to draw revenue and a highly developed tax collecting system, should return a small percentage of its revenues to the money-starved states to use as they wished to meet the problems of their people. But they did not all agree on details: how much should be shared, what special consideration should be given to poorer states and large cities, whether the Federal Government should place "strings" on its aid and whether traditional federal grant-in-aid programs should be trimmed to offset the federal tax rebates to the states. Opponents of the tax-sharing concept contended that such a plan would invite state misuse of funds and would keep money from going to hard-pressed cities and other areas of great need.

Although it was a Democratic professor, Walter W. Heller, later chairman of the Council of Economic Advisers, who gave initial publicity to the tax-sharing concept, the Republican party made it a key point in its program. Most Republican sponsors wanted to make the aid available to the states without strings. Some Democrats countered with proposals that specific amounts be earmarked for large cities or that state and local governments be required to improve their administrative machinery in order to qualify for tax sharing.

The Johnson Administration, which had been cool to the idea even before the 1967 budget squeeze, continued to oppose it. State Governors endorsed the concept, but mayors opposed it, preferring to relay on direct grants from the Federal Government to meet their growing needs. Organized labor lined up with the mayors.

The Advisory Commission on Intergovernmental Relations endorsed the principle of tax sharing in a 1967 report. The Tax Foundation called for further study of the question.

Background

The Federal Government made one direct grant of tax revenues to the states early in its history (in Andrew Jackson's Administration) but the trend has been toward more and larger grant-in-aid programs, each of which imposed certain requirements on the states. Grants-in-aid are for specific purposes, such as road construction or public assistance.

During the Depression of the 1930s, federal grants to states and local governments rose by 650 percent in 11 years, from $147 million in 1930 to $945 million in 1940, most of it for welfare, relief and public works. Grants-in-aid reached $2.9 billion in fiscal 1953, and tripled to $8.6 billion by fiscal 1963. By fiscal 1967 the grants neared $21.9 billion.

The sharp rise in federal grants-in-aid was largely due to the fact that the Federal Government was able to tap far more revenue sources than were state and local governments. Heller wrote in his 1966 book, *New Dimensions of Political Economy:* "At the federal level, economic growth and a powerful tax system, interacting under modern fiscal management, generate new revenues faster than they generate new demands on the federal purse. But at the state-local level, the situation is reversed. Under the whiplash of prosperity, responsibilities are outstripping revenues. As (John Kenneth) Galbraith has suggested, prosperity gives the Federal Government the revenues, and the state and local governments the problems."

The Heller Plan

Walter W. Heller, University of Minnesota economics professor, in a June 1960 speech proposed that part of the rising federal revenues be distributed to the states with few or no strings. In 1964, as chairman of the President's Council of Economic Advisers, he proposed it again and a Presidential task force was appointed to study the idea. Joseph A. Pechman, director of economics at Brookings Institution, headed the task force which showed how Heller's plan might be put into effect. (Although Heller was responsible for generating widespread interest in the proposal, many persons who studied the issue gave Rep. Melvin R. Laird (R Wis.) the credit for having introduced in 1958 the first bill which embodied many of what later were considered the essential principles of revenue sharing. The Laird bill provided for the automatic return of a portion of federal revenues to the states with relatively few conditions attached.)

Heller referred to his proposal as "per capita revenue sharing." He would have the Government distribute to the state 1 to 2 percent of the taxable income reported by individuals, with "next to no strings attached," and over and above federal grant-in-aid for specific purposes. He said the use of taxable income as a base would offer stability, keep the states from having a vested interest in the level of federal tax rates, and would not interfere with the use of federal tax in stabilization policy.

To Provide Financing Assistance to Hard-Pressed States

The money would be distributed to the states on a per capita basis. Some of it, 10 or 20 percent, could be set aside to supplement assistance to states of either low per capita income or high urbanization, he said. States which reduced their own tax efforts would get reduced amounts.

Heller stressed that the states should be "first in line" in getting their "modest share" of federal revenues even if the Government had to bear the brunt of periodic deficit financing. Once begun, revenue sharing should not be tied to federal surpluses, he stressed.

Johnson Reaction. Although President Johnson was reported late in 1964 to be close to adopting the Heller plan, his support was never forthcoming. Reportedly, objections from other Administration officials, mayors and organized labor were instrumental in his decision. Meeting with state Governors in 1966, he in effect rejected their pleas for tax sharing.

Republican Position. In the GOP "State of the Union" message Jan. 19, 1967, House Minority Leader Gerald R. Ford (R Mich.) endorsed a tax-sharing program:

"Republicans reiterate their support for a system of tax sharing to return to the states and local governments a fixed percentage of personal income taxes without federal control. This system would promote a swift improvement in education, law enforcement, community development, mass transit and other essentially local problems...."

"Tax sharing would restore the needed vitality and diversity to our federal system. Revenue sharing could also be accomplished with tax credits."

Group Positions. Generally, state Governors have supported the revenue sharing principle, while most big-city mayors either have opposed it or have questioned whether suburb- and rural-dominated state legislatures would pass along adequate revenue to the cities.

Groups with strong national lobbies, such as the AFL-CIO and the National Education Assn., either have opposed the idea completely or have recommended strict guidelines to ensure that shared federal funds would go for programs which the organizations approved.

Politically, liberals have been divided. Fiscal moderates have been almost unanimously in favor, and fiscal conservatives have seen it as another spending plan.

The Advisory Commission on Intergovernmental Relations, a federally-supported study group, favored the principle in its two-volume, 1967 study, *Fiscal Balance in the American Federal System.*

The Tax Foundation in a 1967 study, *Federal Revenue Sharing With the States*, called for more study, and took a more sanguine view than most observers about the ability of the states to meet their future revenue needs.

The U.S. Chamber of Commerce at its 1967 annual meeting approved a resolution favoring revenue sharing as a substitute for federal grants-in-aid, and warned that safeguards should be written into any plan to keep states from weakening their own tax structures by substituting federal funds for their own efforts.

The President's National Commission on Urban Problems proposed in its 1968 report that the Federal Government provide a system of revenue sharing with states, major municipalities and major urban county governments. The revenue would be a percentage of the federal personal income tax base—incomes of individuals rather than income tax receipts.

Block Grants

Republicans, with their normal inclination to reduce the size and proliferation of federal programs, put their support behind what came to be known as block grants. This approach permitted federal funds to go directly to state officials who would decide how to use it. This removed federal officials from control over the programs and provided enormous new powers for state governments—concepts that were dear to the heart of the GOP. Many Democrats, on the other hand, were opposed to block grants for just those reasons. They tended, generally, to distrust state officials and state governments and were reluctant to see huge sums of money turned over to them without some controls. Democrats contended that the real problems facing the nation were in the cities and surrounding areas and that federal funds should go directly to these governments. They argued that state officials were conservative, rural-oriented persons who did not understand or appreciate the needs of the cities and would not use the federal funds wisely (if at all) in the cities.

Nevertheless, Republicans had moderate success in having the block grant principle written into legislation. Both the Omnibus Crime Control and Safe Streets Act of 1968 (PL 90-351) and the Juvenile Delinquency Prevention and Control Act of 1968 (PL 90-445) contained provisions for block grants for certain purposes. Probably the first use of the concept on a major scale was in the Comprehensive Health Planning and Services Act of 1966 (PL 89-749). That law consolidated the various formulas and project grants formerly made to combat specific diseases and substituted a new system of broad grants for comprehensive public health services. The only major qualification was that at least 15 percent of the funds had to be spent on mental health. Republicans in 1967 barely missed having block grants substituted for the traditional direct categorical grants for aid to education. An intensive Administration lobbying campaign prevented adoption of the GOP plan and retained the provisions of existing law which provided special purpose grants to local school systems based on the number of poor children in the systems. *(Stories on these bills will be found in the chapters on crime and justice, health and education.)*

problem areas that HR 2158 proposed to do." The Council took the position that the Compact would not need Congressional approval, he said, but he believed it would seek Congressional approval when more states had signed up.

HR 2158, as introduced by Rep. Edwin E. Willis (D La.) Jan. 12, was identical to a bill reported by the Committee in 1966 *(See p. 156.)* The Committee in 1967 adopted an amendment further diluting the bill's uniform tax limitations. The amendment allowed states to levy an income, capital stock or gross receipts tax on a small firm that regularly maintained an inventory for sale in its "ordinary course of...business." The 1966 bill allowed taxation of small firms only when the firm owned or leased property within the state or had at least one employee whose service was performed entirely within the state. The amendment was drafted by the National Assn. of Manufacturers, a strong proponent of the bill, which said it had devised the plan in order to blunt the opposition of the state tax administrators.

Tax Adjustments

Congress late in December sent to the President a bill (HR 4765) that provided: (1) tax relief to stockholders of the Financial General Corp., a large holding company; (2) an estimated $22-million tax rebate to American Motors Co., which was in financial difficulties; and (3) a tax adjustment for the Jefferson Standard Life Insurance Co. The President signed the bill into law Dec. 27. (PL 90-225).

HR 4765, as originally passed by the House March 14, provided only the tax relief for Financial General stockholders. The Senate Finance Committee Aug. 3 added amendments to the bill allowing American Motors a $2-million investment tax credit, resolving tax problems of mortgage guaranty insurance companies, permitting a taxfree "spin-off" of stock of a controlled life insurance company (Jefferson Standard) and altering the tax treatment of unfunded pension plans of universities and other tax-exempt groups.

The Senate passed the bill Nov. 9 after adopting three floor amendments. One required that Financial General shareholders pay a capital gains tax when the corporation carried out the divestiture of nonbanking interests required under the 1966 amendments to the Bank Holding Company Act (PL 89-485). The second amendment added a $20-million tax break to the Committee's $2-million provision benefitting American Motors. This permitted the financially troubled company to carry back operating losses for five years, instead of the existing three years. The third amendment limited to one year the effect of the Committee's provision for mortgage guaranty insurance companies.

House-Senate conferees on the bill, in their Dec. 7 conference report (H Rept 1010), insisted on the original House treatment of Financial General stock divestiture, accepted the two American Motors amendments and the life insurance company provision. They dropped the pension plan provision and recommended that the mortgage guaranty insurance company provision be enacted on a permanent basis in a separate bill. This was said to have Treasury Department support and was carried out Dec. 14. *(See below.)*

Financial General Corp. In 1966 Congress amended the Bank Holding Company Act by removing several major exemptions granted by the 1956 Act. One of the largest firms affected was Financial General, which controlled or owned large portions of 26 banks and numerous insurance, mortgage and manufacturing companies. The 1966 law directed Financial General to divest itself of either its banking or its nonbanking holdings by Dec. 31, 1978. The 1956 Act forbade companies which owned two or more banks from simultaneously owning nonbanking businesses, but it permitted numerous exemptions from this restriction. Included was an exemption for certain registered investment companies. Financial General, a Washington, D.C., holding company, was the only firm that availed itself of this exemption.

Investment Credit. Congress, at the urging of the Kennedy Administration, in the Revenue Act of 1962 (PL 87-834) gave businesses the right to claim an investment tax credit for money invested in new machinery and equipment. A company could subtract from its tax bill 7 percent of the funds it invested in modernizing and expanding its production facilities. Limits were placed on the amount of credit that could be claimed and on the number of years over which an investment credit for one year could be spread. In the inflationary period of 1966, the tax credit was suspended, but early in 1967 Congress renewed and liberalized it (PL 90-26).

Mortgage Guaranty Insurance. Since 1960 the Internal Revenue Service (IRS) and mortgage guaranty insurance companies had been unable to resolve the tax treatment of funds that state laws required the companies to set aside as reserves in case of extraordinarily heavy losses. In 1960 the IRS had issued to the Mortgage Guaranty Insurance Corp. of Milwaukee, Wis., (MGIC) and another company a favorable ruling that it subsequently decided was incorrect. Requests by 10 or more other companies for similar rulings were held in suspense pending agreement on uniform tax treatment of funds set aside in contingency reserves. The 1960 ruling favoring MGIC, it was later brought out, was sought by Rep. John W. Byrnes (R Wis.), ranking minority member of the Ways and Means Committee, to whom the company sold stock at a preferential price. Byrnes on Nov. 9, 1963, acknowledged the transaction and promised to sell the stock and devote profits from the sale to college scholarships.

PROVISIONS—As signed into law, HR 4765:

Financial General Corp. Provided that when the company distributed its nonbanking interests to its stockholders, as required by PL 89-485, the distribution would be taxfree if all distributions in kind (i.e., other than in money) were made on a pro rata basis to all shareholders. (The company Dec. 17 announced a plan to distribute its holdings in insurance, industrial and financial fields while retaining its interest in 26 banks and two mortgage-banking companies.)

American Motors. Permitted a company meeting certain qualifications (believed to apply only to American Motors) to carry net operating losses for the taxable years 1967 and 1968 back for five years or forward for three years. (In general, existing law permitted a three-year carryback and five-year carryforward).

Permitted any company to carry back for three years an investment credit that it was unable to use because of carrying back a net operating loss to the year for which the credit was claimed. This applied to losses in taxable years ending after July 31, 1967.

Controlled Life Insurance Companies. Permitted a tax-free distribution of stock after 1966 to a holding company providing the controlled insurance company had been held by the distributing corporation since 1957. (The tax affecting such spin-offs by life insurance companies was imposed in 1959.) The provision was believed to apply only to the Jefferson Standard Life Insurance Co.

MORTGAGE GUARANTY. The Senate Dec. 12 added to an unrelated House bill (HR 1141) the provisions concerning mortgage guaranty insurance companies originally reported by the Finance Committee as an amendment to HR 4765. The House Dec. 14, upon the recommendation of Reps. Mills and Curtis, accepted the Senate amendments by voice vote and sent the bill to the President. He signed it into law (PL 90-240) Jan. 2, 1968.

The provision, which was recommended by the Treasury, validated the tax deductions taken by the mortgage guaranty insurance companies since 1960, the year of the disputed IRS decision. For the future, it allowed such companies to take tax deductions for funds they were required to place in special reserves, providing that the deferred taxes were invested in noninterest-bearing Government bonds for 10 years, after which the money would be restored to income and a tax levied.

1968

Congressional action on taxes was dominated by a single issue in 1968: a 10-percent surcharge on personal and corporate income taxes to help finance the Vietnam war and to reduce inflationary pressures in the U.S. economy. After a bitter and prolonged fight (dating from August of the previous year), Congress in June 1968 finally sent the President the tax increase he said was essential to economic stability. But Congress attached to the legislation mandatory reductions in spending, appropriations and federal employment levels which Mr. Johnson at one point said "would really bring chaos to the Government."

The confrontation between Congress and the President over the surcharge centered on the size of the spending restrictions that were to be attached to the bill. The two sides maneuvered for many weeks in the spring before the White House, in effect, had to give in and accept the stiff restrictions as the price of the tax increase.

Congress was even less cooperative with the other overriding tax-related issue of 1968: the balance-of-payments deficit. After some improvement in 1965 and 1966, the deficit took a bad turn for the worse in 1967 and prompted the Administration in 1968 to propose a wide-ranging program of controls to halt the outflow of dollars. Stiff mandatory controls on foreign investment, replacing voluntary controls that were in existence, were put into effect by administrative action. The President also asked Congress for various pieces of legislation, the primary one being a travel tax, to help reduce the deficit. Congress rejected most of the proposals. Nevertheless, the nation's payments balance improved during the year and showed a slight surplus (in preliminary figures) by one method of accounting that was considered the most comprehensive. (Another method showed an even larger surplus). But it was not certain as 1969 began that the improvements made in 1968 were anything more than temporary changes which would not be repeated.

In other action, Congress restricted the size of industrial development bonds that would be eligible for tax-exempt status. The action occurred because of complaints that the tax-exemption privilege was being abused. The House, but not the Senate, passed the long-delayed interstate taxation bill. But the controversial measure still had not become law when Congress adjourned.

Surcharge

After one of the longest and most bitter battles of the Johnson years, Congress in mid-1968 enacted legislation (HR 15414—PL 90-364) imposing a 10-percent surcharge on personal and corporate income taxes. The struggle over enactment of HR 15414 was one of the most fascinating in the history of Congress. It pitted powerful political forces against one another and cut through to one of the basic issues—Government spending—that was characteristic of the 1960s.

The President eventually won his tax increase, but Congress exacted as its price a $10-billion reduction in projected fiscal 1969 appropriations, a $6-billion reduction in fiscal 1969 spending, an $8-billion recision of unspent prior-year appropriations and an approximately 245,000-man cutback in the number of civilian employees in the Executive Branch. (However, Congress later backtracked and enacted many exemptions. *See separate story p. 180.*)

In passing the tax-increase bill, the Revenue and Expenditure Control Act of 1968, Congress completed action on the first general income-tax increase since the Revenue Act of 1951 (PL 82-183). President Johnson June 28 signed HR 15414 into law in private, without the customary bill-signing ceremonies.

Months of inaction passed on the Administration's tax package (including the surcharge, an excise tax rate extension and an acceleration of corporate tax payments) after it was introduced in late summer of 1967. Suddenly, bypassing the tax-writing House Ways and Means Committee, the Senate in early spring 1968 added the surcharge and the $6-billion spending cut (as well as a dozen other floor amendments) to a comparatively innocuous House-passed bill (HR 15414) extending some soon-to-expire excise tax rates. (Although the Constitution provided that tax legislation had to be initiated in the House, the Senate had authority to amend a House-passed bill.)

It was thought that this was an exercise in futility. Most observers believed that the Ways and Means Committee and its tradition-minded chairman, Wilbur D. Mills (D Ark.), never would agree to accept so major a tax provision which originated in the Senate.

Uncertainty hung over the House and Senate conference on HR 15414. For weeks, Mills and other conferees sought to negotiate a compromise between the widely varying House and Senate versions of the bill. Time passed while conservative Members (opposed to higher taxes) and liberals (opposed to spending cuts) were sounded out for support. More time was lost awaiting indications that President Johnson, who very much wanted the surcharge, was willing to accept a $6-billion spending cut and other restrictions in the bill in order to get the tax increase. Finally, a constitutional challenge was mounted against the bill in the House but was defeated on a 257-162 roll-call vote.

Spring turned into summer before it became clear that what once had been merely a bill to extend automobile and telephone excise taxes had become, through a Senate floor amendment, one of the most important bills of the 90th Congress.

The surcharge amendment (which also included the spending cut and employee cutback) was sponsored by a pair of fiscal conservatives—George A. Smathers (D Fla.) and John J. Williams (R Del.).

The trigger to Congressional action on the tax increase, according to most observers, was a rapidly developing crisis in the international gold market. The crisis became so critical in mid-March (about the same time that the tax increase began to make headway) that the United States was forced to abandon its traditional single-price system for gold and to adopt a new, two-price system. The links between the gold crisis and the tax increase were a rush of gold speculation, a dwindling supply of U.S. gold reserves and a growing and persistent U.S. balance-of-payments deficit. Advocates of a tax increase said it would help reduce the balance-of-payments deficit. (Directly, higher taxes would help dry up excess money available for spending abroad; indirectly, by dampening domestic inflationary pressures, higher taxes would help U.S. goods remain competitive in world markets.)

It was estimated that the bill's tax provisions (the surcharge, excise tax rate extension and accelerated corporate payments) would produce an additional $15.5 billion in Government revenues before their scheduled expiration July 1, 1969. The surcharge was expected to produce about $11.6 billion of the total additional revenue.

In economic terms, the tax increase contained in the Act represented the other side of the fiscal coin of the tax cut contained in the Revenue Act of 1964 (PL 88-272). Taken together, the two bills represented the first complete test of the "New Economics"—a theory that Government fiscal policy should be used to guide the national economy through Budget deficits in a recession and Budget surpluses (or at least smaller deficits) during inflation. Both bills, however, were enacted long after they had been requested. The time-lag between request and enactment of the fiscal measures led President Kennedy in 1962 to ask specifically for standby authority to reduce certain taxes and President Johnson in 1965, 1966 and 1968 to seek to "develop procedures to assure the timely adjustment of fiscal policy..."

The full impact of the 1968 tax increase was not expected to appear in national economic statistics until 1970.

When the tax increase was enacted, the economy was in the 88th month of an unprecedented period of expansion, but strong inflationary pressures were overriding the expansion. The gross national product, which had risen more than $16 billion in the third and fourth quarters of 1967, jumped more than $20 billion in the first quarter of 1968 and an estimated $19.6 billion during the second quarter. Prices were rising steadily (the consumer price

index increased from 116.9 in August 1967 to 119.9 in April 1968). The unemployment rate dropped from 4.1 percent in September 1967 to 3.5 percent in May 1968.

Other provisions of HR 15414—to cut fiscal 1969 spending by $6 billion, to rescind $8 billion of unspent prior-year appropriations and to cut back civilian employment in the Executive Branch—would exert further restraint on the economy. Enactment of the spending and employment cuts represented a victory for fiscal conservatives, led by Rep. Frank T. Bow (R Ohio) and Sen. John Williams, who since 1967 had sought to impose expenditure controls on non-Vietnam federal outlays, in an effort to reduce Budget deficits.

By the time Congress finished work on HR 15414, it had become a highly complex measure with 18 sections broken down among three titles. The bulk of the provisions represented one-time Senate floor amendments. In addition to the provisions dealing with fiscal matters, HR 15414 also: delayed for a year a controversial "freeze" on federal welfare payments to states under the aid to families with dependent children program; ended the existing tax exemption on income from some issues of industrial development bonds; and set a Dec. 31, 1968, deadline for submission to Congress of a comprehensive Administration tax reform program.

LEGISLATIVE HISTORY

The surcharge proposal originally was made by President Johnson in January 1967 as the Government was faced with rising costs of the Vietnam war and of major domestic programs which were producing inflationary pressures in the economy. In August 1967, he sent a specific proposal to Congress and asked for a 10-percent surcharge as well as some other lesser tax measures to raise extra revenues. The bill went nowhere in 1967 but prompted a major debate about the state of the economy and Government spending.

In 1968, Mr. Johnson again asked for the surcharge and warned that failure to act would lead to "an accelerating spiral of price increases, a slump in home building and a continued erosion of the American dollar..." More hearings were held but Mills and his Ways and Means Committee were unmoved, although Mills admitted the Administration had presented a better case for the surcharge than it had in the fall of 1967.

In late February, the Ways and Means Committee reported an Administration-backed bill (HR 15414) to continue excise taxes on autos and telephone service until the end of 1969 and to speed collection of corporate income tax payments. This bill passed the House Feb. 29 by a routine voice vote.

During the floor discussion, Mills took the opportunity of restating both his personal position and the position of the Ways and Means Committee on President Johnson's proposed 10-percent income tax surcharge for individual taxpayers and for corporations. Speaking for the Committee, Mills said that "no decision" had been reached on "possible future action on the surcharge proposal." He emphasized that the Committee's Oct. 3, 1967, resolution which temporarily laid aside the surcharge proposal was still in effect.

Speaking for himself, Mills said he still believed that "any income tax increase should be coupled with actions evidencing firm control over the expenditure side of the

Lobbying by Business Leaders Key to Passage

Passage of the surcharge tax bill was the climax to one of the most vigorous lobbying campaigns in many sessions of Congress. Bankers, businessmen and a variety of other interests teamed up with the Administration to sell the unpopular measure to Congress. By the time the bill cleared, almost every significant business organization in the country had gone on record for it.

The big lobby drive was necessary to offset what many Washington sources believed was a series of miscalculations by President Johnson. Rather than linking the tax to the Vietnam war, the President had emphasized a series of complicated economic arguments beyond public understanding. One key Member of Congress, Rep. John W. Byrnes (R Wis.), ranking GOP member of the House Ways and Means Committee, told Congressional Quarterly it was "impossible to sell that kind of economic argument to the gas station operator. He just couldn't understand why the Administration was seeking a tax increase on one hand and expanding Great Society spending on the other." For more than 10 months, the President resisted efforts to tie a large cutback in federal expenditures to the tax surcharge.

Byrnes and other Congressional sources told CQ they thought the bill would have won easy approval if the President had labeled it as a "war tax." *Newsweek* magazine in its March 11 issue said Ways and Means Committee Chairman Wilbur D. Mills (D Ark.), who pigeonholed the measure for almost a year, had "hinted broadly" that if the bill were labeled a war tax, "it would meet few obstacles in Congress."

Sources also said the White House made a big mistake in its handling of Mills. "I think Mills got upset because we didn't show him more attention," a high Administration official said.

One Administration official said the President made another major miscalculation by terming the tax a 10-percent surcharge (a tax on regular tax liabilities) instead of a 1-percent tax on income. "Although these figures amounted to the same thing," the official said, "it was the 10-percent figure that stuck in the public mind. Although the President began emphasizing the 1-percent figure several weeks after his 1967 tax message, he was never able to rectify his initial miscalculation."

The Administration began lining up its lobby support in 1967; however, public opposition was so strong that the bill never got out of Committee. In May 1968, after the President had reluctantly agreed to a $6-billion cut in Government spending as a move to secure additional votes for the tax increase, the Administration brought all its lobby clout to bear on the issue. "Despite the big cut," one Administration source told CQ, "we were by no means certain we'd get a bill. Most House Members accepted the need for a tax increase but nobody seemed to want to go on record for it." House GOP Leader Gerald R. Ford (Mich.) prom-

ised to deliver a majority of Republican votes only if he was guaranteed the votes of a majority of Democrats.

The thrust of business lobbying for the bill came from the American Bankers Assn. (ABA) and a group of almost 500 prominent business leaders, headed by Henry Ford, chairman of the board of the Ford Motor Co., and Stuart T. Saunders, board chairman of the Pennsylvania Railroad. The ABA, spurred by a May 24 address by Secretary of the Treasury Henry H. Fowler, mobilized local bankers, many of whom made personal calls on Members of Congress to urge their support for the bill.

A week before the final vote, over 100 members of the Ford-Saunders group met with Administration officials in Washington to map out final strategy. Cards listing every Representative and the businesses located in his district were circulated among the leaders, and each was assigned one or more Representatives whose districts included a plant or branch office of his company. One Administration official told CQ the businessmen "went up to the Hill just like Congressional liaison officers. They talked a good game and came back with amazingly accurate vote counts."

Other strong pressures came from the National Assn. of Homebuilders and the Chamber of Commerce of the United States, both of which mobilized their local groups. The Chamber originally had opposed the tax increase but switched its position late in 1967.

One Administration source told CQ that a factor as important as the businessmen's lobbying for the bill was organized labor's decision not to mobilize against it. Although the AFL-CIO strongly opposed the $6-billion spending cut, it favored the tax increase. The result was that the organization did not lobby one way or the other on the final bill. Had it vigorously opposed the bill, the AFL-CIO might have swung a number of Northern Democratic votes.

In addition to the business and Treasury lobbying, the White House assigned Cabinet officers to key Members of Congress and organized a task force of 75 Congressional liaison officers from federal departments and agencies to see additional Members. Each of the liaison officers took four or five Members whom he knew well. On the final vote on the bill, the combined estimate turned in by Administration lobbyists was almost 100 percent correct. The final count showed six Members who said they would vote "yea" but voted "nay" and four who indicated they would oppose the measure but voted for it.

Most of CQ's sources said the "hero" of the lobbying effort was Treasury Secretary Fowler, who literally pursued bankers and businessmen around the world to seek out their support for the measure. One Congressional source said that "without Fowler, there couldn't have been a bill. He was obsessed with the idea that failure to pass the tax increase would spell economic doom for the country, and he seemed to be everywhere at once spreading that message."

Budget both in spirit and deed.'' Although the Administration had made ''some improvements'' in expenditure control, Mills said they were ''not sufficient to justify final consideration of tax increases.''

Mills said that a ''substantial acceleration of war expenditures'' or ''substantial inflationary pressures generated from an excess of demand'' might ''force'' Congress to increase taxes. In either case, however, Mills noted that there would ''still be the need, even intensified as I see it,'' for sharp restraints on domestic federal spending. Any tax increase which was ''not accompanied by rigorous expenditure control'' would have ''questionable value,'' he said. (Mills March 11 added a third contingency to the list when he told a Washington, D.C., meeting of the National Assn. of Life Underwriters that the continuing outflow of gold from the United States was ''part of the overall picture of whether or not (Congress) will be required to take fiscal action'' in 1968.)

Senate Action. When the bill got to the Senate, a campaign was begun to add a surcharge amendment. The proposal was rejected in the Senate Finance Committee (although other major amendments dealing with industrial development bonds and with welfare and medicaid programs were added). But when HR 15414 reached the Senate floor, backers of the surcharge and spending-cut provisions were successful. (In the meantime, the April 1 deadline for an automatic reduction of the automobile and telephone service excise taxes approached without action on the extension bill. When the April 1 deadline passed without final action, the pre-April 1 rates continued in effect under an announcement by the Internal Revenue Service. Shortly thereafter, Congress passed a special bill (H J Res 1223—PL 90-285) to extend the existing automobile and telephone taxes retroactively from March 31 to May 1.)

The surcharge and spending cutback, sponsored by Williams and Smathers, was added to HR 15414 as a floor amendment. Their amendment combined in a single package the Johnson Administration's long-sought 10-percent surcharge and a Republican-favored expenditure cutback, calling for a ceiling of $180.1 billion in fiscal 1969 spending compared with the President's proposed $186.1-billion Budget. In addition, their amendment limited federal employment and required the Administration to propose reductions totaling $10 billion in fiscal 1969 appropriation requests (to achieve the $6-billion spending cutback.) Adoption of the amendment, which cleared the way for action on the bill itself, came on a **53-35** key roll-call vote. Throughout action on the amendment, which included a number of crucial votes, Republicans strongly supported the surcharge-spending cut package.

It was later theorized that Mills was behind Williams' tactic because his Committee could not report out a tax bill including spending cuts (the cuts were under jurisdiction of the Appropriations Committee) and that Mills feared the House might approve a tax increase without the cuts if the two bills were reported separately. If the Senate approved the entire package, Mills would have control over it in conference and could send it to the House floor in a conference report which had to be voted up or down without amendments.

Williams told CQ, however, that he had ''absolutely no contact'' with Mills concerning his ''end-run'' maneuver. Williams did acknowledge that he had a ''hunch''

Mills would go along because he had not informed Williams of his opposition to the tactic even though it was openly known in the Joint Committee on Internal Revenue Taxation that Williams was preparing the package. (Both were members of the Joint Committee.) Williams told CQ that ''I gambled that we'd have a friend in the House and we did.''

CQ learned that the Administration, while cool to the $6-billion spending cut, supported the Williams-Smathers amendment as a means to get the surcharge proposal moving. One Administration official said, ''We didn't worry too much about the $6 billion figure at that point because we thought we could compromise it in conference.'' One key Congressional source told CQ, however, that agreeing to the $6 billion was a serious mistake because the House ''takes great pride in cutting expenditures by a greater amount than the Senate.'' The source said that once the Senate was on record for $6 billion, it was ''impossible to expect'' the House to accept less.

The Senate acted on many other unrelated amendments before passing the bill April 2 by a 57-31 roll-call vote (R 30-3; D 27-28).

Conference Action. Once the bill was passed, the war on nerves began between the White House, the Senate and the House (and more specifically, the Ways and Means Committee). It was not until June 10 that a conference report on the bill was filed. The period between April 2 and June 10 consisted largely of political negotiations—some of it done publicly—between these three powerful political forces. A chronology of developments follows.

May 1—The House Appropriations Committee by a reported 20-0 vote, with Republicans abstaining, approved an Administration-backed ''sense of the Committee'' resolution recommending a $22-billion package of budget reductions. The package included a reduction of not less than $10 billion in Administration-proposed fiscal 1969 appropriations, a recision of not less than $8 billion in unspent prior-year appropriations and a reduction of not less than $4 billion in fiscal 1969 spending. The reduction package reportedly was reluctantly suggested by President Johnson at an April 30 White House meeting of Democratic Congressional leaders. Committee Chairman George H. Mahon (D Texas), who offered the resolution, said that its approval ''will break the deadlock'' in the House-Senate conference on HR 15414, the tax bill.

Action on Mahon's resolution came after the Committee by a reported 21-23 vote rejected a resolution offered by ranking Republican Frank T. Bow (Ohio) recommending a $14-billion reduction in fiscal 1969 appropriations, a $6-billion recision of unspent prior-year appropriations and a $6-billion reduction in fiscal 1969 spending.

May 3—During a nationally televised news conference, President Johnson spoke out sharply against Congressional inaction on the surcharge. The statement was regarded as his strongest public attack on Congress. ''I think that we are courting danger by this continued procrastination,'' Mr. Johnson said. ''I think the time has come for all the Members of Congress to be responsible and, even in an election year, to bite the bullet and stand up and do what ought to be done for their country.'' The President added, ''Don't hold up the tax bill

Can Congress Act Fast Enough on Taxes to Regulate Economy?

Except in times of extreme emergency or immediate danger, Congress tends to move quite slowly on major issues. This is particularly true in the complicated area of taxation because changes in the tax structure can have enormous impact on millions of individuals and organizations. However, if the tax structure is to be used as a tool to influence the economy, swift action often is of the essence.

In the years after President Kennedy took office in 1961, there was increasing public acceptance of the theory that Government fiscal policies—spending and tax actions—were useful tools to help regulate fluctuations in the national economy. Supporters of the theory argued that a decline in economic activity could be partially offset by a tax decrease or a substantial increase in federal spending, both of which make more dollars available for spending throughout the country. Conversely, inflationary pressures could be reduced by increased taxes and reduced spending.

Timing Important

A key to the successful application of the theory was timing. A decision on when to increase or decrease taxes or spending had to be made at just the right time in order to have the effect spread properly through the economy.

President Kennedy said this could be achieved if Congress would provide the President with standby power to change tax rates or increase spending. In 1962, he specifically asked for standby power to temporarily lower individual income tax rates by 5 percentage points, subject to Congressional veto, and standby authority to initiate up to $2 billion in public works spending. Congress, jealous of its taxing and spending powers, took no action.

President Johnson in 1965 urged better procedures to speed tax actions, but did not request standby authority. Congress took no action. In 1966, he urged "background tax studies" to permit "quick decisions and prompt action to accommodate shortrun cyclical changes." A Joint Economic Committee subcommittee in 1966 urged standby authority for quick changes.

Congressional action on tax bills in 1966 gave support to Members who said Congress could act quickly when the need was clear. Early in the year, Congress increased tax revenues by $6 billion by temporarily suspending certain scheduled excise tax cuts and by providing graduated withholding (PL 89-368). Congress completed action by the March 15 deadline set by the President. In the fall, Congress within a two-month period enacted PL 89-800 temporarily suspending the investment tax credit and accelerated depreciation.

In 1967, Congress took 12 weeks to complete action on a measure (PL 90-26) restoring investment tax credits for business. Enactment of the bill could have come much sooner; the House acted very quickly but the Senate became embroiled in a debate, which lasted more than five weeks, over a nongermane rider involving campaign financing.

The three tax measures cited above were enacted relatively quickly. The 1968 income tax surcharge, on the other hand, was subjected to lengthy delays in Congress.

The surtax was first proposed by Mr. Johnson on Jan. 10, 1967, at a rate of 6 percent. On Aug. 3, 1967, he asked Congress for a 10-percent surtax. The surtax measure was not signed into law (PL 90-364) until June 28, 1968, almost 18 months after the idea had first been proposed. (President Johnson in his 1969 Budget Message just before leaving office proposed not only that Congress extend the 10-percent income tax surcharge but also that it give the new President authority to remove the tax entirely or partially "if warranted by developments," subject to Congressional veto. For the long term, Mr. Johnson suggested that Congress give the President limited authority to raise or lower income taxes within a specified range to meet economic conditions. Mr. Johnson's request for flexible Presidential tax authority appeared to be an outgrowth of his experience with the surtax. Mr. Johnson had never before requested administrative taxing authority.)

The fact that Congress acted swiftly on some tax bills in the 1960s did not hide the fact that it acted quite slowly (particularly in terms of economic timing) on other tax measures that were controversial. The outstanding example was the surcharge. But the same was true of the 1964 tax bill (PL 88-272) which required 13 months to become law because of the sections of the bill making reforms in the tax structure. A 1962 tax law (PL 87-834), containing both reductions and reforms, required 18 months to enact.

Major Tax Bills Move Slowly

These experiences suggest that any major tax bill which contains controversial provisions will require a substantial amount of time to enact—probably the better part of an entire Congress covering two years. This amount of time could be too long to produce required changes in economic conditions.

In economic terms, the tax increase contained in PL 90-364 represented the other side of the fiscal coin of the tax cut contained in the Revenue Act of 1964. Taken together, the two bills represented the first complete test of the "New Economics"—the theory that adjustments in fiscal policy—changes in tax rates—should be used to guide the national economy through Budget deficits in a recession and Budget surpluses (or at least smaller deficits) during inflation.

By mid-1969, however, the theory had not yet been proven. The 1964 tax cut was widely believed to have helped spur the economy to greater activity. But it was not clear whether the 1968 tax increase would have the opposite effect.

until you can blackmail someone into getting your own personal viewpoint over on reductions."

May 5—In a letter to House Speaker John W. McCormack (D Mass.) the President said he would accept the $4-billion spending reduction in order to achieve passage of the surcharge and said that further delay on the surcharge was "a ticket to disaster." At the same time, however, the President defended his $186.1-billion Budget as being "tight" and "lean."

May 6—The House Ways and Means Committee by a reported 17-6 vote approved a resolution offered by A. Sydney Herlong (D Fla.) recommending a $10-billion income tax increase "either through a 10-percent surcharge or comparable rate adjustments." The tax increase was to be accompanied by the same reduced appropriations, recision of prior-year appropriations and spending reductions contained in the package approved by the Appropriations Committee. The resolution said the Ways and Means Committee was acting "in the light of the existing critical domestic and international fiscal situation...." Further, the resolution said the tax increase-spending restriction package was "to be embodied" in the conference report on HR 15414.

The Ways and Means resolution marked the first time the Committee had acted favorably on President Johnson's requested 10-percent income tax surcharge since the President submitted the request on Aug. 3, 1967.

Committee approval of the Herlong resolution came after a resolution offered by Byrnes, containing the Republican formula demand for a $6-billion spending reduction, was rejected by a reported 10-15 vote along party lines. There were 15 Democrats and 10 Republicans on the Committee.

May 8—Conferees announced agreement on including in the bill the Senate amendment proposing a 10-percent surcharge on personal and corporate income taxes and a reduction of $6 billion in federal spending in fiscal 1969.

May 9—The conferees announced that all differences between the House and Senate versions of the bill had been resolved and that agreement had been reached to file a report.

May 15—House Majority Leader Carl Albert (D Okla.) announced that consideration of the conference report on HR 15414 was not to begin until the first week of June, or possibly later, because of what he said was difficulty in drafting the precise language of the bill's provisions as agreed to by the conferees.

May 29—The House by a 137-259 roll-call vote rejected a motion by James A. Burke (D Mass.) to instruct the conferees on HR 15414 to reduce the bill's cutback in fiscal 1969 spending from $6 billion to $4 billion. The vote breakdown: R 6-167; D 131-92 (ND 111-29; SD 20-63).

Burke's motion was regarded by Congressional observers as a move by House liberals to lower the spending cutback required by HR 15414 and thus to save what the liberals regarded as being important domestic programs.

Opposition to Burke's motion came from House Republicans and Southern Democrats. Minority Leader Gerald R. Ford (R Mich.) supported the bill's $6-billion cut in spending, calling a $4-billion cutback "just insufficient to meet the crisis the nation faces." Asserting that "today we face a fiscal crisis," John W. Byrnes (R Wis.), ranking Ways and Means Committee Republican, supported

the bill's $6-billion spending cut and urged the President to do so.

The Administration's lobbying effort was highly disorganized during the one-week period that the Burke motion was pending. White House sources said the President was strongly pushing for the motion. However, CQ learned from other sources that the Treasury had adopted a "hands-off" attitude and was not pushing the White House position. Fowler on May 13 had told newsmen that he was "for the (conference) bill," which at that time included a $6-billion spending cut. One Congressional source told CQ that "throughout the discussion of this bill, Fowler had a much better grasp of the mood of the House than the White House did."

Administration sources reported that the White House was strongly behind the Burke motion as a last attempt to save important domestic programs from a severe cutback. Several Congressional sources told CQ, however, they regarded the move as an attempt by the White House to allow liberals to go on record for a lower cut and then vote later for the conference report as a last means to save the tax increase.

May 30—President Johnson told a news conference that he would accept the $6-billion fiscal 1969 spending cut in HR 15414. Until then, the President had said publicly that he would accept only a $4-billion cutback (although he had not said that he would reject a cut of $6 billion). Mr. Johnson's acceptance of the higher cutback was seen as removing a key hurdle to final action on HR 15414.

Citing House rejection of Burke's motion the day before, Mr. Johnson said, "The only choice remaining now is whether the need for a tax increase is so urgent that we must accept a $6-billion reduction. I believe that the need for a tax increase is that urgent." The President went on to say that if Congress agreed to the conference report on HR 15414, "I shall approve it."

June 4—Majority Leader Albert said that he now supported the $6-billion spending cut in the conference report, reversing the stand he took on Burke's motion. "I supported the $4-billion choice (in Burke's motion), but today it is no longer a proper question," Albert said. He continued, "The one clear issue now before us is whether we are resolved to move decisively to protect the economic and financial stability of the United States... I am for this conference report...I urge the House to support it completely as it is."

June 6—Ways and Means Committee Chairman Mills told the House he wanted to delay until June 19 consideration of the conference report on HR 15414 to give Members time to study the report after it was filed.

Final Action. Final action on the surcharge bill came in June. The House June 20 by a **268-150** key roll-call vote adopted the conference report on HR 15414. Voting for the bill were the House leaders of both parties, while an unusual coalition of conservative Members (opposed to higher taxes) and liberal Democrats (opposed to expenditure reductions) voted against the measure. Before approving the report, the House by a 257-162 roll call tabled (killed) a privileged motion by H.R. Gross (R Iowa) which would have returned the report to the Senate on constitutional grounds without any House action. Gross contended the revenue provisions were added by the Senate in violation of constitutional requirements.

The Senate adopted the report June 21 by a 64-16 roll call, clearing the bill for the President who signed it into law June 28 (PL 90-364).

Provisions

As signed into law, the Revenue and Expenditure Control Act of 1968 (HR 15414—PL 90-364) contained the following major provisions:

Excise Taxes. Continued the existing 10-percent excise tax on local and long-distance telephone service through Dec. 31, 1969.

Continued the existing 7-percent excise tax on manufacturers' prices of new passenger automobiles through Dec. 31, 1969.

(The excise taxes were extended retroactively to April 30, the interim expiration date provided by a measure (H J Res 1223) cleared earlier.

Provided for reductions in both excise tax rates to 5 percent during calendar 1970, to 3 percent during calendar 1971, to 1 percent in calendar 1972 with elimination of both taxes scheduled for Jan. 1, 1973.

Corporate Income Taxes. Repealed provisions of existing law which required corporations to file a declaration of estimated tax for the current taxable year.

Raised from 70 percent to 80 percent the portion of corporate income taxes which were to be paid during the year in which the liability was incurred.

Reduced from $100,000 to $40 over a 10-year period the amount of corporate tax liability on which a corporation could postpone payment until April 15 of the year following the year in which the liability was incurred.

Established a 10-year transitional period during which corporations using the existing $100,000 tax deferral provision were gradually to become current in their tax payments. From 1968 to 1972 tax liabilities above $5,500 were to be placed on a current basis; from 1973 to 1977 tax liability above $40 was to be placed on a current basis.

Permitted a corporation to apply for a tax refund immediately after the close of a taxable year if its actual tax payments during the year exceeded a revised tax estimate by at least 10 percent and amounted to at least $500.

Provided that any additional corporate tax payments for 1968 arising from the acceleration of corporate tax payments or the 10-percent surcharge on corporate income taxes *(see below)* were to be made by June 15, September 15 and December 15.

Stipulated that deposits of estimated taxes which were mailed by taxpayers at least two days before the due date would be considered as received on time even if the actual date of receipt by depository banks was later than the due date.

Surcharge. Imposed a 10-percent surcharge on individual and corporate income taxes, effective April 1, 1968, for individuals and Jan. 1, 1968, for corporations.

Exempted from the surcharge the first $1,000 of taxable income of a single person and the first $2,000 of taxable income of a married couple.

Provided that the surcharge was to expire for both individuals and for corporations on July 1, 1969.

Provided that increased withholding would begin 15 days after enactment of the bill.

Excise Tax Timetables

The table below compares the excise tax rates under HR 15414 with the existing schedule of excise tax reductions approved by Congress in the Tax Adjustment Act of 1966 (PL 89-368).

EXISTING LAW

Effective Date	Telephone	Automobile
Current rate	10%	7%
April 1, 1968	1	2
Jan. 1, 1969	0	1

HR 15414

Effective Date	Telephone	Automobile
Current rate	10%	7%
Jan. 1, 1970	5	5
Jan. 1, 1971	3	3
Jan. 1, 1972	1	1
Jan. 1, 1973	0	0

Stipulated that for individuals filing declarations, the increase was to be reflected in declarations filed Sept. 15 in the case of calendar-year taxpayers and that for corporations the surcharge was to be applied before the application of tax credits.

Spending, Budget Reductions. Set a ceiling of $180.1 billion on fiscal 1969 federal spending (compared with the $186.1-billion fiscal 1969 spending estimate in the Budget).

Set a ceiling of $191.7 billion on new obligational authority requested for fiscal 1969 (compared with the $201.7-billion fiscal 1969 new obligational authority requested in the Budget).

Exempted from the spending and appropriation reductions *(above)* spending and appropriations for the Vietnam war, payment of interest on the federal debt, veterans' benefits payments and Social Security benefits payments.

Required the President in submitting the fiscal 1970 Budget to include specific recommendations for legislation to rescind $8 billion in unspent prior-year appropriations.

Federal Employment. Required that until the number of permanent, full-time, civilian employees in the Executive Branch was reduced to the number employed as of June 30, 1966, (2,366,000 persons) not more than 75 percent of the vacancies was to be filled.

Provided that the number of temporary and part-time employees in any Executive Branch department or agency during any one month was not to exceed the number of such employees during the corresponding month of 1967.

Exempted casual employees, persons appointed by the President with the advice and consent of the Senate, employees serving without compensation and employees provided summer work because they were economically or educationally disadvantaged persons between 16 and 22 years old.

AFDC. Postponed from July 1, 1968, to July 1, 1969, the effective date of a provision of the Social Secu-

Population, Government Employment

YEAR	GOVERNMENT EMPLOYMENT				POPULATION	
	Federal executive branch [1] (thousands)	State and local governments (thousands)	All governmental units (thousands)	Federal as percent of all governmental units	Total United States (thousands)	Federal employment per 1,000 population
1942	2,272	3,310	5,582	40.7	135,361	16.8
1943	3,274	3,184	6,458	50.7	137,250	23.9
1944	3,304	3,092	6,396	51.7	138,916	23.8
1945	3,787	3,104	6,891	55.0	140,468	27.0
1946	2,666	3,305	5,971	44.6	141,936	18.8
1947	2,082	3,568	5,650	36.8	144,698	14.4
1948	2,044	3,776	5,820	35.1	147,208	13.9
1949	2,075	3,906	5,981	34'7	149,767	13.9
1950	1,934	4,078	6,012	32.2	152,271	12.7
1951	2,456	4,031	6,487	37.9	154.878	15.9
1952	2,574	4,134	6,708	38.4	157,553	16.3
1953	2,532	4,282	6,814	37.2	160,184	15.8
1954	2,382	4,552	6,934	34.4	163,026	14.6
1955	2,371	4,728	7,099	33.4	165,931	14.3
1956	2,372	5,064	7,436	31.9	168,903	14.0
1957	2,391	5,380	7,771	30.8	171,984	13.9
1958	2,355	5,630	7,985	29.5	174,882	13.5
1959	2,355	5,806	8,161	28.9	177,830	13.2
1960	[2] 2,371	6,073	8,444	28.1	180,684	13.1
1961	2,407	6,295	8,702	27.7	183,756	13.1
1962	2,485	6,533	9,018	27.6	186,656	13.3
1963	[3] 2,490	6,834	9,324	26.7	189,417	13.1
1964	[3] 2,469	7,236	9,705	25.4	192,120	12.9
1965	2,496	7,700	10,196	24.5	194,592	12.8
1966	2,664	8,320	10,984	24.2	196,920	13.5
1967	2,877	8,898	11,775	24.4	199,118	14.4
1968	2,951	9,437	12,388	23.8	201,166	14.7

[1] *Covers total end-of-year employment in full-time permanent, temporary, part-time, and intermittent positions except for summer workers under the President's Youth Opportunity Campaign; member-employees of the Soldiers' Home; merchant seamen on vessels under Federal shipping contracts; and civilian technicians in the Army and Air Force National Guard.*

[2] *Includes piece-rate census workers employed for the decennial census.*

[3] *Excludes 7,411 project employees in 1963 and the 406 project employees in 1964 for the public works acceleration program.*

rity Amendments of 1967 which set the future proportion of children under 18 in each state who could receive federal assistance under the aid to families with dependent children (AFDC) program where the parent was absent from the home at the percentage of AFDC children on the rolls in January 1968.

Allowed a state to include within its base proportion *(above)* those cases added to its rolls by the second quarter of 1969 as a result of court decisions.

Prohibited payments under the AFDC unemployed fathers program during those weeks in which the father was receiving unemployment compensation payments.

Medicaid. Extended from Jan. 1, 1968, to Jan. 1, 1970, the cutoff date for federal matching payments to states under the 1967 Social Security bill's Title XIX medicaid program for medical services which could have been covered under Part B medicare coverage (supplemental medical insurance) if a state had purchased Part B medicare coverage for those persons eligible for medicaid.

Industrial Development Bonds. Ended the existing tax exemption on the interest from industrial development bonds issued on or after May 1, 1968, if the issue exceeded $1 million. (The tax exemption was to remain in effect for small issues. *See p. 177.*)

Provided exemptions from the new taxable status *(above)* for bonds issued for residential property for family units, sports facilities, convention or trade show facilities, various types of transportation facilities, certain public utility facilities, air or water pollution abatement facilities and facilities for industrial parks.

Provided that if substantial steps had been taken before May 1, 1968, on a project to be financed with an industrial development bond issue, the bonds were not to be taxable unless issued after Jan. 1, 1969.

Political Advertising. Allowed a tax deduction for the cost of advertising in a program at a national political convention held to nominate a candidate for President if the cost of the advertising was reasonable compared to the expected business benefits and if the program revenue was to be used solely to defray the costs of the convention.

Joint Hospital Facilities. Exempted from federal taxation facilities operated jointly by tax-exempt hospitals.

Tax Reform. Required the President to submit to Congress by Dec. 31, 1968, a comprehensive program of tax reforms.

Bill Title. Stipulated that HR 15414 was to be named the Revenue and Expenditure Control Act of 1968.

Balance of Payments

The United States' balance of payments improved enough during 1968 to eliminate the deficit that had been characteristic of the problem for a decade. However, the surplus was not substantial on the liquidity basis and may not have reflected a basic improvement in the nation's payments position.

On the liquidity basis, the 1967 deficit of $3.6 billion moved to a 1968 surplus of $187 million based on preliminary figures. On the official settlements basis, the 1967 deficit of $3.4 billion moved to a surplus of $1.7 billion.

Much of the improvement came late in the fourth quarter of the year and may have reflected special circumstances which would not be repeated in the future. Commerce Department officials said repatriations of capital by U.S. corporations played an important part, but noted that this may have occurred in order to bring net capital outflows for direct investments below strict 1968 ceilings set by the Government in January as part of a new program to reduce the overall deficit. Throughout the year, businessmen were critical of these new controls and urged their repeal. But the existence of the controls was widely believed to have helped reduce the deficit and they were expected to be continued for some time after 1968 until other and more basic improvements could be made in the payments accounts.

However, one of the mainstays of the U.S. balance of payments—the trade surplus—dwindled to a dangerously low level in 1968. For the year, the surplus on merchandise trade was only $90 million, based on preliminary figures, compared to the 1967 surplus of almost $3.5 billion. The decline reflected an increase of $6.3 billion in imports and a rise of $2.9 billion in exports. Although the export rise was among the largest in recent years, the import rise was substantially larger than any experienced earlier. Officials attributed about $700 million of the import rise to actual or anticipated strikes. They said the rest reflected higher U.S. prices and better foreign products.

ADMINISTRATION PROGRAM

When it became clear late in 1967 that the U.S. balance of payments positions had not improved as expected from the existing voluntary program and, in fact, had deteriorated badly, the Administration planned a new and much stricter approach to controlling the outflow of dollars. This program, involving both administrative actions and legislation, was announced on Jan. 1, 1968. The administrative actions were put into effect under the powers of the Executive Branch. But Congress rejected most of President Johnson's legislative proposals to shrink the payments deficit.

In general, the program took three distinct courses. One was to discourage increased U.S. expenditures abroad by the Government, by business and by private individuals. The President imposed a series of mandatory controls on private investment abroad (the first time in history this had occurred) and ordered federal agencies to cut down on the number of personnel abroad. The principal legislative proposal along this line called for a tax on U.S. citizens traveling abroad, a tax on airline tickets for foreign travel and a reduction in the amount of purchases a U.S. citizen could bring back duty-free from abroad. The proposal was turned down by Congress.

Secondly, the Administration sought to increase U.S. exports, primarily by implementing the results of the Kennedy Round of tariff-cutting negotiations and by generally trying to promote lower trade barriers. The proposals, embodied in the Trade Expansion Act of 1968, also failed to get through Congress. However, Congress did grant an Administration request to broaden the lending authority of the Export-Import Bank and the Administration was successful in turning back a drive started in late 1967 to increase quotas on imports. Congress did not grant a related Administration request for legislation to expand East-West trade. *(See 1968 chronology in foreign policy chapter for discussion of these measures.)*

Thirdly, the Administration sought to encourage greater numbers of foreigners to visit the United States. The Administration was successful in getting airlines, hotel chains and other tourist businesses to give discounts to foreign visitors to the United States, but Congress did not complete action on an Administration request for legislation waiving visa requirements for certain foreign nationals.

Requests for removal of the remaining gold backing from U.S. currency and to implement the agreement for a new monetary facility (Special Drawing Rights) were approved by Congress. Congress inserted in the

Balance-of-Payments Figures

(in millions)

Balance On:

	Liquidity Basis[1]	Official Reserve Transactions Basis[2]	Changes in U.S. Official Reserve Assets[3]
1946	$ 993		$ — 623
1947	4,210		—3,315
1948	817		—1,736
1949	136		— 266
1950	—3,489		1,758
1951	— 8		— 33
1952	—1,206		— 415
1953	—2,184		1,256
1954	—1,541		480
1955	—1,242		182
1956	— 973		— 869
1957	578		—1,165
1958	—3,365		2,292
1959	—3,870		1,035
1960	—3,901	$—3,403	2,145
1961	—2,371	—1,347	606
1962	—2,204	—2,702	1,533
1963	—2,670	—2,011	377
1964	—2,800	—1,564	171
1965	—1,335	—1,289	1,222
1966	—1,357	266	568
1967	—3,571	—3,405	52
1968[4]	187	1,659	— 880

1 The balance in this column, on the "over-all" or liquidity accounting basis, is measured by changes in U.S.gold and other official reserve assets and in U.S. dollars held by all foreigners.

2 The official settlements balance, first used by the Commerce Department in presenting 1965 figures, measures the payments balance by changes in U.S. reserve assets (gold and others) and in dollars held by official foreign agencies. It differs from the "over-all" measurement primarily by excluding changes in dollar holdings by private foreign parties. The Commerce Department had not prepared figures for the official settlements basis for years before 1960.

3 This covers changes in gold, convertible currencies and the IMF gold tranche position.

4 Based on preliminary figures at the end of 1968.

SOURCE: Commerce Department

Food for Freedom legislation (S 2986) provisions designed to ease the balance-of-payments deficit. *(See foreign policy chapter p. 114 for story on Special Drawing Rights and banking section in this chapter for stories on gold.)*

Private Investment

The centerpiece of the President's program was a series of mandatory controls, effective Jan. 1, 1968, on U.S. private investment abroad. Of the entire balance-of-payments program, this portion was believed likely to have the largest impact; it also was a key portion because the President used what he considered existing authority available to him to implement it whereas other key parts of the program (the travel tax in particular) required Congressional approval which was not forthcoming.

A voluntary balance-of-payments program for corporations had been started in 1965, under which the business community agreed to limit its foreign investment in developed countries, expand exports and repatriate foreign earnings. The Commerce Department in a Jan. 1 statement said the voluntary program had been a "substantial success in achieving the goals set for it," but that the new projected reductions probably could be achieved only through mandatory controls.

"Direct Investor." A "direct investor" subject to the controls was defined as "an individual or company in the United States which owns or acquires an interest of 10 percent or more of the voting power, earnings or capital of a foreign business venture." Generally, the new regulations were imposed on the dealings of a direct investor with each of the ventures in which it had an interest.

Regulations—*New Investment.* New net investment in continental western Europe (except Greece and Finland) was prohibited in 1968. New net investment in other developed countries including Canada, Japan, Australia, Great Britain, and oil-producing nations was limited to 65 percent of the 1965-66 average of investment in those countries. New net investment in developing countries was limited to 110 percent of the 1965-66 average of investment. (Net long-term borrowing abroad for financing overseas investments was not to be counted in the computation of the investment limit.) Officials said a violation of the new controls could lead to a possible criminal prosecution and a maximum fine of $10,000.

They also said that the regulations would bar new foreign investment by a company which lacked an historical record of foreign investment during the 1965-66 base years. The spokesman said, however, that requests for special exemptions from the investment restrictions could be filed.

Repatriation. Each year the direct investor was to repatriate either the same percentage of his share of earnings repatriated during 1964-66, or his share of earnings that exceeded the limit set for new net investment, whichever was greater. Where new net investment was banned, earnings that exceeded 35 percent of the 1965-66 average were to be repatriated. In addition, short-term financial assets abroad not held as direct investments were to be reduced to the 1965-66 level. *EXCEPTION:* Funds made available through depreciation abroad were not required to be repatriated.

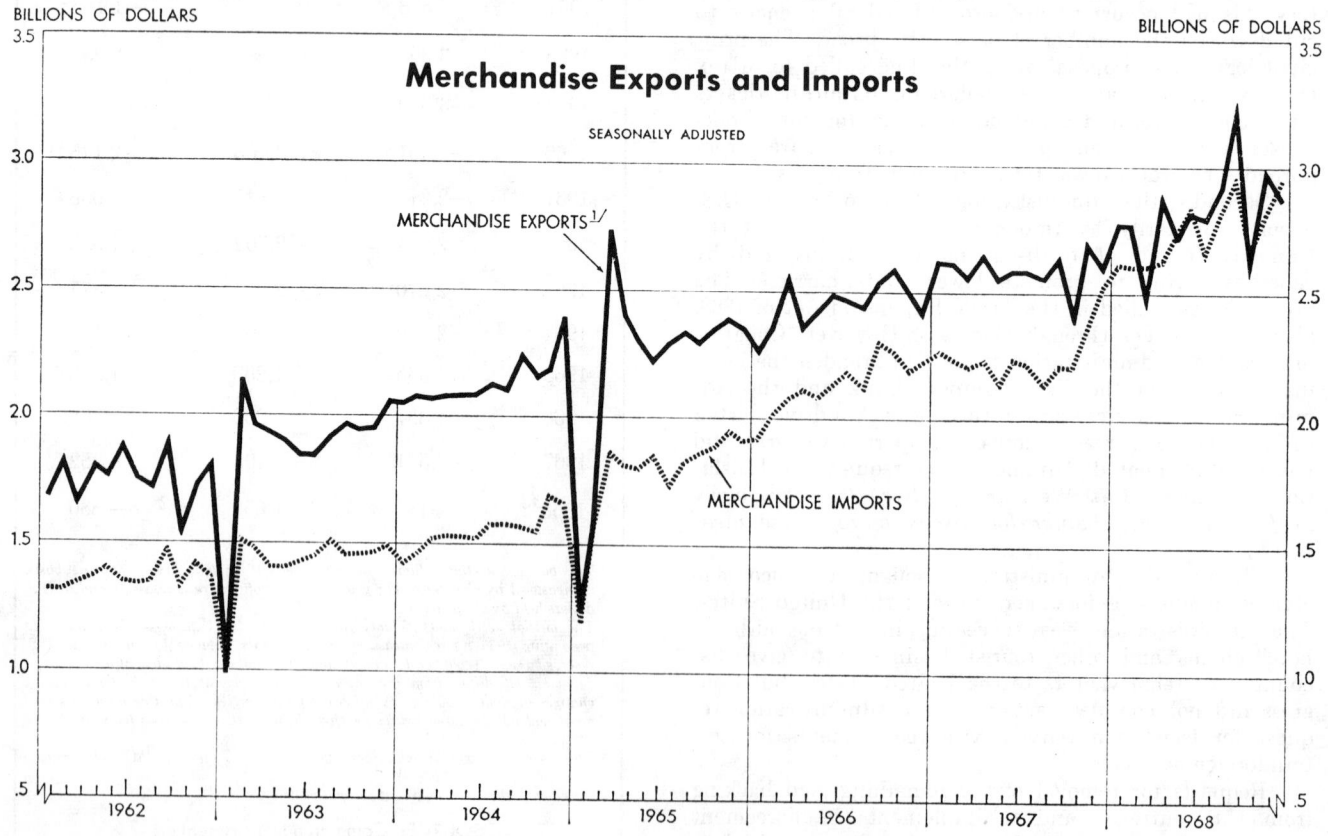

BILLIONS OF DOLLARS

BILLIONS OF DOLLARS

Merchandise Exports and Imports

SEASONALLY ADJUSTED

MERCHANDISE EXPORTS [1]

MERCHANDISE IMPORTS

1962   1963   1964   1965   1966   1967   1968

1 *Total excludes Department of Defense shipments of grant aid military supplies and equipment under the Military Assistance Program.*   COUNCIL OF ECONOMIC ADVISERS

BILLIONS OF DOLLARS   BILLIONS OF DOLLARS

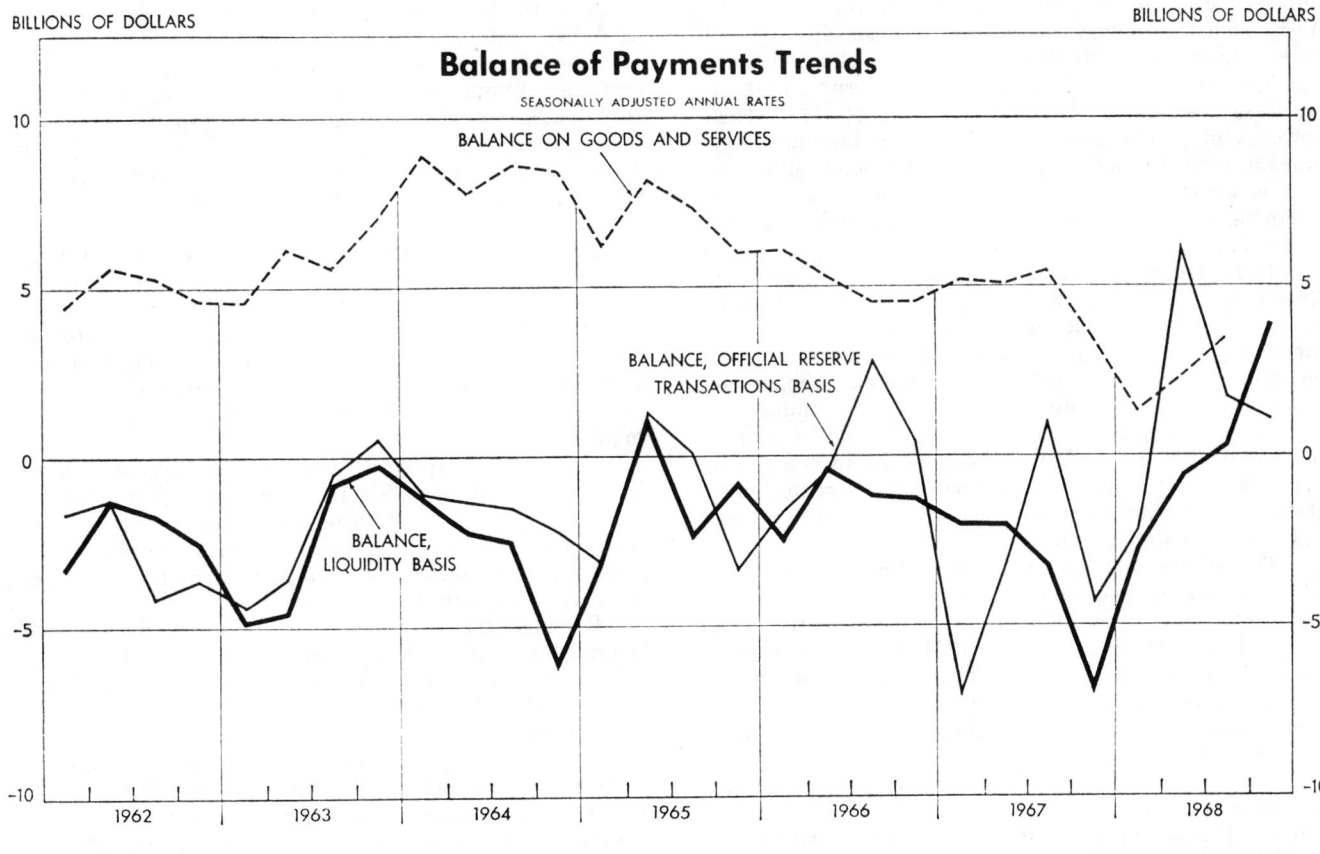

Balance of Payments Trends
SEASONALLY ADJUSTED ANNUAL RATES

BALANCE ON GOODS AND SERVICES

BALANCE, OFFICIAL RESERVE TRANSACTIONS BASIS

BALANCE, LIQUIDITY BASIS

1962   1963   1964   1965   1966   1967   1968

SOURCE: DEPARTMENT OF COMMERCE   COUNCIL OF ECONOMIC ADVISERS

Exclusions. The regulations did not place limitations on current transactions involving goods or services; purchases of portfolio securities when the purchaser's interest was less than 10 percent; direct and annual investments of less than $100,000; or banks in the Federal Reserve foreign credit restraint program.

Proposal. The President directed the Secretary of the Treasury to explore with the chairmen of the House Ways and Means Committee and the Senate Finance Committee the feasibility of legislative proposals to induce or encourage the repatriation of accumulated earnings by U.S.-owned foreign businesses. However, the Administration later decided against requesting legislation on the matter.

Estimated Savings. $1 billion.

Industrial Development Bonds

Industrial development bonds were depression-spawned lures for small industry in rural areas that mushroomed into a nationwide device for cutting factory construction costs. They became an issue in several bills before Congress in 1968. Treasury Department efforts to end the tax-exemption on interest from the bonds led to a Congressional reaction that lasted from spring to fall. In the end, Congress itself limited the size of a bond issue on which interest would be tax exempt. In most cases, the maximum size of a tax-exempt issue would be $1 million, but provision was made for a $5-million ceiling if certain conditions were met; in addition, neither ceiling applied if the bond money was used for certain specified purposes.

Background. Industrial development bonds, also known as industrial revenue bonds, were developed in 1936 in Mississippi as a means to attract industrial concerns to rural areas which had a surplus labor supply and whose residents had low incomes. Use of such bonds spread slowly at first; by 1950 only one other state, Kentucky, in addition to Mississippi authorized the bonds. But in the 1950s, spurred by a 1954 Treasury ruling that interest from the bonds was exempt from federal income tax, 21 other states authorized them. By 1968, 42 states authorized the bonds; and in some other states where they were not authorized outright, similar industrial financing techniques were in use.

How They Worked—Typically, the bonds were issued under the name of a state or local government. Funds from the sale of the bonds normally would be used to construct a facility, such as a factory, that could be used by a private company. In turn, a corporation paid "rent" for the factory at a rate calculated to meet the interest payments on the bonds and to amortize the principal of the bonds. Because of the tax exemption, the bonds could be sold about 1 percent cheaper than normal corporate bonds. The usual results were that the state or community got a new industry (with increased employment and business), the industry got a new plant at a reduced cost and high-income taxpayers who bought the bonds got some tax-free income.

Reaction—As use of the bonds increased, so did criticism of them. Opponents, who included such diverse interests as organized labor and the Investment Bankers Assn., said the bonds were a taxpayers' subsidy for private industry, were driving up the costs of tax-exempt municipal bond issues and were aiding corporations instead of the intended beneficiary—the state or local government. Supporters, mainly state industrial development officials and a segment of the bond-selling industry, denied the opponents' claims and asserted that removing the tax exemption would slow industrial development in poorer, rural areas.

1968 Developments. The Treasury Department in 1968 acted as a catalyst for the growing opposition to the continued tax exemption. In January, it recommended passage of legislation to end the tax exemption on industrial development bonds. In early March, it announced that it was going to issue regulations ending the tax exemption (which it had the power to do). Congress reacted swiftly, partly to the possibility of an end to the tax exemption and partly to the Treasury's effort to change the tax laws by administrative action. Most of the protest in Congress centered in the Senate.

The Senate took three roll calls on the issue in March while considering two separate bills. On each roll call, the Senate took a somewhat different position on the issue than it had on the previous roll call. It finally agreed on a position and added a rider to the income tax surcharge bill (HR 15414) to—in general—end the tax exemption on bond issues over $1 million issued after May 1, 1968. *(See below for exact provision.)*

That is where the issue rested until September when an effort was made to ease the restriction imposed in HR 15414. In acting on another unrelated bill (HR 17324), extending the life of the Renegotiation Board, the Senate added a rider to raise the limit on tax-exempt bonds to $5 million. This was accepted by a 37-34 roll call, the fourth of the year on the issue. Senate supporters of the higher ceiling said the $1-million figure was unrealistic. They were supported by a number of Senators from states where communities had made extensive use of the bonds to attract industry.

In conference, however, the existing $1-million ceiling was retained, but conferees allowed a community to elect to use a $5-million ceiling if it were willing to work within certain restrictions. The key restriction specified that the $5-million figure had to include any tax-exempt bonds issued plus any other capital expenditures which the company benefitting from the bonds made within the borders of the governmental unit issuing the bonds. The purpose was to prevent a company from paying the costs of, say, a $20-million plant partly from a tax-exempt $5-million bond issue and partly from other sources of revenue, such as its own savings or a taxable bond issue of its own. A company also could not build one plant from tax-exempt bonds issued by the community and another plant within the same community from other funds.

The conference agreement on the issue specified that the $5-million ceiling would apply for a six-year period beginning three years before the tax-exempt bonds were issued and ending three years after they were issued. The three-year period following issue meant that a bond issue which originally was tax exempt could lose that status if the company later invested additional money in the area which pushed total capital expenditures above the $5-million ceiling. However, if this happened the in-

terest on the bonds was to become taxable only as of the time the $5-million limit was exceeded.

The basic purpose of the provision was to assure that tax-exempt industrial revenue bonds were used only to assist small businesses in locating in a community. In explaining the agreement, Rep. Wilbur D. Mills (D Ark.) said the $5-million provision in the conference report would continue to provide tax-free interest on about 87 percent of the industrial development bond issues.

Provisions. Following are the provisions on tax-exempt industrial bonds which appeared in HR 15414—PL 90-364 and HR 17324—PL 90-634.

HR 15414, enacted June 28. Ended the existing tax exemption on the interest from industrial development bonds issued on or after May 1, 1968, if the issue exceeded $1 million. (The tax exemption was to remain for smaller issues.)

Provided exemptions from the new taxable status for bonds issued for residential property for family units, sports facilities, convention or trade show facilities, various types of transportation facilities, certain public utility facilities, air or water pollution abatement facilities and facilities for industrial parks.

Provided that if substantial steps had been taken before May 1, 1968, on a project to be financed with an industrial development bond issue, the bonds were not to be taxable unless issued after Jan. 1, 1969.

HR 17324, enacted Oct. 24. Provided an alternative to the existing $1-million limit on the size of an industrial development bond issue on which the interest would be exempt from federal income tax, as follows:

● Specified that a community could elect to issue industrial revenue bonds for use by a private concern up to a level of $5 million without the interest on the bonds being taxable.

● Required, however, that if a community elected to use the higher figure, the $5-million ceiling had to cover the bonds issued by the community for the concern plus any capital expenditures financed from other sources by that concern within that community for a six-year period beginning three years before and ending three years after the bonds were issued.

Interstate Taxation

The House, but not the Senate, passed a bill (HR 2158) to establish uniform limitations on the power of states to tax small out-of-state firms doing business within their boundaries. The House action came May 22 by a 286-89 roll-call vote. It was spurred by small-business pressure and came more than a year after the House Judiciary Committee reported the bill March 7, 1967, and almost ten months after it was granted a rule. The latter delay was particularly unusual; bills which have sufficient support for passage generally are brought to the floor within a month after receiving a rule.

The purpose of HR 2158 was to set uniform jurisdictional standards to determine when a business was subject to taxation in a state where it did business and to provide a uniform federal formula to determine the percentage of income or capital taxable in each state in which liability was found. Supporters of HR 2158 said the bill would, by simplifying tax compliance, stimulate multistate business and result in increased overall tax revenues to the states. Opponents, largely state tax administrators, called it an invasion of states rights and said it would result in reduced state revenues.

During 1967, state tax administrators pushed for approval of a "Multistate Tax Compact" as an alternative to HR 2158. While the Compact provided co-operative interstate machinery to apportion taxable income of interstate businesses, it did not include the restrictions of HR 2158 on taxation of small interstate businesses. Fifteen states had approved the Compact by the May 22 House passage of HR 2158.

Major Provisions. As passed by the House, HR 2158 contained the following major provisions:

Business Location Standard. Established a uniform federal standard for determing circumstances under which a company might be subjected to tax of its interstate business. No state was permitted to impose a corporate net income tax, capital stock tax or gross receipts tax on a business earning less than $1 million average federal net taxable income unless that business (1) owned or leased realty within the state; (2) had at least one employee whose service was performed entirely within the state (except for incidental out-of-state service) and whose duties were more than taking orders; or (3) regularly maintained in the state an inventory for sale in its "ordinary course of...business." Sales or use taxes by states were prohibited unless a business met one of the above three criteria for the income tax *or* unless it made regular house deliveries within the state.

Exemptions. Provided specific exemptions from the business locations formula (thus allowing continuation of existing taxation procedures) with regard to transportation companies, insurance firms, banks and other financial institutions, utilities, companies receiving income in the form of dividends, interest or certain royalties, certain foreign and domestic holding companies, and firms of any kind whose average annual income for federal taxation purposes was in excess of $1 million.

Solicitation of Orders. Broadened the PL 86-272 provision prohibiting imposition of a net income tax on persons soliciting orders for acceptance and filling out-of-state to provide the same prohibition on imposition of capital stock, sales, and use, and gross receipts taxes.

Optional Tax Apportionment Formulas. Gave businesses liable for state income or capital stock taxes and earning less than $1 million average federal net taxable income the option of computing state income or capital stock tax liability (1) in accordance with a federal formula based on two factors, payroll and property; or (2) in accordance with the various existing state formulas based on three factors: payroll, property and sales. No business, however, could be obligated to pay a tax greater than that calculated under the two-factor federal formula.

Other Provisions. Also prohibited states from: (1) requiring any covered business or taxpayer to pay costs of a state audit on interstate business operations; (2) imposing discriminatory sales or gross receipts taxes against out-of-state sellers; and (3) charging a back liability for companies which would not be liable for state taxes subsequent to enactment of the bill.

Continuing Study. Directed the House Judiciary Committee and Senate Finance Committee to conduct, jointly or separately, a continuing study of state taxation of interstate commerce and to propose further remedial measures if substantial progress was not made within four years of the bill's enactment.

FEDERAL SPENDING, JOB CUTS

Congress Fell Short of Tax Bill Goals

Federal spending and employment limitations in the 1968 tax surcharge bill apparently were only partially successful in actually curbing Government spending and employment. *(For story on tax surcharge-spending cuts, see p. 167.)*

Though Congress exceeded the target of $10 billion in reductions in new budget authority (NBA) by about $2.5 billion, it cut only between $3.5 billion and $3.9 billion of the $6-billion spending cut called for in the surcharge bill. The $6-billion goal was established by a fiscal 1969 spending ceiling in the tax bill of $180-billion, compared with January Budget estimates of $186-billion.

NBA was made up of appropriations requests (new obligational authority) and requests for lending authority. No breakdown was yet available on what portion of the $12.5-billion cut was in appropriations and what portion was in lending authority. At least $2.7 billion in authority to issue participations certificates would be included in the latter, however.

How Cutbacks Worked

The Budget Bureau June 28 issued guidelines for implementing the employment controls, three days before they went into effect July 1. Each agency head was made responsible for implementing the controls in his agency. Appointments were not to exceed 75 percent of separations due to resignations, retirements, removals or deaths. The agency head was permitted to fill vacancies, including new positions for new or increasing workloads, without regard to specific positions vacated. (For example, three nurses could be hired for vacancies left by two statisticians and two typists.) Effective Sept. 1, the Budget Bureau allowed only 70 percent of the vacancies to be filled. The balance of five percent of the vacancies was to revert to the Budget Bureau for distribution as needed.

Anticipating attempts to circumvent the controls, the Budget Director prohibited agencies from contracting with outside firms and institutions for personnel services. In addition, agencies were barred from making wholesale substitutions of part-time employees for full-time employees by another provision of the tax bill which limited part-time employment to the level for the corresponding month of calendar 1967.

Each agency was to report monthly to the Budget Bureau on the number of its full-time permanent civilian employees and to report quarterly to the Bureau on the savings realized from the employment controls. In turn, the Director of the Budget was to report quarterly to Congress on the operation of the employment controls.

Total spending would be calculated by adding the estimated spending under NBA, the estimated amount which was to be spent to liquidate contracts entered into in previous years and the amount of previously appropriated but unspent funds which were to be spent. Reductions from Budget estimates could be made in the first two areas but no breakdown was available.

Congress also allowed approximately $5.9 billion in exemptions from the spending ceiling. In addition, it granted an outright "protection" to $3.5 billion education spending.

Congress also exempted a number of agencies from the employment limitations so that in late 1968, approximately one-third of the full-time, permanent civilian Executive Branch employees were exempt from the limitations. The rest of the employees exceeded the target level by about 100,000.

Though it did not formally ask for any of the exemptions to the spending and employment restrictions, the Administration favored all of them except possibly the education protection and the exemption from the spending ceiling of $91 million for school aid to areas "impacted" by federal employment.

A special CQ vote study showed that 53 Senators who voted for the spending and employment limitations (which were part of an amendment to the tax bill adding the 10-percent surcharge) voted for one or more exemptions to the restrictions. The restrictions, which were opposed by the Administration, were accepted by many Members of Congress (and the Administration) as the price for the surcharge.

Accounting for the specific reductions in NBA and estimated spending were difficult, because different groups cited figures that were at least partially contradictory. The figures were compiled by the Joint Committee on the Reduction of Federal Expenditures, the House Appropriations Committee and the Bureau of the Budget.

Both Congressional committees agreed that Congress reduced NBA by $12.5 billion. The Budget Bureau accepted the Committees' figure. But in calculating an estimate of reduced spending (based on reduction in NBA), the two Committees said spending was to be reduced by $3.9 billion, while the Budget Bureau said the reduction would be $3.5 billion. The $400-million difference was caused mainly by differences in accounting interpretations. For example, there were disagreements in estimating spending reductions stemming from cuts in the fiscal 1969 defense appropriations bill and the second supplemental appropriations for fiscal 1968 (since most of the fiscal 1968 supplemental appropriations would lead to spending in fiscal 1969).

Appropriations-Spending Cuts

Congress more than met its responsibility in reducing new budget authority (NBA) and did better than expected in cutting fiscal 1969 spending, according to a staff report of the Joint Committee on Reduction of Federal Expenditures.

The Committee said Congress cut NBA by $12.5 billion and fiscal 1969 spending by $3.9 billion. The Bureau of the Budget concluded that the spending cuts made by Congress totaled about $3.5 billion but emphasized the tentative nature of such estimates. Fiscal 1969 spending figures were not to be complete until some time in fiscal 1970, the Bureau said.

Congress also voted exemptions from the spending ceiling amounting to an estimated $5.9 billion. The exemptions, in effect, raised the ceiling to $186 billion (a combination of the $180.1-billion spending ceiling in the tax bill and the $5.9-billion in exemptions), and Administration spending estimates for fiscal 1969 in November 1968 were set in the area of $185 billion.

However, the $1-billion cushion could prove to be more apparent than real, because of the possibility of unforeseen changes in authorized spending. As a result, the Administration was to earmark spending which could be cut to reach the original $6-billion level.

NBA Reductions. The largest cut in new Budget authority came in the defense appropriations bill (PL 90-580) and amounted to $5.2 billion. It included $1 billion for operation and maintenance and $213 million for a project to equip Polaris missile-carrying submarines with Poseidon missiles.

Another major reduction came in the independent offices-Department of Housing and Urban Development appropriations bill (PL 90-550). Congress cut NBA by $3.1 billion, $1.6 billion of that in participation certificates (PCs).

Agriculture and related agencies were cut by $1.4 billion, including $425 million in PCs, and foreign aid was pared by $1.2 billion.

The total NBA reductions made in appropriations bills was an estimated $13.3 billion, but NBA was increased in several other bills making spending authorizations, leading to a net reduction in NBA of $12.5 billion. Those bills reducing NBA and the amounts by which it was reduced were: the Treasury appropriations bill, $179.2 million; the Interior appropriations bill, $147.4 million; the State-Justice-Commerce appropriations bill, $305.3 million; the Public Works appropriations bill, $300.2 million; the Labor-Health, Education and Welfare appropriations bill, $636.7 million; the Legislative Branch, $10.7 million; the Transportation appropriations bill, $207.8 million; military construction, $273 million; and the first supplemental appropriations bill of 1969, $294 million.

PC Requests Denied. Following is a description of Administration requests for authority to sell participation certificates in fiscal 1969, and the Congressional cuts made in the requests:

Department of Housing and Urban Development—$1.595 billion, including $1.205 billion for the FNMA's own PCs, $80 million for public facility PCs, $285 million for college housing and $25 million for housing for the elderly. The requests were contained in the Independent Office-HUD appropriations bill. Also cut in the bill was a request for authority to sell $515 million PCs backed by Veterans Administration loans. Congress did agree to appropriate directly the $25 million for housing for the elderly.

Small Business Administration—$150 million. The request was contained in the State-Justice-Commerce appropriations bill.

Farmers Home Administration—$425 million. The request was contained in the Agriculture appropriations bill.

Spending Cuts. The Defense Department also took the biggest slice in estimated spending, $1.9 billion. Other reductions expected to come as a result of cuts in NBA were Independent Offices-HUD, $373 million; Agriculture, $339 million; foreign aid, $215 million; Interior $103 million; Labor-HEW, $166 million; Legislative Branch, $10.9 million; military construction, $35 million; public works and atomic energy, $178 million; State-Justice-Commerce, $85 million; Transportation, $254 million; Treasury-Post Office-Executive Office, $129 million; Second Supplemental of 1968, $301.8 million; First Supplemental of 1969, $187.5 million.

The District of Columbia appropriations bill actually increased estimated spending by $3.9 million over the January estimates. The increase came because Congress hiked the federal payment to the District to $90 million from $70 million.

Cuts in appropriations bills produced a reduction of an estimated $4.2 billion in fiscal 1969 spending but a dozen other bills containing authorizations to spend led to increased spending which cut the effective reductions to approximately $3.9 billion, according to the Joint Committee on Reduction of Federal Expenditures.

Exemptions. Congress exempted $5.9 billion in estimated spending from the spending ceiling in the Williams-Smathers amendment. Several exemptions to the spending ceiling were made by Congress, some in the tax bill itself and others in later bills. In addition, a "sense-of-Congress" provision in the Federal Aid Highway Act (PL 90-495) made it clear Congress would look with disfavor upon meeting the spending ceiling by permanently withholding highway trust funds for specific projects.

The tax bill exempted from the $180.1-billion spending ceiling the amounts by which four categories of expenditures exceeded the January Budget estimates. Those categories (and the spending exempted) were defense spending for Vietnam ($2.3 billion), interest on the public debt ($900 million), veterans benefit payments ($400 million) and payments from Social Security trust funds ($700 million).

The first fiscal 1969 supplemental appropriations bill (PL 90-608) exempted up to $907 million in Commodity Credit Corp. (CCC) farm subsidy payments and up to $560 million in public assistance (including medicaid) payments.

A controversial $91 million for aid to schools in areas with high concentrations of children from federally employed families was exempted in the Labor-Health, Education and Welfare appropriations bill (PL 90-557). The Administration had been reluctant to release funds for impacted areas aid, while Congress, especially the Senate, insisted the funds be released. The President Oct. 24 announced the full amount would be released.

In addition, a "protection" for about $3.5 billion in education funds was included in an amendment to the vocational education bill (PL 90-576). In effect, the amendment protected approximately $3.5 billion of education funds. Like an exemption, the "protection" for education funds freed education funds from cuts designed to lower Government spending, but unlike an exemption, spending on education programs still was to be counted as a part of total federal spending.

Employment Limits

The employment limit imposed by the tax bill, unlike the spending ceiling, was permanent and was not to expire at the end of fiscal 1969. When the employment limits became effective July 1, the Administration was faced with the task of reducing full-time, permanent civilian employment by approximately 245,000 to reduce the total to the June 1966 level of 2,366,317.

Soon after the employment restrictions went into effect, the first of a growing list of Executive Branch agencies and departments began seeking exemptions.

Exemptions Granted. Approximately 519,000 Post Office positions were exempted in a bill dealing with assaults on postal workers (PL 90-449), and most Federal Aviation Administration (FAA) employees were exempted in the Transportation Department appropriations bill (PL 90-464).

The omnibus rivers and harbors bill (PL 90-483) exempted most employees of the Tennessee Valley Authority.

The State-Justice-Commerce appropriations bill (PL 90-470) carried an amendment exempting the FBI.

The Defense Department appropriations bill (PL 90-580) exempted up to 150,000 permanent positions in Southeast Asia.

A special type of exemption was granted the Veterans Administration in an amendment to a bill (HR 3593—PL 90-612) to permit partial payment by the Government of nursing home costs of veterans in Alaska and Hawaii. The VA was one of the few agencies which was below the June 1966 level; it was allowed to fill all vacancies until it came up to the ceiling.

Exemptions Denied. Attempts were made to exempt several additional departments and agencies from the employment ceiling, but they were not successful.

Sen. John J. Sparkman (D Ala.) Sept. 23 offered an amendment to a tax bill (HR 2767) to exempt the Department of Housing and Urban Development, the Social Security Administration (SSA), the Division of Indian Health, the Federal Home Loan Bank Board, the Internal Revenue Service and the Tax Court. The amendment was defeated, but the SSA exemption was added to the bill in an amendment by Sen. Russell B. Long (D La.). HR 2767 was not enacted.

Sen. William Proxmire (D Wis.) Sept. 9 tried to exempt the Renegotiation Board from the ceiling, but his amendment to a bill extending the Renegotiation Act (PL 90-364) was defeated.

Exemptions for U.S. attorneys and marshals were deleted from the State-Justice-Commerce appropriations bill.

The House July 11 passed a bill (S 3293) which included a House Armed Services Committee amendment to exempt Navy shipyards from the cutback, but the provision was dropped by conferees.

Employment Pool. One unsuccessful proposal (HR 18985) would have created a 14,000-man employment pool outside the ceiling which the Budget Director could spread around to various agencies. The bill July 31 was reported (H Rept 1832) by the Ways and Means Committee but did not come to the floor for consideration.

A pool of sorts, however, was set up by the Budget Bureau. The tax bill allowed agencies to fill 75 percent of their vacancies until the June 1966 level was met. But Budget Director Zwick said that effective Sept. 1, only 70 percent of the vacancies could be filled. The balance of 5 percent of the vacancies would revert to the Budget Bureau for distribution as needed.

Housing Policy

CONGRESS in the Johnson years enacted four major housing bills. The bills, which became law in 1965, 1966 and 1968, together constituted the most far-reaching achievements in housing and urban development in decades. They were in part a reaction to the crisis that was developing in the nation's deteriorating cities. They were also an indication of Congressional concern for the cities in spite of widespread criticism that most lawmakers neither understood nor cared about urban problems. However, Congress consistently refused to fund the major new programs at anywhere near the maximum levels authorized in the basic laws.

A characteristic of the programs established during this period was a primary concern for low-income Americans and the declining urban areas in which many of these people lived. Much of the national housing effort in the past had been directed at providing adequate homes for millions of Americans who had been uprooted by the Depression and World War II. Some of the biggest Government programs were intended for this purpose (for example, the Federal Housing Administration's mortgage insurance activities). The legislation of the 1960s, particularly the bills enacted from 1966 to 1968, created new methods to assist cities and poor persons.

IN the Johnson years, two of the bills became law in 1965. One of them authorized rent supplements to help poor persons who could not afford decent housing on their own incomes. The second bill established a Department of Housing and Urban Development to give Cabinet-level status to the Government's housing activities and to bring increased importance to federal efforts to solve urban problems. A third law, enacted in 1966, established a model cities program which was intended to pump extra federal funds into needy cities. The fourth law was enacted in 1968 and was designed to promote home ownership by the poor. (In addition, Congress in 1968 enacted a civil rights law which prohibited discrimination in the sale or rental of about 80 percent of the nation's housing. This measure is discussed in the chapter on civil rights.)

The housing bills of 1965 and 1966 were highly controversial. In contrast, the 1968 measure had surprisingly widespread backing—considering the divisions that arose over the earlier bills—and was enacted with little controversy. The central programs of the 1965 and 1966 laws, rent supplements and model cities, were vigorously opposed by Republicans and conservative Democrats. Although they were unable to prevent adoption of the programs, they succeeded fairly well in keeping funding at a low level. The Department of Housing issue had been controversial ever since President Kennedy proposed it early in his term of office.

RENT supplements were the most controversial of all the Johnson housing proposals. It was a key Great Society proposal which, as enacted, authorized the Government to contract with local housing sponsors (which had to be either nonprofit service groups or limited-dividend or cooperative housing organizations) to pay the difference between 25 percent of a poor person's income and his rent in standard housing.

The major argument for rent supplements was that the public housing program alone had not been able to accommodate a large enough portion of the nation's poor and that the rent supplements concept was vastly superior to public housing. Proponents also argued that public housing offered essentially a ghetto existence because it was limited to low-income persons. The supplements program, however, placed subsidized tenants in standard housing with nonsubsidized, higher-income families and gave the former an incentive to increase their income. In public housing, a tenant had to give up his dwelling when his income exceeded a certain level. Another key argument in favor of rent supplements was that the role of private enterprise in sponsoring the projects provided a distinct advantage over local-government sponsorship of public housing.

Opponents of the program characterized it as a "socialistic giveaway." They also contended it would be very costly (the contracts were to run for 40 years) and that it was particularly indefensible to fund the plan at a time when Vietnam war costs were mounting. Perhaps the most important factor working against supplements was that numerous Members of Congress disliked taxing one person to pay another's rent. The racial issue also appeared to play a part. Although it never surfaced in Congressional debate, many Members and employees of Congress said privately that fear that rent supplements might contribute to racially integrated housing had been a major factor in the persistent opposition of numerous Members.

Reference

Housing programs in the period from World War II through 1964 are discussed in *Congress and the Nation, Vol. I, pp. 459-515.*

The model cities program, known at the time of enactment as "demonstration cities," was as important a part of the Great Society concept of President Johnson as was rent supplements. It authorized special federal grants to urban areas for a coordinated attack on blight that would tackle social problems as well as such physical problems as substandard housing. Participating cities were to receive federal grants equal to as much as 80 percent of the financial contribution they were required to make (under existing law) as their share of federally assisted programs included in a model cities plan. The grant funds were to be spent first to finance any new or existing program in the plan which did not receive other federal aid. If any funds remained they were to be used to help pay costs of the local contribution required under the federally assisted programs. The legislation envisioned a restructuring of the total environment of model city neighborhoods. By authorizing additional federal funds which could be used for education, antipoverty and similar social programs, the bill sought to attack the human problems as well as the physical factors causing blight and decay.

The major argument in favor of the program was that the nation's urban areas were desperately in need of a massive attack on blight and that this could be accomplished only through the comprehensive and coordinated federal and local effort contemplated under the cities plan. In addition, proponents argued, the needed therapy could not be accomplished without treating the sociological factors causing decay. The emphasis of traditional urban renewal on removing the physical factors simply was not enough, they said. Opponents contended that the plan could have a substantial effect only if far more federal funds were committed than the level authorized in the legislation. Consequently, they asserted, once the program got started it would mushroom into a multi-billion-dollar commitment.

The model cities program, however, was not as controversial as rent supplements. It had the warm backing of various city officials and housing groups which rent supplements never enjoyed.

BY the time President Johnson left office in 1969, both programs were reasonably well established and were expected to survive. However, even after the precariously close votes on enactment of the basic authorizations, Congress threatened several times to deny funds to implement the programs. Funds were provided but at much lower levels than was authorized. Rent supplements payments were authorized in the basic law at a maximum level of $150 million between fiscal 1966 and 1969, but the Congressional Appropriations Committees, through provisions in their bills, limited the total amount of supplements contracts during the period to $72 million. The lower figure resulted in part from the problems of getting a new program under way; it was questionable whether the Administration could have used the full $150 million authority had it been allowed by the Appropriations Committees. But a much more important reason was the continuing basic opposition in Congress to the entire supplements program. Model cities funding also was off to a slow start in the first two years of the program, fiscal 1968 and 1969, but it was cut less seriously than the supplements program. *(See box on facing page.)* However, the trend for both was encouraging for

their supporters. The funding bills for both programs were put to repeated votes in each session of Congress until 1968; the votes were particularly close in the House where opposition was strongest. But in 1968, funding for both programs went through with relatively little controversy, indicating that they were well on their way toward acceptance. In addition, the 1968 housing bill increased the basic authorization for both programs without creating much controversy.

THE 1968 housing bill was the largest of any enacted during the Johnson period. It contained 17 titles which covered not only housing but also a variety of related activities including interstate land sales, mass transit, and flood insurance. The basic part of the 1968 legislation was directed at home ownership and rental assistance.

Proposals to help low-income families obtain their own homes had received much attention in Congress in 1967. Many bills were introduced, including several major pieces sponsored by Republicans. A home ownership bill was reported but not passed. The Administration had not taken a position on the legislation. The interest in the proposals continued in 1968 and the Johnson Administration, which had been trailing on the issue in 1967, embraced the concept and recommended its own bill. The various proposals eventually were woven together in the mammoth bill that was enacted with surprisingly little difficulty.

The home ownership plan was designed to enable low-income families to purchase their own homes by providing a federal subsidy that could lower the interest cost of the purchaser's mortgage. The subsidy would amount to the difference between 20 percent of the family's monthly income and required monthly payments under the mortgage for principal, interest, taxes, insurance and mortgage insurance premiums. Generally, the program was limited to families with income of $3,000 to $6,500 annually, but exceptions were possible for high-cost areas and for very large families. The plan was expected to help 500,000 families in the following three years. For families that rent, the new program provided indirect subsidies. Nonprofit sponsors of apartment projects would receive a Government subsidy on the interest on their mortgages. The sponsors, in turn, were to pass the savings on to low-income families in the form of lower rents.

Other programs in the 1968 law included: federal underwriting of private insurance against riot losses; a new Federal Housing Administration fund to provide special risk mortgage insurance for low-income persons who cannot meet conventional credit standards; a short-term urban renewal program for neighborhood development programs that were to be carried out on an annual basis; and creation of National Housing Partnerships to work with local builders in providing housing for low and moderate-income families.

The bill also provided prospective land purchasers a measure of protection from fraud, broadened the lending powers of savings and loan institutions, authorized FHA mortgage insurance on vacation homes, established new programs of federal assistance for college housing and mortgage insurance for nonprofit hospitals and provided new spending authorizations for the existing model cities and rent supplements programs.

Chronology

Of Legislation

On Housing

1965

Department of Housing

The Federal Government's role in housing was given Cabinet-level importance in 1965 when Congress—after several years of controversy—established a Department of Housing and Urban Development (HUD). The 1965 legislation (HR 6927;PL 89-174) established the first new department headed by a Cabinet member since the Department of Health, Education and Welfare was created in 1953. (A second new department—Transportation—was to be created during President Johnson's term. *(See Economic Policy, subchapter on transportation policy.)*

Both President Kennedy and President Johnson each year from 1961 to 1964 unsuccessfully proposed creation of a housing department. HUD as established by PL 89-174 was essentially the same as the departments proposed earlier by Mr. Kennedy and Mr. Johnson.

PL 89-174 provided for the establishment of HUD under a Secretary of Housing and Urban Development, appointed by the President with Senate confirmation. The Secretary was given all the powers, functions and duties of the Housing and Home Finance Agency (HHFA) and its components. The HHFA consisted of an Office of the Administrator and five operating units: the Federal Housing Administration (FHA), the Public Housing Administration (PHA), the Federal National Mortgage Assn. (FNMA)—all three of which had specific authorization in law—and the Community Facilities Administration and the Urban Renewal Administration—both of which were administratively created within the HHFA without specific legal authorization. PL 89-174 transferred the FHA as an entity to HUD.

The legislation basically upgraded the existing HHFA (established in 1947) to Cabinet-level status. The new agency was not to administer all federal programs relating to cities and urban problems, although one section of PL 89-174 required a study of the functions of other agencies to determine if any should be transferred to HUD. Supporters of the legislation said PL 89-174 did not change in any substantive way the existing functions and powers of federal housing officials. Opponents said this was only technically true; they argued that a new Cabinet-level department was bound to seek new powers.

PL 89-174 did not attempt to define an urban area or to place a limitation on the size of communities which could benefit from any program handled by HUD, thus bringing both small towns and villages as well as large cities within the agency's scope.

HUD became the 11th Cabinet-level department at midnight Nov. 8, under a provision of the bill ordering it

Model Cities, Rent Supplements Funds

Although Congress enacted major new housing programs in the rent supplements and model cities bills, it did not fund either at anywhere near the authorized level.

Rent Supplements

The rent supplements program authorized the Government to contract with local housing authorities to pay a portion of the rent of a low-income person. The basic law specified that the aggregate contracts for such payments would be limited by appropriations acts, but the actual payments pursuant to the contracts could not exceed $30 million in fiscal 1966; the amount for payments would be increased by the sums shown in Col. 1 for the following fiscal years. Col. 3 shows the amount of contract authority actually granted in appropriations bills and Col. 5 shows the amounts appropriated to make payments under the contracts.

(in thousands of dollars)

Fiscal Year	Basic Authority for Payments [1]		Basic Authority for Contracts [2]		Appropriations for Payments
	Col. 1 Annual	Col. 2 Cumulative	Col. 3 Annual	Col. 4 Cumulative	Col. 5
1966	$30,000	$ 30,000	$12,000	$12,000	$ 100
1967	35,000	65,000	20,000	32,000	2,000
1968	40,000	105,000	10,000	42,000	5,000
1969	45,000	150,000	30,000	72,000	12,000
1970	40,000	190,000	(3)	(3)	(3)
1971	100,000	290,000	(3)	(3)	(3)

1 Contained in 1965 and 1968 omnibus housing laws.
2 Contained in annual appropriations bill.
3 For consideration by Congress in calendar 1969 and following years.

Model Cities

The 1966 model cities law authorized special federal grants *(shown in the middle columns below)* for a coordinated attack on urban blight. The law also authorized planning funds for the projects (left columns) and special urban renewal funds for use in model cities projects (right columns) which were in addition to the basic grants. In each of the three sets of figures, the left column is the amount authorized in the basic law, and the right figure is the actual funding provided in appropriations bills.

(in millions of dollars)

Fiscal Year	Planning		Grants		Urban Renewal	
	Author.	Appro.	Author.	Appro.	Author.	Appro.
1967	$12	$11				
1968	12	12	$ 400	$200.0	$600 [1]	$100.0
1969	12	—	500	312.5		312.5
1970	—	—	1,000	(2)	(2)	(2)

1 Urban renewal funds were authorized to be used for projects which were part of approved model city programs. The 1966 model cities law authorized $250 million for this purpose to be used in and after fiscal 1968. The 1968 housing law added $350 million to that amount for a total $600 million authorization for urban renewal funds.
2 This authorization was to be available for appropriation by Congress in calendar 1969.

created no later than 60 days following the President's approval of the legislation. President Johnson, however, postponed HUD's actual establishment until a special study group completed a report on the Government's role in solving urban problems. On Jan. 13, 1966, he appointed HHFA Administrator Robert C. Weaver as Secretary of HUD.

Background. In 1961, President Kennedy proposed legislation to create a Department of Urban Affairs and

Housing. He promised to make HHFA Administrator Weaver, a Negro, Secretary of the new Department. The bill was reported in both the House and the Senate, but in the Senate a leadership headcount found almost solid Southern Democratic and Republican opposition, ensuring defeat; as a result, the bill was not brought to a vote. In the House, the Rules Committee delayed the bill and in January 1962—by a 6-9 vote—refused to grant a rule for floor action, thus in effect killing the bill.

In response, President Kennedy, using his authority under the Reorganization Act of 1949, submitted Reorganization Plan No. 1 of 1962, proposing to create the Department. The Reorganization Act provided that the plan would take effect in 60 days unless opposed by a majority vote of either the House or the Senate. The House Feb. 21, 1962, rejected the reorganization plan when it adopted a resolution of disapproval by a 264-150 roll-call vote.

(The Reorganization Act of 1949 expired on June 1, 1963. In 1964, Congress extended the Act through June 1, 1965, but only after amending it to prohibit the President from creating a new executive department through use of a reorganization plan. The addition of the provision generally was believed to be a reaction to Mr. Kennedy's 1962 use of the law. In 1965, Congress again extended the 1949 Act, along with the restrictive 1964 provision, through Dec. 31, 1968.

President Kennedy in his 1963 Budget message and President Johnson in his 1964 omnibus housing and Budget messages called for legislation to create a new department of housing, but their requests received no action. In a "Message on the Cities," President Johnson March 2, 1965, called for a Department of Housing and Urban Development "to give greater force and effectiveness to our effort in the cities."

Legislative History. The controversy which had surrounded the housing department proposal in previous years had not subsided by 1965. Conservatives were still opposed and, on Senate and House roll-call votes, a majority of Republicans and Southern Democrats opposed HR 6927. However, the legislation was supported by numerous housing organizations.

The House acted first on the legislation, passing it June 16 by a key **217-184** roll-call vote. Prior to passage, the House rejected by a 141-259 roll call a motion to recommit the bill to the Government Operations Committee with instructions to report back a Republican substitute which would have established an Office of Urban Affairs and Community Development in the Executive Office of the President. Republicans argued that a new department would only give "status to the new Secretary and bureaucracy to be created" and would not give service, economy or efficiency. The GOP approach, they argued, would promote economy and "usefulness" by providing coordination of all Government programs having an impact on urban areas regardless of the department or agency which administered a particular program. Their argument carried little weight with the huge Democratic majority that dominated the 89th Congress; the vote breakdown on the recommittal motion was R 122-5; D 19-254 (ND 0-181; SD 19-73). On the key roll-call on passage it was R 9-118; D 208-66 (ND 170-10; SD 38-56).

The bill passed the Senate Aug. 11 with much less controversy. The roll call on passage was 57-33: R 10-19; D 47-14 (ND 39-2; SD 8-12).

There was one major difference between the House and Senate versions of the bill. The House version transferred the functions of the FHA to the Secretary and designated an Assistant Secretary to administer programs relating to the private mortgage market. The Senate version allowed the FHA to retain its separate identity in HUD under a commissioner appointed by the President and functioning under the supervision of the Secretary. Like the House version, the Senate bill also designated an Assistant Secretary to handle private mortgage market programs. The final bill retained the FHA as a separate entity in HUD under a Federal Housing Commissioner who also was designated an Assistant Secretary.

Provisions. As signed by the President, Sept. 9, 1965, HR 6927, the Department of Housing and Urban Development Act:

Declared that the welfare of the nation required, as a matter of national purpose, sound development of its communities and metropolitan areas. Found that establishment of an executive department was desirable to carry out such a purpose. Said such a department should assist the President in achieving maximum coordination and the best administration of federal programs affecting urban communities; encourage the solution of problems of housing, urban development and mass transportation through state, local and private action; encourage "maximum contributions that may be made by vigorous private home building and mortgage lending institutions" to housing and urban development; and provide for full and appropriate consideration of the needs and interests of the nation's communities.

Established a Department of Housing and Urban Development to be headed by a Secretary of Housing and Urban Development, appointed by the President with Senate confirmation.

Defined the Secretary's function as an adviser to the President with respect to federal programs and activities relating to housing and urban development.

Authorized an Under Secretary, four Assistant Secretaries and a General Counsel, all of whom would be appointed by the President with Senate confirmation; also authorized an Assistant Secretary for Administration, who would be appointed by the Secretary with approval of the President.

Transferred to the Secretary all the functions, powers and duties of the Housing and Home Finance Agency, Federal Housing Administration, Public Housing Administration and the Federal National Mortgage Assn.

Provided for retention of the Federal Housing Administration (FHA) as a separate entity within the new Department. Provided that the FHA would be headed by a Federal Housing Commissioner who would also be an Assistant Secretary. Designated the Commissioner, in addition to his duties as Assistant Secretary and head of the FHA, to administer all other departmental programs relating to the private mortgage market.

Authorized a Director of Urban Program Coordination, designated by the Secretary, to coordinate programs of various agencies of the Government which have "a major impact on community development." Stipulated that the Director, subject to the direction of the Secretary, would establish and maintain close liaison with the federal departments and agencies concerned and would consult with state, local and regional officials and consider their recommendations with respect to such programs.

Authorized the Secretary to provide technical assistance and information to aid state and local governments and to encourage coordinated planning by state and local governments. Authorized him to hold informal public hearings on federal and state development programs.

Directed the Secretary to encourage private enterprise to assume a maximum role in housing and urban development and to achieve the "fullest cooperation" with private enterprise in meeting departmental objectives.

Required the President to undertake a study of functions in other federal agencies that might be transferred to the new Department and to make recommendations to Congress. Stipulated that the outdoor recreation functions of the Department of the Interior could not be transferred or geographically limited without Congressional approval.

Authorized the Secretary to establish a working capital fund for operating various common administrative services in the Department. Provided that the fund would be financed through appropriations and charges against the agencies and offices in the Department for which services were performed.

Stipulated that the act would take effect 60 days from the date of enactment unless the President chose to put it into effect earlier by executive order.

Housing Act-Rent Supplements

At the same time Congress was considering a Department of Housing *(see above),* it also was moving toward enactment of the most far-reaching housing and urban development legislation since the landmark Housing Act of 1949.

The omnibus housing bill (HR 7984—PL 89-117) actually became law Aug. 10, a month earlier than the Housing Department legislation. Taken together, the two bills gave President Johnson the bulk of his housing requests in 1965.

Designed to provide a comprehensive plan of federal assistance over the four-year period of 1966-69, HR 7984 authorized an estimated $7.8 billion to fund a variety of new housing and urban development programs and to extend and broaden existing ones. One major new undertaking was an Administration proposal for federal rent supplements for families or individuals unable to afford standard private housing within their own incomes.

A major impetus for both the Housing Department and the omnibus housing bill came from the increasing demands for better planned and more attractive cities, orderly urban development, and adequate housing for low-income and impoverished individuals. President Johnson in his "Great Society" speech of May 22, 1964, had accorded urban development the role of one of the "three places where we begin to build the Great Society." *(See p. 188.)* In addition, many major existing housing programs were scheduled to expire in 1965.

The bill authorized major new federal efforts to provide good housing for the poor in other than traditional public housing. The major program was rent supplements; it was expected to encourage many private non-profit

Summary of 1965 Housing Bill

In its major provisions, HR 7984:

• Established a new program of rent supplements to low-income families who could not obtain standard housing within their own incomes.

• Extended or increased the funding of numerous housing programs, including ones for moderate-income families, low-rent public housing and direct loans for housing for the elderly. Broadened the public housing program to permit increased use of existing housing which, together with new construction, would provide an additional 60,000 units per year over a four-year period.

• Established a new program of Federal Housing Administration insurance of commercial loans for land development in neighborhoods and subdivisions.

• Authorized a new program of FHA insurance of low down-payment mortgages for veterans who had not already received Veterans Administration (VA) benefits.

• Extended existing FHA home mortgage insurance programs for four years, through Oct. 1, 1969.

• Extended the urban renewal program for four years, through Oct. 1, 1969, and provided an additional $2.9 billion authority for grants.

• Authorized expanded urban renewal code enforcement and rehabilitation activities in order to minimize demolition and clearance in these areas.

• Provided grants to low-income homeowners in urban renewal areas to help them repair their homes.

• Established uniform land acquisition procedures to be followed in connection with the acquisition of land by eminent domain under federally assisted urban development programs.

• Increased the authorization for college housing loans by $300 million a year over the following four years.

• Authorized a new program of matching grants to local public bodies for the construction of basic public water and sewer facilities.

• Authorized grants for up to two-thirds of the cost (three-quarters in some cases) of constructing neighborhood facilities, including health, recreational and community centers.

• Increased grants for open-space land acquisition and provided a new program of grants to provide open space for parks and playgrounds in built-up urban areas.

• Authorized grants to local public bodies to provide programs of urban beautification and improvement.

• Established a new program of insured housing loans for rural areas and broadened an existing loan program to allow persons in any age group to buy previously occupied dwellings, farm service buildings and adequate farm land. (Under existing law, such loans could be made only to elderly persons.)

'Great Society' Speech

Following is an excerpt from President Johnson's May 22, 1964, "Great Society" speech at the University of Michigan in Ann Arbor:

...Many of you will live to see the day, perhaps 50 years from now, when there will be 400 million Americans; four-fifths of them in urban areas. In the remainder of this century urban population will double, city land will double, and we will have to build homes, highways and facilities equal to all those built since this country was first settled. So in the next 40 years we must rebuild the entire urban United States.

Aristotle said, "Men come together in cities in order to live, but they remain together in order to live the good life."

It is harder and harder to live the good life in American cities today. The catalogue of ills is long: There is decay of the centers and the despoiling of the suburbs. There is not enough housing for our people or transportation for our traffic. Open land is vanishing and old landmarks are violated. Worst of all, expansion is eroding the precious and time-honored values of community with neighbors and communion with nature. The loss of these values breeds loneliness and boredom and indifference. Our society will never be great until our cities are great. Today the frontier of imagination and innovation is inside those cities, and not beyond their borders. New experiments are already going on. It will be the task of your generation to make the American city a place where future generations will come, not only to live but to live the good life.

groups to develop housing for low-income individuals who otherwise might seek public housing space. In addition, another provision of the bill authorized the use of federal funds to place low-income individuals in existing private housing at costs comparable to those for providing public housing. This was a modified Republican proposal.

The Administration's rent supplements proposal was the most publicized—and the most controversial— feature of the bill. President Johnson called the proposal "the most crucial new instrument in our effort to improve the American city." Under the provision, an individual was to pay 25 percent of his income for rent in private, non-profit housing and the Government was to pay the balance.

Who would be eligible to receive supplements was a major element in the controversy over the program. Eligibility standards underwent a basic change before the bill became law. The Administration originally proposed that the supplements be made available to persons with income too high to permit them to live in public housing but too low for them to pay rents necessary to obtain good private housing. The proposal specifically excluded persons eligible for public housing. The final bill, however, made eligible for supplements only persons who were also eligible for public housing. In addition, the final bill—as well as the Administration proposal—required a recipient to be either 62 years of age or older, physically

handicapped, displaced by governmental action (highway construction, etc.), or living in "substandard housing." *(See box p. 190.)*

The Administration agreed to the change in eligibility standards when it appeared that its original proposals were headed for defeat. The supplements concept had encountered immediate and sharp criticism from both Republicans and Democrats. In spite of the changes, a Republican move in the House to kill the supplements section was rejected by a narrow **202-208** key roll-call vote. In the Senate, a GOP-sponsored amendment to delete the program was defeated by seven votes. Later in the year, opponents of the program succeeded in blocking a supplemental appropriation to get the supplements program under way.

Housing officials figured that the supplements plan would stimulate the construction of 375,000 units of privately owned housing by 1969. This would compare with only 590,000 units of public housing constructed since that program's enactment in 1937 (HR 7984 authorized construction of an additional 240,000 public housing units during fiscal 1966 through 1969).

The controversy over rent supplements obscured the wide support that much of HR 7984 commanded in Congress. Any large controversies that might have developed over other major programs in the bill were sidetracked by the rent supplements debate.

The bill, in addition to the Administration proposals, embodied several GOP-sponsored programs, including low down-payment federal insurance of home mortgages for veterans, the leasing of existing housing for public housing use, and reduction of interest rates on various housing loan programs from their market-produced level to a flat 3 percent.

One major Administration proposal, which was not enacted was federal assistance to promote the development of entire new towns and new communities. The new towns proposal, which had been requested and turned down in 1964, again encountered opposition from many groups and support from virtually none. *(See 1966 chronology.)*

LEGISLATIVE HISTORY. President Johnson spelled out his housing requests in a March 2 message to Congress.

House Action

The major action on the Administration's requests occurred in the Housing Subcommittee of the Banking and Currency Committee. After hearings in April, the subcommittee May 7 approved a revised version of the Administration's bill. The full Committee reported HR 7984 on May 19; it made no changes in the Subcommittee's work.

Changes from Administration Bill. Following are the major changes made by the Subcommittee:

Rent Supplements. The Administration proposal was modified to permit rent supplements to be paid on behalf of a broader group of people than was possible under the Administration's draft bill. Under the committee proposal, an individual or a family was made eligible for a supplement if he or it was unable to obtain standard private housing at a rent which was equal to or less than one-fourth of his or its income. As in the Administration bill, an individual or family also had to be either displaced by governmental action, at least 62 years old, physically handicapped or occupying substandard housing. The primary effect of the committee change was to make low-income persons who were eligible for public housing also eligible for rent supplements. Persons who could obtain public housing were specifically excluded from supplement aid by the Administration's draft bill.

In addition, the Committee required any person receiving supplement aid to pay 25 percent of his income toward the rent of his dwelling unit; the Administration bill set the amount at 20 or 25 percent depending on whether he was just renting or renting with an option to purchase.

New Towns. A proposal for federal loans to states for land development and subsequent sale of the developed land to private builders was dropped. In addition, the Subcommittee limited FHA land development mortgage insurance to neighborhoods and subdivisions, lowered the ceiling on the amount of mortgages that could be insured in any one project from $25 million to $12.5 million and eliminated the proposal for $500 million in authority for the FNMA to purchase land development mortgages secured by new towns and new communities.

Water and Sewer Facilities. A proposal for grants to growing communities to cover 40 percent of projects for basic water and sewer facilities was broadened to cover all communities and the federal share was raised to 50 percent.

The Subcommittee added provisions for:

• Special FHA home mortgage insurance for veterans who had not already received a GI home loan. The single-family residence loans would cover 100 percent (no down-payment) of the first $20,000 and 85 percent of any additional amount up to a total mortgage of $30,000.

• A 3-percent interest rate on three programs—direct housing loans for the elderly, insured mortgage loans at below-market interest rates for low-and moderate-income families and displaced families, and college housing loans—providing in effect a 1-percent cut in the interest on these programs.

• Public housing authorities to lease existing private housing and make it available to low-income families at normal public housing charges. This was a modification of a GOP "rent certificate" plan under which families eligible for public housing could rent private housing and pay for it with certificates redeemable from public housing authorities.

• Uniform land acquisition procedures to be followed in connection with the acquisition of land by eminent domain under HHFA development programs.

Floor Action. When HR 7984 reached the House floor, it produced one of the biggest—and at times one of the most bitter—battles of the session. Republicans, who were strongly opposed to the rent supplements section, came within six votes of killing the subsidies proposal.

The House passed HR 7984 June 30 by a 245-169 roll call. The vote breakdown: R 26-109; D 219-60 (ND 176-8; SD 43-52).

HR 7984 was passed only after supporters of the bill altered the Administration's rent supplements formula and after the Republican attempt to kill the entire supplements plan was defeated.

Background

The postwar landmark in housing legislation was the Housing Act of 1949. It pronounced a national housing policy, provided for an annual housing census, revived and broadened the public housing program, established the controversial urban renewal program and established a large rural housing program. In later years, the 1949 Act was amended to meet new and special needs, such as aid for college housing (1950), sales housing for the elderly (1956) and rental housing for the elderly (1959). Special aid for public works in small communities was provided for in 1955. The 1961 Housing Act initiated programs for aid to middle-income housing, mass transportation and urban "open spaces" and substantially expanded existing programs to reduce urban blight and congestion and to improve housing for low-income groups.

Although the 1964 omnibus housing bill was called "bare-bones" and considered one which merely extended most housing programs into 1965, it included most of the Administration's proposals and a substantial part of the funds requested. It contained four important new programs: $10 million for construction of low-cost rental housing for domestic farm workers; $10 million in 50-50 matching grants to train local urban development administrators; $1.5 million over three years for graduate training fellowships in city planning and $50 million for low-interest loans to property owners in urban renewal areas to help rehabilitate their property and thereby avoid total demolition and reconstruction (a Republican proposal). The 1964 measure also provided for more ready capital by authorizing the Federal National Mortgage Assn. to pool its mortgages and sell interests in the pool to private investors. In addition, the 1964 bill added handicapped persons to the direct-loan, FHA insurance and public housing programs available to the elderly.

The compromise proposal on the rent section, which was sponsored by Robert G. Stephens Jr. (D Ga.), limited the payment of supplements to persons whose incomes were low enough to make them eligible for public housing. (Public housing eligibility standards varied throughout the nation.) The committee bill covered these persons as well as persons with a somewhat higher income. Stephens' amendment was adopted first by a 190-159 teller vote and later by a 240-179 (R 4-131; D 236-48; ND 182-5; SD 54-43) roll-call vote. Under the provision, an eligible person would pay for rent an amount equal to 25 percent of his income and the government's supplement would cover the remainder.

Although Stephens' amendment carried by large margins, the Republicans tried again just before passage to kill the proposal and nearly succeeded. James Harvey (R Mich.) moved to recommit the bill to the Banking and Currency Committee with instructions to delete the rent supplement section and, in addition, a provision for home improvement grants to homeowners in urban renewal areas. The motion was rejected by a key **202-208** roll-call vote. The breakdown: R 130-4; D 72-204 (ND 21-163; SD 51-41).

Controversial Rent Supplements Retained in Bill

The most publicized feature of the 1965 housing bill—and also the most controversial—was a modified Administration proposal of rent supplements to individuals and families who could not obtain standard private housing within their own incomes. The following is a description of how the program was intended to operate and a summary of the issues that arose during Congressional consideration of the plan.

OPERATION. Eligibility Requirements. Rent supplement payments were to be made only on behalf of individuals or families whose incomes were low enough to make them eligible for public housing. (The income limit varied throughout the country.) Administrative regulations specified that total assets and net worth had to be under $2,000 (or $5,000 in the case of the elderly). In addition, eligibility under the law was limited to individuals who were either physically handicapped, elderly (62 years of age or older), displaced or expected to be displaced by governmental action (code enforcement, highway construction, etc.) or occupants of housing in an area affected by a natural disaster.

Amount of Payment. The amount of any supplement payment was limited to the difference between 25 percent of the applicant's income (which he would pay for rent) and the fair market rental charge for his dwelling. The actual payment was to be made to the housing owner on behalf of the occupant. As the income of the occupant rose, the supplement payment was to decline until he could pay the entire rent; when this occurred, the occupant could continue to live in the same unit without a supplement.

Project Eligibility. Payments were permitted only with respect to new or extensively rehabilitated housing projects sponsored by private non-profit or limited-dividend corporations or by housing cooperatives. Housing project owners were to obtain private, federally insured loans for construction and were to select the tenants.

Types of Structures. Any type of residential structure was eligible for supplement tenants, but safeguards were provided to ensure that they were of "modest design" and cost.

Increase in Income. Required each tenant (except the elderly) to report any increase in income so that there might be a corresponding decrease in the rent supplement payment.

ADMINISTRATION PROPOSAL. In the form originally proposed by the Administration, the rent supplements program provided assistance to persons of moderate and low income, but specifically excluded persons who earned so little that they qualified for public housing. Housing officials said that they hoped to assist what they called "middle-income" families with an "income gap" between public and private housing. By this they meant families or individuals with incomes too high to permit them to live in public housing but too low for them to afford good private housing. Additional eligibility tests were provided, such as age, physical handicap and oc-

cupancy of substandard housing. Under the Administration proposal, the occupant was to pay 20 percent of his income for rent (or 25 percent in the case of a lease with option to purchase) and the Government was to pay whatever additional amount was required for the dwelling unit.

During Congressional hearings on the bill, it became apparent that the proposal had to be drastically modified if it were to be salvaged at all. The powerful public housing lobby, represented by the National Assn. of Housing and Redevelopment Officials, criticized the plan as "administratively cumbersome and socially indefensible." The goal of providing adequate housing for moderate-income families, the association said, could be achieved at lower cost through combined private and public housing developments, federal financing of rehabilitated housing, and traditional public housing. Numerous other civic, labor and business groups asserted that it would be indefensible to subsidize moderate-income housing while a large backlog of low-income families still sought Government aid.

Changes in Plan. Important modifications were made in the Administration plan (primarily the eligibility requirements) before the proposal became law. First, in the House Banking and Currency Committee, eligibility was extended to cover persons who could not obtain standard private housing at rents equal to or less than one-fourth of their income (and also could meet the age and other qualifications noted above.) Later (on the House floor and in the Senate Banking and Currency Committee) the proposal was further modified to permit supplements to be paid *only* on behalf of persons whose income level qualified them for public housing occupancy (and who met the other qualifications). This requirement was enacted. Thus, the person who was made eligible for rent supplements under the final bill was the same person specifically excluded from the original Administration proposal.

Criticism Continued. Even after the modifications that were included in the final bill, opponents of supplements continued to criticize the "gigantic cost" of the rental payments and charged that the program was designed to disrupt the social patterns of the nation. One critic, Sen. John G. Tower (R Texas), said that a major objective of the program was to create "socio-economic integration" which he said would "get low-income, middle-income and high-income groups all living together." (Tower denied that his statement had racial implications.) Rep. Paul A. Fino (R N.Y.) said the program was "a social planner's dream disguised in housing terminology."

Funds Denied. Under renewed criticism, led by Republicans, funds to put the program into operation in fiscal 1966 were denied by Congress at the end of the session. Critics said the Federal Housing Administration, in proposed rent supplement regulations, provided higher income limits for eligibility than was intended by the authorizing legislation.

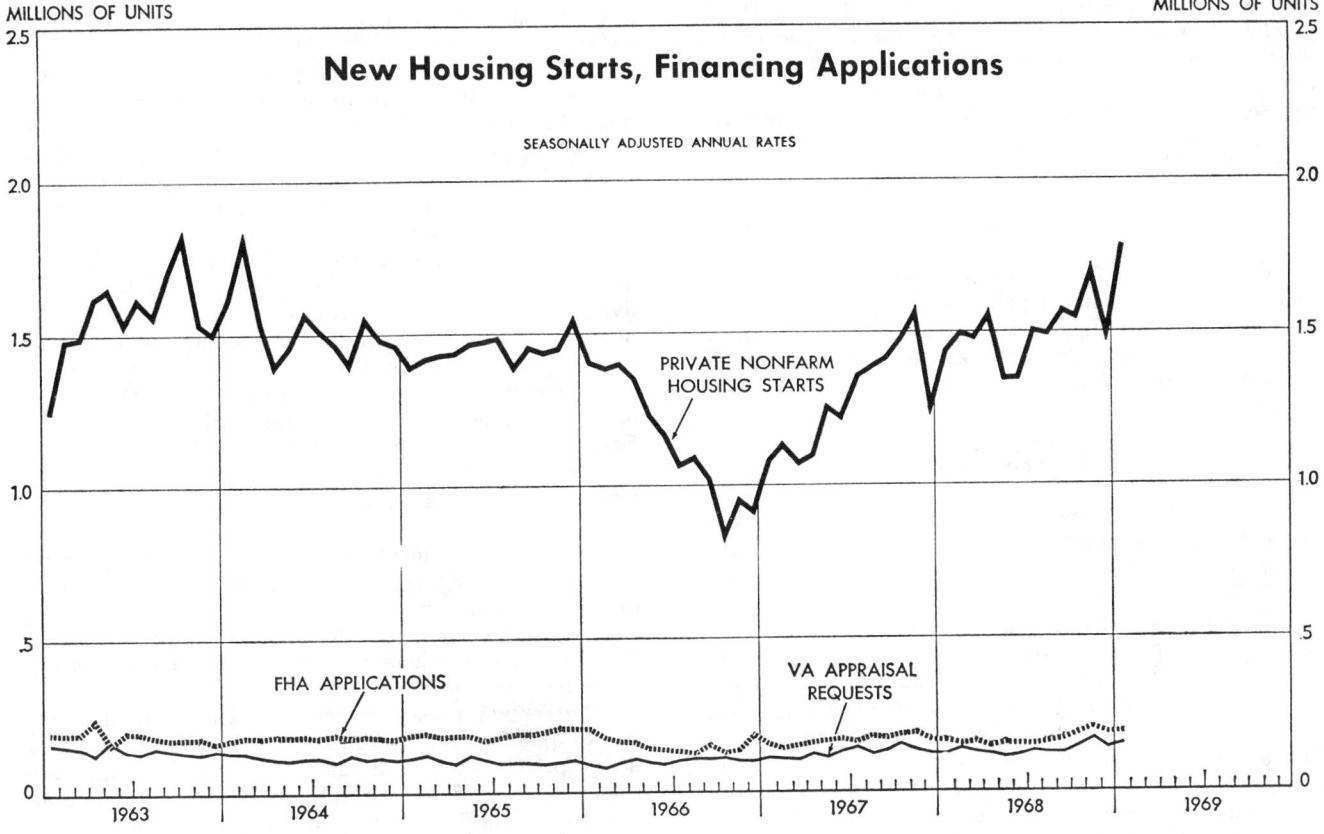

MILLIONS OF UNITS
MILLIONS OF UNITS

New Housing Starts, Financing Applications

SEASONALLY ADJUSTED ANNUAL RATES

PRIVATE NONFARM
HOUSING STARTS

FHA APPLICATIONS

VA APPRAISAL
REQUESTS

1963   1964   1965   1966   1967   1968   1969

SOURCES: DEPARTMENT OF COMMERCE, FEDERAL HOUSING ADMINISTRATION (FHA), AND VETERANS ADMINISTRATION (VA)

COUNCIL OF ECONOMIC ADVISERS

Retaining the rent supplement provision in the bill—even in the modified form finally approved—was one of the most difficult struggles for House Democratic leaders in the 89th Congress. Prior to the voting, there were widespread reports that the supplement program as reported from committee without the public-housing limitation faced certain defeat from a concerted attack by Republicans and numerous Democrats. The likelihood of defeat was the reason that the bill's supporters agreed to modify the controversial rent supplement concept.

However, the narrow six-vote margin by which that provision was retained, and the several days of extremely vigorous and at times acrimonious debate over that and a few other sections, tended to conceal the considerable support the bill in general commanded in the House. An indication of this was seen in Republican voting on the recommittal and passage votes. Even though Republicans led the assault on the rent supplement plan and also voted heavily against passage, a number of GOP members chose to vote for the bill once the supplement issue was disposed of.

Senate Action

Committee Action. Proposed housing legislation was handled by the Housing Subcommittee of the Senate Banking and Currency Committee. The Subcommittee June 4 approved by voice vote a draft bill similar in most respects to the Administration bill. The principal change was the deletion of the Administration's proposal to assist developers of "new towns."

The full Banking and Currency Committee June 24 approved the Subcommittee bill by a 10-4 vote after making several changes in the measure. Voting for approval were 9 of the 10 committee Democrats and one Republican, John G. Tower (Texas).

In addition to approving the Subcommittee changes on new towns, the full Committee made the following changes in the Administration's rent supplements program. The proposal was altered by restricting payments to projects in behalf of persons whose income was low enough to qualify for public housing, as in the House bill. The revised provision retained the categories of eligible persons set by the Administration (physically handicapped, occupying substandard housing, etc.) but added lower-income persons whose homes were destroyed or extensively damaged by a natural disaster. The supplements were to cover the difference between a person's rent and 25 percent of his income. The Committee set aside 10 percent of the appropriations for rent supplements for an experimental program involving rental supplements covering housing built with the aid of the federal below-market interest rate housing loan program and the federal housing-for-the-elderly programs.

Floor Action. The Senate passed its version of the omnibus housing bill on July 15 by a 54-30 roll-call vote. The breakdown: R 7-19; D 47-11 (ND 38-1; SD 9-10).

As in the House, the central issue in Senate debate was rent supplements. An amendment by Tower to delete the program was rejected by a key **40-47** roll-call vote. The breakdown on the vote was: R 24-5; D 16-42 (ND 6-35; SD 10-7). The Senate also defeated an attempt to restrict the supplements program by sharply limiting the funds authorized to carry it out. However, the Senate did cut back the authorization levels approved in committee to the levels contained in the House version of the bill.

Final Action

Conferees reached agreement without unusual difficulty. The conference report was adopted by a voice vote in the Senate July 26. In the House, where opposition remained strong, the report was adopted by a 251-168 roll call on July 27 with majorities of Republicans and Southern Democrats still opposed.

Provisions

As signed into law, Aug. 10, HR 7984, the Housing and Urban Development Act of 1965, contained the following provisions:

Title I: Special Provisions for Disadvantaged Persons. The first title of the bill provided for rent supplement payments to low-income families, provided a four-year extension—to Oct. 1, 1969—of Federal Housing Administration (FHA) mortgage insurance programs for low- and moderate-income persons, authorized a 3-percent interest rate ceiling on the FHA below-market interest rate insurance program, provided rehabilitation grants for owners of substandard housing in urban renewal areas, authorized special programs to aid persons adversely affected by the closing of federal installations and broadened the scope of certain housing programs.

Rent Supplements. Authorized the Administrator of the Housing and Home Finance Agency (HHFA) to make rent supplement payments on behalf of individuals or families who were unable to obtain adequate private housing for rents which were equal to or less than one-quarter of their incomes. Authorized the payments for persons who were determined, under procedures established by the HHFA Administrator, to have incomes less than the maximum amount of income that a person may have and still be eligible for public housing in the area in which he lives. In addition, eligibility was limited to persons who were either physically handicapped, elderly (62 or older), displaced by Government action, occupying "substandard housing," or occupants or former occupants of housing in a locality determined by the Small Business Administration, subsequent to April 1, 1965, to have been affected by a natural disaster.

Limited the amount of any payment to the difference between 25 percent of the occupant's income and the fair market rental charge for his dwelling. (The payment would be made to the housing owner on behalf of the occupant. As the income of the occupant rose, the supplement payment would decline until he could pay the entire rent; when this occurred, the occupant could continue to live in the same unit without a supplement.)

Stipulated that payments would be made only with respect to housing built by private non-profit or limited-dividend corporations or by cooperatives with the assistance of FHA-insured market interest rate mortgages.

In addition, for the purposes of an experimental program, provided up to 10 percent of total rent supplement funds for payments on behalf of eligible tenants in housing projects financed (1) by FHA-insured, below-market interest rate loans for low- and moderate-income families and displaced families, (2) by FHA-insured loans for housing for the elderly and (3) by FHA direct loans for housing for the elderly. In the case of the FHA direct loans, payments could be made only for persons living in existing housing (future construction would not qualify for the supplements program) and would be limited to 20 percent of the dwelling units in an existing project; no similar restriction was provided for other existing or new housing under the experimental-program section. Earmarked one-half of the funds provided by the 10-percent wording for housing built with below-market interest rate loans and one-half for the two other types of housing.

Prohibited payments with respect to projects whose operating costs were greater than those of similar housing in the community.

Authorized the HHFA Administrator to enter into 40-year contracts with housing owners for the purpose of rent supplement payments.

Authorized project owners to select occupants subject to qualifications established by the HHFA, or a public or private agency designated by HHFA, concerning the criteria for eligibility. Authorized occupants to obtain options to purchase rented housing at specified prices when landlords determined the probability of future increases in occupants' incomes.

Directed the HHFA Administrator to establish criteria for determining the continued eligibility of participants in the program. Specifically required the Administrator to provide for recertification of participants' incomes, with the exception of the elderly, at two-year intervals or more frequently as the Administrator desired.

Specified that the aggregate amount of rent supplement contracts would be spelled out in annual appropriations bills. Limited annual payments under the contracts to $30 million in fiscal 1966 but provided that that figure would be increased by $35 million in fiscal 1967, $40 million in fiscal 1968 and $45 million in fiscal 1969. (Additional amounts of $40 million in fiscal 1970 and $100 million in fiscal 1971 were provided in 1968.)

FHA Loan Programs for Low- and Moderate-Income Persons and Displaced Persons. Continued for four years, to Oct. 1, 1969, FHA authority to insure mortgages under these programs.

Established an interest rate ceiling on loan assistance under the FHA below-market interest rate program at the lower of either 3 percent or the existing statutory rate formula, which currently produced a rate of 3-7/8 to 4 percent. (Under this program enacted in 1961, non-profit organizations, cooperatives and public agencies could borrow money from commercial sources, such as banks, at interest rates below those generally prevailing in the housing market. The loans were insured by the FHA. The Federal National Mortgage Assn. (FNMA) then would buy the mortgage from the bank or other lender which normally would agree to the sale in order to avoid tying up funds in low-interest loans. The net effect of the procedures was that FNMA advanced money at low interest rates for construction of housing for this program.)

Pooling of Mortgages for Sale. Amended a section of the Housing Act of 1964 which authorized the FNMA to sell to private investors participations in a trust secured by a pool of mortgage loans held by the FNMA, as follows: in order to encourage inclusion in the pool of mortgages bearing below-market interest rates, the bill authorized appropriations to make up the difference to the FNMA between outlays on participations in a pool and receipts from below-market-rate mortgages. (Appropriations were necessary because mortgage loans that were put into the pool needed to bear interest rates high enough to produce an income that could be used to pay the interest of the participation certificates. As a result, no below-market-rate mortgages had been included in the pool. The sale of participations was designed to draw funds of private investors—rather than Treasury funds—to finance Government mortgage holdings.)

Use of Vacant Units. Authorized local housing authorities to lease vacant units in existing private housing for one- to three-year periods for occupancy by low-income families at rents no higher than those that could be charged for newly constructed public housing units. Limited such leasing to 10 percent of the units in any single structure unless HHFA determined that the limit, in a given case should not apply. Made the program's application in a given locality contingent upon the approval of local governing bodies.

Public Housing for the Handicapped. Amended existing housing law to provide equal treatment of handicapped families and elderly families for low-rent housing purposes by extending to handicapped families all of the special provisions in the law (such as increased room cost limits and special $120 annual contributions per unit for occupied dwelling units) which were currently available to the elderly.

Housing for the Elderly and Handicapped. Increased to $500 million the existing $350 million appropriations authorization ceiling on the program of direct loans to provide housing for the elderly or handicapped, limited the interest rate on such loans to 3 percent (rather than the 3-3/4 - 4 percent that was currently in effect).

Rehabilitation Grants. Authorized grants of up to $1,500 for costs of repairs and improvements of homes in urban renewal areas; specified that a recipient could earn no more than $3,000 annually. Provided smaller grants for homeowners whose incomes exceeded $3,000.

Federal Installations Closings. Provided a moratorium of up to one year on payments of principal, and in some cases, interest, on FHA-insured loans when homeowners were unemployed as the result of the closing of a federal installation.

Authorized the Secretary of Defense to acquire properties for FHA disposal when persons unemployed by the closing of federal installations certified that they were unable to sell their homes on reasonable terms.

Title II. FHA Insurance Operations. Extended FHA loan insurance activities for four years, through Oct. 1, 1969, and authorized the following program:

Mortgage Insurance on Land Development Loans. Authorized FHA insurance of private loans for land acquisition and site development. The maximum FHA insured mortgage could (1) cover up to 75 percent of the estimated value of the developed land or (2) 50 percent of the land value before development plus 90 percent of the cost of the site development, whichever was less. Limited the maximum mortgage for a single land undertaking to $10 million. Eligible costs were the acquisition of the land and its improvement with water and sewer facilities, roads, streets, sidewalks, storm drainage facilities and other similar site work.

Permitted either a public sewer system or an adequately regulated private one on land developed under FHA assistance.

Down Payment Requirement. Reduced the down payment that a person must make on a home valued between $20,000 and $30,000 where the purchase is financed with a mortgage insured under the regular FHA home mortgage insurance program, as follows: required that the payment on that part of the value of insured property which exceeded $20,000 be 20 percent, in place of the existing 25 percent.

Veterans Loans. Established a special FHA home mortgage insurance program for veterans who had not already received benefits under the VA program. Permitted no down payment on the first $15,000 of such insured loan, 10-percent down on the amount between $15,000 and $20,000 and 15 percent on the amount between $20,000 and $30,000, the existing statutory limitation for FHA loan insurance. Limited participation to veterans who had served tours of 90 days or more (or were certified by the Secretary of Defense as having performed extra-hazardous service).

Loans in High-Cost Areas. Authorized the Federal Housing Commissioner to raise the existing ceiling of $10,000 on FHA-insurable home improvement loans by up to 45 percent in high-cost areas.

Mortgages for Servicemen. Increased the maximum amount of a mortgage for a member of the Armed Forces which the FHA would insure from $20,000 to $30,000. Provided for a minimum down payment on such loans as follows: 3 percent on the first $15,000; 10 percent on the amount between $15,000 and $20,000 and 15 percent on the amount between $20,000 and $30,000.

Optional Cash Payment of FHA Insurance Benefits. Authorized the Housing Commissioner at his discretion to pay benefits derived from FHA programs either in cash or in debentures (negotiable, interest-bearing notes) and to borrow from the Treasury for payments as he deemed necessary.

FHA Urban Renewal Housing Programs. Raised the maximum amount of mortgage insurance which a non-occupant mortgagor in an urban renewal area could receive for rehabilitation, purchase or construction for rental purposes of a 1- to 11-family home or other property from 85 percent of the loan amount an owner-occupant could receive to 93 percent of that amount.

Authorized the HHFA Administrator to permit such non-dwelling facilities as he deemed desirable and consistent to be included in FHA-insured multi-family rental housing projects located in urban renewal areas.

Title III. Urban Renewal. Continued the federal urban renewal program for four years by authorizing an additional $2.9 billion for renewal grants, as follows: $675 million upon enactment, $725 million in fiscal 1967 and $750 million each in fiscal 1968 and fiscal 1969.

Directed the Housing Administrator to study and report to the President and Congress on housing and building laws, codes, standards and regulations, zoning and land-use laws, codes and regulations, and federal, state and local tax policies.

General Neighborhood Renewal Plans. Authorized the inclusion of non-renewal areas with "specially related problems" in community development plans so that renewal programs could deal with unfragmented neighborhoods. Provided that all projects in the plan area be initiated in eight years.

Demolition Grants. Authorized grants of up to two-thirds of cost for demolition of unsafe structures in urban renewal areas or other areas which had workable programs and met specified conditions.

Code Enforcement and Rehabilitation. Stipulated that code enforcement and rehabilitation projects (aimed at minimizing the need for demolition and clearance in urban renewal areas) receive a minimum of 10 percent of the aggregate of (1) the $2.9 billion capital grant authority of HR 7984 and subsequent legislation and (2) the authorization for low-interest-rate rehabilitation loans under the Housing Act of 1964.

Doubled the existing $50 million appropriations authorization ceiling provided in the Housing Act of 1964 for rehabilitation loans. Provided for termination of the program on Oct. 1, 1969.

Authorized grants to cities, other municipalities, and counties for programs of concentrated code enforcement in deteriorated or deteriorating areas (rather than only in urban renewal areas, as provided in existing law); grants could be for up to two-thirds of cost, or three-fourths of cost in the case of cities of less than 50,000 population.

Local Grants-in-Aid. Included numerous provisions relating to specific urban renewal projects in various cities throughout the country.

Historic Structures. Authorized an urban renewal project to include the cost of relocating historic structures within the project area.

Workable Program Requirement. Amended the Housing Act of 1949 to require that each workable program for community improvement be sufficiently extensive and detailed to prove the need for a proposed urban renewal project and to demonstrate that the project was in accord with the workable program.

Stipulated that the workable program requirement would be applicable to an Indian tribe, band or nation only to the extent that it had legal jurisdiction and power to carry out the requirement.

Non-Residential Projects. Stipulated that up to 35 percent of the bill's new capital grant authorization for urban renewal activities could be used for projects which were predominantly non-residential both before and after renewal. Stipulated that the existing 30-percent limitation on such projects would remain in force for amounts previously available for such projects but still unused.

Lease Guarantees for Small Businesses. Amended the Small Business Investment Act to authorize the Small Business Administration (SBA) to guarantee payment of rentals under leases entered into by small business concerns displaced by federal or federally aided urban renewal, highway or other construction projects and concerns eligible for loans under the Economic Opportunity Act of 1964. Limited the SBA fee for the guarantee to 2-1/2 percent of minimum annual

guaranteed rental. Established a revolving fund for this program with initial capital of $5 million from SBA's general fund and increased the authorization to the general fund by a like amount.

Other Provisions. Amended the Housing Act of 1954 to authorize the District of Columbia Redevelopment Land Agency to undertake renewal projects in areas which were not residential or predominantly residential.

Expanded and implemented guidelines of existing law regarding relocation assistance programs for persons displaced by urban renewal.

Made economically depressed areas (designated as urban redevelopment areas under the Area Redevelopment Act or similar legislation subsequently enacted) with populations of 150,000 or more eligible for capital grants of three-fourths of the cost of urban renewal projects. (Existing law provided for grants of up to two-thirds of the cost of projects in such redevelopment areas, but up to three-fourths of the cost if the areas had a population of less than 150,000. The provision applied retroactively to Providence, R.I., and could apply to other areas in the fugure.)

Title IV. Compensation of Condemnees. Established uniform land acquisition procedures to be followed in connection with the acquisition of land by eminent domain under the following federally assisted urban development programs: urban renewal, public housing, urban mass transportation, public facility loans, open-space land, basic public works, neighborhood facilities and advance acquisition of land. The uniform procedures required an applicant to make every reasonable effort to acquire property by negotiated purchase before resorting to eminent domain and provided safeguards for the owners of real property against unfair treatment under eminent domain proceedings.

Title V. Low-Rent Public Housing. Extended the low-rent public housing program for four years, to Oct. 1, 1969, and increased the authorization for contracts for this program by $47 million annually during fiscal 1966-69 (the existing authorized total was $366,250,000) in order to provide an estimated 60,000 units per year over the four-year period. (Housing officials said they expected the 60,000 total to include about 35,000 units in new construction, 15,000 units from purchase and—if necessary—rehabilitation of existing housing, and 10,000 units leased from owners for low-rent use.)

Greater Use of Existing Housing. Authorized amortization periods of less than 40 years on public housing indebtedness in order to facilitate the purchase or leasing of older housing for use as low-rent public housing.

Reallocation of Units. Authorized the reallocation of housing units not placed under construction within five years from the date they were reserved for a state, without regard to limits on the amount of units which may be placed under contract in any one state.

Sale of Federally Owned Projects. Authorized the Public Housing Administration (PHA) to sell a federally owned public housing project to a non-profit local group, as well as to a local public housing agency, provided that such project would remain in use as low-rent housing.

Per Room Limitations. Increased the limitations on the cost of construction of low-rent public housing from $2,000 to $2,400 for regular units, from $3,000 to $3,500 for units constructed in Alaska or for the elderly and from $3,500 to $4,000 for units in Alaska for the elderly.

Rental Gap. Exempted disaster victims (as defined under the rent supplements program, above) from a requirement that there be a 20-percent gap between upper-rental limits for admission to public housing and lowest private rents.

Purchase by Tenants. Permitted tenants to purchase detached, semi-detached or row public housing units.

Title VI. College Housing. Extended the college housing loan program for four years, through fiscal 1969. (The existing authorization for the program totaled $2,875,000,000 and was increased by $300 million annually; the $300 million annual increase was to continue during the four-year extension.)

Established an interest rate ceiling on such loans at the lower of either 3 percent or the existing statutory interest rate formula (which currently provided an actual rate of about 3-3/4 - 4 percent). (This encouraged state universities to use the federal program for the first time, since the 3-percent interest rate was lower than that usually paid on state bond issues.)

Stipulated that new colleges were eligible for loans when they provided assurance that they would offer the baccalaureate degree within a reasonable period of time.

Broadened coverage of the loan program to include vocational and technical institutions administered by fully accredited, degree-granting, four-year universities and colleges.

Title VII. Community Facilities. Authorized the HHFA Administrator to make grants to local public bodies and agencies to finance up to 50 percent of the cost of projects to provide basic water facilities (including storage, purification, treatment and distribution) and sewer facilities (other than for "treatment works" eligible for federal aid under the Federal Water Pollution Control Act) in communities of any size. Authorized grants for 90 percent of the cost for a sewer facility in communities under 10,000 population which had an unemployment rate 100 percent above the national average; for the preceding year and in which there was no adequate facility serving "a substantial portion" of the community's inhabitants. Stipulated that before a grant could be approved for a sewer facility, the Secretary of Health, Education and Welfare would be required to certify that any waste material carried by such facilities would be "adequately treated" (in accordance with applicable federal, state, interstate and local standards) before it was discharged into any public waterway. (The grants could be used to construct, expand, enlarge and improve basic public water and sewer facilities, but were not intended for ordinary repair and maintenance expenses of existing systems.)

Authorized the HHFA Administrator to make grants to local public bodies and agencies to finance up to two-thirds of the cost of neighborhood health and recreation centers and similar community services (grants could be for up to 75 percent of the cost in the case of a project located in a "redevelopment area" as designated in the Area Redevelopment Act or a supplementary act). Required such a project to: (1) provide health, recreational, social or similar community services (including a community action program under the

Economic Opportunity Act of 1964), (2) be consistent with community development planning and (3) be located near a "significant portion" of the area's low- or moderate-income residents.

Authorized grants to local public bodies and agencies to assist in the acquisition of land for future construction of public works or facilities; the grant could cover the total amount of reasonable interest charges for five years.

Authorized appropriations for fiscal years 1966-69, as follows: $200 million a year for water and sewer grants; $50 million a year for neighborhood facilities; and $25 million a year for advance acquisition of land.

Title VIII. Federal National Mortgage Assn. Increased by $1,625,000,000 the amount of special assistance the President could authorize the Federal National Mortgage Association (FNMA) to commit for purchases of FHA-insured mortgages financing housing for low- and moderate-income families, for housing activities in urban renewal areas, for housing for the elderly and for other special types of housing, as follows: $100 million in fiscal 1966; $450 million in fiscal 1967; $550 million in fiscal 1968; and $525 million in fiscal 1969.

Provided certain exemptions of FHA below-market interest rate mortgages covering low- or moderate-income housing from the statutory $17,500 limit on the amount of a mortgage that could be purchased by FNMA under its special assistance function.

Authorized FNMA to purchase mortgages covering residential property offered by other federal agencies and other obligations offered by HHFA; provided further authority for FNMA in its fiduciary capacity to deal in any HHFA obligations.

Title IX. Open-Space Land and Urban Beautification and Improvement. Authorized the HHFA Administrator to enter into contracts totaling up to $310 million ($75 million under existing law) for grants to states and localities under Title VII of the 1961 Housing Act to acquire land in and around urban centers to create "open-space" areas for recreational, conservation, scenic and historic purposes. Limited the share of the total amount which could be used for the open-space program in built-up areas (see below) to $64 million and for urban beautification (see below) to $36 million.

Provided that the maximum grant for acquisition of open-space land would be 50 percent of the total cost (existing law allowed up to 20 percent).

Open Space in Built-Up Areas. Authorized the HHFA Administrator to enter into contracts for grants to states and localities to help finance the acquisition of developed land in built-up urban areas which would be cleared and used as permanent open-space land (parks, squares, playground, pedestrian malls, etc.); grants could not exceed 50 percent of the cost of land acquisition and necessary demolition and removal of developments on the sites.

Urban Beautification. Authorized the HHFA Administrator to enter into contracts for grants to states and localities for local landscaping, park improvement and other urban beautification and improvements; grants could not exceed 50 percent of the amount by which the community's activities under the program during any fiscal year exceeded its usual expenditures for comparable activities, except that up to $5 million of the amount authorized for the section (see above) could be used to make grants for up to 90 percent of the cost of demonstration projects of "special value," as determined by the Administrator.

Other Provisions. Limited open-space grants to situations in which they were needed to carry out a unified or officially coordinated program which was part of a comprehensive urban development plan (existing law required that there be comprehensive planning to which the proposed land use is important.)

Permitted up to $50,000 of the funds available for grants under the title for undertaking and publishing open-space surveys and other studies in connection with activities under the title.

Title X. Rural Housing. Authorized the Farmers' Home Administration to make loans to persons in any age group to buy previously occupied dwellings, farm service buildings and adequate farm land. (Under existing law, such loans could be made only to elderly persons.)

Established a new loan program which authorized the Secretary of Agriculture to make and to insure loans for rural home improvement with maximum interest rates of: (1) 5 percent to persons of low- and moderate-incomes and (2) a level comparable to the rates and service charges applicable to loans insured by the FHA to persons of higher incomes. Limited the total amount of loans that could be made or insured in the low- and moderate-income bracket to a total of $300 million annually, but placed no limit on the amount of loans or loan insurance for persons of higher income.

Defined a rural area for purposes of the loan program as a place which was not part of or associated with an urban area and which had: (1) a population not in excess of 2,500; or (2) a population between 2,500 and 5,500, if rural in character.

Increased from $10 million to $50 million the authorization for grants to non-profit sponsors to provide low-rent housing for domestic farm labor.

Extended authorizations for rural housing programs for four years, to Oct. 1, 1969.

Title XI. Miscellaneous. Required the Housing Administrator to report to Congress annually on housing programs under the jurisdiction of the HHFA.

Increased appropriations authorizations on the following existing programs: urban planning grants, from $105 million to $230 million; federal-state urban affairs training programs, from $10 million to $30 million; public works planning advances, from $20 million to $70 million; and low-income housing demonstration grants from $10 million to $15 million.

Authorized loans to private non-profit corporations to finance the construction of water purification, storage and distribution systems and sewer systems for rural areas and small communities.

Authorized savings and loan associations to make loans on the security of buildings to be used as college dormitories, fraternity or sorority houses or for residential purposes by the staffs of community hospitals.

Repealed a provision of the Urban Mass Transportation Act of 1964 (PL 88-365) which required that facilities and equipment used under the program be U.S. manufactured.

Directed the HHFA Administrator to study and report to Congress within one year of the bill's enactment on (1) methods of reducing loss to homeowners whose property depreciates because of proximity to airports and (2) methods of housing construction which would diminish the effect of aircraft noise within such homes.

Authorized federal savings and loan associations to make up to 1 percent of their assets available for overseas housing loans guaranteed under the Foreign Assistance Act of 1961. (Existing law limited participation primarily to national and state banks.)

Rent Supplements Funding

Under a renewed assault on rent supplements by Republicans and dissident Democrats, operating funds to get the program under way during fiscal 1966 were denied during consideration of a supplemental appropriations bill (HR 11588—PL 89-309) approved on the eve of adjournment.

Objectives to funding the program were based on a contention that draft regulations prepared by the Federal Housing Administration (FHA) overstepped the bounds of the original provision by increasing income limits for eligibility.

The appropriation for the program first came under fire in the House Oct. 14, when James Harvey (R Mich.) contended that the regulations would permit families with assets of as much as $25,000 to be eligible for subsidized housing. Supporters of the program vigorously disputed Harvey's calculations but were unprepared for a statistical rebuttal. The House subsequently, by a key **185-162** (R 99-2; D 86-160—ND 24-141, SD 62-19) roll-call vote, approved a Harvey amendment to delete the $6 million in contractual authority for supplements and $180,000 in supplement payments approved by the Appropriations Committee.

Following the House defeat on supplements, Housing Administrator Robert C. Weaver said the maximum amount of permissible assets that could be calculated under the regulations was in the range of $15,000 to $16,000, and this only in the case of large or elderly families in high-cost areas of the nation. In any event, Weaver said, the regulations would be rewritten and lower asset limitations would be formulated.

Although the Senate later restored $12 million in contractual authority for supplements and $360,000 for supplement payments, House-Senate conferees on the measure dropped the entire provision. Conferees, in their report, said their action would provide more time "to develop sound plans and criteria which can be reviewed when funds are sought early in 1966." *(See 1966 chronology.)*

1966

Model Cities

Congress in 1966 enacted broad new programs for community renewal in U.S. cities and for orderly development of metropolitan areas.

The programs were included in an omnibus urban assistance and housing bill, the Demonstration Cities and Metropolitan Development Act of 1966 (S 3708—PL 89-754). It was the second consecutive year that Congress enacted major housing and urban development legislation.

Highlight of the bill was a three-year, $1.2-billion "demonstration cities" plan—a key Great Society measure designed to rebuild entire urban areas by tying together the wide array of existing federal and local programs and new innovations by the participating communities for a coordinated attack on blight. (The program was later renamed "model cities." *See p. 198.*) Participating cities, to be selected under strict federal standards, were to receive federal funds equal to as much as 80 percent of the financial contribution which the cities were required to make (under existing law) as their share of federally assisted programs included in a demonstration plan. Most federal assistance programs, in housing as well as other areas, require a recipient to contribute a certain percentage (which varies with different programs) of the cost of the project. The demonstration cities bill was designed to help cities by providing grants of up to 80 percent of this local contribution. The bill permitted the cities to use the funds coming to them under the 80-percent provision, first, to finance any new or existing program in the demonstration plan which did not receive other federal aid and, second (if any funds were left over from the first purpose), to use them to help pay costs of the local contribution required under the federally assisted programs.

To fund the demonstrations plan, the bill authorized federal grants of $24 million for planning the projects in fiscal 1967 and fiscal 1968, and an additional $400 million in fiscal 1968 and $500 million in fiscal 1969 for carrying out the plans. An additional lump sum of $250 million in urban renewal funds was earmarked for demonstration projects initiated in and after fiscal 1968. Aid to an estimated 60 to 70 cities was contemplated under the bill.

The basic concept of the demonstrations plan came from recommendations by a special Task Force on Urban Problems, appointed by President Johnson late in 1965. The Task Force was headed by Dr. Robert C. Wood, then chairman of the Political Science Department at the Massachusetts Institute of Technology, who Jan. 13, 1966, was appointed Under Secretary of the Department of Housing and Urban Development.

In a departure from the approach of the existing urban renewal program, which emphasized new construction, the demonstrations plan envisioned a restructuring of the "total environment" of the residents of "demonstration" neighborhoods. By authorizing additional federal funds which could be used for education, antipoverty and similar social programs, the bill sought to attack the human problems as well as the physical factors causing blight and decay.

Although the final bill provided essentially the same level of annual funding for demonstrations as requested by the President, it did not provide the long-range program Mr. Johnson had sought. His original request envisioned a $2.3 billion program with one year of planning and five years of implementation (fiscal 1967-72). He subsequently requested an additional $600 million for urban renewal activities in the demonstration cities. An intensive Administration lobbying effort in early summer salvaged the original program in the House Banking and Currency Committee's Housing Subcommittee, but the Administration later was forced to compromise when

---

Purpose of City Demonstrations

A major objective of the "demonstration cities" plan approved by Congress was to set up "showcase" neighborhoods to demonstrate how a coordination of federal and local programs could eliminate urban blight and change the "total environment" of the neighborhood's residents. Relatively few cities were likely to receive aid under the plan; however, many more were expected to benefit from observing new innovations and the example of good coordination which supporters of the bill hoped would be apparent in the "model cities"—the new name given the program. *(See box p. 198.)*

Government officials regarded the coordination example as a vital innovation in the urban rehabilitation effort. An Administration official said that, because of the almost total lack of coordination under existing law, officials of one federal department or agency might be working at cross purposes with those of another, while local officials might be countering both federal and other local efforts.

---

considerable opposition arose in the Senate. Despite the dilutions, the bill came under a strong floor assault by Republicans in both House and Senate, and its outcome was never a certainty in either chamber.

A second major victory for the Administration was inclusion of a new program for federal land development mortgage insurance for developers of entire "new towns." This was a high-priority Administration measure which was killed in committee in 1964 and 1965. The proposal was again blocked by the Senate Banking and Currency Committee's Housing Subcommittee in 1966, but it was approved by the House and sustained by Senate-House conferees. Conferees wrote in restrictive language limiting the program to a six-year duration (terminating Oct. 1, 1972), requiring project approval by governing bodies of adjoining localities and by the state Governor, and limiting to $250 million the maximum amount of all such insured loans that could be outstanding at any one time. *(See box p. 202.)*

A third major Administration program approved in the final bill was a plan for "incentive" grants to encourage comprehensive and current area-wide planning. Cities meeting program standards were to receive supplemental grants of up to 20 percent of project costs normally paid by local communities for such programs as mass transit, sewer and water facilities, highway construction, airport development, open-space land acquisition and acquisition of land and water facilities.

Other important features of the final bill included an Administration-backed program of FHA mortgage insurance to finance and equip facilities for group medical, dental and optometrical practice, a plan revising existing urban renewal laws to authorize preservation of historic sites as an eligible urban renewal cost, liberal Republican-sponsored language requiring the residential redevelopment of any urban renewal area to provide for a "substantial" supply of housing within the means of low- and moderate-income families, and numerous other related programs, including proposals, ad-

'Demonstrations' Program Renamed

Following passage of the 1966 housing legislation, the demonstration cities program underwent an official change in name. On signing the bill Nov. 3, President Johnson termed the program "model cities," rather than "demonstration cities" as was commonly used previously and appeared in the bill's title. "Demonstration Cities and Metropolitan Development Act of 1966." Although officials of the Department of Housing and Urban Development said there was no official directive from Mr. Johnson, they subsequently adopted the new term for all program regulations and official correspondence. Officials declined to explain the change, but it was thought that racial demonstrations in many cities in recent years made the original "demonstration cities" name for the program distasteful to the Administration.

vanced by the Administration and others initiated by Congress.

LEGISLATIVE HISTORY. The President's specific requests were spelled out in a special city development message submitted to Congress Jan 26. Four Administration draft bills eventually formed the basis for the omnibus bill (S 3708) passed by Congress. The four measures included all major Presidential proposals except one banning housing discrimination *(See Civil Rights)* and another providing rent supplement funds.

Senate Action

The Senate Banking and Currency Committee, after hearings in the spring, in August reported three clean bills (S 3700, S 3708, S 3711) embodying most of the pending legislation. (One of these, S 3700, dealt with urban mass transit and is covered in Economic Policy, subchapter on transportation policy p. 227.)

Floor Action. Both bills were passed in August. S 3711 was passed Aug. 12 with little controversy by a 61-3 roll-call vote. The bill dealt with federal housing insurance, urban renewal, college housing and other matters.

S 3708, on the other hand, was controversial because it contained the demonstration cities provisions. It was passed Aug. 19 by a 53-22 roll call. Prior to passage, the Senate by a key **27-53** roll-call vote defeated a move by John G. Tower (R Texas) to delete all funds to implement the demonstrations program, leaving only $24 million for planning purposes. The vote breakdown was: R 17-10; D 10-43 (ND 1-36; SD 9-7).

In calling for acceptance of his amendment, Tower argued that such large domestic spending programs should be deferred until "the days when spending is more in keeping with the supply and cost of money." By the end of the bill's two planning years, he said, "we can hope...Vietnam will only be a blot on history's picture, that the dangers of inflation will have passed, and that we will be in a far better fiscal position to take up billion-dollar expenditures for new programs." Senate Minority Leader Everett McKinley Dirksen (R Ill.),

who directed his opposition to the scope of the program itself, added that the plan had "all the prospects of becoming one of the greatest boondoggles this country has ever witnessed. It will be shot through with waste and corruption and goodness knows what...before we get through."

Edmund S. Muskie (D Maine), the bill's floor manager, retorted that Republicans had invalidated the cost argument by voting for such inflationary but non-controversial programs as college housing. Muskie challenged GOP proponents of the amendment to support the full bill as a measure to "deal with the most explosive domestic issue on the American scene today."

In other action on amendments, the Senate by voice vote accepted seven floor proposals, including important amendments by Tower to limit a single state's share of demonstration cities and "incentive" metropolitan planning grants to 15 percent of total authorizations. None of the seven proposals was debated.

Voting for passage of the bill were 14 Republicans and 39 Democrats. Opposed were 13 GOP Members and 9 Democrats.

House Action

Committee Action. The House Banking and Currency Committee reported two housing and urban development bills. In mid-July, the Committee approved its own omnibus bill (HR 15890), similar to the original Administration package, but only after intensive Administration lobbying. However, after the Senate Aug. 19 passed a more restricted demonstration cities bill, the Committee reconvened in late August and combined the two Senate bills (S 3708, S 3711) into an amended version of S 3708 and made some changes in the enlarged bill.

Administration Lobbying. Approval of the omnibus bill came only after an intensive Administration lobbying effort following reports that the Subcommittee was ready to reduce the $2.3-billion demonstration cities program to $12 million in project planning funds and to eliminate both the new towns and metropolitan planning programs.

An Administration source close to the issue told Congressional Quarterly at the time that such Subcommittee action was forestalled when Vice President Hubert H. Humphrey June 1 telephoned Subcommittee Chairman William A. Barrett (D Pa.) and strongly implied the Administration would not support a planning bill. At the time of the Vice President's call, the source said, the Subcommittee had tentatively approved the diluted measure.

"The Administration decided it couldn't live with a mere 'silhouette' program," the source said. " 'Demonstration cities' was planned to be an ongoing program for the next six years. The funds for it have been provided in the Budget. A truncated bill just wouldn't be acceptable."

The $12-million planning bill was the product of a compromise between Barrett and several Subcommittee Republicans. The source said Barrett and other Democrats feared the original measure could never pass the House during a year when the costs of a war in Asia and various domestic programs were of major concern.

Subcommittee sources later said the panel reversed itself and accepted the full bill because of assurances that the Administration could obtain the votes for passage and because of the Administration's decision to ask for additional urban renewal funds, a request which placated big city mayors.

Committee Reconvenes. After the Senate passed its bill (S 3708), which provided a more restricted demonstration cities program than the President requested ($924 million over fiscal 1967-69 compared to the requested six-year program—1967-72—and an estimated $2.3 billion cost), the Administration requested Barrett to reconvene the Housing Subcommittee and accept the Senate's approach. The Subcommittee was reconvened by Barrett Aug. 25 and late in the day approved S 3708 by a 9-1 vote with amendments that turned the measure into an omnibus housing bill. The major amendment was to add to the bill many of the provisions of S 3711, the separate Senate bill which included provisions on FHA insurance operations, medical facilities, mortgage insurance, urban renewal costs and other subjects. The Subcommittee made some changes in the Senate bill.

In its major changes from the legislation passed by the Senate, S 3708 as approved by the Housing Subcommittee restored the Administration's controversial "new towns" plan and dropped the Senate allotment of an additional $900 million over fiscal 1967-69 for college housing loans.

Floor Action. The House passed the bill (S 3708) on Oct. 14 by a key **178-141** roll-call vote. The vote breakdown: R 16-81; D 162-60 (ND 141-11; SD 21-49).

Before passage, the House by a 149-175 (R 85-11; D 64-164—ND 13-143, SD 51-21) roll call rejected a motion by W.E. Brock III (R Tenn.) to recommit the bill to the Banking and Currency Committee with instructions to delete the $900 million authorization for demonstration city projects (but not the $24 million for planning of the projects), and the entire metropolitan planning title (Title II). The House earlier by non-record votes had rejected floor amendments by Brock to eliminate the authorization for demonstration projects, and by Paul A. Fino (R N.Y.) to eliminate the "metro" planning title.

House passage came after one of the most acrimonious floor debates of the session, during which Fino dominated much of the discussion by repeatedly asserting that the measure was a disguised means of furthering civil rights objectives and federal control over localities. Fino's major contention was that the demonstration cities and "incentive" metropolitan planning programs could be used to require localities to "bus" children into integrated schools and to rewrite school boundaries. "If you vote for this scheme," Fino said, "...you are voting for forced busing, school pairing and redistricting."

Administration forces retorted that nothing in the bill gave the Federal Government any such powers. (They did not deny that localities, when acting on their own incentive, might be able to use funds for such purposes.) In view of the close vote expected on passage, the Administration agreed to amend the measure to specifically prohibit the HUD Secretary from conditioning demonstration cities or "incentive" planning assistance on local agreement to bus children, or from conditioning incen-

tive planning aid on local adoption of any other program to further a racial balance in schools.

Despite House acceptance of the anti-busing amendments, Fino still criticized the measure as the "most far-reaching civil rights bill...that the White House has ever proposed." The amendments were a "red herring," he insisted, because they failed to "prevent the city from being pressured into setting up educational parks or redrawing school district lines," as he said was being contemplated under the "Equal Educational Opportunity Act of 1967," the draft legislation which he asserted was being formulated by the U.S. Office of Education. "If children are bused to such facilities," Fino asserted, "... then such busing would not be covered" by the amendments.

Fino, a member of the Housing Subcommittee, subsequently attempted to amend the bill to require a Justice Department investigation of any "local group" participating in a proposed demonstration city project to ensure they were not connected with "subversive...black power...or any other racist organization." In response to this proposal, Abraham J. Multer (D N.Y.), one of the bill's supporters, said he was "nauseated" by Fino's entire line of opposition. "There is nothing in this bill about 'black power,' " Multer said, "...and no mention of 'local groups.' ...This is one more attempt by him to create some emotional reaction against the bill." Fino's amendment was rejected by voice vote.

In addition to its agreement to prohibit school busing, backers of the bill agreed to an amendment to delete a section authorizing appointment by the Secretary of Housing and Urban Development (HUD) of "metropolitan expediters" to set up liaison between localities and federal agencies in areas demonstrating both a need and a desire for such officials. The National League of Cities, an association of mayors which generally favored the bill, opposed the provision, reportedly contending that the expediters would interfere with municipal affairs. (The provision, in the Senate bill, was included in the final version of the legislation.)

Business Support. In the weeks prior to House consideration of the bill, the Administration reportedly feared that passage of the bill and attempts to delete funds might be decided by margins as narrow as three to five votes. It was thought that a key factor in the wider margin achieved was the endorsement of the measure by 22 leading business executives, including Henry Ford II, Ford Motor Co. president, and David Rockefeller, president of the Chase Manhattan Bank. In a statement issued Oct. 10, the group said that urban blight constituted "the most pressing domestic problem of our time." They termed the demonstrations program an "imaginative" response to the problem and urged its "prompt passage" by the House.

Final Action

Conferees in a single session Oct. 17 resolved differences between the House and Senate versions of S 3708 and agreed tentatively on a compromise version. But conference agreement on a noncontroversial Senate plan to aid purchasers of "seasonal" (vacation) housing raised a procedural quirk which threatened to delay final passage of the bill and, possibly, the adjournment of Congress.

Operation of Model Cities Program Shown in Example

The demonstration model cities program enacted as part of S 3708 provided new federal subsidies for a broad and coordinated attack on urban blight. Participating cities were to receive grants of up to 80 percent of the required local financial contribution to all federally assisted programs approved as part of a demonstration project. They could spend the funds on any new or existing non-federally assisted program approved as part of the demonstration and use the bal-ance of funds to defray costs of the required local share of federal programs in the demonstration. Following is a hypothetical example of how a participating city might compute and spend its grant under the program. In the example, the city uses its funds ($8.8 million) exclusively to finance non-federally assisted programs, and not, as would be possible under the law, to defray costs of the local share of federal programs.

1) The demonstration cities grant is determined on the basis of existing federal grant-in-aid programs which are used as part of the local demonstration program:

Federally Assisted Activities Included as Part of Local Demonstration	Cost of Activity	Federal Share[1]		Local Contribution
		Percentage	Dollars	
Urban Renewal Projects	$15,000,000	66-2/3%	$10,000,000	$5,000,000
Code Enforcement Project	3,000,000	66-2/3	2,000,000	1,000,000
Sewer and Water Project	600,000	50	300,000	300,000
Neighborhood Center	1,200,000	66-2/3	800,000	400,000
Hospital	5,700,000	Varies	2,000,000	3,700,000
Community Action Program	3,000,000	90	2,700,000	300,000
Manpower Development and Training Project	3,000,000	90	2,700,000	300,000
	$31,500,000		$20,500,000	$11,000,000

2) The actual amount of the demonstration grant in dollars is calculated by taking 80 percent of the non-federal contributions to demonstration activities in the program which are assisted under existing federal grant-in-aid programs: 80 percent of $11 million for a grant of $8.8 million.

3) The city might use the $8.8 million grant for the activities listed below. If the city did not plan these or other new or non-federally assisted activities (which were acceptable to the HUD Secretary) on which to spend the $8.8 million, the funds could be applied to the $11 million local contribution for programs listed above.

Grants for rehabilitation of multifamily structures	$2,500,000
Revolving fund for purchase and rehabilitation of housing	2,500,000
Increased level of garbage collection and rodent control in area	400,000
Police-community relations program	300,000
Training unemployed in rehabilitation skills	350,000
Additional "Head Start" activities beyond what is available from Community Action Program	1,750,000
Improving and equipping neighborhood playgrounds	700,000
Other activities	300,000
	$8,800,000

[1] *Under existing law.*

SOURCE: U.S. Dept. of Housing and Urban Development

The problem arose because the seasonal housing plan had been approved as part of S 3711, the collateral Senate housing bill which was not in conference despite House inclusion of most of its provisions. However, the seasonal housing program was not included in S 3708 by the House. If the conferees had included the program in the conference report on S 3708, the report would have been subject to a point of order when it was brought to the floor. Any House Member could have made the point of order and Arch A. Moore (R W. Va.) reportedly said he would do so. Moore voted for the bill when it passed the House Oct. 14, but he also voted for the recommit-tal motion which would have deleted demonstration cities implementation funds.

HUD officials, reportedly told by House Speaker John W. McCormack (D Mass.) that he would sustain a point of order against the seasonal plan (killing the conference report), persuaded Senate conferees to reconvene and drop the provision. Leading Democrats on the House Housing Subcommittee supposedly influenced the decision by promising the program's sponsor, Sen. Edmund S. Muskie (D Maine), they would hold subcommittee hearings on the plan early in the 1967 session. (The provision was enacted in the 1968 housing bill. *See 1968 chronology.*)

The Senate Oct. 18, by a 38-22 roll-call vote, and the House Oct. 20, by a 142-126 roll-call vote adopted the conference report and sent the bill to President Johnson, who signed it into law Nov. 3 (PL 89-754). At the signing ceremony, the President said the bill provided "the tools to reach out into our environment and shape it to our will." He said the measure would provide the housing, community renewal, employment, schools, recreation and other ingredients necessary to "spell the difference between despair and the good life."

Provisions

As signed by the President, S 3708, the Demonstration Cities and Metropolitan Development Act of 1966 (PL 89-754), contained the following major provisions:

Title I.   Comprehensive   City   Demonstration Programs.

Findings, Purpose. Expressed the finding of Congress that improvement of the quality of urban life was "the most critical domestic problem facing the United States." Stated that cities of all sizes did not have adequate resources to deal effectively with urban problems, thus making new means of assistance necessary in addition to urban renewal and other existing federal grant-in-aid programs.

Provided, in accordance with the Congressional finding, a new "comprehensive city demonstration program" providing additional federal assistance to improve the "total environment" of neighborhoods in selected cities through a coordination of federal, state and local programs in the field of housing, welfare, education, transport and related areas. Stated that a major purpose of the program was to provide "additional financial and technical assistance to enable cities of all sizes (with equal regard to the problems of small as well as large cities) to plan, develop, and carry out locally prepared and scheduled comprehensive city demonstration programs containing new and imaginative proposals to rebuild or revitalize large slum and blighted areas."

Stipulated that federal assistance for the program would be channeled through a single "city demonstration agency" designated by the local governing body.

Required that all the activities making up the over-all demonstration program be approved in a single, coordinated package. Stated that the plan might include any new or existing state or local program which furthered the over-all objectives of the plan and also might make use of any federal program which was "closely related to the physical and social problems in the area of the city covered by the program" and could "reasonably be expected to have a noticeable effect upon such problems."

Authorization of Assistance. Authorized federal grants to participating cities of up to 80 percent of the amount which a community must contribute, under existing law, to all of the federally assisted programs approved as part of the plan.

Required the city to spend the funds coming to it under the 80-percent provision first to finance any new or existing non-federally assisted program approved as part of the demonstration and second to help pay the required local share (that is, the community's dollar contribution) of federal programs approved as part of the plans. Funds were to be used first for the new or non-federally assisted programs with any amounts left over

going toward the local share of existing federal programs.

Provided separate grants of up to 80 percent for office and similar expenses incurred in administering new and existing non-federally assisted programs approved as part of a demonstration project (but not administrative costs of programs already receiving federal aid).

Required applicants for demonstration cities projects to submit comprehensive plans for approval of the Secretary of Housing and Urban Development (HUD). Authorized grants of up to 80 percent of costs for formulating such plans.

Directed the HUD Secretary to consider numerous specific criteria in reviewing project plans, including major requirements that: physical and social problems in the project area justified a comprehensive renewal effort; the proposed project was of sufficient magnitude to make a substantial impact on physical and social problems and to remove or arrest blight and decay in entire sections or neighborhoods; the project contributed to the "sound development" of the entire city, making "marked progress" in reducing social and educational disadvantages, ill health, underemployment and enforced idleness"; the project provided educational, health and social services necessary to serve the poor and disadvantaged in the area and envisioned widespread citizen participation in the program and maximum opportunities for employing residents of the area in all of the program's phases; the project contributed toward a well-balanced city, with a substantial increase in the supply of standard housing of both low and moderate cost; all projects within the demonstration be scheduled for initiation within a short period of time; maximum utilization be made of private enterprise and initiative; the program include a plan for relocation of individuals, businesses and other parties displaced because of program activities; the program be approved by the local governing body; local laws and administrative procedures be consistent with objectives of the program; the city or locality assure that it would not reduce, during the period the approved program was carried out, its prior level of aggregate expenditures for activities outside the demonstration project which were similar to those being assisted as part of the demonstration; the project envisioned a high standard of design in housing and building construction, retention of natural and historic sites and "distinctive neighborhood characteristics," and maximum use of new and improved technology and design, including cost reduction techniques.

Authorized the HUD Secretary to impose other eligibility requirements, provided they were essential to carry out the specific provisions of the bill.

Prohibited the Secretary from requiring busing of children into integrated schools as a condition for participation in the program.

Directed the Secretary to consult with other federal Departments and agencies administering grant-in-aid programs before issuing demonstration cities regulations. Also directed the Secretary to consult with each Department and agency affected by each demonstration cities project before approving program funds.

Authorized $12 million in planning funds for the projects in each of the fiscal years 1967 and 1968. Authorized $400 million in fiscal 1968 and $500 million in fiscal 1969 for grants to implement the program. Also autho-

Federal Aid Provided for Construction of New Towns

Along with the new programs launched under the 1966 housing legislation, Congress approved an old Administration proposal—federal mortgage insurance to aid developers of entire new towns and new communities.

Twice before, in his 1964 and 1965 housing messages, President Johnson urged the "new towns" plan as an alternative to urban sprawl. But in each of those years, opposition by big city mayors and urban-oriented homebuilders killed the proposal in committee.

Again in 1966, the program appeared dead when the Senate Banking and Currency Committee dropped it for the third year in succession. However, following a major push by the Administration which was aided by House Banking and Currency Committee Chairman Wright Patman (D Texas), the plan was approved by the House and accepted in modified form by a House-Senate conference. To ease the opposition of mayors, the conference added a provision making aid contingent upon approval by officials of adjoining localities, as well as the state Governor. Conferees also wrote in restrictive language limiting the program to a six-year duration (through Oct. 1, 1972) and limiting to $250 million the total amount of such mortgages that could be outstanding at any one time.

Purpose. The thrust of the new program was to aid private enterprise in establishing well-planned, self-sustaining new communities beyond the periphery of overly populated cities. The communities would have all of the stores, services, schools, public transportation, and—planners hoped—businesses and industry required by the persons living there.

Because of the huge costs of land development, few developers had previously ventured into the new towns field. Under the new program, they could receive Federal Housing Administration mortgage insurance of up to $25 million to finance the costs of land acquisition and improvements (such as water and sewer systems, but not homebuilding and related activities) on any single land project. Although the $25 million limit might provide little more than a start for a large new town, developers considered it more than ample to construct modest-sized communities.

Existing Projects, Development Problems. By mid-1966, five major privately financed new town projects were well under way—El Dorado Hills, Calif., outside Sacramento (projected population: 75,000); Reston, Va., near Washington, D.C. (75,000); Litchfield Park, Ariz., near Phoenix (100,000); Columbia, Md., between Washington and Baltimore (110,000); and Clear Lake City, Texas, outside Houston (180,000).

Although all five of the new communities appeared likely to be a success, each was hobbled by the same problems in early development efforts. These included: (1) the high costs of purchasing large tracts of land reasonably close to established areas; (2) inadequacy of roads and utilities in the development areas; (3) red-tape involved in clearing the projects with county and other local officials; (4) initial difficulties experienced in selling new home buyers on the advantages of "new town" living; and (5) the concessions required to lure in industry before the town was actually thriving.

Future of the Concept. Although federal aid was expected to encourage a substantial increase in the development of modest-sized new communities, it was thought the development of large new towns was dependent upon the effort of major U.S. corporations. Of the five big developments under construction, two were sponsored exclusively by large manufacturing firms—Clear Lake City by the Humble Oil and Refining Co., and Litchfield Park by the Goodyear Tire and Rubber Co. (A third, Reston, was being financed largely by the Gulf Oil Corp. and the John Hancock Life Insurance Co., although sponsored initially by a private developer.) Two other giant companies—the Litton Corp. and the General Electric Co., had, by late 1966, announced their intention to join the city building effort. A key to the trend of future city building was announced by GE, which said it hoped to use its projected new town as a market to test new products it would like to introduce, such as electronic transportation systems.

rized an additional $250 million in urban renewal funds to be used, in and after fiscal 1968, for projects which were part of an approved demonstration.

Limited the amount of funds committed to any one state for approved demonstration projects to 15 percent of the total authorization.

Title II. Planned Metropolitan Development. Expressed the finding of Congress that the national welfare was "directly dependent" upon "sound and orderly" development and organization of metropolitan areas. Stated that the task of current and comprehensive planning was handicapped by the "complexity and scope" of governmental services required in such areas, the "multiplicity" of political jurisdictions and agencies involved, and the inadequacy of administrative arrangements available for intergovernmental cooperation.

Provided, in accordance with the finding, the following provisions to ensure more orderly metropolitan growth:

Cooperation Between Agencies. Authorized the HUD Secretary to obtain from other agencies statistical data, program reports and other material needed to carry out HUD's metropolitan area responsibilities.

Metropolitan Expediters. Authorized the appointment of "metropolitan expediters," in areas demonstrating both a need and desire for such officials, to provide information, data and assistance to local authorities and private persons concerning HUD programs and programs of other federal and state agencies relating to HUD activities.

Stipulated that expediters could be appointed only upon request of local officials of the central city of a metropolitan area and after consultation between the HUD Secretary and local governmental authorities throughout the entire metropolitan area.

Metropolitan Coordination Requirement. Required that, beginning July 1, 1967, all applications for federal assistance in carrying out projects for open-space land, hospitals, airports, libraries, water supply and distribution facilities, sewer facilities and waste treatment works, highways, transportation facilities, or water development and land conservation within any metropolitan area be submitted for review of a metropolitan-wide planning agency; stipulated that such agency should be, to the greatest extent practicable, responsible to the local officials of a unit of areawide government or of the local governments involved. *(See box p. 204.)*

Directed metropolitan-wide agencies to submit their recommendations and comments concerning applications to the appropriate federal authorities, who were required to review such recommendations for the "sole purpose of...determining whether the application is in accordance with the provisions of federal law which govern the making of the loans or grants."

Allowed localities such as a city to submit their applications without the recommendations of a metropolitan-wide agency after the application had lain before the agency without recommendation for a period of 60 days.

Authorized the Bureau of the Budget, or any other agency designated by the President, to prescribe rules and regulations for administration of the new requirement.

"Incentive" Urban Aid Grants. Provided a new program of "incentive" urban and aid grants to supplement existing federal aid in areas demonstrating to the satisfaction of the HUD Secretary that all public and private development having a significant areawide impact was consistent with comprehensive and current metropolitan planning.

Made grants for the program available for up to 20 percent of the local share of costs for the following federally assisted programs: basic water and sewer facilities; library facilities; hospital and medical facilities; construction of sewage treatment works; highway construction (federal-aid primary and secondary systems and urban extensions, but not the Interstate System); airport development; urban mass transportation; open-space land development and acquisition; urban beautification and improvement; historic preservation; acquisition and development of land and waters for recreational purposes; and public works and facilities in redevelopment areas.

Limited the maximum amount of combined federal grants under the new program and existing law to 80 percent of project costs.

Specifically prohibited the HUD Secretary from requiring busing of children or adoption of any other program to achieve a racial balance between school districts in a metropolitan area as a condition for receiving assistance.

Authorized appropriation of $25 million for the grants in fiscal 1967 and $50 million in fiscal 1968. Limited to 15 percent the amount of the total authorization available to any one state.

Stipulated that no specific activities were to receive supplemental assistance under both the "incentive" grant program and the demonstration cities program authorized under Title I.

Title III. FHA Insurance Operations. Broadened the veterans home loan mortgage insurance program authorized by the Housing and Urban Development Act of 1965 (PL 89-117) to make benefits available to veterans who had already received a direct, guaranteed or insured home loan administered by the Veterans Administration.

Waived requirements for economic soundness of loans insured under normal FHA operations to provide a new home mortgage insurance program in areas in which violence or civil disorders had occurred or were threatened. Made property eligible for such assistance when it was deemed an acceptable risk "giving due consideration to the need for providing adequate housing for families of low- and moderate-income in such (an) area."

Authorized the HUD Secretary to issue regulations providing a 25-percent increase in mortgage limits for two-, three- and four-bedroom apartments insured under the FHA rehabilitation housing mortgage loan program.

Increased from $11,000 to $12,500 the mortgage limitation on single-family homes purchased under the FHA mortgage insurance program for low- and moderate-income and displaced families. (The program was widely known as Section 221 Housing—its designation under the authorizing legislation—the National Housing Act.) Also increased the mortgage limit on a two-family residence under the program from $18,000 to $20,000.

Amended the National Housing Act to authorize the FHA to permit occupancy by single persons under 62 years of age of up to 10 percent of the units in a project assisted by the FHA below-market interest rate mortgage insurance program for low- and moderate-income housing. (Existing law limited occupancy in such housing to elderly individuals and families and non-elderly families.)

Provided, for experimental purposes, a new FHA below-market interest rate loan insurance program to assist low-income families in buying rehabilitated homes. Limited the aggregate amount of such insured mortgages that could be outstanding at any one time to $20 million.

Title IV. Land Development and New Communities. Broadened the existing FHA land development insurance program to authorize insurance for developers of entire new towns and new communities.

Increased from $10 million to $25 million the maximum mortgage for a single land development undertaking. Required that private loans for such projects contain repayment provisions satisfactory to the HUD Secretary and have a maturity not to exceed seven years (unless the Secretary at his discretion approved a longer maturity period).

Required that applications for assistance under the title first be approved by the local governing bodies of adjoining localities and by the state Governor.

Limited the program to a six-year duration (terminating Oct. 1, 1972) and limited the maximum amount of all such insured loans that could be outstanding at one time to $250 million.

Areawide Planning Requirement Also Controversial

The controversy over the "demonstration cities" program obscured a provision which some observers thought might require a major change in the administration of urban-oriented federal aid programs.

The provision, Section 204 of S 3708, required local government officials, effective July 1, 1967, to submit to an areawide planning agency for review all applications for federal loans and grants to assist in carrying out activities under ten major aid categories. Included were all activities concerning federal open-space land projects, water development and land conservation programs, and all federal aids for planning or constructing hospitals, airports, libraries, water supply and distribution facilities, sewage facilities and waste treatment works, highways, and transportation facilities. *(See details in provisions, Title II.)*

Although the provision did not allow a planning agency to veto such applications, it directed the agency to submit its recommendations and comments for consideration by the appropriate federal authorities. Critics contended this procedure would lead to complete dominance of the aid programs by the planning agencies. Federal authorities, they said, would seek to avoid the controversies that might be caused by approving programs over the opposition of an areawide agency.

During House debate on the demonstration cities bill Oct. 14, a second criticism of the provision was raised. Although the language of Section 204 did not specifically require the appointment of such agencies where they were not in existence, House Republicans argued it would have that effect. One GOP Member, William C. Cramer (Fla.), contended that the Governor of his state did not have the authority under state law to appoint or designate such agencies, and that unless the state legislature was able to act before the effective date, aid might be cut off for metropolitan areas throughout Florida.

Congressional experts differed in their interpretations of the point raised by Cramer, but most indicated the provision was so vague as to require refinement by additional legislation.

HUD Implementation Blocked. In the following two years, however, Congress blocked HUD from implementing Section 204. In 1967, Congress added an amendment to the HUD appropriations bill for fiscal 1968 (HR 9960—PL 90-121) which prohibited the department from using any part of the bill's funds to administer or implement the requirements of Section 204. The amendment was sponsored in the House by Cramer and accepted by the Senate. It was repeated in 1968 in the HUD appropriations bill for fiscal 1969.

Cramer, in sponsoring the 1967 amendment, said his amendment was necessary because HUD might use the provision to gain more control over local planning decisions. Because of a huge backlog of aid applications, he argued, the areawide agencies would tend to make the kind of recommendations that would be favored by HUD. If they did not, he contended, the applications probably would go to the bottom of the stack.

During debate on the conference report on HR 9960, Cramer said that HUD, following House approval of his amendment in May, had transferred authority over the requirement to the Bureau of the Budget. Since that time, he said, the Bureau had implemented the provision in an orderly manner without prejudice to any local area (including those that lagged in forming an areawide agency). In the meantime, he said, Governors of the states in which metropolitan areas did not have the areawide agencies had designated similar bodies to perform the required review.

Despite his satisfaction with the Budget Bureau's implementation of the provision, Cramer expressed concern that HUD again would assume authority over the requirement after his amendment expired at the end of fiscal 1968. In the interim, he said, the Banking and Currency Committee should study the requirement and consider amendments that would assure "continued local or areawide rather than federal control over planning."

Permitted either a public sewer system or an adequately regulated private one on land developed under the program.

Amended the Housing Act of 1954 to authorize urban planning grants to official government planning agencies in areas where new communities were to be developed with federal mortgage assistance. (Existing law limited such grants to metropolitan areas, depressed areas and federally impacted areas.)

Amended the National Housing Act to make clear that the requirements for encouraging broad participation by builders in all FHA land development mortgage insurance programs envisioned primarily the participation of small builders.

Title V. Mortgage Insurance for Group Practice Facilities. Authorized a new program of FHA insurance for loans to finance and equip facilities for group practice of medicine, dentistry or optometry.

Limited such mortgages to a period of 25 years and to an amount not to exceed the lesser of 90 percent of the value of the facility or $5 million.

Stipulated that although both profit-making and non-profit-making groups could sponsor such clinics, only non-profit groups could actually take out mortgages. Provided a three-year duration for the program, through Oct. 1, 1969.

Title VI. Preservation of Historic Structures. Amended the basic urban renewal law (Title I of the Housing Act of 1949) to provide for recognition of historic and architectural preservation in urban renewal plans and to authorize such planning and actual preservation activities as eligible urban renewal costs.

Authorized the HUD Secretary to make grants to the National Trust for Historic Preservation to cover costs incurred by the Trust in renovating or restoring structures which it considered to be of historic or architectural value and which it would maintain after restoration for historic purposes. Provided an open-ended authorization for the aggregate amount of such grants, but provided a maximum of $90,000 for assistance to any one structure.

Authorized grants to cities, other municipalities or counties for up to two-thirds the cost of surveys of the structures and sites in such localities determined by appropriate authorities to be of historic or architectural value. Directed that such surveys be designed to identify the historic structures and sites in the locality, determine the cost of their restoration or rehabilitation and provide other information necessary to formulate an effective program of historic preservation.

Authorized the HUD Secretary to make grants of up to 90 percent of costs of local projects to demonstrate the effect of modern methods in preserving and restoring historic sites or structures. Limited the total amount of such grants to $10 million. Also authorized the Secretary to make grants of up to 50 percent of the cost of acquisition and restoration of historic sites or structures, without limitation as to the total commitment of grants.

Title VII. Urban Renewal. Authorized localities to credit, toward the local share of urban renewal costs, expenditures totaling the lesser of $3.5 million or 25 percent of costs incurred on (1) facilities used by the public predominantly for cultural, exhibition or civic purposes; (2) city halls or public safety buildings; or (3) facilities constructed or rehabilitated by a public university for the treatment of physical or mental disabilities and illness or for medical research. Stipulated that such credit would be available, however, only when the project was located in or near the urban renewal area, was found to contribute materially to the object of the urban renewal plan, and was not otherwise eligible as a local grant-in-aid.

Permitted air rights sites in urban renewal areas to be used for industrial development if found to be unsuitable for use on low- and moderate-income housing.

Required that the residential redevelopment of any urban renewal area provide a "substantial" supply of standard housing of low and moderate cost and result in "marked progress in serving the poor and disadvantaged people living in slum and blighted areas."

Amended the Housing and Urban Development Act of 1965 to make clear that the Urban Renewal Administration was required to grant a three-fourths rather than two-thirds federal contribution to urban renewal projects initiated in an area suffering from substantial or persistent unemployment; amended the 1949 Housing Act to extend from one-quarter mile to one mile the distance from an urban renewal project a university or hospital could be located and still credit certain expenditures toward the local share of urban renewal costs; and required that plans to redevelop urban renewal areas give "consideration" to development of effective systems for the control of storm and sanitary wastes.

Title VIII. Rural Housing. Amended the Housing Act of 1949 to authorize use of Farmers Home Administration direct housing loans for purchase of newly constructed homes. (Existing law limited the use of such loans to purchase previously occupied dwellings.)

Increased from $1,000 to $1,500 the maximum combination of Farmers Administration loans and grants which could be made to families of low income for essential home repairs.

Broadened the existing rental housing program for rural areas to permit direct loans for housing projects accommodating non-elderly rural residents of low income and insured loans for housing of non-elderly residents of moderate income (non-elderly meant persons under 62 years of age). Also broadened the types of organizations that could receive direct loans to include housing cooperatives. (Existing law limited direct loans to elderly persons of low- and moderate-income and insured loans to any elderly person regardless of income. Direct loans could be executed only by non-profit corporations and consumer cooperatives.)

Eliminated the existing ceiling of $300 million on the amount of rural housing loans that could be insured annually, but limited the duration of the program to Oct. 1, 1969.

Title IX. Urban Information and Technical Assistance Services. Authorized a new program of federal grants to states and metropolitan area agencies of up to 50 percent of cost for establishment of urban information and technical assistance centers.

Required that such facilities provide both state and local bodies and private individuals with information and data needed for the solution of urban problems and provide technical assistance to small communities outside metropolitan areas with respect to the solution of such problems.

Provided an authorization of $2.5 million for the program in fiscal 1967 and $5 million in fiscal 1968.

Title X. Miscellaneous. Increased from 36 months to 60 months the maximum term of lease for private accommodations to be used as public housing.

Authorized appropriation of $10 million for a new program of federal grants and loans to the state of Alaska to assist in providing housing and related facilities to natives and other needy persons. Limited grants to 75 percent of aggregate building costs up to a per unit maximum of $7,500.

Directed the HUD Secretary to conduct two-year studies to test and demonstrate new and improved techniques and methods of applying advances in technology to urban development activities and to formulate methods to improve understanding of environmental conditions necessary for the planning and development of "viable urban centers."

Amended the Housing and Urban Development Act of 1965 to spell out specific terms of Defense Department acquisition (or reimbursement of loss in private sale) of properties held by individuals put out of work by the closing of a federal installation. Stipulated that such homeowners were to receive up to 95 percent of losses incurred in the private sale of such housing or 90 percent of value when the properties were purchased by the Department. (The higher payment for private sale was designed to take into account the additional costs to the homeowner of effecting such sale and also to limit the number of properties that the Defense Department might have to acquire.)

Also amended the 1965 Housing legislation to make available until six months after enactment of PL 89-754 an unappropriated authorization of $100,000 for a study to determine methods of insulating homes located near airports so as to diminish the effects of aircraft noise. (The original authorization expired Aug. 10, 1966.)

Model Cities Appropriations

Congress in 1966 appropriated $11 million for fiscal 1967 for planning demonstration (model) city projects authorized by S 3708. The Administration requested $12 million, the authorized amount.

A request for $12,180,000 to initiate the program of "incentive" grants for metropolitan planning was denied. This was authorized in Title II of S 3708.

The demonstration city funds were provided in a supplemental appropriations bill for fiscal 1967 (HR 18381—PL 89-697) which was enacted shortly before adjournment.

Rent Supplements Funding

After bitter debate, Congress in 1966 provided initial funding for President Johnson's controversial rent supplements program, a major Great Society program that was authorized in 1965 over vigorous Republican opposition. *(See 1965 chronology.)*

The funding came in two pieces of legislation, a supplemental appropriations bill for fiscal 1966 and a regular housing appropriations bill for fiscal 1967. The Administration had requested rent supplements contract authority for these two years totaling $65 million, the maximum amount authorized for payments in the 1965 law. Congress in 1966 provided a total of $32 million: $12 million for fiscal 1966 and $20 million for fiscal 1967. Even these drastically reduced amounts were sustained by the barest of margins in Congress. In addition, Congress added a restrictive rider dealing with local control of the program. *(See below.)*

Funds Denied in 1965. After the rent supplements plan became a law, President Johnson late in 1965 requested funding for fiscal 1966 to get the program under way. However, when Congress was considering this request, criticism developed over preliminary regulations issued for the plan by the Federal Housing Administration (FHA). These guidelines, designed to familiarize housing officials and project sponsors with the program, authorized asset holdings of up to three times the amount of income for the elderly and twice the income for all other tenants. Opponents contended that this proposal circumvented the will of Congress by making supplements available to persons less needy than contemplated under the basic rent supplements law. This controversy caused the House to deny funds for the program.

1966 Action

Guidelines Revised. The FHA Dec. 6, 1965, issued new guidelines which cleared up the biggest objection raised against the supplements plan in the House—that persons with high net assets could live in subsidized housing. The new guidelines deleted the controversial income—asset formulas and provided instead for flat asset limits of $5,000 for the elderly and $2,000 for all other tenants. Revision of the guidelines plus inclusion of the local control rider *(see below)* won over a

number of earlier critics including Rep. James Harvey (R Mich.) who led the fight to kill the initial funding of the program in 1965. Nevertheless, the 1966 battle to obtain the contract authority was difficult and close.

Fiscal 1966 Funding. The crucial action on rent supplements funding came early in the session and produced two key votes. Republicans sought to make the votes "economy-in-Government" issues and nearly succeeded.

Congress provided the initial funding in the Second Supplemental Appropriations Act for Fiscal 1966 (HR 14012—PL 89-426) which became law May 13. The bill provided authority for the Government during fiscal 1966 to enter into contracts with private, non-profit groups totaling up to $12 million for rent supplements payments. It also appropriated $100,000 for actual payments under the contracts in fiscal 1966. In addition, the bill limited the contractual authority and payment of supplements to projects which were either part of a "workable program," such as urban renewal, or had been specifically approved by local officials.

In the House, a Republican-led attempt to delete the $12 million in contract authority and $100,000 for payments failed on a key **190-198** roll-call vote. The vote breakdown: R 125-6; D 65-192 (ND 17-160; SD 48-32). In the Senate, the rent supplements funding was deleted by the Appropriations Committee. However, when the bill reached the floor, the Committee's deletion of the funding was rejected by a key **45-46** roll-call vote, thus returning both the contract authority and the payments appropriation to the bill. The vote breakdown: R 26-5; D 19-41 (ND 7-32; SD 12-9).

The rent supplements vote was the first in 1966 on financing a major domestic program. The GOP "economy" argument was based on the increasing inflationary pressures in the nation and the rising costs of the Vietnam war. Many Democrats were reported to believe that rejection of the supplements funds could lead to other sizable cuts in Administration programs later in the session. Administration lobbyists, including Postmaster General Lawrence F. O'Brien, who was the chief Congressional liaison officer for the White House until late in 1965, campaigned vigorously on Capitol Hill in the days preceding action on the bill to round up votes for the rent supplements provisions.

Fiscal 1967 Funding. Within two months after the bruising battle over 1966 funding, Congress was again locked in combat over rent supplements. This time it was over contract authority and payments for fiscal 1967 which were carried in the Independent Offices-Housing and Urban Development Department appropriations bill for that year.

Mr. Johnson requested $35 million for contracts and $3 million for rent payments in fiscal 1967. Congress provided $20 million for contracts and $2 million in payments. The amounts requested were entirely denied by the House Appropriations Committee. But when the bill (HR 14921—PL 89-555) reached the floor, the reduced amounts ($20 million—$2 million) were added by a 192-188 roll-call vote. The breakdown: R 6-119;, D 186-69 (ND 154-14; SD 32-55). After the first calling of the roll on this vote, four Democrats who opposed the addition of the funds withdrew their "nay" votes and paired with absent Members who favored the funding. The effect was to eliminate a tie vote under which the amendment adding the funds would have been rejected. In the Senate, an amendment to delete the funding was rejected by a 38-51 roll-call vote. This vote showed considerably more support for the program than was evident earlier in the year. The vote breakdown: R 22-8; D 16-43 (ND 6-35; SD 10-8).

As was the case with the supplemental bill for fiscal 1966, the local control rider was added to the fiscal 1967 funding bill.

Local Veto. The local control rider, introduced at the time of the 1965 funding action but obscured in the debate over guidelines, was important to fence-straddling Members who saw it as a way to keep supplements out of areas that did not want them. Specifically, the proviso gave localities an "out" by limiting supplements to projects either approved as part of a "workable program," which meant a joint local-federal blueprint for use of federal housing aids (primarily urban renewal), or approved by the highest elected official or governing body of an incorporated area. Cities or, in some cases, a suburb or section of a city with a workable program could refuse to certify rent supplements as part of the program; other cities and localities without such an arrangement could simply deny approval.

Federal housing officials visualized the rider as posing a twofold threat. In the first instance, officials in suburbs and cities who feared the racial and economic integration contemplated by supplements presumably would keep the program out of their communities. This development would bring on a second problem. In the most feasible area for the plan—downtown sections of large cities—higher land costs would often place mortgage figures far above the per unit limitation of $12,550 (plus a differential of up to 25 percent for high-cost areas) set for the program by FHA. Thus, the over-all effect of the proviso was seen as a severe restriction of the program.

In the strongest statement made against the rider during Congressional debate on supplements, Rep. William F. Ryan (D N.Y.) March 29 said the limitation "clearly...has been written into the bill to block the possible exodus of low-income families into communities outside the central core of our cities. Local officials in these lily-white bedroom suburbs can be expected to exercise this veto power to prevent the have-nots from coming into the community with the haves." The cost ceilings, Ryan added, would further hamper the program by setting a $15,000 limit on per unit construction in high-cost downtown areas where it would take up to $21,500 to construct a comparable unit of public housing. Ryan subsequently introduced an amendment to delete the local control priviso from the fiscal 1966 supplemental appropriations bill, but it was defeated by voice vote of the House.

Political Strategy. Rep. Joe L. Evins (D Tenn.), chairman of the Independent Offices Appropriations Subcommittee, told Congressional Quarterly he had offered the rider during Subcommittee consideration of the fiscal 1966 and fiscal 1967 appropriations bills as a means to "make the impossible possible...to get the program approved."

Rep. Robert G. Stephens Jr. (D Ga.), a leading Congressional authority on housing matters who voted in favor of the rent supplement authorization as well as the two successful 1966 funding attempts, told CQ he

"had no doubt that the amendment eased the feelings of a lot of Congressmen—both North and South." Other sources said that several Southern opponents who withheld their votes on funding would have voted "no" without the proviso.

Rep. Paul A. Fino (R N.Y.), a strong opponent of rent supplements, charged in a floor speech on the fiscal 1966 bill that the Administration had sponsored the local control proviso as a "red herring" to get the supplements program through the House. "The Administration cannot allow rent supplements to be kept out of the suburbs," Fino said. "This is the keystone of the Administration's plans for socio-economic integration. The proviso is a trick—so do not be fooled by it." A Fino aide said that Fino's statement was based on evidence that the Administration had devised the rider in "strategy planning sessions" under the assumption that it would be deleted by the Senate and "dropped quietly in conference."

FNMA Housing Funds

The nation's straining economy, which was attempting to fulfill exuberant consumer and business demand and finance a major war, was causing havoc in the housing industry by 1966 as interest rates soared. The industry was experiencing its second worst year since World War II. *(For a discussion of the economic problems during these years, see introduction to this chapter.)*

In response, Congress enacted legislation (S 3688—PL 89-566) to provide an additional $4.76 billion to the Federal National Mortgage Assn. (FNMA) to enable the agency to replenish the dwindling supply of mortgage money. The bill was passed by almost unanimous roll calls in both chambers of Congress.

Experts blamed the industry's problems on the shortage of money available for mortgage financing—a result of the "tight money" situation that was put into effect in the nation in 1966 to combat inflationary pressures. The homebuilding recession was an ironic by-product of the generally booming economy which had led to the inflationary trend and tight money.

Savings and loan associations were very seriously affected by the tight money conditions and the high interest rates. S & Ls were the principal source of funds to finance new housing construction and the purchase of existing homes, supplying 45 to 47 percent of all housing mortgages. The S & Ls lost funds to commercial banks and to other forms of investment (such as corporate securities) where the financial return to the owner of the funds was considerably higher. As a result, funds available for housing mortgages were substantially diminished in 1966. *(For story on the competition between S & Ls and banks for funds, and legislation that was enacted to help S & Ls, see Economic Policy, subchapter on banking policy, 1966 chronology.)*

As an indication of the reduced funds going to the housing market, Government officials said the net acquisitions of residential mortgages decreased by 25 percent in the first two quarters in 1966. This occurred even though there was significant federal aid. FNMA purchased almost $4.5 billion of mortgages (at an annual rate) during the period and the Home Loan banks provided funds to offset deposit losses of savings and loan associations. In the third quarter, only $9.4 billion (annual rate) went into residential mortgages, more than 40 percent below the amount of a year earlier. Government officials said the net flow into home mortgages from savings and loan associations was "virtually zero."

Although the number of housing starts plunged dramatically, more money was put into private commercial and industrial construction in 1966 than in 1965.

FNMA is a mixed Government-private corporation, one-half of whose stockholders are private. It was created in 1938 to—among other things—provide the housing industry with funds by purchasing from private lenders mortgages which are insured or guaranteed by the Federal Housing Administration or the Veterans Administration, and by selling those mortgages when investment capital is readily available. These were known as FNMA's secondary market operations. (For additional background, *see Congress and the Nation, Vol. I, p. 465.*)

S 3688 as enacted provided FNMA with additional sources of revenue to carry out its purchase functions. FNMA could use the new revenues to purchase additional existing FHA- and VA-insured mortgages from private lenders. This would, in turn, give the lenders more money to make new housing loans. The new revenues were needed because FNMA—in order to help the housing industry—had already bought substantial amounts of mortgages in 1966.

The Administration generally favored legislation to assist the housing industry. However, it opposed one provision, providing $1 billion more for FNMA's special assistance activities, because of its effect on the President's Budget.

Spearheading the effort for legislation was the National Assn. of Home Builders which waged a vigorous lobbying campaign.

Provisions. As signed into law Sept. 10, 1966, S 3688 contained the following major provisions:

Secondary Market Operations Funds. Authorized the Federal National Mortgage Assn. (FNMA) to borrow funds in private capital markets up to 15 times its capitalization (rather than up to 10 times as under existing law), thus providing about $2 billion in new funds for secondary market operations.

Authorized the Secretary of the Treasury to subscribe to an additional $110 million of FNMA preferred stock, thereby providing FNMA authority to borrow another $1.65 billion (under the 15-1 ratio) for a total of $1.76 billion in new funds for secondary market operations.

Special Assistance Funds. Authorized an additional $1 billion for FNMA special assistance functions under which the agency provides financial support for home financing by purchasing selected types of home mortgages.

Specified that purchases with these funds be limited to FHA- and VA-insured or guaranteed mortgages of up to $15,000, except that the amount could be $17,500 ($22,500 in Alaska, Guam or Hawaii) in high-cost areas as determined by the Secretary of HUD.

Limited use of the funds to the purchase of mortgages on new construction.

Specified that $500 million was to come from new borrowing from the Treasury and $500 million was to come from existing FNMA special assistance authority

available to the President. (Existing law authorized the President to buy certain types or classes of mortgages for special purposes; that authority currently had an uncommitted balance of about $1.8 billion. S 3688 took $500 million of that authority and assigned it to the $15,000-or-under special assistance funding provided in the measure.)

Hearings on City Problems

The Senate Government Operations Subcommittee on Executive Reorganization held 26 days of hearings between August and December, 1966, on the problems of American cities. The Subcommittee was headed by Sen. Abraham A. Ribicoff (D Conn.).

In announcing the purpose of the hearings, Ribicoff said cities were being neglected "at our national peril," and that he would conduct an "in-depth" study of the Federal Government's role in solving urban problems, in particular the role of the Department of Housing and Urban Development. The Committee wanted to determine whether HUD was, in fact, exercising its role as coordinator and "meaningful authority" on all federal activities related to urban development, Ribicoff said.

Witnesses who appeared before the Subcommittee included Members of Congress, federal officials, mayors of nine U.S. cities, businessmen, civil rights leaders and two Harlem Negroes, one of whom had spent nearly half his life in jail. He told the Committee that existing "the way I do...you might break the law at any time without intention..."

Riots in several northern cities during the summer months put severe pressure on Congress and the Federal Government to act on the problems of the ghettos. The problems were intensified by the continuing rapid influx of Negroes into the nation's central cities, where they were forming a disproportionately high percentage of the population. In some cities they were rapidly approaching a numerical majority. By 1970, according to one estimate, Negroes would constitute 40 percent or more of the population in 14 of the nation's major cities.

This factor intensified some of the most difficult social and economic problems of the city, presenting possibilities of further erosion of the local tax base, intensified school integration problems, a shortage of decent housing, and less industry moving in because of crowded and rundown conditions.

For Negroes, all these developments could mean an intensification of the major Negro problems—poverty and lack of opportunity, increased joblessness in the central cities, and lack of city funds to pay for welfare programs and other programs needed to break up the ghettos.

Though the problems of the Negro dominated the hearings, Sen. Ribicoff sought to explore many other problems of the city: the flight of the middle classes to the suburbs, the moving away of industry to the suburbs, the rising costs of education.

New York Mayor John V. Lindsay (R) startled the Subcommittee with the statement that New York City needed $50 billion from the Federal Government in the next decade to become "thoroughly livable."

The hearings by Sen. Ribicoff's Subcommittee were held in two sections, between Aug. 15 and Sept. 1 and between Nov. 29 and Dec. 15.

1967 Hearings. Ribicoff's Subcommittee concluded the hearings on June 28, 1967. The panel held seven days of hearings between April and June in 1967, bringing to 33 the total number it had conducted since August 1966. Summing up the hearings, Ribicoff said the problems of the cities were so grave that the need for "quick action" was "especially critical." Contending that "too many of our federal programs offer long-term promises," Ribicoff said this held "little—if any—meaning for the man and woman who need help and assistance today. Neither they nor their children can afford to wait upon our grand design."

1967

Model Cities, Rent Supplements

Two of the Johnson Administration's major urban assistance programs—rent supplements and model cities—were given additional financing by Congress in 1967, but at levels far below those sought by the President.

For new rent supplements contract authority, Congress provided $10 million; President Johnson requested $40 million. For the model cities program, Congress appropriated $312 million; the President requested $662 million.

In addition to the new contract authority for supplements, Congress provided the full $5 million appropriation sought by the Administration for payments under existing supplements contracts. Because the Government was committed to the contracts, the payments were not controversial.

Congress during the 1966 session had approved $32 million for contracts to get the supplements program under way and $11 million to plan the model cities projects (which were called "demonstration cities" in 1966). The full supplements allotment was committed in 1967, but the Government froze the cities funds pending an appropriation to carry out the projects. The initial $11 million in planning money was committed to 63 cities on Nov. 16.

Of the new allotment for the cities program, $12 million was for additional project planning and $300 million for carrying out the plans. The $300 million figure included $100 million for urban renewal in the model cities project areas and $200 million for all the other programs in the projects.

The funding for the two programs constituted relatively small items in one of the larger appropriations bills enacted during the First Session of the 90th Congress. The bill (HR 9960—PL 90-121) covered the Department of Housing and Urban Development (HUD) and various independent agencies for fiscal 1968. HR 9960 appropriated a total of $10,139,473,900. The bulk of the funds in the bill, including more than $6.6 billion for veterans' affairs, aroused little or no controversy. But the items for rent supplements and model cities were at issue throughout the year much as was the case when the programs were enacted in the 89th

Rent Supplements, Model Cities Votes

Following is a list of the five House and three Senate roll-call votes taken on rent supplements and model cities funds in 1967:

House

May 17—Amendment by Glenn R. Davis (R Wis.) to drop the $10 million allotment recommended by the House Appropriations Committee for new rent supplements contracts. Accepted **233-171** (R 163-12; ND 11-132; SD 59-27). This was one of the key votes of the session.

May 17—Motion by Robert H. Michel (R Ill.) to delete $75 million for urban renewal in model city project areas and $150 million in other model city grants (leaving for the program $12 million in planning funds). Rejected **193-213** (R 141-35; ND 5-139; SD 47-39.)

Oct. 24—Motion by Robert N. Giaimo (D Conn.) to concur in Senate amendments increasing the House allotment for the model cities program from $237 million to $537 million. Rejected 156-241 (R 15-159; ND 125-18; SD 16-64.)

Oct. 24—Motion by Sidney R. Yates (D Ill.) to concur in a Senate amendment restoring the full $40 million dropped by the House for new contract authority for rent supplements. Rejected 151-251 (R 15-163; ND 120-24; SD 16-64).

Oct. 26—Motion by Paul A. Fino (R N.Y.) to recommit the second conference report on the bill with instructions to House conferees to insist on disagreement to a $10-million conference allotment for rent supplements. Rejected 184-198 (R 139-35; ND 6-124; SD 39-39).

Senate

Sept. 20—Amendment by Frank J. Lausche (D Ohio) to cut the Appropriations Committee's allotment for rent supplements contracts by $20 million, from $40 million to $20 million. Rejected 34-55 (R 18-13; ND 4-35; SD 12-7).

Sept. 20—Appropriations Committee amendment to provide $40 million in new rent supplements contract authority. Accepted **59-31** (R 17-14; ND 35-4; SD 7-13). This was one of the key votes of the session.

Congress. Moreover, the fact that final action on HR 9960 occurred in October in the midst of an anti-spending fervor in the House of Representatives made it all the more remarkable that Congress provided as much as it did for either program. The bill was cleared Oct. 26. *(For story on budget-cutting efforts, see Budget Policy, p. 135.)*

The difficulty in obtaining financing for the programs was expected when Congress convened. Both were enacted over vocal conservative opposition in 1965 and 1966 in a Congress that was much more liberal than the Congress which convened in January 1967. During

Lobbying Helped Save Model Cities Funds

There were a number of reasons why the House approved funds for model cities and not rent supplements. One was the support of Rep. Louis C. Wyman (R N.H.), the extremely conservative Republican, for model cities but not supplements.

Other important factors were vigorous lobbying efforts in behalf of the model cities plan by big-city mayors and leading business executives and the choice the Administration made concerning which of the programs it wanted most.

Faced with the old adage that the House can't digest more than one controversial issue in a single bill, the Administration focused its lobbying on model cities. Fence-straddling Members who contended they couldn't go on record in favor of both controversial programs were told their vote was needed most on the cities plan. Although the Administration hoped such Members simply would stay away when the roll was called on rent supplements, many of them covered their "aye" votes on cities with a "no" on the supplements test.

With Vietnam war demands increasing, the Administration feared it had to be "now or never" for the model cities plan. Action funds for the program were authorized only for two fiscal years—fiscal 1968 and 1969. Further escalation of the war could mean an even tougher appropriations fight in the next session of Congress, making it conceivable that the cities authorization could expire before the first project ever got under way. On the other hand, the supplements program already was off to a modest start and Congress was committed to it—at least to a limited extent. The Federal Housing Administration already had Congressional approval to enter into 40-year contracts with nonprofit groups to pay up to $32 million a year in supplements.

Mayors. With the exception of the Administration's pressure effort, it was thought the strongest lobbying on the bill was that by big-city mayors in behalf of the model cities plan. Administration sources deemed this support crucial to the salvaging of the appropriation.

Impetus for the mayors' support came from efforts by the "Urban Alliance"—an ad hoc group of organizations which were generally favorable to Administration housing and urban-aid policies. Organized in the summer of 1966 by representatives of the U.S. Conference of Mayors, the Alliance came to include such diverse groups as the AFL-CIO, National League of Cities, National Governors Conference, American Institute of Architects, Mortgage Bankers Assn., National Assn. of Home Builders, numerous civil rights and religious organizations and a number of other groups. Meeting in Washington every Friday morning in the weeks prior to the 1966 model cities authorization fight, the Alliance was highly instrumental in securing passage of the 1966 bill. The meetings continued in 1967 on strategy to gain the appropriations necessary to get the program under way.

On May 12—the Friday morning before Tuesday's House debate on the appropriations bill—the Alliance telegraphed key mayors throughout the nation urging them to pressure their Representatives to support both the cities and rent supplements plans. A source who participated in the Alliance's discussions said the mayors had responded with a "massive" lobby effort in behalf of the cities program but only sporadic support of rent supplements. This, he said, was because a model cities project would have demonstrable benefits for an entire urban area while benefits of the supplements plan would not be so widespread.

Businessmen. Strong pressure for model cities funds also came from a group of 21 of the nation's top business leaders. They issued a statement May 15 expressing disappointment over the Appropriations Committee's cuts and calling on the full House to retain "at least the amount of funds recommended by the Committee." The businessmen signing the statement were: S.D. Bechtel, chairman of the Bechtel Corp.; Fred Borch, president of General Electric: D.C. Burnham, president of Westinghouse Electric; Walter Cisler, chairman of Detroit Edison; former Commerce Secretary John T. Connor, president of Allied Chemical; Donald C. Cook, president, American Electric Power Service Corp.; Russell DeYoung, chairman of Goodyear Tire and Rubber; Ben W. Heineman, chairman of the Chicago and Northwestern Railway Co.; Edgar F. Kaiser, president of Kaiser Industries; David Kennedy, chairman, Continental Illinois National Bank and Trust Co.; former Central Intelligence Director John A. McCone, chairman of the Joshua Hendy Corp.; Cyril Magnin, president of the Joseph Magnin Co.; Robert S. Oelman, chairman, National Cash Register Co.; David Packard, chairman, Hewlett-Packard Co.; Herman H. Pevler, president of the Norfolk and Western Railway; David Rockefeller, president of the Chase Manhattan Bank; Stuart T. Saunders, chairman of the Pennsylvania Railroad; Herbert R. Silverman, chairman of James Talcott, Inc.; Gardiner Symonds, chairman of Tenneco, Inc.; Sidney J. Weinberg, partner, Goldman, Sachs and Co.; and Stanley Marcus, president, Neiman-Marcus Co.

Local Interests. Perhaps the most vigorous lobby effort in behalf of both rent supplements and model cities was that put on by the local civic groups and business interests that stood to gain from the programs. On supplements, this included the local groups that had applied for project sponsorship, the banks which would finance the projects and the construction firms that would build the developments. On model cities, local support came from civic and service groups, banks, businessmen, builders and others that sought a role in the projects.

Sources said the greatest local effort on supplements had come from the prospective sponsors whose applications had not yet been approved.

the 1966 Congressional election campaign, many Republican candidates had promised to try to kill both programs.

Throughout the session, the rent supplements allotment was more in doubt than the model cities financing. The cities program had obtained strong backing from big-city mayors, so funding at some level was expected. Rent supplements, however, had drawn the support of only a handful of special interest groups; moreover, some of these groups did not lobby extensively for the program, according to observers who followed the action on HR 9960 during the year.

Because the aid provided by both programs would benefit a relatively small number of persons, there was no major grass-roots effort to persuade Members of Congress to vote for either of the allotments. On the other hand, some Members said they received considerable mail from residents of suburban areas who opposed the programs.

Another factor working against the cities plan was that aid under the program was contemplated for only 60 to 70 cities. This reportedly made it necessary for the Administration to bargain to obtain the votes of Members from rural and predominantly non-urban areas. Some observers also said HUD's purpose in delaying commitment of the $11 million previously appropriated for planning was to hold as many of the urban Members' votes as possible.

The reluctance to continue the programs—much less expand them—centered in the House. The more liberal Senate was basically receptive to increased financing.

In view of the mood of the House, President Johnson Nov. 3 called the appropriations "a legislative miracle." The President praised the Senate for restoring much of the House cuts but said that in the House-Senate conference the "familiar old voices of reaction and status quo" had prevailed.

Legislative Action

House Action. The model cities and rent supplements battles began in the House Appropriations Committee. The Committee recommended a total of $237 million for all model cities activities, a reduction of $425 million from requests. It cut the $40 million request for authority to enter into rent supplements, contracts to $10 million but provided the full $5 million requested for payments under supplements contracts authorized in each of the two previous years.

Following Committee approval of the bill, Rep. Joe L. Evins (D Tenn.), chairman of the Independent Offices-HUD Appropriations Subcommittee, the panel with original jurisdiction over HUD requests, told newsmen the fact that model cities and rent supplements were kept alive at all was "a great victory for the Administration." Evins said the two programs had been put to "some mighty close votes" in the Subcommittee before funds had been approved. (The Subcommittee allotments were adopted without change by the full Committee.)

Floor Action. When HR 9960 reached the House floor, the Administration suffered a major setback. The House May 17 by a key **233-171** roll-call vote accepted an amendment by Glenn R. Davis (R Wis.) deleting the $10 million in rent supplements contract authority which

Housing Program Restrictions

HR 9960, in which funding was provided for model cities and rent supplements, was a typical example of how Congress sometimes uses appropriations bills to negate or restrict programs which it has authorized earlier in other bills. More often than not, it is the Congressional Appropriations Committees which are using their power to reverse or alter the decisions of other committees. Although these restrictions often originate in the Appropriations Committees, they are sometimes added by floor amendments. The basic laws setting the structure of a program are written by legislative committees. The 1965 and 1966 housing bills, for example, came from the Banking and Currency Committees. The Appropriations Committees provide the money to operate the programs. But in addition, the Appropriations Committees usually add legislative provisions to their bills which restrict or in some way attempt to direct the operation of the program they are funding. On occasion, the provisions simply prevent the implementation of the program.

Following are several legislative provisions added by HR 9960. The first provision is the contract authority for rent supplements, but the second part of it is a rider providing a local veto over the program. The last provision was added by a floor amendment in the House. The provisions were as follows:

HR 9960 provided additional rent supplements contract authority of $10 million, to be available until fully committed. Limited the contracts and the bill's $5 million appropriation for rent supplement payments to projects which either were part of a "workable program," such as an urban renewal project, or had been specifically approved by local officials.

The bill limited the federal share of any grant for an open-space land project to a maximum of 50 percent (in effect rescinding a provision of the 1965 Housing and Urban Development Act which allowed grants of up to 90 percent for projects of "special value").

The bill prohibited use of any part of HR 9960's appropriations to provide for "metropolitan expediters" for liaison between the Federal Government and the cities. This was a section of the 1966 Demonstration Cities and Metropolitan Development Act.

HR 9960 also prohibited use of any part of the bill's funds to administer or implement Section 204 of the 1966 Demonstration Cities and Metropolitan Development Act, which required local officials in a standard metropolitan statistical area to submit their applications for most kinds of federal aid to an area-wide planning agency for review.

had been approved by the Committee. The amendment did not, however, affect the $5 million in rent supplements payments that had been approved by the Committee to honor existing supplements contracts. The vote breakdown: R 163-12; D 70-159 (ND 11-132; SD 59-27).

Model Cities Awards Prompted Charges of Politics

The Department of Housing and Urban Development Nov. 16, 1967, announced that 63 cities had been chosen to draw up plans for the model cities program. The 63 areas—which varied in size from a small Tennessee town to New York City—were to share in the $11 million in planning money appropriated by Congress in 1966.

H. Ralph Taylor, the HUD Assistant Secretary in charge of the model cities program, earlier in the year had said that the recipients of the first $11 million in planning funds would be named around July 1. When the grants were not announced until Nov. 16, the 4½-month delay prompted many Republican opponents of the program to charge that the Administration purposely had withheld the announcement so as not to jeopardize support on the appropriations bill from House Members whose cities had not been chosen. Administration spokesmen countered that complexities of the program had made the selection process long and difficult and that it would be unfair to have cities develop the plans only to learn later that Congress had voted down the funds to carry out the projects.

Republicans also argued that politics apparently had influenced the selection of some of the 63 cities. House Republican Leader Gerald R. Ford (Mich.) Nov. 16 complained that only nine grants, totaling 14 percent of the $11 million in planning money, had gone to Republican districts.

Some of the areas awarded planning funds were in districts of House Members who played a key role in pushing the appropriation through Congress in 1967. These included five cities represented by Members who supported the program on a crucial vote in the House HUD—Independent Offices Appropriations Subcommittee: Smithville, Tenn. (pop. 2,300), represented by the Subcommittee chairman, Joe L. Evins (D); Texarkana, Ark. (21,000), represented by David Pryor (D); Manchester, N.H. (90,000), represented by Louis C. Wyman (R); New Haven, Conn. (151,000), represented by Robert N. Giaimo (D); and Springfield, Mass. (166,000), represented by Edward P. Boland (D).

Funds also went to areas represented by two Democrats who had played major roles in salvaging the Administration's antipoverty program in the House in 1967. These were Pikeville, Ky. (5,000), represented by House Education and Labor Committee Chairman Carl D. Perkins, and Tampa, Fla. (305,000), represented by Sam M. Gibbons.

In addition, funds went to four communities in President Johnson's home-state of Texas: Eagle Pass (14,000), San Antonio (645,000), Texarkana (32,000), and Waco (105,000). Two of these cities were represented by the chairmen of House committees—Texarkana by Banking and Currency Committee Chairman Wright Patman (D) and Waco by Agriculture Committee Chairman W. R. Poage (D). Patman's panel approved the original authorization for the model cities program.

The charges of political considerations were blunted somewhat, however, by the fact that funds went to a city (Charlotte, N.C.) represented by one of the most vigorous House opponents of the cities program—GOP Rep. Charles Raper Jonas. Jonas had strongly opposed the program in the HUD Appropriations Subcommittee and, in a key test on the House floor May 17, had voted in favor of an unsuccessful GOP motion to recommit the bill with instructions to delete all cities money except the $12 million for additional planning. Although 24 other Republicans from applicant districts had voted against the recommittal motion and for the program funds, only seven were "rewarded" with cities planning money.

Four of the areas selected—Newark, Detroit and the Harlem and central Brooklyn areas of New York City—had been the scene of serious racial disturbances. Neither Los Angeles nor Cleveland were chosen, however, even though they had encountered widespread rioting.

It was the first occasion in the 90th Congress on which the conservative coalition—a voting alliance of Republicans and Southern Democrats against Northern Democrats—had formed to defeat a major Administration proposal.

The Administration won a partial victory when the House by a key **193-213** roll-call vote, rejected a recommittal motion by Robert M. Michel (R Ill.) to send the bill back to the Appropriations Committee with instructions to delete all model cities funds except the $12 million allotted for planning. An identical amendment by Michel had been rejected earlier on a 152-160 teller vote.

A factor apparently affecting the vote on model cities was the vigorous lobbying effort staged in behalf of the program by big-city mayors and other urban interests. Rent supplements, by contrast, did not have a strong lobby.

Deletion of the contract authority for rent supplements was the first floor defeat that President Johnson's Great Society program had suffered during the 1967 session.

Factors in House Action. The fact that any funds were provided was a surprise to many Washington observers who expected the Committee to deny the President's requests outright. It was later learned by reporters that the conservative coalition in the House probably would have killed both programs had not one of the coalition's key members defected on the model cities plan. That member—Rep. Louis C. Wyman (R N.H.)—cast the deciding vote that saved the plan in the Subcommittee, and he followed up by rallying crucial votes for it on the House floor. (But Wyman did not support the supplements program, and its funding was killed on the House floor.) Although the model cities plan had other factors working in its favor, including the support of the nation's mayors, the program's funding might well have been denied without Wyman's help.

Administration and GOP sources told reporters that they would have thought Wyman one of the least likely of the GOP Members to support the plan. (Only 35 of 176 GOP Representatives who voted did.) In addition to supporting Barry M. Goldwater, the Republicans' stanchly conservative 1964 Presidential candidate, Wyman had been the only New England Representative to oppose the 1964 Civil Rights Act and had described the 1965 medicare legislation as a "deceptive hoax." He almost always supported the "conservative coalition" before he lost his re-election bid in 1964.

Lobby groups and other sources close to the issue said Wyman's support again was crucial on the House floor. Describing the "unrest" and "acute problems," of the cities, Wyman urged Republicans to give the program a chance. Although the cities plan might not be "precisely the correct program," he said, HUD and Congress could improve it through experience gained once the program got under way. One GOP source said Wyman had influenced "at least 10 to 12 votes." On the 193-213 defeat of Michel's recommittal motion, a shift of 11 votes could have spelled the difference.

Following House action, Wyman said he had supported the plan because it would be a "grievous political error" for Republicans to oppose aid to the nation's cities without proposing a constructive alternative. While rent supplements (which he vigorously opposed) had a generally unpopular connotation in the public mind, he said, the model cities plan was associated with "necessary therapeutic attention for sore and legitimate needs." Other sources attributed Wyman's move to a desire to get away from his "stanch conservative image." Another factor appeared to be the interest of city officials of Manchester, N.H., the largest city in Wyman's district, in applying for model cities funds. On Nov. 16, Manchester was granted planning funds.

Senate Action. The Senate Appropriations Committee restored $300 million of the $425 million the House cut from the model cities program, to provide a total program allotment of $537 million compared to the $662 million requested. The Committee also restored the entire $40 million requested for rent supplements contract authority.

Floor Action. In the major floor action on HR 9960, the Senate Sept. 20 voted to sustain the Committee's restoration of the full Administration request for rent supplements contract authority and its partial restoration of model cities funds. The Senate first rejected by a 34-55 roll call an amendment to reduce the rent supplements allowance to $20 million. It then approved the Committee figure of $40 million by a key **59-31** roll-call vote. The vote breakdown: R 17-14 D 42-17 (ND 35-4; SD 7-13).

A key factor in the outcome on supplements was the shift to support of the program by Senate Minority Leader Everett McKinley Dirksen (R Ill.), who previously had opposed it. Dirksen announced his switch after learning that numerous business leaders had endorsed the program at a recent housing conference in Pittsburgh. Dirksen said: "I now think I understand the program a little better. Now we may be able to get the Government out of public housing." Dirksen made no further comment on the issue on the Senate floor but voted against the amendment which was defeated 34-55 and for the Committee amendment.

The Senate by a 62-38 roll call accepted the Committee figure for the model cities program.

Final Action. House and Senate conferees Oct. 20 filed a conference report on HR 9960 resolving all differences except those on rent supplements and model cities. On these issues, the conferees returned to their respective chambers for further instructions on how to resolve their differences.

Each chamber then voted to reject the allotments provided by the other for rent supplements and model cities. Senate rejection of the House figures was by voice vote. House rejection of the Senate allotments for model cities was by a 156-241 roll call and of the allotment for rent supplements by a 151-251 roll call. The conservative coalition formed in opposition to the Senate figures on both House votes. *(See breakdowns in box p. 209.)*

A new conference then was called to resolve the disputes. On Oct. 25, conferees agreed unanimously to a second conference report providing compromise allotments of $10 million for rent supplements contracts and $312 million in appropriations for model cities. The report was adopted Oct. 26 by voice vote of the Senate and by a 297-88 roll-call vote of the House. Although the House GOP conferees supported the compromise agreements, rank and file House Republicans moved to recommit the report with instructions to drop the rent supplements funds, but their motion was rejected by a roll call of 184-198, the fifth House vote of the session on the supplements.

Low-Income Housing

Government policies for improving housing conditions for low-income families were the subject of a crossfire of Congressional criticism during 1967. The controversy, however, was prologue for enactment in 1968 of one of the most far-reaching housing bills in the nation's history. The major provisions of the 1968 legislation were designed to help low-income persons find adequate housing.

In 1967, conservative critics of Government policies contended that housing officials were jeopardizing the taxpayer's money by insuring housing projects that stood a good chance of ending up in default. At the same time, a group of liberals argued that the Government should take even greater risks in order to achieve the "social goal" of upgrading substandard housing.

The agency absorbing all the criticism was the Federal Housing Administration (FHA)—the Government's primary guarantor of private mortgage loans for the purchase of homes and construction of rental housing. Although the FHA had had its liberal and conservative critics throughout its 33-year history, long-time observers said the 1967 dispute was probably the most heated yet.

The controversy began in June when the Senate Permanent Investigations Subcommittee called on the agency to stop taking what the panel called "excessive risks" in underwriting mortgages on apartment projects. The Subcommittee, headed by John L. McClellan (D Ark.), said substantial numbers of FHA mortgages on low-income housing developments were in financial difficulty if not default, and that insurance reserves for these projects were depleted to the point where a major recession might exhaust them altogether and make it necessary for the taxpayer to foot the bill.

Background on FHA

The FHA was created under the National Housing Act of 1934 as a means to encourage improvement of housing standards, to facilitate the flow of private mortgage money through a system of Government mortgage insurance, and to help keep money markets steady.

For its first 27 years, the agency's sole function was to insure loans on projects that entailed little risk of encountering financial difficulties. The 1934 statute, establishing the basic mortgage insurance program on the purchase of homes (Section 203) and on rental housing (Section 207), required that the FHA deem a loan "economically sound" before insuring it. Attesting to the FHA's strict interpretation of this requirement, the agency over this period built up insurance reserves—the difference between all FHA income (such as appraisal fees, insurance premiums and investments) and insurance losses—of more than $1 billion.

Although the Section 203 and 207 programs remained the centerpiece of FHA activity, the agency in 1961 was given the additional and significantly different task of administering a new program of mortgage insurance (Section 211(d)(3)) on loans to nonprofit and limited divident corporations for sponsorship of apartment development in low- and moderate-income families. (Under certain circumstances, the FHA would arrange for such sponsors to receive subsidized mortgage interest rates.) The FHA's task was further broadened in 1965 with the enactment of the rent supplements program and again in 1966 with the creation of a new mortgage insurance program (Section 221(h)) which provided interest subsidies on private loans to low-income families for the purchase of rehabilitated homes. *(For additional details on these programs, see box in 1968 chronology, p. 217.)*

While the primary purpose of the older FHA activities had been the promotion of economic stability, the objective of this second generation of programs was a social one—the relocation of low-income persons in standard housing. In keeping with this objective, Congress dropped the traditional "economic soundness"doctrine with respect to the new programs and provided instead that projects could be insured on the basis of "acceptable risk."

The other side of the issue took shape in August when Sen. Edward W. Brooke (R Mass.) said it might be necessary to create a new low-income housing division within the Department of Housing and Urban Development (HUD—the FHA's parent agency), unless the FHA began writing insurance for more low-income projects. Brooke, in an Aug. 7 Senate floor speech, said that in the past six years the FHA's "paperwork merry-go-round" had produced only 40,000 units of low-income housing—a figure he called "pitifully inadequate."

As a first step, Brooke, backed by Sens. Thruston B. Morton (R Ky.) and Howard H. Baker Jr. (R Tenn.), moved during consideration of the fiscal 1968 appropriations bill for HUD and independent federal offices (HR

9960) to transfer operational control of the controversial rent supplements program from the FHA to the office of the HUD Secretary. Brooke withdrew his amendment, however, when Senate Banking and Currency Committee Chairman John J. Sparkman (D Ala.) promised to hold hearings on the broader issue posed by Brooke—whether administration of all FHA low-income programs should be shifted.

Brooke Nov. 21 introduced his proposal in the form of a separate bill (S 2681). Because the Sparkman Committee was deliberating over home ownership bills and other measures, it put off consideration of Brooke's bill until 1968. However, in reporting out a home ownership measure (S 2700) on Nov. 28, it approved a key amendment by William Proxmire (D Wis.) that some observers thought would give the FHA a clear mandate to move into the area of low-income housing. (Full Senate action on S 2700 also was deferred until 1968.) Proxmire's amendment permitted the FHA to insure mortgages under all of its programs for projects in "declining urban areas" without regard to the existing statutory requirements of those programs. (Requirements applicable to all programs included such criteria as minimum down payments and maximum mortgage periods. In addition, the traditional home mortgage and rental housing programs included the "economic soundness" requirement, and the social purpose programs the "acceptable risk" standard.)

To ensure that the FHA would implement the plan following its enactment, Proxmire proposed also that losses incurred as a result of the policy set forth in the amendment be made up with federal appropriations. Proxmire intended the amendment as a supplement rather than a substitute for the Brooke proposal; in fact, he later co-sponsored the Brooke bill.

Home Ownership

Congress in 1967 began serious consideration of legislation to aid low-income persons in purchasing homes of their own. Although the legislation did not get very far, the proposals were to lead in 1968 to a major omnibus housing bill that included not only home ownership but numerous related provisions dealing with urban development.

The only substantive action on the issue in 1967 was reporting of a bill (S 2700) by the Senate Banking and Currency Committee. S 2700 provided federal subsidies to lower the interest costs on home mortgages taken out by poor persons. The measure was reported late in the year, Nov. 28, and was not considered on the floor. However, the bill was to form a key part of the 1968 legislation.

Supporters of S 2700 believed it would pass the Senate but doubted that the House would even take it up in the remaining days of the session. Another key factor in the decision of the bill's proponents to defer further action was their hope of gaining Administration support for the measure in 1968. Although Administration officials had helped draft the Committee bill, the Administration never took a formal position on the measure in 1967.

Congress also put off action on most of the Administration's 1967 housing package, which included a new federal rat control program, higher interest rates on college housing loans, new planning grants for rural areas, an additional Assistant Secretary for the Department of Housing and Urban Development (HUD), uniform interest rates on Federal Housing Administration (FHA) mortgage loan insurance for the Agency's various multifamily housing programs, extension of the emergency urban mass transit grant program, and other provisions. The rat control and emergency mass transit grant proposals were approved in modified form in separate legislation; the remainder of the package, however, never moved out of either the House or Senate Banking and Currency Committees. *(For rat control controversy, see story on HR 11000 and HR 6418 in Health, Education and Welfare, subchapter on health; for legislation to extend the transit program, see story on HJ Res 859 in Economic Policy, subchapter on transportation policy.)*

The push for a home ownership bill began early in the 1967 session, when Sen. Charles H. Percy (R Ill.) proposed setting up a private, non-profit corporation with authority to float bonds and use the proceeds to make loans to private sponsors for rehabilitating, buying or constructing homes for eventual resale to low-income persons.

Percy's proposal met with almost uniform Republican support in both the House and Senate but with strong Democratic opposition. The bill was opposed also by HUD Secretary Robert C. Weaver, who said the publicity that the proposal had received had misled poor persons to believe that the bill could meet their housing needs "overnight." "The great danger," Weaver said, "is in overselling the home ownership program" to very poor families who might not be able to carry the burden of owning their own homes.

Following the announcement of Percy's proposal, three Senate Democrats—Walter F. Mondale (Minn.), Joseph S. Clark (Pa.) and Abraham A. Ribicoff (Conn.)—introduced alternate bills to increase the supply of low-income housing through the existing structure of FHA home mortgage insurance. A bitter struggle ensued in the Senate Banking and Currency Committee, and the panel was unable to reach agreement until the closing days of the session.

Although the Committee bill was labeled a "compromise," it was far more like the Mondale proposal than any other. The funding mechanism of the measure was Mondale's proposal for interest subsidies on FHA mortgages. Although the bill retained Percy's proposal for a non-profit corporation to aid in the program, the corporation's duties were limited to providing technical assistance to community agencies sponsoring low-income housing programs and did not include the fund-raising authority sought by Percy.

1968

Home Ownership, Housing Act

A remarkable period in housing legislation culminated in 1968 in the enactment of one of the most far-reaching housing and urban development programs ever adopted by Congress. The legislation (S 3497—PL 90-448) was the third major housing bill enacted during President Johnson's term in office. The earlier bills, passed in 1965 and 1966, included such innovative programs as rent supplements and model cities.

In contrast to the earlier bills, the 1968 measure went through Congress with barely a murmur of dissent. This was all the more remarkable because S 3497 included provisions enlarging the authorizations for the highly controversial rent supplements program and the somewhat less controversial model cities undertaking. Various reasons were cited for the relative ease with which the bill was enacted. One was simply its size and the diversity of its programs; it had 17 titles providing a little something for a large number of people. In addition, many observers believed the Republicans—who would have been expected to be the primary opponents—had been badly embarrassed in 1967 by opposition to a rat control bill and wanted to avoid being labeled "anti-urban" again. *(For discussion of these factors, see box p. 219.)*

S 3497, the Housing and Urban Development Act of 1968, authorized a $5.3 billion, three-year housing program designed to provide more than 1.7 million units of new and rehabilitated housing for low-income families. Major new programs authorized by the measure included federal subsidies to help the poor buy their own homes and rent apartments, federal underwriting of the insurance industry against riot losses, flood insurance for homeowners and new urban renewal programs. The bill also extended and expanded a number of existing housing programs, including rent supplements and model cities.

The bill, which was one of the landmark legislative achievements of President Johnson's Administration, was the first step toward the President's goal of 6 million units of new or rehabilitated housing to replace substandard housing units during the following 10 years. The 10-year goal was announced by Mr. Johnson in a Feb. 22 message to Congress on the cities, in which he requested many of the programs which gained approval in S 3497.

If fully funded by Congress, the eventual price tag of the measure was expected to greatly exceed $5.3 billion. This represented only the three-year cost of the bill, which included many programs that authorized contracts running as long as 40 years.

Home Ownership, Rental Assistance. Highlights of the bill were the home ownership and rental aid programs, both of which went through Congress with surprisingly little controversy.

The home ownership plan, originated by Republicans in 1967 but substantially modified by housing officials before the Administration endorsed it in 1968, was designed to enable low-income families to purchase their own homes by providing a federal subsidy that could bring down the effective interest cost of the purchaser's home mortgage. The subsidy would amount to the difference between 20 percent of the family's monthly income and the required monthly payment under the mortgage for principal, interest, taxes, insurance and mortgage insurance premium. In every case, however, the purchaser would be required to make payments at least equal to the payment that would be required if the mortgage were made at a rate of 1 percent.

Eligibility for the homeowner's program generally would be limited to families with annual incomes of $3,000 to $6,500, but exceptions would be made for

Home Ownership Program Explained

John W., who has an income of $4,200, has applied for federal assistance under the new home-ownership program authorized by the 1968 Housing and Urban Development Act. His income is well within the $6,000 local limitation for program eligibility, so assistance is approved. John goes to a local lending institution and obtains a mortgage loan of $12,000, to be repaid over a 35-year period. The Government draws up a contract with the private lender for payment of a monthly interest subsidy on John's mortgage.

Assuming a market interest rate of 6-3/4 percent, John's required monthly payment is $99.66. As long as his income remains the same, his payment will be $70 (20 percent of his monthly income) and the Government subsidy will be $29.66. His income will be recertified every two years, and appropriate adjustments will be made in the federal assistance payments to reflect any change.

high-cost areas and unusually large families. In general, the maximum mortgage permitted under the program would be $15,000. The plan was programmed to aid 500,000 families over the succeeding three years.

Under the bill's new rental assistance program, low-income families would be aided indirectly by federal subsidies on the mortgage interest costs of apartment projects sponsored by nonprofit organizations. The subsidy would amount to the difference between the market rate mortgage and the amount required on a mortgage bearing an interest rate of 1 percent. The interest savings to the sponsor would be passed on to the tenants in lower rents. The income eligibility requirements for the program were identical to those for the home ownership plan.

When fully operational, the home ownership and rental aid programs would replace the existing program of assistance to apartment construction through below-market interest rate (BMIR) mortgages under Section 221(d)(3) of the National Housing Act. The BMIR program required support from the Federal National Mortgage Assn. (FNMA), which bought up the low-interest mortgages as part of its special assistance function.

In general, the new programs would aid poorer families than those currently assisted under Section 221(d)(3)—a program designed to aid moderate- as well as low-income families. In addition, it was thought the shift to direct interest subsidies would lead to a larger program by attracting private enterprise into the low-income housing field. (The BMIR program was limited to the amount of funds FNMA could commit to buy up mortgages; although the Government eventually got back all but the interest differential, vast amounts of federal money constantly were tied up under the program.) Both the House and Senate Committee reports on S 3497 emphasized that it would be impossible to meet the goals envisioned by the bill without a substantial commitment of funds from the private mortgage market.

Debate on the home ownership and rental aid issues skirted the establishment of the programs themselves and centered on the income levels of the persons to be assisted. The Administration proposed that the Secretary of Housing and Urban Development (HUD) be given the authority to set income limits for eligibility under the programs, with the understanding that the limits would follow those currently used in the below-market interest rate program. Opposition developed in both chambers, however, as Members feared that the programs would not reach the families most in need of assistance. The final bill limited eligibility generally to families whose incomes were no greater than 35 percent above the local income limits for initial occupancy of public housing—a level well below the limits of the BMIR program.

Other Provisions. The bill also required the Federal Housing Administration (FHA) to provide greater opportunities for obtaining FHA insurance on properties in declining urban areas and to make such insurance more available to home buyers who cannot meet ordinary credit standards but are deemed by the Government to be satisfactory risks. To cover losses under the program, the bill provided a new high-risk insurance fund, which was to be financed with federal appropriations.

Another new program established by the measure authorized federal assistance to developers of entire new towns and new communities. The provision authorized the HUD Secretary to guarantee an aggregate of $250 million of bonds and other obligations issued by private developers of such projects. The bill also authorized supplemental federal grants for public facilities built in new communities in which the developer promised to build a substantial number of housing units for low- and moderate-income families. A program embodying the same objectives was approved by Congress as part of the 1966 Demonstration Cities Act; however, the 1966 plan required developers to secure funds from private lenders (which then would be insured by FHA) instead of empowering them to issue the federally insured bonds—an easier means of financing. In addition, the 1966 program did not provide the supplemental financing for public facilities.

Another major innovation provided by S 3497 was a federal reinsurance program to provide the private insurance industry with reinsurance against riot losses and to encourage programs to increase the availability of insurance in ghetto areas. The bill also included a program to make flood insurance available to home owners. The flood insurance provisions were similar to a flood insurance bill (S 1985) passed by the Senate in 1967.

In a broad departure from existing urban renewal law, the bill provided a new renewal program designed to allow for short-term redevelopment projects. The new plan, called the neighborhood development program, provided for planning and carrying out projects on an annual basis. Existing law required detailed and comprehensive planning covering several years.

In its other important features, the bill provided prospective land purchasers a measure of protection from fraud, broadened the lending power of savings and loan institutions, authorized FHA mortgage insurance on vacation homes, and established new programs

Background on HUD Low-Income Housing Activities

Two agencies at HUD were charged specifically with aiding low- and moderate-income families to obtain decent housing: The Housing Assistance Administration (HAA) and the Federal Housing Administration (FHA).

HAA Programs

The HAA was the latest successor to the old United States Housing Authority (USHA) established by the Housing Act of 1937, which authorized the low-rent public housing program to provide homes for those who could not afford decent housing without Government assistance.

Public Housing. The basic HAA program, public housing, resulted in the establishment of 2,200 local public housing authorities. Since 1937 these local agencies had built 680,000 low-rent units. The median income for those occupying the housing was about $2,700 although each housing authority establishes its own eligibility limits.

The bulk of all public housing was provided through the construction by local housing authorities of public housing projects. Each authority received an annual subsidy from the Federal Government to keep rents in the projects low enough to provide housing for very poor persons.

After the passage of the 1965 Housing Act, the HAA put greater stress on rehabilitating existing housing for use as low-rent public housing than on new construction.

Turnkey—Another new approach to expanding the supply of low-rent housing was the so-called turnkey method. Under turnkey, local housing authorities contracted with private developers, builders and rehabilitators to buy, upon completion, housing they had built or rehabilitated. The turnkey method was designed to short-circuit the lengthy delays that often occur when local authorities build housing projects themselves.

Leasing—Another new approach, aimed at speeding up the process of increasing the public housing inventory, was the so-called "rent certificates" program which was approved in the 1965 Housing Act. The program permitted local housing authorities to lease private dwellings for low-income families. The federal contribution makes up the difference in rent that the owner receives and the amount the tenant-occupant is able to pay. The leasing program has been termed a way of providing "instant" housing for poor families who are in acute need.

Housing for Elderly or Handicapped. Another program was long-term, low-interest loans to private, non-profit corporations to provide housing for elderly or handicapped people of moderate income—defined as those with incomes too high for public housing but too low for the private housing market.

FHA Programs

In addition to the HAA, federal assistance for housing low- and moderate-income families was provided through the FHA, the Government's primary guarantor of private mortgage loans. Created in 1934, FHA's chief function through the years was to provide basic mortgage insurance on the purchase of single homes and on rental housing. In recent years, FHA was given jurisdiction over a number of special assistance housing programs.

Section 221(d)(3). In 1961 the FHA was assigned the task of administering a new program of mortgage insurance, known by the numerical designation 221(d)(3), an amendment to the 1934 Housing Act. Section 221(d)(3) authorized both a market-rate and a below-market-rate program. Under the latter, nonprofit organizations, cooperatives and public agencies could borrow money from commercial sources, such as banks, at interest rates below those generally prevailing in the housing market for sponsorship of apartment developments for low- and moderate-income families.

In the case of the below-market interest rate program, the loans are insured by the FHA. The Federal National Mortgage Assn. (FNMA) then buys the mortgage from the bank or other lender which normally agrees to the sale in order to avoid tying up funds in low-interest loans. The effect of the procedure is that FNMA advances money at low interest rates for construction or rehabilitation of housing for this program.

Rent Supplements. The key low-income program in FHA was the rent supplements program. This makes low-income individuals and families who are either elderly, handicapped, displaced by Government action or occupants of substandard housing eligible for admission to FHA 221(d)(3), new or rehabilitated, housing which is owned by a private non-profit, limited-dividend or cooperative mortgagor. The housing owner enters into a 40-year contract with HUD, which promises to pay federal rent supplements to eligible tenants of the housing.

The subsidy payments for any dwelling unit cannot be higher than the amount by which the fair market rental for the unit exceeds 25 percent of the tenant's income. When the tenant has enough income to pay the full rent, he may continue to live in the same unit but without rent supplement payments. Strict limits were placed on the per-unit costs of the rent supplement housing that could be built.

Low-Income Sales Housing. The newest of FHA's special programs was 221(h), which was tacked onto the 1966 Demonstration Cities and Metropolitan Development Act under the sponsorship of Rep. Leonor K. Sullivan (D Mo.), and which in 1968 was operating only on a pilot basis. Under 221(h), the FHA insures mortgages of nonprofit organizations—church groups, nonprofit industries groups, antipoverty community action groups—to finance the purchase and rehabilitation of deteriorating or substandard housing. The nonprofit groups then sell the homes to individuals and families with incomes equivalent to or below the maximum income permitted for those eligible for rent supplements or public housing. The FNMA provides an interest subsidy.

of federal assistance for college housing and mortgage insurance for nonprofit hospitals. The bill also provided a number of new spending authorizations for existing programs, including $1 billion for the model cities program in fiscal 1970, $40 million in additional 40-year contract authority for the rent supplements program in 1970, $100 million more in rent supplements contracts for fiscal 1971, and an additional $265 million in grants for water and sewer facilities in fiscal 1969 and 1970.

Legislative History

Congress in 1967 did not enact major housing legislation despite months of deliberation by the Senate Banking and Currency Committee on proposals to promote home ownership by low-income families. The Committee Nov. 28 reported a compromise bill (S 2700) providing federal subsidies to enable such families to purchase homes, but the measure did not reach the Senate floor in 1967. As reported, S 2700 incorporated provisions of various bills sponsored by Sens. Walter F. Mondale (D Minn.), Charles H. Percy (R Ill.), Joseph S. Clark (D Pa.) and Abraham A. Ribicoff (D Conn.). The home ownership provisions of the measure were not formally endorsed by the Administration in 1967.

In a special message to Congress on urban problems, President Johnson Feb. 22, 1968, detailed his legislative recommendations for housing and other urban-aid programs. In addition to endorsing the home ownership plan contained in S 2700, the President outlined other proposals designed to provide about 6 million housing units for low- and moderate-income families over the next 10 years. The cornerstone of the President's proposed program was the Housing and Urban Development Act of 1968, which was introduced March 4 (S 3029) by Senate Banking and Currency Committee Chairman John J. Sparkman.

S 3029 called for a five-year, $7.5-billion program. With a few exceptions, it covered the same major areas as covered by the final version of S 3497. S 3029 did not include provisions on riot and flood insurance and interstate land sales, all of which were contained in the Senate Banking and Currency Committee's clean bill, S 3497. The Administration's request for a national insurance development corporation to insure private insurance companies against the risk of riots was included in another bill (S 3028) introduced March 4 by Sparkman. S 3029 contained a provision to remove the statutory ceilings on interest rates of mortgages insured by the FHA and the Veterans Administration, but this was included in a separate bill (HR 10477).

Senate Action. The Senate Banking and Currency Subcommittee on Housing and Urban Affairs held hearings in March on S 3028 and S 3029 and various other housing bills. The full Banking and Currency Committee in mid-May reported a clean bill (S 3497) which included the major provisions of S 3029 as well as several new provisions.

The Senate passed S 3497 at the end of May by a key **67-4** roll-call vote. No major changes in the bill were made on the floor. A number of amendments were concerned with aid to riot victims and riot-damaged cities, but a provision that would have made such cities eligible for federal disaster aid was deleted. An amendment to eliminate the provision for federal rein-

surance for insurance companies offering coverage against riot damage was defeated by a 10-62 roll call. An amendment to eliminate aid for development of new communities was defeated by a 27-38 roll call.

House Action. The House Banking and Currency Subcommittee on Housing held hearings in April and March on HR 15624 and HR 15625, the House versions of the Administration bills. The full Banking and Currency Committee at the end of June reported a clean bill (HR 17989) providing home ownership and rent subsidy programs similar to the Senate's. The bills were similar in many other respects also, although the House Committee dropped the provisions on new communities and interstate land sales which were in the Senate version.

The House passed its version of the legislation in July by a 295-114 roll call. The vote breakdown: R 112-66; D 183-48 (ND 145-2; SD 38-46).

The main controversy over the home ownership program centered on income limitations for persons buying houses under that program. After considerable debate, the House by a 271-137 roll-call vote accepted an amendment to limit persons eligible under the home ownership program to those whose income was not more than 30 percent higher than the ceiling for public housing in their area. Under the Committee bill the Secretary of HUD was authorized to set income limits for eligibility and they were expected to be somewhat higher. The conservative coalition formed on this vote; a majority of Republicans and Southern Democrats voted together in opposition to a majority of Northern Democrats. Only eight Republicans opposed the amendment. The breakdown: R 170-8; D 101-129 (ND 31-114; SD 70-15.)

The amendment was offered by John B. Anderson (R Ill.), who said that under the Committee bill the program would not reach those who needed it most. He said, "When we talk in general and ill-defined terms, as we do in this bill, about low-income and moderate-income housing, we are not talking about very much low-income housing. We are talking about a lot of moderate-income housing." The first concern should be the 13 million poor families earning less than $5,000 per year who were looking for assistance in obtaining decent housing, he said. The same limitation was added to the new rent subsidy program.

Final Action. Senate-House conferees had reached agreement on the bill (S 3497) by the end of July.

On the major difference in the bills—the income eligibility limits for the home ownership and rental assistance plans—conferees arrived at a compromise settlement. Eligibility generally was to be limited to families whose incomes were no greater than 35 percent above the local income ceilings for admittance to public housing, plus $300 per minor child. The Senate bill limited eligibility to families whose incomes were less than 70 percent of the local eligibility ceiling for the BMIR program; the House measure limited coverage to families whose incomes were no more than 30 percent greater than the local income ceiling for continued occupancy in public housing (which was higher than the ceiling for admittance).

In another major action, conferees agreed to the Senate provision, dropped by the House, authorizing federal assistance to developers of new towns and new com-

'Rat Debate' and Lobbying Keys to Passage of Housing Bill

Although they did not know it at the time, the Representatives who laughed the Administration's rat control bill off the House floor in the summer of 1967 helped pave the way for passage of the 1968 bill. Although other factors figured in the passage of the bill, Capitol Hill, Administration and lobby sources generally considered the 1967 rat debate to be the "turning point" for massive new programs of federal urban aid.

"The rat debate really dramatized the urban problem," one House Republican said. "At a time when Newark was burning, Congressmen were saying that 'the rat smart thing for us to do is to vote down this rat bill rat now.' After the public outcry over that performance, it would have been political suicide for Republicans to try to defeat the housing bill this year."

Another major reason for the bill's easy passage was the fact that its 17 titles included programs of benefit to a wide array of special interest groups.

Strong bipartisan support for the measure developed when the Senate Banking and Currency Committee, which had studied the bill for almost 18 months, reported out programs similar to proposals originated by Republicans. The heart of the bill—its home owner's assistance program—was originally introduced early in the 1967 session by Sen. Charles H. Percy (R Ill.) and Rep. William B. Widnall (R N.J.), amid much fanfare on Capitol Hill and in the press. Although the Committee substantially reworked the Republican plan, GOP members still claimed credit for giving impetus to the measure. Other major Republican programs in the bill were the flood insurance title and a provision authorizing federal mortgage insurance for private nonprofit hospitals.

A major surprise on the bill was that debate never developed over President Johnson's rent supplements and model cities programs—two controversial Great Society plans which had aroused vigorous GOP opposition in previous sessions of Congress. Although the bill authorized a broad expansion of both programs, neither became the subject of the heated debates of the past. The erosion of GOP opposition was thought to have resulted from malaise over the narrow defeats suffered by Republicans in the past battles over the issue and an increasing awareness that private enterprise would play a major role in implementing both programs.

Income Limits Debate. The only major floor debate in either chamber developed in the House over the income limits for the home ownership and rental assistance programs.

The Administration had proposed that the HUD Secretary be given the authority to set income limits for eligibility under the two programs with the understanding that the limits set would follow those currently used in the below-market interest rate (BMIR) program. The upper range of incomes of persons aided under BMIR was generally around $7,000, but could be considerably higher for large families and families living in high-cost areas. The limits were higher than those envisioned under the original Percy bill.

In consultation with John Williamson, lobbyist for the National Assn. of Real Estate Boards (NAREB), Rep. John B. Anderson (R Ill.), drafted an amendment to limit eligibility under the home ownership program to persons whose income was not more than 30 percent higher than the ceiling for occupancy in public housing in their areas (a level that was not substantially less than the BMIR limitations). The amendment, opposed by the Administration and the National Assn. of Home Builders, carried July 10 by a 271-137 roll-call vote. The House placed the same income limits on the rental assistance program authorized by the bill.

Despite the Administration's opposition, a high HUD official told a reporter that Anderson had "saved the day" by introducing amendments that could give Republicans the opportunity to vote against subsidizing moderate-income families and yet retain a "rather wide spectrum of income eligibility limits."

New Towns. One of the biggest payoffs for Administration strategy came on the provision for assisting developers of new towns and new communities—a proposal that had long been opposed by the U.S. Conference of Mayors. In a calculated move, the Administration neutralized the mayors by making clear that assistance under the program could be provided for additions to the edge of a city as well as entire new towns in the countryside. This wilted the mayors' opposition, which since 1964 had been predicated on fears that the provision would lure middle-income families from the cities, causing them to deteriorate faster.

Reinsurance Provision. One of the biggest lobby victories came on the reinsurance provision, which authorized the HUD Secretary to reinsure private insurance companies against property losses resulting from riots or civil disorders. The provision was proposed by the American Insurance Assn., representing the bulk of the nation's casualty insurers, with an estimated 80-85 percent of outstanding insurance on the nation's urban properties. One staff member on the House Banking and Currency Committee said the insurers "had to get that provision because the state insurance commissioners were really breathing down their necks about canceling so many policies." He said their lobby campaign was a "subtle" one, with local businessmen frequently calling their Representatives and warning that the policies were likely to be cancelled unless the provision went through.

Savings and Loans. Vigorous lobbying by the savings and loan industry resulted in House and conference approval of a provision giving S&Ls broader lending authority, including authority to lend for seasonal homes and for appliances under certain conditions.

munities. Conferees also restored Senate provisions requiring full disclosure in the interstate sale of subdivided undeveloped land and providing interim urban renewal assistance to blighted areas where substantial permanent clearance was planned but not yet under way. Under the latter program, however, the authorization was cut to $15 million per year instead of the Senate's $20 million.

Conferees also accepted a Senate provision, dropped by the House, authorizing FHA mortgage insurance on vacation housing and a provision added by the House after Senate action, which authorized mortgage insurance on nonprofit hospitals. Conferees also agreed to a compromise increase of $150 million for basic water and sewer grants in fiscal 1969 and an extension of the program into fiscal 1970 with a $115-million allotment.

The conference report on the bill was adopted by a voice vote of the Senate July 25. The House the following day, in a key vote, adopted the report by a **228-135** roll call. The vote breakdown was: R 72-92; D 156-43 (ND 124-2; SD 32-41).

Provisions

As signed into law, Aug. 1, S 3497:

Stated that the highest priority and emphasis should be given to providing decent housing for lower income families and that in carrying out such programs the resources of private enterprise and individual self-help techniques should be used as fully as possible.

Required that to the "greatest extent feasible," employment arising from these programs be given to lower income persons residing in the area of such projects. Also required, to the greatest extent feasible, that contracts for work under these programs be awarded to business concerns located in or owned in substantial part by persons residing in the area of the projects.

Stated that emphasis should be given to encouraging good design as an essential component of low- and moderate-income housing.

TITLE I—LOWER INCOME HOUSING

Established a home ownership assistance program for low- and moderate-income families based on an interest rate subsidy. Stipulated that mortgages for housing purchased under the program would be made at market rates of interest and that the Government would pay the interest subsidy directly to the institution making the loans.

Established the following income limits for eligibility under the program: for 80 percent of program funds, participation was to be limited to families whose income was not more than 35 percent higher than the income ceiling for admission to public housing in the area, plus an additional $300 for each minor child. For the remaining 20 percent of program funds, participation was to be limited to families whose income was not more than 90 percent of the area's income ceiling for the below-market interest rate (BMIR) loan program, plus $300 per minor child. Under both the 80 percent and 20 percent provisions, however, the Secretary of the Department of Housing and Urban Development (HUD) was directed to give preference to the lowest income families for whom home ownership was practicable.

Set the amount of subsidy under the program at the difference between 20 percent of the family's monthly income and the required monthly payment under the mortgage for principal, interest, taxes, insurance and mortgage insurance premium. Required, however, that the purchaser make payments at least equal to the payment that would be required if the mortgage were made at a 1 percent rate. Permitted participating families to deduct $300 per minor child from family income for purposes of determining monthly payments as well as income eligibility.

Required a down payment of $200 for participating families whose incomes were less than 35 percent above public housing income eligibility limits and required a 3 percent down payment for all other families.

Set a general limitation on the amount of a mortgage taken out under the program at $15,000, with higher mortgages allowed for high-cost areas and for larger families.

Required that a participant's income be recertified at least every two years and that appropriate adjustments in the assistance payment be made to reflect any changes.

Limited assistance under the program generally to new and rehabilitated housing but provided exceptions for large families, families displaced by governmental action and some other families.

Authorized FHA insurance of mortgages and mortgage payment subsidies for the purchase of housing by nonprofit sponsors or public agencies for subsequent resale to low- or moderate-income home purchasers. (This program was designed to gradually replace the 221(h) program, often called the Sullivan amendment.)

Authorized the Department of Housing and Urban Development (HUD) to provide counseling on care of a home and budgeting of income for persons assisted under the program.

Authorized contracts for annual home ownership assistance payments aggregating not more than $75 million in fiscal 1969, $175 million in fiscal 1970, and $300 million in subsequent fiscal years.

Established a new program to make FHA home mortgage insurance available to low-income families who could not qualify for such insurance under existing FHA programs, because of their credit histories or irregular income patterns, but whom the Department of HUD considered satisfactory risks and capable of home-ownership with the assistance of counseling.

Gave the FHA more flexible authority to provide financing for the repair, rehabilitation, construction or purchase of property located in older, declining urban areas which may not meet normal eligibility requirements.

Established a Special Risk Insurance Fund to insure mortgages under the above programs and under assistance for rental and cooperative housing. Authorized appropriations to the fund to cover any losses. (The Fund was not expected to be operated on an actuarially sound basis.)

Authorized the Secretary of HUD to provide nonprofit sponsors of low- and moderate-income housing with technical assistance and interest-free loans to cover certain preconstruction costs.

Created a National Home Ownership Foundation (a government chartered private nonprofit corporation) to provide technical and limited financial assistance to public and private organizations providing lower income housing.

Authorized the FHA to insure mortgages on large-scale experimental housing projects for lower income families under such programs as home ownership assistance, rent supplements and 221 (d) (3).

Authorized the Secretary of HUD, in cooperation with the private insurance industry, to develop a plan to provide insurance to help home owners meet mortgage payments in periods of personal economic adversity.

Established a National Advisory Commission on Low-Income Housing.

TITLE II—RENTAL HOUSING FOR LOWER INCOME FAMILIES

Established a new program of subsidies for the construction or rehabilitation of rental and cooperative housing by nonprofit sponsors for low-income families. Provided for federal assistance payments to cover the difference between the market rate mortgage and the amount that would be required on a mortgage bearing an interest rate of 1 percent. (This program, when fully in operation, was intended to replace the Section 221(d)(3) below-market interest rate program which relied on support from the special assistance funds of the Federal National Mortgage Assn. (FNMA) rather than subsidies on market rate mortgages.)

Provided that tenants in projects built under this program pay 25 percent of their income as rent up to the full market rental. Required that rental charges collected in excess of the basic charges (calculated on the basis of a 1-percent mortgage) be returned to the Department of HUD. Provided income eligibility limits identical to those under the Title I home ownership assistance program.

Authorized contracts for annual interest assistance payments of not more than $75 million in fiscal 1969, $175 million in fiscal 1970, and $300 million in subsequent fiscal years.

Authorized additional payments under the rent supplements program of $40 million in fiscal 1970 and $100 million in fiscal 1971. (The cumulative authorization for the rent supplements program through fiscal 1969 was $150 million.

Extended assistance under the rent supplements program to projects financed under state or local programs. Existing law limited eligibility to projects financed with federal assistance.

Increased authorization for annual contribution contract authority for the low-rent public housing program by $100 million upon enactment and $150 million in fiscal 1969 and 1970.

Authorized the Department of HUD to enter into grant contracts of up to a total of $45 million through fiscal 1970 with local housing authorities to assist them in upgrading their management and providing tenant services.

Stipulated that high-rise elevator projects could not be approved for low-rent public housing for families with children unless there was "no practical alternative."

TITLE III—FEDERAL HOUSING ADMINISTRATION INSURANCE OPERATIONS

Tightened regulations affecting default on FHA-insured multifamily housing mortgages.

Permitted the Secretary of HUD to insure supplemental loans to finance improvements to multifamily rental projects (including nursing homes and housing for the elderly) and group medical practice facilties financed with an FHA-insured mortgage.

Authorized the FHA to insure mortgages on seasonal homes on an "acceptable risk" basis. Limited the amount of such mortgages to the lower of $15,000 or 75 percent of appraised value.

TITLE IV—NEW COMMUNITY LAND DEVELOPMENT

Authorized the Secretary of HUD to guarantee the bonds, debentures, notes and other obligations issued by private developers to help finance the development of entire new towns or new communities.

Set ceilings of $50 million on the guarantee of any single new development and $250 million in aggregate outstanding obligations.

Authorized supplemental grants of up to 20 percent of the required local cost of federal grant programs to states and localities for assisting new communities with basic water and sewer and open-space land projects. Required, however, that communities using such grants make available a "substantial number" of housing units for low- and moderate-income families as part of the development.

Stipulated that total federal assistance for any facility aided under the supplemental grant program (including the normal federal grant and the supplemental grant) could not exceed 80 percent of the total facility cost. Authorized appropriation of up to $5 million in supplemental grants for fiscal 1969 and up to $25 million for fiscal 1970.

TITLE V—URBAN RENEWAL

Authorized a new program of financial assistance to local public agencies for "neighborhood development programs" under which urban renewal projects were to be planned and carried out on an annual basis. (Existing urban renewal programs required detailed and comprehensive plans covering several years.)

Authorized $1.4 billion for the urban renewal program in fiscal 1970.

Authorized an additional $350 million for urban renewal projects in model cities areas.

Removed existing limitations on the acquisition and rehabilitation of residential properties by a local urban renewal agency. (This limitation reportedly had led to the destruction of salvageable housing and the construction of more expensive housing to replace it.)

Authorized the Secretary of HUD to make grants for the demolition of nonresidential structures that are harborages for rats.

Limited rehabilitation loans generally to borrowers whose incomes were within the local income eligibility limits for assistance under the below-market interest rate loan program.

Authorized grants of up to $15 million a year to provide interim assistance to blighted areas where substantial permanent clearance or rehabilitation is planned but not yet under way.

Broadened rehabilitation loan programs to permit loans to be made outside urban renewal and code enforcement areas and to bring property up to insurance underwriting standards.

Required that a majority of housing units provided in each community's total residential urban renewal projects be for low- and moderate-income families and that at least 20 percent of the units in a project be for low-income families. Permitted the Secretary to waive the 20 percent provision when he determined it was not necessary.

TITLE VI—URBAN PLANNING AND FACILITIES

Authorized a new category of assistance for "district" planning in rural and other areas outside of metropolitan areas. Stipulated that such districts were to include all or part of at least one county and of at least one other general-purpose unit of government, but not any part of a metropolitan area.

Increased the authorization for the over-all urban planning grants program by $35 million in fiscal 1969 and $125 million in fiscal 1970. Specifically earmarked $20 million of the fiscal 1969 authorization and $10 million of the fiscal 1970 authorization for district planning grants.

Extended to the new rural district planning areas eligibility to receive bonus grants of up to an additional 20 percent of project costs under numerous federal grant programs when the HUD Secretary determined that such areas were practicing comprehensive area-wide planning. (Existing law, Section 205 of the 1966 Demonstration Cities and Metropolitan Development Act, limited such assistance to metropolitan areas.) Also continued through fiscal 1970 the availability of the $75 million authorized for the program for fiscal 1967 and 1968 but denied by Congress in appropriations acts for those two fiscal years.

Provided that any funds authorized but not appropriated through fiscal 1969 for basic water and sewer facilities, neighborhood facilities and advance acquisition of land remain available through fiscal 1970. Raised the authorization for water and sewer facilities from $200 million to $350 million in fiscal 1969 and provided an authorization of $115 million for the program in fiscal 1970.

Authorized an additional $150 million for fiscal 1970.

TITLE VII—URBAN MASS TRANSPORTATION

Authorized $190 million for fiscal 1970.

Permitted private transit companies to furnish up to 50 percent of the local share of the project cost of a mass transit project, and up to 100 percent in some cases.

Extended for 20 months, through July 1, 1970, the emergency grant program for mass transportation under which requirements that full area-wide planning be completed were waived.

TITLE VIII—SECONDARY MORTGAGE MARKET

Partitioned the Federal National Mortgage Assn. (FNMA) into two corporations: the Government National Mortgage Assn. (GNMA) and a privately owned Federal National Mortgage Assn. (FNMA).

Provided that the GNMA would operate special assistance and management and liquidating functions and would be administered by the Department of HUD.

Authorized an increase of $500 million in special assistance authority, available July 1, 1969, primarily for the purchase by the GNMA of below-market interest rate mortgages under the 221 (d) (3) program.

Provided that the new FNMA would operate a privately financed secondary mortgage market for government-supported mortgages under general regulation of the Secretary of HUD.

Provided for retiring the current federal capital contribution to the FNMA and transferring control to common stockholders.

Provided new forms of borrowing authority for the FNMA.

TITLE IX—NATIONAL HOUSING PARTNERSHIPS

Authorized the creation of federally chartered, privately funded corporations to plan and carry out the building or rehabilitation of housing for low- and moderate-income families.

Authorized such a corporation to form a national partnership as its vehicle for participating in the provision of low-income housing.

Authorized the national partnership created by the corporation to enter into partnerships, limited partnerships or joint ventures with local builders and investors for the purpose of building low- and moderate-income housing.

TITLE X—RURAL HOUSING

Authorized direct and insured loans with interest rate subsidies to provide housing for low- and moderate-income families in rural areas who are not able to obtain housing under the home ownership or subsidized rental and cooperative housing programs set up under Titles I and II.

Authorized a new program of grants and loans for "self-help" housing in rural areas.

TITLE XI—URBAN PROPERTY PROTECTION AND REINSURANCE

Authorized the Secretary of HUD to set up a program to reinsure insurance companies against property losses resulting from riots or civil disorders. The program was to be terminated in 1976.

Established the new post of Federal Insurance Administrator to administer, under supervision of the HUD Secretary, both the reinsurance program and the flood insurance program established under Title XIII.

Required the Secretary to set reinsurance premiums that would provide an aggregate fund in excess of the estimated amount of insured riot losses during 1967.

Specified that reinsurance would not be offered in states which did not provide, within a specified time, for sharing some of the costs to the Federal Government of covering reinsured losses.

Required insurers reinsured under the program to cooperate with state insurance authorities in establishing and carrying out statewide plans to assure fair access to insurance requirements (FAIR plans). (These plans were designed to ensure that property owners were not denied insurance solely because of the area in which their property was located.)

Provided that state FAIR plans be administered under the supervision of the state insurance authority.

Set minimum requirements for FAIR plans including:

• Property insurance may not be denied without inspection of the property.

• Insurers declining a risk or agreeing to provide coverage only if the property was improved must provide property owners with a statement of reasons for refusal of coverage or improvements required for coverage.

Required state plans to include an all-industry placement facility to help agents and brokers to place insurance up to the full insurable value of a property.

Authorized the Secretary to modify the criteria for state plans.

Authorized the Secretary to borrow up to $250 million from the Treasury to pay reinsurance claims in excess of the aggregate amount of reinsurance premiums received under the program. (The program was expected to be generally self-supporting.)

Directed the Secretary to study means of assuring an adequate supply of burglary and theft insurance.

TITLE XII—DISTRICT OF COLUMBIA INSURANCE PLACEMENT ACT

Authorized the Commissioner of the District of Columbia to establish a joint underwriting association to provide insurance or reinsurance of basic property without regard to environmental hazards. Authorized both federal assistance and an increase in insurance premiums to cover losses.

TITLE XIII—NATIONAL FLOOD INSURANCE

Gave the Secretary of HUD authority to set up a program of flood insurance as a joint federal-private venture and permitted the Secretary to establish an all-federal program in the event that a joint program was not feasible.

Provided that subsidized personal and property insurance would be made available for flood damage to one-to four-family houses and to small business properties in flood-prone areas. Specified that insurance would be available only in states which "evidenced a positive interest" in flood insurance and adopted land use and control regulations before June 30, 1970, to prevent unwise use of flood-prone land.

Established a 15-member Flood Insurance Advisory Committee to assist the HUD Secretary in determining the scope of the program, the premiums to be charged and how the program should be operated. Specified the following maximum liabilities eligible for rates below actuarial cost (subsidized premiums): $17,500 for a one-family dwelling; $30,000 for a multiple-unit dwelling; $5,000 for the contents of each unit; $30,000 for a business

structure; and $5,000 for the contents of each business unit.

Directed the Secretary to encourage private insurers to form a pool to sell and service flood insurance and to share profits and liabilities. Limited insurance outstanding at any time to $2.5 billion.

Authorized the Secretary to make premium equalization payments to the insurers' pool to make up the difference between below-cost premiums paid and the actuarial cost of the insurance. Pledged the Federal Government to back up the private firms by paying any claims in excess of the financial capacity of the privately financed pool.

Directed the Secretary, with other federal agencies, to identify flood zones according to declining risk of disaster and, within five years after enactment, to establish a set of actuarial flood insurance premiums based on the flood-zone statistics.

Created a National Flood Insurance Fund in the Treasury and gave the HUD Secretary borrowing authority of up to $250 million. Rescinded existing authority for Congress to appropriate any amounts the President deemed necessary for flood control. Specified that the Fund would be used to pay premium subsidies to the insurance pool and reinsurance claims when the pool suffered excessive losses. Authorized appropriations to reimburse the Treasury for payments from the Fund.

Authorized the Secretary to develop comprehensive criteria for state and local planning and regulations of land use in flood-prone areas.

TITLE XIV—INTERSTATE LAND SALES

Required that persons selling subdivided undeveloped land in interstate commerce or through the mails file a statement with the HUD Department giving certain required information. Information required included the title of the land, its physical nature, and the availability of roads and utilities.

Required that prospective purchasers be furnished with a property report based on the statement and approved by the HUD Department.

Exempted subdivision of fewer than 50 lots or with lots of more than five acres each.

Authorized the Secretary of HUD to sue for injunctions against violations of this title.

Established criminal penalties of up to $5,000 fine and/or five years imprisonment for violations. Also made persons selling or leasing lots in violation of this title civilly liable.

TITLE XV—NONPROFIT HOSPITALS MORTGAGE INSURANCE

Authorized a new program of FHA mortgage insurance for nonprofit hospitals.

Provided that mortgages could be made for constructing a new hospital, rehabilitating an existing hospital or covering the cost of major items of equipment. Limited the aggregate amount of such mortgages that could be outstanding at one time to $20 million.

TITLE XVI—TEN-YEAR HOUSING GOAL

Stated that the national housing goal of "a decent home...for every American family" should be "substantially achieved" within 10 years by the construction or rehabilitation of 26 million units, 6 million of which would be for low- and moderate-income families.

Required the President to make a report to Congress on or before Jan. 15, 1969, setting forth a 10-year plan to meet national housing needs, together with legislative recommendations for carrying out his plan. Also required the President to make annual reports during each of the 10 years, comparing results for the previous year with the goals set forth in the plan for that year.

Required the Secretary of HUD to report annually to the President on the progress in achieving this goal and to recommend any legislative and administrative measures necessary.

TITLE XVII—MISCELLANEOUS

Authorized $1 billion for the model cities program for fiscal 1970. Authorized $12 million for model cities planning grants in fiscal 1969.

Authorized grants for demonstration projects on the prevention of urban blight to be made to nonprofit organizations (in addition to the public agencies under existing law). Increased the authorization for the program from $10 million to $20 million.

Provided a new program of federal assistance for college housing to supplement the existing direct loan program. Authorized annual grants to cover the difference between the interest an educational institution is required to pay on borrowings from private sources and interest on a direct federal loan (currently 3 percent).

Authorized $10 million in annual contracts in fiscal 1969 and an additional $10 million in fiscal 1970 for the new college housing program.

Authorized appointment of an additional HUD Assistant Secretary with particular responsibilities in the field of urban research and development.

Extended a program of grants to the states to help them provide urban information and technical assistance to communities of less than 100,000 population. Authorized $5 million for fiscal 1969 and $15 million for fiscal 1970.

Provided that savings and loan institutions be given broader lending power, including authority to lend for seasonal homes and for home appliances under certain conditions, and that the Federal Home Loan Bank Board be given greater authority to ensure prompt payment of withdrawals to savers.

Appropriations

After the housing bill became law, the Administration asked Congress to fund the major provisions through a supplemental appropriations bill for fiscal 1969. This was done in HR 20300 (PL 90-608) but at substantially lower amounts than requested for the key home ownership and rent subsidy program.

Home Ownership, Rental Assistance. The Administration came away with much less authority than it sought. The Department of Housing and Urban Development had wanted authorization to enter into contracts of up to $75 million each for home ownership and rental assistance, the amounts authorized in PL 90-448. The House cut the authorizations to $15 million for each program, the Senate approved the full request and the

conferees provided $25 million for each program. The funds would provide 33,000 rental and 33,000 ownership units. Members of both houses urged that more be approved each year.

Flood Insurance. Congress appropriated the $1.5 million requested for the flood insurance program.

Interstate Land Sales. Congress appropriated $625,000 to begin a program of regulation of interstate land sales.

College Housing. Congress authorized contracts for up to $3 million in grants to assist college housing through interest subsidies on private construction loans.

Supplements, Model Cities Funds

In contrast to the previous two years, Congress in 1968 provided additional funding for the rent supplements and model cities programs with relatively little controversy. Funds for both were carried in the fiscal 1969 appropriations bill (HR 17023—PL 90-550) for the Department of Housing and Urban Development, a number of independent agencies and the Executive Office of the President.

Congress appropriated $625 million for the model cities program in fiscal 1969. One-half of this amount, $312.5 million, was designated for urban renewal activities in model cities projects. The Administration had requested a total appropriation of $1 billion. This was the maximum amount authorized and included an increase in the authorization for the urban renewal funds which Congress provided earlier in the year in the omnibus home ownership housing bill. *(See above.)* Although Congress in the omnibus housing bill also authorized an additional $12 million in fiscal 1969 for planning model cities projects, this amount was not appropriated.

For rent supplements, Congress provided new contract authority in fiscal 1969 of $30 million. The Administration had sought $65 million. For payments on rent supplements contracts, Congress appropriated $12 million.

Legislative Action. *House.* The House Appropriations Committee recommended $500 million for model cities, $150 million less than the total authorized at the time the Committee acted. For rent supplements, the Committee recommended $25 million in new contract authority.

When HR 17023 reached the House floor, efforts to reduce the funding for these two programs were rejected. One amendment would have cut the model cities funds to $312 million. It was rejected by voice vote. The amendment on rent supplements would have cut the contract authority to $10 million. It was rejected by a 51-92 standing vote. A second amendment to delete all new contract authority was rejected by a 48-85 standing vote. The fact that none of these amendments came to a roll-call vote indicated that the controversy surrounding the programs in previous years had diminished. Most of the debate, instead, focused on cutting Government spending over-all. The Republican recommittal motion, on which a roll call was possible, provided for an over-all ceiling on fiscal 1969 expenditures by the agencies covered by the bill. It was rejected.

Senate. In the Senate, the Appropriations Committee increased the model cities funds to $1 billion. After House action, the Administration increased its requests to the full amount of the authorization that was being provided in the omnibus housing bill which was in its final stages of enactment in Congress. (All of the increase in the omnibus housing bill was for urban renewal funds in model cities projects. The basic grants authorization from the 1966 law remained at $500 million for fiscal 1969.)

For rent supplements, the Committee provided contract authority of $65 million.

The Senate passed the bill with these figures in it. An amendment to cut $250 million from the model cities funds was rejected by a 21-54 roll-call vote. A majority of both Northern and Southern Democrats opposed the amendment while Republicans split evenly. No effort was made to alter the rent supplements figure.

Final Action. Conferees agreed to the compromise figures of $625 million for model cities and $30 million for rent supplements. The bill was signed into law Oct. 4.

Housing Interest Rates

To help provide relief to the nation's housing industry and to help individuals obtain homes through Government programs, Congress in 1968 enacted legislation (HR 10477—PL 90-301) which allowed higher interest rates.

The bill, which amended Veterans Administration (VA) and Federal Housing Administration (FHA) housing law in several respects, was a response to the tight monetary conditions of the period and the resulting high interest rates throughout the economy. The higher interest rates allowed under the bill were intended to draw mortgage money into the housing market.

The key provision allowed the Secretary of Housing and Urban Development, for a period ending Oct. 1, 1969, to set interest rates on FHA mortgage insurance programs at levels high enough to attract private mortgage money. This provision also allowed the VA Administrator to do the same for interest rates on the VA housing guarantee program so long as the VA rate did not exceed the FHA rate. Existing law limited the rates for both VA and FHA housing programs to 6 percent. Because of the high interest rates throughout the economy, financial institutions with money to lend could earn more in other investments and thus tended to avoid housing mortgages or to make home loans only with special charges that increased the initial purchase price of a house. The authority in HR 10477 to allow interest rates on FHA and VA insurance programs to go above 6 percent was to last until Oct. 1, 1969, when numerous federal housing programs were to expire and would be reviewed by Congress.

A second important provision raised to $12,500 from the existing $7,500 the maximum amount of guarantee for a GI home loan under the VA program. The change was required because of the increasing price of homes. Ceilings on the guarantees were raised over the years.

History of FHA-VA Interest Rates

The following figures show the maximum interest rates permitted by law on Federal Housing Administration and Veterans' Administration housing programs, and the actual rate which was prescribed by each agency within the maximum until the 1968 bill (HR 10477) allowed a flexible ceiling. The ceilings were raised to 6.75 immediately upon enactment of the legislation.

Period	Federal Housing Admin.		Veterans Admin.	
	Pre-scribed	Maxi-mum	Pre-scribed	Maxi-mum
November 1934—June 1935	5-1/2	6	---	---
June 1935—July 1939	5	6	---	---
July 1939—June 22, 1944	4-1/2	6	---	---
June 22, 1944—Aug. 10, 1948	4-1/2	6	4	4
Aug. 10, 1948—April 1950	4-1/2	6	4	4-1/2
April 1950—May 1953	4-1/4	6	4	4-1/2
May 1953—Dec. 3, 1956	4-1/2	6	4-1/2	4-1/2
Dec. 4, 1956—Aug. 5, 1957	5	6	4-1/2	4-1/2
Aug. 6, 1957—April 1958	5-1/4	6	4-1/2	4-1/2
April 1958—June 30, 1959	5-1/4	6	4-3/4	4-3/4
June 30—July 2, 1959	5-1/4	6	4-3/4	5-1/4
July 2—Sept. 23, 1959	5-1/4	6	5-1/4	5-1/4
Sept. 23, 1959—Feb. 1, 1961	5-3/4	6	5-1/4	5-1/4
Feb. 2—May 28, 1961	5-1/2	6	5-1/4	5-1/4
May 29, 1961—Feb. 6, 1966	5-1/4	6	5-1/4	5-1/4
Feb. 7—April 10, 1966	5-1/2	6	---	---
March 3—April 10, 1966	5-1/2	6	5-1/2	6
April 11—Oct. 2, 1966	5-3/4	6	5-3/4	6
Oct. 3, 1966—May 6, 1968	6	6	6	6
May 7, 1968—Jan. 23, 1969	6-3/4	---	6-3/4	---

President Johnson in 1968 requested that the FHA and VA interest ceilings of 6 percent be removed "to allow them to compete on equal terms with other assets" and that the maximum VA home loan guarantee be increased to $10,000.

Provisions. As signed by the President, HR 10477 (PL 90-301):

VA, FHA Interest Rates. Authorized the Secretary of Housing and Urban Development (HUD) until Oct. 1, 1969, to set the interest rate on all single and multifamily FHA mortgage insurance programs (except for home improvement loans) at whatever level was necessary to meet mortgage conditions. (This provision also had the effect of authorizing the VA Administrator to set the interest rate on the VA home guarantee program at whatever level was necessary to meet local conditions so long as the VA rate did not exceed the FHA rate. This was because a provision of existing law (PL 89-358, enacted in 1966) which was not changed permitted the VA rate to be set at the same level—but not higher—than the FHA rate.)

VA Maximum Guarantee. Increased the maximum amount of guarantee on VA-guaranteed home loans from $7,500 to $12,000.

VA Home Price Limit. Permitted eligible veterans to pay a price for a home which was in excess of the reasonable value of the property as determined by a VA appraisal. (Under existing law, the veteran could not pay more than the reasonable value; under the revised law, the VA guarantee still could not exceed the reasonable value of the property.)

Multifamily Housing Interest. Increased to 6 percent the maximum statutory interest rate on four FHA multifamily housing programs: cooperative housing, elderly and handicapped housing, condominium housing and regular rental housing. (The provision made the statutory rate on all FHA programs the same—6 percent; however, as in the case of all other FHA programs, the rate could be set higher during the period until Oct. 1, 1969, if the HUD Secretary used the temporary authority granted to him by the other provision of HR 10477 to make FHA rates competitive.)

Commission. Established a 15-member Commission to study mortgage interest rates and to make recommendations to Congress by April 1, 1969, on: (1) the need for interest-rate controls on Government-assisted mortgages; (2) the level of interest rates necessary to enable low- and moderate-income persons to afford "decent" housing; (3) ways to provide "adequate" mortgage money; and (4) ways to encourage financial institutions to provide more home loan money.

Home Construction Defects. Authorized the VA administrator to extend aid to a veteran who purchased with VA assistance a home which was built under VA or FHA standards and inspection but later developed structural defects. Specified that the VA could correct the defects, pay claims of the owner resulting from the defects or acquire title to the property: Applicable only to loans made or guaranteed after enactment of the bill. Required the home owner to file an application for assistance within four years of the time the mortgage loan on the house was made.

Ceiling Raised. President Johnson May 7 signed HR 10477 into law (PL 90-301). Acting almost immediately, Secretary of HUD Robert C. Weaver announced a new interest-rate ceiling of 6.75 percent.

Transportation Policy

DEVELOPMENT of a coordinated national transportation policy—long a goal of Congress and the Executive Branch—continued to elude the lawmakers in the 1965-68 period. Instead, Congress for the most part contented itself with extending existing programs, which the late President Kennedy once described as "a chaotic patchwork of inconsistent and often obsolete legislation and regulation (evolving) from a history of specific actions addressed to specific problems of specific industries at specific times."

The search for integrated programs intended to promote a diversified transportation system was complicated by a long-standing political struggle affecting all phases of the U. S. transportation problem. Each of the different modes of transportation had some vested interest in existing policies, regulations and legislation. They tended to oppose any changes which would alter these advantages, while often advocating changes designed to improve their own situation.

The problem was compounded by the fact that each of the carriers had its own spokesmen in the Administration and in Congress who tended to support its contentions.

President Johnson in 1966 proposed the creation of a Cabinet-level Department of Transportation as an instrument for the development of a national transportation policy, but the legislation that emerged from Congress was far weaker than the President's proposal.

As the President requested, Congress excluded from the Department all economic regulatory and rate-setting activities of existing federal agencies. But it also imposed an unsought-for decentralization of authority within the new Department, thus effectively denying the Secretary of Transportation independent authority to coordinate or revise existing federal transportation policies and programs among the various transportation modes.

Responding to industry pressure, Congress refused to include the Maritime Administration in the Department. And it limited the Transportation Secretary's authority to establish investment standards for the allocation of federal transportation funds by exempting major programs and by making the authority subject to Congressional approval.

During the 1965-68 period, the Johnson Administration also tried to revamp federal programs in two specific fields: maritime policy and airport aid policy. In both cases its efforts touched off a lively political struggle, and, despite widespread dissatisfaction with the effectiveness of existing programs, no substantial revision was achieved.

Following is an area-by-area summary of key action on transportation issues during the years 1965-68.

TRANSPORTATION DEPARTMENT. Congress in 1966 acceded to President Johnson's requests for creation of a new Department of Transportation (DOT), the 12th Cabinet-level department. However, in enacting the measure, Congress sharply limited its functions, most notably by refusing to grant jurisdiction over maritime activities to the Department. As approved by Congress, DOT had authority over the Coast Guard, Federal Aviation Administration, Federal Highway Administration and Federal Railroad Administration. The bill also established a National Transportation Safety Board—independent of the Secretary and other units—to oversee accident investigations and review license and certificate appeals. The bill approved by Congress established the DOT Secretary chiefly as an administrator of existing policies and programs.

Authority over urban mass transit programs was transferred to DOT in 1968.

MARITIME POLICY. Despite a general agreement among industry spokesmen, union groups and Government officials on the need for a new maritime policy to halt the continuing decline of the U. S. merchant fleet, efforts to write such a policy were stalemated in the 1965-68 period.

President Johnson, who had promised new maritime proposals beginning in 1965, postponed making them until 1968—reportedly because of Administration failure to get industry backing for its program. When the Administration proposals finally were unveiled, Congressional leaders in the maritime field found them unacceptable and decided instead to push their own program. The result was a standoff: Congress did not act on the Administration plan, and the Congressional proposal was first gutted by the House Merchant Marine and Fisheries Committee and then blocked by the House Rules Committee.

Meanwhile, as an expression of dissatisfaction with the Administration approach, Congress approved legislation to establish an independent Maritime Administration within the Executive Branch, but President Johnson pocket vetoed the bill. The President had unsuccessfully urged that the Maritime Administration, currently an arm of the Commerce Department, be included in the Department of Transportation.

Reference

For a discussion of transportation policies in the 1945-64 period, see *Congress and the Nation*, Vol. I, p. 517-561.

Transportation Strikes

Twice in the 1965-68 period Congress considered legislation to deal with a transportation strike.

A 1966 strike of the International Assn. of Machinists (IAM) against five major airlines lasted 42 days and grounded 60 percent of the nation's commercial air traffic. The Senate approved legislation ordering the strikers back to work briefly and authorizing the President to extend the back-to-work order if necessary. The strike was settled before the House acted on the bill.

In 1967, Congress did enact legislation to settle a two-day nationwide railroad strike. The legislation, requested by President Johnson, provided for a compulsory settlement of the controversy if no voluntary agreement had been reached within 90 days. Earlier in 1967, Congress had twice acted to delay the strike.

(For details, see chapter on Labor.)

One of the basic points at issue between the Administration and Congressional maritime proposals was the future of the ship construction subsidy program. The subsidies reimbursed U.S. shipbuilders for the difference between the construction costs in U.S. shipyards and the estimated costs of comparable work in foreign yards. The Administration program contemplated temporary maintenance of ship construction subsidies at existing levels pending development of an alternative approach; the Congressional program called for a massive five-year increase in the construction subsidy program that would allow the building in U.S. shipyards of 35-40 new vessels annually, compared to the current level of 12-13 ships annually. In the absence of an agreement on maritime policy reform, Congress voted a series of stopgap extensions of the existing subsidy program.

AIR TRANSPORTATION. Congestion and safety problems resulting from increasing levels of air travel occupied both Congress and the Administration in the 1965-68 period. However, aside from increased appropriations for safety-related items, no major actions were taken.

Congress in 1966 extended the Federal Airport Act of 1946 through June 30, 1970, and continued the Act's existing $75-million annual authorization for federal grants-in-aid to airports for safety-related improvements. However, it was widely conceded that this program would not meet the growing needs of the national air transport system.

The Johnson Administration in 1968 proposed to supplant the existing matching-grant program with a $1-billion federal loan program. The Senate Commerce Committee countered with a proposal for a five-year extension of the existing grant program, with authorizations doubled from $75 million to $150 million annually. Congress did not act on the Administration proposal and the Commerce Committee bill did not reach the floor. Further, Congress appropriated only $30 million of the $75 million authorized for airport grants in fiscal 1970.

Supersonic Transport. Another air problem remained unresolved as 1968 drew to a close: the future of the trouble-plagued supersonic transport (SST). Congress in 1967 authorized federal participation in the construction of two prototype SST planes, but design problems encountered by the contractors led to delays, and Congress denied funds for fiscal 1969.

Between fiscal 1962 and fiscal 1969, Congress appropriated $623,375,000 for the SST, and $471 million had been obligated by Dec. 31, 1968. It was estimated that the total federal contribution for the SST, through the prototype development phase in 1972, would be $1.24 billion.

HIGHWAYS. Almost from its inception in 1956, the massive Interstate Highway construction program was afflicted with financing problems. Originally it was estimated that by the scheduled 1972 completion date, construction of the 41,000-mile Interstate System would cost nearly $31 billion, with the Federal Government putting up 90 percent of the funds. By 1968, however, total cost estimates for construction of the System had risen to $56.5 billion, basically because of increased land and construction costs and improved design standards. Federal payments for the System were financed by highway user charges, which were channeled through a Highway Trust Fund. And the Fund, which was required by law to operate on a pay-as-you-go basis, did not provide sufficient revenues to meet the increased costs.

In response to this financial crisis, President Johnson in each of the years 1965-68 urged Congress to enact increased user taxes to provide the needed revenues. Congress did not act on this suggestion, but it did stretch out the completion date of the System through fiscal 1974. It also added an additional 1,500 miles to the System, bringing total mileage to 42,500. And, in a departure from traditional highway legislation, Congress included in the 1968 Highway Act provisions recognizing the need to incorporate urban planning in highway construction projects.

RAILROADS. As railroad passenger service continued to decline, Congress in the High Speed Ground Transportation Act of 1965 authorized a research, development and demonstration program to explore the feasibility of high speed ground transportation. The purpose of the legislation was to determine whether such transportation could be made convenient, economical and attractive and meet the increasing transportation requirements of the rapidly expanding urban areas of the United States. Congress in 1968 extended the Act to June 30, 1971.

By 1968, only two projects had been undertaken under the Act, the Washington-New York "Metroliner" service and the New York-Boston "TurboTrain" service. Technical difficulties with the trains delayed both projects, and the first train did not begin operation until 1969.

URBAN MASS TRANSIT. Congress continued and expanded programs begun under the Urban Mass Transportation Act of 1964. The Act authorized matching grants and loans to enable states and localities to construct and improve mass transit facilities. Congress authorized annual appropriations of $150 million in fiscal 1968 and 1969 and $190 million in fiscal 1970.

Originally under the jurisdiction of the Department of Housing and Urban Development, urban mass transit programs were shifted to the Transportation Department in 1968.

Chronology

Of Legislation

On Transportation

1965

Highway Aid

Faced with new, and higher, estimates of the cost of completing the Interstate Highway System, Congress in 1965 enacted only stopgap legislation to keep the program going in fiscal 1967. It took no action on President Johnson's proposals to meet the increasing costs of the program by extending the System's completion date and enacting additional user taxes on trucks.

The Commerce Department Jan. 13 sent to Congress, as required by law, a revised cost estimate for completion of the 41,000-mile Interstate System by 1972. The Department said its cost estimates had increased from $41 billion in 1961 to $46.8 billion, due primarily to improved design standards and higher costs of land acquisition and road construction. The report also recommended the method of apportioning funds authorized for the System among the states in fiscal 1967-69. Congress was required by law to approve the Department's estimate before funds could be apportioned, and approval necessitated an increase in the authorization for the federal share from $37 billion to $42 billion. Further, since the Highway Trust Fund was prohibited from operating at a deficit, additional revenues would have to be provided to pay the additional $5-billion federal share. *(For explanation of highway financing methods, see accompanying box.)*

In order to meet the increased costs, President Johnson proposed (1) extending the completion date of the System by five months, from Sept. 30, 1972 to Feb. 28, 1973, and (2) imposing additional user taxes on heavy trucks.

The House Ways and Means Committee never acted on the revenue proposals, and Congress did not enact a bill (HR 6548) to approve the Commerce Department's 1965 cost estimates, authorize apportionment of funds and increase the existing highway construction appropriations authorization to cover the $5-billion increase in the federal share of the System's higher costs.

However, the Senate Public Works Committee reported a bill (S J Res 81) which simply authorized apportionment of funds in fiscal 1967 on the basis of revenues available under existing taxes. This measure was passed by the Senate May 14 and the House Aug. 2. As enacted (PL 89-139), the bill authorized the appropriation of $3 billion from the Highway Trust Fund for the Interstate System. This was $100 million more than the existing authorization passed in 1961; the increase was based on increased revenue estimates by the Bureau of Public Roads.

S J Res 81 also contained an amendment, sponsored by Rep. John F. Baldwin (R Calif.), specifying that each state "should" have a highway safety program, approved by the Secretary of Commerce, in operation by the end of 1967. *(See chapter on consumers' affairs.)* And it called on the Commerce Department to report to Congress biennially on future U.S. highway needs.

High-Speed Trains

Congress in 1965 enacted an Administration bill (S 1588—PL 89-220), the High Speed Ground Transportation Act, authorizing the Secretary of Commerce to conduct a three-year, $90-million research, development and demonstration program in high-speed ground transporta-

---

Highway Funding

Prior to 1956, authorizations for federal-aid highway programs were made from general revenues of the Treasury. Although there were no clear Congressional guidelines, authorizations were usually made in amounts equal to the revenues collected by the Treasury from certain highway user taxes, such as those on motor fuels, tires and truck weights.

The Federal-Aid Highway Act of 1956 established a Highway Trust Fund into which certain specific highway user taxes were to be channeled and from which funds were to be apportioned to finance the federal share of major highway programs. *(Congress and the Nation, Vol. I, p. 524, 526, 531)*

The law provided that the Highway Trust Fund could not operate at a deficit at any time and stipulated that if the Secretary of the Treasury determined that payment of the full amounts apportioned to the states would create a deficit, the Secretary of Commerce was to reduce apportionments so that obligations could be paid as they came due.

In the face of rising highway construction costs, President Johnson in each of the years 1965-68 proposed legislation to provide additional revenues for the Highway Trust Fund. Congress did not approve the requests.

Two key programs were financed from the Highway Trust Fund. The first was the 41,000-mile Interstate Highway System authorized by Congress in 1956 for completion by 1972. Originally the cost of this program was estimated at nearly $31 billion, with the Federal Government putting up 90 percent of the construction funds and the states the remaining 10 percent. Periodically, revised cost estimates were submitted to Congress, and Congressional approval of these estimates was required before funds could be apportioned. By 1968, the estimated cost of the System had risen to $56.5 billion, with a federal share of $50,640,000,000.

The second program financed from the Highway Trust Fund was construction of federal-aid primary, secondary and urban (ABC) roads. These roads were financed on a 50-50 matching basis with the states. Congress authorized appropriations for the ABC roads on a regular, biennial basis.

Construction of strictly federal roads, such as forest highways and public land highways, was funded from general revenues.

---

tion. The purpose of the legislation was to determine whether high-speed ground transportation could be made convenient, economical and attractive and meet the increasing transportation requirements of the rapidly expanding urban areas of the United States.

The legislation authorized three basic activities:

• Research into and development of different forms of high-speed ground transportation;

• Demonstration projects to test new developments and to learn public response to improved ground transportation;

1965 Maritime Problems

Concern over the U.S. merchant marine continued to grow in 1965 as subsidies increased while the maritime industry declined in size and business. Foreign fleets, especially that of the Soviet Union, continued to expand and to handle more and more of America's foreign commerce.

The Maritime Administration reported that construction subsidies totaled $87,686,365 in fiscal 1965, compared with $73,985,021 in fiscal 1960 and $5,659,000 in fiscal 1955. Gross operating subsidies were $208,588,732 in calendar 1964, compared with $162,966,239 in calendar 1960 and $103,190,611 in calendar 1955. The Maritime Administration said figures on the total cost of the cargo preference program were not available. The President's Maritime Advisory Committee estimated that the cost of the program ran $80 million a year.

The total number of ships in the U. S. merchant marine as of Dec. 31, 1964, was 912, compared with 957 at the end of 1960 and 1,072 at the end of 1955. U. S. ships carried 8.3 percent of America's foreign trade cargo in calendar 1964, compared with 10.5 percent in calendar 1960 and 23.5 percent in calendar 1955.

Defense Requirements. In light of the United States' expanding involvement in the Vietnam war, questions were raised as to whether the merchant marine was adequate to meet existing and future military needs. To help transport supplies to Southeast Asia, chiefly to South Vietnam, the Defense Department in 1965 took seven ships out of the U. S. Navy's reserve fleet and requested the Maritime Administration to reactivate 76 ships from the National Defense Reserve Fleet by the end of fiscal 1966.

Strike. A 75-day strike in 1965 involving eight subsidized shipping lines and three unions added to the confusion in the maritime industry and apparently hardened the position of some Government officials against the subsidy program. (It was about the 25th major strike in the industry since 1934.) The strike, lasting from June 16 to Aug. 29, was ended by an agreement that provided a no-strike guarantee for four years and a 3.2-percent increase in wages and other benefits. The main issue in the strike, the manning of automated vessels, was left to mediation procedures under the direction of AFL-CIO President George Meany and Labor Secretary W. Willard Wirtz.

• A program to improve the collection and availability of transportation statistics.

Regional transportation problems existed or were expected to develop in several major regional urban complexes which were coming into existence in different parts of the nation. The best known and the one with the most serious transportation problem by 1965 was the Northeast Corridor between Maine and Virginia, and the first projects under PL 89-220 were planned for this area. However, other areas faced the prospect of similar problems. These areas included Seattle-Tacoma-Portland on the West Coast, the East Coast of Florida, Milwaukee-Chicago-South Bend-Cleveland, San Francisco-Los Angeles and probably a strip on the Gulf Coast.

When the Department of Transportation was set up in 1967 it assumed responsibility for administering the high-speed ground transportation program. Congress in 1968 extended the program for two years. *(See 1968 chronology.)*

Shipbuilding Subsidies

Congress in 1965 enacted legislation (HR 4346—PL 89-127) extending for one year, through June 30, 1966, the cost-differential subsidy ceiling of 55 percent for new ship construction and 60 percent for reconstruction and reconditioning of passenger vessels. The differential subsidies represented reimbursement of U. S. shipbuilders for the difference between construction costs in U. S. shipyards and the cheaper costs in foreign yards. Without enactment of the bill, the subsidy differentials would have dropped to the permanent figure of 50 percent.

There was little opposition in either chamber to HR 4346, since it was generally recognized that continued subsidy payments were essential to the well-being of the U. S. merchant marine. However, some Senators questioned the feasibility of maintaining the high 55-percent construction ceiling, asking whether it might not lead to even higher subsidies.

Extension of the subsidies was a stopgap measure, pending Administration proposals to revise the subsidy program. President Johnson, in his 1965 State of the Union Message, had promised to recommend a "new policy for our merchant marine." However, the President made no recommendations, apparently because the Administration could not reach agreement on a new program. (The Administration proposals were not unveiled until 1968. *See below.*)

Although Mr. Johnson made no specific recommendations on ship subsidies, numerous proposals were made by various officials, organizations and study groups. The two major sets of proposals—and the most controversial—were by the Maritime Advisory Committee, established by President Johnson in 1964, and the Interagency Maritime Task Force, set up by Commerce Secretary John T. Connor in 1965. The Advisory Committee favored a continuation and extension of the existing subsidy program, while the Task Force called for an entirely new policy, including the elimination of cargo preferences and passenger ship subsidies.

The basic law for the existing program of federal support for private shipping was the Merchant Marine Act of 1936. The Act provided operating and construction differential subsidies to offset lower foreign costs, full Government payment for defense features on vessels and trade-in allowances on old ships to stimulate their replacement. In subsequent amendments and acts, Congress provided certain tax benefits for the shipping industry, Government insurance of construction loans and mortgages and the requirement that at least half of Government-financed, ocean-going cargo be carried in U.S. ships. *(Congress and the Nation, Vol. I, p. 545)*

Other Maritime Bills

WAR RISK INSURANCE. Congress enacted a bill (HR 4526—PL 89-89) to extend for five years, through Sept. 7, 1970, provisions of existing law authorizing the Secretary of Commerce to provide war risk insurance for merchant vessels, cargo and crew. The provisions were added to the Merchant Marine Act of 1936 by amendment in 1950. The initial 10-year authority was extended in 1960 for an additional five years, through Sept. 7, 1965. *(Congress and the Nation, Vol. I, p. 548)*

VESSEL EXCHANGE PROGRAM. Congress enacted a bill (HR 728—PL 89-254) to broaden and extend, through July 5, 1970, the vessel exchange program under the Merchant Marine Act of 1936. Initiated in 1960, the program permitted operators of nonsubsidized merchant ships to exchange obsolete vessels for more efficient ships in the Government reserve fleet. *(Congress and the Nation, Vol. I, p. 551)*

PASSENGER SHIP SAFETY. The House Oct. 5 passed a bill (HR 10327) requiring ship operators to establish financial responsibility to protect passengers from being stranded and losing their fare if a ship failed to sail. The bill also required the filing of certain safety-related information. The bill became law in 1966, after the Senate broadened the scope of the safety provisions. *(See below.)*

Freight Car Shortage

The Senate in 1965 passed a bill (S 1098) which was intended to reduce the national shortage of freight cars. The measure became law in 1966. *(See below.)*

S 1098 authorized the Interstate Commerce Commission to establish daily freight car rental charges (per diem rates), to be paid by railroads using cars owned by other railroads, at a level that would prompt the borrowing line to purchase its own carriers.

The legislation resulted from a continuing and worsening shortage of freight cars in the United States. Existing rental rates were so low that railroads generally found it cheaper to borrow the cars of other lines than to purchase new cars of their own. Relief of some type had long been sought by certain railroads, primarily those in the West, and by a variety of farm organizations and businesses. Legislation was opposed and Congressional action blocked by railroads in the East.

An amended version of S 1098 was reported in the House late in the year (Oct. 20), three days before the session ended. No effort was made to bring the bill to the floor. House backers of the measure later said action was delayed in order to give the railroads further opportunity to resolve the shortage problem themselves.

Shortages of freight cars had become increasingly serious in the years since World War II. Between Jan. 1, 1945, and mid-1965, railroads retired almost 300,000 more cars than were built. Traditionally, the shortages occurred during harvest seasons, but in the postwar period they became chronic. Various conflicting reasons were cited for the shortages, including ownership patterns, improper distribution of existing cars, overdetention by some railroads of borrowed cars, increased emphasis on acquisition of new, special-purpose cars and the problem of origin of shipments versus termination.

Immediately after the war, the ICC attempted to deal with the problem by setting high penalty rates for the use of borrowed freight cars, but federal courts in 1947 ruled that the agency did not possess authority for its action. The ICC then asked Congress to provide the authority. In more recent years prior to 1965, the ICC urged the use of "incentive" charges to induce railroads to purchase their own cars. S 1098 was intended to allow for such "incentive" rates and thereby, in effect, to overturn the 1947 court ruling.

There was no general agreement that the "incentive" approach would alleviate the freight car shortage, but some railroads thought it would be helpful and neither the lines nor their associations presented alternatives.

Under existing procedures, it was estimated that more than 90 percent of all cars carried rental charges of under $3 a day. Actual rates ranged from $2.16 per day to $12.18 for certain special-purpose cars.

Helicopter Subsidies

Congress in 1965 terminated the helicopter subsidy program. The Administration had recommended the termination but opposed efforts made in Congress to cut off the subsidies before the end of the calendar year. The program, which actually provided subsidies to only three helicopter lines, was discontinued Dec. 31, 1965.

The Administration made two separate requests for funds for helicopter subsidies—$942,000 in supplemental appropriations to keep the program going through fiscal 1965 (June 30) and $2.1 million to continue the program through calendar 1965. Congress denied the additional funds for fiscal 1965 and granted only $1.2 million of the other request.

Helicopter Subsidies
(In Thousands)

Fiscal Year	Chicago	Los Angeles	New York
1954	$ 432	$ 684	$ 1,458
1955	423	816	1,417
1956	444	848	1,443
1957	909	941	1,921
1958	1,425	942	2,052
1959	1,644	935	2,281
1960	1,662	1,041	2,227
1961	1,887	1,074	2,577
1962	1,784	1,468	2,529
1963	1,178	1,803	2,019
1964	800	1,600	1,900
1965	625	1,249	1,484
1966*	385	785	——
Total	$13,598	$14,186	$23,308

* Through Dec. 31, 1965, when the subsidy program was discontinued.

SOURCE: Civil Aeronautics Board, Subsidy Division

The program had helped to support helicopter commuter, mail and airport transport service between the center sections of New York, Chicago and Los Angeles and local airports and outlying suburbs.

Certain factions in Congress had sought to eliminate the helicopter subsidy program, arguing that the three subsidized companies would continually require federal financial support and never become self-sufficient and that it was unfair to subsidize only these three lines when 39 other cities also needed the service.

Supporters of the program, generally those representing areas which benefited from the service and Sen. A. S. Mike Monroney (D Okla.), chairman of the Aviation Subcommittee of the Senate Commerce Committee, contended that a system of helicopter transportation would be needed in the future and that the three subsidized lines should be maintained as experiments to prove the value of such transportation.

The Civil Aeronautics Act of 1938 authorized payments by the Post Office to air carriers for transporting mail. These payments amounted to the basic cost of carrying the mail plus a subsidy designed to provide the airline companies with a fair return after they had paid their operating costs. When helicopters began to be used in 1947 to carry mail, they became eligible for the program without the need for additional legislation.

Airmail and subsidy payments were separated in 1953 under President Eisenhower's Reorganization Plan 10. The plan transferred from the Post Office to the Civil Aeronautics Board (CAB) the responsibility of paying all subsidies to airlines that did not involve expenses for carrying mail. The plan also authorized the CAB to set the rates the Post Office was to pay for airmail transportation. The policy took the form of law in 1958 when Congress included it in the Federal Aviation Act. *(Congress and the Nation, Vol. I, p. 539, 541)* From fiscal 1954 until the program ended in 1965, the CAB paid $51.1 million in subsidies to the three helicopter firms. *(See table.)*

In recent years, the House Appropriations Committee had sought to cut back the helicopter subsidy program while the Senate Appropriations Committee tried to increase subsidy funds. Conferees, after reaching a compromise figure, in 1964 warned that "this is the last money to be recommended" and asked "the CAB not to include one penny for these three lines in its budget next year."

Supersonic Transport

President Johnson July 1 called for 18 more months of research on a U. S. supersonic transport (SST) before beginning construction of a prototype plane. Congress in 1965 appropriated (HR 11588—PL 89-309) $140 million to finance the work in fiscal 1966. Meanwhile, the Federal Aviation Agency April 24 announced that its controversial sonic boom tests over Oklahoma City in 1964 indicated that construction of an SST was "clearly warranted" because the test showed that people on the ground "could learn to live with" sonic booms.

The FAA in 1961 decided to study the feasibility of an SST, and Congress had appropriated $91 million prior to 1965. The British and French Governments in November 1962 announced plans for joint development of a supersonic transport. *(Congress and the Nation, Vol. I, p. 543)*

Illegal Transportation

Congress in 1965 enacted a non-controversial Administration-backed bill (HR 5401—PL 89-170) to, among other things, strengthen the Interstate Commerce Act to combat unlawful operations by motor carriers (trucks and buses). Final action on the measure concluded several years of Congressional consideration of the legislation, which initially included more controversial provisions.

HR 5401 was primarily designed to give the Interstate Commerce Commission (ICC), states and shippers more effective tools for coping with illegal for-hire trucking—that is, the transportation of certain commodities in interstate commerce by motor carriers without proper ICC authority. Transportation experts estimated that illegal for-hire business amounted to between $500 million and $5 billion a year, and that it had been a principal factor in what was described in debate as the "erosion" of the ICC-regulated carriers' share of total transport volume.

In its major provisions, the bill permitted the ICC to enter into cooperative agreements with states to enforce transportation laws; authorized the ICC, in cooperation with the National Assn. of Railroad and Utilities Commissioners, within five years to establish uniform state registration standards for motor carriers; extended and increased civil forfeiture penalties for unlawful motor carrier operations; provided that persons injured by an illegal carrier operation could seek a court injunction to prevent further violations; permitted shippers to recover reparations from motor carriers and freight forwarders charging unlawfully high rates; and permitted the ICC or carriers to take action against water carriers who failed to provide transportation.

Legislative proposals similar to those embodied in HR 5401 were endorsed by President Kennedy in 1962 and 1963 and by President Johnson in 1964, and were given extensive hearings in both the House and Senate in 1962 and 1963. A bill (S 2560) covering several of the same provisions was passed by the Senate in 1962, but received no House action. In 1964, several of the provisions were included with highly controversial rate deregulation provisions in a bill (HR 9903) which was reported by the House Interstate and Foreign Commerce Committee. Heavy lobbying for and against the bill prevented enactment. *(Congress and the Nation, Vol. I, p. 556)*

1966

Transportation Department

Congress in 1966 enacted legislation requested by President Johnson creating a Department of Transportation (DOT). When established in 1967, the new Department became the 12th Cabinet-level department.

President Johnson had detailed the scope and functions of the new Department in a March 2 transportation message to Congress. In enacting the measure (HR 15963—PL 89-670), Congress reduced the functions considerably, most notably by refusing to grant jurisdiction over maritime activities to the new Department.

Supporters of the measure as it was enacted, however, contended that it included the tools necessary to carry out the principal purposes of the President's proposal: promotion of transportation safety; development of a national transportation policy; and development of guidelines for the investment of federal funds in facilities and equipment.

As the President requested, Congress excluded from the Department all economic regulatory and rate-setting activities of existing federal agencies. The urban mass transportation programs administered by the Department of Housing and Urban Development (HUD) were also excluded pending further study of their logical place in the Executive Branch. (These programs were transferred to DOT in 1968. *See below.*)

The powers of the Secretary of Transportation were substantially weakened, in comparison with the Administration's proposal, under the final provisions of HR 15963. The Secretary was effectively denied independent authority to coordinate or revise existing federal transportation policies and programs among the various transportation modes. The bill approved by Congress established the Secretary chiefly as an administrator of existing policies and programs.

This was due partly to a desire of Congress to retain its direct influence on transportation activities and partly to the desire of various private transportation groups to preserve to the greatest extent their relationships, built up over many years, with existing federal agencies.

The influence of transportation groups in obtaining their goals was most vividly reflected in complete removal of the Maritime Administration from the Department. It was also seen in the struggle over the Administration's request that the Secretary establish investment standards, subject to Presidential approval, for the future allocation of federal transportation funds throughout the nation. Congress did not want to relinquish its powers to influence transportation investments, just as transportation groups—with good contacts in Congress—did not want to see Congressional influence diminished. Numerous objections were voiced during both House and Senate committee hearings that under the Administration's plan, the Executive Branch would be encroaching on the traditional powers of Congress to determine where federal funds should be spent.

As a result, the final bill permitted the Secretary to develop investment standards, but permitted standards and criteria to be put into effect only after Congressional approval. In some areas, including water resources projects and grant-in-aid programs, the Secretary was flatly prohibited from developing investment standards.

The decentralization of authority within the new Department also was reflected in the final provisions concerning safety functions. The bill established a National Transportation Safety Board—independent of the Secretary and other units—to oversee accident investigations, determine the cause of accidents and review license and certificate appeals. The bill continued the existing separation of aviation safety functions by transferring the Federal Aviation Agency's safety duties to the new Federal Aviation Administrator with his decisions administratively final. The Civil Aeronautics Board's functions, which include accident investigations, probable cause determination and review of appeals, were given to the Safety Board. But on other safety matters, the Secretary was directed to carry out the 1966 auto and highway safety laws; the Federal Railroad and Highway Administrators (not the

---

Boyd Named DOT Secretary

President Johnson named Alan S. Boyd, Under Secretary of Commerce for Transportation, to be the first Secretary of the Department of Transportation. Boyd earlier had been a member of the Civil Aeronautics Board (CAB), serving as chairman in 1961-65. The Senate confirmed Boyd's appointment Jan. 12, 1967, and he was sworn in Jan. 16. The Department officially began operation April 1, 1967.

Secretary) were given statutory authority over the safety functions transferred from the Interstate Commerce Commission; and the Coast Guard was to continue its functions in maritime safety. *(For major components of the Department, see accompanying table.)*

MARITIME ADMINISTRATION. Congressional action on the bill was highlighted by the dispute over the Maritime Administration. In a defeat for the President, the House Aug. 30 voted **261-117**—a key roll call—to exclude the Maritime Administration from the new Department. It then passed the bill, 336-42. The Senate version of the bill, passed by a 64-2 roll call Sept. 29, included the Maritime Administration in the Department. Conferees accepted the House version.

(The House Merchant Marine and Fisheries Committee Aug. 8 reported a bill (HR 11696) to create an independent Federal Maritime Administration, a measure in direct conflict with President Johnson's Transportation Department proposal. The bill was granted a rule for floor action but was not brought up for debate in the 89th Congress. A similar bill was pocket vetoed in 1968. *See below.*)

INVESTMENT STANDARDS. A second controversial feature of the Administration proposal was the investment standards section (Section 7) under which the Secretary would develop general standards for the allocation of federal funds to the various modes of transportation. After approval of the standards by the President, the Secretary would evaluate how funds should be spent for facilities and equipment. The Secretary's recommendations would be presented to Congress.

The standards and criteria were to apply to all proposals requiring investment of funds such as airport construction, water resource projects and maritime subsidies. They also were applicable to transportation programs carried on outside the new Department. The Administration's proposal exempted four groups of investments from the standards. They were (1) Government acquisition of goods for its own use; (2) the Panama Canal; (3) certain projects under the Department of Defense; and (4) foreign aid programs.

According to Charles L. Schultze, director of the Bureau of the Budget, the Secretary's standards would be "broad criteria for evaluating project proposals—what types of benefits are to be considered, what costs are to be taken into account, what noneconomical social advantages are to be weighed and the like." The Administration hoped to evaluate investment proposals on a consistent basis developed for the various modes of transportation in competition with each other for federal money. Section 7 was designed to remedy current executive and legislative practices of judging the various transportation sectors individually without looking at the over-all picture. The hoped-for result would be investments in transportation projects requiring the least financial resources relative to the benefits accruing to the Government and the general public.

Testimony from the affected industry groups disclosed basic fears that a project would be proven unjustified when judged according to uniform standards for the entire transportation field; that the numerous trade associations would no longer exert influence in their personal appeals to Congress for funds; and that the Secretary would eventually replace Congress as the final decision-maker of the allocation of federal funds for projects.

The Administration's goals under Section 7 were dealt a substantial blow by the further exemption of two major transportation sectors—water resource projects and all grant-in-aid programs such as airport construction and highway construction financed out of the Highway Trust Fund. The latter included the 41,000-mile Interstate Highway System and the federal primary, secondary, and urban road construction programs. With Government highway projects and water resource projects ranking high in the allocation of approximately $5.8 billion annually invested in transportation, the exemptions raised serious doubts as to how the Secretary could achieve compatibility in recommending funds if he were deprived of influence in these important areas.

Industry Views

Various segments of the transportation industry reacted differently to the Administration's proposals. Although most industry groups said they favored the idea of a Transportation Department, their general support was often tempered by suggestions for specific changes in provisions of the bill that affected their particular part of the industry. The Board of Directors of the Transportation Assn. of America (TAA) May 10 endorsed the creation of the new Department, as long as no economic regulatory functions were transferred to it from existing independent agencies.

Following is a summary of the positions of major transportation groups on HR 15963:

Railroads. The Assn. of American Railroads supported the plan, but objected to the proposed transfer of boxcar service and safety functions from the ICC to the new Department. The association said these functions could realistically be classified as economic regulation activities and therefore should remain under the ICC. The Railway Labor Executives Assn. wholeheartedly endorsed the legislation, including the transfer of safety regulations, which the association said should be given more attention in the new Department. Both railroad groups—management and labor—actively supported Section 7. The railroads currently received only a small portion of the total Government transportation investment, and therefore had very little to lose and much to gain under the investment standards section.

Truckers. The American Trucking Assns. Inc. (ATA) supported the bill, except for "serious reservations" about Section 7. The trucking groups wanted assurance that the section did not "encroach upon the proper prerogatives of Congress and...other federal agencies." The Private Truck Council of America Inc., like the railroads, opposed the transfer of safety functions from the ICC, but the Private Carrier Council of the ATA supported the transfer provi-

sions. The Teamsters union urged Congress to enact the bill as introduced and to withstand industry efforts to "emasculate" the legislation by amendments designed to weaken the Secretary's authority. The union also said the safety functions of the ICC should be transferred to the new Department, where more attention could be given to safety problems.

Other Highway Groups. The American Assn. of State Highway Officials feared that under the bill authorizations for transportation projects would no longer consider "public desires and convenience" but would be predominantly based on the "investment return concept" which they said would be detrimental to the development of national transportation policies. A second issue raised by the highway groups centered on the possibility that the Secretary might intrude on a current view mutually shared by highway interests and Congress that revenues in the Highway Trust Fund should be used only for construction of highways and not for other purposes such as highway safety or beautification.

Ocean Shipping. Spokesmen for all major international shipping organizations, including the American Merchant Marine Institute Inc., American Tramp Shipowners Assn., Committee of American Steamship Lines and the Shipbuilders Council of America, urged that Congress create a separate and autonomous Maritime Administration. These groups said that if Congress decided—despite industry views—to place maritime affairs in the new Department, the Maritime Administration should be given "full independence within the departmental framework" and a Maritime Subsidy Board should be established within the Department which "would operate in a quasi-judicial manner and whose rulings would not be subject to review by the Secretary of Transportation." These views were shared by the maritime unions, including the AFL-CIO Maritime Committee and the Seafarers International Union.

Coastal Shipping. The Gulf Intercoastal Canal Assn. opposed the bill in its entirety, and said that under Section 7, as proposed, Congress would unwisely "surrender to the Secretary of Transportation alone the right to determine" the advisability of water improvement projects. The Association said Congress, when considering the bill, "will do well to compare the allegations of a better tomorrow in transportation against the facts of a magnificent yesterday and today." The investment standards section was also criticized by the American Assn. of Port Authorities Inc. and the Louisiana Intracoastal Seaway Assn.

Inland Water Carriers. Officials of barge companies and lake carriers unanimously opposed Section 7 of the bill. They contended that since transportation considerations were only a small part of the entire water resource program, which included flood control, water supply, land enhancement and recreation, the criteria for determining investments in water projects should be different from the standards used for investments in other kinds of transportation projects.

The American Waterways Operators Inc. (AWO) cited the current relationship between Congress and the Corps of Engineers as a favorable one of checks and balances, adding that under Section 7, the Secretary could "interpose the decision of his Department to preclude Congress from exercising its prerogatives to determine the practicality, feasibility, and desirability of making water resource improvements for navigation." A spokesman for the Common Carrier Conference of Domestic Water Carriers said that Section 7 possibly could destroy an established "Congressional mandate" that waterway improvements be determined according to public benefit and need and not upon "factors involving intermodal transportation competition."

The AWO July 16 announced that the bill reported from the House Government Operations Committee (HR 15963) "meets to a great extent the objections raised" by the AWO. The committee bill deleted Section 7 altogether.

Oil Pipelines. The Assn. of Oil Pipe Lines urged Congress to keep the safety regulations governing pipe lines under the jurisdiction of the Interstate Commerce Commission (ICC). The group said that safety functions were "so entwined" with economic regulation that these functions should be exercised by an independent regulatory agency.

Air Transport. The Air Transport Assn., representing the airlines, favored the bill, but asked Congress to (1) keep accident investigations in the CAB; (2) "reconsider" Section 7; and (3) keep the FAA "intact" in the new Department as an independent unit. Other air organizations, arguing that air transportation problems were "different" from the problems of other modes and that the "status" of aviation would suffer if the FAA were transferred to the new Department, opposed the Administration bill. These organizations included the Air Line Pilots Assn. International, the National Assn. of State Aviation Officials, the Aircraft Owners and Pilots Assn., the National Pilots Assn., the Air Traffic Control Assn., and the National Business Aircraft Assn.

Shipping Groups. The National Industrial Traffic League, composed of major industrial shippers (but not carriers), supported the Administration bill except for the transfer of boxcar service and safety functions from the ICC to the new Department. The League believed that these functions were inseparable from economic regulation and should not be exercised by the Executive Branch.

Other Groups. The Chamber of Commerce of the United States supported creation of the new Department with the same reservations as the National Industrial Traffic League. The AFL-CIO also endorsed the bill, but suggested amendments to give the Department more authority and to strengthen the safety regulations which the Department would enforce.

Provisions

As signed into law, HR 15963 contained the following provisions:

Policy. Declared that the nation's welfare, economic growth, stability and security required the development of national transportation policies and programs designed to provide "fast, safe, efficient and convenient" transportation at the lowest cost consistent with other national objectives.

Further declared that Congress had found the establishment of a Department of Transportation to be in the public interest and necessary to: (1) assure coordinated and effective administration of federal programs; (2) facilitate development and improvement of coordinated services provided as much as feasible by private enterprise; (3) encourage cooperation in achieving national objectives

among federal, state and local governments, carriers, labor and other interested groups; (4) stimulate technological advances; (5) provide leadership in identifying and solving problems; and (6) develop and recommend to the President and Congress for approval policies and programs to accomplish the above objectives, considering needs of the public, users, carriers, industry, labor and national defense.

Declared a national policy that special effort be made to preserve the natural beauty of the countryside, public park and recreation lands, wildlife and waterfowl refuges and historic sites.

Establishment of Department. Established a Cabinet-level Department of Transportation to be headed by a Secretary appointed by the President with the advice and consent of the Senate.

Established within the Department three operating divisons—a Federal Highway Administration, a Federal Railroad Administration and a Federal Aviation Administration—each to be headed by an Administrator and, in the case of the Federal Aviation Administration, also by a Deputy Administrator. Provided that all four officials were to be appointed by the President with the advice and consent of the Senate. (A fourth operating unit within the Department was to be the Coast Guard; *see transfers, below.*)

Provided that the Administrators and Commandant of the Coast Guard were first to carry out those functions, duties and powers vested in them under the Act, and then such additional duties as prescribed by the Secretary, and were to report directly to the Secretary.

Stipulated that all functions, powers and duties specified by the Act to be carried out by the Administrators could not be transferred elsewhere within the Department unless specifically provided for under an executive reorganization plan.

Directed the Secretary to carry out the provisions of the 1966 Traffic Safety and Highway Acts through a National Traffic Safety Bureau and a National Highway Safety Bureau—each to be established within the Department and headed by a Director appointed by the President with the advice and consent of the Senate. (As an alternative, the bill permitted the President, at his discretion, to carry out the Traffic Safety Act provisions through the Highway Safety Bureau—to continue an option for the Act's administration authorized under the Highway Safety Act.)

Secretary's Duties. *See box on next page.*

Transfers. Provided for the transfer of the following federal agencies and functions into the Department:

• Office of the Under Secretary of Commerce for Transportation and its policy, program, emergency transportation and research staffs.

• Bureau of Public Roads (BPR) and its federal-aid highway programs and functions which were to become a principal part of the Federal Highway Administration. Provided that the Office of Federal Highway Administrator (the existing operating head of the BPR) was to continue operating in that capacity within the new Department with a new title of Director of Public Roads.

• Coast Guard which was to be transferred from the Treasury Department and maintained as a separate unit within the new Department and was to continue operating as part of the Navy in wartime.

(Continued on p. 237)

Division of Duties in Transportation Department

The Department of Transportation bill was criticized frequently for limiting the authority of the new Secretary over federal transportation activities. The criticism stemmed partly from confusion over the duties assigned to each of the principal operating units of the Department—the Secretary, the three Administrations and the National Transportation Safety Board.

The following compilation of the Secretary's duties and the separation of work in the Department is taken in part from provisions in the bill and in part from a memorandum inserted in the *Congressional Record* by Rep. Chet Holifield (D Calif.), floor manager of the bill, which he said demonstrated that the Secretary had "important and very substantial" duties.

Secretary's Duties—*General.*

1. Provide leadership in developing a national transportation policy to be recommended to the President and Congress for implementation.

2. Coordinate and administer transportation programs.

3. Improve and coordinate transportation services.

4. Encourage cooperation among all interested parties and consult with other Government agencies involved in transportation.

5. Identify and solve transportation problems, making recommendations to Congress.

6. Coordinate and reorient research and development activities, including specific measures to reduce noise—particularly aircraft noise.

7. Cooperate with other federal agencies in developing transportation plans and programs that maintain or enhance the natural beauty of lands.

8. Cooperate with the Secretary of Labor in gathering information regarding labor-management contracts and promote industrial harmony and stable employment conditions in all transportation modes.

9. Conduct studies with the Secretary of Housing and Urban Development on urban transportation systems; make recommendations to the President and Congress, including a specific proposal for the best location of mass transportation functions in the Executive Branch.

10. Investigate safety compliance records of applicants seeking operating authority from the Interstate Commerce Commission.

11. Develop standards and criteria which, after receiving Congressional approval, are to be used as general guidelines within the Executive Branch in formulating and evaluating proposals for the investment of federal funds in transportation which will then be submitted to Congress.

Specific Functions

1. Interstate highway program.
2. Federal airport aid program.
3. Operation of the Alaska Railroad.
4. U. S. Coast Guard, except in wartime when it operates as part of the Navy.
5. Highway beautification program.
6. High speed ground transportation program.
7. Army Corps of Engineers bridge and toll functions.
8. Automobile and highway safety programs.

9. Standard time and daylight time administration.
10. National Driver Register Service.
11. St. Lawrence Seaway Development Corp.
12. Great Lakes Pilotage Administration.
13. International aviation facilities program.
14. Aircraft registration and title recording.
15. Development of a civil supersonic transport.

Administrative Duties

1. Control of the budget.
2. Submit legislative recommendations.
3. Establish policy.
4. Hire and fire employees.
5. Administer housekeeping provisions.

National Safety Board's Duties—*Mandatory.*

1. Determine cause or probable cause of accidents.
2. Review license and certification appeals.
3. Investigate aviation accidents.
4. Report and make recommendations to Congress.
5. Ensure that all actions are made public.

Discretionary

1. Conduct safety and accident prevention studies, making recommendations to Department authorities.

2. Ensure that investigation reports adequately state the circumstances, requesting further investigations when necessary.

3. Initiate specific investigations when necessary.

4. Arrange for participation of Board members or staff in investigations.

5. Recommend rules and procedures for conducting investigations.

6. Request notification and reports of all accidents.

Duties of Individual Administrators.

Aviation. The Administrator was given final administrative authority with appeals going to the Safety Board and courts in performing such functions as: controlling navigable airspace; operating air navigation facilities; prescribing air traffic rules and regulations; promulgating regulations for issuance of airman and aircraft certificates; prescribing minimum standards for design, construction and performance of aircraft; and establishing security provisions to permit maximum use of navigable airspace.

Railroads. The Administrator was directed to exercise the Secretary's authority over railroad and pipeline safety functions involving 240 Interstate Commerce Commission personnel and an annual budget of $3.5 million and was given final administrative authority on those functions involving notice or hearings. Functions included those relating generally to safety appliances and equipment, protection of employees and travelers, hours of service of employees, medals for heroism, explosives and other dangerous articles and standard time zones.

Highways. The Administrator was directed to exercise the Secretary's authority over motor carrier safety which involved 160 Interstate Commerce Commission personnel and an annual budget of $1.5 million and was given final administrative authority on those functions involving notice or hearings. Safety functions included qualifications and maximum hours of service of employees and safety of operation and equipment.

• Federal Aviation Agency (FAA) with its functions in safety, promotion, grant programs and development (including development and construction of a civil supersonic transport), which was to become the Federal Aviation Administration.

Stipulated that the FAA's safety functions were to be transferred directly to the Federal Aviation Administrator and that his decisions were to be administratively final with appeals either going to the National Transportation Safety Board *(see below)* or to the courts.

Further stipulated that nothing in the Act was to prevent the appointment of the current FAA Administrator as the new Federal Aviation Administrator. Provided that the FAA transfer was not to affect the President's power to transfer its functions to the Department of Defense in wartime.

• The safety functions of the Civil Aeronautics Board (CAB) which were to be transferred directly to the National Transportation Safety Board whose decisions were to be administratively final with appeals going directly to the courts.

• The safety functions of the Interstate Commerce Commission (ICC) such as inspection and enforcement of safety regulations for railroads, motor carriers and pipelines, but not its boxcar service functions.

Stipulated that safety functions pertaining to railroad and pipeline safety were to be carried out by the Federal Railroad Administrator and safety functions relating to motor carrier safety were to be carried out by the Federal Highway Administrator.

Provided that all decisions made by the two Administrators involving notice and hearings were to be administratively final with appeals going to the Safety Board or to the courts.

• Certain functions of the Army Corps of Engineers, including the authority to prescribe drawbridge and toll bridge regulations.

• Great Lakes Pilotage Administration, Alaska Railroad (currently under the direction and supervision of the Secretary of the Interior), the St. Lawrence Seaway Development Corp. and certain minor transportation-related activities of other agencies.

Safety Board. Established within the Department a bipartisan National Transportation Safety Board to be composed of five members appointed by the President for five-year terms with the advice and consent of the Senate. Provided that the Board was to be independent of the Secretary and the operating units of the Department. *(For duties of the Board, see box.)*

Investment Standards. Directed the Secretary to develop and, as needed, revise standards and criteria consistent with national transportation policies for the formulation and economic evaluation of all proposals for the investment of federal funds in transportation facilities and equipment.

Stipulated that the standards and criteria had to be approved by Congress prior to promulgation by the Secretary.

Exempted from the evaluation standards any proposals concerned with:

(1) acquisition of facilities or equipment by federal agencies for their own use;

(2) the Panama Canal;

(3) Department of Defense activities pertaining to the design and construction of sea, land and civil air transportation projects;

(4) foreign aid programs;

(5) water resource projects; and

(6) grant-in-aid programs (including federal highway and airport construction and improvement programs).

Provided that standards and criteria for evaluating water resource projects were to be developed by the Water Resources Council as authorized under PL 89-80; expanded the membership of the Council to include the Transportation Secretary on matters pertaining to navigation features of the projects. *(See chapter on Natural Resources.)*

Established a definition of primary direct navigation benefits to be used in evaluating water resource projects, thereby restoring by statute the criteria used by the Army Corps of Engineers prior to November 1964, which were more favorable to water transportation than were the criteria used between November 1964 and August 1966.

Other Provisions. Provided that orders and actions of the Secretary, Administrators and National Transportation Safety Board would be subject to judicial review.

Stipulated that the Act did not authorize, without further Congressional action, the adoption, revision or implementation of a national transportation policy of investment standards and criteria.

Highway Aid

Congress in 1966 enacted legislation (S 3155—PL 89-574) authorizing fiscal 1968-72 appropriations totaling $19,816,200,000 for federal highway construction, the Interstate Highway System, Alaskan highways and emergency repair of roads damaged by natural disasters. The Administration had requested $19,281,000,000.

Of the total authorization in the Federal-Aid Highway Act of 1966, $17,085,000,000 was for the Interstate Highway System from fiscal 1968 through fiscal 1972. The Interstate funds, all from the Highway Trust Fund, were composed of $7.2 billion in fiscal 1968-69—$300 million more than requested by the Administration—and $9,885,000,000 in 1970-72—the amount requested by the Administration.

The bill also included a one-year extension of the authorization for the System, from the end of fiscal 1971—as provided in existing law—until the end of fiscal 1972. As planned under existing law, the System was to be completed within about a year following the last authorization. However, most experts connected with the project agreed that it could not be finished by 1972 or 1973 with the funds authorized in the bill because of rising construction costs and improved—and more costly—highway designs. The availability of additional funds, however, awaited enactment of increased as well as new highway user taxes. Administration legislation designed to raise the needed tax revenues was not acted upon by Congress in 1966.

In addition to Interstate funds, S 3155 provided the regular biennial authorization for construction of federal-aid primary, secondary and urban (ABC) roads. The bill authorized $2 billion for this purpose in fiscal 1968-69, $1 billion each year, from the Highway Trust Fund. This was the amount requested.

The bill also authorized appropriations from general tax revenues of $561 million during fiscal 1968-69 ($273 million in 1968 and $288 in 1969) for other federal-domain roads such as forest highways, public lands roads and parkways. These authorizations totaled $165 million above the Administration's requests.

In addition, the bill authorized $14 million from general revenues annually in fiscal years 1968-72 for Alaska for highway development. The extra funds for Alaska were said to be necessary because of the state's size, climatic and seismic conditions and lack of road development prior to statehood. The Alaska funds were not requested by the Administration.

S 3155 contained an Administration-backed provision increasing the funds available annually for emergency repairs to highways damaged by natural disasters from $30 million to $50 million.

The bill signed by Mr. Johnson did not include funds for highway beautification. The House had authorized appropriations of $493 million from general tax revenues, but the Senate did not provide any funds for this purpose. The Administration had requested that the beautification program be financed through the Highway Trust Fund.

The deletion of beautification funds—for landscaping, scenic enhancement, compensation for billboard and junkyard removal and enforcement of controls—meant that almost all beautification programs would end after June 30, 1967, unless Congress renewed their authorization in 1967. Under existing law, only landscaping of federal-aid highway rights-of-way would continue beyond fiscal 1967. This program was financed through the Highway Trust Fund. Beautification programs under the Highway Beautification Act of 1965 were operating in all 50 states in 1966. *(See chapter on Natural Resources.)*

Highway Safety. Congress also enacted the Highway Safety Act of 1966 (S 3052—PL 89-564) authorizing a federal-state-local partnership to combat highway accidents. *(For details of highway safety legislation, see chapter on consumers' affairs.)*

Highway Fund Deferrals. President Johnson Nov. 29 imposed a ceiling of $3.3 billion on fiscal 1967 federal-aid highway obligations, in order to reduce inflationary pressures in the economy. The President described the action as a $1.1 billion spending deferral. The Bureau of Public Roads explained, however, that a "more realistic" estimate of the deferral was $700 million, adding that although Mr. Johnson apparently had used a fiscal 1967 total estimate of $4.4 billion, the level of receipts in the Highway Trust Fund would have limited fiscal 1967 obligations to $4 billion at the most. A similar $600 million deferral was imposed in 1967.

Provisions. As signed into law, S 3155 authorized appropriations for fiscal years 1968-69 as follows:

	Fiscal 1968	Fiscal 1969
From general revenues:		
Forest highways	$ 33,000,000	$ 33,000,000
Public lands highways	14,000,000	16,000,000
Forest roads and trails	170,000,000	170,000,000
Public lands roads and trails	3,000,000	5,000,000
Park roads and trails	25,000,000	30,000,000
Parkways	9,000,000	11,000,000
Indian reservation roads and bridges	19,000,000	23,000,000
Alaskan assistance	14,000,000	14,000,000
Emergency repair fund[1]	20,000,000	20,000,000

	Fiscal 1968	Fiscal 1969
From the Trust Fund:		
ABC roads	1,000,000,000	1,000,000,000
Interstate System	3,400,000,000	3,800,000,000
Emergency repair fund[1]	30,000,000	30,000,000
TOTAL	$4,737,000,000	$5,152,000,000

1 The $50 million total was an increase of $20 million over existing law; see provision, below.

The bill also:

Extended authorizations for the Interstate Highway System by one year through fiscal 1972.

Authorized fiscal 1970-72 appropriations for the Interstate System as follows: 1970, $3.6 billion; 1971, $3.6 billion; and 1972, $2,685,000,000.

Permitted Alaska to use federal-aid highway funds for construction of access and development roads on a federal-aid system for resource development, recreational, residential, commercial, industrial and other purposes.

Authorized for Alaska, from general revenues, an additional $14 million for each of fiscal years 1970-72 for highway construction and maintenance.

Stipulated that the Interstate System's highways have at least four traffic lanes.

Stipulated that appropriations for highway beautification and safety could not come from the Highway Trust Fund unless additional revenues from the general fund or a 1-percent auto excise tax were placed in the Fund specifically to finance those programs.

Provided that parkways, public lands highways and public lands development roads and trails were eligible for 100-percent federal financing of repair or reconstruction of damage due to floods, hurricanes, earthquakes and other disasters over a wide area. (The provision gave these roads equal treatment with other federal-domain roads; currently federal aid was limited to 50 percent of the repair or reconstruction costs for these roads.)

Increased the emergency fund available to assist in the repair or reconstruction of roads seriously damaged or destroyed by disasters from $30 million annually to $50 million annually. Provided that any portion of an annual $50 million authorization not used in that year would be available for use in the following two years. Required that 60 percent of emergency funds come from the highway trust funds and 40 percent from appropriations from general tax revenues. This provision was made retroactive to July 1, 1966 (Funds for the existing $30 million authorization came from the Highway Trust Fund.)

Authorized the Secretary of Transportation to study the advance acquisition of rights-of-way for future construction of federal-aid highways, reporting back to Congress by July 1, 1967.

Declared a national policy that the Secretary was to use maximum effort to preserve federal, state and local government parklands and historic sites and their beauty and historic value. Required the Secretary to cooperate with the states in developing highway plans and programs to carry out the policy and, after July 1, 1968, to approve only those programs and projects which did not require the use of such parks and historic sites, unless a program included all possible planning—including the consideration of alternatives to using the land—to minimize any harm to a park or site resulting from highway use.

Shipbuilding Subsidies

Congress in 1966 enacted legislation (S 2858—PL 89-589) extending for two years, through June 30, 1968, the cost-differential subsidy ceilings of 55 percent for new ship construction and 60 percent for reconditioning of passenger vessels.

The extension of the existing program—regarded as a stopgap measure—resulted from the continued inability of the Executive Branch and Congress to formulate a new federal maritime policy, despite the unanimous feeling among industry spokesmen, union groups and Government officials that a new policy was needed.

The measure encountered little Congressional opposition. Final approval of S 2858 came after House-Senate conferees accepted the House version of the bill (HR 12591) which provided for a two-year extension of the subsidy program. The Senate had voted a one-year extension, after brief debate in which Frank J. Lausche (D Ohio) and John J. Williams (R Del.) objected that the subsidies were not meeting their objective.

Lausche argued that the rationale for the original subsidies was that the cost differential between U. S. and foreign construction would gradually decline. Instead, he said, it had grown larger, and the merchant marine had grown "weaker and weaker," despite payment by the U.S. taxpayers of $2 billion in subsidies over the last 30 years.

The Administration requested only a one-year extension of the subsidy program pending development of a new maritime policy. The House Merchant Marine and Fisheries Committee, however, said that Administration witnesses were unable to indicate when a new policy would be formulated, and the Committee acceded to industry requests for a two-year extension.

A previous stopgap extension was voted in 1965. *(See above.)* Congress approved another one-year extension in 1968. *(See below.)*

Congress in 1966 appropriated $106,685,000 for fiscal 1967 ship construction subsidies, $21,685,000 above the $85 million requested by the Administration. The Administration had said that 13 ships would be built with the $85 million it requested, although some Administration officials in August privately admitted that nine ships was a more realistic expectation.

The effect of the increased appropriations by Congress raised industry estimates of new ships to 12 for fiscal 1967. Press accounts noted that only in 1960 and 1962 had the number of new ships built under the subsidy program dropped as low as 13. The construction program in 1966 reportedly was more than 100 ships behind contract schedule, all because of budgetary cutbacks.

(For fiscal 1966-69 ship subsidy appropriations, see box, p. 248.)

Passenger Ship Safety

Congress in 1966 completed action on an Administration-backed bill (HR 10327—PL 89-777) to provide greater safety on passenger vessels sailing to and from U. S. ports. The measure also required vessel owners to prove financial responsibility in order to prevent losses to passengers through cancellation of cruises after tickets were paid for. HR 10327 was passed by the House in 1965. *(See above.)* Most of the safety provisions were added by the Senate, which passed HR 10327 Aug. 22, 1966. Congress did not include in the bill Administration proposals to repeal current limitations on the liability of shipowners for passenger injuries and deaths.

Enactment of the noncontroversial measure was prompted by a series of ocean cruise ship fires during the previous year—most notably the Nov. 13, 1965, burning and destruction of a 30-year-old Panamanian cruise ship, the SS Yarmouth Castle, in which 90 persons died. In 1966 two more ship fires broke out—one at sea aboard a Norwegian cruise ship, the MS Viking Princess, and the other a few hours before passengers boarded a German flagship, the SS Hanseatic. All three vessels operated in the U. S. cruise trade, carrying a large number of American citizens.

The House version of HR 10327, which was passed before the Yarmouth disaster, required the filing of certain safety-related information with the Federal Maritime Commission, but focused for the most part on requiring ship operators to establish financial responsibility—prior to selling passage on cruises—to protect against passengers being stranded and losing their fare if a ship failed to sail.

After the November 1965 Yarmouth fire, efforts to enlarge the scope of the bill developed during Senate consideration; one of the key problems centered on the existing discrepancies between strict American vessel safety standards and more lenient international safety standards governing foreign ships. The international laws were established under three multilateral treaties known as the Safety of Life at Sea (SOLAS) Conventions. Besides being less strict than American requirements, the SOLAS standards contained the so-called "grandfather clauses" which permitted older vessels such as the Yarmouth Castle, built before the first Convention in 1936, to operate without conforming to the improved standards of the international agreements.

The Senate in 1967 consented to ratification of a series of SOLAS amendments which eliminated the grandfather clauses and tightened other safety standards, as recommended by the Intergovernmental Maritime Consultative Organization (IMCO) in 1966. *(See Foreign Policy chapter, p. 98, 113.)*

Provisions. As signed by the President, HR 10327:

Notification, Promotion. Required owners, operators or agents of foreign and domestic passenger vessels of 100 gross tons or over with accommodations for 50 or more passengers and embarking passengers at U. S. ports, to notify each prospective passenger of the vessel's compliance or noncompliance with existing safety standards.

Required the identical safety information to appear in all promotional and advertising literature distributed within the United States offering passage or soliciting passengers for a voyage.

Noncompliance. Directed the Secretary of Transportation, operating through the Coast Guard, to prevent the departure from a U. S. port of a domestic or foreign vessel carrying American passengers (embarking at that port) upon determining that the vessel did not comply with safety standards established under the 1960 Safety of Life at Sea (SOLAS) Convention, as modified by the amendments proposed by the Maritime Safety Committee of the Intergovernmental Maritime Consultative Organization (IMCO) in May 1966. Applicable to ships of 100 or more gross tons and with accommodations for 50 or more passengers. This provision was to become effective simultaneously with the IMCO amendments, but no later than Nov. 2, 1968.

Financial Responsibility. Required owners and charterers of domestic and foreign vessels accommodating 50 or more passengers and sailing to or from U. S. ports to establish financial responsibility, under Federal Maritime Commission regulations, to meet liabilities as a result of death or injury of passengers.

Stipulated that the amount of financial responsibility was to be based on the number of passenger accommodations as follows: $20,000 for each passenger accommodation up to and including 500; $15,000 for each additional accommodation up to and including 1,000; $10,000 for each additional accommodation up to and including 1,500; and $5,000 for each additional accommodation over 1,500.

Directed the collector of customs at any U. S. port to refuse clearance to any vessel not having evidence of furnishing the required financial responsibility to the Commission.

U.S. Ships. Provided that after Nov. 1, 1968, no U. S. passenger vessel of 100 gross tons or more or accommodating 50 or more passengers could be granted a certificate of inspection by the Coast Guard unless constructed of fire-retardant materials. (Under existing law, the requirement applied to all U. S. vessels except those exempted under the "grandfather clauses" of the SOLAS Conventions.)

Airport Act Extension

Congress in 1966, without controversy, enacted a bill (S 3096—PL 89-647) to extend until June 30, 1970, the current $75-million annual authorization for federal grants-in-aid to airports under the Federal Airport Act of 1946 (PL 79-377). That Act had been amended and extended several times, most recently in 1964. *(Congress and the Nation, Vol. I, p. 536-44)*

The Administration-backed bill extending the Act for three years contained no substantive changes in the current operation of the grant program.

Under the Act, matching grants were available only for airport improvements directly connected with safety. Special funds amounting to $1.5 million annually were available for Hawaii, Puerto Rico and the Virgin Islands. In addition, $7 million annually was reserved for airports which primarily serve general (noncommercial) aviation.

Of the remaining grant funds ($66.5 million annually) 75 percent was apportioned among the 50 states and the District of Columbia on a formula basis, and 25 percent was distributed at the discretion of the Administrator of the Federal Aviation Administration (FAA).

In 1966 Congress transferred the FAA into the new Department of Transportation (DOT), but the Secretary of Transportation was denied authority to interfere with the FAA Administrator's power to make discretionary airport grants under the Federal Airport Act. *(See above.)*

In its fiscal 1967 Budget, the Administration asked for recision of $21 million of the $71 million already appropriated by Congress for fiscal 1967, leaving $50 million available for the year. The Budget also contained only $50 million for the program in fiscal 1968.

During Congressional hearings on the fiscal 1967 Independent Offices appropriations bill, Gen. William F. McKee, administrator of the FAA, attributed the budget cut to "the tightness of the Budget" in general and "the expenditures for the war in Vietnam in particular." McKee said the FAA had not recommended the cut, which indi-

cated that the recision proposal came from the Budget Bureau. "If the money were available we could use it," McKee said.

Congress declined to reduce fiscal 1967 appropriations as the Administration requested. Because S 3096 was enacted so late in the session, no action was taken on the request for fiscal 1968 appropriations. *(For fiscal 1966-70 appropriations for airport grants, see box, p. 250.)*

Provisions. As signed into law, S 3096 extended the Federal Airport Act of 1946 until June 30, 1970, as follows:

Authorized $75 million annually in matching funds for airport development related to safety for fiscal years 1968-70. Annual authorizations were divided as follows:

$66,500,000 for the 50 states and the District of Columbia

7,000,000 for development of general purpose (private, noncommercial) airports

$600,000 additional authorization for Hawaii

$600,000 additional authorization for Puerto Rico

$300,000 additional authorization for the Virgin Islands

Stipulated that 75 percent of total funds reserved for the states and the District of Columbia be apportioned on the basis of state area and population, and 25 percent at the discretion of the Administrator of the Federal Aviation Administration (FAA).

Continued existing provisions barring federal aid for projects not directly related to safety and limiting the federal share to 50 percent except for certain landing aids (75 percent).

Continued an existing provision authorizing the FAA to reimburse airport builders for 50 percent of the costs of advance planning and engineering studies.

Freight Car Shortage

Congress in 1966 completed action on a bill (S 1098—PL 89-430) to help reduce the nationwide shortage of freight cars. The Senate had passed S 1098 in 1965, but House passage was delayed by the opposition of Eastern railroads. *(See above.)* The House passed the bill May 12, 1966, on a 306-27 roll-call vote.

The bill authorized the Interstate Commerce Commission (ICC) to establish freight car rental charges at a level that would prompt lines to buy their own cars rather than borrow them from other lines.

The legislation resulted from a continuing and worsening shortage of freight cars in the United States. Existing rental rates were sufficiently low that railroads generally found it cheaper to borrow the cars of other lines —and frequently hold on to them for extended periods— than to purchase new cars of their own. Shortages frequently developed in Midwestern and Western states where shipments of food commodities and raw materials originated. Relief of some type had long been sought by certain railroads, primarily those in the West, and a variety of farm organizations and businesses.

The bill cleared Congress in 1966 with little opposition. Most House votes against the measure were cast by Members from New York, Massachusetts and Connecticut. In signing the bill, President Johnson said it would help ease the freight car shortage that had "gone from bad to worse in recent years."

Before passage of S 1098, the ICC March 17 acted under existing legislation to ease a critical boxcar shortage in the Northwestern states. The ICC issued a series of orders designed to speed empty boxcars back to their owners.

Provisions. As signed into law, S 1098:

Authorized the Interstate Commerce Commission, after a hearing, to fix rental charges for the use of any type of freight car at a level sufficient to compensate railroads for the expense of owning and maintaining that type of car. (This, in effect, specifically stated the court-interpreted limits of existing law.)

In addition to rental charges based only on ownership costs, allowed the ICC to establish "incentive" charges for any type of car which would be sufficient: to "encourage" railroads to buy and maintain an "adequate" supply of cars to meet national commercial and defense needs; to "contribute" to "sound car service practices," such as promptly returning borrowed cars to the owner company; and to provide fair and reasonable compensation to freight car owners for use of their cars by other lines.

Prohibited the ICC from applying the "incentive" charges to any type of car that was in adequate supply, as determined by the ICC.

Permitted the ICC to exempt from the "incentive" charges any group of carriers where such exemption would be "in the national interest."

Provided that no rental charges established under the bill would take effect before Sept. 1, 1966.

Urban Mass Transit

Congress in 1966 enacted a bill (S 3700—PL 89-562) to continue and expand programs begun under the Urban Mass Transportation Act of 1964 (PL 88-365).

The 1964 Act authorized a three-year, $375-million program of matching grants and loans to enable states and localities to construct and improve mass transit facilities. *(Congress and the Nation, Vol. I, p. 558)*

The 1966 measure authorized annual appropriations of $150 million in fiscal 1968 and 1969 for the program. (Congress in 1968 authorized appropriations for fiscal 1970. *See below.*)

The bill also expanded the 1964 Act by authorizing use of the grant funds for three new purposes: (1) planning and technical studies preparatory to construction and improved operation of mass transit systems; (2) training fellowships for personnel in the mass transportation field; and (3) research on the problems of mass transportation and training of personnel for research or employment in transportation systems.

The bill also directed the Secretary of Housing and Urban Development to prepare within 18 months (by March 1968) a program of research, development and demonstration of new, improved systems of urban mass transit.

Finally, S 3700 allowed a certain amount of leeway in allocation of grants to states with severe transportation problems which had used up their initial federal grants. The 1964 Act stipulated that no state could receive more than 12.5 percent of the total funds appropriated in any year. S 3700 allowed the Secretary to use up to $12.5 million of the funds to make additional unrestricted grants to states which had obligated more than two-thirds of their previous allotments.

President Johnson in his Jan. 26, 1966, city development message had proposed only a one-year extension of the 1964

Act, through fiscal 1968, at the $150-million level authorized for fiscal 1966 and 1967. The President's proposal was contained in the Administration's urban development legislation (HR 12939, S 2977), which included a $95-million authorization for mass transit in fiscal 1968. This amount, when added to $55 million previously authorized but not used, allowed continuation of the $150-million program through fiscal 1968.

Both the Senate and House Banking and Currency Committees decided to report mass transportation bills separately, instead of including them in an omnibus urban development measure as requested by the President. Both also recommended funding at a higher level than requested for fiscal 1968. The Senate Committee recommended a $225-million authorization. The House panel proposed $175 million.

In floor debate, both the House and the Senate adopted amendments, by roll-call votes, to reduce the funds authorized in the committee bills to $150 million a year. Republican proponents of the cut in both chambers argued that expenditures should be held back while the economy was inflated and the Vietnam war was in progress. They also said Congress should not exceed the President's $150-million request without good reason.

As sent to the President, S 3700 substantially retained the provisions of the Senate version of the bill.

Unlike most federal programs, aid for mass transportation is appropriated one year in advance because of the need for advance planning. Congress in 1966 appropriated $125 million for fiscal 1968 urban mass transportation programs, including $55 million authorized in the 1964 Act but not yet appropriated. The $55 million was contained in the fiscal 1967 Independent Offices Appropriations bill (HR 14921—PL 89-555). The Administration asked for an additional $95 million for fiscal 1968 in connection with the Fiscal 1967 Supplemental Appropriations bill (HR 18381—PL 89-697), of which Congress appropriated $70 million. *(For total urban mass transit funds, fiscal 1966-70, see box, p. 251.)*

Provisions. As signed into law, S 3700 amended the Urban Mass Transportation Act of 1964 as follows:

Extended through fiscal 1969 the grant and loan authorization of the Act, scheduled to expire at the end of fiscal 1967, and authorized appropriations of $150 million in each of fiscal years 1968 and 1969. The emergency grant program, however, was not extended past its July 1, 1967, expiration date. (This program was extended in 1967. *See below.*)

From within the over-all appropriations made each year, authorized grants to state and local public bodies to cover up to two-thirds of the cost of planning, engineering, designing and technical studies of urban mass transportation systems to be included in coordinated programs for development of entire urban areas. Activities covered by the grants could include (1) studies related to management, operations, capital requirements and economic feasibility; (2) preparation of engineering and architectural surveys, plans and specifications; and (3) similar activities preliminary to construction, acquisition or improved operation of mass transportation systems.

Also from within the over-all appropriations, authorized up to $1.5 million a year for grants to states and local bodies to provide as many as 100 one-year fellowships for training managerial and technical personnel in the mass transportation field. Each fellowship could not exceed either $12,000 or 75 percent of the sum of (1) the recipient's tuition costs, (2) any additional charges made by the institution for the training involved and (3) the amount by which the recipient's salary is reduced during the training period. Not more than 1.25 percent of the fellowships could be awarded in any one state.

Authorized use of up to $3 million a year, from the over-all appropriations, for grants to institutions of higher learning for (1) comprehensive research on the theoretical or practical problems of urban mass transportation and (2) training of persons to conduct further research or to obtain employment in private or public organizations which plan, construct, operate or manage urban transportation systems.

Continued through fiscal 1969 the $10-million-a-year authorization, from the over-all outlays, for support of research and demonstration projects by bringing the total authorized for this purpose over fiscal years 1965-69 to $50 million by fiscal 1969.

Directed the Secretary of HUD, in consultation with the Secretay of Commerce, to submit to the President and Congress within 18 months of the date of enactment of the bill a program of research, development and demonstration of new systems of urban transportation that could carry people and goods within metropolitan areas speedily, safely, without polluting the air and in a manner that would contribute to sound city planning. The program was to (1) deal with all aspects of new transit systems in metropolitan areas of various sizes; (2) take into account the most advanced technologies and materials; and (3) provide national leadership to efforts of states, localities and other public and private groups.

Modified the existing provision that no state could receive more than 12.5 percent of the total funds appropriated for grants to provide that the Secretary could disregard the 12.5-percent limit and use up to $12.5 million of the total funds to make additional grants to any states which had obligated more than two-thirds of their previous allotments.

1967

Maritime Policy

Despite extensive Congressional hearings and lengthy negotiations between Executive Branch officials and maritime industry spokesmen, no action was taken in 1967 to halt the continuing decline of the U. S. merchant fleet.

Transportation Secretary Alan S. Boyd May 1 outlined the "elements" of a new federal maritime policy before a Senate subcommittee, but Boyd's proposals were not formally introduced as Administration-backed legislation. Administration spokesmen later explained that budgetary considerations (including the 1967 economy drive in Congress) and a lack of unified industry support for Boyd's proposals had contributed to the postponement of the long-delayed policy revision. (The Administration formally made its proposals in 1968. *See below.*)

In the absence of a maritime bill directly sponsored by the Johnson Administration, influential Congressional advocates of a new merchant marine policy Nov. 9 introduced major legislation to strengthen the merchant fleet. The bills (S 2650, HR 13940) were introduced in the Senate

by Commerce Committee Chairman Warren G. Magnuson (D Wash.) and in the House by Merchant Marine and Fisheries Committee Chairman Edward A. Garmatz (D Md.).

The bills authorized $300 million annually for a five-year period for federal construction-differential subsidies to shipbuilders; the amount was sufficient to allow the building in U. S. shipyards of 35 to 40 new vessels annually (compared to the current level of 12 or 13 ships annually).

The Magnuson-Garmatz bill also extended construction subsidies to new classes of companies, such as the tramp steamship operators, and called for unspecified increases and extensions of the existing operating-differential subsidy program.

In an effort to avoid needless controversy, the bill did not touch on the question of the future location of the Maritime Administration, which the Administration wished to transfer from the Commerce Department to the Transportation Department.

Other provisions of the Magnuson-Garmatz bill permitted the subsidized purchase of an unspecified number of nuclear-powered merchant vessels, authorized $125 million over a five-year period for maritime research and development, authorized $30 million for reconstruction of the reserve merchant fleet (mainly decommissioned World War II vessels in mothballs) and expanded the existing capital reserve fund program, under which ship companies could set aside part of their profits (without paying income tax) for future capital improvements to their fleets.

Although the Magnuson-Garmatz plan was not endorsed by the Johnson Administration, Magnuson Nov. 9, 1967, told the Senate that Congressional drafters of the bill had held "a long talk with the President of the United States" during their preparation of the legislation. Further meetings had been held, Magnuson said, with Secretary Boyd, which resulted in "general agreement between all involved...as to most of the provisions of this new program." *(For 1968 action on the legislation, see below.)*

Meanwhile, Congress in 1967 appropriated $143 million for fiscal 1968 ship construction subsidies.

MARITIME AUTHORIZATIONS. President Johnson Sept. 5 signed a bill (HR 158—PL 90-81) requiring for the first time advance authorization of funds for certain programs administered by the Federal Maritime Administration. Enactment of the bill continued a postwar trend in which an increasing number of federal agencies were required to seek annual authorizations for their activities from the appropriate legislative committees, before funds could be appropriated. Before passage of HR 158, continuing authority for merchant marine program appropriations was provided by the Merchant Marine Act of 1936.

No debate on the measure was heard during Senate or House action. The bill was opposed by the Budget Bureau, which said its enactment could cause a heavy expenditure of time by Maritime Administration officials and might interfere with efficient administration.

Provisions. As signed into law (PL 90-81) Sept. 5, HR 158:

Required, after Dec. 31, 1967, that only such sums as specifically authorized by law were to be appropriated for the following activities:

● Acquisition, construction or reconstruction of vessels.

● Payment of construction-differential subsidies (including national defense features of construction).

- Payment of operating-differential subsidies.
- Research and development expenses (including losses from experimental ship operations).
- Reserve fleet expenses.
- Maritime training at the Merchant Marine Academy.
- Federal payments to state marine schools.
- Payments to the Vessel Operations Revolving Fund.

NEW MARITIME AGENCY. In an expression of dissatisfaction with current U. S. maritime policy, the House Oct. 17 by a 326-44 roll-call vote passed a bill (HR 159) to establish an independent Federal Maritime Administration within the Executive Branch. The Senate passed the bill in 1968, but President Johnson pocket vetoed it. *(See below.)*

The principal purpose of the bill, which received broad bipartisan support in the House, was to create a strong new federal agency with sufficient independent authority to bring about basic improvements in the implementation of merchant marine policies. The bill was opposed by the Johnson Administration, which since 1966 had wanted to incorporate the existing Maritime Administration (part of the Commerce Department) into the Transportation Department.

PASSENGER SHIP SUBSIDIES. The House Dec. 4 passed a bill (HR 12639) extending the number of months per year during which U.S. passenger ships could receive operating subsidies for cruises outside their regular trade routes. As passed by the House, the measure carried a three-year time limit designed to assure Congressional review. The bill became law in 1968. *(See below.)*

Urban Mass Transit

Congress in 1967 twice extended the emergency grant provisions of the Mass Transportation Act of 1964 (PL 88-365).

Under the emergency grant program, urban transit authorities received one-half of the "net project cost" for new facilities from the Federal Government, even if area-wide planning for the transit system remained incomplete. Full planning was required for regular program grants, which could be made for two-thirds of the "net project cost"—that is, the portion of total cost which could not be raised through fare box revenues.

Congress in 1966 enacted legislation extending through fiscal 1969 the major provisions of the 1964 Act, but it did not extend the emergency grant program past its July 1, 1967, expiration date. *(See above.)*

The first 1967 extension bill (H J Res 601—PL 90-34) allowed continuation of the program to Nov. 1, 1967, pending Congressional action on a major Administration urban aid-home ownership bill (HR 8068) which was to extend the program for two years. *(See p. 214, 215.)*

The second extension bill (H J Res 859— PL 90-169) was enacted after it became clear that HR 8068 would not be cleared during the 1967 legislative session. H J Res 859 extended the emergency grant program for one year, to Nov. 1, 1968.

Congress further extended the urban mass transportation program in 1968. *(See below.)*

N. S. Savannah

Congress in 1967 successfully resisted an attempt by the Johnson Administration to lay up the N. S. Savannah, the world's first nuclear-powered merchant ship, as an economy measure. The proposed retirement of the vessel, which was announced Jan. 24 by the Maritime Administration, encountered strong resistance among Members of Congress and maritime industry spokesmen. In a complete reversal of Administration policy, Acting Maritime Administrator J. W. Gulick June 12 told a Senate subcommittee that the Savannah "should be kept in operation in fiscal 1968."

In legislative action, Congress in 1967 provided $3.3 million for continued operation of the vessel in fiscal 1968 and specifically denied an Administration request to use $1,350,000 for Savannah layup expenses.

In 1968, Congress appropriated $3.4 million for continued operation of the Savannah and prohibited the use of any of the funds to lay her up.

Construction of the N. S. Savannah was authorized by Congress in 1956. As the first atomic-powered cargo ship, its purpose was to promote the peaceful use of atomic energy. Construction of the vessel was supervised by the Maritime Administration and the Atomic Energy Commission. The Savannah was put into operation May 1, 1962. *(Congress and the Nation, Vol. I, p. 550)*

Aviation Safety

Concern over the dangers of air travel reached a new level of intensity in 1967. Prodded by recent air disasters and by fear of worse to come, the economy-minded 90th Congress appropriated more funds for aviation safety programs than officially requested by the Johnson Administration. For its part, the Administration announced new regulations to make airplanes safer for their occupants.

Congressional Action. Congress in 1967 responded to mounting pressures for an increased federal safety effort by appropriating more than requested by the Administration for safety programs.

A major campaign to increase funds for air navigation facilities and equipment, including radar, instrument landing systems, control towers, approach lights and terminal automation, was led in the Senate by Sen. John Stennis (D Miss.), chairman of the Senate Appropriations Transportation Subcommittee.

In the Senate report on the fiscal 1968 transportation appropriations bill (HR 11456), the Senate Appropriations Committee recommended $27 million above the President's original funding request for FAA operations. The additional funds were to provide more staff positions for safety personnel, the Committee said. Noting that it would take "two years to feel the full effect" of the extra money, the report said it was "imperative to take action...now in order to maintain and improve flying safety standards."

The Committee noted that "passenger miles traveled by air" were expected to "increase by 40 percent by 1972" and that "private plane operation" would rise "35 percent in the next four years." In view of these projected figures, the safety problem would become much more acute, the Committee believed, unless additional funds were "made available now."

The Committee also recommended an increase of $30 million over the President's original request for new airport facilities and equipment. The original request had provided no money for new control towers or radar installations, and the Committee believed that an extra $30 million for these facilities was fully justified.

The Senate accepted without change the recommendations of its Appropriations Committee, but the safety funds in the bill subsequently were reduced by action of the Senate-House conferees.

As signed into law (PL 90-112), the funding bill for fiscal 1968 provided $659.4 million in readily identifiable funds for direct and indirect air safety efforts. The sum was $25.6 million above amended Administration requests, but considerably less than the $1-billion (minimum) annual spending level which was considered necessary by critics of the existing programs.

New FAA Safety Rules. In partial response to criticism of current safety programs, the Federal Aviation Administration Sept. 19 issued extensive new regulations to lessen the risk of injury or death in "survivable" air crashes. The FAA estimated that 174 passengers on commercial airliners had died in "survivable" crashes—at landing or takeoff—in six years, 1961-1966. In the same accidents, 358 passengers had survived the crashes.

Many of the new rules were originally proposed as far back as 1961, after the crash on landing of a United Air Lines DC-8 at Denver. The jet skidded off the runway, struck a truck and began to burn. All 41 first-class passengers escaped, but 16 of the 81 tourist-class passengers were killed. The tourist compartment had only one exit.

The rules included requirements for 90-second evacuation of passenger compartments (compared to a current 120-second maximum), improved emergency exit marking and lighting, more exits, better restraints for cabin baggage, use of fire-resistant materials in compartments and redesign of fuel lines to minimize the danger of fire on impact with the ground. The regulations were to be implemented in four stages, at six-month intervals, beginning Oct. 24, 1967.

SST Appropriations

Congress appropriated $623,375,000 for the supersonic transport (SST) between fiscal 1962 and fiscal 1969. The breakdown of funds:

Fiscal 1962	$11,000,000
Fiscal 1963	20,000,000
Fiscal 1964	60,000,000
Fiscal 1965	None
Fiscal 1966	140,000,000
Fiscal 1967	280,000,000
Fiscal 1968	142,375,000
Fiscal 1969	None*

*The fiscal 1969 Transportation Department appropriation bill (HR 18188) carried no new funds for the SST. In addition, it rescinded $30 million in funds previously appropriated. Sufficient funds remained from previous appropriations to continue the program during fiscal 1969.

Newspaper accounts estimated the total cost of implementing the new regulations at $75 million, to be shared by the air carriers and the manufacturers.

Other Legislation

SUPERSONIC TRANSPORT. In the Department of Transportation appropriations bill for fiscal 1968 (HR 11456—PL 90-112) Congress included legislative provisions which for the first time authorized federal participation in the construction of two prototype SST planes. The bill appropriated $142,375,000 for SST development; this was $55,625,000 less than the Administration requested, but the Appropriations Committees in both chambers made clear that this was merely a bookkeeping cut that would not affect the level of spending for the SST in fiscal 1968. Both the House and Senate defeated efforts at further reductions in the SST appropriation. (In 1968, Congress rescinded $30 million previously appropriated for the SST and denied all funds for fiscal 1969. *See below.*)

During the fiscal 1962-67 period, Congress appropriated $511 million for feasibility and design studies and for initial development of the aircraft. *(See box.)* Of this amount, $311 million was spent by mid-1967.

President Johnson April 29 authorized the Transportation Department to sign contracts with the Boeing Co. and the General Electric Co. for the construction of two prototype aircraft by fiscal 1971. Development costs were to be shared by the Federal Government, the two manufacturing companies and the airlines which had indicated interest in purchasing SSTs.

Supporters of the project argued that a U.S. commitment was necessary because the Anglo-French Concorde and the Soviet Tupolev-144 aircraft—both small supersonic planes—already were under development. The Boeing SST was to carry up to 300 passengers at 1,800 miles per hour. *(See p. 232.)*

PASSENGER TRAINS. The Senate Dec. 1 passed a bill (S 2711) to strengthen Interstate Commerce Commission (ICC) procedures governing discontinuance of passenger trains. There was no further action on S 2711. However, Senate and House subcommittees held hearings in 1968 on similar legislation. *(See below.)*

HIGHWAY AID. Congress in 1967 enacted no major highway legislation. However, it received two reports dealing with anticipated highway problems and requirements of the future.

The American Assn. of State Highway Officials (AASHO) June 5 submitted a preliminary report on future highway needs to the Roads Subcommittee of the Senate Public Works Committee. The report (S Doc 33) anticipated the construction requirements in the 1975-85 decade, following completion of the Interstate Highway System. Future highway programs should concentrate, the report said, on upgrading the "functionally obsolete rural primary highway system" and the non-Interstate urban roads, which had been neglected during the period of Interstate System construction.

Two House Public Works Subcommittees—the Roads Subcommittee and the Special Subcommittee on the Federal-Aid Highway Program—Aug. 24 issued a report (H Rept 597) on the relationship of toll road facilities to the federal-aid highway program. The Subcommittees recommended various actions, including expansion of the Interstate System, to forestall construction of additional toll roads. The report said "a wide extension of toll facilities across our nation" would be "most unfortunate." The report was based on 1966 hearings on the resurgence of toll road planning and construction by states and other non-federal highway authorities.

1968

Highway Aid

In the Federal-Aid Highway Act of 1968 (S 3418—PL 90-495), Congress extended the Interstate Highway System for two years and authorized an additional 1,500 miles for the System. The bill also carried a $12.3-billion authorization for road building and related programs. S 3418 differed from traditional highway legislation in that it focused on the social aspects of highway construction, with special emphasis on urban problems.

President Johnson almost vetoed the bill because it contained a controversial mandate, inserted by the House, requiring that work begin on completion of the Interstate System in the District of Columbia. The mandate required construction to start on four projects named in the bill, including an additional bridge across the Potomac River, within 30 days of enactment.

The D. C. controversy was widely viewed as a dispute between the automotive and road building industry on one side and the supporters of incorporating urban planning into highway construction on the other side. Fighting for inclusion of the mandate in the bill were Rep. John C. Kluczynski (D Ill.), chairman of the Public Works Roads Subcommittee, and Rep. William H. Natcher (D Ky.), chairman of the District of Columbia Appropriations Subcommittee, who blocked funds for a District rapid transit system until the Interstate projects were "beyond recall." The mandate was opposed by various citizens groups and agencies, including the Interior Department and the District Government.

President Johnson finally signed the bill just before the veto deadline. In an accompanying statement the President called the mandate "objectionable" and said it legally could not be carried out. In support of his contention he cited a requirement of federal highway law that proposed projects fit into a comprehensive plan, a condition he implied did not exist with respect to the District projects. The President said he would have vetoed the bill had it been necessary to follow the mandate.

Another disputed area in the bill was the highway beautification program. The Administration had requested a three-year, $255-million authorization and the Senate approved that amount. The House, however, authorized no funds at all. Conferees agreed to authorize $25 million for one year, but when the conference report reached the House floor an attempt to eliminate the authorization failed by only one vote. *(See chapter on natural resources.)*

The bill contained several new provisions affecting the urban highway program. It authorized $400 million for TOPICS, a new program designed to improve traffic

flow in urban areas through traffic movement efficiency procedures rather than new construction. It also required that hearings on proposed route locations consider not only the economic impact of the proposed locations, but also the effect on the community environment. And it directed all states to provide relocation payments to help property owners forced to move because of highway locations, with the Federal Government paying 100 percent of these costs through June 30, 1970.

The bill's total $12,307,500,000 authorization was $290 million below the Budget request of $12,597,500,000. Congress authorized the full $8,340,000,000 requested for the Interstate System. This included increases in existing authorizations for fiscal 1970-72 and new authorizations of $4 billion for fiscal 1973 and $2,225,000,000 for fiscal 1974. The requested increases were based on 1968 estimates that projected the total federal share of completing the system in 1974 at $50,640,000,000.

Major Provisions

As signed by the President, S 3418 provided the following new authorizations shown in the right hand column (years in parentheses are fiscal years):

	Budget Request	Final Authorization
Interstate program (1970-74)	$8,340,000,000	$8,340,000,000
ABC system (1970-7l)	2,000,000,000	2,200,000,000
Primary-secondary non-urban (1970-7l)	---	250,000,000
Urban traffic improvements (TOPICS)	1,250,000,000 (1970-71-72-73-74)	400,000,000 (1970-71)
State-local safety program (1970-71)	125,000,000	175,000,000
Safety research, development (1970-71)	70,000,000	67,500,000
Highway beautification programs	255,000,000 (1969-70-71)	25,000,000 (1970)
Highway beautification administration (1969-70)	5% of authorization	2,500,000
Forest highways (1970-71)	66,000,000	66,000,000
Public lands highways (1970-71)	32,000,000	32,000,000
Forest development roads, trails (1970-71)	250,000,000	340,000,000
Public lands development roads, trails (1970-71)	8,500,000	8,500,000
Park roads, trails (1971)	30,000,000	30,000,000
Parkways (1971)	11,000,000	11,000,000
Indian reservation roads, bridges (1970-71)	60,000,000	60,000,000
Right-of-way advance acquisition revolving fund	100,000,000	300,000,000 (1970-71-72)
TOTAL	$12,597,500,000	$12,307,500,000

The bill also:

Increased the Interstate mileage from 41,000 to 42,500, and extended the completion date from 1972 to 1974.

Retained the 10-percent penalty against construction funds in states which do not have a safety program, but extended the date for having a safety program underway from Jan. 1, 1970 to Jan. 1, 1971.

Established a highway relocation assistance program to aid property owners forced to move because of highway locations, by providing relocation payments.

Federal-Aid Highway Funds

In the annual Commerce Department appropriations bills, Congress authorized appropriations from the Highway Trust Fund to meet federal-aid highway construction obligations. The fund, into which certain highway user taxes were channeled, was used to finance the federal share of major highway programs. Following are the appropriations from the Highway Trust Fund authorized by Congress for fiscal years 1966-69:

Fiscal 1966	$3,898,400,000
Fiscal 1967	3,968,400,000
Fiscal 1968	3,770,872,000
Fiscal 1969	4,155,370,000

Required the Secretary of Transportation and the District of Columbia government to complete part of the Interstate System in the District, including building an additional bridge across the Potomac River.

Directed the Secretary of Transportation to preserve parkland and historic sites considered significant from encroachment unless no "feasible and prudent alternative" was available.

Required equal opportunity requirements to be placed in contracts let for bids, so that concerned parties would be aware of all requirements at the time bids were made.

Established a revolving fund for advance acquisition of rights-of-way, as a means of acquiring land less expensively.

Required setting of standards for bridge inspection, but specified that the states were to make the inspections.

Authorized setting up of fringe parking facilities on a 50-50, federal-local basis.

Retained the 10-percent penalty against construction funds in states which do not have a beautification program, and allowed state and local governments to determine areas as customarily industrial or commercial, although not zoned industrial or commercial, for billboard regulation purposes.

Required hearings on proposed highway route locations to consider proposed locations' impact and effect on community environment, as well as the existing criterion, economic impact.

Required that workers on federally aided highway projects come under the provisions of prevailing wage-rate legislation.

Prohibited impounding of highway funds, except when needed to maintain a sufficient balance in the Highway Trust Fund.

Specified it was the sense of Congress that no highway trust funds be used to pay the administrative expenses of any agency other than the Federal Highway Administration and its Bureau of Public Roads.

Allowed the Secretary of Transportation to pay up to 100 percent of the costs of replacing a transportation facility damaged in a catastrophe.

Required the official concurrence of the Secretary of Transportation before any section of the Interstate System could be constructed as a toll road, and specified that the Secretary should concur only when it was in the public interest.

Instructed the Secretary to make a study of road needs in Guam, American Samoa, and the Virgin Islands.

Instructed the Secretary to complete a study by January 1970 of the nation's highway system, establishing categories according to the function of the highways.

Made provisions of the bill effective upon enactment, except for relocation provisions, which, until July 1, 1970, were to apply to states only so far as they were able under their laws to comply.

Maritime Policy

Three years after President Johnson promised recommendations on a new maritime policy, the Administration in 1968 formally made its proposals. However, the program was strongly criticized, and Congress took no action on it. A bill (HR 13940) originally aimed at providing a new maritime policy and believed to have some Administration backing was reported in the House, but the measure was diluted by the House Merchant Marine and Fisheries Committee and later killed by the Rules Committee.

The Administration maritime program was spelled out by Transportation Secretary Alan S. Boyd in a May 20 appearance before the Senate Commerce Subcommittee on Merchant Marine and Fisheries. The hearing was on the Senate version of the Magnuson-Garmatz bill (S 2650), which had been introduced late in 1967 with the supposed "general agreement" of the Administration. *(See above.)*

In a 13-page prepared statement, Boyd outlined a new Administration plan which bore little resemblance to the proposals contained in S 2650. The Administration had "thoroughly considered the possible alternatives" to the current maritime program, Boyd said, and was "convinced that the future of our merchant marine demands a shift from past policies."

Elements of the plan included:

● Reform of the existing operating-differential subsidy program, including experimentation with new subsidy formulas, emphasis on encouraging innovation and greater productivity, and re-examination of the program to ensure that federal subsidies were being used only to the extent necessary to meet legitimate national defense needs.

● Termination of subsidies for passenger ship operation (affecting 13 currently subsidized vessels).

● Maintenance of ship-construction subsidies at current levels, with the "level and character" of future subsidies to be determined jointly by the Defense and Transportation Secretaries.

● Reforms in ship-construction subsidies to encourage mass production of standardized vessels (on the model of the American aircraft industry).

● Freedom for American ship operators to purchase new vessels in the world shipbuilding market, with elimination of preferential treatment for U. S.-built ships.

● Elimination of the existing capital reserve funds maintained by subsidized shipping companies, so that future capital investments by the companies could come under the same investment tax credit and depreciation guidelines which were applied to other industries.

● Authorization of $30 million for fiscal 1970 to revitalize the mothballed national defense reserve fleet.

● Appropriation of $184 million to fund the Administration's proposed fast deployment logistic ship (FDL) program, designed for flexible military operation.

(Continued on p. 248)

Interstate Highway System Status on Dec. 1, 1968[1]

(Dollars in millions)

State	Mileage[2] Designated miles on system	Total open to traffic	Total under-way	Remaining mileage	Appor-tioned to States	Unpro-gramed balance	Programed only	Projects underway or authorized Construc-tion	Engineer-ing and right-of-way	Projects completed,[3] July 1, 1956, to Dec. 1, 1968 Federal funds	Total cost
Alabama	877.4	484.8	392.6	——	$730.0	$158.2	$16.8	$77.9	$105.9	$378.4	$428.8
Alaska	——	——	——	——	——	——	——	——	——	——	——
Arizona	1,167.3	776.3	390.0	1.0	501.4	64.3	22.1	47.5	28.4	341.4	368.9
Arkansas	518.9	334.5	184.4	——	345.0	33.3	.3	48.2	13.5	255.1	287.4
California	2,164.9	1,403.6	761.3	——	3,244.3	327.7	143.4	483.1	425.3	1,882.7	2,167.1
Colorado	945.5	617.2	200.0	128.3	427.3	62.3	1.7	75.7	27.7	264.6	299.1
Connecticut	295.6	261.3	34.3	——	551.9	85.9	1.6	43.8	69.4	354.9	407.1
Delaware	40.6	22.7	17.9	——	119.1	15.5	5.1	6.1	26.5	68.1	77.1
Florida	1,156.5	689.5	452.8	14.2	750.1	87.2	20.9	72.0	31.1	544.3	620.8
Georgia	1,108.4	621.8	486.6	——	679.4	81.1	5.4	179.0	59.8	362.1	410.3
Hawaii	51.8	12.1	28.1	11.6	230.2	82.2	23.2	52.5	28.5	43.8	49.5
Idaho	608.3	381.6	226.7	——	229.1	31.0	2.9	44.3	12.9	141.4	156.3
Illinois	1,642.3	1,006.8	596.7	38.8	1,882.6	283.5	33.1	260.2	42.4	1,276.6	1,475.7
Indiana	1,115.1	718.0	397.1	——	854.0	77.7	11.8	153.0	69.8	550.0	616.0
Iowa	709.0	510.3	198.7	——	451.4	42.5	19.3	54.5	11.5	330.3	371.8
Kansas	800.9	625.9	174.9	.1	331.9	34.9	.3	48.7	18.0	234.6	266.2
Kentucky	738.6	425.4	313.2	——	689.0	69.0	12.3	96.4	58.3	459.5	519.6
Louisiana	673.3	285.0	388.3	——	894.6	120.9	6.0	185.2	160.5	425.1	476.0
Maine	312.1	275.7	34.6	1.8	191.9	28.4	7.3	4.0	9.3	145.8	165.0
Maryland	354.1	276.4	58.5	19.2	632.3	158.1	55.9	75.2	64.6	282.6	329.5
Massachusetts	451.2	359.2	84.4	7.6	819.0	80.9	33.1	149.1	89.2	472.4	537.1
Michigan	1.081.2	875.6	205.6	——	1,286.9	149.4	32.9	147.1	171.8	797.5	930.6
Minnesota	904.0	404.5	499.5	——	815.0	85.2	2.3	161.6	61.0	511.9	570.9
Mississippi	678.3	453.7	224.6	——	423.4	40.9	23.1	49.3	29.3	286.6	321.5
Missouri	1,119.9	790.3	329.0	.6	896.5	102.1	.4	108.4	63.0	630.8	706.4
Montana	1,186.0	564.8	596.6	24.6	415.2	78.1	22.1	64.0	41.3	215.5	237.8
Nebraska	477.6	334.4	143.2	——	242.8	20.6	.9	23.5	16.0	187.2	210.2
Nevada	534.6	373.4	161.2	——	223.3	33.2	.7	18.2	43.4	131.1	140.6
New Hampshire	214.9	159.5	44.1	11.3	182.0	24.5	10.2	26.5	4.1	119.1	136.5
New Jersey	381.4	170.6	161.6	49.2	955.8	113.5	112.4	150.8	164.6	422.2	478.7
New Mexico	998.4	655.0	305.9	37.5	399.2	48.8	5.7	38.1	10.0	298.0	325.5
New York	1,225.0	1,048.7	153.9	22.4	1,849.1	246.2	.6	383.6	235.0	1,010.5	1,184.6
North Carolina	770.3	446.0	324.3	——	385.4	56.4	(4)	48.6	40.7	247.7	282.8
North Dakota	570.8	392.2	116.0	62.6	197.6	27.4	.6	10.7	5.3	157.0	174.2
Ohio	1,530.6	1,114.7	407.1	8.8	2,113.9	248.4	6.1	383.0	38.7	1,451.8	1,651.9
Oklahoma	797.4	592.1	205.3	——	404.2	44.5	3.1	53.6	61.7	248.0	282.7
Oregon	735.0	648.9	68.0	18.1	615.2	96.3	11.3	62.4	45.4	403.0	460.3
Pennsylvania	1,578.7	1,082.6	459.1	37.0	1,663.4	201.7	5.6	502.0	169.0	803.6	916.2
Rhode Island	70.8	42.9	27.9	——	174.1	20.2	.6	38.6	7.6	109.4	126.5
South Carolina	682.1	392.3	289.8	——	314.0	31.4	12.3	56.4	8.1	210.5	236.0
South Dakota	679.2	415.1	264.1	——	264.3	32.7	4.9	41.7	5.5	183.9	204.5
Tennessee	1,045.1	619.3	411.0	14.8	866.3	94.5	15.5	76.5	86.3	601.6	673.1
Texas	3,027.8	2,032.8	986.6	8.4	1,730.4	233.7	.3	278.6	1.6	1,233.1	1,386.7
Utah	933.8	292.9	590.1	50.8	464.2	61.0	25.0	69.0	58.2	254.4	271.7
Vermont	320.4	144.7	175.7	——	260.8	32.0	13.2	15.4	12.0	190.4	215.1
Virginia	1,059.0	664.6	393.8	.6	1,085.2	121.8	17.6	154.5	99.7	698.0	784.3
Washington	726.7	472.9	205.0	48.8	764.1	117.0	31.5	80.3	61.9	478.6	549.6
West Virginia	514.4	238.4	241.5	34.5	654.2	132.7	63.4	119.3	84.9	258.1	289.5
Wisconsin	458.3	386.6	71.0	.7	387.3	43.7	1.2	14.5	33.7	302.7	341.6
Wyoming	909.8	601.4	212.0	96.4	337.6	37.9	6.0	36.5	9.7	251.2	273.2
District of Columbia	29.6	9.8	9.9	9.9	446.9	151.0	7.5	83.1	79.5	128.2	146.5
Puerto Rico	——	——	——	——	——	——	——	——	——		
Totals	40,972.9	26,508.8	13,704.5	759.6	$35,372.9	$4,651.2	$859.8	$5,451.9	$3,101.7	$21,635.0	$24,538.8
State share							$109.0	$714.3	$387.0		
Total costs							$968.8	$6,166.2	$3,488.7		

Note: Columns may not add to totals due to rounding.
1 Cost data exclude $329.9 million apportioned to States for highway planning and research.
2 Mileage as of Oct. 1, 1968.
3 Includes completed projects authorized prior to July 1, 1956.
4 Less than $0.05 million.

SOURCE: Bureau of the Budget

• Authorization of $25 million annually for five years, beginning in 1970, for increased maritime research.

• Transfer of the Federal Maritime Administration from the Commerce Department to the Transportation Department.

The proper goal of the merchant marine industry, Boyd said, was to provide "a maritime service which is not just barely kept alive by...subsidies, but one able to attract a significant share of our commercial trade."

On the question of nuclear-powered merchant ships, Boyd said there was "serious doubt as to the attractiveness and wisdom of proceeding with a broader nuclear ship program at the present time." On this point, Boyd said he had changed his position since 1967 (when he had called for a limited research program) based on studies by the Atomic Energy Commission.

Reaction. Congressional and industry reaction to Boyd's statement was swift and bitter. After hearing the Secretary's proposals, Subcommittee Chairman E. L. Bartlett (D Alaska) said that "the accord we thought we had reached has been rudely shattered." Bartlett then announced that he was calling up for Subcommittee consideration the House-passed and Administration-opposed bill (HR 159) to create an independent Maritime Administration. *(See below.)*

Commerce Committee Chairman Magnuson, after hearing a description of the Administration plan, said May 20, "I think I'd be in disagreement with 95 percent of it."

In the House, Merchant Marine Committee Chairman Garmatz May 20 said, "You wouldn't be able to print what I have to say about this double-cross." Rep. Frank M. Clark (D Pa.) May 21 urged the Committee to report out the Magnuson-Garmatz bill (HR 13940) and to "ram it down the throat" of the Administration.

Among industry spokesmen, Joseph Curran, head of the AFL-CIO Maritime Committee and president of the National Maritime Union, May 21 described the plan as "inadequate, unimaginative and unsatisfactory" and "designed to kill the United States merchant marine." Curran's remarks were significant, observers believed, because in past years he had tried to conciliate differences over maritime policy.

William T. Moore, chairman of the Committee of American Steamship Lines and board chairman of Moore-McCormack Lines, May 21 called Boyd's program "unrealistic" and "shortsighted."

Garmatz Bill Reported. The House Merchant Marine and Fisheries Committee July 2 reported a diluted version of HR 13940.

In reporting HR 13940, the Committee completely rewrote the Garmatz bill, deleting from it major innovative provisions designed to provide a new national maritime policy. Dropped from the bill by the Committee were provisions for a five-year, federal shipbuilding, construction-differential subsidy of $300 million annually; for an extension of the construction subsidy program to new classes of companies; for increases and extensions of operating-differential subsidies; for the subsidized purchase of nuclear-powered merchant ships; for a five-year, $125-million authorization for maritime research and development; and for a $30-million authorization for reconstruction of the reserve merchant fleet.

Acknowledging the major cuts it made in the Garmatz bill, the Committee said they had been made "in view of the current fiscal strains" in the Budget, and because it was "late in the session and not a time for advancing radical new concepts." Nevertheless, the Committee said its bill would "allow some significant movement" toward improvement of the U. S. maritime industry.

The House Rules Committee July 9 deferred action on HR 13940, thus killing the bill.

Other Maritime Bills

NEW MARITIME AGENCY. Congress Oct. 11—three days before adjournment—cleared a bill (HR 159) to create an independent Federal Maritime Administration within the Executive Branch, but President Johnson pocket vetoed the measure.

Final action on HR 159 came when the Senate passed it in the same form as it had been passed by the House in 1967. *(See above.)* The action was viewed as an expression of Congressional dissatisfaction with existing maritime policy and with Administration reform proposals.

The principal purpose of the bill was to create a strong, new federal agency with sufficient authority to bring about improvements in the implementation of merchant marine policies. Under HR 159, the proposed independent agency would operate along the lines of the existing Maritime Administration. A Maritime Board, responsible for maritime subsidy programs, would be set up within the new agency.

SHIPBUILDING SUBSIDIES. Congress in 1968 enacted legislation (HR 17524—PL 90-572) extending for one year, through June 30, 1969, the cost-differential subsidy ceilings of 55 percent for new ship construction and 60 percent for reconditioning of passenger vessels.

The extension of the existing program—regarded as a stopgap measure—resulted from the continued inability of the Executive Branch and Congress to agree on a new federal maritime policy. Previous stopgap extensions had been approved in 1965 and 1966. *(See above.)*

As passed by the House July 1, the bill provided a two-year extension. The Senate, in passing the bill Sept. 20, amended it to provide only a one-year extension. The House accepted the Senate version.

MARITIME AUTHORIZATION. Congress in 1968 enacted legislation (HR 15189—PL 90-471) authorizing fiscal 1969 appropriations of $429,451,000 for Commerce Department maritime functions, including ship construction and operation subsidies. HR 15189 was the first annual maritime authorization bill, as required by a 1967 law. *(See above.)*

Maritime Subsidies

The following table shows the amounts appropriated by Congress for maritime construction subsidies and operating subsidies for fiscal years 1966-69:

	Construction Subsidies	Operating Subsidies
Fiscal 1966	$132,150,000	$180,000,000
Fiscal 1967	106,685,000	175,000,000
Fiscal 1968	143,000,000	200,000,000
Fiscal 1969	119,800,000	206,000,000

Major interest in the bill centered on efforts to raise the authorizations for ship construction subsidies and for research and development above Administration requests. As passed by the House April 10, the bill carried $237,470,000 for ship construction and $11,000,000 for research and development. The Senate passed the bill June 11, 78-2, after adopting, by a 48-32 roll call, an amendment to cut the ship construction subsidy authorization to the Budget figure of $119.8 million and the research and development authorization to the Budget figure of $6.7 million. The final version provided $200 million for construction subsidies and $10,960,000 for research and development.

The State-Justice-Commerce appropriations bill appropriated $355,852,000 for the Maritime Administration in fiscal 1969. Of this amount $206 million was earmarked for operating subsidies, $119.8 million for ship construction subsidies and $6.7 million for research and development. These were the amounts requested in the Budget. (See box, p. 248.)

FOREIGN-BUILT SHIPS. The House July 15, on a 370-30 roll-call vote, passed a bill (HR 163) to prevent U. S. military cargoes from being carried in ships with major components of their hull or superstructure built or rebuilt outside the United States, or in ships registered in foreign countries until they had been under U. S. registry for at least three years.

The Navy and Commerce Departments opposed the bill.

PASSENGER SHIP SUBSIDIES. Congress in 1968 completed action on a bill (HR 12639—PL 90-358) extending from four to eight months per year the period U.S. passenger ships could receive operating subsidies for cruises outside their regular trade routes. As enacted, the bill also prohibited a passenger ship receiving such subsidies from cruising more than seven months on a route assigned to another U. S.-flag steamship company. The Secretary of Commerce had to approve specific cruises.

As passed by the House in 1967, the bill carried a three-year time limit to assure Congressional review. (See above.) The Senate version, passed April 10, 1968, carried no time limit. Conferees accepted the Senate view.

Under the operating subsidy program, the Government paid the difference between the cost of operating a U. S.-flag ship in certain prescribed trade routes and the estimated cost of operating a foreign flag vessel of the same type along the same routes. (Congress and the Nation, Vol. I, p. 546, 551)

High-Speed Trains

Congress in 1968 enacted legislation (HR 16024—PL 90-423) extending for two years, to June 30, 1971, the High-Speed Ground Transportation Act of 1965. HR 16024 also authorized appropriations of $37.4 million over the two-year period.

As enacted by Congress in 1965, the High-Speed Ground Transportation Act authorized a three-year, $90-million research, development and demonstration program. (See above.) However, Congress actually appropriated only $52 million for fiscal 1966-68.

President Johnson's fiscal 1969 Budget requested a two-year extension and a fiscal 1969 appropriation of $16.2 million. Congress appropriated $13 million.

Penn-Central Merger Upheld

The Supreme Court Jan. 15, 1968 unanimously approved the long-pending merger of the Pennsylvania Railroad Co. and the New York Central Railroad Co. into one massive road, the largest in the history of the nation.

The Court's action came in a 8-0 decision in *The Penn-Central and N&W Inclusion Cases.* Justice William O. Douglas dissented in part. Justice Thurgood Marshall did not participate.

In approving the Penn-Central merger, the Court also approved the inclusion in that system of the rapidly declining New York, New Haven and Hartford Railway Co. The Court also upheld an Interstate Commerce Commission (ICC) order requiring the Norfolk and Western System to acquire, subject to their agreement, three small Eastern railroads— the Boston and Maine, Delaware and Hudson and Erie-Lackawanna railroads, all of which would have suffered financial losses as a result of the Penn-Central merger.

The Pennsylvania and New York Central railroads had applied to the ICC March 9, 1962 for approval of a merger.

During House hearings on the legislation, Transportation Secretary Alan S. Boyd reported on the two demonstration projects undertaken under the 1965 Act, the Washington-New York "Metroliner" service and the New York-Boston "TurboTrain" service. Boyd said both projects had been delayed beyond the original starting times because of the technical difficulties involved in designing and powering the trains.

The Washington-New York Metroliner made its first public run Jan. 16, 1969.

Provisions. As enacted, HR 16024:

Extended for two years the High-Speed Ground Transportation Act of 1965 (from June 30, 1969 to June 30, 1971) and authorized appropriations of $16.2 million for fiscal year 1969 and $21.2 million for fiscal 1970.

Authorized the Secretary of Transportation to acquire sites and provide support facilities necessary for carrying out research, development and demonstration activities, including authority to contract for construction of two suburban railroad stations, one at Lanham, Md., and one at Woodbridge, N. J., without acquiring any property interests in the stations.

Made certain technical changes to reflect the transfer of functions from the Commerce Department as a result of the creation of the Transportation Department and the Department of Housing and Urban Development.

Airport Development

Despite growing alarm over congestion and safety problems, Congress failed to enact far-reaching legislation revising the program of federal aid to airports. In a further blow to aviation, it appropriated only $30 million of the $65 million requested by the Administration for airport grants under the Federal Airport Act of 1946 (PL 79-377) in fiscal 1970. (See box, p. 250.)

Funds for Airport Grants

The following table shows the amounts appropriated by Congress for grants-in-aid to airports for fiscal years 1966-70. The airport grants customarily were funded one year in advance to give the Federal Aviation Administration and the states enough lead time to plan airport improvements.

Fiscal 1966	$75 million
Fiscal 1967	71 million
Fiscal 1968	66 million
Fiscal 1969	70 million
Fiscal 1970	30 million

Congress did not act on an Administration proposal to supplant the existing matching-grant program with a $1-billion federal loan program. The Administration also proposed that aviation users, rather than the general public, pay for a greater share of airport costs through major increases in user taxes on passenger tickets and aviation gasoline. New user taxes were proposed for air freight shipments and jet fuel.

The Senate Commerce Committee July 1 reported a bill (S 3641) which differed in major respects from the Administration proposal. The measure, which had the support of the Air Transport Assn. but was opposed by private aircraft groups, was not taken up on the floor.

As reported, S 3641 extended the Federal Airport Act for five years, through June 30, 1975, and increased the annual authorizations for matching grants from $75 million to $150 million. The bill also set up a new program of federal loan guarantees for airport development.

In other provisions, the Committee accepted the airlines' suggestion for creating a special trust fund, comparable to the existing Highway Trust Fund, to "provide a predictable and increasing amount of funds" for airport development.

The Committee proposed increased and new user taxes to help finance the proposed trust fund, but these were not included in the bill, since tax legislation must originate in the House Ways and Means Committee.

Action on S 3641 followed an intensive two-year review of airport financing problems by the Senate Commerce Committee's Aviation Subcommittee, chaired by A. S. Mike Monroney (D Okla.). In its Jan. 23, 1968 report, the Subcommittee said that by the end of 1975 an additional $6 billion would have to be invested in the national airport system, including runways, terminal areas and access routes. It said passenger travel would triple within the next 10 years and air cargo would increase by six to eight times its current volume. In addition, the report said, 1,000 aircraft would be added, including "jumbo jets" and the SST, "whose speed alone will triple aircraft utilization." The terminal areas would be "the bottlenecks of commercial aviation when the jumbo jets are introduced," the report said.

Other Air Legislation

AIR TRAFFIC CONTROLLERS. Traffic jams at most major airports focused attention during 1968 on the heavy work load of air traffic controllers. A mid-summer work slowdown by the controllers further dramatized the problem.

Acting to remedy the situation, Congress provided 2,399 new positions for the air traffic control system and exempted these positions from the personnel reduction provisions of the 1968 tax surcharge law. The action was taken in the Transportation Department appropriation bill for fiscal 1969 (HR 18188—PL 90-464). The bill also carried $120 million for radar, navigational aids and automation equipment for en route air traffic control. All of the items were intended to increase air safety by relieving air traffic congestion.

Congress also enacted a measure (HR 19136—PL 90-556) changing overtime pay computation standards for federal air traffic safety workers in higher civil service grades. Most of the workers were air traffic controllers.

SUPERSONIC TRANSPORT. Congress denied a $223-million Budget request for development of the supersonic transport, and rescinded $30 million in funds already appropriated for the aircraft. The action was taken in the Department of Transportation appropriation bill for fiscal 1969 (HR 18188). The Department did not oppose the recision because of design problems encountered by the SST contractor and because sufficient funds from previous appropriations were available to continue the program during fiscal 1969. The Administration had announced Feb. 21 that SST construction was to be delayed because of technical problems. *(See 1967, above.)*

AIRCRAFT NOISE. Congress in 1968 enacted a bill (HR 3400—PL 90-411), supported by the Administration, to provide for aircraft noise abatement. The bill, which applied only to non-military aircraft, gave the Federal Aviation Administration (FAA) power to set aircraft noise and sonic boom standards as part of its authority to certify the aircraft for use. Certificate holders were given the same rights of appeal in noise-related actions as they currently held with respect to safety. HR 3400 was passed by the House June 10 and the Senate July 11. The Senate rejected, 12-55, an amendment to ban all non-military, domestic, supersonic flights pending a study of the sonic boom and its effects.

SUPPLEMENTAL AIRLINES. Congress enacted a bill (S 3566—PL 90-514) permitting supplemental (nonscheduled) airlines to transport inclusive group tours. The supplemental carriers had been transporting such tours since 1966, but the Supreme Court in 1968 struck down the inclusive tour authority granted by the Civil Aeronautics Board to supplementals for international travel. Inclusive or "all-expense" tours were those in which the price of a ticket included not only transportation but also accommodations.

The supplementals supported the legislation; the scheduled lines opposed it.

The legislation prohibited the supplementals from selling tickets for inclusive group tours on an individual basis. Tour tickets must be sold by a travel agency, and agencies were prohibited from having close connection with supplementals. The travel agencies were permitted to sell tour tickets on an individual basis.

CAB rules defined an inclusive group tour as one which has at least 40 members, makes at least 3 intermediate stops at least 50 miles apart, lasts a minimum of seven days, includes group transportation and hotel accommodations, and charges at least 110 percent of the fare a regularly scheduled carrier would charge between the same stops.

The rules prevent supplementals from taking away day-to-day travel business from regularly scheduled airlines.

Provisions. As enacted into law, S 3566:

Specified that supplemental airlines could charter their aircraft for inclusive tours.

Prohibited supplemental air carriers from selling individual tickets for inclusive tours to the public, and also prohibited the supplementals from selling tickets indirectly by controlling or being controlled by a travel agency.

Provided that, despite adverse court rulings, CAB certificates and authorizations for supplemental airlines to transport inclusive tours were valid.

Other Legislation

URBAN MASS TRANSIT. President Johnson in 1968 proposed a reorganization plan (Plan No. 2) to shift urban mass transit programs from the Department of Housing and Urban Development to the Department of Transportation. Congress made no effort to block the plan, and it took effect May 7.

Title VII of the Housing and Urban Development Act of 1968 (S 3497—PL 90-448) authorized $190 million for urban mass transportation grants in fiscal 1970. S 3497 also permitted private transit companies to furnish up to 50 percent of the local share of the project cost of a mass transit project, and up to 100 percent in some cases. Finally, it extended for 20 months, through July 1, 1970, the emergency grant program for mass transportation under which requirements that full areawide planning be completed were waived. *(For 1967 extension, see above.)*

In the fiscal 1969 Transportation Department appropriation bill (HR 18188—PL 90-464), Congress appropriated $175 million for urban mass transportation grants in fiscal 1970. The Administration had requested $230 million.

Meanwhile, President Johnson June 12 sent to Congress a 100-page summary report recommending a $980-million research program to develop new sytems of urban mass transportation. The report, "Tomorrow's Transportation: New Systems for the Urban Future," said the program should be phased over a five- to 15-year period. Without endorsing the report's specific recommendations, the President said the document "provides a good foundation" for future decisions on urban transportation.

PASSENGER TRAINS. In the light of Interstate Commerce Commission (ICC) statistics that showed a decline in the number of intercity railroad passenger trains from 1,448 in August 1958 to 590 in May 1968, the ICC May 31 asked Congress to hold hearings that could help stem the erosion of railroad passenger service. Senate and House subcommittees held hearings on bills (S 3861, HR 18212) to strengthen ICC procedures governing discontinuance of passenger trains and to authorize a railroad passenger service study by the Transportation Secretary. No further action was taken. The Assn. of American Railroads opposed strengthening the ICC's power to halt passenger train service.

The Senate passed a similar bill in 1967. *(See above.)*

Urban Mass Transit Funds

The following table shows the amounts appropriated by Congress for urban mass transit grants for fiscal years 1966-70. Grants usually were funded one year in advance to provide lead time for planning.

Fiscal 1966	$130 million
Fiscal 1967	130 million
Fiscal 1968	125 million
Fiscal 1969	175 million
Fiscal 1970	175 million

ICC COURT REVIEW. The Senate Sept. 5 passed by voice vote a bill (S 2687) to make appeals of Interstate Commerce Commission (ICC) orders subject to court review procedures similar to those affecting orders of other federal regulatory agencies. The bill had been requested by the ICC. The House did not act.

In its major provisions, S 2687 shifted jurisdiction over appeals of ICC orders from federal district courts to federal courts of appeals and abolished the automatic right of appeal to the Supreme Court of lower court holdings in ICC cases. Instead the Supreme Court was given discretion as to whether it would review such appeals.

TRUCK SIZES, WEIGHTS. Legislation (S 2658) allowing bigger and heavier trucks on the nation's Interstate Highway System was blocked in 1968.

The bill was passed by the Senate April 4 by voice vote after brief debate. It then moved easily through the House Public Works Committee and was cleared for House floor action by the Rules Committee. But before it was called to the floor, it foundered on adverse publicity which came mainly from articles in the Scripps-Howard Newspapers, a 17-paper group, and from advertisements and lobbying efforts by the American Automobile Assn. (AAA).

The American Trucking Assns. (ATA), chief proponents of the bill, charged Scripps-Howard and the AAA with major distortions of the facts. The ATA also charged that Scripps-Howard had strong ties with the railroad industry, a natural opponent of the bill. Scripps-Howard denied the charge. S 2658 was introduced by Sen. Warren G. Magnuson (D Wash.) and 21 cosponsors Nov. 15, 1967.

In the Federal-Aid Highway Act of 1956 (PL 84-627) Congress had established maximum permissible weights and widths for vehicles operating on the Interstate System. States that permitted greater maximums were to be penalized by the loss of federal funds for their share of the System. However, a "grandfather" clause exempted states which on July 1, 1956, allowed greater widths and weights than specified by the 1956 Act.

In introducing S 2658, Magnuson said the bill's increases in truck size and weight limits were sought by Western states. He said the "freeze"on truck sizes in the 1956 Act caught the Western states "with a considerably lower uniform axle limitation than that which existed in many portions of the country" and which was permissible under the Act's grandfather clause.

Truckers' Campaign Contributions. The *Des Moines* (Iowa) *Register* July 25 reported that the ATA had given "at least $29,000 in campaign contributions the last two years to key members of Congressional committees concerned" with S 2658.

Banking Policy

CONGRESS dealt with a substantial volume of banking and monetary legislation during the Johnson years. Much of the legislation concerned the operations of banks and related financial institutions and was enacted in 1966. Other important bills concerned gold and silver. In addition, the United States and six other nations in 1968 concluded a far-reaching agreement on gold which was prompted by speculation in private gold markets. The agreement established a two-price system for gold.

The major issues and legislation in these areas are discussed below.

GOLD-SILVER. Increasing demand for these precious metals—for different reasons—had been causing problems for several years. This country's gold stock had been declining in years prior to the Johnson Administration as other nations exchanged dollars for the metal. The United States had pledged to sell gold to foreign nations at $35 an ounce. Dollars were accumulating in other countries in large amounts as the U. S. balance of payments ran a steady deficit (meaning that the United States was spending more abroad than foreign nations were spending in this country). Although the U. S. gold stock exceeded $15 billion at the end of 1964, most of it— $13.7 billion—was earmarked by law as backing for the nation's currency and for certain bank deposits held by the Federal Reserve System. The small difference of $1.4 billion was considered insufficient to convince foreign nations that the United States would stand by its pledge to redeem their dollars for gold at $35 an ounce; any likelihood that the price of gold might be increased—thereby decreasing the value of dollars held abroad—would tempt foreign nations to exchange their dollars for gold while the price remained the same. In addition, expansion of the American economy was making it necessary to add to the money supply, which in turn required that more of the limited gold stock be set aside for currency backing.

To help alleviate this situation, Congress acted in 1965 and 1968 to free additional amounts of gold stock from its existing earmarked uses. A bill enacted in 1965 ended the gold backing requirement for the bank deposits held by the Federal Reserve System. This made available $4.9 billion in additional gold. However, the major step was taken in 1968 when Congress—over strong Republican opposition—ended the gold backing for U. S. currency.

The 1968 action came at the time of an international gold crisis which was undermining world confidence in the dollar and thus was raising doubt about the strength of the world monetary system. There had been a rush of gold buying by private purchasers speculating that the United States might have to increase the price of gold to preserve its dwindling gold supply. Speculation that the price of gold would be increased was in effect speculation against the dollar because of the U. S. guarantee of the dollar price of gold. To meet the crisis, the United States and six other nations agreed in March that they would no longer supply gold to private buyers as they had been doing. The effect was to establish a two-price system for gold: the official price for transactions between governments at $35 an ounce and the price for all other transactions. The latter was to fluctuate freely based on supply and demand in the gold market.

Silver—like gold—was undergoing the pressures of limited supply and increasing demand. The demand, however, was from industry and science on the one hand and the nation's coinage on the other. New demands for the metal by private users, particularly the photographic and electronics industries, had developed at the same time that a larger supply of coins was required, particularly for use in vending machines. The increased demand threatened to raise the price of silver so high that the silver in coins would be more valuable than the face amount of the coins. The problem was met by two pieces of legislation enacted in 1965 and 1967. The first removed silver from dimes and quarters and reduced the amount of the metal in half-dollars. A new type of coin was issued which contained nickel and copper (and some silver in the case of the half-dollar). The 1967 legislation accelerated an already planned phase-out of silver backing for silver certificates (mostly $1 and $2 bills).

BANKING, SECURITIES BILLS. Congress considered a variety of banking and securities bills in the 1965-68 period. Some were extremely controversial while others enjoyed wide support.

Bank Mergers. One of the most controversial bills grew out of Supreme Court decisions making bank mergers subject to the antitrust laws. It had been thought that such mergers were governed by another law specifically written to guide federal officials in judging bank combinations. However, when the Justice Department challenged several proposed mergers in court and won, the banking industry sought legislation to exempt mergers from the antitrust laws or at least to make the existing bank merger

---

References

A discussion of banking legislation from 1945-64 will be found in *Congress and the Nation*, Vol. I, pp. 337-395 and 448-450.

law the controlling statute. After a long and bitter battle, Congress in 1966 reached an agreement that attempted to reconcile conflicting views on how to judge a proposed bank merger, but interpretations of the statute differed. It seemed to have little effect on the Supreme Court, which in 1967 ruled that the new law made no major change in the applicability of the antitrust laws to bank mergers.

Bank Holding Companies. Congress in 1966 enacted a bill that repealed certain exemptions from the provisions of an existing law which regulated bank holding companies. The purpose was to prevent possible conflicts of interest in companies controlling both banking and non-banking businesses. However, the bill did not repeal the exemption for one-bank holding companies, thus permitting such companies to continue to engage in both banking and nonbanking activities.

Bank Interest Rates. Another 1966 banking act gave federal bank regulatory agencies temporary power to set different limits on the interest rates which banks and other financial institutions could pay on time deposits. The law was intended to halt a "rate war" between banks and savings and loan associations that was hurting the associations and, in turn, the home mortgage market which depended heavily on the S&Ls. The same act also gave officials the power to control the interest rates that associations could pay on regular savings accounts. Although all the powers were granted for only one year, Congress extended them in 1967 and 1968.

Bank Supervision. Congress in 1966 also enacted a law giving federal officials new authority to prevent unsound financial practices by banks and savings and loan associations. The officials were empowered to issue cease-and-desist orders against unsound practices and to remove bank and S&L officials engaged in such practices. The law also raised the federal insurance on bank and S&L deposits to $15,000 from $10,000.

Mutual Funds. One of the major pieces of proposed legislation in the securities field which Congress did not enact dealt with the mutual fund industry. The bill would have given federal officials new power to control the industry and reduce costs to investors in mutual funds. Strong industry opposition to the main parts of the measure prevented its enactment. The bill was proposed by the Securities and Exchange Commission and received moderate support from the Johnson Administration.

Other Bills. Congress passed a number of other bills dealing with banks and securities. One, enacted in 1968, was prompted by a rise in bank robberies. It required federal banking officials to establish security standards to protect banking institutions against theft and robbery. Another bill, also enacted in 1968, provided increased protection to stockholders in companies that outside groups attempt to take over through cash tender offers. The measure required disclosure of information about the person making the offer, to help the stockholder come to a reasoned decision on whether or not to sell his stock. Another 1968 law revised the Federal Credit Union Act to extend the maturity on secured loans, to raise the limit on unsecured loans, and otherwise to liberalize the lending policy of federal credit unions.

Chronology Of Banking Legislation 1965

Gold Cover

The nation's continuing balance-of-payments problems led to Congressional action to free a larger portion of the U. S. gold stock to meet international claims. The action also allowed more flexibility to increase the nation's money supply as the economy expanded.

The legislation (HR 3818—PL 89-3) eliminated the requirement that each Federal Reserve Bank maintain a reserve of gold certificates valued at not less than 25 percent of the amount of commercial bank deposits it holds. By eliminating the "gold cover" on bank deposits, the act made available about $4.9 billion in Treasury-held gold which the certificates represented. The legislation was requested by President Johnson at the end of January after the stock of gold in excess of the statutory requirements had fallen to only $1.4 billion.

Passage of HR 3818 was the first of two major steps that Congress was to take during the Johnson years to free the U. S. gold stock from much of its traditional role in order to meet international demands that had arisen from years of balance-of-payments deficits. The second step came in 1968 when Congress removed the 25 percent reserve requirement on Federal Reserve notes (currency) which HR 3818 did not affect. *(See 1968 chronology.)*

The Treasury Department was custodian of all monetary reserves held in the form of gold. Reserves of the Federal Reserve Banks were in the form of certificates representing the gold. The Reserve Banks (located in 12 cities) were required to maintain a specified proportion of gold certificates (25 percent) against their liabilities for notes (currency) and against deposits by commercial banks.

Because of the persistent balance-of-payments deficit, the nation's gold supply dwindled from a high of $23.4 billion in 1949 to $15.1 billion at the end of 1964. With a required gold reserve of $13.7 billion at year's end, only $1.4 billion was free to meet potential international claims of $28.9 billion (the amount of dollars held by individuals and institutions outside the United States) and to supply reserve banking for an expanding money supply within the United States. Treasury officials, however, said it was unlikely that large amounts of foreign dollar holdings would be converted during any brief period because of the dollar's role as an instrument of international trade. In addition, existing law permitted—in the event of a monetary emergency—suspension of the domestic gold cover to make the nation's entire gold stock available to meet foreign claims. It was thought, however, that this fact was only dimly understood in European capitals.

The bill was passed with relatively little difficulty, although a majority of House Republicans opposed it.

Supporters of the measure argued that its primary purpose was to gain time for the Administration to take steps to reduce the payments deficit. Republicans contended that the Administration had not taken, and was unlikely to take, the stern financial measures necessary to eliminate the deficit.

Coinage Changes

Increased national demand for silver led to enactment of legislation (S 2080—PL 89-81) eliminating all of the metal from dimes and quarters and reducing the silver content of half-dollars from 90 to 40 percent. The Coinage Act of 1965 constituted the first fundamental change in the country's 73-year-old system of silver coinage. *(See box on following page.)*

S 2080 was enacted in the face of a worldwide silver shortage, the pressure of rising silver prices, and an insatiable demand for coins. The legislation was requested by President Johnson to meet all of these demands and to make more silver available for the increasing needs of industry.

The bill authorized the Treasury Department to mint new dimes and quarters faced with a copper-nickel alloy (75 percent copper, 25 percent nickel), used in the existing 5-cent piece, and bonded to a core of pure cooper. The new half-dollars were to have surfaces composed of 80 percent silver and 20 percent copper and cores composed of 21 percent silver and 79 percent copper. The new coins were designed to have the same electrical properties as the existing coins to make them suitable for use in vending machines. In submitting the Administration's request, President Johnson said: "Silver is becoming too scarce for continued large scale use in coins. To maintain unchanged our high silver coinage in the face of stark reality would only invite chronic and growing scarcity of coins."

Both chambers passed the bill by substantial margins although there was controversy over how much silver should be retained in the coinage. Senators from Western, silver-producing states fought to retain some silver in dimes and quarters. However, an amendment by Frank E. Moss (D Utah) to retain 40 percent silver in dimes and quarters was rejected by a 34-57 roll-call vote; a similar amendment by Howard W. Cannon (D Nev.) to retain 30 percent silver in those coins and the half-dollar was rejected by a 27-52 roll call. In the House, an amendment identical to Moss's was rejected by a 187-218 roll call. On the other hand, Senators from the East sought to eliminate silver in half-dollars, asserting that the additional amounts of metal should be made available to industry.

As finally enacted, S 2080 conformed closely in all major respects to the Administration's original requests.

The new quarters began circulating with the old coins Nov. 1. To discourage the hoarding of silver coins, the Treasury announced that it owned "nearly 900 million ounces" of silver which it could use to keep the price of silver low enough so it would not be profitable to melt silver coinage for its silver content. The Department earlier had announced that the new dimes would begin appearing before "mid-1966" and that the new half-dollars would go into production at a later date.

Provisions. As signed into law July 23, S 2080:

Authorized the minting of new dimes, quarters, and half-dollars. Specified that the dimes and quarters would be faced with a copper-nickel alloy (75 percent copper and 25 percent nickel) bonded to a core of pure copper. Specified that the half-dollar would have a silver content of 40 percent and would be faced with an alloy of 80 percent silver and 20 percent copper, bonded to a core of 21 percent silver and 79 percent copper.

Authorized the Government for a period of five years to purchase domestically mined silver at $1.25 per fine ounce.

Authorized the Secretary of the Treasury to sell excess silver from Treasury stocks at a price not less than $1.29 per fine ounce.

Authorized the Secretary of the Treasury to institute controls over the melting, treating or exportation of coins, and provided that violators would be subject to a fine of up to $10,000 and/or imprisonment for up to five years.

Provided that coins could be inscribed with the year in which they were minted or issued, or—in order to prevent hoarding—with the last preceding year inscribed on coins of the same denomination. Repealed PL 88-580, which provided for the retention of the date "1964" on all coins until an adequate supply was available. Prohibited putting mint marks on the new coins for five years.

Provided that persons convicted of counterfeiting the new coins would be subject to a fine of $5,000 and/or imprisonment of 15 years.

Authorized the President to establish a Joint Commission on the Coinage to study the implementation of the new coinage program and other coinage and silver matters and to make any necessary recommendations.

Prohibited the minting of silver dollars for a five-year period beginning with the date of enactment.

Provided standby authority for the Government to prohibit use of coins as credit or loan collateral.

Bank Mergers

Congress in 1965 was unable to resolve the question of whether the Justice Department, through antitrust action, should try to upset bank mergers approved by an appropriate federal regulatory agency. At issue was the Bank Merger Act of 1960, which was an amendment to the Federal Deposit Insurance Act.

A bill was passed by the Senate but not by the House. It was designed to clarify Congressional intent in enacting the 1960 law. (The legislation was enacted in 1966.)

Background. The 1950 amendments to Section 7 of the Clayton Act prohibited acquisition by one corporation of assets of another corporation subject to the Federal Trade Commission (FTC) jurisdiction if the merger would substantially lessen competition or tend to create a monopoly. Since banks are not subject to the FTC, it was widely believed that Section 7 did not cover most bank mergers.

The Eisenhower Administration, through the Justice Department, asked Congress in 1956 to extend Section 7 to the acquisition of assets by banks. Although the House passed the bill in 1956, the Senate took a different approach and no legislation was enacted. The same situation arose in 1959. In 1960, however, the two chambers agreed on a bill permitting the three federal bank regulatory agencies to approve bank mergers if found to be in the public interest. These agencies were the Comptroller of the Currency, the Federal Reserve Board and the Federal

First Major Change Made in Coinage System

The problem of supplying the nation's silver requirements had reached serious proportions by 1965.

An acute coin shortage had sparked a stopgap Treasury program to double the production of coins, but the consequent depletion of silver stocks threatened to inflate further the price of silver.

Many monetary experts said there were only two practical remedies to the problem: a reduction in or the elimination of the silver content of U. S. coins and the substitution of a cheaper metal alloy, such as nickel or copper. However, the experts said that even partial reduction of the amount of silver in the coins would present delicate political and psychological problems. The silver content of the dime, quarter, half-dollar and silver dollar not only gave the coins high intrinsic value but also helped support public confidence in paper money.

Silver Supply and Prices. Over the previous 15 years, the demand for silver, for both coins and industrial use, increased faster than did the supply. Until 1961, sales from the large Government stockpile of silver, however, had kept the open market price around 91 cents an ounce. With the Treasury silver supply almost exhausted in 1961, President Kennedy directed that Government sales of "free silver" (that portion of the Treasury's holdings not required to back silver certificates) be terminated and that the silver backing of $5 and $10 silver certificates be dropped. On one hand, the action released silver from a monetary reserve fund backing the $5 and $10 denominations and rechanneled it into the production of additional coins. On the other hand, however, the action took the Treasury out of the supply side of the silver market. Thus, with Government sales of free silver no longer keeping a ceiling on the market price, silver prices surged upward to $1 or more an ounce.

In a second measure to release silver for coinage production, President Kennedy in 1963 requested and received legislation (PL 88-36) designed to replace the silver backing of $1 and $2 bills with the gold backing of Federal Reserve notes. At the time, it was estimated that Government redemption of the silver certificates would be carried out over a 15-year period.

As a result of the increased demand for silver and the absence of Government sales, the market price of silver rose sharply in mid-1963. The market price as of Sept. 11, 1963, had risen to a level equal to the monetary value of silver, which is "pegged" by the Government at $1.29 an ounce. The silver content in a silver dollar amounts to .77 ounce, or the equivalent of slightly more than $1. Thus, the Treasury faced the prospect that it might become profitable for the public to melt down coins for the silver in them. However, holders of silver certificates began increasingly to exchange them at the Treasury for silver bullion, in anticipation of further price increases. This influx of bullion served to hold the price of silver at the monetary value.

So long as bullion was available from the Treasury at $1.29 an ounce, the U. S. coinage system would have required no change. But once the Treasury stock had been depleted and it became necessary to buy in the world market to meet coinage needs, the price ceiling could not have been maintained.

Coin Shortage. The Treasury early in 1965 said that the 48 billion coins estimated to be in circulation should be enough for all purposes. But commercial banks, which received coins from the public and gave them back out, were having increasing difficulty in replenishing their coin supplies. Some of the reasons:

• The rising number of sales taxes and toll highways and the increased use of parking meters and vending and coin-changing machines delayed frequency of circulation. Vending machine sales tripled in the 1954-64 decade. At the close of that decade, there were 4.5 million such machines.

• Speculators hoarded coins in anticipation of higher silver prices on the open market. During 1963 and 1964, speculation centered largely on silver dollars, but experts believed it might extend ultimately to smaller coins as well.

• Coin collectors, whose ranks increased from 2 million a decade ago to some 8 million in 1965, took billions of coins out of circulation. It became a popular practice to collect coins by the roll or bagful rather than the piece. This practice apparently was influenced by assumptions that in time the older coins would grow scarcer and could then be sold to other collectors at large profits.

Remedial Action in 1964. The Bureau of the Mint in June 1964 had initiated a program to double the rate of coin production within a year. The mints began operating 24 hours a day, seven days a week. Congress, in the fiscal 1965 Supplemental Appropriations bill (HR 12633—PL 88-635), appropriated $4.5 million to mint 3 billion additional coins. To further increase the productive capacity of the mints, preliminary processing work was delegated to other facilities, additional coin presses and stamping machines were installed and the "proof coin" operation—production of special sets of highly polished coins for collectors—was suspended and the presses converted for production of coins for general circulation. The increase in production was reflected by the fact that the mints in 1964 used 195 million ounces of silver for production of coins in comparison to 111 million ounces in 1963. The Treasury estimated that about 234 million ounces would go into new coins in 1965.

Congress in 1964 appropriated funds for a new mint at Philadelphia with greatly increased capacity. The Treasury projected that the new mint, scheduled to go into operation in 1967, would produce as many coins as the two present mints combined.

To discourage hoarding by coin collectors, Congress enacted an Administration bill (S 2950—PL 88-580) authorizing the mints to inscribe the figure "1964" on all coins minted until adequate supplies were available. Signed by the President Sept. 3, 1964, the measure was designed to "flood the market" with 1964 coins, rendering it pointless to save them.

Deposit Insurance Corp. The House Committee, which authored the compromise, said in its report, "some bank mergers are in the public interest even though they lessen competition to a degree." But it added that "approval of a merger should depend on a positive showing of some benefit to be derived from it." *(Congress and the Nation, Vol. I, p. 449)*

During debate, Sen. J. W. Fulbright (D Ark.), who had been chairman of the Banking and Currency Committee until 1959, said the House and Senate agreed that control of bank mergers should be based on both banking and competitive factors and that the antimerger provisions of the Clayton Act "should continue to be inapplicable to bank mergers."

The 1960 Act required a bank regulatory agency to obtain the views of the Attorney General and the other bank agencies before granting or withholding consent to a bank merger, but it did not give a veto power to the Justice Department. The Act did not expressly exempt bank mergers from the antitrust laws, and its legislative history left unclear whether such exemption was intended.

The Justice Department, however, beginning in 1961 brought suit against seven proposed mergers, contending they violated Section 7 of the Clayton Act or Section 1 of the Sherman Act, or both. The banks involved were the Philadelphia National Bank and the Girard Trust Corn Exchange Bank in Philadelphia; the Manufacturer's Trust Co. and Hanover Bank in New York; the First National Bank & Trust Co. and Security Trust Co. in Lexington, Ky.; the Continental-Illinois National Bank & Trust Co. and City National Bank & Trust Co. in Chicago; the Mercantile Trust Co. and Security Trust Co. in St. Louis; the Crocker-Anglo National Bank of San Francisco and Citizens National Bank of Los Angeles; and the Third National Bank and Nashville Bank & Trust Co. in Nashville, Tenn.

The first proposed merger to be contested by Justice was the one in Philadelphia. The test case was filed Feb. 25, 1961. The Supreme Court, in a June 17, 1963, decision, found the merger would be in violation of Section 7 of the Clayton Act, thus extending the coverage of Section 7 to banks. In 1964 the Court also brought bank mergers under Section 7 of the Sherman Antitrust Act. The decisions, upholding the Justice Department and over-ruling federal bank regulatory agencies, brought consternation to many banking officials.

Of the six other mergers contested by the Justice Department, three were consummated before the Supreme Court decision in the test case June 17, 1963, and three consummated after that date. The Philadelphia merger, blocked by the courts, was never consummated.

Mergers consummated prior to the 1963 decision were those in New York, Lexington and Chicago. Those consummated after the decision were the ones in St. Louis, Nashville and San Francisco and Los Angeles.

Legislative Action

Senate. In an effort to obtain relief for the banks under Justice Department prosecution for violation of the antitrust laws, Sen. A. Willis Robertson (D Va.), chairman of the Senate Banking and Currency Committee, in 1965 introduced a bill (S 1698) which would have prohibited Justice Department antitrust action against any bank merger approved by a federal bank regulatory agency. Robertson said the bill was designed to clarify Congres-

Federal Bank Regulatory Agencies

There are three principal federal bank regulatory agencies:

Comptroller of the Currency—Created by the National Bank Act of 1863, the Comptroller is vested with general supervisory powers over the 4,800 national banks. He issues charters, oversees bank organization and liquidation and conducts examinations. The Comptroller also passes on bank mergers where the resulting institution is a national bank. He is an official of the Treasury Department.

Federal Reserve Board—Created by the Federal Reserve Act of 1913, the "Fed" is vested with examining, auditing and other supervisory authority over the 4,800 national banks and 1,500 state-chartered banks that are members of the Federal Reserve System (FRS). Its chief function is the determination of general monetary and credit policies. The Fed also passes on bank mergers where the resulting institution is a state member bank of the FRS. It is an independent federal agency.

Federal Deposit Insurance Corporation—Created by the Federal Deposit Act of 1933, the FDIC's chief function is to insure deposits in the 4,800 national banks, the 1,500 state-chartered banks that are members of the FRS and also the 7,600 state-chartered banks that are not members of the FRS but that qualify to be insured. The FDIC also acts as receiver for all national banks and certain state banks when placed in receivership. In addition, the FDIC is required to examine all insured banks that are not members of the FRS, and has the discretionary authority to examine any insured bank. It is an independent agency.

sional intent, in the 1960 Bank Merger Act, to exempt approved bank mergers from antitrust laws. Following objections to this blanket exemption by the Independent Bankers Assn. of America, representing mostly small banks, and indications that such legislation would meet strong opposition in the House, the Committee adopted substitute provisions, offered by Sen. William Proxmire (D Wis.), allowing the Justice Department 30 days in which to object to a merger approved by the appropriate federal bank agency. The substitute also exempted from further prosecution the six remaining mergers being challenged by the Justice Department. The Senate passed the bill by voice vote.

House. Although the Senate Committee modified S 1698 reportedly in an attempt to win the support of House Banking Committee Chairman Wright Patman (D Texas), the latter said that, while he was not prejudging the Senate bill, legislation "in any way weakening antitrust law and administration should be viewed...with utmost scrutiny and caution."

The Domestic Finance Subcommittee of the House Banking and Currency Committee, both chaired by Patman, held hearings on S 1698 and other bills in August and September. Attorney General Nicholas deB. Katzenbach called the portion of the bill that exempted approved bank mergers from antitrust actions "outrageous," because, he said, "banking cannot and should not be distin-

Lobbying by Bankers

The American Bankers Assn., representing 98.5 percent of the 14,000 main offices of U. S. banks and most of their branches, conducted a "mass" campaign for S 1698. Three of the merged banks affected by the bill also engaged lobbyists in 1965 to work for passage of the bill. One of the banks' registered lobbyists was ex-Rep. Albert Rains (D Ala. 1945-65), who had been the second-ranking Democrat on the House Banking and Currency Committee until 1965.

American Bankers Assn. president Reno Odlin, in answer to a query by Rep. Patman, wrote Aug. 31, 1965, that the ABA had made a "mass effort" for House passage of S 1698. Odlin said it was the first piece of legislation since the 1962 Revenue Act on which ABA used a "mass communication technique," asking all its member banks "to get in touch" with their Members of the House of Representatives on S 1698. Odlin wrote, "Passage of S 1698 was deemed to be so important to the future of banking that the broadest possible indication of banking's views was sought."

ABA was not registered under the 1946 Federal Regulation of Lobbying Act, but it employed in 1965 six individuals who did register with Congress.

Law firms representing two of the merged banks exempted from antitrust prosecution under S 1698 hired lobbyists to work for the bill. Manufacturers Hanover of New York employed the New York law firm of Simpson, Thatcher & Bartlett, and Continental-Illinois of Chicago employed the Chicago firm of Mayer, Friedlich, Spiess, Tierney, Brown & Platt. The two law firms jointly hired two lobbyists to work for them on the bill—ex-Rep. Rains and Laurance G. Henderson, a Senate committee aide in 1952-54.

The Mercantile Trust Co. of St. Louis, which the House bill would permit to be tried under the new bank merger standards set forth in the bill, hired the Washington, D. C. law firm of Miller & Chevalier to work for the legislation.

All of the law firms above, as well as Rains and Henderson, registered as lobbyists in 1965.

guished from other industries for which no special procedure is proposed." Katzenbach's statement had been cleared with the Budget Bureau, and Patman told James J. Saxon, Comptroller of the Currency, that he considered it to represent the Administration's position. Saxon, who supported the Senate bill, said he "was not aware that Mr. Katzenbach represents the position of the Administration on the bill, if the Administration has a position on the bill." K. A. Randall, chairman of the Federal Deposit Insurance Corp., noted that his testimony (giving qualified support to S 1698) had also been cleared by the Budget Bureau but that he did not "believe there has been an endorsement of my views, just a clearance."

The Subcommittee Oct. 1 approved, by a 7 to 5 vote, a revised version of S 1698 giving the Justice Department 60 days—instead of the 30 days proposed by the Senate—in which to review proposed mergers and exempting the three bank mergers consummated prior to the Supreme Court ruling of June 17, 1963. The effect of this provision was to withhold antitrust immunity from three of the six bank mergers under prosecution by the Justice Department. Under the Senate version, all six mergers would have received retroactive immunity from antitrust prosecution. Patman voted to approve the Subcommittee bill—apparently, observers believed, because it had no chance of passage on the floor.

Meantime, Thomas L. Ashley (D Ohio) Sept. 13 introduced legislation (HR 11011) to require the courts to follow guidelines of the 1960 Bank Merger Act rather than the antitrust statutes in their consideration of bank merger challenges. The guidelines were that the banking agencies must consider the financial history of the banks involved; the adequacy of capital structure, future earnings prospects and character of management of merging and resulting institutions; and the merger's effect on competition and the public interest. Ashley's bill permitted the Justice Department 30 days to contest a proposed merger approved by a bank regulatory agency, but required the Department to follow the 1960 Act's guidelines, instead of basing its case only on the Clayton and Sherman Acts. The measure also exempted from pending antitrust action the three banks merged before the Supreme Court ruling. Including Ashley, 19 Committee members (11 R, 8 D) supported this bill—a majority of the 33-member Committee.

The supporters of the Ashley bill then sought to substitute its provisions for the Subcommittee version of S 1698, but Patman and those who supported him used a variety of delaying tactics to frustrate them. Patman adjourned an Oct. 18 meeting after seven minutes for lack of a quorum when only 13 members (four less than necessary) attended.

The Ashley faction, invoking a rarely used Committee rule requiring regular meetings of the Committee on the first and third Tuesdays of the month, met the next day, Oct. 19, and reported S 1698, amended by substitution of the text of the Ashley bill. Patman denounced the meeting as illegal. The bill was not acted on before the 1965 session adjourned.

Senate-House Bills Compared. As approved by the Senate, S 1698:

Restricted the Justice Department to 30 days in which to contest a proposed merger approved by one of the federal banking agencies.

Exempted from further prosecution under antitrust laws six bank mergers under prosecution by the Justice Department.

As approved by the House Banking and Currency Committee, S 1698:

Required courts to follow guidelines of the 1960 Bank Merger Act rather than the antitrust statutes in their consideration of bank merger challenges. The guidelines were that the banking agencies must consider the financial history of the banks involved; the adequacy of the capital structure, future earnings prospects and character of management of merging banks and the institution to be formed; and the merger's effect on competition and the public interest.

Exempted from pending antitrust action three banks that had merged before the Supreme Court's ruling.

Bank Holding Companies

A movement was begun in 1965 to tighten the provisions of the Bank Holding Company Act of 1956. The legislation was not enacted in 1965 but became law the following year after it was made less strict. *(See 1966 chronology.)* The bill (HR 7371) would have eliminated all major exemptions granted by the 1956 law. It was passed by the House Sept. 23, but the Senate did not act before adjournment.

The bill was designed to prevent conflicts of interest in lending by groups holding both banking and nonbanking businesses. The 1956 law had had the same basic purpose. Congress in that law (PL 84-511) sought to limit holding companies to the ownership and management of banks, to limit their size and to prevent them from controlling nonbanking assets. Proponents of PL 84-511 feared that control of the nation's banking system, with its accompanying influence on the economy, was becoming too highly concentrated. Government bank regulatory officials said that the virtually unrestricted freedom of holding companies in 1956 to increase the number of banking units they controlled made possible the concentration of all commercial banking facilities in an area under single management. Secondly, they said that holding company control of nonbanking enterprises violated the principle that banks should not engage in activities other than banking; such control involved the comparative treatment accorded requests for financing made by a business controlled by a bank's holding company and requests made by businesses operating independently of the bank or holding company. *(See Congress and the Nation, Vol. I, p. 448.)*

Although Congress enacted the 1956 law, it weakened it by allowing many exemptions from the law's provisions.

The House-passed version of the 1965 bill (HR 7371) was much broader than the bill as reported by the House Banking and Currency Committee. The principal effect of the Committee bill would have been to terminate an exemption benefiting only the Florida estate of Alfred I. duPont, which controlled 31 banks with deposits of over $600 million as well as a number of nonbanking businesses, including the Florida East Coast Railway, the St. Joe Paper Mill Co. and real estate interests. The scope of the bill was greatly expanded by House acceptance of a floor amendment by Charles E. Bennett (D Fla.). The amendment, accepted by a 199-178 roll-call vote (R 116-3; ND 30-142; SD 53-33), was strongly backed by the Federal Reserve Board. It provided for withdrawal not only of existing exemptions for long-term trusts like the duPont estate, and exemptions for religious, educational and charitable institutions, but also of an existing one-bank exemption, exemptions for tax-exempt labor, agricultural and horticultural organizations, and exemptions for registered investment companies.

Securities Fees

HR 7169—PL 89-289, an Administration-backed bill, amended the Securities Act of 1933 by doubling the registration fees for offerings of securities and by raising the minimum fee from $25 to $100. Registration fees were increased from 10 cents per $1,000 of securities offered, to 20 cents for each $1,000 of securities. The changes were effective Jan. 1, 1966.

The new law was expected to produce an additional $1,790,000 in fees collected by the Securities and Exchange Commission annually, for a $5,090,000 total annual collection by the Commission. This would equal one-third of the SEC's annual appropriations from Congress. The fees are transmitted to the general fund of the Treasury.

Under the Securities Act of 1933, which set the fees later increased by HR 7169, corporations issuing public offerings of securities are required to file registration statements with the SEC giving financial and other data about the securities offerings.

1966

Bank Interest Rates

An extremely tight policy of credit restraint maintained by the Federal Reserve Board required Congress in 1966 to enact an Administration-backed bill (HR 14026—PL 89-597) giving flexible authority to federal bank regulatory agencies to set different limits on the interest rates banks and other financial institutions might pay on different types and amounts of fixed maturity (time) deposits.

The purpose of the bill was to protect savings and loan associations (S&Ls), traditional source of financing for home building, from the competition of high-interest certificates of deposit (CDs) issued by commercial banks. *(See box p. 260 for explanation of CDs.)*

Despite the Federal Reserve's effort to increase interest rates, a high demand for loan funds prevailed throughout 1966. Consequently, banks and savings and loan institutions began competing vigorously for the savings dollar—a major source of lendable funds.

The banks, in order to acquire funds to meet a high demand for industrial and consumer loans, had begun to offer the certificates in amounts far smaller than in the past and at interest rates higher than S&Ls could afford to pay. The result was that persons with relatively small amounts of money to invest (such as, for instance, a family attempting to put aside some money for future use or for an emergency) were taking their funds out of S&Ls (or not going there in the first place) and instead buying small denomination CDs from banks. This in turn limited funds available to S&Ls and dried up the major source of home financing; a sharp downturn in housing industry activity was one of the most prominent imbalances in the economy during 1966. The shortage of funds for S&Ls, banks, the housing industry and most other groups and organizations was the result of extremely tight monetary conditions put into effect to reduce inflationary pressures throughout the economy.

The "rate war" for savings arose because existing law required federal authorities to set a single general limit on time deposits, with variations permitted only with respect to differing maturities and other related factors. Thus, when banks began offering the CDs in low denominations, authorities could make them less attractive only by lowering the rates on time deposits across the board.

Certificates of Deposit

A certificate of deposit (CD) is issued by a commercial bank as a receipt for funds deposited with the bank for a specific length of time and bearing a specific rate of interest. If it is negotiable, it can be bought and sold like an IOU. Usually it can be cashed at a date earlier than maturity but at a lower interest rate.

Prior to 1961, CDs were issued generally for large amounts ($100,000 or more) and were used by big corporations to put excess cash to work on a short-term basis. In 1961, large New York City banks began issuing CDs for smaller amounts. Savings and loan associations now issue similar "savings certificates" bearing interest at higher rates than passbook savings accounts.

Because this would have included large-denomination CDs, an obligation bought in substantial quantities by major corporations, it would have cut into a major source of funds available to banks for lending.

Although the authority provided by the bill applied only to the rates on deposits left with financial institutions, and not loans by the institutions, some backers of the measure contended it would result in reduction of loan rates as well. If banks were required to reduce rates on deposits, they reasoned, their lower costs in obtaining money would be reflected in lower rates on loans. This contention was disputed by financial experts, however, who feared the lower rates on time deposits might drive funds into higher-yield securities or bonds. This, they said, would keep loan rates high and force banks to curtail lending.

The discretionary rate controls authorized by HR 14026 were to expire one year after the bill's enactment. (However, they were extended throughout the Johnson years.) Agencies given the new powers were the Federal Reserve Board (Fed), the Federal Deposit Insurance Corp. (FDIC) and the Federal Home Loan Bank Board (FHLBB). Together, the three agencies regulated all banks and savings and loan institutions insured by the Federal Government.

Another major provision of the bill gave the FHLBB authority for the first time directly to establish interest and dividend rates which savings and loan institutions could pay their depositors. This authority applied to general savings accounts, as opposed to the CDs—that is, time deposit savings—discussed above. The FHLBB had long sought to obtain this authority over S&L interest rates on general savings accounts. (Federal bank regulatory officials already had this authority over insured commercial banks.) However, this new power of the FHLBB, like the other provisions of HR 14026, was to expire after one year unless extended. (Like the bill's other provisions, this one also was extended during the Johnson years.)

Other provisions of HR 14026 increased the reserves which the Fed could require member banks to hold against time deposits, and enlarged the types of Government securities the Fed could buy and sell. The reserves provision (not subsequently implemented) was designed to make CD purchases even less attractive, while the author-

ity to deal in a broadened portfolio of securities was designed to enlarge the Fed's role in economic management by moving funds in and out of sensitive areas of the economy.

Congressional debate on HR 14026 centered on whether to legislate a rate ceiling on low-denomination CDs or make the rates discretionary with federal banking officials. The version of the bill reported by the House Banking and Currency Committee set a 4.5 percent ceiling on CDs of less than $100,000, while requiring the rate to remain at 5.5 percent for CDs of higher denominations. This approach was defeated on the House floor, however, after the Administration contended it would infringe on the powers of the independent Federal Reserve Board. After brief consideration, the Senate adopted without change the discretionary controls approved by the House.

Provisions. As signed into law Sept. 21, HR 14026 (PL 89-597) contained the following major provisions:

Authorized the Federal Reserve Board (Fed) at its discretion to establish different interest rate ceilings for different types and amounts of time and savings deposits held by banks in the Federal Reserve System. (The provision covered savings accounts, as well as time deposits, although savings were not part of the controversy.)

Extended to the Federal Deposit Insurance Corp. (FDIC) the same discretionary rate-making authority for the commercial banks and mutual savings banks under its jurisdiction as was authorized for the Federal Reserve Board. (The FDIC supervised all insured state banks and mutual savings institutions not in the Federal Reserve System.)

Authorized the Federal Home Loan Bank Board (FHLBB) to establish limits on the rate of interest or dividends paid by insured savings and loan institutions on deposits, shares or withdrawable accounts. Permitted different rates for different types and amounts of deposits.

Prohibited any of the three agencies charged with rate-making authority on time and savings deposits (Fed, FDIC, FHLBB) from setting new interest ceilings without first consulting the other two agencies.

Raised from the existing 6 percent to 10 percent the maximum reserves that the Federal Reserve could require member banks to hold against time or savings deposits. (The provision did not affect the reserve ratio for demand deposits, which remained at a maximum of 22 percent for major banks in large cities and 14 percent for other banks.)

Deleted a provision of existing law stipulating that the Fed's authority to modify reserve requirements was based on prevention of "injurious credit expansion and contraction." (Deletion of the phrase negated the suggestion that the provision prohibited a change in reserve requirements to promote a shift in the pattern of bank deposits and assets, as contrasted to expansion or contraction in the volume of credit.)

Extended the range of government securities that the Fed was empowered to buy and sell in the open market to include all obligations issued or guaranteed by any federal agency. (Existing law prohibited Fed purchase and sale of numerous major issues, including those of the Federal Home Loan Bank Board and Federal National Mortgage Assn. (FNMA).) The provision was designed to allow the Fed to pump in and take away substantial funds from various sectors of the economy, depending upon economic conditions.)

Included a nonbinding sense-of-Congress resolution directing the Secretary of the Treasury, the Federal Reserve Board, the FDIC, and the FHLBB to implement their powers under existing law to bring about a reduction in interest rates to the "maximum extent feasible in the light of the prevailing money market and general economic conditions."

Specified that all provisions would be effective on the date the bill was signed and would expire one year later.

Bank Supervision

Congress in 1966 followed up its 1965 hearings into bank failures by enacting the Administration's Financial Institutions Supervisory Act of 1966 (S 3158—PL 89-695). The Act gave federal bank regulatory agencies temporary new powers to stop or correct unsound financial practices. In addition, it raised from $10,000 to $15,000 per account the amount of federal insurance on insured bank and savings and loan accounts.

The heart of the Act was in its provisions empowering agencies to issue cease-and-desist orders against unsound practices at financial institutions and to remove bank and savings and loan association officials engaged in such practices. A major addition to the Administration bill, made by the House Banking and Currency Committee, was the increase in federal deposit insurance; the House boosted the amount per account to $20,000, but that figure was cut back to $15,000 in conference. In calling for the new supervisory powers in his Jan. 27 Economic Message, President Johnson also urged raising the deposit insurance level, but he offered no specific proposal and the bill contained none when introduced.

The bill applied to banks and savings and loan associations which either had federal charters or federal insurance of deposits and savings left with them. Existing law provided remedies for the financial problems which prompted the legislation, but they were considered either too severe or too cumbersome or time-consuming. The ultimate existing remedy—termination of federal insurance—was a long process which normally could be expected to result in collapse of the bank or association. In the meantime, losses to depositors might continue.

The legislation had the general support of the two major groups representing financial institutions, the American Bankers Assn. and the U. S. Savings and Loan League. The Independent Bankers Assn. of America and the National League of Insured Savings Assns. were opposed. The legislation was supported by the federal agencies involved.

Three provisions of the original proposal became relatively controversial. The first dealt with the power of federal agencies to remove bank officials engaged in unsound practices. Bankers feared that these powers, if used arbitrarily, might result in severe damage to the financial institution and to the reputation of the individual banker concerned. The bill as enacted limited use of this provision to matters involving the personal honesty of the banker.

The second controversy was over whether hearings held under the Act should generally be public or private, with the agency given discretion to rule otherwise in the public interest. The Senate bill provided for private hearings; the House changed that to public hearings; and the conference committee accepted the Senate provision for private hearings.

The third controversy was over the power of the Comptroller of the Currency, acting on his own as an agency, to remove officers or issue cease-and-desist orders in cases involving national banks. The Comptroller had supervisory jurisdiction over these banks. The Senate Committee amended the original bill to vest this power in the Federal Reserve Board, giving the Comptroller a vote on the Board in national bank cases. This was retained in the bill that was enacted.

Provisions. As signed into law Oct. 16, S 3158:

Agencies. Gave identical cease-and-desist and suspension-and-removal powers to the Federal Home Loan Bank Board (FHLBB) and the Federal Savings and Loan Insurance Corp. (FSLIC), in regard to federally chartered savings and loan associations and federally insured state associations; to the Board of Governors of the Federal Reserve System, in regard to national banks and to insured state banks which were members of the System; and to the Federal Deposit Insurance Corp. (FDIC), in regard to insured state banks which were not members of the Federal Reserve System. Specified that in situations involving national banks, the Comptroller of the Currency of the Treasury Department (who normally chartered and supervised national banks) would be a voting member of the Federal Reserve Board in deciding cease-and-desist and suspension-and-removal cases.

Cease-and-Desist Orders. Authorized the agencies to issue temporary and permanent cease-and-desist orders against banks and associations engaged in or about to engage in unsafe or unsound banking and financial practices.

Removal of Officers. Authorized the agencies to issue suspension-and-removal orders against an officer, director or employee of a bank or association if he violated a law; or if he engaged in an unsafe or unsound banking or financial practice which would cause financial damage to his bank or any other bank (or association), or their depositors; or if his act involved personal dishonesty. A person indicted or charged with a felony could be suspended and, if convicted, removed.

State Action. Provided that in cases of cease-and-desist or removal proceedings involving state-chartered banks and associations, federal officials first must notify state supervisory authorities and permit them to take corrective steps before beginning federal action.

Hearing and Review. Provided that all hearings under the Act were to be private unless ordered otherwise by the agency as in the public interest. Temporary orders could be stayed by federal district courts and permanent orders were appealable to federal courts of appeals. Orders were to be set aside if unsupported by substantial evidence.

Deposit Insurance. Increased FDIC insurance on bank deposits and FSLIC insurance on savings and loan accounts from the current $10,000 to $15,000 per account.

Savings and Loan Holding. Permitted holding companies to control more than one insured institution, provided the FHLBB deemed it advisable in order to prevent a failure.

Savings and Loan Reporting. Provided for reporting changes in the control of insured savings and loan associations to the FSLIC. (The requirements for a method of reporting changes were similar to those provided

Developments Leading to Bank Supervisory Legislation

For several years, federal and private banking officials had discussed the central provisions of S 3158: authorizing federal agencies to issue cease-and-desist orders against unsound banking practices and to remove bank and savings and loan (S&L) institution officials engaged in unsound practices. Existing law generally provided only more drastic remedies, such as termination of federal insurance, or time-consuming methods of correcting unsound practices or removing bank officers.

In 1964, Congress enacted a law (PL 88-593) which required federally insured banks to report "promptly" changes in control of voting stock or of loans secured by 25 percent or more of the bank's stock. That law reflected the growing concern with the entry into the banking field of persons seeking to use banks as a means of making quick profits.

House and Senate subcommittees in 1965 investigated the rising incidence of bank failures resulting from purchase of banks by unscrupulous persons and the depletion of bank assets. During hearings, proposals similar to those embodied in S 3158 were put forward.

Administration and industry sources said that the 1966 legislation was prompted by an increasing number of failures of financial institutions and a reportedly substantial number of institutions with financial problems. A key problem was with individuals who obtained control of a bank, through purchase of stock, and then used that bank as a source of revenue. The use might take several forms: the cash could be drawn off in high salaries; assets could be used to buy other banks or savings and loan institutions; loans could be made to friends or front organizations (for example, an $800,000 loan to an accomplice who secures it with only $200,000 in property); cross-loans could be made in which owner of Bank A makes a large, unsecured loan to owner of Bank B in return for a similar loan and both use the loans as ready cash with no intention of repaying them.

This "financial buccaneering," as one federal official called it, had become more conspicuous in recent years, although it was far from being characteristic of the banking industry.

Figures on bank failures in the February 1966 annual audit by the Comptroller General of the Federal Deposit Insurance Corp. (FDIC), which administered insurance of savings accounts in insured banks, showed that in the six months ending Dec. 31, 1963, one insured bank failed; in the six months ending June 30, 1964, two banks failed; in the six months ending Dec. 31, 1964, five banks failed, and in the four months ending April 30, 1965, five banks failed. Between June 30, 1963, and April 30, 1965, a total of 13 banks failed—10 of them in the last 10 months of that period. The FDIC estimated that its total insurance indemnity liability to depositors of the 13 banks would be $39,518,000 while FDIC losses would run to $12,147,000. The biggest single insurance liability was to the Chatham Bank of Chicago, which closed Aug. 23, 1963; the liability was $13,759,000.

For many years, bankers were concerned about unscrupulous activities in their industry on the theory that a key asset of the industry was the confidence of the public. In addition, if banks could not trust one another in their dealings, so often carried only on the books, then reckless actions by one threatened the soundness of others.

Their concern included so-called "problem banks," which was an industry term for banks which were showing signs of internal difficulty, whether through the avarice of their owners or through inept management. For the bank and its depositors, the result often was the same.

The identities of "problem banks" constituted a well guarded secret in federal regulatory agencies, on the ground that public confidence must not be undermined if the bank possibly could be saved. A description of the "problem bank" picture came from Carter H. Golembe, deputy manager and secretary, state bank division, American Bankers Assn. (ABA) in a speech before the South Dakota Bankers Assn. in Aberdeen, S. D. He cited FDIC data submitted to Congress and said they showed that as of June 30, 1965, there were 199 insured (by the FDIC) "problem banks" in the nation, holding deposits of $1.8 billion.

"Of these 199 banks," he said, "37, with total deposits of $300 million, were listed as 'serious problem banks' by the FDIC, and of these 27 were state-chartered and 10 were national. Of the remaining 162 problem banks, holding liabilities in excess of $1.5 billion, 153 were state-chartered and only nine were national. Of the total $1.8 billion of deposits and other liabilities of problem banks, $1.6 billion was in state-chartered banks and $200 million in national banks.

The need for remedial legislation of the sort embodied in S 3158 had been realized by both federal agencies and bankers for some time because of existing "overkill" provisions of federal banking law. Those provisions authorized regulatory agencies to move in and close a bank when certain standards of conduct were breached, but they offered few remedies short of that. Agencies could advise banks and S&Ls to mend their ways, but there was little they could do to head off the "financial buccaneer."

S 3158 sought to fill that void by authorizing agencies to issue cease-and-desist orders, immediately effective and subject to hearing soon thereafter; to remove bank officers and directors, also subject to future hearing; and to appoint conservators to operate a "problem bank" that has gone too far.

The 1966 controversy in Congressional consideration of S 3158 centered on the timing of the hearings—whether any precipitate agency action should be authorized without hearing—and on the nature of offenses for which officers might be removed. The U.S. Savings and Loan League generally endorsed both provisions but sought modifications of the officer-removal provisions to limit removal to officers convicted of a felony involving a breach of trust and to limit suspension to officers indicted for a felony involving a financial institution. As drafted, the bill authorized removal of officers for "unsafe and unsound" banking practices.

in a 1964 law—PL 88-593—for reporting changes in control of banks.)

Expiration Date. Specified that the authority granted by the bill to issue cease-and-desist orders and to suspend and remove officers of financial institutions would expire June 30, 1972. Other provisions were permanent.

Bank Mergers

Legislation to clarify the applicability of the antitrust laws to bank mergers, which was originated in 1965, became law early in 1966, as an amendment to the Bank Merger Act of 1960. However, when final action on the bill (S 1698—PL 89-356) had been taken, it remained uncertain how successful Congress had been in making the intended clarification. The major questions in the controversy went to the Supreme Court for resolution in 1967. *(See box p. 264.)*

As described by its supporters, the bill established uniform standards for bank regulatory agencies, the Justice Department and the courts to determine the legal validity of bank mergers. Most supporters said the bill did not exempt bank mergers from the antitrust laws and still prohibited anticompetitive mergers. They said the bill went a step further in providing that anticompetitive factors in a merger could be overridden if the convenience to the community "clearly outweighed" the anticompetitive nature of the merger.

The bill gave the Justice Department 30 days in which to challenge the proposed merger and, in a key provision, exempted three major mergers which the Justice Department had opposed. Three other major mergers, also opposed by the Department, were not exempted but were brought within the scope of the bill to be adjudged by its new standards.

Thus did Congress attempt to settle a dispute arising from the Bank Merger Act of 1960 over whether the antitrust provisions of the Sherman Antitrust Act and the Clayton Act applied to banks in the same way that they applied to other industries. The 1960 Act had been interpreted differently by different agencies. The Justice Department resolutely maintained that the Act made no exemption for banks and that the legality of bank mergers hinged on their impact on competition. A number of Senators and Representatives disagreed, arguing that it had been the intention of Congress in 1960 to provide for specialized treatment of bank mergers. Bank regulatory agencies—and banks themselves—adopted that view, and something of an internecine war between the agencies ensued. *(For background see 1965 banking chronology p. 256.)*

Following enactment of S 1698, the Justice Department, which had vigorously opposed the bill, stood fast by its contention that the antitrust laws still applied in the same way to bank mergers. It filed suit against two bank mergers, in Texas and Pennsylvania, on the ground that they substantially lessened competition and therefore violated the antitrust laws. Lower courts ruled adversely to the United States in both cases, and the cases found their way to the Supreme Court.

Legislative Action

The bank merger bill had been passed by the Senate in 1965 but was delayed amid much controversy in the

---

Bank Merger Provisions

The key provisions of the Bank Merger Act of 1960 and the 1966 amendments relating to antitrust standards for bank mergers were as follows:

1960. "In the case of a merger, consolidation, acquisition of assets, or assumption of liabilities, the appropriate agency shall also take into consideration the effect of the transaction on competition (including any tendency toward monopoly), and shall not approve the transaction unless, after considering all of such factors, it finds the transaction to be in the public interest."

1966. "A merger transaction which tends to lessen competition may be approved where the probable adverse competitive effect thereof is clearly outweighed in the public interest by the probable effect of such transaction in meeting the convenience and needs of the community to be served."

House and that chamber's Banking and Currency Committee. A faction of the Committee led by Thomas L. Ashley (D Ohio) had reported an amended version of S 1698 which was vigorously opposed by Chairman Wright Patman (D Texas). Patman denounced the action as illegal. No floor action occurred in 1965.

In early 1966, the Justice Department modified its opposition to new bank merger legislation. The Department agreed on the need for the banking agencies, its own lawyers and the courts to follow the same criteria in evaluating bank mergers. But the Department continued to oppose a deadline for antitrust suits against mergers and retroactive approval of contested bank mergers.

Patman called a meeting of his committee on Jan. 18 to consider an amendment to S 1698 embodying the Department's proposal. An attempt to block this action on a point of order that the bill already was reported and could be amended only on the floor was made by Ashley and overruled by Patman. But Patman was reversed by the full Committee by an 18-14 vote. House Speaker John W. McCormack (D Mass.) then intervened and called Patman and Ashley to a private meeting in his office along with eight other Committee members. It was agreed that the Committee would meet the following day and draft a new bank merger bill as a substitute for S 1698.

The Committee met and reached agreement on a compromise providing a single set of standards for the consideration of bank mergers. The standards permitted mergers only if the needs of the community outweighed the anticompetitive effect of the merger. In the most important vote of the meeting, the Committee voted to prohibit a merger which substantially lessened competition unless the anticompetitive factors were "clearly outweighed in the public interest by the probable effect of such transaction in meeting the convenience and needs of the community to be served."

The revised legislation was passed by the House in early February with little opposition and accepted by the Senate later in the month.

Provisions. As signed into law Feb. 21, S 1698 contained these major provisions:

Merger Rules. Directed the federal bank regulatory agency (the Comptroller of the Currency, the Federal Reserve Board or the Federal Deposit Insurance Corp.,

Court Rules Banks Still Subject to Antitrust Laws

A major interpretation of the Bank Merger Act of 1966 (PL 89-356) was made by the Supreme Court March 27, 1967, in the case of *U. S. v. First City National Bank of Houston.* The Court held, in a significant victory for the Justice Department, that the 1966 law made no major change in the applicability of the antitrust laws to bank mergers. Bank mergers, therefore, continued to be open to attack by Justice Department antitrust suits.

The Justice Department took the position that the 1966 law made no substantive change in antitrust law, and it brought suit to test its view. The Department sued to challenge the proposed mergers of the Provident National Bank with the Central-Penn National Bank in Philadelphia and of the First City National Bank of Houston with the Southern National Bank. Then Comptroller of the Currency James J. Saxon had approved both mergers and, when the lawsuits were filed, he intervened, as authorized under PL 89-356, and moved to dismiss on the ground that the Department had sued only under Section 7 of the Clayton Act and not under provisions of PL 89-356. In both cases, federal district judges dismissed the suits on the grounds put forward by Saxon.

Deciding the two cases as one, the Supreme Court reversed the district judges, thus clearing the way for trial on the merits. Justice William O. Douglas, speaking for the Court, said there was "no indication that an action challenging a merger on the ground of its anticompetitive effects is bottomed on the Bank Merger Act rather than on the antitrust laws." He said the 1966 law added a new defense for the banks by enabling them to plead and prove an offsetting convenience to the community. It was not necessary for the Justice Department to raise the issue of convenience to the community, he said, but rather for the banks to do so.

The Court decided another bank merger case on March 4, 1968. This one, *U. S. v. Third National Bank in Nashville,* also upheld the application of the antitrust laws to bank mergers.

In January 1964, a group of prominent Nashville, Tenn., businessmen purchased a controlling interest in Nashville Bank and Trust Co., a bank which had become stagnant and was run by elderly executives. The group promptly proposed a merger with the Third National Bank in Nashville, one of the most vigorous and best managed banks in the nation. Together, the two constituted the largest bank in the county. The merger was opposed by the Federal Reserve Board, the Federal Deposit Insurance Corp. and the Justice Department as anticompetitive. The Comptroller of the Currency nonetheless approved the merger on Aug. 4, 1964. The Justice Department brought suit but lost in a federal district court, prior to the Supreme Court's decision in *U. S. v. First City National Bank of Houston.*

The Supreme Court in the *Third National* decision said the district court erred in its major findings. The merger was anticompetitive because the Nashville Bank, on its own, was still profitable and provided some services different from those of other banks and at different rates. The district court should have inquired into the "convenience and needs" situation on its own, without accepting the findings of the Comptroller. It also should have required the new owners of the Nashville Bank to show that they made reasonable efforts to solve the management problem at that bank before resorting to merger. The key phrase in the 1966 law was "public interest," and Congress insisted in that law that before a merger against the public interest could be approved, a showing had to be made that the gains expected for the community could not reasonably be expected by any other means than merger.

---

depending on the bank involved) to disapprove anticompetitive bank mergers (including consolidations, acquisitions of assets and assumptions of liabilities) unless the agency concluded that the anticompetitive effects of the merger "are clearly outweighed in the public interest by the probable effect of the (merger) in meeting the convenience and needs of the community to be served." Specified that an illegal merger would be one whose effect "may be substantially to lessen competition, or to tend to create a monopoly," or to restrain trade.

Directed the regulatory agencies to prohibit any proposed bank merger, regardless of circumstances, which violated Section 2 of the Sherman Antitrust Act (which prohibited attempts and conspiracies to monopolize trade or commerce).

Required the regulatory agency, in all cases, to consider the "financial and managerial resources and future prospects of the existing and proposed institutions, and the convenience and needs of the community to be served."

Waiting Period. Provided that an approved merger could not take place for 30 days after approval (although in an emergency to prevent failure of one of the banks, the merger could be consummated immediately or within five days), and permitted suits (by the Justice Department, normally) to be filed during this waiting period challenging the merger under the antitrust laws.

Specified that such a suit would prevent the merger, unless the court ordered otherwise, until the case was concluded.

Exempted mergers consummated after the waiting period from antitrust attack except under the antimonopoly wording of Section 2 of the Sherman Act *(see above).*

Directed the courts to apply to any merger proposal challenged in an antitrust suit the criteria established by the bill for use by regulatory agencies in judging proposed mergers.

Permitted any of the federal bank regulatory agencies approving a bank merger to appear in court in an antitrust suit challenging the merger and present its reasons for its action. Permitted any state banking supervisory agency having jurisdiction within the state involved to present its views to the court in an antitrust case.

Pending Cases. Excused from further antitrust prosecution (except under the antimonopoly wording of

Section 2 of the Sherman Act—see above) mergers consummated before June 17, 1963 (the date of a Supreme Court decision applying the Clayton Antitrust Act to bank mergers).

Prohibited prosecution under the antitrust laws (except under Section 2 of the Sherman Act) of mergers consummated after June 17, 1963, and before enactment of the bill if the U. S. Attorney General had not challenged them in court. In any cases not so exempted, directed the courts to apply the merger criteria provided in the bill when judging the merger.

Provided that any application for approval of a merger which was withdrawn before enactment of the bill as a result of objections by the Attorney General could be resubmitted and would be acted upon under the new criteria.

Bank Holding Companies

Action begun in 1965 on a bill to remove several major exemptions from the 1956 Bank Holding Company Act was completed in 1966. The bill (HR 7371—PL 89-485) became law on July 1.

The 1956 law had forbidden companies which owned two or more banks from simultaneously owning a nonbanking business, but had contained a large number of exemptions. Exempt groups could own as many banks as they wished and at the same time as many nonbanking businesses as they wished. The House in passing HR 7371 in 1965 eliminated virtually all the exemptions. But the Senate in 1966 restored many of the exemptions and the Senate's version prevailed and was enacted into law. *(For 1965 action see banking chronology p. 259.)*

The 1956 Bank Holding Company Act (PL 84-511) was designed to halt the growth of potential banking monopolies by preventing the concentration of control over banks in the hands of bank holding companies and by prohibiting such companies, with certain exceptions, from managing or controlling both banks and nonbanking businesses. Under the Act's provisions, a bank holding company was defined as any company owning 25 percent or more of *two* or more banks. Companies qualifying under this definition and not exempted were required to register with the Federal Reserve Board (FRB); to divest themselves of nonbank assets; and to obtain FRB approval before acquiring more than 5 percent of the voting shares of additional banks. The Act contained a large number of exemptions, the most significant of which was the "one-bank" rule.

The final version of HR 7371 eliminated previously existing exemptions for certain long-term investment trusts; certain registered investment companies; companies whose assets were primarily agricultural; and nonprofit religious, charitable and educational groups. These groups would be required within a specified time to divest themselves of either their banking interests or their nonbanking businesses.

The final version left in effect the existing exemption for tax-exempt labor, agricultural and horticultural organizations. The House had sought to end this exemption but the Senate restored it. Moreover, the final bill made no change in the basic language of the 1956 law which required that a company had to own at least two or more banks to be subject to the prohibition against simultaneously owning nonbanking businesses. The House had

---

Robertson Defeated in Primary

The alleged involvement of Sen. A. Willis Robertson (D Va.), chairman of the Senate Banking and Currency Committee and a 10-year veteran of the Senate, in bank lobbying against the bank merger bill became an issue in his primary fight in July with William B. Spong, Jr. Spong won the primary election by 611 votes and went on to be elected to the Senate.

Among the disclosures relating to Robertson and made by newspapers were: a letter from the chairman of the Manufacturers Hanover Trust Co. of New York City (exempted from further prosecution by S 1698) to the bank's 44,000 stockholders urging them to thank Robertson for his support of bank merger legislation; reports of coercion by Virginia bank officials to get employees to wear Robertson buttons on the job and to display his bumper stickers; a "suggested" quota by a leading banker that each of 40 Virginia banks raise $10 per $1 million of assets for Robertson's campaign (which, if reached, would have brought in an estimated $50,000); Robertson's hiring of a registered lobbyist for the banking industry, Charles Emmet Lucey, for his office staff; and the acknowledgement of a Virginia banker's committee that it had raised $30,000 for his campaign.

Robertson said he did not know about the $30,000 or that Lucey was a lobbyist, but added that it did not surprise him that bankers supported him since he knew more about banking than any other Senator or Representative. Lucey said that he had "advised" several banks, including Manufacturers Hanover Trust, on S 1698 but that he did not lobby for the bill as such.

---

changed the basic language so that the law would cover groups owning one or more banks. This change, potentially the most far-reaching in the entire bill, would have extended the prohibitions of the law to possibly 500 or more companies which held only one bank but which also owned nonbanking assets. The Senate, however, eliminated this proposed change.

Because of the Senate's restoration of exemptions, only two major financial groupings were immediately affected by the final bill. They were the Alfred I. duPont trust of Florida and the Financial General Corp., a large investment company. The duPont trust, which controlled 31 banks with deposits totaling over $600 million, as well as many nonbanking businesses including the Florida East Coast Railway, had previously qualified for an exemption as a long-term trust. HR 7371, as signed into law, ended this exemption and required the duPont trust to divest itself of either its banking or nonbanking interests within five years.

Financial General, which controlled or owned large portions of 26 banks in addition to its nonbanking holdings, had previously qualified for exemption as a registered investment company. Under HR 7371, as enacted, registered investment companies were no longer exempt, and Financial General would have to divest itself of either its banking or nonbank holdings by Dec. 31, 1978.

Legislative Action. The Senate Banking and Currency Committee made major amendments in HR 7371. It retained many House provisions but dropped from the bill the sections that would have abolished the one-bank exemption and ended the exemption for tax-exempt labor, agricultural and horticultural organizations. The Senate Committee thus dropped from the bill two of its most far-reaching provisions. The Senate passed the revised bill by voice vote without change. The House, considering the Senate version the best bill obtainable, concurred in the revisions and sent HR 7371 to the President.

Financial Stakes

The stakes in the dispute over HR 7371 were high, running into the billions of dollars. Some exemptions in the 1956 Act applied in practice to only a few small groups. But others were, either already or potentially, of very wide scope. The following information, supplied by the Federal Reserve Board, indicates the number of exemptions in each group:

Long-Term Investment Trusts. The FRB said the exemption for long-term investment trusts, which was repealed in the final version of HR 7371, covered only a handful of existing trusts, most of which were not making use of it. The DuPont trust was the only large financial grouping which lost its exemption as a result of this provision of HR 7371.

Registered Investment Companies. The existing exemption for registered investment companies (companies which had registered before May 15, 1955, under the 1940 Investment Trust Act) was repealed by HR 7371. The FRB said the Financial General Corp. was the only company that would lose its exemption as a result of this change in the law, since it was the only company actually making use of the exemption. It said, however, that about 300 additional companies were potentially eligible for this exemption, and some had been planning to make use of it before it was repealed by HR 7371.

Religious, Charitable, Educational. The FRB said only a handful of groups were eligible for the exemption for nonprofit religious, charitable and educational organizations and most of them were not actually using it. Repeal of this exemption by HR 7371 therefore did not affect many groups.

Primarily Agricultural. Repeal of the exemption for groups whose assets were primarily (at least 80 percent) agricultural had no practical effect, since no company was using it. The exemption had previously been put into the law for the benefit of one company alone—Consolidated Naval Stores of Jacksonville—which was no longer affected by it.

Labor, Agricultural, Horticultural. The final version of HR 7371 left in effect the existing exemption for tax-exempt labor, agricultural and horticultural organizations. The FRB said only three such organizations were currently using the exemption, as far as it knew: the Amalgamated Clothing Workers of America (AFL-CIO), which controlled the Amalgamated Trust and Savings Bank of Chicago and the Amalgamated Bank of New York; the United Mine Workers of America (Ind.), which controlled

the National Bank of Washington (D.C.); and the International Brotherhood of Boilermakers, Iron Shipbuilders, Blacksmiths, Forgers and Helpers (AFL-CIO), which controlled the Brotherhood Bank of Kansas City, Kan. (The UMW and the Boilermakers would still have been exempt under the "one-bank" rule even if the labor union exemption had been repealed, since they controlled only one bank each.)

"One-Bank" Exemption. The basic rule that the 1956 Act applied only to companies owning two or more banks, not to those holding only one bank in addition to their nonbanking holdings, was not changed by the final version of HR 7371. Had it been, the consequences would have been far-reaching. The FRB estimated that over 500 companies with billions of dollars in assets were currently permitted to hold both banking and nonbanking businesses because their bank holdings consisted of only one bank and they therefore were exempt from the 1956 Act. These included the Goodyear Tire and Rubber Co., Macy's Department Store in New York, the C.I.T. Financial Corp. and the Trust Co. of Georgia (holdings in Coca Cola), among others.

Group Positions

The Johnson Administration as such took no position on the bill or on repeal of the "one-bank" exemption. The main supporter of the bill as a whole and of the provision repealing the "one-bank" exemption was the Federal Reserve Board. The FRB's position was set forth at Senate Banking and Currency Financial Institutions Subcommittee hearings. At the same hearings, Comptroller of the Currency James J. Saxon and the American Bankers Assn. vigorously denounced the provision repealing the "one-bank" exemption. The strongest opposition to repeal of the "one-bank" exemption came from banks and companies that would have been directly affected by repeal. Capitol Hill sources said that had the provision not been dropped in the Senate, the whole bill probably would have failed to pass because of industry opposition to repeal of the "one-bank" exemption.

Financial General fought to retain its exemption, but a spokesman for the DuPont trust took a milder position, arguing only that if its exemption were to be ended, all exemptions should be.

Provisions. As signed into law July 1, HR 7371 amended the Bank Holding Company Act of 1956 as follows:

Repealed exemptions from provisions of the Act for: trusts which did not terminate within 25 years or within 21 years and 10 months of the death of beneficiaries; companies registered under the Investment Company Act of 1940 before May 15, 1955; companies with at least 80 percent of their total assets in the field of agriculture; and nonprofit religious, charitable or educational organizations, foundations or funds.

Redefined "bank" as an institution which accepted deposits payable on demand (checking accounts), so as to include commercial banks and to exclude institutions such as industrial banks and nondeposit trust companies.

Exempted so-called agreement corporations which performed banking operations outside the United States under agreements with the Federal Reserve Board pursuant to Section 25 of the Federal Reserve Act.

1967

Provided that a bank holding company was deemed to control indirectly any shares owned or controlled by its subsidiaries or held in trust for its benefit or for the benefit of its shareholders, members or employees.

Required the Board, in acting on applications for the formation or expansion of bank holding company systems, to take into account the same antimonopoly factors specified in the Bank Merger Act (PL 89-356) for bank mergers.

Required companies previously exempted as registered under the Investment Company Act of 1940 to divest themselves of nonbanking interests by Dec. 31, 1978, and other entities previously exempted to divest themselves within five years and to make progress reports to the Board after two years and annually thereafter.

Repealed Section 6 of the Act, which prohibited any subsidiary bank from lending to or investing in its parent or a fellow subsidiary.

Changed from 60 to 30 days the period in which a party aggrieved by an order of the Board could seek review in a circuit court of appeals.

Required the Board to notify the Attorney General immediately of its approval pursuant to the Act of any acquisition, merger or consolidation; specified that any such transaction could not be consummated before 30 days after Board approval; required that any antitrust actions brought against such a transaction must be initiated during that period; provided that at the end of that period or upon termination of such litigation, any such transaction could not thereafter be attacked as an antitrust violation (except for Section 2 of the Sherman Antitrust Act, which made monopolizing trade a federal crime); and provided that such transactions consummated prior to enactment of HR 7371 were conclusively presumed not to have violated antitrust laws with the possible exception of Section 2 of the Sherman Act.

Bankruptcies

The Bankruptcy Act was amended in 1966 to provide limited relief from federal and state back taxes to individuals who went bankrupt. The bill (HR 3438—PL 89-496) was designed to offer relief to the bankrupt individual seeking "rehabilitation" under the Act. Its supporters said that as a practical matter, corporations which went bankrupt were relieved of back tax liability because they were "dead and nonexistent." But bankrupt individuals remained liable for back taxes. They contended this amounted to "invidious discrimination" against individuals.

The bill left bankrupt individuals liable for taxes for the three years prior to bankruptcy. It provided that the individual could be held liable for federal and state taxes before the three-year cutoff only if the government reduced its tax claim to a lien. The theory was to offer the bankrupt individual relief from many years of taxes as later determined by tax officials, but to hold him responsible for taxes of which he was duly and publicly informed through the filing of tax liens.

The bill also provided that forgiveness of back taxes was not available to a bankrupt individual who failed to file an income tax return, who filed a false or fraudulent return or who collected or withheld taxes from others and had not paid them over to the government.

Silver Certificates

A continuing high demand for silver led Congress to follow up 1965 action with new legislation to free more of the metal for industrial and commercial use. The bill (S 1352—PL 90-29) authorized an accelerated phase-out of silver backing for Treasury silver certificates. The certificates were mostly $1 and $2 bills issued before October 1964. The 1965 legislation, the most recent of actions over the years to deal with an increasing shortage of the metal, eliminated silver from new dimes and quarters and lowered the silver content of half-dollars. *(See p. 268 for description of actions to relieve the silver shortage.)*

S 1352 set a one-year time limit on exchanging certificates for silver metal. After June 24, 1968, the Treasury was not required to redeem the certificates for silver metal, although the currency would remain legal tender. The bill was designed to forestall an increase in the price of silver by freeing Treasury supplies (which had backed the certificates) for sales to industrial users at a fixed market price of $1.29 per ounce. Unless the fixed price was maintained, officials feared that higher silver prices would drive many old 90-percent silver coins out of circulation and cause a coin shortage. (A small price increase would make the coins more valuable as silver than as money.)

Acting under a provision of the new law, the Treasury June 30 transferred about 116 million ounces of silver from the supply which had backed certificates to a reserve which was to be used for sales at the fixed price. Despite this action, however, demand for silver soon became so great that the Treasury July 14 abandoned its fixed sales price. The price of silver then rose substantially, forcing many silver coins out of circulation.

Although the measure was reported unanimously by both the Senate and House Banking and Currency Committees, opposition to the bill developed during floor debate in both chambers. Opponents said that the measure was another step in the process which ultimately would eliminate any connecton between precious metals (gold and silver) and the nation's money supply. Some spokesmen for western silver-producing states—areas of traditional support for metal-backed currency—also opposed the bill.

Provisions. As signed into law (PL 90-29) June 24, S 1352:

Established a one-year deadline (from the date of enactment) for the redemption in bullion of all silver certificates currently in circulation, after which period this currency would remain legal tender but without redemption privileges.

Authorized the Treasury Secretary, during the one-year period, to write off on the books of the Treasury an amount, not to exceed $200 million, of the outstanding silver certificates which, in his judgment, were destroyed or irretrievably lost or held in collections, and which therefore would never be presented for redemption in silver bullion.

Required the Treasury to hold for one year, and then to transfer to national defense stockpiles, 165 million ounces of silver.

Background

Congress had attempted repeatedly to deal with the silver shortage problem which developed in the late 1950s. Silver production exceeded consumption until the post-World War II period. During the 1934-1959 period the Treasury was required to purchase any newly mined silver offered it. During that period, 3 billion ounces of the metal were bought and used as backing for silver certificates (currency), in coins and as free silver reserves.

After 1959, however, the increased demand for coins (attributed partly to vending machines, which removed many coins from continuous circulation) and new industrial uses for silver (particularly in photography and electronics) created silver shortages. The excess industrial demand was met for a time by Treasury sales of non-monetized (free) silver, which was not needed to back the outstanding silver certificates. In 1961 such sales were halted because of the persistent drain on Treasury reserves of free silver.

The Administration in 1963 and in 1965 requested enactment of major monetary reform measures to stem the growing shortage of silver and to make additional amounts of the metal available for industrial and other uses.

In 1963, Congress enacted legislation (PL 88-36) which authorized issuance of $1 and $2 bills, with 25-percent gold backing, to replace roughly $2 billion in silver-backed Treasury certificates. (Similar action on silver-backed $5 and $10 bills was taken in 1961 by Executive Order.) The issuance of silver certificates was completely discontinued by the Treasury in October 1964 and the process of retiring the outstanding certificates was begun. As the certificates were taken in, appropriate quantities of silver metal were demonetized by the Treasury, and used for coinage and sold on the free market to help keep the market price of silver down. Withdrawal from circulation of the silver-backed certificates was expected to take about 15 years. (S 1352, by setting a one-year limit on redemption privileges for silver-backed certificates, in effect accomplished the purpose of the 1963 legislation in a shortened period of time.)

In 1965, Congress enacted legislation (PL 89-81) revising the nation's coinage system by eliminating all silver from new dimes and quarters and reducing the silver content in new half-dollars from 90 percent to 40 percent.

Despite these measures, however, demand for silver continued to increase. In May 1967, the Treasury possessed 520 million ounces of silver, of which almost 430 million ounces were held as backing for the approximately $550 million in certificates outstanding. Only 90 million ounces were available for new half-dollars and for sales to stabilize the free market price.

The 1967 legislation was sent to Congress March 14 by the Treasury Department. Its primary purpose was to free additional silver to keep the market price of the metal down, so that the old 90-percent silver coins would remain in circulation sufficiently long to permit minting of enough new coins to serve the needs of the economy.

Repealed the prohibition against using mint marks on coins and permitted the Bureau of the Mint, at its discretion, to reintroduce mint marks.

Mutual Funds

Controversial proposals to increase controls over the mutual fund industry and reduce the costs to investors in mutual funds were considered but not enacted by Congress. The industry strongly opposed the main parts of the draft legislation (S 1659, HR 9510 and HR 9511), which was proposed by the Securities and Exchange Commission (SEC). The SEC and the industry negotiated agreements on several minor points, but controversies over three major provisions were not resolved. Extensive Congressional hearings were held on the proposed legislation, but no bill was reported to either the House or the Senate.

The measure, known as the Investment Company Amendments Act of 1967, was proposed and drafted by the SEC to "provide additional protection for mutual fund shareholders in areas where the tremendous growth of the industry since enactment of the Investment Company Act of 1940 has created needs which were either unanticipated or of secondary importance at the time."

Spokesmen for the mutual funds contended that the proposed legislation would grant the SEC control of the industry's prices and profits.

The Administration gave general, though not specific, endorsement to the measure. President Johnson in his Feb. 16, 1967, message on consumer protection urged Congress to "give careful consideration" to the SEC recommendations, which he said "provide a sound basis for measures which will be beneficial to the investing public and promote the health and stability of the industry itself."

The SEC's proposals were the outgrowth of two studies. One was undertaken for the SEC in 1958 by the Wharton School of Finance and Commerce of the University of Pennsylvania, and submitted to Congress in 1962. The other, a massive staff study authorized by Congress in 1961, was the most exhaustive made of the stock market since the early 1930s. The four parts of the study, which was conducted by a 65-man team, were submitted to Congress in 1963. In sections of the report dealing with mutual funds, sharp criticism was directed at front-end-load plans, at the qualifications of some salesmen and at the practices of some "insiders" who traded in stocks that the mutual funds they represented also were buying or selling. At the request of the SEC, Congress enacted the Securities Act Amendments of 1964 (PL 88-467), which were largely concerned with the qualifications of brokers and dealers and with sales of stock over the counter, or outside the stock exchanges. The new law followed many of the recommendations of the 1963 study. *(Congress and the Nation, Vol. I, p. 383)*

After enactment of the 1964 law, the SEC turned its attention to mutual funds. On Dec. 2, 1966, it sent to Congress a lengthy report on the "Public Policy Implications of Investment Company Growth." This was the genesis of the 1967 legislation.

In broad terms, an investment company is any arrangement by which a number of persons invest funds in a "company" that is itself engaged in investing in securities. Of various types of investment companies, "management" companies dominate the industry. The SEC said that as of June 30, 1966, management companies had 96.5 percent of the $46.4 billion in assets held by all investment companies registered with the SEC. The term "investment companies" usually refers to "management companies."

There are closed-end and open-end investment companies and the open-end variety are known commonly as mutual funds. Closed-end companies issue stock to obtain capital, are not under obligation to buy back the stock, and few make continuous offerings of their own securities. Shareholders sell their stock as they would that of an industrial corporation, through a broker to another investor.

An open-end company is under legal obligation to redeem its stock when shareholders wish to sell. To offset this outflow of cash, the managers of virtually all open-end companies vigorously promote sales of new shares at all times. The mutual funds dominate the industry today.

During the 1920s, mutual funds were few and small and the investment company field was dominated by closed-end companies. After 1929, closed-ends lost much of their former favor with investors, but it was not until 1944 that the aggregate assets of mutual funds exceeded those of closed-end companies.

By June 30, 1966, according to the SEC, the assets of mutual funds were almost six times those of closed-end companies. On that date, there were 379 mutual funds registered with the SEC with total assets of approximately $38.2 billion, as compared to 149 active closed-end companies with total assets of about $6.6 billion. Almost all mutual funds are diversified—that is, they hold securities in several companies.

Growth of Mutual Funds. The first U.S. mutual fund, Massachusetts Investors Trust, was founded in 1924, apparently based on an idea imported from Britain.

In 1940 there were 150,000 investors in mutual funds. By 1966 the number had grown to 4 million. Over the same period, shareholder accounts in the funds grew from less than 300,000 to more than 7,500,000.

Their economic importance could be gauged by SEC figures which showed that in 1965 mutual funds raised almost $5.2 billion through issuance of new shares—a figure more than double the $2.3 billion in new stock sold for cash in the United States by all other corporations.

The assets of mutual funds grew from about $450 million in 1940 to about $38.2 billion on June 30, 1966, according to SEC figures. The growth was particularly striking in the last decade, the SEC said. Mutual fund assets were about $4 billion at the end of 1952; tripled to $13.2 billion by the end of 1958, and nearly tripled again by mid-1966, when they were nine times their 1952 size.

SEC Bill

Points of Controversy. Of the vast number of amendments contained in its 60-page bill, the SEC cited three as particularly important, and these points became the most controversial: (1) Fees paid by the mutual funds to their management and advisory organizations must be "reasonable" and would be subject to court review; (2) a 5-percent ceiling should be placed on the charges levied on investors when they purchase shares in a mutual fund;

(3) there should be a ban on "front-end loads," in which an investor pays in the first year a disproportionately large portion of the amount he would owe over a period of years for shares purchased on the installment plan.

SEC Chairman Manuel F. Cohen, in transmitting the bill to Congress May 1, said: "These legislative proposals recognize...that on the whole the investment company industry reflects diligent management by competent persons, that the industry has provided a useful and desirable means for investors to obtain diversification of investment risks and professional investment management, and that drastic changes are not required. We believe, however, that enactment of these proposals would assure fairer treatment for the millions of Americans, including many of modest means, who have chosen to invest many billions of dollars in investment company securities."

The Investment Company Institute (ICI), which represented mutual funds, their investment advisers and their underwriters, took strong exceptions to the SEC's recommendations. In a memorandum on "Mutual Funds and the Public Interest," the ICI charged that "what the SEC is seeking to control is not dishonesty or mismanagement in the mutual fund industry, but rather prices and profits." Contending there is "vigorous competition in the marketplace," the ICI said "price and performance competition...have brought about improved services and lower costs to the investing public and will continue to do so." The ICI said it was not in the American tradition to prefer government regulation to regulation by the marketplace, nor to substitute rate-making for price competition.

The proposal to abolish front-end-load plans brought strong objections from the Assn. of Mutual Fund Plan Sponsors (AMFPS), which represented mutual funds that use that form of installment-plan stock purchases. The AMFPS contended that the SEC recommendation would wipe out an industry "which has produced large profits for many hundreds of thousands of small investors since the 1940 Act was enacted by Congress, with virtually no complaints from the public since then."

Mutual Fund Procedures

According to the ICI, mutual funds provided the only medium through which millions of investors with limited capital could acquire shares in diversified portfolios of 50 to 100 or more carefully selected securities under professional investment management with immediate redeemability of their shares. Prior to the development of mutual funds, only large investors could afford such diversification and investment management with immediate redeemability serve the economy by helping to broaden public participation in the ownership of American business, tapping new sources of capital for economic expansion and distributing more widely the earnings from American business growth. The ICI described mutual funds as long-term investments which meet the needs of Americans who want to buy common stocks as a "hedge against inflation" but lack the time and financial skills to protect themselves by selecting an adequately diversified portfolio.

Advisers' Fees. The 1966 SEC report said most funds contract out their principal functions to other organizations on a fee basis. The customary fee to the "investment adviser" is one-half of 1 percent of the fund's average net assets during the year. After publication of

Lobbyists Hired

The major opponents of the SEC bill—the Investment Company Institute (ICI), Assn. of Mutual Fund Plan Sponsors (AMFPS) and National Assn. of Securities Dealers (NASD)—hired lobbyists in 1967 to work against the bill or seek amendments to it. The first two groups registered with Congress under the Federal Regulation of Lobbying Act, as did a representative of the NASD and the individual lobbyists mentioned below.

In spending reports filed with Congress, the ICI said it spent $46,125 on its lobbying activities in 1967. The AMFPS did not file spending reports for the last half of 1967 but estimated in its registration statement that expenses would be $35,000 per quarter of the year. Registered lobbyists for the AMFPS filed spending reports as individuals.

Several of the largest mutual funds hired lobbyists to represent them. The Washington, D.C., law firm of Gadsby, Maguire and Hannah registered as representing Massachusetts Investors Trust, the second largest mutual fund, and Insurance Securities, the ninth largest, as well as several smaller companies. Edward N. Gadsby, a partner in the firm, was SEC chairman in 1957-61. Another partner, Richard Maguire, was treasurer of the Democratic National Committee in 1962-65.

A former U. S. Representative, George E. MacKinnon (R Minn. 1947-49), registered as representing the largest fund, Investors Mutual, and the fourth largest, Investors Stock Fund, among others. MacKinnon reported spending $2,173 on his lobbying activities in the fourth quarter of 1967.

---

the Wharton report in 1962, the SEC said, some funds reduced their fee schedules. They paid the traditional rate up to a stipulated asset level, say the first $300 million, and lower percentages, say .4 percent and .3 percent, as the assets increased beyond other levels. A substantial portion of each fund's board of directors and virtually all the fund's officers will normally be associated with or employed by the investment adviser, the SEC said. In most cases the adviser selects the stocks the fund buys and sells, and operates most other aspects of its business. Many advisers organize and manage a number of funds.

The funds constantly buy and sell large blocks of securities, almost always through brokers. If the adviser is an affiliate of a brokerage house, that house normally receives the fund's business. An unaffiliated adviser often gives a fund's business to a broker in exchange for services or research. Most advisers use much of the business to reward brokers and dealers who sell the funds' shares—a form of "extra compensation" for their sales efforts, the SEC said. Furthermore, an adviser can spread the brokerage commissions around because the rules permit commission splitting by the broker who executed the transaction and by other brokers within the same stock exchange who sell the fund's shares, though they did no work on the transaction.

The SEC bill required that fees paid the investment advisers must be "reasonable" and that a shareholder could challenge those fees in court. Opponents said

different courts would set different rates as to what was reasonable in different cases.

The SEC said the close relationship between mutual funds and their advisers precluded bargaining over fees, and that economies to be expected as the funds grew were not always passed on to the funds and the shareholders. But the ICI said the average fee paid by mutual funds with assets of more than $100 million in 1966 was .37 percent. Furthermore, it said mutual fund shareholders usually pay less in management fees than most individuals pay for investment advice from banks or other counselors. The SEC said the fees paid by the funds were higher than those charged by advisers for other types of clients.

Sales Charges. The 1966 SEC report said most funds, in selling new shares, added a sales charge or "load" to the net asset value. Only 60 "no load" funds sold shares without the charges and without salesmen, usually by advertising directed at investors. Some sold through brokers who handled the fund's portfolio business, or on the recommendations of investment counselors. The SEC said the "no load" companies' methods of obtaining business were considerably less effective than the "far more vigorous, personalized selling drives" used by the "load" funds.

Most load funds charged from 7.5 to 8.75 percent of the total purchase price, with 8.5 percent most common, the SEC said. Most funds charged less on larger purchases, providing they were for $10,000 or more.

The SEC said the charge actually amounted to 9.3 percent of the money the investor put into the shares, and the practice of expressing the sales load as a percentage of the total purchase price differed from the way it was expressed in other securities transactions. For example: If an investor spent $1,000 to buy shares, $915 represented investment in the shares and $85 went to the sales organization. The $85 was 9.3 percent of the $915.

"From the small investor's point of view, the sales load is by far the principal cost of a mutual fund investment," the SEC said, and it added, "most mutual fund investors are small investors."

The SEC said an investor buying common stocks directly would pay 1-percent commission when he buys and 1 percent commission when he sells in round (100-share) lots, compared to the 9.3 percent he paid when he bought mutual fund shares. (For less than round lots, the commission was 2 percent.) Mutual funds do not charge when the shares are sold back by the investor. But there also was a broker's commission when the fund buys and sells the common stock in its portfolio, and the burden of those charges fell on the shareholders too, the SEC said.

Chairman Cohen said that during 1965, shareholders in mutual funds paid $130 million in advisory fees, $260 million in sales loads, and in addition incurred more than $100 million of brokerage commissions on the purchase and sale of securities by their funds.

Load fund shares were sold by an external organization known as an underwriter, which usually was the investment adviser or a close affiliate. Therefore, continuous selling of shares benefited not only the underwriter, but also the adviser and broker whose fees were determined by funds' assets and portfolio transactions. The underwriter was usually a wholesaler and he encouraged his retailer dealers to sell the particular fund by increasing the commission and by giving them brokerage business.

Some underwriters employed salesmen who sold directly to customers.

"A high level of direct selling compensation in a price-protected market, coupled with the increased advisory fees and the augmented brokerage commissions that result from new sales, is a strong stimulus to vigorous, intensive, personalized selling effort," the SEC said.

The SEC's proposal that a 5-percent ceiling be placed on sales loads aroused the strongest opposition to its bill. The SEC said the 5-percent figure still would be substantially higher than prevailing charges in the securities market, but the industry contended it would drive many small dealers out of the mutual fund business.

Under the SEC proposal, the 5 percent would be calculated on the amount of money going into shares. The National Assn. of Securities Dealers (NASD) said the ceiling would amount to 4.76 percent of the investor's total expenditure, and asserted that was the traditional way of calculating the percentage in the mutual fund field and in most other types of business.

The SEC said existing law prohibited dealers from selling mutual shares at other than the price established by the underwriter, thus eliminating price competition and leading to competition among underwriters for the "favor" of retail dealers. That had the effect of raising sales prices to investors, the SEC said, but the NASD said any broker who did more than half his business in mutual fund shares—and there were 1,500 firms handling only mutual funds—would find that the 5-percent ceiling had turned his profit-making operation into a loss operation. NASD said investors have a wide range of choice among funds, from those with no loads to those with various sales loads. The ICI said an investor buying and selling $1,240 worth of 20 different stocks on his own would pay a total of 12 percent in commissions.

Front-End Loads. Many investors bought shares in mutual funds on an installment basis, regularly investing small amounts of money—for example, monthly for 10 years. The investor in a "contractual" plan was not legally bound to make all his payments or complete the plan. However, the law permitted as much as half of his first 12 monthly payments to be deducted for sales load, and most plans did that. Unless he completed all his payments, the sales load, set by law at 9 percent, actually would exceed 9 percent and could be as much as 50 percent of the payments actually made.

Plans which provided for payment of most of the sales charges in the first year were known as "front-end loads." Of the 379 mutual funds in 1966, 60 offered this kind of installment-plan purchase system.

In proposing a ban on front-end loads, the SEC said this would protect investors of modest means against enormous sales charges when they did not complete their contractual investment plans. The majority of such investors did not complete their plans, the SEC said, and there the sales charges they incurred amounted to 20 to 50 percent of their total payments.

The Assn. of Mutual Fund Plan Sponsors (AMFPS) said most investors, even if they failed to complete their plans, came out ahead because of equity growth.

In behalf of front-end loads, the AMFPS said the system was necessary to stimulate salesmen to solicit business, just as in the insurance field, and that between 2 and 10 million small investors would never be attracted into the stock programs in the next decade if the contrac-

tual plan were abolished. The AMFPS contended the contractual plan was similar to every other type of installment plan in which a salesman, selling cars for example, gets his commission immediately.

As an example of how the system worked, suppose an investor agreed to buy $3,000 worth of shares in a mutual fund over a period of 10 years in monthly installments of $25. The commission, at 8.5 percent, would amount to $255. But from the investor's $300 payment in the first 12 months, $150 could be deducted against the total sales charge of $255. The remainder of the sales charge would be evenly distributed over the following nine years.

Interest Rate Controls

The 1966 law giving the Government limited control over certain bank interest rates was extended by Congress for a year. The 1966 law gave federal bank regulatory agencies flexible authority to set different limits on the interest rates that banks and other financial institutions could pay on different types and amounts of fixed maturity (time) desposits. *(See 1966 banking chronology.)*

The 1967 bill (S 1956—PL 90-87) extended all of the provisions of the 1966 law for one year, through Sept. 21, 1968. The Administration and the bank regulatory agencies had recommended a two-year extension. No changes were made in the law. The bill was enacted with little controversy.

S&L Holding Companies

The Senate, but not the House, passed a bill (S 1542) to provide additional controls over savings and loan holding companies. (The legislation was enacted in 1968. *See 1968 banking chronology p. 275.*)

S 1542 was called the Savings and Loan Holding Company Amendments of 1967. The purpose of the bill was to give the Federal Savings and Loan Insurance Corp., which was administered by the Federal Home Loan Bank Board, authority to protect savings and loan associations from abuses by parent holding companies.

The legislation was requested by the Administration, which said far greater regulatory problems occurred with savings and loan associations that were controlled by holding companies than with associations not subject to holding company control. The bill required savings and loan holding companies to register and file reports with the FHLBB, tightened restrictions on financial dealings between S&Ls and their parent holding companies or affiliates, required holding companies that controlled more than one S&L to divest themselves of unrelated activities, gave the FHLBB additional control over holding company debt structure and prohibited further creation of interstate holding companies.

Bank Lottery Sales

Federally insured banks and thrift institutions were prohibited from participating in the sale of lottery tickets to the public. The prohibition was contained in a bill (HR 10595—PL 90-203) enacted by Congress over the objections of Members from states which sold lottery tickets through banks.

HR 10595 barred federally insured banks and thrift institutions from selling lottery tickets directly to the public and from distributing them to other sales agents. The bill allowed banks to accept deposits, handle checks or other negotiable instruments and perform other lawful banking services for a state operating a lottery.

The final version of the bill was a compromise between a highly restrictive House measure which prohibited federally insured banks and thrift institutions from having any connection with a lottery and a milder Senate bill which also barred direct sales of lottery tickets by banks but allowed banks to carry on a number of associated banking functions in connection with a lottery.

The bill, sponsored by House Banking and Currency Committee Chairman Wright Patman (D Texas) to "keep banks out of the lottery business," applied to federally insured banks and thrift institutions throughout the country. However, two states, New York and New Hampshire, were affected immediately by the bill. Both states operated state lotteries to aid local education programs, and both states sold tickets for the lotteries through banks. Of the two states, New York was affected more because more of its lottery ticket sales were made through banks.

Provisions. As signed into law (PL 90-203) Dec. 15, HR 10595 contained the following major provisions:

Prohibited federally chartered banks, state banks which were members of the Federal Reserve System or which had federally insured deposits, and federally insured savings and loan associations from selling or otherwise dealing in lottery tickets.

Prohibited such institutions from advertising lotteries and from announcing lottery winners or keeping records of participants or winners as such.

Prohibited the use of the institutions' immediate premises for any of these activities.

Permitted the institutions to perform bookkeeping and recordkeeping chores connected with a lottery and to perform any other "lawful banking services" for a state operating a lottery.

Provided penalties of up to $1,000 in fines, or imprisonment for not more than one year, or both.

Made the law effective April 1, 1968.

Federal Savings Banks

Two days before Congress adjourned in 1967, the House Banking and Currency Committee reported the Federal Savings Institutions Act, a controversial Administration-backed bill (HR 13718) to broaden the lending and investment powers of thrift institutions (savings and loan associations and mutual savings banks). The bill did not reach the House floor before Dec. 15 adjournment.

HR 13718 was designed to make available more funds for housing by enabling the savings and loan (S&L) and mutual savings institutions to obtain more funds to finance housing. Such institutions are the major source of home loan funds.

Under terms of the bill, the thrift institutions were authorized to offer certain bank-type services, such as "certificates of deposit," a type of security yielding higher interest rates than the thrift institutions generally could afford to pay. (They were not, however, authorized to deal in checking accounts or to lend money to commercial firms or industry.) In a provision designed to enable the institutions to pay the higher rates, the measure broadened their investment authority to include a number of specified high-yield, short-term loans, stocks and bonds. (Under existing regulations, they were limited primarily to investment in home mortgages.) Finally, the measure provided for federal chartering of mutual savings banks, which would permit their establishment in all states instead of only the 18 that currently chartered such banks. (S&Ls already were granted federal charters.)

For years, the mutual savings banks had pressed for federal chartering but the move had been opposed by the S&Ls. In his Economic Reports of 1966 and 1967, President Johnson requested legislation to provide for federal charters.

Late in 1967, the S&L industry dropped its opposition and agreed to support the proposal in a new form. The new version allowed both S&Ls as well as the mutual savings banks to perform the expanded services. The U.S. Savings and Loan League, representing about 4,000 S&Ls, voiced its support for HR 13718 late in 1967, although some large S&Ls, already doing well under existing regulations, were slow to support the effort. Qualified support came from the National Assn. of Home Builders, which favored only gradual modification of the requirements regarding investment in home mortgages.

Lobbies for the nation's commercial banks during 1967 launched a strong effort to kill the bill. Leading the attack was the American Bankers Assn., which represented 98 percent of the commercial banks.

1968

Gold Crisis

The United States and six other nations which made up the London Gold Pool announced in Washington, D.C., March 17 that they no longer would supply gold to private buyers as they had been doing. In effect, the decision established a two-price system for gold: the price for official transactions between governments was to remain at $35 an ounce; the price for all other transactions was to be allowed to fluctuate freely based on the normal supply of gold and the demand for it.

The decision came after a rush of gold buying during the first two weeks of March by private purchasers speculating that the United States would be forced to increase the price of gold (currently $35 an ounce) in order to preserve its dwindling gold supply. Similar private speculative buying of gold had followed the British devaluation of the pound sterling in November 1967 and had occurred in December 1967 amid reports that the London Gold Pool was to be modified in some way at that time.

The speculation against gold—which, because of the U. S. guarantee of the dollar price of gold, was in effect speculation against the dollar—was undermining world confidence in the dollar and thus was raising doubts about the viability of the existing world monetary system. This was so because the keystone of the world monetary system had been a pattern of stable exchange rates which had been maintained by foreign central banks (like the

Federal Reserve System in the United States) buying or selling U. S. dollars to maintain the parity of their currencies with the dollar. In turn, the foreign central banks could hold the dollars as part of their reserves (knowing that the dollars were convertible to gold at one ounce of gold for $35) or could convert the dollars into gold and hold gold as their reserves.

London Gold Pool. The London Gold Pool was formed in November 1961 by eight nations: The United States, the Netherlands, Britain, France, Germany, Switzerland, Belgium and Italy. It was designed to maintain the world price of gold at $35 an ounce and to deter private speculation in gold. This was to be done by making available to private London gold dealers through the Bank of England enough gold from government gold supplies (estimated to total about $32.6 billion among the eight nations in 1961) to meet any private speculative demand for gold which could not be met from supplies of newly mined gold or from gold offered for sale by private holders. Without the gold pool arrangement, speculators, faced with a limited supply of commercially available gold, could have forced the gold price above the permissible ceiling of $35.20 an ounce. The theory of the arrangement was that the eight governments could offer a comparatively unlimited supply of gold which would in effect flood the private gold market and thus maintain the stable price of gold. Although there were gold markets elsewhere, the London market was the key one because the main supply of new gold—the output of South African mines—was sold through it. Thus all other gold markets replenished their supplies through London.

The gold pool arrangement worked for a number of years. But beginning in 1966 a series of developments occurred which eroded the foundations of the arrangement:

• The commercial supply of gold declined as the Soviet Union in 1966 stopped offering gold for sale and gold output in the rest of the world leveled off, despite a growing volume of international trade.

• France in June 1967 withdrew from participation in the gold pool arrangement, taking along about $5.2 billion in gold reserves which had been part of the backing of the gold pool. The 9-percent French share of the gold pool operations was picked up by the United States, which had been responsible for a 50-percent share, boosting the U. S. share to 59 percent.

• The U. S. and British balance-of-payments deficits had eaten into their gold stocks available to the gold pool, as part of their gold had been turned over to creditor nations to meet the payments deficits.

• Operations of the gold pool after the British devaluation of the pound sterling in November 1967 further depleted the gold reserves of the remaining seven gold pool nations.

In all, gold reserves of the nations participating in the gold pool dropped from $34.2 billion at the beginning of 1966 to about $26.5 billion at the beginning of 1968.

1968 Gold Speculation. The Treasury Department Feb. 28 reported that a January drop of $62 million in U.S. gold reserves left the total U.S. stock of gold at about $12 billion, its lowest point since 1936. Sen. Jacob K. Javits (R N.Y.) proposed in a Senate speech the same day that the United States halt temporarily automatic sales of U. S. gold to other governments and stop supporting the London gold market through the pool arrangement. Re-

acting to these developments, speculative buying of gold mushroomed, sending volume on the London bullion market to an estimated $300 million for the the first 10 days of March (compared with a normal volume of about $3-$5 million per day, or $30-$50 million for a normal 10-day period).

Basel Statement—In an effort to counteract the speculation, the governors of the seven central banks contributing to the gold pool (including the Federal Reserve) March 10 issued a communique: "The central banks contributing to the London Gold Pool reaffirm their determination to continue their support to the pool based on the fixed price of $35 an ounce of gold." The communique followed a meeting March 9-10 in Basel, Switzerland, of the directors of the Bank for International Settlements. Among the directors were governors of the central banks feeding the gold pool.

In the days that followed the Basel statement, the speculation in gold hesitated briefly—the volume of sales in London March 11 dropped to $30-$40 million compared with about $80 million March 8—but then increased. London sales March 13 reached $165 million and the price of gold pushed through the $35.20 ceiling and varied between $35.20 and $35.25.

March 14—As the volume of gold sales in London reached $440 million and gold sold in Paris at $35.90 an ounce, these developments occurred in the United States:

1. The Senate by a 39-37 roll-call vote cleared a bill (HR 14743) to remove the gold backing for Federal Reserve notes, thus freeing about $10.4 billion in U. S. gold for international transactions. *(See following story.)*

2. Despite an urgent appeal by Treasury Secretary Henry H. Fowler to the Senate Finance Committee to pass within 30 days the 10-percent surtax to maintain "the international monetary system as we know it today," the Committee ordered reported a bill (HR 15414) to extend current excise tax rates on automobiles and telephone service after rejecting an amendment to add the surtax to the bill. The surtax was designed to combat U. S. inflation and thus to help reduce the U. S. balance-of-payments deficit. (The surtax bill was finally cleared June 21. *See Economic Policy, subchapter on tax policy.*)

3. The Federal Reserve Board increased the discount rate it charged member banks from 4.5 percent to 5 percent. The action was designed to curb inflationary pressures and thereby help the U.S. balance of payments.

4. Fowler and Federal Reserve Chairman William McChesney Martin Jr. announced a meeting of the heads of the central banks of the seven gold pool nations for March 16-17 in Washington, D. C.

March 15—The British government ordered a one-day closing of London's international gold market. The move came at the request of President Johnson. The Paris gold market remained open and the price of gold rose to $44.36 an ounce as the volume of sales reached $43.9 million. Amid the financial uncertainty, dealings in foreign exchange were suspended by some countries. Trading in gold elsewhere was at a standstill because of inadequate supplies. American tourists abroad found that they could cash only a limited amoumt of travelers checks for foreign currencies and then usually at premium rates, because some authorities were reluctant to deal in dollars whose value they felt was uncertain.

March 16—The emergency conference opened in Washington, D. C. The key officials were U. S. Federal

Reserve Board Chairman William McChesney Martin, Jr., who served as conference chairman; U. S. Treasury Secretary Henry H. Fowler, Edwin J. Stopper, president of the National Bank of Switzerland; Dr. Jelle Zijlstra, president of the Netherlands Bank; Guido Carli, governor of the Bank of Italy; Gabriel Ferras, managing director of the Bank for International Settlements; Sir Leslie K. O'Brien, governor of the Bank of England; Pierre-Paul Schweitzer, managing director of the International Monetary Fund; Karl Blessing, president of the Bundesbank of West Germany; and Hubert-Jacques Ansiaux, governor of the National Bank of Belgium. No news announcement was made at the end of the first day's session.

March 17—The financial officials issued a post-conference communique. In it they said (1) that the seven nations had agreed to support the existing pattern of exchange rates among currencies; (2) that the seven nations no longer would supply gold to the London market or to any other gold market; (3) that the seven nations "no longer feel it necessary to buy gold from the market"; (4) that the seven nations would not sell gold to a country that sold its gold on a private market; (5) that the seven nations would "cooperate even more closely than in the past to minimize the flows of funds contributing to instability in the exchange markets"; (6) that it had been agreed to supply extra standby credits for Britain to help support the pound which would bring the total to $4 billion, including $1.4 billion that already was available from the International Monetary Fund; and (7) that the seven nations invited the cooperation of other central banks.

In addition, the officials said that a "substantial improvement of the U. S. balance of payments" was "a high priority objective."

The immediate effect of the seven-nation agreement was that the gold pool arrangement had been abandoned, allowing the private market price of gold (as opposed to the official U. S. government price) to fluctuate according to supply and demand. Because the United States agreed to continue to buy and to sell gold for $35 an ounce in transactions with other governments, an effective two-price system for gold had been established. Further, the agreement to stop supplying gold to the gold pool to meet private speculative demand blocked one of the leaks in the U. S.gold supply.

To finance the growing volume of world trade, in view of the agreement by the seven nations to "freeze" their supplies of monetary gold, the seven indicated that they would rely on the plan to create "special drawing rights" (SDRs) in the International Monetary Fund. The SDRs were designed to be a new form of international money for use by central banks (in addition to gold, dollars and pounds sterling) in settling payments among nations.

In London, the Bank of England ordered the London gold market to remain closed until April 1.

March 18—As world bankers watched to see the reaction to the March 17 decision of the seven nations, the price of gold dropped on the Paris and Zurich markets. In Paris, the gold price slipped from $44.36 an ounce on March 15 to $40.10 an ounce. In Zurich, the price dropped from $45 an ounce at the opening of the market to $40 by the close.

April 1—At the first gold-price fixing under free-market conditions, the price of gold in London was set at $38 an ounce. By afternoon the same day the price had slipped to $37.70, or $2.70 above the official U.S.-backed price of $35 an ounce.

Gold Cover

By unexpectedly narrow margins in both houses, Congress voted to remove the remaining gold backing from U. S. currency. The bill (HR 14743—PL 90-269) eliminated the existing requirement that each Federal Reserve Bank maintain reserves in gold certificates of not less than 25 percent of its Federal Reserve notes (currency) in circulation. The certificates were issued by the Secretary of the Treasury against gold held in the Treasury.

The legislation, like similar legislation in 1965, was necessary because of the continued actual and threatened drain on the U. S. gold stock as a result of balance-of-payments deficits. President Johnson requested the legislation in his State of the Union Message.

The current U. S. gold stock was about $12 billion, but approximately $10.7 billion of that total was earmarked to meet the 25-percent backing requirement. The balance was available for sale to foreign countries at $35 an ounce. The Administration said that the $10.7 billion also had to be made available for sale to assure other nations that there would be ample gold available to exchange for dollars which they had been accumulating as a result of the U. S. balance-of-payments deficit. The hope was to encourage these nations to retain their dollars, rather than demand gold, and by so doing, to emphasize that the strength of the dollar depended on the strength of the U. S. economy and not upon a legal 25-percent gold backing for the currency.

The Federal Reserve Act of 1913 required that the 12 Federal Reserve Banks created by the Act maintain a reserve of gold certificates valued at no less than 35 percent of the amount of commercial bank deposits held by each. In addition, it required that Federal Reserve notes issued by the Government be backed by gold bullion holdings amounting to no less than 40 percent of value.

The coinage of gold was ended in 1934, when the United States went off the gold standard as a form of commercial exchange. After that, gold was used chiefly as a reserve for meeting international obligations, with the United States maintaining the gold value of the dollar at $35 an ounce.

The reserve provisions of the 1913 Act remained unchanged until 1945, when both the required Federal Reserve holdings of gold certificates and the gold backing for Federal Reserve notes were reduced to 25 percent. Early in 1965, Congress passed a bill (HR 3818—PL 89-3) which ended the requirement that the Federal Reserve Bank maintain a 25-percent reserve of gold certificates against bank deposits.

Treasury Secretary Henry H. Fowler said prompt action was needed to remove the cover requirement for three principal reasons:

• To allow expansion of cash as a form of domestic money supply.

• To remove all doubt that America's total gold stock was available to maintain the free international convertibility between the dollar and gold at $35 an ounce.

• To reflect in legislation the fact that the strength of the dollar depends upon the strength of the U. S. economy rather than upon a legal 25-percent reserve requirement against Federal Reserve notes.

Fowler said the normal increase in notes would absorb more than $500 million annually, and an additional $150 million or more would be absorbed every year for domestic artistic and industrial purposes. With only $1.3 billion of gold to draw upon under existing conditions, Fowler said, the United States had no more than two years grace before the gold supply ran out, assuming that no gold was needed for international monetary purposes. "Clearly, we cannot proceed on such an assumption," he said.

These arguments were expected to send the bill through Congress with minimal delay and opposition. Although the bill did become law quickly (on March 18), it was passed by surprisingly narrow margins. The House passed HR 14743 by a 199-190 roll-call vote after rejecting a motion to recommit (kill) the bill by a 188-206 roll call. Both votes were along party lines, with Democrats in favor and Republicans opposed. It had been anticipated that Republicans would use the bill as a vehicle to criticize the Johnson Administration economic policies but would vote for passage to free additional amounts of gold in the U. S. stock to meet foreign claims for the metal.

Republicans, however, voted heavily against the measure. The breakdown on the recommittal was: R 151-22; D 37-184 (ND 10-130; SD 27-54). On the passage vote it was: R 25-148; D 174-42; (ND 124-12; SD 50-30). The party division was true even in the dozen Western states where gold production might have been expected to have some bearing on the outcome. South Dakota had been the nation's leading gold-producing state for 20 years. Others were Utah, Arizona, Nevada, Alaska, Washington, California, Colorado, Montana, New Mexico, Idaho and Oregon in that order. The vote in those states on passage was R 3-28; D 29-7.

The removal of the 25-percent gold cover was opposed, mainly by Republicans, as offering only temporary relief for the widespread economic problems which were contributing to the nation's growing balance-of-payments deficit. Concern also was expressed by Members from Western gold-producing states who sought to strengthen confidence in the dollar by stimulating increased gold production.

The House Republican Policy Committee said it was concerned that removing the gold cover might be construed by the Administration as "sanctioning in advance the dissipation of our remaining gold supply in lieu of making the hard decisions which are necessary to restore international confidence in the dollar."

Final action on HR 14743 came March 14 when the Senate passed the bill by a 39-37 roll-call vote without amendment and sent it to the President.

On the passage vote, 30 Democrats and 9 Republicans voted in favor and 14 Democrats and 23 Republicans voted in opposition.

Passage came after three days of floor debate and amid growing concern over record gold-buying in Europe. The near-panic proportions of gold purchasing March 14 caused the closing of the London gold market March 15 and an emergency meeting in Washington March 16-17 of European and U. S. officials to plan major changes in the international monetary system. *(See preceding story.)*

During Senate action, supporters of the Administration bill generally accepted the critics' view that removal of the gold cover was only a stopgap measure that would not solve the country's economic problems. Continued deficits in both domestic and foreign spending were cited in debate as the main reasons for concern about the dollar and for the balance-of-payments deficit.

S&L Holding Companies

Additional federal controls over savings and loan holding companies were provided by legislation (S 1542—PL 90-255) enacted early in 1968.

The purpose of the bill was to give the Federal Savings and Loan Insurance Corp. (FSLIC), which was administered by the Federal Home Loan Bank Board (FHLBB), authority to protect savings and loan (S&L) associations from abuses by parent savings and loan holding companies. S 1542 in effect replaced the existing law dealing with S&L holding companies. That law—the 1959 Spence Act— limited the expansion of holding companies but did not provide strong regulatory powers to control the activities of the industry.

The 1968 legislation was requested several times by President Johnson, most recently in his Feb. 1 Economic Report. S 1542 was passed by the Senate in 1967 and by the House early in 1968.

Administration officials contended that much greater regulatory problems occurred with S&L associations that were controlled by holding companies than with associations not subject to holding-company control. The officials noted that although only about 12.5 percent of all assets of the savings and loan industry were owned by holding companies, the S&L associations which were owned by holding companies accounted for more than 60 percent of the "serious (financial) problem cases" before the FHLBB.

The increased regulatory powers conferred by the bill were said to be necessary to prevent holding companies from ruining S&L associations which they controlled. Holding companies could—and sometimes did—use the assets of controlled S&Ls to pay for activities in other areas. If these other activities ran into financial trouble, the S&L assets could be dipped into more deeply and the associations could be pressured to increase their earnings through financially shaky practices such as investing in speculative real estate. One proponent of the bill, Rep. Henry S. Reuss (D Wis.), contended that holding companies had been known to invest in racetrack and gambling operations. In addition, FHLBB officials said the existing Spence Act did not permit access to holding company books and records, which greatly limited regulation, and was not strong enough even to prevent evasion of the minimal controls that were in force.

Individual accounts at S&L associations were not directly threatened by failures because of FSLIC insurance against default. However, the financial resources of the FSLIC as well as public confidence in the S&L system could be impaired, officials contended.

There was relatively little controversy over the bill. Both Democrats and Republicans supported it, although some GOP House Members were critical of certain parts of the bill.

S&L holding companies were concentrated in a small number of states, primarily California (48), Ohio (14),

Background

Savings and loan associations had been part of the U. S. banking community since before 1900. The industry included federal associations, authorized by the Home Owner's Loan Corp. Act of 1933 (PL 73-43), and state chartered associations. All federal associations and most state associations were mutual organizations owned by savers through purchase of withdrawable shares in the association. Some states permitted stock associations that resembled ordinary business corporations except that the capital represented by the savers' stock was retained in the association as a guarantee for the payment of the savers' withdrawable shares. In recent years holding companies began buying the stock of stock associations at an increasing pace.

Spence Act. The growth of savings and loan holding companies prompted Congress in 1959 to enact a law (PL 86-374), known as the Spence Act after its sponsor, Rep. Brent Spence (D Ky. 1931-63), to halt the accelerating trend of acquisition of stock associations by S&L holding companies. The law prohibited existing S&L holding companies from acquiring any additional stock S&L institutions except in emergency situations to prevent failure of an association; however, new holding companies could be formed to control one association. Certain financial transactions between the associations and the parent holding company or its subsidiaries also were prohibited. The Spence Act did not prohibit an S&L holding company from acquiring additional businesses, such as banks, insurance companies, and real estate development corporations.

Federal officials who oversee S&L companies said that the Spence Act restriction, although helpful, had not been effective in preventing abuses in holding company operations.

FHLBB Report. The Spence Act required the Federal Home Loan Bank Board to survey the S&L holding company industry to determine if new legislation was required.

The FHLBB report was issued in 1960. The findings of the report, combined with the continuing rapid growth of S&L holding companies, led the FHLBB to recommend legislation in the 88th and 89th Congresses. No action was taken on the recommended bills.

President Johnson, in his Economic Messages for 1966, 1967, and 1968, recommended stronger regulation of savings and loan holding companies, but no action occurred. In 1966, however, Congress enacted other legislation (S 3158—PL 89-695) which gave federal officials new regulatory powers over certain financial institutions, including savings and loan associations. One provision of the bill amended the Spence Act to permit holding companies to control more than one federally insured institution, provided the FHLBB deemed it advisable in order to prevent a failure.

Texas (7), Illinois (11) and Colorado (5). These states had 85 of the 98 companies in existence at the end of 1966.

Provisions. As signed by the President, Feb. 14, S 1542 (PL 90-255):

Required S&L holding companies to register with the FHLBB and issue periodic reports; gave the FHLBB investigative and examination authority over the holding companies.

Tightened several loopholes in the Spence Act to prohibit self-dealing financial transactions between a controlled S&L and the parent holding company or its subsidiaries or any affiliate.

Required holding companies controlling more than one S&L to divest themselves of unrelated activities within two years with an additional three-year period allowed upon FHLBB approval. (Twelve of the 98 companies would be affected.)

Gave the FHLBB additional authority over the debt structure of the holding companies by requiring a holding company to obtain FHLBB approval for debts equal to more than 15 percent of the company's net worth. Broadly defined "debt" to include any note or other instrument "commonly used as evidence of indebtedness" or any contract or agreement requiring the eventual payment of money.

Gave the FHLBB in the case of a holding company with only one association and which was primarily in another line of business, authority to exercise a veto over dividends paid by the subsidiary S&L.

Prohibited future holding companies from acquiring S&Ls in two or more states, but exempted three existing interstate holding companies.

Repealed the Spence Act provision restricting the acquisition of S&Ls by holding companies, on the theory it was no longer necessary in view of additional controls given to the FHLBB.

Authorized action in a U. S. district court to enforce compliance with the law or to require divestiture of unrelated activities.

Provided penalties for any company of up to $1,000 in fines for each day a violation of the law continued. Provided penalties for any individual of up to $10,000 in fines and/or up to one year in prison.

Interest Rate Controls

As it had done in 1967, Congress again extended for one year a law (PL 89-597) which gave federal banking regulatory agencies more flexible authority to set interest rates for fixed maturity (time) deposits in banks and savings and loan institutions. The Administration requested the legislation but wanted a longer extension.

The law had been passed at a time when investors were withdrawing their funds from savings and loan institutions, which served the home mortgage market, to invest at higher rates of interest in banks. The law was intended to protect S&Ls, the principal source of home financing.

Except for a minor disagreement over the length of the extension, the only controversy over the bill arose when amendments were proposed in committee in both chambers to direct the Federal Reserve Board to buy directly obligations of Government agencies when such action would aid the housing market. Such activity was permitted but not directed under PL 89-597. The Administration opposed this provision which was dropped from the bill in the Senate by a close 46-45 roll call.

Provisions. As signed by the President, Sept. 21, S 3133:

Extended for one year, through Sept. 21, 1969, the 1966 law (PL 89-597) giving federal bank regulatory agencies flexible authority to set different limits on the interest rates that banks and other financial institutions could pay on different types and amounts of fixed maturity (time) deposits.

Gave the Federal Reserve Board, the Federal Home Loan Bank Board and the Federal Deposit Insurance Corp. added authority to prevent deceptive advertising for time and savings deposits.

Broadened the assets thrift institutions may count in meeting reserve requirements and allowed the Federal Home Loan Bank Board to set reserve requirements ranging from 4 to 10 percent of assets. (Existing law provided a range of 4 to 8 percent.)

Eased prepayment requirements on insurance premiums by insured thrift institutions.

Authorized Federal Reserve banks to accept as loan collateral from member banks the direct obligations of federal agencies.

Made permanent the Federal Reserve Board's authority to purchase on the open market the obligations of any Government agency.

Made permanent the provision of PL 89-597 which set 10 percent as the maximum reserves that the Federal Reserve could require member banks to hold against time or savings deposits (the minimum was 3 percent).

Bank Security Measures

Increasing numbers of bank robberies prompted Congress in 1968 to enact a bill (HR 15345—PL 90-389) authorizing establishment of security standards to protect banking institutions against robbery and theft. President Johnson in his crime message to Congress requested enactment of the legislation.

There had been a continuing increase in bank robberies since World War II. The House Government Operations Committee in a 1964 report called "Crimes Against Banking Institutions" said "there are no federal supervisory agency regulations which specify any standards or requirements for banking institution structures, design, vaults, safes, alarm systems, or for any security procedures, devices or means." The report said federal supervisory agencies considered security of financial institutions matters of industry self-regulation. The report concluded that although the federal supervisory agencies believe "the banking institutions have done a creditable job in the area of crime prevention," that belief "must be viewed in the light of the fact that the bank crime rate keeps rising."

Justice Department figures showed that bank robberies increased 154 percent from 1960 to 1967. The figures also showed a 13.5 percent increase from September 1967 through February 1968 compared to the same period a year earlier. A Federal Bureau of Investigation study showed that "of the 2,551 institutions victimized during 1967 only 374 were equipped with cameras, 18 had microphones and speakers and 142 employed guards." The committee report on HR 15345 said that "the cost of a 'package' of security devices suggested by the Justice Department, including a camera, robbery alarm system,

microphone and speaker system, and ADT (the American District Telegraph Protection Service), would involve an initial installation cost of $2,115 and annual maintenance charges of $475." Total financial losses from violations of the federal bank robbery statute in 1967 were approximately $15 million. During that same year 23 persons were killed as a result of crimes against banks, while an additional 61 persons were injured. About 40,000 institutions would be affected by the rules.

Provisions. As signed July 7 by the President, HR 15345 (PL 90-389), the Bank Protection Act:

Required the Comptroller of the Currency, the Board of Governors of the Federal Reserve System, the Federal Deposit Insurance Corp. and the Federal Home Loan Bank Board each to establish minimum security-system standards for banking institutions under their jurisdictions as a deterrent to robbers.

Required that the standards be set up within six months of enactment of the bill and cover security devices and procedures that were "reasonable" in cost.

Required the agencies to establish time limits for compliance with the standards.

Required the supervisory agencies to determine if reductions of insurance premiums, based on installation of security systems, were feasible, and to report the findings to Congress within two years after the Act passed.

Set a $100-a-day civil penalty for institutions which violated the Act.

Authorized the Federal Home Loan Bank Board to appoint the Federal Savings and Loan Insurance Corp. (FSLIC) receiver of state-chartered savings and loan institutions placed in receivership or closed by state authorities.

Securities Disclosure

Congress passed a bill (S 510—PL 90-439) to give increased protection to stockholders in companies that outside groups attempt to take over through cash tender offers or other purchases of stock. The bill's central provision required disclosure of information by a person making a cash tender offer. The information would have to be of a nature that would help the stockholder in deciding whether to sell.

The cash tender offer has been used with increasing frequency as a method to acquire control of publicly held corporations. In a cash tender offer, a person offers to buy shares of a company, usually at a price above the current market price. Stockholders who accept the offer tender their securities for purchase, and the person making the offer obligates himself to buy all or part of the shares. A key advantage of such a strategy over other means of gaining control, such as a proxy fight, is that the person making the offer is able to operate in total secrecy, using a bank or a brokerage office as an agent for buying the shares. The bill was supported by the SEC and generally by the securities industry.

Provisions. As signed into law July 29, S 510:

Required a person or group making a tender offer to purchase a substantial amount of securities of a corporation to disclose information that would be helpful to stockholders in deciding whether or not to sell their securities. Specified that disclosure was required in cases where purchase of the securities would result in ownership of more than 10 percent of the corporation's securities by the person or group.

Required the Securities and Exchange Commission (SEC) to specify the exact information to be disclosed but provided that it should cover the identity, background and plans of the purchaser and sources of funds. The identity of a bank providing credit could be kept confidential.

Permitted stockholders who accepted the purchase offer to withdraw their acceptance during the seven days after the offer was made. Also permitted withdrawal after 60 days under SEC regulations if the securities were being tied up by a purchaser while he decided whether or not to buy them.

Required any person or group acquiring the ownership of more than 10 percent of a company's securities to disclose similar information.

Authorized the SEC to require a corporation purchasing its own securities on the open market to disclose information which the SEC considered in the public interest. Purchase of shares in a corporation by a pension plan for the company's employees did not come under the act if the plan were operated independently of the corporation.

Specified that the requirements of the bill applied to securities registered under the Securities Exchange Act of 1934.

Credit Union Amendments

Congress enacted legislation (HR 14907—PL 90-375) revising the Federal Credit Union Act to extend the maturity on secured loans from five to ten years, to raise the limit on unsecured loans, and to otherwise liberalize the lending policy of federal credit unions.

The Federal Credit Union Act of 1934 authorized the Federal Government to charter credit unions—cooperative associations of persons with a common bond (located in the same neighborhood, working for the same employer, etc.) designed to serve as a savings and loan facility for members. The Act, which also governed the operating procedure of the federally chartered credit unions, was amended a number of times with major changes occurring in 1959 and 1964.

Provisions. As signed July 5 by the President, HR 14907 (PL 90-375):

Extended the maximum maturity on secured loans made by federal credit unions from five to ten years. (The provision, which did not affect the maximum five-year maturity on unsecured loans, was expected to be used only for large purchase-price items—such as a home improvement—which a credit union borrower would have difficulty paying off over five years.)

Permitted federal credit unions to invest in state-chartered central credit unions which under existing law they were forbidden to do.

Authorized federal credit unions to purchase from any liquidating credit union (such as on a military base that was being closed) the notes of that credit union even though any member whose loan note was being sold would not become a member of the purchasing credit union. Once the note had been repaid, the purchasing union could not extend additional financing to the bor-

rower unless he was within the common bond of the purchasing credit union. Such purchases were to be limited to 5 percent of the unimpaired capital and surplus of the purchasing credit union.

Permitted the board of directors of a federal credit union to delegate borrowing authority to the executive committee.

Authorized a federal credit union to make unsecured loans equal to 2½ percent of its unimpaired capital and surplus up to a maximum of $2,500; specified that small unions with unimpaired capital and surplus of less than $8,000 could make unsecured loans of up to $200. (Existing law limited unsecured loans to 10 percent of unimpaired capital and surplus, up to a maximum of $750.)

Required semi-annual audits of federal credit unions. (Existing law required quarterly audits.)

Authorized the director of the Bureau of Federal Credit Unions to conduct, either directly or indirectly (such as through grants to a college), programs to train persons who will operate credit unions or consumer counseling programs to serve the poor. Authorized demonstration, pilot and similar projects to promote credit unions and consumer counseling services for the poor. Authorized appropriations of $300,000 in fiscal 1970 and $1 million in fiscal 1971. (This provision was intended to allow the continuation of Project Moneywise, a pilot program initiated under a grant from the Office of Economic Opportunity to provide training in consumer counseling and credit union management for selected residents of low-income neighborhoods. The purpose of the training, which was to be given by staff members of the Bureau of Federal Credit Unions, was to place low-income groups seeking credit union charters on a comparable footing with charter applicants from non-poverty areas.)

Permitted the director of the Bureau of Federal Credit Unions to accept unconditional gifts of money. This was to enable the Bureau to obtain money from groups wishing to aid credit unions in low-income areas.

Other Bills

MUTUAL FUNDS. Enactment of legislation to broaden federal regulation of mutual fund sales was blocked by continued opposition from the mutual fund industry. The bill, which had been proposed in 1967 by the Securities and Exchange Commission (SEC), passed the Senate in mid-year but died in the House Interstate and Foreign Commerce Committee. The bill (S 3724) passed by the Senate contained most of the provisions of an SEC draft bill. However, the SEC was not successful in persuading the Senate to prohibit front-end loads—installment plans in which up to one-half of an investor's payments in the first year are deducted for sales charges. Nor did the Senate set a flat 5 percent limit on sales commissions, as the SEC proposed. However, the bill did provide limits on the front-end load and sales commission and allowed shareholders or the SEC to ask a federal court to determine the "reasonableness" of fees paid to investment advisers.

The bill died when the House Interstate and Foreign Commerce Committee in September voted not to consider it. The Committee's Subcommittee on Commerce and Finance had decided a day earlier not to take further action on the bill. House Members had been receiving heavy mail against the proposed legislation; it came mostly from brokers and salesmen who said the bill would drive them out of business. The campaign reportedly was organized by the Assn. of Mutual Fund Sponsors.

INSTITUTIONAL INVESTORS STUDY. A measure enacted in 1968 authorized the Securities and Exchange Commission to make a study of institutional investors and their effect on the stock market. The measure (S J Res 160—PL 90-438) authorized $875,000 for the study, which was to be completed by Sept. 1, 1969.

OVER-THE-COUNTER SECURITIES. An Administration-backed bill (S 1299—PL 90-437) to extend the authority of the Federal Reserve Board over margin requirements to the over-the-counter (OTC) securities market was passed by Congress. The bill was supported by virtually all of the interested federal regulatory agencies and trade associations. The new law had the effect of restricting the previously unlimited amount of credit banks could extend for the purchase of OTC securities—those not listed on an exchange. The Securities and Exchange Act of 1934 gave the Federal Reserve Board power to regulate both the credit that brokers extended on securities registered on an exchange and credit that banks and other lenders extended for the purchase of such securities. At the time the Act was passed, OTC stocks were not considered important because the number traded was relatively insignificant. Since then, the dollar volume of OTC securities had risen from one-sixth to an estimated three-fifths of the dollar volume of listed securities.

Under S 1299, the margin requirement (down payment by the purchaser) was fixed at 80 percent, meaning that the purchaser had to pay at least 80 percent of the value of the stock in order to purchase it. The broker arranged for payment of the remainder as credit. Prior to enactment of the bill, the margin requirement had been 70 percent.

BANKRUPTCY REFEREES. The Senate recommitted to the Judiciary Committee, by a 62-9 roll-call vote, a bill (S 1316) to provide an extended term of office, a fixed retirement age and increased retirement benefits for court-appointed referees in bankruptcy cases. The bill was requested by the Judicial Branch but contained retirement benefits which were objectionable to the Civil Service Commission.

Miscellaneous Economic Legislation

A major effort was made by Congress in 1965 to bring economic development to depressed areas of the nation. Two pieces of legislation were enacted toward this end. One of them, which was the first Great Society measure to clear the 89th Congress, authorized slightly over $1 billion to help the 12-state Appalachian region. Much of the money ($840 million) was for development of highways in the area. A basic transportation system within the region was considered essential to economic development and thus was accorded special attention in the legislation. The second bill authorized help for economic development in other parts of the nation. It authorized $3.25 billion for grants and loans for public works, development and technical assistance and other projects.

Congress was unable to resolve controversies in another important area—copyrights. The legislators considered a bill to revise the existing 1909 copyright statute but did not pass it. The House passed the bill in 1967 but opposition to some provisions was strong enough to prevent the Senate from acting.

Controversy centered, in particular, on provisions dealing with community antenna television systems (CATV). A CATV system involves construction of an antenna to receive distant television signals which then are relayed into the homes of subscribers who pay a fee for the service. The issue was whether CATV owners were liable for royalty fees.

The copyright legislation resulted from more than a decade of studies sponsored by the Copyright Office of the Library of Congress, which also drafted the proposed legislation considered by Congress. The 1909 statute had become an anachronism over the years as radio, television, sound recordings, photocopying, and other new developments came into existence in the half-century following the law's enactment.

Congress also was unable to resolve a controversial problem in the related field of patents. The issue was how to establish a uniform Government patent policy on property rights to inventions and discoveries financed by federal funds.

CONGRESS enacted several pieces of legislation to assist small business. In general, these bills provided additional funding for small business programs. Several bills to give extra aid were passed in 1965. A major bill, passed in 1966, provided both temporary and permanent help needed to keep the Small Business Administration functioning. The permanent aid was extended by ending the existing authorizations used by SBA and creating two new revolving funds: one for most disaster loans and the other for regular SBA activities. The SBA had experienced a heavy financial drain because of an unusually large number of natural disasters in the mid-1960s. In 1966 Congress also passed a bill increasing the SBA's administrative control over small business investment companies (SBICs) which the agency helps to establish. A 1967 bill that was enacted increased the amount of money which SBICs could obtain from the SBA. The same bill also authorized a substantial increase—$650 million—in the funds available to the SBA for regular lending activities.

LEGISLATION enacted in 1967 was intended to provide substantial assistance to noncommercial broadcasting. However, the all-important question of financing was not permanently settled. Until this issue was resolved—and it was not before President Johnson left office—the importance of the 1967 legislation could not be assessed. The bill established a Corporation for Public Broadcasting, a nonprofit and nongovernmental entity, to provide money for noncommercial radio and television. The proposal had wide support in Congress but was controversial because of the fear that the corporation might be influenced by political or governmental pressures.

The main problem was to create a financing mechanism. Many recommendations presented to Congress suggested that the law establish a permanent source of funds—such as a tax on television sales—which would be earmarked for the corporation. Without a permanent and independent source of funds, it was doubted whether broadcasters would feel free to present new and controversial programs which might offend one or another individual or organization and cost them their financing the following year. Congress nevertheless rejected this approach. It decided that financing should be provided, at least initially, through the normal Congressional appropriations process, under which Government activities are subject to review annually by Members of Congress. An appropriation of $9 million was authorized for the first year, fiscal 1968, but the Johnson Administration, moving slowly, eventually had to ask that the authorization be transferred to the following year, fiscal 1969. The Administration said it planned to propose a permanent, long-range financing arrangement, but it failed to do so before leaving office.

In other legislation, Congress extended the Renegotiation Act in 1966 and 1968 and, in the latter year, included numerous riders on the bill. In 1965, it enacted a little-noticed program to help businessmen and industries gain access to the growing body of scientific and technical information available from both federal and private research and development. The legislation was called the State Technical Services Act. Congress also dealt with application of the antitrust laws to professional sports (but enacted only one statute: to exempt a proposed football league merger from the antitrust laws, to newspapers, and to banks which cooperated to reduce the balance-of-payments deficit.

Chronology

of Legislation

(NOTE: The following chronology is organized by subject matter. When action occurred in different years, it is reported entirely within the story about the bill and not in different places in the chronology.)

Copyright Revisions

Congress was unable to agree on major revisions in the nation's copyright laws. A bill to revise the 1909 copyright statute was passed by the House in 1967 but died when the Senate failed to act on it before adjournment of the 90th Congress. *(Congress and the Nation, Vol. I, p. 658.)*

Extensive hearings in 1965 revealed so many conflicting views on how the existing copyright law should be revised that Congress put off action. Although enough changes were made in the pending bill to get it through the House in the 90th Congress, sufficient opposition remained to prevent final enactment.

For lack of a consensus, Congress in 1965, 1967 and 1968 enacted stop-gap legislation which extended the renewal term of any copyright due to expire prior to the date specified in each bill. The 1968 bill extended through Dec. 31, 1969, the renewal term of any copyright scheduled to expire before that time.

Copyright is the right of an author to control the reproduction and dissemination of his work after it has been disclosed. Copyright does not preclude others from using the ideas or information contained in the work; it pertains to the literary, musical, artistic or graphic form in which the concepts are expressed. The primary purposes of copyright legislation are to foster the creation and dissemination of works for the public benefit, and to enable authors to reap due reward for their efforts.

1965-66 Action. A bill drafted by the Copyright Office of the Library of Congress was introduced in early 1965 (S 1006; HR 4347). House Judiciary Subcommittee No. 3 heard more than 150 witnesses during the year. The hearings revealed substantial differences about the bill. *(See box on background for events leading up to 1965.)*

In 1966, the Subcommittee held about 100 hours of closed sessions during which HR 4347 was extensively amended to meet objections raised during the 1965 hearings. The Judiciary Committee reported the bill as amended in October, but no further action occurred

in the 89th Congress. There had been virtually no action in the Senate.

1967-68 Action. A new bill (HR 2512) was introduced in the 90th Congress early in 1967. It was almost identical with HR 4347 and was reported in early March by the Judiciary Committee. The House passed HR 2512 in April by a 379-29 roll-call vote and sent it to the Senate where it was to remain through the rest of the 90th Congress. Controversy over a few provisions, especially those relating to community antenna television (CATV) systems, was the main reason for the inaction.

As in past years, the most serious differences were over the royalty requirements for jukebox owners and CATV stations. The House resolved the jukebox issue, apparently to the satisfiction of all involved. But, at the last minute, the House deleted all provisions on CATV and left that question up to the Senate. A CATV system involves the construction of a sensitive antenna capable of receiving distant television signals which are then relayed into the homes of subscribers who pay a fee for the service. The issue was whether the CATV owners were liable for royalty fees. The issue was not resolved. A 1968 Supreme Court decision, *Fortnightly Corp. v. United Artists, Television Inc.,* held that CATV operators did not infringe on the copyrights of the original broadcasters under the terms of the 1909 law. The effect of the decision was to free CATV operators from any liability for royalty payments unless Congress acted to change the law.)

The major beneficiaries of HR 2512, as it passed the House, appeared to be authors, composers and publishers. For them, the bill: extended the length of copyright protection to the life of the author plus 50 years, as opposed to the existing 56-year total: increased the royalties phonograph record makers must pay composers; required jukebox operators (machine owners) to pay royalties for the first time; relaxed the requirement that nondramatic works by an American must be printed in the United States to qualify for U.S. copyright protection and allowed type for books to be set abroad; removed the blanket exemption for all nonprofit performances of a nondramatic literary or musical work; allowed the accidental omission of copyright indication without loss of protection; and raised the maximum damages for copyright infringement to $20,000. However, the bill removed the author's unlimited protection for an unpublished work.

For educators, the bill codified the doctrine of fair use, the free use of portions of a copyrighted work for such purposes as teaching, research, comment or criticism. It also exempted from copyright protection any work used in classroom activities and specified that damages against a teacher who was guilty of copyright infringement when he honestly believed he was within the bounds of fair use could be remitted.

For scholars, the bill permitted institutions such as libraries to copy unpublished works and to send the reproductions to a similar institution for its archives.

For broadcasters, the bill authorized the making of one copy of a work for subsequent broadcasting and gave certain exemptions from royalties to educational television (ETV).

MAJOR PROVISIONS. The major provisions of HR 2512 as passed by the House were as follows:

Duration of Term. The bill provided for copyright protection during the creator's life, plus 50 years after which the work passed into the public domain. The 1909 law provided for a term of 28 years with a renewal term of another 28 years by the creator of his heirs. The life-plus-50-years provision was in line with the term in most countries of the world, including all of Western Europe. Works in their first 28-year term on Jan. 1, 1969, could renew for an additional term of 47 years, bringing the total protected time to 75 years. Works in their second 28-year term on that date were given an extension without application to bring the total protection to 75 years.

Reversion. Creators were permitted under the bill to terminate a transfer of copyright ownership or right of first publication after 35 years. Under the 1909 law, the copyright reverted to the creator after 28 years, at the time he applied for renewal.

Fair Use. The bill codified the doctrine of fair use for the first time. Before, it was based solely on judicial decisions. An example of a situation in which a question of fair use might arise was the photocopying of copyrighted material by college professors for distribution to their classes. The 1965 bill, as introduced, merely mentioned that "fair use of a copyrighted work is not an infringement of copyright." At the urging principally of educators, HR 2512 defined the elements of fair use to include: "(1) the purpose and character of the use; (2) the nature of the copyrighted work; (3) the amount and substantiality of the portion used in relation to the copyrighted work as a whole; and (4) the effect of the use upon the potential market for or value of the copyrighted work." In addition, the House Judiciary Committee devoted several pages of its report to explaining "legislative intent" in the fair-use doctrine.

The bill also specified that courts could remit damages brought against a teacher who was forced to bear the cost of proving that he believed his infringement was covered by fair use.

Phonograph Records. The bill increased the royalties record makers must pay from 2 cents to 2.5 cents per record or .5 cent per minute of playing time, whichever was greater. The 1965 bill, as introduced, would have raised the royalties to 3 cents or 1 cent per minute.

Jukeboxes. Jukebox operators (the owner of the machine, not the proprietor of the establishment in which the machine was located) were required to pay royalties of $8 per jukebox annually to the Register of Copyrights, who was to turn the money over to a federal court for distribution to the copyright owners.

CATV. All provisions relating to CATV were removed from the bill by a House floor amendment, thus leaving in effect the existing situation that CATV systems were fully subject to copyright liability. (However, a Supreme Court ruling the following year reversed this situation. *See above.*)

Sound Recordings. Sound recordings, as distinct from phonograph records, were added to the list of protected works for the first time. Sound recordings were defined as "an aggregate of musical, spoken or other sounds that have been fixed in a tangible form." The bill provided that the owner of a copyrighted sound recording did not have an exclusive right of public performance but had certain rights against an offender who captured his exact sounds.

Background on Copyright Law

Statutes for copyright protection were among the earliest laws of the United States, the first law having been enacted in 1790. In 1909, all prior statutes were replaced by a single comprehensive copyright law, which expanded the scope of copyright protection from written and dramatic works to musical and pictorial works. The 1909 law was codified and re-enacted in 1947 as Title 17 of the U.S. Code.

That the 1909 law had become anachronistic was indisputable. It took no account of developments over 58 years in such fields as commercial and educational radio and television, motion pictures, sound recordings, photocopying, printing, microfilming and computer storage.

Several futile attempts were made over the years to revise the law in light of new technology. The difficulty in passing any revision came, according to Rep. Robert W. Kastenmeier (D Wis.), House floor manager of the 1967 bill, "because on the copyright law the views became diverse and polarized over the years and because new developments left Congress with few points of reference in the old law."

In addition, a legion of pressure groups developed on every issue within the law. And, to make matters even more difficult, many groups, wary of what would probably be a long wait before another revision of the law, pressed Congress to foresee the future in such barely developed fields as computer storage, community antenna television, educational television and satellite transmissions.

Beginning in 1955, the Copyright Office of the Library of Congress sponsored 35 studies analyzing the major problems. In 1961, the Library of Congress submitted to Congress the Report of the Register of Copyrights on the General Revision of the Copyright Law.

In 1962, Congress extended the renewal term of existing copyrights through 1965, to allow time for consideration of copyright law revisions. The law was extended in 1965, 1967 and 1968 through Dec. 31, 1969.

In light of extensive comments on the 1961 report by consultants and representatives of various interest groups, the Copyright Office substantially revised its recommendations and prepared a preliminary draft revision bill, which was introduced (S 3008, HR 11947) in the 88th Congress for purposes of consideration and comment.

As a result of comments from interested parties, new legislation was drafted by the Copyright Office and introduced (S 1006, HR 4347) in Congress Feb. 4, 1965.

ETV. The bill gave certain limited exemptions from paying royalties to educational television (ETV). The performance had to be nonprofit and "a regular part of the systematic instructional activities of a government body or a nonprofit educational institution." In addition, the transmission had to be intended primarily for reception by: (1) classrooms or "similar places normally devoted to instruction"; (2) disabled persons; or (3) government bodies such as the armed forces. The bill allowed exempt ETV broadcasts to be transmitted over an unlimited area and permitted ETV stations to make an unlimited number of ephemeral recordings.

"Ephemeral Recordings." Commercial broadcasting organizations were permitted to make a single "ephemeral recording" of a copyrighted work for their own subsequent transmission as long as the recording was destroyed or preserved exclusively for archival purposes after six months. An "ephemeral recording" was defined in the report as a copy or record of a copyrighted work made for the purposes of a later transmission by a broadcasting organization legally entitled to transmit the original work. An example given was a recording of a television program for a later showing in a different time zone or as a rerun.

Archives and Collections. The bill added a provision, not in the 1965 bill as introduced, to allow nonprofit archives and similar institutions to copy rare works under certain conditions for deposit in another similar institution. Thus, a university library holding an unpublished manuscript could copy it for deposit in another university's library.

Government Publications. The bill continued the existing prohibition against copyright protection of a work by an employee of the Federal Government within the scope of his official duties. The employee could copyright a work done on his own volition outside his official duties even though it pertained to his official work. The Government was not precluded from receiving or holding copyrights transferred to it.

Foreign Manufacturing. The bill modified but did not eliminate the existing requirement that English-language books and periodicals be manufactured in the United States in order to obtain full copyright protection,

except that a limited number of foreign copies could be imported. The import limit was increased from 1,500 to 2,000 copies. (The 1965 bill as introduced would have raised it to 3,500.) The requirements were made to apply only to nondramatic, literary material, the author of which was an American domiciled in the United States. The bill also clarified what constituted "manufacture in the United States." Works imported for government use or intended for nonprofit scholarly, educational or religious use or written in Braille were exempt from the requirement.

Damages and Infringement. The maximum statutory damages for copyright infringement were raised from $10,000 to $20,000. The maximum penalty for criminal infringement was set at $2,500 and one year in prison for a first offense and $10,000 and one year in prison for a subsequent conviction.

Unpublished Works. All works, published or unpublished, were covered under the bill. This did away with the situation in which unpublished works were covered by "common law."

Notice of Copyright. The requirement that published copies indicate their copyright (name and date) was retained. But the bill provided that accidental omission or error would not forfeit the copyright. Innocent infringers, misled by the omission or error, could not be held liable.

Other Nonprofit Exemptions. The bill removed the blanket exemption from royalty payments for all nonprofit performances of a nondramatic literary or musical work. Instead, it stated that not only was there to be no profit motive but also the performers could not be paid if the performance was to be exempt. The work was exempt, however, if the net proceeds were "used exclusively for educational, religious or charitable purposes," unless the copyright holder forbade such fundraising performances by giving notice of at least seven days. Works in the course of a religious service were exempt from all royalties.

Fees. The bill retained the schedule of Copyright Office fees established in 1965 by PL 89-297. *(See box.)*

Copyright Office Fees

Congress in 1965 enacted a bill (HR 2853—PL 89-297) increasing copyright fees, for the first time since 1948, to enable the Copyright Office to recover a larger share of its costs. The bill was expected to raise the Copyright Office's income to 80 percent of expenditures in the first fiscal year following enactment. (The Office was appropriated $2,021,000 for fiscal 1966.) The percentage of recovered costs was in line with the 75-percent recovery provided in a bill raising Patent Office fees (HR 4185—PL 89-83.)

Provisions. As signed by the President, HR 2853 contained the following major provisions:

Increased the maximum price for an entire set of the Catalog of Copyright Entries from $25 to $75.

Increased the majority of registration fees from $4 to $6.

Increased the fee for renewing a copyright from $2 to $4.

Provided, for the first time, a $3 fee for recording a "notice of intention to use" a musical composition and increased from $2 to $3 the fee for recording a "notice of use" of a composition.

Patent Legislation

Congress in 1965 passed a bill increasing patent fees for the first time since 1932. However, action on proposals to establish a uniform Government patent policy on property rights to inventions and discoveries obtained through the expenditure of federal funds was not completed during the Johnson years. A basic conflict over who should benefit from the Government-financed research was at the heart of the problem.

PATENT OFFICE FEES. Congress passed an Administration-backed bill (HR 4185—PL 89-83) increasing patent fees in order to enable the Patent Office to recover a larger share of its costs and to expedite the patent process. It was estimated that the new schedule of fees would increase from 30 percent to 75 percent the amount of Patent Office costs recouped through patent fees. The new fees were expected to increase the Patent Office's annual income from $8.9 million to $23.4 million.

However, Congress rejected an Administration proposal that part of the income be collected through "maintenance fees," which would be charged at the end of the fifth, ninth and thirteenth year after a patent was issued as a prerequisite for keeping the patent in force for the full 17-year term. Instead, HR 4185 provided for a higher schedule of other fees than recommended by the Administration.

Provisions—As signed into law, HR 4185:

Increased the fees for filing for each original patent or reissue from $30 to $65 and for issuing each original patent from $30 to $100.

Established a new $100 fee for issuing a reissue patent (i.e., republishing a patent to correct technical errors).

Increased the first appeal fee on notice of appeal from $25 to $50.

Required federal departments, agencies and officers to pay the established fees.

Increased the fee for filing an original application to register a trademark from $25 to $35, and increased other trademark fees.

PATENT POLICY. Proposed patent legislation concerned the problem of who should have the ownership and rights to use of inventions and discoveries made through the expenditure of public funds: those who invented or developed an invention or discovery under a federal contract, or the public in general which, through taxes, had financed the research and experimentation.

Those arguing that the contractor should have the principal rights suggested that the added incentive of holding an exclusive license or the patent and the profits derived therefrom would encourage development and rapid marketing of new discoveries.

Those supporting public ownership contended that the former procedure could result in monopoly, unfair advantage for a particular company, and unjustified costs to the public for use of the finished product or service resulting from the discovery or invention.

Prior to World War II most research was financed by private funds. The Federal Government generally retained property rights on inventions arising from research and development which it sponsored and paid for. During the war, however, the Government began granting patent rights to various private companies which were engaged in Government research, while retaining a royalty-free license for Government use of the inventions.

No uniform patent policy existed until 1963, when President Kennedy in a memorandum and statement on Government patent policy established guidelines for all departments and agencies. The guidelines provided generally for giving the patent to the contractor, with the Government retaining a royalty-free license; the Government was to hold the patent on inventions from R & D on products and processes intended for general public use, in public health and welfare, in fields in which there was little privately supported research and in Government-owned research facilities. Various agencies and departments interpreted the memorandum differently, and a variety of patent policies resulted.

The Senate Judiciary Committee in 1966 reported a bill (S 1809), on which hearings had been held in 1965, which generally resolved this dispute in terms of existing policy, i.e., in favor of the contractor. The bill was reported on Aug. 16, rather late in the year to expect House action even if the Senate passed it, and backers

of S 1809 decided not to push for Senate action after Senate Majority Whip Russell B. Long (D La.) announced that he would filibuster rather than let the bill go through. Long for several years had been a critic of what he called the Government's "giveaway" policy on patents arising from research funded in whole or in part by federal money.

A second controversy arose over the standards of patentability. The Supreme Court, for the first time since passage of the Patent Act of 1952, considered several patent cases on the merits and found that the Patent Office and the courts had drifted far apart in the standards they applied to patents. The Office tended to be too lenient in granting patents, the Court said, adding that the monopoly afforded by a patent should be awarded sparingly.

The third major controversy was over the operation of the Office and of the patent system generally. At the end of 1966, the backlog of pending applications at the Office was more than 200,000, and the average time of pendency was two and one-half years, with some applications pending for from five to 10 years. The Office awarded patents on most applications.

On April 9, 1965, President Johnson by Executive Order established a Commission on the Patent System to recommend steps to "ensure that the patent system will be more effective in serving the public interest in view of the complex and rapidly changing technology of our times." It was charged with "determining how well the patent system currently serves our national needs and international goals, with devising possible improvements, and with recommending any legislation required to strengthen the system."

On Dec. 2, 1966, the Commission released its findings and made 35 recommendations for improvement of the patent system. Among the major changes recommended by the Commission were (1) institution of a "first-to-file" system for determining which inventor had priority when two or more applications on the same invention had been filed; (2) institution of informal preliminary filing procedures; (3) requirement that information in an application be disclosed to the public within 24 months from the date of filing; (4) institution of a deferred examining system if the Patent Office could not cope with workloads; and (5) making the life of the patent 20 years from filing of the application rather than 17 years from issuance of the patent. A number of other recommended changes were aimed at making American procedure consistent with foreign practices, with a view toward the establishment of a universal patent. Others dealt with judicial review of patent decisions, infringement and Patent Office operations. The Commission purposely made no recommendations concerning the rights to inventions resulting from Government-financed work. It also recommended that computer programs not be granted patents, and that design and plant patents be discontinued.

Administration Bill. These recommendations were embodied in the Patent Reform Act of 1967, an Administration draft bill. Other proposals of the Commission were not included.

In submitting the draft bill to Congress Feb. 21, 1967, Mr. Johnson said "modernization of the patent system is long overdue. This nation which has reached unparalleled industrial and technological heights is still operating under a patent system that has remained unchanged for the past 130 years." He noted it sometimes took an inventor two and a half years or often much longer to receive a patent, that inventors often faced great expense to secure a patent, that innovations took far too long to benefit the public and that international trade was hindered by lack of uniformity in patent policy. Although draft legislation was introduced in both chambers, it did not progress beyond the hearings stage.

Appalachia Aid, 1965

Passage of S 3, President Johnson's Appalachian Regional Development Act, authorized $1,092,400,000 for development of the economically depressed 12-state Appalachian region. The Act (PL 89-4) was the first Great Society measure to clear the 89th Congress. President Johnson proposed the assistance program in 1964, and at a news conference in November of that year said that Appalachian aid was a high priority item which should receive quick attention in 1965.

Although the Senate approved an Appalachian bill in 1964, by a 45-13 roll call, the House did not act on a companion bill. Supporters in the House said a majority favored the program, but it was not certain that enough members could be produced in the closing days of the 88th Congress to approve the measure. *(Congress and the Nation, Vol. I, p. 1330)*

The 1965 bill, slightly amended in the Senate and passed without change by the House, was opposed by a majority of Republicans in both chambers. In both the Senate and House, the roll calls on passage were among the key votes of the session. In the Senate, the vote was **62-22;** in the House it was **257-165.** Several proposals to expand the bill to other regions were headed off in the Senate by promises from the Democratic leadership that the Administration was working on other regional

APPALACHIA
1965

development proposals that probably would be submitted to Congress in the near future. (Congress later in the year enacted another bill which provided aid to other areas of the nation. *See following story.*)

Republicans called S 3 "a boondoggle" and "pork barrel" and charged that the White House had ordered the Democrats to get the bill through the House without change to avoid having to send it back to the Senate and perhaps to a conference.

The purpose of the Appalachia-aid bill was to help the Appalachia region, one of the nation's poorest, to emerge permanently from a condition of backwardness and poverty. Toward this end, the bill relied on two major approaches: (1) creation of a federal-state regional commission to help draw up coordinated regional economic development plans for the area; and (2) authorization of special federal financial aid to help the area obtain the primary public facilities needed as a basis for economic expansion (such as roads and health facilities), and to help the area restore some of the natural resources ravaged by neglect and misuse (such as timber and water resources and land ruined by strip mining or poor agricultural practices).

S 3 established an Appalachian Regional Commission to coordinate the projects authorized by the bill and to develop an economic program for 360 counties with a population of about 16 million persons. The area covered all of West Virginia and portions of Alabama, Georgia, Kentucky, Maryland, North Carolina, Ohio, Pennsylvania, South Carolina, Tennessee and Virginia. In addition, S 3 allowed the Commission to add 13 New York counties to the program. Inclusion of these counties was announced by the Commission Aug. 18, thus adding a 12th state to the program.

The bill authorized a total of $840 million in federal grants over the six-year period ending June 30, 1971, to pay up to 70 percent of the cost of building 2,350 miles of development highways and 1,000 miles of local access roads in the region. The Appalachian states would contribute a minimum of $360 million for the highways. These highways would be in addition to all other highways built with assistance received under other federal road programs. In addition to the road funds, S 3 authorized a variety of special projects (in addition to any projects which might be undertaken under other existing federal programs) including construction of health facilities and vocational schools, land improvement, reclamation of mining areas and development of timber and water resources. The bill authorized $252.4 million to cover the federal contributions to these projects during the first two years of the program (through the end of fiscal 1967). Additional funds would be authorized later for subsequent years.

The bill provided that the Appalachian Regional Development Act would terminate July 1, 1971. Total federal expenditures for the six-year program (including both the initial $1,092,400,000 authorizations and the additional funds to be sought after fiscal 1967) were expected to be about $2 billion.

President Johnson appointed John L. Sweeney, former chairman of the Federal Development Planning Committee for Appalachia, as federal co-chairman of the Appalachian Regional Commission. Sweeney was confirmed by the Senate April 1. The participating states April 19 named Georgia Gov. Carl E. Sanders (D) as the state co-chairman. He was succeeded as state co-chairman July 1 by Kentucky Gov. Edward T. Breathitt (D).

MAJOR PROVISIONS. As signed into law, March 9, S 3, the Appalachian Regional Development Act, contained the following provisions:

Title I—Appalachian Regional Commission. Created an Appalachian Regional Commission composed of one federal member, to be appointed by the President and confirmed by the Senate, and the Governor or his representative from each state covered by the act. Decisions would require the approval of the federal representative and a majority of the state representatives. The Commission would prepare programs for the economic development of the region, conduct research, formulate interstate compacts, encourage private investment in the area and formation of local development districts, coordinate Appalachian programs, provide a forum for discussion of Appalachian policy and make recommendations to the President and the states regarding the program. The bill provided $2.2 million for the administrative expenses of the Commission through June 30, 1967, after which the expenses would be shared equally by the Federal Government and the states, plus $200,000 for the staff of the federal member (also called the "federal co-chairman"). (These funds would come out of the total of $252.4 million authorized in Title IV, below.)

Title II—Special Appalachian Programs. Authorized appropriations of $840 million over the period ending June 30, 1971, for construction of up to 2,350 miles of development highways in the region and—in addition—up to 1,000 miles of local access road. The Commission would recommend the location of the highways and roads, and state members of the Commission would be required to consult with their state highway departments before voting on road plans. The Secretary of Commerce would approve, reject or modify the recommendations.

Federal aid to any road project could not exceed 50 percent of the cost, except where the Secretary of Commerce determined—on the basis of Commission recommendations—that a higher percentage was needed to further the purposes of the Act, in which case the federal share could go as high as 70 percent.

Authorized various other special programs (as described below) and the amounts shown to cover the costs of such programs through June 30, 1967. (These amounts would come out of the $252.4 million authorized in Title IV, below.)

Authorized up to $41 million in grants for construction of multicounty demonstration health facilities, including hospitals and diagnostic and treatment centers. Grants for construction could not exceed 80 percent of the project cost. Authorized up to $28 million for operation of health facilities during the first two years of operation. Federal grants for operation could cover up to 100 percent of the costs during the first two years of operation and up to 50 percent the following three years. No grants for operation would be made thereafter.

Authorized up to $17 million in grants to control and prevent erosion and sediment damages in the region and to promote the conservation and development of soil and water resources. The Secretary of Agriculture was authorized to enter into conservation agreements of up

Funds Authorized

As signed into law, March 9, 1965, S 3 authorized $1,092,400,000 in federal aid to Appalachia. All the aid funds authorized in the bill were to be in addition to any federal assistance Appalachia-area states and local government agencies were receiving under existing national programs of similar character.

Of the total provided by S 3, $840 million was for special highway construction projects and was intended to cover the entire period (slightly over six years) from the enactment of the law to its expiration on June 30, 1971. (These funds would come from appropriations from general revenues, not from the Federal Highway Trust Fund.)

The remaining $252.4 million provided by S 3 was for a variety of special projects, and was intended to cover the costs of these projects only from passage of the bill to June 30, 1967, a little over two years. Additional authorizations would be required for these projects over the final four years of the Act (June 30, 1967, to June 30, 1971).

The figures below give a breakdown of authorizations in the final bill by purpose and period of time covered. It should be noted that the Administration's initial version of S 3, as introduced, contained authorizations identical to the final ones shown below, with two exceptions: the initial Administration version did not carry $200,000 for the federal co-chairman's staff; and it authorized only $21.5 million for mining area restoration (instead of the $36.5 million carried by the final version of the bill). The final bill, with its total of $1,092,400,000 in authorizations, thus was $15.2 million greater than the initial Administration request of $1,077,200,000.

Purpose of Funds	Period Covered	Total Authorized for Period
Highway construction	To June 30, 1971	$ 840,000,000
Expenses of Appalachian Commission	To June 30, 1967	2,200,000
Federal Co-chairman's staff	To June 30, 1967	200,000
Demonstration health facilities—construction	To June 30, 1967	41,000,000
Demonstration health facilities—operations	To June 30, 1967	28,000,000
Conservation	To June 30, 1967	17,000,000
Timber aid	To June 30, 1967	5,000,000
Mining area restoration	To June 30, 1967	36,500,000
Water resource survey	To June 30, 1967	5,000,000
Vocational education facilities	To June 30, 1967	16,000,000
Sewage treatment works	To June 30, 1967	6,000,000
Grant-in-aid supplements	To June 30, 1967	90,000,000
Expenses of local development districts, research	To June 30, 1967	5,500,000
TOTAL		$1,092,400,000

to 10 years with landowners. Grants to any landowner could not exceed 80 percent of the costs of improving and developing not more than 50 acres of land.

Authorized up to $5 million for fiscal 1966 and 1967 for loans to establish timber development organizations, which would carry out programs to improve timber productivity and quality. The loans would cover up to 50 percent of the initial costs of the organizations.

Authorized up to $36.5 million in grants to states to seal and fill voids in abandoned coal mines, to reclaim and rehabilitate existing strip and surface mines, to extinguish underground and outcrop mine fires and expand and accelerate fish and wildlife restoration projects in connection with mining area restoration. The grants could not exceed 75 percent of the costs and could only be used for projects on publicly owned land. (Reclamation of privately owned strip-mined areas was barred until authorized by law after completion of a study of the problem of strip-mined lands that was provided for in the bill.)

Authorized the Secretary of the Army to prepare a plan for the development, control and efficient use of water and related resources in the region; authorized up to $5 million for the study, which would be completed for submission to Congress by the President by Dec. 31, 1968.

Modifications of Existing Programs

Authorized up to $16 million in grants to supplement Vocational Education Act funds for construction, in the Appalachian region, of vocational schools.

Authorized a supplement of up to $6 million in grants for construction of sewage treatment works authorized by the Federal Water Pollution Control Act.

Amended the Housing Act of 1954 to make the Appalachian Regional Commission an agency eligible to receive comprehensive planning grants under that Act.

Authorized up to $90 million for a special fund to be established by the Secretary of Commerce to increase the federal share under existing grant-in-aid programs to permit Appalachian communities and states to take advantage of the programs. The federal contribution for any of these programs could not exceed 80 percent of the cost. The authorization was limited to those federal programs that provided grant funds for construction and equipment of facilities and acquisition of land and not for operation.

Title III—Administration. Defined the local units to which the Commission would extend assistance through the state governments; provided that local development districts would have to be certified by the state governments.

Authorized up to $5.5 million for initial administrative expenses of local development districts and for research grants to public or private organizations to further the purposes of the Act. Grants to the local development districts could cover no more than 75 percent of their expenses in any one fiscal year and could not be made to any one district for a period in excess of three years.

Title IV—Appropriations and Miscellaneous. Authorized appropriations of $252.4 million in the period from enactment of the bill to June 30, 1967, for the programs enumerated in all the sections of the bill except the section providing highway funds. (The $252.4 million

total figure included $200,000 for administrative expenses of the office of the federal representative on the Commission.)

Designated 360 counties in 11 states as eligible for assistance under the Act.

Provided that the Act would terminate July 1, 1971.

Appalachia Aid, 1967

Congress in 1967 extended and revised the Appalachian Regional Development Act of 1965. The 1967 legislation (S 602—PL 90-103) authorized $886.7 million for all Appalachian development programs, including: (1) $1.7 million for administration in fiscal 1968-69; (2) $715 million for highways in fiscal 1968-71 (including $175 million in new authorizations); and (3) $170 million for non-highway programs in fiscal 1968-69.

The bill, which was requested by President Johnson, was passed by a 68-13 roll call of the Senate. In the House, however, opposition was stronger and the bill passed by only a 189-168 roll-call vote.

As passed, S 602 authorized $93,150,000 less than requested by the Administration to continue the Appalachian aid effort. The 1965 Act was the first—and one of the most successful—of President Johnson's antipoverty bills to be passed by Congress.

The authorizing legislation in 1967 ran into trouble, however, largely because of renewed economy drives in the House which were triggered by increased federal expenditures, a record peacetime Budget deficit, and a considerable increase in the number of economy-minded Members of the House as a result of the 1966 Congressional elections.

The reductions in appropriation authorizations, which affected only the non-highway Appalachian aid programs, originated in the House Public Works Committee and on the House floor. The House conferees on S 602 were successful in retaining a $170-million appropriation ceiling for all non-highway programs in the bill, although the amounts authorized for each individual program totaled $248 million in the final measure. Administration requests for highway construction funds and administrative expense allowances were not altered by Congressional action, however.

In explaining the reduced authorizations to the Senate after completion of action on the conference report on S 602, Public Works Committee Chairman Jennings Randolph (D W. Va.) noted that "our country's extremely heavy commitments in Vietnam," together with the "dark" fiscal situation of the Federal Government, had made the lower authorization figures unavoidable.

In addition to authorizing additional appropriations for Appalachian aid, S 602 provided for direct appropriation of all funds to the President, who was to transfer the money to the Appalachian Regional Commission for actual obligation and expenditures. Under the 1965 Act, Appalachian funds were scattered through the budget requests of several federal departments and agencies.

The bill also contained a $3-million authorization, not requested by the Administration, for a study of mine acid drainage and pollution problems.

S 602 authorized the inclusion of 24 additional counties in the Appalachian area, of which 20 were located in northeastern Mississippi. Other counties were in Tennessee (Cannon), Alabama (Lamar and Pickens) and New York (Schoharie). The Administration had requested inclusion of 26 additional counties—all in Mississippi—in the region.

In addition to the Appalachian provisions of S 602, the bill amended the Public Works and Economic Development Act of 1965 (PL 89-136) and authorized $75 million for the five regional commissions established by that Act for fiscal 1968-69. Funds were to be used for a supplemental grant program, similar to the existing program in the Appalachian region. These provisions were not requested by the Administration.

Provisions. As signed into law (PL 90-103) Oct. 11, S 602 contained the following major provisions:

Appalachian Regional Commission. Authorized $1.7 million for fiscal 1968 and 1969 for administrative expenses of the Appalachian Regional Commission.

Specified that the Federal Government was to pay all administrative expenses of the federal co-chairman of the Commission and his staff, and set the federal share of other administrative costs of the Commission at 50 percent.

Stipulated that no more than $400,000 of the authorization be available for fiscal 1968 and 1969 administrative expenses of the federal co-chairman and his staff.

Highway Programs. Authorized appropriation to the President of $715 million for the four-year period ending June 30, 1971, an increase of $175 million over existing authorizations for the same period.

Increased the authorized length of major development highways from 2,350 miles to 2,700 miles. (The increase permitted construction of new highways in New York and Pennsylvania.)

Increased from 1,000 miles to 1,600 miles the authorization for construction of local access roads, designed to serve specific recreational, residential, educational, commercial or industrial purposes.

Authorized the Appalachian Regional Commission to designate the locations of highway programs and projects and to transmit the designations to the Transportation Secretary for implementation.

Provided for inclusion of the development highways in the federal-aid primary highway system upon completion.

Required the states to bear maintenance costs of all development highways and local access roads in their respective areas.

Authorized the Appalachian states to initiate construction of development highways with their own funds, with the possibility of future reimbursement for up to 70 percent of construction costs by the Federal Government.

Non-Highway Programs. Authorized a fiscal 1968 and 1969 appropriation ceiling of $170 million for all non-highway programs enumerated below and specified that funds be appropriated directly to the President. *(See box.)*

Authorized appropriations of up to $50 million (from within the over-all $170-million ceiling) for an expanded demonstration health program, with new authority for federal support of up to 100 percent of the

Appalachian Aid Authorizations

(excluding highways) [1]

	Authorized by 1965 Act for fiscal 1966 and 1967	Appropriated	Authorized by S 602 for fiscal 1968 and 1969
Millions of dollars			
Administration	$ 2.4	$ 2.4	$ 1.7
Demonstration health facilities	69.0	23.5	50.0
Land stabilization, conservation	17.0	10.0	19.0
Timber development	5.0	1.0	——
Hardwood research	——	——	2.0
Mining area restoration	36.5	24.9	30.0
Water resources study	5.0	3.3	2.0
Housing fund	——	——	5.0
Vocational education	16.0	16.0	26.0
Sewage treatment	6.0	6.0	6.0
Supplemental grants	90.0	75.0	97.0
Local development districts [2]	5.5	5.5	11.0
Totals	$252.4	$167.5	$249.7

1) S 602 authorized $715 million for highway construction for fiscal 1968-71. The 1965 Act had authorized $840 million for fiscal 1966-71, but these amounts were replaced by those in S 602. (See story.)

2) Of which $3 million was for mine acid pollution studies.

operating costs of public or nonprofit medical facilities, including facilities not constructed with Appalachian aid funds.

Authorized up to $19 million in fiscal 1968 and 1969 appropriations for land stabilization and conservation programs.

Eliminated the existing timber development organization program and substituted an authorization for up to $2 million in fiscal 1968 and 1969 for a hardwood research program, emphasizing grants to and contracts with institutions of higher education.

Amended the mine area restoration program to allow states to apply the costs of acquiring private lands needed for restoration to the non-federal share of project costs, and authorized $30 million for fiscal 1968-69.

Authorized the establishment of a $5-million revolving fund for technical assistance grants and loans for up to 80 percent of initial planning and management costs of low and medium-income housing projects.

Authorized appropriations of up to $2 million for water resource programs.

Authorized appropriations of up to $26 million for vocational education programs and provided that grant funds could be used for equipment purchases as well as for facility construction.

Authorized appropriations of up to $6 million for sewage treatment works grants.

Authorized appropriations of up to $97 million for supplemental grant programs, which allowed federal payment of up to 80 percent of projects already covered by grant-in-aid programs.

Authorized appropriations of up to $11 million for local development district grants, of which up to $3 million was authorized for studies of acid mine pollution in Appalachia.

Required the Commission, no later than March 1, 1969, to send the President a comprehensive report and recommendations on acid mine pollution problems.

General Provisions. Added 20 counties in Mississippi, two counties in Alabama (Lamar and Pickens), one county in Tennessee (Cannon) and one county in New York (Schoharie) to the Appalachian region.

Prohibited the Commission from considering any further changes in the Appalachian region unless so directed by the Senate or the House Public Works Committees.

Other Regional Commissions. Included development of comprehensive long-range economic planning among the responsibilities of the five regional commissions established under the Public Works and Economic Development Act of 1965 (PL 89-136).

Established a new program of supplemental grants for the five regions, authorizing federal payments of up to 80 percent of project costs for programs already covered (with a lower percentage of federal participation) by existing grant-in-aid legislation.

Authorized $5 million in fiscal 1968 and $10 million in fiscal 1969 for the supplemental grant programs in each of the five regions (total authorization of $75 million).

Economic Development Act

With the passage of S 1648 (PL 89-136) Aug. 26, 1965, the Public Works and Economic Development Act, the Federal Government launched a major program to help the approximately 27 million people living in economically depressed areas throughout the nation. Depressed areas are areas of chronic, long-term high unemployment and low living standards, usually due to structural faults in the local economy, the absence of basic public facilities needed to sustain commerce and industry, or the decay or obsolescence of formerly active business enterprises.

The Act, requested by President Johnson, provided $3.25 billion over the five fiscal years 1966-1970 for grants and loans for public works, development and technical assistance and other projects, to stimulate long-term and lasting economic growth in areas plagued by chronic unemployment.

As enacted into law, S 1648 relied on three basic federal approaches toward aiding depressed areas:

(1) Encouraging economically depressed communities to draft and carry out economic development plans that would help them emerge into a condition of healthy economic growth. Wherever possible, such plans were to be on a regional or multi-county basis, rather than a single-county basis.

(2) Helping depressed communities to finance construction of the basic public facilities (such as harbors, sewage plants, access roads, industrial parks) that would make the community attractive to private investment and would thus help foster economic growth.

(3) Providing special financial aid to private firms to encourage them to build plants and businesses in depressed areas.

The large-scale spending for public facilities authorized by the bill also had the effect of creating immediate job opportunities in areas of high unemployment and low economic levels.

One important new departure in the bill was the Title IV aid provision to foster the growth of economically sound towns and small cities which had a potential for substantial economic growth that would help nearby depressed areas. It was believed that, in many cases, a depressed area would benefit far more if expansion were encouraged in a nearby area with a potential for "healthy" growth than if Government aid went solely for projects in the depressed area itself.

The final provisions of S 1648 constituted in part a re-enactment and broadening of the Kennedy Administration's 1961 Area Redevelopment Act, which expired Aug. 31, 1965. However, the provisions for construction of public works in depressed areas, particularly the $500 million a year in grants authorized in Title I, also were based on the approach used in the 1962 Public Works Acceleration Act (which had provided $900 million in federal aid for immediate acceleration of job-creating public works projects in high-unemployment areas). In addition, the stress on regional and multi-county economic planning in S 1648 followed a pattern set in the Appalachia-aid bill passed earlier in 1965. (*See stories above.*)

Although S 1648 passed both chambers of Congress by comfortable margins and with relatively few changes from the Administration's initial requests, the bill was sharply criticized by some Republicans as really offering "nothing to correct or solve" regional economic growth problems. They also said it could lead to "pirating" of industry away from established locations into redevelopment areas. They further charged that the Area Redevelopment Program, upon which S 1648 was primarily based, had frittered away federal funds on isolated small projects which had not really led to economic growth in the areas involved.

The bill's supporters responded that the structural economic changes in depressed areas that would be made possible by the bill would, in fact, go far toward helping solve regional growth problems; that precautions would be taken against "pirating" of industry; and that the wasting of funds on isolated small projects would be avoided because of the heavy emphasis in S 1648 on regional and mutli-county economic plans. For the most part, they said, funds under the bill would be available only for projects consistent with economic development plans designed to foster long-term growth. To receive aid for a sewage project, for example, it would not be sufficient that the community merely need such a project for its own uses; it would have to show that the project was consistent with a development plan that would encourage economic growth.

Related Developments

ARA Extension, Expiration. Prior to final enactment of S 1648, Congress June 24 passed a temporary, two-month extension of the 1961 Area Redevelopment Act (HJ Res 541—PL 89-55, approved June 30).

H J Res 541 continued the Area Redevelopment Act until Aug. 31, 1965, at which time it expired. It

Major Programs in Economic Development Bill

Title I, Development Grants. Provided $500 million a year in fiscal years 1966-1969 for federal matching grants to local public agencies and non-profit groups for construction of public works and development facilities that would foster the economic growth of economically depressed areas and help provide job opportunities. Only areas which had drawn up an over-all economic development plan acceptable to the Secretary of Commerce were eligible for aid, and only for projects consistent with the plan.

Title I and the bill as a whole were designed primarily (1) to encourage economically depressed communities to draft and carry out economic development plans that would help them emerge from a depressed condition; and (2) to provide financial aid in the construction of public facilities (the basic economic "infrastructure") that would make the community attractive to private investment.

Examples of public works and development facilities that could be built or obtained with Title I funds: water works, water and sewer lines, waste treatment plants and health facilities; streets and roads needed for commercial and industrial development; harbor facilities, reservoirs, railroad sidings, airports and industrial parks (land improvement and site utilities); tourist facilities; area vocational schools; land for the above. Funds would *not* be available for construction of court houses, town halls, swimming pools unrelated to tourism, or playgrounds.

Title II, Development Loans. Provided $170 million a year in fiscal years 1966-1970 for (1) federal loans for the same purposes, agencies and facilities covered by Title I; and (2) federal loans and loan guarantees to both public and private borrowers for acquisition and development of land, buildings, machinery and equipment for industrial and commercial use in economically depressed areas.

Title III, Technical Assistance. Provided $25 million a year in fiscal 1966-1970 for federal technical assistance, research and informational aid to economically depressed areas and to other areas needing such aid to improve their economic position.

Title IV, Development Districts. Provided $50 million a year in fiscal 1967-1970 in federal grants, loans and loan guarantees for growth projects in towns, small cities and other "economic development centers" which had a population of less than 250,000, which (even if not in a depressed condition themselves) had a potential for economic growth that would aid nearby economically depressed areas, and which were associated with such areas in multi-county economic development districts having over-all development plans.

Title V, Regional Planning. Encouraged the states to set up multi-state regional commissions to plan and foster economic development programs in depressed regions (such as northern New England), and provided $15 million a year in fiscal 1966-1970 for federal technical advice and planning aid to the commissions.

Bills Compared

The Administration version of S 1648 authorized $460 million for fiscal 1966 (the first year of the new program), including $5 million for a special form of aid to depressed areas called "interest-reduction" payments. The $460 million was to rise in stages to a permanent level of $535 million a year as a result of (1) addition in fiscal 1967 of a permanent new authorization of $50 million a year for aid to development districts (Title IV of the bill); and (2) and increase of $5 million each year in the authorization for interest-reduction payments, until a permanent level of $30 million a year was reached.

The Senate version of S 1648 authorized $615 million for fiscal 1966, including interest-reduction payments. The same increases that were in the Administration bill brought the annual authorization in the Senate version to $685 million by fiscal 1970. The larger authorizations in the Senate bill expired at the end of fiscal 1970.

The House and final provisions of S 1648 dropped the interest-reduction payments and authorized funds only for fiscal 1966-1970: fiscal 1966, $710 million; 1967-1969, $760 million a year; 1970, when development grants were to cease, $260 million.

In the chart below, all authorizations expire in the last year shown unless otherwise indicated.

Millions of Dollars

	Johnson Request	Senate Bill	House and Final Bill
Title I (Development Grants)			
Fiscal 1966	$250	$400	$500
1967	$250	$400	$500
1968	$250	$400	$500
1969	$250	$400	$500
1970	$250*	$400	———
Title II (Development Loans)			
Fiscal 1966	$170	$170	$170
1967	$170	$170	$170
1968	$170	$170	$170
1969	$170	$170	$170
1970	$170*	$170	$170
Title II (Interest Reduction)			
Fiscal 1966	$ 5	$ 5	———
1967	$ 10	$ 10	———
1968	$ 15	$ 15	———
1969	$ 20	$ 20	———
1970	$ 25**	$ 25**	———
Title III (Technical Assistance)			
Fiscal 1966	$ 20	$ 25	$ 25
1967	$ 20	$ 25	$ 25
1968	$ 20	$ 25	$ 25
1969	$ 20	$ 25	$ 25
1970	$ 20*	$ 25	$ 25
Title IV (Development Districts)			
Fiscal 1966	———	———	———
1967	$ 50	$ 50	$ 50
1968	$ 50	$ 50	$ 50
1969	$ 50	$ 50	$ 50
1970	$ 50*	$ 50*	$ 50
Title V (Regional Planning Aid)			
Fiscal 1966	$ 15	$ 15	$ 15
1967	$ 15	$ 15	$ 15
1968	$ 15	$ 15	$ 15
1969	$ 15	$ 15	$ 15
1970	$ 15*	$ 15*	$ 15

*And annually thereafter.
**Would eventually level off at $30 million a year permanently.

otherwise would have expired June 30, 1965. In House debate, Wright Patman (D Texas) said the purpose of the resolution was "to prevent a lapse in the economic redevelopment of...a large number of distressed communities" until such time as S 1648, which, in effect, created a successor program, went into effect.

Opposing the extension, William B. Widnall (R N.J.) said, "Neither the ARA's past record nor its present status justify any extension of time for this agency. It is a matter of public record and public knowledge that ARA has done less with more money than almost any other bureaucratic agency in history."

New Agency Created. On Sept. 1, the day after the Area Redevelopment Act finally lapsed and the Area Redevelopment Administration went out of existence, there came into being in the Commerce Department a new agency—the Economic Development Administration—which was, in effect, the successor to the Area Redevelopment Administration and which was charged with responsibility for administering the Public Works and Economic Development Administration Act. The Economic Development Administration took over the personnel of the old Area Redevelopment Administration.

Sports Antitrust

Congress in 1965 considered legislation to extend federal regulation of certain professional sports activities. It took action also to help settle a dispute between two amateur athletic organizations.

The Senate passed a bill (S 950) to bring professional baseball, football, basketball and hockey uniformly under the antitrust laws, with specific exemptions granted for certain activities of the sports. The House passed a bill (HR 8635) designed to rid professional boxing of alleged racketeering. HR 8635 created a Federal Boxing Commission to regulate professional matches televised or broadcast interstate or to other countries. The bill was not enacted, however. The Senate adopted a resolution (S Res 147) authorizing establishment of an arbitration board to settle disputes relating to the conduct of amateur athletics. The board's first job was to help settle the battle between the National Collegiate Athletic Assn. and the Amateur Athletic Union over control of amateur track and field competition in the United States.

The primary legislation considered during the year was S 950. It applied antitrust laws uniformly to professional baseball, football, basketball and hockey, but exempted from such laws the league and team activities believed necessary to preserve a balanced competitive situation. The bill was passed by the Senate but was blocked in the House by advocates of strong antitrust law and enforcement.

Since 1922 the status of baseball and other professional sports with respect to antitrust regulation had been cloudy. In that year, the Supreme Court ruled that organized professional baseball was not subject to antitrust laws *(Federal Baseball Club of Baltimore v. National League).* The Court held that the "reserve clause," a provision in players' contracts that forbade them to contract with another professional baseball team, was not a violation of antitrust regulation.

The Court affirmed baseball's exemption from antitrust laws in 1953 *(Toolson v. New York Yankees).*

George Toolson, New York Yankee farm team player, sued the Yankees on the ground they had blacklisted him after he refused to report to a minor league club. The majority ruled against Toolson, noting that baseball had "been left for 30 years to develop, on the understanding that it was not subject to existing antitrust legislation."

Two years later, professional boxing was refused a similar antitrust exemption. The Court said its baseball decisions "did not hold that all businesses based on professional sports were outside the scope of the antitrust laws" *(U.S. v. International Boxing Club of N.Y.).*

In 1957, William Radovich, a former guard with the Detroit Lions, sued the National Football League on the ground it prevented him from becoming a player-coach in the Pacific Coast League. The Court ruled that professional football was not exempt from antitrust laws *(Radovich v. National Football League.)* It said that the coverage of the Toolson case had been carefully restricted to baseball.

In the Radovich decision, and on previous occasions, the Court indicated that it was a Congressional prerogative to legislate a rule that would apply uniformly to professional sports. "We, therefore, conclude," the Court's majority said in 1957, "that the orderly way to eliminate error or discrimination, if any there be, is by legislation and not by court decision."

Congress was reluctant to act on the Supreme Court's suggestion, although after 1952 it considered sports regulation in several sessions. Only once, in 1961, was a sports antitrust bill passed by both houses of Congress and enacted into law. The law (HR 9096—PL 87-331) was of limited scope. It amended the antitrust laws to authorize professional sports leagues of baseball, football, basketball and hockey to enter into television contracts on behalf of member teams and protected college football from competing telecasts of professional games.

Football Merger Exemption. Congress enacted legislative provisions in 1966 to exempt a proposed merger of two professional football leagues from the antitrust laws. The exemption was added by the Senate as a rider to an investment tax credit bill (HR 17607—PL 89-800) late in the session to get around objections which had been raised to the legislation in the House by Judiciary Committee Chairman Emanuel Celler (D N.Y.). *(See tax policy chapter for story on HR 17607.)*

The football leagues which proposed to merge were the well-established National (NFL) and the newer American (AFL). A major reason for the merger was rapidly rising costs to each league of annually bidding for the services of top college football players. A player drafted by teams in both leagues could negotiate with both and force each to offer large bonuses for signing. The merger called for a common player draft to eliminate interleague bidding. The plan also called for the creation of new franchises, a fact which figured in the enactment of the legislation.

After the merger was announced June 8, 1966, the Justice Department said it would take a close look at the plan to see if it violated antitrust laws. Subsequently, the NFL said it would reconsider merger plans unless Congress granted antitrust exemption. In response, the Senate passed a bill (S 3817) which granted antitrust exemption to a professional football merger agreement if the agreement increased the number of teams in the leagues. The bill was blocked in the House by Celler who was one of Congress' most forceful defenders of the antitrust laws.

In order to get around the House roadblock, supporters of S 3817 had its provisions added as a rider to HR 17607. Minority Leader Everett McKinley Dirksen (R Ill.) offered the bill's provisions as an amendment, which was accepted by voice vote. The tactic reportedly was devised by Senate Majority Whip Russell B. Long (D La.) and House Majority Whip Hale Boggs (D La.) to improve New Orleans' chances of securing a pro football franchise. New Orleans was one of seven cities seeking the NFL's 16th franchise. Both Long and Boggs were conferees on HR 17607. The conference committee retained the Dirksen amendment intact. The conference report said, "The amendment does not seek to resolve any of the antitrust problems of professional football....It is the intent of the conferees...that the new league will commence operations with no greater antitrust immunity than the existing individual leagues now enjoy. The sole effect of this amendment...is to permit the combination of the two leagues to go forward without fear of antitrust challenge based upon a joint agreement between the member clubs of the two leagues to combine in a single league and to conduct their affairs as members of a single league."

The conference report was agreed to by both chambers without change, although Celler argued against the merger provisions. The NFL later in the year announced that New Orleans had been granted the league's 16th franchise.

Antitrust Exemptions

As part of the Government's balance-of-payments program, President Johnson in 1965 proposed and Congress enacted a bill (HR 5280—PL 89-175) providing certain exemptions from the antitrust laws for banks and other institutions which participated in voluntary agreements to help reduce the payments deficit. The voluntary agreements were to curtail the flow of private dollars and credit from the United States to foreign countries. HR 5280 also authorized the President to require reports from institutions participating in the agreements. *(For discussion of U.S. balance-of-payments problems, see chapter on tax policy.)*

The law was to expire 20 months after it became law or upon certification of the President that its provisions were no longer necessary to safeguard the U.S. balance-of-payments position. However, in 1967 Congress extended the law for almost two years, through June 30, 1969 (S 1648—PL 90-62). PL 90-62 did not make any changes in the law other than to extend the expiration date. The 1965 law had expired on May 9, 1967.

'Failing' Newspapers

Congress in 1968 continued an investigation started in 1967 of newspaper mergers and the economics of newspaper publishing. Both chambers held hearings on measures (S 1312, HR 19123) to permit certain newspapers to enter into joint operating arrangements with-

out violating antitrust laws. The Senate bill was approved by a Judiciary Subcommittee, but no further action was taken on either proposal.

Sen. Carl Hayden (D Ariz.) in 1967 introduced a bill (S 1312) to permit an apparently insolvent newspaper to enter into a joint newspaper operating arrangement with a financially sound paper in the same city. The arrangement could consist of combining all business functions, including printing, distribution, advertising and circulation soliciting and bookkeeping. Joint advertising and circulation rates also could be established. A second provision in the bill permitted the "failing newspaper" to merge completely with the solvent paper.

The bill was introduced after an antitrust suit was filed against two newspapers in Hayden's state, the Tucson (Ariz.) *Citizen* and *Star*. The papers had been publishing under a joint operating arrangement since 1940. In 1965, the *Citizen* bought the *Star*, but later stated it planned to sell the paper. The Justice Department ruled the merger and previous operating arrangement in violation of antitrust laws, and the ruling was upheld in federal district court. The Supreme Court Oct. 21 agreed to consider the case. A decision was expected in 1969. (On March 10, 1969, the Court sustained a ruling by the district judge requiring the papers to undo the merger and also abandon the agreement under which they had charged common advertising and circulation rates and pooled profits). Similar operating arrangements existed for newspapers in 21 other cities.

Congressional interest in the financial condition of the newspaper business was aroused in 1967 by the closing May 5 of the New York *World Journal Tribune*, itself the product of a merger, in April 1966, of three papers, the *World-Telegram, Herald Tribune and Journal-American*. The death of the *World Journal Tribune* left only three major daily papers in New York City. On July 8, the 142-year-old Boston *Traveler* also ceased publication.

Small Business Loans

Congress in 1965 authorized increases of $175 million for Small Business Administration (SBA) programs. The increases were authorized in the following bills:

Disaster Loans. S 1796 (PL 89-59) was enacted without opposition in Congress as a stop-gap measure to meet emergency needs for disaster loans. It:

Increased the SBA revolving fund by $50 million, bringing the total SBA authorization to $1,716,000,000, of which $1,375,000,000 was reserved for business and disaster loans. SBA was expected to increase its set-aside for disaster loans to $250 million.

Increased the maximum maturity of disaster loans from 20 years to 30 years.

Gave the SBA Administrator discretion to suspend for up to five years payments on principal and interest on disaster loans to homeowners and small businessmen afflicted by natural disasters and to extend the maturity of 20-year loans for up to five years.

Required the SBA, at the request of a participating lending institution when payment of principal or interest had been suspended, to purchase, or make payments on,

Background on SBA

The Small Business Act of 1953 (PL 83-163) created the SBA for a two-year trial period ending June 30, 1955. The act authorized $275 million for a revolving fund; $150 million was for loans to small businesses that could not get reasonable credit elsewhere, $100 million was to help small businesses finance the procurement of Government contracts, and $25 million was for loans to individuals or businesses of any size damaged by natural disasters. (*Congress and the Nation, Vol. I, pp. 362-63*)

Congress in 1958 made the SBA a permanent federal agency (PL 85-536), with a revolving fund of $650 million. Seven further increases raised the fund to $1,666,000,000 by the end of 1962.

Funds to help get Government contracts were reduced to $25 million in 1958 and in 1961 they were merged with business loans in one authorization. In the 1962 law, funds for disaster loans also were merged with the two other activities. The function of disaster loans was increased several times: in the 1961 Housing Act (PL 87-70), loans were authorized for firms that were forced to relocate by urban renewal or other federally aided construction programs; in 1964, after the Great Lakes fishing industry suffered from the discovery of botulism in commercially sold fish, disasters were redefined to include disease and toxicity; in the same year, in reaction to a serious earthquake in Alaska and flood damage on the West Coast, Congress made the maximum maturity on loans to victims in Alaska, California and Washington 30 years instead of 20.

A new activity for the SBA was authorized in the Small Business Investment Act of 1958 (PL 85-699). It authorized the SBA to charter companies to provide equity capital to small businesses and to make loans to small business investment companies (SBICs). The program began with a $250 million authorization to the SBA revolving fund, which was increased to $341 million in 1962. The program was further expanded in 1964.

loans held by the institution if necessary to avoid default. The borrower was to repay the SBA eventually.

Lease Guarantees. Section 316 of the Housing and Urban Development Act (PL 89-117) added a new title to the Small Business Investment Act of 1958. It permitted the SBA to guarantee rental payments on leases of small businesses that were eligible for SBA loans because they were displaced by urban renewal or other construction or were covered by Title IV of the antipoverty law. A separate revolving fund for the program was established, and $5 million was transferred from the regular SBA revolving fund to the new fund as initial capital. To compensate, SBA's total authority was increased by $5 million, to $1,721,000,000. Fees from the guarantees were expected eventually to permit reimbursement of the regular SBA fund.

Investment Companies. A $120-million increase in available SBA loans to small business investment companies (SBICs) and state and local development companies was signed into law July 21 (HR 7847—PL 89-78.) The increase was requested because loans and commitments from the SBA revolving fund were estimated to exceed the current $341-million statutory limit by mid-June. By June 30, 1966, they were expected to reach the $461-million limit set by HR 7847.

The increased authorization for loans to SBICs required a $120-million increase in the SBA's revolving fund. S 2542, increasing the fund from $1,721,000,000 to $1,841,000,000, was passed without controversy. It was signed into law (PL 89-334) Nov. 8.

Southeastern States. After Hurricane Betsy inflicted heavy damage on Florida, Louisiana and Mississippi, Congress enacted HR 11539 (PL 89-339) which, among other things, provided special SBA disaster loan aid to the area until Jan. 1, 1967. The bill:

Directed SBA, at the borrower's option, to cancel up to $1,800 of that part of any disaster loan in excess of $500, or waive interest for three years. The property loss must not have been covered by insurance.

Authorized disaster loans to private schools and colleges in the affected areas and the waiver of interest and deferral of principal payments for the first three years of the loan. The existing requirement that private financing be sought first was waived.

The bill authorized appropriations of $70 million to provide all aid authorized in the bill and Congress appropriated $35 million before adjourning.

SBIC Regulation

The Small Business Administration's administrative control over small business investment companies it had helped to establish was strengthened in 1966. Legislation (HR 18021—PL 89-779) to give the SBA the new powers was passed without opposition.

Established under the Small Business Investment Act of 1958, small business investment companies (SBICs) were privately operated investment firms which obtained part of their working capital through loans from the Federal Government. Under the law in effect in 1966, the Government could invest (within certain limits) $2 for every $1 of private capital in SBICs. The companies were authorized to make long-term loans to small businesses and to buy stock in small businesses which normally did not have easy access to traditional bank loans. (*For additional background on SBICs, see following story.*)

Evidence of mismanagement of some SBICs led to enactment of HR 18021, which authorized the SBA to take administrative action to correct certain abuses of SBICs and their officers. Previously, the SBA had to go to court, if it wanted to revoke a license or enjoin a malpractice.

Provisions. As signed into law, HR 18021: Gave the SBA the power to: (1) revoke the license of a SBIC after administrative proceedings (previously it had power only to suspend a license administratively); (2) suspend or revoke a license if the SBIC knowingly made a false or misleading statement in connection with any statements required by the SBA or the Act (previously, the SBA could only suspend a license for false statements made in applying for a license); (3) issue cease-

and-desist orders against individuals and SBICs who were about to violate the Act or regulations (previously, orders could be issued only against SBICs, and only after a violation was committed); (4) remove after a hearing and suspend pending a hearing, any officer of SBIC who, in the SBA's view, had willfully and knowingly committed any substantial violation of the Act, regulation or a final cease-and-desist order, or had committed a substantial breach of his fiduciary duty involving his personal honesty.

Prohibited persons convicted of a felony or found civilly liable for fraud from participating in the management of a SBIC except with written consent of the SBA.

Instituted a civil penalty of up to $100 a day against a SBIC which willfully neglected to file required reports on time.

Small Business Funds

A second Small Business Administration bill enacted in 1966 enabled the SBA to meet increased demands for loans. The legislation (S 2729—PL 89-409) was enacted early in May.

Since Oct. 11, 1965, the SBA had been unable to accept applications for regular loans from its revolving fund because it had to divert large sums and personnel to fill an unprecedented demand for disaster loans. It began accepting regular loan applications again on May 26, 1966.

S 2729 was designed to provide both temporary and permanent relief. Until July 1, 1966, it increased by $125 million the amount authorized to be appropriated to the SBA revolving fund and increased by the same amount the total loans the SBA could have outstanding.

To provide permanent relief, the bill, effective July 1, 1966, eliminated the revolving fund and the authorizations and limits on loans outstanding. In its place, two new revolving funds were established: a disaster loan fund to finance all disaster loan functions except displaced-business disaster loans, and a business loan and investment fund for all other SBA activites.

No ceiling was set on the disaster loan fund, either for appropriations or for loans outstanding. For appropriations to the other fund, the bill authorized such sums as were needed. It set three separate limits on amounts outstanding from that fund: $400 million for purchase of certain subordinated debentures and long-term loans; $200 million for loans to state and local development companies; and $1.4 billion for all other activities.

Provisions. As signed into law, S 2729:

Temporary Relief. Increased the authorization for appropriations to the existing SBA revolving fund by $125 million, from $1,841,000,000 to $1,966,000,000.

Increased the authorization for loans and commitments that may be outstanding at any one time under the existing SBA business loan program, disaster loan program, prime contract authority and Title IV of the Economic Opportunity Act of 1964 by $125 million, from $1,375,000,000 to $1.5 billion.

Revolving Funds. Effective July 1, 1966, eliminated the existing SBA revolving fund and the authorizations for appropriations and permissable outstanding loans and commitments. Established two revolving funds to finance SBA activities, as follows:

Disaster Loans. Established a disaster loan fund to finance all disaster loan functions except the displaced business disaster loans; no ceiling was established for outstanding disaster loans. Authorized appropriation of such sums as were necessary.

Regular Activities. Established a business loan and investment fund for the regular business loan program, the displaced business disaster loan program, prime contract authority and the loan programs under the Small Business Investment Act of 1958, the Trade Expansion Act of 1962 and Title IV of the Economic Opportunity Act of 1964.

Set a ceiling of $400 million for the purchase of subordinated debentures (certificates of indebtedness) of Small Business Investment Companies (SBIC) and making long-term loans to SBICs; set a ceiling of $200 million on loans to state and local development companies under the Small Business Investment Act of 1958; and set a ceiling of $1.4 billion on loans under the other regular business loan program, displaced business disaster loan program, prime contract authority and the loan programs under the Trade Expansion Act of 1962 and Title IV of the Economic Opportunity Act of 1964. In addition, limited outstanding loans at any one time under Title IV of the 1964 EOA to $100 million (within the overall $1.4-billion ceiling).

Authorized appropriations of such sums as were necessary.

Small Business, SBIC Funds

A major small business bill (S 1862—PL 90-104) was enacted in 1967. It increased the amount of money the Small Business Administration (SBA) was authorized to have outstanding in loans and gave small business investment companies (SBICs) access to more SBA money. The legislation was requested by the SBA.

The bill increased the SBA's revolving fund for regular lending activities by $650 million (to $2,650,000,000). The SBA said this authorization would enable it to continue its various lending programs until June 30, 1970.

A major purpose of the legislation was to make additional federal money available to the larger SBICs— those with private capitalization in excess of $1 million. SBICs with less private capital would be able to obtain Government backing in about the same amounts as under existing law. The SBA said it preferred to provide backing for the larger SBICs because there was less risk of defaults. For the larger SBICs, the bill (1) increased the ratio of federal dollars that could be contributed for every private dollar, and (2) raised the limit on total federal financing of an SBIC from $4.7 million under existing law to $10 million. The bill also contained incentives for the larger SBICs to invest their money in equity securities of small businesses.

Another important provision of S 1862 liberalized the terms under which SBA financial assistance could be granted to SBICs by providing that all such assistance could be granted through purchase of subordinated debentures.

In 1958, Congress had passed the Small Business Investment Act (PL 85-699). The Act authorized the SBA to charter companies that were organized to provide equity capital or long-term loans to small businesses, and to make loans to such investment companies (SBICs). The legislation was designed to help overcome the handicaps encountered by small business in securing new capital and long-term loans from private sources. Congress in 1966 enacted legislation (PL 89-779) to strengthen the SBA's control over SBICs.

The SBICs obtained money from private sources and from the Federal Government through the SBA. The 1958 Act required an SBIC to have a minimum capitalization of $300,000. At least one-half of this, or $150,000, had to come from private sources. Any remaining balance needed to reach $300,000 could come from the sale of subordinated debentures by SBICs to the SBA. (A debenture is an interest-bearing certificate of indebtedness, which, unlike most bonds, has no collateral. The 1958 Act specified that SBIC debentures sold to the SBA would be subordinate to any other debenture bonds, promissory notes or other obligations issued by an SBIC.)

Federal financial assistance to SBICs through the SBA was provided by two methods. Together they provided a maximum of $4.7 million in SBA aid to an SBIC.

The first of these methods, as noted above, was SBA purchase of SBIC subordinated debentures. Existing law specified that the SBA could purchase up to $700,000 in subordinated debentures from an SBIC, on a dollar-for-dollar matching basis with the private capital obtained by the company. The second method was long-term SBA loans to an SBIC in an amount equal to 50 percent of an SBIC's entire capital (Government plus private funds) to a maximum of $4 million. Collateral was required to assure repayment of these loans.

Although the 1958 Act required a minimum private capitalization of $150,000, the SBA in 1965—by administrative regulation—began to require a $300,000 minimum. SBA held that language of the 1958 Act permitted it to raise the requirement to this level but that any further increase required legislative authorization.

Provisions. As signed into law (PL 90-104) Oct. 11, S 1862 contained the following major provisions:

Small Business Act Amendments

Revolving Fund Increases. Amended the Small Business Act to increase the amount of loans, guarantees, and other obligations or commitments which might be outstanding at any one time from the business loan and investment fund as follows:

$450 million (compared to $400 million under existing law) for the purchases of subordinated debentures (certificates of indebtedness) of small business investment companies; $300 million ($200 million in existing law) for loans to state and local development companies under the Small Business Investment Act of 1958; and $1.9 billion ($1.4 billion in existing law) for loans under the other regular business loan program, displaced business disaster loan program, prime contract authority and the loan programs under the Trade Expansion Act of 1962 and Title IV of the Economic Opportunity Act of 1964 (antipoverty business incentives). In addition, the bill limited outstanding loans at any one time under Title IV of the EOA to $200 million (within the over-all $1.9-billion ceiling) from the existing $100 million.

Loan Maturities. Increased the maturity period for regular business loans made for constructing facilities to 15 years from the existing 10 years.

Small Business Investment Act Amendments

SBIC Capital Requirements. Permitted the SBA administrator to require an SBIC to have more than the existing minimum of $150,000 in private paid-in capital and paid-in surplus in cases in which he determined more was necessary "to assure a reasonable prospect that the company will be operated soundly and profitably, and managed actively and prudently...."

Stipulated that the SBA, in determining whether to license an SBIC, "shall give due regard" to the need and availability for financing small businesses in the geographic area involved, the general business reputation and character of the proposed SBIC owners and management, and the probability of successful operations.

Bank Ownership. Permitted a bank to invest up to 5 percent of the bank's capital and surplus in the stock of SBICs, but prohibited a bank from owning 50 percent or more of any SBIC. (Existing law allowed banks to invest up to 2 percent of their capital and surplus but did not limit ownership in an SBIC.)

SBA Financial Aid to SBICs. Replaced the two existing authorizations for SBA financial assitance to SBICs with the following:

• Authority for SBICs to sell subordinated debentures with up to 15-year maturities to the SBA at interest rates based on the current average market yield on outstanding marketable obligations of the United States, plus an additional charge to cover the costs of operating the program.

Specified that the debentures would be subordinated to other debenture bonds, promissory notes or other debts of the SBIC unless the SBA determined it was prudent to buy debentures that were not subordinated.

• Authority for the SBA to purchase debentures up to 200 percent of an SBIC's private capital, up to a maximum of $7.5 million, thus providing two federal dollars for one private dollar (except under circumstances explained in the following paragraph).

• Authority for the SBA to purchase a larger amount of debentures from an SBIC if that SBIC had more than $1 million in private capital and had invested or legally committed 65 percent or more of its funds in venture capital (such as stocks) of small business concerns. The amount of debentures which the SBA could purchase was $2 million plus 300 percent of the SBIC's private capital above $1 million, up to a total maximum of $10 million for any single SBIC (thus providing a 3-1 ratio of federal funds to private funds above $1 million).

Investment Limit. Changed the computation of the amount of funds an SBIC could lend to a single small business concern from 20 percent of its entire capital (Government plus private funds) to 20 percent of private capital. For SBICs already in operation, the change would go into effect on a sliding scale that delayed full effectiveness until 1972.

SBIC Audits. Required an SBA examination of each SBIC every year, but permitted the SBA administrator to waive the examination in the case of a company whose operations were suspended because the company was involved in litigation or was in receivership.

Lease Guarantees. Provided that all small businesses meeting SBA requirements would be eligible for Government guarantees of rental payments under commercial and industrial leases. The program under existing law had been limited to businesses which had anti-poverty loans or which were displaced by federal activities.

Public Broadcasting

An effort was made during President Johnson's years in office to provide substantial assistance to noncommercial broadcasting. Although legislation was enacted in 1967, the success of the effort was not clear because the all-important issue of financing was not permanently resolved. *(For discussion of federal regulation of broadcasting, see Congress and the Nation, Vol. I, p. 561.)*

The legislation adopted in 1967 (S 1160—PL 90-129) established a public corporation to provide financial assistance for noncommercial educational television and radio broadcasting. The Act authorized $9 million in fiscal 1968, but long-term financing was not provided. In calendar 1968, Congress passed a bill (S 3135—PL 90-294) to carry forward the $9 million from fiscal 1968 to fiscal 1969. S 3135 was enacted because delays in initiation of the corporation's activities made it unnecessary for Congress to appropriate any funds in 1967. The Administration in early 1968 told Congress that it had postponed for at least a year a decision on a long-range financing plan and asked that the fiscal 1968 authorization be made available for 1969. Later in 1968, Congress appropriated $5 million for the corporation under the authorization.

1967 LEGISLATION. The basic authorizing legislation, PL 90-129, contained two major parts. The first, which was Title I of the bill, extended for three years a 1962 law (PL 87-447) which provided federal grants to construct educational television broadcasting facilities. S 1160 also broadened PL 87-447 to include educational radio broadcasting. For these purposes, S 1160 authorized a total of $38 million: $10.5 million in fiscal 1968; $12.5 million in fiscal 1969; and $15 million in fiscal 1970. Title I was not controversial.

The other major part of the legislation, Title II, provided for the establishment of a nonprofit, nongovernmental Corporation for Public Broadcasting. Although the proposal had considerable support in Congress, it was controversial because of the possibility that the corporation's activities might be influenced by political or governmental pressures.

The corporation, a major Administration proposal, was intended to strengthen and improve educational radio and television by providing an independent source of funds to produce programs and operate and interconnect stations.

The bill authorized the corporation to provide financial aid, through grants or contracts, to individuals, noncommercial stations or other groups to produce educational radio and television programs. The corporation also was empowered to make payments to local educational stations to help produce local programs and meet other operating costs. In addition, the corporation was authorized to arrange for systems to connect separate stations regionally or throughout the nation to permit distribution of educational programs.

Financing. Although S 1160 provided the framework within which to assist educational broadcasting financially, the central question of how the funds were to be obtained was not resolved. Thus, future action on financing would determine whether or not S 1160 was a truly significant piece of legislation.

As enacted, S 1160 authorized appropriations of $9 million in fiscal 1968 to finance the activities of the corporation. This was exactly what President Johnson requested in his educational broadcasting proposals that were sent to Congress Feb. 28. The President said he would make further proposals for the corporation's long-term financing in 1968.

The financing provisions of the bill, however, were directly contrary to what many experts in educational broadcasting said should be done to make the corporation a useful source of support for noncommercial radio and television. These experts argued that the paramount need was to assure the corporation a permanent source of funds that was free from political influence. Without permanent financing, they said, educational broadcasters would hesitate to present controversial subjects for fear of losing their financial support in Congress the following year. Various types of permanent financing were suggested: earmarking some form of tax, such as an excise levy on sales of television sets; increasing and earmarking commercial broadcast license fees; or using fees charged commercial stations for the use of a commercial satellite system.

Political Safeguards. In establishing the corporation and providing for its operation, Congress took pains to insulate it from political pressure in all areas except that of financing. In various provisions and in language contained in committee reports, Congress emphasized that control over broadcasting of programs remained entirely with local stations. The corporation established by the bill was to be independent and private. None of the 15 directors could be federal employees. The directors were to be appointed by the President with Senate confirmation, but no more than eight could come from the same political party and each director was limited to two consecutive six-year terms. The corporation was prohibited from owning or operating any television or radio broadcast station, system or network, community antenna television system or interconnection or program production facility. The corporation was allowed to arrange for methods of connecting independent stations for program distribution and live or simultaneous broadcasting on occasions, but the legislative history of the bill as well as certain specific legal language made clear that local stations would not be restricted by any requirement of network programing as was frequently the case in commercial broadcasting.

In one section of the bill, the corporation was directed to function in ways that would assure "maximum freedom" for educational stations from "interference with or control of program content or other activities." Another provision of the bill specifically prohibited any educational broadcasting station from editorializing or supporting or opposing a candidate for political office.

Supporters of the legislation pointed to all of these provisions as safeguards which they said would prevent the corporation from becoming a propaganda agency for either political party or from presenting only a particular point of view. Opponents, nevertheless, contended that

Background on Educational Television Assistance

The Public Broadcasting Act of 1967 sought to fill educational television's (ETV) need for funds. Unable to obtain revenue from advertising in the fashion of their commercial counterparts, ETV stations had existed as "weak sisters" in the television industry.

Funds came from a variety of sources. In fiscal 1966, total income of ETV stations amounted to $56 million. State and local government provided $33.5 million, the Federal Government $8.8 million, the Ford Foundation $8.5 million, fund drives netted $3 million and business corporations gave $2 million.

ETV stations also obtained their programs from diverse sources. Most programs came from National Educational Television (NET), to which most stations belonged; from the individual stations' production facilities; and from business and government.

These funds and programs were funneled to ETV stations, which at the end of 1966 totaled 124. That total included stations attached to school systems, university stations, state-operated outlets and community nonprofit stations in metropolitan areas.

The other branch of educational broadcasting, educational radio, was initiated in 1938 and by 1967 had about 350 stations throughout the country. Such stations had gone on the air at the rate of two new outlets a month during the period between 1962 and 1967. More than 90 percent were FM stations and about 75 percent were attached to colleges or universities and financed by the institutions. Others were connected with local school districts or communities.

Like ETV, educational radio was generally a blend of cultural or informational programing for the public and instructional programing for schools. Much of the programing was originated by the stations themselves, often by students as part of scholastic requirements or extracurricular activities at the schools where the stations were operated. Another five to ten hours weekly was supplied by National Educational Radio, a central program source, to its 165 affiliated stations. National Educational Radio in 1967 operated on a $60,000-a-year budget.

Congressional Action. In both 1958 and 1959, the Senate passed bills to provide assistance for ETV, but the House failed to act on the legislation. The Senate in 1961 passed a bill (S 205) authorizing $51 million over five years in outright grants to the states. Five months later, following Administration requests, the House Interstate and Foreign Commerce Committee reported a bill (HR 132) which authorized $25.5 million for a four-year, matching-grant program.

The House in 1962 passed a slightly amended version of HR 132, and a conference committee reached a compromise on the differences between the House and Senate bills, producing a $32-million, five-year federal sharing plan. A House ban on grants to private nonprofit groups was eliminated. The funds could be used only for certain facilities—towers, transmitters and other transmission equipment—and a limit of $1 million was placed on the amount any one state could receive. President Kennedy signed the bill into law (PL 87-447) on May 1.

Carnegie Commission. In 1965, following a preliminary meeting the year before between the National Assn. of Educational Broadcasters and the U.S. Office of Education, a commission was created by the Carnegie Foundation to study the problems of ETV and recommend solutions. The 15-member Carnegie Commission on Educational Television was headed by James R. Killian Jr., chairman of the Massachusetts Institute of Technology Corp.

The Commission report, released Jan. 25, 1967, contained broad recommendations for strengthening and expanding the existing system of 124 ETV stations into a network of 380 functionally linked but individually operated stations. The Commission urged Congress to extend PL 87-447 and to make funds available for a full range of facilities and equipment rather than limit them (as currently done under PL 87-447) to towers, transmission equipment, cameras and video recording equipment.

The Commission's three major proposals were: (1) creation of a federally chartered, nonprofit corporation to oversee the new public television system; (2) enactment of an excise tax on new TV sets to begin at 2 percent to raise $40 million the first year and to increase to 5 percent to raise $100 million annually; and (3) extension of PL 87-447.

Ford Foundation. Another proposal to assist ETV had been made previously by the Ford Foundation, one of the leading supporters of ETV. The plan, submitted to the Federal Communications Commission (FCC) Aug. 1, 1966, called for the creation of a nonprofit domestic communications satellite for commercial and educational broadcasters. The ETV stations would not be charged to relay their signal via satellite. A certain percentage of the savings realized by the commercial broadcasters from the use of the satellite as opposed to conventional transmission facilities would be earmarked to assist ETV.

Administration Proposals. In his 1967 State of the Union Message, President Johnson said he would submit to Congress measures to "develop educational television into a vital public resource to enrich our homes, educate our families and to provide assistance in our classrooms."

In his education message to Congress Feb. 28, 1967, Mr. Johnson recommended passage of the Public Television Act of 1967, which embodied many of the Carnegie proposals. The Act, he said, would increase federal funds for television and radio facility construction to $10.5 million in fiscal 1968, more than three times the previous year's authorization; create a Corporation for Public Television to support noncommercial television and radio; and provide $9 million as initial funding for the corporation.

The Administration proposals differed from the Carnegie commission proposals in that it included noncommercial radio as well as television and asked Congress to authorize $9 million to finance the corporation for the first year and left the question of future funds open, whereas the Carnegie Commission had proposed an excise tax to raise the funds.

political considerations would influence the corporation's decisions in making grants. One House opponent said that the proposal was equivalent to allowing the Federal Government to select textbooks for local schools. Other opponents said the legislation would take the Government into areas that were better left to private initiative.

As signed into law, the legislation was substantially similar to the Administration's requests. Congress added the restriction that no more than eight of the corporation's 15 directors could be members of the same political party. It also added the provision that no educational station could editorialize or support or oppose a candidate for political office. Congress refused to grant the Administration's request for an extension of the 1962 facilities construction program through 1972 with an open-ended authorization for fiscal 1969-1972. Instead, it authorized specific sums for each of the fiscal years 1968-1970.

Legislative Action. In spite of the criticisms, the legislation commanded wide support in both chambers. The House passed the bill by a 265-91 roll-call vote and the Senate passed it by voice vote. The House by a **167-194** key roll-call rejected a recommittal motion that would have eliminated the provisions establishing the corporation. This motion, one of two attempts to kill the corporation, was made by Samuel L. Devine (R Ohio) and supported by the conservative coalition, a majority of Republicans and Southern Democrats voting together. Devine's motion also would have authorized $5 million to be divided equally among existing educational broadcasting stations. The second attempt to kill the corporation was an amendment by Albert W. Watson (R S.C.) simply to delete the corporation provisions. It was rejected by a 111-120 teller vote.

Provisions. As signed into law (PL 90-129) Nov. 7, S 1160 contained the following major provisions:

Title I. Construction of Facilities. Extended for three years (through fiscal 1970) the Educational Television Facilities Act of 1962 (PL 87-447) and authorized appropriations of $10.5 million in fiscal 1968, $12.5 million in fiscal 1969, and $15 million in fiscal 1970.

Specified that no more than 8½ percent of the annual appropriations could be used for grants in any one state. This limit replaced the existing ceiling of $1 million per state.

Permitted grants to be made for construction of noncommercial educational radio facilities. (The 1962 Act limited grants to construction of television facilities.)

Increased the maximum federal grant to 75 percent of the cost of a project. (Existing law allowed a 50-percent federal grant plus 25 percent of the cost of an existing facility up to a maximum grant of 75 percent of the cost.)

Eliminated a provision of existing law that no more than 15 percent of a grant could be used for equipment to connect two or more stations.

Extended the provisions of the Act to cover the Virgin Islands, Guam, American Samoa and the Pacific Trust Territories.

Title II. Public Broadcasting Corporation. Authorized the establishment of a nonprofit, nongovernmental corporation, to be known as the Corporation for Public Broadcasting, to give financial assistan_ cial educational television and radio.

Prohibited educational broadcasting editorializing or supporting or opposing a political office. (This provision applied t_ tional television stations, including those ass_ Title I.)

Authorized the corporation to make paym_ local noncommercial educational stations to aid in the _ duction of local educational radio and television p_ grams and to help meet other operating costs.

Authorized the corporation to contract with or to make grants to individuals, noncommercial education_ broadcasting stations, and other production groups to produce or otherwise make available educational radio and television programs for national or regional distribution to educational broadcasting stations.

Authorized the corporation, through grants or contracts with public or private groups, to arrange for one or more systems of interconnection for distribution of educational programs to noncommercial educational stations throughout the country.

Authorized the corporation also to maintain a library and archives of noncommercial educational programs, to publish a journal, to encourage the creation of new noncommercial educational stations and to conduct research, demonstrations or training in noncommercial educational broadcasting.

Directed the corporation to function in ways that would assure "maximum freedom" for educational stations from "interference with or control of program content or other activities."

Directed the corporation to maintain "strict adherence to objectivity and balance in all programs or series of a controversial nature."

Prohibited the corporation from owning or operating any television or radio broadcast station, system or network, community antenna television system or interconnection or program production facility.

Provided for a 15-member board of directors for the corporation, appointed by the President and confirmed by the Senate. Not more than eight directors could be of the same political party. Provided for six-year terms and limited directors to two consecutive terms. (One-third of the first group of directors was to be appointed for two-year terms, one-third for four-year terms and one-third for six-year terms. Thereafter, five directors would be appointed every two years for six-year terms.) Prohibited federal employees from serving as directors.

Authorized appropriations for the corporation of $9 million in fiscal 1968, to remain available until expended.

Limited the maximum grant for any one project or to any one station to $250,000 in fiscal 1968.

Required that the accounts of the corporation be audited annually by an independent accountant. Authorized, but did not require, the General Accounting Office to perform such audits for any year during which federal funds had been made available to the corporation.

Definitions. The following definitions, although contained in Title II of S 1160, amended the 1934 Communications Act so as to apply to both the corporation and educational stations assisted under Title I:

al educational broadcast station—A dio station (1) which is eligible under unications Commission rules to be licensed mmercial educational station and which is operated by a public agency or nonprofit undation, corporation or association, or (2) owned and operated by a municipality and ransmits only noncommercial programs for edu-al purposes.

nterconnection—Use of microwave equipment, boost-pace satellites or other equipment for the trans-n and distribution of television or radio programs to n ncommercial educational television or radio broad-cast stations.

• Educational television or radio programs—Programs which are primarily designed for educational or cultural purposes.

Title III. Instructional Broadcasting Study. Authorized the Secretary of Health, Education and Welfare to conduct a study of instructional television and radio and their relation to each other to determine whether federal aid should be provided.

Authorized appropriations of $500,000 for the study. Required that a report be submitted to Congress by June 30, 1969.

State Technical Services

Congress in 1965 enacted a little-noticed program to help businessmen and industries gain access to the growing body of nonproprietary scientific and technical information available from both federal and private research and development. On signing the State Technical Services Act of 1965 (S 949—PL 89-182) into law, Sept. 14, President Johnson called it "the 'sleeper' of the 89th Congress." He said, "If we had had this legislation 25 or 30 years ago, we might have prevented the economic depression that today exists in Appalachia."

The Act provided $60 million over three years—fiscal 1966-1968—for matching federal grants to states which established technical information programs in connection with state universities, land grant colleges, technical institutions and business administration schools. Under the state programs, businesses and industries would be apprised of the opportunities for applying new—or even well-established—scientific information and techniques to create new products, improve sales, administration and production methods, and adjust to coming trends in the economy of their state and region.

(In 1968, Congress extended the law and authorized $26.6 million for the program through fiscal 1971. The bill was enacted in mid-year (S 3245—PL 90-422). It was not controversial.)

In connection with the state programs, the Commerce Department was to provide a central clearinghouse for collecting pertinent scientific and technological information. At the state level, business-oriented scientific and technical libraries and information services were to be established. The states were to sponsor workshops, seminars, field visits and similar means of educating administrators and technical personnel.

Trade secrets and other proprietary information were not to be available for dissemination under the program, Commerce Department officials explained, but there would remain a vast body of information which was freely available but not widely known. As an example, one official said that a company might be unaware of what computer programing can do in pointing to the best methods of inventory control, warehouse location and production scheduling. But the company's administrators could find out if, under the Act, a state university offered seminars in business application of computer technology.

State, Regional Economic Planning. A major feature of the Act was that it required states which wanted federal assistance to set up five-year economic plans for themselves. The plans would identify the economic resources and problems of the state and region, the major businesses and industries and their resources and problems, and proposed methods of attacking the problems.

The Act also promoted a regional approach to providing technical services and to planning by permitting states to combine their programs. It authorized grants to each state of $25,000 a year, with no matching requirement, for planning purposes. The Commerce Department announced that it planned to spend no more than $2 million a year and no less than $150,000 a year in each state that signed up to provide technical services.

In promoting state and regional economic planning, the Act paralleled the Economic Development Act of 1965, which authorized grants to regional planning commissions modeled on the Appalachian Regional Commission.

Provisions. As signed by the President, S 949, the State Technical Services Act of 1965:

Stated that a wider diffusion of science and technology in business, commerce and industry was essential to the growth of the economy, higher levels of employment and the competitive position of U.S. products in world markets; and that the benefits of federally financed and other research must be placed more fully in the hands of American business by means of federally supported state action.

Authorized the Secretary of Commerce to make matching grants of up to $10 million in fiscal 1966, $20 million in fiscal 1967 and $30 million in fiscal 1968 in support of technical service programs approved by the states through designated state agencies. (Planning grants would not require matching.) Permitted him to reserve 20 percent each year for programs which he determined to have special merit or to be otherwise needed.

Defined technical services as "activities or programs designed to enable businesses, commerce and industrial establishments to acquire and use scientific and engineering information more effectively," such as: disseminating technical information by means of reports, computer tapes, microfilms and reviews and the establishment of state or interstate technical information centers; providing a reference service to identify sources of scientific and engineering expertise; and sponsoring industrial workshops, seminars, training programs, extension courses, demonstrations and field visits to encourage more effective application of technology.

Directed the state agency designated as administrator of the technical services program in each state to use the resources of state and private institutions of higher education which offered degrees in science, engineering or business administration in carrying out the Act.

Directed each designated state agency, as a condition for federal grants, to prepare a five-year plan outlining the economic and technological conditions of the state, taking into account the region's business, commerce and industrial potential and identifying the major regional and industrial problems; directed that the plan specify also the general approaches and methods to be used in the solution of these problems and outline the means of measuring the impact of such assistance on the state and regional economy; and directed that the plan specify how technical services would be administered and coordinated. The five-year plan could be revised annually. Each state would get $25,000 in non-matching funds to prepare its plan.

Directed the designated state agency to prepare also an annual plan for technical services, detailing specific services and showing how they would advance the five-year plan, containing a budget and indicating specific responsibilities assigned to various institutions in the state.

Directed that the annual plans and the five-year plans be filed with the Secretary of Commerce after clearance by the state's Governor. Directed the Secretary to reject a plan if the services were in competition with privately available services.

Encouraged interstate agreements by two or more states combining and coordinating their technical services programs. A single agency could administer combined programs.

Directed designated state agencies to appoint advisory boards representing community interests.

Metric System Study

Legislation enacted in 1968 authorized the Commerce Department to undertake a three-year study of the probable effects of increased use in the United States of the metric system of weights and measures. The Senate had passed a similar bill in 1965 but the House Rules Committee refused to act on companion legislation. The 1968 legislation (HR 3136—PL 90-472) was passed by both chambers with little controversy.

Background. U.S. conversion to the metric system had been debated on and off for 175 years. Supporters of the change said the United States should pay more attention to the worldwide trend toward the metric system.

Perhaps the main impetus to renewed debate on conversion was a growing awareness in business and government that the United States might be suffering economically from its position as one of the last major powers to remain on a system of inches, pounds and Fahrenheit degrees. Britain May 24, 1965, announced its intention to convert to the metric system of meters, grams and centigrade degrees over the next 10 years. Canada later announced plans to undertake a feasibility study of conversion to the metric system.

The possibility that the United States might be losing some foreign trade by remaining on non-metric standards had caused some businessmen formerly opposed to conversion to reconsider their position.

Opposition to conversion to the metric system continued to stem largely from major industries mass-producing complicated goods such as machine tools and automobiles. These industries would face elaborate and expensive retooling of machines and redesign of thousands of component parts to conform to metric equivalents. Other opposition came from interests with widespread international agreements based on the American non-metric system, such as those involving the machine screw industry.

The feasibility study was supported by the Commerce Department, which called the study "long-overdue." The Department said that American trade was declining with metric nations but increasing with non-metric nations. Certain scientific, trade and business organizations also voiced support for a feasibility study on the ground that the "metric trend" was moving most foreign nations toward adoption of the metric system.

Provisions. As signed into law Aug. 9, HR 3136:

Empowered the Secretary of Commerce to study the impact on the United States of worldwide use of the metric system, the practicality and desirability of expanding the use of the metric system in the United States, the feasibility of retaining and promoting worldwide use of other engineering and production standards already in use, and the costs and benefits of alternative methods available to the United States.

Provided guidelines for the study which included consultation with industrial, educational, government, military and scientific experts and evaluation of the costs, benefits and problems to each sector of retaining the existing system or switching to the metric system.

Instructed those conducting the study to weigh the changes in packaging or design of important industrial products that would be necessitated by conversion to the metric system; to investigate the extent that U.S. industrial and engineering standards already made use of the metric system; and to recommend means of meeting the costs and difficulties of any changeover.

Ordered the Secretary of Commerce to make reports whenever necessary and after three years to report the conclusions and recommendations of the study.

Authorized the use of $500,000 in general Commerce Department funds in fiscal 1969 for the first year of the study.

Federal Tax Lien Act

Congress in 1966 enacted the Federal Tax Lien Act of 1966 (HR 11256—PL 89-719).

The bill amended the Internal Revenue Act of 1954 with respect to the priority of federal tax liens and brought that Act more into conformity with the lien provisions of the Uniform Commercial Code, which had been adopted by more than 40 states. The Treasury Department supported the bill and the American Bar Assn. assisted in its preparation.

Under current law, a federal tax lien applied against all of a taxpayer's property at the time his tax liability was assessed; once the lien was recorded with local authorities, it was valid against all creditors of the taxpayer except mortgagees, pledges and purchasers of securities or motor vehicles, who were priority creditors.

HR 11256 placed a larger group of creditors on the same footing with priority creditors; among the new categories were persons holding mechanics liens (liens for wages earned but not paid). Its purpose was to place creditors on a more equal basis and to protect small creditors who might not know that the federal tax lien notice had been recorded with local authorities.

Renegotiation Act

On three occasions during President Johnson's term Congress extended the Renegotiation Act of 1951. The Act provided for recapture by the Government of excessive profits realized by private companies on contracts with Government agencies. (*Congress and the Nation, Vol. I, p. 334.*)

The first of these three extensions came in 1964 (HR 10669—PL 88-339) and continued the 1951 law through June 30, 1966. The second came in 1966 (HR 13431—PL 89-480) and extended the law through June 30, 1968. Both of these extensions, the seventh and eighth for the law, were relatively routine, accompanied only by the expected business opposition which had been present since 1951. The 1968 extension, however, included a number of other provisions dealing with both the 1951 law and various other subjects. (*See below.*)

The Renegotiation Act of 1951 (PL 82-9) was enacted during the Korean War to permit renegotiation of contracts with private companies whose minimum annual business with the Government was $1 million or more. (The original figure was $250,000. Congress in 1953 raised the floor on renegotiable contracts to $500,000, and in 1956 to $1 million.) Since 1951, renegotiation by the Board had resulted in savings to the Government of more than $2 billion.

1968 ACTION. The 1968 legislation (HR 17324—PL 90-634) extending the law included riders dealing with the International Coffee Agreement, industrial development bonds, and the International Antidumping Code. As passed by the House in May, the bill dealt only with the Renegotiation Act extension, an Administration request. The riders were added in the Senate in September and retained, in modified form, in the final bill.

Renegotiation. This provision extended the 1951 law for three years, through June 30, 1971, and made various revisions in the section which governed the renegotiability of contracts for items considered to be standard commercial articles. The effect was to assure that items qualifying for an exemption from renegotiation actually were of a commercial nature. The 1951 law, extended for the ninth time in 1968, provided a procedure for federal recapture of excessive profits realized by private companies on contracts with Government agencies.

Extension of the law was considered by many observers in Washington to be a surprising defeat for defense industries. Because of strong industry pressures,

many of the Renegotiation Board's supporters early in the year expected the extension bill to be bottled up in committee until the Board expired June 30 under existing law.

Among the opponents of the Board were such powerful lobby groups as the National Assn. of Manufacturers, the Chamber of Commerce of the United States, the Aerospace Industries Assn., the Shipbuilders Council of America, the National Canners Assn., Financial Executives Institute, American Textile Manufacturers Institute, National Security Industrial Assn., American Institute of Certified Public Accountants, and the Machinery and Allied Products Institute.

As it developed, the lobbyists were outflanked by a surprising groundswell of countervailing public pressures—directed mainly at key members of the House Ways and Means Committee, where the bill originated. Grassroots support for the Board developed after news media began following the efforts of Rep. Henry B. Gonzalez, a low-ranking Texas Democrat who was not a member of the Committee. Beginning early in 1966, Gonzalez made 17 House speeches in favor of the Board before generating any substantial media interest.

Finally, in late 1967, the *Cleveland Plain Dealer* undertook a vigorous campaign to save the Board and expose the dangers of war profiteering. The paper spurred four Members of the Ohio delegation—Reps. Jackson E. Betts (R), Michael A. Feighan (D), William E. Minshall (R) and Charles A. Vanik (D)—into strong support of the measure.

Two of the Ohio Representatives—Betts and Vanik—were members of the Ways and Means Committee. Joined by Reps. James A. Burke (D Mass.), who was under pressure from his home-town newspaper, *The Boston Globe,* and Martha W. Griffiths (D Mich.), a former Government procurement officer, the Ohioans pushed the bill through the Committee.

Lobbyists were not without one victory, however. They succeeded in beating back attempts by Gonzalez to incorporate requirements for a set of uniform accounting standards that could be used to determine costs and profits of negotiated defense contracts. Gonzalez tried several times in 1968 to get the requirement adopted and succeeded only in having a study made by the Comptroller General for Congress in the ensuing year.

Antidumping Code. The Senate, in a move supported by some domestic industries, sought to prevent the United States from participating in the International Antidumping Code, which was negotiated as part of the Kennedy Round trade talks in 1967 and went into effect July 1, 1968. Supporters of the Senate action said the Code conflicted with the U.S. Antidumping Act of 1921, which was a law to prevent injury to American industry from unfair pricing practices involving goods produced abroad and sold in the United States at prices lower than prices charged in the producer's country. The 1921 law provided that if dumping activities which injured domestic industries were established, a special dumping duty, or tariff, would be imposed on the goods being imported. Opponents of the Code said application of the Code would prevent U.S. officials from finding injury in many cases where injury could be established under the 1921 Act. The differences were resolved in the final version of HR 17324 by providing that the 1921 Act would have supremacy in any case where it and the Code were in conflict; the Senate's ban on U.S. participation in the Code was dropped.

Coffee Agreement. This rider, which was not controversial, authorized the United States to continue to participate in the International Coffee Agreement. The provision was required because the Senate June 28 ratified a treaty extending the original International Coffee Agreement of 1962, which was scheduled to expire Sept. 30. The 1962 Agreement was extended for five years, but the implementation was extended by HR 17324 for only two years. Supporters of the shorter extension said it would allow Congress to review operation of the treaty sooner than would otherwise be possible. The International Agreement was designed to keep coffee prices stable.

Industrial Development Bonds. The most controversial rider to HR 17324 reopened the question of federal income tax exemption for municipal development bonds. The bonds were used increasingly by communities to finance the cost of plants for manufacturers moving into their areas. Extensive use of the bonds, which created various problems, caused Congress earlier in the year to limit the size of a bond issue on which the interest would be tax-free to $1 million. The Senate sought to raise the limit to $5 million through a rider on HR 17324. The final bill, however, kept the $1-million ceiling but allowed a community to elect to use a $5-million ceiling if it were willing to work within certain restrictions. The key restriction specified that the $5-million figure had to include any tax-exempt bonds issued plus any other capital expenditures which the company benefiting from the bonds made within the borders of the governmental unit issuing the bonds. The purpose was to prevent a company from paying the costs of, say, a $20-million plant partly from a tax-exempt $5-million bond issue and partly from other sources of revenue, such as its own savings or a taxable bond issue of its own. A company also could build one plant from tax-exempt bonds issued by the community and another plant within the same community from other funds.

The conference agreement on the issue specified that the $5-million ceiling would apply for a six-year period beginning three years before the tax-exempt bonds were issued and ending three years after they were issued. The three-year period following issue meant that a bond issue which originally was tax exempt could lose that status if later company investment in the area pushed total capital expenditures above the $5-million ceiling. However, if this happened, the interest on the bonds was to become taxable only as of the time the $5-million limit was exceeded.

The basic purpose of the provision was to assure that tax-exempt industrial revenue bonds were used only to assist small businesses in locating in a community. In explaining the agreement, Rep. Wilbur D. Mills (D Ark.) said the $5-million provision in the conference report would continue to provide tax-free interest on about 87 percent of the industrial development bond issues. *(For other stories on the subject, see tax policy chapter p. 177.)*

Provisions. As signed into law, Oct. 24, HR 17324 contained the following major provisions:

Renegotiation Act. Extended the Renegotiation Act of 1951 for three years, through June 30, 1971.

Revised the exemptions (from renegotiation) in existing law for standard commercial articles and services to assure that items qualifying for exemption actually were of a commercial nature. The major revisions:

● Provided that at least 55 percent (rather than the existing 35 percent) of total sales of an article be to commercial buyers if an article was to qualify for the standard commercial exemption from renegotiability.

● Repealed an existing provision which allowed the percentages test to be computed from sales in the current year and the preceding year, thereby limiting the test to current-year sales.

● Specified that an article would not qualify for a commercial exemption if the price charged the Government in an otherwise nonrenegotiable sale exceeded the lowest price charged in a comparable commercial sale except when the higher price to the Government was due to "significantly different circumstances" in producing or delivering the article.

● Specified that contractors whose application of the standard commercial exemption brought their annual Government business to below the $1-million renegotiation minimum, must file a report with the Renegotiation Board about the application of the exemption and about renegotiable sales generally. (Existing law allowed the contractor to apply the exemption on his own, making it possible for him to put renegotiable sales below the minimum and removing him from any reporting requirements to justify his actions.)

Antidumping Code. Specified that nothing in the International Antidumping Code would restrict the discretion of the U.S. Tariff Commission in performing its duties under the Antidumping Act of 1921.

Specified that the Tariff Commission and the Secretary of the Treasury must resolve any conflict between the International Code and the 1921 Act in favor of the Act, and could take into account the Code's provisions only insofar as they were consistent with the Act.

Directed the President to report by Aug. 1, 1969, on actions taken under the 1921 Act and the International Code during the period July 1, 1968, to June 30, 1969.

Coffee Agreement. Provided for continued U.S. participation in the International Coffee Agreement for a period of two years, until Sept. 30, 1970.

Provided that U.S. participation in the Agreement would be suspended if the President determined, after an investigation, that U.S. ships were being discriminated against in transporting coffee and the discrimination had not been ended through the use of other methods. Participation would resume once the discriminatory practices ended.

Industrial Development Bonds. Provided an alternative to the existing $1-million limit on the size of an industrial development bond issue on which the interest would be exempt from federal income tax, as follows:

● Specified that a community could elect to issue industrial revenue bonds for use by a private concern up to a level of $5 million without the interest on the bonds being taxable.

● Required, however, that if a community elected to use the higher figure, the $5-million ceiling had to cover the bonds issued by the community for the concern plus any capital expenditures financed from other sources by that concern within that community for a six-year period beginning three years before and ending three years after the bonds were issued.

Technology Report

The National Commission on Technology, Automation, and Economic Progress issued Feb. 2, 1966, a report on its year-long study into the effects of technological change on American life. Established in 1964, the Commission investigated a broad range of problems relating to automation, unemployment and the influence of these factors on the quality of life. Large parts of the report were devoted to ways of sustaining employment, but the section that attracted the most attention dealt with a guaranteed income level for the poor.

Background. Congress in 1964 enacted legislation (PL 88-444) creating the Commission and asking it to (1) identify the impact of technology on production and employment; (2) define community and human needs which the new technologies might meet; and (3) recommend measures to be taken by the Federal Government and local governments which would facilitate adjustment and alleviate problems of displaced workers. President Johnson Nov. 14, 1964, created the 14-member Commission and appointed as its chairman Howard R. Bowen, president of the University of Iowa. Other members were leaders from industry, labor, universities and Negro organizations.

Conclusions. The Commission's final report concluded that failure of the economy to expand rapidly enough, not automation, was the main threat to a continued high level of employment. The severe unemployment following the Korean War was a result, according to the report, of an inadequate growth rate, a fact "firmly supported by the response of the economy to the expansionary fiscal policy of the past five years."

The report distinguished between the general level of unemployment and the displacement of particular workers in particular situations. It said: "Technological change (along with other forms of economic change) is an important determinant of the precise places, industries, and people affected by unemployment. But the general level of demand for goods and services is by far the most important factor determining how many are affected, how long they stay unemployed, and how hard it is for new entrants to the labor market to find jobs. The basic fact is that technology eliminates jobs, not work.

However, the report said, to keep up with the rising rate of productivity (measured by output per man-hour) and the rapid expansion of the labor force, "both unprecedented in our history," there would be a "continuing need for aggressive fiscal and monetary policies to stimulate growth."

The Commission added that Negroes—because of what the report called 300 years of abuse—should be given special consideration in the years ahead, much as returning U.S. servicemen were benefited after World War II. The report cautioned that unless numbers of Negroes were able to move into white-collar jobs, their high unemployment rate would continue because the percentage of unskilled jobs would decrease in the future as a result of technology.

The report noted that while "technology has, on balance, surely been a great blessing to mankind," there also had been "social costs and dislocations flowing from past technological changes." Among such costs, it said, were harmful influences on the physical and community environment, such as pollution and urban blight, and influences on human personality leading to rootlessness, anonymity, insecurity, monotony and even mental disorder. The report contained proposals to attack some of the physical and social ills resulting from modern technology.

Recommendations. Technological change, the report said, must be met with a far-ranging combination of spending programs—public works, research, and aid to the jobless. Observing that automation required increased mobility in the work force, the Commission recommended several measures to match jobs with the jobless, including more extensive education and training, a permanent program of worker relocation assistance (authorized on an experimental basis by the Manpower Development and Training Act through fiscal 1968), federalization of the state employment services, and creation of a national computerized job-man matching system.

Even with the best of fiscal policies, the report said, "there will always be those handicapped in the competition for jobs" by discrimination or lack of skills. For all those able and willing to work the Commission recommended that the Government be an "employer of last resort" by financing a program of public service employment. Since the jobs would provide essential services, such as urban renewal, hospital care and welfare, the report said, no "makework" would be involved. The report estimated that a potential 5.3 million jobs existed in these public service fields. The Commission acknowledged that this employment concept had already been recognized, as in the Neighborhood Youth Corps of the "war on poverty," program, but they recommended that it be "expanded and made explicit as a permanent, long-term program."

Guaranteed Income. The most controversial of the Commission's suggestions was its "income maintenance" plan for persons incapable of working. The Commission said: "We are convinced that rising productivity has brought this country to the point at last when all citizens may have a decent standard of living at a cost in resources the economy can easily bear....The Commission recommends also that Congress go beyond a reform of the present structure and examine wholly new approaches to the problem of income maintenance. In particular, we suggest that Congress give serious study to a 'minimum income allowance' or 'negative income tax' program. Such a program, if found feasible, should be designed to approach by stages the goal of eliminating the need for means-test public assistance programs by providing a floor of adequate minimum incomes."

In a related development, the Advisory Council on Public Welfare, after a two-year study of federally assisted welfare programs, reported to the Secretary of Health, Education and Welfare. It included in its recommendations a guaranteed income for all persons, to be provided by public assistance payments based entirely on need. The 12-member Council was composed mainly of experts in the social welfare field, together with representatives of labor, medicine, business and Negro organizations. The Council was appointed in 1964 by the Secretary of Health, Education and Welfare, acting under a Congressional directive included in the Public Welfare Amendments of 1962.

Labor Dissent. The final report of the Commission was signed by all 14 members, but it contained reservations by the three representatives of labor: Joseph A. Beirne, president of the Communications Workers of America; Albert J. Hayes, former president of the International Assn. of Machinists; and Walter P. Reuther, president of the United Automobile Workers. At the time of an earlier preliminary report (the fourth draft, com-

pleted Dec. 22, 1965), the labor representatives threatened to write a dissent, opposing some of the general and particular conclusions of the report. In an effort to avoid the division, the report was rewritten with some of the controversial sections omitted. Reportedly deleted from the final report was language opposing a shorter workweek, criticizing the seniority system used in labor contracts, recommending changes in collective bargaining, and criticizing labor's record on civil rights. The conclusion of the report that technology does not strongly affect the general level of employment also was said to be unpopular with the labor representatives. However, it was retained in the final version.

Chapter 4—Crime and Justice

Key Votes

In this chapter, key roll-call votes are shown in bold-face type. The party breakdown on each of these votes and the position taken by each Member of Congress may be found in the key vote charts which appear in the appendix to this book.

Crime and Justice

CRIME as a national political issue first surfaced in the 1964 Presidential election campaign. Four years later, in the 1968 elections, "law and order" had become the most emotionally charged, and perhaps the most crucial, of all domestic issues.

To understand the emergence of crime as a political issue, it was necessary to turn first to statistics which recorded a horrifying rise in crime rates during the 1960s. Reliable data were lacking, but the Uniform Crime Reports published annually by the Federal Bureau of Investigation indicated the pattern: more than 3.8 million serious crimes were reported during 1967, a 16 percent rise over 1966 and an 89 percent rise over 1960. Violent crime was up 73 percent over 1960, crime against property up 91 percent.

Nor was that the whole story. Much of the increase in crime was found in the cities, where more and more of the U.S. population was concentrated. Much of it was street crime—the most visible and usually the most violent of the many varieties of crime in the United States. A disproportionate share was committed by young people, and by 1968 almost one-half of all Americans were 25 years of age or younger. The nation's failure to resolve its problems of race, poverty and urbanization contributed to the complexities of the picture. So did urban riots, student rebellions and widespread illegal use of narcotics. Finally, there was assassination: John F. Kennedy, Martin Luther King, Robert F. Kennedy—each the victim of an assassin's bullets.

Although the soaring crime rates bred anxiety, fear and the urge to take remedial action, there was no general agreement on causes and cures. In part this was attributable to ignorance: there had been no major federal study of crime as a national problem since one made by the Wickersham Commission in 1931, and until the 1960s only a handful of scholars and scientists really examined the problem in detail. Even the existing statistics on crime committed were hopelessly inadequate. Thus, the general response to crime tended to be more emotional than reasoned.

References

For Congressional action on crime legislation in the 1945-64 period, see *Congress and the Nation*, Vol. I, p. 1671-1675. For judicial appointments and court legislation, 1945-64, see Vol, I, p. 1441-1454.

The Nature of Crime

"A skid-row drunk lying in a gutter is crime. So is the killing of an unfaithful wife. A Costa Nostra conspiracy to bribe public officials is crime. So is a strong-arm robbery by a 15-year-old boy. The embezzlement of a corporation's funds by an executive is crime. So is the possession of marijuana cigarettes by a student. These crimes can no more be lumped together for purposes of analysis than can measles and schizophrenia, or lung cancer and a broken ankle. As with disease, so with crime: if causes are to be understood, if risks are to be evaluated, and if preventive or remedial actions are to be taken, each kind must be looked at separately. Thinking of 'crime' as a whole is futile."

President's Commission on Law Enforcement and Administration of Justice, 1967 report.

To those who found the causes of crime in a "breakdown of morality" or the "permissiveness" of American society, the solution was fairly simple—more vigorous police action, stiffer court sentences and less rigid regard for procedural technicality. Others held that the root of the problem lay in broader social areas—poverty, ghetto conditions, inadequate police protection and unsuccessful corrections systems.

THROUGHOUT his years in the White House, President Johnson repeatedly pointed to poverty as the breeding ground of crime in big cities. His ultimate solution was "jobs, education and hope."

However, the President also pressed for short-term objectives. Soon after his election in 1964, he began work on an anticrime program which he saw as an integral part of his "Great Society." Much of the program, as it finally emerged, was the work of the President's Crime Commission—more formally the President's Commission on Law Enforcement and Administration of Justice—which Mr. Johnson appointed in 1965. The Commission's February 1967 report was a document of historic importance, the first major federal study of crime since the Wickersham Commission report in 1931. The central conclusion of the 1967 report was that significant reduction in crime was possible despite the inherent difficulties of the problem. It recommended, among other things, the upgrading of state and local police forces, improvement of methods of law enforcement and criminal justice at all levels and compilation of more accurate and comprehensive crime statistics. "We need to know much more about crime," the Commission said. "A national strategy against crime must be in large part a strategy of search."

The Commission also wrestled with the problem of defining the federal role in the war on crime. Traditionally, the Federal Government had remained aloof from local crime matters, viewing them as problems essentially to be dealt with by state and local governments. President Johnson repeatedly said that in his view the nation rejected the idea of a national police force. The Crime Commission also recognized the special state and local responsibility for day-to-day criminal administration, but it proposed a massive program of federal aid for planning, research and training.

Crime Legislation

President Johnson accepted the Commission's views on an enlarged federal role in the attack on crime. Building on the experience of a demonstration law enforcement assistance program which Congress had authorized in 1965, the President in 1967 proposed a "Safe Streets" act to channel federal funds to local police departments

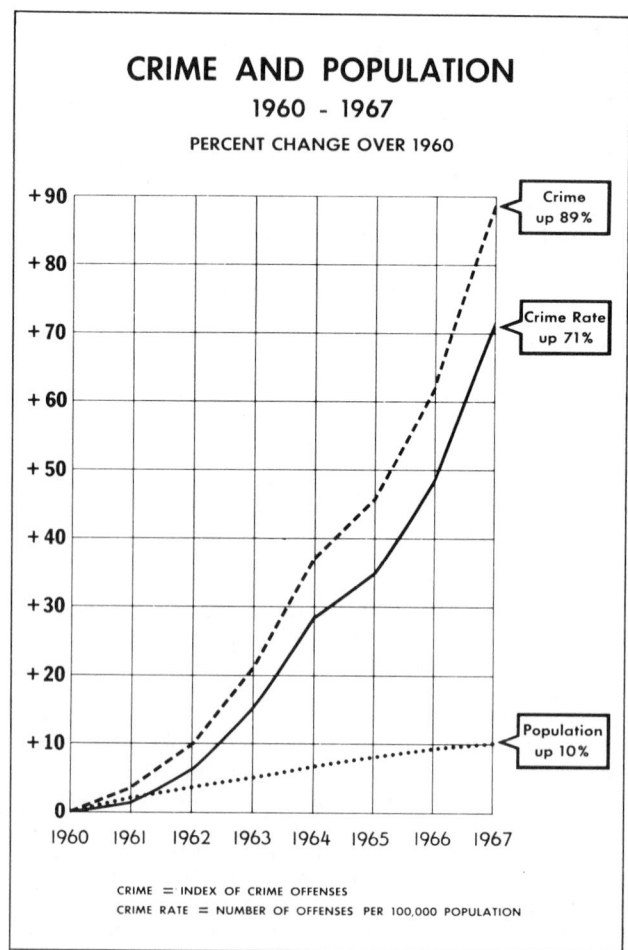

CRIME = INDEX OF CRIME OFFENSES
CRIME RATE = NUMBER OF OFFENSES PER 100,000 POPULATION

FBI CHART

and other law enforcement and correctional agencies. Mr. Johnson was convinced that a direct attack on crimes against property and persons depended on upgrading law enforcement agencies and that large amounts of money—unobtainable by state and local governments—would be needed to accomplish that goal.

Congress did not enact the legislation in 1967 but did so the following year. However, the President paid dearly for it, as Congress loaded the bill with provisions he opposed. It added a section permitting police wiretapping and bugging in a wide variety of criminal cases; this was in direct contradiction to Administration proposals that wiretapping and other forms of electronic surveillance be limited to national security cases. In addition, Congress added a section purporting to overturn three Supreme Court decisions which dealt with the rights of suspects during police interrogation. Congress weakened the President's proposed gun control provisions, making controls applicable only to handguns. Later in the session, Congress enacted another bill extending controls to rifles and shotguns, but it denied the President's request for provisions to require federal registration of guns and licensing of gun owners. (Without the impetus of the King and Robert Kennedy assassinations, it is doubtful that any gun controls would have been enacted in 1968.) Finally even the President's grant program did not emerge unscathed: Congress added the "block grant" approach of sending federal funds to state governments rather than directly to local communities as the President had proposed.

Although the Safe Streets law was the heart of the President's crime program, Mr. Johnson also proposed and Congress enacted a number of other key measures.

Most important of these was a major juvenile delinquency control program designed to channel federal funds to the states to plan and operate projects to prevent juvenile delinquency and to rehabilitate youthful offenders. Here again, Congress added the block grant approach to the President's program.

A landmark bail reform law, enacted in 1966, was designed to facilitate the release of accused persons who were too poor to raise bail. Widely heralded at the time it was enacted, the Bail Reform Act by 1968 was under attack on grounds that it required the release of persons who were likely to commit further crimes before they came to trial.

Other laws were directed toward drug abuse control, prisoner rehabilitation, rehabilitation of alcoholics and narcotics addicts, increased support for the federal judiciary and revision of the federal criminal code. Just as the King and Kennedy assassinations influenced the enactment of gun control legislation, so the specter of urban rioting led to enactment of a variety of antiriot legislation.

In summary, increasing crime rates—and the public alarm they aroused—led to a gradual stiffening of attitudes, both in Congress and the Administration, during the 1965-68 period. Although many leaders continued to see ultimate solutions in broad social terms, they became convinced of the need for a tough immediate attack on the problem. The result was a level of federal action that would have been inconceivable ten years earlier. Thus, as the Presidency passed to Richard M. Nixon in 1969, the Federal Government was committed to a massive and unprecedented role in the war on crime.

Supreme Court on Crime

The Supreme Court in the 1960s embarked on a broad review of the operation of the criminal justice system in America.

It found the system in need of repair.

In a series of landmark decisions, the Court substantially liberalized court procedures, especially in state criminal prosecutions. Reading the 14th Amendment broadly, it made binding on the states more and more of the rights contained in the Bill of Rights, which originally were binding only on the Federal Government.

The hallmark of these decisions was equal treatment by the law—for federal and state defendants alike and for rich and poor alike.

The decisions, especially those having to do with self-incrimination and the right to counsel, were highly controversial. They generated the most severe criticism of the Court in several decades.

Critics contended that the Court was too concerned with the rights of suspects and defendants, and not sufficiently sensitive to the needs of police for some latitude in investigating crime and interrogating suspects. Those critics said the Court was "soft" on criminals and "coddled" them while at the same time "handcuffing" law enforcement. They called for rebalancing the law to provide for more freedom of police action while at the same time preserving the rights of defendants.

Supporters of the Court responded with the arguments that the basic concept of the Constitution was that of restraint on governmental force, including police force. They contended that the police, given proper training and techniques, could operate well and efficiently within the confines of the Bill of Rights.

Apart from legal and constitutional issues involved, critics of the Court's decisions said they generated an atmosphere of "permissiveness" in American society which contributed to the national crime rate increase. Supporters of the Court said the decisions bore no causal relation to criminal activity at all.

The most controversial decision probably was *Miranda v. Arizona* (1966), decided by a narrow 5-4 vote. In an opinion written by Chief Justice Earl Warren, the Court prescribed rules for police to follow in informing suspects of their constitutional rights before proceeding with interrogation.

The *Miranda* decision capped a series of decisions of previous years in which the Court reached farther and farther back along the prosecutorial trail to extend basic rights to state prisoners. That series was highlighted by *Gideon v. Wainwright* (1963), in which the Court held that state defendants were entitled to counsel at trial for non-capital felony offenses even if they were too poor to pay for a lawyer.

The next step came in *Malloy v. Hogan* (1964), in which the Court held for the first time that the 5th Amendment privilege against self-incrimination was binding on the states. In order to make that privilege meaningful, the Court began to combine it with the right to counsel on the theory that the average citizen needed professional legal advice on matters potentially affecting his liberty or life.

Thus, in *Escobedo v. Illinois* (1964), the Court turned its attention from the courtroom to the police station.

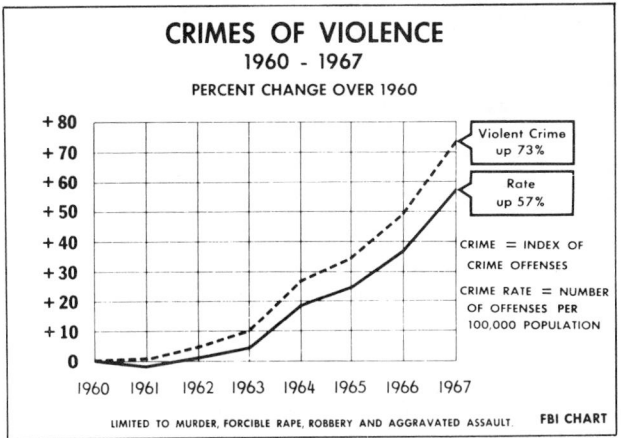

CRIMES OF VIOLENCE
1960 - 1967
PERCENT CHANGE OVER 1960

Violent Crime up 73%

Rate up 57%

CRIME = INDEX OF CRIME OFFENSES

CRIME RATE = NUMBER OF OFFENSES PER 100,000 POPULATION

LIMITED TO MURDER, FORCIBLE RAPE, ROBBERY AND AGGRAVATED ASSAULT.   FBI CHART

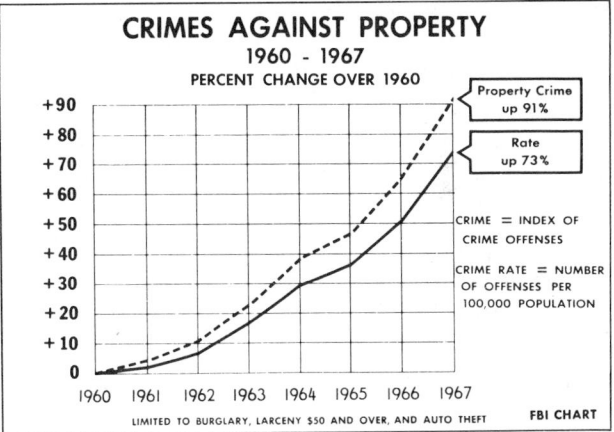

CRIMES AGAINST PROPERTY
1960 - 1967
PERCENT CHANGE OVER 1960

Property Crime up 91%

Rate up 73%

CRIME = INDEX OF CRIME OFFENSES

CRIME RATE = NUMBER OF OFFENSES PER 100,000 POPULATION

LIMITED TO BURGLARY, LARCENY $50 AND OVER, AND AUTO THEFT   FBI CHART

It held that when "investigatory" police interrogation became "accusatorial," the 5th Amendment privilege took effect and the person under arrest was entitled to counsel. The final step came in *Miranda*, which laid down detailed rules for carrying out the *Escobedo* decision.

Hostility in Congress. Strong criticism of the Court's decisions, especially among conservatives, surfaced frequently in Congress, usually in speeches. In 1968, however, it was apparent twice on important issues on which votes were taken. The first was in Senate consideration of the Omnibus Crime Control and Safe Streets Act of 1968, in which Congress accepted Senate amendments attempting to alter some of the Court's decisions. The Senate balked, however, at efforts to limit the Court's jurisdiction to review state criminal law rulings.

The second instance came on Oct. 1, 1968, when the Senate, after acrid debate about the Court, refused to invoke cloture on debate on a motion to consider the nomination of Associate Justice Abe Fortas to succeed Chief Justice Earl Warren, who sought to retire. President Johnson the following day announced he would withdraw the nomination; he formally did so on Oct. 4. Other factors were involved, but the hostility toward the Court was evident.

New Trend. Beginning in 1966, something of a new trend was noticeable in the Court's handling of criminal procedural issues. The Court upheld the use of informants and undercover agents, of the police lineup, of handwriting exemplars and of "stop-and-frisk" practices, and it clarified the constitutionality of wiretapping.

Chronology

Of Legislation

On Crime

1965

Congress in 1965 passed several anticrime and criminal rehabilitation bills. It enacted part of President Johnson's legislative proposals, but it took no action on Administration requests for a gun control law or for a bill providing civil commitment for drug addicts.

While the session produced only a small quantity of anticrime legislation, it marked a turning point in Congressional and Administration views of the crime problem. The emphasis of the session was more on study of the underlying causes of crime than on immediate action and more on prevention and rehabilitation measures than on strictly punitive laws.

The President appointed two commissions, one national in scope and the other concentrating on the District of Columbia, and gave them the task of developing new approaches to solving the generally worsening crime problem. In addition he emphasized his antipoverty and education programs as the long-run solution to crime.

Among bills enacted were those providing for federal assistance in training local law enforcement officers, extending federal control over stimulants and depressants (so-called "pep pills"), renewing existing juvenile delinquency legislation, authorizing new rehabilitation techniques for federal prisoners and providing for a study of manpower needs in the field of correctional rehabilitation.

A new law made it a federal crime to kill, kidnap or assault the President, while another bill made it a federal crime to travel in interstate commerce for the purpose of committing arson. The latter was the so-called "fire for hire" law aimed at professional arsonists and was the major law against organized crime enacted during the session.

The President March 8 outlined his program in a major message to Congress, the first Presidential message ever devoted exclusively to crime.

PRESIDENT'S PROGRAM. President Johnson, in his March 8 message, referred to crime as "a malignant enemy" in America's midst, but he saw its cure more in terms of patient therapy than urgent surgery. He said in that message:

"Plainly, laws are less likely to command the respect of those forced to live at the margins of our society. Stability and order have little meaning and small advantage to those who exist in poverty, hopelessness and despair.

"The long-run solution to this view of crime is jobs, education and hope. This is a goal to which this country is now committed."

The President did, however, ask Congress to enact a number of anticrime laws. He said the Federal Government could act best in four areas: "organized crime, narcotic and drug control, regulation of gun sales and law enforcement activities in the District of Columbia." He added that federal efforts would be useful in juvenile delinquency studies, assistance in training local peace officers and providing comprehensive surveys of crime. The rest—meaning the major burden of combating crime—would fall to state and local governments, he said.

The President March 8 said he would appoint a national commission to study the causes and cures of crime. He subsequently by Executive Order established the President's Commission on Law Enforcement and Administration of Justice, headed by Attorney General Nicholas deB. Katzenbach. The Commission filed its report in 1967. *(See below.)* The President also appointed a crime commission to study law enforcement in the District of Columbia. That group reported in 1966.

Action on Requests

In his message, the President made no specific requests for legislation to combat organized crime. Following is a summary of Congressional action on specific requests in other areas covered by the message:

NARCOTIC AND DRUG CONTROL. The President asked for laws extending federal control over depressant and stimulant drugs, the so-called "pep pills." Congress fulfilled this request by enacting an Administration-backed bill (HR 2—PL 89-74), the Drug Abuse Control Amendments of 1965 to the Food, Drug and Cosmetic Act. The law expanded federal controls over barbiturates, amphetamines and other drugs affecting the central nervous system or producing hallucinogenic effects. *(See chapter on Health.)*

CIVIL COMMITMENT. The President also urged passage of a bill providing for civil commitment of addicts who were "likely to respond to treatment and achieve rehabilitation" and recommended a less restrictive law than the existing one, which specified mandatory minimum sentences without probation or parole. Central feature of the Administration bill (S 2152, HR 9167) was to provide for civil commitment of addicts who were charged with a federal crime. If the rehabilitation of the addict proved successful, he would in effect be excused from prosecution for his crime and would have no criminal record. A House Judiciary subcommittee held hearings on this and other bills, but no action was taken. Congress in 1966 enacted civil commitment legislation. *(See p. 315.)*

GUN CONTROL. Mr. Johnson asked for amendments to the 1938 Federal Firearms Act to prohibit interstate shipment of arms except by dealers licensed by the Treasury (thus halting mail-order sales), to curb imports of surplus military weapons, to place stricter curbs on gun sales by retail dealers and to raise licensing fees.

Extensive hearings were held by the Senate Judiciary Subcommittee on Juvenile Delinquency, headed by Sen. Thomas J. Dodd (D Conn.), and the House Ways and Means Committee, but no bill was reported in 1965. (Gun control legislation was enacted in 1968. *See p. 323, 328.)*

Strong pressures against the legislation were generated by the National Rifle Assn. and other gun and sports groups. Opponents argued that most gun-control proposals would not keep firearms out of the hands of criminals or deranged persons and would impose hardships on legitimate hunters and gun enthusiasts. They also raised constitutional objections to the proposals, citing the 2nd Amendment guarantee of the right "to keep and bear arms."

Earlier hearings on gun control legislation had been held by Dodd's subcommittee and the Senate Commerce Committee in 1963-64. Interest in such legislation had been spurred by the 1963 assassination of President Kennedy with a mail-order rifle. *(For background see p. 324.)*

JUVENILE DELINQUENCY. The President asked for additional funds for federally sponsored study and demonstration projects on juvenile delinquency. The Administration subsequently asked for a two-year extension of the 1961 Juvenile Delinquency and Youth Offenses Control Act, previously extended in 1964. *(Congress and the Nation, Vol. I, p. 1323.)* Congress enacted a one-year extension (HR 8131—PL 89-69), through fiscal 1967, and authorized appropriations of $6.5 million for fiscal 1966 and $10 million for fiscal 1967. (The 1964 extension had not authorized funds for fiscal 1966.)

LAW ENFORCEMENT ASSISTANCE. Mr. Johnson urged enactment of the Law Enforcement Assistance Act of 1965 to supplement such federal training programs for local law enforcement officers as the FBI had conducted for a number of years. The Act was intended to provide training programs and demonstration projects in police work to update and improve the standards of local law enforcement personnel.

The measure (HR 8027—PL 89-197) was passed by the House Aug. 2 and the Senate Sept. 8. During the three-year life of the program, fiscal 1966 through fiscal 1968, Congress appropriated a total of $22 million.

Other Legislation

In addition to the legislation requested by President Johnson in his March 8 message, Congress considered a number of other crime measures in 1965. Following is a summary of these bills and the action taken on them:

ARSON. Congress enacted a bill (HR 6507—PL 89-68) which made it a federal crime to travel in interstate commerce for the purpose of committing arson, a practice called "fire for hire." Such activity could be punished by a maximum $10,000 fine and/or five years in prison. In requesting the law, an amendment to the interstate racketeering law, the Justice Department said that professional arson had become a "profitable business" in organized crime and had cost more than $16 million in insurance claims in the prior 10 years. State law enforcement was frustrated when arsonists fled to another state, the Department said.

BOMB THREATS. Another bill (HR 6848—PL 89-64), requested by the Justice Department, provided a civil penalty of not more than $1,000 against persons who falsely reported bombs aboard planes, motor vehicles, railroads or vessels. The penalty was to be recovered by a civil action brought in the name of the United States. Prior to 1961, the law provided penalties of up to $1,000 fine and/or one year's imprisonment for false bomb threats. In 1961 it was amended to include persons who made such reports without malicious intent; for persons having malicious intent, maximum penalties of fines up to $5,000 and/or five years' imprisonment were provided. The Department said it found it difficult to obtain convictions against persons of good repute who reported bombs as a joke or prank but without malice, as juries were reluctant to render guilty verdicts. HR 6848 eliminated the fine and prison sentences for persons acting without malice, but left the $5,000/five-year penalty for malicious intent intact.

PRESIDENTIAL ASSASSINATION. Congress enacted legislation (HR 6964—PL 89-172) authorizing new federal crime to kill, kidnap or assault the President and certain other high Government officials. *(See chapter on the Presidency for details.)*

PRISONER REHABILITATION. Congress enacted legislation (HR 6964—PL 89-176) authorizing new rehabilitation procedures for inmates of the federal prison system. The new procedures, which had been in effect in some state prison systems for several years, authorized use of "halfway houses" for prisoners about to be released, permitted emergency leaves for prisoners and daytime release for paid jobs or training programs.

The Administration proposed the measure, and Congress made only minor changes in it. These changes reflected the fears of some Senators and Representatives about the impact on the local labor markets of the work release program. The bill was thus amended in the Judiciary Committees of both the Senate and House to stiffen safeguards for local labor pools.

CORRECTIONAL REHABILITATION. The Correctional Rehabilitation Study Act of 1965 (HR 2263—PL 89-178) authorized a three-year study of the nation's needs in manpower and training in the field of rehabilitation of prisoners and delinquents.

HR 2263 amended the Vocational Rehabilitation Act to authorize the Secretary of Health, Education and Welfare to make grants for studies of personnel needs in the correctional field—probation officers, social workers, rehabilitation counselors and the like. The bill authorized appropriations of $500,000 for fiscal 1966 and $800,000 for each of the two succeeding fiscal years to carry out the program.

The bill was supported by the Departments of Justice and HEW, and endorsed by 25 Governors and more than 100 state and local officials in the correctional field.

There was no opposition to it in Congress, and the House and Senate versions of the bill differed in only one respect. The House version specified that advice on the grants should come from the National Advisory Council on Vocational Rehabilitation while the Senate version called for a new Advisory Council on Correctional Manpower and Training to furnish the advice. The House accepted this amendment without controversy.

Congress appropriated the full amounts authorized for the study in fiscal 1966-68.

D.C. CRIME. The House and Senate in 1965 passed differing versions of a bill (HR 5688) revising the District of Columbia Criminal Code. However, the bill did not emerge from conference until 1966, and then the President vetoed it. A somewhat similar bill was enacted in 1967. *(See p. 319.)*

Supporters of the bill contended that the steady rise in the crime rate in the District showed a need for change in existing criminal laws and procedures, especially those permitting police to question suspects.

HR 5688 was passed by the House March 22, on a 251-131 (R 106-11; D 145-120) roll-call vote. The Senate passed the bill Aug. 31, 86-7.

Central points of difference between the House and Senate versions were provisions permitting police interrogation of suspects, authorizing investigative arrests, nullifying the *Mallory* rule (relating to admissibility of confessions) and modifying the *Durham* rule (relating to the defense of insanity).

Passage of HR 5688 was the culmination of efforts in Congress since 1958 to upset two major court rulings affecting the District of Columbia. The rulings were *Mallory v. U.S.*, decided by the Supreme Court in 1957, and *Durham v. U.S.*, decided by the Court of Appeals for the District of Columbia in 1954.

In *Mallory*, the Court held that "unnecessary delay" in arraigning a criminal defendant vitiated his interim confession to police as a violation of Rule 5(a) of the Federal Rules of Criminal Procedure, which required arraignment "without unnecessary delay."

Durham abolished the old right-and-wrong insanity test and enunciated a new test, that "an accused person is not criminally responsible if his unlawful act was the product of mental disease or defect." Previous efforts in Congress to change the *Mallory* rule were unsuccessful. *(Congress and the Nation, Vol. I, p. 1672-73.)*

HR 5688 was essentially the same as an omnibus D.C. crime bill passed by the House in 1963. *(Congress and the Nation, Vol. I, p. 1674.)*

BOXING COMMISSION. The House passed but the Senate did not act upon a bill (HR 8635) establishing a Federal Boxing Commission to rid that sport of racketeering. *(See chapter on Government.)*

BAIL REFORM. The Senate Sept. 21 passed the Bail Reform Act (S 1357), authorizing the release of accused persons prior to trial and making a number of other changes in pretrial procedures affecting, in most cases, the indigent. S 1357 had strong bipartisan backing and the support of the Administration. It became law in 1966. *(See below.)*

PRETRIAL INFORMATION. Subcommittees of the Senate Judiciary Committee held hearings on a bill (S 290) to restrict information released to the press about persons accused of federal crime, but the bill was not reported. The issue of prejudicial pretrial publicity was raised in the Warren Report on the assassination of President Kennedy, a report critical of news media handling of the alleged guilt of Lee Harvey Oswald and Jack Ruby.

1966

Congress in 1966 enacted several anticrime measures, but it deferred action on some key bills and formulated no broad program to cope with the rising crime rate across the nation.

Crime in the streets—the kind most obvious and dangerous for the average citizen—was seen by Congress as largely a matter for local law enforcement. In addition, the Administration presented no comprehensive anticrime program in 1966, preferring to await results of the major crime study undertaken by the President's Commission on Law Enforcement and Administration of Justice. That study, the first of its kind since the 1930s, was initiated in 1965 and completed early in 1967.

The President repeatedly said, however, that the seed-bed of crime was in the slums of cities and that any all-out attack on crime had to encompass an attack on poverty. President Johnson's March 9 Message on Crime and Law Enforcement made few new legislative proposals; most of his requests had been put forward previously in a similar message in 1965.

Congress passed several Administration-backed bills, extending the life of the Office of Law Enforcement Assistance (OLEA), establishing new federal bail procedures, authorizing civil commitment of narcotic addicts and establishing a commission to propose revisions in federal criminal law. It also doubled the appropriations of the Bureau of Drug Abuse Control, which controls distribution of stimulant and depressant drugs, the so-called "pep pills."

Congress took no final action on other Presidential requests for legislation to provide for training local police, to control firearms, to unify the federal correctional system, to provide for immunity of witnesses compelled to testify in racketeering prosecutions and to protect witnesses in federal investigations.

President Johnson received one major setback from Congress when it refused to increase funds for the OLEA, a Justice Department agency which administered a program of grants for experiments and demonstrations in local law enforcement. The OLEA, established in 1965, was the main Administration machinery for stimulating improvement in law enforcement at the state and local levels.

PRESIDENT'S PROGRAM. In his March 9 message, President Johnson repeated several proposals he had recommended in 1965 and outlined some new legislative and administrative actions.

New legislative proposals included establishing a program of study in institutions of higher learning for selected police officers and "forgiving" repayment of National Defense Education Act loans by students who entered law enforcement as a career. The President urged a coordinated federal, state and local effort, led by federal programs to provide new techniques of law enforcement and new incentives to states and communities to upgrade their police and correctional departments.

Action on Requests

LAW ENFORCEMENT ASSISTANCE. The President asked that the budget of the Office of Law Enforcement Assistance be increased from $7.2 million to $13.7 million. Congress later enacted a bill (HR 13551—PL 89-798) extending for two years, until June 30, 1970, the statutory life of the Law Enforcement Assistance Act of 1965 (PL 89-197) and authorizing appropriations of $15 million for fiscal 1967 and $30 million for fiscal 1968 for the OLEA. *(For total appropriations, see p. 313.)*

As originally submitted by the Administration, HR 13551 expanded the scope of the Act to authorize the Attorney General to award scholarships to law enforcement and related personnel and to make cash or honorary awards in the law enforcement fields. The Administration bill also made the loan-forgiveness provisions of the National Defense Education Act of 1958 applicable to law enforcement personnel for study under terms of that Act. These provisions were stricken from the bill by the House Judiciary Committee.

CIVIL COMMITMENT. The President repeated his 1965 request for a law providing for civil commitment of drug addicts in lieu of imprisonment. Congress enacted a bill (HR 9167—PL 89-793), the Narcotic Addict Rehabilitation Act of 1966, which embodied that request.

The Act marked a fundamental change in Congressional policy on the disposition of addicted persons charged with narcotic offenses under the criminal laws. It provided for commitment of such persons voluntarily to medical institutions, instead of prison, for long-term treatment of their affliction. Provision for intensive aftercare was included to assist the former addict in returning to normal life without renewing his habit.

The final version of HR 9167 omitted one key Administration provision. Existing law required stiff mandatory minimum sentences for narcotics violators. The House, on a 198-168 roll call, deleted from the Administration bill language that would have permitted sentencing of young adults under the more flexible provisions of the Federal Youth Corrections Act. The Senate agreed to the omission.

Prior to passage of the Act, federal law generally took a punitive approach to narcotic addiction. The new concept had been advocated by the President's Advisory Committee on Narcotics and Drug Abuse in 1964. *(Congress and the Nation, Vol. I, p. 1186)*

Provisions. The Narcotic Addict Rehabilitation Act of 1966 (PL 89-793):

Provided for commitment to institutional treatment and intensive follow-up care for three classes of addicts: those accused of a federal crime, other than a crime of violence; those convicted of a federal crime; and those charged with or convicted of no federal crime, if the addict or a "related individual" requested such treatment. (The last class was added in a key amendment made by the Senate Judiciary Committee and retained in the final bill.)

Made commitment procedures discretionary with the federal district court before which the alleged addict appeared. A person charged with a crime could voluntarily submit to examination and consequent commitment for up to 36 months; if he successfully completed treatment, the criminal charge would be dropped. A person convicted of crime could be committed by the court involuntarily, for up to 10 years but not for longer than the original sentence he faced upon conviction. A person charged with no crime could be placed in the custody of the Surgeon General for up to 42 months.

Authorized appropriations of $15 million a year for fiscal years 1967 and 1968 for the Surgeon General to assist states and cities in developing narcotic treatment programs.

Authorized consideration of marihuana offenders for parole.

BAIL REFORM. The President asked for enactment of the Bail Reform Act (S 1357), passed by the Senate in 1965. *(See above.)* The House passed the bill June 7 and it became PL 89-465.

The Bail Reform Act of 1966 set up new procedures for the release of federal prisoners charged with noncapital offenses. It was aimed especially at removing inequities in detaining accused persons who were too poor to raise bail. In subsequent years it was attacked on grounds that it required release of persons who were likely to commit further crimes before they came to trial.

The Act represented the first significant reform in federal bail legislation since the basic federal law on bail was established in the Judiciary Act of 1789.

It was the result of growing concern among members of the judiciary and of the bar and among a variety of other observers with the operation of federal bail procedures, especially in relation to the poor. Studies of bail procedures suggested that persons who could afford bail could go free pending trial, irrespective of the actual probability that they would later appear. Persons unable to raise bail, on the other hand, awaited trial in jail and thus were unable to assist in the preparation of their own defense, to help in locating witnesses, to maintain employment and to maintain family ties.

Passage of the Act came after two years of study by the Senate Judiciary Committee and followed pioneering efforts in the field of bail reform by the Vera Foundation of New York City and a growing number of other private and governmental agencies.

Provisions. The Bail Reform Act of 1966 (PL 89-465):

Required release on personal recognizance or on unsecured bond of persons charged with noncapital federal offenses at the time of appearance before a judicial officer unless the officer found that release would "not reasonably assure" appearance as required.

Empowered judicial officers, in lieu of or in addition to such release, to impose one or more of five conditions, the choice to depend upon which condition most reasonably assured the person's appearance. The conditions were: release in the custody of a designated person or organization; restrictions on travel, association or place of abode; appearance bond with no more than 10-percent cash deposit; bail bond or full cash deposit; or "any other condition deemed reasonably necessary to assure appearance as required, including a condition requiring that the person return to custody after specified hours."

Required the judicial officer in setting conditions of release to take into account the offense charged, the weight of evidence against the accused, his family ties, employment, financial resources, character and mental condition, length of residence in the community, prior record of convictions and his record of prior appearances or flights to avoid prosecution.

Permitted persons unable to meet conditions of release or required to return to custody after specified hours to seek review of the conditions by a judicial officer, who was required to present his reasons in writing; if the person was still detained or required to return to custody, he was entitled to ask the court of original jurisdiction over the offense to amend the order; if he was still detained after a rule on that motion, an appeal lay to the appropriate appellate court, which was to affirm the lower court order "if it is supported by the proceedings below." If not so supported, the appellate court could order further hearings in the lower court or could order release of the person.

Required courts to treat persons charged with capital offense or convicted of a crime and awaiting sentence or appeal the same as persons charged with a crime unless the court had reason to believe the person would flee or would "pose a danger to any other person or to the community." Provisions for review of orders detaining persons charged with crime did not apply.

Required the release of material witnesses under the same provisions applying to persons charged with non-capital offenses, provided that release could be delayed for a "reasonable period" to take the deposition of the witness.

Provided penalties for failure to appear as required: forfeiture of all security given or pledged; up to $5,000 fine and five years in prison for persons charged with a felony; up to one year in prison and the maximum fine for the offense for persons charged with a misdemeanor; and up to $1,000 fine and one year in prison for material witnesses.

Provided that the Act did not apply to persons charged with offenses triable by military tribunal.

Required the Attorney General to give credit toward prison sentence for time spent in custody awaiting trial.

Provided that the Act took effect 90 days after enactment and that the credit-toward-sentence provision applied only to sentences imposed on or after the effective date.

LAW REVISION. The President recommended establishment of a national commission to review federal criminal law and to recommend reforms. Congress responded with legislation (HR 15766—PL 89-801) establishing a 12-member National Commission on Reform of Federal Criminal Laws to conduct a three-year study of federal criminal law and to recommend revisions to improve criminal justice. The Commission's report was to be submitted by November 1969.

POLICE TRAINING. The President asked for legislation to establish a program to send selected police officers to institutions of higher learning for a year of "intensive professional study." He also asked for a law to "forgive" repayment of loans under the National Defense Education Act for students who elected law enforcement as a career. These provisions were included in the Administration's draft OLEA authorization bill (HR 13551) but were deleted by the House Judiciary Committee. *(See above.)*

GUN CONTROL. The President repeated his 1965 request for passage of an Administration bill (S 1592) to restrict interstate shipment of firearms, thus curtailing mail-order shipment of guns. In the closing days of the 89th Congress the Senate Judiciary Committee reported a much more limited bill (S 3767) which prohibited the interstate shipment of pistols to persons under 21 years of age. The Administration bill would have extended controls to sales of rifles and shotguns as well as pistols. No further action was taken on the bill. Congress enacted gun control legislation in 1968. *(See p. 323, 328.)*

UNIFIED CORRECTIONS. The President asked that the administration of federal prison, parole and probation functions be unified within the Justice Department instead of being divided between the Department and the Judiciary. House hearings were held on an Administration bill (HR 13549) to accomplish that

consolidation, but the Judiciary Committee did not report the measure.

WITNESS IMMUNITY, PROTECTION. The President urged enactment of a law to grant immunity to witnesses compelled to testify in prosecutions for certain racketeering crimes. The Senate passed such a bill (S 2190) but the House took no action on it. This also occurred in 1967. *(See p. 319.)*

The Senate also passed a companion bill (S 2188) to extend existing law protecting federal witnesses to include potential witnesses such as informants or persons otherwise assisting in a federal investigation. The House did not act. An identical bill became law in 1967. *(See below.)*

DRUG ABUSE. The President said his fiscal 1967 Budget proposed to double funds for the program established by the Drug Abuse Control Amendments of 1965 (PL 89-74), which extended federal control of depressant and stimulant drugs. *(See above.)* Congress had appropriated $2.1 million for the program in fiscal 1966 and increased that appropriation to $5 million for fiscal 1967 for the Bureau of Drug Abuse Control.

DISTRICT OF COLUMBIA. The President urged passage of the District of Columbia Bail Agency Act, which Congress enacted into Law (HR 15860—PL 89-519). The Act established an agency in the District of Columbia to investigate persons charged with crime and to report to the appropriate court on the person's background, financial status and other characteristics bearing on the likelihood of his future appearance in court.

The President asked for an increase in salaries for District policemen, and this increase was authorized in HR 15857—PL 89-810.

The President also asked for a pistol registration law for the District which would prohibit sale of deadly weapons to persons convicted of crimes of violence, and those who had a history of mental instability or chronic alcoholism. The District of Columbia Committees held no hearings on the bill (HR 6745).

Other Legislation

HABEAS CORPUS. Congress enacted two bills dealing with habeas corpus petitions. One bill (HR 5958—PL 89-711) attempted to limit the number of petitions filed by state prisoners in federal courts by introducing a greater degree of finality in court findings regarding the first habeas corpus petition filed. The other bill (S 3576—PL 89-590) permitted prisoners in state prisons to file habeas corpus petitions in the federal districts in which they were tried and convicted as well as in the districts in which they were imprisoned. Existing law permitted only the latter.

D.C. CRIME BILL. Congress cleared an omnibus District of Columbia crime bill (HR 5688) in the closing days of its 1966 session, but President Johnson let the measure die by pocket veto. Congress enacted a D.C. crime bill in 1967. *(See below.)*

The President said the bill raised serious constitutional questions, particularly in its provisions permitting police to detain citizens for questioning and authorizing suppression of allegedly obscene matter. The President said the bill would not diminish crime in the District and would make an already confusing law enforcement situation worse.

The bill had been passed in differing versions by the House and Senate in 1965 (*see above*), but did not emerge from conference until Oct. 17, 1966.

Two conferees—Sens. Robert F. Kennedy (D N.Y.) and Wayne Morse (D Ore.)—refused to sign the conference report on grounds that the bill posed a threat to civil liberties. A third conferee, Sen. Joseph D. Tydings (D Md.), said he signed the report only because House conferees (drawn from the House District Committee) made agreement the "sine qua non" of movement of other District legislation.

The major thrust of the legislation was to ease restrictions on the admissibility of confessions, the so-called *Mallory* rule; to modify the test of insanity developed in the so-called *Durham* rule; and to authorize police to detain and question suspects for up to four hours before releasing or charging them with a crime.

The bill also provided for detention of material witnesses, set mandatory minimum sentences for several crimes and established procedures for obtaining injunctions against indecent matter.

Critics attacked especially the provisions permitting detention of suspects for up to four hours and validating confessions obtained during the first six hours (aggregate, excluding interruptions) of interrogation following arrest. They said these provisions were open to abuse by police.

1967

Crime in 1967 continued its growth as a national problem and as an issue in Congress. After much debate and lengthy hearings, however, Congress enacted three relatively minor bills and deferred action on the major part of the Administration's program.

That program was spelled out by President Johnson Feb. 6 in a special message to Congress on crime. The President adopted virtually intact the recommendations of the President's Commission on Law Enforcement and Administration of Justice, which was made public two weeks later. *(See p. 318.)* At the heart of the program was vastly expanded federal assistance to local law enforcement and criminal justice agencies. At the end of the session, however, Congress had not enacted any part of that federal action program.

The President's key bill, the proposed Safe Streets and Crime Control Act of 1967, providing $50 million in federal money to upgrade local law enforcement, was rewritten by the House before passage and remained stalled in the Senate at the end of the session.

The same route was followed by another major Administration bill, the Juvenile Delinquency Prevention and Control Act of 1967, providing $25 million for local juvenile delinquency programs. Those two measures constituted the President's blueprint for a federal action program to combat the rising crime rate.

No floor action was taken at all on two other major Administration proposals. They were the Right of Privacy Act of 1967, banning all wiretapping and electronic eavesdropping except in national security cases, and the State Firearms Control Assistance Act of 1967, which was aimed at stemming the flow of mail-order rifles and handguns.

The three bills enacted included the controversial omnibus District of Columbia crime bill and bills to establish a Federal Judicial Center and to protect informants and potential witnesses during federal criminal investigations.

PRESIDENT'S PROGRAM. President Johnson, in his Feb. 6 message, outlined a program based on the recommendations of the Commission on Law Enforcement and Administration of Justice.

The heart of the message, contained in the proposed Safe Streets and Crime Control Act of 1967, was a $50-million program intended to stimulate state and local action and spending on crime prevention and control, through updated personnel training, modern equipment and innovative anticrime techniques.

As he had in 1965 and 1966, Mr. Johnson urged passage of a gun control law, and he repeated 1966 requests for a unified federal corrections system and a witness-immunity law. He added requests for Senate ratification of a 1961 international narcotics convention, originally opposed by the Kennedy Administration, and for a new office to make federal court administration more efficient.

Mr. Johnson also proposed the Right of Privacy Act of 1967, which prohibited all public and private wiretapping and other eavesdropping of interstate character except in cases of national security.

In addition, the President called for a new federal program to combat juvenile delinquency in his Feb. 8 message on children and youth.

Action on Requests

SAFE STREETS. The President proposed the Safe Streets and Crime Control Act, to be administered by the Justice Department. As introduced, the Administration measure (HR 5037, S 917) authorized the Attorney General to make grants to state and local law enforcement agencies for up to 90 percent of the cost of preparing master plans for upgrading law enforcement and criminal justice operations, for up to 60 percent of the cost of innovative law enforcement programs, for up to 50 percent of the cost of construction of new facilities and for up to 100 percent of the cost of research and demonstration projects. The bill authorized an expenditure of $50 million in the first year, with expenditures expected to rise to $300 million in fiscal 1969. Governments receiving funds under the bill were required to increase their budgets for law enforcement by at least 5 percent in order to qualify for federal assistance.

The House Aug. 8 by a 378-23 roll-call vote passed HR 5037, after rewriting it on the floor to take most controls over the money away from federal officials. The key amendment substituted block grants to the states for direct grants to local governments. This was adopted by a **256-147 (R 172-4; D 84-143)** key roll-call vote, with support of a majority of Republicans and Southern Democrats. Incorporation of the block grant concept in many federal aid programs was a leading goal of Republican Congressional leaders in 1967 and 1968; this was their first legislative victory. (However, a somewhat similar grant program was included in the 1966 Partnership for Health Law—PL 89-749. *See chapter on Health.*)

President's Crime Commission Reports

The President's Commission on Law Enforcement and Administration of Justice Feb. 18, 1967, reported on its 18-month study of crime in the United States. The 340-page report was entitled "The Challenge of Crime in a Free Society." The Commission was established by President Johnson on July 23, 1965, to undertake the first comprehensive federal survey of crime since the Wickersham Commission reported in 1931.

More than 200 specific recommendations were made by the Commission, ranging from federal action to programs for state and local governments and suggestions for citizens. Generally, the Commission's conclusions coincided with those of President Johnson in his message on crime in America sent to Congress Feb. 6. The draft Commission report had formed the basis of that message. Thus, the Commission agreed with the President that federal aid for training and equipping local law enforcement officers should be undertaken with funding approaching "several hundred million dollars annually." The Commission also agreed with the President on the need for a witness immunity statute, for a gun control law and for a wiretapping law; but it recommended extending police wiretapping to organized crime activities, while the President urged that it be limited to cases involving national security. *(For President's recommendations, see p. 317.)*

Findings. The Commission found that there was "far more crime than ever is reported" in the nation. A survey of 10,000 representative households showed that there were three times as many burglaries, twice as many aggravated assaults and larcenies over $50 and twice as many robberies, in some areas, as ever were reported. In some sections, only one-tenth of the crimes were reported to police. The survey showed that 74 percent of neighborhood businesses did not report employee thefts. A survey of two large cities showed that 43 percent of the persons questioned stayed off the streets at night because of their fear of crime.

In general, the Commission found that law enforcement agencies had fallen behind the times and had failed to make use of new techniques and equipment; and that there was little employment of systems analysis, data processing, modern scientific analysis and new training procedures. The Commission found

that state and local efforts against organized crime were "nonexistent or primitive." It found that criminal justice procedures generally failed to protect society from further violations by the same offenders. It found that most criminal careers began in youth, with 15- and 16-year-olds having the highest arrest rate in the nation.

The report traced the causes of crime to poverty. It said that "crime flourishes where the conditions of life are the worst, and that therefore the foundation of a national strategy against crime is an unremitting national effort for social justice.

"Reducing poverty, discrimination, ignorance, disease and urban blight, and the anger, cynicism or despair those conditions can inspire, is one great step toward reducing crime," the report said.

Recommendations. The Commission "warmly" endorsed federal programs to reduce delinquency and crime and urged that they be intensified. It said that "the Federal Government can make a dramatic new contribution to the national effort against crime by greatly expanding its support of the agencies of justice in the states and in the cities." The recommendations were entitled "A National Strategy." The Commission urged that the federal program be administered by the Justice Department and be addressed to eight major areas of need. Those were: state and local planning; education and training of criminal justice personnel; surveys and advisory services concerning organization and operation of criminal justice agencies; development of coordinated national information systems; development of a limited number of demonstration programs in agencies of justice; scientific and technological research and development; institutes for research and training personnel; and grants-in-aid for operational innovations.

National Crime Conference. The Justice Department March 28 and 29 sponsored a National Conference on Crime Control in Washington, D.C. About 700 delegates attended, representing police, the judiciary and corrections agencies in most of the states. A major purpose of the conference was to discuss methods of implementing recommendations of the Feb. 18 report of the President's Commission on Law Enforcement and Administration of Justice.

The House also increased the appropriation authorization in the bill by $25 million and stipulated that the new funds be used for antiriot programs and efforts to reduce organized crime. Finally, the House added a provision establishing a National Institute of Law Enforcement and Criminal Justice to conduct research and training programs to develop improved methods of law enforcement.

The Senate did not act on the legislation until 1968, but a Senate Judiciary subcommittee approved a heavily amended version of S 917 which included new provisions on wiretapping and confessions, neither of which had been covered in the Administration or House bills.

As finally enacted in 1968, the measure bore little resemblance to President Johnson's original proposals. *(See p. 317.)*

NARCOTICS. The President said he would seek Senate ratification of the 1961 Single Convention on Narcotic Drugs, which was designed to simplify international narcotic control machinery and provide additional controls on such drugs. The Senate ratified the treaty. *(See chapter on Foreign Policy.)*

The President also said he would seek funds to enlarge programs to train local officers in narcotics control. Congress increased appropriations for the Bureau of Narcotics from $6.2 million in fiscal 1967 to $6.5 million in fiscal 1968, and for the Office of Drug Abuse Control from $5.3 million in fiscal 1967 to $7.5 million in fiscal 1968.

GUN CONTROL. The President repeated his earlier requests for gun control legislation. The President's proposal barred private interstate shipment of firearms, over-the-counter sale of handguns to persons under 21 and rifles and shotguns to persons under 18 and import of surplus military firearms (exempting sporting and antique firearms). Senate and House Judiciary subcommittees approved the Administration bills (S 1—Amendment 90, HR 5384), but the full Committees did not act on gun control legislation in 1967. Controls were enacted in 1968. *(See p. 323.)*

UNIFIED CORRECTIONS. The President repeated his 1966 request for legislation unifying federal correctional services in the Justice Department. Congress took no action.

JUDICIAL CENTER. In a new proposal, the President asked for legislation establishing a Federal Judicial Center in the Administrative Office of the United States Courts. Congress enacted the legislation. *(See Court Legislation, p. 338.)*

WITNESS IMMUNITY, PROTECTION. The President repeated requests for enactment of two bills which were passed by the Senate but died in the House in 1966. Congress enacted one bill (S 676—PL 90-123) designed to protect informants in federal criminal investigations. S 676 extended existing law protecting federal witnesses to include potential witnesses such as informants or persons assisting in federal investigations, including investigations by federal agencies or by a committee of Congress. It provided penalties of up to $5,000 in fines and imprisonment for up to five years for obstructing, by means of bribery, intimidation or injury, the communication to a federal investigator of information relating to a violation of federal law.

The other bill (S 677) provided for compelled testimony coupled with witness immunity in certain kinds of criminal cases. The Senate passed S 677, but the House did not act.

WIRETAPPING. The President proposed the Right of Privacy Act, which prohibited all wiretapping and electronic eavesdropping of an interstate character, except in national security cases, and stipulated that wiretap evidence in national security cases was not admissible in court. Sale or advertisement of wiretap or eavesdropping devices in interstate commerce was prohibited. It was Mr. Johnson's first proposal on the subject since he took office. Senate and House Judiciary subcommittees held hearings on the President's bills (HR 5386, S 928) and other measures but took no action.

The second major proposal considered was a bill (S 675) sponsored by Sens. John L. McClellan (D Ark.) and Roman L. Hruska (R Neb.). It was similar to a bill backed unsuccessfully by McClellan in the 89th Congress. S 675 authorized the Attorney General to permit wiretapping in cases of organized crime, capital offenses, narcotics and certain other serious federal crimes. It also authorized states to permit wiretapping in accordance with federal and state law.

The Judicial Conference of the United States in September endorsed legislation to authorize federal and state investigators to tap telephones in organized crime and national security cases if the investigators obtained a court order. That recommendation was substantially the same as the one made by the President's Commission on Law Enforcement and Administration of Justice in its Feb. 18, 1967, report.

Meanwhile, Attorney General Ramsey Clark June 16 issued a memorandum sharply restricting the use of wiretapping and eavesdropping devices by all federal agents except in cases of national security. Previously federal agencies operated under an interpretation of the Federal Communications Act that permitted wiretapping as long as the contents were not disclosed outside the Government. *(See box, p. 320.)*

The Supreme Court in 1967 handed down two decisions relating to wiretapping. *(See p. 334.)*

JUVENILE DELINQUENCY. A new Administration juvenile delinquency program was passed by the House after extensive rewriting on the floor, but it was not acted on by the Senate in 1967. It became law in 1968. *(See p. 330.)*

The program was embodied in a bill (HR 12120), the Juvenile Delinquency Prevention and Control Act, which provided $25 million in federal funds for fiscal 1968 to assist states in developing and improving juvenile delinquency projects and facilities. The bill provided for grants of up to 75 percent of the cost of diagnostic, treatment and rehabilitation programs and of up to 50 percent of the cost of constructing facilities. It also provided for grants for training of juvenile delinquency diagnostic, treatment or rehabilitation specialists. The program was to be administered by the Secretary of Health, Education and Welfare.

Before passing the bill Sept. 26, the House rewrote its major provisions on the floor to provide for block grants to the states instead of direct grants to local agencies. This amendment was adopted with Republican and Southern Democratic backing by a 234-139 roll call. The House earlier in the year had substituted the block grant approach in the Administration's Safe Streets bill.

The Administration juvenile delinquency program was spelled out by President Johnson in his Feb. 8 message on children and youth. It was a more extensive program than that conducted under the 1961 Juvenile Delinquency and Youth Offenses Control Act, which Congress in 1965 extended until June 30, 1967. *(See p. 313.)*

Other Legislation

D.C. CRIME BILL. Congress finally enacted an omnibus District of Columbia crime bill (HR 10783—PL 90-226), the culmination of efforts that began in 1958. As enacted, the bill drew provisions from the omnibus bill which President Johnson pocket vetoed in 1966 *(see p. 316)* and from the President's own proposals, outlined in a special message Feb. 27. The President's D.C. crime proposals were based on the Dec. 31, 1966 report of the Commission on Crime in the District of Columbia.

The most controversial provision of the bill provided for three hours' investigative detention and specified that any statement made during the three hours could not be excluded from evidence at trial solely because of delay in arraignment. This was designed to ease the *Mallory* rule restrictions on admissibility of confessions. The bill did not attempt, as its predecessors had done, to modify the *Durham* rule test of insanity.

Background on Wiretapping

Title III of the Omnibus Crime Control and Safe Streets Act of 1968 (HR 5037—PL 90-351) authorized federal, state and local law enforcement officers to wiretap and eavesdrop in a wide variety of criminal cases. Previously, official wiretapping had been governed by the Communications Act of 1934 and several Supreme Court decisions:

Legislative Background. Until 1968, federal law on wiretapping was embodied in the Communications Act of 1934 (47 U.S.C. 605) which was a general statute aimed at protecting the privacy of citizens using the telephone or telegraph for communications. The Act read in part: "...and no person not being authorized by the sender shall intercept any communication and divulge or publish the existence, contents, substance, purport, effect, or meaning of such intercepted communication to any person...." The statute exempted such matters as routine work by communications workers and transmissions relating to ships in distress.

The Justice Department in 1941 ruled that a violation of Section 605 required both an interception and a divulgence outside the Federal Government; that ruling interpreted the Act as meaning that the Federal Government could wiretap as long as the contents of the communication intercepted were not divulged. The Federal Bureau of Investigation, the Internal Revenue Service and other federal agencies followed that interpretation. As a result, undisclosed wiretapping by the Federal Government was little publicized but relatively widespread.

The amount of state wiretapping was even less publicized. Some states had legislation permitting it, some prohibited it and some had no law at all on the subject.

After World War II Congress in several years considered legislation aimed at restricting the amount of wiretapping but permitting use of wiretap evidence in court in certain instances. The first bills were engendered by the national security concerns of the McCarthy period. The only bill to pass either house was a 1954 measure legalizing use of wiretap information in federal courts in national security prosecutions. It was passed by the House and died in the Senate. *(Congress and the Nation, Vol. I, p. 1659, 1661.)*

The Kennedy Administration in 1961 endorsed proposals for a wiretap law authorizing federal agencies to wiretap in cases of national security, organized crime and other serious crimes and placing no limits on state wiretapping. In 1962, the Kennedy Administration sent a bill to Congress which was somewhat more restrictive: it authorized federal wiretapping in cases of national security, organized crime and other serious crimes; it limited state wiretapping to certain serious crimes; and it outlawed all other wiretapping. Congress took no action on the proposal.

1967 Proposals. President Johnson did not tackle the issue of wiretapping until 1967. In his comprehensive Feb. 6 Message on Crime in America, the President asked for enactment of the Right of Privacy Act of 1967, which prohibited all wiretapping and electronic eavesdropping of an interstate character, except in national security cases, unless one party consented to the wiretap. The legislation enacted by Congress in 1968 rejected this limited approach. *(See Chronology of Legislation, p. 323, 326.)*

Court Decisions. Constitutional law governing federal and state wiretapping and eavesdropping developed considerably through two Supreme Court decisions in 1967.

In *Katz v. U.S.* (Dec. 18, 1967), the Court settled a major question, namely, whether a wiretap or eavesdrop constituted a "search and seizure" within the meaning of the 4th Amendment. By a 7-1 vote, the Court held that a conversation was a "thing" that could be seized by a wiretap and that the wiretap was a "search and seizure" in the constitutional sense. The effect of bringing electronic surveillance within the 4th Amendment was not to ban it but to require police to obtain warrants before placing a tap or bug.

The effect of *Katz* was to overrule two cases of relatively recent vintage. The first was *Olmstead v. U.S.* (1928), which was the Court's first wiretap case. The Court there held by a 5-4 vote that use of wiretap evidence in federal courts did not of itself violate the 4th Amendment protection against unreasonable searches and seizures or the 5th Amendment guarantee against self-incrimination. The second case was *Goldman v. U.S.* (1942), in which the Court found no objection to the use of evidence obtained by a detectaphone placed against the wall of the defendant's room. The Court reasoned that since there had been no physical trespass, there was no violation of the 4th Amendment. That theory was abandoned in *Katz*.

There had been such a physical trespass in *Silverman v. U.S.* (1961), a case in which federal agents used a spike microphone which penetrated the wall of the defendant's home and touched heating ducts, enabling the agents to overhear conversations. The Court held that the recordings thus obtained could not be used in court.

State Wiretapping. In *Berger v. N.Y.* (June 12, 1967), the Court, by a 6-3 vote, struck down as unconstitutional New York's law authorizing police to obtain court orders to eavesdrop. The Court approved of the judicial supervision of the eavesdropping but said the supervision was insufficient.

1934 Act. The Court ruled in *Nardone v. U.S.* (1937, 1939) and in *Benanti v. U.S.* (1957) that the Communications Act of 1934 made it illegal for any third party, public or private, to wiretap on interstate telephone lines and then to divulge the contents of what was learned. The Court said that evidence thus obtained could not be introduced in federal courts.

Regarding state courts, the Court ruled in *Schwarz v. Texas* (1952) and *Pugach v. Dollinger* (1961) that it was up to the states to determine if wiretap evidence obtained in violation of the 1934 Act could be introduced in state courts.

The bill as enacted did not contain Administration provisions for gun control, detention of material witnesses, narcotics addicts rehabilitation or treatment of intoxicated persons. It did include Administration provisions on warrantless arrests, obstruction of justice, citations and law revision.

Provisions. As enacted into law, PL 90-226:

Authorized police to make warrantless arrests for certain misdemeanors.

Required a defendant intending to plead insanity as a defense to inform the court of his intention within 15 days after pleading not guilty.

Authorized investigative detention for up to three hours; provided that any statement made by the arrested person during the three hours could not be excluded from evidence at trial solely because of delay in arraigning the person.

Made obstruction of justice a crime.

Established mandatory minimum sentences for certain specified crimes.

Made it a crime knowingly to sell or distribute obscene materials, or to sell or distribute to minors material considered unsuitable by the adult community.

Authorized police to issue citations in lieu of arrest.

Provided substantial penalties for inciting to riot.

Provided for the revision of the D.C. Criminal Code.

POLICE BENEFITS. The Senate and House passed different versions of a bill (HR 11816, S 798) to provide disability and death benefits for state and local police officers who were injured or killed while enforcing federal laws. The bill was still in conference when Congress adjourned for the year. It became law in 1968. *(See p. 333.)*

APPELLATE REVIEW. The Senate passed a bill (S 1540) permitting the appeal of sentences imposed in felony cases in federal district courts. The measure was supported by the Justice Department. There was no House action.

Under existing law, a sentence could be appealed only if it were unlawful. S 1540 allowed an appeal on the ground that the sentence was excessive.

EVIDENCE SUPPRESSION. The House passed a bill (HR 8654) to provide for an appeal by the United States from decisions sustaining defense motions to suppress evidence. There was no Senate action.

Under existing federal law, if a defendant prevailed in moving to suppress evidence, the Government had to go to trial without the evidence. If the defendant were acquitted, he could not be retried for the same offense. HR 8654 authorized the Government to obtain an appellate ruling on the admissibility of the evidence before trial began. The issue of double jeopardy would not be involved because the trial had not yet been held.

1968

Major developments in federal programs to stem the rising national crime rate took place in 1968.

President Johnson finally succeeded in gaining enactment of the cornerstones of his anticrime program—a law providing federal funds for improving state and local police departments and a law providing federal funds for major juvenile delinquency programs. Congress also enacted new gun control legislation, but it fell short of what the President had sought.

These actions took place in a year in which the nation experienced the shock of two major assassinations and of widespread rioting in urban Negro ghettos.

Violence seemed to be in the ascendancy. There were repeated clashes during the Democratic National Convention in Chicago in August between police and youths protesting the Vietnam war. On dozens of campuses across the nation, students seized buildings, imprisoned university officials, destroyed property and fought with police over a wide range of grievances.

The most stunning events, however, were the two assassinations—the shootings of the Rev. Dr. Martin Luther King Jr. April 4 and of Sen. Robert F. Kennedy (D N.Y.) June 5. In the days and nights following the King assassination, rioting broke out in scores of urban Negro ghettos, including a Negro area of the nation's capital.

Reaction to violence in the nation was varied. Some elements of society expressed fear that the morality of the nation in general was breaking down. They condemned what they described as the "permissiveness" in American life, and traced that characteristic in part to the liberal decisions of the Supreme Court.

Another, and perhaps smaller, element of society saw the issue of crime and violence as a more complicated matter, traceable in part to the conditions of mass living that had developed in the nation's major cities. President Johnson was of this school of thought. While condemning crime and violence, he urged broad programs to strike at what he considered the root of the problem—poverty, ghetto conditions, inadequate police protection and unsuccessful correctional systems.

That diversity of opinion about crime and violence was evident in the Presidential election campaign. Both the Republican and Democratic parties struggled with the problem of defining the "law and order" issue, as it came to be known. Both parties made some effort to separate the issue of crime from the issue of racial unrest, and both contended that an element of justice was necessary if any law enforcement system was to gain the confidence of the population. The third party candidate, George C. Wallace, forthrightly said that police suppression was the most efficacious approach to solving the problems both of crime and racial unrest.

Despite the tendency, in an election year, to oversimplify issues, there appeared to be a growing sophistication in 1968 in analyzing the issues of crime and violence. That was due in part to two new commissions appointed by Mr. Johnson. The first was the National Advisory Commission on Civil Disorders, formed in 1967 to investigate rioting in urban Negro ghettos. That Commission March 2 reported its finding that "white racism" was the fundamental cause of the rioting.

The second was the National Commission on the Causes and Prevention of Violence, formed by Mr. Johnson after the Kennedy assassination. In hearings held in 1968, that Commission explored the history of violence in American life, the implications of congested living conditions, the tendencies of human beings toward violent behavior, the impact of violence depicted on television and in other mass media and a number of other subjects.

PRESIDENT'S PROGRAM. In his fourth annual message on crime, President Johnson Feb. 7 outlined the

Summary of 1968 Action

Following are brief descriptions of the major actions taken by Congress on Administration and other anticrime proposals in 1968. Further details are given in the Chronology of Legislation.

Safe Streets. Congress enacted the President's key bill (HR 5037—PL 90-351), the Omnibus Crime Control and Safe Streets Act. It was the most extensive federal anticrime measure in the nation's history. The law authorized more than $100 million in federal funds for use by state and local governments to upgrade their law enforcement agencies. Congress appropriated $63 million to implement the law.

The bill as passed contained Administration-opposed provisions seeking to alter Supreme Court rulings on the admissibility of confessions in federal criminal trials, on eye-witness testimony and on police lineup procedures. Those provisions were added by the Senate. The Senate refused, however, to accept amendments which would have restricted the jurisdiction of the Court in regard to reviewing state criminal rulings.

Juvenile Delinquency. Congress enacted another major Administration bill (HR 12120—PL 90-445), the Juvenile Delinquency Prevention and Control Act. The law authorized $25 million for fiscal 1969 to begin grants to states to plan and operate projects to prevent juvenile delinquency and to rehabilitate youthful offenders.

Gun Controls. The Safe Streets bill (HR 5037) banned the interstate shipment of handguns to individuals and prohibited the sale of handguns to persons less than 21 years old. In enacting a second piece of legislation (HR 17735—PL 90-618), Congress extended those provisions to rifles, shotguns and ammunition. Congress refused the President's request, however, to enact requirements for federal registration of guns and licensing of gun owners.

Wiretapping. The Safe Streets bill (HR 5037) was amended in the Senate to grant broad wiretapping authority to all levels of government while banning private wiretapping or electronic eavesdropping. The Administration had sought to prohibit all official and private wiretapping and eavesdropping except by federal agencies in national security cases. Congress enacted the Senate amendments, which the President criticized when he signed the measure.

Antiriot Measures. In enacting the Administration's civil rights-open housing bill (HR 2516—PL 90-284), Congress added provisions prohibiting interstate travel to incite to riot. In the Safe Streets bill (HR 5037), Congress added provisions prohibiting persons convicted of riot-related acts from federal employment. In a shift from his position in previous years, the President in his Feb. 7 crime message had asked for limited antiriot legislation, tying it to a gun control measure. The two Presidential commissions investigating disorders and violence also were active in 1968.

Congress in 1968 also enacted several measures intended to bar from federal educational assistance students engaging in activities which disrupted their campuses.

Drug Abuse. The President Feb. 7 announced his plan to consolidate in the Justice Department the Bureau of Narcotics (then part of the Treasury Department) and the Bureau of Drug Abuse Control (then part of the Department of Health, Education and Welfare). Congress passed no resolution against the subsequent Reorganization Plan effecting that shift.

Congress also enacted a bill (HR 14096—PL 90-639), backed by the Administration, which set criminal penalties for the illegal possession of stimulant, depressant or hallucinogenic drugs.

Rights Protection. In the Administration's civil rights-open housing bill (HR 2516—PL 90-284), Congress enacted provisions protecting civil rights workers and others exercising their rights.

Bank Protection. Congress responded to the increase in bank robberies by enacting legislation (HR 15345—PL 90-389) permitting federal banking officials to require the installation of alarm systems and protective devices in banking institutions. The President had requested the measure.

Other Measures. Congress enacted legislation, held hearings or took other action on the following subjects: protection of Presidential candidates; capital punishment; crime statistics; the federal magistrates system; desecration of the American flag; a Joint Committee on Crime; loan-sharking; master keys; obscene telephone calls; assaults on postal workers; and federal benefits for state and local police killed or injured while enforcing federal law.

most comprehensive set of anticrime proposals ever sent by a President to Congress. His 22-point program included requests for more than a dozen separate pieces of legislation.

The President renewed his request for a "Safe Streets" bill to help communities improve their law enforcement capabilities and for a measure to regulate the interstate shipment of firearms. In addition, Mr. Johnson endorsed, for the first time, legislation making it a crime to cross state lines with the intent to incite a riot. He also sought stiffer penalties for illegal use and posses-

sion of narcotics and new laws aimed at gambling and organized crime.

Repeatedly, the President emphasized that "the major effort" against crime "must be made by our cities and towns" and that "state governments must provide maximum support." But he said it was imperative that the Federal Government "deal promptly, firmly and effectively with those who violate federal criminal laws and...assist states and cities in their local efforts."

Following is a summary of action by Congress on the Administration's requests.

Crime Control and Safe Streets Act

Congress enacted the Omnibus Crime Control and Safe Streets Act (HR 5037—PL 90-351), the most extensive anticrime legislation in the nation's history. However, the act bore little resemblance to the legislation President Johnson originally proposed in 1967 and requested again in his 1968 crime message.

HR 5037 did authorize the funds—$100,111,000 to be used in fiscal 1968-69 and $300 million in fiscal 1970—which the President had requested for grants to upgrade state and local police forces and law enforcement methods. But it provided that the funds were to be allocated in block grants to the states, rather than in direct grants to local communities. The block grant procedure, which the Administration vigorously opposed, was favored by Republicans and some Southern Democrats.

Congress added to the law enforcement grant program two titles which the Administration also opposed. One permitted wiretapping in a wide variety of federal and state cases. The other was a criminal law section which purported to overturn three controversial Supreme Court decisions—*Mallory v. U.S.* (1957), *Miranda v. Arizona* (1966) and *U.S. v. Wade* (1967)—which dealt with the rights during police interrogation of suspects accused of federal crimes. *(See box.)*

The bill provided that a confession by a defendant was to be admissible in evidence if it were "voluntary," even if the suspect had not been warned of his constitutional rights. It also permitted police to hold a suspect in custody for up to six hours (or more in certain circumstances) before arraignment and still obtain an admissible confession. And it provided for the admissibility in evidence of eyewitness testimony, even if the suspect had not had a lawyer when he was identified in a police lineup.

In addition, the bill contained firearms control provisions that were substantially weaker than those sought by President Johnson. The measure banned the interstate shipment of handguns to individuals and prohibited the sale of handguns to persons less than 21 years old or to those who did not live in the dealer's state. In subsequent legislation, Congress extended these controls to rifles and shotguns as well. *(See below.)*

Taken as a whole, passage of the bill was a major defeat for the Administration and Congressional liberals. Despite the urging of civil libertarians and a number of liberal Members of Congress that he veto the bill, President Johnson signed it June 19, the last day he could have vetoed it.

Mr. Johnson implored Congress to "repeal" the "potentially dangerous" wiretapping section. Meanwhile, he said, federal officials would continue to observe the guidelines he had set early in his Administration that authorized wiretapping and electronic bugging only in cases of national security.

He said federal law enforcement officials would continue to give suspects warning of their constitutional rights, despite provisions which permitted confessions to be used in court even if the precaution had not been followed. And he called for "more stringent" gun laws.

As passed by the House in 1967, HR 5037 contained only the grant program for law enforcement assistance. The block grant system was inserted in the bill on the

Court Cases Described

Descriptions follow of the three Supreme Court cases which the Senate sought to overturn in Title II of S 917:

Mallory. In *Mallory v. U.S.* (1957), the Court ruled that a 10-hour police interrogation after arrest and prior to arraignment violated Rule 5(a) of the Federal Rules of Criminal Procedure that "arraignment be without unnecessary delay" and violated the Court's supervisory rule, enunciated in *McNabb v. U.S.* (1943), that delay "must not be of a nature to give opportunity for the extraction of a confession."

Miranda. In *Miranda v. Arizona* (1966), the Court held that before interrogation police must advise a suspect that anything he said could be used against him and that he had the right (1) to remain silent; (2) to obtain a lawyer of his choice; and (3) to have a lawyer appointed if he were indigent. The Court said that if these procedures were not followed it would be a violation of the individual's 5th Amendment privilege against self-incrimination.

Wade. In *U.S. v. Wade* (1967), the Court held that identification based on police lineup in the absence of a lawyer, and having no independent origin beyond that, was inadmissible at a trial. The court held that although the lineup did not violate the defendant's privilege against self-incrimination, the absence of a lawyer violated his 6th Amendment right to counsel.

House floor. *(See above.)* A Senate Judiciary subcommittee added the criminal law and wiretapping sections to S 917, the Senate version of HR 5037. The full Judiciary Committee reported the bill April 29, 1958, after adding the gun control provisions by a narrow 9-7 vote and after refusing to delete the controversial criminal law section by an 8-8 tie vote. The gun control vote in Committee was made final April 5, the day after the assassination of the Rev. Dr. Martin Luther King Jr. by a sniper's bullet.

The Senate debated S 917 for three weeks before passing it May 23. Like the House, the Senate substituted block grants for categorical grants in its version of the bill; the block grant amendment was adopted on a 48-29 roll call, with unanimous Republican support.

The Senate rejected a series of efforts by Sen. Joseph D. Tydings (D Md.) to delete provisions relating to confessions and eyewitness testimony, but it accepted a Tydings amendment that removed from the bill provisions denying the Supreme Court jurisdiction to review a determination by a state court judge that a confession was "voluntary" if that decision had been upheld by the state's highest court. The key vote was **52-32 (D 36-17; R 16-15),** with Republicans and Northern Democrats switching to defend the Court's scope of review.

Sen. Edward M. Kennedy (D Mass.) offered an Administration-backed amendment to ban the mail-order sale of rifles and shotguns. In the face of heavy lobbying by the National Rifle Assn., the Senate rejected his amendment on a key **29-53** roll call **(D 20-31; R 9-22),** with Southern and Western Senators lining up against the

(Continued on p. 325)

Background on Gun Control Laws

Interest in strengthening federal laws governing interstate traffic in firearms grew out of a study initiated in March 1961 by the Senate Judiciary Subcommittee on Juvenile Delinquency, headed by Sen. Thomas J. Dodd (D Conn.). The study showed that existing federal and state laws did not restrain mail-order sales of firearms to juveniles and to felons, narcotic addicts and other "undesirables." The study also took notice of a vast increase since 1955 in the number of foreign military-surplus weapons of all varieties—rifles, handguns and even bazookas and antitank guns—that were being imported into the United States. These weapons were easily obtained at low prices from mail-order houses.

Possession of and traffic in firearms in the United States was governed by federal postal, licensing and tax law, state laws and local ordinances. The strict gun-control bills introduced in Congress since 1963 were based on the Federal Government's authority to regulate interstate commerce.

Use of the Mails. Postal law includes ammunition and other explosives among nonmailable injurious objects. A 1927 law banned the mailing of concealable weapons, which by their nature were concealed firearms, such as cane guns and pen guns. Prior to 1968, there was no law or regulation banning the use of the mails to send rifles, shotguns or even larger weapons, provided that the weapons were unloaded and the size of the package was within limits accepted by postal authorities. There was also no ban against sending concealable weapons and ammunition by common carrier, such as railway express. Hand guns could be mailed to authorized federal and state officials, including active and reserve military officers, and to licensed manufacturers and dealers.

'Gangster' Weapons. The 1934 National Firearms Act sought by imposing stiff taxes to curb traffic in and possession of machine guns and other automatic weapons, sawed-off shotguns and rifles, mufflers, silencers and "specialty" weapons, such as cane guns, pen guns and unusual concealable weapons (but not ordinary pistols and revolvers). The law required that all such weapons be registered with the Secretary of the Treasury (by regulation, with the director of the Alcohol and Tobacco Tax Division of the Internal Revenue Service).

Since the Act was based on the taxing power, administration of this law and the subsequent Federal Firearms Act of 1938 (*see below*) was assigned to the Internal Revenue Service.

The National Firearms Act was passed by Congress in the wake of the attempted assassination of President-elect Franklin D. Roosevelt in Miami, Fla., in 1933 and as a reaction to criminal gang killings.

(The Supreme Court Jan. 29, 1968, voided the section of the National Firearms Act that made it a crime to possess an unregistered weapon subject to regulation under the Act on the grounds that the section violated the 5th Amendment protection against self-incrimination. *See p. 334.*)

Federal Firearms Act. In 1938 Congress passed the Federal Firearms Act to regulate interstate commerce in all types of firearms and pistol and revolver ammunition. The law required annually renewable licenses, obtainable from the Internal Revenue Service, for manufactuers and importers of these items. It also required a $1 annual license for dealers in firearms and ammunition. It sought to prevent circumvention of state firearms licensing and registration laws by making it unlawful for a dealer or manufacturer to ship a firearm to other than licensed dealers or manufacturers in a state requiring a permit to purchase a firearm unless the purchaser showed his permit. It also sought to restrict access to firearms by criminals by making it unlawful to ship knowingly any firearm or ammunition to a person convicted of or under indictment for a crime punishable by more than a year's imprisonment or to a fugitive from justice. The latter provision, however, did not prevent criminals from falsifying statements to a dealer in order to obtain a firearm.

Other. Other federal laws dealing with firearms included principally regulations of the State Department dealing with import and export of firearms. These required annual registration with the Department's Office of Munitions Control, for a $75 fee, of manufacturers, importers and exporters of firearms and ammunition (excepting shotguns and rimfire .22-caliber rifles, and their ammunition), plus an export or import license for each shipment; restricted the amount of arms and ammunition that a person might carry into or out of the country for his own use without a license; and permitted license-free importation of firearms manufactured before 1898.

Enforcement. Enforcement of much of the Federal firearms legislation had been less than vigorous. Treasury Department officials acknowledged during 1965 Congressional hearings that only two men and three women were assigned full time to enforcement of both the National Firearms Act and the Federal Firearms Act. A Treasury Department official told Congressional Quarterly he knew of only one conviction in 30 years under the section of the 1938 law that prohibited mailing firearms to individuals in the eight states that required permits for purchasing firearms unless the purchaser produced his permit. The prohibition against shipping a firearm to a known criminal was virtually impossible to enforce.

Congressional Action. In 1963 Sen. Dodd introduced a bill (S 1975) to restrict the mail-order sale of hand guns. Following the assassination of President Kennedy, Dodd amended the bill to cover rifles and shotguns. Hearings were held early in 1963 and mid-1964 by Dodd's Juvenile Delinquency Subcommittee and in late 1963 and early 1964 by the Senate Commerce Committee. The leadership—but not the members—of the National Rifle Assn. (NRA) at first supported the bill, but the NRA shortly became the strongest opponent of firearms control. (*For 1965 and subsequent action, see Chronology of Legislation.*)

proposal. *(For analysis of voting, see box, p. 330.)* Later in the year the Senate enacted legislation prohibiting mail-order sales of long guns. *(See p. 328.)*

Final action on the bill came June 6, the day of the death of Sen. Robert F. Kennedy (D N.Y.), when the House agreed to the Senate changes and sent the bill to the President. Acceptance of the Senate amendments was a defeat for House liberals, who wanted to send the bill to conference in the hope that the criminal law and wiretapping sections could be modified. A motion to send the bill to conference was rejected, 60-318, on June 5, about 12 hours after Kennedy was shot.

The following day, the House voted, **349-40 (R 169-6; D 180-34)** to end debate and prohibit amendments to the resolution (H Res 1197) which provided for acceptance of the Senate bill. It then voted **369-17 (R 172-1; D 197-16)**, to adopt the resolution and thus send the bill to the President. Both were key 1968 votes.

That some Members considered the bill a memorial to Kennedy was ironic in view of the fact that Kennedy was known to oppose many of the key provisions—including those relating to wiretapping, criminal law and block grants—and because there probably was nothing in the bill that could have prevented the sale of the revolver with which he was shot.

Following enactment of HR 5037, the Administration requested an appropriation of $98.6 million to implement the grant program in fiscal 1969. Congress actually appropriated $63 million.

Major Provisions

As signed into law, the Omnibus Crime Control and Safe Streets Act (PL 90-351) contained the following major provisions:

Title I: Law Enforcement Grants

Authorization. Authorized appropriations of $100,-111,000 in fiscal 1969 and $300 million in fiscal 1970, divided as follows in fiscal 1969:
- $25 million for planning grants.
- $50 million for law enforcement assistance grants, of which up to $2.5 million was to educate the public, up to $15 million was for riot control and prevention, up to $15 million was to combat organized crime and up to $10 million was for correction, probation and parole services.
- $25,111,000 for training, education, research and demonstration projects, of which $5,111,000 was for training activities of the Federal Bureau of Investigation (FBI) and up to $10 million was for loans and scholarships to law enforcement students.

Administration. Established in the Justice Department a three-member Law Enforcement Assistance Administration, under the general authority of the Attorney General, to administer the grant programs.

Stipulated that recipients of grants could not be required to achieve racial balance within the police force as a condition for receiving federal funds.

Planning Grants. Authorized block grants to the states for the creation of state planning agencies which, in turn, were to develop a statewide law enforcement plan.

Provided that the members of the planning agency were to be appointed by the Governor.

Specified that at least 40 percent of the planning grant to a state was to be channeled to units of local government.

Set the maximum federal grant at 90 percent of the cost of operating of the planning agency and developing a state plan.

Provided that $100,000 was to be allocated to each state and that the remainder of the appropriation was to be allocated among the states according to population.

Provided that, if a state did not apply for a planning grant within six months of enactment of the law, the funds earmarked to that state would be distributed to units of local government within the state.

Law Enforcement Grants. Authorized block grants to the states to be spent according to the comprehensive statewide plan for the following purposes:
- To develop methods and equipment to strengthen law enforcement.
- To recruit and train police officers.
- To educate the public about crime prevention.
- To construct buildings and other law enforcement facilities.
- To organize and train special units to combat organized crime.
- To organize and train special riot control and prevention units.
- To recruit and train neighborhood youths to improve police-community relations.

Specified that federal grants were to be up to 75 percent of the cost of combating organized crime and controlling and preventing riots; up to 50 percent for construction and salaries; and up to 60 percent for other purposes.

Provided that no more than one-third of any grant could be used for policemen's salaries, except for policemen in training.

Provided that at least 75 percent of the grants were to be channeled by the state to the communities in the state.

Provided that, if a state failed to apply for a grant, the funds were to revert to the Law Enforcement Assistance Administration for distribution to local governments within that state; but required that any local government applying for a grant send a copy of its application to the Governor of the state.

Required that 85 percent of the funds be allocated among the states according to their population, with the remainder to be allocated at the discretion of the Law Enforcement Assistance Administration.

Instructed the Law Enforcement Assistance Administration and state planning agencies to give special emphasis to preventing and controlling riots and to fighting organized crime.

Training and Research. Established within the Justice Department a National Institute of Law Enforcement and Criminal Justice, patterned after the National Institutes of Health, to encourage research and demonstrations in law enforcement methods.

Authorized the director of the FBI to conduct training programs for state and local policemen at the FBI National Academy at Quantico, Va.

Authorized payments to colleges and universities for loans of up to $1,800 a year to persons enrolled in a full-time course leading to a degree in an area related to law enforcement; provided that the loan was to be cancelled at the rate of 25 percent for each year the recipient served as a policeman.

Authorized scholarships of up to $200 per academic quarter or $300 per semester for individuals enrolled in a law enforcement course.

Title II: Confessions and Eyewitnesses

Miranda Case. Provided that in any federal criminal prosecution, a confession should be admissible in evidence if voluntarily given, as determined under the following procedure:

• The trial judge would determine any issue of voluntariness out of the hearing of the jury, and would instruct the jury to give such weight to the confession as the jury felt it deserved.

• In determining voluntariness, the judge would take into consideration the circumstances surrounding the giving of the confession, including: (1) the time elapsing between arrest and arraignment if the confession were given after arrest and before arraignment; (2) whether the defendant knew the nature of the offense with which he was charged or of which he was suspected; (3) whether he had been advised or knew that he was not required to make any statement and that any such statement could be used against him; (4) whether he had been advised prior to questioning of his right to counsel; and (5) whether he was without the assistance of counsel when questioned and when giving the confession;

• No single factor need be conclusive on the issue of voluntariness.

Mallory Case. Provided that in any federal criminal prosecution, a confession made by a person in custody of law officers was not to be inadmissible in evidence solely because of delay in bringing the defendant before a commissioner or other officer empowered to commit persons, if the confession were found to be voluntary, if the weight of the confession were left to the jury and if the confession were given within six hours immediately following arrest. Provided that, if the confession were given after six hours immediately following arrest and the trial judge found further delay to be reasonable considering the means of transportation and the distance to be traveled to the committing officer, the confession could be admissible.

Stated that nothing in this section was a bar to admission in evidence of any confession given voluntarily by any person to any other person without interrogation by anyone or at any time at which the person giving the confession was not under arrest or other detention.

Wade Case. Provided that the testimony of an eyewitness that he saw the accused commit or participate in the commission of the crime for which the accused was being tried was to be admissible in evidence in any federal criminal trial.

Title III: Wiretapping

Illegal Interceptions. Provided that, except as otherwise specified, whoever willfully intercepted wire or oral communications, used wiretapping or electronic bugging devices or disclosed or used such interception

would be fined not more than $10,000 and imprisoned not more than five years.

Exempted switchboard operators, employees of communication common carriers in their normal course of business and employees of the Federal Communications Commission in their normal duties.

Exempted public officials where one party to the communication consented to the intercept.

Exempted anyone if one party consented to the intercept and the communication had to do with any criminal or tortious act.

Exempted intercepts made pursuant to Presidential directive based on national security needs or aimed at efforts to overthrow the Government; and provided that evidence so obtained could be admitted at any trial but would not otherwise be used except as needed to implement the President's power to protect the nation.

Manufacturing. Provided that, except as otherwise specified, whoever sent through the mail, sent or carried in interstate commerce, manufactured or advertised wiretapping or electronic bugging equipment, having reason to know that it would be used for surreptitious interceptions, was to be fined not more than $10,000 and imprisoned not more than five years.

Exempted employees of communication common carriers and all federal, state and local public officials and law officers.

Confiscation. Provided for the seizure by and forfeiture to the United States of equipment made or transported in violation of the foregoing section; and provided for compensation in appropriate cases.

Witness Immunity. Provided, for purposes of this law, that any U.S. attorney, with the approval of the Attorney General, could seek a court order requiring a witness to testify or produce books or accounts or other evidence on condition that the witness not be prosecuted on the basis of evidence he produced; but provided that he could be prosecuted for perjury or contempt.

Prohibited Use. Prohibited warrantless intercepts, except in emergencies, and the use at any trial or hearing of contents of any interception if the disclosure were in violation of law.

Authorized Interceptions. Authorized the Attorney General to apply to any federal judge for a warrant approving wire or oral intercepts relating to a wide range of specified federal offenses punishable by death or imprisonment for more than one year, namely: violations of the Atomic Energy Act; espionage; sabotage; treason; rioting; unlawful payments or loans to labor organizations; murder; kidnaping; robbery; extortion; bribing public officials or witnesses; sports bribes; wagering offenses; influencing or injuring an officer, juror or witness; obstructing criminal investigations; Presidential assassination, kidnaping, or assault; interference with commerce by threats or violence; racketeering offenses; unlawfully influencing an employee benefit plan; theft from interstate shipment; embezzlement from pension and welfare funds; interstate transportation of stolen property; counterfeiting; bankruptcy fraud; narcotics violations; extortionate credit transactions; or any conspiracy to commit such offenses.

Authorizing the principal prosecuting attorney of any state or political subdivision to apply to a state judge for a warrant approving wire or oral intercepts relating to any crime dangerous to life, limb or property and punishable by imprisonment for more than one year.

Authorized Disclosure. Authorized any law officer or any other person obtaining information in conformity with the previous sections to disclose or use it as appropriate.

Provided that no otherwise privileged communication would lose its privileged character.

Provided that information obtained relating to offenses other than those specified in the warrant could be disclosed as appropriate.

Warrants. Required an application for a warrant to identify the investigating officer; contain a statement of facts of the case; specify the offense; describe the nature and location of the communication facilities; describe the type of communications to be intercepted; identify the person, if known, committing the offense; state whether other investigative procedures had been tried; state the period of time of the intercept and state whether previous applications for a warrant had been made; state the results of previous intercepts if applying for an extension.

Authorized the judge to issue a warrant if he determined that probable cause existed that a crime was being, had been or was about to be committed, and that information relating to that crime would be obtained by the intercept.

Required the order issuing the warrant to state the identity of the person involved, if known; the nature and location of the communications facilities; the type of communications to be intercepted; the identity of the law enforcement agency; and the period of time of the intercept.

Limited warrants to 30 days, renewable for 30-day extensions.

Emergency Intercepts. Authorized any federal official designated by the Attorney General or any state or local official designated by the principal prosecuting attorney of his jurisdiction, who reasonably determined that an emergency situation existed relating to conspiratorial activities threatening the national security or involving organized crime, to conduct wire or oral intercepts without a warrant.

Required such an officer to apply for a warrant within 48 hours thereafter.

Recordings. Required, when possible, that intercepts be recorded and kept for 10 years; required that applications for warrants be kept for 10 years.

Inventory. Required the judge issuing or denying a warrant, within 90 days of termination of the intercept, to inform the person whose communications were intercepted of the fact and date of the entry and of the fact that communications were or were not intercepted; permitted the judge to postpone such notice.

Required the prosecution, when possible, to inform a defendant at least 10 days before trial of the fact that an intercept was made and to provide him with a copy of the warrant.

Motions To Suppress. Authorized any aggrieved person to move to suppress the contents of intercepted communications on grounds it was unlawfully intercepted, that the warrant was insufficient or that the intercept was not made in conformity with the warrant; authorized the United States to appeal a ruling granting a motion to suppress.

Reports. Required any judge issuing or denying an application for a warrant, within 30 days of the expiration of the warrant, to report to the Administrative Office of the United States Courts the fact that a warrant was applied for, the action taken and other appropriate information.

Required the Attorney General each January to report to the Office similar information and the number of arrests, trials, motions to suppress and convictions in which intercepts were involved.

Required the director of the Office each April to report a summary of such information to Congress.

Civil Suits. Authorized any aggrieved person to sue the person who made the intercept in violation of law for damages of $100 a day or $1,000, whichever was higher, for punitive damages and for court and attorney's costs; provided that a good faith reliance on a warrant or an emergency intercept was a complete defense to such a suit.

Commission. Established a National Commission for the Review of Federal and State Laws Relating to Wiretapping and Electronic Surveillance.

Provided for four Senators to be appointed by the President of the Senate, for four Members of the House to be appointed by the Speaker and for seven private citizens to be appointed by the President.

Required the Commission to make a comprehensive six-year study of such laws and of the effectiveness of HR 5037; required the Commission to report within one year thereafter.

Title IV: Firearms Control

General Declaration. Stated "that the ease with which any person can acquire firearms other than a rifle or shotgun...is a significant factor in the prevalence of lawlessness and violent crime in the United States" and that "only through adequate federal control over interstate and foreign commerce in these weapons...can this grave problem be properly dealt with and effective state and local regulation of this traffic be made possible."

Declared that it was "not the purpose of this title to place any undue or unnecessary federal restrictions or burdens on law-abiding citizens" and that the title was "not intended to discourage or eliminate the private ownership or use of firearms by law-abiding citizens for lawful purposes."

Mail-Order Sales. Banned the shipment in interstate or foreign commerce of handguns and ammunition to individuals.

Specifically excluded rifles and shotguns from the prohibition.

Permitted a dealer to return a firearm to a person from whom it was received or to replace a firearm of the same type.

Out-of-State Purchases. Prohibited the sale of a handgun, but not a rifle or shotgun, to a person who did not live in the dealer's state; and prohibited a person from purchasing a handgun out of state.

Prohibited the sale of any firearm to a person if it would have been illegal for the person to purchase the same weapon in his own state or community; prohibited the receipt of a firearm by a person if he could not have received it legally in his own state or community.

Banned the transportation in interstate or foreign commerce by an individual of a destructive device (such as a bomb or hand grenade), a machinegun or a sawed-off shotgun.

Other Restrictions. Prohibited the sale of handguns to persons under 21.

Prohibited the sale or delivery of a destructive device, machinegun or sawed-off shotgun to any individual unless he had a sworn statement from the chief law enforcement officer in his community that there was no law which would be violated by the person's receiving the weapon and that the person planned to use the weapon for lawful purposes.

Required a dealer to keep records of the name, age and address of any person to whom he sold a firearm.

Prohibited a dealer from selling a firearm to a person he knew or believed was a convicted felon, a fugitive or under indictment.

Licensing. Required any importer, manufacturer or dealer to obtain a federal license and established a fee schedule for licenses.

Set standards for licensees.

Penalties. Set a maximum penalty of a $5,000 fine and a five-year prison term for violations of the Act.

Set a maximum penalty of a $10,000 fine and 10 years in prison for a person who shipped or received a firearm in interstate or foreign commerce with the intent to commit a felony.

General Provisions. Exempted antique firearms (manufactured before 1898) from mail-order and out-of-state restrictions.

Repealed the Federal Firearms Act of 1938.

Required the Secretary of the Treasury to compile and publish a list of state and local firearms laws.

Permitted the Secretary to prescribe regulations "necessary to carry out the provisions" of the Act.

Provided that the provisions were to become effective 180 days after enactment.

Other Provisions

Federal Employment. Provided that any person convicted of a felony related to a riot or civil disorder was to be disqualified from employment in the Federal Government or the District of Columbia government for five years.

FBI Director. Provided that any individual appointed in the future by the President to be director of the FBI be confirmed by the Senate.

Set the salary of the FBI director at $30,000 a year.

Firearms Possession. Prohibited the possession of firearms by felons, mental incompetents, aliens in the country illegally, former citizens who had renounced their citizenship and veterans with less than an honorable discharge from the armed forces.

Set the maximum penalty for violation of this section at a $10,000 fine and two years in prison.

Evidence Suppression. Permitted the Federal Government to appeal a successful motion by a defendant to suppress evidence.

Warrants. Authorized the issuance of a warrant for the search and seizure of "any property that constitutes evidence of a criminal offense in violation of the laws of the United States."

Extortion. Set maximum penalties for extortion in the District of Columbia at a $5,000 fine and 20 years in prison.

Gun Control

Late in the 1968 session, Congress enacted legislation (HR 17735—PL 90-618) strengthening and extending to long guns and ammunition the restrictions that had been placed on handguns by the Omnibus Crime Control and Safe Streets Act (PL 90-351) earlier in the year. *(See above.)* HR 17735 not only banned most interstate shipment of long guns to individuals but also prohibited individuals with few exceptions from buying guns except in their own states. The two measures were the first pieces of gun control legislation to be enacted since the Federal Firearms Act of 1938. *(For background, see box p. 324; for text of 2nd Amendment, see p. 331.)*

President Johnson, who had proposed strong firearms controls since 1965, responded to the June 5 assassination of Sen. Robert F. Kennedy (D N.Y.) with an additional appeal for legislation. His proposal, sent to Congress June 10, envisioned banning the mail-order and out-of-state sale of rifles, shotguns and ammunition and a prohibition against sales to minors. Two weeks later he escalated his request and called for national registration of every firearm and a license for every gun owner.

Although the final version of HR 17735 did not include the registration and licensing provisions, it was nonetheless a stronger measure than had been considered possible at the beginning of the year. The Senate May 16 had rejected by a 29-53 roll call a long-gun control amendment offered by Edward M. Kennedy (D Mass.) to the Omnibus Crime bill. But a wave of public support for controls arose in the aftermath of the shooting of Robert Kennedy. A subsequent mass-mail lobbying effort directed at Congress by the National Rifle Assn. eroded some of the newly created support for stronger restrictions, notably that for licensing and registration. *(See box, p. 329.)*

The House July 24 passed HR 17735, **305-118 (R 147-39; D 158-79),** after four days of debate during which it rejected, by lopsided nonrecord votes, licensing and registration amendments. *(For voting analysis, see box, p. 330.)* It accepted several amendments to ease restrictions in the bill. The Senate passed HR 17735 Sept. 18 on a **70-17 (D 39-13; R 31-4)** roll call after five days of debate during which the Senate four times rejected amendments which would have required some form of federal registration of guns and/or licensing of gun owners.

The Senate adopted the conference report Oct. 9 by voice vote. The House adopted it Oct. 10 on a surprisingly close 160-129 roll call. The final version did not contain a provision, added by House floor amendment but deleted in the Senate, that would have exempted rifle ammunition, shotgun ammunition and all .22 caliber ammunition from the restrictions of the bill.

Provisions. The Gun Control Act of 1968 (PL 90-618):

Prohibited the mail-order or other interstate shipment of firearms and ammunition to persons who did

NRA and Gun Control Legislation

Enactment of gun control legislation in 1968 marked a significant, though qualified, defeat for the National Rifle Assn. (NRA), which for years had spear-headed a massive lobbying campaign against strong controls.

The NRA, founded in 1871 by National Guard officers to improve its members' marksmanship, had long enjoyed a close relationship with the Defense Department. These ties remained despite the 1967 cancellation of Government support for the NRA-sponsored National Rifle Matches. By 1968, the NRA had a membership of more than 900,000.

The NRA had not registered as a lobbying organization since 1952 on grounds that its functions were primarily educational and that its legislative activities were not a "substantial" portion of its total activities. (Despite these contentions, Franklin L. Orth, the NRA's executive vice president, registered himself as a lobbyist for the organization Dec. 10, 1968. Orth's action followed announcement by the Federal Bureau of Investigation that it was investigating NRA activities to determine whether NRA had violated the Federal Regulation of Lobbying Act of 1946.)

According to Congressional sources, NRA officers were seldom in direct contact with Members of Congress (although they regularly testified at hearings on gun control legislation). But the organization had been remarkably efficient in sending information on gun legislation to its members and in encouraging them to write letters. NRA Secretary Frank C. Daniel told CQ he had no idea how many letters an NRA appeal could generate, but he added that "perhaps half a million would not be too far off." The national organization also encouraged letter-writing campaigns on proposed laws for states and major cities.

The NRA contended that strict gun control laws would not keep weapons out of the hands of criminals but would make it difficult for legitimate sportsmen and collectors to acquire and possess firearms. The NRA proposed, instead, strict penalties for misuse of firearms. In justification of its opposition to gun legislation, the organization cited the 2nd Amendment prohibition on interference with the right to "keep and bear arms." *(See box, p. 331.)*

Nonetheless, nationwide polls suggested there was strong support for a tough gun control law. A January 1967 Gallup Poll said that 70 percent of the persons in a survey believed "laws concerning handguns should be more strict." A Louis Harris Survey published June 17, 1968, found that 81 percent of Americans supported gun registration laws, but the same survey showed that 45 percent of the people felt that "control of guns might not cut down on violence at all."

The effectiveness of the antigun control forces was demonstrated after the 1963 assassination of President John F. Kennedy. Although the alleged assassin had bought the gun through the mail using a false name, the onslaught of letters against a bill banning mail-order sales of handguns and long guns succeeded in having the measure shelved.

In the following years, lobby pressures, notably by the NRA, played a key role in blocking Congressional action on the issue, despite President Johnson's repeated requests for legislation.

However, the fatal shooting of Sen. Robert F. Kennedy (D N.Y.) June 5, 1968, set off an unprecedented wave of public support for strong gun control legislation. Kennedy's murder, two months after the assassination of the Rev. Dr. Martin Luther King Jr., spurred Congress to enact two major gun control measures, the first such laws since 1938.

The day Kennedy died, June 6, Congress cleared the Omnibus Crime Control and Safe Streets Act (HR 5037) which prohibited the interstate sale or shipment to individuals of handguns but imposed no controls on rifles, shotguns or ammunition. *(See p. 323)*

In the week following, Congressional offices were inundated with pro-gun control mail, the NRA's Washington offices were picketed and petition drives were mounted throughout the country by the Council for a Responsible Firearms Policy and other groups.

The NRA June 15 called on its members to write their Senators and Representatives to oppose additional gun laws. "The right of sportsmen in the United States to obtain, own and use firearms for proper lawful purposes is in the greatest jeopardy in the history of our country," NRA President Harold W. Glassen wrote.

Partly as a result of the NRA letter and partly because the outrage following the Kennedy assassination had waned, Congressional offices reported that their mail showed a heavy swing back against controls. One Senator, for instance, said that in the week following the assassination his mail ran 60 percent in favor of stronger gun controls; by the third week, 80 percent of his mail opposed further legislation.

The mail campaign against additional gun controls was not strong enough to block further legislation entirely. Congress enacted a bill (HR 17735) extending the prohibitions in HR 5037 to rifles, shotguns and ammunition. But it rejected President Johnson's request for owner licensing and gun registration requirements, which the NRA emphatically opposed. *(See p. 328.)*

not live in the dealer's state, and prohibited a person from making such a purchase.

Prohibited intrastate mail-order shipment and receipt of firearms unless the buyer submitted to the seller a sworn statement attesting to his competence to purchase the firearm and reciting the essential facts of the transaction. The seller was in turn required to notify the buyer's local law enforcement official.

Prohibited sale of rifles, shotguns or ammunition to persons under 18 and sales of handguns or handgun ammunition to persons under 21.

Modified existing licensing requirements for firearms or ammunition importers, manufacturers and dealers and added licensing requirements for firearms collectors.

Prohibited the importation of foreign-made military surplus firearms into the United States.

Permitted importation of firearms or ammunition upon approval by the Secretary of the Treasury in certain specified circumstances.

Established penalties for violation of the Act.

Extended the scope of the National Firearms Act of 1934 so that its tax provisions would cover destructive devices (defined in the Act) and some other types of weaponry.

Prohibited firearms sale to convicted felons, fugitives, persons under indictment, unlawful users of drugs and mental defectives.

Juvenile Delinquency

Congress enacted the Juvenile Delinquency Prevention and Control Act (HR 12120—PL 90-445), which authorized a three-year, $150-million program of block grants to states to plan and operate projects to prevent juvenile delinquency and rehabilitate young offenders. HR 12120 provided for grants to states and, in some instances, to local governments for the planning and operation of preventive and rehabilitative programs, construction of facilities, training of personnel and research into improved techniques and practices. Congress appropriated $5 million for fiscal 1969.

The legislation was first requested by President Johnson in 1967, and the request was renewed in his 1968 crime message. The President opposed the block grant method of allocation, but the other provisions were generally in line with his requests. As passed by the House in 1967, the bill authorized only a one-year program. *(See above.)*

The major controversy over HR 12120 concerned the method by which the federal grants would be allocated. The original bill had authorized the Federal Government to make grants directly to localities or to private nonprofit agencies according to certain considerations outlined in the bill.

After considerable debate, the House rewrote the original bill on the floor and substituted a system of block grants to the states to be distributed on the basis of population. The House bill required each state to formulate a comprehensive state plan for the use of the funds. The plan was to be submitted for approval to the Secretary of Health, Education and Welfare. Once the plan was approved, all grants were to be made directly to the state for redistribution locally. The only instance in which the Secretary of HEW could make grants directly to local agencies was when a state failed to apply for a grant or to have it approved within nine months of the passage of the law.

The Senate bill, on the other hand, provided for a modified block grant method of allocating the funds. Under the Senate version, the Secretary of HEW was authorized to make grants directly to localities and public and private nonprofit agencies, whether or not a state plan had been approved. But, if a state submitted a

Voting on Gun Controls

Voting on gun control tended to divide along sectional and urban vs. rural lines.

Sectional Voting. The following chart compares two votes: the May 16 vote in which the Senate rejected an amendment to the Omnibus Crime Bill to prohibit the interstate mail-order sale of rifles and shotguns and the July 24 vote in which the House passed HR 17735, which banned such sales and also prohibited most out-of-state purchases of long-guns and prohibited interstate shipment of handgun ammunition. *(For individual voting, see Key Votes in appendix.)*

Senators and Representatives are broken down according to their section of the country.

CQ defines U.S. regions as follows for purposes of its voting studies:

EAST—Conn., Del., Maine, Md., Mass., N.H., N.J., N.Y., Pa., R.I., Vt., W.Va.

SOUTH—Ala., Ark., Fla., Ga., Ky., La., Miss., N.C., Okla., S.C., Tenn., Texas, Va.

MIDWEST—Ill., Ind., Iowa, Kan., Mich., Minn., Mo., Neb., N.D., Ohio, S.D., Wis.

WEST—Alaska, Ariz., Calif., Colo., Hawaii, Idaho, Mont., Nev., N.M., Ore., Utah, Wash., Wyo.

	SENATE		HOUSE	
	For	Against	For	Against
All Members	33%	60%	71%	28%
All Democrats	34%	59%	65%	33%
All Republicans	31%	61%	79%	21%
All East	75%	17%	94%	4%
Democrats	93%	7%	94%	3%
Republicans	50%	30%	94%	6%
All West	8%	88%	75%	23%
Democrats	0%	94%	79%	18%
Republicans	20%	80%	71%	29%
All South	19%	73%	27%	71%
Democrats	19%	76%	22%	76%
Republicans	20%	60%	43%	57%
All Midwest	33%	58%	88%	11%
Democrats	38%	46%	93%	7%
Republicans	27%	73%	85%	14%

Urban Representatives. The nation's 20 largest cities, according to the 1960 census, have a total of 97 voting Representatives in Congress; of these 72 are Democrats and 25 are Republicans.

Eighty-seven of these Representatives (90 percent voted for HR 17735—63 Democrats (88 percent) and 24 Republicans (96 percent).

Eight (8 percent) voted against the bill—seven Democrats (10 percent) and one Republican (4 percent).

Those opposed were: King (D Los Angeles County), Dingell (D Detroit-Wayne County), Hebert (D New Orleans), Cabell (D Dallas), Purcell (D Dallas), Fisher (D San Antonio-Bexar County), Kazen (D San Antonio-Bexar County) and Curtis (R St. Louis County).

Two Representatives—Holland (D Pittsburgh) and Hawkins (D Los Angeles County) did not vote.

statewide plan and if it were approved, grants could also be given in block form to the state, providing the state agreed to pay at least half of the local matching share. The state could also compete equally with the local applicants for federal funds to conduct its own programs. Passage of the Senate bill came July 8 after the Senate narrowly defeated, by a 34-38 roll-call vote, an attempt to insert block grant provisions similar to those passed by the House.

In its final form, the bill contained the House provisions for mandatory block grants for preventive and rehabilitative services, which were expected to consume the major share of funds. However, the conferees retained the Senate provisions allowing grants to be made directly to local agencies for planning, training and research programs.

Provisions. The Juvenile Delinquency Prevention and Control Act (PL 90-445):

Authorized block grants to states for the operation of prevention and rehabilitation projects.

Provided that a state could receive a block grant only if it were willing to pay at least half of the required matching share for the grants.

Stipulated that the funds granted the states in block form were to be distributed statewide according to a comprehensive plan which had been approved' by the HEW Secretary.

Permitted the HEW Secretary to make prevention and rehabilitation grants directly to local agencies only when a state failed to apply for a grant or to have it approved within nine months of enactment.

Authorized direct grants by the HEW Secretary to states and local public and private nonprofit agencies for planning, training and research programs.

Authorized $25 million in fiscal 1969, $50 million in fiscal 1970 and $75 million in fiscal 1971.

Set the federal share of grants at 100 percent for research, demonstration and technical assistance; 100 percent for training; 90 percent for planning; 75 percent for prevention; 60 percent for rehabilitation; and 50 percent for construction.

Miscellaneous Bills

DRUG ABUSE CONTROL. Congress enacted a bill (HR 14096—PL 90-639) providing criminal penalties for the possession of illegally obtained stimulant, depressant or hallucinogenic drugs (including "pep pills," barbiturates and LSD).

The bill also authorized judges to set aside convictions of first offenders after a probationary period (a provision designed to keep young people who experimented with drugs from getting a criminal record) and increased existing penalties for trafficking in illegal drugs.

The legislation, passed by the House July 12 and the Senate Oct. 4, was requested by President Johnson in his 1968 crime message. Its major thrust was to make possession a punishable offense (but to allow an offender to clear his record through corrective behavior) and to increase penalties for those who sold drugs to youths.

Congress previously strengthened federal controls over stimulant, depressant and hallucinogenic drugs in 1965. *(See chapter on Health.)*

DRUG REORGANIZATION. President Johnson Feb. 7 announced he would submit a reorganization plan to establish a new Bureau of Narcotics and Dangerous Drugs in the Justice Department. The new Bureau combined two separate federal agencies for drug law enforcement, the Bureau of Narcotics in the Treasury Department and the Bureau of Drug Abuse Control in the Health, Education and Welfare Department. The President's reorganization plan to bring about the merger took effect April 8. The Senate made no effort to veto the plan; a House resolution of disapproval was rejected April 2 on a 190-200 roll-call vote. There was general support for merging the two bureaus, but opponents of the plan questioned their transfer to the Justice Department.

BANK PROTECTION. President Johnson requested and Congress enacted legislation (HR 15345—PL 90-389) designed to curb the continuing increase in bank robberies throughout the nation. The bill, passed by the House May 6 and the Senate June 19, directed

---

2nd Amendment

"A well regulated Militia, being necessary to the security of a free state, the right of the people to keep and bear Arms shall not be infringed."

Thus reads the 2nd Amendment to the U.S. Constitution. Thirty-five states have similar constitutional provisions (but not New York, California or Illinois, the three largest states). Opponents of guntrol laws contend that such laws are unconstitutional, that the Government cannot take away an individual right to "keep and bear Arms." Supporters of firearms legislation contend that the right is applicable only in the context of a state militia, or in today's sense, the National Guard.

The Supreme Court has never struck down a firearms-control law on the grounds that it violated the 2nd Amendment. But it has upheld such laws. The leading case is a 1939 Supreme Court case, *U.S. v. Miller.* Miller had been convicted of violating the National Firearms Act by transporting an unregistered sawed-off shotgun across state lines. The Court upheld the conviction and said: "In the absence of any evidence tending to show that possession or use of a 'shotgun having a barrel of less than 18 inches in length' at this time has some reasonable relationship to the preservation or efficiency of a well regulated militia, we cannot say that the 2nd Amendment guarantees the right to keep and bear such an instrument." The Court added that the "declaration and guarantee of the 2nd Amendment were made" in order to "assure the continuation and render possible the effectiveness of such forces (militias)." The Amendment the court said, "must be interpreted and applied with the end in view." Proponents of firearms legislation contend that this language is unambiguous.

However, Tacoma, Washington, Superior Court Judge Bartlett Rummel, a past president of the National Rifle Assn. and a frequent writer on the 2nd Amendment, contends that the right to keep and bear arms is a "basic right" to individuals, and he traces the right back to English common law.

Ramsey Clark: Controversial Attorney General

"If we are to restore order and respect for law in this country, there's one place we're going to begin: we're going to have a new Attorney General of the United States of America." Thus spoke Richard M. Nixon, in a speech accepting the 1968 Republican Presidential nomination.

The object of his attack was Ramsey Clark, youthful Attorney General of the Johnson Administration, whom Nixon accused of "leading an official retreat" in the face of rising crime.

Clark was the son of Tom C. Clark, Truman Administration Attorney General (1945-49) and Associate Justice of the Supreme Court (1949-67). The younger Clark joined the Justice Department at the beginning of the Kennedy Administration in 1961 as Assistant Attorney General in charge of the Lands Division, a post he held until he became Deputy Attorney General in 1965. During these years Clark undertook a number of assignments in the field of civil rights; he served at the University of Mississippi (1962), Birmingham (1963) and Selma and Watts (1965). He also helped formulate the Civil Rights Act of 1964 and the Voting Rights Act of 1965. He became Acting Attorney General late in 1966 and was appointed Attorney General by President Johnson early in 1967.

Despite his active interest in civil rights, it was Clark's approach to crime that brought him the greatest criticism and made him an issue in the 1968 campaign. Clark, who held that the root causes of crime lay in social and economic factors, offered no quick and easy solutions to the mounting crime problem. And he was an uncompromising opponent of efforts to maintain order at the expense of due process. It was sometimes said of him that he acted more like a public defender than the nation's number one prosecutor.

Clark consistently opposed wiretapping except in cases of national security. As Attorney General in 1967 he issued a memorandum restricting the use of wiretapping and eavesdropping devices by federal agents to national security cases. When Congress in the 1968 Omnibus Crime Control and Safe Streets Act gave him broader wiretapping authority, he refused to use it.

Similarly, Clark defended Supreme Court rulings on the rights of defendants, most notably *Miranda v. Arizona* (1966), and refused to take advantage of Omnibus Crime bill provisions purporting to overrule them. *(See p. 323.)*

Clark also was a firm opponent of capital punishment, condemned those who advocated the shooting of looters and cautioned against the use of excessive force by police. He thus became a natural target for those who urged a "get tough" policy on crime.

Clark's philosophy was summed up in his 1968 testimony before the Democratic Platform Committee:

"Crime reflects the character of a people. There is no easy solution to America's crime problem. Its causes are as many and diverse as all the needs and aspirations of its people. Oversimplification or demagoguery can only lead to police state practices that destroy freedom and divide a people....

"Criminal justice has been so long neglected that we come to doubt our principles when it is only their implementation that fails. As we build the forces of government to firmly, but fairly, enforce our laws, we must continue with greater diligence our pursuit of equal justice. Every act of justice makes order surer."

---

federal banking officials—the Comptroller of the Currency, the Board of Governors of the Federal Reserve System, the Federal Deposit Insurance Corp. and the Federal Home Loan Bank Board—to establish minimum security-system standards for banking institutions under their jurisdiction as a deterrent to robbers.

MASTER KEYS. In an effort to deter auto thefts, President Johnson requested and Congress enacted a bill (HR 14935—PL 90-560) that prohibited the mailing of master keys for motor vehicles or advertisements for the keys. The bill, passed by the House Feb. 19 and the Senate July 11, was slightly weaker than the measure President Johnson proposed. The President had asked that no exemptions be allowed, but Congress provided that exemptions could be made by the Postmaster General. The bill also included broader police powers for postal inspectors.

ALCOHOLICS REHABILITATION. In his Feb. 7 crime message, President Johnson asked Congress to approve legislation providing rehabilitation, "rather than simple detention," of alcoholics. Congress met this request by enacting the Alcoholic Rehabilitation Act of 1968 as part of a bill (HR 15758) to extend federal participation in regional medical programs.

ANTIRIOT MEASURES. In his crime message, President Johnson called for legislation making it a felony to cross state lines to incite and take part in riots. Congress included such a provision in the Administration's civil rights-open housing bill (HR 2516).

In addition, the Safe Streets bill (HR 5037) barred from federal employment persons convicted of riot-related acts. *(See above.)* Congress also added provisions to a number of measures barring the use of certain federal funds for students and federal workers convicted of riot-related acts. *(See chapter on Education.)*

Committees in both chambers investigated riots and violence, as did the National Commission on the Causes and Prevention of Violence. The Commission, appointed by President Johnson after the shooting of Sen. Robert F. Kennedy (D N.Y.), was headed by Milton S. Eisenhower, president emeritus of Johns Hopkins University and brother of the former President.

Other Legislation

POLICE BENEFITS. Congress completed action on a bill (HR 11816—PL 90-291) providing federal death and disability benefits for state and local law enforcement officers killed or disabled while enforcing federal law. The measure provided benefits equivalent to those in the Federal Employees Compensation Act but stipulated that benefits were to be reduced in proportion to benefits paid by the state or local government.

The Senate and House had passed differing versions of the bill in 1967 *(see above)*; the conference version cleared Congress April 3, 1968.

JOINT CRIME COMMITTEE. The House July 12 passed a bill (H J Res 1) to establish a Joint Committee to Investigate Crime. There was no Senate action and the legislation died with the adjournment of Congress.

CRIME STATISTICS. Congress took no action on a bill (HR 18897) to establish a National Crime Statistics Center. The bill resulted from hearings by the House Post Office and Civil Service Committee's Subcommittee on Census and Statistics, during which witnesses pointed to the need for improved statistical information on all aspects of crime and criminal justice. The inadequacy of existing systems also had been cited by the President's Commission on Law Enforcement and Administration of Justice in 1967.

The Omnibus Crime Control and Safe Streets Act (PL 90-351) authorized the Attorney General "to collect, evaluate, publish and disseminate statistics and other information on the condition and progress of law enforcement in the several states." HR 18897 would have given specific authority for that mission. *(See above.)*

CAPITAL PUNISHMENT. A Senate subcommittee held hearings on a bill (S 1760) to abolish capital punishment in federal crimes and commute all pending death sentences to life imprisonment. There was no further action. Attorney General Ramsey Clark, testifying before the Senate Judiciary Special Subcommittee on Criminal Laws and Procedures, called for total abolition of the death penalty for all federal crimes, including Presidential assassination. He said extensive studies had shown that the death penalty did not deter crime.

"A humane and generous concern for every individual, for his safety, his health and his fulfillment will do more to soothe the savage heart than the fear of state-inflicted death, which chiefly serves to remind us how close we remain to the jungle," Clark said. He added, "Surely the abolition of the death penalty is a major milestone in the long road up from barbarism." Clark continued, "It is the poor, the weak, the ignorant, the hated who are executed. Racial discrimination occurs in the administration of capital punishment."

LOAN SHARKING. The truth-in-lending bill (PL 90-321) contained provisions to fight "loan sharking" by criminals. The bill provided federal penalties for extortionate credit transactions. *(See Consumer chapter.)*

In addition, the Senate Select Small Business Committee held a series of hearings on the role of organized crime in loan sharking.

Major Supreme Court Decisions on Crime

Following is a list of major criminal law cases decided by the Supreme Court beginning in 1957.

Mallory v. U.S. (1957)—The Court unanimously ruled that a 10-hour police interrogation after arrest and prior to arraignment violated Rule 5 (a) of the Federal Rules of Criminal Procedure that "arraignment be without unnecessary delay" and violated the Court's supervisory rule, enunciated in *McNabb v. U.S.* (1943), that delay "must not be of a nature to give opportunity for the extraction of a confession."

Mapp v. Ohio (1961)—By a 6-3 vote, the Court held that the 14th Amendment precluded the use in state prosecutions of evidence illegally seized.

Robinson v. California (1962)—By a 6-2 vote, the Court held that for a state to make it a crime "to use or be addicted to the use of narcotics" constituted cruel and unusual punishment in violation of the 8th and 14th Amendments. The Court called that a "status" crime; the defendant was an addict but had not possessed or used narcotics in California. The decision was the only one in the 1960-68 period in which the Court reversed a state conviction on the basis of substantive criminal law.

Gideon v. Wainwright (1963)—The Court unanimously held that indigent defendants were entitled to counsel at trial in non-capital state prosecutions.

Fay v. Noia (1963)—By a 6-3 vote, the Court held that state prisoners could seek federal court review of their convictions even though they had failed to exercise timely their full rights to state court review.

Malloy v. Hogan (1964)—By a 5-4 vote, the Court held for the first time that the 5th Amendment was applicable to the states.

Escobedo v. Illinois (1964)—By a 5-4 vote, the Court held that at the point at which a police investigation became accusatorial, the suspect was entitled to confer with his counsel.

Miranda v. Arizona (1966)—By a 5-4 vote, the Court held that before interrogating a suspect, state or local police had to advise him: (1) that he need not make a statement; (2) that any statement he made could be used against him; (3) that he was entitled to counsel; and (4) that counsel would be provided if he were indigent and could not retain counsel.

Sheppard v. Maxwell (1966) (1966)—By an 8-1 vote, the Court held that excessive publicity before and during a state trial could be prejudicial to a fair trial and thus vitiated the conviction, requiring retrial.

Lewis v. U.S. (1966)—The Court upheld the practice of a federal narcotics agent misrepresenting his identity in order to purchase marijuana from a suspect. Justice Douglas alone dissented.

Warden v. Hayden (1967)—By an 8-1 vote, the Court held that police in "hot pursuit" of a robber could enter and search his house without a warrant.

Spencer v. Texas (1967)—By a 5-4 vote, the Court upheld the Texas practice of informing the jury of a defendant's prior convictions so that the jury might sentence him under the habitual offender laws.

Washington v. Texas (1967)—By a 9-0 vote, the Court held for the first time that defendants in state criminal trials had the right, through the 6th Amendment, to compulsory process for obtaining witnesses.

In re Gault (1967)—By an 8-1 vote, the Court held that juvenile defendants were entitled to rights under the 5th and 6th Amendments.

Berger v. New York (1967)—By a 6-3 vote, the Court held that New York's permissive eavesdrop statute was unconstitutional since it did not provide for sufficient judicial control over police.

U.S. v. Wade (1967)—By a 9-0 vote, the Court held that identification based on police lineup in the absence of a lawyer, and having no independent origin beyond that, was inadmissible at a trial. The Court held that although the lineup did not violate the defendant's privilege against self-incrimination, the absence of a lawyer violated his 6th Amendment right to counsel.

Katz v. U.S. (1967)—By a 7-1 vote, the Court held that use of an electronic listening device was a "search and seizure" within the meaning of the 4th Amendment, and evidence obtained by it without a warrant was not admissible at trial.

Terry v. Ohio (1968)—By an 8-1 vote, the Court held that police, with reasonable suspicion but without probable cause for arrest, could for their own protection stop citizens briefly on the street and "frisk" them for dangerous weapons.

Powell v. Texas (1968)—By a 5-4 vote, the Court upheld the conviction of a chronic alcoholic for being drunk in a public place. The Court said it lacked sufficient information to conclude, as the defendant argued, that an alcoholic was incapable of controlling his drinking and therefore could not be held criminally liable for his actions.

Haynes v. U.S. (1968)—By a 9-0 vote, the Court held that the registration provisions of the National Firearms Act violated the 5th Amendment privilege against self-incrimination in criminal prosecutions. The Court said that Congress had to find a different method of enforcing the Act.

Marchetti v. U.S. (1968)—By a 7-1 vote, the Court held that the registration provisions of the federal wagering tax statutes violated the 5th Amendment privilege against self-incrimination in criminal prosecutions.

Duncan v. Louisiana (1968)—By a 7-2 vote, the Court held for the first time that the 6th Amendment right to trial by jury applied to the states through the "due process" clause of the 14th Amendment. It applied in state cases in which, if tried in federal courts, the defendant would have the right to trial by jury, the Court said.

U.S. v. Jackson (1968)—By a 6-2 vote, the Court held unconstitutional a provision of the Federal Kidnaping Act that authorized a jury under certain circumstances, to impose the death penalty but did not authorize a judge to impose it. The Court said that provision left the defendant in the position of having to risk his life in order to obtain a jury trial.

Witherspoon v. Illinois (1968)—By a 6-3 vote, the Court held that the death sentence could not be carried out if the jury which imposed or recommended it was chosen by excluding prospective jurors who voiced general objections to the death penalty or who expressed conscientious or religious scruples against its infliction.

The Federal Judiciary

DURING the years 1965-68, interest in the federal judiciary focused on the Supreme Court, which had been under attack since the mid-1950s for a series of "activist" decisions.

President Johnson appointed two Justices to the Court during his term of office. The first was Abe Fortas, long-term Johnson friend and adviser, in 1965. The second was Thurgood Marshall, first Negro ever to be named to the Court, in 1967. Both appointments were confirmed without substantial opposition.

However, in 1968 Mr. Johnson was unsuccessful in his efforts to elevate Fortas to the Chief Justiceship to replace Chief Justice Earl Warren who sought to retire. The Fortas nomination was withdrawn in the face of a Senate filibuster, and Warren agreed to remain in his post through the 1968-69 Court term. Since there was thus no vacancy on the Court, Mr. Johnson's nomination of Homer Thornberry to succeed Fortas as Associate Justice was not acted upon.

Meanwhile, in Congress continuing efforts were made to overturn or modify a variety of controversial Court decisions—most notably concerning crime, reapportionment and school prayer.

Congress enacted several bills dealing with the administration of the federal court system. It created a number of new federal judgeships, established a Federal Judicial Center to promote improvement in court administration and created a new system of federal magistrates to replace the old commissioner system.

Following is a summary of developments in each of these fields for the 1965-68 period. *(For background on the federal judicial system, see Congress and the Nation, Vol. I, p. 1441.)*

Action on Nominations

FORTAS. In 1965, President Johnson nominated Washington lawyer Abe Fortas to be an Associate Justice of the Supreme Court, replacing Arthur J. Goldberg. Goldberg resigned to become U.S. Ambassador to the United Nations. The Senate Aug. 11 confirmed Fortas' nomination by voice vote. Three Republican Senators spoke against the nomination. *(See box, p. 337.)*

MARSHALL. In 1967, President Johnson nominated Solicitor General Thurgood Marshall to an Associate Justiceship to replace retiring Justice Tom C. Clark. Marshall, a Negro and a noted civil rights lawyer long associated with the National Assn. for the Advancement

of Colored People (NAACP) and the NAACP Legal Defense and Educational Fund, had served as Solicitor General since 1965. Previously he had served on the Circuit Court of Appeals. *(See box, p. 339.)*

After fairly protracted hearings by the Senate Judiciary Committee, the Senate Aug. 3 confirmed his nomination on a 69-11 roll-call vote. Ten Southern Democrats and one Northern Democrat voted against confirmation. Senate action followed six hours of debate during which opponents contended that Marshall was a "judicial activist" who would bring the Court into an imbalance favoring liberal rulings.

Marshall Oct. 2 was sworn in as the first Negro ever to sit on the Supreme Court.

FORTAS AS CHIEF JUSTICE. In a stinging defeat for President Johnson, the Senate in 1968 blocked his nomination of Associate Justice Abe Fortas to be Chief Justice. This occurred when the Senate Oct. 1, by a **45-43** roll-call vote, refused to invoke cloture on debate on a motion to consider the nomination. The Senate never took up the nomination as such.

The President Oct. 4 withdrew the nomination at Fortas' request.

A coalition of Republicans and Southern Democrats, called the conservative coalition, formed to defeat the cloture motion. Sen. Carl Hayden (D Ariz.), who was retiring in 1968, cast his first vote for cloture since coming to the Senate in 1927. Breakdown on the vote: R 10-24; D 35-19 (ND 31-4; SD 4-15). Two-thirds (59) of those voting were required to invoke cloture. *(For cloture votes, see Civil Rights chapter.)*

The loss in the Senate was a major personal setback both for President Johnson and for Fortas, whom Mr. Johnson had named to the Court in 1965.

Three other men nominated for the Chief Justiceship never attained it. The Senate by a 10-14 roll-call vote refused to confirm John Rutledge, the nominee of President Washington, in 1795. President Grant's nominations of George H. Williams in 1873 and of Caleb Cushing in 1874 were withdrawn before the Senate could consider them. No nomination of equal importance had been rejected in modern times. The most nearly comparable incident occurred in 1959, when the Senate by a 46-49 roll call rejected President Eisenhower's nomination of Lewis L. Strauss as Secretary of Commerce. *(For precedents, see box and Congress and the Nation, Vol. I, p. 102a.)*

Issues. Several issues began to develop soon after President Johnson nominated Fortas on June 26. Chief Justice Earl Warren June 13 had informed the President of his intention to retire, contingent upon the qualification (confirmation) of his successor. Mr. Johnson also nominated Judge Homer Thornberry of the 5th Circuit Court of Appeals to replace Fortas. *(See below.)* Before going to the Court, Fortas had been a close friend, adviser and counsel to Mr. Johnson.

Freshman Sen. Robert P. Griffin (R Mich.) immediately began a fight against the nomination, a fight he led down to the final vote on cloture. He contended that the nominations were based on "cronyism," referring to long-standing personal and professional relationship of Mr. Johnson and the nominees. Griffin also argued that there was, legally, no vacancy on the Court. Some observers suggested that Griffin's motives were, at least, mixed, and that he really intended to save the nominations for GOP Presidential candidate Richard M. Nixon, if Nixon was elected.

There were other allegations that Warren, whose dislike of Nixon was well known, was trying to assure that his successor would be chosen by a Democratic President. That issue faded, however, and neither Nixon (who was silent on the nominations but did say the Senate should vote on the Fortas nomination) nor Vice President Hubert H. Humphrey, the Democratic candidate for President, figured prominently in subsequent events.

More serious issues developed during hearings held by the Senate Judiciary Committee between July 11 and Sept. 16. One was what appeared to be the continued involvement of Fortas in White House affairs, an involvement frankly admitted to but played down by the Justice in his one appearance before the Committee. There were charges that Fortas had assisted in drafting legislation for the Administration.

More damaging, perhaps, was the disclosure that Fortas had received a fee of $15,000 for giving a nine-week seminar on law at American University during the summer of 1968. The money had been raised by his former law partner from among five former business associates, one of whom had a son involved in a federal criminal case.

During hearings and in subsequent floor debate, however, there was a strong flavor of dislike among many conservatives for the Warren Court. The liberal bent of the Court in general, and the participation of Fortas in some of its decisions, in particular, came under attack. Decisions in the area of criminal procedural law and obscenity were singled out for bitter criticism. During the hearings, opponents of the nomination showed films and books involved in Supreme Court obscenity cases to other Senators and to newsmen.

The opposition to the nomination grew as Griffin pressed the attack relentlessly during the summer. He missed no opportunity to turn the evidence against the nominee. Finally, on Sept. 27, he won his biggest victory, when Senate Minority Leader Everett McKinley Dirksen (R Ill.) reversed his position and announced that he was officially "neutral." Dirksen had been a strong supporter of the nominee, but it was clear that as Griffin's following of Republican Senators grew, Dirksen's control as their leader diminished. On the floor on Oct. 1, Dirksen gave as his reason for voting against cloture the disposition of an Illinois criminal case by the Court. (*The case was Witherspoon v. Illinois.*)

Debate on the motion of Majority Leader Mike Mansfield (D Mont.) to take up the nomination began

on Sept. 25. Republican and Southern Democratic Senators delivered a series of long speeches, often including searing attacks on the Warren Court. But Mansfield made no attempt to keep the Senate in session for long hours during the five-day filibuster. Each day, the Senate set aside time to transact other routine business, and the latest the Senate adjourned during the five days was 5:58 p.m.

Mansfield's cloture motion, eventually signed by 26 Senators, was read to the Senate on Sept. 29, and the vote was set for Oct. 1. After one hour of final debate that day, the roll-call vote was taken.

The next morning, Fortas released his letter to the President requesting that, to avoid further attacks on the Court, the nomination be withdrawn. Terming the action of the Senate "tragic," the President consented.

THORNBERRY. President Johnson's third Supreme Court nomination, that of Homer Thornberry in 1968, was not acted upon by the Senate.

Thornberry, judge of the 5th Circuit Court of Appeals, had served in the House (D 1949-63), representing Mr. Johnson's district in Texas. He was elected to the House in 1948 to fill the vacancy created when Mr. Johnson was elected to the Senate.

The President nominated Thornberry to be an Associate Justice in anticipation of Chief Justice Warren's retirement and the promotion of Fortas to the Chief Justiceship. When the Senate failed to approve the Fortas nomination, Warren did not resign and thus there was no vacancy on the Court for Thornberry to fill.

Efforts to Curb Court

During the 1965-68 period, Congress was the scene of significant efforts to curb the power of the Supreme Court and to reverse or modify several controversial Court rulings.

In only one area did these efforts succeed. Congress included in the Omnibus Crime bill of 1968 provisions designed to reverse three Supreme Court decisions in the field of criminal law. The decisions, which dealt with the rights during police interrogation of suspects accused of federal crimes, were *Mallory v. U.S.* (1957), *Miranda v. Arizona* (1966) and *U.S. v. Wade* (1967). The provisions were added by the Senate. The Senate refused, however, to accept amendments that would have restricted the authority of the Court to review state criminal rulings. *(See p. 323.)*

Congress also attempted to modify two other major Court decisions by the constitutional amendment route. Both efforts were sponsored by Senate Minority Leader Everett McKinley Dirksen (R Ill.), and both failed.

In 1965 and again in 1966 the Senate rejected legislation proposing a constitutional amendment to permit states to apportion their legislatures on the basis of geography and political subdivisions as well as population. The bill was aimed at modifying the Supreme Court's "one-man, one-vote" rule requiring state legislatures to be apportioned on the basis of population only. This rule was enunciated in *Reynolds v. Sims* (1964). In both years Dirksen won a simple majority for his proposal, but each vote fell seven short of the two-thirds majority

Fortas Resigns in 1969

Associate Justice Abe Fortas resigned May 14, 1969, in the wake of renewed controversy over the propriety of his extra-judicial activities. He was the first Supreme Court Justice in history to resign under threat of impeachment.

The controversy was precipitated by a *Life* magazine article which asserted that Fortas in January 1966, three months after becoming an Associate Justice, had accepted a $20,000 fee from a foundation controlled by the family of millionaire industrialist Louis E. Wolfson. In September 1966, Wolfson was indicted for selling unregistered securities. In December 1966, *Life* said, Fortas returned the $20,000.

Wolfson was convicted in September 1967, sentenced to one year in prison, and fined $100,000. The Supreme Court on April 1, 1969, denied an appeal for review of the decision. Fortas took no part in consideration of the case because his former law firm had on occasion represented Wolfson.

In response to the *Life* article, Fortas issued a statement May 4 saying he had been "tendered" a fee by the Wolfson foundation but had returned it after concluding that he could not undertake work for the foundation, which was engaged in promoting racial and religious harmony. The Justice said he did not feel that the fee tender constituted an attempt to induce him to "intervene or make representations on Mr. Wolfson's behalf," and that he had not so acted at any time.

Despite urgings that he amplify his May 4 statement, Fortas in the following days refused further comment. Meanwhile the furor grew.

Some Members of Congress called for a Congressional investigation of the case, while others urged Fortas' resignation or impeachment. Pressure rose for enactment of financial disclosure legislation applicable to the federal judiciary.

It was reported that the Criminal Division of the Justice Department was investigating the Fortas-Wolfson relationship to determine whether there had been any violation of federal law. It was reported also that Attorney General John N. Mitchell met with Chief Justice Earl Warren, supposedly to press for Fortas' resignation. Mitchell allegedly told Warren that "far more serious" information against Fortas would become public unless Fortas resigned. Warren and Mitchell on May 12 confirmed the fact they had met May 7.

Fortas submitted his resignation to President Nixon May 14, and the President promptly accepted it. In a May 14 letter to Chief Justice Warren, Fortas said he had received the $20,000 from the Wolfson Foundation under an arrangement calling for payment of $20,000 a year for life, with like payments continuing to Mrs. Fortas in the event of his death. He said he had decided in June 1966 to sever his relationship with the foundation because his Court work was much heavier than expected, and because of Wolfson's legal difficulties. Following Wolfson's indictment, he returned the $20,000 he had previously received.

Fortas said that since joining the Court he had received no other compensation from Wolfson, his family or his associates, either "directly or indirectly."

Fortas added: "Since I became a member of the Court, Mr. Wolfson on occasion would send me material relating to his problems, just as I think he did to many other people, and on several occasions he mentioned them to me, but I have not interceded or taken part in any legal, administrative or judicial matter affecting Mr. Wolfson or anyone associated with him."

"There has been no wrongdoing on my part," Fortas said. "There has been no default in the performance of my judicial duties in accordance with the high standards of the office I hold. So far as I am concerned, the welfare and maximum effectiveness of the Court to perform its critical role in our system of government are factors that are paramount to all others. It is this consideration that prompts my resignation which, I hope, by terminating the public controversy, will permit the Court to proceed with its work without the harassment of debate concerning one of its members."

Standards of Judicial Conduct. The Constitution, which empowers the House of Representatives to initiate impeachment proceedings against Supreme Court Justices and the Senate to try them, says: "The Judges, both of the supreme and inferior Courts, shall hold their Offices during good Behaviour..." (Article III, Section 1) What constitutes good behavior is not spelled out beyond mention of "treason, bribery or other high crimes and misdemeanors."

Only one Supreme Court Justice ever was impeached: Samuel Chase, in 1804. The House charged Chase with "misconduct in trials impairing the confidence and respect for the courts." He was acquitted by the Senate.

The Canons of Judicial Ethics of the American Bar Assn. offer further guidelines for judicial conduct. Cited in connection with the Fortas case:

Canon 4: A judge's offical conduct should be "free from impropriety" or any appearance of impropriety. A judge's personal, everyday life should be "beyond reproach."

Canon 24: A judge should not undertake duties or obligations—pecuniary or otherwise—which might be inconsistent with or interfere with "his devotion to the expeditious and proper administration of his official functions."

Canon 25: "A judge should avoid giving ground for suspicion that he is utilizing the power or prestige of his office to persuade or coerce others to patronize or contribute, either to the success of private business, or to charitable enterprises."

Douglas Charges. The Fortas controversy brought calls for examination of the relationship of Justice William O. Douglas with the Albert Parvin Foundation, of which Douglas was president and paid director. Following Fortas' resignation, Douglas cut his ties with the Parvin foundation.

required for passage of a proposed constitutional amendment. *(See chapter on Election Law.)*

Dirksen's other proposed constitutional amendment would have authorized local authorities to permit voluntary prayer in public schools and buildings. The Senate in 1966 rejected the Dirksen proposal on a 49-37 vote, nine short of the required two-thirds majority. The vote was the first taken in Congress on school prayer since the Supreme Court decision in *Engel v. Vitale* (1962), which barred the recitation of a state-sponsored prayer in public schools as a violation of the 1st Amendment. *(See chapter on Civil Liberties.)*

Chronology

Of Legislation

On Courts

Following is a summary of legislation, 1965-68, dealing with administration of the federal courts and the judiciary.

1965

FEDERAL JUDGESHIPS. The Senate June 30 passed a bill (S 1666) to establish 44 new federal judgeships to alleviate crowded dockets in a number of federal district courts and circuit courts of appeal. The measure became law after House passage in 1966. *(See below.)*

S 1666 was introduced at the request of the Judicial Conference of the United States, the governing body of the federal judiciary. The last previous increase in federal judgeships came in the Omnibus Judgeship Act of 1961. *(Congress and the Nation, Vol. I, p. 1450)*

JURY COMMISSIONS. The House May 3 passed a bill (HR 5640), requested by the Justice Department, to tighten supervision by federal district court judges over selection procedures for federal trial juries. The bill established a jury commission for each federal judicial district to assist in the selection of jury lists. HR 5640 was endorsed by the Judicial Conference of the United States and the American Bar Assn. There was no further action. *(However, see 1968 action.)*

SUPREME COURT SALARIES. In a controversy that lingered on from 1964, the House March 17 ended a heated debate by rejecting, on a 178-202 roll-call vote, a bill (HR 5374) to restore pay raises for the Chief Justice and eight Associate Justices that were trimmed in the 1964 federal pay raise bill. *(Congress and the Nation, Vol. I, p. 1454)*

HR 5374 was designed to restore the differential between Supreme Court salaries and those of federal judges in lower courts that existed prior to enactment of the omnibus 1964 federal pay raise bill. HR 5374 would have raised the Chief Justices' salary by $3,000 (to $43,000) and the salaries of the Associate Justices by the

same amount (to $42,500). Opposition to HR 5374 centered on such peripheral issues as recent, controversial Court decisions and the personal lives of several of the Justices.

1966

FEDERAL JUDGESHIPS. Congress in 1966 enacted an Administration-supported bill (S 1666—PL 89-372) creating 45 new federal court judgeships. The House passed the bill March 2, on a 371-23 roll-call vote, after adding one additional district court judgeship to the bill which the Senate had passed in 1965. *(See above.)*

As enacted, PL 89-372 authorized 10 new circuit court judgeships and 35 new district court judgeships. Four of the circuit court and five of the district court judgeships were to be temporary—that is, the judges would be appointed to the posts for life but would not be succeeded.

1967

FEDERAL JUDICIAL CENTER. Congress enacted a bill (HR 6111—PL 90-219) to establish a Federal Judicial Center to further the development and adoption of improved judicial administration of the federal courts. The Center was to study court operations, develop recommendations for the Judicial Conference of the United States, stimulate and conduct training programs for judges and other Judicial Branch personnel and provide staff assistance to the Judicial Conference. The legislation was requested by President Johnson in his Feb. 6 crime message.

Retired Associate Justice Tom C. Clark was chosen to be the Center's first director.

MULTIDISTRICT COURT CASES. The Senate Aug. 9 passed a bill (S 159) providing for consolidated pretrial proceedings in multidistrict civil suits in federal courts. The measure became law in 1968. *(See below.)*

FEDERAL JUDGESHIPS. The Senate Nov. 17 passed a bill (S 2349) to create eight new circuit court judgeships and make permanent four temporary circuit court judgeships established in 1966. Congress completed action on the bill in 1968. *(See below.)*

FEDERAL MAGISTRATES. The Senate June 29 passed a bill (S 945) establishing a system of federal magistrates to replace the existing U.S. commissioner system. The bill became law in 1968. *(See below.)*

The 700 commissioners in the nation were the first judicial officers before whom persons arrested on federal charges were brought. Under existing law commissioners were paid by a fee system according to the number and nature of the matters handled. More than a third of the commissioners were not lawyers. And a commissioner's trial jurisdiction was limited to petty offense misdemeanors committed on certain federal property.

S 945 required that all magistrates be attorneys except in extreme circumstances, replaced the fee system of compensation with a system of salaries and gave the magistrates a broader range of duties than the commissioners had.

1968

FEDERAL MAGISTRATES. Congress completed action on the Federal Magistrates Act (S 945—PL 90-578), establishing a system of federal magistrates to replace the existing commissioner system.

The Senate had passed the bill in 1967. *(See above.)* House passage came Sept. 26, 1968. The House rejected, 64-258, a motion to recommit the bill with instructions to amend it to limit the number of magistrates to 250 and to require that they be appointed by the President.

Provisions. As enacted into law Oct. 17, 1968, S 945 —PL 90-578:

Abolished the office of U.S. commissioner and replaced it with the office of U.S. magistrate.

Required that all U.S. magistrates be lawyers except in extreme circumstances when it was impossible for the federal district judge who appointed them to find a qualified lawyer to fill a particular position.

Replaced the fee system of compensation with a system of salaries on a sliding scale according to the anticipated workload.

Set the term of a full-time magistrate at eight years and the term of a part-time magistrate at four years.

Permitted magistrates to be assigned duties by federal district courts such as supervision of pretrial and discovery proceedings and preliminary consideration of certain petitions.

Gave the magistrates an expanded trial jurisdiction over certain minor federal offenses when the defendant waived his rights to trial by a district court and to trial by jury.

Most Controversy Centers on Judicial Nominations

Failure of the Fortas nomination in 1968 marked the first time since 1959 that a Presidential nomination failed of Senate confirmation. In the intervening years, the only major nominations that generated controversy were judicial.

The 1959 rejection involved President Eisenhower's nomination of Lewis L. Strauss as Secretary of Commerce. The Senate by a 46-49 roll-call vote rejected the nomination after months of acrimonious public charges, hearings and debate. *(Congress and the Nation, Vol. I, p. 109a.)*

Five weeks earlier, the Senate by a 70-17 roll-call vote had confirmed the nomination of Potter Stewart as an Associate Justice of the Supreme Court. Justice Stewart had been serving on the Court on a recess appointment and had been a federal judge before. His support of the Court's racial desegregation decisions was well known. All Senators voting against his confirmation were Southern Democrats. *(Congress and the Nation, Vol. I, p. 109a)*

From that time until 1968, four other men were confirmed as Associate Justices. The nominations of three of them—Byron R. White (1962), Arthur J. Goldberg (1962) and Abe Fortas (1965)— were confirmed by voice vote. Only that of Justice Fortas was at all controversial; three Republicans raised objections on the floor that he had "put the United States last" in reportedly asking Washington newspaper editors to delay release of a story that Presidential aide Walter W. Jenkins had been arrested on a morals charge shortly before the 1964 Presidential elections.

The fourth man was Thurgood Marshall. President Kennedy nominated the Negro civil rights lawyer as a judge on the 2nd Circuit Court of Appeals, but the Senate Judiciary Committee held up confirmation for a year. The Senate in 1962 confirmed the nomination by a 54-16 roll-call vote, with all 16 "nays" cast by Southern Democrats. *(Congress and the Nation, Vol. I, p. 111a)*

In 1965, Judge Marshall was confirmed by voice vote and without noteworthy controversy as Solicitor General, a post considered as an "in-house" Presidential position. In 1967, President Johnson nominated him as Associate Justice, the first Negro named to the Court. After criticism from some Senators for his "activist" views on the role of the judiciary, his nomination was confirmed by a 69-11 roll-call vote, with 10 "nays" cast by Southern Democrats and one by a Northern Democrat, Robert C. Byrd (D W.Va.).

Just as the racial issue was involved in the confirmations of Justice Stewart and Judge Marshall, so it was present in the cases of two other nominations to the federal bench. Senate liberals in 1965 opposed the nomination of former Mississippi Gov. James P. Coleman (D) as a judge on the 5th Circuit Court of Appeals for his past segregationist views, but he was confirmed by a 76-8 roll-call vote. In 1966, Constance Baker Motley, the first Negro woman nominated as a federal district judge, was confirmed by voice vote despite the opposition of Senate Judiciary Committee Chairman James O. Eastland (D Miss.), who charged that Mrs. Motley had been linked to the Communist Party 20 years before.

In 1960, the Senate by a 69-15 roll-call vote confirmed the nomination of James R. Durfee as a judge on the United States Court of Claims despite charges that he had violated the Civil Aeronautics Board code of ethics by accepting invitations from airlines while he was Board chairman and that he lacked judicial experience. *(Congress and the Nation, Vol. I, p. 109a)*

In 1965, strong floor opposition developed to the nomination of Francis X. Morrissey, a longtime friend of the Kennedy family, as a federal district judge, on grounds that he was unfit, and the nomination was withdrawn.

Supreme Court Membership, 1965-68

Name	State	Date of Birth	Nominated By	To Replace	Date of Appointment	Date Confirmed	Date Resigned
Hugo L. Black	Ala.	2/27/1886	Roosevelt	Van Devanter	8/12/37	8/17/37	
William O. Douglas	Conn.	10/16/1898	Roosevelt	Brandeis	3/20/39	4/4/39	
Tom C. Clark	Texas	9/23/1899	Truman	Murphy	8/2/49	8/19/49	6/12/67
Earl Warren*	Calif.	3/19/1891	Eisenhower	Vinson	9/30/53	3/1/54	†
John M. Harlan	N.Y.	5/20/1899	Eisenhower	Jackson	1/10/55	3/16/55	
William J. Brennan Jr.	N.J.	4/25/1906	Eisenhower	Minton	10/16/56	3/19/57	
Potter Stewart	Ohio	1/23/1915	Eisenhower	Burton	1/17/59	5/5/59	
Byron R. White	Colo.	6/8/1917	Kennedy	Whittaker	4/3/62	4/11/62	
Arthur J. Goldberg	Ill.	8/8/1908	Kennedy	Frankfurter	8/31/62	9/25/62	7/25/65
Abe Fortas	Tenn.	6/19/1910	Johnson	Goldberg	7/28/65	8/11/65	
Thurgood Marshall	N.Y.	6/2/1908	Johnson	Clark	6/13/67	8/30/67	

*Chief Justice.

†Warren June 13, 1968, announced he would retire upon confirmation of his successor. President Johnson June 26 nominated Fortas to succeed Warren as Chief Justice. He nominated Homer Thornberry to succeed Fortas as Associate Justice. The Senate failed to confirm the Fortas nomination, and Warren continued as Chief Justice for the 1968-69 Court term. Since there was thus no vacancy for Thornberry to fill, the Senate did not act on his nomination.

For Supreme Court appointments, 1789-1964, see Congress and the Nation, Vol. I, p. 1452.

MULTIDISTRICT COURT CASES. Congress enacted legislation (S 159—PL 90-296) providing for consolidated pretrial proceedings in multidistrict civil suits in federal courts. The law authorized such consolidated proceedings where a large number of lawsuits involved one or more common questions of fact.

The purpose of the law was to streamline pretrial proceedings in suits arising from one set of facts, such as an air disaster or antitrust conviction, but which might involve dozens of federal district courts, hundreds of litigants and tens of thousands of claims.

The law established a judicial Panel on Multidistrict Litigation, consisting of seven federal circuit and district judges, selected by the Chief Justice. The panel was authorized to transfer, for purposes of pretrial proceedings only, civil actions pending in different district courts which shared one or more common questions of fact. Antitrust actions in which the United States was a complainant were excluded.

S 159 was passed by the Senate in 1967 (see above) and the House March 4, 1968. It was supported by the Judicial Conference of the United States, the Justice Department and the House of Delegates of the American Bar Assn.

FEDERAL JUDGESHIPS. Congress completed action on a bill (S 2349—PL 90-347) establishing nine new federal circuit court judgeships and making permanent four temporary federal circuit court judgeships established in 1966. (See above.)

The purpose of the bill was to provide more appellate judges in those circuits experiencing backups in their case loads. The House passed the bill June 5, after adding one judgeship to the number approved by the Senate in 1967. (See above.)

The bill was supported by the Justice Department, Budget Bureau and Judicial Conference of the United States.

JURY SELECTION. Congress early in 1968 completed action on legislation to reform procedures for the selection of federal juries (S 989—PL 90-274). The bill provided for random selection of juror names from voter lists and prohibited discrimination in selection. (For details, see chapter on Civil Rights.)

Chapter 5—Civil Rights

Key Votes

In this chapter, key roll-call votes are shown in bold-face type. The party breakdown on each of these votes and the position taken by each Member of Congress may be found in the key vote charts which appear in the appendix to this book.

Civil Rights

THE civil rights movement accomplished more in legislation during the Johnson years than in any previous period in this century, but by the end of 1968 relations between whites and blacks in America had become the most serious domestic problem facing the nation and probably were worse than at any time in a hundred years.

The legislation, which began with a landmark act in 1964, removed legal and traditional barriers which limited Negro opportunities in jobs, housing, education and political expression, restricted Negro access to public facilities and denied them protection from racially motivated violence. The turning point in the legislative phase of the civil rights movement came in 1964 when Congress enacted an omnibus bill which not only fulfilled many emotional needs of the movement, such as ensuring access to public facilities, but also provided a sort of ultimate sanction by denying federal funds to communities which discriminated in federally assisted programs. The withholding of funds was potentially the most effective weapon given the Federal Government to enforce antidiscrimination laws, but in the years immediately following 1964 pressures on the Executive Branch by senior and powerful Southern Members of Congress prevented it from being notably effective.

The 1964 law was a breakthrough also because it was the first time the Senate had invoked cloture on a Southern civil rights filibuster and Congress had enacted a strong rights bill over the objections of Southern Members. This break with previous experience, in which the Southern bloc through its Senate contingent had always held a veto over the legislative action on civil rights bills and thereby was able to dictate the content of the bills, laid the groundwork for two other far-reaching rights measures in 1965 and 1968. These measures also were enacted over Southern opposition after the Senate invoked cloture on Southern-led filibusters. The 1965 law dealt with voting rights and the 1968 law with protection of civil rights workers and open housing.

The enactment in 1968 of a strong law guaranteeing equal access to housing, perhaps the most sensitive civil rights issue of the last 20 years, was unexpected and came in an election year at a time when race relations in the United States were deteriorating rapidly. The passage of the 1968 law capped the 20-year effort of the civil rights movement to remove the legal and traditional barriers to Negro advancement (although some proposals, such as a strong equal employment law, remained to be enacted).

But if one phase of the civil rights movement—enactment of antidiscrimination legislation—was for the most part concluded in 1968, the next phase—actually increasing and improving Negro income, employment, education, and skills—had only begun and was troubled not only with the practical problems implicit in such an undertaking but also with deep-seated emotional issues which had long been associated with relations between blacks and whites in America. The race relations issue was intricately involved in the problems of rioting which had racked major cities for four years, of crime control and police actions, and of rebuilding the nation's increasingly concentrated urban areas into cities that could be inhabited and enjoyed by both races. Solutions to the race problem, which threatened to produce ever deeper divisions between the races for many years, were still not visible when the Johnson Administration prepared to leave office at the end of 1968.

When President Johnson signed the 1968 civil rights bill into law April 11, not long after announcing to a startled nation that he would not seek re-election, it marked the end of the Johnson era in civil rights.

A Southerner, and an opponent of civil rights legislation early in his Congressional career, Mr. Johnson had more to do with enactment of civil rights laws in 1957-1968 than any other man. In 1957, when the first civil rights law since the Reconstruction era after the Civil War was enacted, Mr. Johnson was Majority Leader of the Senate. His skill in shepherding the Civil Rights Act of 1960 through a Senate filibuster enhanced his reputation in the nation at large and contributed to his nomination as Vice President on the John F. Kennedy ticket.

After President Kennedy's assassination, Mr. Johnson took charge of the campaign to enact the 1964 Act as a memorial to the slain President. A Voting Rights Act in 1965 followed, but in 1966 and 1967 President Johnson was rebuffed by Congress in his requests for new civil rights legislation. The major point of contention was his proposal for a federal law banning racial discrimination in the sale and rental of housing. When he repeated this request once more in his 1968 civil rights message Jan. 24, few observers believed there was any likelihood of its enactment. Less than three months later, "fair housing" was the law of the land.

(Continued on next page)

Reference

Discussion of civil rights developments from 1945-64 will be found in *Congress and the Nation, Vol. I, p. 1595-1642.*

In part, enactment of the open housing law was a reaction to the April 4 murder of civil rights leader Rev. Dr. Martin Luther King Jr. and the rioting in ghetto areas that followed. It was also, however, a recognition that in the country as a whole, nondiscrimination was now an accepted principle of law. Whoever might succeed Lyndon Johnson as President would be bound by that national commitment.

The difficulty was that by 1968 the issue of civil rights in the traditional form of breaking down legal barriers to Negro progress (a problem whose focus had been limited primarily to the South, although it existed elsewhere) had broadened to the much more complicated issue of race relations throughout the society in all parts of the country. Elimination of the legal barriers did not quickly lead to elimination of the practices that produced the legalities in the first place; in the opinion of some observers, the issue had become: how much were white Americans ready to grant to Negroes and how quickly were whites prepared to act?

Dropping of legal barriers through civil rights laws clearly had not solved the problems of the Negroes, although there was no question that the laws were a necessary step in that direction. The inadequacy of these civil rights laws was only too clear to Negroes who continued to press their demands (frequently against the desires and sometimes the personal interests of many whites), raised the level of their demands and became much more militant in doing both. The slogan "black power," which came into use as late as mid-1966, became common by 1968 (even to the point of being symbolically expressed at the 1968 Olympics in Mexico by two Negro American athletes during ceremonies presenting them with medals they had won). Although variously interpreted by different Negroes, the slogan seemed to represent at least an aspiration by Negroes for tangible accomplishments to better their lot and for unity in achieving their goals.

As Negroes pressed with militant vigor toward their goals, and white resistance grew, the nature of the race relations problem changed with almost breathtaking speed until it had become the central domestic issue by the end of 1968. From the early days of the 1960s when the efforts of blacks and whites were directed at integration and enacting antidiscrimination laws into 1965 when Congress passed the Voting Rights Act, there were indications of Negro progress and hope for improved Negro-white relations. But the riots in the cities (mostly involving Negroes) became an issue in 1965 at the same time the United States escalated its involvement in the war in Vietnam, thereby draining off enormous sums of federal revenue which might have gone for programs to help Negroes. In the following three years, riots continued and spread, the war dragged on, Negro aspirations, demands and frustrations rose in unison and more whites came to realize that Negro progress might affect them. By the end of 1968 embittered race relations had dimmed the earlier hope of many civil rights advocates of orderly and inevitable Negro progress and of acceptance by white Americans of Negro advances. The most vivid illustration of the low state of race relations probably was the popularity gained by former Alabama Governor George C. Wallace when he ran for President in 1968 as a third-party candidate. He was able to have his name placed on the ballot of all 50 states and fre-

Civil Rights Legislation 1957-1968

Five major civil rights bills were passed by Congress between 1957 and 1968. Highlights of these bills are given below.

1957—The Civil Rights Act of 1957 (HR 6127—PL 85-315) was the first civil rights legislation passed by Congress since the post-Civil War Reconstruction period. The Act prohibited action to prevent persons from voting in federal elections and authorized the Attorney General to bring suit when a person was deprived of his voting rights. It also created a Civil Rights Commission and set up a Civil Rights Division in the Department of Justice.

1960—The Civil Rights Act of 1960 (HR 8601—PL 86-449) strengthened provisions of the 1957 Act for court enforcement of voting rights and required preservation of voting records. It also contained limited criminal penalty provisions relating to bombing and to obstruction of federal court orders (aimed primarily at school desegregation orders).

1964—The Civil Rights Act of 1965 (HR 7152—PL 88-352) prohibited discrimination in public accommodations and in programs receiving federal assistance. It also prohibited discrimination by employers and unions and set up an Equal Employment Opportunity Commission. Enforcement of voting laws and school and public facilities desegregation was strengthened.

1965—The Voting Rights Act of 1965 (S 1564—PL 89-110) authorized the Attorney General to appoint federal examiners to register voters in areas of marked discrimination and strengthened penalties for interference with voter rights.

1968—A civil rights bill (HR 2516—PL 90-284) prohibited discrimination in the sale or rental of about 80 percent of all housing. It also protected persons exercising specified rights such as attending school or working and civil rights workers urging others to exercise their rights. Antiriot provisions also were included.

quently drew large and enthusiastic crowds outside the South. When the votes were cast the predominance of the two-party system was evident as Wallace ran well only in states of the deep South. Nevertheless, he captured 9.8 million votes, 13.6 percent of the total, and 45 electoral votes. The popular vote total, although less than that won by prominent third-party candidates of the past, suggested that Wallace and his philosophy appealed to many voters. Although he couched his appeal to voters in terms of support for states rights, opposition to federal interference in local affairs and promises to reduce crime, Wallace's history as an opponent of racial integration and his acts as Governor of Alabama to prevent it, and the image which he gained as a man opposed to Negro progress, left little doubt that a prime reason for his popularity among whites was racial antagonisms.

The basic domestic issue of race relations which had evolved by 1968 was complicated because it touched on many related problems which lent themselves to relatively more rational discussion, thereby tending to obscure the underlying race problem. These included problems of the inner cities (such as housing conditions), crime (or at least the type of crime that seemed to most distress white America and which went under the general label of crime in the streets and usually involved acts of violence), welfare and the willingness of a person to work, employment opportunities and good education. But each one of these and all the other issues which came to be known as the urban problem were tied in one way or another with the problem of race relations. This was so because Negroes were deeply involved in each: blacks already lived in or were moving to the cities in substantial numbers; they constituted large numbers on the welfare rolls; many were frequently unable to find employment; many were involved in street crimes and confrontations with police; and large numbers of them were participants in riots and looting.

The civil rights legislation of the 10-year period 1957-68, with which Mr. Johnson had so much to do, only indirectly touched these problems in that it chipped away at the legal structure underpinning the discriminatory practices (such as denial of voting rights and inadequate housing) which maintained the Negro in an unequal status in the society and increased his frustrations. Eliminating these practices as well as other conditions damaging to Negroes, such as poor education and inadequate job training which were not illegal in themselves, was another matter and one to which the civil rights movement had to turn in the future. The Johnson Administration already had directed its attention to this new area of civil rights through such noteworthy programs as the war on poverty and federal education assistance to school districts with large numbers of poor families. These programs are discussed elsewhere in this volume; an outline of the probable new directions of the rights movement follows.

New Directions

In his 1968 message President Johnson said: "The more we grapple with the civil rights problem—the most difficult domestic issue we have ever faced—the more we realize that the position of minorities in American society is defined not merely by law, but by social, education and economic conditions." It was these domestic problems that the next President would have to face.

As Congress progressively lowered some of the traditional barriers facing Negroes, such as voting restrictions and "off-limit" public places, there was increasing national awareness that a fundamental barrier to Negro advancement was economic. It was tied to such closely related problems as lack of modern job skills, the unskilled and low-paid work which many Negroes do, poor education, ghetto housing and—basically—inadequate income. That awareness, heightened by the outbreak of riots in many cities, focused mainly on the urban Negro.

The legislation that was expected to bring the greatest benefits to Negroes in the future would be aimed at providing more jobs, job training, low- and middle-income housing and improved schools. It would involve such undertakings as the model cities program to alleviate the "crisis of the cities."

This legislation would differ from traditional civil rights legislation in basic ways. It would not be specifically directed at the Negro but rather at slum residents and rural poor of all races. The extent to which it reduced discrimination and opened jobs and housing to Negroes would depend in substantial part on specific provisions incorporated in the legislation, the amount of money committed to the programs and the skill with which the programs are administered. Secondly, such legislation would require large expenditures and would be particularly sensitive to cuts in the federal Budget—which sharply restricted some programs of this nature in President Johnson's years—and long-standing controversies about the role and size of the Federal Government.

Although economic opportunity and the breaking down of the ghetto walls appeared to be the dominant themes of future legislation, persons who followed civil rights legislation for many years believed that Congress would continue to enact laws to provide legal guarantees of Negroes' civil rights. They pointed to ways in which existing laws such as equal employment and open housing could be expanded and their enforcement procedures strengthened. There also remained a number of areas which were not covered by civil rights legislation, such as state jury selection (which was included in President Johnson's civil rights requests of 1966, 1967 and 1968) and economic coercion and threats.

Rioting

The pace of new economic measures to improve slum conditions and new legal guarantees of civil rights was expected to be affected by the extent of disorders in ghetto areas. That the disorders would not be limited to the "long, hot summers" was seen in April 1968 when serious disorders broke out in Washington, D.C., Chicago, Baltimore and numerous other cities. Following those disorders, however, the remainder of the year experienced fewer racial disturbances than had been expected.

Since the severe rioting in the Watts area of Los Angeles, in August 1965, Congress and much of the nation had been concerned with measures to hold down looting and prevent sniping during disorders.

The civil rights bill of 1968 contained the first new legal provisions directed at civil disorders. It set criminal penalties for traveling in or using the facilities of interstate commerce, such as telephones, to incite a riot. It also provided penalties for manufacturing or teaching the use of firearms or explosives for use in a civil disorder.

The bill was likely to be followed by measures to strengthen local law enforcement agencies through federal grants.

Greater controversy surrounded other legislative proposals to reduce violence in the ghettos. Strict regulation of firearms, though carrying the Johnson Administration's endorsement, aroused the emotional opposition of hunters and gun-lovers, represented by the highly effective National Rifle Assn. The legislation was backed chiefly by Eastern liberals in Congress, while Westerners of all political persuasions led the opposition to it. Nevertheless, some controls on the sale of guns and ammunition were enacted in 1968.

Political conservatives, on the other hand, for years had pushed for legislation to offset what they considered to be the too lenient attitude of the Supreme Court toward criminals. Court-imposed restrictions on police questioning and the use of alleged confessions were the focus of restrictive legislation intended to deter "crime in the streets"—a prominent political issue since the 1964 Presidential campaign of Barry Goldwater (R) and the key issue to many voters in the 1968 elections.

The Johnson Years

In his first address to Congress following the assassination of President Kennedy on Nov. 22, 1963, President Johnson called for "the earliest possible passage of the civil rights bill for which he (Kennedy) fought so long." Although a Southerner, and a former Senate Majority Leader who had sometimes been blamed for the comparative mildness of the 1957 and 1960 Acts, Mr. Johnson was totally committed to passage of the broad bill approved by the House Judiciary Committee. The House passed the bill by a 2-1 margin in February 1964. After a filibuster of almost three months, the Senate took the unprecedented step of voting to close off a filibuster against civil rights legislation. The keys to cloture were pressure on uncommitted Senators and changing the bill to put more emphasis on local enforcement. The House accepted the bill as changed by the Senate, and President Johnson signed it into law in a nationwide television broadcast July 2. Mr. Johnson asked the nation to "close the springs of racial poison" and asked for peaceful compliance. With the help of painstaking preparation by federal and local officials, Mr. Johnson's request for peaceful compliance was largely honored. The civil rights issue, however, became an important element in the 1964 Presidential campaign, contributing to victories for Republican Barry Goldwater, an opponent of the 1964 Act, in several "Deep South" states while President Johnson was sweeping the rest of the country.

A series of voting rights demonstrations in Selma, Ala., in the late winter and spring of 1965 underscored the slow and difficult nature of forcing registration of Southern Negroes under the court procedures provided in the 1957, 1960 and 1964 Civil Rights Acts. The President felt obliged to ask the Congress to pass sweeping new voting rights legislation, including the speedy appointment of federal voting examiners to register would-be voters in areas with literacy tests and low voter turnouts.

President Johnson Aug. 6, 1965, signed into law the Voting Rights Act of 1965, the most comprehensive voting rights legislation to gain Congressional approval in 95 years. When he signed the legislation he emphasized that while the Act was a victory for Negro leadership, it also was "a great challenge to that leadership" to teach Negroes their responsibilities and to lead them to exercise their rights.

In this vein, he noted that he had called a White House Conference "To Fulfill These Rights" for the fall. (A planning session was held in November but the conference itself, the first ever held on civil rights, was not convened until June 1966.) The President first announced plans for the conference in a June 4 commencement

Cloture Votes, 1919-1968

The four cloture votes on the 1968 open housing bill and the single vote on the nomination of Abe Fortas to be Supreme Court Chief Justice brought the total of cloture votes since Rule 22 was adopted in 1917 to 43. Only eight of these were successful. There had been three successful cloture votes on civil rights bills: the omnibus bill of 1964, the Voting Rights Act of 1965 and the open housing amendment in 1968. The successful votes appear below in dark type:

Issue	Date	Vote	Yea Votes Needed
Versailles Treaty	Nov. 15, 1919	76-16	**62**
Emergency tariff	Feb. 2, 1921	36-35	48
Tariff bill	July 7, 1922	45-35	54
World Court	Jan. 25, 1926	68-26	**63**
Migratory birds	June 1, 1926	46-33	53
Branch banking	Feb. 15, 1927	65-18	**56**
Disabled officers	Feb. 26, 1927	51-36	58
Colorado River	Feb. 26, 1927	32-59	61
D.C. buildings	Feb. 28, 1927	52-31	56
Prohibition Bureau	Feb. 28, 1927	55-27	**55**
Banking Act	Jan. 19, 1933	58-30	59
Anti-lynching	Jan. 27, 1938	37-51	59
Anti-lynching	Feb. 16, 1938	42-46	59
Anti-poll tax	Nov. 23, 1942	37-41	52
Anti-poll tax	May 15, 1944	36-44	54
FEPC	Feb. 9, 1946	48-36	56
British loan	May 7, 1946	41-41	55
Labor disputes	May 25, 1946	3-77	54
Anti-poll tax	July 31, 1946	39-33	48
FEPC	May 19, 1950	52-32	64*
FEPC	July 12, 1950	55-33	64*
Atomic Energy Act	July 26, 1954	44-42	64*
Civil Rights Act	March 10, 1960	42-53	64
Amend Rule 22	Sept. 19, 1961	37-43	54
Literacy tests	May 9, 1962	43-53	64
Literacy tests	May 14, 1962	42-52	63
Communications Satellite Act	Aug. 14, 1962	63-27	**60**
Amend Rule 22	Feb. 7, 1963	54-42	64
Civil Rights Act	June 10, 1964	71-29	**67**
Legislative reapportionment	Sept. 10, 1964	30-63	62
Voting Rights Act	May 25, 1965	70-30	**67**
Right-to-work repeal	Oct. 11, 1965	45-47	62
Right-to-work repeal	Feb. 8, 1966	51-48	66
Right-to-work repeal	Feb. 10, 1966	50-49	66
Civil Rights Act	Sept. 14, 1966	54-42	64
Civil Rights Act	Sept. 19, 1966	52-41	62
D.C. Home Rule	Oct. 10, 1966	41-37	52
Amend Rule 22	Jan. 24, 1967	53-46	66
Open Housing	Feb. 20, 1968	55-37	62
Open Housing	Feb. 26, 1968	56-36	62
Open Housing	March 1, 1968	59-35	63
Open Housing	March 4, 1968	65-32	**65**
Fortas Nomination	Oct. 1, 1968	45-43	59

Between 1949 and 1959 the cloture rule required the affirmative vote of two-thirds of the Senate membership rather than two-thirds of those Senators who voted.

address at Howard University, at which time he emphasized the need for moving beyond civil rights programs to those ensuring full social, economic and political participation for Negroes. *(For story about the conference and a partial text of the speech, see p. 392, 397.)*

In 1966 President Johnson suffered his first defeat on civil rights legislation. The Administration's bill was passed by the House but was killed in the Senate when its supporters were unable to muster the two-thirds majority needed to impose cloture and cut off the filibuster against the bill's open-housing provisions.

The emotional impact of the housing proposal was summed up in the phrase, "a man's home is his castle," which was widely used by opponents of the provision. They were aided by effective lobbying against the provision by the National Assn. of Real Estate Boards, which did not want restrictions placed on real estate salesmen and owners. The extent of public antipathy to open housing was seen in Chicago, where Negro marchers were stoned by white residents of segregated areas, and in California, where a referendum to repeal the state's nondiscrimination law won a large majority. (This was later overturned by the U.S. Supreme Court.)

The President resubmitted his proposals in 1967 but again was rebuffed. The omnibus bill was split title-by-title in hopes that each section could be enacted as separate legislation. The tactic was only partially successful.

The least controversial parts of the package were passed by the House—a bill protecting civil rights workers against intimidation and violence, and an extension of the Civil Rights Commission. The latter bill was cleared by the Senate, which also passed the part of the omnibus bill that set standards for the selection of jury panels in federal courts.

President Johnson in his 1968 civil rights message to Congress asked for the passage of all his 1967 civil rights proposals that were still pending. The proposals included protection of persons exercising their civil rights, open housing, enforcement powers for the Equal Employment Opportunity Commission and reforms in the selection of federal and state juries.

At the end of the 1967 session, Senate Majority Leader Mike Mansfield (D Mont.) had made the House-passed bill for protection of civil rights workers the first business for the Senate to consider in 1968. With the effective support of civil rights lobbyists, a bipartisan group of Senators, led by Walter F. Mondale (D Minn.), Hubert Humphrey's successor, and Edward W. Brooke (R Mass.), the only Negro Senator, pressed for an open-housing amendment. After several Senate votes had shown unexpected support for the amendment, the key vote was taken March 4. It imposed cloture on the filibuster against the housing amendment and was adopted by a 65-32 roll-call vote—exactly the two-thirds majority necessary. It was the third successful civil rights cloture vote since Mr. Johnson became President.

A week later the Senate passed the bill, with anti-riot and other amendments acceptable to President Johnson, and the House cleared it April 10.

The action bore out President Johnson's prediction in 1967, after defeat of the earlier open housing bill. He said then that Congress eventually would insist on non-discrimination in housing "because it is decent and right. Injustice must be opposed, however difficult or unpopular the issue."

20 Years of Civil Rights

The first comprehensive civil rights legislation requested by a 20th century President was proposed by President Truman in 1948. In a special message to Congress Feb. 2, Mr. Truman asked for legislation to strengthen the Federal Government's power to enforce civil rights legislation and its machinery to study civil rights problems. He also asked for voting and fair employment legislation, an anti-lynching law, a strengthening of federal civil rights protection laws and a prohibition against discrimination in interstate transportation facilities.

President Truman said, "...there still are examples -- flagrant examples -- of discrimination which are utterly contrary to our ideals.... We cannot be satisfied until all our people have equal opportunities for jobs, for homes, for education, for health, and for political expression, and until all our people have equal protection under the law."

Congress did not pass a civil rights bill until nine years later. The bill which was enacted in 1957 was the first civil rights measure to pass the Senate since 1875. By comparison with later civil rights legislation it was a modest bill providing limited voting rights enforcement and strengthening the Federal Government's organization for enforcing civil rights legislation and examining civil rights problems.

The Civil Rights Act of 1957 opened the way for additional civil rights legislation in 1960, 1964, 1965 and 1968. These later laws were aimed at discrimination in employment, public accommodations, voting, education, and programs receiving federal assistance. The 1968 bill contained provisions protecting persons exercising their civil rights and prohibiting discrimination in the sale and rental of housing. Housing was the last of the major areas of inequality described by President Truman in 1948 to be legislated on by Congress and was perhaps the most politically sensitive of all civil rights issues.

Successive administrations -- both Democratic and Republican -- also worked to reduce discrimination through enforcement of federal civil rights laws and through Executive Orders. Executive Orders affecting segregation in the Armed Forces, discrimination in federal employment and discrimination in federally assisted housing were issued under Presidents Truman, Eisenhower and Kennedy. Segregation in interstate travel facilities was prohibited by the Interstate Commerce Commission.

On the next three pages, there appears a review of major civil rights legislation during the 20 years following President Truman's 1948 proposals. This material is followed by more detailed discussion of civil rights developments from 1965 through 1968.

Voting Rights

Voting rights provisions have been included in all five major civil rights bills passed since 1957 and were a central issue in three of them.

Prior to President Truman's 1948 civil rights message, voting rights legislation focused on the abolition of the poll tax. Poll tax measures were considered by

Congress several times during and after the Second World War but could not be brought to a vote in the Senate because of filibusters by Southern Senators.

President Truman in his 1948 message asked Congress to enact legislation banning the poll tax in elections for federal offices. In the following years the central issue was whether the poll tax should be banned by statute or by constitutional amendment. Many civil rights leaders believed that the constitutional amendment approach favored by states' rights advocates was an admission that Congress had no other method of eliminating abuses in voting laws and would set a bad precedent for other civil rights proposals. The issue was not resolved until 1962 when both chambers of Congress approved a constitutional amendment. When the amendment -- the 24th -- was ratified in 1964 it affected only five states: Alabama, Arkansas, Mississippi, Texas and Virginia.

President Truman placed primary emphasis on prohibiting public officials or private individuals from interfering with the right of qualified citizens to vote, either by intimidation or by "outmoded policies," but Congress did not act on his proposals.

President Eisenhower elaborated on the Truman proposals in his first civil rights request in 1956. His proposals were enacted a year later as the Civil Rights Act of 1957.

The 1957 Act prohibited attempts to intimidate or coerce persons from voting in primary or general elections for federal office. It authorized the Attorney General to seek an injunction when an individual was deprived or about to be deprived of his right to vote and gave federal district courts jurisdiction over such proceedings.

As early as 1959 the U.S. Commission on Civil Rights reported that much stronger methods of enforcement were required to guarantee voting rights. The Commission, which was originally proposed by President Truman, was set up by the 1957 Civil Rights Act with specific powers to investigate allegations that citizens were being deprived of their right to vote because of their race.

The Commission recommended that the President be authorized to appoint a federal registrar to register voters in cases where it was determined that state registrars had refused to register qualified voters because of their race, religion or national origin. The Commission proposal formed the basis of the Voting Rights Act of 1965, but before this proposal for administrative enforcement was enacted two further efforts were made to strengthen court enforcement procedures.

The first of these efforts was made in 1960 when Congress included in the Civil Rights Act of 1960 a modified Administration proposal for court enforcement of voting rights where there were patterns of discrimination. Under this law, if the Attorney General won a suit brought under the 1957 law, he could ask the court for a separate proceeding to determine whether a pattern or practice of such discrimination existed. If the court found that discrimination did exist, Negroes in that area who were qualified to vote could ask the court to order state officials to permit them to vote. The courts were authorized to appoint referees to carry out these provisions. The 1960 Act also required that all federal voting records and registration papers be preserved, thus facilitating investigation of voting discrimination. Further efforts to strengthen court enforcement of voting rights were

made in the Civil Rights Act of 1964 which also barred unequal application of voting registration requirements and made a sixth-grade education a rebuttable presumption of literacy. However, the Commission on Civil Rights reported in 1963 that the 1957 and 1960 Civil Rights Acts had failed to provide "a prompt and adequate remedy for widespread discriminatory denials of the right to vote." An example of the problems encountered in the court enforcement procedure was Selma, Alabama, which was chosen by the Rev. Dr. Martin Luther King Jr. as the focus for his voting right movement. A Federal District Court Nov. 1, 1963, issued a permanent injunction against discrimination by the county registrars as a result of a suit brought by the Justice Department early in 1961. Voting discrimination continued in 1964 and in response to a motion for supplementary relief, the District Court Feb. 4, 1965, ordered the Board of Registrars to speed its voter registration processes, four years after the initial suit was filed.

The Voting Rights Act of 1965, passed in the wake of voting demonstrations in Selma, Alabama, rounded out many years' efforts to strengthen Negro voting rights. It gave the Attorney General the power to appoint federal examiners to supervise voter registration to states or voting districts where a literacy or other qualifying test was in use and where fewer than 50 percent of voting age residents were registered or had voted in 1964. Only eight states were affected in a major way: Alabama, Alaska, Georgia, Louisiana, Mississippi, North Carolina, South Carolina and Virginia.

Other provisions set stiff penalties for interference with voter rights; outlined a limited judicial recourse for the states and prohibited states from imposing new voter qualification laws unless a federal court in the District of Columbia approved.

The 1968 civil rights law included a provision protecting persons who exercised their right to vote or to run for political office from intimidation or injury.

Employment

President Truman, in his Feb. 2, 1948, civil rights message asked Congress to create" a Fair Employment Practices Commission (FEPC) with authority to prevent discrimination by employers and labor unions, trade and professional associations, and Government agencies and employment bureaus." No such Commission was set up until 1964 when Congress established the Equal Employment Opportunity Commission (EEOC). The EEOC's enforcement powers continue to be debated.

President Truman had advocated establishing a permanent FEPC as early as 1945, to replace the President's Fair Employment Practice Committee set up by Executive Order in 1941. FEPC bills did not come to a vote in either House or Senate until 1950 although both the Democratic and Republican party platforms in 1948 included equal-employment planks. In 1950, the House passed a substitute version providing for a voluntary FEPC without any enforcement powers. In the Senate, moves to limit debate on a bill for a compulsory FEPC failed and President Truman refused to compromise for a voluntary FEPC.

President Eisenhower did not include FEPC legislation in either his 1956 or 1959 civil rights programs (which became the Civil Rights Acts of 1957 and 1960). In 1959 he asked Congress to give statutory authority to the President's Committee on Government Contracts which had been set up by Executive Order but this proposal was not included in the 1960 Act.

Until the creation of the EEOC in 1964 responsibility for equal employment practices was vested in committees created by Executive Order. These were limited to barring discrimination in the hiring and treatment of federal employees and to promoting compliance with the anti-discrimination clause in Government contracts. These two functions were held by separate bodies under the Executive Orders of Presidents Truman and Eisenhower but were combined by President Kennedy in 1961 into a single, stronger President's Committee on Equal Employment Opportunity.

President Kennedy did not include fair employment provisions in his major civil rights program presented to Congress in 1963 although he expressed support for fair employment bills pending in Congress. A fair employment provision with court enforcement provisions was added to the Administration's civil rights bill as part of a compromise version.

As enacted, the equal employment section (Title VII) of the Civil Rights Act of 1964 prohibited persons from refusing to hire a person, discriminating against him in the pay or conditions of employment, or segregating him or otherwise depriving him of equal employment opportunities on account of his race, color, religion, sex or national origin. The Act also prohibited unions from refusing or limiting union membership, discriminating in apprenticeships, or attempting to make an employer discriminate because of race, religion, sex or national origin.

Coverage was applied in stages beginning with firms of 100 or more employees and working down to firms with 25 employees. State and local governments were not covered.

An Equal Employment Opportunity Commission was set up to work with state and local agencies and to investigate charges of unlawful employment practices. The EEOC was authorized to attempt to resolve such issues through voluntary conciliation but could not enforce its decisions through administrative action. If EEOC conciliation failed, an individual could bring a civil suit and the Attorney General was authorized to sue where there was a pattern or practice of discriminatory employment practices.

A provision of the 1968 civil rights law provided federal penalties for injuring or intimidating a person because of his race, religion or national origin and because he was working for a state or local government or private employer or joining or using the services of a labor union.

Job Programs. The nation became conscious in the early 1960s that fewer and fewer jobs were available for the unskilled and the semiskilled. The influx of rural Negroes into the cities heightened the problem and the Government began a series of employment training programs. The Manpower and Development Training Act in 1962 and the Economic Opportunity Act of 1964 were the bases on which a complex assortment of work-training programs were built, ranging from programs for teen-age

school dropouts to landscaping jobs for the elderly unemployed.

The ghetto riots of 1965-68 focused attention on a central aspect of ghetto unemployment—the movement of industry away from the central city to the suburbs, where transportation and housing problems made employment of Negroes more difficult. Pending in Congress beginning in 1967 were a number of legislative proposals to encourage businessmen to establish plants in ghetto neighborhoods.

Equal Protection of the Laws

President Truman in his 1948 civil rights message asked for additional protection for the Negro against deprivation of his rights. He asked that existing federal laws against conspiracy to deprive a person of his rights be broadened to include persons acting individually. He also asked that a federal law protecting persons from deprivation of federally secured rights by public officials be made more specific. President Truman's proposals were never enacted but the principles of these proposals were embodied in the civil rights protection provisions of the 1968 civil rights law.

President Truman also asked for a specific federal measure to deal with lynching. Earlier anti-lynching legislation had died in the Senate in 1938 when two cloture motions to limit debate on the bill were defeated. Anti-lynching measures were reported by both House and Senate Committees in 1948 but never reached the floor. Subsequent Administrations did not repeat the request for specific anti-lynching legislation.

President Eisenhower, in his 1956 civil rights proposals, asked for authority for the Federal Government to use civil procedures for the protection of civil rights. The civil remedy approach to civil rights protection continued to be the basis of rights protection proposals until 1966.

President Eisenhower asked for authority for the Attorney General to file civil suits for injunctions against anyone depriving or about to deprive a person of any civil right. This provision, which became known as Part III was rejected by the Senate in 1957 and attempts to add it to the 1960 bill also failed. The House added the Part III provision to the Administration's 1966 civil rights bill which died in the Senate.

Several provisions of the 1964 Civil Rights Act provided for suits by the Attorney General but only in limited types of cases. The 1964 law authorized the Attorney General to sue for the desegregation of state or locally owned public facilities and public schools and colleges if the aggrieved person was unable to do so. A civil suit also was the remedy provided in cases of discrimination in public accommodations and the Attorney General was authorized to bring action when there was a pattern or practice of such discrimination. The 1964 Civil Rights Act also authorized the Attorney General to intervene in private suits where there was alleged denial of equal protection of the laws when the case was of "general public importance."

President Johnson, in his State of the Union Message Jan. 12, 1966, proposed criminal penalties for persons injuring or intimidating civil rights workers or others who were engaging in specified activities such as voting or attending public school or were urging others to do so. This proposal was part of a civil rights bill which died in the Senate in 1966. It became Title I of the 1968 civil rights law after some modifications were made. The criminal penalty approach had been recommended by the Commission on Civil Rights as early as 1961 and was recommended again in a 1965 Commission report.

The 1968 law prohibited injuring or intimidating any person because he was voting or campaigning for office in a public election, serving on a federal jury, working for a federal agency or participating in a federal or federally assisted program or activity. It also prohibited interfering with a person because of his race or religion and because he was attending a public school or college, participating in a state or locally administered program, working for a state, local or private employer, joining or using the services of a labor union, serving on a state jury or using public accommodations. The law protected civil rights workers urging others to engage in these activities. A separate provision provided the same protection to persons buying, selling or renting a house.

Very limited criminal penalty provisions relating to bombing and to obstruction of federal court orders (aimed primarily at school desegregation orders) had been included in the 1960 Civil Rights Act.

Housing

President Johnson was the first President in the 20th century to request open housing legislation. He included this request in the civil rights program which he presented to Congress April 28, 1966. A modified version of this proposal was passed by the House as part of a civil rights bill but died in a Senate filibuster. The housing provision was considered by most observers to be the primary cause of Senate opposition.

President Johnson repeated his request for open housing legislation in 1967 and again in 1968. It was enacted in modified form in the civil rights bill of 1968.

When fully in effect in 1970, the open housing provision was to prohibit discrimination in the sale or rental of 80 percent of all housing including single-family residences. The law exempted from the anti-discrimination prohibitions owner-occupied dwellings of up to four units and privately owned single-family housing if the sale or rental was made without the services of a real estate agent or broker. The prohibition against discrimination extended to financing and brokerage services. The Department of Housing and Urban Development was given authority to receive and investigate complaints of violations and to attempt to achieve voluntary compliance. Enforcement was based on individual civil suits but the Attorney General was authorized to sue in cases where there was a pattern or practice of discrimination.

The major executive action to reduce discrimination in housing was taken in 1962 when President Kennedy Nov. 20 signed an Executive Order prohibiting discrimination in federally assisted housing. The order covered private housing where the mortgages were insured or guaranteed by the Federal Housing Administration or Veterans Administration, federally owned or operated housing, public housing and housing in federally subsidized urban renewal projects and housing constructed with federal loans.

Education

Although education was one of the major areas of discrimination mentioned by President Truman in his 1948 civil rights message, he proposed no legislation to meet the problem. There was no clear federal jurisdiction in an area traditionally financed by state and local government. The first major change came with the 1954 Supreme Court desegregation decision (*Brown v. Board of Education of Topeka, Kan.*).

President Eisenhower, in his 1959 civil rights program, asked for criminal penalties for interference with federal school desegregation orders and certain activities related to school and church bombings, both of which were enacted in modified form. An Administration proposal to provide limited technical and financial aid to areas faced with school desegregation problems was omitted because of Southern opposition.

Under President Kennedy, executive action to encourage desegregation of schools was stepped up. It included entering desegregation suits as a "friend of the court" and the selective use of federal aid for schools in federally impacted areas.

The major legislation affecting discrimination in education was the 1964 Civil Rights Act. It authorized the Federal Government to give technical and financial assistance to public school systems in the process of desegregation. It also authorized the Attorney General to file suit for the desegregation of public schools and colleges in some cases. Another provision of the 1964 Act prohibiting discrimination in federally assisted programs became an important instrument in school desegregation following passage in 1965 of the Elementary and Secondary Education Act which provided federal aid for school districts with children from low-income families.

School attendance was one of the civil rights protected under the civil rights protection provisions of the 1968 civil rights law.

Public Accommodations

The prohibition against discrimination in public accommodations, considered by many to be the heart of the 1964 civil rights bill, was not proposed until 1963. In that year President Kennedy presented Congress with a very modest civil rights bill but later expanded it to include public accommodations and other provisions as Negro demonstrations and boycotts spread throughout the country. Access to public accommodations was a major goal of sit-ins and other civil rights demonstrations.

The public accommodations section of the 1964 Civil Rights Act prohibited discrimination because of race, color, religion or national origin in most restaurants, cafeterias, soda fountains, motion picture houses, theaters, sports arenas, hotels and motels. It permitted persons denied their rights under this provision to sue for relief and authorized the Attorney General to sue where there was a pattern or practice of such discrimination.

The 1968 civil rights law provided criminal penalties for injuring or intimidating a person because of his race, religion or national origin and because he was using or urging others to use public accommodations.

Supreme Court Actions

The Supreme Court played a major role in the advancement of civil rights causes in the years following World War II. Of the three branches of the Federal Government, it was for many years the most active in creating a new status for Negroes in the society. Through its rulings prohibiting racial segregation in schools and public facilities, the Court sought to end the "separate-but-equal" doctrine that had governed race relations in the United States for half a century. Other decisions dealt with discrimination in housing, employment, voting and public accommodations. The rulings provided major support for the civil rights movement as it gained momentum throughout the 1950s and 1960s.

The Court continued during the Johnson years to give support to the civil rights movement through rulings on a variety of subjects. However, in an increasing number of cases involving demonstrations and sit-ins, the Court showed a departure from earlier rulings. Following is a summary of major Supreme Court decisions on civil rights from 1965 through 1968. *(For decisions from earlier years, see Congress and the Nation, Vol. I, p. 1606.)*

School Desegregation. In 1965, the Court in several instances again showed its impatience with the rate of desegregation. On Nov. 15 the Court said that "delays in desegregation of school systems are no longer tolerable," thus finally discarding its 1955 rule for "all deliberate speed." The Court unanimously vacated and sent back to federal district courts for full evidentiary hearings two Virginia suits (*Bradley v. School Board, Richmond, Va.,* and *Gilliam v. School Board, Hopewell, Va.)* on grounds that such hearings on school desegregation plans should have been held in the first place. The district courts had approved the plans without full hearings, and the Court held that the plaintiffs, who argued that faculty members were allocated on a racial basis, were entitled to full hearings on their allegations.

The Court's unequivocal language followed the first full academic year's experience under the desegregation provisions of the 1964 Civil Rights Act. Again on Dec. 6, 1965, the Court moved to speed the pace. In a brief, unsigned opinion in *Rogers v. Paul,* the Court ordered the Fort Smith, Ark., school system to permit the Negro petitioner "immediate transfer" to an all-white high school and said "those similarly situated" might transfer as well. Once more the Court said delays were "no longer tolerable."

On April 17, 1967, the Court once more showed its impatience when it denied a stay sought by six Louisiana school districts from a March 29 court order for six-state desegregation of all grades by the fall of 1967. The petitioners sought a stay to permit full-scale Supreme Court review of the 5th Circuit Court of Appeals' order, which covered schools in Alabama, Florida, Georgia, Louisiana, Mississippi and Texas. The high Court's denial carried no explanation. A request for a review of the decision was denied by the Court on Oct. 9, 1967. The ruling came in desegregation cases in the cities of Bessemer and Fairfield, Ala., in Jefferson County, Ala., and in Caddo, Bossier and East Baton Rouge Parishes, La.

The Court Dec. 4, 1967, in an unsigned order upheld lower court rulings requiring a state to desegregate

(*Wallace v. U.S.; Bibb County Board of Education v. U.S.).* These cases, arising from Alabama, represented the first time that a three-judge federal district court directed a state government to desegregate all of its public schools. The Supreme Court without opinion affirmed that order. Past court orders had been directed to individual, local boards of education.

The district court March 22, 1967, ruled in Montgomery, Ala., that state officials had interfered unconstitutionally with desegregation efforts of local schools; that the state's tuition grant law was unconstitutional; and that Gov. Lurleen B. Wallace, a defendant in the case, and state school officials must place in effect a model desegregation plan developed by the court. The plan allowed students to attend the school of their choice and dealt with school construction, transportation and the integration of faculties. State school officials were directed to inform the 99 local school systems in Alabama that they must follow the model plan.

The *Bibb* case arose from separate efforts by that board of education to challenge the district court order.

In a case decided the following spring, the Court May 27, 1968, held that local school boards were required to come forward with desegregation plans which promised to be effective. The cases were: *Green v. County School Board; Monroe v. Board of Commissioners; Raney v. Board of Education.* *Green* involved the "freedom of choice" plan instituted by the County School Board of New Kent County, Va. *Monroe* involved a variant of that approach, the "free transfer" system instituted by the Board of Commissioners of Jackson, Tenn. *Raney* involved a "freedom of choice" plan used in the Gould School District in Arkansas. Each of the plans permitted white and Negro students to choose the school they wished to attend. In each instance, the integration of the school systems had not progressed appreciably.

Justice William J. Brennan Jr., writing for the Court in the three cases, said that school boards were under an affirmative duty to eliminate segregation "root and branch.... The burden on a school board today is to come forward with a plan that promises realistically to work and promises realistically to work *now.*" (The italics were his and the quotations were from *Green.*)

Justice Brennan said that conclusion was necessitated by the Court's two opinions in *Brown v. Board of Education* (1954, 1955). In *Brown I,* the Court held that the Constitution forbade segregated school systems. In *Brown II,* it required the desegregation of segregated school systems with "all deliberate speed," taking into account the complexity of such a goal. The "freedom of choice" plans not only did not work to desegregate the schools, he said, but placed the burden of dismantling dual school systems on children and their parents, instead of on the school boards.

Sit-Ins, Public Accommodations. A noticeable departure from earlier rulings was evident in this field.

The Court Feb. 23, 1966, by a 5-4 vote reversed the convictions of five Negroes for breach of the peace when they refused to obey a sheriff's order to leave a segregated Clinton, La., public library. Justice Abe Fortas' majority opinion in *Brown v. Louisiana* appeared to enunciate a new constitutional doctrine: peaceful civil rights demonstrations inside public buildings are protected by the 1st and 14th Amendments.

Late in 1966, when the Court convened for its 1966-67

term, its first major ruling on Nov. 14 marked a significant departure from decisions over the previous five years on rights demonstrations. By a 5-4 vote, the Court upheld the trespass conviction of 32 students from Florida A. & M. University who were arrested in 1963 when they staged a protest in front of a Tallahassee, Fla., county jail. The students were protesting the arrest of other students who had demonstrated against segregation in local movie theaters.

Justice Hugo L. Black, in delivering the decision, said the case (Adderley v. Florida) differed from other rights protest cases because the property involved was a jail-house yard, where security was important. Black said that "the state, no less than a private owner of property, has power to preserve the property under its control for the use to which it is lawfully dedicated." While the ruling applied only to publicly owned property, it was apparent that it left uncertain the status of other sites used for demonstrations.

In a vigorous dissent, Justice William O. Douglas said the decision heralded a "great break with the traditions of the Court" and that trespass laws thereafter could be used as a blunder-buss to suppress civil rights.

The Court the following summer (June 12, 1967) upheld the convictions of Negro demonstrators in Walker v. City of Birmingham (Ala.) for contempt in violating an injunction against mass demonstrating. Among the defendants was the Rev. Dr. Martin Luther King Jr. The vote was 5-4.

The Court April 11, 1967, held 8-1 in Pierson v. Ray that 15 white and Negro clergymen, whose convictions for disorderly conduct had been overturned, could not sue the municipal judge who first convicted them or the police who arrested them, for damages. The Court said the judge had absolute immunity and that the police might be sued only if they were found to have acted in bad faith. "This hurts," said Carl Rachlin, the New York civil liberties lawyer who argued the case for the claimants. "If you could sue the judges the police couldn't pull anything."

Picketing. The Court April 22, 1968, by a 7-2 vote, upheld a Mississippi antipicketing law. The case was Cameron v. Johnson.

Civil rights groups began picketing the Forrest County courthouse in Hattiesburg, Miss., on Jan. 22, 1964, to foster increased voter registration of Negroes. They picketed along a "march route" behind barricades set up by the sheriff and in an area designated by him. There was no violence. The state legislature April 8, 1964, cleared the Mississippi Anti-Picketing Law and Gov. Paul B. Johnson (D) signed it into law that day. A messenger took a copy of the law to Hattiesburg where it was read to the pickets April 9, 1964. Arrests began the following day and continued until May 18, 1964, when all picketing was halted. The law prohibited "picketing...in such a manner as to obstruct or unreasonably interfere with free ingress or egress to or from any...county...courthouses..." In an action against Johnson, the defendants sought to have the law declared unconstitutional and their prosecutions enjoined.

Justice William J. Brennan Jr., writing for the Court, said the law was constitutional on its face and as applied to the defendants. The prosecutions, therefore, could continue, he said. The state had the right and the power to enact a law protecting its courthouses, he said, and there was no showing that the law had been applied to the defendants in bad faith.

In dissent, Justice Abe Fortas, joined by Justice William O. Douglas, said the Mississippi law "may fairly be characterized as a directive to the police that the picketing in Hattiesburg should be stopped—forthwith." It was a "rifle-shot law" aimed at citizens exercising their 1st Amendment rights, he said.

1964 Civil Rights Act. By a 5-3 vote, the Court April 8, 1968, reversed a lower court ruling which had dismissed an indictment against several persons on grounds of assaulting Negroes who were attempting to patronize a restaurant. The action sent the cases back for further trial. The case was U.S. v. Johnson. Justice Thurgood Marshall did not participate in the decision.

Title II of the Civil Rights Act of 1964 secured the right of all persons to equal enjoyment of public accommodations. It contained no criminal penalties for violating that right, but it said that "no person" shall intimidate or punish persons attempting to enjoy the right. It provided for civil injunctions through actions brought by the aggrieved person or, in the event of patterns or practices of resistance to enjoyment of the right, by the Attorney General. It said the "remedies provided in this title shall be the exclusive means of enforcing the rights based on this title...."

Another federal law (18 U.S.C. 241), which derived from the Enforcement Act of 1870, punished conspiracies to injure or intimidate any citizen exercising any right secured to him by the Constitution or by any federal law.

Horace Johnson and others were indicted in Georgia on charges of violating Section 241 in that they assaulted Negroes attempting to patronize a restaurant. A federal district judge dismissed the indictment on grounds that Title II of the 1964 Act provided the "exclusive means" of enforcing the right to patronize the restaurant—civil injunction. He held that the defendants might be enjoined from interfering with the Negroes, but could not be prosecuted criminally under Section 241.

Justice William O. Douglas, writing for the Court, said that in enacting the 1964 Act, Congress did not intend to immunize violators of Title II rights from the criminal sanctions of Section 241. The district judge's decision was reversed.

"We refuse to believe that hoodlums operating in the fashion of the Ku Klux Klan, were given protection by the 1964 Act for violating those 'rights' of the citizen that Section 241 was designed to protect," he said.

The exclusive remedy language of Title II of the 1964 Act, he said, referred to proprietors or owners of restaurants covered by that law. By that language, Congress meant they were not to be subject to criminal sanctions before they had a chance to litigate whether their restaurants were subject to the 1964 Act, he said.

In dissent, Justice Potter Stewart, joined by Justices Hugo L. Black and John Marshall Harlan, said that Title II of the 1964 Act in "plain language" made civil injunctions the exclusive remedy to violations of the Title. The Title barred interference or intimidation by any person, including proprietors, owners and third parties, he said.

"The exclusive remedies provided by Congress to protect the rights secured by Title II of the 1964 Act are undoubtedly ineffective in a case like this," he said. "But I cannot, for that reason, join in rewriting the law that Congress so clearly enacted."

Segregated Prison. The Court March 11, 1968, by a 9-0 vote, held in *Lee v. Washington* that Alabama's statutes violated the 14th Amendment to the extent that they required segregation of the races in prisons and jails.

Housing. The major decision in the area of housing came in 1968 when the Court in *Jones v. Mayer* broadly interpreted an 1866 federal statute as barring racial discrimination in the sale or rental of all property. The brief Reconstruction Era statute had never been interpreted fully by the Court before. In the June 17 decision, the Court said the statute did not conflict with the open housing provisions of a civil rights bill which had become law on April 11. *(For details of decision,, see box p. 380.)*

In a case that preceded the far-reaching 1968 decision, the Court in 1967 ruled that a California constitutional provision on fair housing was unconstitutional. The provision said the state could not prohibit a person from discriminating when he sold or rented property. The case was *Reitman v. Mulkey* and was decided May 29, 1967, by a 5-4 vote.

In 1964 California voters voted on a measure known as Proposition 14, which amended the state constitution. The measure was adopted by a vote of 4,526,460 to 2,395,747. It read:

"Neither the state nor any subdivision or agency thereof shall deny, limit or abridge, directly or indirectly, the right of any person, who is willing or desires to sell, lease or rent any part or all of his real property, to decline to sell, lease or rent such property to such person or persons as he, in his absolute discretion, chooses."

The measure exempted state-owned property. It was adopted following considerable controversy over state fair housing laws, especially the Unruh Act (1959) and the Rumford Fair Housing Act (1963), and over the rights of citizens to discriminate in private sales involving Negroes. The California Supreme Court held that Proposition 14, which had become Section 26 of the state constitution, was invalid.

Justice Byron R. White, writing for the majority, said the Court had no good reason for upsetting the findings and holding of the California Supreme Court in interpreting its own state constitution. Therefore, the Court should affirm that state court's decision. Justice White said that Section 26 violated the 14th Amendment in that it was "intended to authorize, and does authorize, racial discrimination in the housing market. The right to discriminate is now one of the basic policies of the state. The California Supreme Court believes that the section will significantly encourage and involve the state in private discrimination. We have been presented with no persuasive considerations indicating that this judgment should be overturned."

In dissent, Justice John Marshall Harlan, joined by Justices Hugo L. Black, Tom C. Clark and Potter Stewart, said the majority opinion generated more problems than it solved. He said that the "electorate itself overwhelmingly wished to overrule and check its own legislature on a matter left open by the Federal Constitution." Justice Harlan said that the Court exceeded its powers in "contriving a new and ill-defined constitutional concept to allow federal judicial interference" in that area.

Justice Harlan warned that the majority opinion was enunciating a new doctrine on the kinds of discriminatory action prohibited by the 14th Amendment. The new doctrine, he said, seemed to hold that the 14th Amendment prohibited state laws which "do nothing more than passively permit private discrimination." He said the 14th Amendment was aimed at state action which was "affirmative and purposeful, actively fostering discrimination," and not at acts of private discrimination. The Court's opinion, he suggested, blurred the difference between the two.

Voting Rights. The major decision in this field upheld the provisions of the 1965 Voting Rights Act. By a unanimous vote March 7, 1966, the Court dismissed a suit challenging the constitutional validity of the major provisions of the Act. The suit *(South Carolina v. Katzenbach)* was filed in September 1965 by South Carolina, and it sought to enjoin Attorney General Nicholas deB. Katzenbach from enforcing the Act on grounds that the law unconstitutionally invaded states' rights to set voter qualifications. In its counter suits, the Justice Department sought to enjoin Alabama, Louisiana and Mississippi from failing to observe provisions of the Act.

Chief Justice Earl Warren, writing for the Court in its March 7 ruling, said: "After enduring nearly a century of widespread resistance to the 15th Amendment, Congress has marshalled an array of potent weapons against the evil, with authority in the Attorney General to employ them effectively." He wrote: "As against the reserved powers of the states, Congress may use any rational means to effectuate the constitutional prohibition of racial discrimination in voting."

Poll Taxes. The 24th Amendment to the Constitution, ratified Jan. 23, 1964, outlawed poll taxes in federal elections. In its first interpretation of the Amendment, the Court in 1965 found in *Harman v. Forssenius* that Virginia had attempted to circumvent the Amendment through a law giving voters in federal elections the choice of paying a poll tax or filing witnessed or notarized certificates of residence at least six months before a federal election. The unanimous Court opinion said the 24th Amendment abolished poll taxes in federal elections absolutely and "no equivalent or milder substitute may be imposed."

Again in 1966, the Court took action on Virginia poll taxes—this time invalidating those required in state elections. By a 6-3 vote in *Harper v. Virginia State Board of Elections* and *Butts v. Harrison* (decided as one case), the Court held that the $1.50 poll tax imposed on citizens desiring to vote in state elections violated the Equal Protection Clause of the Constitution, as stated in the 14th Amendment. The decision struck down Virginia's poll tax and by extension that of Mississippi. (Vermont in 1966, by legislative act, eliminated its poll tax, while three-judge federal district courts declared unconstitutional the poll taxes in Texas and Alabama.)

The *Harper* decision ended a controversy over poll taxes which erupted in Congress during consideration of the Voting Rights Act of 1965 (PL 89-110). In a floor move led by Sen. Edward M. Kennedy (D Mass.), an effort was made to include an outright ban on state poll taxes, although Attorney General Katzenbach warned of constitutional hazards. The Senate May 11, 1965, by a 45-49 roll-call vote rejected the ban. The final version of the Act contained a finding that poll taxes in certain states denied or abridged the right to vote, and it directed the Attorney General "forthwith" to challenge state poll taxes in lawsuits. The Act said Congress predicated that directive on its 15th Amendment powers to ban discrimination in voting on the basis of race. The lawsuits were initiated, and in addition the Solicitor General joined in *Harper*, seeking to have the poll tax declared unconstitutional.

Antimiscegenation. In *Loving v. Virginia*, decided June 12, 1967, the Court by a 9-0 vote held that Virginia's law making it a crime for a white and a Negro to marry violated the 14th Amendment's guarantees of equal protection of the law and of due process.

Demonstrations, Riots

Although Congress enacted two major civil rights bills during the 1965-68 period, this progress in the rights movement was overshadowed by the occurrence of destructive civil disorders in the nation's metropolitan areas. Cities in most parts of the country experienced incidents of some type and many of the larger ones with substantial Negro populations were severely damaged in major riots. Following are the highlights of incidents during the period. *(See Congress and the Nation, Vol. I, p. 1600 for incidents in earlier years.)*

1965-1966

Selma. Civil rights groups in early 1965 selected Selma, Ala., as the focal point of their efforts to secure greater Negro voter registration and dramatize the difficulty Southern Negroes faced in voting. An attempted civil rights march from Selma to Montgomery was broken up March 7 by Alabama state troopers using tear gas, night sticks and whips. Additional hundreds of demonstrators poured into the area. The Rev. James Reeb, a white Unitarian minister from Boston, died of skull injuries March 11 stemming from a beating by white men in Selma March 9. The march to Montgomery again was scheduled for March 21 and President Johnson ordered the Alabama National Guard into federal service to protect the marchers. The march was completed without violence March 25, but Mrs. Viola Liuzzo of Detroit was killed by white ambushers the same night on the road between Selma and Montgomery. Four Ku Klux Klan members were arrested the next day in connection with the murder. Two of them later were convicted on charges of civil rights conspiracy and given 10-year sentences. A third one also was convicted but died before going to prison. The fourth man testified he had infiltrated the group for the FBI.

Los Angeles (Watts district). In terms of death and destruction, the 1965 riot in the predominantly Negro Watts district of Los Angeles was one of the worst racial disorders in the nation's history. Six days of terrorism left 34 dead, 856 injured and damage approaching $200 million. More than 3,100 were arrested. Its effects on the progress of the government's civil rights programs also was significant.

The riot was touched off Aug. 11 when a white California highway patrolman stopped a weaving car and gave its Negro driver a sobriety test. A combined force of 15,000 National Guardsmen and 1,000 law enforcement officers were needed to restore order.

California Gov. Edmund G. Brown (D) Aug. 19 appointed an eight-member panel headed by former Central Intelligence Director John A. McCone to investigate the riot and determine preventive measures. The McCone Commission Dec. 6 reported on finding a sense of despair and a "spiral of failure" among Negroes who migrated to Los Angeles during and after World War II and a complacency within the white community about conditions of Negro life. The report urged a "revolutionary attitude" toward city problems and called for wide-ranging programs to improve jobs, education, and police-community relations.

Riots and Subversives

Whenever riots break out, the issue of outside agitation is raised. Some public officials and news commentators charge that militant "black power" leaders and subversives bear responsibility for igniting the riots; others say these elements merely exploit the disturbances.

The President's Commission on Civil Disorders, in its March 2, 1968, report, said it found "no evidence" that any of the 1967 riots it studied were the result of "any organized plan or 'conspiracy'." However, the Commission blamed the "inflammatory rhetoric of black racists and revolutionaries" for contributing to the troubles. The report said of these militants: "We think it clear that the intolerable and unconscionable encouragement of violence heightened tensions, created a mood of acceptance and expectation and thus contributed to the eruption of disorders."

J. Edgar Hoover, director of the Federal Bureau of Investigation, testified Feb. 16, 1967, about the participation of subversive elements in riots. He told a House Appropriations Subcommittee:

"Although most of the riots and disturbances have been characterized by spontaneous outbursts of mob violence dominated by young hoodlums, the involvement of other violent, lawless, subversive and extremist elements became readily apparent as the rioting grew and spread. Communists and other subversives and extremists strive and labor ceaselessly to precipitate racial trouble and to take advantage of racial discord in this country. Such elements were active in exploiting and aggravating the riots, for example, in Harlem, Watts, Cleveland and Chicago."

He said that Stokely Carmichael, then chairman and later a field worker of the Student Non-Violent Coordinating Committee (SNCC), had been in "frequent contact" with Max Stanford, field chairman of the Revolutionary Action Movement (RAM), a "highly secret all-Negro, Marxist-Leninist, Chinese-Communist-oriented organization which advocates guerrilla warfare to obtain its goals." Hoover also identified the Progressive Labor Party as a "splinter group" of the Communist Party-USA and termed the Nation of Islam (the Black Muslims) "an all-Negro, violently antigovernment and anti-white organization." He said that the Nation of Islam had a membership of 5,500, while RAM had fewer than 50. Carmichael and his successor as SNCC chairman, H. Rap Brown, were most often blamed for instigating violence and burning.

The Watts riot had broad repercussions. In an Aug. 14 statement on the riot, President Johnson said, "To resort to terror and violence...strikes from the hand of the Negro the very weapon with which he is achieving his own emancipation." The President's words were prophetic.

The Watts riot came two months after President Johnson made what many regarded as an historic speech on Negro problems and goals at Howard University, Washington, D.C., and during the planning stage for the first White House Conference on Civil Rights. The speech had been based largely on a Labor Department March 1965 report, "The Negro Family: The Case for National Action," which was compiled under the direction of Daniel P. Moynihan, then an Assistant Secretary of Labor. The Moynihan Report, as it became known, focused attention on a new dimension of the civil rights revolution—the breakdown of the family as a social unit within much of the Negro community. *(See p. 389.)*

Chicago. The year 1965 also saw the worst racial rioting in 13 years in Chicago, Ill., which erupted Aug. 11 after a runaway fire engine killed a Negro woman bystander in a predominantly Negro West Side neighborhood. In a two-day battle between police and Negroes, 80 persons were injured and 123 were arrested; 2,000 National Guardsmen were alerted to prevent a recurrence.

Malcolm X. "Black nationalist" leader Malcolm X was shot and killed Feb. 21 in New York City. He had quit the Black Muslims in 1964 and founded his own group, the Organization of Afro-American Unity. Three Black Muslim members were convicted of his murder in 1966.

Meredith Shooting. James H. Meredith, first Negro to integrate the University of Mississippi, was shot from ambush June 6, 1966, while marching through Mississippi to urge Negroes to register and vote. Meredith, who had left Mississippi in 1965 and entered Columbia University Law School, began the march as a personal undertaking. He suffered buckshot wounds in the back of his head, back and legs but recovered and resumed the march by the end of June. Police almost immediately arrested Aubrey James Norvell, a white man, who pleaded guilty Nov. 21 to assault with intent to kill and was sentenced to five years in jail, with three years suspended. President Johnson June 6 said the shooting was "an awful act of violence which every sensible American deplores."

Summer Riots, 1966. Rioting occurred in Negro sections of Chicago, Cleveland, Jacksonville, Fla., New York City and South Bend, Ind. In Chicago, rights leaders decided to use the city as a testing ground for solutions to "de facto" racial segregation, and a series of rallies led to an Aug. 5 march into an all-white neighborhood where the marchers were attacked by whites. In a Sept. 4 march, two were killed and seven injured, despite the presence of 2,000 National Guardsmen.

In Cleveland, two were killed during July 18-20 riots—the largest disturbances in the city's history. Trouble began in the predominantly Negro Hough district, with mobs setting fires, battling police and shouting, "Black Power."

1967-1968

College Demonstrations. A new kind of demonstration became evident in 1967—violent protests led by Negro college students, often on their college campuses.

In Nashville, Tenn., April 8-10, several hundred Negro students from Fisk University and Tennessee A. and I. State University rioted on three nights after a Negro student at Fisk was arrested by a white policeman; at least 17 persons were injured and 94 arrested. The disturbance started a few hours after Stokely Carmichael spoke to Vanderbilt University students; two of his aides were arrested.

In Jackson, Miss., May 12-14, about 1,000 Negroes at Jackson State College protested the arrest of a Negro student; the National Guard quelled the disturbance in which one Negro was killed.

Hundreds of students at predominantly Negro Texas Southern University in Houston rioted May 16-17 after clashing with police while protesting the arrests of student demonstrators; 487 were arrested; one policeman was killed and two others were shot.

Urban Riots. From June through August, riots or violent demonstrations occurred in 67 cities. The worst were in Newark, N.J., and Detroit, Mich. In Milwaukee, Wis., four persons were killed.

In Newark, riots, with sniping and fire-bombings, took place from July 12-17 after a Negro taxi driver was arrested by white policemen. Twenty-five persons were killed, an estimated 725 injured, 1,462 arrested, and property damage of $15 million was reported. The National Guard and state police were called in to subdue the rioters.

Causes beyond the "triggering" arrest were believed to be the city's high Negro unemployment rate, acute housing shortage and plans to condemn 50 acres of slum area for a new medical school.

The Detroit riots followed within a week. From July 23-28 more than 4,000 fires were set, extensive sniping occurred, 43 persons died and at least 657 were injured. The riot broke out after police raided a Negro "speakeasy." At the request of Gov. George W. Romney (R Mich.), President Johnson July 24 ordered federal troops into the city because police and National Guardsmen were unable to control the situation. It was the first time federal troops had been sent into a state at the request of the Governor since 1943, when race riots occurred in Detroit.

On July 27 the President set up a Commission on Civil Disorders, headed by Illinois Gov. Otto Kerner (D), to investigate the causes of urban riots. *(See p. 398.)*

King Assassination. The Rev. Dr. Martin Luther King Jr. was shot and killed in Memphis, Tenn., April 4, 1968, by a white man. The murder of the preeminent advocate of nonviolence shocked the nation and was followed by rioting and looting in many cities, including Memphis. *(See box on following page.)*

Poor People's Campaign. After King's death, a "camp-in" by poor people to press Congress and the Federal Government to take massive action to help the impoverished was postponed from the April 22, 1968, date King had set. His successor as head of the Southern Christian Leadership Conference, Rev. Ralph David Abernathy, took over plans for the Campaign, and on May 13 he officially opened the camp site on parkland near the Lincoln Memorial. The plywood and canvas shanty-town was given the name of "Resurrection City, USA." Poor white people, Mexican-Americans and American Indians joined Negroes in caravans converging on Washington from all areas of the nation. *(See welfare chapter.)*

<table>
<tr><td>

King Assassination

The Rev. Dr. Martin Luther King Jr. was shot and killed in Memphis, Tenn., in the early evening of April 4, 1968. The 39-year-old apostle of nonviolence was slain as he stood with a few aides on a hotel balcony. King was in the city to lead a march in support of striking sanitation workers. The assassin was later identified as James Earl Ray, a white man who had escaped from a Missouri prison in 1967. Ray was arrested June 8, 1968, in London. He was returned to the United States and was scheduled to go on trial Nov. 12 in Memphis. The trial later was postponed until 1969.

Immediately after the murder, President Johnson went on television to deplore the "brutal slaying" and to ask "every citizen to reject the blind violence that has struck Dr. King, who lived by nonviolence." The President postponed a scheduled trip to Hawaii and met with Negro leaders on the morning of April 5.

Most major Negro organizations and Negro leaders called for others to heed the spirit of nonviolence which King preached. But among many Negroes there was bitterness and anger. Sporadic vandalism and looting erupted in Negro communities in several different cities, among them New York, Washington, D.C., Birmingham, Ala., Raleigh, N.C. and Memphis, Tenn. In the following few days, rioting, burning and looting broke out in Negro districts of more than 100 cities. More than 350,000 National Guardsmen and federal troops were activated; more than 60,000 were deployed in cities to help quell the disturbances.

King first came on the national scene in 1955 when, only 25 years old, he led a year-long bus boycott in Montgomery, Ala. During the boycott King formulated and advanced for the first time his theory of "nonviolence" as the cornerstone of the civil rights protest.

In 1957 King formed the Southern Christian Leadership Conference (SCLC), an integrated organization with headquarters in Atlanta. It specialized in boycotts, demonstrations and sit-ins throughout the South and, later, in the North.

King was a leader of the 1963 March on Washington in which about 200,000 persons participated. In a speech at the Lincoln Memorial he said, "I have a dream that one day this nation will rise up and live out the true meaning of its creed: 'We hold these truths to be self-evident, that all men are created equal.' ...I have a dream that my four little children will one day live in a nation where they will not be judged by the color of their skin but by the content of their character." In 1963 and thereafter King paid increasing attention to Congress and spoke out frequently to urge passage of civil rights legislation.

On Dec. 10, 1964, King was awarded the Nobel Peace Prize for his work.

At the time of his death, King was planning a march of poor people on Washington to pressure Congress into passing legislation to benefit the poor. Some observers felt it was his last chance to prove that nonviolence could work.

</td></tr>
</table>

Chronology
Of Legislation
On Civil Rights

Note: In addition to the bills listed below, other proposals considered by Congress had an important bearing on civil rights. Among them were federal aid to education, antipoverty legislation, and model cities, rent supplements and other urban assistance bills. These are discussed elsewhere in this volume.

1965

Voting Rights

Congress in 1965 responded to a series of Negro demonstrations against voting discrimination in the South by passing the most sweeping voting rights bill in 90 years. The 1965 Voting Rights Act, submitted to Congress by President Johnson March 17 and signed into law Aug. 6, departed from the pattern of civil rights bills of recent years in that it provided for direct federal action to enable Negroes to register and vote, rather than the often-protracted individual legal suits required by previous legislation.

The legislation (S 1564—PL 89-110) suspended the use of literacy tests or similar voter qualification devices and authorized the appointment of federal voting examiners to order the registration of Negroes in states and counties in which voter activity had fallen below certain specified levels. The legislation brought the federal registration machinery to bear on six Southern states (Alabama, Georgia, Louisiana, Mississippi, South Carolina and Virginia), Alaska, 28 counties in North Carolina, three counties in Arizona and one county in Idaho.

Impetus for the Act came from a midwinter series of events in Selma, Ala., when state and local election officials interfered with Negro demonstrations against discriminatory voting practices. *(See below)*. On March 17, as events in Selma reached a climax, President Johnson submitted to Congress a far-reaching bill designed to "strike down restrictions to voting in all elections—federal, state and local—which have been used to deny Negroes the right to vote." Two days earlier, the President had gone before a special, televised joint session of Congress to urge swift enactment of voting rights legislation.

In broad terms, the 1965 Voting Rights Act suspended literacy tests and gave the Attorney General the power to appoint federal examiners to supervise voter registration in states or political subdivisions where a test or similar qualifying device was in force as of Nov. 1, 1964, and where fewer than 50 percent of voting age residents were registered to vote on that date or actually voted in the 1964 Presidential election.

Other provisions established criminal penalties for interference with voter rights, outlined a judicial recourse for delinquent state and local governments (through a three-judge federal district court in the District of Columbia which needed to determine that no racial discrimination in registration and voting practices had occurred for five years), and directed the Attorney General "forthwith" to institute proceedings against the use of state and local poll taxes as a qualification for voting. (Poll taxes were banned in federal elections by the 24th Amendment to the Constitution, which was ratified in 1964. State and local poll taxes were successfully challenged in a case decided by the Supreme Court in 1966. *(See box p. 360 and separate story p. 353.)*

A bipartisan effort, the bill grew out of conferences between Senate Majority Leader Mike Mansfield (D Mont.), Senate Minority Leader Everett McKinley Dirksen (R Ill.), Senate Minority Whip Thomas H. Kuchel (R Calif.), Attorney General Nicholas deB. Katzenbach, and Deputy Attorney General Ramsey Clark.

Comparison with Original Bill. As enacted by by Congress in August, S 1564 was considerably broader than the original bill. While incorporating the major Administration provision—the triggering formula for suspension of literacy tests and appointment of examiners in "massive discrimination" areas—the final bill provided additional machinery for dealing with discriminatory poll taxes, authorized suspension of tests and appointment of examiners by federal courts in voting rights suits initiated by the Attorney General, and waived English language literacy requirements for persons who had completed the sixth grade in a school under the American flag where the language of instruction was other than English.

Key Issues. Congressional sentiment for a strong voting bill was evident from the outset of debate. The only question was the form the bill would take. In the Senate, debate focused on a move by liberals to arm the bill with a flat ban on use of poll taxes as a requirement for voting. In a crucial test May 11, the ban was rejected by a narrow **45-49** roll-call vote, and language similar to the poll tax provision in the final bill was subsequently adopted. With the poll tax issue resolved, the Senate May 25, adopted a debate-limiting cloture motion by a **70-30** roll call, setting the stage for passage the following day. (The vote for cloture was only the second time in history—but the second time in two years—that the Senate voted to end debate on a civil rights bill.

In the House, debate centered on an attempt by Republicans to substitute their own bill (HR 7896) for the Administration measure (HR 6400). At one time, the GOP substitute appeared to stand a good chance of adoption, but it lost some GOP support when Southern Democratic opponents of voting rights legislation threw their support to HR 7896 as the less "objectionable" of the two bills. The House then rejected the GOP substitute and approved the Administration bill.

Implementation. Seeking and receiving voluntary compliance with the Act, the Justice Department appointed federal examiners in only 32 Southern counties by year's end. Justice Department officials said that between the signing of the bill and close of the year, local officials had registered approximately 160,000 new Negro voters in the five Deep Southern states covered by the Act—Alabama, Georgia, Louisiana, Mississippi and South Carolina. Together with 79,593 Negroes listed by federal examiners, Negro registration in these states increased by 40 percent during the first five months of enforcement.

Selma Campaign

The 1964 Civil Rights Act was intended by its proponents to take the civil rights struggle "out of the streets and into the courts." In many respects—notably public accommodations—these intended results had been accomplished with speed. But in several states the Negro was still denied the right to vote, either by strict requirements set by local officials, through administration of a stiff literacy test, or—if he appealed to a court—through unfavorable court action or through litigation periods so slow that in effect he was denied his vote in the election in question.

The Rev. Dr. Martin Luther King Jr., president of the Southern Christian Leadership Conference, decided to take the voting rights movement back into the streets in Selma, Ala., beginning Jan. 18 to "dramatize" to the nation the existing bars to Negro voting in many Southern states. Through the Selma campaign, King and other civil rights leaders hoped to arouse the nation's conscience by pointing out these difficulties.

King chose Selma for a number of reasons. By law, registration took place only two days a month in Dallas County, of which Selma was the county seat. The actual registration process was lengthy because of the detailed requirements involved. An applicant was required to fill in more than 50 blanks, write from dictation a part of the Constitution, answer four questions on the governmental process, read four passages from the Constitution and answer four questions on the passages, and sign an oath of loyalty to the United States and to Alabama. Negro registration in Dallas County lagged substantially behind white registration. Figures from the 1960 census showed that Dallas County was 57.6 percent Negro. Its voting-age population was 29,515—14,400 whites and 15,115 Negroes. Yet when the Selma campaign began Jan. 18, of those 9,877 who were registered to vote, 9,542 were white and 335 were Negro. Between May 1962 and August 1964, only 93 of the 795 Negroes who applied to register were enrolled, while during the same period, 945 of the 1,232 applications from whites were accepted.

On April 13, 1961, the Justice Department had filed a suit to enjoin the Dallas County registrars from discriminating against Negro applicants. A Federal District Court Nov. 1, 1963, issued a permanent injunction against discrimination. In response to a motion for supplementary relief, stating that discrimination still prevailed, Federal District Judge Daniel H. Thomas Feb. 4, 1965, ordered the Board of Registrars to speed its voter registration processes, adding that if all those eligible and desiring to vote were not enrolled by July 1, he would appoint a voting referee under terms of the 1964 Civil Rights Act.

The civil rights leaders, dismayed by the results of previous court orders, continued to protest in the streets and in the courts. Negroes were joined by whites from all parts of the country. Clergymen of all faiths traveled to Selma to participate in the drive. The professed goal continued to be an agreement by the Board of Registrars to remain open every day until all Negroes who wished to vote were registered. However, a larger goal —to arouse public sentiment in favor of a new voter rights law—was also being effectively achieved.

Although the peaceful marches, by their size and frequency, attracted public attention, it was three violent actions which most aroused public sentiment. A 26-year-

Background on Legislation To Protect Voting Rights

The 15th Amendment to the Constitution, the basis for the 1965 legislation, became effective in 1870. It provided that neither the Federal Government nor any state could deny the right to vote because of race, color or previous condition of servitude. In May of that year, Congress enacted a comprehensive piece of legislation to enforce the right to vote. This law repeated the essence of the Amendment, provided criminal penalties for state officials who failed to provide all citizens with equal opportunity to qualify to vote and punished violence, intimidation and conspiracies to interfere with registration or voting. In February 1871, Congress enacted a second statute authorizing federal supervisors of elections. Their duties included inspection of registration books and registration, poll watching on election day, counting ballots and certifying election results. However, enforcement of these statutes proved ineffective and they were largely repealed by 1894.

Civil Rights Acts passed by Congress in 1957, 1960, and 1964 provided Negroes with legal means to obtain the ballot for federal elections when confronted by discriminatory *registration* or voting practices. Another hurdle to the ballot for Negroes was removed in 1964 when the 24th Amendment, outlawing the use of poll taxes as a prerequisite to voting in federal elections, was finally ratified and became part of the Constitution. Following enactment of each measure, however, civil rights groups contended that further legislation was necessary to widen the scope of the laws to include state and local elections and to speed up the pace of litigation in voting rights suits.

1957 Civil Rights Act. The 1957 Act affirmed the right of a citizen to go to court for injunctions to protect his voting rights and empowered the Federal Government, through the Attorney General, to seek injunctions against obstruction or deprivation of those rights. The Act also created a federal Civil Rights Commission with subpena powers to investigate and report to the President and Congress on the violation of voting rights, and established a new Civil Rights Division in the Justice Department.

In its 1959 report, the Civil Rights Commission found that "substantial numbers of citizens qualified to vote under state registration and election laws are being denied the right to register," and "existing remedies...are insufficient to secure and protect the right to vote of such citizens."

1960 Act. The 1960 Civil Rights Act authorized the Attorney General, after winning a civil suit brought under the 1957 Act, to ask the court to hold another adversary proceeding and make a separate finding that there was a "pattern or practice" of depriving Negroes of the right to vote in the area involved in the suit. The court could then, on application from any Negro proving discrimination, issue an order that he was qualified to vote. In its most crucial provision, the 1960 Act authorized the courts to appoint referees to help Negroes register and vote, in order to insure implementation of these provisions.

1962 Action. The Kennedy Administration in 1962 supported two proposals in the voting rights field —a constitutional amendment outlawing the poll tax as a voting requirement in federal elections and primaries and a measure to make anyone with a sixth-grade education eligible to pass a literacy test for voting in federal elections. The poll tax amendment received Congressional approval and finally became the 24th Amendment when ratification of the required 38 states was completed in 1964. (Its only real effect was in the five states which still had a poll tax—Alabama, Arkansas, Mississippi, Texas and Virginia.) The literacy test bill, however, died in a 1962 Senate filibuster, with liberal civil rights forces variously laying the blame on the conservative Southern Democratic-Republican coalition, indifference of civil rights organizations, and lack of aggressive leadership by the Administration.

1963 and 1964 Action. In his first Civil Rights Message of 1963, President Kennedy Feb. 28 called for expanded voting rights measures to correct the "two major defects" of the 1957 and 1960 Civil Rights Acts —"the usual long and difficult delay which occurs between the filing of the suit and the judgment of the court...(and) failure to deal specifically with...abuse of discretion on the part of local election officials who do not treat all applicants uniformly." Mr. Kennedy proposed the following remedies to voter registration practices: (1) prohibit for federal elections all oral literacy tests, unequal application of voting registration requirements, and denial of the right to vote because of errors or omissions on records or applications if these were not material in determining whether a person was qualified to vote; (2) where literacy tests were given, require the presumption of literacy for anyone with a sixth grade education in a public school or accredited private school where the instruction was primarily in English; (3) in areas where less than 15 percent of the Negroes were registered and a voting suit was pending in the courts, permit court-appointed referees to register Negroes who were qualified under state law; (4) provide for preferential and expedited treatment of voting rights suits in federal courts.

President Kennedy June 19, 1963, called for a broadened civil rights bill in his second Civil Rights Message, but the voting rights proposals remained the same.

The bipartisan version of the civil rights bill (HR 7152) reported by the House Judiciary Committee Nov. 20, 1963, eliminated the temporary voting referee formula in favor of special three-judge federal courts which would hear voting rights suits if requested by the Attorney General. (Three-judge court decisions are immediately appealable to the Supreme Court, bypassing the circuit court stage.) The other Kennedy proposals were retained in the reported form of the bill.

The 1964 Civil Rights Act, signed into law by President Johnson July 2, included all the voting rights provisions of HR 7152.

old Selma Negro, Jimmie Lee Jackson, who said he was shot in the stomach and clubbed by Alabama state troopers Feb. 18, died Feb. 26. A white Unitarian minister from Boston, Rev. James J. Reeb, 38, died March 11 of skull fractures inflicted when he was clubbed on the head by white men March 9 in Selma. And state troopers March 7, acting on orders from Gov. George C. Wallace (D Ala.), used tear gas, night sticks and whips to halt a march from Selma to Montgomery, the state capital, severely injuring about 40 marchers.

Attorneys for civil rights groups immediately filed petitions with the U.S. District Court in Montgomery for a temporary restraining order against Wallace and the state troopers. On March 16, Negro leaders presented to the court a detailed plan for the proposed march. On March 17, Judge Frank M. Johnson issued the injunction requested by the Negro leaders. At the same time he denied a Justice Department request for an order to prohibit interference with civil rights demonstrations in addition to the march from Selma to Montgomery, and he denied a petition from Gov. Wallace for an injunction forbidding the march.

In addition to sympathy marches, demonstrations and sit-ins in every part of the country, there were calls for federal action from many groups and individuals. Republicans and Northern Democrats in both houses of Congress urged strong voting rights legislation. The National Assn. for the Advancement of Colored People March 8 called on the President to send troops to Selma to guard against recurrences of brutality against the marchers by state troopers. Several clergymen criticized the President for avoiding federal intervention to assure Negro voting rights as well as freedom from police brutality. The United Steelworkers Union March 12 sent telegrams to Gov. Wallace asking him to protect the rights of all Alabamans and to President Johnson urging him to take all steps necessary to protect lives in Alabama. In front of the White House in Washington, pickets maintained a round-the-clock vigil. There were sit-ins at the Capitol, in the White House and during rush hour across Pennsylvania Avenue in front of the White House, as well demonstrations at the Justice Department. It was against this backdrop that the Administration submitted to Congress its voting rights proposals on March 17.

SENATE ACTION

In the Senate, the President's proposals were embodied in S 1564, which was introduced by 66 co-sponsors on March 18. In voting to send the bill to the Senate Judiciary Committee, the Senate added instructions that the Committee report the bill no later than April 9. This tactic was employed because the Committee, under Chairman James O. Eastland (D Miss.), had never willingly reported a civil rights bill. The Civil Rights Act of 1960 was reported from the Committee on instructions of the Senate; the Senate voted to bypass the Committee altogether in considering the Civil Rights Acts of 1957 and 1964 and the 1962 constitutional amendment barring payment of a poll tax as a requirement for voting in federal elections and primaries.

Battling over liberalizing amendments, the Committee deliberated "down to the wire" and completed action on S 1564 only minutes before midnight April 9.

The bill the Committee reported was substantially stronger than what the Administration had proposed.

The major change was the addition of a ban on the use of poll taxes in state and local elections. (Poll taxes in federal elections had been prohibited by the 24th Amendment to the Constitution, ratified in 1964.)

Other key amendments adopted:

• Made provisions of the bill apply to any area where fewer than 25 percent of voting age Negroes were registered. (This was intended to cover areas where Negro registration was low, but where no discriminatory tests were used);

• Authorized the use of poll watchers to make sure that voters were allowed to vote and that their ballots were counted; and,

• Made private citizens as well as state officials criminally liable for interfering with voter rights.

These amendments were proposed by a nine-man liberal group on the Committee: Sens. Philip A. Hart (D Mich.), Edward V. Long (D Mo.), Edward M. Kennedy (D Mass.), Birch Bayh (D Ind.), Quentin N. Burdick (D N.D.), Joseph D. Tydings (D Md.), Hiram Fong (R Hawaii), Hugh Scott (R Pa.) and Jacob K. Javits (R N.Y.).

One major limitation, proposed by Dirksen, was written into the bill. It allowed states with literacy tests and low voter turnout in 1964 to exempt themselves from coverage if less than 20 percent of the population was "non-white," or by proving in court that at least 60 percent of their voting-age residents were registered. This change was strongly opposed by supporters of the liberalizing amendments who argued that "hard core" discrimination areas could escape coverage by increasing the registration of white voters.

S 1564 was ordered reported by a vote of 12-4. Voting against approval were Committee Chairman Eastland, Sam J. Ervin Jr. (D N.C.), John L. McClellan (D Ark.), and Olin D. Johnston (D S.C.), who was absent but requested to be recorded in opposition.

Cloture Voted

Senate debate on the voting bill began April 22. Southern opponents of S 1564 argued vehemently that the measure was unconstitutional in circumventing a state's rights to impose its own voting criteria. But an expected filibuster never developed. Instead, the Southerners attempted to alter the bill's main provisions by proposing many amendments. Most of these were defeated, some by margins of as much as 2-1 and 3-1.

Debate intensified on the poll tax issue. One group of Senators pushed to retain the flat ban on poll taxes in state and local elections contained in the Committee bill. Another group, which had the Administration's support, contended that a ban might be unconstitutional because of doubtful Congressional powers to ban poll taxes through legislation. To ensure safe constitutional footing, this group proposed to direct the Attorney General to initiate court proceedings against the taxes.

A crucial test on the poll-tax ban came May 11 after Mansfield and Dirksen had deleted it from the bill. By a narrow **45-49** roll-call vote, the Senate blocked a move by Sen. Edward M. Kennedy (D Mass.) to write the ban back into the bill. On May 19, the Senate adopted by a 69-20 roll-call vote another Mansfield-Dirksen proposal, that the Attorney General "forthwith" seek

Controversy Centers on Poll Tax Ban

A major controversy during 1965 action on the voting rights legislation resulted from an attempt by Congressional liberals to include a flat ban on poll taxes in the voting bill.

Sentiment for the ban increased during hearings on the measure when civil rights leaders vigorously criticized the Administration bill for not prohibiting state and local poll taxes. Use of such levies, they said, had prevented thousands of low-income persons from participating in elections.

The Judiciary Committees of both House and Senate later reported bills with the ban. In the Senate, however, the provision was dropped when its constitutionality was questioned. Proponents of the ban attempted to restore it, but their amendment was rejected by a narrow **45-49** roll-call vote.

Outcome of the provision remained in doubt for two weeks while House-Senate conferees sought agreement on a final bill. A compromise provision was finally adopted when civil rights groups urged House conferees to drop the ban and agree to court tests of poll taxes.

The Supreme Court in 1966 ruled that a Virginia poll tax violated the Constitution. The decision was made in *Harper v. Virginia State Board of Elections* and *Butts v. Harrison*, decided as one case. *(For additional details, see story p. 353.)*

Background

The 1965 attempt to include a flat ban on poll taxes in the voting bill marked the first time that Congress had given serious consideration to prohibiting the tax in state and local elections. It was only after 30 years of futile efforts that anti-poll tax forces in 1962 gained approval for a constitutional amendment (ratified as the 24th Amendment in 1964) banning the tax in federal elections. Similar statutes had been passed by the House in 1942, 1943, 1945, 1947 and 1949, but the bills never came to a vote in the Senate.

Twenty-seven states in 1965 imposed a poll tax, but it was used as a voter qualification in only four Southern states—Alabama, Mississippi, Texas and Virginia.

Poll taxes as a requirement for voting in the United States occurred in two different eras. The levies were introduced in some states during the early days of the nation as a substitute for property qualifications, which had been enacted as voting prerequisites. The intent of the early levies was to enlarge the electorate.

These taxes were gradually eliminated, and by the time of the Civil War, few states still had them.

During the second era of the poll tax, which began in the early 1890s, levies were imposed by Southern states as one of a number of devices to restrict suffrage. Poll taxes tied to the right to vote were adopted in 11 Southern states—Florida (1889), Mississippi and Tennessee (1890), Arkansas (1892), South Carolina (1895), Louisiana (1898), North Carolina (1900), Alabama (1901), Virginia and Texas (1902) and Georgia (1908).

The levies were ostensibly adopted to "cleanse" elections of mass abuse, but the records of constitutional conventions held in five Southern states during the period contained statements praising the poll tax as a measure to bar the Negro as well as the poor white from the franchise. Many historians have asserted that these measures were taken to limit the popular base of agrarian revolution inspired by the Populist party.

Since the turn-of-the-century imposition of the poll taxes, seven Southern states dropped the levies. North Carolina, which repealed its poll tax with the granting of womanhood suffrage in 1920, was the first. Other states repealing the tax, all during periods of keen interest in political races, were: Louisiana (1934), Florida (1937), Georgia (1945), South Carolina (1951), Tennessee (1953) and Arkansas (1964). In each of the first six states to drop the tax, voter participation increased sharply in the next election following repeal, decreased in subsequent elections and then rose again. In a widely respected 1958 study entitled "The Poll Tax in the South," Frederic D. Ogden of the University of Alabama political science faculty estimated that 5 percent of the initial increase in each state could be attributed to the repeal of the poll tax.

Of the four Southern states which still levied poll taxes as a voter qualification, attempts had been made in all but Mississippi to repeal or alter them.

Constitutional amendments to repeal poll taxes were rejected by Virginia voters in 1949 and Texas voters in both 1949 and 1963. Alabama voters in 1953 amended the state constitution to reduce the cumulative effect of the poll tax from a maximum of 24 years and maximum payment of $36 to two years with a ceiling of $3. In May 1965, the Alabama State Senate voted overwhelmingly to approve a constitutional amendment repealing the tax. Action on a similar measure in the Alabama House was deferred until a later session. The Texas legislature in May 1965 approved a 1966 referendum to repeal the tax.

federal court orders against the levying of discriminatory poll taxes.

As the debate wore on, Senate leaders tried to limit it and bring the bill to a vote. Mansfield three times sought unanimous consent to limit debate. Each time, his motion was blocked by Sen. Allen J. Ellender

(D La.). Finally, on May 21, a petition for a cloture motion was filed by Hart, floor manager for S 1564. The petition was signed by 29 Democrats and nine Republican (16 signatures were needed). The cloture motion was adopted by a **70-30** roll-call vote on May 25, setting the stage for passage. Approval of the cloture motion marked only the second time in history—but the second time in two years—that the Senate had voted to close off debate on a civil rights issue.

Bill Passed

Passage, by a **77-19** roll-call vote, came on May 26. Voting for passage was a coalition of 30 Republicans and 47 Democrats. Two Republicans joined 17 Southern Democrats in opposing passage.

Four Senators who opposed the Civil Rights Act of 1964 voted in favor of the 1965 bill. They were: Albert Gore (D Tenn.), Norris Cotton (R N.H.), Bourke Hickenlooper (R Iowa) and Milward L. Simpson (R Wyo.). No Senator who voted for the 1964 legislation opposed the 1965 bill.

HOUSE ACTION

House Judiciary Committee Chairman Emanuel Celler (D N.Y.), acting on the request of President Johnson for speedy action, called Judiciary Subcommittee No. 5 into session on the Administration bill (HR 6400) the day after the President's March 17 appeal for the legislation.

As the Senate Committee had done, the House Subcommittee wrote in a poll-tax ban, provided for poll watchers and made private citizens criminally liable for interference with voter rights. The House bill, however, retained the 50-percent formula for "triggering" the federal voter machinery (the percentage of voter turnout determining which states or districts would fall under the bill.)

The Subcommittee April 9 approved an amended version of HR 6400 and voted 10-1 to send the measure to the full Committee. (The Committee declined to identify the lone Subcommittee member who voted against referral.)

Approving these amendments and adding some of its own, the full Committee approved HR 6400 by voice vote on May 12 and the bill was reported to the floor on June 1. A five-week delay ensued before debate, however, while the bill remained in the House Rules Committee under the chairmanship of Howard W. Smith (D Va.).

Sentiment for a strong voting rights bill was clear as debate began July 6. As floor manager for HR 6400, Celler opened debate and said the measure would eliminate the "legal dodges and subterfuges" possible under existing legislation. He called the bill "impervious to all legal trickery and evasion."

Rules Committee Chairman Smith, a leading opponent of civil rights legislation, said the bill was an "unconstitutional" vendetta against the former Confederate states, that it was "dripping in venom" and that its effect was to make of the Attorney General a "czar" with "almost unlimited power to investigate, to prosecute and to try and convict sovereign states...."

The Republican Substitute

The House GOP leadership moved to substitute a bill, HR 7896, for HR 6400, and were nearly successful. The Republican substitute dropped the poll-tax ban, but authorized court action against discriminatory poll taxes and provided for appointment of voting examiners.

Rank-and-file GOP support for HR 7896 appeared to be holding firm until a Southern Democrat, William M. Tuck (Va.), urged in a floor speech that Members opposed to civil rights legislation support HR 7896 as the less "objectionable" of the two bills. Republican defections from support of HR 7896 began as Members feared that alignment with Southerners for the GOP bill would be taken as alignment against civil rights.

Speaker John W. McCormack (D Mass.) estimated that the Tuck speech cost 15 Republican votes for HR 7896. Before that speech, he said, backers of HR 6400 counted on only 10 Republican votes, and of these only three—John V. Lindsay (N.Y.), candidate for mayor of New York City, William T. Cahill (N.J.) and Charles McC. Mathias (Md.)—had publicly announced their support.

GOP leaders needed to hold most of the 141 Republican Members in line and to win over a substantial number of the 99 Southern Democrats to assure passage of HR 7896. This they were unable to do, and the bill was rejected on a 166-215 teller vote.

HR 6400 then survived a motion by Rep. Harold Collier (R Ill.) to recommit to committee, which was defeated by a 171-248 roll-call vote.

The House accepted one amendment to HR 6400 which provided criminal penalties for falsifying voting or registration information or for buying votes in federal elections. Numerous amendments were rejected.

In a roll-call vote on passage July 9, the House approved HR 6400 by a vote of **333-85.** Several Southern Members received standing ovations when they announced before passage that they would support the bill. Voting for passage were 112 Republicans and 221 Democrats. Three Southern Republicans, Cramer (Fla.), Carter (Ky.) and Belcher (Okla.), and 33 Southern Democrats, voted in favor.

Since the House and Senate versions of the voting rights bill differed—especially in the House retention of the poll-tax ban—the measure was sent to a conference committee. HR 6400's provisions were substituted for those of the Senate bill, S 1564, and S 1564 was sent to conference.

CONFERENCE, FINAL ACTION

Stalemate over the poll-tax ban was short-lived. On July 29, the conferees agreed on a final form for the voting rights bill. The poll-tax ban from the House bill was dropped. The Senate proposal that the Attorney General seek court action against enforcement of state and local poll taxes was retained. The compromise included a "finding" that poll taxes were used to discriminate in some areas and that the constitutional right to vote was "denied or abridged" by payment of the taxes as a precondition for voting.

Also included in the final bill were (1) a provision exempting any state or political subdivision where more than 50 percent of eligible Negroes are already registered and where a federal court finds no discrimination and (2) a provision dropping English language literacy requirements for sixth-grade graduates of American schools, a measure benefiting Puerto Rican voters.

The House approved the conference report by a 328-74 vote on Aug. 3. The Senate voted approval on Aug. 4 by a 79-18 roll call.

PRESIDENT SIGNS BILL

President Johnson Aug. 6 signed into law the Voting Rights Act of 1965 (S 1564—PL 89-110).

At the signing ceremony, broadcast by nationwide television from the U.S. Capitol rotunda, President Johnson said that the Act would "strike away the last major shackle" of the Negro's "ancient bonds."

After his speech, Mr. Johnson moved to the President's Room off the Senate chamber to sign the bill. Abraham Lincoln had used the same room on Aug. 6, 1861, to sign a bill freeing slaves who had been pressed into service of the Confederacy.

In a swift series of moves to implement the new Act:
• The Justice Department Aug. 7 filed a suit aimed at striking down the Mississippi poll tax. Similar actions were filed Aug. 10 against the Alabama, Texas and Virginia poll taxes.
• The Justice Department Aug. 7 suspended literacy tests and similar voter qualification devices in the seven states and most of the separate political subdivisions covered by the Act. Tests were suspended in Alabama, Alaska, Georgia, Louisiana, Mississippi, South Carolina and Virginia; 27 North Carolina counties and Apache County, Arizona. Action to suspend tests in seven other North Carolina counties and one county each in Idaho and Maine was withheld pending the outcome of studies to determine levels of voting activity in these areas during the 1964 Presidential election.
• Attorney General Nicholas deB. Katzenbach Aug. 9 designated the first group of counties and parishes in Alabama, Louisiana and Mississippi for the appointment of federal examiners to process Negro voter applicants and order their registration. By Aug. 25, President Johnson was able to announce that 27,385 Negroes in the three Southern states had been registered by federal registrars in the first 19 days of the Voting Rights Act. He said the registrants represented nearly one-third of the potential applicants in the 13 counties included in the first action. The President also said he had received "very heartening" reports of voluntary compliance with the new law in many Southern areas where federal registrars had not been sent.

Voting Rights Act Provisions

Following are the major provisions of the Voting Rights Act of 1965 (PL 89-110):

Voting Examiners

Authorized appointment by the Civil Service Commission of voting "examiners," federal officials who would determine an individual's qualifications to vote and would require enrollment of qualified individuals by state and local officials to vote in all elections: federal, state and local and delegates to party caucuses and state political conventions. Such appointment would be made whenever:
• A federal court, hearing a suit by the Attorney General charging a state or political subdivision with denying or abridging the right to vote on account of race or color, determined that examiners were needed to ensure voting rights. Authorized the appointment of as many examiners as was deemed necessary either during the course of a suit or as part of a final judgment finding voter discrimination.

• The Attorney General certified to the Commission that he had received meritorious complaints from 20 or more residents of a political subdivision of a state (such as a county, parish or other voting district) that they had been denied the right to vote on account of race or color, or that he had determined that general discrimination existed. Examiners would be appointed in these cases only if the area qualified statistically and otherwise as one practicing massive discrimination as defined under the triggering formulas provided in the bill and had not exempted itself through the Act's provision for judicial relief. *(See triggering formula and appeal provisions below.)*

Triggering Formula. Made any state or political subdivision subject to the appointment of federal examiners if: (1) the Attorney General determined that a literacy test or similar device was used as a qualification for voting on Nov. 1, 1964; (2) and the Director of the Census determined that less than 50 percent of the persons of voting age residing in the area were registered to vote on that date or actually voted in the 1964 Presidential Election

Qualifications of Examiners. Authorized appointment of either private citizens or federal officials as examiners. Stipulated that federal officials could be appointed only when the Civil Service Commission consulted with the appropriate department or agency and secured individual consent. Stipulated that private citizens serving as examiners should be appointed, compensated and separated without regard to any civil service law, except the Hatch Act, which prohibits Government employees from engaging in partisan political activity.

Duties. Authorized examiners to interview applicants concerning their qualifications for voting and order appropriate state or local authorities to register all persons they found qualified to vote. Stipulated that the Civil Service Commission, after consultation with the Attorney General, would instruct examiners concerning state laws that would be applicable to the federal registration process. Provided that times, places and procedures for registering and the form for application and removal from eligibility lists would be prescribed by regulations promulgated by the Civil Service Commission.

Stipulated that examiners would require applicants to submit allegations that they were not presently registered to vote. Empowered examiners to administer oaths in processing applicants.

Instructed examiners to certify and transmit lists of qualified voters at least once a month to the offices of the appropriate election officials, with copies to the Attorney General and to the attorney general of the state. Directed such election officials to add lists submitted by examiners to their own official rolls. Directed examiners to provide certificates of eligibility to each voter applicant listed.

Stipulated that any voting lists transmitted by examiners should be available for public inspection on the last business day of the month, and in any event, not later than the 45th day prior to any election. Stipulated that no federally processed voter applicant could be listed after 45 days prior to any election in which he wished to vote.

Directed examiners to remove from eligibility lists federally processed applicants whose qualifications had been successfully challenged *(see below)* or had been determined by examiners to have lost their eligibility to vote under any state voting law still in effect.

Tenure of Examiners. Provided that the appointment of examiners under the automatic triggering formula would be terminated by the Attorney General or a three-judge federal district court in the District of Columbia, when a state or political subdivision had met certain standards stipulated under the Act's procedures for appeal of federal action *(See Appeal Provisions, below).*

Stipulated that the appointment of examiners under federal court order would be terminated only upon order of the authorizing court.

Literacy Tests

Suspended literacy tests or similar voter qualification devices when the Attorney General and Director of the Census determined that a state or political subdivision came within the scope of the Act's automatic triggering formula (*above*). Stipulated that such determinations were not reviewable in any court and were effective upon publication in the Federal Register. (Tests and devices would be suspended for applicants approaching state registrars as well as federal examiners.)

Authorized federal courts, hearing voting rights suits brought by the Attorney General, to suspend tests or devices that it found had been used for the purpose or "with the effect" of discriminating.

Defined "test or device" for purposes of the Act as any prerequisite for registration or voting which required a person to: (1) demonstrate the ability to read, write, understand, or interpret any matter; (2) demonstrate any educational achievement or his knowledge of any particular subject; (3) possess good moral character; (4) prove his qualifications by the voucher of registered voters or members of any other class.

Provided that no tests or device could be suspended if incidents of discrimination had been limited in number and effectively corrected by state and local action, the continuing effect of such incidents had been eliminated and there was no reasonable probability of recurrence.

Stipulated that a person could not be denied the right to vote because of inability to read or write in English if he demonstrated that he had successfully completed the sixth grade (or another grade level equivalent to whatever level of education a state demands) in a school under the American flag that was conducted in a language other than English.

Appeal of Federal Action

Stipulated that any state or political subdivision in which tests or devices were suspended and examiners appointed under the Act's automatic triggering formula could have the tests or devices reinstated and the examiner process terminated by proving in a three-judge federal district court in the District of Columbia that no literacy tests or similar device had been used during the preceding five years for the purpose or with the effect of discriminating. Imposed an absolute prohibition against an exemption from the federal registration machinery (suspension of tests and appointment of examiners) for a period of five years after a finding by any federal court that a state or political subdivision had discriminated against voters.

Stipulated that if the Attorney General had no reason to believe that the petitioning state or local government had used its test or device to discriminate against voters, he could consent to the entry of a judgment freeing the petitioner from the bill.

Stipulated that even if the court freed a petitioner of the charge of discrimination, the court would retain jurisdiction for five years and could reopen the case upon the Attorney General's motion that the state or political subdivision had discriminated.

Also provided the following methods by which political subdivisons could free themselves from the appointment of federal examiners (however, these methods did not provide for reinstating suspended voting qualification tests and devices):

• By successfully petitioning the Attorney General that state and local election officials had enrolled all persons listed by federal examiners as qualified to vote and that there was no reasonable cause to believe that the right to vote would be denied or abridged on account of race or color.

• In the case of political subdivisions in which a Census Bureau survey shows that more than 50 percent of nonwhite voting age population residing in the area was registered to vote, by proving in a three-judge federal district court in the District of Columbia that the same voting condition existed (all eligible persons enrolled and no further discrimination) as political subdivisions petitioning the Attorney General had to show existed in their areas.

Provided that if the federal registration apparatus had been triggered by the order of a federal court in a case instituted by the Attorney General, the appointment of examiners could be terminated and tests and devices reinstated only upon order of the court.

Prior Approval Requirement

Required that new voting laws enacted by state or local governments whose voter qualification laws had been nullified under the bill be approved by the Attorney General or federal courts before they could take effect. In the case of states and political subdivisions in which the automatic triggering formula had been invoked, the affected state or local government would be required to secure the approval of either the Attorney General or a three-judge federal district court in the District of Columbia that the statute did not have the purpose and would not have the effect of discriminating against voters on account of race or color. If the petitioning government chose to submit the new law to the Attorney General and if he objected to it within a 60-day period, the petitioner could still seek the court's approval. In areas to which examiners had been appointed by federal courts in voting rights cases filed by the Attorney General, the petitioning state or local government would be required to secure the approval of either the Attorney General or the authorizing court.

Subpoena Power of D.C. Court. Stipulated that in actions brought by state or local governments in the federal district court for the District of Columbia to obtain approval of new voting laws (or to free themselves from the bill's coverage), subpoenas could be served in any judicial district of the United States, but not at distances greater than 100 miles from the District of Columbia without permission of the D.C. court, which could be secured only upon proper application and presentation of due cause.

Challenges of Voters

Authorized challenges, before hearing officers appointed by the Civil Service Commission, on the qualifications of any applicant listed by federal voting examiners as eligible to vote. Required that such a challenge be filed at offices designated by the Commission and within 10 days after the listing of the challenged person had been made public. Required that such challenge be decided within 15 days of the date it was filed, but provided that challenged voters could participate in any election held in the interim.

Authorized the Commission to subpoena witnesses and documentary evidence and provided enforcement machinery in case subpoenas were ignored. provided that the decision of hearing officers could be appealed within 15 days after the decision of the hearing officer was served upon the petitioning party.

Specifically provided that a challenge would not be basis for a prosecution under the Act's provisions authorizing criminal penalties for voter interference.

Poll Taxes

Included a Congressional declaration that the payment of poll taxes as a condition for voting in certain states denied or abridged the right to vote. Directed the Attorney General to institute "forthwith" in the appropriate federal district courts challenges of poll taxes used as a precondition for voting or against any substitute for such taxes enacted after Nov. 1, 1964. Stipulated that Congress, in directing the Attorney General to proceed against such taxes, was acting under authority of the 14th and 15th Amendments to the U.S. Constitution. (The 14th Amendment prohibits deprivation of liberties without due process of law and guarantees equal protection of the law. The 15th Amendment prohibits denial or abridgement of the right to vote on account of race, color or previous condition of servitude. Both amendments empower Congress to enforce their provisions by "appropriate legislation.")

Stipulated that during the period in which suits by the Attorney General were pending in the courts and following any decision ruling that a poll tax was constitutional, no citizen of a state or political subdivision in which the federal registration machinery was in effect could be denied the right to vote during the first year of his eligibility for the failure to pay a poll tax if he tendered payment of the tax for the current year to an examiner at least 45 days prior to an election.

Authorized examiners to issue receipts for the payment of poll taxes. (Presentation of such receipts might be necessary to actually obtain the ballot for state and local elections in some states.) Directed examiners to transmit "promptly" all poll tax payments to the appropriate state or local officials together with the name and address of the applicant.

Enforcement Machinery

Authorized federal examiners, upon determining that properly registered voters had been turned away from

the polls, to go into a federal district court and obtain an order impounding the ballots until persons entitled to vote had been allowed to do so.

Provided penalties of up to $5,000 in fines and/or five years imprisonment for conviction of vote fraud or of acts to intimidate or otherwise interfere with persons voting or attempting to vote, with persons urging or aiding others to vote or with persons exercising duties provided by the Act.

Provided penalties of up to $10,000 and/or five years imprisonment for conviction of falsifying voting or registration information or buying votes (applicable only to federal elections, the election for the resident commissioner for Puerto Rico and elections in territories or possessions) or for making false or fraudulent statements before a federal examiner or hearing officer (applicable to any election).

Instructed the Attorney General to institute actions for injunctive relief when there were reasonable grounds to believe that any person was about to violate any provision of the Act.

Authorized the Civil Service Commission, at the request of the Attorney General, to appoint poll watchers in political subdivisions to which examiners had been assigned. Stipulated that private citizens, as well as federal officials, could be appointed.

Authorized poll watchers to enter and attend at any place at which voting or tabulation of votes was conducted in order to observe whether all persons qualified to vote were allowed to do so and that their ballots were properly tabulated. Directed such officials to report to the appropriate examiner, to the Attorney General and, if the federal registration machinery was triggered through court action, to the authorizing court.

Stipulated that all criminal contempt cases arising under the Act should be governed by the provisions of the Civil Rights Act of 1957. (That Act provided that the presiding judge in a voting rights case could decide whether the case would be tried by the court alone or by a jury. However, if he tried the case without a jury, the maximum penalty would be a fine of $300 and a jail term of 45 days; if he imposed a greater penalty, the defendant could demand a retrial with a jury.)

Other Provisions

Directed the Attorney General and the Secretary of Defense to make a complete study to determine whether state voting laws or practices discriminated against members of the Armed Forces who seek to vote. Required that these Cabinet members make a joint report to Congress, including their findings and recommendations, by June 30, 1966.

Stipulated that if any section of the Act or its application to any person or circumstances was ruled unconstitutional by the courts, the remainder of the Act and the application of its provisions to other persons not coming under the same circumstances would not be affected.

Authorized the appropriation of necessary sums to implement provisions of the Act.

Equal Employment

Congress did not complete action on a bill (HR 10065) broadening and strengthening Title VII of the 1964 Civil

Rights Act which prohibited employment discrimination based on race, color, religion or national origin. The bill, supported by civil rights groups but not by the Administration in 1965, was reported by the House Education and Labor Committee in August and was scheduled for floor action in October. However, action was postponed until the 1966 session because of the controversial nature of the bill and the leadership's effort to adjourn Congress as soon as possible. *(For provisions of HR 10065 and additional background on equal employment see p. 373.)*

The House took one roll-call vote on the issue before postponing action. On Sept. 13, by a 259-121 roll call, the House adopted an open rule for floor action. Although a roll call seldom develops on this procedural requirement (which is common to most major bills), opponents occasionally will force a vote on the rule for a controversial measure in hopes of defeating the rule and thereby preventing futher action. (Other procedures for floor action are available but normally would not be used because rejection of a rule is considered tantamount to rejection of the bill.) The vote breakdown: R 76-51; D 183-70 (ND 166-2; SD 17-68).

The rule was brought before the House under the special 21-day procedure which permitted a legislative Committee to bring a rule for floor action before the House for a vote if the Rules Committee did not grant a request for a rule within 21 days of the request. It was one of six times the procedure was used in 1965 to bypass the Rules Committee; the procedure was instituted earlier in the session at the insistence of liberals who believed that the Rules Committee was an obstacle to enactment of legislation they favored.

1966

Civil Rights-Open Housing

Congress in 1966 reversed its direction of the previous two years by rejecting a major Administration civil rights bill. The measure survived amendment and attack in the House but died in the Senate.

The Civil Rights Act of 1966 (HR 14765) was not a complicated measure, at least compared to its predecessors of 1964 and 1965. But in its Title IV—the open housing provision—lay the seeds of its own destruction. As introduced, Title IV barred racial discrimination in the sale and rental of all housing.

The rest of the bill was far less controversial: as introduced, it barred racial discrimination in the selection of federal and state jurors, empowered the Attorney General to initiate desegregation suits and protected civil rights workers. The House added provisions empowering the Attorney General to enjoin actions depriving persons of their rights and prohibiting interstate travel for the purpose of inciting riot.

But Title IV, even watered down, so offended Senate Minority Leader Everett McKinley Dirksen (R Ill.) that he led the opposition to the bill. A dozen Republican Senators followed suit, and the civil rights coalition of Northern Democrats and Republicans fell apart in the Senate.

The House had passed the bill Aug. 9 on a 259-157 roll-call vote. The Senate bypassed its Judiciary Committee and put the bill directly on the calendar, but a motion to begin consideration of the bill was blocked by opponents, who indicated they were ready to talk indefinitely. After a week of desultory debate, the Senate Democratic leadership tried to invoke cloture on the incipient filibuster. The leadership failed to rally the two-thirds majority needed to invoke cloture; it was 10 votes short. Five days later the leadership tried again and failed again by the same margin. On that day, Sept. 19, knowing the game was up, Senate Majority Leader Mike Mansfield (D Mont.) moved to adjourn the Senate and thus to kill the bill.

Defeat of the Act was a stunning setback for the Administration of President Johnson and for the civil rights movement. It marked a signal change in the attitude of the same Congress which had passed the historic Voting Rights Act of 1965. The Rev. Dr. Martin Luther King Jr., head of the Southern Christian Leadership Conference and a pre-eminent civil rights leader, Sept. 19 said the Senate vote "surely heralds darker days for this social era of discontent."

The Mood of the Nation

Riots in the seething black ghettos of a dozen cities, Negroes chanting "black power" as they marched along a Mississippi highway, open-housing advocates stoned and spat upon as they paraded down a tree-lined street in a "lily-white" Chicago suburb—that was the civil rights scene in the summer of 1966.

There was more: Southern Negroes by the tens of thousands registered to vote for the first time in their lives; Negro travelers, to their surprise, found public accommodations in the South increasingly open to them; a prominent Negro civil rights advocate was wounded from ambush in Mississippi in June—but another made a trip through that state in November and was welcomed by white politicians and businessmen in the 15 towns he visited.

In the North, the pressures of frustration and desire of slum-dwelling Negroes repeatedly erupted in violence; civil rights leaders condemned the violence, but demanded massive programs to eliminate ghettos; school boards grappled with the problem of "de facto" segregation arising from living patterns of residents; and the relations of police and minority groups were a subject of concern, study and reform.

The year also was a big one for slogans: "black power," "white backlash," "de facto segregation," "de-ghettoization" "burn, baby, burn" and its counterpart "learn, baby, learn." And withal, a Los Angeles strip-teaser billed herself as "Sybil Rights."

A White House Conference "To Fulfill These Rights" was finally convened June 1, a year after it was announced by the President. The Conference, the first on civil rights sponsored by the White House, began in some confusion and ended without clearly defining the new direction of the civil rights movement. *(See p. 392.)* That symbolized the major problem of the movement in 1966: the civil rights revolution had not so much lost its force as it had lost its sense of direction. The movement was becoming more involved in the problems of education, housing, slums, jobs, law enforcement—problems affecting all urban citizens.

In the light of those developments, the mood of the nation in 1966 remained essentially one of sympathy toward the desire of Negroes to improve their lives, tempered by growing concern at the violence fostered by a few spokesmen and slum-dwellers. Negro and white leaders, including the President, unqualifiedly condemned the violence, but the lawlessness of a relatively few thousand Negro rioters generated resentment in a large portion of the nation.

In the South, resentment built up against the efforts of the Department of Health, Education and Welfare to enforce the Civil Rights Act of 1964 by requiring schools and hospitals to desegregate. In the North, resentment built up against efforts of civil rights leaders to bus children to different school districts in order to break down "de facto" segregation and against their efforts to break down the pattern of segregated housing generally. Those activities produced counter-pressures in the white community and resulted in a discernible stiffening of resistance to rapid change. Then, too, the year lacked the kinds of events—a march on Washington, police clubbing Negro marchers to the ground before nationwide television, nightrider slayings, the bombing and burning of churches, a massive march for voting rights—which had helped enact legislation in 1964 and 1965.

Opinion polls in 1966 noted some changes in the attitudes of white citizens. A pre-election Gallup Poll indicated that 52 percent of whites thought that the Johnson Administration was pushing racial integration too rapidly—the highest percentage since the spring of 1962. A Louis Harris Poll, taken about the same time, indicated that 75 percent of whites thought that Negroes were moving too fast, compared to 50 percent two years before.

To a degree that was less than some observers had predicted, this growing uneasiness over the racial situation was reflected in the 1966 elections. The preservation of segregation was an issue in a number of races in the South; open housing was an issue in a number of races in the North. Results in both regions were mixed.

The Mood of Congress

Congress was cool to President Johnson's 1966 civil rights program the moment he announced it in his State of the Union Message Jan 12. Dirksen immediately established himself as spokesman for the opponents of Title IV, contending that it was unconstitutional and an unnecessary invasion of private property rights by the Federal Government.

There was less disagreement about the need for other provisions proposed by the President. His proposal for a law protecting civil rights workers, a proposal which had begun to gain support in 1965, appeared to enjoy widespread backing in Congress. In the weeks following the State of the Union Message, a number of such bills were introduced by Senators and Representatives of both parties.

It was more than three months, however, before the Administration bills (S 3296, HR 14765) were sent from the White House to Capitol Hill. Civil rights leaders were anxious to start the bills moving, knowing that the legislation faced a potential filibuster in the Senate. The Administration offered no explanation for the timing, although it was understood that the Justice Department, which drafted the measure, had waited for two key Supreme Court decisions (*U.S. v. Guest, U.S. v. Price*) which interpreted federal powers to punish acts of vio-

lence against persons exercising their rights. Those decisions were handed down on March 28.

The Administration's proposed total ban on racial discrimination in the sale and rental of housing underwent heavy modification soon after it was introduced. In his first appearance at hearings on HR 14765, Attorney General Nicholas deB. Katzenbach said the Administration would agree to amendments to Title IV exempting certain small landlords—the "Mrs. Murphy" exemption included in the public accommodations section of the 1964 Act. From then on, a major dispute ranged about the nature and extent of exemptions to the bill. The House-passed version of HR 14765 exempted persons in their first two housing transactions in any year and persons occupying their own homes and renting less than three other units in the dwelling. Only through such modification, the bill's supporters reasoned, could enough votes be garnered for House passage.

In reaction against violence and rioting in several major cities, the House overwhelmingly approved an amendment prohibiting interstate travel for the purpose of inciting riot. That provision, like its counterpart, the provision protecting civil rights workers, was the subject of separate legislation introduced but not acted upon in 1966.

Even as overhauled by the House, however, HR 14765 failed to generate enough support in the Senate to survive a filibuster. The Senate Sept. 14 by a **54-42** roll-call vote and Sept. 19 by a 52-41 roll-call vote (two thirds needed) rejected Mansfield's motions to invoke cloture on debate.

Other Setbacks. Defeat of HR 14765 was not the only setback for the civil rights movement in Congress in 1966. Acting on other legislation, Congress imposed curbs on the authority of the Office of Education to defer funds from school districts charged with failure to meet desegregation requirements; restricted the dispensing of anti-poverty funds to persons convicted of promoting riot or activities that resulted in property damage; and deleted from the Demonstration Cities measure a provision aimed at housing and school desegregation. The HEW guidelines on school and hospital desegregation also were the subject of lively hearings.

Brief descriptions follow of major events which bore on the attitude of Congress in 1966:

Riots. Violence erupted in many cities across the nation during the summer; it generally took the form of crowds of Negroes roaming the streets, hurling bottles and other missiles and taunting police. Rioting broke out between July 12 and 20 in Negro sections of Chicago, Cleveland, Jacksonville, Fla., New York City and South Bend, Ind. It was at its worst in Chicago and Cleveland, where the National Guard was called out and where two persons were killed in each city. Riots subsequently broke out in Atlanta, Ga., which had a history of stable race relations, and in San Francisco. In many instances, the crowds chanted "black power" and "burn, baby, burn." The former slogan became identified with the riots. On Dec. 6, 1965, the McCone Commission reported on the August 1965 riots in the Watts section of Los Angeles, the worst riots in the nation in this century. The Commission found a sense of despair and a "spiral of failure" among Watts residents; it called for a "revolutionary attitude" toward city problems and for "many costly and extreme" answers.

(Continued on p. 368)

'Black Power' Enters Civil Rights Movement

A major consequence of the 1966 "Meredith March" through Mississippi was the emergence of the slogan "black power," in the civil rights movement. The meaning and implications of the slogan quickly became the most debated—and debatable—topics among members, observers and opponents of the movement.

That debate erupted in a context of widespread disagreement about a precise definition of "black power." The concept of "black power" generally was regarded as embracing traditional methods of obtaining political power—voter registration, political organization, selection of candidates, campaigning and delivering the vote on election day.

But it was also widely interpreted as embracing much more—antiwhite emotions, rejection of existing political and social institutions, separatism and a desire to meet violence with counterviolence; in short, a neo-racism.

Some observers explained "black power" in terms of the psychology of people first emerging from a long period of inferior status. These observers contended that the wellspring of the concept was a newly discovered sense of pride and self-sufficiency being experienced in the Negro community. Those who found "black power" to reflect a new ethnic integrity among Negroes contended that the aggressiveness and self-assertion implicit in the concept was a logical consequence of the civil rights movement. Virtually impotent in politics when he began his civil rights struggle a decade before, the Negro now was armed with recognition, with the support of the Federal Government and with the right to vote. Thus armed, these observers said, the Negro felt free to express deeper aspirations, to condemn every manifestation of white superiority—including charity—and to press the civil rights movement from a position of strength.

Origin of 'Black Power'

The phrase, "black power," came into wide use during the June march through Mississippi begun by James H. Meredith to demonstrate the need to register Negroes to vote. After Meredith June 6, 1966, was shot in ambush, other civil rights leaders and workers moved quickly to continue the march while Meredith recuperated from his wounds.

One of the first civil rights leaders to arrive after the shooting was Stokely Carmichael, chairman of the Student Non-Violent Coordinating Committee (SNCC), an integrated group of young, militant persons based in Atlanta, Ga. Carmichael then left for organizational activities elsewhere, returning a few days later. Upon his return and upon the arrival of other SNCC workers, the chant of "black power" was taken up with increasing frequency by the marchers; it first appeared in press reports on June 17 and became a dominating element of the march as participants were met in a number of instances with hostile treatment, tear gas and lines of heavily armed law officers.

In speeches at the end of the march at Jackson, Miss., the theme of "black power" overshadowed most others. "Stop being ashamed of being black," Carmichael told an estimated 12,000 to 15,000 persons massed in the state capital. "Black power" was the shouted response from the listeners, most of whom were Mississippi Negroes. Meredith drew a strongly affirmative response when he reminded the crowd that the "issue here is the power structure."

In contrast, Rev. Dr. Martin Luther King Jr., chairman of the Southern Christian Leadership Conference (SCLC), stuck to his philosophy of nonviolence, brotherhood and freedom as the methods and goals of the civil rights movement. (During the march itself, King had stressed the need to exert political power, having been quoted as saying that "power is the ability to make the power structure say 'yes' when it wants to say 'no.'")

In the days following the march, many civil rights leaders, columnists and commentators analyzed the concept of "black power" and many condemned it. The concept was quickly interpreted as racist in nature and, as such, was denounced widely in the press.

The Congress of Racial Equality (CORE), on the other hand, July 4 adopted a resolution at its annual convention in Baltimore endorsing the concept of "black power." CORE was the only civil rights organization to back SNCC on the issue. The National Assn. for the Advancement of Colored People (NAACP) July 5 heard its executive director, Roy Wilkins, denounce the concept at the NAACP annual convention in Los Angeles. Vice President Hubert H. Humphrey July 6 told NAACP delegates that "racism is racism." But the "black power" concept reportedly generated substantial support among members of the NAACP, traditionally a conservative civil rights organization.

Meaning of 'Black Power'

The person generally credited with launching the phrase, "black power," on the civil rights movement, Stokely Carmichael of SNCC, had yet to articulate in any detail what he meant by the concept. During the march through Mississippi, he was quoted as having said:

"Every group in this country owns its own neighborhoods but us. The Jews, the Italians, the Germans. The Irish took over Boston and nobody asked them what they were going to do statewide where they weren't in a majority. Well, we're going to elect sheriffs where we can, where we're in a majority."

Whatever Carmichael's interpretation of the phrase, "black power" had definite appeal among a number of Negroes, in the North and South. The slogan was less important than the aspiration it stood for—the realization and not simply the promise of equal status. The advocates of "black power" were less interested in semantics or in philosophic debate than in concrete results. Their aggressiveness introduced a new element into the civil rights movement.

"Black Power." This phrase rose to prominence during the Meredith March (*see below*) and was attributed then to Stokely Carmichael, chairman of the Student Non-Violent Coordinating Committee (SNCC), a militant civil rights organization. Carmichael said the phrase meant concentrating Negro economic and political strength in order to exercise social and political power. Rep. Adam C. Powell (D N.Y.), a Negro, was the only Member of Congress to embrace the slogan. He said he coined it. On Sept. 3 he convened a meeting of "black power" advocates in Washington, D.C., to discuss the subject. (*See p. 367.*)

Meredith March. James H. Meredith, who in 1962 was the first Negro to integrate the University of Mississippi, June 6 was shot from ambush while marching through Mississippi urging Negroes to register to vote. Civil rights leaders took up the march to Jackson, Miss., while Meredith recovered from his wounds. Aubrey James Norvell, a white man, was arrested immediately and on Nov. 21 pleaded guilty to assault with intent to kill. He was sentenced in Hernando, Miss., circuit court to five years in jail, with three years suspended.

Genesis of the 1966 Bill

The Administration's Civil Rights Act of 1966 was an assemblage of proposals drawn in part from legislation previously rejected by Congress and in part from ideas enjoying varying degrees of currency within the civil rights movement.

The Administration program developed in stages. President Johnson Nov. 16, 1965, announced that he would seek "jury legislation" in 1966, and reform of both state and federal jury selection procedures was embodied in Titles I and II of the Administration bill submitted April 28, 1966. In his Jan. 12 State of the Union Message, Mr. Johnson further said he would seek a federal open housing law (Title IV of his bill) and a federal law protecting civil rights workers and others exercising their rights (Title V of his bill). When the Administration bill was sent to Congress, it contained yet another provision (Title III) which authorized the Attorney General to initiate suits to desegregate public schools and other public facilities. The House added the final provision (displacing Title III, which became Title VI) authorizing the Attorney General to sue to prevent the deprivation of rights. The last two proposals were both legislative leftovers from previous years, having failed of passage during consideration of civil rights laws.

The many-faceted Administration bill, and the months it took to produce it, were indications of the absence of clear-cut goals in the civil rights movement in 1966. In a search for new proposals, Mr. Johnson called together several hundred civil rights experts on Nov. 17-18, 1965, for a Planning Session for the White House Conference "To Fulfill These Rights." The Planning Session report was made public Dec. 14, and the President appeared to draw on it for his proposals for an open housing law and a law protecting civil rights workers. It had been on the eve of that meeting that the President had announced his intention to seek "jury legislation" in 1966. The White House Conference itself, the first ever held on civil rights, was not convened until June 1-2, more than a month after the Administration civil rights bill

Warnings on Open Housing

Civil rights leaders late in 1965 reportedly warned President Johnson that inclusion of Title IV, the open housing provision, could generate substantial and perhaps fatal political opposition. Instead, they argued that Executive Order 11063 should be extended to encompass more housing. The White House subsequently countered that the existing order implemented the maximum Presidential power and that extension could raise constitutional problems. (At least one prominent rights leader agreed. Just before he left office in 1969, President Johnson told a news conference that Clarence Mitchell, Washington director of the National Assn. for the Advancement of Colored People, agreed that open housing could be effectively enforced only if it had the force of a law enacted by Congress.)

Americans for Democratic Action (ADA), a liberal organization which strongly backed civil rights legislation, gave this assessment of the President's handling of Title IV in its Aug. 12 "Legislative Newsletter," after House passage of HR 14765:

"Civil rights advocates did not seek fair housing legislation since, unlike other civil rights issues, housing segregation could be effectively banned by Executive Order. ADA had frequently urged the President to broaden the Executive Order (11063) to cover all federally assisted banks and lending institutions. A primary practical reason for avoiding the statutory route is that housing discrimination is a sensitive political issue. Fair housing referenda have been defeated.... A fair housing provision, to civil rights advocates, would only serve to complicate major legislation on ending segregated justice and deterring violence. Perhaps the very political sensitivity of the fair housing issue resulted in the President placing the responsibility on Congress. Civil rights supporters, having lost the battle to extend the Executive Order, had no choice but to support fair housing legislation. If the legislation were to be defeated, there was no realistic chance of obtaining an Executive Order anyway. By urging legislation, the Administration was precluding a policy of barring housing discrimination by Executive Order."

Other organizations supporting open housing agreed that an extended Executive Order was preferable. The National Committee Against Discrimination in Housing (NCDH) April 28, the day the Administration bill was submitted, called the Administration proposal "totally inadequate in itself to meet today's critical national problem of the explosive racial ghetto." It called for extension of Executive Order 11063.

had been submitted. (*For story on the Planning Session and White House Conference, see p. 392.*)

In addition to that report, the President had available in formulating his 1966 civil rights program the Nov. 14, 1965, report of the Civil Rights Commission. That report, based on a study of law enforcement in the South, recommended a federal law protecting civil rights workers and others exercising their rights.

The 1966 Bill. Unlike 1964 and 1965, the year 1966 produced no central goal for civil rights leaders, and the Administration bill reflected that development. The legislative history of the provisions of the Administration bill was as follows:

Titles I and II. These titles sought to guarantee nondiscriminatory selection of federal and state jurors, respectively. The need for reform in this area was first pointed out on the national level by the Civil Rights Commission in its 1961 report. Civil rights leaders frequently charged that discrimination in the selection of state juries was widespread in the South, and such discrimination was the subject of several Supreme Court decisions over the years. No such reform measures had been included in any recent Administration proposal prior to 1966.

Title III. In the Administration bill, this title authorized the Attorney General to initiate desegregation suits with regard to public schools and accommodations. (It became Title VI of the House-passed version of HR 14765.) It had been put forward in 1959 by House Judiciary Committee Chairman Emanuel Celler (D N.Y.), Sen. Paul H. Douglas (D Ill.) and Sen. Jacob K. Javits (R N.Y.) but had been rejected by Congress when it considered the Civil Rights Act of 1960. A modified version of this title was included as Title III of the Civil Rights Act of 1964; it required the Attorney General to receive a complaint from aggrieved individuals before filing suit and imposed other limitations. Those limitations, which the Administration sought to eliminate, were largely written back into Title VI of HR 14765 by amendments on the House floor.

Title IV. The open housing proposal came as a genuine surprise to Congress. No President in recent years had proposed such a law. An 1866 law purported to equalize the rights of Negroes to buy, sell and rent housing, and the Housing Act of 1949, for example, declared federal policy to be that all Americans were entitled to decent housing. But the only federal action on the issue in recent years had been Executive Order 11063, signed Nov. 24, 1962, by President Kennedy, which prohibited discrimination in federally assisted housing. The order did not apply to conventional loans and mortgages, including those made by institutions regulated or insured by federal agencies.

Congress rejected proposals for a statutory ban on discrimination in public housing when considering the Housing Act of 1949 and on repeated occasions thereafter, in 1950, 1954, 1955 and 1959. Rep. Adam C. Powell (D N.Y.) led the fight for such a provision in 1955 and 1959.

The Civil Rights Commission in its 1959 report urged President Eisenhower to sign an executive order similar to the one Mr. Kennedy later signed; in its 1961 report, it urged a statutory ban on discrimination by federally insured mortgage institutions, in federally assisted urban renewal programs and in programs for persons displaced by clearance under the Highway Acts.

While some participants at the Planning Session in 1965 urged enactment of a federal open housing law, many considered the proposal politically explosive and urged extension of Executive Order 11063 to cover federally insured or regulated banking institutions.

Title V. A law protecting civil rights workers was one urgently sought by civil rights advocates in late 1965 and early 1966. It was perhaps the one provision they considered essential in 1966. While efforts to pass a federal anti-lynching law dated back to the 1930s, a proposal for a general civil rights law to protect security of the person first appeared in the Democratic party platform of 1948. The Civil Rights Commission as early as 1961 and as late as its Nov. 14, 1965, report urged enactment of such a statute. No Administration proposed such a law until 1966, however.

Drafting of Title V was delayed in the spring of 1966 until after the Supreme Court ruled in two cases, *U.S. v. Price* and *U.S. v. Guest* (March 28, 1966). Those cases dealt with the powers of the Federal Government to prosecute for violent acts by private persons as well as by state or local officers against persons exercising their civil rights. By 9-0 votes, the Court gave a broad interpretation to federal powers in this area and sustained the Government's power to prosecute under two existing Reconstruction statutes, 18 U.S.C. 241 and 242, enacted in 1870 and 1866, respectively. Justice William J. Brennan Jr., concurring in *Guest*, said that the "weakness" of Section 241 was that it did not define which rights were protected; he said that "the remedy is for Congress to write a law without this defect." The Administration's Title V was intended to be that remedy. Six Justices said that Congress had power under the 14th Amendment to punish "all conspiracies—with or without state action —that interfere with 14th Amendment rights."

House Title III. The House Judiciary Committee added its own Title III to the Administration bill, renumbering the Administration's Title III as Title VI. The House Title III authorized the Attorney General to bring suits to prevent the deprivation of a person's rights. It first was proposed by President Eisenhower in 1956 but was rejected by Congress when it considered the Civil Rights Act of 1957. As it came up in subsequent years, it was known as "old Part III." It was recommended by the Civil Rights Commission in its 1963 report. A modified version of this provision was included as Title IX of the Civil Rights Act of 1964; that title authorized the Attorney General to intervene in private suits where persons alleged denial of equal protection of the laws.

1966 HOUSE ACTION

Subcommittee No. 5 of the House Judiciary Committee June 16 approved an amended version of HR 14765 and, with the exception of Title IV (the open housing provision), recommended enactment. The Subcommittee included Title IV in its original form and without recommendation.

Reports indicated that Subcommittee Chairman Celler had decided to move the bill along to the full Committee for action on Title IV rather than let the bill become deadlocked in Subcommittee over the title.

The Committee June 28 began consideration of Title IV in executive session, but well before that, pressures were mounting for compromise on the Administration's total ban on discrimination in the sale or rental of housing. Katzenbach May 5 had said in House testimony that some compromise was possible.

A triangle of force developed among supporters, opponents and the Justice Department. Dirksen, the leading opponent, and Attorney General Katzenbach met to discuss the bill on June 15, but both denied making a deal on Title IV. On Friday, June 24, Katzenbach met with Chairman Celler and Republican Committee members William M. McCulloch (Ohio) and Charles McC. Mathias Jr. (Md.). All reportedly assented to the view that, in order to win House passage, Title IV must exempt sales of owner-occupied homes and rentals of small owner-occupied buildings. No details were agreed upon.

By Monday, June 27, a compromise sponsored by Mathias and Rep. James C. Corman (D Calif.) was emerging and was said to be acceptable to the Justice Department. It exempted owner-occupied buildings of up to four dwelling units. The Leadership Conference on Civil Rights met June 27 and decided to press for changes, limiting the exemption to owner-occupied one-family houses and prohibiting real estate brokers from discriminating. The Conference understood that the proposed compromise permitted brokers to discriminate if selling a house for an exempted owner; Mathias subsequently confirmed that interpretation of the compromise. Late on June 27, the Conference communicated its views to the Justice Department, which declined to sponsor the changes for fear they would endanger passage of the bill. The Conference then suggested concentrating on barring real estate brokers from discriminating, but that, too, was turned down.

Meanwhile, Mathias telephoned several key Republican leaders around the nation on the evening of June 27; he won their support for his view that a compromise was better than Republicans being blamed for killing the open housing provision. Among others, he called Pennsylvania Gov. William W. Scranton, New York City Mayor John V. Lindsay, New York Gov. Nelson A. Rockefeller, Michigan Gov. George Romney, a spokesman for Illinois Senate candidate Charles H. Percy and Charles P. Taft.

When the Committee met June 28, the Mathias amendment, as it had come to be known, was rejected. A motion to kill Title IV altogether was narrowly rejected on a 15-17 vote, with 14 Northern Democrats joined by three Republicans—Mathias, William T. Cahill (N.J.) and Arch A. Moore Jr. (W.Va.)—voting "nay." Several amendments designed to weaken the bill were rejected, reportedly by a coalition of liberal civil rights supporters and of Southerners and other opponents, who sought to report such a strong bill that it would encounter opposition on the floor.

A move by Robert W. Kastenmeier (D Wis.) to report the bill without further change was overwhelmingly defeated, and the June 28 meeting ended in deadlock.

Vote on Title IV. The Committee met again the morning of June 29 and found its vehicle for compromise in a slightly revised version of the Mathias amendment, reworked during the night. The amendment was adopted on a 21-13 vote (D 17-6; R 4-7).

The Committee also adopted, 13-4, an Administration-opposed amendment, offered by Rep. John Conyers Jr. (D Mich.) and backed by the Leadership Conference, which created a Federal Fair Housing Board with enforcement powers akin to those of the National Labor Relations Board.

The final housing provision contained certain other minor exemptions: sale of land intended to be used for housing was dropped from coverage, as were transactions by religious, fraternal and educational organizations; and owners and developers engaging in two or less trans-

actions a year were exempted, regardless of whether they occupied the housing involved. However, the main exemption was for sale and rental of owner-occupied one-to-four-family homes.

Following the June 29 meeting, Chairman Celler said that he supported the bill: "All good legislation is the result of a compromise." He added: "At long last we have a fair housing provision. Without it, the civil rights bill would have been like a wine cellar without a corkscrew."

The Committee June 30 reported the bill.

Passage

The House Aug. 9, by a 259-157 (R 76-62; D 183-95) roll-call vote, passed HR 14765 with amendments and sent it to the Senate. Passage came after 12 days of debate, which began July 25, and after action on 77 amendments. Several key amendments were accepted, modifying the open housing provision (Title IV) and adding an anti-riot provision.

President Johnson Aug. 10 lauded the bill as "an important new milestone" for civil rights but expressed regret that the open housing provision was "not as comprehensive as what we proposed and sought." He said that "practically, the House has barred bigotry in all new housing and in apartment houses."

Key Amendments. House passage of HR 14765 followed four roll-call votes on Aug. 9, three of them on key amendments and one on a motion by Arch A. Moore (R W.Va.) to recommit the bill to the Judiciary Committee with instructions to delete Title IV. That motion was rejected by a **190-222** vote.

An earlier vote, on Aug. 3, on an amendment permitting real estate brokers to discriminate when selling or renting the house of an exempt owner (the "Mathias amendment") appeared to end in a 179-179 tie. The presiding officer, Richard Bolling (D Mo.), broke the tie by voting for the amendment.

Key House changes in the bill as submitted by the Administration included the exemptions in the open housing provision, which were added by the Judiciary Committee and a floor amendment offered by Charles McC. Mathias Jr. (R Md.). The Mathias amendment permitted a real estate broker to follow the written instructions of the homeowner, even if discriminatory, in the sale or rental of a home, providing the broker did not solicit the instructions. Another amendment, offered by William C. Cramer (R Fla.), made it a crime to travel in interstate commerce with intent to incite riot or commit an act of violence. The House also added an amendment, offered by Basil L. Whitener (D N.C.), which required the Attorney General to have received a written complaint of denial of equal protection of the laws before instituting a suit to desegregate public schools or facilities. The Mathias, Cramer and Whitener amendments were all accepted in debate and again at the end of debate Aug. 9 by roll-call votes.

Voting. The winning margin on passage was provided by a combination of 183 Democrats and 76 Republicans, who were opposed by 95 Democrats and 62 Republicans. There were 169 Northern Democrats favoring passage (and 17 against) while 78 Southern Democrats opposed passage and 14 favored it. The 14 were: Albert (Okla.), Brooks (Texas), de la Garza (Texas), Farnsley (Ky.), Fascell (Fla.), Fulton (Tenn.), Gibbons (Fla.), Gonzalez (Texas), Grider (Tenn.), Johnson (Okla.),

Pepper (Fla.), Perkins (Ky.), Weltner (Ga.) and Young (Texas). All voted against recommittal except de la Garza and Young, who voted to recommit the bill.

The most lopsided vote was on the Cramer antiriot amendment, which was accepted by a 389-25 roll-call vote. No Republican voted against the amendment and only one Southern Democrat, Gonzalez, opposed it.

The vote on the most controversial amendment, that of Mathias, which permitted real estate brokers to follow discriminatory instructions of their principal, was 237-176; both parties split deeply on the amendment, as Democrats divided 168 for and 107 against and Republicans split evenly, 69 for and 69 against. The amendment was popular with Northern Democrats, who voted 150 for and 33 against. Their intent was to save Title IV from defeat.

Among the Members not voting on any roll call was the most prominent Negro in the House, Adam C. Powell (D N.Y.), chairman of the House Education and Labor Committee. He was paired against recommittal and for passage, however. Powell, who reportedly appeared on the floor only once during debate, Aug. 10 said he did not vote for the bill because it was a "phony carrot stick" which was "aimed solely at the Negro middle-class and does absolutely nothing for the black masses who still are forced to live in rat-infested hovels."

Four of the six Negroes in the House voted for passage and against recommittal. They were: Conyers (D Mich.), Dawson (D Ill.), Diggs (D Mich.) and Nix (D Pa.); Powell and Hawkins (D Calif.) voted on neither roll call.

The entire Republican leadership voted for recommittal of the bill and also for passage, with the exception of Richard H. Poff (R Va.), secretary of the House Republican Conference, who voted for recommittal and against passage. Among the Democratic leadership, only Whip Hale Boggs (D La.) voted for recommittal and against passage.

Lobbying. HR 14765 generated powerful lobbying efforts for and against the bill as it moved to the House floor. The principal efforts were mounted by the Leadership Conference on Civil Rights for the bill and by the National Assn. of Real Estate Boards (NAREB) against it.

As it had done on civil rights legislation in 1964 and 1965, the Conference set up a special Capitol Hill headquarters to coordinate lobbying efforts. The Conference organized visits to House Members by individuals and by delegations from Congressional districts. Two dozen or more regular lobbyists from constituent organizations of the Conference, such as the AFL-CIO, National Assn. for the Advancement of Colored People (NAACP), AFL-CIO Industrial Union Department, Americans for Democratic Action (ADA) and other similar groups also visited House Members.

The Conference July 21 sent out an "urgent bulletin" to constituent groups, appealing for delegations from home areas to visit Members on the Hill and to urge support for the bill. The bulletin urged individuals and groups unable to visit Washington to write to their House Members. The Conference told CQ that it was particularly interested in bringing to Washington influential individuals and local leaders from House Members' home districts.

The Conference also organized a press conference and rally July 26 at the Statler-Hilton Hotel in Washington. Roy Wilkins of the NAACP said the Conference opposed the Mathias amendment and that the bill already had been weakened by the House Judiciary Committee. Celler defended the bill as a necessary compromise.

Wilkins and Clarence Mitchell, the NAACP's Washington, D.C., representative, met with House GOP Leader Ford for an hour on July 28 in an effort to win endorsement of Title IV. The House Republican Policy Committee Aug. 1 formally came out against the title, however.

As the crucial Aug. 3 test vote on Title IV approached, a tactical split developed among the bill's supporters in the civil rights movement. Most spokesmen for major groups in the Conference opposed the new Mathias amendment; they contended that the bill did not have to be weakened beyond the Committee version to assure passage. The United Auto Workers and United Steelworkers of America (both AFL-CIO), for example, sent telegrams to House Members urging defeat of the floor amendment.

Other groups within the Conference—notably the AFL-CIO national headquarters—reportedly took the view that unless the title were "softened" by accepting the Mathias amendment, the entire title might be defeated by conservative opposition. No official pronouncement was made of this position, however. After the Mathias amendment survived the test vote Aug. 3 by one vote (180-179), the Conference indicated that it would support the title as amended despite its official opposition to the Mathias amendment.

The NAREB and its Realtors' Washington (D.C.) Committee meanwhile continued to send out literature to its members urging them to write to House Members to urge defeat of Title IV. The July 18 edition of Realtor's Headlines, a NAREB publication, issued a "Call to Action" to realtors, stating that the housing title of the bill was "full of booby traps" and "restrictions against which you cannot protect yourself...." On the same day, the Realtors' Washington Committee sent a bulletin to local real estate boards calling the House Judiciary Committee version of Title IV "more onerous and more oppressive than the original version" and calling on local realtors to "generate an immediate wave of indignation by all citizens against Title IV."

Provisions—Following are the major provisions of HR 14765, as passed by the House:

Title I. Prohibited discrimination in the selection of federal jurors on the basis of race, color, religion, sex, national origin or economic status.

Provided uniform procedures for selection of federal jurors by a jury commission with jurors to be drawn publicly from a master jury wheel containing the names of at least one-half of one percent of the registered voters in the district.

Excluded persons illiterate in English or charged with or convicted of a crime punishable by imprisonment for more than one year.

Authorized the defendant or the Attorney General to challenge selection procedures and authorized the court to stay criminal proceedings or dismiss the indictment pending selection of a conforming jury.

Title II. Prohibited discrimination in the selection of state jurors on the basis of race, color, religion, sex, national origin or economic status.

Prohibited distinction in selecting jurors on the basis of sex.

Authorized the Attorney General, after notice to local officials, to seek injunctive relief to prevent denial of any defendant's rights.

Authorized federal district courts to suspend state jury qualifications, to require use of objective criteria in selection of jurors, to require maintenance of records and to appoint a master to act as jury official.

If such proceedings were initiated, required state officials to produce records and information on jury selection procedures and required state officials to preserve jury records for at least four years.

Title III. Authorized the potential victim to seek injunctive relief to prevent a person from engaging in any act which would deprive another of a right secured by the Constitution or by federal law on account of his race, color, religion or national origin, including the right to speak, assemble, petition or otherwise express himself for the purpose of securing equal rights. Authorized the Attorney General to bring such suits to end a pattern or practice of resistance to the full enjoyment of such rights.

Title IV. Made it unlawful for any real estate agent or salesman or person engaging in more than two housing transactions within 12 months to discriminate on the basis of race, color, religion, national origin or number or age of children in the sale or rental of any dwelling, in the terms of sale or rental, in written or oral advertising or representations, in showing the dwelling, in representing that the dwelling was unavailable or in providing access to multiple-listing services.

Permitted a real estate broker or his agent to discriminate in the sale or rental of a dwelling on express written instruction to do so from an owner otherwise exempt, provided the broker or agent did not encourage or solicit the instruction.

Made it unlawful for any such person to engage in any act which restricted the availability of housing to any person on the same grounds as listed above; and prohibited inducing sale or lease by representations about the entry into the neighborhood of persons of a particular race.

Exempted persons renting rooms in their own homes, owner-occupants of dwellings of no more than four living units and nonprofit religious, charitable and educational organizations.

Prohibited banks and other institutions, but only those in the business of lending, from discriminating in financing home purchases or improvements.

Authorized any party to seek court relief to enforce the Title; authorized federal district courts to defer to state fair housing agencies before continuing proceedings; and authorized the Attorney General to intervene in such private suits and to initiate suits to prevent patterns or practices of discrimination.

Established a Fair Housing Board to hear charges filed by the Secretary of Housing and Urban Development after the latter's investigation of complaints; authorized the Board to issue orders for appropriate relief and to seek enforcement orders through circuit courts of appeals following procedures used by the National Labor Relations Board.

Directed the Secretary to make a study of discrimination in housing and to publicize the results.

Title V. Made it unlawful to injure or intimidate any person because of his race, color, religion or national origin lawfully engaging in voting, campaigning, poll-watching, attending public school, participating in any publicly administered program, applying for employment or working, engaging in a housing transaction, serving on a jury, using any vehicle or common carrier, participating in any federally aided activity or enjoying goods or services of any public accommodation.

Made it unlawful to injure or intimidate any person in order to discourage him from engaging in such activities or having urged others to participate.

Made it unlawful to injure or intimidate public officials in order to discourage them from affording equal treatment in participating in such activities.

Set penalties at a $1,000 fine and one year in jail; $10,000 fine and 10 years in jail if bodily injury resulted; and any term of years or life in jail if death resulted.

Made it unlawful for any person to move in interstate commerce or use the mails with intent to incite to riot, to commit any crime of violence, arson or bombing or any other felony under state or federal law or to assist or encourage others in commission of such crimes; and set penalties at up to a $10,000 fine and five years in prison.

Title VI. Amended Title III of the Civil Rights Act of 1964 to authorize the Attorney General to bring suit, after notice to local officials and upon written complaint from an aggrieved individual, to desegregate public schools and accommodations.

Provided that desegregation in such suits should not mean the assignment of pupils to public schools to overcome racial imbalance and amended Title VI of the 1964 Act to include a similar proviso regarding racial imbalance.

Title VII. Amended Title III of the Civil Rights Act of 1960 to authorize the Attorney General to permit local election officials to destroy election records.

Title VIII. Authorized an open-ended appropriation to carry out provisions of the Act.

Required the Attorney General to report annually to Congress and the President on enforcement and other activities undertaken pursuant to the various civil rights laws.

SENATE ACTION

Invoking Senate procedure, Majority Leader Mike Mansfield (D Mont.) Aug. 11 intercepted HR 14765, which had passed the House on Aug. 9, and succeeded in having it placed directly on the Senate calendar Aug. 12 without referral to committee. The bill, however, could not be brought up for debate without unanimous consent or a majority vote—if opponents of the measure allowed the motion for debate to reach a vote.

In announcing his intention to bypass the Committee, Mansfield said that because of the press of other legislation he did not expect an effort to be made to bring up the bill for debate until early September. He said the anticipated Southern filibuster against the bill could be broken only with the assistance of Minority Leader Dirksen: "Without him, we can't get cloture," Mansfield said Aug. 11. Dirksen's opposition to the open housing section had already been made clear.

The first effort to call up HR 14765 for debate in the Senate was made Sept. 6 by Philip A. Hart (D Mich.), the bill's floor manager. His request for unanimous consent to consider the bill was blocked by the objection of Sen. Sam J. Ervin Jr. (D N.C.). On Sept. 7, Hart moved to set aside consideration of a pending bill (S 3553—for the relief of Mary T. Brooks) and to consider HR 14765. From that date until Sept. 19, when the second cloture motion failed, all debate was technically on Hart's motion to begin consideration of the civil rights bill. The bill itself was never formally before the Senate.

Before the Southern filibuster began Sept. 8, Hart told a news conference, "If Dirksen delivers the votes this year, we'll have a good bill." This was a reference to the need for Dirksen to support cloture and to bring with him most of his fellow Republicans so that the necessary two-thirds majority could be obtained.

Dirksen, however, was quoted as saying after Hart's press conference, "For all practical purposes, the civil rights bill is dead." The Minority Leader had spoken against the bill in a speech Sept. 7, attacking not only the open housing title but also Titles I and II on the selection of federal and state jurors.

Neither a major debate nor a traditional filibuster fully developed over HR 14765. Adjournment was forced on Sept. 6, 7 and 9 for lack of a quorum. At the beginning of the next week, on Sept. 12, Mansfield filed his first cloture petition. He promised the Senate he would not resort to surprise tactics, and the Senate continued to consider and act upon other legislation during the debate.

As it had been in the House, much of the debate was over the constitutionality of the bill, with opponents arguing that Title IV especially had no constitutional foundation. The bill's supporters denied that, and argued that if Hart's motion were agreed to, the bill then would be subject to amendment.

Several Senators from both sides of the aisle defended Dirksen against what they said were attempts to blame him for the impending defeat of the bill. For himself, Dirksen Sept. 13 said: "I know nobody under the canopy of the bright blue heavens that can say anything to change my mind."

Cloture Rejected Twice

The Senate Sept. 19, by a 52-41 roll-call vote, rejected Mansfield's second cloture motion to limit debate on Hart's motion to consider HR 14765. The motion failed by 10 votes of receiving the two-thirds majority of those voting necessary to adopt a cloture motion. Seven Senators were absent.

Rejection of the cloture motion ended consideration by Congress of civil rights legislation in the 1966 session. It was the first time since 1957, when major civil rights legislation was first enacted in this century, that an Administration civil rights bill had been defeated.

The Senate Sept. 14 by a **54-42** roll-call vote had rejected an identical cloture motion, but Majority Leader Mansfield decided to make one more effort to limit debate and to begin consideration of the bill.

Immediately after the Sept. 19 vote, Mansfield acted to remove the bill from Senate consideration. He moved to adjourn the Senate, in order to kill Hart's pending motion. (A motion to consider a bill has to be renewed at the start of a new legislative day.) The Senate adjourned at 2:59 p.m. and met again in a new legislative day at 3:05 p.m.

Mansfield explained that in view of the two votes on cloture, it would be "futile" to continue efforts to take up the bill. "The attitudes are clear," he said. "The vote on cloture on whether or not to take up can only be interpreted as a vote against civil rights legislation in this session."

Mansfield suggested that "renewed efforts" on civil rights legislation would be made in 1967. "If the prospects for passage are to be improved," he said, "the question of riotings, marches, shootings and inflammatory statements, which have characterized this simmering summer of 1966 in urban areas of the nation, will have to be faced frankly and bluntly."

Dirksen defended his record as a supporter of civil rights legislation in the past, but said that "when conscience and conviction tell me that a bill is full of mischief," he would pursue any course to defeat it. He said he had been trying to "spar for time" to tell the nation about the contents of the bill.

Voting. Mansfield Sept. 15 said in filing the second cloture motion that he hoped to pick up votes over the Sept. 14 roll-call vote, but actually supporters of cloture lost two votes because of absences.

The key vote was that taken Sept. 14 and analysis of that vote, compared to civil rights cloture votes in the two previous years, indicated the crucial importance of Republican support in achieving the two-thirds majority necessary for cloture. That importance was underscored by the President, who on the night of Sept. 13 spent 90 minutes pleading with Dirksen at the White House to alter his position.

On the Sept. 14 vote, 12 Republicans, including Dirksen, who had supported the cloture vote in 1965 voted against the 1966 cloture motion. One Democrat, Lausche (Ohio), also switched from support to opposition.

As voting on the cloture motion ended, Senate Judiciary Committee Chairman James O. Eastland (D Miss.), a longtime foe of civil rights legislation, released a statement in the press gallery which said: "The civil rights advocates who hope to force an interracial society have been completely routed. The old-time coalition of Southern Democrats and Republicans were united and effective." He said that it would not be long before "we can start the fight to repeal those vicious measures," referring to civil rights bills passed in recent years.

Equal Employment

Legislation to strengthen and broaden the federal equal employment law came to a vote in 1966 but was not enacted. It was the only time the issue was brought to a roll-call passage vote in either chamber during the 89th and 90th Congresses. (However, a procedural vote—which could have blocked any final vote—occurred in 1965. *See p. 365.*)

The vote occurred when the House April 27 by a 300-93 roll call passed a bill (HR 10065) which had been awaiting action since late 1965; action was delayed then because of the controversial nature of the bill and the normal end-of-session desire to adjourn. HR 10065 would have revised Title VII of the 1964 Civil Rights Act which prohibited employment discrimination based on race, color, religion or national origin. To carry out this mandate, the 1964 law created an Equal Employment Oppor-

EEOC Membership Changes

The Equal Employment Opportunity Commission was hampered during its early years by the turnover in Commission membership. The 1964 Civil Rights Act establishing the EEOC provided for five commissioners (one of whom was to be chairman) serving five-year terms. (The first five commissioners were appointed to terms of five, four, three, two and one years to establish a rotation.)

One and two commissioner vacancies were in existence during upwards of one-half the time after the EEOC came into existence in July 1965; about 15 months out of the 40 through October 1968. The first vacancy occurred when the Commission's first chairman, Franklin D. Roosevelt Jr., resigned May 11, 1966. All five positions were not filled again until 1968. The Commission operated in 1966 with one vacancy for three and one-half months and two vacancies for four months (including a vacancy in the chairmanship for four months), in 1967 with one vacancy all year and two vacancies for five and one-half months (including a vacancy in the chairmanship for one month), and in 1968 (through October) with one vacancy for five months.

Following is a list of EEOC members and their terms of office. Four Negroes have served as commissioners: Aileen Hernandez, Samuel Jackson, Clifford L. Alexander Jr., and William H. Brown III.

	Length Of Term (Years)	Began [1]	Expired	Resigned
Aileen Hernandez (D)	5	7/2/65	7/1/70	11/10/66
Luther Holcomb (D)	4	7/2/65	7/1/69	
Samuel Jackson [2] (R)	3	7/2/65	7/1/68	
Franklin D. Roosevelt Jr.* (D)	2	7/2/65	7/1/67	5/11/66
Richard Graham (R)	1	7/2/65	7/1/66	
Vincente T. Ximenes (D)	5	5/18/67	7/1/71	
(To replace Graham)				
Stephen N. Shulman* (D)		9/15/66	7/1/67	
(To fill Roosevelt term)				
Clifford L. Alexander Jr.* (D)	5	8/2/67	7/1/72	
(To replace Shulman)				
Elizabeth J. Kuck (R)		1/26/68	7/1/70	
(To fill Hernandez term)				
William H. Brown III (R)[2]		5/6/69	7/1/73	
(To replace Jackson)				

NOTE: Ximenes, Alexander and Brown were named to five-year terms although their Senate confirmations came after the beginning of their terms.

[1] *The first five are the original EEOC members; the date is that on which the law went into effect. The dates by the other five members are those on which the Senate confirmed their appointments.*

[2] *The vacancy created by the expiration of Jackson's term was filled by President Johnson on Oct. 12, 1968, when he appointed William H. Brown III, a Negro, to fill the post. Congress did not act on the appointment before adjournment, but the President—following adjournment—gave Brown an interim appointment. President Nixon renominated Brown in 1969 after taking office.*

* *Chairman of the EEOC. (Luther Holcomb was vice-chairman and acting chairman during the periods when the chairman's position was vacant.)*

tunity Commission. However, the law gave the EEOC no enforcement powers; it invested the agency only with authority to conciliate disputes arising under the title and EEOC guidelines. HR 10065 empowered the EEOC to initiate charges of unlawful discrimination, to issue cease and desist orders and to order hiring or reinstatement, with or without back pay. The bill also increased the pace at which EEOC coverage expanded to smaller

companies and labor unions. It also broadened coverage to include firms or unions with as few as eight employees or members (existing law covered only organizations with 25 or more employees or members).

HR 10065 died when the Senate did not act on it before adjournment of the 89th Congress.

The measure was strongly supported by civil rights groups, which believed that the lack of EEOC enforcement powers made the 1964 law an impotent weapon against discrimination. HR 10065 was endorsed by President Johnson in an April 28 civil rights message, but was not mentioned in the President's State of the Union Message Jan. 12. His endorsement, plus that of the AFL-CIO in 1966 and participants in the White House conference, "To Fulfill These Rights," held June 1-2, gave the bill a push which observers thought would carry it to enactment. But opposition was strong to the controversial legislation. Southerners, as expected, were against it as were many business groups which feared increased federal interference in their operation. Although HR 10065 passed the House with bipartisan support, R 98-32; D 202-61 (ND 179-3; SD 23-58), the House Republican Policy Committee April 26 (the day before the vote on passage) adopted a statement which said the bill would transform the EEOC into an agency rivaling the National Labor Relations Board and that it would diminish the role of the states in unfair employment cases. Many businessmen and numerous Republican Members of Congress had been sharply critical of the NLRB over the years for what they considered improper use of its powers in resolving labor-management disputes and favoritism toward unions at the expense of management.

As the summer progressed, interest in HR 10065 dwindled as the attention and energies of the civil rights groups turned to the major battle over the 1966 Civil Rights Act which included open housing provisions. But the rights groups lost on that bill as well as on HR 10065 as the Senate refused to act.

1967

Omnibus Civil Rights Bill

President Johnson Feb. 15 sent Congress a message proposing enactment of the Civil Rights Act of 1967. Most of the proposals the President put forth were similar to those he unsuccessfully requested in 1966 and, also like 1966, were submitted in a single omnibus bill. Major features of the 1967 package included a prohibition against racial and religious discrimination in the sale and rental of housing, a ban on racial and other types of discrimination in the selection of state and federal jurors, and safeguards for persons exercising or urging others to exercise certain federally protected rights. The proposals also contained two new Administration requests which strengthened enforcement of antidiscrimination employment law and provided for administrative, as well as judicial, enforcement of the housing discrimination ban. The bill was introduced in both the House (HR 5700) and the Senate (S 1026).

Congress, however, never gave serious attention to the omnibus bill and Administration supporters and civil rights advocates did not push the measure. Instead, the Administration's forces tried a new tactic of splitting the omnibus bill and introducing each of the President's proposals as a separate bill. The intent was to avoid the formidable task of obtaining committee action on a package bill. It was generally thought that splitting the package into parts permitted sacrificing the more controversial parts to secure passage of the remainder. As it turned out, only one minor bill—extending the Civil Rights Commission—was enacted in 1967, although ground work was laid for passage of major legislation in early 1968.

The only hearings on the Administration's omnibus civil rights bill (S 1026) were held, after a long delay, by the Senate Judiciary Subcommittee on Constitutional Rights. The bill was not reported in 1967. The House Judiciary Committee did not hold hearings on the House version.

The Senate hearings were insisted upon by Subcommittee Chairman Sam J. Ervin (D N.C.), who had denounced every section of the Administration's bill. Because hearings were going on separately on the separate bills which were introduced after the omnibus measure, Ervin's move was widely interpreted as an attempt to stall action by considering the most controversial provisions, such as open housing, along with the provisions which Congress was considered likely to enact.

Civil Rights Commission

Congress voted in 1967 to extend the life of the Civil Rights Commission for an additional five years (through Jan. 31, 1973). The measure, which originally was Title VI of the Administration's omnibus civil rights bill, was the least controversial of the President's civil rights proposals and the only one enacted in 1967. An amendment, added in the Senate, limited the Commission's expenditures to the fiscal 1968 level—$2,650,000.

The Commission was established under the 1957 Civil Rights Act (PL 85-315) to study civil rights problems in general and to report to the President. Its life was extended several times after that, most recently in 1964 when it was authorized to continue through Jan. 31, 1968.

The extension bill (HR 10805) was passed by the House July 11 by a 284-89 roll-call vote. The Senate Judiciary Committee sent the bill to the floor Oct. 31 over the dissenting votes of four Southerners: Sam J. Ervin (D N.C.), James O. Eastland (D Miss.), John L. McClellan (D Ark.) and Strom Thurmond (R S.C.). It was passed by voice vote of the Senate Nov. 1, and the House Dec. 5 agreed to the Senate amendment limiting funds for the Commission. President Johnson signed the bill into law (PL 90-198) Dec. 14.

In a memorandum submitted to the House Judiciary Committee, the Commission said it hoped to broaden the scope of its work beyond the "hard core" civil rights problems such as the denials of the right to vote, housing discrimination and legally compelled school segregation. It said it had already begun work on "urban civil rights problems, with emphasis on the North"; the "subtler causes of unequal housing opportunity, such as the relationship between minority group income and the availability and location of housing for lower income families"; and school segregation resulting from factors other than legal compulsion. The Commission said it was also examining interrelated problems, such as the relationship

of housing patterns to unequal educational opportunities and the effect of the latter on the lack of employment opportunities for minority groups.

The Commission said it had dealt chiefly with the civil rights problems of Negroes, but there was a need for similar studies of the problems of Mexican-Americans and American Indians.

Civil Rights Workers Protection

A bill (HR 2516) to protect persons exercising or urging others to exercise certain federally protected rights was stalled in the Senate at the end of 1967 because of a threatened end-of-session filibuster. The Administration bill had been passed with amendments by the House Aug. 16 by a 327-93 roll-call vote after two days of delaying tactics by the bill's opponents. It was aimed principally at violent treatment of Negroes and civil rights workers in the South.

The Senate Judiciary Committee Oct. 25 by an 8-7 vote approved a version of HR 2516 which was similar to the Administration bill and omitted most House amendments. A weaker substitute version of the bill, proposed by Sen. Sam J. Ervin Jr. (D N.C.), was defeated when the Administration arranged to fly Sen. Hugh Scott (R Pa.), a liberal Republican, back from England to vote for the Administration version. Scott was lecturing at Oxford University.

Floor consideration of HR 2516 was postponed until 1968 by Senate Majority Leader Mike Mansfield (D Mont.) when a Southern-led filibuster was considered certain and Senate Minority Leader Everett McKinley Dirksen (R Ill.) indicated that he would not vote for a (debate-limiting) cloture motion.

On the last day of the session, Dec. 15, Mansfield quietly got consent of the Senate and made the bill the first business to be considered when the Senate came back to work in 1968. This deprived Southern opponents of the tactic they used in 1966, which was to filibuster against the motion to consider the bill.

When it finally passed the Senate in 1968, HR 2516 had become the vehicle for a strong open-housing amendment and other proposals aimed at rioters.

Provisions—As passed by the House, HR 2516:

Made it unlawful to injure, intimidate or interfere with, or attempt to injure or intimidate anyone because of his race, color, religion, political affiliation or national origin and because he was or had been lawfully engaged in voting, campaigning, pollwatching, attending public school, participating in a publicly administered program, applying for employment or working or joining a union, serving on a jury, using any vehicle or common carrier, participating in any federally aided activity, or enjoying goods or services of any public accommodation.

Made it unlawful to injure, intimidate or interfere with any person in order to discourage him from participating in such activities because of his race, color, religion, political affiliation or national origin, or because he had so participated, or urged others so to participate, or engaged in speech or peaceful assembly opposing any denial of the opportunity so to participate.

Made it unlawful to injure, intimidate or interfere with any public official acting in the performance of his duty to prevent or abate a riot, any policeman making a lawful arrest to prevent or abate a riot or any fireman attempting to extinguish a fire created by a disturbance resulting from a civil rights protest.

Set criminal penalties for these unlawful activities.

Links with Antiriot Bill. Throughout Congressional action on HR 2516 the bill was entangled in efforts to attach to it provisions aimed at rioters. In 1966 the protection bill had been Title V of the civil rights bill passed by the House that year. In acting on the 1966 bill the House added to Title V an amendment by Rep. William C. Cramer (R Fla.) making it illegal to move in interstate commerce to promote a riot or to commit an act of violence. Cramer's amendment was opposed by the floor manager of the civil rights bill, Emanuel Celler (D N.Y.), chairman of the House Judiciary Committee.

The 1966 bill died in the Senate, and in 1967, at the beginning of the new Congress, Cramer introduced an antiriot bill (HR 421) similar to his 1966 amendment. *(See following story.)* The Judiciary Committee took no action on the bill until Cramer on June 14 filed a discharge petition asking the House Rules Committee to relieve the Judiciary Committee of its jurisdiction over the bill. The Rules Committee Chairman, William M. Colmer (D Miss.), a civil rights opponent, soon announced that he would hold hearings on Cramer's discharge resolution.

At this point Judiciary Chairman Celler's Subcommittee No. 5 voted to combine the antiriot bill with the civil rights workers' protection bill (HR 2516). Rep. Colmer, however, vigorously opposed this action and threatened to proceed with Cramer's motion to take the antiriot bill away from the Judiciary Committee. Rep. Celler reluctantly gave in to Colmer and the full Judiciary Committee June 27 voted to report separate bills.

The antiriot bill (HR 421) was the first of the two bills taken up by the House. It was passed July 19. A month later, on Aug. 16, the House passed the bill to protect civil rights workers (HR 2516). Neither was enacted during 1967, however.

Cramer's resolution to force action on HR 421 constituted an unusual procedural move. Only on rare occasions had the Rules Committee exercised its power to report a bill not approved by the Committee to which it was originally referred. The last time such an action was undertaken was in 1964 by Rep. William M. Tuck (D Va.) when the Rules Committee dislodged from the Judiciary Committee Tuck's bill (HR 11926) which denied the Supreme Court and lower federal courts any jurisdiction over state legislative apportionment.

Antiriot Bill

The House on July 19 passed an antiriot bill (HR 421) by a wide margin. The roll call was 347-70. The Senate, however, took no action on the bill other than to hold some hearings. HR 421 prohibited crossing state lines to incite or carry on a riot or other violent disturbance. The bill, which did not have Administration support, was introduced by Rep. William C. Cramer (R Fla.) who had sponsored similar legislation in 1966. *(See preceding paragraph for a discussion of the relationship between HR 421 and another bill (HR 2516) to protect civil rights workers.)*

At the end of 1967, HR 421 was pending before the Senate Judiciary Committee which also was considering a stronger version of the bill. The Committee held 13 days of hearings on the bill in August, focusing on the summer's riots.

In House debate on HR 421 July 19, Cramer said his bill was "aimed at those professional agitators" who travel from city to city, "inflame the people...to violence and then leave the jurisdiction before the riot begins."

Rules Committee Chairman William M. Colmer (D Miss.) said the riots were an "organized conspiracy... backed by the Communists."

Celler, however, said the bill was "a futile gesture, neither preventative nor curative." The "basic reason" for rioting in ghettos, Celler said, "is the discontent of the Negro, his disenchantment as to promises made but not fulfilled, the dreary pace by which he achieves equality." This bill, he said, "will not allay but will, rather, arouse more deeply" the Negroes' anger and frustration.

Don Edwards (D Calif.) said the bill was "offensive to the Constitution and based on dangerous scapegoat thinking." The "underlying assumption" of HR 421 that "riots are caused by professional agitators who travel from state to state...is nonsense," Edwards said, "and all studies to date on riots have failed to substantiate this contention in any way."

Frank Thompson Jr. (D N.J.) charged that HR 421 was "in the nature of a bill of attainder aimed at one man—Stokely Carmichael." He added that it violated the requirements of due process because it "suffers from a vice of vagueness."

Richard D. McCarthy (D N.Y.) attempted to attach the provisions of the Administration firearms-control bill (HR 5384) to the bill, but the Chair sustained a point of order that the amendment was not germane. Lionel Van Deerlin (D Calif.) then offered an amendment making it a crime to furnish or to aid in furnishing a firearm, ammunition or destructive device for use in or in furtherance of a riot. The amendment was defeated by voice vote.

Provisions—As passed by the House, HR 421:

Specified that any person who traveled in or used a facility in interstate or foreign commerce, including the mail, with the intent to incite, organize, promote, encourage or carry on a riot, to commit any act of violence in furtherance of a riot, or to aid and abet any person in such acts, and thereafter performed or attempted to perform such acts was subject to a fine of up to $10,000, imprisonment for up to five years, or both.

Defined a riot as a public disturbance, involving acts of violence by groups of three or more persons, which poses an immediate danger of damage to property or persons.

Defined the term "to incite a riot, or to organize, promote, encourage or carry on a riot" as urging or instigating other persons to riot, but specified that it did not mean "the mere advocacy of ideas or the mere expression of belief."

Jury Selection

The Senate late in 1967 passed and sent to the House a bill (S 989) to prohibit discrimination in the selection of federal juries. The House took no action in 1967. (The bill was enacted early in 1968. *See p. 385.*)

The bill was similar in purpose to Title I of the Administration's omnibus 1967 civil rights package, but its supporters avoided labeling it a civil rights bill. S 989 received the qualified support of Sam J. Ervin Jr. (D N.C.), one of the most outspoken opponents of civil rights legislation on the Judiciary Committee. Only Committee Chairman James O. Eastland (D Miss.) was recorded against reporting S 989. (John L. McClellan (D Ark.), another Committee member and rights opponent, was not present during key sessions when the Committed acted on S 989.) The Senate passed S 989 Dec. 8 by voice vote.

State Jury Reform. Although the Senate passed legislation reforming procedures for the selection of federal juries, it took no action on a bill (S 1318) to prohibit discrimination in the selection of state juries. S 1318 incorporated the provisions of Title II of the Administration's omnibus civil rights bill which banned discrimination in state jury selection on the basis of race, religion, sex, national origin or economic status. It also authorized the Attorney General to sue persons discriminating in jury selection.

Open Housing

The only action taken in 1967 on the Administration's open-housing requests was three days of hearings by a Senate Subcommittee. The open housing requests made by President Johnson were considered the most controversial of his civil rights proposals and an important factor in defeat of the 1966 civil rights bill.

The President, in his 1967 civil rights message to Congress Feb. 15, 1967, noted the 1966 opposition to open housing and said that he was proposing it again because "it is decent and right. Injustice must be opposed, however difficult or unpopular the issue."

The open housing hearings were held by the Housing and Urban Affairs Subcommittee of the Senate Banking and Currency Committee under the chairmanship of Sen. John J. Sparkman (D Ala.). Open housing was also considered in hearings on the Administration's omnibus civil rights bill held by the Constitutional Rights Subcommittee of the Senate Judiciary Committee which had also held hearings on the 1966 bill.

The House took no action on open housing in 1967. Emanuel Celler (D N.Y.), chairman of the House Judiciary Committee and sponsor of the House civil rights bill (HR 5700), indicated Nov. 2 that the House would not act until the Senate had passed open housing legislation. He said that the "reluctance" of the House membership to act was understandable when it had "fought with moments of great bitterness for the open housing section (in the 1966 bill) only to have it killed in the Senate."

The Senate Subcommittee on Housing and Urban Affairs held hearings Aug. 21-23 on an Administration bill (S 1358) and other proposals to prohibit racial discrimination in the sale and rental of housing. S 1358 provided for a graduated, three-stage ban against racial discrimination in housing. The ban would: (1) apply only to federally owned or supported housing until the end of 1967; (2) be extended Jan. 1, 1968, to cover non-owner-occupied houses and those occupied by five or more families; and (3) cover all of the nation's 65 million housing units beginning Jan. 1, 1969, except certain noncommercial developments owned by churches and religious groups for housing persons of their own religious affiliation.

Robert C. Weaver, Secretary of Housing and Urban Development, testified that the fair housing legislation would "fill a void" in the nation's policy against discrimination. He said that progress toward nondiscrimination in housing was "intolerable," with less than 4 percent of the nation's housing supply currently under federal regulation. A significant feature of the Administration bill, Weaver said, was its graduated coverage of housing that would give time for adjustment before full coverage began on Jan. 1, 1969. Weaver estimated that 3.9 million units would be covered on enactment of S 1358; 11.8 million on Jan. 1, 1968; and all housing units, a total of 65 million, on Jan. 1, 1969.

Attorney General Ramsey Clark asserted that there was nothing in S 1358 to substantiate claims by its critics that the bill would constitute "forced housing." He said it would do just the opposite. He said it would "eliminate forced housing where racial minorities are barred from residential areas and confined to the ghetto. Sooner or later," Clark added, "we must manifest our national commitment to open housing.... Delay will prove costly, both in the faith of millions of Americans in our commitment to equal justice and in creation of new segregation."

Roy Wilkins, executive director of the National Association for the Advancement of Colored People, generally supported the Administration bill but criticized its graduated coverage. Wilkins argued for immediate full coverage.

George Meany, president of the AFL-CIO, supported the Administration bill, which he called "absolutely essential" to the achievement of such goals as desegregated schools and equal opportunity.

A spokesman for the National Association of Real Estate Boards (NAREB), testifying in opposition to S 1358, said the "drive for legislation of this nature had exacted its price in denying adequate housing for the poor in our urban ghettos." Declaring there was no "fair method of enforcing an unjust law," he said the NAREB was "convinced that the cause of improved race relations will be retarded, not enhanced, by the enactment of this measure."

Equal Employment

Legislation to strengthen and broaden the 1964 equal employment law (Title VII of the 1964 Civil Rights Act) again failed of enactment in 1967. Proposals received less action than in the 89th Congress when the House passed a bill to give the Equal Employment Opportunity Commission (EEOC) power to halt discriminatory employment practices. In 1967, a bill did not emerge from committee in either the Senate or House.

President Johnson requested the legislation in his Feb. 15, 1967, civil rights message, and a provision to allow the EEOC to issue cease-and-desist orders was included in his omnibus civil rights bill. The provision was later split off and made into a separate bill, partly because supporters thought it would have a better chance if it did not become involved with the entire rights package and partly because of procedural reasons (the EEOC proposal was the responsibility of a different committee than that handling the bulk of the civil rights package). Hearings were held and the bill (S 1308) was marked up by the Senate Labor and Public Welfare Subcommittee on Employment, Manpower and Poverty. But at the end of the session the legislation was still pending before the full Committee. No action was taken on similar proposals (HR 680) in the House.

The 1967 proposals were about the same as the provisions of the legislation passed by the House in 1966 which died in the Senate. The key provision was granting of enforcement powers to the EEOC, authority strongly opposed by Southerners and many businesses.

1968

Open Housing, Rights Protection, Rioting

Congress in 1968 enacted the first open housing law of the 20th Century. The law (HR 2516—PL 90-284) prohibited discrimination in the sale or rental of housing and was expected to cover 80 percent of all housing by 1970, when fully in effect.

The open housing law also included provisions to protect civil rights workers, and others who were exercising specified rights, from injury or intimidation. *(See below.)* Also in the law were a number of antiriot provisions that were added on the Senate floor and a section guaranteeing the constitutional rights of American Indians.

The major components of the bill, open housing, rights protection and antiriot prohibitions, had been considered by Congress in separate bills during the previous two years, but none had been enacted. In 1968, they were brought together in the Senate as one bill.

Final action on the bill came April 10 at a time of heightened racial tension following the assassination of Rev. Dr. Martin Luther King Jr. and the rioting that came in its wake in many cities, including Washington, D.C. The President signed the bill into law on April 11 (PL 90-284).

"Fair housing" had been considered the most sensitive area of civil rights legislation, and it was the last major area on which Congress took action. Congress had not passed open housing legislation since 1866. (The 1866 law, like other Reconstruction-era civil rights legislation, had been largely ignored. The Supreme Court in 1968 upheld the 1866 law. *See box p. 380.*) The opposition arguments were largely emotional and were based on the contention that homeowners had a basic right to sell or rent their homes as they saw fit.

Passage of the bill came as a surprise to many observers who had predicted at the beginning of the year that Congress would not pass open housing legislation in 1968. Congress appeared to be in a more conservative mood than when it had passed the last major civil rights legislation—the Civil Rights Act of 1964 (PL 88-352) and the Voting Rights Act of 1965 (PL 89-110). Although open housing legislation was before the Senate in both 1966 and 1967 leaders were not able to bring it to a vote.

Enforcement Funding. Congress in 1968 appropriated $2 million for fiscal 1969 for enforcement of the open housing provisions of PL 90-284. The Administration first asked $11.1 million (which was denied entirely) but later in the year reduced its request to $8 million. The

funds provided were carried in an end-of-session supplemental appropriations bill.

Previous Action. Congress had considered open housing proposals in 1966 but did not enact them because of a Senate filibuster following House passage. Neither chamber acted on open housing proposals (other than to hold a few hearings) in 1967, although President Johnson repeated his 1966 requests. The House in 1967 passed a bill (HR 2516) which provided protection for civil rights workers. The Senate Judiciary Committee reported this bill Nov. 2. *(For additional details see 1966 and 1967 chronologies, above.)*

Estimated Coverage. The following figures show estimated coverage of the open-housing provisions of PL 90-284.

	Housing by Category		Coverage by Stage (millions of units)		
	Housing Units, in Millions	Percent of Total Housing	Immediately	Dec. 31, 1968	Dec. 31, 1969
Covered					
Federally assisted housing	3.22	5.0%	.9	---	2.32
Multi-unit housing	11.8	18.1	---	11.8	---
2-, 3-, and 4-unit non-owner-occupied housing	8.0	12.3	---	8.0	---
Single-family housing	29.0	44.5	---	---	29.0
Subtotal	52.02	79.9%	.9	19.8	31.32
Percent of total housing, by stage			1.4%	30.4%	48.1%
Exempted					
"Mrs. Murphy" units[1]	5.5	8.4%			
Single-family units sold by owner-occupant	7.0	10.8			
Federally-assisted single-family units sold by owner-occupant	.58	0.9			
Subtotal	13.08	20.1%			
GRAND TOTAL	65.1	100%			

	Housing Units, in Millions	Percent of Housing
Total coverage as of:		
Enactment of HR 2516	.9	1.4%
Dec. 31, 1968	20.7	31.8%
Dec. 31, 1969	52.02	79.9%

[1] *These are dwellings of 2-4 units, one of which is occupied by the owner of the dwelling.*

Summary of 1968 Action

The House-passed civil rights protection bill (HR 2516) became the core of the 1968 legislation. As Congress adjourned Dec. 15, 1967, Senate Majority Leader Mike Mansfield (D Mont.) quietly made the House-passed bill the pending business for the Senate to consider when it returned from its Christmas recess Jan. 15. By this act the possibility of a Southern-led delay over a motion to bring up the bill for floor consideration was averted.

When President Johnson Jan. 24 presented his 1968 civil rights message to Congress, the Senate was in the second week of a leisurely debate on the House civil rights bill and a weakening amendment to it that had been offered by Sen. Sam J. Ervin (D N.C.), a leader of the opposition to the bill.

The President asked Congress to enact the five measures that were still pending from his 1967 request: open housing, civil rights protection, enforcement powers for the Equal Employment Opportunity Commission (EEOC) and reform of federal and state jury selection procedures. The message contained no new legislative proposals.

Most observers expected enactment of only two of the proposals—federal jury reform and the civil rights protection bill. They considered it very unlikely that action would be taken on open housing legislation. There were major stumbling blocks in the path of such legislation.

A coalition of Northern Democrats and Republicans was essential to passage of any civil rights bill in the Senate, as seen in the passage of the Civil Rights Act of 1964 and the Voting Rights Act of 1965. In those two years the Senate leadership was able to muster the two-thirds majority required to vote cloture on Southern-led filibusters when Senate Minority Leader Everett McKinley Dirksen (R Ill.) agreed to support the cloture motions. In 1966, Dirksen strongly opposed open housing legislation, and without his support two cloture votes failed by wide margins and the bill was dropped by the leadership. There was no indication early in 1968 that Dirksen had changed his view.

The House was more conservative than it had been when it passed a modified version of the President's open housing bill in 1966. In the Congressional elections of 1966 the Democratic party lost 47 seats, almost all held by Northerners who supported open housing. House leaders indicated that they would not take up an open housing bill again unless it was first passed by the Senate.

The attitude of the country towards civil rights legislation also appeared to be hardening. The Negro riots which broke out in many cities in the summer of 1967 were probably the most severe of the century.

Although the rioting heightened awareness of the needs of the cities, there were many who felt that rioters should not be "rewarded" with new programs to benefit the poor or the Negro specifically.

The open housing bill and the proposed strengthening of the EEOC were much more sensitive issues for Northern Members of Congress than most earlier civil rights legislation had been. Earlier bills were directed primarily at abuses that were found in the South. The housing and employment proposals also affected the Northern homeowner and labor unionist.

SENATE ACTION

Senate. The first Senate test of the House civil rights protection bill (HR 2516) came on Feb. 6 when the Senate, by a 54-29 (R 19-13; D 35-16) roll-call vote, tabled (killed) the substitute amendment offered by Ervin. His opponents said the bill would be considerably weakened by the amendment, which removed references to racially motivated action.

An open housing amendment was offered to HR 2516 as soon as the Ervin amendment was rejected, and it immediately became the central issue in debate on the

---

Summary of Action and Provisions of 1968 Bill

HR 2516—Reported by House Judiciary Committee June 29, 1967.

HR 2516—Passed by the House by a 327-93 roll-call vote Aug. 16, 1967.

HR 2516—Reported, amended, by Senate Judiciary Committee Nov. 2, 1967.

HR 2516—Debated by the Senate from Jan. 18, 1968, until cloture was voted by a 65-32 roll-call vote March 4, 1968.

HR 2516—Passed, amended, by the Senate by a 71-20 roll-call vote March 11.

HR 2516—House agreed to accept Senate amendments by a 250-172 roll-call vote April 10.

PL 90-284—Signed into law April 11.

PL 90-284 contained the following provisions:

Housing. The law, when fully in effect in 1970, prohibited discrimination in the sale or rental of about 80 percent of all housing. Most housing built with federal assistance, such as public housing and urban renewal projects, was covered immediately on enactment of the bill. Coverage was to be extended Jan. 1, 1969, to all multiple-unit dwellings except for owner-occupied dwellings with no more than four units. Also covered on that date were single-family houses, such as real estate developments, that were not owned by private individuals. Privately owned single-family houses sold or rented by real estate agents or brokers were covered as of Jan. 1, 1970. Private owners selling or renting their house without the services of a real estate agent or broker were exempt. The prohibition against discrimination also applied to financing and brokerage services. The Secretary of Housing and Urban Development was to administer this title.

Other Provisions. The bill provided criminal penalties for injuring or interfering with a person because he was exercising specified rights. These rights included the right to vote, to serve on a jury, to participate in government or government-aided programs, to work, to attend school or college and to enjoy public accommodations. It provided similar protection to civil rights workers urging or helping others to exercise their rights.

Antiriot provisions provided criminal penalties for traveling in or using the facilities of interstate commerce, such as telephones, to incite or take part in a riot. Penalties were also provided for manufacturing or teaching the use of firearms or explosives for use in a civil disorder.

An Indian rights section prohibited tribal governments from making or enforcing laws which violated specified constitutional rights. It also prohibited states from assuming civil or criminal jurisdiction over Indian areas without the consent of the Indian tribes affected.

Supreme Court Interprets 1866 Open Housing Statute

The Supreme Court in 1968 by a 7-2 vote upheld an 1866 law which barred all racial discrimination, private and public, in the sale or rental of property. The June 17 decision came in the case of *Jones v. Mayer* and involved Section 1982 of Title 42, U.S. Code.

Background. Section 1982 was enacted originally as part of the Civil Rights Act of 1866 and was re-enacted in 1870. It read:

"All citizens of the United States shall have the same right, in every state and territory, as is enjoyed by white citizens thereof to inherit, purchase, lease, sell, hold and convey real and personal property."

The 1866 Act was enacted to put into effect the 13th Amendment, which read:

"Section 1. Neither slavery nor involuntary servitude, except as a punishment for crime whereof the party shall have been duly convicted, shall exist within the United States, or any place subject to their jurisdiction.

"Section 2. Congress shall have power to enforce this article by appropriate legislation."

The suit in this case was brought in 1965 by Joseph Lee Jones, a Negro, against the Alfred H. Mayer Co. Jones contended that the company refused to sell him a home in the Paddock Woods community of St. Louis County, Mo., on the sole grounds that he was a Negro. A federal district court dismissed the case and the 8th Circuit Court of Appeals affirmed, on the grounds that Section 1982 applied only to state action and not to the action of private individuals. In reversing the Court of Appeals, the Supreme Court cleared the way for trial on the merits in federal district court.

Opinion. Justice Stewart, writing for the Court, said that Section 1982 was "not a comprehensive open housing law." In "sharp contrast" to Title VIII (open housing) of the Civil Rights Act of 1968, he said, Section 1982 "deals only with racial discrimination and does not address itself to discrimination on grounds of religion or national origin," as did the 1968 Act.

He said that the 1968 Act dealt with discrimination in (1) the provision of services or facilities in connection with the sale or rental of a dwelling; (2) advertising or other representations; (3) financing arrangements; and (4) brokerage services. The 1968 Act, he said, provided for a federal agency (the Department of Housing and Urban Development) to assist aggrieved parties; for intervention in lawsuits by the Attorney General; and for the payment of damages. Section 1982 contained none of those provisions, he said.

Justice Stewart said that, on the other hand, Section 1982 contained "none of the exemptions" included in the 1968 Act. Enactment of the 1968 Act, he said, "had no effect upon Section 1982 and no effect upon this litigation, but it underscored the vast differences between, on the one hand, a general statute applicable only to racial discrimination in the rental and sale of property and enforceable only by private parties acting on their own initiative, and, on the other hand, a detailed housing law, applicable to a broad range of discriminatory practices and enforceable by a complete arsenal of federal authority."

Justice Stewart said that an examination of the legislative history of Section 1982 "persuades us that Congress meant exactly what it said" in enacting the law in 1866. Congress intended to eradicate the Black Codes and to give full force to the 13th Amendment, he said. When President Andrew Johnson vetoed the bill and returned it to Congress, opponents of the measure argued that the bill was too broad in scope. Yet Congress overrode the veto, Justice Stewart said.

"In light of the concerns that led Congress to adopt it and the contents of the debates that preceded its passage, it is clear that the Act was designed to do just what its terms suggest: to prohibit all racial discrimination, whether or not under color of law, with respect to the rights enumerated therein—including the right to purchase or lease property," he said of the 1866 Act.

Justice Stewart said that the 13th Amendment was adopted to remove the "badges of slavery" from the nation, and that discrimination in the sale or rental of housing, as viewed by Congress in 1866, was one such "badge." Thus, he said, Congress had ample power under the 13th Amdndment to enact the law and to apply it to private as well as public actions. He said that "when racial discrimination herds men into ghettos and makes their ability to buy property turn on the color of their skin, then it too is a relic of slavery."

"At the very least," he said, "the freedom that Congress is empowered to secure under the 13th Amendment includes the freedom to buy whatever a white man can buy, the right to live wherever a white man can live. If Congress cannot say that being a free man means at least this much, then the 13th Amendment made a promise the nation cannot keep."

Concurrence. Justice Douglas said that "prejudices, once part and parcel of slavery, still persist. The men who sat in Congress in 1866 were trying to remove some of the badges or 'customs' of slavery when they adopted Section 1982."

Dissent. Justice Harlan, joined by Justice White, said an examination of the legislative history of the 1866 Act disclosed that Congress meant to enact a law aimed at discriminatory practices by states, not by individuals. In addition, he said, the Civil Rights Act of 1968 made available to large numbers of people, although not to Jones (because the law was not yet in effect), legal machinery to combat racial discrimination in housing. Passage of that Act, he said, "so diminishes the public importance of this case that by far the wisest course would be for this Court to refrain from decision and to dismiss" the appeal as improvidently granted.

Related Development. In a June 20 editorial, *The Wall Street Journal* charged that the Court acted like a "legislature" in its decision. Justice Stewart in a letter to the paper July 3 replied: "What would the Court have been if it had held (1) that the law does not mean what it says, or (2) that Congress did not have the power to pass it?" He said Congress still had the power to amend the law.

bill. The housing amendment was sponsored by Walter F. Mondale (D Minn.) and Edward W. Brooke (R Mass.), the Senate's only Negro member. It prohibited discrimination in the sale or rental of about 90 percent of all housing.

The Senate leadership was divided on the question of adding a "fair housing" amendment to the civil rights protection bill. The Leadership Conference on Civil Rights, an organization representing 115 civil rights, church and labor groups, strongly advocated adding such an amendment to any civil rights bill that reached the floor. The organization's view was that in the unlikely event that the Senate Banking and Currency Committee reported out the Administration's open housing bill (S 1358), a motion to take up the bill on the floor was certain to be filibustered.

Mondale agreed Dec. 28, 1967, to sponsor the open housing amendment at a meeting attended by Clarence M. Mitchell, legislative chairman of the Leadership Conference, Philip A. Hart (D Mich.), the leading Senate Democratic sponsor of civil rights legislation, Joseph D. Tydings (D Md.) and representatives of several other Senators. This move was opposed by Majority Leader Mansfield, a strong supporter of open housing legislation, who said Jan. 14 that it would endanger the civil rights protection bill "which is in trouble enough as it is." Hart was skeptical at first but agreed to support the move at the end of January.

Cloture Attempts. The Senate showed unexpectedly strong support for the civil rights protection bill and the open housing amendment to it in two votes on Feb. 20 and 21. A cloture vote Feb. 20 to limit the five-week old debate on the bill and housing amendment was supported by a majority of the Senate (55-37—R 18-18; D 37-19) although it fell seven votes short of the required two-thirds. In a second vote Feb. 21 the Senate rejected, by a **34-58** roll-call vote, a motion to table (kill) the open housing amendment. Mondale, in urging the Senate not to table his housing amendment, said that he would modify his proposal to gain additional support before a second cloture vote, scheduled for Feb. 26, was taken.

Dirksen, who had consistently opposed the housing amendment, criticized Mondale's action but later indicated to supporters of the amendment that he was willing to seek a compromise that would include housing provisions. Observers believed that Dirksen was influenced by the fact that half the Republicans who voted Feb. 20 favored cloture (18-18) and that a majority (19 out of 35) voted against tabling the housing amendment.

The second cloture motion Feb. 26 failed by a narrow margin, 56-36 (R 19-17; D 37-19). Dirksen was instrumental in its defeat but said that his reason for opposing it was to "give us a little maneuvering time."

The compromise that was worked out Feb. 28 became the basis of the final bill. Mondale described the compromise as "a miracle" that included much more than his amendment's supporters had thought possible a few days earlier. Its housing coverage was similar to that in the original amendment with the addition of an exemption for single-family houses that were sold or rented by their owner without the services of a real estate agent or broker. The enforcement provisions were weakened by eliminating the enforcement power given the Secretary of Housing and Urban Development and

---

Senators Never Supporting Cloture

Of the Senators who were Members of Congress when the second session of the 90th Congress adjourned on Oct. 14, 1968, 19 had opposed cloture at every opportunity in their careers. The staunch opponents of cloture lost a long-time ally in 1968 when the dean of the Senate, Carl Hayden (D Ariz.), voted Oct. 1 to end debate on the filibuster that was being conducted against confirmation of Supreme Court Associate Justice Abe Fortas to be Chief Justice of the United States. (The vote, however, was still far short of the two-thirds majority needed to end debate.) Hayden previously had opposed cloture on every occasion since coming to the Senate in 1927. Hayden did not make a statement explaining his vote for cloture, but he let it be known that he did so because he had been a friend of Fortas for 20 years and respected the President's judgment in nominating him. Hayden retired at the end of the 1968 session.

Outside of the South, only Sen. Alan Bible (D Nev.) approached Hayden's record. Bible never supported cloture from the time he entered the Senate in 1954 through the end of the 1968 session. Bible's colleague, Sen. Howard W. Cannon (D Nev.), voted for cloture only twice: on the 1964 civil rights bill (in which he played an important role in obtaining the first cloture on a civil rights bill) and on the 1968 civil rights bill which included the open housing provisions. Cannon became a Senator in 1959. These Senators took the historic position that a filibuster was the ultimate protection for the small states against the superior voting strength of the large.

The view of the Southerners was expressed by their leader, Sen. Richard B. Russell (D Ga.), in 1962 when he told a reporter: "I'll vote to gag the Senate when the shrimp start to whistling 'Dixie'." Of the 26 Senators from Southern states who were Members in 1968, 14 never in their careers voted for cloture.

The list of 14 Democrats and 5 Republicans follows, with the year in which each entered the Senate:

Democrats: Bible (Nev. 1954), Byrd (Va. 1966), Byrd (W.Va. 1959), Ellender (La. 1937), Ervin (N.C. 1954), Hill (Ala. 1938), Hollings (S.C. 1967), Jordan (N.C. 1958), McClellan (Ark. 1943), Russell (Ga. 1933), Sparkman (Ala. 1946), Spong (Va. 1967), Stennis (Miss. 1947) and Talmadge (Ga. 1957).

Republicans: Fannin (Ariz. 1965), Hansen (Wyo. 1967), Murphy (Calif. 1965), Thurmond (S.C. 1954) and Tower (Texas 1961).

---

some changes were also made in the civil rights protection provision.

With Dirksen's sponsorship it was expected that a cloture vote scheduled for March 1 would be adopted by the Senate. Its defeat, 59-35 (R 22-14; D 37-21), four votes less than the necessary two-thirds, was interpreted by some observers as a sign of Dirksen's weakening grip on the reins of power. There were also indications that some Senators felt that they had been asked to vote on the cloture motion before they had had time to study the compromise bill.

The Senate voted cloture on March 4 by exactly the two-thirds required (65-32—R 24-12; D 41-20), thus limiting the debate on the bill which had lasted more than six weeks. Under cloture each Senator is limited to one hour's debate on the bill—in this case, the Dirksen substitute.

As soon as cloture was in effect the Senate turned to voting on amendments which had been offered to the Dirksen compromise. Three attempts to substantially broaden the exemption for single-family houses were defeated, and an amendment proposed by Ervin to eliminate the housing provisions altogether was rejected, 24-64 (R 6-26; D 18-38), March 8.

The Senate accepted amendments by Strom Thurmond (R S.C.) and Russell B. Long (D La.) adding major antiriot sections to the bill. The Senate voted overwhelmingly (82-13) to add criminal penalties for traveling in interstate commerce with intent to incite or take part in a riot. It also voted to prohibit teaching the use of firearms or explosives for use in a civil disorder or manufacturing or transporting firearms or explosives for such use. Several amendments designed to protect law officers and firemen during riots were also accepted.

The Senate added provisions to protect the constitutional rights of Indians in tribal jurisdictions and to prohibit states from assuming civil or criminal jurisdiction over Indian lands without tribal consent. These provisions, which were backed by the Administration, had been strongly advocated by Ervin for several years. They had been passed in the Senate as a separate bill (S 1843) Dec. 7, 1967, but House action appeared unlikely.

Passage. The Senate passed the civil rights bill March 11 by a wide margin **(71-20)**. Only three Republicans joined 17 Southern Democrats in voting against the bill. Much of the opposition seemed to dissipate after adoption of cloture and the antiriot amendments. A second filibuster, although technically possible, was not attempted after adoption of Dirksen's substitute.

HOUSE ACTION

In the House, controversy focused on whether the House should send the bill directly to conference or should first vote on accepting the Senate version without change. Democratic leaders decided to try to avoid sending the bill to conference by proposing a resolution (H Res 1100) to accept the Senate amendments. They feared that the bill would be weakened in conference and that Senate opponents of the bill might be able to delay or obstruct a vote on accepting a conference report, thus killing the legislation.

Republicans were divided on House procedure for handling the bill. Minority Leader Gerald R. Ford (R Mich.) argued that it should be sent to conference because the House had had no opportunity to consider most of its provisions. (Open housing had passed the House in the previous Congress, not the 1967-68 90th Congress.) Ford, who had opposed open housing legislation in 1966, publicly expressed support for the principle of open housing for the first time March 14 but indicated that he

---

House Voting Switches

A number of Members voted differently in 1968 than they did in 1966 on the open-housing issue. For the purpose of this study, a comparison is made between the **229-195** roll-call vote in 1968 and the vote on the motion to recommit the bill in 1966. The votes used in this study, although procedural in nature, were essential to final action and therefore were considered more significant than the passage votes.

The following 25 Members opposed open housing in 1966 but favored it in 1968: Democrats: Boggs (La.), Fallon (Md.), Foley (Wash.), Garmatz (Md.), Gray (Ill.), Hanna (Calif.), Hays (Ohio), Hechler (W.Va.), Hicks (Wash.), Morris (N.M.), Pickle (Texas), Slack (W.Va.), Young (Texas), Zablocki (Wis.). Republicans: Anderson (Ill.), Andrews (N.D.), Betts (Ohio), Broomfield (Mich.), Mize (Kan.), Moore (W.Va.), Nelsen (Minn.), O'Konski (Wis.), Pelly (Wash.), Stanton (Ohio), Wyatt (Ore.). However, four of these Members switched to vote against the bill on the final vote. They were: Fallon, Garmatz, Gray, and Pickle.

The following eight Members voted for open housing in the key vote in 1966 but against it in the key vote in 1968. Democrats: Clark (Pa.), Delaney (N.Y.), Dingell (Mich.), Gibbons (Fla.), Pucinski (Ill.). Republicans: Byrnes (Wis.), Davis (Wis.), Springer (Ill.). Four of these—Clark, Dingell, Byrnes, and Springer—then switched to vote in favor on the final vote.

On the 1968 roll calls, 31 Members voted differently on the key vote **(229-195)** than they did on the final vote. Twenty-two Republicans including Minority Leader Gerald R. Ford (Mich.) and Melvin R. Laird (Wis.) and four Democrats voted, in effect, to send the bill to conference but supported the bill on the final vote. An additional three Democrats who voted against the bill on the key vote did not vote on the final vote. Five Democrats who supported open housing on the key vote opposed it on the final vote.

Party Vote Breakdown. On the key 1968 vote to accept the Senate amendments without change the vote was **229-195**: R 77-106; D 152-89 (ND 140-12; SD 12-77).

On the final vote to accept the Senate version and send it to the President, the vote was 250-172 R 100-84; D 150-88 (ND 137-13; SD 13-75).

---

would like a broader exemption for single-family houses. He rejected the pleas of two Republican Presidential candidates, Richard M. Nixon and Gov. Nelson A. Rockefeller (N.Y.), to accept the Senate version.

Charles E. Goodell (R N.Y.), a member of the House Republican leadership, and Albert H. Quie (R Minn.), assisted by other GOP Representatives, lobbied actively among their colleagues for support of the Senate amendments. Goodell's support for H Res 1100 was credited by some observers with preventing a GOP Policy Committee position in favor of sending the bill to conference.

Rules Committee. The Democratic leadership suffered an initial and unexpected setback in the House Rules Committee. The leaders wanted the Committee to clear H Res 1100 for floor action as quickly as possible so that the real estate lobby, which had been caught off-guard by Senate adoption of the open housing provisions, would not have time to mount a campaign against the bill in the House. The bill's supporters also feared that the Poor People's Campaign, scheduled to begin April 22, would increase opposition to the bill.

The Rules Committee March 19 voted 8-7 to delay voting on the resolution until April 9. Two Northern Democrats who normally supported the Administration—James J. Delaney (N.Y.) and B.F. Sisk (Calif.)—voted with Committee Chairman William M. Colmer (D Miss.) and the five Committee Republicans to delay action.

When the Rules Committee met on April 9 to vote on a rule, the mood of the nation had changed dramatically. The Rev. Dr. Martin Luther King Jr. had been assassinated April 4, and his death had been followed by a wave of rioting in over 100 cities, including Washington, D.C. President Johnson designated April 7 as a national day of mourning. At the time of the Committee vote King's funeral was being held in Atlanta, Ga.

The Rules Committee April 9 defeated, by a 7-8 vote, a motion to send the bill to conference. As Delaney and Sisk continued to favor a conference, the swing vote was provided by a Republican, John B. Anderson (Ill.). Although he originally favored sending the bill to conference, Anderson said, he had decided that procedure was "fraught with some considerable peril." H Res 1100 then was approved by a 9-6 vote, Sisk switching over.

Floor Action. The House accepted the Senate amendments April 10 by a **250-172** bipartisan roll-call vote. The key vote, however, came a few minutes earlier when the House, on a **229-195** roll call, voted to prevent any motion to send the bill to conference with the Senate. A majority of Republicans, joined by most Southern Democrats, voted against this procedural move ("moving the previous question," which prevents amendments and cuts off debate). Lopsided support by Northern Democrats plus 77 GOP votes put the motion across. *(See box p. 382.)*

In floor debate supporters of H Res 1100 said that to send the Senate-passed bill to conference would mean "no civil rights, housing or antiriot bill in the 90th Congress." Minority Leader Ford said that the House should send the bill to conference following "the time-tested principles of parliamentary procedure," but he added that he spoke only for himself. William M. McCulloch (R Ohio), a leading authority on civil rights as ranking Republican on the House Judiciary Committee, urged Congress to accept the Senate amendments. Several opponents, however, warned against "capitulation" to rioters or attempts to "buy off rioters" with legislation.

The effect King's assassination had on the House vote could not be accurately determined. The Leadership Conference told Congressional Quarterly that it had a count of 216 "sure" votes April 2 to accept the Senate bill. However, a count by the National Assn. of Real Estate Boards (NAREB) on the same day indicated that a conference was favored by 224 Representatives. NAREB spokesmen reported they found an increase in support for

---

Who Is Mrs. Murphy?

"Mrs. Murphy" was the mythical owner-occupant of a five-room boarding house. She became known on Capitol Hill during debate on the Civil Rights Act of 1964, when concern abounded in both chambers that the elderly widow, living on Social Security and meager rents from her boarders, might be compelled to take a guest against her wishes.

In response to that concern, Title II of the 1964 Act, which prohibited discrimination in certain public accommodations, contained the "Mrs. Murphy clause" exempting owner-occupied units with five or fewer rooms for rent. The same exemption was put into the 1968 open housing law, except that the size of the dwelling exempted was reduced to one with no more than four (rather than five) units or rooms for rent.

---

the Senate version following the assassination. Most observers agreed that King's death probably widened the margin of the House vote, although the subsequent rioting may have cost H Res 1100 some votes. *(For story on lobbying efforts, see p. 386.)*

Provisions of PL 90-284

Housing Provisions

Prohibited Acts. Prohibited refusal to sell or rent a dwelling to any person, after receiving a bona fide offer, because of his race, color, religion or national origin.

Prohibited discrimination against a person in the terms, conditions or privileges of the sale or rental of a dwelling.

In advertising the sale or rental of a dwelling, prohibited indication of a preference or discrimination based on race, color, religion or national origin.

Prohibited representing to a person, because of his race, color, religion or national origin, that a dwelling was not available if it was.

Prohibited the "blockbusting" technique of inducing or attempting to induce persons to sell or rent a dwelling by representing the entry into the neighborhood of persons of a particular race, religion or national origin.

Prohibited banks or other institutions providing commercial real estate loans from discriminating in the provision or terms of loans. Also prohibited discrimination in the provision of brokerage services. These two provisions were effective Jan. 1, 1969.

Effective Dates. Provided that housing would come under the provisions of the bill in three stages as follows:

• Upon enactment—applicable to federally owned or operated dwellings and to dwellings provided in whole or in part with federal assistance including loans, grants, mortgage insurance, slum clearance, urban renewal and similar activities. This applied only to housing provided under agreements made after Nov. 20, 1962 (the date of President Kennedy's Executive Order prohibiting discrimination in housing built, purchased or financed with federal assistance). In addition, privately owned single-family housing was exempted from immediate coverage, but was covered under a later stage *(see following paragraphs).*

• After Dec. 31, 1968—applicable to multiple-unit housing and to single-family houses owned by contractors (or building firms) or by private individuals (provided the individual owned more than three homes), with certain exemptions *(see below).* This provision was intended primarily to cover most apartments and single-family housing in new subdivisions.

• After Dec. 31, 1969—to all other housing, including privately owned single-family housing, with certain exemptions *(see below).*

Exemptions. Exempted private individuals owning not more than three houses who sold or rented their house without the services of a real estate agent or broker and who did not indicate any preference or discrimination in advertising the sale or rental of the house.

Exempted dwellings of up to four separate living units in which the owner maintained a residence (often referred to as "Mrs. Murphy" housing).

Exempted religious organizations and private clubs housing their own members on a noncommercial basis.

Administration. Provided that the Secretary of Housing and Urban Development (HUD) administer the housing provisions of the bill and provided for an additional Assistant Secretary (there currently were five).

Gave the HUD Department responsibilities for research, education and technical assistance to reduce discriminatory housing practices.

Enforcement. Provided that a person who thought he had been discriminated against could file a complaint with the Secretary of HUD which the Secretary was required to investigate and could attempt to conciliate. Provided that if conciliation failed the person could sue in a federal court for injunctive relief. Provided that state or local remedies, where available, must be sought before federal action was taken. Also provided that a person could sue in federal, state or local courts for relief or damages without filing a complaint with the Department of HUD. Required the burden of proof of discrimination be on the person making the complaint.

Provided that the U.S. Attorney General could bring a civil suit where there was a pattern of discrimination of public importance.

Interference with Sales or Rentals. Provided criminal penalties for injuring, intimidation or interfering with any person, or attempting to injure, intimidate or interfere with any person:

• Because of his race, color, religion or national origin and because he has bought, sold or rented a dwelling.

• Because he has participated without discrimination in the buying, selling or renting of a dwelling.

• Because he has lawfully aided or encouraged a person to participate without discrimination, or has lawfully opposed the denial of the opportunity to participate in buying, selling or renting of a dwelling.

Civil Rights Protection

Provided criminal penalties for injuring, intimidating or interfering with any person or attempting to injure, intimidate or interfere with any person:

• Because he was voting or campaigning as a candidate in any public election, serving on a federal jury, working for a federal agency or participating in a federal or federally assisted program or activity.

• Because of his race, color, religion or national origin and because he was attending a public school or college, participating in a state or locally administered program, working for a state, local or private employer, joining or using the services of a labor union, serving on a state jury or using a common carrier or public accommodations.

• Because he has participated without discrimination in the above activities or because he has helped or encouraged others to participate in them or because he has lawfully opposed any denial of the opportunity to participate.

• During a riot, with any shopkeeper or other person engaged in commerce or business.

Set maximum penalties at $10,000 and 10 years imprisonment if injury resulted, and life imprisonment if death resulted.

Stated that these provisions did not apply to the actions of law enforcement officers, or members of the National Guard or the Armed Forces who were engaged in suppressing a riot or civil disorder.

Provided that the United States could not prosecute an offense under this section except upon the written certification of the U.S. Attorney General or Deputy Attorney General that it was in the public interest and necessary to secure substantial justice. Stated that the section should not be construed to deprive states of their jurisdiction or responsibilities for prosecuting crimes or to limit the authority of federal officers or grand jury to investigate.

Antiriot, Civil Obedience

Riots. Provided federal penalties for persons who traveled in interstate commerce or used the facilities of interstate commerce (such as the mails, telephone, telegraph, radio or television) with intent to incite, organize, encourage, or take part in a riot or assist others to do so and who performed any overt action to incite, organize or further a riot.

Defined a riot as a public disturbance involving an act or threat of violence by one or more persons in an assemblage of three or more persons which created danger of or did result in damage or injury to the property or person of any other individual.

Provided maximum penalties of $10,000 in fines and/or five years imprisonment.

Specified that advocacy of ideas or expression of beliefs would not be considered as action to organize or further a riot so long as a person's remarks did not involve advocacy of violence or an assertion of the rightness of or the right to commit violence.

Civil Obedience. Provided federal penalties for persons who teach the use, application or making of a firearm or explosive with the knowledge or intent that the firearm or explosive would be used in a civil disorder which would obstruct commerce. Also provided penalties for transporting or manufacturing for transportation any firearm or explosive with the knowledge that either would be used in a civil disorder.

Provided federal penalties for obstruction or interfering with a law enforcement officer or fireman performing his official duties during a civil disorder.

Defined civil disorder as a public disturbance involving acts of violence by a group of three or more persons which created immediate danger of or resulted in damage or injury to the property or person of any other individual.

Provided maximum penalties of $10,000 in fines and/or five years imprisonment.

Rights of Indians

Prohibited tribal governments from making or enforcing laws which violated specified constitutional rights. These included freedom of religion, speech and press, protection from unreasonable search and seizures, and a number of rights relating to trials including the right to counsel, to confrontation with witnesses, to trial by jury and to refuse to incriminate oneself. (Indian courts do not have jurisdiction over major crimes and cannot impose penalties of more than a $500 fine and six months imprisonment.)

Directed the Secretary of the Interior to recommend to Congress a model code governing the courts of Indian offenses on Indian reservations. Provided that the code assure that persons tried in Indian courts had the same constitutional rights, privileges and immunities as persons tried in federal courts and that they be made aware of their rights. Required that the code establish qualifications for judges of courts of Indian offenses and make provision for training of judges.

Authorized states to assume jurisdiction over criminal offenses and civil causes in Indian country to the extent to which they had jurisdiction elsewhere in the state but only with the consent of the Indian tribe occupying the area. Provided that this did not authorize the alienation, encumbrance or taxation of Indian property. Repealed a section of the Civil and Criminal Jurisdiction Act of 1953 (PL 83-280) which had authorized states to assume jurisdiction without tribal consent.

Equal Employment

Congress did not act on proposals to strengthen and broaden a 1964 law to prevent discrimination in employment and union membership. A bill was reported by the Senate Labor and Public Welfare Committee May 8 but no further action occurred. Opponents of the bill, and Senate Minority Leader Everett McKinley Dirksen (R Ill.) in particular, said they would filibuster against the measure. Dirksen called the bill "one of the most offensive pieces of legislation that could come before Congress." Senate Democratic leaders said no action would be scheduled until the House passed the bill. There was no House action in 1968.

The Senate bill (S 3465) was a slightly revised version of a bill (S 1308) under consideration in 1967. The legislation was requested by President Johnson in a Jan. 24 civil rights message. Enactment also was urged by the President's Advisory Commission on Civil Disorders. The key provision, as in bills from earlier years, gave the Equal Employment Opportunity Commission authority to enforce rulings against discriminatory practices by issuing cease-and-desist orders. The EEOC currently had only conciliatory powers.

Civil rights forces had attempted in every year since the existing law was passed in 1964 to provide the EEOC with enforcement powers. Death of the 1968 legislation meant they had been unsuccessful in the 89th and 90th Congresses.

Jury Selection

Congress early in 1968 completed action on legislation to reform procedures for the selection of federal juries. The President signed the bill (S 989) into law (PL 90-274) on March 27.

The bill provided for random selection of juror names from voter lists and prohibited discrimination on the grounds of race, color, religion, sex, national origin or economic status.

The Senate passed S 989 in late 1967. There was little opposition to the measure in the House in 1968. On a 307-45 roll-call vote on passage, all 45 opponents were from the South, 44 Democrats and one Republican.

The bill was similar in purpose to Title I of the Administration's omnibus 1967 civil rights package, but its supporters avoided labeling it a civil rights bill. However, S 989 differed in administrative detail from Title I.

S 989 was originally drafted by a committee of the Judicial Conference of the United States. It was supported by President Johnson and the American Bar Assn.

The legislative history of the bill, and particularly the House Judiciary Committee report, indicated that the bill did not require that a jury "accurately mirror community makeup," in the Committee's words, but ensured that the source list for the jury was a cross section of the community.

Provisions—As signed by the President March 27, S 989 (PL 90-274):

Stated that federal juries must be selected at random from "a fair cross section of the community" and prohibited discrimination in jury selection on account of race, color, religion, sex, national origin or economic status.

Required each U.S. district court to draw up a plan for the selection of jurors which met standards set forth in the bill. These included random selection of names from voter lists and clearly defined rules for exclusion or exemption from service.

Required that a person's qualification for jury service be determined solely on the basis of information on jury qualification forms and other "competent" evidence and set criteria based on age, residency, fluency and literacy in English and lack of physical or mental infirmity and criminal record. (However, a juror could be excluded from service if found unsuitable by the court on specified grounds or if challenged on traditional grounds at trial.)

Established procedures for challenging compliance with jury selection requirements.

Raised juror and witness fees.

State Jury Reform. As in 1967, Congress did not act on President Johnson's requests to prohibit discrimination in selection of state juries. A Senate bill (S 1318) never got out of committee.

OPEN HOUSING LAW

Effective Lobbying Put Bill Across

The enactment in 1968 of a major civil rights law with its far-reaching open-housing requirements was one of the most unexpected developments in Congress in many years. In less than three months from the day the 90th Congress began its second session on Jan. 15, open-housing legislation was transformed from a goal which almost no one interested in the subject thought remotely attainable in 1968 to a public law which prohibited racial discrimination in the sale or rental of 80 percent of the nation's housing.

In talks with many of the individuals who followed the three-month battle, Congressional Quarterly learned that the transformation was due in large part to the efforts of Clarence M. Mitchell Jr., the chief lobbyist for the Leadership Conference on Civil Rights. Seldom has an individual lobbyist been accorded so much credit for the outcome of a bill as was Mitchell, who was also Washington director of the National Assn. for the Advancement of Colored People (NAACP). There was considerable agreement among the persons who talked to CQ about the 1968 civil rights battle that Mitchell was the catalyst who organized and kept together the forces that passed the bill.

At the outset of the 1968 session, there was virtually no sentiment in Congress to try to make the year a big one for civil rights. Two years before, an open-housing bill had died in a Senate filibuster, and for most proponents of the legislation the outlook appeared little brighter in 1968. Mitchell, however, refused to accept this prognosis and continued to prod the Administration and Senate liberals until they promised him another big push.

An aide to one Senator who supported the bill told CQ the Senator had decided the measure was worth a try because "he felt Mitchell deserved an effort by Congress to get this thing through.... It demonstrates to the firebrands what moderate Negro leaders like Mitchell and (NAACP President) Roy Wilkins can do."

Despite Mitchell's pre-eminent role, however, there were other key factors in the bill's passage, particularly the substantial support of Republicans and the fact that the nation's real estate interests waited until the bill had passed the Senate to mount their lobbying effort against the measure. This analysis discusses the major factors working for and against the bill and the lobbying activities on both sides of the issue.

Provisions. The law (PL 90-284), when fully in effect in 1970, prohibited discrimination in the sale or rental of about 80 percent of all housing in the nation. The first stage of the law went into effect on enactment. Additional coverage went into effect Jan. 1, 1969 and 1970. *See p. 383 for details.)*

The bill also contained antiriot provisions and provided criminal penalties for injuring or interfering with a person because he was exercising specified rights such as voting or attending school.

Senate

After lobbying fruitlessly for most of 1967, Mitchell scored his first breakthrough Dec. 15 when the Senate leadership made a House-passed bill (HR 2516) protecting civil rights workers the first order of Senate business for 1968. Mitchell and other key officials of the Leadership Conference, an organization of 115 church, labor, civil rights and civic groups, set out to make the bill a vehicle for an open-housing amendment.

The basic strategy on the bill was worked out at a Dec. 28 meeting attended by Mitchell, several other Leadership Conference participants, Sens. Philip A. Hart (D Mich.) (the leading Senate Democratic spokesman for civil rights legislation), Walter F. Mondale (D Minn.), Joseph D. Tydings (D Md.) and representatives of several other Senators. Mondale, who was enthusiastic over the outlook, agreed to cosponsor the housing amendment together with Sen. Edward W. Brooke (R Mass.), who was not present but telephoned his support. The two Senators planned to announce their intentions in a joint press release but were dissuaded by Hart, who was pessimistic about the amendment's chances.

Even more skeptical than Hart were Attorney General Ramsey Clark and Senate Majority Leader Mike Mansfield (D Mont.), who feared the housing rider on HR 2516 would jeopardize chances for any civil rights bill at all. It had even been rumored that Clark was so worried about the outlook for civil rights that he had offered Southern opponents of rights legislation a compromise version of HR 2516.

At meetings held periodically throughout January, support for open housing began to increase. Mitchell commanded better turnouts from the membership of the Leadership Conference, and several other Senators became enthusiastic, including Jacob K. Javits (R N.Y.), Charles H. Percy (R Ill.) and Hugh Scott (R Pa.). Hart, however, remained unconvinced.

Finally, in the closing days of January, Hart decided to give the amendment a try and assumed leadership of the group. One Senate source told CQ Mitchell had persuaded Hart that "it was now or never for civil rights. Hart decided we might as well go for broke."

The group's first show of strength came Feb. 6, when the Senate, by a 54-29 roll-call vote, tabled (killed) an amendment by Sam. J. Ervin Jr. (D N.C.) to limit coverage of HR 2516 to rights guaranteed under the interstate commerce clause (as opposed to a broader approach based on the equal protection clause of the 14th Amendment) and programs involving federal funds. Following adoption of the tabling motion, Mondale and Brooke introduced the open-housing amendment, covering an estimated 91 percent of the nation's homes and apartments. As expected, the Senate's Southern bloc immediately began to filibuster.

The immediate objective for the rights coalition was to gain enough support on an early vote for cloture to convince the Administration that the effort was worth a major White House push. The first step in that direction came Feb. 20, when the group's first cloture motion drew a roll-call vote of 55-37, only seven votes short of the required two-thirds majority of those present and voting. This was considered a reasonable improvement over the 52-41 vote by which cloture was rejected the last time the open-housing legislation was considered in 1966.

In a crucial test Feb. 21, the Senate voted to keep open housing alive when it rejected, by a 34-58 roll-call vote, a motion to table the Mondale-Brooke housing amendment. A second cloture vote Feb. 26 failed by a roll call of 56-36, but the switch of one GOP vote from opposition to support now meant Republicans favored cloture (and thus opposed the position of their Senate leader, Everett McKinley Dirksen—Ill.) by 19-17. The erosion of GOP opposition to cloture, which had been 10-20 on the last cloture vote of 1966, had become a key factor in the consideration of the bill.

Dirksen Switch. Over the holiday weekend following Washington's birthday, Dirksen sent the rights bloc a "feeler" that he might be amenable to a compromise. Javits met with Dirksen that weekend, and in the next few days, a new bill took shape.

To the surprise of the civil rights forces, Dirksen agreed to a plan that would cover about 80 percent of all housing—as compared to the figure of 91 percent in the Mondale-Brooke proposal. The new proposal was agreed to Feb. 28 by Senate leaders, and the Brooke-Mondale amendment was tabled the same day. One strategist in the original civil rights camp told CQ his faction had been ready to "give Dirksen just about anything he wanted. We were astounded at how well we came out." Mondale labeled the compromise "a miracle."

Although it was widely theorized that Dirksen's switch was related to a promise by Democrats to put up a weak slate of candidates in the Illinois elections, authoritative sources told CQ it was more likely that Dirksen feared he was "losing his grip" on the party and "wanted to be on the winning side." It was known that GOP moderates had urged Dirksen to take the initiative in drawing up a compromise to give Republicans a GOP bill to support and to give the party a stronger civil rights record in an election year.

Despite Dirksen's support, however, a third cloture vote March 1 failed by a roll-call vote of 59-35, still four votes short of the needed two-thirds majority. Dirksen was able to take with him only two votes other than his own, those of his son-in-law, Howard H. Baker Jr. (R Tenn.), and Len B. Jordan (R Idaho), who some sources said had indicated before the compromise that he intended to switch.

Within the next three days, the Administration put on its long-awaited pressure effort and cloture finally was invoked March 4 on the fourth try. The roll-call vote on the motion was 65-32, the exact two-thirds margin needed to carry. It was revealed that one of the five Senators switching his vote, Jack Miller (R Iowa), did so in return for Brooke's vote on a weakening amendment Miller later was to offer (unsuccessfully). Several Senate sources told CQ they thought the Administration may have made "deals" with one or two other Western-state Senators, but this could not be substantiated.

Following cloture, the Senate spent another week voting on amendments to the bill before passing it

March 11 by a 71-20 roll-call vote. Several weakening amendments but no strengthening ones were accepted. An aide to one Senate liberal told CQ the proponents of a stronger bill had feared to make the measure any tougher because of concern over the possibility of another Senate filibuster. (This would have been possible because cloture had been invoked only on the Dirksen substitute, which was in the form of an amendment to the bill. The Southerners could have filibustered again on other amendments or on the bill itself.) An aide to a Southern Senator told CQ the Southerners felt it "would not be worth it to go through the whole thing again. We would have lost more Republicans and maybe even some Southern Democrats."

House

Real Estate Lobby. One of the most acrimonious battles of the session developed in the House when the National Assn. of Real Estate Boards (NAREB) directed an intensive lobbying effort toward defeating the Administration's move for quick House acceptance of the Senate bill. NAREB's aim was to get the measure into conference, where it hoped the housing section would be dropped or at least substantially modified.

NAREB, which represents 85,000 members of local real estate boards, was taken by surprise by the Senate's March 4 vote to invoke cloture. "They had no idea the bill could go through the Senate," one Senate aide told CQ. "The whole time we were debating the bill I didn't see a real estate lobbyist or any real estate mail." But when the bill was sent back to the House with the Senate amendments, the NAREB responded vigorously to regain its lost ground.

The thrust of NAREB's effort was to mobilize pressures from its local boards in hope that they could get local homeowners sufficiently concerned to provide a steady flow of mail to Members of the House. NAREB's chief lobbyist, John C. Williamson, told CQ he did very little direct lobbying aside from attending strategy sessions with the opponents of the bill. "My job was to keep the local boards informed," Williamson said, "both with respect to arguments against the bill and the parliamentary situation in the House. After that, it was up to the boards to generate pressure."

Williamson showed CQ a pamphlet called "Freedom of Choice vs. Coercion," which he said he had sent to local boards and other sources. The pamphlet said the housing provision "advances an immoral doctrine because it seeks to reshape human society by invoking the coercive power of the state." Williamson said about 5,000 of the pamphlets had been distributed, including "15 or 20 to key Members of the House."

It was known that NAREB's effort paid off with an avalanche of letters and phone calls advising Members to oppose the bill. One Representative who favored the Senate measure told CQ "the stuff coming in here was not form letters. It was good mail—people's own thoughts on the issue. This is the highest accolade you can pay a lobbying group."

Other Groups. Rep. James G. O'Hara (D Mich.), chairman of the Democratic Study Group, an organization of House Democratic liberals which strongly supported the bill, told the House April 9 that three "extreme right-wing groups" were conducting mail campaigns of "hate, fear, racism and outright lies" against the open-housing provision. O'Hara identified the three organizations as the Liberty Lobby, the Emergency Committee of One Million to Save Our Homes, and the Emergency Committee Against Forced Housing. O'Hara inserted into the April 9 *Congressional Record* copies of letters from all three groups outlining their pressures campaign.

The most vigorous of the three letters was that of the Emergency Committee of One Million, which told recipients that an hour spent to protest the bill "could be the most valuable hour of your life." The letter said that if the bill passed the House, "LBJ's bureaucrats will be swarming over every neighborhood in the United States—setting up Negro-White quotas, forcing homeowners to sell their property, and encouraging vicious gangs of rioters and looters to destroy neighborhoods which dare to resist."

Williamson told CQ that NAREB had made "no contact at all" with the three groups and that he personally was unaware of their pressures effort. Other sources told CQ that NAREB's effort, which they said was conducted on a "somewhat higher plane," probably was hurt by the "excessiveness" of the three groups' "propaganda."

Bill Delayed. The first House test on the Senate bill came March 19, when the Rules Committee by an 8-7 vote approved a Republican motion to delay action on the bill until April 9. The motion was a substitute for a motion by the House Democratic leadership to obtain Rules Committee action April 2 on a resolution (H Res 1100) to permit a House vote on acceptance of the Senate amendments to HR 2516.

In the interim, Mitchell and other civil rights lobbyists worked furiously for rapid House approval of the Senate bill. If action were delayed too long, they feared, the "Poor People's March on Washington" planned by the Rev. Dr. Martin Luther King Jr. for late April might cost them numerous votes in the House. In addition, if the bill went to conference, it might be stripped of its open-housing title or of much of its housing coverage, and there always was the threat of a Senate filibuster over the conference bill. Supporters feared it might be difficult to break another filibuster, particularly if some of the alleged "deals" that produced cloture the first time around did not hold up the second time.

Goodell-Quie Role. One of the key factors in the House outcome was the work done by Republican Reps. Charles E. Goodell (N.Y.) and Albert H. Quie (Minn.) to organize GOP support for the Senate bill. With a target of about 70 GOP votes, Goodell and Quie, assisted by GOP Reps. Clark MacGregor (Minn.), Howard W. Robison (N.Y.), Edward G. Biester Jr. (Pa.), William A. Steiger (Wis.) and Paul Findley (Ill.), divided up the House Republican list and began putting on the pressure. An early assessment in mid-March showed only 37 sure Republican votes. Early in April, the count was up to 57 and then 65. In the critical April 10 vote (to move the previous question and thus consider the resolution to approve the Senate amendments to the bill), a total of 77 House Republicans actually voted "aye."

The significance of the Goodell-Quie effort was twofold: because both Members had records of voting the party line, they enjoyed far greater influence with rank and file party members than did the GOP liberals who

otherwise might have organized the effort; also, because Goodell was a member of the House Republican leadership (chairman of the Republican Committee on Planning and Research), it was believed that his support for the Senate bill prevented a GOP Policy Committee position in favor of sending the bill to conference. Although House Minority Leader Gerald R. Ford (R Mich.) preferred the conference route, he made clear in floor debate April 10 that he then was speaking for himself alone, despite any previous efforts to round up other votes. Had there been a Policy Committee position in favor of a conference, it would have been difficult for GOP Members to vote to accept the Senate provisions without change.

Rules Committee Approval. The Rules Committee April 9 rejected by a 7-8 vote a motion to send HR 2516 to conference with the Senate. The Committee then ordered H Res 1100 reported by a vote of 9-6.

A Republican, John B. Anderson (Ill.), provided the swing vote that blocked the move to send the measure to conference. Anderson, who previously had favored a conference, said he had decided that the full House should have the opportunity to make the choice. Another factor, he said, was the persuasiveness of a statement by Rep. William M. McCulloch (R Ohio) before the Rules Committee, in which McCulloch, the leading House GOP authority on civil rights, attested to the bill's constitutionality. Other sources, however, said Anderson found it easier to vote the way he did since the city council of Rockford, Ill., the major city in his district, had adopted a strong open-housing law the night before the vote took place in the Rules Committee.

Bill Passed. The House April 10 completed action on the bill when it voted by a roll call of 250-172 to accept the Senate amendments. In a key vote minutes before, the House by a 229-195 roll call voted to move the previous question on HR 1100, bringing the resolution (and the Senate amendments) to an immediate and final vote without an opportunity to amend the resolution in order to send the bill to conference with the Senate. President Johnson signed the bill into law the following day (PL 90-284).

The assassination of Dr. King April 4 was thought to have persuaded some House Members to vote for the Senate bill and possibly to have produced a majority for the Senate version, although the riots which followed may have somewhat reduced this support. News stories that Anderson might switch his vote in the Rules Committee were in print before the assassination, however, and leading proponents of the Senate bill told CQ they had a count of 216 sure votes on April 2.

On the other hand, Rules Committee Chairman William M. Colmer (D Miss.) said on the floor April 10 that "on Thursday evening (April 4, just before the assassination) when I went home, in my humble judgment, as well as that of many others, we had the votes to send the bill to conference." A NAREB source told CQ that on April 2, he had been given a count of 224 votes in favor of a conference, but that "because of the assassination," the count had dwindled to 196 by the morning of April 10. Because the latter estimate was only one vote off, the source said, it "attested to the accuracy of the 224-vote count."

THE MOYNIHAN REPORT

A Controversial Study of Negro Problems

In March 1965, the Department of Labor's Office of Policy Planning and Research issued a report, "The Negro Family: The Case for National Action." The report was prepared under the direction of Daniel P. Moynihan, then an Assistant Secretary of Labor in charge of the Planning Office, who also wrote much of the report.

The report, which came to be known as "The Moynihan Report," focused attention on a new dimension of the civil rights revolution—the breakdown of the family as a social unit within much of the Negro community. It offered evidence that only concerted planning and action directed to a new kind of national goal—establishment of a stable Negro family structure—could forestall "a new crisis in race relations."

The report first was issued as a classified document, both because it contained confidential Census Bureau statistics and because it was intended solely as an internal policy paper. It was made public in August 1965.

The main ideas in the report were endorsed by the Administration, and President Johnson incorporated them in his June 4 commencement address at Howard University. The speech was regarded by many as one of the most eloquent pleas ever made by a President on behalf of the Negro. In it the President also called for a White House Conference on civil rights—"To Fulfill These Rights." (See p. 397 and 392.)

Enthusiasm for the report, however, was short-lived. A series of snowballing crises spelled the report's doom. Despite the ultimate discard of Moynihan's proposals, the report continued to be a controversial document. A detailed account of the genesis of the report and the ensuing controversy were the subject of a book published in the spring of 1967, "The Moynihan Report and the Politics of Controversy" (Massachusetts Institute of Technology Press), by two sociologists at Washington University in St. Louis, Lee Rainwater and William L. Yancey. Moynihan, who became director of the Joint Center for Urban Studies of M.I.T. and Harvard University after leaving the Government, wrote his own recapitulation in the February 1967 issue of "Commentary" magazine.

Background of the Report

In their book, Rainwater and Yancey said the report's aim was to show that the Negro family was highly unstable, with female-headed households produced by marital breakups and illegitimacy, and that such instability was the result of a systematic weakening of the Negro male's position—a condition that evolved through slavery, reconstruction, urbanization and unemployment.

The book revealed that while Moynihan did not include recommendations in his report for fear they might overshadow the definition of the problem, he did send the President a memorandum that emphasized the need for planning and suggested several steps for a start. These included: establishment of a government information center to gather relevant data on the Negro's changing situation; top priority for finding jobs for every able-bodied Negro man; income maintenance, perhaps through family allowances; new housing programs, particularly in the suburbs; birth control programs; and greater opportunity for Negro youths to serve in the armed forces, possibly through training programs to help them qualify.

Moynihan's goal, according to Rainwater and Yancey, "was to stimulate a commitment by the Administration to engage in long-range policy planning."

Opposition to the Report

Uneasiness about the report followed the President's Howard University speech. Moynihan, writing in "Commentary," said that when the "welfare bureaucracy" put the report and speech together, "it was instantly perceived that the adequacy of the welfare bureaucracy's efforts and even the integrity of its view of events had been roundly condemned."

The August 1965 Watts riots were regarded by Moynihan, Rainwater and Yancey as the major blow to the report. News accounts of the riots used the report's reasoning on the Negro's internal family plight as a cause of the violence. This angered civil rights leaders. Moynihan said that James Farmer, then director of the Congress of Racial Equality called the report "a massive academic copout for the white conscience." The Administration, becoming more involved in the war in Vietnam, reportedly felt the urban Negro was in direct conflict with law and order. Negro leaders urged eliminating any discussion of "family" from the White House Conference.

Summary of Report

Following is a summary of the Moynihan Report, with quotations from the text.

Introduction

The nation was "approaching a new crisis in race relations." A "new period" was beginning in which Negroes would expect that equal opportunities for them as a group would produce roughly equal results, as compared with other groups. This would not happen unless "a new and special effort is made."

The fundamental problem was the family structure—the evidence was that the Negro family in the urban ghettos was "crumbling." A national effort was needed to give the Negro family structure a stability it traditionally lacked.

The Negro American Revolution

The Negro American revolution was "the most important domestic event" of the postwar period. Its major events—political, administrative and legal—now were past and the Kennedy-Johnson Administration committed the Federal Government to the cause of Negro equality. The 1964 Presidential election "was practically a referendum on this commitment," and President Johnson's overwhelming victory "must be taken as emphatic popular endorsement of the unmistakable and openly avowed course" of Government under him.

"With these events behind us, the nation now faces a different set of challenges, which may prove more difficult to meet, if only because they cannot be cast as concrete propositions of right and wrong."

In the next phase of the revolution, Negroes would seek equality as well as liberty; they would begin to insist that as a group they received proportionate results as well as proportionate opportunities, as other ethnic groups previously had insisted on and received.

"It is increasingly demanded that the distribution of success and failure within one group be roughly comparable to that within other groups.... This is what ethnic politics are all about in America, and in the main the Negro American demands are being put forth in this now traditional and established framework."

Programs such as the Manpower Development and Training Act of 1962, the Economic Opportunity Act of 1964 and the Civil Rights Act of 1964 were aimed at insuring equal opportunity. "They cannot insure the outcome. The principal challenge of the next phase of the Negro revolution is to make certain that equality of results now follow. If we do not, there will be no social peace in the United States for generations."

'The Negro American Family'

"At the heart of the deterioration of the fabric of Negro society is the deterioration of the Negro family. It is the fundamental source of the weakness of the Negro community at the present time."

Probably no single fact of Negro life was so little understood by whites. The white family drew on European traditions of strong family ties and became a highly stable institution. The Negro community was disrupted and "by contrast, the family structure of lower class Negroes is highly unstable, and in many urban centers is approching complete breakdown."

At the same time, a stable middle class Negro group was forming and growing stronger and more successful; it constituted perhaps half of all Negroes. The emergence of this middle class might "beguile the nation" about the conditions of Negro life, and lumping of statistics on all Negroes into one measurement might conceal "the extent of the disorganization among the lower class group. For example, the average monthly unemployment rate for Negro males in 1964 was 9 percent; but during 1964, 29 percent of Negro males were unemployed at one time or another. While 36 percent of Negro children lived in broken homes at any given time, "it is likely that a far higher proportion" lived in broken homes at one time or another.

Statistical analysis showed that:
- Nearly one quarter of urban Negro marriages were dissolved, while the rate was about 8 percent for whites. In the urban Northeast, 25.6 percent of Negro marriages were dissolved (by divorce, separation, etc.).
- About one quarter of Negro births were illegitimate. The rate among whites was 2 percent in 1940 and rose to 3.07 percent in 1963; it was 16.8 percent among Negroes in 1940 and rose to 23.6 percent in 1963.
- Divorces were increasing for both whites and Negroes, but at a faster rate for the latter. Both groups had a divorce rate of 2.2 percent in 1940; by 1964, it was 3.6 percent for whites and 5.1 percent for nonwhites.
- About one quarter of Negro families were headed by females. The percentage of such families among whites was dropping since 1940, and has not exceeded 10 percent since 1949; among Negroes, it was rising, exceeding 20 percent and climbing since 1955.

The breakdown of the Negro family structure led to a "startling increase" in welfare dependency. While 2 percent of white children currently received assistance under the federal Aid to Families with Dependent Children (AFDC), 14 percent of Negro children received such aid. While 8 percent of white children received AFDC at some time in their lives, 56 percent of Negro children received it. Of the 1.8 million nonwhite illegitimate children in the nation in 1961, however, 1.3 million were not receiving AFDC, although a "substantial" number would receive it at some time in their lives.

A chart comparing new AFDC cases with nonwhite male unemployment showed parallel peaks and troughs from 1948 to 1962; as unemployment dropped, so did the number of new AFDC cases. In 1962, however, nonwhite unemployment showed a continuing sharp drop, but new AFDC cases began rising and continued to rise through 1964. Thus, for the first time since 1948, nonwhite applications for welfare were rising despite a drop in nonwhite unemployment.

'The Roots of the Problem'

The first major factor leading to disintegration of the Negro family was the peculiar nature of slavery in America, for it broke up families, did not recognize marriage and downgraded the male. Historically, slaves in other times and in other systems had some legal and social status, albeit at the bottom of society. "In contrast, there was nothing in the tradition of English law or Protestant theology which could accommodate to the fact of human bondage—the slaves were therefore reduced to the status of chattels—often, no doubt, well cared for, even privileged chattels, but chattels nevertheless."

Thus, under American slavery, man, wife and children could be broken up by sale; slaves were not allowed to learn to read or write; they lived in total obedience to and dependence on their masters; and the male lost his role as head of his household. The matrifocal (mother-centered) tradition among Negroes began during the period of slavery.

The institutions of Jim Crow, beginning toward the end of the 19th Century, were directed at the Negro male, who was more of a threat to the white male and who was more likely to use public facilities; the humiliation and submissiveness of segregation were more destructive to the Negro male than to the female.

A more recent factor, in the past two generations, was the rapid migration of Negroes from a rural to an urban basis. Just as a similar migration produced the "wild Irish slums" of the 19th Century, with their "drunkenness, crime, corruption, discrimination, family disorganization, juvenile delinquency," so the recent migration produced the Negro slum—"different from, but hardly better than its predecessors."

Negroes were more urbanized than whites by 1960; 73.2 percent of Negroes and 69.5 percent of whites lived in urban areas. In urban life, the matriarchal pattern intensified among Negroes; while 11.1 percent of rural farm Negro families were headed by a woman, 23.1 percent of urban Negro families were headed by a woman.

As among whites, unemployment and poverty followed recognizable phases in urban life: unemployment of the male head of household led to exhaustion of credit and to the entry of the wife into the labor force, diminishing the standing of the male. That was followed by the appearance of a welfare worker, usually a female, who became the provider and director of family affairs. At that point, either the male obtained work or the family unit began to disintegrate: the "critical element" was not welfare payments, but work for the male, and that was "precisely the one thing the Negro family head in such circumstances has not received over the past generation."

Negro unemployment "has continued at disaster levels for 35 years." In 1963, a "prosperous year," 29.2 percent of all Negro men were out of work at one time or another, almost half of them for 15 weeks or more. Negro families tended to have the largest number of children and the lowest incomes in the nation and because the father so often was absent, unemployed or earning a low wage, the woman worked. While 42 percent of white women worked, 56 percent of Negro women worked.

Meanwhile, the Negro population was growing at the rate of 2.4 percent per year since 1950, compared to 1.7 percent for the population as a whole. The rise was the result of a declining death rate among Negroes and of an increasing fertility rate, especially—as with whites—among families of low income. In seven years, one American in eight would be nonwhite.

The population growth "must inevitably lead to an unconcealable crisis in Negro unemployment," particularly among Negro youth. The Negro teenage unemployment rate stood at 29 percent in 1965, and the nonwhite population over 14 years of age would increase 20 percent by 1970, more than double the white rate.

'The Tangle of Pathology'

"That the Negro American has survived at all is extraordinary—a lesser people might simply have died out, as indeed others have. That the Negro community has not only survived, but in this political generation has entered national affairs as a moderate, humane, and constructive national force is the highest testament to the healing powers of the democratic ideal and the creative vitality of the Negro people."

While circumstances fashioned the Negro community essentially as a matriarchy, the large Negro middle class was stable; its families might be even more patriarchal and protective than white middle class families. "Given equal opportunities, the children of these families will perform as well or better than their white peers. They need no help from anyone, and ask none."

Yet housing segregation made it "immensely difficult" for the stable Negro half to "escape from the cultural influences of the unstable" half, and thus middle class Negro children were likely to be raised in a slum life virtually unknown to white middle class children.

The matriarchal pattern in Negro life reinforced itself in a number of ways: Negro women were better educated than Negro men, performed better in school, held

four times the number of white collar jobs, almost six times the number of professional jobs and about five times the number of technical jobs. In the reversal of husband-wife roles, the daughter rather than the son in a family was chosen to pursue higher education. One study in Elmira, N.Y., showed that a third of Negro youths did not know their father's occupation, and two-thirds did not know their father's father's occupation.

Comparison of IQ tests showed lower performances by Negro children than by white children; even middle class Negro children, "surely (as) a result of housing segregation," performed below their white peers. If the father was not present in the home, IQ scores were markedly lower.

The combined impact of poverty, failure, and isolation among Negro youth has had the predictable outcome in a disastrous delinquency and crime rate." Negroes were present in orphanages in a proportion smaller than their proportion of the total population, but they constituted one-third of youths in training schools for delinquents. Probably a majority of crimes against the person were committed by Negroes. Crime statistics were "unquestionably" biased against Negroes, who were "arraigned much more casually than" whites, but it was doubtful if that bias altered the general proportions of crime data. Most Negro crimes were committed against Negroes.

"The ultimate mark of inadequate preparation for life is the failure rate on the Armed Forces mental test... 56 percent of Negroes fail it. This is a rate almost four times that of the whites." While military service offered life in an "utterly masculine" and truly equal world and was sought by Negro males, it often was beyond their reach. Negro enlistments and reenlistments were proportionately higher than for whites; 16.3 percent of Army sergeants were Negro.

Alienation of Negro males, because of the combination of these factors, was so complete that "large numbers" were withdrawing from society; they could not even be found by census enumerators after 19 years of age. In the 30-34 year age bracket in 1963, there were only 86.6 Negro males per 100 Negro females (compared to 99.2 white males), a biological improbability. An estimated 140,000 nonwhite males probably were not counted in the labor force at all in 1964; had they been, the nonwhite male unemployment rate would have been 11.5 percent instead of the reported 9 percent.

'The Case for National Action'

While "a number of responsible persons" viewed the situation as possibly out of control, "we emphatically and totally disagree." The "tangle of pathology," however, had become self-perpetuating, and a national effort was necessary to strengthen the Negro family to enable it to raise and support its members as did other families. A "militant, organized, and responsible Negro movement exists to join in that effort." The national effort might be stated in these terms:

"The policy of the United States is to bring the Negro American to full and equal sharing in the responsibilities and rewards of citizenship. To this end, the programs of the Federal Government bearing on this objective shall be designed to have the effect, directly or indirectly, of enhancing the stability and resources of the Negro American family."

WHITE HOUSE CONFERENCE

New Ideas for Civil Rights

If the year 1966 produced no new major civil rights legislation in Congress, it did produce an abundance of new ideas for such legislation. Those ideas were the product of two planning groups and the agenda for the first White House conference ever devoted to the subject.

The White House Conference "To Fulfill These Rights" was held in Washington, D.C., June 1 and 2 to discuss means of integrating the Negro American into fuller participation in the nation's social, political and economic life. About 2,600 persons attended, representing business, labor, industry, the arts, sports, the clergy, government at all levels, academia, law enforcement, the professions and civil rights groups. Only the Student Non-Violent Coordinating Committee (SNCC), among the well-known civil rights groups, refused to participate; SNCC contended that the President was insincere about civil rights.

The Conference had its origin in President Johnson's June 4, 1965, speech at Howard University in which he said he would call such a conference to propose ways of moving the Negro American "beyond opportunity to achievement." A Planning Session was held in Washington Nov. 17 and 18, 1965. *(For text of speech, see p. 397.)*

The Planning Session, designed to be a "brainstorming" session, Dec. 8, 1965, sent a list of recommendations to the President in comparatively rough form, without evaluation. *(See recommendations, below.)* The President had sought such recommendations preparatory to drafting his 1966 civil rights program, and all of the proposals he put forward in 1966 were contained in the Planning Session's report.

The next step in preparing for the Conference was taken by a President's Council, established by the President Feb. 23, 1965. This 28-member group drafted a report and agenda for the Conference based on the Planning Session's report. *(See p. 394.)*

The report of the Council became the basic document of the Conference since, more than any other document arising out of the series of planning sessions, it gave form and cohesiveness to the many scattered proposals. A. Philip Randolph, president of the Brotherhood of Sleeping Car Porters (AFL-CIO), was honorary chairman, while Ben W. Heineman, chairman of the Chicago & Northwestern Railway Co., was Council chairman. A full-time staff worked on the report and on final preparations for the Conference, activities which were coordinated with the White House through Clifford L. Alexander, deputy special counsel to the President.

No major action was taken at the conference itself, although 11 of 12 committees endorsed resolutions calling for self-government for the District of Columbia. Efforts pressed by representatives of the Congress of Racial Equality (CORE), a militant civil rights organization, to introduce and pass resolutions calling for withdrawal of American forces from Vietnam gained little other support.

Theme of the Conference

The theme of the Conference remained generally what Mr. Johnson had intended it to be—to develop new methods of bringing a larger proportion of the nation's economy and society into the civil rights effort. Specific proposals, therefore, were aimed at what the Council called "immediate, practical steps to enlist in this cause the great mass of uncommitted, uninvolved Americans."

The Council's agenda, broadly endorsed by the Conference, sifted out major Planning Session proposals in four fields: economic security and welfare, education, housing and administration of justice. In most instances —and in all significant ones—the report supported Administration programs. In many instances, however, it called for extending programs beyond the limits currently set by the Administration.

The implications of the Conference for Congress were modest at best, for the Administration's major programs, including the Civil Rights Act of 1966, had already been introduced by the time the Conference was held. Yet it was clear that Negro delegates were dissatisfied with present opportunities to participate in the "Great Society" and it was clear that they looked to the Federal Government for the key to that participation. It was clear, too, that "Great Society" programs in education, housing and employment and on the right to vote and to use public accommodations, met with the overwhelming approval of the delegates.

Planning Session

A summary of the recommendations of the Planning Session, reported Dec. 8, 1965, follows:

Recommendations

The preliminary reports listed dozens of proposals in random form. No effort was made to evaluate them, although some were designated as of an urgent nature, others were said to have had the support of a consensus of the panel while still others were said to have been suggested by one or more panel members.

Thus, while mentioned only briefly, such programs as birth control information and public legal services in civil cases for indigent persons, were said to have had wide support among panel members.

The panels and their recommendations follow:

Administration of Justice

Urgent Proposal: Provide physical security for Southern Negroes through a Civil Rights Protection Act.

Others. Extend power to remove civil rights cases from state to federal courts, create civil rights criminal offenses, such as making murder of a person exercising his civil rights a federal crime; empower the Attorney General to enjoin discriminatory state prosecutions; make state subdivisions financially liable for violent misdeeds of their officers; use federal officers to protect civil rights workers; enlarge the Civil Rights Division of the Justice Department; and provide for removal of state officers who violate federal rights. (All but the last proposal were advanced by the Civil Rights Commission Nov. 14, 1965.)

Compensate victims of racial violence, possibly by deducting awards from federal grants-in-aid; extend physical security laws to the poor in general; encourage bar associations to accept civil rights litigation; erase discrimination in employment in agencies of justice.

Set federal standards for jury selection in federal and state courts; choose jurors by polling and computers to obtain a cross-section; set federal procedures for selection but not standards for state juries; broaden powers of and stimulate the Justice Department to intervene in jury discrimination cases.

Redefine the role of police as peace-keepers who prevent as well as suppress crime; review discriminatory police procedures, such as "stop-and-frisk"; urge all police departments to establish community relations units; induce Negroes to join the police; federally train Negroes for possible employment by communities nationwide.

Start a massive federal program under the Law Enforcement Assistance Act of 1965; provide grants-in-aid for recruitment, training and community relations and link training and promotion to existing educational institutions; remove administration of this program from the Justice Department and place it "close" to the President.

Encourage civil rights groups and Negroes to assist police in establishing good relations and perhaps to do preliminary investigations on complaints; establish civilian review boards (no agreement among panelists as to their value); establish a general complaint agency, like the Scandinavian Ombudsman; encourage the Office of Economic Opportunity's neighborhood legal aid program and like programs.

Enact a Correctional Bill of Rights to protect persons convicted of crime; encourage work-release programs authorized by Congress.

Community: Institutions and Social Action

Build Negro power in the community; provide jobs and careers for able poor; support mass organizations of low-income persons by (1) making them bargaining agents with "institutions controlled from outside the Negro community," (2) training organizers to lead them and (3) giving them federal funds to operate.

Redirect federal funds toward the neighborhood groups to bypass the "establishment" by (1) giving federal aid directly to these groups, (2) adopting the principle of "maximum feasible participation" for such agencies as the Job Corps and (3) developing new corporate structures such as consumer cooperatives, credit bureaus and the like, utilizing federal subsidies.

Recommendations of one or more panelists: Purchase land with federal funds and underwrite "community neighborhood corporations" for "no-income" and low-income Southern Negroes to help them build homes and businesses; fashion a housing policy to embrace regional planning and "new towns"; enlarge Community Relations Service; establish Cabinet-level Department of Decolonization to transfer "resources" of ghettos to local hands; declare the Negro community a "national disaster" area; initiate massive program of construction and rehabilitation of housing to provide jobs and better housing for Negroes; raise minimum wage; enforce federal contract compliance provisions; place OEO funds only in non-discriminating banks; and institute guaranteed family incomes.

Education

Fully enforce Title VI of the Civil Rights Act of 1964, insisting upon desegregation of schools in the South and in such Northern cities as Boston and Chicago.

Reorganize American education by (1) immediate appointment of a Presidential Task Force to establish goals and make plans for implementing Title VI and for reorganization of the educational system, (2) rejecting evasions of Title VI, such as freedom-of-choice plans and the use of standardized tests, (3) strengthening the Office of Education or establishing a separate office to desegregate schools, (4) heavily investing federal funds to develop new educational methods, such as the educational park, (5) requiring submission of joint proposals by inner city and suburban schools or by white and Negro colleges for federal funds, (6) making special appropriations to poorer states, (7) molding housing policies to effect desegregation, (9) accelerating a movement toward minimum standards of student performance and national norms of academic performance and efficiency in local school systems and (9) providing federal schooling where local government is unwilling or unable to provide non-segregated education.

State and local efforts should include: total reorganization of school systems in terms of goals, curricula, teaching methods, buildings, facilities (including educational parks) and other aspects; extension of pre-school and other compensatory programs; and reorganization of school boards to represent all groups in the community.

The Family: Resources for Changes

Establish programs for: (1) stable family incomes through public works and needed services, (2) family allowances, guaranteed minimum incomes and negative income tax, (3) services to protect family income, (4) housing and housing subsidies for poor and marginal families, (5) Head Start projects for adolescents, adults and older people, (6) family planning, (7) broadening the Negro middle class, (8) helping with internal family problems such as illegitimacy, health and parental control of children, (9) coordinating health, education and welfare services to provide more than merely referral services, (10) using available funds more efficiently, (11) providing more information on existing programs and plugging gaps in state and local programs, (12) reviewing discrimination in services, such as maternity homes, hospitals and juvenile delinquency centers, (13) improving attitudes of welfare workers, (14) placing effective "role models" to be observed by Negro children, for example, by using male teachers in elementary and high schools and in other obvious capacities and (15) drawing the poor into planning, including the June White House Conference.

Health and Welfare

Urgent Proposals: Sufficiently fund Department of Health, Education and Welfare (HEW) to implement Title VI of the Civil Rights Act of 1964 to prohibit discrimination; provide forum to bring together Government officials, local health and welfare officials and recipients, particularly in the South; and establish communications between federal officials and "indigenous people" in the South.

General Proposals: Set federal standards for quality and availability of services; if standards are not met, the Government should contract to provide them; consider birth control programs; involve recipients in decision-making; use trained non-professionals extensively; and establish a universal adult literacy program.

Proposed by one or more panelists: Abolish federal-state grant system and adopt regional planning concept; abolish means and literacy tests; promote mental health programs in the South; integrate boards and staffs of agencies; integrate all HEW staffs; have civil rights groups document infringements of Title VI; place Negro physicians on hospital staffs; recruit young Negroes for health and para-medical programs; base health programs in the neighborhood and use VISTA volunteers in health programs.

Housing and Neighborhood

Urgent Proposals: Extend Executive Order 11063 or promulgate new order to ban discrimination in all federally aided housing; call a White House Conference on Housing; challenge the housing industry to meet the problem; require all federal agencies to promote desegregation; condition federal aid on a regional "workable program" including desegregation; fully implement Title VI of the Civil Rights Act of 1964; require aggressive marketing to Negroes of federally aided housing; fund the rent-supplement provisions of the Housing Act of 1965 and broaden it to include moderate-income groups.

Other Proposals: Reject more large public housing projects; build small projects, widely dispersed; encourage financing provisions (Sections 213, 221) of the Housing Act and reduce interest rates for Section 221 financing, possibly to zero; enact a federal equal housing opportunity law to cover all housing; establish an agency within the Housing Department to purchase metropolitan land for low- and moderate-income housing; supply loans and grants to states for the same purpose; establish federally financed corporations for the same purpose, or finance similar state corporations; amend state laws to permit urban renewal on a regional planning basis; give states a choice of reserving land for development or accepting federal action; adopt housing laws in all states; discourage popular referenda to rescind fair housing laws; develop "new towns" concept; encourage states to assist cities with urban problems; stimulate educators' response to racially transitional areas; encourage civil rights groups to face housing problems; condition federal highway and other aid on state adoption of fair housing laws; sell public housing projects to nonprofit corporations under Section 221; use income supplements as an alternative to rent supplements.

Jobs, Job Training and Economic Security

Develop Government capital and manpower budget; include all agricultural and blue-collar workers under the Fair Labor Standards Act; raise the minimum wage in steps to $2 an hour; stimulate unorganized workers, including those in Government and nonprofit institutions, to organize in unions.

Empower the Equal Employment Opportunity Commission to issue cease-and-desist orders and to initiate action; review Executive Order 11114 to determine if Government contractors' nondiscrimination should not take priority over collective bargaining agreements; attack discrimination in state and local government employment.

Expand the number of junior and community colleges; give tax credits for in-place training; use the Manpower Development and Training Act to train large numbers of Negroes; strengthen and tighten control over the U.S. Employment Service.

Voting, Citizenship Participation

Urgent Proposals: The Government should encourage voter registration; by executive order, establish a Commission on Registration and Voting to coordinate registration activities; and the Attorney General should certify more Southern counties for federal voting examiners.

Other Proposals: Amend the Constitution to set uniform registration and voting laws; establish a national minimum voting age of 18; eliminate residency and literacy requirements and permit registration by mail; establish universal and permanent registration, utilizing computers; eliminate registration altogether.

Protect Southern Negroes who vote under the Voting Rights Act of 1965; use mobile federal voting examiners and use schools, firehouses, libraries and post offices but not police stations or courthouses for registering in the South; use "deputy registrars" as in California to canvass neighborhoods and register on the spot.

Clarify the Hatch Act, which might inhibit potential Negro leaders who are Government workers from entering politics; train Negro leaders in a national Citizenship House; establish programs of voter registration and Citizenship education in schools and neighborhood centers; draw Negroes into policy-making of political parties at the national level; encourage civil rights groups to exert more political pressure on the parties; initiate through OEO a program of political education (some panelists doubted OEO's ability to conduct nonpartisan training); and federally finance neighborhood organizations (some panelists felt it was naive to assume that the Government would support groups seeking political power).

Council's Recommendations

The President's Council, which planned the White House Conference, May 24, 1966, released its report and agenda which became the focal point of the Conference.

Economic Security and Welfare. The report said that "nothing less than a broadly based 'crash' program can significantly improve the life-chances of hundreds of thousands of Negro Americans now trapped in joblessness and poverty." The economic insecurity of the Negro was the most "ugly and urgent crisis" faced by the nation, it said.

Human Resources. The report recommended the establishment of Metropolitan Job Councils in every major urban area with a substantial Negro population to plan and carry out programs to increase the number of jobs. An equivalent Rural Jobs Task Force, appointed by the President, should develop programs for jobs and other economic assistance to impoverished rural Negroes and should report by Sept. 1. Both would coordinate their work with a national-level Comprehensive Human Resource Program under the direction of the Department of Labor. This program would maintain data on the employment status of Negroes and measure the effectiveness of the various other programs.

Guaranteed Jobs. The report recommended a federal program of guaranteed employment through public works and services for persons physically able but unemployable because of their lack of skills. This proposal was stressed at the planning session, particularly as a method of producing jobs while rebuilding slums in Negro ghettos. The National Commission on Technology, Automation, and Economic Progress Feb. 2 recommended this program to provide jobs for 500,000 hard-core unemployed; it estimated the first-year cost at $2 billion.

Other Job Programs. The report recommended a year-round effort to place Negro youths in jobs, an expansion of the Vice President's Task Force on Youth Motivation and expansion of the Neighborhood Youth Corps. It endorsed the main provisions of the Equal Employment Opportunity Act of 1966 (HR 10065), which extended coverage of Title VII of the Civil Rights Act of 1964 to employers and unions with eight or more employees or members and which authorized the Equal Employment Opportunity Commission to issue "cease and desist" orders against discriminatory practices. (The bill was not enacted.)

Existing Programs. The report recommended federalizing the U.S. Employment Service (USES), which was financed by federal funds but operated by the states. It also recommended extending federal labor law protection to agricultural workers.

Public Assistance. The report recommended setting national standards for levels of public assistance, which currently varied widely from state to state, and elimination of the existing five main federal-state categories of public assistance, substituting one category based solely on need.

Guaranteed Income. The report urged "explicit acceptance" of guaranteeing a minimum income "to all Americans." Without suggesting an income level or method of administration, the report said this program should be aimed at those persons unemployable for reasons of age, disability, family responsibility or "other reasons" and who were not adequately covered by "social insurance," presumably meaning welfare programs. The same recommendation, limiting guaranteed income to unemployable and uninsured persons, was made Feb. 2 by the National Commission on Technology, Automation, and Economic Progress. The Commission estimated the cost of the program at $2 to $20 billion, depending on the levels set, and it also called for simultaneous upgrading of welfare programs. One method of administering the "guaranteed minimum income" would be through the Internal Revenue Service, in a so-called "negative income tax" or system of rebates.

Education. The report found that "segregated education is still the general condition" in the South, that de facto education existed widely in the North and West and that a central reason for those conditions was

the failure of state governments to live up to their obligations. The report called for a wide variety of programs to speed up integration of school systems and simultaneously to upgrade public and private education generally. It said the present national average per-pupil expenditure was $553 and suggested a "reasonable goal" of $1,000 per child.

Equal Education Investment. The report recommended increasing allocations under Title I of the Elementary and Secondary Education Act "beyond the newly projected authorization." Title I dealt with funds for disadvantaged children.

Desegregation. The report said federal aid to education should be "contingent on" approval of "area-wide" plans for desegregating school systems.

Compliance. The report said it was "shameful" that Congress appropriated "only $3 million" for the compliance program under Title VI of the Civil Rights Act of 1964, and urged more funds and staff for the Office of Education to carry out the compliance program in Southern school districts.

Teachers. The report recommended efforts to promote desegregation of faculties, as required by HEW guidelines, and implementation of the National Teachers Corps to send teachers into deprived areas.

School Lunch. The report said it was "important to drop the requirement" that the school lunch program apply only to certain deprived children, as requested by the President.

Higher Education. The report recommended a national policy of two years of free post-secondary education, apparently on a voluntary basis, and urged upgrading of predominantly Negro colleges in the interim. The latter provision was included in the 1966 extension of the Higher Education Act.

Housing. The report concentrated on two major efforts in the housing field—eliminating segregated living patterns and providing more adequate housing for more people.

Open Housing. The report endorsed the open-housing provision (Title IV) of the Administration's Civil Rights Act of 1966 (HR 14765), but called for administrative as well as judicial remedies for its enforcement. The bill died in the Senate, but became law in 1968.

Real Estate Dealers. The report called for a statement of policy by the National Assn. of Real Estate Boards (NAREB) and similar groups in favor of open housing. NAREB opposed open housing.

Rent Supplements. The report "strongly endorsed" the Administration's program of rent supplements for low-income families, a key "Great Society" goal. Congress approved the first appropriations for the program in 1966.

Demonstration Cities. The report "strongly endorsed" the Administration's "model cities" program, but asked that approval of local projects be conditioned on development of a "comprehensive metropolitan program." In passing the legislation, Congress included incentives for such comprehensive programs.

Housing Supply. The report called for federal legislation to help stimulate an increase in the rate of production of new homes from about 1.4 million to 2 million a year. Among means suggested were "greatly increased authorizations" under the below-market interest program of the Federal Housing Administration as enacted in the Housing and Urban Development Act of 1965. The report also recommended establishing federally chartered rural housing development corporations to build homes for the elderly or agricultural or migrant workers.

New Towns. The report recommended that the Department of Housing and Urban Development (HUD) be empowered to obtain and "bank" undeveloped land for future development. The report proposed that federal aid to local communities be conditioned on acceptable metropolitan-wide desegregation plans.

Ghettos. The report recommended that "revitalization" of ghettos be made the "cornerstone" of federal housing policy. It said HUD and local authorities should have the power to alter income and rent levels in public housing in order to have a variety of tenants.

Administration of Justice. The report concentrated on three aspects of law enforcement: protection of Negroes and civil rights workers from intimidation, equal justice for Negroes and policy minority group community relations. It endorsed the law enforcement provisions of the Civil Rights Act of 1966.

Legal Aid. The report recommended extending the concept of neighborhood law centers, as currently administered by OEO, to federally sponsored centers providing legal representation to Negroes and civil rights workers.

Cadet Academy. The report recommended establishing a federal police cadet training corps, open to high school graduates, who would train in the federal program before joining local police departments to be employed as clerks or in other capacities until reaching 21 years of age and being hired as regular police officers.

Civil Rights Act. The report supported the Civil Rights Act of 1966 (HR 14765) but recommended adding provisions to: indemnify victims of racial violence; make state and local governments jointly liable with their police officers for such indemnification; provide for removal of civil rights cases from state to federal courts to assure a fair trial; authorize private persons to obtain injunctions against persons exercising 1st Amendment rights; and strengthen existing federal prohibitions against interference by officials with the exercise of constitutional rights.

Conclusion. The report in conclusion called for broadening the base of participation by state governments, cities, public and private groups and citizens in the civil rights movement. It also called for a national conference "in the near future" on health to consider the high infant mortality and lower life expectance rates of low-income Negroes, improvement of health services and drawing Negroes into the health professions.

Community Relations Service Transferred to Justice Department

Congress in 1966 approved a Reorganization Plan submitted by President Johnson that transferred the Community Relations Service (CRS) from the Commerce Department to the Justice Department.

In his message on the reorganization, President Johnson Feb. 10 said this action was "a further step in strengthening the operation and coordination of our civil rights programs." He added that the CRS "was located in the Department of Commerce by the Congress on the assumption that a primary need would be the conciliation of disputes arising out of the public accommodations title (of the 1964 Civil Rights Act).... The need for conciliation in this area has not been as great as anticipated because of the voluntary progress that has been made by businessmen and business organizations."

HUMPHREY PLAN

Background. On Sept. 24, 1965, President Johnson abolished the President's Committee on Equal Employment Opportunity and the similar President's Council and assigned responsibility for nondiscrimination in federal activities to the various departments of the Government (Executive Order 11246). The President's action followed the recommendations of Vice President Hubert H. Humphrey, who had succeeded Mr. Johnson as head of the President's Committee on Equal Employment Opportunity. In his memorandum to the President, Humphrey said responsibility for enforcing nondiscrimination should be as-signed to officials operating the affected programs rather than to interagency committees such as his.

The Executive Order directed the Civil Service Commission to oversee nondiscrimination in Government employment and the Labor Department to oversee nondiscrimination by Government contractors.

At the same time, the President announced that he would send to Congress in 1966 a reorganization plan transferring the Community Relations Service to the Justice Department, as recommended by Humphrey. The Vice President said the Attorney General would be expected to call upon appropriate departments for expert advice when conciliation of disputes was needed.

The plan aroused some opposition, based on the belief it was unwise to combine enforcement and conciliation functions in the same agency.

Concern by some civil rights leaders that moving the CRS to the Justice Department might mean a trend toward acting after racial problems had erupted, rather than preventing their eruption, was mollified somewhat by the announcement Dec. 14 that Assistant CRS Director Roger W. Wilkins was to become Acting Director. Wilkins, a Negro lawyer, was a nephew of Roy Wilkins, executive secretary of the National Assn. for the Advancement of Colored People.

Roger Wilkins was confirmed by the Senate Jan. 29, 1966, as head of the Conciliation Service. When the agency moved to the Justice Department, he was assigned the rank of an Assistant Attorney General.

Partial Text of President's Civil Rights Address at Howard

Following is a partial transcript of President Johnson's June 4, 1965, speech at Howard University, in which he announced plans for the White House Conference on Civil Rights:

...Nothing in any country touches us more profoundly, and nothing is more freighted with meaning for our own destiny than the revolution of the Negro American.

In far too many ways American Negroes have been another nation: deprived of freedom, crippled by hatred, the doors of opportunity closed to hope.

In our time change has come to this nation too. The American Negro, acting with impressive restraint, has peacefully protested and marched, entered the courtrooms and the seats of government, demanding a justice that has long been denied. The voice of the Negro was the call to action. But it is a tribute to America that, once aroused, the courts and the Congress, the President and most of the people have been the allies of progress.

Thus we have seen the high court of the country declare that discrimination based on race was repugnant to the Constitution, and therefore void. We have seen in 1957, 1960, and again in 1964, the first civil rights legislation in this nation in almost an entire century.... The voting rights bill will be the latest, and among the most important, in a long series of victories....

The number of Negroes in schools of higher learning has almost doubled in fifteen years. The number of non-white professional workers has more than doubled in ten years.... But for the great majority of Negro Americans—the poor, the unemployed, the uprooted and the dispossessed—there is a much grimmer story. They still, as we meet here tonight, are another nation. Despite the court orders and the laws, despite the legislative victories and the speeches, for them the walls are rising and the gulf is widening....

First, Negroes are trapped—as many whites are trapped —in inherited, gateless poverty. They lack training and skills. They are shut in slums, without decent medical care. Private and public poverty combine to cripple their capacities.

We are trying to attack these evils through our poverty program, through our education program, through our medical care and our other health programs and a dozen more of the Great Society programs that are aimed at the root causes of this poverty.

We will increase, and we will accelerate, and we will broaden this attack in years to come until this most enduring of foes finally yields to our unyielding will. But there is a second cause—much more difficult to explain, more deeply grounded, more desperate in its force. It is the devastating heritage of long years of slavery; and a century of oppression, hatred and injustice.

For Negro poverty is not white poverty. Many of its causes and many of its cures are the same. But there are differences— deep, corrosive, obstinate differences—radiating painful roots into the community, and into the family, and the nature of the individual.

These differences are not racial differences. They are solely and simply the consequence of ancient brutality, past injustice, and present prejudice. They are anguishing to observe. For the Negro they are a constant reminder of oppression. For the white they are a constant reminder of guilt. But they must be faced and they must be dealt with and they must be overcome, if we are ever to reach the time when the only difference between Negroes and whites is the color of their skin.

Nor can we find a complete answer in the experience of other American minorities. They made a valiant and a largely successful effort to emerge from poverty and prejudice.

The Negro, like these others, will have to rely mostly on his own efforts. But he just can not do it alone. For they did not have the heritage of centuries to overcome, and they did not have a cultural tradition which had been twisted and battered by endless years of hatred and hopelessness, nor were they excluded—these others—because of race or color—a feeling whose dark intensity is matched by no other prejudice in our society.

Nor can these differences be understood as isolated infirmities. They are a seemless web. They cause each other. They result from each other. They reinforce each other.

Much of the Negro community is buried under a blanket of history and circumstance. It is not a lasting solution to lift just one corner of that blanket. We must stand on all sides and we must raise the entire cover if we are to liberate our fellow citizens.

One of the differences is the increased concentration of Negroes in our cities. More than 73 percent of all Negroes live in urban areas compared with less than 70 percent of the whites. Most of these Negroes live in slums. Most of these Negroes live together—a separated people.

Men are shaped by their world. When it is a world of decay, ringed by an invisible wall, when escape is arduous and uncertain, and the saving pressures of a more hopeful society are unknown, it can cripple the youth and it can desolate the man.

There is also the burden that a dark skin can add to the search for a productive place in society. Unemployment strikes most swiftly and broadly at the Negro, and this burden erodes hope. Blighted hope breeds despair. Despair brings indifference to the learning which offers a way out. And despair, coupled with indifference, is often the source of destructive rebellion against the fabric of society.

There is also the lacerating hurt of early collision with white hatred or prejudice, distaste or condescension. Other groups have felt similar intolerance. But success and achievement could wipe it away. They do not change the color of a man's skin....

Perhaps most important—its influence radiating to every part of life—is the breakdown of the Negro family structure. For this, most of all, white America must accept responsibility. It flows from centuries of oppression and persecution of the Negro man. It flows from the long years of degradation and discrimination, which have attacked his dignity and assaulted his ability to provide for his family....

Only a minority—less than half—of all Negro children reach the age of 18 having lived all their lives with both of their parents. Probably a majority of all Negro children receive federally aided public assistance sometime during their childhood.

The family is the cornerstone of our society. More than any other force it shapes the attitude, the hopes, the ambitions, and the values of the child. And when the family collapses it is the children that are usually damaged. When it happens on a massive scale the community itself is crippled.

So, unless we work to strengthen the family, to create conditions under which most parents will stay together—all the rest: schools, and play grounds, and public assistance, and private concern, will never be enough to cut completely the circle of despair and deprivation.

There is no single easy answer to all of these problems. Jobs are part of the answer. They bring the income which permits a man to provide for his family. Decent homes in decent surroundings and a chance to learn—an equal chance to learn —are part of the answer. Welfare and social programs better designed to hold families together are part of the answer. Care for the sick is part of the answer. An understanding heart by all Americans is another big part of the answer. And to all these fronts—and a dozen more—I will dedicate the expanding efforts of the Johnson Administration.

But there are other answers still to be found. Nor do we fully understand even all of the problems. Therefore, I want to announce tonight that this fall I intend to call a White House conference of scholars, and experts, and outstanding Negro leaders—men of both races—and officials of Government at every level.

CIVIL DISORDERS COMMISSION

White Racism Blamed for Urban Riots

President Johnson's National Advisory Commission on Civil Disorders cited "white racism" which has "long permeated much of American life" as the deep, underlying cause of urban riots.

Discrimination and segregation and the lack of concern of "white America" with the problems of the Negro created over the years an "explosive mixture" of poverty, unemployment, inadequate housing, poor education and ghetto life, the Commission said. It found no evidence of a conspiracy or organization behind any facet of the riots.

The Commission released the summary of its findings Feb. 29, 1968, and the full, lengthy report March 2. There was no mincing of words: "This is our basic conclusion: Our nation is moving toward two societies, one black, one white—separate and unequal."

The alternative to this "polarization" was a "commitment to national action—compassionate, massive and sustained." It would be expensive, requiring "unprecedented levels of funding," but "the nation has substantial financial resources...in spite of a war and in spite of current budget requirements." In saying this, however, the Commission avoided any specifics on how much its recommendations would cost.

The 11-member Commission was appointed by President Johnson July 27, 1967, following major riots in Newark and Detroit. Headed by Illinois Gov. Otto Kerner (D) with New York Mayor John V. Lindsay (R) as vice chairman, the bipartisan Commission was instructed to ferret out the causes of the riots and to recommend courses of action. *(For list of members, see box, next page.)*

The report was divided into three parts: What Happened? Why Did It Happen? and What Can Be Done?

What Happened?

There were 164 "disorders" in the first nine months of 1967. The Commission classified eight of them as "major," 33 as "serious" and 123 as "minor." They were typified by "Negroes acting against local symbols of white American society, authority and property in Negro neighborhoods, rather than against white persons." There were 83 deaths, and the "overwhelming majority" of the persons killed and injured were Negroes.

The Commission found that original damage estimates were "greatly exaggerated." It set the damage of the Detroit riot at $45 million ($200-$500 million had been reported following the riot) and the damage in Newark at $10.2 million.

In nearly every case studied by the Commission, tensions mounted over a period of weeks and months as a result of a series of minor incidents and grievances. These culminated in a "final incident," a police action in half of the cases, which triggered the riot. Once the riot began, "no particular control tactic was successful in every situation." Hasty, unnecessary actions by police or National Guardsmen in both Newark and Detroit fanned the

flames of the riots. *(For the Commission's recommendations on controlling riots, see box p. 400.)*

The typical rioter was a teenager or young adult, a high-school dropout who was unemployed or underemployed. The Commission found 12 grievances which were common to nearly every riot area. They were ranked in three levels of intensity:

- First level: police practices; unemployment and underemployment; inadequate housing.
- Second level: inadequate education; poor recreation facilities and programs; ineffective political structure and grievance mechanisms.
- Third level: disrespectful white attitudes; discriminatory administration of justice; inadequate federal programs, with the number of persons aided constituting only a fraction of those in need; inadequate municipal services; discriminatory consumer and credit practices; inadequate welfare programs.

After rioting had taken place, there was little change in the conditions that had precipitated the violent action. Tensions in the ghetto were not reduced, and "in several cities increasing polarization is evident." The Commission noted that in many cities the major response was to "train and equip the police with more sophisticated weapons."

The Commission stated unequivocally that the 1967 riots "were not caused by, nor were they the consequence of, any organized plan or conspiracy. Specifically, the Commission has found no evidence that all or any of the disorders or incidents that led to them were planned or directed by any organization or group, international, national or local." However, the Commission acknowledged that "militant organizations" and "individual agitators" created "an atmosphere that contributed to the outbreak of disorder."

Why Did It Happen?

The fundamental factor leading to the riots, the Commission said, was "the racial attitude and behavior of white Americans toward black Americans."

The frustrations of the ghetto were immense and, to many young Negroes, unbearable. Twenty percent of the total Negro population of all central cities lived "in squalor and deprivation in ghetto neighborhoods." The unemployment rate for Negroes in 1967 was more than double that for whites, and those Negroes who were employed were more than three times as likely as whites to be at the lowest end of the occupational scale.

More than 40 percent of the nation's nonwhites lived below the Social Security Administration's "poverty level" ($3,335 per year for an urban family of four). The result of all this, the Commission stated, was "an environmental jungle characterized by personal insecurity and tension. Children growing up under such conditions are likely participants in civil disorder."

The Commission laid the major share of the blame for these conditions on whites. "What white Americans have never fully understood—but what the Negro can never forget—is that white society is deeply implicated in the ghetto. White instutions created it, white institutions maintain it and white society condones it." The Commission detailed three of the "most bitter fruits" of "white racism."

• Significant numbers of Negroes were excluded from the "benefits of economic progress" because of discrimination and segregation in employment, education and housing. *(For discussion of housing discrimination, see box p. 401.)*

• Growing concentrations of Negroes in the central cities resulted from the black migration to the cities and the white exodus to the suburbs.

• While most whites and many Negroes outside the ghetto prospered, segregation and poverty destroyed opportunity for youth in the ghetto and made failure almost inevitable.

Another factor leading to the riots the Commission said, was the feeling among Negroes that police were the symbol of "white power, white racism and white repression. And the fact is that many police do reflect and express these white attitudes." The result was the widespread belief among Negroes in pervasive police brutality and in the existence of a double standard of law enforcement for whites and blacks.

Reinforcing this fundamental situation was "a climate that tends toward approval and encouragement of violence" and a frustrated feeling among Negroes that they were powerless to change the system by any means other than violence.

Adding to the tensions, the Commission said, was the "inflammatory rhetoric of black racists and revolutionaries.... We cannot measure with any precision the influence of these organizations and individuals in the ghetto, but we think it clear that the intolerable and unconscionable encouragement of violence heightened tensions, created a mood of acceptance and expectation and thus contributed to the eruption of disorders."

What Can Be Done?

"It is time," the Commission said, "to adopt strategies for action that will produce quick and visible progress." The Commission recommended three basic principles: "To mount programs on a scale equal to the dimension of the problems; to aim these programs for high impact in the immediate future in order to close the gap between promise and performance; and to undertake new initiatives and experiments that can change the system of failure and frustration that now dominates the ghetto and weakens our society."

While these actions required "unprecedented levels of funding and performance," the Commission said, "there can be no higher priority for national action and no higher claim on the nation's conscience."

Local Governments. The Commission noted that the riots stemmed from an accumulation of grievances and dissatisfaction, principally at the local level. While the responsibility was basically that of the local government to overcome these conditions, federal and state

---

Commission Members

The members of the National Advisory Commission on Civil Disorders were as follows:

Gov. Otto Kerner (D Ill.), chairman.

New York Mayor John V. Lindsay (R), vice chairman.

Sen. Fred R. Harris (D Okla.).

Sen. Edward W. Brooke (R Mass.).

Rep. James C. Corman (D Calif.).

Rep. William M. McCulloch (R Ohio).

I.W. Abel, president of the United Steel Workers.

Charles B. Thornton, president of Litton Industries Inc.

Roy Wilkins, executive director of the National Assn. for the Advancement of Colored People.

Katherine G. Peden, Kentucky commissioner of commerce.

Herbert Jenkins, Atlanta police chief.

---

support was needed. The Commission recommended that local governments:

• Develop neighborhood action task forces with the aim of improving communication and city services in the ghettos.

• Establish effective grievance-response mechanisms.

• Establish neighborhood outlets for administrative and public service agencies, thus bringing the institutions of local government closer to the people.

• Greatly expand the opportunities for ghetto residents to participate in the formulation of public policy.

State Governments. In addition to recommending the state financial assistance necessary for the local governments to carry out effective programs, the Commission said the states must provide communities with the necessary jurisdictional tools for dealing with their problems and must focus the interest of suburban communities on the problems of the central city.

Police. To improve law enforcement and decrease the potential for riots, the Commission recommended that police administrators and public officials:

• Eliminate abrasive practices by policemen in ghetto neighborhoods.

• Provide more adequate police protection for ghetto residents.

• Establish mechanisms for the redress of grievances against police. (The Commission said the benefits and liabilities of controversial civilian review boards had been "greatly exaggerated.")

• Adopt policy guidelines to help policemen make critical decisions.

• Seek better community support, especially in the ghettos, for law enforcement.

• Recruit more Negroes into local police forces and ensure Negro policemen full opportunity for promotion.

• Establish junior police officers, made up of ghetto youths between 17 and 21, to work in the ghettos. The Federal Government should provide 90 percent of the funds for this program.

News Media. The Commission criticized the press for not giving adequate coverage to Negro communities. It recommended that this be remedied and more Negroes and urban affairs specialists be sought by the press.

Federal Government. "Only a commitment to national action on an unprecedented scale can shape a future compatible with the historic ideals of American society," the Commission said. "The major need is to generate new will—the will to tax ourselves to the extent necessary to meet the vital needs of the nation."

The major goal, according to the Commission, was "the creation of a...single society." To accomplish this goal, the Commission recommended a number of programs as illustrative of "the type and dimension of action needed."

Employment—The Commission noted that unemployment and underemployment were the most persistent grievances in the ghettos. It recommended that the Federal Government:

• Consolidate existing manpower programs to avoid fragmentation and duplication.

• Create 2 million new jobs over the next three years —half in the Government and half in the private sector —with 550,000 of the new jobs created in the first year.

• Establish on-the-job training programs by both public and private employers with the Government reimbursing private employers for the additional cost of training the hard-core unemployed.

• Provide tax and other incentives for businesses to locate in rural poverty areas, thus offering the rural poor an alternative to moving to the cities.

• Remove all discriminatory barriers to employment and promotion; strengthen the Equal Employment Opportunity Commission and implement fully Title VI of the 1964 Act, which permitted the withholding of federal funds from activities which discriminate.

Education—The Commission noted that the "bleak record of public education for ghetto children is growing worse." The Commission supported integration as the "priority education strategy" but noted that there also should be efforts to improve "drastically the quality of ghetto education." The Commission recommended:

• Substantial federal aid for eliminating de facto segregation in schools, with the "desegregation technique best suited to the particular community determined locally."

• Dramatic improvement in schools serving disadvantaged children through increased federal funding of year-round compensatory education programs, better teaching and expanded research and demonstration programs.

• Greater federal support for adult education programs.

• More parent and community participation in school policy and activities.

• Changes in vocational education programs to involve business and industry in work-experience training.

• Increased federal aid for disadvantaged students seeking higher education.

• Revision of formulas to assure greater concentration of federal and state assistance in districts having high proportions of disadvantaged children.

Welfare—The existing welfare system, the Commission said, was "designed to save money instead of

Controlling Riots

The Commission published a supplement on control of disorder. It found among police and fire departments and National Guard units a general lack of readiness to cope with riots. It urged better planning, training and equipping of local police and fire units, more mutual assistance pacts between neighboring communities and more coordination with state police forces, National Guard units and the Army.

The Commission stressed the need for good police judgment in responding to potentially explosive situations. "The way policemen approach an incident often determines whether it is contained or develops into a serious disorder," the Commission said, adding that experienced police witnesses discouraged the use of sirens and flashing lights. "If an incident develops, and a crowd begins to threaten lawlessness and acts of violence," the report said, "the police must act promptly and with a sufficient display of force to make clear their intent and capacity to suppress disorder and ensure the public safety."

Planning. The Commission developed model plans which could be adapted locally. The plans dealt with mobilization of forces and with operations, including command and control, adequate communications (use of emergency radio frequencies and miniaturized radios for officers on foot), intelligence efforts to gather information before and during riots and tactics for coping with rioters. The plan included methods of preparing for the heavy logistical drain on police forces during emergencies, for the massive influx of arrested persons and for protecting fire equipment.

Weapons. The Commission found that "many police forces are inadequately equipped or trained for use of even conventional riot control weapons and material."

"The most serious deficiencies, however, are in advanced nonlethal weaponry," the Commission said. It recommended use of tear gas before resorting to firearms, but it noted that most police departments could not supply even 30 percent of their forces with gas masks.

"The Commission believes that equipping civil police with automatic rifles, machine guns, and other weapons of massive and indiscriminate lethality is not warranted by the evidence," the report said, adding that reports of sniping were "exaggerated." It said: "We should not attempt to convert our police into combat troops equipped for urban warfare."

If the situation were serious enough to warrant National Guard or Army assistance, the report said, even those troops should not use conventional military weaponry as if in combat. They should use nonlethal chemical agents even before fixing bayonets, the report said, adding: "Controlling a civil disorder is not warfare." It recommended against the use of machine guns except in extraordinary circumstances, adding: "Other mass destruction weapons of modern warfare—flame throwers, recoilless rifles, and artillery—have no conceivable place in riot-control operations in densely populated American cities."

Housing Is Last of Rights Covered

Of the major civil rights problems of the country—education, public accommodations, voting rights, employment, housing—the latter was the only one not specifically covered in the 1964 Civil Rights Act. Four years later, however, Congress wrote into law a ban against discrimination in selling or renting new and old houses and apartments. *(See p. 378.)*

The Government's first major step to bar discrimination in housing came Nov. 20, 1962, when President John F. Kennedy signed a long-promised Executive Order which had been recommended in a 1961 Civil Rights Commission Report. The Executive Order forbade discrimination in private housing where the mortgages were insured by the Federal Housing Administration or Veterans Administration; in federally owned or operated housing, public housing and housing in urban renewal projects subsidized by the Federal Government; and in housing constructed with federal loans, such as housing for the elderly, community facilities and college housing.

In practice, the Kennedy order covered only about 18 percent of new housing, principally because it did not include housing financed through savings and loan and commercial bank loans. President Kennedy rejected the 1961 Civil Rights Commission recommendation to the effect that such loans, when made by financial institutions regulated by federal agencies—such as the Federal Home Loan Bank Board, the Comptroller of the Currency, the Federal Reserve System and the Federal Deposit Insurance Corporation—also be subject to nondiscrimination requirements.

Even in areas which the 1962 Executive Order was designed to cover, enforcement was spotty. A new home buyer from a minority group was obliged to "shop around" to find a house being financed by FHA mortgages, a category that covered a decreasing percentage of new housing. Even in public housing projects directly financed by federal revenues, the Government had difficulty in wiping out segregation.

The National Committee Against Discrimination in Housing, a federation of 37 civil rights, religious and labor groups interested in fair housing practices, said that true open occupancy was a distant goal. The NCDH singled out the ghettos "as the rock upon which rests segregated living patterns which pervade and vitiate almost every phase of Negro life and Negro-white relationships."

President Johnson astonished Congress in 1966 when, in his State of the Union Message, he said he would seek a federal open-housing law. Nevertheless, the House on Aug. 9 approved a modified open-housing requirement by a 32-vote margin. The Senate, however, filibustered the bill to death.

In 1968 the Senate about-faced and initiated a fair-housing amendment. The House agreed to it April 10 and President Johnson signed it into law the next day.

---

people and tragically ends up doing neither." The Commission cited two "critical deficiencies": The system excludes a considerable number of persons who are in great need but who are neither aged, handicapped nor parents of young children. And, for those who are eligible, the existing system does not meet the minimum requirements for a "decent level of existence and imposes restrictions that encourage continued dependency on welfare and undermine self-respect."

The Commission recommended:
• That the federal share of welfare costs be raised to at least 90 percent of all payments.
• The repealing of restrictions, adopted by Congress in 1967, that compelled mothers of young children to work and that placed a freeze on the percentage of children in a state that could be covered by federal aid.
• The elimination of all residence requirements for welfare recipients.
• As a long-range goal, the establishment of a "national system of income supplements based strictly on need." (Though the Commission did not say it, this recommendation appeared to be tantamount to controversial proposals for a guaranteed minimum income.)
• Uniform national standards of assistance.
• A requirement that all states receiving federal welfare money participate in the Aid to Families with Dependent Children-Unemployed Parents program.

Housing—The Commission noted the inadequacy of existing federal programs. Only 800,000 units were built in the 31-year history of federal public housing programs.

The Commission recommended:

• The enactment of a "comprehensive and enforceable federal open-housing law to cover the sale and rental of all housing."
• Emphasis in federal programs in placing low-income housing outside the ghetto.
• The construction and rehabilitation of 6 million housing units for low- and moderate-income families in the next five years, beginning with 600,000 units in the first year.
• The use of rent supplements for existing housing, as well as new and rehabilitated housing.
• Expansion and modification of the below-market interest rate program.
• Establishment of a home-ownership program for low-income families.
• Federal interest-rate support on loans to private builders for construction of moderate-rent housing.
• Expansion of the public housing and Model Cities programs.
• Changes in the urban renewal program to give priority to low-income housing.

SCHOOL DESEGREGATION

Attacks on Dual System Increasingly Successful

Dual school systems established by law or custom existed throughout the South. Efforts, first by private litigation and later by the Federal Government, to eliminate the dual system became increasingly successful, but were far from complete by the end of the Johnson years. By the end of 1968, only about 20 percent of Negro children in 11 Southern states attended schools that were at least 50 percent white.

The first major breakthrough came in 1954 when the Supreme Court ruled that "separate but equal" school systems for white and Negro were unconstitutional. In *Brown v. Board of Education of Topeka, Kansas,* the Court found that "separate educational facilities" were "inherently unequal."

The Court did not specify how school desegregation should be achieved. It addressed itself to compliance in a second *Brown* decision in 1955 but stated that because of the varying local problems local school boards would be held responsible for solving the problems. The Court said that the lower courts were responsible for deciding whether local action constituted compliance with the *Brown* decision and that although the lower courts could grant additional time for administrative problems to be worked out, such problems should be solved "with all deliberate speed." *(For Brown and subsequent Supreme Court school desegregation rulings, see Congress and the Nation, Vol. I, p. 1606.)*

The Brown decision paved the way for individual law suits seeking desegregation of individual school districts. Such suits were filed with increasing frequency by such organizations as the National Assn. for the Advancement of Colored People (NAACP). They were given added impetus by the civil rights movement in the early 1960s.

In the ten years following the Brown decision little progress towards school desegregation was achieved in the South. Law suits were time consuming and expensive and often did not effect substantial changes in school districts. Complainants in school desegregation suits were often harassed and intimidated.

Desegregation Legislation. The first federal school desegregation legislation was enacted in 1964 as part of the Civil Rights Act of 1964 (PL 88-352). It authorized the Federal Government, for the first time, to take a major role in desegregating schools. The authority was in several forms: authority to sue, to provide technical assistance and to withhold federal funds. The power to withhold federal funds became the primary tool for achieving school desegregation.

Interpretation and enforcement of school desegregation requirements changed radically after the enactment of the 1964 Act. The first enforcement efforts focused almost entirely on the dual school systems of the South. Freedom of choice plans, which permitted students (primarily Negroes) to choose the school they wanted to attend but did not impose desegregation, were accepted. By 1968, most freedom-of-choice plans were being rejected as inadequate and HEW was investigating segregation in Northern as well as Southern schools.

Freedom of Choice Issue

Under freedom of choice desegregation plans, a student, or his parents, could choose the school he was to attend.

One of the measures of the development of school desegregation enforcement between 1965 and 1968 was the change in the way "freedom of choice" was regarded by supporters and opponents of school desegregation.

In 1965 freedom of choice was seen as a valid means of accomplishing desegregation although HEW guidelines did warn that "the responsibility to eliminate segregation rests with the school authorities and is not satisfied by rules and practices which shift the burden...(to) persons previously discriminated against." The guidelines included specifications, such as requirements for notifying students of their freedom of choice of schools, designed to ensure that a choice of schools was offered to students. By 1968 HEW guidelines ruled out most freedom of choice plans and freedom of choice had become sacrosanct among opponents of school desegregation.

HEW civil rights enforcement officials and other advocates of school desegregation contended that freedom of choice plans were seldom effective in achieving desegregation of dual school systems. In most districts using freedom of choice plans, relatively few Negro children transferred to white schools. In many districts there were instances of economic or physical intimidation of Negro parents or students. Sometimes transfer requests were discouraged or refused. Negro students were also sometimes discouraged from transferring by the staff of Negro schools who felt that their students would not do well in white schools or who feared that Negro schools could be closed down, leaving them jobless. Fear of social isolation or unequal treatment in white schools also deterred Negro students from transferring.

In some cases federal programs were used to discourage Negro pupils from transferring. A number of districts instituted free breakfasts or lunches at Negro schools but not at white schools. Opponents of freedom of choice also argued that such plans placed the burden of desegregation upon Negro pupils and their parents rather than on the school authorities who should bear the responsibility of desegregation. Freedom of choice plans achieved integration only to the extent that Negro students transfer to white schools. White pupils virtually never voluntarily attended Negro schools.

Court Decisions. The courts, in a series of decisions, narrowed the acceptability of freedom of choice plans. The Supreme Court took up the issue of freedom of choice plans in its May 27, 1968, decision on *Green v. County School Board of New Kent County, Va.* It said that although "the general experience" indicated otherwise, there might be instances in which freedom of choice could serve as an effective device for achieving desegregation. But the Court held that "if there are reasonably available other ways, such for illustration as zoning, promising

Basic Desegregation Law Dates from 1964

The basic legislative authority for federal school desegregation activities was enacted in the Civil Rights Act of 1964 (PL 88-352). Provisions affecting school desegregation enforcement also were enacted in subsequent years.

The relevant provisions of the 1964 Act were as follows:

Title IV. Authorized the Office of Education (OE) to give technical and financial assistance, if requested, to local public schools systems planning, or in the process of, desegregation.

Authorized the Attorney General to file suits for the desegregation of public schools and colleges upon receipt of a complaint from individuals who were unable to initiate and maintain legal proceedings provided that the action would "materially further" orderly school desegregation.

Stated that the law did not authorize U.S. officials or courts to issue any order seeking to achieve racial balance in schools by transporting children from one school to another (busing).

Title VI. Prohibited discrimination, under any program or activity receiving federal assistance, against any person because of his race, color or national origin.

Directed each federal agency to issue regulations for carrying out the nondiscrimination provisions of the law in its grants and loan programs.

Required agencies to first seek voluntary compliance but authorized agencies to cut off federal funds for a program, after a hearing, if the particular recipient or political entity did not comply.

Title IX. Authorized the Attorney General to intervene in private suits where persons have alleged denial of equal protection of the laws under the 14th amendment and where he certifies that the case is of "general public importance."

Other legislative provisions affecting school desegregation enforcement are as follows:

• The 1966 amendments (PL 89-750) to the Elementary and Secondary Education Act (PL 89-10) prohibited the Federal Government from requiring the assignment or transportation of students or teachers in order to overcome racial imbalance. They also set a limit of 60 days during which grants under education programs could be deferred for noncompliance without a hearing and required that a decision be issued within 30 days after a hearing.

• The 1967 amendments (PL 90-247) to the Elementary and Secondary Education Act required HEW school desegregation guidelines to be uniformly applied and enforced throughout the 50 states. They stipulated that a school district would be in compliance if it was complying with a court desegregation order.

• The fiscal 1969 appropriations for the Departments of Labor and HEW (PL 90-557) prohibited the withholding of funds in order to force the attendance of a student at any particular school or to force the busing of students or the abolishment of any particular school in order to overcome racial imbalance. They required the Department of HEW to assign as many persons to school desegregation investigation and compliance activities in the other states as in the 17 border and Southern states and to enforce the law on a national basis.

---

speedier and more effective conversion to a unitary, nonracial school system, "freedom of choice must be held unacceptable." It said that the school board must formulate a new plan and "fashion steps which promise realistically to convert promptly to a system without a 'white' school and a 'Negro' school, but just schools."

Earlier, on March 29, 1967, the Fifth Circuit Court of Appeals, sitting *en banc,* had held in *Stout v. Jefferson County Board of Education* that school boards and officials administering public schools in the Fifth Circuit had the "affirmative duty under the 14th Amendment to bring about an integrated, unitary school system." It said that the necessity of overcoming the effects of the dual school system in the Fifth Circuit required the integration of faculties, facilities, and activities as well as students. The Fifth Circuit decision applied to Alabama, Florida, Georgia, Louisiana, Mississippi and Texas.

HEW school desegregation officials said that it was the responsibility of HEW to require desegregation of schools receiving federal aid not only as set out in the 1964 Civil Rights Act but also under the Constitution as interpreted by the courts.

Southern Position. Southern opponents of HEW's enforcement policies contested the Department's assertion that its desegregation guidelines should follow court interpretations of what desegregation was required under the Constitution in addition to the requirements of the

1964 Civil Rights Act. They argued that HEW's desegregation policies should only carry out the intent of Congress and the enforcement of court interpretations which go beyond the intent of Congress should be enforced by the courts.

The original purpose of the 1964 Civil Rights Act was to provide freedom of choice, not desegregation, Southern leaders said. As HEW enforcement policies became more stringent, Southern Members of Congress protested on the basis of the debate on the 1964 Act. In a May 2, 1966, letter to President Johnson protesting newly revised HEW guidelines, Senator Richard B. Russell (D Ga.) and 18 other Senators wrote: "During the entire course of the debate, all of the champions of the bill emphasized that the primary purpose of Title VI was to prohibit racial discrimination by the process of segregation in all programs utilizing federal funds. It was stressed time and again that it was not the purpose of the Act to invoke the federal power to compel integration of the races in the schools."

President Johnson's reply was also cited as an indication that the intent of the law was to provide freedom of choice rather than to ensure integration. The President May 16, 1966, wrote Russell, "The guidelines are not designed to compel desegregation beyond that inherent in a fairly working free choice plan, to strike down freedom of choice, or to achieve 'racial balance'.... In short, the guidelines do not abandon freedom of choice, they seek to guarantee it in fact."

Southern protests against the HEW rejection of most freedom of choice plans conveyed a sense of betrayal. Russell Oct. 8, 1968, in debate on amendments to the Labor-HEW appropriations bill which would have protected freedom of choice plans, said, "The people in my part of the country did not welcome this legislation (the 1964 Act), but they have, in good faith, in practically every instance in my state, undertaken to conform to it. They have undertaken to establish a genuine and bona fide freedom of choice system in the administration of the schools." He said that "there is today not the slightest resemblance on the part of the (HEW) Department to any meaningful freedom of choice in any aspect of its program; instead, the administration of it is marked by bureaucratic coercion and force.... The administrators have abandoned any pretense of the stated objective of the law at the time it was passed, and have undertaken to establish entirely new objectives in their administration of the act."

The HEW desegregation guidelines also placed an unfair burden on local school boards and administrators, in the view of many Southerners. School boards were used by HEW as the Department's agents in implementing school desegregation plans although they were elected by and represented the local community which was generally opposed to such change, Southerners contended. School officials who implemented freedom of choice plans, sometimes at considerable political cost to themselves, were then told that such plans were inadequate, they said.

Although freedom of choice was resisted by most Southern school districts when it was first imposed by the courts and by HEW, it became a "cherished freedom" as school districts attempt to resist further integration.

History of Enforcement

HEW enforcement of the 1964 Civil Rights Act began in 1965 and at first was primarily involved in obtaining "paper compliance" with HEW regulations which went into effect early in January 1965. The regulations stated that elementary and secondary schools would be considered to have satisfied the requirements of Title VI if they were under a U.S. court order for desegregation and provided assurance that they would comply with the order or if they submitted a desegregation plan which was approved by the Commissioner of Education as being adequate to accomplish the purpose of the Civil Rights Act and provided "reasonable assurance that it will carry out such a plan." Those districts which were already in compliance with the regulations could simply file a form (Form 441) stating so.

HEW guidelines for complying with desegregation regulations were not issued until April 1965. School desegregation guidelines, which became one of the main targets of Southern attacks on federal desegregation programs, were originally drafted at the request of Southern school districts, HEW said. A number of districts sought guidance on what was required of them to comply with the HEW regulations.

The guidelines set the Fall of 1967 as the target date for desegregation of all grades and said that school systems must provide for "a substantial good faith start" by desegregating at least four grades by the Fall of 1965.

The guidelines suggested two methods of desegregation—assignment of pupils on the basis of geographic attendance zones or "freedom of choice" so that pupils and their parents could choose among a district's schools.

By the time most classes had begun in the Fall of 1965 almost 90 percent of the school districts in the 17 Southern and Border states had met the federal requirement of integrating at least four classes. The high rate of compliance was an indication of the token nature of the desegregation required in 1965. It was estimated that in the 11 Southern states only about 6 percent of Negro pupils attended schools with whites. Funds for new education programs were deferred only in cases where districts failed to file papers promising compliance. HEW enforcement was criticized in a report of the Civil Rights Commission released Feb. 16, 1966, for failure to effectively monitor implementation of the desegregation provisions of the law.

1966. HEW issued revised guidelines in March 1966 which included provisions for faculty and school staff integration and set a general percentage guide for student transfers to measure the effectiveness of free choice desegregation plans. School districts also were made responsible for ensuring that free choices could be exercised without fear of reprisals or intimidation. The guidelines emphasized that school officials were responsible for eliminating the dual school system and all other forms of discrimination as "expeditiously" as possible and that the most expeditious means was often to close Negro schools, pair them with white schools or set attendance zones on a geographic, nonracial basis. Education Commissioner Harold Howe II said the new 1966 guidelines did not apply to *"de facto"* segregation in cities outside the South, but were aimed at ending segregation in school systems which had maintained separate schools for Negro and white students.

In the fall of 1966, 12.5 percent of Negro students in the 11 Southern states attended school with white students.

1967. New guidelines were issued in December 1966, which were substantially the same as the earlier 1966 guidelines. They called for approximately another doubling of the number of Negro pupils attending classes with white pupils in the 1967-68 school year. They retained the controversial percentages spelling out the pace at which school systems had to move if they were not to lose federal school aid.

Southern leaders continued to fight HEW's desegregation guidelines which they contended were enforced only in the South and were not in effect in the North for political reasons.

Several changes in the administration of school desegregation enforcement were made in 1967 in response to Congressional pressure. All the desegregation activities of HEW were combined in a newly created Office for Civil Rights. The school desegregation program had previously been administered by the Office of Education. Secretary of HEW John W. Gardner, in a letter to Sen. Wayne Morse (D Ore. 1945-68), promised that school districts would be informed by March 1 if they faced possible fund cutoffs for noncompliance in the following school year. The letter, known as the Morse-Gardner compromise, was written to forestall an amendment to the 1967 Elementary and Secondary Education Act that would have prevented HEW from cutting funds off once a school year had begun. HEW officials apparently were reluctant to make such an agreement but in early 1969 said that the

Morse-Gardner compromise was probably an administrative improvement.

The U.S. Commission on Civil Rights issued two reports in 1967 which were critical of racial segregation in the schools of the North and South. The first, "Racial Isolation in the Public Schools," published Feb. 20, said that racial isolation was "intense and increasing" in school systems in large cities in both the North and the South. It said that segregated schools tended to have poorer facilities and teachers, were stigmatized by the community, encouraged students to remain in segregated subcultures and reduced their job opportunities as adults. A second report, "Southern School Desegregation," published Aug. 7, said that the "vast majority" of Negro children in the South were still attending segregated schools.

By 1967 most advocates of school integration had rejected freedom of choice as an effective means of achieving desegregation. Peter Libassi, then Director of HEW's Office for Civil Rights, was quoted by the New York Times Sept. 24, 1967, as saying, "We had to follow the freedom of choice plan to prove its ineffectiveness, and this was the year that it did prove its ineffectiveness."

Freedom of choice plans were also being successfully challenged in the courts. *(See above.)*

1968. A major revision of HEW's desegregation guidelines was made in 1968 in line with recent court decisions and with the concern over the failure of freedom of choice plans to achieve desegregation. The new guidelines, issued in March 1968 said that school systems had "the affirmative duty under law to take prompt and effective action to eliminate segregation or other discrimination" and that "correction of discrimination may require positive action based on the race, color, or national origin of students and professional staff." The guidelines stated that if, under a free choice plan, vestiges of a dual school structure remained, the school system was responsible for taking whatever additional steps were necessary to complete the desegregation of its schools.

The guidelines said that generally school systems should be able to complete the reorganization necessary for compliance by the Fall of 1968 but set the Fall of 1969 as the latest date for bringing about an integrated unitary school system.

The guidelines applied to the North as well as the South for the first time. *(See below.)*

Status of Enforcement

HEW Jan. 16, 1969, released figures showing that 20.3 percent of the Negro children in 11 Southern states were attending desegregated schools in the current school year (1968-69). It defined a desegregated school as one which had a white enrollment of at least 50 percent. It was a marked increase over the previous year when 13.9 percent of Negro children were in desegregated schools. The figures were based on reports from Southern schools accounting for about 85 percent of the total public school enrollment of the 11 Southern states.

The HEW figures also showed that much greater desegregation was being achieved in school districts that were desegregating under voluntary plans than by those which were desegregating under court order. The 718 districts reporting desegregation under voluntary plans

Compliance Procedures

School districts were required to file a form giving assurance that they were in compliance with HEW regulations (Form 441) or, if not in compliance, a plan for desegregating (Form 441-B). In court order cases a copy of the court order and assurance that the district was complying with it were required.

Compliance was reviewed on the basis of reports submitted by the schools and field investigations. HEW officials sought voluntary compliance wherever possible.

If a school district appeared to be out of compliance, HEW had to advise it before March 1 that it could lose its funds for the following school year.

The first formal step towards cutting off funds was a notice of opportunity for a hearing. Hearings were held by examiners who were not part of the Office of Civil Rights and their decisions could be appealed to a reviewing board. The Secretary of HEW could be requested to review a case but was not required to do so.

If a decision to cut off funds was made the House and Senate Committees with legislative jurisdiction over the program had to be notified and a termination order went into effect automatically 30 days after the notification. School districts which came back into compliance became eligible again for federal funds, although not—in cases through 1968—retroactively.

showed 25.6 percent of their Negro pupils in desegregated schools while 297 school districts under court order reported 11.5 percent of their Negro pupils were in desegregated schools.

Integration of 100 percent of Negro pupils in Southern school districts was considered impossible by HEW enforcement officials. In a number of areas Negro pupils outnumbered white and desegregated schools, as defined by HEW, could not be provided for all pupils. However, some HEW officials believed that the proportion of Negro children in desegregated schools in those districts which reported that they were in compliance with HEW regulations was too low. The 553 reporting districts which filed Forms 441 showed 51.6 percent of their Negro pupils in integrated schools. In general, districts filing Form 441 had a much lower proportion of Negroes in their student bodies than other districts.

Most of HEW's enforcement activities involved schools that were desegregating under voluntary plans. Schools that were desegregating under court order came under the jurisdiction of the Justice Department.

Funds had been cut off from 129 school districts, as of Jan. 30, 1969. By far the largest number of such districts were in Mississippi (39) and Georgia (38). Alabama, which had one of the lowest proportions of Negroes in desegregated schools, was under court order. Other districts with more than three termination orders in effect were: South Carolina (15), Arkansas (10), Louisiana (10) and Virginia (10). Sixty additional school districts whose funds were cut off since 1964 had come back into compliance. Of these, 19 were in Alabama, 19 in Mississippi and 15 in Louisiana.

Many of the 1,165 school districts under voluntary desegregation plans by the beginning of 1969 were reviewed by HEW in 1968. Early in 1968, 317 school districts, almost all of which were using free choice plans, were notified that their plans were not achieving desegregation. Three hundred cases was considered to be about the limit that could be handled by the staff of the Office of Civil Rights at one time. The districts were chosen among those that were considered to be making least progress on the basis of annual reports submitted to HEW and other information. The districts were required to submit new plans and all but about 80 did so before negotiations reached the stage of sending out a notice of opportunity for a hearing on a fund cut off. A number of other districts complied before hearings were held.

A second group of over 300 school districts were asked in the summer of 1968 to submit more effective desegregation plans. A number of the districts in the second group were ones that were considered particularly difficult to desegregate because of Negro majorities, the need for new school construction, or for other reasons.

In determining the effectiveness of a desegregation plan, HEW officials reviewed not only enrollment but also faculty desegregation and differences between white and Negro schools in facilities and curriculum.

Southern school officials often accused HEW of forcing them to bus students or to close schools to achieve school desegregation. Schools which were closed were almost always Negro. HEW officials said that they did not force any particular desegregation plan upon school districts but that districts could decide that busing or closing a school might be the best way to achieve integration. HEW is prohibited by law from requiring districts to bus children or to close schools to achieve "racial balance."

Enforcement in the North. Enforcement in the North lagged behind that in the South. In passing the 1964 Civil Rights Act and the 1965 aid to education law Congress emphasized that it was not authorizing HEW to require school districts to overcome "racial imbalance." Racial imbalance was understood to mean *de facto* segregation resulting from housing patterns as opposed to segregation created by a dual school system.

There was, however, deliberate though often subtle discrimination in a number of Northern school districts. Its forms included gerrymandering of school attendance zones, assignment of Negro teachers to predominantly Negro schools and substantial differences in per pupil expenditures between predominantly Negro ghetto schools and predominantly white schools.

The first major HEW involvement with Northern school desegregation enforcement came in 1965 when the Chicago school system was investigated as a result of a complaint filed by a group of civil rights organizations. HEW announced that it would withhold federal funds but the decision was reversed following objections from Members of Congress, Chicago school officials and others.

Although HEW maintained a small staff to investigate Northern school districts, it was not active in this area until 1968 when the Northern compliance staff was substantially increased. The increased activity was in part in response to Congressional requirements that desegregation guidelines be enforced throughout the 50 states.

Revised guidelines were issued in March 1968 which, for the first time, were directed at Northern as well as Southern schools. Although they did not require correction of racial imbalance resulting solely from private housing patterns, they prohibited school systems from denying a student, because of race, religion or national origin, the education "generally obtained" by other students in the system.

The guidelines also said that the responsibility of the school systems to eliminate segregation extended to planning of new schools, renovation of old ones and setting up school zones, feeder patterns and school transportation patterns.

By 1969, HEW was increasing its Northern school desegregation staff in line with the requirement of the fiscal 1969 Labor-HEW appropriations bill which required HEW to assign as many persons to Northern school desegregation enforcement as were assigned to enforcement in the Southern and Border states.

Determining the existence of deliberate noncompliance in Northern schools was generally much more difficult than in Southern schools. A HEW investigation of the Pasadena, Calif., school system, in response to a complaint, took the equivalent of a full year's work for one man.

Several suits were brought against Northern school districts by the Justice Department but HEW had not instigated proceedings against any Northern districts.

Justice Department. School districts which were desegregating under court order were under the jurisdiction of the Justice Department. In January 1969, 355 school districts were under court order including virtually all the school districts of Alabama (which were sued collectively), most school districts in Louisiana and over 40 percent of school districts in Mississippi. The Justice Department was a party to many but not all of the suits.

The Justice Department participated in 207 suits as of Feb. 10, 1969, of which 145 were still active. The largest number of its suits (86) were based on Title IV of the 1964 Civil Rights Act but Title IX also was frequently used (53) and a number were entered as a friend of the court. In a few instances (5) the Justice Department sued districts for their failure to follow their plans filed with HEW under Title VI.

The Justice Department filed its first suit in the North April 25, 1968, and had filed a total of five suits in the North and West by the end of 1968.

The judicial route was considered by many advocates of school desegregation as too slow a method for achieving desegregation. Most court orders provided for freedom of choice plans. Following the *Green* decision the Justice Department moved for abandoning of freedom of choice plans and for bringing court orders in line with the *Green* decision in 68 cases involving 145 districts. Few such revised orders had been made by early 1969.

Chapter 6—Civil Liberties and Internal Security

Key Votes

In this chapter, key roll-call votes are shown in bold-face type. The party breakdown on each of these votes and the position taken by each Member of Congress may be found in the key vote charts which appear in the appendix to this book.

Civil Liberties and
Internal Security

IN THE years following World War II, Congressional preoccupation with civil liberties issues had been closely tied to internal security problems. However, as the anti-Communist pressures of the Cold War era subsided, the focus of civil liberties concern shifted to other areas.

Perhaps the most notable action relating to civil liberties in the 1965-68 period, both in Congress and the courts, took place in the field of criminal justice. These developments are detailed in the chapter on Crime and Justice.

Highlights of other action, 1965-68:

CHURCH-STATE RELATIONSHIPS. The Senate in 1966 came within nine votes of approving a proposed constitutional amendment permitting voluntary prayer in the public schools. The vote was the first taken in Congress on a school prayer amendment since the 1962 Supreme Court decision of *Engel v. Vitale,* which barred the recitation of a state-sponsored prayer in public schools as a violation of the 1st Amendment. Had the amendment been successful, it would have made the first change in the Bill of Rights in the history of the Constitution.

Also in the church-state field, the Senate twice—in 1966 and 1967—passed bills to permit taxpayers' suits in federal court to challenge the constitutionality of certain federal grants and loans to church-related institutions. Efforts to enact such legislation were abandoned in 1968 when the Supreme Court ruled that a federal taxpayer had standing to sue to enjoin the administration of federal programs aiding sectarian schools.

OBSCENITY. Congress in 1967 established a Commission on Obscenity and Pornography to conduct a three-year study of the traffic in obscene matter and ways to control it.

In 1968, Congress enacted legislation making it a federal crime to place abusive, harassing or obscene telephone calls across state lines and within the District of Columbia.

Meanwhile, in the 1960s the Supreme Court was gradually attempting to articulate a standard for the suppression of allegedly obscene material.

VIETNAM WAR PROTESTS. Agitation against the Vietnam war led Congress to enact laws outlawing the destruction of draft cards, in 1965, and the desecration of the U.S. flag, in 1968. These acts were favorite gestures employed by war protestors. The Supreme Court upheld the draft card law in 1968, despite claims that the action was protected by 1st Amendment guarantees of freedom of speech.

The House in 1966 passed a bill aimed at punishing persons who aided the North Vietnamese or Viet Cong or who obstructed military personnel or transportation. The Senate never acted on this measure, which had been brought forth from the House Un-American Activities Committee amid a storm of controversy.

SUBVERSIVE ACTIVITIES. Congress in 1967 enacted legislation designed to revitalize the Subversive Activities Control Board (SACB), an organization set up to determine Communist organizations under the Internal Security Act of 1950. The Board had been inactive since April 1966 because of Supreme Court decisions that had invalidated most of its functions.

The Internal Security Act of 1950 lost most of its teeth during the 1965-68 period. The Supreme Court in 1965 struck down a provision of the Act that required Communist party members to register themselves with the Attorney General. And, after repeated setbacks in the Courts, the Government in 1967 abandoned its efforts to enforce the provision that required the party itself to register.

Also in 1967, the Supreme Court struck down a provision of the Act that barred members of Communist-action organizations from employment in defense facilities.

HUAC. The House Un-American Activities Committee (HUAC) continued in its role as the most controversial committee of Congress. Demonstrators hounded its hearings, opponents called for its abolition and court suits challenged its constitutionality.

The Committee had long been attacked for its limited legislative output. During the 1965-68 period, one bill reported by HUAC was enacted into law. This was the measure to reactivate the SACB. It was the sixth HUAC-reported bill ever to be enacted into law.

By 1968, the Committee was pressing to become the House Committee on Internal Security, in an effort to change both its name and its image. Rep. Edwin E. Willis (D La.), HUAC chairman since 1963, was defeated in 1968; he was to be succeeded in the 91st Congress by Rep. Richard H. Ichord (D Mo.), who sponsored the name-change proposal.

Early in 1969, the House approved the name change.

Reference

Developments relating to civil liberties and internal security in the years 1945-64 will be found in *Congress and the Nation, Vol. I, p. 1645-76.*

Chronology

Of Legislation

1965

OBSCENE MAIL. The House April 5, by a 360-21 roll-call vote, passed a bill (HR 980) to permit a person who received "obscene, lewd, lascivious, indecent, filthy or vile" mail to have the Postmaster General prevent the sender from mailing similar unsolicited material to the addressee or his children.

The Justice and Post Office Departments raised administrative objections to HR 980. The Senate took no action on the bill.

Although the mailing of obscene matter long had been a criminal offense (18 USC 1461), the determination of what was obscene varied greatly. *(For Supreme Court decisions between 1957-62, see Congress and the Nation, Vol. I, p. 123a-127a; between 1964-68, this volume, p. 418, 419.)*

From 1950 on, Congress made a number of attempts to strengthen anti-obscenity laws. Hr 980 was a revision of a bill (HR 319) passed by the House in 1964. HR 319, sponsored by Rep. Glenn Cunningham (R Neb.), would have permitted persons who received mail they considered "morally offensive" to return the mail to the Postmaster General with the request that he notify the sender not to mail them further unsolicited material. HR 319 was opposed by the Administration and the Senate did not act on it. *(Congress and the Nation, Vol. I, p. 1671-74.)*

When the 89th Congress convened in 1965, Cunningham introduced a revised version of the legislation (HR 980) which substituted for the phrase "morally offensive" the language "obscene, lewd, lascivious, indecent, filthy or vile." Under the bill a person could return obscene mail to the Postmaster General and direct him to tell the sender not to mail any more to the individual or his children. Further mailings would allow the Government to seek a restraining order against the sender. Violation of the court order would be punishable as contempt of court.

DRAFT CARD DESTRUCTION. Congress in 1965 enacted legislation (HR 10306—PL 89-152) making it a federal crime knowingly to destroy or mutilate a draft card. The measure was a reaction to calls from various antidraft proponents for young men to destroy their draft cards as a manifestation of their differences with the Johnson Administration's Vietnam policy.

As enacted, HR 10306 amended the Universal Military Training and Service Act of 1951, which previously had outlawed only forgeries, alterations or other changes of draft cards. HR 10306 applied the same penalties for destruction of draft cards—a maximum fine of $10,000 and/or imprisonment for up to five years.

The Supreme Court in 1968 upheld the constitutionality of the measure. *(See p. 418.)*

FREEDOM ACADEMY. The House Un-American Activities Committee July 20 reported a bill (HR 9713) proposing the creation of a Freedom Commission to operate a Freedom Academy to conduct research and train Government personnel, private citizens and foreign students in "advanced techniques" of combating Communism. The Academy was viewed as a means of dealing with Communist political and psychological warfare. No floor action was taken on the bill, which was not cleared by the House Rules Committee. Similar bills had been introduced in every Congress since 1959, and one such measure was passed by the Senate in 1960. The Administration opposed the legislation. *(For 1967 action, see below.)*

1966

School Prayer Amendment

Four years after a storm of controversy broke over a Supreme Court decision dealing with prayer in the public schools, the Senate Sept. 21 rejected a proposed constitutional amendment (S J Res 144) permitting voluntary prayer in public schools. The amendment would have made the first change in the Bill of Rights in the history of the Constitution.

The vote was the first in Congress since the 1962 school prayer decision, *Engel v. Vitale*, although more than 150 measures to reverse the Court's holding were introduced in the 88th Congress. The House Judiciary Committee held extensive hearings on the legislation in 1964, but no bill was reported. The hearings were scheduled after Rep. Frank J. Belcher (R N.Y.) succeeded in obtaining 167 of the necessary 218 signatures on a discharge petition designed to take the bill away from the Committee and bring it to the floor for a House vote. *(Congress and the Nation, Vol. I, p. 1675)*

In the 1966 action, Senate Minority Leader Everett McKinley Dirksen (R Ill.), chief backer of the amendment, carried a majority with him on the crucial roll call Sept. 21, but the vote—**49-37 (R 27-3; D 22-34)**— fell nine short of the two-thirds majority necessary to propose a constitutional amendment. Dirksen's proposed amendment (S J Res 148) had not been reported by the Senate Judiciary Committee so the Minority Leader, to bring the issue to a vote, moved to substitute his amendment for the text of a minor bill then pending (S J Res 144, to honor UNICEF, the United Nations Children's Emergency Fund). The substitution, which needed approval by only a simple majority, was made on a 51-36 roll-call vote. A second substitute, a "sense of Congress" resolution sponsored by Sen. Birch Bayh (D Ind.), was defeated on a 33-52 vote before rejection

---

The 1st Amendment

The 1st Amendment to the Constitution provides: "Congress shall make no law respecting an establishment of religion, or prohibiting the free exercise thereof; or abridging the freedom of speech or of the press; or the right of the people peaceably to assemble and to petition the Government for a redress of grievances."

of the constitutional amendment. President Johnson did not take a position on the prayer amendment.

Major opposition to the Dirksen amendment came from religious leaders of all faiths, especially from national Jewish and Protestant leaders and several prominent Catholics. They warned against unforeseen consequences of modifying the 1st Amendment and of the potential divisiveness in communities attempting to decide which prayer would be used in their schools.

Dirksen stressed the strong grass-roots support for a school prayer amendment, support which even the religious leaders admitted existed across the nation.

Debate and public discussion of the measure raised questions about the precise meaning of the major Court cases involved: *Zorach v. Clauson* (1951); *Engel v. Vitale* (1962); *Abington Township v. Schempp* and *Murray v. Curlett* (1963); and, a case denied review, *Stein v. Oshinsky* (1965). Especially debated was the question whether the cases already permitted "voluntary" prayer, as opponents of the Dirksen measure contended. The Dirksen amendment raised other questions, too—whether any prayer recited in a group in a public school classroom would in fact be voluntary—and about who would choose the prayer to be said, when it would be said or if it would be said aloud. The Bayh proposal specified "silent" prayer or meditation; the Dirksen bill did not.

S J Res 148 was not aimed at the practices condemned in *Engel, Schempp* or *Murray*; in each of those cases, the Court struck down state laws or regulations requiring compulsory Bible reading or prayer in the classroom. Rather, S J Res 148 was aimed more at the administrative practice dealt with in *Stein,* where a school administrator was upheld in barring prayer periods during school hours.

Dirksen's proposed amendment said that nothing in the Constitution prohibited the administrator of a publicly supported school or building from "providing for or permitting the voluntary participation by students or others in prayer." It added that this language did not authorize the administrator to "prescribe the form or content" of any prayer.

Under the bill, local administrators of schools and public buildings could decide for themselves whether prayer would be permitted, and they could "provide" for the practice, presumably by arranging times and places for prayer. But the prayer would have to be "voluntary," a term not defined in the bill. In all likelihood, the Supreme Court would have been called upon to define that term. There was precedent to suggest that "voluntary" prayer by school children already had been upheld by the Court in *Zorach,* where New York's "released time" arrangement for students wishing to attend religious instruction on school time was found to be consistent with the 1st Amendment.

In prohibiting school administrators from prescribing the "form or content" of prayer, Dirksen's bill followed the rule of *Engel,* which held that the state cannot draft a prayer and require children to recite.

The bill did not address itself to other questions raised in the prayer decisions over the use of "In God We Trust" on coinage; the use of prayer to open sessions of Congress, the Court and other bodies; and the maintenance of chaplains in the armed forces. The Court had said in *dicta* that usage of such religious phrases and prayer was largely ceremonial and was fully contemplated by the 1st Amendment; regarding chaplains, it had said that when the nation removes its citizens from society and sends them to military camps or puts them aboard ships as soldiers and sailors, it owes a duty to them to provide ministers, priests and rabbis for their spiritual needs. Justice William O. Douglas, however, had said that all such manifestations of religion in federal action were unconstitutional.

Other Bills

TAXPAYERS' SUITS. The Senate July 29 passed, by voice vote, a bill (S 2097) which permitted civil lawsuits testing the constitutionality of certain federal programs aiding church-related schools and hospitals, but the bill died in the House Judiciary Committee.

The bill was intended to authorize the courts—and ultimately the Supreme Court—to settle the longstanding controversy over federal aid to sectarian institutions. The constitutional posture of such aid, particularly of recent federal education and medical programs, had not been determined.

A central concern of critics and commentators regarding such court tests was that court dockets would be flooded with lawsuits. S 2097, as amended by the Senate Judiciary Committee, sought to meet those objections by requiring that all suits be brought in the District of Columbia federal court and be filed within 60 days of the awarding of a federal grant or loan and by permitting the consolidation of similar suits.

Another concern was over continuation of the federal aid during pendency of the lawsuit. The original bill required the aid to cease when the suit was filed, but the committee version only authorized the court to enjoin the grant or loan at its discretion.

There had been no court tests of the various federal programs aiding religious institutions. A central reason was the Court decision of *Frothingham v. Mellon* (1923) which held that individual taxpayers lacked sufficient financial interest, or "standing," to challenge expenditures out of general tax funds. S 2097 was intended to remove the obstacle of *Frothingham. (Congress and the Nation, Vol. I, p. 1213)*

The Senate passed an identical bill in 1967. *(See below.)* The Supreme Court in 1968 ruled that a federal taxpayer had standing to challenge the constitutionality of federal aid to parochial schools. *(See p. 419.)*

OBSCENE TELEPHONE CALLS. The Senate June 29 passed by voice vote a bill (S 2825) to curb abusive, obscene and threatening telephone calls in interstate commerce and in the District of Columbia. Penalties for violation were set at a fine of $500 and/or a six-month prison sentence. Justice Department officials opposed the bill on grounds that enforcement would be a "staggering burden" on the Department's resources. A similar bill was enacted in 1968. *(See below.)*

OBSCENITY COMMISSION. The Senate July 11 by voice vote passed a bill (S 309) to create a 20-member Commission on Noxious and Obscene Matters and

Committees Study Invasion of Privacy

Several Congressional subcommittees in 1965-66 explored unwarranted invasions of privacy, both by the Federal Government and in the private sector. The most extensive hearings were those conducted by the Senate Judiciary Committee's Subcommittee on Administrative Practice and Procedure. Its investigation ranged from Government wiretapping to electronic snooping kits for suspicious husbands. Other groups considered privacy rights of Government employees and the use of lie detector tests by federal agencies.

Invasion of Privacy. The Senate Judiciary Committee's Administrative Practice and Procedure Subcommittee in 1965 held 22 days of hearings on the question of "invasion of privacy" by the Federal Government. In 1966 the Subcommittee expanded its inquiry to investigate snooping in the industrial and private sectors.

1965 Hearings. A major issue under consideration was the use of "mail covers" by the Post Office Department—a practice which had been strongly criticized by Subcommittee Chairman Edward V. Long (D Mo.). Under existing postal regulations, a postmaster was authorized, at the request of any law enforcement official, to record all information obtainable from mail without opening it. While the provision allowed use of mail covers solely for the purpose of locating fugitives from justice, Long in 1964 said he was "convinced there is wide-open use of this surveillance technique with absolutely no effort at control." He introduced a bill to prohibit it. The issue received extensive consideration early in the 1965 hearings. Long at that time renewed his request for legislation and called for a list of persons whose mail had been under surveillance. However, on March 9 Long announced he would hold his requests "in abeyance" because Postmaster General John A. Gronouski had agreed to "tighten up and centralize controls" over the use of mail covers. Gronouski June 16 announced new postal regulations limiting authority to order mail covers to chief and regional postal inspectors (instead of all postmasters) and providing that law enforcement officials had to request mail covers in writing and show reasonable grounds to justify their use.

Other matters examined during the Subcommittee hearings were the use of electronic eavesdropping devices—from telephone taps to hidden microphones—by the Food and Drug Administration (FDA), Internal Revenue Service (IRS) and telephone companies; Post Office Department use of peepholes to watch for mail theft by employees; and opening of first-class mail by the IRS as an aid in collecting unpaid taxes. Gronouski April 12 wrote Long that he had discontinued the latter practice in 1964, but that, as it was permitted by statute, there was no guarantee that it would not be reinstituted by future Postmasters General. Therefore, the Senate June 15, on an 87-1 roll call, added a prohibition against this practice to the excise tax reduction bill (HR 8371—PL 89-44), and the amend-

ment was retained in conference. *(See chapter on Tax Policy.)*

1966 Hearings. The Subcommittee for the first time heard testimony on methods used by industrial concerns to spy on their competitors. Officials of Bell Telephone affiliates also testified on alleged invasions of privacy caused by the companies' practice of monitoring telephone calls to check on the quality of transmission. Other witnesses told the Subcommittee about methods and electronic equipment used to spy on private individuals.

Government Employees' Privacy. Testing methods used by the Government for job applicants and federal employees were the subject of 1965-66 hearings by the Senate Judiciary Constitutional Rights Subcommittee and the House Government Operations Special Subcommittee on Invasion of Privacy. Sen. Sam J. Ervin Jr. (D N.C.), chairman of the Senate group, sponsored a bill to protect civilian federal employees from "unwarranted invasions" of their privacy, including questions about race, religion and national origin, and psychological and polygraph tests on personal subjects. The Senate passed the bill in 1967. *(See chapter on the Executive Branch.)*

The House Special Subcommittee held hearings in 1966 on the implications of a proposal to create a National Data Center. Subcommittee Chairman Cornelius E. Gallagher (D N.J.) said Congress must "make sure that Government computers do not provide the means by which federal officials can intrude improperly into our lives."

Federal Lie Detector Tests. The House Government Operations Committee in 1965 and 1966 issued reports on the use of polygraph (lie detector) tests by the Federal Government. The Committee's Subcommittee on Foreign Operations and Government Information had been studying polygraphs since 1963. *(Congress and the Nation, Vol. I, p. 1779)*

In its 1965 report, the Committee said there was no "lie detector," either human or machine. "People have been deceived by a myth that a metal box in the hands of an investigator can detect truth or falsehood," the report said. The Committee recommended that the Federal Government begin research on the validity of lie detector tests and prohibit their use except in criminal cases and cases involving "the most serious national security."

In 1966 the Committee said its investigation had brought a "twofold response" from the Executive Branch: the Defense Department had issued a directive "drastically" restricting use of the polygraph and the President had appointed an interagency committee to study the problem. The Committee said the Defense Department directive fell short of Committee recommendations because it still allowed "everyday use" of polygraphs for pre-employment screening of employees of the National Security Agency and Defense Department contractors.

Materials. The Commission was to develop a strategy for coordinating federal, state and local efforts to control the traffic in obscenity. This was the third attempt in as many Congresses to establish such a group. Congress in 1967 enacted similar legislation. *(See below.)*

ANTI-KLAN BILL. The House Un-American Activities Committee reported a bill (HR 16606) making it a federal crime for members of clandestine organizations to use facilities of interstate commerce in order to promote the commission of a crime of violence. The Administration opposed the measure. The Committee reported a similar bill in 1967. *(See below.)*

HR 16606 was an outgrowth of the Committee's 1965-66 investigation of the Ku Klux Klan. During that investigation, the first that HUAC or one of its subcommittees had made in an area not directly related to suspected Communist subversion, the Committee heard 187 witnesses in 37 days of hearings. The hearings resulted in contempt citations—voted by the House Feb. 2, 1966—for seven alleged Klan officials who refused to produce corporate documents from the Klan's files. Among those cited for contempt was Robert M. Shelton Jr., imperial wizard (national leader) of the United Klans of America Inc.

The Committee had announced its investigation of the Klan March 30, 1965—four days after President Johnson, in a sharp attack on the Klan, announced that four of its members had been arrested in connection with the March 25, 1965, slaying of Mrs. Viola Liuzzo, a civil rights worker.

In a Dec. 11, 1967, report, "The President-Day Ku Klux Klan Movement," the Committee delineated the leadership, structure, operations and membership of the Klan organizations in the United States.

The 371-page document was a compilation of information gathered primarily during the Committee's 1965-66 hearings. Much of the information had been made public previously.

The Committee earlier had estimated the number of members in the nation's more than 17 Klan organizations at 15,000 in October 1966. In the Dec. 11 report, the Committee set the number at 16,810 in January 1967. It credited Imperial Wizard Robert Shelton's United Klans of America with 15,075 of those members. "The latest gains appear to have been stimulated to a great extent by riotous situations in northern cities," said HUAC Chairman Edwin E. Willis (D La.) in a foreword to the report.

AID TO VIET CONG. The House Oct. 13 passed, by a 275-64 roll-call vote, a bill (HR 12047) aimed at punishing persons who aided such groups as the North Vietnamese or Viet Cong or who obstructed military personnel or transportation. Consideration of the bill was accompanied by a threatened constitutional crisis and a basic legal challenge to the House Un-American Activities Committee (HUAC).

HR 12047 prohibited anyone subject to the jurisdiction of the United States from soliciting or delivering money or a thing of value for use by any nation or group in armed conflict with the United States. Maximum penalty for this offense was set at a fine of $20,000 and/or 20 years' imprisonment. The bill also prohibited obstruction of the movement of personnel or supplies by

U.S. armed forces in time of armed conflict. Labor disputes were exempted. For this offense the maximum penalty was $10,000 and/or five years' imprisonment.

The bill, sponsored by Rep. Joe R. Pool (D Texas), was reported by HUAC following a series of stormy hearings during which witnesses and spectators, many of them members of the so-called "New Left," shouted protests against the Vietnam war, the hearings, the bill and HUAC itself.

Earlier, a federal district judge, in a move without precedent in American law, had enjoined HUAC from holding hearings on the bill. A three-judge court dissolved his restraining order minutes before a HUAC subcommittee intended to begin hearings in defiance of the order.

The judge acted on a suit, *Krebs v. Ashbrook*, brought by the American Civil Liberties Union (ACLU) on behalf of two plaintiffs, Dr. Allen M. Krebs, president of the Free University of New York, and Walter D. Teague III of New York, chairman of the United States Committee to Aid the National Liberation Front in South Vietnam.

The suit sought an order enjoining HUAC from proceeding with the hearings, at which Krebs and Teague were to testify. It also sought an order convening a three-judge federal court to hear a basic constitutional attack on HUAC. The ACLU contended that HUAC's mandate, given by the House in 1945, to investigate "propaganda" and "propaganda activities" which were subversive or un-American, was in violation of the 1st Amendment guarantee of free speech. *(See p. 416.)*

1967

Obscenity Commission

Congress in 1967 enacted a bill (S 188—PL 90-100) establishing a Commission on Obscenity and Pornography.

The 18-member Commission, appointed by the President, was charged with the duty of studying traffic in obscene materials, with studying the casual relationship between obscene matter and antisocial behavior and with recommending action to control such traffic. It had no extraordinary investigative powers, such as the power to issue subpenas, and it was to go out of existence 10 days after filing its final report, which was due no later than Jan. 31, 1970.

The final version of the bill represented a compromise between S 188 as introduced and a House bill (HR 10347). The Senate passed a similar measure in 1966. *(See above.)*

Subversive Activities Control Board

Congress enacted a bill (S 2171—PL 90-237) designed to revitalize the Subversive Activities Control Board (SACB). The Board had been inactive since April 1966 because of Supreme Court decisions that had invalidated most of its functions. *(See p. 417)* Despite this, the five members of the Board had continued to receive their $26,000-a-year salaries.

S 2171 amended the Internal Security Act of 1950, which had created the SACB and which was passed over the veto of President Truman. *(Congress and the Nation, Vol. I, p. 1645, 1650, 1654.)* The bill redefined the functions of the Board to take into account the Court's rulings.

S 2171 deleted the requirement in the 1950 law that Communist organizations and their members register themselves with the Attorney General—the procedure the Court had ruled unconstitutional—and established instead a procedure under which the SACB would hold hearings on cases referred to it by the Attorney General and would determine whether individuals and organizations were Communist. The names of those found to be Communist would then be placed on a public register.

Most of the provisions of S 2171 were originally contained in a bill (HR 12601) reported by the House Un-American Activities Committee (HUAC). It was only the sixth HUAC-reported bill ever to be enacted into law.

The 1967 controversy over SACB erupted after President Johnson nominated and the Senate confirmed, without debate, Simon F. McHugh as a member of the Board. McHugh, the 29-year-old husband of one of Mr. Johnson's former secretaries, was at the time an employee of the Small Business Administration.

Responding to the McHugh episode, several liberal Members of Congress urged that the SACB be abolished, and the Senate instructed its Appropriations Committee to investigate the Board's functions and activities when it considered funds for the Board. The Committee determined that withholding appropriations from the SACB was "not a solution" to the problem.

Senate efforts to delete SACB funds from the State-Justice-Commerce appropriation bill were unsuccessful, as were efforts to attach S 2171 as a rider to the appropriation bill.

The Senate then began debate on S 2171. In the face of a threatened filibuster by liberal Senators who wanted to abolish the Board, the Senate accepted a compromise amendment providing that the SACB would go out of existence at the end of fiscal 1969 unless proceedings had been initiated before the Board and hearings had been held by Dec. 31, 1968. *(See box.)* The Senate passed the bill Oct. 23, on a 65-10 roll-call vote.

The House Nov. 28, on a 269-104 roll call, passed the much broader HUAC-reported bill (HR 12601) and then substituted its provisions for the Senate-passed bill. The House bill did not contain the termination clause and contained a number of provisions intended to hamper attempts by accused Communists to evade action of the Board by legal maneuvering.

House and Senate conferees accepted a modified version of the Senate termination clause but otherwise adopted the House bill virtually intact.

PROVISIONS. As enacted, PL 90-237:

Registration. Removed the requirement in the 1950 law that Communist organizations and their members register themselves and established instead a procedure under which the SACB would hold quasi-judicial hearings on cases referred to it by the Justice Department and would make determinations as to whether the organizations or individuals were Communist.

Provided that the SACB would keep a public list of individuals found to be members of a Communist-action organization and of organizations found to be Communist action or Communist front.

Specified that sanctions against individuals *(see below)* would be based on the SACB list.

SACB Continued

The Subversive Activities Control Board (SACB) was saved from extinction in 1968 when Attorney General Ramsey Clark gave it some business.

Under terms of PL 90-237, the Board was slated to go out of existence at the end of fiscal 1969 if no proceedings were instituted before it by Dec. 31, 1968.

Clark July 1, 1968 petitioned the SACB to enter orders declaring that seven persons named in the petitions were members of the Communist party. At the time of Clark's request, there was no business pending before the SACB. The Board began hearings on the issue Sept. 11, thereby assuring itself a new lease on life.

Authorized an organization or individual entered on the SACB register to apply once a year for cancellation of the registration.

Permitted the Attorney General to include two or more individuals in a single petition for determination of membership in a Communist-action organization.

Termination of the SACB. Provided that the SACB was to go out of existence on June 30, 1969, unless the Attorney General had initiated a proceeding before the Board and a hearing had been held in the period between enactment of the law and Dec. 31, 1968.

Required the Attorney General to report to Congress by June 30, 1968, on the proceedings he had instituted and required the SACB to report to Congress by that date on the progress it had made in conducting hearings.

Provided that, if the Attorney General had initiated no proceedings, he was to report his reasons for not doing so and that, if the Board had not held hearings, it was to report its reasons.

Specified that similar reports were required of the Attorney General and the SACB by Jan. 10 of each year, beginning in 1969.

Compelled Testimony. Stipulated that an individual could be compelled to testify and produce evidence before the Board and could not claim 5th Amendment protection if the Attorney General granted him immunity from prosecution.

Moot Proceedings. Provided that proceedings against an organization would not be mooted or abated if the organization dissolved itself after proceedings had begun.

Required the SACB to receive evidence and make a determination of the issues even though an organization or individual failed to appear at the proceedings.

Collateral Proceedings. Provided that no court challenge to actions of the Board or of the Attorney General under the Act could be initiated until after Board proceedings were completed and that then any court challenge had to be raised in the court having jurisdiction over enforcement proceedings.

Sanctions. Continued the prohibition against employment in the Federal Government, a labor union or, in some cases, a defense plant by a member of a Communist organization.

Propaganda. Specified that Communist organizations be required to label their public literature and broadcasts as being sponsored by an organization registered as Communist by the Attorney General.

Penalties. Specified that "misbehavior" which obstructed a Board hearing or the administration of the provisions of the Act was punishable as a contempt with a fine of up to $5,000 and up to one year in prison.

Provided that the maximum penalties for a person who accepted employment in a prohibited field or who failed to label propaganda was to be a $10,000 fine and five years in prison.

Definition. Redefined the term "Communist-front" to include an organization that was "substantially directed, dominated or controlled by one or more members of a Communist-action organization."

Tax Deductions. Specified that contributions to organizations on the SACB register were not tax deductible.

Specified that no organization on the register was eligible for consideration as a tax-exempt organization.

Other Bills

AID TO VIET CONG. The House Un-American Activities Committee reported a bill (HR 8) aimed at punishing persons who aided such groups as the North Vietnamese or Viet Cong or who obstructed military personnel or transportation. The bill, known as the Pool bill for its sponsor Joe R. Pool (D Texas), was identical to one passed by the House in 1966. *(See above.)* The House adopted the rule for floor action on HR 8 but did not take up the bill itself in 1967. The Administration opposed the legislation.

ANTI-KLAN BILL. The Un-American Activities Committee reported a bill (HR 7025), the Organizational Conspiracies Act of 1967. HR 7025 amended the Internal Security Act of 1950 to prohibit members of clandestine organizations, such as the Ku Klux Klan, from using interstate commerce facilities in order to promote the commission of a crime of violence. HR 7025 was similar to a bill reported by the Committee in 1966 which the Administration had opposed. *(See above.)*

FREEDOM ACADEMY. The House Un-American Activities Committee reported a bill (HR 735) to establish a Freedom Commission and Freedom Academy to conduct research and educate Government personnel, private citizens and foreign students in the "conflict techniques" of fighting Communism. Similar bills had been introduced in every Congress since 1959, and one such measure was passed by the Senate in 1960. *(See 1965, above.)*

FLAG DESECRATION. The House June 20 passed a bill (HR 10480) making it a crime to desecrate the United States flag. The measure became law in 1968. *(See below.)*

The legislation was prompted by the burning of an American flag in New York's Central Park during a demonstration against the Vietnam war. But through a parliamentary quirk, the key word "burning" was left out of the bill.

As passed by the House, HR 10480 made it a federal crime, punishable by a $1,000 fine and/or a year in jail, to cast "contempt" upon the flag by "publicly mutilating, defacing, defiling or trampling upon it."

Although critics of the bill contended that it violated the 1st Amendment guarantee of free speech, the House passed HR 10480 by a lopsided 387-16 roll call. The Administration did not take a position on the measure.

TAXPAYERS' SUITS. The Senate April 11 passed a bill (S 3) which authorized taxpayers' suits in federal court to challenge the constitutionality of certain federal grants and loans to church-related institutions. There was no House action. S 3 was identical to a bill (S 2097) passed by the Senate in 1966. *(See above.)*

Subsequently the Senate adopted an amendment to the Administration's elementary and secondary education bill (HR 7819) which was virtually identical to S 3, but the amendment was deleted in conference.

The Supreme Court in 1968 ruled that a federal taxpayer had standing to sue to enjoin the administration of federal programs aiding sectarian schools. *(See p. 419.)*

OBSCENE TELEPHONE CALLS. The Senate April 24 passed a bill (S 375) making it a federal crime to place abusive, harassing or obscene telephone calls across state lines and within the District of Columbia. The bill became law in 1968. *(See below.)*

FEDERAL WORKERS' RIGHTS. The Senate Sept. 13 passed a bill (S 1035) to protect civilian federal employees from "unwarranted invasions" of their privacy, including questions about their race, religion and national origin and psychological and polygraph tests on personal subjects. The House did not act on the measure. *(See chapter on Government.)*

1968

OBSCENE TELEPHONE CALLS. Congress in 1968 enacted legislation (S 375—PL 90-299) making it a federal crime to place abusive, harassing or obscene telephone calls across state lines and within the District of Columbia. The bill set a maximum $500 fine and/or six months in prison for a person who made such calls. The Justice Department and Budget Bureau opposed the legislation on grounds that "enforcement of such a penal provision was primarily a matter of state concern and responsibility."

The House passed the bill March 4. The Senate had passed it in 1967. *(See above.)*

FLAG DESECRATION. Congress enacted legislation (HR 10480—PL 90-381) making it a crime to desecrate the United States flag.

The legislation was prompted by the burning of an American flag during a 1967 demonstration against the Vietnam war in New York's Central Park.

The Senate passed the bill June 24 after adding the key word "burning" to the list of acts banned by the bill. The House, which passed the measure in 1967 *(see above)*, had inadvertently omitted the word.

As enacted into law, PL 90-381 made it a federal crime, punishable by a $1,000 fine and/or a year in jail, to "knowingly" cast "contempt" upon the flag by "publicly mutilating, defacing, defiling, burning or trampling

Controversy Continued Over Un-American Activities Committee

The House Un-American Activities Committee (HUAC), long the most controversial committee of Congress, continued in that role in the years 1965-68. As in past years, the Committee's critics continued to disrupt its hearings, challenge its constitutionality and seek its abolition. One bill reported by the Committee became law in this period. Meanwhile, the courts continued to chip away at the provisions of the Internal Security Act of 1950, one of the Committee's proudest legislative achievements. *(See p. 417, 418.)*

LEGISLATION. During the 1965-68 period, only one bill reported by HUAC was enacted into law. This was a measure (PL 90-237), enacted in 1967, to revitalize the Subversive Activities Control Board (SACB). It was only the sixth HUAC-reported bill ever to be enacted into law. The other five:

PL 81-831—Internal Security Act of 1950. Title I, the Subversive Activities Control Act, established complicated machinery for registration of legally determined Communist-action and Communist-front groups. Title II, the Emergency Detention Act, provided for emergency detention of persons likely to commit espionage or sabotage.

PL 83-557—This measure required Communist groups to register their printing equipment.

PL 83-637—Communist Control Act of 1954. The Act had two facets. First, it added to the Internal Security Act a third category of Communist organizations, designated Communist-infiltrated organizations, meant to apply particularly to labor unions. Second, it said the Communist party "should be outlawed," denied it legal standing and made its members subject to the "provisions and penalties" of the Internal Security Act.

PL 87-474—The law repealed a provision of the Internal Security Act that required the Secretary of Defense to publish a list of designated defense facilities.

PL 88-290—The law provided personnel security procedures for the National Security Agency.

In addition, HUAC recommendations were embodied in a number of laws handled by other committees. Notable examples were the Immigration and Nationality Act of 1952, the Espionage and Sabotage Act of 1954 and the Immunity Act of 1954.

FUNDS. Within Congress itself, opposition to the Committee was expressed in votes on resolutions authorizing funds for the group. In some years there also were motions to recommit the fund resolutions to the House Administration Committee with instructions to hold hearings on the justification for the funds. The table shows the amounts authorized, the roll-call votes on those authorizations and recommittal votes, where applicable. (In 1965 there were two authorizations.)

Year	Amount Authorized	Vote	Recommittal
1965	$370,000	360-29	58-333
	50,000	313-43	
1966	425,000	299-24	
1967	350,000	350-43	92-304
1968	375,000	343-45	78-305

These funds were in addition to the funds automatically made available to standing committees under the Legislative Reorganization Act of 1946. *(For previous fund authorizations, see Congress and the Nation, Vol. I, p. 1764.)*

CONTEMPT CITATIONS. In the years 1965-68, 10 persons were cited for contempt of Congress on the recommendation of HUAC. During the years 1945-64, 160 persons were so cited.

NAME CHANGE. Rep. Richard H. Ichord (D Mo.), who was to become HUAC chairman in the 91st Congress, in 1968 proposed changing the name of the Committee to the Committee on Internal Security and redefining its objectives, changing the emphasis from "un-American" activities to "Communist" activities. The House approved the proposal early in 1969.

CONSTITUTIONALITY. Two suits challenging the constitutionality of HUAC's mandate were raised during the 1965-68 period.

The first was *Krebs v. Ashbrook,* brought by the American Civil Liberties Union in 1966 on behalf of two persons called to testify before the Committee during hearings on the so-called Pool bill, regarding aid to the Viet Cong. The ACLU contended that HUAC's mandate, given by the House in 1945, to investigate "propaganda" and "propaganda activities" which were subversive or un-American, was in violation of the 1st Amendment guarantee of free speech.

A three-judge federal court in the District of Columbia Sept. 11, 1967, by a 2-1 vote, ruled that it lacked jurisdiction to rule on the constitutionality of HUAC. Circuit Judge Charles Fahy wrote the opinion in which he said HUAC was established by House adoption of Rule XI, which was not an act of Congress. Only acts of Congress were subject to review by a three-judge court, he said. Chief Circuit Judge David L. Bazelon, in a dissenting opinion, said the House had incorporated Rule XI into the Legislative Reorganization Act of 1946 and it was therefore subject to review. The Supreme Court denied review.

The second suit, *Stamler v. Willis,* was brought by Dr. Jeremiah Stamler, Yolanda F. Hall and Milton M. Cohen. They had refused to testify at 1965 Committee hearings on Communist activities in the Chicago area and were cited by the House in 1966 for contempt of Congress.

The three were indicted by a federal grand jury in Chicago in 1967 on the contempt charges. They brought suit to enjoin the criminal prosecutions and to challenge the constitutionality of Rule XI.

A three-judge federal court in Chicago June 26, 1968, by a 2-1 vote, dismissed the suit. The court ruled that the Members of Congress who were defendants were protected by Article I, Section 6, Clause 1 of the Constitution, which said that "for any speech or debate in either House, they (Members) shall not be questioned in any other place." The Supreme Court first dismissed an appeal, then vacated that action, thus opening the way for further legal steps.

upon it." The definition of "flag" included pictures or representations "which the average person...may believe ...to represent the flag."

FREEDOM ACADEMY. The House Rules Committee April 23 deferred action on, thereby killing, a bill (HR 735) to establish a Freedom Commission and Freedom Academy as a means of combating Communist political and psychological warfare. The bill had been reported by the Un-American Activities Committee in 1967. *(See above.)* In a letter to the Committee included in the report, the State Department said it continued to believe that, as a whole, a Freedom Commission and Academy "will not serve as a useful instrument of national policy."

INTERNAL SECURITY. The Senate Judiciary Internal Security Subcommittee, headed by James O. Eastland (D Miss.), held hearings on an omnibus internal security bill (S 2988) introduced by Eastland and 19 cosponsors. No further action was taken.

The Justice Department opposed virtually all provisions of the bill as being unneeded, self-defeating or unconstitutional. Many of the provisions were aimed at circumventing Supreme Court decisions.

Major Provisions. The omnibus bill prohibited aiding foreign governments or groups engaged in open hostilities with the United States or its forces; extended the life of the Subversive Activities Control Board (SACB); authorized the SACB to hold hearings to determine if groups were Communist-action groups, barred members of such groups from employment in defense facilities or in any public school supported by federal funds and barred union membership to such persons; provided for immunity from prosecution to witnesses compelled to testify or produce records before Congressional committees; eliminated federal court jurisdiction over the actions of committees of Congress; established a Security Administration for Executive Departments (SAED), subordinate only to the President, to oversee all investigations (except those of the FBI) and evaluations in personnel security cases; gave SAED, like the Attorney General, power to initiate cases before the SACB; made it a crime to use interstate commerce facilities to incite a riot; authorized the Secretary of State to impose certain restrictions on the travel of American citizens; established a Communist Defectors Awards Board to oversee the admission of Communist defectors to the United States and payment of annuities to such persons; denied tax exemptions for organizations making donations to subversive organizations or persons; prohibited the importation into the United States of any goods produced by slave labor; and made it a felony to urge, advise, or solicit the use of force or violence to overthrow the United States Government or any political subdivision thereof.

DEFENSE PERSONNEL SECURITY. A bill (HR 15626) to provide new personnel security programs for defense facilities was in effect killed July 9 when the House Rules Committee deferred action on it.

The bill, reported by the House Un-American Activities Committee July 3, was designed to authorize a new personnel security program for defense facilities, since the Supreme Court had struck down the existing authority in *U.S. v. Robel* (1967), and to authorize a maritime security program, since the Court held in *Schneider v. Smith* (1968) that no authority supported certain aspects of the Coast Guard's screening program. *(For Court decisions, see p. 418.)*

FILM CLASSIFICATION. A Senate Commerce subcommittee held a one-day hearing on a proposal (S Res 9) to set up a special Senate committee to study problems of classifying film so as to protect children from unsuitable movies. There was no further action.

FEDERAL WORKERS' RIGHTS. A House Post Office and Civil Service subcommittee held hearings on bills (S 1035, HR 17760) to protect the rights of federal employees, but no further action was taken. S 1035 was passed by the Senate in 1967. *(See above.)*

Supreme Court Decisions

Following is a summary of key Supreme Court decisions in the fields of civil liberties and internal security during the years 1965-68.

1965

COMMUNIST MAIL. The Supreme Court May 24, in *Lamont v. Postmaster General* and *Fixa v. Heilberg*, unanimously struck down a section of the 1962 omnibus postal law (PL 87-793) which required the withholding of "Communist political propaganda" unless the addressee requested delivery. The Court found that the requirement to fill out a Post Office form requesting delivery infringed on the addressee's freedom of speech. *(Congress and the Nation, Vol. I, p. 1490)*

SUBVERSIVE ACTIVITIES. The Court Nov. 15, by an 8-0 vote in *Albertson v. Subversive Activities Control Board*, held that members of the Communist party of the U.S.A. could not constitutionally be required to register as such with the Justice Department under provisions of the Subversive Activities Control Act. The Court said such a requirement violated the members' 5th Amendment right against self-incrimination.

In 1964, the Court had let stand a lower court decision holding that the party itself could not be required to register unless the Government proved that an individual member was willing to waive his 5th Amendment right and register the party. (In a 1965 federal district court case, the Government produced witnesses who said they were willing to register the party, and on Nov. 19 the jury found the party guilty of failing to register. However, efforts to register the party were finally abandoned in 1967. *See below.*)

The 1964 and 1965 Supreme Court decisions removed most of the enforcement provisions of the Subversive Activities Control Act, Title I of the Internal Security Act of 1950. *(Congress and the Nation, Vol. I, p. 1662, 1654.)*

BIRTH CONTROL. The Court June 7, in a 7-2 ruling in *Griswold v. Connecticut*, struck down an 1879 Connecticut law which prohibited the use of, and distribution of information on, contraceptive devices. The Court held the state law to be unconstitutional and in violation of the right to privacy of married couples.

1966

OBSCENITY. The Court March 21 by varying votes upheld two convictions for violation of obscenity laws and reversed a state ruling that the novel "Fanny Hill" be suppressed.

Prior to these rulings the Court had held that the test of obscenity under the 1st Amendment involved three elements: (1) the dominant theme of the material taken as a whole must appeal to a prurient interest in sex; (2) the material must be patently offensive because it affronts contemporary community standards relating to the descriptions or representations of sexual matters; and (3) the material must be utterly without redeeming social value. These standards were set out in *Roth v. U.S.* (1957) and subsequent decisions. *(Congress and the Nation, Vol. I, p. 123a.)*

In its March 21 actions, the Court:

By a 5-4 vote in *Ginzburg v. U.S.*, affirmed the conviction of a New York publisher for violation of a federal statute (18 USC 1461) which prohibited sending obscene matter through the mails. The prosecution conceded and the Court assumed that the publications in question might not have been deemed obscene. The Court ruled, however, that the origin of mailing, the advertising and the promotional matter were proper legal aids in determining the issue of obscenity in "close cases."

By a 6-3 vote in *Mishkin v. N.Y.*, affirmed the conviction of a New York publisher who hired writers, artists and printers to produce paperback books which emphasized sadism, masochism, fetishism and homosexuality.

By a 6-3 vote in *A Book Named "John Cleland's Memoirs of a Woman of Pleasure" v. Attorney General of Massachusetts*, reversed the finding of Massachusetts courts that the book commonly known as "Fanny Hill" was obscene. Writing for the majority, Justice William J. Brennan Jr. said the state court misinterpreted the "social value" criterion of the Roth test in ruling that a book need not be completely without redeeming social value to be deemed obscene.

EXCLUSION OF STATE LEGISLATOR. The Court Dec. 5, by a 9-0 vote in *Julian Bond v. James "Sloppy" Floyd*, held that Julian Bond's exclusion from the Georgia House because of his antiwar statements was a violation of the 1st Amendment. Chief Justice Earl Warren, writing for the Court, said Bond's statements were protected by the 1st Amendment, that he could not constitutionally be prosecuted for making them and that the Georgia House violated Bond's freedom of speech in disqualifying him.

1967

SUBVERSIVE ACTIVITIES. The Court Dec. 11, in a 6-2 ruling in *U.S. v. Robel*, ruled unconstitutional a provision of the Subversive Activities Control Act of 1950 that barred members of Communist-action organizations from employment in defense facilities. Chief Justice Earl Warren, writing for the Court, said the provision

was "an unconstitutional abridgment of the right of association protected by the First Amendment." He added that "nothing we hold today should be read to deny Congress the power under narrowly drawn legislation to keep from sensitive positions in defense facilities those who would use their positions to disrupt the nation's production facilities."

Note: The Government's 16-year effort to enforce the Communist party registration provision of the Internal Security Act of 1950 ended in failure in 1967, after repeated setbacks in the courts. In the final effort, *The Communist Party of the United States v. U.S.*, the Circuit Court of Appeals for the District of Columbia March 3 held that the provision was a violation of the 5th Amendment privilege against self-incrimination in that it required party officers to register. The Justice Department did not appeal the case.

MEDICARE LOYALTY OATH. In *Weiss v. Gardner*, the Court Feb. 13 vacated a lower court order that upheld the loyalty oath requirement for certain applicants for medicare. Federal courts had split as to the constitutionality of this requirement, but Solicitor General Thurgood Marshall Jan. 4 announced that he considered the provision unconstitutional and would not contend the matter in court. Following his suggestion, the Court dismissed the Weiss case as moot.

STATE LOYALTY OATHS. In *Keyishian v. Board of Regents*, the Court Jan. 23 by a 5-4 vote held unconstitutional a loyalty oath required of state university professors under New York's "Feinberg Law."

The Court Nov. 6, in a 6-3 vote in *Whitehill v. Elkins*, struck down a loyalty oath required for Maryland state university employees. Justice William O. Douglas, writing for the Court, said the teachers' loyalty oath was "in the First Amendment field" and that such laws as supported it were "hostile to academic freedom." Justice John Marshall Harlan, joined by two other dissenters, said the oath itself was not unconstitutional since it required only a disclaimer of "actual, present activity, amounting in effect to treasonable conduct."

EXPATRIATION. The Court May 29, in a 5-4 vote in *Afroyim v. Rusk*, invalidated a federal law removing U.S. citizenship for voting in a foreign election. Writing for the majority, Justice Hugo L. Black said the 14th Amendment "was designed to, and does, protect every citizen of this nation against a Congressional forcible destruction of his citizenship, whatever his creed, color or race. Our holding does no more than to give to this citizen that which is his own, a constitutional right to remain a citizen in a free country unless he voluntarily relinquishes that citizenship."

1968

DRAFT CARD BURNING. The Court May 27, by a 7-1 vote in *U.S. v. O'Brien*, upheld the constitutionality of a 1965 amendment to the Universal Military Training and Service Act of 1948, making it a federal crime knowingly to destroy a draft card. The defendant argued that he had burned his draft card intentionally as an act of political protest against the Vietnam war and that this was "symbolic speech," protected by the 1st Amendment. Chief Justice Earl Warren, writing for the majority, did not rule on the applicability of the 1st Amendment to the defendant's action, but said: "This Court has held that when 'speech' and 'nonspeech' elements are combined in the same course of conduct, a sufficiently important governmental interest in regulating the nonspeech element can justify incidental limitations on 1st Amendment freedoms."

OBSCENITY. The Court April 22, in a 6-3 vote in *Ginsberg v. N.Y.,* upheld a New York statute that made it a crime to sell material "harmful to minors" to juveniles less than 16 years of age. The Court said that the statute was sufficiently precise and that it expressed a valid state interest in protecting the well-being of youth. The material involved consisted of "girlie" magazines and admittedly was not obscene for adults.

INTERNAL SECURITY. The Court Jan. 16, in a 8-0 vote in *Schneider v. Smith,* held that Coast Guard regulations inquiring into the past and present associations of persons seeking licenses to serve aboard American-flag vessels exceeded the authority granted by Congress in the Magnuson Act (50 USC 191b). Writing for the Court, Justice William O. Douglas said, "...we hesitate to conclude that Congress told the Executive to ferret out the ideological strays in the maritime industry. The words it used—'to safeguard...from sabotage or other subversive acts'—refer to actions, not to ideas or beliefs." *(Congress and the Nation, Vol. I, p. 1656.)*

TAXPAYERS' SUITS. The Court June 10, by an 8-1 decision in *Flast v. Cohen,* held that a federal taxpayer had standing to sue to enjoin the administration of federal programs aiding sectarian schools. Chief Justice Earl Warren, writing for the Court, said a two-fold test determined whether a federal taxpayer had standing to challenge a federal spending program. "First," he said, "the taxpayer must establish a logical link between the status and the type of legislative enactment attacked.

Thus, a taxpayer will be a proper party to allege the unconstitutionality only of exercises of Congressional power under the taxing and spending clause of Article I, Section 8 of the Constitution. It will not be sufficient to allege an incidental expenditure of tax funds in the administration of an essentially regulatory statute.... Secondly the taxpayer must establish a nexus between that status and the precise nature of the constitutional infringement alleged. Under this requirement, the taxpayer must show that the challenged enactment exceeds specific constitutional limitations imposed upon the exercise of the Congressional taxing and spending power and not simply that the enactment is generally beyond the powers delegated to Congress by Article I, Section 8."

The Court thus removed a bar to taxpayers' suits that had stood since its *Frothingham v. Mellon* decision in 1923. The Senate had considered legislation to permit taxpayers' suits since 1961, and it passed such bills in 1966 and 1967. *(See p. 411, 415.)*

FREE SPEECH. The Court June 3, by a 9-0 vote in *Pickering v. Board of Education,* held that a public school teacher may not be dismissed for criticizing his school board unless the criticism is knowingly or recklessly false. The Court held that the teacher's statements were protected by the 1st Amendment as interpreted by the Court in *New York Times v. Sullivan* (1964), which held that the 1st Amendment protected statements about public officials unless they were made either with knowledge of their falsity or in reckless disregard for their truth or falsity.

The Court April 29, by an 8-1 vote in *St. Amant v. Thompson,* held that failure to investigate the truth or falsity of charges against a public official did not "in itself establish bad faith"—that is, did not meet the reckless disregard test laid down in *New York Times v. Sullivan* in 1964. *(See above.)*

AID TO CHURCH SCHOOLS. The Court June 10, by a 6-3 vote in *Board of Education v. Allen,* held that a state constitutionally could provide textbooks for pupils at sectarian schools in the absence of proof that the textbooks were religious in nature.

Chapter 7—Election Law and Procedures

Election Law and Procedures

The Electoral College

The merits of the venerable electoral college method of electing a U.S. President produced growing national debate during the postwar years. But Congress made no changes, despite—or perhaps because of—the profusion of conflicting proposals to reform the system.

Background

The method of selecting a President was the subject of long debate at the Constitutional Convention of 1787. Several plans were proposed and rejected before a compromise solution, which was modified only slightly in future years, was adopted.

Facing the Convention when it convened May 25 was the question of whether the Chief Executive should be chosen by direct popular election, by the Congress, by state legislatures or by intermediate electors. Direct election was opposed because it was generally felt that the people lacked sufficient knowledge of the character and qualifications of possible candidates to make an intelligent choice. Many delegates also feared that the people of the various states would be unlikely to agree on a single person, usually casting their votes for favorite-son candidates well-known to them. Southerners opposed direct election for the additional reason that suffrage was more widespread in the North than in the South, where Negro slaves did not vote.

The possibility of giving Congress the power to pick the President also received consideration. However, this plan also was rejected, largely because of fear that it would jeopardize the principle of Executive independence. Similarly, a plan favored by many delegates, to let state legislatures choose the President, was turned down because it was feared that the President might feel so indebted to the states as to allow them to encroach on federal authority.

Unable to agree on a plan, the Convention Aug. 31 appointed a "Committee of Eleven" to propose a solution to the problem. The committee Sept. 4 suggested a compromise under which each state would appoint Presidential electors, equal to the total number of its Representatives and Senators. The electors, chosen in a manner set forth by each state legislature, would meet in their own states and cast two votes for President. The votes would be counted in Congress, with the candidate re-ceiving a majority elected President, and the second highest candidate becoming Vice President.

This plan constituted a great concession to the less populous states, since they were assured two extra votes (corresponding to their Senators) regardless of how small their populations might be. The plan also left important powers with the states by giving complete discretion to state legislatures to determine the method of choosing electors.

Only one provision of the committee's plan aroused serious opposition—that giving the Senate the right to decide elections in which no candidate received a majority of electoral votes. Some delegates feared that the Senate, which already had been given treaty ratification powers and the responsibility to "advise and consent" to all important Executive appointments, might become too powerful. Therefore, a counterproposal was made, and accepted, to let the House decide in instances when the electors failed to give a majority of their votes to a single candidate. The interests of the small states were preserved by giving each delegation only one vote in the House on roll calls to elect a President.

The system adopted by the Constitutional Convention was a compromise born out of problems involved in differing state voting requirements, the slavery problem, big-v.-small state rivalries and the complexities of the balance of power between different branches of the government. It also was apparently as close to a direct popular election as the men who wrote the Constitution thought possible and appropriate at the time. Some scholars have suggested that the electoral college, as it came to be called, was a "jerry-rigged improvisation" which really left it to future generations to work out the best form of Presidential election.

Only once since ratification of the Constitution had an amendment been adopted which substantially altered the method of electing the President. In the 1800 Presidential election, the Republican (anti-Federalist) electors inadvertently caused a tie in the electoral college by casting equal numbers of votes for Thomas Jefferson, whom they wished to be elected President, and Aaron Burr, whom they wished to elect Vice President. The election was thrown into the House of Representatives and 36 ballots were required before Jefferson was finally elected President. The 12th Amendment, ratified in 1804, sought to prevent a recurrence of this incident by providing that the electors should vote separately for President and Vice President.

Other changes in the system evolved over the years. The authors of the Constitution, for example, had intended that each state should choose its most distinguished citizens as electors and that they would deliberate and vote as individuals in electing the President. But, as strong political parties began to appear, the electors came to be chosen merely as representatives of the parties; and after 1800 independent voting by electors almost disappeared. (From 1820 through 1968, only nine of the 15,092 electoral votes cast were cast contrary to "instructions." The only such postwar instances occurred in 1948, when Preston Parks, a Truman elector in Tennessee, voted for Gov. Strom Thurmond (D S.C. 1947-51); in 1960, when Henry D. Irwin, a Nixon elector in Oklahoma, voted for Sen. Harry F. Byrd (D Va.); and in 1968, when Dr. Lloyd W. Bailey, a Nixon elector in North Carolina, voted for George C. Wallace.

The original system underwent further change as democratic sentiment mounted early in the 19th century, bringing with it the demand that electors should be chosen by direct popular vote of the people, instead of by the state legislatures. By 1804, the majority of state legislatures had adopted popular-vote provisions.

Initially, most "popular election" states provided that electors should be chosen from districts similar to Congressional districts, with the electoral votes of a state split if the various districts differed in their political sentiment. This "district plan" of choosing electors was supported by the leading statesmen of both parties, including Jefferson, Alexander Hamilton, James Madison, John Quincy Adams, Andrew Jackson, Martin Van Buren and Daniel Webster.

The district plan, however, tended to dilute the power of political bosses and dominant majorities in state legislatures, who found themselves unable to "deliver" their states for one candidate or another. These groups brought pressure for a change and the unit rule system evolved, under which all of a state's electoral votes went to the party which won a plurality of the popular votes statewide.

When some states began to adopt the unit vote, the others soon followed suit. Jefferson explained in 1800: "All agree that an election by districts would be the best, if it could be general; but while 10 states choose, either by their legislatures (or by unit rule popular vote), it is folly and worse for the other six not to follow." A Senate committee report in 1826 said, "When the large states consolidate their votes to overwhelm the small ones, those, in their turn, must concentrate their own strength to resist them. A few states may persevere, for some time, in what they believe to be the fairest system, but when they see the unity of action which others derive from the (unit rule), they cannot resist the temptation of following the same plan."

By 1804, seven of the 10 "popular election" states cast their electoral votes under the unit rule; by 1824, 13 out of 18. By 1836, the district plan had vanished from the scene. However, no mention of unit rule voting was ever written into the Constitution, and the state legislatures retained the power to specify any method of choosing Presidential electors and to determine how their votes would be divided.

Pros and Cons

The existing electoral college system, under which the entire electoral vote in a state is given to the candidate whose electors have won a plurality of the popular vote, has long been a matter of controversy.

Major objections to the current system:

• It has permitted the election of three Presidents who trailed their opponents in the national popular vote.

• The founding fathers never intended that the states would cast their electoral votes en bloc. Under the unit rule, minority popular votes not only are not reflected in a state's electoral votes but are added to those of the majority and given to the candidate against whom they were cast.

• The unit system offers no incentive for a heavy voter turnout in supposedly "safe" states.

• In large states which are fairly evenly divided between the major parties, the unit system inflates the bargaining power of splinter parties and pressure groups.

• The system puts a premium on fraud because juggling of a few votes can swing the electoral votes of an entire state.

• The current electoral system gives state legislatures the power to direct any method they wish of selecting Presidential electors. While moral pressures have forced the legislatures to authorize a popular vote within the respective states, the possibility of abuse of power by state legislatures exists.

• There is no legal way to force an elector to vote for the candidate to whom he pledged himself. In a close election, several electors could be bribed, or simply change their minds, and the selection of the President thus altered.

• If an election is thrown into the House of Representatives because of the failure of a candidate to win a majority of electoral votes, an archaic and totally unrepresentative system goes into operation. Each state has a single vote, in total disregard of its population. Furthermore, the votes of evenly split delegations are not counted at all.

The current electoral system has been defended as follows:

• With minor amendment, it has successfully withstood the test of almost two centuries. Former President Kennedy, defending the current system as a Senator during a 1956 floor debate, said it was one "under which we have, on the whole, obtained able Presidents capable of meeting the increased demands upon our Executive.... No urgent necessity for immediate change has been proven."

• Only once, in 1876, did a man who actually had a majority of the popular vote fail to win the Presidency. The other "minority" Presidents were opposed by men who also failed to win an absolute majority, and probably would have won in run-off elections with their major opponents.

• Any method of electoral reform which preserves the federal system by according each state two extra electoral votes could result in the election of a candidate who did not receive the majority of popular votes. The only alternative would be direct popular election of the President.

• Weighing the composition of the electoral college to give adequate representation to the small and sparsely settled states had been necessary if the authors of the Constitution were to reconcile those states to the idea of federation.

• The choice of President has fallen into the House of Representatives only twice (in 1800 and 1824), a remarkably low average.

• The unit rule's "winner-take-all" feature discourages the growth of splinter parties, which have been an impediment in the path of democratic growth in some European countries.

• The current system's exaggeration of the winner's majority should not be considered an unmitigated evil. After a bitterly fought election campaign, such as that of 1960, the appearance of nationwide backing for the winner of the electoral vote and elimination of doubt about the certainty of his election may help him win broader acceptance of his assumption of the powers of the Presidency.

Reform Proposals

In light of criticism leveled at the existing electoral college, a number of proposals for alternate methods of choosing the President have been suggested. Since Jan. 6, 1797, when Rep. William L. Smith (S.C.) introduced in Congress the first proposed constitutional amendment to reform the electoral college system, hardly a session of Congress has passed without the introduction of one or more resolutions of this nature. The majority of the proposed changes fit into three major categories.

District Plan. The district plan of choosing electors was the most popular reform proposal in the early years of the Republic, having been proposed at one time or another by most of the state legislatures and passed by the U.S. Senate more than once in the early 19th century. Following World War II, the provisions of the district plan were embodied in proposals offered by a number of Senators and Representatives. Those introduced by Rep. Coudert (R N.Y. 1947-59) and Sen. Mundt (R S.D.), known as the Mundt-Coudert plan, became the most widely known but, like the other district plan proposals, were not enacted.

The Mundt-Coudert plan would have preserved the office of elector, but provided that electors be chosen in the same manner as Representatives and Senators. The Presidential candidate with a plurality in each electoral district, the lines of which would be set by the state legislatures, would receive the vote of its elector. The candidate with a plurality in a state would receive the electoral votes equal to its two Senators. The candidate receiving a majority of the total electoral votes would become President; but if no one received a majority, the new Senators and Representatives, sitting jointly and voting as individuals, would choose the President from among the three candidates having the highest number of electoral votes.

Proponents of the district plan argued that it would extend to Presidential elections the same principles of representation that applied to Congressional elections, with popular vote results reflected more accurately in electoral vote totals than under the existing method. Supporters also claimed that the district plan would

'Minority' Presidents

Under the electoral college system, 15 Presidents have been elected, either by the electoral college itself or by the House of Representatives, who did not receive a majority of the popular votes cast in the election. Three of them—John Quincy Adams, Rutherford B. Hayes and Benjamin Harrison—actually trailed their opponents in the popular vote.

The following table shows the percentage of the popular vote received by candidates in the 15 elections in which a "minority" President was elected:

Year	Elected		Opponents	
1824	Adams 30.54	Jackson 43.13	Clay 13.24	Crawford 13.09
1844	Polk 49.56	Clay 48.13	Birney 2.30	
1848	Taylor 47.35	Cass 42.52	Van Buren 10.13	
1856	Buchanan 45.63	Fremont 33.27	Fillmore 21.08	Smith .01
1860	Lincoln 39.79	Douglas 29.40	Breckenridge 18.20	Bell 12.60
1876	Hayes 48.04	Tilden 50.99	Cooper .97	
1880	Garfield 48.32	Hancock 48.21	Weaver 3.35	Others .12
1884	Cleveland 48.53	Blaine 48.24	Butler 1.74	St. John 1.49
1888	Harrison 47.86	Cleveland 48.66	Fisk 2.19	Streeter 1.29
1892	Cleveland 46.04	Harrison 43.01	Weaver 8.53	Others 2.42
1912	Wilson 41.85	T. Roosevelt 27.42	Taft 23.15	Others 7.58
1916	Wilson 49.26	Hughes 46.12	Benson 3.16	Others 1.46
1948	Truman 49.51	Dewey 45.13	Thurmond 2.40	Wallace 2.38
1960*	Kennedy 49.71	Nixon 49.55	Unpledged .92	Others .27
1968	Nixon 43.42	Humphrey 42.72	Wallace 13.53	Others .33

1960 percentages total more than 100 because of double-counted Alabama votes (both under Kennedy and Unpledged columns).

SOURCES: Library of Congress, Historical Statistics of the U.S., and Congressional Quarterly Records

encourage the minority party in currently one-party states by the hope of winning one or more districts. In addition, it was said that the system would give equal weight, based on population, both to rural and urban, and predominantly Democratic and Republican, districts; make it impossible for localized bad weather, vote frauds or other accidental circumstances to swing the entire electoral vote of a state; remove the method of choosing Presidential electors from control of the state legislatures; and mark a return to the system contemplated by the founding fathers.

Opponents of the district plan responded that it might lead to gerrymandering of elector district lines by state legislatures, and that election of a "minority" President would still be possible. They also argued that the district plan might concentrate Presidential campaigns in marginal Congressional districts and minimize the influence of minority groups by isolating them in individual districts. Finally, opponents saw little advantage in substituting a district-wide unit rule for the statewide rule of the existing system.

Proportional Method. Under the proportional method of dividing each state's electoral votes, the office of the elector would be abolished but the electoral vote retained, with each candidate receiving the same proportion of the electoral vote as his share of a state's popular vote. This method was first introduced by Rep. Levi Maish (Pa.) in 1877, when he proposed that each state's electoral votes be divided proportionately, but rounded off to whole numbers. Later in 1877, Rep. Jordan E. Cravens (Ark.) introduced a similar plan but provided for a proportional division of the state's electoral votes to the third decimal place. More recent proportional methods proposals were introduced by Sen. Lodge (R Mass. 1937-53) and Rep. Gossett (D Texas 1939-51), and by Sens. Daniel (D Texas 1953-57) and Kefauver (D Tenn. 1949-63).

The major argument for the proportional distribution of electoral votes was that it would tend to reflect more accurately the popular strength of the various candidates, with the electoral vote count conforming far more closely to the actual vote count than under the existing system. Supporters also contended that it would encourage the two-party system in one-party states because each citizen's vote would have some effect on the national outcome; that state legislatures or individual electors would not have the power to frustrate the will of the people; that the influence of organized minorities would be lessened, inasmuch as their strength would be measured by their numbers rather than their bargaining power; and that accidental circumstances or fraud would be less likely to defeat the choice of the people because the entire electoral vote of a state would not hinge on a few questionable votes. Finally, proponents argued that the proportional plan would set the mode of electing a President on a uniform and permanent principle, at the same time giving the people a feeling that they had a more direct voice in the selection of the President.

Opponents argued that it would still be possible under the proportional method to elect a man who lost in the popular vote. They pointed out that had the system been in effect in 1880, it is probable that Winfield S. Hancock would have been elected, although he trailed James A. Garfield in the popular vote. Likewise, William Jennings Bryan would probably have scored an electoral victory over William McKinley in 1896, even though he received four percent less of the popular vote. Opponents also contended that the proportional

distribution of electoral votes might weaken the power of the major parties by making it relatively easy for minority parties to win electoral votes.

Direct Election. The direct election plan of choosing the President, considered at the Constitutional Convention in 1787, was first introduced in Congress as a constitutional amendment by Rep. William McManus (N.Y.) in 1826.

Supporters of direct election argued that it would be the most simple and direct way of having the President elected by the people. They said that a direct vote for President would sweep away all the possible abuses of the current method, including the right of state legislatures to direct methods of choosing electors, the right of electors to disobey instructions, the advantages of big states over smaller states or small states over big states, and the possibility that the popular vote winner would not become President. Finally, advocates of direct election argued that such a method would promote political activity in the supposedly "safe" states and invigorate the two-party system.

Arguments against the direct vote were that it would deprive the small states of the slight advantage they enjoyed through the two extra electoral votes accorded each state, regardless of size; lead to irresistible pressure for national laws governing qualifications for voting, which would constitute a blow to state power and jeopardize the states' control over voting for all other offices; and be impossible to ratify because of opposition by small states and by Southern states, where many Negroes had been barred from voting in the past and the white population had, in effect, cast the vote for both themselves and the Negroes under the existing system. By the late 1960s, however, several factors—including the widening of suffrage, implementation of the Civil Rights Act and the Voting Rights Act and the growth of effective two-party competition in states where it had previously been weak or nonexistent—were tending to cancel out some of the arguments against direct election of the President.

Congressional Action

None of the proposed reforms of the electoral college was enacted during the postwar period. However, hearings were held on a number of the many bills that were introduced, and several were passed by either the House or the Senate.

1948—Sen. Lodge (R Mass.) and Rep. Gossett (D Texas) introduced legislation (S J Res 200, H J Res 9) calling for a proportional system of electing the President and Vice President. H J Res 9 was reported March 26 by the House Judiciary Committee and S J Res 200 on May 3 by the Senate Judiciary Committee, but no further action was taken in either house.

1950—The Lodge-Gossett proportional-method amendment was passed by the Senate but died in the House Rules Committee. S J Res 2, introduced by Lodge in 1949, was reported by the Senate Judiciary Committee on June 30, 1949. The Senate Feb. 1, 1950, rejected four amendments—including substitute amendments by Langer (R N.D.), rejected 31-60 (D 11-39; R 20-21), and Humphrey (D Minn.), rejected 28-63 (D 13-37; R 15-26)—which provided for election of the

President and Vice President by direct vote. The Senate then accepted by voice vote an amendment by Lucas (D Ill.) making 40 percent of the electoral vote, instead of a majority, the minimum necessary to elect a candidate. If no candidate received at least 40 percent of the electoral vote, the Senate and House in joint session would choose the President from the three candidates receiving the highest number of electoral votes. S J Res 2 was adopted Feb. 1 by a 64-27 (D 46-4; R 18-23) roll-call vote, which was more than the two-thirds majority required for a proposal to amend the Constitution.

H J Res 2, an identical plan introduced by Gossett and approved July 21, 1949, by the House Judiciary Committee, was bottled up in the House Rules Committee. Gossett July 17, 1950, moved to suspend the rules and bring the resolution to the floor, but the motion—which required a two-thirds majority—was rejected 134-210 (D 87-116; R 47-93; Ind. 0-1).

1951—Bills constituting the same Lodge-Gossett plan which had passed the Senate in 1950 were reported in both houses but received no further action. S J Res 52, introduced by Lodge, was reported July 30 by the Senate Judiciary Committee; H J Res 19 (Gossett's) was reported Oct. 17 by the House Judiciary Committee.

1956—S J Res 31, introduced by Sens. Daniel (D Texas) and Kefauver (D Tenn.), was reported May 19, 1955, by the Senate Judiciary Committee and brought to the floor March 27, 1956. The plan, known as the "original Daniel plan," contained provisions similar to the Lodge-Gossett proportional proposals.

By the time S J Res 31 was called up for Senate floor action, supporters of the proportional and the district systems had joined forces in an effort to gain enough votes for passage. Their amendment, known as the "Daniel substitute," would have divided each state's electoral votes by the proportional method, unless the state legislature voted to employ the district method of choosing electors—in other words, giving each state the choice between the Daniel-Kefauver and the Mundt-Coudert plans for casting its electoral vote. The Senate rejected four amendments—including two by Langer (R N.D.), rejected 13-69 (D 11-28; R 2-41), and Lehman (D N.Y.), rejected 17-66 (D 16-25; R 1-41)—providing for direct popular election of the President. The Senate then approved the Daniel substitute by a 48-37 (D 26-18; R 22-19) roll-call vote. This was enough to carry it as a substitute, but was short of the two-thirds favorable vote required for a constitutional amendment. Rather than face defeat on the vote for final passage, Daniel moved, and the Senate voted by voice, to recommit S J Res 31 to the Judiciary Committee, where it died.

Among the leading opponents of electoral reform during the 1956 Senate debate was Sen. John F. Kennedy (D Mass.). Speaking in opposition to changes in the existing system, Kennedy said, "It is not only the unit vote for the Presidency we are talking about, but a whole solar system of government. If it is proposed to change the balance of power of one of the elements of the solar system, it is necessary to consider the others."

By "solar system" Kennedy was referring to the entire governmental structure of the United States—state legislatures, the two houses of Congress and the Presidency. He argued that because the state legislatures and Congress were overweighted in representation by rural areas and the small states, it was proper for the urban areas, with their liberally oriented minority groups, to have a larger role in electing the President. Liberals tended to shift to opposition of electoral reform when it became clear that the consequence could be a weakening of comparatively liberal and minorities voting strengths.

1961—The Senate Judiciary Constitutional Amendments Subcommittee held hearings between May 23 and July 13 on proposals for reform of the electoral college but took no further action. Sentiment for basic reform was expressed by former Presidents Hoover, Truman and Eisenhower, 17 Senators, one state Governor, the chairman of the Republican National Committee, professors of law and political science from a number of universities and several private citizens. However, there was a lack of agreement on how reform should be achieved.

The only principal witnesses opposing a basic overhaul of the current system were representatives of the Kennedy Administration, the chairman of the Democratic National Committee and two Senators. They all recommended some limited type of amendment designed chiefly to prevent individual electors from breaking their pledges to vote for a certain Presidential candidate.

1963—The Senate Constitutional Amendments Subcommittee June 4 held hearings, a continuation of the 1961 hearings. Subcommittee Chairman Kefauver (D Tenn.) said the hearings had been called to assess recent changes in the U.S. political balance of power, including the reduction of conservative-rural influence by rapid state legislature reapportionments in the wake of a 1962 Supreme Court decision in *Baker v. Carr (see below)* and a diminishing of conservative one-party states and areas—all occurring, Kefauver pointed out, without a concurrent change in the unit vote electoral system, which was generally felt to give political priority to the votes of big states with liberally oriented urban populations.

Prof. James MacGregor Burns of Williams College testified that reform of the electoral college, though long a pressing problem, "has proved impossible because politicians have feared that it might upset or threaten political arrangements that they have found congenial or at least predictable and dependable."

1966—The Senate Judiciary Constitutional Amendments Subcommittee again held hearings on electoral reform, with initial emphasis on the proposal of the Johnson Administration—first put forth in 1965 and reiterated by the President in 1966—to abolish the office of elector while confirming the existing state unit vote system of casting electoral votes. But little enthusiasm was expressed for the Administration proposal, which had been sponsored by Subcommittee Chairman Birch Bayh (D Ind.). Most reform advocates considered the Presidential proposal a substitute for true reform since it would "freeze" into the Constitution what they found the most undesirable element of the existing system— the "winner-take-all" system of casting each state's electoral votes. About all the Administration measure would have accomplished would have been to frustrate the Southern "independent elector" strategy. *(See below.)*

The death knell for the Administration plan was apparently sounded May 18 when Sen. Bayh announced he was abandoning his support of it and switching to backing for direct popular election of the President. Bayh said he had changed his position, "after a great deal of soul-searching," because he doubted whether it would be worthwhile to go through the complex steps necessary to amend the Constitution just "to rectify and legalize the status quo" and achieve a reform that was "second best."

Bayh introduced a bill (S J Res 163) providing a constitutional amendment to substitute a direct popular election in which the people would choose between slates of candidates running together for President and Vice President. In the event that no candidate slate received 40 percent of the national popular vote, the Senate and House in joint session would be required to choose, by majority vote, one of the two President-Vice President slates that had received the most popular votes.

Bayh said he was "not speaking for the Administration" and that "at least the Justice Department is not at all happy with this." He said Justice Department officials had asked him why he was shifting to the direct popular vote solution when similar amendments had been soundly beaten on the Senate floor in 1956. Bayh said his reply was that "a lot of history has been made since 1956, and a lot of freedoms given to our people since 1956." Specifically, he noted the 24th Amendment abolishing the poll tax in federal elections, the Civil Rights Act of 1957, 1960 and 1964 and the Voting Rights Acts of 1965. "Today, for the first time in our history, we have achieved the goal of universal suffrage regardless of race, religion or station in life," Bayh said. "Today, we are witnessing a political development in our states where for the first time in decades, legislatures fully represent people.... We have only one election remaining wherein some votes are not equal to others and wherein millions of votes do not count in the final result—and that is in the election of the most powerful political officer in the world, the President of the United States."

Bayh's change of position was only one of several significant developments, all favorable to the direct national vote for President, which took place in 1966 and early 1967:

● The Chamber of Commerce of the United States, following a policy referendum of its member organizations, Jan. 31, 1966, announced it favored abolishing the electoral college and shifting to either a nationwide popular vote or a district system of choosing Presidential electors. The final vote of the Chamber members for approving the new policy position was 3,877 (91.5 percent) in favor and 362 (8.5 percent) opposed.

● The Gallup Poll May 18 reported a heavy majority of the American people would like to do away with the electoral college and substitute a direct vote of the people for President. A nationwide sampling of citizens was asked, "Would you approve or disapprove of an amendment to the Constitution which would do away with the electoral college and base the election of a President on the total popular vote cast throughout the nation?" Results: approve, 63 percent; disapprove, 20 percent; no opinion, 17 percent.

● Sen. Quentin N. Burdick (D N.D.) conducted a poll of all members of the 50 state legislatures and found 58.8 percent in favor of direct election of the President and only 9.7 percent in favor of continuing the existing system. Another 21.2 percent favored a proportional method of casting state electoral votes, while 10.2 percent were in favor of a district system. Results of the Burdick poll showed that in 44 states, direct election was favored by 50 percent or more of the legislators responding. (A constitutional amendment must be ratified by three-quarters of the states—38 of the current 50 states.) Support for direct election was almost as strong among legislators from small states as those from large states.

● A special electoral college commission of the American Bar Assn. Jan. 7, 1967, recommended that the President and Vice President be elected as a team by popular vote of the people, with the entire electoral college mechanism discarded. The commission suggested that the winning candidate must receive at least 40 percent of the vote to be elected. A national runoff election would be held if no candidate reached the 40-percent mark.

The ABA commission called the existing electoral college method "archaic, undemocratic, complex, ambiguous, indirect and dangerous" and said that direct election would ensure election of the popular vote winner, abolish the "anachronism and threat" of the independent electors, "minimize the effect of accident and fraud in controlling the outcome of an entire election" and "put a premium on voter turnout and encourage increased political activity throughout the country." The ABA's House of Delegates Feb. 13, 1967, voted 171-57 to approve the Commission's report.

Recommendations of the ABA were expected to be especially influential, since it was a special 1964 ABA commission that drew up recommendations for a constitutional amendment on Presidential disability which were the chief guidelines for the 25th Amendment to the Constitution, submitted by Congress to the states in 1965 and finally ratified in 1967. Sen. Bayh became the chief Congressional sponsor of the Presidential disability amendment.

1967—The same Senate Judiciary Constitutional Amendments Subcommittee again held hearings on various proposals for reforming or abolishing the electoral college. One proposal, introduced by Sen. Margaret Chase Smith (S J Res 6), called for a direct vote for President and also proposed a national nominating primary for Presidential candidates.

Early 1969—President Nixon, saying he personnally favored direct election of the President but did not believe such a proposal would be ratified by the states, Feb. 20 called on Congress to approve a proportional plan for the casting of electorial votes. However, the House Judiciary Committee May 16 reported a bill (H J Res 681—H Rept 91-253) proposing a constitutional amendment to provide for direct popular election of the President.

Related Developments

Public interest in a change in the electoral college system was spurred on by the close 1960 and 1968 elections, a series of Supreme Court rulings and introduction of unpledged elector systems in the Southern states.

Renewed political and legal challenges to the electoral college stemmed from a series of Supreme Court decisions beginning in 1962. In *Baker v. Carr*, the Court March 26, 1962, ruled that Tennessee citizens had the right to challenge the apportionment of their state legislatures in the federal courts, thus for the first time opening the apportionment and districting established by state legislatures to review by federal courts.

This was followed on June 15, 1964, by a series of decisions in *Reynolds v. Sims* and related cases in which the Supreme Court ruled that the equal protection clause of the 14th Amendment "requires that the seats in both houses of a bicameral state legislature must be apportioned on a population basis," and that while "mathematical exactness of precision" in carving out legislative districts may be impossible, apportionments must be "based substantially on population."

In a March 18, 1963, decision in *Gray v. Sanders*, the Court ruled that Georgia's county unit system of voting in statewide and Congressional primary elections deprived citizens of equal protection of the laws and was therefore unconstitutional. The majority opinion set forth the principle of "one person, one vote," and

went on to refuse to justify Georgia's unit system on analogy to the electoral college, saying that the electoral college was based on a "conception of political equality that belongs to a bygone day."

On Feb. 17, 1964, the Supreme Court declared that Congressional districts must be as equal in population as practicable. In *Wesberry v. Sanders,* in which the Congressional districts of Georgia were challenged, the Court relied on the findings of the *Baker* case to show that districting questions were justifiable and on the *Gray* case to establish the principle of "one person, one vote."

The Court April 7, 1969, in *Kirkpatrick v. Preisler,* ruled that no numerical or percentage population variance between districts within a state could be considered negligible. Any variance—"no matter how small"—must be justified by the state or shown to be unavoidable, the Court said. *(See p. 104.)*

In 1966, Delaware, joined by 12 other states, asked the U.S. Supreme Court to hear a suit challenging the constitutionality under the 14th Amendment of the unit vote—the "winner-take-all" method of casting state electoral votes. Delaware asked the Court to "open the door" to reform by granting a type of interim relief that

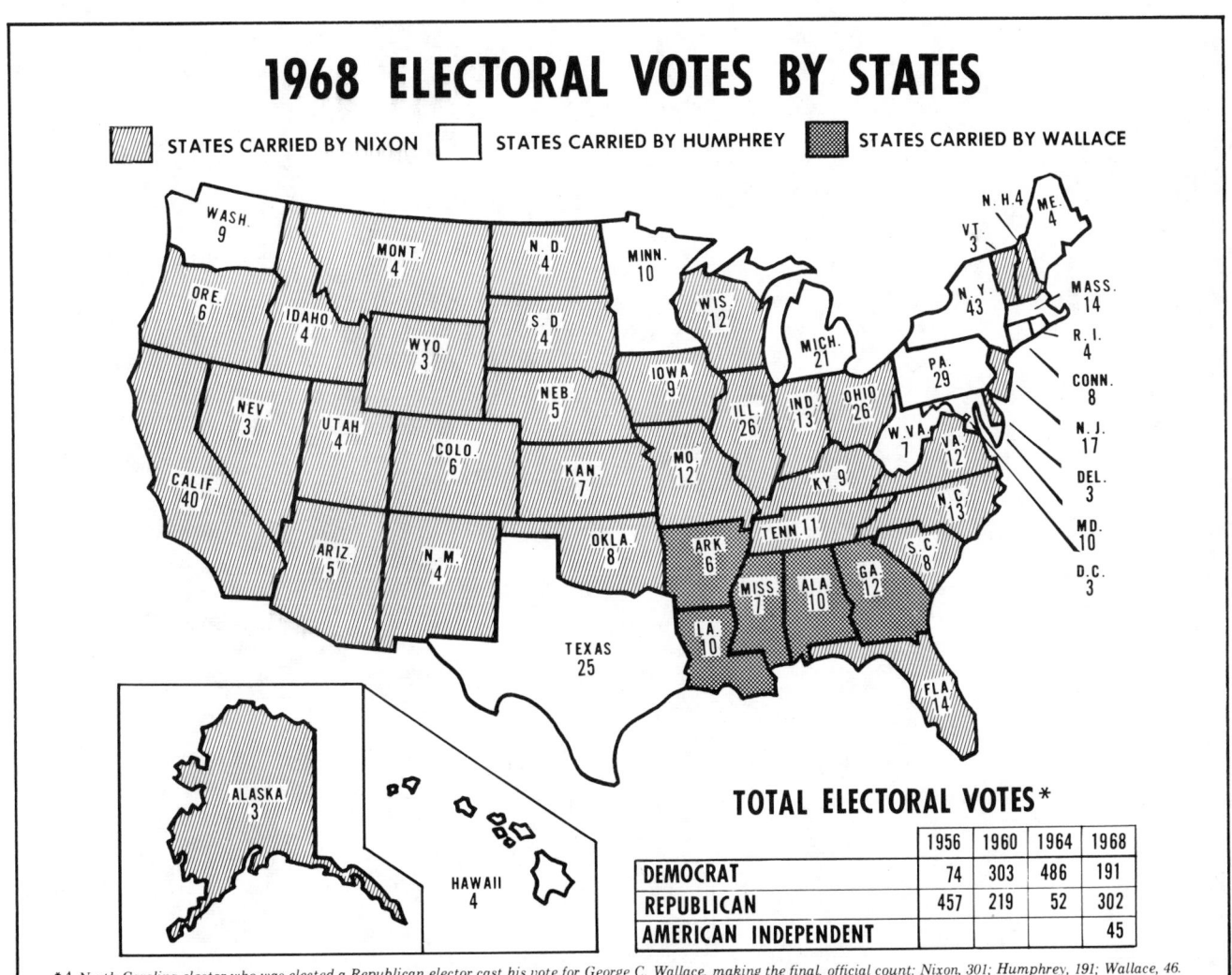

1968 ELECTORAL VOTES BY STATES

STATES CARRIED BY NIXON   STATES CARRIED BY HUMPHREY   STATES CARRIED BY WALLACE

WASH. 9 · MONT. 4 · N.D. 4 · MINN. 10 · N.H. 4 · ME. 4 · VT. 3 · N.Y. 43 · MASS. 14 · ORE. 6 · IDAHO 4 · WYO. 3 · S.D. 4 · WIS. 12 · MICH. 21 · PA. 29 · R.I. 4 · CONN. 8 · NEV. 3 · UTAH 4 · NEB. 5 · IOWA 9 · ILL. 26 · IND. 13 · OHIO 26 · W.VA. 7 · VA. 12 · N.J. 17 · CALIF. 40 · COLO. 6 · KAN. 7 · MO. 12 · KY. 9 · DEL. 3 · MD. 10 · ARIZ. 5 · N.M. 4 · OKLA. 8 · ARK. 6 · TENN. 11 · N.C. 13 · S.C. 8 · D.C. 3 · MISS. 7 · ALA. 10 · GA. 12 · LA. 10 · TEXAS 25 · FLA. 14 · ALASKA 3 · HAWAII 4

TOTAL ELECTORAL VOTES*

	1956	1960	1964	1968
DEMOCRAT	74	303	486	191
REPUBLICAN	457	219	52	302
AMERICAN INDEPENDENT				45

*A North Carolina elector who was elected a Republican elector cast his vote for George C. Wallace, making the final, official count: Nixon, 301; Humphrey, 191; Wallace, 46.

would require the states to divide their electoral votes in a way that would reflect popular vote sentiment. The suit acknowledged that a direct vote would be the only permanent remedy to the inequalities built into the electoral college system. The Court refused to hear the case, giving no reasons for its action. Delaware's brief, however, served to dramatize the shortcomings of the electoral college system when compared with the "one-man, one-vote" standard being required by the courts in the state legislatures and Congressional districts.

Support for changes in the electoral college also increased as a result of postwar efforts to affect the outcome of Presidential elections by means of unpledged electors. The laws of five Southern states—Alabama, Georgia, Louisiana, Mississippi and South Carolina—permitted the election to the electoral college of a slate of independent or unpledged electors. Other states provided a place on the ballot for slates representing new or minor political parties. Some states allowed the use of petition procedures to qualify electoral slates pledged to an independent candidate.

In 1960, an unpledged elector movement was successful in two states—Mississippi and Alabama. In electoral college balloting, all of the Mississippi electors and six of Alabama's 11 electors withheld their votes from both Republican candidate Richard M. Nixon and Democrat John F. Kennedy, casting them instead for Sen. Byrd (D Va.) for President and Sen. Thurmond (D S.C.) for Vice President. Byrd received an additional vote from an Oklahoma elector who had been pledged to Nixon.

In 1968, a North Carolina elector, Dr. Lloyd W. Bailey, who had been elected as a Republican elector, cast his vote for George C. Wallace. Objection to the vote was raised in the Jan. 6, 1969, Joint Session of Congress for the counting of the electoral votes, but the challenge was rejected by a 33-58 roll-call vote of the Senate and a 169-229 roll call of the House.

Apportionment Revolution of the 1960s

During the years 1962-64, the Supreme Court rendered a series of four landmark decisions in the politically sensitive area of Congressional and state legislature apportionment and districting. The precedent-breaking decisions all had a common theme—that "as nearly as practicable, one man's vote...is to be worth as much as another's." By entering the "political thicket" of apportionment and redistricting, the Court extended its authority far beyond its previous scope and seemed certain to cause a revolution in the complexion of state government and the bases of Congressional power.

As recently as 1946, the Court had refused to consider reapportionment cases. In the prevailing opinion in the 1946 case of *Colegrove v. Green,* a challenge to Illinois' greatly malapportioned Congressional districts, Justice Felix Frankfurter had stated that apportionment cases were not "justiciable"—not appropriate for resolution by a court. It was too "political" a question, he said, concluding that "courts ought not to enter this political thicket."

Two developments in the succeeding years caused a reversal of this position by 1962. The first development was the steadily increasing tendency of the Court to extend interpretation of the Constitution to protection of further individual rights, reflected most clearly in the 1954 school desegregation decision. By the early 1960s, the Court had an unmistakably liberal majority. The second development was the population movement from country to city which had been underway ever since the turn of the century. By 1960, there was not a single legislative body in a single state in which there was not at least a 2-1 population disparity between the most and least heavily populated districts. For example, disparity was 242 to 1 in the Connecticut House, 223 to 1 in the Nevada Senate, 141 to 1 in the Rhode Island Senate and 9 to 1 in the Georgia Senate. Studies of the effective vote of large and small counties in state legislatures between 1910 and 1960 showed that the effective vote of the large counties had slipped while their percentage of the national population had more than doubled. The most lightly populated counties, on the other hand, advanced from a position of slight overrepresentation to one of extreme overrepresentation, holding almost twice as many seats as population alone would entitle them to. Predictably, the rural dominated state legislatures resisted every move toward reapportioning districts to reflect new population patterns.

By no means as gross but still substantial was population imbalance among Congressional districts. In Texas, the 1960 Census showed the most heavily populated district had four times as many inhabitants as the most lightly populated. Arizona, Maryland and Ohio each had at least one district with three times as many inhabitants as the most lightly populated. In a majority of cases, it was rural areas which benefitted from Congressional malapportionment. As a result of the postwar population movement out of center cities to the surrounding areas, the suburbs were the most underrepresented.

State Legislature Apportionment

Baker v. Carr. It was against this background that a group of Tennessee city dwellers successfully broke the long-standing precedent against federal court involvement in legislative apportionment problems. For more than half a century, since 1901, the Tennessee Legislature had refused to reapportion itself, even though a decennial reapportionment based on population was specifically required by the state's constitution. In the meantime, Tennessee's population had grown and shifted dramatically to urban areas. By 1960, the House legislative districts ranged from 3,454 to 36,031 in population —a disparity of 23 to 1—while the Senate districts ranged from 39,727 to 108,094—a six-fold disparity. Appeals by urban residents to the tightly rural-controlled Tennessee legislature proved fruitless. A suit brought in the state courts to force reapportionment was rejected on the grounds that courts should stay out of legislative matters.

The urban interests then appealed to the federal courts, stating that they had no redress: the Legislature had refused to act for more than half a century; the state courts had refused to intervene; Tennessee had no referendum or initiative laws. The city dwellers charged that there was "a debasement of their votes by virtue of the incorrect, obsolete and unconstitutional apportionment" to such an extent that they were being deprived of their right to "equal protection of the laws" under the 14th Amendment to the U.S. Constitution. (The 14th Amendment reads, in part: "No state shall...deny to any person within its jurisdiction the equal protection of the laws.")

A three-judge federal court in Tennessee dismissed the case Feb. 4, 1960, citing the *Colegrove v. Green* precedent. The case was then appealed to the U.S. Supreme Court. In March 1961 the U.S. Justice Department intervened in the case as a friend of the court *(amicus curiae),* stating that "numerous states have done nothing with regard to apportionment of their legislatures for 25 or 50 years. The only realistic remedy is federal judicial action." The Justice Department brief urged that the Court exercise jurisdiction and apply 14th Amendment guarantees of equal protection of the laws to prevent "dilution of one's vote by gross malapportionment." The brief said that "in Tennessee, as in many other states, the underrepresentation of urban voters has been a dominant factor in the refusal of state legislatures to meet the growing problems of our urban areas.... Urban governments now tend to bypass the states and to enter directly into cooperative arrangements with the national government in such areas as housing, urban development, airports, defense and community facilities." The brief alluded to the 1955 report of the Kestnbaum Commission, appointed by President Eisenhower to investigate intergovernmental relations, which had warned that state disregard of urban problems would lead to direct city-federal arrangements and an undercutting of state authority.

The Supreme Court March 26, 1962, handed down its historic decision in *Baker v. Carr,* ruling in favor of the

Tennessee city dwellers by a 6-2 margin. In the majority opinion, Justice William J. Brennan emphasized that the federal judiciary had the power to review the apportionment of state legislatures under the 14th Amendment's equal protection clause. "The mere fact that a suit seeks protection of a political right," Brennan wrote, "does not mean that it presents a political question" which the courts should avoid.

In a strong dissent, Justice Felix Frankfurter said the majority decision constituted "a massive repudiation of the experience of our whole past" and was an assertion of "destructively novel judicial power." He said that the lack of any clear basis for relief "catapults the lower courts" into a "mathematical quagmire." Frankfurter said that "there is not under our Constitution a judicial remedy for every political mischief." Appeal for relief, he maintained, should not be made in the courts, but rather "to an informed, civicly militant electorate."

***Reynolds v. Sims* and Related Cases.** The 1962 *Baker* decision left numerous questions unanswered and gave no guidelines for the lower courts to follow in determining whether a state legislature was unconstitutionally apportioned. The major unresolved questions were: How seriously malapportioned must a legislature be to violate the 14th Amendment? Would a "little federal system," with one house apportioned by population and the other by factors such as geography, be constitutionally acceptable? Would state constitutions be overridden to enforce the 14th Amendment's guarantees of equal protection? Would the presence of initiative and referendum laws, or the fact that an apportionment plan has been so approved, affect constitutionality? How would court orders be enforced?

Despite the confusion, countless suits were filed and numerous lower courts undertook to interpret *Baker v. Carr.* Rarely in U.S. history, in fact, had a single decision had such an immediate and far-reaching impact. Within 57 months, court cases or some form of reapportionment action equalizing district populations had been carried out or threatened in all but one of the 50 states. The exception was Oregon, which had been apportioned on a population basis since 1952.

The major questions raised by *Baker* were answered June 15, 1964, when the Supreme Court rendered its most sweeping reapportionment decisions yet in a group of appealed cases. The leading case was *Reynolds v. Sims* from Alabama. Others decided in the group were *Lucas v. 44th General Assembly* (Colorado), *Roman v. Sincock* (Delaware), *Maryland Committee for Fair Representation v. Tawes* (Maryland), *WMCA v. Lomenzo* (New York), and *Davis v. Mann* (Virginia). Salient points of the decisions:

• That the 14th Amendment's equal protection clause "requires that the seats in both houses of a bicameral state legislature must be apportioned on a population basis."

• That "mathematical exactness of precision" in carving out legislative districts might be impossible, but that apportionment must be "based substantially on population."

• That "the so-called federal analogy is inapplicable as a sustaining precedent for state legislative apportionment."

• That it means nothing that the people of a state through referendum or initiative have approved an apportionment based on any other principle than population because a "citizen's constitutional rights can hardly be infringed upon because a majority of the people choose to do so."

In his sweeping decision, joined by five of his colleagues, Chief Justice Earl Warren wrote: "Legislators represent people, not trees or acres. Legislators are elected by voters, not farms or cities or economic interests.... To the extent that a citizen's right to vote is debased, he is that much less a citizen.... Diluting of the weight of votes because of place of residence impairs basic constitutional rights under the 14th Amendment just as much as invidious discriminations based on race or economic status."

Justice Potter Stewart, joined by Justice Tom C. Clark, dissented in part, declaring that the 14th Amendment's equal protection clause did put limits on districting plans but that an apportionment need only be "rational." Stewart said that "the Court's Draconian pronouncement, which makes unconstitutional the legislatures of most of the 50 states, finds no support in the words of the Constitution, in any prior decision of the Court or in the 175-year history of the Federal Union." Clark and Stewart agreed with the Court that the Alabama, Maryland, Delaware and Virginia apportionments were unconstitutional because they strayed too far from a population basis, but they defended the constitutionality of the New York and Colorado apportionments which the Court majority invalidated. Justice John Marshall Harlan differed from the majority in all the cases, saying that "in every accurate sense of the term, (the cases) involved the Court amending the Constitution."

The June 1964 decisions served to quicken the tempo of reapportionment action throughout the country, virtually assuring population-based apportionment in every state within a two- or three-year period.

The decisions also stirred up a storm of criticism in Congress. Many Members felt that the federal analogy, despite the Court's disdain for it, was valid and that within reasonable limits states had a right to apportion their legislatures as they wished. There was special resentment against the Colorado decision, which had invalidated a "little federal plan"—House by population, Senate on a modified population-area base—and was approved by the people of Colorado by an overwhelming margin in a 1962 referendum. Political pressures also contributed to the chorus of protest: from Southerners, as a way to attack the Supreme Court; from Members from all regions, under pressure from home state legislators to help preserve existing apportionments.

Congressional Proposals

Opponents of the decisions first proposed a constitutional amendment to restrict its impact. The most prominent proposal, by Rep. William M. McCulloch (R Ohio), his party's ranking member on the House Judiciary Committee, provided: "Nothing in the Constitution of the United States shall prohibit a state, having a bicameral legislature, from apportioning the membership of one house of the legislature on factors other than population if the citizens of the state shall have the opportunity to vote upon the apportionment."

It soon became evident, however, that there would not be time to win Congressional approval of a constitutional amendment in the 1964 session. Opponents of the Court's decisions decided to try for legislation blocking or at least delaying the judicial intervention in apportionment matters.

A bill (HR 11926) by Rep. William M. Tuck (D Va.), a former Governor of his state, denying the federal courts all jurisdiction whatever in apportionment cases, passed the House Aug. 19, 1964, by a 218-175 roll-call vote (D 96-140; R 122-135).

Meanwhile, Senate Minority Leader Everett McKinley Dirksen (R Ill.) tried to attach as a rider to the pending foreign aid bill (HR 11380) an amendment, co-sponsored by Majority Leader Mike Mansfield (D Mont.), following negotiations with the Justice Department, which would require the courts to delay reapportionment orders until Congress could submit and the states consider a constitutional amendment on the reapportionment problem. Northern liberals, however, staged a month-long filibuster against the Dirksen-Mansfield rider, arguing that the real intent was to preserve rural domination of malapportioned legislatures and block the application of constitutional rights. An impasse was reached when the Senate rejected a Dirksen cloture motion, a liberal substitute for the Dirksen proposal, and the Tuck bill. Mansfield then broke with Dirksen and sponsored a mild, non-binding "sense of Congress" resolution asking the courts to give the legislatures six months to act. This was accepted Sept. 24 by a 44-38 (D 37-15; R 7-23) roll call. But House conservatives, angered at the mildness of the Senate rider, urged their foreign aid conferees to kill the rider—which they did. Thus Congress took no action at all.

Again in 1965 and 1966, Congress was asked to vote on what came to be known as the "Dirksen amendment" (like McCulloch's) to permit a state to apportion one house of its legislature on a nonpopulation basis. In each year, the battle took place almost exclusively in the Senate, and in each year Dirksen saw his proposed amendment win a substantial Senate majority but fall a few votes short of the required two-thirds for a constitutional amendment.

Before the bill (S J Res 2) came to the Senate floor in 1965, Dirksen made several concessions in an effort to pick up support. Controversy had developed over how often the reapportionment plan must be resubmitted to the state's electorate (Dirksen agreed to require submission after each federal census), what factors constituted valid nonpopulation factors (Dirksen agreed to use "geography and political subdivisions"), and whether the electorate should be offered a specific reapportionment plan or simply be asked if a nonpopulation plan was preferred (Dirksen agreed to the former). The Subcommittee also struck from the original bill language giving the "people" of a state the "right and power" to determine the "composition" and "apportionment" of their state legislature. Opponents of this language argued that this would preclude judicial review of state legislature apportionment.

During Senate floor debate, proponents of the Dirksen amendment contended that the people of each state should be permitted to decide for themselves the basis of representation in one house of their legislature. Sen. Paul J. Fannin (R Ariz.) July 23 said, "All this amendment does is restore to the people a right which the Supreme Court has wrongfully taken away from them."

Sen. Thomas H. Kuchel (R Calif.) July 28 argued, "The Dirksen amendment affirms the right of the people to decide how best to determine the composition of their own state legislatures."

Sen. William Proxmire (D Wis.), opposing the amendment, July 28 said the right to vote was so fundamental that measures affecting it should not be open to popular referendum, where the right would be "subject to destruction by the majority." Sen. Clifford P. Case (R N.J.) the same day said, "There are times when a transient majority ought not to be permitted to govern the lives of all the people or any one person.... The real issue here is, shall less than majority be able to control majority actions in the state legislatures?"

In closing days of debate, opponents of the amendment stressed that it could be used to perpetuate discrimination against Negro voters by weighting white-dominated geographical areas or political subdivisions so as to maintain white control of at least one house of a state legislature. Sen. Edward M. Kennedy (D Mass.) Aug. 4 said the "motivation" to disenfranchise Negroes persisted in some states and the amendment would provide the "opportunity." Proxmire said an extreme example of the amendment's potential discriminatory use would be for a state to establish a unicameral legislature and apportion it to assure majority membership from white districts. But Sen. John Sherman Cooper (R Ky.) argued that Supreme Court decisions prohibited drawing voting district lines so as to discriminate against Negroes. Both sides in the debate agreed that drafters of the Dirksen amendment had no intention that it should be used to discriminate against Negroes.

Sen. Paul H. Douglas (D Ill.), who led the opposition to the amendment, Joseph D. Tydings (D Md.) and Proxmire argued on a broader front that the amendment lent itself to preserving the status quo in any state. They said that malapportioned legislatures would be called upon to ratify the amendment and then would draft the reapportionment plans to be submitted to the people, probably so wording the proposition that the "desired" result would be achieved.

On the key vote Aug. 4, 1965, the Senate approved the Dirksen amendment by a 57-39 vote—seven short of the two-thirds majority required.

After his 1965 defeat, Dirksen lost little time in preparing the groundwork for another effort to pass his proposed constitutional amendment. One week later, he introduced a new bill (S J Res 103) that was designed to placate some foes of the ill-fated S J Res 2.

The changes, Dirksen hoped, removed concern among Senators about malapportioned legislatures which might perpetuate themselves, about use of unicameral legislatures to frustrate equality of voting power and about use of geography and political subdivisions in apportionment to dilute the voting strength of Negroes by means of racial gerrymandering.

The key changes were four: (1) when ratifying the proposed constitutional amendment, at least one house of a state legislature must be apportioned on the basis of equal population; (2) a reapportionment plan submitted to referendum by a unicameral legislature must be court-approved; (3) any reapportionment plan submitted to referendum must be accompanied by an alternate plan based on population; and (4) any reapportionment plan based on factors of geography and political subdivisions must be drawn "in order to ensure effective representation in the state's legislature of the various groups and interests making up the electorate."

On April 20, 1966, Dirksen's amendment was again rejected, this time by a 55-38 roll call. The margin of defeat was the same as 1965: with 93 Senators voting, 62 votes were needed for passage and Dirksen supporters were again seven votes short.

Apparently despairing of any hope that Congress would pass such an amendment, Dirksen and his supporters in 1967 pushed for an alternative. The Constitution provided two methods of amendment: (1) Congress with a two-thirds majority could submit amendments to the states; and (2) two-thirds (34) of the states could petition Congress to call a national constitutional convention which would then submit amendments to the states for ratification. The constitutional convention method had never been used in amending the Constitution. As of May 1969, 33 states had submitted petitions

to Congress for calling a constitutional convention, only one short of the required majority. However, prospects for the eventual calling of a convention remained in doubt. There was considerable disagreement as to whether all the petitions had to be worded exactly (they were not) and the procedures to be followed if Congress did not call a constitutional convention.

However, even if the convention movement fails, the almost certain wave of new apportionment following the 1970 census would likely prompt further efforts for passage of some kind of amendment to limit the Supreme Court's decisions.

State Unit Vote Systems. The county unit vote system in the election of statewide officials—a device, like malapportioned legislative districts, to maintain rural control—was struck down by the Supreme Court in a March 18, 1963, decision in the case of *Gray v. Sanders*. The Court held, in this case, that the "unit system" used in Georgia primary elections was unconstitutional since

Definitions of Malapportionment and Gerrymandering

The prevalence of malapportionment and "gerrymandering" in the creation of U.S. Congressional districts was, to many observers, one of the chief evils in the American system during the postwar era. An early end to this evil, however, was promised by a Feb. 17, 1964, U.S. Supreme Court decision declaring that "as nearly as is practicable, one man's vote in a Congressional election is to be worth as much as another's."

MALAPPORTIONMENT

Malapportionment involved creating districts of grossly unequal populations—either through actions of state legislatures in establishing new districts or, as was the more frequent practice, simply by failing to redistrict despite major population movements that result in population inequalities. At the time of the 1964 Supreme Court decision, for instance, Louisiana had not redistricted since 1912, nor had Colorado, Georgia since 1931, or South Carolina since 1932.

Examples of great disparity in Congressional district sizes in recent U.S. history: New York (1930) 776,425 in largest district and 90,671 in smallest district; Ohio (1946) 698,650 and 163,561; Illinois (1946) 914,053 and 112,116; Arkansas (1946) 423,152 and 177,476; Texas (1962) 951,527 and 216,371; Michigan (1962) 802,994 and 177,431; Maryland (1962) 711,045 and 243,570; South Dakota (1962) 497,669 and 182,845.

In 1961 California redistricted but left a disparity of 588,933 and 301,872 between the largest and smallest districts. Other disparities included in 1961-62 redistricting bills: Arkansas 575,385 and 332,844; Florida 660,345 and 237,235; Illinois 552,582 and 278,703; Kentucky 610,947 and 350,839; Mississippi 608,441 and 295,072; New Jersey 585,586 and 255,165; North Carolina 491,461 and 277,861; Pennsylvania 553,154 and 303,026.

The decennial census and ensuing reapportionment of House seats eventually forced reapportionment in most states, although some resorted to the expedient of electing Members at large (like Texas, Hawaii, Ohio,

Michigan and Maryland in 1962) rather than face the process of redrawing district lines.

GERRYMANDERING

Gerrymandering was the name given to excessive manipulation of the shape of legislative districts. The gerrymander was named after Elbridge Gerry, Governor of Massachusetts in 1812 when the legislature created a peculiar salamander-shaped district to benefit the Democratic party to which Gerry belonged.

Like malapportionment, gerrymandering was practiced by both political parties. In 1961, for instance, Republican redistricters in New York created one gerrymander-like creature stretching across the greater part of up-state New York, his head hanging over Albany in the east and his tail reaching for Rochester in the west. Such salamander, tadpole and fishlike creatures sprang to life on the maps of New York City's boroughs. In California, Democrats in control of the Legislature connected two pockets of strong Republican strength in Los Angeles by a thin strip of land to form an unwieldy district running for miles along the coastline. In North Carolina, Democratic redistricters formed an almost-perfect gerrymander shape to throw the state's sole Republican Representative in with a strong Democratic opponent.

The basic intent of practically every gerrymander was political—to create a maximum number of districts which would elect the party candidates or types of candidates favored by the controlling group in the state legislature that did the redistricting. The effect was almost always to increase the political power of the already politically dominant group. Up to the 1950s, this was said to be the Republicans in the North and the Democrats in the South. Growing Democratic strength in many Northern states tended to cancel out the Republican advantage in that part of the country, however, and the reverse could eventually occur in the South.

it deprived city dwellers of equal protection of the laws by giving them less than their fair share of the weighted statewide vote.

The unit vote system, a "miniature electoral college," gave each county a certain number of votes (usually the number of its seats in the state legislature). The candidate who won a county won its unit votes. A candidate could easily win the popular vote but lose the nomination by running poorly in rural areas which had more unit votes. The system permitted rural areas to dominate the Georgia state government and Congressional delegation for more than 50 years.

Only two other states, Maryland and Mississippi, were affected by the decision since they were the only other states with similar nominating systems. All three states subsequently abandoned their unit vote primaries in favor of popular vote primaries. While the decision's immediate impact was limited to these three states, the Court gave a clue to how it would apply *Baker v. Carr.* Justice William O. Douglas' majority opinion said: "The conception of political equality from the Declaration of Independence to Lincoln's Gettysburg Address, to the 15th, 17th and 19th Amendments can mean only one thing—one person, one vote."

Congressional Districts

Wesberry v. Sanders. In a decision certain to have a substantial long-term impact on the composition of the House of Representatives, the Supreme Court Feb. 17, 1964, declared that Congressional districts must be as equal in population as practicable.

Ruling by a 6-3 margin in the case of *Wesberry v. Sanders,* a challenge to the Congressional districts of Georgia, the Court based its decision on the history and wording of Article I, Section 2 of the Constitution, which states that "Representatives shall be apportioned among the states according to their respective numbers" and "chosen by the people of the several states." This language, the Court stated, means that "as nearly as is practicable one man's vote in a Congressional election is to be worth as much as another's."

The majority opinion, written by Justice Hugo L. Black, said that "while it may not be possible to draw Congressional districts with mathematical precision, that is no excuse for ignoring our Constitution's plain objective of making equal representation for equal numbers of people the fundamental goal for the House of Representatives." The Court overturned a June 20, 1962, decision of a three-judge federal court in Atlanta which had ruled against the plaintiffs.

The *Wesberry* decision rested on the findings of the *Baker* case to show that districting questions are justiciable and on the *Gray* case to establish the principle of "one man, one vote." Unlike the previous two decisions, however, the *Wesberry* decision made no attempt to use the 14th Amendment as its justification.

In a strongly worded dissent, Justice John Marshall Harlan—who had also dissented in the *Baker* and *Gray* cases—said that the Constitution did not establish population as the sole criterion of Congressional districting and that the subject was left in the Constitution to the sole discretion of the states, subject only to the supervisory power of Congress. Justice Potter Stewart said he found that the Constitution "gives no mandate to this Court or to any court to ordain that Congressional districts within each state must be equal in population," but disagreed with Harlan in that he thought the matter was justiciable.

Kirkpatrick v. Preisler. The Court April 7, 1969, in *Kirkpatrick v. Preisler* tightened the "one-man, one-vote" principle even further by ruling that no numerical or population variance between Congressional districts within a state could be considered negligible. Any variance, "no matter how small," must be justified by the state or shown to be unavoidable, the Court said.

Only the six states with an at-large U.S. Representative—Alaska, Delaware, Hawaii, Nevada, Vermont and Wyoming—were outside the potential effect of this decision. All other states had districts with maximum population variances ranging from 1.0 percent (West Virginia) to 16.4 percent (Georgia).

According to October 1968 Census Bureau figures (based on 1960 statistics) showing the population of Congressional districts for the 91st Congress, 34 states had a maximum variance from the average district population of 3.0 percent or more. On the basis of the court's ruling, these states could be challenged to justify such variance or redistrict.

The other ten states—Arkansas, Indiana, Maryland, Massachusetts, Michigan, North Carolina, Ohio, Tennessee, Utah and West Virginia—had maximum population variances ranging from 1.0 percent to 2.9 percent. Indiana, Massachusetts, North Carolina, Ohio and Tennessee redistricted for the 91st Congress. These states could also be challenged on the basis of the ruling that no variation was small enough to be considered permissible without justification.

Congress and Districting

Although Congress would constitutionally have the right, through 1968 it had never chosen to exercise directly its power to draw district boundaries. In 1842, Congress provided that states with more than one Representative should establish districts of contiguous territory. The requirement for single districts was dropped in 1852 but reinstated in 1862. In 1872, a requirement was added that districts be as equal in population as practicable; in 1901, a requirement of compactness was added. The 1911 Reapportionment Act provided that Representatives "be elected by districts composed of a contiguous and compact territory containing as nearly as practicable an equal number of inhabitants." All these provisions were dropped, however, to improve prospects for passage of the permanent apportionment Act of 1929, and the Supreme Court ruled them no longer in effect in a 1932 case involving Mississippi's House districts (*Broom v. Wood*).

The anti-gerrymandering provisions were never enforced while they were in effect. In 1901 and 1910, the House rejected moves to deny Members seats on the grounds their districts did not conform to the federal standards.

In several postwar Congresses, House Judiciary Chairman Emanuel Celler (D N.Y.) introduced legislation forbidding the election of Representatives at Large in multi-district states, requiring that districts "be composed of contiguous territory, in as compact a form as practicable," and forbidding any district's population from varying more than 15 percent from the average per-district *(Continued on p. 449)*

The Size of the Franchise

Between 1948 and 1968, the number of persons casting ballots in a Presidential election increased by 24,418,276, from 48,793,286 to 73,211,562. Despite this rather substantial numerical rise, however, the percentage of persons voting in Presidential elections rose by only 9.3 percentage points when the increase in voting-age population—which rose from approximately 94.5 million in 1948 to 120.0 million in 1968—was taken into account.

In addition to the national population increase, other factors—particularly the addition of Alaska. Hawaii and the District of Columbia to the areas whose residents were eligible to vote in Presidential elections and the lowering of the minimum voting age in four states—also helped to swell the potential vote.

At the same time, certain developments tended to increase the number of people who actually went to the polls on election day. Most important were the abolishment of the poll tax as a requirement for voting in federal elections, an easing of requirements and regulations governing absentee voting and an increase in the South in the number of Negroes who registered and voted, particularly in the 1964 and 1968 elections. The greatly increased Negro participating in the South, however, also prompted unprecedented turnouts by white voters in that region.

Negro Voting. One of the most significant developments of the period in terms of voter turnout was the extension of the franchise to a substantial bloc of citizens—the Negroes—who previously had been largely denied their constitutional privilege in many Southern states, where Negroes charged that a pattern of discrimination, kept them from the polls.

In the 90 Congressional districts with the highest percent of Negro population shown by the 1960 census, 64 were in the South, 14 in the East, 10 in the Midwest and two in the West. The heavily Democratic orientation of the "most-Negro" districts was reflected in the 88th Congress: 88 Democrats, 2 Republicans.

The reason for the strong Democratic leaning of these districts appeared to differ sharply, however. The Northern Negro districts were apparently those in which Negroes effectively controlled or influenced the electoral process and were able to elect liberal Democrats in almost every case. The Southern districts with heavy Negro populations were often those in which Negroes had been effectively excluded from voting, districts represented by conservative whites who had consistently opposed civil rights legislation and other measures widely backed by Negroes.

While firm statistics on Negro registration and voting in the South were difficult to obtain, some figures were available which indicated the extent of the failure of Negroes to vote. Statistics compiled by the Republican National Committee in 1957 estimated Negro registrants in the 11 Southern states in the 1952 Presidential election at 1,009,634 and in 1956 at 1,243,759. The 1956 figure was said to represent 23.8 percent of the potential Negroes eligible to register and vote.

The voting rights provisions of the 1957 and 1960 Civil Rights Acts (PL 85-315, PL 86-449) were somewhat successful in increasing the number of Negro voters in 1960. Then, in 1962, a concentrated drive was initiated by the leading civil rights groups to register Southern Negro voters. Their efforts were spurred by passage of the Civil Rights Act of 1964 (PL 88-351) and the Voting Rights Act of 1965 (PL 89-110). The 1964 Act, among other provisions, barred unequal application of voting registration requirements; prohibited denial of the right to vote because of immaterial errors or omissions by applicants on records of application; tightened federal control and supervision over literacy tests; and made a sixth-grade education (if in English) a rebuttable presumption of literacy. The Act went substantially beyond the protections of the right to vote included in the 1957 and 1960 Civil Rights Act.

The 1965 Voting Rights Act was the most sweeping voting rights bill to gain passage in 90 years and departed from the pattern of previous 20th Century civil rights acts in that it provided for direct federal action to enable Negroes to register and vote, rather than the often protracted individual legal suits required by previous legislation. The Act was Congress' response to the violence that had occurred in the Selma, Ala., voting rights demonstrations led by the Rev. Martin Luther King Jr.

The results of these measures can be measured in statistics compiled by both the Southern Regional Council, an Atlanta-based research and information service devoted to improving the Negro's economic status and educational opportunities, and the U.S. Commission on Civil Rights. The Council has estimated that the number of registered Negro voters in the South rose by less than 400,000 between 1952 and 1962 and by 750,000 between 1962 and 1964. But the number of registered Negro voters increased by 938,000 between 1964 and 1968 in the 11 states of the old Confederacy, according to the Council. Perhaps more important than the overall increase, however, was the large jump in Negro voters in such Deep South states as Alabama and Mississippi. In 1964, only 23.0 percent of voting age Negroes in Alabama were registered. In 1968, this figure had risen to 56.7 percent. The increase in Mississippi was even greater—from only 6.7 percent in 1964 to 59.4 percent in 1968.

In voter turnouts, the increase among Southern Negroes and whites was even more dramatic. In 1960, the 11 states of the old Confederacy accounted for only 14.9 percent of the total national turnout (10,271,890 of 68,838,219 votes). By 1968, these 11 states cast 20.2 percent of the national total (14,803,725 of 73,211,562). The national total rose by 4,373,343 between 1960 and 1968, but the increase in the South alone was 4,531,835. In addition to the great increase in Negro voting, the end of the poll tax and the third-party Presidential candidacy of former Alabama Gov. George C. Wallace also accounted for the spectacular increase in voting participation in the South.

Poll Tax. Efforts to prohibit payment of a poll tax as a prerequisite for voting in national elections, either by statute or constitutional amendment, were undertaken in most Congresses beginning in the early 1940s. Five times between 1942 and 1949 bills to ban the poll tax by statute were passed by the House but died in the Senate, three times as a result of Southern filibusters.

One of the chief advocates of a ban on the poll tax was Sen. Holland (D Fla.), who, beginning in 1949, introduced a constitutional amendment to kill the poll tax in every session of Congress. In 1962, the Senate finally took affirmative action on his proposal (S J Res 29), approving the amendment March 27, following a mild Southern filibuster, by a 77-16 (D 47-15; R 30-1) roll-call vote. House approval followed Aug. 27 by a 295-86 (D 163-71; R 132-15) roll call. The state of Illinois Nov. 14, 1962, became the first state to ratify the proposed amendment, which became part of the Constitution as the 24th Amendment Jan. 23, 1964, when South Dakota became the last of the required three-quarters (38) of the states to ratify. At the time of ratification, five states—Alabama, Arkansas, Mississippi, Texas and Virginia—had a poll tax as a prerequisite for voting.

Absentee Voting. Absentee voting laws or lack of those provisions also were responsible for disfranchising many potential voters. Congress in 1942 enacted a law (PL 77-712) establishing absentee voting machinery for members of the armed forces and in 1944 passed a law (PL 78-277) permitting servicemen to vote by absentee ballot in that year's Presidential election. In 1955, Congress passed the Federal Voting Assistance Act (PL 84-296) which repealed the 1942 statute and urged states to enact laws permitting servicemen, federal employees abroad, dependents of both groups and merchant seamen to register for voting by use of uniform postcard applications and to vote by absentee ballot.

By 1964, 16 states still required more than mere absence to qualify for absentee voting, with the result that traveling businessmen, students away at school, vacationers, handicapped and incapacitated persons and others often were unable to vote. Three states—Mississippi, New Mexico and South Carolina—did not provide for civilian absentee balloting of any kind. All states by 1964 allowed absentee voting by members of the armed forces, and 47 states by civilian employees of the Federal Government. However, civilians residing on federal reservations under the exclusive jurisdiction of the U.S. were denied the right to vote in all but three states, and since many of these persons had no state residence, they lost the right to exercise their franchise.

Congress in 1968 passed a bill (S 2884—PL 90-343) amending PL 84-296 to recommend that states provide for absentee voting by otherwise qualified residents who were temporarily living abroad.

Residence Requirements. Millions of persons who would otherwise have been eligible to vote also were barred from the polls because they had moved and could not meet residency requirements, generally one year. The number of voters disfranchised by residency requirements was estimated at 4,000,000 in 1950, 5,000,000 in 1954 and 8,000,000 in 1960. By 1968, however, the number had dropped to 4,800,000.

Two proposed constitutional amendments were introduced in 1961 to limit state residency requirements for voter participation in Presidential elections, but neither was passed. The Johnson Administration in 1967 also backed legislation that would have limited state residency requirements in Presidential elections, but no legislation was passed.

But the trend among the states themselves has been to reduce residency requirements for Presidential elec-

tions and to a lesser extent for other offices. By the time of the 1968 election, 30 states had special rules permitting new residents to vote for President despite the fact that they had not met requirements for voting in state elections. Nine states had adopted legislation permitting old residents to vote if they had not qualified in their new states: Arizona, Connecticut, Michigan, New Mexico, New York, Texas, Vermont, Wisconsin and Wyoming.

Age Limitation. The traditional minimum voting age of 21 was not prescribed in the Constitution, which, for the most part, left establishment of qualifications for voting to the states. Heeding a war-inspired slogan, "Old enough to fight, old enough to vote," Georgia in 1943 became the first state to lower its voting age when voters approved a constitutional amendment setting 18 as the minimum voting age. Only three other states have followed Georgia's example—Hawaii, where the minimum age is 20; Alaska, with a minimum age of 19; and Kentucky, where 18-year-olds may vote. Voters in Nebraska and North Dakota refused to lower the voting age in their states in 1968.

The Senate Judiciary Committee July 1, 1952, reported a bill (S J Res 127) calling for a constitutional amendment lowering the voting age to 18, but the measure never was taken up on the floor. Again on Jan. 22, 1954, the Constitutional Amendments Subcommittee of the Senate Judiciary approved a proposed amendment (S J Res 53) to make 18 the legal voting age, but the measure was not reported by the full committee. The Johnson Administration, with strong bipartisan backing, pushed for passage of a new constitutional amendment in 1967 and 1968, but nothing was passed. The 1968 Democratic Platform called for passage of such an amendment. The 1968 Republican Platform urged the states to lower their voting ages but did not mention support for a constitutional amendment.

Alaska, Hawaii Statehood. Two Congressional actions which had the effect of increasing the size of the franchise in the United States were the granting, in 1958 and 1959 respectively, of statehood to Alaska and Hawaii, thus making residents of the two territories eligible to vote in national elections. In 1958, Congress broke a 42-year legislative deadlock by passing a law (PL 85-508) admitting Alaska into the Union as the 49th state. The last state to be admitted had been Arizona in 1912. The following year, Congress passed a law (PL 86-3) granting statehood to Hawaii.

D.C. Suffrage. Another Congressional action which led to extension of the vote was passage in 1960 of a resolution (S J Res 39) proposing a constitutional amendment that would permit citizens of the District of Columbia to vote in Presidential elections. S J Res 39 was passed by the Senate Feb. 2, 1960, by a 70-18 (D 43-12; R 27-6) roll-call vote, and by the House, amended, June 14 by voice vote. The Senate agreed to the House amendments June 16 by voice vote.

The amendment became part of the Constitution as the 23rd Amendment March 29, 1961, when Kansas became the 38th state to ratify it. The amendment returned to the citizens of the nation's capital the right withdrawn from them upon creation of the District of Columbia, out of land ceded by Maryland and Virginia, in 1802. The last time that citizens of the area covered by the District had voted was in 1800.

1963 Commission

The most comprehensive study of registration and voting during the postwar years was that conducted in 1963 by the President's Commission on Registration and Voting Participation. The 10-man Commission was established March 30, 1963, by executive order of President Kennedy, who named as chairman Census Director Richard M. Scammon, an authority on voting and elections. The group was directed to study the causes for the failure of many Americans to exercise their right to vote, paying particular attention to laws which restricted registration and voting on the basis of residence; absentee voting provisions; and the causes of the failure of qualified voters to cast ballots.

In its report, which was made public Dec. 20, 1963, the Commission placed the blame for low voter turnout in the United States on a number of legal and administrative causes, including inconvenient and burdensome registration and voting procedures; restrictive residence requirements that deprived otherwise eligible voters of their franchise; unreasonable absentee voting provisions; and election-day problems, such as crowded or inaccessible polling places, early closing hours and lengthy ballots that discouraged many citizens from voting. In addition, the poll tax and literacy and other voter qualification tests were mentioned as obstacles to registration and voting by some persons, particularly Negroes in the South.

To overcome these obstacles to higher voter turnout in Presidential and Congressional elections, the Commission recommended these steps, most of which were later implemented.

- Each state should create a commission on registration and voting participation, or utilize some other existing state machinery to survey in detail its election laws and practices.
- Voter registration should be easily accessible to all citizens.
- Residence requirements for voting for state officials should not exceed six months.
- Residence requirements for voting in county and city elections should not exceed 30 days.
- New state residents should be allowed to vote for President, regardless of their length of residence in the new state, if qualified to vote in the state from which they moved.
- States should provide absentee registration for voters who cannot register in person.
- Literacy tests should not be a requisite for voting.
- Voting by persons 18 years of age should be considered by the states.
- The poll tax as a qualification for voting should be eliminated.

The Growing Franchise

YEAR	ESTIMATED POPULATION OF VOTING AGE	VOTE CAST FOR PRESIDENTIAL ELECTORS		VOTE CAST FOR U.S. REPRESENTATIVES	
		Number	Percent	Number	Percent
1920	60,581,000	26,769,000	44.2	25,080,000	41.4
1922	62,984,000	——	——	20,409,000	32.4
1924	65,597,000	29,095,000	44.4	26,884,000	41.0
1926	67,912,000	——	——	20,435,000	30.1
1928	70,362,000	36,806,000	52.3	33,906,000	48.2
1930	72,602,000	——	——	24,777,000	34.1
1932	75,048,000	39,759,000	53.0	37,657,000	50.2
1934	77,215,000	——	——	32,256,000	41.8
1936	79,375,000	45,655,000	57.5	42,886,000	54.0
1938	81,514,000	——	——	36,236,000	44.5
1940	83,512,000	49,900,000	59.8	46,951,000	56.2
1942	85,759,000	——	——	28,074,000	32.7
1944	89,517,000*	47,977,000*	53.6	45,103,000*	50.4
1946	91,497,000	——	——	34,398,000	37.6
1948	94,470,000	48,794,000	51.7	45,933,000	48.6
1950	96,992,000	——	——	40,342,000	41.6
1952	99,016,000	61,551,000	62.2	57,571,000	58.1
1954	101,097,000	——	——	42,580,000	42.1
1956	103,625,000	62,027,000	59.9	58,426,000	56.4
1958	105,727,000**	——	——	45,655,000**	43.2
1960	107,949,000	68,838,000	63.8	64,133,000	59.4
1962	110,266,000	——	——	51,304,000	46.5
1964	113,931,000	70,645,000	62.0	66,044,000	58.0
1966	115,882,000	——	——	52,874,000	45.6
1968	120,006,000	73,211,562	61.0	66,109,209	55.1

*Includes 4,342,000 members of the Armed Forces serving abroad.
**Includes Alaska, which voted for Representative in November, 1958, although it did not achieve Statehood until January, 1959.

(Voting age is defined as resident population 21 years and over, except: 18 years and over in Georgia since 1944; 18 years and over in Kentucky since 1956; 19 years and over in Alaska; 20 years and over in Hawaii.)

Nominating Procedure

The Constitution provides (in Article I, Section 2) for the election of United States Representatives by direct popular vote and, since adoption of the 17th Amendment in 1913, for election of Senators by the same method. It makes no direct reference, however, to the method of nomination—the procedure by which a candidate may qualify for a place on the general election ballot. Until the late 19th century, would-be office holders obtained their party's nomination through means of informal political caucuses or conventions in the districts and states.

The first state laws relating to primary elections were passed in California and New York in 1866. Revulsion against abuses of the convention system mounted during the following decades, and so by 1899 two-thirds of the states had some type of primary law. In that year, the first mandatory primary act was passed in Minnesota, placing the primary on the same plane as the general election and making it uniformly applicable throughout the state. This pioneer law was copied by most other states in the succeeding decades, and by 1927 all but a handful of states had mandatory statewide primary laws that were fairly complete in their provisions.

As of 1968, 44 of the states nominated both U.S. Senators and Representatives by direct primary election. Exceptions were: Indiana (which nominated statewide candidates by convention but House candidates by primary); New York (which used a combination state party committee and primary for statewide candidates but House candidates by a straight primary); Delaware (which nominated both Senate and House candidates by convention); Connecticut and Utah (which used a mixed convention-primary procedure); and Virginia (where statewide candidates were determined in primaries but candidates for the House could be nominated either by primary or convention). In addition, the Republican party nominated by convention rather than primary in three Southern states—South Carolina, Virginia and Alabama. The Republicans in all three states, however, were moving toward use of the primary to nominate their candidates. Between 1956 and 1968, the Republican parties in three states—Arkansas, Georgia and Texas—shifted from the convention to primary method of nomination.

There were 13 states—Colorado, Illinois, Iowa, Massachusetts, Minnesota, Nevada, New Jersey, New York, North Dakota, Ohio, Pennsylvania, Rhode Island and Wisconsin—in which one or both parties, by convention or action of the state committee, often endorsed candidates before the primaries. Advocates of these pre-primary actions said they helped to establish party responsibility while leaving the final decision to the party voters. Only in Colorado and Massachusetts, however, was the practice of endorsing candidates recognized by law. In those states the endorsed candidates were given a special ballot position.

Most U.S. primaries were "closed'—open only to the registered members of the party whose primary was being held. But Alaska, Michigan, Minnesota, Montana, North Dakota, Utah, Vermont, Washington and Wisconsin had "open" primaries in which any citizen could choose at the polling place between casting a Republican or Democratic primary ballot. Alaska and Washington had the so-called "jungle" primary in which voters could vote for any candidate of either party for each office in the primary.

The trend in the late 1950s and early 1960s was generally against the open primary, mainly on the theory that it disrupted party responsibility. Similar arguments were used in winning abolition in 1959 of California's famed "cross filing" primary law, which often resulted in Republicans winning Democratic primaries and the reverse.

Convention Method of Nominating

Reformers of the late 19th and early 20th centuries championed the direct primary as a way to escape from the evils of the "smoke-filled room" method of candidate selection at caucuses or conventions. Some criticism of the convention method continued in more recent years through 1964.

In 1962, for example, the Democratic State Convention in Connecticut was criticized for nominating a politically unknown attorney, Bernard F. Grabowski, for Representative-at-Large, allegedly on the sole basis of his Polish ancestry. The choice of Grabowski, whom most of the convention delegates had never heard of before, was dictated by Democratic State and National Chairman John M. Bailey.

The convention system has been defended by some who say that convention delegates are in a better position than the voters to judge the qualifications of candidates. The convention, its backers have maintained, narrows the responsibility for nomination to a group of delegates and party officials who can then be held accountable. Party responsibility, they say, cannot be established and maintained unless a party has command of its own house.

To bolster their argument, convention backers point to apparent abuses of the primaries, such as the entry of names similar to those of known political leaders in order to confuse the electorate. In 1962 an unemployed 25-year-old salesman named Joseph E. Montoya entered the New Mexico Democratic primary for the U.S. House, reportedly backed by the primary opponent of incumbent Rep. Joseph M. Montoya (D). However, the maneuver failed to draw off any significant number of votes from the total for the incumbent Representative.

Another alleged primary abuse occurred in 1962 when Ohio Democrats nominated Cleveland realtor and handyman Richard D. Kennedy, a political unknown, to oppose Republican Robert Taft Jr. in the Representative-at-Large race. Kennedy ran ahead of an 11-candidate field in the primary, apparently because he had the same family name as the President, but was then defeated by Taft in the general election.

With no direct reference made in the Constitution to the method of nominating House and Senate candidates, however, action with regard to such alleged abuses and to nominating procedures in general was left in the hands of the states.

Presidential Nominating Reform

The 1968 Republican National Convention in Miami Beach took seven hours and 15 minutes of tedious nominating speeches and largely artificial demonstrations before balloting could even begin on a Presidential nominee. The 1968 Democratic National Convention in Chicago was one of the most chaotic in American history. Rulings of the chair often seemed high-handed or even illegal, and there were repeated scuffles between reporters, delegates and security personnel, and even some arrests, on the convention floor. The result: a new push in Congress for basic reform of the way Americans select their candidates for President.

Sen. Gaylord Nelson (D Wis.) Sept. 4, 1968, proposed a special 30-man commission to look into the way that nominees are selected, noting: "It is clear that a majority of the American public, regardless of party, is fed up with our quadrennial party conventions," especially since 1952 when national televised coverage of the conventions began.

Sen. Mike Mansfield (D Mont.) Sept. 5, 1968, reiterated his proposal for a number of basic election law reforms, including a national nominating primary, replacement of the electoral college by a direct vote of the people, lowering the minimum voting age to 18 and limiting the President to one six-year term.

National Debate. If history is a guide, it will take many years—perhaps decades—to effect any basic reform of the system. More than a century-and-a-half of pressure to reform or abolish the electoral college, for instance, has yet to bear fruit. Nevertheless, a lively national debate about the nominating system appeared in the offing—and the idea of a national primary may receive more serious attention in the coming decade.

What would be the impact of a national primary? What problems would arise in instituting it?

Since President Woodrow Wilson first proposed a national primary in a message to Congress in 1913, a quiet debate about the merits of the idea has been going on among politicians and political scientists. Now, that debate may win wide public attention.

Everyone agreed a national primary would give millions of party members a direct and equal voice in choosing nominees. But the idea raised a host of thorny problems.

Independent Voter. The first was the problem of the independent voter. At least in theory, national nominating conventions, anxious to nominate a winning ticket, now take into account the reported desires of independents when they select a nominee. But in a national primary, would independents be allowed to vote? If not, party members alone might make choices unappealing to the broad mass of the country.

But if independents could vote or if there were an open primary like Wisconsin's where the voter can select the primary ballot of either party, unfriendly elements could raid one party's primary to nominate the weaker contender.

Thus, a basic choice would have to be made: have closed primaries (open only to party members) and protect the integrity of the parties while excluding millions of independents from a vital stage in the election process, or have open primaries and run the risk of harming the parties.

One advantage of the open primary system was that it avoided all the problems inherent in any type of federal regulation of party systems and voter registration—a field traditionally left to the states. Many states, for instance, did not even have formal registration by party, and federal rules in this area would probably be required under a closed primary system.

Plurality or Majority. The next problem was whether a majority of the votes cast, or just a plurality, would be sufficient to nominate in a party's primary. If only a plurality were needed, then a widely split field could produce a nominee favored by only 20 or 30 percent of the voters in the primary. If a majority were needed, then runoff primaries might be required in many elections.

There could be a compromise in which a vote of 40 or 45 percent would be the minimum percentage for nomination, with a runoff if no candidate polls that well. There would always be the problem, however, that candidates representing extreme wings of the party would run first and second in a split field and qualify for the runoff, with a moderate contender, who is everyone's second choice but no one's first choice, being eliminated.

'Drafts' Possible? A related problem would arise in years when no candidate succeeds in building a truly national base of support in the pre-nomination period. Under such circumstances, a convention can "draft" a candidate as in the cases of Charles Evans Hughes in 1916 and Adlai E. Stevenson in 1952. In a direct primary, that could not happen.

Also, there was a question whether voter interest and participation could be maintained over three elections—the first primary, the runoff, and—finally—the general election in November.

Then there was the problem of qualifying for the ballot. One easy system to hold down the number of contenders on a national primary ballot would be to require a substantial number of petition signatures—perhaps a million or more—to place a man's name on the ballot.

Next there was the problem of expense in a national primary. Some contend such a contest would escalate the level of campaign costs.

Vice Presidency. Another problem involved the Vice Presidential candidate. If he were nominated in a national primary as well, he might be a political or personal antagonist of the Presidential nominee. The result could be continuing embarrassments in the general election campaign and highly undesirable discord in the next administration.

Under the existing convention system, the Presidential nominee almost invariably selected his own running mate—a sound principle now paralleled in the 25th Amendment to the Constitution, which provides that the President shall nominate a new Vice President, subject to approval of Congress, whenever that office becomes vacant.

One possible way to avoid the problem of incompatible nominees would be for each party to hold a national convention subsequent to the primary. At that convention, the Presidential nominee would be permitted to propose a running mate subject to ratification by the delegates.

Political Contributions and Campaign Spending

The influence of money on politics and politicians has always posed a potential threat to the democratic process, suggesting that elected officials may be "bought" by special interest groups and thus be unable to serve the people who elected them. The immediacy of this possibility increased over the years in proportion to a steady rise in the costs of campaigning for national office, which took a dramatic jump as television grew into a major communications medium.

For about a century, would-be reformers of the U.S. electoral process pressed for laws which would force candidates to make public declarations of the sources of their campaign funds, with the idea that full disclosure would reveal which candidates were unduly indebted to any special interest group so that the voters would be forewarned.

Along with efforts to force disclosure of funds, many reformers sought to place limitations on the amount that candidates and political committees might spend, hoping by such a device to make all major contenders compete on reasonably equitable terms. Suggestions for Federal Government financing of campaigns and for income tax deductions or credits for political giving were also put forward.

State Disclosure Laws

Legislation requiring candidates to reveal their sources of funds was first enacted in New York State in 1890. The New York model was soon copied in many other states. By 1968, 43 states required reports of one nature or another. Of these 43 states, however, a total of only 31 required reports from both candidates and committees, while 12 states required them from candidates only. In four states, the reporting requirements applied only to primaries. The possible weight which such disclosures played in the voters' decision was sharply limited by the fact that only 17 states required filing of reports before primary or general election day. The effectiveness of the reporting laws was further limited by the fact that stiff penalties for violations appeared in the statute books of only a few states, and prosecutions were rare.

Among "model" state campaign reporting laws which were adopted was a 1951 Florida statute requiring each candidate to appoint one campaign treasurer and designate one bank as his campaign depository. Contributions had to be deposited within 24 hours of receipt, with deposit slips showing name, address and amount contributed by each donor. Public reports of expenditures were required by U.S. Senate and gubernatorial candidates every Monday of each week preceding the election and by candidates for other offices once a month before the election.

A widely hailed "tough" disclosure law passed by Massachusetts in 1962 failed to live up to the hopes of many backers. The law stipulated that no candidate could have more than three campaign committees, that each committee must have a bank account and that the banks must make reports of the money deposited and paid out, listing the names and addresses of donors of over $25 and the names and addresses of persons to whom bills were paid.

Backers of the Massachusetts law were pleased that it had revealed the high number of out-of-state contributions to candidates in the 1962 Senatorial race, and that the final reports showed the total campaign outlay for all candidates to be close to $7 million—the first time anything approaching an accurate figure had been available in the state. Other observers were highly skeptical of the filed reports. They pointed out that successful Democratic Senatorial candidate Edward M. Kennedy reported primary expenditures of $100,292.45. Newspaper estimates of what his staff, billboard, television and other expenses would be at normal market rates ranged up to $1 million. Rep. Laurence Curtis (R Mass.), unsuccessful candidate for his party's Senate nomination, reported spending $118,343.08 in the primary campaign, but impartial estimates of his actual outlays ranged up to $300,000.

Federal Control

Pressure for control of campaign spending also built up on the federal level toward the end of the 19th and start of the 20th centuries. After the elections of 1904, a move for federal legislation took shape in the National Publicity Law Assn., headed by former Rep. Perry Belmont (D N.Y. 1881-88). In 1907, the Tillman Act prohibited corporations and national banks from making money contributions for elections.

The first Federal Corrupt Practices Act was passed in 1910, modified in 1911 and finally refined in the Corrupt Practices Act of 1925, which remained in effect at the end of 1968. The Corrupt Practices Act required periodic reports of receipts and expenditures to be filed by national political committees or their subsidiaries, or by other committees seeking to influence elections in more than one state. It also required reports of personal campaign expenses by individual Senate and House candidates.

The Corrupt Practices Act stipulated that reports of campaign receipts and expenditures be filed with the Clerk of the U.S. House or (in the case of Senate campaigns only) with the Secretary of the Senate. No provision was made for publication of the filed reports. Since 1949, however, Congressional Quarterly Service published, on a regular basis, the reported receipt and expenditure figures of all political committees and candidates reporting to the House Clerk or Senate Secretary. Since the reports were withdrawn for purposes of public inspection two years following each election (on orders of the House Clerk), Congressional Quarterly reports constituted the only published source and permanent reference of the reports filed.*

The Corrupt Practices Act was riddled with loopholes, making reported amounts merely indicative and by

---

Following the 1956 election, the Senate Rules and Administration Subcommittee on Privileges and Elections, chaired by Sen. Gore (D Tenn.), undertook a comprehensive examination of campaign spending and printed long lists of reported political gifts and expenditures, based on replies to its own questionnaires. No comparable Congressional study was made after any other U.S. election.

no means complete. For example, the Act did not require reports of contributions or expenditures in either Presidential or Congressional primary campaigns, nor in connection with a party's Presidential nomination. Nor did it require reports by political committees as long as they confined their activities to a single state and were not actual subsidiaries of a national political committee. Frequently, Congressional candidates reported they had received and spent nothing on their campaigns, maintaining the position that the campaign committees established to elect them to office had been working without their "knowledge and consent."

Ceilings on campaign spending were set by the Corrupt Practices Act at $2,500 for candidates for the House and $10,000 for the Senate, although these totals could be raised to a maximum of $5,000 and $25,000 respectively, based upon the number of votes cast in the most recent election. Candidates were able to evade these limitations by channeling most of their campaign expenditures through separate committees which were not required to report federally, thus making the federal ceilings, from a practical standpoint, meaningless.

In 1939, the Hatch Act, named after Sen. Carl A. Hatch (D N.M. 1933-49), was passed, prohibiting active participation in nation politics by federal employees and the use of relief funds for political purposes. In 1940, certain provisions of the Hatch Act were extended and limits were set at $5,000 for annual political contributions by individuals and $3 million for annual spending by political committees in federal elections. In practice, however, the parties evaded this stipulation by forming new committees under various names, each of which was then free to spend up to $3 million.

In the 1943 War Labor Disputes Act, Congress extended the 1907 prohibition on political contributions by national banks and corporations to include certain financial activities by labor unions. This prohibition was made permanent by the Taft-Hartley Labor-Management Relations Act of 1947 and was extended to apply to primaries, conventions and caucuses on federal elections.

The effectiveness of such legal restrictions on corporate and union giving was open to serious question. The prohibition did not extend to campaigns for state and local offices. And while the Taft-Hartley Act banned direct corporate or union gifts to federal campaigns, it said nothing about voluntary contributions of corporation executives or labor union members.

A number of other loopholes existed. For example, corporations could give executives bonuses with which they, as individuals, could make campaign gifts. Expense accounts could serve the same purpose. Corporations were allowed to place advertisements in political journals, even though there was no apparent benefit to the corporations from the ads. Services "in kind" could be furnished—supplying office equipment, lending the services of public relations firms and lawyers or actually permitting corporate officers to spend a substantial amount of their time on political activities. Managers of political campaigns learned to watch for contribution checks drawn directly on corporate funds and to return them to the senders in order to avoid direct violation of the law. Often this money made its way back to the political managers in some other form.

Unions also spend freely from regular union treasury funds for registration drives, get-out-the-vote campaigns,

union newspapers and other communications orienting members on political issues.

Four basic types of labor spending for political purposes appeared:

Free funds, or money obtained through canvasses of labor union members outside the regular union dues structure. Such funds were used almost exclusively for direct contributions to candidates who, organized labor felt, were friendly to its cause.

Nonfederal contributions—the sums spent by labor unions within individual states on campaigns for state and local offices. Usually, such funds came directly from regular union treasuries.

Educational expenditures—money taken directly from union treasuries and used for technically nonpartisan purposes, such as registration drives, encouraging members to vote, or for printing voting records of Members of Congress or state legislatures. Organized labor's registration and get-out-the-vote drives were overwhelmingly in support of Democratic candidates, being keyed to areas where regular Democratic efforts were considered deficient or where an overwhelming Democratic vote was traditionally necessary to overcome a Republican plurality in some other section of the district, state or country.

Public service activities such as union newspapers or radio programs were financed directly from regular union treasuries. As with corporation newspapers and radio programs, a sharply partisan viewpoint could be and often was expressed.

In addition to funds and services donated by individuals, corporations, labor unions and other sources, the political parties began to rely on several new techniques to meet the soaring expenses of campaigning. Major among these in the years prior to 1964 was the political dinner (or breakfast, brunch, lunch and tea), which had been used since the 1930s to fill the party coffers, usually at a charge of anywhere from $25 to $1,000 a plate. (In the 1960s, the $1,000-a-plate affairs became known as "the President's Club.") Perhaps the most productive dinner before 1964 was the "Salute to Eisenhower" held simultaneously at 53 banquets in 37 states on Jan. 20, 1956. These dinners, linked by closed-circuit television featuring President Eisenhower, netted between $4 million and $5 million for the Republican party.

President Kennedy also ranked as an effective fund raiser. Events which he attended between the day of his inauguration, Jan. 20, 1961, and a final dinner in Houston, Texas, the night before he was assassinated, raised well over $10 million for the Democratic party. The most productive of these were the 1961 Inauguration Eve Gala in Washington, D.C., which grossed $1,250,000; a Sept. 20, 1962, dinner in Harrisburg, Pa., that brought in $1,300,000; a $1,000-a-plate dinner and $100-a-ticket gala in Washington, D.C., Jan. 18, 1963, which grossed $1,200,000; and a dinner in Boston in October 1963 that grossed $650,000.

Through the 1968 elections, political dinners continued as a major source of campaign funds and were used extensively by both major political parties and the American Independent party of George C. Wallace. First under President Kennedy and then continued under President Johnson, the "President's Club" became a major source of Democratic funds. By contributing $1,000 or more per year, a "member" supposedly received special privileges, including personal visits with the President. Republicans, who at first attacked the "President's

Club," in 1965 set up their own GOP "Boosters Club" patterned after the Democratic version. The Republican Club raised money for the party's U.S. House candidates.

While these figures gave some indication of the amounts of money needed to conduct a national political campaign, existing loopholes in the laws precluded an exact accounting of both contributions and expenditures. A measure of the incompleteness of the recorded figures was evident in the contrast between the reported total political spending in 1960—$28,326,322—and the $175,-000,000 estimate by political experts of what total spending actually was. In 1962, $18,404,115 was reportedly spent in Congressional races, but Congressional Quarterly estimated that almost $100 million was actually spent. The 1964 campaign expenditures of all candidates and parties were estimated by CQ in the neighborhood of $200 million.

In 1968, campaign committees supporting Vice President Hubert H. Humphrey for President reported total contributions and loans of about $12.6 million. However, Democratic party treasurer Robert Short Jan. 8, 1969, told reporters that at least $3 million in campaign bills had been paid directly by individuals or "nonreporting committees" because "some of these people (who put up the money) obviously don't want to be known." *(See p. 114.)*

Although criminal penalties were provided in law for willful or negligent failure to file campaign spending reports, as of 1968 there had never been a prosecution for failure to report or for false reporting under the Corrupt Practices Act even though reports by news media revealed repeated instances of incomplete filings or complete failure of candidates to report. The stated policy of the Justice Department, spelled out by Attorney General Herbert Brownell in 1954 and confirmed by the Justice Department in a Nov. 19, 1963, letter to Congressional Quarterly, was "not to institute investigations into possible violations of (the Act) in the absence of a request from the Clerk of the House of Representatives or Secretary of the Senate." Those officials, who served at the pleasure of the Representatives and Senators, never made a reference of a violation of the Corrupt Practices Act.

Not once in the postwar period did Congress take any official notice of high expenditures in House or Senate campaigns. In 1927, Sen.-elect William S. Vare (R Pa.) had been barred from taking his seat after reports indicated his campaign had cost $785,000. Sen.-elect Frank L. Smith (R Ill.) was barred from taking his Senate seat the same year on similar grounds. But since then, no public demands for action were made to reprimand Senators, who sometimes spent well over $1 million in their campaigns.

Campaign Expenditures

As political campaigns increased in complexity and costliness, the almost endless variety of expenditures approached the point where they defied a complete categorization. Alexander Heard, in *The Costs of Democracy,** published in 1960, noted just a few:

---

*Alexander Heard, The Costs of Democracy, University of North Carolina, 1960.

"Radio and television broadcasting eat up millions. Thousands go to pay for rent, electricity, telephone, telegraph, auto hire, airplanes, airplane tickets, registration drives, hillbilly bands, public relations counsel, the Social Security tax on payrolls. Money pays for writers and for printing what they write, for advertising in many blatant forms, and for the boodle in many subtle guises. All these expenditures are interlarded with outlays for the hire of donkeys and elephants, for comic books, poll taxes and sample ballots, for gifts to the United Negro College Fund and the Police Relief Association, for a $5.25 traffic ticket in Maryland and $66.30 worth of 'convention liquor' in St. Louis...."

Electronic campaigning—radio and television—came to occupy a greater and greater portion of campaign budgets. In 1956, total expenditures for political radio and TV broadcasting at all levels during the general elections was about $9.8 million. The figure was more than $14 million in 1960 and about $24.6 million in 1964. The three major television networks in 1968 reported political broadcasting charges of $8.9 million for the Presidential primary and general election campaigns that year. The amount was more than double of the 1964 total of $4.1 million. *(For additional figures, see p. 118.)*

Other major expenditures during election campaigns included newspaper advertising, which for a modern statewide campaign was likely to consume 10 to 15 percent of the total budget; public relations firms, which took 40 and 23 percent, respectively, of direct expenditures by the Democratic and Republican national committees in 1960; and public opinion polls. In addition, large sums were needed for campaign materials (buttons, bumper stickers, brochures, etc.); headquarters and staff, which were likely to take between 20 and 30 percent of most campaign budgets; billboards; and expenses of actually getting the voters to the polls on election day, which have been estimated to account for one-eighth of all campaign expenditures.

Proposed Reforms

Congress in the postwar years considered a number of proposals aimed at tightening regulations over election spending and freeing candidates from over-dependence upon large contributors and special interest groups. Little actual action resulted. Following is a year-by-year review of Congressional action.

1948—In its final report on a study of the 1948 Congressional elections, the House Campaign Expenditures Committee recommended a "substantial raise" in existing limits on campaign expenditures, pointing to the increased costs of goods and services, as well as the large population increase since passage of the Corrupt Practices Act of 1925.

1951—The House Special Committee to Investigate Campaign Expenditures, in a report on the 1950 House elections, Jan. 3 said it favored repeal of a number of provisions of the Federal Corrupt Practices Act of 1925 and the Hatch Act (1939). The Committee said it was "patently impossible for a candidate to conduct a Congressional or Senatorial campaign" within the existing limitations of expenditures, and that the "unrealistic"

$3 million annual limitation on the national political committees was "an invitation to criminal violation." The Committee also recommended that primaries be included under political financing regulations, political committees be precluded from receiving and spending funds on behalf of a candidate without his written authorization and that the prohibition against participation in elections by federal employees be eliminated or liberalized.

1953—In a Jan. 24 report, the 82nd Congress Elections Subcommittee of the Senate Rules Committee proposed that the limit on spending for national political campaign committees be increased from $3 million to $10 million a year. The Subcommittee also recommended that the limit for spending by Senatorial candidates be increased from $25,000 to $50,000 or an absolute limit of $250,000, based upon a sliding scale of up to 10 cents for each vote case in the last primary or general election for the office in the candidate's state. On June 10, Sens. Carl Hayden (D Ariz.), Thomas C. Hennings Jr. (D Mo.) and Robert C. Hendrickson (R N.J.) introduced a bill (S 2081) containing these provisions, plus a ceiling of $25,000 (instead of the existing $5,000) on spending by candidates for the House. No action was taken on the bill.

1955—The Senate Rules and Administration Committee June 22 reported a bill (S 636), which had been introduced by Hennings (D Mo.), to include campaign costs in primary elections under the federal regulation limiting expenditures; require all committees active in campaigns for federal office to file financial reports (instead of only those active in more than one state); and increase the spending limit for Senatorial candidates in both primary and general elections to $50,000 and for House candidates to $12,500. The bill also would have raised the existing $3 million limit on spending by national committees, according to a formula based on the number of votes in recent elections, to approximately $12 million. The bill received no floor action in the Senate.

1956—A Select Senate Committee, in an April 7 report, recommended that Congress re-evaluate the Federal Corrupt Practices Act. Specifically, the report suggested that Congress consider the advisability of amending the election laws to require that every candidate for federal office designate a fiscal agent officially authorized to solicit and accept campaign contributions and required to make this information a matter of public record. The Committee also recommended that every person, political committee or organization making more than $5,000 in campaign contributions in any one year be required to file a detailed accounting with the Secretary of State of each state.

1957—A bill (S 2150) increasing the maximum spending limits for political campaigns was reported Aug. 2 by the Senate Rules and Administration Committee but received no further action. As reported, S 2150 would have increased the limit for national committees to a figure equal to 20 cents for each person who voted in the last Presidential election; for Senate and Representative-at-Large candidates to $50,000 or more, depending upon the number of voters in the preceding general election; and for other House candidates to $12,500 or more based on the number of voters.

1960—A bill (S 2436) increasing the limits on campaign spending but tightening provisions for disclosure was passed by the Senate but not acted on by the House. S 2436 was reported July 23, 1959, by the Senate Rules and Administration Committee and passed Jan. 25, 1960, by a 59-22 (D 38-15; R 21-7) roll-call vote. As passed by the Senate, the bill increased the spending limit for Senate and Representative-at-Large candidates to $50,000 or a level established by the number of voters in the previous election; for other House candidates to $12,500, or a sliding maximum based upon the number of voters in the preceding election; and for nominees for President and Vice President at an amount equal to 20 cents times the number of votes cast in any of the three preceding elections, which would have set the ceiling at approximately $12 million and $6 million, respectively, in 1960. The House took no action.

1961—A truncated version of the "clean elections" bill passed by the Senate in 1960 was approved by the Senate Sept. 15, 1961, by voice vote but was not acted upon by the House. As passed, the bill (S 2426) raised the annual limit on campaign spending by political committees to an estimated $14 million, under a sliding scale formula; increased the spending limits for Senate and Representative-at-Large candidates to $50,000, and for other House candidates to $12,500.

Also in 1961, Sen. Maurine B. Neuberger (D Ore.) and four co-sponsors introduced a bill (S 1555) to establish a federal election finance fund which would share up to half of a candidate's radio-television expenses. No action was taken on the measure.

1962—The President's Commission on Campaign Costs April 18 issued a report recommending a series of proposals to encourage greater citizen participation in financing Presidential campaigns. The Commission had been named Oct. 4, 1961, by President Kennedy. Chairman was Alexander Heard, dean of the University of North Carolina Graduate School. Among the Commission's recommendations were that:

- Individuals be given a credit against their federal income tax of 50 percent of political contributions, up to a maximum of $10 per year or, as an alternative, a deduction from taxable income for contributions up to $1,000 a year.
- The current $3 million annual limit on expenditures of interstate political committees and the $5,000 limit on contributions by individuals to those committees be repealed, leaving no limit.
- All candidates for President and Vice President and committees spending at least $2,500 a year be required to report expenditures made in both primary and general election campaigns.
- A Registry of Election Finance be established to help enforce political financing regulations.
- The Government pay the "reasonable and necessary costs" of a President-elect's facilities and staff during the "transition" period between election and inauguration.

President Kennedy May 29 submitted five draft bills to Congress encompassing proposals identical or similar to those made by the Commission. The only bill reported (HR 12479) was one to finance transition costs. This bill was reported by the House Government Operations Committee Sept. 19, but the measure died when Rep. Gerald R. Ford (R Mich.) Oct. 1 objected to consideration of the measure under the Consent Calendar, stating that the

Reported National-Level Political Spending

Year, Man Elected	Expenditures			Total Vote	Cost Per Vote†
1912—Wilson (D)	Total:	$ 2,876,816		15,034,000	19 ¢
	Rep:	1,076,548	37.4%		
	Dem:	1,134,848	39.4		
	Prog:	665,420	23.1		
1916—Wilson (D)	Total:	$ 4,726,155		18,528,000	26 ¢
	Rep:	2,441,565	51.7%		
	Dem:	2,284,590	48.3		
1920—Harding (R)	Total:	$6,887,872		26,769,000	26 ¢
	Rep:	5,417,501	78.7%		
	Dem:	1,470,371	21.3		
1924—Coolidge (R)	Total:	$ 5,366,277		29,095,000	18 ¢
	Rep:	4,020,478	74.9%		
	Dem:	1,108,836	20.7		
	Prog:	236,963	4.4		
1928—Hoover (R)	Total:	$11,598,461		36,806,000	32 ¢
	Rep:	6,256,111	53.9%		
	Dem:	5,342,350	46.1		
1932—Roosevelt (D)	Total:	$ 5,146,027		39,759,000	13 ¢
	Rep:	2,900,052	56.4%		
	Dem:	2,245,975	43.6		
1936—Roosevelt (D)	Total:	$14,116,343		45,655,000	31 ¢
	Rep:	8,951,602	63.4%		
	Dem:	5,164,741	36.6		
1940—Roosevelt (D)	Total:	$26,917,051		49,900,000	54 ¢
	Rep:	18,864,117	70.1%		
	Dem:	8,052,898	29.9		
1944—Roosevelt (D)	Total:	$26,193,311		47,977,000	55 ¢
	Rep:	16,195,376	61.8%		
	Dem:	9,997,935	38.2		
1948—Truman (D)	Total:	$8,771,819		48,794,000	18 ¢
	Rep:	3,686,775	42.0%		
	Dem:	2,266,231	25.8		
	Lab:	1,291,343	14.7		
	Prog:	1,365,389	15.6		
	*SR:	162,081	1.8		
1952—Eisenhower (R)	Total:	$19,421,287		61,551,000	32 ¢
	Rep:	12,229,239	63.0%		
	Dem:	5,121,698	26.3		
	Lab:	2,070,350	10.7		
1956—Eisenhower (R)	Total:	$21,518,260		62,027,000	35 ¢
	Rep:	13,220,144	61.4%		
	Dem:	6,492,634	30.2		
	Lab:	1,805,482	8.4		
1960—Kennedy (D)	Total:	$27,202,155		68,838,000	40 ¢
	Rep:	12,950,232	47.6%		
	Dem:	11,800,979	43.4		
	Lab:	2,450,944	9.0		
1964—Johnson (D)	Total:	$38,079,829		70,645,000	54 ¢
	Rep:	19,314,796	50.7%		
	Dem:	14,948,791	39.3		
	Lab:	3,816,242	10.0		
1968—Nixon (R)	Total:	$56,397,261		73,212,000	77 ¢
	Rep:	29,592,832	52.5%		
	Dem:	12,577,715	22.3		
	Lab:	7,241,259	12.8		
	**AIP:	6,985,455	12.4		

The above figures are the best available summaries of general election campaign spending reported by national-level committees of the Republican, Democratic and major third party groups since 1912, plus labor organization spending since 1948. It should be noted that the figures provide only the roughest guide of spending. Accounting methods of political committees have varied drastically over the years.

In some cases, fund transfers from committee to committee have been counted; and in others, they have not. And some figures include totals of local political groups.

In all cases, funds listed here represent only a fraction of total spending. For example, the figures do not include reports of all national-level committees, of Congressional candidates or on primary and state level campaigns.

†Figures represent total spending divided by the number of votes cast. The actual cost-per-vote figures are higher since the spending figures are not complete.

*States Rights Party
**George C. Wallace's American Independent party

SOURCES: Citizens' Research Foundation, Governmental Affairs Institute, The Two Party System in the U.S. by William Goodman

$750,000 authorization figure for each fiscal year concerned was too high.

1963—President Kennedy April 30 sent to Congress two draft bills to stiffen reporting requirements for campaign finances and to give tax benefits to campaign contributors in order to encourage support of political candidates and committees. Both proposals had been recommended by the President's Commission on Campaign Costs in 1962, but neither was acted upon.

1964—A provision to allow taxpayers to claim a deduction for campaign contributions of up to $50 for individuals and $100 for married couples was added to the Administration's omnibus tax bill (HR 8363—PL 88-272) by the Senate Finance Committee but was dropped in the Senate-House conference.

1966—Reform of U.S. political campaign finances advanced on a number of fronts in 1966. For the first time in U.S. history, Congress approved a form of federal subsidy for the costs of Presidential campaigning. President Johnson sent Congress a comprehensive campaign finance reform law that covered all Presidential and Congressional campaigns, both in the primary and general election stage. Congress also clamped down on corporate tax deductions for advertisements in political journals.

Significant developments of 1966:

• President Johnson, in his Jan. 12 State of the Union address, called for tax incentives to stimulate small contributions to political parties and "make it possible for those without personal wealth to enter public life without being obligated to a few large contributors." He also urged revision of "present unrealistic restrictions on (campaign) contributions—to prohibit endless proliferation of committees, bringing local and state committees under the Act—to attach strong teeth and severe penalties to the requirement for full disclosure of contributions."

President Johnson's draft of a campaign spending reform bill, forwarded to Congress May 26, envisaged sweeping reforms in the field. Not only were primary campaigns, both for President and for Congress, brought under the reporting requirements, but also a provision was added requiring all Members of Congress to report annually all gifts and income from personal services of more than $100 which they received from sources other than Government salary and securities income. Taxpayers were to be allowed to deduct from taxable income up to $100 for contributions to any candidate or political committee—local, state or federal—in each calendar year.

The Senate Rules and Administration Committee refused to hold hearings on the Presidential recommendations, reporting out instead a much weaker reform bill sponsored by Sen. Howard W. Cannon (D Nev.). But in the House Administration Committee, several days of hearings were held and a subcommittee drafted a bill closing loopholes in the Presidential measure and strengthening it in several respects. No House action was taken.

• At the urging of Senate Finance Committee Chairman Russell B. Long (D La.), the Senate added to the Foreign Investors Tax Act, and both houses of Congress approved, a measure establishing a Presidential Election Campaign Fund, to be financed by voluntary $1 tax form checkoffs by the country's taxpayers. The measure was expected to channel $30 million or more into the Presidential campaign chests of each major party in Presidential election years. Though the legislation was criticized

on a number of counts, President Johnson signed it into law and it was expected to act as a catalyst for further Congressional action in financing federal campaigns.

• In the wake of widespread adverse publicity about political journals published by the major political parties with tax-deductible corporate ads at rates of up to $15,000 a page, Sen. John J. Williams (R Del.) persuaded the Senate Finance Committee to attach an amendment to the Administration's excise tax bill totally prohibiting tax deductions for the cost of advertisements in political advertising journals. No move was made to strike the amendment as it went through the House and Senate, and it became law with the President's signature March 15. The amendment deprived national political committees of a growing source of indirect income and cut off a traditional source of funds for state and local political committees, thus adding to pressures for other laws to help the parties with their financing problems.

1967—Congress made inoperative Sen. Long's 1966 measure establishing a Presidential Election Campaign Fund, but the fight over the action (HR 6950) tied up the Senate for more than five weeks.

The Senate passed a bill (S 1880) that extended the reporting requirements of the Corrupt Practices Act to spending in all primaries and conventions for President, Senator or Representative. The bill, the broadest campaign finance reform measure ever to clear a chamber of Congress, also required reports from intrastate political committees, which were exempted by existing law, and removed the existing ceilings on spending by political committees and Congressional candidates.

A subcommittee of the House Administration Committee reported an even more comprehensive bill (HR 11233), sponsored by Reps. Robert T. Ashmore (D S.C.) and Charles E. Goodell (R N.Y.), but the bill remained stalled in the full committee. A coalition of Northern Democrats, who feared restrictions on spending by organized labor, and of Southern Democrats, who opposed the bill's reporting requirements for primaries, blocked full committee approval.

Sen. Long's Finance Committee in November reported a bill (HR 4890) which embodied S 1880 plus a comprehensive plan for federal subsidies to Presidential and Senate campaigns. However, no further action was taken on the measure.

1968—Congress again failed to act on campaign financing and reporting reform. Congress, however, did pass a bill (HR 17325) to permit tax deductions for corporate advertising in Presidential nominating convention programs.

1969—Outgoing Attorney General Ramsey Clark Jan. 17 submitted to Congress proposed legislation that required all committees spending $1,000 or more in support of a candidate for federal office to file reports whether they operated in more than one state or not; placed a $5,000 limitation gift by one individual to a candidate or committees supporting that candidate; repealed the $3-million limitation on spending by a political committee but required more complete reports; required financial reports from persons contributing more than $10 to support a candidate; required reports of committees or groups supporting a national convention campaign; and created a bipartisan commission, appointed by the President, to administer the law.

'Equal Time' Problems Part of TV Impact

Radio and television, which enabled candidates for political office to reach large local and national audiences, played an increasingly important part in the election process during the postwar era. Still in its infancy in 1945, television in particular matured through a series of technological improvements to emerge as a major campaign tool.

In 1952, for the first time, TV audiences across the nation watched sessions of the national conventions of the two major political parties. In 1960, television brought another "first" when the Democratic and Republican Presidential nominees, John F. Kennedy and Richard M. Nixon, faced each other in a series of four televised debates.

While no similar face-to-face confrontations took place in 1964 or 1968 between the Presidential candidates, TV debates were demanded by a number of Senate, House and gubernatorial candidates, and those that took place—or were rejected—were considered major factors in the outcomes of some races.

Section 315(a)

In the Communications Act of 1934, Congress included a provision—Section 315(a)—which stipulated: "If any license shall permit any person who is a legally qualified candidate for any public office to use a broadcasting station, he shall afford equal opportunities to all other such candidates for that office in the use of such broadcasting station...."

This "equal time" provision had not been an acute problem to networks and politicians until 1959, when Lar Daly, a self-described "perennial office-seeker" running as a write-in candidate for mayor of Chicago, demanded as much time on Chicago news broadcasts as had been given to Democratic and Republican candidates. Daly's specific complaint concerned a 20-second news shot of Mayor Richard J. Daley, the Democratic candidate for re-election, greeting a foreign dignitary and a one-minute news report of Daley opening the "March of Dimes" campaign.

The Federal Communications Commission Feb. 19, 1959, ruled, 4-3, that Daly's complaint was justified, interpreting the law as written to apply to newscasts. This decision unleashed a storm of protests, including a March 19 statement by President Eisenhower that the ruling was "ridiculous" and a request by Attorney General William P. Rogers that the FCC "reconsider and reverse" its decision. When the Commission June 16 refused to reverse the ruling, subcommittees of the House and Senate Interstate and Foreign Commerce Committees began hearings on proposals to amend the law.

A bill (S 2424) amending Section 315(a) of the Communications Act of 1934 was passed July 28 by the Senate and Aug. 18 by the House by voice votes, with the conference report (H Rept 1069) agreed to by the House Sept. 2 by a 142-70 standing vote and by the Senate Sept. 3 by voice vote (PL 86-274).

The bill inserted at the end of Section 315(a) the provision that: "Appearance by a legally qualified candidate on any (1) bona fide newscast, (2) bona fide news interview, (3) bona fide news documentary (if the appearance of the candidate is incidental to the presentation of the subject or subjects covered by the news documentary), or (4) on-the-spot coverage of bona fide news events (including but not limited to political conventions and activities incidental thereto) shall not be deemed to be use of a broadcasting station within the meaning of this subsection."

Although panel discussion programs were not explicitly mentioned in S 2424 as enacted, Rep. Oren Harris (D Ark.), floor manager of the bill, asserted in House debate that the exemption applied to panel discussions so long as they were bona fide news interviews. However, the bill did not exempt patently political broadcasts nor those whose major objective appeared to be political rather than news.

Nor, according to a subsequent Federal Communications Commission ruling, did it exempt certain other broadcasts. In response to a query by the Columbia Broadcasting System concerning the effects of PL 86-274, the FCC ruled Oct. 1, 1964, that any radio or television station carrying a live Presidential news conference while the President was a candidate for re-election, or a press conference by a "substantial or significant non-incumbent" nominee, had to grant equal time to all other Presidential candidates, including those running on third-party tickets.

Presidential Debates

Slightly more than a year after passing PL 86-274, Congress enacted another law that enabled the networks to present the so-called "great debates" between the 1960 Presidential candidates of the two major parties, Sen. John F. Kennedy (D) and Vice President Richard M. Nixon (R)—a confrontation that was considered to have had a direct and possibly decisive influence upon the election.

The National Broadcasting Company and the Columbia Broadcasting System April 21, 1960, announced that they planned to offer the Presidential candidates of the major parties free television time for debate before the election. The American Broadcasting Company April 22 said it had set aside time for campaign coverage and that its use depended upon the cooperation of the candidates.

In the meantime, the Senate Interstate and Foreign Commerce Communications Subcommittee had under consideration a bill (S 3171) introduced by Sen. Warren G. Magnuson (D Wash.) which would have required the networks to give free television time to the Presidential candidates of the two major parties for eight weeks beginning Sept. 1 of each Presidential election year. Every network would have had to donate an hour a week to each candidate of a party which received 4 percent of the vote in the last election. While the 4-percent figure appeared low, only the Democratic and Republican parties could qualify in 1960.

In hearings before the Subcommittee, broadcasters opposed S 3171 as compulsory legislation. They asked, instead, that Congress simply relieve them of the requirement to give equal time to minor party candidates. Responding to the views of the networks, the Senate Interstate and Foreign Commerce Committee June 8 reported S J Res 207 as a substitute for S 3171, and the bill was passed June 27 by the Senate by voice vote and Aug. 22 by the House by voice vote, under suspension of the rules (PL 86-677).

As enacted, PL 86-677 suspended Section 315(a) as it related to Presidential and Vice Presidential candidates for the period of the 1960 campaign. Following passage of the bill and statements July 19 and 24 that both Kennedy and Nixon were willing to participate in debates, representatives of the Democratic and Republican candidates and the major networks, including the Mutual Broadcasting System, Aug. 31 released plans for a series of four, hour-long radio and TV debates between the Presidential candidates.

The 1960 debates took place on Sept. 26 and Oct. 7, 13 and 21. Producing them "cost" the broadcast networks in excess of $2 million in loss of commercial time, according to estimates. The number of persons who viewed one or more of the debates on television was estimated at 115,000,000 by the National Broadcasting Company and 120,000,000 by the Columbia Broadcasting System.

As for an exact measurement of the influence of the debates upon the electorate, no precise means of making such a judgment was available. However, it was generally acknowledged that before the debates Nixon was viewed as the candidate casting the "image" of experience and the probable winner of the election; and Kennedy's "image" was the inexperienced, energetic political underdog fighting an uphill battle. When the debates were over, the positions—and to some extent the "images"—had been reversed.

1962 Proposals

Congress next considered, but did not act on, amendments to the "equal time" provision when the Senate Commerce Communications Subcommittee July 10-12, 1962, held hearings on six proposals (S 204, 2035, 3434 and S J Res 193, 196 and 209) concerning the suspension or elimination of Section 315(a). The major proposals were to suspend Section 315(a) for the period of the 1962 Congressional campaign for Congressional candidates (S J Res 196), to suspend the section for the 1962 Congressional and gubernatorial races (S 2035) and to eliminate "equal time" restrictions entirely, without limitations (S 3434).

A Presidential Commission on Campaign Costs, appointed Oct. 4, 1961, by President Kennedy, had recommended in an April 18 report that Congress take some action to allow broadcasters to make their facilities available to nominees of the major parties on an equal basis without having to do so for minor party candidates. President Kennedy May 29 recommended temporary suspension of the "equal time" provision for the 1964 Presidential and Vice Presidential campaign, saying he favored "temporary suspension, rather than permanent repeal...so that Congress can periodically review broadcasting and campaign practices that occur under everchanging conditions."

During the Senate hearings, however, complete repeal drew support from broadcast industry spokesmen, including Robert W. Sarnoff, chairman of the National Broadcasting Company, and LeRoy Collins, president of the National Assn. of Broadcasters. Sarnoff said the public would be better served if broadcasters were free to rely on their "sense of fair play" and their "editorial judgments." Collins agreed, arguing that the "equal opportunities" provision had failed "because it assumes that all candidates are bona fide contenders for public office and because it assumes further that a mathematical formula can be substituted for journalistic judgment."

Lawrence Speiser, Washington director of the American Civil Liberties Union, summed up the argument for a series of opposition witnesses from minor parties and other groups. Permanent suspension, he declared, would give the Democratic and Republican parties "a perpetual monopoly" over television, "the most popular and widely followed medium of communication."

Although Congress failed to act in 1962, face-to-face debates between competitors for public office retained their appeal. Surveying the field of 1962 Senatorial and gubernatorial races, Congressional Quarterly found that direct television encounters between the candidates had been scheduled or suggested in 12 of the year's 39 Senate races. On the gubernatorial level, debates had been proposed in 12 of the year's 35 races.

1964 Debate Issue

Following his inauguration in 1961, one of the first questions President Kennedy was asked, at his second press conference on Feb. 1, was whether he would participate in debates if he were a candidate for re-election in 1964. He answered, "I would, yes."

After Mr. Kennedy's assassination Nov. 22, 1963, attention turned to whether President Johnson would debate as the Democratic nominee. Mr. Johnson, at several news conferences before the Democratic Convention in August, answered that he had not yet been nominated and would "cross that bridge when I come to it."

The prenomination position of the leading Republican contender, Sen. Barry Goldwater (R Ariz.), as expressed in a Jan. 31, 1964, television interview, had been that it was "kind of dangerous to subject a President of the United States to questioning and debate.... He might just slip and say something inadvertently that could change the course of history."

Following his nomination, however, Goldwater's position changed. On July 29, Rep. Jack Westland (R Wash.) announced that Goldwater, then the Republican candidate, had told a group of House Republicans that he was "ready, willing and able" to debate President Johnson and that he hoped Congress would pass legislation making television debates possible. On Sept. 21, speaking in Charlotte, N.C., Goldwater charged that President Johnson "will not face me—he will not face you," and said: "I dare him to face me before the world. I demand of him—debate."

Goldwater's challenge came in the face of the failure of Congress to suspend the "equal time" provision for the 1964 election period, making it impossible, from a practical standpoint, for the networks to offer any candidates television time other than regular news coverage.

A bill (H J Res 247) suspending the "equal time" provision had been passed June 23, 1963, by the House and Oct. 2 by the Senate. The only important differences between the two versions was the number of days preceding the Nov. 3 elections that the bill would have been effective—75 days in the House-passed version and 60 days in the Senate bill.

It was not until Feb. 18, 1964, that the first request for a House-Senate conference was made by Rep. Harris (D Ark.), sponsor of the bill and chairman of the House Interstate and Foreign Commerce Committee which had reported it. The conferees finally met May 7 and on May 19 reported a version of H J Res 247 containing the 60-day suspension included in the Senate bill.

Observers speculated that Harris had postponed calling a meeting of the conference committee at the behest of President Johnson, who, it was felt, might not wish to debate an opponent. Newspaper reports quoted Harris as having told some Committee members that he was "waiting to learn Mr. Johnson's view on the legislation" and that the President's feeling about the bill should be sought "in all fairness" to him.

Apparently at the request of the White House—and over strenuous Republican opposition—the Senate Aug. 18 adopted, by a 44-41 (D 44-12; R 0-29) roll-call vote, a motion tabling (killing) the conference report on H J Res 247, thus settling the question of televised debates between the Presidential candidates for the 1964 campaign.

1968 Debate Issue

After a battle containing strong political overtones and which saw the use of delay tactics in both chambers, Congress in 1968 failed to complete action on a bill (S J Res 175) to permit television debates among the three major Presidential candidates.

Republicans, assuming that President Johnson would seek re-election, early in the year called on the President to debate the eventual GOP nominee. After the President March 31 announced he would not run again, it was presumed that legislation to suspend the "equal time" provision of the Communications Act of 1934 would be acted on favorably.

The Senate passed S J Res 175 May 29. The House, however, did not act on the bill until after the Presidential nominating conventions. The Democratic nominee, Vice President Hubert H. Humphrey, who had side-stepped debates with Sens. Robert F. Kennedy (D N.Y.) and Eugene J. McCarthy (D Minn.) during the campaign for the nomination, in September urged Congress to complete action on S J Res 175. The Republican nominee, Richard M. Nixon, who had made a poor showing in the 1960 televised debates with John F. Kennedy and who was running ahead of Humphrey in the 1968 race according to most polls, reportedly opposed the legislation. Nixon said he would debate with Humphrey but not with third party candidate George C. Wallace.

Through the use of various parliamentary maneuvers, Republicans Oct. 8-9 staged in the House what was the equivalent of a filibuster in an attempt to prevent action on S J Res 175 (although the Republicans said the delay tactics were being used to force action on campaign spending reform and Congressional reorganization bills). After an amended version of S J Res 175 was passed by the House, Senate Republicans then used delay tactics to prevent Senate consideration of the legislation. After the Senate deferred action on the bill, a group of House proponents took up the tactics to delay adjournment in an effort to force Senate action on S J Res 175. However, the move was unsuccessful, and Congress adjourned shortly after it was abandoned.

TV, Radio Political Spending

The Federal Communications Commission Jan. 2, 1969, announced that the three major television networks had reported political broadcasting charges of $8.9 million for the Presidential primary and general election campaigns of 1968. The $8.9 million total was more than double the 1964 total of $4.1 million. Figures for political broadcasting for all offices in 1968 were not expected to be available until mid 1969.

In 1964, a total of $34,610,714 was paid for all political broadcasts on U.S. television and radio stations. The totals were based on almost complete returns from questionnaires sent to the networks and 5,644 commercial broadcast stations (television and radio) in the United States.

Of the total, $10,006,725 was expended by candidates and committees in primary elections and $24,603,989 in general election campaigns. On an over-all basis, Democrats outspent Republicans, $17,841,125 to $15,916,905. (Minor parties spent $852,684.) But in the general election, Republicans outspent the Democrats, $13,032,575 to $11,012,626.

Following is a breakdown of spending in general election campaigns (excluding primaries) for political broadcasts:

	1964	1960	1956
Total	$24,603,989	$14,195,278	$9,818,342
Republican	13,032,575	7,558,809	5,381,891
Democratic	11,012,626	6,204,986	4,120,712
Other	558,788	431,483	315,739

APPORTIONMENT *(Continued from p. 435)*

population of the state. But, as in past years, the bill never went further than the Subcommittee stage. In 1965, however, the bill was reported by the Judiciary Committee and passed by the House March 16 by voice vote. The measure became stalled in the Senate Judiciary Committee, however, and again failed to win Congressional approval.

Spurred by ever-tightening judicial interpretation of what constituted "one-man, one-vote," Congress was moved to action in 1967 on Congressional redistricting.

The House passed a bill setting a 10-percent maximum variation between the largest and smallest district in a single state after the 1970 census but allowing variations of up to 30 percent in the interim.

The Senate refused to accept the House version allowing a 30-percent maximum for the elections of 1968 and 1970 in favor of a straight 10-percent figure applying immediately. The two Houses never were able to come to an agreement, and the only legislation that passed (PL 90-196) was a bill forbidding at-large elections in states with more than one U.S. House seat. The only two states immediately affected by the problem, Hawaii and New Mexico—both with two at-large districts—were exempted from the bill for the 1968 elections. Hawaii must establish districts for the 1970 elections. The legislation was an effort to head off court-ordered at-large elections in states with redistricting problems.

Chapter 8—Veterans

Chapter 8—Veterans

Veterans' Affairs

THE Johnson years marked a renewed congressional interest in veterans. The American military build-up in Vietnam began in 1965 and by the end of 1968 an average of 800,000 servicemen were returning to civilian life yearly. Vietnam veterans numbered 2.7 million, accounting for 10 per cent of all living veterans in the United States.

Since their number was smaller, their impact on society was considerably less than was made by returning veterans of World War II. The return of the "Viet-Vet" was more akin to that of the Korean War (1950-53) veterans. Neither the war in Korea nor war in Vietnam infused public affairs with a veterans point of view.

Preliminary evidence suggests that the Vietnam veteran has been slow to join veterans' organizations and reluctant to identify with them. The war itself was unpopular with many of the Vietnam veterans, as it was with many of his neighbors who stayed home.

Nevertheless, the fighting in Vietnam stirred Congress to enact a set of veterans benefits similar to those extended to the men and women who served in World War II and the Korean War. Congress in 1966 passed a GI Bill of Rights for post-Korea veterans, those who served after Jan. 31, 1955, the officially designated end of the Korean War. The Veterans Readjustment Act of 1966, as the post-Korea GI Bill is formally known, was the centerpiece of veterans' legislation enacted during the Johnson years.

Until 1966, the Johnson Administration had opposed (as had the previous Eisenhower Administration) any special benefits for post-Korea veterans. It contended that such benefits were costly and unnecessary in view of new and existing programs for the general population in matters of health, education, welfare and job training.

As the Vietnam war increased Congressional support for Veterans' programs, President Johnson in 1966 proposed a limited set of educational benefits for veterans in an effort to forestall enactment of more extensive legislation. However, his action dissolved any remaining resistance in Congress to a new GI Bill of considerable scope. The Senate, but not the House, in 1965 had already passed a bill with broader educational benefits than the Administration proposed. The Senate-passed bill quickly received House consideration in 1966 and, with amendment, passed unanimously. The Senate, in turn, accepted the House amendments without dissent. President Johnson signed the post-Korea GI Bill on March 3, 1966, and it became effective June 1.

The major provision of the new GI Bill was that of paying veterans to attend college, a practice patterned on the GI Bills of World War II and the Korean War. Congress in 1967 extended the benefits to include vocational and farm training, and increased the monthly payments to veterans in college. The lawmakers also hoped to entice former dropouts back into high school by authorizing returning veterans to finish high school on the GI Bill without losing any future eligibility for college or vocational benefits.

The response of the Vietnam veteran was disappointing to some of the sponsors of the GI Bill. By the end of 1968 521,000 of the 2.7 million Vietnam veterans—19 per cent of the total—had entered college or other training programs under GI Bill auspices. Participation after World War II was 50 per cent and after the Korean War 42 per cent. However, in the comparable first two and one-half years of those programs, the percentage of enrollees was only 18 and 23, respectively.

Veterans Administration (VA) officials noted that many veterans of the "Vietnam era" (defined by Congress in 1967 as beginning Aug. 5, 1964) were well settled back into civilian life by the time the GI Bill was enacted. They also noted that the monthly payments to veterans for attending college ($130 to $175) were not especially attractive in an affluent age.

The scope of veterans benefits and services range from those of World War II vintage, like aid in starting a civilian career and home buying, to the more traditional ones like disability compensation, pensions, medical care and survivors assistance. For all these activities and their administrative costs, the federal government spent successively more in the 1965-68 years and projected even higher spending in the future. The rising costs reflected a combination of more veterans, new services, and cost-of-living increases in veterans' payments. Despite the higher costs, the share of the federal budget devoted to veterans needs remained a constant 4 per cent through the 1965-68 period.

References

Discussion of veterans affairs from 1945-1964 will be found in *Congress and the Nation*, Vol. I, pp. 1335-1373.

Participants in U.S. Wars

In the statistics below, "deaths in service" includes deaths in battle and deaths from other causes. For wars before the Civil War, estimates vary according to source on the number of participants.

Revolution (1775 - 1784)

Participants:	395,000	
Deaths in Service:	4,000	1.0 percent
Last Veteran Died:	April 5, 1869	

War of 1812 (1812 - 1815)

Participants:	536,000	
Deaths in Service:	2,000	0.4 percent
Last Veteran Died:	May 13, 1905	

Mexican War (1846 - 1848)

Participants:	130,000	
Deaths in Service:	13,000	10 percent
Last Veteran Died:	Sept. 3, 1929	

Civil War, Union Forces (1861 - 1865)

Participants:	2,213,000	
Deaths in Service:	364,000	16.4 percent
Last Veteran Died:	Aug. 2, 1956	

Indian Wars (1817 - 1898)

Participants:	106,000	
Deaths in Service:	1,000	0.9 percent
Living Veterans on Dec. 31, 1968	2	

Spanish-American War (1898 - 1902) [1]

Participants:	392,000	
Deaths in Service:	11,000	2.8 percent
Living Veterans on Dec. 31, 1968	7,000	

World War I (1917 - 1918) [2]

Participants:	4,744,000	
Deaths in Service:	116,000	2.4 percent
Living Veterans on Dec. 31, 1968	1,705,000	

World War II (Sept. 16, 1940 to July 25, 1947)

Participants:	16,535,000 [3]	
Deaths in Service:	406,000	2.5 percent
Living Veterans on Dec. 31, 1968	14,660,000 [4]	

Korean War (June 27, 1950 to Jan. 31, 1955)

Participants:	6,807,000 [3]	
Deaths in Service:	55,000	0.8 percent
Living Veterans on Dec. 31, 1968	5,840,000 [4]	

Cold War (Feb. 1, 1955 to Aug. 5, 1964)

Participants:	3,195,000	
Deaths in Service:	20,000	0.6 percent
Living Veterans on Dec. 31, 1968	3,137,000	

Vietnam War (Aug. 5, 1964 - Dec. 31, 1968)

Participants:	6,232,000 [5]	
Deaths in Service:	54,000	0.9 percent
Living Veterans on Dec. 31, 1968	2,760,000 [6]	

America's Wars
Total Through Dec. 31, 1968

Participants:	40,880,000
Deaths in Service:	1,046,000
Living Veterans	26,656,000

---

1. *Includes also Boxer Rebellion, Philippine Insurrection and activities in the Moro Province to July 15, 1903.*

2. *Includes service in Russia to April 1, 1920.*

3. *Includes 1,476,000 persons who served in both Korean War and World War II.*

4. *Includes 1,257,000 living veterans who served in both Korean War and World War II.*

5. *Includes 887,000 who served in the Korean War.*

6. *Includes 196,000 who served in the Korean War.*

SOURCE: VA; House Veterans Affairs Committee

The benefits have been jealously guarded by veterans organizations. All of the larger ones maintain lobbyists in Washington. These groups were especially active in pushing for passage of the post-Korea GI Bill and in working to block a Johnson Administration plan in 1965 to close 11 VA hospitals, 4 domiciliaries (old soldiers' homes) and 16 regional offices in an economy move. Faced with Congressional opposition, the President later limited the closings to six hospitals, two domiciliaries and nine regional offices.

Chronology
of Veterans'
Legislation

1965

VA Closings

Closings Announced. The VA Jan. 12 announced that it planned to close 11 VA hospitals, 4 domiciliaries, and 16 regional offices throughout the country, with all the closings completed by June 30, in a move to save an estimated $23.5 million a year.

The VA said the hospitals to be closed were selected on the basis of low patient demand, staffing problems, and outmoded structures. It said the functions of the regional offices would be transferred to the nearest VA facility, and all hospital employees would be offered jobs elsewhere.

VA Administrator William J. Driver said the order was in keeping with the "time-tested policy of locating and operating hospitals in close proximity and association with medical schools."

He said that the medical program of the VA employed approximately 4 percent of the nation's physicians and 15,000 of the nation's nurses. In addition, he said it was the largest single employer of persons in several medically oriented professions, and contained almost 8 percent of the nation's hospital beds.

Closings Criticized. The VA announcement brought vigorous protests from Members of Congress. Senate Majority Leader Mike Mansfield (D Mont.) Jan. 13 called the plan "an appalling, backward and insensitive act," and received support in these views from Senate Minority Leader Everett McKinley Dirksen (R Ill.). Sen. Richard B. Russell (D Ga.) Jan. 15 said the closings would "leave a hiatus in large areas where sick or impaired veterans will have to be transported a considerable distance."

VA hospitals were the major focus of Congressional protest; the domiciliary and regional benefit office closings received much less attention.

Hearings Held. The Senate Labor and Public Welfare Veterans' Affairs Subcommittee held hearings on the closing proposals Jan. 22-28. Registering strong protests to Congress were representatives of the National Commanders of the American Legion, AMVETS, Veterans of Foreign Wars, Veterans of World War I, U.S.A., Inc., Disabled American Veterans, and the American Federation of Federal Employees (AFL-CIO).

Hearings were also held Feb. 18-23 by the House Veterans' Affairs Committee. Reps. Joseph Y. Resnick

Federal Budget Outlays for Veterans

Fiscal year	Amount (*in billions*)	% of total federal budget
1970[1]	$ 7.72	4
1969[1]	7.69	4
1968	6.88	4
1967	6.34	4
1966	6.00	4
1965	5.48	4

[1]*Estimates.*

SOURCE: Federal Budgets

(D N.Y.) and Ray Roberts (D Texas) criticized the proposed closings as discriminating against rural areas.

The Budget Bureau and VA defended the proposals, saying they would improve rather than diminish veterans' care.

Confirmation Delayed. One result of the dispute over the VA closings was a brief delay in the confirmation of William J. Driver as VA Administrator. President Johnson Dec. 26, 1964, had announced he would nominate Driver to the job, making him the first VA career official (he was then Deputy Administrator) to be named to the post on a regular, long-term basis (a few had served on an interim basis).

Senate action on the nomination, initially scheduled for Jan. 15, 1965, was deferred. However, on Jan. 26 Sen. Lee Metcalf (D Mont.) withdrew his announced intention to oppose confirmation, (but later changed his mind and voted against Driver), and Mansfield said he was "not opposed to this nomination." Their move was reportedly prompted by Driver's announcement, the day before, that emergency and hardship cases would be accepted in VA hospitals until the final closing date.

The Senate Feb. 2 confirmed Driver as VA Administrator by a 75-7 roll-call vote. But Mansfield and other critics of the closings said their opposition to the VA plans would continue.

Closing Order Revised. In a partial concession to Congressional opposition, President Johnson ordered the closings delayed and, on April 3, appointed a special advisory committee to study the closure proposals. Following its recommendations, Johnson on July 8 ordered the VA to close only 6 of the 11 hospitals, 2 of the 4 domiciliary homes, and only 9 of the 16 regional benefit offices. These closings were completed by the end of August.

Hospitals closed: Tupper Lake, N.Y.; Rutland Heights, Mass.; Fort Bayard, N.M.; Broadview Heights, Ohio; Dwight, Ill.; and McKinney, Texas.

Domiciliary homes closed: Thomasville, Ga., and Clinton, Iowa.

Regional Offices closed: Albany, N.Y.; Syracuse, N.Y.; Wilkes-Barre, Pa., Cincinnati, Ohio; Kansas City, Mo.; Shreveport, La.; Lubbock, Texas; San Antonio, Texas. The Manhattan and Brooklyn, N.Y., offices were consolidated.

Veterans Compensation

Cost-of-Living Increases. Congress provided (HR 168 — PL 89-311) cost-of-living increases averaging 10 per cent in monthly compensation paid to veterans with service-connected disabilities. The increases were payable to 1.8 million veterans who had suffered disabilities in wartime, and 145,000 who had suffered disabilities in peacetime. The increases varied from 5 per cent for the least disabled to 20 per cent for the most disabled.

The new benefit scale set by HR 168 provided total monthly compensation ranging from $21 for a veteran medically judged to be 10 per cent disabled to $300 for a veteran 100 per cent disabled. Even though technically "100 per cent disabled," a veteran could receive added benefits for losses of arms, legs, eyes and so forth—or combinations of disabilities. His total benefits could not exceed $600 a month. Corresponding figures under the old scale were $20, $250 and $525.

Some 300,000 veterans would continue, as before, to receive additional payments to support their dependents. These payments were increased a flat 10 per cent. The total first-year cost of all increases provided in HR 168 was estimated at $176 million.

Hospital Bed Dispute. The only controversial provision of HR 168 was one inserted by the House Veterans' Affairs Committee. It specified that 4,000

Highlights Of GI Bills, 1944-1968

World War II

Title. Servicemen's Readjustment Act of 1944 (PL 346-78).

Benefits. Tuition, fees and other customary school costs up to $500 a year, plus monthly allowance of $50 for single veterans, $75 with dependents, for full-time training (lesser amounts part-time). Increased Dec. 28, 1945, to $75 and $105 ($120 for more than one dependent).

Eligibility. Veterans who served 90 days or more after Sept. 16, 1940, and before July 26, 1947, and discharged other than dishonorably.

Entitlement. One year of full-time training plus a period equal to time spent in service; 48 month maximum. Termination date for education and training, July 25, 1956.

Participants. Some 7.8 million of 15.6 eligible veterans participated, as follows: college, 2,230,-000; below-college education 3,480,000; on-job training 1,400,000; on-farm training 690,000.

Cost. $14.5 billion.

Korean War

Title. Veterans Readjustment Assistance Act of 1952 (PL 550-89).

Benefits. Monthly payments of $110 a month, with no dependents, for full-time institutional training; $135 with one dependent; $160 with more than one dependent (lesser amounts for part-time training.) Veterans paid their own tuition, books, supplies, etc. Allowances for on-job training: $70 a month with no dependents, $85 with one, $105 with more than one. Full-time farm training: $95, $110 and $130.

Eligibility. Service of 90 days or more after June 27, 1950, and before Feb. 1, 1955, with other than dishonorable discharge.

Entitlement. Education and training for a period equal to one and one-half times the veteran's active service. Maximum of 36 months entitlement. Termination date of education and training, Jan. 31, 1965.

Participants. Some 2.4 million of 5.7 million eligible veterans participated, as follows: college 1,213,000; below-college education 860,000; on-job training 223,000; on-farm training 95,000.

Cost. $4.5 billion.

Post-Korea

Title. Veterans Readjustment Benefits Act of 1966 (PL 89-38).

Benefits. Monthly payments of $100 to veterans with no dependents for full-time institutional training; $125 with one dependent; $150 with more than one dependent. (Increased Oct. 1, 1967, to $130, $155 and $175—plus $10 additional for each dependent beyond two). (Lesser amounts for part-time training.) Beginning Oct. 1, 1967, allowances for on-job and farm training were authorized. On-job monthly payments were $80, $90 and $100 during the first six months, reduced proportionally for succeeding six-month periods, with payments of $20, $30 and $40 for fourth and any succeeding six-month periods. Farm training payments were $105, $125 and $145, plus $7 for each dependent over two.

Eligibility. More than 180 days of service, any part of which was after Jan. 31, 1955, with other than dishonorable discharge. Men still in service, after two years of active duty, eligible for lesser benefits while serving.

Entitlement. One month of education for each month of service, with a maximum of 36 months' entitlement. (Changed Dec. 1, 1968, to one and one-half months' entitlement for each month in service; 18 months or more of service after Jan. 21, 1955, qualifies a veteran to full 36-month entitlement.) Veterans must complete education and training by May 31, 1974, or within eight years after separation from service, whichever is later.

Participants. Some 1.2 million of 6 million post-Korea veterans (figures as of March 31, 1969) had participated, as follows: college 701,-200; below-college education 434,300; on-job training 53,100; on-farm training, less than 300.

Cost. $1.14 billion (as of March 31, 1969)

nursing-care beds authorized (by Congress in 1964) for veterans were not to be counted as hospital beds. A ceiling on the number of beds in all veterans' hospitals was set at 125,000 by President Eisenhower in 1959 by administrative action. The Johnson Administration had counted the 4,000 beds as part of the 125,000 limit.

Servicemen's Insurance

New insurance. Administration-backed legislation (S 2127) enacted by Congress (PL 89-214) provided, for the first time since 1956, low-cost group life insurance for all military personnel who wished to purchase it. The insurance paid $10,000 upon death in service, whether from combat or other causes, or $5,000 if the serviceman preferred. Premiums were about $1 a month for $5,000 or $2 a month for $10,000.

Upon leaving service, the policy-holder could convert to a permanent plan of insurance written by one of the companies participating in the group insurance arrangement (administered by the Veterans Administration).

Death gratuity. The legislation also authorized $5,000 death gratuity payments to survivors of servicemen who had died from specified conditions, including action of a hostile force or the "extra hazard of military or naval service," between Jan. 1, 1957, and the effective date of PL 214, Sept. 29, 1965, a period during which no servicemen's insurance was available.

Background. As enacted, the insurance available under S 2127 was basically similar to that available from 1940-51 under the old National Service Life Insurance program. The insurance authorized by the original Senate version of S 2127—before House amendments were added—would have been similar to the insurance issued by the government without charge from 1951 through 1956. (*Congress and the Nation,* Vol. I, p. 1372.)

Substantial monthly benefits already were available to survivors of military personnel who died from service-connected causes after Jan. 1, 1957, under the Dependency and Indemnity Compensation (DIC) system (PL 84-881). For example, under the 1956 law establishing DIC, as amended in 1963, payments for a surviving widow were $112 a month plus 12 per cent of current basic pay for the decreased serviceman's last rank. A separate system of monthly benefits also existed for survivors of those who died from service-connected causes before Jan. 1, 1957 (*Congress and the Nation,* Vol. I, p. 1352.)

Although DIC benefits were generally considered adequate, the following four factors led to enactment of S 2127 in light of the existing world situation: (1) The desire to provide survivors of servicemen killed in action (many of whom were uninsured or uninsurable) with large lump-sum insurance payments in addition to monthly DIC benefits. (2) The unwillingness of most private insurance companies to write life insurance covering servicemen when they were assigned to hostile areas such as Vietnam. (3) The desire to permit servicemen to provide for persons—such as brothers, sisters, grown children, non-dependent parents or friends—other than those eligible for DIC or death compensation. (4) The desire to provide an added inducement for men to seek a service career.

Post-Korea GI Bill

Senate passage. The Senate in 1965, for the second time in six years, passed a Post-Korea GI Bill opposed by the incumbent Administration. The House Veterans' Affairs Committee held hearings on the measure (S 9) and, when the session adjourned, enactment of the bill seemed likely in 1966 in view of the growing U.S. involvement in the war in Vietnam.

S 9 authorized educational and vocational training, and housing assistance to veterans who served in the armed forces between Jan. 31, 1955, when the Korean War GI Bill benefits expired, and July 1, 1967, the date of expiration of the current draft law. Because officially the United States was not at war during this period, those serving were "Cold War GIs." An estimated 5.5

Compensation or Pensions?

Compensation and pensions are frequently confused. Both provide monthly support payments to veterans, but the basis of entitlement is different.

Compensation is paid to a veteran who has a service-connected disability. He is being compensated for losses resulting from injury or disease which he suffered during his military service, whether in time of war or peace.

The amount of compensation is related to the extent of his disability. Highest payments go to those rated 100 per cent disabled for further work. Compensation rates are higher for disabilities suffered during wartime.

Pensions, on the other hand, are not based on service-connected disabilities. They are essentially a welfare payment made available to veterans as a reward for wartime military service in which, at least theoretically, the veteran risked extraordinary danger. Pensions are not and never were payable to veterans whose only service was in peacetime.

The pension system in existence since World War I requires the veteran to be incapacitated for work and in need before he could receive a pension. At least 90 days of military service is another requirement.

Different pension systems applied to veterans of American wars prior to World War I. In some cases, remaining veterans of those wars opted to come under provisions of a new pension law in 1959. That law established a sliding scale of pension payments, depending on the recipient's other income.

PERSONS RECEIVING VETERANS PENSIONS AND COMPENSATIONS

(as of Dec. 31, 1968)

Received by	
Parents	244,376
Widows	997,211
Children	909,379
Veterans	3,170,534

million such veterans were to be covered by S 9 at a cost of between $325 and $400 million annually. The bill, sponsored by Sen. Ralph W. Yarborough (D Texas), was supported by most veterans' lobbies. It was similar to a measure passed by the Senate in 1959 but opposed by the Eisenhower Administration and never enacted into law.

The Johnson Administration, opposed the bill in 1965, citing as reasons for its opposition the cost of the program and the fact that readjustment benefits were traditionally reserved for those who were subject to combat situations. The Administration also said S 9 benefits would overlap those made available to veterans, as well as to others, under such programs as the 1965 Housing Act (HR 7984 — PL 89-117) and the 1965 Higher Education Act (HR 9567 — PL 89-329). The Defense Department opposed the education sections of S 9 on the grounds that they would discourage servicemen from re-enlisting.

1966

Enactment of GI Bill

PRESIDENTIAL ACTION

Johnson change. In response to increased American fighting in Vietnam, and perhaps in an effort to forestall enactment of more costly legislation, President Johnson in 1966 abandoned his opposition to a post-Korea GI Bill. In his State of the Union Message, Johnson declared: "Let us fulfill and improve the great health and education programs of last year, extending special opportunities to those who risk their lives in our armed forces."

Administration proposal. The Administration devised a bill (HR 11985) to provide educational benefits only, for veterans who served after Oct. 1, 1963. It would pay higher benefits to those who had served in such "hot spots" as Vietnam and the Dominican Republic than to those who saw only peacetime garrison duty. The bill was assailed as inadequate and received scant consideration in Congress. The Administration's limited endorsement of new veterans' benefits helped open the door to Congressional enactment of S 9, the so-called Cold War GI Bill which the Senate but not the House had passed in 1965.

CONGRESSIONAL APPROVAL

Final passage. The House passed an amended version of S 9 on a voice vote Feb. 7 (after a prior roll-call vote of 381-0). The House amendments provided a permanent program of GI educational benefits, for those who served 180 days or more on active duty after Jan. 31, 1955, instead of a program expiring June 30, 1967. The House retained Senate provisions to guarantee housing and business loans to veterans, up to specified amounts.

During House debate there was no opposition, but numerous members, mostly Republicans, noted that the amended bill did not provide as much in payments as did the Korean War GI Bill (PL 82-550), which had provided $110 to $160.

Veterans' Benefits and Services			
(In millions of dollars)			
		Outlays	
Program or Agency	1968	1969	1970
	actual	estimate	estimate
Service-connected compensation	2,466	2,600	2,685
Non-service-connected pensions	2,048	2,127	2,183
Readjustment benefits:			
Education and training	447	614	721
Housing	210	252	—86
Other	15	16	18
Hospital and Medical care:			
Medical care and hospital services	1,361	1,458	1,525
Construction of hospital and nursing home facilities	50	59	88
Medical administration, research, and other	59	66	78
Other veteran benefits and services:			
Life insurance benefits	407	652	695
Veterans Administration administration expenses	188	207	223
Other	123	131	80
Deductions for offsetting receipts:			
Interfund and intragovernmental transactions	—5	—6	—6
Proprietary receipts from the public	—487	—484	—480
Total	6,882	7,692	7,724

SOURCE: 1970 Federal Budget

The Senate concurred in the House amendments Feb. 10 on a roll-call vote of 99-0. (Seventeen senators had voted against the original version of S 9 in 1965). President Johnson signed S 9, the Veterans Adjustment Act of 1966, into law (PL 89-358) March 3, and its provisions became effective June 1, 1966.

BACKGROUND

World War II. In a series of laws passed between 1940 and 1944, Congress extended to World War II veterans the traditional, basic veterans' benefits to which veterans of previous wars, and in some cases peacetime veterans, were already entitled. These were: monthly compensation for disabilities suffered in service or resulting from it and death compensation to survivors of persons who died in service or from service-connected causes; free hospital, medical and domiciliary care for veterans with service-connected disabilities; pension for war veterans who subsequently became needy and incapable of work, and for needy survivors of war veterans; and low-cost Government life insurance.

During the same period, Congress also enacted a new category of "readjustment" benefits which: protected the job-rights of drafted persons, provided free vocational rehabilitation with living allowances for veterans, gave veterans preferred status in civil service employment and provided mustering-out pay. Finally, in 1944 Congress passed the Servicemen's Readjustment Act, popularly known as the "GI Bill of Rights" (PL 78-346). This provided veterans with the right to special job-placement services from the United States Employment Service; assistance for up to four years of college (or similar) training, including a living allowance; the right to up to 52 weeks of unemployment insurance; and the right to obtain loans guaranteed by the Veterans Administration for the purpose of buying a home, farm or business. (See *Congress and the Nation,* Vol. 1, pp. 1337-38).

Korea and afterward. In 1950 Congress passed a law making Korean war veterans eligible for vocational rehabilitation, and in 1952 it enacted the Veterans Readjustment Assistance Act (PL 82-550)—the Korean GI Bill of Rights—providing job-placement, education, unemployment insurance, home-loan and mustering-out pay benefits similar to those voted in 1944. (See *Congress and the Nation,* Vol. I, p. 1348).

By 1962, the following readjustment benefits had been extended to certain peacetime veterans as well: reemployment rights for all persons who served in the armed forces in peace or war; unemployment benefits for the same group of veterans; civil service preference for peacetime veterans with service-connected disabilities; and vocational rehabilitation rights to peacetime veterans with service-connected disabilities.

Limited home loans and educational benefits for veterans were enacted by Congress in the 1965 Housing Act and the 1965 Higher Education Act.

1967

Veterans' Benefits

Increases. The Veterans' Pension and Adjustment Assistance Act of 1967 (S 16 — PL 90-77) provided increases in veterans pensions and GI Bill educational allowances. It authorized a cost-of-living increase averaging 5.4 per cent in the non-service-connected pensions of veterans, their wives and children. It specified increases in certain other pensions. (For increases in educational payments to veterans *see table below.*)

Vietnam Era. S 16 also defined the "Vietnam Era" as the period beginning Aug. 5, 1964, and ending on a date to be determined by the President or by concurrent resolution of Congress. Aug. 5, 1964, was the date President Johnson asked Congress to approve the Gulf of Tonkin Resolution, which it did two days later. (see Foreign Policy chapter)

Vocational training. S 16 authorized payments of monthly allowances to veterans enrolled in approved apprenticeship training programs for urban jobs and in agricultural training programs. These programs were in addition to vocational rehabilitation which had been authorized for disabled veterans only since 1943. They were similar in design to vocational training made available to ex-GI's generally in the World War II and Korean War GI Bills. Allowances paid under terms of S 16 are listed in "Highlights of GI Bills." (See p. 454.)

S 16 also authorized aid for veterans taking flight training to qualify for a commercial pilot's license, up to 90 per cent of the tuition costs.

"Educationally Disadvantaged Veterans." Veterans who had never finished high school were authorized to do so by S 16 without their losing any eligibility for subsequent college benefits. About one-fifth of the 2.7 million Vietnam veterans (as of Dec. 31, 1968) had not finished high school.

Post-Korea GI Bill Educational Benefits

Year and public law	Eligibility	Length of benefits	Monthly payments		
			Single	One dependent	More than one
1966 (PL 89-358)	Veterans[1] of more than 180 days service after Jan. 31, 1955.	One month of benefits per month in service; 36-month total benefits.	$100[2]	$125	$150
1967 (PL 90-77)	Same	Same	$130[3]	$155	$175
1968 (PL 90-631)	Extended to include widows of veterans and to wives of totally disabled veterans.	One and one-half month of benefits per month in service; or 36 months of benefits for 18 months or more in service.	Same	Same	Same

[1] Also includes certain servicemen attending classes in off-duty hours, who were eligible to receive up to $100 (later $130) a month.

[2] Rates for three-fourths time attendance were $75, $95 and $115; half-time, $50, $65 and $75.

[3] Three-fourths time, $95, $115 and $135; half-time, $60, $75 and $85. In addition, $10 monthly for every dependent beyond two for full-time attendance; $7 for three-fourths time and $5 for half-time.

1968

Disability Compensation

Increase. Carrying out recommendations of the U.S. Veterans Advisory Commission, Congress passed a bill (HR 16027 — PL 90-493) providing a $100 monthly increase (to $400 monthly) in benefits for totally disabled veterans and an 8 percent increase for partially disabled veterans. All increases became payable Jan. 1, 1969. Two million veterans were eligible for the new increases.

Incentive proposal. President Johnson tried unsuccessfully to attach a provision to the bill to authorize incentive payments to Vietnam veterans who would volunteer to become teachers, firemen or policemen in deprived areas. The proposal was rejected in the House Veterans Affairs Committee. Chairman Olin E. Teague (D Texas) called the Johnson proposal "a radical departure in the veterans program," and one which needed further study.

Other Legislation

Part-time training. Legislation (H 14954 — PL 90-431) enacted in 1968 allowed disabled veterans to receive federal payments for part-time vocational training. It removed a restriction that limited such training to full-time.

Widows and Wives. HR 16025 (PL 90-631) extended educational benefits to widows of veterans and wives of totally disabled veterans for full-time or part-time study. Previously only the minor children of deceased or disabled veterans were eligible for such educational assistance, and then only upon graduation from high school.

Liberalized benefits. GI educational benefits were liberalized in HR 16025 for eligible veterans, to provide one and one-half month of benefits for each month of service, and to provide 36 months of benefits for service of 18 months or more. The effect of the change was to provide four years of college for draftees who were required to serve two years in uniform. A draftee previously could have earned only 24 months of benefits—one for each month he was in service.

Pension safeguards. HR 12555 (PL 90-275) provided that higher Social Security benefits would not affect veterans' pensions until 1970, when pensions would start being adjusted gradually to take into account an increase in Social Security benefits which took effect Feb. 1, 1968. Under previous law it was possible for a small increase in non-pension income to result in a substantial cut in the pension of a veteran or his dependents or survivors.

Housing. HR 10477 (PL 90-301) attempted to make it easier, in time of inflation, for veterans and other eligible persons to obtain housing through existing VA and FHA housing programs. The bill raised to $12,500, from $7,500, the maximum amount of guarantee for a home loan under the VA program. The ceiling on interest rates could be set by the VA administrator acting in conjunction with the FHA administrator.

Since the VA loan-guarantee program had been authorized by the Servicemen's Readjustment Act of 1944 (PL 78-346), ceilings had been fixed by law. However, they had been raised over the years until they stood at 6 per cent in 1968. President Johnson requested that the statutory ceilings on both FHA and VA home loans be lifted "to allow them to compete" for building funds. (See housing policy in Economic Policy chapter.)

Re-employment rights. The Selective Service Act of 1940 guaranteed that men inducted under the Act would get their old jobs back after release from military service. Re-employment privileges already had been extended to reservists called to active duty by the Army Reserve and retired Personnel Act of 1940. Enlistees were brought under the re-employment provisions by the Service Extension Act of 1941. The net effect of these laws, together with certain amendments before World War II ended, was to grant re-employment rights to anyone entering the armed services for active duty after 1940.

The Selective Service Act of 1948, however, limited re-employment rights to those whose absence from their jobs because of military service was no more than three years. The 1951 Universal Military Training and Service Act increased this limit to four years.

President Johnson Aug. 17, 1968, signed into law a bill (HR 1093—PL 90-491) to extend up to two additional years the amount of time a reservist or guardsman could be called back to active duty without losing his right to get his old job back. The extension period for other members of the armed services was set at one year.

The bill also contained a provision protecting reservists and guardsmen against dismissal or denial of promotion because they had to attend weekly drills or summer training camp.

Veterans Administration

The Veterans Administration was created by President Hoover in Executive Order 5398, issued July 21, 1930. It consolidated the functions of three existing agencies—the Interior Department's Pensions Bureau, the National Home for Volunteer Soldiers, and the Veterans Bureau (an independent agency which administered most benefits for World War I veterans). The first VA Administrator was Brig. Gen. Frank T. Hines, who had previously headed the Veterans Bureau. The names and tenure of VA Administrators are as follows:

Administrators of the Veterans Administration

Brig. Gen. Frank T. Hines	7/21/30 to 8/14/45
Gen. Omar N. Bradley	8/15/45 to 11/30/47
Carl R. Gray Jr.	1/1/48 to 6/30/53
Harvey V. Higley	7/22/53 to 12/9/57
Sumner G. Whittier	1/23/58 to 1/20/61
John S. Gleason Jr.	1/30/61 to 12/31/64
William J. Driver	1/2/65 to 5/31/69
Donald E. Johnson	6/5/69 to ——

Chapter 9—Natural Resources and Power

Natural Resources and Power

MANAGEMENT of the nation's resources and power supplies proved a complex task from 1965 through 1968. A growing population and increasing affluence created demands for additional park and recreation land and for more water to meet personal, industrial, agricultural and recreational needs. The trouble was that the supply of both land and water remained constant; thus Congress undertook to establish, to the greatest extent possible, multi-purpose land and water projects.

Congress was particularly active in the field of water management. Legislation enacted in a single year—1965—laid down national standards of purity for all interstate waters; encouraged federal-state cooperation in water resource development of river basins lying within the jurisdiction of two or more states; and provided federal grants for development of water supply and waste-disposal systems in rural areas, where such facilities often were lacking. Capping these measures was a 1968 bill establishing a National Water Commission to develop federal-state plans on water resource development.

Conservation of national land resources also received attention, as shown by the addition of three new national parks to the 32 already in existence. Of more significance, however, was the creation of seven National Recreation Areas to supplement the existing four. A National Recreation Area usually depends for water resources on dams and reclamation projects administered by the Interior Department's Bureau of Reclamation. Such areas, in other words, provide for multi-purpose use of water—for drinking, electric power, and recreation.

Humans are only visitors to National Parks and recreation areas; wild creatures native to the area must live there. Recognizing this, Congress in the 1965 Federal Water Project Recreation Act established a federal-state cost-sharing formula for fish and wildlife improvement features, as well as for recreation facilities, at federal water projects. A 1966 bill, moreover, directed the Secretary of the Interior to take special action to protect species of birds and mammals believed by conservationists to be in danger of extinction.

A new concept—protection of natural beauty—was introduced into federal programs of natural resource development in 1965. In a special message to Congress, President Johnson called for a "new conservation" that would be concerned "not with nature alone, but with the total relation between man and the world around him." This meant, Mr. Johnson said, that "beauty must not be just a holiday treat, but a part of our daily life" available alike to "rich and poor, Negro and white, city dweller and farmer."

This new approach to conservation found expression in the Highway Beautification Act of 1965, which aroused considerable controversy not only prior to passage but also in succeeding years. Many Members of Congress balked at the idea of beautification even though the goals of the Highway Beautification Act were comparatively modest: removal of junkyards and outdoor advertising billboards, and landscaping of areas adjacent to highways. Although no money for highway beautification was appropriated in the three years beginning with 1966, the possibility remained that beautification would become a viable concept when conclusion of the Vietnam war made more federal funds available for domestic programs.

The potentialities of the sea as a source of both food and fresh water was reflected in various bills enacted during the Johnson years. The federal program to develop low-cost methods of desalting sea water, dating from 1952, was extended in 1965 for five years. Legislation approved in 1966 was designed to update and accelerate the nation's oceanography program and at the same time improve the coordination of existing federal oceanography activities.

Two other 1966 bills likewise had to do with exploitation of the oceans. The National Sea Grant College and Program Act was intended to promote the development of "aquaculture" in the same way that the land grant college program had encouraged the development of agriculture. Congress also enacted a bill authorizing federal research and experimentation on the production of fish protein concentrate (a form of flour made from ground-up fish), which held promise of becoming a needed source of protein in overpopulated, underdeveloped countries.

As in past years, most 1965-68 legislation in the field of natural resources and power concerned individual projects benefiting a particular region of the country. Numerous such projects were contained in the annual public works bills and in rivers and harbors legislation. Congress also authorized construction of the huge central Arizona water diversion project and various related water development projects in the Colorado River Basin. The whole represented the largest reclamation program ever authorized in a single piece of legislation. Approval came only after decades of controversy between California and Arizona, the major beneficiaries of the project, and between the states of the Southwest and of the Pacific Northwest. The latter were apprehensive lest water from rivers in their region be diverted to the more arid and more rapidly growing Southwest.

Controversy engulfed the projected Dickey-Lincoln School power project in northern Maine. Authorized in 1965, the Dickey-Lincoln project was designed to provide federal power to the New England region for the first time. Proponents cited New England's electric power rates, which in 1967 were 25 percent higher than the national average. Opponents included the 19 largest private power companies in the six-state region. The project was stalled, at least temporarily, when Congress in 1967 denied all funds for it in the fiscal 1968 public works bill.

Private industry—lumber companies in this case—also fought establishment of Redwood National Park in northern California. Congress nevertheless approved legislation in 1968 creating a 58,000-acre park containing redwood trees up to 2,200 years old, including the two tallest trees in the world.

The stage was set in 1968 for a probable future controversy over the nation's vast oil shale resources. Bills to provide for "the orderly leasing of publicly owned oil shale and associated minerals" were introduced, but Congress took no action. It is estimated that the Green River Formation—which stretches over Colorado, Utah and Wyoming—contains as many as two trillion barrels of oil. Pressure from private industry to develop these resources seemed certain to mount in years ahead.

Parks and Recreation

The 89th and 90th Congresses continued the tradition begun in 1961 of setting aside numerous areas for parks and recreation. Spurred on by President Johnson's warnings that failure to act might condemn the remaining good potential parklands to commercial development, the 89th and 90th were among the most productive Congresses in the field of conservation. President Johnson on Oct. 2, 1968, described the 1960s as "truly an era of conservation in this country." He noted that 2.4 million acres had been added to the National Park System since 1961, compared with 30,000 acres in the previous decade.

MAJOR UNITS AUTHORIZED. Among the park units authorized between 1965 and 1968 were three new National Parks—Guadalupe Mountains, Texas; Redwood, Calif.; and North Cascades, Wash. The Redwood Park, which contained the two tallest trees in the world, was created only after major controversy involving timber interests in the area. The immense North Cascades Park was largely noncontroversial as most of the land was already federally held, but its authorization in 1968 marked the end of a long history; its inclusion in the National Park System had first been proposed in 1906.

A National Park, administered by the Interior Department's National Park Service, is generally an area embodying scenic, historical or scientific features of national significance. The prime purpose in establishing these parks is to preserve such features, and the parks' potentialities for planned recreation activities are usually limited. Hunting, grazing, timber cutting, mineral and mining operations are generally prohibited.

Beginning in 1965, Congress began to put more emphasis on setting aside land which would not be so stringently administered as the National Parks and would permit more recreation possibilities for a growing population with expanding leisure time and financial resources. These areas were called National Recreation Areas. Before 1965 there were only four of them; seven more were added to the system in the next four years. These included the first recreation area in the East, 72,000-acre Delaware Water Gap (Tocks Island), located within driving distance of 30 million people. The National Recreation Areas usually depended for water resources on dams and reclamation projects administered by the Interior Department's Bureau of Reclamation, but the recreation facilities were administered by the National Park Service. Under various conditions hunting, fishing, timber cutting, grazing, mineral and mining operations were allowed in the Recreation Areas.

Among other park units established in the 1965-68 period were two National Seashores and two National Lakeshores. These were generally subject to stricter rules than the Recreation Areas but, unlike the National Parks, permitted such activities as hunting and fishing. One of the National Lakeshores was the Indiana Dunes, a project which had been bitterly opposed for eight years by steel companies located in the area.

In addition to authorizing a large number and variety of parks, recreation areas and seashores (*see table*) the 90th Congress also agreed to President Johnson's requests to establish a National Wild and Scenic Rivers System and a Nationwide System of Trails. Both systems were designed in part to preserve remote primitive areas in their natural state, but many other trails and rivers were near urban areas. Their location reflected a new Congressional interest in providing recreation possibilities near the cities, particularly in the East, where there were few federal parklands. Establishment of the Delaware Water Gap Recreation Area, Indiana Dunes National Lakeshore and several other parks in the East were also a part of the attempt to put more recreation facilities where more of the nation's population lives. This consideration persuaded Congressmen to authorize the areas despite the fact that they involved heavy expenditures because much of the land was privately owned.

Not only was the record of the Johnson Congresses in park legislation substantial; at the end of 1968 only two of the President's requests remained outstanding—Apostle Islands National Lakeshore, Wis., and Potomac Valley Park, Md. (However, three park requests made in 1965-66, which were not agreed on by the Congressional delegations of the states involved, had not been repeated in 1967-68.) The almost clean docket gave rise to speculation that much of the appropriate remaining land had now been set aside in the park system. President Johnson in 1966 talked of completing the National Park System by 1972.

Financing Problems. Many of the park bills of 1965-68 continued the precedent, set in 1961, of creating parks from privately owned lands which had to be acquired through sale or condemnation. During the '60s

---

Reference

For review of origins and development of the National Park System and action by Congress on park legislation in the 1945-64 period, see *Congress and the Nation*, Vol. I, pp. 1074-1093.

Units Added to Park System, 1965-1968

Name and Location	Acres	Date Authorized	Name and Location	Acres	Date Authorized
National Parks			**National Lakeshores**		
Guadalupe Mountains, Texas	77,582	10/15/66	Indiana Dunes, Ind.	8,721	11/5/66
North Cascades, Wash.	505,000	10/2/68	Pictured Rocks, Mich.	67,000	10/15/66
Redwood, Calif.	58,000	10/2/68	**National Monuments**		
			Agate Fossil Beds, Neb.	3,150	6/5/65
National Seashores			Pecos, N.M.	342	6/28/65
			Alibates Flint Quarries, Texas	230	8/31/65
Assateague Island	39,630	9/21/65	Biscayne, Fla.	...	10/18/68
Cape Lookout, N.C.	30,000	3/10/66	**National Historic Sites**		
			Golden Spike, Utah	...	7/30/65
National Recreation Areas			Herbert Hoover Birthplace, Iowa	200	8/12/65
			Hubbell Trading Post, Ariz.	160	8/28/65
Delaware Water Gap, Pa.-N.J.	72,000	9/1/65	Roger Williams National Memorial, R.I.	5	10/22/65
Spruce Knob, W. Va.	100,000	9/28/65	John F. Kennedy Birthplace, Mass.	1/15	5/26/67
Whiskeytown-Shasta-Trinity Calif.	255,000	11/ 8/65	Carl Sandburg Home, N.C.	242	10/17/68
Bighorn Canyon, Mont.-Wyo.	63,300	10/15/66	**National Historical Park**		
Wolf Trap Farm, Va.	96	10/15/66	Nez Perce, Idaho	1,500	5/15/65
Flaming Gorge, Utah-Wyo.	201,253	10/1/68			
Ross Lake, Wash.	107,000	10/2/68			
Lake Chelan, Wash.	62,000	10/2/68			

a serious problem developed concerning price speculation on land authorized to be acquired by the Government. Moreover, the Land Conservation Fund, set up in 1964 to enable the Government to acquire the newly authorized parks, did not function as well as had been expected. In 1968 Congress took steps both to control the land speculation and to provide new financing for the Fund.

Prior to 1961, most park units were created from federally owned lands, donated lands or small areas purchased by the Government. With establishment of the Cape Cod Seashore in 1961, a new precedent was set under which lands for parks were to be acquired mainly by purchase or condemnation of private property. Until 1968 Congress, to acquire an area, first had to pass a bill authorizing establishment of the park within certain boundaries. Congress then appropriated money, usually from the Land and Water Conservation Fund, to purchase the authorized lands.

Often there was a time lag between the authorization and appropriation of funds, and during that time speculators bought up land. The Interior Department, as a result, had to negotiate for purchase of the land. If it failed to work out an agreement with the owner, it could initiate condemnation proceedings in the courts. Condemnation, however, often cost more than outright purchase, even at speculation prices, since courts tended to be generous to the owner and administrative costs were high.

By 1968 the land speculation problem had become so serious that Congress passed two bills aimed to curb it. A bill (S 1401) revising the Land Conservation Fund contain-

ed a provision authorizing Government agencies to enter into financial contracts for the purchase of park land as soon as a park had been authorized and before funds were actually appropriated. The annual amount of such contracts was limited to $30 million. S 1401 was also designed to reduce outlays for park land by permitting the Interior Secretary to acquire non-federal land in a proposed park by exchanging it for federal land.

The bill establishing the Redwood National Park in California (S 2515) likewise contained provisions to hold down costs and speculation; while the provisions were limited to that park, many Congressmen thought they might become precedents. One of these vested ownership of all the large segments of privately owned land authorized for the park in the Federal Government upon enactment of the bill. Owners were to obtain money for the land through negotiation or through litigation in the Court of Claims.

Another provision was highly controversial. It authorized exchange of National Forest Service timber lands for privately owned lands in the park area. The land exchange provision of the land conservation bill (S 1401) caused no controversy; the bill affected the Interior Department, not the Forest Service in the Agriculture Department. The Agriculture Department was "unalterably opposed" to the exchange provision of S 2515.

Coupled with the land speculation problem was the fact that the Land Conservation Fund was not getting the income estimated when the Fund was established in 1964. The Fund was supposed to receive some $140 million annually from three sources: (1) federal surplus property sales; (2) federal motorboat tax receipts; and (3) a new uniform system of fees at federal recreation areas. The fee system brought in only a fraction of the revenue expected and Congress abolished it in 1968. The Administration proposed that new revenues for the Fund be found through receipts from federal gas and oil leases on the outer continental shelf, a suggestion that was highly unpopular in the Senate. Congress finally worked out a compromise authorizing appropriation from general revenues of amounts which would bring the Fund up to $200 million; if Congress did not appropriate enough to bring the Fund to that sum, then receipts from the federal gas and oil leases on the outer continental shelf could be used. It was thought that property sales and motorboat receipts would bring in $100 million, so $100 million more would come from appropriations or continental shelf receipts.

The new Conservation Fund financing provisions and attempts to hold down land costs and speculation appeared to strengthen greatly the position of federal park financing as the Johnson Administration came to an end.

Chronology of

Legislation on

Parks and Recreation

1965

DELAWARE WATER GAP RECREATION AREA. With little debate, Congress in 1965 passed a bill requested by the President establishing the Delaware Water Gap (Tocks Island) National Recreation Area. The authorizing bill (HR 89—PL 89-158) was passed by voice vote in both chambers and was signed by the President Sept. 1.

The new national recreation area, located in Pennsylvania and New Jersey, was the first authorized east of the Mississippi. It was to consist of 72,000 acres of land and water, including several dozen small natural lakes and the 12,000-acre reservoir being formed by construction of the Tocks Island Dam by the Army Engineers.

Delaware Water Gap was to be the first national recreation area created primarily through purchase of privately owned land rather than on land already held by the Government. The bill authorized $37,412,000 for land acquisition plus $18,200,000 for construction of recreational facilities. It was estimated that 30 million people lived within easy driving distance of the park and that it would have 10 million visitors a year.

SPRUCE KNOB RECREATION AREA. Another large national recreation area authorized in 1965 was the Spruce Knob-Seneca Rocks National Recreation Area in West Virginia, in the drainage area of the south branch of the Potomac River. The Administration-requested authorization bill (S 7) was passed by voice vote in Senate and House and was approved by the President on Sept. 28 (PL 89-207).

The new recreation area was to be administered by the Agriculture Department. It was to consist of 100,000 acres, about 82 percent of which were forested. Of the total, 40,000 were federal lands which lay within the existing Monongahela National Forest. An additional 56,000 acres lay within the National Forest but were privately owned. The remaining 4,000 acres were private lands outside of the forest. All of the private lands would be acquired by the Agriculture Department. The bill did not authorize any specific amounts of money, but the estimated cost of the land was $3.5 million and of development of facilities, $16,280,000.

WHISKEYTOWN-SHASTA-TRINITY. A third major national recreation area authorized by Congress was the Whiskeytown-Shasta-Trinity National Recreation Area in northern California. The Administration bill (HR 797) was signed into law by President Johnson Nov. 8 (PL 89-336).

The new recreation area, designed chiefly for water-based outdoor recreation, was to consist of three noncontiguous units—Whiskeytown, Shasta and Trinity—surrounding reclamation reservoirs at the northern end of California's Central Valley, 200 miles north of San Francisco. The Whiskeytown unit would total about 42,000 acres of land and water; the Shasta unit about 129,000 acres and the Trinity unit about 83,500 acres—a grand total of 255,000 acres of land and water. The shorelines of four major reservoirs in the areas totaled 560 miles.

Of the 255,000 acres, about 184,600 were already owned by the Federal Government and 1,250 acres by the State of California. The remaining 70,000 acres, chiefly privately owned, would be acquired by purchase and condemnation. The bill authorized $21.6 million for land acquisition and reserved for the current owners of private lands any interests or right of use deemed appropriate. The bill also authorized $22.7 million for development of recreational facilities. The Interior Department was to administer the Whiskeytown unit; Shasta and Trinity would be administered by the Agriculture Department.

ASSATEAGUE NATIONAL SEASHORE. Another Administration-requested addition to the National Park System was Assateague Island National Seashore, consisting of the 35-mile-long Assateague Island and surrounding waters off the coasts of Maryland and Virginia. The authorizing legislation (S 20) was signed into law (PL 89-195) by the President on Sept. 21.

The new national seashore was to include 39,630 acres of land and water. Of the 19,096 land acres, 9,453 were already owned by the Federal Government, 922 were owned by the states of Maryland and Virginia, and 8,721 were in private ownership. The final bill authorized the Interior Department to acquire the privately owned land, but allowed home owners to retain residence rights for 25 years. The bill authorized $16,250,000 for land acquisition and whatever amounts might prove necessary for development of recreational facilities. Three million visitors a year were expected at Assateague by 1975.

ELLIS ISLAND. President Johnson in May 1965 ended 12 years of uncertainty over the fate of Ellis Island, the former immigration center in New York harbor, by making the 27.5-acre island a part of the Statue of Liberty National Monument. The President's action was taken under the Antiquities Act of 1906, which authorized the

1966

President to set aside federal lands of national monuments by proclamation. In his proclamation, the President asked Congress to authorize funds for development of the island. Mr. Johnson Aug. 17 signed (H J Res 454 (PL 89-129) authorizing $6 million for development of facilities on the island.

NATIONAL PARK CONCESSIONS.

Congress enacted legislation (HR 2091—PL 89-249) putting into statutory form the policies governing concessionaires in areas administered by the Interior Department's National Park Service. Most of the policies outlined in the bill had been followed in practice since Oct. 13, 1950, when the Interior Department issued a formal statement of policy on National Park System concessions.

The key provisions of HR 2091 gave concessionaires a "possessory interest" in buildings and other improvements they constructed with the Interior Department's approval in park areas, and guaranteed them compensation if the property were taken over by the Department or transferred to another concessionaire. The bill also granted various types of preferences to established concessionaires.

MINOR UNITS.

In addition to authorizing four major park units in 1965, Congress added a number of minor units to the park system. Among them were the following:

Hoover Birthplace. A bill signed Aug 12 (HR 8111—PL 89-119) authorized establishment of the Herbert Hoover National Historic Site—a 200-acre area in West Branch, Iowa, containing the cottage in which the former President was born, his grave and the Herbert Hoover Library. The bill authorized $1,650,000 for all basic costs.

Agate Beds Monument. Signed June 5 was a bill (S 339—PL 89-33) authorizing the establishment of a 3,150-acre Agate Fossil Beds National Monument in Sioux County, Neb., to preserve the fossils of animals that lived 15 million years ago. The bill authorized $301,150 for land acquisition and $1,842,000 for development.

Nez Perce Historical Park. A bill signed May 15 (S 60—PL 89-19) authorized the Nez Perce National Historical Park, in the Idaho panhandle, to commemorate historical events connected with the Nez Perce Indians. The bill authorized $630,000 for the purchase of 1,500 acres outright and scenic easements on another 1,500 acres, plus $1,337,000 for development costs.

Other. Also enacted were bills establishing two new national monuments: the 342-acre Pecos National Monument in New Mexico (HR 3165—PL 89-54) and the 230-acre Alibates Flint Quarries and Texas Panhandle Pueblo Culture National Monument (HR 881—PL 89-154); and bills establishing two additional national historic sites and a national memorial: the Golden Spike National Historic Site, commemorating completion of the first transcontinental railroad, in Utah (S 26—PL 89-102), the Hubbell Trading Post National Historic Site in Arizona (HR 3320—PL 89-148), and the Roger Williams National Memorial in Rhode Island (HR 7919—PL 89-293).

INDIANA DUNES.

Congress in 1966 ended one of the most emotional battles in the 50-year history of the National Park Service by passing a bill (S 360) creating the Indiana Dunes National Lakeshore along 13 miles of Lake Michigan shorefront. The bill had been passed by the Senate by voice vote June 21, 1965. The House passed an amended compromise version by a 204-141 roll-call vote Oct. 14, 1966, and the Senate agreed to the amendments Oct. 18. President Johnson signed it into law (PL 89-761) Nov. 5.

Since 1958, Sen. Paul H. Douglas (D Ill.) had been working to get an Indiana Dunes bill passed. However, enactment had repeatedly been blocked by Indiana Members of Congress because the area to be set aside in the proposed lakeshore was desired by steel companies, notably Bethlehem, Inland and National, for expansion of their operations. Former House Minority Leader Charles A. Halleck (R Ind.) had been especially influential in keeping a dunes bill from reaching the House floor.

The way was cleared in 1965 for passage of a dunes bill when Congress in an omnibus rivers and harbors bill (S 2300—PL 89-298) authorized the Burns Waterway Harbor, a project on the Indiana shore of Lake Michigan long sought by the three major steel companies. To assure protection of the remainder of the region, the harbor money was not to be released until both chambers had voted on a dunes preservation bill.

As passed by the Senate in 1965, S 360 excluded from the proposed lakeshore much of the land, included in earlier proposals, sought by the steel companies for expansion. However, the Senate bill included a 750-acre parcel of undeveloped land owned by the Inland Steel Co. The bill as passed by the House reduced the tract to 478 acres, a move agreed to by the Senate.

In other provisions, S 360 as enacted authorized establishment of an 8,721-acre Lakeshore in Porter and La Porte Counties, Ind., 35 miles from Chicago. The Secretary of the Interior was authorized to acquire by sale or condemnation 6,539 acres of land, most of which was privately owned. Owners of residential property could retain right of use for 25 years. The bill authorized $27.9 million for land acquisition. It also authorized the Secretary to include the 2,182-acre Indiana Dunes State Park in the federal park area, but only if the State of Indiana agreed to donate the land.

GUADALUPE MOUNTAINS NATIONAL PARK.

Congress agreed to President Johnson's request to establish Guadalupe Mountains National Park in western Texas. The authorization bill (HR 698) was passed by voice votes in both chambers and was signed into law (PL 89-667) Oct. 15.

HR 698 provided for a 77,582-acre park in Hudspeth and Culbertson Counties, Texas, near 8,751-foot Guadalupe Peak. The area contained extensive and significant fossil reefs. The bill specified that the area was not to be established as a national park until all outstanding subsurface mineral rights, including state-owned rights, had been acquired by the Federal Government. It authorized $12,162,000 for land acquisition and development. Guadalupe Mountains was the second completely new national park authorized by Congress since 1956. The other was Canyonlands, in Utah, established in 1964. *(Congress and the Nation, Vol. I, p. 1089.)*

CAPE LOOKOUT NATIONAL SEASHORE. Another addition to the federal park system was the Cape Lookout National Seashore in North Carolina. The Seashore had been requested by President Johnson in 1965 and the Senate passed the authorization bill (S 251) that year. The House followed suit early in 1966, and the bill was signed into law (PL 89-366) March 10.

S 251 authorized the creation of a 30,000-acre national seashore (of which 10,000 acres would be water) along a 58-mile stretch of the North Carolina coast, beginning at Ocracoke Inlet (just south of the existing Cape Hatteras National Seashore) and running southward to Beaufort Inlet. Most of the North Carolina outer banks were included in the two seashores. Nearly all the land for the new seashore was to be donated by North Carolina. The bill authorized appropriations of $3.2 million to acquire between 1,700 and 2,400 privately owned acres and to defray development costs in the first years.

BIGHORN CANYON RECREATION AREA. Congress completed action on an Administration bill (S 491) establishing the Bighorn Canyon National Recreation Area in south central Montana and north central Wyoming. The bill was signed into law (PL 89-664) Oct. 15.

S 491 set aside 63,300 acres along the Bighorn River covering approximately one-third of the 195-mile shoreline to be created by the reservoir behind the federal Yellowtail Dam, near Hardin, Mont., scheduled for 1966 completion. The land was at the end of Bighorn Canyon, a 47-mile gorge with walls rising from 800 to 2,200 feet above the Bighorn River. More than 90 percent of the land to be included in the recreation area was already federally owned. S 491 authorized $355,000 for acquisition of the privately held land.

HISTORIC SITES. President Johnson Oct. 15 signed into law a bill (S 3035—PL 89-665) designed to encourage preservation of historic sites on the state and local levels and to augment the financing of the National Trust for Historic Preservation.

S 3035 authorized two sets of matching grants to the states on a 50-50 basis, first to help them conduct surveys of historic sites and develop statewide plans for preserving those sites, and then to assist them in financing the actual restoration.

The bill also authorized grants of up to 50 percent to the National Trust for Historic Preservation to increase its capacity to acquire and administer nationally significant properties. As established in 1949 to supplement Park Service work in preserving historic sites, the National Trust had operated entirely with funds donated from individuals and private groups. *(Congress and the Nation, Vol. I, p. 1082.)*

Other provisions of S 3035 required the Secretary of the Interior to maintain a national register of historic properties and established a 17-member National Advisory Council on Historic Preservation to advise on and coordinate restoration activities of federal, state and local agencies. The bill authorized appropriations of

---

Three Parks Not Authorized

The 89th Congress failed to complete action on three major Administration park proposals. In all three cases the Congressional delegations from the states concerned could not agree on a bill. None of the proposals was submitted to the 90th Congress.

Great Basin National Park. President Johnson in 1965 and 1966 asked Congress to authorize establishment of a Great Basin National Park in the Snake Range of eastern Nevada. However, no action was taken on bills (S 499, HR 6122) sponsored by Sen. Alan Bible (D Nev.) and Rep. Walter S. Baring (D Nev.) to create the park. The inaction resulted in part from controversy over differences between the two bills in the size of the proposed park. An additional roadblock was the desire of certain local interests to continue mining and mineral operations, which are almost universally prohibited in national parks.

Oregon Dunes. The House April 19, 1966, passed an Administration bill (HR 7524) authorizing a 30,570-acre Oregon Dunes National Seashore on the Pacific Coast near Coos Bay and Reedsport. The proposal was supported by Sen. Maurine B. Neuberger (D Ore.) and Rep. Robert B. Duncan (D Ore.), in whose district the Seashore would be located. However, Sen. Wayne Morse (D Ore.) opposed provisions permitting acquisition of private land by condemnation. Although the bill was reported to the Senate, it was never taken up and died at session's end.

Sleeping Bear Lakeshore. The Senate Aug. 26, 1965, passed a bill (S 936) authorizing a 46,100-acre Sleeping Bear Dunes National Lakeshore on the eastern shore of Lake Michigan. The bill, a scaled-down version of earlier proposals, was sponsored by Sen. Philip A. Hart (D Mich.) and opposed by Rep. Robert P. Griffin (R Mich.), in whose district the proposed lakeshore was located. Griffin favored a 37,000-acre lakeshore. Criticizing S 936, he said the outstanding bond issues of two school districts might be endangered if part of their taxable land were taken for a lakeshore, and therefore some form of payment in lieu of taxes was needed. He objected also to certain aspects of proposed condemnation proceedings. S 936 was reported to the House in August 1966 but was not called up on the floor.

$2 million in fiscal 1967 and $10 million in each of the three fiscal years 1968-1970.

OTHER PARK UNITS. In addition to agreeing to Administration requests for four major park areas, Congress established two other park units. Neither was requested specifically by the President, but they were endorsed by the Administration.

Pictured Rocks National Lakeshore. A bill (HR 8678—PL 89-668) approved by Mr. Johnson Oct. 15 authorized establishment of the Pictured Rocks National Lakeshore along 39 miles of the south shore of Lake Superior in the Upper Peninsula of Michigan. The park was to consist of two zones: a shoreline of 27,500 acres which would be devoted to recreation uses, and an inland buffer zone of 39,500 acres on which current activities such as timber harvesting would be permitted to continue. Appropriations of $13,223,000 were authorized for land acquisition and development.

Wolf Trap Farm Park. Another bill (S 3423—PL 89-671) established under the National Park Service a cultural center and recreation area of 96 acres at Wolf Trap Farm in Fairfax County, Va., 13 miles from Washington, D.C. It was the first federal park to be devoted primarily to the performing arts. Much of the land plus $1.75 million for an auditorium were donated by Mrs. Jouett Shouse and the American Symphony Orchestra League. The bill authorized $600,000 for additional land acquisition and development.

AUTHORIZATIONS INCREASED. Congress in 1966 had to increase appropriations for two previously established federal parks.

Point Reyes Seashore. Congress in S 1607 (PL 89-666) increased the authorization for the Point Reyes National Seashore, Calif., from $14 million authorized in 1962 to $19,135,000. The additional amount was necessary to cover payments to owners of some 2,100 acres of land to whom the Interior Department already had made commitments. Land values had risen rapidly since the Seashore was authorized in 1962. With the original authorization the Department had been able to acquire only about 16,000 of the 53,850 acres to be included in the Seashore. *(Congress and the Nation, Vol. I, p. 1086.)*

Piscataway Park. Congress increased to $4,132,000 the authorization for appropriations to complete the 1,114-acre Piscataway Park, Md. (HR 13417—PL 89-513). The park was designed to preserve the shoreline opposite Mount Vernon. The original 1961 authorization of $937,000 proved insufficient.

ADMINISTRATIVE ACTIONS. In addition to major bills passed by Congress, the year witnessed several important administrative actions in the field of parks and recreation.

Parkscape U.S.A. In 1966, its 50th anniversary year, the National Park Service initiated a new program, Parkscape, U.S.A. In part the program was designed to assume the responsibilities of Mission 66, an expiring 10-year program to improve park facilities. *(Congress and the Nation, Vol. I, p. 1085.)*

The National Park Service said the new program would consist of (1) identification of those remaining areas that could be brought into the park system; (2) new attempts to exchange park information and experience with states and foreign countries (3) improvement of parklands in urban areas, including a program for Washington, D.C.; (4) improvement of the explanatory programs available in national parks.

Natural Beauty Efforts. President Johnson in May created the President's Council on Recreation and Natural Beauty and the Citizens Advisory Committee on Recreation and Natural Beauty. The Council was charged with reviewing and making recommendations to the President on outdoor recreation and natural beauty programs of the Federal Government. The Citizens Committee was to advise the President and Council on the correlation of federal natural beauty and recreation programs and on local, state and private outdoor recreation and natural beauty activities.

1967

NATIONAL PARK FOUNDATION. Congress passed a bill (S 814—PL 90-209) establishing a National Park Foundation to accept donations of money, securities and real estate from the public to support the programs of the National Park Service. The Foundation was authorized to make its own decisions regarding investments and administration of donations. It was to be composed of the Interior Secretary, the NPS Director and at least six persons from private life. President Johnson approved the bill Dec. 18.

The new Foundation replaced the five-member National Park Trust Fund Board, which was abolished by S 814. The Board had been set up for the same purposes but was dominated by Government officials, had invested its funds mostly in Government securities, and had not managed to attract substantial donations.

Passage of S 814 came at a time when NPS land acquisition programs were threatened by severe shortages of money in the Land and Water Conservation Fund, the Fund created in 1964 to receive federal revenues to finance federal parkland acquisitions. None of the sources of income had come up to expectations, and the Fund was plagued at the same time by steadily rising land prices. *(See below.)*

KENNEDY BIRTHPLACE. A bill (S 1161—PL 90-20) establishing the birthplace of President Kennedy in Brookline, Mass., as a National Historic Site was signed into law May 26. The bill authorized the Secretary of the Interior to acquire the house by donation from the Kennedy family. The site would be maintained with funds from the Land and Water Conservation Fund. The Kennedy home was to be the sixth Presidential birthplace in the national park system. The others were those of George Washington, Abraham Lincoln, Theodore Roosevelt, Herbert Hoover and Franklin D. Roosevelt. The Brookline house and its one-fifteenth acre lot were the only acquisitions authorized for the national parks system in 1967.

1968

LAND CONSERVATION FUND. Congress passed a bill (S 1401) providing new sources of revenue for the Land and Water Conservation Fund. The bill also enabled the Federal Government to hasten acquisition of lands authorized for federal recreation areas, thus avoiding a period of price speculation before the Government took over the land.

Background—The Land and Water Conservation Fund had been established in 1964 to provide financing for accelerated acquisition of outdoor recreation areas. Its supporters said a speedup was urgently necessary because good potential sites were becoming increasingly scarce. The Fund received revenues from several sources: (1) the sale of certain federal surplus real property; (2) the proceeds from the existing federal motorboat tax; and (3) a new system of uniform admission and user fees at federal recreation areas. These three sources were expected to bring in between $140 million and $145 million a year. In addition, Congress was authorized to appropriate repayable funds up to $60 million a year until the Fund was built up.

By 1967 it was clear that the financing system was not generating the expected revenues. Actual receipts for fiscal 1967 were $94.8 million as opposed to the expected $140 million. The major cause of the shortfall was the failure of the new uniform fee system as a revenue producer; of the agencies affected, only the National Park Service had made a serious effort to collect fees, and a $7.00 "Golden Eagle" card admitting the holder to all federal parks had not been popular with tourists. The Interior Department said in 1968 that revenues from the system might not reach 18 percent of the amount estimated when the Fund was established.

Once established, moreover, the Fund had been plagued by soaring land prices. The cost of recreation land in general rose sharply between 1964 and 1968. In addition, there was often heavy price speculation on land which had been authorized for federal recreation but which the Government was not yet able to start acquiring because funds had not been appropriated. Price speculation was a particular problem with two newly authorized National Seashores—Padre Island, Texas, and Point Reyes, Calif.

1968 Legislation. President Johnson requested legislation to provide new revenues for the Fund. As enacted, S 1401 was a composite of Administration, Senate and House provisions.

The final bill increased the Fund's assets by (1) authorizing direct, non-repayable appropriations by Congress from general tax revenues; and (2) providing that if appropriations plus existing revenue sources (motorboat tax and surplus property sales) did not bring the Fund's income to $200 million, then receipts from federal gas and oil leases on the outer continental shelf could be used in an amount necessary to reach $200 million. The bill repealed the uniform admission system (in the future admission funds collected by an agency were to be set aside for its own use) and the 1964 provision authorizing up to $60 million annually in repayable appropriations for the Fund.

In provisions designed to hold down the cost of recreation land to the Government, S 1401 authorized agencies to enter into financial contracts for the purchase of park land as soon as land acquisition had been authorized by Congress and before funds had been appropriated. The annual amount of such contracts was limited to $30 million. The Interior Secretary was also authorized to acquire non-federally owned property within the boundaries of a national park system unit by exchanging federal property (excluding timberlands) under his jurisdiction in the same state.

S 1401 was passed by the Senate April 30. After seven days of debate, the Senate had voted 37-29 to drop the provision making extra revenues available for the Fund out of receipts from gas and oil leases on the outer continental shelf. As passed, the Senate bill provided that the Fund would be brought up to $200 million only through appropriations from general revenues. A companion bill passed by the House May 23 provided that the Fund would be brought up to $200 million through continental shelf oil and gas receipts and that no money would be appropriated from general revenues. Conferees settled on the final compromise permitting use of oil and gas receipts if Congress did not appropriate enough funds to bring

the Fund up to $200 million. President Johnson signed the bill into law (PL 90-401) July 15.

REDWOOD NATIONAL PARK. Congress in 1968 ended a four-year controversy by completing action on a major bill (S 2515) establishing a 58,000-acre Redwood National Park in northern California. The park was to include some 27,500 acres of three state parks and approximately 28,000 acres of privately owned land, much of which was held by lumber companies. The area contained redwood trees up to 2,200 years old, including the two tallest trees in the world.

The final bill included two highly controversial and unprecedented provisions involving the method the Federal Government would use to acquire the land authorized for the park. The first authorized exchange of federally owned Forest Service lands for privately owned land in the park area. The plan, which originated in Congress, was justified as reducing the over-all cost of the park and providing tax revenues to the state. The Interior Department said it "reluctantly would not object" to the provision, but the Agriculture Department was "unalterably opposed." It said the barter would imperil the integrity of the national forest system and "set a very dangerous precedent."

The other controversial provision, which originated in conference, vested ownership of all large segments of private land authorized for the park in the Federal Government upon enactment of the bill. Private owners of the land could recover money through negotiation with the Interior Department or through litigation in the Court of Claims with no provision for jury trial, which is normally provided in federal condemnation proceedings. The provision was designed to halt immediately the cutting of timber on those lands and to avoid the growing problem of land price escalation, which occurred when Congress followed the usual system of allowing a time lag between the time a park was authorized and the time appropriations were made available for land acquisition.

This "legislative-taking" provision did not apply to areas of less than 50 acres held primarily for residential or agricultural purposes. Those areas were to be acquired through negotiation or condemnation, and owners were permitted to retain use of residential property for up to 25 years.

S 2515 authorized appropriation of $92 million from the Land Conservation Fund for land acquisition. However, it was expected that a substantial part of that sum would not be needed because of the land-exchange authorization.

Legislative History—The final form of S 2515 represented a victory for conservationist interests. The bill provided a larger park than was proposed by either Administration or House-passed bills.

President Johnson began to press for establishment of such a park following a Park Service report that only 2.5 percent of the giant redwoods were protected and that they were in danger of extinction. The Administration bill in the 90th Congress, which proposed to establish a 42,000-acre park, mostly in Del Norte County, was attacked as seriously affecting a single lumber company. Moreover, conservationists said it was too small and located too far north.

A Senate bill (S 2515) was passed by a 77-6 roll-call vote Nov. 1, 1967. Designed to meet objections to the Administration bill, it provided for a 64,000-acre park;

shifted the bulk of land to be acquired south to Humboldt County; and spread the impact of the park's establishment over four major lumber companies instead of hitting one hard. The Senate bill also contained the controversial land-exchange provision.

The House July 15, 1968, by a 389-15 roll-call vote passed a severely modified version of S 2515. The House bill excluded most of the disputed private lands and provided for a park of only 28,500 acres.

The final version of S 2515, worked out in conference, was much closer to the Senate than to the House bill. Its 58,000 acres were in the same general areas as the 64,000 acres proposed by the Senate. It included for the first time the legislative-taking provision, which it said would prevent an increase in land values and expedite establishment of the park. The conference report said the provision was requested by one of the lumber companies involved, which wanted to know at once its status in regard to holdings and compensation. On the Senate floor, Sept. 17, Wayne Morse (D Ore.) said he had "great difficulty reconciling the conference report with the 5th Amendment when it comes to the taking of property." He considered the provision "unwise" in departing from the regular procedure by which federal district court juries decide the fair value which the Federal Government should pay for land.

President Johnson signed S 2515 into law (PL 90-545) Oct. 2.

NORTH CASCADES PARK. Congress completed action on a bill (S 1321) creating a 505,000-acre North Cascades National Park in northern Washington, along the Canadian border. The bill established in the same region the Ross Lake National Recreation Area (107,000 acres) and Lake Chelan National Recreation Area (62,000 acres), added to the National Wilderness System the Pasayten Wilderness Area (520,000 acres), and added 10,000 acres to the existing Glacier Peak Wilderness Area. The recreation areas were set up separately to permit continuation of hunting in those regions; no hunting is permitted in national parks.

Because over 99 percent of the 1,204,000-acre region was already owned by the Federal Government the cost of land acquisition was set at only $3.5 million; this sum was authorized in S 1321. Other sections of the bill provided that lands within the recreation areas were to be withdrawn from patent under U.S. mining laws, and authorized a study of public use developments in the region—particularly skiing. The region was to be jointly administered by the Agriculture and Interior Secretaries.

S 1321, passed by the Senate Nov. 2, 1967, and by the House Sept. 16, 1968, was signed into law (PL 90-544) Oct. 2. While S 1321 was the first Administration proposal for a North Cascades park, there had been discussion of establishing a park in that area since 1906. The region has more than 100 mountain peaks and more than 150 active glaciers and glacial lakes. The National Park Service surveyed the area in 1937 and said it "outranked in its scenic, recreational and wildlife values" any existing or prospective park in the country.

NATIONAL TRAILS SYSTEM. Congress completed action on an Administration proposal to establish a nationwide system of trails. The bill as finally enacted (S 827) created three categories of trails: National scenic trails, national recreation trails, and connecting or side trails. The scenic trails would be located in relatively remote areas and would be reserved primarily for hiking and camping. Recreation trails would be located near urban areas and would be developed for various uses, such as bicycling or jogging. Connecting or side trails would provide additional points of public access to the two other types of trails or would provide connections between such trails.

S 827 designated two initial units in the scenic trails system—the Appalachian Trail, stretching from Maine to Georgia, and the Pacific Crest Trail, running along West Coast mountain ranges from Canada to Mexico. It directed the Secretaries of Agriculture and Interior to study 14 other trails, specified in the bill, for possible inclusion in the scenic trails system. The bill provided that scenic trails could be established only by act of Congress and that study of additional scenic trails also would have to be authorized by Congress. National recreation trails and connecting trails were to be designated by the Interior and Agriculture Secretaries.

It was estimated that little federal land acquisition would be necessary for recreation and side trails but that land would have to be acquired for most scenic trails. The bill set forth procedures for land acquisition and land-use agreements. It would permit acquisition by condemnation, if agreement could not be secured within two years, but would limit condemnation to no more than 25 acres in any mile of trail.

The bill authorized initial appropriations, from the Land and Water Conservation Fund, of up to $5 million for land acquisition along the Appalachian Trail and $500,000 for the Pacific Crest Trail, which traversed extensive stretches of federally owned land.

The bill as passed by the Senate July 1, 1968, provided for four scenic trails (the northern sector of the Continental Divide Trail extending from Montana to Wyoming and the Potomac Heritage Trail along the full length of the Potomac River, in addition to the Appalachian and Pacific Crest Trails). The version of the bill passed by the House July 15 provided for only the Appalachian Trail. The conference compromise, placing an East Coast and a West Coast scenic trail in the initial system, was signed into law (PL 90-543) on Oct. 2.

WILD AND SCENIC RIVERS SYSTEM. Congress completed action on a bill (S 119) establishing a National Wild and Scenic Rivers System to preserve outstanding stretches of rivers from incompatible water resource development, pollution or commercialization. The bill established three classifications in the system: Wild river areas, essentially primitive and accessible only by trail; scenic river areas, largely primitive but accessible in places by road; and recreational river areas, areas which may have some developments and are readily accessible by car.

S 119 designated segments of the following eight rivers for inclusion in the system: Clearwater, Idaho; Eleven Point, Mo.; Feather, Calif.; Rio Grande, N.M.; Rogue, Ore; Saint Croix, Minn. and Wis.; Salmon, Idaho; Wolf, Wis. In addition, 27 other rivers were to be studied for possible inclusion by act of Congress, within 10 years. Individual states also were authorized to designate rivers for inclusion in the system.

In its land acquisition provisions, S 119 permitted acquisition by condemnation if negotiation failed, but it limited acquisition by condemnation to 100 acres per mile on both sides of a river and prohibited condemnation if more than one-half of the acreage in proposed areas was already publicly owned. State lands could be acquired only by donation and the appropriate Secretary was authorized to trade federally owned land for land needed for the system. Landowners were permitted to retain homes in river areas for 25 years. The bill authorized appropriation of $17 million from the Land and Water Conservation Fund for land acquisition.

To protect the streams scheduled for inclusion in the system, S 119 prohibited the Federal Power Commission and other agencies from licensing projects which could affect a river in the system, or considered for inclusion in the system, unless Congress specifically agreed. Mining was prohibited within a quarter of a mile of a wild river, but current land-use practice in scenic or wild river areas (such as grazing) were allowed to continue.

A national rivers system had been requested by President Johnson since 1965. The Senate passed the Administration bill in 1966, but the House took no action on the 89th Congress. The Senate passed S 119 Aug. 8, 1967. The House passed a similar but more modest version Sept. 12, 1968, and the differences were compromised in conference. During debate House Interior and Insular Affairs Committee Chairman Wayne N. Aspinall (D Colo.) said the bill would not "lock up the rivers because projects could still be established along the streams if Congress agreed. President Johnson signed the bill into law (PL 90-542) Oct. 2.

FLAMING GORGE RECREATION AREA. Congress passed an Administration bill in 1968 establishing the Flaming Gorge Recreation Area in Utah and Wyoming. S 444 was signed into law (PL 90-540) Oct. 1.

The 201,253-acre recreation area was established on federal land surrounding the Flaming Gorge Dam and reservoir, part of the Upper Colorado River Basin water storage and reclamation project. The area was adjacent to the Ashley Forest and contained a number of dry, rugged buttes noted for scenic value. It was to be administered by the Agriculture Department.

WILDERNESS SYSTEM ADDITIONS. Congress in five bills added more than 800,000 acres of federally owned land to the National Wilderness Preservation System in 1968. These were the first additions to the system since it was authorized in 1964.

The Wilderness System was established by PL 88-577 after eight years of intensive pressure from conservationist groups. The system was set up to protect about 9.1 million acres of federally owned lands in the National Forest System which had not been commercially exploited and were still in a wild state. In addition PL 88-577 authorized the President to recommend additions to the system; in a defeat for conservationists it provided that such additions could be made only by act of Congress. *(Congress and the Nation, Vol. I, p. 1061.)*

The new areas set aside in 1968 were the San Rafael Wilderness, 142,722 acres in Los Padres National Forest, Calif. (S 889—PL 90-271); San Gabriel Wilderness, 36,137

acres in Angeles National Forest, Calif. (S 2531—PL 90-318); Great Swamp Wilderness, 3,750 acres in Great Swamp National Wildlife Refuge, N.J. (S 3379—PL 90-532); Mount Jefferson Wilderness Area, 100,000 acres of a former federal primitive area in Oregon (S 2751—PL-90-548). In addition, PL 90-544, which established the North Cascades National Park in Washington, also established the 520,000-acre Pasayten Wilderness in Washington and added 10,000 acres to the existing Glacier Peak Wilderness area. *(See above.)*

OTHER BILLS. Congress passed the following bills:

Carl Sandburg Home. PL 90-592 established as a National Historic Site the 242-acre farm of poet Carl Sandburg, near Flat Rock, N.C. The bill authorized appropriations of $224,000 for land acquisition and $952,000 for development.

Biscayne National Monument. PL 90-606 (HR 551) authorized establishment of the Biscayne National Monument in Florida. The bill, authorizing $24,575,000 for land acquisition and $2.9 million for development, was strongly supported by conservationists because of great amounts of wildlife in the area.

Padre Island Authorization. PL 90-594 (HR 17787) authorized appropriations of $6.8 million to complete acquisition of land for the Padre Island National Seashore, Texas, originally authorized in 1962. Difficult negotiations and lengthy condemnation proceedings had caused delay in acquiring the land involved. Meanwhile, the total cost of the land had increased from the 1962 estimate of $5 million to more than $16 million. *(Congress and the Nation, Vol. I, p. 1087.)*

FAILURE OF TWO PROPOSALS. At the end of the 90th Congress, all but two of the parks proposed by President Johnson in 1967 and 1968, had been authorized. The two were the Apostle Islands National Lakeshore, which was approved by the Senate, and a Potomac Valley Park, which was not acted upon.

Apostle Islands Lakeshore. The Senate Aug. 21, 1967, by voice vote passed a bill (S 778) establishing the Apostle Islands National Lakeshore on Lake Superior in Wisconsin. The Lakeshore was to include 57,500 acres comprising 22 wild, heavily forested islands and a 30-mile strip along the Bayfield peninsula shoreline. S 778 authorized $13,310,000 for land acquisition and development. The House took no action on S 778, which died at session's end. An Apostle Islands National Lakeshore had first been proposed to Congress in 1965.

Potomac Valley Park. President Johnson in his 1967 Budget message asked Congress to create a Potomac Valley Park along the Potomac River in Maryland, Virginia and West Virginia. In 1968 he asked Congress "to authorize the development of a uniquely historic area—the Potomac National River" and said failure to act "will make us the shame of generations to come." Congress took no action.

Conservation

Conservation of the nation's land, water, mineral and wildlife resources was a matter of continual though not overwhelming concern to Congress from 1965-68. Only one bill enacted in the period could be described as a landmark in its field. Yet the steady flow of conservation legislation testified to the need for constant oversight of the development and preservation of depletable U.S. resources.

The one landmark bill referred to above was the 1965 Highway Beautification Act. This measure set a precedent by establishing maintenance or restoration of natural beauty as a national goal. Passage of the bill was at least partially a Pyrrhic Presidential victory, however. Congress did not appropriate sufficient funds in the Johnson years to fully implement the provisions of the Beautification Act. But the possibility remained that the law would receive new attention once the financial demands of the Vietnam war had ended.

The remaining conservation measures enacted from 1965-68 essentially were extensions or modifications of similar laws of previous years.

A field that received considerable attention during the Johnson Administration was that of oceanography. The existing federal oceanographic program was revised to provide better coordination of activities spread among various federal agencies. At the same time, a program of "sea grant colleges" was approved to foster the development of "aquaculture," as the 1862 Morrill Act had established land grant colleges to encourage progress of American agriculture. A related development was approval of a bill authorizing federal research into production of fish protein concentrate—a food substance that held promise of meeting at least some of the nutritional needs of an increasingly overpopulated world.

Congress failed to take action regarding the exploitation and regulation of federally owned shale oil reserves. This complex issue, involving vast resources of fossil fuel, probably would require years of study before a satisfactory approach could be agreed upon and embodied in legislation. Congress also left unsettled the question of restoring areas despoiled by strip-mining operations. This issue raised indirectly the criterion of beautification contained in the 1965 Highway Beautification Act. Perhaps for that reason, no legislation on strip-mining was enacted.

References

Discussion of various conservation developments from 1945-64 will be found in *Congress and the Nation, Vol. I, p. 971-1010; 1011-1024; 1025-1044; 1045-1063; 1064-1073.*

Ecology and Man

Scientific concern for the future of the human environment has given new prominence to ecology as a branch of scientific learning vital to the survival of man. Ecology as a distinct science is scarcely a century old, but it has ancient forebears in the study of natural science. It is essentially a multiple discipline, calling on the findings of a number of biological and physical sciences. Some knowledge of ecology is essential to modern agriculture, and ecological findings have been a main support of the conservation movement in the United States since the movement got under way in the late 19th century. But only recently has ecology's urgent application to man's fate come forward. Ecologists in general still feel that the public has not altogether awakened to the full import of the connection.

In an address before the American Association for the Advancement of Science on Dec. 27, 1967, LaMont C. Cole, professor of ecology at Cornell University, complained that ecologists had failed to deliver their prime message, which "could hardly be more urgent or important." The message was simply that man "in the process of seeking 'a better way of life' is destroying the natural environment that is essential to any kind of human life at all."

There are some indications that the worries of ecologists are beginning to seep into public consciousness and to affect public policy on environmental protection. Meanwhile, there is concern lest the underdeveloped countries, in their eagerness to take great strides toward a technology-based economy, will repeat and compound the environment-damaging mistakes of the advanced nations. It has been reported that I.B.P.-participating scientists from the poor countries have evinced prime interest in the phase of the International Biological Program that has to do with augmenting productivity. Their interest is natural in view of the difficulty these countries face in providing sufficient food for their rapidly growing populations, and in view of their hunger for other consumer goods as well. But if their efforts to boost productivity in agriculture and industry should follow the old route of indifference to the effects on the environment, the consequences for all mankind might be devastating.

Chronology of

Legislation on

Conservation

1965

President Johnson in 1965 ushered in an era of "new conservation"—a conservation whose concern was "not with nature alone, but with the total relation between man and the world around him." This conservation, the President said in a message to Congress, "must be not just the classic conservation of protection and development, but a creative conservation of restoration and innovation." In other words, conservation must go hand in hand with beautification.

The reaction of Congress to the new approach was mixed—in 1965 and in succeeding years—and on the whole skeptical. Nevertheless, 1965 saw enactment of the Highway Beautification Act, a major presidential request, and Congressional authorization of four of 12 new parks, seashores and recreation areas proposed by Mr. Johnson. *(See Parks and Recreation subchapter.)*

Highway Beauty: Early Efforts

Early efforts to beautify motor car roads were directed chiefly to the treatment of roadsides rather than to the improvement of basic road design. In the early 1920s several states instituted planting projects to prevent or remedy the scarring of roadsides. Massachusetts, Michigan, and Pennsylvania were among the pioneers in state-financed roadside beautification; the Massachusetts highway department operated its own nurseries to supply trees, shrubs and vines for roadside planting.

Roadside beautification proved a popular activity for civic groups, especially the women's clubs and garden clubs. The General Federation of Women's Clubs, conservation-minded since its founding in the late 19th century, endorsed the so-called "good roads movement" in 1912; in its campaign for construction of the transcontinental Lincoln Highway, it spurred local clubwomen to see to it that roadsides were planted with trees and shrubs native to their states.

Some of the early beautification projects proved short-lived, especially when they involved plantings consisting of ornamental shrubs or trees and flowers that required more cultivation than highway departments were able to give them. Roadside planting by volunteers fell into disfavor among highway engineers, who sometimes referred to such projects as "highway prettification." But the early efforts led to scientifically based studies which resulted in the development of sound principles of roadside treatment—for good appearance and for efficient maintenance.

The American Association of State Highway Officials and the Highway Research Board of the National Research Council appointed a Joint Committee on Roadside Devel-

opment in 1930 which initiated and reported on research for roadside design and maintenance. In 1943, the Committee set forth basic principles of good roadside treatment that gave equal emphasis to beauty, economy, safety and utility. "Conservation of stream banks, fine trees, weathered rock ledges, and similar natural features

---

Summary of Revisions

The Highway Beautification Act of 1965, as enacted, was a heavily revised version of the original Administration draft. Following are the major differences between the initial and final bills:

• The final bill financed the programs from the Treasury instead of from the Highway Trust Fund. The purpose of this Congressional change was to make sure that allotments for construction of highways were not cut back to finance scenic beauty.

• Congress totally rejected an Administration provision requiring states to spend one-third of their federal funds for secondary highways ("farm-to-market roads") to construct scenic roads and roads leading to recreational or scenic areas, and for landscaping and roadside development along these highways. Secondary highways covered some 620,000 miles.

• S 2084 authorized the Secretary to withhold 10 percent of a state's highway funds for failure to comply with billboard and junkyard control requirements. Although the original bill had authorized withholding of 100 percent of these funds, the Administration later requested the change to 10 percent.

• The Administration bill would have relied on state police powers (their powers to protect the health, safety and welfare of their citizens) to control billboards and junkyards first and then, if this proved ineffective, would have allowed use of federal funds to compensate owners affected by the control requirements. The federal share would have been 90 percent on Interstate and 50 percent on primary highways. The final bill required federal funds for compensation in all cases, eliminating altogether the use of state police powers, and—at the request of the Administration—set the federal share at a flat 75 percent of compensation costs on both Interstate and primary highways.

• The final bill required control of billboards within 660 feet of the nearest edge of the highway right-of-way, instead of within 1,000 feet of the nearest edge of the pavement. The change was made by the Senate Committee to conform to regulations in effect for states receiving incentive payments for control of billboards under an earlier law.

• Congress added a provision allowing junkyards in industrial areas. The Administration bill had required eventual removal or screening of all junkyards within 1,000 feet of an Interstate or primary highway.

• The final bill provided for judicial review of most of the Secretary's actions which might jeopardize a state's right to its full share of federal highway funds.

is essential to the attainment of beauty in the finished highway," the report stated. "A well-located highway with a streamlined, erosion-proof cross-section, and with well-designed structures, has pleasing and long-lasting qualities which appeal to both the landowner and the motoring public."

PRESIDENT'S PROGRAM. Mr. Johnson's message of Feb. 8, 1965, marked the first time a President had declared enhancement of natural beauty a national goal. In it the President sought legislation to beautify:

• The cities, through new programs for development of open spaces, and through establishment of a community extension program to focus the resources of universities on community problems.

• The countryside, through initiation of a "Parks for America Decade."

• The highways, through control of billboards and junkyards and expanded programs of landscape development.

• The rivers, through preservation of specified streams in their natural state.

• The total environment, through new controls over air and water pollution.

The President also called for administrative actions to control pollution and enhance natural beauty. He said he would call a White House Conference on Natural Beauty to explore and "produce new ideas and approaches for enhancing the beauty of America." Throughout the year the President—and the First Lady—emphasized that beautification must be a continuous process on all levels—federal, state, local and individual.

Highway Beautification Act

The Highway Beautification Act of 1965 (S 2084—PL 89-285) authorized a new program for beautifying the nation's federal-aid highways through removal of junkyards and landscaping of areas adjacent to the highways. Despite the seemingly modest nature of these goals, S 2084 aroused heated controversy, and the final version of the bill disappointed both conservationists and the industries affected by its provisions. In the end, opponents of the bill had their way: Congress refused in 1966, 1967 and 1968 to authorize or appropriate funds to implement the provisions of S 2084 *(see below)*.

The beautification bill, identified with not only the President but also Mrs. Johnson, went through many revisions *(see box)* in Congress before final passage. The Senate passed it Sept. 16 by a roll-call vote of **63-14** (D 47-6; R 16-8); the House gave its approval Oct. 7 by a **245-138** roll call (D 219-49; R 26-89). The Senate accepted the House changes Oct. 13 by voice vote.

Major Provisions

As signed into law Oct. 22, S 2084 (PL 89-285), the Highway Beautification Act of 1965:

Included a declaration of Congress that outdoor advertising in areas adjacent to the Interstate Highway System and the federal-aid primary road system should be controlled to protect the public investment in such highways, to promote the safety and recreational value of public travel, and to preserve natural beauty. (The controls did not apply to federal-aid secondary and urban roads.)

Beautification Pressures

The major amendments of the Highway Beautification Act—both those proposed by the Administration and those initiated in Congress—were chiefly the result of intensive pressure from special interest groups.

The greatest over-all opposition was to the Administration's provisions for financing beautification programs from the Highway Trust Fund instead of the Treasury, and allowing the Federal Government to withhold a state's full federal allotment for failure to comply with the billboard and junkyard controls. Opponents of these provisions included the American Road Builders' Assn., Associated General Contractors of America, Inc., American Assn. of State Highway Officials and the National Assn. of Counties.

Opponents of the billboard control section included the Roadside Business Assn., which asserted that beautification should be a local and state responsibility, and the American Motor Hotel Assn. The largest billboard organization, the Outdoor Advertising Assn. of America Inc., supported most of the section but did not want the Commerce Department alone to decide what were unzoned commercial and industrial areas.

Those opposed to the original junkyard control provisions included the Institute of Scrap Iron and Steel, the National Assn. of Secondary Material Industries and the National Auto and Truck Wreckers Assn.

Proponents of stringent federal control standards (in commercial and industrial areas as well as outside those areas) and of stiff penalties for failure to comply included the Garden Club of America, the National Wildlife Federation and the Izaak Walton League.

Johnson Family Campaign. Both the President and Mrs. Johnson, who undertook a personal campaign in behalf of beautification, took an active interest in the highway bill before and during its legislative journey. Mr. Johnson requested highway beautification legislation in his Feb. 8 message to Congress on natural beauty and later in a May 26 letter accompanying his draft legislation. The fact that S 2084 was enacted at all in 1965 was due almost entirely to intensive Presidential pressure, particularly in the House. When the Public Works Committee, after completing hearings July 22, balked at sending the bill to the floor, the President persuaded the Committee to reopen hearings Sept. 3 and to report the bill Sept. 22, six days after the Senate passed it. Later, when the House threatened to delay final action by one day so that Members could attend Mr. Johnson's "Salute to Congress" on the night of Oct. 7, the President made it clear he wanted the bill passed that very night. Rep. William C. Cramer (R Fla.), ranking Republican on the Committee, Sept. 17 said he had "never before seen such pressures and arm twisting from the Executive Branch...as I have seen with respect to the highway beautification bill." He and other Members expressed similar sentiments on the floor Oct. 7.

Background

Under existing highway laws, the Federal Government shared with the states the costs of construction of the Interstate and ABC (primary, secondary and urban) highway systems. The federal share of these programs (90 percent for Interstate, 50 percent for ABC highways) was paid from the Highway Trust Fund, a separate fund financed chiefly through federal revenues from gasoline, tire and other highway-user taxes. By law, payments from the Trust Fund could not exceed its revenues.

In 1958 Congress enacted two voluntary programs to encourage states to improve the appearance of their highway systems by controlling billboards and landscaping adjacent areas. Both programs were optional and were largely ineffective. Neither applied to the nation's junkyards, which the Commerce Department estimated to number 17,726.

The billboard law, enacted in 1958 (PL 85-381) and extended in 1963 (PL 88-157), gave a bonus to states which agreed to meet federal standards banning billboards within 660 feet of the right-of-way of their portion of Interstate (but not ABC) roads. These states could receive a federal payment of 90.5 percent (instead of 90 percent) of the cost of building the road. When the law expired June 30, 1965, 25 states had signed the agreements necessary to make them eligible for the bonuses, and by October 1965, 10 had actually received bonus payments for control of 209.2 miles of the 41,000-mile Interstate system. Lack of participation was attributed partly to the failure of some state legislatures to pass legislation prohibiting billboards in the prescribed areas and partly to the failure of other states to achieve effective compliance.

The landscaping provision enacted in 1958 (PL 85-767) authorized states to use up to 3 percent of their allotments from the Highway Trust Fund to purchase strips of land alongside highways to preserve their scenic features. Until 1965, this provision was not used at all; in 1965, three states filed applications and funds were allocated to cover about 50 miles. The Commerce Department said that, in general, states preferred to use their entire federal allotment for highway construction and were reluctant to divert money to scenery.

Directed that 10 percent of federal-aid highway funds, payable on or after Jan. 1, 1968, be withheld from any state which the Secretary of Commerce determined had not made provision for effective control (as defined below) of the erection and maintenance along the Interstate System and the primary system of outdoor advertising signs, displays and devices within 660 feet of the nearest edge of the right-of-way and visible from the main traveled way of the system. Authorized withholding of such funds until the state provided for effective control. Provided for reapportionment of the withheld funds to the other states unless a court appeal was pending. Permitted the Secretary to suspend the withholding requirement if necessary in the public interest.

Stipulated that effective control meant that after Jan. 1, 1968, outdoor advertising (except in commercial and industrial areas—see below) would be limited to (1) directional signs pertaining to natural wonders and scenic and historical attractions, so long as they conformed to national standards to be promulgated by the Secretary under the Act; (2) signs, displays and devices advertising the sale or lease of property upon which they were located; and (3) signs, displays and devices advertising activities conducted on the property on which they were located.

Permitted erection and maintenance of off-premise signs, displays and devices—whose size, lighting and spacing, consistent with customary use, were to be determined by agreement between the states and the Secretary —within 660 feet of the nearest edge of the right-of-way adjacent to Interstate and primary roads, within areas zoned industrial or commercial by state law or within unzoned commercial or industrial areas determined by agreement between the states and the Secretary. Stipulated that the states had full authority to zone areas for commercial and industrial purposes and that their actions in that regard would be accepted for purposes of the bill.

Stipulated that removal of outdoor advertising which was in existence along the Interstate or primary system on Sept. 1, 1965, could not be required until July 1, 1970. Stipulated that if other outdoor advertising later was brought under these controls, it need not be removed until the end of the fifth year after it became nonconforming.

Directed the Secretary, in consultation with the states, to designate appropriate areas near interchanges on the Interstate System where signs giving specific information to the traveling public could be erected. Required that such signs conform to national standards promulgated by the Secretary.

Required payment of just compensation, with the federal share 75 percent, on removal of outdoor advertising which was lawfully (1) in existence on the date of enactment of the bill, (2) on any highway made a part of the Interstate or primary system between the date of enactment and Jan. 1, 1968, and (3) erected on or after Jan. 1, 1968.

Directed that all U.S. public lands or reservations adjacent the Interstate and primary systems be controlled in accordance with the bill's requirements.

Stipulated that any state highway department which had entered into an agreement with the Secretary under PL 85-767 (which expired June 30, 1965) for control of outdoor advertising would be entitled to receive the bonus payments for billboard controls set forth in the agreement, but stipulated that no state would receive the payments unless it maintained either the controls under the agreement or the control required in S 2084, whichever was stricter. Made it clear that the bill did not prohibit a state from establishing stricter limitations than those established in the bill, and that it did not exempt from its outdoor advertising control requirements any state receiving bonus payments.

Provided for judicial review of appeals by the states contesting (1) the Secretary's determination to withhold funds for a state's failure to comply with billboard or junkyard control requirements, (2) the Secretary's failure to agree with the state on the size, lighting and spacing of signs, displays and devices, and (3) the Secretary's failure to agree on unzoned commercial or industrial areas in which signs could be erected. Stipulated that funds which the Secretary proposed to withhold from a state could not be reapportioned to the other states while the state's suit was pending. Made funds withheld from apportionment and subsequently apportioned or reapportioned available for three fiscal years after they were apportioned or reapportioned.

Authorized appropriation from the Treasury of $20 million in each of fiscal years 1966 and 1967 to implement the outdoor advertising control provisions.

Junkyards. Included a declaration of Congress that establishment and maintenance of junkyards in areas adjacent to the Interstate and primary systems should be controlled to protect the public investment in such highways, to promote the safety and recreational value of public travel and to preserve natural beauty. (The controls did not apply to federal-aid secondary and urban roads.)

Directed that 10 percent of federal-aid highway funds payable on or after Jan. 1, 1968, be withheld from any state which the Secretary determined had not made provision for effective control (as defined below) of the establishment and maintenance along the Interstate and primary systems of outdoor junkyards within 1,000 feet of the nearest edge of the right-of-way and visible from the main traveled way of the system. Permitted withholding of such funds until the state provided for effective control and provided for reapportionment of the withheld funds to the other states. Permitted the Secretary to suspend the withholding requirement if necessary in the public interest.

Specified that effective control meant that by Jan. 1, 1968, junkyards must be screened by natural objects, planting or fences or other appropriate means so as not to be visible from the main traveled way of the system, or must be removed from sight.

Included definitions of the terms junk, automobile graveyard and junkyard (which included garbage dumps and sanitary fills).

Permitted operation of junkyards, auto graveyards and scrap metal processing facilities within areas adjacent to the highway systems which were zoned industrial under state law or which were not zoned but were used for industrial activities, as determined by the states, subject to approval by the Secretary.

Delayed until July 1, 1970, the removal of any junkyard in existence on the date of enactment of the bill which did not conform to the Act's requirements and which the Secretary found could not be screened.

Made the federal share of landscaping and screening costs 75 percent.

Required payment of just compensation (federal share 75 percent) to the owner for the relocation or disposal of junkyards which were lawfully (1) in existence on the date of enactment of the bill, (2) on any highway made a part of the Interstate or primary system between the date of enactment and Jan. 1, 1968, and (3) established on or after Jan. 1, 1968.

Directed that all U.S. public lands or reservations adjacent to any portion of the Interstate and primary systems be controlled in accordance with the bill's requirements.

Made it clear that the bill did not prohibit a state from establishing standards imposing stricter limitations on junkyards along federal-aid highways than those established in the Act.

Authorized appropriation from the Treasury of $20 million in each of fiscal years 1966 and 1967 to implement the junkyard control provisions.

Landscaping. Authorized the Secretary to approve, as a part of the construction of federal-aid (Interstate and ABC) highways, the costs of landscape and roadside development, including provision of publicly owned and controlled rest and recreation areas and sanitary and other facilities reasonably necessary for the traveling public.

Required allocation to each state of an amount equal to 3 percent of the federal-aid highway funds apportioned to the state annually, without state matching, to be used for landscape and roadside development within the highway right-of-way and for acquisition of interests in and improvement of strips of land necessary to enhance scenic beauty adjacent to the highway, including the authorized rest and recreation areas. Permitted the Secretary to make exceptions if a state showed it did not need the funds.

Authorized appropriations from the Treasury of $120 million in each of fiscal years 1966 and 1967 for these purposes.

General Provisions. Directed the Secretary, in cooperation with state highway departments, to prepare and submit to Congress by Jan. 10, 1967, a detailed estimate of the cost of implementing the bill's provisions, a comprehensive study of the economic impact of the Act's programs on affected individuals and commercial and industrial enterprises, the effectiveness of the programs, and alternate methods of accomplishing the Act's objectives. Required the Secretary, before promulgating standards, criteria and regulations for billboard and junkyard control, to hold public hearings in each state in order to gather all relevant information on which to base them. Required him to report to Congress by Jan. 10, 1967, all standards, criteria and regulations to be applied.

Authorized appropriation of $500,000 to the Secretary for study and coordination of traffic safety programs as authorized in PL 89-139.

Stipulated that nothing in the bill could be construed to authorize the use of eminent domain to acquire any dwelling (including related buildings).

Appropriations

Because S 2084 was not enacted until part way through the fiscal year, the Administration did not ask Congress to appropriate the full amounts authorized for fiscal 1966. The requests totaled $93,040,000 and included $12 million for billboard and junkyard controls (of $40 million authorized); $80 million for landscaping (of $120 million authorized); $750,000 for administrative expenses (no specific amount was authorized for fiscal 1966, although the over-all limit was $5 million) and $290,000 for traffic safety programs (of $500,000 authorized over an indefinite period).

Acting on the requests, Congress in the General Supplemental Fiscal 1966 Appropriations bill (HR 11588—PL 89-309) appropriated a total of $71,040,000 including $10 million for billboard and junkyard controls, $60 million for landscaping, $750,000 for administrative expenses and $290,000 for traffic safety.

Administrative Actions in 1965 to Enhance Natural Beauty

Among the major administrative actions on natural beauty called for by President Johnson in 1965 were: a study by the Interior Department of the desirability of establishing a Redwood National Park in California; a "conservation inventory" by the Secretaries of Defense and Interior to determine what surplus military lands were suitable for "outdoor recreation, wildlife and conservation uses consistent with military requirements"; a study by the Secretary of Interior of the Potomac River basin development plan, with a view toward devising a program for cleaning the river and making it a model for cleaning and developing other rivers for scenic and recreational purposes; evolution by the Secretary of the Interior of a program to encourage a national system of trails; and stepped-up efforts by all federal agencies to "improve measures to abate pollution caused by direct agency operation, contracts and cooperative agreements."

Mr. Johnson directed the chairman of the Council of Economic Advisers to study "the use of economic incentives as a technique to stimulate pollution prevention and abatement." He instructed the Budget Bureau director and the director of the Office of Science and Technology to explore the adequacy of the current organization of pollution control and research activities.

White House Conference. At the President's request, panels of conservationists, industrialists, government officials and private citizens met May 25-26 at a White House Conference on Natural Beauty, chaired by Laurance S. Rockefeller. Among the topics the President proposed for discussion were: a solution to the problems of automobile junkyards; the possibility of underground installation of utility transmission lines; policies of taxation which would "not penalize or discourage conservation and the preservation of beauty"; areas in which the Federal Government could help communities develop their own programs of natural beauty; and the possibility of a tree-planting program.

The most significant legislative program emanating from the Conference was the President's highway beautification plan. In a May 25 speech to the Conference, Mr. Johnson pointed to his Feb. 8 recommendations, many of which were endorsed by the Conference, and said as many of the other Conference recommendations "as feasible" would be included in his next State of the Union Message.

Progress Report. The President Oct. 2 made public a report on beautification efforts by the heads of the Interior, Agriculture, Commerce and HEW Departments, the Office of Economic Opportunity and the Housing and Home Finance Agency. Many of the actions had been recommended by the President or the Conference. Highlights:

All agencies concerned had increased enforcement of existing regulations, issued new guidelines and made efforts to stimulate beautification efforts, particularly by communities and individuals. The Government had begun detailed investigations of 132 surplus defense areas for possible recreation and conservation uses; surveyed the national forest trail system and its accommodations for hikers and riders; and added nine new areas to the National Park System. It had accelerated efforts to clean streams of both natural and industrial debris; expanded research on waste treatment and sewage disposal; and increased research on new processes to make it profitable to use junked motor vehicle bodies for scrap steel. The Federal Housing Administration had issued a regulation requiring home builders to put utilities underground and eliminate overhead wiring where feasible. Concurrently, the Interior Department had scheduled a new research program aimed at reducing the cost of underground transmission. The Department had also initiated studies of use of trash and garbage as fuels for operating desalting plants, with "beautification...a byproduct."

Stipulated that the bill could not be construed to authorize private property to be taken or the reasonable and existing use restricted by such taking without just compensation as provided in the bill.

Authorized appropriation of $5 million from the Treasury for administrative expenses under the bill.

Desecration of U.S. Highways

The most handsomely designed and landscaped road falls short esthetically if the view beyond the right-of-way is marred by incongruous elements. From their earliest days, paved automobile roads attracted two elements which defied the road beautifier's efforts. These were billboards and "commercial stripping." Long before automobile roads became so dominant a feature of the American scene, critics were complaining that billboards injected a vulgar element into countryside vistas or obscured scenes of natural beauty. Even more distressing was the jumble of road signs, garish gasoline stations, ill-kept diners, honky-tonks, junkyards and other establish-

ments which tended to cluster around intersections of main highways or on the approaches to cities. Adding to the confusion was the right of motorists to enter or leave the road at any point where a business establishment (or residential driveway) abutted on the right-of-way.

Roadside clutter on the principal thoroughfares probably reached its peak in the decade before World War II. A survey in the mid-1930s showed that a 47-mile stretch of road between Newark and Trenton, N.J., had 165 intersections and was lined with 472 billboards, 300 gas stations, and 440 other commercial establishments. Wherever better-designed roads were built to replace or supplement over-used routes, the signboards and the commercial establishments soon took over the borders of the new right-of-way.

Development of the limited-access highway under stimulus of the federal-aid road building program has reduced the "roadside mess" along major highways, but the problem remains along many other routes. Results of a state-by-state survey made public in May 1965 showed that 17,726 automobile graveyards, junkyards, scrap metal heaps and similar eyesores were found along 265,000 miles of federal aid primary roads. No fewer than 14,471 of the offenders were graveyards for abandoned automobiles or junkyards where the hulks of stripped cars were rusting in full view of persons passing along the road.

Congress in 1958 gave approval to billboard control along the Interstate system as a matter of "national policy," but the mechanism it created to limit billboards did not prove effective. The law provided that states agreeing to meet federal standards, which forbid placement of billboards (with certain exceptions) closer than 660 feet from the right-of-way, would receive from the Federal Government 90.5 percent of the cost of construction rather than the basic 90 percent.

Miscellaneous Bills

OCEANOGRAPHY PROGRAM. Administration opposition to a key Senate provision blocked final 1965 action on the federal oceanography coordination bill (S 944). The bill was passed by the Senate and the House in different forms, but it did not go to conference in 1965. Where the House and Senate versions differed sharply was on a Senate provision—deleted in the House—to establish a Cabinet-level National Council on Marine Resources and Engineering Development in the Executive Office of the President. The Administration opposed creation of such a council on the ground that the existing Interagency Committee on Oceanography was doing a

good job and need not be supplanted. However, S 944 was enacted in 1966 and it provided for establishment of a National Council *(see 1966 chronology)*.

THREATENED SPECIES. The House passed a bill (HR 9424) directing the Secretary of the Interior to take various special actions to protect species of fish and wildlife threatened with extinction. The Senate did not act on HR 9424 before the 1965 session ended, although the Senate Commerce Merchant Marine and Fisheries Subcommittee held a hearing on a companion Senate bill. Final passage of HR 9424 came in 1966 *(see 1966 chronology)*.

LEAD, ZINC SUBSIDIES. Congress enacted legislation (HR 5842—PL 89-238) extending the Lead-Zinc Small Producers Stabilization Act of 1961 (PL 87-347) for four years, through Dec. 31, 1969.

HR 5842 also provided for stabilization payments in a calendar year on up to 1,200 tons each of lead and zinc for any one producer (current law limited payments to 600 tons of each metal); limited to $2.5 million the total amount of payments in any one year; and redefined "small domestic producers" to simplify administrative procedures, with an additional stipulation that any firm which was a subsidiary of or controlled by a large producer was excluded from the program. The effective date of the bill was Jan. 1, 1966.

Under the 1961 Act, small domestic producers of lead and zinc were paid a subsidy for what they produced

Demise of Passenger Pigeon: Classic Case of Wildlife Extinction

The classic case of wildlife extinction in the 20th century was that of the passenger pigeon. Accounts of the immense flocks of these birds encountered over North America in the early 19th century strain the imagination. John James Audubon estimated that one such flight, which he witnessed, contained well over a billion pigeons. The birds passed over him for hours on end in such concentration that sunlight was almost blotted out. In all directions as far as the eye could see the sky was filled with pigeons, layer upon layer, and all flying at speeds approaching 60 miles an hour. The passenger pigeon probably was the most plentiful bird the world has ever known. By way of comparison, the total bird population of the British Isles is thought to be about 200 million; the single flock observed by Audubon may have contained five times that number.

"A nesting of the passenger pigeon was just as fantastic as its mass flights," Philip Street wrote in *Vanishing Animals.* "A flock would take over a whole forest, and for several hundred square miles there was not a tree without a nest. A hundred or more nests in a single tree was a common occurrence. So great was the weight of these nests and their growing nestlings that quite big branches were broken off, and at the end of the nesting season the forest looked as though it had stood in the path of a tornado. The floor would be covered inches deep in droppings, and all the grass and undergrowth killed, as well as many of the trees. It took years for the forest to recover from one use as a nesting site."

As in the case of the bison, the coming of the white man and the railroads amounted to a death sentence for the passenger pigeon. Since the birds were good to eat, professional hunters amassed huge profits from pigeons sent by rail to major towns and cities. Killing the birds was easy. Firing at a flock on the wing with both barrels of a shotgun often brought down more than 100 birds, and as many as 3,000 roosting pigeons could be trapped in a skillfully laid net. Sometimes the flocks flew so low that large numbers could be knocked down with a pole.

Even so prolific a bird as the passenger pigeon could never survive the annual slaughter of tens of millions such as occurred in the 1860s and 1870s. By the 1880s it was clear that unless immediate preventive measures were taken, the passenger pigeon would be annihilated. Nothing was done. By the early 1900s the few remaining wild specimens had disappeared.

The Cincinnati Zoological Gardens had foreseen the fate of the passenger pigeon. Accordingly, the zoo bought a few pairs of birds in 1879 in the hope of keeping the species alive if it became extinct in the wild state. But the pigeons did not thrive in captivity; only a few young were hatched and reared. One by one they died off until only Martha, hatched in 1885, remained. Martha died in September 1914, and her frozen carcass was shipped to the Smithsonian Institution in Washington, where it is on display today.

based on the difference between the current market price of lead and zinc and the statutory stabilization price of 14-1/2 cents per pound. The current price was 14-1/2 cents per pound or more; therefore, no payments were being made.

The 1961 Act also authorized payments of $16,500,000 over a four-year period; actual payments amounted to $2,132,305 (*Congress and the Nation, Vol. I, p. 989.*) Under HR 5842, payments over the next four-year period would not exceed $10 million.

1966

President Johnson's Feb. 23 message to Congress on natural beauty contained no new legislative requests in the field of conservation and natural resources. Congress completed action on two 1965 bills—wildlife protection and oceanography program reorganization—and enacted legislation authorizing research on production of fish protein concentrate, federal assistance to promote development of marine resources, and a new method of tax deduction for expenditures incurred in mineral exploration.

Economy-minded Republicans in the House struck hard at the $493 million authorized for highway beautification in the Administration's billion-dollar highway construction bill (S 3155—PL 89-574). They lost by two votes Aug. 11 on a motion to delete the funds. The key vote was **173-175** (D 60-170; R 113-5). However, the beautification authorizations for fiscal 1968 and 1969 were deleted from the bill in conference with the Senate.

Oceanography Program

Congress approved legislation (S 944—PL 89-454) to update and accelerate the nation's oceanography program and at the same time improve the coordination of existing federal oceanography activities. Similar proposals had

---

Oceanography Goals

In a Sept. 28 speech Vice President Hubert H. Humphrey, chairman of the Cabinet-level National Council on Marine Resources and Engineering Development, listed the following oceanographic goals and policy:

"To promote international understanding and cooperation;

"To expand domestic fisheries and to help acquire fish protein for the undernourished;

"To supplement continental reserves of fossil fuel and minerals;

"To use oceanic data to improve weather forecasting;

"To diminish hazards of pollution of bays and seashore recreation areas;

"To use the oceans as an immense laboratory for scientific research."

Humphrey said achievement of the policy "must be a joint task of government, business and the academic world."

---

been before Congress since 1960. (*See Congress and the Nation, Vol. I, p. 943-945.*)

S 944 was not enacted in 1965 because of controversy over a Senate provision establishing a permanent National Council on Marine Resources and Engineering Development in the Executive Office of the President to coordinate the widely scattered federal oceanographic activities. The conference version of S 944 provided for establishment of a Council, but with the stipulation that it be a temporary body pending implementation of a plan for a new governmental structure for the federal oceanographic program. The new structure was to be recommended by an independent Commission made up of marine science experts from government, private industry, and scientific institutions involved with oceanography. The bill did not settle the fate of the existing Interagency Committee on Oceanography—presumably to be determined by the independent Commission.

PROVISIONS. As signed into law June 17, S 944 (PL 89-454), the Marine Resources and Engineering Development Act of 1966:

Declared that the purposes of federal oceanographic activities were to accelerate development and knowledge of marine resources; encourage private investment in exploration and development of marine environment; preserve the U.S. role as a leader in the field of marine science; advance education and training in marine science; develop and improve vehicles, equipment and instruments for use in marine studies and development; provide close cooperation among public and private agencies involved in marine activities; and provide for cooperation by the United States with other nations and international organizations in marine science activities.

Established in the Executive Office of the President a National Council on Marine Resources and Engineering Development to be composed of the Vice President, as chairman; the Secretaries of State, Navy, Interior, Commerce, Treasury and Health, Education and Welfare; the chairman of the Atomic Energy Commission; the director of the National Science Foundation; and such others as the President cared to appoint.

Provided that the provisions with respect to the Council expire 120 days after the Commission (*see below*) submitted its recommendations for a governmental organization plan for the oceanographic program.

Directed the President to establish a 15-member Commission on Marine Science, Engineering, and Resources including individuals from federal and state governments, industry, universities, laboratories and other related institutions; provided that not more than five members be from the Federal Government. Provided, in addition, that the Commission shall have four "advisory members" appointed by the President from among Members of the House and Senate.

Directed that the Commission undertake a comprehensive study of "all aspects of marine science" in order to recommend a plan and a federal organization structure for a national oceanographic program with an estimate of its cost.

Directed that the Commission report its findings and recommendations to the President and Congress within 18 months after its establishment and stipulated that the Commission cease to exist 30 days after submitting its report.

Oceans and Man: Growth of Knowledge of the Undersea World

Man's fascination with the sea is old and boundless but his knowledge of it is still relatively new and confined. The ocean depths—95 percent of them still unexplored—are almost as obscure as man's understanding of how the oceans began. The prevailing scientific theory is that they were carved out of the earth by some cosmic accident eons ago and gradually filled under centuries of torrential rains while the planet was still young. There is some belief that the moon is composed of the land mass that once filled the earth's oceans.

Scientists do concur that life on earth had its origins in the oceans. The late Rachel L. Carson suggested that this beginning life may have been in the form of "microorganisms rather like some of the bacteria we know today—mysterious borderline forms that were not quite plants, not quite animals." When this rudimentary stage of life began, and when it began evolving into higher forms, no one is quite sure.

Oceans have been highways of commerce and conquest throughout history, but not until the time of Columbus did seafarers gain a basic understanding of them globally—and then only on the surface. The depths have been investigated in systematic fashion for only the past century or so. Britain and America, two leading maritime nations, made some of the earliest advances in oceanography. The first recorded American oceanographic work of any note was a map of the Gulf Stream that Benjamin Franklin prepared around 1770 on the basis of data collected for him by whaling ships.

Toward the middle of the 19th century new instruments and recording devices enabled seamen to chart ocean currents and wind and storm patterns with greater accuracy and ease than before. Such information was transcribed from ships' logs and compiled by Matthew Fontaine Maury, a naval lieutenant in charge of the Depot of Charts and Instruments, forerunner of the present U.S. Naval Observatory and Hydrological Office. From what he learned, Maury wrote *The Physical Geography of the Sea,* published in 1855, a work which for the first time treated the sea as a distinct branch of science and is recognized today as the first textbook on modern oceanography.

A British scientist, Edward Forbes, had meanwhile made extensive studies of living organisms of the sea. Forbes eventually became leader of a small school of marine biologists, centered during the 1850s in the universities of Scotland. He was the first to observe the relationship of the chemistry, physics and bottom topography of the sea to the nature of marine plants and animals. Another Briton, Sir James Clark Ross, made the first deep-sea soundings in 1840 by dropping a weighted hemp line nearly two miles to the bottom.

Until recent years direct observation of the inner depths was limited to a few feet, then to a few hundred feet beneath the surface; for deeper studies, scientists had to rely on instruments. Since ancient times, man has sought some means of going down to see the underwater world with his own eyes. The earliest diving appliance, known since the time of Aristotle, had a tube for drawing air from the surface. The prototype of the modern diving suit, connected to a surface air pump, was invented in 1819.

The first enclosed craft for deep-sea observation was the bathysphere, invented by William Beebe and Otis Barton and first tested in 1930. It was like an enlarged diving suit with space for two persons—a steel-enclosed sphere with portholes. The bathysphere, raised and lowered by steel cables from a surface ship, made a number of descents, the final one in 1948 to a then-record 4,488 feet.

That year the bathysphere was supplanted by the bathyscape, a device built by the Swiss scientist-engineer Auguste Piccard which could be moved up and down under its own power. Piccard, a balloonist, conceived the idea of attaching a cabin with pressure-resistant hull to a lighter-than-water float, which would sink to the bottom when weighted and rise when the ballast was cast off. Thus, cable attachments to a surface ship were eliminated and the divers freed of an ever-present danger that the cable, buffeted by currents, might break and leave them stranded.

Piccard improved his bathyscape with successive models. The third model, named Trieste, was purchased by the U.S. Navy. It made dozens of dives, reaching on Jan. 23, 1960, a record depth of 35,800 feet (nearly seven miles) at the bottom of the Challenger Deep in the Mariana Trench off Guam. From the Trieste on its record dive, Piccard and Navy Lt. Donald Walsh saw flat-fish and shrimp swimming and squirming at the bottom, clear evidence of currents that bring oxygenated water down from near the surface.

The Trieste is considered the "Model-T" of a wide variety of "submersibles" already under water or on the drawing board. At least 30 types of maneuverable underwater craft, aside from military submarines, are known. Counting foreign-built craft, the number is 40 or more. One of the first in this new breed of deep-sea vehicles was the Aluminaut. The Reynolds Metals Co. had it built of high-strength aluminum alloys for exploration down to 15,000 feet. The craft, 51 feet in length, extends two claw-like arms nine feet outside to pick up objects from the ocean bottom. Searchlights on the craft penetrate the eerie darkness of the great depths.

The Deep Quest, built by Lockheed Missiles & Space Co., in February 1968 made the deepest dive to date for a research submarine, some 8,310 feet under the Pacific off the Southern California coast. The Deep Quest, 40 feet long and weighing 50 tons, can hover in place or tilt up to 30 degrees fore and aft or 10 degrees sideways. It carries a four-man crew and permits divers to leave and return.

Lockheed is the Navy's prime contractor for building a prototype Deep Submergence Rescue Vehicle designed for removal of crewmen trapped aboard submarines in distress. The rescue vehicle would extend an escape hatch into the submarine. Perhaps the most dramatic underwater mission of recent years occurred off the coast of Spain in early 1966 when the tiny research submarine Alvin located and recovered hydrogen bombs lost in the aerial collision of two U.S. Air Force planes.

Directed the President to transmit to Congress an annual report on federal oceanographic activities.

Wildlife Protection

Congress enacted without controversy an Administration-backed bill (HR 9424—PL 89-669) directing the Secretary of the Interior to take special actions to protect around 35 species of mammals and 30 to 40 species of birds which conservationists believed would otherwise become extinct. Among the animals and birds considered threatened were the whooping crane, trumpeter swan, prairie chicken, California condor, Kenai moose, Kodiak bear, Key deer, fur seal and American bison. Conservation groups including the National Audubon Society, National Wildlife Federation, Wildlife Management Institute, Sport Fishing Institute, and Defenders of Wilderness, Inc., supported the legislation.

PROVISIONS. As signed into law Oct. 15, HR 9424 (PL 89-669):

Steam Bill Vetoed

Congress in 1966 passed and President Johnson pocket-vetoed a bill (S 1674) authorizing the Federal Government to issue leases for private commercial development of geothermal steam and associated resources on public lands. Geothermal steam is generated within the earth by the high temperatures present there. A major use of such steam is in generation of electricity.

In the United States, geothermal resources are concentrated in the Western states. Recent exploration was conducted mainly in California, but Nevada was thought to have even more extensive resources. Without legislation, those interested in developing geothermal resources could use only private lands. Because so many of the resources were located on public lands, some individuals and corporations had attempted to acquire rights to them through use of existing laws such as mining and mineral lease statutes. S 1674 was intended to provide clear authority for private development of geothermal resources on public lands.

In his Nov. 14 memorandum of disapproval, the President said S 1674 was "flawed by six major provisions which ran counter to sound public policy": (1) it provided unlimited "grandfather" rights to current holders of mineral and mining leases on the land involved (current holders were given preference in obtaining the new geothermal leases); (2) it provided for leases covering as much as 51,200 acres, with the result that a single developer could monopolize the geothermal resources of entire states; (3) it provided that royalties were repayable only on steam "sold or utilized," encouraging waste; (4) it failed to provide clear authority for the Government to readjust the terms of the lease; (5) it provided for perpetual leases if steam were produced in commercial quantities; and (6) it gave the developer 20 years in which to begin production—a period which was too long and which would encourage speculation.

Declared it the policy of Congress that the Secretaries of the Interior, Agriculture, and Defense and their Departments shall seek to protect endangered fish and wildlife species, including migratory birds, and where practicable and consistent with the primary purposes of their Departments, shall preserve the habitats of threatened species on lands under their jurisdiction.

Directed the Secretary of the Interior, after consultation with the affected states and various scientific groups having expertise in the field, to designate species of fish and wildlife that are regarded as threatened with extinction.

Directed the Secretary to use existing law (the Migratory Bird Conservation Act, the Fish and Wildlife Act of 1956, and the Fish and Wildlife Coordination Act) to conserve, protect, restore and propagate endangered species through such activities as research, studies and land acquisition.

Gave the Secretary, in addition to land acquisition authority in existing laws, new authority to acquire any other lands or interests in lands necessary to conserve, protect, restore and propagate species of native fish threatened with extinction.

Specifically authorized use of funds from the Land and Water Conservation Fund to acquire lands and waters and interests in lands and waters for the purposes of the legislation.

Designated as the "National Wildlife Refuge System" the areas administered by the Secretary as wildlife refuges, areas for the protection and conservation of fish and wildlife threatened with extinction, wildlife ranges, game ranges, wildlife management areas, and waterfowl production areas.

Sea Grant Colleges

Congress enacted an Administration-supported bill (HR 16559—PL 89-688) authorizing a program of federal assistance to promote the development of marine resources. HR 16559 was intended to encourage the development of "aquaculture" in the manner that the land grant college program had encouraged the development of agriculture. As in the land grant program, federal funds could not be used to build or repair physical facilities; rather, the money was to finance educational and research expenses at existing institutions. (For explanation of land grant program, see *Congress and the Nation, Vol. I, p. 1196.*)

As sent to the President, HR 16559 amended PL 89-454, the Marine Resources and Engineering Development Act of 1966, which had been cleared earlier. During floor consideration of HR 16559 in both chambers of Congress, Members expressed concern that the Soviet Union had trained manpower and developed technology for exploiting marine resources to a greater extent than had the United States.

PROVISIONS. As signed into law Oct. 15, HR 16559 (PL 89-688), the National Sea Grant College and Program Act of 1966:

Declared that the development of marine resources, and of manpower and equipment to exploit those resources, could provide a significant asset for the United States, and that therefore such development should be supported by the Federal Government.

Authorized the National Science Foundation to initiate and support programs of education and research in fields relating to the development of marine resources, and programs to disseminate information that could be of use in the development of such resources. Authorized the NSF to support the programs through grants to or contracts with participating institutions.

Specified that such programs were to be initiated and conducted at "suitable public or private institutions of higher education, institutes, laboratories, and public or private agencies" which already were engaged in activities relating to the development of marine resources. Provided that an institution of higher education receiving a grant under the bill was to be known as a "sea grant college."

Specified that a federal grant or contract under the bill could not finance more than two-thirds of the total cost of each program being aided.

Limited payments within any one state to no more than 15 percent of total annual appropriations.

Directed the Foundation to consult with other federal agencies in administering the programs, and specifically with the Office of Education in matters relating to education, and to seek advice from the National Council on Marine Resources and Engineering Development.

Directed the National Council on Marine Resources and Engineering Development, if the President so requested, to advise the Foundation on policy, grants and contracts; and to make annual reports to Congress on its activities relating to implementation of the Act.

Other Legislation

FISH PROTEIN. Congress enacted a bill (S 2720—PL 89-701) authorizing federal research and experimentation on the production of fish protein concentrate (a form of flour made from ground-up fish). The bill was initiated by Members of Congress from Atlantic and Pacific coastal states and endorsed by large food and research companies and the Administration. Sponsors hoped that a process could be developed that would be acceptable to people in underdeveloped countries. They planned to use fish, such as those in the hake family, that are widely available but not often served as food.

Provisions. As signed into law Nov. 2, S 2720 (PL 89-701):

Authorized the Secretary of the Interior to make grants to and contracts with public and private agencies for studies, research and experiments to develop fish protein concentrate production methods and to conduct similar research within the Department.

Authorized the Secretary of the Interior to construct one experiment and demonstration plant for production of fish protein concentrate and to lease one other plant for the same purpose. Specified, however, that the Secretary could not construct or lease a plant until after the Secretary of Health, Education and Welfare certified that fish protein concentrate produced from the whole fish was safe for human consumption and complied with the provisions of the Food, Drug and Cosmetics Act.

MINE EXPLORATION. Congress enacted legislation (HR 4665—PL 89-570) providing a new method of tax deduction for expenditures made in exploration for minerals in the United States. The bill was intended to

Fish Flour Dispute

There had been a continuing struggle since 1960 over certification of fish protein concentrate (fish flour) as fit for domestic consumption in the United States. It was not thought that the concentrate would be used widely in the United States if certified, but certification was considered essential prior to large-scale export to underdeveloped countries. Fish protein concentrate was considered highly valuable as a low-cost additive to increase the nutritional value of food—a service urgently needed in underdeveloped countries. However, the Government was reluctant to export a commodity that had not been deemed fit for consumption in the United States, because it feared the Communists would use such action as propaganda against the United States.

In the late 1950s, Ezra Levin, president of the VioBin Corp. of Monticello, Ill., developed a processing method utilizing the whole fish—including the head, tail and internal organs. This method was more efficient and less costly than previous techniques using only parts of the fish.

The Food and Drug Administration (FDA) early in 1961—in response to inquiries from Levin—issued an informal opinion that fish protein concentrate made from the whole fish was not considered fit for domestic consumption. The FDA based its decision on the ground that use of the whole fish was aesthetically undesirable. The National Fisheries Institute, in an action backed by Levin, then sought a formal opinion from the FDA on the subject. On Sept. 15, 1961, it filed a proposed "standard of identity" order which would have permitted use of the whole fish in the production of fish flour for domestic consumption.

The FDA Jan. 25, 1962, amended the proposed order—approving production from fillets of fish only. The amended order never took effect, but it nullified the proposed order filed by the Institute.

Proponents of the process took a new approach in 1966, when they requested approval of a "food additive petition" which would declare fish protein concentrate produced from the whole fish—but in a certain manner for certain purposes only—safe for domestic consumption. Two such petitions were filed —one in February by the Interior Department (which had developed its own process using the whole fish) and the other by Levin, in April. No action had been taken on the petitions by the end of 1966.

The Interior Department's Bureau of Commercial Fisheries had begun research on fish flour in 1962 in an attempt to develop a process using the whole fish that could win approval by the FDA. A spokesman for the Bureau said late in 1966 that the FDA no longer disapproved whole-fish concentrate on aesthetic grounds but that it had several specific objections to the process developed by the Bureau. The objections included the amounts of isopropyl alcohol, lead and fluoride residues that remained in the finished product. Efforts were being made to meet the FDA's objections, the spokesman said.

supply incentives for exploration. This was done by establishing an alternative schedule of tax deductions for possible use by large companies that had reached existing deduction limits.

Provisions. As signed into law Sept. 12, HR 4665 (PL 89-570):

Authorized taxpayers to deduct expenditures for exploration of minerals other than gas or oil either (1) without limit or (2) under provisions of existing law which limited deductible amounts to $100,000 annually and a total of $400,000 for all taxable years.

Provided that if the taxpayer elected to take deductions without limitation, the Government would recover the amount saved by the deductions when the mine reached the producing stage or when the mining property was sold or otherwise disposed of. (If the existing-law method was elected, there was to be no recovery.)

Required that after a taxpayer had made an election (which he had not revoked within the time permitted) as to whether he would be covered by the existing system or the new system, he could not thereafter seek coverage under the other system.

Limited the taxpayer's right to elect which coverage he would come under (or to revoke a previous election) to a period ending three years after the filing of a return by the taxpayer in which exploration expenditures were deducted for the first time after the enactment of HR 4665.

Established rules for type of coverage where there were mergers or other similar combinations or divisions of corporations or partnerships which had chosen differing types of coverage.

WEATHER MODIFICATION. Congress did not complete action in 1966 on an Administration-backed bill (S 2916) authorizing $82 million for a three-year program of coordinated federal research and engineering in weather modification. The Senate passed the bill but the House took no action. As passed by the Senate, S 2916 authorized weather control projects to be undertaken by the Commerce Department, Federal Aviation Administration, Interior Department, Agriculture Department, Health, Education and Welfare Department, and National Science Foundation.

1967

President Johnson, in a Jan. 30 message on "Protecting Our National Heritage," proposed a "sound financing plan" for the highway beautification program enacted in 1965. Beautification projects had "started well," the President said, adding: "Now, we must provide for their continued financing. We must do this so that our children, and their children, can enjoy the benefits of a vast highway network that we cared enough about to improve and protect and make safe and scenic."

The financing device recommended by Mr. Johnson was a special Highway Safety and Beauty Trust Fund to be financed with the receipts from two percentage points of the excise tax on new automobiles. No bill to create the trust fund was introduced in 1967. Moreover, Congress failed to complete action on an amended Administration-backed bill authorizing appropriation of funds in fiscal

1968 to finance projects under the Highway Beautification Act of 1965. In consequence, no funds were available after June 30, 1967, for beautification projects authorized by the 1965 act. Congress also failed to complete action on Administration-requested legislation to develop geothermal steam resources.

Highway Beautification

S 1467, authorizing appropriations of funds to carry out Highway Beautification Act projects in fiscal 1968, was passed by voice vote of the Senate and was reported favorably by the House Public Works Committee. The Committee approved the bill by a strictly party-line 18-14 vote, however, with all Republicans in opposition. The House Democratic leadership, fearing defeat on the House floor, decided not to schedule S 1467 for debate during the remainder of the 1967 session.

Lobbying Efforts

Despite press reports in 1967 that the outdoor advertising interests were primarily responsible for Congressional inaction on the extension of beautification programs, Capitol Hill sources reported that the effect of the lobbying effort had been overemphasized. The billboard industry testified before both House and Senate Committees that the BPR's proposed billboard control rules were "unfair" and "unreasonable" and asked Congress to "either persuade the Department of Transportation to rescind" the standards or to "clearly set forth...that these criteria are...unworkable and in no way reflect the intent of Congress."

On the other side of the issue, conservation groups and garden clubs in 1967 asked Congress to repeal the provision in the 1965 Act which called for mandatory compensation to sign owners for billboards removed under the advertising control program. The conservation groups said that removal could be accomplished by the states, through the use of general police powers, without compensation to the owners. This position was so extreme, however, that even its proponents recognized that it was an unrealistic demand. The Citizens Council on Natural Resources, testifying June 29 before a Senate Subcommittee, noted that it was "politically impossible" to change this provision of the 1965 Act.

Because of the rigidity of the beautification supporters on this issue, one highly placed Congressional source described the beauty lobby as "their own worst enemies" during the efforts to extend the programs. A spokesman for a national conservation group Sept. 11 conceded that advocates of beautification "probably took the wrong line" in urging stiffer controls in 1967, rather than endorsing the simple extension of the existing program.

The major result of lobbying efforts, therefore, was to deprive the existing program of major support, both in and out of Congress. Essentially, the only major proponent of the BPR blueprint for billboard control was the Bureau of Public Roads itself.

Although the 1965 Act established three separate highway beautification programs—outdoor advertising control, junkyard control, and landscaping and scenic enhancement along federal-aid highways—the advertising control provisions provoked by far the most controversy. Obligational authority for the three programs expired June 30, 1967.

The scenic enhancement program, to which no opposition was expressed during 1967 Congressional hearings, was the most costly of the three phases of the beautification effort. According to Bureau of Public Roads (BPR) statistics, the fiscal 1966 and 1967 apportionments to states for scenic enhancement purposes totaled $128,500,000, while the junkyard control apportionment for the same two years was $11,545,854 and billboard control funds totaled $2,722,980.

During lengthy House hearings in 1967 on the progress of beautification efforts, many House Members expressed serious concern about the content and administration of the programs. Some Members advocated a complete overhaul of the basic beautification program law, but neither the Administration proposal nor the Senate-passed bill (S 1467) contained substantive changes in the 1965 Act.

Washington observers believed that the lack of strong feelings about continuing the programs was attributable to a combination of factors, including widespread dissatisfaction with the 1965 Act and its administration by

Surface Mining

President Johnson July 3 sent Congress an Interior Department report which proposed a national program for regulating surface mining operations and for reclamation of lands already damaged by unwise surface mining techniques. The study was authorized by the Appalachian Regional Development Act of 1965 (PL 89-4). Much of the surface mining area was located in Appalachia.

In a letter to Congressional leaders, Mr. Johnson said that damage from bad mining practices was "seen in water pollution, soil erosion, flooding and safety hazards." The report indicated, Mr. Johnson added, that "present...practices can and must be improved.... Many constructive actions...can be taken by mining operators, by the states and by the Federal Government."

The Interior Department study recommended the following major steps by the Federal Government: (1) development of federal standards and reclamation requirements to prevent future damage to land and water resources, regardless of their ownership; (2) reclamation of damaged lands through cost-sharing agreements between the Federal Government, state and local governments and private land owners; (3) authority to acquire privately owned lands where necessary to promote good conservation practices; and (4) support for surface mining research.

The President directed all federal agencies to review "their policies dealing with surface mining on lands under their jurisdiction." He said he would submit specific legislative requests, but they were not expected until 1968.

The Cost of Beauty

The Bureau of Public Roads on Jan. 10, 1967, issued an 84-page report on beautification which included cost estimates for long-range implementation of the 1965 Highway Beautification Act, a study of the economic impact of billbaord and junkyard removal, and revised standards and regulations ("report standards") governing outdoor advertising. The report was required by the 1965 Act. The report standards were generally considered to lie between the original draft standards and the interim standards in strictness.

Under the proposed report standards, 839,000 existing billboards located on Interstate or primary federal-aid highways outside commercial or industrial areas would be removed by July 1, 1970.

The report estimated that approximately 178,000 of the 261,000 existing signs located in commercial or industrial areas violated the proposed size and spacing requirements and would also require removal. Of these, 50,000 would come down in 1970 and the remaining 128,000 by 1973.

The total cost of removing the 1 million signs and compensating their owners, as provided in the Act, was estimated at $558,610,000, of which the federal share would be $418.5 million.

The cost of screening or relocating approximately 17,500 junkyards was estimated at $121,518,000. The cost of the scenic enhancement programs, the report said, would range from a minimum figure of $991,605,000 to a maximum of $2,065,385,000 to complete "all work which is desirable."

the BPR, the rigid attitudes of some lobbying groups, growing pressures to trim President Johnson's fiscal 1968 Budget, and a noticeable lack of pressure from the White House for action in 1967 on the beautification programs.

Status of Program. Because S 1467 was not enacted into law, no funds were available after June 30, 1967, for the beautification projects authorized by the 1965 Act. Congressional inaction did not affect another program, however, which provided limited funds for landscaping and improvement of highway rights-of-way along federal-aid highways, including the Interstate Highway System. These projects were financed directly by the Highway Trust Fund. (Under the 1965 Act, funds also were available for beautification of scenic strips located outside the rights-of-way.)

During the last six months of 1967, the BPR reached agreement with eight states and the District of Columbia on precise spacing, size and lighting standards for outdoor advertising signs within each state. The states were: Connecticut, Hawaii, Kentucky, Minnesota, New York, Rhode Island, Vermont and Virginia.

A BPR spokesman in January 1968 stressed that negotiations with states on billboard control standards were still in progress, despite the failure of Congress to approve additional funds to implement the federal-state agreements and despite the fact that no billboards could be removed unless Congress made money available to compensate billboard owners. All provisions of the 1965 Act remained in force, the spokesman said, except authoriza-

Ocean Space Development

The House Foreign Affairs Subcommittee on International Organizations and Movements issued a report Dec. 7 on "The United Nations and the Issue of Deep Ocean Resources."

The Subcommittee found unresolved questions and conflicts in the field of international law relating to the use of the seas and exploitation of ocean resources. And, it said, a 1966 United Nations proposal to internationalize the seabed and the ocean floor cut across such a broad spectrum of scientific, economic, political and security considerations that the proposal could "profoundly affect" the entire structure of private, national and international marine undertakings.

"We are strongly of the opinion that hasty action (in vesting title to the ocean floor) can create more problems than it will solve or avert," the report said. It recommended that the U.S. Government actively discourage an immediate decision on the vesting of titles to the seabed, ocean floor or ocean resources, and that it proceed with the greatest caution so as not to limit or prejudice U.S. interests in the exploitation of ocean resources. The report recommended that studies being conducted under the Marine Resources and Engineering Act of 1966 (PL 89-454) and a December 1966 United Nations General Assembly resolution be pursued to their conclusions.

In separate views, Reps. Donald M. Fraser (D Minn.) and Benjamin S. Rosenthal (D N.Y.) said, "The United Nations is the proper assembly for a careful and lengthy consideration of the various national and international issues related to ocean space development." They said the alternative was a continuing "haphazard exploitation" of the ocean resources.

Senate Hearings. The Senate Foreign Relations Committee held hearings Nov. 29 on three bills (S J Res 111, S Res 172 and S Res 186). S J Res 111, introduced by Norris Cotton (R N.H.), opposed vesting title to the ocean floors in the United Nations. S Res 172 and S Res 186, introduced by Claiborne Pell (D R.I.), urged the United Nations to study principles for governing activities of nations in oceanic research and development.

An Administration spokesman told the Committee that the Administration did not believe it would be helpful for Congress "to go on record" with any of the resolutions. "We have made it clear that we are only at the beginning of what will certainly be a lengthy process of national and international deliberation," he said. "In such a situation we see great advantages in keeping open every desirable option." No further action was taken on the bills.

tion of program funds. Because money for administering existing beautification projects still was available, the spokesman explained that significant cutbacks in federal beautification personnel were not expected in the near future.

Other Legislation

PUBLIC LAND LAW. Congress enacted a bill (HR 12121—PL 90-213) extending the life of the Public Land Law Review Commission for 18 months, until Dec. 31, 1970, and authorizing additional appropriations of $3,390,000 to complete the Commission's work. The additional authorization brought the total to $7,390,000. The Commission was created in 1964 to study federal management and disposal statutes and regulations for the approximately 770.8 million acres of land owned by the Federal Government. The purpose of the review was to provide guidelines to help Congress overhaul outmoded laws and unsnarl the often conflicting regulations governing use and sale of federal lands. The Commission was to have gone out of existence June 30, 1969.

WETLANDS PRESERVATION. Congress cleared a bill (HR 480—PL 90-205) extending for eight years, through fiscal 1976, the period during which Congress could make advance appropriations for acquisition of wetlands for migratory bird conservation. The final bill continued an existing-law authority for a state Governor to veto acquisitions in his state. The Administration had requested that the veto provision be dropped from the existing law.

Background

The original 127 million acres of wetlands in the 48 contiguous states was reduced to about 74 million acres by 1955. Only 22.5 million acres of the total in 1955 were important for migratory waterfowl use. Of the 22.5 million acres, 10 million acres were expected to remain in private ownership, leaving 12.5 million acres for public control. Five million of the 12.5 million acres were to come under state control, leaving 7.5 million acres to be acquired by the Federal Government; by 1961, 5 million acres had been obtained through purchase or donations, leaving 2.5 million to be acquired.

The 1961 Wetlands Loan Act (PL 87-383), which HR 480 amended, authorized advance appropriations of $105 million over a seven-year period (through fiscal 1968) to accelerate the Interior Department's program of acquiring wetlands. During the period from enactment in 1961 (and including) fiscal 1968, only $46 million of the total authorization was actually appropriated. Of the 2.5 million acres expected to be acquired by 1968, only 750,000 had been purchased by 1967. Interior Department spokesmen attributed the delays to (1) a slow start in acquiring land (Congress made its first appropriation for the program in fiscal 1963); (2) state and local opposition during 1964 and 1965 which was subsequently quelled when the Federal Government awarded local governments a higher proportion of revenues from the national wildlife refuge system beginning in fiscal 1966; and (3) the rising cost of land to be acquired under the program.

1968

Congress in 1968 enacted legislation embodying one of President Johnson's major requests in the field of conservation. In a March 8 conservation message to Congress, Mr. Johnson asked for additional sources of revenue for the Land and Water Conservation Fund so that the fund's income would reach the level of $200 million a year. Congress granted this request virtually in full.

Only token funds were provided for the highway beautification program that was a favorite project of both the President and Mrs. Johnson. The House on July 10 considered an amendment to the House version of the Federal Aid Highway Act of 1968 (HR 17134) to strike out all funds for highway beautification projects. The House accepted the amendment by a **211-145** vote in a victory for the conservative coalition (ND 21-102; SD 46-27; R 144-16). The Senate restored a $255 million, three-year program. As enacted, however, the measure (S 3418—PL 90-495) contained only $25 million for highway beautification for fiscal 1970.

Conservation Fund

President Johnson signed into law a bill (S 1401—PL 90-401) to provide additional revenue, up to an annual total of at least $200 million, for the Land and Water Conservation Fund. The Fund, established by Congress in 1964, was intended to finance acquisition of parks and recreation areas. However, revenue for the Fund authorized in the 1964 law had fallen far short of expectations. Moreover, land prices were rising rapidly throughout the country.

PROVISIONS. As signed into law July 15, S 1401 (PL 90-401):

Repealed effective March 31, 1970, the provision of the Conservation Fund Act which authorized a uniform system of admission and user fees at federal recreation areas. Stated that until that date, admission and user fees should continue to go into the Fund.

Stipulated that responsibility for fixing and collecting admission and user fees be returned to individual federal agencies and provided that all such fees (except ones earmarked for special purposes) be placed in a special Conservation Fund account for appropriation to the collecting agencies for any authorized outdoor recreation function without prejudice to appropriations from other sources for the same purpose.

Authorized additional revenues for the Land and Water Conservation Fund from fiscal 1969 through fiscal 1973 as follows:

1. Direct appropriations were to be made from general tax revenues in an amount sufficient to make the income of the Fund at least $200 million a year.

2. To the extent that direct appropriations did not bring total annual Fund income to $200 million, revenues from federal oil and gas leases on the outer continental shelf were to be credited to the Fund in an amount sufficient to provide the difference.

Authorized federal agencies covered by the Conservation Fund Act, within limitations prescribed by the Interior Secretary, to enter into contracts for the pur-

Surface Mining Hearings

In his March 8 message to Congress on conservation, President Johnson asserted that the country needed "a nationwide system to assure that all land disturbed by surface mining in the future will be reclaimed." To that end, he proposed adoption of the "Surface Mining Reclamation Act of 1968" to correct abuses outlined in a 1967 report by Interior Secretary Stewart L. Udall.

The report said that surface mining in the United States already had affected 3.2 million acres of land and that it was estimated that it would have affected more than 5 million acres by 1980. About one-third of the total acreage disturbed by surface mining had been reclaimed adequately, according to the report. The report declared, "Elementary principles of resource management dictate that our nation put a stop to unnecessary damage from future mining, and begin an orderly program to repair damage from past mining."

The Senate Interior and Insular Affairs Committee's Subcommittee on Minerals, Materials and Fuels held hearings in May on three bills providing for regulation and reclamation of surface mining areas. S 3132, the Administration bill, required the states to submit for approval by the Secretary of the Interior within two years plans for reclamation of current and future (but not past) surface-mining areas; gave the Secretary authority to determine if enforcement of state plans was being carried out; and provided that if state plans were not being enforced, the Secretary could withdraw approval of the state standards and issue federal regulations.

S 3126 was similar in most provisions to S 3132 but differed in that it also provided for reclamation of previously surface-mined land. S 217 differed from the Administration bill in that it applied only to coal surface-mining areas (which were covered along with other surface-mining areas in the Administration measure). Like S 3126, S 217 provided for reclamation of previously mined areas.

Testifying before the Subcommittee, Secretary Udall in prepared remarks said that reclamation of surface-mined land was "an issue to which most of us awakened only in recent years." Udall said every state had some surface-mining activities within its boundaries. But only 14 states had surface-mining reclamation laws and 5 of these applied solely to coal surface-mining reclamation. The Secretary added that "Our first task is to ensure that tomorrow's inventory of damaged lands is no larger" than at present. Thus S 217 and S 3126 were appropriate subjects "for later consideration."

In other testimony, Henry M. Caudill, chairman of the Congress for Appalachian Development and a spokesman for the Sierra Club, said "none of the pending bills come near to meeting the challenge" to control surface mining. On the other hand, Joseph S. Abdnor, speaking on behalf of the American Mining Congress, said federal controls were "unnecessary, undesirable and impractical." Aside from the Subcommittee hearings, no further action was taken on any of the surface-mining bills in 1968.

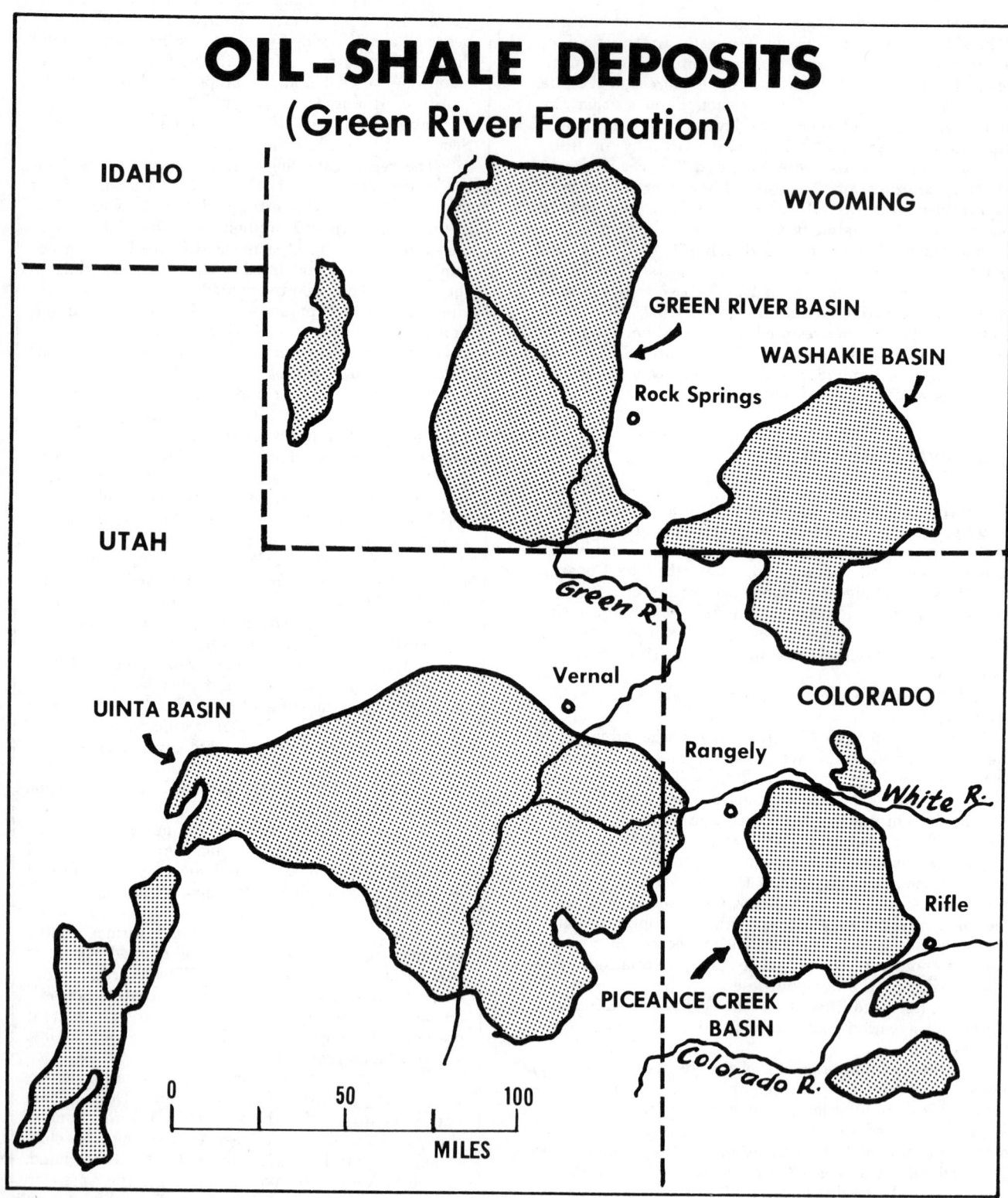

OIL-SHALE DEPOSITS
(Green River Formation)

IDAHO

WYOMING

GREEN RIVER BASIN

WASHAKIE BASIN

Rock Springs

UTAH

Green R.

UINTA BASIN

Vernal

COLORADO

Rangely

White R.

Rifle

PICEANCE CREEK BASIN

Colorado R.

0   50   100

MILES

Oil Shale: Debate on How to Develop an Untapped Resource

Bills aimed at providing "the orderly leasing of publicly owned oil shale and associated minerals" were introduced in 1968, but Congress took no action in the field. The most significant development was a decision by the Department of the Interior to lease some of the Government-owned oil shale lands.

The Interior Department May 28 released a detailed 134-page report on the prospects for oil shale development in Colorado, Utah and Wyoming. The report estimated it would be "at least five years" before significant private leasing of Government-owned oil shale lands would be "possible or desirable."

Meanwhile, the report proposed competitive bidding for two "test leases." One lease would be in the midst of thick oil shale beds and the other in thinner formations. Covering a few thousand acres combined, the "test leases" would be designed to test the market for the development of an oil shale industry at an investment of $140 million-$200 million for each lease. The proposal represented an effort to encourage oil shale research and production before committing the Federal Government to large-scale leasing.

The Department Sept. 9 announced that three Government-owned sites in Colorado would be opened for competitive bidding by private companies. The sites were in the Piceance Creek Basin of Rio Blanco County in northwestern Colorado.

Potential bidders were allowed to drill a limited number of core holes on the sites. The sale of leases was tentatively set for 1968. The plan brought on some Congressional protest, notably from Sen. William Proxmire (D Wis.)

The Department of the Interior May 7 ruled that 5,200 mining claims in Utah and Colorado based on the discovery of dawsonite, a source of aluminum, were invalid. The ruling was subject to appeal. The claims were made on shale lands which contained vast deposits of oil. Under a 1930 Presidential order, shale land claims for oil were not eligible for leases. Critics contended that the dawsonite claims were filed by speculators seeking in some way to gain an interest in the oil deposits in the shale lands.

Background. All the public-policy debate on oil shale focuses on the arid mountains and valleys of northwestern Colorado, northeastern Utah and southwestern Wyoming—a broad area known to geologists as the Green River Formation. It is the site of ancient lakes, bogs and swamps which, perhaps 50 million years ago, began to ensnare tiny creatures which in due course decayed into a waxy substance called kerogen. Kerogen is the source of oil—albeit a synthetic oil—in shale.

The quality of shale oil is judged in terms of gallons of recoverable oil per ton of shale. The calculation of two trillion barrels of oil in the Green River Formation is made on the basis of all shale that is likely to yield 10 gallons per ton or more. But mining engineers tend to believe that it is more realistic to speak in terms of shale bearing at least 15 gallons—and in deposits at least 15 feet thick. By that reckoning, the estimate of the formation's potential

supply of oil drops to 1.7 trillion barrels. Going further, a Geological Survey spokesman has said that 80 billion barrels are sufficiently accessible for mining "under present conditions...by demonstrated methods." Eighty billion barrels, though only 4 percent of two trillion, still represent twice the proved reserves of conventional oil deposits in the United States.

Shale oil deposits are not uniformly distributed or equally accessible. Some are just below the surface and others are thousands of feet deep. About three-fourths of the known deposits are within the Piceance (pronounced Pea-ance) Creek Basin of Rio Blanco and Garfield counties in Colorado. *(See map, opposite.)*

1967 Developments. Interior Secretary Stewart L. Udall announced Jan. 27, 1967, a five-point Administration program to promote oil shale development. This action prompted the Senate Antitrust and Monopoly Subcommittee to hold hearings on the possibilities of meaningful competition within the oil industry in oil shale development under the Udall program and under alternative methods of exploitation.

In their detailed form released May 7, the Udall proposals envisaged consolidation of private and public holdings of oil shale lands into convenient units for commercial production. Government leases for specific research and development projects would be available on relatively small acreages for individuals, corporations or municipalities. Upon successful completion of the proposed research, the Department would make larger acreages available to the leasees for commercial production. The federal land to be devoted to the lease program was limited to 30,000 acres.

The question of leasing federal oil shale lands was made more immediate by the testimony before the Senate Antitrust and Monopoly Subcommittee of The Oil Shale Corp. (TOSCO). The company stated that the first commercial production facility would begin operations in 1970 with a daily output of 58,000 barrels of oil. The plant would use existing mining and retorting technology, the company said, on privately owned land. Details of the technical process were not disclosed, and some close observers of the industry privately expressed doubts that TOSCO had developed an economically feasible process.

The pressure for Government leasing of oil shale lands to private corporations, represented by the position of TOSCO and many larger oil companies, was countered during the Senate hearings by proposals to turn the enormous task of development over to a quasi-public corporation modeled after the Communications Satellite Corp. or to a government body like the Tennessee Valley Authority.

The Senate Interior and Insular Affairs Committee also held hearings on the oil shale question in 1967. Former Sen. Paul. H. Douglas (D Ill., 1949-67), testified that he had uncovered numerous oil shale claim abuses on a visit to Colorado. Douglas later announced formation of an oil shale watchdog committee, called the Public Resources Assn., to study the economic and political aspects of the question.

chase of park, recreation and similar land as soon as the land acquisition had been authorized by Congress and prior to appropriation of funds for this purpose.

Limited the amount of the contracts which could be entered into by all federal agencies combined to $30 million in fiscal 1969 and $30 million in fiscal 1970.

Authorized the Interior Secretary to acquire options on lands and waters within boundaries of areas authorized by law for inclusion in the national park system; limited the option authority to expenditure of not more than $500,000 in any one year.

Authorized the Interior Secretary to sell or lease tracts previously acquired for inclusion within a unit of the national park system, but not needed for public facilities or public use; required that use of such land after being sold or leased be consistent with the purpose for which the general recreation area was authorized. Provided for the sale or lease of such tracts to the highest bidder at not less than market value.

Authorized the Interior Secretary to acquire non-federally owned property within the boundaries of a unit of the national park system by exchanging federally owned property (excluding timberlands owned on a sustained-yield basis) under his jurisdiction if such property was situated in the same state.

Provided that proceeds from the sale, leasing or exchange of property be credited to the Conservation Fund.

Other Legislation

GREAT LAKES COMPACT. Congress enacted legislation (S 660—PL 90-419) approving, with some limitations, creation of a Great Lakes Commission. The purpose of the Commission was to study and make recommendations regarding the use and development of the Great Lakes. Congressional approval of interstate compacts is required by the Constitution (Article I, Section 10), which provides that no state shall, without consent of Congress, enter into any agreement or compact with another state.

Member states of the Commission were Illinois, Indiana, Michigan, Minnesota, New York, Ohio, Pennsylvania and Wisconsin. The Commission was funded by the member states. The Commission's powers included the gathering and publication of information making recommendations with respect to the orderly and balanced development, use and conservation of the water resources of the Great Lakes Basin; considering ways of improving fisheries and navigation; recommending legislation to the states; and cooperating with the Federal Government and other bodies.

FISHERIES RESEARCH. Congress completed action on a bill (S 3866—PL 90-551) extending the grant provisions of the Commercial Fisheries Research and Development Act of 1964 (PL 88-309) for four years, through fiscal 1973. S 3866 authorized total appropriations of $23 million during the four-year period, for the same purposes and in the same annual amounts as under the existing law. The grant provisions of the 1964 law were to expire at the end of fiscal 1969. They authorized: (1) appropriation of $5 million a year for grants to promote state commercial fishery research and development projects, (2) appropriation of $650,000 a year for restora-

tion of commercial fisheries affected by disasters, and (3) appropriation of $100,000 a year for use in developing new state commercial fisheries.

ESTUARY PRESERVATION. Congress completed action on an Administration-backed bill (HR 25—PL 90-454) authorizing initiation of a program to preserve the nation's estuaries. The areas to be preserved included coastal marshlands, bays, sounds, seaward areas, lagoons and the land and waters of the Great Lakes. HR 25 authorized appropriations of $250,000 for fiscal 1969 and $250,000 for fiscal 1970 for a study and report by the Interior Department on how best to preserve estuaries and to determine whether a national system of estuarine areas should be established. The Department's report was due by Jan. 30, 1970, and was to include recommendations for further action, including legislation. No acquisition of land by the Government was authorized. A second major portion of the bill authorized the Secretary of the Interior to enter into agreements with any state or locality for the permanent protection of estuarine areas already publicly owned. Under such an agreement, the states or localities were required to share the costs of preservation "in an equitable manner."

SEA GRANT COLLEGES. Congress enacted legislation (HR 13781—PL 90-477) to extend the National Sea Grant College and Program Act of 1966 *(see 1966 chronology)* to June 30, 1970. The bill authorized appropriations of $21 million through fiscal 1970 ($6 million in fiscal 1969, $15 million in fiscal 1970).

Fishing Legislation

Congress in 1965 enacted two bills which provided financial backing and protective conservation measures for the U.S. fishing industry.

S 998, signed into law July 24 (PL 89-85), extended for five years the Interior Department's loan program for the commercial fishing fleet. HR 23, signed into law Oct. 30, (PL 89-304), authorized the initiation of a cooperative conservation and development program for the nation's anadromous fishery resources.

A third bill, S 1734, designed to protect domestic fishery resources in coastal waters and on the high seas against depredations by Japanese fishermen, was passed only by the Senate.

Fishing Boat Loans

The Administration-backed S 998 authorized an appropriation of $20 million to extend the fishery loan program administered by the Interior Department's Bureau of Commercial Fisheries through June 30, 1970.

The bill also expanded the scope of the program to permit loans to be made regardless of whether the applicant intended the vessel to replace an existing boat, as had been required previously.

Background—The U.S. fishing fleet suffered a steady decline in the years following World War II, due chiefly to its antiquated condition and high costs compared with the fleets of other nations. *(Congress and the Nation, Vol. I, p. 1068-1072.)*

In the Fish and Wildlife Act of 1956 (PL 84-1024) Congress authorized $10 million to start a revolving loan fund from which the Bureau of Commercial Fisheries could provide U.S. commercial fishermen with 10-year loans for the improvement, replacement and repair of fishing vessels and equipment. *(Congress and the Nation, Vol. I, p. 1069.)*

In 1958, Congress (in PL 85-888) increased the revolving fund to $20 million for the remaining seven years of the program.

Closely related to the loan fund was the Interior Department's fishing vessel subsidy program, which was first set up in 1960 and reinstated in 1964.

The U.S. Fishing Fleet Improvement Act of 1960 (PL 86-516) authorized the Secretary of the Interior to provide a maximum subsidy of one-third the cost of constructing fishing vessels in domestic shipyards. The subsidies were considered necessary because American fishermen by law must use vessels built only in U.S. shipyards. These are substantially more expensive than vessels built abroad, giving foreign competitors a cost advantage that enables them to operate more cheaply. *(Congress and the Nation, Vol. I, p. 1070.)*

Pl 86-516 expired June 12, 1963. In 1964, Congress passed the Fishing Vessel Construction Subsidy Act (PL 88-498) which renewed and expanded the 1960 law by increasing the maximum subsidy from one-third to one-half the construction costs. The new five-year program authorized a $10-million appropriation annually and repealed a provision of the 1960 Act which had in effect limited the subsidies to the New England fishing fleet. *(Congress and the Nation, Vol. I, p. 1072.)*

Anadromous Fish Conservation

HR 23 authorized the Secretary of the Interior to initiate with states or other non-federal interests a cooperative program for the conservation, development and enhancement of the nation's anadromous and Great Lakes fishery resources. The bill authorized $25 million in federal funds over the period ending June 30, 1970, to pay up to one-half the cost of projects. Not more than $1 million could be spent in any one state annually.

HR 23 also required the Secretary to make recommendations to the Secretary of Health, Education and Welfare concerning the control of polluting substances detrimental to fish and wildlife interstate and navigable waters.

Background—HR 23 was designed along the general lines of the broader Commercial Fisheries Research and Development Act (PL 88-309) passed by Congress in 1964. PL 88-309 authorized a five-year, $28,250,000 program to promote commercial fisheries research and development projects for all species of fish.

Anadromous fish were included under the 1964 law for their commercial value. Legislators, however, felt there was need for a separate program authorizing additional funds to redevelop anadromous fish resources from the sporting as well as the commercial standpoint. The fish had been depleted in recent years by pollution, dams, channel improvements, ship traffic and over-fishing.

U.S. Fishery Resources

The unwillingness of Japanese fishermen to agree to limit substantially their catch of North Pacific salmon led to Senate passage of S 1734. The bill authorized the President to increase the duty on fishery imports from any country up to 50 percent above July 1, 1934, levels when the Secretary of the Interior determined that that country's fishing vessels were being used in such manner as to diminish the effectiveness of U.S. fishery conservation programs. The House refused to accept the bill on the ground that, because of its tarriff provisions, it should have originated in the House in compliance with the revenue-raising section of Article I of the Constitution. There was no further action on the bill in 1965.

Background—Earlier legislation authorizing the President to impose economic sanctions on nations violating fish conservation agreements was passed in 1962 in the Trade Expansion Act (PL 87-794) and in Pl 87-814, amending the 1959 Tuna Conventions Act. *(Congress and the Nation, Vol. I, p. 1072.)*

In 1964 Congress enacted a law (PL 88-308) imposing penalties on foreign vessels that fished within U.S. territorial waters or took shellfish and other fish from the U.S. Continental Shelf. *(Congress and the Nation, Vol. I, p. 1070.)*

Fisheries Zone

Congress in 1966 passed a bill (S 2218) to extend the U.S. fishing zone nine miles beyond the existing three-mile belt of territorial waters for the exclusive use of U.S. fishing fleets and vessels of other nations with traditional fishing rights in these waters.

In 1964, Congress had passed a law (PL 88-308) which authorized the Federal Government to impose severe penalties on foreign vessels fishing in U.S. territorial or related waters. *(Congress and the Nation, Vol. I, p. 1070.)* The provisions of the 1966 bill (S 2218—PL 89-658) would be enforced under the 1964 law.

Final Provisions—As signed into law, Oct. 14, S 2218 (PL 89-658):

Established a fisheries zone, contiguous to the territorial waters of the United States, in which the United States would exercise the same exclusive fishing rights as it had currently in its territorial sea.

Provided for the continuation of such "traditional fishing by foreign states" within the new zone as the United States may recognize.

Defined the new zone as a strip of water extending nine nautical miles beyond the existing three-mile-wide territorial sea.

Authorized the President to change the established limit if he determined that "a portion of the fisheries zone" conflicts with the territorial waters or fisheries zone of another country.

Stipulated that coastal states would continue to regulate fisheries within the three-mile limit, but that the Federal Government would regulate the new nine-mile zone.

Jellyfish Control

Congress in October 1966 enacted legislation (HR 11475)—PL 89-720) authorizing $2,250,000 over a three-year period for matching grants to states to control or eliminate jellyfish and other coastal water pests. There currently was no effective method to control or eradicate jellyfish.

The measure authorized appropriations of $500,000 in fiscal 1968, $750,000 in fiscal 1969 and $1 million in fiscal 1970. The funds were to be granted to states on a 50-50 matching basis and could be used for (1) studies on the abundance and distribution of jellyfish and other water pests and their effect on fish and shellfish and water recreation; (2) studies to control such pests and floating seaweed; and (3) actual programs to control or eliminate such pests and seaweed.

The Department of the Interior was to administer the grants program. Under existing law, the Department had authority to conduct research on problems created by jellyfish but had not sought funds for a study. *(Congress and the Nation, Vol. I, p. 1067.)*

Fishing Rights

On July 26, 1968, the President signed into law a bill (S 1725—PL 90-427) prohibiting foreign ships to engage in activities supporting a foreign fishing fleet while within U.S. territorial waters or the U.S. 9-mile contiguous fishing zone.

The bill tightened provisions of a 1964 law (PL 88-308), which forbade fishing by foreign vessels within the 9-mile territorial zone contiguous to the three-mile belt of U.S. territorial waters. Although the existing law prohibited such activities it was considered vague in regard to vessels which were transferring fish from one ship to another and in regard to vessels which transferred men, fishing supplies or fuel to another ship engaged in illegal fishing. *(Congress and the Nation, Vol. I, p. 1070.)*

Fishing Vessel Seizure

The President Aug. 12, 1968, signed into law a bill (S 2269—PL 90-482) designed to guarantee to owners of U.S. fishing boats reimbursement for losses and costs incurred due to what the United States considered illegal seizure of the boats by a foreign country.

Final action on S 2269 came after a two-year effort to enact such legislation. The effort included S 2269 as well as its companion bill in the House (HR 4451). At one time, the House in 1967 refused to suspend the rules and pass HR 4451 and the Senate Foreign Relations Committee rejected S 2269. At issue was a provision which ordered a temporary cutback in foreign aid to a nation which seized a U.S. vessel.

Under existing law, enacted in 1954, compensation was provided by the Government to fishermen whose vessels had been seized in territorial waters not recognized by the United States and who had been required to pay fines to secure their release. Other losses connected with the seizures were not covered by the law, however. These included damage to the ships or their contents and spoilage or confiscation of the fish cargo.

Final Provisions—As enacted, PL 90-482:

Provided an open-ended authorization for the Government share of the program.

Provided that the program was to become effective 180 days after enactment and was to remain in effect for two years.

Included license fees, registration fees and other direct charges among the penalties to be reimbursed by the Government.

Authorized the Secretary of State to take appropriate action to recover from the seizing government U.S. costs under the program.

Provided that foreign aid funds for the current fiscal year equal to a U.S. claim for costs were to be withheld from the seizing country, pending payment of the claim, if the claim was not paid within 120 days.

Authorized the Interior Secretary to make agreements with fishing vessel owners to guarantee payment of certain costs resulting from seizure or detention of the vessel by a foreign government, including damage, destruction, loss or confiscation of the vessel, its gear or equipment; of the market value of spoiled or confiscated fish; of up to 50 percent of the estimated gross income lost because of such action (based on the expected daily fish catch.)

Authorized the Interior Secretary to establish fees to be paid by vessel owners to meet at least one-third of the cost of the program.

Water and Power

MOUNTING demands on the nation's limited water supplies led to an intensive search in the Johnson years for ways to expand, conserve and purify this most vital natural resource. Use of water to generate electric power also received attention, but the primary emphasis was on personal, industrial, agricultural and recreational uses.

Differing regional needs shaped the approach of Congress. In the East and South, where water is relatively abundant, pollution—and means of combating it—was a major concern. West of the Mississippi, however, the simple availability of water was of overriding importance. But even there opinion was divided. The states of the Pacific Northwest, with an abundance of water and a relatively small population, were apprehensive lest fresh water from rivers in their region be diverted to the more arid and more rapidly growing states to the south. This Northwest-Southwest dispute delayed until 1968 approval of the Central Arizona Project, which settled a decades-old dispute between California and Arizona over allocation of the waters of the Colorado River Basin.

The 89th and 90th Congresses were notable for passage of a number of landmark bills on federal water policy. One of the first—and perhaps the most important—was the Water Quality Act of 1965, which laid down nationwide standards of purity for all interstate waters. A complementary law, the Clean Waters Restoration Act of 1966, provided substantial amounts of federal money to help communities defray the costs of meeting the standards established in 1965.

Another 1965 law, the Water Resources Planning Act, encouraged federal-state cooperation in development of water resources of river basins lying within the jurisdiction of several states. The 1968 law approving the Central Arizona Project could be considered a prime example of the type of cooperation envisioned in the Water Resources Planning Act.

A continuing concern of Congress, dating from 1952, was the saline water program—exploration of methods to convert salt and brackish water into fresh water pure enough to drink. No single saline water conversion plant or method was devised to produce fresh water in large quantities or at costs competitive with those of water drawn from rivers or underground reservoirs. Neverthe-

Reference

For Congressional action on water, irrigation and power legislation in the 1945-64 period, see *Congress and the Nation, Vol. I, pp. 769-969.*

Water: Supply and Demand

A sort of Malthusian law of supply vs. consumption applies to water as well as to food; that is, water use has been growing more than in proportion to the rise in population, while the supply of fresh water has remained virtually constant. Of the approximately 300 million cubic miles of water on earth, about 97 per cent is in the oceans. Two-thirds of the remainder lies frozen in the Arctic and Antarctic. Thus, only one per cent of the earth's water is both fresh and readily accessible—in streams, lakes, and underground reservoirs, all dependent on rainfall for replenishment.

Water consumption in the United States is well on the way to equaling the potential supply, only half of which has been exploited to date. Every day, an average of 4.4 trillion gallons of water fall on the continental United States in the form of rain or snow; about 1.1 trillion gallons of that amount enter the country's streams, lakes and reservoirs, the balance returning to the atmosphere through evaporation or being absorbed by vegetation. At the turn of the century, water consumption in America aggregated around 40 billion gallons a day. In 1965, daily consumption totaled about 360 billion gallons, and by the year 2000 the country will be using some 880 billion gallons daily.

The average human being is said to drink about four pints of water a day, but he consumes indirectly much more—between 300 and 2,500 gallons. Indirect consumption represents the water needed to grow food. For example, it takes about 500 pounds of water to produce one pound of wheat, and 500 more to turn the pound of wheat into a loaf of bread. Approximately 700 gallons of water are needed to remove the juice from a ton of oranges, and 13 gallons to brew one gallon of beer. An acre of irrigated farmland uses 1.6 million gallons of water in a single growing season.

Big industries, particularly oil, steel, chemical and paper manufacturers, are prodigious water users. Between 17,000 and 65,000 gallons of water go into the making of a ton of steel, while 700 tons of water are needed to produce a ton of paper. In 1950, industrial water consumption averaged 560 gallons a day per capita; by 1975, it is expected to rise to nearly 1,200 gallons a day per capita.

less, the long-range need for additional sources of water was so great that Congress provided for substantial expansion of federal research into desalination methods.

The multitude of uses to which water is put was reflected in the diversity of legislation on the subject. The 1965 Federal Water Project Recreation Act, for example, established a uniform cost-sharing formula for recreation facilities and fish and wildlife enhancement features at federal water projects. The bill served as a reminder that a lake or reservoir created by a dam at a federal hydroelectric power project can provide, in addition to water and electric power, swimming and boating facilities and a haven for fish and waterfowl.

Numerous federal water projects—some with power features—were authorized and funded in the Johnson years, as in years past. Occasionally some individual project became a subject of intense controversy. This proved to be the case in 1965-68 with the Dickey-Lincoln School project, a proposed hydroelectric power development in Northern Maine that was designed to furnish federal electric power to the New England region for the first time. Authorized in 1965 despite objections by private power companies and organized labor, the Dickey-Lincoln School project was set back when Congress refused in 1967 and 1968 to appropriate any additional funds for it.

Because more than 50 federal agencies are concerned with water resource problems, President Johnson proposed for three consecutive years, starting in 1966, that Congress establish a National Water Commission to develop coordinated, long-range plans on water resource development. Congress finally did so in 1968. In addition, Congress in the Water Resources Planning Act established a Federal Water Resources Council, composed of the Secretaries of Interior, Agriculture, Army, and Health, Education and Welfare. It also authorized an international conference on water.

Congress took little action of broad significance in the field of power in 1965-68. Aside from various hydroelectric power projects contained in the annual public works bills, the major new start authorized in the period was a third power plant at the Grand Coulee Dam in Washington. Several bills were introduced to exempt rural electric cooperatives and certain public utilities from jurisdiction of the Federal Power Commission, but none was enacted.

Both water and power tend to be taken for granted as inexpensive, readily available necessities of life in most parts of the country. But at least two events in the 1965-68 period showed that unforeseeable disasters can curtail water and power supplies. The Northeast drought entered its fourth (and, as it turned out, virtually final) year in 1965. Communities in the densely populated Northeastern states imposed restrictions on water use, and the Federal Government took a number of remedial actions. A massive power blackout that struck the same part of the country late in 1965 led to federal inquiries into the causes of the failure with a view to preventing similar blackouts in the future.

Although both the drought and the blackout were confined to a single area of the country, they constituted a lesson of nationwide import: Rising population and widespread prosperity were creating ever greater demands on water and power resources; to meet these demands would require constant attention by Congress as well as by state and local governments.

Chronology of

Legislation on

Water and Power

1965

Congress completed action in 1965 on an unusually large number of major bills dealing with water policy. It passed five Johnson Administration measures of broad national significance, plus numerous bills authorizing and funding specific water projects.

Of the five pieces of general legislation, three were aimed directly at solving one of the nation's most urgent natural resource problems—the need to assure an adequate supply of clean water for rapidly growing national needs of all types.

The three were the Water Quality Act, authorizing enforceable water purity standards to be set for all interstate waters, in order to combat pollution; the Water Resources Planning Act, providing for the creation of federal-state river basin planning commissions and giving statutory authority to the existing Federal Water Resources Council, with the over-all aim of maximizing existing water resources through coordinated development; and a bill stepping up the existing federal program of research on ways to convert salt water to sweet water and thus enlarge the water supply. Of these bills, the Water Quality Act was the most important; in fact, it was probably the single most important natural resource measure of any type enacted in 1965.

The two other general water bills passed in 1965 were the Federal Water Project Recreation Act, establishing, for the first time, a formal local cost-sharing requirement for recreation and fish and wildlife enhancement features of federal water projects built by the Army Engineers and Bureau of Reclamation; and a measure creating a new federal aid program for rural water supply and waste disposal systems.

Federal Installations

President Johnson Nov. 17, 1965, signed an Executive Order which required the head of each federal department and agency to examine all facilities under his jurisdiction and present to the Budget Bureau no later than July 1, 1966, "a phased and orderly plan for installing such improvements as may be needed to prevent water pollution." The order also required that provisions for pollution control be included in construction plans for all new federal installations. A bill (S 560) containing similar pollution-control requirements relating to both air pollution and water pollution from federal installations was passed by the Senate by voice vote, but there was no further action in 1965.

Congress took little action in 1965 in the related field of power. The omnibus river-harbor-flood control bill authorized four new federal hydroelectric power facilities, all of which were opposed by the private power industry and the United Mine Workers of America. A proposal by President Johnson to authorize a third hydroelectric power plant at Grand Coulee Dam in Washington State gained Senate but not House approval. Congress considered two bills to clarify or change the jurisdiction of the Federal Power Commission over electric power sales, but neither was enacted. The FPC, meanwhile, handed down a landmark decision establishing a maximum price for natural gas produced from new wells in the Texas-New Mexico Permian Basin. In addition, the Commission and the House and Senate Commerce Committees undertook investigations of the electric power failure that plunged much of the Northeastern part of the country into darkness Nov. 9-10.

Water Quality Standards

Congress passed an Administration-endorsed bill (S 4—PL 89-234) significantly strengthening the federal anti-water-pollution law. Supporters of the bill called it a major new weapon to combat water pollution, one of the nation's most serious natural resource and environmental health problems.

The key section of S 4 required the states, in effect, to establish and enforce water quality standards (purity levels) for all interstate waters within their boundaries. If a state failed to take action by June 30, 1967, or if it set standards that the Department of Health, Education and Welfare considered too weak, then the Department would move in and set federal standards.

The establishment of water quality standards was designed to prevent pollution before it occurred. The existence for the first time of clear, prior standards of water purity would make it possible to determine, definitely and relatively easily, whether actual or proposed discharges of wastes and sewage by industrial plants, municipalities and others were causing or would cause unacceptable pollution in a given river or other interstate body of water. Preventive or abatement action could then be taken, either voluntarily or under state or federal compulsion. Under previous law, there were no pre-established purity levels. As a result, abatement action was not usually taken until the pollution had already reached an advanced stage—a far more costly and difficult process. Sponsors of S 4 said that by establishing prior purity standards that would make it possible to determine comparatively easily whether a discharge would cause (or was causing) pollution, they hoped to encourage voluntary compliance and thus reduce the need for federal and state government compulsory abatement proceedings.

The Senate rejected an amendment offered by John G. Tower (R Texas) that would have substantially weakened S 4. The Tower amendment proposed to substitute for the provisions of S 4 the provisions contained in a similar water pollution control bill reported to the House in 1964. The 1964 bill contained many of the same provisions as S 4, but it did not give the HEW Secretary authority to promulgate standards of water quality as did S 4; it authorized him only to recommend standards. The key

---

Types of Pollutants

Water pollutants can be divided into three major general categories: municipal wastes, industrial wastes and land run-off. Municipal wastes (including some wastes from industrial plants) are largely organic domestic sewage and synthetic organic chemicals such as detergents. Industrial wastes include a variety of items, but mostly inorganic chemicals and mineral substances resulting from mining, manufacturing and oil refining processes. In addition, the increased temperature of water which has been used for industrial cooling purposes contributes to pollution in that it has harmful effects on fish and aquatic life. Land run-offs include pesticides, fertilizers and chemicals used on highways to give traction in bad weather. Pollution has several general effects on water: it makes the water unfit for wildlife, unhealthy and/or unsavory, thus necessitating expensive treatment before the water involved is fit for use. Polluted water can become unfit for any or all of the following uses: drinking, industrial purposes, water sports and recreation, fishing and hunting, or aesthetic appreciation.

---

vote was **15-62**. President Johnson took no position on the amendment.

The House version of S 4 in 1965 favored state action only and would have given states the right to exclude all standards, whether state or federal. A deadlock over the standards section tied up the bill in conference for more than four months. A similar dispute had helped to kill a water pollution control bill—the one referred to in the Tower amendment—in the 88th Congress (1963-64).

Provisions. As signed into law Oct. 2, S 4 (PL 89-234), the Water Quality Act of 1965, amended the Federal Water Pollution Act as follows:

Directed each state to file with the HEW Secretary a letter of intent, within one year following passage of the bill, stating that it would, by June 30, 1967, (1) establish water quality standards for interstate waters or portions thereof within the state and (2) adopt a plan for implementation and enforcement of the standards.

Provided that the state standards would go into effect for the waters concerned if the Secretary found that they were adequate to protect the public health and welfare and that they met certain other criteria (see below for criteria).

Provided that if a state failed to establish and enforce such standards, or if the Secretary or the Governor of any affected state desired a revision in state standards, the HEW Secretary could propose water quality standards for interstate waters within the state following an informal conference with all parties concerned.

Provided that the federal standards would not take effect for six months and that during that period, the state involved could establish its own standards (which would have to be approved by the HEW Secretary as consistent with the definition below) or the state could ask for a public hearing on the federal standards. (The request could be made as late as 30 days after the end of the six-month period.)

Significance of Standards

The water quality standards authorized in S 4 were to be purity criteria against which streams could be checked regularly. Once the standards were established, federal and state authorities could move through various proceedings, including court action, to stop an individual, an industry, or a state or local government agency or municipality, from discharging matter into a stream which reduced the water quality below the established purity level. Under the previous law, there were no fixed standards of water quality. The absence of pre-established purity levels usually meant that abatement action was not instituted until pollution had reached a fairly advanced stage, and that what constituted pollution had to be determined on a case-by-case basis.

Under the water quality section of S 4, states were given initial jurisdiction over standards of all interstate bodies of water within their boundaries. However, if any state did not take acceptable action (as judged by the Department of Health, Education and Welfare) by June 30, 1967, the responsibility to establish standards for interstate waters within the state's boundaries automatically would be assumed by the Federal Government. The final bill did not give the states the alternative of choosing not to have water quality standards at all (as had been provided in the House version). The Federal Government was required to set standards if a state failed to do so.

S 4 was the latest in a long series of steps, beginning in 1948, to combat water pollution. Congress in 1948 gave the Federal Government the authority to take court action (following a formal governmental hearing) against anyone polluting an interstate body of water (defined as waters flowing from one state to another or forming the boundary between two or more states), provided the Governor of the state where the pollution originated consented to such action. In 1956, an informal conference was added to the abatement procedures and federal court action was permitted with prior consent either of the state of origin of pollution or of any state affected, instead of just the state of origin. In 1961, the requirement for state consent was dropped in any action where the pollution endangered the health and welfare of persons outside the state where the pollution originated, and the legislation was broadened to cover coastal and navigable waters, including navigable intrastate streams. If the pollution endangered only persons in the state where it originated, then the state's consent was required before the Federal Government could seek court action to compel abatement.

The 1965 bill streamlined enforcement procedures by providing for precise purity levels which could be used to check streams regularly. Violation of the standards would automatically lead to the institution of abatement procedures. Water quality standards would differ from stream to stream and even for parts of the same stream, but for the first time there would exist a clear, recognizable standard for all cases arising in a specific region. Water quality standards were intended to serve as both a warning and a goal to all potential polluters.

Required that the hearing be conducted before a board of at least five members, appointed by the HEW Secretary and made up of representatives of the Federal Government and the state. Provided that the state affected, the Department of Commerce and other affected federal agencies each would name one member of the board. Specified that a majority of the board could not be from the Department of HEW.

Directed the hearing board to make findings on the proposed federal standards and to approve or modify the standards. The standards, as approved or modified by the board, would become those applicable to the interstate waters of the state.

In the event that matter was discharged into the waters which reduced the water quality below the standards set by the Secretary or by a state under the procedures in S 4, the Secretary was authorized to use existing abatement procedures (informal conference, formal hearing and finally a federal court injunction), to halt the discharge. Where the case went as far as the courts, the latter were given the power to review the standards and to determine the "practicability" and "physical and economic feasibility" of the standards. Required that before abatement procedures were begun, the Secretary would have to notify the persons involved and allow 180 days for voluntary compliance.

Required that water quality standards established under S 4, either by a state government or by the Secretary, be such as to "protect the public health or welfare, enhance the quality of water and serve the purposes of this Act," taking into account the use and value of the water for water supply, fish and wildlife propagation, recreation, agriculture, industrial and other legitimate uses.

Authorized the Secretary to use all existing federal pollution abatement procedures, without having to obtain the consent of the Governor of the state involved, against pollution of any waters subject to the Water Pollution Act, if the pollution was causing dirty shellfish and thereby resulting in substantial economic injury to the marketing of shellfish in interstate commerce.

Authorized establishment in the Department of Health, Education and Welfare of a new Federal Water Pollution Control Administration, and the appointment of an additional Assistant Secretary of HEW to supervise it.

Authorized appropriations of $20 million a year in the fiscal years 1966-1969 for federal matching grants to states, municipalities and interstate or intermunicipal agencies for projects to develop improved methods of preventing untreated sewage and wastes from being discharged into bays, rivers, etc., from storm sewers or from combined storm and sanitary sewers.

Increased the existing $100 million-a-year federal grant program for construction of community sewage treatment plants to $150 million a year, starting in fiscal 1966.

Water Resources Planning

Congress in midsummer enacted legislation (S 21—PL 89-80) which provided for federal and regional coordination of plans for water resource development. President Johnson, who had requested S 21 in his 1965 Budget Message, called the measure "a valuable tool for planning what we are going to have to do at every level, federal, state and local." He added: "I think the day is past when the nation can afford to listen to, or laugh smugly with, those who have gone about slandering our water resources projects throughout the years as pork barrel and boondoggle."

Supporters of S 21 said that proper utilization of the nation's water resources was vital because demand for water for industrial, municipal, recreation and agricultural purposes was expected to double in the next 15 years. The House report on the bill said that "as our limited water supplies dwindle in relation to our national needs, choices among alternative uses will have to be made."

Both President Johnson and his predecessor, John F. Kennedy, had requested legislation similar to S 21 in earlier years. They argued that, in view of increasing demands for water, it was necessary to assure the best use of existing water resources through coordinated development and planning, instead of permitting federal, state, local and private groups each to proceed with its own (sometimes conflicting) projects.

Provisions. As approved July 22, S 21 (PL 89-80), the Water Resources Planning Act:

Established a Federal Water Resources Council, composed of the Secretaries of Interior, Agriculture, Army, and Health, Education and Welfare and the Chairman of the Federal Power Commission. The Council chairman would be designated by the President.

Directed the Council to assess biennially the adequacy of water supplies in each region of the United States; evaluate regional and river basin plans in relation to water needs; coordinate the administration of federal water programs; and establish standards and procedures for federal water projects.

Authorized the President to establish regional federal-state river basin commissions to prepare and keep up-to-date comprehensive water resource plans.

Directed each commission to coordinate federal, state, interstate, local and private water development plans for the basin; to prepare and keep up-to-date a comprehensive joint development plan, including an evaluation of alternative programs; and to establish priorities for the collection of basic data and for the planning and construction of projects. The comprehensive plans were to be submitted to the Water Resources Council.

Desalination Program

At the request of President Johnson, Congress approved legislation (S 24—PL 89-118) to increase substantially the research program to develop low-cost water desalination methods. On signing the bill, Johnson said he was determined on a "great breakthrough" in the program before 1970. Congress, however, did not vote the funds he requested for the five-year program.

The Senate version of S 24 extended the desalination program for five years, from fiscal 1968 through fiscal 1972, and authorized the additional $200 million Mr. Johnson requested for the program. The House, however, insisted on a year-by-year review and approved only a $10 million increase for the last year of the existing law, fiscal 1967. In conference, the Senate agreed to a one-year, $15 mil-

Background

Proposals for a central national water planning agency and for regional natural resources development or planning agencies, including river basin commissions, had a long history. During New Deal days, the National Resources Planning Board functioned from 1933-43 as federal coordinator of natural resource needs and plans for resources development, but it was killed by Congress in 1943 for fear of excessive centralization of power. Also during the New Deal period, a regional water development agency was set up for one area—the Tennessee Valley Authority, authorized in 1933. Despite President Roosevelt's "Seven TVAs" message of June 3, 1937, and repeated requests by President Truman for establishment of similar agencies for the Columbia, Missouri and other river basins, no further regional development agencies were created by Congress. The states feared encroachment on their water rights and powers; and both they and conservative groups feared increased centralization of power in the Federal Government.

Nevertheless, attempts were made to provide some form of coordinated water planning, at least for federal projects. On Dec. 29, 1943, a Federal Inter-Agency River Basin Committee was established, consisting of the heads of the major federal water agencies. The Committee was, in effect, an ad hoc grouping which attempted to coordinate the water projects and planning activities of the different federal water agencies. Its name was changed in 1954 to the Inter-Agency Committee on Water Resources. On Oct. 6, 1961, President Kennedy ordered the establishment of a Federal Water Resources Council, which he hoped would eventually become a real central water planning agency rather than just an ad hoc coordinating group. But in the absence of a Congressional funds authorization and specific statutory authority, the Council had no staff of its own and did not perform the functions of a true central planning agency.

In the meanwhile, numerous special study commissions, beginning with President Truman's Water Resources Policy Commission in its December 1950 report, recommended the establishment of river basin planning commissions. The latest such recommendation was that of the Senate Select Committee on National Water Resources in January 1961.

Bills to establish a national water resources council and create river basin commissions, as recommended by the Senate Select Committee on National Water Resources in 1961, were requested by President Kennedy in 1961 (S 2246, HR 8177) but received no action in 1961 or 1962. However, after the measures were revised to permit the states to select their own members of the commissions (instead of having the President choose all river basin commission members), the Senate passed the new version of the bill (S 1111) Dec. 4, 1963. Though reported in the House Sept. 2, 1964, and endorsed by President Johnson, S 1111 failed to receive a rule for floor debate and died when the 88th Congress ended.

Background

The federal saline water program began in 1952. In that year, Congress authorized $2 million in appropriations for a five-year program of research on converting sea and brackish water into fresh water. Administration of the new program was assigned to the Secretary of the Interior, who created an Office of Saline Water within the Department to carry out the new program.

Legislation enacted in 1958 authorized $10 million for the construction of five federal saline water demonstration plants, which were subsequently built and put into operation.

The five plants were constructed by the Interior Department for $6,378,428. The states contributed $900,000 of that total. Three plants were to demonstrate sea water conversion, and the two others, brackish water conversion.

The first plant, dedicated in 1961 at Freeport, Texas, cost $1,255,712. It converts 1 million gallons per day of sea water by long-tube vertical distillation.

A 250,000 gallon-per-day plant was built at Webster, S.D., in 1961 for $433.470. It converts brackish water by electrodialysis and produces all of the city's water.

In 1962, a plant was dedicated at San Diego, Calif., to convert sea water by multistage flash. The $1,663,246 plant, converting 1 million gallons per day, was dismantled in 1964 and taken to the U.S. Naval Base at Guantanamo Bay, Cuba, after the water supply at the base was cut off by the Cuban government.

In 1963, a plant to convert brackish water was dedicated at Roswell, N.M. Costing $1,794,000, the plant was designed to convert 1 million gallons of water per day by vapor compression.

A sea-water conversion plant was completed in 1964 at Wrightsville Beach, N.C. The $1,232,000 pilot plant was designed to convert 200,000 gallons per day by direct freezing.

---

lion increase and won approval of the five-year extension but without specific authorization of funds for those years. The President's program was approved "for planning purposes," the conferees said. Subsequently, Congress appropriated $23,151,000 for the Interior Department's Office of Saline Water in fiscal 1966, almost a 50 percent increase over fiscal 1965 funds.

Provisions. As signed into law Aug. 11, S 24 (PL 89-118):

Extended the federal saline water program from June 30, 1967, through June 30, 1972.

Increased the existing fiscal 1967 authorization by $15 million (an additional $20 million previously authorized was still available for appropriation).

Required specific authorizations in the future for fiscal 1968-1972 funds but, by setting a maximum $185 million for this period, indicated approval of the broad five-year plan submitted by the Administration.

Amended the basic law to permit testing and development of modules and components for desalination plants

(existing law mentioned only testing by laboratory or pilot plant).

Water Project Recreation

Congress passed an Administration bill (S 1229—PL 89-72) establishing, for the first time, a uniform federal-local cost-sharing formula for recreation facilities and fish and wildlife enhancement features at federal water projects. The formula applied only to projects built by the Interior Department's Reclamation Bureau and by the U.S. Army Corps of Engineers—the nation's two major water project construction agencies. Sponsors said projects of other agencies were not suited to the type of cost-sharing provided by the bill.

S 1229 had two major objectives: to provide a uniform federal-local cost-sharing formula; and to shift a substantial portion of recreation and fish and wildlife enhancement costs at federal water projects to the states and localities, in order to reduce the burden on the Treasury. It had long been accepted that local residents and users, who enjoyed easy access and therefore benefited most from inclusion of recreation and fish and wildlife enhancement features, should bear a portion of their cost. However, while the Army Engineers and Reclamation Bureau in recent years had frequently been including such facilities in their projects, often at great cost, there were no uniform cost-sharing requirements. The two agencies operated under rules that differed not only as between the agencies, but in some cases for different projects built by the same agency. In most cases, there was little or no substantial local cost-sharing. S 1229 was an attempt to fix federal-local cost-sharing requirements that would apply uniformly both to Army Engineers and Reclamation Bureau projects; that would be fair to the localities, and that would require the localities, nevertheless, to bear a substantial portion of the costs. If local public groups did not wish to assume a fair share of the costs of recreation and fish and wildlife enhancement facilities at federal water projects, the bill said (in effect), then the Federal Government simply would not provide the facilities.

Provisions. As signed into law July 9, S 1229 (PL 89-72), the Federal Water Project Recreation Act:

Provided that recreation, and fish and wildlife enhancement, be given "full consideration" for the investigation and planning of any federal water project.

Directed federal construction agencies, prior to the authorization by Congress of any new federal water projects, to seek written agreements from non-federal public bodies to share the cost of developing the recreation and fish and wildlife enhancement potential of the projects and to undertake administration of the resulting recreation and fish and wildlife areas.

Provided that when a non-federal public body made such an agreement: (1) The federal construction agency would take into account the economic benefits of recreation and fish and wildlife enhancement in determining the cost-benefit ratio of the project. (The costs attributable to the two purposes could not exceed 50 percent of the total project cost except in the case of projects for the enhancement of anadromous fish—salt-water fish that breed in fresh-water streams—and shrimp, and the conservation of migratory birds protected by treaty.) (2) The federal construction agency would bear all of the joint costs allocated to recreation and fish and wildlife enhancement, and up to half the separable costs of these items. (3) The non-federal public body would pay the remaining portion of the separable costs, plus all subsequent operation and maintenance costs.

Permitted the non-federal public body to make its payments for its share of the separable costs in the form of cash, land, or facilities.

Effective July 1, 1966, barred the Interior Department from preparing feasibility reports on reclamation projects unless the report was first authorized by Congress.

Rural Water Systems

A new program of $55 million in grants for development of water supply and waste disposal systems in rural areas was passed by Congress. The measure (S 1766—PL 89-240) also increased the loan insurance limit of the Farmers Home Administration from $200 million to $450 million annually. The latter action was taken because of the existing backlog of applications, many of which were for water systems. After S 1766 was enacted, the Budget Bureau recommended an appropriation of $17 million for the grant program in fiscal 1966. The Senate, however, voted $30 million for grants in the General Supplemental Appropriations Bill. This was reduced to $20 million in conference.

Provisions. As signed into law Oct. 7, S 1766 (PL 89-240):

Authorized $50 million annually in matching grants to soil and water associations and local public agencies for construction of water supply and sewage disposal systems in rural areas where the population does not exceed 5,500.

Limited the federal share to no more than 50 percent of the cost of a project, required that grant applications be submitted to the local government for comment, gave applications by local government priority over requests by non-governmental groups serving the same area, and required that projects comply with state and federal water pollution control standards. (The Agriculture Department subsequently set the federal share at one-third of the cost of each project.)

Authorized an additional $5 million a year in grants to help public agencies prepare comprehensive plans for development of water supply or sewage disposal systems in rural areas.

New Water Projects

Congress approved an omnibus bill (S 2300—PL 89-298) authorizing construction by the U.S. Army Corps of Engineers of nearly $2 billion in new federal water projects. The bill also authorized the Army Engineers, in cooperation with other federal, state and local agencies, to draw up a long-range plan for reservoirs, aqueducts and water purification facilities to meet the needs of the drought-ridden Northeast.

S 2300 was the first omnibus bill authorizing new Army Engineers river, harbor, flood control, beach erosion

Major Projects

Following is a list of major projects (costing more than $25 million) authorized in S 2300:

Navigation

San Francisco Bay to Stockton, Calif.	$ 46,853,000
Burns Waterway, Ind.	25,000,000
New York Harbor anchorages, N.Y.	44,852,000
Trinity River, Texas (initial funds)	83,000,000
Newport News-Norfolk Harbor, Va.	25,600,000

Flood Control   (a (p) indicates power projects)

Gila River at Phoenix, Ariz.	58,310,000
Lazer Creek, Lower Auchumpkee Reservoirs, Flint River, Ga. (p)	88,653,000
Wabash River, Ind.	44,800,000
Wabash River, Ind. and Ill.	72,900,000
Walnut River, Kan.	66,036,000
Big Sandy River, Ky.	51,491,000
Lake Pontchartrain, La.	56,235,000
St. John River, Maine (p)	227,000,000
Mississippi River and tributaries, Ark., Miss., Mo., La., Ill. Ky., Tenn.	181,109,000
Grand River, Mo. and Iowa	218,009,000
Platte River, Mo. and Iowa	26,889,000
East Rockaway Inlet and Jamaica Bay, N.Y.	32,620,000
Cheat River, W.Va. (p)	133,548,000

and hurricane protection projects since a similar 1962 measure. The final bill contained projects for all except 10 states. Of the 149 authorizations in the bill for new projects or major modifications of existing projects, nearly a score had estimated total costs of $25 million or more. (*See box.*)

Four of the projects authorized by the bill contained new federal hydroelectric power facilities, and for that reason were opposed by the private power industry and the United Mine Workers of America. The four projects were the $227 million Dickey-Lincoln School project on the St. John River, Maine (794,000 kilowatts installed capacity); the $88.7 million Lazer Creek (87,000 KW) and Lower Auchumpkee (81,000 KW) reservoirs on the Flint River, Ga.; and the $133.6 million Rowlesburg dam and reservoir project on the Cheat River, W. Va. (provisionally authorized to contain a 350,000 KW pumped-storage system).

The bill specified that the federal pumped-storage power system at Rowlesburg reservoir was to be built only if the Federal Power Commission turned down a pending application by the Monongahela Power Co. to build and operate the pumped-storage system itself as a private power plant. (Under the Federal Power Act, any non-federal entity wishing to build a hydroelectric power project must first obtain approval of the FPC.) If the FPC, on the other hand, granted the company's application for private construction of the pumped-storage power facility, then the Army Engineers would build the Rowlesburg dam and reservoir, but without the power facility; and in that case, the bill specified, the authorization would be only $88.4 million instead of $133.6 million.

Northeast Blackout

A massive Northeastern electric power failure Nov. 9-10, 1965, led President Johnson to request an emergency investigation by the Federal Power Commission. The blackout, worst in the nation's history, began at 5:16 p.m. Nov. 9 and lasted from a few minutes in some areas to more than half a day in others.

New York City, the worst-hit area, was totally without electric power in nearly all areas for periods ranging from 8-1/2 to 13-1/2 hours. The blackout, affecting 30 million people, covered 80,000 square miles, encompassing all of New York State, Connecticut, Massachusetts and Rhode Island, parts of Vermont and New Hampshire, a substantial portion of the province of Ontario, and fringe areas of New Jersey and Pennsylvania.

In a Dec. 6 report to the President, the FPC said it had found no evidence that sabotage was responsible for the blackout, as some had feared. Instead, the power failure had been set off by a faulty electric switch at the Ontario Hydroelectric Power Commission's Sir Adam Beck hydroelectric generating plant on the Niagara River. Malfunctioning of the switch had caused a series of failures and overloads which had eventually knocked out all the other power systems in the affected states, which were tied together in a partially integrated power grid called CANUSE (Canada-U.S. East).

(A large-scale power grid is a system of electric power transmission lines tying extensive areas into a single interconnected power system, so that, for example, it is possible to transmit power generated at Niagara Falls to New York City, New England, and points along the way, and vice versa.)

The FPC stated that it did not believe the blackout had demonstrated that large-scale and regional power grids were undesirable. The Commission pointed out that the CANUSE grid was only partially integrated and hence lacked some of the equipment and coordinating devices which any fully integrated system should possess and which would have substantially reduced the likelihood of a massive power failure.

The FPC report made the following recommendations, among others, for action by power companies to help prevent power failures: (1) reexamination by all utilities, "individually and collectively," of the "overall design and operation of their power systems"; (2) closer working relationships between Canadian and U.S. power operators and between governmental organizations of the two countries; (3) an "acceleration of the present trend toward stronger transmission networks within each (power) system and stronger interconnections between systems"; (4) additional studies of the stability of the systems under emergency conditions; (5) a "thorough review of training procedures for emergencies."

Provisions. As signed into law Oct. 27, S 2300 (PL 89-298), the Flood Control, River and Harbors Acts of 1965, authorized:

Navigation projects (49 projects)	$ 343,338,000
Beach erosion projects (9 projects)	6,681,000
Flood control projects (91 projects)	1,635,766,000
TOTAL (149 projects)	$1,985,785,000

The bill also:

Authorized the Corps of Engineers, in cooperation with federal, state and local agencies, to prepare a long-range plan in accordance with the Water Resources Planning Act (PL 89-80), to meet the water needs of the Northeastern United States. The plan could entail major reservoirs, water conveyance facilities between river basins and purification works.

Stipulated that no funds could be appropriated for construction of the Burns Waterway harbor until establishment of the Indiana Dunes National Lakeshore had been voted on by both the House and Senate in the same congress.

Increased from $200,000 to $500,000 the maximum size of small navigation projects on which the Army Engineers, under authority granted by the 1960 River and Harbor Act, could undertake work without specific authorization of the project by Congress.

Increased from $400,000 to $500,000 the maximum size of small beach erosion projects which the Engineers, under authority granted in the 1962 River and Harbor Act, could undertake without specific authorization of the project by Congress.

Miscellaneous Bills

PUBLIC WORKS. Congress enacted the annual public works-Atomic Energy Commission appropriations bill (HR 9220—PL 89-299), which included $1,307,955,500 for river, harbor and flood control projects of the Army Corps of Engineers; $324,480,000 for similar projects of the Interior Department's Bureau of Reclamation and $113,765,000 for the Bonneville Power Administration, a power marketing agency of the Interior Department. HR 9220 provided funds for at least one project in every state.

The water project appropriations included funds for 68 new construction starts—62 under the Corps and six under the Bureau of Reclamation. Five of the new starts contained major power features. These were the Corps' Jones Bluff Lock and Dam, Ala.; New Melones Reservoir, Calif.; Joanna Dam and Reservoir, Mo.; Libby Reservoir, Mont.; and the Reclamation Bureau's Central Utah project. Funds appropriated to the Atomic Energy Commission included $474,450,000 for nuclear reactor development.

SOUTHERN NEVADA PROJECT. Congress enacted legislation (S 32—PL 89-292) authorizing construction by the Reclamation Bureau of the Southern Nevada Project, at a cost of $81,003,000. The project was to provide the populous Las Vegas area with municipal and industrial water drawn from Lake Mead (the reservoir behind the Hoover Dam) and was to include recreation and fish and wildlife enhancement features. A controversial provision of S 32 in effect protected the water-usage rights

FPC Issues Landmark Permian Basin Rate Ruling

The Federal Power Commission, in a landmark decision on natural gas rate regulations, Aug. 5, 1965, set 16.5 cents per thousand cubic feet as the maximum price which producers in the Texas-New Mexico Permian Basin natural gas area could charge interstate pipelines for natural gas produced from new natural gas wells. A new natural gas well, according to the terms of the FPC ruling, was one which produced natural gas only, not oil and gas together, and whose production was contracted for interstate sale on or after Jan. 1, 1961.

The Permian Basin rate decision—the FPC's first ruling in an "area rate proceeding"—was one of the most important FPC natural gas rulings of recent years.

Until 1954, the FPC did not regulate interstate sales of natural gas made by independent natural gas producers. In that year, however, the Supreme Court, in the *Phillips Petroleum* case, ruled that the FPC could regulate the rates charged by independent producers to interstate pipelines. The decision produced a storm of protest from producers, who contended that because of the character of the natural gas industry, utility-type regulation was entirely inappropriate. Under utility-type regulation, which is used to regulate prices charged by interstate gas pipelines, the FPC determines each company's costs and capital, allows a certain amount for return on capital (usually around 6 percent) and fixes rates on that basis. The natural gas producers argued that because of the costs of exploration and because of the fact that wells costly to find might produce very little while wells which cost little to find might yield large amounts of gas, fair utility-type regulation was not possible. Repeated attempts to enact legislation reversing the *Phillips* decision and thus freeing

independent natural gas producers from FPC regulation failed. *(See Congress and the Nation, Vol. I, p. 980.)* The FPC, meanwhile, had not developed a system of rate regulation for independent gas producers.

On Sept. 28, 1960, the FPC ruled that individual rate calculations for each natural gas producing company would be unworkable. Subsequently, it decided to fix prices on the basis of area rate proceedings—that is, setting some uniform price for an entire natural gas producing area based on various factors such as average costs, depreciation, depletion and so forth. The Permian Basin case was the first such proceeding to be decided. The Permian Basin was chosen as the initial proceeding because of the great importance of the Permian Basin deposit, which accounts for about 11 percent of all gas moving into interstate markets.

The Permian Basin proceeding involved 336 producers, and, technically, the new maximum rates applied only to them. However, the FPC in a separate action indicated it would apply the same price limits to other producers in the Permian Basin.

The Permian Basin ruling was considered particularly significant in indicating the FPC's approach to natural gas producer price regulation—an approach that might eventually be applied to areas other than the Permian Basin. From this point of view, the key elements in the decision were the fixing of a higher maximum price for gas from new gas wells than from other sources, designed to encourage a search for new gas reserves; the use of costs as the primary factor in establishing the price; and the fixing of the price at a level substantially below that sought by producers.

---

of Basic Management Inc., a group of four industrial concerns in Nevada *(see 1966 chronology for further action)*. The Southern Nevada Project was made possible by a 1963 Supreme Court decision *(Arizona v. California)* which determined how much water Arizona, California and Nevada were entitled to draw from the Colorado River.

COULEE POWER PLANT. A bill favored by President Johnson to authorize a third hydroelectric power plant at the Reclamation Bureau's Grand Coulee Dam on the Columbia River in Washington passed the Senate but was not reported in the House. S 1761 had three main purposes: to avoid a power shortage predicted for the Pacific Northwest by 1973; to provide additional peaking power for the Southwest through the Pacific Northwest-Pacific Southwest interties; and to enable the U.S. to take full advantage of additional water storage resulting from construction of dams under the 1961 Columbia River Treaty with Canada.

FPC JURISDICTION. Congress gave major attention to two bills (S 1459, S 218) to clarify or change the jurisdiction of the Federal Power Commission over electric power sales, but neither bill was ultimately enacted. S 1459, which exempted all nonprofit rural electric cooperatives from FPC jurisdiction, was passed by the Senate. S 218, which substantially reduced FPC jurisdiction over interstate sales of electricity by private power companies, was neither passed nor reported in either the House or the Senate.

1966

Congress in 1966 enacted far-reaching and costly legislation to control water pollution. Enactment of the Clean Waters Restoration Act of 1966, following passage in 1965 of the Water Quality Act, made the 89th Congress the most important in history in dealing with this increasingly serious national problem.

In his State of the Union Message, President Johnson said: "We must undertake a cooperative effort to end pollution in several entire river basins...." Mr. Johnson expanded this request in a subsequent message to Congress outlining his conservation and anti-pollution proposals, which he said would set a course to "a natural America restored to her people," whose "promise is clear rivers, tall forests and clean air."

The President's major proposal was establishment of a "Clean Rivers Demonstration Program" to unite federal, local and state pollution control activities in entire river basins. The demonstration projects were to begin in a "few basins whose states and communities are prepared to begin," Mr. Johnson said, and later expand to other basins as they qualified.

The Administration's draft legislation, the "Clean Rivers Restoration Act of 1966," was introduced by Sen. Edmund S. Muskie (D Maine), chairman of the Senate

Public Works Subcommittee on Air and Water Pollution, and by Rep. George H. Fallon (D Md.), chairman of the House Public Works Committee. The emphasis in the Administration bill, as in the President's messages, was on organization for careful anti-pollution planning in river basins. A modified version of the river-basin approach was added to a bill (S 2947) that had been introduced earlier by Muskie and 47 cosponsors. S 2947, based in large part on recommendations of the Senate Air and Water Pollution Subcommittee, eventually was enacted as the Clean Waters Restoration Act.

Congress also approved legislation authorizing numerous water and power projects, but it failed to pass a bill authorizing the $580 million Central Arizona Project—the largest single water project considered in 1966.

Clean Waters Restoration

The Water Quality Act of 1965 *(see 1965 chronology)* had required that purity standards be established and enforced for interstate waters and had authorized the Federal Government to take such action if the states did not. The 1966 legislation (S 2947—PL 89-753) provided substantial amounts of money to help communities pay the costs of abiding by the standards and offered financial incentives to the states to establish purity standards on intrastate waters.

S 2947 was enacted with little controversy; all three roll calls taken on the bill were unanimous. The measure which Mr. Johnson signed into law was shaped by Congress as much as, if not more than, by the Administration. Although Administration support was made known early in the session, its recommendations were quite limited in scope and cost compared to proposals that were being considered independently by Congress. The Administration later expanded its own proposals, at least partly in response to the widespread support that was evident in Congress for the more far-reaching proposals.

Provisions. As signed into law Nov. 3, S 2947 (PL 89-753), the Clean Waters Restoration Act of 1966:

Authorized appropriations totaling $3,550,000,000 during fiscal years 1967-71 for grants for construction of sewage treatment plants. Eliminated existing dollar ceilings on the amount of a single grant.

Provided that a federal grant could pay for 30 percent, 40 percent, or 50 percent of the construction costs of a sewage treatment plant. Both the 40-percent and the 50-percent grants were conditional on state participation in the financing of treatment plants, and the 50-percent plan was also conditional on establishment by the state of quality (purity) standards for bodies of water within its boundaries—that is, non-interstate waters.

Established new programs of federal grants for research on industrial water pollution and on advanced

---

Federal Action Taken to Alleviate Northeast Drought

A fourth successive year of drought in the Northeast brought federal action to help relieve severe water shortages. The federal assistance took the form of financial and technical aid; a speedup of work on several federal water projects; and the initiation of several long-range water studies for the area.

Background. The Northeast drought started in October 1961. It was marked by below-average rainfall in much of the 13-state area from Maine to Virginia. With rainfall proving inadequate to replenish reservoirs depleted by heavy summertime use, water reserves dropped progressively. By the summer of 1965, water shortages became critical in parts of New York, Pennsylvania, New Jersey, Delaware and several other states. Some of the hardest-hit areas, like New York City and Philadelphia, adopted water-saving schemes, such as campaigns to plug leaks or to limit the use of water for car-washing, watering of lawns and air conditioning.

While these efforts resulted in substantial savings of water, experts said that a fifth summer of drought conditions might have disastrous consequences for some of the areas involved unless additional steps were taken to capture and conserve all existing and potential supplies of water. Moreover, many contended, with population rising rapidly, long-range plans should be drafted to assure adequate water supplies through new reservoir construction, the cleaning up of polluted rivers and related methods.

Emergency Actions. President Johnson July 14, 1965, directed the Federal Water Resources Council to undertake a rapid survey of ways to relieve the Northeast water shortage. After receiving reports from the

Council and from its chairman, Interior Secretary Stewart L. Udall, Mr. Johnson summoned to Washington the Governors of New York, Pennsylvania, New Jersey and Delaware, and the mayors of New York City, Philadelphia, Newark, Camden and Jersey City for an emergency water conference. The conferees agreed on a number of water-conserving actions, including an accord between New York City and Philadelphia to hold 200 million gallons of water in reservoirs on the upper Delaware River as a "water bank" for use by either city if critically needed. The President designated portions of the states represented at the conference as disaster areas. That action made the areas eligible for special aid from the Office of Emergency Planning for a variety of municipal water-supply projects.

Long-Range Requests. To help meet the long-term water needs of the Northeast, the President said he would ask Congress for special funds to enable the Army Engineers to speed up construction or planning of several federal reservoirs on the Delaware River and its tributaries. The objective was to make more water storage capacity available sooner. Mr. Johnson requested a total of $1.25 million in special funds, and Congress provided the full amount in the public works appropriations bill. In related actions, the President (1) initiated a North Atlantic Regional Framework Study of the water problems of the Northeast and (2) directed Dr. Donald F. Hornig, Director of the Office of Science and Technology, to prepare studies on water pollution control and "the potential of desalting" (saline water conversion plants) in the Northeast.

Water Pollution Control Grants Authorized by S 2947

(Fiscal years; millions of dollars)

	1967	1968	1969	1970	1971	Totals
Treatment Plant Construction Grants	$150 [5]	$450	$700	$1,000	$1,250	$3,550
Waste Treatment Demonstrations Grants [1]	20	20	20			60
Industrial Pollution Demonstrations Grants [2]	20	20	20			60
Research and Demonstrations Grants, Contracts [3]	20 [6]	20 [6]	20 [6]			60
Interior Department Antipollution Research	5 [7]	60 [7]	65			130
Pollution Control Plans [4]	5 [8]	10 [8]	10	10	10	45
Study of Pollution in Estuaries	1	1	1			3
	$221	$581	$836	$1,010	$1,260	$3,908

1 Grants for demonstrations of advanced waste treatment and water purification methods, and of new methods for joint treatment of municipal and industrial wastes.

2 Grants to industries for projects, having industry-wide application, to demonstrate new or improved ways to control industrial water pollution.

3 Grants and contracts for waste treatment demonstrations and for industrial pollution demonstrations (to supplement separate specific authorizations for these activities), and for demonstrations of improved methods of controlling discharge into bays, rivers, etc., of inadequately treated wastes from storm sewers or from combined sewage and storm water sewers.

4 Grants to states and interstate agencies for costs of developing and administering water pollution control plans.

5 Authorized in existing legislation.

6 These funds were authorized in existing legislation but were earmarked for sewers demonstrations only.

7 Existing legislation authorized appropriations of not more than $5 million in any fiscal year for this program, with total program appropriations not to exceed $25 million and with no specified duration for the program.

8 Existing legislation authorized appropriations of $5 million a year for this program, ending with the fiscal year 1968.

waste treatment and water purification methods; and greatly increased authorizations for general Interior Department water pollution research. Total research authorizations were $313 million in fiscal 1967-69.

Authorized federal grants to assist river basin planning organizations, and increased grant authorizations for assistance to state or interstate water pollution control agencies.

Gave the Interior Secretary new investigative powers for use at pollution abatement conferences or hearings, and extended pollution abatement procedures to cases of international water pollution.

Other Legislation

PUBLIC WORKS. The public works-Atomic Energy Commission appropriations bill (HR 17787—PL 89-689) included direct appropriations of $1,290,595,000 for river, harbor, and flood control projects of the Army Corps of Engineers; $323,943,000 for similar projects handled by the Interior Department's Bureau of Reclamation; $126,010,000 for the Bonneville Power Administration, a power marketing agency for the Interior Department.

The water project appropriations included funds for 63 new construction starts—58 under the Corps and five under the Bureau of Reclamation. Of the 63 starts, 29 were requested in the President's Budget (25 for the Corps, four for the Bureau) and 34 were added by Congress (Corps: 33, Bureau: one). The largest unbudgeted starts in the bill were the Lost Creek Reservoir, Ore., with an estimated total federal cost of $83.1 million, and the Snettisham power project, Alaska, $41.5 million, both added by the Senate; and the Chatfield Reservoir, Colo., $74 million, and the Raystown Reservoir, Pa., $49 million, both added by the House.

Five of the Corps and Interior new starts contained major power features. These were Interior's budgeted new starts on the Auburn-Folsom South unit of the Central Valley project, Calif., and on the third power plant at the Grand Coulee Dam, Wash.; the Corps' budgeted new start on additional power units at The Dalles dam and lock, Wash. and Ore.; and the Corps' unbudgeted new starts on the Snettisham and Lost Creek projects. In addition, the bill provided funds for initiation of construction by the TVA on the Tellico Dam.

HR 17787 also contained an unbudgeted $500,000 to initiate planning on one highly controversial project—the proposed Lake Erie-Ohio River Canal. Attempts to delete funds for the project failed in both chambers of Congress. If actually built, the canal was expected to cost at least $1 billion. *(See box.)* Atomic Energy Commission appropriations included $465,296,000 for nuclear reactor development.

WATER RESOURCES RESEARCH. Congress completed action on Administration-requested legislation (S 22—PL 89-404) to amend Title II of the Water Resources Research Act of 1964 (PL 88-379) by sharply increasing authorizations for grants to support research into water problems relating to the Interior Department's responsibilities and by eliminating certain restrictions attached to grants made under the title.

Title II grants, contracts and other types of financial aid were to go to colleges, states, individuals and private firms for research projects that bore upon the Interior Department's water responsibilities. PL 88-379 had authorized $1 million annually in fiscal years 1965-74. S 22 increased the fiscal 1967 authorization to $5 million and provided that the annual authorization would increase by $1 million each year until it reached $10 million in fiscal 1972, and that it would remain at the $10-million level through fiscal 1976.

S 22 satisfied a Presidential request by taking away the power of the Interior and Insular Affairs Committee of either chamber of Congress to veto Interior Department grants made under Title II. (The power was granted to the Committees by PL 88-379.) The bill provided that any grant proposal was to lie before each committee for at least 60 days before it was effected, but the Committees were to have no veto power.

COULEE POWER PLANT. A bill (S 1761—PL 89-448) to authorize construction of a third hydroelectric power plant at the Interior Department's Grand Coulee Dam on the Columbia River in Washington, requested by President Johnson in 1965, was enacted by Congress. The bill also changed accounting procedures on power and irrigation projects in the Northwest.

The new plant was to contain 12 generators of 300,000 kilowatts electric generating capacity each. It thus would add 3.6 million kilowatts of capacity to the 2 million kilowatts already in operation at Grand Coulee. The 5.6 million kilowatt total capacity would be larger than that of any other hydroelectric generating dam in the world. Sponsors of the bill said the benefit-cost ratio of the third plant was 3-1. The 12 new generators were to be added in stages. The bill authorized $390 million in appropriations for construction of the plant, specifying that appurtenant works and a visitors' center should also be built, and required that construction costs of each stage of the plant be repaid with interest within 50 years of the time that stage began commercial production of power.

A controversial provision of S 1761 established a partial basin-wide account and consolidated financial state-

---

Change in Waterway Formula Brings Favorable Report on Canal

The only major controversy that arose in connection with HR 17787 concerned appropriation of $500,000 (not requested by the Administration) to begin planning of the proposed Lake Erie to Ohio River canal, which would run 120 miles through Ohio and Pennsylvania. Debate centered on the over-all merits of the $1-billion project; its supporters claimed that it was a needed addition to the nation's inland water transportation system, and its opponents contended that it was not needed and an immense waste of tax dollars.

Funds for the project could not have been provided unless Army Corps of Engineers studies showed that the benefits accruing from use of the waterway would outweigh its construction costs—expected to exceed $1 billion. A major underlying facet of the controversy was the method used by the Army to compute the benefit-cost ratio of the canal—and of all other inland waterway proposals. The Board of Engineers for Rivers and Harbors had used two different methods of making this computation in recent years. An issue in 1966 was which of the two methods the Corps should use in the future.

Until November 1964, the Board figured the potential benefits of a proposed project by comparing the costs of shipping goods on the waterway with the costs of shipping the goods overland at the rates that overland transportation agencies in the area were charging. But in November 1964, under a Budget Bureau directive, the Board switched to figuring benefits on the basis of "water-compelled rates," which took into account rate decreases that probably would be put into effect as a competitive measure by land transportation carriers if the water project in question were built. In almost all cases, the benefits that a water project would produce were smaller under the water-compelled system of figuring because this sytem counted on less traffic in the proposed waterway as a result of land transportation rate decreases. No major projects were approved while the system was in effect.

The American Waterways Operators and other groups conducted a strong lobbying campaign against the water-compelled system. The Budget Bureau Aug. 24, 1966, announced that the system had been discontinued, and that the old way of figuring waterways benefits was back in effect—at least temporarily. It

indicated that other methods of making the benefit-cost ratio computation were under study.

The Board of Engineers for Rivers and Harbors, which passes on proposals for Army Corps projects, Sept. 9 announced that it had approved the Lake Erie-Ohio River canal. It said that the estimated total cost of the canal system, which would include 10 dams with dual locks along its route, was $1,012,000,000, of which $95 million would be paid by non-federal interests. It said the benefit-cost ratio, calculated under the system that was reinstated Aug. 24, was 1.3 to 1. This meant that for every dollar spent, $1.30 in benefits would be realized. The Board had not made a final benefit-cost ratio finding under the water-compelled rates system, an Army Corps source said.

The Senate Appropriations Committee, in its Oct. 3 report on HR 17787, said that the Budget Bureau currently was considering adopting a new and "unrealistic" formula for computing the benefit-cost ratio for waterway projects.

The report pointed out that the Senate had added to the bill to establish a new Department of Transportation (HR 15963) a provision to write into law the formula that was reinstated in August. The report said this provision would prevent adoption of the "unrealistic" formula that was being considered by the Budget Bureau.

The Senate-approved provision was retained in the Transportation Department bill as enacted Oct. 15. It specified that computation of the benefit-cost ratio was to be made by comparing the expected costs of moving goods on the proposed waterway with "the freight rates or charges prevailing at the time of the study for the movement by the alternative means." This wrote into law the computation formula used until November 1964.

The provision had originated in the Senate Government Operations Committee. In its report (S Rept 1659), the Committee said the provision was "deemed necessary in order to ensure that future projects will be evaluated on the same basis as those which have resulted in the development of this nation's outstanding system of inland navigation which has served so well in peace and war."

ment for revenues and payout on federal irrigation and federal hydroelectric power projects in the Columbia River basin. The new accounting system provided that revenues from the sale of electric power at all federal dams in the Columbia River basin be used to help pay for those portions of the capital costs of irrigation projects in the area which could not be covered by proceeds from the sales of irrigation water.

RIVERS AND HARBORS. Congress approved an omnibus bill (HR 18233—PL 89-789) authorizing construction by the Army Corps of Engineers of 40 federal water projects, at an estimated cost of $669,075,000 as the Federal Government's share. HR 18233 was the smallest omnibus bill of its kind in many years. However, it followed by only one year enactment of a similar measure that authorized nearly $2 billion for new federal water projects. *(See 1965 chronology.)*

The final bill contained river, harbor, flood control, beach erosion or hurricane protection projects for 25 states: Arkansas, California, Connecticut, Florida, Georgia, Idaho, Illinois, Iowa, Kansas, Kentucky, Louisiana, Massachusetts, Michigan, Mississippi, Missouri, New Jersey, New York, North Carolina, Ohio, Oklahoma, Pennsylvania, South Carolina, Texas, Washington, and West Virginia. Of the 40 authorizations in the bill for new projects or major modifications of existing projects, only five had estimated total costs of $25 million or more.

Two of the projects authorized by the bill contained new federal hydroelectric power facilities: the $132.9 million Marysville dam and reservoir on the Yuba River, Calif. (50,000 kilowatts installed capacity), and the $84.9 million Trotters Shoals project (dam and reservoir) on the Savannah River, Ga. and S.C. (310,000 kw). *(See box.)*

FEASIBILITY STUDIES. Congress enacted Administration-supported legislation (S 3034—PL 89-561) authorizing the Interior Department to proceed with or to initiate feasibility studies on 140 water development projects in the 17 Western states (and Alaska) served by the Bureau of Reclamation. The bill also included provisions regulating the timing and amounts of financial assistance that could be given to irrigation projects in the Columbia River Basin from revenues accruing from the sale of power produced at federal dams in the basin. These provisions were intended to ensure that irrigation assistance would not cause an increase in the power rates charged by the Bonneville Power Administration, the marketing agency for federal power produced at hydroelectric dams on the Columbia River and its tributaries.

S 3034 was the first bill ever passed by Congress to authorize Bureau of Reclamation feasibility studies. In the past, the Bureau had undertaken such studies without Congressional authorization; but under the provisions of the Federal Water Project Recreation Act of 1965 (PL 89-72), authorization was required. *(See 1965 chronology.)* Although Congress refused to authorize a few studies requested by the Bureau in its draft legislation and added others, there was little controversy on the measure. The bill did not authorize appropriations to defray Bureau of Reclamation expenses in conducting the studies. But later in the year, in the fiscal 1967 Public Works Appropriations Act (HR 17787), Congress provided $15,075,000 for the Bureau's general investigations of water projects. Approximately 36 percent of this amount, according to the Bureau, was for feasibility studies authorized by S 3034 for fiscal 1967.

Trotters Shoals Dispute

Authorization of the Trotters Shoals project ended a controversy of several years' duration over development of a stretch of the Savannah River, between Georgia and South Carolina. Essentially, the dispute was between Georgia, which wanted federal development of the Trotters Shoals site, and South Carolina, which wanted to protect use of the river for the Duke Power Company, a private concern. The solution in the bill allowed for both federal and private development. In addition to authorizing the federal Trotters Shoals project, the bill authorized the Duke Power Company to build a small dam at Middleton Shoals, 19.5 miles upstream from Trotters Shoals. The Duke dam was to divert water from the Savannah to cool a large thermal power plant that Duke planned to build on the South Carolina bank of the river. South Carolina had opposed authorization of the federal project for several years, fearing that it might not be compatible with the Duke plan.

TVA REVENUE BONDS. Congress passed without amendment an Administration-requested bill (HR 15225—PL 89-537) raising the ceiling on the amount of revenue bonds which the Tennessee Valley Authority (TVA) could sell to finance construction of new TVA electric power generating and transmission facilities. The TVA, a federal agency, is the principal producer of electric power in the Tennessee Valley Region. (For background on TVA, see *Congress and the Nation, Vol. I, p. 908-931.*)

HR 15225 increased the amount of revenue bonds which the TVA could have outstanding at any one time by $1 billion, to a total of $1,750,000,000. In requesting the legislation in a message to Congress, President Johnson said, "Without an increase in borrowing authority, TVA cannot continue to carry out its responsibility to meet the growing demand for electric power in the Tennessee Valley." He said the power needs of the TVA marketing area would double over the next decade, and the added $1 billion in borrowing authority would be sufficient to finance new TVA power facility construction for about seven years. The increase was the only provision in HR 15225.

SMALL IRRIGATION PROJECTS. Congress completed action on a bill (S 602—PL 89-553) increasing the total appropriations authorization for the 1956 Small Reclamation Projects Act from $100 million to $200 million. Under the Act, the Federal Government gave loans and grants to local water users' organizations in the West to help pay for construction of small water projects, usually for purposes of irrigation. S 602 also raised the dollar ceiling on the amount of aid the Government could give to such a group. And it provided that recreation and fish and wildlife enhancement features at any project built with federal aid under the Act be governed by the cost-sharing rules established by the Federal Water Project Recreation Act of 1965. *(See 1965 chronology.)*

RIO GRANDE CANAL. Congress enacted legislation (S 2747—PL 89-584) authorizing conclusion of an agreement between the United States and Mexico for joint construction, operation and maintenance of a drainage canal in the lower Rio Grande Valley to reduce

Objections to Committee Veto Power

President Johnson in 1966 objected to provisions of three laws authorizing appropriations for small water projects whose construction had been approved by the Executive Branch and by Congressional committees, but not by Congress as a whole. Mr. Johnson said the procedure requiring Congressional action only on the committee level violated the constitutional separation of powers between the Executive and Legislative Branches. His Administration, warning that it would delay the construction programs in 1967 by refusing to use the committee approval procedure, requested legislation to give Executive agencies greater freedom of action. Under the Administration proposals, the power to veto Executive plans was to be stripped from the committees, although it would remain with Congress as a whole. The laws were:

• The Small Reclamation Projects Act, under which the Bureau of Reclamation could make loans or grants to local groups for construction of small irrigation projects. The Bureau was required to submit loan or grant proposals to the House and Senate Interior and Insular Affairs Committees, either of which could veto the proposal within 60 days. (None had ever been vetoed.) *(See Congress and the Nation, Vol. I, p. 853.)*

• The Small Watershed Act, under which the Soil Conservation Service could make loans or grants to local groups for construction of small water projects. All but the smallest projects had to be approved by resolutions of the House and Senate Agriculture Committees or Public Works Committees, depending on the size of the project. *(See Congress and the Nation, Vol. I, p. 1021.)*

• The 1965 Flood Control, River and Harbor Acts, under which the Army Corps of Engineers could build water projects costing less than $10 million, if they were approved by resolutions of the House and Senate Public Works Committees.

The Administration forwarded small reclamation project proposals to the Interior and Insular Affairs Committees throughout the year. No small watershed projects, however, were forwarded to the Committees until July 25, 1966, when under Congressional pressure the Budget Bureau released a backlog of 56 projects. Small projects of the Army Corps of Engineers were also held up until late in the session, and when they were forwarded to the Public Works Committees, the Administration said it would not consider them authorized (and presumably would not spend money to build them, even if money were appropriated) unless they were included in a River, Harbor and Flood Control authorization bill. This was subsequently done, in the 1966 omnibus water bill (HR 18233—PL 89-789).

Late in 1966 the President asked deletion of similar committee-veto provisions in two other laws: the Public Buildings Act of 1959, in which buildings proposed for construction by the General Services Administration had to have committee approval; *(See Congress and the Nation, Vol. I, p. 1467);* and the Bankhead-Jones Farm Tenant Act, which required committee approval for rural renewal loans.

in 1965, Mr. Johnson vetoed two major public bills on similar grounds.

salinity in the Rio Grande River. The bill empowered the Secretary of State to complete plans with Mexican officials to build a 23-mile drainage channel to carry saline water from the El Morillo River to the Gulf of Mexico, bypassing the Rio Grande. Under the provisions of the bill, the United States and Mexico were to share equally the $1.38-million total cost of construction and an annual maintenance cost of $40,000. The bill authorized appropriations of $690,000 for the U.S. share of construction costs and of $20,000 a year for operation. Before the United States could participate, however, it was required to obtain assurances that half of its actual costs would be paid by private citizens or a local group. The Lower Rio Grande Water Committee, formed in response to the bill's requirements, promised in a letter to the Secretary of State to pay half the U.S. costs.

SOUTHERN NEVADA PROJECT. Congress cleared the way for construction of the Southern Nevada water diversion project by enacting a bill (S 2999—PL 89-510) amending a controversial section (Section 6) of the Southern Nevada Project Act of 1965, to satisfy an Administration request. S 2999 amended Section 6 to specifically protect the water usage rights of Basic Management Inc., a group of four water-using industrial concerns in Nevada. As originally enacted, the section had been intended to serve the same purpose, but it was couched in general language which the Administration feared might have application beyond the intent of Congress. Because of its objections to the section as originally written, the Administration had not requested appropriation of funds to begin construction of the $81,003,000 water diversion project. But after enactment of S 2999, Congress in the fiscal 1967 Public Works Appropriations bill (HR 17787) appropriated $1 million to initiate pre-construction planning on the project.

NUCLEAR DESALTING PLANT. Congress enacted an Administration bill (S 3807—PL 89-648) authorizing the Atomic Energy Commission (AEC) to participate in the development of a very large nuclear power and desalination project in Southern California. S 3807, approved Oct. 13, authorized appropriation of $15 million as the AEC's share of the project's costs. The project was to be built in cooperation with the Interior Department, the Metropolitan Water District of Southern California, and three California power utilities, at a total cost of $444.3 million. At full capacity, it would produce 150 million gallons of desalted water per day—much more than was produced at any existing desalting plant—and would have an installed capacity of 1.8 million kilowatts. The desalting plant would be the first to produce water that was commercially competitive with natural fresh water.

The Southern California project offered the prospect of the first large-scale application of nuclear energy to the desalting process, the first big joint power and desalination plant, and the production of an unprecedented volume of commercially competitive desalted water. The project was not seen as the solution to all the technological problems that the desalination program had encountered, but it was a major step in that direction. The huge size of the new project would cause the cost of water it produced to be low; technology had yet to be developed that would make small desalting plants economically attractive.

TIJUANA RIVER. A bill (S 2540—PL 89-640) authorizing conclusion of an agreement between the United States and Mexico for a joint flood control project on the Tijuana River at the international boundary was approved by Congress. It authorized appropriations of $12.6 million for construction of the U.S. portion of the project and such sums as were needed for operation and maintenance. The project authorized was an 8.4-mile, concrete-lined channel on the lower reaches of the Tijuana, which flows from Mexico through Southern California to its outlet at San Diego. The Mexican government was to build and maintain 2.7 miles of the channel. The cost to the United States of constructing the remainder was estimated in 1965 at $15.4 million, of which San Diego had agreed to pay about $4.5 million. The $12.6 million authorized in the bill allowed for cost increases expected during the period of construction.

WATER CONFERENCE. Congress enacted an amended Administration bill (SJ Res 167—PL 89-799) authorizing Government officials to plan for and to hold an International Conference on Water for Peace, in Washington, D.C., in 1967. The House passed the bill over the opposition of a conservative faction. A spokesman for House opponents predicted that the conference would be a "booze" party at the expense of taxpayers. Supporters said that a great conference would focus attention on mankind's need for water and would stimulate international cooperation in meeting the need. The sum of $900,000 was appropriated to defray conference expenses.

Miscellaneous Bills

POWER LINES STUDY. The Senate passed an Administration-backed measure (SJ Res 189) directing the Secretary of Housing and Urban Development (HUD) to study the economic and scenic effects of overhead power lines. The bill, passed without debate, was reported by the Commerce Committee following hearings on several related bills. The House took no action on SJ Res 189 or on any of the related bills.

WATER COMMISSION. Congress failed to enact an Administration bill (S 3107) establishing a nonfederal National Water Commission to review U.S. water resource problems and to identify possible solutions to the problems. The Senate passed S 3107 without controversy, but in the House the issue became embroiled in a dispute over Western water problems and never reached the floor.

Growth of Regional Power Systems in the United States

Many residents of the Northeast were surprised to learn that their lights could go out because of a relay failure in Canada. The fact is that electric power facilities within the United States and between the United States and adjoining countries—Canada and Mexico—have become increasingly interconnected. U.S. systems are linked to Canadian systems at a number of points; the six most important interconnections are at the St. Lawrence Seaway Dam, Niagara Falls, Windsor-Detroit, and three points in the Northwest near Nelway, B.C., and Blaine, Wash. International interties are scheduled to increase in the future. Under a treaty whose ratification was completed in 1964, for example, Canada is to build three dams on the Columbia River in British Columbia. The dams will make possible increased hydroelectric production at American plants downstream, and Canada is to have the right to one-half of the additional power.

Within the United States itself, 97 percent of total power generation is hooked into five regional systems, although the degree of interconnection within the systems varies widely. In a National Power Survey, published in 1964, the Federal Power Commission noted that the extent of the interconnections ranges "from fully integrated pools in which the capacity of several power systems is planned and built to meet the combined needs of the entire interconnected group to situations in which two systems merely have joined in a low capacity for emergency purposes only."

The largest assemblage of interconnected systems, involving more than one-half of the nation's generating capacity, covers all of the United States east of the Rockies except Texas, plus two provinces in eastern Canada. The network is made up of three groups: (1) the Canada-U.S. Eastern Interconnection, or CANUSE, the system involved in the November 1965 power failure; (2) the Pennsylvania-New Jersey-Maryland Interconnection; and (3) the Interconnected Systems Group, which includes the Middle West and the South. Each of two other major networks—the Northwest Interconnected Systems Groups covering all of six states and parts of seven additional states, and the Pacific Southwest Interconnected Group, connecting the systems of four states—supplies about 11 percent of the country's total electric power production. In addition, there are two small power pools, the Texas Power Pool and the Rio Grande-New Mexico pool.

Within the five large systems, the 3,600 electric utility companies in the United States are joined into a number of groups and power pools. With federal encouragement, the number of pools and interconnected systems is growing. The rationale behind development of regional systems and inter-regional links is economic. Electricity cannot be stored for use when the customer needs it; an electrical system must have sufficient generating capacity to meet demands on it at the times of peak usage. At other times much of this capacity lies idle. But the peak loads of individual customers within a system occur at different times, just as the peak loads in different cities occur at different times.

In a country that spans a continent, peak load patterns exhibit the greatest diversity and offer broad opportunities for making the most efficient use of power generating capacity. The peak load in New York City occurs during morning and evening rush hours; but these hours precede rush hours in Chicago. Similarly, peak seasonal loads in the Pacific Northwest occur during the winter, when regional generating capacity, which is largely hydroelectric, is at its lowest because of reduced river flow. In Texas and the Southwest, however, loads are greatest during the summer due to the demand for electric energy for air conditioning.

President Johnson had formally proposed establishment of a National Water Commission in his 1966 message to Congress on conservation. *(See 1968 chronology.)*

COLORADO BASIN PROJECT. Congress failed to enact a bill (HR 4671) authorizing the Interior Department's Bureau of Reclamation to build several large water development projects in the Colorado River Basin, at a total cost of more than $1.7 billion. The primary purpose of the bill was to authorize construction of the Central Arizona Project, a $580 million plan to divert water from the Colorado River into central Arizona. Additional provisions, inserted in the bill as the price exacted by other Colorado River Basin states for their support of the Central Arizona Project, expanded HR 4671 into an ambitious and expensive regional water development plan. The resulting controversy blocked passage of the measure. *(See 1968 chronology.)*

1967

No water or power legislation of broad national significance was enacted in 1967. In his message to Congress on pollution, resources, and road safety, President Johnson made only one legislative recommendation: to establish a National Water Commission which would "examine our major water problems and develop recommendations, guidelines, and long-range plans for the most effective use of available water resources." As in 1966, Congress failed in 1967 to enact legislation creating such a commission. A number of water and power projects—but many fewer than in 1965 or 1966—were authorized.

PUBLIC WORKS. After months of controversy over federal funding of a proposed hydroelectric power project in Maine, Congress enacted the annual public works and Atomic Energy Commission appropriations bill (HR 11641—PL 90-147), which provided funds for construction of public works water development projects by the Army Corps of Engineers and the Bureau of Reclamation; for the Federal Water Pollution Control Administration; for several independent federal agencies including the Tennessee Valley Authority; and for Interior Department power agencies such as the Bonneville Power Administration.

Appropriations for Corps of Engineers public works projects totaled $1,298,129,000 for fiscal 1968. That sum included funds for 34 new construction starts with a total estimated federal cost of $177.8 million. There was only one new start whose total estimated federal cost exceeded $25 million: New York Harbor anchorages ($47.5 million). The $177.8 million figure for new starts was unusually low. In fiscal 1967, Congress had provided money for 58 Corps of Engineers new starts with a total estimated federal cost of $935.3 million. Also unusual was the fact that none of the Corps' new starts contained major power features. Atomic Energy Commission appropriations included $507,458,000 for nuclear reactor development.

The Public Works-AEC funding bill for the first time included appropriations ($295.8 million) for the Federal Water Pollution Control Administration, which was transferred in 1966 from the Health, Education and Welfare Department to the Interior Department. Another major Interior Department agency funded by HR 11641, the

Bureau of Reclamation, received $314,047,000 for its fiscal 1968 irrigation and power activities.

Final action on HR 11641 came after the Senate accepted a House amendment to delete all funds for continued planning of the much-debated Dickey-Lincoln School power project in Maine. The Senate action came after the House had rejected a motion to accept a compromise figure of $875,000 for the project. The Dickey-Lincoln School controversy, in which public power advocates (supported by the Johnson Administration) were successfully opposed by a coalition of conservationists and private power spokesmen, was one of several issues which had delayed swift passage of the fiscal 1968 appropriation bill. *(See box.)*

SALINE WATER. Congress completed action on an amended Administration bill (HR 6133—PL 90-30) authorizing additional appropriations for the saline water conversion program. The bill also authorized the Office of Saline Water (OSW) to construct "test bed" facilities and clarified existing provisions of law relating to the sequence of water conversion facilities to be constructed by the OSW.

Congress denied an Administration request for continuing the saline water program authorization for three years, through fiscal 1970. The bill's supporters argued that the program should be subjected to annual scrutiny by the appropriate legislative committees. Therefore, Congress extended the authorization for only one year—fiscal 1968.

As a result of action on HR 6133, the OSW was authorized appropriations totaling $26,782,000 (the figure requested by the Administration) for its research program in fiscal 1968. That figure was composed of $23,282,000 in authorized but unappropriated funds, and $3.5 million in previously appropriated but unobligated funds. In the end, a total of $19.8 million was appropriated for the OSW in fiscal 1968—$9.8 million in the Interior Department appropriations bill (HR 9029—PL 90-28) and $10 million in the first supplemental appropriations bill (HR 14397—PL 90-239).

NUCLEAR DESALTING PLANT. Congress cleared an Administration-backed bill (S 270—PL 90-18) authorizing the Interior Department to participate in construction of a huge nuclear power and water-desalting plant in Southern California. S 270, approved May 19, authorized appropriations of $57.2 million as the Interior Department's share of a total project cost of $444.3 million. The plant was to be built in cooperation with the Atomic Energy Commission (AEC), the Metropolitan Water District of Southern California and three California power utilities. Congress in 1966 had enacted legislation authorizing appropriations of $15 million as the AEC's share of the project's cost. The Southern California project offered the prospect of the first large-scale application of nuclear energy to the desalting process, the first large combined power and desalting plant and production of an unprecedented amount of commercially desalted water. At full capacity—to be reached in 1977—the plant was to produce 150 million gallons of desalted water daily, far more than was produced by any existing plant, and it was to have a power generating capacity of 1.8 million kilowatts. (The project was killed by Congress in 1968.)

SAN FELIPE PROJECT. Congress completed action on an amended Administration-backed bill (S 1111—PL 90-72) authorizing the Interior Department to construct

Controversial Dickey-Lincoln Power Project Stalled by House

The most controversial item in the fiscal 1968 Public Works-Atomic Energy Commission appropriation bill (HR 11641) was planning funds for the Dickey-Lincoln School power project in northern Maine. In the final bill, Congress denied all requested funds for the Corps of Engineers power project after the Senate unsuccessfully tried to compromise with the House to retain a token amount for the project.

Instrumental in the successful effort to delete the funds was a vigorous lobbying campaign conducted by New England private power company spokesmen. Almost all House Republicans, joined by some Democrats, voted against the public power project funds. The project was supported by public power groups and a majority of Northern and Southern Democrats on two of three votes; a majority of Southerners joined Republicans on the third.

Since its authorization by Congress in 1965 (PL 89-298), the controversial project had received a total of $1.9 million in planning funds for fiscal years 1966 and 1967.

The final defeat for Dickey-Lincoln School supporters in 1967 occurred when the House rejected for the second time a compromise appropriation of $875,000 for fiscal 1968 planning. The Administration had originally requested $1,676,000. It was the third 1967 House roll call on the issue. On each occasion the House by a substantial margin refused further support for the project.

Following the House vote, the Senate yielded to House wishes and approved HR 11641 by voice vote, without Dickey-Lincoln School funds, and cleared the measure.

Although project supporters, led by Sen. Edmund S. Muskie (D Maine), insisted that the legislative defeat was a "strategic retreat" until a more favorable time, other Members believed that the project might be delayed indefinitely. Sen. George D. Aiken (R Vt.), ranking Senate Republican and a project backer, noted that when Congress "dropped a project from the public works bill," it normally was "awfully hard to get back in future years."

Background. The Dickey-Lincoln School project, authorized in 1965 amid intense controversy, was designed to furnish federal electric power to the New England region for the first time. The project was approved despite the objections of private power companies which contended that it was unnecessary and represented subsidized competition for their own power.

The major issue in 1965—and again in 1967—was whether federal facilities should be built in New England to provide a "yardstick" for all power rates in the entire six-state area. Such "yardsticks" existed in every other part of the nation. Proponents of the project pointed to New England electric rates, which in 1967 were 25 percent higher than the national average, as justification for constructing the project. Opponents claimed, however, that higher rates were necessary in New England because of the natural shortage of abundant water power and coal, the principal sources of power to generate electricity.

Congress in 1965 and 1966 appropriated the first planning funds for the Dickey-Lincoln School project, under the 1965 authorization. By early 1967, 30 percent of planning studies were completed. Appropriations for planning were $800,000 for fiscal 1966 and $1.1 million for fiscal 1967.

As authorized, the project included construction of the Dickey Dam, containing a 760,000 kilowatt hydroelectric generating plant, on the Upper St. John River, and the Lincoln School Dam, with a 34,000 kilowatt generating plant, on the St. John River 11 miles downstream from the Dickey Dam. The cost of high-voltage transmission facilities to distribute peaking power produced by the two dams was not included in the $227-million authorization. The transmission lines were estimated in 1965 to require an additional $76 million.

Project Review. The House Appropriations Committee in 1966 ordered a staff study of the Dickey-Lincoln School project, with emphasis on its "economic feasibility and soundness." The Committee was prompted by private power company claims that recent developments in nuclear power plant construction had made further work on Dickey-Lincoln unnecessary. However, the results of the study, presented to the Committee in 1967, were generally favorable to proceeding with the project. The report contained revised estimates of total costs, setting the amount of funds needed at $229,313,000, exclusive of transmission facilities.

Action. The Appropriations Committee recommended $1,676,000 (as requested) for continued fiscal 1968 planning, but the House deleted the funds by a roll-call vote on an amendment offered by Robert N. Giaimo (D Conn.), a leading House opponent of the project.

After the Senate Oct. 10 passed HR 11641 with the full amount requested, conferees agreed to an $875,000 compromise figure. This was rejected in the House by a roll-call vote.

Finally, the House reiterated its position against the compromise figure by another roll-call vote, thus creating an impasse which the Senate ended by accepting the House position.

Lobby Groups. During Senate discussion of the Dickey-Lincoln School project, Muskie noted that Members of Congress "have told me...they cannot recall a more vicious lobbying campaign against any single project."

The 1967 lobbying drive was organized by the Electric Coordinating Council of New England, an association of chief executives of the 19 largest private power companies in the six-state region. Major companies included: Maine Public Service Co., Central Maine Power Co., Bangor (Maine) Hydro Electric Co., Public Service Co. of New Hampshire, Boston Electric Co., New England Electric System, Connecticut Light and Power Co., Hartford Electric Light Co. and United Illuminating Co. (Conn.).

Water Pollution Hearings

Senate and House Committees in 1967 held hearings to investigate the progress of federal water pollution control programs. Under the Water Quality Act of 1965 and the Clean Waters Restoration Act of 1966 *(see 1965 and 1966 chronology)*, all states were to submit proposed quality standards to the Federal Water Pollution Control Administration by June 30, 1967. In addition, the 1966 Act provided for federal grants to aid in the construction of waste treatment facilities. The Act authorized $450 million for such grants in fiscal 1968. Congressional criticism was aroused when the Administration's fiscal 1968 Budget request included only $200 million for waste treatment facility construction.

House. In hearings held by the House Public Works Subcommittee on Rivers and Harbors, Interior Secretary Stewart L. Udall defended the request for reduced fiscal 1968 funds. "I don't feel that the severity of the reduction is in the ratio of $200 million to $450 million as many seem to assume," Udall said. Some states still had fiscal 1967 funds available, Udall explained, while other states had not yet established water purity standards which would enable them to receive 50 percent grants for facility construction.

New York Gov. Nelson A. Rockefeller (R) commended the Subcommittee for holding the hearings and said that progress in pollution control might be threatened by the "unwise" proposed reduction in budgeted funds for construction grants. The pollution problem was so serious, Rockefeller said, that even the appropriation of all currently authorized funds would cause New York to "fall behind in meeting...urgent needs." He estimated that the cost of constructing treatment plants to clean up the nation's water—reckoned at $20 billion through 1972—would increase to $31 billion if the program were stretched out another decade by budget cuts.

Senate. In hearings held by the Senate Public Works Subcommittee on Air and Water Pollution, Udall said he expected "acceptable standards for almost all interstate and coastal waters" to be approved "no later than the end of this year," which would complete "the first phase" of the federal pollution control effort. The "second and continuing phase," the Secretary said, was "even more challenging and demanding" because "in this second step we must monitor water quality to assure that...implementation...is carried out." In the absence of state action to enforce compliance with established pollution abatement timetables, he added, federal regulation would be applied.

Frank C. DiLuzio, Assistant Secretary of the Interior for Water Pollution Control, testified that new kinds of water pollution, such as the overheating of streams by electric power generating plant discharges, necessitated development of a "whole range of options" for pollution abatement.

and operate the San Felipe addition to the Central Valley water project in California. The multipurpose San Felipe unit was designed to ensure future water supplies—for irrigation, industrial and municipal uses, wildlife conservation and recreational purposes—in portions of four California counties (Santa Clara, San Benito, Santa Cruz and Monterey) situated south and west of San Francisco Bay. S 1111 authorized appropriations of $92,380,000 for the San Felipe project.

Specific features of the project included: (1) a canal, tunnel and pipeline system to transport water into the four-county area from the Sacramento-San Joaquin Delta, with storage facilities at the existing San Luis reservoir; and (2) construction of several pumping plants, three small regulatory reservoirs and distribution facilities. Construction of the San Felipe unit was required by depletion of the natural underground water supplies of a region which in recent years had experienced substantial growth in population and industrial activity.

Miscellaneous Bills

POLLUTION CONTROL. The Senate passed an omnibus water pollution control bill (S 2760) to combat lake, mine, and oil pollution, but the House did not act on it in 1967. S 2760, the Federal Water Pollution Control Act Amendments of 1967, authorized pilot programs to prevent and control lake pollution and acid or other mine water pollution. Authorization of a comprehensive program to fight oil pollution, modeled after the Oil Pollution Act of 1924, also was included in the bill.

CENTRAL ARIZONA PROJECT. The Senate passed an Administration-backed bill (S 1004) authorizing construction of the Central Arizona Project and five other water projects in the Colorado River Basin. The House took no action. Bills to authorize the project had been considered by Congress since 1948 and twice before had passed the Senate, in 1950 and 1951. *(For eventual passage of the Central Arizona Project bill and background, see 1968 chronology.)*

WATER COMMISSION. For the second year in a row, Congress failed to enact an Administration-requested measure to establish a nonfederal National Water Commission to review U.S. water resource problems and to identify possible solutions. The Senate and the House each passed a bill (S 20) to establish a National Water Commission, but the bills differed in a number of provisions. As the first session of the 90th Congress ended, S 20 was pending in the Senate, awaiting a decision whether to ask for a conference with the House or to accept House amendments. *(For passage of bill, see 1968 chronology.)*

POWER REGULATION. Congress did not act on a bill (S 1365) to prohibit the Federal Power Commission (FPC) from regulating electric utilities whose operations were conducted substantially within a single state. S 1365 also specifically exempted all rural electric cooperatives from FPC regulation. The Senate Commerce Committee held hearings on the bill, but it was not reported by the Committee.

1968

Two of President Johnson's three major requests for water legislation were granted by Congress in 1968. After more than two decades of controversy, action was completed on a bill authorizing construction of the huge Central Arizona water diversion project and various other water development projects in the Colorado River Basin. The total cost of the authorized projects would be around $1.3 billion, making this the largest reclamation program ever authorized in a single piece of legislation. In a message to Congress on conservation, the President had described it as "a plan...that will require no dams on the Colorado River, preserve its scenic values, and at the same time permit the immediate construction of essential water supply facilities."

For the third consecutive year, Mr. Johnson urged Congress to adopt legislation establishing a National Water Commission, and in 1968 Congress did so. However, no action was taken on a third Presidential request—passage of the proposed Safe Drinking Water Act of 1968. The overriding goal of the proposed legislation was that "Every glass of drinking water drawn from America's public water supply systems will meet proper health standards." As in previous years, Congress in 1968 authorized a host of individual water and power projects.

Colorado River Project

Passage of the bill (S 1004—PL 90-537) authorizing construction of the Central Arizona Project and related water projects on the Colorado River was of immense importance to the arid states of the Southwest. Thousands of acres of land in the region were in danger of becoming barren wasteland as underground sources of water were depleted. S 1004, however, held promise of eliminating this danger, or of at least postponing it for many years, during which time additional measures for meeting the water needs of the area could be proposed and implemented. Because of its significance to a large and fast-growing region of the country, S 1004 became the center of the most intensive lobby pressures of any public works bill in recent memory.

The Central Arizona Project was a 400-mile system of aqueducts, dams and associated works to divert water from the mainstream of the Colorado River to the arid areas around Phoenix and Tucson in the central and southern parts of the state. Power for pumping the water was to be obtained through a unique plan for federal acquisition of an interest in a joint public-private thermal power plant. The cost of the Central Arizona Project and the power purchase arrangement was put at $892 million.

Also authorized were five reclamation projects on the Western Slope of Colorado, with a total cost of $392 million. Three of the five projects in 1966 had received unfavorable reports from the Budget Bureau, which is usually enough to block authorization. All of the projects were located in the fourth Congressional District of Colorado, represented by Chairman Wayne N. Aspinall of the House Interior and Insular Affairs Committee. That committee had jurisdiction over S 1004.

Other provisions of S 1004 gave California an important water usage guarantee, relieved the Colorado River Basin states of responsibility for financing works to provide water due to Mexico under a 1944 treaty, and protected the Northwest—for 10 years—from studies of plans to divert some of its water to the arid Southwest.

The Interior Department's Bureau of Reclamation, created under the Reclamation Act of 1902, was responsible for developing the water resources of 17 Western states so as to provide irrigation for arid areas, as well as flood control and hydroelectric power. Over the years, because water was scarce in the Southwest, allocation of water resources became a major economic and political issue in the area. The Colorado River, the Southwest's main source of water, was at the center of most of the controversies; of primary concern was the fact that, by late in the 20th Century, the river's annual flow would not suffice to serve the areas that depended on it.

Under a 1922 compact, the seven Colorado River Basin states agreed to divide the river's water evenly between the Upper Basin states (Colorado, Wyoming, Utah and New Mexico) and the Lower Basin states (California, Arizona and Nevada). Each part of the Basin was allotted 7.5 million acre-feet of water annually. (An acre foot is the amount of water needed to cover one acre of land to a depth of one foot, or 325,900 gallons.)

In 1944, the United States signed a treaty guaranteeing that Mexico would receive 1.5 million acre-feet a year from the Colorado River. That brought allocated annual usage up to 16.5 million acre-feet. But the river's average annual flow from 1922-67 was only about 13.7 million acre-feet.

The first proposal to construct the Central Arizona Project was made in 1947. The Senate twice passed a bill, in 1950 and 1951, that included the Central Arizona Project and a dam at Bridge Canyon near the Grand Canyon. But the House Interior and Insular Affairs Committee in 1951 voted to put off the bill until the continuing dispute over apportionment of the Lower Basin's share of the water was resolved. With that, Arizona in 1952 filed suit in the Supreme Court to resolve the water allocation dispute, and legislative activity ceased.

It was not until 1963 that the Court rendered its decision in the case of *Arizona v. California.* Among the various apportionment formulae advanced, the Court chose the one set forth in the Boulder Canyon Project Act of 1928, which had divided the Lower Basin's 7.5 million acre-feet as follows: California, 4.4 million; Arizona, 2.8 million; Nevada, 300,000; this apportionment never had been agreed to by the three states involved. The Court also said that the Secretary of the Interior had broad discretion on how to allocate reductions among the states in cases of shortages of water.

Following the Supreme Court decision, efforts were renewed to enact Central Arizona Project legislation. In 1963, Secretary of the Interior Stewart L. Udall proposed

---

Lobbying on Bill

The Colorado River Project was the subject of the most intensive lobby pressures of any public works bill in many years. For details, see separate story at the end of this subchapter.

---

his Southwest Water Plan, an ambitious regional development scheme that included the Central Arizona Project, two dams on the stretch of the Colorado River that runs through Arizona, and various other features. In 1964, the Senate Interior and Insular Affairs Committee reported a bill embodying those three main features, but it did not receive further action.

Hearings were held in 1965 on the Southwest water bills, and the seven basin states conducted intensive negotiations late in the year. Those negotiations brought concessions and compromises among the states. The compromises provided for intensive study of plans for

---

Background

Congress since 1948 had considered proposals to divert Colorado River water from western Arizona to the area around Phoenix and Tucson in south-central Arizona. This region faced the prospect of severe water shortages. No authorizing legislation had been enacted, however, largely because Members of Congress from other Western states feared that the Arizona diversion project ultimately would create water shortages elsewhere. The problem was that the Colorado River did not contain enough water to satisfy the demands of its users.

The Colorado long has been a major source of water for many of the areas it touches, including the arid states of Arizona and (Southern) California. It was estimated that the river had about 13-15 million acre-feet of mainstream water available for various uses in each year.

In 1922, the seven states of the Colorado River Basin drew up the Colorado River Compact, allocating use of the river's water. The compact divided the river into the Upper Basin (Colorado, New Mexico, Utah and Wyoming), and the Lower Basin (Arizona, California and Nevada). The compact allocated the use of 7.5 million acre-feet of water annually to each of the two basins. States within each basin were allocated a certain portion of the 7.5 million acre-feet. In addition, a 1944 treaty provided that 1.5 million acre-feet of Colorado River water was to be delivered annually to Mexico. An additional 1 million acre-feet was lost annually in the Lower Basin through evaporation. Thus, the total legal allocations of river water amounted to 17.5 million acre-feet annually, compared to the 13-15 million acre-feet of water which actually was available for allocation.

Until recent years, the disparity between legal allocations and the actual water supply seemed academic because all the Colorado River Basin states (especially the Upper Basin states) were not using all the water to which they were entitled. Currently, Lower Basin states were using about 6.5 million acre-feet annually, Upper Basin states used about 3 million acre-feet, 1.5 million acre-feet went to Mexico under the 1944 treaty, and 1 million acre-feet were lost through evaporation. But the total annual use of 12 million acre-feet was nearing the river's annual average flow of 13-15 million acre-feet and this fact raised problems of future water shortages.

inter-basin transfers to supplement the Colorado's water (insisted on by the Upper Basin states and California) and gave California a guarantee that it would not have to cut back its water usage to below 4.4 million acre-feet in the event of shortages. In 1966, the compromises were embodied in a bill (HR 4671) which was endorsed by all seven Governors of the Basin, marking the first time that unanimity among the Basin states had been achieved. The House Interior Committee held hearings in May on HR 4671, but waited until August to report it. During that interval, the Sierra Club, an influential San Francisco-based conservation organization, had time to mount one of the most intensive lobbying efforts in the history of the conservation movement in opposition to the proposed construction of two hydroelectric dams on the section of the Colorado River that runs through the Grand Canyon. The Administration initially supported construction of both dams.

After the Sierra Club's lobbying had generated an extensive letter-writing campaign against the dams, the Administration during 1966 hearings on the bill indicated that it might be willing to accept only one of the dams. Finally, in 1967, Udall dropped both of the dams and proposed the plan for the Government to buy an interest in a joint public-private thermal power plant. This was the plan that Congress eventually approved.

During its lobbying campaign, the Sierra Club distributed copies of expensive, glossy books on the Grand Canyon and Glen Canyon to every Member of Congress, and paid for full-page advertisements in *The New York Times* and other newspapers attacking the dams. The Internal Revenue Service in 1966 removed the Sierra Club's right to receive tax deductible contributions on the ground that it was violating laws prohibiting nonprofit organizations from lobbying, but that only served to give the Sierra Club and its cause increased publicity.

The Sierra Club's victory in the biggest conservation lobbying battle in more than a decade was a singular defeat for the states of the Colorado River Basin. The dams were needed, their proponents said, not only to provide hydroelectric peaking power, but also to provide revenues for the basin's development fund, established under the bill. The development fund was to provide a source of money for future works to augment the supply of water in the Colorado River.

The matter of augmentation, quite aside from the financing of augmentation, was an issue of high controversy. Proposals for a detailed study of the feasibility of importing water into the Colorado River Basin from other basins were bitterly fought by Members of Congress from the Pacific Northwest, who feared that the Southwest had its eye on the two major rivers in the Northwest: the Columbia and the Snake. The Northwest opposed any detailed importation study until completion of a general study of water availability and need on a regional basis. California and the Upper Colorado Basin states believed that quick action on augmentation was imperative in light of the dwindling supply of Colorado River water.

The Northwest's position prevailed in the end, as S 1004 put a 10-year moratorium on any importation studies and ordered a general study of water availability and needs. That this region's view had prevailed over the unanimous position of the far more populous Southwestern states with their large voting bloc in the House was due in no small part to the fact that the Northwest's chief

COLORADO RIVER BASIN PROJECT

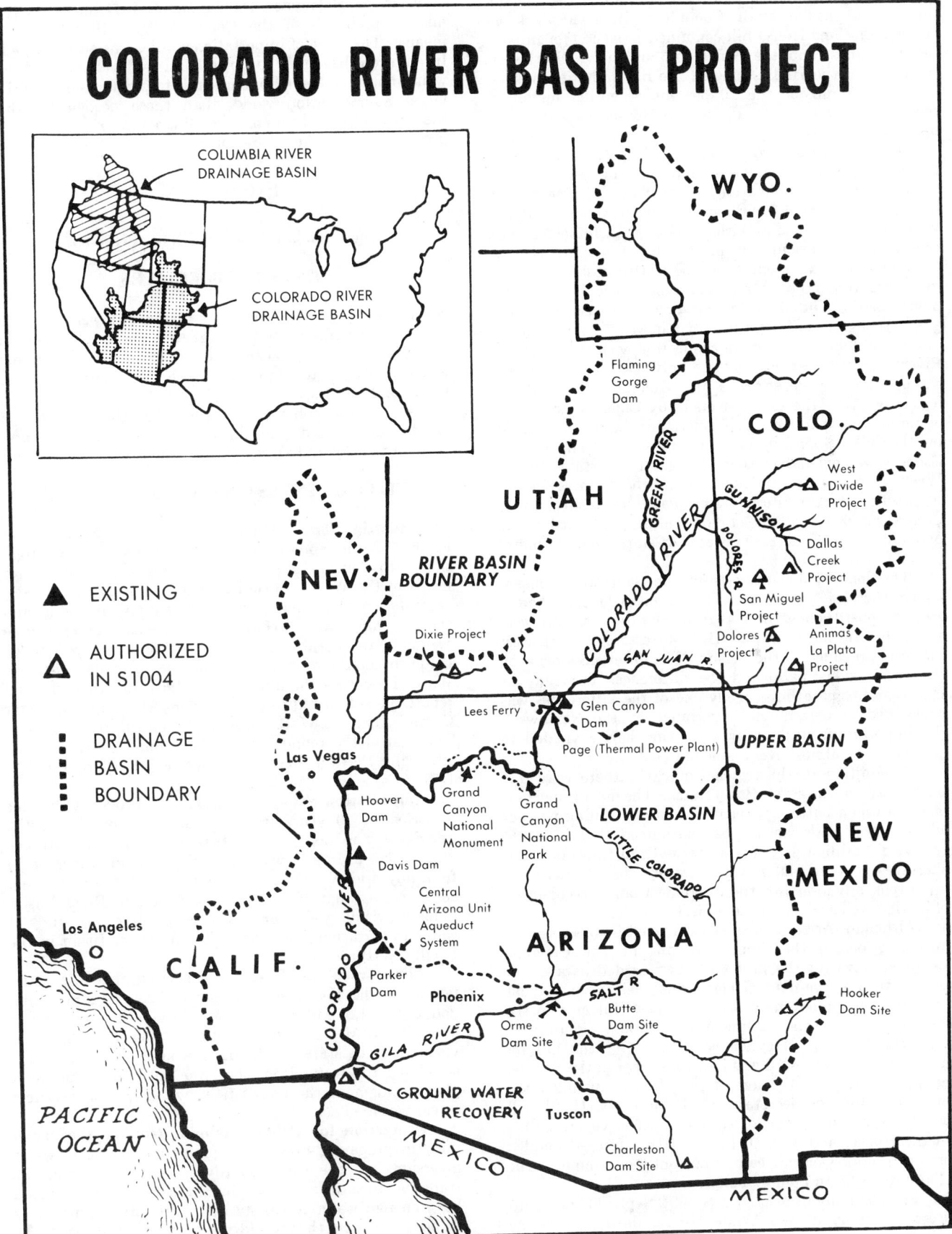

spokesman on the issue was the chairman of the Senate Interior and Insular Affairs Committee, Henry M. Jackson (D Wash.). The House bill contained provision for importation studies, and the Senate bill did not. Northwest Members in the House opposed the bill and tried unsuccessfully to muster the 20 percent of voting members required to force a roll-call vote on House passage of the bill May 16.

The Northwest also put up some opposition to a controversial provision which declared as national, rather than regional, an obligation incurred in the 1944 treaty to provide Mexico 1.5 million acre-feet of Colorado River water annually. The provision was of great importance to the Southwest because it meant that the costs of any Colorado River augmentation works attributable to satisfying the treaty obligation would be borne by the taxpayers of the United States, not just of the Basin states.

Although the Sierra Club's battle was the most widely publicized lobbying effort in connection with the Colorado River legislation, it was not the only one. It was known throughout consideration of the Colorado River Basin legislation that the decision made by Congress would be of immense economic significance, and interests affected by the bill responded with that in mind. The biggest issues were regional ones involving all the states in the West. Accordingly, the Governors of those states, particularly the Southwestern states, came to testify before Congress and sent dozens of representatives to Washington periodically; in some cases, states or state agencies maintained full-time lobbyists in the Capital.

The lobbies for interests in the Southwest concentrated their efforts on the House, because they had a greater constituency there than in the Senate, and were successful in most cases. By contrast, the Northwest interests prevailed in the Senate. The differences between the two regions paralleled the differences between the House and Senate bills. Only one of the differences was considered of paramount importance by the Northwest: the importation study provisions; the Senate yielded in conference on almost every issue but that one.

In addition to the regional quarrels, there were disputes between the seven Basin states. The most important of these was a battle between Arizona and California over whether the latter should be guaranteed that it would receive 4.4 million acre-feet a year even in times of water shortages. California prevailed in this dispute, as Congress took advantage of the Supreme Court's recognition of its right to legislate on the subject.

Although Arizona made many concessions to gain authorization for the Central Arizona Project, Congressional approval of the proposal was regarded as a credit to the state's five-man Congressional delegation. That delegation included one of the most powerful men in the Senate, the chairman of the Appropriations Committee, Carl Hayden (D). Hayden had fought for the bill for many years, and in 1968 was in his last year in the Senate; he was retiring at the age of 90. It also included the brother of Interior Secretary Udall, Morris K. Udall (D), widely regarded as one of the more effective legislators in the House, and John J. Rhodes (R), a former member of the Interior Committee and currently chairman of the House Republican Policy Committee.

President Johnson signed S 1004 Sept. 30 in a full-dress ceremony at the White House, during which he called the measure "a landmark bill" and proclaimed the

occasion "Carl Hayden Day." But S 1004 did not solve all the problems of the Colorado River Basin by any means. The issue of importation studies was only delayed. In addition, because the Lower Basin's development fund would not have enough money in it to pay for significantly larger augmentation works than those needed for the Mexican treaty burden, the financing of the works promised to provoke future controversy.

Provisions

As signed into law Sept. 30, S 1004 (PL 90-537):

TITLE I—OBJECTIVES

Stated that the objectives of the bill were: (1) to provide for comprehensive water resource development in the Colorado River Basin; and (2) to provide additional and adequate water supplies in both the Upper and Lower Colorado River Basins.

Stated the policy of Congress that the Secretary of the Interior should continue to develop a regional water plan for the Colorado River Basin.

TITLE II—INVESTIGATIONS, PLANNING

Investigations. Directed the Interior Secretary to conduct "full and complete reconnaissance investigations" to develop a plan for meeting the future water needs of the West. Specified that the study was to concentrate on the long-range water supply available and the long-range water requirements in each water resource region of the area. Provided that the study was to be made in coordination with studies being made under the Water Resources Planning Act of 1964 and that biennial reports be submitted to the President, the National Water Commission, the Water Resources Council and Congress. The first of the reports was to be submitted by June 30, 1971, and the final reconnaissance report before June 30, 1977. **Importation Study Moratorium.** Provided that for a period of 10 years from the date of enactment, the Secretary was not to undertake reconnaissance studies of any plan to import water into the Colorado River Basin from any drainage basin lying outside of those portions of seven states that lay within the Colorado River Basin. (This provision was intended to block immediate study of water importation from the Columbia River Basin in the Pacific Northwest.)

Mexican Water Treaty. Declared that the satisfaction of the 1944 Mexican Water Treaty (guaranteeing delivery of 1.5 million acre-feet of Colorado River water annually to Mexico) was a national obligation, but provided that the states of the basin would have to continue supplying the water from the river until such time as a plan to augment the river's flow by 2.5 million acre-feet a year was in effect.

Protection for Other Basins. Required the Secretary, in preparing any future plan for inter-basin water diversion into the Colorado River Basin, to protect the states or areas of origin by making sure that they would have enough water to satisfy their ultimate requirements at prices to users that would not be higher because of the diversions. Granted states of origin a perpetual priority of right to use of water diverted from them, unless otherwise provided by interstate agreement.

Authorized appropriation of such funds as necessary (estimated at $10 million) to implement the provisions of Title II.

TITLE III—AUTHORIZED UNITS

Central Arizona Project Works. Authorized construction, operation and maintenance of the Central Arizona Project to divert water from Lake Hasavu, behind the Parker Dam on the Colorado River, to the areas in and around Phoenix and Tucson. Associated works included three regulating dams along the diversion aqueducts (Orme, Butte and Charleston), reservoirs, canals, pumping plants, hydroelectric power plants and electric transmission facilities. Also authorized was the Hooker Dam on the Gila River in Western New Mexico, which was to provide water storage for the New Mexico area in lieu of Central Arizona Project water to which the area was entitled.

Size of Aqueduct. Provided that the Central Arizona Project's aqueduct system could have a capacity for diversion of up to 3,000 cubic feet per second or any lesser amount found to be feasible. Specified that any capacity in excess of 2,500 cubic feet per second could be used only when Lake Powell (the Upper Basin's lowest storage reservoir, behind the Glen Canyon Dam) was full or under certain other circumstances. Further specified that any capacity built into the aqueduct in excess of 2,500 cubic feet per second would have to be paid for by Arizona, unless there were enough money in that part of the basin's development fund *(see Title IV)* which was available to Arizona. (The full 500 extra cubic feet per second capacity would cost $53 million, it was estimated.)

California Usage Guarantee. Gave California a guarantee that it would not have to cut back its water usage to below 4.4 million acre-feet a year in the event of water shortages in the Lower Basin. Also provided that existing or authorized usages in Arizona and Nevada (amounting to about 1.7 million acre-feet) would be senior in right to the Central Arizona Project.

Power Plant. Directed the Secretary to conclude studies and to recommend the most feasible plan for the construction and operation of hydroelectric facilities large enough, or the purchase of power in sufficient quantity, to provide for pumping Central Arizona Project water. Barred construction of any dams on the Colorado River between Hoover Dam and Glen Canyon Dam (the section of the river which runs through the Grand Canyon).

Required the Secretary to submit his recommended plan within one year of enactment. To become effective, the plan had to be approved by Congress, except that Congressional approval was not required if the Secretary recommended a specified plan for acquisition of a portion of the generating capacity in a thermal plant whose construction (at Page, Ariz.) was being planned by a combine of private and state utilities.

Provided that in the event the Secretary decided to acquire an interest in such a thermal generating plant, the Federal Government would pay for a share of construction, operation and maintenance costs that would be proportional to the generating capacity it would use.

Other. Permitted acquisition of Indian lands needed for the Orme Dam and Reservoir and allowed payment of up to $500,000 for relocating Indian structures there.

Directed the Secretary to offer to contract for the use of up to an average of 18,000 acre-feet per year of Gila River water in New Mexico, over and above New Mexico's entitlement to Gila River water under *Arizona v. California.* Provided that such use would not be permitted until there was Colorado River water available in sufficient quantities to replace the water currently used by Arizonans drawing on the Gila River. Permitted the 18,000 figure to be raised to 30,000 when augmentation of the Colorado River's flow allowed use in Arizona of more than 2.8 million acre-feet a year.

Provided that water provided California, Arizona and Nevada through augmentation should not cost them any more than mainstream Colorado River water, to the extent that such water was used to bring the states up to their full legal entitlements to mainstream water. (After a state reached its legal entitlement, augmentation water would cost more than mainstream water.)

Provided that Central Arizona Project water could not be made available for irrigation of lands unless the lands had a recent irrigation history.

Reauthorized the Dixie Project in Utah, increased authorizations for the project from $42.7 million to $58 million and integrated it into the Colorado River Basin Project to permit it to participate financially in the Lower Colorado River Basin Development Fund established under Title IV.

Authorized $832,180,000 for construction of the Central Arizona Project; authorized an additional $100 million for construction of distribution and drainage facilities.

TITLE IV—LOWER COLORADO RIVER BASIN DEVELOPMENT FUND

Basin Development Fund. Established a Lower Colorado River Basin Development Fund into which was to be paid: (1) all appropriations for the Central Arizona Project and the Dixie Project; (2) all revenues from the Central Arizona Project and the Dixie Project; (3) all revenues from the Boulder Canyon and Parker-Davis Projects after they were paid for; and (4) all revenues from the Arizona-Nevada portion of the Pacific Northwest-Pacific Southwest power intertie, after other repayment obligations had been met.

Uses of Fund. Provided that money in the fund (except for some of the revenues from Hoover and Parker-Davis, *see below*) could be used to construct, maintain and operate the projects in the bill, and for payments to Arizona water users to compensate them for losses caused by lower power production at Coolidge Dam (estimated at $5,000 annually). Provided that revenues not used for these two purposes be transferred annually to the Treasury to repay with interest that portion of the costs of the Central Arizona Project and the Dixie Project which was allocated to irrigation, commercial power, municipal or industrial water supply, within a period of 50 years from completion of these features.

Provided that the percentage of revenues in the fund that came from sale of Hoover and Parker-Davis power in California and Nevada (after the projects were paid off) be earmarked for future works to augment the Colorado River's flow. (This amounted to 77 percent of power sales; the remaining 23 percent was sold in Arizona, and so 23 percent of the power revenues could be used for the Central Arizona Project outlays (as described in the previous provision).

Mexican Treaty Works. Provided that in the event of construction of augmentation works, the part of the cost attributable to satisfying the Mexican Treaty obligation was to be nonreimbursable. (It would take 1.8 million acre-feet to satisfy the obligation, making allowance for 300,000 acre-feet in evaporation.) Cost of any additional augmentation water was to be reimbursable from the development fund and other sources. The cost of construction and operation of augmentation works was to be divided between the Treaty obligation and the additional capacity on a pro rata basis.

Reports. Required the Secretary to submit annual reports on Jan. 1 of each year stating the status of costs and revenues of each Lower Basin project; also required submission of annual development fund budgets.

TITLE V—UPPER COLORADO RIVER BASIN

Upper Basin Projects. Authorized $392 million for construction of five (Upper Basin) reclamation projects on the Western Slope of Colorado: Animas-La Plata, Dolores, Dallas Creek, West Divide and San Miguel. Directed the Secretary to proceed with construction of the projects so they would be completed not later than the Central Arizona Project.

Provided that construction of the Animas-La Plata project could not begin until Colorado and New Mexico had ratified an interstate compact.

Conditionally authorized, in the Upper Basin, the Uintah unit of the Central Utah Project, subject to future Congressional approval of a feasibility report.

Power Compensation. Provided that revenues from the sale of power at Hoover Dam were to be used (at a rate of $500,000 annually) to repay the Upper Basin Fund for payments it had made to compensate Hoover Dam power contractors; any deficiency remaining as of June 1, 1987, was to be transferred to the Upper Basin Fund from the Lower Basin Fund. (The compensations were needed because the upstream impounding of water to fill Lake Powell, behind Glen Canyon Dam, had caused power generation deficiences at Hoover.)

TITLE VI—GENERAL PROVISIONS

Directed the Secretary to report to Congress at five-year intervals, beginning with the five-year period starting on Oct. 1, 1970, on water usage and losses in the Colorado River.

Provided that any state affected by the legislation could file suit in the U.S. Supreme Court if any federal agency or official failed to comply with any provision of the Act.

Required the Secretary, in consultation with each of the seven Colorado River Basin states, to set up criteria for coordinated long-range operation of reservoirs constructed under this Act, the Colorado River Storage Act and the Boulder Canyon Project Act.

Specified that the criteria should provide basically for storage of the river's water in Upper Basin reservoirs, and established the following priorities for release of water from Lake Powell in the Upper Basin to Lake Mead in the Lower Basin:

(1) Releases to satisfy one-half of the deficiency in deliveries of treaty water to Mexico, if a deficiency existed.

(2) Releases to ensure that the Lower Basin states received the 7.5 million acre-feet a year they were entitled to. (In the event of augmentation, the level would be reduced.)

(3) In the event of surpluses of water after the above priorities had been met, releases for domestic and agricultural use in the Lower Basin (except that such releases were not to be made from Lake Powell when the level of active storage water there was lower than active storage at Lake Mead), releases to equalize storage levels between Lake Powell and Lake Mead, and releases to prevent spillage at Lake Powell.

Directed the Secretary to submit proposed criteria to the Governors of the basin states by Jan. 1, 1970, and to publish them in the Federal Register by July 1, 1970, and required annual reports on operations under the criteria beginning in 1972.

Removed the Grand Canyon stretch of the Colorado River from the hydroelectric facility licensing authority of the Federal Power Commission, until otherwise provided by Congress.

Water Commission

Congress completed action on an Administration-backed bill (S 20—PL 90-515) authorizing the establishment of a National Water Commission to make a non-federal comprehensive study of water resources problems. The commission's purpose was to examine major water problems and to develop recommendations, guidelines and long-range plans for effective use of available water resources.

Many federal agencies deal with water resources and almost every agency is affected by federal water policy, and it was thought by the sponsors of S 20 that various studies being conducted by these agencies would reflect parochial interests. For this reason, among others, the legislation required that all seven Commission members be appointed from outside Government ranks. Interior Secretary Stewart L. Udall, in testimony before the House Interior Committee, said the Commission should be made up of individuals who "can detach themselves from the vested interests that Government agencies have." It was hoped that the new Commission could develop a coordinated federal water policy that would generally chart a future course for the more than 50 federal agencies dealing with water resources.

President Johnson had urged establishment of the commission in 1966, 1967 *(See earlier chronology)* and again in 1968. Many observers thought that the National Water Commission legislation had been delayed because of the dispute over western water problems. Members of Congress from the Northwest, for example, feared that the Commission would set out to study the possibility of diverting water from the Columbia River Basin in their region to the Colorado River Basin in the arid Southwest.

However, the issue of importation studies was resolved, at least temporarily, with passage of S 1004, the bill authorizing the Central Arizona Project and other development in the Colorado River Basin. (S 1004 and S 20 were cleared on the same day.) S 1004 put a 10-year moratorium on any Interior Department study of water importation for the Colorado River. The Interior Department would be equipped to handle such a detailed study, whereas the new Commission would not; furthermore, the Commission's legislative mandate was a more general one and its life was only five years.

Provisions. As signed into law Sept. 26, S 20 (PL 90-515):

Established a seven-member National Water Commission, named by the President, and excluded federal employees (other than retired federal employees) from appointment.

Gave the Commission a five-year life and authorized appropriation of $5 million to finance it.

Directed the Commission to consider various ways of meeting U.S. water requirements, including more efficient use of water, reduction of water pollution, interbasin transfers of water, and various technological advances, such as desalting and weather modification. The Commission also was to "consider economic and social consequences of water resource development" and to advise on projects submitted to it by the Administration.

Other Legislation

SALINE WATER CONVERSION. Congress enacted legislation (S 2912—PL 90-297) authorizing fiscal 1969 appropriations of $24,556,000 for the saline water program, administered by the Office of Saline Water in the Department of the Interior. In addition, S 2912 reorganized the authorization section of the existing law to provide for the traditional type of annual authorization. The existing law authorized appropriations through fiscal 1972 of $105,782,000, plus whatever additional sums Congress authorized from year to year up to a maximum of $169,218,000. This "declining balance" approach was considered unnecessarily complicated.

PUBLIC WORKS. The annual public works-Atomic Energy Commission appropriations bill (HR 17903—PL 90-479) included funds for construction of public works water development projects by the Army Corps of Engineers and the Bureau of Reclamation and for the Federal Water Pollution Control Administration. In addition, HR 17903 appropriated money for several independent federal agencies, including the Tennessee Valley Authority, and for Interior Department power agencies such as the Bonneville Power Administration.

Appropriations for Army Corps of Engineers public works projects totaled $1,214,772,500, or $86,921,500 less than in fiscal 1968. Congress provided money for only 11 new starts on construction of water projects, and three of these were solely for land acquisition. As in 1967, the highly controversial New England power project, the Dickey-Lincoln School dam and reservoir, received no funds. The Senate provided money to begin planning on the project, but the House did not; and the House prevailed in conference. Atomic Energy Commission appropriations included $465,270,000 for nuclear reactor development. One of the most controversial AEC projects was the proposed 200-billion electron volt nuclear accelerator at Weston, Ill., for which $7.1 million was appropriated in HR 17903 for continued planning—a cut of $17.9 million from the Budget estimate of $25 million *(See box)*.

Saline Water Expenditures

The following figures show the total amount of money spent on the saline water conversion program since its beginning in fiscal 1953. The information was provided during House Appropriations Committee hearings March 4 on the fiscal 1969 Budget request of the Office of Saline Water.

(Figures in thousands of dollars)

Fiscal year	Total	Salaries and expenses	Operation and maintenance	Construction, operation, and maintenance	Prototype desalting maintenance
Actual expenditures					
1953	$ 70	$ 70			
1954	180	180			
1955	422	422			
1956	503	503			
1957	499	499			
1958	780	780			
1959	1,084	1,084			
1960	1,423	1,192		$ 231	
1961	3,346	1,870		1,476	
1962	4,113	2,035		2,078	
1963	8,674	5,843	$ 816	2,015	
1964	9,494	7,017	1,392	1,085	
1965	11,468	9,533	330	1,605	
1966	12,955	12,280	1,084	—409	
1967	16,820	13,397	1,763	1,660	
Total actual	$ 71,831	$ 56,705	$5,385	$ 9,741	
Estimated expenditures					
1968	$ 26,084	$ 21,881	$2,000	$ 453	$ 250
1969*	30,090	26,840			4,750
Total estimated	$ 56,174	$ 48,721	$2,000	$ 453	5,000
Total actual and estimated	$128,005	$105,426	$7,385	$10,194	$5,000

* *The S.&E. and O.&M. appropriations have been consolidated into the saline water conversion appropriation.*

HR 17903 allotted to the Interior Department's Bureau of Reclamation $273,351,500 for its fiscal 1969 irrigation and power activities. Like the Army Engineers, the Bureau received less money than in fiscal 1968. It was not allowed any new starts. The Federal Water Pollution Control Administration, an Interior Department agency, received $302,838,000, of which $214 million was earmarked for the waste treatment construction grant program.

RIVERS AND HARBORS. Congress completed action on an omnibus bill (S 3710—PL 90-483), approved Aug. 13, authorizing construction by the Army Corps of Engineers of nearly $1.8 billion in new federal water projects. The bill also raised appropriations authorizations for ongoing construction on federal water projects in 13 river basins by a total of $469 million. The bill involved eventual expenditure totaling more than $2.2 billion on public works projects. S 3710 was the first omnibus bill authorizing new Army Engineers river, harbor, flood control, beach erosion and hurricane protection projects since a similar 1966 measure.

The rivers and harbors and flood control project authorizations would involve construction in 38 states. In practice, many of these projects would not be started for years, and, once started, their construction (and therefore the associated expenditure of federal dollars in the proj-

Weston Accelerator

The proposed Weston, Ill., accelerator drew national attention in 1965 and 1966 as officials searched for a construction site. Sharp competition developed among communities across the nation for the laboratory, because its presence was expected to boost the local economy and lead to development of other science research facilities nearby. At one point, 200 possible sites in 46 states were under consideration. Midwesterners particularly sought the accelerator to help offset the drain of talented scientists to major science installations on the East and West Coasts. The AEC Dec. 16, 1966, announced Weston as the site.

Controversy surrounded the Weston authorization in 1967 because of alleged housing discrimination in the area. The village Feb. 15 passed an open housing ordinance, but the Illinois Legislature June 17 turned down a proposed state open-occupancy law. Some Congressional leaders, including Joint Atomic Energy Committee Chairman John O. Pastore (D R.I.) opposed the authorization because of the Illinois Legislature's action. Floor amendments to delete the authorization were defeated in both chambers of Congress.

ects' districts) would stretch out over several years. During debate on S 3710, it was estimated that there were already $10 billion in authorized projects that had not been started. Raising the appropriations authorizations in the 13 river basins made possible additional construction on projects in 24 states. In practice, the funds authorized for the basins would be appropriated and spent within the next two years for work on ongoing construction projects.

All in all, the bill authorized construction, either on new projects or on ongoing projects, in 42 states. The eight states not covered were Arizona, Maine, Maryland, Nevada, New Jersey, New Mexico, Vermont and Wyoming. Two of the projects authorized by the bill contained new federal hydroelectric power facilities. They were the Salem Church dam on the Rappahannock River in Virginia (89,000 kilowatts installed capacity) and a project on the Cooper River in South Carolina (84,000 KW).

PALMETTO BEND RECLAMATION. Congress enacted legislation (HR 5117—PL 90-562) authorizing the Interior Department's Bureau of Reclamation to construct the first stage of the Palmetto Bend reclamation project in Texas. The project was to dam the Lavaca and Navidad Rivers near Edna, Texas, to regulate the flow of those streams so as to provide a dependable water supply. The first stage called for a dam across the Navidad River to be built at an estimated cost of $34,077,000. The bill also authorized appropriation of an additonal $2.7 million for land acquisition for the second stage.

POWER PROJECT RELICENSING. Congress completed action on an Administration-backed bill (S 2445—PL 90-451) simplifying the Government's procedures for reviewing and relicensing privately operated hydroelectric power projects that were subject to federal recapture under the Federal Power Act of 1920.

The Federal Power Act of 1920 authorized the Federal Power Commission (FPC) to issue licenses for development and operation of hydroelectric power facilities on rivers under federal jurisdiction. Licenses could not be issued for more than 50 years. The law provided that when the original FPC licenses expired, they were to be reviewed for relicensing (either to the original licensee or to a new party). In the case of projects operated by private groups, if the FPC decided that relicensing was not desirable, and Congress concurred, then the Government could institute proceedings to recapture the project in question. Projects operated by public power groups such as municipally owned electric systems were not subject to federal recapture, although they did have to go through relicensing procedures.

At the end of fiscal 1967, some 270 licensed hydroelectric projects were subject to recapture or relicensing at the expiration of their license terms. These projects had a total estimated cost of about $8.2 billion and estimated installed generating capacity of $29.3 million kilowatts. Sixty-seven licenses were due to expire in the next five years.

Existing procedures for review of the expiring licenses were deemed unnecessarily complicated by the FPC, and so the agency conceived S 2445 to ease the burden of review that fell both on itself and on Congress. The existing procedures provided for FPC consideration of an expiring license several times during a period that could stretch over several years, and provided that Congress must separately consider each project up for relicensing. The FPC proposal, which was enacted without substantial change, eliminated duplicative stages of agency review and gave the Commission authority to relicense, without specific Congressional action, any project where federal recapture had not been recommended. Under the bill, Congress would consider only those projects where recapture had been recommended either by the FPC or by another federal agency. Of course, Congress could act on its own initiative when it thought that the FPC had not acted equitably in relicensing any individual project.

MISSOURI RIVER BASIN. Congress completed action on a bill (S 6—PL 90-453) authorizing the Interior Department's Bureau of Reclamation to construct the first stage of the Oahe irrigation project on the Missouri River in South Dakota, at an estimated federal cost of $191,670,000. Construction, however, would not begin until Congress provided funds for the project, and none were included in the fiscal 1969 public works appropriations bill.

Miscellaneous Bills

POWER REGULATION. The Senate Commerce Committee rejected a bill (S 1365) which sought to exempt from Federal Power Commission (FPC) jurisdiction rural cooperatives and certain public utilities operating within a single state. It was the third time in as many Congresses that such a measure had been introduced—and the third time that it had been rejected. The earlier bills differed, however, in that they sought the withdrawal of FPC jurisdiction over wholesale rates charged by private power companies which operated primarily in a single state "even though part of the electricity was generated or transmitted outside the state."

NUCLEAR ELECTRIC POWER. The Joint Atomic Energy Committee held hearings on identical Senate and House bills (S 2564, HR 13828) to give public and private electric power companies access to the economies of large-scale nuclear generation of electric power. However, no further action was taken on the measures.

The bills prohibited the granting of a license for a nuclear electric generating plant unless certain specific conditions were satisfied. Among the conditions were ones that required the license applicant to have offered "all other interested persons" (including small power companies and electric cooperatives) an opportunity either to join in ownership of the proposed nuclear generating plant or to purchase a share of the electric output to be generated by the plant. Also, the bills required the Atomic Energy Commission, before granting a license, to seek advice from the Federal Power Commission, the Water Resources Council and the U.S. Attorney General on the compatibility of the proposed generating plant with efficient power generation, with comprehensive development of water and related regional land resources, and with antitrust laws.

WATER POLLUTION. A comprehensive and heavily amended water pollution control bill (S 3206) narrowly lost a race against the adjournment clock and thereby died with the close of the 90th Congress. Although the House and the Senate had passed different versions of the bill, they were unable to reconcile their differences prior to adjournment.

The bill, which was considered twice on the floor of each chamber, was acted on last when the House rejected controversial Senate amendments which extended pollution controls to offshore oil installations and gave the Secretary of the Interior increased power to control interstate water pollution by licensees of federal agencies. The House then returned the bill to the Senate, but it did not arrive in time for consideration.

House rejection of the Senate amendments and the subsequent death of the bill were attributable at least in part to a concerted lobbying effort by oil interests and by federal licensees, principally electric power companies. The American Petroleum Institute was reported to have worked with individual oil companies to block acceptance of the Senate amendments extending controls to offshore installations.

Colorado Bill Lobbying

When Congress on Sept. 12 cleared the $1.3 billion Colorado River bill (S 1004), it marked the end, at least for the time being, of a dispute that had raged in the West for half a century. The bill authorized construction of the huge Central Arizona water diversion project and of various other water development projects that would draw on the Colorado River, and construction of these projects would mean that practically all of the river's annual flow of water had been spoken for. Just how that flow would be divided up among the seven states of the Colorado River Basin was a matter of enormous economic consequence, and of political controversy.

The long fight over the Colorado River made a fascinating tale of politics in the West, of judicial battles over the course of four decades, and of heavy lobbying of Congress in the late 1940s and the succeeding 20 years.

The simple fact that made the matter so controversial was that the Colorado River did not contain enough water to serve the rapidly expanding needs of the arid Southwest. It was estimated that by late in the twentieth century, water uses in the Basin would begin to outstrip water availability.

The Colorado River is the main source of water for sections of seven Western states, which between them contain about one quarter of the entire land area of the United States. Under a 1922 compact, the seven states agreed to divide the water in the river evenly between the Upper Basin (Colorado, Utah, Wyoming, New Mexico) and the Lower Basin (California, Arizona, Nevada).

Regional Disputes. Over the years since the compact, there were various disputes between the two basins,

---

Major Projects

Following is a list of major projects (projects costing at least $25 million each) authorized in S 3710. (A (p) indicates a power project):

Navigation

Gulf Intracoastal Waterway, St. Marks to Tampa Bay, Fla.	$ 40,000,000
Cal-Sag Bridges, Ind.	33,265,000
Red River Waterway, La., Texas, Ark. and Okla.	50,000,000[1]
Detroit River, Trenton Channel, Mich.	31,300,000
Yazoo River, Miss.	52,147,000
Cooper River, Charleston Harbor, S.C. (p)	35,381,000

Flood Control

Tanana River, Alaska	$111,700,000
Cucamonga Creek, Calif.	26,300,000
Mad River, Calif.	38,600,000
Bear Creek, South Platte River, Colo.	32,314,000
Park River, Conn.	30,300,000
Water resources, Central and Southern Fla.	58,182,000
Wabash River, Ind.	50,000,000[2]
Little Blue River, Mo.	38,492,000
Papillion Creek, Neb.	26,800,000
Licking River, Ohio	32,953,000
Aquilla Creek watershed, Texas	23,612,000
Navasota River, Texas	119,707,000
Rappahannock River (Salem Church Reservoir), Va. (p)	79,500,000

River Basins. Alabama-Coosa River, $29 million; Arkansas River, $108 million; Columbia River, $193 million; Missouri River, $38 million; Ohio River, $35 million.

1 Total estimated federal cost: $471,223,000.
2 Total estimated federal cost: $152,840,000.

notably on the question of whether major tributaries in the Lower Basin were to be counted as part of the Lower Basin's allotment of river water. But disputes that were even more bitterly contested occurred between the states of the Lower Basin, whose land was the most arid in the nation. While the amount of water in the area showed signs of decreasing, the population was growing rapidly. Government demographic statistics showed that from 1960-66, while the over-all population of the United States increased at an average annual rate of 1.4 percent, the population of Nevada increased at an annual rate of 7.4 percent, Arizona 3.5 percent and California 3.0 percent. No other state showed an average annual increase of more than 2.9 percent.

A continuing dispute between Arizona and California led to four Supreme Court cases in the 1930s, none of which conclusively settled the issues raised. One of the cases, decided in 1935, provided a clear indication of how strongly the states felt about apportionment of the river's water. The case was brought by the Federal Government against Arizona, which had sent troops to the Colorado to block construction of the Parker Dam, and was threatening use of military force if an attempt was made to build the structure. In this case, the Supreme Court upheld Arizona's contention that the dam was not properly authorized under law, but Congress in the same year enacted an authorization law and the dam was built.

Attempts to enact authorizing legislation for the Central Arizona Project began in 1947, and the Senate twice passed an authorization bill, in 1950 and 1951. But then the continuing dispute between Arizona and California was once again thrown into the Supreme Court, and legislative activity stopped until the Court handed down its decision in 1963.

Lobbying. In 1963 the lobbies that had existed in Washington in the late 1940s came back to life, and new ones also were formed. The most active lobby groups were those representing California and Arizona interests. The other states affected by the legislation did not have permanent lobbies in Washington, although they frequently delegated state officials and others to testify before Congress.

Many of the lobbyists and other spokesmen for the Western states were attorneys, and some of them had been involved in Colorado River disputes for decades. One such attorney was Northcutt Ely; he had dealt with Colorado River problems ever since 1929, when he became an assistant to Interior Secretary Ray Lyman Wilbur. Ely urged California's case before the Supreme Court in the early 1960s and continued to speak for California before Congress thereafter.

Ely pointed out in interview that there exist three methods of settling interstate water disputes: by interstate compact, by litigation in the Supreme Court, and by Congressional action. He noted that all three methods had been used in the case of the Colorado River. And Ely characterized the lobbying on the Colorado River matter as a "collision of advocates"—attorneys who confronted each other repeatedly in all phases of the dispute.

Aside from the lawyers, other men who were influential in developing arguments for the states were mostly expert technicians—hydrologists and engineers.

For the most part, the Colorado River bill was not lobbied in a conventional sense. Large industry organiza-

tions and trade associations did not become intimately involved. Rather, the bill's sponsors were subject to intense regional pressures that grew from the enormous economic stakes that the Western states had in the legislation. No single group of men were as aware of those stakes as were the Members of Congress from the region. Although they were subject to some industry pressures, they were most responsive to the demands of the citizens of their states; they were the spokesmen in Congress for states' positions that had been formulated over the years and that were supported by the majority of constituents and the governments of their states.

In a sense, then, the Members of Congress from the states in the Colorado River Basin were the primary lobbyists for the Colorado River bill. It fell to them, as a minority of the membership of Congress representing less than 15 percent of the votes in the House and Senate, to persuade the majority of their colleagues to support their position. And this could be done only after the Members from the Basin had reached substantial agreement among themselves on the many controversies among their own states. That agreement was reached in 1966 after decades of disputes and negotiations, and it held together for the most part through 1968. Before House floor action on the legislation, the Members of Congress from the Basin states set up their own whip system and personally contacted practically every one of their colleagues.

Only two important parts of the Basin agreement failed to gain enactment. One was authorization for intensive study of importing water into the Colorado River Basin from sources outside its natural drainage area. The Northwest, fearing that the Basin states had their sights set on the major rivers of the Northwest, succeeded in eliminating that section from the legislation. The second part involved construction authorization for two hydroelectric dams on the stretch of the Colorado that runs through Northern Arizona and the Grand Canyon.

Battle of the Dams. The dams were eliminated from the Colorado River bill after a widely publicized lobbying effort by the Sierra Club and other conservation groups, which felt that the dams would ruin the scenic beauty of the free-flowing Colorado and the Grand Canyon.

The Sierra Club paid for full-page advertisements in large-circulation newspapers and magazines, and they generated a massive mailing campaign to Congress and the Administration. The Administration until 1966 had supported construction both of the Hualapai (Bridge Canyon) dam downstream from the Grand Canyon National Park and of the Marble Canyon dam upstream from the park. But in 1966 it said it would drop one of the dams, and early in 1967 it dropped both of the dams and proposed instead to acquire the power needed to pump water through the Central Arizona project by participating in a joint public-private thermal power plant. This was the plan eventually adopted, and it was a defeat for the Basin states, which lobbied for the dams.

Conservation Groups

The most widely publicized lobbying campaign in connection with the Colorado River legislation was the battle waged by conservation organizations against the proposed inclusion in the bill of construction authorization for two large hydroelectric dams on the stretch of the river that runs through the Grand Canyon in Northern Arizona. The fight was led by the influential San Francisco-based Sierra Club, which generated a large-scale mailing campaign by placing full-page advertisements in big-circulation daily newspapers and magazines.

It was the most intensive conservation campaign in more than a decade, and it aroused considerable bitterness among supporters of the dams on Capitol Hill. The Sierra Club's activities led the Internal Revenue Service to revoke its right to receive tax-deductible contributions on the ground that the Club had violated provisions of the tax law that prohibited certain nonprofit tax-exempt organizations from lobbying. The IRS acted against the Club with unprecedented speed, and that speed gave rise to charges that the IRS move was politically inspired—an allegation that the IRS firmly denied.

The Sierra Club took on—and defeated—a powerful coalition of interests which included the Interior Department's Bureau of Reclamation, the Colorado River Assn. and like-minded lobbies in the Southwest, the American Public Power Assn. as well as several large private power companies. The Club was also opposing the united position of the seven Basin states, with their 51 seats in the House and 14 seats in the Senate. This coalition argued that the dams were needed for two primary purposes. One was to provide additional hydroelectric "peaking" power for use in the Southwest during periods of high demand for electricity, for example in the evening when the demand for electricity for lighting jumps and in the summer when air conditioning requires large amounts of electricity. The other was to provide a source of revenue from the sale of power, that eventually would help finance works to augment the amount of water available in the area. The groups further said that lakes formed behind the dams would provide recreational opportunities for many more people than the few who annually made the grueling trip down the Colorado River in its current free-flowing state.

After the Supreme Court case had been settled, Interior Secretary Stewart L. Udall in 1963 proposed his ambitious Southwest Water Plan, a regional water development scheme that included construction of the two hydroelectric dams at the two best remaining dam sites on the river: Bridge Canyon below the Grand Canyon National Monument and Marble Canyon above the Grand Canyon National Park. The Plan was revised in 1964, but still included the dams. *(See Congress and the Nation, Vol. I, pp. 886, 894.)*

Opposition developed quickly among conservation groups, although it did not reach an intense level until 1966. The Sierra Club displayed evidence of growing concern about the Grand Canyon as early as 1964. In that year, the Club published an expensive ($25) glossy book in its Exhibit Format series, "Time and the River Flowing," on the Grand Canyon. The book, which extolled the beauty of the Colorado River in its natural state and of the Grand Canyon, was later sent to every Member of Congress.

In February 1965, the Club published in its monthly Bulletin an editorial entitled "The Chips are Down for Grand Canyon," which advocated that readers write to their Members of Congress and others, opposing the dams. The Bulletin was distributed to all Members of Congress, all members of the California legislature, hundreds of

persons in the news media, as well as to members of the club.

It was in 1965 that the Club's director, David R. Brower, first testified in Congressional hearings on the legislation; he testified numerous times in later years. In August 1965, the Club published a special 20-page Bulletin reproducing Brower's testimony in opposition to the dams and advising readers to write their Congressional Representatives, the President, Secretary Udall, and certain influential Members of the House and Senate Interior and Insular Affairs Committees. The special Bulletin was entitled "Dams in the Grand Canyon—A Necessary Evil?"

In early 1966, it was evident that negotiations between the seven Basin states would result in an agreement for Colorado River legislation that would include the dams, and the Sierra Club stepped up its activities. The peak of its campaign against the dams came on June 9, 1966, when the Club paid for a full-page advertisement in *The New York Times* and *The Washington Post* attacking the dams.

The IRS reacted quickly. On June 10, its district director in San Francisco notified the Club's headquarters that the IRS would no longer guarantee that contributions to the Club would be tax deductible, and on June 13 it announced its action publicly in a press release. The public advance notice of possible action against the Sierra Club was unprecedented; usually the IRS makes no public announcement of its decisions in such matters, let alone public announcement of its intention to investigate.

In spite of the IRS action, the Sierra Club did not stop its campaign against the dams. All of the advertisements were striking to the eye and provocative to the emotions. They resulted in what Sen. Thomas H. Kuchel (R Calif.) July 15, 1966, called "one of the largest letter-writing campaigns which I have seen in my tenure in the Senate." And the campaign resulted in what must be reckoned as a complete victory for the Sierra Club: the elimination of both dams from the bill.

Looking back over the fight in a recent interview, Morris Udall said of the conservationists, "I can't think of any group in this country that has had more power in the last eight years," and he credited Brower with "cleverly exploiting it." He pointed out that there had existed substantial unanimity on the dams among conservation groups, that each group has its own newsletter which is mailed to thousands of members.

Positions of Other Conservation Groups. Because the tax exemptions of their own organizations might be endangered by lobbying, leaders of conservation groups in the mid-1950s formed two new organizations, legally separate from the conservation groups themselves, to carry on direct lobbying. These were the Citizens Committee on Natural Resources and the Trustees for Conservation. Although the groups conducted some lobbying activities against the dams, the leadership role in the fight was assumed by the Sierra Club.

The position of the Sierra Club, if not its legislative activities, was supported by a wide range of other conservation groups, almost all of which testified in Congressional hearings on the legislation. They included some with national constituencies, such as the Wilderness Society, the National Audubon Society and the Izaak Walton League, and others with more regional or local focus, such as the Federation of Western Outdoor Clubs, the Grand Canyon Workshop of the Colorado Open Space Coordinating Council, and Save the Grand Canyon Committee and Arizonans for Water Without Waste. The last three Western groups were organized on an ad hoc basis to combat the proposed dams.

Hooker Dam Controversy. A second conservation controversy that arose in connection with S 1004 concerned the proposed construction authorization for the Hooker Dam on the Gila River in New Mexico. The Hooker site was near the Gila Wilderness, established in 1924 as the first component of the nation's wilderness system, and construction of a dam there would have backed up water a short distance into the wilderness area. Conservation organizations, led in this instance by the Wilderness Society, opposed a dam at the Hooker site. The Wilderness Society claimed that other wilderness areas would be "in great jeopardy" if the dam were built there, and suggested other sites in New Mexico for the dam. In a February 1967 bulletin to its members, the Society listed all members of the House Interior and Insular Affairs Committee, and suggested that readers might write them as well as their own Representatives.

The controversy was resolved in Congress by authorization of a dam at the Hooker or a suitable "alternative" site.

Lower Basin: Arizona

Congressional Delegation. Arizona relied mainly on its Congressional delegation during its 20-year battle to secure authorization for the Central Arizona Project. The lobbyists and other individuals who helped in the fight for the most part took their directions from the delegation, which over the years attained influence in Congress that was remarkable for such a small state.

Back in the late 1940s, when Central Arizona Project legislation was first considered, and in the early 1950s, when the Senate twice passed a Central Arizona bill, Sen. Ernest W. McFarland (D 1941-53) was an influential member of the Arizona delegation. McFarland was Senate Majority Leader from 1951-53.

In the 1960s, the five-man Arizona delegation was headed by Sen. Carl Hayden (D), the chairman of the powerful Senate Appropriations Committee. It also included an influential Member of the House on each side of the aisle: John J. Rhodes (R) and Morris K. Udall (D). In the 89th and 90th Congresses, when the Colorado River legislation was making its painful way through the House and Senate, Rhodes was not only chairman of the House GOP Policy Committee, but also was the ranking minority member of the House Appropriations Public Works Subcommittee, the group which decides where to allocate money among politically popular "pork barrel" public works projects. Udall, an able politician who was very knowledgeable about the Colorado River dispute, was the brother of Stewart L. Udall, the Secretary of the Interior under Presidents Kennedy and Johnson. (The Interior Department was the agency which would build the Central Arizona Project.)

Central Arizona Project Assn. There was only one full-time lobby for Arizona interests in Washington. It was the Central Arizona Project Assn., an organization started in Arizona in 1946 to push for construction of the

water diversion project. Members of the group included towns, industries and small businesses in the area, farmers and banks; in general, what was a representative cross-section of the community of Central Arizona. The organization's first lobbyist, Howard J. Smith, registered in Washington in 1947, and the group was active from that year until 1951, when the whole dispute over the Colorado River was thrown into the Supreme Court.

At that point the Central Arizona Project Assn.'s office was closed, and it did not reopen until 1964, the year after the Supreme Court had handed down its decision. The chief agent for the Assn. in Washington in the later years was Morley E. Fox, who registered on May 15, 1964. Fox, with offices in the Congressional Hotel, just across the street from one of the three House office buildings, was one of the chief coordinating agents in the drive by Arizona to line up support for the bill.

The primary objective of the Central Arizona Project Assn. was to secure authorization and then appropriations for construction of the water project. But like the rest of the Lower Basin, the Assn. was also strongly in favor of establishment of a Lower Basin development fund that would accrue enough money to finance water augmentation works in the future.

The Central Arizona Project Assn.'s Washington operation served as a liaison and information agency for the state's Congressional delegation. Fox, aided from time to time by experts in Arizona, developed information needed in Congressional hearings and by the delegation and performed similar tasks. One project of interest that the group completed was the preparation of loose-leaf "floor books" an inch thick, for the Arizona Congressional delegation to use in debate over passage of the legislation.

In Arizona, the Central Arizona Project Assn. raised money to finance its Washington operation and its office in the state. In 1967, the last year for which figures were available, the group reported lobby spending of $78,867, ranking it 12th among the 280 organizations which listed their spending that year. In the previous year it had ranked eighth among 296 groups, with spending of $117,300. (Fox pointed out that lobby spending reporting requirements were notoriously lax, that many organizations which lobby did not report any expenses, and said his organization reported "even the paper clips" used in Arizona.)

In 1966, part of the money raised by the group was spent to finance a series of lunches for Members of Congress, newsmen, and Congressional staffers. One purpose of the sessions was to counteract the unfavorable publicity generated by the Sierra Club on the Grand Canyon dams. The sessions included a steak lunch and a 30-minute talk by a member of the Arizona delegation, who in making his point about the dams could illustrate it by pointing to a huge table relief model of the Grand Canyon. Morris Udall told CQ that almost every Member of the House had attended at least one of the luncheons.

Arizonans Who Helped. Although Arizona did not have the number of permanent lobbyists in Washington that California did, the state periodically sent a task force of experts to testify in Congressional hearings and to help Arizona's cause in other ways. The basic task force, in addition to Fox, consisted of Roger C. Ernst, an Assistant Secretary of Interior under President Eisenhower who later became an official in the Arizona Public Service Co., a large private power utility; Frank G. Scussel, an official in the Salt River Project, the biggest water agency in the state; William S. Gookin, formerly State Water Engineer, representing the state's water agency, the Arizona Interstate Stream Commission; and J. A. Riggins, a member of the law firm of Jennings, Strouss, Salmon and Trask of Phoenix and Washington, D.C., who was the Salt River Project's chief lawyer.

Groups, Industries That Helped. Arizona's Congressional delegation and other Arizonans influential in the fight for the bill also met from time to time with representatives of industries, trade associations and labor groups which had a stake in the legislation. Among these industries were several mining concerns, the Goodyear Tire & Rubber Co., which has large land holdings around Phoenix, Motorola, Inc., and American Airlines.

Trade associations included the American Public Power Assn. and the National Rural Electric Cooperative Assn. Both of these groups had a substantial stake in the legislation because of the Federal Government's policy of giving a preference for purchase of federal power to public power systems (municipal, rural electric and other such systems) over private electric utilities. The Hualapai and Marble Canyon dams would have added significantly to the amount of federal power available to such systems in the area.

Sources also said that coal industry and labor groups helped somewhat on the bill. There are large coal deposits in Northern Arizona, and the coal groups stood to benefit from the increased use of coal from these deposits at the huge thermal generating plant whose construction was proposed at Page, Ariz.

Arizona Strategy. For the most part, Arizona's Congressional delegation attempted to make the Central Arizona Project a part of a broad regional water development scheme. But there was no question that even if the regional compromise had fallen apart completely, Arizona would have pushed for a bare-bones authorization bill containing only the water diversion project. In fact, through the years there was a conservative faction in Arizona which wanted the state to push for such a bare-bones bill or to build the project itself without any federal assistance.

California

The state of California, as the largest user of the Colorado's water, had the biggest stake in disposition of the dispute over water allocation. It had had a number of registered lobbyists in Washington since the late 1940s, some of them representing the interests of the state as a whole, either in a legal or a public relations capacity, and others representing the interests of individual water-using groups in the state.

Congressional Delegation. Like Arizona, California had some members of its 40-man Congressional delegation also in positions of influence during the 1960s. Sen. Thomas H. Kuchel (R), for example, was ranking minority member of both the Senate Interior and Insular Affairs Committee and the Appropriations Committee's Public Works Subcommittee, which performs the same functions as the House Subcommittee of the same name. Kuchel was also the Senate Minority Whip during the 1960s (he was elected Whip in 1959). California's Rep. Harold T. Johnson (D) was chairman of the House Interior and Insular Affairs Committee's Irrigation and Reclamation Subcommittee, the panel which had jurisdiction over the Colorado River bills.

Northcutt Ely, Supreme Court Case. The chief lobbyist for California over the course of several decades was Northcutt Ely, a partner in the firm of Ely and Duncan of Washington, D.C. The importance of Ely's role in stating California's position over the years, and in explaining the technical and legal points that arose, is hard to overstate. Ely first registered as a lobbyist in 1947, and he registered for no less than five water agencies in California. Ely was appointed a special assistant attorney general of the state in 1953 (he still retained that status in 1968), and he was among those who led California's battle through the years of litigation leading up to oral arguments before the Supreme Court in 1962 and 1963, and thereafter through Congressional approval of S 1004. But his role in the legislation went back to the early 1930s when, as an executive assistant to the Secretary of the Interior, he helped draft contracts for sale of power to be generated at the Hoover Dam. Although when Gov. Ronald Reagan (R) took over the statehouse in California he delegated high state officials to help Ely represent the state before Congress, for years, in the words of a lobbyist who worked with Ely, "What Mike Ely said was California's position."

Ely was one of the leaders of the huge legal team that represented California before a special master appointed by the Supreme Court in some three years of hearings in San Francisco over the period 1956-58. The transcript of the hearings filled about 26,000 pages and there were an additional 4,000 pages of exhibits. Several hundred witnesses were heard. Arizona had a similarly large legal staff in San Francisco. The special master filed his opinion on Dec. 5, 1960, and California filed exceptions to it. The Supreme Court in 1962 and in 1963 heard a total of 22 hours of oral arguments on the case, an amount of time that it had not devoted to a single case since the Civil War. Ely argued for California in the case. When the Supreme Court handed down its decision in *Arizona v. California* (1963), it for the most part upheld the position of Arizona, although it overruled certain parts of the special master's opinion.

The primary issue considered by the Supreme Court was the matter of how to divide the waters of the Colorado among the states of the Lower Basin. When the Court chose the formula set forth in the Boulder Canyon Project Act of 1928, there was little controversy. But more controversial issues had been whether or not the waters of one of the Colorado's chief tributaries, the Gila in Arizona, should be counted against Arizona's share. On this point, the Court held in favor of Arizona; the Gila was not counted and so Arizona had a right to more mainstream Colorado River water than would otherwise have been the case. The Court did overrule in California's favor an opinion of the special master that in cases of water shortages the cutbacks on water usage would be prorated among the states. Instead, the Supreme Court gave the Secretary of the Interior authority to apportion cutbacks as he saw fit.

Other Lobby Groups. Another agency, the Colorado River Assn., also had a registered representative in Washington to represent California's interests. Described by its representative as a nonpartisan nonprofit citizens group, the Colorado River Assn. essentially represented the same agencies and their interests as did the so-called Six Agency Committee. It was the public relations arm of the Colorado River Board of California. John U. Terrell, the Colorado River Assn.'s first lobbyist, registered in March of 1948.

The Metropolitan Water District of Southern California, one of the six California agencies, had a bigger stake in settlement of the Colorado River problem than any of the others, and it sent its own representatives to Washington. The District was particularly concerned because under Western water law, agencies with first claims on water use take precedence in case of cutbacks over later claimants. The District's claim was junior to those of the three Agricultural agencies using the river, and if California had to cut back its over-all use of the river to 4.4 million acre-feet, the District stood to suffer a 55 percent cut in its current use of water.

While the lobbies for California interests were active in the late 1940s and early 1950s, their role in Washington ended for more than a decade when in 1951 the House Interior and Insular Affairs Committee voted to put off consideration of Colorado River bills until the dispute over apportionment of the water in the Lower Basin had been settled by the Supreme Court. After the Court handed down its decision in 1963, the groups reopened their Washington offices and became very active in the 89th and 90th Congresses. While Northcutt Ely continued to represent the Colorado River Board of California and the Six Agency Committee, the Metropolitan Water District sent Robert P. Will, a lawyer who first registered in February 1964, to represent it in Washington, and the Colorado River Assn. was represented by Joseph D. Phelan, who first registered in May 1965.

Upper Basin States

The states of the Upper Colorado River Basin— Colorado, Utah, Wyoming and New Mexico—had little to gain from construction of the Central Arizona Project. Indeed, they feared that they had much to lose. The increased use of Colorado River water that would result from construction of the project would mean that the Lower Basin would increase its uses to a level substantially above the 7.5 million acre-feet allotted to it, and the Upper Basin feared that it would be difficult to force Lower Basin projects to cut back water usage in years of shortage. Thus, while the Upper Basin acknowledged Arizona's need for the Central Arizona Project and supported its authorization, at the same time it insisted on a regional approach to the problems of the Colorado River Basin. Key to the regional approach were provisions for declaring satisfaction of the 1944 Mexican Water Treaty a national obligation and for finding a way to augment the Colorado River's flow to compensate for anticipated shortages.

For these reasons, the Upper Basin states found themselves aligned with the position of California, which also insisted upon augmentation provisions. On the other hand, Arizona in 1967 and 1968 was willing to settle for a simple project authorization, dropping controversial provisions for augmentation and for the two dams near the Grand Canyon which would have provided power revenues to finance the augmentation.

This represented a shift in the alignment of the Basin states on questions involving use of the river. In the early 1940s, when the Roosevelt Administration was negotiating the water treaty with Mexico, all seven Basin states supported an approach that would have guaranteed a percentage of the river's annual flow to Mexico. But when the State Department negotiated a flat guarantee of 1.5 million acre-feet a year, the Basin coalition fell apart. Arizona and the Upper Basin states continued to support the treaty, along with Texas, which was given benefits on the Rio Grande. But California and Nevada actively opposed it; the California legislature appropriated $50,000 for expenses incurred in opposing the treaty. In addition, the Colorado River Water Users Assn. was organized to oppose the treaty. It included water users from all of the seven Basin states.

The Arizona-Upper Basin coalition continued through the 1950s. In 1956, Arizona supported authorization of the $760-million Upper Colorado River Storage Project, which included construction of four large dams and various irrigation projects in the Upper Basin. California opposed it.

The shift came in 1963, after the Supreme Court's action in *Arizona v. California* made possible renewed Congressional consideration of Central Arizona Project bills. At that time, the Upper Basin found its uses of Colorado River water rapidly increasing.

Without a doubt, the most influential spokesman for the Upper Basin was Rep. Wayne N. Aspinall (D Colo.), chairman of the House Interior and Insular Affairs Committee which had jurisdiction over Colorado River legislation. Another man who was important in stating the Upper Basin's position was Ival V. Goslin, executive director of the Upper Colorado River Commission, a compact-created, interstate administrative agency representing all of the four Upper Basin states. Goslin came to Washington on several occasions to work on the legislation and to testify before Congressional committees.

In 1965 and 1966, Aspinall had helped develop a regional compromise which, on July 5, 1966, gained the support of all the Governors in the Basin, marking the first time that such unanimity had existed. From the Upper Basin's point of view, the key features of the compromise were provisions: (1) directing the Interior Department to make a comprehensive feasibility study of importing water into the Colorado from sources outside its drainage basin; (2) declaring the Mexican Water Treaty a national obligation; (3) specifying how the dams on the river were to be operated, thus protecting the Upper Basin against excessive draw-downs on its reservoirs by the Secretary of the Interior and setting priorities for release of water from the Upper Basin to the Lower Basin; (4) authorizing construction of five water projects in Colorado. Associated with the first feature was construction authorization for the Hualapai and Marble Canyon Dams in Arizona so that their revenues would produce enough money to help pay for importation works.

Colorado. The state of Colorado had the biggest stake among Upper Basin states in any legislation affecting allocation of river water; it was allocated 51.25 percent of the amount of water available for use in the upper Basin. Of the five projects (total cost: $392 million) in the bill for Colorado, three had not been endorsed by the Budget Bureau. The Bureau's approval usually is a prerequisite for Congressional authorization. Since

Aspinall represented the entire Western Slope of Colorado, all of them were in his district. One source said that even if the three questionable projects were not constructed, Aspinall's objective had been attained for the time being. That objective, the source said, was to establish Colorado's claim to its share of the Upper Basin's water; Colorado was not currently using a substantial part of the amount it was entitled to.

By early 1968, when Aspinall's Committee was preparing to report the Colorado River bill, the two dams had been eliminated from the legislation. But the other features of importance to the Upper Basin, especially to Colorado, were still intact.

Colorado did not maintain full-time lobbyists in the capital. But Aspinall, in his position of Committee chairman, was immensely influential. And the state sent representatives periodically to Washington to testify and to contact Members of Congress. One man who came to Washington several times over the years was Felix L. Sparks, director of the Colorado River Conservation Board, the state water agency.

Between the time that the House Interior Committee reported the Colorado River bill on April 24 and the beginning of floor debate on May 15, the state sent many people to Washington to work for favorable House action, as it had done before passage of the Upper Colorado River Storage bill in 1956. Among them were several well-known political figures: former Gov. Stephen L. R. McNichols (D 1957-63), former Sen. Edwin C. Johnson (D 1937-55) who was also Governor in 1933-37 and 1955-57, and former Rep. J. Edgar Chenoweth (R 1941-49, 1951-56).

Utah. In addition to the benfits it would receive from the provisions of the legislation affecting all the Upper Basin states, Utah stood to gain construction authorization for two new projects: the Uintah unit of the big Central Utah project and the Dixie Project, in the Southwestern part of the state, a part that is actually in the Lower Basin.

Utah's position was stated by, in addition to its Congressional delegation, the state water agency, the Utah Power and Water Board and its director, Jay R. Bingham. The board financed a reception and steak dinner, hosted by members of the delegation, for 23 members of the House Interior Committee on March 20, 1968. A film was shown and two Ute Indian chiefs, imported from Utah, spoke in an effort to point up the benefits of the first stage of the Central Utah project and the potential benefits of the second stage.

Northwest's Position

The position of the Pacific Northwest states (Washington, Idaho, Oregon) with regard to the Colorado River legislation was simply stated. These states were adamantly opposed to proposals advanced by the Southwest to initiate detailed feasibility studies of importing water into the Colorado River Basin from sources outside its drainage area. They feared that the Southwest had its eye on the two major rivers in the Northwest: the Columbia and its big tributary, the Snake. The Northwest states were particularly opposed to such a study by the Interior Department's Bureau of Reclamation, because they feared that the Bureau was already committed to the principle of importation, as opposed to other augmentation methods such as desalting or weather modification. They further believed that it would be difficult for the Bureau to report unfavorably on such a huge project, when the Bureau itself would be the agency that would construct the importation works.

The Northwest argued that no detailed feasibility study should be undertaken until a comprehensive impartial study of water availability and need in the Northwest had been completed. The Northwest states themselves were conducting such studies, and they further supported enactment of a bill to create a National Water Commission, composed of private citizens, to make another such study.

The Northwest had a powerful spokesman in Sen. Henry M. Jackson (D Wash.), the chairman of the Senate Interior and Insular Affairs Committee which had jurisdiction over the Colorado River bill. What Jackson accomplished in the final version of the bill was a ten-year moratorium on any Interior Department study, even a limited reconnaissance study, of importation schemes. After the ten-year period was over, the Department presumably could proceed with a reconnaissance study without Congressional authorization. However, it could not begin a detailed feasibility study—a prerequisite to construction of any federal water project—without specific Congressional authorization. Under a 1965 law, all such studies needed authorization, and any authorization bill would go through Jackson's Committee.

Legislative Strategy

The Members of Congress and the lobbies from the seven Basin states concentrated their efforts on the House. They lost their battle to secure authorization for the Hualapai and Marble Canyon dams when the Administration, under pressure from conservation forces, in 1966 and 1967 withdrew its support first for one of the dams and then for both. But the Basin worked hard for other provisions of the legislation which it considered important, notably a commitment for intensive study of the feasibility of importing water into the Basin from other river basins. In the House, the Basin had a powerful spokesman in Aspinall, whereas in the Senate it had to contend with the chief Northwest spokesman, Jackson, who was opposed to importation studies.

The Southwest expended considerable effort and money in 1966, when the Colorado River bill was reported, with the dams, by Aspinall's Committee, and it appeared that the bill might be brought to the floor for a vote. But when conservation opposition to the dams gained a large following in the House, Aspinall decided against floor action in 1966.

In 1967, the Southwest's activity subsided somewhat, as most action was taking place in the Senate, which passed a limited Colorado River bill that year. (One indication of this was the fact that the Central Arizona Project Assn.'s reported spending dropped from $117,300 in 1966 to $78,867 in 1967.)

Late in 1967, Aspinall promised that his Committee would act on the Colorado River legislation early the next year, and the Basin interests geared themselves for a big effort. What followed was an extraordinary effort by the Basin, especially by its Representatives in the House, to ensure favorable action by the full House on the bill. Rep. Laurence J. Burton (R Utah) said in an Oct. 8 interview, "It was the best job of lobbying I've ever seen." The most intense period of activity was between April 24, when Aspinall's Committee reported the bill, and May 15, when House floor action began. Because the reported bill contained provisions important to all of the Basin states, the effort was a united one.

Key to the strategy in the House was the belief of the bill's prime backers that a roll-call vote on the measure should be avoided. They feared that Representatives, who would under normal circumstances support the $1.3-billion bill, would be constrained to vote "nay" if they were forced to go on the record. Representatives in this category, the bill's sponsors thought, included the conservative budget-cutting economy bloc in the House and also some liberals who would resent authorizing huge public works expenditures while social welfare programs were being curtailed for lack of funds. Members of the economy bloc told the bill's strategists that, for the sake of consistency, they would have to vote "nay" on a record vote. They conceded that the bill did not actually appropriate money for expenditure in the current year, but said the distinction between an authorization bill and an appropriation bill would be a difficult one to explain to constituents in an election year, especially with Government spending a significant issue in many campaigns.

With this thought in mind, Morris Udall proceeded to set up his own whip system in the House. In an interview, Udall said his tactic was similar to the tactic used in the House before passage of the 1964 Civil Rights Act, when some members of the regular Democratic whip system were Southerners who opposed the bill. Udall and his colleagues from the Basin divided up the House and began contacting Representatives to ascertain their position on the bill. Members of the whip system, the regular Washington lobbyists for the bill and other individuals who had come to town in large numbers to help with House passage, met every evening in the Congressional Hotel, across the street from the House office buildings, to assess their progress. There they rated the position of their colleagues in five categories: firm support, probable support, undecided, probable opposition and definite opposition.

Burton said that in some instances, members of the whip system were assigned members of their Congressional "class"—who were first elected to Congress in the same year. In other instances, Representatives were contacted by key members of the whip system who held positions of influence in the House—for example, Harold T. Johnson (D Calif.), chairman of the subcommittee which passes on construction of irrigation projects in the West, or John J. Rhodes (R Ariz.), ranking minority member of the Appropriations subcommittee, which performs a similar function, and chairman of the House GOP Policy Committee. Of this technique of contacting colleagues, Burton said, "Maybe they needed a project, or a park, in their district a while back. You are aware that they talked to you about their bill a couple of months ago and now you need their support for the Colorado River project."

Udall and the bill's other strategists knew that Representatives from Northwest states would try to force a roll-call vote on the bill, since these Representatives were opposed to its provision for detailed study of inter-basin water transfers. A roll-call vote can be forced under two circumstances in the House: one, if a quorum is not present in the chamber and a roll call on passage is demanded; two, if a quorum is present and one-fifth of the Members present demand the record vote. Udall told CQ that by the time House floor action began, the whip system was so highly organized that at a signal from him on the House floor, 180 phone calls could be made to colleagues' offices within six or seven minutes.

It was this system that made it possible to attain a quorum in the chamber before the vote on passage of the bill. A further tribute to the persuasiveness of the whips was the fact that when the Northwest Representatives attempted to secure a roll-call vote, after the fact that a quorum existed had been established, they were unable to do so; one-fifth of the Members present did not support them in their desire for a record vote.

Chapter 10—Space Activities

Space

THE American space program came of age in the years 1965-1968 with spectacular successes in the skies, culminating in a manned moon landing July 20, 1969. *(See box, p. 534.)* But on earth the program's expenditures and objectives were being questioned in Congress, by the public and the scientific community. As Vietnam war demands and city problems increased. Congressional outlays for the National Space and Aeronautics Administration dwindled. Annual appropriations fell below $5 billion and then below $4 billion.

The high priority that NASA gave to manned flight during these years was frequently criticized as a wasteful and costly race with the Russians for national prestige. But manned flight received the greatest public attention, and progress in space tended to be judged by this standard. At long last, the Apollo project for putting a man on the moon had begun bringing in the successes in manned space flight that American space officials hoped for.

As 1968 drew to a close, three astronauts in the Apollo 8 spaceship became the first humans in history to circle the moon. Their dramatic flight at Christmas time was so successful that NASA soon named a crew and date for the lunar landing in 1969.

A moon landing "before the decade is out" was urged by President Kennedy and endorsed by Congress in 1961. Despite setbacks and a late start, the American space program was within sight of that goal when Kennedy's successor, Lyndon B. Johnson, also a strong advocate of space exploration, left the White House.

The timetable set in 1961 speeded up the space race— a race which neither the United States nor Russia would acknowledge officially but which had existed in fact since the Soviets launched Sputnik I into orbit around the earth, Oct. 4, 1957. That single deed at once ushered in the space age and humbled American pride.

Further humiliation came as Russia scored one "first" after another. It placed in space the first man (Yuri A. Gagarin), the first woman (Valentina V. Tereshkov), the first two-man and three-man crews and the first "space walker" (Aleksei A. Leonov). But after early 1965, when this country's two-man Gemini flights began, Americans supplied the momentum. Gemini, a predecessor of the three-man Apollo spacecraft, could maneuver to change orbit, rendezvous in space, and "dock" (link up) with Agena target vehicles. Using the Agena as a pusher rocket, American spacemen in 1966 flew as high as 851 miles above the earth, a record until surpassed by the 233,000-mile flight of Apollo 8 astronauts in 1968.

Both the American and Russian space programs suffered tragedies—and delays—in 1967. Preparing for the first manned Apollo flight, three astronauts died on

Kennedy's Space Goal

"I believe that this nation should commit itself to achieving the goal, before the decade is out, of landing a man on the moon. No single space project in this period will be more impressive to mankind, or more important for the long-range exploration of space; and none will be so difficult or expensive to accomplish. In a very real sense, it will not be one man going to the moon—it will be an entire nation."
—John F. Kennedy, in a message to Congress, May 25, 1961.

the launching pad at Cape Kennedy, Fla., Jan. 27, when a flash fire swept through their spacecraft. Two months later (April 24), Soviet cosmonaut Vladimir Komarov suffered fatal injuries when his spacecraft—the first manned flight in Russia's new Soyuz series— went out of control on returning to earth and crashed in the Ural Mountains. Komarov's death was the first known to have occurred in space flight.

By some estimates, the Soviet and American manned space programs were set back almost two years by the accidents. Neither country sent men into space again until October 1968. The Russians did not succeed in getting off the manned circumlunar flight that many people expected before the 50th anniversary of the Soviet revolution. But during 1968 they sent two unmanned capsules around the moon, and they were the first to be recovered on earth—with cameras and biological specimens intact.

The relative size of the American and Soviet space programs has been hard to determine because of Russian secrecy. In terms of money and manpower, the American space effort reached a peak in the middle 1960s and then tapered off. The Soviet space program was believed still climbing, perhaps reaching a point in 1968 where the American program had been when it crested.

The American space program seemed likely to be governed in the future as much by cost factors—and therefore by what the public would support—as by tech-

Reference

Discussion of space developments from 1945-1964 will be found in *Congress and the Nation*, Vol. I, pp. 237-334.

History of NASA Funding
(in millions)

Fiscal Year	Administration Request	Appropriation	Percent Cut
1959	$ 280.5	$ 222.8	20.6
1960	508.3	485.1	4.6
1961	964.6	964.0	.1
1962	1,940.3	1,825.3	5.9
1963	3,787.3	3,674.1	3.0
1964	5,712.0	5,100.0	10.7
1965	5,445.0	5,250.0	3.6
1966	5,260.0	5,175.0	1.6
1967	5,012.0	4,968.0	.9
1968	5,100.0	4,588.9	10.0
1969	4,370.4	3,995.3	8.6
1970 [1]	3,757.0	——	——
1970 [2]	3,712.0	——	——

1 *Johnson Administration budget.*
2 *Nixon Administration budget.*

nical limitations. American spending for both civilian and military exploration, and the support programs, approached $50 billion by the end of 1968. The civilian program, run by NASA, accounted for more than two-thirds of the total. NASA's spending began to taper off after reaching a peak in fiscal 1966. *(See table.)*

The Apollo project alone employed about 420,000 persons in aerospace industries and government in the mid-1960s but fewer than half that number in early 1969. The prior level of Apollo employment suggested that a total of 700,000 Americans were then directly engaged in space work. The figure had dropped to 500,000 or under by 1969.

As early as 1963, some Republicans in Congress complained that the moon project detracted from important military objectives in space. The Senate GOP Policy Committee asserted that year that it would be a "fatal error" to let the Soviet Union dominate the atmosphere "while we seek to put a man on the moon." This thought recurred in the 1968 Republican platform, which deplored the "failure of the Johnson-Humphrey administration to emphasize the military uses of space for America's defense."

It was suggested that United States military and civilian space programs should be combined, as they had been before 1958. There was speculation that President Nixon might name Bernard Schriever, a retired Air Force lieutenant general, to succeed James E. Webb, who resigned as NASA administrator Oct. 7, 1968, in apparent protest at repeated reductions in the space agency's budget. Nixon, however, named Dr. Thomas O. Paine, who had been acting administrator since Webb's departure. Paine had argued strongly for bigger civilian space spending and for a continuation of manned space flights beyond the moon.

Civilian and military space programs were separated by the National Aeronautics and Space Act of 1958 (PL 85-568). The Act created NASA, a civilian organization, to administer the principal parts of the space program. A major segment was left to the Defense Department, with

the Air Force as its chief agent. Other parts of the program were assigned to such agencies as the Atomic Energy Commission (nuclear rocket propulsion) and Commerce Department (weather satellites).

The separation at times proved more theoretical than actual. Space shots conducted by civilian authorities often had potential military applications, and vice versa. The Army's Jupiter rocket was used to place America's first satellite in orbit, Jan. 31, 1958. The following year President Eisenhower transferred to NASA the rocket team headed by Dr. Wernher von Braun, then working for the Army Ballistic Missile Agency. (Von Braun and his team were to build the Saturn V rocket, believed to be the world's most powerful.) Forty-two of the 66 astronauts chosen by NASA were military and naval officers. (As of April 1969, 52 astronauts remained; six had resigned or transferred and eight had been killed.)

Of some 455 successful American space launches between 1958 and 1968, 278 were conducted by or for the Defense Department. Cape Kennedy was the major launch site for manned, lunar, planetary and communication satellites; Vandenberg Air Force Base, Calif., for military polar orbit flights and for weather and navigation satellite launchings; Wallops Island, Va., for certain small satellites; and White Sands Proving Grounds, N.M., for short-range testing.

Military Aspects

The military aspects of space took on added importance when Robert S. McNamara, then Secretary of Defense, disclosed in November 1967 that the Russians were working on a Fractional Orbital Bombardment System—known by its initials FOBS. The 1968-69 edition of Jane's *All the World's Aircraft,* authoritative aerospace reference book, estimated that the Soviets had tested at least 12 rocket carriers for FOBS since Jan. 25, 1967. FOBS is a nuclear bomb designed to rocket into orbit at about 100 miles above earth. It can be called down onto a target before it completes one orbit. The low altitude, compared with the 700-mile height reached by an Intercontinental Ballistic Missile, would presumably cut warning time sharply. The McNamara disclosure became an issue in policy debate in Washington over whether to build an Anti-Ballistic Missile System (ABM). *(See chapter on National Security.)*

John S. Foster, Jr., director of defense research and engineering for the Defense Department, disclosed in a speech in Dallas, Dec. 13, 1967, that the United States was developing a spacecraft—which he described as a "space bus"—that could carry several thermonuclear warheads and drop them off one at a time as it passed over enemy cities. The new weapon, known also as the MIRV (for multiple, independently targeted re-entry vehicles), would be sent into space by either the Minuteman-3 intercontinental ballistic missile or by the submarine-borne Poseidon missile.

Foster described MIRV as "a major breakthrough in missile technology." He said that after it is launched and the main booster has cut off, it "keeps making minor adjustments to its speed and direction, and after each adjustment it ejects another warhead."

Under the 1967 treaty on outer space, the United States and Russia promised to abstain from placing weapons of mass destruction in space, but work on the development of such weapons was not barred. The two nations also promised under the 1963 test-ban treaty to refrain from nuclear testing in outer space.

Some advocates of greater military emphasis on space contended that it might improve the prospects for world peace. They noted that "spy" satellites might entirely replace electronic surveillance ships and airplanes and reduce the chances of war from an accidental intrusion into enemy territory. If the Russians and Americans agreed upon strategic arms limitations, satellites might become the means by which one side policed the other. Moscow had always balked at suggestions of on-site inspections or plane flyovers. But Russian and American satellites were already in the skies, taking pictures of the earth below without regard for national boundaries. The two countries were believed about on a par in terms of "spy" satellite capability.

President Johnson said in 1967, in what was intended as an "off-the-record" remark, that Samos reconnaissance satellites yielded intelligence worth 10 times what the United States had spent on space. A proposal under discussion in 1968 to set up a network of reconnaissance satellites was described as consisting of 100 or more satellites using the latest refinements in communications, electronics and photography. Their cameras could detect from a distance objects less than one-foot wide, and their radars could "see" objects six feet wide.

MANNED ORBITING LABORATORY

A key element of the proposed network, according to the Air Force Association's *Air Force and Space Digest* (March 1968), would be a Manned Orbiting Laboratory (MOL)—the first manned military excursion in space. Engineering work on the MOL began in 1967 and was intended to be airborne in the early 1970s. As envisioned by its planners, crews would remain in orbit 30 days at a time conducting military experiments with complex equipment.

They would be launched into orbit in a Gemini B spacecraft and transfer from the Gemini to the laboratory, where they could work in a "shirt-sleeve" environment unencumbered by space suits. To return to earth, they would re-enter the Gemini B and descend into the atmosphere for an ocean landing and recovery—while a replacement crew was being sent up.

NASA envisioned similar permanent stations in orbit around the earth from which astronauts could shuttle back and forth. This was part of a package of projects called Apollo Applications to be pursued in the 1970s after a series of moon landings. But Congress had been wary of duplicating MOL, and for that reason, and others, sharply reduced NASA's requests in 1967 and 1968 for Apollo Application funds. As the year closed, the agency's post-moon space goals were uncertain. The Defense Department announced June 10, 1969, that it had ordered the MOL program cancelled as a "major step" toward reducing the military budget. The cancellation, together with the success of the Apollo shots, brightened prospects by mid-1969 of continued congressional support of NASA programs.

United States Space Spending

Fiscal year	NASA[1]	Defense	Other[2]	Totals
	(millions of dollars)			
1955	$ 73.8	$ 1.5	——	$ 75.3
1956	71.1	16.5	12.5	100.1
1957	76.1	47.5	26.5	150.1
1958	89.2	135.5	24.2	248.9
1959	145.6	341.0	34.1	520.7
1960	401.0	518.1	41.1	960.2
1961	744.3	710.0	64.3	1,518.6
1962	1,257.0	1,028.8	131.9	2,417.7
1963	2,552.3	1,367.5	194.3	4,114.1
1964	4,171.0	1,563.5	235.0	5,969.5
1965	5,092.9	1,591.8	259.3	6,944.0
1966	5,933.0	1,637.4	223.4	7,793.8
1967	5,425.7	1,673.1	227.5	7,326.3
1968	4,723.7	1,890.2	181.2	6,795.1
1969[3]	4,249.7	2,095.0	150.5	6,495.2
	$35,006.4	$14,617.4	$1,805.8	$51,429.6

1 *Includes amounts for non-defense space technology before NASA was established in 1958.*
2 *Atomic Energy Commission, National Science Foundation, Departments of Agriculture, Commerce and Interior.*
3 *Estimate for year ending June 30, 1969.*

SOURCE: Bureau of the Budget, President's 1968 Report to Congress on Aeronautics and Space Activities.

New Space Goals

Presidential science adviser Lee A. DuBridge announced Feb. 13, 1969, that a summer study would be conducted to draw up plans for the nation's space program during the next decade. The study, DuBridge said, would be conducted jointly by his office, the National Aeronautics and Space Council, the National Aeronautics and Space Administration and the Department of Defense. A report to President Nixon was due about Sept. 1, 1969.

The National Aeronautics and Space Council is a five-man body set up to coordinate and give over-all direction to the nation's space effort. Established in 1958 under President Eisenhower, the Council was revised in 1961 by President Kennedy to consist of the Vice President, the Secretaries of State and Defense and the heads of NASA and the Atomic Energy Commission.

In making the announcement, DuBridge said that personally he would like to see a balanced space program in the future rather than a program committed primarily to one project. The existing space program had been criticized as being over-committed to the Apollo manned mission.

Dr. George E. Mueller, associate administrator of NASA, disclosed at the Manned Spacecraft Center in Houston March 13, 1969, that NASA advocated 11 manned landings on the moon, at the rate of two or three a year through 1974.

Apollo 11 Mission Completed...

The Mission:

A manned moon landing, the goal of the American space program since 1961, came at 4:17 P.M. EDT, July 20, 1969. Astronauts Neil A. Armstrong and Edwin E. Aldrin Jr. of the Apollo 11 mission descended in their lunar module, the "Eagle," to a level rock-strewn plain near the southwestern edge of the moon's arid Sea of Tranquility.

The first words spoken by man on the moon were Armstrong's, radioed to Mission Control at the Manned Spacecraft Center, Houston, Texas, and heard by listeners around the world: "Houston, Tranquility Base here. The Eagle has landed."

Armstrong had been designated in advance to be the first man actually to set foot on the lunar surface. He did so six and one-half hours later, at 10:56 P.M. EDT. A television camera attached to the lunar module recorded the event "live" for viewers on earth. They saw the astronaut—a ghost-like figure in his bulky, white spacesuit—slowly crawl backwards down a ladder fixed to one of the lunar module's four legs. "That's one small step for man, one giant leap for mankind," he said as he stepped onto the moon.

Armstrong gingerly tested the firmness of the finely grained, grayish lunar soil and found that it supported him. Shallow footprints marked his steps. The moon's gravity, only one-sixth as strong as the earth's, permitted relatively free body movement despite the cumbersome spacesuit and back pack.

Science Tasks. Within 20 minutes, Aldrin became the second human in history to plant a foot on the moon. He joined Armstrong at 11:14 P.M. EDT. Their moon exploration continued about two hours, until they reentered the Eagle at 1:09 P.M. EDT. In that time they conducted a number of tasks on behalf of science and erected an American flag on a metal staff—while providing television pictures and a running commentary. They placed rocks and lunar soil in sealed boxes for the return trip to earth, where, it was hoped, scientists might examine the specimens free of exposure to the earth's environment. They left behind two scientific instruments—a package of seismometers to detect moonquakes and a reflector to bounce laser pulses back to earth.

Armstrong's first step onto the moon was planned originally to come about five hours later than it did. Part of the intervening time after the Eagle's landing was scheduled for sleeping. But after making sure that their rocket engines could be refired for departure, the two astronauts decided to forgo rest. Houston concurred in their decision. They slumbered for a few hours after returning to the Eagle, but only fitfully, according to signals received in Houston from medical monitoring devices.

The Eagle blasted off the moon at 1:55 P.M. EDT, July 21, as flawlessly as it had alighted almost 21 hours earlier. It rejoined the command module, Columbia, at 5:35 P.M. EDT. The Columbia had been manned by the third Apollo 11 astronaut, Michael Collins, since the two spacecraft separated—"undocked"—shortly after 1:50 P.M. EDT the previous day. Collins circled the moon 31 times in all—on about half of the orbits he was without companions and was out of radio contact with anyone while on the moon's far side. His vigil has been described as man's loneliest venture into space.

For several minutes after undocking, prior to the moon landing, Columbia and Eagle flew only a few feet apart in their moon orbit. Then Collins maneuvered the Columbia away while the Eagle began the first phase of its descent, from an altitude of 65.5 miles. At around 50,000 feet above the moon surface, about the lowest point reached by Apollo 10 in May 1969, the Eagle began descending in a steadily steepening trajectory toward the landing site 250 miles away. In the final minutes before landing, Armstrong took control manually when he saw that the computer-operated automatic control was guiding the craft down onto a football-field-size crater studded with large boulders. He flew the Eagle to a smoother site nearby and touched down with only enough descent fuel left in the engine's reservoir to fly 30 seconds more.

Departure for Earth. Upon leaving the moon, Eagle rejoined Columbia in orbit so surely that only one mid-course correction was required. The reunited crew of Apollo 11 fired the propulsion rockets of their command ship and broke out of moon orbit at 12:56 A.M. EDT, July 22, for the return trip of about 245,000 miles. The astronauts splashed down in the Pacific at 12:50 P.M. EDT, July 24, eight days after their launching from atop a Saturn V rocket at Cape Kennedy, Fla.

The launching came precisely on schedule at 9:32 A.M. EDT, July 16. It was witnessed by Vice President Spiro T. Agnew, former President Lyndon B. Johnson, hundreds of Members of Congress, space officials, foreign dignitaries and by countless thousands of curiosity seekers who lined nearby beaches, highways and waterways. Millions more saw the launching on television.

President Nixon was aboard the aircraft carrier Hornet to welcome the astronauts after their recovery from the sea. Their spacecraft splashed down some 210 miles south of tiny Johnston Island and 920 miles southwest of Honolulu. Nixon had previously congratulated the Apollo 11 crew by radio-telephone during their moon walk, July 20, and on the day of the launching he had proclaimed the following Monday, July 21, a "National Day of Participation." The President decreed that most federal workers would receive the day off, and he urged that other employers excuse their workers that day. The proclamation stated that "...we on earth will want, as

...Man Sets Foot Upon the Moon

one people, to be with them in spirit to share the glory and the wonder and to support them with prayers that all will go well."

Astronaut Quarantine. The returning astronauts were unable to greet the President directly, because of precautions taken to guard against the remote chance that they might be carrying some disease-producing organism from the moon. Elaborate plans had been made for a 21-day quarantine of the astronauts after their return to earth. While still in their spaceship afloat at sea, awaiting rescue, they each zipped into a covering garment designed to shield others from any contamination. Upon reaching the Hornet, the three astronauts entered isolated living quarters—a mobile van that resembled a house trailer.

When the carrier reached Honolulu, the astronauts in their van were placed aboard a cargo jet and flown to Houston, where they were transferred to specially built quarters at the Manned Spacecraft Center for the remainder of the quarantine. They underwent detailed medical examinations.

The lunar materials that the astronauts brought back had meanwhile been flown ahead to an adjoining laboratory at the Manned Spacecraft Center for examination by scientists under conditions designed to keep the specimens free of earthly contamination. These were among the greatest scientific prizes of all time. After study at the laboratory, some pieces of lunar rocks were due to be sent to scientists in several foreign countries. The bulk of the moon materials would remain in the laboratory.

The Astronauts:

Neil A. Armstrong. A civilian test pilot and former Navy combat flier, he was among the second group of astronauts chosen, Sept. 17, 1962. Armstrong was born in Wapakoneta, Ohio, Aug. 5, 1930, and received a bachelor of science degree in aeronautical engineering from Purdue University in 1955. He was command pilot of the Gemini 8 mission, backup command pilot of Gemini 5 and Gemini 11, and commander of the Apollo 11 lunar module. He is married and has two children.

Edwin Eugene ("Buzz") Aldrin Jr. An Air Force colonel, he was born in Montclair, N.J., Jan. 30, 1930, and was graduated from West Point in 1951 with a bachelor of science degree. Aldrin entered the Air Force and completed work on a doctor of science degree in astronautics at Massachusetts Institute of Technology in 1963. Among the third group of astronauts chosen, Oct. 8, 1963, he was pilot for the backup crew of Gemini 9, pilot for Gemini 12 and lunar module crewman for

Apollo 11. He is considered expert in orbital rendezvous techniques. He is married and has three children.

Michael Collins. An Air Force lieutenant colonel, he is the son of a career Army officer. Collins was born in Rome, Italy, Oct. 31, 1930, and was graduated from West Point in 1952 with a bachelor of science degree. He entered the Air Force and, along with Aldrin, was among the third group of astronauts chosen. He was backup pilot for Gemini 7, pilot for Gemini 10, and command module pilot for Apollo 11. He is married and has three children.

Lunar Module:

The lunar module (LM or "lem") is like no other contraption flown by man. It has the appearance of a gigantic mechanical bug with Rube Goldberg-like fixtures jutting out at odd angles. It weighs 16 tons and stands on four legs of 10-foot length.

Streamlining was not necessary in the LM design because the moon is airless and thus offers no airflow resistance to moving vehicles. For its passage through the earth's atmosphere, the legs and antennas retract. The lunar module rode into space between the third, or topmost, stage of the Saturn V rocket and the Apollo 11 command module ("mother ship").

Upon descending to the moon, the LM shielded the two astronauts inside with its featherweight covering of insulation—25 layers or so of ultrathin aluminized sheets. This shielding offered the crew protection from temperature extremes and from showers of micrometeorites before they put on their spacesuits.

Spacesuits:

For their moon walk, Armstrong and Aldrin wore pressurized and inflated spacesuits made of 26 layers for protection against radiation, heat and cold, and the lack of pressure in an environment that is almost a vacuum. The suits, together with backpack, each weighed 180 pounds on earth but only 30 on the moon. They provide moon explorers with an "earth environment" for two and one-half hours—water to drink and oxygen to breathe—and radio contact with each other and with earth.

The outer layer of the spacesuit was a milky-white heat-resistant glass fabric that was coated with a tough plastic. On the shoulder was sewn an American flag. Thick boots—"lunar overshoes"—and a helmet of clear and unbreakable plastic completed the Apollo 11 astronauts' outfits.

NASA Administrators

James E. Webb resigned as Administrator of the National Aeronautics and Space Administration, effective Oct. 7, 1968. In leaving the post he had held since February 1961, Webb told newsmen that repeated reductions in the space agency's budget had allowed the Soviet Union to build up a commanding lead in space exploration. "We are going to be in second place for some time," he said on Sept. 16 when he announced his resignation.

President Johnson named Dr. Thomas O. Paine, the deputy administrator of NASA, as acting administrator. President Nixon nominated, and the Senate confirmed, on March 4, 1969, Paine as Administrator, the third man to head NASA since the agency's founding.

NASA Administrators (date of Senate confirmation in parentheses):

T. Keith Glennan	(Aug. 15, 1958)
James E. Webb	(Feb. 9, 1961)
Thomas O. Paine	(March 4, 1969)

Communications Satellites

GLOBAL SYSTEM

The world's first commercial communications satellite, the American-built Early Bird, was launched from Cape Kennedy, April 6, 1965. It immediately began relaying telecasts across the Atlantic and soon had increased trans-Atlantic telephone capacity by two-thirds. The 85-pound satellite was placed in synchronous orbit—timed to the speed of the earth's rotation—so that it had the effect of hovering (from a height of 22,300 miles) over a fixed point off the eastern coast of Brazil near the equator. Placement near the equator increased the range of its signals, because of the curvature of the earth.

Similar satellite communications were extended across the Pacific with the launching, Oct. 26, 1966, of the Pacific One ("Lani Bird") satellite, the first of a bigger and more powerful series known as Intelsat II. It succeeded in transmitting television broadcasts from Australia to Britain for the first time and between the United States and Japan. But it never reached the desired orbit and had only limited use when supplanted Jan. 11, 1967, by the Pacific Two satellite. A second Atlantic satellite was added March 22, 1967, and another Pacific satellite went up Sept. 27, 1967.

The first of the still more powerful intelsat III series of satellites was put into orbit over the Atlantic, Dec. 18, 1968, and the second over the Pacific, Feb. 5, 1969. Two additional launchings in this series were planned in the first half of 1969. Plans were afoot for these new satellites to be followed in 1971 by an Intelsat IV series, each with a capacity of 3,000 to 10,000 telephone circuits. In contrast, the Early Bird, which was phased out of service after 43 months of commercial operation, had only 240 circuits. Each Intelsat III had 1,200 and weighed almost four times as much as Early Bird. By early 1969 all of the airborne satellites radiated signals over one-third of the earth's surface.

INTELSAT AND COMSAT

The communications satellites and their ground facilities were owned jointly by member nations of the International Telecommunications Satellite Consortium (Intelsat). The United States was represented in Intelsat through the Communications Satellite Corporation (Comsat). Comsat also acted as Intelsat agent by contracting with the National Aeronautics and Space Administration (NASA) to launch the communications satellites.

Congress declared in the Communications Satellite Act of 1962 (PL 87-624) that it was "the policy of the United States to establish, in conjunction and in cooperation with other countries, as expeditiously as practicable a commercial communications satellite system, as part of an improved global communications network, which will be responsive to public needs and national objectives...."

The same act authorized the creation of Comsat as the American segment of the global system. Comsat was to be established as a private corporation for profit, subject to government regulation, including responsibility to the State Department to establish service to foreign points that might be deemed unprofitable. Shares would be sold in the new corporation, one-half to the public generally and one-half to a group of American-owned communications carriers, of which American Telephone & Telegraph Co. was by far the largest. The act provided for a 15-member board of directors, three to be named by the President, six elected by public shareholders and six by corporate shareholders (amended by Congress in February 1969 to provide for eight public and four corporate directors—reflecting changes in stock ownership).

The stock, issued in 1964, was promptly oversubscribed. In the same year, the United States and 18 other nations formed Intelsat by signing interim agreements in Washington allocating among them the ownership and financing of the space portion (in contrast to ground facilities) of the communications satellite system. The quotas were subject to change as new members were added. Intelsat had 68 members by April 1969. (See box.)

The original agreements specified that the U.S. share of the total ownership would never be less than 50.6 percent. At the beginning of the 1965-68 period the American share was 61 percent and at the end 53 percent.

Voting rights were allocated accordingly, and exercised through a 12-member international committee. Because the United States would always have more than 50 percent control, the rules originally required a 73.5 percent (later 66 percent) majority vote to make policy decisions. The United States thus did not have absolute voting power, but it did hold veto power.

SOVIET CHALLENGE

American dominance of the satellite communications system was being challenged by Russia and by Western Europe as the time approached for reaching permanent agreements on Intelsat. The interim agreements were due to expire in 1970. The Soviet Union in 1968 proposed a rival system of satellite communications called Intersputnik and recruited seven other potential members: Bulgaria, Cuba, Czechoslovakia, Hungary, Mongolia, Poland and Rumania. The Russians had no synchronous satellites in orbit, but there was no doubt about their ability to put them up. Intersputnik, if developed, would be an extension of the Cold War into circumterrestial space.

Signals from rival satellites in orbit would be likely to interfere with one another. For that reason or others, Russia had begun in late 1968 to indicate that it was weighing a standing offer to join Intelsat. A Russian observer attended a month-long conference of member nations that met in Washington on Feb. 24, 1969. Moscow was understood to be demanding a "one nation, one vote" formula as a condition for entering the organization. The United States appeared unwilling to go that far, but some compromise appeared in the offing to still Western European criticism of American dominance. France, in particular, sought to have areas of regional control provided within Intelsat. An international committee, designated at the Washington meeting, set out to draft proposed language for permanent agreements which would be submitted for ratification at another meeting in Washington, in November 1969.

COMSAT PROBLEMS

The communications satellite program was beset by political problems at home as well as abroad. During the 1965-68 years a controversy developed between proponents of communications satellites and interests with big investments in older systems of communications. In a series of controversial decisions, the Federal Communications Commission generally defined Comsat's function as that of a "carrier's carrier." In essence, it would be limited to leasing satellite circuits to its would-be competitors for resale to the ultimate consumer. As created by Congress, Comsat was a corporate anomaly in that its potential competitors—AT&T and Radio Corporation of America, for example—had a voice in its operation.

The 1962 Act was written on the assumption that, for the immediate future, the only system that could be operational would be one using low- or intermediate-altitude satellites, such as AT&T's "Telstar." Because such a global system would require numerous satellites and expensive mobile tracking equipment, only a few visionary technicians thought satellites soon would be competitive with surface communications.

By mid-1963, Hughes Aircraft Co. had developed and perfected a new satellite that could be placed high enough (22,300 miles) to make its orbit synchronous with the rotation of the earth. Completion of the global system required only three synchronous satellites. Thus competition with surface communications came quickly.

Domestic applications of Comsat were left unclear in the 1962 law. It stated only that they were not "precluded...if required to meet unique governmental interests." In December 1966, the FCC reversed an earlier tentative decision which would have allowed Comsat to become the sole owner of satellite ground stations in the United States and its possessions. The final ruling required a 50-50 ownership of the stations by Comsat and private communications carriers.

A major controversy over domestic satellite applications developed in 1965, when the American Broadcasting Co. (ABC) applied to the FCC for permission to operate its own domestic satellite system to handle its TV service. (Network TV was being transmitted over coaxial

---

Intelsat Member Nations

Signers of the original 1964 agreements: United States, Australia, Austria, Belgium, Britain, Canada, Denmark, France, West Germany, Ireland, Italy, Japan, the Netherlands, Norway, Portugal, Spain, Sweden, Switzerland, and Vatican City.

Subsequent members: Algeria, Argentina, Brazil, Ceylon, Chile, Colombia, Ethiopia, Greece, Guatemala, India, Indonesia, Iran, Iraq, Israel, Jamaica, Jordan, Kenya, South Korea, Kuwait, Lebanon, Libya, Liechtenstein, Luxembourg.

Malaysia, Mexico, Monaco, Morocco, New Zealand, Nicaragua, Nigeria, Pakistan, Panama, Peru, Philippines, Saudi Arabia, Singapore, South Africa, South Vietnam, Sudan, Syria, Taiwan, Tanzania, Thailand, Tunisia, Turkey, Uganda, United Arab Republic, Venezuela and Yemen.

---

cable by AT&T at a total cost to the three networks of about $65 million a year. AT&T in 1968 filed with the FCC for an increase to $85 million.) The FCC dismissed ABC's application on technical grounds but invited comments from all interested parties on the issues raised by the proposal.

Most of the controversy centered on a subsequent proposal by the Ford Foundation to create a nonprofit satellite television system (operated by a new entity—not the Foundation) which would use profits from commercial television service to finance new instructional TV networks into a coast-to-coast system. (Despite the satellite savings, the commercial networks would continue to pay the old rates. The resulting profits would be "social dividend" for educational TV.)

Both Comsat and AT&T strongly opposed the plan and submitted their own proposals. The proposals submitted by Comsat and AT&T were essentially the same. Both would provide for a multipurpose system that would handle telephone and data transmission as well as TV; both would provide channels for educational TV, but not for free as under the Ford plan.

COMMUNICATIONS POLICY STUDY

President Johnson in 1967 named a Task Force on Communications Policy to conduct what White House officials described as "the most comprehensive review of international and domestic communications policy since the Communications Act of 1934."

Johnson sent a special message to Congress, Aug. 14, 1967, announcing the Task Force of top governmental officials headed by Eugene V. Rostow, Under Secretary of State for Political Affairs. The President directed the group to study a number of pressing questions, including (1) whether the nation was making full use of the electromagnetic frequency spectrum; (2) the feasibility of a domestic satellite system; (3) whether a domestic system should be general-purpose or specialized and whether there should be more than one domestic system; and (4) how these and other developments would affect Comsat and the international communications carriers.

Developments in the Space Race 1957-68

Robert H. Goddard, an American physicist drawn to space flight in part by Jules Verne's fictional *From the Earth to the Moon* (1865), launched the world's first liquid-fuel rocket on March 16, 1926, at Auburn, Mass. NASA historian Eugene M. Emme calls the 184-foot flight "as significant to space flight as the flight of the Wright Brothers...was to aviation." Goddard's work long went little noted in this country, but it provided a basis for the work of German scientists, including Werner Von Braun, who built the V-2 rocket during World War II.

The United States and the Soviet Union raced in the 1950s to build intercontinental ballistic missiles capable of delivering thermonuclear (hydrogen) warheads across the oceans.

The Russians concentrated on building large thrust boosters, while the Americans developed compact warheads which required a less powerful missile. The Atlas, Minuteman and Titan ICBMs, major bulwarks in this country's strategic defense, followed. The Soviets, capitalizing on an overly large rocket which had been designed to carry massive uranium-fission warheads, had an advantage over the Americans when the space race got under way.

The space age opened Oct. 4, 1957, when the Soviets' Sputnik I was lofted into an elliptical orbit around the earth. Circling the globe every 96.2 minutes, the 184-pound sphere reminded Americans for three months that their opponents had scored the first major technological triumph on the new frontier of space—and one the United States could not then match.

The Soviets followed up on Nov. 3, 1957, with the second man-made earth satellite, Sputnik II. It weighed 1,120 pounds and carried a dog, Laika, which lived a week. The first American satellite launch effort originally scheduled as a test firing in the non-military Vanguard series, collapsed with explosion of the booster before a national television audience.

It was Jan. 31, 1958, before the United States orbited Explorer I, its first earth satellite, under Army auspices. The satellite's discovery of the Van Allen radiation belts around the earth was called in some quarters the most significant finding of the International Geophysical Year (July 1957-December 1958). Critics noted, meanwhile, that Sputnik I weighed six times as much and Sputnik II 36 times as much as the 31-pound Explorer. The Americans' Vanguard I satellite, orbited March 17, 1958, showed that the earth was pear-shaped.

Such achievements led United States spokesmen to claim, with considerable justification at the time, greater sophistication for American space efforts and a broader scientific base. American results were shared with the world; the Soviets kept theirs largely to themselves. But the Soviets capitalized thereafter on their running start and the capability for the spectacular provided by their powerful first-stage booster rockets. The headlines went to the sensational. Premier Nikita S. Khrushchev said the Soviets had "outstripped the U.S. in science and technology." The Soviets hit the moon with Luna II on Sept. 13, 1959, two days before

Khrushchev visited the United States. Their Luna III circled the moon and radioed the first photographs of its hidden side.

In the first four years of the space age, the United States launched 55 satellites and space probes (as against the Soviet Union's 16) and sent Alan B. Shepard Jr., and Virgil I. (Gus) Grissom on sub-orbital rides into space. But the Soviets had launched Yuri Gagarin into the first manned earth orbit on April 12, 1961, three weeks before Shepard's flight. Each country had placed two satellites in orbit around the sun.

President Kennedy told Congress on May 25, 1961, that it was time "for this nation to take a clearly leading role in space achievement." Urging a national commitment to a manned moon-landing by 1970, the President said: "No single space project in this period will be more impressive to mankind, or more important for the long-range exploration of space." With Gagarin's recent orbit and the prospects raised by Shepard's flight fresh in mind, Congress set the moon as a national goal and opened a generous line of credit.

A rapid buildup began with acceleration of some existing projects. Congress doubled NASA's appropriation for 1962 and again for 1963, nearly doubled it again the third year. The Mercury man-in-space series, a 25-flight program authorized Oct. 7, 1958, six days after NASA was organized, reached its primary objective on Feb. 20, 1962, when John H. Glenn Jr. flew the first U.S. orbital flight in Friendship 7. Work was already in progress on the next step of the manned push into space—Gemini. Development of the Saturn rocket began in 1958; its first launch on Oct. 27, 1961, signified America's entry into the large booster field.

In other activity instrumented spaceships flew deep into space. Mariner II passed within 21,594 miles of Venus. Mariner IV flew past Mars. Ranger VII struck the moon after sending back 4,316 quality pictures of the surface. The United States still trailed the Soviets in some ways, but its space program was clearly in high gear.

Death struck the American space effort without warning at a Cape Kennedy missile pad on Jan. 27, 1967. Fire engulfed the oxygen environment of the Apollo moon capsule during ground tests preparatory to an orbital test flight. Three astronauts were trapped with no chance to escape—veteran Virgil I. (Gus) Grissom, "space walker" Edward H. White and Roger B. Chaffee. The tragedy shocked the nation, touched off investigations, and launched the civilian space agency on the stormiest stage of its career just three months before the Soviets lost their first cosmonaut.

Investigators criticized many aspects of NASA's program, but Administrator James E. Webb rode out the storm, as did the agency he headed. NASA made personnel changes and ordered major engineering improvements in the Apollo capsule. The worked-over moon capsule received its first manned flight test in the Apollo 7 mission of October 1968 and was pronounced fit. The way was clear for the spectacular manned moon flights to come.

The study group issued a report to the White House in the closing weeks of the Johnson Administration but it was not made public. It was understood that the Task Force members reflected the sharp disagreements found in industry and government over some basic policy matters and that no real consensus emerged.

The report did contain a number of recommendations, the news media learned. *Telecommunications Reports*, a weekly publication covering the communications field, reported Dec. 9, 1968, that the Task Force had concluded "that a single entity for international transmission" would be the most effective because it would have no vested interests in any particular technology and thus would be in a better position than existing companies to make impartial decisions. The creation of such an entity would presumably entail the consolidation of some AT&T and Comsat facilities.

As for the domestic use of satellites, the Task Force was said to have urged establishment of a pilot program in which Comsat would have primary responsibility. In discussing Intelsat, the report took the position that the United States should be willing to adjust its structure to gain world cooperation.

Chronology

Of Space

Activities

1965

CONGRESSIONAL ACTION

Funds Reduced. For the first time, funds requested for and appropriated to the National Aeronautics and Space Administration dropped below the level of the previous year. The largest single cuts made by Congress in the Administration's requests were for the manned lunar landing program, Project Apollo. In the NASA authorization bill for fiscal 1966 (HR 7717—PL 89-53), Congress set a ceiling of $5,190,396,200 on NASA appropriations—a $69.5 million cut in the request, of which $38.9 million was cut from Apollo. In the Independent Offices Appropriations Act for fiscal 1966 (HR 7997—PL 89-128), Congress made a slight additional cut, leaving $5,190,305,200. NASA officials and the President, however, subsequently asserted that the United States still intended to achieve the previously established goal of landing a man on the moon by 1970.

Amendments Defeated. The Senate rejected an amendment by Sen. William Proxmire (D Wis.) to reduce NASA appropriations further—by 5 percent ($259.5 million). Proxmire called the space effort "one program in which there has been a lot of waste" and said NASA was "the prime example" of an agency "whose expenditures Congress has difficulty in controlling, let alone fully

---

X-15 Astronaut-Pilots

The X-15 was a research aircraft that could fly at hypersonic speeds (over 4,500 miles per hour) and reach heights of over 350,000 feet. The X-15 program was a joint NASA-Air Force project which was canceled in December 1968.

By Air Force directive any pilot who flies to an altitude of 50 miles or more is eligible to receive astronaut rating. The military men involved in the project who qualified for the astronaut label were given astronaut wings: the civilians who achieved the title received no wings but were given the astronaut rating.

The X-15 pilots were: Maj. Michael J. Adams; Neil A. Armstrong; A. Scott Crossfield; William H. Dana; Capt. Joe H. Engle; Maj. William J. Knight; John B. McKay; Capt. Forest Petersen; Lt. Col. Robert A. Rushworth; Milton O. Thompson; Joseph A. Walker; Lt. Col. Robert M. White.

Armstrong and Engle left the program to become NASA astronauts. Adams left the Defense Department's Manned-Orbiting-Laboratory program to become a pilot for the X-15 program.

---

understanding." He contended NASA activities were consuming "too great a proportion of our national resources...monetary, material and manpower resources." Wayne Morse (D Ore.) described the space program as "the most elaborate, costly and uneconomical venture of our lifetime, all for the purpose of gratifying our national ego."

The amendment was strongly opposed by John Stennis (D Miss.), who called the proposed cut a "lick in the dark" and argued that the United States could not, in terms of national security, afford to let "anyone else become superior" to it in space.

Manned Orbiting Laboratory. President Johnson announced on Aug. 25 that he had directed the Defense Department to proceed "immediately" with development of a $1.5 billion manned orbiting laboratory. It would be the Defense Department's first manned space assignment. All previous manned space activities had been assigned to NASA. The President said unmanned test flights of the MOL were scheduled for late 1966 and early 1967, to be followed by manned flight late in 1968.

In the Defense Department Appropriations Act for fiscal 1966 (HR 9221—PL 89-213), Congress earmarked $150 million of the Air Force research and development funds in the bill for the MOL program.

SPACE FEATS

Major achievements of the U.S. space program in 1965 were five two-man Gemini flights of increasing length and complexity, and close-up photographs of Mars transmitted by a space probe, Mariner IV. The purpose of the Gemini flights was to perfect devices and techniques for Project Apollo, designed to carry men to the moon before the end of 1969. The photographs of Mars revealed, in the view of most scientists, the improbability of the existence of life on that planet. Generally, in the 1965 Gemini flights, men performed far above expectations, while machines proved fallible. The flights and what they achieved:

Gemini 3. Manned by astronauts Virgil I. Grissom and John W. Young, Gemini 3 was the first maneuverable space craft. The craft March 23 made three orbits in four hours, 53 minutes.

Gemini 4. Astronauts Edward H. White II and James A. McDivitt June 3-7 orbited the earth 62 times in Gemini 4. During the flight, White left the spacecraft and maneuvered himself in space for 23 minutes, the first American astronaut to take a "walk in space."

Gemini 5. In a flight lasting 190 hours and 56 minutes and orbiting the earth 120 times, astronauts L. Gordon Cooper Jr. and Charles Conrad Jr. broke the previous record for number of orbits (81) and time in space (119 hours) set in 1963 by a Russian cosmonaut. At the end of six orbits it was feared the mission would be ended, but the astronauts cut electricity use to a minimum, nursed the electrical system back to the point of normal power and continued the flight on a day-to-day basis.

Gemini 6 and 7. A meeting Dec. 15 of two space ships 180 miles above the earth represented the greatest success up until that time in the U.S. program to land a man on the moon. Gemini 7, flown by astronauts Frank Borman and James A. Lovell Jr., was launched Dec. 4. Gemini 6, manned by astronauts Walter Schirra Jr. and Maj. Thomas Stafford, was launched Dec. 15 and reached the point of rendezvous with Gemini 7 in four orbits. The space ships flew in formation for four hours, separated at one time by only one foot. Gemini 6 was only 26 hours aloft, descending Dec. 16, but Gemini 7 remained aloft for 330 hours and 35 minutes, longer than any previous space flight. It came down Dec. 18.

Mariner IV. After a 325-million-mile flight that began Nov. 28, 1964, the Mariner IV space probe July 15 transmitted the first close-up photographs of Mars. The plannet "fly-by" brought Mariner IV within 6,118 miles of the planet. The photographs, the first close-up photographs of another planet, showed a crater-pocked landscape lacking any sign of water erosion or other indication that life might be sustained on Mars. President Johnson said July 29, "It may be, it just may be, that life as we know it with its humanity is more unique than many have thought, and we must remember this."

Ranger Shots. The Ranger 8 unmanned craft Feb. 20 crash-landed in the moon's Sea of Tranquility after transmitting 7,137 pictures of the lunar surface. Ranger

9, launched March 21, transmitted 5,814 pictures before crashing only four miles off target in the Alphonsus crater.

Soviet Feats. A Russian cosmonaut, Aleksei A. Leonov, March 18 was the first man to step outside a space craft and float in space. Russian viewers saw the maneuver and other activities of Leonov and his fellow cosmonaut on television. The flight lasted 26 hours 17 orbits. Russia July 16 demonstrated a powerful new booster rocket, Proton I, that lifted into orbit the heaviest payload, 26,000 pounds. The heaviest payload lifted by the U.S. was 19,000 pounds. Dr. George E. Mueller, chief of manned flight for NASA, said it would take "a great number of years" for the U.S. to achieve first place in space.

1966

LEGISLATION

NASA Funding. For the first time in four years, Congress in 1966 appropriated less than $5 billion for the space agency. It appropriated $4,968,000,000 for fiscal 1967 after having authorized $5,000,419,000. The authorization was $11.6 million below the administration request —itself the smallest amount President Johnson had ever asked for the space program.

Johnson's View. Specific mention of the U.S. space program was conspicuously absent from President Johnson's Jan. 12 State of the Union Message. The President pledged his support for the program, however, on accepting the 1966 Goddard Trophy Award March 16. He said, "...I want to declare once again that so long as I am in public office, I am going to do everything within my power and my capability to prevent us from falling behind. We intend to land the first man on the surface of the moon, and we intend to do this in the decade of the '60s."

In other 1966 statements, President Johnson expressed an awareness of the cost of the space program and its impact on the U.S. economy. In a news conference March 22, he said that the slightly lower space budget in fiscal 1967 "will free many highly skilled workers that are now in tight supply. They estimate we will have between 50,000 and 100,000 people that will be freed unless we accelerate that budget."

SPACE FEATS

The U.S. space program in 1966 successfully concluded its two-man Gemini flights, preparatory to Project Apollo, designed to place a man on the moon. Unmanned U.S. spacecraft provided space planners with detailed knowledge of the lunar surface. Though NASA planners promised only that they would land astronauts on the moon by the end of the decade, it appeared that they were aiming for a landing in 1968.

Gemini 8. Astronauts Neil A. Armstrong and David R. Scott March 16 achieved the first linkup in space of a manned spacecraft and a separately launched target vehicle. Shortly after docking, however, the astronauts lost maneuverability of their capsule and were forced to make an emergency landing in the Pacific.

Gemini 9. Astronaut Eugene A. Cernan made one-and-a-half orbits of the earth outside the Germini 9 spacecraft during its June 3-6 flight. A target orbited for

---

Orbits or Revolutions?

Space officials describe the number of times a spacecraft circles the earth in terms of orbits or revolutions—to the confusion of laymen.

The word revolution denotes how many times a spacecraft passes over a fixed point in the sky; orbit denotes how many times it passes over a fixed point on earth. Because the earth is moving, the spacecraft completes one more orbit than revolution every 24 hours.

In the early days of space exploration, NASA officials tended to speak in terms of orbits. The later tendency has been to talk of revolutions.

Record of Manned Space Flights

Crew	Date	Spaceship	Revolutions	Weight (lbs.)	Duration (hrs.; mins.)	Distance from earth (miles)
Yuri A. Gagarin	April 12, 1961	USSR Vostok 1	1	10,419	1:48	203
Alan B. Shepard Jr.	May 5, 1961	U.S. Mercury 3	0	2,845	:15	117
Virgil I. Grissom	July 21, 1961	U.S. Mercury 3	0	2,836	:16	118
Gherman S. Titov	Aug. 6, 1961	USSR Vostok 2	16	10,432	25:18	159
John H. Glenn Jr.	Feb. 20, 1962	U.S. Mercury 6	3	2,987	4:55	162
M. Scott Carpenter	May 24, 1962	U.S. Mercury 7	3	2,975	4:56	167
Adrian G. Nikolayev	Aug. 11, 1962	USSR Vostok 3	60	10,412	94:22	156
Pavel R. Popovich	Aug. 12, 1962	USSR Vostok 4	45	10,425	70:57	157
Walter M. Schirra Jr.	Oct. 3, 1962	U.S. Mercury 8	6	3,028	9:13	176
L. Gordon Cooper Jr.	May 15-16, 1963	U.S. Mercury 8	22	3,033	34:20	166
Valery F. Bykovsky	June 14-19, 1963	USSR Vostok 5	76	10,408	119:06	139
Valentina V. Tereshkova	June 16-19, 1963	USSR Vostok 6	45	10,392	70:50	144
Vladimir M. Komarov Konstantin P. Feoktistov Boris G. Yegorov	Oct. 12, 1964	USSR Voskhod 1	15	11,731	24:17	254
Aleksei A. Leonov Pavel I. Balyayev	Mar. 18-19, 1965	USSR Voskhod 2	16	12,529	26:02	307
Virgil I. Grissom John W. Young	Mar. 23, 1965	U.S. Gemini 3	3	7,111	4:53	139
James A. McDivitt Edward H. White II	June 3-7, 1965	U.S. Gemini 4	62	7,879	97:56	184
L. Gordon Cooper Jr. Charles Conrad Jr.	Aug. 21-29, 1965	U.S. Gemini 5	120	7,947	190:56	215
Frank Borman James A. Lovell Jr.	Dec. 4-18, 1965	U.S. Gemini 7	206	8,076	330:35	203
Walter M. Schirra Jr. Thomas P. Stafford	Dec. 15-16, 1965	U.S. Gemini 6 [1]	16	7,817	25:51	189
Neil A. Armstrong David R. Scott	Mar. 16-17, 1966	U.S. Gemini 8	7	8,351	10:41	185
Thomas P. Stafford Eugene A. Cernan	June 3-6, 1966	U.S. Gemini 9	44	8,268	72:21	205
John W. Young Michael Collins	July 18-21, 1966	U.S. Gemini 10	43	8,248	70:47	476
Charles Conrad Jr. Richard F. Gordon Jr.	Sept. 12-15, 1966	U.S. Gemini 11	44	8,509	71:17	851
James A. Lovell Jr. Edwin E. Aldrin Jr.	Nov. 11-15, 1966	U.S. Gemini 12	59	8,297	94:34	188
Vladimir M. Komarov [2]	Apr. 23-24, 1967	USSR Soyuz 1	17	16,000	26:40	139
Walter M. Schirra Jr. Donn F. Eisele R. Walter Cunningham	Oct. 11-22, 1968	U.S. Apollo 7	163	45,374	260:09	279
Georgy Beregovoi	Oct. 26-30, 1968	USSR Soyuz 3	60	16,000	94:51	156
Frank Borman James A. Lovell Jr. William A. Anders	Dec. 21-27, 1968	U.S. Apollo 8	2 earth 10 moon	96,260	147:00	231,000
Vladimir A. Shatalov Aleksey S. Yeliseyev Yevgeiy V. Khrunov	Jan. 14-17, 1969	USSR Soyuz 4	45	16,000	71:14	157
Boris V. Volynov Aleksey S. Yeliseyev [3] Yevgeiy V. Khrunov [3]	Jan. 15-18, 1969	USSR Soyuz 5	46	16,000	72:46	157
James A. McDivitt David R. Scott Russell L. Schweickart	Mar. 3-13, 1969	U.S. Apollo 9	151	95,099	241:01	313
Thomas P. Stafford Eugene A. Cernan John W. Young	May 18-26, 1969	U.S. Apollo 10	31 moon 2 earth	107,230	192:03	240,000
Neil A. Armstrong [4] Edwin E. Aldrin Jr. [4] Michael Collins	July 16-July 24, 1969	U.S. Apollo 11	31 moon 2 earth	96,698	195:18	244,000

1 Flight postponement caused Gemini 6 launching to come after Gemini 7.
2 Komarov died in the crash of his spacecraft in the Ural Mountains.
3 Yeliseyev and Khrunov transferred from Soyuz 5 to Soyuz 4 in flight.
4 Armstrong and Aldrin land on moon, July 20, 1969.

NASA Launch Record

Year	No. of Launches	Vehicle Results Success	Failure	Mission Results Success	Failure
1958	4	0	4	0	4
1959	14	8	6	8	6
1960	17	10	7	9	8
1961	23	16	7	15	8
1962	27	23	4	20	7
1963	13	12	1	11	2
1964	30	26	4	25	5
1965	31	27	4	26	5
1966	36	33	3	26	10
1967	27	25	2	25	2
1968	21	16	3	17[1]	3
10-Year Totals	243	196	45	182	60

[1] *Includes two satellites launched on one vehicle.*

docking maneuvers could not be used because a protective shroud failed to fall away.

Gemini 10. John W. Young and Michael Collins July 21 completed a three-day trip which carried them 43 times around the earth. The astronauts docked their Gemini 10 capsule with a target vehicle and used the power of the target to propel them to a higher orbit. They also closed their capsule with another rocket, still in orbit from the Gemini 8 mission.

Gemini 11. Charles Conrad Jr. and Richard F. Gordon Jr., during a four-day flight launched Sept. 12, rendezvoused with an Agena rocket, rose to an orbit reaching 851 miles above the earth and carried out docking maneuvers.

Gemini 12. James A. Lovell Jr. and Edwin E. Aldrin Jr. splashed down Nov. 15 at the end of a mission which began Nov. 11. Gemini 12 docked with an Agena rocket in the capsule's third orbit. By the end of the flight, astronaut Lovell had logged a total of 7.3 million miles in space—5.7 million miles in the two-week Gemini 7 flight and 1.6 million miles in the Gemini 12 mission.

Surveyor 1. Launched May 30, the unmanned capsule made a soft landing on the moon (touching down at eight miles an hour), demonstrating that men would be able to land on the moon without vanishing into lunar dust. The capsule's cameras returned 11,237 pictures.

Lunar Orbiter 1. The first U.S. spacecraft to circle the moon, Lunar Orbiter 1 transmitted 414 pictures. Weighing 853 pounds, it was launched Aug. 10.

Lunar Orbiter 2. Pictures variously described as "incredible" and "the most spectacular" were transmitted by Lunar Orbiter 2 whose cameras were turned on Nov. 18. Taken as the capsule skimmed the lunar surface at 150,000 feet, the photographs showed the Crater Copernicus surrounded by a mountain lunar landscape.

Orbiting Astronomical Observatory (OAO). Lofted April 8, the 3,900-pound capsule was the most complicated unmanned spacecraft ever orbited by the United States. Data obtained by 10 telescopes, scanning the universe from above the earth's atmosphere, were processed by computer and portrayed on charts.

Soviet Achievements. The Soviet Union achieved two space "firsts" in 1966: its Luna 9 capsule Feb. 3 became the first vehicle to land gently on the moon, and Luna 10 in April became the first vehicle to orbit the moon. The unmanned spacecraft supplied a wealth of scientific data. The U.S.S.R. in 1966 lofted dogs into space in its Cosmos series but had not put a man in space since March 1965.

OTHER DEVELOPMENTS

Moon and Space Treaty. Multilateral negotiations for the peaceful exploration of outer space and celestial bodies began July 12 under the auspices of the United Nations Committee on the Peaceful Uses of Outer Space. The negotiations were an outgrowth of a proposal for a celestial treaty made by President Johnson May 7. The President said, "We want to make sure that our astronauts and those of other nations can freely conduct scientific investigations of the moon" and that the "results of these activities...(will) be available for all mankind."

The treaty, President Johnson said, should provide for the free exploration and use of celestial bodies by all countries and for the prohibition of claims of sovereignty; freedom and cooperation in scientific investigations; studies to avoid harmful contamination; permission for astronauts to help colleagues of other nations; and the banning of weapons of mass destruction, weapons testing and maneuvers on any celestial body.

U.S. Ambassador to the United Nations Arthur J. Goldberg said Aug. 8 that although disagreements remained on the "moon treaty," he believed they could be resolved and that the Soviet Union would sign it despite the Vietnam war. Mr. Johnson at a Sept. 9 news conference said that he had been told by Goldberg that "much of the substance of (the) treaty has been resolved." Asked at a Sept. 23 news conference if he remained hopeful that the treaty could be signed in the fall, the President replied in the affirmative. Negotiations, still in progress in December, were described by a spokesman for the U.S. Arms Control and Disarmament Agency as proceeding favorably.

Post-Apollo Program. The Space Sciences Board of the National Academy of Sciences issued reports in December 1965 and January and February 1966 with recommendations for U.S. space exploration in 1970-1985, after completion of the Apollo project to land a man on the moon's surface.

The Board recommended planetary exploration "as the most rewarding scientific objective." It proposed three priorities: unmanned exploration of Mars; detailed investigation of the lunar surface; and unmanned exploration of Venus. No decision, however, had been made on a post-Apollo program by the end of the year.

1967

OUTER SPACE TREATY

Senate Action. The Senate April 25 gave its unanimous consent to the ratification by the President of a treaty governing the peaceful exploration and use of outer space (Exec D, 90th Congress, 1st Session). The resolution of ratification was adopted by an 88-0 roll-call vote.

Major Space 'Firsts'

UNITED STATES

Event	Satellite	Launch date
Science		
Van Allen radiation belts	Explorer 1	1/31/58
Earth shape measured	Vanguard 1	3/17/58
Orbiting solar observatory	OSO 1	3/7/62
Data from Venus	Mariner 2	8/27/62
Geodetic satellite	Anna 1B	10/31/62
Lunar close-up pictures	Ranger 7	7/28/64
Mars pictures	Mariner 4	11/28/64
Micrometeorite satellite	Pegasus 1	2/16/65
Lunar orbit pictures	Orbiter 1	8/10/66
Lunar trenching	Surveyor 3	4/17/67
Color picture of full Earth face	DODGE	7/1/67
Lunar soil chemical analysis	Surveyor 5	9/8/67
Point-stabilized Orbiting Astro-Observatory	OAO 2	12/10/68
Live lunar TV broadcast	Apollo 8	12/21/68
Applications		
Active communications	Score	12/18/58
TV pictures from space	Explorer 6	8/7/59
Weather satellite	Tiros 1	4/1/60
Navigation satellite	Transit 1B	4/13/60
Missile detection	Midas 2	5/24/60
Passive communications	Echo 1	8/12/60
Nuclear explosion detection	Vela Hotel	10/17/63
Manned viewing of lunar far side	Apollo 8	12/21/68
Bio and Manned Flight		
Manned orbital maneuver	Gemini 3	3/23/65
Controlled extravehicular activity	Gemini 4	6/3/65
Manned space rendezvous	Gemini 6, 7	12/4/65
Manned docking	Gemini 8-Agena	3/16/66
Manned lunar orbit	Apollo 8	12/21/68
Manned lunar return re-entry	Apollo 8	12/21/68
Manned earth escape	Apollo 8	12/21/68
Manned moon landing	Apollo 11	7/20/69
Space Flight and Propulsion		
Multiple spacecraft Payload recovery	Transit/Solrad	6/22/60
Payload recovers	Discoverer 13	8/10/60
Synchronous satellite	Syncom 2	7/26/63
Hydrogen rocket orbited	Centaur 2	11/27/63
Docked spacecraft maneuver	Gemini 10-Agena	7/18/66
Lunar lift-off	Surveyor 6	11/7/67
Lunar-velocity re-entry	Apollo 1	11/9/67
Constant deceleration re-entry	Apollo 8	12/21/68
Auxiliary Power Systems		
Solar cells	Vanguard 1	3/17/58
Isotope power	Transit 4A	6/29/61
Nuclear reactor in orbit	Snapshot 1	4/3/65
Fuel cell	Gemini 5	8/21/65

UNION OF SOVIET SOCIALIST REPUBLICS

Event	Satellite	Launch date
Science		
Orbiting geophysical lab	Sputnik 3	5/15/58
Farside lunar picture	Luna 3	10/4/59
Cosmic ray measurements	Proton 1	7/16/65
Lunar surface pictures	Luna 9	1/31/66
Lunar surface bearing test	Luna 13	12/21/66
Venus atmospheric probe	Venera 4	6/12/67
Applications		
Bio and Manned Flight		
Biosatellite	Sputnik 2	11/3/57
Recovery, orbited animals	Korab	8/19/60
Recovery orbited man	Vostok 1	4/12/61
Multi-manned spacecraft	Voskhod 1	10/12/64
Extravehicular activity	Voskhod 2	3/18/65
Recovery, circumlunar live animals	Zond 5	9/21/68
Transfer crew between ships	Soyuz 4-5	1/14-1/15/69
Space Flight and Propulsion		
Space flight	Sputnik 1	10/4/57
Earth escape spacecraft	Luna 1	1/2/59
Lunar impact	Luna 2	9/12/59
Orbital platform launch	Sputnik 5	2/12/61
Venus flyby	Venera 1	2/12/61
Mars flyby	Mars 1	11/1/62
Venus impact	Venera 3	11/16/65
Lunar soft landing	Luna 9	1/31/66
Lunar orbiter	Luna 10	3/31/66
Automatic docking	Cosmos 186/188	10/27-29/67
Recovery, lunar payload	Zond 5	9/21/68
Auxiliary Power Systems		
Battery power	Sputnik 1	10/4/57

OPERATIONAL COMMUNICATIONS SATELLITE EARTH STATIONS
AND SATELLITE COMMUNICATIONS COVERAGE AREAS

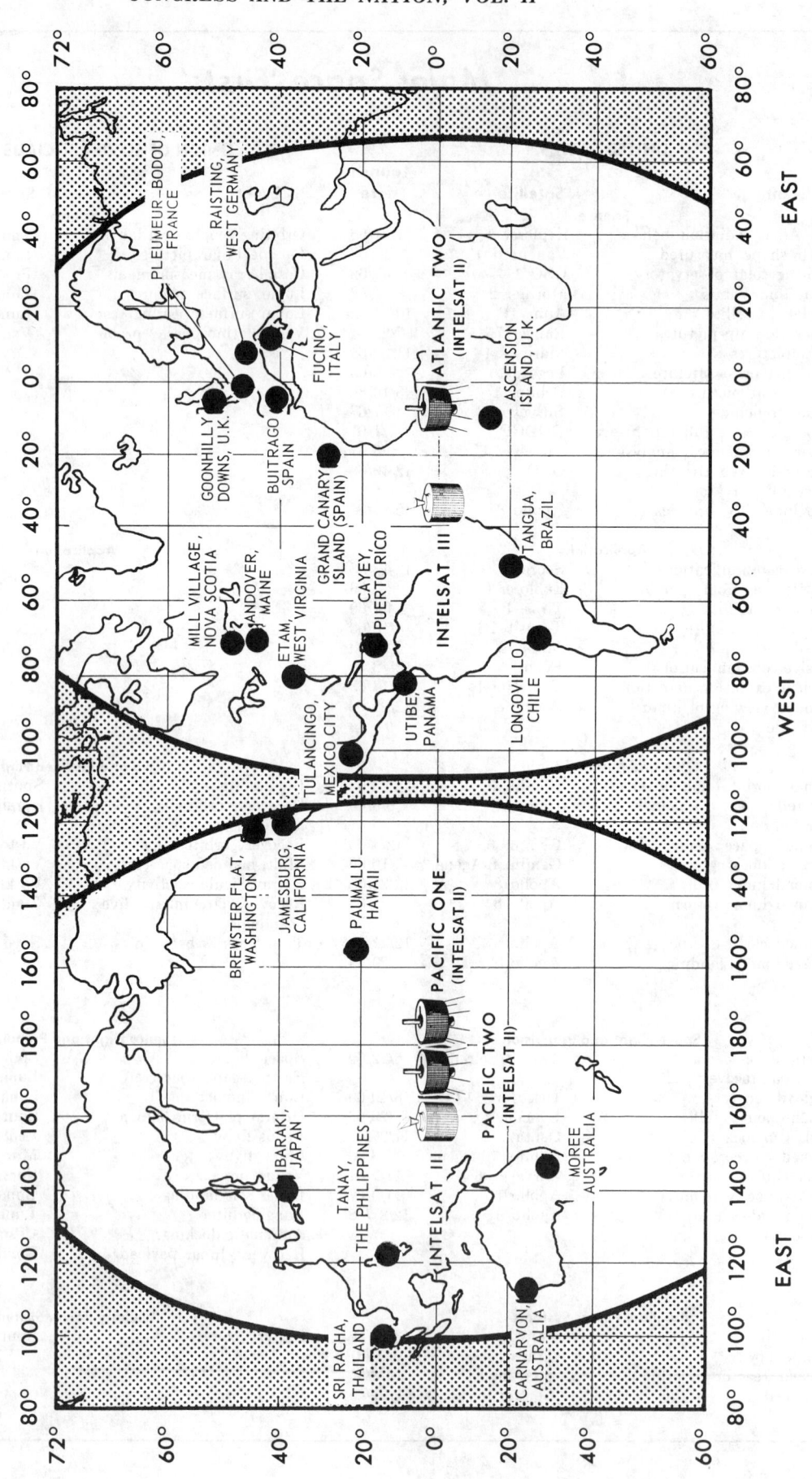

The treaty went into force Oct. 10 when 13 nations deposited notices of ratification in a White House ceremony. Although the treaty was multilateral, major negotiations were conducted by the United States and the Soviet Union. Therefore, the treaty was seen as a step forward in U.S.-Soviet relations.

Provisions. The treaty, in addition to establishing general principles for the peaceful international exploration and use of outer space (including the moon and other celestial bodies), contained provisions for arms control in outer space, suspension of claims of national ownership or sovereignty, and the protection of astronauts.

A key provision of the treaty obligated signatory nations not to station in space or place into orbit any object carrying nuclear or other weapons of mass destruction (such as chemical or biological devices). The same provision also prohibited weapons testing and military bases, fortifications and maneuvers on celestial bodies.

To verify the peaceful use of space, the treaty provided for the right to inspect installations and space vehicles on the moon and on other celestial bodies. Controversy focused on the fact that the inspection provisions did not apply to orbiting objects. This major objection was apparently overcome by statements by U.S. military leaders that they saw no danger to national security in the treaty and that they preferred to rely on military detection systems rather than grant other nations inspection rights and access to U.S. spacecraft.

Background. Similar to the 1959 Antarctic Treaty, the space treaty was seen as a significant step toward preventing the extension of nationalistic competition into space. The Johnson Administration called it the most important arms control agreement since the 1963 limited test ban treaty. Others saw the space treaty as an important part of the Administration's "bridge-building" program to reduce East-West tensions, which included approval earlier in the year of the U.S.-Soviet Consular Convention. Although the pact officially was a product of the United Nations, the major negotiations were conducted by the Soviet Union and the United States.

President Eisenhower in 1958 recommended that the United Nations adopt a resolution endorsing peaceful exploration of outer space. Under President Kennedy, the United States and the Soviet Union in 1963 separately issued pledges that they would not station in outer space nuclear or other weapons of mass destruction. These assurances were officially endorsed by the United Nations.

President Johnson May 7, 1966, proposed a treaty on the peaceful exploration of the moon and other celestial bodies. A U.S. draft treaty was submitted to the United Nations on May 9, and a similar draft by the Soviet Union May 31. Negotiations were begun in July—chiefly between the two major space powers—under the auspices of the UN Outer Space Legal Subcommittee. The treaty's provisions were agreed upon by 28 members of the UN Outer Space Committee and were endorsed Dec. 19, 1966, by the UN General Assembly.

The United States, the United Kingdom and the Soviet Union signed the treaty Jan. 27, 1967, with 57 other countries. President Johnson on Feb. 7 submitted the space treaty to the Senate for its advice and consent to ratification. In his message, the President described the treaty as an "interim achievement" in the diplomacy of space—"a significant but not a final step forward."

Orbiting Nuclear Weapons

The Treaty on Principles Governing the Activities of States in the Exploration and Use of Outer Space, including the Moon and Other Celestial Bodies, known also as the Space Treaty, went into effect Oct. 10, 1967. Both the United States and the Soviet Union were signatories. Article IV of the Treaty stated in part:

"States Parties to the Treaty undertake not to place in orbit around the Earth any objects carrying nuclear weapons or any other kinds of weapons of mass destruction, install such weapons on celestial bodies, or station such weapons in outer space in any other manner...."

CONGRESSIONAL ACTION

Space Program Funds. Congress in 1967 appropriated $4,588,900,000 for the nation's space program in fiscal 1968. The amount in the NASA appropriations bill (HR 12474) represented a cut of $511,100,000 from President Johnson's request—the largest reduction Congress ever made in the recommended space budget.

The space program suffered a serious blow Jan. 27 when three Apollo astronauts *(see box)* died in a flash fire at the Cape Kennedy launch pad. However, the cuts made by Congress appeared to reflect a drive for economy rather than dissatisfaction with the stewardship of the space program. The appropriations bill denied funds for the Voyager program of unmanned investigation of the moon and sharply reduced funds for Apollo Applications, a program designed to avoid a hiatus in manned space flights after a manned moon landing.

Investigation of Launch-Pad Fire. Two Congressional groups charged with overseeing NASA investigated the causes of the Jan. 27 launch-pad fire. They were the Senate Aeronautical and Space Sciences Committee and the House Science and Astronautics Subcommittee on NASA Oversight.

NASA Administrator James E. Webb told the Senate panel on May 9 that the tragedy could delay a moon landing by six to eight months and might increase program costs by $200 million to $500 million. However, he said it did not rule out a lunar landing before 1970.

Members of both committees criticized NASA for not informing Congress of alleged shortcomings in the Apollo program prior to the 1967 tragedy. A focal point of this discussion was the controversial "Phillips Report"—a 1965 memorandum in which the Apollo project director, Maj. Gen. Samuel C. Phillips, informed North American Aviation, Inc., the prime contractor, of what he considered to be engineering deficiencies and management laxity on the part of the company's conduct of the project. After NASA refused to furnish copies of the report to Congress, Rep. William F. Ryan (D N.Y.) obtained them through other channels and made them public.

Assessment of Hearings. At the close of the House probe May 11, Subcommittee Chairman Olin E. Teague (D Texas) said his panel would not seek a scapegoat on which to pin the blame for the Jan. 27 tragedy. "We were all to blame," Teague said.

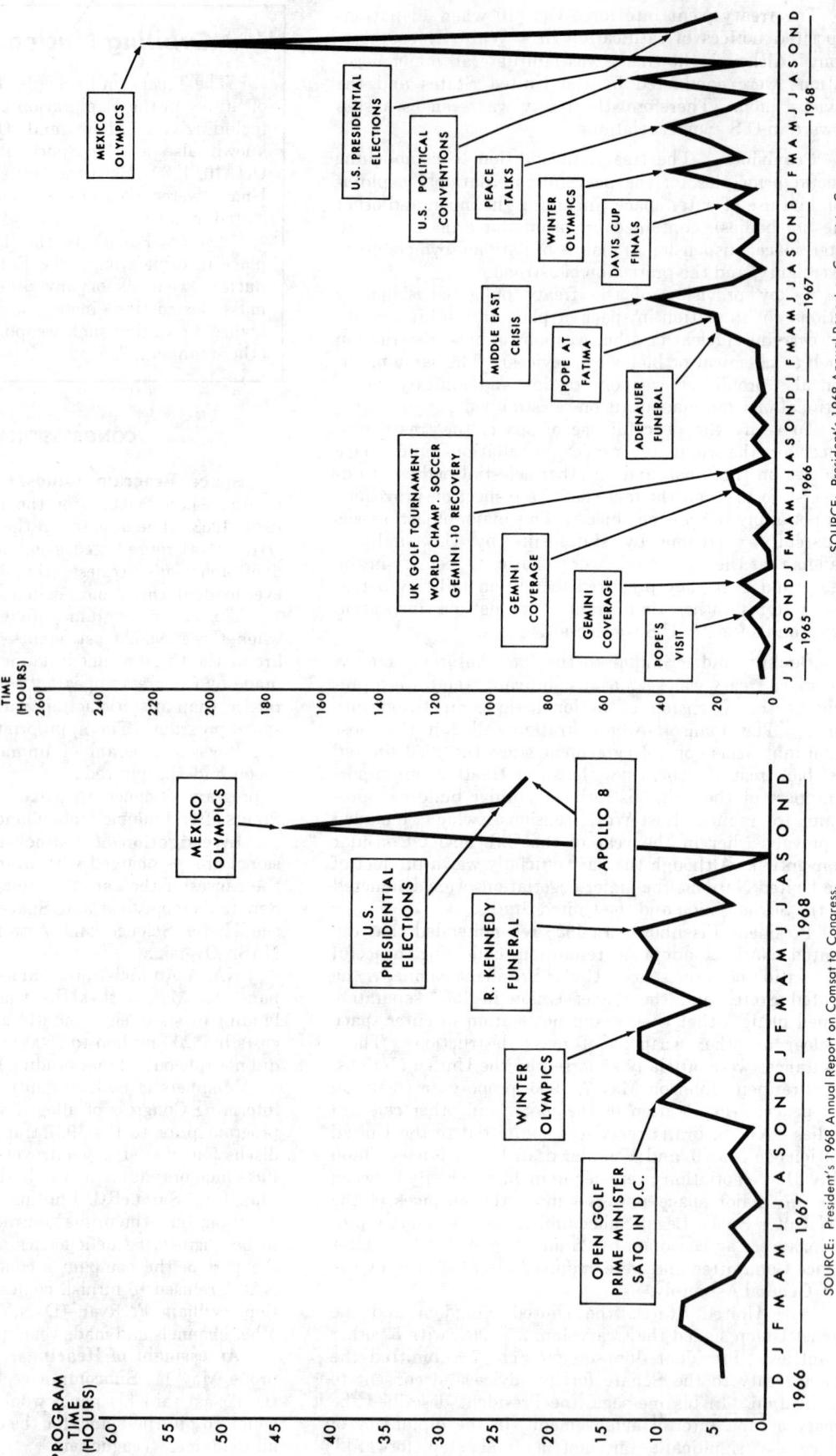

Trans-Pacific Satellite Telecasts of Major Events

(December 1966 through December 1968)

Trans-Atlantic Satellite Telecasts of Major Events

(June 1965 through December 1968)

SOURCE: President's 1968 Annual Report on Comsat to Congress.

SOURCE: President's 1968 Annual Report on Comsat to Congress.

Sen. Clinton P. Anderson (D N.M.), chairman of the Senate panel, May 12 issued a statement placing most of the blame on complacent program management and administration. "An admitted mood of overconfidence by NASA and North American, based on past successes, proved fatal," he said. Anderson added that the ultimate responsibility for the tragedy lay with NASA, but North American "surely had a direct responsibility to exercise the kind of sound management and quality control for which it was selected."

In September, Rep. George P. Miller (D Calif.), chairman of the House Science and Astronautics Committee, outlined a plan which he said he had worked out with NASA Administrator Webb to keep the Committee more fully informed on NASA activities.

SPACE FEATS

The year 1967 began with a major tragedy, the death of three astronauts in a launch-pad fire. No Americans were launched into space that year, and a cosmonaut's death marred the only reported manned space flight conducted by Russia in 1967. However, the successful test flight of the gigantic Saturn 5 moon rocket in November ended the year on a note of triumph for the American space program. The Soviets had meanwhile achieved another space "first" by soft-landing an unmanned craft on the planet Venus.

Moon Rocket. A three-stage U.S. Saturn 5 moon rocket Nov. 9 made a successful first-test flight from Cape Kennedy, Fla. The mission showed that the 363-foot high, 3,100-ton rocket carrying an Apollo spacecraft could fly and that the Apollo capsule could withstand the heat, estimated at about 5,100 degrees, that it would encounter on a return flight from the moon.

The Apollo capsule, still attached to the third stage of the rocket, orbited the earth twice at altitudes between 110 and 119 miles. As the second orbit ended, the third-stage rocket was refired, sending the capsule to an altitude of 11,286 miles. The capsule plunged back toward the earth at speeds nearing 25,000 miles per hour compared to the 18,000 mile-per-hour speeds encountered in return from a regular earth orbit. Eight hours, 36 minutes and 54 seconds after blast-off, the capsule, charred but intact, landed in the Pacific Ocean about 10 miles from its target point.

Lunar Orbiter 3. Launched Feb. 5, the unmanned spacecraft returned pictures detailing six primary sites for the landing of a manned Apollo capsule. The craft also returned pictures partially mapping six other secondary landing sites.

Lunar Orbiter 4. Seven days after launch, Lunar Orbiter 4 on May 11 began transmitting photos of the moon's surface. High resolution photos of over 99 percent of the front side of the moon were transmitted.

Lunar Orbiter 5. Beginning Aug. 1, this, the last and most ambitious Lunar Orbiter mission, completed the mapping of the entire lunar surface. Specifically, the mission provided complete information on 36 scientific sites and five Apollo landing sites.

Surveyor 3. The unmanned capsule achieved a soft landing on the moon April 19. Information transmitted from the capsule indicated its landing site had a bearing strength of 10 pounds per square inch, a strength considered ample for the planned landing of an Apollo lunar craft.

Astronauts' Deaths

The three astronauts designated to fly the first Apollo spacecraft into orbit were killed in a flash fire in the craft on the launch pad at Cape Kennedy, Jan. 27, 1967. They were rehearsing for a scheduled launching Feb. 21.

They were Air Force Lt. Col. Virgil I. (Gus) Grissom, Air Force Lt. Col. Edward H. White II, and Navy Cmdr. Roger B. Chaffee.

Grissom, 40, was one of the original seven Mercury astronauts. He had been the pilot aboard the Mercury capsule Liberty Bell 7 in a suborbital flight and the command pilot of Gemini 3, the first two-man spaceship orbited by the United States. White, 36, was the first American, and second person, to "walk" in space. Chaffee, 31, had not made a space flight.

The fire started at 6:31 P.M. and the spacesuit-clad astronauts were unable to open the spacecraft's single hatch in time to escape. They were dead when ground crewmen got to them five minutes later. An autopsy found that the astronauts had died of "asphyxia due to inhalation of toxic gases due to fire" and that "a contributory cause of death was the thermal burns."

An investigative report issued April 9 by a NASA-appointed review board concluded that "some minor malfunction or failure of equipment or wire insulation" most probably caused the fire. The fire flared in the artificially created pure-oxygen atmosphere inside the Apollo spacecraft. Unlike the outside air, which is four-fifths nitrogen, pure oxygen can be ignited.

The astronauts had entered the spacecraft, situated 218 feet above Cape Kennedy's Launch Complex 34 (atop an un-fueled Saturn 1 rocket) at 1 P.M. to begin pre-launching tests. They presumably were reclining in their flight positions when they detected the fire.

Five other astronauts had been killed—four in airplane crashes and one in an automobile accident—from the time the program started through April 1969.

Theodore C. Freeman, an Air Force captain, was the first astronaut killed, Oct. 31, 1964, in the crash of a T-38 jet trainer near Ellington Air Force Base, Houston, Texas. Charles A. Bassett II, an Air Force major, and Elliott M. See Jr., a civilian, died in a T-38 crash at Lambert Municipal Airport, St. Louis, Feb. 28, 1966. Edward Givens Jr., an Air Force major, died in an automobile accident near Houston, June 6, 1967. Clifton C. Williams, a Marine Corps captain, was killed in a T-38 crash near Tallahassee, Fla., Oct. 5, 1967.

In the same period of time, Soviet cosmonaut Vladimir Komarov encountered trouble on his second trip into space and died, April 23, 1967, in the crash of his Soyuz I craft in the Ural Mountains; and Soviet Col. Yuri Alexeyevich Gagarin, the first man to make an orbital flight (April 12, 1961), was killed March 7, 1968, in the crash of his jet plane about 40 miles northeast of Moscow. Gagarin and a Red Air Force test pilot killed in the same crash were accorded a state funeral March 30 and their ashes were interred in the Kremlin wall.

UNMANNED

Launch Date	Spacecraft Name	Weight (pounds)	Cumulative National Weight (pounds)	Mission	Results
1958					
Aug 17	Pioneer 0	84	84	Orbit	Fail—Exploded 10 miles up.
Oct. 11	Pioneer 1	84	168	Orbit	Fail—Climbed 70,700 miles, fell back over South Pacific.
Nov. 8	Pioneer 2	86	254	Orbit	Fail—Climbed 1,963 miles, fell 7,500 miles away over Africa.
Dec. 6	Pioneer 3	13	267	Strike	Fail—Climbed 63,580 miles, fell back over Africa.
1959					
Jan. 2	Luna 1	797	797	Strike	Fail—Missed moon by 3,100-3,720 miles, entered solar orbit.
Mar. 3	Pioneer 4	13	280	Strike	Fail—Missed moon by 37,300 miles, entered solar orbit.
Sept. 12	Luna 2	860	1,657	Strike	Succeed—Struck 270 miles from visible center.
Sept. 24	Pioneer (P-1)	375	655	Orbit	Fail—Exploded in static test on pad.
Oct. 4	Luna 3	959	2,615	Photo far side	Succeed—Passed within 4,373 miles of moon, returned pictures.
Nov. 26	Pioneer (P-3)	372	1,027	Orbit	Fail—Shroud failure, payload fell near Africa.
1960					
Sept. 25	Pioneer (P-30)	387	1,414	Orbit	Fail—Second stage failed, fell in South Africa.
Dec. 15	Pioneer (P-31)	388	1,802	Orbit	Fail—Exploded 8 miles up.
1962					
Jan. 26	Ranger 3	727	2,529	TV before hard land	Fail—Missed moon by 22,862 miles, entered solar orbit.
Apr. 23	Ranger 4	730	3,259	TV before hard land	Fail—Timer failed, fell on far side of moon.
Oct. 18	Ranger 5	755	4,014	TV before hard land	Fail—Missed moon by 450 miles, entered solar orbit.
1963					
Jan. 4	Unannounced	3,100 ?	5,716	Soft land	Fail—Earth orbit only.
Apr. 2	Luna 4	3,136	8,852	Soft land	Fail—Missed moon by 5,281 miles, entered barycentric orbit.
1964					
Jan. 30	Ranger 6	804	4,818	TV before strike	Fail—On target, but TV failed.
July 28	Ranger 7	807	5,625	TV before strike	Succeed—Returned 4,308 pictures.
1965					
Feb. 17	Ranger 8	809	6,434	TV before strike	Succeed—Returned 7,137 pictures.
Mar. 12	Cosmos 60	3,200 ?	12,052	Soft land	Fail—Earth orbit only.
Mar. 21	Ranger 9	808	7,242	TV before strike	Succeed—Returned 5,814 pictures.
May 9	Luna 5	3,255	15,307	Soft land	Fail—Retrofire ineffective, struck moon.

LUNAR FLIGHTS

Launch Date	Spacecraft Name	Weight (pounds)	Cumulative National Weight (pounds)	Mission	Results
1965					
June 8	Luna 6	3,180	18,487	Soft land	Fail—Missed moon by 100,000 miles, entered solar orbit.
July 18	Zond 3	2,000 ?	20,487	Photo far side	Succeed—Returned 25 pictures, entered solar orbit.
Oct. 4	Luna 7	3,321	23,808	Soft land	Fail—Retrofire came early, struck moon.
Dec. 3	Luna 8	3,422	27,230	Soft land	Fail—Retrofire came late, struck moon.
1966					
Jan. 31	Luna 9	3,491	30,721	Soft land	Succeed—Returned 27 pictures.
Mar. 1	Cosmos III	3,500 ?	34,221	Orbit	Fail—Earth orbit only.
Mar. 31	Luna 10	3,588	37,809	Orbit	Succeed—72 degrees inclination.
May 30	Surveyor 1	2,194	9,436	Soft land	Succeed—Returned 11,237 pictures.
July 1	Explorer 33	206	9,642	Orbit	Fail—Excessive speed precluded capture, entered barycentric orbit.
Aug. 10	Lunar Orbiter 1	853	10,495	Orbit	Succeed—12 degrees inclination, returned 414 pictures.
Aug. 24	Luna 11	3,616	41,425	Orbit	Succeed—27 degrees inclination, returned no pictures.
Sept. 24	Surveyor 2	2,204	12,699	Soft land	Fail—Stabilization failed, struck moon.
Oct. 22	Luna 12	3,600 ?	45,025	Orbit	Succeed—Equatorial inclination, returned pictures.
Nov. 6	Lunar Orbiter 2	861	13,500	Orbit	Succeed—12 degrees (later 17 degrees) inclination, returned 422 pictures.
Dec. 21	Luna 13	3,600 ?	48,625	Soft land	Succeed—Returned pictures and soil density measures.
1967					
Feb. 5	Lunar Orbiter 3	850	14,410	Orbit	Succeed—21 degrees inclination, returned 307 usable pictures.
Apr. 17	Surveyor 3	2,283	16,693	Soft land	Succeed—Returned 6,315 pictures and dug soil with shovel.
May 4	Lunar Orbiter 4	860	17,553	Orbit	Succeed—86 degrees inclination, returned 326 pictures.
July 14	Surveyor 4	2,287	19,843	Soft land	Fail—Signals ceased at last moment before touchdown.
July 19	Explorer 35	230	20,073	Orbit	Succeed—Returning data.
Aug. 2	Lunar Orbiter 5	860	20,933	Orbit	Succeed—85 degrees inclination, returned 424 pictures.
Sept. 8	Surveyor 5	2,216	23,149	Soft land	Succeed—Returned 18,006 pictures and made chemical analysis of soil.
Nov. 7	Surveyor 6	2,223	25,372	Soft land	Succeed—Returned 30,065 pictures and made chemical analyses of soil.
1968					
Jan. 7	Surveyor 7	2,293	27,660	Soft land	Succeed—Returned 21,274 pictures, dug soil, and made chemical analyses of soil.
Apr. 7	Luna 14	3,600 ?	52,225	Orbit	Succeed—Returned data on lunar mass distribution.
Sept. 15	Zond 5	16,000	68,225	Moon orbit	Succeed—Biological specimens and photographs. Recovered.
Nov. 10	Zond 6	16,000	84,225	Moon orbit	Succeed—Same.

Surveyor 5. Launched Sept. 8, Surveyor 5 made a soft landing on the moon two days later. (Surveyor 4 had soft-landed on the moon but stopped transmitting at touchdown.) Findings from the first chemical analysis of the lunar surface indicated the landing area had a composition roughly similar to that of basalt found on the earth. Components of the surface included oxygen, silicon and aluminum. The spacecraft transmitted a total of 19,049 pictures, 18,006 of which were of high quality.

Surveyor 6. On Nov. 9, Surveyor 6 completed a successful soft landing on the moon three miles from its aiming point and began sending back television pictures of a rugged area never before photographed at close range. Surveyor 6 was launched Nov. 7 and was aimed for Sinus Medii-Central Bay, almost dead center in the face of the moon. Flight controllers said Surveyor 6 performed flawlessly during its three-minute landing sequence to slow down from a speed of 6,000 miles per hour to three miles per hour 13 feet above the moon.

Mariner V. Launched June 14, the Mariner V capsule achieved a Venus "flyby" Oct. 19, coming within 2,500 miles of the planet. Preliminary data from the spacecraft indicated that Venus had a weak magnetic field and a relatively heavy atmosphere composed of approximately 72 percent carbon dioxide. This contradicted information obtained by the Soviets from the first successful soft landing on Venus.

Soviet Achievement. The Soviets Oct. 18 achieved another space "first" when they soft-landed an unmanned craft on the planet Venus. The Venus 4 spacecraft transmitted information during its descent to the planet's surface but fell silent before touchdown. A short time later, however, signals were received indicating the craft had made a successful landing. Information from the Soviet craft recorded no magnetic field but found an atmosphere 15 times as heavy as the earth's and composed almost entirely of carbon dioxide.

Soviet Tragedy. The only reported Soviet manned space flight in 1967 ended in tragedy April 24. Vladimir Komarov, the first Russian cosmonaut to make two trips into space, piloted Soyuz I into orbit April 23 on orders to link up with a six-man spacecraft to be launched later. Komarov ran into trouble, began tumbling, apparently righted himself, then cut short his flight on ground command and re-entered the atmosphere. Then Komarov's craft apparently got tangled in its parachute cords and plunged four miles in the Ural Mountains. The cosmonaut's death was the first reported by the Russians during their space program.

1968

CONGRESSIONAL ACTION

Space Funds. Economy pressures and shifting Administration priorities combined in 1968 to bring about the fourth straight budget reduction and the lowest appropriation since 1963 for the National Aeronautics and Space Administration. In providing $3,995,273,000 for NASA in fiscal 1969, Congress pared $375,127,000 from what the agency had described as a "bare-bones request."

The Apollo Applications program was the most severely affected by the budget cuts. Apollo Applications is a composite of many projects and experiments intended to increase the activities of men in space after the man-on-the-moon mission. The post-moon program had been an object of dispute in Congress for some time because of parallels between its objectives and those of the Manned Orbiting Laboratory (MOL) program conducted by the Air Force.

Congress dropped the Voyager planetary program, which eventually would have cost $2.4 billion, in favor of a far less expensive Mariner program. The scaled-down program envisioned sending instrument packages in orbits around Mars in 1971 and the placement of "rough landers" on the Martian surface in 1973 for a total cost of $500 million.

Astronaut Treaty. The Senate consented Oct. 8, by a 66-0 roll-call vote, to the ratification of a treaty (Exec J, 90th Congress, 2nd Session) providing for the safe return of astronauts who land in foreign countries. The Astronaut Assistance and Return Agreement, signed by 74 countries, went into effect Dec. 3. It provided that:

Any party to the treaty who learns of an accident involving a manned flight will immediately inform the launching authority; that a party to the treaty will take immediate steps to rescue and lend all necessary assistance to an astronaut who lands in its territory; that a foreign astronaut, once rescued, will be returned safely and promptly to his country; and that a launching authority will have the right to obtain the return of an object landing from space in foreign territory.

UNITED NATIONS

Space Resolutions. The General Assembly unanimously approved two resolutions Dec. 20 dealing with the peaceful uses of outer space. The first resolution commended the results of the Conference on the Exploration and Peaceful Uses of Outer Space, held in Vienna, Aug. 14-27. The resolution also welcomed the decision of the Committee on the Peaceful Uses of Outer Space to examine proposals for U.N. activity in the field.

The second resolution welcomed the coming into force of the Astronaut Assistance and Return Agreement. It also reaffirmed mankind's common interest in the further exploration of space and urged the Committee on the Peaceful Uses of Outer Space to prepare a draft agreement on the liability for damage that might be caused by the launching of objects into outer space.

PRESIDENTIAL CAMPAIGN ISSUE

Nixon Speech. Richard M. Nixon said in a presidential campaign speech in Houston, Sept. 6: "I would have this clearly understood...I consider the space program as one of our national imperatives, that it must be supported at a level assuring efficient and steady progress, that the ups and downs of recent times in planning, programing and financing must be brought to a halt, and that as President I will make certain our country retains leadership in this great endeavor."

Political Platforms. The Republican 1968 platform asserted that the party "shares the sense of urgency manifested by the scientific community concerning the exploration of outer space." It further deplored the "failure of the Johnson-Humphrey Administration to emphasize the military uses of space for America's defense" and regretted "that the Administration's budgetary management has forced sharp reductions in the space program."

The Democratic Party platform stated: "We shall continue to work for our goal of leadership in space."

OTHER DEVELOPMENTS

Sciences Board. The Space Sciences Board of the National Academy of Sciences urged Aug. 14 an increase in unmanned flights to the planets. In its report to NASA, the 23-man board said "we do not believe man is essential for scientific planetary investigation at this stage." It opposed proposals that a manned fly-by of Mars should be the next major space goal of the United States. The report was based on studies by a committee of scientists under the leadership of Dr. George J. F. MacDonald of the Institute for Defense Analyses.

Moon Research. NASA announced Jan. 4 the opening of an Apollo Lunar Exploration Office in Washington to unify America's manned and unmanned programs for scientific exploration of the moon. Lee R. Scherer, a retired Navy captain, was named director of the new office.

SPACE FEATS

For the first time in history, humans circled the moon in 1968. The three members of the Apollo 8 crew beamed live television pictures to earth during their 10 trips around the moon Dec. 24-25.

Surveyor 7. The most fully equipped scientifically of all Surveyor probes, Surveyor 7 soft-landed on the moon Jan. 9, two days after its launching from Cape Kennedy. It landed almost exactly at its aiming point north of the crater Tycho in the moon's southern hemisphere.

Apollo 7. Three astronauts conducted the first manned test of the Apollo spaceship, Oct. 11-12, in earth orbit. Their 260-hour journey was the first trip by Americans into space since November 1966. Walter M. (Wally) Schirra Jr., 45, the oldest man to make a space flight and the first to go into orbit for a third time, was commander of Apollo 7. Donn F. Eisele, 38, was navigator, and R. Walter Cunningham, 36, monitored controls and handled communications. All three suffered head colds during the flight but the illness did not mar their performance.

Apollo 8. The crew of Frank Borman (commander), James A. Lovell Jr. and William A. Anders circled the moon 10 times Dec. 24-25 and returned from their six-day trip into space with a safe splashdown in the Pacific, Dec. 27. They established these records: It was the first time men had flown so far (about 231,000 miles) from the earth; the trip was man's longest space flight (about 550,000 miles round-trip); it was the first time that men had gone into orbit around the moon or reached its vicinity (within 70 miles of its surface); it was the first time that men had reached the place where the gravitation of an astronomical body other than earth was dominant; and

Manned Space Flight Costs

The manned space flight programs, Mercury, Gemini, and currently Apollo have consumed an increasing percentage of the NASA budget over the last decade. Although recent economy pressures have reduced funds for collateral programs, the Apollo man-on-the-moon program has been virtually untouched. A self-imposed interim operating plan issued by NASA Aug. 8, 1968, continued this trend by proceeding with the Apollo program at the authorized level while cutting operations in other areas to about $163.4 million below authorized 1969 levels.

The table below shows the percentage of NASA's research and development funds which have been spent each year directly for manned space flight programs.

FY	Annual NASA R&D funds	Manned Flight Funds	Percent spent on Manned flight Programs
	(in millions)		
1959	$ 195.3	$ 49.7	25.4%
1960	305.3	119.4	39.1
1961	617.7	296.3	48.0
1962	1,145.2	538.0	46.9
1963	2,509.7	1,502.0	59.8
1964	3,977.4	2,717.9	68.3
1965	4,285.3	2,961.0	69.9
1966	4,486.3	3,199.5	71.3
1967	4,175.7	3,024.0	72.4
1968	3,967.6	2,789.0	70.2
1969	3,370.0 [1]	2,280.7 [1]	67.7

1 Authorized level.

the astronauts were the first men to see the far side of the moon.

Russian Achievements. Zond 5, an unmanned lunar probe launched by Russia Sept. 15, flew around the moon Sept. 18 and then returned to earth. It splashed down in the Indian Ocean Sept. 21 and was recovered by a Soviet ship the next day. It was the first time that a space vehicle had been recovered from a moon orbit. *Pravda* reported Nov. 15 that Zond 5 had carried two live turtles, fruit flies, plant seeds, bacteria and other specimens. The turtles were reported alive and apparently well on landing, though they had lost 10 percent of their weight and changes had taken place in their liver cells and spleen structure.

Zond 6 followed on Nov. 10-17 and was also recovered (in Russia) after orbiting the moon. *Tass* and the Soviet press reported that Zond 6 and its predecessor flights had shown that Russians could protect cosmonauts from cosmic radiation during a lunar flight and recover them on earth. *Izvestia* reported Nov. 25 that Zond 6 had recorded a radiation level "almost 100 times less than the permissible level."

Chapter 11—Agriculture

Agriculture

THE broad directions of basic U.S. farm policy changed very little during the period 1965-68.

Farm production continued in most areas to be highly mechanized, with heavy use of fertilizers and chemicals, steady increases in yields, a trend toward larger, more consolidated farms.

The farm population continued to decline, as it had been doing for generations, and reached a new low of just over 5 percent of the population. Yet so great was the efficiency of U.S. producers that each farm worker on the average produced enough food in 1967 for more than 42 other persons.

Two central problems occupied farm policymakers —overproduction and low rural income.

For some of the nation's most important crops, like feed grains, wheat and cotton, there was continual danger that farmers, pouring on the fertilizer and insecticides, using the most modern production methods, would produce more than could be sold at a profit. When that happened, it was feared, prices would drop precipitously, eventually driving some farmers out of business, speeding up the rural migration to the cities to create new welfare problems, and endangering the whole economy with a farm-initiated depression.

The traditional Democratic answer to this threat was a system of production controls and income aids, first tried in the 1930s and kept in effect continuously (except in wartime, when controls were not needed) since then. It applied to about a dozen and a half of the most important crops.

Production controls, in the form of acreage limitations, helped to limit oversupply and prevent price breaks. At the same time, the Government, through standing ready to buy or offer loans at a fixed price on farm produce, with the latter as collateral, could peg the price received by the farmer at some desired rate.

President Johnson in 1965 helped put through Congress a revision of the system of production limitations and price support devices. One problem to be faced was that if price supports were set too high, U.S. products might not be able to compete on the international market. But if they were set too low, some of the less efficient, smaller farmers might find them inadequate to sustain their income at decent levels.

The 1965 basic legislation was designed to reduce surpluses of cotton, corn and wheat. It asked farmers to retire a certain portion of their cropland from production of these surplus crops and put it to soil-conserving uses. In return, they were made eligible for a price support on their crops plus special, direct cash payments of different types.

The price support was to be fixed at a level that would result in a market price competitive with overseas prices, but the farmer's income was maintained by giving him the additional direct payments. Thus the U.S. surplus crops could find markets without dropping the farmers' incomes to a disastrously low level.

This system, a new and more sophisticated variation of the basic price support system in effect since New Deal days, was put into effect by the Johnson Administration with the assurance that it would reduce surpluses of wheat, cotton and corn to manageable proprotions without costing too much.

By 1968, sponsors of the program were boasting that it had achieved much of what it set out to do. Corn and wheat surpluses had dropped sharply—aided in the case of wheat by heavy donations to hungry peoples overseas—and cotton surpluses had dropped even more sharply, though a major factor here was a drought which dropped 1967 cotton production to the lowest level (7.4 million bales) since 1895.

At the same time, sponsors said, farm income was at a high level (though dropping somewhat after 1966) and the cost of the over-all program was not excessive, running about $2 billion to $4 billion a year—a cheap enough price to pay to guarantee an abundant supply of food and fiber and avoid the dislocations that would occur if too many farmers went broke.

Many Republicans and the nation's biggest farm organization, the American Farm Bureau Federation, sharply disagreed with this diagnosis. They believed that the system of production controls, based on historical acreage rights, had the effect of freezing some of the most inefficient production patterns and preventing expansion of some farms to more efficient sizes.

They saw the Johnson program as a complicated system of market rigging, designed to sustain the income of farmers who could not otherwise successfully compete.

In the long run, they argued, it would be better to move toward a system where the market was the basis for economic decisions. With production controls

Reference

For history of agricultural policy and legislation from 1945-64, see *Congress and the Nation*, Vol. I, pp. 665-767.

off and price supports lowered to a level where at best they would merely be a safeguard against disaster—not a market-fixing mechanism or guarantor of high income—supply and demand would automatically adjust and the surplus problem would disappear. The marginal and inefficient farmers would gradually retire or move out of farming. And the $2 billion to $4 billion a year which the Government was now spending on price support and production control programs would be saved.

Opponents of the Johnson program contended also that it had not really achieved what it set out to do: farm income was beginning to fall off, new surpluses of wheat were threatened as overseas production rose and export possibilities declined, and people were still leaving farming at a pretty steady rate.

Problem of Low Rural Income

The problem of low rural income was related in part to agricultural price and surplus policy. The price and production programs backed by the Democratic Administration were designed to sustain farm income, but chiefly for the 1.8 million farms with sales of $2,500 a year or more, which could be considered viable economic enterprises. (Even some of these clearly were operating on the margin of disaster.)

A whole additional category of farmers, about 1.3 million, had sales of under $2,500 a year and could not be considered commercial farms. Some persons in this category were actually gentleman farmers or part-time farmers with small holdings. But a large group of them, particularly in the South, were simply impoverished farmers with insufficient land, equipment, credit or skills, and were clearly in no position to make a living from agriculture.

For these farmers, and for some of those in the lower echelons of the 1.8 million commercial farm class, Government policies were sometimes more welfare-oriented than farm-oriented.

Government credits for housing for the rural poor, for retraining, for local economic planning, and for basic water and sewer facilities were among the policies continued in the 1965-68 period.

Some of the Government credits were plainly welfare-type aids. Others were designed to give commercial farmers who needed it the chance to strengthen their operations by acquisition of new land, machinery and stock.

Another aspect of rural poverty was the hired farm labor force—a group of about 1 million persons whose pay and living standards were among the lowest in the nation, especially in the case of migratory farm workers. Some welfare programs for these workers were enacted, and about one-third of them were finally given Federal minimum-wage protection in 1966, albeit at low pay levels. But attempts to bring them under Federal laws protecting the right to organize unions and strike did not succeed.

While the broad outlines of basic policy did not change much during the 1965-68 period, there were a number of new trends on a smaller scale.

There was a clear upsurge of resentment among urban Congressmen against the large amounts of money being spent on price supports—particularly when it was shown that many really big farm enterprises got payments of $1 million or more a year from the Government. One received as much as $4.1 million. (See 1968 chronology, below.)

Urban Congressmen resented these payments because some of the farm-area Congressmen on committees with jurisdiction over school lunches, food stamps and other Government feeding programs for the poor were holding down appropriations for those programs.

In an attempt to impose a $20,000 annual payment limitation per farm, members of Congress from the cities made common cause with some Republican rural-area Congressmen who opposed the whole system of price supports and production controls. The latter believed that imposition of an annual payment limitation would help kill the existing system. Their attempts did not succeed but appeared to portend further efforts of the same sort in the future.

Food for Hungry

Two important sets of agricultural programs were reoriented in the 1965-68 period. Food programs for the hungry had been run for many years as dumping areas for surplus farm goods or as adjuncts to attempts to boost farm income. In a series of massive legislative fights during the period 1965-68, Northern Congressional liberals, backed by welfare, labor and philanthropic organizations, made hunger in America a key public issue. They succeeded in winning apparent acceptance of the idea that the problem of hunger deserved to be solved regardless of agricultural surplus problems.

One result was that projected spending on anti-hunger programs was expected to reach about $1.5 billion in fiscal 1970—nearly double the 1965 outlay.

A similar reorientation occurred for the overseas food donation program (PL 480)—the so-called Food for Peace or Food for Freedom plan. It had been started in 1954 as a means of getting rid of surplus production by "selling" it overseas for local, tied (and often unusable) currencies.

In 1966, the program was revised to focus on meeting hunger needs among developing nations rather than just getting rid of surpluses. At the same time, it sought to encourage developing nations to improve their own agricultural production and to limit their population increase.

One program in which there was almost no basic change at all was the Sugar Act, that microcosm of agricultural protectionism. First enacted in 1934, the Act sustains high prices for domestic beet sugar growers and cane sugar growers by limiting both domestic production and imports from abroad. Without the import limits, foreign sugar could easily undersell the domestic product.

At the same time, big coastal refineries are protected by the rule that nearly all imports must be in the form of raw sugar, which is then refined in this country. The standard dispute over the Sugar Act is how to divvy up the loaf, with U.S. mainland beet and cane getting an ever larger share of the total. In 1965, the Sugar Act was extended through Dec. 31, 1971, with Cuba's share of the import quota suspended and the mainland cane and beet producers getting increased shares.

Over-All Economic Trends

During the 1965-68 period, American agriculture continued to be highly productive, a heavy user of fertilizers, insecticides and machinery which helped push up yields per acre.

The number of farms and farm population declined, and about two-fifths of the 3,146,000 farms had sales so small (under $2,500 a year) that they could not be classified as commercial farms.

Wheat, cotton and corn (with related feed grains) remained the Big 3 crops, with soybeans (the number one export market crop) joining them to make it a Big 4. Livestock and dairy products accounted for about two-thirds of all cash sales, however, with cattle and calves alone (the single biggest source of cash sales) constituting 24.9 percent. The feed grain economy underlay all livestock products: a heavy portion of feeds was not sold but fed on the farm to cattle, hogs and other livestock. Thus, while the Government price support program did not include livestock directly (though it did include dairy products), it nevertheless had profound influence through supports and production controls on feeds.

Federal outlays for programs attributable to agriculture, according to the fiscal 1970 Budget document, averaged about $5 billion a year over the fiscal 1965-68 period, with a large part of the total going to support prices, make direct crop payments to farmers or otherwise stabilize farm income. (The Agriculture Department appropriations bill includes some programs which, functionally, are allocated to non-agricultural objectives, like Food for Peace; for this reason, figures in the Budget document as given below may not correspond to annual appropriations in Agriculture appropriations bills.)

OUTLAYS TO STABILIZE FARM INCOME

Year	Agricultural Outlays (billions)	Portion for Stabilizing Farm Income
1959	$5.365	$4.057
1964	5.186	3.803
1965	4.807	3.234
1966	3.679	1.932
1967	4.376	2.536
1968	5.944	3.934
1969	5.448	4.509

If the Food for Peace outlays, plus certain other items were added, the cost of agriculture programs to the Federal Government came to from $6 billion to over $7 billion a year.

The cost-price squeeze continued to press farmers in the 1965-68 period—i.e., the cost of the things they must buy tended to rise at least as fast as the prices of the things they sell. The farmers' net income as a proportion of his gross fluctuated at around 30 percent for most of the 1960s, dropping to an all-time low of 29 percent in 1967 (compared with a 50 percent figure during the boom years of the World War II Period).

Another measure of the cost-price squeeze was the drop in the parity ratio, a measure of "fairness" in farm prices and costs based on historical precedents. A parity ratio of 100 meant that the relationship between the farmer's costs and prices was 100 percent fair; a ratio of 80 meant that the prices the farmer received were less favorable in relation to his costs than they had been during the pre-World War I period used as the historical base.

The parity ratio—in the 80s during the 1950s—dropped to the low 70s (see Income from Farming chart) in the 1965-68 period. Farm income, however, rose, and per-operator annual income in terms of constant 1957-59 dollars was substantially higher than in earlier years. Following are some of the statistical measures of these developments.

Relation to Economy. While farming was one of the biggest, if not the single biggest, occupation in the nation as compared with individual industries like steel, autos, etc., it produced directly only 3 percent of total national income in 1967, the remainder coming from non-farming activities. And the per capita personal income of the farm population from all sources—including not only agriculture but dividends, off-farm part-time employment, pensions, etc.—was about 73 percent of the personal income per capita of the population as a whole.

Farm Population. Both the number of farms and the farm population declined steadily over the 1965-68 period, continuing a trend which had been going on steadily since well before World War II.

Year	Farms	Farm Population	As % of Total Pop.
1935	6,814,000	32,161,000	25.3%
1940	6,350,000	30,547,000	23.1
1945	5,967,000	24,420,000	17.5
1950	5,648,000	23,048,000	15.2
1955	4,654,000	19,078,000	11.5
1960	3,962,000	15,635,000	8.7
1965	3,340,000	12,363,000	6.4
1966	3,239,000	11,595,000	5.9
1967	3,146,000	10,817,000	5.4

Size of Farms. The average size of farms increased steadily. In 1940, it was 174 acres per farm. By 1950, it had risen to 215.3 acres, by 1959 to 302.4 acres, and by 1964 to 351.5 acres.

Productivity. The long-term trend of rises in farm productivity, due to use of more machinery, fertilizer, lime and insecticides, continued in 1965-68. Corn yields, which averaged 32.7 bushels an acre in 1945 and 68.3 bushels over the 1962-66 period, reached 78.5 bushels an acre in 1968. Sorghum grain, a feed similar to corn, had average yields of 15.2 bushels an acre in 1945, 47.4 bushels over 1962-66 and 52.9 in 1968. Wheat rose from 17.0 in 1945 to 25.8 bushels an acre in the 1962-66 period and 28.4 bushels in 1968.

Agriculture continued to use heavy machinery inputs. The value of assets per farm worker (land, machinery, etc.), which already in the 1950s was greater than in manufacturing, rose from $27,367 in 1964 to $45,872 in 1968.

Fertilizer use jumped enormously even in the brief 1965-68 period. In 1950, some 2,772,000 tons of the fertilizer nutrients nitrogen, phosphorus and potassium were used; in 1960, 5,643,000 tons. The 1964 figure was 8,093,000 tons, and by 1968 the total had jumped to 11,649,000.

Importance of Government Payments. Government payments were an important part of farm receipts. They increased as a result of the 1965 Food and Agriculture Act, which reduced price support loan levels but gave farmers direct payments to compensate for the lower loan levels. Direct Government payments totaled $1.493 billion in 1961, $2,181 billion in 1964 and $3,079 billion in 1967. Direct payments under the cotton, feed grain and wheat programs amounted in 1967 to $932 million, $865 million, and $731 million respectively. The soil bank, the agricultural conservation program, cropland retirement, and a few other programs made up the remainder.

Division of Market. The larger commercial farms continued to increase their share of the market. In 1959, some 2.8 percent of the nation's farms had sales of $40,000 or more annually and accounted for 31.2 percent of total farm income from sales. By 1964, farms in the $40,000 or more annual sales class constituted 4.5 percent of all farms and accounted for 42.3 percent of all sales. By 1967, they made up 5.8 percent of all farms, with 47 percent of all sales by

value. Agriculture Department figures divided farms in 1967, according to gross annual sales, as follows:

Class	Number	% of All Farms	% of All Sales
$40,000 and over	183,000	5.8	47.0
$20,000 to $39,999	318,000	10.1	20.8
$10,000 to $19,999	492,000	15.6	17.3
$5,000 to $9,999	446,000	14.2	8.1
$2,500 to $4,999	360,000	11.5	3.4
Under $2,500	1,347,000	42.8	3.4
Total	3,146,000	100.0	100.0

Chronology Of Legislation On Agriculture

1965

The most important farm legislation of the 1965-68 period was enacted in 1965. That year saw passage of the Food and Agriculture Act, establishing price support and production control programs for the major crops for four years; a new Sugar Act to govern sugar production, imports and marketing through 1971; and a new system of tobacco controls.

The Food and Agriculture Act represented, on the whole, a major victory for the President and for the traditional Democratic policy of trying to maintain farm income through a system of relatively generous price supports and other income aids combined with production cutbacks.

Farm Bill

Congress gave the President and Secretary of Agriculture Orville L. Freeman a major victory with enactment of the Food and Agriculture Act of 1965 (HR 9811—PL 89-321).

Although the final bill was not in all respects what the Administration had sought, provisions for the major crops (cotton, wheat and feed grains) were in accord with the general philosophy of the President and Mr. Freeman.

The provisions called, in effect, for a system of production controls, price supports and direct Government payments to cooperating farmers that would (1) maintain relatively high farm income; (2) prevent production of surpluses of major crops, thereby simultaneously reducing Government stockpiles and avoiding depression of market prices by oversupply;

INCOME FROM FARMING

(in millions of dollars)

	Realized Gross Income	Production Expenses	Realized Net Income		Per farm, 1957-59 dollars*	Parity Ratio**
			Amt.	% of Gross		
1930	$11,472	$ 6,944	$ 4,528	39.5%	$1,384	83
1940	11,059	6,858	4,201	38.0	1,574	81 (88)
1950	32,271	19,410	12,861	39.9	2,648	101 (102)
1960	38,088	26,352	11,736	30.8	2,904	80 (81)
1965	44,926	30,933	13,993	31.1	3,916	77 (82)
1966	49,597	33,404	16,193	32.6	4,545	80 (86)
1967	49,061	34,820	14,241	29.0	4,005	74 (79)
1968	50,752	35,900	14,852		N A	73 (79)

*Dollars, not millions

**Adjusted parity ratio, reflecting Government payments, shown in parentheses.

(3) avoid an excessively high market price and thereby encourage both exports (world prices for many U.S. farm goods were lower than U.S. prices) and domestic consumption of such items as cotton, which otherwise could not compete with lower-priced synthetics and imports.

The bill, in general, was a continuation of the policies initiated by Presidents Kennedy and Johnson since 1961.

Major Provisions

Following is a summary of major provisions, compared with Administration requests.

COTTON. Established a new system for the 1966-69 cotton crops, which, the Administration hoped, would reduce production significantly from the 15 million bales grown in 1965, reduce the market price to mills and overseas buyers, and enable the Government to interfere with actual market operations less than under the existing program. Cotton was then in massive oversupply; carryover had risen from 7.8 million bales in 1962 to 14.3 million in 1965.

The system was based upon a national minimum cotton acreage allotment of 16 million acres. Under the new law, a part of each farm's regular cotton allotment was designated as a "domestic allotment." For 1966, the "domestic allotment" constituted 65 percent of the regular allotment.

A grower wishing to participate in the program would be required to idle at least 12.5 percent of his regular allotment. In return he would receive:

(1) Price supports on all the cotton he produced, at 90 percent of the world market price (about 21 cents).

(2) A special direct payment subsidy—9.42 cents a pound in 1966—on the portion of cotton grown on his smaller "domestic allotment."

(3) Diversion payments of about 10.5 cents a pound in 1966 on the cotton that would have been produced on the idled acres. (A farmer choosing to idle more than 12.5 percent of his acreage would get added payments.)

Special provisions allowed very small cotton farmers to receive most of these benefits without reducing their acreage.

Estimated first-year cost of the program was about $800 million. It was hoped the special bonuses for compliance would encourage farmers to participate in the program, thus reducing cotton surpluses. At the same time, the market price of cotton both in the United States and in overseas sales—instead of 29 cents, as in 1965—would be around the world market price of 21 cents, assuring that U.S. cotton would not be priced out of the market. (In 1965, the cotton market price was 29 cents and the U.S. direct subsidy 4.35 cents, for a total return to the farmer of 33.35 cents. In 1966, under the new program, the market price was 21 cents and the direct payment 9.42 cents.)

An additional special provision of the bill allowed farmers choosing to sell their entire crop in the export market to plant up to 150 percent of their allotments. But they would not be eligible for diversion payments or special direct subsidy payments. This provision was designed for big farms, chiefly in the West, whose best economic course lay in a large volume of production.

The Johnson Administration did not propose the cotton program, but it accepted it after it was drafted by the House Agriculture Committee.

WHEAT. Established a program for the 1966-69 wheat crops similar to one in effect in earlier years of the Kennedy-Johnson Administrations, but with some significant changes.

Under the new program, farmers planting within their acreage allotments (based on a national figure set at 47.8 million acres by the Secretary for 1966) would be eligible for a return equal to the full parity figure (then $2.57 a bushel) on about two-fifths of their crop (the portion attributable to domestic human consumption). On the remainder of their production they would get the market price of about $1.25 a bushel.

Receipt of the full parity figure on two-fifths of the crop was more than farmers had been receiving. The $2.57 guarantee would be fulfilled as follows:

(1) Complying wheat farmers could sell their wheat on the market at $1.25 or, alternatively, obtain price support loans of about $1.25 a bushel.

(2) On the portion of the wheat coming under the $2.57 guarantee, they would receive, in addition to the $1.25 sale price (or support loan), a direct Government payment of 57 cents, plus a special bonus payment of 75 cents a bushel. The bonus payment would be made by millers purchasing the wheat to be processed for human consumption, for they would be required to redeem, at the 75-cent rate, "certificates" distributed by the Government to wheat farmers participating in the program.

Farmers who chose to reduce wheat acreage below their permitted allotments could also receive special diversion payments.

The estimated first-year cost of this program to the Government was $1.25 billion. It was believed, however, that it would keep production down while maintaining high farm income and a market price for wheat low enough to allow it to move into world mar-

---

Farm Lobbies

Literally dozens of farm organizations were active on the legislative scene during the 1965-68 period, but the most influential were the three general farm organizations—the conservative American Farm Bureau Federation, which claimed 1.8 million "farm families" as members, the more liberal National Farmers Union, which claimed 225,000 "farm families," and the National Grange, with 750,000 individual members.

The NFU and the Grange supported much of the price support and production control legislation proposed by the Johnson Administration. The Farm Bureau generally favored moving toward a system where the marketplace would have more influence over prices than at present, with production controls removed and price supports reduced to a level where at best they would serve as a floor against disaster.

kets and be used for feed in the United States when not needed for food uses.

These provisions were basically the plan sought by the Administration with one major exception. The Administration did not want the $2.57 price to consist partly of a direct Government payment. It preferred that the millers pay the entire difference between the market price of $1.25 and the full-parity guarantee of $2.57. It therefore proposed that the certificates to be purchased by millers for wheat used for domestic consumption cover the full spread between $1.25 and $2.57. This would have shifted from the Government to the millers about $300 million in costs. However, a strong lobbying campaign by bakery unions, milling groups, bread and macaroni companies, the Teamsters union, and the American Farm Bureau Federation—calling the proposal a "bread tax"—killed the initial Administration plan.

FEED GRAINS. The bill continued through 1969 with some changes the basic feed grains program that had been in effect for several years. It asked farmers to retire and devote to conservation practices at least 20 percent of the feed grain acreages based on their past history of production. Compliers would be eligible for price support loans (set for corn at $1 a bushel for 1966) plus direct subsidy payments (30 cents a bushel on corn in 1966), plus diversion payments at the Secretary's discretion on production lost on the idle

acreage. The first-year cost of the program was estimated at $1.4 billion.

RICE. The Administration proposed a certificate program for rice similar to the one for wheat. Instead of Government supports at $4.50 a hundredweight, rice growers complying with production controls would have received $3.50 in supports (the world market level) plus a certificate worth another $3. Both rice growers and millers opposed this plan and it was dropped.

Instead, the bill provided for acreage reduction payments in 1966-69 if needed to keep rice growers' income at 1965 levels.

WOOL. The bill instituted new wool supports through 1969 under which the Government, instead of paying producers the difference between the lower market price and 62 cents on each pound of wool, would pay the difference between the market price and 65 cents in 1965 and 66 cents in 1967. Further changes depended on a cost-of-living formula. (The 1968 figure was 67 cents; 1969, 69 cents.) The Administration had sought a complicated formula change to give small producers the highest rate of subsidies, but that proposal was killed by Congress.

DAIRY. The Administration made no dairy proposals. The final version of HR 9811 authorized establishment of individual quotas for sales of Class I milk under federal milk marketing orders. Currently

Acreage allotments:
Acreage by crops, United States, 1954-68

Crop year	Wheat[2]	Corn (commercial area)	Cotton		Peanuts	Rice	Tobacco	
			Upland	Extra long staple			Flue-cured	Burley
	1,000 acres	*1,000 acres*	*1,000 acres*	*1,000 acres*	*1,000 acres*	*1,000 acres*	*1,000 acres*	*1,000 acres*
1954	62,000	46,996	21,379	41	1,610		1,053	399
1955	55,000	49,843	18,113	46	1,731	1,928	1,007	309
1956	55,000	42,281	17,391	45	1,650	1,653	888	309
1957	55,000	37,289	17,585	89	1,611	1,653	711	309
1958	55,000	38,818	17,555	83	1,612	1,653	712	309
1959	55,000		17,330	71	1,612	1,653	713	309
1960	55,000		17,525	65	1,612	1,653	713	309
1961	55,000		18,458	64	1,612	1,653	714	329
1962	55,000		18,102	100	1,613	1,818	745	349
1963	55,000		16,250	150	1,612	1,818	708	349
1964	49,500		16,200	112	1,613	1,818	638	316
1965	49,500		16,200	78	1,613	1,819	607	287
1966	47,800		16,200	81	1,613	2,001	607	250
1967	68,195		16,200	70	1,613	2,001	607	250
1968	59,300		16,200	70	1,613	2,401	607	250

1 National acreage allotments proclaimed by the Secretary of Agriculture under the Agricultural Adjustment Act of 1938, as amended. In most years, allotments were accompanied by marketing quotas.

2 Excludes increases in allotments granted under special legislation, as for durum for years 1954-57 and 1962, and for small wheat farms, 1964-66.

producers selling under federal milk marketing orders were paid a "blend" price representing their share of the pooled receipts of the sales of all Class I (drinking) milk, which commanded premium prices, and all manufacturing milk, which commanded only the minimum support price. The dairy title provided that, if approved by producers in a referendum, the producers in a market order area would each be assigned a specific quota for Class I sales.

In addition, authorized marketing orders for manufacturing milk, provided for individual voting (instead of block voting) in the farmer referendums, provided access for new producers in the case of increased consumption or forfeited bases, and permitted transfer of Class I bases among farmers.

The aim of the Class I quota plan was to reduce incentives to overproduction of milk. Under this plan, a farmer increasing his production could only receive the lower manufacturing price for the excess; the amount of milk he could sell at the higher price would be fixed.

CROPLAND RETIREMENT. The bill incorporated an Administration program designed to retire 40 million acres of land from production—thus reducing surpluses—through 5 to 10-year contracts with farmers. No more than $225 million in new contracts could be signed in any year. Payments on the contracts would be up to 40 percent of the annual market value of the crop that would have been produced on the land. Contracts could be entered into between 1965 and 1969.

LEGISLATIVE HIGHLIGHTS

House. The House passed HR 9811 on a 221-172 (R 19-104; D 202-68) roll call Aug. 19. In order to win urban Democratic support for the bill (many urban Members opposed the farm programs as costly and tending to boost consumer food prices), the Democratic leadership linked it to a liberal-supported measure repealing state authority to pass right-to-work laws.

The latter passed July 28 with the support of some farm-area Congressmen, and the big farm bill, in turn, got backing from many urban Democrats.

The most bitter debate involved cotton. Some cotton-area Congressmen, like Thomas G. Morris (D N.M.) and Thomas G. Abernethy (D Miss.) criticized the cotton provisions, saying the direct payments smelled like a dole, which farmers disliked, while the low price-support loan level would not please them.

Other congressmen criticized the wheat certificate provisions. Republicans, particularly, were critical of the "bread tax" proposal as were many urban Democrats.

The debate was marked, also, by disenchantment with the whole farm program, which John S. Monagan, (D Conn.), for example, called "expensive" and "wasteful" as currently run.

Senate. The Senate passed the measure Sept. 14 on a 72-22 roll call after adding the Class I milk plan, 57-27; substituting for Committee provisions new cotton and wheat titles similar to those finally enacted into law, in place of more costly programs; and re-

jecting on roll calls of 33-56, 42-49 and 42-50 amendments by Daniel Brewster (D Md.) and John J. Williams (R Del.) to limit over-all aid to any one farmer to $25,000, $50,000 or $100,000 a year, respectively. Sponsors said program costs were so high that aid should be limited to the amount needed by small and middling farmers, and should not enrich giant farm enterprises.

In signing the bill into law Nov. 3, President Johnson predicted that the low support levels would make for greater exports and thus reduce surpluses, while the direct payments would help keep up farm income. Over the next several years the cotton surplus did drop, but the reduction was due in part to bad growing weather. Wheat surpluses also dropped for two or three years, but rising foreign wheat production, resulting in part from U.S.-introduced new strains in Asia, cut into this country's overseas markets toward toward the end of the 1960s and threatened new and serious grain surpluses.

Sugar Act

Congress in 1965 enacted legislation fixing new domestic and foreign sugar quotas—action it had been unable to take in 1964 because of a deadlock within the U.S. sugar industry. The new quotas established by HR 11135 (PL 89-331) were to run through Dec. 31, 1971. They replaced existing domestic quotas, set in 1962, which otherwise would have remained in effect until Dec. 31, 1966, and foreign quotas (also set in 1962) which had expired at the end of 1964.

The Sugar Act is designed primarily to protect the domestic sugar industry. The Act creates an artificially high price for sugar by setting quotas limiting the total amount of sugar that can be sold in the United States. Under the Act, domestic sugar growers are guaranteed a large share of the market. The remainder is assigned to foreign countries. The latter are anxious to obtain quotas because the protected U.S. sugar price is normally higher than the world price. In mid-1965, for example, the New York price of delivered raw cane sugar was 6 cents a pound, while the world market price was only 2 cents.

Key Features of HR 11135

The key feature of the 1965 Sugar Act amendments was an increase in the share of the U.S. market guaranteed to domestic sugar producers.

Under the previous law (the 1962 Sugar Act Amendments), domestic producers (mainland beet sugar producers, mainland cane sugar producers and Hawaiian, Puerto Rican and Virgin Islands cane producers) were granted the right to supply 5,810,000 tons of sugar a year to the U.S. market—or approximately 60 percent of the over-all normal market supply of 9.7 million tons a year. The remaining 3,890,000 million tons were to be supplied by imports from foreign countries.

Under HR 11135, the domestic producers' figure was raised by 580,000 tons—to 6,390,000 tons (66 percent)—and foreign suppliers were reduced correspondingly, to 3,310,000 tons a year. The entire 580,000-ton increase was divided among mainland beet (375,000

Sugar Quotas

As signed into law, HR 11135 set up the following annual quotas fixing the amount of sugar to be provided to the U.S. market by different producing areas during calendar years 1966 through 1971. The figures reflect basic quotas plus proration to other foreign countries of Cuba's suspended 1.1 million-ton quota, and are based upon a U.S. consumption level of 9.7 million tons of sugar annually. When consumption rises about 9.7 million tons, quota amounts increase (see Provisions).

A. Domestic Suppliers	Annual Quota, Tons
Mainland U.S. beet sugar	3,025,000
Mainland cane sugar	1,100,000
Hawaii	1,110,000
Puerto Rico	1,140,000
Virgin Islands	15,000
Total, Domestic	6,390,000

B. The Philippine Islands	1,050,000(a)

C. Western Hemisphere	
Mexico	348,501
Dominican Republic	340,925
Brazil	340,925
Peru	272,013
British West Indies	136,000
Ecuador	49,770
French West Indies	42,970
Argentina	40,000
Costa Rica	40,000
Nicaragua	40,000
Colombia	36,000
Guatemala	34,000
Panama	25,134
El Salvador	25,000
Haiti	18,731
Venezuela	17,000
British Honduras	10,000
Bahamas	(b)
Bolivia	4,054
Honduras	4,054
Cuba	(c)
Total, Western Hemisphere	1,825,077

D. Other Foreign Countries	
Australia	162,152
Republic of China	67,431
India	64,861
South Africa	48,000
Fiji Islands	35,489
Thailand	15,000
Mauritius	14,985
Malagasy Republic	7,492
Swaziland	6,081
Southern Rhodesia	6,081 (d)
Ireland	5,351 (e)
Total, Other Countries	432,923

GRAND TOTAL	9,700,000

(a) Philippine quota fixed by treaty, but increases when U.S. consumption exceeds 9.7 million tons.

(b) The Bahama Islands were granted a 10,000 ton annual quota starting in 1968. After the Bahamas quota became effective, figures for countries in groups C and D were reduced very slightly in order to provide the Bahamas' 10,000 tons.

(c) Cuba's quota of approximately 1,130,000 tons suspended until U.S.-Cuban relations improve. Figures for other foreign nations shown in the table include reallocations from the suspended Cuban quota.

(d) Southern Rhodesia's 1966 quota was suspended and reallocated following that country's break with Great Britain, which occurred after the bill was passed.

(e) Ireland's quota is stationary and does not increase as the national U.S. consumption level goes up.

tons) and mainland cane producers (205,000 tons). The Administration endorsed these changes.

Other key features of the 1965 legislation were the continued suspension of the basic Cuban quota and its reassignment to other nations, pending restoration of good relations between the United States and Cuba; the absence of any special import fees on foreign sugar; and the return to a statutory system of country-by-country quotas for foreign suppliers, instead of partial use of a first-come, first-served system for foreign suppliers, as had been the case during 1963 and 1964.

Basic Pattern of Amendments

The Sugar Act amendments made by HR 11135 set up the following basic pattern for the U.S. sugar quota system:

• Estimated the normal national consumption level at 9.7 million tons of sugar a year and contained provisions allocating quotas based upon that amount.

• Provided for a 580,000-ton increase in the domestic mainland producers' annual share of the U.S. market, allocated as follows: The mainland beet sugar share was increased by 375,000 tons (to a new total of 3,025,000 tons a year) and the mainland cane sugar share was increased by 205,000 tons (to a new total of 1,100,000 tons a year). In the eyes of mainland producers, this was the key section of the bill because the 580,000-ton increase—which was deliberately made retroactive to Jan. 1, 1965—permitted them to dispose of surpluses accumulated in recent years and enlarge their share of the market.

• Assigned the following quotas to domestic offshore producers: Hawaii, 1,110,000 tons; Puerto Rico, 1,140,000 tons; and the Virgin Islands, 15,000 tons. These were the same amounts as under the previous legislation.

• Assigned the Philippines a quota of 1,050,000 tons. This amount, guaranteed by treaty, was the same as under previous legislation.

• Divided the remaining 2,260,000 tons among 32 foreign nations, including Cuba. However, Cuba's share continued to be suspended and reassigned to the other nations. (See box.)

• Reduced Cuba's permanent legal share—currently suspended and reassigned—from 57.77 percent to 50 percent of the 2,260,000-ton foreign total (exclusive of small amounts set aside for Ireland and the Bahamas).

• Permitted the Secretary to raise the annual national total quota above 9.7 million tons if he believed U.S. consumption needs required it, and provided that all increases in national consumption between 9.7 million tons and 10.4 million tons be assigned to foreign countries—10.86 percent to the Philippines and the rest divided among other foreign nations with quotas. All increases above 10.4 million tons would be filled 65 percent by mainland U.S. cane and beet sugar producers, and the remainder by foreign nations.

• Did not reinstate either a "recapture" import fee or the "global quota" concept (distributing Cuba's suspended share on a first-come, first-served basis instead of reallocating it to specific nations). The import fee and the "global quota" were written into the Sugar Act in 1962 and expired Dec. 31, 1964. The import fee, designed to "recapture" for the U.S. Treasury some of the difference between the normally low world market price and the normally higher Government-pegged U.S. price, was opposed by Latin American countries.

The "global quota" was blamed for causing U.S. shortages during the 1963 sugar crisis. Critics of the global quota said that country-by-country quotas, by guaranteeing foreign producers a long-term share of the lucrative U.S. market, encouraged them to maintain their shipments to the United States (in order to maintain their future quota rights) even on those rare occasions when world sugar shortages drove the world market price higher than the domestic U.S. price of sugar.

The critics of the global quota said that during 1963, when world production was down because of bad crops, some countries hesitated to continue selling sugar in the United States because at that time they could get a better price on the world market. By failing to provide these countries with the guarantees of future sales afforded by country-by-country quotas, the critics charged, the global quota system had left them little incentive to sell to the United States when the world market price was higher.

The same general argument was made against import fees. By taking away part or all of the "quota premium" (the difference between the normally high U.S. price and normally low world market price) through imposing an import fee, the 1962 law, it was contended, had reduced the incentive to foreign producers to sell in the U.S. market and had thus made it more difficult to obtain a dependable supply of foreign sugar. (Backers of import fees said the "quota premium" was simply a handout to foreign producers, but they failed in attempts to restore the fees.) The final version of HR 11135 rejected both the global quota concept and the use of "recapture" import fees. The final provisions were in accord with the Administration position.

Major Dispute

The main dispute between the House and the Senate in 1965 was over the size of individual foreign quotas.

The Administration approach, backed by the Senate, was that quotas should be based on deliveries to the United States during the sugar crisis years of 1963-64, thus rewarding the countries that had stuck by the United States at the time when the world market price had gone up. The House approach, spelled out in an Agriculture Committee print, "The Development of Foreign Sugar Quotas in HR 11135," was that quotas should be based upon deliveries during more normal years such as 1962 and upon certain other factors. These included a nation's ability to produce enough to meet its quota reliably and to carry reserves for emergencies; the need for ready availability of sugar from nearby sources (hence a House revision of the Administration's proposed country-by-country quotas to favor Latin America more); and the need to aid friendly nations.

Critics of the House quotas said lobbyists for foreign countries exerted undue influence upon the de-

liberations of the House Agriculture Committee. These charges were vigorously denied by Chairman Harold D. Cooley (D N.C.). Unsuccessful efforts were made on the House floor to write an anti-lobbyist amendment into the bill. Ultimately, the House prevailed on most individual country quotas, as had been the pattern in recent years.

There was no disagreement between the House and the Senate over increasing domestic quotas. Both chambers approved identical domestic provisions, which, in effect, continued the historic increase in the share of the market reserved for the mainland beet and mainland cane producers. Domestic quotas were a key factor in insuring favorable action on the over-all package. Members from mainland beet and cane producing areas were anxious to reach agreement on foreign quotas and enact a sugar bill in 1965 so that the 580,000-ton increase in mainland quotas could be retroactive to Jan. 1, 1965, and could also be fully effective throughout 1966. The increase would allow them to dispose of surplus stocks of sugar built up when production was expanded to meet the shortage during the 1963-64 crisis, and would also give them a long-range increase in their basic quotas.

Lobbying

Lobbyists for both domestic and foreign interests were extremely active during 1965 Congressional action, and many received sizable fees for their efforts. Twenty-seven foreign countries were represented by United States-based lobbyists. In addition, all major domestic interests were represented by lobbyists—some of whom sat in on Administration and House Agriculture Committee sessions—and some private concerns with interests in foreign countries hired lobbyists.

Tobacco Controls

A significant change in the method of controlling tobacco production was made in 1965 when Congress enacted a bill authorizing acreage-poundage marketing quotas in place of the existing acreage allotment system, if approved by a producers' referendum.

The Administration-backed bill (HR 5721—PL 89-12) applied only to flue-cured tobacco in 1965 and to all tobacco beginning in 1966. If approved by two-thirds of the farmers voting in referendums, the new programs would be binding for three successive crop years following the vote. Under the new system farms would be assigned both acreage allotments and poundage quotas (based upon histories of production) in a manner designed to reduce surpluses.

The change was viewed by the Agriculture Department and most tobacco interests as a solution to problems caused by the drive for increased yields per acre in recent years. Steadily rising yields had negated reductions in acreage allotments, causing surpluses to remain high and tobacco quality to decline.

Main opposition came from small growers in Georgia and Florida who maintained they were being penalized because of surpluses produced by large North Carolina and Virginia growers, and from Republicans who said the bill established a precedent (yield per acre control) that could be carried over to other crops. Spokesmen for the Georgia and Florida interests also said the new system should not take effect until 1966 because the 1965 crop had already been planted.

Both houses passed bills that were basically similar. Their differences were in the manner of administration rather than in the over-all approach taken. The major difference settled in conference was the formula for determining individual farm quotas under the new acreage-poundage system. The House version was more favorable to high-yield producers than the Senate bill and the House language, with some modifications, prevailed in conference.

Secretary of Agriculture Orville L. Freeman May 1 announced the following controls for the 1965 flue-cured tobacco crop year under the new system: national acreage allotment—607,335 acres; national marketing quota—1,126,000,000 pounds; and national average yield goal—1,854 pounds per acre. Growers in a May 4 referendum approved the new system of controls for 1965, 1966 and 1967.

Electric Co-Op Funds

The National Rural Electric Cooperative Assn. Aug. 5 unveiled a three-part plan to provide new, supplementary funding for the nation's rural electric cooperatives. The plan, based on a study by the NRECA and the investment consulting firm of Kuhn, Loeb and Co., was intended to help the co-ops expand their facilities to serve future markets.

The NRECA said existing financing for co-ops— 2-percent, 35-year loans from the federal Rural Electrification Administration to help cooperatives provide service in areas not receiving central station service—was inadequate for two reasons: (1) Congress probably would not provide as much money ($8.1 billion from 1965-80) as the co-ops believed they needed for expansion (in recent years, Congressional appropriations for the loans had run only $300 million to $400 million a year); and (2) existing REA-imposed or Congressionally imposed limitations on the use of REA loans would prevent the co-ops from building large-size generating and transmission systems with the REA funds. There was no Congressional action in 1965 on the NRECA financing proposals.

Details of Proposals. Following were the details of the Aug. 5, 1965, NRECA proposals:

(1) The existing federal 2-percent, 35-year loans should be continued, chiefly for the benefit of the weakest rural electric cooperatives—those serving very sparsely settled areas having few financial resources and unable to remain in existence without receiving very low-cost Government loans.

(2) A new federal revolving loan fund should be created. It would make 50—year loans to cooperatives at an interest rate equal to the average cost to the Government on its total borrowings over the past 20 years (the rate would be 3-4 percent at present). Loans from this fund would be chiefly for cooperatives having substantial resources of their own and a strong financial position, would not be subject to the existing re-

strictions on the size of generating facilities that could be built with Government-loaned money, and would be used primarily to permit "generating and transmission" cooperatives to build their own, large-scale generating facilities. The NRECA said this loan fund should be financed by channeling into it repayments by cooperatives on loans made under the existing 2-percent program. At present, REA loan repayments simply go into the Treasury.

(3) Some method of channeling private investment funds into loans to cooperatives should be found. One way would be to set up an REA-administered Federal Bank for Rural Electric Systems patterned on the Farm Credit Administration banking system. The Bank, to be funded by the sale of stock to the Government ($500 million perhaps) and to borrowers, and by borrowings in the commercial money market, would make loans to cooperatives.

Private Power Comment. President Robert T. Person of the Edison Electric Institute, principal private power spokesman, said, "One of the NRECA proposals involves the use of Government borrowings at the cost of money to Government. . . While this is better than the 2-percent rate, it is still less than what people want for the use of their money when it is invested through the free market in the electric power business." He said nearly all needs for rural power had been met, and "providing below-cost money and freedom from taxes to co-ops to build generating plants and transmission facilities is wasteful and unnecessary."

Pesticide Research

Congress in 1965 passed a bill increasing the authorization for pesticide research funds; however, it failed to act on a major Administration request to increase controls over the manufacture of pesticides to assure their safety and to prevent pollution by the disposal of waste in the manufacturing process.

S 1623, signed into law on Oct. 1 (PL 89-232) increased authorizations for Interior Department research on the effects of pesticides on fish and wildlife from $2,565,000 to $3.2 million for fiscal 1966 and authorized appropriations of $5 million a year for fiscal 1967 and 1968.

Pesticide Controls

President Johnson asked for legislation to tighten Government controls over the manufacture and use of potentially dangerous agricultural chemicals. But an Administration bill (S 2470), introduced by Sen. Abraham A. Ribicoff (D Conn.), received no action by the Senate Agriculture Committee.

Background. Congress took a major step toward control of pesticides in 1947 with passage of the Federal Insecticide, Fungicide and Rodenticide Act. The Act, which required labels of all pesticides to be registered with the Agriculture Department, with proof that they conformed to safety standards, allowed products considered unsafe by the Department to be sold in the market until a final judicial determination on the issue. Congress in 1964 passed a law (PL 88-305) permitting the Department to keep off the market an unsafe product but setting up an appeals process by which the manufacturer could establish the safety of the pesticide.

1965 Proposals. President Johnson Feb. 8, in his special message to Congress on natural beauty, said the Secretary of Agriculture would submit "legislation to tighten control over the manufacture and use of agricultural chemicals (pesticides), including licensing and factory inspection of manufacturers, clearly placing the burden of proof of safety on the proponent of the chemical rather than on the Government." Under existing procedures, manufacturers had to submit proof that their products conformed to Government standards on safety for pesticides and that labels properly specified the safe use and the effectiveness of the product. The Government, however, had no authority to inspect the actual manufacturing process.

Interagency disagreement over wording of the bill (S2740)—accounting for the delay in introduction—and Congressional preoccupation with broader legislation, such as the Administration's air and water pollution bills, were generally regarded as the reasons for inaction in 1965

'Silent Spring' Criticism. The surveys and investigations staff of the House Appropriations Committee April 19 released a report on the effects of agricultural pesticides on public health which challenged the conclusions drawn in the book "The Silent Spring" by Rachel Carson. The Carson book, published in 1962, alleged that chemical pesticides had contaminated the "air, earth, rivers and sea with dangerous and even lethal materials" resulting in a "chain of poisoning and death." Public concern over pesticide use generated by the Carson book resulted in the House investigation, which began in June 1964. Rep. Jamie L. Whitten (D Miss.), chairman of the House Appropriations Subcommittee on Agriculture, said the study was undertaken because "we must not permit anyone or any group to saddle our sources of food and fiber with the burden of the unknown."

The report was based on interviews with "over 185 outstanding scientists and 23 physicians," state and local officials, and representatives of conservation groups and private industry. The report said the Carson book was "superficially scientific in that it marshals a number of accepted scientific facts," but it was "unscientific in drawing incorrect conclusions from unrelated facts and making implications that are based on possibilities as yet unproved." The report said that Miss Carson had magnified the amount of environmental pollution resulting from pesticides and had made unsubstantiated statements that pesticides would produce cancer, sterility and cellular mutations in human beings and eventually extinguish all plant and animal life. "The book," the report alleged, "created an atmosphere of panic, foretold an impending disaster, and barely mentioned the immensely useful role played by pesticides in the U.S. economy . . . ."

The report said, however, that the Carson book had performed a service in alerting the general public to "the dangers of misuse of chemical pesticides in and around the home and on the farm" and had increased public support for pesticides research programs.

CCC Supplemental

Early in 1965, Congress passed legislation providing funds to reimburse the Agriculture Department for price support outlays (HJ Res 234—PL 89-2, signed into law Feb. 11). It became the vehicle for several basically unrelated disputes.

Passage of H J Res 234 provided $1.6 billion in fiscal 1965 supplemental appropriations to reimburse the Agriculture Department's Commodity Credit Corporation (CCC) for losses on price supports and other activities. One controversial provision prohibited the Agriculture Department from using funds in the bill to finance shipments of surplus farm products to the United Arab Republic (Egypt) under Title I of PL 480 (the Agricultural Trade Development and Assistance Act of 1954), unless the President deemed it in the "national interest." Other disputed provisions barred the closing of 31 Veterans Administration facilities and 20 agricultural research stations before May 1, 1965. (See below for details.)

Congress was under some pressure to complete action on the bill rapidly, in order to keep the farm price support program and other activities financed by the CCC in operation. Secretary of Agriculture Orville L. Freeman Nov. 24, 1964, had said he would have to ask Congress for supplementary funds to keep the commodity programs going through fiscal 1965. Freeman said Feb. 9, 1965, the CCC had no more price support funds and therefore needed the funds in H J Res 234 in order to keep making payments under the price support programs.

In debate, House Republicans complained about the federal farm programs and their costs and the periodic requests for funds to reimburse the CCC.

MAJOR CONTROVERSIES

Food Shipments to Egypt. A major foreign policy controversy arose when the House, before passing H J Res 234 Jan. 26, added to the bill wording which specified that appropriations in the measure could not be used to finance the export of farm commodities to Egypt under Title I of PL 480 (sales of U.S. farm goods for foreign currencies). The action was taken in retaliation for anti-American incidents in Egypt. However, the Administration strongly opposed this wording, saying it could tie the President's hands in deciding whether to permit shipment of about $37 million worth of food constituting the final installment under an Oct. 8, 1962, Title I agreement with Egypt that was due to expire June 30, 1965.

President Johnson on Jan. 27 sent Secretary of State Dean Rusk to a special Capitol Hill meeting to brief Senators on relations with Egypt. Rusk said that surplus food shipments provided one of the few remaining levers left in U.S. relations with Egypt. As a result, the Senate relaxed the House ban by writing in language that gave the President discretionary authority to continue PL 480 Title I shipments to Egypt with funds in the bill, provided he found such shipments were in the U.S. national interest. At a press conference Feb. 4, Mr. Johnson urged the House to accept the Senate version, calling it a matter of the "highest importance" that he "have freedom of action to act in the best interest" of the nation.

The House finally complied and approved the Senate language leaving discretionary authority with the President. Subsequently, the State Department June 22 announced that the President, exercising the discretionary authority given him in the bill, had approved the final $37 million shipment to Egypt. The discretionary authority left with the President in the final version of H J Res 234 corresponded to the way the problem of aid to Poland and Yugoslavia had been handled in the past.

Later in 1965 the House, acting on the fiscal 1966 agriculture funds bill (HR 8370), rejected proposals to insert provisions barring use of funds in the bill for PL 480 Title I shipments to Egypt and Indonesia. (See below.)

VA Closings. Another controversy on H J Res 234 involved a provision, inserted in the Senate, barring the Veterans Administration from carrying out a plan announced Jan. 12 to close down 11 veterans' hospitals, four old soldiers' (domiciliary) homes and 16 regional benefit offices. The Administration insisted on its right to close these installations if it wished, and as a result the final version of H J Res 234 placed a ban on the closings only until May 1, 1965 (enough time, some claimed, for Congress to study the matter). Subsequently, the dispute was compromised when the President June 8 announced that only six of the hospitals, two of the old soldiers' homes and nine of the regional benefit offices would be closed.

Farm Research Closings. A similar controversy on H J Res 234 arose when the Senate added a provision barring the proposed closing of 20 agricultural research facilities and curtailment of projects at many other such facilities. The final version of H J Res 234 placed a prohibition on the closings only until May 1, 1965, but the Administration later agreed to rescind some of the proposed closings and curtailments. (See Funds Bill, below.)

Funds Bill

The regular Agriculture Department appropriations bill for fiscal 1966 (HR 8370—PL 89-316) appropriated $6.2 billion.

During consideration of the measure, Congress refused to accept two Administration economy moves. One called for the closing of 15 agricultural stations and the curtailing of research at 36 other sites, at an annual saving of $5,151,000. The other proposed to slash the advance authorization for agricultural conservation to $120 million. Congress finally agreed to the closing of 8 research stations and the curtailing of work at 21 others, for an annual savings of $2,761,100. But it added 20 unbudgeted research projects to HR 8370 at a cost of $3,369,000.

The final advance authorization for the Agricultural Conservation Program was set at $220 million. Congress has repeatedly refused to cut or kill the program. It provides limestone for farmers to replenish depleted soil and is popular in the South.

On another issue, Administration forces in the House May 26 narrowly defeated, 187-208, a Republican motion to recommit HR 8370 to the Appropriations Committee with instructions to add a ban on food shipments to the United Arab Republic (Egypt) and Indonesia.

Pressure from the Senate forced the Administration to increase by $500 million its request for funds to repay borrowing by the Commodity Credit Corp. (CCC) to cover 1964 losses incurred in price support and food distribution programs. The original request for CCC reimbursements was $2.3 billion, almost $1 billion under the actual amount of losses. The final version of the bill set reimbursements at $2.8 billion.

PROVISIONS—As signed by the President, Nov. 2, HR 8370 appropriated:

General Activities

Agricultural Research Service	$ 200,922,000
Cooperative State Research Service	54,795,000
Extension Service	89,135,000
Farmer Cooperative Service	1,141,000
Soil Conservation Service	(223,485,000)1
Conservation operations	106,373,000
Watershed planning	5,721,000
Watershed protection	65,671,000
Flood prevention	25,417,000
Great Plains conservation program	16,000,000
Resource conversation and development	4,303,000
Economic Research Service	11,536,000
Statistical Reporting Service	13,755,000
Consumer and Marketing Service	(417,942,000)1
(Formerly Agricultural Marketing Service)	
Consumer Programs	76,192,000
Payments to states	1,750,000
Special milk program	103,000,000
School lunch program	157,000,000
Food stamp program	80,000,000
Foreign Agricultural Service	20,574,000
Commodity Exchange Authority	1,169,000
Stabilization and Conservation Service	(618,778,500)1
Expenses, ASCS	126,278,500
Sugar Act program	95,000,000
Agricultural conservation program	220,000,000
Conservation reserve program	146,000,000
Cropland conversion program	7,500,000
Emergency conservation	24,000,000
Rural Community Development Service	625,000
Office of Inspector General	10,491,000
Office of General Counsel	4,184,000
Office of Information	1,689,000
National Agricultural Library	8,699,000
Office of Management Services	2,483,000
General Administration	3,848,000
Subtotal, general activities	**$1,685,251,500**

Credit Agencies

(for loan authorizations, see below)

Rural Electrification Administration	$ 11,934,000
Farmers Home Administration	(50,700,000)1
Rural housing for domestic farm labor	3,000,000
Rural renewal	1,200,000
Rural housing for elderly revolving fund	2,500,000
Salaries and expenses	44,000,000
Subtotal, credit agencies	**$ 62,634,000**

Corporations

Federal Crop Insurance Corporation	$ 8,000,000
Commodity Credit Corporation	2,800,000,000
PL 480	(1,658,000,000)*1*
Sales for foreign currencies	1,144,000,000
Emergency famine relief	298,500,000
Long-term supply contracts	215,500,000
International Wheat Agreement	27,544,000
Subtotal, corporations	**$4,493,544,000**

Related Agencies

National Commission on Food Marketing	$ 1,500,000
GRAND TOTAL	**$6,242,929,500**

1 Subtotal of items immediately following (indented).

The bill also:

Authorized the following transfers of Section 32 funds to various agencies to be spent for their programs in addition to amounts provided through direct appropriations: Agricultural Research Service, for research, $18.1 million; Cooperative State Research Service, $400,000; school lunch program, $45 million; Foreign Agricultural Service, $3,177,000.

Authorized $20 million left over from the fiscal 1965 appropriations for the food stamp program to be used for the program in fiscal 1966, in addition to the new appropriations provided.

Authorized the transfer of $81,933,500 from the Commodity Credit Corp. for expenses incurred by the Agricultural Stabilization and Conservation Service, in addition to funds included in direct appropriations for the same purpose.

Continued a 1963 and 1964 provision barring use of federal funds to influence legislation or the vote on a referendum, or to pay salaries of members of county and local farmer committees for other than prescribed functions.

Authorized $220 million for the Agricultural Conservation Program in calendar 1966.

Authorized $462 million in REA loans: $365 million for electrification loans (including a reserve of $60 million) and $97 million for telephone loans (including a reserve of $15 million).

Authorized $375 million to be spent from Farmers Home Administration direct loan account: $75 million for real estate loans and $300 million for operating loans (including a reserve of $50 million).

1966

There was no major price support and production control legislation in 1966, since a four-year program had been passed the previous year. By far the most important enactment was an overhaul of the overseas "surplus disposal" law—the Agricultural Trade Development and Assistance Act of 1954 (known as PL 480), also called "Food for Peace."

The program was reshaped in an atmosphere influenced by droughts overseas, reduced supplies of commodities at home and fears of massive starvation abroad. PL 480 was originally created to get rid of U.S. surplus crops like wheat and feed grains. In 1966, the program was reoriented at the Administration's request to emphasize the need to combat world hunger, even if this meant loosening production restrictions in the United States and bearing a larger cost of overseas shipments.

At the same time, the new law heavily stressed the requirement that recipient nations undertake self-help efforts to boost their own agriculture and to control population increase.

Also noteworthy in 1966 was the report of the National Commission on Food Marketing, which concluded that the widening spread between farm market prices and retail prices for agricultural products resulted in part from new packaging and promotional devices, and in part from the cumulative effects of inflation which boosted retail prices more than farm market prices.

Food for Peace

Congress in 1966 passed legislation (HR 14929—PL 89-808) extending, reorganizing and adding major new provisions to the Agricultural Trade Development and Assistance Act of 1954 (PL 480), which authorized the U.S. Food for Peace program. HR 14929 extended the Act for two years, through calendar 1968, and authorized a new expenditure commitment of $2,533,000,000 for each year.

Until enactment of HR 14929, PL 480 had been considered mainly a means for disposing of U.S. farm surpluses by sending them overseas, either for sale—primarily for inconvertible foreign currencies—or as donations. The new bill changed the emphasis of the program from surplus disposal to foreign aid. In addition, it provided for shifting the bulk of payments from local currencies to dollar sales under long-term credit agreements. The new bill also, for the first time, placed heavy stress on the need for recipient countries to carry out "self-help" programs to increase their own food production. The effectiveness of these programs was made a criterion for receiving goods under the Act. The change in emphasis came about as U.S. surplus stocks of a number of commodities (notably wheat) were dwindling, while current and projected demands from underdeveloped countries for PL 480 food were increasing.

Surplus Concept Eliminated. In 1965 and 1966 the United States succeeded in controlling to a substantial extent its long-standing problem of farm surpluses. This meant that PL 480 was no longer needed to fulfill its stated function as a vehicle for surplus disposal. Therefore, the Administration asked, and Congress in HR 14929 provided, that the PL 480 program be continued and considered as a means of combatting world hunger. The change had major implications for overall agricultural policy. It meant that production controls on U.S. farmers would have to be substantially loosened to meet commitments under the Act. (Under the 1965 omnibus Food and Agriculture Act the Agriculture Secretary already had authority to take administrative action to increase production—*see box.*)

Production Increases Ordered

Agricultural experts in 1966 warned increasingly of a potential "world food crisis." It was estimated that by 1980 the world hunger problem would be so great the the United States alone could not meet it even if domestic agricultural production controls were abandoned. In addition, U.S. officials reportedly felt that the U.S. aid program had discouraged needy countries from developing their own agricultural production facilities and programs sufficiently. Accordingly, officials began to put more emphasis on the need for agricultural self-help.

David E. Bell, then Administrator of the Agency for International Development, Nov. 19, 1965, in a speech to the U.S. National Commission for the UN Educational, Scientific and Cultural Organization, dwelt on the role recipient nations must play: "Unless self-help measures are undertaken, foreign aid is only a crutch, which helps a developing country avoid its problems, not solve them." He said "the application of scientific and technical knowledge to raising food" was especially important because developing nations were "beginning to reach the margins of new land available for cultivation" and increased food output must, therefore, come from higher yields per acre. Bell said developing nations must give a higher priority to agriculture.

The Department of Agriculture took the following administrative actions during calendar 1966 to increase production of commodities needed for shipments under PL 480:

Rice—Increased 1966 rice acreage allotments by 10 percent.

Soybeans—Exercised an option granted under the 1965 omnibus farm bill to allow soybeans to be grown on feed grain "permitted" acres (part of a farm's feed grain base).

Wheat—Increased 1967 wheat acreage allotments—15 percent on May 5 and another 15 percent on Aug. 8, 1966.

Feed Grains—The Agriculture Department in late October announced the specifics of the feed grain program for 1967. To encourage production, the Department increased the price support loan from $1 to $1.05 a bushel on corn and provided that there would be no diversion payments except for small farms (25 acres or less).

Elimination of the surplus disposal concept also had the effect of broadening the Agriculture Secretary's discretion as to what crops could be programed under PL 480, because the food to be furnished would not have to be in surplus.

Self-Help Emphasized. PL 480 formerly emphasized building markets for U.S. agricultural commodities. The major emphasis in the new bill was on encouraging underdeveloped countries to take steps to remedy their own food problems—both in terms of boosting agricultural production and controlling population—and on providing assistance for these self-help efforts.

For the first time, Congress in HR 14929 required that countries must carry out self-help measures to improve their own agricultural production to qualify for food shipments under the Act. These provisions were a result of concern about the projected "world food crisis" and concern that U.S. food aid had kept underdeveloped nations from working to solve their agricultural problems.

In its provisions relating to self-help, HR 14929 required the President, before entering into PL 480 sales agreements, to consider the extent to which the recipient country was undertaking self-help measures in nine specific areas. The bill required that at least 20 percent of foreign currencies acquired under PL 480 were to be loaned back to the recipient country to help finance agricultural self-help programs. It also authorized $33 million annually for a new farmer-to-farmer technical assistance program designed to encourage self-help efforts.

HR 14929 specified that efforts by underdeveloped countries to control their own population was one of the factors to be considered by the President when he determined which countries would receive food shipments under the Act. In addition, the bill authorized the use of U.S.-owned foreign currencies obtained under the Act for (1) grants to foreign countries to conduct birth control programs and (2) programs carried out by the United States, in cooperation with foreign countries, to promote population control.

Administration Request. Although the Administration request in 1966 included changing the emphasis of the program to foreign aid and stressing self-help, the final version of HR 14929 was very different from the President's original proposal. Mr. Johnson had asked for an entirely new statute—entitled "Food for Freedom"—with a five-year life and $3.3 billion in new authorizations for each year. Congress however chose to rewrite the existing law, enacted a two-year program and voted a new authorization of $2,533,000,000 per year. In addition, the self-help provisions in HR 14929 were more specific and stiffer than those requested by the Administration.

In proposing a new statute, the Administration had hoped quietly to rid itself of many of the restrictions that had been written into PL 480 since it was first enacted in 1954. However, the House, in choosing to amend the old Act, kept many of the restrictions, and the Senate and final bills went further, adding most of the old restrictions which the House had omitted. The final bill also included stiffer new terms which had not been requested by the Administration, such as requirements that 5 percent of the cost of goods sold under PL 480 be paid for immediately in hard currencies and that most shipping costs of food to be sold (not donated) be paid in dollars on receipt of goods.

Program Expenditures. According to the Agriculture Department, total expenditures under PL 480 in fiscal 1966 were $2.16 billion. This compared to a projected expenditure of $2.02 billion for fiscal 1967. HR 14929 authorized the expenditure of up to $3,733,000,-000—$2.5 billion in new authorizations and $1.2 billion in carryover funds—during each of calendar 1967 and calendar 1968. Expenditures on the program during these years were not expected to approach the total authorization level—primarily because of domestic budgetary considerations—but were expected to be in excess of previous levels.

PROVISIONS

Policy. Eliminated reference to use of U.S. "surplus" commodities. Emphasized that countries receiving commodities under the Act should show a determination "to improve their own agricultural production."

Title I—*Sales.* Combined the existing Title I (sales for local currencies) and the existing Title IV (sales for dollars under long-term credit agreements) into a new Title I covering all sales.

Authorized a maximum annual expenditure commitment of $1.9 billion, plus any unused previous authorizations, for both types of sales during each of calendar years 1967 and 1968.

Terms of Sales. Required the President, in entering into either kind of sales agreement, to "take into account efforts of friendly countries to help themselves toward a greater degree of self-reliance, including efforts to meet their problems of food production and population growth."

Directed the President, before entering into a sales agreement, to consider the extent to which the recipient country was undertaking self-help measures in nine specific areas of agricultural development, including production of needed food rather than nonfood crops; development of fertilizer, farm equipment, transportation and other necessary industries; training of farmers in agricultural techniques; construction of storage facilities; improvement of marketing systems; creation of a favorable environment for private investment; establishment of government policies to ensure adequate incentives to producers; establishment and expansion of institutions for adaptive agricultural research; and allocation of adequate resources for these purposes. Provided for termination of the agreement if the President found the self-help program inadequate.

Required the President to conduct the Title I program in a manner to ensure a progressive transition from sales for foreign currencies to sales for dollars, to be completed by Dec. 31, 1971.

Continued the payment terms for long-term dollar credit sales at 20 years after a two-year grace period but, in cases where a transition by Dec. 31, 1971, from local currency sales to sales for dollars was not possible, allowed countries to pay for food in local currency which would be convertible to dollars at the end of the same length of time permitted for repayment of development loans under Section 201 of the Foreign Assistance Act (currently 40 years).

Banned food sales under Title I to nations selling any goods to North Vietnam or transporting any goods to or from North Vietnam.

Imposed a similar ban on nations selling and transporting goods to or from Cuba but provided that the President, if he determined such action would be in the national interest, could waive the ban for countries selling and transporting—but not for countries

simply transporting—certain goods (medical supplies, nonstrategic raw materials for agriculture and nonstrategic agricultural or food commodities). Required the President, whenever he waived the ban, to inform the Senate and House of his reasons for doing so and to publish his reasons in the Federal Register.

Broadened the ban on local currency sales to the United Arab Republic (Egypt), unless the President "determines that such sale is in the national interest," to include dollar sales as well.

Directed the President, when practicable, to require that no less than 5 percent of the purchase price of any commidity sold under Title I be paid upon delivery in dollars or hard currencies.

Required the President to obtain, from countries purchasing food under Title I, commitments that this food will be marked or identified at the point of distribution or sale as being provided on a concessional basis through the generosity of the American people and that the recipient countries will publicize widely to their people that the commodities are being provided on a concessional basis through the friendship of the American people as food for peace.

Foreign Currency Requirements. Made foreign currency acquired by the United States under Title I sales subject to the appropriations process (1) when spent by the United States in foreign countries for payment of U.S. obligations or for one of five other types of U.S. uses itemized in the bill (such as developing new markets for U.S. agricultural products and financing international educational and cultural exchanges) and (2) when spent by the United States in foreign countries for economic development grants and for the purchase of goods or services for other friendly countries. In the latter instance, the requirement did not apply in the case of nations for which the United States owned currencies in excess of its needs for a two-year period.

Revised the list of purposes for which foreign currencies acquired under Title I sales could be used by (1) adding grants to foreign countries for programs of maternal welfare, child health and nutrition and—where participation is voluntary—programs sponsored either by the United States or recipient nations related to population growth problems; and (2) adding co-operatives to the types of U.S. and foreign businesses eligible for "Cooley loans." Required that at least 20 percent of the foreign currencies be loaned back to the foreign countries (with certain exceptions) and allocated for programs in the nine specific areas of agricultural development in which the President was directed to weigh progress prior to signing sales agreements.

Required that foreign currencies be convertible to dollars at least to the extent necessary to (1) meet U.S. obligations to the importing country and (2) ensure an adequate supply to cover all normal expenditures of American tourists in the importing country. Earmarked up to 25 percent of funds for the latter purpose.

Required recipient countries to pay food transportation costs in dollars, but permitted the Commodity Credit Corp. (CCC) to finance that part of the cost that was higher than would otherwise be the case because of a requirement that goods be transported in U.S.-flag vessels.

Title II—Donations. Combined the famine relief programs of Title II and the sections on donations through international agencies in Title III into a new Title II.

Authorized an annual expenditure commitment of $600 million, plus any unused previous authorizations, for Title II programs during each of calendar years 1967 and 1968.

Required that, as far as practicable, all commodities furnished under Title II be "clearly identified by appropriate marking on each package or container . . . as being furnished by the people of the United States."

Authorized the CCC to pay, in addition to the cost of acquisition, the costs of packaging, enrichment, preservation and fortification of commodities under Title II.

Stated the sense of Congress that the President should encourage other advance nations to make increased contributions for the purpose of combating world hunger and malnutrition, particularly through the expansion of international food and agricultural assistance programs.

By deleting the stipulation that food for donation programs had to be provided from the CCC's own stocks (obtained through price-support programs), gave the CCC the authority to go into the open market to purchase commodities for these programs.

Title III. Deleted several sections which were incorporated in the new Title II and left unchanged the section of PL 480 which allowed barter of goods for foreign-produced strategic products.

Title IV. Substituted for the existing Title IV (sales for dollars, which became part of Title I above) a new title containing miscellaneous provisions.

Authorized the Secretary of Agriculture to establish and administer a program of "farmer-to-farmer" assistance to enable U.S. farmers to help farmers in developing countries to increase food production and distribution and to improve the effectiveness of their farming operations.

Authorized the Secretary to enter into contracts or other cooperative agreements with, or make grants to, land grant colleges and other institutions of higher education for recruitment and training of Americans to participate in the program. Also authorized him to arrange for the exchange of farm workers with developing countries and for training of foreign farm workers either in the United States or abroad.

Authorized appropriation of up to $33 million in any fiscal year for the program.

Prohibited the sale (under Title I) and the donation (under Title II) of alcoholic beverages and the donation (under Title II) of tobacco and tobacco products.

Permitted supplying of fish concentrate as well as other fish products, under the Act, subject to the availability of appropriations.

Other Provisions. Prohibited the CCC from selling any commodity for which there was a voluntary support program (except wheat) in the open market at less than 115 percent of the current support price whenever carryover of it was less than 25 percent. (The crops affected were corn, feed grains and cotton.)

In the case of wheat, prohibited such sales at less than 115 percent of the current support price whenever carryover was less than 35 percent and at less than 120 percent of the current support price whenever carryover was less than 25 percent.

Food for India

With little debate, Congress early in the year passed legislation (H J Res 997—PL 89-406) endorsing a March 30 Presidential request for U.S. participation in an international effort to prevent famine in India. The over-all cost of U.S. donations, which would be handled under the Food for Peace program, was estimated at $500 million. It covered: 3.5 million tons of food grains, mainly wheat (in addition to 6.5 million tons already scheduled); 200,000 tons of corn; 150 million pounds of vegetable oil; 125 million pounds of powdered milk; 325,000 to 700,000 bales of cotton; and 2 to 4 million pounds of tobacco to free India's own foreign exchange resources for more imports of food and fertilizer.

Food Marketing Report

In a year of increasing agitation over rising food prices, the National Commission on Food Marketing published in June a report on "Food from Farmer to Consumer." The 15-member Commission, established by Congress in 1964, wrote its report after an 18-month study of price and organizational structures in the food industry.

Of the 15 Commission members (five Senators, five Representatives and five Presidential appointees), nine approved the June 27 report; the minority filed lengthy views in opposition.

The purpose of the Commission's study was to appraise the marketing structure of the food industry and to find reasons for the growing disparity between retail food prices and farm earnings. The report concluded that inflation was a primary cause of the gulf created since 1950; it affected costs and prices on the retail level far more than it did farm prices. The latter were kept down by the combination of rapid improvements in farm technology combined with inadequate controls over the farm surpluses that resulted. The Commission said, "The comparative stability of farm food prices during a period when most other prices and costs were rising meant a decline in the farmer's share of the consumer's dollar."

The report laid a portion of the blame for higher food prices on retailers whose advertising and promotion budgets had increased costs, especially in large chains. The report found that the middleman's share of the food industry's profits, although it had increased, was not evidence of excessive profit-taking in that sector of the industry. The increases, the Commission said, in large part reflected the exercise of consumer choice— for example, a housewife's decision to buy prepared French-fried potatoes instead of a sack of raw potatoes.

The large retailers had almost unanimously claimed that sales profit margins were dwindling below the margins of other consumer industries, an argument

Value of U.S. farm products shipped under Public Law 480 compared with total exports of U.S. farm products, July 1, 1954 through December 31, 1968 [1]

(In millions of dollars)

Calendar Year	PUBLIC LAW 480								TOTAL AGRICULTURAL EXPORTS		
	Sales for foreign currency	Long-term dollar and convertible foreign currency credit sales	Government-to-government donations for disaster relief and economic development	Donations through voluntary relief agencies	Barter [2]	Total Public Law 480	Mutual security (AID) [3]	Total government programs	Commercial sales [4]	Total agricultural exports	Public Law 480 as per-cent of total
1954 July-December	—	—	28	20	22	70	211	281	1,304	1,585	4
1955	263	—	56	186	262	767	351	1,118	2,081	3,199	24
1956	638	—	65	187	372	1,262	449	1,711	2,459	4,170	30
1957	760	—	39	175	244	1,218	318	1,536	2,970	4,506	27
1958	752	—	43	159	65	1,019	214	1,233	2,622	3,855	26
1959	731	—	32	111	175	1,049	158	1,207	2,748	3,955	27
1960	1,014	—	49	124	117	1,304	157	1,461	3,371	4,832	27
1961	878	1	93	151	181	1,304	179	1,483	3,541	5,024	26
1962	1,007	42	81	178	137	1,445	35	1,480	3,554	5,034	29
1963	1,162	52	99	160	38	1,511	11	1,522	4,062	5,584	27
1964	1,232	97	62	186	35	1,612	23	1,635	4,713	6,348	25
1965	899	152	73	180	5	1,309	26	1,335	4,894	6,229	21
1966	815	239	79	132	41	1,306	47	1,353	5,528	6,881	19
1967	736	201	108	179	13	1,237	33	1,270	5,113	6,383	19
1968	539	385	101	150	3	1,178	11	1,189	5,039	6,228	19
July 1, 1954 through December 31, 1968	11,426	1,169	1,008	2,278	1,710	17,591	2,223	19,814	53,999	73,813	24

1. Export market value.
2. Annual exports have been adjusted for 1963 and subsequent years by deducting exports under barter contracts which improve the balance of payments and rely primarily on authority other than Public Law 480. These exports are included in the column headed "Commercial Sales."
3. Sales for foreign currency, economic aid, and expenditures under development loans.
4. Commercial sales for dollars include, in addition to unassisted commercial transactions, shipments of some commodities with governmental assistance in the form of short- and medium-term credit, export payments, sales of Government-owned commodities at less than domestic market prices, and, for 1963 and subsequent years, exports under barter contracts which benefit the balance of payments and rely primarily on authority other than Public Law 480.
5. Partly estimated.

that was corroborated by the Commission. The report also noted, however, that the retailers' share of the consumer dollar rose from a 1954 range of 15 to 17 percent to a range of 19 to 22 percent in 1964. Another facet of the food industry's profit picture was revealed in a study by the First National City Bank of New York. After a review of 59 of the largest retail chains in 1965, the Bank found that while the claims showed an average net profit of 1.3 percent on sales, they showed a 12.5 percent return on their investment. The rate of investment profit compared favorably with returns for most other consumer industries. Moreover, in the Commission's words, "the large chains almost never lose money."

The report concluded that the food industry was generally efficient and progressive but noted that closer surveillance by the Federal Government would be needed to keep prices down.

Legislative Recommendations. The Commission report recommended legislation requiring Government notification prior to the merger of companies in the food industry and giving regulatory agencies power to issue temporary cease and desist orders to halt mergers; establishment of regulatory agency guidelines to discourage many such mergers; a study of possible revision of the Robinson-Patman Act (prohibiting discrimination in prices offered purchasers of commodities): legislation establishing consumer grades for various food products; legislation creating a centralized consumer agency in the Executive Branch; legislation authorizing federal marketing agreements and orders for all agricultural commodities; legislation guaranteeing farmers' rights to form bargaining associations and cooperatives; and a number of other changes in existing procedures governing food marketing.

Minority Views. In a joint statement, Commission members William M. Batten, chairman of the board, J. C. Penney Co., Sen. Roman L. Hruska (R Neb.) and Sen. Thruston B. Morton (R Ky.) charged that the conclusions of the report were drafted first and that the "report was contrived to give the 'conclusions' credibility." They added that the majority "ignored or misread the evidence" in some cases.

In another statement of minority views, Albert K. Mitchell, a New Mexico rancher, Rep. Catherine May (R Wash.) and Rep. Graham Purcell (D Texas) said that the Commission, by making conclusions which proposed new legislation, "deliberately violated and exceeded our statutory authorization." They added that the report, "rather than analyzing and responding to particular problems developed in our studies—advocates broad legislative proposals, some discarded by the Congress years ago." The minority referred specifically to grade labeling for products, rejected as early as the New Deal and again in 1943, and to the perennial issue of compulsory pre-merger notification.

The Commission report included a study, made in February 1966 by the Bureau of Labor Statistics in six U.S. cities, which showed that the buying habits of low-income persons led them to pay more for food than did shoppers in high-income neighborhoods. For example, the Bureau said, patrons of stores in low-income areas generally purchased smaller amounts of certain grocery items and, as a result, paid higher unit costs.

RELATED DEVELOPMENTS

Food Costs. Food prices rose steadily during 1966 to highs unprecedented in the postwar period, according to Department of Commerce figures. The high point for the year was reached in August, when housewives paid $11.58 for groceries that cost $10 in the 1957-59 base period used by the Bureau of Labor Statistics. The figure was almost 50 cents higher than the peak reached in July 1965, when food cost $11.09.

The House Agriculture Subcommittee on Wheat held hearings Aug. 8-11 on bread costs, which had doubled since 1949. The Subcommittee Aug. 11 absolved all levels of the bread industry of taking "an unconscionable profit" from the price rise.

Agriculture Secretary Orville L. Freeman Aug. 14 maintained that the farmer was not responsible for rising food prices. He said that a study he was preparing for the Senate Agriculture and Forestry Committee would show profiteering by middlemen in the food industry. "Somewhere along the line from farmer to consumer," he said, "someone is getting more than a reasonable fair share for services rendered."

The Agriculture Department announced in November that the farmer's share of the consumer's food dollar climbed from 39 cents in 1965 to 40 or 41 cents in 1966. The Department said, however, that the cost of bringing food from the farm to supermarket shelves rose at a rate of 3 to 4 percent during 1966. The increase, coupled with an expected decline in average farm prices, the Department predicted, would lower farm earnings during 1967.

Housewives Boycott. In Denver, Colo., there was active protest against rising prices in mid-October when housewives picketed the city's supermarket chains. The movement spread across the country and into Canada as woman shoppers organized in local groups to encourage selective buying of low-priced meats and groceries. Supermarket bingo games and trading stamps, which the housewives claimed raised the price of food, became a major focus of the protests.

The retailers argued, in return, that they were operating on the narrowest possible margin of profit and reminded the housewives that the higher prices they were charged paid for the greater quality, variety and convenience of the supermarkets' food supply. Both the National Association of Food Chains and the Grocery Manufacturers of America, in formal statements, blamed higher prices on general inflation in the American economy. George W. Koch, president of the grocery manufacturers group, absolved the food industry and placed the principal guilt for higher prices on the fact that the nation was at war and that its economy was inflated.

Meat Inspection Fees

President Johnson's proposal to shift the cost of meat and poultry inspection from the Federal Government to processors through the institution of inspection fees got nowhere in 1966.

Opposition to the proposed fees came from processors who would have to pay them and from some producer groups, such as the American Farm Bureau Federation, who felt the cost of the fees eventually would be passed on to either the producer or the consumer. One processor organization, the American Meat Institute, hired an experienced lobbyist, Michael B. Deane, to oppose the measure in 1966. Deane was a Commerce Department official from 1936-53.

REA Financing

A highly controversial Administration proposal to create a new source of financing for rural electric co-operatives provoked the only major public vs. private power struggle in the second session of the 89th Congress. After lengthy consideration, the House Agriculture Committee declined to report a bill (HR 14837) to set up a bank, partially capitalized by the Government, to make intermediate- and higher-interest loans to the co-ops. The loans were to finance expansion of power generating, transmission and distribution facilities.

Cotton Promotion

Congress enacted a bill (HR 12322—PL 89-502) providing for a cotton research and promotion program financed by a $1-a-bale assessment on cotton growers. The program was to go into effect only if approved in a nationwide referendum of the growers. (Growers approved it in December 1966.)

The bill faced stiff opposition in the House from Members representing small Southern growers. They objected to a provision in the House bill which specified that approval in the referendum could be determined in two ways: (1) if two-thirds of the cotton farmers voting in the referendum approved the research-promotion program or (2) if farmers who accounted for two-thirds of the cotton produced by those voting approved the program. Southerners argued that the latter method of ratification would permit a minority of the total growers to commit all producers.

The measure was backed primarily by large growers from the West who said the program was necessary because of competition from synthetic fibers. The large growers previously had spearheaded a voluntary promotion effort which was not highly successful.

The Senate Agriculture and Forestry Committee subsequently altered the bill to provide that the latter method of ratification would be valid only if at least a majority of the growers—though less than two-thirds—had voted for ratification. The House accepted the Senate version.

Funds Bill

The regular Agriculture Department appropriations bill (HR 14596—PL 89-556), signed into law Sept. 7, provided $7 billion in appropriations.

The debate during the year was marked by squabbles over budget-tightening cuts made by the Administration in a number of programs—school milk and lunches (proposed cut $101 million); agricultural conservation; rural electric loans; agricultural research, and insect and pest control.

Congress eventually restored most of these cuts, but the final bill ended up $28 million under Mr. Johnson's over-all requests because Congress cut $150 million from the $200 million request for the land retirement program authorized in the 1965 omnibus farm bill. With surpluses down and agricultural controls being loosened to provide supplies to combat hunger overseas (see above, Food for Peace), retirement of cropland to reduce surpluses was considered less urgent.

Mr. Johnson said he would not veto the bill because of fund restorations which he opposed, but complained that it added $312.5 million more to present or future spending than he wished. (Advance authorizations for the agricultural conservation programs and rural electric cooperatives would show up in later years when commitments contracted in 1967 would have to be met.) He also objected to a provision, added in the House, flatly banning all PL 480 aid to countries furnishing goods to North Vietnam.

Rep. Jamie Whitten (D Miss.), chairman of the House Agriculture Appropriations Subcommittee, reduced to $637,000 the Administration request for $3,468,000 for a big expansion of the Rural Community Development Service created by executive action in the Agriculture Department in 1965. Whitten said he feared it would take over functions dealing with rural poverty which rightly should be handled by the Farmers Home Administration. The final bill provided only $637,000. Shortly afterward, Secretary Freeman took away from the RCDS its "outreach program" of added aid to the rural poor and gave it to the Farmers Home Administration.

In the Senate, an amendment by Daniel Brewster (D Md.) to limit agricultural aid to any one farm to $50,000 a year was rejected by a 28-53 roll call.

PROVISIONS—As signed by the President, HR 14596 appropriated the following (figures in parentheses are subtotals):

General Activities

Agricultural Research Service	$ 208,166,400
Cooperative State Research Service	58,740,000
Extension Service	92,824,000
Farmer Cooperative Service	1,175,000
Soil Conservation Service	(234,105,000)
Conservation operations	109,235,000
Watershed planning	6,142,000
Watershed protection	70,000,000
Flood prevention	25,654,000
Great Plains conservation program	18,500,000
Resource conservation and development	4,574,000
Economic Research Service	12,132,000
Statistical Reporting Service	13,511,750
Consumer and Marketing Service	(412,486,000)
Consumer programs	83,881,000
Payments to states	1,750,000
Special milk program	51,000,000
School lunch program	165,855,000
Food stamp program	110,000,000
Foreign Agricultural Service	21,218,500
Commodity Exchange Authority	1,398,000
Stabilization and Conservation Service	(634,058,000)
Expenses, ASCS	128,558,000
Sugar Act program	80,000,000
Agricultural conservation program	220,000,000

Appalachian conservation program	3,000,000
Cropland adjustment program	50,000,000
Cropland conversion program	7,500,000
Conservation reserve program	140,000,000
Emergency conservation	5,000,000
Rural Community Development Service	637,000
Office of Inspector General	11,254,000
Packers and Stockyards Act	2,502,000
Office of General Counsel	4,325,000
Office of Information	1,851,000
National Agricultural Library	2,412,500
Office of Management Services	2,600,000
General administration	3,959,000

Subtotal, general activities $1,719,355,150

Credit Agencies

(for loan authorizations, see below)

Rural Electrification Administration	$ 12,202,000
Farmers Home Administration	(81,257,000)
Rural water and waste disposal	26,000,000
Rural housing for farm labor	3,000,000
Rural renewal	1,200,000
Salaries and expenses	51,057,000

Subtotal, credit agencies $ 93,459,000

Corporations

Federal Crop Insurance Corporation	$ 8,446,000
Commodity Credit Corporation	3,555,855,000
PL 480	1,617,000,000

Subtotal, corporations $5,181,301,000

Related Agencies

National Advisory Commission on Food and Fiber	$ 475,000
	$6,994,590,150

The bill also:

Authorized the following transfers of Section 32 funds to various agencies to be spent for their programs in addition to amounts provided through direct appropriations: Agriculture Research Service, for research, $25 million; special milk program, $53 million; school lunch program, $45 million; Foreign Agricultural Service, salaries and expenses, $3,117.000.

Reappropriated $30 million in unused fiscal 1966 funds for the food stamp program to be used for the program in fiscal 1967, in addition to the new appropriations provided.

Authorized the transfer of $75,803,600 from the Commodity Credit Corp. for expenses incurred by the Agricultural Stabilization and Conservation Service in addition to funds included in direct appropriations for the same purpose.

Continued a provision from previous years barring use of federal funds to influence legislation or the vote on a referendum, or to pay salaries of members of county and local farmer committees for other than prescribed functions.

Authorized $220 million for the Agricultural Conservation Program in calendar 1967.

Authorized $492 million for Rural Electrification Administration loans: $375 million for electrification loans (including a $30-million reserve authorization) and $117 million for telephone loans (including a $15-million reserve authorization).

Authorized $440 million for the Farmers Home Administration direct loan account: $90 million for real estate loans and $350 million for operating loans (including $25 million reserve authority).

Authorized the use of $15 million from funds deposited in the rural housing direct loan account for rural housing loans.

Authorized the Government to enter into cropland adjustment agreements in fiscal 1967 that would require payments during calendar 1967 of no more than $80 million.

Prohibited the use of funds in the bill to administer PL 480 (Food for Peace) local currency or dollar sales to any nation transporting or selling goods to North Vietnam while that country is governed by a Communist regime.

Limited future budget estimates for transfers of Section 32 funds for agricultural research to $15 million.1

1967

There was little agricultural legislation enacted in 1967. The President made few major requests, and the most important farm bill enacted was actually a consumer measure—requiring states either to set up adequate inspection systems for meat that did not move across state lines or have the Federal Government take over the inspection. Another emergency food program for India was also enacted. (For meat inspection bill, see chapter on Consumer Legislation. For India food measure, see chapter on Foreign Policy.)

Dairy Indemnities

Congress cleared a bill (S 1657) extending through fiscal 1968 the authority of the Secretary of Agriculture to make indemnity payments to dairy farmers ordered to remove their milk from commercial markets because it contained pesticides registered and approved for use by the Federal Government. The President signed the bill Sept. 28 (PL 90-95).

The original dairy indemnity authority, contained in the Economic Opportunity Act of 1964 (PL 88-452) and extended by Congress three times, expired June 30, 1967.

Food and Fiber

The National Advisory Commission on Food and Fiber submitted a report to President Johnson July 14 urging that the Government revise its agricultural policies to take greater advantage of the market's own ability "to allocate resources and distribute incomes."

The Commission, appointed by the President in 1965 to conduct a long-range appraisal of U.S. farm policy, split sharply on the question of how best to achieve such a "market-oriented agriculture."

A 16-member majority of the Commission contended that federal commodity programs should be continued, while a 13-member minority argued that the programs "interfere too greatly with the structural adjustment needed in agriculture." The majority consisted mostly of producers and farm economists, while food and fiber business executives formed the minority.

The panel was in general agreement in recommending the following modifications of present policy: establishment of price supports at levels moderately below the moving average of world prices; greater reliance on direct payments to farmers instead of high price supports, export subsidies and import quotas; and development of a new standard for comparing farm and nonfarm incomes to replace the parity price index.

The panel also urged that acreage allotments and marketing quotas be made negotiable or transferable to meet market demands, that public subsidies for capacity-increasing farm practices be discontinued and that a national security food reserve be established.

Regardless of domestic farm policy, the report said, it was expected that by 1980 the United States would need one-third fewer farm workers. The Commission outlined federal programs to aid displaced farm workers and their families.

One of the most significant factors affecting U.S. domestic farm policy, the Commission said, was the growing commercial export demand. The report recommended that the United States: seek further liberalization of world trade, particularly in farm products; lead in eliminating export subsidies and import quotas, substituting other methods for protecting farmers' incomes; and put trade with the U.S.S.R. and Eastern Europe in nonstrategic foods under the same set of rules as applied to the rest of the world.

Rural Electric Disputes

Electric Bank. For the second consecutive year, Congress failed to approve a highly controversial Administration proposal to provide additional sources of financing for rural electric and telephone cooperatives.

The Administration's bill (HR 1400) called for setting up two banks, capitalized in part by the Government, to make low-cost loans to the co-ops. In the case of the rural electric co-ops, the loans would finance expansion of power generating and transmission and distribution facilities.

HR 1400 was introduced by Rep. W. R. Poage (D Texas), chairman of the House Agriculture Committee, who called it the most important measure before his Committee in 1967. As in 1966, the bill was strongly opposed by private power interests, which said that rural co-ops were encroaching on suburban markets.

After lengthy consideration, Poage's Committee in June reported a clean bill (HR 10190)—a feat it had not accomplished in 1966. But concessions made by the Committee to private power demands aroused the opposition of the National Rural Electric Cooperative

Assn. (NRECA). The NRECA, which was the prime force behind the bill, said it would prefer no legislation to the bill reported by the Committee. Private power spokesmen, also opposed the clean bill.

HR 10190 was referred to the House Rules Committee. But that panel refused to give the bill a rule permitting floor action, and that killed the bill for 1967.

The Rules Committee action prompted Poage to introduce the relatively noncontroversial provisions of HR 10190 that related to financing of telephone co-ops in a separate bill (HR 12066). The Agriculture Committee reported out that bill in October.

Poage Oct. 9 asked the Rules Committee to give HR 12066 a rule for floor action, but the Committee did not act on the request before Congress adjourned Dec. 15.

Co-op Regulation. The Federal Power Commission (FPC) Jan. 5 held that it had no authority to regulate rural electric cooperatives. The decision resolved a lengthy case involving the Dairyland Power Cooperative, LaCrosse, Wis., a second large generating and transmission (G&T) cooperative and a large distribution co-op. The case was initiated July 22, 1963, by the FPC to test its jurisdiction. Of primary importance was the question of the FPC's authority to regulate rates charged by G&T co-ops for wholesale electricity. FPC regulation of co-ops was strongly opposed by the politically powerful National Rural Electric Cooperative Assn. (*Congress and the Nation,* Vol. I, p. 889, 891.)

Feed Grains Problems

Secretary of Agriculture Orville L. Freeman Oct. 26 announced the restoration in 1968 of voluntary acreage reductions for feed grains in an effort to reduce "this year's 2- to 3-percent overproduction to a 2- to 3-percent underproduction."

Under the 1968 program, farmers were to be required, as in 1967, to divert 20 percent of feed grain acreage without payment to be eligible for the price support program, which in 1968 was to be maintained at 1967 loan levels. In addition, farmers were to be permitted to divert another 30 percent of their acreage on a voluntary basis, as in 1966. The Department of Agriculture estimated that farmers would make use of the increased diversion option to retire 30 million acres, 10 million more than in 1967.

Freeman expressed the hope that the increased diversion to be allowed in 1968 would result in a considerable boost in feed grain prices. Without it, he said, 1968 feed grain production would be "well in excess of requirements," and returns to producers would be about 30 percent less than in 1967. The 1967-68 marketing year began Oct. 1 with a 37-million ton "carry-over" of U.S. feed grain stocks, according to Department estimates.

GRAIN RESERVES BILL

The House Agriculture Subcommittee on Livestock and Feed Grains voted down, Nov. 1, a controversial bill (HR 12067) designed by the Administration to boost sagging grain prices.

The measure would have authorized Government purchases of more than $1 billion in wheat, feed grains,

Committee Rebukes Rep. Resnick . . .

The functions and activities of the American Farm Bureau Federation (AFBF) in 1967 were the subject of a one-man investigation by Rep. Joseph Y. Resnick (D N.Y.), chairman of the House Agriculture Committee's Rural Development Subcommittee. Other members of the Subcommittee disassociated themselves from the investigation, as did the full Committee.

The controversy began June 21 when John C. Lynn, the Farm Bureau's legislative director, appeared before the Subcommittee, which was conducting hearings on the effects of federal programs on rural America. The Farm Bureau July 7 in a letter to Committee Chairman W. R. Poage (D Texas) said that Lynn had hardly begun reading his statement at the hearing when Resnick "challenged the propriety" of the statement and charged that "the Farm Bureau is not a farm organization but a large group of insurance companies without primary interest in the welfare of the agricultural community."

Lynn did not complete his statement and on June 28 Roger Fleming, secretary-treasurer of the Farm Bureau, appeared before the Subcommittee.

Resnick June 27 and 28 on the House floor charged that the Farm Bureau had "not been representing the American farmer" but had "been using him to build one of the largest insurance and financial empires in the United States, an empire . . . bringing great profit to a select handful of men."

COMMITTEE REACTION

The House Agriculture Committee July 12 by a 27-1 vote, rebuked Resnick by disassociating itself from charges he had made against the AFBF. The action by the full Committee stemmed from a resolution offered by the other five Subcommittee members, stating that the Committee "does in no manner endorse, condone or support the personal attack launched" by Resnick against the Farm Bureau.

In their statement dated July 12, the Subcommittee members disassociated themselves "from charges" against the Farm Bureau or "any other general farm organization which carries on service programs for its membership." They recommended that the Committee "likewise disassociate itself from these strictly personal activities" of Resnick.

The Committee meeting, a rare closed session, lasted more than 90 minutes. But Resnick left after it had been under way for only 10 minutes. He later charged that the Committee action was "a conspiracy masterminded by the Farm Bureau," that the five members of his Subcommittee "reacted like puppets on a string" in response to a Farm Bureau request, and that Committee members had opened themselves to conflict-of-interest charges because "the ma-

jority . . . are also Farm Bureau members." He threatened to seek an investigation by the recently organized House Committee on Standards of Official Conduct to determine whether the Agriculture Committee was to be "controlled by powerful outside interests."

Eligio de la Garza (D Texas), a member of the full Committee but not of Resnick's Subcommittee, was the only one to vote against the action of the Committee.

In a speech on the House floor, James G. O'Hara (D Mich.) described the Committee's action as "unprecedented" and said it set "a dangerous precedent when a subcommittee chairman cannot question the activities of one of the largest lobbies that operates in Congress."

The Farm Bureau Federation is the country's largest and most conservative general farm organization. Of 296 organizations which filed lobby spending reports for 1966, the Farm Bureau ranked fifth in the amount of money spent. It listed $133,944.

RESNICK CHARGES

On July 18, Resnick recalled that "as a result of facts uncovered in the intervening week," he questioned Fleming's right to appear as a representative of the interests of farmers. Resnick said the Farm Bureau "had a substantial nonfarm membership" and "conducted widespread financial and commercial activities," unrelated to farmers.

"My investigation has revealed the shocking fact that (the Farm Bureau) is a gigantic interlocking, nationwide combine of insurance companies with total assets of over $1 billion. I have evidence that the granting of membership in the Farm Bureau is purely and simply a device for selling insurance and other services," Resnick charged.

Resnick contended that perhaps half the Farm Bureau's membership had no agricultural interest whatsoever, that the Farm Bureau had misrepresented itself to obtain a tax exemption, that it had used the American farmer to build one of the largest insurance and financial empires in the nation, that the directors and officers of the Farm Bureau were also directors and officers of insurance companies directly controlled and owned by various state farm bureaus, and that the Farm Bureau might have been in violation of antitrust laws. (Resnick pointed out earlier that Charles B. Shuman, president of the Farm Bureau, was also president of the American Agricultural Mutual Insurance Co. and Farm Bureau Mutual Funds Inc.)

Resnick further charged that the Farm Bureau took advantage of its tax-exempt status to expand its business activities into insurance, real estate, shopping centers, fertilizer, mutual funds, gasoline stations, oil wells, grain storage, petro-

... for Attack on Farm Bureau Federation

leum refineries and a variety of others. Resnick said the Farm Bureau had misrepresented itself, therefore, in statements to Congressional committees.

He also charged that, being tax exempt, the Farm Bureau improperly competed in commercial activities with private tax-paying business concerns.

The Farm Bureau "torpedoed" the American farmer by posing as a representative of his interests while actually engaging in commercial activities, including some that sell to and buy from the farmer, which put the Bureau in a position antagonistic to farmers' interests, Resnick said.

He also said the Farm Bureau's commercial activities generated funds which found their way illegally into political and lobbying activities.

FARM BUREAU POSITION

Fleming, in the July 7 letter to Poage, said Resnick used his position to engage in a "personal vendetta." "We view his assault as an attack on all voluntary, nongovernment organizations. If a farm organization's purpose is not to serve its members' needs, then what is it? This attack on Farm Bureau members for having developed their own insurance companies to serve their own needs would appear to be an attack on the self-help efforts of any and all organizations," Fleming wrote. He also countered that the Farm Bureau insurance companies did in fact act independently of each other.

The Farm Bureau, he said, had nothing to hide. It would cooperate in any responsibly conducted Congressional inquiry into its operations and those of other farm organizations, Fleming declared. He added, "We do not believe Chairman Resnick's Subcommittee is the proper setting for such an investigation," and termed Resnick's charges "reckless."

In the interest of justice and fair play, Fleming wrote, the Farm Bureau urged the Committee to consider Resnick's charges and if the Committee believed there was a basis for the charges, to conduct a full-scale, in-depth investigation of all farm organizations. Otherwise, Fleming said, the Committee should disassociate itself from Resnick's attacks.

Fleming noted, "It has been suggested that the hearings be terminated forthwith and that the report . . . not be published. From our point of view, this would be a most unsatisfactory approach to resolving the matter. . . ." Resnick July 15 said the Farm Bureau was behind a move to block publication of the hearings. He insisted July 18 that only the Farm Bureau "is doing the suggesting since this idea never existed until it came up in their letter."

Fleming told CQ that Shuman headed six other organizations, in addition to those men-

tioned by Resnick: American Agricultural Insurance Agency Inc., American Agricultural Marketing Corp., American Farm Bureau Trade Corp., American Farm Bureau Service Co., American Farm Bureau Research Foundation, and American Farmer to Farmer Corp. Fleming said the only organization listed by either Resnick or himself from which Shuman drew compensation was the American Farm Bureau Federation.

FURTHER INVESTIGATION URGED

Resnick Sept. 8 urged the full Agriculture Committee to undertake a full-scale inquiry into the functions and activities of all farm organizations "at the earliest possible time."

The request, made in a letter to Committee Chairman Poage, was prompted by testimony at ad hoc hearings, Resnick said, which along with over 2,000 letters "established . . . that the American Farm Bureau Federation exercises a powerful and dangerous control over many aspects of life in much of rural America and pursues policies which seriously violate the interests of a great majority of our farmers."

The hearings, held in August in Chicago, Omaha and Washington, D.C., were conducted by Resnick alone and with personal funds after the full Committee had voted to disassociate itself from charges he had made against the Farm Bureau in the earlier hearings before his Subcommittee.

In a speech Aug. 17 on the House floor, Resnick said each Member had the right to hold ad hoc hearings on his own on any organization whose activities were questionable. "When the organization is the fifth largest lobby in Washington and enjoys the privilege of tax exemption, I feel such an investigation is my duty," he added. The Farm Bureau boycotted the hearings, saying it would cooperate only with an official inquiry by the full Committee.

In addition, Resnick pointed to "possible fraud" by Bureau cooperatives which he said issued patronage dividends in the form of certificates which had no value. (Resnick Aug. 31 asked the Internal Revenue Service to investigate charges that farmers were receiving "worthless stock" instead of profits from an Ohio cooperative.)

Fleming Statement. AFBF Secretary-Treasurer Fleming Dec. 12 at a Farm Bureau meeting in Chicago said Resnick's announcement of his intention to seek the Democratic nomination for the U.S. Senate seat held by Jacob K. Javits (R N.Y.) made it "easier to put together the pieces of the 'Resnick affair' puzzle." Fleming described the situation as a "headline-hunting exercise by this multi-millionaire industrial tycoon from the Catskills of New York state."

Advisory Commission Criticizes Aid Programs for Rural Poor

The National Advisory Commission on Rural Poverty, appointed by President Johnson Sept. 28, 1966, to undertake a year-long study of rural poverty, released the results of its study Dec. 9, 1967.

Its report was highly critical of current federal programs to aid the rural poor. It recommended a broad new government attack on the problems of 14 million poor rural Americans, including massive birth control programs, federally assured income and revisions in the federal food stamp program.

The 160-page report was called "The People Left Behind." Chairman of the 25-member commission was Kentucky Gov. Edward T. Breathitt (D).

The report, submitted to President Johnson in September, said the urban riots of 1967 had their roots in considerable part in rural poverty, because a high proportion of the people crowded into city slums came there from rural slums. Unemployment, which was as high as 37 percent among farmworkers, compared to a national average of about 4 percent and a rate of about 18 percent in rural areas generally, was seen as a major problem, along with hunger, disease and poor schools.

The report said that instead of raising the incomes of rural people, some rural programs helped create wealthy landowners. It noted that changes in technology increased farm output by 45 percent between 1950 and 1965, while reducing farm employment by the same amount, causing a great exodus to the cities. The same percentage changes were expected in the next 15 years, the report added.

The Commission was unanimous in the conviction that effective programs for solving the problems of rural poverty would contribute to the solution of urban poverty.

"The Commission is convinced that the abolition of rural poverty in the United States, perhaps for the first time, in any nation, is completely feasible," the report said. "The nation has the economic resources and the technical means for doing this. What it has lacked thus far, has been the will."

RECOMMENDATIONS

In its call for action by all levels of government — local, state and federal — as well as by private individuals and groups, the Commission recommended:

(1) that the Federal Government put into effect immediately a policy designed to give rural Americans equal access to jobs, medical care, housing, education, welfare and other public services enjoyed by other citizens.

(2) that the national policy of full employment, adopted in 1946, be made effective for rural residents by assuring that to the extent that private enterprise did not provide employment for all those willing and able to work, government would do so;

(3) that changes be made in public assistance programs, including expansion of the food stamp program to permit the poorest to receive stamps without cost;

(4) that manpower programs and policies be overhauled to deal effectively with rural unemployment and under-employment;

(5) that extensive changes be made in the rural education system to bring rural schools up to par with urban schools;

(6) that health manpower be expanded and community health centers be established to focus on the health needs of rural people;

(7) that family planning programs be developed and expanded for the rural poor;

(8) that immediate action be taken to provide housing in rural areas by public agencies; that a rent-supplement program be established for the rural poor; that a single unified housing agency be made responsible for housing programs in rural areas and that credit terms be made more responsive to need; also, that a substantial increase be made in appropriations for Indian housing;

(9) that multicounty districts, cutting across urban-rural boundaries, be created to plan and coordinate programs for economic development;

(10) that increased attention be given to involving the poor in the affairs of the community, on both local and areawide levels;

(11) that the Federal Government re-examine its commercial farm programs to make sure that adjustments in the supply of farm products were not made at the expense of the rural poor;

(12) that changes be made in program development and administration to facilitate and encourage the effective involvement of local, state and federal governments.

---

soybeans and rice for placement in a permanent strategic grain reserve. Purchases were to be made by the Commodity Credit Corp. in bumper crop years such as 1967 to shore up prices. Reserves thus acquired could be sold in years of low production. (A related measure was defeated by the full Committee in 1966.)

Major objections to the bill were its cost and the fear, expressed by grower groups and grain traders, that the Government in the future might dump acquired reserves on the market to drive prices down.

Rural Development

Both Secretary of Agriculture Freeman and the Republican Coordinating Committee (the latter in a July report entitled "Revitalizing Our Rural Areas") expressed grave concern in 1967 that bad economic conditions on American farms were exacerbating urban problems by causing a half million or more farm people a year to migrate to the cities.

Several Senate bills to help create more job, housing, credit and educational opportunities in rural areas failed to pass the House in 1967 (though some were eventually enacted in 1968). The bills introduced in 1967 included:

• S 645, an Administration bill passed May 9 by the Senate, to help pay for the drafting of economic development plans in rural areas.

• S 1504, passed by the Senate Aug. 28, to provide a variety of housing and other credits for rural areas.

• SJ Res 64, passed by the Senate Oct. 27, to set up a Commission on Balanced Economic Development to study rural and urban problems.

Farm Funds

A bill (HR 10509 - PL 90-113) granting $4,952,-945,700 in direct appropriations in fiscal 1968 for the Department of Agriculture and related agencies was cleared by Congress Oct. 10.

The amount of appropriations was $2,069,625,750 below appropriations made for fiscal 1967. The drop, however, did not result from fewer or smaller farm programs; it was caused almost entirely by omission of sums to reimburse the Commodity Credit Corp. (CCC) for losses which the agency incurred in previous fiscal years for price supports, commodity storage and export and similar programs. Congress eventually must make up losses by the CCC if the agency's programs are to continue. The Administration, in its request for fiscal 1968, asked only for funds sufficient to meet anticipated CCC activities the following year; the amount requested and provided in HR 10509 ($1.4 billion) was almost $1.6 billion under the actual losses for fiscal 1966 and almost $2.2 billion less than Congress provided in the fiscal 1967 agriculture appropriations bill to reimburse CCC losses for fiscal 1965 and previous years.

Outside of the decrease in CCC funds from fiscal 1967 to 1968, the bill made few other reductions in programs; amounts for most activities were higher than in fiscal 1967.

Attempts in both Senate and House to limit Government payments to any one producer failed. The House on June 6 overwhelmingly rejected an amendment by Paul Findley (R Ill.) to limit annual payments to a single recipient to $25,000 under certain specified programs.

House Agriculture Committee Chairman W. R. Poage (D Texas) said "when those large farmers cease to be a part of the program and produce without any limitation . . . the amount of production is going to destroy the income of these small farmers."

The Senate on July 13 rejected an amendment by John J. Williams (R Del.) limiting to $10,000 the amount that any individual farmer could collect in direct cash subsidies. (The amendment did not apply to price support loans.)

Williams was supported by Daniel B. Brewster (D Md.) who said he could "think of no reason why the Federal Government should give five producers over $1 million apiece annually and 11 producers over $500,000 apiece, when the average farmer gets only $831 a year. . . ."

John Sherman Cooper (R Ky.) said the amendment would expand production, drive down farm prices and hurt the farm economy and the nation's economy. In opposing the amendment, he said, he was speaking for the small farmer "because the production control and price-support programs, including both small and large farms, assures them fair prices."

The final bill did not grant an Administration request for $52.2 million in authority to sign cropland retirement contracts in fiscal 1968, as authorized by the 1965 omnibus farm bill. The House felt the retirement of acreage was not needed and its view prevailed.

PROVISIONS—As signed into law (PL 90-113) Oct. 24, HR 10509 appropriated the following (figures in parentheses are subtotals):

General Activities

Agricultural Research Service	$ 231,077,500
Cooperative State Research Service	63,113,000
Extension Service	96,602,000
Farmer Cooperative Service	1,304,000
Soil Conservation Service	(238,121,000)
Conservation operations	113,500,000
Watershed planning	6,000,000
Watershed protection	70,403,000
Flood prevention	25,753,000
Great Plains conservation program	16,336,000
Resource conservation and development	6,129,000
Economic Research Service	12,421,000
Statistical Reporting Service	13,830,500
Consumer and Marketing Service	(435,685,000)
Consumer programs	89,310,000
Payments to states	1,750,000
School lunch program	182,825,000
Food stamp program	161,800,000
Foreign Agricultural Service	22,141,500
Commodity Exchange Authority	1,491,000
Stabilization and Conservation Service	(650,435,400)
Expenses, ASCS	137,935,400
Sugar Act program	80,000,000
Agricultural conservation program	220,000,000
Cropland adjustment program	84,500,000
Conservation reserve program	123,000,000
Emergency conservation measures	5,000,000
Rural Community Development Service	450,000
Office of Inspector General	11,993,000
Packers and Stockyards Act	2,569,300
Office of General Counsel	4,325,000
Office of Information	1,928,000
National Agricultural Library	2,608,500
Office of Management Services	2,667,000
General administration	4,487,000
Subtotal, general activities	$1,797,249,700

Credit Agencies

(for loan authorizations, see below)

Rural Electrification Administration	$ 12,457,000
Farmers Home Administration	(104,356,000)
Payment of sales insufficiencies, participation certificates	13,268,000
Rural water and waste disposal grants	30,000,000
Rural renewal	1,600,000
Rural housing for domestic farm labor	3,500,000

Salaries and expenses	55,988,000
Subtotal, credit agencies	$ 116,813,000

Corporations

Federal Crop Insurance Corporation	$ 10,208,000
Commodity Credit Corporation	1,400,000,000
PL 480	1,605,500,000
Bartered materials for stockpile	23,000,000
Subtotal, corporations	$3,038,708,000

Related Agencies

National Advisory Commission on Food and Fiber	$ 175,000
GRAND TOTAL	$4,952,945,700

The bill also:

Authorized the following transfers of Section 32 funds to various agencies to be spent for their programs in addition to amounts provided through direct appropriations: Agricultural Research Service, for research, $15 million; special milk program, $104 million; school lunch program, $45 million; Foreign Agricultural Service, for salaries and expenses, $3,117,000.

Reappropriated $2 million in unused fiscal 1967 funds for research salaries and expenses of the Agricultural Research Service in fiscal 1968, in addition to the new appropriations.

Authorized the transfer of $275,000 from the Commodity Credit Corp. appropriation to the Agricultural Research Service for cotton research.

Limited future budget estimates for transfers of Section 32 funds for agricultural research to $15 million.

Authorized use by the Soil Conservation Service of $7.5 million from the direct loan account of the Farmers Home Administration: $5 million for watershed protection, $1 million for flood protection and $1.5 million for resource conservation and development.

Reappropriated $23.2 million in unused fiscal 1967 funds for the food stamp program to be used for the program in fiscal 1968, in addition to the new appropriations.

Authorized the transfer of $58,608,600 from the Commodity Credit Corp. for expenses incurred by the Agricultural Stabilization and Conservation Service in addition to funds included in direct appropriations for the same purpose.

Authorized the Government to enter into cropland adjustment agreements in fiscal 1968 that would require payments during calendar 1968 of no more than $52.2 million.

Provided an advance authorization for the 1968 agricultural conservation program of $220 million.

Authorized $434,600,000 for Rural Electrification Administration loans: $314 million for electrification loans and $120.6 million for telephone loans.

Authorized the sale of $750 million of participation certificates in outstanding loans of the Farmers Home Administration.

Authorized $410 million for the Farmers Home Administration direct loan account: $110 million for real estate loans and $300 million for operating loans.

Authorized $15 million for the Farmers Home Administration rural housing direct loan account.

Authorized the transfer of $2,250,000 from the agriculture credit insurance fund and of $500,000 from miscellaneous program funds for salaries and expenses of the FHA.

Limited administrative expenses of the Commodity Credit Corp. to $31,500,000.

Prohibited the use of funds in the bill to administer PL 480 (Food for Peace) local currency or dollar sales to any nation transporting or selling goods to North Vietnam while that country is governed by a Communist regime.

Authorized $1.6 million of administrative and operating expenses of the Federal Crop Insurance Corp. Fund to be paid from premium income.

Limited administrative expenses of the Farm Credit Administration to $3,224,000.

1968

The key bills of 1968 were a one-year extension of the basic omnibus farm bill of 1965, a two-year extension of the Food for Peace program, and enactment of some rural development programs. A farmer cooperative bargaining bill also was passed, as was a Clean Poultry bill for birds not moving across state lines. (See chapter on Consumer Legislation for poulty measure.)

Possibly the most important development of the year was a powerful upsurge of sentiment for some kind of payments limitation on Government aid to each individual farmer. Tables put into the Congressional Record by Rep. Paul Findley (R Ill.) showed that payments in excess of $20,000 to any one farmer were heavily concentrated in the cotton states and sugar areas.

Agriculture Department figures showed that one California recipient, the J. G. Boswell Co., had received $4.1 million in Government payments of all types (but excluding price support loans) such as diversion payments, special direct subsidies and so forth; Rancho San Antonio of California had received $2.9 million and many others had received in the hundreds of thousands of dollars, with several over $1 million.

The tables showed that 24 Hawaiian sugar companies had received payments ranging from $181,540 to $1.4 million in 1967.

The Mississippi plantation of Sen. James O. Eastland (D Miss.), chairman of the Senate Judiciary Committee, received $158,000, while Eastland and a relative were listed separately as receiving $22,314.

Findley and several other Members gathered around them an unusual coalition. The coalition included Northern urban Congressmen, Democratic as well as Republican, who resented the enormous spending on subsidies for giant farms when funds for hunger and poverty were so scarce in the Federal budget, and some farm area Republicans, many of whom believed that to impose a tight upper limit on Government payments to any individual farmer would cause the "big boys" to turn against the existing farm program and kill it. Numerous farm area Republicans, with the backing particularly of the American Farm Bureau Federation, opposed production controls and what they saw as "market rigging" inherent in Democratic farm programs. They preferred to move toward a free market and believed that making the farm programs unprofitable for big companies would hasten such a move.

Southern Democrats and the Agriculture Department contended, however, that the purpose of existing farm programs with their special payments was to restrict production and thus avoid price-breaking surpluses. If the biggest farms with the biggest production were forced to drop out of the program by a payment limitation of $20,000, their production would soar and the surplus probably would crack the whole market, with disastrous consequences for all. (The big farms could not afford to stay in the production control programs if there were a $20,000 payment limit, because in that case they would have to restrict their production sharply in return for what, to them, would be practically nothing.)

The coalition nevertheless succeeded in getting the House for the first time to approve a $20,000 annual limit on payments to any one farmer (see Omnibus Bill, below), but the provision was dropped by House-Senate conferees on the bill.

Omnibus Bill

After much maneuvering, Congress cleared a compromise bill (HR 17126 - PL 90-559) extending the Food and Agriculture Act of 1965 for one year, through calendar 1970, without changes. President Johnson signed the bill into law Oct. 11.

Although Mr. Johnson had asked for permanent extension and the Agriculture Department had indicated it would settle for four years, extension for more than a year was probably never a real possibility. With a chance to win the Presidency, as they subsequently did in November, Republicans were in no mood to vote for legislation that would prevent them for at least four years from rewriting the whole farm program along lines oriented more toward a free market, as traditionally favored by the party. A one-year extension—to the end of 1970—would give a new Republican President enough time to study the program but still guarantee him a crack at amending it during his term of office.

All major farm organizations except the American Farm Bureau Federation supported extension of the Act. Programs extended were: milk, feed grains, cotton, wheat, wool, rice and cropland adjustment.

No change was made in the operation of the farm program, despite the fact that both the original House and Senate bills contained changes. The most controversial proposed change was the House amendment adopted July 31 by a 230-160 (R 137-30, D 93-130) roll call, which would have limited federal payments to individual farmers to $20,000 a year. This, like the other changes, were eliminated in the final bill.

Rep. Paul Findley (R Ill.), one of the authors of the limitation, three times (July 31, Aug. 1, Sept. 4) blocked unanimous consent motions to send the farm bill to conference with the Senate. Findley said he felt that any delay on the bill would give his colleagues more time to understand the reasons for his limitation amendment. Finally, on Sept. 10, the House Agriculture Committee voted to make a motion to send the bill to conference. Such a motion does not require un-

animous consent, and it was adopted by the House by a 223-85 roll-call vote on Sept. 17.

Findley intended to offer a motion instructing the House conferees to insist in conference on the limitation amendment immediately after the conferees were appointed on Sept. 17. But the Republican leadership believed that this motion, if it carried, might have the ultimate effect of killing the bill and said this would not be in the party's interest. So, the leadership approved a motion by Rep. Wiley Mayne (R Iowa) to instruct the conferees to insist that the program be extended only for one year. Since conferees can only be instructed on one point, this motion effectively blocked instruction to the conferees regarding the payments limit.

On Sept. 17, shortly before House consideration of the Agriculture Committee's motion, Rep. Dan Kuykendall (R Tenn.) sent a telegram to his fellow Republicans informing them of GOP Presidential candidate Richard M. Nixon's support for the one-year extension and urging them to block the Findley motion. It was feared that if a GOP-sponsored limitation provision prevented final passage of the farm bill, the bill's failure might lose votes for the GOP in the November elections. As a result of these maneuvers, the $20,000 limit was finally dropped in conference, and left out of the bill as enacted.

HR 17126 was one partner in what was called a "shotgun wedding" between the farm bill and a bill extending the food stamp program. The two bills went hand in hand through the Congressional process, with supporters of a larger food stamp program threatening to make an attempt to defeat the farm bill if the food stamp measure failed. Led by Rep. Leonor K. Sullivan (D Mo.) they had blocked granting of a rule on the farm bill on May 21 and forced the leadership to withhold the bill from the floor until the House Agriculture Committee approved a food stamp measure.

Food for Peace

The President July 29 signed into law a bill (S 2986 —PL 90-436) extending for two years the Food for Peace program (also called PL 480 and Food for Freedom). Mr. Johnson had favored a simple three-year extension.

Besides the two-year extension, S 2986 contained provisions designed to ease the U.S. balance-of-payments deficit and to prevent any private grain companies engaged in trade with North Vietnam from benefiting from export business under PL 480. Also, the bill encouraged population control and mutual educational and cultural exchange activities.

PROVISIONS—As sent to the President, S 2986:

Extended the program for two years through Dec. 31, 1970.

Continued annual authorizations of $1.9 billion for Title I (sales of U.S. commodities for local currencies and for dollar credits) and $600 million for Title II (famine relief and food donations); and continued the availability of funds previously authorized but not used.

Required the President to determine the amounts of foreign currencies needed by the United States for various expenses in foreign countries. Nations buying

PL 480 commodities under long-term contracts would be required to make immediate payments in local currencies of the amounts needed for U.S. expenses. (This provision was designed to ease U.S. balance-of-payments problems.) The enumerated expenses included: (1) payment of U.S. obligations, (2) development of U.S. agricultural markets, (3) financing international educational and cultural exchanges, (4) cost of translation and dissemination of scientific and technological information, (5) money for the lease or rental of buildings, (6) funds for purchase of foreign books and periodicals, (7) defense grants, (8) loans to U.S. business and (9) money for financing, at the request of the foreign country, programs for voluntary family planning, maternal welfare, child health and nutrition.

Directed the President to take steps to assure that the United States obtained a fair share of any growth in commercial agricultural markets in developing nations which were purchasing agricultural commodities under PL 480.

Permitted excess foreign currencies generated by PL 480 sales to be sold at discount at mutually agreed upon rates (up to 50 percent of any future sales agreement) for the purpose of paying wages of U.S. or foreign public works contractors in countries receiving PL 480 commodities.

Permitted the United States to exchange up to 50 percent of foreign currencies for dollars from any future agreement with U.S. importers for materials or commodities located in countries making PL 480 purchases.

Authorized the use of foreign currencies to the maximum extent practicable for carrying out rodent, insect, weed and plant and animal pest control programs.

Prohibited the Commodity Credit Corp. from financing the sale and export of agricultural commodities for any exporter which currently, or in the six months prior to an application for such financing, engaged (directly or through a subsidiary or affiliate) in any sales, trade or commerce with North Vietnam.

Required at least 5 percent of total sales proceeds to be made available for voluntary population control programs, if requested by the foreign country.

Included voluntary programs to control population growth as among the self-help measures to increase per capita production which the President should consider before entering into an agreement to aid a needy nation.

Authorized use of foreign currencies for any activities assisting cultural and educational exchanges or strengthening educational agencies for international studies and research. Required that at least 2 percent of total sales proceeds received each year in each country be used to finance such educational activities.

Class I Base Plan

Congress in 1968 failed to complete action on bills (HR 19910, S 4064) to encourage more dairy farmers to participate in marketing plans for fluid milk. The marketing plans first were authorized in the Food and Agriculture Act of 1965; the authorization later was extended through calendar 1970 in the 1968 farm bill (HR 17126). HR 19910, introduced by Lloyd Meeds

(D Wash.), passed the House Oct. 7. The Senate Agriculture and Forestry Committee held hearings on S 4064, but took no action before adjournment.

The fluid milk marketing plans, called Class I base plans (Class I milk was for drinking), established quotas for dairy farmers so that those who increased their production beyond the quota would receive for the surplus only the lower price for "manufacturing" milk—milk used to make milk products. The purpose of the plans was to encourage farmers to hold down their production and to relieve the Government of the need to buy up dairy products.

The aim of HR 19910 and S 4064 was to add flexibility to the quota plan and thus to make it more attractive to dairy farmers, who had to approve it in a referendum before it could take effect.

Since 1965, only one federal milk marketing order area, around Puget Sound in Washington, out of 75 such areas had implemented the quota system. It was thought that some procedures of the system, plus its temporary nature, made it unattractive to large groups of dairy farmers.

Futures Markets

Congress cleared for the President's signature an Administration-backed bill (HR 13094) amending the 1936 Commodity Exchange Act to strengthen regulation of the commodity futures markets, including livestock and livestock products. President Johnson signed the bill Feb. 19 (PL 90-258).

The bill authorized the Agriculture Secretary to disapprove bylaws and rules of contract markets and issue cease-and-desist orders under certain conditions, but it did not cover trading in coffee and sugar futures, as had the original Administration proposal.

Co-Op Dealings

Congress cleared for the President's signature an amended bill (S 109), the Agricultural Fair Practices Act, prohibiting unfair trade practices affecting procedures of agricultural products. The Administration strongly supported the original version of S 109, introduced by Sen. George D. Aiken (R Vt.), but opposed Senate amendments to the bill which many farm groups felt discriminated against farm co-operatives. The Administration reluctantly supported the final version, which contained House amendments softening the language, but not the legal impact, of the Senate bill. President Johnson signed S 109 April 16.

PROVISIONS—As signed, S 109 (PL 90-288):

Prohibited canners, packers and other purchasers of farm products from using discrimination, coercion, intimidation, bribery, falsehood or conspiracy to discourage growers from joining producer cooperatives.

Prohibited associations of producers from using such tactics to increase their membership. (This was the language to which farmer groups objected.)

Declared that nothing in the Act prevented handlers and producers from selecting their customers for any reason other than a producer's membership in, or contract with, a cooperative, nor required a handler to deal with a cooperative.

Exempted producers of cotton and tobacco from provisions of the bill.

Co-Op Haulage

President Johnson July 26 signed into law a bill (S 752—PL 90-433) that limited to 15 percent of the total any tonnage transported in interstate commerce by farm cooperatives for nonmembers, including the Federal Government; prohibited such an organization from hauling more nonmember than membership business; required a cooperative planning to haul nonmember traffic to notify the Interstate Commerce Commission (ICC) in advance; and authorized the ICC to inspect cooperatives' books.

Under existing legislation, trucks operated by farm cooperatives were exempted from ICC rate regulations. It was developed through Congressional testimony that trucks operated by some farm co-ops were hauling regular freight shipments (on return runs after hauling farm product to markets, for example) in apparent violation of existing conditions for their ICC exemption.

As introduced, S 752 limited exempt farm cooperative hauling to farm traffic. This restriction was opposed by the Agriculture Department as impairing legitimate hauling operations by cooperatives. The thrust of the legislation was aimed at curtailing cooperatives' nonmember traffic, especially shipments for the Defense Department which competed with normal carriers.

Pesticide Research

A bill (HR 15979—PL 90-394) to extend an Interior Department pesticide research program was signed into law by the President on July 11.

HR 15979 continued for three years, through fiscal 1971, the program established by a 1958 law for research on the hazardous effects of pesticides and other poisonous chemicals on fish and wildlife. The bill authorized appropriations of $3.5 million each year for the research by the Interior Department.

Expenditures under the Interior Department's pesticide research program since the program began were as follows, in thousands of dollars:

1960	$ 280.0	1965	$ 2,329.2
1961	386.5	1966	2,351.0
1962	678.9	1967	2,795.7
1963	809.8	1968	2,994.0
1964	1,071.8	Total	$13,696.9

Dairy Indemnities

Congress cleared a bill (S 3638) to extend through June 30, 1970, authority for the Agriculture Secretary to compensate dairy farmers for milk accidentally contaminated by federally approved pesticides. The President signed the bill into law (PL 90-484) Aug. 13.

Since authority to indemnify dairy farmers for milk losses first was provided as part of the Economic Opportunity Act of 1964, the program had cost $978,043, according to the House Agriculture Committee.

Sen. Joseph M. Montoya (D N.M.) said that when the authority for the indemnification was extended in 1967, the Department of Agriculture had indicated steps were being taken to remedy the situation. He said there had been, at that time, "reasonable prospect that the problem would have diminished" so that a further extension of the authority would not be necessary. But it did continue, he said, "and it appears that it will continue for the foreseeable years to come."

Animal Drugs

The House agreed to Senate amendments to a bill (HR 3639) providing a single procedure for the pre-marketing clearance of new animal drugs by the Food and Drug Administration. The action cleared the Administration-backed bill for the President, who signed it July 13 (PL 90-399).

Rural Development Aid

Congress completed action on a bill (S 1504) expanding federal assistance for rural areas. The Senate had passed it by voice vote Aug. 28, 1967, and the House passed an amended version of the measure Aug. 2, 1968.

In a major provision, S 1504 authorized the Farmers Home Administration (FHA) to make loans to farmers for projects that would supplement family income. The Agriculture Department said the projects might include such small nonfarm enterprises as repairing farm or automotive equipment, processing locally produced commodities and establishing woodworking, leather or handicraft shops. S 1504 also authorized loans to help farmers convert all or part of their acreage to outdoor recreational purposes. These provisions were intended to benefit families which were unable or barely able to support themselves from farming alone.

PROVISIONS—As signed into law (PL 90-488) Aug. 15, S 1504 amended the Consolidated Farmers Home Administration Act of 1961 as follows:

Water, Sewer Grants. Increased to $100 million from $50 million the maximum annual amount of matching grants which the Farmers Home Administration could make to soil and water associations and local public agencies for construction of water supply and sewage disposal systems in rural areas where the population did not exceed 5,500. Increased to $15 million from $5 million the annual amount of grants which the FHA could make to help public agencies prepare comprehensive plans for development of water supply or sewage disposal systems in rural areas.

FHA Loan Provisions. Authorized FHA loans to operators of family-type farms (1) to finance small nonfarm enterprises to supplement family income and (2) to finance development of outdoor recreational enterprises or conversion of their farms to recreational uses. Specified that the loans could be either for real estate transactions or operating purposes.

Removed the statutory 5-percent ceiling on the interest rate of operating loans and established a flexible formula for calculating the rate, based on the cost of money to the Government.

Removed the existing $450 million annual limit on the FHA's authority to insure loans and specified that the loan insurance authority would expire on Oct. 1, 1971.

Increased from $50 million to $100 million the amount of loans in the insured loan program that could be held in the agricultural credit insurance fund pending sale to private investors.

Removed a provision of existing law which specified that 75 percent of operating loans must be for $15,000 or less. (Loans, however, could not be for more than $35,000.)

Rural Housing

Some of the rural housing and rural planning authorizations which President Johnson had been seeking for a number of years were included in the omnibus Housing and Urban Development Act of Aug. 1, 1968 (S 3497—PL 90-448).

The bill authorized $20 million in fiscal 1969 and $10 million in fiscal 1970 for rural district planning; provided subsidized interest to encourage construction of low and moderate-income rural housing; authorized a program to provide housing and training facilities for rural trainees; and provided other rural aids. (For details, see Chapter on Housing)

Farm Credit System

The President Oct. 17 signed a bill (S 3986—PL 90-582) designed to expedite the retirement of Government capital in the Federal Intermediate Credit Banks, the Banks for Cooperatives and the Production Credit Assns.

The action would virtually free the Farm Credit Administration programs from direct federal control and make future federal Budgets more accurate and predictable. Currently, through the Government's holdings of approximately $148,214,720 of the capital of the three programs was less than one-eighth of the estimated worth of the capital stock, the entire $771 million of estimated fiscal 1969 net lending of the programs showed up in the Budget. Once the sale of Government stock is completed, only that percentage of net lending which occurred while the Treasury still held some stock will appear in the Budget.

Farm Funds

The regular fiscal 1969 appropriations bill for the Department of Agriculture (HR 16913—PL 90-463) provided $6.1 billion—an ostensible cut of nearly $1.3 billion from the Administration request.

But most of the reduction was more of an accounting device than anything else, since $600 million of it came from PL 480 Food for Peace reimbursements and $400 million from reimbursements to the Commodity Credit Corp., which finances the price support programs.

Both Food for Peace and price support programs operate—in effect—by the advance contract authority method. Obligations to the maximum amounts authorized under PL 480 and under the price support laws are incurred as necessary to keep the programs going; the amounts in appropriate bills merely pay off these obligations. If money to handle them is not included in one appropriations bill, it must and invariably is provided in the next or in a supplemental.

In accord with the ritual observed for well over a decade, Congress denied the Administration request to slash the agricultural conservation program to a level of $100 million. It provided $195 million. Congress denied $55.5 million in advance contract authority sought for the cropland retirement program authorized in the 1965 Food and Agriculture Act. The House Appropriations Committee said dwindling surpluses of many crops made land retirement under this program unnecessary at present.

Some of the major disputes on the bill came over the food programs. (For details, see following section of this chapter, Feeding the Hungry.)

PROVISIONS—As signed into law Aug. 8, HR 16913 appropriated the following for activities of the Agriculture Department (figures in parentheses are subtotals):

	Budget Request	Final Appropriation
General Activities		
Agricultural Research Service	$ 237,620,600	$ 220,257,800
Cooperative State Research Service	62,179,000	59,105,000
Extension Service	97,629,000	96,988,000
Farmer Cooperative Service	1,848,000	1,341,000
Soil Conservation Service	(196,968,000)	(229,314,000)
Conservation operations	116,313,000	114,893,000
Watershed planning	6,224,000	6,165,000
River basin surveys	8,780,000	8,780,000
Works of improvement	33,368,000	57,220,000
Flood prevention	12,395,000	20,000,000
Great Plains conservation program	13,414,000	16,000,000
Resource conservation, development	6,474,000	6,256,000
Economic Research Service	13,964,000	12,789,000
Statistical Reporting Service	14,674,000	14,326,000
Consumer and Marketing Service	(531,039,000)	(521,488,500)
Consumer programs	119,846,000	116,264,500
Payments to states	1,750,000	1,750,000
School lunch program	184,443,000	178,474,000
Food stamp program	225,000,000	225,000,000
Foreign Agricultural Service	22,414,500	21,541,300
Commodity Exchange Authority	1,584,000	1,530,000
Stabilization and Conservation Service	(526,433,700)	(617,031,400)
Expenses	143,933,700	141,031,400
Sugar Act program	82,300,000	82,000,000
Agricultural conservation program	100,000,000	195,500,000
Cropland adjustment program	85,700,000	84,500,000
Conservation reserve program	109,500,000	109,000,000
Emergency conservation measures	5,000,000	5,000,000
Rural Community Development Service	469,000	463,000
Office of Inspector General	12,867,000	12,426,000
Packers and Stockyards Administration	3,166,000	2,815,300
Office of General Counsel	5,033,000	4,611,000
Office of Information	1,997,000	1,997,000
National Agricultural Library	3,419,000	3,292,750
Office of Management Services	2,910,000	2,841,600
General administration	4,664,000	4,614,000
Subtotal, general activities	$1,740,878,800	$1,828,772,650

Credit Agencies
(for loan authorizations, see below)

	Budget Request	Final Appropriation
Rural Electrification Administration	$ (436,937,000)	$ (461,805,000)
Electrification loans	304,000,000	329,000,000
Telephone loans	120,000,000	120,000,000
Salaries and expenses	12,937,000	12,805,000
Farmers Home Administration	(517,982,000)	(91,830,000)
Participation sales authorization	425,000,000	denied

Payment of sales insufficiencies	indefinite	denied
Rural water and waste disposal	27,250,000	28,000,000
Rural renewal	1,600,000	1,600,000
Rural housing for domestic farm labor	5,000,000	4,250,000
Salaries and expenses	59,132,000	57,980,000
Subtotal, credit agencies	$ 954,919,000	$ 553,635,000

Corporations

Federal Crop Insurance Corporation	$ 12,000,000	$ 11,243,500
Commodity Credit Corporation	3,298,039,000	2,837,645,500
PL 480	918,143,000	300,000,000
Subtotal, corporations	$4,228,182,000	$3,148,889,000
CCC (appropriations to liquidate contract authorizations)	$ 350,467,000	$ 350,467,000
Agricultural conservation program (liquidating appropriation)	195,500,000	190,000,000
GRAND TOTAL	$7,469,946,800	$6,071,763,650

The bill also:

Authorized the following transfers of Section 32 funds to various agencies to be spent for their programs in addition to amounts provided through direct appropriations: Agricultural Research Service, for research, $15 million; special milk program, $104 million; school lunch program, $64,325,000 (*also see below*); Foreign Agricultural Service $3,117,000 (total: $186,442,000).

Authorized $362,900,000 for the Farmers Home Administration (FHA) direct loan account: $83 million for real estate loans, $275 million for operating loans and $4,900,000 for soil conservation loans.

Authorized $30 million for rural housing loans of the FHA.

Placed in reserve $13,440,250 of the appropriation for consumer protective, marketing and regulatory programs of the Consumer and Marketing Service, to be released "only after the inspection activities of this service have been fully coordinated and placed on an efficient and economical operating basis."

Placed in reserve $25 million of the appropriation for the food stamp program, to be used "only to the extent required during the current fiscal year after various corrections are made in the handling of the program."

Authorized the Agriculture Secretary to spend up to $45 million in Section 32 funds to provide direct distribution of food to needy children and low-income persons determined by him "to be suffering, through no fault of their own, from general and continued hunger resulting from insufficient food." (The Secretary was to consider the age, income, locations and income of parents (if a minor) and employability. Such funds could be used whether or not needy cases occurred in areas already being served by the food stamp program or by the commodity distribution program.)

Prohibited the use of funds in the bill to administer PL 480 (Food for Freedom) local currency or dollar sales to any nation transporting or selling goods to North Vietnam while that country was governed by a Communist regime.

Prohibited use of funds in the bill to pay salaries of any federal employee convicted in any federal, state or local court of competent jurisdiction of inciting, promoting or carrying on a riot, or any group activity resulting in material damage to property or injury to persons in violation of federal, state or local laws.

Feeding the Hungry

Despite budgetary pressures resulting from the Vietnamese War, Federal programs to feed the nation's hungry—estimated to number at least 11.5 million persons early in 1969—were among the fastest-growing outlays in the entire U.S. budget during the years 1965 through 1968.

Over-all Federal budget authority for food-stamp aid, direct distribution of commodities to the poor, school lunches and related feeding programs was about $836.7 million in fiscal 1965. By the end of 1968, projected authority had risen to $1.5 billion for fiscal 1970 but was nevertheless being sharply criticized as too little by men such as Sen. George S. McGovern (D S.D.), chairman of a newly created Senate Select Committee on Nutrition and Human Needs, and organizations like the Urban Coalition, the National Council on Hunger and many urban-based Negro groups.

The new interest in waging a war against hunger had a number of sources:

• The steady, cumulative work of some Members of Congress—Rep. Leonor K. Sullivan (D Mo.) is one of the most notable examples—in publicizing the appalling diets and living conditions of many of the nation's poor.

• The feeling of Negro and labor leaders, that the broad war on poverty launched by the Johnson Administration in 1965 was petering out because of inadequate funding. The growing "white backlash" to Negro riots and the uncovering of financial scandals in connection with funding of some of the poverty programs also helped diminish public support for the war on poverty. A new fallback issue, which would also help the poor but which would be more sentimentally compelling and less vulnerable to attack, therefore was sought, and hunger was a politically ideal choice.

• Massive publicity given the hunger issue by CBS in a May 21, 1968, television documentary; by the Poor People's Campaign in the nation's capital in the spring and summer of 1968; and by a nationwide study, "Hunger, U.S.A.," organized by the Citizens Crusade Against Poverty (a Walter Reuther offshoot). Despite disclaimers from Congressmen, particularly those on the Agriculture Committees, that hunger was not really a serious problem, the evidence that it was started to pile up heavily in the form of statistics, photographs and studies. The public was put face to face with the fact that whatever the precise figure—6 million persons, 8 million, 12 million—there were millions of persons in the United States suffering from malnutrition, poor diet and hunger.

Fights in Congress

Over the period 1965 through 1968, there were repeated fights in Congress over enlargement of the existing anti-hunger programs and, in the end, advocates of a more generous stand began winning. Conservative congressmen were able to chop down funding in committee and in appropriations action but, over-all, the programs got bigger.

Nevertheless, leaders of the anti-hunger fight argued that even the projected $1.5 billion ticketed for fiscal 1970 was grossly inadequate, guaranteeing food only for school lunches and for about 8 million persons in poor families while at least 10 or 12 million were in need. They talked in terms of raising the figure to $3 billion or more a year.

Opposition to expanded hunger programs came from several sources: simple disbelief that the need was as great as pictured; fiscal conservatism; budget-tightening due to the war; and fear on the part of some Congressmen that feeding programs which had originated as devices to move agricultural surpluses off the market might be converted into welfare mechanisms pure and simple and lose their agricultural impact. Questions were raised, too, as to the balance between welfare aid and food aid. A powerful body of opinion believed it might be far better to give the hungry poor more cash—possibly a guaranteed annual income—and let them buy what food they needed and wanted.

Others favored maintaining a substantial amount of food in aid to the poor, on the theory that giving them the food would guarantee they did not use for other purposes cash intended for food.

Developments during 1965-68 were marked by a proliferation of new food-aid programs: special food packages for nursing and expectant mothers; a big expansion of low-cost or no-cost food for poor children participating in the school lunch program; school breakfasts for poor children; and larger bonuses of food stamps under that program. Late in 1968 a new food-stamp payment schedule was announced under

---

Reference

Discussion of the federal feeding programs for the poor from 1945-64 will be found in *Congress and the Nation*, Vol. I, p. 739-40.

---

which a poor family—with under $30 a month income—could get $58 worth of food stamps for $2, with the Federal Government paying for the $56 "bonus" portion.

The Agriculture Department estimated that if the entire $1.5 billion requested for fiscal 1970 were made available by Congress, about 8 million persons in hungry families would be receiving food under the food stamp or direct food distribution program, and about 1 million expectant and nursing mothers and small children would be receiving special nutrition supplement packages.

It further estimated that under the regular school lunch program, which is available to all children in those schools choosing to participate, about 19.8 million children would be receiving lunches; while 6.6 million poor children (which it said was the number in school needing reduced rate or no-cost lunches) would be receiving school lunches free or at less than cost.

A conflict which marked the entire 1965-68 period arose from the fact that the child-feeding programs and the direct distribution program had nearly all been started for the basic purpose of making use of surplus agricultural commodities and of helping clear surpluses from the market.

The conservative Agriculture Committees, as a result, had jurisdiction over the programs and the Agriculture Department administered them. In some cases, these groups tended to view the programs as still designed to clear away agricultural surpluses. Members of Congress from areas producing perishable commodities without regular price supports, for example, strongly opposed the idea of earmarking funds derived from Section 32 of a 1935 law (giving the Secretary of Agriculture 30 percent of U.S. customs receipts) for food purchases for the poor. This demand was made by the Poor People's Campaign in 1968, but it was resisted by many Congressmen, on the ground that tying up of the funds in food programs for the poor would make them unavailable when needed for spot purchases of perishables to avoid price-depressing surpluses.

These Congressmen had no objection to giving the purchased fruits and vegetables to the poor once they had been obtained in surplus clearance activities, but they wanted the money held unobligated and ready for use in surplus clearance.

Spokesmen for the poor and the needy directed bitter criticism against the Agriculture Department for not making use of Section 32 funds in more programs to supplement the diets of the poor, but the Department's basic answer under Agriculture Secretary Or-

ville L. Freeman was that it could not act without the agreement of Congress, which so far was not forthcoming.

Chronology
Of Legislation
On Food for Hungry
1966

Child Nutrition Act

President Johnson in his Jan. 24 Budget Message asked a reorientation of the two basic child-feeding programs, school lunches and school milk, to focus them more on poor children and less on the general run of children, many of whom were receiving adequate diets and did not really need school lunch and school milk aid. At that time, it was estimated that about 18 million children were receiving regular school lunches and about 2 million needy children were receiving below-cost or no-cost lunches. It was estimated also that at least several million more children—out of some 9 million in schools not participating in the lunch program—were needy and would benefit from free or reduced-rate lunches.

The President asked also for a pilot summer food program for needy children at playgrounds and child-care centers; a pilot breakfast program for schools in poor areas; and aid for kitchen and service equipment for schools in poor areas, to help them participate in the child-feeding programs.

A coalition of dairy state Members of Congress and other farm area spokesmen sharply opposed the proposed new orientation, fearing that milk purchases, particularly, would eventually shrivel to almost nothing. (Mr. Johnson's budget requests (*see below*) called for a cutback in milk outlays under the programs.)

In the end, Congress passed the Child Nutrition Act, which left the school milk and lunch programs basically as they were, without the President's requested changes. The summer food program was dropped, but the breakfast program and the kitchen equipment programs were adopted.

LEGISLATIVE ACTION

The House and Senate both rejected the reshaping of the milk and lunch programs along the lines suggested by the President. The Senate passed its version (S 3467) of the Child Nutrition Act without a dissenting vote, July 12, after rejecting, 37-42, an amendment by Abraham A. Ribicoff (D Conn.) to establish a special summer lunch program for children 3 to 18. (The House later passed a separate summer lunch bill, but it died without Senate action.)

The House version of the Child Nutrition Act was passed Sept. 1, and the conference report was cleared by the two chambers a month later.

Major Provisions

As signed into law Oct. 11, S 3467 (PL 89-642):

Special Milk Program. Authorized appropriations of $110 million in fiscal 1967, $115 million in 1968, $120 million in 1969 and $120 million in 1970 to "encourage consumption" of fluid milk in nonprofit schools and other institutions that train and care for children.

Stipulated that the special milk program be administered in the same manner as in fiscal 1966.

School Breakfast Program. Authorized appropriations of $7.5 million in fiscal 1967 and $10 million in 1968 for a pilot program of grants to the states for breakfast programs in schools.

Specified that in allotting funds, states give first consideration to schools with students from poor economic areas and to schools with a "substantial proportion" of students who traveled long distances.

Specified that the breakfasts be served without charge or at a reduced charge only to children unable to pay the full costs, as determined by local school authorities. (Other students could participate, but would pay for their meals.)

Provided that disbursement of funds to schools by the states would be on the basis of rate-per-meal or such other basis as was set by the Secretary of Agriculture. In cases of severe need, where the normal disbursement formula would be inadequate, permitted the Secretary to pay up to 80 percent of the operating costs of a school's program.

Nonfood Assistance. Authorized appropriations of $12 million in fiscal 1967, $15 million for fiscal 1968, $18 million for fiscal 1969 and $18 million in fiscal 1970 to aid public and nonprofit private schools in low-income areas in acquiring equipment to establish programs for the storage, preparation, transportation and serving of food in connection with federally aided school lunch and breakfast programs.

Other Provisions. Authorized the Secretary of Agriculture to extend school food assistance to pre-school programs operated as part of a school system.

Directed that all federal school food programs be administered by the Secretary of Agriculture.

Directed other federal agencies administering school food programs to transfer funds for these activities, "to the extent practicable," to the Agriculture Department.

Authorized such sums as were needed for the new administrative expenses of the state agencies and the Secretary of Agriculture under the Act.

Funds Fight

The President, as part of his budget-tightening actions resulting from the war in Vietnam and in accord with his requests (*see above*) to reshape food programs to concentrate on hungry children, asked Congress to slash school milk funds for fiscal 1967 from the fiscal 1966 figure of $103 million to only $21 million. He also asked a cut in funds for school lunches

---

Basic Food Programs

School Lunches. Started in 1936 under special authority, permanently authorized by National School Lunch Act of 1946. Provides Federal matching cash grants to the states for nonprofit school lunches. Agriculture Department often supplements foods obtained by states by giving them donations of actual commodities from Government stockpiles or special Government purchase programs designed to clear surpluses from the market. A 1962 amendment authorized a much broader program of special below-cost meals for needy children.

Special Milk. Authorized in 1954, designed to help clear surplus milk from the market through Government purchase and donation to schools.

Food Stamps. Started in 1961 on experimental basis, made permanent by 1964 legislation. Poor persons in counties and cities which choose to participate may buy food stamps, which are redeemable in participating grocery stores for more in food than the stamps cost. The Federal Government pays the difference.

Direct Distribution. Counties and cities not participating in the food stamp program may, under authority of the 1949 Agricultural Act, obtain surplus food from federal stockpiles and donate them to the hungry poor, who come to a central depot to pick up supplies at specified intervals. Many consider this program inferior to food stamps because it appears more like a handout and, until recently, was limited to only a handful of commodities available from the stockpile. (Supplementation of the food packages under this program was providing 22 different foods by early 1969.)

Section 32. A 1935 law authorized 30 percent of U.S. customs receipts each year for the use of the Secretary of Agriculture for various purposes, including increasing domestic consumption. Several hundred million dollars are usually available. Part of the money is used to buy up fresh fruits, vegetables and other perishables in areas threatened by a surplus. These items are then donated to the direct distribution program, to school lunches and to institutions.

---

from $157 million the previous year to $138 million (plus $45 million in transfers from Section 32 funds). In addition, he asked that the entire food stamp program—$150 million—be financed from Section 32 funds instead of from new appropriations.

Congress, in the Agriculture Funds bill (HR 14596 —PL 89-556), refused to grant these requests. It provided $104 million for school milk (partly from Section 32 funds); $165.9 million in appropriations and $45 million in Section 32 funds for school lunches; and $140 million in direct appropriations and carryovers for food stamps, with a notation in the conference report that it appeared the original food stamp act forbade use of Section 32 funds to finance food stamps.

The provision forbidding use of Section 32 funds to finance food stamps—unless Congress should give its express approval—was sharply criticized by the Poor People's Campaign in 1968.

1967

Food Stamp Extension

After a three-month deadlock, Congress gave final approval to a bill (S 953) continuing the food stamp program for two years and authorizing appropriations of $200 million for fiscal 1968 and $225 million for fiscal 1969.

Controversy had developed when the food stamp program came up for renewal, posing a threat that it would not be continued. One issue was the length of the new authorization and the level of funding. The House favored a one-year extension (fiscal 1968) at a level of $195 million, while the Senate supported a three-year continuation (fiscal 1968-70) with a total authorization of $675 million.

These Senate-House differences in the end were compromised down the middle.

A second controversy was over a proposal to force states to foot a larger share of the program's cost. In this case the Administration scored a victory when the House by a 173-191 roll-call vote rejected an amendment by its Agriculture Committee to require states that participated in the program to contribute 20 percent of the costs beginning July 1, 1969. Existing law did not require states to make any contribution other than for administrative expenses.

Opponents of the cost-sharing provision, especially Leonor K. Sullivan (D Mo.), sponsor of the original Administration food stamp bill, contended that to require states to meet 20 percent of the total costs of the program would force many poor states, already hard pressed to meet existing welfare program costs, to drop out of the stamp plan entirely. Mrs. Sullivan indicated she believed the Committee amendment was tacked on in an effort to scuttle the entire program.

Agriculture Committee Chairman W. R. Poage (D Texas) said; "There is not a state in this Union that is so poor that it cannot pay $1 out of $5 to feed these poor people."

Page Belcher (R Okla.), ranking minority member of the Committee flatly opposed continuing the food stamp plan. Belcher, along with eight other Committee Republicans and one Democrat, feared the program was turning into a nationwide federal welfare activity, destroying state and local initiative, failing to help agriculture and doing little to help the truly destitute. House and Senate conferees reported on Sept. 19 that they were unable to agree. But on the same day, with the Senate acting first, both chambers agreed to accept a compromise solution providing for the two-year continuation.

PROVISIONS—As signed into law (PL 90-91) Sept. 27, S 953:

Provided a two-year extension of the food stamp program by authorizing appropriations of $200 million for fiscal 1968 and $225 million for fiscal 1969.

Directed that the program be financed from the Treasury's general fund, thus barring use of any funds from Section 32 of PL 74-320 for the program.

(Sen. Spessard L. Holland (D Fla.) explained on the Senate floor that he regarded Section 32 funds as an "insurance program" for agriculture that should not be tied down in other commitments.)

Nutrition Study

A little-noticed provision of the Public Health Service Amendments (HR 6418—PL 90-174) directed the Department of Health, Education and Welfare to study malnutrition and hunger and related health problems in the United States. As of the beginning of 1969 the study, headed by Dr. Arnold Schaefer, was operating in about 10 states and, according to Schaefer, had produced definite evidence of serious hunger problems in the United States.

Funding of Programs

The Administration did not ask big cutbacks in any of the food programs in 1967, and there were no big disputes over funds. In the Agriculture funds bill (HR 10509—PL 90-113) the food stamp program received $185 million in new appropriations and carryovers (with Congress once again rejecting a request for financing from Section 32 funds) compared with a request for $195 million; school milk $104 million (all from Section 32 funds); school lunches $227.8 million (a cut of about $15 million in the request); and funds were provided for the pilot school breakfast program and for school lunch equipment.

Poverty Funds

The Senate Labor and Public Welfare Subcommittee on Employment, Manpower and Poverty held highly publicized hearings in the summer of 1967 on poverty and hunger in Mississippi. The outgrowth was introduction by Sen. John Stennis (D Miss.) of a bill (S 2138) authorizing $10 million for emergency food and medical services for the poor.

It was eventually incorporated into the 1967 anti-poverty authorization bill (S 2388—PL 90-222), providing $25 million to the Office of Economic Opportunity in fiscal 1968 and $50 million in fiscal 1969. Actual appropriations provided by Congress, however, were far smaller: $12.8 million for fiscal 1968 and $16.9 million for fiscal 1969.

1968

The last year of the Johnson Administration was perhaps the most active and controversy-ridden of any in history on the subject of hunger. For the first time, hunger became a truly national issue as two major citizens' reports and a nationwide television program focused on it.

The Poor People's Campaign, an encampment in Washington of Southern Negroes, sponsored by the Southern Christian Leadership Conference of the recently assassinated Dr. Martin Luther King Jr., made the satisfaction of hunger one of its major demands. The Senate created a special committee to investigate it and Mrs. Leonor K. Sullivan (D Mo.) won an astonishing victory over House conservatives in legislative fighting over the food stamp authorization bill.

All the while the Agriculture Department came under increasing fire for not doing enough to satisfy hunger needs, although it had steadily been improving the program over the years. Charges were frequently heard that to fuel the Vietnamese war, the Administration had gone too slowly on improving the national feeding programs.

The year ended with the Johnson Administration, in its final, outgoing budget, asking for $1.446 billion in budget authority in 1970 for food programs, compared with $1.243 billion provided for fiscal 1969, and the Agriculture Department announcing several important new administrative revisions in its anti-hunger programs.

Child Feeding Bill

Congress April 17 cleared for the President's signature a bill (HR 15398) extending and expanding food service programs for children. Final action came when the Senate by voice vote passed HR 15398 as approved by the House March 5. The President signed the bill May 8 (PL 90-302).

The bill amended the National School Lunch Act to provide federal support for lunches to children in public or private nonprofit child-care institutions. Day-care centers, settlement houses, playgrounds, summer day-camps and centers for the handicapped would be eligible for aid. Under existing law, only children enrolled in school activities were eligible for food services. The new program applied only to children from impoverished areas or those with high concentrations of working mothers.

HR 15398 authorized $32 million a year for fiscal 1969, 1970 and 1971 for the day-care lunch program. Congress had made available $227.8 million in fiscal 1968 for the lunch program in schools (plus an additional $104 million for the special milk program).

The bill also extended for three years the pilot program of breakfasts in schools in impoverished areas which had begun in fiscal 1967. The bill authorized federal contributions of $6.5 million in fiscal 1969, $10 million in fiscal 1970 and $12 million in fiscal 1971. (The fiscal 1968 authorization had been $10 million but only $3.5 million was appropriated.)

PROVISIONS—As passed by Congress, HR 15398:

Amended the National School Lunch Act to authorize a pilot program of lunches for children in public or private nonprofit child-care institutions from areas where poor economic conditions existed or where there were high concentrations of working mothers.

Authorized $32 million annually for the program in fiscal 1969, 1970 and 1971.

Provided a basic grant to each state, not to exceed $50,000, with the remainder to be allotted according to the ratio of the number of children in each state aged 3 to 17 in families with incomes of less than $3,000, to the number of children in all the states.

Reserved 2 percent of total funds for U.S. territories.

Allowed states to use up to 25 percent of their funds to pay up to 75 percent of the cost to institutions for purchase or rental of equipment to store, prepare or transport food.

Provided that in circumstances of severe need, up to 80 percent of the operating costs of the day-care lunch program could be funded under the Act.

Required that meals be served at no cost or at a reduced cost to children unable to pay the full cost.

Authorized for the school pilot breakfast program $6.5 million in fiscal 1969, $10 million in fiscal 1970 and $12 million in fiscal 1971.

Public Reports

Reports by two citizen groups and a television documentary in 1968 severely criticized Government food assistance programs as inadequate, poorly funded and poorly administered:

SCHOOL LUNCH INQUIRY. The Committee on School Lunch Participation in an April 16 report said that the school lunch program "was failing to meet the needs of poor children." Members of the Committee represented Church Women United, National Catholic Women, the National Council of Jewish Women, the National Council of Negro Women and the National Board of the Young Women's Christian Association. The group's report, "Their Daily Bread," resulted from more than 1,500 personal interviews across the nation conducted by housewives using a 35-page questionnaire.

The Committee cited the following "facts" about the school lunch program: (1) Of 50 million public elementary and secondary school children, only about 18 million participated in the National School Lunch Program; (2) Fewer than two million, just under four percent, were able to get a free or reduced-price school lunch, even though there were six million school-age children from families at the "rock-bottom of poverty," that is, whose parents earned less than $2,000 a year and/or were receiving aid to families with dependent children (AFDC); (3) Whether or not a child was eligible for a free lunch was determined "not by any universally accepted formula, but by local decisions about administration and financing which may or may not have (had) anything to do with the need of the individual child—and, generally speaking, the greater the need of children from a poor neighborhood, the less the community (was) able to meet it."

The Committee pointed to what it considered "basic inadequacies" of the current program. First, was inadequate financing. The report called "unjust and harmful" the formula for state and local financing which allowed states and localities to contribute little or no financial support to the program. In many states, the report said, federal money and federal commodities paid for one-third of the child's lunch and the children themselves paid for two-thirds. The Committee argued that a lack of a uniform method of determining who should be eligible for a free or reduced price lunch resulted in "unequal and unfair" decisions on the local level. Finally, many older schools did not participate in the program because they were built without kitchens or cafeterias. Other schools contended it would not pay to have a kitchen or cafeteria, that is, the children's payments could not cover the cost of the program. Both types of schools almost invariably were located in slums, the report added.

Recommendations: Recommendations by the Committee included the "short-run objective" of reducing the price of the school lunch to place it within reach of the majority of children, preferably a maximum price of 20 cents. This could be accomplished, the Committee said, by: increasing the federal contribution to nine cents per meal "as a preliminary 'step'"; requiring states to match the federal contribution on a one-to-one basis from state appropriations out of state revenues (not the children's fees); requiring local school districts to pay for local administration, labor and equipment (again, not from children's fees); and maintaining the cash value of donated commodities at a steady and dependable level.

The Committee urged that a local public school district should be the unit which contracted to participate in the program, not the individual school. "Lack of facilities, the enrollment of large numbers of poor children, or the fact that a school is a neighborhood school where children can go home for lunch should not be considered valid reasons for excluding schools from the program," the Committee argued.

Other major recommendations included: (1) higher reimbursement rates and increased special assistance funds for schools which served a high proportion of needy children; (2) uniform standards for determining a child's eligibility for a free or reduced price meal; and (3) a universal free school lunch program as part of a coordinated plan for better nutrition for all children.

FOOD PROGRAMS INQUIRY. The Citizens Board of Inquiry into Hunger and Malnutrition in the United States in an April 22 report, "Hunger, USA," based on nine months of study, was highly critical of all Government food aid programs. The 25-member Board was formed in the summer of 1967 at the request of Walter Reuther, acting in his capacity as chairman of the Citizens Crusade Against Poverty and followed reports of cases of malnutrition among poor Mississippians.

The report said Agriculture Department officials "confirmed" that Secretary Orville L. Freeman had the power to spend excess Section 32 funds for the poor, "but they emphasized that Section 32 has come to have a one-sided application to further other interests," such as "to maintain producers' markets, and consequently, profits."

The 100-page report said over 300 of the poorest counties in the United States had no food assistance of any kind and that between 10 million and 14.5 million Americans were seriously underfed. The Board criticized the Agriculture Department's administration of food programs.

Recommendations. Major recommendations included: providing some food program (either food stamps or commodity distribution) in every county; eliminating restrictive eligibility requirements; providing adequate quantities and varieties of food necessary to insure proper nutrition; and improving the distribution system to make foods more accessible.

Food Stamp Program. The Board argued that food stamp prices were set at prohibitively high levels, while food stamp bonuses were set too low to provide the purchasing power necessary to secure an adequate diet. Families with no income were treated as nonexistent and irrational discrepancies were built into both the schedule of prices to be paid for stamps and the size of bonuses different households of different sizes could obtain, according to the report. Lump sum payments, continuing review of eligibility, delays in certification of eligibility, gaps between the termination of the commodity program and the initiation of the food stamp program (which could not operate in the same county)—all were cited as producing "massive drops" in participation and "substantial individual suffering."

New Proposals. The Board urged that free food stamps be provided families and individuals living alone who had no income or available cash. Where payment was required, the Board said, it should be low enough to promote rather than to discourage participation. Also, prices should be adjusted to allow for variation due to seasonal fluctuations in income. State-imposed barriers to eligibility of any persons deemed poor under federal standards of poverty should be prohibited, the Board said. Eligibility procedures should be simplified; and certification should be made upon applicants' affidavit alone, it said.

Reaction. The House Agriculture Committee June 16 issued a "Hunger Study" containing statements by county officials which the Committee said "lead to the unmistakable conclusion that there is very little actual hunger in the United States, but widespread malnutrition caused largely by ignorance as to what constitutes a balanced diet." The few instances of borderline starvation and hunger referred to in the statements were blamed mostly on parental neglect of infants, and most of those involved mentally retarded fathers and mothers, the Committee added.

The statements were cited as a rebuttal of the Board's report, which was highly critical of county officials and the Congressional Agriculture Committees as being unresponsive to the needs of the poor.

House Agriculture Committee Chairman W. R. Poage (D Texas) concluded that "the report was quite inaccurate and misleading to put it mildly. There seems to be little or no evidence that any substantial hunger in this country exists as the result of the refusal of assistance agencies, public and private, to give needed aid to those who are "unable to work." (The Board's report cited cases in which counties discontinued food distribution programs during harvest seasons as a coercive device to force the poor to provide abundant labor at subsistence wages.)

In a May 27 letter to Chairman Carl Perkins (D Ky.) of the House Education and Labor Committee, Agriculture Secretary Orville L. Freeman called a

May 21 CBS documentary, "Hunger in America," a "biased, one-sided, dishonest presentation of a serious national problem." (The program presented generally the same picture as the Board of Inquiry.)

While the program said 1,000 counties had no food programs, Freeman said the number was only 600. He called "a lie" the producers' charge that the Department "protects farmers, not consumers, and especially not destitute consumers." In the past 7-1/2 years the Department distributed 7.9 billion pounds of food at a cost of $1,320,560,000 and $279.7 million worth of bonus food stamps to needy families, according to Freeman.

Senate Nutrition Committee

The Senate July 30 by voice vote adopted a resolution (S Res 281) establishing a 13-member Select Committee on Nutrition and Human Needs. The Committee, to include members of the Committees on Labor and Public Welfare and on Agriculture and Forestry, was to report by June 30, 1969, on hunger in America. Sen. George S. McGovern (D S.D.) was appointed chairman.

Hearings. The Labor and Public Welfare Subcommittee on Employment, Manpower and Poverty held hearing on S Res 281 late in May.

The Rev. Ralph Abernathy, president of the Southern Christian Leadership Conference and head of the Poor People's Campaign, testifying May 29, said, "We cannot let Americans starve because Agriculture Committees choose to dislike the poor." He said the poor were in Washington "to say that hunger in America must be abolished, and we cannot compromise on that fact."

Abernathy outlined the following demands "as a minimum of immediate action": (1) establishment of federal food commodity programs in all of the poorest counties now deprived of them; (2) inclusion of foods making an adequate and balanced diet; (3) free food stamps to families having no income or lacking money to buy stamps. Abernathy said he preferred the food stamp program to the commodity distribution program, whose "emphasis on starches increases the incidence of so much malnutrition, illness, infant mortality and so forth amongst the poor."

Food Stamps

The House on Sept. 25 and the Senate Sept. 26 adopted the conference report on an Administration-backed bill (S 3068) extending the Food Stamp Act of 1964 for one year, through calendar 1970, and authorizing appropriations for the program.

The food stamp program repeatedly encountered stiff opposition from House Republicans and Southern Democrats. Republicans and Southern Democrats made up the controlling faction on the House Agriculture Committee, which has jurisdiction over the program, and so supporters of the program continually tried to extend its authorization for several years in order that the Agriculture Committee would not have to consider the question every year.

Early in 1968 President Johnson requested an increase of $20 million over the authorized appropriations for fiscal 1969. The Senate on May 17 passed the Administration bill without debate, increasing the authorization from $225 million to $245 million.

In the House, a bill-swapping move had been launched by Mrs. Sullivan in May. She and others who believed that the food stamp program should be expanded and extended for several years pressured the Rules Committee to delay action on the Administration's bill (HR 17126) extending basic farm programs until the Agriculture Committee reported the food stamp measure. The farm bill remained in the Rules Committee until June, and then was held off the floor by Democratic leaders until the food stamp bill was approved in committee in July.

Although Agriculture Secretary Freeman told the Committee the Administration now favored an open-ended authorization, the Agriculture Committee July 2 reported the food stamp bill providing only for a $20-million increase in fiscal 1969. The Committee had rejected an amendment proposed by Mrs. Sullivan which would have extended the program through 1972 with an open-ended appropriations authorization.

In a major victory for House liberals, the House July 30 voted to reverse its Committee's action by accepting Mrs. Sullivan's amendment. The House vote on the Sullivan amendment came after several weeks of pressure by the Poor People's Campaign and recommendations by the Citizens Board of Inquiry into

Costs and Beneficiaries

(Projected for Fiscal 1970)

Program	Cost million $	Beneficiaries
Families		
Food Stamps	$ 340.0	3,900,000
Direct Distribution	365.0	4,100,000
Nutrition Supplements to Nursing Mothers, etc.	34.5	1,000,000
Nutrition Aides (Education on Food Use)	15.0	N.A.
Institutions (For elderly, etc.)	53.8	2,700,000
Child Feeding		
Regular School Lunch	168.0	19,800,000
Reduced Rate School Lunches for Needy Children	105.8	6,600,000
School Breakfasts for Needy Children	11.0	450,000
Equipment for School Feeding Programs	15.0	—
Commodity Donations to School Feeding Programs	301.6	23,700,000
Non-School Child Feeding (Day Care Institutions, etc.)	10.0	100,000
Milk for Children	20.0	N.A.
Administration		
For Federal Costs	3.9	
For State Costs	2.7	
TOTAL	$1,446.3	

Hunger and Malnutrition for an expansion of the food stamp program.

But in conference, House Agriculture Committee conferees agreed to fix dollar limits on the program, despite adoption of Mrs. Sullivan's amendment on the floor.

Before adopting the conference report Sept. 25, the House rejected, on a 158-187 roll call, a motion by Rep. Charles M. Teague (R Calif.) to restore a Teague-sponsored House provision, dropped in conference, that would have barred strikers and students from participating in the food stamp program.

PROVISIONS—As signed into law (PL 90-552) Oct. 8, S 3068:

Extension. Amended the Food Stamp Act of 1964 to extend it through December 31, 1970.

Authorization. Increased fiscal 1969 appropriations authorization from $225 million to $315 million and authorized appropriation of $340 million for fiscal 1970 and $170 million for the first half of fiscal 1971.

Report. Required the Secretary of Agriculture to submit an annual report on operation of the Act to Congress by Jan. 20 of each year.

Program Funding

Appropriations action in 1968 yielded the following results for major feeding programs:

The Agriculture Department appropriation bill (HR 16913—PL 90-463) provided the requested $104 million in Section 32 funds for the school milk program; $242.8 million for school lunches, part cash and part in Section 32 fund transfers; and $225 million for the food stamp program. (The supplemental appropriation bill, HR 20300—PL 90-608, increased this food stamp figure to $280 million later in the year.)

In addition, the Agriculture Department funds bill provided $45 million to the Department, not tied to any one program, to be used as a special fund for direct distribution of food to needy children and the poor. The $45 million was to be drawn from Section 32 funds; it was a compromise of an amendment offered by Sen. Jacob K. Javits (R N.Y.) and adopted, 31-30 by the Senate May 29, which would have lifted all restrictions on the use of Section 32 funds for feeding programs. The Javits amendment was dropped in conference and the $45 million provided instead.

The bill also provided funds for the school breakfast program for poor children and for the special low-cost or no-cost meals for poor children in the school lunch program.

Ten million dollars to start the child-feeding program in institutions and day-care centers, authorized earlier in 1968, was provided in the Second Supplemental for Fiscal 1968 (HR 17734—PL 90-392). Only $5.75 million was actually used.

Administrative Actions

Spurred by the hunger reports, the Poor People's Campaign and pressure from citizen groups and some members of Congress, the Agriculture Department took a number of highly significant actions on hunger in 1968.

It added six new commodities to food packages available under the direct distribution program, bringing the total to 22 and providing recipients with a more rounded diet.

It instituted the program authorized earlier in the year for needy children in non-school centers like day-care facilities (see PL 90-302 and program funding, above).

By October 1968, it completed the program of getting family food programs—either food stamps or direct distribution—into all the nation's 1,000 poorest counties.

It began developing the food-package program for nursing and expectant mothers, and put the program into effect on an experimental basis; it was scheduled to rise to $34.5 million and reach 1 million persons in fiscal 1970.

It announced late in the year (and put into effect on Feb. 1, 1969) a new schedule of bonus payments under the food-stamp program, which gave greatly enlarged bonuses to the very poor—for example, families of four with monthly incomes of $60 or less. Such a family could now get $58 worth of stamps for a payment of $2 a month.

At the end of 1968, it was estimated that about 480 of the nation's 3129 counties and independent cities had no family feeding program—neither food stamps nor direct distribution. And the programs in a large number of counties and cities were inadequate, with monthly benefits far below the $100 to $120 considered adequate for a family of four by the Department's own reckoning.

Farm Labor

Despite passage of legislation providing a minimum wage for some farm workers and health, education and welfare aids for migratory farm workers, the nation's 1.2 million hired farm workers remained among the least privileged and most needy groups of society during the period 1965-1968.

Per hour wage rates in agriculture averaged $1.21 in 1968. Migratory farm workers employed in agriculture for 25 days or more totaled 194,000 in 1967 and earned an average of $1555 for both farm and nonfarm work combined.

Although the regular Mexican farm labor program died in 1964 (Mexican contract workers were brought into the United States in large numbers under this program), domestic farm workers—about one-third of them Negroes and Americans of Mexican descent—still faced competition from holders of "green cards". These were chiefly Mexicans holding permanent resident alien cards, making them migrants and permitting them to work in this country, returning over the border at night or living in the United States.

Labor and welfare groups had long contended that the availability of foreign contract labor and green card workers, often at relatively low wages, undermined the wage structure for native American farm workers and helped keep them in a perpetual state of poverty.

These labor and welfare groups worked to engineer a Congressional situation in which the Mexican farm labor program was allowed to die.

At the same time, Congress, with the farm bloc in the lead, defeated all efforts to give U.S. farm workers the protection to organize and strike, under the National Labor Relations Act, that was enjoyed by most other workers.

The argument against strikes by farm workers—as expressed, for example, at the 1968 convention of the American Farm Bureau Federation—was that perishable commodities like fruits and vegetables were uniquely vulnerable to work stoppages, and a farmer's entire year's work could be destroyed by only a brief work shutdown.

Nevertheless, a farm worker organizing group in California had some success in organizing grape workers. Led by Cesar Chavez, in 1966-68, it signed up some of the biggest farms—the Christian Brothers, Schenley and pressed a national consumer boycott against table grapes which received support from labor unions and welfare groups.

The farm labor force as a whole averaged 4.7 million a month in 1968, but of these, 3.5 million were family workers on their own farms. Only the remaining 1.2 million were hired workers. California, with its huge fruit and vegetable industries, was the largest user of hired farm labor.

The total number of green card holders was estimated in 1967 at 40,000 Mexicans and 10,000 Canadians. Additional foreigners—chiefly West Indians and Canadians—were allowed into the United States for farm work under special temporary-labor provisions of the basic immigration laws. About 15,000 entered for temporary farm work in 1968—a vast fall-off from the heyday of the Mexican farm labor program, when in some years of the 1950s as many as 450,000 foreign workers entered for farm work under special conditions.

Administrative action to lessen the competition from imported foreign labor was taken on several occasions by Secretary of Labor Willard Wirtz. In 1964, Wirtz ruled that before farmers could apply to import foreign contract workers under the special provisions of the immigration law, they would first have to seek to hire native American workers by offering them at least $1.15 to $1.40 an hour (depending on location), beginning April 1, 1965, and various minimum-hour, housing, transportation and insurance benefits.

Wirtz revised this scale upward in 1967 and 1968.

Chronology

Of Legislation

On Farm Labor

1965

Wirtz Regulations

In December 1964 Secretary of Labor Willard Wirtz had made it clear that he did not intend to let large numbers of foreign farm workers enter the United States under the general immigration laws, now that the Mexican farm labor program had expired.

On Dec. 19, he had put into effect regulations requiring that before farmers sought to bring in foreign labor, they must attempt to recruit native American farm workers by offering them between $1.15 and $1.40 an hour and various other benefits.

The regulation outraged many farmers, particularly in Florida and California, who had depended heavily on the Mexican labor program or on West Indian or Bahamian workers. They insisted that not enough native workers would be available to harvest their crops.

Wirtz early in 1965 sought to ward off criticism by launching a special recruiting job for American farm workers through the Bureau of Employment Security, and he even went so far as to begin, on May 4, a special effort to recruit high-school students for summer farm work. The youths were organized in "A-Teams" (Athletes in Temporary Employment as Agricultural Manpower) and used primarily in Western states.

The program met with only moderate success; a number of the youths quit after several weeks because of the difficulty of the work or because of poor housing or food.

Wirtz's difficulties reached a peak in September, when the Senate Agriculture Committee added to the omnibus farm bill (HR 9811) a provision to transfer authority over importation of foreign farm workers for temporary work from the Secretary of Labor to the Secretary of Agriculture. The latter official was expected to be more sympathetic to the growers demands.

In one of the key votes of the 1965 session, the Senate killed this provision and thereby backed Wirtz's position.

The amendment to drop the provision was offered Sept. 13 by Sen. Ross Bass (D Tenn.) and adopted 46-45 (D 43-17; R 2-28). The 46th and tie-breaking vote in favor of the amendment was provided by Vice President Hubert H. Humphrey, after the initial balloting had come out 45-45. (A tie vote, under Senate rules, is equivalent to a negative vote, so without Humphrey's vote the amendment would have failed.)

Wirtz refused to back down on his regulations and only about 50,000 foreign contract laborers entered the country in 1965, compared with 200,000 the year before, when the Mexican farm labor program was in effect. However, green card workers (who are, in effect, simply regular immigrants) were available in many areas.

Migrant Aid Bills

Three existing laws to provide health, housing and related aid to migrant farm workers were extended in 1965.

OEO Grants. An authorization for aid to migrants for child care, sanitation, housing and education, first enacted in the 1964 anti-poverty bill, was extended in the 1965 anti-poverty bill (HR 8283—PL 89-253). The same program, administered by the Office of Economic Opportunity, was subsequently again extended in the 1966 and 1967 anti-poverty bills, which provided authorizations through June 30, 1969. Obligations under

---

Reference

For history of farm labor legislation from 1945-64, see *Congress and the Nation*, Vol. I, p. 756-767.

---

this program totaled $14.9 million in fiscal 1965; $25.4 million in fiscal 1966; $32.9 million in 1967; $26.5 million in 1968; and $27.3 million in 1969.

Migrant Housing. Grants for low-rent housing for farm labor, first enacted in 1964, were increased from $10 million to $50 million in the omnibus housing bill (HR 7984—PL 89-117) and the over-all amount was made available for expenditure through Oct. 1, 1969. But according to the Senate Migratory Labor Subcommittee, only about 20 percent of the authorization was actually funded over the 1965-68 period.

Migrant Health Services. The Community Health Services Extension Amendments of 1965 (S 510—PL 89-109) authorized $24 million over fiscal 1966-68 for health services and hospital care for migratory farm workers. In 1968, in the regional medical care bill (HR 15758—PL 90-574), Congress authorized $9 million to continue the program in fiscal 1969 and $15 million to continue it through the end of fiscal 1970.

1966

Minimum Wage

The Fair Labor Standards Amendments of 1966 (HR 13712—PL 89-601) imposed for the first time a minimum wage for agricultural labor, but it covered only about 400,000 of the nation's 1.2 million farm workers and provided them with a minimum that was 30 cents an hour lower than that guaranteed for workers in other occupations.

The final bill covered only those farms which used at least 500 man-days of agricultural labor (about 7 men) per calendar quarter of the year—about 29,000 farms in all. For these workers, the minimum rate was set at $1 an hour Feb. 1, 1967; $1.15 Feb. 1, 1968; and $1.30 Feb. 1, 1969.

The bill exempted from coverage members of the employers' families; hand-harvest piece-workers; those employed in agriculture for less than 13 weeks the previous year; those who commuted daily from their permanent residences to the farms on which they were employed; and those principally engaged in production of livestock on a range. Also exempted were children of migrant workers who were under 16 and worked as hand-harvest workers; paid on a piece-rate basis; paid at the same piece rate as those over 16 on the same farm; or employed on the same farm as their parents.

Except on their parents' own farm the bill barred children under 16 from working in agricultural jobs which the Secretary of Labor considered hazardous. (Wirtz on July 1, 1967, issued a list of hazardous occupations.)

Migrant Children

The 1966 school-aid bill (HR 13161—PL 89-750) contained an amendment to the basic school-aid law providing for special grants to the states for education of children of migrant farm workers. This program, extended through fiscal 1970 in the 1967 omnibus education bill (HR 7819—PL 90-247), became the major source of education aid to migrant children. In fiscal 1967, about 80,000 children participated in the program and the federal outlay was $9.5 million; in fiscal 1968 the figures were 228,000 children and $37.7 million.

1967

In April, Secretary of Labor Wirtz put into effect new requirements on wages and conditions of work that farmers would have to offer domestic farm workers before they could seek to obtain foreign contract workers for temporary farm employment. Instead of $1.15 to $1.40 an hour, depending on location, the scale went to $1.35 to $1.60.

1968

In April, the $1.35 to $1.60 scale set in 1967 was raised to $1.45 to $1.68.

Farm Unions

The House Education and Labor Committee on April 3 reported a bill (HR 16014) guaranteeing farm workers the right to organize unions, bargain collectively with employers, and conduct strikes. It covered only farms employing more than 12 persons at any time during a year or farms where direct wage costs were over $10,000 a year—about 30,000 farms in all. The bill was criticized by the American Farm Bureau Federation and the House Agriculture Committee, and it was killed by the House Rules Committee.

Chapter 12—Labor

Key Votes

In this chapter, key roll-call votes are shown in bold-face type. The party breakdown on each of these votes and the position taken by each Member of Congress may be found in the key vote charts which appear in the appendix to this book.

Labor Legislation

THE Johnson Administration early in its career produced one of the most fruitful legislative periods in American history from the viewpoint of organized labor. This appraisal by union leaders rested on the fact that the goals of major labor unions and those of President Johnson's "Great Society" coincided in many respects. And for a time those goals found a highly responsive Congress. The American Federation of Labor-Congress of Industrial Organizations (AFL-CIO) called the 89th Congress "the most outstanding Congress in the history of this nation." Paradoxically, it was nonlabor legislation which evoked the plaudits of the AFL-CIO and other leading elements of organized labor.

The lawmakers' actions in the fields of civil rights, anti-poverty, education and other social welfare areas under Mr. Johnson's energetic and experienced leadership generally followed the unions' longstanding stance on social legislation. The forces of organized labor comprised a major bulwark in the coalition which produced what was sometimes termed the legislative and political "consensus" of the early Johnson years. Those years, particularly 1965, were marked for the quantity and variety of legislation enacted in the health, education and welfare categories which was supported and in many instances strongly pushed by labor. From the mid-sixties on, Congress and the Administration—like the American people at large—became increasingly preoccupied with problems created by the growing U.S. involvement in the Vietnam War, inflation, racial upheaval in American cities and campus unrest. Both social and labor legislation met rising competition in the lawmaking and budgetary arenas.

Several head on confrontations between business and labor interests occurred during Mr. Johnson's Presidency. In contrast to organized labor's high batting average in the field of social legislation, its record on labor matters was mixed.

Two developments long held the limelight in the field of labor legislation. One was the proposed repeal of Section 14(b) of the Taft-Hartley Act, which permitted states to enact laws banning the union shop. Repeated attempts to repeal 14(b), commonly known as the "right-to-work" issue, generated considerable controversy both on Capitol Hill and among opposing pressure groups throughout the country. The Senate twice rebuffed repeal attempts by the Administration and organized labor, although the issue was used to provide political leverage on other legislation. In each case Southern Democrats and Republicans joined forces in successful filibusters which prevented the repeal measure from coming before the Senate.

By contrast, the other major piece of proposed labor legislation produced an important victory for the labor unions. This was a bill proposed by the Administration providing far-reaching extension of minimum wage coverage and increases in the pay floor.

Business forces and their allies emerged victorious over both the labor unions and the Administration with Congress' refusal to enact laws expanding unemployment compensation and lifting restrictions on construction site picketing by striking unions.

The period also saw Congress and the Administration faced with the recurrent problem of how to deal with work stoppages which disrupted the nation's economy. The issue arose twice during the Johnson Administration, each time in the area of transportation. Congress followed the President's lead in requiring compulsory arbitration, over the objections of labor leaders, to avert a threatened nationwide railroad walkout. A strike which grounded more than half the nation's commercial air carrier service for several weeks, on the other hand, was permitted to run its course without decisive intervention on the part of either Congress or the President.

The rail dispute, whose roots went back several years, involved prolonged negotiations and required intermittent attention in Congress. Centering on "featherbedding"— a term applied to the practice of hiring more employees than actually required for the given work—the controversy focused national attention on the dislocations and unemployment which could result from technological advances.

The difficulties in two basic areas of mass transportation stimulated renewed discussion on the Government's proper role in labor disputes of a national emergency nature. The wide impact of national strikes in essential industries, with possible injury to many nonparticipants, presented officials with a dilemma: how to protect the public's interests without interfering unduly with the processes of collective bargaining.

The expansion of mechanization and computer applications suggested that automation and other forms of scientific development would in the future present increasing challenges to policymakers of the legislative and executive branches.

Reference

For Congressional action on labor legislation in the 1945-1964 period, see *Congress and the Nation*, Vol. I, p. 563-657.

Chronology

Of Legislation

On Labor

Note: In addition to the legislation mentioned below, other proposals considered by Congress involved matters of interest to labor. These are dealt with in other chapters. For developments relating to migratory farm labor, see chapter on agriculture; for manpower training and vocational rehabilitation, see chapter on education; for guaranteed income, see chapter on welfare.

1965

Congress in 1965 produced what the American Federation of Labor-Congress of Industrial Organizations (AFL-CIO) called "the most productive Congressional session ever held." But the appraisal by the AFL-CIO, whose affiliated unions totalled approximately 13 million members, was based on Congress' actions on health, welfare, education and related measures rather than on labor legislation.

In a session notable for its high batting average on Presidential programs, Congress handed the President one of his two major setbacks on organized labor's top priority measure: a bill (HR 77) to repeal Section 14(b) of the 1947 Taft-Hartley Act. (Mr. Johnson's other major defeat was his failure to obtain enactment of "home rule" for the District of Columbia.) The bill to repeal Section 14(b), which permitted states to enact laws banning the union shop, bogged down in a Senate filibuster at the end of the session and was laid aside by a weary Congress eager for adjournment.

A second disappointment for the Administration in labor legislation was Congress' failure once more to approve a bill (HR 10518, HR 8259, others) to expand minimum wage coverage. The AFL-CIO called this "the single most important measure in our war on poverty." Congress did enact, however, a bill (HR 10238—PL 89-286) to set minimum standards of pay and fringe benefits for employees of companies working on Federal Government contracts.

An Administration bill (HR 5883—PL 89-216) which became law substituted in place of the "faithful performance" bond required of union officials by existing law a requirement that they be bonded only against loss due to fraud or dishonesty.

Among proposals left hanging at the end of the session was a union-backed bill (HR 10027) to permit "common-site" picketing by unions employed on construction jobs. The AFL-CIO was deeply disappointed by Congress' inaction on that bill and on Section 14(b) repeal, as well as on an unemployment insurance reform bill (HR 8282).

Congressional hearings were held in the autumn on administration of the nation's first peacetime compulsory arbitration law (PL 88-108), in connection with a nation-wide rail strike threatened for 1966. A Senate committee urged negotiators to resume bargaining talks.

Migratory farm labor was much discussed, but there was little new legislation on the subject in 1965. The principal topic of discussion was the decision of Secretary of Labor W. Willard Wirtz, upon the expiration of the Mexican farm labor program (PL 78) on Dec. 31, 1964, to severely limit the number of foreign workers who could be employed on U.S. farms in 1965. This was described as an effort to open more jobs to domestic farm workers and improve their wages and working conditions. The move was backed by unions seeking to organize farm workers and opposed by some growers. (*See agriculture chapter.*)

'Right to Work'

President Johnson's 1965 legislative program suffered one of its few defeats late in the session when Senators conducted a successful filibuster against a bill (HR 77) to repeal Section 14(b) of the 1947 Taft-Hartley Act. The controversial bill, which would have had the effect of outlawing state "right to work" laws, was passed by the House, but by a much narrower margin than most major 1965 Administration bills.

Under the 1947 "right to work" provision of the Taft-Hartley Act, the union shop contract was legal and permissible throughout the United States, except in those states which passed "right to work" laws forbidding the union shop. A union shop contract is one requiring employees to join a union within a specified time after being hired. Employees who refuse to do so must be dismissed. Fourteen states enacted "right to work" laws in 1947, and by 1965 there were 19 states with such laws—10 in the South, the rest in the Midwest, Rocky Mountain area and Southwest. No industrial state had a "right to work" law.

The effect of HR 77 would have been to nullify all 19 state "right to work" laws, to forbid future enactment of such laws, and thus to make the union shop permissible throughout the country. The bill did not require employers to conclude union shop agreements; it permitted union shop contracts where the union, through collective bargaining or other legal methods, was able to get the employer to agree to such a contract.

Since the 1940s the issue of "right to work" laws had been an emotional one. Labor unions bitterly resented the tag name of "right to work," saying it was a misnomer for antiunion laws. Supporters said workers should be free to join or not to join unions.

Text of Section 14(b)

Following is the text of the section of the Taft-Hartley Act which authorizes state "right-to-work" laws:

"Nothing in this Act shall be construed as authorizing the execution or application of agreements requiring membership in a labor organization as a condition of employment in any state or territory in which such execution or application is prohibited by state or territorial law."

SUMMARY OF 1965 ACTION

While committed to working for repeal of Section 14(b) in 1965, President Johnson delayed sending the proposal to Congress. An Administration spokesman said in January the President wished to see such measures as medical insurance for the aged under Social Security, his education program and the Appalachia bill well on their way to passage before Congress tackled the controversial labor issue. An AFL-CIO spokesman was quoted as saying, "The measures he wants are things we want too, and we are willing to wait."

It was believed there was a majority for repeal of Section 14(b) in the Senate but a less favorable outlook in the House. The Administration therefore engineered a marriage of convenience between certain urban and rural Democratic Congressmen. Under this arrangement, some farm state Democrats voted for HR 77 in return for subsequent votes from Northeastern Democrats for the Administration's omnibus farm bill. HR 77 was unpopular with many farm state constituents and the farm bill was unpopular with Easterners because wheat provisions foreshadowed a rise in bread prices, but Administration forces argued that Congressmen could afford to displease their constituents on one bill if this assured passage of the other. The coalition worked, as party voting was extremely tight, and the House passed HR 77 by a narrow margin and with the help of 21 Republican votes.

On the day the Senate Labor and Public Welfare Committee reported HR 77, Sen. Dirksen announced he would help organize "extended debate" designed to block passage.

On Oct. 4 Senate debate began on a motion by Majority Leader Mike Mansfield (D Mont.) to make HR 77 the Senate's pending business. The filibusterers immediately began to talk against this motion and after seven days of debate Mansfield sought to impose cloture—cut off debate—on his motion. Cloture, if adopted, would have permitted the Senate after 100 hours of debate to proceed with consideration of the bill. The cloture motion was substantially defeated Oct. 11, **45-47** (a two-thirds majority was necessary to invoke cloture). Mansfield the following day announced that the leadership was abandoning its effort to pass HR 77 in 1965. Mr. Johnson pledged renewal of the fight for 14(b) repeal in 1966. "Just as we had to come back last year to finish the unfinished battle for Medicare," Mr. Johnson wrote, "we will come back in the next session to remove this divisive provision."

LOBBYING EFFORTS

A direct, clear-cut confrontation between labor and business groups was the key feature of the extensive 1965 pressure campaign on HR 77.

The campaign for repeal of the "right to work" provision was led by the AFL-CIO national headquarters and supported actively by most of the large unions in the labor federation, particularly the industrial unions. The International Brotherhood of Teamsters, an independent union, also was active. While a large number of non-labor groups gave public endorsement to repeal of Section 14(b), all of the really hard lobbying for repeal was done by the various unions and the Johnson Administration.

Unions' Views of 1965 Session

AFL-CIO. The AFL-CIO executive council said the "highlights" of the session were enactment of: Medicare (HR 6675—PL 89-97), the Voting Rights Act (S 1564—PL 89-110), the Elementary and Secondary Education Act (HR 2362—PL 89-10), the Higher Education Act (HR 9567—PL 89-329), "a stepped-up war on poverty" (HR 8283—PL 89-253), the omnibus housing bill (HR 7984—PL 89-117), the bill establishing a Department of Housing and Urban Development (HR 6927—PL 89-174), a "new regionally based public works program" (S 1648—PL 89-136), the highway beautification bill (S 2084—PL 89-285), "a sweeping new attack on health problems" (the regional medical bill, S 596—PL 89-239; the mental health staffing measure, HR 2985—PL 89-105; and others).

The AFL-CIO also supported the repeal of the national origins immigration quota system (HR 2580—PL 89-236), the excise tax reduction (HR 8371—PL 89-44), the manpower training amendments (S 974—PL 89-15), the Older Americans Act (HR 3708—PL 89-73), the Water Quality Act (S 4—PL 89-234), foreign aid (HR 10871—PL 89-273), Appalachia aid (S 3—PL 89-4), a bill to ease bonding requirements for labor officials (HR 5883—PL 89-216), and several others. The AFL-CIO also counted as a legislative victory the defeat of the Dirksen (R Ill.) reapportionment amendment (S J Res 2, S J Res 103).

AFL-CIO Building & Construction Trades Department. (About 3.5 million members.) Considered 1965 to be one of Congress' "best years" because of enactment of the various health, welfare and education measures backed by the AFL-CIO as a whole, as well as the Building & Construction Trades Department. But was deeply disappointed because "no labor legislation passed other than the bonding bill" (HR 5883—PL 89-216). Gave its strongest support to the "right to work" repeal bill (HR 77) and the common-site picketing bill (HR 10027), neither of which passed in 1965.

American Federation of Teachers (AFL-CIO). (125,000 teachers.) Said Congress in 1965 "produced more and better educational and social legislation than any Congress in our history." The "big one" which received AFT backing was the Elementary and Secondary Education Act (HR 2362—PL 89-10). AFT also supported the Higher Education Act (HR 9567—PL 89-329) and a bill establishing the National Foundation on the Arts and Humanities (S 1483—PL 89-209).

International Brotherhood of Teamsters (Ind.). (1.8 million workers.) Said "Congress did very well by every segment of our society except labor....Labor wound up with a goose-egg." Among the measures strongly supported by the Teamsters but not receiving final Congressional approval in 1965 were: the "right to work" repeal bill (HR 77); the minimum wage bill (HR 10518); and the unemployment compensation bill (HR 8282). Major non-labor bills for which the Teamsters worked in 1965 included Medicare (HR 6675—PL 89-97) and the Elementary and Secondary Education Act (HR 2362—PL 89-10).

The campaign against repeal was conducted by a coalition of business organizations, the most active of which were the National Right to Work Committee (a citizens' organization with a strong business coloration), the Chamber of Commerce of the United States, the Associated General Contractors and the National Assn. of Manufacturers.

Union Arguments. Union spokesmen contended that "right to work" laws were largely responsible for the slow growth of unions in the South and in many of the other states with such laws. The requirement that new employees join a union, union leaders said, had the effect of strengthening unions financially by adding to dues collected; of winning to unionism through daily contact workers who were indifferent when they first came to work; and of blocking attempts by employers to "break" unions through hiring of antiunion personnel and related devices. All these advantages were absent where union shop contracts were forbidden by state laws.

Union spokesmen further argued that, in many parts of the South, "right to work" laws were only one of a battery of antilabor devices designed to keep unions weak, keep wages low and keep business taxes (for such items as unemployment insurance) low—thereby creating a "favorable business climate" in order to "pirate" industry from other areas.

Finally, unions contended that antiunion business groups often put forward "right to work" proposals in state legislatures not only for their own sake but also in order to absorb the attentions and resources of unions in a fight against the proposals, thus diverting the unions from pushing favorable welfare and tax legislation through the state legislatures. AFL-CIO President George Meany told a House hearing in May 1965, "In the last eight years alone—from the beginning of 1958 to the present time—we in the AFL-CIO have engaged in more than 40 significant battles over so-called 'right to work' laws...." He called this effort on both sides of the issue "a staggering waste of money and manpower."

Also cited by some proponents of repeal was the argument that non-union employees obtained a "free ride" at the expense of dues-paying union members. Labor Secretary W. Willard Wirtz expressed it like this to the House Special Labor Subcommittee: "The central argument is that all who receive the benefits of union representation should contribute to its support, particularly its financial support."

Opposing Views. Opponents of 14(b) repeal, led by the National Right to Work Committee, denied that state "right to work" laws were favored by business simply as antiunion devices in order to break unions or prevent their growth (as many union spokesmen charged). The Committee advanced a number of arguments in favor of "right to work" laws: that it was repugnant to American conceptions of personal freedom to require a man to join a union as a condition of earning a living if he did not wish to join; that unions in many cases were corrupt, practiced racial discrimination or were Communist dominated, and that to force an individual to join such unions, as a result of a union shop agreement, was morally wrong; that the decision on whether to permit union shop agreements should remain with the states; that the growth of the union shop would retard economic growth because of restrictive union practices.

The Committee also hit hard on the argument that increased union dues which would result from a rise in union shop agreements would be used as a political slush fund by "union bosses who are bent on dominating the nation's political and economic life." The group's newsletter said union membership in the 19 "right to work" states would automatically rise from about 1.7 million to about 2 million, an increase of over a quarter-million, if the federal "right to work" provision were repealed. "With compulsory dues averaging $60 a year per worker, the AFL-CIO income in the 19 'right to work' states will surpass $120 million. This money will be used primarily for political action," the newsletter said.

During hearings, the Seventh Day Adventists, Mennonite Church, National Assn. of Evangelicals, Plymouth Brethren, Old German Baptists and several similar groups requested special provision for persons who, for personal religious reasons, did not wish to join unions. These representations led to Senate insertion in HR 77 of the Wayne Morse (D Ore.) amendment, permitting such persons not to join unions, even where a union shop was in effect, if they paid the equivalent of dues to charity or made some similar arrangement.

HOUSE

The House Education and Labor Committee ordered HR 77 reported on a 21-10 vote in which 19 Democrats favored the bill and 2 opposed it, while 2 Republicans favored it and 8 were opposed. Besides repealing Section 14(b), HR 77 made two related changes in existing law to ensure that states could not enact "right to work" laws.

Discrimination Tie-In. Committee Chairman Adam C. Powell announced he would not ask the Rules Committee to grant a rule for floor consideration of HR 77 until the House had passed legislation strengthening federal curbs on racial discrimination by unions. Spokesmen for the AFL-CIO and the National Assn. for the Advancement of Colored People opposed Powell's position and contended that the two issues should be dealt with separately. Powell then backed away from his position.

Rules Committee Bypassed. Powell filed a resolution June 23 to bring the bill to the House floor for debate in the event the Rules Committee failed to grant it a rule. Under a new rule approved by the House in 1965, the chairman of a committee which reported a bill could bring it directly to the floor (with the Speaker's approval) if the

---

State "Right to Work" Laws

The "right to work" law is a law which prohibits labor-management agreements requiring union membership as a condition of getting or keeping a job. The state "right to work" law, in effect, outlaws the closed shop and the union shop.

As of Jan. 1, 1969, a total of 19 states had in effect "right to work" laws, or constitutional provisions, or both, of general application. Six other states had in the past enacted similar legislation but had subsequently repealed it. *(For a list of states with legislation in effect, see Congress and the Nation, Vol. I, p. 600. That list was unchanged as of Jan. 1, 1969.)*

Rules Committee had not approved a regular rule for debate within 21 days.

The Rules Committee was divided 6-9 against HR 77. Those opposed included customarily pro-Administration Democrats James W. Trimble (Ark.) and John Young (Texas), from "right to work" states. (However, they subsequently voted with the majority of the House to adopt the 21-day rule.)

The 14(b) repeal issue provided the first use of the new 21-day procedure. The test vote came on a procedural motion by Powell to move the previous question, ending debate and bringing the rule to a vote. The motion was adopted by a 248-171 roll-call vote July 26. The rule then was adopted by voice vote.

The rule allowed five hours of debate and was worded to permit only amendments which the presiding officer held germane. As a result, all amendments except one to make HR 77 effective Dec. 31, 1965, rather than the date of enactment, were ruled out of order. That amendment by William H. Ayres (R Ohio) was defeated on a 74-126 standing vote.

Bill Passed

The House July 28 passed HR 77 by a **221-203** (D 200-86; R 21-117) roll-call vote and sent it to the Senate. Prior to passage a motion by Robert P. Griffin (R Mich.) to recommit (kill) the bill was defeated by a 200-223 roll call.

Provisions. As passed by the House, HR 77:

Amended Section 8(a) (3) of the Taft-Hartley National Labor Relations Act of 1947 to declare that no state could prohibit union security arrangements permitted under federal law.

Repealed Section 14(b) of the Taft-Hartley Act which permitted states to enact laws outlawing union shop contracts.

Repealed Section 705(b) of the Labor-Management Reporting and Disclosure Act of 1959 which permitted states to outlaw union shop contracts in the building and construction industry.

Farm-Labor Coalition. To ensure House passage of HR 77, members of the Johnson Administration had sought to form a farm-labor coalition in which Northern Democrats from industrial areas would support the 1965 omnibus farm bill (HR 9811—PL 89-321) in return for support for Section 14(b) repeal from farm state Democrats.

Because the Administration was less sure of passage of HR 77 than of the farm bill, HR 77 was scheduled first. This put the pressure squarely on the Midwestern Democrats: had HR 77 been defeated because they failed to support it, passage of the farm bill would have been threatened because the Northern industrial bloc would have opposed it.

The House passed HR 77 July 28 on a 221-203 roll-call vote. It passed HR 9811 Aug. 19 by 221-172. Only three Midwestern and four Western Democrats opposed HR 77, whereas only four Republicans from the Midwest and one from the West voted for it.

Votes for passage were supplied by 21 Republicans, largely from the industrial Northeast and Midwest, and by 18 Democrats from states with "right to work" laws; 15 of these 18 votes came from Members representing Midwestern and Southern states where much opposition to 14(b) repeal existed. *(For state-by-state voting, see chart.)*

Background on Section 14(b)

The basic federal law governing labor-management relations was the National Labor Relations (Wagner) Act of 1935, as amended by the 1947 Labor-Management Relations (Taft-Hartley) Act and subsequent laws. The depression-bred Wagner Act was highly favorable to labor organizations. The Taft-Hartley Act, which was bitterly fought by labor, nullified and modified some Wagner Act provisions and, in so doing, gave rise to state "right to work" laws. *(For details on labor law prior to 1965 see Congress and the Nation, Vol. I, p. 565.)*

Among other things, the Taft-Hartley Act forbade the closed shop and the closed shop hiring hall, a union-run employment service which referred only union members to employers. The Act permitted union-shop contracts, but in Section 14(b) allowed states and territories to pass "right to work" laws forbidding them. (A closed shop agreement is one in which the employer agrees to hire only persons who are already union members before being hired; a union shop agreement is one in which the employer agrees that anyone hired must join the union within a specified period of time—usually 30 to 60 days.)

Though the 1960 Democratic party platform pledged repeal of authorization for state "right-to-work" laws, no legislation to that effect went to Congress from the Kennedy-Johnson Administration of 1961-64. The 1964 Democratic platform said: "The industrial democracy of free, private collective bargaining and the security of American trade unions must be strengthened by repealing Section 14(b)...."

The 1960 Republican platform said it supported "the right of employers and unions freely to enter into agreements providing for the union shop and other forms of union security" authorized by the 1947 Act, but it did not ask repeal of state laws forbidding the union shop. The 1964 GOP platform mentioned neither union security nor "right-to-work" laws.

During the 1964 election campaign, the AFL-CIO's Committee on Political Education (COPE) endorsed 350 House candidates, of whom 234 were elected. A COPE spokesman: "I think it is safe to say that every Congressional candidate we backed was checked out on the matter" of repeal of Section 14(b).

Following the overwhelming Democratic victory in the November 1964 national election, labor leaders made repeal of Section 14(b) their first order of business. In his January 1965 State of the Union Message, Mr. Johnson said that by changes in Taft-Hartley he hoped "to reduce conflicts that for several years have divided Americans in various states of our union."

The farm bill received 51 votes from Eastern Democrats and only two votes from Republican Easterners. Following is a breakdown of the voting on the two bills:

		East	South	Midwest	West
Democrats:	14(b)	77-1	18-78	63-3	42-4
	Farm	51-23	63-28	55-9	33-8
GOP	14(b)	16-23	0-19	4-54	1-21
	Farm	2-33	4-13	12-41	1-17

SENATE

The Senate Labor and Public Welfare Committee approved HR 77 in September with an amendment permitting a person opposed to union membership on religious grounds to be exempted by paying the equivalent of union dues into a charitable fund.

Filibuster Threat. Several Senators raised the possibility of a filibuster while HR 77 was before the Committee. Senate Minority Leader Everett McKinley Dirksen (R Ill.) told reporters in August that when the bill reached the Senate floor there would be "uninhibited discussion" which was "likely to be extended." The next day President Johnson reiterated his support for HR 77 and told reporters he "certainly" considered its passage a major goal in 1965.

Among those reported active in organizing a filibuster bloc were Sens. Carl T. Curtis (R Neb.), Paul J. Fannin (R Ariz.), Strom Thurmond (R S.C.) and John G. Tower (R Texas). Dirksen Sept. 9 announced that he would help organize "extended debate" to block HR 77 from coming to a vote. By then, according to CQ's sources, Dirksen had in his possession a list of 26 Senators who agreed to undertake speaking assignments in a filibuster against HR 77.

Floor Action. Senate Majority Leader Mike Mansfield (D Mont.) Oct. 1 moved to make HR 77 the pending business of the Senate. On Oct. 4, debate began on the Mansfield motion, and a coalition of Republicans and Southern Democrats began a filibuster against the motion which was essentially a filibuster against the bill. Mansfield said he would not hold the Senate in around-the-clock session in order to reach a vote based on "physical endurance."

Opening the filibuster, Dirksen said, "If this body repeals Section 14(b) we shall never retrieve it." He added, "In my book probably the most basic case that could be made is the fact that it (repeal) would be a rupturing of the federal-state fabric which accounts for the greatness of this country."

Paul H. Douglas (D Ill.), arguing for repeal, said "an agreement for the union shop is not perpetual; it can be revoked at any time if a majority of the workers become dissatisfied with it." He said 14(b) gave states "a hunting license to prohibit employers and employees from coming to a voluntary agreement to establish the union shop under free collective bargaining." Many of the state "right to work" acts, Douglas said, "were basically passed because of malapportioned state legislatures."

To test Senate sentiment, Mansfield announced he would make a motion Oct. 8 to table (kill) his own motion to take up the bill. He said he would vote against the tabling motion but that Senators who opposed considering HR 77 should vote for the tabling motion. He said there were "various currents" in the Senate, apart from the issue of Section 14(b), among them the question of whether there was a "more appropriate time" for considering HR 77, the question "of the relative weight to be given this issue...among many issues" of importance, and the desire of some Senators for the 1965 session to adjourn.

Mansfield's hope for a real test was nullified, however, when Dirksen told his followers to vote against the tabling motion. The motion was defeated on a 0-94 roll call Oct. 8, giving no indication of how many Senators would vote for or against repeal of 14(b).

Mansfield then petitioned to invoke cloture (shut off debate) on his motion to make HR 77 the Senate's pending business.

Senate Rejects Cloture

The Senate Oct. 11, by a **45-47** roll-call vote, rejected the cloture motion. A two-thirds majority was necessary to invoke cloture. Five absentees were paired in favor of cloture, and informed sources agreed that at least 52 Senators favored 14(b) repeal on the merits.

Five Senators from states having right-to-work laws voted for cloture. They were Democrats Ross Bass (Tenn.), Quentin M. Burdick (N.D.), Gale W. McGee (Wyo.), Frank E. Moss (Utah) and Ralph Yarborough (Texas). Thirty Senators from the 19 right-to-work states voted against cloture.

Final Action. On Oct. 12, Mansfield announced that the leadership was abandoning its effort to pass HR 77. Dirksen asked assurance that no effort would be made during the rest of the session to attach HR 77 to another bill as a rider. Mansfield replied that as far as he was concerned, "no such attempt" would be made.

That day Mansfield moved that the Senate adjourn until Oct. 13. This move—adjourning instead of recessing as was usual with a bill under consideration—killed the Majority Leader's pending motion to take up HR 77. The adjournment motion was adopted by voice vote. *(For concise summary of all cloture votes, see chapter on civil rights, p. 343.)*

Minimum Wage

Congress in 1965 for a second consecutive year failed to enact Johnson Administration proposals to extend federal minimum wage and overtime provisions to some workers not already covered and to increase the overtime pay rate. Mr. Johnson in a May message asked extension of minimum wage and overtime coverage to an additional 4.6 million workers and an increase in certain overtime pay from the existing time-and-a-half to doubletime.

A bill (HR 10518) providing even broader minimum wage provisions (but no provision for increase of the overtime rate) was reported by the House Education and Labor Committee, but floor action was deferred in the absence of the strong Administration support believed needed to ensure passage.

President's Proposals. President Johnson submitted legislation to extend provisions of the 1938 Fair Labor Standards Act (FLSA) to employees in construction, laundering and cleaning establishments, hotels and motels, restaurants, hospitals and nursing homes, logging operations, taxicab companies, agricultural processing and other industries.

The President proposed that workers in these areas receive the same minimum wage and overtime protection—a minimum of $1.25 an hour with overtime pay after 40 hours a week—as the 29.6 million workers already subject to the FLSA. Mr. Johnson also recommended payment of double wages for all worked hours over 48 per week, effective for one year after enactment. Then three annual steps would reduce the cutoff to 45 hours. Time-and-a-half pay would apply, as it had since 1938, to hours worked in excess of 40 up to the point at which the proposed new doubletime provision took effect. *(See box.)*

Mr. Johnson said that "Congress should consider carefully the effects of higher minimum wage rates...." While he made no specific recommendations to raise the existing $1.25 hourly minimum wage, the President said that "as average wages rise, the minimum wage level should be increased periodically. The question is not whether the minimum wage should be increased but when and by how much."

The Administration bill extended protection in two ways: (1) by removing exemptions from the FLSA which applied to employees in certain industries and (2) by amending the definition of an "enterprise engaged in commerce or the production of goods for commerce" and subject to the FLSA to include all such enterprises which have employees engaged in these activities and which have an annual gross volume of sales of at least $250,000. The measure did not alter the existing exclusion of so-called "mom and pop" establishments which were operated by their owners or members of their immediate families.

The Department of Labor said almost half of the nation's wage and salary workers were outside the Fair Labor Standards Act. A Department fact sheet said the proposed premium overtime pay rate was "certain to lead to a reduction in...overtime and the creation of additional job opportunities."

The Administration proposals were contained in bills introduced in the Senate (S 1986) by Sen. Pat McNamara (D Mich.) and in the House (HR 8259) by Rep. Adam C. Powell (D N.Y.). George Meany, president of the AFL-CIO, told House hearings there were "no more important legislative proposals before this Congress."

Opposing Views. Spokesmen for business organizations expressed doubts that the legislation would accomplish its stated objectives. Dr. Richard S. Landry of the Chamber of Commerce of the United States said the job-increase effect of the doubletime premium would be "slight at best. But the cost-increase and stimulus-to-automate effects could be considerable." Landry said that with each extension of the minimum wage to additional job classifications, thousands of people were denied job opportunities. This was due, he said, to "the fact that the minimum wage rates together with the costs of fringe benefits exceed the economic value of the workers with lowest productivity."

Action. Though the House Education and Labor Committee reported a bill (HR 10518), the Democratic majority on the Committee agreed to postpone action until 1966. Committee Chairman Adam C. Powell (D N.Y.) said the Democrats had decided to withhold action because chances were slim that such controversial legislation could be passed late in the session without dismembering amendments. Powell said the Democratic leadership told him Oct. 6 that only about 100 of the 292 House Democrats favored 1965 action on HR 10518.

Government Service

Congress passed without controversy a bill (HR 10238—PL 89-286) to set minimum standards of pay and fringe benefits for employees of companies under contract to perform services for the Federal Government.

The bill covered contracts of $2,500 or more to furnish laundry, drycleaning, custodial, janitorial, guardian, food and other such services to the Government. Contractors

---

Minimum Wage Background

The first successful federal attempt to regulate working hours and establish a "floor" for wages was the 1938 Fair Labor Standards Act (FLSA). This law, which provided the basis for all subsequent legislation, set a minimum hourly wage for covered workers of 25 cents, to be raised to 40 cents in 1945. It also made 40 hours the normal workweek for most covered workers and required employers to pay time-and-a-half for overtime.

Congress raised the minimum to 75 cents in 1945 and to $1 in 1955. However, the majority of American workers did not receive protection, and efforts to amend the Act to bring more workers under its protection failed through 1960.

In 1961 Congress concluded a bitter struggle by passing landmark legislation raising the hourly minimum wage and, for the first time, extending the categories of coverage. The Fair Labor Standards Amendments of 1961 (PL 87-30) extended the minimum wage and (with some exceptions) the overtime provisions to an estimated 3.6 million additional workers. The Act also raised the minimum wage for workers already covered from $1 an hour to an eventual $1.25 an hour. The newly covered workers were to reach the $1.25 hourly minimum and the 40-hour standard work week in three steps over four years.

President Johnson sent Congress draft legislation in 1964 to extend minimum wage and overtime pay protection to more workers and to authorize a double-time rate for overtime in industries where it was determined that such a rate would increase employment without boosting costs excessively. Hearings were held on both bills in the House, but neither measure was reported.

---

and subcontractors were required by PL 89-286 to pay wages and fringe benefits at least equal to those prevailing in their locality for similar work. In no case could they pay wages below those applicable to private employees under the federal minimum wage law (Fair Labor Standards Act).

Earlier legislation had covered employees of companies performing contract construction work and of companies supplying materials to the Federal Government under contract. *(See Congress and the Nation, Vol. I, p. 634.)*

The Johnson Administration endorsed HR 10238, facilitating its passage. The Budget Bureau in 1964 had opposed a similar bill (HR 11522). One change in 1965, which substantially reduced opposition from various sources, was removal of 1964 language that would have required contractors on service jobs to pay their employees wages and fringe benefits based on federal rates of pay and fringe benefits for similar work. This language had met strong opposition on grounds it established an entirely new concept of requiring private employers to match federal wages. HR 10238 required service contractors merely to pay prevailing area wages and fringe benefits.

Another factor aiding in passage was the allaying of the fears of some construction unions that the legislation might foster the performance of painting and alterations under service contracts rather than construction contracts. HR 10238 specifically excluded from its coverage contracts for painting, construction and alteration work.

The House passed the bill by voice vote on Sept. 20 without floor amendments. Sponsor James G. O'Hara (D Mich.) said that in the Education and Labor Committee the bill "was enthusiastically supported by both sides." The Senate passed the bill Oct. 1 by voice vote, approving minor committee amendments with which the House concurred. The President signed the law Oct. 22, saying "many of the employees who will benefit are among the lowest paid workers in our society."

Provisions. As signed, PL 89-286:

Applied to contracts over $2,500 for furnishing services to the Federal Government.

Specified that wages for employees working under such contracts be no lower than the prevailing local rate, and in no case lower than the federal minimum wage.

Provided that fringe benefits for such employees be no less than the prevailing local fringe benefits, and that work be performed in safe and sanitary surroundings.

Authorized the Secretary of Labor to determine what were prevailing local wages and fringe benefits.

Provided that certain fringe benefits should be excluded in computing overtime pay.

Required that provisions satisfying minimum wage, fringe benefit and working conditions requirements specified above be included in service contracts and bid specifications.

Permitted withholding from contractors of amounts necessary to pay workers if the act were violated, plus cancellation of the contract, exclusion of the contractor from further federal contracts for three years, and suits by the Federal Government to obtain from the contractor any back benefits owed.

Covered guards, watchmen, and any persons working at a recognized trade or craft or other skilled mechanical craft, or at unskilled labor, in all 50 states, the District of Columbia, Puerto Rico, the Virgin Islands, Outer Continental Shelf lands, Samoa, Guam, and Wake Island, Eniwetok, Kwajalein and Johnston Islands.

Exempted from the bill contracts for construction, alteration and/or repair, including painting and decorating of public buildings and public works; any work done under the Walsh-Healey Public Contracts Act; any contract subject to the Communications Act of 1934; any contract for carriage of freight or personnel where published tariff rates were in effect; direct services; any contract for public utility services; and any contract with the Post Office Department for operation of postal contract stations.

Union Official Bonding

Congress in 1965 passed an Administration-backed bill (HR 5883—PL 89-216) amending provisions of the 1959 Labor-Management Reporting and Disclosure Act (Landrum-Griffin Act) which required union officials to be bonded for faithful performance of duties in the handling of union money and property.

HR 5883 substituted a requirement that officials be bonded only against loss through fraud or dishonesty on their part. Sponsors said "faithful performance" bonding had led to higher bonding rates due to uncertainties as to losses the bonding companies would be liable for under existing law. They said substitution of a more familiar type of bonding covering only acts of fraud or dishonesty would give union members substantially the same protection at about 25 percent lower cost.

Critics, led by Rep. Robert P. Griffin (R Mich.), a sponsor of the 1959 legislation, said the change would reduce union members' protection by limiting bonding protection to fraud and dishonesty. Carelessness and negligence on the part of union officials would go uncovered. Administration spokesmen and others contended that there was legal doubt as to whether the costlier "faithful performance" bonds covered such acts. They said fraud and dishonesty presented the major dangers.

The new law made bonding requirements for union officials handling money and property the same as those adopted in 1962 for persons handling union welfare and pension plan funds. (*See Congress and the Nation, Vol. I, p. 617.*) The House passed HR 5883 in May; the Senate did so in September. Both actions were by voice vote.

Provisions. As signed into law Sept. 29, HR 5883:

Required union officials handling union funds and property to obtain bonding that would protect the union against loss due to acts of fraud or dishonesty on the part of the official, directly or through connivance with others. Eliminated the requirement that the official be bonded for "faithful discharge of his duties." (The bill did not change existing provisions of the Labor-Management Reporting and Disclosure Act of 1959 which set the amount of the bond for each official at 10 percent of the funds handled by him in the year preceding the one for which he was being bonded, up to a maximum of $500,000 on the amount of the bond.)

Authorized the Secretary of Labor to exempt unions from the requirement that they obtain their bonding only from surety companies on a Treasury list of approved companies, if, in the Secretary's opinion, the union had made other bonding arrangements which would provide the protection sought by the bonding requirement; but made clear that this provision was not intended to sanction self-insurance on the part of unions.

Required any surety companies issuing the bonds required above, or similar bonds under the Welfare and Pension Plans Disclosure Act, to file annual reports with the Secretary of Labor describing premiums, claims paid, expenses and related information; and provided that such reports would be made available for public inspection and examination.

Communist Union Officials

In a related development, the Supreme Court June 7, 1965, struck down the section of the 1959 Landrum-Griffin Act which made it illegal for a Communist to serve as a union officer (*U.S. v. Brown*). The Court ruled that the provision "is void as a bill of attainder." Chief Justice Earl Warren, for the majority, said the Constitution barred bills of attainder as "trial by legislature." Bills of attainder were enacted by the British Parliament in the 16th to 18th centuries against persons threatening to overthrow the government.

In dissent, Justices Byron R. White, Tom C. Clark, John Marshall Harlan and Potter Stewart said the law was not a bill of attainder because it involved regulation instead of punishment.

Railroad Dispute

Congressional hearings were held on the problem of "featherbedding" in railroad jobs, which in 1965 was once more threatening a possible nationwide railroad strike for the following year. A 1963 law which required compulsory arbitration of a dispute over eliminating most firemen and helpers on railroads and prohibiting strikes or lockouts in the meantime was to expire March 31, 1966. A strike could result then if a solution had not been reached.

The Senate Commerce Committee held 18 days of hearings in August and September on the administration of PL 88-108, the nation's first peacetime compulsory arbitration law. The Brotherhood of Locomotive Firemen and Engineers (BLF&E) had charged that the law, enacted in 1963, was not being administered properly. Following the hearings, the Committee adopted a resolution urging the carriers and the operators' unions to return to the bargaining table.

The key issue remained the future of the locomotive firemen on diesel or electric engines. Under terms of the 1963 arbitration award, virtually all of these positions were eliminated on freight and yard engines, and by October 1965 almost 18,000 firemen had lost their jobs.

Meanwhile, a joint carriers-union board to study administration of the arbitration award (National Joint Board) convened in Washington, and the Supreme Court was asked to rule on the question of whether state safety laws requiring a fireman in the locomotive cab were preempted by PL 88-108.

The Court ruled in 1966 that PL 88-108 did not supersede state "full-crew" laws requiring specified train crew sizes for safety purposes. The decision left such laws in force in seven states. *(See box.)*

Background. The "featherbedding" dispute between the carriers and the unions, serious since the late 1950s, appeared headed for a nationwide rail strike in 1963. The issue was the presence of firemen or helpers in the locomotive cab; the carriers argued that these employees were unnecessary while the unions responded that for the purposes of safety, the firemen were indispensable.

Congress met the strike threat by enacting PL 88-108. Under its provisions, Arbitration Board No. 282 was established, consisting of union, carrier and neutral representatives. This board made its award Nov. 26, 1963, the union members dissenting, and held that almost all (up to 90 percent) of the approximately 35,000 firemen should be eliminated by stated procedures. The law prohibited strikes or lockouts for disputes over provisions of the award. It covered all railroads except Southern Railway.

A dispute over so-called "secondary issues" raised the specter of a nationwide strike in 1964. The dispute involved such issues as paid holidays, expenses when away from home, a wage raise and the size of yard crews. In a dramatic nationwide television broadcast April 22, 1964, President Johnson disclosed that a settlement had been reached between the carriers and the operators' unions on these issues. The settlement was considered a personal triumph for the President, who noted in his announcement that a strike would have idled six million workers and cut the gross national product by 13 percent while driving up prices.

Another strike threat in 1964 was averted when Mr. Johnson invoked the 60-day cooling off period provisions

Supreme Court Test

The Supreme Court was asked during the 1965 efforts at preventing a threatened railroad strike to rule on a key aspect of PL 88-108, the 1963 compulsory railroad arbitration law. The question was whether state legislation requiring certain crew sizes—the so-called "full-crew laws"—were preempted by PL 88-108 and were therefore inapplicable.

The case, *Brotherhood of Locomotive Engineers v. Chicago, Rock Island and Pacific Railroad Co.,* involved the conflict between PL 88-108 and the Arkansas full-crew law which required a fireman on every train and a crew of six men on every train, with some exceptions. The Arkansas laws were adopted in 1907 and 1913. The case arose when six railroads sued to enjoin state prosecuting attorneys from continuing to enforce the Arkansas statutes. The BLE intervened, a three-judge federal district court ruled that the state law was in "substantial conflict" with PL 88-108 and therefore had to yield to the federal law, and the BLE appealed the case to the Court. The Brotherhood argued in its brief that the state law was aimed at safety and thus did not conflict with PL 88-108, which was aimed at economic problems, and further that the arbitration award under PL 88-108 merely established minimum crew make-ups and did not preclude states from increasing crew sizes. The state of Wisconsin, with a similar law, filed a brief in support of the BLE.

1966 Decision. The Supreme Court Jan. 31, 1966, by a 7-1 vote held that PL 88-108 and Arbitration Award No. 282 did not supersede state "full-crew" laws which required specified train crew sizes for safety purposes. Such laws were in effect in seven states (Ark., Ind., Mass., N.Y., Ohio, Wash. and Wis.).

Justice William O. Douglas dissented and Justice Abe Fortas, whose former law firm represented parties in the case, did not participate. Justice Hugo L. Black wrote the Court's opinion for the case, which consolidated two suits, *BLE v. Chicago, Rock Island and Pacific Railroad Co.* and *Hardin v. Chicago, Rock Island and Pacific Railroad Co.*

Justice Black wrote that Congress sought in enacting PL 88-108 to deal specifically with a labor issue and did not intend to extend the law's impact into the area of state safety laws. Justice Douglas said Congress did not intend PL 88-108 to be effective in some states but not in others—those having "full-crew" laws.

of the Railway Labor Act. This dispute involved the carriers and the nonoperators' unions, who represented about 300,000 clerks, telegraphers, signalmen, maintenance workers and dining-car employees. The settlement was based on the carriers' acceptance of the principle of attrition in reducing work forces and the unions' acceptance of management's right to transfer workers between areas. Final settlement of the outstanding issues was arrived at on Feb. 7, 1965.

In the continuing dispute over firemen and crew makeup, however, the BLF&E and the Brotherhood of Locomotive Engineers (BLE) pressed the issue vigorously.

Private Pension Plans

Tightening of tax law provisions for private pension plans was recommended in January 1965 by a committee appointed in 1962 by President Kennedy. Changes proposed by the President's Committee on Corporate Pension Funds and Other Private Retirement and Welfare Programs required fuller funding of private pension plans and minimum standards giving employees pension rights even though they left a company (known as "vesting").

Secretary of Labor W. Willard Wirtz headed the Committee, which included the Secretaries of Treasury and Health, Education and Welfare, the chairmen of the Federal Reserve Board, Council of Economic Advisers and Securities and Exchange Commission, and the director of the Budget Bureau.

No legislation on the subject was sent to Congress, and the Ways and Means Committee, with jurisdiction over tax matters, took no action. The report to the President was widely criticized in the business community.

According to the report, private pension plans covered about 25 million workers, or half those employed in private nonfarm enterprises, and by 1980 were expected to cover 60 percent. The report said plans currently were paying almost $2,750,000,000 annually to some 2.5 million retired workers.

Under existing tax laws, employers could take tax deductions for payments into pension funds and the income earned through investments by the fund was not taxed until it was distributed as benefits to employees. The President's Committee recommended that the law require larger payments into the funds to meet commitments promised to workers. It also proposed that, to qualify for tax deductions, plans must provide a minimum amount of vesting for employees.

Pensions for the Self-Employed. A report issued in June by the Subcommittee on Employment and Retirement Incomes of the Special Senate Committee on Aging recommended amendment of the 1962 Self-Employed Individuals Tax Retirement Act (PL 87-792). *(Congress and the Nation, Vol. I, p. 1324.)* The report said testimony at March 1965 hearings indicated that only 15,000 persons were covered by the Act, compared to 7 million self-employed who could be covered. "The least progress in providing private pension coverage," the report said, "has been made in businesses with the fewest employees, most of which are owned and managed" by self-employed persons.

The 1962 Act gave self-employed persons a tax deduction of 50 percent of contributions made to their own retirement plans. Contributions were limited to the lesser of 10 percent of earned income or $2,500. The 1965 subcommittee report recommended 100 percent tax deductions and removal of the contribution limit, so long as the employer gave comparable retirement benefits to his employees. These changes would encourage more employers to set up retirement systems, the report said. They were incorporated in a bill (HR 10) introduced by Rep. Eugene J. Keogh (D N.Y.) and endorsed by the American Bar and Medical Assns. Keogh had sponsored the 1962 law.

They were themselves battling for representation dominance in the industry. By October 1965, almost 18,000 firemen had been discharged under terms of the arbitration award. The methods by which they were discharged and the particular employees discharged were the subjects of the Senate Commerce Committee hearings. *(For further background, see Congress and the Nation, Vol. I, p. 553, 618, 620.)*

Hearings. Alan S. Boyd, Under Secretary of Commerce for Transportation, testified that between 1947 and 1963 railroad employment dropped almost 50 percent, for a net loss of 672,000 jobs. Under the arbitration award, he said, the number of locomotive firemen and helpers had been halved in little more than a year. He suggested, among other things, that the narrow jurisdictions of the various unions inhibited flexibility in moving displaced workers to new jobs within the transportation industry.

H. E. Gilbert, president of the BLF&E, said there had been a sharp rise in railroad accidents since the firemen were eliminated. This was challenged by railroad management spokesmen. Ralph T. Seward, chairman of the arbitration board, testified that in regards to safety, "the evidence convinced us that the need for a fireman was very rare, but it did not convince us that such a need was nonexistent." J. E. Wolfe, chief negotiator for the carriers, urged extension of PL 88-108 and maintenance of the status quo under the arbitration award for two years. Of 17,250 firemen jobs eliminated in freight and yard service, Wolfe said, 8,675 were eliminated by natural attrition or promotion of firemen to engineers. Another 4,465 were abolished when firemen chose severance pay averaging $5,600 rather than comparable jobs while another 950 firemen accepted comparable jobs and the remaining 3,160 firemen—18.3 percent of the total—were released with severance pay since they had less than two years' seniority.

Following the hearings, the Committee adopted a resolution urging the carriers and unions to return to collective bargaining to resolve their disputes. It noted a Committee "dislike for legislating solutions to labor-management disputes" and called attention to "the obvious dangers of repeated Congressional intervention in this field." The resolution said the public interest would be served if the carriers and the BLF&E and the BLE returned to the bargaining table, and it called on the National Mediation Board and the Secretary of Labor to assist in bringing the parties together.

Common-Site Picketing

An Administration-endorsed bill (HR 10027) to permit "common-site" picketing by unions employed on construction jobs was reported late in the session by the House Education and Labor Committee. At adjournment the bill was awaiting clearance for floor action by the House Rules Committee.

The legislation, which the AFL-CIO Building and Construction Trades Department called its top goal in the 89th Congress, was opposed by the Associated General Contractors of America and other major employer groups. The bill was forced to compete for union legislative priority with the controversial 14(b) repeal measure. It marked another in a series of labor attempts to overturn a 1951

Supreme Court ruling. In *NLRB v. Denver Building and Construction Trades Council*, the Court ruled that a union could not throw a picket line around a construction site in a strike against one employer if the intent and effect were to keep out workers employed at the site by other subcontractors or contractors. The ruling held that such a shutdown would constitute an illegal secondary boycott under the Taft-Hartley Act of 1947. Reversal of the ruling's impact, through legislation, was endorsed by the Eisenhower, Kennedy and Johnson Administrations.

The unions argued that where a number of employers were working together on a single construction job, and were linked by contractual or similar arrangements, the companies were helping one another and should be considered as a single employer for purposes of the secondary boycott prohibitions of the Taft-Hartley Act.

Building industry spokesmen countered that the bill would permit the smallest, most irresponsible union to shut down a whole construction job. They said that despite the link of subcontractual relationships, one subcontractor on a job often had little influence over the labor policies of the others, and should not be made to suffer for the others' sins. The Chamber of Commerce of the U.S. and others also said the bill would make construction stoppages at military and missile bases easier and thus could endanger the national security.

The Taft-Hartley Act outlawed secondary boycotts by labor unions. The Act made it an unfair labor practice for a union to get workers to strike against an employer not directly involved in the primary dispute, in order to pressure him to stop doing business with the company engaged in the primary dispute with the union.

The House Education and Labor Committee in reporting HR 10027 in September said it removed "present unfair restrictions...on the right to strike and picket peacefully." In minority views, Reps. Robert P. Griffin (R Mich.), Dave Martin (R Neb.), Glenn Andrews (R Ala.) and Edward J. Gurney (R Fla.) opposed the bill and said it was expressly designed to permit undesirable secondary boycotts and the closing down of whole jobs at construction sites.

1966

A "guns versus butter" debate in 1966, as Congress reflected growing public concern over inflation and rising United States involvement in Vietnam, produced several legislative setbacks for organized labor. These were partly offset by one major triumph—a far-reaching new minimum wage law.

The AFL-CIO called the 89th Congress as a whole "the most outstanding Congress in our history," despite rejection of several labor priorities, including a renewed attempt to repeal Section 14(b) of the Taft-Hartley Act.

In its appraisal the labor organization agreed with President Johnson, who predicted that historians would rate the 89th Congress "the best Congress in the history of this nation" on its two-year record in 1965 and 1966.

At the same time, the defeat or revision of some major labor union proposals in 1966 contributed to a U.S. Chamber of Commerce spokesman's assessment of the session as "a fairly good legislative session." And the National

Small Business Assn. called 1966 "a year of great legislative accomplishment for the small business community."

In an important victory for the Johnson Administration and for organized labor, Congress in 1966 enacted legislation (HR 13712—PL 89-601) which the AFL-CIO told *Congressional Quarterly* it considered "the most important and best minimum wage law that has ever been passed." It raised the $1.25 an hour nonfarm wage floor by stages to $1.60 and extended minimum wage coverage to an additional 9.1 million employees, including certain agricultural workers for the first time.

For the second time in two years a Senate filibuster blocked Administration and union efforts to push through a bill (HR 77) to repeal Section 14(b) of the Taft-Hartley Act which permitted states to ban the union shop. The Senate twice rejected motions to invoke cloture (cut off debate).

Both houses passed a bill (HR 15119) based on a major Johnson Administration proposal to revise the federal-state unemployment compensation system. House and Senate conferees were unable to resolve differences between respective versions of the bill, however, and the legislation died with the 89th Congress in a major defeat for organized labor.

Another union setback occurred when the long-sought bill (HR 10027) to permit construction union "common site" picketing was pigeonholed by House Education and Labor Committee Chairman Adam C. Powell (D N.Y.). He said in May he would block action on HR 10027 until the Senate passed the fair employment practices bill (HR 10065), as well as the picketing measure. HR 10065 did not pass the Senate.

Congress refrained from any decisive action in an airline strike which lasted 42 days and grounded 60 percent of the nation's commercial air traffic. An Administration-backed bill (S 2974) to strengthen the U.S. Employment Service cleared the Senate but died in the House.

Minimum Wage

In an important victory for the Administration and for organized labor, Congress in 1966 enacted legislation (HR 13712—PL 89-601) substantially broadening federal minimum wage and overtime pay protection and increasing the minimum wage.

As signed into law, HR 13712 increased the existing $1.25 an hour nonfarm federal wage floor by stages to $1.60, and extended minimum wage coverage to an estimated 9.1 million additional employees, *(see box p. 612)*, including, for the first time, certain agricultural workers. The bill also extended overtime protection to an estimated 6 million additional employees and established a minimum wage of $1 an hour for newly covered farm workers, to be increased in steps to $1.30.

Under the bill's timetable, effective dates for the full minimum were to vary according to whether a worker was covered by the existing wage law. Those covered under the existing statute were to receive an increase to $1.40 on Feb. 1, 1967, and to the full $1.60 on Feb. 1, 1968. Newly covered workers, both in agricultural and nonagricultural occupations, were to receive a minimum of $1 on Feb. 1, 1967, and $.15 annual increases culminating in the $1.30 agricultural wage floor on Feb. 1, 1969, and in the $1.60 nonfarm wage requirement on Feb. 1, 1971.

On balance, HR 13712 provided the most far-reaching revision of the federal minimum wage concept since its inception as part of the 1938 Fair Labor Standards Act. The AFL-CIO regarded the wage bill as its only major legislative victory of the session.

President Johnson said in signing the bill that the new wage law would "bring a larger piece of this country's prosperity, and a greater share of personal dignity to millions of our workers...."

Coverage. The new coverage provided by HR 13712 brought to an estimated 41.4 million the number of employees to whom the minimum wage applied. The categories of employment to which the wage floor was extended were as follows: certain retail and service firms; laundering and dry-cleaning establishments; clothing or fabric repair shops; transit and taxicab systems; hotels and motels; restaurants and food service establishments; agricultural processing firms; logging enterprises; certain agricultural workers (approximately 1 percent of all workers on U.S. farms); construction firms; hospitals and related institutions; certain employees of the Federal Government; federal service contract employees; and nonprofessional employees of elementary and secondary schools and of colleges and universities.

Enterprises covered by the law were broadened to include, by Feb. 1, 1969, most businesses having annual gross sales of $250,000 or more. Existing law had exempted most businesses with annual sales below $1 million.

Some workers under the new law were to receive the minimum wage regardless of their employer's volume of sales or business. These included workers in laundries, dry-cleaning establishments, clothing or fabric repair shops, construction firms, hospitals and related institutions, schools and colleges, and the covered employees of the Federal Government and those employed under federal contract. A family-run business was exempted.

Facts and Figures, 1966 Minimum Wage Bill

Following are the major features of the 1966 minimum wage legislation together with the bill's expected cost to employers:

Changes in minimum wage coverage:

1) Total number of workers covered by the Fair Labor Standards Act prior to the 1966 amendments: 32.3 million.
2) After the 1966 amendments: 41.4 million.

Thus, the amendments extended minimum wage protection to 9.1 million workers not previously covered. (At the time of the bill's passage, coverage was estimated at 8.1 million. The higher figure was attributable to a recomputation of the labor force at the end of 1966.)

Breakdown of new coverage:

- 2 million employees of hospitals and nursing homes.
- 1.3 million workers in educational institutions (public and private)
- 1.7 million in retail trade
- 600,000 in construction
- 500,000 in laundries
- 500,000 in restaurants
- 300,000 in hotels
- 400,000 in agriculture
- 700,000 federal nonsupervisory employees
- 1.1 million other employees

Minimum Wage Increase:

1) For workers covered prior to enactment of 1966 legislation: from the existing level of $1.25 an hour to $1.40 an hour on Feb. 1, 1967, and to $1.60 on Feb. 1, 1968.
2) For newly covered nonfarm workers: a minimum of $1 an hour on Feb. 1, 1967, to increase in annual $.15 increments to a level of $1.60 on Feb. 1, 1971.
3) For newly covered agricultural workers: a $1 minimum on Feb. 1, 1967, to increase in steps to $1.30 by Feb. 1, 1969.

Most of the 41.4 million workers covered by the revised Act were already earning more than the new 1967 minimums; however, an estimated 4.7 million employees were earning less (estimates were not available for the number of covered workers earning less than the final phase, $1.60 floor.)

Included in the 4.7 million figure were:

1) 3.7 million previously covered workers whose wage would be increased from $1.25 to $1.40.
2) 838,000 newly covered employees whose wage would be raised to $1.

1967 Cost of Increase:

1) The payroll for the 3.7 million workers who were to go from $1.25 to $1.40 under the 1966 legislation was expected to increase by $800 million.
2) The payroll for the 838,000 newly covered workers eligible for the $1 minimum wage was expected to increase by $281 million.

Total number of establishments covered as of Feb. 1, 1967: 1.9 million, divided as follows—
- Agriculture, forestry and fisheries—42,800
- Mining—26,500
- Contract construction—319,000
- Manufacturing—257,000
- Transportation, communications, utilities—126,100
- Wholesale trade—279,900
- Retail trade—222,700
- Finance, insurance, real estate—181,700
- Services and government—419,000

SOURCE: Wage and Hour Division, U.S. Department of Labor.

Overtime pay provisions applied, with certain exceptions, to the same categories of employees covered by the minimum wage.

Administration-Labor Involvement. Enactment of HR 13712 came after months of bitter wrangling between Congressional backers of the legislation, the Administration, and the AFL-CIO. The bill which resulted was the product of a compromise.

President Johnson, wary of any inflationary push on wages, had reportedly opposed any increase above $1.40 an hour until late 1968. AFL-CIO President George Meany had publicly insisted on an increase to $1.40 by Sept. 1, 1966, and a further increase to $1.60 a year later. Congressional leaders were generally split between the two positions. After numerous bargaining sessions, an accord was reached March 10. Under the compromise, the $1.40 minimum was to go into effect in February 1967, followed by an increase to $1.60 in February 1968. President Johnson officially announced his support for the new wage and wage timetable in a May 23 address before the International Labor Press Assn.

The Administration and organized labor lobbied intensively for the agreed-upon measure, with their Congressional supporters repulsing repeated Republican-led attempts to dilute it. Although the House voted a year's delay—from 1968 to 1969—in the effective date of the full wage floor, Administration-labor lobbying paid off in Senate restoration of the original timetable and its acceptance in the final bill by the House-Senate conferees and by the House itself. *(For background on minimum wage legislation and events leading to the 1966 action, see p. 606.)*

Provisions

As signed into law, HR 13712 (PL 89-601), the Fair Labor Standards Amendments of 1966, made the following major revisions in the Fair Labor Standards Act of 1938 (FLSA):

MINIMUM WAGE COVERAGE. Extended federal minimum wage protection to an estimated 9.1 million non-professional employees not covered by minimum wage requirements under existing law. Made the new coverage effective in two steps: Feb. 1, 1967, and Feb. 1, 1969.

1967 Coverage. Provided expanded coverage in three different ways:

(1) Covered additional employees by amending the definition of an "enterprise engaged in commerce or the production of goods for commerce" and subject to the FLSA to cover businesses which had lower annual sales or business than those covered under existing law. (Under the existing statute, most businesses with an annual gross sales or business volume of less than $1 million were exempt from the minimum wage requirement. HR 13712 reduced this $1 million sales volume cutoff to $500,000 on Feb. 1, 1967. Certain categories of employment which had lower sales volume cutoffs under existing law were not affected by the provision, nor were the previously exempted categories whose exemptions were not specifically removed by the bill.)

(2) Covered additional employees by further amending the commerce definition to cover certain enterprises specifically exempt from coverage under existing law. Coverage, depending upon the applicability of the sales volume test *(see above)*, was extended to the following types of enterprises: certain retail and service firms; transit and taxicab systems; hotels and motels; restaurants and food service establishments; agricultural processing firms; logging enterprises; and farm workers (those employed by farmers who used more than 500 man-days of agricultural labor in any calendar quarter of the preceding year—roughly equivalent to the use of seven fulltime hands). Coverage of the following additional categories was provided, regardless of sales volume: laundries, dry-cleaning establishments, clothing or fabric repair shops, construction firms, hospitals and related institutions, and nonprofessional employees of colleges and similar higher education schools (e.g., janitors, cafeteria employees, etc., but not professors or academic administrative personnel).

(3) Provided specific new coverage for certain employees of the Federal Government, federal service contract employees, and nonprofessional employees of elementary and secondary schools.

1969 Coverage. Further lowered the sales volume test *(see above)* to provide that businesses or enterprises covered by the law would be subject to minimum wage requirements if they had gross sales or business of $250,000 or more annually. (Certain enterprises, such as laundries and hospitals—*see above*—continued to be covered regardless of sales volume.)

'Mom and Pop' Establishments. Stipulated that strictly family-run enterprises were to remain exempt from coverage regardless of the volume of sales or other criteria.

Exemptions from Agricultural Wage Floor. Exempted from the agricultural wage floor workers otherwise covered who: (1) were members of the agricultural employer's immediate family; (2) were employed as hand-harvest workers on a piece-rate basis; (3) had been employed for less than 13 weeks during the preceding year in agriculture; (4) commuted daily from their permanent residence to the farm on which they were employed; or (5) were principally engaged in production of livestock on a range.

Also exempted from the wage floor were children of migrant workers who were: (1) 16 years of age or under and employed as hand-harvest laborers; (2) paid on a piece-rate basis; (3) employed on the same farm as their parents; and (4) paid the same piece rate as employees over 16 were paid on the same farm.

Child Labor Prohibition. Prohibited employment of children below the age of 16 in an agricultural occupation determined by the Secretary of Labor to be "particularly hazardous" (unless such children were employed by their parents on their parents' own farm).

Handicapped Labor. Required that handicapped persons in sheltered workshops be paid wages commensurate with those paid nonhandicapped workers in the vicinity for essentially the same type and quality of work. Stipulated, however, that, effective Jan. 1, 1967, no such worker was to receive less than half the prevailing minimum wage for newly covered employees.

Authorized the Secretary of Labor to establish special rates of compensation for handicapped workers whose physical or mental handicap was so severe as to make their productive capacity inconsequential.

Also directed the Secretary to study and report to Congress by July 1, 1967, on the feasibility of raising wage payments in sheltered workshops.

Age Discrimination. Directed the Secretary of Labor to submit to Congress by Jan. 1, 1967, legislative recommendations for eliminating employment discrimination based on old age.

WAGE RATE. Increased the federal minimum wage from the existing $1.25 an hour to the level specified in the following table:

Employees	Hourly Rate	Effective Date		
Presently Covered (32,300,000)	$1.40	Feb.	1,	1967
	1.60	Feb.	1,	1968
Newly Covered:				
Nonfarm (8,000,000)	1.00	Feb.	1,	1967
	1.15	Feb.	1,	1968
	1.30	Feb.	1,	1969
	1.45	Feb.	1,	1970
	1.60	Feb.	1,	1971
Agriculture (400,000)	1.00	Feb.	1,	1967
	1.15	Feb.	1,	1968
	1.30	Feb.	1,	1969
Federal employees (700,000)	1.40	Feb.	1,	1967
	1.60	Feb.	1,	1968
Federal Service Contract (number undetermined)	1.40	Feb.	1,	1967
	1.60	Feb.	1,	1968

Tipped Employees. Provided that the minimum wage rates would be reduced for tipped employees (those customarily receiving $20 or more a month in tips) by an amount representing all or a portion of tips received. Specified that in no case could an employer credit tips (in order to reduce the actual wages he had to pay) in an amount that was larger than 50 percent of the prevailing minimum wage. (The restriction meant that an employer had to pay at least 50 percent of the prevailing minimum wage regardless of how much an employee earned in tips.)

Permitted an employer to estimate the amount of tips received by a covered employee. Provided safeguards for the employee, however, by (1) authorizing him to demonstrate to the satisfaction of the Secretary of Labor that the amount of tips received was less than stated by his employer and (2) authorizing the Secretary to direct the employer to adjust the wage by the amount of the difference.

OVERTIME. Extended overtime protection of the FLSA to the same categories of employment provided new minimum wage coverage, with the exception of retail auto, truck, trailer and farm implement salesmen; mechanics; individuals principally engaged in selling or servicing farm implements; operating employees of transit systems whose annual volume of sales or business was less than $1 million; farm workers; employees of restaurants, food service establishments, hotels, motels, bowling alleys and sugar and syrup processing concerns. Also provided new overtime coverage for gasoline service station employees (already covered by minimum wage) and reduced from two to one the 14-week overtime exemption periods authorized each year for certain canneries and other seasonal industries.

Made coverage effective Feb. 1, 1967, or Feb. 1, 1969, concurrent with the effective dates of the expanded minimum wage protection. (Overtime coverage of gas station employees, not keyed to the bill's minimum wage coverage, also was made effective Feb. 1, 1967.)

Hours Limitation. Stipulated that newly covered employees were to receive compensation at not less than one and one-half times the regular rate for hours of employment in excess of 44 hours a week as of Feb. 1, 1967; in excess of 42 hours as of Feb. 1, 1968; and 40 hours as of Feb. 1, 1969.

Overtime Study. Directed the Secretary of Labor to undertake a study of present overtime practices in industries under the FLSA, including the extent to which overtime work impeded the creation of new job opportunities, and report his findings and recommendations to Congress by July 1, 1967.

HOUSE

The House passed HR 13712 by a 303-93 roll-call vote May 26 and sent it to the Senate. Passage was never in doubt, but Republican Members staged a vigorous effort to dilute the measure—with respect both to coverage and to the effective date of the $1.60 wage floor.

Just before passage, the House rejected by a 167-232 roll-call a motion by Rep. Dave Martin (R Neb.) to delete the sections pertaining to farm coverage and to include new language giving canneries and other seasonal industries broader exemptions from the 40-hour standard work week.

Backers of the Administration-labor compromise bill suffered a setback, however, when the House accepted, by a 205-194 roll call, an amendment to hold the wage floor for presently covered workers at $1.40 for an additional year—delaying the $1.60 wage increase for such workers until Feb. 1, 1969.

As drafted by its sponsor, Thomas G. Morris (D N.M.), the amendment held the wage floor at $1.40 for an additional two years (until Feb. 1, 1970) rather than one. The House accepted the lesser postponement after Committee Chairman Adam C. Powell (D N.Y.) agreed with Morris on a one-year extension.

Some House Members reportedly saw Powell's move as an attempt to prevent a longer delay in the $1.60 wage increase; others interpreted it as an open affront to AFL-CIO President George Meany, who had been critical of Powell's refusal to seek floor action on a bill (HR 10027) sought by labor to extend picketing rights of construction unions. (*For picketing controversy, see p. 610, 618.*)

As passed after floor amendment, HR 13712 increased the hourly minimum wage for nonfarm workers by stages to $1.60 and extended minimum wage coverage to an estimated 9.1 million additional employees. It extended overtime protection to the same categories of employment granted new minimum wage coverage, with certain exceptions.

SENATE

The Senate Aug. 26, by a 57-17 roll-call vote, passed HR 13712, amended to make the $1.60 wage floor effective Feb. 1, 1968, and sent the measure to conference. As in the House, debate centered on an attempt by Republicans and Southern Democrats to reduce the bill's coverage and postpone the effective date of the $1.60 minimum wage. Administration supporters defeated most major amendments.

Sen. Paul J. Fannin (R Ariz.), sponsor of an amendment to restore the House timetable, argued that too rapid a transition to the higher wage "would cause severe hardship on the very people it purports to protect—the unskilled, the uneducated, and especially our youth.... The result of a minimum wage going too far too fast, will be to further increase the national problems in our welfare programs." Senate Labor Subcommittee Chairman Ralph W. Yarborough (D Texas), the bill's floor manager, retorted that even the $1.60 wage "barely provides a poverty level of living today....Dare we wait to 1969 to bring it up to that level?" Fannin's amendment was rejected by a 40-42 roll call.

The GOP-Southern coalition moved to delete coverage beginning in 1969 of retail and service firms with an annual volume of gross sales of less than $500,000. The amendment, sponsored by Senate Minority Leader Everett McKinley Dirksen (R Ill.), was rejected on a 41-41 tie vote. Then, the coalition's strategists redrafted the proposal to eliminate 1969 coverage of firms with less than $350,000 business, and the revised amendment carried on a roll call of 41-38. Its adoption meant exemption of about 185,000 workers from the bill's provisions.

The GOP-Southern contingent attempted to delete the bill's extension of coverage to approximately 400,000 agricultural workers, but was defeated by a 37-51 vote.

As passed by the Senate, HR 13712 contained essentially the same provisions as the House-passed bill, with exceptions which were resolved in conference.

FINAL ACTION

The conference report was adopted by the House Sept. 7, by a 260-89 roll-call vote, and by the Senate Sept. 14, by a 55-38 vote. The actions sent the measure to the White House.

The House, by a **163-183** (ND 11-147; SD 51-18; R 101-18) key roll-call vote, rejected a motion by William H. Ayres (R Ohio) to recommit the measure to conference with instructions to House conferees to insist on delaying the effective date of the $1.60 minimum a year beyond the 1968 date set by the Senate.

'Right to Work'

A renewed attempt by President Johnson in 1966 to obtain repeal of Section 14(b) of the 1947 Taft-Hartley Act was defeated by a Senate filibuster. As in 1965 "uninhibited discussion," as Minority Leader Everett McKinley Dirksen (R Ill.) once called it, prevented the House-passed bill (HR 77) from becoming the Senate's pending business. Two attempts to impose cloture (limit debate) on the leadership's motion that the Senate consider HR 77 failed by large margins to receive the necessary two-thirds vote. A cloture attempt in 1965 also had fallen short. *(For background on the issue and 1965 action, see p. 602.)*

The bill repealed the Taft-Hartley section permitting states to pass "right to work" laws banning the union shop. The emotional issue pitted the Johnson Administration and organized labor against a coalition of business groups. Dirksen led the filibuster against consideration of HR 77. The Senate floor struggle occupied eight days in 1965 and 15 days in 1966. Results showed that even with a 2 to 1 Democratic margin in the Senate and support from the White House, there were not enough votes to overcome a determined filibuster by Republicans and Southern Democrats.

During the 15 days that Majority Leader Mike Mansfield's (D Mont.) motion to consider HR 77 was under debate, relatively little time was devoted to speaking on the issue. As is the practice in a filibuster, the bulk of the speeches were made by opponents of the legislation.

Dirksen said the issue was not right-to-work laws but rather "the sovereign authority of the 50 states to legislate in this field if they so desire." Sen. Karl E. Mundt (R S.D.) said: "So long as there is even one right-to-work state in the United States, it will tend to serve as a warning to labor leaders who are inclined to engage in excesses...that if they go too far and become too tough or steal too much or sell us out...it is possible for any of the other states to write right-to-work legislation to prevent that kind of influence...."

Sen. Wayne Morse (D Ore.) said: "The repeal of 14(b) will apply the federal law governing union security agreements, which authorizes the union shop, to all 50 states, instead of to 31 of them." In the 19 right-to-work states, he said, "union-organized workers will have the legal right to ask for a union shop if they want to, to negotiate with their employer on the subject, and sign such a contract if the employer agrees to it....Their freedom will be greater, not less." And Sen. Joseph S. Clark (D Pa.) said, "The phrase 'right-to-work' has, I am certain, been responsible for 99.44 percent of the opposition generated by the anti-union lobbies....Repeal of Section 14(b) will not mean the establishment of compulsory unionism."

The cloture motions, each requiring 66 affirmative votes, were defeated Feb. 8 by 51-48 and Feb. 10 by 50-49. After the second defeat the Democratic leaders abandoned efforts to bring repeal of Section 14(b) to a Senate vote in the 89th Congress.

Reaction. In a speech interpreted as labor's reaction to the Administration's failure on HR 77 and its controversial wage-price guidelines, AFL-CIO President George Meany March 22 announced that organized labor would give its support only to those Members of Congress who voted in sympathy with labor's interest. Meany told an AFL-CIO conference that labor did not need the Democratic party. "I'm sure it is the other way around," he said. He charged that the Democratic party did not "deliver" on labor legislation and that the Republican party appeared to be under the control of "financial interests."

President Johnson, in a speech two months later to the International Labor Press Assn., said he "did my best" to get HR 77 passed but Dirksen defeated it. "I talked to 61 Senators that I thought we could influence...and most of them were ready to support the measure," Mr. Johnson said. "We will have to try again, and try again we will."

Most observers believed that opposition from constituents of many on-the-fence Senators doomed the bill. The two-week strike of subway and bus workers that tied up transportation in New York City in January also seemed to stiffen the opposition to HR 77. Mayor John V. Lindsay (R), who as a Representative had voted for HR 77 in 1965, said Jan. 10: "Many view this strike as a death warrant for the repeal of Section 14(b)...which authorizes antiunion right-to-work laws." Secretary of Labor W. Willard Wirtz Jan. 26 said the strike had damaged chances for HR 77. He said the walkout "left a very bad taste in most people's mouths about organized labor."

Related Development. The President in October vetoed a "right-to-work" bill enacted by the Guam legislature. The bill had previously been vetoed by Guam Gov. Manuel Guerro and then repassed over his veto. Guam's organic act empowered the President to veto legislative actions within 90 days without possibility of being overridden.

Unemployment Compensation

Major Administration proposals for a broad overhaul of the 31-year-old federal-state unemployment compensation system again failed of enactment by Congress in 1966. Changes had been sought by Presidents Kennedy and Johnson since 1961. *(See box.)*

These changes came the closest to enactment in 1966. Both the Senate and the House passed a bill (HR 15119) but with numerous differences. The legislation died at the end of the 89th Congress when Senate-House conferees were unable to resolve the differences.

Johnson Plan for Jobless Benefits

President Johnson asked a broad revision of the unemployment compensation system in 1965 and 1966. His program was embodied in HR 8282 introduced in the House and S 1991 in the Senate.

The Administration legislation included minimum federal standards for the level and duration of state unemployment benefit payments (a minimum benefit of 50 percent of a worker's wages, up to a limit of 50 percent of the average statewide wage, for a period of 26 weeks), and an extension of coverage to 4.7 million additional workers. It also included an additional benefit period of up to 26 weeks for workers who had exhausted their entitlements under existing state law, federal grants to cover two-thirds of unusually high payments of unemployment benefits in any one year, an increase in the taxable wage base for the federal unemployment tax from the current level of $3,000 to $5,600 in 1967 and to $6,600 in 1971, a .15-percent increase in the tax (to 3.25 percent) and other changes.

A highly controversial feature of the original Administration bill was a proposal to reduce the amount of unemployment tax payable by firms in the state to a level reflecting the actual cost of the state's program. The existing statute required that the amount of rate reduction be computed specifically on the basis of a firm's individual record of employment stability. This provision, known as "experience ratings," meant that if the firm had a low level of unemployment and consequently had few workers leaving and applying for benefits, it received a sizable reduction in its tax rate. The Administration bill eliminated this requirement, leaving states free to drop the tax to a uniform level for all firms in the state based on the average state cost of the entire program. Elimination of the existing "experience rating" section was strongly opposed by firms whose employment stability records allowed them tax reductions. *(For "experience rating," see Congress and the Nation, Vol. I, p. 1292.)*

The key obstacle to agreement by the conferees was a controversial Administration proposal for minimum federal standards for unemployment compensation, both with respect to the amount of state benefit payments and to the duration of the payments.

The House Ways and Means Committee, after considering the plan for more than a year, refused to approve the federal standards; it reported HR 15119, providing modest revisions in the system. The House passed the committee bill unamended, by a 374-10 roll-call vote. The Senate Finance Committee restored the federal standards and the Senate, after a bruising floor battle, approved the standards with some revisions by a 53-31 vote.

However, efforts by Senate supporters to get the bill to conference were ignored by the House for more than two months. Conferees finally met twice shortly before adjournment but were unable to agree, primarily because neither would retreat from its position on federal standards.

The conference stalemate over standards prevented enactment of several Administration proposals approved in modified form in both the House and Senate bills. These included provisions for expanded coverage, a new program of extended unemployment benefits for workers who had exhausted their original entitlements (modified by both the House and Senate to become effective only during periods of national or state recession) and a higher tax on employers to defray the resulting costs. In a minor consolation to the Administration, however, the stalemate also killed an Administration-opposed provision granting states the right of judicial review of decisions by the Secretary of Labor holding state unemployment compensation laws, or the operation of such laws, not in conformance with federal requirements. The judicial review section originated in the House Ways and Means Committee and was sustained by both House and Senate.

Congress' refusal to enact the standards proposal was a major defeat for organized labor and an important victory for business interests, both of which conducted major lobbying efforts on the legislation. AFL-CIO pressures were focused mainly on the White House, while the business pressure centered on the House Ways and Means Committee. Adamant positions by both groups were reflected in the refusal of House and Senate conferees to agree on a compromise bill. The U.S. Chamber of Commerce, one of the leading business pressure groups, reportedly said it would settle for nothing less than complete rejection of the standards, while the AFL-CIO reportedly urged the President to veto any bill not containing standards. *(For background, see Congress and the Nation, Vol. I, p. 1289.)*

Airline Strike

For the second time in three years, Congress in 1966 was faced with the prospect of passing legislation to deal with a transportation strike. Although Congress in 1963 acted swiftly to block a threatened nationwide railroad strike, in 1966 an airline strike that continued for 42 days during the summer did not prompt decisive Congressional action.

The strike was called July 8 by the International Assn. of Machinists (IAM) against five major U.S. air carriers: Eastern Airlines, National Airlines, Northwest Airlines, Trans World Airlines and United Airlines. About 35,400 IAM members—engaged in mechanic, ramp and store, flight kitchen, dining service, plant protection and related classifications—walked off their jobs. The strike grounded 60 percent of the nation's commercial air traffic.

For three days beginning Aug. 2, the Senate debated the politically sensitive issue of whether to act at all and if so, whether Congress or the President should order the machinists back to their jobs. It finally passed, by a 54-33 roll call, a compromise bill (S J Res 186) ordering the strikers back to work immediately for a short period of time and giving the President the authority to extend the back-to-work order if necessary. The House had the bill under consideration, but was spared the burden of voting on it when the machinists ratified a strike settlement on Aug. 19.

S J Res 186 was supported by the airlines, but bitterly opposed by organized labor. The Administration did not declare a national emergency, and repeatedly refused to take a position on the bill. Administration officials worked behind the scenes to bring about a negotiated settlement.

The final contract, which included a cost-of-living escalator clause, was attacked by the Administration as inflationary and as being clearly in violation of its 3.2 percent wage-price guidelines. *(See box, p. 618.)*

As the strike wore on, pressures developed for enactment of new legislation to deal with emergency strikes. The President had proposed such a measure in his State of the Union Message. However, the Administration did not submit a draft emergency antistrike bill in 1966, nor did Congress take independent action on the matter.

Other 1966 Airline Disputes. Presidential creation of Emergency Boards, under the provision of the Railway Labor Act, averted two other threatened airline strikes in 1966. President Johnson July 27 appointed an Emergency Board in a dispute between American Airlines and the Transport Workers Union, thus putting into effect the 60-day cooling-off period of the Railway Labor Act. He took similar action on Sept. 30 in a dispute between Pan American Airways and the TWU. Both disputes were settled by collective bargaining. *(For background on National Emergency Strike Laws, see Congress and the Nation, Vol. I, p. 626.)*

Employment Service

An Administration-backed bill (S 2974) to update and strengthen the U.S. Employment Service (USES) was passed by the Senate with numerous amendments in 1966 but died in a House committee. Parts of the bill were strongly opposed by private employment agencies who argued that expansion of USES functions would infringe upon their area of responsibility. Some opposition was based on federal-state relationships.

The purpose of S 2974 was to enable the federal-state employment service to play a more active and effective role in connection with the new training and anti-poverty programs enacted in recent years. Although it had been intended that the 2,000 local offices of USES would be used to implement much recent legislation in the manpower field, they were bypassed to a large extent, partly because of their inadequate personnel and partly

---

Meany Position

During House committee hearings on a Senate-passed bill (S J Res 186) ordering striking airline workers back to their jobs, AFL-CIO President George Meany called a press conference after being refused permission to testify.

Meany said Members of Congress would "regret for the rest of their lives" passage of antistrike legislation. "There is much more involved here than 35,000 machinists and five airlines," Meany said. "If Congress votes to end this legal non-emergency strike by a federal law forcing the men back to work, it will deliver a crippling blow to the whole labor movement, and, more than that, to the liberty of every American who works for wages." He said antistrike legislation would "take us down the road to socialism." Meany said that "without the promise of Congressional help, the airlines will settle and settle quick."

Meany's comments came Aug. 10. Five days later, on Aug. 15, Assistant Labor Secretary James J. Reynolds emerged from a marathon bargaining session at 6:22 a.m. and said "we've got a settlement." The agreement was ratified by union members Aug. 19.

---

because their employment policy tended to be passive—waiting for the jobless to come to them. The new bill gave USES clear instructions to search out the disadvantaged and to serve the employed as well as the unemployed; it required new professional standards for its personnel. The bill also stressed the need for better exchange of job information over large geographical areas and set up interstate centers for information and for placement and relocation help.

As amended by the Senate, S 2974 provided funds from general revenues for USES in addition to the usual amount (about $250 million annually) from the Unemployment Trust Fund.

The Administration's original bill (HR 13362) was largely based on recommendations by a labor-industry task force assigned by Labor Secretary W. Willard Wirtz. The task force reported Dec. 29, 1965, that the USES should expand its role by actively reaching out to the jobless and offering them professional job counseling of high standards. It also suggested that the USES begin helping employed persons find better jobs. The task force recommendation for financing of the expanded activities from general revenues was not incorporated in the Administration bill.

The Senate-passed bill permitted a cutoff of funds in the federal-state program, subject to court review, if the state program violated the state's federally approved plan. (The USES, while federally financed, was a state-run operation.) The bill also authorized a loan program to help pay relocation costs of unemployed persons who found jobs outside their communities.

The legislation received joint hearings in March by the Select Subcommittee on Labor of the House Education and Labor Committee and the Subcommittee on Employment and Manpower of the Senate Labor and Public Welfare Committee. The Senate passed S 2974 by voice vote late in June.

Wage Guidelines Exceeded

The contract settlement which ended the strike by the International Assn. of Machinists against five major airlines substantially exceeded the Administration's wage guideposts. *(See figures, below.)*

The wage guideposts were a central part of the controversy surrounding the long strike. The guideposts generally sought to limit annual wage increases (including fringe benefits) to the national trend of increase in output per man-hour. The Administration contended that the nationwide productivity increase was 3.2 percent and that larger wage settlements would have inflationary consequences. The guideposts also included noninflationary standards for establishing prices. Although the guideposts were voluntary, the Administration exerted pressure in a number of wage and pricing controversies—including the airline strike—to keep contract settlements and price changes within the standards. *(For background on guideposts, see p. 000.)*

The ability of the airlines to pay for a contract that was substantially in excess of the guideposts never was contested. However, airlines spokesmen cited the guideposts in arguing that initial union demands were inflationary. Union spokesmen, by contrast, said that productivity increases among the airlines were far in excess of the national average, and that wage increases in the airline industry should be tied to the productivity of that industry.

Three strike settlements were formally proposed. The first was proposed June 5 by an Emergency Board headed by Sen. Wayne Morse (D Ore.), and never was subjected to a vote of the union membership. The second was developed through joint negotiations after President Johnson had intervened personally in the strike. It was announced by the President July 29 and rejected by the IAM membership July 31. The third settlement—also developed through collective bargaining—was announced Aug. 15 and ratified by the union Aug. 19.

The figures below show estimates of the cost to the airlines of the three settlements, and the annual percentage increases that they represented. The figures were given to Congressional Quarterly by **William J. Curtin,** a Washington lawyer who was chief negotiator for the five airlines during the strike. Labor Department officials told CQ that department policy prevented the release of official Government estimates of the cost and percentage increases of the three settlements. These officials, however, said that the Department's estimates were very close to those provided by Curtin. The first settlement proposed a 42-month contract, whereas the second and third settlements provided for 36-month contracts.

Settlement Proposal	Cost to Airlines	Increase for Employees [1]
	(3 or 3½ years)	*(annual)*
June 5	$76 million	3.6%
July 29	$73.4 million	4.7%
Aug. 15	$85.8 million	5.0%

[1] The size of the increase for employees includes the higher wages and other benefits included in the package.

Rep. Elmer J. Holland (D Pa.) Oct. 4, in a speech on the House floor, said his Labor subcommittee had not yet reported a manpower services bill and the legislation probably would not be acted on before the end of the session. He criticized the "kind of pressure campaign the private agencies have mounted this year," citing in particular the objection to "recruitment" as a function of USES.

Contending that the Wagner-Peyser Act had set up the USES to aid all jobseekers, Holland quoted a 1964 report of the Senate Appropriations Committee which said: "Members of the Committee have recently been the recipients of a barrage of communications attacking the public employment system. It is repeatedly asserted that the placement of employed workers should be the prerogative of the fee-charging agencies and that the public employment service should be arbitrarily restricted to serving unemployed workers. Congress in framing the Wagner-Peyser Act in 1933 stipulated that a placement service be provided for all persons 'who are legally qualified to engage in gainful occupations.' Accordingly, the employment service must operate on the basis that its services are to be available to all. It cannot deny service to a certain portion of the public...."

Common-Site Picketing

Organized labor suffered a defeat when Congress took no action in the 89th Congress on a bill (HR 10027) to ease restrictions on construction site picketing. Enactment of the bill was a prime objective of union officials. The measure was reported in the House in 1965; however, it was removed from the House calendar on May 4, 1966, because of opposition from Education and Labor Committee Chairman Adam C. Powell (D N.Y.).

House floor consideration was blocked by two factors. Powell told reporters he would block action until the Senate had passed the bill and also had passed the fair employment practices bill (HR 10065). The latter was passed by the House in April but did not pass the Senate. In addition, many freshman Democrats in the House, facing a stiff fight for re-election, did not want to go on record in support of the labor-backed "common-site" picketing bill only to see it die in the Senate. Like Powell, they wanted the Senate to act first. The Senate held no hearings on the subject during the 89th Congress. *(For background, see p. 610.)*

1967

A reduced emphasis on legislation directly affecting labor became noticeable during the first session of the 90th Congress. With national attention centered on the war in Vietnam, domestic economy matters and city problems, President Johnson sent few labor requests to Congress. Those which he sent, however, received favorable action from the Administration viewpoint.

The most notable development in the labor area in 1967 was the first nationwide railroad strike in more than 20 years. The President's request for legislation providing for compulsory settlement if the parties failed to agree in 90 days was enacted by Congress. The labor unions opposed the position adopted by the President and Congress.

Congress enacted a bill requested by Mr. Johnson which barred employment discrimination on the grounds of age. It covered employees between the ages of 40 and 65.

Legislation to permit "common-site" picketing by construction unions once more failed to reach the House floor after receiving committee approval.

Rail Strike

A two-day nationwide railroad strike ended July 17, as Congress acceded to President Johnson's request for legislation to settle the dispute. The bill (S J Res 81—PL 90-54) provided for a compulsory settlement of the controversy if no voluntary agreement had been reached within 90 days.

Congressional action had been required twice before in 1967 to delay the strike of six railroad shopcraft unions against most of the nation's major lines. The parties had been unable to agree on terms of a new contract and the President had twice asked Congress to delay the strike deadline in the hope that the parties could resolve their differences.

The first Congressional action, on April 11, delayed the strike, scheduled for April 13, for 20 days until May 3 (S J Res 65—PL 90-10). The second move occurred May 1 when Congress set a new deadline of June 19 on the talks, with the understanding President Johnson would offer a plan to settle the controversy "within a few days" (H J Res 543—PL 90-13). On May 4 the President outlined his plan in a message to Congress and the measure was introduced in Congress by Sen. Wayne Morse (D Ore.) and Rep. Harley O. Staggers (D W.Va.).

The plan proposed a 90-day status-quo period during which a mediation board would seek to bring about an agreement. As a last resort, the board would prepare a settlement based on April 22 recommendations made by a special mediation panel headed by retired Judge Charles Fahy. The final solution would take effect on the 91st day if no agreement was reached between the parties.

The President, the Secretary of the Department of Transportation, the Secretary of Defense and Members of Congress had said a railroad strike was intolerable because it would disrupt the nation's economy and interfere with shipments of defense material headed for Vietnam.

Organized labor and its supporters argued that the plan was compulsory arbitration, something alien to American democracy. The unions had rejected the recommendations of the Fahy panel and a previous board. Their offer to move all defense items during a strike was rejected by the Government.

The Senate on June 7, by a 70-15 vote, passed S J Res 81, the Presidential plan to end the controversy. The House on June 15 deleted provisions for an imposed settlement and approved, by voice vote, only the 90-day mediation section with its extension of the no-strike period.

After the House vote the unions announced they would postpone their walkout pending a Senate-House conference to resolve the differences in the two bills. However, when the conferees still had not reached agreement on July 13, union representatives withdrew their no-strike pledge and the walkout began July 16.

Chronology of 1967 Rail Dispute

Jan. 13—National Mediation Board terminates efforts to achieve settlement of dispute between major carriers and six shopcraft unions.

Jan. 28—President creates emergency panel under Railway Labor Act to study dispute.

March 10—Panel reports, recommendations rejected by unions. Strike set for April 13.

April 10—President asks Congress to extend cooling-off period strike deadline for 20 days to May 3.

April 11—Congress approves 20-day extension.

April 12—President signs bill (PL 90-10), appoints Fahy panel to recommend settlement.

April 22—Fahy panel reports, its proposals rejected by unions and carriers.

April 28—President requests further 45-day extension, says he will offer legislation to settle dispute.

May 1—Congress approves 47-day extension, to June 19.

May 2—President signs bill (PL 90-13).

May 4—President proposes legislation to settle dispute. Plan calls for creation of board to mediate and, if necessary, impose settlement.

June 7—Senate approves President's proposal.

June 15—House approves amended version of President's plan, drops binding settlement provision. Unions say they will postpone walkout pending Senate-House conference on bill.

July 13—Conferees still deadlocked, unions say they will withdraw no-strike pledge at midnight, July 15.

July 16—Strike begins.

July 17—Senate and House approve Senate version of President's plan. President signs bill (PL 90-54).

July 18—President names Morse board to mediate dispute and impose settlement if necessary.

Sept. 15—Board recommends settlement.

Oct. 15—Board's recommendations become effective.

The conferees reported the bill in disagreement July 17, and the same day both chambers gave final approval to the Senate version of S J Res 81 providing for an imposed settlement. Senate action came on a **68-21** rollcall; the House acted on a **244-148** roll call.

The President signed S J Res 81 July 17 (PL 90-54) and the following day he appointed a five-man board headed by Sen. Wayne Morse (D Ore.) to mediate the dispute and impose a settlement if necessary.

Efforts to achieve a voluntary settlement failed, and the Morse board's recommendations went into effect Oct. 15. The railroads opposed the terms of the settlement, but a union official described them as "what could reasonably be expected under the restrictions imposed by the special legislation."

The panel recommended wage increases for members of six shopcraft unions of 11 percent over a two-year contract and an additional increment of 20 cents an hour for skilled workers, to narrow the gap between the skilled rail hands and comparable workers in other industries. Presi-

Permanent Legislation

Debate on the 1967 rail strike bills was marked by increasing Congressional resentment at being called upon, for the third time in four years, to take emergency action in collective bargaining disputes. Many Members complained that President Johnson had failed to propose permanent anti-strike legislation as he said he intended in his 1966 State of the Union Message. The request was not repeated in the 1967 message.

Senate Majority Leader Mike Mansfield (D Mont.) was quoted June 20 as saying the President would welcome action by Congress to write permanent legislation dealing with emergency strikes. "He has endeavored to find a formula," Mansfield said of the President, "but so far has not been able to achieve much. He would not be adverse to the labor committees (of both chambers) starting consideration of proposals they think applicable."

Many bills were introduced, but only one received any action. That was a bill (S 176), sponsored by Sen. George A. Smathers (D Fla.), to establish a United States Court of Labor-Management Relations with jurisdiction over strikes "that adversely affect the public interest of the Nation to a substantial degree." The Senate Judiciary Subcommittee on Improvements in Judicial Machinery held hearings in October on S 176, but took no further action.

---

dent Johnson endorsed the decision as "one of the finest products" of any Presidential panel. Although the recommendation was unanimous, Frederick R. Kappel, former board chairman of the American Telephone & Telegraph Co. and a panel member, criticized the terms. He said he was "very dissatisfied," adding that the final terms were close to meeting the union demands and were inflationary.

The unions had sought a 7-percent general pay increase plus an additional 15-cent-per-hour "wage compression" increase for skilled men, effective Jan. 1, 1967, and a 5-percent general increase and a further 15 cents for the skilled men, both as of Jan. 1, 1968.

The railroads involved in the dispute included most of the major lines in the country, accounting for more than 95 percent of the total railroad mileage in the United States. The unions were the International Assn. of Machinists and Aerospace Workers; the International Brotherhood of Boiler Makers, Iron Ship Builders, Blacksmiths, Forgers & Helpers; the Sheet Metal Workers' International Assn.; the International Brotherhood of Electrical Workers; the Brotherhood of Railway Carmen of America; and the International Brotherhood of Firemen & Oilers. The unions represented approximately 137,000 shopworkers, mostly journeymen mechanics, their helpers and apprentices, powerhouse workers and railway shop laborers.

Age Discrimination

In response to President Johnson's call for legislation to widen job opportunities for older citizens, Congress in 1967 enacted a bill (S 830—PL 90-202), the Age Discrimination Act of 1967, which barred discrimination against

workers or potential workers between the ages of 40 and 65 because of age.

The major change in the bill as requested by the Administration was a reduction from 45 to 40 years in the lower age limit in the definition of older workers. The investigation and enforcement provisions of the bill were similar to those of the Fair Labor Standards Act.

The House passed a bill of its own (HR 13054) by a roll-call vote of 344-13, then substituted its provisions for those of the bill (S 830), an essentially similar bill passed earlier by the Senate. The Senate subsequently accepted the House version of S 830, with a minor amendment accepted by the House by voice vote.

PROVISIONS. As enacted PL 90-202:

Prohibited employers, employment agencies and labor organizations from engaging in discriminatory practices on the basis of age against any worker or potential worker between 40 and 65 years old. Employers and labor unions covered by the bill were those employing or having as members more than 50 persons before June 30, 1968, or more than 25 persons after that date.

Barred employers, employment agencies and labor unions from indicating in advertisements a preference based on age.

Authorized the Secretary of Labor to carry on an education program to reduce the barriers to employment for older workers. Directed the Secretary to make recommendations to Congress, six months after enactment, regarding adjustments of the age limits provided in the bill and to make an annual report thereafter.

Authorized an individual, as well as the Secretary, to bring court action against violators if the Secretary failed,

Railway Labor Act

Congressional intervention in the threatened nationwide strike of train shopworkers marked the third time in recent years that Congress had to step in after the machinery of the Railway Labor Act had run its course and failed to produce a settlement.

In 1963, a railroad dispute over the elimination of certain jobs required Congress to enact a special compulsory arbitration law (PL 88-108). It was the first time that compulsory arbitration was imposed by Congress in peacetime in a major labor dispute.

In 1966, Congress was in the process of ordering striking machinists, members of one union that was also involved in the 1967 railway conflict, back to work in a dispute between the organization and five major airlines, when the parties reached a settlement ending a strike that lasted 42 days.

The Railway Labor Act of 1926 is one of two general laws that deal with the strikes that represent a potential national emergency. The other is the Taft-Hartley Act of 1947 which is not applicable to industries that are covered by the Railway Act. By 1967 the Railway Labor Act had been used well over 100 times in disputes since the end of World War II. *(For background on the two laws, see Congress and the Nation, Vol. I, p. 626.)*

Provisions of 3 Laws

Congress acted three times in response to President Johnson's requests for legislation to deal with the 1967 railroad strike by six shopcraft unions.

FIRST STRIKE DELAY. Congress cleared a bill (S J Res 65—PL 90-10) prohibiting until May 3 the scheduled walkout. This delayed the strike for 20 days. President Johnson April 10 requested the emergency legislation to forestall "the threat of a crippling and paralyzing nationwide railroad strike." He said studies indicated such a strike would do "incalculable" damage to the nation by snarling shipments for the war in Vietnam. The vote was nearly unanimous in both houses.

Provisions. As signed into law (PL 90-10) April 12, S J Res 65:

Extended for an additional 20 days, from April 13 until May 3, 1967, the 60-day "cooling off" period of the Railway Labor Act which prohibited a strike or change in work rules in the current labor dispute between six shopcraft unions and the railroad carriers, represented by the National Railway Labor Conference. (The bill extended the law only for the current dispute.)

SECOND STRIKE DELAY. Congress May 1 passed a second bill (H J Res 543—PL 90-13) asked by the President which postponed the work stoppage for 47 days. The President assured key Congressmen he would offer legislation to settle the controversy "within a few days." The House passed H J Res 543 by a 302-56 roll-call vote and the Senate later in the day passed the House measure by a 72-2 roll-call vote.

Provisions. As signed into law (PL 90-13) May 2 H J Res 543:

Extended the railroad strike deadline for 47 days, from May 3 to June 19, by amending the legislation passed three weeks before (PL 90-10).

SETTLEMENT. Congress ended the strike by approving a Presidential plan imposing a settlement if the parties had not agreed by the end of a 90-day mediation period. Mr. Johnson had made the plan public May 4. He called it "a procedure to complete collective bargaining, not to replace it." He also indicated the search for general strike legislation would continue. The President signed the measure (S J Res 81—PL 90-54) two hours after passage.

Provisions. As signed into law (PL 90-54) July 17, S J Res 81:

Authorized the President to create a Special Board to mediate the rail dispute for the first 30 days of a 90-day period from enactment of the bill.

If the parties did not reach agreement in the first 30 days, directed the Board to hold hearings on the proposals made April 22 by the special mediation panel headed by retired Judge Charles Fahy.

Ordered the Board to make recommendations based on the April 22 report if no accord were reached by the 60th day, and to submit them to the President and Congress.

If the parties had not reached agreement by the 91st day, directed that the Board's terms take effect. They were to remain in effect until the parties settled their dispute or until Jan. 1, 1969, at the latest. (The Board's settlement terms could be enforced by order or injunction of federal courts in the District of Columbia, under terms of the bill.)

Permitted either party to seek from the Board clarification of any disagreement on terms.

Barred either party, pending a settlement, from changing existing conditions except by mutual agreement.

---

within a specified period of time, to bring voluntary compliance through conciliation.

Excluded from coverage situations where age was a "bona fide" qualification for the job, where differentiation was based on factors other than age or where hiring an older worker would violate the terms of a "bona fide" employee benefit plan. Specified that older workers could be discharged or disciplined for "good cause."

Authorized appropriations of not more than $3 million annually.

"Common-Site" Picketing

For the second year in a row, legislation to permit "common-site" picketing by construction unions failed to reach the House floor after receiving committee approval. Pushed in Congress since 1965 by organized labor elements, the legislation failed in both 1966 and 1967 partly because of reluctance of many House members to go on record for the controversial measure only to see it die in

the Senate. A House committee reported the bill (HR 100) in May. The Rules Committee, acting on the request of Democratic leaders, voted in October to delay consideration until after the Senate acted. The Senate did not consider the bill in 1967. *(For background, see p. 610.)*

1968

Congress enacted no significant labor legislation in 1968. Major labor goals—including farm labor under the National Labor Relations Act, permitting common site picketing and establishing national standards for occupational safety—were considered in committee but never reached the floor.

Although job training was considered by many to be a key to reducing poverty, Congress did not vote to increase funds for most federal job training programs. The most substantial increases were expected in a new program (JOBS) to subsidize job training in the business sector. Congress also extended existing manpower programs.

Trust Funds

The House in 1968 passed two bills amending the Taft-Hartley Act to permit employer contributions to jointly administered labor-management trust funds, but they were not passed by the Senate.

HR 15198 permitted contributions to trusts for promotion of products in the construction industry. HR 14314 permitted contributions to trust funds to provide scholarships and child care centers for dependents of employees.

NLRB Hearings

A Senate Judiciary subcommittee held intermittent hearings on Congressional oversight of the independent administrative agencies of the Federal Government. The National Labor Relations Board (NLRB) was the only agency under study in this phase of the hearings. Sen. Sam J. Ervin Jr. (D N.C.), chairman of the subcommittee on separation of powers, said the study was intended to find more effective ways for Congress to oversee agency activities rather than to recommend changes in labor laws. No action resulted.

Pension Plans

The House Education and Labor Committee reported with amendments a bill (HR 6498) establishing fiduciary standards of conduct, responsibility and obligation for those charged with administering private employee pension and welfare funds. The bill provided sanctions for violations. The Committee said in its report that the assets of employee welfare and pension funds totaled about $100 billion and were increasing by about $7 billion a year. It predicted that by 1980 such assets would comprise "the greatest single block of the U.S. economy." The Labor Department supported the bill as reported. No major opposition was announced. The bill died without House action.

Chapter 13—The Presidency and the Executive Branch

The Presidency, 1965-68

WHEN Lyndon B. Johnson won a four-year White House term in his own right in 1964, he amassed the largest vote of any Presidential candidate in history. The victory made him a "consensus President"—both in his own eyes and in the public view of his conduct of the nation's affairs. "Consensus politics" became a term used to describe the Johnson Administration; "consensus" increasingly became a key to the President's mode of operation.

Johnson's performance as President in 1965 resulted in an outpouring of major programs, many of which his predecessors had written off because of unwilling and uncooperative Congresses. Johnson seized the momentum provided by his 1964 landslide victory and the resulting large Democratic majorities in Congress to get his "Great Society" program off to an impressive start.

The monumental record of the first session of the 89th Congress stands as a lesson in Presidential power and leadership. Among the landmark legislative accomplishments of 1965 were medical care for the aged, the first comprehensive plan of federal aid to elementary and secondary education, a historic voting rights act and the first significant reform in immigration legislation in four decades. In 1964, the "war on poverty" was begun.

But by 1966, the "status of the consensus" was a matter of national debate. It was also a matter of grave concern to the President. His motives and policies had undergone increasing questioning and challenge in the face of escalation of the war in Vietnam, a growing economic inflation, and the approaching mid-term Congressional elections.

As the second session of the 89th Congress progressed, the rosy glow of the Johnson courtship waned. During the first session, Johnson had gone further than any recent President in cultivating a harmonious relationship with Congress. Both personally and through the White House legislative liaison staff, he had kept in close touch with Democratic Members. But in 1966, many freshmen Representatives who faced hard re-election battles became increasingly reluctant to bow to White House pressure to support controversial mea-

Reference

Discussion of the Presidency and the Executive Branch in 1945-64 will be found in *Congress and the Nation*, Vol. I, pp. 1432-1438, 1455-1459.

Boxscore Records—1953-1968

Following are listed the Presidential Boxscore records for President Eisenhower in the 83rd Congress (1953-54, Republican), 84th Congress (1955-56, Democratic), 85th Congress (1957-58, Democratic) and 86th Congress (1959-60, Democratic); for President Kennedy in the 87th Congress (1961-62, Democratic); for Presidents Kennedy and Johnson in the 88th Congress (1963-64, Democratic); and for President Johnson in the 89th Congress (1965-66, Democratic) and the 90th Congress (1967-68, Democratic):

Year	Proposals Submitted	Approved by Congress	Percent Approved
1953	*	*	*
1954	232	150	65%
1955	207	96	46
1956	225	103	46
1957	206	76	37
1958	234	110	47
1959	228	93	41
1960	183	56	31
1961	355	172	48
1962	298	133	45
1963	401	109	27
1964	217	125	58
1965	469	323	69
1966	371	207	56
1967	431	205	48
1968	414	231	56

Figures for 1953 are not comparable to those for subsequent years. Before 1954, CQ used a different system, grouping Presidential requests in relatively broad categories.

sures when there was no assurance that the Senate would support them.

In the Senate, the escalation of the war in Vietnam had led to questions about the administration's judgment and veracity. From 23,000 American military personnel in Vietnam at the end of 1964, the number rose to 181,000 by the end of 1965 and on to 400,000 by the end of 1966. Sen. J. W. Fulbright (D Ark.), chairman of the Senate Foreign Relations Committee, and Sen. Mike Mansfield (D Mont.), the Majority Leader, had begun to criticize war policies. The Senate Foreign Relations Committee in the spring of 1966 held public hearings on the conduct of the war, providing a forum for many leading critics of the war. Fulbright charged that the United States planned to stay indefinitely in Asia to counterbalance Communist China. The Senator said he regretted that he had helped to persuade Congress, in August 1964, to approve the "Gulf of Tonkin" resolution (PL 88-408), which buttressed the legal foundation for American involvement in the war.

Newspapers of Sept. 23, 1966, noted on that date Johnson's occupancy of the White House equaled that of President Kennedy—1,037 days. Newsmen, looking ahead to what they called the "second thousand days," made two major points: the President's mood was one of optimism and "buoyancy"; and the shadow of the slain President—the "Kennedy myth"—still lay heavily upon Johnson despite his accomplishments.

Reviewing Johnson's "thousand days" in office, Chalmers Roberts of the *Washington Post* wrote that "People profess to have seen qualities in the late President that they could not find with a microscope when he was alive." He added: "One of the reasons they delude themselves is surely that the qualities they see in Lyndon Johnson disappoint them." The approbation that marked President Johnson's ability to carry on after the 1963 assassination of President Kennedy and the landslide victory of 1964 was being marred by rising criticism and dissent. "Teach-ins" against the war were being conducted on college campuses and almost daily the President's credibility was being questioned in print or on the airways. Senate Republican Leader Everett M. Dirksen (Ill.) on Oct. 14, 1966, summed up his feelings on the state of the nation: "Today, what appeared to be a golden glow only two years ago has been broken by rolls of thunder . . . and uncertainty, queasy doubts, bewilderments, have spread across the country."

President Johnson took the criticisms as a personal affront. Eric Goldman, a Princeton professor who had become "intellectual-in-residence" at the White House, resigned from the Johnson staff in September 1966, declaring that he could not promote real cooperation because the President was increasingly suspicious of the views and motives of scholars and artists. Goldman said that while he regarded Johnson as a brilliant "consensus President," the Chief Executive was hindered by excessive feelings of insecurity and by deep resentment over his inability to evoke the response he desired from the academic community.

One explanation of the breach between the President and the intellectuals was offered by columnists Rowland Evans and Robert Novak in their book *Lyndon B. Johnson: The Exercise of Power*. They wrote: "The conflict between objective and performance, between the public posture of the President and the private manipulations of the politician, is the essence of the Johnson paradox. The lofty goal and the hard use of power to achieve it are essential components for any successful Presidency, but Johnson often overstates the goal and overuses his power to achieve it."

"This ponderous, protean Texan, with the forbidding look of a chain-gang boss, knows more about the sources of power in the political world of Washington than any President in this century," they observed. "He can be as gentle and solicitous as a nurse, but as ruthless and deceptive as a riverboat gambler, with the veiled threat in his half-closed eyes."

In his continuing search for public approval, President Johnson became, according to one writer, "the first U.S. President to retain a private polling firm which reports to him on a continuing basis." William H. Honan said in the *New York Times Magazine*, Aug. 21, 1966, that Johnson had "assigned a personal aide to the job of official poll watcher and Presidential poll adviser."

Both the public opinion polls and the electoral polls became less pleasing to Johnson from 1966 onward. The Democrats lost 47 House seats and three Senate seats in the Congressional elections that November, though still retaining a sizable majority in both chambers. The President in midsummer 1966 had begun a nationwide pre-election campaign trip. His theme was that Americans "never had it so good," and that United States forces were in Vietnam only because this country had a commitment to "stand up for freedom, whatever the price."

His speeches covered almost every facet of domestic policy, as well as foreign affairs, and brought comments that the first round of the next Presidential campaign had already begun. The 1968 election intruded several times into the 1966 campaign. Public opinion polls indicated that Sen. Robert F. Kennedy (D N.Y.) scored higher than the President in midsummer as the favorite to head the Democratic ticket. In some Congressional districts, Johnson appeared to be a liability to the local Democratic Congressmen. He cut short his political campaigning by leaving Washington Oct. 17 for a 17-day tour of Asia—his first extended overseas journey since assuming the Presidency. It included attendance at the Manila Conference of nations allied with the United States in the war in Vietnam and an unannounced visit to the U.S. supply base at Cam Ranh Bay. There, some 50 miles from the nearest fighting, Johnson spent two and a half hours among 7,000 U.S. troops. It was the first visit by an incumbent President to a foreign battle zone since Franklin D. Roosevelt received U.S. troops in Casablanca in 1943. "I came here today for one good reason," Johnson told the troops, "simply because I could not come to this part of the world and not come to see you."

When the President returned from his Asian trip, a week before the Nov. 8 election, he announced he would undergo abdominal and throat surgery. This meant that he could not undertake the anticipated last-minute campaigning for Democratic candidates. Whether his support would have helped or not was debatable; Republican gains in the election marked a resurgence of the G.O.P. after its bad defeat in 1964.

President Johnson underwent surgery successfully the morning of Nov. 16, 1966, at Bethesda (Md.) Naval Hospital for the removal of a non-malignant polyp from his throat and for repair of a ventral hernia. The Johnson family physician, Dr. James C. Cain, said later the same day that the President had "tolerated this surgery very beautifully." He recovered fast enough to leave the hospital Nov. 19 and go to his Texas ranch.

However, friends and other observers noted that several months passed before he recaptured his old vigor.

In 1967 it became increasingly clear that the nation had to choose in budgetary matters between "guns" and "butter." The words described a policy choice between a stepped-up war effort and an expansion of "Great Society" domestic programs. When Congress began to debate the "guns-versus-butter" issue in 1966, the President maintained that the country could afford both. But Congress in 1967 and 1968 did not agree; it cut more deeply into the funding of new social legislation as war costs rose.

The President nevertheless persuaded Congress to pass consumer-oriented legislation, including a strong meat-inspection bill, in 1967. The Senate in 1967 and the House in 1968 passed a comprehensive truth-in-lending bill requiring creditors to disclose the true cost of borrowing. A civil rights open-housing bill, proposed by the President in 1966 and 1967, became law in 1968 during a time of racial disorders and riots in many American cities. The disorders followed the assassination of Dr. Martin Luther King Jr., the civil rights leader, in Memphis, April 4, 1968.

Johnson Bows Out

New successes in Congress were not enough to overcome the President's waning popularity throughout the country. When President Johnson bowed out of the Presidential race, March 31, 1968, the country was divided as never before during his Presidency. "I shall not seek, and I will not accept, the nomination of my party for another term as your President," he said at the conclusion of a nationally televised policy statement on Vietnam in which he announced restrictions on the bombing of North Vietnam in the hope of getting peace talks started.

Johnson's decision not to run again was preceded by the strong showing of a war critic, Sen. Eugene J. McCarthy (D Wis.), in the New Hampshire Democratic Presidential primary election, March 12. Four days later, Sen. Robert F. Kennedy announced his candidacy for the Democratic Presidential nomination, saying: "I run to seek new policies—policies to end the bloodshed in Vietnam and in our cities, policies to close the gap that now exists between black and white, between rich and poor, between young and old . . . I run because it is now unmistakably clear that we can change these disastrous, divisive policies only by changing the men who are now making them." Kennedy insisted, however, that his candidacy reflected "no personal animosity or disrespect" toward President Johnson.

After making his withdrawal speech, President Johnson told reporters that he had taken into account the "dissension in the country" and he said that the Kennedy candidacy had "added to the general situation." The President maintained, however, that the primary factor in his decision was his desire to seek peace in Vietnam without "the aura of a political campaign." "I don't want to get involved in partisan politics while there are a half-million men out there in

Text of Johnson's Withdrawal

Key paragraphs from President Johnson's address March 31, 1968, announcing that he would not seek re-election.

Tonight, I renew the offer I made last August—to stop the bombardment of North Vietnam. We ask that talks begin promptly, that they be serious talks on the substance of peace. . . .

So, tonight, in the hope that this action will lead to early talks, I am taking the first step to de-escalate the conflict. We are reducing—substantially reducing—the present level of hostilities. . . .

I have ordered our aircraft and our naval vessels to make no attacks on North Vietnam, except in the area north of the Demilitarized Zone where the continuing enemy buildup directly threatens allied forward positions and where the movements of their troops and supplies are clearly related to that threat. . . .

We have no intention of widening this war.

But the United States will never accept a fake solution to this long and arduous struggle and call it peace.

No one can foretell the precise terms of an eventual settlement.

Our objective in South Vietnam has never been the annihilation of the enemy. It has been to bring about a recognition in Hanoi that its objective—taking over the South by force—could not be achieved.

We think that peace can be based on the Geneva Accords of 1954—under political conditions that permit the South Vietnamese—all the South Vietnamese—to chart their course free of any outside domination or interference, from us or from anyone else.

So tonight I reaffirm the pledge that we made at Manila—that we are prepared to withdraw our forces from South Vietnam as the other side withdraws its forces to the North, stops the infiltration, and the level of violence thus subsides. . . .

For 37 years in the service of our nation, first as a Congressman, as a Senator and as Vice President and now as your President, I have put the unity of the people first. I have put it ahead of any divisive partianship. . . .

With America's sons in the fields far away, with America's future under challenge right here at home, with our hopes and the world's hopes for peace in the balance every day, I do not believe that I should devote an hour or a day of my time to any personal partisan causes or to any duties other than the awesome duties of this office—the Presidency of your country.

Accordingly, I shall not seek, and I will not accept, the nomination of my Party for another term as your President. . . .

Vietnam giving their lives . . . Now is the time to remove yourself from any selfish actions and try to turn in as good a result as the men out there are turning in. I'm doing what I think is right."

Johnson's goal of bringing about a peace settlement before he left office proved elusive. American and North Vietnamese negotiators began peace talks in Paris, May 11, 1968. By the time Johnson left the White House, Jan. 20, 1969, no settlement was in sight. The war which had eroded his domestic programs and blemished his Presidency, frustrated him to the end.

Presidential Power:

Concepts Change

When Richard M. Nixon was elected President of the United States on Nov. 5, 1968, he succeeded to the most powerful office in the world. The Presidency is not one office but several: The President is Chief Executive, Commander in Chief of the armed forces, Head of State, and head of his party. He is also the government's chief public information officer.

The power of the Presidency is such that it may no longer be meaningful to classify Presidents as "weak" or "strong." In the modern era, the President is vir-

tually forced to be a strong executive. The powers of the office are not only those spelled out in Article II of the Constitution but also those established by precedent or authorized by Congress. Only about one President in three, according to Edward S. Corwin, the author of a landmark study of the Presidency, has contributed to the development of executive power. However, "Precedents established by a forceful or politically successful personality in the office are available to less gifted successors, and permanently so because of the difficulty of amending the Constitution." [1] (See footnotes p. 635.)

Presidents themselves often contend that their power is more potential than real. Harry S. Truman, envisioning in 1952 the problems that Dwight D. Eisenhower would encounter if elected President, said: "He'll sit here and he'll say, 'Do this! Do that!' *And nothing will happen.* Poor Ike—it won't be a bit like the Army. He'll find it very frustrating." [2] President Johnson once exclaimed: "Power? The only power I've got is nuclear—and I can't use that." [3]

Critics of the Presidency nevertheless maintain that the President is overburdened and possessed of too much power, and that his burdens and powers should be lightened or shared with others. A representative view, expressed by Marcus Cunliffe, a professor of American studies at the University of Sussex (England), holds that "The Presidency works badly." He says: "Among other things it embraces a paradox. The President has at once too much prestige and—in domestic affairs—not enough real executive leeway. His frustrations match those of his countrymen. In the sphere of foreign policy he and the Executive Branch possess too much capacity to commit the nation to disaster. Liberal advocates of an aggrandizing Presidency now sense uneasily that they have created a Frankenstein; an executive which, in the name of leadership and patriotism, may respond to the demand for spectacular Presidential direction by acting in the only untrammeled way open to it—belligerently." [4]

A number of proposals have been advanced to remedy the alleged defects of the Presidency. Among other things, it has been suggested that (1) Legislation be enacted putting specified limits on the size of forces committed to war abroad when there is no declaration of war by Congress; (2) the functions of head of state and head of government be divided between two men; (3) several Vice Presidents, instead of only one, be elected or appointed to look after specific areas of government; (4) the United States adopt some sort of parliamentary government, in which the President would be elected by members of the majority party in Congress. Such proposals have been put forward off and on for years, with no result. Although they are not likely to fare better, they reflected widespread discontent with the condition of the Presidency in the 1960s.

Scope of President's Powers

The powers of the President derive from Article II of the Constitution, which has been described as "the most loosely written chapter" of the nation's fundamental law. "To those who think that a constitution ought to settle everything beforehand it should be a nightmare; by the same token, to those who think that constitution-makers ought to leave generous scope for the future play of political forces it should be a vision realized."[5]

The ambiguity of Article II is evident in its opening sentence: "The executive power shall be vested in a President of the United States of America." These words can be interpreted as comprising a grant of power or a mere designation of office. The former interpretation has been generally accepted, but it is vitiated somewhat by the more specific grants of power in the ensuing sections of Article II. Arthur M. Schlesinger Jr. is of the opinion that "The drafters (of the Constitution) knew they were writing a document not just for their own generation, but for generations to come." He adds: "With their masterly instinct for ambiguity, they bequeathed a series of vital questions to the future. Thus the language of the Constitution did not end the debate over whether the executive should be weak or strong. It only settled the context in which subsequent phases of that debate would take place."[6]

The powers enumerated in Article II are relatively few. Section 2 provides that "The President shall be Commander in Chief of the Army and Navy of the United States, and of the Militia of the several States, when called into the actual Service of the United States." The section also empowers the President (1) to grant reprieves and pardons for federal offenses, except in cases of impeachment; (2) to make treaties, provided two-thirds of the Senators voting concur, (3) to nominate and, by and with the advice and consent of the Senate, to appoint ambassadors, other public ministers and consuls, justices of the Supreme Court, and other officers of the United States.

Section 3 of Article II requires the President "from time to time" to give Congress information on the State of the Union and to submit to Congress "such measures as he shall judge necessary and expedient." It goes on to state that the President "may, on extraordinary Occasions, convene both Houses, or either of them and in Case of Disagreement between them with Respect to the Time of Adjournment, he may adjourn them to such Time as he shall think proper; he shall receive Ambassadors and other public Ministers; he shall take Care that the Laws be faithfully executed, and shall Commission all the Officers of the United States."

Presidents of the past quarter-century have been criticized mainly for their handling of foreign affairs — a field in which the Chief Executive exercises disproportionate power vis-a-vis Congress. Franklin D. Roosevelt came under attack after his death for his part in the Yalta Conference; Truman was assailed for his handling of the Korean War; Eisenhower for the U-2 affair; Kennedy for the abortive Bay of Pigs invasion; and Johnson for the Vietnam war.

Criticism of Johnson

Johnson's troubles on Vietnam stem from adoption by Congress in August 1964 of a joint resolution authorizing the President to "take all necessary measures" to stop aggression in Southeast Asia. The resolution was adopted soon after North Vietnamese PT-boats had twice attacked American destroyers in the Gulf of Tonkin. It was to remain in force until such time as "the President shall determine that the peace and security of the area is reasonably assured by international conditions created by action of the United Nations or otherwise, except that it may be terminated earlier by concurrent resolution of the Congress."

The Johnson administration contended that the Tonkin Gulf resolution was the "functional equivalent" of a declaration of war. Under Secretary of State Nicholas deB. Katzenbach, testifying before the Senate Foreign Relations Committee, Aug. 17, 1967, asserted that the resolution was "an authorization to the President, and in my judgment it [was] as broad an authorization of war so-called [as it] could be in terms of our internal constitutional process." A member of the committee, Sen. Eugene J. McCarthy (D Minn.), told a reporter after Katzenbach had testified: "This is the wildest testimony I ever heard. There is no limit to what he says the President could do. There is only one thing to do—take it to the country."

The Tonkin Gulf resolution set no precedent. Congress in 1955 had adopted a joint resolution authorizing President Eisenhower to "employ the armed forces of the United States as he deems necessary" for protection of Taiwan and the Pescadores Islands against armed attack. As in the case of the later Tonkin Gulf resolution, the Taiwan resolution provided that expiration of the granted authority should await the President's report to Congress that the "peace and security of the area is reasonably assured." A similar resolution, embodying the "Eisenhower Doctrine," was adopted with respect to the Middle East in 1957.

Power of Congress

Strong Presidents, it has been observed, store up trouble for themselves and their successors. This is what happened to President Johnson, and not solely because of Vietnam. The unusually active 89th Congress, elected with Johnson in 1964, proceeded to approve legislation that had been stalled for as long as 20 years. Major laws enacted in 1965 included medical care for the aged under Social Security; aid to primary and secondary schools; immigration reform; protection of Negro voting rights; excise-tax reduction; aid to urban areas, and others. This burst of activity in a single session led seasoned Washington observers to compare the 89th Congress with the 73rd Congress of 1933-34 (the first two years of the F. D. Roosevelt administration) and the 63rd Congress of 1913-14 (the first two years of the Woodrow Wilson administration).

The second session of the 89th Congress was notably less productive than the first. The 90th Congress often displayed outright hostility to Presidential proposals, even though both houses were controlled by the President's party. For example, the President's request for a 10 per cent surcharge on individual and corporation income taxes was approved only after the administration reluctantly agreed to a provision calling for a $6 billion reduction in budget estimates for fiscal 1969 non-Vietnam spending.

Johnson's experience was far from unique. Every activist President has been accused of being domineering; most have been succeeded by men who took a more cautious approach to the exercise of executive power. Thus, Lincoln was succeeded by Grant; T. R. Roosevelt by Taft; Wilson by Harding; Truman by Eisenhower.

Founding Fathers' View

Delegates to the Constitutional Convention in Philadelphia in the summer of 1787 faced a dilemma when they took up the problem of creating a "national executive." On one hand, the majority of the framers wanted an executive power capable of penetrating to the remotest parts of the Union, not only for the purpose of enforcing national laws, but also—a lesson from Shay's Rebellion—for the purpose of bringing assistance to the states in grave emergencies of domestic disorder. On the other hand, the framers wanted also to avoid stirring up the widespread popular fear of monarchy.

Roger Sherman of Connecticut was the foremost proponent of an executive subordinate to the legislature. According to James Madison's *Notes,* Sherman "considered the Executive magistracy as nothing more than an institution for carrying the will of the legislature into effect," and he "wished that the number [of executives] might not be fixed, but that the legislature should be at liberty to appoint one or more as experience might dictate." James Wilson of Pennsylvania was the spokesman for those delegates who favored a "strong executive." He preferred, Madison records, "a single magistrate, as giving most energy, dispatch, and responsibility to the office." Wilson was also for rendering the executive "independent of the legislature," and to this end proposed that he be elected by the people at large and be vested with an absolute veto on acts of the legislature. "Without such a defense," he said of the latter proposal, "the legislature can at any moment sink it [the executive] into nonexistence." Wilson was supported by Charles Pinckney, who proposed the title "President," and by Alexander Hamilton, who wanted to see the "governor" chosen for life and vested with the power to appoint the governors of the states.

Wilson, as it turned out, was appointed chairman of the Committee of Detail, which was charged with producing a comprehensive draft of the new Constitution. Article X of the Committee's draft began: "The Executive Power of the United States shall be vested in a single person." The article went on to provide that this person should be chosen by the national legislature for one term of seven years and not be eligible for a second term. He was to be charged with executing the laws and be empowered to appoint officers in all cases not otherwise provided for by the Constitution (but Article IX would have given the Senate power to appoint ambassadors and Supreme Court justices). The executive was to be Commander in Chief of the armed forces, have the power to receive foreign ambassadors (but Article IX gave the Senate power to make treaties), and convene and adjourn the legislature. He was to be subject to impeachment; and, in case of removal, disability, or death, the President of the Senate was to exercise the executive's

powers and duties. In addition, Article VI would have given the executive power to veto acts of the legislature and the legislature power to override such vetoes by a two-thirds vote.

Constitutional Compromises

The Committee of Detail's draft represented progress for advocates of a strong executive. But several provisions, notably those giving Congress authority to elect the executive, make treaties, and appoint high officials, still made for the clear subordination of the executive to the legislature. All of these matters, and others, were debated by the convention for five weeks. Finally, on Sept. 8, 1787, a Committee on Style was appointed to write a final draft. Schlesinger holds that Gouverneur Morris, chairman of this committee, "was probably the main author of the text submitted on Sept. 12, and he undoubtedly took full advantage of the opportunity to strengthen the Presidential prerogative."

Article II of the final draft constituted a further victory for the supporters of executive autonomy and authority. In the most important change of all, the final draft took the election of the President away from the national legislature and assigned it to electors designated in whatever manner each state legislature might direct. This provision, urged principally by Madison, is believed to have been a key consideration in adoption of the entire article.

The new draft shortened the Presidential term to four years and removed the ban on re-eligibility. It transferred to the President the authority to make treaties, though with the advice and consent of the Senate. It transferred to him authority to appoint all government officials, including ambassadors and Supreme Court justices, though again with the Senate's advice and consent. In case of removal, disability, or death, his powers and duties would now devolve on the Vice President; Congress was authorized to make provision by law for succession beyond the Vice President. And it added a definition of the conditions of Presidential eligibility.

The changes provoked surprisingly little debate. The Constitution of the United States, including Article II, was adopted by the convention after only three days of consideration. The delegates may have accepted the new provisions on executive power because, as Pierce Butler of South Carolina later wrote, "many . . . cast their eyes toward General Washington as President; and shaped their ideas of the Powers to be given to a President, by their opinions of his Virtue."

Ebb and Flow of Power

Washington, the first President, turned out to be almost exactly the kind of executive the framers of the Constitution had envisaged. He understood the importance of the precedents he would be setting.

Washington presided over a Cabinet of such strong and clashing intellects as Hamilton and Jefferson. Nevertheless, the President's subordinates cleared major decisions with him and obtained his approval. "By staying somewhat above the battle Washington

Presidents of the United States

Vice-President and Terms

President and Vice President		Service			
1. George Washington	April	30, 1789 - March	3, 1797		
John Adams (F)	April	30, 1789 - March	3, 1797		
2. John Adams (F)	March	4, 1797 - March	3, 1801		
Thomas Jefferson (AF)	March	4, 1797 - March	3, 1801		
3. Thomas Jefferson (D-R)	March	4, 1801 - March	3, 1809		
Aaron Burr (D-R)	March	4, 1801 - March	3, 1805		
George Clinton (D-R)	March	4, 1805 - March	3, 1809		
4. James Madison (D-R)	March	4, 1809 - March	3, 1817		
George Clinton* (D-R)	March	4, 1809 - April	20, 1812		
Elbridge Gerry* (D-R)	March	4, 1813 - Nov.	23, 1814		
5. James Monroe (D-R)	March	4, 1817 - March	3, 1825		
David D. Tompkins (D-R)	March	4, 1817 - March	3, 1825		
6. John Quincy Adams (N-R)	March	4, 1825 - March	3, 1829		
John C. Calhoun (N-R)	March	4, 1825 March	3, 1829		
7. Andrew Jackson (D-R)	March	4, 1829 - March	3, 1837		
John C. Calhoun** (D-R)	March	4, 1829 - Dec.	28, 1832		
Martin Van Buren (D-R)	March	4, 1833 - March	3, 1837		
8. Martin Van Buren (D-R)	March	4, 1837 - March	3, 1841		
Richard M. Johnson (D-R)	March	4, 1837 - March	3, 1841		
9. William Henry Harrison* (W)	March	4, 1841 - April	4, 1841		
John Tyler (W)	March	4, 1841 - April	4, 1841		
10. John Tyler (W)	April	6, 1841 - March	3, 1845		
11. James K. Polk (D)	March	4, 1845 - March	3, 1849		
George M. Dallas (D)	March	4, 1845 - March	3, 1849		
12. Zachary Taylor* (W)	March	5, 1849 - July	9, 1850		
Millard Fillmore (W)	March	5, 1849 - July	9, 1850		
13. Millard Fillmore (W)	July	10, 1850 - March	3, 1853		
14. Franklin Pierce (D)	March	4 1853 - March	3, 1857		
William R. King* (D)	March	4, 1853 - April	18, 1853		
15. James Buchanan (D)	March	4, 1857 - March	3, 1861		
John C. Breckinridge (D)	March	4, 1857 - March	3, 1861		
16. Abraham Lincoln* (R)	March	4, 1861 - April	15, 1865		
Hannibal Hamlin (R)	March	4, 1861 - March	3, 1865		
Andrew Jackson (D)	March	4, 1865 - April	15, 1865		
17. Andrew Johnson (D)	April	15, 1865 - March	3, 1869		
18. Ulysses S. Grant (D)	March	4, 1869 - March	3, 1877		
Schuyler Colfax (R)	March	4, 1869 - March	3, 1873		
Henry Wilson* (R)	March	4, 1873 - Nov.	22, 1875		

President and Vice President		Service			
19. Rutherford B. Hayes (R)	March	4, 1877 - March	3, 1881		
William A. Wheeler (R)	March	4, 1877 - March	3, 1881		
20. James A. Garfield* (R)	March	4, 1881 - Sept.	19, 1881		
Chester A. Arthur (R)	March	4, 1881 - Sept.	19, 1881		
21. Chester A. Arthur (R)	Sept.	20, 1881 - March	3, 1885		
22. Grover Cleveland (D)	March	4, 1885 - March	3, 1889		
Thomas A. Hendricks* (D)	March	4, 1885 - Nov.	25, 1885		
23. Benjamin Harrison (R)	March	4, 1889 - March	3, 1893		
Levi P. Morton (R)	March	4, 1889 - March	3, 1893		
24. Grover Cleveland (D)	March	4, 1893 - March	3, 1897		
Adlai E. Stevenson (D)	March	4, 1893 - March	3, 1897		
25. William McKinley* (R)	March	4, 1897 - Sept.	14, 1901		
Garret A. Hobart* (R)	March	4, 1897 - Nov.	21, 1899		
Theodore Roosevelt (R)	March	4, 1901 - Sept.	14, 1901		
26. Theodore Roosevelt (R)	Sept.	14, 1901 - March	3, 1909		
Charles W. Fairbanks (R)	March	4, 1905 - March	3, 1909		
27. William H. Taft (R)	March	4, 1909 - March	3, 1913		
James S. Sherman* (R)	March	4, 1909 - Oct.	30, 1912		
28. Woodrow Wilson (D)	March	4, 1913 - March	3, 1921		
Thomas R. Marshall (D)	March	4, 1913 - March	3, 1921		
29. Warren G. Harding*	March	4, 1921 - Aug.	2, 1923		
Calvin Coolidge (R)	March	4, 1921 - Aug.	2, 1923		
30. Calvin Coolidge (R)	Aug.	3, 1921 - March	3, 1929		
Charles G. Dawes (R)	March	4, 1925 - March	3, 1929		
31. Herbert C. Hoover (R)	March	4, 1929 - March	3, 1933		
Charles Curtis (R)	March	4, 1929 - March	3, 1933		
32. Franklin D. Roosevelt* (D)	March	4, 1933 - April	12, 1945		
John N. Garner (D)	March	4, 1933 - Jan.	20, 1941		
Henry A. Wallace (D)	Jan.	20, 1941 - Jan.	20, 1945		
Harry S. Truman (D)	Jan.	20, 1945 - April	12, 1945		
33. Harry S. Truman (D)	April	12, 1945 - Jan.	20, 1953		
Alben W. Barkley (D)	Jan.	20, 1949 - Jan.	20, 1953		
34. Dwight D. Eisenhower (R)	Jan.	20, 1952 - Jan.	20, 1961		
Richard M. Nixon (R)	Jan.	20, 1953 - Jan.	20, 1961		
35. John F. Kennedy* (D)	Jan.	20, 1961 - Nov.	22, 1963		
Lyndon B. Johnson (D)	Jan.	20, 1961 - Nov.	22, 1963		
36. Lyndon B. Johnson (D)	Nov.	22, 1961 - Jan.	20, 1969		
Hubert H. Humphrey (D)	Jan.	20, 1965 - Jan.	20, 1969		
37. Richard M. Nixon (R)	Jan.	20, 1969 -			
Spiro T. Agnew (R)	Jan.	20, 1969 -			

*Died in office

**Resigned to become
U.S. Senator

consolidated the people's support for him, lent his name and prestige to the new republic, and ultimately helped convert his charismatic appeal and authority into the popular and constitutional legitimacy so badly needed" by the new country, James MacGregor Burns writes. [7]

With Hamilton's support, Washington took a series of steps asserting presidential conduct of foreign policy-making. He exercised sole discretion in the reception of envoys and hence in the recognition of nations; he rejected a request from the House of Representatives for papers relating to negotiation of the Jay treaty with Great Britain; and he issued a proclamation of neutrality in 1793 on his own responsibility. A crucial incident occurred on Aug. 22, 1789, when President Washington arrived at the Senate to consult with it on a proposed Indian treaty. A motion was made that the papers submitted by the President be referred to a committee of five, whereupon Washington "started up in a violent

fret," exclaimed "This defeats every purpose of my coming here," and withdrew "with a discontented air."[8] Burns comments: "The Senate may have won that skirmish, but it lost the war, for the President never again collaborated directly with the Senate in the treaty-making process and thus the Senate lost an opportunity to affect the shape of treaties at the critical stages."

Jacksonian Activism

John Adam's conception of the Presidency closely resembled that of Washington, but Thomas Jefferson, the third President, took a different approach. "What we encounter in Jefferson for the first time," Corwin writes, "is a President who is primarily a party leader, only secondarily a Chief Executive." The tone of his messages to Congress was uniformly deferential. But

Jefferson undertook to guide the opinion of Congress through the party caucus, which enabled the Republicans to present a united front on the floor. With the withering of the Federalist party, the Republican caucus became the "Congressional Caucus," by which James Madison and James Monroe were successively put in nomination for the Presidency. John Quincy Adams, though not the nominee of the caucus, was virtually elected by it when the election of 1824 was thrown into the House. Thus, for 20 years after Jefferson, the Presidency was in decline.

This trend was suddenly reversed under Andrew Jackson, who, Schlesinger says, "revolutionized the Presidential office and may be said to have invented the modern Presidency." Jackson was the first President in American history to appeal to the people over the heads of their legislative representatives. In this spirit, he dominated the Cabinet and the Executive Branch; expanded Presidential powers of initiation and control in Congress; [9] and made it impossible for the states to nullify federal legislation.

Jackson's view of the relationship of the executive, legislative and judicial branches of the Federal Government is contained in a message of July 10, 1832, vetoing Henry Clay's bill for rechartering the second Bank of the United States. "The Congress, the Executive, and the Court," Jackson wrote, "must each for itself be guided by its own opinion of the Constitution."

Jackson's opponents in Congress, led by the two greatest Senators of the time, Henry Clay and Daniel Webster, denounced him as a tyrant. "The President," Webster said, "carries on the government; all the rest are sub-contractors." Clay asserted that "We are in the midst of a revolution, hitherto bloodless, but tending rapidly towards a total change of the pure republican character of the government, and to the concentration of all power in the hands of one man." Clay and Webster were among the founders of the Whig party, which was dedicated to the thesis of a strong Congress and a weak, one-term President.

The Whig philosophy—though not the party itself—remained dominant for a quarter-century after Jackson left office. With the exception of James K. Polk, all of the eight Presidents [10] who served between Jackson and Abraham Lincoln are today considered weak executives. One reason why the Presidency went into temporary eclipse during this period was emergence of the slavery issue. Congress, through the devices of compromise and negotiation, was better qualified to handle this question than was the President.

Lincoln's Concept of Executive Power

Abraham Lincoln was the last President of the 18th century to add to the powers of the office. Lincoln's contribution was to enlarge the meaning of the "Commander-in-Chief" clause, the "forgotten clause of the Constitution." He wedded this provision to the clause which makes it the duty of the President to "take care that the laws be faithfully executed" and fashioned from them the President's "war power."

Altogether, Lincoln's exercise of the war power asserted for the President, "for the first time in our history, an initiative of indefinite scope and legislative in effect in meeting the domestic aspects of a war emergency." In his study on the *President and Congress* (1947), Wilfred E. Binkley wrote that the Lincoln administration represented "the high-water mark of the exercise of executive power in the United States" because "No President before or since has pushed the boundaries of executive power so far over into the legislative sphere."

Lincoln's administration was followed, as it had been preceded, by a period in which Congress was dominant and the office of President was held by a series of relatively weak executives. Woodrow Wilson, writing in 1885, asserted that "Congress is fast becoming the governing body of the nation, and yet the only power which it possesses in perfection is the power which is but a part of government, the power of legislation." Wilson added:

> But the prestige of the presidential office has declined with the character of the Presidents. And the character of the Presidents has declined as the perfection of selfish party tactics has advanced. . . .
>
> I am disposed to think, however, that the decline in the character of the Presidents is not the cause, but only the accompanying manifestation, of the declining prestige of the Presidential office. That high office has fallen from its first estate of dignity because its power has waned; and its power has waned because the power of Congress has become predominant. [11]

James Bryce, writing on the same subject three years after Wilson, suggested that the President had lost ground to Congress because "Men come and go, but an assembly goes on forever." In other words, "A weak magistrate comes after a strong magistrate, and yields what his predecessor had fought for; but an assembly holds all it has ever won."

Roosevelt-Wilson Vs. Taft-Harding

Theodore Roosevelt brought new vigor to the Presidency when he succeeded to the office in 1901. He assured the independence of Panama from Colombia, late in 1903, by ordering the Navy to prevent landing of Colombian troops to put down a revolt on the isthmus. And under the so-called Roosevelt Corollary to the Monroe Doctrine, he asserted the right of the United States to intervene in other Caribbean countries to maintain public order. At home, Roosevelt launched a broad attack on abuses stemming from the concentration of industrial power.

Roosevelt governed by what he called the "stewardship theory" of the Presidency. He described the theory in his *Autobiography* as follows:

> I declined to adopt the view that what was imperatively necessary for the nation could not be done by the President unless he could find some specific authorization to do it. My belief was that it was not only his right but his duty to do anything that the needs of the nation demanded unless such action was forbidden by the Constitution or by the laws. Under this interpretation of executive power I did and caused to be done many things not previously done by the President and the heads of the departments. I did not usurp power, but I did greatly broaden the use of executive power.

William Howard Taft, Roosevelt's successor as President, took a diametrically opposed view of the Presidency. Writing in 1916 on *Our Chief Magistrate and His Powers,* Taft rejected the notion that the President had any constitutional warrant to attempt the role of "a Universal Providence." He asserted that "The true view of the executive functions is . . . that the President can exercise no power which cannot be fairly and reasonably traced to some specific grant of power or justly implied and included within such express grant as proper and necessary." Taft thought Roosevelt's theory of "a residual executive power" to be "unsafe."

Woodrow Wilson was an activist President in both domestic and foreign affairs, and he was also the first President to become a recognized world leader. In the domestic field, Wilson proposed and Congress approved tariff reform, the Federal Reserve Act, the Federal Trade Commission Act, the Clayton (antitrust) Act, and the Adamson Act (establishing an eight-hour day for railroad employees), among other measures. Although a non-doctrinaire pacifist, Wilson twice ordered the invasion of Mexico, and he sent the Marines to Haiti (1915), the Dominican Republic (1916) and Cuba (1917).

As Commander in Chief in World War I, Wilson drew on the precedents established by Lincoln. One week after war was declared, for example, the President created by executive order a Committee on Public Information, under whose direction a system of voluntary news censorship was established and various government publicity services were organized. Congress, moreover, conferred upon Wilson sweeping control of the American economy.

After the war ended, new Republican majorities in Congress reasserted the prerogatives of the Legislative Branch. Feelings on Capitol Hill were ruffled by Wilson's failure to include Senators in the American delegation to the Paris Peace Conference. The Senate twice refused, in 1919 and again in 1920, to ratify the Treaty of Versailles. Repudiation of the treaty ushered in an era in which Congress exerted commanding influence over foreign policy.

Warren G. Harding, who succeeded Wilson as President, shared the widely held feeling against vigorous use of executive power. "During the anxieties of war, when necessity seemed compelling," Harding declared in his first annual message to Congress in December 1921, "there were excessive grants of authority and an extraordinary concentration of powers in the Chief Executive."

F.D.R. and Postwar Presidents

Franklin D. Roosevelt in the midst of the Great Depression marked a return to the activist Presidency personified by Lincoln, T. R. Roosevelt, and Wilson. Corwin remarks on reviewing F.D.R.'s accomplishments, "We perceive again the immense reinforcement which recognized 'emergency' is capable of bringing to Presidential leadership." Confronted with emergency, "Congress feels at once the need for action and its inability to plan the action needed; so it turns to the President."

Roosevelt saw the Presidency as "pre-eminently a place of moral leadership." This aspect of the office gained new importance after World War II. The President today is a leader who must acquaint himself with other world leaders and win the acceptance and confidence of peoples everywhere.

The postwar expansion of Presidential power in foreign affairs was accompanied by enlargement of the Chief Executive's domestic powers and duties. For example, the Labor-Management Relations [Taft-Hartley] Act of 1947 empowered the President to name boards of inquiry to investigate labor disputes which, in his opinion, "imperil the national health and safety." After the board has reported, the President may direct the Attorney General to petition a federal district court to enjoin an actual or threatened strike or lockout. The Employment Act of 1946, which created the Council of Economic Advisers, required the President to submit an annual economic report to Congress. Moreover, the President was expected, under terms of the act, to recommend legislation and policies to foster free competitive enterprise and maintain employment, production and purchasing power at maximum levels.

Sen. John F. Kennedy outlined his views on the Presidency and its powers 12 days after he had announced his candidacy for the 1960 Democratic Presidential nomination. In a speech at the National Press Club in Washington, Jan. 14, 1960, Kennedy declared that "The American people in 1960 have an imperative right to know what any man bidding for the Presidency thinks about the place he is bidding for—whether he is aware of and willing to use the powerful resources of that office." During the Eisenhower administration, he said, "Our needs and our hopes have been eloquently stated, but the initiative and follow-through have too often been left to others." This "restricted concept of the Presidency" was no longer good enough; the next President "must be prepared to exercise the fullest powers of his office—all that are specified and some that are not."

A similar speech was made by Richard M. Nixon on Sept. 19, 1968. Nixon said in a nationwide radio broadcast that "The days of a passive Presidency belong to a simpler past." He added: "The next President must take an activist view of his office. He must articulate the nation's values, define its goals and marshal its will." *(See box, p. 634.)*

Proposals for Reform

Criticism of the Presidency is usually directed at the immense burdens as well as at the powers of the office. The President is so constantly preoccupied with trivial matters, it is said, that his ability to exercise his powers on important decisions is bound to be impaired. "The Presidency may no longer be manageable by any single individual, however wise and resourceful," Norman Cousins wrote in the *Saturday Review*, April 13, 1968. "No one can stand up against that type of pounding, or deal with such powerful cross-currents, or have the emotional and physical resiliency to cope with the demands of the office."

Every President starting with Washington has complained of overwork. The higher duties of the of-

Nixon Gives Concept of Presidency

Following are excerpts from Sept. 19, 1968, remarks over nationwide radio by Richard M. Nixon on his conception of the Presidency:

"The next President must unite America. He must calm its angers, ease its terrible frictions, and bring its people together once again in peace and mutual respect. He has to take hold of America before he can move it forward . . . The first responsibility of leadership is to gain mastery over events, and to shape the future in the image of our hopes. The President today cannot stand aside from crisis; he cannot ignore division; he cannot simply paper over disunity. He must lead. . . .

"The President is trusted (by the people), not to follow the fluctuations of the public-opinion polls, but to bring his own best judgment to bear on the best ideas his administration can muster. There are occasions on which a President must take unpopular measures. But his responsibility does not stop there. The President has a duty to decide, but the people have a right to know why. The President has a responsibility to tell them—to lay out all the facts, and to explain not only why he chose as he did but also what it means for the future. Only through an open, candid dialogue with the people can a President maintain his trust and leadership. . . .

"When we debate American commitments abroad, for example, if we expect a decent hearing from those who now take to the streets in protest, we must recognize that neither the Department of State nor of Defense has a monopoly on all wisdom. We should bring dissenters into policy discussions, not freeze them out; we should invite constructive criticism, not only because the critics have a right to be heard, but also because they often have something worth hearing.

"And this brings me to another, related point: The President cannot isolate himself from the great intellectual ferments of his time. On the contrary, he must consciously and deliberately place himself at their center. The lamps of enlightenment are lit by the spark of controversy; their flames can be snuffed out by the blanket of consensus.

"This is one reason why I don't want a Government of yesmen. It's why I do want a government drawn from the broadest possible base—an administration made up of Republicans, Democrats and independents, and drawn from politics, from career Government service, from universities, from business, from the professions—one including not only executives and administrators, but scholars and thinkers.

"While the President is a leader of thought, he is also a user of thought, and he must be a catalyst of thought. The thinking that he draws upon must be the best in America—and not only in Government. What's happening today in America and the world is happening not only in politics and diplomacy, but in science, education, the arts—and in all areas a President needs a constant exposure to ideas that stretch the mind. . . .

"When we think of leadership, we commonly think of persuasion. But the coin of leadership has another side. In order to lead, a President today must listen. . . . The President is the only official who represents every American—rich and poor, privileged and underprivileged. He represents those whose misfortunes stand in domestic focus and also the great, quiet forgotten majority—the nonshouters and the nondemonstrators, the millions who ask principally to go their own way in decency and dignity, and to have their own rights accorded the same respect they accord the rights of others. . . .

"The Presidency has been called an impossible office. If I thought it were, I would not be seeking it. But its functions have become cluttered, the President's time drained away in trivia, the channels of authority confused. When questions of human survival may turn on the judgments of one man, he must have time to concentrate on those great decisions that only he can make. One means of achieving this is by expanding the role of the Vice President—which I will do. I also plan a reorganized and strengthened Cabinet and a stronger White House staff than any yet put together. The people are served not only by a President, but by an administration, and not only by an administration, but by a Government. The President's chief function is to lead, not to administer; it is not to oversee every detail, but to put the right people in charge, to provide them with basic guidance and direction and to let them do the job. . . .

"Another change I believe necessary stems directly from my basic concept of government. For years now, the trend has been to sweep more and more authority toward Washington. Too many of the decisions that would have been better made in Seattle or St. Louis have wound up on the President's desk. I plan a streamlined federal system, with a return to the states, cities and communities of decision-making powers rightfully theirs. The purpose of this is not only to make government more effective and more responsive, but also to concentrate federal attention on those functions that can only be handled on the federal level.

"The Presidency is a place where priorities are set and goals determined. We need a new attention to priorities, and a new realism about goals. We are living today in a time of great promise—but also of too many promises. . . . A President must tell the people what cannot be done immediately as well as what can."

fice, James Monroe wrote, were "sufficient to employ the whole mind, and unceasing labors, of any individual." James K. Polk noted in his diary in December 1848 that "The public have no idea of the constant accumulation of business requiring the President's attention." Entrusting minor matters to subordinates resulted in errors, Polk found; hence he preferred "to supervise the whole operations of the government" himself. President Buchanan remarked that in the brief period of four years Polk had assumed the appearance of an old man.

Parliamentary System Suggested

It has been suggested from time to time that the burdens and powers of the Presidency be reduced by adopting some sort of parliamentary government in which the President would act as Prime Minister. Such a change was recommended as early as 1884 by Henry C. Lockwood in a book called *The Abolition of the Presidency*. Lockwood maintained that there was no effective check on Presidential power, for "The sentiment of hero worship, which to a great extent prevails among the American people, will endorse him." However, "With the destruction of Presidential and the establishment of representative Congressional government, we could, with impunity, place any man at the head of the Executive Branch, were he never so bad, ambitious, and inefficient, for it would then be known that at any moment he could be relieved from the cares of state."[12]

A similar proposal was made recently by Dwight MacDonald, political columnist for *Esquire*. MacDonald urged adoption of a constitutional amendment which would (1) abolish the office of the President and transfer the duties described in Article II to a chief executive "who shall be known as the Chairman"; (2) provide for election of the Chairman by members of the majority party in Congress; (3) establish a six-year term for the Chairman, unless his party should lose a major vote in Congress. In that event, the Chairman would resign and national elections for both houses of Congress would be held. MacDonald asserted that his proposal would, if adopted, respond "more flexibly to changes in public opinion and . . . [reduce] the prestige our President now commands because he is directly elected by the whole country."[13]

Proposal to Create Vice Presidents

Herman Finer, in a book on the "crisis and regeneration" of the Presidency, suggested in 1960 that the President and a Cabinet of no fewer than 11 Vice Presidents be elected on the same ticket every four years, without limit on the continued eligibility of any or all of them. Finer proposed, in addition, that members of the House and of the Senate be elected to four-year terms, which would run concurrently with those of the President and Vice Presidents. None of the Vice Presidents would serve as the presiding officer of the Senate. "Their attention and experience will be concentrated on executive responsibility."[14]

The purpose of Finer's proposal is to ease the burdens, not to diminish the powers, of the Chief Executive. He chose the number of 11 Vice Presidents as the "minimum number of men required to handle the most important government departments" and to afford "cogent discussion in cabinet." Some of the Vice Presidents, under the Finer plan, would not be assigned to a specific department but would be deputies of the President, concerned with policy formulation.

Proposals to reform the Presidency have not fared well in the past, regardless of their merits. The only substantive change that has been approved since World War II is the 22nd Amendment to the Constitution, which limits any person to two four-year terms as President. Efforts in the 1950s in behalf of the so-called Bricker amendment to revise and clarify the treaty power were inspired as much by fear of United Nations encroachment on American domestic law as by desire to restrict the President's prerogatives. Failure of those efforts made it seem more probable than ever that, for the foreseeable future, the only restraints on executive power would be those exercised by the holder of the office himself.[15]

Footnotes

1. Edward S. Corwin, *The President: Office and Powers* (1948 edition), p. 38.
2. Quoted by Richard E. Neustadt. *Presidential Power—The Politics of Leadership* (1960), p. 9.
3. Quoted by Saul K. Padover, *Commonweal*, Aug. 9, 1968.
4. Marcus Cunliffe, "A Defective Institution?" *Commentary*, February 1926, p. 32.
5. Edward S. Corwin and Louis K. Koenig, *The Presidency Today* (1956), p. 2.
6. Arthur M. Schlesinger, Jr., "The Constitution: Article II," *An American Primer* (1966), Daniel J. Boorstin, ed., p. 108.
7. James MacGregor Burns, *Presidential Government: The Crucible of Leadership* (1966), pp. 8-9.
8. *Journal of (Sen.) William Maclay*, Edgar S. Maclay, ed., pp. 128-133.
9. Jackson vetoed more bills, for example, than all his predecessors put together and secured the Presidential right to veto clearly constitutional measures.
10. In order, Martin Van Buren; William Henry Harrison (died in office); John Tyler; Polk; Zachary Taylor (died in office); Millard Fillmore; Franklin Pierce, James Buchanan.
11. Woodrow Wilson, *Congressional Government* (1885), pp. 301, 41-43.
12. Henry C. Lockwood, *The Abolition of the Presidency* (1884), pp. 191-182, 195.
13. Dwight MacDonald, "The Constitution of the United States Needs to Be Fixed," *Esquire*, October 1968, p. 144.
14. Herman Finer, *The Presidency: Crisis and Regeneration* (1960), p. 304.
15. This study was adapted from "Presidential Power," published Oct. 2, 1968, by Editorial Research Reports, an affiliate of Congressional Quarterly, Inc.

President's War Powers

The Vietnamese War reminded Congress that its constitutional power to declare war counts for little in today's world. It can be argued, in fact, that the President acting alone can exercise his power to make war.

Only five of this country's 11 serious and extended engagements with force against another country or countries have been accompanied by a declaration of war—and then only in response to the President's acts or recommendations.[1] *(See footnotes p. 640.)* Beginning with the Spanish-American War of 1898, a declaration of war by Congress has taken the form, not of an outright declaration, but of recognition of an existing state of war.

Congress virtually abdicated the power to declare war in Vietnam when it adopted, in August 1964, the

Tonkin Resolution Text

Following is the text of the "Gulf of Tonkin" resolution (PL 88-408) adopted by Congress in August 1964 following North Vietnamese attacks on U.S. ships:

Whereas naval units of the Communist regime in Vietnam, in violation of the principles of the Charter of the United Nations and of international law, have deliberately and repeatedly attacked United States naval vessels lawfully present in international waters, and have thereby created a serious threat to international peace;

Whereas these attacks are part of a deliberate and systematic campaign of aggression that the Communist regime in North Vietnam has been waging against its neighbors and the nations joined with them in the collective defense of their freedom;

Whereas the United States is assisting the peoples of Southeast Asia to protect their freedom and has no territorial, military or political ambitions in that area, but desires only that these peoples should be left in peace to work out their own destinies in their own way; Now, therefore, be it

Resolved by the Senate and House of Representatives of the United States of America in Congress assembled, That the Congress approves and supports the determination of the President, as Commander in Chief, to take all necessary measures to repel any armed attack against the forces of the United States and to prevent further aggression.

SEC. 2. The United States regards as vital to its national interest and to world peace the maintenance of international peace and security in Southeast Asia. Consonant with the Constitution of the United States and the Charter of the United Nations and in accordance with its obligations under the Southeast Asia Collective Defense Treaty, the United States is, therefore, prepared, as the President determines, to take all necessary steps, including the use of armed force, to assist any member or protocol state of the Southeast Asia Collective Defense Treaty requesting assistance in defense of its freedom.

SEC. 3. This resolution shall expire when the President shall determine that the peace and security of the area is reasonably assured by international conditions created by action of the United Nations or otherwise, except that it may be terminated earlier by concurrent resolution of the Congress.

Gulf of Tonkin resolution authorizing the President to "take all necessary measures" to stop aggression in Southeast Asia. The measures taken have included, among others, a tenfold increase in the number of American troops in Southeast Asia. If Congress had been able to foresee this development, it might have added a number of qualifications to the 1964 resolution. A future resolution of this kind might very likely con-

tain language specifying the measures which Congress deemed appropriate for use by the President.

The framers of the Constitution vested most of the Federal Government's war powers in the Legislative Branch. Article II, Sec. 2 provided that the "The President shall be Commander in Chief of the Army and Navy of the United States, and of the militia of the several states, when called into the actual service of the United States." Congress, however, was given the sole power "to declare war, grant letters of marque and reprisal, and make rules concerning captures on land and water." Also:

To raise and support armies, but no appropriation of money to that use shall be for a longer term than two years.

To provide and maintain a navy.

To make rules for the government and regulation of the land and naval forces.

To provide for calling forth the militia to execute the laws of the Union, suppress insurrections and repel invasions.

To provide for organizing, arming, and disciplining the militia, and for governing such part of them as may be employed in the service of the United States, reserving to the states respectively the appointment of officers, and the authority of training the militia according to the discipline prescribed by Congress.

During the debates in the Constitutional Convention of 1787, Pierce Butler of South Carolina was for "vesting the power [to declare war] in the President, who will have all the requisite qualities, and will not make war but when the nation will support it." Elbridge Gerry of Massachusetts retorted that he "never expected to hear in a republic a motion to empower the Executive alone to declare war"; George Mason of Virginia was "against giving the power of war to the Executive, because [he was] not safely to be trusted with it." A motion by Charles Pinckney of South Carolina to strike out the clause giving Congress sole power to declare war was rejected.[2]

The early Presidents made little use of such war powers as they had received. John Adams went so far in 1798, at the time of the undeclared naval war with France, as to divest himself of the title of Commander in Chief and confer it upon George Washington. The Senate approved that action unanimously. Three years later, President Jefferson forbade the Navy to attack the Tripoli pirates on the ground that Congress had not declared war. Alexander Hamilton ridiculed Jefferson for inaction. He said the Constitution meant "that it is the peculiar and exclusive province of Congress, when the nation is at peace, to change that state into a state of war." But "when a foreign nation declares or openly and avowedly makes war upon the United States, they are then by the very fact already at war and any declaration on the part of Congress is nugatory; it is at least unnecessary."[3]

President Madison followed the example of his predecessor rather than the advice of Hamilton. In his war message to Congress, June 1, 1812, Madison noted "on the side of Great Britain, a state of war against the United States; and on the side of the United States, a state of peace towards Great Britain." He added: "Whether the United States shall continue passive under these progressive usurpations . . . or, opposing force to force in defense of their nationla rights, shall commit a just cause into the hands of the Almighty Disposer of events . . . is a solemn question, which the Constitution wisely confides to the legislative department of the government." The proposed declaration of war was finally approved June 18, by a vote of 19 to 13 in the Senate and 79 to 49 in the House.

James K. Polk perceived that the war powers of the Chief Executive were potentially far greater than the Founding Fathers had intended them to be. One of his major ambitions as President was to acquire Texas and California to provide room for the extension of slavery. With the boundary between Mexico and the independent Republic of Texas in dispute, and with California belonging to Mexico, Polk reckoned that war with Mexico was necessary; "and a good deal of ingenuity went into bringing it about in such a way that the Mexicans would appear to be the aggressors." [4]

Polk sent an army detachment into Texas in May 1845; seven months later, Texas was annexed to the United States. It was not until April 1846, however, that the Mexicans responded by crossing the Rio Grande and attacking an American cavalry unit. Polk asked Congress for a declaration of war on May 11; the House complied within hours and the Senate the following day.

The President had got his way despite the fact that the Whig minority in Congress and a number of leading Democrats opposed the Mexican adventure. Secretary of State James Buchanan also expressed deep misgivings. [5] In the end, Congress had no choice; the President, through exercise of his power to conduct foreign policy, had made war inevitable.

Lincoln's Improvised Powers

In the early days of the Civil War, Lincoln used not only the war powers at his disposal but also some of the powers reserved to Congress. Without Congressional authorization, he issued a proclamation, May 3, 1861, increasing the size of the Regular Army and the Navy and calling for 80,000 volunteers. Moreover, he ordered 19 vessels added to the Navy and directed the Secretary of the Treasury to advance $2 million to three citizens to cover military and naval requisitions. When Congress convened, July 4, 1861, the President declared that some of his emergency measures, "whether strictly legal or not, were ventured upon under what appeared to be a popular demand and a public necessity, trusting then, as now, Congress would readily ratify them."

Congress validated Lincoln's actions by adopting a resolution, Aug. 6, 1861, providing that "All the acts, proclamations and orders of the President respecting the Army and Navy of the United States and calling out or relating to the militia or volunteers . . . are hereby approved and in all respects made valid . . . as if they had been issued and done under the previous express authority and direction of the Congress of the United States."

The Supreme Court, in a group of actions at law called the Prize Cases, (67 U.S. 1863) gave its blessing to another of Lincoln's improvised war powers. Early in the war, the President had proclaimed a blockade of Confederate ports to prevent the South from selling cotton to England and importing supplies. Vessels attempting to run the blockade were seized and condemned as "prizes"—that is, they were confiscated for having defied the President's order. The owners sued for redress on the ground that no war had ever been declared between North and South.

The Court observed that declarations of war were almost unknown in rebellions and insurrections. The President, charged with seeing that the laws be faithfully executed and armed with the powers of Commander in Chief, was entitled to treat the rebellious states as belligerents, to attack them, and to blockade them. The Court said:

"By the Constitution, Congress alone has the power to declare a national or foreign war . . . [The President] has no power to initiate or declare a war either against a foreign nation or a domestic state. . . . If a war be made by invasion of a foreign nation, the President is not only authorized but is bound to accept the challenge without any legislative act. And whether the hostile party be a foreign invader or states organized in rebellion, it is none the less a war although the declaration be 'unilateral.'"

On the other hand, the Court took a dim view of Lincoln's order authorizing various military commanders to suspend the writ of habeas corpus. Chief Justice Roger Brooke Taney, sitting as a federal circuit judge at Baltimore in 1861, ordered John Merryman released from military detention to stand trial in civil court. If the President had the power to suspend habeas corpus, Taney argued, "the people of the United States are no longer living under a government of laws, but every citizen holds life, liberty and property at the will and pleasure of the army officer in whose military district he may happen to be found." The Supreme Court supported Taney in *Ex parte Milligan,* a case decided in 1866 (71 U.S. 2). It ruled that civilians might be tried by military tribunal only where civil courts could not function because of invasion or disorder.

Delegation of Powers to Wilson

Woodrow Wilson had no need during World War I to resort to actions beyond the law, but he amassed greater powers than those employed by Lincoln. Many of the extraordinary powers exercised by President Wilson came by delegation from Congress. However, he drew also upon his constitutional powers to implement plans for which Congress denied or delayed legislative authorization.

A week after war was declared, the President used his authority as Commander in Chief to create by executive order the Committee on Public Information, under whose direction a system of voluntary news censorship was established and various government publicity services were organized. On April 28, 1917, again acting as Commander in Chief, he imposed stringent cable censorship, which was later extended to other forms of communication with foreign countries under authority of the Trading With the Enemy Act of Oct. 6, 1917.

Wilson appointed Herbert Hoover as Food Administrator on May 19, 1917. Then, on June 12, two months before passage of the Food and Fuel Control Act of Aug. 10, 1917, the President gave Hoover "full authority to undertake any steps necessary" for the conservation of food resources. The functions of the War Industries Board, created originally by the Council of National Defense, were expanded and vested almost exclusively in its chairman, Bernard M. Baruch, by a letter of the President to Baruch on March 4, 1918. By an executive order of May 28, 1918, Wilson formally established the War Industries Board as "a separate administrative agency to act for me and under my direction." Although created without statutory authority, the board was able to exert wide control over industry; behind its "requests" stood the President's power to commandeer factories or withhold fuel and transportation priorities.

The sweeping control of the economy acquired by Wilson during the war constituted, in the opinion of Rexford G. Tugwell, "the most fantastic expansion of the Executive known to American experience." The numerous powers conferred upon the President by Congress included power:

To take over and operate enemy vessels for use in the war.

To regulate and prohibit exports.

To take over and operate the railroads.

To regulate priorities in transportation.

To regulate by a licensing system the importation, manufacture, storage, mining or distribution of any necessaries.

To requisition foods, fuels, and other supplies necessary for any public use connected with national defense.

To fix a reasonable guaranteed price for wheat based upon a statutory minimum.

To fix the price of coal and regulate the method of its production, sale, shipment, distribution and storage.

To prohibit or license transactions in the United States by foreign insurance companies.

Reaction in Congress

Congress was willing to delegate the foregoing powers to the President because it recognized that modern warfare required singleness of direction, unity of command, and coordination of vital resources. After the war ended, new Republican majorities in Congress reasserted the prerogatives of the Legislative Branch. Feelings on Capitol Hill were ruffled by Wilson's failure to include Senators in the American delegation to the Paris Peace Conference. The Senate twice refused, in 1919 and again in 1920, to ratify the Treaty of Versailles. Repudiation of the treaty ushered in an era in which Congress exerted commanding influence over foreign policy.

The prevailing mood of isolationism in Congress and the country during the latter 1930s sharply limited President Roosevelt's freedom of action in foreign affairs. This mood found expression in such laws as the Neutrality Acts of 1935 and 1937, which prohibited shipments of arms, ammunition or implements of war to belligerent nations. A resolution introduced by Rep. Louis L. Ludlow (D Ind.) in 1935 and again in 1937 would have restricted the war powers of Congress as well as of the President. The resolution proposed a constitutional amendment to require submission of a declaration of war to a popular referendum. Although the Ludlow resolution was pried from committee by a discharge petition, Dec. 14, 1937, a motion to bring it to the House floor for a vote failed to carry.

Following Roosevelt's proclamation of a limited national emergency on Sept. 8, 1939, a week after the outbreak of war in Europe,[6] the United States began to drift from neutrality to engagement. An act of June 15, 1940, authorized military assistance to any Latin American republic that requested it. Almost three months later, on Sept. 3, 1940, the President announced that the United States had entered into an agreement under which Great Britain would receive 50 "over-age" (but, reconditioned and recommissioned) destroyers in return for the right to construct U. S. naval bases on certain sites in British territory in the western Atlantic. The Attorney General defended the constitutionality of the transaction on the ground that the President's power as Commander in Chief enabled him to "dispose" the armed forces of the United States.

Roosevelt cited the same power in 1941 as his authority for ordering American troops to Greenland and Iceland; Congress was not consulted on either occasion. In a special message to Congress, July 7, 1941, the President asserted that the occupation of Iceland by Germany would constitute a serious threat to Greenland and North America, to North Atlantic shipping, and to the steady flow of munitions to Britain. While the establishment of bases in Greenland and Iceland was not an act of war, it reflected this nation's hostility toward Germany, which declared war on the United States four days after Pearl Harbor.

Entry of this country into World War II was accompanied by concentration of virtually all war power in the President's hands. Under his power as Commander in Chief and using powers delegated by Congress, Roosevelt created many new emergency agencies and made them responsible to him rather than to existing departments or independent regulatory agencies. By V-J Day, no fewer than 29 war agencies were grouped under the Office for Emergency Management, which had been created by an administrative order of May 25, 1940.

New Problems in Postwar Era

President Truman, unlike President Wilson, encountered little Congressional interference in foreign policy in the early postwar years. The foundation of Truman's policy was the so-called Truman Doctrine, outlined in an address before a joint session of Congress, March 12, 1947. The doctrine called for containment of Communism throughout the world; as a first step, Truman requested $400 million for assistance to Greece and Turkey. Congress approved the full amount.

Scope of Executive Emergency Powers and Plans

The United States has lived in a continuous state of national emergency since the Roosevelt proclamation of Sept. 8, 1939. The Truman proclamation of 1950 has never been rescinded. Hence the President today has at his disposal many of the emergency powers employed by President Truman in the Korean War. He need not seek prior approval of Congress to wield these powers, which give him broad authority over military manpower and the civilian economy.

Under existing authority, the President can increase—and has increased—draft calls of men between the ages of 19 and 26. Moreover, he can establish draft priorities on the basis of marital, educational or occupational status. By proclaiming a new national emergency, the President could call to active duty up to one million Ready Reservists and National Guardsmen.

Congress in 1966 granted the President special temporary call-up authority for any Ready Reserve unit without an emergency declaration. President Johnson used this authority Jan. 25, 1968, to order 16,000 reservists to active duty, following North Korea's seizure on Jan. 23 of the U.S. intelligence ship Pueblo. All of those called up were due to be released by mid-1969.

The Defense Production Act of 1950, as amended, authorized the President "to purchase metals, minerals, and other (strategic) raw materials . . . for government use or for resale" and to store, process and refine those materials. Moreover, it empowered the President to require that performance under certain contracts or orders deemed essential to national defense shall take priority over performance under any other contract or order and to allocate materials and facilities in any manner that national defense may dictate. These powers are not to be used unless the President finds that a material is both essential and scarce, and that defense requirements cannot otherwise be met.

To expedite production and deliveries under government contracts, the Defense Production Act authorized the President to extend loans to private business enterprises for expansion of capacity, development of technical processes, or production of essential materials. If the Secretary of Agriculture or the Secretary of the Interior certifies that a particular material is likely to be in short supply in time of war or national emergency, the President may initiate programs for the development of substitute materials.

A number of war powers employed by the President in past wars have expired by limitation and could not be exercised unless reinstated by Congress. Among these are price, wage and rent controls; food, clothing, gasoline and consumer product rationing; news censorship; installment credit restrictions; production and building controls. The Office of Emergency Preparedness (formerly the Office of Emergency Planning) has prepared drafts of legislation that would restore these powers if such action becomes necessary. The OEP, in addition, has drawn up a National Plan for Emergency Preparedness covering every conceivable type of emergency from international tension to all-out nuclear war. The plan outlines the measures that it would be necessary to take during and following the various kinds of emergency. Power to take the necessary measures would be derived from diverse sources. The Office states: "In crises requiring extraordinary measures by the United States, the President or Congress might formally declare a national emergency, limited or unlimited, or a civil defense emergency in order to provide authority for certain actions. These authorities are available through standby statutes, executive orders, delegations, and directives."

Immediately after a nuclear attack, the President would issue an order (a draft of which has already been prepared) freezing all prices, rents and wages for at least five days. To thwart speculators, the order would close the stock exchanges. It would also prohibit retail sale of gasoline, non-perishable foods and other essentials except for emergency needs. Meanwhile, state governments would print and issue ration cards and coupon books, using reproduction plates already supplied by Washington. The overall objective would be to provide each survivor with 2,000-2,500 calories of food a day, an amount deemed sufficient to support "a reasonable degree of health and vigor for a limited time."

The Federal Government would operate from around 100 secret headquarters not far from Washington, D.C., in a half-dozen states. These emergency centers, constructed years ago, contain duplicates of official records. More than 50 of them are manned permanently on a year-around basis. Telegrams would be sent from the centers to undamaged war plants to activate standby munitions contracts. Then, as the country slowly recovered, the harsh controls originally imposed would be relaxed or rescinded.

Congress did not mount a serious challenge to Truman's war powers until 1951. At issue then was the President's authority to dispatch troops to Korea and to Western Europe. Sen. Robert A. Taft (R Ohio) opened a three-month-long "great debate" on Jan. 5, 1951, by asserting that Truman had "no authority whatever to commit American troops to Korea without consulting Congress and without Congressional approval." Moreover, he said, the President had "no power to agree to send American troops to fight in Europe in a war between the members of the Atlantic Pact and Soviet Russia."

The debate revolved principally around the troops-to-Europe issue. It came to an end—April 4, when the Senate adopted two resolutions approving the dispatch of four divisions in Europe. One of the resolutions stated that it was the sense of the Senate that "no ground troops in addition to such four divisions should be sent to Western Europe . . . without further Congressional approval." But neither resolution gained the force of law, for the House took no action.

Truman never asked Congress for a declaration of war in Korea, and he waited until Dec. 16, 1950—six months after the outbreak of hostilities—to proclaim the existence of a national emergency. In defense of this course, it was argued that the Russians or Chinese or both had violated post-World War II agreements on Korea, and that emergency powers authorized during World War II could still be applied.

Truman overstepped his powers as Commander in Chief when he relied on them, April 8, 1952, to take possession and control of all facilities, plants and properties of 86 steel companies involved in a dispute with the United Steelworkers. Congress ignored the President's request to approve the seizure order. Then, on June 2, the Supreme Court ruled that his action was without statutory authority and that it violated the concept of separation of powers by usurping functions of Congress. The Court rejected the argument that "The Commander in Chief of the armed forces has the ultimate power as such to take possession of private property in order to keep labor disputes from stopping production."[7]

Presidents since Truman have made frequent use of their war powers, sometimes in cooperation with Congress. For example, President Eisenhower asked Congress, Jan. 24, 1955, for advance approval of the use of American armed force in the event of a Communist attack on Formosa or the Pescadores. A resolution to that effect was adopted by both Senate and House within a week. However, Eisenhower sent troops to Lebanon in July 1958 strictly on his own authority. In a special message to Congress, July 15, he said this action was designed to protect American lives and "to assist the government of Lebanon in the preservation of Lebanon's territorial integrity and independence, which have been deemed vital to U.S. national interests and world peace."

President Kennedy, responding to Soviet threats to Allied rights in West Berlin, asked Congress on July 26, 1961, for authority to call up Ready Reservists and to extend the enlistments of men already on active duty. Such authority was granted in a joint resolution signed by the President on Aug. 1. Kennedy could not wait for Congressional approval of his actions in the Cuban missile crisis of October 1962. Confronted with a buildup of Soviet missile bases in Cuba, Kennedy ordered an immediate naval quarantine of Cuba to prevent delivery of additional Russian missiles. More than any other crisis in the postwar period, the Cuban episode illustrated the vast sweep of Presidential power in times of great emergency. [8]

The 'Credibility Gap'

President Johnson and his administration suffered from what the press and opposing politicians called a "credibility gap"—to express their doubts about official truthfulness. Walter Lippmann, a critic of the Johnson war policy, contended that the term was a euphemism akin to the Victorian habit of speaking of limbs rather than legs. Two Washington newspapermen observed in a book on the topic: "Newspaper reporters began talking about the Credibility Gap in the mid-1960s when they were too shy to speak of lies—the lies that increasingly, alarmingly emanate from the Government through its official spokesmen, including the President of the United States. [1] (*See footnotes p. 644.*)

Other Presidents, including all the recent ones, suffered credibility gaps under different names. "What sets the Johnson Administration apart from its predecessors," the newsmen wrote, "is merely that the dissemination of half-truths and untruths has become a matter of day-to-day routine."

President Johnson and his staff were sensitive to credibility-gap criticism and appeared perplexed by its prevalence. The President alluded to it in news conferences, such as one on Nov. 1, 1967, when he said to a questioner: "First, I want to correct you before you get a credibility charge." White House Press Secretary George Christian told a national television audience Dec. 31, 1967: "The question of the credibility gap is something that puzzles me as much as it does anyone. This has happened to other Presidents. It is, in a political sense, a smart thing to do, to discredit your President." Christian denied that he had ever deliberately misled a reporter, but he acknowledged that "there are mistakes on both sides."

The origin of the administration's credibility problem was traced by one observer to the first news conference held by Johnson after he succeeded to the Presidency. When asked on Dec. 7, 1963, about the size of the federal budget then being prepared, the new President pointed out that President Kennedy's last budget had been $98.8 billion. Then he said that about $3.5 billion would have to be added to that figure to cover "built-in" increases.

Reporters came away with the impression that the new budget would be between $102 billion and $103 billion. A few days later, the spending total changed again. At the President's Texas vacation headquarters,

Footnotes

1. *Congress declared war in the War of 1812, Mexican War, Spanish-American War, World War I and World War II. No declaration was made or requested in the Naval War with France (1798-1800), First Barbary War (1801-1805), Second Barbary War (1815), Mexican-American clashes of 1814-17, Korean War, Vietnamese War.*

2. *"Debates in the Federal Convention of 1787 as Reported by James Madison," Documents Illustrative of the Formation of the Union of the American States (1927), pp. 561-563.*

3. *James Grafton Rogers, World Policing and the Constitution (1945), p. 36.*

4. *Rexford G. Tugwell, The Enlargement of the Presidency (1960), p. 124.*

5. *Later, as President, Buchanan stressed the separation of executive and legislative war powers in his first three annual messages to Congress and in a special message on Feb. 18, 1859.*

6. *An unlimited national emergency was proclaimed on May 27, 1941. At that time the President ordered naval vessels to sink on sight any foreign submarines found in this country's "defensive waters."*

7. *Youngstown Sheet & Tube Co. v. Sawyer, 343 U.S. 579 (1952).*

8. *This study was adapted from "War Powers of the President," published March 14, 1966, by Editorial Research Reports, an affiliate of Congressional Quarterly, Inc.*

officials spread the word that the new budget would be about $100 billion. . .But when it was submitted to Congress it was none of these figures. . .It was $97.9 billion, and this was later reduced to $97.3 billion. Johnson had his victory. He had kept spending under the Kennedy level. And the reporters and the public had their first lesson in what to expect from the new President: calculated confusion. [2]

Fiscal affairs remained a source of criticism of the Johnson Administration on the credibility score. In an editorial in February 1968 calling for the resignation of Secretary of the Treasury Henry H. Fowler, *Fortune* magazine assigned to the Treasury "some of the blame for the dissembling, the secrecy, and the last-minute improvisation in economic and fiscal matters that have become standard Johnsonian practice." In the opinion of *Fortune,* it was "partly the Treasury's fault that the public was deceived on the true costs of the Vietnam War for more than a year following the 1965 decision to mount a major U.S. military effort."

Louis Harris reported in December 1967 that in a public opinion poll he conducted among potential voters, 51 per cent felt that President Johnson had not been candid in saying how many troops would be sent to Vietnam. A Gallup poll one month earlier found that 70 per cent of the persons interviewed thought the government had not told them all they should know about the war.

Newsmen generally agree that President Johnson's credibility troubles were rooted mainly in the Vietnam War. "Though the 'credibility gap' was almost daily on display before the major escalations of 1965," Richard H. Rovere wrote, "he [Johnson] was in no serious trouble; ever since, he has been in trouble." Rovere explained: "People normally indifferent as to whether a President misleads them about the exact size of the deficit he plans to incur or about his choice for an Under Secretary of the Interior are by no means indifferent when they are deceived about what they properly regard as a matter of life or death." [3]

Statements on Vietnam War

American foes of the war cited a statement President Johnson made during the 1964 election campaign. He told an audience at Akron (Ohio) University on Oct. 21, 1964: "We are not about to send American boys nine or ten thousand miles to do what Asian boys ought to be doing for themselves." Yet within six months the United States had doubled the size of its forces in South Vietnam to 34,000, the beginning of a military buildup which reached 542,000 by the time he left office.

Unfulfilled predictions of victory, differing justifications for American policy, and doubts about the sincerity of Washington's professed desire to negotiate peace—all were advanced in support of further claims that the public had been misled. "The major part of the military task can be completed by the end of 1965," Secretary of Defense Robert S. McNamara and Gen. Maxwell D. Taylor said in a joint statement issued by the White House, Oct. 2, 1963, upon their return from an inspection trip to Vietnam.

Having been stung, officials later grew reluctant to predict when hostilities would end. But optimistic reports on the war's progress kept coming. After the U.S. commander in Vietnam, Gen. William C. Westmoreland, appeared before the Senate Foreign Relations Committee, Nov. 16, 1967, Sen. Albert Gore (D Tenn.) was moved to complain: "This is about the 13th optimistic report we've had."

America's war policy was repeatedly defended by government spokesmen, including President Johnson, as necessary to protect the right of the South Vietnamese people to political self-determination. This point was emphasized when South Vietnam conducted presidential and legislative elections on Sept. 3, 1967. However, the next month Secretary of State Dean Rusk appeared to put the American war commitment in terms of this country's self-interest. He told a news conference on Oct. 12 that the United States must stand by South Vietnam lest other nations of Southeast Asia conclude that they can expect no help from America and therefore seek accommodation with Communist China. Rusk warned that "Within the next decade or two there will be a billion Chinese on the mainland, armed with nuclear weapons, with no certainty about what their attitude . toward the rest of Asia will be."

On the matter of negotiations, critics of the administration were wont to say its professed desire to hold peace talks could not be taken seriously as long as the United States continued to build up military strength in South Vietnam and refused to halt bombing in the North. Government pronouncements on many other aspects of the war also were in dispute. Casualty figures always seemed to show heavier losses on the other side. And they often purported to give a precise "body count" of the enemy dead even during the course of battle. McNamara was questioned closely on NBC's "Meet the Press," Feb. 4, 1968, about U.S. claims that Communist forces had lost 15,000 men killed in a week of attacks on South Vietnamese population centers. McNamara acknowledged that the figures were a "reasonable approximation of the price the enemy is paying" and that "to some degree they may be overstated."

Sen. J. W. Fulbright (D Ark.), chairman of the Senate Foreign Relations Committee, in time would question whether President Johnson had all the facts he needed about North Vietnamese attacks on U.S. Navy destroyers in the Gulf of Tonkin in August 1964 to justify an immediate request to Congress for a sweeping joint resolution to back up Presidential action in Southeast Asia. The so-called Gulf of Tonkin resolution, approved by both houses almost without dissent on Aug. 7, voiced support of "the determination of the President . . . to take all necessary measures to repel any armed attack against the forces of the United States and to prevent further aggression" in Southeast Asia. This resolution became, in effect, the legal foundation for Presidential measures escalating the war in Vietnam.

Pentagon Cover Stories

When North Korean patrol boats seized the U.S. Navy intelligence ship Pueblo on Jan. 23, 1968, the Administration was asked by a number of news publications to say frankly whether the ship was or was not spying in North Korean territorial waters prior to its capture and why it was not better protected. The *Washington Post,* which tended to support the Administration's Vietnam policy, commented editorially the following day: "The Administration must realize that public tolerance in this country of the unexplained and the inexplicable is wearing thin. . . . A public which was lied to over the U-2 [spy plane], confused, if nothing else, by the Tonkin Gulf [resolution], and misled, to say the least, in the affair of another intelligence ship attacked by the Israelis last year, cannot be satisfied or reassured by the same old coverups." (Official statements referred to the seizure in "international waters." McNamara said on NBC-TV, Feb. 4, however, that he could not be completely certain that the ship had not intruded into North Korean waters during the Jan. 10-21 period prior to capture. To free the surviving crewmen, the U.S. Government Dec. 12, 1968, signed a statement affirming the "confessions" made by some of the crewmen from prison that the ship had intruded into North Korean waters. But at the same time the Government formally repudiated its own statement — with the explanation that it had been signed only to obtain release of the crew. Upon their release, Dec. 22, crewmen said that their "confessions" had indeed been false, having been made only after repeated beatings and threats of death.)

The *Washington Post* was referring to a Pentagon "cover story" when the U.S.S. Liberty was attacked and damaged by Israeli naval and air units in the Mediterranean during the Arab-Israeli war in June 1967. When newsmen asked why the ship was close to the war zone, Defense Department officials said the ship was there in order to use the moon as a passive reflector for its communications.

That explanation was soon followed by another saying the Liberty was "sailing approximately 15 miles north of the Sinai Peninsula . . . to assure communications between posts in the Middle East and to assist in relaying information concerning the evacuation of American dependents and other American citizens" caught in the war zone. But it soon became known that the Liberty was an electronic eavesdropper, or "ferret ship," whose job is to gather information rather than to relay communications.

Defense of Administration

Some leading officials of the Administration tended to believe it had become the whipping boy of a waspish press, which itself reflected discontent over the Vietnam War. The London *Economist* viewed the problem of Johnson's credibility as "a problem of the gap between the man's buccaneering manner and the real substance of the ideas that lie beneath the manner." It said:

"The Americans themselves have been slow to realize this. Mr. Johnson came to the Presidency in the worst of all possible circumstances. . .The Americans, after a half-rational love affair with John Kennedy, were disposed to be suspicious of any successor. . .Mr. Johnson has been the victim of a bad case of straight prejudice. . . .The last of the frontier Presidents cannot turn himself into a megalopolis American of 1968. It is going to be a problem for him right up to November." *4*

Max Frankel, White House correspondent for the *New York Times,* looked at the credibility gap in another light. He reported that Johnson liked to keep his "options open" until the last minute before he made a decision. "It is here," Frankel wrote, "in his quest for time before decision and commitment, that Mr. Johnson most often seems to the public to be domineering, querulous and secretive. . . . He has delayed or even canceled decisions or appointments that were prematurely revealed without his consent. . . . Mr. Johnson's habitual prudence and secretiveness, combined with his emphasis on results and neglect of appearances, have produced the celebrated 'Credibility Gap,' at which his Administration has taken so many casualties."

The high cost of operating as he does, Frankel recounted, was demonstrated when Johnson set out to create a more effective system of famine relief for India. India's friends around the world bitterly resented the delay of new American commitments, and they said so while Johnson let pass one "absolute deadline" after another.

The United States' wheat stockpiles were dwindling and Congressional support for all foreign aid was declining. He therefore pressed the Indians to demonstrate that they were doing everything possible in their own behalf and spurred them into action to help him force greater contributions of wheat, fertilizer or cash from other nations . . . He stood fast as the villain of the piece, without every publicly blaming other nations for the slowness of their response, until he had created an entirely new system of relief of presumably greater benefit to the Indians, at less cost to the United States and thus with more solid support in Congress.[11] The President earned little credit for that exercise. "More often than most of his critics would grant," Frankel added, "Mr. Johnson has thus sacrificed effect for effectiveness."[5]

On questions of Vietnam policy, the Administration denied that it had shifted ground regarding war aims. First, it pointed out that containment of Communism has characterized American foreign policy for two decades. President Kennedy gave that rationale for Vietnam when he said at a news conference on Sept. 12, 1963: "We want the war to be won, the Communists to be contained, and the Americans to go home. . . . But we are not there to see a war lost, and we will follow the policy which I have indicated today of advancing those causes and issues which help win the war."

Credibility Gaps in Other Times

American history is replete with doubts cast on Presidential credibility. A notable example involved the country's entry into the Mexican War (1846-48), a conflict which, like Vietnam today, was unpopular with large sectors of the population. President Polk sent U.S. troops into a disputed border region between the Nueces River and the Rio Grande. The Mexican government considered their presence an act of aggression and its forces shelled an advanced American position.

Polk thereupon proclaimed that American blood had been shed on American soil and thus persuaded Congress to declare war. However, the President was repeatedly challenged by the Whig opposition to produce evidence that the attack occurred on American

'Freedom of Information' Law

Congress in 1966 passed a bill (S 1160—PL 89-487) designed to make federal agencies disclose more information to the public. The bill largely rewrote Section 3 of the 1946 Administrative Procedure Act, the law governing agency information disclosure, which had been criticized for vagueness since its enactment. Known as the Freedom of Information bill, S 1160 affected information policies of the entire Executive Branch.

Like the original Section 3, S 1160 required agencies to publish procedures and rules in the Federal Register; and to make publicly available all final opinions, statements of policy and staff manuals, and to maintain an index of these. However, where the old law had permitted agencies at their discretion to exempt from this rule matter "required for good cause to be held confidential," S 1160 permitted exemption only of matter which met one of nine specific requirements (such as that relating to national defense or confidential financial information). In addition, S 1160 for the first time provided a court procedure by which an aggrieved person could move against an agency it thought was improperly withholding records, and federal courts were authorized to punish responsible agency officers for contempt. Also for the first time, S 1160 required agencies to keep public records of final votes on proceedings.

Legislation similar to S 1160 had been before Congress since 1947. It was supported by the press, the American Civil Liberties Union, the American Bar Assn. and some legal scholars, all of whom contended that existing law was being used inconsistently by agencies, often as an excuse to withhold information to which the public had a right. The legislation was opposed by the affected agencies and, to some extent, by business interests, although the final version had been amended to meet some objections by business. In 1965 testimony on the proposal, Administration representatives said that it would be unwise to substitute a stringent rule for flexible Executive Branch judgments. The President himself refrained from taking a position on the proposal until after its enactment. Then, in a statement accompanying signing of the bill, he praised it as a product of a free society and said it provided for Government confidentiality when necessary, while at the same time protecting the public's right to information.

Most of the provisions of S 1160 were the same as those of a bill passed by the Senate in the 88th Congress, and the 89th Congress made no changes in the bill after it was first reported by the Senate Judiciary Committee in October 1965.

soil. Abraham Lincoln, then a young Congressman, introduced a number of resolutions demanding to know the exact spot. He rejected Polk's claim as "sheerest deception."

Standards of credibility can be affected by the values of the time. President McKinley said he prayerfully searched his soul before deciding to keep the Philippines in American possession—in order to uplift and Christianize the inhabitants. His explanation might be hooted down today, but at the turn of the century it seemed thoroughly credible to a great part of the public.

White House credibility was openly questioned in the last months of Woodrow Wilson's Administration. The President lay ill, felled by a stroke, and the country was unsure whether he or someone else was performing the duties of his office. Franklin D. Roosevelt was criticized for the devious tactics he employed to aid Britain and France against Nazi Germany by all means short of American entry into World War II. Roosevelt believed that a Nazi victory would be disastrous, but the United States was officially neutral and much of its public sentiment was isolationist.

James MacGregor Burns recounted that in the 1940 election campaign Roosevelt "compromised on the issue throughout the whole campaign, stressing his love for peace and neutrality and his record on defense rather than expounding his crucial policy of aiding Britain even at the risk of war."[6] Roosevelt's Republican opponent, Wendell L. Wilkie, had scored heavily by saying that the President's re-election would mean war within six months. Roosevelt's advisers and Democratic party chieftains pleaded with him to reassure the voters.

The President demurred at first, but in the end he told a campaign audience in Boston: "I have said this before, but I shall say it again and again and again: Your boys are not going to be sent into any foreign wars." Roosevelt had indeed said the same thing before, but always with the proviso "except in case of attack." This time he left out the proviso. After the United States found itself in World War II, the statement was to be flung in Roosevelt's face repeatedly. To this day it is cited against the credibility of politicians.

Perhaps the most embarrassing single incident involving the veracity of the American government was the U-2 affair in 1960. When an American U-2 spy plane was shot down over Russia on May 1, the United States issued a cover story which the Kremlin soon was able to expose to the world as a lie. (*See Congress and the Nation*, 1945-64, p. 123-124, 1753-56.)

The Kennedy Administration suffered similar embarrassment in 1961 over the Bay of Pigs. Washington officially tried to portray the abortive invasion of Cuba, which was planned and financed by the Central Intelligence Agency, as solely a Cuban refugee undertaking. There was evidence that the Kennedy Administration not only misled the American public but also Adlai E. Stevenson, U.S. Ambassador to the United Nations, who denied Cuban charges of American complicity. Arthur M. Schlesinger Jr. wrote later *(A Thousand Days)* that Stevenson had been poorly informed by his own government and was unaware of the U.S. role in Cuba.

During the Cuban missile crisis of October 1962 the Defense Department deliberately issued false information and its chief spokesman later defended such action on the ground that "the government had the right, indeed the duty, to lie if necessary to mislead the enemy and protect the people it represented." Arthur Sylvester, then Assistant Secretary of Defense for Public Affairs, issued a news release saying the Pentagon had "no information indicating the presence of offensive weapons in Cuba," when in fact it was aware of Russian missiles on the island and busy mapping ways to remove them. Upon learning about the missiles, President Kennedy interrupted a political tour in Chicago to return to Washington—on the pretext that he had a cold.

Government-Press Conflicts

The founding fathers recognized the connection between democratic government and an informed public. But their acceptance of the principle of freedom of the press did not bring tranquillity to the relations between newspapers and politicians. Washington went to his grave hating the press, and his Presidential successors have had trouble with it up to the present day. "The conflict between the men who make and the men who report the news is as old as time," James B. Reston of the *New York Times* has written. "News may be true, but it is not truth, and they never see it the same way. . . . In the old days, the reporters or couriers of bad news were often put to the gallows; now they are given the Pulitzer Prize, but the conflict goes on." [7]

Bill Moyers, former press secretary to President Johnson and now a newspaper publisher, has commented:

As a journalist I am quick to say 'tell us more.' But as one who has had some experience in crisis management, I can understand why silence is sometimes the wisest policy. . .What I am speaking of is the necessity for a President to refrain at times from telling all he knows—and to resist commenting on a situation until he can be certain his words will produce the intended result. Some of us will not hesitate to hustle a President's priorities if we can; unfortunately we forget far more quickly than a President can afford to forget, that diplomacy and political maneuvers, like film, can curl up up and die from exposure." [8]

"Every sophisticated newsman knows the Federal Government puts its best, not its worst, foot forward," Arthur Sylvester observed. "The newsman's best friend, his club, his business, his city, county and state government all do things that way. That being so, it is

his function to penetrate this protective coloration behind which all men attempt to mask their errors." Sylvester asserted that the press liked to explain its shortcomings by blaming the Johnson Administration for a credibility gap. "If there is a credibility gap," he contended, "it measures the failure of newsmen to do their job." [9]

The Cuban missile crisis of 1962 graphically pointed up the difficulties involved in a conflict between the government's obligation to preserve national security and the public's right to be informed. Clearly, the highest authorities in government felt they had a right to lie at that time, although Arthur Sylvester was the only one to admit it explicitly. But his "right to lie" thesis was roundly criticized in the press. The very nature of this controversy tends to put the press and government on opposite sides. "Confidence is a fragile and precious asset of government," Walter Lippmann wrote, [10] "—in fact the supreme asset of a democratic government. The widespread feeling that the Federal Government in Washington cannot be believed is enough to make responsible men shudder." [11]

The 'Bobby Baker Case'

The "Bobby Baker Case" involved an ethics issue in Congress at the time Lyndon B. Johnson was Senate Majority Leader, but it came to light only a short time before he assumed the Presidency. The case had political overtones reminiscent of scandals during the Truman and Eisenhower Administrations. Disclosures about the wide-ranging activities of Robert G. (Bobby) Baker were embarrassing to Johnson because, as Senate Majority Leader, his chief staff assistant was Baker. Baker was Secretary to the Senate Majority, a $19,600-a-year post, from 1955 until he resigned under fire Oct. 7, 1963. He bore a reputation as Johnson's protege and came to be characterized by Republicans in Congress as the Senate's "most powerful employee."

Revelations of Baker's numerous "improprieties" while a Senate aide also exposed the Senate as a whole to criticism and prompted a review of Congressional ethics. The Baker case, ultimately, had little significant impact on the Johnson Presidency. Johnson did not suffer noticeably in the 1964 re-election campaign from Republican attacks on his well-publicized connections with Baker.

The Senate Rules and Administration Committee investigated Baker's activities from the standpoint of Congressional ethics and issued reports in June 1964 and June 1965. In the first report, the Committee's Democratic majority found Baker guilty of "gross improprieties." The Republican minority objected that the investigation was incomplete and a "whitewash."

On Sept. 1, 1964, Sen. John J. Williams (R Del.) said in a Senate speech that an insurance man who had figured prominently in the earlier investigation had charged that Baker and Matthew H. McCloskey conspired to contribute $25,000, illegally, to the 1960 Democratic campaign when McCloskey was prime contractor for the District of Columbia Stadium (since

Footnotes

1. *Erwin Knoll and William McGaffin, Anything But the Truth (1968), p. 13.*
2. *James Deakin, "The Dark Side of L.B.J.," Esquire, August 1967, p. 135.*
3. *Richard H. Rovere, "Letter from Washington," New Yorker, Sept. 23, 1967, pp. 158-159.*
4. *"Lyndon's Year," The Economist, Dec. 30, 1967, p. 1271.*
5. *Max Frankel, "Why the Gap Between L.B.J. and the Nation," New York Times Magazine, Jan. 7, 1968, pp. 42-44.*
6. *James MacGregor Burns, Roosevelt: The Lion and the Fox (1966) p. 448.*
7. *James B. Reston, "The Press, the President and Foreign Policy," Foreign Affairs, July 1966, p. 555.*
8. *Speech before the Foreign Press Association of America, Nov. 27, 1967.*
9. *Arthur Sylvester, "The Government Has a Right to Lie," Saturday Evening Post, Nov. 18, 1967, p. 15.*
10. *Walter Lippmann, "The Democrats in 1968," Newsweek, Jan. 1, 1968, p. 9.*
11. *This study was adapted from "Credibility Gaps and the Presidency," published Feb. 7, 1968, by Editorial Research Reports, an affiliate of Congressional Quarterly Inc.*

renamed Robert F. Kennedy Stadium). The disclosure caused the Senate to reopen the Rules Committee investigation.

In June 1965 the Committee issued a report on the second phase of its inquiry. The majority views covered the allegations involving the stadium contract and five other major issues investigated in both phases. The majority in effect found Baker and McCloskey "not guilty." Most of the statements on the other issues tended to back up conclusions in the first report. The minority views were sharply critical of the majority's conclusions in the stadium case and repeated earlier objections to the majority's handling of the investigation.

Both the majority and minority views in the 1964 and 1965 reports called for rules requiring financial disclosure statements by Members of Congress and their employees. The Senate in July 1965 appointed members to a Senate Select Committee on Standards and Conduct, which it had established 12 months earlier. When the Committee met, it postponed formal operations until 1966. In 1968, the Senate and House adopted separate but similar rules requiring their members to disclose outside income above fixed amounts.

Baker's Conviction

In the meantime, Baker had been indicted Jan. 5, 1966, by a federal grand jury and convicted in the U.S. District Court for the District of Columbia, Jan. 29, 1967, on seven counts of income tax evasion, one count of theft, and one count of conspiracy to defraud the Federal Government. The trial before a jury of six men and six women, all of them present or past federal employees and all Negro except one white woman, lasted 14 days.

Judge Oliver Gasch, who had presided at the trial, sentenced Baker to prison April 7, 1967, for one to three years on each count, the sentences to run concurrently. The maximum sentence would have been 48 years in prison and a fine of $47,000. Baker's attorney, Edward Bennett Williams, appealed, and Baker remained free on $5,000 bond pending the outcome of the appeal.

The disclosures about Baker's activities which ultimately led to his trial and conviction began in 1963, when a civil suit was filed against him charging that he had used influence to obtain contracts in defense plants for a vending machine concern, the Serv-U Corp. The action was brought by a business competitor, Ralph L. Hill, president of Capitol Vending Co. (*Congress and the Nation,* Vol. I, p. 1773-1778.)

Highlights of Trial

Two California savings and loan association executives testified Jan. 12 that in 1962 they gave Baker about $66,000 for campaign contrbutions to seven Senators and one House Member, Ways and Means Committee Chairman Wilbur D. Mills (D Ark.). Mills and one of the Senators, Foreign Relations Committee Chairman J. W. Fulbright (D Ark.), testified that they had received none of the funds. Defense counsel Edward Bennett Williams stipulated that none of the

other six Senators had received any of the funds. The six Senators were: President Pro Tempore Carl Hayden (D Ariz.), Minority Leader Everett McKinley Dirksen (R Ill.), Wallace F. Bennett (R Utah), Frank Carlson (R Kan.), Thruston B. Morton (R Ky.) and George A. Smathers (D Fla.). One of the savings and loan executives testified that Baker told him the California savings and loan associations could improve their standing in Congress with a "very impressive" contribution to certain Senators and House Members and could "win friends" in Congress at a time when a bill was pending to increase taxes on the associations.

The trial involved the following charges:

1. Counts 1 and 2 charged Baker with evading more than $1,500 in income taxes in 1961 and more than $21,000 in income taxes in 1962.

2. Counts 3 through 7 charged him with larceny after trust, grand larceny and transporting stolen money in that he collected about $99,600 from a group of California savings and loan executives but, instead of forwarding it as campaign contributions, as was intended, kept about $80,000 for himself.

3. Counts 8 and 9 charged Baker with fraud, with making false statements and with conspiracy in that he assisted an associate, Wayne L. Bromley, in preparing a false income tax return for 1963 and that he conspired with Bromley and on one occasion with former Nevada Lt. Gov. Clifford A. Jones to defraud the Government on taxes.

Counts 4 and 6 were for larceny after trust. When Baker was convicted of grand larceny, he was automatically acquitted of counts 4 and 6 since, as a matter of law, he could not be guilty of both. (Grand larceny involved an intention to misappropriate funds at the time of receiving them; larceny after trust involved an intention to misappropriate funds sometime after receiving them.)

Only the ninth count dealt with matters reported by the Senate Rules Committee. The count charged a conspiracy to defraud the Government in its income tax collection in regard to $5,000 allegedly received by Baker after a federal charter was granted in 1962 to the Redwood National Bank in San Rafael, Calif.

Presidential Disability: The 25th Amendment

A decade of Congressional concern over the issue of Presidential disability was eased in 1967 by the ratification of the 25th Amendment to the Constitution. The Amendment provided for the first time for continuity in functions of the Presidency in the event of Presidential disability and for filling a vacancy in the Vice Presidency. The Amendment was ratified and became part of the Constitution when the Nevada state senate voted at 10:44 a. m. (PST), Feb. 10, to make that state the 38th to approve the proposal.

In a race to be last, Nevada had ratified the Amendment on Feb. 8, but nullified that action when it learned it was only 37th at that point. Ohio, North Dakota and Montana reportedly also were vying for the distinction of being 38th. The Minnesota legislature acted at 11:31 a.m. (CST) on Feb. 10, becoming the 37th state, and Nevada, in a time zone two hours earlier than that in Minnesota, made its decisive move one hour and 13 minutes later.

Congressional consideration of the question of Presidential disability had been prompted by former President Eisenhower's heart attack in 1955. But ambiguity of the language of the disability clause, Article II, Section 1, Clause 6 of the Constitution, had pro-

Text of 25th Amendment

Section 1. In case of the removal of the President from office or his death or resignation, the Vice President shall become President.

Sec. 2. Whenever there is a vacancy in the office of the Vice President, the President shall nominate a Vice President who shall take office upon confirmation by a majority vote of both houses of Congress.

Sec. 3. Whenever the President transmits to the President pro tempore of the Senate and the Speaker of the House of Representatives his written declaration that he is unable to discharge the powers and duties of his office, and until he transmits to them a written declaration to the contrary, such powers and duties shall be discharged by the Vice President as Acting President.

Sec. 4. Whenever the Vice President and a majority of either the principal officers of the Executive departments or of such other body as Congress may by law provide, transmit to the President pro tempore of the Senate and the Speaker of the House of Representatives their written declaration that the President is unable to discharge the powers and duties of his office, the Vice President shall immediately assume the powers and duties of the office as Acting President.

Thereafter, when the President transmits to the President pro tempore of the Senate and the Speaker of the House of Representatives his written declaration that no inability exists, he shall resume the powers and duties of his office unless the Vice President and a majority of either the principal officers of the executive departments or of such other body as Congress may by law provide, transmit within four days to the President pro tempore of the Senate and the Speaker of the House of Representatives their written declaration that the President is unable to discharge the powers and duties of his office. Thereupon Congress shall decide the issue, assembling within forty-eight hours for that purpose if not in session. If the Congress, within twenty-one days after receipt of the latter written declaration, or, if Congress is not in session, within twenty-one days after Congress is required to assemble, determines by two-thirds vote of both houses that the President is unable to discharge the powers and duties of his office, the Vice President shall continue to discharge the same as Acting President; otherwise, the President shall resume the powers and duties of his office.

voked occasional debate ever since the Constitutional Convention of 1787. At that time there was no settlement as to how far the term "disability" extended or who would be the judge of it.

Clause 6 provided that Congress should decide who was to succeed to the Presidency in the event that both the President and the Vice President died, resigned or became disabled. Congress enacted succession laws three times. By the Act of March 1, 1792, it provided for succession (after the Vice President) of the President pro tempore of the Senate, then of the House Speaker, but if those offices were vacant, states were to send electors to choose a new President.

That law stood until passage of the Presidential Succession Act of Jan. 19, 1886, which changed the line of succession to run from the Vice President to the Secretary of State, Secretary of the Treasury and so on through the Cabinet, in order or rank.

Sixty-one years later, the Act of July 18, 1947 (still in force), placed the Speaker of the House and the President pro tempore of the Senate ahead of Cabinet officers in succession after the Vice President.

Prior to ratification of the 25th Amendment, no provisions had been made to define procedures in the event of Presidential incapacity. Two Presidents sustained serious disabilities—President Garfield after he was shot in 1881 and President Wilson after he suffered a stroke in 1919. In each case the Vice President did not assume any duties of the Presidency for fear he would appear to be usurping the powers of that office.

Nor had any provisions been made to fill the Vice Presidency if that office became vacant. The United States had been without a Vice President 16 times for a total of 37 years, either when the elected Vice President succeeded to the Presidency, died or, on one occasion, resigned. (John C. Calhoun resigned as Vice President Dec. 28, 1832, to become a U.S. Senator.)

Ratification of the 25th Amendment established procedures that clarified these areas of uncertainty in the Constitution.

The Amendment provided that the Vice President should become Acting President under either one of two circumstances. If the President informed Congress that he was unable to perform his duties, the Vice President would become Acting President until the President could resume his responsibilities.

If the Vice President and a majority of the Cabinet, or other body designated by Congress, found the President to be incapacitated, the Vice President would become Acting President until the President informed Congress that his disability had ended. Congress was given 21 days to resolve any dispute over the President's disability.

Whenever a vacancy occurred in the office of Vice President, either by death, succession to the Presidency or resignation, the President was to nominate a Vice President to be confirmed by a majority vote of both houses of Congress.

Congressional Action

Sen. Birch Bayh (D Ind.), chairman of the Senate Judiciary Committee's Subcommittee on Constitutional Amendments, introduced the proposed 25th Amendment (S J Res 1) on Jan. 6, 1965. House Judiciary Committee Chairman Emanuel Celler (D N.Y.) had introduced a companion resolution (H J Res 1) two days earlier.

President Johnson on Jan. 28, 1965, officially endorsed both measures, urging Congress "to approve them forthwith for submission to ratification by the states."

The Senate's joint resolution was adopted on a 72-0 roll-call vote, Feb. 19, 1965, and the House Resolution April 13, 1965, on a **368-29** key vote.

Senate-House conferees took two months to resolve the differences. The primary difficulty was in deciding whether to set a time limit for decision by Congress in the event a Vice President and majority of the Cabinet challenged a formal assertion by the President that his inability had ended. The House had set a 10-day limit, the Senate none. Conferees finally agreed to a 21-day time limit.

The House on June 30, 1965, adopted the conference report by voice vote, and the Senate adopted it by a **68-5** key vote on July 6. The proposed Amendment was then sent to the states for ratification.

When notified of the ratification of the 25th Amendment, Feb. 10, 1967, Bayh declared, "It's a happy day. A constitutional gap that has existed for years has finally been filled."

Informal Disability Agreements

After President Eisenhower's series of illnesses in 1955, 1956 and 1957, the President and Vice President Richard M. Nixon had entered into an agreement to provide for an orderly, temporary transfer of power should the President again become incapacitated. Nixon would have become Acting President after "such consultation as it seems to him appropriate under the circumstances."

President Kennedy and then-Vice President Lyndon B. Johnson made the same agreement in 1961, adding that "consultation" should include the Cabinet. After President Kennedy's assassination, President Johnson and House Speaker John W. McCormack (D Mass.), next in line to succeed to the Presidency, entered into the same agreement. President Johnson and Vice President Hubert H. Humphrey signed virtually the same agreement just prior to President Johnson's Jan. 20, 1965, inauguration.

The legality of these informal arrangements was questioned by some but no occasion arose for a test in the courts.

Johnson's Operations

The matter of temporary Presidential disability was raised twice during the Johnson years, when the President underwent surgery in 1965 for removal of his gall bladder and in 1966 for the removal of a nonmalignant polyp from his throat and for the repair of a ventral hernia.

The matter clearly was one of highest concern to the President himself in announcing the pending op-

---

Text of Johnson-Humphrey Agreement

The following procedures, which are identical to the procedures adopted by President Eisenhower and Vice President Nixon as well as President Kennedy and Vice President Johnson, have been agreed upon by President Johnson and Vice President Humphrey:

(1) In the event of inability the President would—if possible—so inform the Vice President, and the Vice President would serve as Acting President, exercising the powers and duties of the office until the inability had ended.

(2) In the event of an inability which would prevent the President from so communicating with the Vice President, the Vice President, after such consultation as seems to him appropriate under the circumstances, would decide upon the devolution of the powers and duties of the office and would serve as Acting President until the inability had ended.

(3) The President, in either event, would determine when the inability had ended and at that time would resume the full exercise of the powers and duties of the office.

---

erations. After describing the necessity for surgery and the steps taken to ensure proper diagnosis, the President stated that he had consulted with the Vice President, members of the Cabinet, Congressional leaders and former President Eisenhower and assured the public that doctors "expect there will be minimal time during which I will not be conducting business as usual."

Before his first operation, Johnson referred to his pre-election agreement with Vice President Hubert H. Humphrey concerning the devolution of duties and powers of the Presidency in the event of disability. He noted that the agreement was virtually the same as that made by Eisenhower and Vice President Richard M. Nixon, who originated the practice in 1958. Finally, the President assured the public that the Vice President, top Cabinet officers ("particularly the Secretary of State and the Secretary of Defense") and the White House staff would remain in communication with the Vice President, that the Vice President would be in Washington on the day of the operation and that Humphrey and the top Cabinet officers were fully informed on all major policy matters.

While the President was described as in good health and the operations as routine, Johnson had a medical history which included a massive heart attack, suffered July 2, 1955, when he was Senate Majority Leader. He took a six-month leave from those duties to recover, describing the attack as one "as bad as you can have and still live." A heavy smoker before the attack, Johnson gave up tobacco and went on a "reasonably" low calorie diet.

Johnson's gall bladder operation Oct. 8, 1965, was performed by a team of eight doctors at the Naval Medical Center in Bethesda, Md. It lasted two hours and 15 minutes. In addition to removing Mr. Johnson's gall bladder, the doctors found two kidney stones and removed one of them. Tests showed no indications of malignancy, doctors said, adding that the operation was a "complete success". Five hours after the operation began, Mr. Johnson walked a few steps beside his hospital bed and later in the afternoon conferred with staff members. The next day he was signing legislation and attending to other Presidential matters, but for more than two months he remained on a restricted work schedule.

The President left the hospital Oct. 21 and after two days at the White House flew on Oct. 23 to his ranch in Texas to recuperate. He remained there, except for a trip Nov. 14-19 to Washington, until Dec. 13, when he returned to Washington for a series of conferences with foreign leaders. He spent the Christmas holidays at the ranch in Texas. By the end of 1965, Johnson's recovery appeared to be satisfactory and virtually complete.

The second operation, Nov. 16, 1966, was also performed at Bethesda. The Johnson family physician, Dr. James C. Cain, said later the same day that the President had "tolerated this surgery very beautifully." He recovered fast enough to leave the hospital Nov. 19 and fly to his Texas ranch. There he remained 20 days before returning to Washington.

Disabled Presidents

Three earlier Presidents suffered extended periods of disability:

• In 1881, President James A. Garfield performed only one official act in the 80 days between the time he was shot and his death. The Cabinet wanted Vice President Chester A. Arthur to act in his stead, but no action was taken, partly from fear that Garfield could not reclaim his office once he had surrendered it.

• President Woodrow Wilson did not meet with his Cabinet from the time his illness began in September 1919 until April 13, 1920. He was able to resume only a few of his official duties before his term ended March 4, 1921. A move to install Vice President Thomas R. Marshall as Acting President during this period was rejected on the ground of disloyalty to Wilson.

• President Eisenhower's 1955 heart attack and June 9, 1956, ileitis operation kept him from bearing a full workload for lengthy periods. During Eisenhower's illnesses Vice President Nixon presided over meetings of the Cabinet and the National Security Council, as he did again after the President suffered a mild stroke Nov. 25, 1957.

Presidential Security

Carrying out a recommendation of the Warren Commission, which made an exhaustive inquiry into the assassination of President Kennedy, Congress in 1965 made it a federal crime to kill, kidnap or assault the President of the United States or any other federal official and prescribed penalties for violations of the law (PL 89-141).

Because murder of a President was not then a federal crime, neither the Secret Service nor the Federal Bureau of Investigation had jurisdiction over Lee Harvey Oswald after he was captured and charged with the killing of President Kennedy in Dallas, Nov. 22, 1963.

The Warren Commission, appointed by President Johnson Nov. 29, 1963, and headed by Chief Justice Earl Warren, was directed to investigate all circumstances relating to the Kennedy assassination and to report its findings and conclusions to the President. In addition to determining that Oswald was the assassin, the Commission's report of Sept. 27, 1964, criticized then existing measures for protecting the President.

Among its recommendations on which action was taken were: overhaul of Secret Service facilities for better advance detection of potential threats to the President; improvement of Secret Service protective measures in the planning and conducting of presidential motorcades; closer relationship of the Secret Service with other federal and with local law enforcement agencies; enlargement of Secret Service personnel and resources; and a law to make it a federal crime to assassinate a President.

In addition, Congress enacted legislation in 1965 authorizing the federal government to acquire all items of evidence considered during the Warren Commission's investigation (PL 89-318); authorizing Secret Service agents to make arrests without a warrant in certain situations (PL 89-218); and extending the period in which Secret Service protection should be available to former Presidents and their widows (PL 89)186).

Dillon Committee

The Warren Commission report was critical of the Secret Service, as well as of other federal agencies concerned with Presidential protection, for "insufficient liaison and coordination of information." It also said the Secret Service arrangements for the "identification and elimination of possible sources of danger to the President," prior to President Kennedy's assassination, were "seriously deficient." As a result, the Commission recommended measures for improving protection of the President, many of which were based on suggestions of the Secret Service itself in an August 1964 report to the Commission.

In response to the Commission's recommendations, President Johnson Sept. 27, 1964, named a four-man committee headed by Treasury Secretary Douglas Dillon, the Cabinet officer responsible for the Secret Service, to advise him on "execution of the recommendations." The Dillon Committee submitted a formal report to the President in February 1965 and then disbanded. Although the report was not made public, the Committee had previously disclosed that it had rejected a Commission recommendation to create a post of special assistant to the Treasury Secretary to be charged with supervision of the Service and recommendations, on which the Warren Commission had not taken a position, to transfer the Service's investigative functions to the FBI and to limit the Service's responsibility to the physical safeguarding of the President.

The Dillon Committee announced Nov. 27, 1964, that it had recommended a $3-million plan for modernization of the Secret Service during fiscal 1966 and the immediate appointment of 75 additional personnel—50 agents, 20 clerical assistants and 5 automatic data processing (ADP) consultants. The Budget Bureau promptly approved a fiscal 1965 deficiency appropriation of $810,000 for the Service to increase its personnel and to launch an ADP feasibility study.

Secret Service Budget

The President's fiscal 1966 Budget called for an appropriation of $8,750,000 for the Secret Service—an increase of only $440,000 over fiscal 1965 appropriations. Most of the increase was for the 75 additional personnel provided in the fiscal 1965 deficiency appropriation.

During hearings before the House Treasury-Post Office Appropriations Subcommittee, however, Dillon requested a fiscal 1966 Secret Service appropriation of $12,627,000—$3,877,000 above the President's requests. Dillon said the increase was based on the recommendations of his Committee and would provide $2,187,000 for the employment of 183 additional agents and 76 additional clerical and administrative assistants, $541,000 for additional support costs and $1,149,000 for additional equipment, including two Presidential armored vehicles.

The fiscal 1966 Treasury-Post Office appropriation bill (HR 7060) was passed by the House carrying the full $12,627,000 request. The Senate passed HR 7060 June 8, 1965, appropriating $12,105,000. The Senate reduced Secret Service funds by $522,000 on the recommendation of Treasury Secretary Henry H. Fowler, who had replaced Dillon April 1. The Senate Appropriations Committee said Fowler withdrew the . . . $522,000 for two Presidential armored vehicles. It was made clear to the Committee that the President did not approve the original request for these vehicles and that if they were built he would not use or condone their use in his protection." The House and Senate June 28 adopted the conference report on HR 7060 that upheld the Senate reduction.

Secret Service Actions

In testimony before the House Appropriations Subcommittee Feb. 23, 1965, Secret Service Chief James J. Rowley said the funds in HR 7060 would enable the Service to modernize its operations as well as improve on changes in procedures already effected administratively in line with the recommendations of the Warren Commission and the Dillon Committee.

Rowley cited the following examples:

Personnel. He said approval of the 259 additional positions in HR 7060 would increase total service employment to 920—644 agents and 276 clerical and administrative assistants. Rowley said the 183 new agents would all be assigned to the Service's 65 field offices to assist in the Service's investigative and counterfeiting activities. The number (which is classified information) of agents personally assigned to the President and the 225-man White House Police would not be enlarged, Rowley added.

Motorcade Protection. Rowley testified that since President Kennedy's assassination the Service had "completely revised" preparations made in advance of Presidential trips. He said the Service had conducted numerous surveys designed to pinpoint dangerous locations in most of the nation's major cities and had instituted a new system of building inspections along motorcade routes.

Criteria and Liaison. Rowley said the Service had developed specific "criteria" which it transmitted to other federal agencies concerning the procedures to be used in furnishing the Service with information pertaining to potential as well as actual threats to the President. Such agencies included the FBI, CIA, the State Department and Military and Naval Intelligence. The criteria were also provided to state and local authorities. Rowley said that a formal agreement setting forth the new criteria had already been consummated with the FBI and that agreements were being negotiated with other parties.

Rowley told the Subcommittee that the Kennedy assassination "opened a new vista to us, that included subversives, defectors, and so forth." Previously, he said, the Service primarily investigated only known actual threats to the President, most of which were relayed from the White House mailroom. However, as a result of the new criteria and improved liaison, Rowley said, the Service's Protective Research Section was currently receiving about 6,000 pieces of information monthly "from sources outside of the Service" and that during fiscal 1965 about 14,000 pieces of information would be forwarded to the Service's regional offices for "priority investigation." He said this new influx of information compared with only 125 pieces received in September 1963.

Modernization, Advance Detection. Rowley explained that the employment of five ADP consultants was done in order to advise the Service on transferring its files from manual to computer operation. The first phase of an ADP feasibility study had already been launched, he added. He said the consultants "will program the operation so that if the President is going, say, to the Midwest or Far West, you would press the button and determine what dangerous persons we have in the file that would require immediate attention, and those (agents) that would be in the field . . . would be the ones who would proceed to investigate or locate and neutralize such persons." Rowley said the Service's files currently contained 130,000 names, 240,000 index cards and 55,000 dossiers. A special index, known as the "trip" file, contained 800 names of persons considered most dangerous. This file had grown from 200 to 800 names "in the last year," he said. He added that there were about 550 daily manual searches in the indexes, or an annual total of approximately 150,000 searches.

Reorganization. The Treasury Department Nov. 10 announced that the Secret Service would be reorganized into four divisions: protection forces to guard the White House, Vice President, former Presidents

'Great Society' and 'Creative Federalism'

In a single speech, May 22, 1964, at the University of Michigan, President Johnson introduced two phrases that in time became identified with his Administration—"Great Society" and "creative federalism." The former gained wider currency than the latter.

"For in your time we have the opportunity to move not only toward the rich society and the powerful society, but upward to the Great Society," the President said that day. "The Great Society rests on abundance and liberty for all. It demands an end to poverty and racial injustice, to which we are totally committed in our time. But that is just the beginning.

"The Great Society is a place where every child can find knowledge to enrich his mind and to enlarge his talents. It is a place where leisure is a welcome chance to build and reflect, not a feared cause of boredom and restlessness. It is a place where the city of man serves not only the needs of the body and the demands of commerce, but the desire for beauty and the hunger for community.

"It is a place where man can renew contact with nature. It is a place which honors creation for its own sake and for what it adds to the understanding of the race. It is a place where men are more concerned with the quality of their goals than the quantity of their goods. But most of all, the Great Society, is not a safe harbor, a resting place, a final objective, a finished work. It is a challenge constantly renewed, beckoning us toward a destiny where the meaning of our lives matches the marvelous products of our labors."

Johnson referred in the speech to the problems of relations among the different levels of government—federal, state and local. He said intergovernmental relations posed a challenge to "creative federalism." He used the term in subsequent Great Society proposals and in political speeches. He further defined it, in a speech Oct. 15, 1964, before the New York Liberal party as "the cooperation of the state and the city, and of business and labor, and of private institutions and of private enterprise." The dimensions of "creative federalism" remained uncertain, however, and in later years President Johnson tended to speak instead of a federal-state "partnership."

and Mrs. John F. Kennedy and her children; a protective intelligence unit to handle threats to those guarded; an investigations section to carry out the agency's work against counterfeiting and forgery; and an administrative division to handle budgetary, personnel and similar problems.

Secret Service Legislation

Arrests. HR 6294 (PL 89-218) authorized Secret Service agents to make arrests without a warrant for federal offenses which were committed in their presence or which they had "reasonable grounds to believe" had been or were being committed. The arrest authority was currently exercised by FBI agents and U.S. marshals. Administration spokesmen contended that it was "anomalous" for the Service to have authority to protect the President without being authorized to arrest anyone who harmed or threatened to harm him.

HR 6294 was requested by the Treasury Department, approved by the Justice Department and supported, though not specifically recommended, by the Warren Commission.

Protection. S 2420 (PL 89-186), also requested by the Treasury Department, authorized the Secret Service to protect a former President and his wife during the former President's lifetime and to protect the widow and minor children of a former President for four years after he left or died in office, unless the protection was declined. The bill extended the protection offered former Presidents and their wives from the "reasonable period" provided in existing law, which had been interpreted to mean six months. It also extended for two years the protection afforded Mrs. John F. Kennedy in 1963 (PL 88-195), which was due to expire Dec. 11, 1965.

The President's Cabinet

The President's Cabinet is a creature of tradition and necessity, dating back to George Washington's Presidency. By custom, it is made up of the heads of the executive departments, which now number twelve with the creation of the Departments of Transporation in 1966 and Housing and Urban Development in 1965. The Vice President, not formally considered a Cabinet member, participates in meetings. During the Kennedy Administration, the U.S. Representative to the United Nations was given nominal Cabinet rank.

Cabinet members are not elected and, as a body, have no Constitutional basis or legal powers. Still, the group can be a highly influential one, depending on the use made of it by the President.

The Constitution states in Article II, Section 2, the President "may require the opinion . . . of the principal officer in each of the executive departments," but furnishes no details on how such "opinions" should be obtained. President Washington secured it through meetings of his Secretaries of State, War and Treasury—the heads of the original executive departments—and his Attorney General.

The Cabinet has since become a fixture, but many of Washington's successors have thought less than he did of its collective wisdom. President Jackson took much counsel from trusted friends (his "kitchen cabinet") and President Lincoln once polled his Cabinet and determined, "Seven noes, one aye—the ayes have it."

Recent Presidents have used the Cabinet to varying extent. President Franklin Roosevelt was said to have turned more to outsiders than to his Department heads for advice. President Truman described the Cabinet as a "board of directors" which could help a President "by offering advice, whether he liked it or not." President Eisenhower made Cabinet meetings formal, named a Cabinet secretary, circulated an advance agenda and attempted, though not always with success, to elicit major policy decisions from the group. Under President Kennedy, discussion and formulation of policy usually evolved from the counsel of smaller clusters of Department heads, or more often, sub-Cabinet officials or White House aides with specialized knowledge of the problem at hand. Kennedy called his Cabinet together only eight times in 1963.

The Johnson Cabinet

President Johnson made some innovations in Cabinet procedure. He kept the Eisenhower tradition of a formal agenda and assigned a Special Assistant to function as Cabinet Secretary. The Cabinet reportedly discussed such vital subjects as the war in Vietnam and economic problems. Sessions lasted as long as three hours. On occasion, the President called reporters in afterward to make announcements or have Cabinet members themselves report to the press. Those who attended meetings described them as providing "insight" into what the President wanted, or as being a kind of "locker room fight talk" by the President for promoting solidarity on his administrative team.

Often summoned to Cabinet sessions were officials who might be said to rival or surpass Cabinet members in importance to the Administration. Such officers included the Director of the Budget Bureau, and the Chairman of the President's Council of Economic Advisers (both prime advisers on economic policy and the legislative program generally).

It is obvious from the size and complexity of government today that no single collection of men could effectively help a President over every policy hurdle. In the area of national security, a separate high-level group, the National Security Council, exists to advise the President on national security objectives, commitments and policy. It is often argued that the Cabinet is an "antique," which cannot now perform an important advisory function, but that its members may prove highly influential as individual advisers. A full-dress Cabinet session, with 15 to 20 men seated around a long table in a room near the President's office, may not seem an appropriate place for shirt-sleeve policy discussions. In the past, Cabinet members have hesitated to dissent from the President's position or to open their views to attack by their colleagues. They have preferred to put their problems directly to the President in private.

Why do Presidents bother with Cabinet meetings? The answer may lie in the Cabinet's potential as a supportive group—a team which can back up a President, help him promote an image of solidarity in his Administration, and help see him through a national emergency or over a legislative hurdle.

New Cabinet Posts, Changes

In 1966, President Johnson proposed, and Congress approved, a 12th Cabinet-level Department of Transportation to coordinate principal transportation policies, functions and operations of the Federal Government. Congress the previous year had voted to increase the number of executive departments to eleven with the establishment of the Department of Housing and Urban Development. That move was the first addition to the Cabinet-level departments since 1953, when the Department of Health, Education and Welfare was created.

Three of the 10 cabinet members whom President Johnson inherited from the Kennedy Administration remained in their posts until his departure from office Jan. 20, 1969. They were Secretary of State Dean Rusk, Secretary of the Interior Stewart L. Udall and Secretary of Agriculture Orville L. Freeman. All three had been among Kennedy's original Cabinet appointees. They took office Jan. 20, 1961.

Upon assuming the Presidency Nov. 22, 1963, Johnson asked the ranking officials of the Kennedy Administration to remain. All the Cabinet members did so for several months. The slain President's brother, Attorney General Robert F. Kennedy, was the first to leave. He resigned Sept. 3, 1964, to seek a Senate seat from New York.

Nicholas deB. Katzenbach, Kennedy's deputy at the Justice Department, was elevated to Attorney General in January 1965, the first of our new Cabinet members to be confirmed that year. Henry H. Fowler replaced Douglas Dillon as Secretary of the Treasury; Lawrence F. O'Brien succeeded John A. Gronouski as Postmaster General; John W. Gardner succeeded Anthony J. Celebrezze as Secretary of Health, Education and Welfare.

In 1966, President Johnson filled the two newest Cabinet posts. Robert C. Weaver became the first Secretary of Housing and Urban Development and Alan S. Boyd became the first Secretary of Transportation. In the same year, Katzenbach resigned as Attorney General to become Under Secretary of State, replacing George W. Ball, who resigned.

Ramsey Clark, who had served as Acting Attorney General after Katzenbach's departure from Justice, was confirmed as Attorney General in 1967. His father, Associate Justice Tom C. Clark, resigned from the Supreme Court in June, during the closing days of its 1966-67 term, to avoid any conflict of interest involving his son.

Alexander B. Trowbridge became Secretary of Commerce in 1967, replacing John T. Connor, who left the Government to return to private business. The post changed hands again in March 1968, when C. R. Smith succeeded Trowbridge. Other Cabinet changes during the final year of the Johnson Administration were those of W. Marvin Watson to replace O'Brien as Postmaster General; Wilbur J. Cohen, the Under Secretary of HEW, to replace Gardner as Secretary; and Clark M. Clifford to succeed Robert S. McNamara, an original appointee of President Kennedy, as Secretary of Defense.

The final change in the Johnson Cabinet occurred when Fowler resigned Nov. 8, 1968, and was succeeded by the Under Secretary of the Treasury, Joseph W. Barr.

Biographies of Key Cabinet Members, 1965-68

Robert S. McNamara, former president of the Ford Motor Co., was appointed Secretary of Defense in the original Kennedy Cabinet. A chief decision maker in the Vietnam war, McNamara was considered the most influential member of the Johnson Administration and was perhaps second only to Robert Kennedy in terms of influence among Kennedy Cabinet members. McNamara's application of computer-based business techniques to defense operations made possible some economies and more centralized control of the Department, but won him the enmity of many high military officers. He also was unpopular with some Congressmen for closing down military bases he judged obsolete, and with some businessmen for a controversial decision involving the contract for the TFX fighter plane in 1962. After service with the Air Force, McNamara went to Ford in 1946 with nine other young ex-military officers, offering to revamp the company. Hired with the others, McNamara rose quickly and assumed the presidency of Ford Nov. 9, 1960. He is a registered Republican but has often supported Democratic political candidates. Born June 8, 1916, in San Francisco; graduate, University of California (Phi Beta Kappa in his sophomore year), Harvard Business School; taught at Harvard; World War II veteran; married, two daughters, one son.

Dean Rusk left his job as president of the Rockefeller Foundation to become Secretary of State in the original Kennedy Cabinet. He breasted crises in Cuba, Panama, Southeast Asia and the Dominican Republic; at home he faced widely circulated reports that "Kennedy was his own Secretary of State" and that, according to Arthur Schlesinger Jr., Kennedy had planned to replace Rusk after the 1964 election. There was also speculation that Rusk, a "hard-liner" on the Vietnam war, would resign after President Johnson adopted a conciliatory stand March 31, 1968. But Rusk served to the end of Johnson's term, holding the office a full eight years, the longest tenure of any Secretary of State since Cordell Hull (1933-44). Rusk became head of the State Department's Office of Special Political Affairs in 1947 and moved up to be Deputy Under Secretary of State in 1949. When the Department's Asian policies came under heavy attack in 1950, Rusk volunteered to leave his higher post to direct the Far Eastern Affairs division, which he headed at the outbreak of hostilities in Korea. He was a forceful advocate of UN intervention in Korea and, as State Department spokesman in May 1951, enunciated the policy of U.S. recognition of the Chiang Kai-shek government as the legitimate government of China. He became president of the Rockefeller Foundation in 1952. Born Feb. 9, 1909, in Cherokee, Ga.; graduate, Davidson College, Rhodes Scholar; World War II veteran (decorated infantry officer); teacher, dean of faculty, Mills College; married, two sons, one daughter.

Henry H. Fowler became Secretary of the Treasury April 1, 1965, succeeding Kennedy-appointed Douglas Dillon. Fowler had alternated private law practice with Government service under Democratic presidents since 1933. "Joe" Fowler began government work as a lawyer for the Tennessee Valley Authority, served the War Production Board in World War II and headed the Defense Production Administration during the Korean War. A staunch Democrat, he was appointed Under Secretary of the Treasury by Kennedy in 1961. He served as an important link between the Administration and businessmen, lining up support for the 1964 tax cut and helping to organize (after leaving Treasury in mid-1964) the National Independent Committee for Johnson-Humphrey, which drew many normally Republican businessmen into the Democratic ranks. Born Sept. 5, 1908, in Roanoke, Va.; graduate, Roanoke College, Yale Law School (L.L.B., J.S.D.); married, two daughters.

John W. Gardner succeeded Anthony J. Celebrezze as Secretary of Health, Education and Welfare in July 1965. A Republican, Gardner was president of the Carnegie Corp., one of the country's largest philanthropic organizations, and of its educational arm, the Carnegie Foundation for the Advancement of Teaching. In these influential posts, he served as a leading adviser on educational policy to both Presidents Kennedy and Johnson and was chairman of the 1965 White House Conference on Education. His appointment was interpreted as a sign that education would, for the first time, assume primary importance at HEW. Gardner joined the Carnegie Corp. in 1946 and became president in 1955. Before World War II, he taught psychology at Connecticut College for Women and Mount Holyoke College. Born Oct. 8, 1912, in Los Angeles; graduate, Stanford University, University of California (Ph. D.), holds 12 honorary degrees; World War II veteran; married, two daughters.

Stewart L. Udall, Secretary of the Interior, was a well-known supporter of conservation, reclamation and national park improvement legislation during three terms in the U.S. House (1955-61). One of Kennedy's first Cabinet appointees, he served until the end of Johnson's term. Udall added significantly to his Department's role in water planning, outdoor recreation and national parks programs. Udall entered Congress on his first try for elective office in 1954. In the House, he helped sponsor "seminars" for freshman Representatives and was a member of the Democratic Study Group of liberal Democrats working to facilitate Congressional action on their proposals. Born Jan. 31, 1920, in St. Johns, Ariz. (descendant of Mormon pioneers); graduate, University of Arizona Law School; World War II veteran (enlisted gunner in the Air Force); lawyer; married, four sons, two daughters.

Orville L. Freeman, Secretary of Agriculture in the original Kennedy Cabinet, also served until the end of Johnson's term. Freeman at first carried out the New Frontier policy of higher farm supports and strict controls until a series of legislative defeats brought about a shift to less stringent production controls. As Minnesota's governor for six years (1955-61), Freeman was perhaps best known among his state's Democrats for advancing health and welfare measures and, among Republicans, for raising taxes. He made the nominating speech for Kennedy at the 1960 Democratic National Convention, helped Democrats carry the state afterward, but lost his own bid for a fourth term as Governor. He rose through state Democratic politics working with Hubert H. Humphrey, whom he had met on the University of Minnesota campus. City born, Freeman worked on a farm as a boy. Born May 9, 1918, in Minneapolis; graduate, University of Minnesota (magna cum laude, Phi Beta Kappa); World War II veteran (survived a serious bullet wound in the jaw at Bougainville); lawyer; married, one son, one daughter.

W. Willard Wirtz joined the Kennedy Administration as Under Secretary of Labor in 1961, was appointed Secretary in August 1962 and remained through the Johnson years. He figured in several critical labor-management confrontations and, in 1965, drew fire from farmers and fruit growers by reducing the number of foreign laborers they could import for harvest. A former law associate of the late Adlai Stevenson in Chicago, Wirtz preferred to write his own speeches. During and immediately after World War II, he served on a number of Federal emergency wage and labor boards and committees. In 1946, he was chairman of the National Wage Stabilization Board which dealt with wage controls. In private law practice, he arbitrated numerous labor-management conflicts and taught labor law at Northwestern University. Born March 14, 1912, in DeKalb, Ill.; graduate, Beloit (Wis.) College, Harvard Law School; married, two sons.

Lawrence F. O'Brien, an important White House political strategist for Presidents Kennedy and Johnson, was nominated Postmaster General by Johnson in August 1965. He resigned April 10, 1968, to become chairman of the National Democratic Committee. As a special Presidential aide, O'Brien turned his considerable political talents to advantage, working to secure passage of the Administration's programs in Congress. O'Brien helped John F. Kennedy get elected to the Senate (won his praise as "the best election man in the business"), and was director of campaign organization for the Kennedy-Johnson campaign of 1960 and the Johnson-Humphrey campaign of 1964. Gregarious and popular, O'Brien smiled when asked about "logrolling" and "arm-twisting" in his former job, insisted "it just didn't exist." Born July 7, 1917, in Springfield, Mass.; graduate, Northeastern University Law School; real estate and public relations; married, one son.

Robert C. Weaver, the Government's top housing official since 1961, was sworn in as a Johnson Cabinet member (Secretary of the Department of Housing and Urban Development) in January 1966. President Kennedy's desire to make Weaver the first Negro in the Cabinet was thought largely responsible for the early defeat of bills to set up a housing department. Weaver, who holds a doctorate in economics and is a former college professor, began his career in his native Washington with various New Deal and wartime (World

War II) agencies. He was later New York rent administrator and was named administrator of the Housing and Home Finance Agency in 1961. Born Dec. 29, 1907, in Washington, D.C. (the son of a postal clerk); honors graduate (M.A., Ph.D.) Harvard University; taught at Columbia, New York Universities, among others; married. *(Full listing of Cabinet members, 1933-69, in Appendix).*

White House Staff, 1961-68

Forty-one men and two women served as special assistants, special counsel, legislative counsel, administrative assistants or special consultants to President Johnson after he was sworn in Nov. 22, 1963, following the assassination of President Kennedy.

These men and women were the key figures in the White House Office, performing many of the detailed activities incident to the immediate office of the President.

Johnson inherited a staff that had been assembled by Mr. Kennedy. In one of his first acts as President, Johnson asked members of the Kennedy staff to remain in the White House to advise him. At first, many of President Kennedy's aides stayed on, but gradually they began to drift away. Theodore C. Sorensen, special counsel to the President, was the first of the Kennedy aides to resign, leaving the staff in January 1964. By late in 1968, only one member of the Kennedy staff, Mike N. Manatos, administrative assistant, remained as a Presidential adviser.

The average tenure of President Johnson's top assistants was 28 months. Each year after 1963, at least six aides resigned. Some were appointed to other Government posts, others returned to private life.

The two women who served as advisers were Esther Peterson and Betty Furness, both appointed by President Johnson to advise him on consumer affairs.

1968 Staff

SPECIAL ASSISTANTS. President Johnson's special assistants during his last year in the White House were:

Joseph A. Califano Jr., 36, New York, directed the development and implementation of the President's domestic programs. His duties included coordination of policies on domestic issues with department heads, direction of staff work on Presidential messages and management of the President's legislative program. Formerly special assistant to the Secretary of the Army (1962-63) and the Secretary of Defense (1964-65), Califano joined the White House staff in July 1965. He graduated from Holy Cross College and Harvard Law School (1955).

Walt Whitman Rostow, 51, New York, staff adviser on national security and foreign affairs. Rostow, a former deputy special assistant (1961) and chairman of the State Department's Policy Planning Council (1961-66), directed White House liaison and coordination with the Departments of State and Defense after his appointment in April 1966. An economic historian, Rostow is a graduate of Yale University (Ph.D., 1940) and was a Rhodes Scholar at Oxford University.

George E. Christian, 41, of Austin, Texas, White House press secretary and chief adviser on press relations. A former newsman and adviser to several Texas governors, Christian was appointed administrative assistant on the White House staff in May 1966, became a special assistant in December 1966, and press secretary in February 1967. Christian had a wide range of activities, including attendance at almost all Presidential meetings and conferences. He attended the University of Texas.

William Leonhart, 49, a Foreign Service officer with the rank of ambassador, became in May 1967 special assistant in charge of peaceful reconstruction in Vietnam. A native of West Virginia, Leonhart is a graduate of the University of West Virginia and Princeton University (Ph.D., 1943).

E. Ernest Goldstein, 49, of Pittsburgh, Pa., joined the White House staff in September 1967. As Cabinet secretary, his duties ranged over organizational and legislative matters. He acted as liaison for the White House with the heads of all departments. A graduate of Georgetown University Law School and the University of Wisconsin (1956), Goldstein formerly was a member of a Paris law firm.

James R. Jones, 28, the youngest special assistant, joined the White House advisers in early 1965 as deputy to Marvin W. Watson, then a special assistant. Jones, a native of Oklahoma and a 1964 graduate of Georgetown University Law School, assumed Watson's duties as schedule director and appointments secretary when Watson was appointed Postmaster General in April 1968.

Three of the special assistants dealt with highly specialized areas. **Donald F. Hornig,** 49, served as special assistant for scientific affairs from 1964. A former professor at Princeton University, Hornig also was director of the Office of Science and Technology. **Roger L. Stevens,** chairman of the National Endowment for the Arts, had been special assistant to the President on the arts since 1964. **Miss Betty Furness** succeeded Mrs. Esther Peterson in March 1967 as special assistant on consumer affairs. Mrs. Peterson returned to her duties as Assistant Secretary of Labor.

LEGISLATIVE COUNSEL. Harold Barefoot Sanders Jr., 45, Dallas, Texas, served as legislative counsel to the President from May 1967, when he succeeded another Texas lawyer, E. Jake Jacobsen, who had held the post since early 1965. Sanders, in addition to duties as counsel, acted as Congressional liaison. Before his White House appointment, Sanders was Assistant Attorney General in charge of the Civil Division of the Department of Justice (1966). He is a graduate of the University of Texas LLB., 1950).

SPECIAL COUNSEL. Harry C. McPherson, Jr. and **Larry Eugene Temple** were special counsel to the President. McPherson, 38, formerly Assistant Secretary of State for Educational and Cultural Affairs (1964-65) directed legal review of all executive orders, proclamations and enrolled bills. A native of Tyler, Texas, he became assistant counsel in August 1965, succeeding to the post of special counsel in March 1966 when the President appointed special counsel Lee C. White chairman of the Federal Power Commis-

sion. McPherson is a graduate of the University of the South and the University of Texas LLB., 1956).

Temple, 32, was named special counsel in October 1967. Temple, from Plainview, Texas, and a graduate of the University of Texas (LLB. 1959), had served as law clerk to former Supreme Court Justice Tom C. Clark and as executive assistant to Texas Gov. John B. Connally.

ADMINISTRATIVE ASSISTANT. Mike N. Manatos, 53, was the veteran of the White House aides, having served as administrative assistant at the White House since 1961. Manatos directed most Congressional liaison, primarily with the Senate. Henry H. Wilson Jr., who resigned in 1967 to become president of the Chicago Board of Trade, had managed White House liaison with the House since 1961.

SPECIAL CONSULTANTS. Among the President's special consultants was former Chairman of the Joint Chiefs of Staff (1962-64) and former Ambassador to Vietnam (1964-65) **Gen. Maxwell D. Taylor,** since 1965 special consultant on military affairs. **Charles S. Murphy,** a former chairman of the Civil Aeronautics Board, (1965-67) advised the President on regulatory matters. **George E. Reedy** returned to the White House in March 1968 as a special consultant.

McGeorge Bundy, Special Assistant (1961-66), currently president of the Ford Foundation, was named a special consultant in mid-1967. **James A. Lovell Jr.** one of America's astronauts, was special consultant on physical fitness.

Staff Changes

Many former White House aides moved to other Government positions.

Lawrence F. O'Brien (Special Assistant, 1961-65) was appointed Postmaster General from the White House staff and then was selected Democratic National Chairman. W. Marvin Watson (Special Assistant, 1965-68) was appointed from the White House to succeed O'Brien as Postmaster General.

Robert W. Komer (Special Assistant, 1966-67) and Ralph Dungan (Special Assistant, 1961-64) both left the White House to serve abroad with the rank of ambassador. Komer went to Saigon; Dungan to Chile. Lee C. White was appointed chairman of the Federal Power Commission after five years at the White House (Special Counsel, 1961-66); and Charles Murphy (Special Consultant) joined the staff in 1967 after serving as chairman of the Civil Aeronautics Board.

Clifford L. Alexander, formerly deputy special counsel, became chairman of the Equal Employment Opportunity Commission in June 1967. Robert H. Fleming, deputy press secretary, was appointed in September 1968 to the post of assistant director of the United States Information Agency.

Former White House aides Pierre Salinger (1961-64), Theodore C. Sorenson (1961-64) and Kenneth P. O'Donnell (1961-65) remained active in politics, while other former assistants returned to private life as lawyers, businessmen or professors. Richard N. Goodwin (1963-65) and John P. Roche (1966-68) returned to academic life. Goodwin in 1968 took part in the Presidential campaigns of Sens. Robert F. Kennedy (D

N.Y.) and Eugene J. McCarthy (D Minn.). Bill D. Moyers (1963-67) became publisher of *Newsday,* a Long Island newspaper. Jack Valenti (1963-66) assumed the presidency of the Motion Picture Assn. of America. Henry H. Wilson (1961-67) became president of the Chicago Board of Trade. E. Jake Jacobsen (legislative counsel, 1965-67) and Myer Feldman (1961-65) returned to the private practice of law.

Executive Branch

Reorganization

Congress in 1932 empowered the President to reorganize agencies of the Executive Branch without obtaining prior authorization. But his action is subject to a veto by House or Senate within a 60-day period.

The Reorganization Act of 1949, which grew out of recommendations of the first Hoover Commission, gave the President much greater latitude than earlier legislation. It eliminated exemptions for specific agencies and permitted the creation of Cabinet-level departments. But Cabinet-level departments were again exempted in 1964, following a controversy over President Kennedy's plan to create a Department of Housing and Urban Affairs.

Congress in 1965 extended through 1968 the President's authority, under the Reorganization Act of 1949, to reorganize agencies of the Executive Branch and the District of Columbia government. Under the act, Presidential reorganization plans went into effect automatically 60 days after being submitted to Congress, unless either chamber disapproved the plan by a majority vote.

Unlike a bill, a reorganization plan cannot be amended by Congress. It can be rejected only if the House or Senate adopts a resolution disapproving the plan. Any member of Congress may file a resolution of disapproval; the Government Operations Committee of that chamber then has 10 days to send a report on the resolution to the floor. If the committee does not report the resolution, the sponsor may move to have it discharged and brought to the floor for a vote.

Johnson's Reorganization Plans

Between 1949 and the end of 1968, 85 reorganization plans were submitted to Congress. Of these, 66 became effective and 19 were rejected. President Johnson did not send any until 1965. Sixteen of the 17 he submitted to Congress in 1965-68 went into effect. However, it was reported that he refrained from sending others to Congress when it became apparent they would run into trouble.

1965

President Johnson submitted five reorganization plans to Congress in 1965. All five went into effect.

Customs. This plan abolished 53 offices in the Bureau of Customs which had been filled by Presidential appointment. The effect of the plan was to

Staff Members

Following is a list of the 41 men and two women who served President Johnson after Nov. 22, 1963, as special assistants, special counsel, legislative counsel, administrative assistants or special consultants.

Position and Name	Appointed	Resigned
Special Assistant		
Pierre Salinger	1961	1964
Arthur M. Schlesinger Jr.	1961	1964
Jerome B. Wiesner	1961	1964
Ralph A. Dungan	1961	1964
Kenneth P. O'Donnell	1961	1965
Lawrence F. O'Brien	1961	1965
McGeorge Bundy*	1961	1966
Richard N. Goodwin	1963	1965
Bill D. Moyers	1963	1967
Jack J. Valenti	1963	1966
Walter W. Jenkins	1964	1964
George E. Reedy*	1964	1966
David Lawrence	1964	1966 *(died)*
Horace Busby, Jr.	1964	1965
Esther Peterson	1964	1967
Donald F. Hornig	1964	--
Roger L. Stevens	1964	--
S. Douglass Cater Jr.	1964	1968
W. Marvin Watson	1965	1968
Joseph A. Califano Jr.	1965	--
Robert W. Komer	1966	1967
Robert E. Kintner	1966	1967
Walt W. Rostow	1966	--
George E. Christian	1966	--
Betty Furness	1967	--
William Leonhart	1967	--
E. Ernest Goldstein	1967	--
James R. Jones	1968	--
Special Counsel		
Theodore C. Sorensen	1961	1964
Myer Feldman	1961	1965
Lee C. White	1961	1966
Harry C. McPherson Jr.	1966	--
Larry Eugene Temple	1967	--
Legislative Counsel		
E. Jake Jacobsen	1965	1967
Harold Barefoot Sanders Jr.	1967	--
Administrative Assistant		
Henry Hall Wilson Jr.	1961	1967
Mike N. Manatos	1961	--
Special Consultant		
Eric Goldman	1963	1966
Stan Musial	1964	1967
Gen. Maxwell D. Taylor	1965	--
John P. Roche	1966	1968
McGeorge Bundy*	1967	--
James A. Lovell Jr.	1967	--
Charles S. Murphy	1967	--
George E. Reedy*	1968	--

Held more than one position.

place the Bureau on a career, civil service basis. (In the past, appointments generally were made on Senators' recommendations.) The offices affected were those of the customs collector, customs controller, merchandise appraiser, and customs surveyor. The plan also transferred to the Secretary of the Treasury any functions vested by law in officials of the Customs Bureau. The plan was estimated to produce savings totaling $9 million a year. Of this amount, approximately $1 million a year represented salaries of the abolished political appointee positions.

The plan itself did not cover another aspect of the proposed Custom Bureau reorganization which could be accomplished administratively by the Treasury Department (of which Customs was a part). It involved reorganization of the service into six regional offices with about 25 subordinate district offices. They were to replace 113 existing independent field offices. The regional offices were placed in Boston, New York, Miami, New Orleans, San Francisco and Chicago.

The Customs Bureau announced subsequently that Baltimore, Houston and Los Angeles would also become regional Customs headquarters, and that the number of subordinate district offices would be increased to 42. Regional offices were to assume the over-all principal supervisory responsibilities and functions of the abolished offices.

E.S.S.A. The plan consolidated the Coast and Geodetic Survey, the Weather Bureau and the Central Radio Propagation Laboratory of the National Bureau of Standards into a single new agency in the Department of Commerce to be known as the Environmental Science Services Administration. In an accompanying message to Congress May 13, the President said the reorganization would "enhance our ability to develop an adequate warning system for the severe hazards of nature." Savings were estimated to reach $700,000 by the end of the third year.

Railroad Safety. The plan coordinated the work of railroad safety personnel with that of locomotive inspectors to eliminate duplication of inspection activities. The effect of this plan was to transfer to the Interstate Commerce Commission all federal locomotive inspection activities which had been operated by Presidential appointees since 1911. Savings were estimated at $170,000 a year through more efficient operation.

Abolition of Committees. The plan abolished nine statutory committees, transferring their functions to existing officials or agencies, and abolished the National Housing Council, the National Advisory Council on International Monetary and Financial Problems, the Board of Examiners of the Foreign Service and the Civilian-Military Liaison Committee established by the National Aeronautics and Space Act. The functions of the latter groups were transferred to the President, who was given authority to provide for their performance.

In addition, this plan abolished the Advisory Council on Group Insurance, the Loan Policy Board of the Small Business Administration, the Bonneville Power Advisory Board and the Atomic Weapons Awards Board. The functions of these groups were assigned to agency heads.

National Science Foundation. The plan eliminated all eight advisory committees of the National Science Foundation. The Foundation originally had three divisions, each with an advisory committee as required by the National Science Foundation Act of 1950. With the growth of the Foundation to eight divisions, each with its own committee advising the Director, it was felt there was overlapping in some of the program areas. Exact savings were not identified, but the annual cost of supporting each committee was $14,000 to $15,000.

1966

President Johnson in 1966 submitted five reoganization plans to Congress, and all five took effect. Approval of the five plans in 1966 brought to 10 the number of reorganizations put into effect in the Johnson Administration.

The 1966 plans all involved the transfer of federal agencies or their functions:

Community Relations Service. Transferred from the Commerce Department to the Justice Department. The Community Relations Service aids local communities by conciliating disputes involving racial discrimination.

Water Pollution Control Administration. Transferred from the Department of Health, Education and Welfare to the Department of the Interior.

Public Health Service. The plan transferred to the Secretary of Health, Education and Welfare all the functions of the Public Health Service previously vested in the Surgeon General, and authorized the Secretary to reorganize the agency.

In his message on the reorganization plan April 25, President Johnson said: "Today the organization of the Public Health Service is clearly obsolete." He noted that since 1953 more than 50 new programs had been placed in PHS, and that its budget had increased from $250 million to $2.4 billion in the past 12 years. The current PHS structure was "adequate" when the agency's functions could be "neatly compartmentalized," but the many new health programs called for an "integrated attack" on disease by combining health services, state and local aid and research. "Our health problems are difficult enough without having them complicated by outmoded organizational arrangements."

President Johnson said integrating PHS agencies would not "go far enough," because the HEW Secretary lacked the "essential authority" over PHS needed to secure the highest possible level of health services for the American people.

National Zoo. Transferred to the Smithsonian Institution from the District of Columbia Board of Commissioners certain responsibilities for the National Zoological Park.

Capital Planning Council. Abolished the National Capital Regional Planning Council and transferred its responsibilities to the Metropolitan Washington Council of Governments.

Other Proposals. Reorganization proposals advanced in 1966 which the Administration did not submit to Congress included plans to move the independent Small Business Administration into the Commerce

Department; to give the President authority to designate the chairman of the Interstate Commerce Commission from among its members, instead of the existing annual rotating system; and transfer of the Community Action Program from the Office of Economic Opportunity to the Department of Housing and Urban Development.

Republican leaders were critical of reorganization attempts in their annual "State of the Union Report." House Minority Leader Gerald R. Ford (R Mich.), who participated in the Jan. 17 report, said the Executive Branch "needs reform—not Presidential repatching or piecemeal creation of new departments." Ford said the Executive Branch had become "a bureaucratic jungle" and "the time has come to explore its wild growth and cut it back." The report called for "a new independent bipartisan commission" to recommend "substantial reforms" in the Executive Branch.

Congress in 1966 did approve establishment of a 12th Cabinet-level post—the Department of Transportation. In 1965, it had approved a new Cabinet post, the Department of Housing and Urban Development. Both these departments were set up by statute.

1967

President Johnson in 1967 submitted three reorganization plans to Congress, two of which went into effect. Rejected was a plan aimed at strengthening the operations of the U.S. Tariff Commission. The two approved plans:

Ship Documents. Transferred the authority to approve the surrender of certain ship documents—certificates of ownership, declarations of citizenship and other papers for vessels covered by preferred mortgages or owned by the Government—from the Secretary of Commerce to the Secretary of Transportation.

D.C. Government. Provided the first reorganization of the District of Columbia government in 89 years. The plan took effect Aug. 11, two days after the House rejected by a 160-244 roll-call vote a resolution (H Res 512) to disapprove the plan. The resolution was pushed by members of the House District of Columbia Committee who believed they should have jurisdiction over any changes in the D.C. government. No disapproval resolutions were introduced in the Senate.

Under the plan, the three D.C. commissioners were replaced by a single commissioner, or "mayor," and a nine-member city council, all nominated by the President and confirmed by the Senate.

Tariff Commission. The rejected plan concerned a transfer of powers within the U.S. Tariff Commission from the six commissioners to the chairman. Included was the authority to hire and fire personnel, distribute and communicate policies to the staff, manage and reorganize the Commission, carry out functions under the Budgeting and Accounting Act and allocate and use funds.

The Senate May 15 by voice vote and without debate adopted S Res 114 disapproving the plan. In

submitting the plan March 9, President Johnson described the proposed reorganization as "long overdue," and noted that the principle of a single executive authority had been applied successfully to other Government commissions, including the Federal Trade Commission, the Securities and Exchange Commission and the Civil Service Commission.

In its report May 11, the Government Operations Committee said it agreed with the stated objectives of the plan and expressed its willingness to support changes necessary to promote administrative efficiency while preserving the integrity and impartiality of the Commission on trade and tariff matters. But the Committee said the plan as presented would "seriously endanger the independence and impartiality of the Tariff Commission."

1968

Four reorganization plans submitted by President Johnson to Congress in 1968 all went into effect.

Congress, however, rejected a Presidential request to extend the President's authority to reorganize Government departments, subject to a veto by either chamber of Congress within 60 days. The authority, provided by the Reorganization Act of 1949, expired Dec. 31, 1968. (*Congress and the Nation,* Vol. I, p. 1455.)

Drug Enforcement. Plan No. 1, which established the new Bureau of Narcotics and Dangerous Drugs in the Department of Justice, combined two separate federal agencies for drug law enforcement, the Bureau of Narcotics in the Treasury Department and the Bureau of Drug Abuse Control in the HEW Department. The House April 2 by a 190-200 roll-call vote rejected a resolution (H Res 1101) to disapprove Plan No. 1. No disapproval resolutions were introduced in the Senate; the plan went into effect April 8.

Opposition to the reorganization plan focused on giving the Justice Department jurisdiction over the new drug law enforcement agency. There was general support for merging the two bureaus but opponents of the Plan argued that further studies were needed to determine which department would best be able to administer the program. Voting on the disapproval resolution was largely along party lines (R 166-8; D 24-192).

Mass Transit. Plan No. 2 shifted urban mass transit programs from the Department of Housing and Urban Development to the Department of Transportation. The proposal created an Urban Mass Transportation Administration within the Transportation Department. The plan went into effect May 7.

District of Columbia. Both Plan No. 3 and Plan No. 4, which gave the D.C. Commissioner (mayor) greater authority, went into effect May 23. Plan No. 3 brought recreation programs under the Commissioner's authority by abolishing the autonomous D.C. Recreation Board and the Office of the Superintendent of Recreation. Plan No. 4 gave the Commissioner authority to appoint all five members of the autonomous Redevelopment Land Agency Board and to prescribe rules governing the conduct of business of the Board.

Federal Personnel Activities

Hatch Act Review

Congress in 1966 cleared a bill (S 1474—PL 89-617) establishing a bipartisan Commission on Political Activity of Government Personnel. The action authorized the first review in 27 years of federal laws, notably the 1939 Hatch Act, that limit participation by Government employees in political affairs on both the national and local level.

The last supplemental appropriations bill (HR 18381) of the 89th Congress included $75,000 for the Commission's activities in fiscal 1967. The amount was cut from the Administration request of $200,000.

The commission was composed of 12 members of which no more than six could be from either of the two major political parties. The President was directed to choose two members from the Executive Branch; the Vice President to choose two members of the Senate, and the Speaker of the House, two Representatives. Each of the three officials was to name also two private citizens. President Johnson in January 1967 named Frank Pace Jr., former Budget Bureau director and former Secretary of the Army; Arthur S. Flemming, president of the University of Oregon and former Secretary of Health, Education and Welfare; Assistant Attorney General Frank Wozencraft; and Roger W. Jones, assistant to the Budget Bureau director and former chairman of the Civil Service Commission. Named by Vice President Hubert H. Humphrey were Austin Ranney, political science professor at the University of Wisconsin; Malcolm Loos of the Ford Foundation, former assistant to President Eisenhower; and Sens. George Murphy (R Calif.) and Daniel B. Brewster (D Md.). Brewster was the author of S 1474. Speaker John W. McCormack (D Mass.) appointed ex-Rep. Robert Ramspeck (D Ga. 1929-45), former Civil Service commissioner; Charles O. Jones, professor of government at the University of Arizona; and Reps. Ancher Nelsen (R Minn.) and Arnold Olsen (D Mont.). The Commission was to name its chairman.

Vice President's Residence

Congress in 1966 authorized the General Services Administration to design and construct an official residence for the Vice President on 10 acres at the U.S. Naval Observatory in Washington. The legislation (PL 89-386) authorized an appropriation of $750,000 to plan, construct and furnish the residence.

However, in 1969 the House Appropriations Committee deleted a Nixon administration request of $150 million for designing the residence. Committee Chairman George H. Mahon (D Texas) asserted that the deletion of design funds was not directed against Vice President Spiro T. Agnew. Even if the $150 million had been appropriated, he said, the house could not have been completed before 1972, the last year of Agnew's present term.

PROVISIONS. The law directed the Commission to study federal laws "which limit or discourage the participation of federal and state officers and employees in political activity with a view to determining the effect of such laws, the need for their revision or elimination, and an appraisal of the extent to which undesirable results might accrue from their repeal."

It required that a report and recommendations be made within one year following enactment of the bill, and it empowered the Commission to hold hearings and subpoena witnesses and documents. It further required federal agencies to provide information requested by the Commission in connection with the study.

When President Johnson signed the bill into law Oct. 3, 1966, he said the Commission "must resolve three important questions: (1) how strictly should the Government control the political activities of federal employees, (2) how tightly should the Federal Government control the political activities of state employees who work primarily in programs financed by federal funds, and (3) what penalties should be attached to violations of the political activities statutes. . . ." The President said, "These issues are as old as the Republic itself." Mr. Johnson indicated Oct. 4 that the Commission's study would be part of a "thorough review" of legislation on campaign contributions by federal employees.

BACKGROUND. The Hatch Political Activities Act of 1939 restricted partisan political activities of most federal employees and of state and local employees working in federally aided programs. The Act had remained without major change. It included legislation dating as far back as the Civil Service Act of 1883. The 1939 law extended coverage beyond classified employees to include most other employees of the District of Columbia Government and certain state officials working on federally financed projects. The Act gave partial exemption for political activity to employees living in "privileged" communities where the majority of voters were federal workers. Among the privileged areas were the Maryland and Virginia suburbs of Washington; the District of Columbia, however, was not included in the exemption clause.

During Senate debate in 1965, Sen. Daniel B. Brewster (D Md.), the bill's sponsor, said that in the years since 1939 "there have been changes in Government programs and relationships." He added that the changes "may have produced conditions which call for modifications in the methods and degree" of the Hatch Act's restrictions.

Recommendations. The Commission in December 1967 recommended a general easing of restrictions on political activities of most federal workers, but also a general tightening of provisions intended to protect public employees from coercion by their superiors. The Commission said that the "crux" of its assignment was to "reconcile constitutional freedom with controls against political excesses. It drafted legislation which would, in its major provisions:

Permit public employees to express their opinions freely in private or in public on any political subject or candidate.

Prohibit certain activities, including partisan political fund raising, engaging in political activity while on duty, becoming a candidate for other than local office, managing a campaign, acting as an official at any polling place or serving as an officer in a political organization at the city level or above; and specifically permit all other political activity.

Make the Civil Service Commission solely responsible for enforcement; direct it to study the feasibility of a plan of voluntary political contributions by public employees; and direct it to study the feasibility of establishing an Office of Employees' Counsel to which federal employees could report instances of political coercion, intimidation, misuses of official authority or other alleged violations of law.

Distinguish between local political offices for which federal employees could run on the basis of the nature of the office, rather than with reference to a "partisan" or "nonpartisan" distinction or to the geographic area where the employee lived, as was currently the case.

Add administrative sanctions and procedures to existing criminal penalties for violation of the law.

Apply to state employees administering federally aided programs the same prohibitions that apply to federal employees; encourage states to develop their own systems of controlling political activities.

Authorize an appropriation of $1 million and fund the enforcement program in that amount, rather than in the amount of $100,000 or less appropriated annually since 1939.

None of the foregoing provisions were enacted into law in 1968.

Federal Workers' Privacy

The Senate passed a bill (S 1035) in 1967 to prohibit federal officers from requiring government employees or job applicants to answer certain personal questions or to take part in or contribute to activities not directly related to their work. The activities included political events, charitable contributions and savings bond drives. The bill proposed to set up a Board of Employees' Rights to handle complaints and to authorize employees to take civil action in a federal court without exhausting administrative remedies.

The House Subcommittee on Manpower and Civil Service, a unit of the Post Office and Civil Service Committee, held hearings in 1968 on S 1035 and on another bill (HR 17760) sponsored by the subcommittee chairman, Rep. David N. Henderson (D N.C.). John W. Macy Jr., chairman of the Civil Service Commission, testified June 13, 1968, that the Commission endorsed the objectives of S 1035 but said that it would be a "mistake" to create a new agency, the Board of Employees' Rights, to hear appeals while lacking jurisdiction in other matters of employee-management relations in government.

Sen. Sam J. Ervin Jr. (D N.C.), sponsor of S 1035, criticized HR 17760 as protecting no rights and providing no remedies. "The order has gone out to kill S 1035," he declared, "and we can only marvel at the equanimity with which the Administration's troops

---

Woodrow Wilson Memorial

A memorial to Woodrow Wilson, 28th President of the United States (1913-21), was authorized by Congress in 1968. A bill passed by Congress and signed into law Oct. 24 by President Johnson authorized an appropriation of $500,000 to plan for the creation of a Woodrow Wilson International Center for Scholars, within the Smithsonian Institution.

The Center was to be constructed in Washington, across Pennsylvania Avenue from the National Archives at 8th Street, N.W. It would be maintained and administered by a 15-member board of trustees, of whom eight were to be appointed by the incumbent President from private life and seven from within the government.

A special commission recommended the memorial to Congress in 1966 after conducting a five-year study.

A memorial to James Madison, the fourth President (1809-17), was authorized by Congress in 1965—a third building of the Library of Congress to be built and named for him. But by the end of 1968 Congress had not appropriated money to begin its construction. *(See Chapter on Government.)*

---

have carried out their orders. . . They have obediently marched up Capitol Hill and back down . . ." Neither bill was approved by the subcommittee and both died when the 1968 session of Congress ended.

Riots and Federal Workers

The Omnibus Crime Control and Safe Streets Act (HR 5037—PL 90-351) of 1968 (*see Chapter on Crime and Justice*) contained a provision to bar any person from employment in the federal government or the District of Columbia government for five years if he had been convicted of a felony related to a riot or civil disorder.

Information Agency Personnel

An Administration-backed bill (S 633—PL 90-494) authorized a career system for certain personnel of the United States Information Agency comparable to that of Foreign Service officers in the State Department. The bill passed both chambers of Congress on voice votes and with little debate, the Senate in November 1967 and the House in August 1968. President Johnson signed the measure into law, Aug. 20, 1968.

From its establishment as an independent agency in 1953, the USIA had never had a career system for its overseas professional officers. Foreign Service Reserve officers of the USIA were limited by statute from serving more than 10 years, although some had served longer through a rider to the Agency's appropriation bill.

The House Foreign Affairs Committee held hearings on S 633 in 1968 and reported an amended bill (H Rept 1632) which limited the appointment of Foreign Service Reserve officers in the USIA and the State Department to five years. After that time, a Reserve officer had to be released unless he received appointment as a Foreign Service officer, or a Foreign Service information officer, or a Foreign Service reserve officer with unlimited tenure, or a Foreign Service staff officer. The amendment was adopted by the House and Senate.

S 633 also authorized USIA Foreign Service staff personnel with more than 10 years' service to participate in the Foreign Service retirement and disability system.

Background. The House in 1967 passed an Administration-backed bill (HR 6277) to establish a single personnel system within the State Department, the United States Information Agency, and the Agency for International Development. AID was attached to the State Department, but USIA was an independent agency. Each of the three foreign affairs agencies operated under two personnel systems. The Classification Act of 1949 governed their federal civilian career employees (the so-called "classified" or Civil Service workers), and the Foreign Service Act of 1946 governed career diplomatic corps officers and some others subject to overseas duty. HR 6277 proposed to shift all employees of the three agencies, over a period of time, to the Foreign Service. The bill was supported by the Civil Service Commission but opposed by federal employees' unions and veterans' groups.

The Senate Foreign Relations Committee in 1966 rejected the proposed legislation and also returned to President Johnson the nominations of some 700 USIA officers for appointment as regular Foreign Service Officers. The nominees held Reserve Officer status in USIA and the change would have given them career rather than temporary appointments. The appointments would have enlarged the Foreign Service Officer Corps by about 20 per cent. The Subcommittee on Foreign Service felt it was "inappropriate" to bring in that many officers and it also anticipated legislation in 1967 to create a career service within USIA.

Chapter 14 — Health, Education and Welfare

Key Votes

In this chapter, key roll-call votes are shown in bold-face type. The party breakdown on each of these votes and the position taken by each Member of Congress may be found in the key vote charts which appear in the appendix to this book.

Health, Education and Welfare

THE most enduring legacy of the Johnson Administration may well be the wide range of innovative social programs initiated under the banner of the "Great Society." The years 1964-68 saw the enactment of piece after piece of landmark social legislation that promised to have an impact on the nation for generations to come. Some of this legislation, such as general education aid and medical care for the aged, had been bottled up in Congress since the Truman Administration. Other programs bore Mr. Johnson's personal stamp.

Mr. Johnson's most important independent initiative was the "war on poverty," which he "declared" in his first State of the Union Message and later expanded into the cornerstone of the "Great Society." The basic antipoverty legislation, the Economic Opportunity Act of 1964, established 10 programs—among them Head Start, the Job Corps and VISTA—which amounted to the first concerted attack on poverty since New Deal days. In spite of increasing opposition, Congress extended the programs in 1965, 1966 and 1967 and appropriated more money each year.

Other major programs followed: Medicare and Medicaid, federal aid for elementary and secondary education, federal scholarships for college students, the Partnership for Health program and an assortment of consumer protection laws. Much of this legislation, which together with housing formed the heart of the "Great Society," was enacted during the 89th Congress (1965-66); huge Democratic gains in the 1964 Congressional elections provided the margin of votes for passage. In the last years of the Johnson Administration, the economic drain of the Vietnam war—and the disillusionment the war produced—caused the pace to slacken. New proposals often were not acted on, and programs already enacted were funded well below authorized limits.

Health

A major expansion of federal health programs occurred under the Johnson Administration, as the focus of the federal role shifted from research and training to more direct efforts to provide improved health care for the general population.

Aside from Medicare and Medicaid *(see Welfare, below)*, major new legislation enacted included the Partnership for Health program, which provided for a coordinated federal-state attack on health problems, and the Heart Disease, Cancer and Stroke Amendments, which provided grants for specialized research and training and for demonstrations of patient care.

Other programs were extended and expanded: community mental health and retardation, air pollution control and educational assistance for doctors, nurses and other health specialists.

Reacting to two current social problems, drug abuse and the population explosion, Congress strengthened federal controls over stimulant, depressant and hallucinogenic drugs and authorized federal aid for family planning services.

No action was taken on proposals for increased federal aid to modernize deteriorating hospitals in urban areas. Instead, Congress enacted a simple extension of the Hill-Burton program which provided grants for hospital construction, primarily in rural areas.

Education

The federal role in the field of education also expanded dramatically in the mid-1960's. Federal support of education had been growing piecemeal since the Morrill Act of 1862, but until 1965 no aid program was enacted which could be considered a general subsidy program for education or for college students.

The Elementary and Secondary Education Act of 1965, however, launched a federal program so broad in application as to constitute the first general aid-to-education program ever passed by Congress. The Act provided aid to school districts on the basis of the number of children from low-income families in the area. Thus, although 95 percent of the nation's counties were expected to be eligible for aid, the bulk of the money was to be concentrated on the inner city and impoverished rural areas where the neediest children lived. "Aid to children" under the 1965 Act included aid to private school children through special programs such as shared-time services and through the loan of federally financed textbooks.

A second 1965 law further broadened the federal role in education. In the Higher Education Act, Congress for the first time in the nation's history authorized federal scholarships for college undergraduate students in a

---

Reference

For a discussion of health, education and welfare legislation in the years 1945-64, see *Congress and the Nation*, Vol. I, p. 1111.

The "Great Society"

"....Your imagination, your initiative and your indignation will determine whether we build a society where progress is the servant of our needs, or a society where old values and new visions are buried under unbridled growth.

"For in your time we have the opportunity to move not only toward the rich society and the powerful society, but upward to the Great Society. The Great Society rests on abundance and liberty for all. It demands an end to poverty and racial injustice, to which we are totally committed in our time. But that is just the beginning.

"The Great Society is a place where every child can find knowledge to enrich his mind and to enlarge his talents. It is a place where leisure is a welcome chance to build and reflect, not a feared cause of boredom and restlessness. It is a place where the city of man serves not only the needs of the body and the demands of commerce, but the desire for beauty and the hunger for community.

"It is a place where man can renew contact with nature. It is a place which honors creation for its own sake and for what it adds to the understanding of the race. It is a place where men are more concerned with the quality of their goals than the quantity of their goods. But most of all, the Great Society is not a safe harbor, a resting place, a final objective, a finished work. It is a challenge constantly renewed, beckoning us toward a destiny where the meaning of our lives matches the marvelous products of our labor."

President Johnson in a May 22, 1964 speech at the University of Michigan in Ann Arbor.

position of "exceptional financial need." The same Act also authorized federal interest subsidies on private loans to middle-income students. Another key program established in the Act was the Teacher Corps, a program designed to provide a corps of skilled teachers to improve school education in slums and other impoverished areas.

These were the major laws on education enacted during the Johnson Administration, and they are considered in this chapter. Two other aspects of education policy are treated elsewhere in this volume. Federal action on school desegregation is discussed in the chapter on Civil Rights; veterans' education benefits are covered in the chapter on Veterans.

Welfare

Certainly the most dramatic development in the field of welfare during the 1965-68 period was the enactment of the Medicare program in 1965. Medicare, a program of hospital insurance for the aged financed through the Social Security System, had been a major goal of liberal forces throughout the postwar period, and the Democratic gains in the 1964 elections provided the votes needed to write it into law. As enacted, the Medicare program contained not only the basic compulsory Medicare hospital plan, but also a voluntary supplementary plan covering doctor bills and related services.

Also in 1965, Congress established a new "Medicaid" program of aid to the poor for medical expenses. Experience with the Medicaid program showed that it cost far more than Congress had intended, and efforts to trim costs continued throughout the Johnson Administration.

Widespread dissatisfaction with the effectiveness of the existing welfare system led, in 1967, to important and controversial changes in public assistance programs. The changes included a mandatory work-training program for all recipients under the Aid for Families with Dependent Children (AFDC) program and a freeze on the amount of federal aid for AFDC assistance when the father was absent from the home. Proposals for a guaranteed minimum annual income were discussed but not acted on. Meanwhile, Congress continued to expand traditional welfare programs.

President Johnson's major 1964 legislative success, the antipoverty program, was a source of controversy throughout the remainder of his Presidency. Republicans were unsuccessful in their efforts to dismantle the Office of Economic Opportunity and transfer the various elements of the program to old-line agencies, but growing criticism of the program did lead to efforts to tighten its administration. Despite the criticism, the program was expanded and the authorization steadily increased.

Consumers

Consumer issues became a subject of major public concern during the Johnson Administration, and much important consumer legislation was enacted during the period.

Congress in 1966 enacted auto safety and highway safety bills in an effort to curb the growing incidence of death and injury on the nation's highways. The auto safety bill gave the Federal Government power to establish motor vehicle safety standards, while the highway safety bill required states to establish federally approved highway safety standards or lose some of their federal highway aid dollars.

Two major pieces of disclosure legislation were enacted during the Johnson Presidency. The 1968 truth-in-lending law required lenders and companies extending credit to make available, in a consistent manner, information on the costs of financing they provided. The 1966 truth-in-packaging law required manufacturers to provide consumers with specific information about a commodity's content to enable them to make price and other comparisons between products.

Meat and poultry inspection laws, enacted in 1967 and 1968, were designed to protect consumers against low-quality meat sold in intrastate commerce. The bills required states to set up inspection systems at least equal to the existing federal system (for meat shipped in interstate commerce) or have the Federal Government take over the inspection of plants handling meat sold only in intrastate commerce.

Other bills enacted included measures to protect consumers from dangerous household items, flammable fabrics and articles emitting radiation. Congress also enacted a gas pipeline safety bill.

Consumers won an increased voice in national affairs through the appointment of special Presidential assistants on consumer affairs and through the establishment of various consumer advisory groups.

Health Programs

A MAJOR expansion of the Federal Government's role in the field of health occurred in the 1965-68 period.

The federal commitment in this area had been growing rapidly since the end of World War II, but prior to 1965 the primary emphasis was on research, training of health and research personnel, and the construction of hospitals and medical and research facilities. In the mid-1960s, the focus shifted to more direct efforts to provide improved health care for the general population.

President Johnson pointed the way in his 1965 message to Congress on health legislation. Noting that "our advances, thus far, have been most dramatic in the field of health knowledge," the President said: "We can—and we must—strive now to assure the availability of and accessibility to the best health care for all Americans, regardless of age or geography or economic status." Accordingly, Mr. Johnson's health program placed special emphasis on health care, and Congress enacted many of his proposals.

The most dramatic of the new health care programs enacted during the 1965-68 period were the Medicare program of health insurance for the aged and the Medicaid program of aid for the medically needy. Although most health programs of the Health, Education and Welfare (HEW) Department were administered by the Public Health Service (PHS), Medicare was under the Social Security Administration (SSA) and Medicaid was under the Social and Rehabilitation Service (SRS). These and other welfare-oriented health programs are described in the chapter on Welfare.

Major health care programs also were initiated under the jurisdiction of the Public Health Service. Programs administered by PHS are described in the following pages. These are the highlights:

Health Care and Services. In the Heart Disease, Cancer and Stroke Amendments of 1965, Congress authorized federal grants to promote the establishment of regional medical programs to fight heart disease, cancer, stroke and related diseases. The purpose of the legislation was to make widely available to doctors and patients the latest advances in diagnosis and treatment of these diseases, which cause seven of every ten deaths in the United States.

In the Partnership for Health program (the Comprehensive Health Planning and Services Act of 1966 and its 1967 amendments), Congress attempted to match health needs and health resources on a state- or area-wide basis. The law gave new emphasis to planning and setting priorities in health programs at both state and community levels. It authorized funds for comprehensive

health planning and consolidated many existing formula and project grants into grants for comprehensive health services to make possible greater flexibility in planning and administration.

The Partnership for Health program was expected to result in fundamental changes, over a number of years, in state and local administration of federally aided health programs. The planning required by the program was seen as leading to the provision of more comprehensive health services. Area-wide planning was encouraged by the legislation and was expected to produce a more rational allocation of resources and more effective control over problems, such as environmental health, which crossed local government boundaries.

Congress also established grant programs to provide for construction and staffing of facilities to treat and rehabilitate narcotics addicts and alcoholics. It extended existing programs for vaccination of children against childhood diseases and for health care services for domestic migratory workers.

Mental Health and Retardation. Congress extended the program of federal grants to help build community mental health centers under the Community Mental Health Centers Act of 1963. Additional grants to help staff the centers also were provided; Congress had denied a request for staffing grants in 1963. Staffing grants were also authorized for mental retardation facilities in the 1967 extension of the Mental Retardation Facilities Construction Act of 1963.

Education and Training. Responding to a continuing shortage of doctors, nurses and other health specialists, Congress expanded its educational assistance programs. In 1965 it amended the Health Professions Educational Assistance Act of 1963 to extend and expand existing programs of student loans for health professionals and of federal grants to help professional schools increase their student capacity. The bill also authorized new programs of scholarship aid and improvement grants to professional schools. In 1966 Congress authorized a three-year program of grants to improve training of technical personnel to assist doctors, dentists and other health professionals. The bill authorized a limited pro-

---

Reference

For details of federal action in the field of health for the years 1945-64, see *Congress and the Nation,* Vol. I, pp. 1122-1194.

gram of opportunity grants for needy nursing students and revised the existing loan program for health professionals. The Health Manpower Act of 1968 extended and revised the programs for technical personnel. It also extended and enlarged scholarship and loan programs in the health professions and created a new nursing scholarship plan.

Hospital Construction, Modernization. Under the Hill-Burton hospital construction program, the Federal Government since 1946 had provided matching grants for construction of hospitals, primarily in small towns and rural areas. By the 1960s, however, deterioration of existing hospitals in major urban areas had become a more pressing problem. Beginning in 1964, Congress authorized limited use of Hill-Burton funds to modernize hospitals in large cities, but the modernization grants were not sufficient to meet urban needs. President Johnson in 1966 proposed a massive, 10-year aid program for hospital modernization, but Congress did not act on his request and the President did not repeat it in 1967. Instead, he appointed an advisory commission to study the Hill-Burton program, and Congress in 1968 approved a simple extension of the 1946 Act.

PHS Reorganization. Two reorganizations of the Public Health Service, undertaken in 1966 and 1968, were designed to help PHS meet the demands of its new and expanded responsibilities and to tighten the HEW Secretary's control over decisions on health policy.

The reorganizations fundamentally altered the PHS. It was expanded to include the previously independent Food and Drug Administration but lost much of its own historic independence. The PHS, tracing its beginnings back to 1798, was traditionally a relatively independent agency even after it became part of the Department of HEW in 1953. Its head, the Surgeon General, was always selected from among the career officers of the Service's Commissioned Corps; he reported directly to the Secretary but retained final authority in a number of areas. The reorganization placed the PHS under a political appointee, the Assistant Secretary for Health and Scientific Affairs. The Assistant Secretary was given responsibility also for over-all health policy direction and coordination of HEW's other health programs.

The activities of the Service were shuffled and reshuffled to give greater emphasis to newly emerging concerns of the Service. Among those concerns were the support of health manpower training, the provision of health services, environmental health activities and consumer protection.

Cigarette Labeling. A lobbying campaign by the cigarette industry paid off in 1965 as Congress enacted a bill which not only required a health-hazard warning statement on cigarette packages and cartons ("Caution: Cigarette Smoking May Be Hazardous to Your Health"), but also prohibited any other health warning requirement on the packages and prohibited until July 1, 1969, any requirement that cigarette advertising include a similar statement. The bill was Congress's response to the 1964 declaration of the Surgeon General's Advisory Committee on Smoking and Health that "cigarette smoking is a health hazard of sufficient importance...to warrant appropriate remedial action." The bill superseded a 1964 promulgation by the Federal Trade Commission that both cigarette packages and advertising carry a warning of the health hazards of smoking. It also prevented states and localities from requiring a stronger warning on cigarette packages.

Drug Abuse Controls. Mounting concern over the illegal use of drugs, especially by young people, led Congress in 1965 to strengthen federal controls over stimulant, depressant and hallucinogenic drugs. The 1965 law was directed chiefly against illegal traffic in these drugs, including pep pills and LSD. Failure of the 1965 law to curb illegal drug use led to enactment in 1968 of legislation providing criminal penalties for illegal possession of such drugs.

Birth Control. President Eisenhower in 1959 said he could not imagine a subject less fit for governmental action than population control, but by 1965 he as well as other national figures were urging federal efforts to curb the worldwide population explosion. Sen. Ernest Gruening (D Alaska) led a continuing campaign to promote more aggressive Government action on population control, and Congress in the 1965-68 period added to a variety of bills amendments authorizing family planning aid. President Johnson also came out in favor of federal aid for birth control activities. As a result, about one million women in the United States received federally aided family planning services in fiscal 1968, and the Government obligated more than $35 million for international family planning activities.

Air Pollution. Congress extended and expanded the grant program for state, local and regional air pollution control activities under the Clean Air Act of 1963. The 1965 air pollution bill also established automotive exhaust emission standards and authorized a national research program for disposal of solid wastes. In the Air Quality Act of 1967, Congress authorized federal enforcement of regional air quality standards if the states failed to act.

Health Research. Although federal spending for health research activities consumed a declining share of the federal health dollar, actual federal outlays for health research continued to increase. The largest sources of federal medical research support were the National Institutes of Health (NIH) and the National Institute of Mental Health (NIMH), which together accounted for more than 62 percent of federal health research expenditures. For fiscal 1947-68 their research outlays were about $6.6 billion, of which 60 percent was spent in fiscal 1964-68.

Chronology Of Health Legislation

1965

The record of Congress in 1965, President Johnson said Oct. 22, "is impressive in every field—and monumental in the field of health."

Signifying the priority he attached to health legislation, the President had sent his health proposals to Congress Jan. 7—preceding all other messages except the traditional State of the Union report. The message said: "Our first concern must be to assure that the advance of medical knowledge leaves none behind. We can—and we must—strive now to assure the availability of and accessibility to the best health care for all Americans, regardless of age or geography or economic status." The President added: "Our advances, thus far, have been most dramatic in the field of health knowledge. We are challenged now to give attention to advances in the field of health care—and this is the emphasis of the recommendations I am placing before you."

Topping the list of recommendations was the medical-care-for-the-aged program to be financed under the Social Security system—a plan sought and denied for 20 years prior to 1965. The Medicare bill also carried additional aged health care programs not proposed by the President, and a wide range of child health care programs, most of which were requested by Mr. Johnson. *(For details of these programs see chapter on Welfare.)*

In addition, the message included a variety of proposals, sought previously but denied, which were enacted in 1965: scholarships for needy medical and dental students, grants for initial staffing of community mental health centers, and the first overhaul of the vocational rehabilitation program since 1954.

There were also some new proposals. The President asked authority to launch a nationwide attack on heart disease, cancer and stroke—the major killers in the United States—in regions throughout the country. And he asked Congress to enlarge the federal effort to control the illicit distribution and use of psychotoxic drugs. Congress responded favorably.

Finally, there were proposals for extensions, and often substantial expansions, of existing programs—vaccination of preschool children against childhood diseases, health care services for domestic migratory workers, grants to encourage cures for mental retardation, programs under the Health Research Facilities Act and the Health Professions Educational Assistance Act (including scholarships), and grants for general and special health programs. All these were enacted.

Only a few requested programs failed of enactment: new requirements for labeling of hazardous substances and for pre-marketing examination of the safety of cosmetics and therapeutic devices; an increased federal share for specialized national or regional research

---

White House Conference

President Johnson invited 850 health specialists to a Nov. 3-4, 1965, White House Conference on Health. Major preliminary recommendations:

Health Professions Education. Find new methods to develop medical manpower. Establish pilot projects in hospitals and universities to explore and demonstrate solutions to health problems and to serve as centers for community education and continuing education of health personnel. Subjects should include: (1) providing incentives to attract personnel, especially the under-privileged; (2) analyzing needs for health personnel and then tailoring education programs to meet them; (3) developing guidelines for financing services provided by medical schools, such as free care for indigents, with a view toward making support of "education for health manpower...an integral part of the cost of health care"; (4) expanding use of physician assistants (human and electronic).

Health Care. Assure dissemination of the results of health research. Require every medical school to plan for delivery of health care services, using the community as a laboratory for research and demonstration of comprehensive health care. Encourage group practice, to stabilize costs without curtailing services. Expand health insurance to cover comprehensive care wherever needed—"at the hospital, outpatient clinic, office or home."

Health Protection. Eliminate additional waterborne, foodborne, animal and communicable diseases, including those caused by open dumps, junkyards and solid wastes. Provide for surveillance and testing of drugs before merchandising. Prevent fatalities and injuries in industrial and residential accidents. Improve driver training, set higher driver licensing standards, improve highway design and build more crashworthy vehicles with restraining devices, stronger door locks and safer steering assembly and interior surfaces. Prevent "alcohol-related" fatalities. Prevent (rather than cure) mental illness. Increase commitment of public and private resources to providing family planning services, as a routine part of medical practice, for those who desire them.

---

facilities; funds to increase the modernization of older hospitals; direct loans and loan guarantees for constructing and equipping group practice facilities; and a variety of pesticide control measures.

Congress generally acted favorably on requests for funding both old and new health programs. In a few cases—notably the National Institutes of Health—the budgeted amounts were increased by Congress. (NIH funds exceeded $1 billion, for the first time, in fiscal 1966). In other cases, most cuts were minimal.

Heart Disease, Cancer, Stroke

In the Heart Disease, Cancer and Stroke Amendments of 1965 (S 596—PL 89-239), Congress authorized a new three-year program of federal grants to encourage and aid localities in planning and establishing regional medical programs throughout the country for a specialized attack on heart diseases, cancer, stroke and related diseases. The bill authorized appropriations totaling $340 million over the fiscal years 1966-68. Congress extended the program in 1968. *(See below.)*

The regional medical programs contemplated by S 596 were intended to serve as a framework for dissemination of the most advanced medical knowledge throughout the country to practicing physicians and their patients who were suffering from heart disease, cancer and stroke —the major killers in the United States. The programs were to provide for research and training and for demonstrations of patient care related to the research and training.

The broad aim of the legislation was eventually to save lives by providing higher-quality diagnosis and care for heart, cancer and stroke patients. The immediate objectives of the bill were (1) to improve the nation's health manpower by training new specialists in heart, cancer and stroke problems and by providing for continuing education of medical personnel; and (2) to upgrade heart, cancer and stroke health facilities by encouraging renovations and replacement of obsolete equipment.

The federal grants authorized in S 596 were to cover up to 100 percent of the costs of local planning for establishment of coordinated arrangements—among existing local institutions (medical schools, research institutions,

---

Key Health Officials, 1965-68

Following is a list of Health, Education and Welfare Department officials with major responsibility in the field of health during the 1965-68 period. *(For a similar list for the years 1945-64, see Congress and the Nation, Vol. I, p. 1120.)*

HEW Secretaries

Anthony J. Celebrezze, 1962-65
John W. Gardner, 1965-68
Wilbur J. Cohen, 1968-69

Assistant Secretary for Health and Scientific Affairs (new position)

Philip R. Lee, 1965-69

Surgeons General of the U. S.

Luther L. Terry, 1961-65
William H. Stewart, 1965-

Commissioners, Food and Drug Administration

George P. Larrick, 1954-65
James L. Goddard, 1966-68
Herbert L. Ley, Jr., 1968-

Directors, National Institutes of Health

James A. Shannon, 1955-68
Robert Q. Marston, 1968-

---

hospitals)—for research, training and patient-care demonstrations in the fields of heart disease, cancer and stroke. Once the plans for such regional medical programs were drawn up, additional federal grants would be available for actual establishment and operation of the regional programs, including grants covering up to 90 percent of the costs of alteration, major repair, remodeling and renovation of existing buildings and replacement of built-in equipment.

Johnson Proposals Modified. The final bill was a modified version of legislation proposed by President Johnson to implement the 1964 recommendations of the President's Commission on Heart Disease, Cancer and Stroke. The Commission concluded that "by bringing to all the people the full benefit of what is now known of prevention, detection, treatment and cure, we could save each year a number of lives equal to the population of a major city."

The Commission recommended establishment of 450 "stations" across the country to provide such services as screening, diagnosis and outpatient care and training of physicians, and 60 regional medical centers for more complex research and treatment of patients. Estimated cost of the five-year program recommended by the Commission was $2.94 billion.

The Administration draft bill did not include the "stations." Instead, it proposed grants for planning and establishment of an unspecified number of regional "complexes" affiliated with medical schools, hospitals and medical centers, to provide for diagnosis and treatment of patients along with research and training. The grants could be used for construction of new facilities if necessary to achieve a coordinated program. Total contemplated authorizations for grants were not stated directly in the bill, but they had previously been estimated by the Public Health Service at $1,150,000,000 over the five-year period.

The Senate version of S 596 was similar to the Administration bill except that it limited authorizations to $650 million over four years (fiscal 1966-69) and eliminated authority for the construction of wholly new facilities. The House (and final) version further limited the program, providing authorizations over three years (fiscal 1966-68) totaling $340 million (about the same amount as for the first three years of the Administration and Senate proposals), and making certain other changes which gave the final legislation the character more of a pilot program than of a permanent long-range program. In contrast to the original Administration proposal, which had envisioned a large-scale construction program, the final bill was designed primarily to encourage a start on local planning of regional medical programs and to get pilot projects under way, so that at the end of three years Congress could study the results and determine whether to go ahead with a broader type of program, such as proposed by the Commission and the Administration.

AMA Position. The most significant opposition to establishment of the regional medical complexes came from the American Medical Assn. (AMA) and resulted in the extensive amendments which reduced the scope of the legislation.

At its June 20-24 national convention, the AMA adopted a resolution opposing those portions of the report of the President's Commission which proposed creation of the regional medical centers. The resolution said "immense strides" had been made under "existing patterns of research and medical practice."

Late in August, after the Senate had passed S 596, the AMA requested President Johnson to defer action on the bill until 1966 "because the likelihood of its passage was jeopardizing AMA's attempts" to cooperate with the Health, Education and Welfare Department in implementing the newly enacted medical care for the aged bill (PL 89-97), which the AMA had also opposed.

The President refused to delay the bill. However, he directed the new HEW Secretary, John W. Gardner, to work with the AMA committee to develop amendments to make the bill less objectionable to the AMA. Subsequently, the House Interstate and Foreign Commerce Committee adopted numerous amendments which became part of the final bill. Several were amendments worked out at meetings between the HEW and AMA spokesmen. Others were added by the Committee on its own or suggested by other groups. Although the Administration did not like all the changes, it accepted them as the price of getting the legislation enacted. The AMA Sept. 2 said it still could not support the bill, but the changes "certainly make the bill much less objectionable."

The House Committee, in adding a provision which strengthened a Senate-inserted ban on construction of wholly new facilities, said the provision was designed to make absolutely clear that the bill was not intended to finance a massive federal construction program of medical complexes but only to help existing local hospitals, medical schools, etc., to coordinate their efforts.

Provisions

As signed into law, Oct. 6, S 596:

Declared that the purposes of the legislation were: to encourage and assist, through grants, in the establishment of regional cooperative arrangements among medical schools, research institutions and hospitals for research and training (including continuing education) and related demonstrations of patient care in the fields of heart disease, cancer, stroke and related diseases; to enable the medical profession and medical institutions to make available to their patients the latest advances in the diagnosis and treatment of these diseases; to improve generally the health manpower and facilities available to the nation; and to accomplish these ends without interfering with existing patterns, or methods of financing, of patient care or professional practice or with administration of hospitals, and to accomplish them in cooperation with practicing physicians, medical center officials, hospital administrators and representatives of appropriate voluntary health agencies.

Authorized the Surgeon General to make grants, on the basis of applications from local groups, to assist public and nonprofit private universities, medical schools, research institutions and other public and nonprofit private institutions and agencies in planning, conducting feasibility studies and operating pilot projects for the establishment of regional medical programs to implement the purposes of the Act. Provided that the grants might cover up to 100 percent of the costs of planning and up to 90 percent of the costs of construction or providing built-in equipment. *(See definition below.)*

Stipulated that the grants not be used to pay the cost of hospital, medical or other care of patients except

when such care was incident to research, demonstration or training activities. Stipulated that no patient be furnished such care unless he had been referred to the facility by a practicing physician.

Authorized a total of $340 million over fiscal years 1966-68 for the grants, broken down as follows: $50 million in fiscal 1966, $90 million in fiscal 1967 and $200 million in fiscal 1968.

Defined a regional medical program as a cooperative arrangement among a group of public or nonprofit private institutions or agencies engaged in research, training, diagnosis and treatment relating to heart disease, cancer, stroke and, at the option of the applicant for the grant, related disease or diseases. (The definition was designed to emphasize that the new regional medical programs would be limited in scope and intended primarily to facilitate arrangements among existing institutions.)

Defined construction as alteration, major repair, remodeling and renovation of existing buildings (including initial equipment of the buildings) and replacement of obsolete, built-in equipment of existing buildings (thereby prohibiting any new construction during the three years of the program authorized by the bill).

Established a 13-member National Advisory Council on Regional Medical Programs, chaired by the Surgeon General, to advise and assist the Surgeon General in preparation of regulations and policy for the programs and to review and make recommendations on applications for grants.

Required the Surgeon General, after consultation with the Council, to prescribe general regulations for approving grant applications and for coordination of programs assisted by the grants.

Stipulated that grants could be made only on approval of applications by the Surgeon General on the recommendation of the Advisory Council.

Stipulated that laborers or mechanics employed for construction financed under the Act would be paid prevailing wages under the Davis-Bacon Act.

Directed the Surgeon General to establish and maintain on a current basis a list of facilities in the United States equipped and staffed to provide the most advanced methods and techniques in the diagnosis and treatment of heart disease, cancer or stroke, along with other information including the availability of advanced specialty training in such facilities, and to make the list and information readily available to licensed practitioners and others.

Community Mental Health Centers

The Administration-endorsed Community Mental Health Centers Act Amendments of 1965 (HR 2985—PL 89-105), authorized a new seven-year (fiscal 1966-72) program of grants to public or nonprofit private organizations or agencies to help pay the initial costs of professional and technical personnel at community mental health centers. The grants were to be available during the first 51 months of operation of a new center or of new services in existing centers. They could cover a portion of the staffing costs ranging from 75 percent during the first 15 months to 30 percent in the final 12 months. After the end of the 51 months, the full staffing costs were to be borne by the local community.

The staffing grants were sought by President Johnson in his Jan. 7 health message. A similar program had been sought by President Kennedy in 1963 as part of the Community Mental Health Centers Act (PL 88-164), but Congress denied his request. *(Congress and the Nation, Vol. I, p. 1147.)*

The bill made specific authorizations of $19.5 million in fiscal 1966, $24 million in fiscal 1967 and $30 million in fiscal 1968 for initial staffing grants to eligible centers. After fiscal 1968, no additional centers could receive staffing grants, but those centers which had received grants during the first three years would be eligible to receive follow-up grants to cover staffing during the remainder of the full 51 months. The bill authorized appropriation of whatever amounts were necessary during fiscal 1967-72 to finance the follow-up grants. The estimated total cost of all the initial and follow-up grants from fiscal 1966-72 was $224,175,000.

Explaining why Congress had approved the staffing grants in 1965 although it had denied them in 1963, the House Interstate and Foreign Commerce Committee said experience since 1963 had indicated that the community mental health centers covered by the 1963 legislation could not get under way properly without financial aid for staffing from the Federal Government.

In addition to authorizing the staffing grants, HR 2985 extended for three years, with increased authorizations, existing programs (1) for training of teachers of mentally retarded and other handicapped children; and (2) for otherwise improving educational opportunities for these children through grants for research and demonstration projects. President Johnson had requested the extensions.

Congress in 1967 enacted a further extension of the community mental health program. *(See below.)*

Provisions. As signed into law, Aug. 4, HR 2985 contained the following provisons:

Mental Health Staffing. Amended the Mental Retardation Facilities and Community Mental Health Centers Act of 1963 (PL 88-164) to authorize the Secretary of Health, Education and Welfare to make grants for the compensation of professional and technical personnel in community mental health centers.

Limited the grants to the first 51 months of operation of a new center or of new services in existing centers; and to 75 percent of staffing costs in the first 15 months, 60 percent in the subsequent 12 months, 45 percent in the next 12 months and 30 percent in the following 12 months.

Directed the Secretary, in making the grants, to take into account the relative health and financial needs and the populations of the states.

Provided that grants be made only upon application by public or nonprofit private agencies or organizations, and in accordance with specified criteria.

Directed the Secretary, after consultation with the National Advisory Mental Health Council, to prescribe regulations for the determination and approval of grants.

Limited grants after June 30, 1968, to facilities which had received an initial grant on or before that date.

Authorized appropriations of $19.5 million in fiscal 1966, $24 million in fiscal 1967, and $30 million in fiscal 1968 for initial grants under the program, and of such sums as were necessary for fiscal years 1967-72 for grants to centers which had previously received initial grants.

Teacher Training. Amended PL 88-164 to extend from fiscal 1966 through fiscal 1969 the program of grants to states and higher education institutions for training teachers of mentally retarded and other handicapped children. Authorized $29.5 million in fiscal 1967, $34 million in fiscal 1968 and $37.5 million in fiscal 1969 (in addition to the existing authorization of $19.5 million for fiscal 1966).

Expanded the existing definition of a state to include Puerto Rico, the Virgin Islands, the District of Columbia, Guam and American Samoa.

Education of Children. Amended PL 88-164 to extend from fiscal 1966 through fiscal 1969 the program of grants to states and public and private colleges and universities for research and demonstration projects to improve educational opportunities for handicapped children.

Increased the existing fiscal 1966 authorization for this program from $2 million to $6 million and authorized $9 million in fiscal 1967, $12 million in fiscal 1968 and $14 million in fiscal 1969.

Amended PL 88-164 to authorize the Commissioner of Education to make grants to institutions of higher education for the construction, equipping and operation of a facility for research and demonstration in the field of education of handicapped children.

Special Fund. Established in the Treasury a special account without fiscal year limitation into which the Secretary of Health, Education and Welfare could pay sums set aside for certain grants and from which he could make payments of the grants as needed.

Community Health Programs

The Administration-requested Community Health Service Extension Amendments of 1965 (S 510—PL 89-109) extended the life of four federal health grant programs. *(Congress and the Nation, Vol. I, p. 1143, 1145.)* Three of the four programs subsequently were absorbed by the Partnership for Health program, enacted in 1966; the fourth program, which provided health services for domestic migrant workers, was extended in 1968. *(See below.)*

Provisions. As signed by the President, Aug. 5, S 510:

Immunization Grants. Extended for three years, through June 30, 1968, the existing program (PL 87-868) of grants to the states and local communities to buy vaccine to immunize children against polio, diphtheria, whooping cough and tetanus. Added to the diseases covered measles and any other infectious diseases which the Surgeon General decided represented a major public health problem. Authorized appropriations of $11 million in each of the fiscal years 1966-68. Permitted use of the grants for purchase of vaccines for all preschool-age children (rather than only for children under five).

Migratory Workers Health Services. Extended for three years, through June 30, 1968, the existing program (PL 87-692) of grants to public and nonprofit private agencies for health services to domestic migrant workers. Authorized $7 million in fiscal 1966, $8 million in fiscal 1967 and $9 million in fiscal 1968. Included hospital care for migrant workers and their families among the other benefits financed with federal aid under the program.

Public Health Grants. Extended for one year, through June 30, 1967, the existing program (PL 87-395) of matching grants to the states to provide general public health services. Within the existing over-all $50-million annual authorization, increased from $2.5 million to $5 million the appropriations authorization for grants to schools of public health.

Community Health Services. Extended for one year, through June 30, 1966, the existing program (PL 87-395) of grants to states, local communities and nonprofit private organizations for studies, experiments and demonstration of new methods of out-of-hospital care.

Total New Authorizations. For all four programs, added a total of $117 million in appropriations authorizations over fiscal 1966-68, as follows (in millions of dollars by fiscal year):

	1966	1967	1968
Immunizations	$11	$11	$11
Migrants Health	7	8	9
Public Health	1	50	——
Community Health	1	10	——
Total	$18	$79	$20

1 *Previously authorized*

Health Research Facilities

The Health Research Facilities Amendments of 1965, (HR 2984—PL 89-115) extended and expanded the existing program of matching grants for construction of health research facilities at medical schools, universities, hospitals and other institutions. The existing program, with a $50-million annual authorization, was scheduled to expire at the end of fiscal 1966. HR 2984 authorized appropriations for construction totaling $280 million in fiscal 1967-69. (Congress voted a further extension in the 1968 Health Manpower Act. *See below.*)

In addition, the 1965 Act provided a three-year (fiscal 1966-68) authorization for the Public Health Service to enter into research contracts. Since 1957, the PHS had received temporary research contract authority from language inserted in annual appropriations bills: HR 2984 wrote this authority into the basic PHS organic act. No limit was set on funds, which were expected to increase to $94 million in fiscal 1966.

Finally, HR 2984 authorized appointment of three additional Assistant Secretaries of Health, Education and Welfare. Another was authorized later in the year in the Water Quality Act of 1965 (PL 89-234), bringing the total to seven.

Expansion of the health research facilities construction program was requested by President Johnson in his Jan. 7 health message. He also asked special authority to construct and operate specialized national or regional health research facilities, but this was denied by the House and in the conference version of HR 2984.

The Health Research Facilities Act (PL 84-835) became law in 1956, under a $30-million annual authorization. Congress in 1961 extended the Act until June 30, 1966, and increased the authorization to $50 million a year (PL 87-395). (*Congress and the Nation, Vol. I, p. 1138, 1143.*)

Study Group Praises NIH

A special Presidential committee concluded in 1965 that the activities of the National Institutes of Health (NIH) were "essentially sound" and that the NIH budget was, "on the whole, being spent wisely and well in the public interest." It reported that NIH-supported research, which accounted for 40 percent of all biomedical research in the United States, was of "high quality." The committee warned, however, that unless organizational and procedural changes were made in NIH's operations, "substantial problems will arise in the future."

The 13-member committee, appointed by President Johnson in 1964, was composed of scientists, industrialists and educators and was chaired by Dr. Dean E. Wooldridge of the Thompson Ramo Wooldridge electronics firm.

The report said that NIH's "most important organizational need" was in the area of policy and planning. To meet this need, the committee recommended creation of an advisory Policy and Planning Council to operate at the level of the Director of the Institutes. It also recommended that the autonomy of the separate institutes, such as the National Cancer Institute and the National Heart Institute, be "diminished" and that the authority of the Director be "increased." This re-balancing of authority, the report said, should also occur with respect to the Director's "access" to the "higher councils of the Department of Health, Education and Welfare."

Procedural changes, the committee recommended, should be aimed at enhancing the responsibility and authority of executives of universities conducting research under the auspices of NIH.

Provisions. As signed into law Aug. 9, HR 2984:

Amended the Public Health Service Act to extend the existing program for construction of health research facilities for three years, from fiscal 1967 through fiscal 1969, and authorize appropriations totaling $280 million for grants for the program.

Authorized the Public Health Service to enter into contracts for research during fiscal 1966-68.

Authorized the President to appoint three additional Assistant Secretaries of Health, Education and Welfare (for a total of six). Abolished the existing office of Special Assistant to the Secretary of HEW for Health and Medical Affairs.

Health Training Aid

At the request of President Johnson, Congress in 1965 enacted amendments to the Health Professions Educational Assistance Act, extending two old programs and establishing two new programs to aid schools and students of medicine, dentistry and other specified health professions. The legislation, like the original 1963 Act, was designed to increase the number of students in these professions as well as improve the quality of their education. (*Congress and the Nation, Vol. I, p. 1148*)

The bill (HR 3141—PL 89-290) authorized a new four-year program of scholarships for students of medicine, dentistry, osteopathy, optometry, podiatry and pharmacy, and established a new four-year program of "improvement grants" to professional schools to help pay their basic operating expenses and improve teaching. It extended (fiscal 1967-69) and expanded existing programs of student loans and federal construction grants to help schools increase their student capacity.

The final bill, similar in its major provisions to the Administration request, provided specific authorizations of $480 million for construction grants; $76.5 million for loans to students and institutions; $200 million for improvement grants; nearly $27 million for scholarships; and $4 million for operation, review and record-keeping.

President Johnson, in his Jan. 7 health message to Congress, outlined the need for the legislation, saying that, "In all sectors of health care, the need for trained personnel continues to outstrip the supply.... To begin to meet the nation's health needs, the number of new physicians graduated each year must increase at least 50 percent by 1975, and the output of new dentists by 100 percent."

President Johnson said the improvement grants were needed because many existing schools could not meet their operating costs and that many had "borne heavy financial burdens at the expense of academic standards."

The new improvement grants program, providing $200 million over a four-year period to help professional schools cover their operating costs, was the only program which provoked opposition. It was opposed by the American Medical Assn. (AMA) and the Republican Policy Committee in the House, the latter charging that it was "outright federal subsidy" for almost any school, instead of the "selective assistance" provided in the past. During floor debate in the House, Albert H. Quie (R Minn.) attempted to strike out the improvement grants, but the motion was defeated on a 21-69 standing vote. There were no further efforts to delete the provision.

HR 3141 also contained a provision, added on the House floor, permitting "forgiveness" of up to 50 percent (10 percent annually) of loans to students subsequently practicing in an area in which there was a certified shortage of health personnel. A similar loan forgiveness proposal was approved by the Senate but defeated by the House in 1964. Earlier in 1965, the Senate had passed a separate loan forgiveness bill (S 576).

Provisions

As signed into law, Oct. 22, HR 3141 amended the 1963 Health Professions Educational Assistance Act (PL 88-129) as follows:

Quality Improvement Grants. Authorized a new four-year program of grants, beginning in fiscal 1966, to assist non-profit schools of medicine, dentistry, osteopathy, optometry and podiatry in improving the quality of their educational programs. Authorized $200 million as follows: $20 million in fiscal 1966, $40 million in fiscal 1967, $60 million in fiscal 1968 and $80 million in fiscal 1969.

Authorized part of these funds for basic improvement grants. Limited the grants for each school in fiscal 1966 to $12,500 plus a sum equal to $250 multiplied by the number of full-time students, and in fiscal 1967-69 to $25,000 plus a sum equal to $500 multiplied by the number of full-time students.

Authorized use of the additional funds not required for basic improvement grants for special improvement grants. Stipulated that grants to any school for special improvements could not exceed $100,000 in fiscal 1966, $200,000 in fiscal 1967, $300,000 in fiscal 1968 and $400,000 in fiscal 1969.

Provided that, to receive a basic or special improvement grant, a school would guarantee to expend non-federal funds equal to the average amount spent during the previous three years; and required that a special improvement grant be recommended by the National Advisory Council created by the bill.

Established in the Public Health Service a 12-member National Advisory Council on Medical, Dental, Optometric and Podiatric Education to advise the Surgeon General on policy and administration of the two new programs—scholarships and improvement grants.

Scholarships. Authorized a new four-year program of scholarship grants to schools of medicine, osteopathy, dentistry, optometry, podiatry and pharmacy.

Limited the total scholarship grants to any school to $2,000 multiplied by one-tenth the number of full-time first-year students in fiscal 1967; first-, second- and third-year students in fiscal 1968; and total students in fiscal 1969. Authorized sufficient grants in fiscal 1970-72 to enable a school to continue scholarships to students receiving them prior to fiscal 1970.

Authorized the scholarships for first-year students in fiscal 1966, first- and second-year students in fiscal 1967, first-, second- and third-year students in fiscal 1968 and first-, second-, third- and fourth-year students in fiscal 1969.

Directed that the scholarships be awarded to students from low-income families who otherwise could not pursue the course of study. Stipulated that a scholarship could cover the portion of a student's tuition, fees, books, equipment and living expenses which his school determined he needed, but not more than $2,500.

Construction Grants. Extended for three years, through fiscal 1969, the existing program of federal grants for training physicians, pharmacists, optometrists, podiatrists, professional public health personnel and dentists.

Authorized $480 million for the grants over fiscal 1967-69 but stipulated that not more than $160 million would be available for grants before July 1, 1967, and not more than $320 million would be available before July 1, 1968.

Student Loans. Extended for three years, through fiscal 1969, the existing program of loans for students of medicine, dentistry, osteopathy or optometry and allowed it to be phased out in the following three fiscal years. Made eligible for the loans, in addition, full-time students of podiatry, pharmacy or surgical chiropody.

Increased the maximum amount of a loan from $2,000 to $2,500 per student each year.

Authorized $25 million in each of fiscal years 1967-69 and such sums as were necessary in fiscal 1970-72 for completing the loan program.

Authorized forgiveness of up to 50 percent (10 percent annually) of student loans (plus accrued interest) for medical, dental, or optometric students subsequently practicing in an area certified as having a shortage of health personnel under regulations drawn up by the Secretary of Health, Education and Welfare.

Provided that the interest rate on the first loan received under the Health Professions Educational Assistance Act or the Nurse Training Act of 1964 (PL 88-581) would apply in the case of all subsequent loans made to the student.

Authorized up to $1.5 million to enable the Surgeon General to make loans to schools to establish loan funds.

Nurse Training Amendments. Amended the Nurse Training Act to provide that nursing schools would be eligible for grants for expansion and improvement and for assistance to nursing students if they were, as under existing law, approved or accredited by a recognized body approved by the Commissioner of Education (currently, only the National League for Nurses was so recognized) or were accredited directly by the Commissioner of Education. *(Congress and the Nation, Vol. I, p. 1149)*

Medical Libraries

Congress in 1965 enacted a bill (S 597—PL 89-291) authorizing $105 million for a four-year program of federal matching grants to build medical library facilities and a five-year program of grants to expand medical library services, establish regional medical libraries and provide other assistance.

The Administration-backed legislation, which met with almost no opposition in Congress, provided funds for the matching grant program over the fiscal 1966-70 period to cope with the tremendous expansion of knowledge in the field of medical science. The legislation was designed to furnish space, facilities and trained personnel to deal with the massive body of published information and to advance new methods of collecting and disseminating material needed by health professionals.

S 597, as enacted, contained the provisions of a substituted House bill (HR 3142) which differed from the original Senate bill mainly in the amounts authorized.

Provisions. As signed into law, Oct. 22, the Medical Library Assistance Act (S 597):

Required the Board of Regents of the National Library of Medicine (part of the Public Health Service) to advise the Surgeon General in preparing regulations and in policy matters arising in administration of the Act. Required Board approval of an application for a grant for construction of a medical library facility before the grant could be made.

Defined "sciences related to health" to include medicine, osteopathy, dentistry, public health, and fundamental and applied sciences related to these fields.

Construction of Facilities. Authorized $40 million—$10 million annually in fiscal 1967-70—for grants to aid construction or improvement of nonprofit medical library facilities. Authorized the Surgeon General to award grants for up to 75 percent of the construction costs. Required that the library be intended for use as a medical library facility for at least 20 years, that sufficient matching funds be available for construction and operating costs, and that contractors pay prevailing wages as determined by the Davis-Bacon Act.

Training in Medical Library Sciences. Authorized $5 million—$1 million annually in fiscal 1966-70—for grants to individuals and nonprofit institutions for training and retraining in medical library science and in the field of communication of information.

Special Scientific Projects. Authorized $2.5 million —$500,000 annually in fiscal 1966-70—for assistance, through fellowships to physicians and scientists, in the compilation of existing and the creation of original contributions relating to advancements in sciences related to health.

Research and Development. Authorized $15 million —$3 million annually in fiscal 1966-70—for grants or contracts for research and investigations in medical library science and related activities, and for the development of new techniques, systems and equipment for processing, storing, retrieving and distributing information pertaining to health sciences.

Improving and Expanding Basic Resources. Authorized $15 million—$3 million annually in fiscal 1966-70—for grants of money and materials to nonprofit medical libraries and related scientific communication organizations to expand and improve their basic medical library or related resources (books, catalogues, duplicating equipment, film projectors, etc.). Provided that no grant in a single year could exceed $200,000.

Establishment of Regional Medical Libraries. Authorized $12.5 million—$2.5 million annually in fiscal 1966-70—for grants to enable existing nonprofit medical libraries to serve as regional medical libraries for the geographic areas in which they are located.

National Library of Medicine Regional Branches. Authorized $10 million—$2 million annually in fiscal 1966-70—for the establishment, as a branch of the National Library, of a regional medical library in locations where no existing library could be feasibly developed into a regional library.

Support of Biomedical Scientific Publications. Authorized $5 million—$1 million annually in fiscal 1966-70—for grants or contracts for up to three years to nonprofit institutions of higher education or individual scientists to support nonprofit biomedical scientific publications and the compilation of reviews, abstracts, handbooks, indexes and related matter pertaining to scientific works and development.

Drug Controls

Congress in 1965 enacted an Administration-backed bill (HR 2—PL 89-74) expanding federal controls over depressant and stimulant drugs. The bill was intended to reduce illegal distribution and use of barbiturates, amphetamines and other drugs affecting the central nervous system or producing hallucinogenic effects.

Under existing law, it was already illegal to sell barbiturates and amphetamines at retail without a prescription. HR 2 strengthened and broadened this prohibition by setting up, in effect, a permissible "chain of distribution," beginning with the manufacturer, and making it illegal for anyone not in the chain to possess the drugs except for his own use or that of members of his household or his pets. The bill also made it unnecessary for the Government to prove that the drugs had moved in interstate commerce before it could seize illegal supplies or proceed against violators. In addition, it increased the record-keeping required of manufacturers and distributors (including both drug wholesalers and retail pharmacists), strengthened the powers of federal inspectors and enforcement agents, and limited prescription refills. Although the new controls in the bill applied specifically only to barbiturates and amphetamines, the bill permitted the Secretary of Health, Education and Welfare to bring under the new controls by administrative regulation any other drugs which he found to have the same effects.

HR 2 was similar to, but stronger than, a bill (S 2628) which was passed by the Senate in 1964, but which received no hearings by the House Interstate and Foreign Commerce Committee. *(Congress and the Nation, Vol. I, p. 1194)*

In addition to imposing sharper controls on barbiturates and amphetamines, HR 2 also strengthened federal prohibitions against the counterfeiting of trademarked, brand-name or any other drugs.

President Johnson Jan. 7, 1965, in a special health message to Congress, called for legislation to bring barbiturates, amphetamines and other "psycho-toxic" drugs under more effective controls. Mr. Johnson repeated these requests in his March 8 crime message.

In 1968, Congress further strengthened controls over stimulant, depressant and hallucinogenic drugs. *(See below.)* In 1967, the Senate ratified the 1961 Convention on Narcotic Drugs. The Convention was designed to simplify international narcotic control machinery and to provide additional controls. *(See chapter on Foreign Policy.)*

Provisions

As signed into law, July 15, HR 2, the Drug Abuse Control Amendments of 1965, amended the Food, Drug and Cosmetic Act as follows:

Declared that additional regulation of depressant and stimulant drugs was required regardless of whether the drugs moved in interstate or intrastate commerce.

Defined depressant or stimulant drugs as barbiturates, amphetamines or any substances determined and designated by the Secretary of Health, Education and Welfare to be habit forming or to have potential for abuse because of their stimulant or depressant effect on the central nervous system or their hallucinogenic effect.

Prohibited the manufacture, compounding or processing of any depressant or stimulant drug except by: manufacturers, compounders and processors registered with the Health, Education and Welfare Department and otherwise qualified under local laws who engaged solely in legitimate activities spelled out in the bill; suppliers of these persons; wholesale druggists registered with the Department, pharmacies, hospitals, clinics and public health agencies operating in conformity with local laws regulating the practice of pharmacy and medicine; practitioners licensed to prescribe or administer such drugs; persons using the drugs in research, teaching or chemical analysis and not for sale; employees of these persons or organizations acting in the course of their employment; and government employees acting in the course of their official duties.

Prohibited the selling, delivery or disposal of any depressant or stimulant drug except by those named above or by a common or contract carrier or warehouseman acting in the course of his employment.

Prohibited to all other persons possession of these drugs except for use by the possessor for himself or a member of his household or for administration to an animal owned by him or by a member of his household.

Required those manufacturing, compounding, processing, selling, delivering or otherwise disposing of any such drug (except licensed practitioners—see below) to prepare and keep for three years a record of all stocks of each such drug on hand. Required those manufacturing, compounding or processing such drugs to prepare and keep for three years a record of the kind and quantity of each drug prepared. Required those selling, delivering or otherwise disposing of the drugs to prepare and keep for three years a record of the kind and quantity of each drug received, sold or delivered, the name and address of the person receiving it, and the person's registration number, if any, assigned by the Government.

Directed that every person required to keep these records permit an inspector designated by the HEW Secretary to have access to and copy the records, at reasonable times. Permitted the inspector to inspect, at reasonable times, any facility in which a drug was held, manufactured, compounded, processed, sold, delivered or otherwise disposed of, and to inventory stock and obtain drug samples, giving the owner a receipt describing the sample obtained. Exempted from inspection all financial, sales, pricing, personnel or research data.

Exempted from the record-keeping and inspection requirements licensed practitioners (who by law may prescribe or administer depressant or stimulant drugs in their professional practice). The exemption would not apply if the practitioner regularly dispensed the drugs to patients and charged for them.

Prohibited filling or refilling of prescriptions for depressant or stimulant drugs more than six months after the date of issuance and prohibited refilling of such prescriptions more than five times, unless the practitioner issuing the prescription renewed it in writing or orally if it was promptly reduced to writing and filed by the pharmacist filling it.

Permitted the Secretary to exempt a drug from application of the requirements when he determined they were not necessary for the protection of the public health. Required him to exempt any depressant or stimulant drug which under the Act (1) could be sold over the counter without a prescription or (2) included one or more substances not producing a depressant or stimulant effect on the central nervous system or a hallucinogenic effect if these substances were present in such concentration as to prevent the substances producing such effects from becoming habit forming or from having a potential for abuse because of their effect on the central nervous system or their hallucinogenic effect.

Permitted the Secretary to appoint advisory committees of experts to advise him on such exemptions and on which drugs, not specifically named in the Act, should be classified as depressants, stimulants or hallucinogens and thus made subject to the Act by administrative action.

Required any persons wholesaling, jobbing or distributing any depressant or stimulant drug to register with the HEW Secretary their names, places of business and all establishments where they operate. Under existing law, the premises of any person so registered were subject to inspection by the Food and Drug Administration and must be inspected at least once every two years. Existing law also required persons (with certain exceptions) manufacturing, compounding or otherwise preparing drugs to register with the Secretary. HR 2 required those persons who were manufacturing or preparing depressant or stimulant drugs to indicate this fact on their registrations. (Note: The registration requirement did not apply to retail druggists, doctors, nurses, researchers or teachers.)

Permitted seizure and condemnation of any drug involved in a prohibited act under the bill, any counterfeit drug, or any container or equipment used in their manufacture.

Provided that any persons over 18 years of age who disposed of drugs covered by the bill (by selling, delivering, etc.) to anyone under 21 was subject to imprisonment of not more than two years and/or a fine of up to $5,000 for the first conviction and imprisonment of not more than six years and/or a fine of up to $15,000 for subsequent convictions. (The existing Food, Drug and Cosmetic Act provided more lenient penalties for persons violating other specified parts of the Act.)

Authorized an inspector or investigator designated by the HEW Secretary to examine or investigate depressant or stimulant drugs or counterfeit drugs to carry firearms; serve search and arrest warrants; execute seizure; make arrests without a warrant if the offense was committed in his presence or, in the case of a felony, if he had probable cause to believe the person had committed such an offense; and make seizures even before obtaining a court order or instituting legal seizure proceedings.

Made it a federal crime to forcibly assault, resist or interfere with any HEW employee conducting an investigation or inspection under the Food, Drug and Cosmetic Act.

Strengthened existing controls over counterfeit drugs (which could be deemed misbranded and seized) by no longer requiring the Government to prove that the drugs moved in interstate commerce and by authorizing the seizure and condemnation of equipment used in the manufacture of the drugs. Defined counterfeit drugs as drugs which, or the containers or labeling of which, bore the identifying mark of a drug manufacturer, processor, packer or distributor other than the person or persons who in fact manufactured, processed, packed or distributed it.

Asserted there was no intent to supersede state laws on drugs unless there were a direct conflict with the federal law, and no intent to prevent enforcement of state criminal laws on drugs covered by the bill.

Cigarette Health Warning

The Federal Cigarette Labeling and Advertising Act (S 559—PL 89-92) required that as of Jan. 1, 1966, all cigarette packages and cartons sold in the United States and its possessions bear the following statement: "Caution: Cigarette Smoking May Be Hazardous to Your Health." The bill applied to imported as well as domestically produced cigarettes.

The bill was Congress's response to the conclusion of the Jan. 11, 1964, Surgeon General's report on smoking and health that cigarette smoking was "a health hazard of sufficient importance in the United States to warrant appropriate remedial action."

Although it required a health-hazard warning on cigarette labels, S 559 specifically prohibited until July 1, 1969, any requirement by any government agency, whether federal, state or local, that cigarette advertising

include a similar statement. It also prohibited any government agency from imposing any health labeling requirement other than that contained in S 559.

While the new health-hazard warning on cigarette packages was the first ever required by Congress, spokesmen for some major health and consumer organizations actually considered S 559 a victory for the cigarette industry because the bill superseded far stricter health warning regulations promulgated in 1964 by the Federal Trade Commission. The FTC regulations, which were nullified by S 559, would have required that as of July 1, 1965, both cigarette packages and *cigarette advertising* on radio, television, newspapers and other media carry a health-hazard warning. *(Congress and the Nation, Vol. I, p. 1184)*

The industry had threatened court suits challenging the FTC's authority to issue such regulations, but in the meantime it took its case to Congress. In S 559, the industry was granted exactly what it sought from Congress: a uniform federal labeling requirement which precluded a multiplicity of similar requirements by federal, state or local bodies and was not expected to have a serious effect on sales, and provided protection for four years at least from any advertising requirements, which clearly would have been more harmful to the industry economically.

The industry's success was due in part to the failure of the President to make any personal endorsement of the proposed FTC regulations or any similar strong regulatory proposals, and to the failure of the pertinent Executive agencies to agree on a suitable, uniform formula for action.

But it was also the result of an effective lobbying campaign which deemphasized the possible connection between smoking and illness and, instead, attempted to win the support of individual Congressmen by pointing up the alleged economic and ideological dangers of the proposed FTC advertising regulations. Industry spokesmen stressed the lack of scientific evidence for the conclusion that smoking was a major cause of disease; raised the possibility that the FTC regulations could set a precedent for other regulatory actions by the Government in other fields; and emphasized the potential economic impact of the regulations not only on the entire tobacco industry but on the advertising industry and others heavily dependent on advertising revenues, and on governments at all levels which obtained revenues from tobacco taxes.

The news and broadcasting industries, which received nearly $260 million in advertising revenues from tobacco companies in 1964, supported the tobacco industry's position in opposition to the FTC advertising regulations. Their argument was that free speech would be violated. But some observers charged their real fear was loss of advertising revenues.

Also bolstering the industry's cause was its voluntary imposition of a ban on certain types of cigarette advertising that might encourage young people to smoke or contain health claims not supported by valid scientific data. The code took effect on Jan. 1, 1965.

In passing S 559, the House and Senate were essentially in agreement on the provisions of the bill. The major difference between the two versions was that the House permanently prohibited any requirement for a health-hazard warning in cigarette advertising, while the Senate banned it for only three years. The final version compromised on a four-year ban.

President Johnson signed the bill into law July 27. He made no statement. White House Press Secretary Bill D. Moyers read an announcement saying the bill made "a real contribution to the efforts to bring to the attention of all smokers and potential smokers the scientific and medical data indicating the health hazards in cigarette smoking." Moyers said that after considering both the bill and the reports of his advisers, the President had decided that "the benefits of the bill far outweighed any deficiencies or disadvantages." Moyers did not indicate whether the President looked with favor or disfavor on the nullification of the FTC regulations. Several Members of Congress had asked him to veto the bill as too weak.

The FTC July 28 announced it had canceled its regulations requiring a health-hazard warning in cigarette labeling and advertising. It said, however, that during the four-year moratorium on advertising regulations, it would continue to monitor cigarette advertising and promotion and take any action consistent with the provisions of S 559 to prohibit any advertising which it deemed unfair or deceptive.

The only other action taken by Congress in this field in 1965 was appropriation of funds to establish a National Clearinghouse on Smoking and Health in the Public Health Service. Congress had denied the funds in 1964. In 1965, in the bill providing funds for the PHS (HR 7765—PL 89-156), it voted the full $2 million requested.

Surgeon General Luther L. Terry formally established the Clearinghouse Sept. 29. He said it would continue research currently under way on the behavioral aspects of smoking, and would undertake new functions including collection and distribution of all available materials on the subject, consultation with other federal agencies and private professional organizations, and additional behavioral studies designed to determine methods of helping people resist pressures to smoke.

Provisions. As signed by the President, S 559, the Federal Cigarette Labeling and Advertising Act:

Declared that the policy of Congress was to establish a federal program on smoking and health whereby the public would be "adequately informed" of the possible health hazards of cigarette smoking, and commerce and the national economy would not be impeded by diverse cigarette labeling and advertising regulations.

Required that as of Jan. 1, 1966, all cigarette packages, cartons and containers for sale in the United States bear the following statement: "Caution: Cigarette Smoking May Be Hazardous to Your Health," to be located in a "conspicuous place" on every package and appear in "conspicuous and legible type" in contrast with other printed matter on the package.

Stipulated that no other statements on smoking and health could be required on cigarette packages and that, until July 1, 1969, no statement on smoking and health could be required in the advertising of cigarettes labeled in conformity with the Act's provisions.

Stipulated that except as otherwise provided in the Act, nothing in the Act could be construed to limit, restrict, expand or otherwise affect the authority of the Federal Trade Commission with respect to unfair or deceptive acts or practices in cigarette advertising, nor to affirm or deny the FTC's holding that it had the authority to issue trade regulation rules or to require an affirmative statement in any cigarette advertising.

Required submission to Congress within 18 months after the effective date of the Act and annually thereafter of reports (1) from the Health, Education and Welfare Department on current information on the health consequences of smoking and recommendations for legislation and (2) from the FTC on the effectiveness of cigarette labeling, current practices of cigarette advertising and recommendations for legislation.

Imposed a fine of $10,000 on anyone violating the provisions and provided that the Attorney General would enforce the Act.

Birth Control

Acknowledging growing public concern over population problems, Congress in 1965 for the first time turned its attention to the controversial issue of birth control. A Senate subcommittee held extensive hearings intended to pave the way for an open dialogue on the problems posed by the worldwide population explosion and on the possible responsibility of governments to hold down population expansion. Meanwhile, the Federal Government began to enlarge its activities in the birth control field, and President Johnson became the first American President to indicate that federal support for population control was being contemplated. Finally, the Supreme Court struck down a Connecticut law banning the use of, and distribution of information on, contraceptive devices.

Hearings. Under the leadership of Sen. Ernest Gruening (D Alaska), the Senate Government Operations Subcommittee on Foreign Aid Expenditures held hearings on Gruening's bill (S 1676) to establish Offices for Population Problems in the Departments of State and Health, Education and Welfare. The Offices were to collect and disseminate, upon request, information on family planning programs and population growth. The bill, which did not impose any federal controls on population matters, also called for a White House Conference on Population, to be preceded by state conferences.

Witnesses testified on the consequences of uncontrolled population growth and on the success of various family planning programs. A spokesman of the U.S. hierarchy of the Roman Catholic church condemned all government support for birth control programs.

In a letter to Subcommittee Chairman Gruening, former President Eisenhower urged Congress to authorize the Government to cooperate with private organizations in programs for "slowing down and finally stabilizing the growth in the world's population." Mr. Eisenhower said he had joined former President Truman as co-chairman of the honorary sponsors of Planned Parenthood—World Population "in order to demonstrate my recognition of the urgency of the entire problem and the alarming consequences that are certain to follow its neglect." This was a reversal of position for Mr. Eisenhower, who as President in 1959 had said he could "not imagine anything more emphatically a subject that is not a proper political or governmental activity or function or responsibility."

Federal Action. Before 1965 the Federal Government participated in birth control programs only on an indirect basis. Federal funds and technical assistance, both at home and abroad, went for research and training in demography and reproductive biology rather than for information on birth control and actual provision of contraceptive materials. State and local governments carried out the only public activities. According to officials of the Department of Health, Education and Welfare, federal funds authorized by the public assistance provisions of the Social Security Act of 1935 had been used by health and welfare agencies for birth control programs since the late 1930s, particularly in several Southern states, but there was no explicit or direct authority for a Government role in family planning assistance.

1965 Changes. During 1965 the Government took a more active though still largely indirect role in domestic family planning programs, notably through the federal antipoverty program. Early in the year the Office of Economic Opportunity (OEO) indicated it would provide funds for local birth control projects, if locally approved, and by the end of November 1965 OEO had approved 17 grants for family planning services. Funds were used for information, mobile clinics and medical supplies including contraceptives. OEO policy stipulated that the projects must assist married women only.

At the same time the Interior Department June 19, 1965, became the first federal agency to offer direct birth control advice and services. Aid was provided to certain groups under the Department's jurisdiction: American Indians on reservations, natives of the Pacific Trust Territory, and Indians, Eskimos and Aleuts in Alaska.

Other birth control aid was provided in 1965 through the maternal and child care programs of the Health, Education and Welfare Department. This was effected by grants to state and city hospitals and clinics which carried out local birth control services.

President's Statements. In 1965 Mr. Johnson became the first President to indicate that federal support of population control was under consideration. In his Jan. 4 State of the Union Message he said, "I will seek new ways to use our knowledge to help deal with the explosion in world population and the growing scarcity of world resources." He went further in a June 25 speech marking the 20th anniversary of the United Nations, when he appealed to the UN to "face forthrightly the multiplying problems of our multiplying populations and seek the answers to this most profound challenge to the future of the world. Let us act on the fact that less than $5 invested in population control is worth $100 invested in economic growth."

The President's position was buttressed by former President Dwight D. Eisenhower, who conceded a change of position on birth control in 1965. *(See above.)*

President Kennedy, the first Catholic U.S. President, had said in 1963 that Government-sponsored studies in reproductive biology were "important" and information on the subject should "be made available to the world so that everyone can make their own judgment...."

Supreme Court Ruling. In a 7-2 ruling June 7, the Supreme Court struck down an 1879 Connecticut law which prohibited the use of, and distribution of information on, contraceptive devices. The case arose when Estelle T. Griswold, executive director of the Planned Parenthood League of Connecticut, offered birth control counseling to married couples in a deliberate effort to test the validity of the law. She was convicted and fined $100.

Population Growth

Several 1965 statistical studies predicted explosive population growth rates. The United Nations Population Commission in 1965 predicted that world population could, at the current rate of growth, more than double by the year 2000—rising from 3.3 billion to 7.4 billion. The Commission estimated that in 1964 world population had increased by 2.1 percent, the largest increase in history. In the less-developed countries, the increase was approximately 2.5 percent, a rate which, if it remained constant, would double the population every 28 years.

The Population Reference Bureau in 1965 estimated that U.S. population, currently at 194.5 million and growing at a 1.5-percent rate annually, would reach 245 million by 1980 and 338 million by the year 2000. A May 1965 report by the National Academy of Sciences on "The Growth of U.S. Population" contrasted the U.S. family in the 1930s and the 1950s. "By the 1930s, the spread of family limitation in the American population had reached the point where, on the average, women were bearing only a little more than two children," the report said. By the 1950s, the average family size had increased by 50 percent, to more than three children per family. The report assigned two reasons for this increase: a preference, among couples who plan their families, for moderate-size instead of small families; and "the lack of effective limitation of family size among the underprivileged, relatively impoverished and less-educated Americans" of all races.

In *Griswold v. Connecticut*, the Court held the state law to be unconstitutional and in violation of the right to privacy of married couples. Speaking for the majority, Justice William O. Douglas said the 1st Amendment had a "penumbra where privacy is protected from governmental intrusion."

Hospital Closings

Congress in 1965 forced the Johnson Administration to reduce the scope of proposed shutdowns of Public Health Service hospitals and of Veterans Administration hospitals and related veterans' facilities.

The Administration claimed that the planned closings were not intended to reduce the level of services provided by the Government, but simply to consolidate services and thus bring about savings of money. But Congressional protests eventually led the Administration to compromise. Where it had originally proposed closing 11 VA hospitals, 4 domiciliary homes (old soldiers' homes) and 16 VA regional benefit offices, the Administration finally agreed to close only 6 of the 11 hospitals, only 2 of the 4 domiciliaries and only 9 of the 16 regional benefit offices. Where it had originally proposed to close 7 (out of a total of 12) PHS general hospitals, the Administration finally agreed to close only 2 of the 7 immediately, leaving 2 for restudy and the other 3 open.

Despite the closings, both the VA and PHS retained substantial hospital capacity. On June 30, 1965, before any of the VA installations were closed, there were 168

VA hospitals with 118,896 beds available for use. Six months later, on Dec. 31, 1965, after the closings had been made and other changes had taken place, there were 165 VA hospitals with 116,857 beds available for use. Over the same six-month period, as a result of the closings, the number of VA domiciliaries dropped from 18 to 16, and the number of VA regional benefit offices from 66 to 57. The total of PHS general hospitals dropped from 2 to 10 as a result of the closings.

The Jan. 12 VA announcement of the proposed hospital closings was followed by a series of Congressional actions designed to block the move. Hearings were held in both the Senate and the House, and major veterans' organizations testified in opposition to the proposal. The dispute led also to a brief delay in the Senate confirmation of William J. Driver as VA Administrator. *(See chapter on Veterans.)* The Senate inserted in a supplemental appropriations bill (H J Res 234—PL 89-2) an amendment which prohibited the VA from going ahead with the closings. After consultation with Administration officials, conferees on H J Res 234 accepted a provision to delay the closings only until May 1. This and other legislative efforts to block the closings led President Johnson April 3 to appoint a special advisory committee to restudy the VA closure proposals; the recommendations of that committee resulted in the final compromise.

In a related action later in 1965, Congress in the Veterans' Disability Compensation bill (HR 168—PL 89-311) gave statutory authority to a 125,000 limit—set by President Eisenhower administratively in 1959—on the number of beds in VA hospitals, and specified that the 125,000 hospital beds should be in addition to 4,000 nursing-care beds authorized in 1964. Some supporters of this provision interpreted it as intended to push the Administration into constructing enough new hospital facilities to increase its total beds to 125,000 in the very near future. But the House Veterans' Affairs Committee said the objective was not to force any immediate increase in the number of beds to 125,000, but rather to make clear by statute that the 4,000 nursing-care beds authorized in 1964 were not intended to be included in the 125,000 hospital bed limitation, and that the latter applied to hospital beds only, not nursing-care beds—in case the matter should arise in the future. The Committee said the Budget Bureau had contended that the 125,000 limit included both hospital and nursing beds. The HR 168 provision made clear that this was not so. *(See chapter on Veterans.)*

The Senate June 4 had adopted a resolution (S Con Res 13) expressing the sense of Congress that the 125,000-bed ceiling should be raised to 130,000. The House took no action on the measure.

Auto Pollution,

Waste Disposal

Congress in 1965 enacted a bill (S 306—PL 89-272) to control air pollution caused by automotive exhausts and to authorize a national research program for disposal of solid wastes. The bill provided also for procedures (culminating in legal action) to be taken against international air pollution originating in the United States.

The measure essentially was two separate bills—the air pollution section which became a new title in the Clean Air Act of 1963 and the solid waste section.

The car exhaust provisions at first were opposed by the Administration, which preferred to have the latitude to reach agreements with the automobile industry on control of exhausts and objected to the time schedule in the original version of the legislation. The Administration subsequently altered its position and supported the entire bill. The final version of the bill contained no deadline for implementation of the standards. Mr. Johnson had called for solid waste legislation Feb. 8 in his message on natural beauty.

The new law authorized the Secretary of Health, Education and Welfare to set standards limiting the amount of carbon monoxide, hydrocarbons or other air pollutants that could be contained in the exhaust from gasoline or diesel-powered cars, trucks and buses. The standards were to apply only to new vehicles. (Manufacturers were expected to install "blowby" devices or make engine modifications in order to meet the standards.) The Secretary March 29, 1966, set standards for most gasoline vehicles *(see below)*, but—as intended by the bill's sponsors—delayed setting diesel standards pending further knowledge of diesels.

The solid waste section represented the first major legislation in this particular area. It authorized an expenditure of $92.5 million during fiscal 1966-69 for research into developing better methods of disposing of solid wastes—discarded matters such as garbage, rubbish, ashes, demolition debris, abandoned automobile hulks, old refrigerators and the wastes from slaughterhouses, canneries, and manufacturing plants.

The international pollution provision added a new dimension to federal pollution abatement. It permitted use of existing procedures (previously limited to interstate and intrastate pollution) for abatement of international pollution originating in the United States. An HEW spokesman said the legislation had been sought by Canada to enable the United States to take action to curb pollution affecting that country. The main pollution problem was in Windsor, Ont., which is directly across the Detroit River from Detroit.

Background. In 1963, Congress passed the Clean Air Act (PL 88-206) providing for an expanded and strengthened program. It provided a series of steps, culminating in legal action, which a state, municipality or the Federal Government could take to bring an end to air pollution; but in the case of intrastate pollution, the Federal Government could act only at the request of a state's governor. The legislation authorized $95 million for matching grants to state, local and interstate agencies through 1967. The grants were for establishing and improving programs of air pollution prevention and control. *(Congress and the Nation, Vol. I, p. 1136-1150.)*

Congress in 1967 strengthened federal powers to combat air pollution. In 1968, it extended the waste disposal law. *(See below.)*

Provisions

As signed into law, Oct. 20, PL 89-272 contained the following major provisions:

Motor Vehicle Air Pollution Control Act. (This was designated as Title II of the Clean Air Act of 1963.) Directed the Secretary of Health, Education and Welfare to establish as soon as practicable standards applicable to emission of substances from new motor vehicles or new motor vehicle engines which caused or contributed to, or were likely to cause or contribute to, air pollution endangering the health or welfare of humans. Required the Secretary to take into consideration technological feasibility and economic cost in establishing standards.

Prohibited the domestic sale, manufacture for domestic sale, or importation of any vehicle or vehicle engine not in conformity with the regulations. Provided fines of up to $1,000 for each new motor vehicle or new motor vehicle engine which was manufactured or sold in violation of the regulations.

Provided that sample vehicles or engines could be submitted to the HEW Secretary, who would conduct tests and, if the sample passed the tests, issue a certificate of compliance to cover all vehicles or engines of the same production model.

In cases of air pollution affecting a foreign country, directed the Secretary to call a conference of state and local air pollution agencies in the area where the pollution originated and to invite the affected foreign country to participate in the conference; authorized a legal suit to be brought to abate air pollution affecting another country.

Authorized accelerated federal research to reduce sulfur oxide emissions from fuel combustion sources (such as heating plants in buildings and electric generating plants), and to extract sulfur from fuels.

Authorized appropriations of $470,000 in fiscal 1966, $845,000 in fiscal 1967, $1,195,000 for fiscal 1968 and $1,470,000 in fiscal 1969 to carry out the Motor Vehicle Air Pollution Control Act.

Solid Waste Disposal Act. Specified that the purpose of the new Act was to begin a national research and development program for new and improved methods of solid waste disposal and to provide technical and financial aid to state and local governments in developing, establishing and conducting solid waste disposal programs.

Split responsibility for the solid waste disposal program between the Departments of HEW and the Interior with Interior having responsibility over problems of solid waste resulting from the extraction, processing, or utilization of minerals or fossil fuels, and the HEW Secretary having jurisdiction over all other aspects of the program.

Defined "solid waste" as garbage, refuse and other discarded solid materials, including solid-waste materials resulting from industrial, commercial and agricultural operations and from community activities; specified that it did not include solids or dissolved material in domestic sewage or other significant pollutants in water resources.

Authorized grants to (or contracts with) public and private agencies and institutions and individuals for research, training projects, surveys and demonstrations, including construction of facilities (but limited grants for construction to no more than two-thirds of the project's cost).

Authorized grants to state and interstate agencies for up to 50 percent of the cost of making surveys of solid-waste disposal practices and problems within the jurisdictional areas of such states or agencies and of developing solid-waste disposal plans.

Authorized appropriations of $7 million in fiscal 1966, $14 million in fiscal 1967, $19.2 million in fiscal 1968, and $20 million in fiscal 1969 to the Secretary of HEW to implement the Act.

Authorized appropriations of $3 million in fiscal 1966, $6 million in fiscal 1967, $10.8 million in fiscal 1968, and $12.5 million in fiscal 1969 to the Secretary of the Interior to implement the Act.

Required that all information, uses, processes, patents and other developments resulting from activities financed by a grant under the Act be readily available on fair and equitable terms to industries involved in solid-waste disposal or waste-disposal equipment manufacturing.

Other Pollution Action

FEDERAL SITES. The Senate March 25 passed a bill (S 560) authorizing the Secretary of Health, Education and Welfare to set air and water pollution control standards for all federal installations. The House did not act.

A heated controversy surrounded the 1965 efforts to establish the federal-installation standards by administrative action. The Bureau of the Budget in July 1964 issued a directive requiring that design and construction estimates for new federal buildings include air and water pollution control systems. The directive could not be put into effect, however, until standards were approved. Toward this end, the Public Health Service in December 1964 drafted air pollution control standards and submitted them to the Budget Bureau for approval. The proposed standards, regarded by the coal and oil industries as unnecessarily stiff, drew considerable criticism and the Budget Bureau took no action on them during 1965. (However, President Johnson Nov. 17 issued an Executive Order establishing water standards at federal sites.)

STANDARDS FOR GOVERNMENT CARS. The General Services Administration, the Federal Government's main purchasing agent, Jan. 26, 1965, published an order specifying that, beginning with the 1967 model year, motor vehicles purchased by it would have to have exhaust pollution control equipment and 16 safety features listed in the order. The only other large Government purchase of automobiles was the military—not covered by the order. Legislation enacted in 1964 (PL 88-515) authorized the standards for vehicles purchased by the Federal Government. *(Congress and the Nation, Vol. I, p. 1149.)*

The GSA requirement on exhaust emissions was based on standards set in 1964 by California. The final version of the GSA standards was published June 30.

AUTO SAFETY, POLLUTION TAX. An unsuccessful attempt was made in the Senate in June to force automobile control devices in all cars beginning with the 1968 model year. The attempt was made by Sen. Abraham A. Ribicoff (D Conn.) during consideration of a bill (HR 8371) to reduce or eliminate $4.7 billion in federal excise taxes, including those on the purchase of automobiles. The Administration had proposed eliminating the 10 percent automobile tax. The Senate adopted a Ribicoff amendment to make elimination of 4 percent of the existing tax conditional upon the installation by manufacturers of the same safety and pollution-control devices as those required by the General Services Administration in January on automobiles purchased by the Federal Government. Ribicoff's amendment was dropped from the final bill by Senate-House conferees.

POLLUTION TAX PROPOSED. The President's Science Advisory Committee Nov. 5 recommended that the Federal Government consider instituting a tax on those who pollute the country's air, water and land. The Committee suggested a system of "effluent charges" to tax polluters and a tax on junked automobiles to cut down on the number of auto junkyards.

WATER POLLUTION. Legislation was enacted in 1965 to strengthen controls over water pollution. The bill (S 4—PL 89-234) provided for the establishment—by states or by the Federal Government if the states failed to act—of water quality standards for interstate streams. Once standards were established, authorities could move through various proceedings including court action to prevent individuals or industries from discharging matter into a stream that would lower the water quality below the established purity level. The bill, which was requested by President Johnson, also increased federal financial aid for construction of community sewage projects and created a new federal water pollution control agency. *(See chapter on Water and Power for details.)*

Mine Safety

COAL MINE SAFETY. For the fourth time in the 1960s, Congress failed to enact legislation to extend to small coal mines the mandatory federal inspection requirements of the 1952 Federal Coal Mine Safety Act. The 1952 Act exempted mines that regularly employed 14 or fewer persons underground. *(Congress and the Nation, Vol. I, p. 995.)*

The 1965 bill (HR 3584), a major legislative goal of the United Mine Workers of America (Ind.), was passed by the House June 1, on a 336-42 roll call. The bill finally became law in 1966. *(See below.)*

The Senate had passed a small coal mine bill in 1960. Similar House bills were blocked in 1961 and 1963 by the House Rules Committee.

METALLIC MINE SAFETY. The House Sept. 2 passed an Administration-backed bill (HR 8989) extending federal health and safety regulations to include mining and milling operations in the metal and non-metallic mineral industries. The bill became law in 1966. *(See below.)*

HR 8989 excepted from its coverage coal and lignite mining (most of which was already covered under the Federal Coal Mine Safety Act, *above*) and petroleum and other materials extracted in liquid form unless extraction required employment of workers underground. Enforcement was left to the Secretary of the Interior, but he could delegate enforcement powers to any state which submitted an acceptable mine safety plan.

The bill was a major legislative goal of the International Union of Mine, Mill & Smelter Workers (Ind.). The union was unsuccessful in seeking inclusion of smelters and refineries in the bill.

1966

Partnership for Health

Congress in 1966 enacted an Administration bill (S 3008—PL 89-749) providing new authority to plan for public health services on the state level and revising the federal grant programs for public health services of the states to permit greater flexibility in tackling health programs. Described by the Administration as Partnership for Health, S 3008 was officially the Comprehensive Health Planning and Public Health Services Amendments of 1966. President Johnson requested the legislation in a March 1 message on health and education.

S 3008 authorized comprehensive planning and coordination of public health services on a state- and area-wide basis. The planning was designed to identify imminent and pressing public health problems and establish priorities for health services. The bill carried $9 million in new authorizations for planning in fiscal 1967 and retained a $5-million authorization under Section 318 of the Public Health Service Act. It authorized $15 million for fiscal 1968. Congress in 1967 extended and expanded the program. *(See below.)*

In the interest of flexibility in dealing with health problems, the bill consolidated the various formula and project grants currently made to combat specific diseases and substituted a new system of broad grants for comprehensive public health services, effective in fiscal 1968. Formula grants are allotted to states on the basis of a formula which takes into consideration population, extent of need, and state per capita income; project grants are specific grants to an applicant (a state or local health agency or nonprofit private organization) which requests a federal grant for a specific project or program. Existing law authorized formula grants in the fields of cancer, chronic illness, dental disease, general health services, heart disease, home health services, mental illness, radiological health and tuberculosis. Project grants were made in the areas of cancer, chronic illness, mental retardation, neurological diseases, tuberculosis and venereal diseases. Grants made for a specific purpose could not be used to combat any other health problem, no matter how great the need. For fiscal 1967, however, the project and formula grants to combat specific diseases were left in effect.

S 3008 authorized $125 million, divided equally, for formula and project grants under the revised program in fiscal 1968.

Although the final version of S 3008 failed to meet the Administration request for a six-year bill, it did provide immediately for new, broader planning and coordination of health programs and, beginning in fiscal 1968, for flexibility in the grant-in-aid program, as requested by the Administration. In addition, the House and Senate Committee chairmen both said they would consider additional funding early in the 90th Congress.

Background. The forerunner of S 3008 was the Public Health Service Act of 1944 (PL 78-410) and its subsequent amendments. Section 314 of that Act and subsequent authorizations provided annual formula grants to the states for general public health services and the control of specific diseases. It also authorized the

Surgeon General to train personnel for state and local health work and authorized $5 million in fiscal 1967 for assisting nonprofit schools of public health for professional training, specialized consultative services and technical assistance in public health and administration of state or local health programs.

Section 316 and subsequent amendments authorized annual project grants to state, other public and nonprofit health organizations for developing new methods of providing out-of-hospital health services, and Section 318 authorized $5 million in fiscal 1967 for public health services planning. *(Congress and the Nation, Vol. I, p. 1129-1149.)*

Provisions. As signed by the President, Nov. 3, S 3008 contained the following major provisions:

General Provisions. Specified that federal funds be directed to support the marshaling of national, state and local health resources to assure comprehensive, high-quality health services for every person, but without interference with existing patterns of private practice of medicine and dentistry.

Planning. Authorized $2.5 million in fiscal 1967 and $5 million in fiscal 1968 for formula grants to the states for planning comprehensive health services. Federal funds could cover all costs of the planning, if the U.S. Surgeon General approved.

Required each state to set up one agency to administer the planning programs and to encourage cooperation among public and private health organizations in the planning.

Authorized $5 million in fiscal 1967 and $7.5 million in fiscal 1968 for grants to cover up to 75 percent of the costs of projects to develop regional or local plans for coordination of health services.

Authorized $1.5 million in fiscal 1967 and $2.5 million in fiscal 1968 for grants to public or nonprofit agencies for training or demonstration projects to develop improved comprehensive health planning.

Comprehensive Health Services. Authorized $62.5 million in fiscal 1968 for grants to state health authorities to help them establish and maintain adequate public health services under plans approved by the Surgeon General.

Repealed Section 314 of the Public Health Service Act, which authorized formula grants to the states for general public health services and control of specific diseases, effective July 1, 1967.

Directed that state plans promote local health services and use federal funds to augment existing services.

Stipulated that at least 15 percent of a state's allotment was to go to the state's mental health authority.

Provided that the federal share range from one-third to two-thirds of total costs for the services, depending on relative state per capita income.

Health Services Development. Authorized $62.5 million in fiscal 1968 for grants to public and nonprofit agencies to cover part of the cost of (1) providing services to meet health needs of limited geographic scope, (2) stimulating new health services and (3) undertaking studies or training to improve methods of providing health services.

Repealed Section 316 of the Public Health Service Act, which authorized project grants for developing new methods of providing out-of-hospital health services, effective July 1, 1967.

Personnel Interchanges. Authorized exchanges of personnel between the states and the Department of Health, Education and Welfare to improve federal-state cooperation.

Authorized the Surgeon General to train personnel for state and local health work.

Public Health Schools. Authorized $5 million in fiscal 1968 for grants to nonprofit schools of public health for professional training, specialized consultative services and technical assistance in public health and administration of state or local public health programs. (Under Section 314 of the Public Health Service Act, which was to remain in effect through fiscal 1967, $5 million was authorized for this purpose annually.)

Health Training Aid

Congress in 1966 authorized a three-year program of grants to improve training of allied health professions personnel. The legislation, which was requested by President Johnson, was designed to meet an urgent need for technical personnel to assist doctors, dentists and other health professionals. The bill (HR 13196—PL 89-751) also authorized limited grants for nursing students and revised the existing loan program for health professionals.

There was little controversy over the aid program for allied health personnel. The bill authorized federal grants for construction and rehabilitation of allied health training centers at universities, colleges and junior colleges. It also authorized grants to improve allied health curriculums and to provide traineeships (tuition, fees and a stipend) for persons receiving advanced allied health training which would enable them to teach or do supervisory and other specialized work in the field.

The most controversial provisions of the bill were those relating to the loan program for health professionals. Existing laws dating from 1963 (PL 88-129, the Health Professions Educational Assistance Act) and 1965 (PL 89-290 *(see above)* authorized direct federal grants to schools for lending to students of medicine, dentistry, osteopathy, optometry, podiatry, pharmacy and surgical chiropody. Similar loans were authorized for nurses in a 1964 law (PL 88-581). Schools had to provide 10 percent of the loan funds needed by their students; the Federal Government provided the other 90 percent. *(Congress and the Nation, Vol. I, p. 1148-1150.)*

President Johnson in 1966 proposed that the direct federal loans be replaced by a Government-subsidized and guaranteed program of loans from private sources, such as banks. The House adopted the new proposal but also continued the existing program as an alternative. After House passage of HR 13196 and indications that private loans would not be available on a sufficient scale (partly because of a very tight money market at the time) the Administration submitted a revised plan under which federal loans were to be provided to schools for lending, in turn, to students, but also under which the loan notes from the participating schools were to be pooled and participation certificates sold to private investors. The existing program was also continued, but the new program contained incentives designed to encourage schools to use it rather than the existing one. (The primary incentive was elimination of the 10-percent matching requirement.) This revised plan was incorporated into the Senate version of the bill and later agreed to by the House.

The Administration in 1966 proposed similar revisions in the college student loan program, but Congress did not approve the proposals, chiefly because sales of participation certificates had been suspended for the remainder of 1966. *See chapter on Education; for detailed explanation of participation certificates, see chapter on Budget.)*

Total Authorization. HR 13196 authorized $29,350,000 is fiscal 1967, $31,850,000 is fiscal 1968 and $44.1 million in fiscal 1969. In addition, existing law authorized $25 million annually in fiscal 1967-69 for direct federal grants to schools for lending to students of health professions (doctors, dentists, etc.). Existing law also authorized the following amounts for grants for nursing loans: $16.8 million in 1967, $25.3 million in 1968, $30.9 million in 1969 and such sums as were necessary in fiscal 1970-72.

Provisions

As signed by the President, Nov. 3, HR 13196 contained the following major provisions:

Aid For Allied Health Professions

Allied Health Professions. Established a three-year program of grants to help improve the training of allied health professions personnel at junior colleges, colleges and universities through June 30, 1969.

Construction Grants. Authorized appropriations of $3 million in fiscal 1967, $9 million in 1968 and $13.5 million in 1969 for grants to construct, rehabilitate or replace training centers for allied health professions.

Stipulated that funds appropriated in one fiscal year were to remain available for grants until the end of the next fiscal year.

Required that training centers assisted with federal funds be used for at least 10 years for training in the allied health professions and not be used for sectarian instruction or as a place for religious worship. Provided for recapture of grants when the use of facilities violated these requirements.

Required centers that received grants to maintain an enrollment in the 10 years after construction at least 5 percent higher than the highest enrollment in any of the five years preceding construction. Provided that the increase was to be in addition to the enrollment increase required for recipients of basic improvement grants where applicable. *(See below.)*

Stipulated that, in awarding grants, consideration be given to an equitable geographical distribution of opportunities for training for allied health professions.

Limited federal grants to two-thirds of the construction costs of a new training center or new training facilities for major expansion of a center, and to one-half of the cost of replacement or rehabilitation of existing facilities.

Improvement Grants. Authorized appropriation of $9 million in fiscal 1967, $13 million in 1968 and $17 million in 1969 for grants to centers to develop new or improved curriculums for the training of allied health professions personnel and to "otherwise improve" educational programs.

Authorized basic improvement grants for training centers totaling $5,000 for each allied health professions curriculum plus $500 for each full-time student receiving training at the center.

Stipulated that recipients of basic improvement grants increase their enrollment in each year for which a grant is made by at least 2.5 percent over the highest enrollment during the five years from July 1, 1961, through July 1, 1966, or by three students, whichever is greater. Permitted the requirement to be waived if physical facilities were inadequate to handle the additional students. Provided that the increase was to be in addition to the increase required for construction grants, where applicable. *(See above.)*

Authorized special improvement grants for training centers which improved the special functions which the center served or which provided at least three allied health professions curriculums.

Limited special improvement grants for any one training center to $100,000 each fiscal year.

Traineeships. Authorized appropriations of $1.5 million in fiscal 1967, $2.5 million in fiscal 1968 and $3.5 million in fiscal 1969 to provide traineeships to train allied health professionals (1) to teach others in the field, (2) to become supervisors or administrators or (3) to serve in specialized professions which require advanced training.

New Methods Development. Authorized appropriations of $750,000 in fiscal 1967, $2,250,000 in fiscal 1968 and $3 million in fiscal 1969 to develop, demonstrate or evaluate new curriculums for new types of health technologists.

Other Provisions. Limited assistance to public and nonprofit private allied health professions training centers.

Defined allied health professions training centers as those which provide training for at least 20 persons in allied health professions curriculums and offer associate, bachelor or higher degrees in allied health professions specified by regulations.

Aid for Health Professions

Forgiveness of Federal Loans. Provided that doctors, dentists and optometrists who had obtained federal loans for their education (as permitted under existing law) and who later practiced in a rural area with low family income (as determined by the HEW Secretary) could have the entire loan, and the interest on it, canceled at a rate of 15 percent of the loan for each year he practiced in the rural area. (Existing law, which was not changed, permitted loan forgiveness at 10 percent a year up to one-half the total loan for doctors, dentists, optometrists and osteopaths who practiced in an area in which members of their profession were in short supply.)

Revision of Loan Program. Revised the existing program of loans for students of medicine, dentistry, nursing and other health professions by providing a new method of financing college loan funds (the revisions did not affect the manner in which students themselves obtained loans or the terms applicable to the loans).

Established two new revolving funds, the health professions education fund and the nurse training fund, to provide loans to medical and health schools which were in turn to provide loans to students. Specified that the federal loans would provide the complete amount needed by an institution for its loan fund. (The bill did not change the existing program of federal capital contributions—essentially grants—established under the Health Professions Educational Assistance Act of 1963 and the Nurse Training Act of 1964 in which schools had to provide 10 percent of the funds.)

Provided that each revolving fund would consist of (1) appropriations authorized in existing law for the direct federal loan capital contributions (in fiscal 1967: $25 million for health professions and $16.8 million for nursing; these funds were to be available either for loans to schools under the new program or direct contributions to schools under the existing program); (2) appropriations specifically authorized by HR 13196 for the revolving funds *(see next item)*; (3) repayments of loans and interest on loans and (4) money received from the sale to the public of participations in the assets of the funds.

Specifically authorized appropriations of $10 million in fiscal 1967 for the health professions revolving fund and $2 million in fiscal 1967 for the nurse training revolving fund.

Authorized the sale of participations in the loans made from the revolving funds.

Authorized the Secretary of Health, Education and Welfare to reimburse institutions (or, in other words, to write off or cancel specified amounts of federal loans), as follows:

(1) For 90 percent of the loss from loan defaults; (2) for the difference between the interest paid by the institution on loans from the revolving funds and the interest paid to the institution by student borrowers; (3) for certain administrative expenses and (4) for the amount of principal canceled under loan forgiveness provisions of the law.

Specified that the maximum amount of loans to schools each year from each fund would be specified in appropriations acts, with an over-all ceiling (for each fund) of $35 million minus whatever direct federal capital contributions were made to schools using that method of financing their loan funds.

Nursing Opportunity Grants. Authorized appropriations of $3 million in fiscal 1967, $5 million in fiscal 1968 and $7 million in fiscal 1969 for grants to schools of nursing for scholarships ("educational opportunity grants") to undergraduate students of "exceptional financial need."

Limited the amount of each scholarship to the lesser of $800 or one-half the amount of financial aid provided the student by the college or a state or private scholarship program, including assistance under Title IV of the Higher Education Act of 1965 *(see chapter on Education)*, but excluding aid under work-study programs. Prohibited scholarships of less than $200. Authorized a $200 bonus to scholarship students who in their preceding college year placed in the upper half of their class.

Required that the scholarships be granted to persons of exceptional financial need who without the grant would be unable to pursue a course of study at such school.

Required the Secretary to allot to each state an amount which bears the same ratio to the total amount appropriated as the number of persons in that state enrolled on a full-time basis in schools of nursing bears to the total number of persons enrolled on a full-time basis in all states. Permitted the Secretary, when he determined the sums available to an individual state exceeded the state's need, to reallot the excess as he wished.

Authorized appropriations of not to exceed $100,000 annually for contracts with state and local educational agencies and other public or nonprofit organizations and institutions to devise programs to encourage young people to enter nursing.

Hospital Modernization

Congress in 1966 failed to approve an Administration request for a new 10-year, $4.8-billion program of federal grants, loans and loan guarantees for the modernization of hospitals. The Administration program provided also for planning grant assistance and development grants for public and nonprofit private groups for research on improvements in hospital service. A Senate subcommittee held hearings on the Administration proposal; there was no House action.

The Administration bill proposed that the Federal Government guarantee commercial loans to private hospitals for up to 90 percent of the cost of a modernization project, or make direct loans if the hospitals could not obtain private financing on reasonable terms; that direct federal loans be made to public hospitals for 90 percent of the cost of a modernization project; and that in both cases the Government pay the amortization costs of the first 40 percent of the loan—in effect, this would be a federal grant covering 40 percent of the cost of a project.

The allocation formula provided in the Administration program would have permitted commitment of a higher proportion of the funds to city hospitals in the North than had been possible under the Hospital Survey and Construction (Hill-Burton) Act, which placed greater emphasis on aid to low-income states.

The Hill-Burton Act, authorizing federal matching grants for hospital construction, was enacted in 1946 and extended and expanded periodically thereafter. In the 1964 extension, Congress for the first time authorized grants for hospital modernization as well as construction. *(Congress and the Nation, Vol. I, p. 1130, 1148.)*

Failure of the 1966 Administration hospital modernization program was attributed in part to the opposition of the American Hospital Assn. and the U.S. Conference of Mayors. Both groups said they would have too great difficulty raising funds to meet the terms for federal aid specified in the bill, and both said the federal share of the cost of modernization projects should have been greater. *(For subsequent action on hospital modernization, see 1967 and 1968, below.)*

GROUP PRACTICE FACILITIES. Congress enacted a program to provide Federal Housing Administration loans to finance group medical practice facilities. The program was included in the omnibus demonstration cities and urban development bill (S 3708—PL 89-754). *(See chapter on Housing.)*

Birth Control

The Federal Government in 1966 continued to expand its role in the controversial field of birth control. Spurred by 1965-66 Senate hearings under the leadership of Sen. Ernest Gruening (D Alaska), several executive departments, by administrative actions, liberalized their policies and expanded their small programs. The executive initiatives were supplemented by enactment of several significant pieces of legislation affecting the Government's birth control activities both domestically and abroad.

President Johnson in 1966 moved to open endorsement of federal aid for birth control activities. He requested help through U.S. foreign aid programs for nations trying to control their populations, and in his March 1 domestic health and education message made a strong statement on the need for Government support of domestic programs. "We have a growing concern to foster the integrity of the family," he said, " and the opportunity for each child. It is essential that all families have access to information and services that will allow freedom to choose the number and spacing of their children within the dictates of individual conscience." He said his fiscal 1967 Budget included "a sizable increase" in funds for research, training and services in this field. "The National Institute of Child Health and Human Development will expand its own research and its grant program to study human reproduction. The Children's Bureau and the Office of Economic Opportunity will support family planning in the maternal and infant care programs in local communities when requested. State agencies will be aided by federal welfare funds to provide family planning services to mothers."

Hearings. In January 1966 the Subcommittee on Foreign Aid Expenditures of the Senate Government Operations Committee resumed its hearings on Gruening's bill (S 1676) creating offices of population problems in the State Department and the Department of Health, Education and Welfare (HEW). In April three Administration witnesses, Secretary John W. Gardner of HEW, Administrator David E. Bell of the Agency for International Development (AID) and Under Secretary of State Thomas C. Mann testified in opposition to S 1676. Gardner said getting the job done was more important than titles and "organizational boxes." All witnesses said existing law gave them sufficient authority to carry out population control activities.

Gruening, the Subcommittee chairman, criticized the witnesses for not taking more aggressive action and for not having bigger staffs for population control. He said there were fewer than 20 persons in the Government working full time on population problems. Although he did not plan to report his bill, Gruening continued the hearings for a total of 28 days, reportedly to dramatize the population problem.

Legislation. Several measures enacted by Congress in 1966 contained provisions relating to birth control:

● A bill (S 3008—PL 89-749) providing federal grants to states for comprehensive health service programs, including family planning. Grants for special health problems, including birth control, were also authorized to public and private nonprofit organizations, such as hospitals and voluntary groups. In an Oct. 20 letter to Sen. Joseph D. Tydings (D Md.), who had introduced similar legislation early in the session, Wilbur J. Cohen, Under Secretary of Health, Education and Welfare, said the Department planned to spend $20 million in fiscal 1968, $25 million in fiscal 1969 and $30 million in fiscal 1970 for family planning under S 3008. *(See above.)*

● Two amendments to the Economic opportunity Act (HR 15111—PL 89-794), (1) giving the local community action agency, rather than the federal antipoverty office, the authority to determine whether unmarried women should be eligible for family planning information, and (2) authorizing $61 million for neighborhood health centers, which could include family planning services. *(See chapter on Welfare.)*

● Appropriation in HR 14745—PL 89-787 of $2.5 million more than the President requested for the National Institute of Child Health and Human Development to conduct research on "population dynamics with particular emphasis...on contraceptive devices."

● An amendment to the Food for Peace bill (HR 14929—PL 89-808), permitting use of U.S.-owned foreign currencies for activities "related to the problems of population growth" in countries requesting such aid. The provision was initially a separate bill proposed in the House by Rep. Paul H. Todd Jr. (D Mich.) *(See chapter on Agriculture.)*

● An amendment to the foreign aid authorization bill (HR 15750—PL 89-583) permitting use of excess U.S.-owned foreign currencies for voluntary family planning programs, including dissemination of "information, medical assistance and supplies," in countries requesting such aid. *(See chapter on Foreign Policy.)*

Executive Action. Following is a summary of action by Executive agencies in 1966:

Foreign Aid. AID for several years had helped foreign countries in such areas as demographic research and surveys on population growth related to economic problems. The agency announced in 1965 that it would consider requests for assistance in family planning activities from governments which were undertaking their own programs, if such programs were based on freedom of choice for the persons involved. On June 21, 1966, in a sharp break with the past, the agency announced its first development loan for technical assistance to a birth control program in a developing country. Turkey would receive, it said, a $3.6-million loan to purchase 1,400 jeeps to carry family planning education programs to its villages and audiovisual equipment for mobile birth control teams. No contraceptives were provided.

The U.S. foreign aid program would spend about $10 million in fiscal 1967 for family planning activities, AID Administrator David E. Bell told the Subcommittee on Foreign Aid Expenditures. He said the amount was $5.5 million in fiscal 1966 and $2 million in 1965. This included funds for research and training of public health personnel.

Domestic Programs. HEW Secretary John W. Gardner Jan. 24, 1966, sent a memorandum to the heads of Department agencies saying the Department would dispense birth control information and devices to anyone requesting such aid, whether married or unmarried. The memorandum, which was made public March 31, set policy guidelines similar to those set forth by the President March 1. *(See above.)*

The memorandum stated also that Dr. Philip R. Lee, Assistant Secretary for Health and Scientific Affairs, would be in charge of birth control programs. On May 5 a new post, Deputy Assistant Secretary for Science and Population, was established under Lee.

Dr. Lee emphasized that the memorandum did not set new policy but clarified and stated for the first time existing policy. He said he did not know whether any unmarried women received assistance under the Department's programs, because the decision was left to local agencies and individual doctors.

HEW officials said an estimated $3 million in maternal and child health and maternity and infant care funds was spent in fiscal 1966 for family planning programs in 32 states, in contrast to 13 states in 1964. An estimated $5 million would be spent in fiscal 1967, they said. In addition, Gardner told the Senate Foreign Aid Expenditures Subcommittee, $6.5 million was being spent in fiscal 1966 for applied research in population studies. About $2 million would be spent in fiscal 1966 for research directly related to fertility regulation, about double the amount in fiscal 1965, he said. He said $1.7 million was being spent for personnel training in fiscal 1966. Gardner said 165 professional and technical staff members were working on population matters in the Department.

The Office of Economic Opportunity also liberalized slightly its policy on aid to unmarried women. It announced Jan. 14 that they would be eligible to receive information on birth control methods, but not contraceptive devices themselves. There was no restriction on the use of non-federal funds for antipoverty programs.

State and Local Programs. State and local governments, through their health departments and hospitals, entered the birth control field long before the Federal Government did. In the 1940s they began to set up public birth control services. Their efforts were aimed primarily at promoting family planning among welfare recipients and low-income families.

By the end of 1963, there were 21 states, mostly in the South, offering some publicly financed birth control help to low-income families. In 1964, the number rose to 35.

Gruening July 31, 1966, released a printed record of the 1965 hearings by his Subcommittee on the population crisis. An appendix contained the results of a state-by-state survey of birth control activities, which showed that:

• Twenty-one states had state-operated family-planning programs: Alabama, Arkansas, California, Colorado, Delaware, Florida, Georgia, Illinois, Iowa, Kansas, Kentucky, Maryland, Michigan, Mississippi, Nevada, North Carolina, Oregon, South Carolina, Tennessee, Virginia and Washington.

• Nine states had some local governmental or private programs but no state programs: Idaho, Minnesota, Missouri, Montana, Nebraska, North Dakota, Ohio (private programs only), Utah and Wyoming.

• Seven states were studying a program or anticipated one in the near future: Alaska, Arizona, Hawaii, Maine, Pennsylvania, Texas and West Virginia. (Arizona and West Virginia had one local program each.)

• Four states only referred patients to private physicians: New Mexico, New York, Vermont and Wisconsin.

• Nine states had no state or local programs and no state study under way: Connecticut, Indiana, Louisiana, Massachusetts, New Hampshire, New Jersey, Oklahoma, Rhode Island and South Dakota.

• The District of Columbia, Puerto Rico, American Samoa and the Virgin Islands each had centralized programs.

Catholic Position. The Roman Catholic church still remained the strongest opponent of Government birth control activities in 1966. Although some interpreters of the Ecumenical Council's documents saw hope for a modified position, and a February 1966 Gallup Poll showed that 56 percent of Catholics polled favored a change in the church's position, no relaxation was apparent.

Pope Paul VI Feb. 13, 1966, reaffirmed the church's stand that the rhythm method was the only acceptable form of family planning for Catholics. On March 3, the Pope named Alfredo Cardinal Ottaviani, a conservative, to head a reorganized papal commission studying the church's stand on birth control. The commission's report was made public in 1967. *(See below.)*

In the United States the Catholic clergy continued to speak out strongly against Government involvement in birth control. At the annual gathering of the American hierarchy in November, more than 200 prelates issued a unanimous statement saying that "Government activities increasingly seek aggressively to persuade and even coerce the underprivileged" to limit the size of their families. The organization, known officially as the National Conference of Catholic Bishops, said, "Health and welfare assistance should not be linked, even indirectly, to conformity with a public agency's views on family limitation or birth control."

Birth Control Lobby. Support for population control continued to come from private organizations such as the Planned Parenthood Federation, the Ford Foundation (which in 1966 gave its first grants for direct birth control aid in the United States), and the Population Crisis Committee formed in 1965 to carry out lobbying activities. William H. Draper Jr., national chairman of the Committee, said in an April 1966 article that the only way to reach the millions of women who want help is through governments. He said, "In this country, the goal for the next year or two should be the addition of birth control facilities to every tax-supported hospital and health clinic throughout the fifty states. This movement has gotten under way recently and is fast becoming a tidal wave."

Narcotic Addict Treatment

Congress in 1966 enacted a major Administration bill (HR 9167—PL 89-793), the Narcotic Addict Rehabilitation Act of 1966. The Act marked a fundamental change in Congressional policy on the disposition of addicted persons charged with narcotic offenses under the criminal laws. It provided for commitment of such persons to medical institutions, instead of prison, for long-term treatment of their affliction. Prior to passage of the Act, federal law generally took a punitive approach to narcotic addiction. *(For details of legislation, see chapter on Crime and Justice.)*

Drug Controls

In a March 21 message on consumer interests, President Johnson requested enactment of a Drug Safety Act that would authorize the Government (1) to require records and reports on the effects of drugs and to require labeling changes on any drugs whether old or new (rather than only on antibiotics and new drugs); (2) to require certification of all drugs whose potency or purity could mean life or death to a patient (thus extending a certification requirement currently applying only to insulin and antibiotics), and (3) to control the unsolicited distribution of drug samples.

Congress took no action on the President's proposals, but a House subcommittee held hearings on drug safety and the Food and Drug Administration (FDA) stepped up its drug safety activities. *(See below.)*

The President also recommended expanding the FDA's training programs for nonfederal officials, with the goal of strengthening and enlarging state and local professional staffs. The House Oct. 17 passed a bill (HR 13884) embodying the President's request, but the Senate took no action.

FDA Activities. FDA operations in 1966 came under the supervision of a new Commissioner, Dr. James L. Goddard, and the agency immediately intensified its work in the regulation of drugs. When Goddard took office Jan. 10, he promised to use all of the agency's wide authority in the drug field to crack down on those drugs of doubtful safety or efficacy, and on those drugs which had not been properly handled in testing. He immediately took actions that brought protests from the pharmaceutical manufacturers and the American Medical Assn. (AMA). The FDA's heightened surveillance also led to hearings by a House Government Operations subcommittee.

Goddard was appointed by President Johnson to succeed George P. Larrick, who resigned as commissioner in December 1965, after heading the agency since 1954.

International Health

The International Health Act of 1966 (HR 12453, S 2873), requested by President Johnson in a Feb. 2 message to Congress, did not reach the floor of either the House or the Senate in 1966. The bill authorized a three-year program to build a core of U.S. medical personnel trained to deal with health problems in other countries. It faced stiff Republican opposition in the House on the ground that it would drain critically needed health personnel from the United States.

HR 12453 was reported to the House, but the Rules Committee denied a rule for floor consideration. Although a resolution was filed to bypass the Rules Committee and bring the bill to the floor under the 21-day-rule procedure, the Democratic leadership did not call up the resolution, reportedly because of the GOP opposition. No action was taken in the Senate.

PHS Reorganization

President Johnson in 1966 submitted to Congress a reorganization plan (Plan No. 3) to give the Secretary of Health, Education and Welfare full authority over the health functions of the Public Health Service and the power to reorganize PHS. Senate and House subcommittees held hearings on the proposal, but Congress did not attempt to block the plan and it became effective June 24. (A further reorganization took place in 1968. *See below.*)

PHS had been part of HEW since 1953, when a reorganization plan recommended by President Eisenhower transferred to the newly established HEW Department all the components of the Federal Security Agency (FSA), which was abolished. Under the 1953 plan, creation of HEW represented an attempt to coordinate and unify control over the health, education and welfare agencies by giving them departmental rank. In effect, the new Department had no administrative unity, but served as a kind of "holding company." PHS had four basic units, set up by the Public Health Service Act of 1943: National Institutes of Health, Bureau of State Services, Bureau of Medical Services and Office of the Surgeon General. Under the 1944 Public Health Service Act, that organization was continued intact. The 1944 Act served to codify all PHS functions and it also vested in the Surgeon General authority to administer the service, subject to the FSA Administrator. *(Congress and the Nation, Vol. I, p. 1120, 1129.)*

President's Message. In his message on the reorganization plan, President Johnson April 25 said: "Today the organization of the Public Health Service is clearly obsolete." He noted that since 1953 more than 50 new programs had been placed in PHS, and that its budget had increased from $250 million to $2.4 billion in the past 12 years. He said the current PHS structure was "adequate" when the agency's functions could be "neatly compartmentalized," but the many new health programs called for an "integrated attack" on disease by combining health services, state and local aid and research.

President Johnson said integrating PHS agencies would not "go far enough," because the HEW Secretary lacked the "essential authority" over PHS needed to secure the highest possible level of health services for the American people.

Provisions of Plan. Reorganization Plan No. 3 made the following changes in the PHS:

• Transferred to the Secretary of HEW the health functions previously vested in the Surgeon General.

• Abolished the four PHS bureaus—Medical Services, State Services, Office of the Surgeon General and the National Institutes of Health (NIH).

• Authorized the Secretary to assign the functions transferred to him to the PHS or other agencies.

HEW Secretary John W. Gardner said he would delegate the functions transferred to him to the Surgeon General and create five new bureaus in the PHS:

1. Bureau of Health Manpower, to coordinate all federal functions of medical education, training and construction.

2. Bureau of Health Services, to coordinate direct federal health services such as PHS hospitals, Indian health programs and medical care for federal prison inmates.

3. Bureau of Disease Prevention and Environmental Control, to pull together federal activities to prevent and control diseases, injuries and health hazards. Among such activities were air pollution control and the Communicable Disease Center in Atlanta, Ga. A separate office was set up to handle Comprehensive Health Planning and Services, as authorized in the Comprehensive Health Planning and Services Act (PL 89-749).

4. National Institutes of Health (NIH), which would remain substantially unchanged except for a new National Environmental Health Sciences Center for research, and removal of the National Institute of Mental Health (NIMH).

5. National Institute of Mental Health (NIMH), to become a new bureau because it had operational as well as research functions.

Gardner Plan. Gardner Oct. 11 announced he had approved reorganization of the PHS into eight component parts, as recommended by Surgeon General William H. Stewart. Under this plan the Office of the Surgeon General was expanded and strengthened to give it more responsibility for directing programs and setting over-all policy for PHS; the National Library of Medicine and National Center for Health Statistics, which were closely related to the Office of the Surgeon General, were continued as independent units; and the Bureaus of State Services and Medical Services, along with NIH, were reorganized into the new divisions Gardner previously had set up.

Air Pollution

Congress in 1966 enacted a bill (S 3112—PL 89-675) expanding the existing program of federal grants for state, local and regional air pollution control activities authorized under the Clean Air Act of 1963.

The final measure embodied most of the changes sought by the Administration. There was no opposition to the bill in either chamber and the Administration did not object to changes made during consideration of the bill.

The measure authorized a new program of grants to state, local and regional (intermunicipal and interstate) air pollution control agencies to help them maintain pollution control programs. Maintenance grants to state and local agencies could provide up to one-half the cost of the programs; those to regional agencies could cover up to three-fifths of the cost.

The maintenance grants program was to supplement existing programs of federal grants for developing, establishing and improving (but not maintaining) air pollution prevention and control programs.

The bill also removed the existing limitation that no more than 20 percent of the total amount appropriated under the Act each year could be used for grants to support state, local and regional air pollution control programs. Other federal air pollution activities—currently receiving 80 percent of funds appropriated under the Act—included federal research, training of air pollution control personnel (including grants to universities), technical assistance to states, administrative action (conferences and in some cases court action) to abate interstate air pollution and the establishment and enforcement of national standards regulating pollution from automobile exhausts.

The bill also altered eligibility standards for federal grants by providing that federal officials could disregard nonrecurrent expenditures of participating pollution control agencies in deciding whether or not an agency could receive federal aid the following year. The existing law required that an agency had to maintain its previous year's level of expenditure in nonfederal funds in order to obtain a federal grant the next year. The new provision was intended to complement the new maintenance grant program; over a period of years, an agency's nonrecurring costs, such as for major facilities, could cause wide fluctuation in its year-to-year spending. A related provision specified that federal grants were not to be used to supplant state or local contributions to air pollution control agencies.

In another provision, the bill combined two separate authorization sections in the existing Clean Air Act and set the total authorization for all activities under the Act at $46 million for fiscal 1967, $66 million for fiscal 1968 and $74 million for fiscal 1969. The separate authorizations in the existing Act totaled $35,845,000 for fiscal 1967, $1,195,000 for fiscal 1968 and $1,470,000 for fiscal 1969 (the latter two amounts for automobile pollution activities only.)

The Clean Air Act was enacted in 1963 (PL 88-206) and was expanded in 1965 (PL 89-272) by the addition of a new title (Title II) dealing with control of air pollution from cars. *(See above.)*

Further air pollution legislation was enacted in 1967. *(See below.)*

Provisions. As signed into law, Oct. 15, S 3112:

Consolidated into one section authorizations to carry out the Clean Air Act (provided in two sections under existing law) and set the authorization for fiscal 1967 at $46 million, for fiscal 1968 at $66 million and for fiscal 1969 at $74 million.

Authorized the Secretary of Health, Education and Welfare to make grants to state, local and regional (intermunicipal or interstate) agencies for maintenance of air pollution control programs, as follows: for state programs, up to one-half of the cost of maintaining the programs and, for regional programs, up to three-fifths of the cost of maintaining the programs.

Removed the limitation that no more than 20 percent of the total amount appropriated annually under the Act could be used for grants to support state, local or regional air pollution control programs.

Provided that in determining an agency's eligibility under the provision of the Act which prohibited grants to agencies spending less in nonfederal funds than in the previous fiscal year, the HEW Secretary was not to consider nonrecurrent expenditures of the agency during the previous year.

Specified that no grant was to be made to an air pollution control agency unless the Secretary of HEW determined that the grant would not supplant state or local funds that normally would be available to the agency, and that it would supplement and if possible increase amounts of available nonfederal funds.

Provided that in the case of a grant to an interstate agency, the HEW Secretary would determine the portion of the grant chargeable to the maximum amount (12-1/2 percent of appropriations) of the total grants that any one state could receive.

RELATED DEVELOPMENTS

Exhaust Standards. The Department of Health, Education and Welfare (HEW) March 29 published final standards limiting discharge of two air pollutants from the exhaust systems of new motor vehicles or motor vehicle engines. The standards applied to most new gasoline-powered motor vehicle engines, beginning with the model year 1968. The standards did not apply to (1) motor vehicles with an engine displacement of less than 50 cubic inches, (2) motorcycles or (3) commercial vehicles with cargo capacity of more than half a ton. HEW and automobile industry spokesmen estimated that devices to control pollution emission would add from $10 to $50 to the price of 1968 models, depending on engine size and the control device adopted by individual manufacturers.

Federal Installations. President Johnson May 26 signed an Executive Order (Exec Order 11282) requiring heads of all federal agencies to develop phased plans for installing equipment to control air pollution at facilities operated by their agencies. The order was similar to one issued in 1965 requiring heads of federal agencies to develop water pollution control plans for federal installations.

Water Pollution. For the second consecutive year, Congress enacted far-reaching legislation to step up the Federal Government's water pollution control activities. *(For details, see chapter on Water and Power.)*

Investment Tax Credit. In action on a bill (HR 17607—PL 89-800) suspending existing tax incentives for business investment, Congress exempted air and water pollution control facilities from the temporary suspension of the 7-percent investment tax credit. The Administration had not requested the exemption. *(See chapter on Tax Policy.)*

Coal Mine Safety

After eight years of controversy, Congress in 1966 enacted a bill (HR 3584—PL 89-376) extending mandatory federal inspection and safety requirements under the 1952 Federal Coal Mine Safety Act to previously exempt small coal mines.

Senate passage of HR 3584 on March 14 cleared the bill for the President's signature and brought to a close the long-standing debate over the exemption of mines employing 14 or fewer workers underground from certain mandatory provisions of the 1952 Act. Those provisions authorized federal inspectors to order large mines to close down in cases of imminent danger or violation of other safety regulations which the mines did not correct.

The repeal of the exemption under HR 3584 represented a victory for large mine interests led by the United Mine Workers (Ind.). The bill was expected to affect about 7,000 small mine operators, most of whom opposed the legislation. HR 3584 also strengthened federal safety controls applying to all coal mines. (HR 3584 was passed by the House in 1965. *(See above.)*

Provisions. As signed into law, March 26, HR 3584:

Extended the mandatory federal inspection and safety requirements of the Federal Coal Mine Safety Act to previously exempt small mines—those regularly employing fewer than 15 persons underground. The authority to close mines where accidents were imminent was to take effect upon enactment of the bill. On safety violations not involving immediate danger, the small mines were given six months to meet federal standards.

In provisions affecting all mines, HR 3584:

Permitted closing of mines when inspectors found an "unwarrantable failure" by operators to comply within 90 days with orders to remedy safety violations that could lead to accidents.

Authorized federal grants of $500,000 annually, to be matched by the states, for coal mine safety education programs.

Strengthened provisions for federal-state cooperation on safety enforcement.

Ordered an Interior Department study of the sufficiency of federal coal mine safety standards and a report to Congress within one year.

Directed the Secretary of the Interior to familiarize all mine operators and workers with the provisions of the bill.

Raised the membership of the Coal Mine Safety Board of Review from three to five members, with representatives of large and small mine operators and workers as members, and, as before, a mining engineer as chairman.

Metallic Mine Safety

Congress in 1966 enacted legislation (HR 8989—PL 89-577) authorizing federal safety standards for metallic and other non-coal mines. The Senate passed the bill June 23, on a 57-18 roll call. House passage came in 1965. *(See above.)*

The new law, called the Federal Metal and Non-Metallic Mines Safety Act, applied to all metal mines and other types of mining operations except (1) coal and lignite mines, which were already covered by the existing Coal Mine Safety Act; (2) natural gas and minerals extracted in liquid form (such as oil), unless the extraction required the use of underground workers, in which case the mining operation would not be exempt.

Though similar in some respects to the Coal Mine Safety Act, the new law differed substantially in that it permitted the states, if they chose, to set and enforce their own mine safety standards in lieu of federal standards and federal enforcement. The Coal Mine Safety Act did not give the states that option. *(For 1966 amendments to Coal Mine Safety Act, see above.)*

The option granted to the states to set and enforce their own mine health and safety standards under HR 8989 was to operate as follows:

• In states which chose not to adopt their own health and safety standards for mines covered by the bill, the Federal Government—acting through the Interior Department's Bureau of Mines—was empowered to (1) inspect all mines (annual inspection was required for all underground mines); (2) establish health and safety standards for the mines; (3) enforce compliance with the standards and shut down mines which failed to comply, even if conditions in the mine did not present an immediate danger to health and safety; (4) shut down mines in which there was an immediate danger to health and safety.

• In states which chose to adopt mine health and safety standards of their own which were accepted by the Interior Department as being substantially as strong as the federal standards, the state was to perform all the four basic functions listed above. However, even where such a state safety plan was in effect, the Bureau of Mines would still be authorized to make its own inspection of all mines (including the required annual inspections of underground mines) and to shut down mines in which it found an immediate danger. But the Bureau could not, in those states, set any health and safety standards or participate in their enforcement in the absence of an immediate danger.

The bill provided that where the Bureau, through its inspections, found that a state was not adequately enforcing the state's own health and safety standards, federal approval of the state safety plan would be withdrawn and the Bureau would then apply and enforce federal standards instead.

In practice, most of the states with mines covered by the bill were expected to exercise the option and set up their own standards and enforcement systems. Federal inspections were expected to be confined mainly to underground mines, leaving inspection of above-ground mining operations pretty much to the states. Some observers said that with its small staff of inspectors, the Bureau of Mines would be hard pressed to fulfill even the requirement for annual inspection of all underground mines.

The President, in signing HR 8989, said it would protect about 250,000 workers.

Compromise Enacted. The final version of HR 8989 was a compromise. The initial House bill, passed in 1965 and preferred to the Senate version by Western mine operators, had provided that where a state established a mine safety plan acceptable to the Interior Department, the Federal Government could make its own inspections but could not establish or enforce safety standards or shut down mines, even if there was an immediate danger.

The Senate version, preferred by mine labor unions and the Interior Department, had authorized basically an all-federal safety system patterned on the Coal Mine Safety Act, without any option for the states to take over standard-setting, enforcement or shutdowns to the exclusion of the Federal Government, although with state participation in federal inspections.

The final version of HR 8989 was similar to the House version in allowing the states to set up their own plans, but gave the Federal Government a stronger role than the House version in several important respects. For example, it permitted federal closure of mines where there was an immediate danger, even in states having state safety plans, and it made final the Interior Department's decision to disapprove, or to withdraw approval from, a state safety plan, dropping a House provision for court review.

The final bill was accepted by the Administration and the unions. The United Mine Workers Journal said that despite the shortcomings of the final version, "it was acceptable to the labor groups who were supporting it as at least getting their foot in the door."

Provisions. As signed into law, Sept. 16, HR 8989:

Health, Safety Standards. Authorized the Secretary of the Interior, with the aid of advisory committees appointed by him, to establish and publish in the Federal Register health and safety standards for metal and non-metallic mines and related facilities (roads, equipment, milling facilities, machinery, structures).

Exempted from the bill (1) coal and lignite and (2) natural gas and minerals extracted in liquid form such as oil or mercury, unless workers were employed underground for extraction.

Permitted any party, such as a mine operator, who would be adversely affected by any mandatory standard established by the Secretary, to appeal it to the federal courts within 20 days of its issuance, but not if the standard was one which had been specifically recommended by an advisory committee.

Permitted the Secretary to decline to assert jurisdiction over any class or category of mines with a good safety record and with little effect on interstate commerce. (This allowed the Secretary to exclude certain types of surface mines, such as the thousands of small gravel pits and sand pits near construction jobs, and thus avoid the impossible task of inspecting them with a small inspection force.)

Inspection. Authorized the Secretary at any time to inspect any mine subject to the Act to determine (1) whether it presented an immediate danger to health and safety, or (2) whether it was complying with health and safety standards, or (3) whether—in cases where state health and safety standards were in effect in place of federal standards *(see State Plans, below)*—the state standards were being properly enforced.

Required the Secretary to inspect all underground mines at least once a year (including those where state health and safety standards were in effect).

Enforcement. Authorized federal inspectors to shut down any mine in which they found an immediate danger to health or safety. (The mine could reopen when the danger was eliminated.)

Authorized federal inspectors to require mine operators to comply with the mandatory federal health and safety standards even if there was no immediate danger, and empowered them to shut down a mine if it refused to comply with the standards within a specified time. (The mine could reopen after it complied.)

Authorized a mine operator dissatisfied with an order issued by federal inspectors under either of the two above enforcement provisions to appeal to the Secretary.

Mine Review Board. Established a five-member Federal Metal and Non-Metallic Mine Safety Board of Review, to be appointed by the President, subject to Senate confirmation, for staggered five-year terms. Two members were to represent the mining industry, two members were to represent mining unions, and the chairman was to represent the public.

Authorized the Board to hear appeals against orders by federal inspectors. A mine operator receiving a shutdown or correction order from a federal inspector could appeal it directly to the Board, bypassing the appeal to the Secretary described above, or could first appeal to the Secretary and then appeal the Secretary's decision to the Board. In either case, the Board could confirm, annul or revise the order being appealed or the Secretary's decision.

Made decisions of the Board appealable to the U.S. Circuit Courts, which could confirm, annul or revise them, and ultimately to the Supreme Court.

Penalties. Authorized the Secretary to enforce the Act by seeking federal court civil injunctions, but provided that where an operator's refusal to shut down a mine or correct a fault created or left in effect an immediate danger of death or serious physical harm, criminal penalties of up to 60 days in jail and/or fines of $100 to $3,000 would be applicable.

Other. Required mines subject to the Act to submit to the Secretary annual reports on accidents, injuries and occupational diseases. Authorized the Secretary to undertake expanded education and training programs in mine health and safety, and required him to make annual reports on the Act to Congress.

Required the Secretary to place major responsibility for carrying out the Act in the Bureau of Mines.

Provided that the enforcement provisions and criminal penalties should go into effect one year after publication in the Federal Register of the mandatory health and safety standards. Other provisions were effective immediately on passage of the Act.

State Plans. Authorized the states, if they chose, to submit health and safety plans to the Secretary covering mines subject to the Act.

Required the Secretary to approve the plans if they provided for (1) mine health and safety standards substantially as effective as the federal standards; (2) annual inspection of all underground mines subject to the Act; (3) adequate enforcement with qualified personnel; (4) reasonable safeguards against loss of life or property arising from mines closed or abandoned; and (5) regular reports to the Secretary.

Provided that once a state plan was approved by the Secretary, the state health and safety standards would be applicable for mines in that state in place of federal standards. The state alone would enforce the standards and could also conduct its own inspections and shutdowns of mines (all in accord with terms of the approved state plan); but provided that the Secretary could also carry out inspections in that state (including the required once-a-year inspection of all underground mines) and could also shut down mines in which there was an immediate danger.

Provided that the Secretary could cancel approval of a state plan if, on the basis of his inspections and the state reports, he determined it was not being enforced properly. (In that case, the Bureau of Mines would move in and could apply and enforce the federal standards.) Made the Secretary's decision on whether to approve or withdraw approval of a state plan final—not subject to court review.

1967

Partnership for Health

The most important Administration health bill enacted by the first session of the 90th Congress was the Partnership for Health Amendments of 1967 (HR 6418—PL 90-174).

The bill authorized $589 million in fiscal 1968-70 for grants to the states for comprehensive health planning and services and included a $40-million authorization intended, but not earmarked, for rat-control projects in fiscal 1968-69.

The final provisions of HR 6418 were almost identical to those of the Senate-passed bill except that the conferees dropped authorization to create the position of Under Secretary of Health in the Health, Education and Welfare (HEW) Department.

Although President Johnson had requested open-ended authorizations through fiscal 1972, the House provided specific authorizations through fiscal 1971. The Senate deleted the fiscal 1971 funds, and the House conferees accepted this action. In reporting HR 6418, the Senate Labor and Public Welfare Committee said fiscal 1971 authorizations had been "postponed" because "the Committee will not have the benefit of the information assembled through comprehensive health planning until 1969 or 1970."

Partnership for Health was a name given by the Administration to the Comprehensive Health Planning and Public Health Services Amendments of 1966 (PL 89-749). The Act authorized grants to the states to be used for whichever health services each state deemed most important and a comparable amount for special projects meeting specialized or regional needs or initiating new services. The Act also provided for statewide and areawide planning and research grants. *(See above.)*

HR 6418 extended these programs at expanded authorization levels. It also initiated a new program of federal licensing of clinical laboratories dealing in interstate commerce and established a program of grants for research and demonstrations to develop more efficient health services and facilities. The bill also included a Senate provision directing the HEW Secretary to conduct a survey of the extent of serious hunger and malnutrition in the United States and to make recommendations to Congress within six months.

HR 6418 authorized an additional $48.5 million for fiscal 1968. Under the 1966 law, $157 million was already authorized for that year.

Rat Control. The House Sept. 20, on a 227-173 roll-call vote, accepted an amendment offered by Reps. Henry S. Reuss (D Wis.) and Charles McC. Mathias Jr. (R Md.) providing an additional $20 million in each of the fiscal years 1968-69 for project grants. Although the funds were not earmarked for rat-control projects, it was clear from the debate that Congress intended them for that purpose. The Reuss-Mathias amendment gave House Members a chance to reverse the action they took July 20 when, amid derisive remarks about passing a "civil rats bill...rat now," they refused formal consideration of the Administration's separate rat-control bill.

Forty-five Republicans changed their votes to provide the margin by which the July position on rat control was reversed Sept. 20. However, as in the previous vote, the program was opposed by the "conservative coalition"—a majority of Republicans and Southern Democrats voting against a majority of Northern Democrats. *(For action on separate rat control bill, see below.)*

Provisions

As signed into law (PL 90-174) Dec. 5, HR 6418 included the following new authorizations, in millions of dollars. (Sums already authorized in the 1966 Act for fiscal 1968, totaling $157 million, are in parentheses.)

	1968		1969	1970	Total New Auth.
Research, demon-strations	$ 8	($12)	$ 40	$ 60	$108
Grants to schools of public health		(5)	6	7	13
Planning grants:					
State planning	2	(5)	10	15	27
Areawide planning		(7.5)	10	15	25
Training, studies, demonstrations		(2.5)	5	7.5	12.5
Health service formula grants	7.5	(62.5)	90	100	197.5
Health service project grants	27.5	(62.5)	95	80	202.5
Experimental facilities	3.5	—	—	—	3.5
TOTAL	$48.5	($157.0)	$256	$284.5	$589

In addition to the new money authorizations above and the extension of existing programs through fiscal 1970, the bill:

Research-Demonstrations. Authorized a new program of grants for research and demonstration projects to develop more efficient physical plants and methods of delivering health services in medical facilities including long-term care facilities.

Specified that the grants could be used for health-manpower research and demonstration projects.

Limited the federal share of each project to 50 percent, except in unusual circumstances.

Laboratories. Authorized the Secretary of HEW to license clinical or other diagnostic laboratories that solicited or received specimens in interstate commerce. (An estimated 1,000 laboratories were involved.)

Required the Secretary to establish standards for maintenance of quality-control programs and for the professional qualifications of the supervisory personnel of the licensed laboratories.

Authorized the Secretary to bring court action against any licensed laboratory that represented an imminent danger to public health.

Exempted from the licensing provisions laboratories accredited by the Joint Commission on the Accreditation of Hospitals, the American Osteopathic Assn., the Commission on Inspection and Accreditation of the College of American Pathologists or any other national accreditation body approved by the Secretary which had standards equal to or more stringent than the federal regulations.

Other Provisions. Required that, beginning in fiscal 1970, the states pay 25 percent of the cost of planning their comprehensive health programs.

Required states, effective in fiscal 1969, to devote at least 70 percent of their grants for comprehensive health services and mental health programs to services in the local communities.

Authorized the HEW Secretary to make agreements with health schools, hospitals and other medical training facilities for the interchange and cooperative use of personnel, facilities, services and information.

Authorized the Secretary to make cooperative planning agreements with medical facilities and community health facilities to solve health problems resulting from disasters.

Authorized a loan of $3.5 million, at 2.5-percent interest, for an experimental intensive-care unit at the Georgetown University Medical Center. (The sum is included in the table above.)

Instructed the HEW Secretary to conduct a six-month survey of the extent and location of serious hunger and malnutrition in the United States.

Rat Control

The House July 20 refused to consider an Administration-backed bill (HR 11000) establishing a $40-million federal grant program to aid localities in controlling and exterminating rats.

Rejection of the bill occurred when the House, by a **176-207** key roll-call vote, rejected a resolution that would have permitted formal House debate and action on HR 11000. A majority of Republicans and Southern Democrats voted against the resolution.

In the discussion of the resolution opponents of HR 11000 attacked the bill with ridicule, terming it the "civil rats bill" and contending that the measure would create a "rat bureaucracy," "rat patronage" and a "high commissioner of rats."

The House action drew sharp criticism from President Johnson, who termed the program one of the most important of the Administration's new proposals to improve substandard living conditions in the nation's urban areas. The President said he hoped the House would reverse its action and "vote to defend the children who are now menaced by rats."

The Leadership Conference on Civil Rights, a coalition of 112 civil rights, labor, religious and civic organizations, called the House action "an act of shocking irresponsibility" which could only add to the "sense of hopelessness" of the "millions of poor in our large cities."

House refusal to act on the rat control bill came one week after serious ghetto rioting in Newark, N.J., and one day after the chamber had voted overwhelming approval of a bill to prohibit use of interstate facilities with the intent to incite a riot. Supporters of the rat bill contended it was inconsistent to attempt riot control by use of federal powers while rejecting measures which would attack the conditions which they said had led to the rioting.

The House Sept. 20 reversed its position on rat control when, on a 227-173 roll call, it added a rat-control amendment to the Administration's Partnership for Health bill (HR 6418). The amendment, which was enacted, authorized $40 million that was intended—though not earmarked—for rat-control projects in fiscal 1968 and 1969. *(See above.)*

Republicans provided the margin by which the July position on rat control was reversed Sept. 20, although the program again was opposed by the "conservative coalition"—a majority of Republicans and Southern Democrats voting against a majority of Northern Democrats. In all, 51 Representatives (45 of them Republicans) switched from opposition in July to support of rat-control funds in September. While four Southern Democrats switched to support, eight others switched to opposition. A comparison of the party breakdowns on the two votes:

July—Defeated 176-207: R 22-148; SD 27-52; ND 127-7.

Sept.—Adopted 227-173: R 68-110; SD 25-60; ND 134-3.

Widespread public outrage over the frivolous House approach to HR 11000 was credited with helping to pave the way for enactment of the massive 1968 housing bill. *(See chapter on housing.)*

Health-Care Report

A special advisory commission reported to President Johnson in 1967 that sweeping changes in the nation's health-care system—including reforms in existing practices of physicians, hospitals, medical schools and insurance companies—were needed to extricate the country from the current "health crisis."

The National Advisory Commission on Health Manpower, appointed by the President in May 1966, found that while the cost of medical care was skyrocketing the quality of the care was not increasing proportionately.

Taken as a whole, the report was a severe indictment of existing medical practices. The current "crisis" was brought about, the Commission said, by a lack of leadership and an unwillingness to change within the health establishment.

President Johnson said the report was to be "required reading by all of the Cabinet members."

The report warned that an individual's average yearly medical expenses could be expected to rise by 140 percent by 1975. If the spiral in medical costs was not checked by then, hospital costs would rise 250 percent; physicians's services by 160 percent; dental care by 100 percent; and drug prices by 65 percent.

Although it was necessary to have more doctors and other health professionals, the report stated, "the crisis is not simply one of numbers. Unless we improve the system through which health care is provided, care will continue to become less satisfactory, even though there are massive increases in cost and in numbers of health personnel."

Among the more than 50 recommendations to combat the "crisis" were the following:

• Such massive Government programs as Medicare and Medicaid should institute a new system for paying hospitals that would reward them for efficiency and quality care and penalize them for inefficiency.

• Doctors and dentists should undergo periodic relicensing and refresher courses to maintain their skills.

• Communities should establish a system of "peer reviews" in which local medical groups would evaluate the activities and services of doctors, insurance companies and hospitals.

• Direct federal loans should be given medical and dental students during their study, internship and residency, and these students should have the option to repay the loan in cash over a long term or to serve two years, excluding time required by the draft, in national service.

Medical Costs Conference. HEW Secretary John W. Gardner June 28 told a meeting of health experts in Washington, D.C., that all groups involved in delivering health care must participate in devising new approaches to stem the rising costs of medical care. Otherwise, he said, Government would have to shoulder more than its share of "corrective measures." The participants at the two-day National Conference on Medical Costs were told that the medical care cost index rose 6.6 percent during 1966—twice the rise of the consumer price index.

The conference was called at the direction of President Johnson, who said in a Feb. 28 education and health message that the average per-patient, per-day hospital charge of $45 was more than triple the cost in 1950.

Mental Retardation Centers

Congress enacted the Administration's Mental Retardation Amendments of 1967 (HR 6430—Pl 90-170). There was little controversy over the measure, which was passed by the House Sept. 20 and the Senate Nov. 6.

The bill extended two grant programs for construction of mental retardation facilities, authorized a new program of grants for staffing the centers, extended for an additional year—through fiscal 1970—an existing program of training teachers of the handicapped, and initiated a new program for training teachers in physical education and recreation for the handicapped.

As signed by the President, Dec. 4, HR 6430 authorized a total of $281.8 million in fiscal 1968-70, including $19 million in new authority for fiscal 1968. (Under existing law, $30 million for fiscal 1968 was already authorized for constructing community mental retardation centers, and $71.5 million was authorized in fiscal 1968-69 for training teachers of the handicapped.)

The House version called for $216.8 million. The Senate increased the total by $83 million by adding $73 million for training teachers of the handicapped and for research into education of the handicapped in fiscal 1970, and $10 million in fiscal 1968-70 for training physical education and recreation personnel for the handicapped. The conferees cut the Senate figure by $18 million by deleting the funds for research.

The bill extended through fiscal 1970 two programs originally created by the Mental Retardation Facilities Construction Act of 1963 (Title I of PL 88-164). One of them provided grants for construction of public and private nonprofit community mental retardation centers.

The other authorized grants for construction of clinical mental retardation facilities associated with a college or university *(Congress and the Nation, Vol. I, p. 1147.)*

President Johnson did not request, and Congress did not authorize, extension of a program established by the 1963 Act for construction of research centers. Instead HR 6430 initiated a major new grant program to help the communities staff their centers.

HR 6430 also extended through fiscal 1970 a program for training teachers of handicapped children. The program was authorized by Title III of the 1963 Act and was extended through fiscal 1969 by the Mental Health Centers Act Amendments of 1965. *(See above.)*

The new program for training persons to teach physical education and recreation to the handicapped was sponsored in the Senate Labor and Public Welfare Committee by Sen. Edward M. Kennedy (D Mass.).

President Johnson, in his Feb. 28, 1967, message on education and health, asked for an extension of authorizations for grants for university and community retardation centers and recommended a new program of grants to help staff the community centers. While not requesting new funds for research centers, the President asked for an extension of the Community Mental Centers Act, Title II of PL 88-164. Congress enacted the legislation. *(See below.)*

Provisions. As signed into law (PL 90-170), HR 6430 authorized the following funds, in millions of dollars: (Funds already authorized are in parentheses; "continuations" are staffing funds for projects originally funded in a previous fiscal year.)

	1968	1969	1970	1971	1972	1973	Total New Auth.
University-affiliated construction	$10	$20	$ 20				$ 50
Community centers construction	(30)	30	50				80
Staffing:							
New grants	7	10	14				31
Continuations		5.6	12.2	$20	$12.4	$5.6	55.8
Training Teachers of handicapped	(34)	(37.5)	55				55
Training recreation teachers	2	3.5	4.5				10
TOTAL	$19	$69.1	$155.7	$20	$12.4	$5.6	$281.8

In addition to authorizing new funds, HR 6430:

Authorized the use for research activities of a portion of the university facilities constructed under the bill.

Provided that staffing grants were to be made as follows: The Government was to pay up to 75 percent of staff costs for the first 15 months the center was in operation. The Government contribution was to be reduced to 60 percent for the next 12 months, 45 percent for the next 12 months, and 30 percent for the next 12 months. No federal contributions were to be made after the center had been operating for 51 months. The grants were limited to the cost of staffing new services at existing facilities or services at new centers.

Stipulated that funds for construction of university-affiliated facilities for the mentally retarded could be used for planning grants. The grants could not exceed 75 percent of the planning costs of $25,000 for a single project.

Permitted a state to use 2 percent of its federal grants for construction of community mental retardation centers, or $50,000, whichever was the smaller sum, to pay up to one-half of the costs of administering the program at the state level.

Specified that $4 million of the funds for training physical education and recreation teachers were to be used for demonstration projects in this area.

Community Mental Health Centers

Congress enacted Administration-requested legislation (HR 6431—PL 90-31) to extend through fiscal 1970 authorizations for federal contributions to the costs of building and staffing community mental health centers.

The program, initiated under the Community Mental Health Centers Act of 1963 (Title II of PL 88-164), previously was extended in 1965. The 1965 extension authorized grants to help staff the centers; Congress had denied a request for staffing grants in 1963. *(See above.)*

HR 6431 authorized appropriations of $180 million in fiscal 1968-70 for the construction grants program and $58 million in fiscal 1969-70 for the program to help pay the salaries of the staff at the centers. Existing law already authorized $30 million in fiscal 1968 appropriations for the staffing program. Thus, specific appropriation authorizations for fiscal 1968-70 totaled $268 million —$238 million in HR 6431 and $30 million in existing law.

Additional appropriations could be provided under an open-ended authorization for follow-up staffing grants to centers that had previously received such grants under the specific staffing authorizations. HR 6431 extended this open-ended authorization through fiscal 1974—two years beyond the cut-off date provided by existing law.

Except for extending authorization for federal grants to mental health centers, the bill made only minor changes in existing law.

Congress made few changes in the Administration's proposed bill. The Administration asked for extension through fiscal 1972 of the mental health centers program, with open-ended authorizations for fiscal 1969-72. Congress declined to provide any authorizations for the last two fiscal years, and provided specific, not open-ended, authorizations for fiscal 1969-70. All changes were made by the House Interstate and Foreign Commerce Committee and were later endorsed by the Administration.

Provisions. As signed into law June 24 (PL 90-31), HR 6431:

Construction. Extended federal grants for the construction of community mental health centers for three years, through fiscal 1970, and authorized appropriations of $50 million in fiscal 1968, $60 million in fiscal 1969 and $70 million in fiscal 1970.

Amended the definition of the term "construction" in existing law to permit use of construction grants for acquisition of existing structures. (Under existing law, these grants could be used to erect new buildings, or to expand, remodel or alter—but not acquire—existing ones.)

Staffing. Extended for two years, through fiscal 1970, federal grants for staffing community mental health centers, and authorized $26 million in fiscal 1969 and $32 million in fiscal 1970.

Extended for two years, through fiscal 1974, authority to make follow-up staffing grants to mental health centers that had recieved initial staffing grants under the specific authorizations. Appropriation of such sums as were necessary was authorized for the follow-up grants.

Other. Required, effective July 1, 1969, that state mental-health-center plans provide for enforcement of minimum operation and maintenance standards for the centers. (Existing law made submission of the plans a condition of participation in the construction grants program.)

Amended Title V of the Public Health Service Act to allow the Public Health Service to give research, training or demonstration project grants to federal hospitals on the same terms as grants were given to nonfederal institutions.

Hospital Modernization

Proponents of federal aid to overcrowded, obsolete urban hospitals failed in their 1967 efforts to provide a stepped-up program of loans for hospital modernization.

The basic federal hospital-aid law, the Hospital Survey and Construction (Hill-Burton) Act of 1946, gave a preponderance of funds to rural states for construction of new hospitals. Beginning in 1964, limited funds were authorized also for hospital modernization, with a preference given to urban hospitals. President Johnson in 1966 proposed a massive, 10-year hospital modernization program, but Congress did not approve the request. *(See above.)*

Mr. Johnson did not renew his request in 1967. Instead, he appointed a 15-man National Advisory Commission on Health Facilities to consider "the future of the Hill-Burton program" and to "make recommendations for financing the construction and modernization of health facilities."

In 1967, the House Interstate and Foreign Commerce Committee adopted an amendment to the Partnership for Health bill (HR 6418) authorizing $58 million for hospital modernization, but the amendment was rejected on the House floor Sept. 20. *(See above.)*

The $58 million was merely a token, not recommended by the Administration and opposed by some hospital officials as inadequate. It was intended as a stopgap measure until Congress in 1968 considered extension and modification of the Hill-Burton Act. But the debate, in which rural Members called the bill a "bonanza for a few big cities," was indicative of the difficulties faced by urban hospitals in their efforts to obtain federal funds.

Over the years a leader in the successful efforts to keep Hill-Burton a strictly rural-oriented program was Sen. Lister Hill (D Ala.), cosponsor of the original bill. Hill was chairman not only of the Labor and Public Welfare Committee, which set Hill-Burton authorizations, but also of the Appropriation subcommittee which determined Hill-Burton funding.

In 1967, however, Hill introduced a bill (S 2251) which, according to American Hospital Assn. officials met many of the demands of urban hospitals. The bill authorized direct federal loans, at low interest rates, for modernizing hospitals and earmarked one-third of new funds under the Hill-Burton Act for modernization projects. There was no action on the bill.

Congress in 1968 voted a two-year extension of the Hill-Burton program. *(See below.)*

Birth Control

Congress took no action on birth control in 1967, although a Senate Government Operations subcommittee headed by Sen. Ernest Gruening (D Alaska) held a one-day hearing on family planning activities of the Health, Education and Welfare Department.

A report critical of HEW implementation of its stated family planning policy was released at the hearing. The report, "Implementing HEW Policy on Family Planning and Population," was made at the request of the Department by Oscar Harkavy of the Ford Foundation in collaboration with other outside consultants. The report stated that the HEW Department had made "some progress" in support of family planning but that "it is clear that none of the HEW regional offices or operating agencies presently places high priority on family planning, or is certain what precise functions it is expected to carry out in the field." It said the Secretary must give a "clear signal" that "vigorous support of this field is an integral part of HEW business." The report called for greatly increased funds and professional staff and said the Department had fewer than 10 professionals working full time on family planning activities.

It called also for training programs and an intensified research effort. It said the Department should require adequate family planning components in all applicable health programs.

In testimony, Dr. Philip R. Lee, Assistant Secretary of HEW for Health and Scientific Affairs, said the Department's goal was to make family planning services available by 1973 to the estimated five million women who did not currently have access to them. Katherine B. Oettinger, who was appointed Aug. 14 to the newly created post of Deputy Assistant Secretary for Population and Family Planning, said at least $100 million would be needed to achieve this goal.

Vatican Commission Report. A majority of the members of the Papal Commission on Birth Control, in a report made public April 19, recommended that the Roman Catholic Church accept "decent and human means" of contraception.

Health Agency Reports

The House Government Operations Committee in 1967 issued two reports critical of the administrative practices of Government agencies.

One report (H Rept 800) charged the Public Health Service (PHS) and especially its research arm, the National Institutes of Health (NIH), with "inadequate administrative performance" and "inept handling of payments" in its health research grants. The NIH, the report stated, "should not be 'fumbling around,' as one of its officials expressed it, when awarding substantial amounts of public money."

The other report (H Rept 801) said the Food and Drug Administration (FDA) had "demonstrated a serious lack of concern for economy and efficiency" in its selection of a site for a $17-million laboratory.

The two reports were based on studies by the Committee's Intergovernmental Relations Subcommittee headed by Rep. L.H. Fountain (D N.C.).

Cigarette Health Warning

The Executive Branch in 1967 stepped up its efforts to curb cigarette smoking or make it safer, both through administrative actions and through requests to Congress for legislation. Congress, however, took no new steps, beyond appropriating money for research.

Pending in the House and Senate at year's end were more than a dozen bills and resolutions to set new requirements for cigarette labeling and advertising. During the year the Senate Commerce Committee held three days of hearings on progress toward development of a safer cigarette, but no further action was taken by Congress.

The Government had assumed an important role in the antismoking campaign in 1964 with issuance by the Public Health Service of a report by the Surgeon General's Advisory Committee on Smoking and Health stating that "cigarette smoking is a health hazard of sufficient importance in the United States to warrant appropriate remedial action." The report contained statistics and other data to support the statement.

Congress responded in 1965 by passing the Cigarette Labeling and Advertising Act of 1965 (PL 89-92) requiring that labels on all cigarette packages carry the warning, "Caution: Cigarette Smoking May Be Hazardous to Your Health." The law, however, prohibited any other requirements for warnings on package labels and also prohibited until July 1, 1969, any requirement that cigarette advertising carry a similar warning. *(See above.)*

Passage of the 1965 law limited the Executive Branch's powers to impose new requirements. Nonetheless, during 1967 Executive agencies released several new findings, including data compiled by the Surgeon General and a report that the 1965 law had had little effect on smokers. New legislation was proposed and a number of new research efforts got under way. Following are the major developments:

● President Johnson, in a Feb. 28 message to Congress on health, directed the Secretary of Health, Education and Welfare to appoint a task force on lung cancer. Dr. Kennedy M. Endicott, director of the Public Health Service's National Cancer Institute, Aug. 16 announced the formation of a 10-member task force to study lung cancer and smoking and the development of a safer cigarette.

● U.S. Surgeon General William H. Stewart July 13 released a report summarizing research findings and conclusions made since the 1964 Surgeon General's report was issued. The 1967 report confirmed and strengthened the findings of the earlier study.

● HEW Secretary John W. Gardner July 13 called on Congress to strengthen the warning labels on cigarette packages required under the 1965 Act; require that the warning appear in advertising as well as on labels; and require that both labels and advertising identify the tar and nicotine levels in cigarettes. Congress did not enact the legislation.

● Secretary Gardner Jan. 10 sent to Commerce Committee Chairman Warren G. Magnuson (D Wash.) a report on the significance of tar and nicotine in cigarette smoke.

The PHS study concluded that "the lower the tar and nicotine content of cigarette smoke, the less harmful would be the effect on the smoker." The PHS recommended that the Surgeon General encourage research to bring about a "progessive reduction" of the tar and nicotine content of cigarette smoke and thus produce a safer cigarette.

• The Federal Trade Commission (FTC) in July filed a report with Congress on the impact of the first 18 months of the 1965 Act on the smoking habits of Americans and the advertising practices of the tobacco industry and the media. There was "virtually no evidence," the report stated, that the warning label on cigarette packages had had "any significant effect."

• Sen. Magnuson Nov. 27 released the results of tests by the FTC of 59 brands of cigarettes. The report marked the first time the Government had made public its own evaluation of the tar and nicotine content of cigarettes. The test results were attacked as meaningless by the Tobacco Institute Inc., a major industry group.

• The Federal Communications Commission (FCC) June 3 ordered radio and television stations to allow time—but not necessarily equal time—for antismoking advertisements.

Industry Activities. The tobacco industry—through its major Washington lobby group, Tobacco Institute Inc.—continued to oppose the Government's antismoking efforts. In addition to its own research, the industry issued press releases challenging the announcement of almost every Government research finding in the field of smoking and health.

Earle C. Clements (D Ky.—House 1945-48; Senate 1950-57), lobbyist for the Tobacco Institute Inc., was considered a strong influence on Members of Congress because of his earlier position as Senate Democratic Whip under Lyndon B. Johnson. In an article which appeared in January 1967 in an industry publication, Clements said, "The industry's position is clear: We do not pretend to know the causes of such diseases as lung cancer and heart disease. Nor do we believe the critics of smoking know the causes."

Air Pollution Control

Spurred by an increasingly serious national air pollution problem, Congress enacted the Air Quality Act of 1967 (S 780—PL 90-148) to strengthen federal powers to combat air pollution in the absence of meaningful state action.

President Johnson, in a Jan. 30 message to Congress, called for an increased federal role in air pollution control, but the legislation that emerged differed substantially from his requests. *(For previous action on air pollution, see 1965 and 1966, above.)*

S 780 was passed in somewhat different versions by the Senate July 18 and the House Nov. 2, by unanimous roll-call votes. The conference version cleared Congress No. 14.

As signed by the President, No. 21, S 780 authorized $428.3 million for federal air pollution control efforts in fiscal 1968, 1969 and 1970. Of the total authorization, $125 million was earmarked for fiscal 1968 and 1969 research on pollution caused by fuels combustion (including automobile emissions). The total authorization was the same as approved by the House. The Senate had recommended $700 million for the three-year period. Of the $428.3-million authorization, $140 million was reauthorization of existing spending authority.

New Federal Powers. S 780 greatly enlarged the existing federal responsibility for air pollution control, although in most cases the Federal Government was not to step in unless the states failed to act. The bill did not authorize the Federal Government to set national uniform emission standards for specific pollutants, as President Johnson had requested. This authority was a key feature of the original Administration proposal, but it was strongly opposed by various industry groups, including coal and steel producers and electric power companies. However, the bill authorized a two-year study of the impact of national emission standards.

S 780 authorized the HEW Secretary, in time of "imminent and substantial" danger to public health from air pollution, to seek a court injunction to halt further emissions into the atmosphere. The authority was not requested by the Administration.

Other provisions of S 780, which amended the Clean Air Act of 1963 (PL 88-206) and its subsequent amendments, authorized the HEW Secretary to designate air quality control regions throughout the nation, provided full federal financing for regional control commissions to be established by state Governors, and empowered the Secretary to enforce air quality standards in the control regions, if the regional commissions failed to enforce an air pollution plan that conformed to or was more stringent than guidelines for air purity which were to be supplied by the HEW Department. (Since air pollution conditions varied from region to region, the Department was to supply specially tailored guidelines for each region.)

Automobile Emissions. In addition to the $125-million study of fuels combustion, which included automobile emissions, D 780 required the registration of all fuel additives with the HEW Secretary, as requested by President Johnson. Moreover, fuel manufacturers were required to notify the Secretary of the type, concentration and purpose of all additives which were used in their fuels.

The bill provided that automobile exhaust standards could be issued only by the Federal Government, except for California, which was permitted to enforce its own (and more stringent) control standards. No other state was given this authority. The California exemption was retained in the final bill after the House refused to accept the position of the auto industry that one national standard for automobile emissions was preferable to different standards for California, which forced the auto industry to install special pollution control devices on cars destined for sale in that state. The California House delegation unanimously supported the exemption for their state from federal standards, which they said were not strict enough to meet the pollution problem.

In addition, S 780 provided federal support for state programs for inspection of automobile pollution-control devices.

Provisions

As signed into law (PL 90-148), S 780 contained the following major provisions:

Authorized the expansion of existing federal grants to states and local governments to assist in planning the implementation of air quality standards.

Provided 100-percent federal financing for the first two years of operation of interstate planning agencies established by state governors to develop air quality standards for air quality control regions.

Authorized the HEW Secretary to define the "atmospheric areas of the nation" within one year after enactment of the bill.

Required the Secretary to designate, within 18 months of enactment of the bill, air quality control regions based on existing jurisdictional boundaries, urban-industrial concentrations and other factors, in order to provide adequate implementation of air quality standards.

Authorized the Secretary, after the 18-month period, to revise the designation of such regions and to designate additional regions.

Authorized the establishment of federal interstate air quality planning agencies if the states failed to act.

Authorized the Secretary to set ambient air quality standards in any air quality region, if states failed to adopt such standards and an acceptable pollution abatement plan within 15 months after receipt of air quality criteria and recommended control measures from the HEW Department.

Authorized the Secretary, in time of "imminent and substantial" danger to public health from air pollution, to seek a court injunction against the continued emission of such pollutants as might be necessary to protect the public.

Authorized the Secretary to go to court to enforce any violation of quality standards in any air quality region, after 180 days' notice of such violation.

Directed the Secretary to continue existing enforcement procedures, if necessary, to protect public health during the period of standards development, and provided for pollution abatement conferences between interested parties in particular cases.

Specified a three-step development of air quality standards, including: (1) designation of air quality control regions by the Secretary; (2) expansion of existing provisions for the development of air quality criteria, stating the health effects of pollutants and combinations of pollutants required; and (3) publication of information on the control techniques required to achieve various levels of air quality.

Authorized an expanded research and development program for the control of pollution from fuel combustion and automobiles, including authority for research grants to non-profit organizations, with specific authorization of $35 million for fiscal 1968 and $90 million for fiscal 1969.

Provided that standards for automobile exhaust emissions could be established only by the Federal Government, except for states which had set their own criteria prior to promulgation of federal standards (designed to benefit California).

Established a 15-member President's Air Quality Advisory Board, headed by the HEW Secretary or his designate, and authorized the creation of other advisory committees to assist the Secretary.

Authorized a two-year study of the concept of national emission standards for various industries and pollution sources, including a study of the economic impact of pollution control.

Authorized federal assistance to states for development of automobile emission-device inspection systems.

Required the registration of fuel additives with the HEW Secretary and required fuel manufacturers to dis-

close to the Secretary the type, concentration and purpose of each additive used.

Provided for comprehensive reports to Congress on the progress of air pollution control efforts.

Authorized appropriations of $74 million in fiscal 1968, $95 million in fiscal 1969 and $134.3 million in fiscal 1970 for all programs other than research on fuels and vehicle emissions. (Total authorizations, including fuels research, amounted to $428.3 million for fiscal years 1968 through 1970, including reauthorization of $66 million for fiscal 1968 and $74 million for fiscal 1969.)

RELATED DEVELOPMENTS

HEW Department Actions. The HEW Department carried forward its air pollution control program in a series of 1967 developments and announcements.

The Department Feb. 24 announced additional standards to control automotive pollution, effective in the 1969 model year. The new standards limited evaporative losses from fuel tanks and carburetors. Previous standards, applicable only to exhaust emissions, took effect in the 1968 model year.

The Department March 22 released a report on "Air Quality Criteria for Sulphur Oxides," the first in a series of studies on all major air pollutants. The report was prepared under provisions of the Clean Air Act of 1963. Almost all major U.S. cities, the report said, were exposed regularly to unhealthy amounts of sulphur dioxide, which is a by-product of the combustion of coal and fuel oil. Publication of the report was vigorously opposed by the coal industry and by Senators from coal-producing states.

The HEW Department March 21 announced regulations to control sulphur dioxide emissions at 154 federal installations in the New York, Chicago and Philadelphia areas. HEW Secretary Gardner said that "federal agencies must take the initiative" in reducing pollution from this source.

Oil Import Rules. In other action designed to reduce air pollution, Interior Secretary Stewart L. Udall July 17 announced changes in oil import regulations to encourage the use of fuel oil with low sulphur content.

Environmental Health Task Force. A special task force on environmental health June 12 released a report which recommended a $2.5-billion five-year federal program to deal with problems such as air and water pollution, urban congestion and the development of new products potentially hazardous to man. The report, which outlined 10 immediate goals and a number of long-range proposals, described the "danger to environmental quality" as one of the most important current domestic problems.

The six-member study group, headed by Ron M. Linton, former staff director of the Senate Committee on Public Works, was appointed by HEW Secretary John W. Gardner to advise the Department on ways to combat the problems of environmental health.

Electric-Powered Autos. Commerce Secretary Alexander B. Trowbridge Oct. 18 issued a report by a 16-member advisory panel which recommended steps to reduce automotive air pollution and included a status report on the development of electric-powered vehicles. The current state of technology did not indicate large-scale marketing of improved electric vehicles during the next decade, the report said.

During 1967 Senate hearings on proposals to promote the development of electric-powered vehicles, Administration witnesses opposed federal support for electric vehicle research.

Water Pollution. For 1967 developments see chapter on Water and Power.

1968

Health Manpower

Congress Aug. 2 completed action on the Administration's Health Manpower Act of 1968 (S 3095—PL 90-490), extending and revising major existing health manpower laws. The bill was designed to expand and improve the training of medical and allied health personnel, provide construction and other improvement grants for training and research facilities, and broaden health student loan and scholarship programs. It authorized new appropriations of almost $1.2 billion over the period of fiscal 1970-71.

The bill amended provisions of five existing health laws: the Public Health Service Act of 1944, the Health Research Facilities Act of 1956, the Health Professions Educational Assistance Act of 1963, the Nurse Training Act of 1964 and the Allied Health Professions Personnel Training Act of 1966.

Under the programs extended and revised by S 3095, grants were provided to many kinds of medical and nursing schools for construction of new facilities, rehabilitation of old ones, improvement of their curriculums, or development of new approaches to teaching in the health professions—including devising ways to shorten the lengthy course that doctors must pursue before they can practice. New conditions in the grants programs were calculated to serve as incentives for medical and nursing schools to increase their enrollments. The bill also extended and enlarged scholarship and loan programs in the health professions and created a new nursing scholarship plan. The legislation was requested by President Johnson in a March 4 message on health.

The Administration requested an extension of the above programs for four years, with authorizations totalling $2.6 billion. As enacted, S 3095 provided for a two-year extension of the programs (with the exception of the Allied Health Profession Personnel Training Act, which was extended for only one year) and authorizations of about $1.2 billion. The Senate version approved a three-year extension with authorizations totalling $1.9 billion. Final action came when the Senate Aug. 2 by voice vote and without debate agreed to the House version of the bill, which was similar to the Senate's except that it did not contain authorizations for fiscal 1972.

Both the House and Senate committee reports on the bill said the need for increased manpower in the health professions and in nursing was urgent. The Senate Labor and Public Welfare Committee said there currently were 311,000 active physicians and 100,000 active dentists, in the United States, and that an additional 80,000 physicians and 25,000 dentists would be needed by 1975.

The Health Professions program was the largest of the health manpower programs. In this program, between 1963 and 1968, construction grants were awarded to a total of 114 schools, providing teaching facilities accommodating 4,200 additional students at new schools and 12,000 students through the expansion of existing schools. In the same period, the grants maintained the enrollment capacity for 35,000 students through the modernization and replacement of obsolete facilities. Grants were also made for schools to improve and expand educational capabilities, develop new courses and to improve teaching methods.

Student loans were awarded to 25,000 or 39 percent, of the enrolled students in the 1963-68 period. The average award was $1,050. Scholarships were awarded to 8,000 students at an average cost of $903.

The Senate Committee said that about 660,000 nurses were currently practicing, and that an additional 190,000 would be needed by 1970. Under the Nurse Training Act, 13 new schools were under construction in 1968, which would provide space for 10,600 students. These schools, plus schools that were to be built or renovated, would provide space for 24,400 students. About one-fourth of students enrolled in schools participating in the loan program received loans.

Provisions

As signed by the President, Aug. 16, S 3095 (PL 90-490):

Title I—Health Professions. Extended for two additional years, through fiscal 1971, the Health Professions Act of 1963 and authorized appropriations of $338 million for fiscal 1970 and $444.8 million for fiscal 1971.

Added schools of pharmacy and veterinary medicine to the types of schools eligible to receive grants.

Construction Grants. In the grants program for construction of teaching facilities, authorized the Secretary of Health, Education and Welfare to increase from one-half to two-thirds the federal share of construction costs in cases where a school was experiencing financial difficulties because of heavy expenses on projects such as major revisions in curriculum, replacing obsolete facilities or moving to new locations. Existing law allowed the federal share to be increased from one-half to two-thirds only in the case of a new school or a school planning a major expansion of training capacity.

Permitted the Federal Government to recover a proportionate share of federal grants if, within 20 years, the recipient school lost its eligibility by ceasing to be a public or nonprofit private school or failing to meet other conditions. Existing law provided for a 10-year recovery period.

Basic Improvement Grants. Revised an existing condition for basic improvement grants so as to provide the following condition: that the Secretary receive assurance from a recipient school that, in the fiscal year of the grant and in each succeeding year when a grant was made, its freshman year enrollment would exceed by 2½ percent or by five students, whichever was greater, the average of the school's two highest years' freshman enrollment of full-time students during the 5-year period July 1, 1963-July 1, 1968. Permitted the Secretary of Health, Education and Welfare to waive this requirement in cases where he determined that an enrollment increase would cause overcrowding and thereby diminish the quality of training provided. (Basic improvement grants were given to schools to improve and expand their educational capabilities, develop new courses and improve teaching methods.)

Altered the existing allotment formula for basic improvement grants so as to provide bonuses for schools that increased their enrollments. The new formula provided that each recipient school be allotted a minimum of $25,000, and that the remaining available appropriations be distributed among the schools with those schools showing the greatest increases in enrollment receiving the greatest share of funds. These provisions were to be effective beginning in fiscal 1970, and S 3095 provided that no school was to receive less in fiscal 1970 or 1971 than it received in fiscal 1969.

Special Project Grants. Permitted special project grants to be awarded for projects that offered promise of expanding and improving the national capacity for training health manpower, including experimental approaches to the training of physicians and dentists, such as programs that would reduce the time required for the first professional degree, or programs to develop training for new levels or types of health personnel. Existing law permitted special project grants only for the carrying out of nationally important specialized functions and to maintain or provide a school's accreditation; these grant purposes were continued by the bill.

Removed existing per-project grant limitations in the special project grants program.

Student Aid Programs. Made several changes in the loan programs for students in the health professions, the most important of which: (1) established a uniform interest rate of 3 percent on student loans; (2) required a student to begin repaying his loan within one year after ceasing full-time study; and (3) provided that a student would not have to make payments on his loan during periods (up to five years) of advanced professional training, including internships and residencies. Existing law set a formula for the interest rate which could result in rates as high as 6 percent, did not require a student to begin repayment until three years after ceasing full-time study, and allowed loan recipients to defer repayment only for service in the armed forces or the Peace Corps (for periods not to exceed three years). S 3095 continued the loan repayment deferral provisions for service in the armed forces and the Peace Corps.

Permitted a school to transfer up to 20 percent (or more if approved by the HEW Secretary) of federal scholarship grants from its scholarship fund to its loan fund, or 20 percent of federal student loan grants to the scholarship fund.

Report. Required the Secretary of HEW to submit a report to the President and to Congress on the administration of the programs to aid in the training of allied health professions personnel by July 1, 1970.

Title II—Nursing. Extended for two additional years, through fiscal 1971, the Nurse Training Act of 1964 and authorized appropriations totaling $115 million for fiscal 1970 and $145 million for fiscal 1971.

Construction. Permitted increases in the ceiling on the permissible federal share of grants for nursing school construction similar to the increases authorized in Title I.

Basic Improvement Grants. Permitted these grants to be made to collegiate and associate degree nursing schools as well as to diploma schools. Only diploma schools were eligible under existing law.

Required the same assurances of enrollment increases as a condition for improvement grants (and provided the Secretary of HEW with the same waiver authority) as set forth in Title I.

Provided for a $15,000 minimum grant to recipient schools, and established the same formula for enrollment bonuses as provided in Title I.

Special Project Grants. Expanded the scope of activities for which these grants could be made, in the same manner as in Title I. Allowed grants to be made to any public or nonprofit private organization for projects to improve nursing curriculums, etc. (Previously only nursing schools were eligible for these grants. Retained provisions allowing grants to nursing schools to help meet accreditation requirements.

Student Aid Programs. Established a new program of grants to nursing schools for scholarship funds. Established a per-student ceiling of $1,500 annually on the amount of a scholarship. (The annual ceiling in the health professions scholarship program was $2,500. Previously no formal nursing scholarship program existed, although a small "opportunity grants" program that was similar to a scholarship program was enacted in the 1966 health training bill. *(See above.)*

Raised the annual ceiling on the nursing loan program from $1,000 to $1,500. Established a uniform interest rate of 3 percent, required a student to begin repaying the loan nine months (instead of a year) after ceasing studies, and established the same loan repayment deferral provisions as in Title I.

Continued provisions of existing law which allowed 50 percent of the loan to be canceled at the rate of 10 percent for each complete year of full-time employment as a professional nurse in a public or nonprofit institution. Added new provisions specifying that the entire loan would be canceled at the rate of 15 percent a year for full-time employment in such an institution located in an area designated by HEW as having a substantial shortage of nurses.

Provided the same authority to transfer money between loan and scholarship funds as was provided in Title I.

Accreditation. Altered the existing provisions under which nursing schools were accredited for purposes of becoming eligible for federal aid. Deleted the authority of the Commissioner of Education to accredit programs of nurse education directly and redefined an "accredited" school of nursing as any institution accredited by a recognized accreditation body, as designated by the Commissioner of Education, or any school of nursing at an accredited hospital, junior college or college.

Report. Required the Secretary of HEW, in consultation with the National Advisory Council on Nurse Training, to submit a report to the President and to Congress on the administration of the nurse training program by July 1, 1970.

Title III—Allied Health. Extended for one year, through fiscal 1970, the provisions of the Health Professions Personnel Training Act of 1966, authorizing grants for the construction of new training facilities and the improvement of existing facilities, for the expansion of traineeship programs and for the development of new methods of training health technologists. The authorization was for $39.5 million for fiscal 1970.

Public Health. Extended for two years, through fiscal 1971, the provisions of the Public Health Service Act of 1944, authorizing project grants for graduate training in public health and traineeships for professional public health personnel. The authorizations were for $18.5 million for fiscal 1970 and $26 million for fiscal 1971.

Title IV—Research Construction. Extended for two years, through fiscal 1971, the Health Research Facilities Act of 1956, authorizing grants to public and private nonprofit institutions for the construction of research facilities in the health sciences. The authorizations were for $20 million for fiscal 1970 and $30 million for fiscal 1971.

Allowed the federal share of research facilities construction projects to be increased from one-half to two-thirds for projects that the HEW Secretary determined had special regional or national significance. Specified that not more than 25 percent of funds appropriated could be used for such special grants.

Health Service Amendments

In the Public Health Service Amendments of 1968 (HR 15758—PL 90-574), Congress extended a variety of existing health programs:

• A two-year extension of federal grants for regional medical programs for heart disease, cancer and stroke. The program was initiated in 1965. *(See above.)*

• A two-year extension of a program of grants for health services for domestic migratory agricultural workers. This was the second extension of a program established by the Migrant Health Act of 1962 (PL 87-692). A previous extension was voted in the Community Health Services Extension Amendments of 1965. *(See above.)*

• A two-year extension of the grant program for the rehabilitation of narcotics addicts. The program was initiated under the Narcotic Addict Rehabilitation Act of 1966. *(See chapter on Crime and Justice.)* In HR 15758, the program was combined with a new rehabilitation program for alcoholics and transferred to the Community Health Centers Act. *(See below.)*

• A two-year extension of the Hill-Burton hospital construction and modernization program. Not included in the final bill were provisions added by the Senate to increase Hill-Burton authorizations and to establish a new program of loans and loan guarantees for hospital modernization. *(For previous action on hospital modernization legislation, see 1966 and 1967, above.)*

• A one-year extension of the Solid Waste Disposal Act of 1965, which was scheduled to expire June 30, 1969. *(See above.)* This provision was added by Senate floor amendment.

In addition to extending existing programs, HR 15758 established a new grant program to provide for construction and staffing of facilities to treat and rehabilitate alcoholics. Such programs were to be an integral part of community mental health centers where they existed. Title III of HR 15758, the Alcoholic and Narcotic Addict Rehabilitation Amendments of 1968, placed both alcoholic and narcotic addict rehabilitation programs under the Community Mental Health Centers Act, as amended in 1965. *(See above.)*

HR 15758 authorized total appropriations of $576.5 million: $89 million for fiscal 1969 and $487.5 million for fiscal 1970.

President Johnson, in his Feb. 7 message on crime, requested adoption of the rehabilitation program for alcoholics. In his March 4 message on health, he requested a five-year extension of the regional health center program. In his March 8 conservation message, he requested a one-year extension of the Solid Waste Disposal Act. The President did not ask for extension of the Hill-Burton Act; he was believed to be waiting for the recommendations of the National Advisory Commission on Health Facilities, which he had appointed in 1967. That group reported in December 1968.

Hospital Mortgage Insurance. Title XV of the omnibus 1968 housing bill (S 3497—PL 90-448) authorized a new program of FHA mortgage insurance for the construction or rehabilitation of nonprofit hospitals. *(See chapter on Housing.)*

Provisions

The Public Health Service Amendments of Oct. 15, 1968 (PL 90-574):

Heart, Cancer, Stroke. Extended through June 30, 1970, programs of federal grants to regional medical programs for treatment of heart disease, cancer and stroke.

Authorized $185 million for such programs—$65 million for fiscal 1969 and $120 million for fiscal 1970.

Extended regional medical programs to Guam, American Samoa and the Pacific Trust Territory.

Provided that funds appropriated under the provision would be available to any public or nonprofit agency or institution for services of "substantial use" to any two or more regional medical programs.

Migrant Workers. Extended through June 30, 1970, the grants to public and non-profit agencies for health services to domestic agricultural migratory workers.

Authorized appropriation of $9 million for such grants in fiscal 1969 and $15 million in fiscal 1970.

Alcoholic and Narcotic Addict Rehabilitation. Declared that alcoholism should be treated not so much as a criminal problem but as a health problem.

Noted that programs to treat and control alcoholism should, whenever possible, be community based; provide a comprehensive range of services, including emergency treatment under proper medical auspices on a coordinated basis; and be integrated with and involve the active participation of a wide range of public and non-governmental agencies.

Amended the Community Mental Health Centers Act (PL 88-164) to authorize grants to construct and staff facilities—including specialized facilities such as halfway houses—for the treatment and rehabilitation of alcoholics.

Required the Secretary of Health, Education and Welfare to assure that no individual would be made the subject of research under the grants unless he agreed to become a research subject.

Limited the federal payment for construction projects to two-thirds of each project's costs, and payments for professional staff to 51 months, with the initial federal share set at 75 percent and declining gradually to 30 percent in the final year.

Transferred the narcotic addict rehabilitation program from the 1966 Narcotic Addict Rehabilitation Act to the Community Mental Health Centers Act.

(Continued on p. 702)

Health, Education and. . .

(Comparable budget authority

	FY 1966	FY 1967	FY 1968	FY 1969
CONSUMER PROTECTION AND ENVIRONMENTAL HEALTH SERVICE				
A. Food and Drug Administration	$55,009	$64,666	$67,956	$70,444
B. National Air Pollution Control Administration	25,808	39,145	63,109	87,960
C. Environmental Control Administration	53,933	64,770	71,162	62,831
1) Solid waste management	3,849	11,505	13,350	16,113
2) Occupational health	5,118	6,077	6,667	7,466
3) Radiological health	16,798	16,934	16,261	16,183
4) Community environmental management, water hygiene, and program direction	28,168	30,254	34,884	23,069
D. Service-wide management and facilities construction	11,742	14,115	8,839	5,830
Total, CPEHS	**$146,492**	**$182,696**	**$211,066**	**$227,065**
HEALTH SERVICES AND MENTAL HEALTH ADMINISTRATION				
A. Comprehensive health planning and services program	119,122	129,411	153,578	187,359
1) Partnership for health grants	112,208	115,975	137,800	171,132
a) Planning	5,000	5,000	15,000	18,500
b) Formula	57,550	55,250	60,300	66,032
c) Project	49,658	55,725	62,500	86,600
2) Migrant health program	3,500	8,000	8,100	8,100
3) Standard-setting, resource development, and program management	3,414	5,436	7,678	8,127
B. National Center for Health Services Research and Development	30,897	28,583	32,472	41,907
C. Regional medical programs	42,286	63,705	78,229	83,133
1) Planning and operational grants	24,000	43,000	53,900	56,200
2) Chronic disease control and program management	18,286	20,605	24,329	26,933
D. Medical facilities construction	263,241	273,528	283,696	258,289
1) Hill-Burton grants	260,000	270,000	280,000	254,400
2) Technical assistance and program management	3,241	3,528	3,696	3,889
E. Operation of the PHS hospital system and related activities	50,875	65,621	73,062	71,998
F. Indian health program	81,294	90,448	101,175	112,438
1) Operations	67,198	75,959	84,327	94,282
2) Direct construction	14,096	14,489	16,848	18,156
G. National Communicable Disease Center	38,516	42,533	45,263	39,084
H. National Institute of Mental Health	269,522	305,740	337,953	346,303
1) Support and conduct of research	86,964	92,583	100,684	114,178
2) Manpower development	93,031	99,042	109,205	122,781
3) Support of State and community programs	56,991	80,260	91,454	71,396
4) Service activities and program management	22,246	23,684	25,861	24,568
5) Operation of St. Elizabeths Hospital	10,290	10,171	10,749	13,380
I. National Center for Health Statistics	7,127	8,059	8,203	8,109
J. Administration-wide management, facilities construction and related activities	17,452	26,192	21,067	21,642
Total HSMHA	**$920,332**	**$1,033,720**	**$1,134,698**	**$1,170,262**
NATIONAL INSTITUTES OF HEALTH				
A. Health manpower education	225,822	374,946	389,104	275,671
1) Institutional support	25,881	54,884	71,550	96,646
2) Student assistance	40,912	77,517	56,490	63,349
a) Traineeships	16,412	18,762	20,120	20,820

...Welfare Program Funding

in Thousands of Dollars)	**FY 1966**	**FY 1967**	**FY 1968**	**FY 1969**
b) Loans	24,300	54,225 [1]	24,170	24,810
c) Scholarships	200	4,530	12,200	17,719
3) Facilities construction	146,000	223,500	241,750	93,200
a) Teaching facilities	90,000	160,000	203,000	84,800
b) Health research facilities	56,000	56,000	35,000	8,400
c) Medical libraries	——	7,500	3,750	——
4) Manpower requirements, utilization and program management	13,029	19,045	19,314	22,476
B. National Library of Medicine	9,685	12,692	17,773	18,009
C. Categorical Research Institutes and Divisions	883,683	996,651	1,055,740	1,078,551
1) Research grant awards	521,301	588,819	617,086	616,812
2) Research manpower development programs	171,895	183,053	187,143	197,727
3) Intramural research	64,543	71,777	77,421	85,554
4) Collaborative research and development	82,462	102,443	111,561	121,306
5) Supporting services and program management, including facilities construction	43,482	50,550	62,529	57,152
Total NIH	**$1,119,190**	**$1,384,289**	**$1,462,617**	**$1,372,231**
Special foreign currency program	**$5,000**	**$10,000**	**$15,000**	**$15,000**

SOCIAL AND REHABILITATION SERVICE

	FY 1966	**FY 1967**	**FY 1968**	**FY 1969**
A. Grants to States for Medical Assistance	830,000	1,180,567	1,832,219	2,396,322
1) Payments for medically indigent receiving maintenance payments	500,000	625,066	849,977	1,196,100
2) Payments for medically indigent not receiving maintenance payments	300,000	532,117	909,796	1,115,122
3) State and local administration	30,000	51,632	76,918	98,100
4) Adjustments	——	-28,248	-4,472	-13,000
B. Maternal and child health programs	131,670	167,566	178,358	209,200
1) Maternal and child health and crippled children's services	88,822	99,250	99,354	107,000
2) Maternity and infant care	24,156	27,744	29,645	48,000
3) Health of school and preschool children	14,715	31,677	36,779	39,000
4) Training and research	3,977	8,895	12,580	15,200
Total, SRS	**$961,670**	**$1,348,133**	**$2,010,577**	**$2,605,522**

SOCIAL SECURITY ADMINISTRATION (trust funds) [2]

	FY 1966	**FY 1967**	**FY 1968**	**FY 1969**
A. Hospital insurance for the aged	915,695	3,073,730	3,902,418	5,368,161
B. Supplementary medical insurance	1,256,018	1,384,734	1,353,179	1,910,324
Total, SSA	**$2,171,713**	**$4,358,464**	**$5,255,597**	**$7,278,815**
GRAND TOTAL, DHEW	**$5,324,397**	**$8,317,302**	**$10,089,555**	**$12,668,565**

1 Includes $12 million for initial capitalization of student loan revolving funds.
2 Under the new consolidated budget approach, budget authority for trust fund accounts reflects tax receipts into the fund. The Social Security Administration outlay accounts are broken down between benefit payments and administrative expenses and construction. The breakdown for outlays follows:

	FY 1966	**FY 1967**	**FY 1968**	**FY 1969**
A. Hospital insurance for the aged	$ 64,491	$2,596,713	$3,814,994	$4,471,150
1) Benefit payments	——	2,507,773	3,736,322	4,367,000
2) Administrative expenses and construction	64,491	88,940	78,672	104,150
B. Supplementary medical insurance	995,769	798,943	1,532,267	1,750,837
1) Benefit payments	861,000	664,261	1,389,622	1,567,000
2) Administrative expenses and construction	$134,769	$ 134,682	$142,645	$183,837

SOURCE: Health, Education and Welfare Department

Authorized construction and staffing grants under the same matching requirements as alcoholic grants.

Authorized $15 million for fiscal 1969 and $25 million for fiscal 1970 for the construction and staffing of facilities for alcoholics and narcotic addicts.

Hospital Construction and Modernization. Extended through June 30, 1970, the Hill-Burton Act program of federal grants for hospital and other medical facility construction and modernization.

Authorized appropriation of $295 million for these grants in fiscal 1970.

Veterans Educational Benefits. Provided that students could receive grants or loans under the Public Health Service Act without losing eligibility for veterans' educational benefits.

Gorgas Laboratory. Authorized an additional $500,000 for the work of the Gorgas Memorial Laboratory, the medical-research component of the Gorgas Memorial Institute of Tropical and Preventive Medicine located in Panama City, Panama.

Solid Waste Disposal. Authorized appropriations of $32 million for a one-year extension of the program of research and demonstrations in the field of solid waste disposal in fiscal 1970.

National Eye Institute

Congress enacted legislation (HR 12848—Pl 90-489) to create an independent National Eye Institute in the National Institutes of Health.

The new institute was to consolidate existing programs in the National Institute of Neurological Diseases and Blindness dealing with visual disorders and blindness. Supporters of the bill, which included the American Medical Assn., the American Foundation for the Blind Inc., and the American Assn. of Ophthalmology, asserted a separate eye institute was needed because of the unique medical problems of visual disorders. Opponents of the measure, including the Health, Education and Welfare Secretary, the Surgeon General and the director of the National Institutes, said the new institute could lead to over-isolation of eye-disorder research.

As signed by the President, Aug. 16, the bill authorized the Health, Education and Welfare Secretary to create the new institute and establish an advisory council dealing with the Eye Institute. The bill provided for research and training fellowships in visual disorders. In addition, the name of the National Institute of Neurological Diseases and Blindness was changed to the National Institute of Neurological Diseases.

The HEW Department estimated that the new institute would entail additional administrative expenses of about $800,000.

Drug Abuse Control

Congress enacted legislation (HR 14096—Pl 90-639) providing criminal penalties for the possession of illegally obtained stimulant, depressant or hallucinogenic drugs (including "pep pills," barbiturates and LSD).

The bill also authorized judges to set aside convictions of first offenders after a probationary period (a provision designed to keep young people who experimented with drugs from acquiring a criminal record) and increased existing penalties for trafficking in illegal drugs, especially for those who sold drugs to youths.

HR 14096 amended the Drug Abuse Control Amendments of 1965 (PL 89-74), which expanded federal controls over stimulant, depressant and hallucinogenic drugs. *(See above.)* The 1965 law's failure to stem the illegal flow of drugs led President Johnson, in his 1968 crime message, to request legislation making the illegal manufacture, sale or distribution of such drugs a felony and illegal possession a misdemeanor.

Provisions. As enacted into law, Oct. 24, HR 14096:

Prohibited the possession of stimulant, depressant or hallucinogenic drugs—including amphetamines, barbiturates and LSD (lysergic acid diethylamide)— unless they were obtained directly from a physician or by prescription.

Made illegal possession a misdemeanor punishable by a $1,000 fine and/or up to one year's imprisonment for the first and the second offense, and up to three years in prison and/or a $10,000 fine for subsequent offenses.

Permitted courts to suspend the sentences of first offenders and to place them on probation and, if they did not violate probation, to set the conviction aside to leave them with no criminal record.

Increased the 1965 Act's penalties for selling stimulant, depressant or hallucinogenic drugs illegally as follows: for selling to adults, a maximum five-year prison term and/or a $10,000 fine for sale to minors under 21, by persons over age 18, up to 10 years in prison and/or a $15,000 fine for a first offense and for subsequent convictions, 15 years and/or a $20,000 fine.

Declared it the sense of Congress that priority should be given to federal information programs designed to educate the public, especially young persons, regarding the dangers of drug abuse.

Extended coverage of the bill to the Canal Zone.

Changed the name of the National Institute of Neurological Diseases and Blindness to the National Institute of Neurological Diseases and Stroke.

Executive Branch Reorganization

PUBLIC HEALTH SERVICE. Dissatisfaction with the results of the 1966 reorganization of the Public Health Service *(see above)*, led to a further reorganization in 1968. Under the 1968 plan, responsibility for overall health policy direction was vested in the Assistant Secretary for Health and Scientific Affairs, a political appointee. The Surgeon General, who as head of the PHS previously had reported directly to the HEW Secretary, was made a deputy of the Assistant Secretary with responsibility for day-to-day PHS operations.

Three new administrations were created within the PHS by the 1968 reorganization:

• National Institutes of Health—NIH activities were expanded to include medical education as well as research, and the Bureau of Health Manpower and National Library of Medicine were included in the new administration.

• Health Services and Mental Health Administration—This administration drew together major aspects of public health relating to health services and individual health, including the Partnership for Health program and the National Institute of Mental Health.

• Consumer Protection and Environmental Health Service—This new service was created by Executive

Order of the President July 1. It included the Food and Drug Administration, which had reported directly to the HEW Secretary until the 1968 reorganization. It included also the Environmental Control Administration, the National Air Pollution Control Center, the National Center for Radiological Health and the National Center for Urban and Industrial Health.

DRUG ENFORCEMENT AGENCY. President Johnson submitted to Congress a reorganization plan (Plan No. 1) to establish a new Bureau of Narcotics and Dangerous Drugs in the Justice Department. The Bureau combined two separate federal agencies for drug law enforcement, the Bureau of Narcotics in the Treasury Department and the Bureau of Drug Abuse Control in the HEW Department. The plan took effect April 8. *(For details, see chapter on Crime and Justice.)*

Birth Control

The fiscal 1969 foreign aid authorization bill (HR 15263—PL 90-554) authorized the use of up to $50 million from over-all economic aid funds to assist voluntary family planning activities either through foreign governments or through the United Nations or private non-profit organizations. *(See chapter on Foreign Policy.)*

Sen. Ernest Gruening's (D Alaska) Government Operations Subcommittee on Foreign Aid Expenditures continued its hearings, begun in 1965, on the population crisis and on Gruening's proposal to establish Offices for Population Problems in the State and HEW Departments. William S. Gaud, administrator of the Agency for International Development (AID), said three of the important steps he had taken in 1967 relating to population matters were establishment of a Population Service in the Office of the War on Hunger, removal of AID's self-imposed restriction against aid for buying or manufacturing contraceptives, and a November 1967 directive to all missions to give highest priority, along with food production, to family planning programs in developing countries.

Birth Control Panel. President Johnson July 16 appointed an 18-member committee to study the Government's role in birth control. The President appointed Wilbur J. Cohen, Secretary of Health, Education, and Welfare, as head of the committee. John D. Rockefeller III was named cochairman.

Papal Encyclical. Pope Paul VI July 29 upheld the Roman Catholic prohibition of all artifical means of contraception. In an encyclical letter, "Of Human Life," he reaffirmed that Roman Catholics might limit the size of families only by the rhythm method or by abstinence. The encyclical was met with strong protest throughout the Catholic Church. A group of 87 U.S. Roman Catholic theologians issued a statement in Washington, D.C., July 30, asserting that the encyclical was not binding on Catholics.

Other 1968 Health Action

MEDICAL SCIENCE COMMISSION. A Senate Government Operations subcommittee held hearings on a bill (S J Res 145) to create a 15-member Presidential Commission on Health Science and Society, but the measure was not reported out of committee.

COAL MINE SAFETY. President Johnson on Sept. 11 sent Congress proposals for a Federal Coal Mine Safety and Health Act. Mr. Johnson said that since passage of existing coal mine safety legislation in 1952 (PL 82-552), thousands of miners had died from "black lung" disease. Congress took no action.

Interior Secretary Stewart L. Udall said June 13 that safety critic Ralph Nader was correct in charging that the Bureau of Mines was lax in protecting the health of coal miners. Udall added that the Bureau would accept responsibility from that date in the field of health.

SMOKING REPORTS. The Department of Health, Education and Welfare (HEW) and the Federal Trade Commission (FTC) released reports to Congress July 1 calling for restrictions on cigarette advertising and linking cigarettes more directly to diseases. The reports were required annually until 1969 under a provision of the 1965 cigarette labeling act (PL 89-92).

HEW Secretary Cohen forwarded to Congress the Surgeon General's 1968 Supplemental Report on the Health Consequences of Smoking and recommended more widespread and strongly worded warnings of the hazards involved in cigarette smoking. Cohen asked Congress to require a warning to appear in all cigarette advertisements and on vending machines as well as cigarette packages, which were currently required to carry a warning. Further, Cohen called for rewording of the current warning to make it stronger.

Cigarette advertising was also challenged by the FTC in its annual report to the Senate Commerce Committee. In a 3 to 2 decision, the FTC voted to recommend a ban on all cigarette advertising on radio and television. This was the FTC's third annual report, and the first in which a majority of the members supported such a ban. Sen. Warren G. Magnuson, (D Wash.), chairman of the Senate Commerce Committee, said the Committee would give the recommendation "serious consideration."

The FTC also renewed its 1965 demand that all forms of cigarette advertising carry warnings of the health hazards involved in smoking. In 1965, the FTC recommended that a strongly worded warning appear on all cigarette packages and in all cigarette advertising. However, the bill enacted by Congress (PL 89-92) required only a weak warning on cigarette packages, and it stipulated that no other statement be required to appear on packages or in advertising before June 30, 1969. *(See above.)*

In an Aug. 16 report, the Surgeon General's Task Force for Smoking and Health charged that the tobacco industry was "encouraging death and disease" by its advertising practices. The report cited the "inability or unwillingness of the cigarette industry to face up to the health hazards of cigarette smoking or even to admit that they exist."

The Tobacco Institute Inc., spokesman for the major tobacco companies, replied that the report was "a shockingly intemperate defamation of an industry which has led the way in medical research to seek answers in the cigarette controversy." The Institute asserted that Task Force members were "biased against cigarettes."

Pollution Developments

Congress in 1968 continued to study the problems of pollution but enacted no significant legislation in the field.

Both the Senate and House passed a comprehensive water pollution bill but failed to complete action on the measure before adjournment of the 90th Congress. *(See chapter on Water and Power.*

In other Congressional action, a House Science and Astronautics subcommittee held hearings on pollution of the environment and the science resources available to support environmental quality.

A Senate Public Works subcommittee held hearings on air quality standards promulgated by the Secretary of Health, Education and Welfare under the Air Quality Act of 1967. *(See above.)*

Air Quality Board. President Johnson July 25 named 15 members of an Air Quality Advisory Board, which was established under provisions of the Air Quality Act of 1967 (PL 90-148). Wilbur J. Cohen, Secretary of Health, Education and Welfare, was designated as chairman. Members included representatives of state and local governments and of groups interested in air pollution and its prevention.

Air Pollution. The creation of a three-year, $10-million research program designed to gain new knowledge of air pollution by automobiles was announced Feb. 14. John T. Middleton, director of the National Air Pollution Control Center in Washington, D.C., said the costs of the program would be shared by the Federal Government, the American Petroleum Institute and the Automobile Manufacturers Assn. He said the study would be directed by the Coordinating Research Council. The Council was sponsored by the Society of Automotive Engineers and the American Petroleum Institute.

Drug Pricing Controversy Highlights Health Investigations

Mounting Congressional concern over the high cost of prescription drugs was reflected in the 1967-68 hearings of the Senate Select Small Business Subcommittee on Monopoly, under the chairmanship of Sen. Gaylord Nelson (D Wis.). The Small Business Committee is not a legislative committee and cannot send bills to the Senate; however, its investigation prompted a variety of legislative proposals, none of which was enacted by the 90th Congress.

1967 Action

The Nelson subcommittee's 1967 hearings focused chiefly on the comparative cost and effectiveness of generic and trade-name drugs.

It was generally conceded that trade-name drugs tended to be more expensive than their generic equivalents, but drug industry representatives attributed the higher prices to better quality controls and to research and development expenses. Further, it was argued that drugs with different trade names but the same generic equivalent did not necessarily offer the same therapeutic value. Other witnesses contended that drug industry profits were unduly high, in part because of manufactures' promotion of brand-name drugs, and that there was no real competition among the big drug manufacturers. Dr. James L. Goddard, Commissioner of the Food and Drug Administration, warned against over-simplification of the issue of generic versus trade-name drugs.

Meanwhile, the Senate Nov. 21 went on record as favoring generic, rather than trade-name, prescribing under federally financed programs. The action came during Senate consideration of the Social Security Amendments of 1967 (HR 12080) when the Senate adopted, on a 43-37 roll call, an amendment sponsored by Finance Committee Chairman Russell B. Long (D La.). The amendment required the Government to provide reimbursement under federal-aid programs for drugs prescribed and dispensed chiefly by their generic or established name rather than by trade name. The amendment, however, was deleted in conference. *(See chapter on Welfare.)*

Congress had not shown so much interest in drug costs since the Kefauver drug investigation of 1960 and enactment of the Drug Amendments of 1962. *(Congress and the Nation, Vol. I, p. 1181.)* Renewed Congressional interest was prompted by two developments.

First, with the passage in 1965 of the Medicare law, the Federal Government became more actively involved in financing drug purchases. Through the hospital insurance aspect of Medicare, reimbursement was provided to the aged for all drugs dispensed in hospitals and nursing homes. Coupled with this, the Title XIX Medicaid program substantially enlarged Government medical aid to the needy, thereby increasing not only federal but state expenditures on drug purchases.

Second, there was growing Congressional support for legislation that would expand the Medicare program to provide reimbursement for all drugs purchased by the elderly, not simply those dispensed to Medicare patients in institutions. It was estimated that such an expansion of Medicare would obligate the Federal Government to an additional $200 million a year in drug costs. An amendment to provide this coverage was offered during Senate action on the 1967 Social Security bill but was rejected, 37-33, on a tabling motion.

Powerful pressure groups were involved in the drug debate. The Pharmaceutical Manufacturers Assn. (PMA) and the American Medical Assn. (AMA) were wary of any increased federal action dealing with drugs. The PMA was especially apprehensive about possible federal control over drug prices. The AMA feared federal efforts to dictate how drugs should be prescribed by doctors. Together the two constituted a well funded and vigorous lobby.

Arrayed on the side of greater federal participation both in improving coverage of drug purchases and in bringing down prices were the same groups that lobbied so long for the passage of Medicare. Chief among them were labor, represented by the AFL-CIO and the United Auto Workers, and the elderly, especially the labor-supported National Council of Senior Citizens. Furthermore, the retail druggists' organization and the American Pharmaceutical Assn., representing 44,000 pharmacists, enthusiastically supported expanding Medicare to cover outpatient drugs.

1968 Action

In early 1968, the Subcommittee narrowed its field of inquiry to concentrate on the use and misuse of the wonder drug chloramphenicol, marketed by Parke-Davis under the brand name of Chloromycetin since 1949. According to experts, the drug's first and best use was for treatment of typhus and salmonella infections. On Feb. 6 and 8, the Subcommittee heard testimony from doctors who said that the drug was being "overprescribed." Doctors were using the potent wonder drug for minor illnesses, such as colds and acne, the testimony showed. In addition, evidence was presented that Chloromycetin could cause aplastic anemia by attacking the victim's bone marrow, where blood cells are made. In spite of this, the witnesses said, Parke-Davis had continued to tout the drug although U.S. Food and Drug Administration (FDA) warnings appeared prominently on its labels.

Late in the year, the panel's hearings centered on the sales and promotion practices of the drug industry.

Dr. Philip R. Lee, Assistant Secretary of the Department of Health, Education and Welfare (HEW), testified Sept. 25 that "most of the drug information received by practicing physicians comes from the advertising and promotional activities of drug companies—from printed and graphic advertisements and from drug salesmen...."

He said that "currently the drug industry is spending nearly $500 million on drug research and an estimated $600 million on drug advertising, drug detailing, and other forms of promotion. The sheer amount of this material has reached super-saturation proportions and contributes, I am certain, to increasing confusion among doctors."

Lee recommended that a federal drug compendium be issued on all drugs "with some indication of relative costs," and also called for "the Federal Government (to) either publish or support publication of a journal which would provide up-to-date guidelines on drug therapy."

Lee also said that a task force he headed which was studying the problems involved in extending Medicare to out-of-hospital prescription drugs had determined that "—except in rare instances—drugs which are chemically equivalent, and which meet all official standards, can be expected to produce essentially the same biological or clinical effects." That finding backed up the argument for the use of generic names in precribing drugs, he said. *(For task force report, see below.)*

In a statement issued Sept. 25, the Pharmaceutical Manufacturers Assn. (PMA) said that the hearings were planned "to create a climate of public acceptance for price control legislation on prescription drugs."

Related Developments

Compendium. President Johnson March 4 asked Congress to authorize the publication of a U.S. compendium of drugs to be circulated among doctors, pharmacists and hospitals. Congress did not act on the proposal (HR 15759, S 2944).

Drug Report. A report on prescription drugs released Sept. 13 by the Department of Health, Education and Welfare (HEW) challenged many of the drug industry's arguments for the current system of drug manufacture, pricing and prescribing. The report was an interim report of the Task Force on Prescription Drugs headed by Dr. Lee.

The report said that the difference between the effectiveness of brand-name drugs and chemically equivalent drugs sold under their generic names had been "grossly exaggerated as a major hazard to public health."

Recommendations. The report recommended that HEW continue to give high priority to current clinical trials to determine the biological equivalency of important chemical equivalents. It said also that the establishment and "rigid enforcement" of quality control standards in drug production were essential to ensuring clinical equivalency and recommended that the necessary inspections for such a program be carried out through the FDA.

The report also contained a number of recommendations designed to improve the prescribing practices of physicians. It said that the ability of an individual physician to make sound judgements in view of the great number of drugs available and large amounts of promotional advice from drug companies was "a matter of serious concern to leading clinicians, scientists and medical educators." The report said that the most effective way to improve physicians' prescribing practices was to improve medical education, particularly in the area of clinical pharmacology, and supply practicing physicians with objective data on drugs. To achieve these ends, the Task Force recommended expanding aid to medical schools, HEW support of a publication providing "objective, up-to-date information and guidelines on drug therapy" and the publication of a drug compendium listing all prescription drugs with dosage forms, recommedations for use and price information on each product.

Drug Prices. The Task Force said drug prices reflected research and development costs that were "rel-atively high in comparison with other industries and included "a substantial degree of effort" put into producing drugs similar to ones already on the market. Prices also included high promotion costs directed primarily at physicians. It said that "the exceptionally high rate of profit which generally marks the drug industry is not accompanied by any peculiar degree of risk, or by any unique difficulties in obtaining growth capital, and that industry profits have not been significantly reduced by new governmental regulations concerning drug safety, drug efficacy, or drug advertising."

Patents. The Task Force proposed no changes in existing laws involving drug patents and trademarks but called for a joint study by a number of Government departments to consider permitting new drugs to be marketed only under their generic names and shortening the patent life on drugs from the current 17 years.

Medicare. Wilbur J. Cohen, Secretary of HEW, in a statement Sept. 13 on the Task Force report, said it "does not yet answer the question of how prescription drugs can be included in the Medicare program. I have already proposed that such drugs should be covered as a Medicare benefit, but the details of a program—the reimbursement methods, the administrative techniques, the financing approaches, and other significant matters— are still under study."

Other Health Investigations

DOCTORS AND MEDICAL SALES. The Senate Judiciary Subcommittee on Antitrust and Monopoly, under the chairmanship of Sen. Philip A. Hart (D Mich.) held hearings in 1965 and 1967 on the propriety of physician ownership of pharmacies, drug repackaging concerns, optical dispensaries and the like. In 1968, the Subcommittee's hearings focused on the dispensing of diet pills.

The question of a possible conflict of interest on the part of physicians who owned companies that sold products they prescribed first came to the attention of Congress as a result of the hearings on the Kefauver-Harris Drug Amendments of 1962. *(Congress and the Nation, Vol. I, p. 1181.)*

The Subcommittee held hearings in 1964 on doctor-owned pharmacies and drug repackaging companies and issued a report on its investigation in 1965. The report said about 140 physician-owned repackaging companies in more than 30 states had been identified by the Subcommittee. In addition, the report said, many doctors owned shares in pharmacies.

The Subcommittee in 1965 also held hearings on physicians who dispensed eyeglasses. Hart subsequently introduced a bill to prohibit doctors from profiting from the sale of products they prescribed, but Congress took no action.

In 1967, Hart introduced a new measure (S 260) to prohibit physicians from selling drugs, eyeglasses or other devices, from receiving rebates from companies that sell precriptions, and from having a financial interest in a pharmacy or optical dispensary. No action was taken on the bill, which was opposed by the American Medical Assn. (AMA).

Dr. James Z. Appel, immediate past president of the AMA, stated the AMA position that dispensing drugs and devices was "a privilege granted to physicians in order that they may best serve the public interest." He said the bill would "withdraw the privilege entirely, regardless of its benefits for the many, because it is abused by the insignificant few." Patients were not being exploited, he said, if they obtained from their doctor "devices needed for their medical treatment at prices no higher than...elsewhere...with equal or greater convenience and with equal or greater confidence." He acknowledged that the AMA position on doctors who own pharmacies had been altered over the years through the "democratic processes" of its house of delegates. He contended that S 260 would give "to pharmacists and other suppliers a virtual monopoly in the sale of drugs and devices" and, therefore would increase "exploitation" by reducing competition. "The key factor," he said, was "to preserve the freedom of choice of the patient." As for eye care, he said the bill would create the "peculiar situation" that an opthalmologist was trusted in treatment and surgery of his patients' eyes but not in the dispensing of glasses or contact lenses.

In 1968, the Subcommittee turned its attention to the diet pill industry and the practices of "obesity doctors." Hart said Americans spent $250 million a year in obesity specialists' offices and another $120 million on the diet pills prescribed by the doctors. The 1968 hearings were highlighted by testimony from Susanna McBee, a Washington correspondent for *Life* magazine, who related her experiences while on assignment from *Life* to write a story about the diet pill industry. Miss McBee said she visited 10 obesity doctors from whom she collected a total of 1,479 tablets and capsules. All of the pills prescribed for Miss McBee were either sold to her at the doctor's office or at a pharmacy specified by the doctor, she said.

Dr. James L. Goddard, FDA Commissioner, told the Subcommittee that "there are no drugs which can safely control the problem of obesity." He announced that the FDA would move "momentarily" to seize supplies of a combination thyroid-digitalis drug, sold by about 25 drug companies and widely used by obesity doctors. Goddard said the FDA had felt for almost a decade that use of the combination drug was "irrational and hazardous." It was not until 1967, he continued, that the agency received a report of a death associated with use of the drug, which enabled the FDA to institute proceedings against companies producing the drug. The combination, Goddard said, had been on the market since 1938.

Criticized by Hart for slowness in moving against the drug, Goddard said "it seems to me that more aggressive action could well have been justified at an earlier date."

MEDICAL COSTS. In other 1968 action, the Senate Government Operations Subcommittee on Executive Reorganization held hearings on medical costs and the organization of health care. Several witnesses called for greater coordination of health services to improve medical care. Gov. Nelson A. Rockefeller (R N.Y.) proposed a federal program of universal health insurance "coupled with hospital cost controls."

Federal Education Programs

SUPPORT of elementary and secondary education is primarily a local responsibility; college education traditionally has been furnished by the states and private citizens. Yet in the 1967-68 school year, the Federal Government provided 7.2 percent of all funds spent on elementary and secondary education and 24 percent of higher education funds—more than the states' 22.8 percent contribution. *(See box on next page.)*

Direct federal contributions to education date back to the Morrill Act of 1862, establishing land-grant colleges in the states. But federal involvement grew slowly over the next 100 years. A dramatic change occurred in the middle 1960s—a landmark period in American education.

By 1966, the Federal Government was aiding education at all levels, from pre-school through graduate school to adult education for those bypassed along the way. From nursery schools to university campuses, it would be hard in the late 1960s to find a single pupil, teacher or classroom not in some way affected by the Federal Government's interest and assistance.

From the Morrill Act which helped establish colleges to the Smith-Hughes Act of 1917 which supported vocational training at the high school level, the Government moved piecemeal into the education field. In the 1940s and 1950s Congress authorized the Government to buy school lunches, to supply funds to improve the teaching of science, mathematics and foreign languages, to lend colleges money to build dormitories, to educate veterans and to grant funds for school construction, operation and teachers' salaries in areas "impacted" by tax-free federal property and the school-age children of federal employees.

Until 1965, however, no aid program was enacted which could be considered a general subsidy for education or for college students. The Elementary and Secondary Education Act of 1965 launched a federal program so broad in application as to constitute the first general aid-to-education program ever adopted by Congress. In the same year the Government for the first time assumed responsibility, in the Higher Education Act, to pay for a college education for talented but needy students.

Reference

For Congressional action on education legislation in the 1945-64 period, see *Congress and the Nation*, Vol. I, p. 1195-1224.

Elementary and Secondary Education

Until the 1940s it was a truism that responsibility for the lower levels of education rested entirely in the states and local communities. But growing financial strains on local and state governments and the greater taxing power of the Federal Government led to slowly rising support in Congress for some general kind of federal contribution to education. A key portent was the conversion of the pre-eminent leader of conservative Republicanism, Sen. Robert A. Taft (R Ohio 1939-53). Taft declared in 1946 that the nation's schools no longer could provide an adequate education for all without federal assistance.

Two years later, the Senate for the first time passed a general school aid bill, but the House remained opposed to the concept. It did not give in until 1960, only to see final action on the legislation stymied by the Rules Committee, which refused to let the House-passed bill be sent to conference with the Senate. Five years later, the first broad general-aid bill was enacted.

Over the years, opposition to general aid was based primarily on the contention that federal aid meant federal control of the schools, particularly if teachers' salaries and textbooks were part of the aid package. Two other basic issues added to the controversy: the Government's position with regard to racially segregated schools and church-related schools.

The segregation issue reached its peak after the Supreme Court's 1954 decision outlawing the doctrine of "separate but equal" schools. It was largely resolved by the Civil Rights Act of 1964, which authorized federal court suits for desegregation of schools and the withholding of federal funds from institutions that practiced segregation. *(See chapter on Civil Rights.)*

The church-state issue, based on the First Amendment's ban on federal laws concerning religion, was not resolved until 1965. Legislation in the late 1940s had proposed to let the states spend federal education funds as they did their own tax revenues, supporting public schools and, in some states, parochial schools as well. Opposition to this proposal was too strong to overcome, and in the next decade Congress considered legislation that would specifically prohibit aid to private schools. Opposition then came from the Roman Catholic church and its spokesmen in Congress. The impasse continued until, in the 1965 Act, federal aid was focused on disadvantaged children no matter what kind of school they attended.

Elementary and Secondary
Education Act (ESEA)

This Act, the first general aid to education law (PL 89-10), was signed by President Johnson April 11, 1965, outside the former one-room schoolhouse at Stonewall, Texas, where he first attended classes. The President, a former school teacher himself, said no measure he had "signed, or will ever sign, means more to the future of America."

Enactment of the law took only three months—largely because old controversies were stilled by the new emphasis on aid to children, not schools, and because the Democratic party had achieved huge majorities in Congress in the November 1964 elections. To make sure there was no hang-up in conference, the Senate accepted the bill exactly as the House had passed it, which was almost as submitted by the Johnson Administration.

The heart of the Act was Title I, which directed its funds to school districts on the basis of the number of children from low-income families in the area. Thus, although 95 percent of the nation's counties were eligible for aid, the bulk of the money was to be concentrated on the inner city and impoverished rural areas where the neediest children lived.

The appeal to all geographical segments was underlined by Title I's formula for providing federal funds,

which was based on each state's average spending per student and its number of children from low-income families. Thus it appealed to the poorer states by taking into account their many poor children and to the richer states by recognizing their higher expenditures per child. The formula was made more generous to the poorer states in 1966 by permitting them to use the national average expenditure per child instead of their own, smaller figure.

The church-state controversy which had blocked so many school bills in the past was overcome by ESEA's focus on aid to needy children rather than schools. The school districts were directed to include private school children in compensatory programs and to lend (but not give) federally funded school books to needy private school children. Such aid was not comprehensive enough to offend powerful opponents of private school aid and was satisfactory to lobbyists for aid to parochial schools.

Summary of ESEA Provisions

Following are the main provisions of the Elementary and Secondary Education Act (ESEA) as passed in 1965 and amended in 1966 and 1967. Technically, the entire Act was an amendment to the "impacted area" school law of 1950 (PL 81-874), but it is generally treated as an entirely separate law.

Title I. This title allocated funds to local school districts (through state agencies) under a formula that multiplied the number of school children from low-income families (under $2,000 a year or on public assistance) by one-half of the state's average expenditure per school child. In 1966 Congress raised the low-income figure to $3,000, to take effect in fiscal 1968, but the next year this provision was made conditional upon the availability of sufficient appropriations to fulfill the goal. With appropriations for fiscal 1968 and 1969 falling far short of amounts authorized in the revised formula, the new income level was not put into effect.

The 1966 amendments to ESEA made another change in the formula, one that greatly benefited the poorer states. It allowed any state to use the national average expenditure per school child, instead of its own expenditure figure, in determining its Title I allotments. As a result, most Southern states received a substantial increase; the poorest state, Mississippi, went from $23.5 million in fiscal 1967 to $44.8 million in fiscal 1968.

"Incentive" grants were authorized but not funded. They were to go to states that spent a larger share of their resources on education than the national average.

The purposes for which Title I funds could be used were largely left up to the local school districts. The Act said only that the money was for programs "designed to meet the special educational needs of educationally deprived children." The schools could reduce their class sizes, hire remedial reading teachers, buy special equipment, serve breakfasts at school—the possibilities were endless.

Private school children, however, had to be included in some of the programs. The Act said the local school agency must make provision for special services (such as dual enrollment, educational TV programs or mobile educational facilities) in which private school children could participate.

Spending by Educational Institutions and Sources of Funds

(in billions)

	School Years		
	1957-58	**1963-64**	**1967-68**
Total Spending, all levels	$21.1	$36.2	$54.6
Elementary, secondary schools	$15.8	$24.9	$35.8
Sources of funds			
Public schools:			
Federal	.7 (4.1%)	1.0 (4.0%)	2.6 (7.2%)
State	4.8 (30.4)	8.1 (32.5)	12.0 (33.5)
Local	8.4 (53.5)	12.5 (50.2)	17.0 (47.5)
Other	.0	.1	.1
Nonpublic schools			
Nonpublic sources	1.9 (12.0)	3.2 (13.3)	4.1 (11.8)
Higher Education	$ 5.3	$11.3	$18.8
Sources of funds			
Public institutions:			
Federal	.4 (7.5%)	1.1 (9.7%)	2.2 (11.7%)
State	1.4 (26.4)	2.5 (22.1)	4.2 (22.3)
Local	.1 (1.9)	.3 (2.7)	.5 (2.7)
Other	1.2 (22.6)	2.5 (22.1)	4.3 (22.9)
Nonpublic institutions:			
Federal	.3 (5.7)	1.1 (9.7)	2.3 (12.2)
State, local	.0	.1 (0.9)	.1 (0.5)
Other	1.9 (35.8)	3.7 (32.7)	5.2 (27.7)

SOURCE: Department of Health, Education and Welfare

Significant Federal Aid-to-Education Laws

1862. The **Morrill Act** provided for grants of federal land to each state for establishment of colleges specializing in agriculture and mechanical arts. These became known as "land-grant colleges." The original Act authorized grants to the states of 30,000 acres of land, or the equivalent in scrip, for each U.S. Representative and each U.S. Senator to which the state was entitled in 1860. The proceeds from the grants were to be used for support of the colleges. After several land-grant colleges had been in operation for a number of years, and the states were having difficulty supporting them, Congress in the second Morrill Act of 1890 authorized annual federal grants to the states for the operation of the colleges. The purpose of the Morrill Acts was to provide both liberal and practical education for the working classes.

Unlike later education laws, federal grants under the Morrill Act remained small. In the 1960s they amounted to $14.5 million a year, spread among 67 land-grant colleges in the 50 states and Puerto Rico.

1917. The **Smith-Hughes Act** set up the first program of federal grants-in-aid to promote vocational education in the public schools below college grade. Funds were provided for courses and teacher training in the fields of agriculture, home economics, trades and industries. This was extended and expanded over the years.

1940. The **Lanham Act** authorized federal aid to local governments for construction, maintenance, and operation of facilities, including schools. Aid was given to communities with populations swollen by increased military personnel and defense workers. This was the forerunner of temporary legislation between 1946 and 1950 for "emergency" school aid and, beginning in 1950, "impacted" areas aid.

1944. The servicemen's Readjustment Act **GI Bill of Rights** set up a program of educational benefits for World War II veterans which was unprecedented in scope. A more limited program was provided for veterans of the Korean war, and in 1965 a similar bill for "Cold War GIs" was enacted.

1950. The **National Science Foundation** was established to promote scientific research, through extensive grants to scholars, and the education of future scientists, through scholarships and graduate fellowships. The emphasis was on the physical sciences, mathematics and engineering.

1958. The reaction to Russia's achievements in space, the **National Defense Education Act** was drawn up to encourage the study of science, mathematics, engineering and foreign languages at all levels of the education system. It provided the first general federal loan program for college students (NDEA loans).

1963. Colleges and universities, facing severe financial pressures and a swiftly growing student population, began receiving massive amounts of aid for construction of classroom buildings in the **Higher Education Facilities Act** of 1963.

1964. The **Economic Opportunity Act**, President Johnson's vehicle for his war on poverty, launched the Head Start program for pre-school children and a smaller program of adult education.

1965. The 89th Congress enacted two historic education bills in 1965, the **Elementary and Secondary Education Act**, whose main focus was on disadvantaged children in city slums and rural areas, and the **Higher Education Act**, which furnished federal scholarships for needy students, financed college library books and established the Teacher Corps to help out in overburdened schools.

Reviewing the first three years of the program, HEW Secretary Wilbur J. Cohen said in January 1969 that the trend among participating schools was to put "increasing stress on activities most directly serving the student's needs: improving the quality of instruction and offering such services as medical care, guidance and counseling, and food." The percentage of money spent on construction and equipment had dropped sharply from the first year, while the proportion spent on instruction and, to a much smaller extent, services had increased, Cohen said.

Over 9 million children participated each year in Title I programs, about 500,000 of whom were private school students. In addition, children of migrant farmworkers, residents in state institutions for neglected, handicapped or delinquent children, and those attending Indian schools received separate Title I allotments.

The failure to appropriate up to the level authorized, however, meant a reduction in per capita spending over the first three years. The number of poor children covered in the formula went up from 5,600,000 to 6,670,000 be-tween 1966 and 1968 while the amount spent per child declined from $210 to $173. (The other children included in the 9 million Title I total were attending the same schools as the "formula" children but were from families with incomes above the Act's poverty definition.)

Authorizations under the formula rose from $1 billion for fiscal 1966 to $2.7 billion for fiscal 1969, but appropriations stayed close to the original $1 billion, reaching only $1,123,000,000 in fiscal 1969, a slight drop from fiscal 1968.

Title II. Unchanged since its enactment in 1965, Title II authorized federal grants to the states for school library resources, textbooks and other printed material for the use of children and teachers in public and private schools. To avoid conflict with the First Amendment's clause on religion, the ESEA specified that title and control of all materials furnished under Title II must remain with a public agency and that all materials, including books, must have been approved for use in public schools.

Because many states and school boards provide free textbooks for their schools, the emphasis under Title II has been on library resources. Almost $300 million was appropriated for the program in ESEA's first three years.

Title III. This title was designed to introduce innovative programs into the schools. Federal grants were provided for supplementary educational centers and services that could serve as models for regular school programs or as centralized supplements to the curricula of individual schools.

The Act specified a number of different services that might be offered, including: specialized equipment and instruction for students in advanced scientific subjects and foreign languages; art and music courses; production of educational radio and TV programs; special services for people in rural areas, including mobile units; and counseling and social services to encourage dropouts and adults to resume their education.

Originally, grants were made directly from the U.S. Commissioner of Education to the agencies applying for funds, although there was a general allotment of funds by state, based on their population.

In 1967 Congress rewrote the program to give most of the control to state education agencies. State plans for use of the funds were to be drawn up, and after fiscal 1969 the state agencies would distribute all of the money. However, 15 percent of the funds were to be spent on special programs for handicapped children. (Title VI of ESEA, which was added in 1966, was directed entirely at handicapped children.)

Authorizations for Title III programs, like those for Title I, increased sharply over the years but appropriations remained relatively stable. The program began with a $100 million authorization and jumped to $500 million for fiscal 1968 and $528 million for fiscal 1969. Appropriations for the last two years, however, were only $208 million and $165 million, respectively, a drop reflecting dissatisfaction with results under the program.

Title IV. The Cooperative Research Act of 1954, providing federal construction aid for educational re-

School-Aid Authorizations for Fiscal Years

	1966	1967	1968	1969	1970
Elementary and Secondary Education Act:					
Title I—Educationally deprived children			$2,563,067,584	$2,725,959,699	$2,862,175,945
Special incentive grants			——	50,000,000	50,000,000
Title II—Libraries and textbooks			154,500,000	167,375,000	206,000,000
Title III—Supplementary education			515,000,000	527,875,000	566,500,000
Title IV—Cooperative research	$100,000,000 [1]	——[1]	——[1]	——[1]	——[1]
Title V—State education departments	25,000,000	30,000,000	65,000,000	80,000,000	80,000,000
Title VI—Handicapped children:					
Regional resource centers	——	——	7,500,000	7,750,000	10,000,000
Deaf-blind children	——	——	1,000,000	3,000,000	7,000,000
Recruitment	——	——	1,000,000	1,000,000	1,000,000
Captioned films	3,000,000	3,000,000	8,000,000	8,000,000	10,000,000
Grants to states	——	50,000,000	154,000,000	167,375,000	206,000,000
Title VII—Bilingual education:					
Aid to school districts	——	——	15,000,000	30,000,000	40,000,000
Teacher training	——	——	11,000,000	10,000,000	10,000,000
Title VIII—					
Rural area information	——	1,500,000	3,500,000	3,700,000	4,000,000
Dropout prevention	——	——	——[2]	30,000,000[2]	30,000,000
Adult Education Act	30,000,000[3]	40,000,000	60,000,000	70,000,000	80,000,000
Impacted areas:					
Construction	50,000,000	85,000,000	62,000,000	66,000,000	66,000,000
Operation-maintenance	365,000,000	419,000,000	477,384,000	510,000,000	545,000,000
TOTALS			$4,097,951,584	$4,458,034,699	$4,773,675,945

1 Funds available for five-year period.
2 Funds available for fiscal 1968 as well as fiscal 1969.
3 Appropriation.

search facilities, had funded research centers on a pilot basis at four universities. In 1965 the program was written into ESEA as Title IV and was expanded to permit contracts or grants to various kinds of research groups. A five-year authorization of $100 million for cooperative research construction was provided, but only $32 million was appropriated through fiscal 1969 and very little of that sum was spent.

Title V. To strengthen state departments of education, Title V of ESEA authorized direct federal grants for such purposes as statewide planning, reporting of educational data and programs to improve the competence of employees of educational agencies and of teacher training efforts.

Originally, 85 percent of each appropriation was to be alloted directly to the states and 15 percent reserved for allotment by the U.S. Commissioner for experimental projects or services that might help state agencies on a regional or nationwide basis. In 1967 the Commissioner's share was reduced to 5 percent. About $30 million a year was appropriated under the title although the authorization permitted $65 million in fiscal 1968 and $80 million the next year.

Title VI. Enacted in 1966, this title authorized federal funds to assist the states in the education of mentally and physically handicapped children. It was expanded in 1967 to include funds to improve the recruitment of personnel for the field, to establish regional resource centers and model centers for deaf-blind children.

Under the state grant program a number of services were provided for the first time: mobile units for rural areas, work-study programs, and special transportation arrangements, for example. Nearly 225,000 children were helped under the program in its first years.

Title VII. At the initiative of Congress, particularly the delegations from California and Texas, a program to improve the education of children from non-English-speaking families was authorized in 1967. About 3 million children of school age were expected to benefit from special programs funded under this Bilingual Education title.

However, although $40 million was authorized for aid to school districts and teacher training in fiscal 1969, the appropriation—the first granted under the program—was only $7.5 million. By contrast, the states had submitted requests for over $40 million, proposing projects in 17 different languages. The emphasis, however, was on teaching children of Mexican and Puerto Rican background.

Title VIII. Two other Congressionally initiated programs were added to this title in 1967. One authorized grants for local programs to prevent school dropouts. The demonstration programs were to focus on schools which have a high concentration of children from low-income families and a high dropout rate. The authorization was for $30 million a year, but the first appropriation, granted in fiscal 1969, was for only $5 million, which was expected to finance five projects.

The second new program in Title VIII authorized a small technical assistance project for rural schools to help them apply for federal aid. In 1968 this was replaced by a more general provision for collection and dissemination of information which was written into the Vocational Education Amendments of 1968.

Federal Control. The 1965 Act stated that there was to be no federal control over the curriculum, selection of books or personnel of any school aided by the ESEA, nor was there to be any payment of funds for religious worship or instruction.

Desegregation. After a bitter battle in 1966, Congress wrote into the law language prohibiting the Federal Government from requiring the assignment or transportation of students or teachers to overcome racial imbalance—in other words, to alter de facto segregation. The provision left intact the Government's authority to require desegregation of schools that were run on a discriminatory basis; it also permitted school districts, if they wanted, to use federal funds for busing students in order to improve the racial balance of their schools.

A time limit was set for determination by the U.S. Commissioner of Education of a district's compliance with the nondiscrimination requirements of the 1964 Civil Rights Act. Title VI of that Act authorized the Commissioner, after holding hearings, to withhold federal funds from any school district found in noncompliance with the Act.

Adult Education. The community action program authorized in the 1964 Economic Opportunity Act, the basic antipoverty law, included as one of its many undertakings projects to upgrade the education of adults. In 1966 Congress transferred this activity to the U.S. Commissioner of Education. Specific authorization of funds for the program was made, and the Federal Government's share of the cost of each local undertaking was set at 90 percent. Most of the money was to go to state agencies for distribution, but 20 percent was reserved for experimental projects funded directly by the Commissioner.

Advance Appropriations. In 1967 Congress granted a request urgently sought by school superintendents. It authorized approval of appropriations one year in advance of the time at which the funds were be be obligated. The purpose was to help school administrators to plan their programs for the next school year. Previously, appropriations often were not available until the school year was well under way, making the hiring of teachers and planning of courses difficult and inefficient.

Teacher Corps

The National Teacher Corps was first proposed in 1965 by Sens. Edward M. Kennedy (D Mass.) and Gaylord Nelson (D Wis.). Kennedy had noted the success of trained volunteers who taught Negro students in Prince Edward County, Va., when the public schools were closed to avoid integration. Nelson was impressed with the impact of former Peace Corps volunteers who participated as teacher interns in ghetto schools in Washington, D.C.

The two Senators offered their Teacher Corps proposal as an amendment to the Higher Education Act. The idea was quickly endorsed by President Johnson and became labeled a Great Society program.

The National Teacher Corps was created by Title V, Part B of the Higher Education Act of 1965 (PL 89-329). The Corps had no difficulty in the Senate, but it survived in conference with the House only after a motion by Albert H. Quie (R Minn.) to delete it was rejected on a 152-226 roll-call vote of the House.

The Corps was designed to improve elementary and secondary education in city slums and impoverished rural areas by sending in teams of an experienced teacher and several young college graduates to strengthen local school programs. The Act authorized the Commissioner of Education to recuit teachers and interns to serve in the Corps for up to two years.

There were two stages in the program—a three-month summer training period at a designated college, followed by an in-service period during which a team was assigned to a local school. The interns had their tuition paid for part-time graduate work at a nearby university.

The primary goal of the program was to improve public education in poverty areas. But the program was also intended to encourage idealistic college graduates to enter training in the country.

PL 89-329 authorized $36,100,000 for fiscal 1966 and $64,715,000 for fiscal 1967. In 1967, in PL 90-35, the Teacher Corps was extended for three years, through fiscal 1970, and the word "National" was removed from its name. Authorizations for the Corps were set at $33 million in fiscal 1968, $46 million in 1969 and $56 million in 1970.

Appropriations for the Corps came slowly and were far below the authorized amounts. The first appropriation was not granted until six months after the Teacher Corps was approved by Congress; it appropriated $9.5 million. For fiscal 1967, $11.3 million was appropriated in two segments. The next year, President Johnson asked for $33 million for the Corps and Congress allowed only $13.5 million. Finally, in 1968, Congress put its stamp of approval on the program, approving with little controversy two-thirds of the money requested; the fiscal 1969 appropriation was $20.9 million compared to the request for $31.2 million.

Opposition to the Teacher Corps was always something of a mystery. It was extremely popular with school authorities; it provided direct assistance to the neediest schools while at the same time training young school teachers to cope with the most difficult of educational problems. To overcome opposition, Congress specified that not only the local schools but also the state agencies must request the assignment of Teacher Corpsmen and that 10 percent of their salaries must be furnished by the schools they were serving. The opposition came from the "conservative coalition" of Republicans and Southern Democrats and was generally based on the need to economize in federal spending.

Impacted Area Schools

Although no general school aid program was approved by Congress until 1965, from 1950 on there were two highly popular programs of federal grants to build and operate schools and pay teachers in federally "impacted" areas. The programs were begun as the outgrowths of federal commitments in the Lanham Act of 1940 to provide school aid in areas where federal activities brought in more families and reduced taxable property. Amendments raising the amount of federal support and liberalizing the qualifications for aid over the following 10 years led to a broad program which some Congressmen, mainly those from recipient areas, said merely honored a federal commitment to supplant lost taxes, and which others, mainly those from non-recipient areas, and those who supported general school aid, said had developed into a massive, "pork barrel."

Repeatedly, Presidents Eisenhower, Kennedy and Johnson were rebuffed in attempts to cut back the impacted areas program to what they said would represent more accurately the need of each "impacted" district.

The two 1950 laws (PL 81-815 and 81-874) authorized federal grants to areas "impacted" by tax-free federal property and installations, Indian reservations or Government contractors. PL 815 authorized federal payments for school construction; PL 874 authorized federal payments for building maintenance and teachers' salaries. The two laws did not authorize specific money appropriations but set criteria for determining whether a school district was entitled to assistance and, if so, how much it could receive.

Under PL 874 the Government paid 100 percent of the local share of the cost of educating each child whose parents both lived and worked on federal property (Section A). It paid 50 percent of the local share of the cost of educating children whose parents lived or worked on taxable property (Section B). It also authorized payments of 100 percent the first year and 50 percent the second where there were sudden increases in federal contract activity (Section C).

Under PL 815, the Government paid 95 percent of the cost per pupil of construction for Section A children, 50 percent for Section B children and 45 percent for Section C children.

Section A of both laws was permanent; the others carried expiration dates.

College and Graduate Education

Unlike the elementary and secondary field, federal aid to institutions of higher education was well established before 1965. But the period 1965-68 produced a dramatic new emphasis on aid to college students, especially those from families who could not afford a college education for their children.

Federal scholarships were authorized in the Higher Education Act of 1965, though they were disguised as "educational opportunity grants," not scholarships. The same Act also authorized interest subsidies on private loans to middle-income students and transferred the anti-poverty agency's work-study program for college students to the Office of Education.

Federal financing of direct loans to students dated back to the 1958 National Defense Education Act (NDEA); the subsidized-interest program was intended to replace NDEA loans, but Congress insisted on retaining both programs. As interest rates zoomed up in 1966 and again in 1968, the private, subsidized program fell far below expectations in the number of students it helped. A plan, popular with some Congressmen and endorsed by the Republican party, to offer tax credits for college education costs never was authorized.

The principal laws aiding colleges and universities were:

College Housing

The 1950 Housing Act authorized 40-year, low-interest Government loans to public and private colleges and universities for construction of dormitories and infirmaries. The program was operated through a revolving fund administered by the Housing and Home Finance Agency, which became the Department of Housing and Urban Development. The agency was authorized to borrow $300 million from the Treasury to set up the fund, and this authorization was regularly reviewed. In 1965 a flat 3 percent interest rate was set on the loans. To avoid the costs involved, the Administration asked Congress in 1968 to phase out the direct loan program in favor of subsidized interest on private loans. Congress assented but also demanded continuation of the regular loan program. By July 1, 1968, the direct loan revolving fund amounted to $3,775,000,000.

Classrooms

A more controversial program of federal aid for college classroom construction was included in the Higher Education Facilities Act of 1963. The Act authorized $1.2 billion over three years in federal grants and loans for facilities at public and private colleges and universities. The funds for grants were earmarked for libraries and classrooms where science, engineering, mathematics or modern language courses were taught.

When the program was extended in 1965, these categorical restrictions, similar to those in the original NDEA law, were removed.

By fiscal 1969, annual authorizations for the program had reached $936 million for grants for undergraduate facilities, $120 million for graduate facilities and $400 million in loans.

National Defense Education Act (NDEA)

Enacted in 1958 in reaction to Russian achievements in space technology, symbolized by the 1957 orbiting of the first earth satellite (Sputnik), and in awareness of the country's need for more scientists, the NDEA focused on encouraging the study of science, mathematics and foreign languages. All school levels were covered by the Act. Its major titles provided equipment for elementary and secondary schools; financed loans for college students; and authorized three-year graduate fellowships, with preference for prospective college teachers.

By the end of 1968, after several extensions, NDEA's focus on limited, mainly scientific, categories was ended and aid for study of almost all subjects was authorized under the Act. For the principal programs the 1968 extension authorized: $130 million in fiscal 1970 for purchase of equipment for lower schools, plus an additional $160 million for schools receiving ESEA Title I funds (those in disadvantaged areas); $275 million for student loans; and 7,500 new graduate fellowships a year, with matching payments to the graduate schools of $3,500 per fellow.

The NDEA student loans grew out of a proposal by President Eisenhower in 1958 for 10,000 federal scholarships a year. The House Education and Labor Committee reported a bill providing 23,000 scholarships and, in addition, $220 million for a federal student loan fund. The scholarship provision was stripped from the bill on

Aid to College Students

Following are the major federal financial programs enabling students to attend college. All are administered by the Office of Education with the exception of the Cold War GI Bill, which is administered by the Veterans Administration.

Cost figures are in *millions* of dollars.

	Fiscal 1968		Fiscal 1969	
	Students	Cost	Students	Cost
Educational opportunity grants	292,600	$131.4	258,600	$133.8
NDEA direct loans	429,000	181.8	442,000	193.4
Insured loans	515,408	39.9	750,000	71.2
Work-study grants	375,000	133.8	375,000	146.1
Special programs for the disadvantaged:				
Upward Bound	25,368 }	$ 35.4	26,000 }	33.8
Talent Search	115,000 }		115,000 }	
Cold War GI Bill	471,696	$428.7	605,008	$619.4

SOURCE: Federal Budget, fiscal 1970, and Veterans Administration.

the floor, and the $120 million authorized for the scholarships was added to the loan fund. The Senate version was accepted in conference and became law. Under its provisions, the Federal Government provided 90 percent and the individual schools 10 percent of the money in loan funds set up and administered by each participating college.

Under NDEA, undergraduates were eligible for loans of up to $1,000 a year, not to exceed $5,000 during a student's undergraduate years. The 3-percent interest rate did not go into effect until the repayment period began, nine months after the student left college. The repayment could be deferred up to a total of three years while the recipient was attending graduate school or serving in the armed forces, the Peace Corps or Volunteers in Service to America (VISTA). Repayment could extend over a 10-year period.

If the borrower became a full-time school teacher or college professor, half of the loan was cancelled at 10 percent for each year of teaching. If he taught at designated "hardship" schools in low-income areas or was a teacher of handicapped children, he could have the additional 50 percent cancelled at 15 percent a year.

To receive a loan, students had to sign an oath of loyalty to the United States.

Since the loans were made directly by the institutions, students applied directly to their colleges.

Office of Education figures showed that through the end of the 1966-67 college year, one million students had borrowed more than $1 billion since the program began.

Work-Study Program

The Economic Opportunity Act of 1964 (PL 88-452), the basic anti-poverty law, authorized grants to colleges to pay 90 percent of the wages of students with part-time jobs in the college or other nonprofit institutions. The grants were to support students from low-income families.

The Higher Education Act of 1965 transferred the work-study program to the Office of Education, removed the requirement that students be from low-income families and permitted colleges to provide their matching share through services and equipment, including tuition and books. The Act authorized $129 million in fiscal 1966, $165 million in fiscal 1967 and $200 million in fiscal 1968. A further extension was made in 1968, raising the authorization to $285 million by fiscal 1971 and setting the federal matching share at 80 percent of the grants.

The work-study program was administered by the colleges, which passed upon the applications of their students and received the matching funds from the Government.

Work under the program was limited to an average of 15 hours a week while classes were in session and 40 hours a week during summers and vacation periods. The on-campus work could be anything from running the soda fountain in the student union to acting as faculty aides or laboratory assistants. Many students spent their summers working in youth programs or as tutors.

The average work-study program provided the student with about $450 a year. Of all the federal programs, work-study was most often used as part of a "package plan" of financial assistance.

Higher Education Act of 1965

Enacted with wide bipartisan support in Congress, the Higher Education Act (PL 89-329) was revolutionary in several aspects, particularly in its student aid provisions. For the first time in U.S. history Congress approved federal scholarships for undergraduate students. The $70 million authorized annually for first-year scholarships was estimated to provide 140,000 students of "exceptional financial need" with scholarships each year. Scholarships had been approved by the Senate in past years only to die in the House. When HR 9567 was first debated by the House, an amendment to remove scholarships from the bill was defeated on a 58-88 standing vote. No further efforts were made to delete the provision.

Another new aid program for college students was insurance on loans, with federal subsidies on interest payments. Federally insured loans had been proposed by President Johnson when he was in Congress, and were subsequently requested by President Kennedy in 1963. Insured loans and scholarships, combined with the expanded work-study program also authorized by the Act, were expected to help students from middle-income as well as low-income backgrounds. They were designed to supplement NDEA loans.

Five titles of the 1965 Act provided aid for colleges and universities. For the first time, funds were voted ($50 million a year) to buy library materials, including books. Other programs in the Act provided grants to develop university extension courses related to community problems and funds to raise the academic quality of impoverished small colleges. The latter program was authorized for only one year because the Senate insisted

on making junior colleges eligible, and the House was opposed.

Another key program established by the Act was the Teacher Corps (*see above*).

HIGHER EDUCATION ACT PROVISIONS

The principal programs in the Act, as amended by Congress in 1966 and 1968 were:

Title I. Matching grants to the states were authorized for community service programs conducted by public or private nonprofit colleges and universities. They were to give particular emphasis to urban and suburban problems, including housing, poverty, employment, transportation, health and other local issues.

Beginning at a $25 million level, the grants rose to an authorized $60 million for fiscal 1971, with the states required to pay one-third of the costs, a reduction from the original 50 percent.

Title II. The library title of the Act, this section authorized basic grants for college library books and materials, special purpose grants for colleges with special needs, training grants to increase the supply of college librarians and to develop new techniques, and a small amount for the cataloging service of the Library of Congress. The 1968 extension of the Act authorized $75 million for this title in fiscal 1970 and $90 million in fiscal 1971.

Title III. Colleges which "are struggling for survival and are isolated from the main currents of academic life," defined as "developing institutions," received special help under this title. The colleges, many of them small, largely Negro institutions in the South, could apply for federal grants to raise the academic quality of their programs. Faculty and student exchange programs with more established colleges were part of the offering, along with national teaching fellowships for graduate students and junior faculty members who wished to strengthen the developing colleges' faculties. Two-year colleges and technical institutes were eligible for aid as well as institutions that grant B.A. degrees. For fiscal 1970 and 1971, $70 million and $91 million, respectively, were authorized for this title of the Higher Education Act.

Title IV. The Student Assistance title of the Act authorized federal scholarships ("educational opportunity grants"), federally insured loans and subsidies on interest for full-time college students and transferred the work-study program authorized in the 1964 Economic Opportunity Act to the Office of Education.

The scholarships section authorized (in Part A) $70 million annually in fiscal 1966-68 for grants to institutions of higher education for first-year scholarships to full-time students "of exceptional financial need," plus whatever sums were necessary to continue scholarships beyond the first year.

It limited the amount of each scholarship to the lesser of $800 or half the amount of financial aid provided the student by the college or a state or private scholarship program, including loans and scholarships under the Act but excluding aid under work-study programs. (To be eligible for a federal scholarship, a student had to receive an equal amount of other financial aid.) A $200 bonus could be awarded scholarship students who in their preceding college year placed in the upper half of their class. In 1968 the bonus was dropped and the maximum scholarship was raised to $1,000.

Scholarship funds were allotted to the states according to the ratio of the number of each state's college students to the number nationally. The colleges receiving funds were forbidden to cut back their other student aid below the average amount furnished in the preceding three years.

Funds were provided for 123,000 first-year students in the 1966-67 school year, for 132,000 in the next year and 140,000 in 1968-69. However, in the fiscal 1969 appropriation bill, covering the 1969-70 school year, the figure dropped to 31,300 students when Congress cut the budget request by $16 million, appropriating $124.6 million. (Scholarships beyond the first year are not included in these figures.)

Upward Bound—A provision in the 1965 Act authorized the U.S. Commissioner of Education to contract with public or private groups for the singling out of talented students who needed encouragement to attend college. This program, known as Talent Search, was directed in the 1968 law to take over, beginning in fiscal 1970, the better known Upward Bound program of the Office of Economic Opportunity, which had similar goals. Funds for the merged programs, including special services to help disadvantaged students stay in college, were set at $56.7 million for fiscal 1970 and $96 million for fiscal 1971.

Guaranteed Loans—Part B of Title IV established a guaranteed, interest-subsidized loan program designed for middle-income families. The program was proposed by the Johnson Administration in the hope that private loans could replace the direct federal cost of NDEA student loans, but Congress clung to the popular NDEA program as well as approving the new program.

The new program sought to encourage state and private nonprofit insurance for student loans and authorized the Federal Government to pay the interest costs while a student was in college and 3 percent during the repayment period on loans made by private sources at a maximum rate of percent. The subsidy was available to families with net income, before taxes, of less than $15,000.

In its first three years, the program fell far below its predicted scope as banks and other lenders found the interest rate too low and the administrative details too cumbersome to be profitable. By the end of 1968 the number of students receiving loans under the program was about 750,000 whereas the goal for the first year alone had been 950,000.

In 1968 Congress set the maximum interest rate at 7 percent and removed the interest subsidy during the after-college repayment period.

Work-Study—The work-study program, originally part of the antipoverty law, became Part C of the Higher Education Act of 1965. (*For description of the program, see above.*)

Cooperative Education—In 1968 Part D was added to Title IV. Entitled Cooperative Education, the program was to encourage alternate periods of full-time study and full-time employment. Beginning in fiscal 1970, grants of $8 million the first year and $10 million the second year could be made to colleges and universities to plan and carry out these programs.

Title V. This title established the Teacher Corps (described in the preceding section on Elementary Education) and a number of programs to improve teacher education, mainly by fellowships for graduate study.

The title was expanded in 1967 and given the name of the Education Professions Development Act. It added special grants for the educational upgrading of persons teaching or preparing to teach in elementary and high schools, and for the recruitment of qualified personnel in areas of critical teacher shortages.

In fiscal 1969, grants to the states of $15 million provided for recruitment and training of about 9,000 persons, one third of them as teacher aides. Grants to institutions to improve the quality of teaching and teacher training benefited 31,725 persons at a cost of $80 million.

Title VI. This title, the equipment section of the Higher Education Act, authorized 50-50 matching grants to the states for laboratory and audiovisual equipment and closed-circuit television equipment. The program was generally funded at $10 to $15 million a year.

Title VII. This title increased the grants for construction of classrooms and other academic facilities and removed the restrictions that limited the kind of facilities to scientific, engineering and library activities. It also set the interest rate on construction loans at a flat 3 percent.

Title VIII. Added to the Act in 1968, this title was given the name Networks for Knowledge. It was intended to encourage colleges to share educational facilities and resources such as closed-circuit TV, computers and special library collections. The Commissioner of Education was authorized to make contracts to facilitate such sharing. Planning funds were authorized for fiscal 1969, plus grants of $4 million in fiscal 1970 and $15 million the next year.

Title IX. Three new programs to encourage professional training were authorized in 1968. Title IX authorized grants to educational institutions for graduate-level courses to train students for careers in state, local and federal governmental service and to provide fellowships. Total grants authorized were $5 million in fiscal 1970 and $13 million in 1971.

Title X. This title provided grants to improve training at the Ph.D. level, authorizing $5 million in fiscal 1970 and $10 million in fiscal 1971. The universities were required to pay one-third of the cost of these projects.

Title XI. The third program authorized contracts with law schools to pay 90 percent of the cost of programs providing clinical experience for law students. The hope was to train more trial lawyers. The authorization was $7.5 million annually in fiscal 1970 and 1971.

Title XII. As in other education acts, this title specified that nothing in the Act authorized any federal control over curriculum or personnel or any aid to religious instruction or departments of divinity. In addition, it specified that there was to be no federal control over college organizations, such as fraternities, which were financed entirely by private funds and whose facilities were not owned by the college.

National Science Foundation

The National Science Foundation was established by Congress in 1950 (PL 81-507) to promote basic scientific research and education of future scientists and to establish and coordinate national scientific policies.

The 1950 Act directed the NSF to "develop and encourage the pursuit of a national policy for the promotion of basic research and education in the sciences." The NSF was authorized to (1) make grants and loans for basic research in the mathematical, physical, medical, biological, engineering and other sciences; (2) undertake military research for national defense; (3) award scholarships and graduate fellowships to U.S. citizens; (4) aid the interchange of information among scientists in the United States and other countries; (5) correlate its programs with private and other public research projects; and (6) maintain a roster of scientific and technical personnel and in other ways provide a central clearinghouse for information on such personnel in the United States.

The Act authorized appropriation of $500,000 to establish the Foundation and get its program under way, and eventual appropriations of $15 million. In the first year of operation, fiscal 1951, the NSF received an appropriation of $225,000. In 1953, the $15-million ceiling was removed, but total appropriations did not exceed that level until 1956. In the next 11 years, appropriations increased rapidly until, in fiscal 1968, they reached a total of $495 million, reflecting a vast enlargement of the Foundation's activities. In fiscal 1969, however, over objections in the Senate, NSF appropriations dropped to $400 million.

Only minor amendments to the 1950 Act were made between 1952 and 1959. Major changes came in 1962, by Presidential initiative, and in 1968, by Congressional order. President Kennedy's 1962 Reorganization Plan No. 2 established a new Office of Science and Technology in the Executive Office of the President and transferred to the new Office the NSF's responsibility for shaping, evaluating and coordinating Government scientific policy Under the Plan, the NSF could continue to originate policy proposals and make recommendations, but the policy was actually set by the Office.

Because the NSF authority had been granted on a permanent basis, the principal Congressional review of the Foundation's operations had come during the annual appropriations process and was conducted by the Appropriations Committees of both chambers. In view of the increasing importance of science, the House in 1959 established a Science and Astronautics Committee and gave it legislative jurisdiction over the NSF, as well as over other scientific matters. Senate jurisdiction was in the Labor and Public Welfare Committee, which handles education bills.

The House Subcommittee on Science, Research and Development, headed by Rep. Emilio Q. Daddario (D Conn.), began the first comprehensive legislative review of the NSF late in 1964. The review resulted in proposed legislation to expand NSF's scope. The House passed the bill in 1966 and again in 1967, only to have the Senate fail to act.

1968 Action. The Senate in 1968 passed a bill that closely followed the language of the 1967 House bill in updating operations of the NSF. It gave the Director greater authority over NSF management, although the National Science Board, to whom he would continue to report, remained responsible for overseeing NSF policies. The bill also enlarged the Foundation's scope so that it could support applied science as well as basic science, and research in the social sciences as well.

A Senate provision required that henceforth the NSF must seek an annual authorization from Congress for its activities. This was the traditional way for Congressional legislative committees to influence an agency's policies and also to inform Appropriations Committee members (sometimes in vain) of emphases the legislative committee members felt should be given to programs.

The House accepted the Senate amendments to its 1967 bill and it became law (PL 90-407) July 18, 1968.

Foundation on Arts and Humanities

After several years of growing Congressional and private support for federal aid for the study, development and presentation of the arts and humanities, Congress in 1965 established a National Foundation on the Arts and Humanities. The final bill was based on an Administration proposal, which was submitted after Congressional hearings had begun on a number of bills introduced in the Senate and House. Earlier attempts to win Congressional approval for federal support of the arts had met with failure, most often because action was blocked in the House.

The National Foundation established in PL 89-209 consisted of two autonomous subdivisions, a National Endowment for the Arts and a National Endowment for the Humanities. Each endowment had a chairman and a 26-member advisory council—one on the arts and one on the humanities. Each endowment was authorized to make grants—most of them to be matched—for a wide range of activities. The operations of the National Foundation were to be coordinated with other federal activities through a nine-member Federal Council on the Arts and the Humanities, made up of representatives of various agencies.

In addition to establishing the Foundation, Pl 89-209 (S 1483) authorized two small programs of financial assistance to be carried out by the Office of Education. These were to help schools buy equipment for teaching the humanities and the arts and to finance training institutes for teachers of these subjects.

The bill authorized appropriations for each endowment of $5 million for each of three fiscal years, 1966, 1967, and 1968. An additional annual maximum of $5 million for the Humanities Endowment and $2.25 million for the Arts Endowment were authorized to match gifts or bequests. Another $2.75 million was authorized for the Arts Endowment for matching grants to state arts agencies of $50,000 annually to each state. States without such an agency could receive a one-time grant of $25,000—without matching requirements— to establish arts councils.

As enacted, S 1483 authorized total appropriations of $63 million from fiscal 1966 through 1968.

In 1968 Congress extended the Foundation for two years. PL 90-348 (HR 11308) authorized appropriations of $34 million over the two years, plus sums to match up to $13.5 million in private gifts to the Foundation.

In contrast to the funds finally enacted, the figures initially recommended by the House Education and

Labor Committee totaled $135 million over two years. In the first of many signs of "economy fever" in Congress, the House initially rebuffed the Committee by reducing the first-year authorization to $11.2 million and entirely deleting the second-year authorization. The Senate put back the two-year authorization and the House went along with it.

Appropriations for the Foundation in its first four years remained around the $10-million level annually. These were the figures (carried in the annual appropriations bill for the Interior Department and Related Agencies, one of which had for years been the Commission on Fine Arts): Fiscal 1966, $10.7 million; 1967, $9 million; 1968; $12.2 million; 1969, $11.5 million.

Support for the Foundation. Pressure for federal support of the arts and humanities was, in part, a reaction to the Government's concentration on advancing scientific activities. Efforts in behalf of artistic fields got under way some years before promotion of the humanities was undertaken.

Congress in 1910 established the Commission of Fine Arts, which reviews and comments on architectural and urban design affecting federal areas within the District of Columbia. In 1958 federal land was donated for a National Cultural Center in Washington, D.C., to be built by private donations. After President Kennedy's assassination, Congress in 1963 authorized federal matching contributions for the center and renamed it for Mr. Kennedy.

This was a recognition of the late President's sponsorship of federal support for the arts. In 1961 he backed legislation to establish a Federal Advisory Council of the Arts, as President Eisenhower had done in 1955. The Kennedy bill was defeated in the House Sept. 21, 1961, on a 166-173 roll-call vote. In 1962 President Kennedy appointed August Heckscher as his Special Consultant on the Arts. At their urging, the Senate in 1963 passed a bill to establish a National Arts Foundation to make grants to the states and to professional groups to encourage and support the arts. The bill was not passed by the House, but in 1964 Congress did establish an advisory body, the National Council on the Arts, in the Executive Office of the President.

To promote the humanities, a private group, the National Commission on the Humanities, was established in 1963 by the American Council of Learned Societies, the United Chapters of Phi Beta Kappa and the Council of Graduate Schools in the United States.

In a 1964 report, the Commission called for the establishment of a National Humanities Foundation to support study, teaching and research in the arts and humanities through federal grants and fellowships and through assistance in construction and expansion of libraries, classrooms, etc. The report said that the United States faced "a crisis of national leadership" because the development of the humanities lagged far behind science and technology.

Although President Johnson had expressed support for a foundation on the humanities in 1964, he asked in his January 1965 State of the Union message only for a foundation on the arts. However, numerous bills introduced in Congress called for both foundations and in March the President submitted a bill to establish the dual National Foundation on the Arts and the Humanities. Over considerable opposition in the House (an

effort to kill the bill lost in the House on a 128-251 roll-call vote), the legislation was enacted in September 1965. It had the support of a great many educators, artists, musicians and actors as well as their private patrons.

The top officials appointed to the Foundation in 1965 were: S. Dillon Ripley, Secretary of the Smithsonian Institution, as chairman of the Federal Council on the Arts and the Humanities; Barnaby C. Keeney, retired president of Brown University and chairman of the private commission on the humanities, as chairman of the National Endowment for the Humanities; and Roger L. Stevens, chairman of the National Council on the Arts established in 1964, as chairman of the National Endowment for the Arts.

Chronology of Legislation on Education, 1965-68

1965

Congress in 1965 authorized over $2 billion for revolutionary new education programs to help students and schools at the elementary, secondary, college and graduate levels. Although the first session of the 88th Congress in 1963 (labeled by President Johnson the "Education Congress") and the second session in 1964 had produced important new education legislation, the 89th Congress outdid its predecessor by enacting controversial programs that had been voted on and rejected off and on for 20 years.

For the first time, Congress approved a general aid to education bill, the Elementary and Secondary Education Act, providing an initial $1.3 billion for the nation's elementary and secondary schools. Different versions of a general school aid program had been before Congress since World War II. Also enacted for the first time was a program of federal scholarships for college students. In the past, both of these programs had bogged down in bitter controversies, religious, racial and partisan.

The scholarships were part of numerous new programs authorized in the Higher Education Act. Included in the Act were guaranteed loans to college students, grants for library books and materials and for university extension programs to combat urban problems, and funds to help small colleges.

Teachers, too, were singled out for special help. The Act contained a graduate fellowship program for experienced and future teachers, and authorized a national Teacher Corps to improve classes in impoverished schools. As in the past, when conservatives regarded direct aid to teachers as a possible instrument for federal control of education, House Republicans opposed the Teacher Corps. The Corps was the only part of the entire education program which was blocked; though authorized for two years, it received no appropriations in 1965.

Later in the year, with Presidential endorsement, Congress established the National Foundation on the Arts and the Humanities, providing federal grants to these fields of cultural and educational interest.

Poverty Theme. Passage of the Elementary and Secondary Education Act was attributed to the power of the large Democratic majority in Congress and the skill with which the Administration and Congressional leaders skirted the controversy over disbursing federal aid to parochial schools. Supporters of the bill successfully avoided the religious issue by emphasizing that aid would go to school children in needy areas and not to schools. The Administration's hand was also strengthened by the absence of the racial issue which had provoked additional opposition in the past. This issue had been settled by passage of the 1964 Civil Rights Act, which forbade federal aid to schools that practiced racial discrimination.

Much of the credit for this achievement went to the "teacher who became President." President Johnson built his education program around the theme of poverty, drawing support from public concern over the problem of the poor in an affluent society. "Poverty has many roots," the President said in his education message, "but the taproot is ignorance."

The major share of funds under the elementary-secondary bill was to be distributed according to the numbers of impoverished pupils in school districts (although 95 percent of the nation's counties were eligible). The college scholarship program was for exceptionally needy students. The pre-school Project Head Start was actually part of the antipoverty program, enacted in 1964. The Teacher Corps was aimed at improving schools in impoverished areas. The aid program for small colleges was directed principally at impoverished Negro colleges.

Appropriations for the Office of Education in fiscal 1966 doubled the fiscal 1965 sum, rising from $1.5 billion to $3 billion.

Elementary and Secondary Education

Elementary and Secondary Education Act. Congress and the President in 1965 broke through the impasse that had long stymied legislation to provide federal aid to elementary and secondary schools. The Elementary and Secondary Education Act that resulted (HR 2362—PL 89-10) authorized the first general school aid in the nation's history.

The President's victory was made possible after he abandoned the traditional proposals—across-the-board aid for school construction and teachers' salaries for all of the public school systems—in favor of general aid to districts with many children from low-income families. Furthermore, private schools were permitted to share in some of the federally aided services through special programs such as shared-time projects and educational television.

By using the "aid-to-children" approach and by providing some help to private school children, the bill avoided much of the crossfire over aid to church-related schools that had helped to kill past bills. The heavy Democratic majorities in Congress were able to overcome traditional Republican opposition to federal aid to education.

The ideas for the Administration bill were contained in a report by a Presidential task force headed by John W. Gardner, then president of the Carnegie Corporation and later in the year appointed Secretary of HEW. Before the bill was sent to Congress, Administration officials held many meetings with representatives of the National Education Assn., which for years had opposed any aid to private schools while seeking broad federal support for public schools, and with Catholic and other interested groups. The Administration aim was to win their prior approval of the bill so that it might go smoothly through Congress.

The President requested enactment of the bill in an education message Jan. 12. Acting swiftly, the House Education and Labor Committee held hearings and reported the bill favorably March 8, with minority views by all but two of the Republican members.

The House passed the bill March 26 by a **263-153** roll-call vote. It was opposed by the majority of Republicans and Southern Democrats but the large Northern Democratic contingent prevailed.

Within two weeks, the Senate Labor and Public Welfare Committee reported the bill without amendment, and three days later the Senate passed it and sent it to President Johnson for signature. The Senate vote April 9 was **73-18**, with all three political groups supporting passage despite defeat of a number of Republican and Southern Democratic amendments.

Major Provisions—As enacted, the Elementary and Secondary Education Act (ESEA) contained five major titles. Total first-year cost of the bill was estimated at $1.4 billion. Of this, an estimated $1.1 billion was to be spent under Title I, which was designed to aid school districts with impoverished children. (It was expected that this would affect 95 percent of the nation's counties.) The program provided federal grants to the states (which would in turn distribute the funds to school districts) on the basis of the number of children from low-income (under $2,000 a year) families times 50 percent of each state's average expenditure per school child. The school districts could spend the funds in any way approved by state and federal educational agencies, but they had to take into account the needs of children who attended nonpublic schools.

The other four titles of HR 2362: authorized grants to states for purchases of textbooks and other library materials under which such books could be loaned to private schools; authorized grants for supplementary community-wide educational centers to provide services that individual schools could not provide; expanded the 1954 Cooperative Research Act to authorize grants for new research, training and research centers; and authorized grants to strengthen state departments of education.

The groundwork for enactment of the bill had been laid so well that Congressional debate focused on the formula for providing aid rather than on the broad issue of providing federal aid for the first time. The major controversy was over the formula in Title I.

Throughout the legislative action, opponents said the Administration method of multiplying half of a state's average expenditure per school child times the number of "low-income" pupils discriminated against the poorer states. They said it would be particularly hard on Southern school districts, which needed the most aid. Support-

White House Conference on Education, 1965

The need for better quality teaching in American schools, a shakeup of hidebound methods and a closer link between educational programs and social problems were the major themes of the 1965 White House Conference on Education, held July 20-21 in Washington, D.C.

The conference, the first in 10 years, was attended by 650 delegates from throughout the nation. Its chairman was John W. Gardner, president of the Carnegie Corp., who was named by President Johnson one week later as Secretary of Health, Education and Welfare.

By design of its organizers, the conference was set up to preclude it from formally adopting any policy resolutions. President Johnson told the delegates the purpose of the meeting was to "stimulate some fresh thinking, not just talk about old ideas." Mr. Johnson said the chief problem in American education was "not merely more classrooms and more teachers, although we need them and we are going to have them," but "a fundamental improvement in the quality of American education....We are far too easily satisfied when we know that a child has a desk in a classroom with a teacher to instruct him. But it is what happens inside that classroom that really counts, and this is finally what is really important. And far too often what does happen is sadly unequal to what we have a right to expect."

During panel discussions, there was relatively wide agreement that education in the United States, to a far greater extent than could be considered acceptable, suffered from lack of imagination, lack of innovation and failure to develop new methods and approaches to meet emerging social problems. Many of the panelists agreed that the hidebound, unimaginative quality of much of American education left educators incapable of coping effectively with some of the most urgent problems of the day. The schools were said to be providing little leadership, in the North and South, in racial integration; they lacked both money and developed techniques for educating underprivileged and culturally deprived children, and were not doing enough for either gifted or handicapped students.

Some observers of the conference reported that the delegates were markedly more optimistic in their assessment of possible improvements than delegates to the 1955 conference had been.

---

ers of the Administration formula responded that it provided for larger percentage increases in Southern school budgets, and that because it was much more expensive to educate a child in the North such a formula was necessary to aid school children in Northern slums. Opponents in both chambers offered floor amendments to substitute a straight $200 grant for each impoverished child. In the House this was defeated on a 149-267 roll-call vote, and in the Senate it lost on a vote of 38-53.

Impacted Area Laws, Disaster Aid. ESEA technically was an amendment to the 1950 law (PL 81-874) that provided federal aid for school operations and maintenance in school districts "impacted" by the presence of federal installations and their employees and families. *(See above.)*

The least controversial section of the Elementary and Secondary Education Act law extended PL 874 for two years, through June 30, 1968. A related law (PL 81-815, authorizing funds for school construction) was scheduled to expire in 1966.

Late in 1965, Congress enacted the School Disaster Aid Act (HR 9022—PL 89-313), which included a major amendment of the impacted area laws. The amendment made a number of large cities eligible for funds by removing the requirement that school agencies with enrollments of more than 35,000 had to have 6 percent of their children "federally connected" to qualify for impact aid. Agencies with fewer than 35,000 students could qualify with 3 percent federally connected children, and PL 89-313 applied this percentage to all school districts. Among the cities that qualified under this provision were Boston, Baltimore, St. Louis, New Orleans and Los Angeles.

The disaster provisions of the law authorized federal funds to repair or rebuild public schools damaged in a federally recognized major disaster. Funds to help operate the schools for up to five years also were authorized. The program covered disasters between Aug. 30, 1965 and July 1, 1967.

Teacher Corps. Part B of Title V of the Higher Education Act of 1965, the Teacher Corps was the most controversial part of the huge new college-aid bill *(see below).* The idea of a corps of skilled teachers and young teachers-in-training who could be assigned to improve education in slum schools was first advanced by Sens. Edward M. Kennedy (D Mass.) and Gaylord Nelson (D Wis.). It was picked up by President Johnson, who incorporated it in his July 17 program to upgrade the training of elementary and secondary school teachers by federally financed fellowships.

Provisions for a Teacher Corps were added to the House-passed higher education bill (HR 9567) by the Senate. When the Corps was accepted by Democratic House conferees, the Republican House conferees refused to sign the conference report. They said the Corps would enable the Government to exercise control over local schools.

During floor debate on the conference report, Rep. Albert H. Quie (R Minn.) moved to send the bill back to the conference committee with instructions to delete the Teacher Corps. The motion was defeated Oct. 20 by a 152-226 roll-call vote, with Republicans supporting the motion 111-7 and all but 41 Democrats opposing it.

When appropriations for the programs in the Higher Education Act were considered late in 1965, the Senate included $13.2 million for the Teacher Corps. The House conferees on the supplemental appropriations bill refused consent for any funds for the Corps and the bill was enacted without money for the Corps.

Higher Education

Higher Education Act. Featuring extensive aid for poor and middle-class students who wished to attend college, and new programs of graduate study for public school teachers, the Higher Education Act of 1965 was an eight-title $840-million bill. It embodied numerous requests of President Johnson, including the Teacher Corps he endorsed, and two programs initiated by Congress, raising funds authorized in 1963 for construction of college classrooms and granting financial aid to colleges for the purchase of classroom equipment.

The student-aid provisions authorized: federal scholarships of up to $800 a year for exceptionally needy students (the scholarships were called educational opportunity grants); funds to encourage state and private insurance programs for loans to students made by commercial lenders, with the students' interest costs subsidized by the Government if their family income was less than $15,000 a year; transferred the work-study program for college students from the Office of Economic Opportunity to the Office of Education and removed the requirement that participating students must come from low-income families.

The teacher-aid provisions authorized federal fellowships for graduate study below the Ph.D. level for teachers, prospective teachers and other school personnel, including librarians, social workers and guidance specialists, among others. The number of fellowships was to begin at 4,500 a year and move up to 10,000 a year. To strengthen the universities' teacher education programs, the Act provided payments to the institution of $2,500 per student, less fees charged him.

Other sections of the Act authorized funds for: community service programs focusing on urban problems, to be conducted by colleges and universities; grants to improve college libraries and train librarians; a program to raise the academic quality of developing institutions— mainly small Negro colleges and semi-professional technical institutions—through federal grants and faculty exchanges with well-established colleges and universities; and equipment grants to improve classroom instruction in the sciences, humanities, arts and education.

NDEA. Included in the Higher Education Act were provisions amending the National Defense Education Act. The student loan section was amended to permit cancellation of loan repayments ("forgiveness") by students who taught in public or private schools eligible for federal aid under Title I of ESEA (schools with many children from low-income families). Fifteen percent of a loan could be forgiven for each year the student taught in such schools. Another amendment increased authorized funds under Title III of NDEA (which authorized equipment grants to lower schools for the teaching of specified subjects) to a total of $100 million, and added economics as a qualifying subject.

A third major amendment increased funds for Title XI (financing advanced teacher-training institutes) to a total of $50 million and made teachers of economics, civics and industrial arts eligible for the institutes.

College Classrooms. Title VII of the Higher Education Act amended the Higher Education Facilities Act of 1963. It removed the categorical restrictions of that Act which had made federal funds available for contruc-

tion only of classrooms and libraries in which science, mathematics, modern foreign languages or engineering were taught or studied. It also permitted transfers of allotments between junior colleges and four-year colleges within a state (the original Act set aside 22 percent of the appropriations for exclusive use of two-year institutions) and reduced the interest rate on future classroom loans to a maximum of 3 percent (the going rate was then 3-7/8 percent). In addition, Title VII doubled the fiscal 1966 authorizations for undergraduate and graduate facilities grants.

College Housing. The interest rate on loans for construction of college dormitories (as well as classrooms, *above*) also was set at a maximum of 3 percent, over the objections of the Administration and the Budget Bureau. The dormitory provision was in the Housing and Urban Development Act of 1965 (PL 89-117), which also authorized annual increases of $300 million for the college housing loan fund through fiscal 1969. The reduction of the interest rate, formerly about 3-7/8 percent, encouraged state universities to use the program for the first time, as 3 percent was lower than the rate then paid on state bond issues.

Programs for the Deaf. Two new laws for the deaf were enacted: a National Technical Institute for the Deaf (PL 89-36) and a program providing new educational media for the deaf (PL 89-258). (PL 89-36 authorized funds for construction and operation of a college to prepare deaf students for jobs in industry and other fields where special skills are required. PL 89-258 expanded a loan program of captioned films for the deaf to include other educational media, such as educational television with captions.

Arts and Humanities. Congress established a National Foundation on the Arts and the Humanities in order to develop for the first time a national policy of support for these activities. The Act (PL 89-209) provided $20 million in fiscal 1966 to be granted to organizations and individuals engaged in the creative and performing arts, and to be granted or loaned for scholarships or research in the humanities. Part of the money was to match private donations. Similar amounts were authorized for fiscal 1967 and 1968.

The Foundation was a three-part body. A Federal Council on the Arts and the Humanities, composed of nine federal officials (headed by the Secretary of the Smithsonian Institution), was to advise the chairmen of the arts and humanities endowments (who were members of the Council) and to coordinate their activities with other undertakings of the Federal Government.

The endowments were autonomous organizations, each headed by a chairman, with an advisory council to help him. The National Council on the Arts, which Congress had established as an advisory group in 1964, became the advisory council of the National Endowment for the Arts.

The legislation, which was similar to a bill passed by the Senate in the previous Congress, had the support of President Johnson and passed the Senate by voice vote in June. Considerable opposition to it developed in the House.

It was reported by the House Education and Labor Committee over the opposition of 8 of the 10 Committee Republicans. Their minority views suggested that direct federal subsidies to the arts would lower the nation's "cultural level" and possibly lead to "attempts at political control of culture." Furthermore, they described the Foundation as "an impenetrable thicket of duplication and overlapping."

The bill was held up in the House Rules Committee from July until September, when it was brought to the floor under the 21-day rule then in force, which allowed a legislative committee to bring a bill up for debate by majority vote if the Rules Committee had not granted a rule for debate within 21 days. After sharp arguments on the merits of the bill, the House Sept. 15 rejected on a **128-251** roll-call vote a motion by then-Rep. Robert P. Griffin (R Mich.) to recommit (or kill) the bill. The "conservative coalition" of Republicans and Southern Democrats voted to kill the bill but Northern Democrats voted overwhelmingly for it.

The Senate accepted the House version of the bill Sept. 16, and President Johnson signed it into law (PL 89-209) Sept. 29. The first appropriation for the Foundation was $10.7 million, more than $7 million less than the amount requested by the President.

1966

Congress in 1966, at President Johnson's request, enacted a measure (PL 89-750) expanding the Elementary and Secondary Education Act of 1965. The Act's strongest supporters in Congress were disappointed at the Administration's efforts to hold down education costs in view of the budgetary demands of the Vietnam war, and Congress went beyond the President's proposals in several instances. The major Presidential request that Congress rebuffed was an effort to cut in half the authorization for funds under the two 1950 programs (PL 81-815, 874) providing federal aid for schools in "impacted" areas. The Administration sought $206 million for the program in fiscal 1967; Congress appropriated $439 million.

Late in the session, Congress enacted a $3.6-billion measure (PL 89-752) designed to increase aid for construction of college facilities, strengthen "developing institutions" and enlarge student loan programs. The Higher Education Amendments of 1966 corresponded closely to the President's proposals, except that Congress turned down his request to move away from direct federal funds for student loans.

The first funds for the Teacher Corps were appropriated.

Elementary and Secondary Education

ESEA. The most important changes made by the 1966 legislation in Title I or ESEA expanded the scope of the program and made it more costly. In view of Vietnam costs, however, the changed formula was not to take effect for one year—in fiscal 1968. (Actually, only a part of the more generous formula, that helping the 15 poorest states, did take effect. *(See 1967 chronology.)*

One of the major changes in the 1966 amendments permitted any state to use the national average per pupil expenditure, if the national average were higher. This benefited the poorer states, which had sought a similar privilege when the Act first was before Congress. It was expected to provide $343 million more to the poorer states in fiscal 1968. The second major change, the one

that did not take effect, expanded the Title I program to include children whose families earned up to $3,000, rather than the existing limit of $2,000 a year. Unlike the first change, this was requested by the President. It was expected to provide Title I funds for an additional 300,000 children.

The 1966 law also increased authorizations for the other titles of ESEA, established a new program to aid in the education of handicapped children, and transferred the adult education activities of the Office of Economic Opportunity to the Office of Education in HEW.

Other changes repealed the Act's incentive grant program, which authorized additional funds to school districts which substantially increased their educational spending (repealed on the ground it was not related to the poverty-orientation of the Act), and provided special programs for children of Indians and migratory workers.

Congress also expanded Title I by including inmates of homes for neglected and delinquent children and children in foster homes and by requiring that in fiscal 1967 the most recent data be used to determine the number of children in a district who were covered by the Aid to Families with Dependent Children welfare program.

The 1966 bill weathered a sharp debate on school desegregation in the House. Southerners used it as a vehicle to express their opposition to guidelines for the desegregation of schools that had been issued by Education Commissioner Harold Howe II. An amendment by Rep. L.H. Fountain (D N.C.) prohibiting the Commissioner from deferring federal grants to a school district until he had held hearings and established the district's noncompliance with desegregation rules was adopted on a 220-116 roll-call vote. The House also adopted an "anti-busing" amendment to ban any federal requirement for transporting children to achieve racial balance in schools. The Administration said it had no busing plans, that such decisions were entirely up to local communities.

In the House-Senate conference on the bill, the "anti-busing" amendment was accepted and the desegregation amendment was modified considerably. It authorized deferral of funds for 90 days while a school district's alleged segregation practices were investigated and a decision on compliance reached.

As enacted, PL 89-750 authorized fiscal 1967 appropriations of $1.9 billion, but Congress followed up by actually appropriating only $1.4 billion.

Impacted Area Laws. The ESEA Amendments (PL 89-750) further liberalized the impacted area school laws instead of cutting them back as the Administration proposed. The changes made districts with 400 federally connected children eligible for federal support of school operations under PL 81-874, even though they might not meet the law's requirement that 3 percent of the district's children be federally connected.

Also, the PL 81-815 construction law was extended through fiscal 1967 and its eligibility standards eased.

President Johnson had proposed amendments to the two laws that would have cut authorizations to $206 million. Instead, Congress authorized $490 million and appropriated $439 million.

Teacher Corps. The Corps received its first appropriation—$9.5 million—in May of 1966, plus a second appropriation, $7.5 million, in November for the fiscal year that began July 1, 1966. In the six months between the two appropriations, the future of the Corps was in great doubt, and it did not get its first director, Richard A. Graham, until November, when its life seemed more assured.

The House Appropriations Committee, in approving the first funds for the Teacher Corps, put two restrictions on its operations which Congress went on to ratify: (1) schools requesting the services of Corps members must have the approval of the state's education agency; and (2) federal financing must not exceed 90 percent of Corpsmen's salaries, with the local or state agency paying the remaining 10 percent.

Higher Education

College Classrooms. The Higher Education Amendments of 1966 (PL 89-752) authorized expenditures for undergraduate and graduate facility grants and loans in fiscal 1967-69. By fiscal 1969, 24 percent of the undergraduate grants had to be allotted to two-year community colleges or technical institutes.

NDEA. President Johnson, in his 1966 education message, proposed that NDEA student loans, which were a direct charge on the Budget, be replaced by the 1965 Act's federal interest subsidies and guarantees for loans from private lenders. The House rejected this proposal, and the Administration then offered a new plan, based on sale of participations in federal loans. Under this plan, funds from the sale of participation certificates to private investors were to be merged with funds for regular NDEA loans. This proposal was accepted by the Senate but dropped in conference, largely because sales of participations in Government-held loans had been suspended for the remainder of 1966 because of high interest rates in the private market.

Dropping the revised loan program meant that the existing NDEA program, which financed college loans to students at 3-percent interest, continued unchanged. Existing law authorized appropriations of $190 million in fiscal 1967 for direct student loans and Congress appropriated the full amount. In addition, it authorized an increase in the fiscal 1968 authorization for loans, from $195 million to $225 million.

Another NDEA amendment in PL 89-752 permitted total "forgiveness" of loan repayments if the recipient became a full-time teacher of handicapped children. Still another amendment added industrial arts as a subject qualifying for federal aid under the equipment grant section (Title III) of NDEA.

Student Veterinarians. PL 89-709, enacted Nov. 2, made students of veterinary medicine eligible for student loans under the Health Professions Educational Assistance Act of 1963. Veterinary schools also were made eligible for construction grants.

OTHER BILLS

Higher Education Act. The 1966 Amendments (PL 89-752) extended the Developing Institutions section (Title III) of the 1965 Act through fiscal 1968. Only $5 million had been appropriated for the title's first year, fiscal 1966; the new law authorized $85 million for the next two years.

Library Assistance. 1966 brought a five-year extension of the Library Services and Construction Act of 1964. It also increased the Act's authorizations for matching federal grants for library services and construction and added new grant programs for cooperative library networks within states and regions and for state institutions other than colleges and libraries.

The 1964 Act had made federal funds available for the first time for urban libraries and for construction in both rural and urban areas. The 1966 extension (PL 89-511) increased the authorizations for services and construction (for which $55 million was appropriated in fiscal 1966) to $75 million in fiscal 1967, with annual increases of $20 million until the sum of $155 million was reached in fiscal 1971. The new grant programs in the Act were much smaller. They were to start at $13 million and reach $37 million in fiscal 1971.

Appropriations in the first three years of the 1966 Act did not reach authorized levels. In fiscal 1969, for example, the appropriation was $65 million compared to the authorized $140 million.

International Education. Congress, in the International Education Act of 1966 (HR 14643—PL 89-698), voted a $131-million program to strengthen international studies at American colleges and universities. But the program was killed by the House Appropriations Committee, which refused to approve funds to institute it in 1967, although the Senate approved a small sum.

The Act was proposed by President Johnson, who said it would increase American students' awareness of foreign nations and their interest in serving abroad. Grants were to help establish or improve graduate centers of international studies and develop new courses at the undergraduate level.

HR 14643 was passed by the House June 6 on a 195-90 roll-call vote after opponents contended it was an opening move in an attempt to erase illiteracy in foreign lands. The bill's sponsor, Rep. John Brademas (D Ind.), emphasized that it dealt only with domestic education programs. There was no opposition in the Senate, where it passed by voice vote.

President Johnson signed the bill into law Oct. 29 at a ceremony held at a university in Bangkok, Thailand. He described PL 89-698 as "the first step" toward extending the goals of "the Great Society" to the rest of the world.

Cold War GI Bill. After seven years of consideration, Congress enacted the Veterans' Readjustment Benefits Act (PL 89-358), known as the Cold War GI Bill. It authorized a permanent program of educational and other benefits for veterans who served in the armed forces after Jan. 31, 1955. By its third year, the Act was providing more federal support of college students than all other programs combined.

1967

Elementary and secondary education became entangled in the question of state vs. local planning of education programs, with the Federal Government cast as the whipping boy. Republicans proposed that funds for ESEA's largest programs be allotted as "block grants" to state departments of education, rather than directly to local school agencies that applied to the federal Office of Education. After big-city school superintendents and Catholic spokesmen joined Administration forces to defeat the original block grants amendment of Rep. Albert H. Quie (R Minn.), a compromise was agreed to that affected only the innovative programs of Title III.

Several new programs were added to the Act, including aid to children whose native language is not English, and dropout prevention activities; appropriations one year in advance of the school year were allowed for future education budgets. The bill as enacted (PL 90-247) authorized appropriations of more than $9.2 billion over a two-year period, including funds for federally impacted areas. Appropriations, however, turned out to be only half of what was authorized.

With far less controversy, Congress extended the Teacher Corps and expanded existing programs for teacher education. The Administration's proposals for phasing out NDEA student loans in favor of greater reliance on private loans did not get beyond the hearing stage. The controversial plan to grant tax credits for the cost of college education won approval by the Senate for the first time, only to be dropped when the provision got caught in a parliamentary tangle with other, unrelated matters.

Elementary and Secondary Education

ESEA. Congress Dec. 15 cleared the largest school assistance bill in the nation's history, the Administration's Elementary and Secondary Education Amendments of 1967 (HR 7819—PL 90-247). The bill authorized appropriation of a total of $9,249,860,644 for fiscal 1969 and 1970 and added $132,884,000 to existing authorizations for fiscal 1968. Final Congressional action came, barely an hour before adjournment of the session, when the conference report was approved by both chambers.

The bulk of the funds authorized in HR 7819—an estimated $2.7 billion in fiscal 1969 and $2.9 billion in fiscal 1970—was for federal aid to disadvantaged children under Title I of ESEA. The bill also extended authority for a number of existing programs, such as adult education, school library assistance and aid to state school departments, and it created several new programs, including additional grants for special education of handicapped children and aid to districts with non-English-speaking children.

HR 7819 provided that appropriations under the Act could be made a fiscal year in advance. Thus, it authorized Congress in 1968 to vote appropriations for fiscal 1970 as well as fiscal 1969. The advance funding provision was designed to meet the objections of local school agencies that the school year was usually well under way before they knew how much federal money they would receive.

The scope of the bill far exceeded the original Administration requests. However, the Administration supported most of the changes, and passage of HR 7819 was one of President Johnson's major legislative accomplishments in the 1st session of the 90th Congress.

The bill had a rocky path through Congress. It was delayed for weeks in both chambers while major controversies were resolved.

Controversies—In the House, HR 7819 became the vehicle for a Republican attempt to substitute block grants to the states for the traditional direct categorical grants to the localities. Led by Rep. Albert H. Quie

Group Stands on Quie Amendment

The Republican "block grant" amendment to the elementary school bill evoked comment from a wide range of interest groups and individuals. The Administration conducted a strong campaign against the measure, which was offered by Rep. Albert H. Quie (R Minn.).

Generally, the Quie amendment was opposed by national education groups, civil rights and some religious organizations as well as by school officials of large cities.

Supporting the amendment were many state school officials and school superintendents from small and middle-sized towns.

OPPOSED TO QUIE AMENDMENT

National Education Assn. (NEA)

U.S. Catholic Conference, Msgr. James C. Donohue, head of the education department. (The presidents of the National Council of Churches and Synagogue Council of America joined Donohue in a telegram opposing the amendment.)

Education bodies of the Baptist, Evangelical United Brethren, Episcopal and United Presbyterian Churches and the United Church of Christ.

American Council on Education (because there had not been hearings on the proposal)

National Congress of Parents and Teachers (PTA)

AFL-CIO Executive Council and American Federation of Teachers.

Citizens for Educational Freedom (representing parents of private school children, a large percentage of them Catholic)

Leadership Conference on Civil Rights

National Assn. for the Advancement of Colored People (NAACP)

American Assn. of University Women

Americans for Democratic Action (ADA)

Two former HEW Secretaries in the Eisenhower Administration, Arthur S. Flemming and Marion B. Folsom

New York City Mayor John V. Lindsay

New York State Commissioner of Education

California State Board of Education

California Assn. of School Administrators

School superintendents of New York City, Chicago, Detroit, Baltimore, San Francisco, Cleveland, Minneapolis, Atlanta and other cities.

SUPPORTING QUIE AMENDMENT

Council of Chief State School Officers

U.S. Chamber of Commerce

Governors of California, Colorado, Massachusetts, Montana, Nevada, Minnesota, South Dakota, Washington and Wisconsin (all Republicans)

State school superintendents of Arkansas, Colorado, Florida, Indiana, Kansas, Maine, North Dakota and Pennsylvania.

President of the Minn. Assn. of School Administrators.

National Union of Christian Schools (representing 280 Protestant schools)

Numerous school officials of small and medium-sized towns.

(R Minn.), a member of the House Education and Labor Committee, the Republicans contended that state education departments were better able to determine the needs of local school children than was the U.S. Office of Education and that red tape could be eliminated by channeling money through the states. The Administration argued that state agencies were not sufficiently staffed to handle the massive grant programs and that these agencies were unlikely to give urban areas their fair share. Furthermore, they said local school agencies were in the best position to plan their programs.

The Republicans received support in their efforts from the Council of Chief State School Officers and the U.S. Chamber of Commerce. But Administration forces were able to muster powerful support from big-city school officials, labor and civil rights organizations and—most importantly—church groups.

Defeat of the Quie block-grant amendment could be traced directly to the fact that it raised the specter of the church-state issue, the very issue which had delayed passage of an aid-to-education bill for more than a decade. Catholic Church leaders feared that laws in many states prohibiting aid to church schools would keep parochial school pupils from benefiting from the federal-aid programs if the money were channeled through the states. Catholic organizations and the church hierarchy lobbied heavily against the Quie proposal.

Quie's block-grant amendment was rejected May 24 by a 168-197 nonrecord (teller) vote when the Republicans failed to pick up substantial support from Southern Democrats. The amendment would have given money under Titles I, II (library and textbooks), III (supplemental centers) and V (strengthening state agencies) to the states, to be distributed by the state departments of education according to a statewide plan. Quie would have changed the apportionment of Title I funds by allocating 50 percent, instead of the law's 80 percent, to areas with concentrations of children from low-income families.

After defeat of Quie's amendment, Republicans got behind amendments by Rep. Edith Green (D Ore.) placing all control of Title III and Title V funds in the state education departments.

Southern Democrats played a key role in the voting. They helped defeat the Quie amendment and a GOP recommittal motion, supported Mrs. Green's amendments, and won several other votes of direct interest to the South. The latter included amendments that prohibited the Government from withholding new funds from school districts on segregation charges until after a hearing and a ruling of violation; changed the formula for Title I grants to impoverished school districts so that the poorer states would get more money; and directed that desegregation guidelines be applied uniformly in the North and South.

Anticipating that appropriations for Title I programs would be smaller than was authorized under the 1966 revision of the formula, the House May 24, by a 222-194 roll-call vote, adopted an amendment to the authorization bill that awarded more money to the 15 poorer states at the expense of the 35 richer states. The amendment, sponsored by Sam M. Gibbons (D Fla.) retained one part of the 1966 revision, overruling the Education and Labor Committee which had voted to delay both parts of the revision. Gibbons' amendment permitted state allotments for Title I funds to be computed on the basis of one-half the state average expenditure per pupil or one-half the national average, whichever was higher, multiplied by the number of pupils from families making less than $2,000 a year.

Thirty-five states, including Florida, were entitled to less money under the Gibbons amendment than they were under the Committee bill. And six of them actually were to receive less appropriated money than they received in fiscal 1967.

However, the Labor-HEW Appropriation bill (HR 10196), passed the next day, provided that no state was to be allotted less money than it received in fiscal 1967. Since the fiscal 1968 Title I appropriations in HR 10196 were $137.6 million more than fiscal 1967 funds, most states received a small increase over 1967 and most Southern states received a substantial increase. The largest single increase in funds was in Mississippi, which received $23.5 million in funds in fiscal 1967 and $44.8 million in fiscal 1968.

Senate Action—On Nov. 6, more than five months after House passage, the Senate Labor and Public Welfare Committee reported the ESEA Amendments bill. The Committee provided for advanced appropriations, reinstated a program of incentive grants to states that spent more than the national average for education and included a number of new programs, among them additional grants to aid handicapped children, school dropouts and children from non-English-speaking backgrounds. These later were accepted by the House.

The Senate Committee watered down Mrs. Green's block grant amendment for Title III funds, which HEW Secretary John Gardner and Education Commissioner Harold Howe II had vigorously opposed. On the Senate floor, an effort by Sen. Strom Thurmond (R S.C.) to get the Green amendment adopted without change was narrowly defeated, 35-38. In conference with the House, the Senate accepted the amendment, effective in fiscal 1970.

The bill was delayed for one month in reaching the floor by a threatened filibuster to reinstate a House anti-desegregation amendment sponsored by Rep. Fountain (D N.C.) and a proposed anti-busing amendment by Minority Leader Everett McKinley Dirksen (R Ill.). Eventually, both issues were compromised by agreement with the Administration.

Major Provisions—Amendments to Title I allowed states to use the national expenditure per pupil in determining their allotments; set out priorities if appropriations fell short of the full amount allowed under the formula (handicapped or migrant children and those in state institutions were to receive their full entitlements); and re-authorized incentive grants for states that spent above-average proportions of their revenues for education, effective in fiscal 1969.

Title III grants for supplementary centers were to be made according to state plans and, as of fiscal 1970, were to be entirely allotted by the state education agency. All but 5 percent of the funds under Title V were to be allocated by state agencies.

New programs established in the 1967 law authorized: a bilingual education project for children from non-English-speaking backgrounds, with additional fellowships awarded for teachers of these children; pilot projects to develop effective programs to prevent school dropouts; and technical assistance to rural schools that wished to apply for federal aid.

Other amendments to ESEA: authorized advance appropriations for programs under the Act; required that 15 percent of Title III funds be spent on programs for handicapped children; authorized a small number of service centers for children who were both deaf and blind; and continued indefinitely the Federal Government's 90 percent share of the cost of adult education projects.

Impacted Area Laws, Disaster Aid. The ESEA bill extended the two impacted area laws (PLs 81-815 and 874) and the disaster relief law (PL 89-313), with minor amendments, through fiscal 1970.

Teacher Corps, Fellowships. The House June 27 and the Senate June 28 passed, and the President signed into law the next day, an Administration-backed bill (HR 10943—PL 90-35) extending the Teacher Corps through fiscal 1970. Called the Education Professions Development Act, the Act extended Title V of the Higher Education Act of 1965, including the Teacher Corps and a teacher fellowship program, and created four new teacher-training programs effective in fiscal 1969.

The rapid-fire action of House passage, Senate passage and the President's signature on successive days resulted from the urgency of authorizing the Teacher Corps before June 30, the end of fiscal 1967.

Congress May 25 had approved $3,823,700 for the Corps in the Second Supplemental Appropriations Act for fiscal 1967 (HR 9481). But HR 9481 specified that the funds would lapse if the Corps were not authorized for fiscal 1968 before June 30.

For the first time in its uncertain life, the Teacher Corps was supported by a majority of House Republicans. A key roll-call vote was taken on a motion that would have killed the Corps; the motion lost, **146-257**, with Republicans divided **83-95**. Committee amendments ensuring local control of the Corps played an important part in reducing opposition to the program, and inclusion of other teacher-training projects in the bill helped to gather support for it.

HR 10943 authorized $135 million for the Corps in the fiscal years 1968-70. In addition, it authorized $435 million in the fiscal years 1969-70 for the Higher Education Act's graduate fellowships for elementary and secondary school teachers and grants to colleges and universities to help them improve their graduate education facilities.

HR 10943 authorized also four new programs to begin in fiscal 1969: (1) grants to assist local education agencies, under a state plan, to carry out programs to attract and qualify teachers and teacher aides in areas that were short of teachers; (2) grants for preservice and in-service training of persons in elementary and secondary education; (3) fellowships and other training for college and university teachers and administrators and (4) a small program of grants for the purpose of attracting qualified persons into the field of education. With the exception of the first (teacher shortage) program, all of these programs were proposed by the Administration. The teacher shortage program was added to the bill on the initiative of the House Special Subcommittee on Education.

Later in the year, in the annual appropriations bill for the Departments of Labor and HEW, Congress pro-

vided $13.5 million for the Teacher Corps in fiscal 1968. The House, which passed the appropriations bill before the Teacher Corps authorization had cleared Congress, provided no money. The Senate later voted $18.1 million, after narrowly defeating, on a 43-45 roll-call vote, an amendment to provide the full $33 million the Administration had requested. The compromise $13.5 million figure was arrived at by House-Senate conferees.

House Controversy—The Education Professions Development Act (HR 10943) was put together by a subcommittee headed by Rep. Edith Green (D Ore.), a past critic of the Teacher Corps but an ardent friend of the teaching profession. The bill included several provisions designed to "localize" control of the Corps.

When the bill was brought to the floor June 27, the House defeated, by a 62-108 teller vote, an amendment offered by Edward J. Gurney (R Fla.) eliminating the Teacher Corps provisions from the bill. Later it rejected, by a 146-257 roll-call vote, a Gurney motion to recommit the bill to the Education and Labor Committee with instructions to delete the Corps provisions. Gurney, a member of the Committee, charged that Republicans had "helped put a dress of respectability" on the Teacher Corps, but it was still "the miniskirt and bikini bathing suit of the Great Society—in other words...a federally oriented elite group of teachers financed by federal money."

However, Gurney was opposed by a bipartisan majority. Rep. Albert H. Quie (R Minn.), a Committee member, said he had opposed the Teacher Corps in the past because of the control over it held by the U.S. Commissioner of Education. But he could support it now, Quie said, because the bill shifted control to the states and local school districts.

Major Provisions—As enacted, PL 90-35 authorized $33 million in fiscal 1968, $46 million in fiscal 1969 and $56 million in fiscal 1970 for the Teacher Corps. Had the full funds been appropriated, this would have provided for 6,000 volunteers in fiscal 1968, 7,500 in fiscal 1969 and 9,600 in fiscal 1970.

The provisions designed to "localize" the Teacher Corps deleted "National" from the title; provided that local agencies, rather than the Commissioner, were to "recruit, select and enroll" the volunteers; specified that local districts were to pay at least 10 percent of the Corps members' salaries; assured that no more volunteers than were requested would be sent into any state; required the approval of the state education agency before Corps members were sent to a local district; and set the salary for teacher interns at $75 a week plus $15 for each dependent, or the lowest rate paid a teacher in the school district, whichever was less (experienced teachers in the Corps received their regular salaries).

Higher Education

Tax Credit for College Costs. For the first time in three tries, the Senate in 1967 voted to allow a tax credit for expenses of a college education. Adopted by a 53-26 vote, the amendment was attached to an unrelated House bill that became so encumbered with Senate amendments that it was recommitted to committee and stripped of all extraneous amendments, including the tax credit. Thus the House had no opportunity to vote on the question.

Opposing Views on College Tax Credit

Senate debate on Ribicoff's amendment brought out the following contentions:

Pros. Those in favor of a tax credit for college students argued it would be the most effective way to help meet college expenses. "Fairness demands that the Congress recognize the need to give a tax break to the ordinary American taxpayer who faces today's enormous cost of higher education," Ribicoff told the Senate April 14. He said opinion polls had shown the public overwhelmingly in favor of such legislation.

Ribicoff said the revenue loss in fiscal 1968 would be less than $600 million and "might rise to $1.3 billion" by 1970. He contended this money would be more than paid back to the Government in years to come since the educated recipients could be expected to earn a higher income and thus pay higher taxes than they otherwise would pay.

The proponents said a tax credit would aid the institutions as well as the students by allowing the colleges to raise their tuition. They said it also would encourage persons not related to a student to help one through college since a tax credit could be claimed. Further, Ribicoff contended, it would free graduates of the indebtedness that causes many to take jobs on the basis of immediate pay and would encourage teachers and others to take graduate training.

Cons. The Administration and its supporters opposed the tax credit on four grounds: (1) The Treasury estimated it would cost $1.1 billion in lost taxes in the first year and up to $1.5 billion by the third year. In the face of an expected budget deficit of nearly $10 billion in fiscal 1967 and $8 billion in fiscal 1968, the nation was said not to be able to afford the additional revenue loss. (2) The individual taxpayer would not be helped in the long run because institutions would immediately increase tuition charges beyond what they felt they currently could demand. (3) The Ribicoff bill amounted to "class legislation" because it applied only to those with sufficient means to pay taxes. (4) The $325 maximum would hardly make a dent in student expenses.

For several years Congressional Republicans had advocated a tax credit for college expenses. The party's 1964 platform pledged enactment of "tax credits for those burdened by the expenses of college education."

Democratic Administrations opposed the idea, both for budgetary reasons and for its alleged discrimination in behalf of the more prosperous parents of students.

The House Ways and Means Committee never acted on tax credit bills, but the issue was voted on in the Senate in 1964, 1966 and 1967. Each time the chief sponsor was Sen. Abraham A. Ribicoff (D Conn.), who was President Kennedy's first Secretary of Health, Education and Welfare (1961-62).

Ribicoff introduced his 1967 bill (S 835) Feb. 6, with 46 cosponsors. Realizing that its best chance of enactment would be by attachment to a House-passed bill wanted by the Administration, Ribicoff April 14 offered it as an amendment to the House-passed bill (HR 6950) restoring the tax credit on business investments.

Ribicoff's amendment was agreed to by the Senate on a 53-26 roll-call vote. The party breakdown on the vote was: R 25-5; D 28-21 (ND 22-12; SD 6-9). It was the first time in three votes on the proposal that a majority of Northern Democrats supported the tax credit. Republicans had overwhelmingly supported it each time and Southern Democrats regularly opposed it. When the tax credit was first voted on, in 1964, it lost on a 45-48 vote. In 1966 the margin of defeat was larger, 37-47.

Under Ribicoff's bill, students, their parents or others who helped pay their way through college were entitled to deduct up to $325 a year from their income tax payments. The tax credit was on a sliding scale that allowed deduction of 75 percent of the first $200 of college expenses, 25 percent of the next $300 and 10 percent of the next $1,000. The credit was to be reduced by 1 percent of the taxpayer's adjusted income over $25,000 so that there would be no credit for persons with income over $57,500.

A substitute proposal by Sen. Winston L. Prouty (R Vt.) that would have given a proportionately greater credit to poorer taxpayers was defeated on a 16-63 vote.

Ribicoff's amendment was subsequently deleted from HR 6950. So many extraneous amendments had been attached to the bill that Senate Majority Leader Mike Mansfield (D Mont.) moved to send it back to committee with instructions that all amendments be stripped from it. The Senate agreed to Mansfield's motion April 25.

In the House, more than 60 college tax credit bills were referred to the Ways and Means Committee in 1967. Most of these were introduced by Republicans.

Library Services. A one-year extension of full federal financing of the three new library programs authorized in 1966 was provided in PL 90-154. The programs were for interlibrary cooperation, state institutional libraries and services for the physically handicapped.

The 1966 law had required the state and local governments to pay 50 percent of the costs of the programs after June 30, 1967. PL 90-154 extended the effective date to June 30, 1968. Committee reports noted that many states had not had time to complete plans for matching the federal contributions.

For fiscal 1968 Congress appropriated $5,815,000 for the three programs.

Work-Study Program. A stop-gap bill (PL 90-82) was enacted setting the federal share of the cost of college work-study grants for 1968-1970. Had the legislation not been enacted, the federal share would have dropped from 90 percent to 75 percent, beginning Aug. 20, 1967.

PL 90-82 set the federal share at 85 percent until Aug. 20, 1968, at 80 percent for the next year, and at 75 percent thereafter. (This was changed in 1968.) The bill also allowed some variation in students' work periods by setting the maximum as an average of 15 hours a week per semester.

1968

Concerned at the rising federal budget deficit, and outraged at violent disturbances on college campuses, Congress in 1968 zigged and zagged on education programs. It cut appropriations for assistance to underprivileged elementary, secondary and college students but went beyond the budget request for the popular "impacted area" programs. Then it barred the Executive Branch from reducing education expenditures to meet the over-all spending ceiling Congress imposed on the entire Government.

Reacting to campus riots, Congress enacted three conflicting provisions forbidding federal aid to students who took part in disturbances. The resulting confusion left administrators in a quandary as to how the three laws should be enforced.

For the first time in four years, no new elementary or secondary school programs were enacted, but an extensive higher education bill was passed. Experimental programs to help handicapped children of pre-school age were authorized in a separate bill. Legislation on the National Science Foundation and arts and humanities also was enacted.

Elementary and Secondary Education

ESEA Funds. Appropriations for Title I of ESEA, the key section aiding disadvantaged school children, dropped below the previous year's level. Congress had appropriated $1,191 million for Title I in fiscal 1968; for fiscal 1969 the total fell to $1,123 million, $77 million less than the budget request. For the entire ESEA appropriation Congress approved $1,477 million, a cut of $200 million below fiscal 1968 figures. Two programs authorized in 1967 received their first appropriations: bilingual education, $7.5 million, and dropout prevention, $5 million.

The advance appropriation for Title I, first authorized in the 1967 law, was carried in the fiscal 1969 appropriation bill (HR 18037—PL 90-557). The bill provided $1,010 million for fiscal 1970, in the expectation that more could be added the following year when the regular fiscal 1970 appropriations were considered.

School Desegregation—A serious attack on HEW's authority, under the Civil Rights Act, to withhold funds from school districts clinging to segregation was barely beaten off in the House. In the end, the House narrowly reversed its position on an amendment by Rep. Jamie L. Whitten (D Miss.) to protect Southern "freedom of choice" plans from HEW efforts to require full desegregation of schools. On June 26 the House adopted Whitten's amendment by a 137-101 teller vote. After the Senate rejected the amendment, the House retreated from its position and on a key **167-156** roll-call vote, Oct. 3, accepted the Senate's milder language. Congress, however, required HEW to assign as many desegregation investigators to Northern states as it did to the 17 Southern and border states.

Impacted Areas. Once again the President sought to reduce the burden of aid to schools in federally impacted areas. That aid, he said, failed to reach some of the neediest school districts while assisting some that least needed federal help. Mr. Johnson proposed an appropriation of $410 million, $120 million less than the fiscal 1968 figure; Congress appropriated $521 million.

Handicapped Children. In HR 18763—PL 90-538, Congress authorized experimental programs to help handicapped children of pre-school age. Committee reports said that funds for education of handicapped children as authorized in Title VI of ESEA were not used in many states, or could not be used under state laws, for children of pre-school age.

PL 90-538, the Handicapped Children's Early Education Assistance Act, authorized the U.S. Commissioner of Education to make contracts with public or private non-

---

ESEA Appropriations Gap

In the amendments to ESEA the Congressional committees with jurisdiction over the Act have shown a zeal for greatly expanded spending that both the Executive Branch and the Congressional appropriation committees resisted, with success.

The figures below contrast the authorized amounts for ESEA programs in fiscal 1969 with the amounts actually appropriated (in millions).

ESEA Titles	Authorized	Appropriated
I—Educationally deprived children	$2,776	$1,123
II—Library resources, textbooks	165	50
III—Supplementary education centers	528	165
V—Strengthening of state education departments	80	30
VI—Handicapped children	179	31
VII—Bilingual education	30	7
VIII—Dropout prevention	30	5
Adult Education Act	70	45
TOTALS	$3,858	$1,456

In contrast, the programs for federally impacted areas, which the Executive Branch hoped to cut back substantially, received appropriations of close to 90 percent of authorized amounts in fiscal 1969.

Impacted Areas Aid	Authorized	Appropriated
Maintenance and operation	$561	$506
Construction	80	15
TOTALS	$641	$521

SOURCE: House Education and Labor Committee

---

profit agencies for experimental programs. The Federal Government would pay 90 percent of the costs of each project. The law authorized appropriations of $1 million in fiscal 1969, $10 million in fiscal 1970 and $12 million the next year.

Higher Education

Higher Education Amendments. Late in the year, Congress cleared the Higher Education Amendments of 1968 (S 3769—PL 90-575), which extended through fiscal 1971 the various titles of the Higher Education Act, the National Defense Education Act (NDEA) and the Higher Education Facilities Act. There was little controversy over the bill; proposals to penalize riotous students consumed most of the debate.

Earlier in the year a stop-gap bill (PL 90-460) extended the guaranteed loan program for students, which was due

Authorized Federal Aid to Colleges and Students

(in millions)

	Fiscal 1969	1970	1971
Higher Education Act			
Community services	$ 10	$ 50	$ 60
Library assistance	43	114	139
Developing institutions	35	70	91
Work-study grants	225	255	285
Education opportunity grants	70	100	140
Advances for insured loans	13	—	—
Vocational student loans	1	1	1
Talent Search, other aid	10	57	96
Educational Professions Development:			
Recruitment	4	5	5
Teacher Corps	46	56	56
Teacher upgrading	50	65	65
Teacher fellowships	205	250	250
School personnel training	—	—	90
College personnel training	22	36	36
College equipment	15	70	70
Cooperative education	1	9	11
Networks for Knowledge	*	4	15
Public service education	*	5	13
Dissemination of information	—	2	—
Program planning	1	2	—
Improved graduate programs	*	5	10
Law school clinical experience	*	8	8
National Defense Education Act			
Student loans	210	275	300
Equipment grants, loans	110	120	130
Equipment for ESEA Title I	84	160	—
State supervision	10	10	10
Guidance, testing	25	40	54
Language development	16	30	39
Higher Education Facilities Act			
Undergraduate facilities grants	936	936	936
State planning	7	7	7
Graduate facilities grants	120	120	120
Academic facilities loans	400	400	400
Grants to reduce borrowing costs	5	7	14
International Education Act	90	90	90

* *Less than $500,000.*

SOURCE: House Report 1919, 90th Congress

to expire June 30. It also raised the maximum interest on guaranteed loans to 7 percent. These provisions were continued in the three-year Higher Education Amendments bill (PL 90-575).

Higher Education Act—All titles of the Act were extended and four new titles were added: Networks for Knowledge, encouraging colleges to share their educational facilities and equipment (Title VIII); Education for the Public Service, graduate training for governmental jobs (Title IX); Improvement of Graduate Programs, encouraging training at the Ph.D. level (Title X); and Law School Clinical Experience, to train more trial lawyers (Title XI).

In addition, a new program was added to Title IV of the Act, the student assistance section. The new program provided grants to encourage colleges to establish cooperative education programs. These were defined as programs providing for alternate periods of full-time study and full-time employment so that students could earn money to continue their education and gain job experience at the same time.

Other amendments to Title IV: raised the maximum educational opportunity grant (federal scholarship) to $1,000 and removed the $200 bonus allowed students who placed high in their class; set the federal share of work-study grants at 80 percent; transferred the Upward Bound program from the Office of Economic Opportunity to the Office of Education, effective July 1, 1969; authorized grants to colleges to provide special services (such as tutoring) to help disadvantaged students stay in college, and consolidated the two programs with the Office of Education's Talent Search program, which encouraged disadvantaged youths to attend college or take other post-high-school training.

The insured loan program in Title IV also was amended. The permissible interest rate was raised to 7 percent, the federal subsidy allowed to students after they completed college was removed, and a new federal guarantee program to cover 80 percent of any losses on student loans insured by nonfederal agencies was authorized.

In amendments to other titles of the Act, PL 90-575 raised the federal share of community service projects (Title I) to two-thirds of the cost instead of one-half, and authorized grants to retired professors who wished to teach at small developing institutions (Title III).

NDEA—The NDEA student loan program, equipment grants, guidance and testing, and language development programs were extended with minor changes. The fellowship program's cost-of-education grants to universities were raised to a maximum $3,500 per fellowship to correspond to payments allowed under the Higher Education Act.

A large new equipment grant program was added to Title III. This was earmarked for schools with large concentrations of poor children, those eligible for aid under Title I of ESEA. This program was authorized for only two years, through fiscal 1970.

Title VII of NDEA, grants for educational media, was allowed to expire.

College Classrooms—The grant and loan provisions of the Higher Education Facilities Act were extended until fiscal 1971 and a new program of federally subsidized interest on private loans for construction was authorized. For the grant programs the federal share of costs was raised to 50 percent (it was previously 40 percent for junior colleges and 33-1/3 percent for four-year colleges).

International Education—PL 90-575 extended the International Education Act of 1966, which had never been funded, through fiscal 1971, at $90 million annually.

Other Provisions—The 1968 Amendments also carried three general provisions of importance. They:

● Called for a Presidential report on the feasibility of making post-secondary education available to all who were qualified and wanted it.

• Permitted higher education funds to be appropriated one year in advance of the fiscal year in which they would be used.

• Required colleges and universities to deny federal aid to students who engaged in substantial disruption of the institution. *(See section below for a discussion of conflicting anti-riot provisions in other bills.)*

College Housing. The Housing and Urban Development Act of 1968 (PL 90-448) authorized a new program to relieve the Government of the growing demand for federal loans for college housing. It authorized annual grants subsidizing the difference between interest on a loan secured from private sources and the 3 percent rate charged on direct federal loans. The HUD Department could sign contracts for up to $10 million annually with colleges and universities for interest subsidies in fiscal 1969 and 1970, subject to limits set in appropriation bills.

Higher Education Appropriations, Teacher Corps. In appropriating almost $1 billion for higher education programs in fiscal 1969 Congress followed the President's lead in cutting back funds from the fiscal 1968 level. Although the total was $282 million less than the previous year's, a few programs were given increased funds. One was the Teacher Corps, which went up from $13.5 million to $20.9 million. The President had requested $31,235,000.

Educational opportunity grants (federal scholarships) received a severe cut. Of the $159.6 million requested by the President, Congress appropriated only $124.6 million. This meant a cut of 75 percent in the number of freshmen who could receive federal grants in the next school year, because the appropriation had to cover the second, third and fourth years of college for those who already had received grants. The number of freshmen receiving grants was expected to go down from 144,600 to 31,300.

National Science Foundation. The Senate in 1968 passed with minor changes a bill (HR 5404) which the House had passed the previous year. It became law (PL 90-407) July 18.

The bill clarified the organizational structure of the NSF, expanded the scope of its activities, and required that each year Congress pass an authorization bill for the agency before appropriating funds for it. This practice was followed for other scientific agencies, such as the Atomic Energy Commission and the space agency, NASA.

PL 90-407 allowed the NSF to support applied—as well as basic—research, and research in the social sciences as well as the natural sciences. The Foundation was directed to keep track of the whereabouts of all federal funds allocated for scientific research and to make an annual report.

The Director of the Foundation was given authority over all management and operations of the NSF, with the Foundation Board relieved of its authority over operations but kept responsible for overseeing broad policies.

PL 90-407 authorized appropriations of $525 million for the NSF in fiscal 1969. However, the Independent Offices appropriation bill (HR 17023—PL 90-550) allowed the agency only $400 million, which was $100 million less than the President's request.

Arts and Humanities. The House Education and Labor Committee tried in 1968 to give the National Foundation on the Arts and the Humanities a large increase in funds, but the final result was a two-year extension at about the funding level of previous years (HR 11308—PL 90-348).

The House Committee's bill authorized federal grants of $135 million for the two fiscal years 1969 and 1970, but the authorization was decimated on the House floor. By a 118-65 teller vote, the House accepted an amendment reducing the authorization to $11.2 million for one year. There was little opposition to the Foundation's activities; it was the economy issue that carried the day.

The Senate raised the authorization to $34 million for a two-year period, and the House agreed to this figure on a 194-166 roll-call vote June 5. In addition, the bill authorized the Government to match up to $13.5 million in private gifts to the Foundation.

The appropriation for the Foundation in fiscal 1969, carried in the Interior Department and Related Agencies bill (PL 90-425), was $11.5 million, half of what the President had requested before passage of HR 11308.

A related program, authorizing HEW grants for equipment to be used in the study of the arts and humanities, was extended for three years at an annual authorization of $500,000. The provision was in the Higher Education Amendments (PL 90-575).

Restraints on Students

Congress in 1968 enacted five measures designed to cut off federal aid to students engaging in crimes or other activities which disrupted the operations of institutions of higher learning. Three of the laws had conflicting provisions.

The action came in response to a number of disorders on university campuses, notably at Columbia University. The sentiment in Congress apparently overwhelmingly favored condemnation of the student demonstrators; but there was far less agreement on how best to express that sentiment.

Conservatives adopted a hard line and sought to enact provisions requiring the cutting off of federal aid to students engaged in the prohibited activities. Liberals tended to give academic institutions some discretion in determining when aid should be withheld. The Senate leaned more toward the liberal view on that issue and the House leaned more toward the conservative view.

Another point at issue was whether the institution or the federal agency administering the aid program should oversee administration of the aid cut-off provisions. Still another was whether a hearing should be afforded the student before his aid was withheld.

As a consequence, Congress enacted various forms of the aid cut-off provisions. Some measures provided for hearings, others did not; some placed the burden of administration on the university, others on the federal agency; some required that the student be convicted of a crime, while others said he need be found only to have disobeyed a lawful regulation or order of the university resulting in disruption of its operations; and one measure, the NASA authorization (PL 90-373), cut off funds to colleges prohibiting on-campus recruiting by armed forces representatives. Only one such college (Oberlin) appeared to have such regulations.

Civil libertarians contended that constitutional issues of academic freedom and free speech were raised by the aid cut-off provisions. They said that the provisions were unconstitutionally vague, failed to provide for due process and delegated uncontrolled discretion to university officials. A number of university presidents spoke out in opposition to the measures.

Student Unrest. From Berkeley in 1964 to Columbia in 1968, students forcefully made their presence felt on many college campuses across the country. They were bothered by impersonalization at large institutions, angered by American involvement in Vietnam and concerned about racial problems in the cities. They also demanded a greater voice in determining university policies.

Unruly demonstrations began on the Berkeley campus of the University of California in 1964 when students protested campus restrictions on political activities. During the next four years the student movement mushroomed, and within the first two months of the 1967-68 academic year, the National Student Assn. reported 71 student protests on campuses across the country. By the end of the school year more than 100 demonstrations had been held.

Possibly the worst eruption occurred at Columbia University where student occupation of buildings and a student strike kept the campus in turmoil most of the time from late April through May. Ostensibly the issue involved construction of a new gymnasium on the edge of a city park used by residents of nearby Harlem, but underlying it was the demand for more student participation in university policy decisions. Before the university quieted, 897 students were arrested and 216 students, faculty members and policemen were injured.

Conflicting Bills. Three bills enacted in 1968 had conflicting provisions on student rioters. They were the Independent Offices-HUD appropriations bill (PL 90-550), which carried funds for National Science Foundation grants, the Labor-HEW Departments appropriations bill (PL 90-557), which provided funds for college student loans and scholarships, and the Higher Education Amendments of 1968 (PL 90-575), extending student-aid programs for three years. In addition, the defense appropriations bill carried the same language as the Labor-HEW bill, and

the NASA authorization, referred to above, was concerned with colleges that barred recruiters for the armed forces.

Action on the bills with conflicting provisions is described below.

NSF Funds—In fiscal 1968, more than 14,000 graduate students received grants, loans, scholarships or fellowships from the National Science Foundation.

When the House considered the Independent Offices-HUD appropriations bill, which carried funds for the NSF, Rep. Louis C. Wyman (R N.H.) won acceptance May 8 of an anti-rioter amendment. The amendment prohibited payment of NSF funds to any student "who willfully refuses to obey a lawful regulation of the university or college which he is attending."

In reporting the bill July 9, the Senate Appropriations Committee toned down the Wyman amendment by requiring that a hearing be afforded students before funds could be stopped. Also added were sections placing the burden of withholding funds on the university, rather than on the scholarship or loan funding agency, and stipulating that the student's actions must have been of a serious nature and must have contributed to the disruption of the administration of a university.

In September the Senate version was agreed to by both chambers.

Higher Education Amendments—The Senate Labor and Public Welfare Committee reported S 3769 July 11 with a provision urging universities to "take immediate and prompt action to apply disciplinary measures, whether by withholding financial aid offered through federal programs, by other measures, or by both." The report stated that the right to withhold funds and the duty of maintaining discipline should be vested in the college itself, not in the Federal Government.

In considering HR 15067 (S 3769), the House July 25 by a **260-146** roll-call vote accepted an amendment by William J. Scherle (R Iowa) requiring colleges to withhold

---

Federal Spending on Education and Manpower Programs

(in millions, by fiscal year)

	1959	1965	1966	1967	1968	1969 [1]
Elementary and secondary education	$ 259	$ 478	$1,646	$2,286	$2,430	$2,182
Higher education	225	413	701	1,159	1,392	1,368
Vocational education	38	132	136	250	265	252
Manpower training	4	336	731	940	1,263	1,511
Science education and basic research	106	309	368	415	449	480
Other education and manpower aids	451	850	925	1,097	1,227	1,386
Veterans readjustment benefits	864	50	211	596	673	881
Deductions for offsetting receipts	-3	-9	-11	-11	-16	-14
TOTALS	$1,944	$2,559	$4,707	$6,732	$7,683	$8,046

1. Estimated

SOURCE: Bureau of the Budget

funds, rather than giving them the option to cut off aid, from students disrupting campus activities. Other restrictions also were added by the House. An effort to delete the entire restrictive section was defeated by an 18-109 vote.

S 3769 was reported out of conference Sept. 25 and passed by both chambers with substantial changes softening the House-imposed restrictions on student aid and on payments to employees of the institution. It provided that the burden of cutting off funds be placed on the university, rather than the Federal Government; that the university afford notice and opportunity for a hearing before aid was withheld; that the student or employee be convicted in court of a crime involving use of force, or be found to have disobeyed a lawful regulation or order of the institution, resulting in disruption of the university; and that funds be denied such a student or employee for a two-year period.

HEW Funds—Appropriations for all programs of the U.S. Office of Education and HEW health activities were carried in the Labor-HEW bill.

As reported by the Appropriations Committee and passed by the House June 26, it was specified that no funds appropriated by the bill could be used to aid any student convicted of using force to disrupt a college or university.

In Senate floor consideration of the bill Sept. 6, debate focused on where power should be vested for cutting off student aid funds. Jacob K. Javits (R N.Y.) and Wayne Morse (D Ore.) each sponsored amendments delegating power to the universities, rather than to the funding agency. The Javits amendment, defeated by a 25-35 roll-call vote, gave universities discretion in withholding funds, rather than requiring that they do so.

After defeat of the Javits amendment, Morse proposed acceptance of the language included in the Higher Education Amendments bill, which made the universities accountable to the Federal Government in cases of withholding aid. The Morse amendment was accepted on a close 28-26 roll call.

House-Senate conferees were unable to reconcile the differences between the two chambers' positions and reported the anti-riot section in disagreement. After a week of further disagreement, however, the Senate receded and accepted the House version Oct. 9.

In debate before final action, Javits pointed out that Congress had already enacted two different versions of anti-disturbance legislation (in the NSF and Higher Education bills) and urged that the Senate give serious thought before approving a third version. "I do not think it adds to our majesty when we are seen to be wandering all over the lot on three different bills," he said. "I do not see that our action builds up the confidence of the students in the fact that we in Congress know what we are doing."

Job Training and Rehabilitation

The period of 1965-1968, which produced high levels of employment, turned the job spotlight on the most disadvantaged of the labor force, the hard-core unemployed. Usually semi-literate, with physical and social disabilities, and more often than not of brown or black skin, the hard-core included not only the chronically unemployed of middle age or older, but also a large number of teen-agers. When clustered in the inner cities, the out-of-work teen-agers constituted the most combustible element in urban life and the source of soaring crime rates.

More than any other group, jobless youth became the focus for new manpower-training developments of 1965-68.

The figures below contrast the unemployment rates for teen-age males with the rates for young male adults. They are average yearly rates representing unemployed males who were actively seeking work, and thus exclude full-time students.

	National Average	Age 18-19 White	Age 18-19 Nonwhite	Age 25-34 White	Age 25-34 Nonwhite
1965	4.0%	11.4%	20.2%	2.6%	6.2%
1966	3.2	8.9	20.5	2.1	4.9
1967	3.1	9.0	20.1	1.9	4.4
1968	2.9	8.2	19.0	1.7	3.8

The training emphasis on the hard-core unemployed began with the Economic Opportunity Act of 1964 and its Job Corps and Neighborhood Youth Corps. These were essentially pre-employment training programs, putting more emphasis on getting young people oriented toward jobs (work experience) than on training them in specific skills.

The Manpower Development and Training Act took on a similar emphasis in 1966, and the longer-established vocational education and vocational rehabilitation programs followed suit in 1968.

The Hard-Core, the Unemployed and Underemployed. In prosperous 1966, the Labor Department conducted a survey of the nation's big-city slum areas and measured, for the first time, not only the unemployment rates but also the underemployment rates. The study showed a subemployment rate in these areas of 32.7 percent—nearly a third of all ghetto residents over 16. This figure included the 9.3 percent who were unemployed (persons who looked for jobs but did not find them) and the 23.4 percent who were underemployed (persons who worked only seasonally or part-time, who worked full-time but made less than $3,000 a year or who had given up and were no longer looking for a job).

In the nation as a whole in 1966, 2.5 million individuals were unemployed for 15 weeks or longer; 1.3 million looked for but did not find any work during the entire year; another 1.3 million men between the ages of 25 and 64 did not even seek work; and more than 5 million persons worked for less than the federal minimum wage. Thus, the hard-core unemployed were only part of the national problem.

The Labor Department defined the hard-core unemployed as poor persons (income of less than $3,130 a year for a family of four) who do not have suitable employment and who are either school dropouts, under 22, over 45, handicapped or "subject to special obstacles to employment" such as racial discrimination or a prison record.

The National Advisory Commission on Civil Disorders, (better known as the Kerner Commission) calculated that 20 percent of the participants in the 1967 riots did not have jobs and that many of those who were employed were in unskilled, low-status, dead-end jobs below their ability and educational level. Unemployment and underemployment, the Civil Disorders Commission noted, are "inextricably linked to the problem of civil disorder."

The persons in the most critical need of help, the Commission said, were the 500,000 "hard-core unemployed" within the nation's central cities. These individuals, the vast majority of them Negroes, were simply unable to cope with the problems of performing a job, the commission said. They lacked even a basic education. They had no experience of living on a schedule, of following the directions of supervisors, of working at a task to its completion or of managing money. Even more important, unlike the immigrants who performed the lowest-level jobs in past decades, they were not imbued with the tradition of supporting a family.

Added to these handicaps were racial discrimination in hiring and promotion, still prevalent in many industries and labor unions, and discrimination in housing which forced Negroes to live outside areas where new jobs were located.

'Mix' of Manpower Programs. By 1968, when the Kerner Report was issued, the Government was spending over $1.2 billion on manpower-training programs. Yet a leading expert in the field, Prof. Garth Mangum, wrote that the United States was "without a federal manpower policy." The programs were piled one on top of another, without any real reference to each other. The result was a duplication in some services and a situation in which many programs did not have enough funds to carry out their aims, Mangum and others said.

There were several reasons for the disjointed approach. Congress seemed willing to grant more money for

11 Major Federally Supported Manpower Programs

PROGRAM	TRAINEES	AUTH-ORITY	AGENCY	ADMINIS-TERED BY	FY 1968 APPROP.	FY 1969 APPROP.	SLOTS FY 1968	SLOTS FY 1969
Manpower Development Training (MDTA -- on-the-job training, institutional training)	unemployed and underemployed adults and youths	PL 87-415 (1962)	Labor Dept.	Labor Dept. (Manpower Adm.) HEW (Office of Education)	$386,207,000	$400,000,000	275,000	274,000
Vocational Education	state deter-mined	PL 88-210 (1963)	HEW	HEW (Office of Education)	$262,900,000	$248,216,000	(enrollees) 8,150,000	(enrollees) 9,250,000
Vocational Rehabili-tation	physically, men-tally handicapped	PL 89-333 (1965)	HEW	HEW (Vocational Rehab. Adm.)	$287,000,000	$346,000,000	(rehabltd.) 208,000	(rehabltd.) 230,000
Work Incentive Program	Aid to Families with Dependent Children recipients	Social Security Amendments PL 90-248 (1967)	HEW	Labor Dept., state welfare agencies HEW (Child care)	$ 35,000,000	$100,000,000 $ 17,500,000		102,000
Neighborhood Youth Corps	poor as well as un-employed youths	PL 88-452 (1964) amended, PL 90-222 (1967)	Office of Eco-nomic Oppor-tunity (OEO)	Labor Dept. (Bu-reau of Work Programs)				
in-school summer program } out-of-school	poor youths in school unemployed youths				$ 48,300,000 91,000,000 141,700,000	$ 46,000,000 125,000,000 130,000,000	74,800 220,000 52,900	100,000 291,000 48,000
Operation Main-stream (formerly Green Thumb)	chronically unem-ployed adults in rural areas	PL 89-253 (1965) amended, PL 90-222 (1967)	OEO	Labor Dept. (Bu-reau of Work Programs)	$ 34,300,000	$ 41,000,000	9,300	10,800
New Careers	unemployed, poor youths in urban areas	PL 89-794 (1966) amended, PL 90-222 (1967)	OEO	Labor Dept. (Bu-reau of Work Programs)	$ 27,700,000	$ 18,600,000	6,500	5,100
Concentrated Em-ployment Program (CEP)	hard-core unem-ployed in selected cities	OEO Amend-ments PL 90-222 (1967)	OEO	Labor Dept. (com-munity prime sponsors)	$ 55,000,000 (OEO and MDTA)	$ 83,000,000 (OEO) $ 31,800,000 (MDTA)	54,000	100,000
JOBS (Job Opportu-nities in the Business Sector)	hard-core unem-ployed in 50 largest cities	PL 90-222 (1967)	OEO & Labor	Labor Dept.	$ 53,000,000 (OEO and MDTA)	$152,000,000 (OEO) $ 48,000,000 (MDTA)	15,000	66,700
Special Impact	adult & youth slum residents in JOBS cities	PL 89-794 (1966) amended, PL 90-222 (1967)	OEO	Labor Dept. (Bu-reau of Work Programs)	$ 10,000,000	$ 10,000,000	3,500	4,000
Job Corps	poor school dropouts	PL 88-452 (1964)	OEO	OEO	$285,000,000	$280,000,000	35,000	38,800

SOURCES: Office of Economic Opportunity, Labor Department

a number of separate programs than for a few programs with a broader scope. The Congressional appropriation process forced manpower administrators to return to Congress to ask for funds for the next fiscal year shortly after they had received funds for the current fiscal year. This meant that they were asked to show that an existing program was successful when it was barely under way. Perhaps more significant was the fact that there was no real concept in or out of the Government of what kinds of programs produced the best results.

There were no available statistics on how many individuals actually were aided by Government employment programs. The Labor Department kept personnel figures on the manpower programs it funded. But the Office of Economic Opportunity (OEO) evaluated its programs solely in terms of "slots" rather than in terms of men. *(For a list of the slots in each Government manpower program, see next page.)*

A slot is a training position over a period of time, normally a year. Several individuals can be trained in one slot. For instance, if one person can be trained in 13 weeks, four persons can be trained in this one slot over a year. The concept can be explained in terms of a desk in a classroom. The desk would be the slot. Several students could sit at the desk during the course of a school day.

Government officials contended it was necessary to talk in terms of slots because individuals take different amounts of time to be trained, while the number of job-training openings (the "desks") have to be budgeted ahead of time.

Following is a description of some of the Government's major manpower programs.

Office of Economic Opportunity

Title I of the Economic Opportunity Act, the basic antipoverty law, was entitled Work Training and Work-Study Programs. It authorized the Job Corps and Comprehensive work and training programs, which included three aspects of the Neighborhood Youth Corps and other special programs. Only the Job Corps was operated by OEO; the Labor Department operated the others under delegation from OEO. Brief descriptions follow; for more detailed discussion, see this book's separate section on the Antipoverty Program.

Job Corps—The Job Corps was based on the assumption that it was necessary to remove young people from an unsuitable environment before they could be properly trained. It created residential conservation camps and job training centers in rural and urban areas where men and women 16 to 21 could receive educational counseling and health services as well as work experience. Most of the enrollees were school dropouts, mainly unemployed and unemployable.

Neighborhood Youth Corps—This program provided work experience and training in local communities for three categories of men and women 16 to 21—poor youths in school, poor youths during their summer vacation from school, and unemployed school dropouts. The program was designed to increase the employability of youngsters or to enable them to earn money so they could stay in school.

Most of the local work programs provided jobs in public or in nonprofit private facilities, but some were in private industry.

Other Antipoverty Programs—New job programs to put slum residents to work were authorized by the antipoverty amendments of 1966 and 1967. Two programs —one called Special Impact and the other called New Careers—were coordinated in 1966 with an existing adult work-experience program called Operation Mainstream and delegated by the OEO to the Labor Department. Special Impact sought to employ slum residents in rehabilitating slum housing. New Careers sought to train the poor to be aides in such fields as education, welfare, health and public safety, thereby creating new subprofessional jobs. Operation Mainstream, formerly called Green Thumb, was designed to employ chronically unemployed adults, many of them elderly, in beautification projects.

The Social Security Amendments of 1967 (HR 12080— PL 90-248) required all adult recipients of aid to families with dependent children (AFDC) to participate in a work-training, work-incentive program. The law specified that an attempt was first to be made to find jobs for welfare recipients who were employable. Others were to be trained and given a $30-a-month incentive payment. *(See welfare section.)*

Vocational Education

The basis for federal aid to occupational training lies in the Smith-Hughes Act of 1917 and the George-Barden Act of 1946 which authorized grants to the states for vocational education in public schools. The Acts limited federal assistance to specific occupations, principally agriculture and home economics and, to a lesser extent, trade and industrial occupations. Vocational education aid is dispensed through HEW's Office of Education.

A breakthrough was achieved in the Vocational Education Act of 1963, which greatly increased federal contributions and permitted use of federal funds to train for any occupation not requiring a four-year college education. This brought training in office work under the program for the first time.

Previously, home economics had enrolled most of the girls in vocational schools. Three years after passage of the 1963 Act, the sharp emphasis in vocational training, which included a sharp percentage growth in health training (practical nurses, dental assistants, X-ray technicians, etc.), was clearly apparent. *(See table.)*

A new direction was ordered yet again in the 1968 Act, which ordered priority attention for the handicapped, both the physically and the economically disadvantaged. This was in response to findings of the National Advisory Council on Vocational Education, which reported to Congress on the need to expand programs reaching "residents of slum and ghetto neighborhoods," and especially high-school dropouts.

The Act (PL 90-576) required the states to devote certain portions of their federal grants to education of the physically, mentally and culturally disadvantaged. It also enlarged programs that combined study with on-the-job experience.

The Act also emphasized the growing need for vocational training beyond the high school level, requiring the states to allot portions of their federal grants for post-secondary programs.

ENROLLMENTS IN FEDERALLY AIDED VOCATIONAL-TECHNICAL EDUCATION

Field of Education	Number (thousands)		Percent distribution		Percent change,
	Fiscal year 1964	Fiscal year 1967	Fiscal year 1964	Fiscal year 1967	Fiscal year 1964-67
TOTAL	4,566	7,048	100.0	100.0	54.4
Agriculture	861	935	18.9	13.3	8.6
Distributive	334	481	7.3	6.8	44.0
Health	59	115	1.3	1.6	94.9
Home economics	2,022	2,187	44.3	31.0	8.2
Office	——	1,572	——	22.3	——
Technical	221	266	4.8	3.8	20.4
Trades and industry	1,069	1,491	23.4	21.2	39.5

Note: Detail may not add to totals due to rounding.

SOURCE: Office of Education

Vocational Rehabilitation

Authorized in 1920, and slowly expanded since then, the Vocational Rehabilitation Act provides federal grants to state rehabilitation agencies for services that will enable the disabled to gain employment. The grants are administered by HEW's Rehabilitation Services Administration.

At first, the program concentrated on the physically handicapped. 1965 amendments brought the mentally handicapped into the program in large numbers, and in 1968 a new category was added—the "socio-economic disadvantaged," in other words the hard core.

Major increases in federal funding of the Act accompanied these amendments. The first specific authorization, $30 million, was enacted for fiscal 1955. Ten years later the appropriation had grown to $137 million and in fiscal 1969 it was $369 million.

The caseloads increased proportionately: 298,000 in 1960 compared to 670,000 in 1968, with the number of persons actually rehabilitated increasing from 88,000 to 208,000 in that period. The services that could be provided included: comprehensive medical and psychological evaluation, with medical treatment where needed; counseling and guidance in vocational adjustment and job training; limited allowances for maintenance and transportation; and, finally, job placement and follow-up.

Manpower Training

A key achievement of the Kennedy Administration, the Manpower Development and Training Act of 1962 was the first comprehensive effort by the Federal Government to help the unemployed and the underemployed get training in skills which were needed and for which jobs were available. In its first years the majority of trainees were unemployed family men who had at least three years of previous employment.

Rapidly, as the Act (known as MDTA) was amended and extended in 1963, 1965, 1966 and 1968, the emphasis shifted to younger men with little or no working experience. In 1963, basic literacy training was authorized as an adjunct to work training, and allowances were paid to young persons between 16 and 21.

A formal redirection of the program was announced in 1966. Approximately 65 percent of MDTA training efforts would be directed at the hard-core unemployed, and 35 percent would be focused on training for skills in short supply. As experience with the program grew, the early tendency to establish one-shot training programs diminished, and in 1968 priority was given to establishing Manpower Training Skills Centers. These were centralized facilities giving training of various kinds and providing the supporting services needed by disadvantaged trainees. In 1968 there were 55 such centers.

From the beginning, the MDTA provided both institutional and on-the-job training. Most of the institutional training—which enrolled more than two-thirds of the trainees—was in vocational education schools and was administered by the HEW Department. The Labor Department was in over-all charge of the entire MDTA program, however.

From its start in 1963 through fiscal 1968, MDTA enrolled more than 1 million persons, over 600,000 of whom completed their training courses. The Labor Department said over 75 percent of these were employed when last contacted by the Department.

A new emphasis was given to on-the-job training in 1968 with the JOBS program, operated by private employers and financed in part by the Federal Government. The goal was to have 500,000 hard-core on the job by June 1971, employed and trained by the private sector, with the Government paying only for above-normal training costs (literacy training, counseling, health services, for example). In practice, a number of businessmen shunned government payments and financed all training, but there was some question about the number of truly hard-core trained without Government contract.

Tax Credit Pros and Cons

A tax credit permits a taxpayer to subtract the amount of the credit from what otherwise would be his total tax liability. Proposals for tax credits for businesses which hire and train the unemployed had the endorsement of the Republican party hierarchy, the U.S. Chamber of Commerce and most business leaders. The President's Advisory Commission on Civil Disorders found that tax credit proposals held "promise." Tax credits were opposed by the Johnson Administration and by Rep. Wilbur D. Mills (D Ark.), chairman of the House Ways and Means Committee.

Pros. The basic argument in favor of tax credits was that they provided a greater financial incentive for industry to participate in manpower programs than did direct Government payments. Businessmen believed tax credits would involve less red tape than direct payments. Also, they preferred not to have to wait for Government reimbursement of training costs.

Cons. Opponents of tax credits for manpower programs argued that they would be an enormous drain on the Treasury and would open the door to similarly expensive credits in other areas. In addition, Government officials believed that under such a system they would have less control over the training programs set up by industry than they would if they had to approve the direct payments.

The JOBS program (officially, Job Opportunities in the Public Sector) was established under authority of the 1967 Economic Opportunity Act Amendments (PL 90-222) and funded jointly from OEO and MDTA appropriations.

Another spin-off from the 1967 Amendments, also jointly financed, was the Concentrated Employment Program. This was designed to bring together a variety of manpower services and focus them in a unified effort in designated target areas. Administered by the Labor Department's Manpower Administration, CEPS usually were controlled by OEO-funded community action agencies, acting as the prime local sponsor.

During the years 1966-68 two proposed additions to the range of manpower programs received considerable attention but neither Administration support nor Congressional passage. One, sponsored by liberal Members of Congress and urban organizations, advocated a Public Service Employment program, to subsidize employment of the hard-core by local and state agencies and nonprofit organizations. Impetus for the idea came from the 1966 report of the National Commission on Technology, Automation and Economic Progress. The Presidentially appointed group recommended that "the Government be an employer of last resort, providing work for the 'hard-core unemployed' in useful community enterprises."

The other proposal, backed by conservatives in Congress and business groups, called for a tax credit for businesses that hired the unemployed. The Republican proposal, endorsed in the 1964 and 1968 party platforms, was titled the Human Investment Act. It offered a tax credit of 10 percent for an employer's training costs and was not limited to the hard-core or to areas of high unemployment. *(See box.)*

Chronology

Of Legislation

On Job Training

1965

The first major changes in the Vocational Rehabilitation Act in 12 years were made, with overwhelming support, by the first session of the extremely productive 89th Congress. The changes had first been requested by President Kennedy in 1963 and endorsed by President Johnson in 1964.

A three-year extension of the Manpower Development and Training Act (MDTA) also was authorized by Congress with almost no opposition. It made no major innovations but lengthened permissible training periods and increased the allowances paid those taking training.

As a complementary measure to the insured loan program for college students authorized in the Higher Education Act, Congress extended the same program to students in post-secondary vocational schools.

Vocational Rehabilitation. HR 8310—PL 89-333, the Vocational Rehabilitation Act Amendments of 1965, made the first major changes in the Act since 1954. The amendments were intended to produce a dramatic increase—from 120,000 to 200,000—in the number of physi-

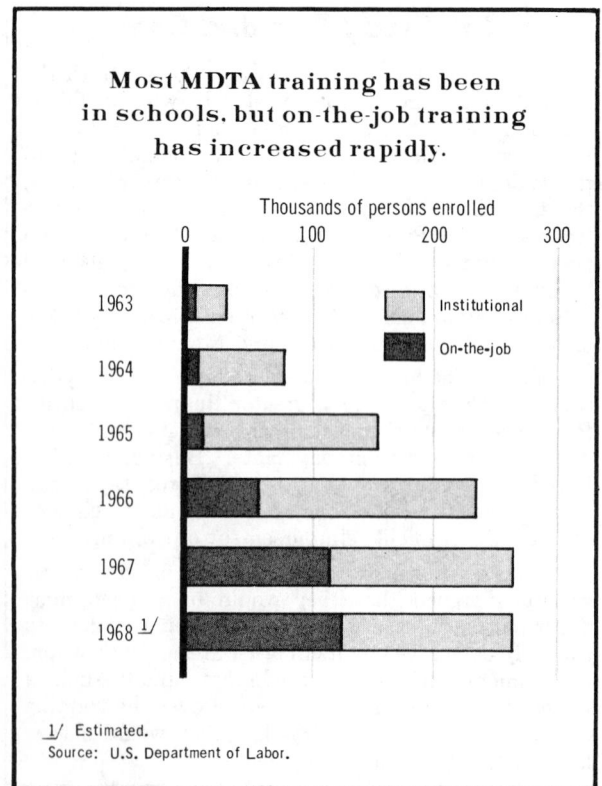

Most MDTA training has been in schools, but on-the-job training has increased rapidly.

Thousands of persons enrolled

1/ Estimated.
Source: U.S. Department of Labor.

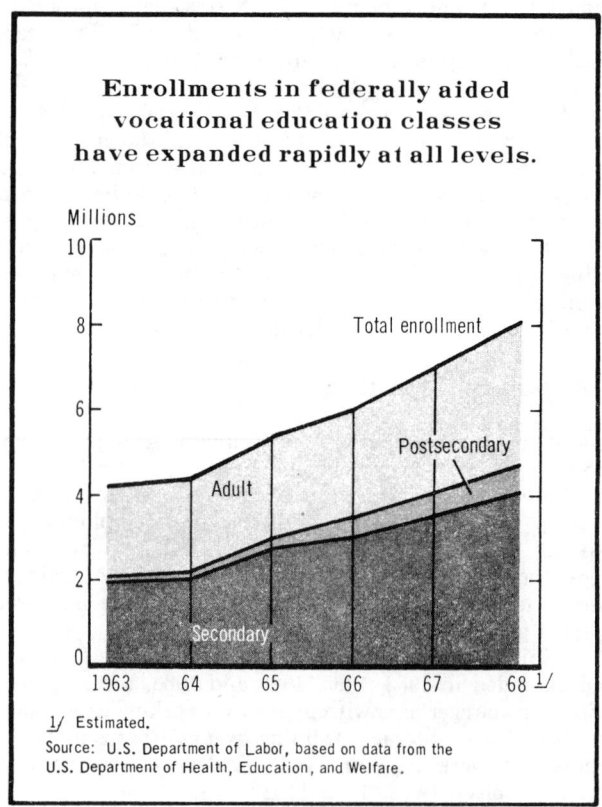

Enrollments in federally aided vocational education classes have expanded rapidly at all levels.

1/ Estimated.
Source: U.S. Department of Labor, based on data from the U.S. Department of Health, Education, and Welfare.

cally and mentally handicapped individuals who could be rehabilitated annually and permitted to pursue a useful and gainful vocation. The bill was also designed to improve the quality of services provided and to encourage rehabilitation of new groups of disabled persons, with particular emphasis on the mentally retarded and severely handicapped.

The main approach of the bill was the enlargement—both in dollar amounts and in scope—of several existing federal grant programs for vocational rehabilitation, and the creation of several wholly new grant programs as well. The major new activities for which the bill provided financing were: development of new rehabilitation methods and of new or expanded services for the severely handicapped, special programs to increase the number of persons rehabilitated; planning for development of programs aimed at making services available to all handicapped individuals in a state by 1975; training and traineeships for rehabilitation personnel in a variety of new fields and for longer periods of study; construction of workshops and facilities; initial costs of staffing rehabilitation facilities; determination of future state needs and planning to meet them; training in occupational skills and allowances for trainees; and projects to analyze and improve the professional services of workshops.

In addition, the bill specifically permitted rehabilitation services for extended periods of time for mentally retarded or other handicapped individuals if necessary to determine their rehabilitation potentialities. This had a major effect on the number of mentally handicapped who could receive rehabilitation services.

HR 8310 was a modified version of legislation requested by President Johnson in his Jan. 7 Health Message. As enacted, it contained every major provision of the Administration draft bill. In addition, however, it included a number of new financing provisions added by the House which, in general, eased state matching requirements, set dollar ceilings on most of the existing and new programs, and provided spending authorizations only for fiscal years 1966-68. The existing programs had been permanent since 1958, with spending limited only through the Congressional appropriations process and by the states' abilities to match federal funds.

HR 8310 authorized a vast enlargement of federal spending for vocational rehabilitation. Federal expenditures for the vocational rehabilitation program in fiscal 1965 totaled $137 million. HR 8310 authorized federal spending of $388.25 million in fiscal 1966, $477.25 million in fiscal 1967 and $549.25 in fiscal 1968, for a total of $1,414,750,000 over the three-year period. State and local matching contributions would push over-all expenditures substantially higher. In addition, HR 8310 authorized $1.5 million over fiscal 1966-68 for the President's Committee on Employment of the Handicapped.

By far the largest programs in the bill were the basic grants to the states (starting at $300 million and rising to $400 million) and the grants to public and private non-profit organizations for special projects (starting at $80 million and rising to $117 million).

The major change initiated by Congress was raising the federal share of rehabilitation costs from a sliding scale of 50 to 70 percent to a flat 75 percent.

The bill passed both the House and Senate by voice votes, without floor amendments. It became law (PL 89-333) Nov. 8, 1965.

MDTA. Congress with little controversy enacted an Administration bill amending and extending for three years, through June 30, 1969, the Manpower Development and Training Act of 1962. The bill (S 974—PL 89-15) authorized $454 million for the program in fiscal 1966 and such sums as were necessary thereafter. The funds would be set in annual appropriations bills.

The 1965 bill continued in the direction of the 1963 amendments by increasing the period during which persons could receive training, thereby benefiting the least educated, by increasing the training allowances, by relaxing eligibility requirements for training allowances, by providing additional benefits for trainees, by postponing for one more year (through fiscal 1966) requirements that states help pay the costs of training programs, and by increasing the federal share of financing in subsequent years above that provided in the existing law. The bill also expanded and authorized additional experimental and demonstration programs. Training programs conducted by the Area Redevelopment Administration were brought under provisions of the MDTA.

The provisions on training programs authorized payment of allowances for up to two years, replacing the previous limit of one year for occupational training plus 20 weeks of basic education. The prohibitions against allowances for single persons without dependents and for more than one person in a family were removed.

The legislation passed both chambers with bipartisan support and little controversy. There were only two major differences between the House and Senate versions—the expiration date of the MDTA and a limit on appropriations. The three-year extension was a compromise. The Senate version, calling for four years, survived a Republican effort to limit the extension to only one year. This amendment, offered by Sen. Winston L. Prouty (R Vt.), lost on a 35-49 roll-call vote March 16, after which the bill was passed on a 76-8 roll call.

The House bill, which extended MDTA for two years without an appropriations limit, passed on a 395-0 vote.

The new law's authorization of $454 million replaced the fiscal 1966 authorization of $285 million that had been enacted in the 1963 Amendments.

S 974 was signed into law April 26. Earlier in the month, Secretary of Labor W. Willard Wirtz had issued an annual report on MDTA. The April 1 report said that occupational training projects for nearly 200,000 unemployed workers were approved under the MDTA during 1964, a 79 percent increase of 1963. Total number of individuals approved for training or other vocation services under the MDTA was close to 400,000 at the end of 1964. About one-half of 1964 participants had been unemployed for more than 15 weeks; almost a third had been jobless for more than six months. These individuals were considered hard-core, long-term unemployed. Participants with less than a grade school education more than doubled in 1964 and the number of nonwhite workers enrolled increased to more than one-quarter of the total number of trainees, Wirtz said. About 37 percent of the 1964 participants were unemployed workers 21 years of age or younger. At the end of 1964, there were 700 occupations for which training had been approved, up 200 from 1963.

Indian Vocational Training. President Johnson April 22 signed into law a bill (HR 4778—PL 89-14) amending the Indian Vocational Training Act of 1956.

The bill increased the authorization for the Indian training program to $15 million annually. A 1963 amendment to the Act had raised the annual authorization from $7.5 million to $12 million.

The President said, "The program is open to Indian men and women between the ages of 18 and 35 who live on or near reservations. They may receive up to two years of vocational training at Government expense." He said "Indian trainees come from reservation areas where unemployment is six to seven times the national average—where industrialization is just beginning—and where population pressures on the land base have led to prolonged and extreme poverty." He said that since the program's inception, more than 13,000 Indians had received training, "nearly 10,000 of them in the past four years."

HR 4778 was passed by voice votes of the House April 5 and the Senate April 9.

Vocational Loan Insurance Act. Congress in 1965 enacted an Administration-backed bill (HR 7743—PL 89-287) providing insured loans and federal interest subsidies for students in post-secondary business, trade, technical and other vocational schools. The bill was designed to encourage state and private efforts to insure loans for students in public and private vocational schools and to provide federal insurance if no local programs were available. In addition, it authorized direct federal loans for post-secondary vocational students who could not otherwise obtain loans at reasonable interest rates. The plan was identical to the college loan insurance feature of the Higher Education Act. *(See Education section.)*

The vocational loan provisions originally were part of the Administration's higher education bill but Congress decided to treat them separately.

Under the law the Commissioner of Education was allowed to insure up to $75 million a year in loans during fiscal 1966-68 and to make direct loans totaling $1 million to students who could not get loans from state or private sources at reasonable interest (gernerally 6 percent).

The bill was passed by a 300-0 roll-call vote in the House June 21, by voice vote of the Senate Sept. 28, and became law Oct. 22.

1966

In a year when unemployment fell to the lowest rate in 13 years—3.8 percent—Congress made only minor changes in MDTA. When the Act became law in 1962, the unemployment rate was 5.5 percent. In subsequent years it was 5.7, 5.2 and 4.5 percent.

In his March 8 manpower message, President Johnson said that despite the low unemployment figures, there were still 3 million unemployed, and "the unemployed and underemployed are not fully matched with the jobs available." He ordered the Labor Department's Bureau of Labor Statistics to include information on labor shortage situations in its monthly reports. Later the Joint Economic Committee of Congress recommended that the Government gather and publish comprehensive national job vacancy statistics.

MDTA. HR 16715—PL 89-792, signed into law Nov. 7, authorized training programs in skills in which there were critical shortages of workers. This was envisioned primarily as an upgrading program for already employed workers. They could receive $10 a week allow-

ance for training after their regular working hours. As the upgraded workers moved into more highly skilled jobs, it was hoped that unemployed persons would fill the resulting vacancies.

Other new departures in HR 16715 authorized special programs to counsel and train older unemployed workers, 45 years and older, and to train prison inmates for employment after their release. The latter, an experimental program, was authorized for two years only.

1967

Action on job training was taken during Congressional consideration of the 1967 antipoverty bill. OEO's various training programs were ordered consolidated, and the Senate debated, and ultimately defeated, a $2.5 billion emergency job program that stemmed, in part, from severe riots in the ghettos of Detroit and Newark.

Although programs in the 1965 Vocational Rehabilitation Act were authorized through fiscal 1968, Congress in 1967 acted a year in advance to assure the states of increases in their basic grants.

Vocational Rehabilitation. HR 12257—PL 90-99, extending basic grants through fiscal 1970 at increasingly higher levels, was an Administration bill passed by Congress without significant change. It included two new programs, one for migratory farm labor families and the other authorizing a National Center for Deaf-Blind Youths and Adults.

The authorization for basic grants to the states, which was $400 million in fiscal 1968, was raised by the bill to $500 million in fiscal 1969 and $600 million the next year. These sums were estimated to increase the number of rehabilitated persons from 173,000 in 1966 to 247,000 in 1969 and 278,600 in 1970, if the amounts authorized were appropriated in full.

The Senate Labor and Public Welfare Committee's report on the bill said that each dollar invested in rehabilitation yielded about $5 in income taxes paid by the person rehabilitated. At the time they were accepted for rehabilitation, almost one-fifth of the persons served were on public assistance or in public institutions and three-fourths were unemployed, the Committee said.

The program for migrant farm workers authorized project grants to state or private nonprofit agencies with the Government paying 90 percent of the costs of each project. A provision in the bill directed the states by July 1, 1969, to provide services to the handicapped without regard to how long the person had resided in the state. It was pointed out that most migrant workers were "noncitizens" of any state, so that they had not been eligible for rehabilitation services under previous programs.

OEO Job Programs. Consolidation of OEO's job-training programs was ordered as a part of the Economic Opportunity Amendments of 1967 (S 2388—PL 90-222). Programs to be consolidated by July 1, 1968, included the Neighborhood Youth Corps, New Careers and Operation Mainstream. *(For details, see separate section on the antipoverty program.)*

During Senate consideration of S 2388, bitter controversy developed over the Labor and Public Welfare Committee's recommendation for a $2.5 billion, two-year emergency job program. The funds were to support "labor intensive" projects (those providing a large number of jobs for the investment) in low-income areas with severe unemployment problems (mainly big-city ghettos). The first-year authorization of $1 billion could provide over 200,000 jobs in private industry and public agencies, the sponsors said.

The Johnson Administration opposed the program, though it was largely a Democratic plan, reportedly because it feared it would endanger enactment of the antipoverty bill. Also, the Administration, which had asked Congress to enact a 10 percent tax surcharge, was under strong pressure to hold down federal spending.

The emergency job program was the focus of much of the debate during the two weeks in which the Senate considered S 2388. When it became clear that the Committee's plan could not pass, attention centered on a compromise one-year, $925 million substitute offered by Sen. Winston L. Prouty (R Vt.). This was an amalgam of existing manpower training activities, public service jobs and elements of the Republicans' tax credit proposal for the training expenses of businesses. The substitute was rejected Oct. 4 on a key **42-47** roll-call vote (R 16-18; ND 24-13; SD 2-16). The Committee's $2.5 billion plan then was recommitted (killed) on a 54-28 roll call.

Other manpower votes taken during Senate action on S 2388 included: a proposal by Sens. Abraham A. Ribicoff (D Conn.) and Charles H. Percy (R Ill.) to transfer 2 percent of non-defense appropriations to a special fund to be used by the President for public service jobs, defeated 14-73; an amendment by Carl T. Curtis (R Neb.) to abolish the Job Corps and increase vocational training funds by $195 million, defeated 30-49; and a Prouty amendment authorizing $200 million to pay up to 15 percent of company costs in hiring and training the hard-core unemployed, defeated 28-57.

Simultaneously with Senate action on the antipoverty bill, the Administration announced an experimental program, to cost $40 million in five cities, to encourage businessmen through training subsidies to hire the hard-core in ghetto areas.

1968

Amendments to the Vocational Education and Vocational Rehabilitation Acts put new emphasis on preparing the disadvantaged for productive work, markedly increasing federal funds for this purpose. MDTA programs also were extended.

The major innovation of the year was achieved through Presidential directive. It was a joint Government-industry effort to hire the hard-core unemployed, and grew out of the experimental program started in five cities late in 1967.

President Johnson described the plan, called JOBS— Job Opportunities in the Business Sector—in his Jan. 23 manpower message. He said it would be run by the National Alliance of Businessmen, an organization created especially for the program and headed by Henry Ford II, chairman of the board of the Ford Motor Co.

Operating in the 50 largest cities, the program was to put 100,000 hard-core to work by June 1969 and 500,000 by June 1971, the President said.

The companies participating in the program were to furnish jobs and bear the normal cost of training, while the Government agreed to underwrite additional costs such as literacy training, transportation, health services and counseling. The federal subsidy per worker was to be negotiated separately with each company. It was estimated that an average subsidy would be about $3,500 a year, but it could run as high as perhaps $5,000.

The program needed no new authorization. The 1967 antipoverty amendments (PL 90-222) specified that the Government could pay private businesses for their manpower efforts. The JOBS program was funded out of both OEO and MDTA appropriations.

If it attained its goal of employing 500,000 by June 1971, the program still would not meet the need for jobs estimated by the Kerner Commission and other urban specialists. The report of the Commission on Civil Disorders, headed by Illinois Gov. Otto Kerner (D), called for 2 million new jobs by 1971, half in the public sector, half in the private.

Sen. Joseph S. Clark (D Pa.) and other liberal Senators sponsored a bill (S 3063) which placed the initial emphasis on creating public service jobs. During hearings in April before Clark's Subcommittee on Manpower, Employment and Poverty, the bill was endorsed by the National League of Cities, the U.S. Conference of Mayors and former Health, Education and Welfare Secretary John W. Gardner, the new chairman of the National Urban Coalition.

The Clark bill provided for job training and employment for 2.4 million low-income, unemployed persons in both the public and private sectors by 1972. It envisioned 450,000 participants in the first year. The bill authorized no specific sums of money, but Clark estimated the total cost at $10.3 billion.

Participants were to be provided with community service jobs in such fields as maintenance, recreation, conservation and neighborhood improvement and at the same time were to undergo training and education to prepare them for placement in jobs in the private sector.

Private employers were to be paid stipends to cover the cost of training and of special services for the hard-core unemployed. Each private employer was to be required to have a training plan based on regulations prescribed by the Secretary of Labor.

Clark hoped that the public service employment concept could be added to the pending bill extending MDTA (S 2938), but that bill was withheld from Senate debate until the leadership received assurance that the Clark proposal would not be offered as an amendment. The Senate had debated the issue for two weeks in 1967 before killing a similar proposal.

Vocational Education. The Vocational Education Amendments of 1968 (HR 18366—PL 90-576), passed by unanimous votes in House and Senate, was an amalgam of proposals by Congressional committees and by the Administration, which had submitted a bill called the "Partnership for Learning and Earning Act." Enacted just before Congress adjourned, HR 18366 included a number of apparently overlapping programs.

Basic grants to the states for vocational education were greatly increased from the $225 million level of fiscal 1968 *(see table)*, but the states were required to devote 40 percent of the funds for education of the physically handicapped and the disadvantaged and for post-high school courses.

Vocational Education Authorizations, Fiscal 1969-72

(In millions)

PRESENT PROGRAMS	Fiscal 1969 Authorization	Fiscal 1970 Authorization	Fiscal 1971 Authorization	Fiscal 1972 Authorization
General [1]	$355	$565	$675	$675
Work-Study	35	35	—	—
Demonstration Residential Schools	25	30	35	35
Homemaking	[2]	25	35	50
Natl. Advisory Council	.1	.15	.15	.15
TOTAL	$415.1	$655.15	$745.15	$760.15
NEW PROGRAMS				
Disadvantaged	40	40	—	—
Exemplary	15	57.5	75	75
Cooperative Work-Study	20	35	50	75
Residential	15	15	—	—
Residential Loans	5	10	—	—
Curriculum Development	7	10	—	—
Teacher Development	25	35	—	—
TOTAL	$127	$202.5	$125	$150
GRAND TOTAL	$542.1	$857.65	$870.15	$910.15

1 *Basic state program plus training and research.*
2 *Included in general authorization.*

SOURCE: House Education and Labor Committee

The work-study program, which was terminated in fiscal 1969 because it duplicated the in-school program of the Neighborhood Youth Corps, was extended, with its provision for 80 percent federal funding. In addition, a new program, cooperative work-study, was added, with the costs 100 percent federally funded. Unlike the old work-study program, students in the new program had to take on-the-job training in work related to their education course.

Special programs were authorized for persons with academic, socio-economic or other handicaps that prevented them from succeeding in regular vocational courses. One-third of funds spent on homemaking and consumer education courses were ordered spent in economically depressed areas.

Several efforts were made to upgrade vocational education courses. A new program of exemplary, or innovative, programs was authorized. This was intended to establish model programs in a few schools in each state to test new approaches. The aim was to braoden the occupational ambitions of school children, beginning at the elementary level and ending with job placement at the conclusion of high school. Additional funds for research, curriculum development and teacher training also were authorized. The Labor Department was directed to con-duct manpower projections to help the schools plan up-to-date training programs.

The states were required to fully match the federal funds for basic grants, but in actual practice most put up $3 for each $1 in federal funds. Appropriations by Congress for vocational education since fiscal 1964 were, in millions of dollars:

Fiscal 1964	$ 34.8	Fiscal 1967	$268.0
Fiscal 1965	166.3	Fiscal 1968	259.3
Fiscal 1966	235.7	Fiscal 1969	248.2

Indian Vocational Training. S 306—PL 90-252, which became law Feb. 3, increased the authorization for vocational education of Indians to $25 million, $10 million above the level first authorized in 1965. The Interior Department's Bureau of Indian Affairs, which administered the program for reservation Indians, said in 1967, in requesting enactment of the bill, that there was a backlog of more than 900 requests from Indians to take the training courses.

Vocational Loan Insurance. The insurance program for loans to students in vocational schools was merged with the program for college students in the Higher Education Amendments of 1968 (S 3769—PL 90-575).

Vocational Rehabilitation. Enlarged scope for rehabilitation was authorized in HR 16819—PL 90-391, which amended the Vocational Rehabilitation Act to permit assistance to disadvantaged—as well as physically and mentally handicapped—persons. The bill broadly defined a disadvantaged person as one hampered by such factors as youth, advanced age, poor education, police record or ethnic or cultural conditions.

Under the new provisions for the disadvantaged, state rehabilitation agencies were authorized to conduct extensive evaluations of an individual to determine the sources of his handicaps and the extent of his limitations. Services were authorized to develop work attitudes and behavior patterns suitable for holding a job. The Federal Government would pay 90 percent of the cost of the new effort. The bill authorized appropriations for the program of $50 million in fiscal 1969, $75 million in fiscal 1970 and $100 million in fiscal 1971.

HR 16819 also extended through fiscal 1971 the Act's existing programs for the physically and mentally handicapped. The bill authorized a total of $1,399,200,000 for fiscal years 1969-71. It also made certain changes in existing programs such as increasing the federal share from 75 to 80 percent for basic rehabilitation grants to the states. The Special Projects Section of the Act was expanded to include three new programs: contracts with business to provide handicapped individuals with work-training in a realistic setting; grants to recruit or train individuals for careers in vocational rehabilitation; and grants to train the handicapped for public service employment.

Basic support grants, already authorized through fiscal 1970, were set at $700 million for fiscal 1971, an increase of $100 million. The second largest program, Special Projects, was given fiscal 1969-71 authorizations of $80 million, $115 million and $140 million.

The bill passed through Congress without controversy and was signed into law July 7.

MDTA. A rather routine extension of MDTA was cleared by Congress Oct. 10 after the Senate leadership held up floor action on the bill until the last days of the session. S 2938 was reported by the Senate Labor and Public Welfare Committee July 20 but not called up for debate on Oct. 7 until sponsors of controversial amendments agreed not to offer them. Among the controversial proposals that were pigeonholed were a public service employment program, coverage of farm workers under the National Labor Relations Act, and an Economic Opportunity Corporation to stimulate business investment in poverty areas.

Another controversial provision omitted from the bill was a House directive that at least 65 percent of MDTA funds be spent on institutional training, principally vocational education courses.

The House bill (HR 15045) was passed unanimously Sept. 5 and the Senate bill (S 2938) Oct. 7, after it was reworded to conform closely to the House bill. This cleared the way for House acceptance of the Senate bill Oct. 10. It became law Oct. 24 (PL 90-636).

The bill did not authorize specific amounts for MDTA programs. The fiscal 1969 appropriation was $407,492,000.

As enacted, the bill extended basic MDTA programs (institutional and on-the-job training) through fiscal 1972 but limited to fiscal 1970 the extension of several pilot programs (training for prisoners, labor mobility, and placement).

Other provisions: increased allowances for youths taking training from $20 a week to the average unemployment compensation payment in the state; earmarked 2 percent of MDTA appropriations for training special personnel, such as counselors and administrators of skill centers, and another 2 percent for publication of comprehensive labor market information; and provided federal payment of 75 percent of the cost of supplemental state programs coordinating manpower activities.

Summer Jobs. The spring of 1968 saw a long controversy over additional funds to provide summer jobs for needy teen-agers. The Senate voted four times for $75 million for Neighborhood Youth Corps summer jobs, but House Appropriations Committee members remained opposed for four months. They finally agreed to allow $13 million, which was included in the conference report on the Second Supplemental Appropriations Act (HR 17734—PL 90-392), signed into law July 9, 1968.

Welfare Legislation

THE last four years of the Johnson Administration witnessed major events in the field of welfare legislation. Chief among these was passage of "medicare"—a program of hospital insurance for the aged financed through the Social Security System. A major goal of liberals throughout the postwar period, enactment of medicare was finally ensured in 1965 by the big increase of liberals in Congress as a result of the 1964 elections. As enacted, the medicare program contained not only the basic compulsory medicare hospital plan, but also a voluntary supplementary plan covering doctor bills and related services.

There were other important expansions of the 1935 Social Security Act during the 1965-68 period. Over-all retirement benefits were raised twice, by 7 percent in 1965 and by 13 percent in 1967.

The trend of easing Social Security eligibility requirements continued. In 1965 Congress also established a new "medicaid" program of aid to the poor for medical expenses; rapidly rising costs under this program were to trouble Congress for the rest of the Johnson Administration. Funds for child welfare programs also were substantially increased.

BUT while Congress continued to expand Social Security programs, in 1967 it also made a dramatic attempt to change the nature of U.S. public assistance programs. The provisions, which originated in the House, included a mandatory work-training program for all recipients under the Aid for Families with Dependent Children (AFDC) program, and a freeze on the amount of federal aid for AFDC assistance when the father was absent from the home. The bill also took the first major step toward involving the Federal Government in family planning for welfare recipients.

Although some liberals were adamantly opposed to the AFDC freeze and mandatory character of the job training program, there was a growing feeling during the Johnson Administration that welfare programs as set up by the Social Security Act were no longer appropriate for the conditions of the 1960s. One aspect of this was increasing discussion of controversial proposals for a guaranteed annual income for everyone.

The other major welfare measure of the Johnson Administration was the Economic Opportunity Act of 1964, the authorization for the antipoverty program. In succeeding years the Act was heavily amended in Congress, partly as a result of conservative opposition to the program, partly because of a genuine effort by liberals to revise the program to meet continuing criticisms. Despite the criticisms the program was expanded and the authorization steadily increased.

Medicare

The long effort to enact medicare legislation came to an end in 1965 when Congress established a medical care program for the aged under the Social Security System. The program covered up to 90 days of hospital care, 100 days of nursing home care and 100 home health care visits. In addition, Congress authorized a supplementary program under which persons over 65 could pay $3 a month for a voluntary health insurance plan covering 80 percent of doctor bills, laboratory tests and related services. This sum was matched from general federal revenues.

Liberals had worked for passage of the basic plan throughout the postwar period, but during most of that time it had appeared to be a very remote goal. Most had not even dreamed of enactment of the supplementary plan, which was initiated in Congress and considered for the first time in 1965.

Throughout the years the medicare proposal had been one of the most fiercely lobbied issues to come before Congress. Preeminent among its opponents was the American Medical Assn., which waged a vigorous and unflagging campaign right up to enactment. Among its major arguments were the contentions that the program would lead to socialized medicine and would greatly increase the cost of medical services. On the evidence of the first three years of the program the AMA was wrong on the first score, but correct on the second.

Once medicare got underway there appeared to be little public support for extending the program to other segments of the population. The only proposal put forward was a 1967 Administration request to extend medicare to the disabled who were covered by the Social Security Act, and this was immediately rejected as too expensive by both House and Senate committees.

But within a year after the inception of the program it became clear that medicare was contributing to a major increase in medical costs in the United States. During extensive hearings on the omnibus 1967 Social Security bill, many witnesses told Congress that hospital costs were increasing dramatically and might go up by as much as 15 percent a year in each of the next few years, posing

---

Reference

Discussion of welfare policies and legislation from 1945-64 will be found in *Congress and the Nation*, Vol. I, p. 1225-1330.

Fiscal 1965-69 Funding of OEO Programs

(in millions)

Programs Administered by OEO

	ACTUAL OBLIGATIONS				NEW OBLIGATIONAL AUTHORITY
	Fiscal 1965	1966	1967	1968	1969
COMMUNITY ACTION	($236.7)	($630)	($816)	($847)	($939)
made up of the following:					
Neighborhood Service Systems	a	72	100	132	136
Indians j		(12)	(20)	(24)	(25)
Employment Services	a	18	20	22	22
Education Services	a	22	22	13	14
Housing Activities	a	3	6	10	12
Neighborhood Health Centers	—	1	51	33	60
Narcotic Addiction programs b	—	—	—	—	—
Family Planning	a	2	4	9	13
Other Health Services	a	9	10	13	17
Legal Services	.9	20	25	36	42
Upward Bound c	.3	25	28	30	30
Head Start	103	198	349	333 d	348 d
Foster Grandparents	—	—	10	10	9
Staff Training		13	12	12	13
Research & Demonstration	38.2	18	34	34	31
"Versatile" CAP Funds (for locally designed projects)	94.3 a	186	136	187	192
MIGRANTS	15	25	33	25	27
JOB CORPS	175	306	209	282	280
VISTA	2.6	16	26	29	32
GENERAL DIRECTION & ADMINISTRATION	6.3	11	14	14	15

Programs Delegated by OEO to Other Agencies

	Fiscal 1965	1966	1967	1968	1969
HEALTH, EDUCATION AND WELFARE DEPARTMENT					
Adult Basic Education e	4.4	21	—	—	—
Work Study f	55	—			
Work Experience g	111.9	111	100	44	10
LABOR DEPARTMENT (TOTAL)	(132)	(269)	(460)	(471)	(639)
Neighborhood Youth Corps h	132	269			
Out-of-School			148	96	130
In-School			69	59	46
Summer			133	114	125
Special Impact	—	—	7	20	22
Operation Mainstream	—	—	26	22	41
New Careers	—	—	17	8	19
Concentrated Employment Programs	—	—	49	74	84
JOBS	—	—		60	152
DOL Support	—	—	11	18	20
AGRICULTURE DEPARTMENT					
Rural Loans (revolving fund) i	21.2	35	24	17	6
OTHER (Transfers)	—	66	2	10	—
Unobligated	—	10	4	7	—
TOTAL APPROPRIATION	$760.1	$1,500	$1,688	$1,773	$1,948

a In fiscal 1965 the OEO allocated $94.3 million to a number of community action programs for which spending was not listed individually. The $94.3 million included funds for locally designed programs later designated as "versatile CAP" funds.

b A demonstration program which was given funds for fiscal 1967 only.

c The Higher Education Amendments of 1968 (PL 90-575) transferred Upward Bound to the Office of Education as of July 1 , 1969.

d Includes Head-Start Follow-Through.

e The Elementary and Secondary Education Act Amendments of 1966 (PL 89-750) transferred the Adult Basic Education program to the Office of Education.

f The Higher Education Act of 1965 (PL 89-329) transferred the Work Study Program to the Office of Education.

g The Work Experience program was to be phased out by June 30 , 1969 because of a similar program (Work Incentives) passed by Congress in the Social Security Amendments of 1967 (PL 90-248) , also to be administered by HEW.

h Funds for Neighborhood Youth Corps were not broken down into the three components of the program (Out-of-School , In-School and Summer) for fiscal years 1965 and 1966.

i The rural loan program operates as a revolving fund. When money comes back into the fund , it can be loaned again. Therefore , the actual loan levels for fiscal years 1967 , 1968 and 1969 are higher than the amounts shown on the chart which are new obligational authority. The actual loan levels were: fiscal 1967 , 31.9 million , fiscal 1968 , 26.9 million and fiscal 1969 , 15.0 million (estimated).

j Although there is no specific OEO Indians program , the agency estimates it has spent these amounts on Indian poverty through various community action programs.

SOURCE: OFFICE OF ECONOMIC OPPORTUNITY

a threat to medicare financing. Representatives of the American Hospital Assn. said that hospital expenses per patient day were $57.93—30.2 percent higher than on Sept. 30, 1965.

A fraction of the 1967 increase in the Social Security tax was earmarked for medicare, and the Department of Health, Education and Welfare April 1, 1968, raised the premium rate for the supplementary medicare plan from $3 to $4 a month. In his March message to Congress on health, President Johnson listed as one of five major goals dealing with "the soaring cost of medical care." He said he had directed the HEW Secretary to begin extensive tests on incentives to reduce the cost of medical care. He asked Congress to authorize the HEW Secretary to employ new methods of payment under medicare and other federal health programs if they lowered costs, and to establish a reasonable cost range for reimbursement of drugs. Congress took no action on either proposal, postponing action on an issue which seemed certain to continue in the Nixon Administration.

Welfare Issue

An important feature of the over-all Social Security program was the public assistance or welfare program—a broad category of federal-state public charity for the needy.

Under all welfare programs—old-age assistance (OAA) aid to the needy blind (AB), aid to families with dependent children (AFDC), aid to the permanently and totally disabled (ATPD) and medical assistance to the aged (MAA)—the states had wide latitude in shaping policy. The states made cash payments to the eligible needy in each category, with the Federal Government reimbursing the states for part of their cost. *(Congress and the Nation, Vol. I, p. 1225.)*

The history of the welfare programs during the postwar era had been a steady expansion, but the programs developed very much in the mold in which they had been put in 1935. In 1967 Congress made important and controversial changes in the direction of the programs. The major change was a mandatory work-training program for all adult AFDC recipients, including mothers, who were required to put small children in day care centers. It was estimated that there were about 5.1 million persons on AFDC in 1967, about 1.1 million of them mothers.

Under the new program, Congress for the first time set up an incentive system. It allowed those taking training a $30 monthly allowance, and permitted recipients to keep $30 a month plus one-third of their income over $30 without a reduction in welfare payments. Senate liberals objected bitterly to the mandatory nature of the program, but the House Ways and Means Committee, which originated the provisions, said it had become "very concerned" about the growth of the AFDC program. It said the number of recipients had doubled in 10 years, and that work-training, while very costly at first, was necessary to reverse the trend.

An even more controversial provision in the 1967 bill froze at the January 1968 level the percentage of children with an absent parent which could be on AFDC rolls in each state. This was a severe blow to states which were experiencing an influx of poor migrants from other states,

Social Security Tax, Wage Base Increases

Here is a comparison of the taxable wage bases and combined health care payroll tax and Social Security payroll tax that workers would pay annually under former (1961) law, under the 1965 medicare bill and under the 1967 Social Security amendments. The maximum annual payment is made by the employee and matched by the employer. Self-employed persons are taxed at a different rate.

| Year | 1961 LAW | | | 1965 LAW | | | 1967 LAW | | |
	Taxable Base	Rate *	Maximum Payment	Taxable Base	Rate *	Maximum Payment	Taxable Base	Rate *	Maximum Payment
1966	$4,800	4.1%	$198	$6,600	4.2%	$277	———	———	———
1967	4,800	4.1	198	6,600	4.4	290	$6,600	4.4%	$290
1968	4,800	4.6	222	6,600	4.9	290	7,800	4.4	343
1969-70	4,800	4.6	222	6,600	4.9	323	7,800	4.8	374
1971-72	4,800	4.6	222	6,600	5.4	323	7,800	5.2	406
1973	4,800	4.6	222	6,600	5.4	356	7,800	5.65	441
1974-75	4,800	4.6	222	6,600	5.4	356	7,800	5.65	441
1976-79	4,800	4.6	222	6,600	5.45	360	7,800	5.7	445
1980-86	4,800	4.6	222	6,600	5.55	366	7,800	5.8	452
1987 and after	4,800	4.6	222	6,600	5.65	373	7,800	5.9	460

* Rates include taxes for OASDI and medicare benefits.

and in 1968 Congress postponed the effective date of the freeze until July 1, 1969.

The same bill also sought to hold down the number of potential welfare recipients by involving the Federal Government in family planning. The bill required the states to offer family planning services on a voluntary basis to all appropriate AFDC recipients and earmarked 6 percent of all appropriations for maternal and child health for family planning. Congress also in 1967 authorized a family planning program as part of the antipoverty effort. HEW expected to spend about $30 million on the welfare family planning program in fiscal 1969 and the Office of Economic Opportunity had programmed about $13 million.

While many liberals were concerned about the specifics of the 1967 welfare provisions, there was general agreement that the existing welfare system was out of date. President Johnson in 1968 said it was "in need of major change" and appointed a Commission on Income Maintenance to recommend improvements and perhaps a complete revamping of the system. The report was expected sometime in 1969.

Guaranteed Income. One feature of the new debate on the welfare system was increasing discussion about various proposals for a guaranteed minimum annual income. Broadly, the theory of guaranteed income was that instead of a traditional welfare system, the Government would guarantee that every person received a certain level of income each year. The income would bridge whatever gap existed between a predetermined breakeven point for an acceptable standard of living and the amount of money a family earned.

During 1968 Congressional hearings on guaranteed income, a number of alternative proposals were considered. These included an outright cash payment up to a specified income; the "negative income tax" under which a family

with a low or no income would receive a percentage of the amount between the amount the family earned and a breakeven figure; and a "children's allowance" in which a stipulated amount would be paid for every child in every U.S. family, present children's income tax exemptions would be eliminated, and the allowance itself would be taxed.

All of these plans would be expensive, and general acceptance of such a system appeared to be a long way off. However, the OEO had begun a $4.5-million experimental pilot program with nine different guaranteed income plans, and political debate on the issue seemed likely to increase.

Other Social Security Changes

Other Social Security amendments adopted during the Johnson Administration were more traditional. In addition to providing two increases in Social Security retirement benefits, the 1965 and 1967 omnibus bills continued the tradition of liberalizing the retirement test and bringing under the System more of the few remaining groups still outside it. For the first time persons with no Social Security coverage were allowed to receive benefits at age 72.

These various liberalizations forced further increases in the Social Security tax rate. Whereas existing (1961) law had foreseen an employer-employee tax rate of 4.6 percent in 1987 and a taxable earnings base of $4,800, the 1965 bill took the rate to 5.65 percent and the base to $6,600, and the 1967 bill took the rate to 5.9 percent and the base to $7,800. *(See chart.)*

Testimony during House hearings in 1967 revealed that the Administration believed that the Social Security payroll tax rate was in danger of reaching its maximum level. The Administration said it would favor in the future a lower payroll tax on a larger amount of earnings. A number of witnesses testified that the time was near when Social Security benefit increases should be financed through general revenues rather than "regressive" higher payroll taxes. Later in the year, an attempt was made in the Senate to move in the direction of general revenue financing of Social Security, but it failed by a wide margin.

Medicaid. In 1965 Congress wrote a new Title XIX to the Social Security Act designed to substitute a single system of medical assistance for the many existing fragmented services administered through welfare programs. In addition, it gave the states the option of extending the 1961 program of assistance to the "medically needy" aged (persons who were poor but not poor enough to qualify for welfare) to other needy persons who were not elderly. Under medicaid, federal money was based on the total cost of the program within each state. A formula for federal cost sharing was based on a state's per capita income, with the highest federal share going to the poorest state. The percentage of federal money made available varied between 50-83 percent.

Title XIX increased substantially the number of persons who were eligible for federal aid to pay medical bills. In 1965, prior to medicaid's enactment, a total of $1.35 billion was spent for medical assistance payments by the states and Federal Government, with $600 million of the total in federal funds. In 1966, after the first calendar year of medicaid, the Federal Government's share was $975 million of $2 billion spent to pay medical bills for welfare recipients and needy persons.

Within a year after medicaid was implemented, it became obvious that the program was costing far more than Congress had intended. A major factor was the rising cost of medical care. A second factor was the flexibility in the law which permitted states to define the medically needy, sometimes providing coverage for persons with incomes substantially higher than welfare levels.

In an attempt to cut federal costs under medicaid, Congress in 1967 set income levels for eligibility of the medically needy at 33-1/3 percent of the qualifying income level for AFDC welfare payments. It was estimated that the medicaid program would cost the Federal Government $1.7 billion in fiscal 1969. However, by early 1968 medicaid costs had increased enough to require a budget request of $2.1 billion, and by October they had increased by another $300 million. In the Senate an amendment to reduce the federal share was added to an unrelated bill, but was later dropped on threat of a Senate filibuster. However, the issue seemed certain to reappear in the Nixon Administration.

Medicare Figures

Fiscal 1966 to 1969 figures for hospital insurance for the aged and supplementary medical insurance will be found on p. 701 as part of a table showing budget outlays for health programs.

Antipoverty Program

President Johnson's major 1964 legislative success—the antipoverty program—was among the most controversial legislation considered during the remaining four years of his Presidency. Throughout this period Republicans made an unsuccessful but unremitting effort to dismantle the Office of Economic Opportunity and transfer the various elements of the program to old-line agencies. The program was also plagued from the beginning by charges of "boss rule" and rule by the militant poor at the local level, of rioting and excessive costs in the Job Corps and of excessive salaries in the OEO and local agencies. Such reports distressed both liberals and conservatives, and eventually led Congress to take a strong hand in molding the program.

In 1965, Congress in lengthy hearings heard criticism of various antipoverty programs, but took little action. The only major legislative action that year was a successful fight to dilute the Governor's veto power over certain programs. But in 1966 Congress began to try and tighten up the program. A number of administrative restrictions were made, and provisions were more precisely defined. Congress began to authorize and initiate programs, and funds for individual programs were earmarked for the first time.

Despite the changes in the 1966 bill, and a cessation of criticism in some areas, opposition to the antipoverty program in the House was so strong in early 1967 that many observers thought the authorization was likely to be killed. Instead, Congress added more provisions to tighten administration and made a major change in the operation of local community action programs. Largely because of this change, the authorization at year's end emerged remarkably intact. Moreover, Congress in 1967 agreed to a two-year authorization for antipoverty programs, saving the administration another fight in 1968.

Although passage of the antipoverty legislation was a long battle for the Administration in both 1966 and 1967, and the level of criticism of the program was always high, appropriations were increased in every year. In 1965 the sum ($1,500,000,000) was almost double the amount of the original appropriation ($800,000,000). Thereafter Congress voted $1,612,500,000 in 1966, $1,773,000,000 in 1967 and $1,948,000,000 in fiscal 1968.

Job Corps. Probably the most unpopular antipoverty program with Congress was the Job Corps, a program to take unemployed and poorly educated youths away from their home environments either to residential conservation camps or training centers. Controversy began in the first year with reports of riots among enrollees at several camps, and friction between Job Corps members and townspeople of the communities in which the centers were located. Private contractors running Job Corps centers were charged with poor administration, and critics said sloppy and politically motivated recruiting led to a 13 percent drop-out rate in the first year.

Despite heavy criticism of the program both in and out of Congress, Members made no efforts to alter it in 1965. But in 1966, amidst charges in the House that the Job Corps had 'failed more noticeably than any other single poverty program," it added a number of amendments which attempted to improve the Corps. These included establishment of specific, enforceable standards of behavior for members. After an OEO report setting the annual cost per enrollee at $9,945, Congress limited the cost to $7,500 and limited Corps enrollment to 45,000. Moreover, a new Congressional requirement earmarking money for specific antipoverty programs further cut the amount the Administration had wanted for the Corps. However, a Senate amendment to transfer the Job Corps to the Labor Department was rejected, 27-38.

The 1966 Job Corps amendments were all initiated by Congress. The Administration in 1967 acknowledged trouble with the program by promising "tighter cost controls, firmer discipline and more effective recruitment." The Senate Labor and Public Welfare Committee added amendments defining eligibility requirements more precisely and providing for better job placement after training. The House agreed to these amendments, and added amendments further reducing per enrollee costs to $6,500 per annum and setting up a new program of nonresidential Job Corps centers. The final bill set the per enrollee cost at $6,900.

While many GOP members continued to oppose the Job Corps, liberals seemed less unhappy with it by the end of the Johnson years. The House Education and Labor Committee in 1967 found that "the Job Corps is, on balance, a substantial success, with noticeable improvements in this year's program. We are convinced that the Job Corps is making a significant contribution towards eradication of poverty."

Local Community Action. Title II of the OEO authorization contained both highly popular and highly controversial antipoverty programs. The popular programs were "national emphasis" programs such as Head Start; the controversial were the "versatile" community action programs which were to be handled at the local level. The purpose of the latter programs was debated for three years until Congress in 1967—partly for ideological reasons, partly for political—made major revisions in their structure.

As versatile community action was originally set up, local agencies were to be established in low-income rural and urban areas to run a number of locally-developed social programs for the poor. The original OEO authorization specified that the activities of the local community action agencies (CAAs) were to be "developed, conducted and administered with the maximum feasible participation of residents of the areas and members of the groups served." This provision contained the seeds of trouble that were later to plague the community action program. Members argued for three years over whether it meant that community action programs were simply to involve the poor, or to be run by the poor.

Under the original community action program, the Federal Government provided up to 90 percent of the cost (100 percent in the very poorest communities) of antipoverty programs developed and administered by either public or private nonprofit community action agencies. About 80 percent of all local CAAs were private organizations. Locally developed programs ranged from remedial reading, homemaking services and literacy campaigns to direct action to improve housing conditions or transportation services.

During much of 1965 and 1966 debate intensified over who should have the major responsibility for running community action programs—the poor or local political leaders. In many cities a tug of war took place between the militant poor and City Hall with the OEO in the uncomfortable position of mediator.

Congress in 1966 attempted to clarify the role of the poor in community action. Among the amendments was the requirement that at least one-third of the members of local CAAs be representatives of the poor, chosen by residents in poverty-stricken neighborhoods. Also, to ensure stricter administration, Congress set a $15,000 ceiling on the amount of federal money that could be paid a CAA employee, and established tougher auditing rules for community action grants.

Despite the 1966 amendments, the controversy over who should run community action deepened in 1967. Early in the year Rep. Sam M. Gibbons (D Fla.), antipoverty bill manager in 1965 and 1966, said the concept of the involvment of the poor was good, but that the "concept got all messed up." He said he did not think "you should turn over the whole war on poverty to the poor any more than you should turn the hospitals over to the sick." He said community action had worked best where "the city government is responsible enough, strong enough and imaginative enough to put it to work."

Provisions of the 1967 authorization as passed by the Senate were largely intended to increase the involvement of the poor. But the House version of the bill, worked out in unusual open committee sessions, made major revisions in the program which placed it in the hands of local public officials.

The new provisions required that a CAA actually be the state or local government or a public or private agency designated by the state or local government. On each CAA board one-third of the members would have to be public officials, one-third poverty area representatives and one-third representatives of business, labor, civic and charitable groups. The committee report said there had been "weaknesses and deficiencies in the manner in which the community action program has been administered to date." It cited instances of administrative laxity, situations where CAAs "have indulged in political activities of questionable propriety," and cases of "insufficient attention to special problems of rural areas and the elderly."

Although the new community action provisions were bitterly attacked by Senate liberals, they were included in the final bill with a modification providing that the OEO could fund private groups as CAAs if public officials failed to carry out a program satisfactorily. Senate leaders said it was necessary to accept the provisions in order to get any bill at all. The new CAA provisions almost certainly aided in getting the bill through the House, which earlier in 1967 had shown so much hostility to the OEO that it had taken the unusual move of eliminating pay raises for OEO employees from a general federal pay bill (a move dropped in conference). But while political motivations certainly contributed to passage of the new provisions, there was also an element of real concern on the part of many of their supporters for the direction and problems of the community action program.

National Community Action. The first nationwide community action programs were started by the OEO without Congressional authorization. In 1965 it set up the highly successful Head Start program for preschool children, a Legal Services program and the Upward Bound program to assist able, poor youths to prepare for college. Congress in 1966 provided legislative authority for these

How the Original Poverty Program Worked

The first major legislation originated by President Johnson was the omnibus antipoverty bill (S 2642—PL 88-452), the Economic Opportunity Act of 1964. Enacted almost as the President had wanted it, the bill authorized a combination of programs encompassing different approaches and intended for different low-income groups. The programs were put under the supervision of a new Office of Economic Opportunity (OEO) in the Executive Offices. This original antipoverty legislation authorized $947.5 million to carry out the first year's activities, and provided general authority, but no funds, for the next two years. Congress later appropriated $800 million for the first year of the program.

In 1964, two changes in the Administration bill provoked controversy. One was an amendment designed to win Southern support for the bill by permitting Governors to veto proposed Job Corps, community action, work-training adult basic training and volunteer (VISTA) programs. The other required Job Corps enrollees and any other individuals receiving antipoverty payments to sign an affidavit disclaiming support of any organization favoring violent overthrow of the Government. Both provisions were modified in later years.

Following is a title-by-title run-down of the programs set up under the original antipoverty act:

Title I. Title I authorized $412.5 million in fiscal 1965 for three programs to aid impoverished youths.

Job Corps—The Job Corps was intended for school drop-outs who were felt to need a total change in environment to improve their way of life. They would live for two years in job centers away from home, either as members of a "Youth Conservation Corps" in conservation camps on federal land where they would gain work experience or in training centers in urban areas where they would learn specific job skills. All centers would provide basic education courses.

Work-Training Program—This program authorized federal assistance for state and local programs which would enable underprivileged youths to do work beneficial to their own communities. The aim was to encourage them to continue or resume schooling. The Federal Government was to pay up to 90 percent of costs for the first two years , and 50 percent thereafter.

Work-Study Programs—Under this program, the Government would aid colleges in paying students from low-income families for part-time work either on or off the campus. The OEO was to pay 90 percent of the program cost for the first two years, and 75 percent thereafter. (This was transferred to the Office of Education in 1965.)

Title II. Title II authorized $340 million in fiscal 1965 for programs of federal grants to state or local programs.

Community Action—Under the community action programs, the Government was to provide both financial and technical assistance for locally designed and operated programs. The programs could be run either by a group of local government officials or a private non-profit organization. Funds could be used for a wide variety of purposes—trips for slum children, remedial reading, job counseling, day care services etc. Emphasis was to be put on helping the poor to help themselves by participating in the local action programs. Funds would be distributed to the states by a formula determined largely by the number of unemployed and public assistance recipients in the state.

Adult Education—Grants were authorized to the states for local programs to teach persons over 18 to read and write adequately. (This was transferred to the Office of Education in 1966.)

Voluntary Assistance for Needy Children—The OEO Director was authorized to establish an office to help volunteers to locate and give financial assistance to needy children.

Title III. This title authorized programs to help raise the income and living standards of poor rural and migrant families.

Loans—The OEO Director was authorized to make 15-year loans of up to $2,500 to low-income rural families who could not get credit elsewhere. In addition, 30-year repayable loans were authorized to local processing or marketing cooperatives.

Migrant Workers—The act authorized $35 million for loans and grants in fiscal 1965 for development of programs to aid migrant workers in housing, sanitation, education and day care of children.

Title IV. *Business Incentives*—Title IV authorized the Director to make or guarantee 15-year repayable loans to establish or strengthen small businesses and help them to employ the long-term unemployed. The borrower was required to participate in a management training program. (This was transferred to the Small Business Administration in 1966.)

Title V. *Work Experience Programs*—The bill authorized $150 million which could be used by the Health, Education and Welfare Secretary for pilot projects to employ and train heads of families receiving help under the Aid to Families with Dependent Children program. (This was later phased out because of a similar program in the 1967 welfare amendments.)

Title VI. This title authorized establishment of the OEO in the Executive Offices and authorized the VISTA program.

Volunteers in Service to America—The act authorized $10 million in fiscal 1965 for recruitment and training of volunteers to combat poverty on the local level. Volunteers were to work in rural or urban poverty areas, Indian reservations, migrant camps, hospitals for the mentally ill and retarded and similar areas. Volunteers were to be provided with living and other allowances and a stipend of up to $50 per month. The program grew out of proposals for a "domestic peace corps."

Title VII. *Public Assistance*—The bill granted exemption of payments to individuals under the poverty program from provisions of the Social Security Act which required that incomes of a public assistance recipient be taken into account in determining need and the amount of public assistance payment.

programs and added another—Comprehensive Health Services.

In the 1967-68 authorization bill Congress added four more national community action programs: Follow Through, an extension of the Head Start program to the early school years; Emergency Food and Medical Service; Family Planning, a voluntary program for the poor; and Senior Opportunities and Service, a program for needy persons over 60. Showing its frustration with problems in the antipoverty programs, Congress in 1966 had earmarked specific amounts for each national program. But the following two-year authorization eliminated earmarking, and left the distribution of funds ($950 million for all local and national community action programs) up to the OEO.

Work and Training Programs. The manpower activities of the antipoverty program were considerably less controversial than the community action provisions and the Job Corps. These provisions included the Neighborhood Youth Corps, one of the original OEO programs *(see box p. 746)*, "Operation Mainstream," a 1965 program to employ the chronically unemployed on community beautification projects; "New Careers," a 1966 program to train the poor to be aides to professionals in such fields as education, health and welfare; and a 1967 concentrated employment program. Congress in 1967 combined all of these activities in Part B of Title I. The Senate Labor and Public Welfare Committee, which initiated the consolidation, said it would give participants an unbroken sequence of services to help them obtain and hold a job.

Other Programs. Other OEO programs were relatively uncontroversial. From the original 1964 authorization, these included the VISTA program (the domestic peace corps) and programs directed specifically at rural and migrant families. Noncontroversial programs added to the Act after 1964 included a 1966 Title I Special Impact Program to employ residents of slum neighborhoods in projects aimed at rehabilitating those neighborhoods; a 1966 Emergency Family Loan Program; and a 1967 Day Care program.

Administrative Restrictions. While Republicans were never successful in their continuing effort to dismember the OEO, the ambivalent Congressional attitude toward the anti-poverty programs was reflected in a number of administrative restrictions imposed on the programs for several years. Other restrictions grew out of widespread criticisms, especially in the area of salaries.

Among such actions were 1966 amendments requiring the OEO to give Congress a list of local antipoverty officials earning more than $10,000 a year; providing that no CAA or Job Corps official earning over $6,000 could earn more than 20 percent over his previous salary; providing that no new supergrade jobs (GS 16-18) could be created by the OEO in the fiscal year; and temporarily limiting administrative expenses for the OEO to 10 percent of the total funds authorized under the Act. Further restrictions in 1967 required public announcement of OEO contracts, prohibited use of OEO funds for partisan or nonpartisan political activities (such as voter registration), and limited the length of time a consultant could be employed by the OEO.

Chronology Of Legislation On Welfare

1965

Medicare

CONGRESS in 1965 passed the bill which was not only the most important welfare legislation of the Johnson Administration, but was also generally considered the most important welfare measure since passage of the original Social Security Act in 1935. The bill (HR 6675—PL 89-97) established a medical care program for the aged under the Social Security System, a goal of liberals throughout the postwar period. But the 'medicare' program finally enacted was much more far-reaching than the plan which liberals had proposed unsuccessfully for years. Moreover, HR 6675 made a multitude of other changes in Social Security law, including a 7-percent increase in retirement benefits.

The medicare program which had been sought by liberals in the Kennedy-Johnson Administrations had been limited in an attempt to win more support for enactment. Essentially, that program called for compulsory hospital insurance for the aged covering spells of hospital and post-hospital care, financed through an increase in the Social Security tax. Surgical and other doctor bills were deliberately not included in an effort to counter the American Medical Assn.'s (AMA) charge that the program would lead to "socialized medicine." At the outset of 1965, medicare backers would certainly have been content with enactment of this program alone, and it was only this program that was proposed by President Johnson when the 1965 session began (HR 1, S 1).

But the final bill, in addition to that basic Social Security hospital care plan, also provided for a second, voluntary, Government-administered plan covering surgical and other doctor bills, laboratory tests and other services. Ironically, the broader bill was a result of the AMA's last-ditch stand against medicare. Ascertaining that a large percentage of the population thought the Administration bill would cover doctor costs and approved of this, the AMA began an intensive campaign attacking the Administration bill largely on the grounds that doctor bills were not included. The AMA proposed its own alternative plan which covered doctor bills. This plan, dubbed "eldercare," called for voluntary comprehensive medical insurance for the aged which would be optional with the states and which would vary in cost according to the income of recipients.

The eldercare program did not win the support of Congressional Republicans, but it prompted the drafting of another bill (HR 4351) which was introduced by ranking minority Ways and Means Committee member John W. Byrnes (R Wis.) with the blessing of the GOP leadership. This was also voluntary and covered 80 percent of doctor bills and most other costs of illness to the aged, but was administered by the Federal Government. When the Administration plan came before the Ways and Means Committee for consideration, a majority of the committee voted to report a clean bill which included both the basic medicare hospitalization plan and the essence of the Byrnes bill without hospitalization provisions, which medicare rendered unnecessary. Administration officials and long-time medicare backers were delighted with the new two-pronged program, but the original proponents of the voluntary plan refused to support the revised bill. (House action on medicare bills was crucial because the legislation had to originate in that chamber.

Summary of HR 6675

BENEFITS

Basic Health Plan. Benefits about 19 million aged; provides up to 90 days of hospital care, 100 days of nursing-home care and 100 home health-care visits and outpatient diagnostic services. Some deductions required.

Supplementary Health Plan. Benefits about 16.9 million aged; pays 80 percent of the cost of a variety of health services, including services of doctors, after a $50 annual deduction.

Kerr-Mills. Medical assistance to the needy aged was extended to needy persons under all public assistance programs, and federal funds for the programs increased. About 8 million persons would be benefitted.

Child Health Care. Federal funds increased for existing programs, and new programs added.

Social Security. Cash benefits for about 20 million persons increased by 7 percent, and regulations liberalized to provide further benefits. Coverage extended to self-employed doctors and to tips.

Public Assistance. Federal funds increased, and income exemptions liberalized.

EFFECTIVE DATES—Increased Social Security payments—retroactive to Jan. 1, 1965. Most of the other Social Security benefits—effective Sept. 1, 1965. Increased federal funds for most child health care programs—retroactive to July 1, 1965. Increased federal funds for the new Kerr-Mills program and the public assistance programs—available Jan. 1, 1966. Most benefits under the basic and supplementary health plans—effective July 1, 1966, with the remainder becoming effective Jan. 1, 1967.

FINANCING—Increased Social Security benefits and most of the basic health program—financed by payroll taxes. The supplementary health plan—financed by contributions from participants and general revenue. All other benefits in the bill—to be financed by general revenue. First full year cost of operation (1967): basic health plan $2.5 billion; supplementary health plan $1.2 billion; Kerr-Mills $200 million; Social Security benefits $2.3 billion; child health and public assistance $339 million; grand total $6.5 billion. Sources of financing: $4.5 billion from payroll taxes; $1.4 billion from general revenue; $600 million from contributions from individuals.

For a discussion of the key role played by the House Ways and Means Committee see box p. 756.)

Once the proposal reached the House floor, where it was considered under a rule that prohibited floor amendments, it moved through Congress with little controversy and great ease. The House passed it April 8 by a key **313-115** roll-call vote. The only House provision that was opposed by the Administration transferred from the basic hospital insurance plan to the supplementary plan coverage of services furnished by specialists in radiology, anesthesiology, pathology and physical medicine.

The Senate passed the bill July 9 by a key **68-21** roll-call vote. Before passage it returned the services of specialists to the basic plan and made numerous other changes. None of the amendments altered the basic structure of the bill, although several were very important. Some of these eliminated the 60-day hospitalization period under the basic plan (to provide for catastrophic illness), made further increases in payroll taxes and lowered the retirement age for Social Security cash benefits. The only amendment accepted over opposition of the Democratic leadership substantially expanded the disability insurance program for the blind. In all, the Senate changes increased the annual cost of the bill by about $1.4 billion, to $7.6 billion.

House-Senate differences were resolved in six meetings of the conference committee. One-year costs under the final bill were estimated at $6.5 billion, and the provisions were very similar to the original House version—conference chairman Wilbur D. Mills (D Ark.) said over 95 percent of them came from the House. The only major Senate amendment retained in the final bill was the additional increase in payroll taxes to finance medicare and the enlarged Social Security benefits. Hospitalization benefits were also longer than those under the House version (90 days), but were not unlimited. Services of specialists were placed in the supplementary plan.

President Johnson signed HR 6675 into law (PL 89-97) July 30, proclaiming that, "No longer will older Americans be denied the healing miracle of modern medicine." He said the bill had a few defects, "such as the payment of certain specialists," but that he was confident they would be quickly remedied.

In October the AMA ended months of suspense on the subject by making clear that it would not sponsor an organized boycott of the medicare program. In a sense it signaled acceptance of the program by resolving to participate in advisory committees "and to contribute whatever advice and suggestions are deemed advisable and necessary in the formulation and revision of regulations."

Comparison With Earlier Votes. As with much of the other liberal legislation passed by the 89th Congress, the key reason for the ease with which medicare was enacted in 1965 was the big Democratic victory in the November 1964 elections. Although the already heavily Democratic Senate gained only two more Democrats in the 1964 elections, the margin in favor of medicare on the 1965 key vote was far wider than on the favorable 1964 vote—68-21 contrasted with 49-44 the previous year. The new margin of support was widely believed to be a recognition that the 1964 elections had shown the popular appeal of medicare.

Medicare passed the House in 1965 by a whopping **313-115** roll-call vote. But a more revealing roll call was the **191-236** vote by which the Byrnes (GOP) plan to substitute a voluntary program for the Administration bill was defeated. The closeness of that vote gave some substance to speculation that medicare could not have passed the House prior to 1965 even if the Ways and Means Committee had permitted it to come to the floor for a vote.

1965 Request

Failure of medicare in 1964 had been one of President Johnson's few serious legislative defeats. In 1965 he took no risks. It was assigned the numbers HR 1 and S 1, and the President's first special message to the 89th Congress dealt with health legislation. In the message he called 1965 the year "when, with the sure knowledge of public support, the Congress should enact a hospital insurance program for the aged.... In this way, the spectre of catastrophic hospital bills can be lifted from the lives of our older citizens."

The 1965 hospital care bill was very similar to the bills proposed by the Kennedy-Johnson Administrations since 1961. The major difference was that the new bill provided coverage for a flat 60 days of hospital care instead of a benefit option of 180, 90 or 45 days with varying deductibles. Other major provisions called for the following additional benefits: 60 days of nursing home care, 240 home health-care visits, and outpatient hospital diagnostic services. The program would cover all persons 65 and over, except Government workers with federal insurance and certain aliens. It would be financed mainly by increases in the Social Security tax rate, which would reach 7.8 percent in 1971. The taxable annual earnings base would be increased to $5,600. The money would go into a separate trust fund within the Social Security System. Total costs were estimated at $2 billion in the first full year of operation.

HR 1 and S 1 also included a bipartisan-backed provision for a general 7-percent increase in Social Security benefits, retroactive to Jan. 1, 1965. It brought self-employed physicians into the Social Security System (a move opposed by many doctors) and required that Social Security taxes be paid on tips.

Alternative Proposals. With most political observers predicting that the landslide Democratic victory in the 1964 elections ensured enactment of the medicare plan, the American Medical Assn. came forth with the most vigorous campaign of its years of opposition to the proposal. In its last-ditch stand against medicare, the AMA switched its major argument against the program. In previous years anti-medicare advertising had stressed that the plan would "lead the country down the road to socialized medicine." In 1965, the AMA apparently decided that its most effective argument against the bill was not that it would go too far, but that it would accomplish too little. A Jan. 2 Gallup Poll had shown that only 23 percent of persons questioned knew that fees of doctors, surgeons and dentists would not be covered under the Administration's proposal. Of those who thought doctors' fees would be covered, 73 percent approved of the program. Of those who thought such fees would not be covered, 56 percent approved. Building on the idea of more comprehensive coverage, the AMA in January mobilized an intensive campaign of newspaper and television advertising attacking the Administration bill and proposing a new, alternative "eldercare" plan.

The eldercare plan was introduced Jan. 27 in the House (HR 3727, 3728) by Ways and Means Committee members Thomas B. Curtis (R Mo.) and A. Sydney Herlong Jr. (D Fla.). It called for a voluntary comprehensive medical insurance program which would be available to persons over 65 if their state government signed up for the program. The program would be financed by matching federal-state funds and by variable contributions from recipients.

Instead of endorsing the AMA proposal, the House Republican Leadership set forth its own bill (HR 4351) introduced by the ranking minority member of the Ways and Means Committee, John W. Byrnes (R Wis.). Like the eldercare program, HR 4351 provided a voluntary health insurance program for all persons over 65, which would cover a large proportion of most costs of illness in old age. Unlike the eldercare plan, it would be administered by the Federal Government. It would be financed by a graduated premium contribution based on the individual's ability to pay, by contributions from states and by an annual appropriation from the Federal Government. Supporters estimated that the program would cost $3.4 billion annually with full participation.

House Action

The Ways and Means Committee Jan. 25 decided not to hold public hearings on HR 1, the Administration medicare bill, on the grounds that it had heard extensive testimony on similar proposals in recent years. It then began holding regular executive sessions on the 1965 proposals which continued until March 24 when it ordered reported a clean bill (HR 6675) that was broader in scope. Whereas HR 1 had been introduced by second ranking Ways and Means Committee member Cecil R. King (D Calif.), the new bill was introduced by Committee Chairman Wilbur D. Mills (D Ark.), once medicare's most influential opponent. President Johnson praised Mills "for his statesmanlike leadership in working out, on a sound and practical basis, a solution to one of the most important problems which has been pending before the Congress for nearly 15 years."

Major Provisions, Changes. The basic hospital care plan included in HR 6675 was similar to that in HR 1, but provided somewhat different and slightly fewer benefits. The basic hospital coverage remained the same (60 days) but post-hospital care was changed from a flat 60 days to 20 days plus additional time for each day a person's hospital stay had been less than 60 days; the number of home health-care visits was reduced from 240 to 100 a year. Social Security tax rates for medicare were somewhat higher than contemplated in HR 1 and the Social Security taxable earnings base was increased to $6,600 in 1971 as opposed to $5,600 in 1966 under HR 1. In line with Chairman Mills' concern about keeping the Social Security retirement and hospital funds separate, the Committee report on HR 6675 said "the hospital insurance program will in no way impinge upon the financial soundness of the Old-Age, Survivors and Disability Insurance trust funds." It said this separation would be assured through such devices as separate trust funds and a separate statement of the hospital insurance tax on W-2 tax forms. Also, unlike the OASDI system, the hospital insurance system would be financed on the assumption of rising earnings levels and rising hospitalization costs (in-

Medicare Enactment Ends 20-Year Issue

President Truman in 1945 made the first proposal for enactment of a federally operated health insurance program. The Truman plan would have covered the entire population, not just the elderly. The proposal immediately brought forth the lobbying might of the American Medical Assn., the organization which was chief opponent of federal hospital insurance through the years. The AMA was joined in opposition by the insurance industry and conservative business groups. Labor unions and liberal organizations worked for enactment of the Truman proposal and the more limited medicare plan that followed, but there was no one organization that was as important in support of a medicare program as the AMA was in opposition.

The lobbying campaign for and against the Truman proposal reached a peak when the President pushed for Congressional action in 1949-50. Hospital insurance became one of the major issues of the session; when Congress adjourned without taking any action, the AMA was considered to have won a notable victory. Its warnings that national health insurance would mean "socialized medicine" and Government interference in medical practice were generally credited with being the major factor in the outcome. The campaign had been costly; in 1949-50 the AMA filed the two highest lobby spending reports ever.

After 1950 the issue subsided for awhile; the Eisenhower Administration, which came to office in 1953, opposed any such plan. But in 1957 the issue returned to public prominence with introduction by Rep. Aime J. Forand (D R.I.) of a bill which covered hospital and surgical costs of the aged under the Social Security retirement system. This became a major part of the legislative program of the AFL-CIO and the AMA began another nationwide publicity campaign in opposition. This marked the start of the struggle which ended with enactment of medicare in 1965.

By 1960 the Forand bill (as medicare was then tagged) had become a very hot political issue. However, the rules of the House were such that the proposal could not be brought to the House floor for debate unless it was reported by the House Ways and Means Committee. The Committee in 1960 voted 17-8 against the proposal, and was never to vote in favor of it until 1965. *(For box on the crucial role of the Ways and Means Committee, see box, p. 756.)*

With House action blocked, medicare supporters worked on getting the bill through the Senate, even though there seemed to be little chance of enactment.

Kennedy Administration bills covered only hospital and post-hospital costs; not surgical bills as proposed by Forand. Medicare produced another major Senate fight in 1962. Concessions were made to win five Republican votes, but the Administration nevertheless suffered a stunning defeat when the plan was tabled, 48-52. Medicare finally passed the Senate for the first time in 1964, as an amendment to a House-passed bill raising Social Security retirement benefits by 5 percent. But the bill died in conference when a majority of House conferees opposed any medicare plan and a majority of Senate conferees held firm in favor. As the 1964 bill died, President Johnson spoke of hopes for a mandate in the November election, and pledged that he would try again for medicare in 1965.

Chronology

Following is a chronology of the major legislative landmarks in the drive for medicare up to 1965:

1935—The report of President Roosevelt's Committee on Economic Security, which formed the basis of the Social Security Act passed later that year, endorsed the principle of compulsory national health insurance.

1943—Sens. Robert F. Wagner (D N.Y.) and James E. Murray (D Mont.) and Rep. John D. Dingell (D Mich.) introduced the first "Wagner-Murray-Dingell" bill, proposing a broadening of the entire Social Security Act, including a compulsory national health insurance system financed by a payroll tax.

1945—President Truman's message on health legislation proposed a comprehensive, prepaid medical insurance plan for persons of all ages to be financed by raising the Social Security tax.

1949-50—President Truman's health insurance proposals were among the hardest-fought of all issues before Congress, but no action resulted.

1954—President Eisenhower's plan to help meet the cost of health care proposed that the Government reinsure private insurance companies against unusually heavy losses on health insurance.

1957—Rep. Aime J. Forand (D R.I.) introduced a bill proposing that Social Security payroll taxes be raised to provide hospital care for old-age assistance beneficiaries.

1960—Democratic Presidential nominee John F. Kennedy (D Mass.), who had sponsored a Senate version of the Forand bill, announced in July 1960 that its enactment was one of his chief legislative goals for Congress' post-convention August session. Sen. Clinton P. Anderson (D N.M.) proposed a revised version of the Forand-Kennedy bill as a floor amendment to the omnibus Social Security bill. Opposed by President Eisenhower, the amendment was defeated 44-51 Aug. 23. The medical care provisions later added to the bill, and called the Kerr-Mills program after its sponsors, established a state-administered, flexible matching grant program for medical aid to needy persons not poor enough to qualify for public assistance.

1962—President Kennedy's 1961 medical care proposal, sponsored by Sen. Anderson and Rep. Cecil R. King (D Calif.), died in the House Ways and Means Committee. When Sen. Anderson offered a revised amendment to the Public Welfare Amendments bill, it was tabled (defeated) by a 52-48 Senate vote.

1963-64—Mr. Kennedy's 1963 proposals for health care were again introduced by King and Anderson. The Administration achieved a major but temporary victory Sept. 2, 1964, when a medicare amendment to the Social Security Amendments bill passed the Senate, 49-44. The amendment, sponsored by Sen. Albert Gore (D Tenn.), and similar to the Administration bill, died in conference.

stead of level-earnings assumptions) and the estimates would be for a 25-year period rather than 75 years.

In its other major change in the Administration bill, HR 6675 removed from the basic plan coverage of the costs of hospital services of radiologists, pathologists, physiatrists and anesthesiologists and included such coverage in the supplementary plan *(below)*.

The Committee bill created a voluntary additional plan which would pay for a large proportion of physicians' and surgical services, psychiatric costs on a limited basis, laboratory tests and prosthetic devices and home health care. The plan would be financed by $3 monthly premiums from participants and matching contributions from general federal revenues. This plan, never before considered in connection with a medicare proposal, was a modification of the GOP's bill for health care of the elderly (HR 4351). (Under HR 4351, hospitalization costs had also been covered under the voluntary plan, and there were no Social Security provisions.)

The bill also included a number of OASDI changes, many of which had been proposed by the Administration. These included: the retroactive 7-percent increase in retirement benefits; the requirement that self-employed physicians and employees' tips be brought under the system; exemption from the system for religious groups (such as the Amish) morally opposed to insurance; liberalization of requirements for disability benefits; extension of insurance payments to certain children attending school to age 22 instead of 18.

In addition to all of these major provisions, HR 6675 also included most of the provisions of another Administration bill (HR 3699) expanding the Kerr-Mills medical program for the needy aged to persons under the dependent children, blind and disabled programs, and increasing federal funds for maternal and child health, crippled children and mental retardation programs. HR 6675 brought together in one new title of the Social Security Act (XIX) all medical assistance provisions affecting the indigent aged, dependent children, blind and disabled, and made other minor liberalizing changes in those programs.

The estimated cost of HR 6675 was $6 billion in its first full year, broken down as follows: $2.2 billion for the basic health care plan, $1 billion for the supplementary health care plan, $2.3 billion for increased Social Security cash benefits and $500 million for the liberalization and expansion of the public assistance programs.

House Passage. The House passed HR 6675 April 8 by a key **313-115** roll-call vote. The bill had been debated for two days. It was considered under a closed rule barring floor amendments.

Before passage the House rejected by a key **191-236** roll-call vote (R 128-10; ND 3-188; SD 60-38) a motion to recommit HR 6675 to the Ways and Means Committee with instructions to substitute the text of a bill (HR 7057) introduced by Byrnes April 1. The new Byrnes bill contained the fully voluntary elderly health program first set forth in HR 4351 plus all of the OASDI, Kerr-Mills, child health and public assistance benefits of HR 6675.

During debate, opponents of HR 6675 said they could not support the Social Security hospital care plan because it was compulsory, would be financed by a "regressive" payroll tax and would endanger the current Social Security retirement cash benefits program. Byrnes said his "primary concern" in offering his substitute was to

protect the Social Security retirement program. But Mills said he was "thoroughly convinced" that the hospital fund would be completely separate and was actuarially sound. He said the health care provisions of HR 6675 represented "a satisfactory and reasonable solution of an entire problem."

Senate Action

The Senate Finance Committee held hearings on HR 6675 between April 29 and May 18. It then went into executive session and approved HR 6675 June 24 with numerous amendments. The Committee approved the bill by a 12-5 vote (D 10-1; R 2-4). While the Committee added many amendments to HR 6675, it made no basic revisions in the bill. Estimated cost of the Committee version was $6.8 billion in the first full year, as opposed to $6 billion under the House bill.

The most important Committee amendments involved the basic hospital care program. The Committee raised the limit on inpatient hospital services from 60 to 120 days; raised the limit on post-hospital extended care to 100 days; raised the number of home health care visits after hospitalization from 100 to 175; placed inpatient psychiatric hospital service under the basic plan with a lifetime limit of 210 days (the House put it under the supplementary plan and set the limit at 180 days). The Senate also made the one basic change in the House bill which had been requested by the Administration. This covered the services of radiologists, anesthesiologists, pathologists and physiatrists under the basic, not the supplemental, plan. To finance the hospital care plan, the Senate bill raised the taxable Social Security wage base to $6,600 beginning in 1966 instead of 1971. The employer-employee tax rate also was slightly higher under the Senate bill.

Other major Senate amendments increased the amount an individual could earn a year without losing Social Security benefits, and continued at a reduced rate benefits to widows age 60 and over and widowers age 62 and over who remarry. The Senate also made numerous other smaller changes in HR 6675. Almost all of such changes were dropped from the bill in conference.

Senate Passage. The Senate July 9 passed HR 6675 by a key **68-21** roll-call vote and sent it to conference with the House. Thirteen Republicans joined 55 Democrats to vote for passage. Passage by a wide margin had been assured earlier that day when a motion to delete both the basic hospitalization and supplementary plan was defeated, **26-64**, in another key vote.

The Senate accepted 29 additional amendments to HR 6675, increasing the annual cost of the bill to $7.6 billion. It rejected other amendments to expand the bill even further, as well as several attempts to kill the medical care programs.

The most important amendments accepted eliminated the time limit on the basic hospital care plan entirely and lowered the retirement age for Social Security cash benefits to 60. The only floor amendment accepted over the opposition of the leadership expanded the disability insurance program for the blind by liberalizing the definition of blindness and lifting the limit on earnings by a blind recipient. Most of the other floor amendments were not of a major nature and most were dropped in conference. The only committee amendment that ran into opposition on the Senate floor was the proposal that tips be considered as self-employment income for Social Security purposes. Senators tried unsuccessfully but persistently to reinstate the House provision classifying tips as wages.

Ways and Means and Mr. Mills

Because the medicare proposal amended the Social Security Act, it was classified as revenue-raising legislation. The Constitution provides that revenue-raising bills must originate in the House, a provision usually interpreted as meaning a bill had to pass the House before the Senate if it was to be enacted. And because non-germane amendments cannot be offered on the House floor, a measure such as medicare had to be reported from committee before the House could vote on it. Thus the approval of the House committee with jurisdiction over medicare—the Ways and Means Committee—was all-important.

Until 1965, the Ways and Means Committee kept any medicare proposal from reaching the House floor. In 1960, the last year of the Eisenhower Administration, the Committee voted 17-8 (D 7-8; R 10-0) to table (kill) that year's medicare bill. The vote was particularly discouraging to medicare supporters because the Committee's influential chairman, Wilbur D. Mills (D Ark.), was among the opponents.

When the pro-medicare Kennedy Administration took office in 1961, it took every opportunity to place medicare supporters on the Committee. By 1963 the margin of opposition had shrunk to one vote. The Committee stand on medicare stayed at 12-13 (D 12-3; R 0-10) until 1965. At the beginning of the 1965 session, the Ways and Means Committee ratios were revised from D 15-R 10 to D 17-R 8, reflecting the heavy new Democratic ratio in the House. The new Democratic committee seats were filled by medicare supporters, and Committee approval of the program was assured.

One reason it took so long to develop a pro-medicare majority on the Committee was that the American Medical Assn. concentrated lobbying might in the home districts of Ways and Means Committee members. But perhaps a more important reason was the firm opposition of Chairman Mills, who had considerable influence over his colleagues. Until 1965, when there was a clear majority for the measure without his vote, Mills refused to discuss any kind of compromise. In 1964 he had issued a statement expressing some sympathy with prepaid health insurance for the elderly, but said he could not support it because such a program would overtax the Social Security System. Many observers believed, when Mills finally switched to support of medicare in 1965, that his previous objections had probably gone deeper than concern for the Social Security System. The 1965 bill did contain some new provisions designed to protect the System, but they were not far-reaching and could have been added in previous years. It seemed to many that the major reason for Mills' about-face was unwillingness to be on the losing end of the issue.

Conference Action

The conference report on HR 6675 was filed July 26. During subsequent House debate, Rep. Mills said it represented over 95 percent of the House's original version. The first full-year cost was estimated as $6.5 billion. This would be financed by $1.4 billion in general revenues, $4.5 billion in additional payroll taxes (to finance the compulsory basic health insurance program and increased Social Security benefits) and $600 million in contributions from participants in the voluntary supplementary medical care plan.

As enacted, the basic hospital care plan called for 90 days of hospitalization, as opposed to 60 under the House bill and unlimited hospitalization voted by the Senate. It included the Senate's extended care provisions (100 days) and the House home health-care provisions (100 visits). The Administration-requested Senate amendment transferring services of radiologists, anesthesiologists, pathologists and physiatrists from the supplementary plan to the basic plan was dropped, but the limited provision for psychiatric care was placed under the basic plan as proposed by the Senate. Senate financing provisions setting the taxable Social Security earnings base at $6,600 Jan. 1, 1966, were accepted.

In the OASDI provisions, conferees split the difference between the House and Senate bills on the amount an individual could earn yearly without losing benefits. They provided that employees receiving tips would pay taxes at the employee rate but that the employer would pay no tax. (The House provided that both employee and employer pay taxes, while the Senate made tips subject to higher self-employment taxes.) The Senate provision for 50-percent benefits to certain widows and widowers who remarried was accepted. Senate floor amendments lowering the retirement age for cash benefits to 60 and liberalizing the blind disability program were dropped.

The House adopted the conference report July 27 by a 307-116 roll-call vote. In brief debate, John W. Byrnes (R Wis.), who had led a floor fight against passage, urged its opponents "to bury any disagreements or animosities" and "do their utmost to make the program work as well as possible."

The Senate adopted the conference report July 28 by a 70-24 roll-call vote, sending HR 6675 to the White House. During July 27-28 debate on the report Majority Leader Mike Mansfield (D Mont.) described the bill as "a new milestone in the history of American social legislation." Much of the rest of the debate consisted of Senators complaining that their amendments had been rejected in conference. Majority Whip Russell B. Long (D La.) indicated he agreed with some of the complaints, saying, "I have been to conference with a House bill that the Senate had amended, and the attitude of the House conferees was that we had no right whatever to amend it except...in keeping with something the House had put in its bill in the first place."

Bill Signed

President Johnson July 30 signed HR 6675 into law (PL 89-97). The signing took place in Independence, Mo., in the presence of former President Truman, the first President to seek Government medical care legislation.

In signing the bill Mr. Johnson said, "No longer will older Americans be denied the healing miracle of modern medicine. No longer will illness crush and destroy the savings that they have so carefully put away over a lifetime so that they might enjoy dignity in their later years. No longer will young families see their own incomes, and their own hopes, eaten away simply because they are carrying out their deep moral obligations to their parents, and to their uncles, and to their aunts."

Provisions of HR 6675

As signed into law, PL 89-97:

Added a new title (XVIII) to the Social Security Act to provide for persons over 65 a basic hospital and related care insurance plan and a voluntary supplementary insurance plan covering medical and other costs. Major provisions of the Health Insurance for the Aged Act follow.

Basic Health Insurance Plan

Eligibility. Provided a basic health insurance plan for all persons 65 and older, except active or retired federal employees enrolled in the federal health benefits program, federal employees who were eligible for the federal health benefits program after Feb. 16, 1965, aliens who had not been lawfully admitted for permanent residence or who, though admitted for permanent residence, had not lived in the United States for at least five consecutive years and persons convicted of certain subversive crimes.

Benefits. Provided that the plan would pay:

• Inpatient hospital services for up to 90 days for each spell of illness, with the patient paying a deductible amount of $40 for the first 60 days and $10 a day for the next 30 days. Services covered included those ordinarily furnished by a hospital for its inpatients, except the services of radiologists, anesthesiologists, pathologists and physiatrists. Payments would not be made for private-duty nursing or hospital services of physicians, except services provided by dental and medical interns and residents under approved teaching programs. Psychiatric hospital care would be subject to a lifetime limit of 190 days and 60 days per spell of illness.

• Post-hospital care for up to 100 days in each period of illness after at least three days in the hospital, with the patient paying $5 a day after the first 20 days. The post-hospital facilities, such as nursing homes, must have arrangements with a hospital for the timely transfer of patients and for furnishing medical information on the patients or, in certain cases, must have sought such transfer agreement with a hospital. Christian Science nursing homes would be limited to providing 30 days of services to a patient during a period of illness with a $5 deduction.

• Outpatient diagnostic services with the patient paying the first $20 for diagnostic services provided by the same hospital during a 20-day period and 20 percent of the remaining costs. The $20 deduction would be credited against the annual $50 deduction required under the supplementary health plan. *(See below)* If the deduction for the supplementary plan had already been paid, then the diagnostic services deduction would be reimbursable under the supplementary plan.

• Up to 100 home health-care visits (such as by a nurse but not a doctor) after discharge from at least a three-day stay in hospital, or from an extended-care facility, and before the beginning of a new period of illness.

Defined a period of illness as beginning when a patient entered a hospital or nursing home and ending when the patient had not been an inpatient of a hospital or nursing home for 60 consecutive days.

Provided that the deductions required for the various services would be increased if necessary to meet rising health care costs but that no increases would be made before 1969.

Provided that payments to providers of the services would be "the reasonable cost" of the services.

Effective Date. Provided that post-hospital, extended-care benefits would become effective Jan. 1, 1967, and the other benefits July 1, 1966.

Financing. Provided a payroll tax, which would apply equally to employers, employees and self-employed persons, of: 0.35 percent in 1966; 0.50 percent in 1967-72; 0.55 percent in 1973-75; 0.60 percent in 1976-79; 0.70 percent in 1980-86; 0.80 percent in 1987 and thereafter.

Set the taxable annual earnings base for the health insurance payroll tax at $6,600, effective Jan. 1, 1966.

Provided that general revenue would finance the plan for persons not covered by Social Security or the Railroad Retirement Act.

Provided that the health insurance payroll taxes and the general revenue for the plan would go into a separate Hospital Insurance Trust Fund in the Treasury.

Administration. Gave the Secretary of Health, Education and Welfare (HEW) the main responsibility for administering the plan. Provisions were included for the Railroad Retirement Board to assist in the administration of benefits for its beneficiaries and to collect the Hospital Insurance Trust Fund taxes from its beneficiaries if the Board increased its taxable earnings base to equal that of the base for the health insurance payroll tax. (This was done in PL 89-212. *See story p. 762.)*

Provided that the Secretary would use appropriate state agencies and private organizations to assist in the administration.

Provided that an Advisory Council would be created to advise the Secretary on administration of the plan.

Supplementary Medical Care Plan

Eligibility. Provided the same eligibility requirements as those for the basic plan (above).

Enrollment. Provided that persons at least 65 years of age before Jan. 1, 1966, could enroll between Sept. 1, 1965, through March 31, 1966. Persons reaching 65 after Dec. 31, 1965, would have a seven-month initial enrollment period beginning three months before reaching 65. Future general enrollment periods would be from Oct. 1 to Dec. 31 in each odd year. The first such period would begin Oct. 1, 1967.

Provided that no person could enroll after three years from the close of the first period in which he could have enrolled. Persons who dropped out of the plan could re-enroll only once, and this must be done within three years after dropping out.

Provided that states could enroll and pay the premiums for their public assistance recipients.

Benefits. Provided that the plan would pay 80 percent of the patient's costs after an annual deduction of $50 on the following:

• Services of physicians, surgeons, radiologists, anesthesiologists, pathologists and physiatrists and certain services of dental surgeons, regardless of whether these services were provided in a hospital, clinic, office or home.

• Up to 100 home health-care visits each calendar year.

• Other medical and health services, whether provided in or out of a medical institution, including x-rays, laboratory tests, electrocardiograms, basal metabolism readings, radium and radioactive isotope therapy, certain ambulance services, certain surgical dressings, splints and casts, braces, artificial legs, arms and eyes, and rental of certain medical equipment. Payment for out-of-the-hospital treatment of mental, psychoneurotic and personality disorders would be limited in each calendar year to $250 or 50 percent of the costs, whichever was smaller. Payments would not be made for routine physical examination, dental care, eyeglasses or hearing aids.

Required that payments to institutional providers of care be based on reasonable costs and payments to doctors and non-institutional providers be based on reasonable charges.

Effective Date. Provided that the benefits would be effective July 1, 1966.

Financing. Provided that persons enrolled in the plan would pay monthly premiums of $3 each. The premiums would be deducted from the monthly retirement benefits received by those persons under the Social Security, railroad and civil service retirement systems.

Provided that the Federal Government would match from general revenue the $3 monthly premium paid by each enrollee, and make a preliminary appropriation to establish an operating fund.

Required that the individual and Government contributions go into a separate trust fund for the supplementary plan.

Authorized a Government appropriation equal to $18 per aged person to provide an operating fund when the plan took effect.

Provided that premium rates could be increased—but not before 1968—as medical costs rose and also by 10 percent for each year out of the program for those persons who delayed enrollment until after the first period when enrollment was open to them and for persons who re-enrolled after dropping out.

Income Tax. Reinstituted for persons 65 and older the income tax provisions limiting medical expense deductions to amounts in excess of 3 percent of adjusted gross income and drug expenses in excess of 1 percent. (Under existing law, the limits applied only to persons under 65.)

Provided a separate income tax deduction for one-half of the cost of premiums on medical care insurance, with the deduction not to exceed $150 a year.

Removed all ceilings on income tax deductions for medical expenses. (Existing law provided a $10,000 ceiling for a single taxpayer, $20,000 for a married taxpayer or a single disabled taxpayer 65 and over and $40,000 for a married disabled taxpayer 65 and over.)

Administration. Provided that the HEW Secretary would contract with private carriers to perform the major administrative functions, such as determining rates of payments and disbursing funds.

Kerr-Mills Program

Provided a new title (XIX) to the Social Security Act to combine all the medical provisions for the needy covered in five titles of the existing Act.

Coverage. Extended the Medical Assistance for the Aged (MAA) program for the indigent aged to needy persons under the dependent children, blind and permanently and totally disabled programs (dependent children under 21 must be covered by July 1, 1967); if a state so provided, also made eligible for medical aid needy children who did not qualify for public assistance. Existing provisions of the Act covering medical assistance programs would terminate upon adoption of the new program by a state but not later than Dec. 31, 1969. The MAA program for the "medically needy" aged not on public assistance continued to be optional with the states, but if a state adopted the program it must also make it available to those in comparable need under the blind, disabled and dependent children programs.

Effective Date. Provided that the combined program would take effect Jan. 1, 1966.

Benefits. Required states participating in the new program to provide inpatient and outpatient hospital services, laboratory and x-ray services, skilled nursing home services and physicians' services. States could provide additional benefits.

Required that needy persons on the state programs be provided with assistance to meet the deductible amounts imposed by the federal basic health plan.

Means Test. Required states to provide a "flexible" income test to determine eligibility of the needy elderly for the program. The program could not be based on rigid income standards which adversely affected persons with large medical bills.

Financing. Increased the federal share over existing MAA matching so that states with an average per capita income would receive 55 percent (rather than the existing 50 percent) and states with the lowest level of per capita income could receive up to 83 percent (rather than 80 percent).

Provided a 75-percent federal share for compensation to and for the training of professional medical personnel used in the programs and a 50-percent federal share for other administrative expenses.

Provided that states would not receive additional federal funds unless they continued their own expenditures for the programs at their existing rate.

Administration. Provided that any state agency could be designated to administer the new program as long as the eligibility requirements were established by the agency administering the old-age assistance program.

Child Health Care

Increased federal funds for the maternal and child health services and for the crippled children's services by $5 million for fiscal 1966 and by $10 million in each succeeding fiscal year. This would bring total federal funds for each of the two programs to $45 million in fiscal 1966, $50 million in 1967, $55 million in 1968-69, and $60 million in 1970 and after.

Increased to the same authorizations as above the federal funds for the child welfare services program. Removed the $10 million limit on day-care services under the program.

Authorized $5 million in fiscal 1967, $10 million in fiscal 1968, and $17.5 million in each succeeding fiscal year for grants to schools for training personnel for care of crippled and mentally retarded children.

Authorized $15 million for fiscal 1966, $35 million for fiscal 1967, $40 million for fiscal 1968, $45 million for fiscal 1969 and $50 million for fiscal 1970 for grants to states, medical schools and hospitals to pay up to 75 percent of the cost of programs of providing comprehensive health care services, including dental work, to children in low-income families.

Authorized $2,750,000 in fiscal 1966 and in fiscal 1967 in grants to states to implement programs to combat mental retardation authorized by previous legislation.

Authorized $500,000 annually for fiscal 1966-67 for grants for research in emotional illness in children.

OASDI Changes

Benefits. Provided a 7-percent across-the-board increase in Old-Age, Survivors and Disability Insurance benefits, retroactive to Jan. 1, 1965, with a minimum monthly increase of $4. The monthly benefit range would be increased in 1965 from the existing $40-$127 to $44-$135.90. The maximum monthly payment would increase to $149.90 in 1966 and to $167.90 in 1971. The maximum benefits payable to a family would increase from the existing $254 to $312 in 1965 and to $368 in 1971. About 20 million persons would receive additional benefits of $1.4 billion in 1965.

Permitted children's insurance benefits for those eligible to continue from age 18 through 21 if the child was attending school full-time after reaching 18. An estimated 295,000 children were expected to receive annual benefits of $195 million under this provision, which was retroactive to Jan. 1, 1965.

Permitted widows to receive benefits at age 60, rather than 62, although at an actuarially reduced rate. The provision would take effect in September 1965. For 1966, it was estimated that 185,000 widows would take advantage of this provision and receive additional benefits of $165 million.

Provided that an insured worker would be eligible for disability benefits if his disability had lasted or was expected to last for 12 consecutive months. (Existing law required that the disability must be expected to result in death or be of long duration.) The new provision would take effect in September 1965. An estimated 60,000 disabled workers and dependents would be affected and would receive about $40 million in annual benefits.

Required that disability benefits be offset by payments under workmen's compensation laws when combined payments would exceed 80 percent of the beneficiary's average monthly pay before disability.

Provided reimbursement from Social Security funds to states providing vocational rehabilitation services to persons entitled to disability insurance benefits or a disabled child's benefits. The reimbursement funds could not exceed 1 percent of the Social Security disability benefits paid in the previous year.

Liberalized eligibility requirements to provide benefits to persons 72 and older with only three to five quarters of work in covered employment (instead of the existing minimum of six quarters). A worker or widow who qualified would receive a monthly benefit payment of

$35, and a qualified wife would receive $17.50. About 355,000 persons would receive an estimated $140 million annually under the change, which would take effect in September 1965.

Authorized wife's and widow's benefits to a divorced wife 62 or older if she had been married to an eligible worker for at least 20 years. This provision would take effect in September 1965.

Continued benefits to widows 60 and over and to widowers 62 and over who remarry. (Under existing law, the benefits stopped when the survivor remarried.) The benefits for a remarried person would be 50 percent of the deceased spouse's primary insurance amount rather than the 82.5 percent received by widows and widowers not remarried. The change would take effect in September 1965.

Exempted the first $1,500 that an individual could earn a year without losing Social Security benefits; provided a $1 reduction in benefits for each $2 of earnings between $1,500 and $2,700 and for each $1 of earnings above $2,700. (Existing law exempted the first $1,200 and applied the $1-for-$2 ratio to earnings between $1,200 and $1,700 and the $1-for-$1 ratio to earnings above $1,700. It also exempted those 72 and over from the reductions.) Certain royalties from copyrights and patents would not be counted as earnings. The new provision would become effective in 1966 and would provide additional benefits of $295 million to about 750,000 persons.

Provided disability benefits to a person becoming blind before age 31 if he had worked in Social Security covered jobs for six quarters or half the time between 21 and the age when he became blind, whichever was greater. (Existing law provided that a blind person must have worked five years during the 10 years preceding his blindness.) Provide disability benefits to a person 55 and older who became blind if he was unable to work in his past occupation. (Existing law prohibited benefits to blind persons of all ages who were able to work in any substantial gainful job.) These provisions would benefit about 7 million persons at an annual cost of $5 million.

Continued orphan's benefits to a child legally adopted by a brother or sister.

Coverage. Extended compulsory OASDI coverage to self-employed physicians in 1965 and to interns in 1966.

Provided that waiters and other employees receiving tips would pay Social Security taxes—at the employee rate—on tips received after 1965. The employer would withhold from the employee's wages the Social Security taxes and income taxes on tips reported by the employee if they exceed $20 a month. The employer would not be required to pay the matching employer Social Security tax on the tips.

Provided that farmers with annual gross earning of $2,400 (instead of the existing $1,800) or less could report either their actual net earnings or two-thirds of their gross earnings. Farmers with gross earnings above $2,400 would report actual net earnings if over $1,600 (rather than $1,200).

Added Alaska to the list of states which could bring state and local government employees under the Social Security system. Coverage was extended to certain hospital employees in California whose positions were removed from the state or a local government retirement system and to employees of the District of Columbia not already covered by a retirement system.

Exempted self-employed members of certain recognized religious sects—such as the Amish—from Social Security taxes and coverage. The sect must have been in existence since Dec. 31, 1950, and must teach conscientious opposition to acceptance of benefits from insurance or Social Security.

Financing. Increased the Social Security annual taxable base from the existing $4,800 to $6,600 beginning Jan. 1, 1966.

Increased the employer-employee tax rate from the existing 3.6 percent each to 3.85 percent in 1966; 3.90 percent in 1967-68; 4.40 percent in 1969-72; 4.85 percent in 1973 and thereafter.

Increased the self-employed tax rate from the existing 5.4 percent to 5.8 percent in 1966; 5.9 percent in 1967-68; 6.6 percent in 1969-72; 7.0 percent in 1973 and thereafter.

Administration. Required the Social Security Administration, upon request by a local or state public assistance agency, to disclose the last known address of a person who had failed to support his or her destitute children under age 16. The information must be transmitted through a welfare agency, an actual public assistance case must be involved, a court order for support issued, and non-disclosure provisions must be complied with.

Public Assistance Programs

Revised matching formulas to increase the federal share under all state public assistance programs by an average of about $2.50 a month for the aged, blind and disabled and by an average of about $1.25 for needy children, effective Jan. 1, 1966. The additional federal funds would total about $150 million a year.

Extended the old-age and medical assistance programs to the needy aged and needy blind and disabled in mental or tuberculosis institutions, effective Jan. 1, 1966. Federal funds would be available only if states increased their support of mental health programs. This would cost the Federal Government an estimated $75 million a year.

Increased earnings exemptions under the Old-Age Assistance Program and the Aid to the Permanently and Totally Disabled Program so that a state could exempt the first $20 and one-half of the next $60 of a recipient's monthly earnings in deducting benefits. This would become effective Oct. 1, 1965.

Permitted states, in deducting benefits under the aid for dependent children program, to exempt up to $150 a month earned by dependent children under age 18 in the same home, with a $50 limit per child. The provision was retroactive to July 1, 1965.

Permitted states to disregard up to $5 a month in increased income, above other exemptions, before reducing public assistance payments.

Permitted states taking part in the Title XIX program to determine the federal share in the non-medical public assistance programs by using the matching formula provided in Title XIX for the medical assistance programs.

Non-Communist Pledge Required

In December, when application forms for participation in the basic health insurance plan were sent out, it was discovered that language in the medicare law required persons not covered by Social Security to swear that they were not members of Communist organizations. PL 89-97, in a section not discussed in the committee reports on the medicare bill or in floor debate, said the basic health plan was not available to any member of organizations "referred to in Section 210a (17) of the Social Security Act." The Section barred Social Security coverage for employees of Communist organizations.

Revelation of this previously unnoticed ban in PL 89-97 brought demands from some Members of Congress for repeal of the requirement for non-Communist affidavits.

Antipoverty Program

President Johnson's major 1964 legislative success, the antipoverty program, was—like medicare—aided in 1965 by the big increase of Northern liberals in the new Congress. Most Republicans remained bitterly opposed to the program, Southern Democrats were cool, but the appropriation ($1.5 billion) was double the fiscal 1965 figure. Moreover, the fiscal 1966 authorization bill (HR 8283—PL 89-253) whittled down the chief concession made to Southerners in 1964—the veto right given Governors who disapproved of certain antipoverty programs proposed in their states. *(Congress and the Nation, Vol. I, p. 1326.)*

In other respects, HR 8283 was a comparatively simple piece of legislation, especially when contrasted with the yearly authorization bills that would follow it or the original authorization in 1964. In its main provisions, it authorized funds loosely, title by title, leaving the Office of Economic Opportunity to decide how they should be programmed. The bill extended for a year the date on which financing by the Federal Government was due to drop from 90 to 50 percent of the cost of most projects.

In 1965 the antipoverty program authorization, unlike that for succeeding years, left to the OEO the development of most specific programs under the Title II community action authorization. Congress did initiate one program—federal grants to enable chronically unemployed poor adults to work on federal beautification projects. Congress, at the President's request, also transferred one program—the Title I college work-study program—entirely to the Office of Education.

But the simplicity of the 1965 authorization bill was deceptive. In that year the program was coming under attack not only from Congressional conservatives, but from militant urban groups and the mayors of a number of cities. Militant groups contended that the poor were inadequately represented on community action planning boards and that the program was largely political pork barrel concentrating on excessively high salaries for local officials. Taking the opposite tack, some mayors in 1965 accused OEO Director R. Sargent Shriver Jr. of "fostering class struggle" and "creating tensions" among the poor by insisting on greater participation of the poor in planning community action programs. This policy, they said, failed to "recognize the legal and moral responsibilities of local officials who are accountable to the taxpayers for expenditures of local funds."

Acknowledging that a program of such scope was bound to have difficulties, President Johnson said at an April 1965 news conference, "I don't know of any national program in peacetime that has reached so many people so fast and so effectively." While Shriver was criticized for remaining as head of both the poverty office and the Peace Corps, President Johnson kept him on in both jobs through 1965. Early in 1966 Shriver resigned as director of the Peace Corps.

House Action

The House passed HR 8283 July 22 by a 245-158 roll-call vote, twice the margin by which the original Economic Opportunity Act was approved in 1964. The bill was passed over strong opposition from Republicans, while Southern Democrats divided almost evenly: R 24-110; D 221-48 (ND 176-2; SD 45-46).

The House-passed bill authorized $1,895,000,000, almost $400 million more than the Administration request. In addition, the House version permitted the poverty program director to overrule a state Governor's veto of projects in three antipoverty programs: community action, work-training and adult education (the veto right over the Job Corps and VISTA program was left untouched). The veto privilege had been written into the 1964 act as a concession to Southerners but its repeal was not requested by the Administration in 1965. During three days of debate before passage, Republicans fought unsuccessfully for the absolute veto's retention. An amendment to kill the sections on the veto and cut back authorized funds to the 1965 level failed on a key roll-call vote, **178-227**.

The House rejected numerous other amendments. One which produced particularly acrimonious exchange would have retained in the law a requirement that individuals receiving federal payments under the Act sign an affidavit saying they did not support any organization advocating the overthrow of the Government. The provision had been inserted in the Act on the House floor in 1964. In 1965 the Administration requested its deletion, and the House agreed. Another amendment rejected by the House would have prohibited the OEO Director from holding another Government position. The amendment was designed to prevent OEO Director Shriver from also heading the Peace Corps.

Senate Action

As passed by the Senate Aug. 19, 61-29, the bill authorized $1,650,000,000. During four days of heated debate preceding passage, Republicans made seven unsuccessful attempts to retain all or part of the Governor's veto power. The efforts were defeated by narrow margins, twice by tie votes, and the Senate bill went farther than the House in repealing entirely a state Governor's veto over work-training, community action and adult basic education programs. Republicans also failed in an attempt to cut the program back to the 1964 level and set up a joint Congressional committee to oversee it. The motion was rejected Aug. 18, **39-48**, in a key vote.

Conference Action

Senate-House conferees accepted the Senate's absolute repeal of the Governor's veto, but the House refused to go along with the action. On Sept. 15, by a 209-180 roll-call vote, it recommitted the conference report with instructions that House conferees insist on the House Gov-

---

OEO Develops Title II Programs

The original Economic Opportunity Act gave the OEO substantial flexibility in developing and funding Title II community action programs. In 1965 it set up the following programs:

Project Head Start. A nationwide effort called Project Head Start was launched in summer 1965 to assist preschool children from deprived families to enter kindergarten or first grade in September 1965. The Project offered health services, social services (i.e. child-care counseling for parents) and "pre-learning" experiences to enrollees. Local Head Start programs were run by colleges, schools, local government or private non-profit organizations.

The original Head Start summer program enrolled more than five times as many children (561,-359) than the OEO had originally anticipated, and the program became one of the most popular antipoverty measures with Congressmen. President Johnson Aug. 31, 1965, announced a substantial expansion of the program, including establishment of year-round centers and "follow-through programs" such as field trips and home visits.

Upward Bound. The OEO in summer 1965 also began project "Upward Bound" to prepare talented, poverty-stricken youths for college. It was aimed at youths who could not qualify for college because of psychological, physical and social conditions.

Legal Services. In the spring of 1965, the OEO began a program of federally financed Neighborhood Legal Service centers to provide free legal counsel on civil matters in the nation's slum areas.

Foster Grandparents. President Johnson Aug. 28 announced a new Foster Grandparents program to train unemployed elderly poor in work caring for neglected and mentally retarded children, and bed-ridden sick persons. This program was to be operated in cooperation with the Department of Health, Education and Welfare.

---

ernor's veto provision. The House Sept. 23 agreed to the new conference report by voice vote. The Senate adopted the revised report Sept. 24, on a 46-22 roll-call vote, clearing the bill for the President. The final bill authorized appropriations of $1,785,000,000—$285 million over the President's request. Congress Oct. 21 cleared a supplemental appropriations bill (HR 11588—PL 89-309) appropriating $1.5 billion, the exact amount of the President's request.

Bill Signed. President Johnson signed HR 8283 into law Oct. 9 (PL 89-253).

Provisions. As signed by the President, HR 8283 made the following major changes in the Economic Opportunity Act of 1964:

Title I. Authorized appropriations of $700 million in fiscal 1966 for all three Title I youth programs.

Deleted a provision of the 1963 Act which required Job Corps enrollees to sign an affidavit that they did not support violent overthrow of the Government.

Extended for one year—through Aug. 20, 1967—the existing authority for 90 percent federal financing of work-training (Neighborhood Youth Corps) programs instead of 50 percent federal-50 percent state sharing of costs; required the 50 percent sharing thereafter.

Authorized the OEO Director to override a Governor's veto of proposed work-training programs.

Also extended through Aug. 20, 1967, the existing authority for 90 percent federal financing of college work-study programs instead of 75-percent federal, 25 percent state sharing; required the 25-percent state contribution thereafter. (The Higher Education Act of 1965 (PL 89-329) transferred this program to the Office of Education.)

Title II. Authorized appropriations of $850 million in fiscal 1966 for all Title II programs.

Extended for one year, through Aug. 20, 1967, existing authority for 90 percent federal financing of community action and adult basic education programs, instead of 50 percent federal-50 percent state sharing of costs; required the 50 percent state contribution thereafter.

Authorized a new program of jobs on beautification projects on federal, state and local lands.

Authorized the OEO Director to override a Governor's veto of proposed community action and adult basic education programs.

Title III. Authorized appropriations of $55 million for all Title III programs in fiscal 1966.

Title IV. No changes.

Title V. Authorized $150 million in fiscal 1966 for work-experience programs.

Title VI. Authorized $30 million in fiscal 1966 for VISTA programs.

Railroad Retirement

Congress in 1965 in HR 10874 voted to raise the taxable wage base for the Railroad Retirement System from $450 to $550 a month, and made other changes in the Railroad Retirement Act. The increase brought the wage base to $6,600, the same rate that had been established for the Social Security System by the medicare bill. *(See p. 751.)* Financial interchange between the two systems required that the wage base be the same for both. Moreover, other provisions of the bill, which had the effect of increasing many spouse's annuities, also necessitated a rise in the wage base.

Another provision of HR 10874 temporarily reduced the railroad retirement tax rate in order to soften the new tax burden resulting from the wage base increase. The temporary reduction caused the Assn. of American Railroads to switch from opposition to support of the bill.

HR 10874 was passed by the House Sept. 14 and by the Senate Sept. 15 by voice votes. President Johnson signed it into law (PL 89-212) Sept. 29. It was similar to a bill (HR 3157) passed by both chambers earlier in the session which the House later objected to because the Senate had added certain tax provisions which House Members contended had to originate in their chamber. The Budget Bureau also objected to HR 3157 on grounds that the contemplated $14 million increase in the actuarial deficit of the Railroad Retirement Fund was too high. It did not object to HR 10874, which increased the deficit from approximately $20 million to $29.5 million.

Major Provisions. HR 10874, effective Jan. 1, 1966, raised the maximum creditable and taxable compensation (wage) base for the Railroad Retirement System from $450 to $550 a month. The higher wage base would

result in higher revenues for the Railroad Retirement System and higher monthly retirement benefits.

HR 10874 also reduced the railroad retirement tax rate for employers and employees from 7-1/4 percent each to 6-1/4 percent each during the period Oct. 1 to Dec. 31, 1965, in order to soften the immediate tax burden resulting from the increase in the taxable wage base. However, the bill provided that the tax rate would later be restored to 7-1/4 percent by annual increases of one-quarter of 1 percent—the first to become effective Jan. 1, 1966, the last Jan. 1, 1969.

HR 10874 also extended to railroad employees, beginning in 1966, the right to count tips totalling over $20 a month as wages for the purpose of calculating employee tax payments and Railroad Retirement System benefits (thus yielding a higher retirement benefit). Only the employee would pay the taxes on such tips, not the employer. (Similar rights were granted for non-railroad employees in the 1965 Social Security amendments.)

Finally, HR 10874 permitted the spouse of a retired railroad employee to receive, simultaneously, both the spouse's retirement annuity, and also Social Security or railroad retirement benefits earned in his or her own right, without a reduction in the spouse's annuity. Under the previous law, the spouse of a retired railroad worker received a monthly annuity equal to 50 percent of the retired husband's or wife's annuity, up to a maximum of $69.90. However, this annuity was reduced by amounts equal to payments of Social Security and railroad retirement benefits earned by the spouse.

Administration on Aging

Congress in 1965 passed a bill (HR 3708—PL 89-73) taking responsibility for federal activities relating to the aging away from the Health, Education and Welfare Department's Commissioner of Welfare. It established an Administration on Aging in HEW whose Commissioner was directly responsible to the HEW Secretary. The existing Office of Aging, which had been under the jurisdiction of the Welfare Commissioner, was abolished.

HR 3708, the Older Americans Act, also authorized a five-year program designed to coordinate federal activities related to the elderly and to improve and expand programs for the aging on both the federal and state level. It authorized federal grants totaling $17.5 million in fiscal 1966 and 1967 to states and to public and private non-profit organizations for developing programs for the elderly.

HR 3708 was passed by the House on a 395-1 roll-call vote March 31. During debate, a number of representatives said a separate agency for the elderly, not associated with welfare, was long overdue. The Senate passed the bill by voice vote May 27, without debate. The House July 6 agreed to minor Senate amendments by voice vote, and President Johnson signed the bill into law (PL 89-73) July 14.

Provisions. As enacted, HR 3708:

Created an Administration on Aging in the Department of Health, Education and Welfare, directed by a Commissioner on Aging appointed by the President and confirmed by the Senate. The Administration would serve as a clearinghouse for information on problems of the aged, assist the HEW Secretary on matters concerning the aging, administer grants under the Act, provide technical assistance to state and local governments, develop and arrange for research and demonstration programs, prepare educational materials and statistics on aging and "stimulate more effective use of" existing programs for the aging.

Authorized appropriations of $5 million for fiscal 1966 and $8 million for fiscal 1967 for grants to states for community planning and coordination of programs for the aged, establishing or expanding programs and training of specialized personnel to carry out the programs. Appropriations for fiscal 1968-70 would have to be authorized later by Congress. No funds could be used for construction in establishing or expanding programs, except for "minor alterations and repairs." States would receive specified allotments plus grants based on a state's population of persons 65 or older.

Authorized appropriations of $1.5 million for fiscal 1966 and $3 million for fiscal 1967 for grants or contracts with public or private non-profit organizations and agencies for study, development, demonstration and evaluation projects related to the needs of the elderly and for specialized training of persons to carry out the programs for the aged. Appropriations for fiscal 1968-70 would have to be authorized later by Congress.

Created a 16-member Advisory Committee on Older Americans, with the Commissioner on Aging as chairman and other members to be from outside the Government, to advise the HEW Secretary on matters involving the aging.

1966

Antipoverty Program

Unlike 1965, criticism of the antipoverty program in 1966 began to catch up with the legislation. The Administration bill was heavily amended, as Congress attempted to change the program to deal with reports of lack of discipline and high costs in the Job Corps, and poor administration of the local community action programs.

While the final appropriation ($1,612,000,000) was more than the amount voted the year before, it was substantially below the Administration request. In addition, Congress in the fiscal 1967 authorization bill (HR 15111—PL 89-794) for the first time earmarked funds for specific OEO programs. The result was to provide more than the Administration wanted for certain popular programs, such as Head Start, and to provide substantially less than the request for local community action and less than the request for the Job Corps.

Congress in 1966 also wrote a variety of restrictive amendments into the authorization, such as ones limiting salaries of antipoverty officials and placing a ceiling and per-enrollee cost limit on the Job Corps. It transferred the small business loan program from the OEO to the Small Business Administration and transferred the Adult Basic Education program to HEW. It also sought to keep a firmer hand on the OEO by giving unsought statutory authority to existing programs and originating new programs. The new programs were: emergency family loans; subprofessional jobs; special impact program for areas

with severe unemployment; and a neighborhood health services authorization which included a narcotics rehabilitation program.

President Johnson's 1966 poverty request was brief. On Jan. 24 he asked Congress to appropriate $1,750,000,000 and to extend for one more year expiring provisions for a high federal share of the costs of Neighborhood Youth Corps, community action and adult education projects. The bill was passed Sept. 29 by the House and Oct. 4 by the Senate, and signed into law Nov. 8. The appropriations bill (HR 18381—PL 89-697), carrying $138 million less than the amount antipoverty officials called the "irreducible minimum" for continued progress, was cleared Oct. 21.

House Action

The House Education and Labor Committee June 1 reported a clean bill (HR 15111) embodying its changes in the Administration request. As the Administration had asked, the bill provided $1.75 billion; however, the Committee set statutory minimum authorizations for a number of specific programs in Title I and Title II. The result was to provide only what funds were left over after earmarking for the Title I Job Corps and Title II versatile community action programs; this meant a cut in the amount the Administration wanted for the Job Corps and a substantial cut in community action funds. The committee also wrote into the 1964 Act new programs of narcotic rehabilitation, emergency $300 family loans, and subprofessional jobs for the poor. The committee bill also reduced the federal share of most community action programs from 90 to 80 percent, dropped the 100 percent federal share of work experience programs to 80 percent and extended indefinitely the 90 percent federal share for the neighborhood youth corps. It set a $12,500 limit on federal contributions to salaries of local community action officials, and wrote a number of other restrictions into the 1964 Act.

There was a delay of almost four months between the time HR 15111 was reported and the date (Sept. 26) that it was brought to the House floor. The delay was attributed partly to a lack of pressure by the Administration and partly to an attempt by Committee Chairman Adam C. Powell Jr. (D N.Y.) to use the bill as a lever to get concessions on other legislation. The delay was connected closely to a subsequent revolt by Committee members against Powell's leadership.

The House passed HR 15111 Sept. 29 by 210-156 (R 15-105; ND 167-5; SD 28-46) roll-call vote. No changes were made in the committee's provisions on funds, but a number of substantive amendments were adopted. These included transfer of the small business loan program to the Small Business Administration, a requirement that at least one-third of the members of local community action boards be representatives of the poor and limitation on the number of "supergrades" (GS 16-18) that could be hired by the OEO to one per 100 employees. Dissatisfaction with the Job Corps program was reflected by floor amendments setting a ceiling of 45,000 on the number of Job Corps enrollees and setting a per-enrollee cost ceiling of $7,500.

Prior to passage the House by a 162-203 (R 115-5; ND 9-162; SD 38-36) roll call rejected a motion to recommit the bill and substitute for it the Republican's "Opportunity

Crusade" which dispersed much of the poverty program throughout several of the older federal agencies. Earlier Sept. 29 the House by a key **156-208** (R 107-15; ND 5-159; SD 44-34) roll-call vote rejected a motion offered by Paul A. Fino (R N.Y.) to strike the enacting clause and kill the bill entirely.

Senate Action

The day HR 15111 was passed by the House, the Senate Labor and Public Welfare Committee reported its own version (S 3164). The Committee bill authorized $2,496,000,000—an increase of $746 million over the $1.75 billion requested by the Administration and approved by the House. It earmarked funds for specific programs only in Title I (the youth programs) of the Act. As the Administration had requested, expiring 90-10 federal-state formulas for funds were extended.

The Committee authorized two new programs: (1) job creation projects in urban areas with high concentrations of unemployment and (2) a subprofessional job provision similar to that of the House. It did not include most of the House restrictions, or the new narcotics rehabilitation and emergency family loan programs. However, it gave statutory authority to and expanded the neighborhood health centers program.

The Senate passed HR 15111 Oct. 4 by a 49-20 roll-call vote. Prior to passage it adopted amendments reducing the authorization to the Administration and House figure of $1.75 billion. In its only other major differences from the Senate committee bill, the measure earmarked funds for Head Start under Title II and laid the groundwork for the transfer of the Adult Basic Education program to the Office of Education.

Conference

The Senate adopted the conference report on HR 15111 Oct. 18 by voice vote. The House adopted the report Oct. 20 by a 170-109 roll-call vote, sending the bill to the White House.

The final bill went farther than both the House and Senate in earmarking specific amounts for all programs under Titles I and II. It did not alter the 1964 provision permitting limited transfer of funds from title to title, but specified that "under no circumstances" could the $211 million for the Job Corps be increased. Expiring federal share provisions were continued indefinitely, in some cases at a slightly reduced rate.

Conferees adopted all of the new programs initiated by the House and Senate. The narcotic rehabilitation program was included under the Neighborhood Health Centers program which had already been begun by the OEO. They followed the House in giving statutory authority to Head Start and legal services for the poor. They also accepted the House floor amendment transferring the small business loan program from the OEO to the Small Business Administration. They followed the Senate approach of not authorizing money for the Adult Basic Education program on the assumption that it would be transferred to the Office of Education by other pending legislation.

Conferees included the major restrictions written into the bill by the House, including the specific directions on the operations of the Job Corps, and the requirement that

at least one-third of the members of local community action boards be representatives of the poor. They modified the House limit on the federal share of salaries paid local antipoverty officials from $12,500 to $15,000. The House floor amendment limiting the number of "super-grades" in the OEO office was changed to a stipulation that no additional "supergrades" could be created or filled for the rest of the fiscal year.

Bill Signed. President Johnson signed HR 15111 into law Nov. 8 (PL 89-794.)

Provisions. HR 15111 extended the antipoverty program through 1970, authorized $1.75 billion in fiscal 1967 and made the following major changes in the Economic Opportunity Act of 1964:

Title I. Authorized appropriations of $696 million in fiscal 1967, earmarked as follows: Job Corps $211 million, Neighborhood Youth Corps, $410 million; and Impact Programs, $75 million.

Set a ceiling of 45,000 on the number of persons in the Job Corps and specified that a minimum of 23 percent of the persons in the Job Corps were to be women. Limited the cost of the Job Corps to $7,500 per enrollee for camps in operation more than nine months.

Made a number of other requirements concerning Job Corps operations, including establishment of standards of conduct for Job Corps centers and procedures to ensure that transfer of Job Corps enrollees from local jurisdiction would not violate parole or probationary procedures.

Required the OEO to undertake four pilot demonstration projects providing youth employment and training on a combined residential and nonresidential basis.

Rewrote the work-training section of Title I to make a clear distinction between programs designed to provide employment for students and those to provide work experience for the unemployed.

Authorized indefinitely a federal payment of 90 percent for the Neighborhood Youth Corps.

Added a new section which authorized special impact programs to provide employment to adults and youths in urban areas with high concentrations of unemployment. They would perform such work as the rehabilitation of slum housing.

Title II. Authorized a total of $846 million in fiscal 1967 *(for distribution, see below)*.

Versatile Community Action— Authorized $323 million.

Added a number of new requirements including the following: a person serving on a community action board was to live in the geographic area he represented; one-third of local board members were to be representatives of the poor; the elderly and rural poor were to be able to petition for representation on local boards if they felt current representation was inadequate; local community action employee salaries were to be no more than $15,000 a year from federal funds; representatives of the poor were to be paid for attending board meetings.

Provided that beginning July 1, 1967, the federal share of the costs of most community action programs would be 80 percent, replacing an existing provision which reduced the federal share from 90 to 50 percent.

Public Service Employment— Authorized a new program of subprofessional public service employment for hard-core unemployed adults, and earmarked $36.5 million for the program in fiscal 1967. This became known as the new careers program.

Earmarked $36.5 million in fiscal 1967 for the program of jobs on beautification projects begun in 1965.

Emergency Family Loans—Authorized a new program of small loans (not to exceed $300 for one person and bearing a 2-percent annual interest rate) to persons from low-income families confronted with financial emergencies, and earmarked $8 million in community action funds for this purpose in fiscal 1967.

Head Start—Gave legislative authority to the Head Start program and earmarked $352 million for it in fiscal 1967.

Legal Services—Also gave legislative authority to the legal services program, and earmarked $22 million in fiscal 1967.

Health Centers—Authorized the OEO to make grants to or to contract with public or private nonprofit agencies to operate neighborhood health centers (eight were already funded) and to conduct a narcotic rehabilitation program. Earmarked $61 million for this section.

Adult Literacy—Added a new adult literacy program, similar to, but on a narrower basis than, the existing Adult Basic Education program (transferred to the Office of Education in separate legislation). Earmarked $7 million for the new program.

Title III. Increased the ceiling on loans to low-income rural families from $2,500 to $3,500. Authorized $57 million for Title III programs in fiscal 1967.

Title IV. Transferred the small business loan program from the OEO to the Small Business Administration, but retained in the OEO the power to make grants to or contract with nonprofit agencies to pay costs of screening, counseling, management guidance and other assistance to small business concerns. Authorized $5 million for this purpose in fiscal 1967.

Title V. Restructured the work experience program, splitting its operation between the Labor Department and HEW.

Authorized an 80-percent federal share of the costs of work-training programs beginning July 1, 1968 (instead of the current 100 percent).

Title VI (Administration). Authorized appointment of an assistant director of the OEO for programs benefitting the elderly poor.

Required a list of local antipoverty program employees earning more than $10,000 a year.

Provided that no additional supergrade (GS 16-18) could be created or filled in fiscal 1967.

Title VIII (VISTA). Removed the Volunteers in Service to America (VISTA) program from Title IV.

Authorized appropriations of $31 million for the program in fiscal 1967.

Aids to Elderly

For the most part, 1966 saw a pause between the big Social Security bills of 1965 and 1967 in terms of legislative aids to the elderly. However, a provision of the Tax Adjustment Act of 1966 (HR 12752—PL 89-368) gave persons who had reached 72 years of age and were not eligible for Social Security a monthly payment of $35 from Social Security funds. A spouse 72 or above was to receive $17.50 a month. Payments were to be reduced by the amounts of benefits from Government pensions or public welfare payments. The final provision was a much modified version of a Senate floor amendment.

Other Senate amendments for aids to the elderly, added to a different bill, did not survive a House-Senate conference. The amendments, tacked on to a tax bill (HR 13103) would have (1) given the elderly full tax deductibility for medical expenses; and (2) authorized federal payment of part of the cost of drug purchases by outpatients under the supplementary medicare plan.

Railroad Retirement

Congress in 1966 voted to increase annuities for certain pensioners covered by the Railroad Retirement Act and also to establish a supplementary pension program for all railroad employees. The bill (HR 17285—PL 89-699) was passed by the House Oct. 13, passed by the Senate Oct. 14, and signed into law Oct. 30.

The 1965 Social Security-Medicare bill (PL 89-97) raised the level of Social Security cash benefits, thereby also increasing Railroad Retirement pensions for about two-thirds of pensioners. This was because the credits of any railroad worker who retired with less than 10 years of service were transferred to the Social Security System and his benefits were then paid through that System. HR 17285 therefore gave a 7 percent increase to those retirees whose funds had not been transferred to Social Security. The new benefits were to be financed by an additional one-quarter percent tax on railroad employees and employers.

The supplemental plan established by HR 17285 gave minimum extra annuities of $45 a month to any individual over 65 with at least 25 years service. The annuities were to be financed by an excise tax of two cents for each man-hour of work, and would be paid for by the employer. The new program was an outgrowth of collective bargaining agreements between railroad management and labor.

In a related development, President Johnson Oct. 30 signed into law a bill (HR 14355—PL 89-700) amending the Railroad Retirement Act to provide benefits for surviving children ages 18 to 21 who were full-time students. PL 89-97 contained similar provisions for Social Security beneficiaries.

Medicare Developments

Most of the provisions of the landmark 1965 medicare bill took effect during 1966. At year's end some 19.5 million aged were covered by the basic medicare hospital plan and 17.5 million had enrolled in the voluntary supplementary program which covered a large proportion of doctor, laboratory and related costs. Congress in 1966 made several minor changes in the medicare law and considered, but did not enact, two more important ones.

Deadline Extended. President Johnson April 8 signed into law a bill (HR 6319—PL 89-384) extending the sign-up deadline for the voluntary plan from March 31 to May 31, 1966. He said the extension would enable an additional 1.3 million persons to sign up for medicare.

Nursing Home Profits. Mr. Johnson Nov. 2 signed into law a bill (HR 6958—PL 89-713) permitting proprietary nursing homes a profit of roughly 7-1/2 percent on services to medicare patients. The conference committee report said it expected that nonprofit nursing homes would receive bonuses of 2 percent above actual costs, and that nursing homes organized for profit would receive a 1-1/2 percent bonus.

Drug Costs. Senators in 1966 made several proposals to reduce drug costs to medicare and welfare recipients, but none was enacted. Dropped in conference was a Senate amendment to the Foreign Investors Tax Act (HR 13103) requiring federal payment of part of the cost of outpatient drug purchases under the supplementary medicare program.

A proposal (S 3614) that drugs purchased under federally aided programs be prescribed on the basis of generic (chemical) name, rather than brand name, saw no action.

Medicaid Funding. The new Title XIX of the Social Security Act, authorized by the 1965 medicare bill, permitted state and federally financed medical aid to the "medically needy"—persons who were not quite poor enough to be on public assistance, but met all other requirements for welfare aid. (Before 1965 this category had been limited to the elderly.) In 1966 Congressmen became concerned that some states were making such a liberal definition of "medically needy" that enormous federal contributions were required. A bill (HR 18225) cutting from the program any adult between 21 and 65 who was not eligible for public assistance was reported by the House Ways and Means Committee late in the session, but got no further.

Loyalty Oath. The Justice Department in 1966 conceded that the provision in the medicare law requiring medical applicants not covered by Social Security to disclaim Communist affiliation was unconstitutional. The provision, contained in the medicare authorization without the knowledge of most Congressmen, caused a major controversy at the time of its discovery. *(See p. 760.)*

1967

Antipoverty Program

For a time in 1967 Congressional objections to the antipoverty program were so strong that it looked as if the program might be killed altogether. However, the final authorization bill (S 2388—PL 90-222) provided a two-year authorization and only slightly less money ($1,980,000,000) than the Administration had requested for fiscal 1968. The fiscal 1968 appropriation was $1,773,000,000. Funds were earmarked less strictly than in 1966.

The reason for this major 1967 Administration success was adoption of a House Education and Labor Committee amendment drastically revising the Title II community action programs. The controversial new provision required that all local community action funds be controlled by public officials. Previously, about 80 percent of the more than 1,000 local community action agencies were run by private, nonprofit organizations, with public officials playing no specific role. Instead, the emphasis of the original community action program was on the involvement of the poor.

The new local-control feature, called the Green amendment after its sponsor, Rep. Edith Green (D Ore.) was written into the bill to make the program more palatable to Southerners and also to appease representatives

of some northern cities where militant antipoverty groups had come in conflict with the city administration. The final version of S 2388 contained a "bypass" provision permitting direct OEO administration of programs if public officials did not develop a satisfactory plan. The Green amendment was nevertheless bitterly attacked by some Northern liberals, although others insisted it was necessary to ensure enactment of any bill at all in 1967.

Other major provisions of the final bill attempted to tighten the Job Corps program further, although in general there was less criticism of the program than in 1966. The new bill also consolidated all work and training programs in Title I, and contained four new national community action programs—a new program for the elderly, an emergency food and medical services program, a family planning program and a "Follow Through" program for children after Head Start. Congress also added a new migrant worker aid program to Title III and a new day care program to Title V. As in 1966 Congress wrote various administrative restrictions into the programs—such as a tight limit on administrative costs of local community action programs—but some of the strongest restrictions, added on the House floor, were dropped in conference.

The President made his 1967 antipoverty request in March. His message acknowledged widespread criticism of the program by stressing tighter administration of existing programs rather than the development of major new efforts. Despite the President's approach, it soon became clear that the newly-elected House was in an austerity mood, and that the over-all program could be in real trouble. Action was delayed on the antipoverty bills to permit a cooling-off period in the aftermath of violent summer riots in city after city.

The Senate antipoverty bill finally reached the floor in late September. After 10 days of desultory debate, during which an Administration-opposed $2.8 billion emergency job program was killed, the bill was passed by a lopsided 60-21 roll-call vote. For the first time, a majority of Senate Republicans voted for the measure.

Subsequent House Committee mark-up sessions on S 2388 saw very little progress. Finally the Committee took the unusual action of holding public mark-up sessions; during this time the controversial new local community action provisions were adopted. The strategy of adding the Green amendment was successful. The bill was quickly approved and S 2388 passed the House Nov. 15 without major damage except for a cut in funds. Republicans apparently lost Southern support for their own attempts to dismember the poverty program by labelling the Green amendment "the bosses and boll weevil" amendment.

After 11 meetings with House conferees, Senate conferees reluctantly accepted the Green amendment in order to get final approval of the bill. House conferees, for their part, gave in on the higher authorization figure, and permitted a two-year authorization, saving the Administration another major struggle in 1968.

Request. President Johnson March 14 recommended a 25-percent increase in antipoverty funds—a $2.06 billion authorization for fiscal 1968. More than half of the increase was earmarked for new programs, including a "Follow Through" program to sustain the benefits of Head Start, and an intensified program to find work for 100,000 hard core unemployed in 19 cities.

The heaviest emphasis in the President's message was on stricter administration of antipoverty programs. In the troublesome Job Corps program, the President promised "tighter cost controls, firmer discipline and more effective recruitment." For community action programs, he recommended amendments to improve planning and personnel systems of local community action agencies and give public officials a greater voice on community action boards.

Senate Action

The Senate Labor and Public Welfare Committee did not report its version (S 2388) of the Administration proposal until September, apparently to allow a cooling-off period after summer rioting in many major cities. The Committee increased the fiscal 1968 authorization by $198 million, to $2,258,000,000, provided an open-ended authorization for fiscal 1969 and added on an additional $2.5 billion two-year emergency job program to support labor intensive projects in slum areas with severe unemployment problems and $300,000 for loans tied to the job program in fiscal 1968. The report said, "The poverty program, because it has never been funded at a level commensurate with needs, at its best is barely scratching the surface of community relations, and the remedies will be far costlier and much more difficult than the limited efforts so far underway."

The Committee bill also made other major changes in the antipoverty program. In Part A of Title I it followed the Administration's wish in substantially tightening the Job Corps program—improving the selection, counseling and job placement processes. The Committee went far beyond the Administration bill in completely rewriting the work-training section and consolidating all manpower activities authorized in the Economic Opportunity Act—the Neighborhood Youth Corps, Operation Mainstream (formerly Green Thumb, the 1965 community beautification employment program), the 1966 new careers program and a new concentrated employment program. The report said the director of the OEO could delegate administration of the comprehensive program to the Labor Department. It said the comprehensive program would give participants an unbroken sequence of services to help them obtain and hold jobs.

In Title I, Part C, the Committee expanded the special impact program authorized in 1966. It called for the development of a variety of special programs in communities with a high concentration of poor people, and authorized $83 million more than the Administration request.

In Title II, the community action section of the Act, the Committee agreed to Administration requests to improve planning and personnel systems. It also added provisions to further involve the poor in community action. It expanded from four to seven the number of specific Title II programs, adding to Head Start, Legal Services, Comprehensive Health Services and Upward Bound three others—a program for the aged, a family planning program and the "Follow Through" program requested by the Administration. Community action funds were not specifically earmarked for these programs as in 1966; instead the bill required that at least half the Title II funds were to be used for locally selected programs; the rest could be allocated as the OEO saw fit.

In other major changes, the Committee in Title III authorized a new program for migrant workers, in Title V set up a new day care program, and in Title VIII established a demonstration project utilizing VISTA volunteers for the rehabilitation of juvenile delinquents.

Floor Action. The Senate Oct. 5 passed S 2388 by a 60-21 roll-call vote.

The Senate-passed bill included the $2,258,000,000 authorization voted by the Committee, but did not include the additional $2.8 billion two-year emergency employment program. The emergency program was dropped from the bill on a 54-28 (R 24-6; ND 14-20; SD 16-2) roll-call vote. A compromise one-year, $925 million program was then defeated on a narrow **42-47** key roll-call vote (R 16-18; ND 24-13; 2-16). The program was opposed by the Administration, which reportedly feared that inclusion of the large new program would jeopardize the legislative future of the poverty program.

The Senate-passed bill was substantially the same as the bill recommended by the Committee. The most important Senate floor changes further tightened screening requirements for the Job Corps and VISTA; set a 15-percent ceiling on administrative costs of local community action programs; and limited the fiscal 1969 authorization to $2.4 billion.

The Senate also rejected a number of important floor amendments. On a 35-54 roll-call vote it defeated a GOP attempt to transfer the Head Start program from the OEO to the HEW Office of Education. This was the only attempt made in the Senate in 1967 to dismantle the OEO and transfer programs it administered to old-line agencies. A proposal to abolish the Job Corps was defeated by a 30-49 roll-call vote. The Senate also rejected, by a 41-45 roll call, an amendment to provide a limited Governor's veto over migrant assistance programs.

House Action

The House Education and Labor Committee Oct. 16, after more than four weeks of closed meetings during which little progress was made on the antipoverty bill, took the unusual move of beginning open mark-up sessions. It then completed work on the bill in four days. In this period it wrote into the bill controversial and far-reaching provisions which substantially altered Title II, the community action section.

The new provisions required that all local community action funds be channeled through public officials. Currently about 80 percent of local community action agencies were run by private, nonprofit organizations with representatives of the poor; public officials played no specific role. The Committee amendment required that the community action agency would be the state or local government or an agency designated by them. The agency would run its program through a community action board consisting of one-third public officials, one-third poverty area representatives and one-third representatives of business, labor and charitable groups. The provisions were written into the bill partly to make the program more palatable to Southern Democrats, and partly to solidify Northern Democratic support. (In some cities there had been bitter conflict between local poverty groups and the city government.) As a concession to Northern Democrats who opposed the change, the Committee included a "bypass" amendment permitting direct funding of community action programs to a nonprofit agency if the local government refused to participate in the poverty program.

In other changes from the Senate bill, the House measure authorized the $2.06 billion requested by the Administration, and specified that the fiscal 1969 authorization could not exceed that. It reduced per-enrollee costs for the Job Corps from the current $7,500 per annum to $6,500 and established nonresidential Job Corps centers.

In its other major provisions, the House Committee version followed the lines of the Senate bill. It also provided for stricter Job Corps administration. It added to the seven specific Senate Title II programs an eighth— an Emergency Food and Medical Services Program to combat malnutrition and starvation. A special Title III migrant program and VISTA juvenile delinquency demonstration program were not included.

Floor Action. The House Nov. 15 passed S 2388 by a 283-129 roll-call vote (R 97-79; ND 145-5; SD 41-45). However, before passage it adopted a recommittal motion cutting the authorization to $1,600,000,000. The reduction was made on a key **221-190** roll-call vote (R 148-28; ND 9-141; SD 64-21).

Much of the debate between Nov. 7 and 15 concerned the Committee changes in the community action programs. Republicans charged that the Committee had "carved the heart" out of community action in order to pick up enough Southern votes to pass the bill. They said the new provisions would result in city hall domination of community action, and a loss of the program's innovative quality. The local-control feature of community action was dubbed by Republicans the "bosses and boll weevil amendment"—a taunt that irritated Southerners.

The new community action provisions did indeed appear to have given the Administration Southern support it had not had in previous years. All of the Republican proposals to transfer individual poverty programs to existing Government agencies were soundly rejected as Southern Democrats joined Northern Democrats in opposition.

While Republicans were totally unsuccessful in reshaping the basic structure of the poverty program, they were able to push through a number of administrative restrictions. Among these were provisions barring use of Legal Service program funds to defend persons who organized civil disturbances, limiting "supergrade" antipoverty employees to one for every 100 employees, barring antipoverty employees from participating in demonstrations and riots, and abolishing the OEO's authority to hire consultants. Another floor amendment eliminated the fiscal 1969 authorization.

Conference

The conference report on S 2388 provided a two-year authorization of $1,980,000,000 for fiscal 1968 and $2,258,000,000 for fiscal 1969. The minor differences between Title I in the two versions were compromised, with the per-enrollee Job Corps cost set at $6,900. The House provision for nonresidential centers was accepted.

In the most controversial provisions of S 2388, the Title II community action authorization, conferees accepted the new House concept of community action with a modification. They broadened the bypass provision to allow the Director to bypass an agency that failed to

carry out its program in a satisfactory manner. Conferees also accepted a provision in the original Senate bill giving the poor a chance to petition for better representation on a community board. Conferees rejected the Senate provision that at least 50 percent of community action funds be used for locally selected community action programs. They accepted a Senate amendment prohibiting earmarking of Title II funds for specific community action programs.

Conferees agreed to eight special impact programs eligible for community action funding. They accepted a modified House amendment prohibiting Legal Services aid to persons indicted for a crime. The Senate's special Title III migrant program and VISTA juvenile delinquency demonstration program were agreed to. House floor amendments limiting antipoverty supergrades and banning OEO consultants were rejected, and a House antiriot floor amendment was modified. The Senate floor amendment limiting administrative costs of local community action programs to 15 percent of the total was accepted.

Final Action. The Senate Dec. 8 adopted the conference report by a 62-16 roll-call vote. In debate GOP Sen. Jacob K. Javits (N.Y.) bitterly attacked the community action provisions. He said they destroyed the concept that the poor themselves would have a role in the development of antipoverty programs. He said "a deal was made to get the votes for this program." Floor manager Joseph S. Clark (D Pa.) said "it was necessary to accept the amendment if we wanted any bill" and that the bypass provision was strong.

In the House, the conference report was adopted Dec. 11 by a 247-149 roll-call vote, sending the bill to the President.

Appropriations. The fiscal 1968 antipoverty appropriation was contained in the first supplemental appropriations bill for fiscal 1968 (HR 14397), cleared Dec. 15. The final bill carried $1,773,000,000 for antipoverty programs. It did not specify how the funds should be divided. The Senate had voted $1,980,000; the House provided $1,612,500,000.

Provisions of S 2388

As signed into law (PL 90-222) Dec. 23, S 2388 amended the Economic Opportunity Act of 1964 as follows:

Funds. Authorized $1,980,000,000 for antipoverty programs for fiscal 1968 and $2,180,000,000 for fiscal 1969. The fiscal 1968 section allocated for Title I programs: $295 million to the Job Corps, $476 million for adult and youth work and training programs, and $60 million for special slum job and development programs; for Title II to VIII programs: $950 million for community action, $47 million for rural loan and migrant programs, $10 million for technical assistance to small businesses in slums, $70 million for work experience programs, $25 million for a day-care program, $16 million for administrative expenses and $31 million for the VISTA program.

Fiscal 1969 funds were not broken down by program.

Title I—Job Corps. Tightened the screening process to assure that Job Corps enrollees would be able to perform successfully in the program. In the case of a potential enrollee with a history of antisocial behavior, required the OEO Director to obtain a professional finding that participation of such enrollee would not hurt the program. Required the assignment of an enrollee to the center nearest his home that has a vacancy. Provided for the establishment of nonresidential Job Corps centers. Required that 40 percent of male enrollees be assigned to conservation centers to be called Civilian Conservation Centers. Provided that each enrollee receive a personal allowance of not more than $50 a month. Provided for the establishment of community advisory councils to improve communication between a Job Corps center and the local community. Required the OEO Director to undertake a systematic evaluation of the Job Corps program to determine the best method of training enrollees. Authorized the Director to undertake an experimental program involving the operation of community vocational education schools and skill centers in urban areas. Permitted the Director to cooperate with states in the administration of state-operated Job Corps centers.

Special Limitations—Limited the capacity of residential centers in fiscal 1968 to 45,000 and required that the per-enrollee cost not exceed $6,900 a year. Required that by June 30, 1968, 25 percent of the enrollees be women and set 50 percent as the future goal. Prohibited any Job Corps enrollee or employee from taking active part in political campaigns.

Work and Training Activities—Consolidated into a single, comprehensive work and training program various training programs for adults and youths such as the Neighborhood Youth Corps, the "new careers" program and Operation Mainstream. Provided that the new concentrated program take effect July 1, 1968. Specified that assistance for such work and training activities be channeled through a "prime sponsor," which would be a public or private nonprofit agency. Specified that among the eligible activities were part-time employment, on-the-job training and work experience for students; special programs for the unemployed or underemployed in either urban or rural areas having a large concentration of unemployed, low-income persons; supportive and followup services in addition to job training; and incentives to private employers to train or employ low-income persons. Provided that the incentives not be used as a subsidy for the normal operations of a company. Barred assistance to any work and training program where the person running the program was a member of the Communist Party. Authorized the OEO Director to undertake pilot projects and to design programs to deal with long-term unemployment among persons 55 years old and over. Authorized federal assistance of up to 90 percent for such programs.

Special Impact Programs—Established a special program (consolidating several new programs of 1966) that was directed at particular urban neighborhoods with a high concentration of low-income persons and at rural areas suffering a substantial migration to urban areas. Directed that the programs attempt to alleviate the critical problems of chronic unemployment, "rising community tensions" and "dependency." Authorized special economic and business development efforts to lure businesses into impoverished urban and rural areas and proposed intensified community development and manpower training activities. Specified that the federal share of such special impact programs would be 90 percent unless the neighborhood or local area was unable to provide its full 10-percent share. Specified that at least 7 percent of the funds appropriated for Title I be spent on special impact programs.

Title II—Community Action. Redefined a community action agency, requiring that it be a state or local government or a nonprofit agency (public or private) designated by a state or local government. In the event, however, that the state or local government failed to establish or designate a community action agency, or failed to submit to the OEO Director or carry out a satisfactory plan for a community action program, the Director was authorized to designate a nonprofit agency as the community action agency.

Required that a local community action agency which was the state or local government have a community action board to administer the policies set by the controlling government. Required that community action agencies designated by the local or state government or the OEO have a governing board to establish program, fiscal and personnel policies for the agency.

Specified that community action boards and governing boards could not have more than 51 members, one-third of whom would have to be public officials (unless that many were not available to serve), one-third poverty area representatives democratically selected, and the remainder representatives of business, labor, civic and charitable groups.

Provided that each community action board should have a "full opportunity" to participate in the development and implementation of all programs and projects designed to serve the poor.

Required the OEO Director to promulgate ground rules for community action agencies and required local agencies to set up procedures by which representatives of the poor who believed they were inadequately represented on the board could petition for better representation.

Specified that existing community action agencies could continue to receive funds through June 30, 1968, and set Feb. 1, 1969, as the date on which all community action agencies not meeting the new definition would cease to exist.

Defined community action program to include a sufficient number of community based and operated programs to make an impact on the causes of poverty.

Required each community action agency to foster the establishment of housing development and service organizations to focus on the housing needs of low-income persons.

Financial Assistance—Prescribed the nature of community action programs which were eligible for financial assistance under Title II. Eliminated the earmarking of funds for programs authorized under Title II. Required non-federal matching of 20 percent for community action, with the 20 percent being either in cash or kind.

Special Programs—Enumerated eight "special programs" that could be funded through community action. They included the ongoing Head Start, Upward Bound, Legal Services and Comprehensive Health Services programs. Added were: Follow Through, an extension of the Head Start program to the early school years; Emergency Food and Medical Services, for which $25 million in fiscal 1968 and $50 million in fiscal 1969 was made available for emergency aid to persons who were starving; Family Planning, a voluntary program for the poor; and Senior Opportunities and Services, a program to aid those 60 years old and over. (A provision in Title VI directed the OEO Director to recommend to the President and Congress any legislation needed for programs to aid the elderly poor.)

Required that the Follow Through program be run by the Department of Health, Education and Welfare; that local and state bar associations get a chance to make recommendations about Legal Services programs prior to approval of such projects and that only in "extraordinary circumstances" could Legal Services funds be used to defend a person indicted for a crime; that Comprehensive Health Services include treatment of narcotic addiction and alcoholism; and that the Emergency Food and Medical Services program be run by the Secretaries of Agriculture and HEW, through community action agencies where feasible.

Provided that residents of poverty areas be given maximum employment opportunities in all community action programs and required the OEO Director to encourage the development of neighborhood centers.

Provided that a local community action agency or local governing officials be given an opportunity to pass on proposed pilot or demonstration programs, although local disapproval could be overridden by the OEO Director. Directed him to develop and carry out programs aimed at aiding the elderly, stemming migration from rural areas and developing new techniques dealing with narcotics addiction. Provided that no more than 15 percent of community action appropriations be allocated to research and pilot programs and that one-third of that amount be devoted to a program to stem the migration to urban areas from the countryside.

Required the OEO Director to carry out continuing evaluations of the community action program. Tightened the auditing procedures for community action programs. Provided two new OEO positions—assistant director for community action in rural areas and assistant director for community action in urban areas. Required more emphasis on rural-aid programs and more equitable division of funds between rural and urban areas.

Special Limitations—Prohibited federal matching funds for salaries of community action program personnel above $15,000 a year except in large metropolitan areas, at the Director's discretion. Limited administrative costs of local community action agencies to 15 percent of total costs.

Title III—Rural Areas. Enlarged the program of federal assistance to state and local agencies, private nonprofit agencies and cooperatives to develop and carry out programs to aid migrant farm workers.

Title IV—Small Business Aid. Specified that under the Small Business Administration's economic opportunity loan program, special attention be given to urban and rural areas having a high concentration of unemployed and low-income persons. Required that at least 50 percent of the loans each year go to small businesses in urban slums or to small businesses owned by low-income persons. Authorized a new program of technical assistance and management training to small business concerns in both urban and rural areas with high unemployment. Directed that the Small Business Administration carry out the program but gave the President authority to transfer all or part of it to the Secretary of Commerce.

Title V—Day Care Projects. Established a new day care program with the aim of enabling low-income parents to work, take vocational training or continue their educa-

tion. Provided 90 percent federal matching for these projects, which could be carried out by public or private agencies, labor unions or companies.

Title VI—Administrative Restrictions. Limited to 100 days the length of time a consultant could be retained by the OEO Director on a per diem basis.

Authorized the Director to transfer up to 10 percent of the funds from one OEO program to another.

Prohibited the use of antipoverty funds for partisan or nonpartisan political activities, including voter assistance or registration.

Required the OEO Director to make a public announcement of any contract entered into for research and demonstration and of the results of the project.

Provided, in a section on the "voluntarily poor," that a person could not receive benefits under the poverty program "if his lack of income results from his refusal, without good cause, to seek or accept employment commensurate with his health, age, education and ability."

Prohibited community action employees from planning, initiating, aiding or participating in any "unlawful demonstration, rioting or civil disturbance."

Coordination—Revised and staffed the Economic Opportunity Council in the Executive Office of the President to promote better coordination among the antipoverty programs of the OEO and other federal agencies. Directed the OEO Director to prepare a five-year national poverty "action plan" listing estimated expenditures needed to eliminate poverty. The plan was to be updated annually and presented to Congress.

Directed the OEO Director to study ways of improving the operation of the Information Center.

Title VII—Public Assistance. Gave the states until July 1, 1969, to comply with the title's requirement to disregard portions of poverty funds paid to welfare recipients in establishing eligibility for assistance.

Title VIII—VISTA Program. Authorized the OEO Director to assign VISTA volunteers to their own or nearby communities; directed him to set up and encourage a program for part-time volunteers; tightened screening of volunteers; established demonstration projects to provide youthful criminal offenders with education, training and counseling by volunteers and Teacher Corps members; provided that the participation of older persons as volunteers should be encouraged; prohibited the use of VISTA funds for any labor or anti-labor activities.

In an additional title to the bill, directed the Comptroller General to undertake an investigation of both federally run and locally administered antipoverty programs and to report to Congress by Dec. 1, 1968.

Social Security Amendments

Congress in 1967, as in 1965, enacted a bill raising Social Security benefits and making major changes in the Social Security System. But whereas the 1965 bill only liberalized and expanded programs, the 1967 measure (HR 12080) also wrote major new restrictions into the welfare program.

Initiated by the House, the new welfare provisions applied mainly to assistance under the aid to families with dependent children (AFDC) program. The bill established a mandatory work-training program for all AFDC recipients. Mothers of preschool children would have to

Social Security Programs Steadily Enlarged

The 1935 Social Security Act, the most important welfare legislation ever passed by Congress, contained a number of programs, all of which were amended and enlarged during succeeding years. Following is a brief discussion of those programs which were amended in 1967 by HR 12080.

Old Age Insurance. The most important program established by the original Social Security Act was old-age insurance, a giant national pension system financed by a federal payroll tax imposed equally on employers and employees. At first the program covered only industrial and some white-collar workers, but over the years it was expanded so that, as of July 1, 1967, 17.2 million of the 19.3 million Americans aged 65 and over were eligible for Social Security. In addition, Congress in 1966 began providing special benefits for persons over 72 who did not meet Social Security requirements.

Over the years probably the most important changes were: (1) 1939 amendments bringing dependents and survivors of covered workers under the system; (2) 1950 amendments extending coverage to the self-employed and agricultural, domestic and state and local government workers; (3) 1956 amendments adding a disability insurance system for the long-term and permanently disabled (these amendments also changed the name of the program to Old-Age Survivors and Disability Insurance (OASDI). In addition to enlarging the scope of the system, Congress through the years steadily eased eligibility requirements. As the cost of living rose, benefits were increased. The maximum per person benefit in 1940 (the first year benefits were paid) was $85. In 1967 the maximum benefit was $149.90 and this was scheduled to rise to $167.90 in 1971.

OASDI Financing—The original Social Security Act provided a tax of 1 percent each for employers and employees on the first $3,000 of annual earnings. Through the years, as benefits increased, the tax and wage base were steadily increased also. The 1965 medicare-Social Security bill raised the wage base to $6,600, and the 1967 bill was to take it still higher. Under the 1965 bill the Social Security employer-employee tax was scheduled to reach 5.65 percent by 1987; this was also increased by HR 12080. *(See box p. 747.)*

The Social Security Act set up a special trust fund to receive the proceeds of the payroll tax, and separate funds were later set up for the disability insurance system and medicare. Assets of the funds were required to be invested in federal securities of various types.

Public Assistance. The original Social Security Act set up three charity programs designed to aid the indigent aged (OAA), blind (AB) and dependent children (ADC). These programs were to be administered by the states, state participation was optional, and the federal authorization for matching grants was open-end. During the post war period a fourth program, aiding the

disabled (ATPD), was added (in 1950). This period saw a steady increase in the federal matching share of total program costs and introduction of formulas under which federal reimbursements to the states varied in accord with state per capita income. The last increase in federal matching for the public assistance programs was made in 1965. Before that, there were increases in 1962 and 1958. *(See story p. 751; also Congress and the Nation, Vol. I, p. 1273ff.)*

Kerr-Mills, Medicaid—An important aspect of the evolution of public assistance programs was provision for medicare care of the indigent through a system of vendor payments (federal reimbursement to the states for medical aid outlays). The vendor payment system was established in the Social Security Amendments of 1950. In 1960, the so-called Kerr-Mills bill (named for Sen. Robert S. Kerr (D Okla.) and Rep. Wilbur D. Mills (D Ark.)) increased federal matching for vendor payments for medical care under the existing Old Age Assistance program. In addition, it created a new program called Medical Assistance for the Aged (MAA) under which the Federal Government would reimburse the states for 50 to 80 percent of their costs of providing medical care to the "medically needy" aged. The "medically needy" were defined as persons not poor enough to qualify for OAA, but judged too poor (by a means test) to be able to pay their medical costs. State participation was optional.

A major expansion of this program took place in the 1965 Social Security-medicare Act. The MAA program was extended to comparably poor blind and disabled and persons covered by the dependent children program. The federal share was increased and the states were given authority to provide a "flexible" income test to determine eligibility of the needy for the program. In succeeding years federal costs were substantially higher than anticipated under the new program (medicaid) and Congress tried—not entirely successfully—to reduce them. *(See p. 751, 758.)*

Child Welfare Programs. One title of the 1935 Social Security Act contained three separate grant programs to meet health and welfare needs of children. These were: (1) the Maternal and Child Health program providing grants to states for pre-natal clinics and related service; (2) the Crippled Children's Services program, providing grants to the states for locating, diagnosing and treating crippled children; and (3) the Child Welfare Services program, authorizing grants for state welfare services for neglected and delinquent children. After initiation of the programs, state matching requirements were imposed. The federal share was steadily increased. Originally the highest authorization was less than $4 million. Before 1967 all the authorizations were scheduled to rise to $50 million; the 1967 Act made the child welfare and maternal and child health authorizations much higher.

put them in federally subsidized day-care centers and attend job training. This feature of the bill drew howls of protest from the Administration and Congressional liberals, as did a provision freezing the amount of federal aid to states for AFDC assistance. But modifying amendments adopted by the Senate were dropped from the bill and the restrictions became law containing the most controversial provisions. Defending these, Ways and Means Committee Chairman Wilbur D. Mills (D Ark.) said, "Is it in the public interest for welfare to become a way of life.... We want the states to see to it that those who are drawing welfare checks...take training and then work.... Is that not the thing we should do?"

In its other provisions, HR 12080 provided a 13-percent across-the-board increase in Social Security benefits (the Administration had wanted 15 percent). It also raised the monthly minimum benefits, liberalized the retirement test and liberalized the definition of blindness for disability payments. The first full year (1969) cost of the bill was put at $3.7 billion.

The bill also made changes in the medicare program. Some extra days of hospitalization were provided, and hospital outpatient diagnostic services were transferred to the supplementary medicare plan. Another provision of the bill attempted to limit federal participation in the fast-growing "medicaid" program for the "medically needy" poor who did not qualify for welfare payments. The bill also made substantial increases in maternal and child health and child welfare authorizations and earmarked at least 6 percent of all maternal and child health appropriations for family planning services.

The final bill did not include a number of major provisions requested by the Administration, including extension of medicare to the 1.5 million disabled who received Social Security benefits but who were under 65, and a new system of tax treatment for the elderly. Also missing from the final bill were a number of costly Senate floor amendments such as a big increase in the amount a person could earn and still receive Social Security, liberalized medicare reimbursement to hospitals and nursing homes and restoration of the full income tax deduction for medical expenses of the elderly. As the running controversy on drug costs continued in 1967, the Senate, in a major surprise, had also adopted a floor amendment requiring the Government to adopt a method for bringing down the cost of drugs purchased under federally-aided programs. This too was knocked out in conference.

The Social Security benefits increase was requested by President Johnson in his first special message to the 90th Congress. It was passed by the House Aug. 17 by a 416-3 roll-call vote and passed by the Senate Nov. 22 by a 78-6 roll-call vote. The conference report was cleared for the President Dec. 15, the final day of the 1967 session, after a threatened filibuster by Senate liberals against the welfare provisions was averted. President Johnson signed the bill into law (PL 90-248) Jan. 2, 1968. He said, "Measured in dollars of insurance benefits, the bill...is the greatest stride forward since Social Security in 1935." But he criticized the welfare restrictions, said the welfare system was "outmoded" and in need of major change, and appointed a commission to look into it.

Johnson Request

President Johnson's first special message to the 90th Congress called for a 15-percent across-the-board increase

in OASDI benefits and numerous other changes in the Social Security Act. OASDI changes recommended by the President included: a raise from $44 to $70 in the minimum monthly benefit; a special minimum benefit for long-service workers; cash benefits for disabled widows under 62; liberalization of the retirement test, an increase from $125 to $140 a month in the amount a beneficiary could earn without loss of benefits; coverage for 500,000 farm workers who did not meet existing requirements; an increase from $35 to $50 a month in benefits for those over 72 who did not meet Social Security work requirements. The OASDI benefits were to be financed by a gradual rise in the 4.4 percent payroll tax to 5.8 percent in 1987. The tax would be applied to the first $10,800 of annual salary (up from $6,600) by 1974.

The President's message called for changes in medicare which would: bring 1.5 million persons under 65 who received disability benefits under the program at an estimated annual cost of $325 million; require coordination of hospital depreciation payments under medicare with over-all state health planning; include nonroutine podiatrists' services under the supplementary medical insurance program; repeal provisions of the 1965 medicare authorization requiring medicare applicants not covered by Social Security to disclaim Communist affiliation.

The President also proposed changes in the Title XIX medicaid program, established in the 1965 Social Security bill, which permitted federal-state aid to the "medically needy"—persons who were not quite poor enough to be on public assistance, but met all other requirements for welfare aid. The President's changes limited federal participation to those state programs where medical payments were provided to individuals and families whose incomes did not exceed by more than 50 percent the income levels set for eligibility for cash welfare assistance, and allowed a 75-percent federal share of the cost of training and paying all personnel to administer a state medicaid program.

Changes in other Social Security welfare programs recommended by the President included: a requirement that all states raise cash welfare payments to the level they set as the minimum for subsistence; a new work incentive program for welfare recipients; voluntary work-training programs for welfare recipients; expanded child welfare programs.

In addition to these extensive changes in Social Security law, President Johnson's message proposed income tax reform for those over 65. The key feature replaced the current system of numerous exemptions for the elderly with a single flat exemption of $2,300 for an individual and $4,000 for married couples when both are over 65.

The President's proposals were embodied in a bill (HR 5710) introduced in the House Feb. 20 by Ways and Means Committee Chairman Wilbur D. Mills (D Ark.).

House Action

The House Ways and Means Committee held extensive hearings on the Administration bill between March 1-April 11. It did not act until Aug. 7 when it reported a clean bill (HR 12080) increasing Social Security benefits by 12.5 percent. The new bill did not include many important Administration proposals, and made major new restrictions on welfare payments.

The most important proposals rejected would have: provided a special minimum benefit for workers with long-term Social Security coverage; extended OASDI coverage to 500,000 farm workers; extended medicare to 1.5 million disabled under 65; required coordination of hospital depreciation payments under medicare with state health planning; repealed the loyalty oath provisions in the medicare act; required states to raise public assistance payments to the level set as the minimum for subsistence; replaced the existing complex system of taxing the elderly with a flat deduction.

Not only did the House committee turn down or modify most of the major Administration requests, but it added many completely new provisions. On OASDI, it increased the minimum monthly benefit only to $50 and increased to only $40 a month benefits for persons over 72 who did not meet OASDI work requirements. Improved benefits were financed by raising the payroll tax by steps to 5.9 percent in 1987 and increasing the taxable base to $7,600 in 1968.

New medicare provisions increased the number of days of hospitalization from 90 to 120; transferred hospital outpatient diagnostic services to the supplementary plan; and made other less important changes in the program which had not been requested by the Administration.

The Committee agreed to the Administration requests limiting federal participation in the medicaid program. The report said the Committee had not intended, in approving Title XIX, that the Federal Government would become responsible for subsidizing the medical care "of a considerable portion of the adult working population of moderate income."

The most far-reaching Committee proposals were in the field of public welfare. It required every state to set up mandatory work-training programs for unemployed parents and children over 16 who received aid under the aid to families with dependent children (AFDC) program. (States were required to set up day-care centers to enable mothers to take job training.) It increased the amount welfare recipients could earn while retaining welfare payments. It limited the future proportion of children in each state who could receive AFDC because the father was absent to the percentage of AFDC children on the rolls in January 1967. The Committee required all states to offer birth-control information to welfare recipients requesting it. The Committee said its new approach to public welfare would be costly at first—by 1972 new AFDC program costs could be $930 million; however, it estimated the new programs could also mean a reduction of 400,000 children on the rolls. The Committee said it had "become very concerned" about the continued growth of the AFDC program, and that the time for a new approach to the problem had arrived.

House Passage. The House Aug 17 passed HR 12080 by a roll-call vote of 416-3. The bill was debated under a closed rule prohibiting floor amendments.

Most of the debate centered on the controversial new welfare provisions. In defending the Committee action, Mills said Congress faced a taxpayers revolt if mounting welfare costs were not reduced. For that reason, he said, "We on our Committee felt the time had come when the taxpayers want us to be rough and do not have any doubts in your mind about it, we intend to be rough

in a constructive manner.... We intend that anyone capable of working be made to work where possible."

A number of Northern liberals spoke against the welfare measures. Particular objection was directed at the provision limiting the future proportion of AFDC recipients whose fathers were absent from the home.

Senate Action

The Senate Finance Committee held hearings on HR 12080 Aug. 22-Sept. 26. On Nov. 14 it reported a heavily amended bill which restored many of the Administration requests and modified the House welfare provisions.

Senate OASDI provisions provided a 15-percent increase in cash benefits and raised the monthly minimum to $70, as requested by the Administration. The Committee also increased to $50 the amount of the special payment for persons over 72 who did not meet Social Security requirements. Among its new OASDI provisions was one permitting retirement at age 60 (instead of 62) at reduced benefits. To finance the changes, the Committee raised the taxable base to $10,800 in stages in 1972.

Among the Committee's medicare provisions was the Administration request requiring coordination of hospital depreciation payments under medicare with over-all state health planning. The Committee also liberalized the House plan for additional days of hospitalization, and permitted reimbursement under the doctor-bill plan on the basis of an itemized but unpaid bill.

The public welfare provisions of the Senate bill established a more elaborate work-training program than that provided by the House, but did not make it mandatory for mothers with small children. Trainees were to be given a $20 a week incentive payment in addition to the regular welfare payment. It also permitted more liberal earnings exemptions for welfare recipients who were placed in jobs. The controversial freeze in the proportion of children receiving AFDC was eliminated. Child welfare authorizations were increased. The Committee agreed with the House provision requiring dissemination of birth-control information. Moreover, it provided that 20 percent of all maternal and child health funds would be earmarked eventually for family planning services.

Floor Action. The Senate passed HR 12080 Nov. 22 by a 78-6 roll-call vote. During six days of debate it added 29 amendments to the bill, increasing its estimated cost to about $7 billion, almost double the House figure. On Nov. 21 the Senate on a **22-58** key vote rejected a Republican proposal substituting the benefits and financing provisions of the House-passed version for the Committee bill. (The vote breakdown: R 17-9; ND 0-37; SD 5-12).

Major floor amendments that increased the cost of the Committee bill by nearly $1 billion raised the retirement test for OASDI beneficiaries, liberalized medicare reimbursement to hospitals and nursing homes, restored the full income tax deduction for the drug and medical expenses of the elderly (which had been ended by the 1965 medicare authorization), and exempted Social Security increases from computation of veterans' benefits. Two other costly amendments made it mandatory for all states to provide AFDC assistance to families with an unemployed father in the home and established a new program of federal aid to children under foster care. The Senate also further eased the work-training requirements for mothers. In a major surprise, it voted 43-37 to require the Government to provide reimbursement under federal-aid programs for drugs prescribed and dispensed chiefly by the generic rather than trade name. Russell B. Long (D La.), the bill's sponsor, said it could cut Government drug costs by $100 million in state medicaid programs alone.

Conference

The conference report on HR 12080 was filed Dec. 11. All of the major Senate floor amendments were dropped from the bill, and the mandatory character of the work-training program was restored. Conferees split the difference between many of the other House-Senate provisions.

For OASDI, conferees agreed on a compromise across-the-board benefit increase of 13 percent and a compromise of $55 for the minimum monthly benefit. The House figure for special benefits for persons 72 or over was accepted, and the Senate provision for age 60 retirement was dropped. Conferees agreed on a compromise increase in the amount of earnings subject to the tax.

In the medicare provisions, conferees rejected the Senate amendment requiring coordination of hospital depreciation payments with state health planning and accepted the Senate provision permitting reimbursement under the doctor-bill plan on the basis of an unpaid bill. They compromised on provisions for extra days of medicare hospital coverage.

Conferees agreed to the specifics of the Senate work-training plan, but made the program mandatory for all recipients, including mothers of small children. They decreased the training allowance voted by the Senate, and accepted the House provision on the amount a welfare family could earn without loss of benefits. The controversial freeze on the level of federal participation in AFDC assistance to homes with absent fathers was included, as were the lower House child welfare authorizations. Conferees earmarked 6 percent of maternal and child health funds for family planning services.

Final Action. The House adopted the conference report Dec. 13 by a 390-3 roll-call vote. Mills said it was "substantially" in the form of the House-passed measure. Referring to criticisms of mandatory work-training, he said, "You would think the American way of life was built on a dole system..." He said he had never felt stronger about any proposition than the desirability of training and finding jobs for welfare recipients.

The Senate adopted the conference report Dec. 15 by a 62-14 roll-call vote, sending the bill to the White House. Adoption of the report came over the vigorous objection of Senate liberals who opposed the bill's welfare provisions. They particularly objected to mandatory training for mothers of preschool children and the freeze in AFDC funds where the father was absent from the home. Liberals threatened to filibuster the bill but were out-maneuvered by bill manager Russell B. Long (D La.). Noting the absence of those who opposed HR 12080 most strenuously, he asked that the report be adopted. It was then agreed to by voice vote. Long later agreed to a request for reconsideration, but stipulated that the report be put to a vote Dec. 15, thereby precluding the possibility of a filibuster.

Bill Signed. HR 12080 was signed into law (PL 90-248) Jan. 2, 1968.

Provisions

As signed into law PL 90-248 amended the 1935 Social Security Act as follows:

OASDI. Provided an across-the-board increase of 13 percent to all beneficiaries under the old-age, survivors and disability insurance (OASDI) programs, effective Feb. 1, 1968. Raised the monthly minimum benefits from $44 to $55. The first full year (1969) cost of all improvements in benefits was estimated at $3.7 billion.

Increased the special benefits to persons 72 and over who had not met Social Security requirements from $35 to $40 a month for a single person and from $52.50 to $60 a month for a couple. The annual cost was about $50 million.

Liberalized the retirement test, allowing a beneficiary to earn $1,680 a year, or $140 a month, instead of $1,500 a year, or $125 a month, without loss of benefits. The 1969 cost was $220 million.

Provided graduated cash for some 65,000 disabled widows or widowers between 60 and 62 years old at an estimated cost of $60 million for the first 12 months. Provided a stricter definition of disability. Liberalized the definition of blindness for purposes of disability.

Provided $83 million in additional benefits for 175,000 dependent children whose mother was covered by OASDI but died, retired or became disabled.

Provided cash benefits for some 100,000 young workers who were disabled before age 31 and had been covered by OASDI for at least six quarters. The first year cost was $70 million and improved benefits for children adopted by disabled persons.

Financing. Financed higher benefits and other changes in OASDI through existing trust funds and increases in Social Security tax payments. Raised the taxable base to $7,800 from $6,600, beginning Jan. 1, 1968. Raised the 4.4-percent payroll tax which the employee and employer each contributed to the employee's OASDI and medicare benefits to 4.8 percent in 1969, 5.2 percent in 1971, 5.65 percent in 1973, 5.7 percent in 1976, 5.8 percent in 1980 and 5.9 percent in 1987 and thereafter. *(See box p. 747.)*

Medicare. Permitted medicare reimbursements under the doctor-bill plan to a doctor or directly to a patient on the basis of an itemized bill, whether paid or unpaid, submitted by a patient. Permitted medicare payments for certain ancillary hospital and extended care facility services which previously were not reimbursable. Included coverage of podiatrists' services for non-routine foot care under medicare.

Allowed full "reasonable charges" for inpatient radiological and pathological services. Permitted reimbursement for outpatient physical therapy services and out-patient diagnostic x-rays.

Permitted an annual enrollment period for the supplementary plan rather than enrollment only in odd-number years. Permitted a person becoming 65 in 1968 to be covered by medicare if he has three quarters of Social Security coverage. This requirement would increase by three quarters each year for persons becoming 65 after 1968.

Provided each medicare beneficiary with a total "lifetime reserve" of 60 days of added hospital coverage to be used whenever the 90 days covered in a "spell of illness" had been exhausted. The patient would pay $20 a day for each day of the additional protection.

Transferred hospital outpatient diagnostic services to coverage under the supplementary insurance plan, subject to a $50 annual deductible and a 20-percent coinsurance provision.

Required the Secretary of Health, Education and Welfare to make a study of the cost of including under medicare reimbursement of all prescription drugs and the establishment of a method of controlling the cost and quality of drugs purchased under federally aided programs. The report was due Jan. 1, 1969. The Secretary also would study ways to improve the earnings test and the feasibility of increasing payments on delayed retirements.

Medicaid. Limited federal participation in the Title XIX medicaid program. Stipulated that beginning July 1, 1968, the Federal Government would not provide matching funds to any state where the medicaid eligibility requirements permitted a medically needy person to earn more than 150 percent of the state's income standard for assistance under the aid to families with dependent children program. This percentage limit would drop to 140 percent in 1969 and 133-1/3 percent in 1970. Fiscal 1969 savings due to these provisions was put at $329 million.

Allowed states to purchase supplemental medical insurance under medicare for the medically needy elderly and not just for those on welfare.

Increased from 50 to 75 percent the federal share of the cost of physicians and medical personnel working in state medicaid programs.

Allowed medicaid recipients (those who were not cash assistance recipients) to be reimbursed directly for the costs of physicians' and dentists' services they received.

Allowed a state to establish different income levels for eligibility under medicaid based on variations in the cost of housing in urban and rural parts of a state.

Stipulated that only nursing homes meeting certain specifications could be used for public assistance recipients under medicaid. Permitted federal matching for medicaid beneficiaries in intermediate care facilities (facilities which provide more services than boarding houses but less than skilled nursing homes).

Required states to make sure that unnecessary services were not provided under medicaid—and to assure that payments did not exceed "reasonable charges," including payments for drugs.

Public Welfare. Required every state to participate in a work-training work-incentive program for all recipients under the aid to families with dependent children (AFDC) program to be administered by the Department of Labor. Specified that state welfare agencies would decide who was an appropriate candidate for training but excluded from participation children under 16 or those going to school; any person with an illness or incapacity or those persons whose presence was needed at home because of the illness or incapacity of another member of the household.

Required that an attempt first be made to find jobs for those who were employable; required that those in need of training be trained and given a $30 a month incentive payment; provided for the establishment by state employment offices of special work projects to employ in public service jobs those who after training were

unable to find work in the private economy. Provided that those who refused to accept work or undertake training would lose their welfare benefits.

Provided that day-care centers be set up to take care of the preschool children of those mothers who take training or hold a job. Provided 80 percent federal matching for the cost of the work-training program and the day care program. Fiscal 1969 cost of work-training was $129 million and day-care costs $35 million.

Required an earnings exemption for those getting AFDC assistance of $30 a month, plus one-third of all monthly income over $30. Required a full earnings exemption for a child who was a full-time or part-time student and not working at a full-time job. Fiscal 1969 cost of these provisions was $20 million.

Provided that under the AFDC program where there was un unemployed parent in the home, federal matching would be available only for the children of unemployed fathers and not unemployed mothers. Gave the Secretary of HEW authority for setting standards for determining what was unemployment.

Limited the future proportion of children under 18 in each state who could receive federal assistance under AFDC where the parent was absent from the home to the percentage of AFDC children on the rolls in January 1968.

Required all states to offer family planning services to all appropriate AFDC recipients. Stipulated that at least 6 percent of all maternal and child health appropriations be earmarked for family planning services.

Liberalized the federal matching funds that were available for the care of children who were placed in foster homes beginning July 1, 1969. Authorized up to 30 days of emergency aid to dependent children and their families, including migrant workers with dependent children.

Permitted states, in determining assistance for aid to the blind, aid to the aged and aid to the totally and permanently disabled, to exempt up to $7.50 a month any income earned by persons receiving such aid.

Consolidated all child welfare services in a single title of the Social Security Act and increased the fiscal 1969 authorization from $55 to $100 million and increased the authorization for later years from $60 to $110 million. Increased from $2 million to $4 million the annual funds for demonstration projects.

Required all states by July 1, 1969, to train and use welfare recipients as community services aides in public assistance, child welfare and health programs authorized by the Social Security Act.

Required the Internal Revenue Service to make available information that might lead to the location of runaway parents of children receiving AFDC.

Authorized $5 million for fiscal 1969 and $5 million for each of three succeeding fiscal years for grants to colleges to develop programs for training social workers.

Provided up to 50 percent federal matching funds for repairs (up to $500) to homes owned by public assistance recipients.

Combined several separate sections of the Social Security Act dealing with child health and authorized $250 million for fiscal 1969 and up to $350 million for fiscal 1973 for the broad category of maternal and child health. Provided that 50 percent of the total authorization would be for formula grants, 40 percent for project grants and 10 percent for research and training.

Older Americans Act

President Johnson July 1 signed into law a noncontroversial bill (HR 10730—PL 90-42) extending for two years and increasing the grant provisions of the Older Americans Act of 1965. Other provisions of the 1965 Act ran through 1970. The Act authorized programs to expand and improve federal and state activities relating to the elderly. *(See story p. 762.)*

HR 10730 passed the House June 19 by a 333-0 roll-call vote, carrying only a one-year authorization. The Senate added the fiscal 1969 authorization and several other provisions to HR 10730, and passed the bill by an 83-0 roll-call vote June 28. The House agreed to the Senate amendments June 29 by voice vote.

Major Provisions. As signed into law, the Older Americans Act Amendments of 1967:

Authorized appropriations of $10,550,000 in fiscal 1968 and $16 million in fiscal 1969 for grants to states for community planning and coordination of programs for the aged, establishing or expanding programs and training specialized personnel to carry out the programs.

Authorized appropriations of $6.4 million in fiscal 1968 and $10 million in fiscal 1969 for grants to or contracts with public or private nonprofit organizations and agencies for study, development, demonstration and evaluation projects and for personnel training.

Authorized the Secretary of Health, Education and Welfare to study the need for trained manpower in the field of aging and report by March 31, 1968.

1968

Antipoverty Program

Because Congress had provided a two-year antipoverty authorization in 1967, major controversy over the program was avoided in 1968. The fiscal 1969 Labor-HEW appropriation bill (HR 18037) provided $1,948,000,000 for the Office of Economic Opportunity, the highest amount in the history of the program. The sum was $170 million more than Congress appropriated in 1967, but $232 million below the budget request and authorization. The bill did not earmark funds for specific OEO programs, but the House committee report said the OEO had an obligation to inform Congress when any significant change in allocation of funds was contemplated.

The House passed HR 18037 by voice vote June 26, carrying $1,873,000,000 for the antipoverty program, $307 million below the Administration request. Earlier that day by a **181-220** key roll-call vote it rejected an amendment cutting another $100 million from OEO funds. The vote breakdown: R 110-64; ND 11-132; SD 60-24.

HR 18037 was passed by the Senate Sept. 6 by a 45-8 roll-call vote. Before passage the Senate, by a **37-26** key roll-call vote, accepted an amendment increasing the OEO appropriation by $215 million, to $2,088,000,000. Opponents of the increase said the OEO was a wasteful agency, with poor auditing procedures. The vote breakdown: R 8-14; ND 27-1; SD 2-11.

Conferees agreed on the compromise figure of $1,948,000,000 for the OEO, HR 18037 was cleared by the Senate Oct. 9 by a 56-3 roll call, and by the House by voice vote Oct. 10. President Johnson signed it into law (PL 90-557) Oct. 11.

In related developments, Congress in the Higher Education Amendments of 1968 (PL 90-575) transferred the Upward Bound program for college preparation for poor youths to the Office of Education as of July 1, 1969. In 1968, plans also were made to phase out the Title V Work Experience Program for pilot projects to train heads of families receiving assistance under the Social Security Aid to Families with Dependent Children program. The decision was made because of the similar work training provisions of the Social Security Amendments of 1967 (PL 90-248.)

Poor People's Campaign

In 1968 representatives of the poor in America tried to put their welfare goals before the country through a massive lobbying effort known as the "Poor People's Campaign."

Originally conceived by the Rev. Martin Luther King Jr. before his assassination, the campaign was led by King's successor as head of the Southern Christian Leadership Conference, Rev. Ralph David Abernathy. Participants in the Campaign constructed "Resurrection City," a plywood and canvas shantytown campsite on a portion of the Washington Monument grounds, which eventually housed more than 3,000 people.

The camp-in ran from April 29 until June 23, when the Interior Department refused a further extension of the "Resurrection City" permit. On June 14 more than 50,000 people, about half of them white and the vast majority of them middle-class, marched at the Washington Monument and Lincoln Memorial in an orderly demonstration of support for the demands of the nation's poor.

Other aspects of the campaign included visits by Campaign leaders to Cabinet members to present legislative demands. These were followed by a series of demonstrations against Cabinet Departments, Congress and the Supreme Court. The demonstrations led to a number of arrests, most of them peaceable; 400 demonstrators, including Abernathy, were arrested as police closed down "Resurrection City" June 24.

The arrival in Washington of the first demonstrators met with generally adverse reaction. President Johnson warned of "inherent dangers" in the camp-in, and Congressmen were skeptical both of the chance of keeping the demonstration nonviolent and the outlook for favorable Congressional action on the demands. A June 10 public poll also indicated considerable public disapproval of the aims of the campaign.

The Campaign had three major legislative priorities. Among these was repeal of the welfare restrictions added to the 1967 Social Security Act—particularly the freeze on the number of aid to families with dependent children (AFDC) recipients and a new compulsory work program. The freeze was postponed one year *(see p. 778)*, but the work program was unchanged. The other two legislative priorities were passage of an emergency employment bill (S 3063) and passage of the Administration housing bill (S 3497). Only the latter was enacted, and funds were reduced. *(See education, housing chapters.)*

Fundamental Welfare Revisions Proposed by Nixon

In a nationwide speech President Nixon Aug. 8, 1969, proposed radical transformation of the nation's welfare system. He called the existing system a "colossal failure" which breaks up poor families, often penalizes work, robs recipients of dignity, distributes benefits unequally, lures thousands into overcrowded inner cities, and rapidly increases the numbers of dependent families and the costs.

Outlining his new system in an Aug. 11 message to Congress, the President said it would "make it more attractive to go to work than to go on welfare, and will establish nationwide minimum payment to dependent families with children." The welfare proposals were part of a package of reforms which also included a new job training and placement program, a revamping of the Office of Economic Opportunity, and the sharing of federal tax revenues with the states.

The welfare program would provide direct federal payments to all families with children with family incomes below stipulated amounts. Aid would thus be available to families with fathers, whose exclusion from benefits in many state plans encouraged the breakup of families.

The new program would also permit families to continue to receive welfare payments while earning up to a specified maximum income based on the size of the family. All families would be allowed to "disregard" earnings up to $60 per month; above that amount benefits would be reduced by 50 percent of earnings. The purpose of this provision was to remove disincentives to work embodied in welfare programs in which the "working poor" were deprived of benefits available to the unemployed.

Under the new proposals, a family of four with no earnings would receive federal payments of $1,600 per year, $500 per person for the first two family members and $300 for each additional family member. A family of four would remain eligible for welfare payments until its annual income reached $3,920. The following table shows how total income would vary in relation to earned income for a four-member family:

Earned Income	Benefit	Total Income
0	1600	1600
720	1600	2320
1000	1460	2460
1500	1210	2710
2000	960	2960
2500	710	3210
3000	460	3460
3500	210	3710
3920	—	3920

To receive payments, employable persons would be required to accept available work or training. Training and child care services were to be expanded, but mothers with pre-school children would be exempted from the work requirement.

In the 30 states in which the basic federal payments would be less than the present level of combined federal-state payments, the states would be required to supplement federal benefits so that payments would not fall below current levels. The program would be administered by the Social Security Administration, but separately from other Social Security programs.

The President's proposals also would establish a federal minimum payment level of $65 per month for aid to the blind, the disabled and the aged, and combine the administration of these three programs.

Cost of the entire program in its first full year of operation was estimated at $4.0 billion, in addition to the current level of federal spending for public assistance, estimated at $4.2 billion in fiscal 1970.

Related Developments

As part of the "New Federalism" proposed in his Aug. 8 speech and spelled out in subsequent messages to Congress, President Nixon combined with his welfare revision the three following related proposals:

• An expanded Manpower Training Act which would combine and coordinate existing programs, provide "flexible funding" geared to demands of labor and industry, and shift administration from Washington to the states and localities. The proposed Act would also revise allowances for trainees, provide them with tailored career development plans, establish a national computerized job bank, and authorize use of the manpower training system appropriations as an economic stabilizer.

• Conversion of the Office of Economic Opportunity to a "laboratory agency" which would concentrate on developing and testing new approaches to social problems. When these proved successful, they would be "spun off" to other departments or agencies for wider implementation.

• The sharing of federal revenues with the states, beginning with $500 million in the last half of fiscal 1971 and increasing in stages to $5 billion in fiscal 1976. The size of the fund distributed among the states would be based on a percentage of personal taxable income, allocated among the states on the basis of population with adjustments for the state's revenue efforts, and shared with local governments according to prescribed formulas. The states would determine the purposes for which the funds would be spent. *(For background on revenue sharing proposals, see p. 164.)*

Among its requests to Government agencies were three for the Office of Economic Opportunity. The Campaign asked the OEO to hire a specific number of subprofessionals from persons who show skill in working with the poor, devise guidelines for participation of the poor in antipoverty programs, and actively support additional funds for Head Start and summer jobs. The OEO at year's end said it was working on the first two requests; it was expected that the higher authorization in the 1968 antipoverty bill would go in part to Head Start and summer job programs.

Hunger in America

While Congress passed little welfare legislation per se in 1968, it passed a number of bills which grew out of a new controversy about hunger in the U.S. *(For details of the legislation, see agriculture chapter.)*

The controversy arose from reports by two citizens' groups and a television documentary which severely criticized Government food assistance programs as inadequate and poorly administered.

The Committee on School Lunch Participation April 16 issued a report charging that the school lunch program failed to meet the needs of poor children. The report included many objections ranging from the fact that eligibility for the program was determined by local administrative decisions which had nothing to do with the needs of the children, to the fact that many slum schools had no cafeterias and could not participate in the program.

The Citizens Board of Inquiry into Hunger and Malnutrition in an April 22 report was highly critical of Government food programs. It found that over 300 of the poorest U.S. counties had no assistance at all, and estimated that between 10 million and 14.5 million Americans were seriously underfed.

A May 21 CBS documentary, "Hunger in America," accused the Agriculture Department of protecting "farmers, not consumers, and especially not destitute consumers." The program reported cases of serious malnutrition in the South. Agriculture Secretary Orville Freeman said the program was a "biased, one-sided, dishonest presentation of a serious national problem."

Welfare Freeze Postponed

The Administration's big tax surcharge bill (HR 15414—PL 90-364) contained a provision postponing for one year, until July 1, 1969, an important and controversial provision of the 1967 Social Security Amendments (PL 90-248). The provision had set the future proportion of children under 18 who could receive federal assistance under the aid to families with dependent children program (AFDC) where the father was absent from the home at the percentage of AFDC children on the rolls in January 1968. HR 15414 also allowed a state to include within its base proportion those cases added to its rolls by the second quarter of 1969 as a result of court decisions.

Another provision of HR 15414 extended from Jan. 1, 1968, to Jan. 1, 1970 the cutoff date for federal matching

payments to states under the Social Security Title XIX medicaid program for medical services covered under the supplementary medicare plan if a state had purchased the supplementary medicare plan for residents eligible for medicaid.

As originally passed by the House, HR 15414 contained no Social Security provisions. The Senate Finance Committee added the above medicaid provision and repealed the welfare freeze entirely. It said the repeal was necessary because court decisions were forcing states to increase the number of AFDC recipients above the freeze level and putting a heavy financial burden on the states. The compromise one-year postponement of the freeze and inclusion of cases added to the rolls by the courts was worked out in conference. Several other minor Senate relaxations of 1967 welfare provisions were dropped or severely modified in conference.

Railroad Retirement

Congress in 1968 voted to increase annuities for the one-third of railroad pensioners who received benefits under the Railroad Retirement System rather than the Social Security System. The increase was equal to 110 percent of the amount of increases that other railroad pensioners had already received under the 1967 Social Security Act amendments. Pensions under the Railroad Retirement Act were also raised in 1966 to provide a commensurate increase with the 1965 Social Security benefits raise.

The bill (HR 14563) also provided benefits for disabled widows between the ages of 50 and 60 and liberalized the earnings test for persons eligible for disability benefits. It increased sickness benefits but eliminated maternity benefits as such. The bill did not call for an increase in the Railroad Retirement contribution base or contribution rate, and was not expected to affect the actuarial condition of the Railroad Retirement System.

HR 14563 was passed by the House Jan. 25 by a 321-0 roll-call vote, and passed by the Senate Jan. 30 by voice vote. President Johnson signed it into law (PL 90-257) Feb. 15.

Conference on Aging

President Johnson Sept. 28 signed into law a bill (H J Res 1371—PL 90-526) providing for a White House Conference on Aging in 1971 to consider such subjects as health, employment, housing and retirement income for the elderly. The bill directed that the national conference was to be preceded by state conferences, and authorized $1.9 million for the state conferences and 1971 meeting.

In a related development, the House in 1968 passed a bill (HR 19747) to amend the 1965 Older Americans Act. Major provisions authorized federal grants of up to 90 percent for projects to permit persons over 60 to help children in child-care centers and elderly persons unable to care for themselves. The Senate did not act on the bill before adjournment.

Consumer Legislation

CONSUMER legislation commanded more interest and sympathetic attention from Congress during the Johnson years than in any previous period.

Consumer issues were a major subject of concern to Members of Congress both on their own merits and because of their value as a means of attracting the support of voters. Business interests opposed much of the legislation, as they had in the past, but the consumer movement nevertheless achieved a momentum that produced remarkable success in Congress—particularly considering the ineffective efforts of consumer advocates in previous years.

The increased Congressional interest in consumer matters spanned the Presidencies of John F. Kennedy and Lyndon B. Johnson. Mr. Kennedy brought to the Presidency a concern for the welfare of the consumer, and he sought to make the consumer's voice as clearly heard and as influential in Washington decisions as were the voices of business, labor and other special interests. Mr. Kennedy did not accomplish much of what he sought; many proposals from the Kennedy years were not enacted until President Johnson was in the White House, while still other recommendations remained for future Congressional consideration.

Even allowing for the failures, the period from 1961 to 1969 was marked by over-all success. William G. Kaye, executive director of the President's Committee on Consumer Interests, writing in a magazine article in 1969, called the eight-year span "the greatest single period of concentrated consumer activity in the history of the nation." Kaye said that 20 major federal consumer laws had been enacted during the period.

The two Presidents also increased consumer representation in the Federal Government through appointments and through the creation of official groups. Mrs. Esther Peterson and Miss Betty Furness served as special assistants for consumer affairs. Consumer Advisory Councils were named and the President's Committee on Consumer Interests, a Cabinet-level policy coordinating committee, was established. (The momentum created by these appointments was carried on by President Nixon in 1969 when he named Mrs. Virginia H. Knauer as his special assistant for consumer affairs. Mrs. Knauer was an outspoken advocate of consumer interests.)

The legislation enacted during Mr. Johnson's term ranged widely in purpose from prohibiting business from doing certain things to simply providing useful information to the consumer. The two most important and strongest laws enacted covered both prohibitions and information disclosure. They were the auto safety and truth-in-lending bills.

Following is a summary of the major legislation considered during the 1965-68 period.

Auto Safety. Congress enacted two bills in this area which were designed to launch a comprehensive attack on the increasing number of deaths and injuries on the nation's highways. The auto safety bill and the highway safety bill covered all phases of the traffic safety problem. The most important part of the program was the auto safety bill which gave the Federal Government power to establish motor vehicle safety standards. The highway safety bill required states to establish federally approved highway safety programs or lose some of their federal highway aid dollars. Originally, the deadline for the states to act was Dec. 31, 1968, but this was later pushed back a year to the end of 1969. Both bills were enacted in 1966. *(See 1966 chronology below.)*

Truth in Lending. As opposed to the auto safety measures, which gave the government power to order companies to do certain things, the truth-in-lending bill was primarily a disclosure law. It was intended to help consumers who were seeking either loans or credit in order to purchase an item to have useful information about the costs of the financing they were seeking. Moreover, the information had to be presented in a consistent manner by all lenders or companies extending credit so that the consumer could make valid comparisons about the cost of borrowing or using credit. Comparisons on the basis of information that most companies disclosed under existing practices were at best very difficult. The bill was enacted in 1968 after almost a decade of controversy and delay. *(See 1968 chronology below.)*

Truth in Packaging. This bill was a companion to the truth-in-lending proposal, but was a less stringent measure—primarily because of industry opposition. It also dated from the early 1960s but was enacted only after its sponsors made important concessions. As enacted, it was intended to aid consumers in making price-per-unit comparisons and other comparisons for the thousands of household and personal goods usually sold in supermarkets and drug stores. The bill required manufacturers to provide consumers with specific information about a commodity's content, including a clear statement of the net quantity

---

Reference

A discussion of consumer legislation in earlier years will be found in *Congress and the Nation*, Vol. I, p. 1159-1185.

---

expressed in ounces if the quantity were less than four pounds or one gallon. However, the measure did not give the Government power to establish standard package sizes, which would have further eased the task of consumers in making comparisons. It did allow federal officials to urge industry to develop standard-sized packages and directed the officials to seek new legislation if the voluntary approach did not work. The bill became law in 1966.

Meat, Poultry Inspection. These two bills, enacted in successive years, were designed to improve consumer protection against low-quality meat. A key part of the bills directed the Secretary of Agriculture to work with state agencies to upgrade state inspection systems to federal levels so as to assure that only high quality meat would be sold in intrastate commerce. Meat and poultry products shipped between states had federal inspection, but such products not shipped out of a state were under state inspection systems, which in many states meant that there was little or no governmental regulation of the quality of products used or the conditions under which the products were prepared for human consumption. The bills required states to set up inspection systems at least equal to the federal system or have the Federal Government take over the inspection of intrastate plants. Federal financial assistance was provided to help the states meet the requirements. The meat inspection bill became law in 1967, after a vigorous battle between consumer advocates and the meat packing industry, while the poultry measure was passed in 1968 with considerably less controversy.

Child Protection. Despite the name of this bill, it was a broad-ranging measure designed to protect not only children but also adults who might come into contact with potentially dangerous household items. The bill required improved labeling on dangerous household items (including toys) and allowed the Government to ban from sale items that were too dangerous for use regardless of how carefully they were labeled. The measure was enacted in 1966.

Flammable Fabrics. This bill gave consumers increased protection against harm from dangerously flammable fabrics. It authorized the Government to establish improved flammability standards for clothing and other fabrics and related materials such as plastics. It also authorized federal research on flammability of fabrics. It was enacted in 1967.

Radiation Emission. After considerable publicity about dangerous radiation emissions from color television sets, Congress enacted a bill to authorize limitation of such emissions under federal standards for electronic products. The measure applied to other electronic products as well as color television sets. It was enacted in 1968 after the electronic industry won important concessions on some issues.

Gas Pipeline Safety. A highly controversial bill, much weaker than safety advocates sought, authorized federal standards for gas pipelines. The bill included provisions allowing states to supervise observance of the standards within their borders. States could simply certify that the facilities complied with federal standards; this was a major victory for the industry, which lobbied extensively to avoid strong federal controls. The final provision put the burden of proof of compliance on a state if the Federal Government challenged its certification. The legislation was enacted in 1968.

Product Safety Commission. A National Commission on Product Safety was established in 1967 to conduct a formal study of hazardous household products. The Commission was to review only categories of products, thereby preventing any list of hazardous products by brand name.

Chronology
Of Legislation
On Consumer Issues
1965

Congress in 1965 took little action on consumer legislation bearing on prices, business malpractices and frauds. Administration-endorsed truth-in-lending and truth-in-packaging proposals did not clear either chamber; nor did a wide variety of proposals for the creation of special councils and study groups on consumer interests receive Congressional approval.

A bill extending the National Food Marketing Commission another year was passed by Congress, however, and some administrative actions benefiting consumers were taken by federal regulatory agencies.

Mr. Johnson did not submit a special consumer message to Congress in 1965, as he had the previous year. He did endorse the concept of truth-in-lending and truth-in-packaging legislation in his Jan. 28, 1965, Economic Report. But some observers said the President did not convey to Congress any sense of urgency about passage of these measures, for fear—it was alleged—of provoking business hostility.

Although Congress did little on bills to help force down consumer prices and give consumers better product information and clearer bases for choice between products, it did act on related proposals in the field of consumer product safety, notably control of harmful barbiturates, amphetamines and counterfeit drugs. It also passed legislation dealing with pesticide research, cigarette health labeling and automobile exhaust.

Action on specific measures in 1965 is outlined below.

Actions Taken in 1965

Food Marketing Commission. The President May 15 signed an Administration-backed bill (HR 5702—PL 89-20) extending for one year, to July 1, 1966, the scheduled date of the final report of the National Food Marketing Commission. The Commission was created in 1964 to study, among other things, the reasons why retail prices of farm goods were so much higher than the prices received by farmers.

Barbiturates, Amphetamines. Congress passed legislation (HR 2—PL 89-74) that complied with President Johnson's Jan. 7 request for stronger controls over the illegal sale of barbiturates, amphetamines, other psychotoxic drugs and counterfeit drugs. *(See Health chapter.)*

Pesticide Research. Funds for Interior Department research into the effect of pesticides on fish and wildlife were increased from an authorization of $2,565,000 a year to $3.2 million for fiscal 1966 and $5 million a year for the following two years in an Administration-backed bill (S 1623—PL 89-232).

Cigarettes, Health Labeling. Congress passed a mild cigarette health labeling bill (S 559—PL 89-92). But most consumer spokesmen considered the bill a victory for the cigarette industry because the measure forestalled the imposition of far stronger administrative regulations. *(See Health chapter.)*

Excise Tax Cut. President Johnson, in an Oct. 15 message to the President's Consumer Advisory Council, said the 1965 excise-tax cut bill (HR 8371—PL 89-44) was a major boon to consumers.

Automobile Exhaust. The President Oct. 20 signed a bill (S 306—PL 89-272) authorizing the Secretary of Health, Education and Welfare to set standards limiting air pollution from automobile exhaust. *(See Health chapter.)*

Administrative Actions. *Auto Safety*—In an administrative action, the General Services Administration Jan. 26 published a list of 17 auto safety devices to be required on new cars purchased by the GSA. The action was taken under a 1964 law. The requirements included seat belts, padded dashboards, impact-absorbing steering wheels, recessed steering columns, and similar features.

New FTC Division—The Federal Trade Commission Oct. 14 announced the creation of a new Federal-State Relations Division to "develop programs of effective cooperation between the FTC and agencies of the 50 states responsible for enforcing state antitrust, deceptive practice and consumer protection laws." In another action, the FTC July 19 set up an office of consumer complaints (the first) in the District of Columbia to handle consumer complaints in that locality.

Measures Not Enacted in 1965

Truth in Lending. In his Jan. 28 Economic Report, the President endorsed the concept of truth-in-lending legislation (requiring a full statement of interest charges on loans). But there was no 1965 action in the House or Senate Banking and Currency Committees on truth-in-lending bills.

Truth in Packaging. The Senate Commerce Committee held intermittent hearings on an Administration-backed bill (S 985), sponsored by Sen. Philip A. Hart (D Mich.), to curb deceptive packaging. The President in his Jan. 28 Economic Report endorsed the concept of truth in packaging, which was the main objective of S 985, and Administration witnesses at the hearings testified for S 985 (with proposed amendments). But some observers said President Johnson did not indicate to Congress any real urgency about passage of the measure, for fear of antagonizing the business community.

Automobile Safety. Aside from the automobile exhaust legislation and the GSA safety-device requirements for automobiles described above, there was no favorable action in 1965 on bills to improve automobile safety. The Senate Commerce and Senate Government Operations Committees held hearings on several automobile safety measures, but none was reported.

Non-Prescription Drugs. In his Jan. 7 health message, President Johnson asked Congress to amend the Food, Drug and Cosmetic Act of 1938 to impose stronger federal regulation over "non-prescription drugs, medical devices, cosmetics and food." However, the Administration never sent a draft bill on this subject to Congress and there was no action.

"Quality Stabilization." The 1965 version (S 1484, HR 7841) of the perennial fair-trade bill, permitting manufacturers to fix retail price minimums on their goods, was opposed by the President's Consumer Advisory Council as anti-consumer, and received no action.

Consumer Councils. A number of bills were introduced in both chambers in 1965 proposing to establish either an independent governmental agency for consumers or a joint Senate-House committee to deal with consumer problems. None won favorable action.

Trading Stamps. Rep. Lester L. Wolff (D N.Y.), on his own initiative, held five days of meetings from July to September on the impact of trading stamps on consumer prices. Food chain spokesmen appeared at the meetings, held in federal buildings in New York and Washington, D.C., but trading stamp representatives refused to appear. No legislation resulted.

1966

By 1966, consumer legislation had become a popular issue in Congress. The rather meager list of bills passed in the first session of the 89th Congress (1965) was substantially fattened in the second. In 1966 and the following two years, Congress enacted a wide range of consumer legislation ranging from relatively weak bills which had been diluted under industry and business pressure to a few very strong statutes.

The 1966 legislation provided important safeguards for consumers against deceptive packaging-labeling practices, dangerous children's toys and other articles, and unsafe motor vehicles. The latter bill, the auto safety law, became one of the most publicized issues of the year after the auto industry, and General Motors Corp. in particular, made a heavy-handed effort to discredit the critics of car safety. The bill which became law, although criticized as inadequate by many safety advocates, was to lead in several years to the addition of many useful safety features to newly manufactured automobiles.

Congress did not, however, enact numerous other proposals relating to credit loans, drug safety, mail frauds, creation of a Cabinet-level Department of Consumers and expansion of training programs for food and drug control personnel.

Two of the most controversial consumer proposals in past Congressional sessions met with opposite fates in 1966. Congress enacted, in weakened form, a long-sought truth-in-packaging bill giving the Federal Government more control over methods of labeling food and other household goods. But Administration-backed truth-in-lending proposals continued to lie dormant in Senate and House committees.

Although many consumer bills failed of enactment in 1966, several factors appeared during the year which indicated a trend toward increased consumer activity in Congress. These included a major consumer message by President Johnson, establishment of subcommittees in the

House and Senate to deal with consumer matters, increased demands by consumer interest groups and a report by the President's Consumer Advisory Council with recommendations for action on a wide range of consumer affairs.

Presidential Requests

In a March 21, 1966, consumer interests message to Congress, President Johnson repeated requests made in his 1964 consumer message and his 1965 Economic Report for truth-in-lending and truth-in-packaging legislation. In addition, Mr. Johnson called for enactment of three new measures—a Child Safety Act, a Drug Safety Act and legislation expanding the Food and Drug Administration's (FDA) training programs for nonfederal officials. The President added that new controls on cosmetic and medical devices might be needed, pending the outcome of a study by the Secretary of Health, Education and Welfare. None was proposed, however.

Following is a summary of the President's specific proposals, their background and 1966 Congressional action or inaction:

Truth in Lending. Pointing out that about $75 billion in new installment credit was extended to consumers in 1965, the President recommended legislation requiring lenders "to state the full cost of credit, simply and clearly, and to state it before any credit contract is signed."

Truth-in-lending legislation had been sponsored in Congress by Sen. Paul H. Douglas (D Ill.) since 1959. A Senate Banking and Currency Subcommittee in 1964 approved a bill (S 750) on truth in lending, but the full Committee did not act. In 1965, when Douglas again introduced truth-in-lending legislation (S 2275), it received no action.

S 2275 required merchants or finance and loan dealers extending credit to disclose all interest and other charges on loans, including the annual interest rate, a point which the President endorsed in his 1964 consumer message but which he did not mention specifically in his 1966 message. Despite the President's failure to endorse a specific bill, however, Administration spokesmen said the Douglas bill would "do the job." They simply did not, they said, want to rule out the possibility of alternate methods of accomplishing truth in lending. In 1966, as in 1965, the Senate Banking and Currency Committee took no action on S 2275. (The proposal was enacted in 1968.)

Truth in Packaging. In passing a truth-in-packaging bill (S 985—PL 89-755), Congress granted several of the President's specific requests. The final bill, however, did not include provisions prohibiting the marketing of commodities in deceptively shaped boxes or those carrying misleading pictures. In addition, instead of allowing Government officials to establish weight and quantity standards to govern package sizes, S 985 authorized the officials only to request manufacturers to develop such standards voluntarily. If no voluntary action was taken, the officials were required to seek additional authority from Congress.

Child Safety Act. Mr. Johnson endorsed legislation to: (1) bring all hazardous substances, regardless of their labels, under the Federal Hazardous Substances Labeling Act; (2) bar from commerce those household substances that are so hazardous that warning labels are not adequate safeguards; (3) ban the sale of toys and other children's articles containing hazardous substances, regardless

of their packaging; (4) require that labels warn consumers against possible injury from drugs and cosmetics and from food in pressurized containers; (5) limit the amount of children's aspirin available in retail packages; and (6) require that certain patent drugs attractive to children have safety closure caps. The first three requests were subsequently enacted in S 3298 (PL 89-756). The others were dropped by Congress.

Drug Safety Act. The President recommended a new drug act authorizing the Government: (1) to require records and reports on the effects of drugs and to require labeling changes on any drug whether old or new (rather than just on antibiotics and new drugs); (2) to require certification of all drugs whose potency and purity can mean life or death to a patient (i.e., extend the certification requirement, which currently applies to insulin and antibiotics, to drugs such as anticoagulants); and (3) to control the unsolicited distribution of drugs. No action was taken on the President's proposals, but a House subcommittee held hearings on drug safety and the Food and Drug Administration stepped up its drug safety activities.

FDA Training Program. Mr. Johnson recommended expanding the FDA's training programs for nonfederal officials, with the goal of strengthening and enlarging state and local professional staffs. The relatively small staffs had been said to hamper the activities of the FDA.

An Administration bill (HR 13884) embodying the President's recommendations was passed by the House Oct. 17 by voice vote. However, the Senate took no action on the measure before Congress adjourned five days later.

As passed by the House, HR 13884 would authorize the Secretary of Health, Education and Welfare to provide training programs for state and local food, drug and cosmetic personnel, and to pay travel expenses and a reasonable per diem allowance to state and local personnel while they were receiving training under the program.

The House Interstate and Foreign Commerce Committee held five days of hearings on HR 13884 between June 24 and Sept. 19 before reporting the bill Oct. 7. In its report, the Committee noted that although the FDA had provided formal training opportunities for state and local officials in the past, the bill would provide financial assistance to the trainees, many of whom had been unable to attend because of lack of state funds for use in traveling.

Cosmetic and Medical Devices. The President announced that he had requested the Secretary of Health, Education and Welfare to study existing authority in the control of cosmetics and medical devices and to recommend any measures needed to close loopholes.

Existing cosmetic controls had been criticized because: (1) coal tar dyes could be used in hair dyes if a cautionary label was used; (2) cosmetics were not subject to a premarketing test but instead could go on sale untested except for color additives; and (3) cosmetics were subject only to weak labeling requirements which did not include the obligation to identify any of the chemical ingredients. (*Congress and the Nation, Vol. I, p. 1167.*)

Auto, Traffic Safety

With unexpected determination and swiftness, Congress in 1966 enacted far-reaching legislation enabling the Federal Government—for the first time—to launch a comprehensive attack on the mounting number of deaths and injuries on the nation's highways.

Passage of two related bills—the National Traffic and Motor Vehicle Safety Act and the Highway Safety Act—initiated a major campaign to increase the safety performance of motor vehicles, tires, drivers and roads. The unexpected unity of Congress in approving the measures served to accentuate the influence of an awakened public's demands for action and the surprising ineffectiveness of a reluctant automobile industry's protests.

As pressure mounted for a solution to the traffic safety problem, which was exemplified by the more than 52,000 estimated traffic deaths in 1966, the response was varied. To advocates of safety legislation, such as Sen. Abraham A. Ribicoff (D Conn.), traffic deaths were a "new type of social problem that springs from affluence and abundance rather than from crisis and convulsion." To others, such as Business Council President William B. Murphy, the country was "on a safety kick. It is a fad, on the order of a hula hoop.... We are going through a cycle of overemphasis on safety." While auto critic Ralph Nader, author of a best-selling book entitled "Unsafe At Any Speed," pushed for strong legislation making safety features mandatory, Detroit officials attempted to ward off a major role for the Federal Government in motor vehicle safety. The Johnson Administration called for action, but at a much more cautious pace than that at which Congress was prepared to proceed.

Enacted Bills

As enacted, the National Traffic and Motor Vehicle Safety Act (S 3005—PL 89-563) and the Highway Safety Act (S 3052—PL 89-564) were designed to cover all phases of the traffic safety problem by providing specific tools to deal with and improve the performance of each participating factor—the vehicle, the tire, the driver and the road. While the programs were to be temporarily administered by the Department of Commerce, they were transferred to the newly created Department of Transportation under legislation (HR 15963—PL 89-670) establishing the Cabinet-level unit.

The Traffic Safety Act required the establishment of interim federal motor vehicle standards by Jan. 31, 1967, and revised safety standards by Jan. 31, 1968, to be effective on all new domestic and imported foreign cars, buses, trucks, cycles and other motor vehicles within 180 days to one year after publication. The interim standards, therefore, were required on 1968 model vehicles. S 3005 also provided for a tire safety program—based on a bill (S 2669) passed by the Senate in March 1966, authorizing federal standards for tires, requiring safety information on tire labels and directing the Secretary to establish a uniform quality grading system for tires within two years after enactment. In addition, the Traffic Safety Act authorized federal standards for used cars within two years; federal safety research and development; a study to determine the need for a research and test facility; and expansion of a national driver register service (established in 1960) to record the names of drivers with suspended or revoked licenses.

The Highway Safety Act required each state to set up federally approved highway safety programs by Dec. 31, 1968, or face the penalty of losing 10 percent of their federal-aid highway construction funds. (A highway aid bill enacted in 1968—PL 90-495—extended this deadline one year, until the end of 1969.) The bill authorized $267

million over fiscal years 1967-69 for grants to establish the state programs and specified that 40 percent of the federal funds granted to each state were to be allocated to communities to set up their own highway safety programs. The Highway Safety Act also authorized $55 million over the three fiscal years for federal safety research and development activities.

The final bills, as signed by the President, were stronger than the Administration's original traffic safety package. The major strengthening features of the traffic safety bill, and those which most affected the automobile industry, were the provision that setting of federal motor vehicle safety standards was mandatory (rather than optional) and the requirement that they be effective as early as the 1968 model year. The Administration had proposed originally to give the industry a chance to establish standards voluntarily, by authorizing the Secretary of Commerce to establish uniform standards only if, after two years, he determined that no such standards existed or were being complied with. The prominent strengthening sections added by Congress to the highway safety bill were the requirement that the states set up safety programs and the penalty for failure to do so. The Administration bill had simply encouraged the states to act.

Background on Traffic Safety Bills

The factors and forces coming together in 1966 to induce passage of the traffic safety bills included both the visible efforts of certain groups and individuals and the more intangible influence of their actions upon the public and Congress as a whole. The participants worked against a background of sharply rising highway deaths in the 1960s

Motor Vehicle Deaths, 1950-68

Year	No. of Deaths	Per 100,000 Population	No. of Vehicles (millions)
1950	34,763	23.0	49.2
1951	36,996	24.1	51.9
1952	37,794	24.3	53.3
1953	37,955	24.0	56.3
1954	35,586	22.1	58.6
1955	38,426	23.4	62.8
1956	39,628	23.7	65.2
1957	38,702	22.7	67.6
1958	36,981	21.3	68.8
1959	37,910	21.5	72.1
1960	38,137	21.2	74.5
1961	38,091	20.8	76.4
1962	40,804	22.0	79.7
1963	43,564	23.1	83.5
1964	47,700	24.9	87.3
1965	49,000	25.3	91.3
1966	53,041	27.1	95.9
1967	52,924	26.7	98.9
1968	55,200	27.6	102.1

SOURCE: National Safety Council

following a relatively stable period in the 1950s. According to the National Safety Council, 49,000 Americans were killed in motor vehicle accidents in 1965, 1.8 million were disabled and another 1.8 million suffered minor injuries. The aggregate cost of the accidents was estimated at $8.5 billion in property damages, wages lost, medical expenses and insurance payments. The publication of statistics, however, was not startling enough in itself to produce action by the Federal Government.

Nader's Stand

Breaking into the traffic safety inertia was the publication in November 1965 of "Unsafe At Any Speed," a book written by Ralph Nader, a 32-year-old Connecticut lawyer who had served as a consultant for the Department of Labor and a Senate subcommittee in 1964-65. House Speaker John W. McCormack (D Mass.) Oct. 21, 1966, credited the final outcome of the traffic safety bill to the "crusading spirit of one individual who believed he could do something...Ralph Nader."

In his book, Nader cast the automobile industry in a role of having placed style, horsepower, comfort and sales over safety. He contended that there was no economic incentive for the manufacturers to institute safety features because the costs and penalties of auto casualties were borne by the driver.

Nader attacked the accepted theory that the best corrective approach to the safety problem was to study all of the components (car, driver and road) instead of focusing on one area to initiate action. Nader argued that much could be done to make cars safer, whereas drivers would always be prone to error. And he contended that safer cars had to be produced at a more rapid pace than that at which Detroit had proceeded voluntarily. He rejected the driver-at-fault theory on the basis that human failure could be offset through proper engineering and design of a motor vehicle. Many of Nader's contentions were based on the "second collision" approach—that no matter what caused the accident, the injuries and deaths usually resulted from the occupant colliding with the car (steering wheel, instrument panel or other features) or being thrown from it. He reasoned that even if motor vehicle accidents continued to occur at the current rate, there would be a substantial reduction in injuries and deaths if safety features were required on motor vehicles.

In addition, Nader spoke out against what he considered limited research and development efforts on the part of the automobile industry and against secrecy on the part of both the industry and Government. In testimony to the Senate Commerce Committee in 1966, Nader cited examples of the secrecy, including: (1) automobile companies—until 1966—withholding announcements of recalls of certain models to be checked for safety defects; (2) automobile insurance companies withholding data that could help delineate the accident-and injury-producing characteristics of various makes of automobiles; and (3) the Division of Accident Prevention at the Department of Health, Education and Welfare refusing to release results of a $170,000 study, under a federal grant, designed to identify relationships between vehicles and accident rates.

Industry Position—Nader Investigation

Until 1966, the automobile industry—and in particular four leading manufacturers (General Motors Corp., Ford Motor Co., Chrysler Corp. and American Motors Corp.)—enjoyed the unique position, compared to other major transportation industries, of having a large measure of freedom from federal regulation. For that reason, the industry, until 1966, had not found it necessary to build a strong communications link with Washington. The impending signs of change, however, appeared in 1965 when Detroit officials were called to testify on automobile safety before the Senate Government Operations Subcommittee on Executive Reorganization chaired by Sen. Abraham A. Ribicoff (D Conn.).

The testimony emerging from the hearings revealed a conflicting set of views on the part of the manufacturers. While never questioning the importance of safer motor vehicles, the Detroit spokesmen contended that automobiles could not be separated from the entire traffic safety picture; that if any one factor should be focused upon, it was the driver behind the wheel; that the industry could improve the safety of cars without the Government stepping in; and that additional research was necessary before substantial changes could be made on a grand scale in the performance characteristics of cars.

The auto industry's problems grew in March 1966 with the public disclosure of harassment of its outspoken critic, Ralph Nader. As depicted in magazines and newspapers nationally, Nader had been followed by a private investigator in Des Moines, Iowa, Philadelphia and Washington, approached by women and bothered by late-hour telephone calls. He had also received reports of agencies inquiring into his background—on the pretense that he was being considered for a new job—with questions on his sex life and whether he was anti-Semitic, a member of a left-wing political group, a licensed driver and profesionally competent. General Motors Corp., in a March 9 announcement, admitted conducting what it called a "routine" investigation of Nader to determine whether there was a connection between the auto critic and lawyers suing GM in pending Corvair design litigation. (The Corvair was a small car built by GM's Chevrolet division. Some critics—including Nader—said its design made it inherently unsafe. A number of people injured in Corvair accidents were suing GM on these grounds.) GM said the investigation did not include harassment. Sen. Ribicoff's Government Operations Subcommittee on Executive Reorganization called on GM President James M. Roche March 22 to testify on the alleged harassment. During the nationally televised hearing, Roche apologized to Nader "to the extent that General Motors bears responsibility" for what happened. Roche accepted responsibility for GM's actions, but said the investigation had been initiated, conducted and completed without his knowledge or the consent of GM's governing committee.

The impact of the Nader incident was twofold: the publicity seemed to bring Nader, his book and beliefs prominently to public attention, strengthening the position of Congressional advocates of a strong traffic safety bill; it also put the auto industry in an extremely unfavorable light.

Whereas the industry in 1965 had opposed any federal standards for motor vehicles, its views slowly evolved during the 1966 action on the traffic safety bill: first, it favored a voluntary industry approach; next, it endorsed a combined industry-state partnership in developing standards; then it supported discretionary federal standards; finally, it reluctantly accepted the final bill. During the 1966 hearings, the manufacturers attempted to present a united front through their trade association, the Automobile Manufacturers Assn. (AMA). On April 22, 1966, Lloyd N. Cutler, of the Wilmer, Cutler & Pickering firm in Washington, registered as a lobbyist for the AMA, and was on hand to represent the industry's interests through every step of the legislative process. Counterbalancing Cutler was Ralph Nader, who made himself available to the committees and Members in working for a strong measure. On Sept. 2, shortly after final passage of S 3005, an American Motors Corp. executive announced the appointment of Thomas C. Mann, a recently resigned Under Secretary of State for Economic Affairs, as president and chief executive officer of the AMA. One of Mann's first duties was to represent the industry in Washington on the formation of federal auto safety standards.

Congressional Action

The first Congressional hearings on traffic safety were held in July 1956 by a special subcommittee of the House Interstate and Foreign Commerce Committee. The subcommittee was headed by then-Rep. Kenneth A. Roberts (D Ala. 1951-65), one of the early Congressional safety advocates. Although a decade was to pass before Congress enacted the 1966 bills, several measures were written into law during the 10 years, partly contributing to the favorable climate for safety legislation in 1966. In 1959, for example, the House passed a bill requiring certain safety standards on Government-purchased automobiles, but no action was taken by the Senate. The three basic arguments against the measure were that the industry could voluntarily build in safety features without being required to do so; that the cost to the Government would be prohibitive; and that the Government—under the bill—would have too much say on the design of automobiles. In 1960, Congress directed the Commerce Department to maintain a national driver register service. The register included persons whose driver permits were revoked for drunken driving or for conviction of traffic offenses involving death. Furnishing of the names, however, was voluntary on the part of state and local authorities, who in turn were authorized to consult the register.

From 1962-64, Congress enacted three bills applicable to some aspect of auto safety. The bills required that hydraulic brake fluid used in motor vehicles meet certain Government specifications; required that seat belts used in motor vehicles meet standards set by the Secretary of Commerce; and prohibited the Government from purchasing passenger-carrying motor vehicles unless they were equipped with reasonable safety devices set by the General Services Administration (GSA).

It was not until 1965, however, that Congress, led by Ribicoff and other safety spokesmen, began a full-scale study of all aspects of traffic safety. While the Senate Commerce Committee held hearings on a tire safety bill (S 1643) and related measures, the Senate Government Operations Subcommittee on Executive Reorganization, chaired by Ribicoff, studied the efforts of federal agencies in promoting and improving highway traffic safety and heard testimony on a bill (S 2162) authorizing the GSA to design and test a prototype safety automobile. Although no measures were enacted, the comprehensive efforts underscored a growing Congressional concern over traffic safety and a determination to take stronger steps in 1966.

Johnson Administration

As safety advocates within and outside the Government looked to the second session of the 89th Congress as a potential setting for federal legislation, the need for support from the White House took on importance. That President Johnson was willing to give some measure of backing became evident in his Jan. 12, 1966, State of the Union address, which included a "Highway Safety Act of 1966" among the proposed programs. In a speech to the American Trial Lawyers Assn. Feb. 2, the President urged that the country stop "the slaughter on our highways." Citing statistics showing substantially more American deaths on the highways than U.S. casualties in all American wars, the President described the carnage as the "gravest problem before this nation—next to the war in Vietnam."

Mr. Johnson gave his strongest official support to traffic safety legislation in his March 2 transportation message to Congress. Noting that existing government and private safety programs were "widely dispersed...without effective coordination," the President cited the need for a "clear assignment of responsibility at the federal level" and for private industry and government officials concerned with automotive transportation to make "safety first among their priorities." Specifically, the President called for enactment of a six-year, $700-million Traffic Safety Act of 1966 to include federal grants to states for comprehensive highway safety programs, improvement of automobile safety performance and expansion of federal highway safety research. The President also endorsed the tire safety bill (S 2669) under consideration in the Senate. In calling for immediate Congressional action, the President said that Congress had not "hesitated to establish rigorous safety standards for other means of transportation (such as airlines, railroads, trucks and buses) when circumstances demanded them," and therefore should not hesitate to do so in preventing future traffic deaths.

While the President willingly became the catalyst in presenting a traffic safety package for Congress to consider, the Administration during the ensuing months gave only cautious support as Congress strengthened the proposals. After enactment of the bills, the President was publicly criticized by Senate Commerce Committee Chairman Warren G. Magnuson (D Wash.) for requesting only $26 million in fiscal 1967 appropriations to finance the safety programs while Congress had authorized more than $91 million in the first year. While Administration spokesmen said the reduction was due to the time that had already passed in the 1967 fiscal year, Magnuson expressed "near disbelief" that so little was being asked for the problem earlier described by the President as the gravest "next to war in Vietnam."

LEGISLATIVE HISTORY

The Administration's bill was submitted March 2—the day the President called for the legislation in his transportation message. In its major provisions, it authorized the Secretary of Commerce to issue federal safety standards for motor vehicles if, after two years, he determined that the automobile industry had not initiated adequate standards on its own or was not complying with existing standards. The bill also provided a national research and test center and provided federal grants to states to set up highway safety programs. The bill also contained other provisions of lesser importance. In general, the bill was far less stringent than the advocates of auto safety legislation wanted Congress to enact and, from that standpoint, was a disappointment to them. However, Congressional sentiment was overwhelmingly for a stronger bill than the Administration recommended; this sentiment made it relatively easy for advocates of tough legislation to strengthen the Administration's bill.

Senate Action. The bill (S 3005) was reported by the Senate Commerce Committee June 23 and passed the following day by the Senate by a 76-0 roll-call vote. The principal strengthening amendment adopted by the Committee required—rather than permitted, as the Administration proposed—the Secretary of Commerce to establish federal safety standards. It also directed him to place interim standards in effect by Jan. 31, 1967, and revised standards a year later. Also, the standards were to go into effect 180 days after publication; the Administration bill had not required any standards which the Secretary of Commerce found necessary (after the initial two-year period of industry self-regulation) to go into effect up to two years after their issuance. Thus, the Administration bill provided for a possible delay of up to four years before any Government standards would take effect.

The Committee also placed numerous restrictions on manufacturers. It required them to notify owners of vehicles and the Government of safety defects, repair safety defects on new vehicles at their own expense, notify the Government of information given to dealers about safety defects and certify that their cars met safety standards. The bill also required the Government to publicize all information about safety defects and set a maximum civil penalty of $400,000 for a series of related violations in addition to the Administration's maximum $1,000 for a single violation.

The latter point—penalties—was an issue when the bill reached the floor. Some safety advocates wanted the bill to provide criminal penalties—as well as civil penalties—for a willful violation of the safety standards by industry officials. An amendment to add criminal penalties to the bill was rejected by a 14-62 roll call; it was sponsored by Vance Hartke (D Ind.).

House Action. In the House, the Interstate and Foreign Commerce Committee considered its version (HR 13228) of the Administration's draft bill. It acted after the Senate had completed consideration of S 3005; HR 13228 was reported on July 28.

Differences from Senate Bill—As reported, HR 13228 was stronger than the Senate bill in two major respects. It included under the federal mandatory standards those trucks and buses already regulated by the Interstate Commerce Commission (ICC) and stipulated that the ICC's standards would be effective only if they were stricter than the Secretary's requirements. In addition, HR 13228 went beyond the Senate bill's requirement that the Secretary conduct a used car safety study by directing the Secretary to prescribe uniform safety standards for used vehicles within one year after reporting to Congress on the study.

HR 13228, however, was weaker in its enforcement and investigatory provisions. It did not include Senate provisions for: civil penalties for manufacturers' failure to notify owners and dealers of safety defects or to certify that a new vehicle met federal standards; on-site inspec-

tion of manufacturers' premises by the Government; or penalties for failures to comply discovered during such inspections.

HR 13228 placed two requirements on the manufacturer not specified under the Senate bill. It stipulated (1) that notification of a defect must be made not only to the first purchaser of a vehicle, but also to any subsequent purchaser to whom the warranty was transferred; and (2) that the manufacturer must provide the Secretary with safety performance and technical data and, if required by the Secretary, provide the same information to the original purchaser of a vehicle or item of equipment.

Additional changes made by the Committee included establishment of a 13-member National Motor Vehicle Safety Advisory Council, to be appointed by the Secretary to advise him in promulgating standards, and creation of a National Traffic Safety Agency in the Commerce Department, to be headed by an administrator appointed by the President, to administer the bill's provisions.

Tire Safety—In another major difference, HR 13228 embodied a three-year, $5.8 million tire safety program, similar to that authorized in the bill (S 2669) passed by the Senate March 29, 1966. HR 13228 directed the Secretary to establish federal tire standards, under the same procedures stipulated under the bill for motor vehicles, and—within two years after enactment—to establish and publish a uniform quality grading system for tires. Unlike the Senate bill, HR 13228 applied to tires for all motor vehicles, instead of only for passenger cars and station wagons.

HR 13228 also directed the Secretary—as in S 2669— to require that tires be permanently and conspicuously labeled with safety-related information and include the identification of the manufacturer or retreader. It went beyond S 2669, however, in requiring additional information on tire labels including the composition of material used in the ply of the tire, the actual number of plies, the maximum permissible load of the tire and certification that the tire conformed to federal minimum safety performance standards. The Committee added a new section not included in the Senate bill to require motor vehicle manufacturers to equip new vehicles with tires that met the maximum permissible load standards when the vehicle was fully loaded with the number of persons it was designed to carry as well as a "reasonable" amount of luggage.

Bill Passed—As in the Senate, the auto safety bill passed the House overwhelmingly. In one of the session's key votes, the measure was passed Aug. 17 by a **371-0** roll-call vote. However, the unanimous vote was possible only because of a compromise engineered by Interstate and Foreign Commerce Committee Chairman Harley O. Staggers (D W.Va.). The Committee's bill had been sharply criticized by safety advocates as falling short of the necessary minimum to assure that the auto manufacturers would comply with safety standards. The relatively weak enforcement and inspection provisions had come under sharp attack and a floor fight to strengthen them was promised by Members who wanted strong sanctions. It appeared quite possible that these Members would win, but a fight never proved necessary. Staggers offered a series of amendments to strengthen the enforcement and inspection sections and they were accepted by voice vote. Acceptance of these changes resolved most of the major differences between the Senate and House bills.

Tire Safety Requirements Added to Auto Bill

As part of the far-reaching attack on automobile safety problems, Congress in 1966 enacted provisions to protect the public against unreasonable risk of highway accidents occurring as a result of tire failure and to reduce confusion in the marketing of tires. The Senate in March passed its own bill (S 2669). Although the House took no action on S 2669, an expanded version of the bill, covering tires on all motor vehicles, was added in the House to the auto safety bill which became law (S 3005—PL 89-563).

Public and Congressional concern over the need for uniform tire safety standards—both for tires on new cars and for replacement tires—mounted in the 1960s as U.S. highways became increasingly crowded with a greater number of travelers taking longer and more frequent trips. At the same time, a highly competitive horsepower race among Detroit automobile manufacturers, coupled with state laws permitting higher maximum rates of speed, placed more and more stress on vehicle tires, thus increasing the risk of traffic accidents.

Original Equipment Tires. Many critics of the quality of tires in new cars, testifying before the Senate Commerce Committee in 1965, blamed the auto industry for demanding style, speed and comfort in their cars while ignoring the safety of the tires.

Tire industry spokesmen contended that the decision as to what kind of tire was placed on new automobiles was made in Detroit. One small tire manufacturer said that in 1964, auto manufacturers bought approximately 35 million new passenger car tires, making them "very important customers" with a great deal of power over the types of tires manufactured. Another said that for several years the tire industry's Tire and Rim Assn. Inc. had attempted to set maximum tire carrying-capacity weights, but for the most part Detroit had ignored the standards in equipping new cars. Other spokesmen cited the auto manufacturers' reaction to a new type of tire, the radial ply, which, because of a different type of cording, was cited by many observers as safer than most conventional tires. Although the tire had been popular in Europe for the past 10 years, American manufacturers reportedly hesitated to introduce the radial ply tire in the U.S. market because it gave a rougher ride—particularly at low speeds—than other types of tires.

Replacement Tires. When it came to replacing the original tires on his car, the consumer was easily overwhelmed. In 1966, there were 14 tire manufacturing companies in the United States producing about 950 different types of tires for sale to Detroit or to the public, plus an additional 120 types for small marketing companies to sell. Tire prices ranged from less than $8 to more than $100. While it was generally held that buyers willing to pay a higher price for a better grade of tire would receive a safer tire, criticism was directed toward the problem of choosing a safe tire from the hundreds available; the standards of safety used in manufacturing the so-called "cheapie" tires (low-price replacement tires usually sold under the unfamiliar brand name of the marketer) which constituted a major part of replacement tire sales; and the quality and safety of retreaded tires offered as replacements. One of the most perplexing problems cited by consumers was the confusing and sometimes misleading terminology used by marketers and manufacturers to rate the tires. Because no uniform system of grading tires existed, the consumer often was forced to make value judgments according to one marketer's use of such terms as "premium," "first line," "second line" and "100 level," without knowing whether another marketer's use of the same terms was comparable or implied different values.

Existing Standards. By the beginning of 1965, three groups—one federal, one interstate and one private—had attempted to establish tire standards, but none had uniform application. In January 1965 the General Services Administration (GSA), a federal agency acting under authority granted by Congress in 1964 (PL 88-515), issued standards for tires on Government-purchased vehicles. By the end of 1965, the interstate Vehicle Equipment Safety Commission (VESC), which in 1966 was made up of 44 member states and the District of Columbia, and the Rubber Manufacturers Assn. (RMA) each had issued revised minimum safe performance standards for tires.

At the request of Senate Commerce Committee Chairman Warren G. Magnuson (D Wash.), the National Bureau of Standards in January 1966 submitted the results of a study of the existing standards. It concluded that the VESC and RMA standards were not as stringent as the GSA specifications (which applied only to Government vehicles) and were not based on adequate research and testing. The Federal Trade Commission (FTC), which also studied the standards, pointed out that enforcement was almost impossible because it depended on voluntary compliance by manufacturers or by the states. By May 1966 only four states had adopted the VESC standards, and the FTC suggested that even if every state adopted them, there was "no assurance that the standards will be enforced equally in each state."

The amendments authorized on-site inspections of factories and warehouses by federal authorities; provided civil penalties if a manufacturer failed to permit the inspections; and set penalties for manufacturers' failure to notify owners and dealers of safety defects and to certify that new motor vehicles and equipment met the federal standards.

Final Action. As a result of Staggers' amendments, the differences between the Senate and House bills were relatively minor and were easily resolved. In general, conferees on the bill accepted the House version of differing provisions. The bill was cleared for the President on Aug. 31.

Bill Signed, Director Named. President Johnson signed the bill (S 3005) into law (PL 89-563) on Sept. 9. He announced the appointment of William Haddon Jr., former safety expert for the Commerce Department and New York State Department of Health, to be administrator of the new National Traffic Safety Agency. In October, Mr. Johnson also appointed Haddon as head of the new

Highway Safety Agency, established under the Highway Safety Act of 1966, in a move to combine the administration of the two safety programs under one person.

PROVISIONS

As signed by the President, S 3005, the National Traffic and Motor Vehicle Safety Act of 1966:

Established a three-year traffic and motor vehicle safety program in the Department of Commerce to be transferred to the new Department of Transportation when it came formally into existence in 1967.

TITLE I. MOTOR VEHICLE STANDARDS. Directed the Secretary of Commerce to establish federal minimum safety standards for the performance of all motor vehicles manufactured for use on the public highways, including automobiles, trucks, buses and cycles, and of all motor vehicle equipment either originally manufactured to replace or improve any part of a motor vehicle.

Directed the Secretary to prescribe interim motor vehicle safety standards on or before Jan. 31, 1967, and new or revised federal motor vehicle standards on or before Jan. 31, 1968. Provided that all standards were to be effective within 180 days to one year after publication, unless the Secretary prescribed an earlier or later date.

Required the Secretary, in establishing interim and revised standards, to:

(1) Consider relevant available safety data, including the results of research activities conducted under the Act;

(2) Consult with the Vehicle Equipment Safety Commission and other appropriate state and interstate agencies;

(3) Consider whether any proposed standard for a particular type of motor vehicle or piece of equipment was "reasonable, practicable and appropriate" and the extent to which it would contribute to traffic safety; and

(4) Specify the date each standard would become effective. Permitted the Secretary to prescribe an earlier or later effective date upon finding that it was in the public interest and served a good cause, and upon publishing his reasons for doing so.

Permitted the Secretary to amend or revoke any safety standard established under the Act. Required the change to become effective within 180 days to one year after publication unless made earlier or later by the Secretary.

Prohibited state and local safety standards applicable to the same aspect of performance of a motor vehicle or piece of equipment that differed from the federal standards, except where such requirements—including other federal standards—were more stringent than the Secretary's standards solely for the purpose of the Government's own procurement.

Prohibited safety standards established by the Interstate Commerce Commission (ICC) that differed from the Secretary's standards, except where the ICC imposed a standard requiring a higher level of performance after a vehicle was manufactured than the performance required by the federal standard at the time the vehicle was manufactured.

Provided that within 60 days after publication of a standard any person adversely affected could petition for judicial review of the standard.

Advisory Council. Directed the Secretary to establish a National Motor Vehicle Safety Advisory Council, of which the majority of members were to be representative of the general public, including state and local governments, and the remainder were to be representative of vehicle manufacturers, equipment manufacturers and dealers.

Required the Secretary to consult with the Council on motor vehicle standards under the Act.

Research and Development. Directed the Secretary to conduct research, testing, development and training for traffic safety purposes to include, but not be limited to:

(1) data collection designed to determine the relationship between the performance characteristics of motor vehicles and equipment and (a) motor vehicle accidents and (b) death and injuries resulting from such accidents;

(2) procurement of experimental or other vehicles and equipment for research and testing; and

(3) sale or disposal of test vehicles and equipment, using the proceeds to reimburse the existing appropriation available to carry out the Act.

Authorized the Secretary to make grants to states, interstate agencies and nonprofit institutions for research, testing, development and training purposes.

Provided that patents, processes, uses and other information developed with more than "minimal" federal aid be freely and fully available to the general public.

Required the Secretary to utilize the services, research and testing facilities of public agencies whenever possible to avoid duplication.

Authorized the Secretary to advise, assist and cooperate with federal, state, public and private departments and agencies in the planning and development of safety standards and methods for inspection and testing to determine compliance with the standards. (See Inspection, below.)

Used Vehicles. Stipulated that the safety standards to be established by the Secretary did not apply to used motor vehicles and equipment.

Directed the Secretary to conduct a study on the adequacy of state safety standards and inspection requirements and procedures applicable to used vehicles, and the effect of the Act's programs upon such standards, requirements and procedures.

Required the Secretary to report the results of the study and recommendations for additional safety legislation to Congress within one year after the Act became effective.

Directed the Secretary, within one year after submitting his used vehicle report and after consulting with the Advisory Council and other public and private agencies, to establish uniform safety performance standards for all used motor vehicles. Permitted the Secretary to amend or revoke the used vehicle safety standards.

Manufacturer Requirements. Required all manufacturers of motor vehicles and equipment and persons importing vehicles or equipment for resale to:

(1) Maintain records, make reports and provide information as required by the Secretary to enable him to determine if the manufacturer is complying with the safety standards.

(2) Permit inspection by the Secretary of appropriate books, papers, records and documents to facilitate determination of compliance with the standards.

(3) Provide the Secretary and, if required by the Secretary, provide the original purchaser of a motor vehicle or piece of equipment with the necessary performance and technical data to carry out the purposes of the Act.

(4) Notify by certified mail the purchaser (where known by the manufacturer) of a motor vehicle or piece of equipment containing a safety-related defect, making such notification within a "reasonable" time after discovering (or being informed by federal officials of) the defect. Also notify by certified mail any subsequent purchaser to whom the warranty was transferred, and by certified mail or other "more expeditious means" the dealer to whom the vehicle or equipment was delivered. Include in the notification a clear description of the defect, an evaluation of the risks to traffic safety, and a statement of the measures to be taken in making repairs.

(5) Furnish the Secretary with a copy of all communications with dealers and purchasers regarding safety defects, an evaluation of the risks to traffic safety, and a statement of the measures to be taken in making repairs.

(6) Furnish the dealer or distributor at the time of delivery with a certification that each vehicle or piece of equipment conforms to all applicable safety standards. In certifying vehicles, attach a permanent label or tag to each vehicle, and in the case of equipment, place a label or tag either on the equipment or on the outside of a container in which it is delivered.

Inspection. Authorized the Secretary to conduct inspections and investigations to enforce the safety standards, including on-site inspection of factories, warehouses and other manufacturing, distributing and sale establishments—providing that proper credentials and a written notice are presented at the time of entry and such inspections are conducted at reasonable times, within reasonable limits, in a reasonable manner and with reasonable promptness.

Required the Secretary, upon discovering noncompliance with the standards, to notify the Attorney General, and in certain cases the Secretary of the Treasury for appropriate action.

Stipulated that all information received by the Secretary through inspections and reports provided by the manufacturer which contained trade secrets was to be disclosed only to those officers or employees concerned with carrying out the Act and the appropriate committees of Congress.

Required the Secretary, upon discovering—through testing, inspection, investigation, research, inspection of reports or otherwise—noncompliance with the standards or a safety-related defect, to: notify the manufacturer of the findings; provide the manufacturer with an opportunity to present his views; and, if he then concludes that the noncompliance or defect exists, direct the manufacturer to notify the purchaser of the motor vehicle or equipment.

Repairs of Defects. Required the manufacturer or distributor, when a motor vehicle or piece of equipment sold to a dealer or distributor (but not yet resold to a customer) failed to comply with the safety standards or contained a safety-related defect, to:

(1) Repurchase the vehicle or item at the price paid by the dealer or distributor and pay all transportation charges plus a reimbursement of not less than 1 percent of the original price for each month from the date of notification of the nonconformance to the date the vehicle or equipment is repurchased; or

(2) Deliver to the dealer or distributor, in the case of motor vehicles, the corrective parts, paying the costs of installment, plus a reimbursement of not less than 1 percent of the original price for each month of delay from the time of notification of the nonconformance to the date the vehicle is corrected—provided that the dealer or distributor installs the corrective parts with "reasonable diligence" after receiving such parts.

Provided that a dealer or distributor could bring suit in district court within three years of a manufacturer or distributor's refusal to correct a defect to recover damages for the breach of the obligation, including court costs and attorneys' fees.

Penalties and Injunction. Established civil penalties for any violation of the Title I requirements pertaining to safety standards compliance, access to and inspection of records and premises, reports to the Secretary, certification and notification.

Provided penalties of up to $1,000 for each violation and up to $400,000 for a related series of violations.

Authorized the Secretary to compromise any civil penalty, and in determining the amount of a penalty, to consider the size of the business of the violator and the gravity of the violation.

Exempted from the penalties any person who established that he did not have reason to know that a vehicle or piece of equipment was not in conformity with federal standards or any person holding a certificate issued by a manufacturer or importer stating that a vehicle or piece of equipment conforms to federal standards, unless the person knows that the vehicle or equipment does not conform.

Authorized the Attorney General or any appropriate U.S. attorney to seek injunction in district court against a violation and to restrain the sale of any vehicle or equipment failing to conform to the standards.

Required the Secretary, whenever practicable, to notify the person against whom injunction was sought, giving him an opportunity to present his views and, except in cases of knowing and willful violations, giving him a "reasonable" opportunity to achieve compliance.

Directed the Secretary and the Secretary of the Treasury by joint regulation to refuse entry into the United States of any motor vehicle or piece of equipment not conforming to the safety standards.

Provided that the Secretaries could by joint regulation permit entry of such nonconforming vehicles or equipment if ensured that the vehicles or equipment would either be brought into conformity, exported or abandoned to the United States.

Provided that the Secretaries could permit temporary entry into the United States of a nonconforming vehicle or piece of equipment not intended for resale.

Safety Agency. Directed the Secretary to administer the provisions of the bill through a National Traffic Safety Agency to be established within the Department of Commerce and to be headed by an Administrator appointed by the President. (However, the highway safety bill, S 3052, provided a similar agency to administer that law and specified that the President could have the auto safety law administered through the highway agency. Managers of the highway bill said it was the intent of Congress that both laws be administered through the highway safety agency.)

Antitrust Application. Stipulated that the bill neither exempted from antitrust laws any conduct otherwise unlawful under the laws nor prohibited any conduct that would be lawful under the laws.

Additional Provisions. Authorized the Secretary to issue, amend and revoke any rules and regulations deemed necessary in carrying out the Title I provisions.

Stipulated that compliance with the safety standards would not exempt any person from common law liability.

Required the Secretary to submit an annual report to the President and Congress on March 1 containing a detailed account of the administration of the Act and recommendations for additional legislation for the improvement and strengthening of national traffic safety programs.

Authorized three-year appropriations for the implementation of Title I as follows: $11 million for fiscal 1967; $17 million for fiscal 1968; and $23 million for fiscal 1969.

TITLE II. TIRE SAFETY. Directed the Secretary to establish federal minimum safe performance standards for all motor vehicle tires under the same procedures as stipulated under Title I.

Directed the Secretary to require that tires be permanently and conspicuously labeled with safety-related information to include: (1) the identification of the manufacturer or retreader—unless the tire contained a brand name other than the manufacturer's name in which case it was required to bear a code mark permitting the seller of the tire to identify the manufacturer if requested to do so by the purchaser; (2) the composition of material used in the ply of the tire; (3) the actual number of plies; (4) the maximum permissible load of the tire; and (5) a statement or an appropriate mark or symbol prescribed by the Secretary indicating that the tire conforms to federal standards.

Permitted the Secretary to require that additional safety-related information be provided to the purchaser when buying a tire.

Directed the Secretary to require that each motor vehicle be equipped—either by the manufacturer or by the purchaser at the time of the first purchase for purposes other than resale—with tires which meet the maximum permissible load standards when the vehicle is fully loaded with the number of persons it was designed to carry and a "reasonable" amount of luggage.

Directed the Secretary to establish and publish a uniform quality grading system for tires within two years after enactment of the bill. Stipulated that the order establishing the system specify the date the system would become effective, which was to be within 180 days to one year after publication.

Required the Secretary to cooperate with industry and the Federal Trade Commission to eliminate deceptive and confusing tire nomenclature and marketing practices.

Established civil penalties, as described under Title I, for the sale or delivery in interstate commerce of any tire or any motor vehicle equipped with a tire which had been regrooved (producing a new tread by cutting into the tread of a worn tire). Exempted from the penalties the sale of regrooved tires or motor vehicles with such tires which the Secretary determined to be designed and constructed so as to ensure safe performance.

Authorized three-year appropriations for the implementation of Title II as follows: $2.9 million for fiscal 1967; and $1,450,000 for each of fiscal years 1968 and 1969.

TITLE III. RESEARCH AND TEST FACILITY. Authorized the Secretary to make a complete investigation and study of the need for facilities to conduct research, development and testing in traffic safety. Required him to report back to Congress by Dec. 31, 1967, with information on existing capabilities, recommendations, preliminary plans and the estimated costs.

Authorized $3 million in appropriations to finance the investigation, study and report.

TITLE IV. REGISTER SERVICE. Directed the Secretary to expand and maintain a national driver register service, containing the names, furnished by states, of individuals whose licenses had been suspended or revoked, except for revocations of less than six months based on a series of nonmoving violations.

Directed the Secretary to make available information contained in the register only at the request of a federal, state or local department or agency and only with respect to an application for a vehicle operator's license or permit.

Highway Safety Bill

A vital segment of the 1966 traffic safety package—authorizing a federal-state-local partnership to combat hgihway accidents—won overwhelming Congressional endorsement in passage of the Highway Safety Act of 1966 (S 3052—PL 89-564).

As signed into law, the revised Administration bill required each state to establish a highway safety program, in accordance with uniform Government standards covering such areas as driver education, licensing, pedestrian performance, accident recordkeeping, accident investigations, vehicle registration and inspection and highway design and maintenance. The bill authorized $267 million in fiscal years 1967-69 for grants to the states for highway safety programs. Each state was required to match the federal funds it received with an equal amount, and to reallocate at least 40 percent of its federal funds to local communities to set up their own safety programs. In addition, S 3052 stipulated that a state could lose 10 percent of its federal-aid highway funds and would not be entitled to receive additional highway safety funds under the bill if, by Dec. 31, 1968, it had failed to implement an approved program. (The deadline later was extended to Dec. 31, 1969.) A complementary feature of the bill authorized appropriations of $55 million over the three-year period for federal research and development, state and local training grants, highway safety fellowships and related activities.

Like the auto safety law also enacted in 1966 (S 3005—PL 89-563), the highway safety law was to be administered temporarily by the Secretary of Commerce until the newly created Department of Transportation began formal operation and took it over in 1967.

The strongest features of S 3052—the penalties for a state's failure to implement an approved safety program by a specified date (Dec. 31, 1968)—were added by Congress. The Administration bill had proposed only to offer federal funds, on a 50-50 matching basis, to encourage the states to establish or strengthen highway safety programs. Congress also added emphasis on local, as well as state, programs by requiring each state to allocate 40 percent of its federal funds to localities. In addition, Congress changed the method of financing the program by authorizing appropriations from general revenues, rather than from the Highway Trust Fund as proposed by the Administration.

Although S 3052 authorized appropriation of $67 million for state highway safety programs and $10 million for research and development in fiscal 1967, the Administration at the end of the year requested only $26 million for activities under both S 3052 and the auto safety bill (S 3005). Congress appropriated $10 million for state highway safety programs and $10 million for both the auto safety programs and research and development activities under both bills.

Background. The first stirrings of Congressional interest in highway safety legislation appeared in an amendment to the 1956 Federal Aid Highway Act (PL 84-627) directing the Secretary of Commerce to make a study of highway safety and report to Congress by March 1, 1959. A more concrete step was taken with the 1958 adoption of a resolution (PL 85-684) under which Congress gave advance consent to interstate compacts in traffic safety. Two compacts emerged from the new authority—the first seeking to protect the public from unsafe or poor-risk drivers (adopted by nine states as of 1966) and the second establishing a Vehicle Equipment Safety Commission designed to ensure adoption of uniform standards for new or improved automobile safety equipment.

The most significant federal effort before 1966 was evidenced in the 1965 Baldwin amendment—offered by Rep. John F. Baldwin (R Calif. 1955-66) to a bill (PL 89-139) authorizing funds for the Interstate Highway System. Although watered down in its final form, the amendment specified that each state, after Dec. 31, 1967, "should" have a highway safety program approved by the Secretary of Commerce.

LEGISLATIVE HISTORY

The highway safety bill passed Congress in 1966 with relatively little controversy—almost as an afterthought to the auto safety bill. The Administration's proposals were contained in President Johnson's March 2 transportation message. The President called for appropriation of $580 million over six years from the Highway Trust Fund for grants to assist and encourage states to establish highway safety programs in accordance with uniform national performance standards issued by the Government. All grants to the states were to be matched with an equal amount.

The bill (S 3052) was reported June 23 by the Senate Public Works Committee with amendments. A major amendment reduced the proposed six-year program to three years. However, it increased funding for the initial three-year period from $215 million to $375 million. The Administration's proposal to finance the program from the Highway Trust Fund also was rejected by the Committee. The Senate passed the bill the following day by a voice vote after adding $90 million to help states initiate and improve motor vehicle inspection and driver training programs.

In the House the Public Works Committee amended its version of the bill. A key change authorized $270 million for the safety package—$195 million less than the Senate provided. It strengthened the bill in two major respects. It required all states to establish safety programs by Dec. 31, 1967. After that date, a state would lose 10 percent of its highway aid dollars. The second strengthening feature required the Government to report to Congress by Jan. 10, 1967, all uniform standards to be

promulgated initially. The Senate bill contained no deadline. The House passed the bill in mid-August by a 317-3 roll-call vote.

In conference, agreement was reached by the end of August. In major action, conferees agreed to a three-year, $322-million program—$52 million higher than authorized by the House but $143 million less than the Senate. The final version was essentially the same as the House-passed version. The conferees accepted the House 10-percent highway funding penalty provision but made the cutoff date one year later—Dec. 31, 1968—than the House proposed. The bill was sent to the President on Sept. 1.

Mr. Johnson signed the measure on Sept. 9. On Oct. 20, the President named William Haddon Jr. administrator of the National Highway Safety Agency established under S 3052. Haddon had been appointed Sept. 9 to head the National Traffic Safety Agency established under S 3005.

PROVISIONS

As signed by the President, S 3052, the Highway Safety Act of 1966:

Established a three-year highway safety program in the Department of Commerce to be transferred to the new Department of Transportation upon formal operation of the new Department in 1967.

State Program. Required each state to establish a highway safety program approved by the Secretary of Commerce designed to reduce traffic accidents and resulting deaths, injuries and property damage.

Authorized appropriations of $67 million in fiscal 1967, $100 million in fiscal 1968 and $100 million in fiscal 1969 for establishment of the state programs. Required each state to match its federal allotment with an equal amount.

Specified that the programs should be in accordance with uniform standards promulgated by the Secretary of Commerce. The standards were to cover (but not be limited to) such subjects as driver education, driver testing to determine ability to operate a vehicle, physical and mental testing of drivers, driver licensing, pedestrian performance, accident record systems, accident investigation, vehicle registration, vehicle operation and inspection, highway design and maintenance, traffic control, vehicle codes and laws, surveillance of traffic for detection and control of potentially high accident locations and emergency services.

Permitted the Secretary to amend or waive standards on a temporary basis for the purpose of evaluating new or different highway safety programs instituted on an experimental, pilot or demonstration basis if he found that the public interest would be served by such an amendment or waiver.

Prohibited the Secretary from approving any state highway safety program which failed (1) to make the Governor responsible for administering the program, (2) to authorize localities to carry out programs related to their area in accordance with federal standards, (3) to provide that at least 40 percent of a state's portion of the federal funds be spent by the localities (unless the Secretary determines that there is an insufficient number of local highway programs to justify the expenditure), (4) to maintain state and local expenditures in the field at a point at least equal to the average level of such expenditures in the two years preceding enactment of the bill, or (5) to provide comprehensive driver training programs, including the initiation (or "significant expansion and improvement") of a state driver education program in the schools, the training and certification of driver education instructors for schools, regulation and licensing of other driver training schools, adult driver training programs including the retraining of selected drivers, and development and procurement of practice driving facilities, simulators and other teaching aids.

Required that 75 percent of the funds be apportioned among the states on the basis of population and 25 percent at the discretion of the Secretary for fiscal 1967-69. Required the Secretary by Jan. 1, 1969, to recommend a nondiscretionary apportionment formula for years after 1969. Permitted up to 5 percent of the authorized appropriations to be used for administration of the state program provisions.

Directed the Secretary to reduce by 10 percent the amount of federal-aid highway funds to which a state would normally be entitled if the state, after Dec. 31, 1968, failed to implement an approved highway safety program. Permitted the Secretary to suspend any reduction in funds required by this provision if such action was "in the public interest." Directed the Secretary not to provide any highway safety funds, after Dec. 31, 1968, to any state which had not implemented an approved program by that date.

Required the Secretary, in developing uniform standards, to cooperate with the states, their political subdivisions, appropriate federal departments and agencies and other appropriate public and private organizations.

Stipulated that the section providing for state programs did not authorize funds for highway construction, maintenance or design (other than design of safety features of highways to be incorporated into standards for highway research and development) or for research and development.

Research and Development. Authorized appropriations of $10 million in fiscal 1967, $20 million in fiscal 1968 and $25 million in fiscal 1969 for safety research and development.

Permitted the Secretary to use the funds, independently or in cooperation with other federal agencies, for grants to state and local entities for training or education of highway safety personnel; research fellowships in highway safety; development of improved accident investigation procedures; and emergency service plans, demonstration projects and related activities.

Advisory Committee. Established in the Department of Commerce a National Highway Safety Advisory Committee composed of the Secretary, or an officer of the Commerce Department appointed by the Secretary, serving as chairman, the Federal Highway Administrator and 29 other members appointed by the President for three-year terms, of whom no more than four could be federal officers or employees. Directed that the 29 members be selected from among representatives of state and local governments; public and private interests contributing to, affected by or concerned with highway safety; other private and public agencies, organizations or groups demonstrating an interest in highway safety; and research scientists and other experts in the field.

Directed the Committee to advise, consult with and make recommendations to the Secretary on highway

safety, to review research projects and to review and make recommendations on federal highway safety standards.

Other Provisions. Stipulated that all facts contained in any report of any federal department or agency relating to any highway traffic accident must be available for use in civil, criminal or judicial proceedings arising out of the accident and that any federal officer, employee or agent may be required to testify in such proceedings concerning the facts developed by the investigation.

Repealed the "Baldwin amendment" to a 1965 law (S J Res 81—PL 89-139) apportioning funds for the Interstate Highway System, which specified that each state, after Dec. 31, 1967, "should" have a highway safety program approved by the Secretary of Commerce.

Directed the Secretary to establish in the Department of Commerce a National Highway Safety Agency, headed by an Administrator appointed by the President, to administer the provisions of the Act.

Authorized (but did not require) the President to carry out the provisions of the National Traffic and Motor Vehicle Safety Act of 1966 (S 3005) through the National Highway Safety Agency and Administrator.

Directed the Secretary to report to the President and Congress by March 1 of each year on the administration of the act and to recommend additional legislation if necessary.

Directed the Secretary to report to Congress by July 1, 1967, on the uniform standards to be initially applied to state programs.

Directed the Secretary to make a study of the relationship between the consumption of alcohol and highway safety and to report the results of the study to Congress by July 1, 1967, with recommendations for legislation if warranted.

Directed the Secretary in making grants to the states under the federal-aid highway systems to give priority to projects which provide for improved safety standards.

Directed the Secretary to make a detailed estimate of the cost of carrying out the provisions of the Act and to make a report on the estimated costs and recommendations for federal, state and local matching funds to Congress by Jan. 10, 1968.

Truth in Packaging

A long-sought consumer protection measure, the truth-in-lending bill, was enacted by Congress in 1966 (S 985—PL 89-755).

Enactment of the Administration-backed measure culminated an effort initiated in 1961 by Congressional consumer legislation leaders and consumer interest groups to obtain stronger federal controls to guard against deceptive packaging and labeling practices. The purpose of the bill was to aid consumers in making price-per-unit and broader value comparisons of some 8,000 household and personal goods usually sold in supermarkets and drug stores.

As signed into law, S 985 required manufacturers to provide consumers with specific information about a commodity's contents, including a clear statement of the net quantity expressed in ounces if the quantity were less than four pounds or one gallon. However, unlike the original version of S 985 as introduced by Sen. Philip A. Hart (D Mich.) and the version passed by the Senate, the final bill did not authorize the Government to establish standard-package sizes which would have further eased the task of consumers in comparing products.

The absence of authority for federal package-size standards represented a major victory for the good industry, which vigorously opposed giving federal officials the ultimate power to determine how many and what sizes a commodity could be packaged in. The primary argument credited for the manufacturers' victory was the threat of increased costs to consumers if producers were forced to convert operating equipment to meet the proposed requirements.

However, the final bill permitted Government officials to request manufacturers to develop standard package sizes on their own and to seek legislation later if the voluntary approach did not work. The voluntary vs. mandatory approach to package size was the key difference between the Senate and House bills. Both versions authorized federal officials—upon determining that a proliferation of package sizes impaired product comparisons by consumers —to request a commodity's manufacturers to participate in the development of voluntary weight and quantity standards to reduce the number of package sizes. If after one year, industry failed to develop such standards or if voluntary regulations were not being adhered to, the Senate version authorized the federal officials to establish Government package standards. The House and final versions, on the other hand, required the officials to seek additional legislative authority from Congress.

In its other major provisions, S 985 directed the Secretary of Health, Education and Welfare (HEW) and the Federal Trade Commission to issue regulations requiring clear and accurate statements on package labels regarding the commodity's identity, manufacturer, and, if the number of servings were given, the net quantity that constituted a serving. The bill also gave the federal officials discretionary authority to regulate the use of package characterizations such as "family" and "jumbo" size, and advertising and promotional claims such as "cents-off" offers; to require a listing of the commodity's ingredients; and to prohibit "slack-filling" practices when packages were not filled to capacity for reasons other than protecting the contents or using a certain type of machine to enclose the product.

Several stronger provisions originally proposed but left out of the final version included prohibiting, instead of regulating, package advertising claims; prohibiting the use of misleading illustrations or pictorial matter; and preventing the distribution of packages in sizes and shapes deceptive to the consumer.

BACKGROUND

Truth-in-packaging proposals had been under consideration in the Senate and supported by the Kennedy and Johnson Administrations since the 87th Congress. The House, however, took no action on the proposals until 1966.

1961-62. The Senate Judiciary Antitrust and Monopoly Subcommittee held hearings in 1961-62 on packaging and labeling practices affecting consumers. After the hearings, Sen. Philip A. Hart (D Mich.), sponsor of the inquiry, introduced a bill (S 3754) to prohibit restraints of trade through deceptive packaging. In his 1962 consumer message, President Kennedy said that the Administration planned to submit recommendations in the near

future for package-standards legislation. In July 1962, the President appointed a 12-member Consumer Advisory Council to represent consumer needs and demands. No further action was taken.

1963. The Senate Antitrust and Monopoly Subcommittee held hearings in 1963 on a similar Hart bill (S 387) and approved it June 13 by a 5-3 vote. However, the bill was never reported by the full Judiciary Committee. S 387 was supported by the Consumer Advisory Council in its Oct. 8 consumer legislation recommendations, but there was no further action.

1964. Although the idea of federal truth-in-packaging legislation was endorsed by President Johnson in his Feb. 5 consumer message to Congress, the only action before the close of the 88th Congress was the issuance of a report Nov. 11, 1964, by the Antitrust and Monopoly Subcommittee urging enactment of S 387.

1965. In his Jan. 28 Economic Report, President Johnson endorsed the concept of truth-in-packaging legislation and on Feb. 3, Hart introduced a new bill (S 985). Major provisions of the bill authorized the Food and Drug Administration and the Federal Trade Commission to issue regulations requiring prominent statements of net quantity on packages; providing reasonable standards for weights, quantities, sizes, shapes and dimensions of packages; and prohibiting statements offering a product at less than the customary retail price and deceptive pictures on packages.

S 985 differed from the earlier Hart bill in two major respects. Instead of amending the 1914 Clayton Act as had S 387, and thus being technically classified as an antitrust bill, S 985 prohibited deceptive packaging and labeling in interstate commerce. The change was designed to transfer jurisdiction of the bill from the unresponsive full Judiciary Committee to the Senate Commerce Committee. The second change was the replacement of criminal sanctions under the earlier bill with civil penalties. Criminal enforcement had been objected to by the Department of Commerce in 1963 while the Department of Health, Education and Welfare in 1965 requested that the criminal penalties be put back in.

After S 985 was introduced in the Senate, a dispute developed Feb. 19 over which Senate committee should consider the bill. By voice vote, the Senate supported Hart who contended that the bill should be sent to the Commerce Committee. Senate Minority Leader Everett McKinley Dirksen (D Ill.), who argued that the bill should go to the Judiciary Committee because of its "antitrust characteristics" in dealing with the standardization and price competition, promised he would move to have the bill sent to the Judiciary Committee if and when it ever reached the Senate floor.

During 10 days of hearings from April 28 to May 18, 1965, the Senate Commerce Committee heard opposition to the bill from the packaging, food and grocery industries. The spokesmen specifically objected to federal standards for weight measures and packaging sizes, definitions of a "serving" of a food commodity and requirements for ingredient information on the package label. They also objected to provisions prohibiting the placement of "cents-off" advertising on package labels. There was no House action on related bills in 1965.

LEGISLATIVE HISTORY

Johnson Requests. President Johnson supported truth-in-packaging legislation in his Jan. 12, 1966, State of the Union message and Jan. 27 Economic Report. On March 21, the President sent Congress a consumer interest message in which he proposed fair packaging and labeling legislation to: (1) require each package to provide simple, direct, accurate and visible information as to the nature and quantity of its contents, including ingredients when important; (2) keep off the shelves packages with deceptively shaped boxes, misleading pictures, confusing or meaningless adjectives, inappropriate size or quantity markings and promotional gimmicks that promised non-existent savings; and (3) provide for the establishment of reasonable and appropriate weight standards to facilitate comparative shopping. While the President did not specifically endorse the Hart bill (S 985), Administration spokesmen said that it would be an acceptable means of dealing with the problem. In his consumer message, Mr. Johnson said that federal regulation would not "make packaging less attractive...less efficient" and would not "prevent economies of scale in packaging, nor...impose costly restrictions."

Senate Action. The Senate Commerce Committee reported S 985 in late May after amending it. The bill, in its key and most controversial provision, authorized the Secretary of Health, Education and Welfare and the Federal Trade Commission to establish "reasonable" weights and quantities for commodities on a product-by-product basis after first providing the affected industry the opportunity to develop voluntary standards under procedures administered by the Commerce Department. A proposal by Norris Cotton (R N.H.) to delete this provision was defeated by a 7-11 committee vote.

Floor Action—The Senate passed S 985 in June by a 72-9 roll-call vote. Debate and key floor amendments centered on the bill's provisions authorizing establishment by Government officials of package weights and quantities following procedures for industry self-regulation. There was considerable agreement on the other provisions dealing largely with content and placement of information on package labels.

Prior to passage, Republicans made a series of unsuccessful attempts to delete various sections of the bill. The most important vote, one of the key votes of the session, came on an amendment by Cotton to delete the controversial package weights and quantities section. It was rejected by a **32-53** roll call (R 25-4; D 7-49).

The Senate also rejected by voice votes a series of amendments by Minority Leader Everett McKinley Dirksen (R Ill.) to delete most other sections of the bill. Dirksen also sought unsuccessfully to have the bill sent to the Judiciary Committee.

Senate debate, spreading over six days, centered on the Cotton amendment with supporters contending that the packaging section would give too much power to "bureaucrats" to standardize packaging; would increase costs to the consumer because of the expense of making changes; and would "stifle competition." Opponents of the amendment, in turn, argued that its adoption would remove the "core" of the bill, which was to help the consumer to make informed choices in the supermarket by providing the necessary information for price comparisons.

House Action. In the House, a bill (HR 15440) nearly identical to the Senate bill was introduced in early June. The major difference was that the House bill permitted Government officials to prohibit the sale of packages upon determining that their size, shape or dimensional proportions were likely to deceive purchasers as to the actual quantity of the contents.

Hearings consumed much of the rest of the summer until September when the Committee acted on the bill.

The Committee finally approved HR 15440 late in September, but only after an effort by a conservative Southern Democrat to kill the measure nearly succeeded.

The Committee Sept. 13 by a 12-7 vote adopted a motion offered by John Bell Williams (D Miss.) to table (kill) the bill. The surprise move, supported by all Republicans attending the session, was successful in large part because several members either were out of town to participate in primary elections or arrived late at the meeting, after the vote was taken. The Committee was composed of 22 Democrats and 11 Republicans.

Immediately following the tabling vote, John D. Dingell (D Mich.), a supporter of the bill, initiated a move to save it by switching his vote on the tabling motion from "nay" to "yea," thereby enabling him to offer a motion that the bill be reconsidered. House rules stipulate that only a member of the voting majority can move for reconsideration.

The motion to resume consideration was then adopted Sept. 20 by a 17-14 vote. All of the 17 supporters were Democrats, while five Democrats and nine Republicans opposed it. Two Republicans, Glenn Cunningham (Neb.) and Tim Lee Carter (Ky.) were absent. The Committee went on to approve the bill Sept. 22.

As approved by the Committee, HR 15440 contained most of the Senate bill's requirements for clear labeling of packages. Additional provisions, which were slightly varied between the two versions, dealt with the requirement that the net quantity be expressed in ounces; the use of the term "servings" on the label; the requirement for certain ingredient information on labels; and a new prohibition against nonfunctional slack-filling of packages.

The major difference between the two measures lay in the Committee's elimination of a section permitting Government officials to establish standards governing the weights and quantities in which products could be marketed. The House version authorized the Secretary of Commerce, upon determining that proliferation of package sizes impaired consumer price comparison, to request the packaging industry to develop, voluntarily, its own product standards. If, after one year, no standard had been worked out or a voluntary standard was being violated, the Secretary was required to go to Congress to seek additional regulatory authority. The Senate bill, on the other hand, permitted the HEW Secretary and the FTC to establish federal standards without additional authority from Congress if the industry failed to develop its own.

The Commerce Department agreed to the compromise provision after the Senate passed its bill, so as to overcome industry opposition and thereby speed enactment of the bill in 1966. The Committee, in explaining the change, said the substitution of an entirely voluntary procedure was desirable to meet the "recurrent objections raised by industry that mandatory standards would result in greatly increased cost to the consumer and would stifle packaging innovations."

Floor Action—The House passed the bill in early October by a 300-8 roll-call vote.

The bill was brought to the floor under suspension-of-the-rules procedure—generally reserved for noncontroversial legislation. The fact that it passed easily under the procedure was a reflection of the elimination by the Interstate and Foreign Commerce Committee of controversial provisions in the Senate version which gave the Government a large measure of control in regulating the package industry.

Harley O. Staggers (D W.Va.), chairman of the Interstate and Foreign Commerce Committee, said the bill would accomplish the "twin objectives of protecting the American consumer without hurting American industry." He said the major reason for eliminating federal power over package sizes was a predominance of testimony indicating that standardization of package sizes would increase manufacturers' costs and consequently the cost to the consumer.

Leonor K. Sullivan (D Mo.), who had championed consumer legislation since she came to Congress in 1953, said she would vote for S 985 "and if it passes we can all voice a very mild cheer—for very little." She contended that "there is so little in the bill which does anything of any great importance that opposition to it, in my opinion, is tilting at windmills."

Conference Action. Senate conferees conceded to the House version on all major differences including acceptance of a weaker packaging-standards section authorizing the Secretary of Commerce to request manufacturers to develop their own standards, but requiring him to return to Congress for additional authority.

On other differences, the Senate conferees accepted the House terminology to facilitate "value comparisons" by consumers instead of the Senate's "price comparisons." Senate conferees agreed to House provisions requiring the statement of net quantity, if less than four pounds or one gallon, to be expressed both in terms of ounces, and when applicable, in quarts or pounds with the remainder either in ounces or a fraction of the whole unit. Also adopted were House provisions not contained in the Senate bill dealing with net quantity for random packages and packages labeled in terms of area or linear measure. The conferees accepted the House version's requirement that if a representation was made on the package as to the number of servings of the commodity, it would have to show the net quantity of each serving. The conferees also agreed to House provisions requiring a commodity's ingredients to be listed on the package label in order of decreasing predominance and prohibiting slack-filled packages, and a House stipulation that the Act would supersede those state laws that were either less stringent or required different information from the federal laws.

PROVISIONS

As signed into law Nov. 3, S 985, the Fair Packaging and Labeling Act:

Declared the intent of Congress to assist consumers and manufacturers in ensuring that packages and labels provide accurate information as to the quantity of their contents so as to facilitate value comparisons.

Prohibited the distribution in commerce by a producer or manufacturer of any packaged or labeled "consumer commodity" not conforming to standards and regulations provided by or under authority of the bill. Exempted the wholesaler and retailer unless such person was part of the packaging and labeling process.

Specifically defined "consumer commodity" to mean any food, drug, device or cosmetic as defined in the Federal Food, Drug and Cosmetic Act, and any other article or product customarily sold for consumption, use or personal care by individuals or to perform household services and which normally was consumed or used-up (that is, nondurable goods).

Exempted certain commodities already under federal law including meats, poultry, tobacco, alcoholic beverages, certain drugs and seeds.

Authorized the Secretary of Health, Education and Welfare (working through the HEW Department's Food and Drug Administration) and the Federal Trade Commission (FTC) to establish standards and regulations for package information and identification, and to encourage the voluntary development of package size standards by manufacturers.

Vested authority in the HEW Secretary for most foods, drugs and cosmetics, and in the FTC for other household (generally kitchen and bathroom) commodities.

Mandatory Regulations. Required the HEW Secretary and the FTC to establish labeling standards which require on packages:

(1) Identification of the commodity, its manufacturer and the place of business;

(2) A separate and accurate statement of the net quantity in a uniform location on the principal display panel of the label; defined the principal display panel as that part of the label most likely to be displayed or shown under normal or customary conditions.

(3) The net quantity to be expressed:

(a) if on a package containing less than four pounds or one gallon, *both* in terms of ounces and, if applicable, in pounds for weight with any remainder in ounces or fractions of a pound, or in the largest whole unit for liquids (quarts, quarts and pints or pints) with any remainder in fluid ounces or fractions of a pint or quart;

(b) if on a "random package" (defined as one of a lot, shipment or delivery of packages of the same consumer commodity, but with no fixed weight pattern) in terms of pounds and fractions of the whole units;

(c) if on a package labeled in terms of linear measure, both in terms of inches and the largest whole unit with the remainder in inches or fractions of the foot or yard; and

(d) if on a package labeled in terms of area measure, both in terms of square inches and the largest whole square unit with the remainder in square inches or fractions of the square foot or square yard;

(4) The net quantity to appear in "conspicuous" typography contrasting distinctly with the rest of the package;

(5) The net quantity to be stated in a type size established by the Government "in relationship" to the principal display panel and to be uniform for all other packages of substantially the same size;

(6) The statement of net quantity to be "generally" parallel to the base of the package;

(7) That no qualifying words or phrases accompany the primary statement of net quantity on the label. Permitted such qualifying words to appear with a supplemental statement of net quantity elsewhere on the package, providing the modifiers did not exaggerate the

amount of the net contents (thus permitting a phrase such as "6 oz. of fast acting detergent" but prohibiting "6 jumbo oz. of detergents.");

(8) A statement of the net quantity (in terms of weight, measure or numerical count) constituting a serving when such a designation of the number of servings appeared on the label or package.

Permitted the HEW Secretary or the FTC to exempt a commodity from the mandatory requirements upon finding that because of the nature, form or quantity of a particular commodity, full compliance was not necessary to adequately protect consumers.

Discretionary Regulations. Permitted, but did not require, the HEW Secretary and the FTC, upon finding it necessary to prevent the deception of consumers or to facilitate value comparisons, to establish additional regulations on a product-by-product basis to:

(1) Establish and define standards to characterize the size of packages, such as small, medium or large, specified that this provision did not authorize any limitation on the size, shape, weight, dimensions or number of packages which could be used to enclose a commodity;

(2) Control the use by manufacturers or producers of statements on the label (such as "cents-off" advertising and "economy size" claims) to indicate that the commodity is offered for retail sale at a price lower than the regular price or that a price advantage is available to the consumer because of the size or quantity of the package.

(3) Require that the label of a package containing a nonfood commodity bear the common or usual name of the commodity and when it consists of two or more ingredients, the common or usual name of each ingredient listed in order of decreasing predominance, but not the disclosure of trade secrets. (The requirement was already applicable to food under the 1938 Federal Food, Drug and Cosmetic Act);

(4) Prevent the nonfunctional slack-filling of packages, defined as packages not "substantially" filled to capacity, unless for reasons of protecting the contents or employing a particular type of machine to enclose the contents.

Packaging Standards. Directed the Secretary of Commerce, upon determining that an undue proliferation of weights, measures or quantities of a commodity impaired the ability of the consumer to make "value" comparisons, to request the manufacturers, packers and distributors of the commodity or commodities involved, to participate in developing a voluntary product standard for the commodity under Commerce Department procedures.

If after one year the Secretary determined that the manufacturers had not developed a standard or such a voluntary standard was not being observed, directed him to promptly report to Congress with recommendations as to whether new legislation was necessary to provide the needed authority to deal with the situation.

Other Provisions. Provided that a food, drug, device or cosmetic which violated regulations issued under the bill would be deemed misbranded and thus subject to seizure under the Federal Food, Drug and Cosmetic Act. Provided that violations for other consumer commodities would constitute "unfair or deceptive acts or practices in commerce," which are illegal, and would be subject to "cease and desist" orders by the FTC.

Specified that there would be no criminal penalties for violations of regulations under the bill.

Provided that control over imported items would rest with the Secretary of the Treasury.

Provided for judicial review of regulations issued by the HEW Secretary and the FTC.

Authorized the HEW Secretary and the FTC to cooperate with federal, state and local departments and agencies in carrying out the Act.

Exempted from the bill all packages and reusable glass containers for beverages in the process of orderly disposal from inventories as of the effective date of the regulation.

Directed all Government authorities involved in establishing regulations to transmit a report to Congress each January on their activities during the preceding year.

Stipulated that copies of all regulations were to be furnished to the Secretary of Commerce who, in turn, was required to transmit copies to state officers and agencies and furnish to such officers and agencies information and assistance to promote uniformity in state and federal labeling regulations.

Stated the intent of Congress to supersede any state or local laws concerning labeling of net quantity which were less stringent than or required different information from the federal regulations.

Provided that the Act would become effective July 1, 1967. Permitted the HEW Secretary or FTC to postpone the effective date an additional year for a commodity when such postponement would be in the public interest.

Child Protection

Congress in 1966 enacted a bill (S 3298—PL 89-756) which expanded federal control over hazardous substances and articles. The legislation, called the Child Protection Act, was intended to provide increased safeguards not only for children who might come in contact with dangerous toys but also for adults who might use potentially dangerous household items.

S 3298 permitted federal officials to require a warning label on all hazardous household items (instead of only those that are packaged) and on hazardous toys and children's articles. It also allowed the Government to ban from sale household items and children's toys if they were found to be too dangerous for general use, regardless of whether a warning label was attached. It included in the definition of hazardous articles any items containing dangerous substances such as pesticides or other poisonous residues.

The bill included many of the recommendations made by President Johnson in a March 21 message on consumer interests. It did not, however, cover his requests for legislation to limit the amount of children's aspirin available in retail packages, require safety caps on other medicines or require labels warning of injury in drugs, cosmetics and pressurized cans. The requests, particularly the limit on children's aspirin, were strongly opposed by the drug industry, and Congress dropped them in response to pleas from the industry that it be allowed time to act voluntarily.

In November 1966 the Food and Drug Administration (FDA) met with drug industry representatives and reached an agreement that beginning June 1, 1967, bottles of children's aspirin would be limited to 36 tablets each and the potency of each tablet would be limited to 1.25 grains.

Most bottles currently contained 50 tablets, and some tablets ranged as high as five grains in potency.

S 3298 amended the Federal Hazardous Substances Labeling Act of 1960. That Act permitted the Secretary of Health, Education and Welfare (HEW) to ban from interstate commerce packaged hazardous substances designed for household use, such as cleaning agents, detergents or inflammable ornaments, which did not contain adequate warning statements on their labels. The Act did not otherwise permit the Secretary to prohibit the sale of a substance regardless of how dangerous it might be, and it applied only to articles which were packaged. It was administered by the Food and Drug Administration.

The bill modified the 1960 law in several major respects.

S 3298 clarified the FDA's authority to declare as a hazardous substance any article which contained a residue of an insecticide, fungicide, pesticide or similar chemical. Under the 1960 law, poisons used as insecticides, fungicides and pesticides could not be classed as hazardous substances. Instead they were controlled under the Federal Insecticide, Fungicide and Rodenticide Act of 1947, which authorized the Agriculture Department to require proper labeling of such chemicals and to ban from interstate commerce those poisons which were too dangerous for general use. Later laws extended federal control over residues from such poisons in fresh fruits and vegetables. There was, however, no legislation concerning the control of dangerous residues in other articles, and there was some question about whether the FDA could act in such cases in light of the Agriculture Department's authority under the 1947 law and the prohibition of the 1960 law. S 3298 specified that the FDA had such authority.

S 3298 also extended the authority of the HEW Secretary to deal with hazardous substances and articles which are not packaged. It required that a written, printed or graphic display be attached directly to the hazardous article. This permitted the FDA to require warnings to be printed directly on such items as blasting caps or on tags attached to items which are sold singly and unpackaged.

The bill also permitted the Secretary to ban from sale in interstate commerce children's toys and articles and household articles when they were too dangerous for general use, even if properly labeled. Certain exceptions were, however, permitted. This was a new authority not contained in the 1960 Act. It permitted the Secretary to ban substances and articles because of their intrinsic danger rather than because of any improper labeling. FDA Commissioner James L. Goddard, in testimony on the bill Aug. 24, supported the right to ban dangerous children's articles, noting that it "makes no sense to label a toy, 'Keep out of the reach of children.' " As examples of items which might be banned under this provision, Goddard mentioned "cracker-balls," small torpedo-like firecrackers which look like candy and cannot be individually labeled, and jequirity beans, seeds of Indian licorice which can cause death in hours if eaten. The beans were used as dolls' eyes and as decorations on swizzle sticks. Turning to dangerous household substances, Goddard mentioned X-33, a water repellent, which was more explosive than gasoline and caused a number of deaths and injuries despite its labeling.

For toys that were less dangerous but still hazardous, S 3298 required warning labels as were already required for household items by the 1960 law.

LEGISLATIVE HISTORY

The bill was passed by both Senate and House with little controversy after the main issue involving children's aspirin was resolved. Both chambers passed the bill by voice votes.

PROVISIONS—As signed by the President Nov. 3, S 3298 changed the title of the 1960 Federal Hazardous Substances Labeling Act by deleting the word Labeling. The bill also:

Definition Revisions. Made articles bearing or containing an economic poison (such as an insecticide or pesticide) which forms a hazardous residue subject to the provisions of the 1960 Act as amended by S 3298 regarding hazardous substances.

Unpackaged Articles—Redefined the term "label" in the 1960 Act to require not only that a display of written, printed or graphic matter be upon the container of a hazardous substance (as required by the 1960 Act), but also that, in the case of unpackaged articles or articles not in a container, the same display be upon the hazardous article itself or on a tag or other suitable material attached to the article.

Labeling of Hazardous Toys—Replaced the terms "misbranded package" or "misbranded package of a hazardous substance" as used in the 1960 Act with the term "misbranded hazardous substance." Defined the new term to include toys or other articles intended for use by children which were made of a hazardous substance or contained a hazardous substance that was accessible to children but which did not have the required warning label. The bill also defined the new term (as did existing law for the old terms) to include a hazardous substance which was intended for household use but did not have the required warning label.

Extremely Hazardous Toys, Household Items—Added to the 1960 law the term "banned hazardous substances" to cover articles and substances which, regardless of the presence of a warning label, were so dangerous that the public health and safety could be protected only by keeping them out of interstate commerce. *(See Prohibited Acts, below.)*

Defined "banned hazardous substances" to include toys or other articles intended for use by children or substances intended for household use.

Permitted the Secretary of Health, Education and Welfare to exempt from the coverage of "banned hazardous substances" articles, such as chemistry sets and common fireworks, which were designed for older children and contained a cautionary label and instructions, if he determined that they could be adequately labeled for safe handling.

Prohibited Acts. Expanded the section of the 1960 Act which defined the types of acts that were prohibited and which thereby subjected a manufacturer to penalties and his product to seizure and destruction, as follows:

(1) Amended the 1960 Act to prohibit the sending or receipt in interstate commerce of the new categories of "misbranded hazardous and banned hazardous substances."

(2) Amended the 1960 Act to prohibit the alteration, mutilation, destruction, obliteration or removal of any label which results in a hazardous substance becoming a misbranded hazardous or banned hazardous substance.

(3) Amended the 1960 Act to prohibit entrance of foreign articles as imports if they fell within the misbranded or banned hazardous substances definitions.

1967

Truth in Lending

After almost a decade of delay, legislation to help the consumer make sense of interest rates and similar charges began to move through Congress in 1966. By the end of the year, a surprisingly strong truth-in-lending bill had passed the Senate and was well on its way toward enactment by the House. The bill (S 5) became law in 1968 and was heralded as one of the strongest consumer protection statutes ever enacted. *(For 1968 action and complete provisions, see below.)*

The legislation, which originated in Congress in the late 1950s, was a priority item on President Johnson's list of consumer protection bills.

Truth in lending was a label which described bills that required lenders and other consumer creditors to provide their customers full, honest and—most importantly—comparable information about the cost of the credit the consumers were buying. The heart of these bills was a requirement that buyers be told the cost of loans and installment purchase plans in terms of an annual rate calculated under certain specified procedures by all lenders. The resulting uniformity was intended to enable consumers to make valid cost comparisons between the lending rates or installment plans of different stores or lending institutions.

Only Massachusetts, Washington, Connecticut and Maine had state laws comparable to the legislation envisioned by supporters of a federal credit statute. However, only Massachusetts' truth-in-lending laws, enacted in 1966, were considered comprehensive enough to provide a guide to the workability of credit disclosure on a national scale.

The need for federal legislation, its supporters believed, was established during seven years of Senate hearings on truth-in-lending bills. The testimony indicated that disclosure of credit costs in terms of dollars-and-cents or a monthly rate was not sufficient to inform consumers of the range of credit plans available on the open market. Testimony before the Senate Banking and Currency Committee showed that uninformed borrowers sometimes involved themselves in credit contracts which required them to pay 200 or 300 percent interest.

The inequities of some credit practices affected not only the poor and uneducated but also consumers experienced in credit buying. The intricacies of computing the interest rate on a loan or an installment plan—with all the added carrying charges and insurance costs—confused even the wariest credit purchaser.

The credit industry, however, opposed credit disclosure legislation on the ground that stating an annual rate cost would only confuse consumers. The industry also feared that customers who discovered they were paying, say, a 36-percent annual rate—instead of a 3-percent monthly rate—would decide against buying the credit, and eventually ruin the credit business.

Supporters of truth in lending argued in return that the legislation was not intended to restrain the credit market. It was meant only to give consumers a full, free choice in an open market. The supporters did concede that in the long run the effect of the legislation could be to lower interest rates because consumers would choose the lowest rate available to them.

These arguments, and technical questions of how best to make credit disclosure work, kept truth-in-lending advocates and the credit industry at loggerheads for seven years. From 1960 until 1967 credit disclosure bills were locked in the Senate Banking and Currency Committee, where Sen. Paul H. Douglas (D Ill. 1949-67) adamantly maintained his position that a "simple" annual rate should be disclosed by all creditors. Douglas's bills were strongly opposed by the industry.

Four factors contributed to the action taken on the bill in 1967 and 1968.

First was Douglas' defeat in the 1966 election. Second was the defeat in a 1966 primary election of Sen. A. Willis Robertson (D Va.); Robertson was chairman of the Senate Banking and Currency Committee and an adamant opponent of truth-in-lending legislation. The uncompromising and diametrically opposed views of Douglas and Robertson were major reasons that truth-in-lending bills never were reported by the Banking and Currency Committee before 1967.

A third factor was President Johnson's strong endorsement in his Feb. 16, 1967, consumer affairs message of annual rate disclosure and other consumer credit protections which Douglas had supported. The fourth factor was the willingness of William Proxmire (D Wis.), who replaced Douglas as the champion of the legislation, to bargain with the credit industry to write a bill the industry felt would be workable. Proxmire on Jan. 11, 1967, introduced S 5, the bill the President endorsed.

1967 Action. The Senate July 11, by a **92-0** roll-call vote, passed S 5. The bill required disclosure of annual rate costs—and the methods of determining them—for money lenders and installment plan creditors. In a compromise move, the bill exempted from the yearly rate provisions those creditors who offered retail revolving charge accounts; these retailers were required to disclose only the monthly rate of interest. Charge accounts which were similar to installment plans, under criteria set forth in S 5, were required to disclose an annual rate.

The House Banking and Currency Committee Dec. 13 reported a bill (HR 11601) which incorporated the Senate provisions and added new ones. HR 11601 banned certain wage garnishments, required disclosure of annual rates in credit advertising, contained new enforcement procedures and established a National Commission on Consumer Finance. The Committee's report was filed two days before the close of the first session, too late for floor action in 1967.

A major disagreement developed in the House Committee over the type of disclosure that should apply to revolving credit. The Committee eventually voted 17-14 to drop the bill it was considering a requirement that the cost of such credit be expressed as an annual rate. Once that issue was resolved (although the resolution was only temporary because the decision was successfully challenged on the floor in 1968), the bill was approved and reported by the Committee. The sponsor and prime mover behind the House measure was Rep. Leonor K. Sullivan (D Mo.).

Meat Inspection

Legislation enacted late in the year made broad changes in the 60-year-old federal meat inspection system. The bill (HR 12144), called the Wholesome Meat Act of 1967, updated and greatly strengthened existing federal standards and applied them to plants in interstate commerce and, under certain conditions, to plants doing business within state borders. President Johnson Dec. 15 signed HR 12144 into law (PL 90-201). It was the most important consumer bill enacted in 1967.

The most far-reaching portion of HR 12144 was aimed at helping—or, if necessary, forcing—states to strengthen their own meat inspection systems. The Secretary of Agriculture was authorized to provide assistance (ranging from advice to funds covering 50 percent of the cost) to states for the purpose of bringing their meat inspection standards to a level "at least equal" to those in HR 12144. In addition, HR 12144 directed the Secretary to actually assume the costs and duties of inspection in plants doing business within a state if he determined, two years after enactment of HR 12144, that the state had not developed and activated an inspection system "at least equal" to the federal system. Finally, the Secretary could require federal inspection of any intrastate plant which he found produced meat dangerous to the public health if he notified state officials first and they failed to act.

The major provisions of HR 12144 strengthening existing federal standards applied to inspection of animals. The bill made inspection before slaughter mandatory instead of leaving it to the discretion of the Secretary. Animals to be inspected were cattle, sheep, swine, goats, horses, mules and other equines yielding meat or meat products "capable of use as human food." (Existing law covered meat "prepared for human consumption"—a narrower range of coverage.) The Agriculture Department could seize meat it believed had not been inspected or was adulterated or misbranded. Certain animal products not intended as human food were exempted from the inspection requirements, but the processors had to denature them or identify them to deter their use as food. In most cases, the purity requirements imposed on domestically produced meats were applicable also to imported meats.

In addition, the bill required meat processors to keep records of their transactions and to make the records available to federal inspectors for examination. It also authorized the Secretary to require registration of processors. The Secretary could extend the record-keeping and registration requirements to intrastate businesses if he found the state involved as not exercising comparable authority.

President Johnson requested meat inspection legislation in his Feb. 16 message to Congress on consumer protection. "It should be our goal," Mr. Johnson said, "to provide full assurance of the wholesomeness of all meat products offered for sale to the housewife. This assurance can best be developed through a federal-state partnership for consumer protection." The Administration draft bill, however, did not provide for federal inspection of plants doing business only in intrastate commerce. This portion of HR 12144 was initiated by Congress but was added to the bill with the strong endorsement of the Administration.

Pressures on Meat Inspection Bill

Pressure groups representing meat packers and industry union groups were intensely active during Congressional consideration of the Wholesome Meat Act.

Meat packing groups and the powerful National Assn. of State Departments of Agriculture, for the most part, opposed the portions of HR 12144 extending federal standards to intrastate meat plants. As feeling in Congress began to swing toward the more comprehensive bill passed by the Senate, however, the meat packers announced stands more favorable to the proposed new system. The union groups, chiefly the Amalgamated Meat Cutters and Butchers Workmen of North America (AFL-CIO), laid on a strong campaign for regulation of plants in intrastate commerce.

The meat packers' position was probably hurt, observers felt, by an incident which cropped up just after HR 12144 was passed by the House.

The *Des Moines Register* revealed Nov. 1 that the Western States Meat Packers Assn. Inc. had begun to raise a "Congressional campaign fund" among its 600 members in mid-September—just as HR 12144 was reaching a critical stage in its consideration by the House Agriculture Committee.

The *Register* said that L. Blaine Liljenquist, president and general manager of the Western States Meat Packers Assn. Inc. had sent letters Oct. 28 to the group's 600 members asking for contributions in the form of personal checks to a "Congressional campaign fund" for Senators and Representatives of both parties. The checks, the letter advised, should range "between a $25 minimum and a $99 maximum." (Federal law required candidates to list the source of contributions only if the amount were above $100.)

Although the letters did not mention HR 12144, Liljenquist circulated the solicitation at a time when Reps. Neal Smith (D Iowa) and Thomas S. Foley (D Wash.) were seeking support for a stronger meat inspection bill than the one the House Agriculture Committee reported Aug. 16. The Smith-Foley proposal would have placed an additional 6,000 meat plants under federal inspection regulations. The meat packers favored the less-inclusive Committee bill (HR 12144), which extended the modernized inspection regulations to plants in interstate commerce.

Liljenquist's letter came to the attention of Rep. W. R. Poage (D Texas), chairman of the Agriculture Committee. In identical letters sent Oct. 6 to Liljenquist and to two other major packer groups, Poage said he was "shocked" to learn of the solicitation and demanded that it be stopped. The campaign, he said, could "prove deeply embarrassing" to Members "who are honestly and objectively trying to deal with the problems of the meat industry before Congress." Liljenquist, in an Oct. 11 letter to Poage, denied that the fund had any improper political implications but added that he had ordered the campaign closed and donations returned.

The meat inspection bill was aimed at instituting uniform standards for product quality and inspection practices in the nation's approximately 17,000 slaughter and packing plants. About 2,000 of these plants were covered under the 1907 meat inspection law and were already being inspected by federal inspectors because their products were sold in interstate commerce. These operations produced about 85 percent of the meat eaten by American consumers. The other 15,000 plants—many of them small or on seasonal slaughter schedules—produced the remaining 15 percent of the meat. Since this meat was sold only within the state in which it was produced, these plants were required only to meet state meat inspection regulations or, in seven states, no regulations at all.

In 1967, 29 states had mandatory regulations of varying degrees of stringency applying to slaughter and, in most cases, processing; another 12 states had voluntary inspection of slaughter and, with four exceptions, processing operations; 7 states had no inspection at all; and 2 had very limited statutes.

Revelations in the press and during committee hearings about slaughter and packing practices at some state plants made meat inspection the most emotional consumer issue of 1967. Early in the year it appeared that the Wholesome Meat Act of 1967 would be no more than a routine updating of standards affecting interstate operations. This was essentially what the Johnson Administration proposed. But public outcry encouraged the Administration and Members of Congress, who supported stiffer inspection regulations, to seek legislation covering state plants as well as those in interstate commerce.

LEGISLATIVE HISTORY

The bill passed by the House Oct. 31, by a 403-1 roll-call vote, differed little from the measure the Administration had requested. It authorized a program of federal-state cooperation to bring state meat inspection systems to a level "comparable" to the federal system. HR 12144 also brought inspection procedures and standards in line with broad changes in the meat industry since 1907. Before passage, the House rejected, by a 98-104 teller vote, an amendment offered by Reps. Neal Smith (D Iowa) and Thomas S. Foley (D Wash.) which would have authorized actual federal inspection of plants doing more than $250,000 of business a year in intrastate commerce.

The failure of the Smith-Foley plan was a significant one. Instead of burying the issue of intrastate inspection once and for all, the controversy the amendment raised served to polarize the opinions of pressure groups and Members on the question of federal regulations for state plants. Although the powerful Western States Meat Packers Assn. Inc. continued to support the House-passed bill, the American Meat Institute and meat industry union groups expressed support for some form of federal control over state inspection systems.

Another factor which contributed to the growing controversy over the bill was the Administration's eleventh-hour switch from support of the weaker bill, reported by the House Agriculture Committee, to support for the Smith-Foley amendment. The announcement was made by Betty Furness, President Johnson's special assistant for consumer affairs, on Oct. 30—the eve of the House vote on HR 12144.

The Senate, taking its cue from the rejected Smith-Foley amendment and from the Administration, passed its own bill Nov. 28 by an 89-2 roll-call vote. The Senate measure—substituted directly after passage for the provisions of HR 12144—included the basics of the House-passed bill but also required states to initiate inspection systems "at least equal" to the federal requirements. If a state failed to design and enforce such a program within two years, the Agriculture Secretary was authorized to assume actual inspection of the state plants doing intrastate business. The Senate version also authorized a state Governor to waive the two-year interim and come directly under the federal system, relinquishing both the costs and the responsibility of inspecting state plants to the Federal Government.

The Senate bill was the result of a compromise between Sens. Joseph M. Montoya (D N.M.) and Walter F. Mondale (D Minn.), chief strategists in the Senate campaign for a stronger meat bill.

Intrastate inspection was the major issue separating the House-Senate conferees on HR 12144. Southern Democrats in the House were against the Senate measure because they felt it was an unwarranted invasion of states rights. Leading the opposition to the stronger bill was Rep. W. R. Poage (D Texas), chairman of the House Agriculture Committee, who was to lead the House conferees. To assure that the bill would not die in a deadlocked conference, Smith and Foley Nov. 29 offered a motion instructing the House managers to accept the Senate version. The move was rejected by a 166-207 roll-call vote. In spite of the motion's failure, the House conferees agreed to all of the major Senate amendments but one—the provision that a Governor might waive the two-year period and bring his state directly under the federal system.

The Senate approved the conference report by voice vote Dec. 6. The House, pressed to a record vote on the issue by the continued opposition of Poage, adopted the conference report the same day by a 336-28 roll-call vote.

President Johnson Dec. 15 signed the Wholesome Meat Act into law (PL 90-201) at a White House ceremony attended by Upton Sinclair, 89, whose novel *The Jungle* prompted Congress to pass the first federal meat inspection law in 1907.

Background. The Meat Inspection Act of 1907 was passed in response to the public outcry that followed the publication of Upton Sinclair's novel *The Jungle*. The book graphically descibed methods used by stockyards and packing houses to process meat from the time the animal was slaughtered until its entrails were packed into sausage.

The 1907 Act required the Agriculture Department to inspect every red meat animal—before and after slaughter—whose carcass moved in interstate commerce. The Department could set standards of cleanliness for both the animals and the slaughter houses, prevent the use of chemical additives, and require truthful labeling of meat packages. Without the Department's approval, the meat could not be shipped or sold.

From 1907, the Act stood—with one change—until 1967. In his 1964 message on consumer affairs, President Johnson requested legislation to ensure "that all meat and poultry in the United States—instrastste as well as interstate—is inspected for safety and wholesomeness, either by the Department of Agriculture or in cooperation with state authorities." An Administration bill was introduced in the 89th Congress but again no action was taken.

Provisions

As signed into law (PL 90-201) Dec. 15, HR 12144, the Wholesome Meat Act of 1967:

Declared it "essential in the public interest that the health and welfare of consumers be protected by assuring that meat and meat food products distributed to them are wholesome, not adulterated, and properly marked, labeled and packaged."

Title I—Inspection Requirements. Amended the 1907 Meat Inspection Act by modernizing definitions of what constituted adulterated and misbranded meat and meat derivative products.

Definitions—Specified that the Act covered all meat products "capable of use as human food."

Applied the term "adulterated" to any carcass, part of a carcass, meat or meat food product which (1) bears or contains any poisonous or deleterious substance injurious to health; (2) has had any poisonous or deleterious substance added to it (such as a pesticide, food additive or color additive) which makes it unfit for human food; (3) consists of any filthy, putrid or decomposed substance; (4) has been prepared, packed or held under insanitary conditions; (5) comes from an animal that died by some means other than slaughter; (6) is packed in a container composed of any substance that could make the contents injurious to health; (7) has been intentionally subjected to radiation (except under certain supervised conditions); (8) has been changed by removal of any valuable constituent, substitution of any substance, concealment of damage or inferiority, or addition of any substance so as to increase bulk or weight, reduce quality or stength or make it appear of greater value; or (9) is margarine made with animal fat containing a filthy, putrid or decomposed substance.

Applied the term "misbranded" to any carcass, part of a carcass, meat or meat product if (1) its labeling is false or misleading or does not contain certain required information; (2) it is offered for sale under the name of another food; (3) it is an imitation of another food, unless its label so states; (4) its container is so made, formed or filled as to be misleading; (5) it is in a container without a label showing the name and place of business of the manufacturer, packer or distributor and an accurate statement of the quantity of the contents; (6) any word or information required on the label does not appear in such size and terms as to make it likely to read by the ordinary individual; (7) it purports to be a food for which the Secretary has set certain standards of composition but does not meet those standards; (8) it purports to be a food for which standards of fill of container have been set but its does not meet those standards; (9) it purports to be for special dietary uses but its label does not bear specified information on its vitamin, mineral and other dietary properties; or (10) it contains or bears any artificial flavoring or coloring or chemical preservative unless this is stated on the label.

Inspection—Directed the Secretary of Agriculture to require inspection of all cattle, sheep, swine, goats, horses, mules and other equines before they could enter any slaughtering, packing, rendering or similar establish-

ment. Required that any such animals with symptoms of disease be slaughtered separately and be subject to careful inspection after slaughter. (Existing law contained similar provisions but the pre-slaughter inspection was not mandatory.)

Required that all carcasses, meat and meat food products inspected under the authority of the bill and found to be not adulterated be labeled in conformity with provisions of the bill.

Authorized the Secretary to prescribe regulations for the storage and handling of meat and meat food products.

Made imported meat subject to the inspection and purity requirements imposed on domestic products and stipulated that the foreign plants would have to comply with U.S. sanitation and construction standards. Required the Secretary to certify in an annual report to Congress that U.S. inspection of foreign plants was being carried out.

Forbade use of the official federal inspection mark without the Agriculture Secretary's authorization and outlawed forgery of the mark.

Exempted from the inspection requirements persons slaughtering animals for family consumption and persons purchasing less than 50 pounds of meat abroad and bringing it into the United States.

Title II—Meat Processors. Exempted from the Title I inspection requirements any processors of carcasses or animal products not intended for use as human food, but required that any such articles be denatured or otherwise identified to deter their use as human food.

Required processors to keep records of their transactions and to open the records as well as their facilities to federal inspectors for examination at reasonable times. Applied the requirement to anyone slaughtering, preparing, freezing, packaging or labeling any meat products for use as human or animal food; persons buying, selling, importing or storing such products; and person buying, selling or importing any dead, dying, disabled or diseased (4-D) animals.

Authorized the Secretary to require registration of persons engaged in various forms of meat processing, including those processing 4-D meat.

Prohibited dealers from engaging in any transactions involving 4-D meat except in conformance with regulations prescribed by the Secretary to ensure that no part of the meat would be used for human food purposes.

Permitted the Secretary to extend to intrastate business his authority to require record-keeping and registration and to prohibit certain transactions by 4-D meat dealers when he determines that the state or territory involved does not have or is not adequately exercising comparable authority.

Title III—Federal-State Cooperation. Authorized the Secretary to initiate a program of cooperation with the states to strengthen their meat inspection programs so the programs would be "at least equal to" those in HR 12144.

Specified that the cooperation might take the form of advisory assistance in planning and developing an adequate state program under the state law; technical and other aid for administration. Allowed the Federal Government to contribute up to 50 percent of the cost of the cooperative program in any one year.

Directed the Secretary—if after consulting with the Governor he determined that a state had not developed and activated an inspection system, within two years of enactment of the bill, "at least equal" to the federal system—to assume the costs and duties of inspection in plants doing business within that state. Specified that if the Secretary determined, after two years, that the state would complete such a program within an additional year, he could allow the state a third year to develop an acceptable system.

No matter what the status of the inspection program in the state, directed the Secretary to require actual federal inspection of any intrastate plant which he found produced meat dangerous to the public health—but only if he notified state officials and they failed to act first. Authorized the Secretary to continue inspecting the plant until he was satisfied that the state was prepared to enforce proper regulations.

Directed the Secretary to review annually all state inspection programs and to report annually to the House and Senate Agriculture Committees on their status.

Title IV—Enforcement. Authorized the Secretary to refuse meat inspection service under Title I for any applicant he determined was unfit to engage in the meat business on the basis of convictions for violation of federal or state food handling laws.

Authorized administrative detention of meat and 4-D articles believed to be adulterated or misbranded or uninspected.

Authorized judicial proceedings for seizure and condemnation of meat and 4-D articles subject to the Act. Set penalties for failure to comply with the Act.

Authorized appropriation of whatever sums were needed to implement the Act.

Made the Act effective on enactment, except the provisions dealing with processors of 4-D animals and imported meat, which were to take effect 60 days later.

Flammable Fabrics

Congress in 1967 passed a bill (S 1003—PL 90-189) to provide consumers with increased protection against harm from dangerously flammable fabrics.

S 1003 amended and strengthened the 1953 Flammable Fabrics Act in the following major respects:

• It provided Government officials with flexible authority, which they did not have, to establish flammability standards for clothing and other fabrics and related materials such as plastic. Merchandise which was more flammable than the standards permitted could be forced off the market.

• It directed the Government to conduct research on the flammability of fabrics to obtain information on which to base the standards.

• It broadened the 1953 Act to cover all wearing apparel and home and office interior furnishings made of fabrics or related materials.

President Johnson requested the legislation in his Feb. 16 message to Congress on consumer affairs and again in Nov. 20 remarks on signing a bill to establish a Product Safety Commission. *(See following story.)*

The bill updated legislation enacted in 1953 after a number of deaths and serious injuries from fires involving children's cowboy chaps and sweaters. The sweaters became known as "torch" or "exploding" sweaters because of their extreme flammability.

However, the 1953 statute wrote the flammability standards into law. The standards covered highly flammable clothing articles but not other, less dangerous articles commonly in use; an act of Congress was required to change the standards. S 1003 allowed the Secretary of Commerce flexible authority to issue new standards limiting the flammability of fabrics.

In addition, S 1003 extended the Act to cover interior furnishings in order to provide protection against dangerously flammable blankets, bedding, drapes, upholstery and other products. The 1953 law did not cover interior furnishings.

Legislative Action. S 1003 was passed by both the Senate and House with little controversy. The bill was strengthened on the House floor by authorizing the Secretary of Commerce to issue standards for the flammability of hats, gloves and footwear. These items were covered in the Senate bill but had been exempted by the House Interstate and Foreign Commerce Committee.

Provisions. As signed into law, S 1003 contained the following major provisions:

Definitions—Defined wearing apparel as any costume or article of clothing worn, or intended to be worn, by individuals. (This provision deleted an existing-law exemption for hats, gloves and footwear.) Stipulated that interior furnishing meant any type of furnishing made wholly or partly of fabric, or a related material (paper, plastic, rubber and various synthetics), and used in homes, offices and other places of assembly or accommodation.

Standards—Directed the Secretary of Commerce to issue standards for the flammability of fabrics found necessary after an investigation *(see below)* to protect the public against unreasonable risk of injury, death or property loss. Specified that the standards must be reasonable, technologically practicable and appropriate. (Existing law prohibited the Secretary from issuing standards, except those specifically authorized in the 1953 Act, without action by Congress.)

Provided that a standard would become effective 12 months after it was promulgated by the Secretary. Permitted the Secretary, however, to specify an earlier or later effective date if circumstances in the industry or the consumer field required a change in effective date. Authorized the Secretary to exempt fabrics or materials held in inventory at the time the standard became effective unless he found them dangerous to consumers, in which case he could limit or withdraw the exemption granted to the inventory fabrics.

Procedure—Authorized the Secretary to subpena testimony, books, records and other information in making his flammability determinations, but provided that any information relating to a trade secret would be kept confidential.

Required standards and regulations to be issued under the provisions of the Administrative Procedure Act which are designed to afford fair treatment to persons involved through requirements on evidence, hearings, relevant information and similar issues.

Provided for judicial review of standards and regulations.

Directed the Federal Trade Commission (FTC) to establish rules for record-keeping necessary to enforce the Act. Specified that violation of FTC regulations in administration and enforcement of the Act would constitute an unfair and deceptive act in commerce subject to prosecution under the FTC Act.

Imports—Authorized the Treasury Secretary to demand return, to the country of origin, of imported fabrics which fail to conform to flammability standards under the Act.

Investigation and Research—Directed the Secretary of Health, Education and Welfare (HEW), in cooperation with the Commerce Secretary, to conduct a continuing study and investigation of the deaths, injuries and economic losses resulting from accidental burning of fabrics and related materials.

Authorized the Secretary of Commerce to: (1) conduct research into the flammability of products, fabrics, and materials; (2) conduct feasibility studies on reduction of flammability of these items; (3) develop flammability test methods and devices; and (4) offer training in the use of flammability test methods and devices.

Required the HEW Secretary to report annually to the President and Congress on these activities.

Exports—Stipulated that the provisions of the Act would not apply to fabrics labeled for export and, in fact, sent abroad—except for products shipped to U.S. installations overseas (PX's and commissaries).

National Committee—Established a National Advisory Committee for the Flammable Fabrics Act, composed of at least nine members representing the industry and the consuming public. Members were to serve for two years.

Required the Secretary to consult with the Committee before promulgating standards under the Act.

Existing Law—Stipulated that the Act was intended to supersede any state or local law.

Provided that standards of flammability currently in effect would remain in effect until superseded or modified by the Commerce Secretary.

Appropriations—Authorized appropriations of $1.5 million for fiscal 1968 and $2,250,000 for each of the fiscal years 1969 and 1970.

Product Safety Commission

A formal study of hazardous household products was authorized in 1967 when Congress established (S J Res 33—PL 90-146) a National Commission on Product Safety.

The Commission's seven members were directed to review categories of products used in or around American households to determine whether or not the products were hazardous. The requirement that "categories" be studied prevented the Commission from listing hazardous products by brand name.

Among the household items which the bill's supporters said might be studied were kitchen ranges, boilers, portable heaters, dehumidifiers, blenders, food disposals, power tools, electric fans, lawnmowers and other appliances.

The Commission also was directed to study the extent and adequacy of existing measures—such as industry self-regulation and current laws—to protect consumers against injuries from dangerous household products.

A report was due by Nov. 20, 1969.

Legislative Action. The bill met little opposition in the Senate but narrowly escaped defeat in the House.

In the Senate, Commcerce Committee Chairman Warren G. Magnuson (D Wash.), floor manager of the bill, said Congressional action on safety legislation had been "characterized by reaction to tragedy—specific, preventable tragedy." The work of the National Commission on Product Safety, he explained, would help prevent this cycle from repeating itself with regard to products used in American households.

Roman L. Hruska (R Neb.) offered six amendments to the resolution, all of which were accepted by voice votes. His chief amendment exempted guns and other firearms from the categories of products which the Commission might study. Before the amendment was accepted, Magnuson and Hruska agreed that review of the safety of BB guns and zip guns would be within the province of the Commission.

The House passed S J Res 33 by a 206-102 roll-call vote, under suspension of the rules. Suspension passages require the approval of two-thirds of those present and voting—204 in the case of SJ Res 33. Helping to preserve the slim, two-vote margin for passage of the resolution was Speaker John W. McCormack (D Mass.) who—as Speaker—rarely voted. It was the only vote cast by McCormack in 1967. A House official explained that McCormack voted in order to protect the majority against subsequent vote changes.

A narrow majority of Republicans (69-74) voted against passage of S J Res 33. The opposition was led by Reps. H.R. Gross (R Iowa) and Durward G. Hall (R Mo.) who said that the Commission was unnecessary.

Provisions. As signed into law (PL 90-146) Nov. 20, S J Res 33:

Established a seven-member National Commission on Product Safety, to be appointed by the President. Stipulated that no more than four Commission members could be affiliated with the same political party.

Directed the Commission to identify *categories* of household products which may present an unreasonable hazard to consumers; to determine the effectiveness and extent of industry, federal, state and local laws and other requirements protecting the consumer from hazardous products; to report its findings and recommendations to Congress and the President not later than two years after S J Res 33 was enacted (therefore, by Nov. 20, 1969).

Required the Commission to publish "as soon as practicable" a list of categories of products that it proposed to study and to allow interested persons to submit views concerning any category on the list.

Authorized the Commission to hold hearings and subpena witnesses and documentary material. Permitted the Commission to receive information from federal agencies and to contract for studies in connection with its inquiry.

Required the Commission, prior to the publication of information about a product category, to notify all known manufacturers of the product of the planned publication and to allow the manufacturers 30 days in which to submit views on the publication to the Commission.

Exempted from review by the Commission products regulated under the National Traffic and Motor Vehicle Safety Act of 1966; the Flammable Fabrics Act;

the Federal Food, Drug and Cosmetics Act; the Federal Hazardous Substances Labeling Act; the Federal Cigarette Labeling and Advertising Act; the Federal Insecticide, Fungicide and Rodenticide Act; the Federal Firearms Act and the National Firearms Act.

Defined household products as products customarily produced or distributed for sale through retail agencies for use by a consumer or his family in or around the household.

Authorized an appropriation of $2 million to carry out the provisions of the resolution.

Auto Safety

The implementation of major new federal programs of automobile and highway safety was begun in 1967, following the enactment of landmark safety legislation by Congress in 1966.

Final standards covering motor vehicles, automobile tires and state highway safety programs were issued in 1967 by the National Highway Safety Bureau (NHSB). Two Senate committees also held hearings on automobile safety standards and highway safety programs. In legislative action, President Johnson Nov. 24 signed a bill (S 1522—PL 90-150) which made minor changes in the Highway Safety Act of 1966. The Senate also approved a bill (S 2029) to exempt certain limited-production vehicles from compliance with some of the federal safety requirements, but the House did not act.

Safety Agencies Consolidated. In a 1967 development which affected all federal safety efforts, President Johnson June 6 by Executive Order consolidated the National Traffic Safety Agency (NTSA) and the National Highway Safety Agency (NHSA) into a new bureau: the National Highway Safety Bureau (NHSB). Under the Department of Transportation Act of 1966 (PL 89-670), the President was authorized to combine the two agencies into a single unit which operated (after April 1, 1967) as part of the Transportation Department. Mr. Johnson also named William Haddon Jr., who previously had headed both safety agencies, as director of the new NHSB.

Auto Safety Standards. NTSA Jan. 31 issued 20 revised automobile safety standards for 1968 model-year cars. Of the 23 draft standards originally proposed Nov. 30, 1966, by the agency, three were omitted from the revised list, 14 were amended more or less extensively and adopted as final standards and six were amended and provisionally adopted, subject to further change after consultation with the automobile industry. Both domestic and foreign car manufacturers had claimed they would be unable to meet many of the original standards because of engineering difficulties and lack of sufficient "lead time."

Changes from Draft Standards—Major revisions of the original proposals included:

• Standards for pneumatic tires, tire selection and rims and installation of head restraints were "temporarily withdrawn" by the agency, pending further study and testing. *(For tire standards, see below.)*

• The mandatory deadline for compliance with all except one of the 20 standards was moved back from Sept. 1, 1967, to Jan. 1, 1968. The deadline for mandatory seat belts, March 1, 1967, was unchanged.

• Most foreign cars were excluded from requirements concerning windshield wiping, washing and defrosting systems and lighting systems. The agency announced, however, that standards for these vehicles would be adopted in the future.

• Special purpose vehicles, such as jeeps and campers, were placed in a special category so that all standards did not apply to them.

• Proposed measures to protect unrestrained children in cars were dropped from the final standards.

• Technical performance standards for a wide variety of specific construction and engineering details were lowered in the revised standards. These specifications ranged from the maximum permissible rearward displacement of the steering column in an accident, increased from three to five inches, to the degree of effectivness of outside rearview mirrors.

Reaction—Although NTSA Administrator Haddon defended the standards as "a major step" in reducing highway deaths, other reactions were less enthusiastic. Auto safety critic Ralph Nader, a key figure in the passage of 1966 safety legislation, called the revised standards "virtually meaningless." Nader said he thought Congress should investigate why the NTSA "performed so poorly."

Related Development—William I. Stieglitz, an NTSA consultant on auto safety who helped draft the original standards, resigned from the agency Feb. 2 in protest against what he called the "totally inadequate" revised standards. Stieglitz said the altered requirements were "so weakened from the proposed standards that...they do not establish an acceptable minimum level of safety." Haddon said that Stieglitz had proposed "completely unsound" standards and did not take seriously the legal requirement that standards "be practical." Haddon added that Stieglitz wanted to force industry to build cars that in some ways "approached or exceeded the performance of a Sherman tank."

Auto Industry Response—The general reaction to the safety requirements by the automobile industry was unfavorable. The companies asked for further changes or deletions covering 18 of the 20 standards, but the NTSA denied their requests, except for "minor technical amendments." The agency did agree, however, to hold public hearings on a controversial standard requiring interior impact protection for automobile occupants.

Interior Impact Protection—In later developments, Lowell K. Bridwell, the new Federal Highway Administrator, on Aug. 11 announced modification of the interior impact protection requirement which the auto companies said was impossible to meet before the Jan. 1, 1968, deadline. The standard was considered by some experts to be one of the most important of the 20 requirements issued Jan. 31.

The modified standard called for increased padding of car interiors, additional arm rests and energy-absorbing sun visors, but omitted requirements for extra knee and leg impact protection and for changes in interior knobs and handles. In his Aug. 11 announcement, Bridwell said the NHSB was "beginning work immediately on a substantially stronger standard" which would "be applied to automobiles sold in future years."

Tire Safety. Transportation Secretary Alan S. Boyd Nov. 10 announced final approval of two automobile tire safety standards which were formulated by the

National Highway Safety Bureau (NHSB) under the provisions of the National Traffic and Motor Vehicle Safety Act of 1966 (PL 89-563).

The standards, which applied to all types and sizes of new passenger car tires, were to become effective in three stages, beginning Jan. 1, 1968. One standard applied to tire manufacturers, while the other covered requirements for automobile manufacturers. Each standard contained several provisions.

In issuing the tire standards, Boyd said he was "confident" that the new regulations, together with the 20 auto safety standards previously approved by his Department, would "bring us closer to the day when... injury and death on the road...will largely be the result of human error and not of design or equipment deficiencies.

The standards included the following provisions, effective on the dates indicated:

Jan. 1, 1968—Required temporary labels or tags to be affixed to tires manufactured on or after this date disclosing the size designation, maximum inflation pressure, composition of the tire material, number of plies in sidewall and tread areas and other information, including the marking "DOT" which showed compliance with applicable federal standards.

April 1, 1968—Required passenger cars built on or after this date to be equipped with tires suitable for the maximum loaded weight of the vehicle. Specified wheel rim standards to ensure that in case of a blowout at 60 miles an hour, the tire could be held on the rim until the car was stopped. Required new cars to carry a permanent placard on the glove compartment door (or similar convenient place) listing recommended tire size, optimum tire inflation pressure for maximum loads, designated seating capacity and the maximum load that the original tires on the car were designed to carry.

Aug. 1, 1968—Required tires manufactured on or after this date to have the information listed in the Jan. 1, 1968 labeling requirement molded permanently into both sidewalls of all tires. Required tires to be equipped with a tread wear indicator showing clearly when only one-sixteenth inch of tread remained.

Highway Safety. Transportation Secretary Alan S. Boyd on June 27 issued 13 final standards for state highway safety programs, under the Highway Safety Act of 1966 (PL 89-564). Except for one major change, the standards were subtstantially the same as tentative draft standards which were announced Feb. 16 by the Department of Transportation.

One of the 13 draft standards, requiring annual state inspections of all vehicles, was changed in the final version to allow a state to substitute experimental or pilot inspection plans, subject to approval by the Transportation Secretary. The proposed mandatory annual inspection was opposed by states—including California— which already used a "spot check" inspection system. The requirement also was opposed by the American Automobile Assn., which urged "substantial changes" in the 13 draft standards.

Under the 1966 Act, federal funds for state programs were available on a 50-50 matching basis. The Act also provided for a possible 10-percent reduction in federal-aid highway construction funds for any state which had failed to incorporate the federal standards in state safety programs.

Major safety measures included in the standards were:

• Annual inspection of all motor vehicles and additional inspections when vehicles were sold, resold or registered in another state, except a state with an inspection program approved by the Transportation Department.

• Re-examination of all licensed drivers at least every four years, with more frequent testing of persons under 25 years of age and over 65.

• Requirement that states prohibit persons from driving if the alcohol concentration in their blood equals or exceeds one-tenth of 1 percent. The standard also required drivers to submit to alcohol blood tests.

• Establishment of driver training programs for all high school students, with state licensing of driving instructors.

Other standards required uniform traffic laws throughout a state, standardized highway markers and traffic signals, coordination of statewide emergency medical services, central motor vehicle registration, central traffic court records and a uniform accounting system for fines, statewide traffic data systems, identification and improvement of highway localities with a high accident rate, maintenance of existing highways in safe condition and special regulations for motorcycle safety.

Highway Safety Act Amendments. In a related development, President Johnson signed into law on Nov. 24 an amended bill (S 1552—PL 90-150) increasing the size of the National Highway Safety Advisory Committee which was established under the Highway Safety Act of 1966. S 1552 authorized the appointment of 35 members to the Advisory Committee, instead of 29 members as originally provided by the 1966 Act. The additional members were to represent major highway user organizations, such as the American Automobile Assn. and the American Trucking Assns. These groups currently were not formally represented on the Advisory Committee. The Committee's function was to consult with the Transportation Secretary on highway safety programs and projects.

The legislation was opposed by the Transportation Department and the Budget Bureau. Both agencies believed that sufficient latitude existed in the 1966 Act to permit the appointment of spokesmen for highway user groups to the Advisory Committee.

Auto Insurance

Increasing concern about the nation's automobile insurance system came to Congressional attention in 1967. Events in 1967 led in 1968 to formal Congressional authorization of a federal study of the auto insurance industry.

The major 1967 development occurred in November when the House Judiciary Committee voted 17-14 to recommend a "full-scale, intensive investigation" of auto insurance company practices by the Federal Trade Commission. (However, the study authorized in 1968 was assigned to the Transportation Department.)

Background. Growing Congressional concern in 1967 over the automobile insurance industry was prompted by increasing numbers of public complaints about the rising cost of insurance and the difficulty of obtaining—and maintaining—insurance coverage.

The Federal Government currently exercised little regulatory jurisdiction over the insurance industry, which was exempted from effective coverage of federal anti-trust laws by the McCarran-Ferguson Act of 1945 (PL 79-15). The 1945 Act made insurance companies subject to antitrust laws only to the extent that they were not regulated by state law. Much of the criticism in 1967 of company practices was directed at the alleged inadequacy of state regulation. *(For the 1945 Act, see Congress and the Nation Vol. I, 454.)*

Judiciary Committee Action. The House Judiciary Committee endorsed the recommendation of a five-member ad hoc subcommittee on auto insurance. In a Nov. 16 press statement, Committee Chairman Emanuel Celler (D N.Y.) said there was "no question about the need" for a thorough investigation, adding that "the existing system of state regulation of the...industry...does not ...adequately protect the public."

The Judiciary Committee's interest in auto insurance began July 25, when Celler asked the staff of Judiciary Subcommittee No. 5, which deals with antitrust matters, to prepare a study of the auto insurance industry. The 183-page staff report, which was highly critical of industry practices, was completed Sept. 30 and released to the public Oct. 24.

In his Sept. 30 letter of transmittal to Judiciary Committee members, which accompanied the staff report, Celler noted that "a broad cross section of the American driving public" was "gravely disturbed by allegedly unfair and arbitrary insurance company action."

Report—The staff report concluded that "by any objective standard, performance of the automobile insurance business...is unsatisfactory. The system is slow, incomplete and expensive." The study recommended that the Federal Trade Commission be empowered to conduct a full-scale examination and analysis of the industry.

The materials for the Subcommittee report included answers to a questionnaire sent to a selected sample of 19 automobile insurance companies and three insurance rating organizations, investigation of complaints received by the Judiciary Committee and comprehensive data on current state regulatory practices. The information gathered made it "abundantly clear," the report said, that a comprehensive long-range study was needed. "Virtually all interests...recognized," the staff noted, "that changes are needed in the present system."

The report contended that current insurance protection was inadequate to meet the need for coverage. Citing a "comprehensive" 1964 Michigan study, the Subcommittee noted that "in the aggregate, reparation for...accident losses amounted to roughly one-half...of the economic losses" caused by accidents. A major defect of the existing system, the report added, was that "the injured victim deals not with his own insurance company, but with the... company, if there is one, of the person who caused his injury." The system encouraged recourse to the courts to settle negligence cases, the Subcommittee found, which "threaten to overwhelm the court system." Studies indicated that the average delay in bringing cases to trial in major urban areas was more than 31 months, with average delays of more than 69 months in Cook County, Ill. (Chicago).

The report also criticized state regulation of insurance companies. State regulating agencies, which often were hampered by low salary levels and inadequate personnel, placed "too great a reliance on an industry that is all too willing to assist in the processes of its own regulation," the

study concluded. The cost of automobile insurance in many areas rose "more than 30 percent" in the 1960-66 period, the study showed, while the consumer price index rose only 10 points in the same period.

The report also cited individual "case studies" in which private persons had been denied insurance coverage or refused continuation of coverage for seemingly trivial reasons. Some of the cases required "further investigation and consideration," the report said. These cases included "allegations of fraud, kickbacks and rebates" in automobile repair shops and alleged improper activities of "private investigators in the insurance business."

Gas Pipeline Safety

Gas pipeline safety, a consumer issue which had been on the back burner for many years, was given serious consideration by Congress in 1967. The Senate passed a bill (S 1166) to improve pipeline safety but the House did not complete action until 1968. The legislation was subjected to intense lobbying by the gas industry, which did not want increased federal regulation.

S 1166 as passed by the Senate authorized the Transportation Secretary to set minimum standards for safety of some 800,000 miles of gas pipelines across the United States. The bill specified that standards would not apply to existing pipelines unless the Secretary found that a "potentially hazardous situation" existed. Coverage of existing pipelines was a major issue because the industry feared it would be burdened with heavy expenses of repairing or replacing lines if strict safety standards were applied to them.

The Senate passed S 1166 by a 78-0 roll call.

Fire Safety

Congress did not complete action in 1967 on bills (S 1124, HR 11284) authorizing a federal program of research and development into ways of lessening the death and destruction caused by fire in the United States. Action was completed in 1968.

The Senate passed its version (S 1124) by voice vote in August. The House Science and Astronautics Committee reported a House bill (HR 11284) but the House Democratic leadership did not schedule it for a vote in 1967.

President Johnson requested the legislation in his Feb. 16 message to Congress on consumer protection. He said the Act would be part of a "major national effort to reduce our shameful loss of life and property from fires."

Bills carrying out what Mr. Johnson outlined in his message were introduced in the House and Senate. They authorized a program of contracts and grants to state and local governments and to nonprofit private organizations to conduct: comprehensive investigations into the nature and causes of fires; public education programs in fire prevention; a clearinghouse for information on fires; training programs for fire services; and demonstration projects in fire prevention and control. The program would be administered by the Commerce Department's National Bureau of Standards (NBS) at a Fire Research and Safety Center. The NBS would be authorized to pay up to 100 percent of the cost of these projects.

The bills passed by the Senate and reported in the House contained these provisions and, in addition, incorporated provisions establishing a National Commission on Fire Prevention and Control to evaluate existing fire control programs at the federal and local levels and to recommend new programs.

Other Bills

RADIATION EMISSION. Hearings were held in both the House and the Senate during 1967 on bills authorizing establishment of federal standards regulating the radiation emission from consumer electronic devices. No further action was taken, but legislation was enacted in 1968.

President Johnson in his Feb. 16 message on consumer protection asked Congress to establish radiation standards to ensure the safety of certain medical devices, including X-ray equipment—a purpose which the bills introduced in 1967 would have accomplished.

MAIL FRAUDS. Congress considered but did not complete action on a bill (HR 1411) to protect consumers against deceptive mail-order schemes. Action was requested by President Johnson to put a stop to fraudulent mail-order land sales—a purpose HR 1411 would have helped to accomplish. *(See following story.)*

The House passed HR 1411 in October. The Senate passed it in December but first added an unrelated amendment authorizing the Civil Service Commission to add 129 new supergrade (GS 16-18) positions to its roster for distribution among federal agencies hard-pressed for high-level personnel. In the House, an economy advocate, Durward G. Hall (R Mo.), objected to the supergrade amendment and prevented House action on the issue before adjournment. The bill was passed in 1968, but without the supergrade amendment.

LAND SALE FRAUDS. The Senate Banking and Currency Committee's Securities Subcommittee held two days of hearings on a bill (S 275) to prevent frauds in interstate land sales. The legislation was requested by President Johnson in his Feb. 16 consumer protection message. In his message, Mr. Johnson noted that many elderly persons had been swindled by mail-order land offers.

In its major provisions, S 275 required an interstate developer of a subdivision (25 lots or more) to file with the Securities and Exchange Commission a registration statement containing a legal description and other pertinent information about the property. The developer was to supply buyers a prospectus disclosing the same information.

S 275 was not enacted in 1967. However, in 1968 Congress in an omnibus housing bill (S 3497—PL 90-448) added a title (Title XIV) which was similar to the 1967 proposal. Title XIV required the developer to file information with the Housing and Urban Development Department. Information required included the title of the land, its physical nature, and the availability of roads and utilities. Prospective purchasers had to be provided the same information. The HUD Secretary could sue for injunctions against violations of the title. Criminal penalties of up to $5,000 fine and/or five years imprisonment were provided. Civil liabilities against persons selling or leasing lots in violation of the title also were provided.

1968

Truth In Lending

Congress in 1968 enacted into law a truth-in-lending bill (S 5—PL 90-321) to help consumers make informed decisions when they obtain credit.

The legislation was one of the toughest and most far-reaching consumer bills enacted by Congress in many years. Enactment came in the 90th Congress after almost a decade of controversy which kept the legislation buried in committee. The first truth-in-lending bill was introduced by Sen. Paul H. Douglas (D Ill. 1949-67) in 1959. Although Douglas was no longer a Member of Congress when the proposals he championed were approved in 1968, the bill that was signed into law by the President May 29, 1968, included the essence of his earlier measures: disclosure to consumers of useful information about credit transactions.

Truth in lending was a label which described bills that required lenders and other consumer creditors to provide their customers full, honest and—most importantly—comparable information about the cost of the credit the consumers were buying. The heart of these bills was a requirement that buyers be told the cost of loans and installment purchase plans in terms of an annual rate calculated under certain specified procedures by all lenders and creditors. The resulting uniformity was intended to permit consumers to make valid cost comparisons between the lending rates or installment plans of different stores or lending institutions just as they could compare the prices of, say, automobiles or washing machines manufactured by different companies. This generally was not possible from the mish-mash of rates and lending conditions cited by creditors under current conditions in the marketplace unless the consumer went to considerable pains by using complex mathematical formulae to make different quoted figures comparable.

Another key section of the legislation required the lender or businessman to tell the customer the total cost in dollars of the credit that was being extended.

The law did not in any way fix a minimum or maximum charge for credit. It was designed only to assure the customer that he had adequate information about the charge. In addition, the law did not cover all types of credit. Exempted from the law were business and commercial credit other than for agricultural purposes, credit transactions of more than $25,000 (other than transactions secured by real estate which were covered regardless of the amount), transactions in securities or commodities with a broker-dealer registered with the Securities and Exchange Commission, and some types of transactions with regulated public utilities.

The law thus was aimed strictly at consumer credit which was defined as credit offered or extended to a person primarily for personal, family, household or agricultural purposes and for which a finance charge is or may be imposed or which is repayable in more than four installments.

The Federal Reserve Board was given the task of drafting regulations to implement the law. The Board issued its regulations (Regulation Z) on Feb. 10, 1969. The Board said the regulations applied to banks, savings and loan associations, department stores, credit-card

Background

The first truth-in-lending bill was introduced by Sen. Paul H. Douglas (D Ill. 1949-67) in 1959. That bill and others introduced in the 87th, 88th and 89th Congresses all failed of enactment.

86th Congress (1959-60). S 2755 was approved in 1960 by the Banking and Currency Subcommittee on Production and Stabilization which Douglas headed. The disclosure procedure, outlined in the bill, required that the consumer know both the dollars and cents cost and the "simple annual rate"—a percentage based on all the charges over and above the purchase price of the item or the principal of the loan. Douglas' bill was opposed by the Eisenhower Administration. The full Committee took no action on S 2755.

87th Congress (1961-62). Douglas in 1961 introduced a bill (S 1740) that was similar in most respects to his earlier bill, S 2755. In hearings on S 1740, opponents argued that a simple annual rate would be difficult to apply to revolving credit accounts offered by many retail stores. The critics argued that because the balance owed under such plans was continually shifting through purchases and payments, the requirement for a simple annual rate would mean a merchant would have to compute a new yearly rate every time a customer bought a new item.

These objections, and others raised in the 1961 hearings, prompted new hearings in 1962 to consider amendments to S 1740. Among the amendments was a provision directing that a merchant disclose a simple annual rate on two occasions: at the time the customer entered into a revolving plan agreement and on every monthly statement.

President Kennedy endorsed truth-in-lending legislation. However, the bill was unanimously condemned by credit industry spokesmen who claimed it would create "fear, doubt and distrust."

The Subcommittee, by a 4-5 vote, rejected S 1740.

88th Congress (1963-64). Douglas' third truth-in-lending bill (S 750) required the same disclosures outlined in his previous bills. However, the bill contained a provision which, in effect, exempted the revolving credit accounts from the bill by permitting merchants to express the finance charges in terms of a monthly rate. S 750 was endorsed by President Kennedy's Consumer Advisory Council and, as before, opposed by representatives of business and the credit industry. In his 1964 consumer message, President Johnson urged that the bill be enacted.

Douglas' Subcommittee approved S 750 by a 5-4 vote in 1964. However, Sen. A. Willis Robertson (D Va.), chairman of the full Committee and an opponent of truth-in-lending legislation, was long in placing the bill on the Committee's calendar. After a bitter exchange of letters and floor speeches between Robertson and Douglas, the Committee voted 8-6 to recommit the bill to the Production and Stabilization Subcommittee, thus in effect killing it.

89th Congress (1965-66). Although Douglas again introduced a truth-in-lending bill (S 2275), no action was taken in either the House or the Senate. President Johnson in 1965 and in 1966 endorsed truth-in-lending legislation.

issuers, credit unions, automobile dealers, consumer finance companies, residential mortgage brokers, craftsmen such as plumbers and electricians, doctors, dentists, hospitals and any other individuals or groups which extend or arrange for consumer credit.

Although the Board was assigned to write the regulations, enforcement was spread through nine different federal agencies including the Board. *(See provisions for a list of agencies.)*

Summary of Major Provisions

The heart of S 5 was the requirement for disclosure of information about credit. But the bill contained a number of other provisions, most of which were added in the House and which greatly strengthened S 5 as it had passed the Senate in 1967.

Following is a summary of the bill.

Truth in Lending. The major part of the legislation was contained in Title I which covered credit disclosures and was entitled the Truth-in-Lending Act (the entire bill was called the Consumer Credit Protection Act).

Title I required creditors such as a store or loan company to give the consumer in writing certain specified information about the extension of credit. This had to be done before the credit was given. The most important information that had to be disclosed was the finance charge and the annual percentage rate.

The *finance charge* was the total of all costs imposed by the creditor and paid by the consumer as a condition of obtaining credit. It included such items as interest, service or carrying charges, loan fees, points, appraisal fees, charges for investigations or credit reports (except in real estate transactions), and premiums for credit life insurance that are required by the creditor before credit will be given. Items which could be excluded from the finance charge, if itemized and separately disclosed to the consumer, included: taxes not included in the cash price of the article; license, certificate of title and registration fees imposed by law; the premium paid for insurance in lieu of allowing the creditor a security interest in the property, but only up to certain limits; and fees paid public officials under law for such things as title and mortgage searches. In addition, certain charges paid in connection with real estate transactions could be excluded if they are reasonable in amount and do not destroy the purpose of the disclosure requirements of the law. These could include charges for title examination and insurance, surveys, deed preparation and settlement payments, appraisal fees and credit report charges.

The *annual percentage rate*, the second of the two key elements in the required disclosures, represented the relationship of the total finance charge to the total amount financed. It had to be computed to the nearest one-quarter of 1 percent. The rate had to be in terms of what is commonly called the "true" annual interest rate. This is the rate on the amount of money that a consumer actually has available for his use over the repayment period.

In a commonly cited example, it would work like this: if a consumer borrowed $100 with a finance charge of $6 and repaid the loan in 12 months in equal installments, he would have had the use—on the average—of approximately one-half of the original amount of credit over the course of the year. Under existing conditions, lenders usually would say the loan was made at 6 percent. However, under the requirements in S 5, the rate would be measured against the declining amount or the amount actually in use and this would produce a "true" annual percentage rate of about 11 percent; this is the figure that would have to be given to the consumer.

In practice, the rates cited to consumers were expected to be obtained from standard tables prepared under Government supervision. But in any event, the figures cited would be comparable from one store or bank to another.

Until Jan. 1, 1971, the rate cited to consumers could be expressed—if the creditor desired to do so—in dollars per hundred. Thus in the above example the rate would be cited as $11 per $100. This was to avoid any possible conflict with state usury laws which frequently limited interest to amounts lower than those expected to be cited to consumers under current market conditions. It was assumed that states would change their laws by 1971, when the rate would have to be expressed as an annual percentage—11 percent in the example.

The disclosure requirements were to go into effect on July 1, 1969.

An exemption from the disclosure requirements was provided for small amounts. The annual percentage rate did not have to be given if the finance charge was no more than $5 on amounts up to $75 and was less than $7.50 on amounts above $75.

Revolving Credit. A major controversy which delayed enactment of S 5 involved the treatment of the increasingly popular open-ended credit arrangements. These were better known as revolving charge accounts. They usually were offered by department stores and central credit agencies serving numerous small businesses. The accounts typically had an interest charge of $1\frac{1}{2}$ percent a month on the balance owed. The Senate required only that the monthly rate be stated, but the House required that this be translated into the nominal annual rate—18 percent in the case of $1\frac{1}{2}$-percent monthly charges.

The final bill required that both the periodic (usually monthly) and the nominal annual rate be stated. This was a victory for the House and for advocates of a strong truth-in-lending provision on revolving credit. But in addition, the final bill allowed an optional third interest rate to be given the consumer. This was to be the average effective annual interest rate earned or expected to be earned by the store on its revolving account business. This usually would be somewhat less than the nominal rate because it would take account of the "free-time" which customers have (usually a month) before they are charged interest.

As a result of this compromise, a typical revolving charge-account bill received each month by a consumer could have three interest rates stated on it: the monthly rate, the nominal annual rate, and the effective annual rate on the store's revolving account business.

Credit Advertising. The bill required that advertisements for credit which gave some details on the terms provide enough information to be meaningful. The information which had to be included, if any was given at all, was spelled out in the bill. The provisions also required an advertiser to be able to meet the claims he made in an ad.

Mortgages. First mortgages generally were brought under the disclosure requirements of the bill. However, home lenders were not required to provide the total dollar cost of the financing charge on a mortgage. The interest charge over the life of a home mortgage often is as much as or more than the cost of the home itself, and mortgage lenders feared that disclosure of this fact might frighten away some potential home buyers. Generally, the home mortgage business already stated interest rates as a true annual percentage rate. Thus, it was expected that S 5 would have relatively little effect on the home loan industry.

The bill imposed new restrictions aimed at ending fraudulent second mortgage practices which had bilked many low-income persons in recent years. Typically, fast-talking salesmen selling everything from color television sets to home intercom systems would get these home-owners to sign second mortgages on their property without explaining the nature of the papers that were signed. Frequently, the home-owners, unable to meet the payments on the improvements or products they had purchased, would lose their homes.

The second mortgage provisions of S 5, which were a Republican proposal sponsored in the House by Rep. William T. Cahill (R N.J.), gave the home owner three days in which to cancel any agreement into which he had entered involving a second mortgage. In addition, any security interest in property must be clearly explained to the consumer as involving a mortgage or lien. The consumer was given the right to cancel absolutely and unconditionally even if the mortgage paper had been sold to another person who was not aware of the fraudulent nature of the transaction.

Garnishment. A provision of the bill, which was added in the House, imposed restrictions on the amount of money that a creditor could garnishee from the paycheck of a consumer who was in debt to him. No more than 25 percent of the worker's take-home pay (after deductions for taxes and the like) would be garnisheed. A flat $48 weekly exemption from garnishment was provided for low-income workers even if that was more than 75 percent of their take-home pay.

Loan Sharking. The final bill also included a Republican proposal sponsored by Rep. Richard H. Poff (R Va.) to fight "loan sharking" by criminals. In the bill, the section was called extortionate credit transactions. Making or financing extortionate extensions of credit and attempting to collect any extension of credit by extortionate means was made a federal offense subject to maximum penalties of $10,000 and 20 years' imprisonment. "Extortionate" was defined to mean the use of violence to collect the amounts due on the loans. In order to avoid the problem of witnesses who are reluctant to testify because of their fear of personal harm, the bill provided that extortion would be presumed to exist if certain conditions were proved. They were spelled out in the provisions.

Republicans said the provisions were aimed at organized crime, which was said to profit greatly from extortionate credit.

LEGISLATIVE HISTORY

The long deadlock over truth in lending was broken in 1967 when Sen. William Proxmire (D Wis.) took charge of the legislation following the 1966 election defeat of Sen. Paul H. Douglas (D Ill.), the original chief backer of the proposal.

Proxmire was more willing than Douglas to bargain with the credit industry to write a bill the industry felt it could live with. The more flexible approach taken by Proxmire permitted a bill (S 5) to be passed by the Senate by mid-1967. A key compromise was to exempt revolving credit from the requirement of annual rate disclosure. Retailers using this form of credit were required to give only the periodic (usually monthly) interest rate.

In the House, the Banking and Currency Committee was working on its own bill, HR 11601. The Committee accepted the basic disclosure requirements of S 5, including an exemption from disclosure of an annual interest rate for revolving accounts. In addition, the Committee added various features to the bill which the Senate did not consider. The bill was reported Dec. 13, 1967.

When HR 11601 came to the House floor in late January 1968, support for the revolving credit compromise had declined. This was attributed in part to lobbying efforts by banks and other lenders who had to disclose annual interest rates under the bill and did not want any exemptions for revolving credit. In addition, several major department stores had switched their positions to oppose the revolving credit exemption. As a result, the House struck the exemption from the bill, added provisions on second mortgages and loan sharking and passed it Feb. 1 by a **383-4** key roll-call vote.

A recommittal motion offered by James A. McClure (R Idaho) to kill HR 11601 was defeated by voice vote. Voting against passage were McClure, Thomas G. Abernethy (D Miss.), G. V. Montgomery (D Miss.) and Robert G. Stephens Jr. (D Ga.).

House passage of S 5 was preceded by three days of debate beginning Jan. 30.

Revolving Accounts, $10 Exemption. The focus of the debate was Leonor K. Sullivan's (D Mo.) effort to strike from HR 11601 annual rate disclosure exemptions for revolving charge accounts and for loans on which the finance charge came to less than $10. The House Jan. 31 by a 19-131 standing vote, rejected a Committee amendment exempting retail revolving accounts from providing annual rate disclosures. The small-loan amendment, also contained in the Committee bill, was rejected the same day by voice vote.

Mrs. Sullivan, floor manager of the bill, said the two exemptions were "special interest, anticonsumer...loopholes" which had been "lifted almost verbatim from the Senate bill." There was no reason to include the exemptions in HR 11601 "other than to weaken the legislation," she said.

Her appeal to vote down a Committee amendment excluding revolving charge accounts from annual disclosure, Mrs. Sullivan said, was "the moment of truth for truth-in-lending."

Business support for the revolving charge exemption, she said, had crumbled to almost nothing. She reported that she had received telegrams Jan. 29 from representatives of three of the largest catalogue houses—Spiegel's, Montgomery Ward and Sears Roebuck—all of which offered revolving charge plans and had supported the exemption in hearings before the Committee. All three, Mrs. Sullivan said, now opposed the annual rate exemption.

No support was expressed for the $10 finance charge exemption—even by members of the Committee which had written the amendment into HR 11601.

Loan Sharking. The House Jan. 31, by voice vote, accepted an amendment—later confirmed Feb. 1 by a

383-5 roll-call vote—placing severe federal penalties on loan sharks and their associates who charge interest rates in excess of the usury levels set in most states.

The amendment, offered by Richard H. Poff (R Va.), was identified by Minority Leader Gerald R. Ford Jan. 30, as part of a GOP anticrime program announced in December 1967.

Poff explained that the "thrust of this amendment is to fix a federal definition of the crime of usury." Patterned on the "anti-racketeering" sections of the Criminal Code (Title 18), the amendment would make it a federal crime, with a $10,000 penalty, to practice loan sharking. The term was defined to mean the lending of money at rates prohibited by state usury statutes. Poff said the amendment also would "activate the investigating arm of the Federal Government" to help enforce the usury laws of state and local governments. (Usury laws, in effect in 43 states, set a limit, generally 6 percent, on interest. Some states, however, had usury limits of up to 240 percent.)

In the 383-5 roll-call vote, accepting Poff's amendment, the five who voted against it were Reps. Emanuel Celler (D N.Y.), chairman of the Judiciary Committee, Bob Eckhardt (D Texas), Frank E. Evans (D Colo.), Henry B. Gonzalez (D Texas) and James H. Scheuer (D N.Y.).

Conference Action. Conferees on the bill did not reach agreement until May 15, primarily because of disagreement over the revolving charge account section. The conference report was filed May 20 and was adopted by voice votes of the House and Senate May 22.

Conferees required disclosure of interest rates on all revolving charge accounts on both an annual and monthly basis (such as 18 percent a year and 1½ percent a month). In addition, the bill gave stores the option of disclosing an "effective" interest rate to be calculated by dividing total annual income from revolving credit by annual earnings from interest rates on revolving accounts. This meant a store which earned $100,000 in interest on revolving charge accounts that took in a total of $1 million from those accounts could indicate an "effective" interest rate of 10 percent. As a result of this provision, a monthly department-store bill for a revolving charge account might show three different interest rates.

Conferees accepted a Republican-sponsored House floor amendment aimed at combating fraudulent second mortgage practices which had bilked many low-income persons in recent years. The compromise measure also prohibited the "extortionate extension of credit," originally contained in the House bill as an amendment prohibiting loan sharking.

Provisions

As signed into law, S 5, the Consumer Credit Protection Act, contained the following major provisions:

TITLE I—TRUTH-IN-LENDING ACT

Open-End Consumer Credit (Revolving Credit). Required a creditor to disclose the following information about an open-end consumer credit account on every bill sent out to cover a payment period:

• The outstanding balance at the beginning of the period; the amount and number of purchases charged to the account; and the amount of any finance charge added to the account during the period.

• The periodic rate used to compute the finance charge and the corresponding annual percentage rate, determined by multiplying the periodic rate by the number of periods in a year (typically, this would be 1½ percent a month and 18 percent a year).

• The balance on which the finance charge was computed and a statement of how the balance was determined; the outstanding balance in the account at the end of the period; and the date by which a payment must be made to avoid an additional finance charge.

Permitted the creditor at his discretion to state—in addition to the periodic and annual rate—a third rate: the average effective annual percentage rate actually or expected to be earned by the company on the type of accounts covered by this section of the bill.

Exempted from the interest-rate disclosure requirement finance charges of 50 cents or less a month on small balances. (In a typical situation where a store charges 1½ percent a month, the finance charge would be 50 cents on a $33 balance. If the balance dropped below $33 and the store charged a minimum of 50 cents, the actual rate would rise above the usual monthly rate but this higher rate would not have to be stated by the store.)

New Accounts—Required a store before opening a new account for a customer to disclose substantially the same information about billing procedures, finance charges and interest rates as he must include on regular bills.

Consumer Sales Not Under Open-End Credit Plans. Required a creditor to disclose the following information to a customer before he extended credit for the purchase of property or service:

• The cash price of the property or service minus any downpayment, and any charges other than the finance charge which are part of the credit extended.

• The total amount to be financed and the amount of the finance charge expressed in dollars and cents (except that the finance charge on the purchase of a house did not have to be stated).

• The finance charge expressed as an annual percentage rate except if the charge did not exceed (1) $5 on an amount financed up to $75 and (2) $7.50 on an amount financed above $75. Specified that a creditor could not divide the credit into two or more sales to avoid disclosure of the interest rate.

• The number, amount and due dates or periods of payments; the default, delinquency or similar charges resulting from late payments; and a description of any security interest required by the creditor.

Provided methods to meet these requirements in the case of mail order or telephone sales.

Consumer Loans Not Under Open-End Credit Plans. Required a lender to disclose the following information to a customer before he made a consumer loan:

• The amount of credit which will be actually available to the consumer, any charges other than the finance charge included in the credit extended and the resulting total amount to be financed.

• The amount of the finance charge, expressed in dollars and cents (except that the finance charge did not have to be disclosed in the case of a loan for the purchase of a house).

• The finance charge expressed as an annual percentage rate, except if the charge did not exceed (1) $5 on a loan of up to $75 and (2) $7.50 on a loan of more than $75.

Specified that a lender could not divide the loan into two or more parts to avoid disclosure of the interest rate.

• The number, amount and due dates or periods of payments; the default, delinquency or similar charges resulting from late payments; and a description of any security interest required by the lender.

Provided methods to meet these requirements in the case of loans made by mail or telephone.

Finance Charge. Required that a finance charge which must be disclosed to the consumer include all direct and indirect charges paid by the consumer to obtain the credit, including such items as interest, amounts payable under a point or discount system, service or carrying charges, loan fees, investigation or credit report charges and premiums protecting the creditor against loss.

Required that charges for credit life, accident or health insurance be included in the finance charge unless the coverage was not required to obtain the credit and this was disclosed in writing to the consumer, and the consumer indicated his desire to have the coverage after receiving written disclosure of the cost.

Required that charges for property and liability insurance be included in the finance charge unless the creditor discloses to the consumer in writing that the consumer may obtain the insurance from a source other than the creditor.

Excluded from the finance charge were certain specified items such as legal fees paid to public officials, taxes, and charges usually made in connection with the purchase of a home or other real property (such as deed preparation, title examination, etc.).

Annual Percentage Rate. Specified the methods to be used to determine the annual percentage rate on the types of credit covered by the bill so as to provide consumers with figures that were comparable from one store or lending institution to another.

Authorized the use of rate tables to determine annual percentage rates.

Permitted annual percentage rates cited to consumers under methods approved by federal officials to vary slightly from a rate based on precise mathematical calculations.

Permitted any percentage rate required by the bill to be stated in dollars per hundred until Jan. 1, 1971, after which it would have to be expressed as a percentage figure. (Thus a 9½-percent interest rate on a loan could be expressed as $9 per $100 until 1971. This was to avoid any possible conflict with state usury laws, many of which limited interest to smaller percentages. Presumably, the states would change their laws by 1971.)

Penalties. Provided criminal penalties of up to $5,000 in fines and/or one year imprisonment for violation of the disclosure requirements of the bill.

Provided civil penalties as follows: any creditor who fails to disclose information to a consumer as required by the law is liable to the consumer for (1) twice the amount of the finance charge, with a minimum payment of $100 and a maximum payment of $1,000 and (2) the costs, including an attorney's fee, to enforce the liability.

Provided a grace period of 15 days for a creditor to correct an error in disclosure of information without suffering liability. Permitted a creditor to avoid liability by proving an error was not intentional.

Credit Advertising. Provided that advertisements of credit meet certain disclosure requirements, as follows:

Credit Other Than Open-End (Revolving) Plans—
Provided that if an advertisement stated the rate of a finance charge, it must express the rate as an annual percentage rate.

Provided that if an advertisement stated the amount of a downpayment, the amount of an installment payment, the dollar amount of a finance charge or the number of installments or the period of repayment, then it must also state all of the following: (1) the cash price or the amount of the loan; (2) the downpayment; (3) the number, amount and due dates or period of payments; and (4) the rate of the finance charge expressed as an annual percentage rate.

Specified that this section applied to a consumer credit sale, loan or other credit extension other than open-end credit, but exempted advertisements for residential real estate except to the extent that the Federal Reserve Board may require by regulation.

*Open-End (Revolving) Credit Plans—*Required that any advertisement for this type of credit which gave any specific terms of the plan or the effective interest rate earned by a store on this type of credit must also state all of the following information: (1) the time period for repayment without incurring a finance charge; (2) the method of determining the balance upon which a finance charge is based; (3) the method of determining a finance charge, including any minimum charge; (4) any periodic rate (if that is used) expressed as an annual percentage rate; and (5) such other information as the Federal Reserve Board may require to allow adequate comparison of credit costs between different plans.

*Downpayment, Installment Advertising—*Prohibited advertising claims of consumer credit amounts, installment amounts or downpayments unless the creditor "usually and customarily" meets the claims set forth in the advertisement. (This provision was intended to halt the practice of bait-and-switch advertising.)

*Exemption—*Exempted publications and other media from liability under the advertising section.

Second Mortgages. Allowed a consumer three days in which to cancel a consumer credit agreement in which an interest in any real property used as his residence is obtained by the creditor as security for the credit. Provided that the three-day period for recision would follow consummation of the agreement or the delivery of disclosures required under the law.

Required the creditor clearly and conspicuously to disclose the rights of the consumer under this section, and the fact that a security interest in property involved a second mortgage or lien.

Specified that the three-day cancellation privilege did not apply in the case of an ordinary purchase of a home through a first mortgage.

Regulation, Enforcement. Provided that regulations to carry out the law would be prescribed by the Federal Reserve Board.

Specified that enforcement would be carried out by the courts and by those federal agencies with specific responsibility for separate segments of the credit industry or other segments of commerce, as follows: the Federal Reserve Board for state banks which are members of the Federal Reserve System; the Federal Deposit Insurance Corp. for other insured state banks which are not members of the Federal Reserve System; the Comptroller of the Currency for national banks; the Federal Home Loan Bank Board for institutions insured by the Federal Savings and Loan Insurance Corp. and for members of the FHLB System other than those insured by the FDIC; the Bureau of Federal Credit Unions; the Interstate Commerce Commission for industries it regulates; the Civil Aeronautics Board for airlines; the Agriculture Department for creditors under the Packers and Stockyards Act, and the Federal Trade Commission for all other creditors including department stores and other retailers.

Exempted Transactions. Specified that Title I did not apply to (1) business or commercial credit transactions, governmental agencies or organizations; (2) securities or commodities transactions by a broker-dealer registered with the Securities and Exchange Commission; (3) transactions in which the amount to be financed exceeds $25,000; and (4) transactions for public utility services which are under state regulation.

State Laws. Specified that Title I did not annul or alter any state law not inconsistent with the federal law, or exempt any creditor from complying with state laws on the same subject.

Reports. Required the Federal Reserve Board and the Attorney General on Jan. 3 of each year after 1969 to report to Congress on the administration of Title I.

TITLE II—EXTORTIONATE CREDIT TRANSACTIONS (LOAN SHARKING)

Definition. Defined extortionate extension of credit as the extension of any credit in which both the creditor and the debtor understand when the credit is extended that delay in repayment or failure to repay could result in the use of violence or other criminal means to cause harm to the person, reputation or property of any individual.

Charging Extortionate Credit. Provided that any person making extortionate extension of credit would be subject to fines of up to $10,000 and/or 20 years in prison.

Specified that extortion would be presumed to exist if the prosecution in a court case could prove all of the following four factors: (1) The lender was legally unable to collect the amount due under state laws; (2) the interest rate on the loan was more than 45 percent on an annual basis; (3) the lender had a reputation for extortion in the community of which the borrower was a member; (4) the loan was more than $100.

Collection of Credit by Extortion. Provided penalties of up to $10,000 in fines and/or 20 years' imprisonment for any person who uses extortionate means to collect or attempt to collect on any loan or to punish another person for nonrepayment of any loan. (This provision was aimed at the use of extortion to collect a loan regardless of how the indebtedness arose.)

Financing Credit Extortion. Provided penalties of up to $10,000 in fines and/or 20 years' imprisonment for any person who willfully advances money or property with "reasonable grounds to believe" that the money or property would be used to make extortionate extensions of credit.

Compulsory Testimony. Authorized the Government, in any court or grand jury case involving a violation of this section, to require the testimony of a witness who claims the 5th Amendment against self-incrimination. Permitted testimony to be required only by a court order on application by the U.S. Attorney General, and granted immunity from prosecution to the witness on matters on which he was compelled to testify.

Preemption. Specified that this title did not preempt any state laws on the same subject.

TITLE III—GARNISHMENT

Exempted from garnishment either 75 percent of a persons's weekly disposable earnings or an amount equal to 30 times the national minimum wage, whichever amount was the larger. (Under the existing minimum wage of $1.60 an hour, a worker would have at least $48 of his disposable earnings exempted from garnishment.) Provided that the Secretary of Labor would arrange by regulation for pay periods longer than a week.

Defined "disposable earnings" as the amount of a person's total earnings remaining after deductions required by law.

Provided that the restrictions on the amount of a garnishment did not apply to court orders for support of any person, court orders dealing with bankruptcy proceedings or any state or federal tax debt.

Prohibited an employer from firing an employee because of a single incidence of garnishment. Provided penalties of up to $1,000 and/or one year imprisonment for violation of this restriction.

Directed the Wage and Hour Division of the Labor Department to enforce this title.

Defined garnishment as any legal or equitable procedure through which the earnings of any individual are required to be withheld for payment of any debt.

TITLE IV—CONSUMER FINANCE COMMISSION

Established a nine-member National Commission on Consumer Finance composed of three Members of the Senate, three Members of the House and three persons appointed by the President from private life.

Directed the Commission to study the functioning and structure of the consumer finance industry and consumer credit transactions generally.

Required the Commission to report on (1) the adequacy of existing arrangements to provide consumer credit at reasonable rates; (2) the adequacy of existing arrangements to protect the public from unfair practices and insure the informed use of consumer credit; (3) the desirability of federal chartering of consumer finance companies or other federal regulatory measures.

Required the Commission to submit its report and recommendations by Jan. 1, 1971.

Provided the Commission with subpoena powers.

Authorized appropriations of $1,500,000 for the Commission.

EFFECTIVE DATES

Provided that the disclosure requirements for open-end credit, consumer sales credit and loans take effect on July 1, 1969.

Provided that the restrictions on credit advertising take effect on July 1, 1969.

Provided that the garnishment requirements take effect on July 1, 1970.

Provided that all other provisions take effect upon enactment of the legislation.

Gas Pipeline Safety

Congress in 1968 completed action on a highly controversial bill (S 1166—PL 90-481) to improve the safety of gas pipelines. The bill as enacted was much weaker than safety advocates wanted and was the subject of intense lobbying by the gas industry to prevent stronger safety standards.

The legislation authorized the Secretary of Transportation to set up interim standards, and then continuing standards, for 760,000 miles of transmission and distribution lines and for a small mileage of gathering lines in residential or commercial areas. It included provisions for the states to supervise the standards for facilities within their borders, penalties for violations, and authorization of appropriations for the costs of the program.

A key provision allowed the states simply to certify that they complied with the federal standards. This provision, originally put in by the House and sharply criticized by safety advocates as negating the purpose of the bill because of alleged state laxity in pipeline safety matters, was somewhat strengthened by the addition of language which put the burden of proof of compliance on a state if the Federal Government challenged its compliance.

In general, however, the House version was considered much weaker than the Senate bill by supporters of strong pipeline safety legislation. An extensive fight took place on the House floor to rewrite the bill to Senate standards, but it was largely unsuccessful. The conference bill was closer to the House version than the Senate version.

A second major provision dealt with existing lines. The bill gave very limited powers to the Government to require improvements in these lines even though they posed the most important safety problem because of their age. Many of the existing pipes had been in the ground for years.

BACKGROUND

In 1967-68, there were more than 800,000 miles of gas pipelines in the United States. The figure included 63,000 miles of gathering lines, reaching from the wellheads to transmission points; 224,000 miles of transmission lines; and 536,000 miles of distribution lines. The pipe sizes ranged between one-inch gathering pipe and 42-inch distribution lines. In some of the large pipes, pressure along the pipe walls amounted to 93 tons per square foot. Many of these high-pressure lines ran under heavily populated areas.

The gas industry claimed accidents were rare and of minor importance along their lines. But in March 1965 escaping gas ignited and incinerated a 13-acre area in Natchitoches, La.; the holocaust melted cars and rock with flames that reached 2,500 degrees Fahrenheit. Seventeen people were killed. The accident prompted Sen. Warren. G. Magnuson (D Wash.), chairman of the Senate Commerce Committee, to request a study by the Federal Power Commission (FPC). The investigation showed that between 1950 and the time of the FPC inspection, accidents had occurred along gas lines at a rate of one every five days.

The standard for existing state regulation was the 1963 code of the U.S.A. Standards Institute (USASI) for Pressure Piping. This set of voluntary regulations, adopted in various forms by 40 states, applied chiefly to new pipe and not to pipe already under ground. According to FPC Chairman Lee C. White, old pipe was a major safety concern.

Gas Line Safety Bill Shows Marks of Lobbying Battle

The Natural Gas Pipeline Safety Act bill (S 1166—PL 90-481) carried the marks and scars of three years of legislative lobbying battles. The final version of S 1166 was in some ways stronger than the gas pipeline industry—or at least a segment of the industry—wanted and in many ways weaker than supporters of strong safety legislation wanted. But generally the measure was one the industry "can live with."

The bill started out March 17, 1965, as S 1553, a one-sentence amendment to the Natural Gas Act giving the Federal Power Commission (FPC) authority to set standards for the safe transmission of natural gas. Between the time the proposal was introduced as a bill of less than 50 words giving the FPC authority to issue safety regulations for pipelines and the time it emerged as a detailed federal-state arrangement for administration of pipeline safety, the measure underwent wholesome changes and was the subject of legislative and lobbying fights.

INDUSTRY BACKS OWN CODE

By 1967, it appeared that Congress eventually would pass some type of gas pipeline safety legislation, despite the industry's belief that the status quo—regulation by the states—should be maintained. If the status quo could not be maintained, the industry wanted the state regulatory agencies to have as big a role as possible in setting standards and enforing them.

It wanted the industry's code to be adopted as the federal standards. It wanted existing pipe excluded from the standards. It wanted to have a dominant voice on any pipeline standards committee and wanted the committee to have strong powers.

It did not want criminal penalties included in the legislation, and it did not want large civil penalties. It wanted a grace period, giving it time to correct a deficiency before a penalty could be ordered. It did not want to have to deal with both federal and state regulations.

The transmisssion lines wanted the federal government to pre-empt regulatory authority if there was to be federal regulation. The gathering lines wanted to be excluded from coverage under the bill. The basis for their bid for exclusion was that less than 2,000 miles of about 63,000 miles of gathering lines were in urban areas.

The distribution companies also faced a special problem—they were in the retail business, selling an energy fuel in competition with oil and electricity. They did not want Congress to pass legislation singling out their product as dangerous, because it could hurt them in the marketplace. The distribution companies were divided into two groups, investor-owned and municipal-owned. The municipal-owned distribution companies wanted the law to exempt them from coverage because of the nature of their ownership by cities.

The National Assn. of Regulatory and Utilities Commissioners (NARUS) opposed legislation which would dilute its members' authority over pipeline safety and enhance federal authority.

During Senate consideration of S 1166, the interests involved—the industry and its segments, the Government agencies, the consumer spokesmen—followed the usual lobbying practices. They testified before the appropriate committees and appealed for help from certain Members of Congress. But after the Senate passed the bill in November 1967, the fight intensified.

Industry pressure to change the bill more to the industry's liking was concentrated on the House Interstate and Foreign Commerce Committee's Communications and Power Subcommittee. The major lobbying groups seeking changes in the bill were:

The American Gas Assn. (AGA), an organization of about 350 distribution companies, located in many of the towns and cities of America.

The Independent Natural Gas Assn. of America (INGAS), an association of interstate pipeline companies.

The American Petroleum Institute's Natural Gas Committee (API), joined by the Independent Petroleum Assn. of America, Mid-Continent Oil and Gas Assn. and Western Oil and Gas Assn.; API, with about 8,000 individual and 250 corporate members, was concerned mainly with gathering line facilities.

The American Public Gas Assn. (APGA), an association of about 175 municipally owned distribution companies.

The Natural Gas Processors Assn. (NGPA), an association of firms that use gathering lines and processing facilities.

The National Assn. of Regulatory and Utility Commissioners (NARUC), an association of state regulatory commissioners.

The AFL-CIO and various individual labor unions.

Also seeking changes in the bill were the Department of Transportation, individual Representatives and several gas companies, including the Columbia Gas System Service Corp., New York; Union Gas Co., Brooklyn, N.Y.; Pacific Gas and Electric Co., San Francisco, Calif.

The Subcommittee held hearings for five days, and then went to work rewriting a bill. There reportedly was bitter fighting within the subcommittee, with its chairman, Torbert H. Macdonald (D Mass.), trying unsuccessfully to preserve the consumer-oriented aspects of the Senate-passed bill against strong moves by a majority of subcommittee members to make some of the changes the industry wanted.

Efforts in the full Committee to reverse the work of the Subcommittee failed; and when the bill was reported out May 15, it showed the effectiveness of the industry's lobbying.

BILL CRITICIZED

Four members of the Committee, all of whom signed a minority report opposing the changes, wrote a letter to *The New York Times* May 3 saying, "In our opinion the bill was essentially gutted at the behest of the gas pipelines lobbies, most of whose proposals were adopted verbatim." The four were Reps. Richard Richard L. Ottinger (D N.Y.), John E. Moss (D Calif.), John D. Dingell (D Mich.) and Brock Adams (D Wash.).

Rep. Joseph P. Vigorito (D Pa.), an early supporter of pipeline safety, used the words "industry sell-out" to describe his feelings about the bill, and said "the House version is so weak and so industry-oriented that it would be better to have no bill at all than to sign this one into law." In a May 16 statement, he said "Lobbyists for the natural gas industry succeeded in rewriting the bill so as to weaken it in several important respects."

A legislative assistant said lobbyists for the industry "were in the office day after day, with copies of the amendments they wanted."

Lobbyists frequently stressed the need to reduce appropriations, in line with the surcharge tax bill, as a reason for lowering the authorization for enforcing the bill.

Boyd did not publicly criticize the lobbying efforts, but he called the House bill "worse than an empty gesture. It is a dangerous deception."

The code was not legally binding and its provisions were drawn up in such a way that members of the industry might veto rulings they did not like. The FPC, under the 1938 Natural Gas Act, had the authority to investigate accidents but not to keep continued watch over the industry's safety practices. *(Congress and the Nation Vol. I, p. 980.)*

Gas pipeline safety legislation was first introduced in 1951. The issue did not raise concern in Congress, however, until the Natchitoches tragedy. Then Magnuson requested the FPC study and introduced a bill (S 1553) which would have assigned administration of gas safety to the FPC. Hearings were held by the Commerce Committee but no further action was taken. Creation of the Department of Transportation in 1966 also provided an impetus because the new agency regulated oil pipelines and possessed the administrative expertise to oversee gas pipeline safety.

President Johnson, in his Feb. 16, 1967, message to Congress on consumer protection, urged that the new Department be given responsibility for gas pipelines and requested passage of legislation in 1967.

LEGISLATIVE HISTORY

The Senate passed S 1166 in 1967 and the House Interstate and Foreign Commerce Committee began consideration of the measure but did not complete action.

The House Committee held additional hearings in early 1968 and approved a drastically amended version of S 1166 in mid-May.

The House Committee's major change concerned adoption of standards by the states. It permitted the states to certify their compliance with the standards and procedures set as minimum by the Secretary, rather than, as the Senate bill provided, prove that they had established standards and procedures that were on a par with federal standards.

On this point, the Committee report said, "If the Secretary is not satisfied with the state's performance of the role, he is not bound by the state's certification but may reject it."

The House Committee also widened the Senate's limited exemption for existing pipelines. Rather than let the Secretary apply standards to a "potentially hazardous situation," as the Senate provided, the House Committee version said that when he found "a particular facility to be hazardous," he was to require the operator of that facility to remedy the hazard.

Secretary of Transportation Alan S. Boyd denounced the Committee version of the bill. Boyd said the Committee's action "was worse than an empty gesture," for it went so far as "encouraging violation of the very standards" the Administration considered essential to protect the public.

Boyd said the bill "repudiated" what President Johnson had sought "and what the Senate bill had done." He pledged his support, within legal bounds, of efforts by the dissenting Committee members to strengthen the bill on the House floor.

Floor Action. The House by a 351-14 roll-call vote passed S 1166.

The crucial vote came on accepting the Committee's substitute for the Senate version. It was accepted on a 247-125 "conservative coalition" roll call, with most Republicans and Southern Democrats voting for the Committee version and Northern Democrats voting 18-111 against it. The Committee bill had the support of the House Republican Policy Committee, and only seven Republicans defected on the vote.

The House rejected five amendments designed to toughen the bill to Senate standards or stronger. The key amendment, substituting Senate provisions on enforcement for the House Committee provisions, was offered by Communications and Power Subcommittee Chairman Torbert H. Macdonald (D Mass.) and supported by the chairman of the full Committee, Harley O. Staggers (D W.Va.). It was rejected by a 36-83 standing vote and a 59-112 teller vote.

Points in Dispute—Major points of difference involved the relationship between the states and the Secretary of Transportation in enforcing safety standards, inclusion of gathering lines, treatment of potentially hazardous situations, penalties, and funds to implement the bill's aims.

The point considered most important was the federal-state relationship.

Regarding this, Macdonald said that in the House version, "the authorization is given to any state which has a clerk who can type merely to set forth the fact, whether it is a fact or not a fact, that the state, whatever state it is, is in compliance with the bill."

This was disputed by supporters of the House version, who argued that the Secretary could reject or withdraw any state's certification if he believed the state was not in compliance. But supporters of the Senate version said it would be almost impossible for the Secretary to determine whether or not a state was in compliance, especially with the small amount of funds authorized in the bill.

The correction of potentially hazardous situations, some involving thousands of miles of existing lines, many of them old and in urban areas, was another controversial point. It was resolved to a degree by creating legislative history on it.

Critics said under the House language, the Secretary would have to determine that there was a potential hazard in each specific, particular case, before correction could be ordered. So if the Secretary found a specific type of pipe in a specific type of soil was a potential hazard after 20 years, he could not order all such pipe removed, but would have to do it on a location-by-location basis, the opponents said.

Supporters of the House wording who wanted to forestall unnecessary, large-scale replacement of pipeline systems, argued there was no major difference between the House and Senate language. They agreed to make their view a matter of legislative history, and with that done, John E. Moss (D Calif.) withdrew his amendment to restore the Senate provisions.

Richard L. Ottinger (D N.Y.) sought to amend the House bill to restore more than 60,000 miles of gas gathering lines to the bill's coverage. Gathering lines, which run from the well to the transmission line, were added to S 1166 on the Senate floor.

Brock Adams (D Wash.), a supporter of the Senate version, offered an amendment to restore the higher civil penalties of the Senate bill. The amendment also eliminated a House Committee provision requiring the

Secretary to warn violators and allow them time to correct violations before he could impose penalties. Adams said the House version "might be called a 'mad dog' type of statute, because what it says is that everybody is entitled to one bite before you can do anything about it." Supporters of the House provision said the Senate version would produce more litigation than corrections. Adams' amendment was rejected by voice vote.

The House also rejected amendments to impose criminal penalties, which were not in the Senate bill.

Conference. The conference version was closer to the House version than the Senate version.

Certification—A major point of difference was the relationship between the Secretary of Transportation and the states regarding certification of the state to supervise gas lines within its borders. Under the Senate bill, the Secretary could work out agreements with the states allowing the state to supervise intrastate lines, if the state adopted federal standards and compliance procedures acceptable to the Secretary. Under the House bill, states could certify themselves in compliance with the Secretary's standards, and the burden was placed on the Secretary to prove that a state was not in compliance in order to withhold its certification.

The conferees retained the House certification system but added a provision making "it clear that when the Secretary moves to reject a certification the burden of proof is on the state agency to show that it is in compliance." The conferees also agreed that as a condition of certification, the state's pipeline legislation include provisions for obtaining injunctions in pipeline violation cases and for civil penalties.

Penalties—The Senate bill set civil penalties at a maximum of $1,000 a day, with a total maximum of $400,000. The House bill set them at $500 a day, with a $100,000 total maximum. The conferees agreed on $1,000 a day and a total maximum of $200,000, and exempted facilities in existence on the date of the legislation's enactment from civil penalties for a year from that date.

Appropriations—The Senate authorized appropriations of $10 million for fiscal 1969, $13 million for fiscal 1970 and $15 million for fiscal 1971. The House had authorized appropriations of $500,000 for fiscal 1969, $2 million for fiscal 1970 and $3 million for fiscal 1971. The conferees agreed on $500,000 for fiscal 1969, $2 million for fiscal 1970 and $4 million for fiscal 1971.

A Senate provision allowing the Secretary to charge the industry reasonable fees to help defray the costs of the pipelines safety program was eliminated in the conference.

Old Pipelines—A controversial point that supporters of strong pipeline legislation had wanted strengthened in the conference concerned the Secretary's authority to deal with existing hazards in old lines. The Senate bill was written so that if the Secretary found a certain type of pipe in a certain type of soil was hazardous after a certain number of years, he could order all such pipe replaced. The House bill required the Secretary to find a "particular" situation hazardous before he could order corrective measures at the particular facility under question. Conferees accepted the House version, although there was disagreement over the meaning of the language.

Gathering Lines—The inclusion of gathering lines, the lines that run from the wells to the transmission lines, was also a point of difference between the House and Senate. The Senate had included them, and the House had excluded all gathering lines, except those in residential and commercial areas. The Secretary was authorized to determine which pipes were in residential or commercial areas. The conferees accepted the House amendment.

PROVISIONS—As signed into law, Aug. 12, S 1166:

Authorized the Secretary of Transportation to issue interim safety regulations within three months, and guiding standards within two years after enactment, covering gathering, transmission and distribution of natural gas.

Exempted gathering lines in rural areas outside of the limits of any residential or commercial area.

Specified that existing pipelines were not subject to standards for design, installation, construction, initial inspection and initial testing unless the Secretary found a particular facility to be hazardous to life or property. In that case he was empowered to order the removal of the hazard.

Allowed states to certify their compliance with the Secretary's standards, but required each state to have legislation including injunctive powers and civil penalties. Gave the states two years for legislatures to enact the penalty provisions. Required the burden of proof of compliance to be on the state if the Secretary challenged its compliance.

Set civil penalties at $1,000 a day maximum, with a total maximum of $200,000, and exempted facilities in existence on the date of the Act's enactment from civil penalties for a year afterward.

Authorities appropriations of $500,000 for fiscal 1969, $2 million for fiscal 1970, and $4 million for fiscal 1971.

Authorized the Secretary to pay up to 50 percent of the costs of state programs to bring pipeline safety up to federal standards.

Directed the Secretary to set up a 15-member Technical Pipeline Safety Standards Committee made up of persons experienced in gas transportation safety, required the Secretary to submit all proposed standards to the technical committee and allowed the Secretary to reject their conclusions upon publication of his reasons.

Fire Safety

Early in 1968, Congress completed action on a bill (S 1124—PL 90-259) authorizing a two-year, $5-million federal program of research on the causes of fire and the methods of reducing loss of life and property from fire and establishing a 20-member National Commission on Fire Prevention and Control.

The bill had been passed by the Senate in August 1967. The House passed it in February by a 269-78 roll call over the protests of economy-minded Republicans who argued that the government could not afford to spend $5 million on such a "minor" program.

BACKGROUND

The Federal Government was prepared to extend its influence in the traditionally local field of fire safety because of what one federal official called a "compelling need" for better knowledge of how fires started and how to put them out. Local fire stations, often staffed by volunteers, had been unable to keep up with the training and technology required to protect growing communities. In 1965, the year for which the most recent estimates were available, there were 12,100 deaths by fire in the United States and property losses amounting to $1,741,300,000.

Fire Research Programs. Federal fire research and prevention activities had been supported in recent years by an average annual appropriation of $6 million, divided among several agencies. The most active agencies were the Agriculture Department's Forest Service and the Defense Department, notably its civil defense office.

Most of the federal research was aimed at specific rather than broad problems, according to Allen V. Astin, director of the National Bureau of Standards (NBS). In addition, most of the fire programs related to Federal Government problems alone. For example, the General Services Administration's Federal Fire Council dealt only with projects directly related to federal buildings and installations. The Interagency Fire Research Committee, established late in 1966, also concentrated solely on Government fire losses.

The NBS—the focus of the Administration's proposed new program—had been concerned with fire research and safety in a modest way since 1904. In that year, a huge conflagration in Baltimore, Md., was allowed to burn almost untended because the hose couplings of the city's several fire companies did not match the hydrant fittings in the vicinity of the fire. Consequently the NBS's first fire safety task was to set a uniform hose coupling size recommended for city fire departments. In 1931, the NBS published a monumental compilation of building construction standards that was still used in 1967 as the basis for many state and local building codes.

The NBS maintained what Astin called a "reasonably stable and nonexpanding" fire research program at a spending level of about $200,000 a year. Most of the Bureau's work, he said, was devoted to studying the properties of building materials and their resistance to fire.

Some research into the causes of fires and ways of putting them out was conducted in university laboratories. But the studies were generally of such a specialized nature that the researchers "make little contact with the working world of fire prevention and suppression," according to Astin. A Commerce Department report on the proposed Fire Research Act said there was a "major research gap" between the universities' advanced studies and the operation of fire departments.

Information on Fires. There was no accurate system in the United States—public or private—for collecting full data on the causes, number and results of household and industry fires. The most extensive data-gathering work was done by the National Fire Protection Assn. (NFPA), a nonprofit, Boston, Mass., organization founded in 1896. The NFPA was supported by membership dues, sale of its publications and by contributions; the professional membership was about evenly divided between fire service groups—fire chiefs and fighters—and the insurance industry.

Fire Training and Organization. Published figures showed there were currently about 25,000 fire departments in the United States; only about 1,600 of them were staffed by fully paid professionals. The remainder were staffed by volunteers or a combination of volunteers and professionals. A spokesman for the NFPA estimated that "there are actually a little more than 100 well-mannered, quality fire departments in the United States that are fully capable of handling almost any kind of firefighting situation."

A statement on the need for the Fire Research Act, printed in the *Congressional Record* when Sen. Warren G. Magnuson (D Wash.) introduced the bill Feb. 28, made these points: "Most professional fire personnel lack sufficient training" in commanding and controlling large disaster operations and major fire. Most states had training courses for fire fighters and officers but the programs varied widely in their effectiveness. Whether or not the courses were given often depended on the availability of local funds.

University participation in advanced fire training was small. Only two universities offered four-year degree courses in fire engineering.

In general, NBS Director Astin told a Congressional committee in 1963, local and industry fire-control efforts are "diffuse." None of the three, he said, was capable of mounting "the concerted effort necessary to create a technical basis" for fire engineering and suppression.

Earlier Federal Plan. The Administration's Fire Research and Safety Act of 1967 was not an entirely new idea. In 1963 the National Bureau of Standards asked Congress for an increase from $200,000 to $1.2 million for its fire research centers and administrative expenses. The request caused what House Appropriations Subcommittee Chairman John J. Rooney (D N.Y.) called "an uproar."

Although one major pressure group—the Assn. of Fire Chiefs—supported the NBS's plans, most lobby groups and private organizations, including the National Fire Protection Assn., were opposed to an increased role for the NBS. They maintained, as one NBS source put it, that "the Federal Government was out to federalize all the fire departments." Data collection organizations like the NFPA, the source continued, insisted that the Government intended "to take over a lot of private activities and put (the private organizations) out of business." The NBS request died in the House Subcommittee.

In the course of the House hearings, Astin and other NBS staff members outlined reasons why the Federal Government should be in the firefighting and research business. They said that a coordinated adequately funded program could reduce the incidence and effects of man-made fires. The success of the Forest Service fire control program, in operation since 1905, was frequently cited. Improvements in fire-fighting techniques and in fire spotting decreased the Service's land loss from man-made fire from 423,319 acres in 1947 to 45,183 acres in 1965. The Service also conducted a public information program through Smokey the Bear, a cartoon bear in a forest ranger's hat.

Pressures. Contrary to their reactions in 1963, when an increased role for the NBS was proposed, all of the major fire service organizations testified in 1967 Congressional hearings in support of the Administration's new program and the National Commission on Fire Prevention and Control.

PROVISIONS—As signed into law, March 1, S 1124:

Declared that "a comprehensive fire research and safety program is needed in this country to provide more effective measures of protection against the hazards of death, unjury and damage to property." Added that the

Secretary of Commerce should establish a fire research and safety center to coordinate the activities described in the bill.

Amended the 1901 National Bureau of Standards Act to authorize the Secretary of Commerce to conduct—directly or though grants to nonprofit organizations—(1) investigations of fires to determine their causes, frequency and other factors; (2) research into the nature of fires and development of improved methods of prevention and control; (3) educational programs; (4) fire information reference services to collect and disseminate data related to prevention and control; (5) training programs for fire fighters and (6) demonstration projects.

Authorized the Secretary to make grants to educational institutions to develop engineering and scientific courses in fire protection and instructional material.

Specified that grants might cover up to 100 percent of the cost of a project.

Directed other federal agencies to assist the Secretary in carrying out the research program but stipulated that nothing in the Act would affect the status or operation of existing federal fire research and safety programs.

Authorized an appropriation of $5 million for fiscal 1969 and 1970 to carry out the research and development programs.

Established a 20-member National Commission on Fire Prevention and Control to include the Secretaries of Commerce and Housing and Urban Development, 18 members appointed by the President, and four Congressional advisers. Specified that the members should include a spectrum of industry, academic, trade and government representatives.

Directed the Commission to undertake a comprehensive study of practicable means of reducing fire losses, including technology, communication techniques, suggestions for standardizing fire equipment, training of personnel, administrative problems of local fire services and state, local and federal responsibilities in reducing fire losses.

Directed the Commission to report to the President and Congress within two years.

Radiation Emission

Late in the year, Congress sent to the President a bill (HR 10790—PL 90-602) intended to protect consumers from dangerous radiation from electronic products.

Although the legislation applied to all electronic products, it had received public attention because of the revelation in 1967 that some color television sets manufactured by General Electric gave off potentially dangerous amounts of radiation. It was later determined that excessive color television radiation was an industry-wide problem. (The director of the National Center for Radiological Health estimated April 1, 1968, that from 5 to 10 percent of the 14 million color television sets in the United States emitted excess radiation. James G. Terrill said the estimates were made from surveys.)

The bill applied, with few exceptions, to all kinds of electronic products. It authorized the Secretary of Health, Education and Welfare (HEW) to prescribe performance standards for electronic products to limit radiation emission, required manufacturers to certify that their products conformed to such standards, prohibited importation of nonconforming products, and required manufacturers to repair or replace defective products or to re-

fund the customer his money. Besides TV sets, the bill covered such terms as lasers, microwave ovens and other electronic products.

Legislative History. The House acted first on HR 10790, passing it March 20. The Senate Oct. 3 passed the bill with strengthening amendments. The most controversial of these were ones that permitted seizure of defective products and granted the Secretary of HEW broad powers to inspect plants producing electronic products.

Strong lobbying in the House, however, by electronics interests was successful in causing the defeat of Senate-favored provisions on plant inspections and seizure of defective products.

The bill was nearly killed on the morning of Oct. 10 when a House-Senate conference meeting, the second in two days, broke up over several major differences on which neither House nor Senate conferees were willing to compromise. House conferees, headed by Paul G. Rogers (D Fla.), opposed Senate language which would have permitted seizure of defective products under some circumstances, extended protection to workers on factory assembly lines, and granted the Secretary of HEW broad powers to inspect plants producing electrical products.

Rogers, who held proxy votes for absent Members of the House conference committee, was adamant in his refusal to accept the Senate language. Believing that Congress was to adjourn the 11th, and that the bill, if it were to pass, would have to be reported out of conference by midnight on the 10th, Senate conferees decided to concede the disputed points to the House. Accordingly, the conferees reconvened late on the afternoon of Oct. 10 and agreed to the weakened provisions.

A strong lobbying effort, financed by the Electronic Industries Assn., and headed by former Postmaster General J. Edward Day (1961-63), was credited with having created much of the opposition to the stronger provisions passed by the Senate. A staff member of the Senate Commerce Committee, which handled HR 10790, told Congressional Quarterly that Day had concentrated his efforts on three or four major provisions, and had submitted language which the Electronic Industry Assn. felt was preferable to that contained in the Senate bill. In the case of the provision regarding inspection of plants, the language of the final bill paralleled almost exactly the languages submitted by Day.

Provisions

As signed by the President, Oct. 18, HR 10790:

Performance Standards. Authorized the HEW Secretary to set performance standards to control the level of radiation emission from electronic products where the Secretary felt such standards were necessary for the protection of the public health and safety.

Required the Secretary to consult with appropriate interested persons including representatives of affected industries in formulation of the standards.

Required that the Secretary in setting a standard consider the reasonableness and the technical and economic feasibility of its application.

Required that the first of such standards be prescribed prior to January 1970.

Authorized the inclusion in any performance standard of provisions for measuring radiation emissions of products and the inclusion of requirements for the attachment of accessories, warning signs, and labels. Also authorized the inclusion in any standard of requirements for instructions regarding the installation, operation and use of products.

Permitted the Secretary to amend or revoke any standard prescribed under the act.

Provided for judicial review of standards.

Exemptions. Permitted the Secretary to exempt from application of the performance standards certain electronic products of a type used solely by departments or agencies of the Federal Government and for which certain procurement specifications had been prescribed.

Permitted the Secretary to exempt from prohibitions of the bill electronic products used in research, investigations, studies, demonstrations, training or for reasons of national security.

Stipulated that performance standards were not to apply to any product intended solely for export, if the product's container bore an export marking and if the product met all the applicable requirements of the country to which it was being sent.

Effective Dates. Required that standards prescribed by the Secretary take effect not less than one year or more than two years after they were issued.

Advisory Committee. Required the Secretary to establish a 15-man Technical Electronic Product Radiation Safety Standards Committee, five members of which were to be selected from the Federal Government, five from affected industries and five from the general public.
general public.

Required the Secretary to consult the advisory committee before prescribing performance standards, but left the manner and method of consultation to the discretion of the Secretary.

Industry Testing Review. Directed the Secretary to review and evaluate industry testing programs to assure that safeguards against hazardous radiation were adequate and to assure that products complied with standards set under the act.

Product Certification. Required manufacturers of electronic products to attach a label to each product certifying that the product conformed to standards.

Prohibited the importation of products not tagged and certified in accordance with tests meeting the same criteria as those applied to domestically produced products.

Notification. Required a manufacturer to notify dealers, distributors, first purchasers and subsequent transferees of defects or noncompliance with standards that might cause a product to be unsafe because of emissions of electronic product radiation.

Required a manufacturer to notify immediately the Secretary of any such defect discovered by the manufacturer.

Required a manufacturer to notify subsequent purchasers or transferees of a defective product even though they did not hold a manufacturer's warranty.

Relieved a manufacturer of notification duties if he could satisfy the Secretary that the defect or the noncompliance did not create a significant risk of injury.

Repair or Replacement. Required a manufacturer, in the event notification was required concerning a non-conforming or defective product, either to remedy the defect, replace the product with an equivalent non-defective product, or refund the product's cost. The obligation to repair, replace or refund was to extend only to products manufactured after the date of enactment of the bill.

Required that a manufacturer, in notifying a dealer, a distributor, purchaser or subsequent transferee, inform the notified party of his right to receive above remedies.

In-Plant Inspection. Authorized the Secretary to make inspections of establishments in which electronic products were manufactured, used, repaired or maintained to determine whether facilities and procedures related to radiation safety were adequate to ensure that its products would confirm to safety standards.

Limited inspections to the area of the factory in which the manufacturer's radiation emission tests were carried out.

Required that, before the Secretary could make such an inspection, he must have good cause to believe such procedures and facilities to be inadequate. (The bill specified that the sale of a product which failed to meet prescribed standards was to constitute good cause.)

Reports. Required that accident and investigation reports made by the HEW Department and reports on demonstration or research projects be public information.

Permitted accident and investigation reports to be available for use in any judicial proceeding arising out of the accident to which the report related.

Dealer Recordkeeping. Authorized the Secretary to require dealers and distributors of electronic products to furnish the manufacturer with information necessary to identify and locate the ultimate purchaser of a product in the event notice of a defect or noncompliance needed to be given.

Exempted dealers and distributors from recordkeeping provisions for all products costing less than $50.

Required the manufacturer to preserve the information furnished him by a dealer or distributor.

Permitted a dealer or distributor to delay transmission of the required information until advised of the need for notification. And required that dealers and distributors electing to delay transmission of such information immediately inform the manufacturer of that fact.

Prohibited Acts. Prohibited a manufacturer from producing or importing any electronic product which did not comply with an applicable standard prescribed under the act.

Provided that persons must furnish notification or information required under the Act and make appropriate records accessible.

Prohibited a manufacturer from failing to certify or from falsely certifying that a product conformed to a prescribed standard.

Investigation and Research. Authorized the Secretary to conduct the following studies and to make a report on the results by Jan. 1, 1970:

• A study of present state and federal control of health hazards from electronic product radiation and other types of ionizing radiation.

• A study to determine the necessity for the development of standards for the use of nonmedical electronic products for commercial and industrial purposes.

• A study of the development of practical procedures for the detection and measurement of electronic radiation emitted from products manufactured or imported prior to the effective date of any standard prescribed under the Act.

Penalty. Set $300,000 as the maximum civil penalty which would be assessed for a series of violations under the act.

Annual Report. Directed the Secretary to prepare an annual report on the administration of the radiation control program and a thorough analysis of the incidence of biological injury from electronic product radiation.

Poultry Inspection

Congress in 1968 enacted an Administration-backed bill, the Wholesome Poultry Products Act (HR 16363—PL 90-492) to extend federal poultry inspection standards to poultry sold only within a state.

The bill, similar to the Wholesome Meat Act of 1967 (PL 90-201), authorized the Agriculture Secretary to work with state agencies to establish poultry inspection programs which were to be at least equal to federal standards. An estimated 1.6 billion pounds of poultry slaughtered in the United States each year without federal inspection was expected to be covered by provisions of the bill.

The bill was requested by President Johnson in a Feb. 6 message to Congress on consumer interests. The legislation provoked substantially less controversy than the similar meat inspection bill did a year earlier. The poultry bill was enacted with relatively little controversy. The major dispute was over a proposal to allow sale in interstate commerce of poultry products which were inspected under state inspection programs which met federal standards. This proposal was not included in the final bill.

The bill was passed by the House in June and the Senate in July by overwhelming roll-call vote margins. It was signed into law on Aug. 18.

Background. Under authority granted in the 1957 Poultry Products Inspection Act (PL 85-172), the Federal Government for a decade had been inspecting poultry prepared and sold in interstate commerce. The Act provided for compulsory post-mortem inspection on a bird-by-bird basis and for ante-mortem inspection if the Agriculture Secretary found it necessary. Diseased and unclean birds were barred from the market. The Act directed the Secretary to set sanitation and construction standards for plants and to regulate the use of chemical additives in poultry. Certain labeling requirements were also written into the Act. All of these regulations applied to imported as well as domestically produced birds.

In addition to the interstate provisions, the Act permitted the Secretary to designate "major consuming areas" which included several states—the New York metropolitan area, for example—and to apply federal inspection to plants in these areas. Federal regulations were to apply even if the poultry did not move in interstate commerce. However, this provision had never been implemented.

By 1968, some 87 percent of the poultry consumed by Americans was federally inspected. The remaining 13 percent was subject to state inspection laws of varying effectiveness. The Agriculture Department reported that 12 states had a mandatory ante- and post-mortem inspection law and 4 had effective enforcement programs; 5 states had voluntary inspection programs; and 33 states regulated poultry quality in general food purity laws. Federal inspection was available to plants which volunteered to receive federal inspectors.

Provisions. As signed by the President, HR 16363:

Authorized the Secretary of Agriculture to work in cooperation with state agencies to set up inspection programs for poultry shipped intrastate, with standards for the programs equal to or higher than federal standards for inspection of poultry shipped interstate. Allowed the states two years to establish a program, and permitted a one-year extension for states in the process of setting up a program at the end of the two-year period.

Required the program to include poultry inspection both before and after slaughter, regular inspection of facilities and personnel in the poultry business, and establishment of sanitation requirements for facilities.

Extended federal inspection to poultry production in states which do not establish a federal level program.

Required registration of various previously exempted segments of the poultry industry, including dealers in dead, dying, diseased and disabled poultry, and authorized regulation of previously exempted dealers.

Exempted producers of 5,000 turkeys or an equivalent amount of other poultry (calculated at four other birds equaling one turkey) from all except the sanitary standards of the bill, and exempted producers of less than 250 turkeys (or their equivalent) from all provisions of the bill.

Extended record-keeping requirements to additional segments of the poultry industry.

Established criminal penalty provisions for persons convicted of violating the Act, setting the penalties at up to $1,000 and a year in jail, or both, but allowed penalties of up to $10,000 and three years in jail, or both, for cases involving attempts to defraud and involving distribution of adulterated articles.

Included penalties of up to $5,000 and three years, or both, for persons who interfere with officials enforcing the Act, and extended that penalty to $10,000 and 10 years, or both, to persons who use a deadly or dangerous weapon in the courses of the interference.

Authorized regulation of storage of poultry.

Authorized standards for labeling of poultry and required the labels to be uniform.

Authorized denial of inspection services to persons with previous convictions which demonstrated "callous disregard for the public welfare."

Authorized federal sharing of costs with the states up to a maximum of 50 percent.

Auto Insurance

The Department of Transportation was directed by Congress to conduct a comprehensive study of the automobile insurance industry and—in particular—the existing compensation system for motor vehicle accident losses. President Johnson had requested the legislation

(S J Res 129—PL 90-313) in a consumer message to Congress.

The assignment of the study to the Transportation Department foreclosed the possibility of several separate Government studies which were under consideration in 1967 when the proposal first received considerable publicity.

S J Res 129 as signed into law, May 22, required that a final report be made to Congress within two years of enactment, and authorized appropriations of $2 million for the study.

The study was prompted by increasing discontent among consumers over the existing automobile insurance system. Critics of the system had charged that it was unnecessarily cumbersome and expensive, discriminated against certain drivers because of their race, age or place or residence, and was frequently unfair in awarding judgments.

Numerous reform proposals had been made in recent years, but both Congress and the Executive Branch believed that additional information about the system's operation had to be gathered before reform legislation could be formulated.

The proposal that attracted the most attention in 1967 and 1968 was the Basic Protection plan suggested in 1965 by Professors Robert E. Keeton and Jeffery O'Connell in their book *Basic Protection for the Traffic Victim.* The plan would replace the existing system of establishing fault in a traffic accident with a system to compensate all persons injured without regard to who was at fault. The plan embodies two key principles. First, it would require compulsory basic-plan insurance for every driver. The insurance would pay up to $10,000 per person and $100,000 per accident to compensate an individual for out-of-pocket losses such as medical expenses and wage losses. This compensation would come from the driver's own insurance company. Second, a driver would be exempt from liability in an accident to the extent that the injuries suffered by the other person involved did not exceed $10,000 in out-of-pocket losses and $5,000 in damages for pain and suffering. The existing liability system would be preserved to the extent that an injured person could go to court to recover damages from another person in excess of the $10,000-$5,000 exemption. An injured driver could not expect to recover the first $5,000 of damages for pain and suffering. Optional insurance would be available for purchase to protect a driver against other damages such as claims above the $10,000-$5,000 exemption and property and collision damage.

Under the Basic Protection plan, payments to compensate for economic losses normally would be paid to the injured driver in monthly installments rather than a lump sum. In addition, compensation would be paid only to the extent that losses were not covered by other insurance; duplicate insurance would not be permitted.

Keeton and O'Connell said that their solution would reduce the excessive court caseload by limiting trials to only the most serious lawsuits. They also maintained that their plan would be cheaper for consumers. A New York state study estimated that a "no-fault" system such as Basic Protection would cost between 15 and 20 percent less than the current liability system.

AUTO SAFETY EXEMPTIONS. In a related development in automobile legislation, Congress enacted a bill (S 2029—PL 90-283) temporarily exempting limited-production motor vehicles from certain safety standards required under Title I of the National Traffic and Motor Vehicle Safety Act of 1966 (PL 89-563). The Department of Transportation favored the bill.

The purpose of S 2029 was to protect an estimated 11 small companies, usually with limited financial resources, from experiencing economic hardships in meeting auto safety standards set under the 1966 Act. S 2029 allowed safety exemptions to be granted for up to three years. A major financial cost of meeting safety standards came from testing requirements, particularly tests which required the total destruction of a vehicle. The bill defined a limited-production car as one produced by a manufacturer whose total vehicle production did not exceed 500 vehicles annually. It also limited any exemption to three years from the date it was issued and the Secretary's authority to issue exemptions to three years from the date of enactment.

Occupational Safety

The President's 1968 proposed legislation to provide federal standards for employee safety and health died in the House Rules Committee. The proposal had been strongly opposed by business interests.

As a result of criticism of the Administration bill (HR 14816, S 2864), which empowered the Secretary of Labor to issue mandatory standards for employee health and safety and to close down plants if he found that "imminent harm" existed, the House Education and Labor Committee reported a clean bill (HR 17748) limiting the Secretary's authority to that of promulgating standards adopted by established safety organizations and providing judicial review of the Secretary's determinations. However, business groups continued to oppose the measure and the Rules Committee never cleared the bill for floor action.

The Senate Labor and Public Welfare Committee held hearings on S 2864 but took no further action.

A scaled-down version (HR 2567)—applying only to federal-aid construction projects—was later reported, but that also failed to pass.

Assistant Labor Secretary Esther Peterson in October said a "flood of propaganda" spread by the Chamber of Commerce of the United States and the National Assn. of Manufacturers and the lack of support by the National Safety Council helped defeat the occupational safety bill.

Prior to introduction of the Administration bill, laws in the field were the Walsh-Healey Act of 1936, which established certain safety criteria for workers on federal contracts; the Longshoremen's and Habor Workers' Act amendment of 1958, which required employees to maintain safe conditions; and Mine Safety Act provisions enacted in 1941, 1947 and 1952 authorizing safety inspections of mines. According to Mr. Johnson in his Jan. 23 address, "The Federal Government offers the worker today only a patchwork of obsolete and ineffective laws." He observed that the Walsh-Healey Act was more honored by its breach than its observance, that the other laws covered only specialized workers and that state coverage was inadequate.

Lobbying. The President's occupational safety proposal came under sharp assault by powerful business interests. A broad front of business groups, including the Chamber of Commerce of the United States, the National Assn. of Manufacturers (NAM), American Iron and Steel Institute, American Medical Assn., Manufacturing Chemists' Assn., and others, lobbied hard against the bill and succeeded in watering the measure down considerably in the House Education and Labor Committee and keeping it bottled up altogether in the Senate Committee on Labor and Public Welfare.

Despite the House Committee's changes, business groups still opposed the bill. The Chamber of Commerce, regarded as the leading opponent of the measure, issued a position paper asserting that "...the changes have not turned a poor bill into a good bill." The only satisfactory solution, the Chamber indicated, would be to knock out the Secretary's authority altogether. The Chamber and other groups based their attack primarily on a contention that the federal standards invaded an area that traditionally had been the domain of the states.

Throughout the spring and summer, business lobbyists paid frequent visits to key members of the House and Senate committees, and a flood of constituent mail reflecting material printed in Chamber and other business publications, was reported. A Chamber spokesman told *Congressional Quarterly* that the groups opposing the bill maintained "close contact" but that there was no "master plan or master plan strategy."

Senate supporters of the Administration bill criticized the Chamber for assigning William J. Fannin, son of Sen. Paul J. Fannin (R Ariz.), a member of the Labor and Public Welfare Committee, to help in the Chamber's effort to keep the measure bottled up. The younger Fannin told CQ, however, that he had not "lobbied at all" against the bill but only had conducted his "usual" duties of keeping the Chamber posted on Committee actions on "any bill in which we have an interest." He said the Labor panel was only one of "six or seven committees that I have to watch." Fannin had been employed by the Chamber for four years.

Rep. James G. O'Hara (D Mich.) said April 11 that many Members of the House were receiving form letters from members of the Chamber of Commerce of the United States throughout the nation opposing HR 14816. "Once again the U.S. Chamber of Commerce has taken the lead in advocating action later on a problem we face now." O'Hara said.

Rep. Elmer J. Holland (D Pa.) said May 21 he had received a large number of letters "ranging from the merely outraged to the downright abusive" opposing HR 14816. But he said "support had begun to appear" for the measure.

Holland inserted into the *Congressional Record* letters of support from the National Consumers League, the National Education Assn., the International Union of Operating Engineers and state nursing associations in Maryland, Florida, Vermont and West Virginia.

In a related development, 50 representatives of the National Council of Senior Citizens on May 31 picketed the U.S. Chamber of Commerce in Washington to protest the Chamber's opposition to the pending bill.

The Administration's big ally in the battle was the AFL-CIO.

Other Bills

MAIL FRAUDS. Congress in 1968 completed action on a bill (HR 1411—PL 90-590), acted on in differing forms by both chambers in 1967, which amended the postal civil fraud statute to protect consumers against deceptive mail-order schemes.

Final action on the bill had been delayed by a Senate amendment to allow appointments to new supergrade positions in the Federal Government. These were the top three levels (GS 16-18) in the Government's career civil service. The House bill contained no similar provision. Final action on HR 1411 came when the Senate agreed to drop its supergrade amendment.

Under existing law, the Postmaster General could require a local postmaster to return to the sender mail addressed to a promoter only if the Post Office could prove that (1) the promoter was using advertising to seek property or money through the mail, (2) the advertising used contained representations which were material and false as a matter of fact and (3) the advertising was used by the promoter with "false or fraudulent pretenses, representations or promises." HR 1411 rewrote the latter provision to eliminate the requirement that the Postmaster General first prove the promoter's intent to defraud.

The protection HR 1411 offered was authority for the Post Office to return mail, usually containing checks or money orders, to consumers cheated by a promoter's schemes.

DOOR-TO-DOOR SALES. An Administration-backed bill (S 1599) to allow the customers of door-to-door salesmen 24 hours in which to reconsider their purchases and to cancel them if they wished was reported in the Senate in 1968, but no further action was taken on the measure.

The bill also required the salesmen's firms to bear the cost of shipping any rejected merchandise back to the warehouse. Purchases costing less than $25 were exempted.

DECEPTIVE SALES. The Senate passed and sent to the House an amended Administration-backed bill (S 3065), the Deceptive Sales Act, which expanded the powers of the Federal Trade Commission. There was no House action.

The bill authorized the FTC to seek injunctive relief against methods of competition in commerce or acts or practices in commerce which were unfair or deceptive to the consumer.

Currently, the FTC had power to seek injunctions only in cases involving alleged false advertising of food, drugs, devices or cosmetics. It had no such authority in enforcing Section 5 of the FTC Act, which contained the broad prohibition against "unfair methods of competition in commerce, and unfair or deceptive acts or practices in commerce." In enforcing Section 5, the FTC was required to file a complaint, hold hearings and then, if justified, issue a cease-and-desist order, which was enforceable by federal court order. That administrative remedy often took up to three years to achieve.

WHOLESOME FISH. Both the House and Senate in 1968 held hearings on an Administration proposal to improve and expand fish inspection procedures, but no further action was taken.

Government inspection of fish and fishery products currently was carried out under two basic programs. The Food and Drug Administration (FDA) sampled fish in retail stores as part of its regular food inspection efforts. The Interior Department's Bureau of Commercial Fisheries offered a voluntary continuous inspection service of shore fishery establishments.

President Johnson in his message to Congress on consumer protection called inspection of fish and fishery products "virtually nonexistent" and proposed a Wholesome Fish and Fishery Products Act of 1968.

The Administration measure (S 2958) was to impose the same kind of continuous inspection for fish and fishery products as was to be applied to meat under the Wholesome Meat Act of 1967 (PL 90-201).

Under S 2958, the Secretary of Health, Education and Welfare (HEW) was to develop and to issue regulations on standards of manufacturing and storage practices, including sanitation and quality control standards.

Complying firms were to be issued certificates of registration which could be revoked if a firm violated the standards. Fishing vessels and fish processing plants were to be inspected, and an official mark was to be used on products subject to continuous inspection. Federal grants-in-aid were to be offered to states for the development of their own inspection systems, but the Secretary two years after enactment of the bill was to be able to apply standards in the bill to locally processed products if he found that a state either had failed to develop or was not enforcing an inspection service that was at least equal to the federal inspection service.

Imported fish and fishery products were to be subject to the same requirements as were domestic products.

OTHER ACTIONS. In other consumer actions, Congress held hearings on bills to authorize federal grants to states for developing and implementing programs for youth camp safety standards and for a study of laws governing operation of youth camps. There was no further action.

Congress held hearings also on the use of games of chance in gasoline marketing and on bridge safety. The latter hearings followed the death of 45 persons in the collapse on Dec. 15, 1967, of a bridge over the Ohio River between Point Pleasant, W. Va., and Gallipolis, Ohio.

Congress considered but did not act on an Administration-backed bill (HR 15223) authorizing the Secretary of Transportation to set safety standards for the design, construction, materials and performance of boats and related equipment. The bill prohibited the manufacture or sale of any boat or equipment which did not meet the federal standards. The bill was opposed by the Boating Industry Assn.

CONGRESS AND THE NATION, VOL. II

Chapter 15—National Security Policy

Key Votes

In this chapter, key roll-call votes are shown in bold-face type. The party breakdown on each of these votes and the position taken by each Member of Congress may be found in the key vote charts which appear in the appendix to this book.

National Security Policy

NATIONAL security policy in the Johnson years was marked by an intense battle among Pentagon planners over the course of U.S. policy in the Vietnam war and the share of the nation's resources that should be made available for a new generation of costly and sophisticated weapon systems.

Central figures in this struggle were Defense Secretary Robert S. McNamara and the Joint Chiefs of Staff, backed by the powerful military and appropriations committees of Congress. McNamara sought to hold down military spending and limit the nation's objectives in Vietnam—courses that sparked bitter opposition from the Joint Chiefs and their Congressional allies.

By late 1967, it appeared that Pentagon "hawks" had won. Under instructions from the White House, McNamara announced plans for deployment of an antiballistic missile (ABM) system, a key program on the "wish lists" of the Joint Chiefs and one which McNamara had long opposed. Less than three months later, McNamara announced he would leave the Pentagon early in 1968 (after seven years in office) to assume the presidency of the World Bank. *(See p. 863)*

But by early 1969, a number of developments appeared to have diminished the military influence. To the surprise of many Washington observers, McNamara's successor, Clark M. Clifford, a prominent Washington attorney who had represented some of the nation's leading defense contractors, urged President Johnson to turn down the military's requests for escalation of the Vietnam war and to set his objectives on attaining a negotiated peace. After reported bitter in-fighting in the President's Cabinet, Clifford won the President's support for his position. By early 1969, increasing public distrust of the military's role in the war, concern over the nation's pressing domestic problems, dissatisfaction over the inflation and higher taxes wrought by increased defense spending, and doubts over the efficacy of the ABM and other weapon systems had resulted in greatly increased pressure on Congress for a larger amount of Congressional scrutiny over the military's purse-strings in the years ahead.

McNamara-Military Battles

VIETNAM STRATEGY. McNamara's celebrated drive for Pentagon efficiency carried over to the air war against North Vietnam and made him a reluctant partner in Administration decisions to bomb North Vietnamese targets which he considered to be of questionable military significance. Unlike the military, McNamara saw little likelihood that the North Vietnamese could be bombed to the conference table.

McNamara's disagreements with the Joint Chiefs (JCS) over the bombing became so heated that they were twice aired in public. The first indication of the dispute came Jan. 23, 1967, in conflicting testimony from the Secretary and Army Gen. Earle G. Wheeler, JCS chairman, before the Senate Armed Services Committee. McNamara said the bombing had not reduced infiltration from North to South Vietnam. Wheeler said it had.

The second airing of differences came in a series of closed hearings that began on Aug. 9, 1967, before the Senate Armed Services Preparedness Investigating Subcommittee. In a report released Aug. 31, the panel said that it found "a sharp difference" between McNamara and the military witnesses on the use of air power against North Vietnam. Despite a Sept. 1 statement by President Johnson that "there is no deep division" of views, a number of North Vietnamese targets previously off limits to U.S. planes were brought under attack, raising speculation that the division did exist and that the President had overruled McNamara and had sided with the military experts.

Another sharp dispute between McNamara and the Chiefs was touched off by the Secretary's plan to construct an infiltration barrier along the demilitarized zone (DMZ) in Vietnam, which McNamara announced Sept. 7, 1967. Emplacement of the barrier raised questions as to whether U.S. military strategy was shifting from mobile to static operations, and thus was opposed vigorously by the JCS. The barrier went into operation early in 1968 but was never developed as fully as McNamara had intended. It was dropped entirely by the Nixon Administration in 1969.

WEAPON ISSUES. Throughout the Johnson years, Congress provided almost anything the Administration sought for defense, and in fact, often approved additional funds that had been requested by the military and turned down by McNamara. Amid assertions that McNamara was endangering the nation's security, Con-

---

Reference

For discussion of national security developments in the 1945-64 period, see *Congress and the Nation,* Vol. I, pp. 237-334. A more detailed discussion of Vietnam policy during the Johnson years will be found in the foreign policy chapter of this volume beginning on p. 49.

gress added funds for advanced bomber development, procurement of a nuclear-powered surface fleet and deployment money for the ABM system a year before the Administration asked for it. In each of these cases, McNamara simply refused to spend the money.

Underlying these disputes were two important differences of view on defense policy—one strategic and the other a matter of economics.

'Mutual Deterrence.' In the era of strategic policy, McNamara advocated a balance of forces between the United States and the Soviet Union (disparagingly termed "parity" by its critics), under which each superpower would deter the other from nuclear attack. This doctrine was deemed unthinkable by the Joint Chiefs and their backers on Capitol Hill, who thought the nation should settle for nothing less than outright superiority over Soviet nuclear arms.

McNamara's "mutual deterrence" doctrine, as enunciated in his 1963 "defense posture" statement, held that both the United States and the Soviet Union had deployed strategic forces powerful enough to absorb a surprise attack and still destroy the other nation as a viable, modern society. Any major strategic buildup by either nation, he said, would only lead to offsetting weapon developments

by the other. This was the rationale for McNamara's argument against the deployment of the ABM system and his reluctance to forge ahead at the pace sought by the military for development of an advanced manned bomber and other strategic weapons. (In keeping with this logic, however, when it appeared that the Soviets were developing their own ABM system, McNamara responded by ordering development of missiles that could carry multiple warheads—a weapon that could overwhelm the Soviet ABM and thus retain mutual deterrence. *(See p. 869.)*

Elaborating on his doctrine, McNamara said in the 1963 posture statement, "Even if we were to double and triple our (retaliatory) forces, we would not be able to destroy quickly all or almost all of the hardened ICBM bases...and the enemy's missile-launching submarines at the same time. We do not anticipate that the United States or the Soviet Union will acquire that capability in the foreseeable future." Therefore, McNamara said, "We are approaching an era when it will become increasingly improbable that either side could destroy a sufficiently large portion of the other's strategic force, either by surprise or otherwise, to preclude a devastating retaliatory blow" accompanied by casualties "in the tens of millions."

Whether this prospect spelled "mutual deterrence" (as the Secretary asserted) or "strategic stalemate" (as Air Force partisans claimed), the real issue concerned McNamara's continuing veto of projects which military professionals deemed essential to preserving the "superiority" of the nation's defense posture.

Cost Control. The economic consideration that led to controversy was McNamara's strenuous effort to place cost controls on the defense budget. The military and their enthusiasts on Capitol Hill argued that the cost of a weapon should be a secondary issue if expert military opinion had determined the weapon vital to the national security.

McNamara, upon assuming office in 1961, was quick to assert the full authority of his office to achieve unprecedented control over weapon costs and military procurement decisions. Among his first acts in office, the Secretary instituted a new system for evaluating military budget requests in terms of functions rather than service, thereby comparing the costs and advantages of such similar-purpose weapon systems as the Navy's Polaris missile, the Air Force's Minuteman and the RS-70 bomber. The new system, supervised by a staff of civilian experts in the Office of the Secretary of Defense, allowed development of a master plan that down-played the traditional roles and the "balanced forces" thinking of the separate services.

The system was christened the "planning-programming-budgeting" (PPB) system, and was applied to the fiscal 1963 defense budget and to each thereafter. PPB was the application of systems analysis to federal programs; its purpose was to assist decision-makers by developing a basis for systematic and, if possible, quantitative comparison of the cost and benefits of alternative programs and by making such comparisons part of the decision-making process.

Another cost-cutting tool inaugurated by McNamara was the "Cost Reduction Program," introduced in 1962 to encourage the identification and realization of savings through improved management procedures and actions. Savings asserted to have been identified under the pro-

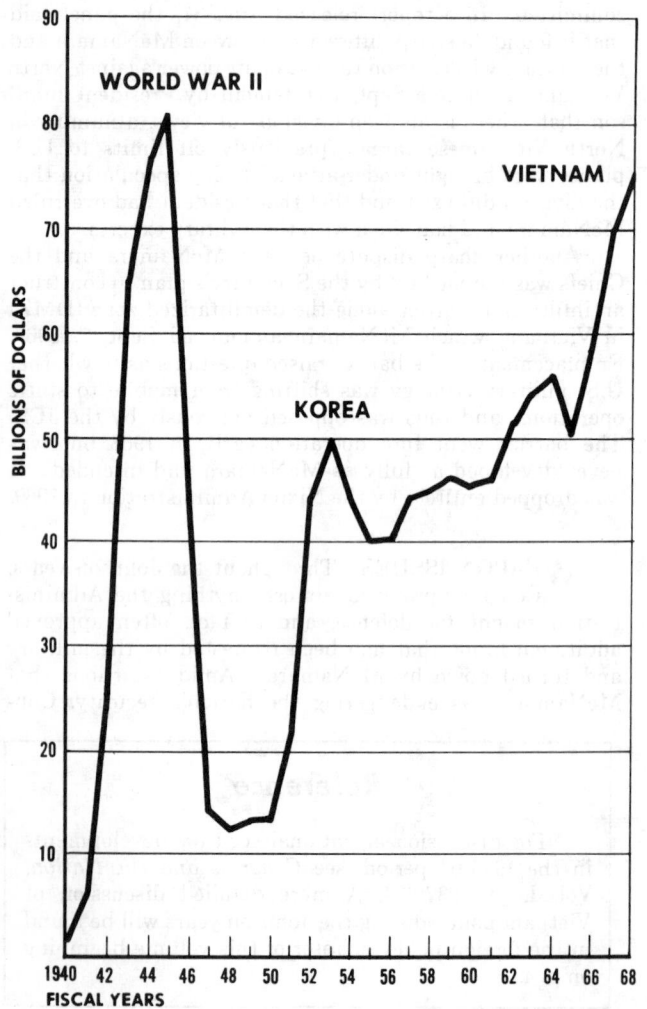

Federal Expenditures for National Defense, 1940-1968

BILLIONS OF DOLLARS

WORLD WAR II

VIETNAM

KOREA

1940 42 44 46 48 50 52 54 56 58 60 62 64 66 68
FISCAL YEARS

gram totaled more than $15 billion over the period fiscal 1962-68.

PPB and the cost reduction program became major irritants to the military committees on Capitol Hill, particularly the House Armed Services Committee and its outspoken chairman, L. Mendel Rivers (D S.C.). In its 1966 report on the fiscal 1967 defense procurement bill, Rivers' committee complained that "sound military recommendations (on matters including procurement of manned bombers and Navy nuclear surface vessels) have been overruled by the Secretary of Defense." While conceding "much brilliance" among civilian directors of the Pentagon, the Committee said: "Too often, it is feared, the almost obsessional dedication to cost effectiveness raises the specter of a decision-maker who...knows the price of everything and the value of nothing."

The cost-effectiveness studies influenced McNamara's decisions to deny procurement of the services' coveted bombers, the nuclear surface fleet and the ABM system. They also led him to adopt the controversial idea of a common fighter aircraft (TFX) for the Air Force and Navy, to propose that fast deployment logistic ships (FDLs) be procured in a single package from one shipyard (rather than the usual practice of dividing the contract between several firms), and to call for a merger of the Army Reserve and the Army National Guard under Guard management. All these proposals sparked vigorous opposition from Congress.

Other Issues

DRAFT. One major battle with Congress that McNamara managed to avoid was that of draft reform, in which President Johnson himself chose to take the lead. Amid widespread discontent over alleged inequities in the drafting of youth for service in Vietnam, the President called in 1967 for comprehensive draft reform, including a random selection system or "draft lottery," and other measures, some of which he said he would order himself under existing statutory authority. But after a bitter fight, Congress passed a four-year extension of the draft which retained most features of the present law and sharply restricted the President's authority to order reforms, including the lottery. Two leading proponents of draft reform, former Assistant Attorney General Burke Marshall, who headed an advisory panel on the draft for President Johnson, and Sen. Edward M. Kennedy (D Mass.), who led the fight for reforms in the Senate, argued that the new law made the system even more inequitable than it had been before. *(See p. 879.)*

DEFENSE COSTS. Spiraling costs of the war, which increased from $100 million in fiscal 1965 to an estimated $29.2 billion in fiscal 1969, pushed the defense budget to a fiscal 1969 level of $81.0 billion, a postwar high. The swelling defense outlays and the inflationary toll they took on the economy led to increasing public and press criticism of the military and its spending programs— a criticism buoyed by disclosures that some weapon systems were costing far more than anticipated, performing short of expectations, or both.

Defense Spending—1960-69

Following is a breakdown of U.S. defense spending over fiscal years 1960-68, with estimated spending for fiscal 1969. Expenditures related directly to the war in Vietnam are included in the totals, and are also isolated in the third column. All figures are expressed in terms of the "unified" budget, which first went into effect in fiscal 1969.

(in billions of dollars)

Fiscal Year	Amount *	Vietnam
1960	$45.9	
1961	47.4	
1962	51.1	
1963	52.3	
1964	53.6	
1965	49.6	$ .1
1966	56.8	6.1
1967	70.1	20.6
1968	80.5	26.8
1969 (est.)	81.0	29.2

* Department of Defense military functions including Vietnam costs and foreign military assistance, all Atomic Energy Commission activities and national defense activities of other agencies.

SOURCE: Fiscal 1970 U.S. Budget

Against this background, the military and other Government officials (of both the Johnson and Nixon Administrations) were making pronouncements that little of the $25 billion-$30 billion a year that the nation was spending for the Vietnam war could be spared for tax cuts or domestic programs once the war was over. These officials said the bulk of the Vietnam money would be needed for procurement of new weapon systems deferred for the last several years because of the high war costs. Military planners indicated that a good part of this spending would be for acceleration of some of the programs currently under attack, primarily the antiballistic missile system.

ABM System. The focal point of the defense cost controversy was the ABM system, which if fully deployed would probably be the most expensive weapon ever purchased by the United States or any other nation. Opposition to the system crystallized behind the efforts of some of the nation's most eminent scientists and several Congressional military experts, including Sens. Margaret Chase Smith (R Maine) and Stuart Symington (D Mo.), a former Air Force Secretary (1947-1950). *(For arguments for and against the system, see p. 872.)*

The system McNamara had ordered into production in 1967 was a "thin" antimissile net designed to intercept missiles that might be launched by Communist China when it attained a "primitive" intercontinental missile capability in the mid-1970s. (Initial investment cost of the "thin" system, christened "Sentinel," was estimated at $5 billion.) By mid-1968, however, Congressional backers of the system, including Senate Armed Services Committee Chairman Richard B. Russell (D Ga.), had begun to stress that the real value of Sentinel was to serve as a building block for a "thick" system to defend U.S. cities against a Soviet missile attack. McNamara had estimated the costs of a "thick" system at $40 billion. But other opponents pegged the costs much higher, with Symington coming up with the all-time high estimate of $400 billion.

After long and acrimonious debate, Congress in 1968 beat back attempts of House and Senate liberals to cut funds for the system, but by year's end, informal polls showed that the anti-ABM forces in the Senate had apparently picked up enough strength to place the outcome in real doubt for 1969.

After an outburst of opposition from citizens in some of the cities planned for ABM deployment, President Nixon withdrew the "Sentinel" plan early in 1969 and substituted a "Safeguard" program which emphasized the protection of offensive missile sites rather than cities (thus eliminating the "building block" for later expansion of the system into a "thick" city net, Administration officials said).

TFX. The cost experience and performance of the once-heralded F-111 (TFX) fighter-bomber also added fuel for the critics of excessive military spending. But here, McNamara rather than the military got the blame.

Approved by McNamara over military objections, the F-111 was plagued from the beginning (1963) by the problem of producing a single aircraft for two services whose tactical air requirements called for distinctly different missions. *(See p. 875.)*

The Navy, which long had feared that its version (the F-111B) was too heavy for aircraft carrier use, asked Congress in 1968 to kill the F-111B program, and Congress readily obliged. By the time the F-111B was scuttled, its estimated costs per copy had risen from an original figure of $4 million to more than $9 million. At the Navy's request, Congress provided funds for accelerated development of a substitute, solely Navy aircraft, the VFX-1, which some Pentagon cost analysts thought would cost far more and perform only slightly better than the F-111.

Although the Air Force expressed satisfaction with its version of the craft (the F-111A), losses in 1968 of three of the first six F-111s sent to Vietnam for combat tests cast serious doubt over the future of the Air Force's F-111 program. In total, 14 of the F-111s had crashed by early 1969: 12 F-111A models and 2 CF-111Bs. The Air Force program also experienced cost overruns. The original per copy cost estimate for the F-111A, made in 1965, was $3.1 million; by 1968, it had risen to $7 million.

C-5A. Another major program that ran into serious cost difficulties was the Air Force's giant C-5A transport aircraft, which was designed to give the nation a new capability for instant deployment of large tactical ground forces in the 1970s. Hearings before the Joint Economic Committee late in 1968 revealed that costs of the craft had increased by some $2 billion over the original estimated cost of $3.3 billion for 120 planes, engines and spare parts. The Air Force ran into further difficulties when the Committee obtained an Air Force document which mapped out a plan for firing A. E. Fitzgerald, an Air Force cost expert who had revealed the cost over-runs under questioning by the Committee. Although Fitzgerald was stripped of his Civil Service tenure (job protection), he still was on the job as of mid-1969.

Congressional Reaction. Despite public concern over the level of defense spending, the military and appropriations committees of Congress still were reluctant to forego military advice on weapons. Although Congress cut the fiscal 1969 defense appropriations bill by $5.2 billion, Congressional leaders made clear that the cuts amounted to deferments of weapon programs not scheduled for actual spending in 1969 and did not constitute actual denial of funding. The cuts were taken to comply with limitations on Government spending made mandatory by the 1968 tax surcharge bill—limitations that President Johnson once called "phony paper" cuts.

Determination of the Congressional military establishment to maintain the strongest possible defense posture—come what may—was indicated in the remarks of Senate Armed Services Committee Chairman Richard Russell in presenting the fiscal 1969 defense appropriations bill to the Senate: "There is no hesitation in my mind," Russell said, "in stating that we cannot continue to support a war, be capable of honoring our commitments abroad, and maintain an adequate defense posture without substantially increasing the size of our defense budget in the near future. As reluctant as Congress will be to accept that statement, I make it unequivocally and without fear of contradiction."

CIA. While the military succeeded in keeping most of its program intact, the Central Intelligence Agency (CIA) had somewhat lesser luck. Responding to press reports that unraveled an account of CIA secret subsidization of organizations in education, law, journalism, labor and religion, President Johnson in early 1967 ordered a halt to secret Government financing of all private voluntary organizations.

Allegations that the CIA was playing a major role in the formulation of national policy (instead of merely carrying out that policy) led to a bitter Senate floor debate in 1966, when Members of the Foreign Relations Committee called for creation of a new Committee on Intelligence Operations, whose nine members would be drawn equally from the Foreign Relations, Armed Services and Appropriations Committees (at that time, Senate oversight of the Government's intelligence operations was by senior members of the Armed Services and Appropriations Committees, meeting as one group). Although the proposal was rejected by the Senate, its backers achieved their objective when Armed Services Committee Chairman Richard Russell announced early in 1967 that he would ask three members of the Foreign Relations Committee to attend the meetings of the CIA oversight panel, of which he was chairman.

* * * *

Details of national security policy over the 1965-68 period appear on the following pages in chronological order. Included in the discussion are highlights of Congressional action on defense authorization and appropriation bills, reorganization plans and other defense-related legislation. Detailed articles on three major defense issues—deployment of an antiballistic missile system, procurement of the F-111 (TFX) fighter aircraft and extension of the military draft appear at the end of the chronologies. Vietnam war developments, while described briefly in this chapter, are covered in detail in the chapter on foreign policy, which begins on p. 49.

Chronology of

National Security

Legislation

1965

President Johnson's hopes to stabilize the defense budget and divert more funds to important domestic programs were shattered at mid-year when Mr. Johnson made the decision to order a massive buildup of U.S. forces in Vietnam.

The year began with the President emphasizing that U.S. power was sufficient to meet any threat from the Communist world and that the defense budget could be stabilized through cost reduction efforts, elimination of unnecessary forces and improved management procedures. The President called for a military budget of $47.4 billion for fiscal 1966, a reduction of $1.3 billion from the amount appropriated in the previous fiscal year. But this projected saving was quickly wiped out when the President asked, and Congress provided, supplemental appropriations of $2.4 billion (including $700 million in additional fiscal 1965 funding and $1.7 billion for fiscal 1966) to support the Vietnam buildup.

Major developments in the non-Vietnam weapons budget included cutbacks in the planned level of the Minuteman ICBM force, retirement of the oldest B-52 bombers and a decision to delay deployment of an antiballistic missile system while continuing the ABM research effort on a priority basis. The President also hoped to save money by merging the Army Reserve and Army National Guard under Guard management and closing a number of unneeded military bases.

The cuts in strategic forces met with surprisingly little Congressional opposition but the Guard-Reserve merger and base closure plans touched off two of the bitterest Congressional debates of recent years. After prolonged wrangling, Congress succeeded in blocking the merger proposal but the President won out on his base closures plan when he vetoed legislation that required prior Congressional review before any base could be closed.

In other action, Congress provided a pay raise for the military services which was more than twice the level requested by the Administration. It also granted the Atomic Energy Commission's request to place increased emphasis on civilian rather than military uses of atomic energy—a development reflecting President Johnson's assessment that the U.S. nuclear arsenal was sufficient to meet any Communist threat.

Defense Budget

The President's budget for fiscal 1966, submitted Jan. 25, 1965, estimated that the Defense Department would spend $47.9 billion in the coming fiscal year and would need new obligational authority (appropriations) of $47.4 billion. (Both the spending and appropriations figures

were exclusive of military assistance, activities of the Atomic Energy Commission and defense-related functions of other agencies, which came to another $3.7 billion).

Mr. Johnson set what he hoped would be the tone for the year's defense program in a special Jan. 18 message to Congress, in which he emphasized that the "United States today is stronger militarily than at any other time in our peacetime history" but that "arms alone can not assure the security of any society or the preservation of any peace." Pointing to the needs of his "Great Society" program of domestic social legislation, the President added: "The health and education of our people, the vitality of our economy, the equality of our justice, the vision and fulfillment of our aspirations are all factors in America's strength and well-being."

The arms buildup that began in 1961, the President said, had succeeded in providing "an indisputable margin of superiority for our defenses." Over that period, he pointed out, U.S. strategic nuclear power on the alert had increased threefold, Special Forces eightfold, combat-ready Army divisions by 45 percent, the Marine Corps by 15,000 men, and tactical Air Force airpower and airlift capacity by 100 percent.

In line with the President's assessment that U.S. strategic nuclear forces had attained sufficiency, the new defense budget omitted plans made in 1964 to increase the Minuteman ICBM force by 200 missiles, which would have brought it to a total force level of 1,200 (as compared with the Air Force's request of 1,800). In other cutbacks in the strategic forces area, the President decided to dismantle all 126 Atlas intercontinental ballistic missiles and half the 108 Tital ICBMs by mid-1965, and to retire 30 of the oldest B-52 bombers in fiscal 1966, leaving a force of 600. Mr. Johnson also denied funds to begin production of the Nike-X antiballistic missile system, although he approved $400 million to continue its research and development on an urgent basis.

Despite these cuts, the budget included money to begin development of a variety of new programs in both the strategic and tactical force areas. These included a new submarine-launched missile called Poseidon, which was capable of mounting multiple warheads rather than the single, larger warhead carried by Polaris missiles; a new air-to-ground missile called SRAM (short range attack missile) to enable the B-52 bomber to attack a larger number of targets from greater distances; and two new weapon systems which would work hand-in-hand to improve the mobility of U.S. land forces: a giant transport aircraft, the C-5A, capable of carrying 750 passengers (about one-tenth of an Army division), and a large fast deployment logistic ship (FDL) to rush heavy combat equipment to trouble spots where it would be "married up" with troops flown in by the C-5A.

Authorization. On April 2, the Senate Armed Services Committee reported a bill (S 800) authorizing $15,283,800,000 for defense procurement and research—a total of $13.4 million less than the Administration had sought for these activities. (Under legislation that became effective in 1961, prior authorization was required for major procurement and research items; other portions of the defense budget, such as procurement of small arms and ammunition, personnel costs and operations and maintenance could be appropriated without prior authorization.)

Major specific cuts made by the Committee included $99.8 million for procurement of 10 E-2A Hawkeye planes,

(Continued on p. 834)

Creation of Nuclear-Powered Surface Fleet for Navy

One of the major defense controversies during the McNamara era was over McNamara's go-slow approach on the issue of a nuclear-powered surface fleet.

Advocates in the Navy and Congress of nuclear propulsion compared the difference between nuclear and oil power plants for ships to the differences between oil and coal or coal and sails. A thoroughly nuclear fleet, they said, would provide increased range, responsiveness, staying power and reduced vulnerability to enemy attack.

McNamara's reluctance to move too rapidly toward nuclear power was influenced by studies on the part of his systems analysts that questioned whether additional benefits of nuclear-powered surface ships were worth their additional costs, which were substantial. "As a general rule," he told the Joint Committee on Atomic Energy in 1963, "I am interested in achieving the most efficient possible naval forces, defining efficiency as achieving the most beneficial military results for a given expenditure."

Nuclear Surface Warships

For nearly 20 years the Navy and the Atomic Energy Commission (AEC) had been engaged in a program to design, develop and utilize a family of nuclear power plants in Navy ships, ranging from submarines to surface, capital ships.

Work on a submarine reactor began in April 1948. The Nautilus, the first atomic submarine, was included in the fiscal 1952 shipbuilding program. The concept of a nuclear submarine, however, encountered intense opposition based on arguments that the military advantages of nuclear power were not worth the extra cost. Work on a reactor for a surface ship began in 1950, was canceled by the Defense Department in 1953, but was reinstated in 1954.

Following is a chronology of the development of nuclear surface warships:

1956—Congress included funds in the fiscal 1957 shipbuilding program for the first nuclear surface warship, the guided missile cruiser Long Beach (commissioned in 1961). The ship had been requested by the Defense Department.

1957—The nuclear carrier Enterprise, requested by the Navy and the Defense Department, was included in the fiscal 1958 shipbuilding program. The Enterprise also was commissioned in 1961.

1958—The Navy and the Defense Department requested the first nuclear frigate (DLGN), the Bainbridge, which Congress included in the fiscal 1959 shipbuilding program. The Bainbridge was commissioned in 1962.

1959, 1960—No nuclear surface warships were requested by the Defense Department. The Navy had requested nuclear power for the carrier America.

1961—The Navy had included two DLGNs in its fiscal 1962 request, which were turned down by the Defense Department. Congress authorized one DLGN, the Truxton, commissioned in 1967.

1962—The Navy and the Defense Department for fiscal 1963 requested one DLGN, which was to be equipped with a new surface-to-air missile (SAM) system called Typhon. Congress authorized the DLGN, but the SAM system proved unsuccessful for shipboard operations, and the Defense Department first canceled the SAM system and then canceled the DLGN. In addition, the Navy had requested a nuclear carrier. The request was denied and the Defense Department instead requested a conventional carrier, the John F. Kennedy.

1963, 1964—In 1963, the Navy and Congress continued to urge nuclear power for the Kennedy, creating a major controversy and sparking an intensive review of Navy nuclear propulsion systems. However, the Defense Department insisted on conventional power for the carrier. No nuclear or conventional surface warships were requested for construction or were added by Congress.

1965—The Navy requested a DLGN for fiscal 1966, but the request was turned down by the Defense Department which asked for no new surface warships. Congress, however, included $150.5 million for a DLGN in the fiscal 1966 military procurement authorization bill (PL 89-37), but appropriated only $20 million (PL 89-213) for long leadtime procurement.

1966—The Navy requested one DLGN but was turned down by the Defense Department. The Defense Department requested funds for a second nuclear carrier, the Chester W. Nimitz, and said it would ask for two more nuclear carriers in later years. Two conventional guided missile destroyers also were requested by the Defense Department. Congress in the fiscal 1967 military procurement authorization (PL 89-501) approved funds for the three Administration-requested ships. In addition, Congress earmarked $130.5 million as reauthorization for the unappropriated balance of the $150.5 million authorized in PL 89-37 for a DLGN and earmarked $20 million for long leadtime procurement for another DLGN. Moreover, Congress stipulated that the contract for the construction of the DLGN authorized in fiscal 1966 and reauthorized in fiscal 1967 was to be entered into "as soon as practicable" unless the President advised Congress that its construction was not in the national interest. This DLGN became known as the fiscal 1967 DLGN.

In the fiscal 1967 Defense appropriation bill (PL 89-687), Congress appropriated funds for the nuclear carrier and the two DLGNs (although it deleted language in the final conference on the bill that had specifically earmarked the bill's funds for the DLGNs only for that activity). No funds were appropriated for the two conventional guided missile destroyers.

1967—In his annual posture statement, McNamara said he had "decided to proceed with construction" of the fiscal 1967 DLGN.

The Administration requested (and Congress approved) $50 million for procurement of long leadtime items for a third nuclear carrier, currently designated CVAN-69. The Navy, in addition to requesting the carrier, requested one DLGN and two conventional guided

Was a Major Defense Controversy During McNamara Years

missile destroyers. The Department of Defense approved only the request for the conventional destroyers, but Congress refused to provide funds for them. Instead, Congress in the fiscal 1968 military procurement authorization (PL 90-22) earmarked $249.6 million in Navy funds for use only in construction of two DLGNs. Only one new DLGN, however, was involved in the fiscal 1968 bill. The bill provided that the $249.6-million authorization was to be combined with the $20-million fiscal 1967 appropriation for long leadtime procurement of a DLGN to meet the full $269.6-million cost of two DLGNs. In PL 90-22 Congress again stipulated that contracts for the two DLGNs were to be entered into "as soon as practicable" unless the President advised Congress that their construction was not in the national interest.

In his posture statement, McNamara proposed $30 million for contract definition of two newly designed escort ships. One was designated the DX and was to be primarily an antisubmarine warfare (ASW) ship. The other was designated DXG and was to be both an ASW and anti-air warfare (AAW) ship. Congress approved funds (PL 90-22) for contract definition of the two new ships.

Congress in the fiscal 1968 Defense appropriations bill (PL 90-96), appropriated $135 million for procurement of one DLGN and $20 million for long leadtime procurement of another DLGN. Congress also appropriated the $30 million authorized for contract definition of the DX and DXG class ships.

1968—President Johnson April 1 declared that construction of one of the two nuclear frigates (DLGNs) authorized by Congress for fiscal 1968 in PL 90-22 was not in the national interest. (The other was not fully funded and did not yet require a decision.) The President thus met a provision of PL 90-22 that contracts for the DLGNs be entered into "as soon as practicable" unless the President found that their construction was not in the national interest.

In action on the fiscal 1969 defense procurement bill (PL 90-500), Congress agreed to the full Administration request of $246 million for five conventionally powered guided missile destroyers (DX), $82.4 million for further long-leadtime procurement of the new nuclear carrier, CVAN-69; $39.3 million for spare parts for the nuclear systems of the three nuclear carriers; and $52 million for long leadtime parts procurement of nuclear-powered guided missile destroyers (DXGN) or nuclear frigates (DLGN).

McNamara Arguments

McNamara in 1963 spelled out over-all policy toward Navy procurement in memorandums to the Secretary of the Navy and in testimony before the Joint Committee on Atomic Energy.

Nuclear Carriers. During the 1963 arguments over nuclear versus conventional power for the Kennedy, McNamara testified before the Joint Committee. "My own analysis," he said, "is that in certain quite unusual

situations where long steaming time is involved for very limited types of response, a nuclear powered carrier has substantial advantage over a conventional powered carrier." He added, "In extended operations, again in quite exceptional circumstances, where frequent refuelings would be required of a conventional powered carrier, a nuclear powered carrier has advantages." And he concluded, "Translated into the contingency that we face, these would occur very infrequently."

The Secretary in 1966 explained to the House Appropriations Subcommittee on Department of Defense Appropriations that he recommended nuclear power for the fiscal 1967 carrier, the Nimitz, when he had opposed nuclear power for the Kennedy, because "we have gotten the cost down to the point where we are justified in installing nuclear power in carriers."

Escort Ships. The Defense Secretary also talked about nuclear escort ships in his 1963 appearance before the Joint Committee. "The real choice we face," he said, " is not between a given number of conventional ships for one sum of money and the same number of nuclear ships for a larger sum. The choice is between a given number of conventional ships and a smaller number of nuclear ships at the same total cost." In a 1965 letter to House Armed Services Committee Chairman Rivers, McNamara said that "the question" was "whether these advantages in numbers...do or do not offset the advantages of nuclear propulsion."

Proponents' Arguments

Joint Atomic Energy Committee. In a 1963 report on nuclear power in Navy surface warships, the Joint Committee on Atomic Energy, a strong Congressional supporter of nuclear power, concluded that cost-effectiveness studies of nuclear surface warships by the Defense Department had underestimated the military advantages and overestimated the additional costs. The Committee said the studies had included an assumption that in war, logistic support forces (such as fuel and ammunition ships) would be able to operate unhampered and without losses as they did in peace. The Committee asserted that the assumption was "a fundamental weakness" in the studies that "negates their validity."

Rickover. Vice Adm. Hyman G. Rickover, director of the Naval Reactors Division of the AEC, in 1965 told the House Appropriations Subcommittee on Department of Defense Appropriations. "The danger in continuing to make these extensive cost analyses...is that this diverts attention from the real issues...." Rickover added, "I would rather have fewer good warships that are the best we can build than have inferior weapons just because the initial cost looks cheaper...."

Ignatius. Reviewing Navy studies of nuclear propulsion, Navy Secretary Paul R. Ignatius Oct. 27 concluded: "It is clear that *all* escort ships should not be nuclear powered because their additional costs are not offset by operational advantages in some of the missions to be performed. It is equally clear to the Navy, however, that *some* of its escort ships should be nuclear powered."

a carrier-based early-warning aircraft, and $64.2 million for two fast deployment logistic ships (the Administration requested four). The cuts were largely offset, however, by Committee additions of $133.6 million for two more nuclear-powered attack submarines (the Administration requested four) and $82 million for accelerated development work on a manned bomber, the AMSA (for a total allotment of $97 million). (The AMSA succeeded the cancelled B-70 as the Air Force's hoped-for new bomber for the 1970s.)

In explaining the additional funding for AMSA, the panel noted that "consistently has emphasized the importance it attaches to the continued availability of effective manned bombers and its concern over the aging of the B-52 force." It added, however, that even if full-scale development of a new bomber were begun immediately, it "could not be produced and deployed in substantial numbers before the expiration of the estimated useful life of the older models of the B-52." Alternative proposals by McNamara to develop a bomber version of the F-111 (TFX) fighter plane, the Committee said, would result in a plane with less payload and less range capacity than desired. The Senate April 6 passed the bill without change by an 85-0 roll-call vote.

As approved by the House Armed Services Committee April 29, HR 7657, the House version of the authorization bill, carried a total of $19.6 million more than the figure approved by the Senate.

Arguing that the Defense Department had "both procrastinated and vacillated in its approach to nuclear-powered surface ships," the panel added $150.5 million for an unbudgeted nuclear-powered guided missile frigate, a large carrier-escort ship. In other major actions, the Committee restored the Senate cuts in the Hawk-eye aircraft and the FDL programs but dropped the two nuclear-powered attack submarines which had been added above Administration requests. The panel also cut the Senate add-on for AMSA development from $82 million to $7 million.

The House May 5 passed HR 7657 without change by a 396-0 roll-call vote. By subsequent voice vote, it substituted the text of HR 7657 for that of the Senate-passed bill, S 800, and sent the measure to conference with the Senate. Prior to passage, Armed Services Committee Chairman L. Mendel Rivers (D S.C.) expressed the Committee's intention to fight McNamara over the Secretary's opposition to a nuclear-powered surface fleet. "To my mind," Rivers said, "...Congress has been shunted aside by the Pentagon over the past several years in determining our defensive and offensive military structure. We have been invited to sit at the table but we have not been invited to join in the meal, so to speak. This time is over. We are going to carve the roast for ourselves from now on."

House and Senate conferees agreed to the Senate provision for two unbudgeted nuclear attack submarines, the House provision for an unbudgeted nuclear frigate, the Senate action dropping two of the four FDLs that were requested and the House allowance of an unbudgeted $7 million (for a total allotment of $22 million) for bomber development, instead of the Senate add-on of $82 million. During brief Senate debate May 27, the bill's floor manager, John Stennis (D Miss.), said the Senate accepted the House figure for bomber development because "with the passage of time and the absence of a decision to proceed to the program definition phase, it is clear that all of the

$82 million...could not be effectively expended in fiscal 1966." As approved by voice votes of the House May 26 and the Senate May 27, S 800 (PL 89-37) authorized appropriations of $8,958,300,000 for aircraft, missile and ship procurement and $6,444,500,000 for defense R & D, a total allotment of $15,402,800,000.

Appropriation. Sufficiency of the defense budget to cover costs of the U.S. buildup in Vietnam was the centerpiece of debate on the fiscal 1966 defense appropriations bill (HR 9221—PL 89-213), which carried $46,887,163,000 including a supplemental appropriation of $1.7 billion to support activities in Vietnam.

The bill's $1.7 billion allotment for Vietnam, requested in August after House action on the bill was complete, was the second supplemental appropriation provided for the war during the 1965 session. Congress May 6 cleared another bill (HJ Res 447—PL 89-18) making fiscal 1965 supplemental appropriations of $700 million for support of Vietnam operations. Final action on the fiscal 1965 bill came less than 53 hours after President Johnson appealed to Congress to show "prompt support of our basic course: resistance to aggression, moderation in the use of power, and a constant search for peace," by enacting the appropriation. It was the first occasion that the Administration had asked for an appropriation specifically for Vietnam, in addition to the regular defense budget.

Throughout the discussion of HR 9221, House Republicans charged that the Administration was deliberately holding down requests for Vietnam and presenting a "phony" budget. They argued that the nation could not afford both "guns and butter" and implied that the Administration was not disclosing the true cost of Vietnam because it did not want to endanger its ambitious program of domestic legislation.

Democrats in Congress supported the Administration's level of funding the war, arguing that the armed forces currently had sufficient supplies and funds, and that it was best to wait until 1966 to see what more was needed. They pointed out that the Defense Department already had the authority to spend whatever funds necessary to support needed increases in military personnel, to transfer funds from low-priority to high-priority programs and to make use of the substantial amount of funds saved from prior years. However, Sen. Stennis, chairman of the Senate Armed Services Preparedness Investigating Subcommittee, which conducted year-long hearings on the equipment and readiness of Army forces, warned in August that the drain on Army supplies created by the Vietnam war had become "critical."

On June 17, several weeks prior to President Johnson's buildup of forces for Vietnam, the House Appropriations Committee reported a version of HR 9221 carrying $45,188,244,000, or $60.6 million less than Administration requests. Although the Committee added $250.9 million to the bill, it cut $311.5 million (including cuts of $185.5 million made mandatory by the reductions in the authorization bill).

In a comment on the measure's adequacy to meet Vietnam requirements, the Committee said: "Our reserve stocks and equipment levels are presently such that all our general purpose forces would be able to engage in combat for sustained periods of time." The report said that, in addition, the Department possessed "staggering totals" of unobligated appropriations approved in prior years that could be used for currently unforeseen combat contingencies.

In major specific actions, the Committee added $133.6 million for two additional nuclear-powered submarines, $20 million for long-leadtime items for a new nuclear-powered frigate authorized by S 800 at a cost of $150.5 million, and $7 million for development of a new manned bomber. The panel also added $45 million to the bill to provide funds for a separate Army Reserve and Army National Guard, rather than the merged Reserve-Guard force envisioned by the Pentagon, and inserted language earmarking the $150 million requested for the Air Force's manned orbiting laboratory (MOL) program for use only for that program.

In a procedure unusual on an appropriations bill, the three Republicans on the Defense Appropriations Subcommittee, Reps. Melvin R. Laird (Wis.), Glenard P. Lipscomb (Calif.) and William E. Minshall (Ohio), said they supported the bill but felt "compelled" to point out certain defense policies which they said gave "cause for concern." They said the bill provided "inadequate funding" for the Vietnam war, that testimony by defense officials reflected "an approach falling far short of what we believe must be done" to advance development of antisubmarine warfare and military uses of space, and that an Army program called STEP, to give special training to rejected draftees was "ill conceived" and duplicated the Job Corps and other programs. The three GOP Members also stated that they had "grave reservations" about the Administration's basic defense policy, which was "more of a policy of seeking to achieve a balanced deterrent rather than ensuring a decisive superiority."

Laird again questioned the adequacy of funds for Vietnam when the measure came to the House floor June 23. He argued that the fiscal 1966 defense budget had been made up on the basis of guidelines established in 1963, well before a Vietnam buildup was contemplated. He implied that the Administration was unwilling to revise its defense spending plans to reflect the greater cost of the Vietnam effort because it wanted to keep fiscal 1966 spending below "the much-publicized $100 million budget ceiling." Republicans, Laird said, "will not refrain from telling the American people of their extreme displeasure at the cavalier way in which this Administration sees fit to inject political considerations into its defense proposals." No effort was made to increase the bill's funds, however, and the measure passed the House without change by a 407-0 roll-call vote on June 23.

Before the Senate Appropriations Committee acted on HR 9221, the Administration submitted its request for the additional $1.7 billion in fiscal 1966 appropriations to meet part of the costs of the Vietnam buildup. On Aug. 18, the panel reported the bill, appropriating $46,877,063,000, some $1,688,819,000 more than had been approved by the House and $95.8 million less than the revised Administration requests. Except for addition of the special Vietnam funds (which were called the Southeast Asia Emergency Fund) the panel's main change in the House bill was to restore language, not included in the House version, requiring that at least 35 percent of the funds in the bill for repair, alteration and conversion of naval vessels be allocated to private shipyards. The Senate Aug. 25 passed the bill without further change by an 89-0 roll-call vote.

Conferees agreed to a bill carrying $46,887,163,000, which was more than was provided under either the House or Senate versions of the measure. The Senate's shipyard amendment, which was the only major variation in the two bills, was resolved in favor of the House. Conferees stipulated in their report, however, that the Defense Department should make the "most effective, practical use of both public and private shipyards" and should inform Congress quarterly of its efforts to distribute vessel work between public and private yards "on a reasonable and equitable basis." The conference report was adopted by the House Sept. 17 by a 382-0 roll-call vote and by the Senate Sept. 21 by voice vote.

As enacted, HR 9221 appropriated $10,973,094,000 to the Army, $13,957,200,000 to the Navy and Marine Corps, $17,519,600,000 to the Air Force and $4,437,269,000 to defense agencies. In other provisions, the bill authorized, in addition to the amounts appropriated, transfer from stock and industrial funds of $470 million, earmarked $150 million for the Air Force's manned orbiting laboratory (MOL) program and $22 million for development of an advanced manned strategic aircraft and directed that the Army National Guard be programmed to attain an end strength of 380,000 in fiscal 1966 and the Army Reserve an end strength of 270,000.

Reserve-Guard Merger

Angered by McNamara's failure to seek its prior approval, Congress in 1965 successfully blocked a major Pentagon plan to reduce the size and improve the readiness of the Army Reserve and Army National Guard by merging the two components under Guard management.

Under terms of the proposed plan, outlined by McNamara on Dec. 12, 1964, the combined 700,000-man authorized paid-drill strength of the Guard and Reserve would be reduced by 150,000 men, resulting in a new authorized strength of 550,000, all under the Guard. The plan, which was designed to save about $150 million a year, authorized the outright elimination of 21 low-priority divisions—15 Guard and 6 Reserve—for which adequate equipment was not available. The plan was to go into effect July 1, 1965.

The plan, which had the full backing of President Johnson, came under attack from the House Armed Services Subcommittee No. 2, headed by Rep. F. Edward Hebert (D La.), and by the Senate Armed Services Preparedness Investigating Subcommittee, headed by Sen. John Stennis (D Miss.). The plan received qualified support from the National Guard Assn. and most states. It was sharply opposed by the Reserve Officers Assn., a powerful Washington, D.C., lobby group, as well as by Members of Congress who were reservists and by a handful of state legislatures and Governors.

As originally proposed, the plan would have been implemented under the Defense Secretary's existing statutory authority to effect reorganizations within the defense establishment. The only Congressional action required would have been to accept the proposed reduction in the authorized paid-drill strength of the Army reserves and to agree to a single appropriation for the merged forces.

Following a hostile reception of the plan in Congress, however, Defense Secretary McNamara in May held a joint press conference with Hebert to announce that the merger would be delayed to permit a thorough Congressional review of the plan and enactment of technical

Abolishment of Capitol Hill Reserve Units Draws Fire

One of the features of Secretary McNamara's reserve reorganization plan that upset Congress was a proposal to bar any person holding a "key assignment" in the Federal Government, including Members of Congress, from participation in the ready (active) reserve forces. The plan also placed sharp restrictions on travel by Members of Congress at the invitation of the military services.

In announcing his plan on Dec. 12, 1964, McNamara said a recent survey had shown that about 150,000 federal personnel were reservists, and that about 5,000 of these, in addition to Members of Congress, held jobs in which they would be more valuable to the nation's security, in case of mobilization, than they would be on active duty. He said elimination of these personnel from the ready reserves would free positions for other reservists who could be called to active duty in case of need.

Affected reservists with less than 18 years of combined active and ready reserve service would be placed on standby status; they would not be entitled to draw drill pay and would lose eligibility for promotion and retirement benefits as long as they remained on standby status. Reservists with 20 years of service would be automatically retired, but those with between 18 and 20 years of service would be permitted to remain in active reserve status until they had served 20 years and so become eligible for retirement benefits.

The ruling applied to 79 Senators and Representatives and 240 Congressional staff assistants who were active reservists at the time of the announcement. Those Members affected by the change who were on either the Senate or House Armed Services Committees or the Senate or House Defense Appropriations Subcommittees were: Sens. Howard W. Cannon (D Nev., Brig. Gen., Air Force Reserve), Barry Goldwater (R Ariz., Maj. Gen., Air Force Reserve), Daniel K. Inouye (D Hawaii, Maj., Army Reserve), Henry M. Jackson (D Wash., Lt. Col., Army Reserve) and Strom Thurmond (R S.C., Maj. Gen., Army Reserve); Reps. William H. Bates

(R Mass., Cmdr., Navy Reserve), Charles E. Chamberlain (R Mich., Cmdr., Coast Guard Reserve), O. C. Fisher (D Texas, Lt. Col., Air Force Reserve), Ed Foreman (R Texas, Capt., Air Force Reserve), Durward G. Hall (R Mo., Col., Army Reserve), George M. Huddleston Jr. (D Ala., Cmdr., Navy Reserve), Richard H. Ichord (D Mo., Capt., Air Force Reserve), Joe M. Kilgore (D Texas, Col., Air Force Reserve), Glenard P. Lipscomb (R Calif., Lt. Col., Army Reserve), Robert L. F. Sikes (D Fla., Maj. Gen., Army Reserve), Robert T. Stafford (R Vt., Cmdr., Navy Reserve) and Samuel S. Stratton (D N.Y., Capt., Navy Reserve). Goldwater, Foreman, Huddleston and Kilgore did not serve in the 89th Congress.

The Defense Department Jan. 16, 1965, issued an official order carrying out the plan and abolishing the Capitol Hill reserve units.

In debate on the defense appropriations bill April 6, Cannon tried but failed to win approval of an amendment to block the Jan. 16 order. Cannon said his amendment would not reverse the disbanding of the Capitol Hill reserve units but would permit the individuals affected by the order to continue their reserve careers. He said the Defense Department should not be allowed to "unilaterally abrogate" their reserve contracts. But when sufficient support did not develop, Cannon withdrew the amendment.

Congressional Military Travel. McNamara in his Dec. 12, 1964, announcement also said that, effective immediately, all future defense survey trips by Congressmen and Congressional staffs at the invitation of the individual military departments would be subject to regulations issued by his office. The regulations, he said, would ensure a more equitable distribution of Congressional travel between the various services and would provide Congressmen "a fuller view" of military activities in the field in all the services. McNamara noted that there was a wide "disparity" between the departments in the amount of travel authorized for Congressmen.

"supporting" legislation. The House Subcommittee subsequently held brief hearings on this legislation (HR 8243), then deferred action. In August, it issued a statement declaring the plan to be not "in the national interest" in view of the Vietnam buildup.

In line with the House Subcommittee's action, Congress in the annual defense appropriations bill (HR 9221—PL 89-213) appropriated funds for separate components rather than for the merged force requested by the Defense Department (see above). The legislation also required the Reserve to be programmed to attain a total strength of 270,000 men by the end of fiscal 1966 and the Guard a strength of 380,000—a slight drop from the 700,000-man combined strength authorized for fiscal 1965. In addition, the law stated that the required strengths would cease to be effective only upon enactment by Congress of legislation authorizing a reserve reorganization and prohibited the Secretary from transferring funds appropriated in the bill to carry out a reorganization that did not have Congressional approval.

Despite the stand taken by Congress, McNamara by year's end accomplished many of the objectives of his original merger proposal by creating a 100-percent combat-ready, 150,000-man "select" force of separate Reserve and Guard units and by eliminating certain obsolete Reserve units. McNamara said the new plan did not violate Congressional guidelines set in PL 89-213.

The Defense Department also studied plans to merge the Air Force Reserve and Air National Guard, but deferred a decision in 1965.

According to some observers, the refusal of Congress to endorse the Reserve-Guard merger in 1965 was due not so much to specific objections to the plan itself as to anger at McNamara's "arrogance" in initially attempting to press the reorganization without full Congressional advice or authorization. They said that Congress had in the past reacted strongly against proposals to reduce the size of the Army reserves. Also they noted that the merger proposal was one of several issues in 1965 where Congress sought to assert its authority over defense affairs, others being military pay, where Congress provided pay increases more than double the ones requested by the Defense Department, and the attempt to gain veto power over base-closure plans. *(See below.)*

Spokesmen for the Reserve Officers Assn., the chief opponent of the merger plan, said that these factors, while evident, were not the real reason for the position taken by Congress. They asserted that the hearings had shown that the Administration proposal was a "bad plan" which Defense officials were unable to justify. Moreover, they contended that, in the proposed transition period during which the merged force would have taken shape, morale and combat readiness would have been very low. In face of the Vietnam situation, they stated, Congress could have ill-afforded to endorse a proposal which would have resulted in an immediate, though temporary, loss of readiness.

Observers noted that the Administration would have had to obtain the approval of all state Governors, as well as of Congress, in order to achieve a consolidation of the reserves by reducing the size of the National Guard and building up the Reserve.

Base Closures

With the aid of a Presidential veto, the Pentagon won its other major dispute with Congress in 1965—a plan by McNamara to close or phase out 95 military installations in the United States or abroad.

Fearful of the economic consequences the closures posed for Members' districts (the plan envisioned elimination of 63,401 military and civilian jobs at estimated annual savings of $477 million), Congress added a proviso to the annual military construction authorization bill (HR 8439) requiring the Secretary of Defense to submit plans for closing military installations to Congress for review. Terming the proviso a "fundamental encroachment" on powers of the Executive Branch, President Johnson vetoed it on Aug. 21. Congress did not attempt to override the veto and instead, passed a new bill (HR 10775—PL 89-188) with a watered-down reporting requirement acceptable to the President.

The controversial provision which brought the veto of HR 8439 originated in the House Armed Services Committee and appeared to be a challenge by the Committee's new chairman, L. Mendel Rivers (D S.C.) to the "unilateral" decisions made by McNamara to close bases. McNamara's closure plan, announced Nov. 18, 1964, affected facilities in 34 states and numerous Congressional districts.

As originally approved by the House, HR 8439 provided a formula under which any base-closure plan would be subject to a veto by either chamber of Congress; this provision was deleted by the Senate altogether. In conference, a compromise was reached which dropped the authority for a Congressional veto and instead required the Secretary of Defense, between Jan. 1 and April 30 of each year, to submit base closure plans to Congress for a 120-day review. After HR 8439 was vetoed, Congress replaced the bill with HR 10775, which included a provision giving Congress 30 days to review base-closing plans submitted by the Secretary. A procedural move on the House floor to get a vote on overriding the veto of HR 8439 was blocked by a 323-19 roll-call vote.

After Congress went out of session and the dispute died down, McNamara Dec. 6 announced the closing or consolidation of an additional 126 domestic and 23 overseas military bases at an estimated savings of $410 million a year. McNamara explained Dec. 8 that most of the base reductions were related to a Defense Department decision to cut back the Strategic Air Command's bomber fleet between 1965-71.

Construction Funds. In both HR 8439 and HR 10775, Congress authorized identical sums of $1,780,062,000 for various military construction projects, $173.1 million less than Administration requests. The figure was cut back an additional $23.4 million in the military construction appropriation bill (HR 10323—PL 89-202), which appropriated $1,756,635,000.

Military Pay Raise

Congress Aug. 12 cleared a bill (HR 9075—PL 89-132) authorizing pay increases for the military services worth $1,048,029,000 a year—more than double the $504.3 million level of increase sought by the Administration.

Of the total authorized, $880.4 million was for basic pay increases, averaging an over-all 10.4 percent and effective Sept. 1, 1965. The pay of enlisted men with less than two years' service was increased for the first time since 1952. The remaining $167.6 million was for such items as Social Security payments, terminal leave payments, retired personnel benefits, new hostile fire pay rates and new re-enlistment bonuses. The increases were applicable to active duty and retired members of the military services, plus uniformed personnel of the reserves, Coast Guard, the Public Health Service and the Coast and Geodetic Survey.

HR 9075 was a slightly revised version of a bill (HR 5725) introduced earlier in the session by House Armed Services Committee Chairman Rivers. The legislation, according to Rivers, was designed to give military personnel a substantial pay boost in order to "correct" the current "inequitable" lag between military and federal civilian employees' pay scales. Rivers also introduced the Administration's draft bill (HR 8714), but called its pay recommendations "disgracefully inadequate" and "paltry."

Upon signing HR 9075 into law Aug. 21, President Johnson said that, while the measure provided pay raises of more than $540 million above what he sought, "In this critical period...in light of the alternatives available to me, I have concluded that the public interest will best be served by signing the bill."

Enactment of HR 9075 constituted the third major military pay increase since 1963. PL 88-132, signed Oct. 2, 1963, authorized pay increases of $1.2 billion, including 17-percent raises for all active duty personnel with two or more years of service. PL 88-422, signed Aug. 21, 1964, authorized increases of $207.5 million, including 2.5-percent raises for all active duty personnel except enlisted men with less than two years of service.

Congress in 1965 also enacted legislation (HR 3044—PL 89-149) increasing the pay of enlisted men by $55 a month and of officers by $110 a month while serving on flight deck crews of aircraft carriers. The increase was estimated to cost $5.3 million annually.

Servicemen's Insurance

In another move to make service careers more attractive, Congress in 1965 enacted Administration-backed legislation (S 2127—PL 89-214) permitting all military personnel to purchase $10,000 in low-cost group life insurance to protect them against the risk of death in service, whether from battle or other causes not connected with combat in any way. The bill also authorized $5,000 death gratuity payments to survivors of servicemen who died under certain conditions between Jan. 1, 1957, and the effective date of S 2127—the period during which no servicemen's insurance was available.

The insurance provisions of S 2127 authorized the Administrator of the Veterans Administration (VA) to purchase group life insurance policies from one or more participating life insurance companies. Each individual entering the armed forces would be eligible for the $10,000 coverage unless he affirmatively elected not to receive it or elected instead to receive insurance in the amount of only $5,000. The policy would be effective only for the duration of the individual's term of service. During his period of coverage, however, the individual could—upon application, payment of the required premium, and without medical examination—convert to a permanent plan of insurance written by one of the participating companies which would remain in effect after the individual was discharged from the service.

The premium rates for servicemen under the group plan would be determined by the VA. They were estimated at about $2 a month for $10,000 policies and $1 a month for $5,000 policies, amounts believed sufficient to make the program, including VA administrative costs, self-sustaining.

The bill's death gratuity provisions authorized retroactive payments to survivors of military personnel dying from certain specified causes, including action of a hostile force of the "extra hazard of military or naval service." The total cost of the gratuity program was estimated at about $46 million.

The final version of S 2127 was based largely on amendments added in the House which made the bill acceptable to the Administration. The Senate version, which the Administration opposed, was more selective in its coverage than the final version and would have authorized free, Government-financed $10,000 "special indemnity insurance" benefits for survivors of military personnel who were killed on duty in "combat zones."

Draft Developments

Card Burners. Reacting to a wave of demonstrations against U.S. involvement in the Vietnam war, Congress Aug. 13 approved a bill (HR 10306—PL 89-152) making it a federal crime to destroy or mutilate a draft card. The legislation was a reaction to calls from various antidraft proponents for young men to destroy their draft cards as a manifestation of their opposition to the war.

As enacted, HR 10306 amended the Universal Military Training and Service Act of 1951, which previously had outlawed only forgeries, alterations or other changes of draft cards. Penalties provided for forgeries, etc., were also applied to destruction of draft cards—a maximum $10,000 fine and/or imprisonment for up to five years.

The legislation was passed by Congress after brief debate and little controversy. Only one person was recorded against the measure—Rep. Henry P. Smith III (R N.Y.), who objected to the severity of the punishment for offenders. Proponents said the bill was aimed at the "beatniks and so-called 'campus-cults' " who made up much of the antidraft movement and had urged draft card burnings. Enactment of the bill, House Armed Services Committee Chairman Rivers said during House debate, was "the least we can do for our men in South Vietnam fighting to preserve freedom, while a vocal minority in this country thumb their noses at their own Government."

Six individuals were arrested for violating the new law in 1965; none had come to trial by the end of the year.

Unpublished Draft Study. The doubling of draft calls and the reactions to the increasing manpower needs in Vietnam brought to an unpublished end a special Pentagon study of alternatives to the draft, which was initiated by President Johnson in 1964. According to one Pentagon official, the importance of the study had been "overtaken by events" such as the military buildup in Vietnam. Certain of the study group's conclusions, however, were leaked to the press. The group, according to May reports, estimated that under normal conditions it would cost between $3 and $5 billion a year in higher recruitment and pay costs to end the draft and provide sufficient incentives for enlistment to maintain projected military strengths over the coming decade.

Establishment of the study group had done much to blunt Republican calls during the 1964 election campaign for an outright end to the draft system. Opening his bid for the Presidency Sept. 3, 1964, Republican candidate Sen. Barry Goldwater (Ariz.) had promised that, if elected, "Republicans will end the draft, and as soon as possible." In reply, Democratic Vice Presidential candidate Sen. Hubert H. Humphrey (Minn.) Sept. 3 said that to end the draft "at this time (before all alternatives were thoroughly studied) would be premature and irresponsible. The draft is still necessary to our national security...."

National Stockpiles

The two houses of Congress and the Executive Branch were unable to agree in 1965 on a major overhaul of stockpiling laws. A bill (S 28), passed Feb. 9 by the Senate, was unsatisfactory, for different reasons, to the Administration and to Members of the House.

Involved in the stockpiling issue were both national security—the acquiring of materials essential in case of war—and the impact of government actions on the national economy—the disposal of unneeded items from the stockpile without disrupting the private economy.

Late in 1965 the Administration used the threat of unloading aluminum from the stockpile to persuade aluminum producers to rescind a price increase and announced the sale of a large quantity of copper to ease a shortage of that metal.

S 28 would have consolidated the three existing U.S. stockpiles into two stockpiles, one containing materials sufficient to meet stockpiling objectives to be set by the President, and the other consisting of excess materials. Materials from the excess inventory could be sold provided neither house of Congress vetoed the action. It was hoped to dispose of $4.5 billion worth of excess items without disrupting domestic markets or relations with U.S. allies.

Three Members of the House, testifying at hearings held by the House Armed Services Committee, objected that S 28 would transfer to the Executive Branch power over disposal of materials which had been largely vested in Congress. The Members, all from districts with mineral interests, were Wayne N. Aspinall (D Colo.), chairman of the Interior and Insular Affairs Committee, Laurence J. Burton (R Utah) and Ed Edmondson (D Okla.). Officials of the Bureau of the Budget and Justice Department, on the other hand, objected that the provision for disapproval of a disposal action by one house of Congress violated the principal of the separation of powers.

S 28 provided that the General Services Administration, under the President, would administer the stockpiles. Existing law vested the authority in the President, who had delegated responsibility to the Office of Emergency Planning. The OEP, at the House Armed Services Committee hearings, recommended that S 28 be amended to vest authority to administer the stockpiles in the President.

Atomic Energy

New Emphasis. In a broad departure from previous year's policies, the program sought by the Atomic Energy Commission and approved by Congress in 1965 envisioned a reduction of funds for military purposes and increased amounts for civilian atomic energy projects.

While in fiscal 1965, 60 percent of AEC funds was spent for military purposes and 40 percent for civilian ones, the $2.6 billion program authorized for the AEC for fiscal 1966 (HR 8122—PL 89-32) envisioned a split between these activities of roughly 50-50. Although the public works appropriation bill (HR 9220—PL 89-299) reduced this figure by $143 million (for a total cut of $179.5 million from Administration requests), it provided for the same shift in emphasis.

Outlining the AEC's new program, Commission Chairman Glenn T. Seaborg told the Joint Atomic Energy Committee Jan. 27 that it would be "possible in 1966, without in any way jeopardizing our national security, to make further significant reductions" in AEC programs "most directly related to military requirements."

Weapons production costs in fiscal 1966 would be about $705.4 million, down from $753.3 million in fiscal 1965, Seaborg said, in line with changing stockpile objectives. He said AEC weapons facilities would be closed in 1966 at Medina Base, San Antonio, Texas, and at Clarksville, Tenn. and that the Oak Ridge, Tenn., Y-12 plant would be reduced by 1,000 employees during calendar 1965.

Seaborg requested an increase in the program for development of civilian and military nuclear reactors. Included under the reactor program, he said, would be increased development of "those advanced reactor concepts which will achieve near-or low-gain breeding," and development of uses of nuclear energy for desalination of sea water.

He also sought increases for various civilian programs, such as biology and medicine, and a $5 million increase, to $17.9 million, for the "plowshare" program to develop peaceful uses of atomic energy. Emphasis would be placed on developing a nuclear excavation technology, Seaborg said.

As cleared by Congress, the total authorized by HR 8122 was $69,016,000 less than the amount appropriated to AEC for fiscal 1965. The decrease resulted primarily from reductions in raw materials costs and in cutbacks in production of fissionable materials and nuclear weapons.

HR 8122 reflected a shift in emphasis of the reactor development program from work on low conversion ratio reactors to more advanced reactors, designed to improve the efficiency of nuclear fuels. The bill authorized AEC to enter into cooperative arrangements, under the cooperative power reactor program, for development of a large seed-blanket reactor (LSBR) and a high-temperature gas-cooled reactor (HTGR). Both were advanced reactors designed to use thorium as a fuel in addition to uranium. The LSBR, moreover, was intended to be a breeder reactor, creating as much as or more fuel than it consumed.

AEC Powerlines. In another important measure involving the AEC, Congress passed a bill (HR 8856—PL 89-135) to make clear that the Commission was not subject to local and state government laws, regulations or authority when carrying out the functions assigned to it by federal law, such as constructing, contracting for and operating nuclear facilities for defense, research and related federal purposes.

The immediate effect of the bill was to block attempts by two local government units in California to prevent construction of an extra-high-voltage overhead electric power transmission line to supply electricity to the AEC's Stanford linear accelerator. The two local agencies had objected to the overhead line as unsightly, preferring that the AEC arrange for construction of a more costly underground transmission line. They had refused to grant zoning for the overhead line. When the Federal Government brought suit to compel the granting of an easement for construction of the overhead line, the refusal of the California communities had been upheld by a federal appeals court on grounds that a provision of the Atomic Energy Amendments of 1954 made the AEC subject to state and local laws and regulations in matters of this type, despite the doctrine of federal supremacy which ordinarily would have applied.

HR 8856 revised the 1954 provision to make it clear that the AEC was not subject to the laws and regulations of state and local government units; it could, for example, obtain federal court condemnation orders, regardless of local government opposition, in order to provide itself with land needed for the construction of AEC installations. The bill thus had the simultaneous effect of overturning the appeals court's general interpretation of the disputed provision and of destroying the legal basis for the efforts of the two California local government units to prevent construction of the overhead powerline for the Stanford accelerator. Proponents of the bill said that, had the appeals court's ruling been allowed to stand, any county or city government would have been able to delay or prevent AEC activities of all types and thereby make it impossible for the AEC to carry out its responsibilities.

Nuclear Indemnities. Congress in 1965 also cleared legislation (S 2042—PL 89-210) providing for gradual lowering of federal indemnification guarantees of private nuclear reactors and extending the Price-Anderson Act, the basic authority for providing indemnification, for another 10 years.

S 2042 amended the Price-Anderson Act to cover the lifetimes of nuclear reactors licensed before Aug. 1, 1977, instead of before the current date of Aug. 1, 1967. It also altered the formula on which federal liability was based.

That liability was accepted by the Government in 1957 when the Price-Anderson Act added Section 170 to the Atomic Energy Act of 1954. Section 170 provided that the Federal Government would pay up to $500 million in indemnities for damage claims arising from a nuclear accident at private atomic energy facilities licensed by the Atomic Energy Commission. The federal indemnity was over and above commercial insurance required of the licensees which was available from insurance pools to an amount of $60 million.

The purpose of the legislation, named for its sponsors, Rep. Melvin Price (D Ill.) and Sen. Clinton P. Anderson (D N.M.), was to promote the growth of the private atomic energy industry, especially in the production of electricity, by shifting to the Government much of the risk of liability for catastrophic nuclear accidents. It was assumed that the risk of major incidents was small, if not minute, but even the theoretical possibility of catastrophe combined with the unavailability of heavy insurance was said to be a deterent to expansion of the industry.

S 2042 maintained the theory of federal indemnification and required AEC licensees to continue to carry as much commercial insurance as was available, an amount still about $60 million per facility. But the bill discarded the strict federal liability of $500 million and substituted a sliding scale of limited liability. Under the S 2042 formula, the Government liability was limited to the difference between the amount of commercial insurance available and $560 million. Currently that difference was $500 million, but as the amount of available commercial insurance rose, the federal liability was to gradually diminish. S 2042 also limited all liability for such nuclear incidents to $560 million.

1966

Both the war in Vietnam and Secretary McNamara's clash with Congress escalated sharply in 1966. By year's end, the nation's troop commitment to the war had increased to 385,300 from 184,300 on Dec. 31, 1965. *(See box p. 53.)* War costs continued to rise, increasing from $6.1 billion at the end of fiscal 1966 (mid-calendar 1966) to $20.6 billion a year later. *(See box p. 829.)*

Growing Congressional concern that McNamara was not pursuing the war vigorously enough (mainly by denying military requests to expand the list of North Vietnamese targets that could be bombed) undercut McNamara's prestige and gave military leaders new leverage to take their arguments with McNamara on other defense issues for resolution on Capitol Hill.

After the Joint Chiefs of Staff told a house Subcommittee that McNamara had overruled their unanimous recommendations that development of an advanced manned bomber should be accelerated, Congress responded by appropriating the full amount for this program that the Joint Chiefs sought.

Under reported heavy lobbying by the Navy, Congress also appropriated funds for purchase of an unrequested nuclear-powered guided missile frigate and advance purchase of parts for a second such vessel. The House adopted language specifically requiring the Pentagon to buy the two ships but was dissuaded by the Senate.

In another major variation from McNamara's policies, Congress appropriated $167.9 million for initial deployment of an antiballistic missile system—a weapon McNamara hoped to keep in the research stage until there was conclusive evidence it would work effectively. Support for the ABM, which would affect plants and installations in many Congressional districts, continued to build up throughout the session.

The other major defense controversy of the year was over a Senate-proposed expansion of the President's authority to mobilize the military reserves. The new authority, which was not requested by the White House, would permit the President to call up reservists without first taking the unsettling step of declaring a national emergency—a requirement under existing law. The proposal ran into trouble in the House and was modified in conference to tone down tough new language giving the President the added authority to call individual reservists out of reserve units. The authority was extended in following years through June 30, 1969. (The authority was used by President Johnson in 1968 during the crisis over North Korea's seizure of the U.S. Navy intelligence collection ship Pueblo. *See p. 103.*)

Defense Budget

The President's determination to maintain the level of non-Vietnam forces while providing the funds necessary to support the war was indicated in his fiscal 1967 defense budget, which proposed spending of $57.2 billion and new obligational authority of $58.9 billion.

"So long as cold war tensions persist," the President said in his budget message, "large sums will continue to be required to maintain...superiority over the forces of any potential aggressor." Neither this nor the Vietnam objective could be slighted, he said.

For Vietnam, the President requested $10.3 billion over the 1966 regular spending levels (which the Pentagon could not specifically identify) and also indicated he would ask for fiscal 1966 supplemental defense appropriations of $12.8 billion for Vietnam as the bulk of a $13.1 billion defense supplemental. Although spending figures for non-Vietnam programs were down by $1.5 billion, new obligational authority for these programs (a better measure than spending since NOA includes complex weapons which take several years to produce after commitments are signed) was the same as the previous year, $48.6 billion.

Authorization. The first step toward Congressional approval of ABM deployment came April 25 when the Senate Armed Services Committee reported a version of the annual defense procurement and research authorization bill (S 2950) that carried an unbudgeted $167.9 million for pre-production activities leading to ABM installation.

The panel commented that the funds, if used, could save almost one year in the time required between a decision to deploy the system and attainment of operational capability. This, it said, was "reasonably priced insurance when one considers the consequences of being attacked without any protection."

"After nine years of research and development effort," the Committee continued, "the Nike-X system... has progressed to such an extent that the Committee believes it can afford significant protection against many types of ballistic missile attack....Even a modest ballistic missile defense might save millions of American lives in the event of an enemy attack."

In other action, the Committee denied an Administration request of $145.1 million for two conventionally powered guided missile destroyers and provided instead for the reauthorization of a $150-million unrequested nuclear-powered guided missile frigate which had been fully authorized but only partially funded ($20 million for advance parts) in 1965. The Senate passed the bill without change by voice vote April 28.

When the bill came before the House Armed Services Committee, it became a forum for that panel's most vigorous assault yet on the policies of Secretary McNamara.

After sustaining the Senate's unbudgeted nuclear frigate and adding a second similar frigate, the Committee put language in the bill directing the Secretaries of Defense and of the Navy to proceed with construction of these two unrequested vessels "as soon as practicable." "If this language constitutes a test as to whether Congress has the power to so mandate," the report said, "let the test be made and let this important weapons system be the field of trial."

In a second proposed restriction on the Defense Secretary's decision-making authority, the panel added a new title to the bill prohibiting the Secretary from approving plans to eliminate any major weapon system without first reporting "all the pertinent details" to Congress while it was in session. Armed Services Committees of the House and Senate then would have 90 days to formulate their recommendations to the Secretary on the proposed action. While noting that the proviso was the "direct result" of the panel's belief that the B-58 bomber system should not be phased out, the report said the "fundamental purpose of the language is to ensure that such a situation will not again occur in the future without the Congress being aware of all the pertinent details upon which such a decision was based."

Commenting further on these two restrictive provisions, the Committee forecast a "new era" of Congressional participation in military policy-making. In the past, the statement said, Defense Secretary Robert S. McNamara had not only overruled "sound military recommendations" by the Joint Chiefs of Staff, but had sought to mislead Congress as to what the Chiefs had recommended. In addition, it said, his "almost obsessional dedication to cost effectiveness raises the specter of a decisionmaker who...knows the price of everything and the value of nothing."

In other changes in the bill, the Committee included a new title increasing the basic pay of all armed services personnel by 3.2 percent, effective July 1, 1966 (Administration officials estimated full costs of the pay increase, which was not requested, at an annual $356.8 million); restored the $145.1 million dropped by the Senate for two conventional destroyers and increased research and development allotments for the three services by $363.4 million, including $80 million in Air Force R&D funds (a total of $230 million) for a manned orbiting laboratory (MOL) to conduct military experiments in space and $11.8 million in additional funding for an advanced manned

bomber (a total of $22.8 million). The House passed the bill by a 356-2 roll-call vote June 14 with only minor changes.

Most of the conference action on the measure focused on the policy statements added to the bill by the House. Under pressure from the Senate, the provisos were amended to avert the Constitutional clash that some Senators thought certain if the language went through unchanged. The amendment to direct the Pentagon to move immediately to purchase the nuclear frigates was changed to stipulate that the contract for one of the vessels was to be entered into "as soon as practicable" unless the President advised Congress that the ship's construction was not in the national interest. The proviso blocking the Defense Secretary from eliminating weapon systems without informing Congress was watered down to knock out the 90-day waiting period during which the Armed Services Committees could formulate recommendations on the Secretary's actions.

In other actions, conferees accepted the House action providing for two nuclear-powered frigates and two conventionally powered destroyers but reduced the allotment for the second frigate from $130.5 million down to $20 million for procurement of long-leadtime parts. Conferees also agreed to the House's addition of the military pay increase, the House provision of an additional $11.8 million for advanced bomber development and to $50 million of the $80 million House increase for MOL (a total of $200 million).

The report was adopted July 12 by a 359-2 roll-call vote in the House and an 81-1 roll call in the Senate. As signed by the President, S 2950 (PL 89-501) authorized $17,480,759,000, a total of $533.9 million more than Administration requests.

Appropriation. Debate on the $58.1 billion defense money bill (HR 15941) skirted the major programs funded under the measure and centered on a late-session move by the Senate to broaden the President's discretionary authority to mobilize the reserves.

Although the House agreed with the need for a more flexible callup authority (which would permit the President to mobilize reservists without declaring a national emergency), the two chambers differed sharply over how far the new authority should go. (Existing law permitted mobilization of units and individual reservists not in units if the President declared an emergency. The President did not request but also did not oppose the new authority.) The Senate wanted to let the President reach into the units and pull out individuals who had served short active-duty stints, but the House felt this would be disruptive to the units. After a seven-week battle that delayed passage of the bill until the final week of the session, the two Houses agreed to a compromise provision which permitted the callup without declaring an emergency but limiting the new authority for calling individuals out of units.

The Senate's callup proviso, sponsored by Armed Services Committee Chairman Richard B. Russell (D Ga.) and the Committee's ranking Republican member, Leverett Saltonstall (Mass.) had been designed to achieve what the two Senators called "equality of service"—equity between Vietnam-assigned draftees and persons who had put in short stints on active duty but were exempt from the draft because of their membership in the reserves. As accepted by the Senate Aug. 17, the proviso empowered the President, without declaring an emergency, to mobilize any individual member of a reserve component (including those participating in Reserve or National Guard units) who had not yet served on active duty or had served for less than two years.

Conferees in an Aug. 24 report agreed to a compromise plan that included the basic Senate provision but directed that consideration be given to preserving the "identity and maintenance" of whole units wherever possible. After accepting most provisions of the conference bill, the House rejected the callup proviso Aug. 25 by a 39-162 standing vote.

After a prolonged round of additional discussions, conferees agreed Oct. 10 to a second conference report including a considerably altered reserve callup plan. Under the final provision, the President could mobilize entire reserve units, individual reservists (with less than two years' service) who were not attached to units, and unit members who were members of the Reserve Enlistment Program (REP)—a plan which allowed a draft-eligible man to enter a reserve unit while awaiting his six-month active duty training stint, then return to the unit to complete a total of five and one-half years' reserve service, all the while exempt from the draft. The authority was to expire June 30, 1968. The Defense Department estimated that if the provision was fully utilized it could affect approximately 789,000 reservists.

With little further debate, the second conference agreement was sustained by the House Oct. 11 by a 305-42 roll-call vote and the Senate the same day by voice vote. In brief remarks prior to Senate acceptance, Russell said he was sure the House would have accepted his original amendment except for "strong lobbying efforts" by Reserve and National Guard pressure groups which had contended Russell's plan would disrupt units.

In other differences between the House and Senate bills, conferees accepted a Senate floor amendment prohibiting commitment of any funds in the bill for purchase of the Navy's F-111B fighter aircraft, agreed to a Senate add-on of an additional $50 million for the manned orbiting laboratory (MOL) program (bringing the appropriation up to the full authorization level of $200 million) and agreed to House action denying $145.1 million for two conventionally powered guided missile destroyers.

As signed by the President (PL 89-687), the bill appropriated $58,067,472,000 for the Defense Department in fiscal 1967. The sum represented an increase of $403.1 million above Administration requests, including $167.9 million for deployment of an ABM system, $130.5 million for purchase of a nuclear-powered guided missile frigate, $20 million for advance parts for a second such frigate, an additional $11.8 million for development of an advanced manned bomber (for a total of $22.8 million), and smaller increases for a variety of other programs.

Vietnam Supplemental. At the request of the President, Congress passed a bill (HR 13546—PL 89-374) making supplemental fiscal 1966 defense and foreign aid appropriations totaling $13,135,719,000, including $12.8 billion for Vietnam and the rest for the pay increase enacted the year before and for increased costs of veterans benefits. The final amount approved in the measure was the same as the White House sought. *(See p. 69-70 for other details.)*

Manned Bomber Issue

One of the sharpest controversies of the year came when a House Subcommittee studied McNamara's plans to retire much of the manned bomber fleet.

In December 1965 McNamara announced plans to retire 345 early-model B-52 strategic bombers and all 80 B-58 supersonic strategic bombers, leaving 255 late-model B-52s in service. The retirements would take place over five years. To replace some of the losses, but not all, he announced plans to buy 210 models of a bomber version of the F-111, a supersonic swing-wing aircraft developed as a tactical fighter for the Air Force and Navy.

The House Armed Services Committee, Subcommittee No. 2, held hearings Jan. 25 - Feb. 2 on this plan. On April 25 it released a report on the plan which charged (1) that the FB-111 did not have sufficient range or payload to qualify as a substitute for late model B-52s, but was merely an interim weapon system; (2) that the useful life of the late model-B-52s would end in the mid-1970s; (3) that the Joint Chiefs of Staff were unanimous in recommending the development of an advanced manned strategic aircraft (AMSA); (4) that the Chiefs did not concur in the decision to retire the B-58; (5) that Defense Secretary McNamara was virtually alone in seeing no "clear need" for a follow-on to the late-model B-52s.

The Subcommittee recommended that $11.8 million be added to the fiscal 1968 defense program for AMSA. This was a sum recommended by the Chief of Staff of the Air Force to begin the "contract definition" phase of development. Under Defense Department ground rules, however, "contract definition" depends on a decision by the Defense Secretary to pursue full development with an eye to procurement—in this case, commitment to a $4-billion program. The Subcommittee also recommended that the Defense Department be required to seek the "advice" of Congress in advance of setting in motion plans to retire any major weapons system. Congress appropriated the $11.8 million and adopted a modified version of the latter recommendation. *(See sections on military authorization and appropriation bills, above.)*

CIA Oversight

After bitter debate, the Senate in July rejected a proposal, largely backed by Vietnam war critics, to permit members of the Senate Foreign Relations Committee to participate directly in Senate oversight of U.S. intelligence operations.

A resolution (S Res 283), drafted in the Foreign Relations Committee and brought to the floor by Sen. J. W. Fulbright (D Ark.), Committee chairman, called for the creation of a Committee on Intelligence Operations whose nine members would be drawn equally from the Armed Services, Appropriations and Foreign Relations Committees. Currently, Senate oversight of the Government's intelligence operations was by senior members of the Armed Services and Appropriations Committees, meeting as one group.

The proposal was made by the Foreign Relations Committee on the ground that the Central Intelligence Agency (CIA) played a policy-making role in U.S. foreign relations. It was opposed in an attack led by members of the Armed Services and Appropriations Committees chiefly on the ground that expanding the current Senate CIA "watchdog" group would increase the risk of "leaks." Prominent in the dispute, moreover, was a contending for authority on the part of senior members of major Senate committees.

The Senate July 14, following an unusual secret session, by a 61-28 roll-call vote in effect rejected the resolution. The roll call was on a point of order that S Res 283 involved subject matter predominantly under the jurisdiction of the Armed Services Committee and should, therefore, be referred to that Committee. Since there was little expectation that the Armed Services Committee would approve S Res 283, a vote to sustain the point of order amounted to a vote to reject the resolution.

The resolution was not reported by the Armed Services Committee in 1966 but on Jan. 7, 1967, Chairman Richard B. Russell (D Ga.) announced that for the 90th Congress he would ask three members of the Foreign Relations Committee to attend the meetings of the Senate CIA oversight committees, of which he was chairman.

Russell said he had asked Fulbright, Bourke B. Hickenlooper (Iowa), the ranking Republican member of the Foreign Relations Committee, and Majority Leader Mike Mansfield (D Mont.), third ranking member of the Committee, to attend the meetings. They would have full right to participate in questioning of intelligence officials and to consider appropriation matters involving the secret agencies, Russell said.

Base Closures, Construction Funds

In a renewal of the long-standing controversy over closure of military bases, Congress added a proviso to the fiscal 1967 defense construction bill (S 3105—PL 89-568) tightening its 1965 requirement for a Congressional review of the Pentagon's base closure plans. The new provision stipulated that plans for closures would have to be submitted to Congress for a 30-day review while Congress was in session. The 1965 requirement stipulated only that the Pentagon could not close bases until 30 days after informing Congress, which left open the possibility that bases could be closed between sessions without a review being conducted.

As signed by the President, the construction authorization measure carried $1,005,842,000 for military base construction and family housing in fiscal 1967. In a subsequent base construction money bill (HR 17637—PL 89-744), Congress appropriated $979,570,000, a cut of $135,377,000 from Administration requests.

Reserve-Guard Merger

For the second year in a row, Congress rejected a controversial Defense Department proposal to merge the Army Reserve and the Army National Guard into a single reserve force under Guard management. Following the procedure used to block the plan in 1965, Congress wrote language into the defense appropriations bill (HR 15941) requiring that any realignment or reorganization of the two reserve components during the current fiscal year be specifically authorized by law. The merger plan, first proposed in late 1964, was designed to increase combat effectiveness while providing a substantial reduction in costs, according to supporters.

A plan to permanently block the merger by setting required annual strengths for both the Reserve and Guard was approved by the House as part of a reserve reorganization and call-up bill (HR 17195), but the measure died for the 89th Congress when House and Senate conferees agreed to a call-up plan written into the defense appropriations bill. *(See above.)*

Renegotiation Act

With little debate, Congress June 24 cleared a bill (HR 13431—PL 89-480) providing a two-year extension of the Renegotiation Act of 1951, through June 30, 1968. The Act provided for the recapture by the Government of excessive profits realized by private firms on contracts with the Pentagon and other Government agencies. The Administration had asked for a six-year extension, but the term was cut by the House Ways and Means Committee in order to permit Congress to decide in the relatively near future whether the renegotiation process was still necessary.

Military Draft Hearings

Rising draft calls resulting from the Vietnam war buildup generated criticism of the draft system on college campuses and in Congress. On June 22 the House Armed Services Committee opened hearings on the Selective Service System. The major complaints were about the system of deferments, especially for students, and the system of choosing from among those eligible for the draft. Several witnesses urged adoption of a lottery-type selection process. Lt. Gen. Lewis B. Hershey, director of Selective Service, urged retention of the existing system. The Committee considered many suggestions but no bill. The President July 2 established a 20-member National Advisory Commission on Selective Service to study the draft and to report recommendations to him by Jan. 1, 1967. Defense Secretary Robert S. McNamara Aug. 23 announced a new program to draft and "salvage" borderline rejects through a special training program.

Military Medical Benefits

Congress enacted legislation (HR 14088—PL 89-614) extending for the first time eligibility for outpatient care in civilian hospitals to spouses and children of active-duty U.S. military personnel (they were already eligible for inpatient care). The bill also made military retirees and their spouses and children eligible for both inpatient and outpatient care at civilian facilities for the first time. For mentally retarded and physically handicapped spouses and children of active-duty personnel, the bill created a new program of Government-subsidized care.

Costs of the care provided in the bill were to be shared between the patient and the Government, with the latter bearing up to 80 percent of costs. First-year cost of the bill was estimated as $142 million. The Administration supported the bill, although Congress made its provisions take effect sooner than the Administration would have liked, thus increasing the President's fiscal 1967 budget estimate.

Atomic Energy Program

The Johnson Administration in 1966 asked Congress to provide $2,407,470,000 in funds for the Atomic Energy Commission in fiscal 1967. Responding to the request with very few changes, Congress in the Atomic Energy Commission Authorization Act (HR 14732—PL 89-428) subsequently authorized $2,259,958,000 in new appropriations for the AEC, with the understanding that additional amounts needed to fulfill the over-all AEC request for $2.4 billion in fiscal 1967 would come from appropriations left over from previous years and from revenues received by the AEC from the sale of goods and services.

Later, in the Public Works Appropriations Act for fiscal 1967 (HR 17787—PL 89-689), Congress appropriated actual funds for the AEC in fiscal 1967. Because unobligated balances from prior years and revenues from sales were somewhat higher than had been anticipated earlier in the year when the authorization bill (HR 14732) was passed, it was not necessary to provide new appropriations as high as previously thought necessary. Instead, Congress in HR 17787 provided $2,199,030,000 in new appropriations for fiscal 1967, plus authority to use $223,635,000 in unobligated appropriations from previous years and revenues from sales. The total—$2,422,665,000—actually gave the AEC about $15 million more in funds for fiscal 1967 than the Administration had initially sought. The increase was chiefly for underground testing of nuclear weapons.

As compared with fiscal 1966, the total of $2,422,665,-000 made available in HR 17787 for fiscal 1967 was nearly $100 million lower because of cuts in amounts for production of raw materials, fissionable materials and nuclear weapons. Other programs remained at about the same levels, with few innovations. Because of Administration desire to hold the line on Government spending, very few AEC program levels were increased.

A notable feature of the 1966 authorization bill (HR 14732) was the emphasis on the fast breeder reactor in the civilian power reactor development program. Funds for the fast breeder for fiscal 1967 were boosted by more than $10 million above the fiscal 1966 spending level of $34 million. The fast breeder offered prospects for a cheap and readily available source of energy for the future. Fast breeder reactors would continuously produce amounts of fissionable material in excess of that consumed, thus providing a new source of reactor fuel and reducing the cost of producing electricity.

1967

Inability to conclude the Vietnam war continued to undermine McNamara's position in 1967.

With McNamara becoming a political liability, his prestige with the President suffered. Despite the Secretary's well-known opposition, Mr. Johnson ordered the ABM system deployed. Two months later, in November, the White House announced that McNamara would be leaving the Pentagon early the next year to take over the presidency of the World Bank. Although McNamara said he had mentioned the Bank post to the President as a possible long-range objective, he appeared surprised by Mr. Johnson's timing.

Throughout the year, McNamara suffered a round of rebuffs from Congress, including denial of funds for a fleet of fast deployment logistic ships to move equipment rapidly in the event of new brushfire wars, a sharp curtailment of the F-111B (TFX) aircraft program, a permanent blocking of the Reserve-Guard merger, and a restriction against buying Navy minesweepers overseas. The latter restriction negated a reciprocal agreement with Great Britain under which the British were to buy F-111 aircraft in return for construction of the U.S. minesweepers in British yards.

The nation's posture in Vietnam was summed up by R. W. Apple Jr. of *The New York Times* in an Aug. 6 report from Saigon: "In the opinion of most disinterested observers, the war is not going well. Victory is not close at hand. It may be beyond reach. It is clearly unlikely in the next year, or even in the next two years, and American officers talk somberly about fighting here for decades."

Defense Budget

Mounting costs of the war were reflected in the President's fiscal 1968 defense budget, which called for spending of $72.3 billion and new obligational authority of $74.7 billion.

The President estimated in his budget message that $21.9 billion would be spent for the war in fiscal 1968 and that a Vietnam supplemental of $12.3 billion would be needed to complete requirements for fiscal 1967.

As in the previous year's budget, the President stressed that the Vietnam buildup would not come at the expense of non-Vietnam forces. The budget envisioned new obligational authority of $54.1 billion for non-Vietnam programs, an increase of $2.7 billion over the President's revised estimates of NOA for fiscal 1967. "Today," the President emphasized, "our military requirements are dictated by two fundamental realities. We must continue to counter aggression in South Vietnam. We must also continue to enhance our ability to meet changing threats to our freedom and security elsewhere. The 1968 budget will ensure that our forces remain equal to both these tasks."

Barring unforeseen developments, the President said, the Vietnam funds sought for the new fiscal year should be adequate and another supplemental should not be needed. He said the fiscal 1967 supplemental had become necessary because the "most rapid phase" of the Vietnam buildup had occurred while the fiscal 1967 budget was in preparation (late in 1965) and that it had been difficult to determine the requirements a full 18 months in advance. "Rather than request an amount not based on firm requirements," he added, "it was decided to defer the request for the additional funds until those requirements became better known."

For the first time, the President requested standby funds for possible deployment of the ABM system in the event negotiations with the Soviets on ABM limitation failed. The budget said that of a total of $782.2 million in requested ABM appropriations, about $375 million was related to deployment of the system and the rest for continued research.

Authorization. Controversy on the $21.1 billion defense procurement and research authorization (S 666) focused on McNamara's request for a fleet of fast deployment logistic ships (FDLs), a new class of very large supply vessels designed to give the United States a rapid deployment capability for intervention in future brushfire wars. Not only did Congress deny McNamara's request for $233.5 million for five of the vessels, but it also rescinded the previous year's appropriation of $67.6 million for two FDLs.

The program first encountered difficulties in the Senate Armed Services Committee because some Members were unwilling to consider it as a mere request for five additional ships but rather saw it as a move by the Administration to secure tacit Congressional approval of all 30 vessels ultimately contemplated for the FDL fleet. This was because the Navy intended to contract immediately for the entire 30-ship package with a single shipbuilding firm instead of the usual practice of parceling out the order in increments to several different firms. This new contract procedure was called "total package procurement," and McNamara hoped to use it for all major new weapon purchases.

Critics also contended that the $1 billion cost for 30 of the ships was excessive and that the vulnerability of the 880-foot craft would necessitate spending of another $1 billion or more for antisubmarine and antiaircraft protection. Some of the ships were to be deployed fully loaded off potential trouble spots while others, partially loaded, were to be stationed on the U.S. coasts.

Another problem for the FDLs was a vigorous lobbying effort against the plan by many of the nation's maritime interests. Shippers contended they would lose lucrative military cargo contracts, while seamen's unions argued their members would lose jobs. Some of the nation's shipbuilders also were opposed, contending that the "total package" contract with one firm might cost them much of their usual business.

Probably the most significant opposition to the plan, however, was that of Senate Armed Services Committee Chairman Richard B. Russell (D Ga.), who argued that the ships might encourage U.S. intervention in more situations like Vietnam. Congressional and other sources close to the issue told Congressional Quarterly that the impact of Russell's argument and his personal influence on defense matters were largely responsible for the program's defeat. With Russell leading the opposition, the FDLs were dropped in the Senate and again in conference after the House had acted to restore part of the program funds.

Highlight of the bill's military hardware and research authorization was the standby financing it provided in the event the Administration decided to install the ABM. The bill authorized $291 million for this purpose. In addition, it carried $421.3 billion for continued research on the project for a total ABM authorization of $712.3 billion.

Although installation of the ABM did not become a major floor issue in either the House or Senate, Armed Services Committees of the two chambers differed on the question in their reports accompanying the bill. The House panel called for immediate deployment of a "thin" system to defend U.S. cities and missile sites against Chinese attack or an accidental Soviet firing, while the Senate group adopted the Administration's view that the decision on deployment should await the outcome of U.S.-Soviet talks.

In other actions on the bill, Congress added $294.7 billion for procurement of additional aircraft for the Air Force, Navy and Marine Corps and for modifications of existing Air Force craft; provided an additional $83 million

for two nuclear powered guided missile frigates (costing $249.6 million) instead of the two conventionally powered destroyers requested by the Administration; and provided an additional $25 million (a total of $51 million) for advanced bomber development.

In addition to its funding provisions, S 666 included language establishing, effective in 1969, a four-year term of appointment for the Chiefs of Staff of the Army and the Air Force and the Chief of Naval Operations. Existing law required the four-year term only for the Commandant of the Marine Corps, allowing appointments for any period of up to four years for the other three Chiefs. The fixed four-year term for the Chiefs, which originated in the House Armed Services Committee, was designed to assure the Chiefs a long enough tenure in office to put their ideas to a full test. The provision was opposed by the Administration, which preferred the flexible authority provided under existing law. It was widely believed the Administration's opposition was based on concern that the provision might encourage a bid by the military to diminish civilian control of the Pentagon.

As signed by the President, S 666 (PL 90-22) authorized $21,168,032,000 for defense procurement and research in fiscal 1968, a total of $101.6 million more than the Administration sought.

Appropriation. The long-standing battle over the F-111 (TFX) aircraft resumed when the House took up the $70.5 billion defense appropriation bill (HR 10738).

In reporting its version of the bill June 9, the House Armed Services Committee pared $78.2 million from the $287 million requested for procurement of F-111Bs. The Committee allotment was sustained by the full House but cut by the Senate to $115 million, $172 million less than Administration requests. Conferees agreed to a compromise figure of $147.9 million but emphasized in their report that the funds should be used only for procurement of eight of the aircraft to support the continuing research effort and for purchase of no more than $10 million worth of engines to support a possible future buy. Conferees stressed that they considered the project strictly in the developmental stage and that their approval of the eight aircraft should not be interpreted as a Congressional decision to move toward full production.

In the last few days of the bill's consideration, an intense House-Senate dispute developed over a House floor amendment which prohibited construction in a foreign shipyard of any naval vessel funded under the bill. The amendment, deleted by the Senate, was returned to the House for a separate vote after House and Senate conferees were unable to work out a solution. The House then voted overwhelmingly to retain the amendment and the Senate followed suit rather than subject the entire bill to a long delay.

The purpose of the proviso, which had been sponsored by Rep. John W. Byrnes (R Wis.), was to block the Defense Department from permitting Great Britain to bid on seven prototypes of a new ocean minesweeper as part of a reciprocal U.S.-British arms purchase arrangement. The British in 1965 had committed themselves to purchase $2.6 billion in U.S. equipment—primarily the F-111 aircraft— in return for a U.S. pledge to purchase $325 million in British arms. The Defense Department had not agreed to earmark any specific items for construction in Britain but agreed to allow the British to bid competitively with U.S. firms for a number of U.S. requirements. Defense Secre-

(Continued on p. 848)

Noninterventionists, Shipping Interests Combine to Defeat . . .

The Administration's request for a fleet of fast deployment logistic ships (FDLs) provided the major item of controversy during Congressional consideration of the fiscal 1968 defense procurement and research authorization bill (S 666). Defense Secretary Robert S. McNamara suffered complete defeat in his battle to secure authorization for five FDLs. Not only were the five craft he requested for fiscal 1968 deleted, but also an existing appropriation for two of the vessels was rescinded. (The Administration's 1968 request of $183.6 million for four of the vessels was also denied, leaving the future of the program very much in doubt.)

The purpose of the mammoth vessel—which would weigh over 40,000 tons and almost equal the length of three football fields—would be to move in the waters off potential trouble spots with all the heavy equipment and combat supplies needed by ground forces for rapid intervention. Fifteen of the vessels (half the proposed FDL fleet) could supply all of an infantry division's heavy equipment and enough supplies and rations to sustain it for a 15-day period. For swift movement, the ships would be equipped with the fastest engines of any supply vessel in either the U.S. merchant or naval fleets.

Under the Pentagon's plan, FDL vessels would cruise off foreign shores until called on to "marry up" with a troop contingent, which would be airlifted to the scene. After a Vietnam peace, for instance, four of the vessels might be stationed off the coast of Southeast Asia as a deterrent to a new outbreak of war. Four more might be deployed in the Caribbean, while several others were shuttled through the Mediterranean and around the African coast. The remainder would be partially loaded and would remain in ports on each U.S. coast—ready to move as soon as the U.S. intervened.

The Administration was practically the only source of strong support for the FDL concept during 1967 and 1968. Many Members of Congress—the most influential was Richard B. Russell (D Ga.), chairman of the Senate Armed Services Committee—feared that the FDL concept would encourage U.S. intervention in more situations like Vietnam. These noninterventionists were joined in opposition to the FDLs by a strong array of shippers and merchant seamen who feared loss of lucrative military cargo contracts and civilian jobs and of shipbuilders who saw grave portents in the way the vessels were to be procured.

Background

The FDL concept was developed during 1964-65 as the result of joint Army-Navy studies on global logistic problems likely to confront the United States during the 1970s. Defense Secretary McNamara approved the plan early in 1965 and sought $131.8 million in fiscal 1966 appropriations for the first four FDLs. Largely because of the experimental aspects of the plan, Congress in the fiscal 1966 Defense Procurement Act (PL 89-37) reduced the authorization to $67.6 million—providing for only two of the craft. Funds for the two vessels were appropriated in the fiscal 1966 Defense Appropriations Act (PL 89-213).

After action on PL 89-213, McNamara decided to wait for more program funds and then to use the FDL to test his newly devised "total package procurement" approach, which he previously had tested only for relatively small ship contracts. Under this approach, which would conform to current aircraft procurement techniques, a contract for the entire FDL package—including design, construction and possibly even maintenance—would go to a single firm.

The Pentagon assumed that competition for the huge contract would touch off a wave of needed shipyard improvements because the added efficiency would cut long-range costs. Such modernization, it thought, would go a long way toward solving the chronic U.S. maritime crisis. But for most U.S. shipbuilders it meant that only a modicum of their number would get the contracts for all of the Navy's ships. Their opposition to the total package approach intensified when competition for the FDL award was narrowed to three companies engaged primarily in the aerospace field—Litton Systems Inc., Lockheed Co., and the General Dynamics Corp.

Support for FDLs

ADMINISTRATION. Administration arguments for procurement of the FDLs were outlined by the Defense Department in a special pamphlet made public Nov. 14, 1966. These arguments were repeated by Administration witnesses during testimony before the House and Senate Armed Services Committees in early 1967. Witnesses included McNamara, Navy Secretary Paul H. Nitze and Gen. Harold K. Johnson, Chief of Staff of the U.S. Army. Following were the Administration's major contentions.

Deterrent Effect. The FDL's capability to support fast and heavy deployment of U.S. combat forces, the pamphlet said, would have the "same deterrent effect as large, costly occupation forces...." FDLs would provide the United States with a "demonstrated ability to move forces rapidly" which could "cause potential enemies to have serious doubts about their chances of military success in remote areas of the world."

Advantage Over Use of Merchant Shipping. Because FDL vessels would be "loaded and in position" prior to an emergency, the Department asserted, the FDL concept had "no counterpart" in the merchant marine. To charter merchant ships in an emergency would "invoke the very deployment delays these ships are designed to overcome." (Gen. Johnson during House hearings said it had taken merchant shipping 56 days to move the first U.S. division from the United States to Korea following the outbreak of the Korean war. By contrast, he said, a combination of FDLs and the new C-5A transport aircraft could land an even greater force in Korea in less than two weeks.)

The capability of the FDL for rapid unloading once a beachhead was secured and its facilities for "controlled humidity" storage also could not be equalled by U.S. merchant vessels, the statement asserted. The Department also pointed to other special features of the

... *Administration Request for Fleet of Mammoth Supply Ships*

FDL such as its accommodations for a large contingent of military personnel to perform maintenance on the cargo and its facility to store together both a division's heavy weapons and all its ammunition and other necessary items.

The Department's statement contained assurances that FDLs in no way would diminish the existing military supply role performed by the U.S. merchant fleet. "At no time will they be available for cargo-carrying in competition with the merchant marine," the statement asserted. And because FDLs would be manned in many instances by civil marine crews, it added, the program would create an estimated 1,000-2,000 additional seagoing jobs.

McNamara in January 1967 offered to write into the authorization act a restriction against use of the FDLs for transportation of any point-to-point cargo during peacetime.

Airlift Alternative. Where equipment could not be stored on land in readiness for an emergency, a massive airlift would be the only alternative to use of the FDL, the statement said, and this would be prohibitively expensive. While 15 FDLs moving from the West Coast could fully supply an infantry division in Southeast Asia within 13 days, it would take over 200 of the huge C-5A jet transports to deliver the same load within the same time, the Department said.

NON-ADMINISTRATION. In addition to the support of the three aerospace firms in the running for the FDL contract, the Administration gained support for the plan from the Industrial Union of Marine and Shipbuilding Workers (AFL-CIO). During House hearings, a spokesman for the union noted that the FDLs would be built, loaded and operated by American workers.

Opposition to FDLs

Seamen. Capt. Lloyd W. Sheldon, president of the International Organization of Masters, Mates and Pilots, a major merchant marine union, early in January termed the FDL a "power grab" which if successful would knock "both the unions and private business...out of the military end of the shipping business." Instead of investing in FDLs, Sheldon said, Congress should support a policy giving the United States a merchant marine that could meet both commercial and military needs.

Shipbuilders. Daniel D. Strohmeier, a spokesman for the shipbuilding division of Bethlehem Steel Corp., assailed the contention of FDL supporters that competition among shipbuilders for a "total package procurement" contract would revitalize the shipbuilding industry by encouraging construction of new shipyards or modernization of existing ones. He urged an expansion of the existing Government subsidy programs for replacement of aging merchant vessels.

Ship Owners. Ralph E. Casey, president of the American Merchant Marine Institute, an organization representing 33 companies that owned and operated merchant ships, said that—assurances of the Defense Department to the contrary—there was a strong possibility that FDLs would operate in "direct competition" with the privately owned merchant fleet. Casey said he could "well envision some future period of temporary or permanent peace" when Congress would balk at "the chartering and use of commercial vessels for military cargo when these vastly expensive supply ships float aimlessly about."

Criticizing the prospective cost of an FDL fleet, Casey said the construction and operating funds necessary to support one FDL would equal the construction and operating subsidy for five modern commercial ships, meaning the cost of the entire 30-ship FDL program (estimated cost per ship: $35 million) would be roughly equivalent to 150 commercial vessels. "When it is considered that the construction subsidy brings forth an equal amount of private capital which then goes into the economy," Casey asserted, "it is apparent where the benefit to the taxpayer really lies."

Congressmen. During the 1967 House Armed Services Committee hearings, both the chairman, Edward A. Garmatz (D Md.) and the ranking minority member, William S. Mailliard (R Calif.), of the House Committee on Merchant Marine and Fisheries opposed the FDL concept. Other Congressional opponents of the plan contended that the 30 FDLs would cost about $1 billion and that the vulnerability of the ships would necessitate expenditure of another $1 billion or more for antisubmarine and antiaircraft protection. They also feared that approval of five additional FDLs in effect would commit Congress to approval of the entire 30-ship package, since the Navy intended to contract immediately with a single shipbuilder for procurement of all 30 vessels.

Russell. Of all the opposition to the bill, probably the most significant was that of Senate Armed Services Committee Chairman Richard B. Russell (D Ga.), who feared that the vessels would encourage U.S. intervention in more situations like Vietnam.

During floor debate on the procurement bill, Russell said there was "reason to think (because of the forward positioning of combat supplies and equipment)...that if it is easy for us to go anywhere and do anything, we will always be going somewhere and doing something." Russell also said he feared the worldwide deployment of the "huge floating arsenals" would be taken as an intimidation by numerous countries throughout the world.

Although he did not repeat this contention on the Senate floor, Russell during committee hearings indicated that a controlling factor in his opposition had been concern that the FDLs might be used to enforce sanctions against segregationist regimes in Rhodesia and South Africa. "I know I am suspect when there are any racial problems," Russell, a long-time opponent of civil rights legislation, asserted. "But no matter what races were involved, I would say we had no business going into Rhodesia....Some persons will keep making speeches and building up sentiments in this country until it will not be long before we have...another pretty good-sized Vietnam on our hands."

Marksmanship Subsidies Ended

Government subsidies for the National Rifle Assn. (NRA) civilian marksmanship program came under fire in 1967 from Congressional supporters of gun control legislation. Opponents of the subsidies objected particularly to the annual National Rifle Matches, the major event of the NRA program, for which the Government supplied weapons, ammunition and lodging for participants. The matches tied up an entire military reservation, Camp Perry, Ohio, for more than a month.

Although Congressional critics of the subsidies were unsuccessful in efforts to block the 1967 matches (they were held Aug. 3-Sept. 1 at Camp Perry), Army Secretary Stanley R. Resor Nov. 1 announced cancellation of Government support for the 1968 event. The Pentagon said the move would save more than $2 million. The NRA Dec. 5 said the Army had agreed to permit it to hold the 1968 matches at Camp Perry, without Army participation or supplies.

The move to eliminate Government subsidies of the NRA was led by Sen. Edward M. Kennedy (D Mass.) and Rep. Richard D. McCarthy (D N.Y.). In June, Kennedy wrote Defense Secretary Robert S. McNamara that it was "impossible to justify" the Government subsidy in view of other budgetary needs. McCarthy wrote McNamara that the NRA was open to members of extremist groups and that it had advocated "vigilantism" in calling for the "armed citizen" to counter rioting.

Franklin L. Orth, executive vice president of NRA, June 17 said the subsidy was needed because "it has been definitely shown that the young man who receives marksmanship training prior to entering the service stands a much better chance of survival." McCarthy retorted that a 1966 Defense Department study showed that only 3 percent of Army trainees had been members of NRA clubs.

Both Kennedy and McCarthy offered amendments to curtail the subsidies during floor consideration of the fiscal 1968 defense appropriations bill (HR 10738), but they were unsuccessful.

tary McNamara had identified the new ocean minesweeper as one of the programs on which the British would be permitted to bid.

A total of nine of the minesweepers were funded in the fiscal 1966 and 1967 shipbuilding programs, but their construction was deferred when McNamara decided to seek seven more of the craft for fiscal 1968 and then contract for the entire 16-vessel package. Byrnes did not oppose the construction in Britain of the first nine ships but said the seven others should be constructed in the United States so that U.S. yards would have a capability for producing the vessels if the British supply source ever were cut off. (The British cancelled their F-111 orders in early 1968.)

Aside from the estimated $20 billion that the bill provided for Vietnam (the rest of the Vietnam allotment was to come in other measures), its most controversial appropriation was an allowance of $718.9 million for the ABM

system, including $421.3 million for continued development work and $297.6 million in standby financing for deployment. Although HR 10738 did not include language directing that the funds be spent, both the House and Senate Appropriations Committees urged in their reports on the bill that the Administration move ahead with deployment of a "thin" system to protect against a Chinese attack.

As cleared by Congress, HR 10738 (PL 90-96) appropriated $69,936,620,000 for the Defense Department in fiscal 1968, a total of $1,647,380,000 less than Administration requests. Of the net reductions, $467.7 million represented requests that had been disallowed during consideration of the procurement bill (S 666). Of the further reductions of $1,179,680,000, the major cuts were $139.1 million for procurement of the F-111B, $123 million for the first ship of a new type of amphibious assault vessel, $103 million from the requested allotment of $326 million for the Air Force A-7D ground-attack aircraft, $64.1 million for additional civilian employment and $52.7 million for implementation of a new Defense Department accounting system.

(Total Congressional reductions in Administration requests came to more than $2 billion. These were partially offset by a number of add-ons, however, including the following major items: $114.8 million for procurement of one nuclear-powered guided missile frigate and $20 million for purchase of long-leadtime items preparatory to construction of a second such craft; $106.7 million for purchase of additional EA-6A (low-level attack) fighter aircraft for the Marine Corps; $60 million for purchase of additional C-130 transport aircraft for the Air Force; and $21 million for accelerated development work on an advanced manned bomber (for a total of $47 million).

Vietnam Supplemental. For the third year in a row, Congress acceded to Administration requests for supplemental appropriations to carry on the war in Vietnam. On March 21, it cleared a bill (HR 7123—PL 90-8) appropriating $12,196,520,000 in additional Vietnam funding for fiscal 1967. The funds were $79,350,000 less than Administration requests. *(For details, see p. 81.)*

ABM Deployment Decision

After considerable pressure from the military committees of Congress, Secretary McNamara announced Sept. 18 that the Administration had decided to install a limited, $5-billion system to protect against the threat of a missile attack by Communist China in the 1970s.

Announcing the decision in a carefully worded San Francisco speech, McNamara warned against pressures to expand the light system into a heavy Soviet-oriented one. He said such a system could not be effective against an all-out Soviet attack and could only lead to higher Soviet spending on offensive weapons and a similar response by the United States. *(For additional details, see special article on ABM, p. 869.)*

The Administration's decision to install the limited system, to be called "Sentinel," came three months after Communist China announced that it had successfully exploded its first hydrogen bomb. After the Chinese announcement, pro-ABM sentiment in Congress increased markedly, particularly among Republicans, who threatened to make it a campaign issue in 1968.

Although he had opposed the concept of an anti-Chinese system in the past, McNamara said in his speech that there now were "marginal" grounds for concluding that the light deployment was "prudent." Although an attack by Communist China would be "insane and suicidal," he said "one can conceive conditions under which China might miscalculate. We wish to reduce such possibilities to a minimum." McNamara's speech was somber and unenthusiastic, which led many observers to conclude that he had not compromised on the issue but had been overruled completely by the President.

ABM Hearings. After the ABM deployment decision was announced, the Joint Atomic Energy Committee's Subcommittee on Military Applications held four days of hearings in November on ABM defense. Since McNamara on Nov. 3 had announced that the Soviet Union was thought to be developing an orbital bomb (called FOBS for fractional orbital bombardment system), the hearings focused mainly on that issue.

John S. Foster Jr., director of defense research and engineering, told the panel that the proposed U.S. ABM system could be modified to cope with a FOBS. Foster said the United States decided not to build a FOBS in 1963, about the same time the Russians decided to build theirs. Instead, the United States decided to develop "over-the-horizon" radar systems which gave early warning of an incoming FOBS, Foster said. He said the United States planned to spend "tens of millions of dollars" in the next couple of years to improve the over-the-horizon radar. The FOBS delivery route reduced payload by one-third to one-half, decreased accuracy and made it difficult to launch a coordinated attack, Foster said.

Questioning Foster and another Administration witness, Deputy Secretary of Defense Paul H. Nitze, Subcommittee Chairman Henry M. Jackson (D Wash.) raised the issue of whether Soviet development of a FOBS was a violation of Article IV of the Space Treaty which banned the orbiting of nuclear weapons in outer space. Jackson said, "At a minimum, there is a 'good faith' violation of the treaty. If the Soviet Union tests and stockpiles this kind of weapon, the treaty won't be worth the paper it's written on....The point I'm trying to make is, with all the talk of an arms limitation agreement, we're off to a bad start with the Soviet Union having a weapon capable of being placed in orbit. It's a terror weapon, and that's the whole point of the treaty." Nitze replied, "It is no more a terror weapon than an intercontinental ballistic missile—less so." Nitze said there was no violation of the Treaty because the Treaty only precluded the stationing of nuclear weapons in orbit and did not prevent the development of such a weapon.

Dr. Philip E. Mosely, director of the European Institute at Columbia University, testified that as the world military balance shifted between the United States and the Soviet Union, Russia would be "tempted to undertake a more extensive, more acute and more dangerous range of risks in order to pursue its declared long-range ambition to reshape the world according to its own dogma." Mosely said the military apparently had taken control in China and warned that it was possible that the split between China and Russia could close after the death of Chairman Mao Tse-Tung.

Dr. Thomas W. Wolfe, senior staff member of the Rand Corp., said that Russia appeared to consider the "thin" U.S. ABM system aimed at China "merely the first step in a more extensive deployment aimed at the Soviet Union, which the China rationale simply serves to camouflage." He continued, "While the military merits of ABM systems may or may not come to fully justify their deployment, these systems have probably become already too potent a symbolic element in the strategic equation to be readily discarded. Once started down the ABM road, neither superpower can afford to forgo a means of defense which might afford a meaningful measure of protection and which at the same time helps to symbolize its rank order as a superpower and sets it off from lesser powers." He said that ABM deployment could set off a new arms race and "may well restore the premium on a first strike and destabilize the deterrent balance...."

Alice Langley Hsieh, senior staff member in the social science department of the Rand Corp., said that Chinese thinking concerning a nuclear war with the United States was "entirely defensive." She said it was more likely that the Chinese would concentrate on development of intermediate range missiles rather than on ICBMs. "There are no indications to date," she said, "that when China is in

(Continued on p. 852)

McNamara Explains FOBS

Defense Secretary Robert S. McNamara Nov. 3 told a news conference of "the possible development by the Soviet (Union) of something we have called a fractional orbital bombardment system, or FOBS." He said an orbital bomb differed in a number of ways from an intercontinental ballistic missile (ICBM). An ICBM followed a trajectory like a bullet, reaching "a peak altitude of perhaps 800 miles," McNamara said. An orbital bomb was fired "into a very low orbit about 100 miles above the earth," he said. "At a given point—generally before the first orbit is complete—a rocket engine is fired which slows down the payload and causes it to drop out of orbit. The payload then follows a re-entry path similar to the re-entry of a ballistic missile," McNamara said. He said that because of their relatively low altitude "some trajectories of a FOBS would avoid detection by some early warning radars, including our BMEWS (Ballistic Missile Early Warning System). Also the impact point can not be determined until ignition of the rocket engine that deboosts the payload out of orbit... and the flight path can be much as 10 minutes shorter than an ICBM." An orbital bomb also was capable of being launched against the United States from the Southern Hemisphere, it was said. Regular Soviet ICBM boosters, the SS-7 and SS-8, were used to launch an orbital bomb, it was said. It was reported that nine tests of Soviet short-duration flights were conducted between Sept. 17, 1966, and Oct. 28, 1967. McNamara told the news conference, "Even now it is impossible to be certain of what these tests represent. It is conceivable that the Soviet Union has been testing space vehicles for some re-entry program. But we suspect the Russians are pursuing the research and development of a FOBS." After outlining the capabilities of a FOBS, McNamara cited U.S. counter-capabilities and a number of disadvantages of an orbital bomb, and concluded, "I am not concerned."

House Panel Criticized Army for M-16 Rifle Jammings;

Reports that U.S. troops were dying needlessly in Vietnam because of jamming of the newly developed M-16 rifle brought the Army under severe criticism from a House Subcommittee in 1967.

The House Armed Services Committee's Special Subcommittee on the M-16 Rifle Program issued a report Oct. 19 confirming that both the Army and Marines had experienced "serious and excessive malfunctions" with the weapon in Vietnam. The panel attributed the problem mainly to faulty ammunition and called the Army's failure to correct it "unbelievable" and bordering on "criminal negligence."

The report was signed by all three members of the Subcommittee: Richard H. Ichord (D Mo.), chairman, Speedy O. Long (D La.) and William G. Bray (R Ind.). In accepting the report, L. Mendel Rivers (D S.C.), chairman of the Armed Services Committee, said he was "in full accord with the views and recommendations of the Subcommittee."

Among its recommendations, the Subcommittee suggested audits by the General Accounting Office (GAO) of the contracts held by Olin Mathieson Chemical Corp., manufacturer of powder used in the M-16 cartridge, and Colt Industries Inc., manufacturer of the rifle. The GAO Oct. 23 announced it would undertake the audits but its findings were never made public.

By the end of the year, the Pentagon announced that all M-16s in Vietnam had been overhauled to reduce the chances of jamming. According to Defense Department spokesmen, there were few additional complaints of jamming throughout the next year.

Background

BACKGROUND—The M-16 was the basic rifle for all Army combat units in Vietnam and for the Marines. The rifle was designed in 1957 by Eugene M. Stoner, chief engineer of Armalite, a division of the Fairchild Engine and Airplane Corp. The rifle was a 5.56-millimeter, magazine-fed, gas-operated, air-cooled, shoulder weapon. It was a lightweight, high-velocity system, capable of both automatic and semi-automatic fire, designed to fire a .223-caliber cartridge.

Reports that the newly developed rifle jammed frequently in combat became public in May 1967 when Rep. James J. Howard (D N.J.) read to the House excerpts from a letter sent by a Marine to his family after a fire fight in which many of the M-16s jammed. "Practically every one of our dead was found with his rifle thrown down next to him where he had been trying to fix it," the Marine had written.

The Special Subcommittee on the M-16 Rifle Program was established May 3, 1967. Hearings were held between May 15 and Aug. 22. The Subcommittee conducted a number of field investigations at military posts in the United States and among U.S. troops in South Vietnam.

Findings

FINDINGS. The report issued by the Subcommittee contained 31 findings and recommendations.

Powder. The Subcommittee said the rifle "as initially developed was an excellent and reliable weapon." Modifications later were made in the rifle and its ammunition which the Subcommittee said in at least some cases were unnecessary, were not supported by test data, increased the unit cost or reduced the performance. One of the modifications was a switch from the original firing powder, manufactured by E. I. du Pont de Nemours Inc., to powder manufactured by Olin Mathieson. The new powder left a greater amount of carbon residue in the chamber and around the working parts of the rifle than the original powder, the report said. The Subcommittee called the new powder "the major contributor" to combat malfunctions of the weapon. The most common malfunction was failure to extract the spent cartridge. The Subcommittee said the malfunctions were "serious and excessive." It added, "Shortages of cleaning equipment, lack of proper training and instructions contributed to the excessive malfunction rate." Other modifications made in the weapon were addition of a bolt closure device, chrome plating of the barrel chamber, changing of the barrel twist, and addition of a buffer to slow the rate of fire.

Suppliers. Powder for the M-16 cartridge was supplied by Olin Mathieson. The rifle was made by Colt Industries. The new powder manufactured by Olin Mathieson was less expensive than the original powder manufactured by E. I. du Pont de Nemours Inc. Since 1955 the Army had been providing Olin Mathieson with excess obsolete propellant from which Olin Mathieson extracted a main ingredient used in its powder. The change in 1964 to the new powder "was not supported or justified by test data," the Subcommittee said. "The sole-source position enjoyed by Olin Mathieson on ball propellants for many years and their close relationship with the Army may have influenced the decision makers of Army Munitions Command, Army Weapons Command and the Army Materiel Command," the Subcommittee said. It recommended an audit by the General Accounting Office (GAO) of the Olin Mathieson contract to produce the new powder.

Stoner said in an Oct. 19 interview with United Press International that the Army had only consulted with him twice about the modifications for the weapon. He said he had urged the Army to proceed "very cautiously" in making any changes but that despite his warnings, the powder the Army selected was "really not compatible."

Said U.S. Troops Dying Needlessly from Failure of Weapon

The Subcommittee said Colt apparently had enjoyed "an excessive profit" on M-16 production contracts. Colt had a fixed-price contract on a 10-percent profit rate basis. The Subcommittee said it found profits of 19.6 percent for calendar 1965, 16.8 percent for calendar 1966 and 13.4 percent for the first four months of calendar 1967. A GAO audit of Colt military contracts to determine the actual profit rates was recommended by the Subcommittee.

Conflict of Interest. Maj. Gen. Nelson M. Lynde Jr. was commanding general of the Army Weapons Command throughout negotiations for the first Army procurement of the M-16 rifle. He approved the terms of the contract negotiated by his subordinates, the Subcommittee said. The initial contract was awarded Nov. 4, 1963. Lynde retired from the Army March 1, 1964. He was hired by Colt as an executive consultant on Aug. 1, 1964. The Subcommittee called the arrangement "at least unethical." It added, "Without passing judgment on the legality of Gen. Lynde's activities since becoming associated with the company producing a rifle contracted for by his immediate command while he was on active duty, the Subcommittee does seriously question the wisdom of such action in view of the suspicion aroused by this type of association."

Weapons Development. The Army system of development, production and introduction of a new weapon "should be thoroughly reviewed," the Subcommittee said. It said that management of the Army rifle program was "unbelievable," that the command structure was "either inadequate or inoperative," and that it was "almost impossible to pinpoint responsibility." An independent test of the M-16 weapon system, including the rifle and its ammunition, was urged by the Subcommittee to determine whether proposed modifications would eliminate the type of malfunctions plaguing the weapon in Vietnam. "There is substantial evidence of lack of activity on the part of responsible officials of highest authority" to correct deficiencies in the rifle and its ammunition, the Subcommittee said. The Subcommittee suggested that "internal politics and jealousies" between the Army Weapons Command and the Army Munitions Command might be "roadblocks" to management of new weapons systems.

1968 Procurement Controversy

The M-16 came into the limelight again in 1968 when reports in the press disclosed that the Pentagon was paying excessive prices for M-16 production orders it had placed outside Colt in an effort to broaden the production base for the weapon.

The Army April 19 announced the awards of two contracts for 240,000 rifles to General Motors Corp.'s Hydramatic Division in Ypsilanti, Mich., for $56 million, and to Harrington and Richardson Co. of Worcester, Mass., for $42 million. According to press reports, Colt had been manufacturing M-16 rifles at an average cost of $104 apiece. In the first year of the two-year contracts, the average cost of a GM rifle would be $316, while a Harrington and Richardson rifle would be $250. The costs would drop in the second year.

Two companies were eliminated from competition before price data were requested, according to the reports. One of these firms, the Maremont Corp. of Saco, Maine, the sole supplier of M-60 machine guns, had prepared a $36.5 million bid for 240,000 rifles ($152 per rifle) but on advice of the Pentagon did not submit it. This brought criticism from Sen. Edmund S. Muskie and Rep. Peter N. Kyros, both Maine Democrats. The fourth firm, the Cadillac Gage Co. of Warren, Mich., was considering a proposal of $38.8 million.

The Army's primary explanation for the contract decisions was that it had "greater confidence" in General Motors and Harrington and Richardson than it did in Maremont and Cadillac Gage. Another explanation was that the contracts were subject to renegotiation if the costs were less than anticipated. Sen. George McGovern (D S.D.) responded that, "The possibility of renegotiation cannot and never should be employed as an excuse for failure to exercise due diligence and good businesslike dealings in the process of negotiating and awarding contracts...."

COMMITTEE REPORTS

Reports by both the House and Senate Armed Services Committees were extremely critical of the Army's contract decisions for the additional M-16s.

The House Armed Services Special Subcommittee on the M-16 Rifle Program said in a Sept. 26 report that it viewed the awards as "an exercise of extremely poor judgment from the standpoint of procurement policy and practice, and in callous disregard of the interest of the taxpayers of the United States."

The Special M-16 Rifle Subcommittee of the Senate Armed Services Preparedness Investigating Subcommittee concluded Sept. 2 that the purchase was "a most inept performance." "The removal of price as a factor is not even plausibly supported by the reasons advanced by the Army," it said. The panel added that it was too late to cancel the awards but that "this should be the last time that any defense agency conducts a procurement in such an awkwardly, unreasonable manner."

possession of a nuclear delivery capability, whether regional or intercontinental, she will be more prepared than at present to engage in a high-risk military policy." She added that China might decide to launch a satellite before testing an ICBM because of the national prestige inherent in a satellite launch capability.

Draft Extension

Congress in 1967 approved an Administration-requested bill (S 1432—PL 90-40) extending the military draft and related statutes for four years, through July 1, 1971.

Although Administration forces and private interests had pushed hard for comprehensive draft reform in 1967, S 1432 in its final form provided little more than a simple extension of the draft. The only major reform the bill permitted was a plan to reverse the current "oldest first" order of induction and call 19-year-olds before older men. (The President did not implement this authority through 1968.)

As passed by Congress, S 1432 included a restrictive amendment specifically prohibiting a plan by the President to institute a random selection system to ensure that all registrants within a given age group stood an equal chance of induction. Another prohibited the President from ending college undergraduate deferments except for unusual manpower needs.

Final action on S 1432 came after more than a year of vigorous public debate over alleged draft inequities, which critics said had the effect of sending underprivileged youths to fight in the Vietnam war while youths from more affluent families received educational deferments. Former Assistant Attorney General Burke Marshall, who headed an advisory commission on the draft for the President, said the new law "made the system worse than it was before." *(For additional details, see special article on draft, p. 879.)*

Military Bases Funds

Congress Oct. 4 cleared a bill (HR 11722—PL 90-110) authorizing $2,333,255,000 for military construction and family housing in fiscal 1968. Appropriations of $2,093,362,000 were made for these purposes in the fiscal 1968 military construction appropriations bill (HR 13606—PL 90-180), cleared Nov. 21. The sum appropriated was $843,638,000 less than Administration requests but $489,292,000 greater than the amount appropriated for these same programs in fiscal 1967.

The appropriation bill carried the full $64 million allotment sought by the Administration for construction of facilities to support deployment of the ABM system, which Secretary McNamara announced Sept. 18. Approval of the construction funds brought to almost $1 billion the total allotment Congress had appropriated in fiscal 1967 and 1968 to get ABM deployment under way.

Military Pay

Congress Dec. 12 cleared a bill (HR 13510—PL 90-207) increasing military pay for the fifth consecutive year. The bill, which was retroactive to Oct. 1, increased the monthly pay of servicemen (including basic pay, quarters and subsistence) by 4.5 percent. The increase, requested by the White House, corresponded to a 4.5 percent pay boost in federal civilian classified salaries that was also approved Dec. 12.

In addition, the bill provided automatic military pay raises in the future that would correspond to salary increases for federal civilian employees—unless Congress took separate action on military salaries. This automatic increase provision was opposed by the Administration.

CIA Secret Financing

The Central Intelligence Agency (CIA) made front page news across the country in February 1967 as the press unraveled an account of CIA secret subsidization of organizations in education, law, journalism, labor and religion.

President Johnson responded by ordering a halt to secret financing of private voluntary organizations by the CIA and other Government agencies.

At the same time, the President announced he was ordering a study on establishing a quasi-public agency to channel federal funds openly into the overseas activities of organizations deemed worthy of support in the national interest. Heading the study panel was Secretary of State Dean Rusk. (The White House in August 1969 said no report was ever submitted.)

The tangled web of secret CIA links with private organizations came under a spotlight of publicity when a former officer of the National Student Assn. (NSA) gave *Ramparts* magazine the story of the NSA's ties with the CIA. The NSA-CIA story triggered a snowballing account in which such diverse groups as Radio Free Europe, the National Council of Churches and the National Education Assn. were linked to the CIA. News reports identified at least 50 foundations believed to have been used by the CIA in an involved method of funneling funds to private organizations.

The NSA, the largest college student organization in the United States, Feb. 13, 1967, admitted that it had received funds from the CIA since 1952. In disclosing the subsidy, NSA President Eugene Groves said the funds were used to help finance international activities, including sending representatives to student congresses abroad and funding student exchange programs. The association, formed in 1947, had chapters on more than 300 campuses.

President Johnson Feb. 15 directed "a careful review" of the matter by a three-member committee headed by Acting Secretary of State Nicholas deB. Katzenbach, who, in a statement for the President, said: "The President believes strongly that the integrity and independence of the educational community must be preserved. He has directed a careful review of any Government activities that may endanger this integrity and independence. He has further directed me, in consultation with Secretary of Health, Education and Welfare John W. Gardner and CIA Director Richard Helms, to formulate a policy that will provide necessary guidance for Government agencies in their relationship to the international activities of American education organizations."

The statement added, "At the same time, the President recognizes the great need of America's private organizations to participate in the world community....He has asked me to explore means for assuring that United States organizations play their proper and vital role."

Reserve-Guard Merger

Congress Nov. 16 cleared a bill designed to block permanently the Defense Department's plans to merge the Army Reserve and Army National Guard, which had been a matter of continuing dispute since it was first proposed in late 1964.

The bill (HR 2—PL 90-168) created a "Selected Reserve Force" in each component of the Ready Reserve, including the Army Reserve and the Army National Guard, and required the Selected Reserve in each component to consist of some organized units. By specifically establishing separate Selected Reserve components in the Army Reserve and Army National Guard and requiring that the Selected Reserves consist in part of units, the bill in effect blocked the attempt to merge the two components.

In addition, the bill required Congress in each fiscal year to specifically authorize the size of each of the components of the Selected Reserve as a prior condition for appropriations. A similar requirement for authorizations prior to appropriations already existed for aircraft, missiles, ships and other military equipment. To strengthen the voice of the reserves in Pentagon planning, the bill created in the office of the Assistant Secretary of Defense for Manpower a statutory post of deputy with specific responsibility for the reserves.

Ironically, the Johnson Administration in 1967 had not again proposed the merger plan, which Reserve officers opposed. It achieved some of the aims of the merger in 1967, however, by putting into effect a new realignment plan that envisioned the elimination of most of the combat units from the Army Reserve and a number of logistic and other support units from the Guard.

Atomic Energy Program

Congress in 1967 authorized appropriation of $2,633,876,000 for the Atomic Energy Commission (AEC) in fiscal 1968. The amount provided in the annual authorization bill (HR 10918—PL 90-65) was $4,381,000 less than AEC requests.

Later, in the public works and AEC appropriations bill (HR 11641—PL 90-147) Congress appropriated $2,509,133,000 for the AEC in fiscal 1968. However, because of AEC revenues from sales of radioactive materials and the availability of prior year appropriations which remained unobligated, the total fiscal 1968 program level of the AEC was to be $2,603,507,000, compared to $2,433,326,000 in fiscal 1967. Of the $170,181,000 increase over the previous year, $52 million was for nuclear weapons development and $93,103,000 was for plant and capital equipment. The authorization bill (HR 10918) included $7,333,000 for planning on the proposed $400 million 200-Bev (billion electron volt) proton accelerator and accompanying laboratory to be built in Weston, Ill., about 30 miles southwest of Chicago. The authorization was $2,667,000 less than the $10 million requested by the AEC.

The proposed accelerator drew national attention in 1965 and 1966 as officials searched for a construction site. Sharp competition developed among communities across the nation for the laboratory because its presence was expected to boost the local economy and lead to development of other science research facilities nearby. At one point, 200 possible sites in 46 states were under considera-tion. Midwesterners particularly sought the accelerator to help offset the drain of talented scientists to major science installations on the East and West Coasts. The AEC Dec. 16, 1966, announced Weston was the site.

Controversy surrounded the Weston authorization in 1967 because of alleged housing discrimination in the area. The village Feb. 15 passed an open housing ordinance, but the Illinois Legislature June 17 turned down a proposed state open occupancy law. Some Congressional leaders, including Joint Atomic Energy Committee Chairman John O. Pastore (D R.I.) opposed the authorization because of the Illinois Legislature's action. Floor amendments to delete the authorization were defeated in both chambers of Congress.

The full authorization of $7,333,000 was appropriated in the public works bill.

1968

A year that began well for proponents of greater military spending ended amid considerable apprehension.

At his confirmation hearing in January, Secretary McNamara's successor, Clark M. Clifford, had charmed the Senate Armed Services Committee with promises that he would seek outright U.S. "superiority" over Soviet nuclear arms (instead of the McNamara concept of "parity"), and that he favored the advanced manned bomber and continued separate status for the Army Reserve and Army National Guard. After seven years of domination by McNamara, it appeared that the Pentagon was back in military hands.

But by year's end, the changes had gone almost full circle. A complex array of factors, including public distrust over the military's aims in Vietnam, doubts by leading scientists that the ABM system would work effectively, and exposure of massive cost overruns in the C-5A and other weapons programs, led to a ground swell of public pressures to cut back on Pentagon spending. By early 1969, alleged "fat" in the defense budget had become a major political issue, and huge cuts appeared almost certain.

The proponents of budget cuts had gained leverage in the summer of 1968 when President Johnson ruled that the Pentagon should absorb half the $6 billion cut in spending and $10 billion reduction in new obligational authority required by Congress as the price for its approval of the Administration's tax surcharge request. Although the House and Senate Armed Services Committees made clear the funds would be made up in later years, the admission that the money could be defrayed at all led critics to wonder if there weren't more "fat" in the defense budget.

Despite Clifford's rhetoric at his confirmation hearing, his one year in office marked little change from the basic policies of McNamara. Although Clifford pushed hard to win funds for the ABM system, he refused to accelerate the manned bomber program and defended the nation's existing strategic forces as more than sufficient for deterrence. Clifford reportedly spent most of his time on the Vietnam war, where he dealt Pentagon hawks a further blow by persuading President Johnson to reject military demands for another 200,000 troops and to begin looking toward de-escalation.

In his successful campaign for the Presidency, Republican candidate Richard M. Nixon looked on the growing defense debate with alarm. McNamara's treatment of the military, he said, had led to a "security gap," which could become a "survival gap" if not bridged by the early 1970s. Stepped-up funding for the advanced bomber and other controversial programs reflected his thinking in 1969, but the defense budget appeared headed toward its most searching Congressional review since the close of World War II.

Defense Budget

Increased spending for Vietnam, the F-111 aircraft program and the ABM system were reflected in President Johnson's fiscal 1969 budget, which proposed Pentagon

---

Cheyenne Helicopter Controversy

During House debate on the procurement bill (S 3293) controversy broke out when Rep. Otis G. Pike (D N.Y.) told the House that the Lockheed Aircraft Corp. had won the contract on the Cheyenne helicopter at a time that a former Lockheed vice president was serving in a high Army post closely associated with the contract award.

The official Pike cited—though he never named him—was Willis M. Hawkins—who left Lockheed Oct. 14, 1963, to become Assistant Secretary of the Army for Research and Development. In June 1966, the year after the research contract was awarded, he returned to his post at Lockheed.

The day of the House debate, June 11, Hawkins released a statement that he never participated in or influenced the contract decision.

"Throughout the Army's consideration of the proposal from 12 contractors," he said, "I excluded myself from all participation in the evaluation process. The final decisions on the basis of recommendations from the Army's Source Selection Board were made by the Secretary of the Army and the Deputy Secretary of Defense. I had no part in these decisions nor influence upon them."

During the debate, Pike asked House Armed Services Committee Chairman L. Mendel Rivers (D S.C.) to investigate the extent of Hawkins' role in the contract, but Rivers declined. By a non-record vote of 47-121, the House June 11 rejected a Pike amendment to knock out $137.9 million in Army procurement funds to start buying operating models of the helicopter. (Lockheed also had won the production contract, but the bulk of production orders were cancelled early in 1969 amid reports of large cost overruns and unsatisfactory performance of the helicopter—a heavy assault craft designed to provide covering fires for attacking ground forces.)

Almost a year later, in May 1969, columnist Drew Pearson contended he had evidence that Hawkins had actually signed the Army document granting the research and development contract to Lockheed. Hawkins denied this but affirmed that he had as an Army official assisted in preparing presentations to the Department of Defense "justifying the mission for which the vehicle was to be designed."

---

spending of $76.7 billion, an increase of $3 billion over the levels projected the previous January for fiscal 1968. Requested new obligational authority totaled $79.1 billion.

Of the proposed increase in spending, $1.3 billion was for Vietnam and $1.7 billion for other defense programs. The Budget estimated Vietnam spending at $25.8 billion, and non-Vietnam outlays at $50.9 billion, including $1.1 billion for ABM development and deployment, $2 billion for Air Force and Navy F-111s, and $183.6 million for four fast deployment logistic ships.

The defense spending estimate had been pared from Service requests of $101 billion—a figure described by one defense official as "the largest amount of money ever requested from anybody by anybody in the history of the world."

Authorization. What amounted to the death knell for the controversial F-111B Navy aircraft program was sounded March 28, when the Senate Armed Services Committee voted 11-2 to drop all F-111B funds from the fiscal 1969 defense authorization bill (S 3293). Anticipating that the Committee's position would be sustained in the final bill, the Defense Department cancelled the program July 10. (See special article, p. 875.)

The panel's scuttling of the F-111B project came a day after the Defense Department had sought a compromise under which only eight of the planes would have been procured and the research effort would have been cut back proportionally. Only Sens. John G. Tower and Howard W. Cannon (D Nev.) supported the Defense Department on the crucial Committee vote.

In the face of heavy Navy lobbying, the Committee April 2 approved a substitute authorization of $287 million for development of an alternative plane, known as the VFX-1 (and later as the F-14) to replace the F-111B. The Committee said the replacement aircraft would cost about the same as the F-111B program (although this was disputed by some Defense Department civilian analysts who said it would cost far more) and that the new plane would be entering the fleet 18 to 24 months after the 1971 target date for its ill-fated predecessor. The VFX-1 was to be an interim fighter to bridge the gap until the Navy's projected "air superiority" fighter, VFAX, was ready in the mid-1970s.

In other actions on the procurement bill, the Committee added $139 million for purchase of eight electronic countermeasure aircraft, the EA-6B, and dropped $28 million requested for modification of the existing F-106 Air Force interceptor into a new version called the F-106X for use in a proposed new anti-bomber system. Altogether, the Committee reduced the Administration's $22.4 billion budget request by $383 million.

When the bill came to the Senate floor April 18, foes of the ABM system made their first of several vigorous efforts during the session to block or delay deployment. By a 17-41 roll-call vote, the Senate rejected an amendment by Gaylord Nelson (D Wis.) to knock out the entire $342.7 million in Sentinel procurement money. Later in the day, by a surprisingly close margin of 28-31, the Senate rejected an amendment by John Sherman Cooper (R Ky.) to prohibit deployment until the Defense Secretary certified that the system was "practicable" and that its costs were known with "reasonable accuracy." The Senate passed the bill the next day by a 54-3 roll-call vote.

The House Armed Services Committee went along with the Senate's substitution of the VFX-1 for the F-111B but dropped the entire $183.6 million request figure approved by the Senate for four FDLs. In other actions, the panel restored the $28 million for F-106 modifications and added $50 million for stepped-up efforts in antisubmarine warfare research. In all, the panel added $295.2 million to the Senate-passed bill.

The House July 11 passed the measure 363-15 without further change. During the course of debate, several opponents of the bill or critics of some of its programs called for huge cuts in view of the reductions that were being imposed in Congressional action on key domestic programs. James H. Scheuer (D N.Y.) termed the bill a "laundry list of unnecessary and superfluous military programs...." But supporters insisted that many programs had been delayed too long, awaiting the possibility of an East-West detente that had never come. In the meantime, they said, the Soviet Union had made significant strides in the development of aircraft, submarines, and ABM systems.

House and Senate conferees on S 3293 agreed to the House cut of the entire $183.6 million for FDLs and the Senate cut of $28 million for F-106 modification but accepted $38 million of the $50 million in unbudgeted antisubmarine money added to the bill by the House. The conference report, adopted by the House Sept. 10 and the Senate the next day, authorized $13,832,013,000 for military procurement and $7,793,737,000 for defense R&D, a total of $21,625,750,000.

Callup Authority Extended. In a little noticed provision of the bill, Congress extended for one year, through June 30, 1969, the temporary authority granted in 1966 for the President to order military reservists to duty without declaring a national emergency.

Appropriation. The Pentagon came in for an unaccustomed blast from Congress July 18 when the House Appropriations Committee approved an amended version of the defense appropriations bill (HR 18707), carrying $72,239,700,000, or $4.8 billion less than requested. In a strongly worded report, the panel criticized defense planners for conducting "business as usual" despite the Government's severe fiscal crisis. What was needed, the report said, was a "tightening up" of defense procedures to eliminate "waste and mismanagement."

Despite its tough statements about waste, however, the Committee made clear that a large part of the cut was made necessary by restraints imposed under the Federal Revenue and Expenditure Control Act of 1968 (PL 90-364), which coupled a 10-percent tax surcharge with a $6 billion spending reduction.

Passage of PL 90-364, the Committee said, "was an implicit recognition that the basis for a strong national defense is a strong and stable economy." But, it added, the Committee's $4.8 billion slash would result in a reduction of only about $1.7 billion in projected fiscal 1969 spending because many of the cuts were on long-range weapon programs where contracts might have been let in fiscal 1969 but spending held over until later fiscal years.

Among the Committee's major cuts were $987 million from the general area of operating expenses, $755.4 million in substitution of carryover funds, previously appropriated, to finance fiscal 1969 programs, $329 million for military personnel appropriations, $163.7 million in recovered balances from programs failing to receive further authorization, $677 million in a recom-

mended slowdown of production for the Air Froce F-111D and FB-111 aircraft, and $55 million for equipment procurement for the proposed Army Sixth Infantry Division.

Despite the enthusiasm the House and Senate Armed Services Committees had shown for the VFX-1 Navy fighter—proposed successor to the F-111B—the panel approved only $30 million of the unbudgeted $287 million authorized for the program in the procurement bill. In its evaluation of the new aircraft project the Committee urged scrutiny "lest the nation encounter another F-111B-type program." Among the features of the VFX-1 program which disturbed the Committee were the inclusion of the Phoenix missile, the engine and the sophisticated anvionics (guidance and control) system, all of which had caused the F-111B to be overweight: the high cost resulting from use of exotic lightweight materials to overcome the weight problem and the optimistic timetable for activation of the aircraft. The Committee suggested the possibility of eliminating the VFX-1 and moving on to a later VFX-2 aircraft. The House approved the bill Sept. 12 without change.

The VFX aircraft program fared better in the Senate Appropriations Committee, which added $100 million to the House's $30 million allotment. But on balance, the Committee cut $352.8 million from the House-passed bill, including an additional $113.4 million for military personnel and $279.1 million of the $482.6 million request and House figure for conversion and arming of Polaris submarines with Poseidon missiles.

In floor action on the measure, the Senate rejected attempts to cut funds for the ABM system and decisively beat back a series of amendments by Joseph S. Clark (D Pa.) to cut other defense programs.

An expected floor battle over the level of U.S. troops in Europe did not materialize. Sen. Stuart Symington (D Mo.) did not follow up on plans announced earlier in the year to introduce an amendment to cut off funds for all but 50,000 of the 337,000 U.S. troops in Germany and other NATO countries. Symington never publicly explained why he withheld the amendment (which at one point commanded strong support), but it was clear that the Soviet invasion of Czechoslovakia in August had changed the temper of the Senate regarding NATO troop cuts.

After adopting two minor amendments which did not affect the bill's appropriations, the Senate passed the measure Oct. 3 by a 55-2 roll-call vote.

Conferees on the measure agreed to the Senate allotment of $130 million for the VFX-1 aircraft program, a compromise figure of $269.5 million for Polaris submarine conversion and the Senate's cut of an additional $113.4 million in military personnel appropriations. But in a footnote on the VFX program, conferees emphasized that none of the bill's funds could be utilized for airframe development until 15 days after the Secretary of Defense had informed Congressional Appropriations Committees of the costs and design characteristics of the aircraft selected.

The conference report was adopted Oct. 11 by a 213-6 roll-call vote of the House and voice vote of the Senate. As approved, the bill appropriated $71,869,828,-000, a reduction of $5,204,172,000 from Administration requests. It carried $23,215,429,000 for the Army,

$20,368,939,000 for the Navy and Marines, $24,320,724,000 for the Air Force, and $3,964,736,000 for defense agencies. cies.

Military Construction. Congress July 11 cleared a bill (HR 16703—PL 90-408) authorizing $1,800,151,000 for military construction and family housing in fiscal 1969. The allotment, $95,848,000 less than the Administration requests, was reduced by an additional $41,775,000 in the military construction appropriation bill (HR 18785—PL 90-513), which appropriated $1,758,- 376,000.

Both bills carried an allowance of $227.3 million for construction relating to deployment of the Sentinel antiballistic missile system. In a key vote on the appropriations bill, the Senate, Aug. 1, rejected by a **27-46** roll-call vote an amendment by Gaylord Nelson (D Wis.) to knock out all $227.3 million for the ABM (R: 5-14; D: 22-32—ND 20-15, SD: 2-17). Nelson said that arguments used by ABM opponents during previous Senate debates had not been refuted but that nevertheless "like the lemming, we have all joined together in a vast mob, rushing off to nonsense land, waving the flag, and shouting slogans about national defense and communism while we proclaim our unbounded faith in peace in the world."

C-5A Hearings

The first of what was to be an array of disclosures of shocking cost overruns in key weapon programs was revealed Nov. 13 when a high-ranking Pentagon official told the Joint Economic Committee that costs of the C-5A jet transport aircraft were running almost double the Air Force's original estimates.

Under questioning by the Committee, A.E. Fitzgerald, deputy for management systems in the office of the Assistant Secretary of the Air Force, confirmed that costs of procuring all 120 C-5As would now run $5.3 billion, or $2.0 billion above the initial projections. The Pentagon disputed Fitzgerald's figures but admitted that costs had escalated to $4.3 billion by late 1968. (In July 1969 the Department estimated program costs at $5.1 billion.)

Fitzgerald, who had been instructed not to testify at the hearing, which was on the broad topic of military procurement procedures, received word Nov. 25 that his civil service tenure (job protection) had been removed. The Pentagon said the tenure had been granted erroneously due to a "computer error" and was not in retaliation for Fitzgerald's appearance at the hearing. Fitzgerald told Congressional Quarterly it was "conceivable" that the Air Force was right about his tenure but that it seemed "highly probable" that it was his testimony that prompted a review of his status.

In response to questions by Sen. William Proxmire (D Wis.), the Committee chairman, Fitzgerald said at the hearing that cost of the C-5A airframes being manufactured by the Lockheed-Georgia Corp. could exceed its target cost by about 100 percent and that engines produced by the General Electric Co. might also run well above estimates.

Fitzgerald attributed the added cost to a number of factors, including increased manufacturing costs, overly optimistic cost estimates by the company, poor cost control and planning and "corporate strategy." He ex-

plained the latter term as a willingness by the company to absorb a loss on the initial production in order to take advantage of a unique "repricing formula" which would permit a renegotiated price on later production runs that would more than cover the original losses.

Asked by Proxmire "what kind of pressure" there would be on the Government to pay off the additional $2 billion, Fitzgerald listed "the desire to obtain the aircraft" and "an understandable desire to keep the production base active at this particular plant." Beyond this, he said, "I can only speculate on pressures that might be generated through elected representatives..." The primary Lockheed C-5A production facility was located in Georgia, home of Richard B. Russell (D Ga.), the chairman of the Senate Armed Services Committee and of the Defense Appropriations Subcommittee.

Despite his loss of tenure, Fitzgerald was still in his Air Force job as of early 1969, although he said he had been stripped of all important responsibilities.

The Joint Committee resumed its probe into military procurement activities in 1969, obtaining documentation and testimony revealing cost overruns on numerous other weapon systems, including the SRAM (short range attack missile), the Minuteman III intercontinental ballistic missile, the Sheridan tank and the electronics system for Air Force versions of the F-111 aircraft. Together with public concern over the cost and efficacy of the proposed antiballistic missile system, the hearings provided considerable leverage for opponents of excessive military spending.

War 'Profiteering' Controls

Congress in 1968 passed three bills aimed at ensuring the public against war profiteering by defense contractors, but stopped far short of the comprehensive overhaul of contractor accounting procedures that one determined House member sought. Rep. Henry B. Gonzalez (D Texas), charging that profiteering was "rampant," pushed hard throughout the session for uniform accounting procedures that would prevent contractors from using accounting "gimmicks" to make their profits appear low.

His efforts attracted considerable attention and some support, but in the end, Congress approved only limited controls.

Defense Production Act. Congress June 27 cleared a bill (HR 17268—PL 90-370) extending the Defense Production Act of 1950 for two years and requiring a study of the feasibility of instituting uniform cost accounting procedures in most defense contracts.

The Defense Production Act of 1950 (PL 81-774) was a Korean War measure designed to assure a sufficient supply of national resources for defense needs. The 1950 Act also gave the Federal Reserve Board authority to curb consumer credit. This authority lapsed June 30, 1953. *(Congress and the Nation, Vol. 1, p. 356.)*

As introduced in the House, HR 17268 required uniform accounting standards to be formulated and put into effect within one year. In the face of vigorous pressures against this proposal by defense industries, however, the House Banking and Currency Committee amended the bill to require the Comptroller General to devise standards for negotiated defense contracts above $100,- 000 and to recommend legislation within one year. The

House passed the bill without change after rejecting an amendment by Gonzalez to require uniform accounting standards.

In reporting the bill June 25, the Senate Banking and Currency Committee knocked out the House provision requiring the Comptroller General's proposals. On the floor, however, the Senate overrode the panel and accepted an amendment to provide for a study of the feasibility of Gonzolez's uniform accounting proposal.

The amendment was introduced by William Proxmire (D Wis.), who called his proposal a "modest" one which would find whether uniform accounting procedures would be workable, save money and be fair to defense contractors. He was opposed by Charles H. Percy (R Ill.), who said experts had concluded that uniform accounting procedures could not be established successfully and that they would serve no useful purpose. The House June 27 accepted the Senate changes by voice vote, clearing the bill for the President, who signed it July 1.

Provisions—As signed by the President, HR 17268:

Extended the Defense Production Act (PL 81-774) for two years, from June 30, 1968, to June 30, 1970.

Required the Comptroller General, in cooperation with the Director of the Bureau of the Budget and the Secretary of Defense, to study the feasibility of applying uniform cost accounting standards to all negotiated prime defense contracts and subcontracts of $100,000 or more.

Instructed the Comptroller General to consult with the accounting profession and the defense industry during his study and ordered him to report the findings of his study to the Congressional Banking and Currency and Armed Services Committees within 18 months of the enactment of the bill.

Increased the amount authorized for the operations of the Joint Committee on Defense Production from $85,000 to $100,000 for any fiscal year.

Truth-in-Negotiations. Congress Sept. 11 cleared a bill (HR 10573—PL 90-512) amending the Truth in Negotiations Act of 1962 (PL 87-653) to give the Government authority to examine contractor pricing records for those defense contracts which are not put up for competitive bidding. Such contracts totaled about $5 billion a year.

The 1962 law required defense agencies in negotiating contracts of more than $2,500 to solicit bids from the largest possible number of qualified buyers (though the agencies are not required to accept the lowest bid) and provided that pricing data must be submitted by the bidder for any contract over $100,000. It also increased the number of categories for which written justification was required when negotiation rather than competitive bidding was involved.

The Pentagon was lukewarm to efforts to amend the law but did not oppose the bill. The change was supported by the General Accounting Office.

Provisions—HR 10573 amended PL 87-653 to authorize the Government to inspect within three years after final payment on a defense contract, to examine all books, records, documents and other data of a contractor or subcontractor related to the negotiation, pricing or performance of the contract or subcontract.

Renegotiation Act. Congress Oct. 10 sent to the President a bill (HR 17324—PL 90-634) extending the Renegotiation Act, which set up a procedure for federal recapture of excessive profits realized by private firms on contracts with Government agencies.

The final bill included riders (nongermane amendments) dealing with the International Coffee Agreement, industrial development bonds and the International Antidumping Code. The riders were added by the Senate after House passage of the renegotiation bill and were retained in modest form in the final version of the measure. *(For discussion of riders, see banking chapter p. 253.)*

The bill's renegotiation provisions extended the 1951 law for three years, through June 30, 1971, and made various revisions in the sections which governed the renegotiability of contracts for items considered to be standard commercial articles. The effect was to assure that items qualifying for an exemption from renegotiation actually were of a commercial nature.

Rep. Gonzalez had sought to establish the Board on a permanent basis, but his floor amendment to achieve this purpose was rejected by the House. Ways and Means Committee Chairman Wilbur D. Mills (D Ark.) said he "would feel more secure as to this type of operation which involves so much judgment, if it were extended periodically." Some observers thought, however, that the mere extension of the Act was a victory for Gonzalez.

Because of massive industry pressures, many of the Renegotiation Board's supporters early in the year expected the House Ways and Means Committee to keep HR 17324 bottled up until the Board expired June 30 under existing law. Although the Johnson Administration favored a permanent extension of the Board, sources close to the issue told Congressional Quarterly that Administration pressure for extension was nowhere evident on Capitol Hill.

Among the opponents of the Board were such powerful lobby groups as the National Assn. of Manufacturers, the Chamber of Commerce of the United States, the Aerospace Industries Assn., the Shipbuilders Council of America, the National Canners Assn., Financial Executives Institute, American Textile Manufacturers Institute, National Security Industrial Assn., American Institute of Certified Public Accountants, and the Machinery and Allied Products Institute.

As it developed, the lobbyists were outflanked by a surprising groundswell of countervailing public pressures—directed mainly at key members of the Ways and Means Committee. Grassroots support for the Board developed after news media began following Gonzalez's efforts to save the bill. Although he was not a member of the Ways and Means Committee, Gonzalez made 17 House speeches in favor of the Board in 1966 and 1967.

Finally, late in 1967, the Cleveland *Plain Dealer* undertook a vigorous campaign to save the Board and expose the dangers of war profiteering. The paper spurred four Members of the Ohio delegation—Reps. Jackson E. Betts (R), Michael A. Feighan (D), William E. Minshall (R) and Charles A. Vanik (D)—into strong support of the measure.

Two of the Ohio Representatives—Betts and Vanik—were members of the Ways and Means Committee. Joined by Reps. James A. Burke (D Mass.), who was under pressure from his home town newspaper, *The Boston Globe,* and Martha W. Griffiths (D Mich.), a former Government procurement officer, the Ohioans pushed the bill through the Committee.

Floor debate against the bill was led by Rep. Charles S. Gubser (R Calif.), who called the Board "unnecessary, obsolete and wasteful." Gubser, whose district included 12 major defense plants and installations, said the Board cost more than it brought in, duplicated the functions of Pentagon procurement officers, and constituted an "unnecessary harassment" that caused small firms to get out of the Government market.

Gonzalez replied that the Board should be strengthened and that it had recovered almost $2 billion while having an operation cost of about $50 million.

Provisions—Following are the bill's major provisions applying to the Renegotiation Act. (for other provisions, see banking chapter.)

Extended the Renegotiation Act of 1951 for three years, through June 30, 1971.

Revised the exemptions (from renegotiation) in existing law for standard commercial articles and services to assure that items qualifying for exemption actually were of a commercial nature. The major revisions:

• Provided that at least 55 percent (rather than the existing 35 percent) of total sales of an article be to commercial buyers if an article was to qualify for the standard commercial exemption from renegotiability.

• Repealed an existing provision which allowed the percentage test to be computed from sales in the current year and the preceding year, thereby limiting the test to current-year sales.

• Specified that an article would not qualify for a commercial exemption if the price charged the Government in an otherwise nonrenegotiable sale exceeded the lowest price charged in a comparable commercial sale except when the higher price to the Government was due to "significantly different circumstances" in producing or delivering the article.

• Specified that contractors whose application of the standard commercial exemption brought their annual Government business to below the $1-million renegotiation minimum, must file a report with the Renegotiation Board about the application of the exemption and about renegotiable sales generally. (Existing law allowed the contractor to apply the exemption on his own, making it possible for him to put renegotiable sales below the minimum and removing him from any reporting requirements to justify his actions.)

Draft

Implementing plans he had announced the year before, President Johnson Feb. 16 abolished draft deferments for most male graduate students and men in "critical" occupations. The National Security Council, of which the President was chairman, recommended the new policy, and it was relayed to all state draft directors by Selective Service Director Lewis B. Hershey. While the local boards continued to have discretion to grant deferments as they saw fit, Hershey's recommendations generally were expected to be followed.

The recommendations did not alter the existing policy of drafting the oldest eligible men first. College undergraduates continued to receive deferments, as did medical, dental and divinity students. (Doctors and dentists were subject to a special draft when they completed their training.)

The policy also did not affect men who were in their second or subsequent year of graduate school on Oct. 1, 1967, and were continuing toward a degree. These men were to continue to be deferred.

The statement of policy affected about 650,000 male graduating seniors, men completing one year of graduate school and men receiving graduate degrees; 340,000 men with job deferments; and 40,000 apprentices. According to most estimates, more than half of these men still would not be susceptible to call-up, either because their local boards decided to continue their job deferments, because they were overage, because they were veterans or for other reasons.

The remaining men, whose deferments were to lapse, were likely to be the first to be called beginning in July because nearly all of them were older than the 20 years and three months at which men were currently being drafted.

Mrs. Betty Vetter, executive director of the Scientific Manpower Commission, a private agency supported by scientific and academic organizations, estimated that "99 to 100 percent" of the draftees beginning in July would be college graduates.

The new policy was immediately assailed by educators, who predicted that graduate school enrollments would be cut in half for the 1968-69 school year, thus placing a huge financial burden on universities and sharply reducing the number of graduate students serving as undergraduate instructors.

Despite the educators' pessimism, however, a survey printed by *The Washington Post* Oct. 6 reported that the draft changes had only a "relatively minor effect" on the institutions. Early reports indicated a small decline in enrollment in several schools across the country, it said, but in only a few instances was the drop the 50 percent level that educators had predicted.

Wheeler Reappointment

President Johnson June 15 signed into law (PL 90-342) a bill (HR Res 1224) which waived an existing limitation on the length of service by a chairman of the Joint Chiefs of Staff. The bill enabled the President to reappoint Gen. Earle G. Wheeler to an additional one year term. The bill applied only to Wheeler.

Final Congressional action occurred when the Senate June 3 by a 52-2 roll-call vote passed the bill and cleared it for Mr. Johnson's signature. The votes against passage came from Stephen M. Young (D Ohio) and Lee Metcalf (D Mont.). The House had passed H J Res 1224 by a voice vote May 14 after Rep. Paul Findley (R Ill.) on May 7 had blocked an attempt at passage under a procedure requiring unanimous consent. Only limited opposition was voiced in each house.

The purpose of the legislation was to amend a law (PL 81-216) restricting the chairman of the Joint Chiefs to two two-year terms except during a Congressionally-declared war. President Johnson and Secretary of Defense Clark M. Clifford had sought the action so Wheeler could be reappointed for a year when his term expired July 2, 1968.

Findley argued that Wheeler had "presumably been a major architect of" or silent against the Vietnam war policy of "gradualism" which he called "morally indefensible and militarily self-defeating." Young, a strong

(Continued on p. 860)

Congress, Defense in Hassle Over New Nuclear Subs

Throughout 1968 a controversy raged between Congress and the Defense Department over the development of a new generation of nuclear attack submarines.

The battle began when Defense Secretary Robert S. McNamara, in the defense posture statement accompanying the fiscal 1969 defense budget, indicated that construction on nuclear attack submarines would be halted after fiscal 1970 when the United States acquired a fleet of 60. Although McNamara considered that level to be sufficient, Navy officials reportedly thought a fleet of at least 100 was necessary. Attack submarines are vessels designed to track and destroy other submarines.

In reaction, nearly every Congressional committee connected with defense, military funding and atomic energy stepped into the debate. Fortified with the testimony of Vice Adm. Hyman G. Rickover, head of the Navy's nuclear submarine program, these groups urged a general stepping up of nuclear submarine development beyond 1970.

In addition, they stressed the need to develop two controversial submarines. One was a high-speed craft that would double the speed of existing submarines. The second was an electric-drive submarine that would be quieter and thus less susceptible to detection by enemy antisubmarine forces. The cost of the quiet sub was estimated at $100 million and the price of the fast vessel was put at $185 million.

Defense Secretary Clark M. Clifford, who succeeded McNamara, July 11 announced the Department would go ahead with the high-speed vessel but would study further the need for the quite submarine, on which work was halted in May. He finally approved the quiet sub on Oct. 25.

In addition to speaking out on the matter, Congress also provided additional funds to continue the development program. The Navy had requested $18 million for advanced procurement on two such submarines. Congress appropriated $9 million for one vessel plus $22.5 million in items for a new type of submarine and $20.4 million for research on other new vessels, including $16.4 million to be spent after fiscal 1970 to assure continuation of the program.

Following is a chronology of the 1968 highlights in the controversy:

February. The Joint Committee on Atomic Energy held hearings Feb. 8, 1968, and Feb. 25 issued a transcript of the inquiry. In a foreword to the transcript, the Committee urged "immediate and major improvement" in the nuclear submarine program lest the United States find "itself unable to counter the rapidly increasing Soviet submarine threat." At that time the Soviet Union was believed to possess 55 nuclear subs and to be adding five each year. Rickover, during the hearings, predicted the Soviet Union would surpass the United States in numbers of submarines within five years.

April 10. The Senate Armed Services Committee in reporting the defense procurement authorization bill (S 3293) criticized the nuclear submarine cur-

tailment planned for 1970. It termed such plans "highly dangerous," and urged a construction program beyond 1970. It also added funds to those requested by the Administration for nuclear submarines and added $16.4 million to be spent after fiscal 1970 to assure continuation of the program.

May 21. A special House Armed Services investigating subcommittee headed by Samuel S. Stratton (D N.Y.) recommended continuation of the atomic submarine program beyond fiscal 1970. If did not recommend the precise number of submarines it felt necessary but noted that Navy officials had sought 100 to 110.

June 21. The Joint Atomic Energy Committee, concerned about the lack of response from the Pentagon on the submarine issue, held further hearings. It claimed new intelligence information showed the Soviet Union was progressing at a more rapid pace than had been anticipated.

July 4. The Senate Armed Services Prepardness Investigating Subcommittee released testimony of March hearings on nuclear submarine development. In his appearance, Rickover asserted that Director of Defense Research and Engineering John S. Foster was trying to kill the quiet submarine project. He said the Navy had agreed to the program in December 1967, but that Foster kept asking for reviews. Subcommittee Chairman John Stennis (D Miss.), said the Soviet Union had a "very substantial numerical superiority in attack submarines." Stennis said the United States had a total of 146 submarines, including 41 Polaris ballistic missile subs which he said were no more than missile platforms, and 105 attack subs, 33 of which were powered and 72 were diesel-driven. The Russians were said to have an overall total of more than 350 submarines, 250 of which were attack submarines.

July 11. Defense Secretary Clifford announced that the Navy would proceed with the new high-speed nuclear attack submarine. But he said the question of going ahead on the quiet sub would be studied further. Clifford said, "Submarines constitute only one facet of the defense we have against enemy submarines. We have sea-based planes; we have land-based planes; we have destroyers; we have destroyer escorts; and we have other means by which we can contend against enemy submarines."

July 25. After Clifford announced further delay for the quit submarine, the Joint Atomic Energy Committee decided to hold its third hearing of 1968 into the situation.

In a foreword to the transcript, the Committee said that "by holding up projects once authorized and supported by major committees of Congress, such as the electric-drive submarine, and then delaying decisions for interminable periods, the nation is deprived of important military capabilities."

Oct. 25. Following further charges of a submarine and security gap by GOP Presidential candidate Richard M. Nixon, Clifford approved the construction of a prototype quiet submarine costing from $150 million to $200 million. One Defense Department planner opposed to the vessel labeled it "First of the Nixon Class."

critic of U.S. policies in Vietnam, said it would be tragic to "saddle" a new President coming into office in the middle of Wheeler's proposed term with a Joint Chiefs chairman "whose advice over the past four years had been so discredited."

Military Justice

Congress Oct. 10 approved a bill (HR 15971) making extensive reforms in the system of military justice. The measure was supported by the Defense Department.

Final action came when the House by voice vote accepted several major amendments added to the House bill in the Senate Oct. 3. Many of the significant provisions in the bill were added in the Senate. The House had originally passed the bill June 3.

President Johnson signed the bill into law (PL 90-632) Oct. 24, saying it granted the armed forces a first-class system of justice to accompany the other outstanding services they received.

The legislation created an independent military judiciary outside the pressure and control of base commanders and empowered these military judges with new authority to bring them more closely in line with civilian judges and to expedite courts martial. It also required legal counsel and judges in cases where they were not required in the past and allowed a defendant to be freed pending an appeal of a court martial decision. It further sought to remove pressure from commanders on courts martial by prohibiting performances by members of the armed forces on courts martial from being evaluated in individual efficiency or fitness reports.

The House bill was limited to expanding the role of law officers, who served in a quasijudicial role, and granted some additional rights to defendants, such as two-year right of appeal in serious cases and access to legal counsel in some cases.

However, the Senate expanded the bill to include all the final provisions. Senators said the House managers of the bill had been consulted and approved the amendments as did the Department of Defense. They also indicated that further revisions in the system of military justice would be sought in the future.

The bill amended the Uniform Code of Military Justice (PL 81-506), which had been enacted in 1950 following years of efforts to reform the existing courts martial system following World War II. Despite the Code's expansion of the rights of the accused, critics felt a further overhauling was needed, primarily to ensure that base commanders could not exert pressure on cases that accused servicemen would be assured of trained legal counsel in any court-martial proceeding.

Provisions. As signed by the President, HR 15971 contained the following major provisions:

Redesignated the law officer of a military court-martial as a military judge, and empowered him to make certain legal and procedural decisions in a trial.

Provided that a defendant in a general or special court-martial could request his case be heard by a military judge alone.

Prohibited a general court-martial consisting only of a military judge from deciding a case in which the death penalty may be adjudged.

Specified that the accused in a special court martial or in a case where a bad-conduct discharge may be ad-

judged be given legally trained counsel and required a military judge in the latter cases.

Provided that a serviceman may refuse trial by a summary court martial consisting of one commissioned officer.

Provided that a serviceman desiring to have enlisted men serve on his court martial shall make such request before the end of a pretrial session.

Created an independent military judiciary of commissioned officers who were members of the federal bar or of the bar of the highest court in a state to preside over special and general courts-martial and provided that the secretary of each service establish the requirements for these military judges.

Strengthened prohibitions against command influence over members of a court martial by providing that the performance of a serviceman as a member of a court martial could not be evaluated in preparing an effectiveness, fitness or efficiency report.

Permitted the deferment of sentences to confinement pending appeals and allowed two years to petition for a new trial.

Redesignated board of review as courts of military review to review court martial cases and also authorized the Judge Advocate General, because of new evidence, error or fraud, to modify findings, or sentence of a court martial which has not yet been reviewed.

National Guard Technicians

Congress in 1968 passed a bill (S 3865—PL 90-486) to grant federal employee status to National Guard technicians. Final action came when the House passed the bill as approved by the Senate.

The bill was similar to a deleted portion of "The Reserve Forces Bill of Rights" (HR 2—PL 90-168) which passed Congress in 1967. The provisions for Guard technicians were withdrawn from HR 2 by the Senate which wanted to study them further and promised to act on them in 1968. A clarification in the status of National Guard technicians was deemed desirable because such persons were full-time employees of the Guard under state jurisdiction but were paid by the Federal Government without having the normal benefits of other federal workers.

Provisions. As signed by the President, S 3865 contained the following major provisions:

Converted National Guard technicians from their previous indefinite status to noncompetitive Federal Government employees to be hired and administered by state adjutants general.

Gave such technicians full credit for past Guard employment in computing leave, death and injury compensation, health and life insurance and other fringe benefits and 55 percent credit for computation of retirement benefits.

Gave technicians the option of staying on the state retirement program or joining the federal program.

Established a ceiling of 42,500 on the number of Guard technicians employed at any one time.

Made the bill effective Jan. 1, 1969.

Atomic Energy

Authorization. The budget-cutting made necessary by the Government's fiscal crisis did not spare programs of the Atomic Energy Commission, which were pared by almost $300 million in the annual AEC authorization bill. The measure (HR 16324—PL 90-289), cleared April 8, authorized $2,618,301,000. The cuts were absorbed by the agency's civilian programs, with military applications actually showing an increase. The measure carried about $1.7 billion for military purposes, up $306 million from fiscal 1968. The increase in weapon programs was attributed largely to decisions to deploy the Sentinel antiballistic missile system and to intensify work on the Navy's Poseidon missile, although precise figures for the two projects were classified.

The largest single reduction in the bill came in the Administration's $242.7 million request for construction funds for the 200-Bev (billion electron volt) accelerator at Weston, Ill. The project was cut by $217.7 million to $25 million for continued design and engineering work and site preparation. In cutting the funds, however, the Joint Atomic Energy Committee said the accelerator was "of the utmost importance to the nation's scientific effort" and said it expected full project authorization in fiscal 1970.

The bill included an add-on of $8.5 million above Administration requests for naval propulsion to allow the AEC to proceed with a new nuclear propulsion plant for an advanced nuclear attack submarine. The action, initiated by the Committee after it heard testimony from Vice Adm. Hyman G. Rickover that pictured major new Soviet submarine efforts, was designed to continue the nuclear attack submarine construction program past the fiscal 1970 cutoff date proposed by the Department of Defense.

Appropriation. Funds for the AEC were cut by an additional $47.4 million in the Public Works-AEC appropriations bill (HR 17903—PL 90-479), approved July 30. The measure appropriated $2,570,874,000 for the

AEC in fiscal 1969. The main cut in the bill came in the Weston accelerator project, which was trimmed down from the $25 million authorization figure to $12,074,000. Both the House and Senate Appropriations Committees made clear that they supported the project but could not justify funding it in view of the Government's fiscal situation.

Other Bills

Civil Defense. Congress May 29 cleared a bill (HR 15004—PL 90-336) to extend for four years, through fiscal 1972, three civil defense financial assistance programs. The programs extended by the bill (1) provided financial assistance to states for state and local civil defense personnel and administrative expenses, (2) procured and maintained radiological equipment for use by states for loans or grants and (3) made payments for travel and per diem expenses of trainees in civil defense schools. In reporting the bill March 11, the House Armed Services Committee estimated that the cost of the financial assistance programs extended by the bill was to be $22,430,000 in fiscal 1969, $28,350,000 in fiscal 1970, $30,240,000 in fiscal 1971, and $31,740,000 in fiscal 1972.

Coast Guard Authorization. Congress May 27 sent the President a bill (HR 15224—PL 90-334) authorizing $136 million to procure and improve Coast Guard ships and facilities in fiscal 1969. The authorization was $29 million above the Administration's request of $107 million. The extra funds were added in the House and were to provide for three high-endurance cutters instead of the one cutter requested by the Coast Guard. Other provisions of the bill authorized procurement of various other types of vessels, improvements on existing vessels, procurement of nine medium-range helicopters, and construction at shore installations and other facilities.

THE McNAMARA ERA

Control of Pentagon Brought Revolution in Defense Policy

Seldom in U.S. history has a Cabinet official attained as much influence or aroused as much controversy as did Defense Secretary Robert S. McNamara.

McNamara, who resigned in 1968 to become president of the World Bank, wrested an unprecedented measure of control of the Pentagon from the military establishment. In so doing, he revolutionized U.S. defense policy, both with respect to the kinds of weapons the services could buy and the ways in which they could use them. *(See below.)*

During his tenure of almost seven years at the Pentagon (the longest on record), McNamara became the most influential Cabinet adviser to both the Presidents he served. Because of his keen intellect and broad experience as a business executive, his advisory role far transcended defense matters alone. President Johnson so appreciated his versatility that he reportedly considered McNamara for 1965 openings in two other key Cabinet posts—the Secretaryship of either the Department of Housing and Urban Development (HUD) or of the Department of Health, Education and Welfare (HEW).

Clashes With Congress. McNamara's firm control of the Pentagon and his computerized solutions to defense problems caused considerable resentment in Congress. Throughout the years, Congress voted billions of dollars for weapons systems that the military endorsed but that McNamara opposed. In almost every case, McNamara simply refused to spend the money.

Although Congress was able to thwart some of McNamara's proposals (notably the Army Reserve-National Guard merger and a fleet of fast deployment logistic ships), Pentagon officials regarded these developments as only minor setbacks. Richard Fryklund, Deputy Assistant Secretary of Defense (Public Affairs) told Congressional Quarterly that there had been only three important failures during McNamara's entire term (none of them inflicted by Congress). These included (1) his inability to win the Vietnam war; (2) his failure to persuade U.S. allies in the North Atlantic Treaty Organization (NATO) to build up the alliance's tactical defenses; and (3) his inability to develop a doctrine for use of tactical nuclear weapons that would not provoke a full-scale nuclear war.

Political Ramifications. Because McNamara was widely regarded as a moderating influence on U.S. Vietnam policy, his departure touched off speculation that the conflict soon would be escalated. President Johnson said, however, the U.S. policy was "firmly set" and that no major changes were contemplated. At the urging of McNamara's successor, Clark M. Clifford, de-escalation began in 1968.

Similarly, press reports that several members of the Joint Chiefs of Staff had threatened to resign if McNamara stayed on as Secretary were described by a Presidential Assistant as "a damned lie." Fryklund told CQ that no member of the Chiefs had contemplated resignation "for a flickering second," and, to the contrary, all had found it "exhilarating that McNamara always can make a decision and get things done."

World Bank Post. McNamara's interest in the World Bank position or in a similar job first became apparent during a 1966 speech in Montreal, in which he said there could be "no question that there is an irrefutable relationship between violence and economic backwardness" in nations throughout the world. (The primary role of the Bank, whose formal title is the International Bank for Reconstruction and Development, is to provide development loans for poor countries. The challenge of McNamara's new position would be to persuade affluent nations to commit more funds for lending through World Bank auspices.)

The fact that McNamara's pending appointment to the Bank leaked to the press before any official announcement spurred rumors that he was being eased out of the Cabinet. The President did not comment on the nomination until two days after the story first appeared. McNamara himself appeared surprised, and he said later that he had mentioned the Bank post to the President as only a possible long-range objective.

In his official statement, the President said McNamara was "obviously highly qualified" for the World Bank job and was "certainly entitled to appointment to any appropriate post in which he is interested and to relief from the extraordinary burdens he has been carrying...." The Bank approved the nomination Nov. 29, 1967, and McNamara announced his acceptance the same day. He assumed his new post April 1, 1968.

McNamara remained a controversial figure long after leaving office. By 1969, when it was revealed that large cost overruns were being experienced on some of the major weapon systems developed during the McNamara era, the former Secretary's critics hastened to blame McNamara's computerized approach to weapon purchases. McNamara's defenders retorted that these weapons, such as the mammoth C-5A transport aircraft, the F-111 (TFX) fighter and the Minuteman III intercontinental missile, involved unprecedented complexity and would have cost far more except for McNamara's management techniques.

Flexible Response, Cost-Cutting

President Kennedy epitomized the defense posture that he and McNamara sought for the nation when he said July 25, 1961, that "we intend to have a wider choice than humiliation or all-out nuclear action." In their search for more "options," Mr. Kennedy and his Defense Secretary emphasized three major objectives: the earliest possible attainment of a relatively invulnerable second-strike (retaliatory) capability in the form of solid-fuel ballistic missiles in mobile and hardened bases; increased non-nuclear capabilities—in terms of man-

Secretaries of Defense

The position of Secretary of Defense was established by the National Security Act of 1947, which made the Secretaries of the three services subordinates of the Defense Secretary. McNamara was the eighth Secretary of Defense.

James V. Forrestal (9/17/47 - 3/27/49)
Louis Johnson (3/28/49 - 3/19/50)
George C. Marshall (9/21/50 - 9/12/51)
Robert A. Lovett (9/17/51 - 1/20/53)
Charles E. Wilson (1/28/53 - 10/8/57)
Neil H. McElroy (10/9/57 - 12/1/59)
Thomas S. Gates Jr. (12/2/59 - 1/20/61)
Robert S. McNamara (1/21/61 - 3/1/68)
Clark M. Clifford (3/1/68 - 1/20/69)
Melvin R. Laird (1/22/69 -)

Defense Chiefs, Civilian and Military: 1961-69

Secretary of Defense
Robert S. McNamara (1/21/61 - 3/1/68)
Clark M. Clifford (3/1/68 - 1/20/69)
Melvin R. Laird (1/22/69 -)

Deputy Secretary of Defense
Roswell L. Gilpatric (1/24/61 - 1/20/64)
Cyrus R. Vance (1/28/64 - 6/30/67)
Paul H. Nitze (7/1/67 - 1/23/69)
David Packard (1/24/69 -)

Secretary of the Army
Elvis J. Stahr Jr. (1/24/61 - 6/30/62)
Cyrus R. Vance (7/5/62 - 1/28/64)
Stephen Ailes (1/28/64 - 7/1/65)
Stanley R. Resor (7/7/65 -)

Secretary of the Navy
John B. Connally (1/25/61 - 12/20/61)
Fred H. Korth (1/4/62 - 11/1/63)
Paul H. Nitze (11/29/63 - 6/30/67)
Paul R. Ignatius (9/1/67 - 1/29/69)
John H. Chafee (1/30/69 -)

Secretary of the Air Force
Eugene M. Zuckert (1/24/61 - 9/30/65)
Harold Brown (10/1/65 - 1/29/69)
Robert C. Seamans (1/30/69 -)

Chairman, Joint Chiefs of Staff
Gen. Lyman L. Lemnitzer (10/1/60 - 8/9/62)
Gen. Maxwell D. Taylor (8/9/62 - 7/2/64)
Gen. Earle G. Wheeler (7/3/64 -)

Chief of Staff, U.S. Army
Gen. George H. Decker (9/30/60 - 8/9/62)
Gen. Earle G. Wheeler (8/9/62 - 7/3/64)
Gen Harold K. Johnson (7/3/64 - 7/1/68)
Gen. William C. Westmoreland (7/2/68 -)

Chief of Naval Operations
Adm. George W. Anderson (8/1/61 - 8/1/63)
Adm. David L. McDonald (8/1/63 - 8/1/67)
Adm. T. H. Moorer (8/1/67 -)

Chief of Staff, U.S. Air Force
Gen. Curtis E. LeMay (6/30/61 - 2/1/65)
Gen. John P. McConnell (2/1/65 - 7/31/69)
Gen. John D. Ryan (8/1/69 -)

Commandant, U.S. Marine Corps
Gen. David M. Shoup (1/1/60 - 12/31/63)
Gen. Wallace M. Greene Jr. (1/1/64 - 12/31/67)
Gen. Leonard F. Chapman Jr. (1/1/68 -)

power, airlift and weapons—to cope with any form of aggression short of direct nuclear attack; and improved "command and control" equipment and procedures to give leaders as much time as possible to choose a response to aggression, thus lessening the chance that hasty action might provoke all-out nuclear war. In doctrinal terms, these revisions amounted to the abandonment of the Eisenhower "massive retaliation" doctrine as an all-purpose deterrent in favor of the "flexible response" long advocated by Gen. Maxwell D. Taylor and others.

In pursuit of these objectives, the Kennedy Administration moved immediately to a higher level of defense spending than its predecessor, but all considerations of cost were not abandoned. On the contrary, McNamara in the interests of efficiency and economy effected important reorganizations within his Department and applied innovative systems analysis techniques to decision-making and budget-cutting in the Pentagon.

Flexible Response Doctrine. Implementing the doctrine of flexible response involved changing both military hardware and defense contingency planning.

In 1961 and 1962, McNamara and President Kennedy found that they had neither the equipment nor the contingency plans to deal with international incidents that might justify U.S. intervention, such as the Communist insurgency in Laos in those years. By the time of the Cuban missile crisis in October 1962 a flexible response plan was in effect. When the presence of Soviet missiles and jet bombers on the island was learned, the President first warned the Soviets to withdraw them and then imposed a naval blockade around Cuba to stop shipment of further weapons. The third step was the stopping by the Navy of two Soviet ships on the high seas. Twelve other Soviet ships turned back from the blockade. The fourth step would have been bombing of the missile sites; but that was not necessary, as the Soviet Union agreed to withdraw its weapons from Cuba.

McNamara took many steps to increase the ability of the armed forces to respond to aggression in limited warfare. The Army's counterinsurgency training program was greatly expanded, and large numbers of helicopters were procured to give Army land forces more mobility in difficult terrain like that of Vietnam. A multitude of new tactical weapons was developed, including a new type of tank, a new supersonic swing-wing fighter aircraft (the TFX) and short-range tactical nuclear rockets. McNamara hoped that the proposed fast deployment logistics ship would add significantly to U.S. ability to respond to limited war situations, but that plan was blocked by Congress.

McNamara also supervised the shift of the country's strategic offensive strike force from reliance on manned bombers to reliance on intercontinental ballistic missiles as a deterrent force. About 1,000 Minuteman II and III ICBMs were placed in "hardened" underground silos and a fleet of 41 submarines was equipped with nuclear Polaris missiles. Procurement of a new and better submarine-launched missile, the Poseidon, began in 1967. McNamara refused to procure a new long-range bomber (the RS-70), thus thwarting the desires of the Joint Chiefs of Staff and powerful Members of Congress. He angered the same group by refusing until 1967 to deploy any form of defensive antiballistic missile system, although that decision was reversed in September, three months after Communist China detonated a test hydrogen bomb.

These forces, plus comprehensive contingency plans developed by the Pentagon, added up to a capability for flexible response. But where that concept worked in the Cuban crisis, it did not work in Vietnam. Gradualism there expanded into major warfare and pushed the United States into vast expenditures and toward what some in and out of Congress feared was an inevitable confrontation with China. If McNamara's flexible response failed it was certainly in dealing with guerrilla warfare.

Centralization of Command, Cost-Cutting. McNamara was quick to assert the full authority of his office to achieve a greater degree of centralization and control over the services than had ever existed before. In 1961, he established the Defense Intelligence Agency and the Defense Supply Agency, raising to five the number of centralized agencies designed to perform functions common to all of the services. In later years, he created a sixth such agency, the Defense Contract Audit Agency, established a new office of systems analysis and reorganized the technical services of the Army, Air Force and Navy.

Of longer range significance was the introduction in 1961 of a new system for evaluating military budget requests in terms of function rather than service, thereby comparing the costs and advantages of such similar-purpose weapon systems as the Navy's Polaris missile, the Air Force's Minuteman and the RS-70 bomber. The new system, supervised by a staff of civilian analysts in the Office of the Secretary of Defense, allowed development of a master plan for defense that down-played the traditional roles and ran counter to the "balanced forces" thinking of the separate services.

The system was devised by Charles J. Hitch, Pentagon comptroller, and by Alain Enthoven who was in charge of weapons systems analysis—two of the brilliant civilians McNamara attracted to the Pentagon. It was christened the planning-programming-budgeting (PPB) system, and was applied to the fiscal 1963 defense budget and to each thereafter. PPB was the application of systems analysis to federal programs. Its purpose was to assist decision-makers by developing a basis for systematic and, if possible, quantitative comparsion of the cost and benefits of alternative programs, and by making such comparisons part of the decision-making process.

In part, PPB was a cost-cutting tool. Another was the "Cost Reduction Program," introduced by McNamara in 1962 to encourage the identification and realization of savings through improved management procedures and actions. Savings asserted to have been identified under the program totaled more than $15 billion in fiscal 1962-1968.

Elements in Congress, including the Armed Services Committees, sometimes took a dim view of PPB and the cost reduction program. In its 1966 report on the fiscal 1967 defense procurement bill, the House Armed Services Committee said that "sound military recommendations (on matters including procurement of manned bombers and Navy nuclear surface vessels) have been overruled by the Secretary of Defense." While conceding "much brilliance" among civilian directors of the Pentagon, the Committee said, "Too often, it is feared, the almost obsessional dedication to cost effectiveness raises the specter of a decision-maker who, as it has been said, knows the price of everything and the value of nothing."

McNamara's cost-effectiveness studies influenced him to abandon or defer several weapons systems that had strong support from the Joint Chiefs of Staff and Congress (a nuclear surface fleet, a nuclear-powered aircraft, the RS-70 strategic bomber and an antiballistic missile system). The studies and his goal of providing a flexible response capability led him to adopt the controversial idea of a common fighter aircraft (TFX) for the Air Force and Navy, to propose that fast deployment logistic ships be procured in a single package from one shipyard (rather than under the usual practice of dividing the contract among several firms), and to call for a merger of the Army Reserve and the Army National Guard under Guard management.

Vietnam War

The U.S. commitment of military advisers to South Vietnam, which began in 1955 under President Eisenhower, was six years old when McNamara became Defense Secretary in 1961. Despite the new Administration's emphasis on strengthening the ability to counter guerrilla warfare, progress against the Viet Cong and North Vietnamese was slow, and the United States seemed inexorably drawn deeper into the war. From 600 U.S. advisers in 1961, the U.S. commitment grew by 1967 to more than 525,000 servicemen in the war area, costing about $2.5 billion per month and producing 62,000 U.S. casualties.

Overseeing U.S. military operations in the war, McNamara came to symbolize the Johnson Administration's determination to stand fast in Vietnam. By 1964, with no conclusive results in hand despite the growing U.S. involvement, the Vietnam conflict had become "McNamara's War" in the words of Sen. Wayne Morse (D Ore.). "I don't object to its being called 'McNamara's War,' " the Secretary replied. "I think it is a very important war, and I am pleased to be identified with it and do whatever I can to win it." It was clear by 1967 that no one person was responsible for the continuing conflict, and the phrase "McNamara's War" was merely a memory.

McNamara in 1967 grew increasingly aware of the growing antiwar feeling in the country. He told a Sept. 7, 1967, news conference, "I think there is a concern...a frustration in the country with the unpredictable character of the war." This was "dangerous," he said, "because impatience can lead to irrational, irresponsible action, actions which can have the result of widening the war."

Air War. McNamara's celebrated drive for efficiency carried over to the air war against North Vietnam and made him a reluctant partner in Administration decisions to bomb targets in North Vietnam which he considered to be of questionable military significance. He rejected the view that North Vietnam could be bombed to the negotiating table. McNamara's doubts about the effectiveness of bombing North Vietnam targets led to a disagreement with the top military experts of the Pentagon which surfaced twice during 1967. The first indication of the dispute came Jan. 23 in conflicting testimony from the Secretary and Gen. Earle G. Wheeler, JCS chairman, before the Senate Armed Services Committee. McNamara said the bombing had not reduced infiltration from North to South Vietnam. Wheeler said it had.

The second indication of the dispute, suggesting that it still was unresolved months later, came in a series of closed hearings that began Aug. 9 before the Senate

Armed Services Preparedness Investigations Subcommittee. The Subcommittee Aug. 31 said in its report that it found "a sharp difference" between McNamara and the military witnesses on the use of air power against North Vietnam. Despite a Sept. 1 statement by President Johnson that "there is no deep division" of views, a number of North Vietnam targets previously off limits to U.S. planes were brought under attack, raising speculation that the division did exist and that the President had overruled McNamara and had sided with the military experts.

DMZ Barrier. The Sept. 7 announcement by McNamara that the United States would contruct an infiltration barrier along the demilitarized zone (DMZ) raised questions as to whether U.S. military strategy was shifting from mobile to static operations. The Secretary described the barrier as a system of barbed wire, mines, and sophisticated electronic devices which would be in operation by late 1967 or early 1968. The barrier was interpreted by some as a further example of McNamara efficiency in which hardware would replace manpower in an area exposed to North Vietnamese artillery fire. "No obstacle system can stop the infiltration of men or supplies from North to South," the Secretary's announcement said. The barrier was designed to make the infiltration "more difficult," he explained. The barrier was abandoned by Defense Secretary Melvin R. Laird in 1969.

War Assessments. McNamara commented on progress of the war after strategy meetings with U.S. commanders and inspection trips to Vietnam, and before Congressional committees. In 1963, McNamara and Gen. Maxwell D. Taylor, JCS chairman, Oct. 2 reported to President Kennedy "that the major part of the U.S. military task can be completed by the end of 1965, although there may be a continuing demand for a limited number of...training personnel." The regime of South Vietnam Premier Ngo Dinh Diem was overthrown in November 1963, setting off a succession of Saigon governments, and by March 1964 McNamara's earlier optimism had faded. "In short," he said March 26, 1964, in an Administration white paper, "the situation in South Vietnam has unquestionably worsened at least since last fall....The road ahead in Vietnam is going to be long, difficult and frustrating." Eleven months later, the Secretary Feb. 19, 1965, told House Armed Services Committee, "The present situation in South Vietnam is grave but by no means hopeless." McNamara March 4, 1966, speaking of the possible length of the war, told the Senate Foreign Relations Committee, "No answers framed in terms of years or months have validity, because so much will depend on North Vietnam's estimate of our own determination."

In his annual "posture statement," McNamara Jan. 23, 1967, presented a mixed picture of success and failure in the war. He called search-and-destroy operations "an unqualified success" but said that clear-and-secure operations had not shown satisfactory progress. He said that the number of Viet Cong killed, captured, and defecting was increasing and that enemy infiltration had leveled off. U.S. air operations, he said, "by and large...have produced the results that we expected from them."

European Policies

Major changes in the U.S. conception of the military role of the North Atlantic Treaty Organization (NATO) took place while McNamara was Defense Secretary. Faced in 1961 with a NATO strategy inherited from the Eisenhower years that stessed tactical nuclear weapons over conventional forces, the Kennedy Administration was determined to place greater emphasis on conventional forces. It used the Berlin crisis of 1961 as an opportunity to increase the size and strength of U.S. forces in Europe and called on its allies to follow suit. McNamara Jan. 30, 1963, told the House Armed Services Committee, "We must be in a position to confront (a Soviet attack in Europe) at any level of provocation with an appropriate military response. The decision to employ tactical nuclear weapons should not be forced upon us simply because we have no other way to cope with a particular situation." The response by other NATO countries, however, was disappointing to McNamara.

Seeking to discourage development of a French nuclear force independent of NATO and to meet the allies' pressures for a share in their nuclear defense, the Kennedy Administration supported through 1964 a multilateral nuclear force (MLF) of 25 surface ships armed with Polaris missiles and manned by multinational crews. The MLF proposal languished for diplomatic reasons, and in 1965 the United States shifted its attention from a "hardware solution" of NATO nuclear problems to increased consultation with its allies on nuclear planning in the defense of Europe.

The easing of cold war tensions and growing affluence of Europe led McNamara in his Jan. 30, 1963, House Armed Services Committee testimony to see "a new power center" developing "inevitably" on the European continent. This would mean, he said, "some basic changes in our present arrangements with our NATO partners." He spelled out what the changes might be in June 21, 1966, testimony before the Senate Foreign Relations Committee: "I think that we might well consider adjustments in our force structure as the Europeans contribute more to their own force and as technical changes make it possible for us to modify our deployments without really reducing our military capabilities." NATO could "play a vital role in the political evolution that is beginning in Europe," the Secretary said Jan. 23, 1967, in his annual defense posture statement.

Another important NATO change was the French decision in 1966 to "terminate her participation in the 'integrated' commands, and no longer place forces at the disposal of NATO," in the words of President Charles de Gaulle. The decision was a major jolt to U.S. policy in Europe, but McNamara June 21, 1966, said the effect of de Gaulle's actions "on the military posture of the Alliance will be in no way disabling."

Skybolt. McNamara's 1962 decision to cancel the procurement of the Skybolt missile—a nuclear-tipped missile for use on bomber aircraft—touched off a wave of resentment in Great Britain. The United States had pressured Britain to buy the missile in order to retain its independent nuclear deterrent. After a long deliberation, Prime Minister Harold Macmillan had agreed to the purchase in the face of vigorous criticism from the opposition Labor Party.

McNamara had decided that the Skybolt was unnecessary to U.S. needs because of the greater efficiency of landbased Minuteman and seaborne Polaris missiles. He had not informed the British that he was considering termination, however, and the first Macmillan learned of it was at a December conference on Nassau after the decision already was final. MacMillan's role in the project was widely criticized in Britain, and some observers thought it a major reason for the defeat of the Conservative Government in the 1964 Parliamentary elections. *(Congress and the Nation, Vol. I, p. 315)*

German Arms Agreement. West German resentment against McNamara's policies was aroused in 1966 when the Defense Secretary reportedly threatened to reduce the level of U.S. troops in the Federal Republic unless the Germans honored previous agreements to purchase a total of more than $4 billion in U.S. armaments. Because of a recession in the West German economy, the government of Chancellor Ludwig Erhard sought to postpone some scheduled purchases, but McNamara was unsympathetic to the request. According to some reports, the fall of the Erhard Government in 1966 was partly caused by the U.S. refusal to be more flexible on the arms question.

Defense Spending Under McNamara

Federal expenditures for military functions of the Department of Defense (including military construction, family housing and civil defense, but excluding military foreign assistance) rose from $46.8 billion in fiscal 1962 to $80.5 billion in fiscal 1968. The 1968 figure was the second highest military spending level in U.S. history.

Effect on National Economy. As Secretary of Defense, McNamara wielded more direct and indirect control over the course of the U.S. economy than any other official except the President himself. Defense Department expenditures generated at least 7 percent of the gross national product (GNP) during each year of McNamara's tenure. In calendar 1967 alone, Congress appropriated $84,226,502,000 in supplemental fiscal 1967 and regular fiscal 1968 funds for defense, authorizing spending that would affect every segment of the economy.

Under the pressures of rapidly mounting defense spending—and in the continued absence of higher taxes

to take money out of the economy—the consumer price index jumped from 111.0 percent in January 1966 to 117.5 percent in October 1967.

Biography

Robert Strange McNamara was born on June 9, 1916, in San Francisco, Calif.

Education: University of California, Berkeley, B.A., 1937; Harvard Univ. Graduate School of Business Admin., M.B.A., 1939.

Military: Planned and conducted courses for U.S. Army Air Corps officers at Harvard Univ. 1940-43; served as special consultant to the Air Corps on the establishment of a statistical system to control the flow of materiel, money and personnel; in 1943 went to England to set up a statistical control system for U.S. Eighth Air Force; entered U.S. Air Force as captain, serving in England, India, China and the Pacific, winning Legion of Merit; discharged as lieutenant colonel, 1946; later, colonel in U.S. Air Force Reserve.

Family: Married Margaret McKinstry Craig, Aug. 13, 1940; three children: Margaret Elizabeth (Mrs. Barry Carter), Kathleen and Robert Craig.

Religion: Presbyterian.

Party Affiliation: Republican.

Profession: Teacher and business executive: assistant professor of business administration, Harvard Univ., 1940-43; Ford Motor Co. executive, 1946-61, serving as controller, 1949-53; assistant general manager, Ford division, 1953-55; vice president and general manager, Ford division, 1955-57; group vice president of car divisions, 1957-60; president, Nov. 9, 1960; accepted President Kennedy's offer of post of Secretary of Defense, Dec. 13, 1960; sworn in on Jan. 21, 1961.

DEPLOYMENT OF ABM

A Major Defense Controversy During Johnson Years

Aside from the Vietnam war, the most controversial defense issue during the Johnson years was whether the United States should deploy an antiballistic missile (ABM) system to defend the nation against the possibility of an intercontinental missile attack. It was the only occasion since World War II on which a substantial part of the public and their representatives in Congress questioned the wisdom of the Defense Department on a major weapons issue.

Throughout his years in office, Defense Secretary Robert S. McNamara (1961-68) vigorously opposed the system as too costly, possibly ineffective and a measure sure to provoke a new arms race with the Soviet Union. But under White House orders, McNamara announced late in 1967 that the nation would deploy a limited ABM net which might defend effectively against the threat of a relatively unsophisticated Communist Chinese missile assault. McNamara showed no enthusiasm for the decision, noting that it had been made on only "marginal" grounds.

Doubts over the efficacy of the system and pressures to divert more arms spending to meet pressing domestic needs combined in 1968 to produce a year-long Senate debate on the issue. Although the Administration won all the ABM money it sought, opponents lost one of the Senate tests by only three votes—a surprising show of strength against an Administration position on a matter the White House considered vital to national security. (The issue was not as hot in the House, where ABM funds sailed through.) By the end of the year, widespread opposition from citizens in some of the areas where the system was to be installed had given the ABM opposition group in the Senate hope that it might be able to defeat the additional funds that would be requested for the system in 1969.

History of ABM

The debate over whether to construct an antiballistic missile system was a long-standing controversy waged between the military and its supporters on one side and Congressional liberals and some scientists on the other. (For pro and con arguments, see end of article.)

Discussions about ABM defenses trace back to World War II and the introduction of German V-2 rockets. Medium-range missiles were developed in the early 1950s. Russia in 1958 produced intercontinental ballistic missiles (ICBMs) capable of flights of 4,000 to 5,000 miles. The United States deployed its first ICBM, the Atlas, in 1959 and followed it with the Titan and then the Minuteman. (Congress and the Nation, Vol. I, p. 1583.)

Beginning with President Eisenhower in 1960, three Presidents rejected military requests to deploy ABM systems to counter the Soviet ICBM threat. Nevertheless, the United States from 1954 to 1968 spent about

$3 billion on research and development for such systems, and by 1967 an estimated 15,000 military and civilian persons were working on these efforts.

In 1954 the Army began a research program which developed through stages known as the Nike-Ajax, Nike-Hercules, Nike-Zeus and Nike-X programs. In 1957, tests indicated missiles could be intercepted by an anti-missile missile. The same year Congress approved $137 million more than the Administration sought for research on the Nike-Zeus. From then on, pressure to begin production increased. In his last Budget, President Eisenhower provided for $287 million in research funds but warned against starting production until tests were fully completed. Soon after he came into office, President Kennedy was subjected to heavy pressure to launch production—a pressure he was always able to withstand.

Pressure for deployment again built up in 1966. Early in the year Congress boosted the Defense budget $167.9 million to prepare for production of the Nike-X system. This was in addition to the $417 million the Administration sought for research. (But no funds were ever used for production.) In November Defense Secretary McNamara announced that Russia had begun to deploy an antimissile system around Moscow and President Johnson was said to be considering ordering production of the Nike-X system. (Earlier reports that the Soviet Union was constructing an ABM led in 1965 to a U.S. decision to start development work on multiple warhead missiles. The U.S. intelligence community later came to substantial agreement that the earlier Soviet system, called Tallinn, was only a sophisticated antiaircraft system. But intelligence sources generally agreed that the 1966 system, called Galosh, was an ABM with capabilities similar to the U.S. Nike-Zeus, which was scrapped in the early 1960s. About 70 of the Galosh missiles were thought to be in place by late 1968, but it was believed at that time that the Soviet deployment effort on that system had been slowed or even stopped.)

Although in his 1967 State of the Union Message President Johnson said the United States had made no decision on whether to deploy an ABM system, he nonetheless requested standby funds for production awaiting the outcome of approaches at negotiating an arms agreement with the Soviet Union. Congress appropriated $291 million for construction and $421.3 million for research.

Congressional committees differed on their approach to ABM deployment at that time. The Senate Armed Services Committee suggested that while efforts should be made to negotiate an arms limitation agreement with the Soviet Union, procurement of Nike-X should begin if such an accord were not reached within a reasonable time. It also urged consideration of a "thin" system against China. The House Armed Services Committee went farther, urging immediate deployment of a "thin" ABM net.

Conflicting Testimony. Congressional testimony released in 1967 also revealed a wide gulf between De-

Sentinel—Complex Array of Missiles, Electronics Gear

The "Sentinel" ABM deployment announced by the Pentagon in 1967 was not a single weapon but a coordinated array of missiles, radars and computers. It was composed of two types of missiles and two types of radars responding and feeding impulses to a computerized central nervous system.

The first type of radar was a Perimeter Acquisition Radar (PAR)—a long-range detection and tracking mechanism with a beam which could be moved from one direction in the sky to another in a few millionths of a second so that it could virtually scan the horizon instantly.

The other radar was a Missile Site Radar (MSR) designed to track incoming targets at shorter ranges than the PAR and to combine with computers to guide the system's defensive missiles to their encounter with the attacking missiles. (The components of the Nixon Administration's "Safeguard" system were the same except for additional radars which could detect submarine-launched missiles and fractional orbiting bombs whose comparatively low trajectories might evade detection by the PARs and MSRs.)

The two types of missiles envisioned for the system were called Spartan and Sprint. The Spartan, a three-staged rocket, was to have a range of several hundred miles and would be used to intercept enemy missiles above the atmosphere. Its purpose was to provide long-range defense of broad areas of the country (the 15 to 20 sites planned for the system were expected to provide an area defense that would protect the entire nation against the Chinese missile threat). The Sprint, a smaller, two-staged rocket, was designed to provide last-ditch protection against enemy missiles that got past Spartan. Capable of extremely rapid acceleration, Sprint was assigned the primary role of providing close-in protection for the ABM's radars, but it could perform the same mission for cities or offensive missile sites. Both the Spartan and Sprint were to use solid propellants and both would be launched from underground silos.

Mode of Operation. As envisioned, the Sentinel network would gear up for action when incoming missiles were spotted by the long-range radar (PAR) over a thousand miles away. The PAR would track missiles for a minute or two to establish their trajectory and feed the data to a computer. A Spartan missile would then be triggered to intercept the enemy missiles at a computer-determined point hundreds of miles in outer space. The Spartan would fly at about 5,000 miles an hour and at its nearest point to the enemy rocket would explode its hydrogen warhead with the impact of millions of tons of TNT. Although the missiles would not collide, the H-blast of the Spartan would destroy its targets in a wide swath in the vacuum of outer space. Any enemy weapons penetrating Spartan's shield would encounter the short-range Sprint deployed upon radar warning that missiles had gotten through. The Sprint would employ the same procedure as the Spartan to destroy its targets but its warhead would be smaller and the contact and explosion would be within the atmosphere, about 20 miles in the air.

According to plans, about six PAR radars would be installed along the northern U.S. border and in Hawaii and Alaska. Each would require a 297-acre site and be housed in a concrete building 330 feet wide and 140 feet high. According to published data, the MSR radars and the Spartan sites would need 282-acre plots.

Surveys were conducted in 1968 for ABM sites near Boston, Chicago, New York, Detroit, Albany, Ga., Dallas, Salt Lake City, Seattle and in North Dakota and Hawaii. Other sites were to be surveyed later. The Sentinel plan called for eventual purchase of 360 Spartan and 672 Sprint missiles. The system was expected to become fully operational by fiscal 1975.

Defense Department estimates of the cost of the Sentinel system were put at $3.5 billion in early 1967 and $5 billion by McNamara when he announced deployment at the end of that year. (The Nixon Administration's Safeguard was expected to cost $6 to $7 billion.) All of these figures were initial investment costs and did not include costs of operating the system, which reliable industry sources placed at a minimum of $500 million a year.

Among the top subcontractors for the Sentinel system were the Western Electric Co. (manufacturing and supply unit of the American Telephone and Telegraph Co.), prime contractor; McDonnell Douglas Corp., Spartan missile; Martin Marietta Corp., Sprint missile; Raytheon Corp., missile site radars; General Electric Co., perimeter acquisition radars; Sperry Rand Corp., data processing equipment; and General Research Corp., Hercules Inc., Honeywell Inc., Kaman Sciences Corp., Lear-Siegler Inc., Lockheed Aircraft Corp., Microwave Associates, Motorola Inc., Philco-Ford Corp., RCA, Sandia Corp., Texas Instruments, Inc., Thiokol Corp., TRW Systems, and Varian Associates, Inc., for lesser but still important roles.

Limited Purpose. The Sentinel was designed to protect against small or relatively unsophisticated attacks or an accidental launch. The system would not be effective against more sophisticated and elusive attacks using rockets with multiple warheads, radar interference devices, low-trajectory missiles which elude the radar, such as attacks from missile-firing submarines and fractional orbiting bombs. Massive attacks that Russia might launch would overwhelm the Spartans and Sprints.

Proponents of the system argued, however, that it could be fully effective against the strike force that China was expected to possess for the first several years after developing an ICBM capability in the early 1970s. China was expected to produce about 20 missiles in the first year or two, building up to an arsenal of 50 to 100 missiles by the mid-1970s. Protection against these missiles by the Sentinel could save 20 to 30 million American lives, according to proponents of the system.

Opponents claimed the Sentinel's effectiveness could not be predicted with such certainty and that it was doubtful that the Chinese would risk destruction of their entire country merely to lob a few ICBMs at the United States.

fense Secretary McNamara and the Joint Chiefs of Staff on the ABM issue.

Testifying Jan. 26 before the Senate Armed Services Committee, McNamara said the Russians "have this almost religious fanaticism toward the subject of defense, and I think that is what has led them to deploy an ABM defense." This defense would be "wasteful and ineffective," he said.

"In the short run," McNamara argued, "if we put the Nike-X in, and they don't react immediately, if we slipped it in before they could react, which is very unlikely, then perhaps we would enjoy some advantage. However, in the longer run we could expect that they would retarget their missiles, increase the danger to our other cities, and probably end up with the capability to inflict essentially the same total fatalities on the United States as they would have if we hadn't put the system in."

Gen. Earle G. Wheeler, chairman of the Joint Chiefs of Staff, took a different view of the ABM problem in testimony the same day. Wheeler told the Committees that the Joint Chiefs "believe that a measure of defense achieved on our part is an added deterrent to the initiation of nuclear war; in other words, that we should not in this era depend purely upon a strike force for our deterrent, but instead should also have a measure of defense for our population, our industry, and perhaps our missiles." He said that the Soviet Union would be faced with "grave uncertainties associated with targeting against an ABM-defended nation."

Wheeler also argued that if "the Soviets come to believe that their ballistic missile defense, coupled with a nuclear attack on the United States, would limit damage to the Soviet Union to a level acceptable to them, whatever that level is, our forces would no longer deter, and the first principle of our security policy is gone."

'Sentinel' Decision

On Sept. 18, 1967, three months after the announcement that China had detonated its first hydrogen bomb, McNamara announced that the United States would proceed with a "thin" ABM deployment against Communist China. But McNamara, whose tone indicated he was more apologetic than enthusiastic about the deployment he was announcing, said the decision was made on "marginal" grounds which held that the Chinese might risk destruction of their entire nation in order to strike the United States with the few ICBMs it was thought they would have by the mid-1970s.

The major part of McNamara's address was devoted to warning the nation about the temptation of expanding the system into a "heavy Soviet-oriented" one which would provide "no adequate shield at all against Soviet attack" and would merely induce the Soviets to build up their own offensive strength. McNamara emphasized, as he had on many occasions before, that America's best deterrent was a strong offensive force.

Nuclear physicist Ralph E. Lapp said in his 1968 book, *The Weapons Culture*, that McNamara had "stubbornly and courageously" opposed military and industry demands for the system but that in the end, the pressure of election-year politics had proved "irresistible." Following the disclosure late in 1966 that the Soviet Union was deploying an ABM system, Lapp wrote,

"prominent Republicans—Presidential 'hopefuls' among them—strongly advocated immediate action on U.S. ballistic missile defense. With this issue now given a political slant, the White House became vulnerable to a 1968 campaign attack that the incumbent Administration had failed to provide adequately for the nation's security. Such Republican 'missile attack' involved political warheads whose punch was measured in megavotes, not megatons."

1968 Action. To implement the decision to construct the "thin" ABM, which became known as "Sentinel," the Defense Department requested a total of $1,195,600,000 in fiscal 1969 funds for it and continuing development work on improved ABM systems. A total of $227.3 million was designated for construction of the ABM facilities, $342.7 million for procurement of defensive missiles and other components, $312.9 million for further research and development of the Sentinel, $268 million for testing of other ABM systems such as Nike-X, and a total of $44.7 million for ABM operation, maintenance and personnel. *(For details of the Sentinel deployment, see box, p. 870.)*

While some ardent backers of an antimissile system expressed disappointment over the decision to deploy only a limited ABM, there was no substantial pressure to build a full version. These parties limited themselves to indicating that the Sentinel was merely a first step toward the full project, Nike-X, which had won the endorsement of the Joint Chiefs of Staff. However, opponents of the ABM concept who had previously enjoyed backing from the Johnson and other Administrations attacked the funding requests vehemently. This opposition surfaced almost each time bills bearing funds for the Sentinel appeared. Attempts were made to delete the funds four times in the Senate and twice in the House in 1968.

The first battle came when the Military Procurement Authorization bill (S 3293) was discussed in the Senate in April. Led by John Sherman Cooper (R Ky.), opponents sought to knock out $342.7 million for Sentinel procurement or to delay deployment. An amendment by Gaylord Nelson (D Wis.) to delete these funds altogether was rejected by a 17-41 roll call April 18 (R 3-20; D 14-21—ND 13-11, SD 1-10). Then the Senate rejected by a 28-31 roll call a Cooper amendment to delay deployment until the Secretary of Defense certified it was "practicable" and that the costs were known with "reasonable accuracy" (R 11-11; D 17-20—ND 16-10, SD 1-10).

Debate was renewed with even greater intensity June 25 when ABM opponents sought to delay for a year the $227.3 million contained in the Military Construction Authorization bill (HR 16703). Speaking out against the authorization were Sens. Philip A. Hart (D Mich.), Stuart Symington (D Mo.), Margaret Chase Smith (R Maine) and Mike Mansfield (D Mont.). An amendment by Cooper and Hart to delay ABM construction funds for a year was defeated on a 34-52 roll call (R 12-23; D 22-29—ND 20-13, SD 2-16). A second amendment by Stephen M. Young (D Ohio) to delete the ABM authorization was rejected by a 12-72 roll-call vote (R 4-30; D 8-42—ND 8-24, SD 0-18). The defense was led by members of the Armed Services Committee and by Defense Secretary Clark M. Clifford, who wrote that the delay would impair the project.

When the defense procurement authorization (S 3293) reached the House floor another fight erupted over the $342.7 million for ABM procurement. A proposal by Robert L. Leggett (D Calif.) to remove that amount from the bill was defeated on a 40-147 standing vote July 11.

On July 29 the House again rejected an attempt to delete funds for ABM construction in the Military Construction Appropriation bill (HR 18785). The action came on a standing vote of 37-106 on an amendment by Jeffery Cohelan (D Calif.) to remove the full $263.3 million for acquisition of property and construction of related facilities.

Acting on the construction appropriation bill Aug. 1, the Senate again took an ABM vote. Although leading ABM opponents had decided not to press the issue of construction and planned instead to wait for an all-out thrust against the full Defense Department appropriation bill (HR 18707), Sen. Nelson introduced an amendment to delete the funds. The Senate rejected the amendment on a **27-46** roll-call vote (R 5-14; D 22-32—ND 20-15; SD 2-17).

The final test of the year came in the Senate Oct. 2 during consideration of the defense appropriations bill. After an unusual closed-door session in which the Senate heard classified material presented by opponents of the system, the chamber rejected by a 25-45 roll-call vote an amendment to delay construction of the project by a year (R 8-20; D 17-25—ND 15-12; SD 2-13).

The amendment sought to block the ABM deployment by deleting $387.4 million in Sentinel procurement, personnel and operating funds. The proposal, which would have left intact an allotment of $312.9 million for ABM research and development, was introduced by Sens. Cooper and Hart and cosponsored by 10 others.

In the Oct. 2 showdown, the forces opposing the Sentinel deployment gained the backing of three Senators who had not previously voted against the ABM—Charles E. Goodell (R N.Y.), who shortly before had been appointed to the seat vacated by the death of Robert F. Kennedy (D N.Y. 1965-1968); Albert Gore (D Tenn.) and Winston L. Prouty (R Vt.). The ranks of the ABM foes, however, were depleted by the absence of 16 Senators who had previously voted against the program but were not present for the Oct. 2 vote. However, even if the 16 had been present and had voted for the ABM delay, the anti-ABM effort still would have fallen five votes short of success.

Site Controversy. In the process of implementing the decision to begin installing the Sentinel system, the Army by year's end had run into stiff citizen opposition at some of the sites being considered (the plan called for installation of Sentinel batteries in or near 15 to 20 cities around the country). In Boston, Chicago and Seattle, where work was at an advanced stage, opposition was particularly vigorous, with citizens frequently holding protest demonstrations and placing considerable pressure on their representatives in Congress.

The opposition to the Sentinel sites rose for a variety of reasons. The most serious of the complaints was that location of the sites near populous areas posed a potential nuclear hazard and made the community a more probable enemy target. In other cases, the opposition came from residents who objected to a military installation near their residential neighborhood in the fear that the character of the neighborhood would be altered, that property values would tumble, that insurance rates

might climb or that television reception would be damaged by the ABM's high-powered radars. However, one Army spokesman minimized these Sentinel protests as typical of those encountered whenever any sort of military facility was proposed for an area. Persons facing the possibility of such a facility frequently objected and asked, "Why here?," he said.

Opposition from the cities intensified in early 1969 and apparently was a factor in a decision by President Nixon to reconfigure the system. His new ABM plan, called "Safeguard," removed all sites from around cities (with the exception of Washington, D.C., which was to get one under the Safeguard plan but not under Sentinel) and placed them either in the countryside or around U.S. offensive missile sites. In so doing, Pentagon planners hoped to give the nation's strategic deterrent a new measure of protection against a Soviet attack, while still providing an area defense for the whole nation against a Chinese assault.

In announcing the new deployment March 14, President Nixon said the "primary purpose" of the system was to "prevent war." This, he said, was "why the emphasis on this system is on protecting our deterrent, which is the best preventive for war." A city defense, he said, would be "more provocative" to the Soviet Union. "I want no provocation which might deter arms talks."

The President's new strategy was a significant shift away from that of the Sentinel system, which was designed to serve as a building block for a "thick" ABM net in the event such a deployment were ever deemed feasible. ABM sites under Sentinel had been planned for emplacement in or near cities, so that the system could be thickened later by merely adding more Sprint.

High Administration officials told reporters in remarks not for attribution that the new deployment meant the "permanent" foregoing of the thick system—a project long favored by the Joint Chiefs of Staff—because it would be too expensive to come back later and build new missile site radars (MSRs) for the cities in order to provide thick protection (a thick defense relied on the Sprint missile for close-in protection and the Sprint, effective for only a 30-40 mile radius from the MSR, could not reach into many cities from the proposed new deployment sites); also, these officials said, it was doubtful that a successful thick defense could ever be developed, regardless of cost. In announcing his rejection of the Sentinel deployment, President Nixon said "there is no way that we can adequately defend our cities without an unacceptable loss of life."

ABM Pros and Cons

Following are the major arguments that were made for and against the ABM system in Congressional debates over the years and in statements by Administration officials and outside scientists:

System Effectiveness. Perhaps the most important argument against an ABM system was the question of whether it would be effective. In his 1967 speech announcing the Sentinel deployment, McNamara said that if the nation could build "a genuinely impenetrable shield over the United States, we would be willing to spend not $40 billion, but any reasonable multiple of that amount that was necessary." Expressing doubts over the efficacy of such a system, however, McNamara added, "There is clearly no point...in spending $40 billion if it is not going to buy us a significant improvement in our security. If it is not, then we should use the substantial resources it represents on something that will."

Other defense officials who opposed any current ABM deployment told Congressional Quarterly late in 1968 that they doubted whether the ABM would be effective against sea-launched missiles; missiles with multiple warheads, decoys or other evasive devices; orbiting ICBMs or planted hydrogen mines. Summarizing this argument Rep. Charles S. Joelson (D N.J.) commented, "I do not believe the enemy is going to be so cooperative and considerate as to deliver the kind of attack that we have a defense for."

The Federation of American Scientists issued a statement stating that the system "can easily be neutralized by the Chinese using relatively simple and cheap penetration aids or by developing different means of weapons delivery." An observer commented, "to assume that Chinese scientists will not, indeed have not already, initiated such devices would be irresponsible."

Reply—In response, ABM proponents argued that the defense provided by the Sentinel would be sufficient to defend against the expected Communist Chinese threat for at least the next decade. Paul H. Nitze, Deputy Secretary of Defense, observed: "We are confident that this sophisticated defense can provide us with high assurance of denying damage to the United States from the type of attack the Chinese People's Republic will be able to launch in the mid-1970s. With further foreseeable improvements we believe we can maintain such protection at least until the 1980s." Dr. John S. Foster Jr., Director of Defense Research and Engineering, called the Sentinel "very effective" against the type of small and unsophisticated attack the Chinese would be capable of. Rep. Robert L. F. Sikes (D Fla.) commented, "Any defense against an enemy weapon can be better than no defense at all."

Inadequate Testing. Opponents also challenged the effectiveness of the Sentinel on the grounds that because of the test-ban treaty, which prohibited nuclear tests in the atmosphere, the missile components were relatively untested. In addition, they said that the system would be obsolete before it was constructed.

Jerome B. Wiesner, provost of the Massachusetts Institute of Technology and a former science adviser to President Kennedy, stated: "I am skeptical that any ABM system based on the present approach will ever work at its calculated effectiveness." Both Wiesner and former Deputy Secretary of Defense Cyrus R. Vance said that if the Nike-Zeus system had been installed as proposed in the early 1960s, it would have been obsolete by the time work could have been completed. Ohio's Sen. Young, a member of the Senate Armed Services Committee, asserted that since World War II, the United States had spent almost $19 billion on missile systems that either were never finished or were obsolete when completed.

Reply—The response by ABM proponents was that the $3 billion research effort for the system has resulted in extensive tests for components, even if the entire system had not been assembled for testing.

Secretary of Defense Clark M. Clifford wrote in a June 18, 1968, letter to the Senate, "I believe that the time has arrived when we can no longer rely merely on continued research and development but should proceed with actual deployment of an operating system." He called a delay of production of a few months or a year a "serious mistake" that could retard the readiness of the system by as much as two years.

Rep. Sikes claimed that the system had proved for several years that it was capable of knocking down incoming missiles. "I can state categorically the Sentinel system will not be obsolete or ineffective because it is constantly being modernized," he said. Rep. Melvin Price (D Ill.) warned, "We cannot wait until the first missile arrives before we start building."

Expansion of System. Another key issue was whether the "thin" ABM system proposed was an end in itself or merely the first step toward a fullscale ABM costing $40 billion or more.

Critics frequently cited McNamara's warning, in announcing the program that: "There is a kind of mad momentum intrinsic to the development of all nuclear weaponry. If a weapon works—and works well—there is a strong pressure from many directions to procure and deploy the weapon out of all proportion to prudent levels required."

Sen. Cooper noted that defenders of the system were expanding its scope in their arguments. "Is it our purpose to install a 'thin' system at an estimated cost of $6.5 billion, or is it to lay a foundation to install what has been admitted to be an ineffective system against the Soviet Union at a minimum cost of $40 billion?" Majority Leader Mansfield saw the "thin" system as a first installment on a thick one. "We are launching another multibillion dollar enterprise on grounds as flimsy as the arguments made for Vietnam," Sen. Nelson said.

Reply—Although the official Johnson Administration policy was that the Sentinel would be limited to an anti-Chinese defense and that an effective anti-Soviet deployment was not feasible, many ABM supporters went beyond that. They expressed confidence that the proposed system was indeed only the first step in a "thick" ABM.

Sen. Henry M. Jackson (D Wash.), a top spokesman for the pro-ABM forces, said some had "taken too literally the public rationale for the Sentinel system previously given by officials of the Defense Department." He said the "thin" system would provide a limited degree of protection against a Soviet attack and was a "crucial" part of our continuing efforts of and experimentation to achieve, if we can, an effective defense against a fullscale Soviet missile attack."

Arms Race. ABM opponents contended that deployment would merely touch off a Soviet arms buildup and would kill any chances for a U.S.-Soviet arms limitation agreement. For their most eloquent spokesman, they again turned to McNamara, who tempered his 1967 ABM announcement with the warning: "If we...opt for heavy ABM deployment—at whatever price—we can be certain that the Soviets will react to offset the advantage we would hope to gain." McNamara also said: "It is futile for each of us to spend $4 billion, $40 billion or $400 billion—and at the end of all the spending, and at the end of all the deployment and at the end of all the effort, to be relatively at the same point of balance on the security scale that we are now."

Sen. Wayne Morse (D Ore.) put it vehemently when he called requests for ABM funds "legislative fraud," making the United States "the leader in the armaments race." Other critics argued that an ABM system against Soviet missiles would seem to unbalance the strength of the two nations and make the Soviets less likely to accept an arms freeze.

Reply—ABM proponents, such as Assistant Secretary of Defense Paul C. Warnke, argued that "the modest scope of the Sentinel deployment—clearly insufficient to deny the Soviets an attack capability—should not alarm them."

Jackson and other Congressional proponents said the race for new defensive capability was started by the Russians. Jackson said the U.S. ABM was needed to offset the Soviet increase in ICBMs, which he said would soon give them more land-based missiles than the United States, the deployment of the Russian ABM system and the emergence of Communist China as an H-bomb power.

ABM backers, pointing out that the Soviets agreed to discuss arms control with the United States two days after the Senate rejected attempts to delete the $227.3 million for Sentinel site construction, saw a direct relationship between the two events. Sen. Richard B. Russell (D Ga.) said the U.S. ABM would be a "very strong card" for U.S. negotiators at disarmament talks. And Sen. John Stennis (D Miss.) added, "I have never heard a more absurd way in which to approach negotiations with the Soviets than by announcing in advance that we will remove a big part of bargaining strength from the agenda by not going forward with the ABM program."

Other Criticism. Among other points raised by opponents of the program was the belief that the United States already possessed a sufficient deterrent against China. They also said that in addition to initial costs, millions would have to be spent to maintain the Sentinel system.

Assistant Secretary Warnke gave some ammunition to this argument when he said "the prime deterrent against Chinese nuclear aggression will remain for the foreseeable future our overwhelming strategic retaliatory capability...." An expert on Chinese affairs commented that all pro-ABM arguments "add up to one thing, that the Chinese are prepared to commit suicide."

Reps. Sidney R. Yates (D Ill.) and Henry S. Reuss (D Wis.) called the ABM "false security" and a "Maginot line." Rep. Richard L. Ottinger (D N.Y.) said its real purpose was "insurance for our defense contractors" and Sen. Symington warned that it was a needless expense that could "cripple our society."

Reply—Sen. Jackson stated that the ABM would help maintain the credibility of the U.S. deterrent power for potential enemies and reassure U.S. allies.

Backers frequently replied to general attacks with assertions that the ABM system would save countless American lives. They also noted that military officials had sought the system for many years and that they were the experts entrusted with U.S. defense responsibilities. At one point, Sen. Strom Thurmond (R S.C.), while saying that this was not the prime consideration, indicated that the ABM development would provide employment for many workers who might have lost their positions with defense and aerospace firms because of cuts in the U.S. space budget.

F-111B PROGRAM KILLED IN CONGRESS

McNamara, Navy Clash Over Fighter Plane

A bitter six-year dispute between the Navy and Defense Secretary Robert S. McNamara ended in the Navy's favor when Congress denied funds in 1968 for procurement of the F-111B Navy fighter aircraft (formerly the TFX) and substituted money for a new Navy plane.

In one of his most controversial decisions in office, McNamara in 1961 denied Air Force and Navy requests for separate fighters and ordered development of a single aircraft which he said would serve the needs of both services. Development of a single plane, McNamara said, would save taxpayers $1 billion over the cost of separate Navy and Air Force fighters.

Although the Air Force officially expressed satisfaction with its version of the plane (the F-111A), losses of three of the first six of the craft sent to Vietnam in 1968 cast serious doubt over the future of the Air Force's F-111 program. In total, 12 of the F-111A and two of the F-111Bs had crashed by early 1969. At the end of the 1968 session of Congress, Sen. Stuart Symington (D Mo.), a former Secretary of the Air Force and an influential member of the Senate Armed Services Committee, said Congress should give "serious consideration" to cancelling the Air Force version.

Background

The F-111, once called the TFX for Tactical Fighter Experimental, was a swing-wing aircraft designed to be used as a fighter, bomber or reconaissance plane. It could "tuck in" its wings for flights at supersonic speeds or extend its wings and hover over targets at low, subsonic speeds. The Navy version of the craft was designed for carrier use, while the Air Force version could take off and land on short, unpaved runways.

The TFX was conceived in the late 1950s as a means of improving on the tactical fighters that were still in use by the late 1960s, the Navy's F-4H and the Air Force's F-105. Navy and Air Force requirements for an updated plane, however, were distinct and separate. The Navy's requirement was for a carrier-based aircraft capable of employing a projected new and sophisticated missile system, the Phoenix, and providing fleet air defense by "loitering" at high altitudes on a perimeter about 150 miles from the fleet. On the other hand, the Air Force's need was for a heavy fighter-bomber that could plunge within several hundred feet of the ground for a 400-mile supersonic dash beneath enemy radar screens to deliver nuclear bombs.

Although it was traditional for both services to have separate aircraft programs to meet their specific requirements, the popularity of the swing-wing design with both the Air Force and Navy gave Defense officials an opportunity to phase out the separate programs by utilizing essentially a single airplane for both services, with minor modifications to satisfy particular needs.

Pressure within the Defense Department for a single, sophisticated, multimission aircraft came from the Office of Defense Research and Engineering, which was headed in the early 1960s by Harold Brown, who later became Secretary of the Air Force. Although the concept was opposed by the young systems analysts that Defense Secretary Robert S. McNamara had brought with him to the Pentagon, they were not then in a position to conduct a running battle with Brown. At the time, the Office of Systems Analysis was subordinate to the Pentagon comptroller which was one level below Brown.

The most effective opposition to the common approach came from the Navy, which long had held a close relationship with several aircraft companies whose operations were geared mainly to Navy work. As the price of getting the Navy to go along, the Defense Department agreed to give the Navy the costly and not yet developed Phoenix missile system and to propel both the Navy and the Air Force planes with engines from the Pratt and Whitney Aircraft Division of United Aircraft Corp., one of the Navy's favored firms.

Even then, the Navy sought to gain control of the entire program on grounds that only Navy management could ensure that the planes would be carrier-suitable. Because of the rigorous demands of the Air Force's low-level dash requirement and the fact that the Navy would be getting only about 15 percent of all F-111s, the Air Force was given over-all program management.

Selection of Contractor. Contract competition on the TFX began in October 1961, when proposals for a swing-wing aircraft were requested from 10 companies. Proposals were returned by six companies, and in December 1961 the initial evaluation by the Military Source Selection Board concluded that designs by the Boeing Co. and the General Dynamics Corp. best met military requirements. In April 1962, $1 million was allotted to each to refine their proposals before beginning the final phase of competition for design study contracts. In November 1962, the contract was awarded to General Dynamics.

Although the Military Source Selection Board, in the final analysis, found the Boeing design preferable, civilian Defense Department officials awarded the contract to General Dynamics primarily on the basis of probable long-term costs. Agreeing that both designs would produce savings by phasing out the two separate aircraft programs, the civilian officials concluded that the greater degree of "commonality"—greater percentage of identical parts—in the General Dynamics Navy and Air Force versions would produce more savings by allowing for the same structural design, same logistics, same maintenance, etc.

At stake in the awarding of the contract was an aircraft program for which production orders were estimated eventually to be worth more than $6.5 billion and involve 20,000 jobs and 1,700 planes—the largest tactical airplane contract since World War II. The ini-

F-111—Pros and Cons

Following are the major arguments for and against the F-111, as asserted by industry sources, Members of Congress, the aerospace press and Air Force and Navy officials:

Pros. Proponents of the F-111 characterized the craft as the fastest and most versatile fighter-bomber in the world. As the plane's high points, they listed its abilities to:

• Land or take off in distances less than 3,000 feet and from unimproved runways.

• Fly up to 3,300 nautical miles without refueling.

• Strike at two and one-half times the speed of sound at high altitudes.

• Fly supersonically at sea level.

• Remain on fleet air patrol hours longer than any existing fighter aircraft.

• Operate at altitudes in excess of 60,000 feet.

• Carry a payload of nuclear or conventional weapons, or a combination of both, six times heavier than that of a World War II strategic bomber.

• Perform in any weather, day or night.

Cons. Following are shortcomings most often cited by opponents of the F-111:

• The plane's unusually high investment costs and even higher operating costs.

• Enormous complexity of operation and questionable operating capability in the event the plane's sophisticated systems did not work.

• An assertion that the multimission capability had diminished the plane's ability to perform any single one of its missions.

• The questionable necessity of purchasing a supersonic aircraft to perform the "static" mission of Navy fleet air patrol.

• Inability of the plane to dogfight successfully with some existing aircraft because of its weight and other shortcomings.

• Payload and range far below that advertised.

---

tial $28 million contract, for which Boeing and General Dynamics were bidding, involved 22 developmental planes for testing, to be delivered within two and one-half years. (The Defense Department on May 10, 1967, announced the signing of the first definitive production contract with General Dynamics for 493 F-111s at a total cost of $1,821,938,561. The contract called for production of 419 Air Force and Navy craft for U.S. use as well as 24 craft ordered by Australia and 50 ordered by Britain. The British order was canceled early in 1968.)

TFX Investigation. The Permanent Investigations Subcommittee of the Senate Government Operations Committee in 1963 conducted a long and stormy probe of the TFX contract award. Hearings were held on 46 days between Feb. 26 and Nov. 20. (*Congress and the Nation, Volume I, p. 1766.*)

The Subcommittee's hearings, chaired by Sen. John L. McClellan (D Ark.), were initiated in response to allegations that the contract might have been awarded as a result of political or regional pressure—possibly in conflict with national security interests. General Dynamics planned to build the aircraft at its Convair plant at Ft. Worth, Texas, and to subcontract the assembly work for the F-111B to the Grumman Aircraft Engineering Corp., located at Bethpage, Long Island, N.Y. Boeing, whose headquarters was in Seattle, Wash., planned to build the aircraft at its Wichita, Kan., plant.

Sen. Henry M. Jackson (D Wash.), a member of the Subcommittee, proposed that it look into the circumstances of the award, and McClellan decided on a full-scale investigation.

During the long investigation, suggestions of political pressure were made concerning Jackson, Rep. K. William Stinson (R Wash.), of Seattle, Rep. James C. Wright Jr. (D Texas) of Ft. Worth, the Kansas Congressional delegation and then Vice President Lyndon B. Johnson among others.

Speaking to a Ft. Worth audience Nov. 22, the morning of his assassination, President Kennedy said award of the TFX contract to General Dynamics ensured that the "same basic plane" would serve both the Air Force and Navy, "saving the taxpayers at least $1 billion in costs" as compared with separate aircraft development programs for both services.

Development Problems. From the beginning of development work on the F-111, the Air Force's requirement for a craft rugged enough and with sufficient fuel capacity to sustain the 400-mile low-level dash was the controlling factor in the program. Consequently, the weight of the craft ballooned to more than 46,000 pounds (weight empty)—about 8,000 pounds more than the weight limit that had been promised the Navy. Admirals began to complain that the craft would be too heavy for carrier operation. Although heavier planes were being operated from aircraft carriers, the Navy claimed that weight of aircraft inevitably grew as new modifications were added and that the 46,000 pound figure was far too high for the mere outset of the program.

To solve the weight problem, General Dynamics and Grumman undertook vigorous and expensive efforts known as WIP (weight improvement program) and SWIP (super weight improvement program) to pare as many excess pounds as possible without jeopardizing the Air Force mission. Despite considerable redesign work, the WIP and SWIP programs succeeded in cutting out only about half the 8,000 excess pounds. In addition, about 1,200 more pounds were added later in the form of more sophisticated electronics systems, primarily at the request of the Office of Defense Research and Engineering.

Another major problem was encountered with the Pratt and Whitney engines, which burned more fuel than had been contemplated and did not work properly when placed in the airframe of the F-111. At high altitudes, top speeds or in hard turns, the engine frequently stalled or delivered sudden bursts of power. (Pratt and Whitney blamed airframe inlet deficiencies, while General Dynamics blamed Pratt and Whitney for inadequate engine performance.) Significant problems and large-scale cost overruns also were encountered with the Navy's Phoenix missile system. Ironically, however, the most revolutionary feature of the plane, its swing wing, worked to perfection.

The redesign work and other problems resulted in long delays and a steep escalation of costs. Cost estimates of the Air Force plane rose from the original figure of about $3.1 million per copy to over $7 million. Cost projections of the Navy plane, which was far more expensive because of the Phoenix missile system and a more complex version of the Pratt and Whitney engine, soared from about $4 million to about $9 million. (The comparisons are from 1965 to 1969.)

Because of the problems of making the Navy plane carrier-suitable, developing the complex Phoenix missile system, improving the engine and overcoming the delaying tactics of the Navy's anti-F-111 faction, development of the Navy craft lagged far behind that of the Air Force version. Congress in 1966 provided funds to begin production of the F-111A and followed it up with another appropriation in 1967. However, renewed attacks on the Navy plane by McClellan and other Capitol Hill opponents, urged on by the admirals, resulted in Congress' providing only enough money to continue the F-111B's development program. In the meantime the admirals, reportedly upset over the continued Air Force domination of the program, began searching for an alternative.

New Navy Proposals

Russian display of several new swing-wing fighter aircraft at the Moscow air show in the summer of 1967 touched off new Navy fears that Soviet aerospace technology was making greater strides than that of the United States. Late in the year, Grumman confirmed the Navy's fears in a study which found that the F-111B was not maneuverable enough to cope with the new generation of Russian fighters in fast-moving aerial dogfights.

Along with the study, Grumman submitted a proposal (widely known as the "303") for an alternative aircraft to take the place of the F-111B. The plane, which would be an interim fighter to bridge the gap between the F-4 and the VFAX, the Navy's projected "air superiority" fighter for the mid-1970s, would incorporate the Phoenix missile system and the Pratt and Whitney P-12 engine, together with a lighter airframe and a swing wing. Other proposals, subsequently were submitted by three other companies with long records of service to the Navy— the McDonnell Douglas Corp., Ling-Temco-Vought Inc. and the North American Rockwell Corp. All the proposals reportedly emphasized that the substitute craft could be introduced to the fleet by 1972—only a year beyond the current target date for the F-111—if early approval were granted.

Secretary of the Navy Paul R. Ignatius and Chief of Naval Operations Adm. Thomas H. Moorer Jan. 22, 1968, issued a statement acknowledging that the four proposals were under study but emphasizing that the result of the Navy's assessment "will not be available for several months." In the meantime, the statement said, the Navy would continue to support the "on-going" aircraft programs, including the F-111B.

The emphasis given the new proposals prompted a new call by McClellan to drop the F-111B. Speaking on the Senate floor Jan. 22, McClellan said: "It is now conclusive that all of the tinkering, fixing, engineering patching, and the exorbitant spending of funds for research and development have not produced a Navy plane that is capable of performing the combat missions required by the Navy." McClellan added that the airplane was "a flop" and that it could "result in a national defense tragedy" if approved for production.

According to civilian sources in the office of the Defense Secretary (OSD) the new designs probably signaled the death knell for the F-111B. "The Navy is the one service McNamara never really brought under control," said one OSD source. "They have enormous power on Capitol Hill. Even if they were to testify in favor of the F-111, it's what they say to Senators over drinks later on that counts."

This source, who himself was anti-F111, said he thought the new proposals were "even more preposterous than the F-111. They retain the two worst components of the F-111B concept, the P-12 engine and the Phoenix missile system. The admirals probably will escalate a lot of the F-111's sophisticated electronic gadgetry too and wind up with an aircraft that would cost substantially more than it would cost to continue with the F-111." Asked about the possible weight advantage of the new craft, the source said "the F-111 doesn't weigh too much more than the new aircraft would. This argument about the F-111's weight is something the Navy cooked up to try to get the program killed."

Navy-Defense Department 'Deal.' On March 27, 1968, high Defense Department officials approached members of the Senate Armed Services Committee with a proposal that the F-111B program for fiscal 1969 be scaled back from 30 to eight aircraft and that funds be provided for accelerated development work on a possible successor aircraft, the VFX-1. The Defense Department said the purpose of the move was to give the Navy more time to solve the problems that had plagued the F-111. Dissident Pentagon officials associated with the program told Congressional Quarterly, however, that the Navy and Defense Department had worked out a "deal" whereby the F-111B would be "quietly dropped" after the 1968 elections and the Navy would then get a full go-ahead on the VFX-1. These officials said the cutback proposed to the Committee was only a "guise" to spare the Administration the embarrassment of having the project killed on the eve of the 1968 elections.

But on the following day, March 28, the Committee spurned the new proposal and by an 11-2 vote adopted a motion to knock all F-111B funds from the defense procurement bill (S 3293). The following week, the panel approved $287 million for development of the VFX-1. The action was sustained by the full Senate April 19 and by the House in its version of the bill, which was passed July 11.

Anticipating the House action, the Defense Department had officially canceled the F-111B the previous day. Congress in the fiscal 1969 defense appropriations bill provided $130 million for VFX development.

In explaining the Senate Committee's rapid rejection of the "deal," one Defense Department official said that all the panel had been waiting for was "word for the Navy that it could afford slippage—any slippage at all—in the timetable for deploying the Phoenix missile system." When the terms of the "deal" indicated it could, he said, "the Committee jumped in like wolves to kill the F-111."

Air Force Developments

Despite its problem with crashes of F-111As in Vietnam, Air Force officials continued to express high praise for the plane throughout 1968. But another headache by year's end—the discovery of a crack in the structural part of the aircraft that holds the wings to the fuselage—

loomed large in considerations about the plane's future. Early in 1969, President Johnson cut back on the planned purchase of FB-111 strategic bombers (another Air Force version of the TFX) and President Nixon eliminated the purchase altogether. (One important element in the outcome of the F-111A, however, was whether President Nixon would follow up on the campaign promise he made in Texas in 1968 to continue procuring the Texas-built plane.)

Brig. Gen. Ralph G. Taylor (USAF), commander of the Tactical Fighter Weapons Center at Nellis Air Force Base, Nev., where the F-111 was undergoing further tests in 1968, told CQ early that year that his pilots had encountered "unprecedented success with the F-111A as compared to the rest of the jet fleet at this time." Taylor listed eight categories in which the F-111A showed a significant improvement over existing craft. They included its greater fuel capacity, greater bomb load, capability of its sophisticated radar system to locate obscure targets, greater capability to fly in poor weather, ability to sustain the low-level dash at supersonic speeds (although the actual range capability is thought to have

fallen as much as 75 percent short of the original 400-mile specification), a terrain-following radar device that permits the pilot to fly at low levels on automatic controls, ability to loiter at low speeds and ability to operate from short and unpaved runways.

Col. Ivan H. Dethman, commander of Operation Harvest Reaper, the F-111A's Vietnam combat test, told CQ in 1967 that the F-111A compared "most favorably with any airplane I've ever flown. I'd say it's a big jump forward in the state of the art." Asked about the plane's reported inability to hold its own in a dogfight, Dethman said "the guys in my outfit say this plane can whip any other."

However, sources in the office of the Defense Secretary said the Air Force had been under instructions "not to bad mouth the F-111A," probably because of the Air Force's responsibility for the basic design of the overall F-111 system and Air Force Secretary Harold Brown's role in pushing the proposal through the Defense Department. "There's a lot of discontent about the Air Force plane that you just won't hear in public," one of these sources said.

U.S. MILITARY DRAFT SYSTEM

Congress Rejects President's Bid for Comprehensive Reform

Another of the major defense issues that marked the Johnson years was a spirited public debate over the fairness of the nation's military draft. Critics argued that the system was riddled with inequities which resulted in sending underprivileged youths to fight the Vietnam war while youths from more affluent families received educational deferments.

Public pressures for change in the draft system resulted in a major Administration push for draft reform in 1967, but most of the President's program foundered in Congress, largely as a result of action by the House Armed Services Committee.

Eleven days before the draft was to expire, Congress on June 20, 1967, cleared a bill (S 1432—PL 90-40) extending the draft and related statutes for four years, through July 1, 1971. The bill in its final form provided little more than an extension of the existing draft law.

The only major reform that S 1432 permitted was a plan to reverse the current "oldest first" order of induction and call 19-year-olds before older men. (This was not to include college students, however, who were to receive deferments automatically for fulltime undergraduate study.) Following the measure's enactment, one leading proponent of draft reform, former Assistant Attorney General Burke Marshall, who headed an advisory commission on the draft for President Johnson, said the new law "made the system worse than it was before."

Presidential Proposals. President Johnson in a special March 6, 1967, Message to Congress announced his intention to reverse the order of call and make other draft reforms through issuance of Executive Orders under authority granted him by existing law. The final bill, however, contained language restricting all of these proposals except his authority to reverse the order of call. The restrictions were adopted by the House following Senate action on the bill and were accepted in similar form by a House-Senate conference.

The major proposal blocked by S 1432 was a plan to institute a random selection system or "draft lottery" to ensure that all registrants within a given age group stood an equal chance of induction. Under terms of the final bill, the President could institute the plan only when he received the specific approval of Congress. This left in force the existing procedure of inducting the oldest registrants first within a given age group (such as 19-year-olds) in filling monthly quotas for the draft. The President had hoped to replace this system with the lottery by Jan. 1, 1969.

In a second major restriction on the President's discretionary authority, Congress adopted a provision prohibiting the President from ordering an end to college undergraduate deferments unless he found it necessary to draft the students in order to meet the armed forces' manpower needs. Although the President had not indicated an intention to end the deferments, the Administration was reportedly unhappy over this restriction on its flexible authority.

Although Congress did not restrict the President's authority to curtail graduate deferments, which he had proposed to limit to students in medical and dental courses, it added language directing the National Security Council (NSC) to study and advise the Director of Civil Service on the areas of study where deferments should be continued. Although the President controlled both the NSC and the Selective Service Director, it was thought that this move indicated a Congressional intent that areas of study other than medicine and dentistry should retain deferments.

Local Boards. In another defeat for proponents of draft reform, Congress in the final bill watered down a GOP-sponsored House provision which directed the President to recommend national criteria for classification of draft registrants and required that local draft boards apply the criteria uniformly to all registrants throughout the country. House and Senate conferees modified the provision to make establishment of the criteria optional with the President and their observance optional with local boards. The effect of the final provision was to leave unchanged the authority of local boards to make classification decisions on the merits of individual cases. The President did not take a position on either the House or final version of the provision.

Draft Violations. In a move reflecting the mounting public criticism of antidraft demonstrations and draft evasion, Congress added provisions (1) directing the Justice Department, at the request of the Selective Service Director, to move as "expeditiously as possible" to prosecute alleged draft violations and (2) directing the courts to give such cases precedence on their dockets over other types of cases. The Administration opposed the provisions, contending it was impractical for the Justice Department and the courts to give priority to one type of case regardless of the importance of all others.

Other Amendments. Other controversial amendments approved in the final bill included a provision that sought to narrow the basis for draft exemptions based on conscientious objection and a provision to end exemptions for doctors who entered the Public Health Service (PHS) in lieu of serving in the military and spent their active duty in assignments outside PHS, such as the Peace Corps and the Office of Economic Opportunity. The Administration did not take a position on the conscientious objectors amendment but opposed the curtailment of exemptions for the PHS doctors.

Reversal of Call, Undergraduate Deferments. Despite the Congressional action to block the other

History and Operation of Selective Service System

Following is an account of the history and operation of the U.S. military draft prior to enactment of S 1432. S 1432 extended the draft law for four years and changed it in some respects, notably in provisions restricting the President's authority to institute a draft lottery and to control draft deferments.

Draft Law History. The nation's first peacetime selective service law was the Selective Training and Service Act of 1940. Most of the current characteristics of the military draft, however, had been established in the Selective Service Act of 1917, enacted to meet U.S. commitments in World War I.

During World War II, the Selective Service System registered about 50 million men. Problems of deferments during the war produced several instances of conflict between the System and Congress. In 1942, for example, Congress provided for a conditional exemption of agricultural workers. On Dec. 5, 1942, President Roosevelt by Executive Order placed the System under the War Manpower Commission, but Congress amended the law Dec. 5, 1943, to make the System an independent agency, which it remained.

Congress did not extend the 1940 Act when it expired March 31, 1947, and the nation was without a conscription law until enactment of the Selective Service Act of 1948 on June 24, 1948. The Universal Military Training and Service Act of 1951, enacted during the Korean War, extended the draft until 1955. The 1951 Act was extended three more times by Congress until July 1, 1967.

Registration and Deferments. The draft law provided for the registration of all males as they became 18 years of age. While the law provided for a few specific exemptions and deferments, those affecting the largest number of registrants were left to the discretion of the President, who in turn was authorized to delegate authority in draft matters to the director of the Selective Service System.

Deferments were in the areas of industry, agriculture, education and dependency. Draft boards based occupational deferments on a List of Essential Activities and Critical Occupations drawn up by a committee comprising officials of the Departments of Commerce and Labor. The Commerce Department identified essential activities and the Labor Department identified critical occupations. There also were deferments for persons physically, mentally or morally unacceptable for military service, with standards in those categories by law set by the Secretary of Defense and not by the Selective Service System. By adjusting standards and changing regulations on deferments, the President could expand or contract inductions to meet changing needs of the armed forces.

Selective Service System. The System was administered by the director and his staff, located in the District of Columbia, and by about 4,000 local draft boards in the states. The local draft boards were under the supervision of a state director. Draft calls originated with a request of the Defense Department for a given number of men, based on projected enlistments and needs. The System then determined which states would provide the men, basing its decision on a credit-debit procedure reflecting the number of men from each state already in the military. Each state then was assigned a quota of inductees, and the state director proceeded to provide the men through the state's local draft boards.

The entire System operated under regulations drawn at the national level, but these left local boards with considerable latitude in selecting men for service. Some draft boards, for example, imposed more stringent requirements on student deferments in the liberal arts field than on such deferments in the sciences or medical arts, having determined at the local level that the production of doctors and scientists, for example, was more important to the national interest than was the production of lawyers or English professors.

draft reforms, some observers thought the most significant development on the bill was that Congress had not prohibited the President from calling 19-year-olds before older men. Because the Administration estimated that only one in seven registrants in the 19-year-age group would be drafted under normal peacetime circumstances, a registrant would be reasonably safe from the draft after he reached his 20th birthday. This, observers pointed out, would enhance his opportunities for employment and allow him to plan his life without giving major consideration to his possibilities of being drafted.

(An Executive Order issued by the President June 30, 1967, to implement the provisions of S 1432 did not include a reversal in the order of call. Officials said the reversal probably would not be necessary as long as the Vietnam war continued because the draft pool was being drained of older men so profusely that the average age of draftee induction currently was between the ages of 20 and 21. The military preferred to induct men anywhere in the 19-21 age range. There still had been no reversal in the sequence of call by the end of 1968.)

The bill also provided an equitable means to assure that college students who were in a deferred status when they were 19 did not ultimately receive more protection from the draft than persons who did not attend college. Under terms of the measure, any student who did not subsequently receive a graduate, occupational or hardship deferment under strict rules established by the bill was to be placed in the age pool facing maximum exposure to the draft at the time of: (1) his graduation; (2) his dropping out of school; or (3) his 24th birthday, whichever came first. He would remain in the maximum exposure pool for one full year and then, if not drafted, would be placed in the pool with persons of his own age until he reached the age of 26 (or, if he received a graduate or other deferment, until he reached the age of 35). (This procedure, under terms of S 1432 would not pertain to students who received their undergraduate deferments prior to enactment of the bill. The President under existing law, however, would have discretionary authority to place such students in the maximum exposure pool, and it was thought he would do so if he later ordered the drafting of 19-year-olds first.)

In a development that worked in the student's favor, however, Congress provided that undergraduate deferments no longer could be granted at the discretion of a local draft board but would have to be given automatically upon a student's request. In addition, the bill provided that the deferments were to continue regardless of the level of the student's class standing so long as he remained enrolled in a full-time course of instruction. The effect of the provision was to block an existing procedure under which draft boards sometimes based deferments on test scores or inducted students not performing satisfactory work.

Lottery. The assurance of what amounted to a near draft-exempt status for persons who had survived the 19-year-old pool without being drafted became a factor that worked to the detriment of the proposed draft lottery. Opponents of the lottery system argued that the lottery, when combined with the drafting of 19-year-olds first, might cut back on enlistments as well as on officer procurement. Once a 19-year-old found he had survived the lottery, opponents said, he would be less likely to enter the ranks or enroll in a college officer training course. (Participants in the advanced division of the Reserve Officers Training Corps (ROTC) normally enrolled before the end of their sophomore year, or while they were 19.)

Other considerations, however, were equally important in the Congressional decision to block the lottery plan. Because alleged inequities in the draft had been confined to the classification of an individual's draft status rather than the method of his selection once he was classified, opponents said there was no need to change the present system. In addition, they argued, Congress should be able to make a thorough review of the proposed new system before it went into effect, and the Administration currently had not worked out a specific lottery proposal.

Background

The military draft, which was due to expire July 1, 1967, became a subject of considerable controversy in 1966, when increasing numbers of persons drafted for the 1965 buildup in Vietnam, were becoming combat casualties. Though criticism of the draft system became commingled, especially on college campuses, with protests of the Vietnam war, there was considerable opposition to the system itself. Some critics called for a broad overhaul of the present system to correct alleged inequities, while others contended that the draft should be abolished altogether and replaced by a highly paid, all-volunteer force.

Reform Proposals. Following lengthy studies of the problem, four major proposals for draft reform were announced early in 1967. These were contained in S Con Res 12, a "sense of Congress" resolution introduced Feb. 23 by Sens. Edward M. Kennedy (D Mass.) and Joseph S. Clark (D Pa.); in a Feb. 28 report by a House Armed Services Committee advisory panel headed by Gen. Mark W. Clark (USA ret.); in a March 4 report by President Johnson's National Advisory Commission on Selective Service; and in a March 6 special message sent to Congress by Mr. Johnson.

All four of the proposals supported a four-year extension of the existing draft law, due to expire July 1; an end to deferments from the draft for graduate students (except those in critically important fields); and a reversal in the current order of draftee induction, with 19-year-old men called into service before older men. All proposals except that of the Mark Clark panel recommended that the order of call within a given age category be determined through a system of "random selection"—or national lottery. The Clark panel argued in favor of retaining the current method of drafting by date of birth sequence within the various age brackets, with quotas assigned to the states in relation to the size of their draft-eligible pool.

The proposals differed significantly in some other particulars, however, notably in their recommendations with regard to continuation of undergraduate student deferments. The Presidential Commission called for abolishing such deferments, while the Mark Clark panel and Kennedy-Joseph Clark proposal recommended their continuation. The President did not take a position on the issue.

Most of the proposals under study could be implemented by the President through issuance of an Executive Order. Legislation was required, however, to extend the basic draft law and to implement less signifcant changes outlined in the four basic proposals. (Of the four proposals, the final bill most closely followed the Clark panel report.)

Details of proposals:

National Advisory Commission. The Commission, appointed by Mr. Johnson in 1966 and headed by Burke Marshall, made the following recommendations:

Order of Induction—The Commission recommended that the current "oldest first" order of call be reversed, with 19-year-old men being called to duty before older men. At the age of 18, all men would register and, as soon as possible, would be given tests to determine if they were fit for military service. Those qualified would be put in a pool of draft eligibles, and at age 19 they would undergo a year of maximum vulnerability to the draft. Order of call within the draft eligible pool would be determined "through a system of impartial random selection." If the registrant were not called during his year of maximum eligibility, he would be relatively "safe" from the draft, although still eligible for call in case of unexpectedly large manpower needs.

Deferments—No further student or occupational deferments should be granted, the Commission said. (A sizable minority of the Commission announced at the time of the report that they had favored continuing the deferments for college undergraduates.) Persons who were in deferred school or apprentice training programs when the Commission's plan went into effect would be allowed to complete those programs, but then would be placed into the draft eligible pool with 19-year-olds regardless of their age. Men who were chosen for induction at age 19 would be allowed to complete their sophomore year in college before beginning active duty. The Commission recommended an immediate study of the feasibility of giving 18-year-old men the opportunity to choose the time when, between the ages of 19 and 23, they would serve.

Organization and Appeal—The Commission recommended that the national headquarters of Selective

Service issue policies concerning draft classifications, exemptions and deferments, which would be applied uniformly throughout the country. The national policy would be administered by eight regional offices, and by 300-500 area offices. The local draft board, composed of volunteer citizens, would serve as a draft registrant's first court of appeals. This would take considerable autonomy away from the 4,000 or so local boards.

Reserves—The Commission said that "direct enlistment into Reserve and National Guard forces should not provide immunity from the draft for those with no prior service except for those who enlist before" they were classified draft-eligible at age 18.

Negroes—The Commission's report said that participation by the Negro in the armed forces "is in several ways inequitable." The inequities reflected "social and economic injustices which are older by far than the operation of the Selective Service System," it said.

President's Message. In his message to Congress, President Johnson endorsed many of the Commission's recommendations. He said he would seek legislation to implement some of them, and would put some into effect by Executive Order. Other Commission recommendations would be studied before decisions on their merits were made, the President said.

Order of Induction—The President said he would issue an Executive Order to reverse the order of induction so that 19-year-old men would be drafted first. Selection of men from the pool of 19-year-olds would be made by a "Fair and Impartial Random (FAIR)" system, to be developed by the Defense Department and the Selective Service and to be "fully operational before Jan. 1, 1969."

Deferments—Mr. Johnson said he would issue an Executive Order directing that no more education deferments be granted to postgraduate students, except those in medical and dental courses. The President said he would make no immediate recommendation regarding deferments for college undergraduates but called for an extensive public debate prior to his making a final decision on whether to recommend their continuation or abolishment.

Draft Structure—Mr. Johnson said a Government task force would be established to study the Commission's proposals to reorganize the structure of the Selective Service System. Meanwhile, he said, actions would be taken to improve the System's appeals and information procedures, and to make sure that local draft boards were "truly representative."

Reserves—The President asked Congress to enact legislation providing (1) permanent authority to order to active duty, without declaring a national emergency, obligated reservists who were not assigned to or participating satisfactorily in Reserve or National Guard units and (2) standby authority to draft men into Reserve and Guard units whenever the authorized strength of such units could not otherwise be maintained. Congress in 1966 granted the President the former authority temporarily (through June 30, 1968). President Johnson used the authority in 1968 to call up reservists during the Pueblo crisis. *(See p. 103.)*

Other—Mr. Johnson said that he would request a military pay raise. The last such pay raise had been enacted in 1966. (The pay raise was not subsequently considered as part of the draft legislation.)

Clark Panel. The Mark Clark panel commissioned by the House Armed Services Committee recommended that 19-year-olds be drafted before older men but that the present method of drafting the oldest registrant first within a given age group be retained. It said that college undergraduate student deferments should be continued, with students, after they had graduated, reverting into the draft pool on a level with 19-year-olds. Post-graduate and occupational deferments would be granted only for persons in critically important fields. The panel also called for: (1) a narrowing of the definition of conscientious objectors to permit exemptions only for objection based on religious belief; (2) imposition of "severe and expeditious" punishment on draft card burners and draft evaders; (3) creation of a National Manpower Resources Board under the National Security Council to advise the Director of Selective Service on which critical skills should be granted occupational and graduate deferments; (4) retention of autonomy by local boards; (5) creation of "watchdog" subcommittees of the two Armed Services Committees to review operation of the draft; (6) mobilization of some reservists "to spread the burden of the Vietnam war more equitably"; and (7) permanent authority for the President to call up individual reservists without declaring a national emergency.

Kennedy-Clark Resolution. The Kennedy-Joseph Clark proposal (S Con Res 12) also recommended that 19-year-olds be drafted first. It said that the order of call should be based on random selection. While the proposal called for a continuation of deferments for college undergraduates, it stipulated that such deferments should be dropped during a national emergency declared by the President. Other features of the proposal called for establishment of national criteria for draft classification, uniform administration of draft criteria, and a revision of physical and mental standards for military service so that persons who did not meet the standards necessary for combat service might be inducted in a noncombat capacity.

Administration Bill. An Administration bill (S 1432) extending the draft provisions of the Universal Military Training and Service Act of 1951 through June 30, 1971, was introduced in the Senate April 5 by Armed Services Committee Chairman Richard B. Russell (D Ga.). In addition to the draft extension, the measure renamed the draft law the Selective Service Act of 1967. It also included the President's proposals for: (1) permanent authority to call up obligated Reservists and National Guardsmen who were not assigned to or not participating satisfactorily in a Reserve or Guard unit and (2) standby authority to draft men into Reserve and National Guard units.

Senate Action

The President's proposals emerged virtually unscathed in the version of the bill reported by the Senate Armed Services Committee May 4. The Committee bill included only one major amendment—language dropping the Administration's request for standby authority to induct men into Reserve and National Guard units; instead, the Committee provided standby authority to permit voluntary enlistment in a Reserve or Guard unit up to the time of an individual's induction. Although the Committee criticized some of the President's proposed changes in the draft it did not put in language to block them.

The Committee endorsed the President's proposal to eliminate graduate school deferments and his proposal for a reversal in the current order of induction, with 19-year-old men inducted before older men. Although it expressed doubt about the President's proposal for a draft lottery to determine the order of call within a given age category, the panel said it was not so opposed as to recommend prohibition of the plan. In other important recommendations the panel applauded a proposal by the Mark Clark group to continue college undergraduate deferments (with the student going into the draft pool with 19-year-olds when he was graduated or reached age 24) and criticized a plan by the President's commission to dilute the powers of local boards.

On balance, the Committee's recommendations most closely followed the proposals of the Clark panel report although they did nothing by way of legislation to see that the proposals were implemented. The only variation was that the Committee was willing to give the draft lottery a trial while the Clark panel recommended outright rejection of the lottery. The Committee's position differed most significantly from the report of the President's commission, which, in addition to the proposal for consolidation of local boards, had called for the draft lottery and elimination of deferments for undergraduates. The President himself had not yet taken a position on the issues of the local boards and undergraduate deferments.

BILL PASSED

The Senate May 11 passed S 1432 without change by a 70-2 roll-call vote.

Most of the debate centered on an amendment by Mark O. Hatfield (R Ore.) calling for a transition from the draft to a system of voluntary enlistment to raise and maintain personnel for the armed forces. The Senate rejected the Hatfield amendment by a 9-69 roll-call vote, and by similarly lop-sided votes, rejected amendments to extend the draft law for two years rather than four, to prevent draftees from being sent to Southeast Asia unless they volunteered for it, to reduce the length of service for draftees, to make the draft "more uniform" throughout the nation, to defer men while they served in the Peace Corps or similar groups, and to permit registrants to have lawyers when objecting to their draft classifications.

Volunteer Army. Hatfield, in what was the freshman Senator's first proposal offered on the floor, introduced an amendment which stated, "Whenever...reassessment reveals that a system of involuntary inductions can be replaced by a system based on the free choice of individuals at an over-all cost the nation can reasonably afford, Congress should act to facilitate the prompt termination of involuntary inductions and a transition to an effective voluntary system for the procurement of military manpower."

He stressed he was not advocating abolition of the draft immediately but was asking Congress to go on record as seeking the objective of a voluntary system as soon as feasible. "I believe that it is an unfair indictment against our youth to imply that young people do not have sufficient patriotism and love for country to create a desire and an incentive on their part to respond to our country's needs," Hatfield said.

Volunteer Army—Pros and Cons

Following are the major arguments for and against the concept of abolishing the draft and substituting an all-volunteer military force, as asserted by Defense Department officials and Members of the House and Senate during debate on S 1432.

Pros. Proponents of the all-volunteer force argued that the concept would:

- Produce a more highly skilled, highly motivated, professional corps.
- Save money because of a lower turnover in military personnel (largely because of a reduction in training costs).
- Replace a system that they said was riddled with inequities.

Cons. Opponents argued that such a force would:

- Cost too much, despite the argument of proponents, because pay would have to be raised considerably to attract sufficient numbers of volunteers.
- Result in a disproportionate number of low-income persons, particularly Negroes, joining the service.
- Curtail the President's foreign policy options if he thought an unpopular commitment might result in resignations or a cutback in new enlistments.
- Almost certainly require continued drafting of doctors, lawyers and other highly paid specialists.
- Lead to dismemberment of reserve forces (which depend largely on persons with a military obligation.)
- Run the risk of creating a separate institution which might try to assert itself politically.

Hatfield said "coercive conscription" should be used only as a last resort, when vast numbers of men are needed during a national emergency. To maintain the level of manpower needed after Vietnam, he said, only five of every 100 young men in the manpower pool need be recruited.

Hatfield called for higher and "realistic" pay for servicemen, replacement of combat-trained soldiers by civilians for nonmilitary jobs (typists, bartenders) in the armed forces, better housing, educational opportunities and cultural opportunities such as found in civilian life.

He said the Government would save money by the lower turnover in military personnel. He quoted an Army authority as saying that at no time did more than 43 percent of the Army have more than one year's experience, and that 95 percent of the draftees left the service as soon as they can. Hatfield also called for "adjustments" of physical and educational qualifications to permit enlistments by persons who could not meet existing rigid standards but who could perform many duties which did not require "1-A's."

Edward W. Brooke (R Mass.), the only Negro in the Senate, rejected arguments that a voluntary system would create a "poor man's Army" and a "Negro Army." He said persons of middle and high income groups might consider a military career, too. He said he had found there was not a disproportionate number of Negroes drafted or enlisted in the Army, but a disproportion did exist because of re-enlistments by Negroes who found they could do better in military than civilian life.

Views on Draft Clash at House and Senate Hearings

Extensive hearings held on the draft by three Congressional committees in 1967 indicated a sharp difference of view on what, if anything, should be done to change the law. Hearings were held by the Senate Armed Services Committee April 12-19; the Manpower, Employment and Poverty Subcommittee of the Senate Labor and Public Welfare Committee (which did not hold jurisdiction over draft legislation), March 20-April 6; and the House Armed Services Committee, May 2-18. Highlights of testimony:

Lottery. Presenting the case for President Johnson's draft lottery proposal, Thomas D. Morris, Assistant Secretary of Defense for Manpower, told the House Armed Services Committee May 2 that under normal peacetime conditions, only about 110,000 of the 730,000 19-year-olds in the 1-A draft eligible pool each year would be drafted. "How do you take one in seven and be fair?," Morris asked.

Lt. Gen. Lewis B. Hershey (USA ret.), director of Selective Service, told the Manpower Subcommittee March 20 that he saw no problems in working out the President's lottery plan even though he personally had long opposed it. In announcing his shift to support of the lottery, Hershey said: "I am an operator. I've never played in the backfield much. I wasn't too good on the line. But when the quarterback calls the signals, that is the way I play them."

Gen. Mark W. Clark (USA ret.), who directed a panel that prepared one of the major draft studies, told the Senate Armed Services Committee April 12 that his group had found the concept of a draft lottery "unwise and retrogressive." Clark said a "primitive drawing" used as far back as the Civil War had met with "charges of fraud, manipulation and favoritism."

Undergraduate Deferments. Burke Marshall, general counsel of International Business Machines Corp. and chairman of the Presidential commission on the draft, told the Manpower Subcommittee March 22 that the way the draft had operated during the Vietnam war had raised a "compelling need for fairness" on the matter of deferments. "It seems to me," he said, "that you can't explain to someone who doesn't have the means or the skill or the intelligence that in a time of war you're taking him and allowing someone else to stay on a campus." Responsibility to fight a war, he asserted, "should fall equally on all segments of society."

U.S. Commissioner of Education Harold Howe II called April 5 for an end to college undergraduate deferments. In testimony before the Manpower panel, Howe noted that the Administration hoped to keep the question of deferments open to discussion but that he personally felt that deferments were "no longer justified." He termed any interruption that might be involved in such a policy "sustainable."

In testimony before the Senate Armed Services Committee April 12, Gen. Clark took issue with the Marshall panel's recommendation to end the undergraduate deferments. Although critics called such deferments discriminatory, Clark said, statistics for recent years showed that 60 percent of the college student group had served in the armed forces, whereas only 57 percent of the non-college students had served.

Encouragement of Draft Evasion. Assistant U.S. Attorney General Fred M. Vinson Jr., testifying on enforcement procedures of the draft law, told the House Armed Services Committee May 5 that anti-draft statements, no matter how "outrageous," had not violated the law. Despite an existing statute that provided imprisonment for obstruction of recruitment, Vinson said, vocal protests alone were protected by the free speech clause of the 1st Amendment unless they presented a "clear and present danger." Thus far, he said, no antidraft statement fit that category. Following Vinson's explanation, Rep. F. Edward Hebert (D La.), a senior member of the Committee, asserted that the Justice Department should "forget the 1st Amendment" and make an effort to prosecute offenders. This, he said, would "show the American people that the Justice Department and Congress were trying to clean up this rat-infested area." (Hebert later said that he had not intended to infer that the 1st Amendment should be disregarded but only that the Justice Department should leave the interpretation up to the Supreme Court.) In an appearance before the House panel May 9, Clark testified that if existing law were too weak to deal with persons encouraging draft evasion, Congress should pass legislation "making it a very serious punishable offense." Following Clark's remarks, Committee Chairman L. Mendel Rivers (D S.C.) said the Justice Department "hasn't got the nerve to prosecute those people." This, he suggested, was because the Department feared it would be overruled by the Supreme Court. "Let the digrace fall on the Supreme Court," he said. "There are plenty of provisions in the laws under which they could be prosecuted now."

Senate Armed Services Committee Chairman Richard B. Russell (D Ga.), who opposed the amendment, said a professional army of volunteers might contain no serious drawbacks when the force was small, but that problems could exist in a large military establishment. He called it "a healthy thing" to have an in-and-out flow of civilians who served a brief period. He said the nation could hardly have raised the money necessary to attract the 650,000 persons added to the military after the intensification of the Vietnam war.

Russell and others criticized a paragraph in the amendment which called the draft an "invasion of the liberties of America's young men." Russell said such language would hurt morale of draftees serving in Vietnam as well as men just being drafted. He also questioned how the military would obtain physicians and dentists. Finally, Russell noted that in a professional army, a man's devotion sometimes turns primarily to the army, rather than to the nation.

Edward M. Kennedy (D Mass.) suggested that with a volunteer system, a President would have to consider the popularity of action he might want to take in a foreign venture. Russell said a volunteer system would "disarm the President so that he could not fight a war."

House Action

The President's authority to order draft reform was sharply restricted in a version of the bill reported May 18 by the House Armed Services Committee.

Lottery. In its most far-reaching change, the Committee added language prohibiting the President from instituting a draft lottery or other random selection system unless he found the new method "in the national interest" and gave Congress at least 60 days advance notice. At the close of the 60-day period the new system would take effect automatically unless Congress had enacted a resolution disapproving it.

The Committee said it had adopted the restrictions on the lottery because it could determine no advantage in random selection over the existing method of drafting the oldest registrant first with a given age group. Noting that alleged inequities in the draft had been confined to the classification of an individual's draft status rather than the method of selection once he was classified, the Committee said it was "unable to identify the specific inequities which the so-called random system...would eliminate." Because the existing system had worked "effectively and impartially" in more than 26 years of use, the panel's report said, the Committee was reluctant to endorse a system "which would have no particular advantage but could create significant problems." This was especially true, the panel said, in light of the fact that the Administration had not yet agreed on a specific lottery proposal.

Undergraduate Deferments. In another major change, the Committee adopted an amendment prohibiting the President from ending college undergraduate deferments unless he found their restriction or termination necessary in view of armed forces manpower needs. The Committee also added language specifically providing that, unless a student received a further deferment for graduate study under rules established by the bill *(see below)*, he was to be placed in the draft pool with the age group facing maximum exposure to the draft at the time of (1) his graduation; (2) his failure to pursue a fulltime course of instruction satisfactorily; or (3) his 24th birthday, whichever came first. As with the lottery, the Senate Committee had recommended a similar course but had not written it into the bill.

In comments on this amendment, the Committee said it had taken steps to ensure that such deferments would be continued because their continuation was "clearly in the national interest." If student deferments were abolished and most inductees taken from the pool of 19-year-olds, the report said, potential doctors, lawyers and other specialists would fulfill their military obligation before attaining their professional training. Such specialists could not be expected to re-enter the service, the report said, and there was no other source but the draft pool from which to obtain them. The report added that similar difficulties would be encountered in officer procurement.

As to the equity of deferments, the report said that numerous government and private loan and scholarship programs currently available ensured that any needy student who was serious about a college education could obtain one. "Therefore, despite the protestations to the contrary," the report said, "a properly motivated young man desiring a college education need not be deterred because of financial considerations.

Occupational, Graduate Deferments. The Committee added to the bill a new section establishing an independent National Manpower Resources Board which, in conjunction with the National Security Council, would determine the critical skills which should warrant occupational and graduate school deferments. The Committee in its report said the provision contemplated that the Board would be expected to recommend deferments for apprentices in a skilled trade—an area which did not qualify for deferments under existing draft regulations. The Senate Committee endorsed apprentice deferments while opposing graduate deferments, but again, neither was reflected in the Senate bill.

Conscientious Objectors. The Committee adopted a provision eliminating the existing requirement that the "religious training and belief" on which draft exemptions for conscientious objection were based must be belief in a "Supreme Being." (Although the language of the amendment appeared at first glance to be broadening the test for conscientious objectors, its intended effect was just the opposite. Its intent was to knock out the basis for the Supreme Court's broad interpretation of permissible grounds for conscientious objection. The interpretation came on the basis of the "Supreme Being" clause in the 1965 case of *U.S. v. Seeger.*) There were no comparable Senate recommendations or provisions. *(For additional details, see final provisions and conference action.)*

The Committee also adopted a new provision requiring that conscientious objectors who chose to perform two years of critical civilian work in lieu of serving as a noncombatant in the armed services actually be inducted into the military and then furloughed into their civilian jobs. The intent of the provision was to provide a measure of military control which would ensure that the objectors performed the required civilian work.

Draft Violators. The Committee approved an amendment directing the Department of Justice to proceed "as expeditiously as possible" to prosecute draft law violations, when prosecution was requested by the Director of the Selective Service System. Existing law left the decision to prosecute up to the Attorney General. There was no comparable action or comment in the Senate.

Other Changes. In other variations from the Senate bill, the Committee adopted amendments: (1) changing the Administration-proposed name of the new Act from the Selective Service Act of 1967 to the Military Selective Service Act of 1967; (2) dropping Administration-proposed language granting permanent authority for the President to mobilize Reservists or National Guardsmen not participating in an organized unit; (3) providing that a potential draftee who prolonged litigation of his draft classification beyond the age of 26 would remain liable for the draft for a like period if he later was determined qualified for induction; (4) directing the President to establish national criteria for the draft and, to the extent "consistent with the national interest," require that the criteria be administered uniformly by local draft boards; (5) limiting a person's service on a local board to 25 years, requiring a board member's retirement at age 75, and prohibiting discrimination against women in the selection of board members; and (6) ending exemptions from the draft for doctors who entered the Public Health Service (PHS) in lieu of the military and spent their active duty in assignments outside the PHS, except for those detailed to the Coast Guard, who would remain exempt.

Positions of Organizations on Military Draft Extension

During Congressional hearings on the 1967 military draft extension bill, representatives of religious, professional and other groups took the following positions on the major issues under consideration.

DRAFT LOTTERY

Issue: Establish a random selection system or draft lottery to determine which registrants within a given age group would be inducted into the service.

FOR—American Council on Education; American Veterans Committee; National Committee for a Sane Nuclear Policy; University Christian Movement.

AGAINST—American Legion; Chamber of Commerce of the United States; National Assn. of Evangelicals; National Guard Assn.; Reserve Officers Assn.; Veterans of Foreign Wars.

REVERSAL OF CALL

Issue: Reverse the current "oldest first" order of call and induct 19-year-olds before older men.

FOR—AFL-CIO; American Council on Education; American Veterans Committee; Chamber of Commerce of the United States; United States Youth Council.

AGAINST—None.

UNDERGRADUATE DEFERMENTS

Issue: Retain student deferments for college undergraduates enrolled in a full-time course.

FOR—American Academy of Microbiology; American Council on Education; American Dental Assn.; American Legion; American Medical Assn.; American Optometric Assn.; American Society for Engineering Education; American Veterinary Medical Assn.; Chamber of Commerce of the United States; Federation of American Societies for Experimental Biology; Manufacturing Chemists' Assn.; National Guard Assn.; Engineering Manpower Commission; National Society of Professional Engineers; Scientific Manpower Commission.

AGAINST—AFL-CIO; American Civil Liberties Union; American Veterans Committee; National Committee for a Sane Nuclear Policy; University Christian Movement; Veterans of Foreign Wars.

GRADUATE DEFERMENTS

Issue: Retain deferments for graduate students enrolled in studies critical to national security. Same positions as taken on undergraduate deferments.

OCCUPATIONAL DEFERMENTS

Issue: Retain deferments for persons employed in critical occupations.

FOR—American Council on Education; American Veterans Committee; Chamber of Commerce of the United States; Corn Refiners Assn.; Engineering Manpower Commission; Farm Bureau Federation; Manufacturing Chemists' Assn.; Scientific Manpower Commission.

AGAINST—National Committee for a Sane Nuclear Policy; Veterans of Foreign Wars.

NATIONAL DRAFT CRITERIA

Issue: Establish national criteria for draft classification and require local draft boards throughout the country to apply them uniformly.

FOR—AFL-CIO; American Civil Liberties Union; American Council on Education; American Veterans Committee; Jewish War Veterans; United States Youth Council.

AGAINST—American Legion; Chamber of Commerce of the United States; Farm Bureau Federation; National Assn. of Evangelicals; National Guard Assn.; Reserve Officers Assn.; Veterans of Foreign Wars.

CONSCIENTIOUS OBJECTORS

Issue: Write into law a provision allowing exemption for conscientious objection to the draft based on philosophical and other nonreligious beliefs.

FOR—American Civil Liberties Union; American Ethical Union; Church of the Brethren; Friends (Quakers) Committee on National Legislation; Jewish Peace Fellowship; Methodist Board of Christian Social Concerns; National Collegiate Conference on Selective Service Reform; National Committee for a Sane Nuclear Policy; National Council of Churches; Unitarian Universalist Assn.; United Presbyterian Church; Washington Friends Joint Peace Committee; Women's International League for Peace and Freedom; Women Strike for Peace.

AGAINST—Allegheny Mennonite Conference; American Legion; National Assn. of Evangelicals.

Issue: Permit exemptions for conscientious objection to a particular war as well as to war in general.

FOR—American Civil Liberties Union; American Ethical Union; Church of the Brethren; Disciples of Christ; Friends of Committee on National Legislation; Methodist Board of Christian Social Concerns; National Collegiate Conference on Selective Reform; National Committee for a Sane Nuclear Policy; National Council of Churches; United Church of Christ; United Presbyterian Church; University Christian Movement; Washington Friends Joint Peace Committee; Women's International League for Peace and Freedom; Women Strike for Peace.

AGAINST—Allegheny Mennonite Conference; American Legion; Jewish War Veterans; National Assn. of Evangelicals.

DRAFTING MEN INTO RESERVE

Issue: Provide standby authority for the President to draft men into the Reserve and National Guard when necessary to maintain the strength of those components.

FOR—None.

AGAINST—National Guard Assn.; Reserve Officers Assn.

DOCTORS' EXEMPTIONS

Issue: End draft exemptions for doctors who entered the Public Health Service (PHS) in lieu of the military and spent their active duty in assignments outside PHS (such as the Peace Corps, Office of Economic Opportunity, Food and Drug Administration, etc.).

FOR ABOLISHMENT—American Medical Assn.

AGAINST—None.

Committee Views—Volunteer Army. The Committee in its report on S 1432 said it had conducted an "intensive" study of alternatives to the draft and had come to the conclusion that "the hard realities in the world in which we live require a continuation of the draft law." It said it had chosen a four-year extension over a shorter one because it could "see no lessening of the likelihood of the need" for the draft over the entire four-year period. To approve a shorter extension, it said, would be to create an element of uncertainty for youth as to whether they would be needed after the draft next expired.

The Committee said that no issue raised during its deliberations had received "greater and more thorough" consideration than the proposal to eliminate the draft in favor of a highly paid all-volunteer force. The panel said it had determined that such an alternative would be too costly, however, and that even the incentive of higher pay might not ensure enough enlistments to meet full manpower needs. A particular problem, the Committee said, would be the enlistment of doctors and other professional personnel, who would demand pay far in excess of that provided the rest of the military and the Civil Service structure. In addition, the panel said, the removal of the draft obligation would vastly diminish the strength of reserve forces. The report estimated it would be necessary to increase Reserve and National Guard compensation by at least $1 billion a year to maintain their strength at current levels.

BILL PASSED

The House May 25 passed S 1432 by a 362-9 roll-call vote and sent the measure to conference with the Senate.

Prior to passing the bill, the House by voice vote accepted one major floor amendment—a proposal by Armed Services Committee Chairman L. Mendel Rivers (D S.C.) to rewrite one of the committee provisions regarding conscientious objectors. Although the amendment retained the existing requirement that conscientious objectors perform two years of civilian work, which was re-enunciated in the bill, it deleted the Committee's requirement that objectors be inducted into the armed forces and furloughed by the military into civilian jobs. Deletion of the new procedure had been urged by Quaker, Amish, Mennonite and other traditional "peace" churches, which objected to military authority as well as to war.

In other major actions, the House by a 41-140 standing vote rejected an amendment by Otis G. Pike (D N.Y.) to eliminate the bill's retention of undergraduate student deferments and rejected, by a 77-160 standing vote, a proposal by Donald Rumsfeld (R Ill.) extending the draft law for two, rather than four, years. The Rumsfeld amendment was designed to retain the draft only long enough to give Congress time to conduct an extensive study of the alternative of an all-volunteer force.

The nine Members who voted against passage of the bill all were Democrats. They were: Brown (Calif.), Burton (Calif.), Conyers (Mich.), Foley (Wash.), Gonzalez (Texas), Hicks (Wash.), Kastenmeier (Wis.), Rees (Calif.) and Ryan (N.Y.). The only Republican to go on record against the bill was O'Konski, who was paired against passage. (The House Republican Policy Committee May 24 had issued a statement supporting the Committee bill in its entirety.)

All-Volunteer Force. Much of the debate on S 1432 centered on the Rumsfeld amendment to shorten the draft extension, making 1969 consideration possible for the alternative of an all-volunteer force.

Opponents of the four-year draft contended that Congress was moving toward another long extension of conscription without giving sufficient study to alternatives. This was particularly true, they said, with regard to the all-volunteer force. Because the plan had received short shrift in Congress, they argued, it had been only dimly understood.

Proponents of the Rumsfeld amendment were particularly critical of the Defense Department's estimate that the additional costs of the force would be in the range of $4 billion to $17 billion. Assuming a 2.7-million man military, Rumsfeld said, the $17 billion figure would average out to a pay increase of more than $6,000 per man. "No one," Rumsfeld asserted, had "even begun to suggest" such a figure. William S. Moorhead (D Pa.), another proponent of the proposal, added that the Defense Department's estimate also had not contemplated the substantial reduction in training costs which should be realized by a stable, all-volunteer establishment.

Rogers C.B. Morton (R Md.) criticized both the nation and Congress for accepting the draft "as an unalterable fact of American life." Conscription should be used only as a "stopgap" measure, he said, while Congress studied the entire concept of mandatory service, not only as it affected military posture but as it related to the nation's "long-range development" as well.

Rivers, who led the opposition to the proposal, argued that the world was in an "uproar," necessitating the "long-range planning" made possible by the draft. Alton Lennon (D N.C.), another opponent of the amendment, said the all-volunteer force would put the Government "in a morally untenable position if its international policies in defense of freedom were in any way equated with the ability to buy sufficient forces." Clarence D. Long (D Md.) said he saw in the proposal "an unholy alliance...between certain liberals and the representation of the upper middle class" to "shrug off" responsibilities for defending the country "onto the poor or the patriotic."

Undergraduate Deferments. Debate also centered on the bill's provision to retain deferments for college undergraduates. Robert L. Leggett (D Calif.), who had opposed the deferments in the Armed Services Committee report, reiterated his argument that it was indefensible to require a poor laborer to go to war while a college student from a higher income family received a four-year deferment. "If young men had elected a four-year deferment (had they been available) in 1861, 1898, 1914 and 1941," he said, "the whole effort would have been over" before the student could have been available for service. Leggett also emphasized recent statistics by the Department of Health, Education and Welfare which showed that of the lower 50 percent of high school graduates, only 19.6 percent of students from homes with annual incomes of $3,000 entered college in contrast to a 49.7-percent entrance figure for students from the $12,000 bracket.

Alexander Pirnie (R N.Y.), a proponent of the deferments, argued that the mere deferral of service in no way constituted an inequity. "There is no way of saying whether the numerical probability of service or the risks of such service will not be greater four years from now than it is today. Young men deferred to attend college in 1963 are undoubtedly leading platoons in Viet Nam today."

Conference, Final Action

House and Senate Conferees worked out a final version of S 1432 and filed a conference report June 8.

The conference version retained almost all of the House limitations on the President's authority to order draft revisions, a development reflecting stern bargaining by House conferees. Of the 16 major differences between the bills, language identical or similar to House provisions prevailed on all but three occasions. On one major item— the draft lottery—conferees not only accepted the House argument that restrictions were needed but agreed to language that went beyond that provided by the House bill. In its final form, the bill flatly prohibited the President from ordering a draft lottery or similar means of random selection unless the proposed new system received the specific approval of Congress. The House bill permitted the lottery unless Congress enacted a resolution specifically disapproving it; the Senate bill did not restrict the President's existing discretionary authority.

In another major change from both bills, conferees compromised on a House provision, not in the Senate bill, which sought to narrow the tests for conscientious objection by knocking out language of existing law stipulating that the "religious training and belief" on which exemption was based must be belief in a "Supreme Being." At the insistence of Senate conferees, the conference committee reinserted language, which was already in existing law but was deleted under the House bill, which stipulated that the term "religious training and belief" for purposes of the exemption could not include "essentially political, sociological or philosophical views or a merely personal moral code." Senate conferees argued that reinsertion of the language would better clarify Congressional intent in knocking out the "Supreme Being" clause. This intent apparently was to exclude exemptions for conscientious objection not based on a belief which had some foundation in religious training, whether that training came in the home or in more formal courses of instruction. (The Supreme Court in the 1965 *Seeger* decision had interpreted the "Supreme Being" clause as allowing exemption for any religious belief which was sincere and meaningful and occupied a place in the objector's life parallel to a belief in God. The belief had to be "religious" in nature, although not necessarily conforming to that held by any organized religious group. Political, sociological or philosophical views or a merely personal moral code, which were not "religious" in nature, were not grounds for exemption. It was open to question how the courts would interpret the new provision. Some observers thought that deletion of the "Supreme Being" clause would enable the courts to broaden the definition of "religious training and belief," thus liberalizing the grounds for conscientious objection. However, the conference report said the intent of Congress was "to more narrowly construe the basis" for conscientious objection.)

FINAL ACTION. The conference report was adopted by the Senate June 14 by a 72-23 roll-call vote and by the House June 20 by a 377-29 roll call. The actions sent the measure to the White House.

Senate. Prior to final Senate action, Edward M. Kennedy (D Mass.), one of the leading Senate advocates of broad draft reform, conducted a long and vigorous opposition to the conference report on grounds that the compromise bill represented an entirely new measure which failed to revise the draft and "make it a fair, just and predictable system." Kennedy, in order to work up his case against the conference bill, secured a two-day delay in the final vote on the measure.

Arguing that acceptance of the conference report would amount to "an abrogation of responsibility by the Senate," Kennedy urged Senators to defeat the report and to instruct Senate conferees to seek a one-year rather than four-year extension of the draft. Kennedy said he would prefer to instruct conferees also to delete some of the restrictions added in conference but that the "exigencies as to termination of the Selective Service Act" on July 1 would make it impossible to take adequate time to work out another compromise bill. The one-year extension, he said, "would at least give us a chance to review in considerable detail next year a number of questions which have come up."

Kennedy's major objections to the final bill centered on five categories of provisions adopted in conference: the prohibition against the draft lottery; the removal of draft exempt status for Public Health Service doctors detailed to the Peace Corps and various other agencies; the provisions directing the Justice Department to expedite prosecution of alleged draft violations and directing the courts to give precedence to such cases on their dockets; the narrowing of the test for exemption of conscientious objectors; and the vesting in the National Security Council of the responsibility of identifying and recommending the critical skills which should warrant graduate or occupational deferments. Together, Kennedy said, these changes made the bill "less satisfactory than the existing law."

Russell Position. Senate Armed Services Committee Chairman Richard B. Russell (D Ga.), who led the Senate conferees in the House-Senate conference, agreed with Kennedy that the Senate-approved version would have been preferable but said Kennedy had "vastly overstated" his objections to the compromise bill.

With respect to Kennedy's move for the one-year draft extension, Russell said the proposal probably would be subject to a point of order in either chamber because both bills had provided the four-year extension period. Consequently, Russell said, the delay that might be caused by acceptance of Kennedy's position would mean "gambling with the security of this country." Russell said the Defense Department already had announced plans to draft 39,000 men in July and that there would be no other means to obtain the necessary manpower if draft extension were delayed beyond that date.

House. A brief House debate centered on the conference decision to delete the provision for mandatory national standards on classification of draft registrants and replace it by discretionary authority for the President to promulgate the criteria and discretion for the local boards to follow them. Don H. Clausen (R Calif.), a leading proponent of the mandatory standards, argued it would be unjust to ask the nation's youth "to run the risk of sacrificing their lives in military conflict and then leaving their selection for duty to the discretion of boards of citizens with authority to fix their own policies and procedures." Clausen added that he could not see how uniform criteria "would, in any way, impair the discretion of local boards to consider such case on its merits."

BILL SIGNED. President Johnson June 30 signed S 1432 into law (PL 90-40). He issued the same day an accompanying Executive Order (11360) implementing sections of the law.

The Executive Order placed a moratorium on the ending of graduate deferments. It stated that any registrant enrolled for his first year of post-baccalaureate study in a graduate or a professional school by Oct. 1, 1967, would be deferred for a 12-month period following the beginning of his course of study. Registrants who were already enrolled and participating satisfactorily in a master's degree program could be deferred for one additional year. Those who were enrolled and participating satisfactorily in a course of study leading to a professional or doctoral degree could be deferred for one additional year or for a total of five years, including years already completed, whichever was greater.

Although it had been widely believed that the President would order induction of 19-year-olds before older men, he did not do so in the Executive Order. Officials said such action had not been necessary at the present time because the demands of the Vietnam war had drained the draft pool of older men so profusely that the average age of draftee induction currently was between the ages of 20 and 21. As long as the war continued, officials added, this likely would remain the case. Thus it was expected that an order to call 19-year-olds first would be issued only during peacetime circumstances.

Draft Law Provisions

As signed by the President S 1432—PL 90-40—contained the following major provisions:

Draft Law Redesignation and Extension. Changed the name of the 1951 Universal Military Training and Service Act (commonly known as the Draft Act) to the Military Selective Service Act of 1967.

Extended for four years, from July 1, 1967, to July 1, 1971: (1) the authority to induct men between the ages of 18-½ and 26, or up to 35 for those who had received deferments; (2) the authority to issue special calls for physicians, dentists, and allied specialists to age 35 when they had been deferred for professional education; (3) the suspension of permanent limitations on the active duty strength of the armed forces (statutory permanent ceiling: about 2.3 million; ceiling under S 1432: 5 million; estimated actual current strength: 3.4 million); (4) the authority to pay a quarters allowance to all enlisted members of the armed forces with dependents, irrespective of the rank of these members, if the dependents were not furnished Government quarters; and (5) the authority to pay physicians and dentists up to an additional $350 a month (based on their length of service) and to pay veterinarians an additional $100 a month, regardless of their period of service.

Draft Lottery. Prohibited the President from instituting a draft lottery or other means of random selection of draftees without the specific approval of Congress. (The President under existing law could institute the change under his discretionary authority to order revisions in draft procedures.)

Undergraduate Deferments. Prohibited the President from ending college undergraduate deferments unless he found that restriction or termination of such deferments was necessary in view of the armed forces' manpower needs. Specifically provided, however, that unless a student later received a graduate or occupational deferment, or unless his induction would cause "extreme hardship to dependents" *(see parental deferments section below),* he was to be placed in the draft pool with the age group facing maximum exposure to the draft at the time of: (1) his graduation; (2) his withdrawal or expulsion from school; or (3) his 24th birthday, whichever came first.

Stipulated that undergraduate deferments were to be granted automatically upon request of any student enrolled in a full-time course of instruction and were to continue despite the level of the student's class standing so long as he remained enrolled. (The provision had the effect of blocking an existing procedure under which draft boards sometimes inducted students not performing satisfactory work.)

Parental, Marital Deferments. Eliminated the existing draft regulation which allowed students who had received undergraduate deferments to receive subsequent parental deferments. Under terms of S 1432, they would be granted the parental deferments only if they could prove exteme hardship to dependents. (Fathers who did not receive the undergraduate deferments would continue to receive the parental deferment without proof of extreme hardship as would registrants who received their undergraduate deferments prior to enactment of S 1432.) Retained the existing regulation which prohibited married registrants without children from receiving deferments for being married unless they could prove extreme hardship.

Occupational, Graduate Deferments. Restated the President's existing authority to prescribe criteria for the granting of graduate and occupational deferments. Directed the National Security Council, however, to assume the responsibility of identifying and periodically advising the Director of Selective Service on the critical skills which would warrant occupational graduate deferments. Directed the Council in making its recommendations to consider the needs of both the armed forces and the civilian economy.

Public Health Service Exemptions. Removed draft-exempt status for doctors who entered the Public Health Service (PHS) in lieu of serving in the military and spent their active duty in assignments outside the PHS, such as the Peace Corps, Food and Drug Administration and the Office of Economic Opportunity. Specifically retained the exemption, however, for PHS doctors detailed for active duty to the Coast Guard, the Bureau of Prisons and the Environmental Science Services Administration. Made the removal of the other exemptions effective with all assignments made after enactment of the bill.

Conscientious Objectors. Took action which had the intended effect of invalidating a 1965 Supreme Court decision that broadened the grounds on which persons could be exempted from the draft because of conscientious objection to participation in war. Existing law permitted such exemptions for persons opposed to war on grounds of "religious training and belief," which was defined by the law as meaning belief in a "Supreme Being." The Supreme Court, in the 1965 case of *U.S. v.*

Seeger, interpreted the "Supreme Being" clause as including any belief which was sincere and meaningful and occupied a place in the objector's life parallel to a belief in God. Congress in S 1432 knocked out the reference to a "Supreme Being," thus deleting the language on which the Supreme Court relied for the *Seeger* decision. (The legislative history of the provision made it clear that Congress hoped that deletion of the "Supreme Being" clause would result in a new Supreme Court interpretation which would exclude exemptions for conscientious objection not based on a belief which had some foundation in religious training, whether that training came in the home or in more formal courses of instruction.)

Draft Violations. Directed the Department of Justice, upon request of the Director of Selective Service, to proceed "as expeditiously as possible" to prosecute draft law violations (which included such acts as draft evasion, counseling others to evade or obstructing their compliance, and, in the case of conscientious objectors, refusing to perform two years of "critical" civilian work in lieu of military service). Required the Justice Department, in the event it failed to honor the Selective Service Director's request, to inform Congress in writing as to its reasons for failing to do so. (Prosecution of such violations under existing law was left to the discretion of the Attorney General.)

Required that cases involving violations of the draft law be given precedence on the dockets of federal courts over other types of cases. (Existing law gave the Attorney General discretionary authority to request that such cases be given precedence.) Also clarified language in the Draft Act to make clear that the existing statute prohibited court review of a registrant's draft classification until after the registrant had been ordered to report for induction and had responded either affirmatively or negatively to the order.

Congressional Review of Draft. Required the Director of Selective Service to report to Congress semiannually on operations of the Selective Service System, to include state breakdowns on the number of persons registered, inducted and deferred from the draft, the rea-

sons why deferments were granted and "such other specific kinds of information" as Congress might request.

National Classification Criteria. Authorized the President to recommend national criteria for classification of draft registrants and, to the extent that the President deemed such action "consistent with the national interest," to recommend that such criteria be administered uniformly "whenever practicable" by local draft boards.

Reserve Enlistment Alternative. Provided standby authority for state Governors (in the case of the National Guard) and the President (with regard to the other reserve components) to allow persons to enlist in those components, in lieu of being drafted, at any time prior to the date they were scheduled for induction. Stipulated that this authority could not be used, however, unless a state Governor and/or the President previously had affirmed that it was not otherwise possible to maintain the statutory personnel strength of the applicable component.

Reserve Call-Up Authority. Granted permanent authority for the President, without declaring a national emergency, to order to active duty obligated reservists who had not yet completed a total of two years active duty and were not currently assigned to, or participating satisfactorily in, a Reserve or National Guard unit.

Other Provisions. Provided that a potential draftee who prolonged litigation of his draft classification beyond the age of 26 would remain liable for the draft for a like period if he later was determined qualified for induction.

Permitted reserve officers on inactive duty to serve as Government appeals agents and counselors to registrants.

Permitted the special induction of alien physicians and dentists to age 35 years even if they were older than age 26 when they entered the country.

Changed the designation of "chief clerk" of local draft boards to "executive secretary" of the board and limited the tenure of such officials to 10 years, unless reappointed. Also limited a board member's total service to 25 years, required members to retire at age 75 and prohibited discrimination against women in the selection of board members.

Chapter 16—Congress and Government

Key Votes

In this chapter, key roll-call votes are shown in bold-face type. The party breakdown on each of these votes and the position taken by each Member of Congress may be found in the key vote charts which appear in the appendix to this book.

Congress

REFORM pressures swept Congress in the 1965-68 period, and Congress responded in characteristic fashion. As in the past, it showed little disposition to effect the bold reforms its critics demanded, but some modest changes were achieved.

The most decisive action came in the area of greatest criticism, Congressional ethics. Haunted by the case of Robert G. (Bobby) Baker, former Secretary to the Senate Majority, and confronted by ethical charges against two of its Members, Rep. Adam C. Powell (D N.Y.) and Sen. Thomas J. Dodd (D Conn.), Congress attempted to provide itself with written rules of ethical behavior, and ethics committees were created in the Senate and House. Both chambers approved limited financial disclosure requirements but rejected the more stringent disclosure proposals of the reformers.

In other areas, reform proposals made less headway. Congress did not complete action on a comprehensive legislative reorganization bill, and attempts to liberalize the Senate cloture rule ended in failure. However, efforts to curb the obstructive power of the House Rules Committee enjoyed some success. Highlights of action:

ETHICS. One of the late House Speaker Sam Rayburn's (D Texas 1913-61) often-quoted rules of politics was that the ethics of a Member of Congress should be judged not by his peers in the House but by the voters once every two years. By the mid-1960s, it had become clear that neither Congress nor the public felt this was enough.

Demands for action on Congressional ethics intensified in 1963 with charges that Robert G. (Bobby) Baker had used his office as Secretary to the Senate Majority to promote outside business interests.

Largely because of embarrassments caused by the Baker case, the Senate in 1964 established a Select Committee on Standards and Conduct to investigate "allegations of improper conduct" by Senators and Senate employees.

The Committee's first inquiry began in 1966. It involved charges by syndicated columnists Drew Pearson and Jack Anderson that Sen. Thomas J. Dodd (D Conn.) had misused political campaign funds contributed to him and had committed other offenses. The Committee in

Reference

For a discussion of Congress in the Postwar Years (1945-64), see *Congress and the Nation*, Vol. I, p. 1407; for lobbying activities, 1945-64, see Vol. I, p. 1545.

Public Laws

In 1968, a total of 391 bills became public laws. This was 142 more than the 1967 total but 70 fewer than in 1966. The highest number of public laws for any one year since 1950 was 638 in 1956. The lowest number was the 1967 figure. Following is a list of the number of public laws enacted since 1961:

Congress	Public Laws	Congress	Public Laws
1968	391	1964	409
1967	249	1963	257
1966	461	1962	484
1965	349	1961	401

April 1967 recommended that the Senate censure Dodd for misuse of political funds and for double-billing for official and private travel. The Senate censured Dodd on the first charge by a **92-5** roll-call vote but refused, by a 51-45 vote, to censure him on the second charge. The action marked the seventh time in its history that the Senate had censured one of its members.

MEANWHILE, ethical storms were raging in the House over the activities of Rep. Adam C. Powell (D N.Y.). The controversial Harlem Negro came under fire on a variety of counts, ranging from a libel action against him in New York state to charges of misusing Government funds. However, his downfall began in 1966 as the result of a revolt in his own committee over legislative business.

Following preliminary investigation by a House subcommittee, Powell was stripped of his chairmanship of the Education and Labor Committee and temporarily denied a seat in the House. Subsequently, Powell was investigated by a Select Committee, which recommended that he be seated but censured, stripped of his seniority and fined $40,000—unprecedented punishments for a Member of Congress. Rejecting the recommendations of the Committee, the House March 1, 1967, excluded Powell from the 90th Congress. He was re-elected at a subsequent special election but did not present himself for swearing in.

Re-elected to the 91st Congress in 1968, Powell was seated in January 1969, although he lost his seniority and was fined $25,000. The Supreme Court in 1969 ruled that the House had acted unconstitutionally in excluding Powell in 1967.

Pressures generated by the Powell and Dodd cases led first to the creation in 1966 of a temporary House Select Committee on Standards and Conduct that lacked the investigative powers of its Senate counterpart. In the 90th Congress, the House created a stronger standing Committee on Standards of Official Conduct.

Acting upon that Committee's recommendation, the House in 1968 approved a new Code of Official Conduct for the House. And it added to the Rules of the House requirements for limited disclosure of outside income by Representatives and top employees.

In the Senate, the Select Committee on Standards and Conduct in 1968 also recommended new rules to guide the ethical conduct of Members and employees. These rules were approved by the Senate without substantial change.

The ethics rules adopted by the two chambers differed considerably. Only the Senate restricted outside employment and political fund-raising by its employees. The House rule on financial disclosure, however, made more information public than the Senate rule, which covered only certain campaign contributions and honoraria of more than $300.

LEGISLATIVE REORGANIZATION. The 90th Congress failed to complete action on a major legislative reorganization bill. The measure, the first full-scale attempt at Congressional reform since the Legislative

Reorganization Act of 1946, was the outgrowth of a two-year study by the Joint Committee on the Organization of the Congress.

The bill would have made reforms in committee procedure and established several new standing committees; provided for fuller budgetary data and for new procedures on appropriations bills; increased committee staffs and provided committee minorities with staff members; made changes in job services, Capitol police, pages and appointment of postmasters; and strengthened the Regulation of Lobbying Act.

The bill did not touch on the most controversial areas of reform, such as the seniority system and the Senate and House rules.

The Senate passed the reform bill early in 1967, but it never reached a vote in the House. The measure died in the House Rules Committee in 1968 despite a late-session move by some dissident Members to force it to the floor. The bill was supported by the Republican leadership and reform-minded Democrats in the House, but it was opposed by many committee chairmen and other senior House Members who were against changes that would tend to dilute their authority.

CURBS ON OBSTRUCTION. Repeated efforts to curb legislative obstruction, long a favorite cause of the liberal forces in Congress, continued during the 1965-68 period. In the Senate these efforts centered on attempts to revise Rule 22, the anti-filibuster rule. In the House the focus was on efforts to limit the power of the Rules Committee, where for many years conservative Southern Democrats and Republicans had been able to block or delay legislation sought by the Democratic majority.

Rule 22. Both in 1965 and 1967 a bipartisan group of liberal Senators tried to achieve a revision of Rule 22 that would make it easier to shut off debate by invoking cloture. Both efforts failed.

The chief purpose of those who favored Rule 22 reform was to make it easier to pass civil rights legislation. It had long been considered impossible to impose cloture on civil rights legislation, but in 1964, 1965 and 1968 cloture votes on civil rights bills succeeded. This development took some of the steam out of the Rule 22 reform efforts.

House Rules Committee. At the beginning of the 89th Congress in 1965, the heavily Democratic House adopted the so-called 21-day rule to curb the power of the Rules Committee to bottle up legislation. The 21-day rule made it possible for a legislative committee to bring directly to the House floor a bill that had not been cleared for floor action by the Rules Committee. The rule was employed successfully only eight times in 1965 and 1966, but the threat of its use apparently helped to ease the way for other legislation.

At the beginning of the 90th Congress in 1967, following Republican gains in the mid-term elections, the House repealed the 21-day rule. Despite this move, the Rules Committee maintained a moderate posture in the 90th Congress. That posture resulted in part from the 1966 election defeat of veteran Committee Chairman Howard W. Smith (D Va.), a House conservative leader, and the adoption of a set of rules to limit the power of his successor.

Congress Sets Roll-Call Vote Record

The 90th Congress (1967-68) took 1,074 roll-call votes on legislation (excluding quorum calls), the largest number in at least two decades. The high for a single year was 1967, when 560 roll calls were taken. Second was 1968, when 514 were recorded. Both chambers set individual highs in 1967:

Year	House	Senate	Total
1968	233	281	514
1967	245	315	560
1966	193	235	428
1965	201	258	459
1964	113	305	418
1963	119	229	348
1962	124	224	348
1961	116	204	320
1960	93	207	300
1959	87	215	302
1958	93	200	293
1957	100	107	207
1956	73	130	203
1955	76	87	163
1954	76	171	247
1953	71	89	160
1952	72	129	201
1951	109	202	311
1950	154	229	383
1949	121	227	348
1948	79	189	268
1947	84	138	222

Ethical Problems

Public concern over the activities of Rep. Adam C. Powell (D N.Y.) and Sen. Thomas J. Dodd (D Conn.) played a key role in the development of Congressional codes of ethics and related actions in the 1965-68 period. These and other cases involving ethical problems are summarized below. Following this summary is a Chronology of Legislation, in which general action on ethical standards is detailed.

Powell Case

One of the stormiest episodes of modern Congressional history was the precedent-shattering case of Rep. Adam C. Powell (D N.Y.).

The flamboyant Harlem Negro, first elected to the House in 1944, had long been under fire on a variety of issues—his involvement in court cases concerning income tax evasion and libel; his numerous well-publicized trips at Government expense; and his employment of his wife as a $20,578-a-year clerk while she lived in Puerto Rico. All of these things were an embarrassment to some of Powell's fellow Representatives, but his downfall began in 1966 as the result of a revolt in his own Committee over legislative business.

As developments unfolded, Powell in 1967 first was stripped of his chairmanship of the House Education and Labor Committee, then temporarily denied a seat in the House pending an investigation of his activities. A special House committee set up to investigate Powell recommended that he be seated but censured for "gross misconduct." It also recommended stripping Powell of his seniority and levying a $40,000 fine—punishments never before prescribed for a Member of Congress. The House, however, overruled its committee and instead voted to exclude Powell from the 90th Congress. On only five previous occasions had the House excluded a Member, most recently in 1919.

In a special election to fill the resulting vacancy, Powell, who did not campaign, was re-elected with 86.1 percent of the vote. He did not attempt to take his seat, however. Instead, he remained at his vacation retreat in the Bahamas while a lawsuit to reverse his exclusion from the House began its career in the courts. The suit contended that the House exceeded its powers in excluding Powell because he met the constitutional requirements for membership.

That suit was not decided by the Supreme Court until 1969. The Court then held that the House had acted improperly in excluding Powell.

Meanwhile, Powell easily won re-election to the House in 1968. He was seated by the House at the beginning of the 91st Congress in 1969, although he was stripped of his seniority and fined $25,000.

Background

Adam Clayton Powell was first elected to the House of Representatives from New York's 18th Congressional District in 1944, and from then on was regularly re-elected by large majorities. In 1961 he became chairman of the Education and Labor Committee, the second Negro chair-

---

Bribed Congressman Decision

The Supreme Court Feb. 24, 1966, by a 7-0 vote, held that in prosecuting a former Member of Congress, the Executive Branch may not constitutionally inquire into his motives for making a speech on the floor of Congress, even though the speech was made for a bribe and was part of an unlawful conspiracy.

The holding in *U.S. v. Johnson* left Members of Congress immune from prosecution for their words and legislative deeds on the floor of Congress, with one exception reserved by the Court—prosecution under a "narrowly drawn" law enacted by Congress itself "to regulate the conduct of its Members." Members of Congress already were immune from libel suits for speeches made on the floor.

The *Johnson* case arose out of the conviction of former Rep. Thomas F. Johnson (D Md. 1959-63) on June 13, 1963, by a federal jury in Baltimore. The Government charged that Johnson, former Rep. Frank W. Boykin (D Ala. 1935-63) and two officers of a Maryland savings and loan company then under indictment, J. Kenneth Edlin and William L. Robinson, entered into a conspiracy whereby Johnson and Boykin would approach the Justice Department to urge a "review" of the indictment and Johnson would make a speech on the floor of the House defending savings and loan institutions. Johnson made the speech June 30, 1960, and it was reprinted by the indicted company and distributed to the public. Johnson and Boykin allegedly received money in the form of "campaign contributions," Johnson's share being more than $20,000. *(Congress and the Nation, Vol. I, p. 1420)*

Johnson was convicted on seven counts of violating the federal conflict of interest law (18 U.S.C. 281) and on one count of conspiring to defraud the United States (18 U.S.C. 371); the others were convicted of the same charges. President Johnson Dec. 17, 1965, granted Boykin a full pardon.

The 4th Circuit Court of Appeals Sept. 16, 1964, set aside Johnson's conspiracy conviction on the ground that it was unconstitutional under provisions of Article I, Section 6: "...for any speech or debate in either House, they (Senators and Representatives) shall not be questioned in any other place." The court ordered a new trial on the other counts on the ground that evidence taken about Johnson's speech on the conspiracy count "infected" the entire case.

The Supreme Court affirmed the lower court's ruling, thus foreclosing further prosecution on the conspiracy count but permitting retrial on the other counts.

Johnson Jan. 26, 1968, was convicted for the second time on the conflict of interest charges by the U.S. District Court in Baltimore, Md. He was sentenced to six months in prison.

---

man in Congress. His position as a powerful Negro in Government (there were only six Negro Members of Congress in 1966) and his often flamboyant actions and public statements led to considerable publicity about his activities.

Powell's Travels. Powell's travels at Government expense particularly embarrassed other Members, partly because they were well-publicized and directed attention to the extensive travels of Members and to their use of counterpart funds. Powell regularly took a midsummer trip to Europe, officially as a Congressional Adviser to the U.S. delegation at the annual International Labor Organization meeting in Geneva. Publicity about his patronage of night spots in European capitals with female staff members while traveling on Government business provoked considerable comment both within and without Congress.

Congressional critics also accused Powell of using Committee funds to make frequent vacation trips to his beach house on Bimini island, in the Bahamas. The fact that Powell made many of the trips with a female staff member, Corinne A. Huff, who was not his wife, also embarrassed Congressmen.

Over the years, coupled with publicity about Powell's travels was publicity about his unusually high House absentee record.

Tax Problems. Powell in 1958 was indicted on three counts of tax evasion by a federal grand jury. In 1960, two counts were dismissed and the trial on the remaining count ended in a hung jury. The Federal Government continued efforts to obtain back taxes from Powell. On June 8, 1966, Powell's attorney announced that Powell had paid $27,833.17 in back taxes and penalties and the Government had withdrawn fraud charges against him.

Libel Suits. Extensive publicity was given to two suits accusing Powell of libel and to his maneuvers to avoid paying a libel judgment. The suits were brought by Mrs. Esther James, a Harlem widow, whom Powell—in a March 6, 1960, television interview—described as a "bag woman," or graft collector, for New York City police. Mrs. James pursued Powell relentlessly through the courts in an effort to collect the judgment. By the end of 1966, Powell had been held in contempt of court on four separate occasions—three times for civil contempt and once for criminal contempt. He ultimately satisfied the civil judgments against him, but the criminal contempt case was still in the courts in mid-1969.

Nepotism. From the time of their marriage in December 1960 Powell employed his Puerto Rican wife—Yvette Marjorie Flores—as a paid member of his own Congressional office staff. She remained in Puerto Rico after the birth of a son in 1962, but continued to draw a $20,578 annual salary as a clerk whose job was to answer mail to Spanish-speaking constituents. The House in 1964 had adopted a resolution (H Res 294) aimed specifically at that situation; it forbade Members from hiring employees who did not work either in the Member's home district or in Washington, D.C. That provision was readopted as part of the Legislative Branch appropriation (PL 89-90) in 1965. Mrs. Powell, however, remained in Puerto Rico.

Civil Rights. Powell's civil rights stands at times got him into trouble with both liberals and conservatives. He spoke out frequently in favor of "black power" and criticized the national civil rights leadership for cooperating too much with whites. He failed to vote on the civil rights bills of 1965 and 1966. Before that, he had helped kill several liberal-backed bills when he insisted on stringent antidiscrimination riders. Such riders became known as the Powell amendment.

Tactics as Committee Chairman. As chairman of the Education and Labor Committee, Powell angered Congressmen and organized labor by delaying Committee action on bills or by "ransoming" bills in return for House action on other measures. In 1966 he announced that he would not call up for debate a Committee-reported bill which permitted "common-site picketing" unless certain conditions were met. They were not met, and he got the bill withdrawn from the House calendar. *(See chapter on Labor.)*

Also in 1966 Powell was considered largely responsible for a four-month delay between the time the poverty program authorization was reported and the date it came to the House floor. During June, after the bill was reported, he attended the ILO conference. He then spent most of the summer fishing off Bimini.

In Powell's absence, and in a highly unusual move, the House Rules Committee July 14, 1966, reported a resolution providing for an open rule for debate on the poverty program authorization, but not specifying that the appropriate committee chairman—in this case, Powell—would be in charge of the majority's debate. This rule had the effect of authorizing the Speaker to bypass Powell and to recognize any majority member of the Education and Labor Committee to manage debate on the bill. The Rules Committee also included a statement highly critical of Powell for refusing to appear before it. Debate on the bill was scheduled for July 20, but was postponed on the 19th. The delay continued to Sept. 26, when the House adopted the Rules Committee rule for debate. Powell, who had filed a 21-day rule in order to bypass the Rules Committee, withdrew his opposition to the Rules Committee rule and was recognized by the Speaker after its adoption. The House passed the poverty bill Sept. 29. *(See chapter on Welfare.)*

It was within that context that the members of the Education and Labor Committee quietly organized to change the rules to limit much of Powell's power as chairman.

1966 Developments

Committee Revolt. The Education and Labor Committee Sept. 22, 1966, by a 27-1 vote, adopted new Committee rules which limited Powell's power as chairman. The rules left the initiative for action with Powell in most cases, but eliminated his power to block action desired by a majority. One rule provided that if the Chairman failed to act, the six subcommittee chairmen could take the necessary steps to bring a bill to the floor for a vote. The rules provided also for the preparation of a Committee budget for each session which was to be approved by members of the majority party on the Committee. The chairman was required to submit a monthly detailed accounting of all Committee expenditures, which was then to be approved by the full Committee.

Hays Subcommittee Investigation. The protests of the Committee dissidents led the House Administration Committee's Special Subcommittee on Contracts Sept. 26 to begin an investigation of Powell's use of Committee funds. The Subcommittee, headed by Wayne L. Hays (D Ohio), between Sept. 26 and Dec. 30 held public and closed hearings. Powell refused an invitation to testify and Mrs. Powell did not answer a subpoena.

The House Administration Committee Jan. 3, 1967, approved a report containing the 12 conclusions and eight recommendations of the Hays Subcommittee. The report concluded that Powell and some members of his Committee staff had used assumed names on airline flights to cover up use of Committee funds for unofficial travel. It also found a "strong presumption" that Mrs. Powell had not performed services that entitled her to the $20,578 annual salary she received.

The Committee recommended that she be dropped from the House payroll immediately, and the action was taken Jan. 3. Other recommendations were for stronger controls over spending and travel by House committees, to be closely audited by the House Administration Committee.

1967 House Action

Removal from Chairmanship. The House Democratic Caucus, meeting in closed session Jan. 9, 1967, by voice vote removed Powell from the chairmanship of the Education and Labor Committee for the duration of the 90th Congress. The Democratic Caucus consisted of all Democratic Members of the House. Just before each Congress convened, it met to select its candidates for House offices and to designate committee chairmen.

Powell's removal resulted from adoption of a resolution which said simply that the Caucus favored naming Rep. Carl D. Perkins (D Ky.) to the chairmanship. Powell, who attended the meeting of the Caucus, described the action as "a lynching—Northern style."

Temporary Denial of Seat. On the opening day of the 90th Congress Jan. 10, the House by a 365-65 roll-call vote adopted a resolution (H Res 1) denying Powell his seat pending the result of a five-week investigation by a Special Committee. The resolution was offered by House Minority Leader Gerald R. Ford (R Mich.) as a Republican substitute for a less drastic Democratic leadership resolution. All 65 votes against H Res 1 were cast by Democrats.

That action followed rejection of the Democratic resolution by a 126-305 roll call (R 0-186; D 126-119). The Democratic resolution, offered by Rep. Morris K. Udall (D Ariz.), proposed to seat Powell pending the result of a committee investigation.

The Republican substitute, as adopted, provided that a nine-member Special Committee of House Members (five Democrats and four Republicans) was to investigate and report on Powell's "right" to be sworn in as a Member of the 90th Congress. Until Congress acted on the report of that Committee, Powell was to continue to receive his salary and to retain his staff and offices. Because the final vote on seating Powell would come before he was sworn in, the issue would be decided by a simple majority of the House. Had the Udall resolution been adopted and Powell temporarily seated, he would have been subject to the provision of the Constitution (Article I, Section 5) requiring a two-thirds vote to expel a sworn Member.

Lobby Action. The most noteworthy aspect of lobby action in the Powell affair was the lack of a concerted effort in Powell's behalf by the organized civil rights lobby. He did not receive strong backing from the movement despite the fact that in his public statements, Powell himself sought to treat the exclusion issue largely as a civil rights matter.

The lack of coordinated support seemed to be a result of two factors. First, apparently neither Powell nor civil rights leaders thought exclusion likely; this assumption

---

Precedents on Deposing Chairmen

The House and the Senate both have been reluctant to tamper with the prerogatives of seniority by removing chairmen from their positions.

The most recent precedent in the House deposing Committee chairmen came in 1925 when the 69th Congress opened. In that case, the reason was party disloyalty. John M. Nelson and Florian Lampert, both Wisconsin Republicans, were stripped of seniority rights along with the nine other members of the Wisconsin delegation, for campaigning as LaFollette Progressives in the 1924 elections. Nelson was chairman of the Committee on Elections and Lampert of the Patents Committee. All of the mavericks were stripped of their seniority and dropped to the bottom of the list or moved to less important committees.

A much earlier precedent—one not connected with party politics—was set in 1807, when John Randolph of Virginia lost the chairmanship of the Ways and Means Committee for what the records say was eccentric and arbitrary behavior. What he had done was not described, but several years later he brought a brace of hunting dogs into the chamber. Speaker Henry Clay evicted him.

---

was also held by many Democratic Members and Capitol Hill observers. Second, the Leadership Conference on Civil Rights—a coordinating body of 112 Negro, labor, religious and civic organizations—found itself so badly split on the Powell issue that a unified drive was impossible. The latter fact was itself apparently a result of Powell's erratic support of civil rights legislation.

After the Jan. 10 vote, Roy Wilkins, executive director of the National Assn. for the Advancement of Colored People (NAACP), observed: "The truth of the matter is that Powell never called on the civil rights movement. He never invited their help....Only Adam's office knew of the tremendous volume of mail received by Congressmen against Powell. If we had known this, we could have done something."

Committee Investigation, Report. The Select Committee to investigate Powell was appointed Jan. 19 by House Speaker John W. McCormack (D Mass.). Judiciary Committee Chairman Emanuel Celler (D N.Y.) was named chairman.

Powell appeared in response to a Committee invitation at a public hearing Feb. 8. On the advice of his lawyers, he responded only to questions relating to the constitutional requirements for House membership—age, citizenship and inhabitancy.

The Select Committee's Feb. 23 report recommended that Powell be sworn in as a Member of the House, but it also called for his censure for "gross misconduct" and recommended that Powell be stripped of his seniority and fined $40,000—punishments never before prescribed for a Member of Congress.

Chairman Celler said the Select Committee had not recommended expulsion because "Mr. Powell's wrongdoing does not rise to the heights of such malevolence."

Findings. Following are the Committee's major findings:

Constitutional Requirements. Powell was over 25 years of age, a citizen of the United States for over seven years and an inhabitant of the state of New York on Nov. 8, 1966 (the day he was elected to the 90th Congress). He therefore met the constitutional qualifications for membership of age, citizenship and inhabitancy, and he held a certificate of election from his state.

The Courts. Powell had "repeatedly asserted a privilege and immunity from the processes of the courts of the state of New York not authorized by the Constitution." There were outstanding against Powell, in New York courts, one criminal and two civil contempt charges for his failure to appear in court as ordered. His "contumacious conduct" towards the courts had reflected "discredit upon and (brought) into disrepute the House of Representatives and its Members."

Public Funds. As a Member of Congress and chairman of the Education and Labor Committee, Powell had "wrongfully and willfully" appropriated public funds totaling $44,934. Of the total, $44,186 was drawn between Aug. 31, 1964, and Jan. 1, 1967, as salary for Y. Marjorie Flores (Mrs. Powell) as an employee of his office staff, whereas she was "not an employee in that she performed no Congressional duties" and did not work either in Powell's New York office or in his Washington office as required by law. The remainder of the funds were used by Powell to pay for domestic help at his Bimini vacation retreat and to pay for seven airline tickets for his son, personal friends and a staff member, none of whom was on official Committee business. He also "falsely certified" for payment vouchers for travel by other members of his Committee staff "when in fact the chairman...and a female member of the staff had incurred such travel expenses as a part of their private travel to Bimini and the Bahamas." Finally, Chairman Powell "made false reports on expenditures of foreign exchange currency (counterpart funds) to the Committee on House Administration."

Failure to Testify. Powell's "refusal...to cooperate with the Select Committee and the Special Subcommittee on Contracts of the House Administration Committee in lawful inquiries authorized by the House...was contemptuous and was conduct unworthy of a Member."

Further Action. The hearings, records and report of the Select Committee were forwarded to the Justice Department "for prompt and appropriate action, with the request that the House be kept advised in the matter."

Recommendations. The resolution (H Res 278) proposed by the Committee provided that:

• Powell be permitted to take the oath and be seated as a Member of the House.

• Powell "by reason of his gross misconduct be censured and condemned" by the House.

• Powell, "as punishment," pay the Clerk of the House $40,000, to be deducted from his salary at the rate of $1,000 a month, to "offset any civil liability of Mr. Powell to the United States."

• Powell's House seniority commence as of the date he would be sworn in as a Member of the 90th Congress.

• If Powell did not take the oath of office by March 13, 1967, his seat would be declared vacant, and the Governor of New York would be notified of the vacancy.

The Committee also recommended that:

• The House direct the Clerk to terminate "forthwith" the salary payments of Corinne Huff, a Powell staff member.

• The House "make a study in depth to determine whether or not existing procedural and substantive rules

are adequate in cases involving charges of breach of public trust which have been lodged against any Member."

• The House Administration Committee be directed by the House to file annually a report of audit of expenditures by each House committee.

House Votes Exclusion. In a surprise move, the House March 1, 1967, rejected the resolution proposed by the Select Committee and instead adopted an amended version of H Res 278 which excluded Powell from membership in the 90th Congress. The House had been expected to accept the Select Committee's recommendations. Powell was not present for the 4 ½ hours of debate and the five roll-call votes.

House adoption of H Res 278, amended, was by a 307-116 roll-call vote, but this was not the decisive vote of the day. The crucial votes came—first—on a parliamentary issue which technically opened H Res 278, as reported from committee, to amendment but which had the practical effect of approving or rejecting the Committee recommendations, and—second—on a proposal by Thomas B. Curtis (R Mo.) to flatly bar Powell from the 90th Congress. It was Curtis' proposal which the House favored—by a surprisingly large margin of 72 votes—and which was the language of H Res 278 as finally approved. The action occurred March 1 as follows:

The House debated H Res 278 as reported and the issues involved in the Powell case for more than two hours. At the end of the debate, Emanuel Celler (D N.Y.), floor manager of the bill and chairman of the Select Committee on Powell, moved the previous question. This was the parliamentary device to end debate and bring the resolution, as reported, to an immediate vote without amendment. It was, in addition, the first and basic test of House sentiment toward Powell. The previous question was rejected by a 202-222 (R 71-113; D 131-109) roll-call vote; this vote opened H Res 278 to amendment.

Curtis was recognized by Speaker John W. McCormack (D Mass.). Curtis offered an amendment to H Res 278 which deleted the provisions recommended by Celler's Select Committee and instead simply stated that Powell "is excluded from membership in the 90th Congress." It also directed the Speaker to notify the New York Governor of the vacancy. After further debate, Curtis moved the previous question to cut off discussion and proceed to a vote on the substitute he had offered. The House adopted Curtis' motion, first by a 151-66 standing vote and then by a 263-161 roll call. Immediately afterward the House accepted the Curtis substitute by a **248-176** (R 125-59; D 123-117) key roll-call vote. This was the second crucial vote of the day.

H Res 278, as amended by the Curtis substitute, then was adopted by the 307-116 roll-call vote.

On the last roll call of the day, the House voted 311-9 to move the previous question on the preamble originally included in H Res 278 as reported—a section which embodied the findings of the Select Committee. The preamble was then adopted by voice vote.

In voting to prevent Powell from taking his seat, the House rejected the advice of its leadership, both Republican and Democratic. On the two decisive votes—moving the previous question on the Committee resolution and acceptance of Curtis' substitute—Majority Leader Carl Albert (D Okla.), Majority Whip Hale Boggs (D La.), Minority Leader Gerald R. Ford (R Mich.) and Minority Whip Leslie C. Arends (R Ill.) all were on the losing side.

The debate on punishing Powell involved a tangle of constitutional and parliamentary questions. Members cited portions of debate at the 1789 Constitutional Convention, the Federalist papers and dozens of examples in Cannon's and Hind's Precedents of the House of Representatives. Some Representatives argued that the House did not have the authority to bar Powell from his seat, while others contended that nothing less was acceptable because the integrity of the Congress was at issue.

Several Members referred to a heavy mail campaign on the Powell question. Most of the mail, which was described as having a racist flavor, was said to favor Powell's exclusion. After Powell's ouster, Celler said on television he "saw an element of racism in the vote...accompanied by the hysteria that had resulted from the climate of public opinion due to Mr. Powell's antics and peculiarities and swagger and defiance." When criticized for the statement by Curtis, Celler reaffirmed it on the House floor. He then referred to the mail on the issue as "uninhibited expressions of hate and vindictiveness" and said "some of the Members succumbed to the pressure of this mail."

Powell Re-Elected. In a special election held April 11 to fill the vacancy created by Powell's exclusion from the House, Powell was re-elected with 86.1 percent of the vote. Because he could not return to New York state without facing arrest on a criminal contempt charge, he did not campaign but remained at his Bimini vacation retreat.

Following his election, Powell did not attempt to take his seat but remained on Bimini while his lawsuit to overturn the earlier denial of the seat began its career in the courts.

Powell Suit for Readmission. Powell March 8, 1967, filed suit in federal district court in the District of Columbia to regain the House seat denied him March 1. The suit, *Powell v. McCormack*, was the first of its kind in the history of American law and raised constitutional issues of the highest order.

The central legal issues in the Powell suit were:

● Could the House add to the Constitution's three "qualifications" for House membership? The three were that the Member be at least 25 years old, have been a U.S. citizen for at least seven years and be, when elected, an inhabitant of the state from which he was elected.

● Could the courts properly examine the actions of the House in such cases, order the House not to add to the Constitution's qualifications, and enforce this order?

District Judge George L. Hart Jr. ruled April 7, 1967, that he had no jurisdiction in the case and dismissed the suit.

The Court of Appeals for the District of Columbia on Feb. 28, 1968, affirmed the action of the lower court in dismissing the suit. The Court of Appeals held that the lower court did have jurisdiction over the subject matter but that the case involved a political question, which, if decided, would constitute a violation of the separation of powers and produce an embarrassing confrontation between Congress and the courts.

The Supreme Court by a 7-1 vote on June 16, 1969, reversed the lower courts. Chief Justice Earl Warren, delivering the opinion of the Court, ruled that the House had improperly excluded Powell, a duly elected Representative who met the constitutional requirements of age, residence and citizenship.

Exclusion Precedents

Prior to the exclusion of Adam C. Powell, five Members-elect had been excluded from the House. They were:

John Young Brown (D Ky.)—In 1867 he was excluded from the House after an investigating committee had found that he aided the Confederacy during the Civil War. It was judged he was "not entitled" to a seat or to take the Test Oath. *(See below.)*

John D. Young (D Ky.)—In 1867 he was excluded from the House "for giving aid and comfort to the enemies of the Government." The resolution adopted by the House stated that Young was "not entitled" to a seat or to take the Test Oath. *(See below.)*

B. F. Whittemore (R S.C.)—In 1870 he was excluded from the House by a 130-76 roll-call vote after he had resigned earlier in the same session to escape expulsion proceedings against him for having sold appointments to the U.S. Military Academy. The majority report which recommended exclusion stated that "where the House has the right to expel for a violation of its rules or of some existing statute it has the same power to exclude a Member from its body."

Brigham H. Roberts (D Utah)—In 1900 Roberts was excluded from the House. Before his election he had been convicted of violating the 1882 Edmunds Act prohibiting polygamy and had served a prison term. Although the minority members of an investigating committee argued that he should be sworn and then expelled, the House, by a 268-50 roll-call vote, excluded him.

Victor L. Berger (Socialist, Wis.)—In 1919 he was excluded from the House by a 309-1 roll-call vote. He had been convicted of sedition under the wartime espionage act. Front-runner in a special election to fill the vacancy caused by his own exclusion, Berger was again denied the seat in January 1920. The Supreme Court reversed his conviction a year later, and he was elected to the House in 1922 and seated at the first session of the 68th Congress in 1923.

Test Oath

Most Congressional precedents in the Civil War and Reconstruction periods were considered not binding. However, the "iron-bound oath" of loyalty to the Federal Government, required of Members of Congress by law in 1862, was cited in three of the exclusion cases above as precedent for placing an additional qualification on Members-Elect. In the Brown and Young cases, a minority contended that the addition of a loyalty oath was contrary to the Constitution. It was argued in 1867 that "A power to add new qualifications is equivalent to a power to vary or change (the Constitutional requirements of age, citizenship and inhabitancy)." In the 1900 Roberts case, the majority report recommending exclusion stated that the precedent of the Test Oath permitted the House "by the same reasoning" to add qualifications to those prescribed in the Constitution. The Test Oath was repealed in 1884.

Powell Seated in 1969. Powell was sworn in as a Representative Jan. 3, 1969, on the opening day of the 91st Congress. He had won re-election in 1968 with 80.8 percent of the vote.

Before permitting him to be seated, however, the House by a 254-158 roll-call vote adopted a resolution (H Res 2) fining Powell $25,000, purportedly for at least partial recovery of about $40,000 in Congressional funds which Powell allegedly misused, and stripping him of seniority.

The House, in adopting H Res 2, showed that its feelings about Powell had moderated considerably since 1967. In 1969, those who were influential in developing the compromise H Res 2 never even proposed that Powell be censured, and those wanting to exclude him again were clearly a small minority.

The deciding vote came after five hours of debate and parliamentary maneuvering, during which the House took five roll calls.

There were unsuccessful efforts to seat Powell outright, a move led by Celler, and to exclude him pending an investigation, a move led by Rep. Clark MacGregor (R Minn.). Rep. H. R. Gross (R Iowa) spoke for the forces uncompromisingly opposed to the seating of Powell.

During the debate, Powell either was off the floor or waited in the back of the House chamber, smoking cigars. As soon as H Res 2 had been adopted, he walked to the well and was sworn in by the Speaker. He then held a press conference, at which he said: "I'll behave as I always have."

Dodd Censure

For the seventh time in its history, the Senate in 1967 censured one of its Members, Sen. Thomas J. Dodd (D Conn.). Dodd's troubles began in 1966, when columnists Drew Pearson and Jack Anderson charged that he had misused political campaign funds contributed to him and had committed other offenses. Dodd requested the Senate Select Committee on Standards and Conduct to investigate the charges, which it did in its first official inquiry. The Committee April 27, 1967, recommended that the Senate censure Dodd for misuse of political funds and for double-billing for official and private travel. The Senate June 23, 1967, censured Dodd on the first charge by a **92-5** roll-call vote but refused, by a 51-45 roll-call vote, to censure him on the second charge.

A summary of developments:

1966 Action

Pearson-Anderson Charges. Beginning in January 1966, Pearson and Anderson wrote frequent columns on the activities of Dodd, and Dodd on Feb. 23 asked the Senate Select Committee on Standards and Conduct to investigate their charges. On Feb. 25, Chairman John Stennis (D Miss.) announced that the Committee would consider Dodd's request.

The Pearson-Anderson columns which prompted Dodd to ask for the investigation charged that Dodd had used his position as Senator to do favors for Julius Klein, a Chicago public relations man with extensive West German

accounts. The columns also claimed that Dodd had taken favors in return from Klein and from at least one Connecticut contracting firm which Dodd had allegedly helped to get Government contracts. Subsequent columns charged Dodd with misuse of political and Senate funds.

Pearson and Anderson compiled the substance of their columns from 6,000 letters and documents from Dodd's Senate office files. The files were taken from the office between May and December 1965 by three former employees of the Senator and by the office manager, Michael V. O'Hare, who remained on the staff until Jan. 31, 1966. The others who participated in the removal of the files—which were photocopied by Pearson and Anderson and returned to the office—were James P. Boyd Jr., administrative assistant to Dodd for 12 years; Mrs. Marjorie Carpenter, personal secretary; and Miss Terry Golden, a secretary.

Hearings. The Select Committee held hearings June 22-24 and 27 and July 19 on Dodd's relationship with Klein. In a statement June 20, Chairman Stennis said the stolen documents would not be admitted as evidence; they were "stigmatized," he said.

Boyd testified June 22 that Dodd had traveled to West Germany in April 1964 ostensibly on business for the Senate Judiciary Committee. In fact, Boyd said, Dodd had made the trip at Klein's insistence to help patch up Klein's relations with some of his clients connected with the Bonn government, whom Klein was afraid he was losing. Dodd had used the Senate business explanation for his trip, Boyd maintained, as a "cover-up."

Dodd testified June 27 that he had not made the trip primarily to help Klein. He admitted having brought up the matter of Klein's accounts when he talked with West German Chancellor Konrad Adenauer. But Dodd said, "I wasn't his (Klein's) advocate or agent." The principal purpose of the trip, the Senator stated, was to check on the Communist terror apparatus by interviewing B. N. Stashynsky, a Soviet citizen imprisoned in West Germany. Dodd also denied he had ever received gifts from Klein.

Klein, in testimony July 19, said he had asked Dodd to intercede with West German officials to help save his public relations contracts in West Germany. Klein told the Committee "I have a right to ask any Senator to see anybody."

1967 Action

Hearings. The Select Committee's 1967 hearings, held March 13-17, focused on charges that Dodd had misused political funds and double-billed for his travel. Before the hearings began, Dodd and the Committee agreed to and released a list of stipulations (facts agreed by both parties to be true), which included statements that funds raised at testimonial dinners for Dodd had in some cases been used for personal expenses and that there had been instances of double billing. In testimony before the Committee, Dodd contended that his continuing financial problems were well known to his constituents and that persons who bought tickets to testimonial affairs did so on the understanding that he would use the money as he saw fit. Dodd also denied that he had ordered members of his office staff to bill twice for trips he made. Michael V. O'Hare, Dodd's former office manager, had testified that Dodd had ordered the double billing. Dodd called O'Hare's testimony "a sickening experience."

"My conscience is clear," Dodd said. "I do not believe that anybody can look me in the eye and say I did wrong."

Committee Report. The Select Committee April 27 reported a resolution (S Res 112) censuring Dodd for "his conduct which is contrary to accepted morals, derogates from the public trust expected of a Senator and tends to bring the Senate into dishonor and disrepute."

Specifically, the resolution censured Dodd for "exercising the influence and power of his office as a United States Senator" from 1961-65 to "obtain, and use for his personal benefit, funds from the public through political testimonials and a political campaign" and "to request and accept reimbursements for expenses from both the Senate and private organizations for the same travel."

In its report, the Committee drew the following major conclusions as the basis for its recommendation:

Testimonials. Dodd or his representatives received a total of $450,273 from seven testimonial events between 1961 and 1965 and from contributions to the Senator's re-election campaign. Of the sum, Dodd used "at least" $116,083 for personal expenses. Dodd "exercised the influence and power of his office as a U.S. Senator to directly or indirectly obtain funds from the public through testimonials which were political in character....Not one solicitation letter, invitation, ticket...or other written communication informed the public that the funds were to be used for personal purposes." Sponsors of a 1961 dinner in Hartford represented the affair as a "testimonial dinner" for the Senator "without stating any further purpose." The six other events were represented, in either sponsors' solicitation letters or in contemporary press reports, as being held for "political campaign purposes." Because of "the preoccupation of the organizers with Sen. Dodd's apparently political indebtedness, and the partisan political nature of the printed programs, Sen. Dodd's knowledge of the political character of these events must be presumed."

Double Billing. On seven trips between 1961 and 1965 Dodd "requested and accepted reimbursements from both the Senate and private organizations for the same travel." (In 1963 and 1964, the Committee noted, Dodd had made six other trips, none of them official, for which he was reimbursed from both his political campaign funds and private sources.)

Relations with Klein. The "relationship of Sen. Dodd with Julius Klein was indiscreet and beyond the responsibilities of a Senator to any citizen," but there was not "sufficient evidence of wrongdoing" to warrant disciplinary action by the Senate. Beyond "repeated use" by Dodd of a hotel suite Klein rented in New York City, the Committee could not establish the "validity" of evidence that Dodd had accepted favors from Klein for performing services. "With the exception of Sen. Dodd's admission that he briefly mentioned...Klein" to West German Chancellor Konrad Adenauer during his trip to Germany in 1964, "there is no direct evidence that...Dodd intervened with German officials or clients of Klein in Klein's behalf." Evidence "suggested" that Dodd made the trip under Klein's influence, but because of the recent death of Adenauer and the unavailability of other evidence, the Committee "could not pursue this phase of the case further." The Committee noted that Dodd did not file a report on his interview with a Soviet spy—which he said was the purpose of the trip—until 11 months after he returned from

Censure Procedures Contrasted

The two censure proposals of 1967—the Senate resolution to censure Thomas J. Dodd (D Conn.) and the plan, rejected by the House in March, to censure Adam C. Powell (D N.Y.)—illustrated the vast differences in the procedures used by the two chambers in punishing Members. The oddity of a censure proceeding in each chamber in the same year highlighted these differences. Before 1967, only six Senators, 17 Representatives and one Delegate had been censured.

The Senate's courtly observance of the accused Member's privilege contrasted sharply with the tradition of the House, where a censured Member is treated like a felon hearing his sentence pronounced by a judge. Even this harshness was not enough for the House when it considered Powell's case; censure was rejected in favor of the stiffer penalty of exclusion.

Senate. By tradition, Senate censure proceedings were carried out with the moderation which earned that body its reputation as a private gentlemen's club. The accused Senator was considered equal in privilege to his colleagues before and after the censure vote. He had the choice of being present or not, and he was always granted the privilege of debate. The only formal announcement of censure came when the tally clerk stated that the censure resolution had been adopted. After the vote was taken, the issue was closed. Though he suffered the condemnation of his colleagues, the censured Senator suffered no further punishment such as loss of seniority or committee assignments.

The six men censured by the Senate before 1967, the date of the action and the cause were:

Senator	Date	Cause
Timothy Pickering (Fed.Mass.)	1811	Security breach
Benjamin Tappan (D Ohio)	1844	Security breach
Benjamin R. Tillman (D S.C.)	1902	Assault
John L. McLaurin (D S.C.)	1902	Assault
Hiram L. Bingham (R Conn.)	1929	Unethical acts
Joseph R. McCarthy (R Wis.)	1954	Abuse of Senators

Only two of the six—Pickering and Tillman—were re-elected following their censure.

House. As in the Senate, most accused House Members had the choice of being present for the debate on the censure resolution or not. In Powell's case, he was allowed to speak in his own defense, but many other Members were denied this privilege. In most instances, if the censure resolution was adopted, the Member was in effect under arrest until the Speaker "pronounced" censure. Almost all the resolutions after 1875 included a dramatic injunction that the Member "be brought to the bar of the House in the custody of the Sergeant-at-Arms and there publicly censured by the Speaker in the name of the House." The Powell censure resolution which the House rejected included this clause as well as a course of action unprecedented in House tradition: a requirement that he pay a $40,000 fine and a provision stripping him of his 22-year seniority.

The House by 1967 had censured 17 Members and one Delegate. Ten of the 18 were re-elected.

Germany, and the report "contained little that was not available to him before the trip."

Referral of Possible Violations. The Committee referred the following matters, revealed during the investigation, to the Justice Department to be reviewed "for possible violations of law": an $8,000 International Latex Corp. contribution to Dodd in 1964 and the loan of three cars to the Senator by Connecticut businessman David P. Dunbar. The Committee referred to the Internal Revenue Service the following: the International Latex contribution, which the corporation had listed as an "industrial relations expense"; the taxability of campaign funds received by Dodd and used for personal purposes; and the taxability of funds received by the Senator from the seven testimonial events.

Removal of Dodd's Files. In a supplement to the report, the Committee concluded that Dodd's four former employees "collaborated" in removing filed documents from Dodd's office.

The Committee noted that it had agreed not to accept the photocopied documents as evidence and instead had uncovered evidence in the Dodd case by separate investigations. The Committee said the theft and return of the files "constitutes a breach of the relationship of trust between a Senator and his staff (and) is an invasion of... privileged communications between a Senator and his correspondents." Since all four responsible for the removal of the files were no longer employed by the Senate, the Committee said disciplinary action against them by the Senate was impossible. It referred the thefts to the Justice Department.

Senate Votes Censure. The Senate June 23, by a 92-5 roll-call vote, censured Dodd for using political funds for his personal benefit. Dodd thus became the seventh Member in the history of the Senate to suffer official censure.

Prior to final action on the censure resolution (S Res 112), the Senate, by a key **92-5** roll-call vote, agreed to the first count of the resolution, censuring Dodd for his misuse of political funds. It then voted, 51-45, to strike out the double-billing charge from the resolution as reported by the Select Committee.

Adoption of S Res 112 followed nine days of debate and six roll-call votes. Dodd's side of the case was defended in emotional speeches by the Senator himself and in remarks by his self-appointed defense attorney, Sen. Russell B. Long (D La.). Proposals by Long and John G. Tower (R Texas) to soften the language of the censure resolutions were defeated by wide margins.

The 92-5 roll calls on approval of the fund misuse section and on final adoption of S Res 112 were identical. On both of these roll calls, Dodd voted "no." Joining him were Long, Tower, Strom Thurmond (R S.C.) and Dodd's Connecticut colleague Abraham A. Ribicoff (D). Dodd was the first of the seven censured Senators to vote on the outcome of his own case.

Provisions. As adopted by the Senate, S Res 112:

Declared it the judgment of the Senate that Sen. Dodd, "for having engaged in a course of conduct...from 1961 to 1965 of exercising the influence and power of his office as a United States Senator...to obtain, and use for his personal benefit, funds from the public through political testimonials and a political campaign, deserves the censure of the Senate; and he is so censured for his conduct, which is contrary to accepted morals, derogates

from the public trust expected of a Senator, and tends to bring the Senate into dishonor and disrepute."

Long Investigation

In 1967, the Senate Select Committee on Standards and Conduct investigated charges that Sen. Edward V. Long (D Mo.) had used his position to aid imprisoned Teamster Union President James R. Hoffa and had accepted fees for his efforts from one of Hoffa's lawyers.

The investigation of Long's activities was generated by a *Life* magazine story in the issue of May 26, 1967, contending that Long, chairman of the Senate Judiciary Subcommittee on Administrative Practice and Procedure, had misused his investigating Subcommittee "first as an instrument for trying to keep Jimmy Hoffa out of prison; subsequently, for trying to get Hoffa's conviction reversed."

To support its charge, *Life* said that Long was paid $48,000 for legal services by Morris A. Shenker, a close personal friend and chief counsel for Teamster President James R. Hoffa, during 1963 and 1964, the years immediately preceding the opening of Long's Senate hearings on invasion of privacy. The payments for legal services were made, the magazine said, despite the fact that the Senator said he had not practiced law since the mid-1950s.

Life charged that Long was "strongly influenced" to take up his Subcommittee probe of Government investigative practices, including wiretapping, by friends high in the hierarchy of the Teamsters Union. *(For privacy hearings, see chapter on Civil Liberties and Internal Security.)*

Select Committee Chairman John Stennis (D Miss.) announced Oct. 25 that the Committee had voted unanimously to exonerate Long of the *Life* charges. The Committee's report said the cases referred to Shenker's firm, for which Long received referral fees, "had no relationship whatsoever to Mr. Hoffa or the Teamsters Union." *Life* then carried another article calling the Committee findings a "whitewash" and claiming that "far from exonerating Long, they brought even more ominous questions about Long's connections and his sources of income."

Long himself defended the legal fees received from Shenker in telling the Senate May 23, 1967, that "some people apparently value my legal advice and are willing to pay for it." And he stated that "not a cent of these legal fees has come either directly or indirectly from Jimmy Hoffa."

Long ran for re-election to the Senate in 1968 but was defeated in the primary.

Gallagher Charges

The House Committee on Standards of Official Conduct did not investigate 1968 charges by *Life* magazine that Rep. Cornelius E. Gallagher (D N.J.) was a "tool and collaborator" of Joseph Zicarelli, a reputed Mafia figure in New Jersey. *Life* also linked Gallagher with another reputed Mafia figure, Harold Konigsberg.

In a subsequent *Life* article, Gallagher was charged with receiving legal fees in 1962-63 from Anthony "Tino" DeAngelis. In 1965 DeAngelis was convicted of fraud and conspiracy in a $150-million salad oil swindle and was sentenced to 20 years' imprisonment.

Gallagher called the allegation contained in the first article a "monstrous lie." He declared that he was the "victim of a malicious assault by a mammoth publishing empire." After the second article he added that "all through this campaign they *(Life)* have had their tools, collaborators and lackeys harassing my family, my friends and myself as well as the voters of this district."

Despite Gallagher's statement that he would welcome a Congressional investigation of the charges, the Committee on Standards of Official Conduct took no action. Committee Chairman Melvin Price (D Ill.) said "there was no proof of any violation of the code (of ethics) which the Committee had adopted." Gallagher easily won re-election to the House in 1968.

House "Ghost" Voting

A controversy over "ghost" voting in the House arose in 1968 following newspaper reports of alleged irregularities in some House roll-call voting procedures.

The House Committee on Standards of Official Conduct on Oct. 1 authorized a preliminary inquiry into the charges. The Committee action came after Speaker John W. McCormack (D Mass.) requested it to consider allegations involving Rep. Bob Wilson (R Calif.) and two House employees, tally clerk Thomas Cooke and Republican pair clerk Walter Kennedy. House voting records had shown Wilson voting on six roll-call votes taken Sept. 9, 10 and 16, when he was in California. A newspaper reporter who knew that Wilson had been in California on the dates in question asked House Clerk W. Pat Jennings Sept. 17 why Wilson was recorded as having voted. Jennings began to look into the incidents the next day. On Sept. 19, Wilson requested from the House (and was granted) permission to have the voting records changed to show that he had not been present Sept. 9, 10 and 16. On Sept. 23, after talking with Cooke, who had been the tally clerk on the days of the voting incidents, Jennings relieved Cooke of his tally duties.

Summarizing the findings of his inquiry, Jennings wrote McCormack that Cooke said he had marked Wilson "present and voting in order to 'help out at the request of Walter Kennedy.' " Kennedy on Sept. 30 told newsmen, "I made no such request."

As the Committee met Oct. 1, Wilson wrote Chairman Melvin Price (D Ill.), "I have no idea how these errors occurred." In addition, Wilson said he would pledge his "fullest cooperation in this investigation."

In an Oct. 11 speech to the House, Wilson said: "I would hope that this matter could be resolved at the earliest possible moment, not only because of the unfortunate timing and subsequent political implications but primarily because of my understandable personal concern that my integrity as a Member of Congress has been challenged before this great body."

Staff members of the House Committee on Standards of Official Conduct began an investigation of the voting discrepancies, and in a staff report to Committee Chairman Melvin Price Nov. 1 stated that "to date absolutely no evidence whatsoever has been disclosed that any of the Members of Congress...either directly or indirectly caused improper recording of their votes in the House." The report added that it was at that time "impossible to reach

a final conclusion as to the specific cause or causes of the tally discrepancies," and that the investigation would continue.

After the Wilson investigation had begun, there were reports of a few other cases in which Representatives were recorded as present and voting when in fact they were absent. CQ records showed that most roll-call vote corrections are made because Members of Congress are recorded as having not voted when in fact they had voted, rather than as having voted when they had not been present.

Chronology

Of Legislation

On Congress

1965

House Rules Change

On the opening day of the 89th Congress, Jan. 4, 1965, House Democrats succeeded in changing the House rules to curb the power of the Rules Committee.

The most important of the new rules, the 21-day rule, limited the Committee's power to bottle up legislation through refusal to grant a rule for floor consideration. The 21-day rule provided a method by which a legislative committee could circumvent the Rules Committee and bring its bill directly to the House floor. The 21-day rule was abandoned in 1967. *(See below.)*

The second rules change curbed the Committee's power to block a conference on a bill passed by the Senate and House in different versions. The new rule made it possible to send a bill to conference by majority vote of the House. Under the old rules, bills usually were sent to conference either by unanimous consent or by House adoption of a resolution reported by the Rules Committee.

A third rules change removed the power of a single House Member to delay final action on a bill.

Background. Adoption of the 21-day rule was the latest in a series of steps to curb the power of the Rules Committee, where for many years conservative Southern Democrats and Republicans had been in a position to block or delay legislation sought by the Democratic majority. The House had adopted a 21-day rule in 1949, but it was repealed in 1951 after the Democrats lost 29 seats in the 1950 elections.

At the beginning of the Kennedy Administration in 1961, House Democrats, led by then Speaker Sam Rayburn (D Texas 1913-61), enlarged the membership of the Committee and filled the new seats in such a way as to give Administration supporters a one-vote majority. But Administration forces on the Committee did not always

Record of Long Sessions

The first session of the 90th Congress (1967), which lasted 340 days, was one of the longest sessions in recent years. Comparative figures for the other sessions of the 1965-68 period: 89th Congress, first session (1965)—293 days; 89th Congress, second session (1966)—286 days; 90th Congress, second session (1968)—274 days (the shortest session since 1961). Below are the 20 longest sessions in the history of Congress.

Congress	Session	Convened	Adjourned	No. of days
76th	3rd	Jan. 3, 1940-Jan. 3, 1941		366
77th	1st	Jan. 3, 1941-Jan. 2, 1942		365
81st	2nd	Jan. 3, 1950-Jan. 2, 1951		365[1]
80th	2nd	Jan. 6, 1948-Dec. 31, 1948		361[2]
88th	1st	Jan. 9, 1963-Dec. 30, 1963		356
65th	2nd	Dec. 3, 1917-Nov. 21, 1918		354
79th	1st	Jan. 3, 1945-Dec. 21, 1945		353[3]
80th	1st	Jan. 3, 1947-Dec. 19, 1947		351[4]
78th	1st	Jan. 6, 1943-Dec. 21, 1943		350[5]
77th	2nd	Jan. 5, 1942-Dec. 16, 1942		346
40th	2nd	Dec. 2, 1867-Nov. 10, 1868		345[6]
78th	2nd	Jan. 10, 1944-Dec. 19, 1944		345[7]
90th	1st	Jan. 10, 1967-Dec. 15, 1967		340
83rd	2nd	Jan. 6, 1954-Dec. 2, 1954		331[8]
63rd	2nd	Dec. 1, 1913-Oct. 24, 1914		328
50th	1st	Dec. 5, 1887-Oct. 20, 1888		321
51st	1st	Dec. 2, 1889-Oct. 1, 1890		304
31st	1st	Dec. 3, 1849-Sept. 30, 1850		302
89th	1st	Jan. 4, 1965-Oct. 23, 1965		293
67th	2nd	Dec. 5, 1921-Sept. 22, 1922		292

1 Congress recessed from Sept. 23 to Nov. 27.
2 Congress recessed from June 20 to July 26 and Aug. 7 to Dec. 31.
3 The House was in recess from July 21 to Sept. 5 and the Senate from Aug. 1 to Sept. 5.
4 Congress recessed from July 27 to Nov. 17.
5 Congress recessed from July 8 to Sept. 14.
6 No business was transacted after July 27. Congress took three recesses between July 27 and Nov. 10.
7 Congress recessed from April 1 to 12, June 23 to Aug. 1 and Sept. 21 to Nov. 14.
8 The House adjourned sine die on Aug. 20. The Senate was in recess from Aug. 20 to Nov. 8 and from Nov. 18 to Nov. 29, and adjourned sine die on Dec. 2.

hold together, and several Administration bills were lost as a result. *(Congress and the Nation, Vol. I, p. 1424.)*

House Action. The House Jan. 4, by voice vote, adopted a resolution (H Res 8) reinstituting the rules of the 88th Congress with an amendment incorporating the three rule changes, which had been approved by the Democratic Caucus two days earlier.

The decisive vote came on a motion to consider the previous question, thereby preventing amendments and ending debate on the resolution. The motion was adopted by a **224-202** key roll-call vote (D 208-79; R 16-123). Southern Democrats cast 75 of the Democratic "nay" votes. The roll call was closer than had been generally expected in the heavily Democratic House (the line-up: 295-140).

Provisions. H Res 8 adopted the House rules of the 88th Congress for use in the 89th Congress, with the following changes:

21-Day Rule. The most important of the new rules was the 21-day procedure whereby a chairman, or any other member, of a committee which had favorably re-

ported a bill could bring a rule (permitting House action on the bill) directly to the floor for adoption by a majority vote. This was permitted on the second or fourth Monday of the month, if the Rules Committee had not granted clearance for the bill within 21 calendar days after a resolution to call up the bill had been filed by the legislative committee. Discretion remained with the Speaker to recognize the member from the committee, so that it was highly unlikely, if not impossible, for a bill to come up successfully through this procedure without leadership approval.

The 1965 version of the 21-day rule differed in this respect from the 1949 version. The 1949 rule required the Speaker to recognize the Member who was calling up a 21-day resolution.

Conference Rule. The second rule adopted permitted the Speaker, at his discretion, to recognize a Member to offer a motion that would permit the sending of a bill to conference by majority vote. The action had first to be approved by the committee with jurisdiction over the bill. Previously, to send a bill to conference with the Senate required either unanimous consent of the House or majority consent to a rule obtained from the Rules Committee. In the absence of a rule or unanimous consent, the only other way to send a bill to conference was under suspension of the rules, which required approval by a two-thirds majority. This method was seldom used.

Engrossing a Bill. The third rules change removed the power of a single Member to demand an engrossed copy of a bill before it was passed. This is the final copy of a bill with the text as amended by floor action and certified by the Clerk of the House. Members opposed to a bill sometimes demanded an engrossed copy to delay action, usually overnight, while it was printed.

Use of 21-Day Rule. The 21-day rule was employed successfully only eight times in the 89th Congress: six times in 1965 and twice in 1966. However, most observers believed that the threat of its use was instrumental in bringing about the release of other bills from the Rules Committee. In four cases in 1966, for example, the Committee granted regular rules to bills after a 21-day rule resolution had been filed but not voted upon.

Senate Cloture Rule

Following a biennial pattern, a bipartisan group of liberal Senators attempted in 1965 to ease the Senate cloture rule (Rule 22), and once again the effort failed. Rule 22 was supposed to provide a means of limiting debate and choking off filibusters.

The 1965 fight was expected to produce a filibuster as in previous years. But the prospect of a long debate that would have tied up action on President Johnson's legislative program was averted when two resolutions aimed at easing Rule 22 were referred to the Rules and Administration Committee Jan. 8 after only two days' debate. The Committee reported the resolutions adversely March 9, ending the 1965 fight.

The most recent revision of Rule 22 occurred in 1959. It provided for limitation of debate by vote of two-thirds of the Senators present and voting, two days after a cloture petition was submitted by 16 Senators. Thereafter, debate was limited to one hour for each Senator on the bill itself and on all amendments and motions affecting it. No new amendments could be offered except by unanimous consent. Amendments that were not germane to the pending business, and amendments and motions clearly designed to delay action, were out of order. The rule applied both to ordinary business and to motions to change the Senate rules. *(Congress and the Nation, Vol. I, p. 1426.)*

Liberal Senators, whose chief purpose in trying to ease Rule 22 was to make passage of civil rights legislation easier, found in 1964 and 1965 that they had the votes to impose cloture on civil rights bills even under the two-thirds majority requirement of the existing rule. In 1964 the Senate voted for cloture to shut off debate on the Civil Rights Act. On May 25, 1965, a cloture motion limited debate on the Administration-backed voting rights bill (S 1564). These were the first times in the history of Rule 22 that cloture was successfully invoked to close off debate on civil rights legislation. *(For listing of cloture votes, see chapter on Civil Rights.)*

The 1965 attempt to liberalize Rule 22 was marked by little bitterness compared with former efforts. Having discovered that it was possible to impose cloture on civil rights legislation under the existing rule, liberal Senators in 1965 waged their war against the rule less vigorously than in other years.

Legislative Reorganization

Congress in 1965 established a Joint Committee on the Organization of the Congress to study the operation and organization of Congress. Establishment of the Committee represented the first major attempt at Congressional reform since the Legislative Reorganization Act of 1946. *(Congress and the Nation, Vol. I, p. 1408, 1418.)*

The membership of the Joint Committee was set at 12, evenly divided between the Senate and House members. The resolution (S Con Res 2) establishing the Committee gave it specific authority to study and make recommendations on a variety of subjects, including the relationship between the two chambers and between Congress and other branches of Government; the employment and pay of Members of Congress and Congressional employees; and the structure of and relationship between committees.

There was little opposition to establishment of the Joint Committee, but certain Members of both chambers failed in attempts to remove a provision prohibiting any recommendations by the Committee on the rules, parliamentary procedure, practices and precedents of the Senate or the House. The Committee, however, in an April 13 statement interpreting the scope of its authority, noted that the same restriction had been placed on the 1945 Joint Committee that wrote the Legislative Reorganization Act of 1946. The statement also disclosed that the Committee felt the restriction applied "only to the recommendations the Committee could make" and not "to the scope of the study authorized."

Sen. A. S. Mike Monroney (D Okla.), cosponsor of the 1946 Act, was named co-chairman of the 1965 Joint Committee along with Rep. Ray J. Madden (D Ind.), a close associate of House Speaker John W. McCormack (D Mass.). Although Sen. Monroney's credentials as a reform architect were well established, a number of prime reform backers, including Sen. Joseph S. Clark (D Pa.), Rep. Richard Bolling (D Mo.) and Rep. Chet Holifield (D Calif.),

---

Mississippi Representatives Challenged

The House in 1965 rejected a challenge to the seating of the entire five-man Mississippi House delegation. The challenge, prepared by the Mississippi Freedom Democratic Party (MFDP), was based on the contention that eligible Negroes had been systematically excluded from participation in the 1964 election.

The MFDP was formed in 1964 with the initial purpose of challenging the seating of the all-white regular Democratic Mississippi delegation to the 1964 Democratic National Convention. *(Congress and the Nation, Vol. I, p. 57.)*

The MFDP had attempted to place three House candidates on the ballot in the regular November 1964 Mississippi election. When that failed, the MFDP sponsored its own extra-legal election. It then declared its own candidates duly elected; however, Gov. Paul B. Johnson (D) issued certificates of election to the regularly elected candidates.

When the 89th Congress convened Jan. 4, 1965, the three MFDP contestants for Mississippi seats were barred from the House floor, and the House voted to seat the regular delegation.

Subsequently the MFDP presented a formal challenge, and after months of delay the House Administration Committee by a 19-5 vote on Sept. 15, reported a resolution (H Res 585) recommending rejection of the petition to unseat the Mississippi delegation. The House adopted the resolution Sept. 17 on a 228-143 roll-call vote. The vote breakdown: R 87-34; D 141-109 (ND 54-109; SD 87-0).

Other Seating Challenges. In addition to the 1965 challenge to the seating of the Mississippi delegation, the House in 1965 and 1967 rejected four other seating challenges. The 1965 challenges involved Reps. Richard L. Ottinger (D N.Y.) and H. R. Gross (R Iowa); the 1967 challenges involved Reps. Benjamin B. Blackburn (R Ga.) and Fletcher Thompson (R Ga.).

---

were not named to the Committee. However, two of the Republicans who had strongly supported reform in recent years, Rep. Thomas B. Curtis (R Mo.) and Sen. Clifford P. Case (R N.J.), were given Committee seats.

The Committee held hearings on Congressional reform between May 10 and Sept. 23, taking testimony first from Members of Congress and then from political scientists, representatives of various organizations and persons with special interests in or knowledge of reform.

The Committee filed its report in 1966. The Senate in 1967 passed a bill embodying most of the Committee's recommendations, but the House never acted on it. *(See below.)*

Members' Allowances

Congress in 1965, in the legislative appropriations bill for fiscal 1966 (HR 8775—PL 89-90) and in three separate bills, increased Members' allowances for travel, telephone service, postage and maintaining offices in their home states or districts. The House, but not the Senate, pro-

---

Party Disloyalty

House Democrats in 1965 punished two of their members for party disloyalty in the 1964 campaign. It was the first such action since 1911.

By a secret ballot of 157-115, the Democratic Caucus voted Jan. 2 to censure two Southern party members, John Bell Williams (Miss.) and Albert W. Watson (S.C.), for publicly supporting the Republican Presidential candidate in the 1964 election. Both men were stripped of seniority rights but continued to be recognized as Democrats.

Watson lost little seniority, but Williams, a Member since 1947, lost his place as second-ranking Democrat on the Interstate and Foreign Commerce Committee. He would have succeeded to the chairmanship in 1966, upon the retirement of Oren Harris (D Ark.), if he had retained his seniority.

Watson on Jan. 12 switched to the Republican party and later resigned in order to seek election as a Republican. In a special election June 15, he defeated his Democratic opponent to become the first Republican to win a South Carolina House seat since the Reconstruction era. He was re-elected in 1966 and 1968.

Williams in 1966 won re-election to the 90th Congress as a Democrat, but the Democratic Caucus on Feb. 1, 1967, refused to restore his seniority. He resigned from the Caucus and refused to accept committee assignments. Subsequently, he ran for Governor of Mississippi and, following his election to that post, resigned from the House Jan. 16, 1968.

---

vided funds to permit its Members to hire college students for a summer Congressional "intern" program.

HOME OFFICES. The legislative appropriations bill raised from $600 to $1,200 annually the rental allowance a Senator could receive for an office in his home state when suitable space was not available in a post office or other federal building. Later in 1965 the House passed a bill increasing from $1,200 to $2,400 a year the total amount allowed a Representative for rental of either one or two offices in his home district. When the Senate considered the bill, it made the same provisions applicable to Senators (HR 10014—PL 89-211).

TRIPS HOME. Allowances for Senators' trips home during a Congressional session were increased from two to six in the legislative appropriations bill. House Members' compensable round trips were increased from three to five by HR 9947 (PL 89-147). The bill also provided an optional formula whereby Members from districts within commuting distance of Washington, D.C., could elect to take a lump sum of $300 instead of actual payments for the five trips.

A Senate amendment to HR 9947 repealed a prohibition in existing law against payment of travel expenses to Senators returning to their home states and to Representatives returning to their districts unless the trips were (1) specifically authorized by law, (2) for official participation in the funeral of a deceased Member, or (3) for official business while Congress was not in session. The provision, which was adopted in 1960 as an anti-junket device, was considered unfair since it prohibited travel payments, for example, to a Member attending committee hearings in his own district. *(Congress and the Nation, Vol. I, p. 1430.)*

HR 9947 allowed round trips to a Member's district for two staff members once or for one staff member twice in a calendar year, while the legislative appropriations raised to six (instead of four) the number of paid trips for the staffs of Senators from the six states with a population of 10 million or more.

TELEPHONES, POSTAGE. House Members received a 20-percent increase in the amount of charges for long-distance calls for which they could be reimbursed from Government funds (in HR 10139—PL 89-131). Senators received similar increases in the legislative appropriations bill, plus raises in their postage allowances.

SUMMER INTERNS. The House June 16, by a 229-153 roll-call vote, adopted a resolution (H Res 416) permitting each Representative to hire a college student for two and a half months in the summer at a salary of $300 per month. The Senate failed to act on a similar measure (S Res 139) for employment of summer interns by Senators. (The intern program was canceled in 1967. *See below.*)

Other Action

HOUSE DISTRICT STANDARDS. For the first time in 54 years, Congress in 1965 seriously considered proposed legislation to set population standards for U.S. House districts. The House on March 16 passed a bill (HR 5505), sponsored by Judiciary Committee Chairman Emanuel Celler (D N.Y.), setting at 15 percent the maximum permissible deviation from a state's average Congressional district population. Later in the year, the Senate Judiciary Committee approved an amended version of the bill which reduced the maximum variation to 10 percent. There was no further action on the bill. *(For 1967 action, see below.)*

Celler had been pressing for district standards legislation for 12 years. His case was strengthened by the 1964 Supreme Court decision in *Wesberry v. Sanders.* *(See chapter on Election Law.)*

MADISON MEMORIAL LIBRARY. Congress in 1965 authorized a third building for the Library of Congress, to be named in honor of James Madison, fourth President of the United States. The final version of the legislation (S J Res 69—PL 89-260) contained a House provision authorizing construction of the library by the Capitol Architect. The Senate version would have entrusted the construction to the General Services Administration. The Senate bill reflected criticism of recent construction by Capitol Architect J. George Stewart. *(Congress and the Nation, Vol. I, p. 1428.)*

Congress subsequently denied funds for the proposed library. *(See 1967 chronology, below.)*

JOINT BUDGET COMMITTEE. The Senate passed a bill (S 2) Jan. 27 to establish a Joint Committee on the Budget, with membership drawn from the Senate and House Appropriations Committees. It was the seventh time since 1952 that the Senate had passed such legislation, but the House never approved it. *(Congress and the Nation, Vol. I, p. 1423.)* The Senate passed an identical bill in 1967. *(See below.)*

1966

Legislative Reorganization

The Joint Committee on the Organization of the Congress on July 28 reported its recommendations for Congressional reform. Bills embodying the recommendations were introduced in both chambers but there was no floor action on them during the remainder of the 89th Congress. Similar legislation was passed by the Senate in 1967, but the House did not act on it. *(See below.)*

Major recommendations included: a committee "bill of rights" to curtail the power of House and Senate committee chairmen; realignment of existing committees and creation of several new ones; revision of committee procedures to make committee sessions open to the public more often and to make the results of committee action, such as votes on amendments and bills, available to the public; limitations on Senate committee assignments designed to decrease the workload of individual Senators; alteration of the Congressional work schedule to provide for five-day work weeks and mandatory August vacations; removal of certain positions, such as postmasters, from patronage status; steps for improved Congressional evaluation of the Budget; and strengthening of the federal lobbying law.

The Committee provided the following summary of its recommendations:

Committee procedures should be strengthened to provide:

1. For a committee "bill of rights" to give a majority of the committee the right to call meetings, to eliminate proxy voting, and to give a majority the right to require a chairman to report legislation.

2. That committee *hearings* should be public to the maximum extent possible and may be broadcast or televised at the option of the committee.

3. That committee *meetings* should also be open except for necessary executive sessions, and results of all committee action should be made public.

4. That the Legislative Reference Service prepare concise legislative histories of bills scheduled for hearings.

5. That committee hearings should be announced publicly at least two weeks in advance and witnesses should submit written statements at least two days in advance of their appearance.

6. That the minority be given at least one day to call witnesses of its choice.

7. That daily summaries of hearing testimony should be prepared by staff.

8. That committee reports should be circulated among all Members at least two days prior to filing with the opportunity for submission of supplementary and minority views. Floor votes should not be taken until committee reports and hearings have been available for at least three days.

9. That committees should be permitted to conduct hearings during floor sessions by consent of the majority and minority leadership and should schedule their business on a 5-day work week.

10. That subcommittees should follow the rules of their parent committees and should be funded by a single annual resolution of the full committee.

Committee jurisdictions should be realigned by:

1. Division of the House Committee on Education and Labor into a Committee on Education and a Committee on Labor and Public Welfare and creation of a Senate Committee on Education with redefinition of the jurisdiction of the Senate Committee on Labor and Public Welfare.

2. Redesignation of the Senate Aeronautical and Space Sciences Committee as the Committee on Science and Astronautics and expansion and redefinition of the jurisdictions of the Science and Astronautics Committees of both houses.

3. Redesignation of the House and Senate Banking and Currency Committees as the Committees on Banking, Housing and Urban Affairs.

4. Creation of a Senate Committee on Veterans' Affairs.

Committee assignments of Senators should be limited to:

1. Membership on two major committees and one minor, joint, select, or special committee.

2. Membership on not more than one of the following committees: Appropriations, Finance, Foreign Relations, and Armed Services.

3. One committee chairmanship and the chairmanship of not more than one subcommittee of any major standing committee.

Committee staff resources should be augmented by:

1. An increase of professional staff positions under the 1946 Act from four to six.

2. Assignment of two professional staff positions and one clerical position to the minority on their request, and equitable treatment to the minority in the staffing of subcommittees.

3. Authorization to employ outside consultants to supplement permanent staff.

4. Authorization to provide supplemental training or education for professional staff.

Review of the administration of existing laws should be strengthened by:

1. Redesignation of the term "oversight" to "review" for better public understanding.

2. A full-time review specialist for each standing committee in addition to other authorized professional staff.

3. An annual report on review activities by each standing committee.

4. Provision for committee hearings on major reports required of the Executive.

Conference committee procedures should be modified to provide that:

1. Senate conferees should prepare an explanatory statement in connection with the conference report.

2. The minority should have the right to half the allotted time in floor debate on the conference report.

Fiscal controls should be strengthened by:

1. The use of automatic data processing of budget information.

2. Reorganization of the General Accounting Office to participate in the establishment of a standard classification code of activities and expenditures, to assist in locating budget information, to provide expert assistance in the analysis of cost-effectiveness studies, and to prepare tabulations of budget data.

3. Improvement of the budget document to include multiple-year financial projections for ongoing programs, better descriptions of carryover balances, updating of budget summaries on June 1, and more detail on financial assumptions underlying the budget totals.

4. Requiring an appearance before the full Appropriations Committee of each house of the Director of the Bureau of the Budget, the Secretary of the Treasury, and the Chairman of the President's Council of Economic Advisers within 30 days after the submission of the budget.

5. Modifying the appropriations process to include examination of multi-agency programs, open hearings (except in national security matters), yea and nay votes on all appropriations bills, and more comprehensive reports on supplemental and deficiency bills.

6. Requiring more uniform distribution of GAO audits and reports, and reference to those reports in agency budget justifications.

7. Greater participation by the legislative committees through a projection of costs on new legislation in committee reports, review of fixed obligation and grant-in-aid programs, and authorization of programs in such a manner that they will be subject to annual appropriations review.

Office staff and allowances should be improved by:

1. Creating the position of legislative assistant for each Member.

2. Increasing the maximum allowable salary for one position on the House Member's office staff without increase in the total clerk-hire allowance.

3. Increasing the transportation allowances available to Members and Members' staffs.

4. Studying the feasibility of a Capitol-wide leased-line telephone service and consolidation of present telephone and telegraph allowances under the unit system.

The Legislative Reference Service of the Library of Congress should be strengthened by:

1. Redesignation of the Service as the Legislative Research Service.

2. Creation of a new reference division to handle routine reference inquiries.

3. Authorization to employ outside consultants and research organizations on a temporary basis.

4. Better liaison between the Service and committees of Congress.

5. Provisions for closer supervision of the Service by the Joint Committee on the Library through approval of the Director of the Service by the Joint Committee, an annual report by the Service to the Joint Committee and provision for a review specialist on the Joint Committee to oversee the Service.

6. Abolition of the Office of Coordinator of Information of the House of Representatives and the transfer of its functions to the Service.

The Congressional Record should be improved by recommendations to the Joint Committee on Printing to:

1. Limit the body of the Record to germane insertions and verbatim remarks actually delivered, with provision for special time periods during which insertions will be permitted.

2. Print nongermane debate separately in the body of the Record.

3. Utilize modern printing techniques for greater readability and more frequent indexing.

A Joint Committee on Congressional Operations should be established to:

1. Conduct a continuing study of the organization and operations of the Congress.

2. Study and recommend the use of automatic data processing for Congressional purposes.

3. Absorb the functions of the Joint Committee on Disposition of Executive Papers.

4. Identify court proceedings and actions affecting Congress as an institution and provide for appropriate legal representation.

5. Consolidate functions lending themselves to central supervision.

To deal with the problem of ethics, the House of Representatives shall:

Create a Committee on Standards and Conduct similar to the Senate Committee on Standards and Conduct.

Capitol housekeeping functions should be improved by:

1. Providing greater authority for the elected officers of each house to supervise the activities of Capitol employees under their jurisdiction.

2. Creating a professional Capitol Police force operating as a division of the Metropolitan Police Department.

3. Creating an Office of Personnel and Office Management to assist Members and committees in filling job vacancies and to render assistance on office management practices.

4. Limiting the appointment of pages to persons who have completed high school.

5. Placing the Capitol Guide Service under the Joint Committee on Congressional Operations.

6. Repealing the House Classification Act (for employees).

The Lobbying Regulation Act should be strengthened by:

1. Broadening its scope to require registration by individuals and organizations who solicit or receive funds and have influencing of legislation as a "substantial purpose."

2. A requirement for a more complete disclosure of expenditures for influencing legislation.

3. Transfer of the responsibility for the maintenance and publication of lobby registration records to the General Accounting Office.

4. Stringent requirements for disclosure of arrangements for contingent fees for purposes of influencing legislation.

Scheduling of the business of Congress should be improved by:

1. Scheduling committee and floor business on a 5-day work week.

2. Requiring a majority roll-call vote in each house to extend the session beyond July 31.

3. Providing for no session in August except in time of war.

Appointment and confirmation of postmasters and recommendation of rural carriers should be by the Post Office Department with no Congressional participation.

Four-Year House Terms

A move to extend the terms of Members of the House of Representatives from two to four years gained temporary momentum early in 1966 after President Johnson urged the extension in his State of the Union message Jan. 12. Following brief committee hearings, however, the proposal failed to emerge from the House and Senate

Amending the Constitution

An untried method of amending the Constitution came to prominence in 1967 as a result of Senate Minority Leader Everett McKinley Dirksen's (R Ill.) campaign to overturn a Supreme Court decision on apportionment of state legislatures.

• Article V of the Constitution offers two methods of proposing amendments to the Constitution, both subject to ratification by three-fourths of the states:

• "The Congress, whenever two thirds of both Houses shall deem it necessary, shall propose amendments to this Constitution...." This was the process that had always been used.

Congress, "on the application of the legislatures of two-thirds of the several states, shall call a convention for proposing amendments...."

The convention route toward amendment never had been used successfully since the Constitution was ratified in 1788, and legislation to implement it never had been enacted by Congress. There was no precedent on how Congress might convene the convention and none for setting the agenda for such a convention.

The possibility of a constitutional convention, called by Congress on application of the states, arose following the Supreme Court decision in *Baker v Carr* (1962). In that case, the Court held that the judiciary could entertain lawsuits challenging malapportionment of state legislatures. In *Reynolds v. Sims* (1964), the Court elaborated on that holding and enunciated its "one-person, one-vote" doctrine, applying that doctrine to both houses of state legislatures.

Reaction to those decisions was negative among a number of Members of Congress. In 1964 the House passed a bill which denied federal courts jurisdiction over state reapportionment, but the Senate did not approve the measure.

In 1965 and 1966, Senate Minority Leader Dirksen led a fight in the Senate to propose an amendment to the Constitution giving states the power to apportion one house of their legislatures on a basis other than population, such as geography and political subdivisions. Dirksen was defeated both times, seven votes short of the two-thirds necessary to propose an amendment to the Constitution. The vote was 57-39 in 1965 and 55-38 in 1966.

In the meantime, a campaign was under way, under the general leadership of Dirksen, to encourage states to petition Congress for a constitutional convention to consider the issue of apportionment.

Between 1963 and 1967, 32 states—two short of the two-thirds required to initiate such a convention—so petitioned Congress. *(See chapter on Election Law.)*

With this situation in mind, Sen. Sam J. Ervin Jr. (D N.C.), chairman of the Senate Judiciary Subcommittee on Separation of Powers, in 1967 introduced a bill (S 2307) establishing procedures for the convention method of constitutional amendment. Ervin's Subcommittee held hearings on the bill but never reported it.

S 2307 in essence would have authorized states to establish their own procedures for petitioning Congress on a constitutional convention but limited the scope of that convention strictly to specific amendments proposed by the states. Congress would call a convention when 34 states had petitioned for consideration of an amendment on the same subject. Each state would have as many delegates at the convention as it had Members in the House, but each state would have only one vote on any question submitted to the convention. Congress would set the terms of ratification by the states. A state legislature's petition for a constitutional convention would remain effective for six years.

Ervin said the major question in enacting such legislation was whether Congress had the power under the Constitution to pass such a bill in order to "define the processes for amendment by convention. I certainly believe that it does, but I nevertheless recognize the existence of the problem."

Ervin said the "second over-riding question" was whether the process of amendment by convention could be limited to specific amendments or must authorize an open convention empowered to rewrite the Constitution as a whole. He said his own reading of history convinced him that the framers of the Constitution contemplated a process of individual amendment, notwithstanding "Jefferson's notion of a revolution every generation or so."

Judiciary Committees and was dead for the 89th Congress.

President Johnson's endorsement of a four-year House term in his State of the Union address was unexpected. It received more applause than any other part of his speech. But enthusiasm soon evaporated as opponents stressed the President's insistence that four-year terms coincide with the Presidential terms. This would create a House of "coattail riders," critics said, and end the minority party's traditional gains in non-Presidential election years. The fear of diminishing the independence of the House appeared to be the principal factor that killed the proposal.

The constitutional amendment proposed by the President was to take effect, if approved by Congress and three-fourths of the states, in the November 1972 elec-

tions—when Mr. Johnson, if still President, would be ineligible to seek another term. His proposal also specified that Representatives in mid-term could not run for the Senate without resigning from the House 30 days before the election. This was to allay Senators' fears that Representatives who were in the middle of a four-year term could seek to unseat a Senator without jeopardizing their House seats if unsuccessful.

The Administration's draft bill (S J Res 126, H J Res 807) was introduced in the Senate by Birch Bayh (D Ind.), chairman of the Senate Judiciary Subcommittee on Constitutional Amendments, and in the House by Frank Chelf (D Ky.), third-ranking member of the House Judiciary Committee. The President's approach differed substantially from a 1965 resolution (H J Res 394), sponsored by Chelf and favored by Bayh, under which one-half of the House Members would be elected every two years for four-year terms.

Arguments Pro and Con. Advocates of the four-year House term argued that the increasing Congressional workload and longer sessions of Congress required Members to spend more time than before in mastering legislative problems. Under these conditions, they contended, the two-year term placed formidable strains on the Representatives' time, requiring them to be constantly campaigning. In addition, mounting campaign costs forced legislators to spend additional time raising funds. A four-year term would cut campaign costs and improve legislative expertise, it was argued. It might also attract better-qualified candidates, some supporters contended.

Defenders of the two-year term—many of them representing "safe" districts where re-election was not difficult—stressed that it helped keep the House independent of the Executive Branch. They said that it was designed by the founding fathers with the specific intent of keeping the Representatives responsive to the people's wishes and that midterm elections served as a kind of national referendum on Presidential policies.

The issue of whether the House should be more responsive to the President's leadership, or more independent of it, was the crux of the dispute over the four-year term. Advocates of the proposal suggested that it would help to advance stronger Executive-Legislative party unity by forcing Members to campaign on national issues and, once elected, making them more responsive to Presidential programs. Criticizing this as an argument for riding on the President's "coattails," opponents asserted that such a dependency on the President would destroy the traditional checks and balances ensured by the Constitution and would transform the Members into Presidential puppets, no longer representative of their constituents.

The suggestion that half of the membership be elected in Presidential years and the other half in non-Presidential years was opposed by President Johnson. Mr. Johnson said staggered terms would create a "wholly unfair division" in the House, "condemning half its membership to a shrunken electorate"—a reference to the fact that "off-year" elections bring out many fewer voters than do Presidential-year elections.

While most reports indicated substantial Congressional backing for the four-year House term, it was clear that in 1966 such a proposal could not have gained the necessary two-thirds majority of each chamber required for approval of a constitutional amendment.

House Ethics Committee

The House in 1966 created a bipartisan Select Committee on Standards and Conduct but gave the Committee almost no power.

A resolution (H Res 1013) which would have created a Committee comparable to the one in the Senate—with authority to investigate the conduct of Members and recommend disciplinary action—was substantially weakened on the House floor. The resulting measure, adopted by the House Oct. 19, empowered the Committee only to draft a code of conduct for House Members and employees.

The 12-member Committee, created in October only for the remaining two months of the 89th Congress, took little action other than to recommend that it be reconstituted by the 90th Congress and granted the power denied it by the 89th Congress. Its draft of a code of ethics was not completed because of a shortage of time and funds.

Early in 1967, the House created a standing Committee on Standards of Official Conduct to recommend an enforceable code of ethics for House Members and employees. *(See below.)*

Background. The Senate created a Select Committee on Standards and Conduct in 1964, following an investigation of the activities of Robert G. (Bobby) Baker, former Secretary to the Senate Majority. *(For background on Senate Committee, see 1967 chronology, below.)*

The Joint Committee on the Organization of the Congress in 1966 recommended creation of a similar committee in the House. Controversy over the activities of Rep. Adam C. Powell (D N.Y.) contributed to the pressure for establishment of a House ethics committee. *(For review of Powell case, see Ethical Problems, above.)*

Capitol West Front

A controversy over plans to reconstruct the West Front of the U.S. Capitol arose during consideration of the fiscal 1967 legislative appropriations bill (HR 15456— PL 89-545). Similar controversy occurred in the 1950s over extension of the East Front. *(Congress and the Nation, Vol. I, p. 1428.)*

The problem arose because the West Front had deteriorated to such an extent that temporary wood shoring had been erected to keep it standing. There was no question that it must be repaired. The argument was chiefly over whether it should be rebuilt along its existing lines or expanded as well, to provide space for restaurants, offices, a tourist center and other facilities.

Congress in 1965 appropriated $300,000 for preliminary plans and cost estimates for rebuilding and extending the West Front. The Commission for Extension of the U.S. Capitol on June 17, 1966, advanced a plan to rebuild the West Front, altering its appearance and adding about 4.5 acres of space, at an estimated cost of $34 million.

Proponents contended that the extension was necessary to provide badly needed facilities at the Capitol. Opponents said the proposal was unnecessarily expensive and destructive of esthetic and historic features of the existing structure. Others directed their criticism at the Architect of the Capitol, J. George Stewart, who was not in fact an architect. Many felt that the opinions of professional organizations such as the American Institute of Architects should be solicited before Congress appropriated funds either to rebuild or to extend the West Front.

The Senate version of HR 15456 contained a provision designed to ensure that no further steps were taken until Congress had a chance to examine the existing plans thoroughly. The Senate provision was dropped in the final bill after House and Senate conferees agreed that no funds for continuing the project would be provided during the 1966 session, either in HR 15456 or in a supplemental bill.

Congress subsequently denied funds for the project. *(See 1967 chronology, below.)*

Finance Committee Staff

The Senate in 1966 approved a resolution (S Res 224) to increase the Senate Finance Committee staff from 10 to 22 members. The resolution was effective upon its adoption by the Senate.

The increase was sought by Finance Committee Chairman Russell B. Long (D La.), who succeeded Harry Flood Byrd (D Va.) as chairman late in 1965. Long said the Committee had to borrow professional help when it considered complex legislation.

The Committee's clerical staff was increased in 1967. *(See below.)*

1967

21-Day Rule Repeal

On the opening day of the 90th Congress Jan. 10, the House voted to repeal the 21-day rule it had adopted in 1965. It adopted all other permanent rules of the House, including the two other rules that had been instituted in 1965. *(See above.)*

The vote for repeal was 233-185. A total of 157 Republicans joined 69 Southern Democrats to vote down the 21-day rule, while 26 Republicans and only 18 Southern Democrats supported the rule. Almost all of the 59 Republican freshmen, elected in the 1966 GOP resurgence, voted for repeal.

Despite repeal of the 21-day rule, the Rules Committee assumed a moderate posture in the 90th Congress. It held back only 10 bills for which rules were requested in 1967. Of the 10, most were of minor importance and none provided for major Administration programs. In addition, the Committee took no action on three bills which had been referred directly to it; the most important of these was the Legislative Reorganization Act (S 355). *(See below.)*

Several factors contributed to the Committee's less conservative posture. First, it had lost its chairman, Howard W. Smith (D Va.) as a result of his defeat in a 1966 primary election. Smith, chairman since 1955, was a skilled parliamentarian and the acknowledged leader of the House conservative coalition—a voting alliance of Republicans and Southern Democrats against Northern Democrats. He was replaced as chairman by Rep. William M. Colmer (D Miss.), also a conservative Southerner, but Colmer was prevented from exerting the high degree of control over the fate of legislation that had characterized Smith's 12-year tenure as chairman.

Two liberal members had been added to the Committee, thus creating a more secure liberal majority, and a set of rules had been introduced to govern Committee procedure, the first such rules in the Committee's history. The new regualtions took from the chairman the right to set meeting dates—a power Smith frequently had used postpone or thwart action on bills backed by liberals

or the Administration. The rules also required the consent of a majority to table a bill and set limits on proxy voting by members.

Senate Cloture Rule

Senate liberals failed in their biennial attempt to amend Rule 22, which allowed two-thirds of the Senators present and voting to shut off debate by invoking cloture. The liberals threw their support behind a resolution (S Res 6) that would have allowed three-fifths of the Senators present and voting to end a filibuster. This resolution never reached a vote, and the issue was decided on procedural grounds.

Background. The 1967 fight involved a question with which the Senate had wrestled for years: Was the Senate, since one-third of its membership was elected every two years, a continuing body with a continuing set of rules, or should it adopt new rules by general parliamentary procedure—majority vote—at the beginning of each Congress?

If the Senate was a continuing body, rule changes could be talked to death unless two-thirds of the membership was willing to invoke cloture under Rule 22. If it was not a continuing body, a filibuster could be stopped by majority vote at the beginning of a new Congress and the substantive proposals for changes in the rules could come to a vote. Proponents of rules changes, who had never succeeded in invoking cloture in a Rule 22 fight, held the latter view.

In 1959, at the time of the most recent revision of Rule 22, the Senate also added to Rule 32 the following language: "The rules of the Senate shall continue from one Congress to the next unless they are changed as provided in these rules." This language buttressed the position of those who maintained the Senate was a continuing body, but liberal opponents of the filibuster never conceded the point. *(For previous action on the cloture rule, see 1965 chronology, above; see also Congress and the Nation, Vol. I, p. 1426.)*

1967 Action. After several days of debate on a motion to consider S Res 6, Sen. George McGovern (D S.D.), sponsor of the resolution, made a motion Jan. 18 based on the assertion that the Senate had a constitutional right to adopt new rules by majority vote. McGovern's motion provided that debate on the pending motion to take up S Res 6 be brought to a close in the following manner: the Senate would immediately vote on the McGovern motion; upon adoption of the McGovern motion by majority vote of the Senators present and voting, the Senate would debate the motion to take up S Res 6 for two hours; at the end of the two-hour debate, the Senate would vote on the motion to take up S Res 6.

Senate Minority Leader Everett McKinley Dirksen (R Ill.) raised a point of order against the McGovern motion, claiming that "it amounts to nothing more than an effort to shut off debate" without a two-thirds vote.

Supporters of the move to revise Rule 22 had hoped for favorable rulings from the Presiding Officer of the Senate, Vice President Hubert H. Humphrey, who, as a Senator, sought changes in the cloture rule to make it easier to shut off debate.

Humphrey, however, instead of ruling on Dirksen's point of order, put the matter up to the Senate. Explaining his view, Humphrey said: "The point of order made by the Senator from Illinois involves or raises the question of the constitutionality of the motion of the Senator from South Dakota. On many occasions questions have been raised regarding the constitutional right of the Senate to act in a given manner, and the precedents are uniform. The Chair, on all these occasions, has submitted such questions to the Senate for its consideration.

Humphrey then submitted to the Senate the following question: "Shall the point of order made by the Senator from Illinois be sustained?" Humphrey also said the question was debatable and, in answer to a parliamentary inquiry, that the point of order could be subjected to a tabling motion. A motion to table is not debatable and can be accepted or rejected by majority vote. McGovern moved to table the Dirksen point of order. Acceptance of the tabling motion would have validated the constitutionality of the McGovern motion, but the Senate rejected the tabling motion by a 37-61 roll-call vote. It then sustained the Dirksen point of order against the motion by a 59-37 roll-call vote. Thus, the Senate found McGovern's motion unconstitutional.

When the liberals lost in the two votes on procedural motions, they attempted, as in the past, to invoke cloture on debate on the rules change. This effort failed by a 53-46 roll-call vote—a majority, but 13 votes less than the required two-thirds of those present and voting. The margin of defeat was wider than it had been in the 1963 cloture vote on consideration of Rule 22 changes.

Legislative Reorganization

The Senate in 1967 passed a legislative reform bill (S 355) based on the 1966 recommendations of the Joint Committee on the Organization of the Congress. *(See above.)* However, the House failed to act on the measure, which remained bottled up in the House Rules Committee for the remainder of the 90th Congress.

Major provisions of S 355 made reforms in committee procedures and established several new standing committees (Title I); provided for fuller budgetary data and for new procedures on appropriations bills (Title II); increased the committees' professional staff and provided the minority with staff members (Title III); made changes in job services, Capitol police and pages and appointment of postmasters (Title IV); and strengthened the Regulation of Lobbying Act (Title V).

The bill did not touch on the most controversial areas of reform, such as the seniority system and Senate and House floor rules. It was hoped by supporters that this limitation would ease passage of the legislation.

Senate Action. The Senate passed S 355 March 7, on a 75-9 roll-call vote, after 17 days of debate and 31 roll-call votes. The Senate considered 75 amendments, of which 36 were accepted.

The bill survived most efforts to water down its provisions, a vote to recommit it to committee and a vote to delete Title V, the new lobby registration title. However, the original bill's total ban on proxy voting in committee was virtually eliminated, a number of "grandfather clauses" were added to protect the positions of incumbent Senators, and provisions dealing with the conduct of

committee meetings were substantially altered. The Senate made no changes in provisions dealing with the House alone.

Much of the story of the debate had to do with Joseph S. Clark (D Pa.) who sought to make many changes in Senate rules and procedures, using the bill as a vehicle. Twenty-four of his amendments were rejected by the Senate, 11 of them on roll calls. Only one of his amendments, cosponsored by Ralph W. Yarborough (D Texas), was accepted.

Clark's major efforts were to eliminate the filibuster, and technical machinery which permitted filibusters to begin and to continue, and to enact what became known as the "Bobby Baker" amendments, a reference to Robert G. Baker, former secretary to the Senate Majority, who was convicted Jan. 29 on seven counts of income tax evasion, theft and conspiracy to defraud the Federal Government. *(See chapter on Executive Branch.)*

Clark's amendments would have restricted the outside employment of Senate employees, required Senators and employees to file financial statements and prohibited joint ventures between Senators and lobbyists or the receipt of gifts of more than $100 by Senators from lobbyists. John J. Williams (R Del.) introduced an amendment requiring Senators and employees to make financial disclosures, but that, too, was rejected. (Later in the session Clark also tried unsuccessfully to add a disclosure amendment to the Election Reform Act of 1967. *(See below.)*

Many of Clark's amendments were tabled on motions by A. S. Mike Monroney (D Okla.), floor manager and co-author of the bill, frequently on the ground that they dealt with Senate rules alone and went beyond the scope of the bill.

Two major tests for the bill were the motion to recommit it to committee for further study, made Feb. 7 by Majority Whip Russell B. Long (D La.), which was rejected by an 18-70 roll-call vote, and the move to delete Title V, the lobby registration title, which was made March 7 by Roman L. Hruska (R Neb.) and Minority Leader Everett McKinley Dirksen (D Ill.). That move was rejected by a **30-53** key roll-call vote. *(For background on lobby law revision, see box.)*

The ban on proxy voting in committee first was restricted to votes to report bills, by an amendment offered by Monroney. The Senate then accepted a Long amendment permitting proxies on votes to report bills, provided the absent Senator was informed and had requested to be so recorded.

House Action. S 355 promptly ran into opposition in the House, principally because of its provisions affecting committee procedures. Senate-approved concessions to committee minorities were bitterly disputed.

The first difficulty occurred when House Speaker John W. McCormack (D Mass.), acting on the advice of veteran House Parliamentarian Lewis Deschler, referred the bill to the Rules Committee. It was argued that the bill changed House rules and, since it contained a number of provisions added by Senate amendments that had not been considered by any committee, some study of the bill was needed before it went to the floor.

By contrast, in 1946, then-Speaker Sam Rayburn (D Texas 1913-61) held the Senate-passed Legislative Reorganization Act of 1946 at his desk for nearly six weeks without referring it to committee at all. He held the bill

Loopholes in the Lobby Law

Lobbying in its broadest sense means any attempt to influence actions of government. In its narrowest, it means the relative handful of people and organizations who are required to register and report by the Federal Regulation of Lobbying Act of 1946.

Concerned about lobbying ebbs and flows, Congress first began to worry about regulating it during the early years of this century. Not until 1946 was legislation passed which attempted to deal generally with lobbying. And the 1946 Act, more loophole than law, has been narrowly construed by the courts. Attempts since to pass tighter regulations have failed; yet with the growth of government, the efforts and influence of lobbyists have increased.

The 1946 Act has not seriously restricted lobbyists. Its theory is that if their activities and affiliations are made public, that's enough. It requires anyone hired for the principal purpose of lobbying Congress to register with the Clerk of the House of Representatives and the Secretary of the Senate and to file quarterly financial reports. Organizations which solicit or receive money for the principal purpose of lobbying Congress don't necessarily have to register, but they do have to file quarterly financial reports.

Even these modest disclosure requirements are seldom met. For example:

Loophole. Groups or individuals who spend their own funds to influence legislation don't have to register unless they solicit, collect or receive funds for that purpose.

Loophole. Many organizations, including large ones such as the National Assn. of Manufacturers and the U.S. Chamber of Commerce, say that since influencing Congress isn't the principal purpose for which they collect or receive money, they don't have to report what they do spend lobbying.

Loophole. The courts have held that the 1946 Act doesn't apply unless a lobbyist contacts Members of Congress directly. Thus lobbyists who stir grass roots interest in legislation—which usually results in pressure on Congress—aren't covered.

Loophole. The law says testifying before Congressional committees isn't lobbying and the courts say preparing testimony for someone who isn't either. Then there's a gray area. Some lobbyists say their contacts with Members of Congress aren't intended to influence but merely to inform—and thus aren't lobbying.

Loophole. Groups and individuals can determine more or less for themselves what part of their total expenditures is spent for lobbying. An organization with a large Washington budget can decide that only a small part of it should be charged to lobbying—that most of it is spent to inform the public or for research. Another organization may reverse this ratio and appear to spend much more for lobbying, when in fact the activities of the two organizations are about the same.

Loophole. The 1946 Act requires the Clerk of the House and the Secretary of the Senate to receive registrations and reports but doesn't require them to investigate the truthfulness of the reports or require anyone to register. The Justice Department can prosecute violators but has no authority to investigate reports. Thus the Justice Department acts only when it gets a complaint. There have been only four prosecutions since 1946.

Title V of the Legislative Reorganization Act of 1967 (S 355) constituted the first full-scale Congressional effort in 21 years to strengthen the 1946 Act. During Senate action on S 355, an attempt to strip Title V from the bill was defeated on a **30-53** key roll-call vote. President Johnson "strongly" endorsed Title V and urged the House to approve it, but S 355 never reached the House floor.

Basically Title V would have:

• Required those whose "substantial purpose" is to influence legislation (rather than "principal purpose" as required in the 1946 Act) to register and report.

• Required organizations which say they cannot separate lobbying expenditures from total expenditures to report total expenditures and estimate the lobbying portion.

• Transferred responsibility to receive and file lobbying registrations and reports to the General Accounting Office. The GAO would also have been given modest lobbying enforcement authority.

• Required lobbyists whose fee depends on whether particular legislation passes or is defeated to state the terms of these contingent fees in detail.

• Given television and radio the same exemption as newspapers and other periodicals to advocate or oppose legislation without being classed as lobbyists.

(For complete background on the 1946 Lobbying Act and its implementation, see Congress and the Nation, Vol. I, p. 1557. Highlights of lobby registration and spending reports for the years 1964-68 are summarized at the end of this chapter; for earlier years, see Congress and the Nation, Vol. I, p. 1585. More detailed information is available in annual CQ Almanacs.)

until changes he wanted were worked out informally. *(Congress and the Nation, Vol. I, p. 1418.)*

The Rules Committee held one hearing on S 355 but never reported it. Attempts to force House action in 1968 failed. *(See below.)*

Major Provisions

As passed by the Senate, S 355 contained the following major provisions:

Title I. Committees. Authorized the majority of a committee to call a meeting (if the chairman in 10 days had not heeded their request for one).

Required that all meetings be open, except executive sessions to mark up bills or to vote.

Required announcement of all record votes taken in committee in the committee report, unless previously announced.

Authorized a majority of members to force a bill to be reported which had been ordered reported.

Required reported bills to lie over for three days before being voted on on the floor.

Exempted the Appropriations Committees. *(See below.)*

Hearings. Provided that hearings would be open except when dealing with national security matters or matters which tended to reflect adversely on the reputation of the witness or any other individual.

Exempted the Appropriations Committees. *(See below.)*

Proxies. Permitted the use of proxies except that on a vote to report a measure, proxies were permitted only when the absent member was informed of the matter and affirmatively requested to be so recorded (thus prohibiting general proxies).

Authorized committees to prohibit the use of any proxies on the vote to report a measure.

Specified that the restrictions did not apply to subcommittees.

Review. Provided that standing committees must conduct legislative review of programs in their areas of jurisdiction, and could employ a review specialist on their staff for that purpose.

Conference Reports. Required that conference reports be printed as a report of each house, with an explanatory statement by conferees from both the House and Senate, and with individual statements, if any.

Senate Committees. Retitled the Committee on Banking and Currency as the Committee on Banking, Housing and Urban Affairs.

Established a new Senate Veterans Committee, drawing jurisdiction largely from the Finance Committee.

Limited each Senator, with some exceptions, to membership on two major committees and one minor, joint, select or special committee; but provided that no current Senator should be displaced from a major committee assignment by this limitation.

Limited Senators to service on only one of the following committees: Appropriations, Armed Services, Finance and Foreign Relations; but exempted current Senators.

House Committees. Retitled the Banking and Currency Committee as the Committee on Banking, Housing and Urban Affairs.

Split the Education and Labor Committee into Committees on Education and on Labor and Public Welfare.

Established a Committee on Standards and Conduct.

Title II. Fiscal Controls. Directed the Comptroller General, the Secretary of the Treasury and the director of the Budget Bureau to establish a standardized information and data processing system for budgetary and fiscal data.

Directed the Comptroller General to prepare summary tables of data for any Member or committee.

Directed the Comptroller General to make available to the General Accounting Office and to Congress information on the cost effectiveness of federal programs.

Directed the Comptroller General to report to Congress on changes made in the President's Budget by enactment of appropriations or changes in expenditures.

Budget. Required the President every June 1 to submit a supplemental summary of his Budget reflecting changes caused by revisions of estimated revenues and expenditures or by appropriations enacted.

Required the President every June 1 to submit summaries of estimated expenditures for the next four fiscal years.

Appropriations. Required the Appropriations Committees to hold open hearings, except when dealing with matters which affected national security, which might reflect adversely on the character of the witness or any other individual, or which were confidential.

Required hearings on the Budget within 30 days after it was submitted.

Required the yeas and nays on passage of any appropriations bill (except conference reports) and on bills increasing the compensation of Members of Congress.

Required legislative committees reporting bills to include estimates of the cost of the legislative program for the next six fiscal years.

Title III. Sources of Information. Authorized six professional and six clerical staff members for each standing committee.

Authorized the majority of the minority of each committee to select two professional and one clerical employees.

Equalized Senate and House committee staff salary ceilings at $25,890.

Authorized a legislative assistant for each Senator.

Raised from six to seven the number of trips a Senator might take to his home state, and from four to seven the number a Representative might make to his home district, at Government expense each year. These trips were in addition to one separately authorized round trip to and from the session annually.

Streamlined operations of the Legislative Reference Service of the Library of Congress and changed its name to Legislative Research Service.

Abolished the Office of Coordinator of Information of the House.

Provided for the study of a Senate public address system.

Title IV. Congress as an Institution. Established a Joint Committee on Congressional Operations, to consist of five Senators and five Representatives, to make a continuing study of the operation of Congress and to recommend improvements.

Established an Office of Placement and Office Management to recommend employees for Senators and Representatives.

Converted the Capitol Police into a professional police force.

Required Senate and House pages to have completed high school.

Provided that House employees be paid on a gross rate basis. (House employees currently were paid on a basic rate basis. They received a basic rate of pay, established some years ago, plus percentage increases of that basic rate granted by Congress from time to time since. Thus, their total salaries—basic rate plus percentage increases—were higher than appeared from the basic rate alone.)

Authorized the Senate Appropriations Committee to study the possibility of converting the pay rates of Senate employees to a gross rate.

Adjournment. Required Congress either to adjourn sine die (indefinitely) by July 31 or, by a roll-call vote, to a specified day after Aug. 31, unless a state of war existed pursuant to a declaration of Congress. (Only in the case of a war declaration could Congress legally meet in August. Existing law required adjournment by July 31, but the provision had been ignored for many years.)

Patronage. Provided that the Postmaster General would appoint all postmasters.

Title V. Regulation of Lobbying. Vested administration of the Regulation of Lobbying Act in the Comptroller General, instead of in the Clerk of the House.

Congress Enacts Some Provisions of S 355 Piecemeal

Several provisions of the Legislative Reorganization Act (S 355) were enacted, with some variation, in other bills in 1967. Some were "sweeteners"—provisions that had been included in S 355 to make it more palatable to reluctant Members of Congress.

Following is a summary of major provisions that were enacted separately:

Clerks. The fiscal 1969 legislative appropriations bill (HR 10368—PL 90-57) was the vehicle for most of the action. The Senate July 10, on a 48-31 roll-call, accepted an amendment to HR 10368 to increase each Senator's clerk hire allowance for fiscal 1968 by $23,400. S 355 allowed a legislative assistant for each Senator at that salary. Floor debate on the amendment made clear that it was designed to provide a legislative assistant, as provided in S 355, although the funds were not limited to that use alone. A.S. Mike Monroney (D Okla.), cosponsor of S 355, opposed the amendment as removing a major incentive for enactment of S 355.

Pay Rates. The Senate also included in HR 10368 language converting the pay rates of Senate employees to a gross rate basis. S 355 had requested the Senate Appropriations Committee to formulate a conversion plan.

Telephones. Another provision added to HR 10368 by the Senate permitted the consolidation of telephone and telegraph allowances of Senators in one account. S 355 had directed the formulation of a consolidation plan.

Capitol Police. The Senate also added to HR 10368 funds for 46 additional positions in the Capitol Police. This was accepted by the House, although on May 11 it had adopted, by a 334-16 roll call, a resolution (H Res 464) creating 78 new positions in the Capitol Police. Neither chamber provided for the conversion of the Police to a merit force, as provided in S 355.

Information Coordinator. A House provision of HR 10368 abolished the House Office of Coordinator of Information by providing funds for a "phase-out" of the Office by Oct. 1, 1967. The Office also was to be abolished by S 355.

House Travel. Increased travel allowances for House Members, for which provision was made in S 355, was the subject of separate legislation. S 355 provided an increase from four to seven in the number of trips a Representative could take to his district at Government

expense each year, in addition to one annual trip to and from the session. The House Aug. 21 passed, by voice votes, a bill (HR 9837—PL 90-86) which increased the number of round trips to one for each month Congress was in session, plus one annual trip to and from the session. The bill also increased from $300 to $750 the lump sum payment which Members within commuting distance of Washington, D.C., could elect to take in lieu of actual payments for the five trips. It further provided that unused entitlements could not carry over from year to year.

Ethics. The House April 13 adopted a resolution (H Res 418) establishing a Committee on Standards of Official Conduct for House Members and employees. S 355 provided for a House Committee on Standards and Conduct. (*See below.*)

Committee Rules. Several House committees in 1967 adopted rules to curb the power of the chairman and to protect minority party rights.

Other Measures

The following four measures, which did not deal directly with provisions of S 355, were acted upon in 1967:

House Telephones. The House May 11 by a 189-157 roll-call vote adopted a resolution (H Res 161) providing for an additional $1,200 annually for Members' telephone expenses in their home districts. Unused funds would lapse.

Senate Finance. The Senate Feb. 17 by voice vote adopted a resolution (S Res 21) providing for six additional clerical assistants for the Senate Finance Committee. The Senate first rejected by an 11-53 roll-call vote an amendment to reduce the number from six to four.

House Bill Sponsorship. The House April 25 by voice vote adopted a resolution (H Res 42) permitting up to 25 Members to introduce a bill or resolution jointly. Previously, House Members supporting the same legislation had to introduce separate bills. Cosponsorship of legislation was an accepted practice in the Senate.

Joint Budget Committee. For the eighth time since 1952, the Senate May 11 passed a bill (S 538) to establish a Joint Committee on the Budget. There was no House action.

House Clerk Replaced

The House in 1967 replaced Clerk of the House Ralph R. Roberts, who had held the post since 1949. His successor was ex-Rep. W. Pat Jennings (D Va. 1955-67), who was defeated for re-election in 1966.

Roberts had been criticized for using the chauffeur and limousine that go with the Clerk's job for trips to his home in Indiana and to the race tracks. Before becoming Clerk, Roberts had served as doorkeeper of the House, 1943-47, and as minority clerk, 1947-49.

The Clerk's job paid $27,500. The Clerk had a staff of over 200 and a $94-million annual budget.

Required the Comptroller to maintain records for five years, instead of the current two.

Changed the Act to require registration of groups having as a "substantial" instead of "principal" purpose the influencing of legislation.

Extended to broadcasting stations the provisions applying to newspapers and magazines (which exempted editorials but required registered lobbyists to report on material they had caused to be published).

Directed the Comptroller to refer to the Justice Department information relating to the failure to register or to the filing of false, improper or incomplete information.

House Ethics Committee

The House in 1967 took a first step toward establishing a workable guide for the official conduct of House Members. It set up a 12-member, bipartisan standing House Committee on Standards of Official Conduct to recommend an enforceable code of ethics for House Members and employees.

Unlike the comparable Senate committee, which was established in 1965, the House panel had no powers of enforcement; its sole functions were to recommend a code and to suggest what powers the Committee might be given for enforcement of the code. The Committee was appointed shortly after its creation, with Melvin Price (D Ill.) as chairman, and it set to work holding hearings. No code of ethics was recommended by the end of the year.

The Committee was established April 13 when the House adopted the authorizing resolution (H Res 418) by an unusually large unanimous vote of 400-0. During debate on the proposal a number of Representatives said creation of the Committee was the very least the House should do in the area of ethics in 1967, and voiced hopes that the Committee would quickly recommend an enforceable set of rules. This attitude was in strong contrast with past House reluctance to adopt self-policing measures. Even as late as 1966 attempts to come to terms with the issue of House ethics resulted only in creation of weak temporary Committee on Standards and Conduct whose life was too short to enable it to fulfill its mandate. (See above.)

The House adopted a code of ethics in 1968. (See below.)

Senate Ethics Committee

The Senate Select Committee on Standards and Conduct in 1967 concluded its first investigations and made its first recommendations. Like its House counterpart, however, it did not complete its formulation of a code of ethics.

Most of its attention during the year centered on the case of Sen. Thomas J. Dodd (D Conn.), who subsequently was censured by the Senate on the recommendation of the Committee. The Committee also investigated charges against Sen. Edward V. Long (D Mo.). (See Ethical Problems, above.)

The Select Committee was established in 1964 in the wake of an investigation into charges that Robert G. (Bobby) Baker had used his office as Secretary to the Senate Majority to promote outside business interests. The proposal was a substitute, adopted on a 50-33 roll call, for more stringent ethical reforms proposed by the Rules and Administration Committee. (Congress and the Nation, Vol. I, p. 1430, 1773.)

The six-member, bipartisan Committee was authorized to receive and investigate complaints of unethical and illegal conduct by Senators and employees of the Senate; to recommend disciplinary action; and to draw up a code of ethical conduct.

The Committee members were not selected until July 9, 1965. Sen. John Stennis (D Miss.) was elected chairman and Sen. Wallace F. Bennett (R Utah) vice chairman. The Committee's first undertaking was its investigation of Dodd, which began in 1966.

The Senate in 1968 adopted a code of ethics based on recommendations made by the Select Committee. (See below.)

Financial Disclosure

Concern in Congress over the ethical conduct of its Members rose in 1967. Before the year was half over, Rep. Adam C. Powell (D N.Y.) had been excluded from the House for misusing public money and Sen. Thomas J. Dodd (D Conn.) had been censured by his colleagues for misusing political funds.

In the Senate the year's events prompted growing support for financial disclosure. Three times in 1967 the Senate defeated proposals to require disclosure of Senators' financial assets, but the margin of disapproval slipped from 15 votes in February to four in September.

The issue of disclosure was first raised in February during debate on the legislative reorganization bill (S 355), when the Senate voted to table two amendments requiring financial reporting.

The first, tabled Feb. 8 by a 45-30 roll-call vote, was called the "Bobby Baker" amendment by its sponsor, Sen. Joseph S. Clark (D Pa.); it provided for disclosure of assets, liabilities, income and capital gains by Senators and Senate employees earning more than $10,000 a year. Sen. A. S. Mike Monroney (D Okla.), floor manager of S 355 and a member of the Senate Select Committee on Standards and Conduct, objected to the amendment because, he said, the Committee was already preparing a code of ethics and would be considering the matter of financial disclosure.

Sen. John J. Williams (R Del.) Feb. 8 offered a second amendment, tabled by a 57-18 roll call, which he said had "teeth" in it. The amendment required disclosure of income tax returns and a full financial statement to the U.S. Comptroller General and the Select Committee. The information would be kept confidential.

The third vote came on an amendment proposed by Clark to the Election Reform Act of 1967 (S 1880).

The key vote on the second Clark proposal was **42-46**, the most substantial show of support in Congressional history for disclosure legislation.

Clark's disclosure amendment would have applied both to Members of and candidates for Congress. It required periodic listing of their assets, liabilities, income, securities, gifts and fees for professional services. Clark pointed out that it represented an expanded version of the disclosure requirements for Members of Congress recommended by President Johnson in 1966 but not repeated in 1967. Clark's move earned the disapproval of Senate Minority Leader Everett McKinley Dirksen (R Ill.), a long-time foe of financial disclosure. Dirksen called the proposal "an inpertinence and an outrage."

Although bills to require financial disclosure by Members of Congress had been introduced since at least 1946, the first thorough Senate discussion of the subject came in 1964 in the wake of the Baker scandal. During July 1964, the Senate five times rejected disclosure proposals by lopsided roll-call votes. (*Congress and the Nation, Vol. I, p. 1774.*)

The Senate approved a limited financial reporting rule in 1968. (*See below.*)

Nepotism

Congress included in the postal rate-federal pay increase bill (HR 7977—PL 90-206) a provision to curb nepotism in federal employment. The provision prohibited public officials, including Members of Congress, from appointing or influencing the appointment of relatives in the agency in which the official served. The ban covered all officials, including the President, but did not cover relatives already employed. The language of the provision did not prevent an official in one agency or chamber of Congress from seeking to obtain employment for a relative in another agency or chamber.

The ban had been added to the bill on the House floor when few Representatives were present. Rep. Neal Smith (D Iowa), author of the provision, said his amendment was aimed mainly at conditions in smaller post offices where "many postmasters...will not take a permanent clerk unless their wife is on the eligible list."

House District Standards

Congress in 1967 wrestled with the Supreme Court's "one man, one vote" doctrine as applied to Congressional districting, but its efforts ended in stalemate.

Although both the House and Senate endorsed the principle of a maximum 10-percent population variation between the largest and smallest districts in a state, they failed to agree on how soon to apply such a rule.

In the end, the only legislation enacted was a ban on at-large elections in states with more than one U.S. Repre-

sentative. This was an effort to head off court-ordered at-large elections in states with redistricting problems. Hawaii and New Mexico were exempted from the ban for the 1968 elections only (HR 2275—PL 196).

The ban on at-large elections was all that remained of a bill (HR 2508), sponsored by Rep. Emanuel Celler (D N.Y.), that would have established strict standards for Congressional districts beginning in 1972, after the 1970 Census. The original purpose of the Celler bill was to secure in each state non-gerrymandered districts of close to equal population. As passed by the House April 27, the bill permitted no more than a 10-percent variation in population between the smallest and largest districts in any state beginning with the 1972 elections but allowed a 30-percent variation until 1972.

The Senate Judiciary Committee accepted the maximum 10-percent variation for 1972 and beyond but amended the bill to permit a 35-percent variation in 1968 and 1970. However, the Senate June 8, in passing a revised version sponsored by Edward M. Kennedy (D Mass.) and Howard H. Baker Jr. (R Tenn.), strengthened the bill's provisions by putting the 10-percent variation into effect immediately and by tightening the requirement that districts be as "reasonably compact...as is practicable."

The first conference report on the bill, filed June 27, omitted standards for the 1968 and 1970 elections, retained the 10-percent variation for 1972 and thereafter, prohibited court-ordered redistricting on the basis of 1960 Census figures, but omitted a ban on at-large elections in 1968 and 1970. This omission brought a flurry of objections and on June 28 the bill's sponsor, Rep. Celler, moved for recommittal of the conference report. The House quickly agreed to his motion.

On its second try, the conference committee was unable to reach agreement on permanent standards and recommended instead a compromise banning at-large elections in 1968 and 1970 (with Hawaii and New Mexico exempted) and providing that no state could be required to redistrict before the 1970 Census unless the results of a special federal census were available. The House Oct. 26 accepted the conference version, 241-106, but the Senate Nov. 8 rejected it on a 22-55 roll-call vote. The same day, the Senate amended a House-passed private bill (HR 2275) to include a simple ban on at-large elections in all states, including Hawaii and New Mexico. The House Nov. 28 insisted on exemptions for both states in the 1968 elections, and the Senate Nov. 30 concurred.

Congressional action on district standards legislation was a study in conflicting pressures. Celler, sponsor of the measure, had long advocated legislation to ban gerrymandering and establish equal-population districts. Defenders of the status quo resisted such action. (*For 1965 action, see above.*)

Some Members of Congress, anxious to establish Congressional authority in a field they feared the courts were preempting, wanted Congress to set up standards for House districts to keep the courts from ordering redistricting or at-large elections.

Others charged that the bill was simply an effort to deny the "one man, one vote" doctrine. They feared that the establishment of temporary standards would thwart current court rulings on redistricting and also contended that the temporary standards proposed by the bill were far too broad. Opposition to temporary standards came from those who felt that the 1960 Census figures were too

---

Otepka Case

Secretary of State Dean Rusk in 1967 demoted Otto F. Otepka, former State Department security evaluator who had turned over classified documents to a Senate subcommittee.

Rusk reprimanded Otepka Dec. 9 and assigned him to a nonsecurity post after receiving a hearing examiner's report on the controversy, which stemmed from 1961-63 hearings on State Department security conducted by the Senate Judiciary Internal Security Subcommittee.

The Department had dismissed Otepka, Nov. 5, 1963, but he had appealed and remained on the Department payroll pending the conclusion of an administrative review. *(Congress and the Nation, Vol. I, p. 1771.)*

President Nixon in 1969 appointed Otepka to membership on the Subversive Activities Control Board.

---

outdated to be useful redistricting guides and that Congressional guidelines should not apply until the reapportionment of the House following the 1970 Census. The ban on at-large elections was pushed by Representatives who feared that the courts might order at-large elections in states where redistricting of House seats was either being sought or challenged.

Finally, party considerations also played a vital role. Sen. Baker was widely credited with marshaling Republican opposition to the conference report on HR 2508 by circulating a statistical study indicating that equal-population districting would lead to the election of more Republicans to the House in 1968.

Capitol Hill Demonstrations

Increasing problems with demonstrators on Capitol Hill led Congress in 1967 to enact legislation (S 2310—PL 90-108) strengthening laws governing conduct within the U.S. Capitol buildings and grounds.

The bill, passed by the Senate Oct. 5 and the House Oct. 19, was signed by President Johnson Oct. 20 on the eve of a major peace march on Washington.

Earlier in 1967, incidents involving demonstrators at the Capitol had included forcible entry into the House gallery by supporters of a rat extermination bill, dropping of anti-war leaflets onto the Senate floor from the gallery and a demonstration by welfare recipients at a committee hearing.

S 2310 was designed to supplement and clarify existing laws (dating back to 1892) governing conduct within the area of the Capitol. Clarification had been urged by the U.S. Court of Appeals in 1967, when it reversed the convictions of two demonstrators at the Capitol who had been sentenced under the general disorderly conduct statute applicable to the District of Columbia. The court, in *Feeley v. District of Columbia*, said the "defendants could not be required to select from the maze of small statutes here potentially applicable the course probably to be chosen by the prosecutor." The "maze" consisted of:

A 1946 statute which prohibited demonstrations, loud or abusive language and the discharge of firearms on the Capitol grounds but specifically excluded the Capitol buildings from coverage of its provisions;

An 1892 statute covering disorderly conduct in public buildings belonging to the U.S., including the Capitol.

A general disorderly conduct statute applicable to the District of Columbia.

Each of the statutes had different penalties.

Some observers felt that the passage of S 2310 was given impetus by a peace demonstration scheduled to be held in Washington Oct. 21-22. Rep. William M. Colmer (D Miss.), a supporter of the bill, said Oct. 19 it was brought about by "the fact that there is another one of the numerous marches upon Washington anticipated here within the next few days." However, House Speaker John W. McCormack (D Mass.) sternly denied a charge by Jerome R. Waldie (D Calif.) that the bill was "aimed at one weekend."

Opposition to S 2310 focused on the bill's failure to amend a provision of the 1946 act which banned any kind of unauthorized demonstration on the Capitol grounds. Opponents said the ban violated 1st Amendment rights.

Provisions. As signed into law Oct. 20, PL 90-108:

• Made it a felony, subject to a $5,000 fine and/or five years' imprisonment, for unauthorized persons to:

Carry or discharge firearms and other dangerous devices in the Capitol grounds or buildings. (The House report made it clear that Members keeping guns for display, protection or sporting use would be exempted under regulations to be drawn up by the Capitol Police Board.)

Knowingly, with force and violence, enter or remain upon the floor of either house of Congress.

• Made it a misdemeanor, subject to a $500 fine and/or six months' imprisonment, for unauthorized persons willfully and knowingly to:

Enter or remain on the floor of either house or the cloakrooms, lobbies, or other private rooms, or in the gallery of either house in violation of the rules.

Enter or remain in any room in the Capitol buildings with intent to disrupt the orderly conduct of official business.

Utter loud or abusive language or engage in disorderly conduct on the grounds or in the buildings with intent to disrupt official business.

Obstruct passages or engage in acts of violence in the buildings or grounds or to picket or demonstrate within the Capitol buildings. (A 1946 provision which prohibited standing or moving in processions on the Capitol grounds or displaying the banners of any party, organization or movement except on authorized occasions of "national interest" was left unchanged.)

Congressional Interns

Congress in 1967 put an end to the controversial House summer intern program after a number of college-age participants in it engaged in protests against the Vietnam war. Under the program, authorized in 1965, each Representative was entitled to draw $750 annually from the contingency fund to employ one student for a 10-week period or two students for five-week periods. The Senate had no formal program, but a number of Senators individually hired students during the summer. *(For origin of program, see 1965 chronology, above.)*

In an apparent reaction to the interns' war protest activities, the House Appropriations Committee inserted in a supplemental appropriations bill (HR 14397—PL 90-239) a provision specifying that fiscal 1968 House contingency funds could not be used for the intern program. The provision did not affect funds for fiscal 1969 or later years, nor did it prevent Representatives from paying summer interns from regular clerk-hire funds as was the practice in the Senate.

Congress in 1968 continued the ban on funds for the intern program in the fiscal 1969 legislative appropriations bill (HR 18038—PL 90-417).

Capitol Hill Construction

Haunted by the presence of the $100-million-plus Rayburn House Office Building, Congress in 1967 faced with deeply divided feelings the prospect of two new Capitol Hill construction projects, and for the second consecutive year it denied funds for their construction. Meanwhile, pressure mounted for the creation of a master plan for Capitol Hill development to replace the existing piecemeal approach.

Authorized and only needing funds to move ahead were a $34-million extension of the West Front of the Capitol (the central portion facing the Mall and the Washington Monument) and a $75-million annex to the Library of Congress, to be known as the James Madison Memorial Library.

Congress in 1965 authorized construction of the Library annex. The five-member Commission for Extension of the U.S. Capitol approved the West Front project in 1966. *(See above.)*

Congress considered but did not recommend appropriations for the projects in either the 1968 Legislative Branch Appropriations Bill (HR 10368—PL 90-57) or the first fiscal 1968 supplemental appropriations bill (HR 14397—PL 90-239). Although the Senate-passed version of HR 14397 contained $2.8 million for the James Madison library annex, the funds were deleted in conference.

The dispute over the two building projects was only part of a broader debate on Capitol Hill development. The Senate May 18 adopted a resolution (S J Res 74) which directed the Capitol Architect, in consultation with the National Capital Planning Commission, to select a firm to prepare a long-range master plan for Capitol Hill development. The lack of a plan had come under fire from several Members of Congress. The House never acted on S J Res 74.

Congress in 1968 continued to refuse funds for the construction projects.

1968

Legislative Reorganization

The Senate-passed legislative reorganization bill (S 355) died in the House Rules Committee despite last-minute efforts to bring it to the House floor. The death blow came July 23, when the Rules Committee, reportedly by unanimous vote, deferred action on the bill.

House proponents late in the session used parliamentary stalling tactics in an attempt to force action on the bill, but the move failed. *(For details, see below.)*

The Rules Committee action came after several abortive attempts at compromise between those favoring a strong reform bill and those wanting no bill at all.

On the one hand were Republicans and reform-minded Democrats who advocated changes in committee procedures and Congressional operations designed to broaden minority rights and staffing and generally to increase the efficiency of the Legislative Branch.

On the other hand was the existing power structure, which opposed any changes in the status quo. As one observer put it, "They're still here after 20 years—and that's the proof of the pudding."

The July 23 Rules Committee action followed a last-minute reform push by those who held that some reform was better than none. A compromise bill (HR 18039) that was "not objected to" by committee chairmen and other opponents of S 355 was introduced June 20, but the measure proved unacceptable to the reform faction. Republican proponents of S 355 called the compromise a "phony" reform bill and a "can of worms."

Meanwhile, Senate backers of S 355 studied the possibility of salvaging certain provisions of the bill for Senate reorganization alone. They abandoned the effort as being too complex so late in the session.

S 355, the first major attempt at Congressional reform since 1946, was the outgrowth of a two-year study by the Joint Committee on the Organization of the Congress. It was passed by the Senate in 1967. *(For details of Joint Committee recommendations, see 1966 chronology; for Senate action and provisions of Senate-passed bill, see 1967 chronology.)*

Delaying Tactics Fail

Delaying tactics that became the equivalent of a Senate filibuster were used in the House in 1968 in behalf of three pieces of legislation. The stalling maneuvers delayed adjournment a few days and at one point kept the House in continuous session for 32 hours and 17 minutes, the longest in 93 years.

The bills involved were the legislative reorganization bill (S 355), a campaign spending reform measure (S 1880, HR 11233) and a bill (S J Res 175) to permit television debates among the three major Presidential candidates. Like S 355, S 1880 was passed by the Senate in 1967 but killed by the House Rules Committee in 1968. *(For stories on the campaign spending and TV debate bills, see chapter on Election Law.)*

The principal delaying effort came Oct. 8 and 9 when Republicans—saying they sought action on the reform measures—forced the House to stay in the third longest session in history before it finally passed the TV debate bill. When Senate Republicans—also using delaying maneuvers—succeeded in having the measure killed, a group of House Democratic liberals then used stalling tactics to hold up adjournment from Oct. 10 to Oct. 14 in an unsuccessful attempt to force the Senate to act on S J Res 175.

The stalling tactics were first used in early September by a small group of Republicans and Democrats in an unsuccessful effort to force the House leadership to bring the two reform bills to the floor for action.

Discharge Petition

The discharge petition is a little-used device designed to permit a majority of Representatives to bring to the House floor legislation blocked by a legislative committee or the Rules Committee.

The modern discharge rule was first adopted in 1910. The present form of the rule, adopted in 1935, permits a majority of the House (218 Members in the 89th Congress)—by signing a motion to discharge a committee from consideration of a bill (popularly called a discharge "petition")—to bring to the House floor after a complicated series of parliamentary steps: (1) any public bill that has been before a standing committee of the House for 30 days; or (2) any committee-approved bill that has been before the House Rules Committee for seven legislative days without receiving a special "rule" for floor debate.

In addition, the discharge rule permits dislodging of a special rule from the Rules Committee for debate on a bill that has been before a standing committee for 30 days—a combination of the first two procedures.

The following table shows the extent to which the discharge petition was used between its adoption in 1910 and the close of the 90th Congress in 1968. Although 23 bills were pried loose from committee by the discharge method and 19 of those ultimately passed the House, only two were eventually enacted into law: the Fair Labor Standards Act of 1938 and the 1960 federal pay raise bill. The only successful use of the discharge method in the 1965-68 period was on a bill to provide home rule for the District of Columbia. That bill never went to conference.

Congress	Petitions Filed	Bills Discharged	Discharged Bills That Passed House
61 (1909-10)	223		
62-67 (1911-22)	241	figures not available	
68 (1923-24)	4	1	0
69 (1925-26)	4	0	0
70 (1927-28)	2	0	0
71 (1929-30)	5	0	0
72 (1931-32)	12	1	1
73 (1933-34)	31	1	1
74 (1935-36)	33	2	0
75 (1937-38)	43	3	2
76 (1939-40)	37	2	2
77 (1941-42)	15	1	1
78 (1943-44)	21	3	3
79 (1945-46)	35	1	1
80 (1947-48)	20	1	1
81 (1949-50)	34	3	3
82 (1951-52)	14	0	0
83 (1953-54)	10	1	1
84 (1955-56)	6	0	0
85 (1957-58)	7	1	1
86 (1959-60)	5	1	1
87 (1961-62)	6	0	0
88 (1963-64)	5	0	0
89 (1965-66)	6	1	1
90 (1967-68)	4	0	0
TOTAL	823	23	19

The Republican group, led by Donald Rumsfeld (R Ill.), initially sought floor action on both bills, but later concentrated its efforts on the campaign spending measure.

The Democrats, led by Thomas M. Rees (D Calif.), centered their effort from the start on the Congressional reorganization bill.

The Republicans Sept. 11 began their effort. Relying on seldom-used parliamentary maneuvers, they held up routine House business for more than two hours, as they said, "to dramatize the need for House consideration and, hopefully, House action" on the two bills. Later they sought to use a method known as Calendar Wednesday to bring the campaign spending bill to the floor. Still later, they talked of using a discharge petition. *(For descriptions of these procedures, see boxes.)*

The Democrats Sept. 12 began their effort, introducing a resolution to seek Rules Committee consideration of the Congressional reorganization bill. The Democratic resolution was the first step in filing a discharge petition. About 17 Members took central parts in the effort; four of them were freshmen.

The House Democratic leadership appeared to try to stay aloof from the issue. Speaker John W. McCormack (D Mass.) Sept. 12 said he was for a Congressional reorganization bill, but said a difficulty was reconciling differing views toward the existing bill.

The House Republican leadership supported the effort by Rumsfeld's group. On Oct. 8 Rumsfeld and his group—this time without advance notice—combined full reading of the *Journal*, 33 quorum calls, three roll-call votes and other tactics to delay proceedings for 20 hours before the House considered the TV debate bill. Democrats asserted that Republican Presidential candidate Richard M. Nixon did not want to debate Vice President Hubert H. Humphrey, while the Republicans responded that they were concerned with the two reform measures.

During the entire 32-hour, 17-minute Oct. 8-9 session, 45 roll calls (37 quorum calls and eight record votes) were taken. The doors of the House were closed during quorum calls for the first time since 1950 and later were locked for the first time since 1917. Passage of S J Res 175 came 27 hours into the session.

After threats of a Senate Republican filibuster led Senate Majority Leader Mike Mansfield (D Mont.) to move to postpone indefinitely that chamber's action on S J Res 175, a group of House Democrats led by James G. O'Hara (D Mich.) Oct. 10 announced they would prevent adjournment by demanding the presence of a quorum and then absenting themselves from the chamber when the roll was called. The House met again on Oct. 11 and 12, and on the latter day O'Hara repeated his intention to block adjournment. Finally, on Oct. 14 O'Hara said he was abandoning the attempt to force Senate consideration of the "equal time" bill, thus removing the last obstacle to final adjournment.

According to the Legislative Reference Service of the Library of Congress, the Oct. 8-9 session was surpassed in length twice. The longest session was 46 hours and 25 minutes Jan. 27-29, 1875, when the House was debating a civil rights bill. Previous to that, the longest session had been on May 11-12, 1854, when a 35 and a half hour debate culminated in passage of the Kansas-Nebraska bill, repealing the Missouri Compromise of 1820-21 (compromise on admission to the union of slave and free states). Both of these debates were delayed by roll-call votes on motions to adjourn and by other dilatory tactics; 101 votes and two quorum calls were taken during the 1854 debate.

Senate Conduct Code

Concern over ethical problems led in 1968 to Senate adoption of a code of conduct for Senators and Senate employees. The action came March 22, when the Senate, by a 67-1 roll-call vote, adopted a resolution (S Res 266) providing four new Senate rules of ethical conduct. Although nearly two dozen amendments were adopted during the five days of debate, the final version of S Res 266 did not differ significantly from the version recommended by the Select Committee on Standards and Conduct March 15.

George D. Aiken (R Vt.), dean of Senate Republicans, was the only Member who voted against the resolution. He said the rules were "a farce" and that he refused to "be a party to the perpetrating of a fraud upon the American people...."

The Senate rejected several amendments which would have strengthened the rules. The first of these, rejected March 20 by a **40-44** key roll-call vote, would have required detailed public disclosure of Members' and employees' assets, liabilities and business relationships. The amendment was offered by Joseph S. Clark (D Pa.) and Clifford P. Case (R N.J.).

The two Senators won an unexpected victory March 21 when the Senate, by a 41-40 roll call, adopted an amendment which overturned a recommendation of the ethics committee and barred use of political contributions to pay Senate office expenses. The ban was partly rescinded the next day when the Senate adopted another amendment, by a 43-28 roll call, permitting the use of contributions for travel home, for reprinting speeches and other specified expenses.

In an opening statement in support of the four-point Committee resolution, Chairman John Stennis (D Miss.) said that the resolution would "add rules (but)...not replace that great body of unwritten but generally accepted standards that will, of course, continue in effect." Stennis pointed out that the resolution contained no provisions for punishing a violator. Censure of Senators and dismissal of employees, he said, would continue to be the remedies.

The strongest criticism of the resolution came from Minority Leader Everett McKinley Dirksen (R Ill.), a vehement opponent of financial disclosure. Repeating his charge that disclosure would make him a "second-class citizen," Dirksen announced March 20 that he intended to offer 18 to 20 amendments to "interlard (the resolution) with limitations and restrictions."

Clark-Case Amendment. The Senate March 20 rejected, by a **40-44** roll-call vote, the Clark-Case amendment, widely regarded as the most serious challenge to the confidential financial reporting recommended by the Committee.

The amendment, similar to ones Clark had offered in 1964 and twice in 1967, required that Senators and employees earning more than $15,000 a year list annually the market value of each asset and liability and the source and amount of each capital gain and each item of outside income or gift over $100. Also required, under the amendment, was a detailing of associations with businesses and other firms and the identity of any client

represented by the firm before the Federal Government. The margin of defeat was the same as on the previous disclosure amendment, which lost, 42-46, on Sept. 12, 1967. *(See above.)*

Office Expenses. Case, arguing for a ban on the use of contributions for office expenses, said March 21 that the Committee's proposed rule would give "official sanction" to the practice and would postpone action by the Senate Rules and Administration Committee to increase office allowances. The Committee's recommendations, he added, "not only provide no guide but open the door wider to political pressures."

Stennis agreed that the Rules and Administration Committee ought to review Senate office allowances. He said, however, that "it would be unreasonable and wrong to cut a Senator off and prohibit him from using funds that come into his hands in good faith to be spent in connection with his office." The receipt of such funds, he pointed out, would have to be disclosed.

Howard W. Cannon (D Nev.), however, referred to it as "a rich man's amendment," for he pointed out that wealthy Senators could afford to pay for office expenses not covered by official allowances. The amendment was accepted on a 41-40 roll call.

The Case ban was softened the next day when the Senate, by a 43-28 roll-call vote, adopted a second amendment permitting the use of contributions to pay certain politically related office costs. Offered by Jacob K. Javits (R N.Y.) and Ralph W. Yarborough (D Texas), the amendment permitted Senators to use contributions to pay for travel to and from their states, for printing speeches and newsletters to constituents, for radio and television time, telephone, stationery and other expenses over their allowances, and for subscribing to home-state newspapers.

Political Fund-Raising. The Senate March 21, by a 43-37 roll-call vote, adopted an amendment permitting aides, designated by their Senator and earning more than $10,000 a year, to solicit and distribute campaign funds. Each Senator was required, under the amendment, to file with the Secretary of the Senate the names of the aides he had authorized to deal with political funds; these records were to be open to the public. The other restrictions in S Res 266, banning political fund-raising by other Senate employees and committee staff members, were retained.

The amendment was offered by Clinton P. Anderson (D N.M.). He explained that Senators rely on their assistants to take part in fund-raising activities because they "know who these (donors) are, whether they are lobbyists or not, and whether one could accept their gifts appropriately or not." The alternative course—detaching the assistant from his Senate salary during a campaign—would be distasteful, Anderson said, because it would mean that the aide would lose insurance and health insurance benefits associated with his Senate salary.

Stennis opposed the amendment. The Committee's version, he said, although "drastic," was "the only way to have absolute control" over money-raising by Senate employees. He added that "it would be a mighty good move for a Senator who is a candidate...to let someone else take care of campaign funds and not use people paid for by the Federal Government for such purposes."

Edmund S. Muskie (D Maine) and George Murphy (R Calif.), chairmen, respectively, of the Democratic and GOP Senatorial Campaign Committees, urged adoption of the Anderson amendment.

Candidates. The Senate also accepted, by a 45-37 roll-call vote, an amendment requiring candidates for the Senate to comply with the proposed rules restricting the use of contributions and providing for financial disclosure.

The amendment was offered by Cannon, who argued that "to deny to an incumbent the right to know as much data about his opponent as is required by (the resolution) from the incumbent would be obviously unfair and discriminatory." Stennis opposed the amendment. He said the Senate had no power to decide "what the pre-election campaign qualifications will be for someone who wants to run for an office...." He predicted that the amendment, if adopted, would be overturned in the courts, making the Senate "look a little foolish."

Outside Employment. The Senate, by voice vote March 22, adopted an amendment to the proposed rule restricting outside employment by Senate employees. Offered by Javits, and subsequently modified by Stennis, the amendment deleted a requirement in the resolution that a Senator or supervisor give his permission to an employee to take an outside job. Javits' original amendment had simply stricken the phrase requiring a Senator's permission. Stennis, however, rewrote the amendment, with Javits' approval, to make the Senator or supervisor responsible for preventing a conflict of interest in the employee's activities. As reported by the Committee, Javits said, the rule would have implied disrespect for Senate employees and might prove "onerous and embarrassing."

Provisions

As adopted by the Senate, S Res 266:

Declared that a Senator should use the power entrusted to him by the people "only for their benefit and never for the benefit of himself or of a few."

Amended the Rules of the Senate to provide the following new rules:

Rule 41. Stipulated that no officer or employee of the Senate might engage in any other employment or paid activity unless it was not inconsistent with his duties in the Senate. Directed employees to report their outside employment to specified supervisors, including Senators, who were to take such action as they considered necessary to avoid a conflict of interest by the employee.

Rule 42. Directed that a Senator and a declared candidate for the Senate might accept a contribution from a fund-raising event for his benefit only if he had given express approval before funds were raised and if he received a full accounting of the sources and amounts of each contribution. Official events of his party were exempted from these restrictions.

Permitted a Senator or candidate to accept contributions from an individual or an organization provided that a complete accounting of the sources and amounts were made by the recipient.

Specified that a Senator or candidate might use such contributions for the expenses of his nomination and election and for the following purposes: travel expenses to and from the Senator's home state; printing and other expenses of sending speeches, newsletters and reports to his constituents; expenses of radio, television and other media reports to constituents; telephone, postage and stationery expenses not covered by Senate allowances; and subscriptions to home-state newspapers.

Required disclosure of gifts, from a single, non-family source, of $50 or more under the provisions of Rule 44. *(See below.)*

Rule 43. Prohibited employees of the Senate from receiving, soliciting or distributing funds collected in connection with a campaign for the Senate or any other federal office. Exempted from the rule Senators' assistants who were designated to engage in such activity and who earned more than $10,000 a year. Required that the Senator file the names of such designated aides with the Secretary of the Senate, as public information.

Rule 44. Required each Senator, declared candidate and Senate employee earning more than $15,000 a year to file with the U.S. Comptroller General, by May 15 each year, a sealed envelope containing the following reports:

• A copy of his U.S. income tax returns and declarations, including joint statements.

• The amount and source of each fee of $1,000 or more received from a client.

• The name and address of each corporation, business or professional enterprise in which he was an officer, director, manager, partner or employee, and the amount of compensation received.

• The identity of real or personal property worth $10,000 or more that he owned.

• The identity of each trust or fiduciary relation in which he held a beneficial interest worth $10,000 or more and the identity, if known, of any interest the trust held in real or personal property over $10,000.

• The identity of each liability of $5,000 or more owed by him or his spouse jointly.

• The source and value of all gifts worth $50 or more received from a single source.

Specified that the information filed with the Comptroller General would be kept confidential for seven years and then returned to the filer or his legal representative. If the filer died or left the Senate, his reports would be returned within a year.

Provided that the Select Committee on Standards and Conduct might, by a majority vote, examine the contents of a confidential filing and make the file available for investigation to the Committee staff. Required that due notice be given to an individual under investigation and an opportunity provided for him to be heard by the Committee in closed session.

Required each Senator, candidate and employee earning more than $15,000 a year to file with the Secretary of the Senate by May 15 each year the following information, which was to be kept for three years and made available for public inspection:

• The accounting required under Rule 42 of all contributions received in the previous year (amounts under $50 might be totaled and not itemized).

• The amount, value and source of any honorarium of $300 or more.

Uniform Disclosure. Declared the sense of the Senate that appropriate action be taken by the House, the Executive and Judicial Branches to impose uniform ethical requirements like those in S Res 266 on all sections of the Federal Government.

House Conduct Code

The House, like the Senate, adopted a code of ethical conduct in 1968. The code had been recommended by the Committee on Standards of Official Conduct in a unanimous March 14 report.

The House April 3 adopted a resolution (H Res 1099) embodying the Committee's recommendations on a 406-1 roll-call vote. The dissenting vote was cast by Rep. Peter H. B. Frelinghuysen (R N.J.), who said the resolution's disclosure rule was meaningless and unclear.

H Res 1099 established a Code of Official Conduct for Members and employees of the House and added to the Rules of the House requirements for limited disclosure of outside income by Representatives and top employees. It also continued the Committee on Standards of Official Conduct as a permanent standing committee, with increased powers.

The only amendment accepted to H Res 1099 was a minor Committee amendment recommended by the House Rules Committee. It permitted the Committee on Standards to require anyone wishing to examine the public financial reports to give the reason for his inquiry. Two other amendments proposed from the floor would have required full, public disclosure of income, assets and liabilities, but these were defeated on voice votes after brief debate.

Provisions

As adopted by the House, H Res 1099:

Standing Committee. Established the Committee on Standards of Official Conduct as a permanent standing committee of the House with 12 members, divided equally between the political parties.

Authorized the Committee to: recommend action to enforce the Code of Official Conduct; investigate alleged violations of law or of the Code by any Member, officer or employee of the House; and render advisory opinions on ethical matters.

Required approval by a majority of the Committee before it could issue recommendations or initiate investigations. An investigation could be undertaken on the Committee's initiative, or upon a sworn, written com-

---

Hayden Retirement

Sen. Carl Hayden (D Ariz.), the dean of the Senate, retired in 1968 at the age of 91. Hayden gave up his job as a county sheriff to become Arizona's first Representative in 1912. He was sworn in Feb. 19, 1912, five days after Arizona became a state, and served in the House for 15 years. In 1927 he moved to the Senate where he served seven six-year terms. At the time of his retirement, Hayden was president pro tempore of the Senate and chairman of the Senate Appropriations Committee. With nearly 57 years of continuous service in the House and Senate, he had served as a Member of Congress longer than any other person in history.

(For earlier landmarks in Congressional service, see Congress and the Nation, Vol. I, p. 1423.)

---

plaint submitted by a Representative or, if three Representatives declined in writing to submit a complaint, at the request of any individual. Before recommending disciplinary action to the House, the Committee was required to give notice and a hearing to the person investigated.

H Res 1099 added the following to the Rules of the House:

Code of Official Conduct (Rule 43). Established an 8-point Code, which, in part: forbade a Member or employee to use his official position improperly to receive compensation; prohibited the acceptance of gifts of "substantial value" from an individual or group with a direct interest in legislation before Congress; prohibited acceptance of honorariums of more than "the usual and customary value" for speeches and articles; required Representatives to keep campaign funds separate from personal funds and not to convert campaign funds to personal use; required that unless the purpose of funds raised at testimonial events was made clear in advance, the funds must be treated as campaign contributions (and thus be subject to the reporting requirements and spending limits of the Corrupt Practices Act); required that employees paid from the clerk-hire allowance of Members perform the work for which they were paid.

Financial Disclosure (Rule 44). Required Members and officers of the House, their principal assistants and professional staff members of committees to file with the Committee on Standards by April 30 each year a report naming the sources of certain financial interests—which were to be available to the public—and a sealed report on the amount of income from each source. The sealed report could be opened by the Committee only if it determined that it was essential to an investigation. The first filing was not required until 1969.

The public listing of financial interests was to include: the name of any business in which the filer had a financial interest of over $5,000 or from which he derived income of $1,000 or more, but only if it did substantial business with the Federal Government or was under federal regulation; (2) the name and type of practice of any professional organization from which the filer received income of $1,000 or more, but only if the filer or his spouse was an officer, director, partner or adviser; (3) the source of income exceeding $5,000 from a service rendered (except to the Government) or a capital gain (except sale of the filer's home) and of reimbursement for expenditures exceeding $1,000.

These reports were to be available for public inspection under regulations to be set by the Committee, which could require full identification of the person making the examination and the reason for it and was to notify the Member involved.

The confidential reports were to give the fair market value of the business holdings reported and the amount of income from each source reported publicly.

Required persons without financial interests that must be reported to file statements to this effect.

Congressional Pensions

The House Foreign Affairs Committee on June 4 reported a routine retirement bill for officers of the Foreign Service (HR 16903), with an amendment to increase pensions for Members of Congress. There was no further action on the bill.

The amendment, sponsored by Committee member Wayne L. Hays (D Ohio) and approved by a 24-3 Committee vote, would have permitted Members of Congress to retire at full pension (currently $24,000) after 24 years of service instead of 32. The bill raised Members' contributions to the Civil Service Retirement Fund to 10 percent of their salaries. Under existing law they contributed 7½ percent. In each case the Government matches the Member's contribution.

The bill also based pensions on 3½ percent of a Member's final salary before retirement times the number of years he served in Congress, the Federal Government and the military. The existing rate was 2½ percent of the "average pay" over a five-year period. At a salary of $30,000, and under the law's provisions limiting the maximum pension to 80 percent of the salary, the bill authorized the top pension of $24,000 after 24 years of service. The sliding scale of benefits for service of five to 24 years remained in effect.

The bill required the 10-percent deduction for Members entering Congress after enactment of the bill but made the increase optional for current Members and retroactive to Jan. 1, 1967. Increases in salaries for Members of Congress were currently under study by a Presidential commission on executive salaries. The commission was authorized by the Federal Salary Act of 1967. *(See chapter on federal pay-postal rates.)* Early in 1969 Congressional salaries were increased from $30,000 to $42,500 annually.

Stationery Allowances

Congress included in the fiscal 1969 legislative appropriations bill (HR 18038—PL 90-417) a provision limiting the use of Senate stationery funds. The provision, offered on the Senate floor by John J. Williams (R Del.) and accepted by voice vote, required that stationery allowances of Senators be used only for stationery and that any unused funds be returned to the Treasury rather than turned over to the individual Senators for personal use as was currently the practice.

Williams had offered similar amendments in the past, but they had applied to Representatives as well as Senators and had been rejected in conference.

HUAC Name Change

The House did not complete action on a proposal to change the name of the House Un-American Activities Committee (HUAC) to the House Committee on Internal Security. The proposal was sponsored by Rep. Richard H. Ichord (D Mo.), who was to become chairman of the Committee in the 91st Congress. The change was approved early in 1969. *(See chapter on Civil Liberties and Internal Security.)*

Senate Office Building

In a rare departure from Congressional tradition, the House Sept. 26 rejected a Senate-passed bill (S 2484) authorizing acquisition of land for future expansion of the new Senate Office Building.

Defeat of S 2484 by a roll-call vote of 144-162 climaxed lengthy arguments in regard to authorization of $1,250,000 to acquire the additional land. The Senate had passed the bill April 30 on a 42-33 roll call.

Rep. Kenneth J. Gray (D Ill.), House floor manager for S 2484, argued that while the Senate had spent nothing for itself, the House had spent $200 million in recent years to expand its facilities. He cited the Senate's need of space, skyrocketing land prices, and the traditional "rule of comity" by which each House gave routine assent to the "housekeeping" requests of the other. Gray also stated that the Senate did not intend to request any funds in the present fiscal situation, but only wished to serve notice to present owners of its intention to acquire the land.

Opposition to S 2484 was led by James C. Cleveland (R N.H.). Cleveland asserted that S 2484 was the first step toward a project that would cost at least $30 million. He cited assertions by Sen. John J. Williams (R Del.) to the effect that the Senate should cut its subcommittees and its staffs rather than expand its office space.

Lobby Spending Highlights

The Federal Regulation of Lobbying Act of 1946 required registration with the Clerk of the House and the Secretary of the Senate of persons who received pay to lobby Congress. It also required such persons, plus any organizations that lobbied Congress, to file quarterly reports giving certain financial information and describing how much they spent for lobbying.

Since 1946, Congressional Quarterly has recorded lobbyist registrations and lobby spending reports filed under the 1946 Act. However, the reports give only a partial indication of how much lobbyists spend in their efforts to influence Congress on legislation. Loopholes in the lobby law and differing methods used by lobby groups in compiling reports obscure the total spending picture. *(For lobby registration requirements and loopholes, see box in 1967 chronology, above.)*

The following information based on CQ records is given below:

• A list of top lobby spenders for each of the years 1964 through 1968.

• A box showing yearly spending totals, 1946-68.

• A box showing yearly lobby registration totals, 1946-68.

(For background on the 1946 Act and its implementation, see Congress and the Nation, Vol. I, p. 1557; for highlights of lobby spending reports for the years 1946-63, see Congress and the Nation, Vol. I, p. 1585. More detailed information on lobby registration and lobby spending is available in annual CQ Almanacs.)

Yearly Spending Totals

Total spending reported by organizations under the Federal Regulation of Lobbying Act for each full year since the law's enactment:

Year	Spending	Year	Spending
1968	$4,298,387	1957	$ 3,818,177
1967	4,751,145	1956	3,957,120
1966	4,656,871	1955	4,365,843
1965	5,484,413	1954	4,286,158
1964	4,223,277	1953	4,445,841
1963	4,223,605	1952	4,823,981
1962	4,211,304	1951	8,771,097
1961	3,986,095	1950	10,303,204
1960	3,854,374	1949	7,969,710
1959	4,281,468	1948	6,763,480
1958	4,132,719	1947	5,191,856

Lobby Registration Totals

The 1946 Federal Regulation of Lobbying Act required any person or group (except public officials) who, for pay, attempted to influence federal legislation to register with the Clerk of the House and the Secretary of the Senate. The law did not provide any specific way to withdraw a registration once it was filed, and it was vague on other procedural points. Some lobbyists follow the practice of registering anew each session, even if they still represent the same client. Others register only once for each client.

The year-by-year breakdown of all registrations (including duplications) since the law was enacted is shown below. Prior to 1964, years are calendar years unless otherwise indicated. Since 1964, the adjournment of Congress has marked the end of each year's total.

Year	Registrations	Year	Registrations
1946*	222	1960	236
1947	731	1961	365
1948	447	1962	375
1949	599	1963	384
1950	430	Jan. 1, 1964-	
1951	342	Oct. 3, 1964	255
1952	204	Oct. 4, 1964-	
1953	296	Oct. 23, 1965	450
1954	413	Oct. 24, 1965-	
1955	383	Oct. 22, 1966	332
1956	347	Oct. 23, 1966-	
1957	392	Dec. 15, 1967	449
1958	337	Dec. 16, 1967-	
1959	393	Oct. 14, 1968	259
		TOTAL	8,641

* Last four months only.

Top Lobby Spenders, 1964-68

1964

Coordinating Committee for Fundamental American Freedoms Inc.	$319,825
AFL-CIO (national headquarters)	153,542
United Federation of Postal Clerks (AFL-CIO)	131,913
Council for a Livable World	123,982
American Legion	123,914
American Farm Bureau Federation	123,645
International Assn. of Machinists, District Lodge #44 (AFL-CIO)	123,569
United States Savings and Loan League	98,233
National Housing Conference Inc.	88,224
National Farmers Union	80,946
International Brotherhood of Teamsters, Chauffeurs, Warehousemen & Helpers of America	73,196
National Federation of Independent Business Inc.	67,143
American Trucking Assns. Inc.	64,271
Committee for Study of Revenue Bond Financing	63,720
National Assn. of Letter Carriers (AFL-CIO)	60,931
National Education Assn., Division of Federal Relations	60,009
National Rivers and Harbors Congress	59,776
National Rural Letter Carriers' Assn.	59,364
National Restaurant Assn.	55,499
Investors Diversified Services Inc.	51,572
National Reclamation Assn.	51,376
National Assn. of Home Builders of the United States	49,725
American Textile Manufacturers Institute	47,189
American Medical Assn.	45,515
American Petroleum Institute	45,465

1965

American Medical Assn.	$1,155,935
United Federation of Postal Clerks (AFL-CIO)	175,365
AFL-CIO (national headquarters)	148,344
American Legion	139,538
Committee for Automobile Excise Tax Repeal	116,394
American Farm Bureau Federation	115,846
U.S. Savings and Loan League	105,840

International Assn. of Machinists, District Lodge #44 (AFL-CIO)	104,767
National Housing Conference Inc.	95,534
National Farmers Union	87,352
Brotherhood of Locomotive Firemen & Engineers Grand Lodge (AFL-CIO)	86,945
International Brotherhood of Teamsters	86,429
National Federation of Independent Business Inc.	80,747
National Education Assn., Division of Federal Relations	79,214
Council for a Livable World	76,983
Central Arizona Project Assn.	74,065
American Trucking Assns. Inc.	70,961
National Assn. of Letter Carriers (AFL-CIO)	66,487
AFL-CIO Industrial Union Department	60,143
Iron Ore Lessors Assn. Inc.	58,077
American Library Assn.	56,041
National Federation of Federal Employees	54,929
National Assn. of Home Builders of the United States	54,854
National Reclamation Assn.	52,502
National Rural Letter Carriers Assn.	51,124
Wheat Users Committee	51,056

1966

United Federation of Postal Clerks (AFL-CIO)	$286,972
Brotherhood of Locomotive Firemen & Enginemen, Grand Lodge (AFL-CIO)	199,262
AFL-CIO (national headquarters)	169,705
American Legion	137,193
American Farm Bureau Federation	133,944
U.S. Savings and Loan League	120,899
National Assn. of Real Estate Boards	118,289
Central Arizona Projects Assn.	117,301
International Brotherhood of Teamsters	100,525
National Housing Conference Inc.	94,444
Council for a Livable World	90,597
National Federation of Independent Business Inc.	90,244
National Farmers Union	87,679
National Assn. of Home Builders of the United States	73,577
National Education Assn., Division of Federal and State Relations	73,055

American Transit Assn.	72,084
American Trucking Assns. Inc.	67,443
International Assn. of Machinists, District Lodge #44 (AFL-CIO)	65,077
Assn. of American Railroads	63,117
American Library Assn.	62,686
National Assn. of Letter Carriers (AFL-CIO)	58,478
National Cotton Council of America	57,249
Iron Ore Lessors Assn. Inc.	55,675
National Automobile Dealers Assn.	53,973

1967

United Federation of Postal Clerks (AFL-CIO)	$277,524
AFL-CIO (national headquarters)	165,505
Record Industry Assn. of America Inc.	139,919
American Legion	139,527
National Assn. of Letter Carriers (AFL-CIO)	133,877
American Farm Bureau Federation	133,777
United States Savings and Loan League	108,485
National Automobile Dealers Assn.	101,707
National Federation of Independent Business Inc.	96,701
National Housing Conference Inc.	91,995
National Farmers Union	86,994
Central Arizona Project Assn.	78,867
Retired Officers Assn.	78,213
Council for a Livable World	77,470
National Committee for the Recording Arts	77,040
National Education Assn., Division of State and Federal Relations	73,612
American Library Assn.	73,132
Assn. of Mutual Fund Plan Sponsors Inc.	70,402
American Trucking Assns. Inc.	61,718
National Assn. of Electric Companies	61,382
Liberty Lobby Inc.	61,341
American Hospital Assn.	61,283
American Medical Assn.	58,378
American Textile Manufacturers Institute Inc.	57,394
Brotherhood of Locomotive Firemen & Enginemen, Grand Lodge (AFL-CIO)	56,109
International Brotherhood of Teamsters, Chauffeurs, Warehousemen & Helpers of America	54,091

National Tax Equality Assn. 53,527
Brotherhood of Railway, Airline
& Steamship Clerks, Freight
Handlers, Express and Station
Employees (AFL-CIO) 53,352
National Assn. of Home
Builders of the United States 53,244

1968

United Federation of Postal
Clerks (AFL-CIO) $170,784
AFL-CIO (headquarters) 154,466
Council for a Livable World 154,022
American Farm Bureau
Federation 147,379
American Legion 141,134
American Trucking Assns. Inc. 121,399

United States Savings & Loan
League 119,784
Record Industry Assn. of
America Ind. 111,394
National Federation of Indepen-
dent Business Inc. 102,455
National Housing Conference
Inc. 96,935
National Farmers' Union 95,639
Brotherhood of Railway, Airline
& Steamship Clerks, Freight
Handlers, Express and Station
Employees (AFL-CIO) 93,456
Laborers' Political League* 90,214
National Education Assn., Divi-
sion of State and Federal
Relations 84,146
Assn. of Mutual Fund Plan
Sponsors Inc. 78,608

Liberty Lobby Inc. 75,807
National Assn. of Home Builders
of the United States 70,095
Central Arizona Project Assn. 66,542
National Assn. of Letter
Carriers (AFL-CIO) 63,797
American Textile Manufac-
turers Institute Inc. 58,378
National Council of Farmer
Cooperatives 57,832
National Federation of Federal
Employees 57,148
American Medical Assn. 56,374
National Assn. of Electric
Companies 54,182
American Hospital Assn. 50,199

* *Campaign contributions reported by mistake.*

Federal Pay

THE Johnson years closed the gap between federal civilian pay scales and those of private enterprise, with the final move accomplished by executive order in mid-1969.

President Nixon, in compliance with a three-stage federal pay increase approved by Congress in 1967, ordered pay raises effective in the first pay period after July 1, 1969. The raise increased the average white-collar worker's paycheck by 9.1 percent. Military pay also was increased to correspond to the civilian increases, as specified by Congress.

The 1969 executive action completed a process, first given official recognition in 1962 legislation and set on its final course in 1967, based on the principle that federal pay should be comparable to that of other workers. Since World War II, Congress had steadily increased federal pay levels. The trend persisted through the years of the Johnson Administration.

Pay increases were approved in 1965, 1966 and 1967. In an unprecedented move, Congress in 1967 not only set higher salary levels to take effect promptly, but also provided for automatic increases in 1968 and again in 1969 based on scales determined by the President. Mr. Johnson urged the three-stage action as what he called the final step "to achieve full comparability with private industry...."

The various pay hikes during the period raised the scale of the lowest-paid General Schedule (GS) federal worker from $3,385-$4,420 prior to Oct. 1, 1965, to $3,889-$5,057 after July 1, 1969. Pay of mid-range GS-9 employees rose in that period from $7,220-$9,425 to a range of $9,320-$12,119. Similarly, GS-13 workers went from $12,075-$15,855 in 1965 to $15,812-$20,555 in 1969.

Parallel increases occurred in the postal service and in other categories of federal employment, as well as in the military. In some instances, employees also bene-fited by advancement on the GS scale.

The costs of the Vietnam War and rising inflation caused increasing concern in governmental circles. Some Members of Congress noted that both the numbers of federal employees and employment costs were soaring to record levels. There were contentions that the Government was contributing to inflationary pressures by high spending levels, including the continuing pay increases for its employees.

Mr. Johnson himself referred to this factor on several occasions and either vetoed or threatened to veto legislation which he considered inflationary. In 1965 the President told Congress in his January budget message that pay raises in the preceding three years had "moved us much nearer to realizing the principle that civilian pay rates should be comparable to those in private enterprise for the same levels of work and that changes in pay and allowances of members of the uniformed forces should keep pace with advances in the general economy." While this principle should continue to be followed, he said, it was equally essential to assure that further action "be compatible with our national wage and price objectives"—a reference to his desire to adhere to guide-posts set up by the Council of Economic Advisers to curb inflation.

A year later, in 1966, Mr. Johnson told Congress in a message proposing increased benefits for federal workers: "If our Government is to exercise continued leadership in the fight for price stability, then we must continue to practice what we preach."

Federal civilian employment continued to rise. In December 1967, for a brief period, it edged above the 3 million mark for the first time since World War II. That figure, however, included temporary and part-time workers; full-time permanent employees then totaled 2.6 million.

Congress in 1968 imposed a ceiling on federal employment. In the Revenue and Expenditure Control Act of 1968 (PL 90-364), which imposed a 10 percent surcharge on federal income taxes and a $6 billion cut in fiscal 1969 spending, Congress required reduction of civilian employment. The number of full-time, permanent employees in the Executive Branch was to be pared from the mid-1968 level of about 2.6 million to the 2.4 million-man level of June 30, 1966.

The cutback was to be achieved gradually by leaving 25 percent of upcoming vacancies unfilled. Agencies began asking special exemption from the cutback on the ground that they needed a full roster of employees because of their particular responsibilities.

By the end of 1968, Congress had voted exemptions for so many agencies that nearly one-third of the federal workers were exempt from the economy measure. Employment settled below the 1967 level, nevertheless. But the built-in pay increases at all levels of federal civilian and military agencies kept over-all Government employment costs, including fringe and insurance benefits, on the upswing to new record levels.

Reference

Discussion of federal pay policy and legislation in the 1945-64 period will be found in *Congress and the Nation*, Vol. I, p. 1471-1494.

Chronology

of Legislation

On Federal Pay

1965

Congress enacted pay increases for federal employees and military personnel in 1965, in each case exceeding the limits recommended by President Johnson in the light of inflationary pressures.

Classified employees of the Federal Government received their 12th raise in pay since 1945. The implied threat of a Presidential veto held the increase considerably below that urged by employee unions.

The military pay raise voted by Congress was more than double the figure recommended by the Administration. It raised the pay of enlisted men with less than two years' service for the first time in 13 years.

Federal Pay

Congress late in 1965 passed legislation (HR 10281— PL 89-301) providing a 3.6-percent across-the-board pay increase for about 1.8 million federal career, postal, legislative and judicial employees, retroactive to Oct. 1, 1965.

The bill also liberalized postal overtime and relocation allowances; granted substitute postal workers time-and-a-half for overtime for the first time; and established, for the first time, a severance pay system applicable to nearly all federal civilian workers. Pay provisions of the measure were estimated to cost $488.2 million a year; fringe benefit provisions, $153.3 million a year, a total of $641.5 million a year for the bill as a whole. The increases were the 11th pay raise received by postal workers and the 12th received by classified employees since 1945.

Congress was under heavy pressure from federal employee and postal worker unions to grant a far more costly pay increase than finally enacted. They sought a 7-percent raise. An increase of that general magnitude, they argued, would be necessary to maintain the principle of "comparability" established in the 1962 federal pay bill, namely, that federal salaries should be comparable to those paid in private industry for the same level of work.

President Johnson, on the other hand, on the basis of April 15 recommendations of a special pay panel he had established, recommended a 3 percent increase in a May 12 message to Congress.

Mr. Johnson, in statements at various times, indicated that a 3 percent raise would be consistent with his desire that wage and price increases in the economy conform with "guideposts" aimed at avoiding inflation which were established by the Council of Economic Advisers in 1962 and repeated in documents accompanying Mr. Johnson's 1965 Economic Report. According to the guideposts, in order to avoid inflation, wage increases should not

exceed the average increase in worker productivity nationally over the previous five years. The Council said this productivity rate in 1964 was 3.2 percent.

Mr. Johnson indicated that because of the possible inflationary effect, he strongly opposed any federal pay increase exceeding the limit derived from the wage-price guideposts. In several statements, he gave Congress reason to believe that he would veto any federal pay increase bill granting raises much in excess of his 3 percent recommendation. *(See box.)*

When the House, acting first on the pay raise bill, passed by a 370-7 roll-call vote a version granting a 4 percent increase as of Oct. 1, 1965, with an additional automatic increase ranging from 3 to 8 percent to take effect a year later, it appeared that Congress and the President were on a collision course.

During House floor action Sept. 30, debate centered on Administration opposition to the 4.5 percent pay raise then proposed and on Members' opposition to a provision authorizing an automatic pay increase, effective January 1967, for Members of Congress and federal executives and judges equal to percentage increases granted in the future to top classified employees (GS 18) or the over-all average increases granted all classified employees, whichever was greater. The House reduced the over-all pay raise to 4 percent by a 107-33 standing vote and deleted the automatic pay increase by a 238-140 roll call.

The Senate's Post Office and Civil Service Committee reduced the first-step pay raise to 3.6 percent and eliminated the proposed second-step automatic raise approved by the House. The Committee said it made the changes on the ground that the Federal Government must abide by Administration wage-price guidelines "if it expects private industry to abide by them." The Senate passed the amended bill by a 67-0 roll-call vote.

Some Members urged the House to reject the Senate version and stand firm behind its own proposal, arguing that the Senate bill would bring salaries close to comparability only at the lower grades and not at the middle and higher grades which were furthest from comparability. The House bill, they said, would bring federal workers closer to the comparability goal. But Chairman Morris K. Udall (D Ariz.) of the House Post Office and Civil Service Compensation Subcommittee said that, although the Senate version was "a watered down, toothless, illegitimate, emaciated outrage," leaders of the federal and postal employees unions preferred to accept a 3.6-percent raise in 1965 rather than risk a veto by the President of a bill containing a larger raise. Consequently, the House agreed by voice vote to the Senate version and the President signed the measure into law Oct. 29.

Provisions

As signed by the President, PL 89-301, the Federal Employees Salary Act of 1965:

Pay Raises. Authorized an across-the-board, 3.6 percent federal pay increase, retroactive to Oct. 1, 1965, for persons covered by the Classification Act of 1949, the Postal Field Service Compensation Act of 1955 and related Acts, the Foreign Service Act of 1946, the Medicine and Surgery Salary System of the Veterans Administration and the Agricultural Stabilization and Conservation Service's County Committee salary system; for officers and employees of the Legislative and Judicial Branches; and for federal and District of Columbia officers and employees whose salaries were fixed administratively, other than in accordance with prevailing wage rates.

Provided that no federal employee salary rate shall exceed that of Level V of the Federal Executive Salary Schedule ($26,000).

Increased from $30,000 to $35,000 annually the salaries of the Majority and Minority Leaders of the Senate and the House of Representatives.

Limited maximum salaries for officers and employees of the Senate, whose rates were not fixed by law, to $23,770 annually, and reserved to each Senator the authority to determine whether the pay increases would apply to his own employees.

Fringe Benefits. Required the heads of departments and agencies, "to the maximum extent practicable," to schedule all official travel away from an employee's official duty station within his regularly scheduled workweek.

Established a basic workweek of five eight-hour days for all postal workers and required, "to the maximum extent practicable," the assignment of senior regular employees to a basic workweek, Monday-through-Friday.

Provided that substitute postal employees would be paid at time-and-a-half rates (that is, at 150 percent of their regular rate) for overtime and for work on Christmas day, but at straight-time rates for work on other holidays.

Provided that regular postal employees would receive time-and-a-half pay for overtime if in postal grade 7 or below, and either time-and-a-half pay or compensatory time if in grade 8 or above. (Previously, employees in grade 8 or above could receive only compensatory time.)

Provided that regular postal employees would receive double-time pay (twice the normal rate) for holiday work if in grade 7 or below, and either double-time pay or compensatory time for work on holidays if in grade 8 or higher. (Previously, those in grade 7 or below received either double-time pay or compensatory time for holidays, and those in grade 8 or above received only compensatory time.)

Gave the Postmaster General discretion, in applying the two provisions described immediately above, to determine whether compensation for overtime by employees of grade 8 and over should take the form of time-and-a-half pay or the form of compensatory time.

Provided that regular postal employees would be paid at 2½ times their regular rate for work on Christmas day. (Same as before.)

Provided that regular postal employees would be paid for Sunday work, if falling within their basic workweek, at the rate of 125 percent of the regular hourly wage for their level. (Previously, they merely received their regular rate of pay.)

Authorized the Postmaster General, retroactive to July 1, 1965, to grant postal employees required to relocate by the Department (1) a per diem allowance for each member of his family while en route to his new location, (2) subsistence expenses for each member of his family for not to exceed 30 days while occupying temporary quarters at his new location and (3) five days of extra leave with pay.

Increased from $100 to $125 annual allowances for all federal employees required to wear a uniform.

President's Position

While the 1965 pay raise legislation was under consideration by the Post Office and Civil Service Committee in the House, President Johnson pressed his insistence on a non-inflationary increase. He did so on the occasion of signing a bill (HR 1771—PL 89-116) providing a five-day workweek for postmasters. He said, "I do want to say to all of you that it is going to be pretty difficult for the President of the United States to be the first person to be the chief wrecker of a non-inflationary wage and price policy." He also said, "I hope that the postmasters who will benefit from what we are doing today, and the other federal employees who will benefit from the recommendations that we have made on all this legislation this year, will not ask for any special privileges over and above what we ask the rest of the country to follow."

In his press conference Aug. 25, nine days after the Committee reported HR 10281, President Johnson was asked if he thought the pay increases in the bill, which far exceeded 3 percent, violated the wage-price guideposts. Mr. Johnson answered, "I do think that it would violate the guidelines. I do hope that the Congress will carefully and thoroughly consider the destructive effect it would have if we should pass the bill in its present form." He said the Committee bill would be "very disastrous to our price-wage stability policy in this country."

A day after signing HR 10281 into law Oct. 29, President Johnson commented, "In Government, as in industry, rapid change will continue to cause dislocations in employment...I am pleased that this bill enables the Government to provide severance pay to federal employees whose jobs are eliminated." He also said, "Above all, the benefits conferred by this bill are made possible within the wage-price guideposts developed by the Council of Economic Advisers."

Established, effective upon enactment, a system of severance pay, for nearly all federal employees losing their jobs through no fault of their own and not entitled to immediate civil service retirement benefits, of an amount equal to the sum of (1) one week's pay for each of the employees' first 10 years of service, plus (2) two weeks' pay for each year of service beyond 10 years, plus (3) 10 percent of the basic severance allowance (the sum of 1 and 2) for each year the employee was over age 40 (total severance pay could not exceed the equivalent of one year's pay).

Allowed a federal employee whose in-grade raises were denied by his agency because of poor performance on the job to appeal the denial to the Civil Service Commission. (Under the 1962 federal pay bill, employees not performing at an "acceptable level of competence" could be denied in-grade raises until their work improved. There was no appeal beyond the head of their own agency. HR 10281 now permitted an appeal to the Civil Service Commission.)

Federal Retirement Pay

In 1965 Congress enacted Administration-backed legislation (HR 8469—PL 89-205) increasing pensions received by retired federal employees and Members of Congress and revising the method of determining future cost-of-living pay increases for retirees. The bill did not affect retirement contribution rates, which remained at 6.5 percent of salary for employees (7.5 percent for Members), matched by an equal amount contributed by the Federal Government. The bill was estimated to cost $101.9 million a year.

In its major provisions, HR 8469 increased by 11.1 percent (6.5 percent plus an estimated 4.6 percent which represented the increase in the cost of living between 1962 and September 1965, as gauged by the Consumer Price Index) the amount of pensions received by persons who had retired on or before Oct. 1, 1956. It also boosted by 6.1 percent (1.5 percent plus the 4.6-percent cost-of-living increase) the amount of pensions received by persons who retired after that date but prior to Dec. 1, 1965. (The latter date was changed to Dec. 31 in PL 89-314—see below.) The same provisions applied to pensions received by survivors (mostly widows) of these retirees. The bill also increased by 15-percent or $10, whichever was less, the monthly payments for survivors of federal employees who died prior to the date that formal survivor pensions were begun in 1948 (PL 80-426).

The increases provided by HR 8469 were designed to partially remove the difference in benefits received by pre-1956 and post-1956 retirees. In 1956, Congress in PL 84-854 voted benefit increases averaging 20 percent for future retirees but did nothing to improve the position of persons already on the retirement rolls. In 1958, Congress in PL 85-465 provided benefit increases averaging 10 percent for pre-1956 retirees, thus closing about half the gap created by the 1956 law.

In addition, HR 8469 changed the method of determining future cost-of-living pay adjustments for retirees by providing automatic pension increases whenever the Consumer Price Index rose 3 percent for three consecutive months in place of the existing requirement of an average 3 percent rise for an entire calendar year. According to the House Committee, the cost-of-living adjustment principle, adopted in 1962 (PL 87-793), was producing "disappointing" results.

For example, the Consumer Price Index rose by an average of only 2.6 percent in 1964 (not enough to warrant a retiree pay adjustment) even though it reached 3 percent in November 1964 and increased steadily to 3.7 percent in May 1965 and to 4.6 percent in September 1965. Under existing law, a retiree had to wait until three months after the end of 1965 to receive the cost-of-living adjustment. Under HR 8469, the retiree would have received the adjustment soon after the increase averaged 3 percent over three consecutive months. (An identical provision was adopted in 1965 for military retirees. *(See story below.)*

Related Development. Congress enacted a bill (HR 11303—PL 89-314), signed Nov. 1, extending the terminal date for benefit increases under HR 8469 from Dec. 1 to Dec. 31, 1965. The extension was designed to retain, during the 1965 Christmas season, the services of numerous employees (mostly postal workers) who had planned to

retire prior to Dec. 1 in order to receive the benefit increases. (Retirees eligible for the new benefits in 1965 received pension increases of 8.1 percent—6.1 percent as provided by HR 8469 plus a 2 percent "bonus" provided in the 1962 law (PL 87-793) for all retirees leaving Government service during calendar 1965.)

According to the Civil Service Commission, an estimated additional 20,000 federal civilian employees took advantage of the benefit increases, electing to retire during the period November-December 1965. The normal monthly retirement rate was 5,000.

Military Pay Raise

By unanimous roll-call votes of both chambers, Congress in 1965 enacted an Administration-opposed bill (HR 9075—PL 89-132) authorizing basic pay and related pay increases for active duty and retired members of the uniformed military services, plus uniformed personnel of the Reserves, Coast Guard, Public Health Service and Coast and Geodetic Survey. The bill was estimated to cost $1,048,029,000 a year, more than double the $504.3-million pay increases recommended by the Administration. Raises went to about 4.1 million uniformed military personnel.

Of the total authorized, $880.4 million was for basic pay increases, averaging an over-all 10.4 percent and effective Sept. 1, 1965. The pay of enlisted men with less than two years' service was increased for the first time since 1952. The remaining $167.6 million was for such items as Social Security payments, terminal leave payments, retired personnel benefits, new hostile-fire pay rates and new re-enlistment bonuses.

HR 9075 was a slightly revised version of a bill (HR 5725) introduced earlier in the session by House Armed Services Committee Chairman L. Mendel Rivers (D S.C.). The legislation, according to Rivers, was designed to give military personnel a substantial pay boost in order to "correct" the current "inequitable" lag between military and federal civilian employees' pay scales.

The Senate made a net $4.3 million cut in the House-approved total. Among other changes, the Senate approved an Administration proposal to provide for future cost-of-living pay increases for all retirees. This provision was identical to that adopted for federal civilian employees in 1965. *(See above.)* The House concurred in the Senate amendments by voice vote.

Upon signing HR 9075 into law Aug. 21, President Johnson said that, while the measure provided pay raises of more than $540 million above what he sought, "In this critical period...in light of the alternatives available to me, I have concluded that the public interest will best be served by signing the bill."

Enactment of HR 9075 constituted the third major military pay increase since 1963. PL 88-132, signed Oct. 2, 1963, authorized pay increases of $1.2 billion, including 17 percent raises for all active duty personnel with two or more years of service. PL 88-422, signed Aug. 21, 1964, authorized increases of $207.5 million, including 2.5 percent raises for all active duty personnel except enlisted men with less than two years of service.

Congress in 1965 also enacted legislation (HR 3044—PL 89-149) increasing the pay of enlisted men by $55 a month and of officers by $110 a month while serving on flight deck crews of aircraft carriers. The increase was estimated to cost $5.3 million annually.

PROVISIONS—As signed by the President, PL 89-132:

Authorized military pay increases totaling $1,048,-029,000 for an estimated 2.7 million uniformed personnel on active duty, 1 million reservists and 505,000 retired personnel.

Basic Pay Costs. Of the total, $809,855,000 was for basic pay increases for active duty armed forces personnel of the Defense Department, broken down as follows:

• $136.6 million for officers with more than two years' service, for a flat 6 percent increase. The basic pay of a first lieutenant with four years' service would rise from $477 a month to $505; the pay of a brigadier general with 28 years' service, from $1,266 a month to $1,342; the pay of a chief of staff, from $2,019 a month to $2,140.

• $493.1 million for enlistees with more than two years' service, for a flat 11 percent increase. The basic pay of a corporal with five years' service would rise from $210 a month to $233; the pay of a sergeant first class with 18 years' service, from $379 a month to $421.

• $28.9 million for officers with less than two years' service, for a flat 11 percent increase. The basic pay of a second lieutenant would rise by 22.2 percent, from $241 a month to $295; the pay of a captain by 21 percent, from $354 to $428.

• $151.2 million for enlistees with less than two years' service, for an average 17.3 percent increase. The basic pay of a recruit would rise 12.7 percent, from $78 a month to $88; the pay of a sergeant by 33.6 percent, from $145 a month to $194.

In addition, the bill authorized basic pay increases totaling $53,536,000 for reservists and approximately $17 million for uniformed personnel of the Coast Guard. Public Health Service and Coast and Geodetic Survey and officer candidates.

Additional Costs. The remaining $167.6 million of the $1-billion increase went for such items as Social Security, re-enlistment bonuses, hostile-fire pay, terminal leave payments and retired personnel benefits.

The bill also:

Permitted variable re-enlistment bonuses of up to four times current rates for personnel possessing critically needed skills.

Authorized a $10 monthly increase (to $65) in hostile-fire pay.

Granted free first-class postage for servicemen in areas designated by the President as combat zones.

Authorized a "bonus" increase in retirement pay for personnel retired prior to the effective date of HR 9075 equal to the percentage by which the Consumer Price Index rose from the 1962 average to August 1965 (about 4 percent).

Provided for future cost-of-living pay increases for all retirees whenever the Consumer Price Index rose 3 percent for three consecutive months in place of the existing requirement of an average 3 percent rise for an entire year.

Established a procedure requiring the President to review the "adequacy" of military pay each year and report to Congress and requiring the President to review the "principles and concepts" of military pay each four years.

Set the effective date of the pay raises on the first day of the month following the date of enactment (Sept. 1, 1965).

Servicemen's Insurance

Congress enacted Administration-supported legislation (S 2127—PL 89-214) in 1965 permitting all military personnel to purchase $10,000 in low-cost group life insurance to protect them against the risk of death in service, whether from battle or other causes not connected with combat in any way. The bill also authorized $5,000 death benefit payments to survivors of servicemen who died under certain conditions between Jan. 1, 1957, and the effective date of S 2127—the period during which no servicemen's insurance was available.

The insurance provisions of PL 89-214 authorized the Administrator of the Veterans Administration (VA) to purchase group life insurance policies from one or more participating life insurance companies. Each individual entering the armed forces would be eligible for the $10,000 coverage unless he affirmatively elected not to receive it or elected instead to receive insurance in the amount of only $5,000. The policy would be effective only for the duration of the individual's term of service unless he converted it to a permanent plan.

The premium rates for servicemen under the group plan would be determined by the VA. They were estimated at about $2 a month for $10,000 policies and $1 a month for $5,000 policies, amounts believed sufficient to make the program, including VA administrative costs, self-sustaining. Premiums were to be deducted from servicemen's pay.

The final version of S 2127 was based largely on amendments added in the House which made the bill acceptable to the Administration. The Senate version, which the Administration opposed, was more selective in its coverage and would have authorized free, Government-financed $10,000 "special indemnity insurance" benefits for survivors of military personnel who were killed on duty in "combat zones."

Rationale of Bill. A system of substantial monthly benefits already existed for survivors of military personnel killed in action or dying from other service-connected causes from Jan. 1, 1957, on. It was called the Dependency and Indemnity Compensation (DIC) system (PL 84-881). Under that 1956 law establishing DIC, as amended in 1963, for example, payments for a surviving widow were $112 a month plus 12 percent of current basic pay for the deceased serviceman's last rank. The payments, however, were available only to certain classes of beneficiaries: spouses, unmarried children under 18 or dependent parents. A separate system of monthly benefits also existed for survivors of those dying from service-connected causes before Jan. 1, 1957. It was called "death compensation." *(Congress and the Nation, Vol. I, p. 1352.)*

Although DIC benefits were generally considered adequate, the following four factors led to enactment of S 2127 in light of the existing world situation: (1) The desire to provide survivors of servicemen killed in action (many of whom were uninsured or uninsurable) with large lump-sum insurance payments in addition to monthly DIC benefits. (2) The unwillingness of most private insurance companies to write life insurance covering servicemen when they were assigned to combat areas such as Vietnam. (3) The desire to permit servicemen to provide for persons—such as brothers, sisters, grown children, non-dependent parents or friends—other than those eligible for DIC or death compensation. (4) The desire to provide an added inducement for men to seek a service career. As enacted, the insurance available under S 2127 was basically similar to that available from 1940-51 under the old National Service Life Insurance (NSLI) program.

Provisions—As signed by the President Sept. 29, (PL 89-214):

Life Insurance. Authorized the Administrator of Veterans Affairs to purchase from private insurance companies group life insurance policies to cover members of the armed forces on active duty.

Provided that each member of the armed forces would be insured against death in the amount of $10,000 unless (1) he stated in writing that he did not want the insurance or (2) he chose to be insured in the amount of $5,000. Allowed a person refusing the insurance or choosing the lower amount to obtain the full coverage later upon proof of good health and meeting any other requirements specified by the Veterans Administration.

Provided that the insurance policies authorized under the legislation would terminate 120 days after a member's separation or release from active duty or upon a member's being absent without leave for a period of more than 31 days. Provided that a member, at any time during the period he was covered, could convert the insurance policy to permanent, regular insurance without medical examination.

Stipulated that premiums, as determined by the Veterans' Affairs Administrator, would be deducted from each member's monthly "basic or other pay" until his separation or release from active duty (amounts previously paid would cover the final 120-day period).

Stipulated that the VA would pay each month to the participating insurance companies the costs traceable to "extra hazards" such as currently existed in Vietnam. (The cost would be determined on the basis of the "excess mortality" suffered by recent and former armed services' members insured under the legislation above the mortality incurred by the U.S. civilian male population of the same age as the median age of armed services' members).

Authorized the insured to designate anyone he desired as beneficiary.

Provided that the group insurance would be in addition to any United States Government Life Insurance, National Service Life Insurance or other benefits that the insured might hold or that survivors might be eligible to receive.

Established an Advisory Council on Servicemen's Group Life Insurance consisting of the Secretary of the Treasury as chairman, the Secretaries of Defense, Commerce and Health, Education and Welfare, and the Director of the Bureau of the Budget, to meet annually or more often the call of the Administrator and to assist the Administrator in matters relating to activities carried out under the legislation.

Provided that the insurance would take effect on a date designated by the Administrator (Sept. 29, 1965).

Death Gratuity. Authorized a $5,000 retroactive "death gratuity" payment to survivors of armed services' members who died under specified conditions on or after Jan. 1, 1957, and before the effective date of the insurance provided by S 2127.

Stipulated that death must result from (1) action of hostile forces, (2) a military or naval aircraft accident, (3) "the extra hazard of military or naval service," as determined by the VA, or (4) service for which special pay or hazardous duty pay was authorized.

Provided that the payment would be made only if applied for within one year after enactment of S 2127 and if the person receiving the gratuity waived all future death compensation and DIC payments.

Required that the amount of the gratuity be reduced by the amount of any death compensation, DIC, National Service Life Insurance or U.S. Government life insurance payable as a result of the death of the armed forces' member.

Provided that a gratuity payment could go only to a widow or widower, a child or children of the veteran (in equal amounts), or the parents of the veteran, in that order. (The gratuity was designed to aid certain special categories of survivors, namely, those ineligible for DIC and death compensation benefits, such as married children, children over 18 and non-dependent parents, plus any person whose monthly DIC or death compensation benefit was very small—for example, a parent receiving the minimum single-person DIC payment of $17 a month).

1966

Congress increased the pay of most federal employees in 1966 for the 13th time in 21 years. It also raised the basic pay of all military personnel.

The federal pay legislation based on President Johnson's recommendations provided a 2.87 to 2.9 percent across-the-board pay increase, retroactively effective as of July 1, 1966, for about 1.8 million federal career, postal and foreign service employees and employees of the Legislative and Judicial branches. It also included health and retirement provisions.

The military pay raise was added by the House to the defense procurement and research authorization bill. It increased the basic pay of all armed services personnel by 3.2 percent, effective July 1, 1966.

President Johnson approved both measures, but he noted that Congress had made the increases effective six months earlier than he had sought, adding almost half a billion dollars to the fiscal 1967 budget. The President said: "Taken alone, this addition...does not spell the difference between fiscal responsibility and irresponsibility, or between stable prices and inflation...But should it be followed by other actions which add sharply to our spending, the over-all result could seriously jeopardize our efforts to maintain sound economic growth without inflation."

Those remarks, made July 18 when he signed the federal employees pay bill, underscored the Administration's frequently expressed concern over rising inflation. In his request for increased employee benefits falling within the 3.2 percent limit suggested as a guidepost by the Council of Economic Advisers, Mr. Johnson had said March 7:

"If our Government is to exercise continued leadership in the fight for price stability, then we must continue to practice what we preach. The Government has the added responsibility of not contributing to inflation by its own actions."

Mr. Johnson vetoed a bill to increase life insurance coverage for federal employees, calling the measure inflationary. He told newsmen that "at a time when we are making every effort to reduce low-priority federal spending in other areas, this bill cannot be justified." *(See below.)*

Federal Pay

The Federal Salary and Fringe Benefits Act of 1966 (HR 14122—PL 89-504) granted workers in the classified civil service their 13th pay raise of the post-World War II era. It also gave postal workers their 12th pay raise in that period.

The bill contained an across-the-board increase of about 2.9 percent, retroactive to the first pay period beginning on or after July 1, 1966. The 2.9 percent figure, one of the lowest percentage increases ever granted, applied to all persons covered by the bill except employees in the top three Government salary grades (GS 16-18, PFS 18-20, etc.). The latter received somewhat smaller increases as low as 2 percent in most cases. The bill also provided increased fringe benefits, health benefits and retirement benefits. The total cost of the final bill was estimated at $620.4 million a year.

The raises in HR 14122 applied to some 1.8 million of the Government's 2.5 million employees. These included persons covered by the four major statutory federal pay systems (Classification Act, Postal Field Service Compensation Act, Foreign Service Act, Veterans' Administration Medicine and Surgery Salary System), plus employees of Congress and the Judicial Branch, employees of the federal wage boards, persons subject to the Agricultural Stabilization and Conservation Service's County Committee Salary System, and certain other minor categories of federal employees.

The bill did not increase the salaries of federal judges, Members of Congress, top appointive federal officials (such as Cabinet and sub-Cabinet officials and those subject to the Federal Executive Salary Schedule), or federal blue-collar workers (engaged in building construction, shipbuilding, etc.).

Costs, Guideposts. A key factor in debate on the bill was the wage-price "guidepost" concept. First enunciated by the Council of Economic Advisers in 1962, it was designed to prevent inflation. According to this concept, the total increases in wages and fringe benefits in any year for any group of employees in the economy— federal or private—should not exceed over-all percentage increases in labor productivity. On this basis, the Council calculated that no employee increases should exceed 3.2 percent in 1966.

The President, in requesting 1966 enactment of a federal pay raise bill, asked Congress to stay within the 3.2 percent guidepost figure. However, the Administration did not base its calculations on the cost of all benefits in the

---

Johnson on Comparability

In asking pay increases and new fringe benefits for federal employees in 1966, President Johnson said in a March 7 message to Congress:

"In recent years, we have moved steadily to compensate these men and women equitably and competitively for their quality performance in the public interest. To that end, the Administration prepared and the Congress enacted, the Federal Salary Reform Act of 1962. We established the principle that Government workers are entitled to a pay scale which compares favorably with pay in private industry.

"Such a pay scale is as much in the national interest as it is in the interest of Government employees. I said when signing the Government Employees Salary Reform Act of 1964:

" 'America's challenges cannot be met in this modern world by mediocrity, at any level, public or private. All through our society we must search for brilliance, welcome genius, strive for excellence.'

"We have been true to the principle of comparability. Since 1961, the pay of federal employees has increased by over 16 percent. In the brief period since I have been President, employees of the Federal Government have enjoyed pay increases amounting to nearly 12 percent. These increases have done much to close the gap between compensation for Government employees and those in private enterprise.

"The increases in basic pay, however, were not accompanied by any significant benefits in forms other than salary. Yet pay, retirement, and other fringe benefits are all parts of an employee's total compensation. Recognition of this basic fact is crucial in developing a rational and equitable system of compensation...."

---

bill, but only on a portion of the costs. On this basis, the Administration calculated that the total annual costs of the bill should not exceed $485 million for those pay raises and fringe benefits subject to the guideposts. The Administration also calculated that certain additional benefit increases which were to be included in the bill, but for which guidepost figures were not calculated, would add $100 million to $110 million a year to the total cost of the legislation. (The additional benefit increases included all raises and benefits for legislative and judicial employees, on whose salaries the Executive Branch normally defers to Congress and therefore did not calculate guidepost figures.)

The President reportedly indicated that he would veto any pay measure if its costs for items subject to the guideposts substantially exceeded $485 million.

The House, in passing HR 14122, provided increases of $518.6 million for portions of the bill subject to the guideposts. The Senate reduced the figure to $505.8 million a year, only $20 million more than the Administration figure and close enough to the guideposts to satisfy the President. The Senate figure was accepted by the House.

The final bill thus provided $505.8 million a year in wage and fringe benefit increases subject to the guideposts, plus $114.6 million a year in increases not subject to the guideposts.

It should be noted that while the Government's total increase in obligations as a result of the bill was $620.4 million a year, not all of that would be reflected in annual budget outlays, since some $52 million a year would come out of the civil service retirement fund and $30-odd million would represent interest owed to the civil service retirement fund by the Government but not actually paid. Actual estimated new budget outlays for the entire bill were expected to come to $532 million in fiscal 1967.

Changes in Administration Bill. The final version differed in several major respects from Mr. Johnson's proposals. One change made the raises effective July 1, 1966—six months earlier than the Jan. 1, 1967, date "urgently" requested by the President. As a result, the raises were to be in effect throughout all of fiscal 1967, instead of only the last half. The increases would thus raise federal spending for civilian pay by nearly $300 million more in fiscal 1967 than Mr. Johnson had previously calculated.

A second major change provided for a flat 2.9 percent across-the-board increase in pay, in place of Mr. Johnson's proposed graduated scale of increases rising from 1 percent at the lower pay levels to 4.5 percent at the higher levels. Administration spokesmen said federal pay scales at the lower job levels were already equivalent or nearly so to comparable jobs in private industry, whereas pay at the higher job levels was substantially below that in private industry. Therefore, they argued, the middle and upper level jobs should receive larger percentage pay increases.

In another major change, the final bill failed to grant the President's request for authority to force a person in GS 13 or a higher level job to retire at age 55 after 30 years of service.

The House passed HR 14122 by a 393-1 roll-call vote, the Senate by an 81-0 roll-call vote. The Senate by a 9-71 roll-call vote rejected an amendment by Frank J. Lausche (D Ohio) to postpone the effective date of the bill until Jan. 1, 1967, as asked by President Johnson. It rejected by an 18-62 roll-call vote an amendment by John J. Williams (R Del.) to increase Government and employee contributions to the Civil Service Retirement Fund from 6.5 to 7 percent. By a 48-33 roll-call vote, the Senate tabled (killed) a Williams amendment prohibiting representatives of political committees from soliciting contributions from civil service employees. Williams said the amendment would close a loophole in existing law.

Provisions

As signed by the President July 18, PL 89-504, the Federal Salary and Fringe Benefits Act of 1966:

Title 1—Federal Employee Salaries. Authorized 2.9-percent pay increases for persons under the Classification Act of 1949, the Postal Field Service Compensation Act of 1955 and related Acts, the Foreign Service Act of 1946, the Medicine and Surgery Salary System of the Veterans Administration and the Agricultural Stabilization and Conservation Service's County Committee salary system and for assistant U.S. attorneys and federal and District of Columbia officers and employees whose salaries are fixed administratively, other than in accordance with prevailing wage rates.

Permitted heads of departments, in certain circumstances, to appoint exceptionally qualified individuals to steps above the minimum entrance step in GS 11 (rather than 13 as in existing law) and above, with the approval of the Civil Service Commission.

Made the pay increase effective the first pay period beginning on or after July 1, 1966; made the other provisions effective upon enactment.

Title II—Federal Judicial Salaries. Authorized pay increases for Judicial Branch employees to be comparable with the proposed raises for Executive Branch employees governed by the Classification Act (above).

Made the pay increase effective the first pay period beginning on or after July 1, 1966.

Title III—Federal Legislative Salaries. Authorized a 2.9-percent increase in the gross rate of compensation for officers and employees of the Legislative Branch.

Provided that the total annual compensation of the Clerk of the House and the Sergeant at Arms of the House, respectively, equal the total annual compensation of the Secretary of the Senate and the Sergeant at Arms of the Senate, respectively.

Stipulated that the increase not apply to student interns in the House and employees covered by the House Wage Schedule under the House Employees Position Classification Act.

Permitted a Senator to deny his office employees the increase.

Raised from $23,770 to $24,460 the maximum annual gross compensation allowed most Senate officers and employees.

Prohibited a salary increase in an amount which would provide an employee (other than specified above) with a salary greater than the salary currently or thereafter in effect for level 5 of the Federal Executive Salary Schedule (currently $26,000).

Made the pay raise effective the first pay period beginning on or after July 1, 1966.

Title IV—Miscellaneous Benefits. Authorized the Postmaster General to appoint or advance employees transferred with their jobs from other federal agencies and departments to the postal service to a point in the salary scale which would protect them against a loss of salary.

Authorized overtime pay for classified employees (except scientific and engineering personnel and employees above GS 10, step 1, for whom the first 40 hours of work constitutes the "basic work week") and wage board employees who work more than eight hours in a single day.

Required overtime compensation to take the form of money, rather than compensatory time, for Postal Field Service employees in grade PFS 10 or lower and for classified employees in grade GS 10, step 1, or lower.

Authorized compensation of classified and wage board employees at a rate of the regular salary plus 25 percent of the regular salary for an entire eight-hour period of work, any part of which falls on Sunday (midnight Saturday to midnight Sunday), providing the work is not considered overtime.

Required (rather than permitted) federal agencies and departments to provide allowances for uniforms where authorized by law. Increased uniform allowances.

Fixed the Salary of the Director of the Federal Mediation and Conciliation Service at level III of the Federal Executive Salary Schedule ($28,500), instead of level IV ($27,000).

Title V—Civil Service Retirement. Broadened the definition of "child" to extend benefit entitlement to a child survivor of a deceased federal employee, providing the child is attending school, until the end of the school year following the child's 22nd, rather than 21st, birthday.

Permitted a Government official or employee on leave without pay to work as an officer or employee of a recognized employees' organization and to continue to receive full retirement credit providing he arranges to pay both his and the agency's contribution to the retirement fund.

Permitted federal employees (except Members of Congress) to retire with full annuities at age 55 after 30 years of service or at age 60 after 20 years of service.

Permitted surviving spouses of employees or retired employees (except Members of Congress) to continue to receive their survivor annuities (55 percent of the employee's annuity) if they remarry after age 60. Under existing law, these benefits terminated upon remarriage.

Permitted surviving spouses of employees and retired employees to regain benefits if a remarriage which took place before they reached 60 years of age terminates in death of the partner or divorce.

Increased by 10 percent the annuity paid to the surviving spouse of a deceased Member of Congress or federal employee who died or retired before Oct. 11, 1962.

Made provisions effective upon enactment unless otherwise provided.

Title VI—Health Benefits. Extended from 21 to 22 years the age limit for health insurance coverage for children of federal employees.

Authorized biweekly Government contributions of $1.62 (rather than $1.25-$1.75) for individuals and $3.94 (rather than $3.00-$4.25) for an individual with a family for health benefits. (The actual effect was to increase the Government contribution.)

Provided that, if these amounts were more than twice the amount the individual contributed, the Government would pay 50 percent of the total premium, as of the first pay period beginning on or after July 1, 1966.

Coverage. The civil service retirement system covers all major civilian pay groups in the Government except Foreign Service Officers, who have a retirement system of their own. Therefore, the new retirement benefits of Title V would apply to all classified, postal, VA Medicine and Surgery, legislative and judicial employees, plus some of the smaller pay groups, plus any State Department employees not eligible for the Foreign Service Officers' separate retirement system. The health benefits in Title VI would go to all the same groups, plus any State Department employees who had opted to be covered by the general Government-wide health insurance in place of several existing Department plans.

Military Pay Increase

Congress approved a 3.2 percent increase in basic pay of all armed services personnel, effective July 1, 1966. Administration officials estimated costs of the action at an annual $356.8 million. The provision was added to a bill (S 2950—PL 89-501) authorizing appropriations to the Defense Department for weapons procurement and research and development by the House Armed Services Committee. The Committee report said the increase was necessary to raise military pay commensurate with the 2.87 to 2.9 percent over-all federal civilian pay increase embodied in legislation (HR 14122) then pending in the Senate following passage by the House.

The pay increase affected active and reserve military personnel, as well as those who retired after the bill went into effect. Special allowances were unchanged. The military pay provision as adopted by the House was agreed to by the House-Senate conference committee and included in the $17.5 billion authorization bill signed by President Johnson July 13.

Federal Insurance

President Johnson Sept. 12 vetoed a bill (HR 6926) increasing life insurance for federal employees. He said it would cost the Government nearly $90 million a year, instead of the $12 million which the Administration's proposals on the subject would have cost. The President said that to increase federal spending that much above Administration proposals was unjustified and would have inflationary effects, particularly in view of the fact that Congress "at the request of the (federal)employee unions" had just passed a federal pay raise which was to go into effect six months earlier than the President wanted and therefore would add "almost $300 million more than I requested" to the Government's fiscal 1967 outlays. (*See above.*)

To make up a deficit in the insurance program which then amounted to $31.6 million a year, the Administration in 1966 proposed that federal employees' biweekly contribution be increased from 25 cents to 30 cents per $1,000 of insurance. The Government contribution, meanwhile, would rise from the existing 12.5 cents to 15 cents. This would cover the deficit, maintain the existing 2-1 ratio of employee contributions to Government contributions, and increase Government costs by $11 to $12 million a year.

As passed by voice vote in both chambers and sent to the President, the bill changed the basic insurance, as compared to existing law, from an amount equal to the individual's annual pay, with a limit of $20,000, to an amount equal to 1-1/3 times the individual's annual pay, plus $2,000, with a limit of $42,000. This raised annual program costs by about $147 million. HR 6926 further provided that henceforth, employee and Government contributions should be sufficient to meet all costs, leaving no annual actuarial deficit; and that, instead of the existing 2-1 contribution ratio, employees would pay only 60 percent of program costs and the Government would contribute the remaining 40 percent. The net effect of the added $147 million in costs for the new benefits in the bill, the requirement that the deficit (now estimated at $35 million a year) be wiped out, and the change in the contribution ratio, was to increase Government contributions by $88.1 million a year above the existing level. Employees would have to increase their contributions by about $95 million.

Neither House nor Senate attempted to repass the bill after the President vetoed it on budgetary grounds.

Other Legislation

Supergrade Jobs. The President Oct. 8 signed into law an Administration-endorsed bill (S 2393—PL 89-632) creating 300 new positions in the supergrades (GS 16-18) of the classified system. As initially passed by the Senate Sept. 1, 1965, the bill was a stopgap measure authorizing 100 new supergrade jobs which the Civil Service Commission said were urgently needed to staff new agencies or functions. Subsequently, however, long-range staffing needs were studied and the House passed S 2393 June 6, 1966, with amendments raising the total of new positions to 456.

The final version, cleared Sept. 21 by the House and Sept. 22 by the Senate, authorized 300 new supergrade positions, as follows: 177 for the Civil Service Commission "pool," to be distributed among various federal agencies at the direction of the Commission (this raised the total in the pool to 2,577); 28 for the Library of Congress (which previously had no statutory supergrade jobs, and depended entirely on the CSC pool); 25 for the General Accounting Office (raising its total to 64); 35 for the Federal Bureau of Investigation (raising its total to 110); 5 for the National Security Agency (raising its total to 70); and 30 new scientific and professional jobs which were the equivalent of supergrades for the National Security Agency (raising the total of such jobs to 90).

Workmen's Compensation. Congress in 1966 enacted a bill (HR 10721—PL 89-488) increasing the benefits payable under the Federal Employees Compensation Act of 1916—the law providing workmen's compensation for federal employees. HR 10721, the 18th amendment to the 1916 Act, removed the existing ceiling of $525 a month on benefits paid to federal employees and their dependents when such employees are injured in the performance of their duties, and substituted a ceiling based on 75 percent of the salary paid in the highest step of GS 15 of the classified schedule. The bill also provided for automatic increase in benefit payments equal to the cost-of-living increase when the cost of living as measured by the Consumer Price Index rose 3 percent or more for three consecutive months. Other compensation provisions of the Act were also liberalized.

Upon signing the bill into law July 4, 1966, the President "strongly" urged "each state, in the light of these new federal amendments to examine its workmen's compensation law and act to assure that workers disabled by work injuries are properly compensated for the loss of their earnings."

CLAIMS PROCEDURES

President Johnson in July signed into law four Administration bills that he said were "long overdue reform measures" advancing "equal justice under the law." The bills were enacted without controversy. They were:

HR 13650—PL 89-506 (July 18). Amended the Federal Tort Claims Act to authorize heads of federal agencies to settle claims up to $25,000 and, with approval of the Attorney General, above that amount. Previously, only the Attorney General could settle claims, after suit was filed.

HR 13651—PL 89-508 (July 19). The Federal Claims Collections Act of 1966 authorized agency heads to attempt collection of Government claims against citizens and to settle such claims up to $5,000. Previously, only when claims were referred to the Attorney General for suit could they be settled.

HR 13652—PL 89-505 (July 18). Set a six-year statute of limitations for actions brought by the United States involving contracts, three years for actions involving a tort, and six years for actions involving money erroneously paid. Previously, most Federal Government claims were not subject to a statute of limitations.

HR 14182—PL 89-507 (July 18). Authorized courts to award costs to the prevailing party in actions involving the United States. Previously, costs were seldom awarded against the Government when it lost.

1967

Congress approved 4.5 percent pay increases in 1967 both for federal civilian employees and for military personnel. In a major departure from previous practice, it provided also for pay raises in 1968 and 1969 which would require no further legislation. The latter action, taken at President Johnson's request in the case of the civilian but not the military increases, was aimed at completely closing the gap between federal civilian pay and that of other workers.

In the Federal Salary Reform Act of 1962, Congress for the first time had officially adopted the principle that pay of federal civilian workers should be comparable to that of nongovernment workers performing the same types of duties. While that principle had long been among factors applied in determining pay scales, it had never before been proclaimed as policy by Congress. (*Congress and the Nation, Vol. I, p. 1471.*)

The civilian and military pay increases were among Mr. Johnson's few major victories in Congress in 1967, with the Democratic margin in the House cut to 47 seats by the 1966 elections and the so-called "conservative coalition" of Republicans and Southern Democrats victorious a record 38 times out of 54 legislative attempts.

The pay provisions originally were submitted as a separate bill but were attached to a much-needed revenue bill after the President threatened to veto salary increases costing more than his requests. The bill as finally enacted also established a liberalized life insurance program for federal employees estimated to cost $35.4 million a year more than the current plan.

The Federal Government's civilian employment costs had reached an all-time high of $20.5 billion in fiscal 1967, the Joint Committee on Reduction of Nonessential Federal Expenditures reported. The House Post Office and Civil Service Committee said the chief thrust of the pay provisions in the 1967 legislation was toward achievement of comparability between federal civilian salaries and those in private enterprise "without aggravating the critical budget problems of most immediate concern to the Administration and the taxpayers."

The Committee said the pay raises were "well below many employee group requests, but in their entirety represent the most liberal salary package proposed in many years."

Federal Pay

The new pay increases in 1967 of 4.5 percent for federal civilian employees, including Legislative and Judicial Branch employees, were incorporated in a bill (HR 7977—PL 90-206) signed into law Dec. 16. As requested by the Administration, the raises were made retroactive to Oct. 1.

The final version of HR 7977 combined these measures—the Administration-backed Postal Revenue Act of 1967 (HR 7977), a federal pay bill (originally HR 8261) and a federal employee life insurance plan which was attached to HR 7977 in the Senate. Pay increases in HR 7977 exceeded his budgeted costs by $63 million in fiscal 1968. When fully effective, the pay provisions were expected to cost $2.6 billion annually.

In a major departure, the bill provided automatic future pay increases that would not require Congressional action. On July 1, 1968, postal workers were to receive a 5-percent pay increase and nonpostal employees were to receive half the difference between their salary levels and comparable private enterprise salary levels (based on the June 1967 Bureau of Labor Statistics salary survey), but not less than 3 percent. A third-stage adjustment was to be made July 1, 1969, to close the "comparability gap" between salaries of private employees and Government workers, including both postal and classified employees.

(For details relating to postal pay and rates, see postal pay section.)

Pay Commission—Another, and more controversial, aspect of HR 7977 was the establishment of a "quadrennial commission" to recommend rates of pay for judges, Administration executives and Members of Congress. The commission was to include three members appointed by the President, two by the President of the Senate, two by the Speaker of the House, and two by the Chief Justice of the United States. Beginning in fiscal 1969, the commission was to submit its recommendations to the President, who was to recommend in his Budget the exact rates of pay "he deems advisable" for federal executives, judges and Members of Congress. His recommendations could be either higher or lower than those of the commission, or he could propose that salaries not be altered. The recommendations would take effect within 30 days unless Congress either disapproved all or part of them or enacted a separate pay bill. (Past salary commissions have had to submit their proposals in bill form, requiring positive action by Congress.)

Provisions establishing the commission, strongly pushed by the House and reportedly backed by the Administration, relieved Members of Congress of the politically uncomfortable task of raising their own salaries.

HOUSE

Before the House passed HR 7977 Oct. 11 by a bipartisan 319-89 roll-call vote and sent it to the Senate, it defeated by a 199-211 roll-call vote a recommittal motion by H.R. Gross (R Iowa) designed to knock out provisions for automatic second- and third-stage pay increases in July 1968 and April 1969 and for a commission to recommend future increases in salaries of Members of Congress, top Executive Branch officials and federal judges. "There is no reason whatsoever why the Congress

Johnson on Federal Pay

In asking a 4.5 percent pay increase for federal civilian employees in 1967, two additional automatic increases in 1968 and 1969 and a 4.5 percent increase for military personnel in 1967, President Johnson said in an April 5, 1967, message to Congress:

"We have made great progress recently toward a pay scale which approaches that of private industry. Since 1962, civilian employees have received pay increases amounting to more than 23 percent. We have improved retirement and other fringe benefits so that they now compare favorably with benefits in private industry. There have been corresponding increases in military pay, and fringe benefits have been improved substantially.

"Yet we still fall short of comparability with private industry....To close this gap in one year would require an average pay increase of 7.2 percent. With a similar increase for the armed forces, the cost would be more than $2.5 billion per year....I recommend that the Congress take the final step this year to achieve full comparability with private industry....

"The pay and postal rate increases I recommend in this message are essential if we are to have a government of responsive and talented people and an efficient postal system.

"Delay in attaining comparability...is inexcusable. To neglect—and thus impair—the public service would be far more expensive for the American people in the long run...."

should abdicate its authority over federal salaries to any President," Gross argued.

Morris K. Udall (D Ariz.), floor manager of the pay section, countered that Congress would be delegating its salary-fixing authority not to the President but to an independent group. Udall termed the commission "the critical reform if we are ever to get out of the annual struggle on pay that we are fighting today, with people and (postal) clerks lobbying in our offices."

Expressing its displeasure with the antipoverty agency, the House by an 86-68 standing vote accepted an amendment by Edward J. Gurney (R Fla.) eliminating pay raises for all employees of the Office of Economic Opportunity (OEO). Gurney argued that the OEO had too many supergrade personnel (GS 16-18).

SENATE

The Senate passed HR 7977 Nov. 29 by an 85-2 roll-call vote and sent it to conference with the House. Major changes from the House version included a change in the date of the final adjustment of the "comparability gap" between Government and private salary schedules to July 1, 1969; deletion of the quadrennial commission; reinstatement of OEO employees in the bill, and adding of a new life insurance program for federal employees not included in the House bill.

The Senate rejected by a 27-60 roll-call vote an amendment by John J. Williams (R Del.) "to write into

Executive Branch Civilian Employment, Fiscal 1965-1968

Federal civilian employment costs reached an all-time high of $22,400,000,000 in fiscal 1968—$1,900,000,000 more than in fiscal 1967 and $5,200,000,000 more than in fiscal 1965. The fiscal 1968 total included

$13,000,000,000 in civilian agencies and $9,400,000,000 for civilian employees in military agencies.

The following table shows the numbers employed in the major employing agencies.

	Fiscal 1965	Fiscal 1966	Fiscal 1967	Fiscal 1968
Agriculture Dept.	113,027	118,585	121,871	122,715
Health, Education and Welfare	87,316	99,810	105,600	117,115
*Interior Dept.	70,738	74,985	76,770	77,545
Post Office	595,512	675,423	716,603	730,977
*Treasury Dept.	88,765	91,365	89,496	89,125
Veterans' Administration	167,059	170,228	173,474	175,668
†All other civilian agencies	351,906	369,460	393,680	402,623
Total civilian agencies	1,474,323	1,599,856	1,677,494	1,715,768
Defense Dept.	1,033,796	1,138,191	1,302,665	1,317,049
TOTAL	2,508,119	2,738,047	2,980,159	3,032,817

* Agencies involved in transfers to new Department of Transportation.
† Includes General Accounting Office and Government Printing Office, agencies of the Legislative Branch.

SOURCE: Joint Committee on Reduction of Nonessential Expenditures

law" a Sept. 20, 1966, Executive Order freezing federal civilian employment at the July 1, 1966, level. Exempted were the Defense and Post Office Departments, the Federal Bureau of Investigation and Central Intelligence Agency. Since the order had been issued, Williams said, the President had added 185,393 more employees.

A.S. Mike Monroney (D Okla.), chairman of the Senate Post Office and Civil Service Committee, called the Williams proposal "a typical operation for a quickie amendment to vitally affect, in a dangerous way, the economy and the operation" of the Government. If Congress wished to roll back the federal employment ceiling, he added, "let us do it with a surgeon's scalpel and not with a meat ax."

Conference. House-Senate conferees agreed upon a July 1, 1969, effective date for the third stage of salary increases. They accepted House provisions for a commission to recommend top salaries every four years and agreed on Senate provisions for a liberalized life insurance plan. The House accepted the conference report by a 327-63 roll-call vote, the Senate by a 72-0 roll-call vote.

PROVISIONS—As signed into law (PL 90-206) Dec. 16, the sections of HR 7977 relating to federal pay and insurance:

Title II—Federal Pay. Increased federal civilian pay as follows:

Changed the existing 20-level postal field service salary schedule to a 21-level schedule and advanced employees one salary level (a 6 percent pay raise), retroactive to the first pay period in October 1967.

Granted 4.5 percent pay increases to employees subject to the General Schedule (classified), Foreign Service

Officer and Staff Schedules, Veterans Administration medical and surgical salary ranges, Agricultural Stabilization and Conservation county committee pay schedule, and Judicial and Legislative Branch pay rates, effective the first pay period in October 1967.

Provided second-phase increases in July 1968—a 5 percent raise for postal employees and a raise for other employees equal to one-half the difference between their salary levels and comparable private enterprise salary levels (based on the June 1967 Bureau of Labor Statistics salary survey), but not less than 3 percent. (The necessary adjustments for these other employees were to be made by the President without further legislative action.)

Called for a final, third-phase adjustment in July 1969 to bring all federal civilian employees' salaries up to par with private enterprise salaries, as determined by the June 1968 BLS survey. (This also was to be determined by the President without further legislative action.)

Increased salaries for executive levels III, IV and V from $28,500, $27,000 and $26,000 to $29,500, $28,750 and $28,000.

Established a so-called "quadrennial commission" to determine proper levels for Executive, Legislative and Judicial salaries once every four years, beginning in fiscal 1969. The Commission was to submit its recommendations to the President, and he was to recommend in his Budget the exact rates of pay for federal executives, judges and Members of Congress. The recommendations would take effect within 30 days unless Congress enacted a separate pay bill or vetoed all or part of the President's plan within that period.

Prohibited any federal or District of Columbia officer or employee (including the President and Members of Congress) from appointing or recommending for appointment or promotion a relative to serve in the same agency or department as the public official.

Increased the maximum amount of office expense funds available for payment of staff members of former Presidents from $65,000 a year to $80,000 with a limitation that no employee could receive more than executive level II salary.

Extended to wage board employees the right to appeal to the Civil Service Commission when their positions are reclassified by their agency.

Authorized federal employees, including wage board and postal workers, to count time spent in actual travel outside regular hours of work for overtime, Sunday or holiday pay purposes. Such travel was to be by the most expeditious means practicable and to conform to the duties of the employee involved.

Title IV—Life Insurance. Provided a liberalized federal employee life insurance program, granting a minimum coverage of $10,000 and a maximum of $32,000, guaranteeing all employees at least $2,000 more protection than currently provided, effective 60 days after enactment. The employee would continue to pay two-thirds of the cost and the employing agency one-third.

Provided optional insurance up to $10,000 additional to employees wishing to purchase it at their own expense, effective between 90 and 180 days after enactment. (The amount was not to exceed the employee's salary.)

Military Pay

The 1967 military pay bill (HR 13510—PL 90-207), signed into law Dec. 16, increased the monthly pay of servicemen, retroactive to Oct. 1, 1967, by 4.5 percent for "regular compensation," which included basic pay, quarters and subsistence allowances. The increase, proposed April 5 by President Johnson, corresponded to the 4.5-percent boost in federal civilian classified salaries.

In addition, HR 13510 provided automatic military pay raises in the future that would correspond to similar increases for federal civilian employees—unless Congress took separate action on servicemen's salaries. Under this automatic increase provision, which was opposed by the Administration, military pay costs could rise by as much as $2.7 billion by fiscal 1970.

HR 13510 also authorized "continuation pay" to career physicians and dentists in the Army, Navy and Air Force in critical specialty categories. The Defense Department had requested the authority only for physicians.

In other major provisions, HR 13510 provided travel and transportation allowances for servicemen who were authorized convalescent leave if such leave resulted from illness or injury incurred while the member was performing duty which made him eligible for hostile fire pay. Such transportation was estimated to cost a maximum of $2.7 million annually.

The House passed HR 13510 Oct. 26 by a 386-2 roll-call vote. It accepted a change made by its Armed Services Committee which said it deleted "any reference to what might be construed as Presidential discretion" in the establishment of future military pay increases. The Committee substituted language ensuring

Federal Salaries: Old, New Rates

LEVEL	OLD RATE*			NEW RATE**		
General Schedule (Classification Act) Employees (GS)						
GS - 1	$ 3,385	-	$ 4,420	$ 3,889	-	$ 5,057
2	3,680	-	4,805	4,360	-	5,665
3	4,005	-	5,220	4,917	-	6,393
4	4,480	-	5,830	5,522	-	7,178
5	5,000	-	6,485	6,176	-	8,030
6	5,505	-	7,170	6,882	-	8,943
7	6,050	-	7,850	7,639	-	9,934
8	6,630	-	8,610	8,449	-	10,987
9	7,220	-	9,425	9,320	-	12,119
10	7,900	-	10,330	10,252	-	13,330
11	8,650	-	11,305	11,233	-	14,599
12	10,250	-	13,445	13,389	-	17,403
13	12,075	-	15,855	15,812	-	20,555
14	14,170	-	18,580	18,531	-	24,093
15	16,460	-	21,590	21,589	-	28,069
16	18,935	-	24,175	25,044	-	31,724
17	21,445	-	24,445	28,976	-	32,840
18	24,500	-		33,495	-	——
Postal Field Service Schedule (PFS)						
PFS - 1	$ 3,945	-	$ 5,375	$ 4,522	-	$ 6,183
2	4,270	-	5,810	4,889	-	6,682
3	4,615	-	6,320	5,286	-	7,222
4	5,000	-	6,815	5,715	-	7,805
5	5,345	-	7,325	6,176	-	8,442
6	5,735	-	7,825	6,675	-	9,128
7	6,140	-	8,190	7,216	-	9,867
8	6,650	-	8,630	7,802	-	10,402
9	7,190	-	9,350	8,434	-	10,963
10	7,830	-	10,215	9,101	-	11,828
11	8,650	-	11,305	10,110	-	13,143
12	9,570	-	12,495	11,233	-	14,599
13	10,575	-	13,860	12,478	-	16,222
14	11,660	-	15,305	13,864	-	18,022
15	12,885	-	16,890	15,404	-	20,021
16	14,240	-	18,695	17,114	-	22,244
17	15,755	-	20,705	19,011	-	24,717
18	17,450	-	22,940	21,122	-	27,458
19	19,345	-	24,070	23,467	-	30,505
20	21,445	-	24,445	26,071	-	32,154
21	——	-	——	28,976	-	32,840
Foreign Service Officer Schedule (FSO)						
FSO - 8	$ 6,050	-	$ 7,250	$ 7,639	-	$ 9,169
7	7,010	-	8,420	8,916	-	10,698
6	8,395	-	10,005	10,608	-	12,732
5	9,945	-	12,015	12,848	-	15,416
4	12,075	-	14,595	15,812	-	18,974
3	14,860	-	17,950	19,704	-	23,646
2	18,295	-	22,105	24,867	-	29,841
1	22,650	-	24,500	31,705	-	33,495
Foreign Service Staff Schedule (FSS)						
FSS -10	$ 4,480	-	$ 5,830	$ 5,522	-	$ 7,178
9	5,010	-	6,495	6,158	-	8,003
8	5,490	-	7,155	6,865	-	8,926
7	6,205	-	8,050	7,655	-	9,950
6	6,755	-	8,780	8,536	-	11,092
5	7,480	-	9,775	9,517	-	12,370
4	8,295	-	10,860	10,608	-	13,794
3	9,945	-	13,050	12,848	-	16,700
2	12,075	-	15,855	15,812	-	20,555
1	14,860	-	19,495	19,704	-	25,617

* *Effective prior to Oct. 1, 1965.*
** *Effective the first pay period beginning on or after July 1, 1969. This scale represented the ultimate outcome of pay increases legislated in 1965, 1966 and 1967, the latter including a 1967 increase and automatic increases by executive action in 1968 and 1969.*

Military Pay Raises

The military pay increase enacted in 1967 (HR 13510—PL 90-207) provided the fourth major military pay increase since 1963. PL 88-132, signed Oct. 2, 1963, authorized pay increases of $1.2 billion, including 17 percent raises for all active duty personnel with two or more years of service. PL 88-442, signed Aug. 12, 1964, authorized increases of $207.5 million, including 2.5 percent raises for all active duty personnel except enlisted men with less than two years of service. PL 89-132, signed Aug. 23, 1965, authorized military pay increases totaling $1,048,029,000 for an estimated 2.7 million uniformed personnel on active duty, 1 million reservists and 505,000 retired personnel. This provided a flat 6 percent increase for officers with more than two years' service and a flat 11 percent increase for enlistees with more than two years' service and officers with less than two years' service.

automatic increases in military pay to correspond with future boosts in federal classified employees' pay. The amendment did not prevent Congress from increasing military pay, the Committee emphasized, but would ensure comparability between federal civilian and military pay in case specific future action were not taken.

Major floor debate centered around the automatic future pay boosts provided. H. R. Gross (R Iowa) said he refused to support "a pay bill that places a huge mortgage on the unknown economic future of this country....It would be grotesque gratitude to pay our debt to our fighting men by providing that for those who return it will be to a land of galloping inflation." William M. Tuck (D Va.) said he had voted against the federal civilian pay bill for the same reason, but that since it had passed the House with future raises provided, "it is only fair...to vote for a pay increase for the servicemen who are making such a sacrifice for the salvation of our country...."

The Senate passed HR 13510 by an 83-0 roll-call vote Nov. 29 with some changes. Its Armed Services Committee report called provisions for automatic future increases to correspond with civilian pay raises a form of "legislative insurance, in the event circumstances beyond the control of either the Executive or Legislative Branches preclude timely action on military compensation legislation during 1968."

Differences were ironed out in conference, with both chambers adopting the conference report by voice votes. In House discussion of the report, Rep. L. Mendel Rivers (D S.C.), floor manager, said the Pentagon opposed the automatic future pay increases because future increases were under study. "Our committee has come to realize that when the Department of Defense says that something is 'under study' it means no decisions, so we did not accept this...gimmick and we wrote our own bill" to ensure that servicemen receive pay increases that parallel those provided classified employees, Rivers said.

PROVISIONS—As signed into law (PL 90-207) Dec. 16, HR 13510:

Increased the rates of basic monthly pay of members of the uniformed services to provide a 4.5 percent increase in "regular compensation" (which included basic pay, quarters and subsistence allowances.) The increase was retroactive to Oct. 1, 1967.

Provided a monthly increase of $4.80 to $7.50 in the allowances of personnel in pay grades E-1 through E-4 (with less than 4 years completed service) who are not provided Government quarters and who have up to two dependents.

Authorized payment of a basic allowance for quarters to a member (E-4 and above without dependents and with 4 years or more of service) for the period spent in travel or on leave between permanent duty stations.

Permitted payment of a dislocation allowance to a member without dependents when he is transferred to a permanent station where he is not assigned to Government quarters. (The dislocation allowance was to equal one month's basic allowance for quarters.)

Granted senior noncommissioned officers $150 per month more than the highest enlisted basic pay in the bill.

Provided a refinement in the formula for computing future increases in the retired pay of uniformed services personnel in response to changes in the consumer price index.

Provided for automatic adjustments in military pay comparable to increases in civilian federal employees' salaries.

Entitled those military personnel who are injured or become ill while serving in an area where they receive hostile fire pay, and who are sent to a medical facility in the United States, to transportation at Government expense to their home for convalescence and back to the facility.

Authorized "continuation pay" (in annual or semiannual installments) to doctors and dentists in critical specialist categories, which would permit a bonus of from one to four months of basic pay for each year an eligible officer agreed to extend his service.

Required an annual written report on the operation of the continuation pay program to the Congressional Armed Services Committees.

Other Military Bills

Congress in 1967 cleared two bills providing further benefits to military personnel:

Military Trailer Transportation. Congress Dec. 15 cleared an Administration-backed bill (HR 3982—PL 90-246) to increase the reimbursement to servicemen for shipping their trailers and household effects when transferred to another duty station. The bill was signed Jan. 2, 1968.

Leave. Congress Dec. 15 cleared a bill (HR 1341—PL 90-245) granting up to 90 days' leave to military personnel who served more than 120 days in a foreign hostile area. (Existing leave was 60 days.) President Johnson signed the bill Jan. 2, 1968.

Veterans. Congress in August enacted the Veterans Pension and Readjustment Assistance Act of 1967 (S 16—PL 90-77), which provided an average 5.4 percent cost-of-living increase in the pensions of veterans and their dependents; an expanded program of medical benefits; compensation at full wartime rates and pensions for veterans of the Vietnam war; and larger educational allowances and new training programs for veterans attending school under the Cold War GI Bill. The first-year cost of the expanded program was expected to be $285.6 million—some $115 million beyond the Administration's expectations. President Johnson had proposed many of the benefits provided in S 16 in a special message to Congress Jan. 31.

Federal Insurance Veto

President Johnson Aug. 12 vetoed a bill (HR 11089) increasing life insurance for federal employees. The President said it would cost the Government $61 million in the first year instead of the $13 million which the Administration's proposals on the same subject would have cost.

Mr. Johnson in 1966 vetoed a somewhat more costly insurance bill on similar grounds. The Aug. 12 veto was the President's first during the 90th Congress and his 23rd since he assumed office.

There were no efforts to override the veto. Mr. Johnson said in his veto message that he had asked Administration officials to begin working "immediately" with the appropriate Congressional committees "toward an acceptable program." He indicated he would accept a provision of HR 11089 raising the minimum coverage to $10,000. This would increase the Administration proposals to $30.2 million.

Subsequently, a liberalized federal employee life insurance plan was added to the postal rate-federal pay increase bill (HR 7977) in the Senate. The life insurance plan under HR 7977 was estimated to cost $35.4 million a year more than the existing plan. President Johnson signed the bill Dec. 16.

1968

Action on federal civilian and military pay in 1968 fell into the executive rather than the legislative realm, due to the automatic raises provided for in the 1967 legislation.

President Johnson issued executive orders June 11 ordering pay increases averaging about 5 percent for more than two million federal civilian employees and for more than three million members of the armed forces. Effective the first pay period in July, the raises were estimated to cost about $1.6 billion annually.

The 1967 law (PL 90-206) required the President in 1968 to boost the pay of non-postal civilian employees by half the difference between their salary levels and comparable private enterprise salary levels, but not less than 3 percent based on the June 1967 Bureau of Labor Statistics salary survey. Postal workers were to receive a 5 percent pay increase.

Another 1967 bill (PL 90-207) required the President in 1968 to raise military pay to correspond to salary increases for federal civilian employees.

Rates of Monthly Basic Military Pay Effective July 1, 1969

COMMISSIONED OFFICERS (ARMY)

Pay Grade	Years of Service	
	2 or less	Over 10
General*	$1,810.20	$1,945.80
Lt. Gen.	1,604.40	1,724.10
Maj. Gen.	1,453.20	1,646.40
Brig. Gen.	1,207.20	1,425.30
Col.	894.60	1,047.60
Lt. Col.	715.50	926.10
Major	603.60	890.40
Capt. †	561.00	848.10
1st Lt. †	449.70	676.50
2nd Lt. †	386.40	534.00

* *While serving as Chairman of the Joint Chiefs of Staff, Chief of Staff of the Army, Chief of Naval Operations, Chief of Staff of the Air Force, or Commandant of the Marine Corps, basic pay for this grade is $2,807.10 regardless of cumulative years of service computed under section 205 of this title.*
† *Does not apply to commissioned officers who have been credited with over 4 years' active service as enlisted members.*

ENLISTED MEMBERS (ARMY)

Pay Grade	Years of Service	
	2 or less	Over 10
Sgt. Major*	——	$648.90
1st Sgt. or Master Sgt.	——	559.80
Platoon Sgt., Sgt. 1st Class or Spec. 7	$342.30	484.80
Staff Sgt. or Spec. 6	294.90	433.20
Sgt. or Spec. 5	254.70	395.70
Corporal or Spec. 4	214.20	321.00
Private 1st Class	155.10	246.30
Private	127.80	179.10
Recruit	123.30	163.80
Recruit (Under 4 months)	115.20	——

* *While serving as Sergeant Major of the Army, Master Chief Petty Officer of the Navy, Chief Master Sergeant of the Air Force, or Sergeant Major of the Marine Corps, basic pay for this grade is $1,016.10 regardless of cumulative years of service computed under section 205 of this title.*

SOURCE: *Federal Register, Vol. 34, No. 117—June 19, 1969*

Postal Policy

"**T**HE United States Post Office faces a crisis," reported the Kappel Commission on Postal Organization in 1968. "Each year it slips further behind the rest of the economy in service, in efficiency and in meeting its responsibilities as an employer. Each year it operates at a huge financial loss." Postmaster General Lawrence F. O'Brien put it even more bluntly: the postal system, he said in 1967, was "in a race with catastrophe."

A dramatic illustration of the growing postal crisis occurred in October 1966 when the Chicago post office, the world's largest postal facility, suffered a total breakdown that paralyzed postal service for nearly three weeks. The Kappel Commission attributed the Chicago crisis to breakdowns in management authority and in physical plant and warned of the danger of similar incidents elsewhere in the country.

The postal crisis could be traced to one fundamental problem. Although the Post Office was one of the nation's largest businesses, it was not run as a business. Up to 1958, the Post Office Department was instructed to operate on a "businesslike" basis, but not necessarily at a profit. The Postal Policy Act of 1958, however, established that the Post Office was a public service, not a business, and that public service costs should be borne by the Government and non-public service costs should be met by periodic adjustments in rates.

The Post Office Department's net operating loss in fiscal 1968 was more than $1 billion, of which $591 million was attributed to public service costs. The remaining $430 million, which according to law should have been covered by postal revenues, was termed the postal fund deficit.

Because of its interconnection with the country's development, operation of the Post Office historically has been shaped by tradition and a patchwork of changes in the law. Congress retained control of the operating and capital budgets. It dispensed pay raises and set postage rates, controlled appointments of postmasters and rural letter carriers, legislated labor-management relations and even limited the types of transportation available for moving the mails. The money the public spent on postage and other services went back to the U.S. Treasury and not to the Post Office itself.

By the beginning of 1969, the Post Office Department had grown to a point where it employed more than 725,000 employees handling more than 82 billion pieces of mail a year; Post Office appropriations for fiscal 1969 amounted to nearly $7.13 billion.

Postmaster General O'Brien first proposed converting the Post Office Department into a corporation in a speech made April 3, 1967, to a group of magazine editors and publishers. He outlined a plan in which a board of directors, appointed by the President and confirmed by the Congress, would hire top management officials. The corporation would bargain collectively with employees to set wages and benefits, and it would be empowered to issue bonds to raise money for new buildings and equipment. "I have concluded that there are so many existing and formidable barriers to efficient management that the ultimate solution to the problems of the postal service lies in taking the Department out of its present context entirely. I think the effort to patch a fabric so full of holes is yielding diminishing returns," O'Brien said.

Five days later, President Johnson established a 10-man Commission on Postal Organization, headed by Frederick R. Kappel, former chairman of the board of the American Telephone & Telegraph Co. The Commission was given a mandate to review the corporation proposal and other suggestions for reform.

Kappel Commission Report

The Kappel Commission issued its report, "Towards Postal Excellence," July 16, 1968. The Commission made five major recommendations, the first of which was the establishment of a Government-owned corporation to operate the postal service on a self-supporting basis. "Piecemeal changes to the present system will not do the job: a basic change in direction is necessary," the report stated. The other recommendations were:

● The corporation should act immediately to improve the quality and kinds of services offered, the means of providing those services and the physical conditions under which employees work. It should place the Post Office on "a sound financial footing" through operating efficiencies and increased revenues.

● Appointments and promotions should not be influenced by politics.

Reference

For a discussion of postal legislation in the years 1945-64, see *Congress and the Nation*, Vol. I p. 1473.

• Postal employees should be transferred to a new career service which would retain their wage scales and accrued civil service benefits. The Commission recommended the establishment of collective bargaining by law and suggested compulsory arbitration, but not the right to strike.

• The board of directors of the corporation should be empowered to set rates, which would go into effect unless vetoed by a concurrent resolution of Congress within 60 days. Congress should establish broad policy criteria for rates but not the "intricacies."

The corporation envisioned by the Commission would be run by a nine-man board of directors. Six part-time members of the board would be nominated by the President and confirmed by the Senate; they would select the other three members, who would be full-time executives of the corporation. The corporation would have full control over postal revenues and expenditures; it could sue or be sued, enter into contracts, acquire and dispose of property and borrow from the public. The report recommended allowing the corporation to issue up to $2 billion in bonds and debentures to finance capital outlays. During the transition, it noted, some subsidies would still probably be needed but Congress could consider arrangements for reimbursing the Government. Eventually the Post Office would be self-sustaining as a whole, although "not necessarily class by class," the report stated.

SAVINGS CITED

More efficient operation of all aspects of mail service, the Commission estimated, could cut costs by 20 percent, thus freeing "well over a billion dollars a year of our Federal Budget for the urgent social purposes of our time." A series of recommendations for employees included increased opportunity for advancement through training and education and an improved grievance system. Wages and benefits should be comparable to private enterprise, and recruiting procedures, work conditions and opportunities for advancement should be improved, according to the report.

The postal corporation proposal was endorsed by President Johnson and a number of business organizations. It was opposed by the labor unions representing postal employees. Reaction on Capitol Hill was mixed. Although there was no action on the Commission report in 1968, it provided a basis for future debate on postal reform.

Meanwhile, in the face of rising postal deficits, Congress in 1967 increased postal rates for the fourth time since World War II.

Postmasters General, 1963-69

The following persons served as Postmaster General during the Johnson Administration:
    John A. Gronouski, 1963-65
    Lawrence F. O'Brien, 1965-68
    W. Marvin Watson, 1968-69

Chronology
Of Legislation
On Postal Policy

1966

Parcel Post Revisions

Congress in 1966 enacted legislation (HR 14904—PL 89-593) to increase postage rates on most parcels and on fourth-class catalogs and to liberalize many existing size and weight restrictions on packages in steps over a five-year period. The bill was designed to put the parcel post system on a break-even basis through increased rates and increased business.

When fully effective in 1971, the bill was expected to produce $108.6 million a year in additional revenues for the parcel post system. The deficit of the system in fiscal 1965 was $107.1 million.

The prospect of a balanced parcel post budget allowed continued operation of the Post Office Department, which was prohibited by law from withdrawing funds from the Treasury after June 30, 1966, unless it certified that the parcel post system's revenues and operating expenses were within 4 percent of balancing or that steps had been taken to promote such a balance.

Beginning Jan. 15, 1967, rates on most packages were increased by an average of 10 cents per package, and rates on catalogs were increased by about 3.3 cents. The combined rate increases were expected to produce about $76.6 million a year in additional revenue.

In addition, the maximum size and weight limits on packages sent between two first-class post offices were raised gradually between July 1, 1967, and July 1, 1971, when the maximum limits were to be 40 pounds and 84 inches in length and girth combined. The higher limits were expected to generate an additional $32 million a year from increased business after the July 1, 1971, changes were made. *(For details of package standards, see box.)*

The rate changes applied only to zone-rated parcels, which comprise about 80 percent of all packages mailed. They did not apply to preferentially rated items such as books, library materials, materials for the blind and educational materials. Furthermore, the new size and weight limits did not affect the existing higher limits on packages sent to or from second-, third- and fourth-class post offices. The limits on these packages remained at 70 pounds and 100 inches.

The results of the bill were twofold: (1) it provided relief for the chronic deficit of the parcel post system and (2) it eliminated in part the confusion resulting from the existing package standards.

Package Standards Controversy. The only controversy over the bill concerned the proposals for liberalizing package standards. The existing standards had been set by Congress in 1951 to protect the Railway Express Agency and other private carriers. Before 1951, packages weighing up to 70 pounds and measuring up to 100 inches could be mailed anywhere in the United States. Congress in 1951 restricted the size and weight of all packages sent to or from first-class post offices. The size was limited to 72 inches, and the weight limit differed according to whether the post offices were less than 150 miles apart (40 pounds) or more than 150 miles apart (20 pounds).

Postmaster General Lawrence F. O'Brien asked Congress Jan. 27 to enact a two-part package increasing parcel post rates and easing package restrictions.

In proposing changes in the standards, O'Brien contended that failure to liberalize them would place further protection for special interests above the public interest, which he said involved both eliminating confusion and reducing the deficit. The need to allow mailing of more parcels was particularly important in cutting the deficit, he said, because increased rates alone merely resulted in lower volume and higher unit costs.

The proposals, however, brought cries of protest from REA and other private carriers who said that easing of the standards would bankrupt them by allowing operation of the parcel post system as a Government-subsidized, unfair and unnecessary source of competition for the carrying of large and bulky parcels.

The strength of the opposition to the liberalized standards manifested itself after the bill was reported from the House Post Office and Civil Service Committee. First, the House Rules Committee refused to grant HR 14904 a rule for floor consideration and the Post Office and Civil Service Committee was forced to bring the bill up under the 21-day rule. This was the first of two occasions on which the 21-day procedure was used in 1966. *(For details of 21-day rule, see chapter on Congress.)*

Then, the House added an amendment on the floor requiring the Post Office Department to hire any employee from a private parcel operation who was displaced from his job by the bill within two years of enactment. Postmaster General O'Brien, during Senate hearings on HR 14904, agreed to the provision. He said the Post Office would not have to make jobs for these persons because increased business made it necessary for the Post Office to hire additional personnel annually. The Senate Post Office and Civil Service Committee, however, modified the bill to make the new size and weight restrictions effective in steps over a five-year period and to establish an Advisory Commission to study the situation and report to the President and Congress by Jan. 1, 1969, on the effect of the size and weight changes on private parcel carriers. If at that time the Commission found that the new package standards would seriously endanger private carriers, the 91st Congress was directed to consider eliminating the remaining weight modifications scheduled to go into effect later. The Senate Committee deleted the House floor amendment as unnecessary in view of the new safeguards contained in the gradual modification of package standards and the establishment of the Commission. The Senate version of HR 14904 was subsequently agreed to by the House.

Provisions. As signed into law, Sept. 20, 1966, HR 14904:

Rates. Established a new postage rate schedule for all zone-rated parcels, based on their weights and the zones to which they are sent. Fourth-class parcel post rates were increased by an average of 10 cents per package, rounded off to the nearest five cents. In addition, the bill made packages of less than 10 pounds in weight, but 84 to 100 inches in length and girth combined, subject to a minimum rate equal to the rate for a 10-pound package being shipped to the same destination. (The new rates did not apply to preferentially rated books, library materials, materials for the blind and educational materials.)

Established new rate schedules for fourth-class catalogs, based partly on the zones to which they are sent. Rates for individual catalogs of 24 or more pages (at least 22 of which are printed) and of one to 10 pounds were increased by an average of 3.2 cents (10 percent.) The bill also provided a bulk rate, composed of a pound weight and a piece rate, for these catalogs if they were mailed in quantities of 300 or more, were individually addressed and met other requirements set by the Postmaster General. The bulk rate was increased by an average of 3.3 cents (12 percent.)

Stipulated that the new rates were subject to modification if the Postmaster General used his authority *(below)*

Package Standards

The changes in size and weight limits set by HR 14904 applied only to packages sent from one first-class post office to another.

Under existing law, the size of any package mailed between two first-class post offices was limited to a maximum of 72 inches in length and girth combined. Permissible weights, however, depended on the distance between the offices. Packages sent between two first-class post offices *more* than 150 miles apart were limited to 20 pounds, whereas those sent between first-class post offices *less* than 150 miles apart could weigh up to 40 pounds.

Weight Changes. HR 14904 provided that beginning July 1, 1969, the maximum allowable weight of packages mailed between *all* first-class post offices (regardless of distance) would be 40 pounds. That weight limit, however, was to be reached in three steps:

Existing law	20 pounds
July 1, 1967	25 pounds
July 1, 1968	30 pounds
July 1, 1969	40 pounds

Size Changes. Beginning July 1, 1970, the maximum sizes were to be increased for packages sent between *all* first-class post offices, while the weights remained at 40 pounds, as follows:

Existing law	72 inches
July 1, 1970	78 inches
July 1, 1971	84 inches

to petition the Interstate Commerce Commission for rate changes.

Made the new rates effective Jan. 15, 1967.

Certification. Repealed the existing provisions requiring certification that fourth-class revenues and costs were within 4 percent of balancing and authorizing the Postmaster General to petition the ICC for reforms to achieve such a balance, and replaced them with similar, permanent provisions. Authorized the Postmaster General to request the ICC to increase or decrease fourth-class rates and/or to reclassify mailable articles or modify the zone structure when he found that the postage rates, classification or zone structure: (1) prevented the acceptance of mail which otherwise would be acceptable, (2) caused the revenue from fourth-class mail to be greater than or less than the cost of providing the service or (3) resulted in any other condition which impaired the efficient or economical operation of the service. Reclassification of mailable articles could not include revisions of the size and weight limits *(below)*, and rate changes could not include rates on preferentially rated items.

Specified that the Postmaster General's request would be considered approved after 30 days unless the ICC rejected the request or ordered an investigation, which had to result in action within 180 days or the request automatically took effect.

Required the Postmaster General to certify annually to the Secretary of the Treasury, before funds could be withdrawn for the Post Office Department, that parcel post rates and revenues were within 4 percent of balancing; that he had requested consent of the ICC to raise rates or modify classifications to achieve the balance; or that the most recent cost ascertainment report of his Department estimated that the anticipated revenue from the complete effect of the size and weight modifications over the five-year period would achieve the proper balance.

Made the new certification provisions effective Jan. 15, 1967.

Package Standards. For details of changes in package standards made by the bill, see box. The bill also:

Retained the 70-pound and 100-inch limit currently provided for mailings: (1) to and from smaller than first-class post offices, (2) of certain agricultural products, (3) of certain books and films, (4) to or from servicemen outside the United States, (5) of records and books for the blind, and (6) to and from Puerto Rico, Alaska, Hawaii and certain other U.S. possessions.

Zones. Changed the method of measuring zone distances by substituting sectional centers for local post offices.

Stipulated that the new zones and methods of determining them were subject to modification if the Postmaster General used his authority to petition for changes in the zone structure *(above.)*

Advisory Commission. Established a five-member Advisory Commission on Parcel Distribution Services, to be appointed by the President, to make a full and complete study of small parcel distribution services including the parcel post service. Required the Commission to make an interim report to the President and Congress by Jan. 1, 1968, and a full report with recommendations by Jan. 1, 1969. If the Commission found that modifications in parcel size and weight limitation set by the Act seriously endangered private parcel carriers, the 91st Congress

was to consider eliminating the increase in maximum package size from 78 to 84 inches scheduled to become effective July 1, 1971.

Postal Savings System

Congress in 1966 completed action on a bill (HR 8030—PL 89-377) to discontinue the Postal Savings System. The System provided facilities, at designated post offices, for the deposit of savings. These savings drew interest and were guaranteed by the U.S. Government. The Administration recommended discontinuance on the ground that the system was no longer needed and was not worth the cost. Both President Johnson and Postmaster General Lawrence F. O'Brien recommended that persons with money in the System transfer the savings into United States savings bonds.

In its major provisions, HR 8030 provided that no deposits or new accounts under the Postal Savings System would be accepted after 30 days of enactment of the bill and that interest on investments would cease to accrue on the anniversary date of each savings certificate during the year following the closing date. The Postmaster General was given from the closing date (30 days after enactment) through the fiscal year beginning after the closing date "to terminate the business, settle and pay the accounts, liquidate the assets, discharge the obligations and otherwise wind up the affairs of the Postal Savings System."

The Postal Savings System was established by Congress in 1910. According to a May 4 release by Postmaster General O'Brien, the original purposes of the System were "to (1) get money out of hiding, (2) attract the savings of immigrants who were accustomed to saving at post offices in their native countries, (3) provide safe depositories for people who had lost confidence in private banks, and (4) provide more convenient depositories for savings of working people who were unable to bank during regular banking hours."

From 11,918 depositors and $677,145 in deposits in 1911, the System grew to include 4,196,517 depositors with a balance of $3,392,772,461 at its peak year of 1947. By June 30, 1965, depositors had declined to 997,029 with a balance of $344,233,788. The maximum deposit for any one account was $2,500.

The Post Office Department in 1965 recommended abolition of the Postal Savings System as part of President Johnson's campaign to eliminate unnecessary departmental and agency programs in order to reduce Government costs.

The House passed HR 8030 July 12, 1965, without amendment. Senate passage come March 14, 1966.

1967

Postal Rate Increases

Responding to a growing postal crisis, Congress enacted legislation (HR 7977—PL 90-206) increasing postage on all classes of mail.

The final version of HR 7977 combined three measures—the Administration-backed Postal Revenue Act of 1967 (HR 7977), a federal pay bill and a federal employee life insurance plan. The federal pay bill was added to the much-needed revenue measure after President Johnson threatened to veto salary raises costing more than his budgeted amount. Pay increases in HR 7977 exceeded his budgeted costs by $63 million in fiscal 1968. *(For details of action on salary increases, see chapter on federal pay.)*

HR 7977 increased the cost of mailing a first-class letter from 5 cents to 6 cents and the cost of mailing an airmail letter from 8 cents to 10 cents, effective Jan. 7, 1968.

Postage increases on all classes of mail were expected to produce $885.9 million-$914.6 million in new revenues when fully effective, or a maximum of about $90 million more than requested by the President. However, the Post Office Department estimated that it had lost considerable revenue in fiscal 1968 due to delay in enacting the bill. The Administration had proposed that certain rate increases take effect July 1, 1967. *(For new rates, see table.)*

Major controversy centered on regular third-class bulk rate increases (mainly advertising matter often referred to as junk mail). As cleared, HR 7977 increased regular bulk rates to 3.6 cents minimum per piece from Jan. 7, 1968, until June 30, 1969. On July 1, 1969, the rate under HR 7977 was to go to 3.8 cents minmum per piece for the first 250,000 pieces mailed, and to 4 cents minimum per piece for all pieces in excess of 250,000. The House had set a single rate—3.8 cents, the Administration request—effective Jan. 7, 1968. The Senate had increased the rate to 3.6 cents Jan. 7, 1968, and to 4 cents Jan. 1, 1969. The six-month delay in the 4-cent rate was agreed to in conference. *(For third-class mail lobby activity, see box.)*

The revenues from the new rates, when fully effective, were expected to cover 72 percent to 75 percent of the costs of handling the regular third-class bulk mail. Existing rates covered about 61 percent of the costs.

Background. Postal revenues had not met costs since fiscal 1945, and the cumulative deficit for the period 1946-66 totaled nearly $12.5 billion. The deficit was attributed to substantial increases in the volume of mail handled and the number of employees needed to handle it, to "subsidies" through below-cost rates for certain categories of mail users, and to the multiplication of Post Office activities. Deficits also were caused by hikes in postal employees' pay unaccompanied by postal rate increases.

In almost every year since World War II the Administration urged Congress to take on the politically unpopular task of increasing postal rates. The requests usually accompanied pay increase proposals for postal workers. Congress responded affirmatively only three times. Partly to offset postal employees' raises, comprehensive postal rate increases were enacted in 1951, 1958 and 1962. *(Congress and the Nation, Vol. I, p. 1479, 1485, 1489.)*

1967 Action. In an April 5 message to Congress, President Johnson said existing postal rates did not even cover normal operating costs, much less provide sufficient funds for necessary improvements in postal facilities and equipment. The President proposed postal rate increases designed to increase postal revenues by $825 million a year when fully effective. *(See table.)*

Third-Class Mail Lobby

During Congressional consideration of HR 7977, the activities of lobbyists for third-class mailers generated considerable controversy and probably helped the cause of Members of Congress who sought to raise the postal rates for those mailers.

In its July 23 issue, *The Washington Post* said that J. Don Kerlin, registered representative for Time Inc., the Reuben H. Donnelley Corp. and certain other mailers, had "walked out of" a closed session of the House Post Office and Civil Service Subcommittee on Postal Rates while it was drafting HR 7977. The Subcommittee recommended that third-class bulk rates (mainly advertising matter) be raised less than 1 cent over a three-year period.

The full Committee Aug. 3 unanimously adopted a resolution denying the newspaper report. The Committee thereupon rejected the Subcommittee recommendations and approved the Administration request for a 1-cent increase in 1968.

The Senate then boosted regular bulk third-class rates in two steps to 4 cents per piece. The difference was estimated to cost bulk mailers an additional $28 million annually over the House rate. In debate on HR 7977, Senate Post Office and Civil Service Committee Chairman A.S. Mike Monroney (D Okla.) accused bulk mailers of "some of the most vicious lobbying activities it has been my experience to witness in some 29 years in Congress."

President of the Associated Third Class Mail Users, Harry Maginnis, then wrote Monroney that he was not responsible for such activities. (The group includes about 800 organizations, among them the Billy Graham Evangelistic Assn., shopping guides with about 17 million circulation, Time Inc. and other magazines, and the Boy Scouts of America.)

In his letter, hand-delivered to certain members of the conference committee on HR 7977, Maginnis recalled previous favors he had performed for Monroney, such as contributing "$1,900 of my personal funds" in 1966 toward the "ill-fated campaign" of Monroney's son, Mike Monroney Jr., for a Congressional seat from Maryland's 8th District. The tone of the letter reportedly only strengthened Monroney's opposition to the mailers' pleas for lower rates.

When conferees approved the higher rate provided by the Senate, Rep. H.R. Gross (R Iowa) charged that the House was "the victim of a running feud involving a third-class mailer lobbyist." Monroney, he said, had delivered an ultimatum to conferees to either approve the 4-cent rate or stay in conference "until hell freezes over."

Meanwhile, Rep. Ken Hechler (D W.Va.), a leading opponent of third-class 'subsidies,' Dec. 11 told the House that a "prominent citizen" in his district "was offered by an intermediary a political war chest in excess of $100,000 to try and eliminate me from Congress in 1968....If the junk mailers can afford to raise over $100,000 in order to launch a political campaign, surely they can afford to pay postage rates which are not subsidized by the taxpayers and mailers of first-class mail."

Postal Rates: Existing, Administration Proposal, Enacted

MAIL CLASSIFICATION	EXISTING RATES	ADMINISTRATION PROPOSAL	HR 7977 [7]	NEW REVENUES (millions)	COST COVERAGE [6]	
					Existing Law	HR 7977
First Class: [1]						
letters	5¢ oz.	6¢ oz.	6¢ oz.	$493.2 ⎫		
drops	4¢ oz.	5¢ oz.	6¢ oz.	2.2 ⎬	103%	110%
cards	4¢ each	5¢ each	5¢ each	23.0 ⎪ $518.4 ⎭		
Airmail						
letters	8¢ oz.	9¢ oz.	10¢ oz.	$ 56.3 ⎫	105	119
cards	6¢ each	7¢ each	8¢ each	0.6 ⎬		
parcels	1st class and zone rates		zone rates	- 7.2 ⎭ $ 49.7	175	157
Second Class:						
regular [2]	advertising 4.2-14¢ lb. non-advertising 2.8¢ lb. minimum per piece 1¢	advertising 5.1-17¢ lb. non-advertising 3.4¢ lb. minimum per piece 1.3¢	advertising 5.2-17¢ lb. non-advertising 3.4¢ lb. minimum per piece 1.3¢ [3]	$ 26.1 ⎬	29	33
nonprofit	1.8¢ lb; 1/8¢ minimum per piece	2.1-2.8¢ lb.; 0.2¢ minimum per piece	2.1¢ lb.; 0.2¢ minimum per piece advertising at zone rates, 5.1-12¢	4.2	7	9
classroom	60% of regular rates	60% of regular rates	60% of regular rates	.4	18	20
in-county	1 1/4¢ lb.; 1/8¢ minimum per piece	1.5¢ lb.; 0.2¢ minimum per piece	1.5¢ lb.; 0.2¢ minimum per piece	2.0	13	14
transient	4¢ first 2 oz.; 2¢ each additional ounce	5¢ and 1¢	5¢ and 1¢	.5 $ 33.2	92	91
Third Class:						
single piece	4¢ first 2 oz.; 2¢ each additional ounce	5¢ and 2¢	6¢ and 2¢	$ 69.8	86	103
bulk regular	12 and 18¢ lb.; 2 7/8¢ minimum per piece	16 and 22¢ lb.; 3.8¢ minimum per piece	16 and 22¢ lb.; 3.6 and 4¢ minimum per piece [4]	$154.1-182.8 [5]	61	72-75
bulk nonprofit	6 and 9¢ lb.; 1 1/4¢ minimum per piece	8 and 11¢ lb.; 1.9¢ minimum per piece	50% of bulk lb. rate; 40% of bulk minimum per piece	12.1 $236.0-$264.7	27	31
Controlled Circulation:	13 1/2¢ lb.; 1¢ minimum per piece	15¢ lb.; 3.8¢ minimum per piece	15¢ lb.; 3.8¢ minimum per piece	$ 6.4	58	68
Fourth Class:						
general	10¢ first lb.; 5¢ each additional	16¢ first 2 lbs.; 6¢ each additional	12¢ first lb.; 6¢ each additional	$ 11.5	45	49
library	4¢ first lb.; 1¢ each additional	8¢ first 2 lbs.; 3¢ each additional	5¢ first lb.; 2¢ each additional	1.1 $ 12.6	16	24
Government Mail	applicable class rates	applicable class rates	applicable class rates	$ 29.6	105	115
TOTAL REVENUE GAINS				$885.9-$914.6	83%	87-88%

1 All first-class mail exceeding 13 ounces and all airmail exceeding 7 ounces will be carried as one class on a "most expeditious" basis, subject to a single air parcel schedule.
2 Authorized agricultural publications will retain the current 4.2 cents advertising pound rate for zones 1 and 2.
3 The current 0.5-cent minimum charge for publications mailing fewer than 5,000 copies outside the county of publication will be 0.6 cent in 1967, 0.7 cent in 1969, and 0.8 cent thereafter.
4 HR 7977 provided a new rate of 3.6 cents minimum per piece from Jan. 7, 1968, until June 30, 1969. On July 1, 1969, the rate under HR 7977 was to go to 3.8 cents minimum per piece for the first 250,000 pieces mailed, and to 4 cents minimum per piece for all pieces in excess of 250,000.
5 Exact effect of lower rate for first 250,000 pieces not determined.
6 The percent of costs to the Post Office incurred in the handling of a certain class of mail which are covered by revenues from postage charged to that class. There are two types of mail which are not expected to fully cover their costs -- those receiving preferred rates due to their "public service" (economic and educational) value and those receiving slower delivery. The losses on such mail are paid either from Treasury funds or from excess revenues from other classes of mail -- primarily first class and airmail.
7 The new postal rates shown in the chart under HR 7977 are those that will be fully effective in 1973. Some of the rates increase in steps over the 1968-73 period. However, the first class and air mail rate increases, among others, occur entirely in 1968. (See provisions.)

In reporting HR 7977, the House Post Office and Civil Service Committee added to the postal rate increase bill provisions of a separate federal salary measure that also had been requested by President Johnson. HR 7977 was passed by the House Oct. 11 and by the Senate Nov. 29. The life insurance provisions were added to the bill in Senate committee. Congress completed action on HR 7977 Dec. 12, three days before adjournment of the session. Mr. Johnson signed the bill into law Dec. 16.

Provisions

The Postal Revenue Act of 1967 (Title I of HR 7977) increased postal rates and made other changes as follows:

First-Class—Raised letters to 6 cents per ounce, postcards to 5 cents—up 1 cent each.

Eliminated the special "drop letter" rate. (A drop letter was one picked up by the addressee at the office where deposited.)

Airmail—Raised letters to 10 cents per ounce, postcards to 8 cents—up 2 cents each.

Placed in the air parcel post category first-class letters over 13 ounces and airmail over 7 ounces; provided a single rate of 80 cents for all zones for matter weighing 1 pound or less.

Created a new category of airlift mail for parcels of no more than 30 pounds sent to or from any Armed Forces post office at low surface postage rates.

Extended the airlift for news publications (currently furnished only to combat areas) to "isolated, hardship or combat support areas overseas, or where adequate surface transportation is not available."

Second-class—Raised regular rates over a three-year period as follows: from 2.8 cents to 3.4 cents for the nonadvertising portion; from 4.2-14 cents to 5.2-17 cents per pound (depending upon the zone) for the advertising portion; and from 1 cent to 1.3 cents minimum per piece.

Established separate rates for advertising and nonadvertising portions of nonprofit publications as follows: from 2.35-3.5 cents per pound (depending upon the zone) in 1968, to from 5.1-12 cents in 1973 (six annual steps starting Jan. 7, 1968); from 1.9 to 2.1 cents per pound in three stages for the nonadvertising portion; and from 0.13 to 0.2 cents minimum per piece. (Qualified nonprofit publications with 10 percent or less advertising would pay postage based on the nonadvertising rates.)

Established a second-class airmail category (on a space available basis) at regular postage plus additional charge, with the total to be not less than 4 cents per piece.

Required all bills and statements of account (not including subscription renewal notices) to be mailed at first-class rates.

Eliminated special local rates for mailings at additional entry points (mailings at post offices outside the county of publication).

Increased rates on the following: publications of less than 5,000 mailed copies; within-county mailings, controlled-circulation and transient mail. *(See table.)*

Continued classroom publications at 60 percent of the regular rate.

Authorized the Postmaster General to require publishers and news agents "to separate, make up, and address second-class matter in such manner as he directs in accordance with a five-digit ZIP code system."

Third-class—Raised to 6 cents the single piece rate for the first 2 ounces (a 2-cent increase) and retained the current 2-cent charge for each additional ounce.

Increased regular bulk rates as follows: from 12 to 16 cents per pound (books); from 18 to 22 cents (circulars); and from 2.875 to 3.6 cents minimum per piece on Jan. 7, 1968, and to 4 cents on July 1, 1969, except that the rate for the first 250,000 pieces mailed by any one mailer in one year would cost 3.8 cents per piece.

Set bulk nonprofit rates at 40 percent of the minimum regular bulk charge of 3.6 and 4 cents per piece.

Entitled third-class mail (limited in weight to less than 16 ounces) to special handling upon payment of a fee to be fixed by the Postmaster General.

Fourth-class—Raised the general rate for books, films, records and other special items from 10 cents for the first pound and 5 cents for each additional pound to 12 cents and 6 cents.

Increased the special library rate from 4 cents for the first pound and 1 cent for each additional pound to 5 cents and 2 cents.

Permitted invoices "whether or not also serving as bills, if they relate solely to the matter with which they are mailed" to be enclosed with fourth-class matter.

Authorized the Postmaster General to require large-scale mailers using the fourth-class educational materials postage rate (principally book and record clubs) to prepare material mailed in quantities of one thousand or more "in the manner directed by him."

Other—Extended free mailing privileges currently provided for matter mailed to the blind to other persons who cannot use or read conventionally printed material because of physical handicaps.

Increased the rate for keys and other small articles from 6 cents for each two ounces to 14 cents for the first two ounces and 7 cents for each additional two ounces.

Prohibited the mailing of solicitations for orders or services prepared in a form to mislead the addressee into believing that the solicitation actually was a bill for goods or services previously rendered.

Clarified the application of mailing privileges for servicemen to those in the Canal Zone.

Directed the Postmaster General to furnish change of address information to senders of all classes of mail at a rate covering handling costs (subsequently set at 10 cents). (Under existing law, such information was available to mailers operating from mailing lists and to second- and third-class mailers requesting notification when mailing pieces were undeliverable as addressed. Postmasters also were authorized to provide change of address information for a $1 fee.)

Effective Dates—The following increases were to become effective Jan. 7, 1968: first class, airmail, in-county publications minimum per piece rate, transient second class, single piece third class, special rates on keys and identification devices, regular and nonprofit third-class per pound bulk rates, and all fourth class rates. The following increases were to become effective in three steps (Jan. 7, 1968, Jan. 1, 1969, and Jan. 1, 1970): in-county pound rates, regular second class, classroom publications, nonadvertising and minimum rates for nonprofit second class and controlled circulation. Special advertising rates for nonprofit publications were to become effective in six annual steps beginning Jan. 7, 1968, and ending Jan. 1, 1973. Per piece bulk rates for both regular and nonprofit third class were to become effective in two steps—Jan. 7, 1968, and July 1, 1969.

Post Office Corporation

Postmaster General Lawrence F. O'Brien in March 1967 warned Congress that the nation's postal service was "in a race with catastrophe" due to burgeoning mail volume and an "inadequate, badly located and aging" physical plant. In an April speech, he said the Post Office reminded him of "the classic definition of an elephant: A mouse built to Government specifications."

O'Brien proposed April 3 that the Post Office Department be removed from the President's Cabinet and be converted into a nonprofit corporation.

Speaking before a meeting of magazine editors and publishers in Washington, D.C., O'Brien recommended that the postal service be operated by a board of directors appointed by the President and confirmed by Congress and be managed by a professional executive appointed by the board.

Congress would determine what services the corporation should provide and establish a general rate formula for mail service. O'Brien urged that members of management and employees be paid "according to standards of comparable industries" and that employees be offered "more incentive and scope as well as a wider area for collective bargaining."

Many existing statutory restrictions on appropriated funds would be avoided by establishment of a Government corporation, O'Brien said. He said that "the corporation would issue bonds to provide a capital fund with which to build appropriately designed and well equipped office structures, which could also be self-amortizing through rental income."

Progress in improving postal service has been "painful and difficult" because of "the restrictive jungle of legislation and custom that has grown up around the Post Office Department in the 138 years" that it has been part of the President's Cabinet, the Postmaster General contended. He concluded that "there are so many existing and formidable barriers to efficient management that the ultimate solution to the problems of the postal service lies in taking the Department out of its present context entirely." He pointed out that a number of proposals had been made in Congress to alter some aspects of the postal service. "While all are well intentioned," he argued, "they are only props for the tottering structure we now inhabit so uneasily. I believe the time for props is past. I think we must stop tinkering and begin constructing."

Study Group Named. President Johnson April 8 established by Executive Order a 10-member Commission on Postal Organization, to be headed by Frederick R. Kappel, former chairman of the board of the American Telephone & Telegraph Co.

The Commission was to determine the "feasibility and desirability" of transferring the postal service from the Post Office Department to a Government Corporation, "or such other form of organization as the Commis-

Mail Classes

First Class and Airmail. First-class mail must be processed by the Post Office within two hours after its deposit. The same is true of airmail, which then must be transported by air. Included in the letter rate for these categories are messages, bills and checks. The card rate applies to utility bills and government and picture postcards. HR 7977 included in the air parcel post category first-class letters over 13 ounces and airmail over 7 ounces.

Second Class. Has following subclasses:

Regular—All publications (except reduced-rate publications) mailed for delivery outside counties of publication. Major users are mass circulation magazines, business publications and some hometown papers.

Nonprofit—Publications of religious, educational, scientific, philanthropic, agricultural, labor, veterans, fraternal organizations and Rural Electrification Administration cooperatives.

In County—All publications delivered to subscribers in home counties. Major users are hometown newspapers in rural areas.

Classroom—Scholastic papers for class use.

Transient—Publications mailed by individuals which do not qualify for publishers' bulk rates.

Controlled Circulation. Publications which do not qualify for second class because addressees do not pay a subscription price—mainly trade, technical and industrial publications and some shopper guides.

Third Class. Contains three sub-classes:

Regular Bulk—Quantity mailings of circulars, newsletters, shopper guides, booklets, small catalogs, seeds, merchandise samples, coupons and other matter weighing less than 1 pound per piece. Major users are advertisers, seed and plant wholesalers and state and local governments. According to the Post Office, this subclass is "largely a mass-advertising medium. But many small business firms use direct mail as their only economical advertising medium."

Nonprofit Bulk—Quantity mailings for fund raising appeals, institutional newsletters, reports, booklets and meeting notices. Major users are religious, educational, scientific, philanthropic, agricultural, labor, veteran or fraternal organizations not organized for profit.

Single Piece—Includes greeting cards, small parcels, printed matter, booklets and catalogs and all mail weighing less than 1 pound not included in any other mail class. Major users include mail order companies for small parcels and single catalog mailings and the general public for greeting cards and small parcels.

Fourth Class. This is a special-rate class for books, sound recordings, manuscripts, academic theses, printed music, films, slides, microfilms and other educational materials. Major users are book publishers, book and record clubs and book dealers. Also libraries and educational institutions, which pay lower rates.

Government Mail. Includes franked and penalty mail—free mailings by Members of Congress for which the Government reimburses the Post Office.

sion may consider desirable." The panel's conclusions were reported in 1968. *(See below.)*

Postal Lease Authority

Congress enacted legislation (S 1039—PL 90-15) extending through June 30, 1972, the authority of the Postmaster General to make 30-year leases for post office buildings. The authority was needed so that the Post Office Department could acquire new postal facilities where Government construction was not feasible, such as on municipal lands.

Had Congress failed to renew the program, which expired April 30, the Department would have been left with only 20-year leasing authority provided under permanent law. Supporters of the bill contended that the 30-year term saved the Government money because it attracted investors who were willing to accept a lower annual rent in return for the longer term agreement.

The Post Office Department also would have lost its land acquisition authority, which Postmaster General Lawrence F. O'Brien said had "proved invaluable" in assembling sites with multiple ownership; sites where owners demanded unreasonable prices; sites to which the title was defective; and those where the owner, such as a municipality, lacked authority to sell.

1968

Postal Corporation

The 10-member President's Commission on Postal Organization on July 16 urged creation of a Government-owned corporation to operate the postal service as a self-supporting business free from politics. Noting much "public concern over the quality of mail service," the Commission concluded that the current "outmoded" postal system "cannot keep pace with the demands of our society unless it is given a basic change in direction."

Benefits from the adoption of modern management practices would include "not only greatly improved mail service but the early elimination of the postal deficit and far better career opportunities and working conditions for the individual postal employees," the Commission said in a 212-page report to President Johnson.

The Commission had been appointed by Mr. Johnson in 1967. *(See above.)*

Recommendations. Under the Commission's plan, the corporation would be run by a nine-man board of directors. Six would be appointed by the President to serve on a part-time basis. These directors would appoint the remaining three—one of whom would serve as chief executive officer and two as corporate officers.

The directors would be authorized to set postal rates after hearings. Rates would be based on "actual costs of service, value to those served and changing market demands."

New rates would become effective after 60 days unless vetoed by Congress. The Commission contended

that Congress should not "deal with the intricacies of postal rates." The report suggested that Congress find some "more efficient and visible" way of helping non-profit and educational groups than through special postal rates.

Postal employees would be transferred to a new career service in the corporation, which would appoint and promote workers on a nonpolitical, merit basis. Local postmasters and rural carriers would be removed from the patronage system, which the report said "not only forecloses career opportunities for many potential managers, but prevents the successful postmaster from being promoted...."

Employees could bargain with the board on wages and working conditions. However, they would be required to observe the Government's ban on strikes by its employees. The President would settle any disputes between the board and its employees.

Cost. The Commission warned against expecting any "overnight miracles" from adoption of its proposals, noting that an initial heavy investment would be necessary. The investment would be made by appropriations and bond issues. However, cost savings of at least 20 percent—or more than $1 billion—could be achieved in a few years, the report said.

Administration Reaction. President Johnson did not immediately endorse the Commission's recommendations. Instead, he said the report "renders a sobering judgment on what is required for excellent postal service in the years ahead."

In his final Budget, submitted in January 1969, Mr. Johnson urged Congress to approve the Commission's recommendations.

Manpower Cutback, Postal Assaults

Congress enacted a bill (HR 15387—PL 90-449) designed to protect postal workers from assault, after amending it to exempt certain Post Office Department employees from the manpower cutback provisions of the Revenue and Expenditure Control Act of 1968. That Act provided that full-time, permanent employment in the Executive Branch was to be reduced from the mid-1968 level of about 2.6 million persons to the 2.4-million-man level of June 30, 1966. *(See chapter on Tax Policy for details.)*

The postal exemption was added to HR 15387 by the Senate Post Office and Civil Service Committee after Postmaster General W. Marvin Watson said the cutback order would require him to reduce employment in his Department by 83,238 persons, which would force a curtailment of some postal services.

Provisions. As enacted into law, HR 15387:

Authorized the Postmaster General to discipline a postal employee who assaulted another postal employee.

Made it a federal crime to assault postal employees.

Exempted employees of the postal field service (except those in regional offices) and employees in the Department's Bureau of Research and Engineering from the manpower cutback of the Revenue and Expenditure Control Act of 1968.

District of Columbia and Island Dependencies

The Johnson years brought partial self-government to three dependencies of the federal government—the District of Columbia, Guam, and the Virgin Islands—thus continuing a postwar trend that has resulted in statehood for Hawaii and Alaska and commonwealth status for Puerto Rico. In two other dependencies, self-government was not in immediate prospect. The Pacific Trust Territory was administered by the United States under a United Nations mandate, while the Ryukyu Islands desired to rejoin Japan.

The only heated battle in Congress over self-government concerned the city which is the seat of Congress. Despite intense pressure from the White House and despite large Democratic majorities in both House and Senate, Congress failed to enact legislation providing home rule for the District of Columbia (Washington, D.C.).

Some of the opposition in Congress to home rule legislation stemmed from fear that Washington, about 65 per cent of whose inhabitants were Negroes, would elect a predominantly black government. In the end, President Johnson established a modified form of home rule through executive action. To head the new District government Mr. Johnson chose a Negro as mayor and appointed five Negroes to the nine-man city council.

Reference

Discussion of developments on statehood and territories from 1945-64 will be found on *Congress and the Nation,* Vol. I, p. 1497-1516.

I—District of Columbia Home Rule

The District of Columbia in 1967 achieved partial self-government through a reorganization plan drawn up by President Johnson. It was the first time since 1874 that residents of the Nation's Capital had exercised any control over the running of their city. *(For history of D.C. self-government in the 19th century, see box.)*

Between 1874 and 1967, Washington had been governed by the U.S. Congress and by a three-member Board of Commissioners. Two commissioners were civilians, residents of the District, appointed by the President with the advice and consent of the Senate for three-year terms. One of the two, designated president of the board, functioned as the ceremonial "mayor" of the city. The third commissioner, also nominally appointed by the President, was actually assigned by the Chief of Army Engineers. He was always a brigadier general of engineers or a colonel eligible for promotion. Residency in the District was not required. A nine-member Citizen's Advisory Council was established by the Commissioners in 1952 as a guide to local opinion.

Congress was left to enact, for the District, laws usually handled by a municipal government. The Federal Government also supplemented the District budget with annual payments. Every minor bill affecting the city was required to complete all procedures for major legislation, passing the House and Senate District of Columbia Committees and the House and Senate Appropriations Committees, as well as the floors of both chambers. Home rule advocates insisted that it was ridiculous for the national legislature to concern itself with such municipal

minutiae as whether or not to raise dog-license fees from $3 to $5. Others objected that more important local problems suffered neglect because Congress could not spare enough time from national affairs to perform adequately the duties of a city council.

Defenders of the existing order pointed out that Washington had escaped the municipal corruption common in other big cities. They also suggested that Congress might refuse to approve a federal contribution to the District budget if it did not exercise full control over District affairs. The basic issue, however, was racial. Southern Members of Congress and many white Washingtonians were afraid that the Negro majority would win control of a local government. The District population was more than one-half Negro.

After self-government was temporarily withdrawn from Washington in 1874, Congressmen offered numerous and varied proposals to restore home rule. They received no legislative action until the late 1940s. In persistent efforts to provide local government for the city, the Senate five times between 1949 and 1959 passed different home rule proposals, only to see them die in the Southern-dominated House District of Columbia Committee. Only in 1948 did a House bill reach the floor, and it was killed by Southern delaying tactics.

Home rule legislation was requested by Presidents Truman, Eisenhower, Kennedy and Johnson. All the proposals received bipartisan support in both chambers and were almost unopposed in the Senate. But the House District Committee was so successful in blocking the leg-

Founding Fathers' Views

The original intent of the founding fathers concerning the District of Columbia is reasonably clear. Article I, Section 8, of the Constitution provided:

"The Congress shall have power...to exercise legislation in all cases whatsoever over such District (not exceeding 10 miles square) as may, by cession of particular states and the acceptance of Congress, become the seat of the government of the United States."

Notwithstanding the comprehensiveness of this grant of power to Congress, self-government in local affairs was not precluded; rather, it seems to have been taken as a matter of course. James Madison indicated in No. 43 of *The Federalist Papers* what was in the minds of the drafters of the Constitution:

"The indispensable necessity of complete authority at the seat of government carries its own evidence with it. It is a power exercised by every legislature of the Union, I might say of the world, by virtue of its general supremacy. Without it, not only the public authority might be insulted and its proceedings interrupted with impunity; but a dependence of the members of the general government on the state comprehending the seat of the government, for protection in the exercise of their duty, might bring on the national councils an imputation of awe or influence, equally dishonorable to the government and dissatisfactory to the other members of the confederacy. This consideration has the more weight, as the gradual accumulation of public improvements at the stationary residence of the government would be both too great a public pledge to be left in the hands of a single state and would create so many obstacles to a removal of the government, as still further to abridge its necessary independence....

"As the inhabitants will find sufficient inducements of interest to become willing parties to the cession; as they will have had their voice in the election of the government which is to exercise authority over them: *as a municipal legislature for local purposes, derived from their own suffrages, will of course be allowed them;* and as the authority of the legislature of the state, and of the inhabitants of the ceded part of it, to concur in the cession, will be derived from the whole people of the state, in their adoption of the Constitution, every imaginable objection seems to be obviated." (Italics added.)

Events preceding and following adoption of the Constitution suggest that the object of setting apart a federal district was to forestall conflicts between state and federal interests. There was no plan to deny local residents the right to manage their own affairs.

islation that in the 87th and 88th Congresses (1961-64) no serious attempt was made to pass a new bill in the Senate.

Although no home rule legislation was enacted, Congress did make two concessions to proponents of suffrage in the District. A 1955 act gave District residents not claiming the right to vote in any other jurisdiction the privilege of electing delegates to the nominating conventions of the major parties. In 1960 and 1961 Congress approved and the states ratified the 23rd Amendment to the Constitution, providing for Presidential election voting in the District.

1965 LEGISLATIVE ACTION

Congress in 1965 failed to complete action on a bill to provide home rule for the District of Columbia. The Senate approved the Administration's draft bill (S 1118) with only minor changes, but the House passed an entirely new proposal. Backers of home rule hoped that somehow the differences between the two versions could be resolved, but at the end of the year there was great doubt that House and Senate conferees could reach agreement.

President Johnson Feb. 2 sent Congress a special message stating that "the restoration of home rule to the citizens of the District of Columbia must no longer be delayed." He said the people of the District were "ready and eager to join fully in the democratic process" as shown by the fact that "more than 90 percent of the registered voters went to the polls" in the 1964 Presidential election. He said that the citizens of the capital should no longer be "taxed without representation."

Accompanying the message was a draft bill, the District of Columbia Charter Act, which created a representative local government consisting of a locally elected Mayor and 15-member city council. The bill permitted District residents to elect a non-voting Delegate to the House of Representatives, and preserved existing powers of Congress and the President by permitting Congress to repeal or modify acts of the local council, permitting the President to veto such acts if they were contrary to federal interests, and providing for supervision of local fiscal affairs by the General Accounting Office. To provide for a D.C. budget, Mr. Johnson proposed: a permanent annual federal appropriation to the District equal to the real estate, personal property and business income taxes which the Federal Government would pay if it were a taxable entity; and a loan limit equal to 12 percent of the value of the property (including federal property) in the District. Limits on loans and payments are currently set by Congress and subject to annual appropriation.

Senate Action. The Senate District of Columbia Committee June 29 unanimously reported S 1118 (S Rept 381) with minor amendments. Contingent upon approval of its provisions by District of Columbia voters in a special referendum, the bill provided for election of a mayor, a partisan 19-member District Council, a nonpartisan Board of Education and a non-voting Delegate to the U.S. House of Representatives. It authorized the annual federal appropriation based on federal property in the District, which was requested by the President, and also the Administration formula for determining the limit on D.C. borrowing.

The Committee amended the Administration bill as follows: provided for five-at-large council members in addition to one from each ward; increased the council's terms of office from two to four years and provided for staggering of terms; provided for appointment by the Mayor of a City Administrator to be his managerial aide; provided for election on a nonpartisan basis of a 14-member Board of Education (the Administration bill abolished the Board and transferred its functions to the council); stipulated that no more than three of the five at-large council members could be members of the same political party; provided for recall of any elected officer of the District (instead of only the Mayor); authorized D.C. voters to initiate and enact legislation relating to the District, independent of the Mayor and council.

The Senate July 22 passed S 1118 without amendments by a roll-call vote of 63-29 and sent it to the House. Southerners voted against the bill by a 3-1 margin. Before passage the Senate July 21 rejected seven amendments, including a potentially crippling proposal to make the federal payment to the District subject to annual appropriation by Congress.

House Action. Despite the President's home rule request Feb. 2, a subsequent plea in a Feb. 15 District of Columbia Development message, and the Senate's July 22 passage of S 1118, the House District of Columbia Committee made no move to hold hearings on home rule proposals.

On Aug. 4 President Johnson, in a letter to House Speaker John W. McCormack (D Mass.), made another strong appeal for home rule, saying, "For much too long this nation has tolerated in the District of Columbia conditions that our ancestors fought a revolution to eliminate. For much too long we have imposed on many hundreds of thousands of citizens who live in the District a badge of inferiority—the stigma of unworthiness to guide their own affairs. For much too long we have denied at our Nation's Capital the principles of representative government for which we stand throughout the world." Mr. Johnson urged that the House "be given the opportunity, and promptly, to restore the basic rights of democracy at the very heart of the greatest constitutional system in the world."

Discharge Petition. Rep. Abraham J. Multer (D N.Y.) Aug. 11 filed a discharge petition to relieve the House District of Columbia Committee of jurisdiction over HR 4644, the Administration bill, and bring it to the floor. The petition required 218 signatures, a majority of the House membership. *(For mechanics and history of discharge petitions, see box p. 920.)* Home rule supporters hoped to gain the signatures by Sept. 2 and thereby bring the bill to the floor by Sept. 13. (Under House rules, a discharged bill can be called up only on the second and fourth Mondays of each month, except during the last six days of the session, and must have been on the discharge calendar seven legislative days before being brought up.) The following day, Aug. 12, the District Committee announced that hearings on HR 644 and related bills would start Aug. 18.

Two weeks after the discharge petition was filed, President Johnson began a vigorous campaign on behalf of home rule. On Aug. 24 he urged Congressional leaders to do everything possible to bring the measure to a vote. The following day, in a highly unusual move, Mr. Johnson urged House members to sign the discharge petition. He said "it is an irony and disgrace that having extended self-government already to the Philippine Islands and to Puerto Rico...some people seem to be afraid to trust almost a million American citizens with the management of their own affairs here in the District of Columbia....No one doubts the outcome once that bill finally gets to the floor of the House...But what is needed this morning is a commitment...to the only practical means of getting the bill on the floor, and that seems to be the petition

to discharge the House District Committee from further delay of the bill."

The petition nevertheless had only 197 signatures as late as Sept. 2, when White House aides began calling Members and urging them to sign. By the end of the day, all except one of the needed signatures had been collected. The same day the House District Committee, in an effort to stop the discharge proceedings, ordered reported a greatly modified home rule bill (HR 10115) *(see box).*

On Sept. 3 the petition gained the last signature, allowing the bill to be brought up on Sept. 27, the next date on which the Administration bill could be called up on the Discharge Calendar of the House. Of the 218 members who signed the petition, 192 were Democrats (ND 169, SD 23) and 26 were Republicans. The petition

---

Committee Home Rule Bill

The House District of Columbia Committee Sept. 3 reported a modified "home rule" bill (HR 10115—H Rept 957), a combination of two bills sponsored by Rep. Joel T. Broyhill (R Va.) and Rep. B. F. Sisk (D Calif.). The Committee ordered the bill reported late Sept. 2, after the home rule discharge petition had reached 217 signatures. Under HR 10115 the Government would retain jurisdiction over only the old Federal City of Washington, as it existed from 1791 to 1871. The remaining area of the District, including a majority of its inhabitants, would be offered to Maryland, and if the state rejected the area the eligible voters of the rejected area would then hold a referendum on the issue of establishing a board to draft a home rule charter. If approved, the charter would be sent to Congress, subject to amendment, and would go into effect in 90 days unless disapproved by either house.

The Committee report called the formula for an automatic, annual federal payment as proposed in HR 4644 unconstitutional and charged that the federal payment would tax all the people of the U.S. for the District without representation. The report said, "United States taxpayers would pay the District $4.4 million for the Capitol...nothing but a levy by local District officials on the sacred halls of Congress."

President Johnson Sept. 4 in a letter to House Committee Chairman John L. McMillan (D S.C.) said that the Justice Department had found that the payment formula did not permit the city to tax federal property and "does not impose an unconstitutional delegation of the appropriation power of Congress."

The Committee bill was scheduled for House action on the next "District Day," Sept. 13, preceding the discharged bill (HR 4644) by two weeks. However, House Speaker John W. McCormack (D Mass.), the Administration bill's floor leader, blocked floor action on the Committee bill by inviting action on any one of seven other bills under the new 21-day rule by which the Speaker may recognize a Member to bring up a measure for House consideration if it had been before the Rules Committee for 21 days without having been granted a rule.

Self-Government in the Nation's Capital, 1802-1874

It is not generally known that the District of Columbia enjoyed self-rule of one sort or another for more than 70 years, and that for a time it had a non-voting delegate in the House of Representatives.

The decision to locate the nation's capital on the Potomac was reached in July 1790, after Maryland and Virginia had consented to cede any territory required. The actual ten-mile-square site was marked out by President Washington.

Congress and the outgoing President, John Adams, took up residence in the new City of Washington in November 1800. The implicit promise of self-government for the District of Columbia was fulfilled with little delay. A charter adopted on May 3, 1802, established an elective council of two chambers and provided for appointment of a mayor by the President. Jurisdiction of the new local government extended only to the City of Washington, not to other parts of the District of Columbia. Alexandria and Georgetown continued to be governed much as before. As for Washington, provision was made in 1812 for election of the mayor by the council, and from 1820 until 1871 the mayor was elected biennially by popular vote.

The eclipse of self-government in the District resulted largely from partisan conflict between District residents and the Radical Republican majority in Congress immediately following the Civil War. There had been earlier quarrels. When the city elected a Whig mayor in 1840 and rubbed it in by erecting a Harrison log cabin and a 100-foot liberty pole in the center of town, the still dominant Van Buren forces in Congress suspended the corporate privileges of District banks. A bill to abolish the city charter, moreover, got as far as a third reading in the Senate.

1846 Retrocession. It was a continuation of this crossfire which led in 1846 to retrocession of Alexandria to Virginia. By this time, Tyler had come and gone as President, and the Democrats were again in control. Unable to get funds from Congress for needed improvements and still rankled by the bank action, both Georgetown and Alexandria sought to be ceded back to their respective states. The Maryland legislature, not wanting to assume added financial burdens, refused Georgetown's overtures, but Virginia was willing. When Alexandria voters approved the transfer, 3½ to 1, a bill retroceding all that part of the District on the Virginia side of the Potomac was passed through Congress.

Throughout the pre-Civil War period, relations between the District of Columbia and Congress were complicated by the slavery question and by the city's predominantly southern attitudes. A move in Congress to abolish slavery in the District almost carried in 1840. The slave trade, though not slavery, was forbidden in the District as a part of the Compromise of 1850. Washington was early a gathering place for freed Negroes. When slavery in the District was finally abolished in April 1862, the influx of Negroes began in earnest. By 1866, some 30,000 ex-slaves had come to the city.

The District quickly became a testing ground in the drive of the Radical Republicans to establish Negro suffrage. It was likewise a focal point in the struggle

for power between the Radicals and President Andrew Johnson. An act passed over Johnson's veto on Jan. 7, 1867, conferred the elective franchise on citizens over 21 years old without distinction of race or color who had lived in the city one year before an election.

When the first city election under the new suffrage law was held in June 1867, many whites refrained from voting. Negroes, however, trooped to the polls to back the party which had given them freedom. The resulting near-sweep put the Republicans in control of both chambers of the council and set the stage for contention with a carryover Democrat left in the mayor's office. The situation was reversed when white voters streamed back to the polls at the election of 1868. The Republican candidate for mayor, Sayles J. Bowen, won a narrow victory.

Financial Troubles. Projects launched by Mayor Bowen to open up new areas of the city put the District promptly into financial trouble. A Republican landslide in the local election of 1869 did not help matters. The new council took up integration problems to the neglect of financial problems. Factionalism broke out in Republican ranks, and Bowen was shown to have made payments to contractors.

Alexander Shepherd, prominent local business leader, stepped into the breach with a proposal for a modified territorial form of government. The Bowen forces were overwhelmed in the ensuing elections, and in February 1871 Congress passed a territorial bill after only brief debate. The act abolished the separate status of Georgetown, provided for an appointed District of Columbia governor, an elected non-voting delegate to the House of Representatives, and a territorial assembly with one elected and one appointed chamber. The bill also established a five-member Board of Public Works. Shepherd was named to the board and quickly became its moving force.

Shepherd's leadership proved arbitrary and costly. Determined to modernize the City of Washington at one stroke, he and his colleagues tinkered with the debt limit and the valuation rolls to finance their projects. Matters were only aggravated when Grant in September 1873 named Shepherd to succeed Henry D. Cooke as governor. A memorial from aggrieved taxpayers resulted in appointment of a joint Congressional committee to investigate District affairs. The committee turned up an incredible tale of financial mismanagement and maladministration. It recommended that the District be placed temporarily under three commissioners appointed by the President, with an Army engineer in charge of public works. The territorial assembly and the post of delegate to the House of Representatives were to be abolished. A bill to carry out these recommendations passed on June 18, 1874, only two days after the committee had reported. Although it was clear that permanent suppression of representative government was not intended, the changes then made were incorporated in the act of June 11, 1878, which established the government of the District of Columbia essentially as it remained until 1967.

was signed by the chairman of seven of the 20 House standing committees. Except for Wayne N. Aspinall (Colo.), chairman of the Interior and Insular Affairs Committee, all chairmen who did not sign were Southerners.

Compromise Moves. Even having won the victory on the discharge petition and forestalled earlier action on the Committee's counter-proposal, Administration forces were clearly uncertain of the votes needed to pass HR 4644. Many petition signers indicated they would not vote for the bill unless it was amended in several respects. And the House GOP Policy Committee Sept. 21 issued a policy statement which suggested "essential safeguards" which "must be included in any home rule legislation" including nonpartisan D.C. elections, retention of Hatch Act provisions and appropriation by Congress of the annual federal payment to the District.

In view of the objections, Multer Sept. 22 introduced a bill (HR 11218) which he said would offer as a substitute amendment to HR 4644 when it reached the floor Sept. 27. HR 11218 contained the provisions of S 1118 as passed by the Senate, with these major changes: (1) it provided for annual Congressional appropriation of the federal payment to the District (while retaining the flexible formula for determining the payment ceiling); (2) it provided for election of the Mayor and all Council members for four-year terms in even-numbered non-Presidential election years, instead of staggering the terms of the Council with half elected every two years (this was designed to overcome some objections to holding partisan elections and waiving Hatch Act requirements); (3) it required that D.C. voters be 21 years old (instead of 18) and be residents for one year (instead of six months); and (4) it authorized the President to use federal troops or take over local police if necessary to protect the federal interest or to maintain order. While knocking out the automatic federal payment feature, which President Johnson had termed the "heart" of the bill, proponents of the substitute hoped to retain the partisan election feature.

Floor Action. The House Sept. 29 passed and returned to the Senate a completely new version of S 1118. Under the House version, if D.C. voters determined in a referendum that they wanted home rule, a 15-member D.C. Charter Board elected on a nonpartisan basis would be given seven months to prepare a charter which would then be submitted to D.C. voters in another referendum. If accepted, it would go into effect in 90 days unless disapproved by either house of Congress.

House approval of the substitute was considered a smashing defeat for the Administration and a serious blow to the prospects for home rule. The choice in the House was between the Charter Board plan, sponsored by Rep. B. F. Sisk (D Calif.), and the Multer version of the original Administration bill which contained compromises *(see above)* designed to gain support for passage.

The crucial decision on the legislation came near the end of three days of heated debate and parliamentary maneuvers on a vote on the Sisk substitute. The amendment was accepted by a 198-139 teller vote—later confirmed by a key **227-174** roll call (ND 50-134; SD 72-17; R 105-23) on which a large number of Midwestern and Western Democrats left the Administration ranks. Only five or six Republicans voted against the Sisk substitute on the teller vote, despite the fact that House

Minority Leader Gerald R. Ford Jr. (R Mich.) had announced that he would support the compromise Administration bill. The crucial vote actually was the teller, not the roll call, because the parliamentary situation was such that the leadership had to defeat the Sisk amendment on the teller vote in order to bring the Multer substitute to a vote.

Many members who had signed the discharge petition under pressure from the White House were unwilling to support the Administration on the House floor and voted for the Sisk proposal. Of the last 26 petition signers, some of whom reportedly had been annoyed by the Administration's heavy-handed tactics, 15 voted in favor of the Sisk substitute on the confirming roll call.

House Maneuvering. At the beginning of debate Sept. 27, Multer moved to discharge the Rules Committee from further consideration of H Res 515, an open rule (permitting amendments) which provided for five hours of general debate on HR 4644 and five minutes on each amendment, followed by one motion to recommit the bill with or without instructions and then an immediate vote on final passage of the bill (with amendments adopted previously). The motion was agreed to. The House then adopted the rule (H Res 515) and agreed to a motion by Multer that the House resolve itself into the Committee of the Whole House for consideration of HR 4644. A majority of Republicans and Southern Democrats opposed all three votes.

Debate then began on HR 4644 and continued for the five hours allowed under the rule. At the end of that period, Multer Sept. 28 submitted his amendment substituting the provisions of his bill (HR 11218) for those of HR 4644 *(see above)*. Sisk immediately offered his Charter Board plan as a substitute for the Multer substitute. Both proposals were then open for discussion and amendment simultaneously.

Debate began Sept. 29 on the substitutes and other amendments to them. Alphonzo Bell (R Calif.) offered an amendment to the Multer proposal which required nonpartisan elections for all District officers except the Delegate to the U.S. House. In a last-ditch—but futile—attempt to gain GOP support, Multer accepted the amendment "in furtherance of that bipartisan effort" to "perfect a good home rule bill." The amendment was first rejected on a standing vote but then accepted on a teller vote.

The next move caught Administration forces off guard. Wayne L. Hays (D Ohio) moved to strike the enacting clause of HR 4644, which would have killed the bill entirely. The motion was first agreed to on a 144-140 teller vote, but was later rejected on a 179-219 roll call. After this, N. Neiman Craley Jr. (D Pa.) offered an amendment to the Sisk substitute which eliminated a requirement that a majority of registered voters in the District must vote in the referenda and election. This was accepted by voice vote.

Finally, Sisk's substitute came to a vote. It was accepted by a teller vote, and the Multer substitute as amended by the Sisk substitute (which had the effect of killing Multer's proposal) was accepted by a teller and subsequently by a roll call. This concluded consideration of amendments, and under the rule, the previous question (preventing amendments and bringing HR 4644 to a vote) was ordered. The only hope for the Administration forces would have been to offer the one

Free D.C. Movement

A new element in the form of the Free D.C. Movement became involved in the home rule struggle in 1966. The movement, headed by Marion Barry Jr., director of the Washington Office of the Student Nonviolent Coordinating Committee, said it would work to counteract the opposition of the Washington Board of Trade, an organization of Washington businesses. The Board in November 1965 sent letters to newspapers across the United States stating that many Washingtonians were opposed to home rule and, according to the Movement, planned to raise $100,000 to fight home rule in 1966. A spokesman for the Board, however, said the letters were referring to the Administration bill and not to the Sisk bill and that there were no plans to raise $100,000. The Movement was supported by several other groups, including the Washington Urban League and, for a time, the D.C. Coalition of Conscience and the Washington branch of the National Assn. for the Advancement of Colored People. The Coalition and NAACP branch later took the position of a number of other Washington groups: they favored home rule but not all the Movement's tactics.

The Movement originally planned to ask D.C. merchants to sign a petition in support of home rule, to send telegrams supporting home rule to the President and certain Members of Congress, to display "Free D.C." stickers and to make a contribution to a fund which was to be used to lobby for home rule. If a merchant refused, he faced a possible buyers' boycott and picketing. The plan to seek contributions provoked cries of blackmail, intimidation, coercion and extortion and charges that the move would be a violation of a federal anti-racketeering law. The Movement dropped its initial requirement that a contribution be made in order to avoid the boycott and picketing. The Movement, however, announced that it would accept voluntary contributions, and a permit to solicit funds was granted under the District's charitable solicitations law. The group eventually picketed several Washington stores, but the consensus was that merchants were not noticeably affected by the Movement's activities.

Many Members of Congress—both opponents and proponents of home rule—agreed that the Free D.C. Movement "pulled the rug out from under" the Senate three-member committee and harmed the chances of passage of home rule legislation in 1966. Some felt the Movement's activities were irresponsible in that they sought to put pressure where it could not be effective rather than on Congress. Sisk said that if the boycott were representative of potential leadership in the District, "I am going to reassess my thinking as to whether there is the kind of responsible enough leadership in the District for home rule."

recommittal motion permitted under the rule and to include instructions that the District Committee report back the Administration bill. But under House rules a minority member opposing the bill is given the first chance at recommittal. Alvin E. O'Konski (R Wis.) moved to recommit HR 4644 without instructions (kill the bill), which was rejected by a roll call. The House passed the bill by a roll call and then substituted its provisions for those of S 1118 as passed by the Senate.

1966 DEVELOPMENTS

Congress in 1966 did not complete action on home rule legislation for the District of Columbia. Differences between the House and Senate home rule bills passed in 1965 proved irreconcilable. Between sessions, however, home rule supporters worked to break the impasse. Three basic strategies were advanced—one using the House bill and the others using the Senate bill as the vehicle for compromise.

The first plan was evolved by Rep. Sisk and Senate District Committee Chairman Alan Bible (D Nev.). They agreed that the Senate should amend the Sisk bill and then return the amended version to the House for final approval. The other two plans—both using the Senate bill as the compromise vehicle—were proposed by Joseph L. Rauh Jr., chairman of the D.C. Democratic Central Committee and a vice chairman of Americans for Democratic Action. Both plans were aimed basically at bypassing the House District Committee.

Rauh's first plan was to attach the provisions of the Senate bill, modified to eliminate the automatic federal payment features, to a high-priority House-passed bill which came under the jurisdiction of a House chairman in favor of home rule. By tradition, the chairman of the House committee with jurisdiction over a bill recommends whether or not to agree to a conference requested by the Senate and which Members to appoint as conferees.

Rauh's other plan was to send both versions to conference in hopes that at least a modified version of the Senate bill would emerge. To make this outcome possible, however (assuming the House agreed to hold a conference), House Speaker John W. McCormack (D Mass.) would have to break tradition by appointing conferees favorable to immediate home rule, rather than those recommended by the House District Committee.

Senate Moves. President Johnson, in his Jan. 12 State of the Union Message, implied that he preferred the Senate version of the home rule bill. At a news conference the following day the President confirmed this impression, but he added that home rule was "a matter for the Congress to work out." After Mr. Johnson's statements, House Speaker McCormack reportedly told Bible that the next move was up to the Senate. This was interpreted to mean that McCormack was not willing to participate in the proposals to bypass the House District Committee. The Senate District Committee Jan. 25 appointed three of its members—Bible, Robert F. Kennedy (D N.Y.) and Winston L. Prouty (R Vt.) to confer with the President and McCormack on ways of passing home rule legislation in 1966.

The three Senators met Feb. 24 with McCormack and Rep. Abraham J. Multer, who had filed the discharge petition in 1965, to discuss the home rule outlook. After the meeting, Bible again expressed belief that the best chance for passage of home rule legislation was in working within the provisions of the House-passed bill.

The Senate District Committee, however, March 29, voted 5-1 to send the problem to conference.

The dissenting vote was cast by Wayne Morse (D Ore.), who, as he did earlier, contended that the move was useless. The Senate April 5 formally disagreed to the House amendments to S 1118 and asked the House for a conference. All seven members of the Senate District Committee were appointed as conferees.

Observers speculated that the Senate action resulted from the likelihood that Morse would filibuster any type of charter board bill brought to the floor and from the possibility that the D.C. community might misinterpret Senate rejection of an amended Sisk bill, especially if home rule opponents joined a Morse filibuster. Others felt that the Senate, believing home rule lost for the term, decided to send the problem back to the House where opposition to the proposal had been strongest and where many Senators were thought to feel that the blame for the failure in passage should lie.

Bible April 5 said he would appeal to House District Committee Chairman John L. McMillan (D S.C.), a staunch opponent of home rule, to send the problem to conference, and McMillan said he would consider the request.

The House District Committee May 11 by a 10-13 vote rejected a motion by Rep. Frank Horton (R N.Y.) asking that conferees be appointed. McMillan said he did not see "how we can get together on two absolutely different bills." He contended that the Committee "should wait and see if the Senate agrees with us" on five other District bills ready for conference.

Further Attempts. With home rule blocked in the House District Committee, Morse July 8 announced that he would seek Senate approval of a home rule rider to the college aid bill (HR 14644), which had been passed by the House May 2. *(See below.)* The rider was drafted in June, with House Education and Labor Committee Chairman Adam C. Powell (D N.Y.), an ardent backer of home rule, promising Morse his full cooperation. If the Senate agreed to the Morse rider, the bill then could be considered in conference by members of Powell's Committee, most of whom were friendly to home rule.

Meanwhile two efforts were made for separate enactment of the provisions in S 1118 for an elected D.C. school board with independent taxing powers. Rep. Edith Green (D Ore.), chairman of the House Education and Labor Subcommittee on Special Education, June 7 gained unanimous Subcommittee approval of a school board amendment to a vocational rehabilitation bill (HR 14323). However, the Subcommittee June 16 decided to try to add the school board proposal to the more important elementary-secondary education bill (HR 13161). But Chairman Powell blocked the amendment during consideration of HR 13161 by the full Committee. An aide said Powell had received no support for the school board amendment from D.C. citizens and that he did not want the issue to cloud any new Senate efforts to enact home rule.

An amendment similar to that of Rep. Green was offered in the Senate Sept. 21 to the D.C. college bill (S 293) by Sen. Peter H. Dominick (R Colo.). The amendment was rejected by a 22-54 roll-call vote.

In final 1966 action, Morse Oct. 7 introduced a home rule rider to the college aid bill (HR 14644) as planned. His rider was a modified version of S 1118 designed to meet House objections by: allowing for a federal con-

tribution toward the cost of running the city based not on federal property holdings, but on revenues raised through city taxes; providing for nonpartisan elections; establishing a nonpartisan school board without independent taxing powers; and authorizing the President to assume command of the police in case of civil disorders.

Majority Leader Mike Mansfield (D Mont.) minutes later filed a cloture petition to halt a threatened Southern filibuster on the issue. Mansfield, who said he "personally" opposed using the rider tactic, gained 22 signatures on the petition, including that of Minority Leader Everett McKinley Dirksen (R Ill.). Richard B. Russell (D Ga.), leader of the Southern opposition, said the attempt to close off debate before it started amounted to "legislative lynching." The cloture motion was rejected Oct. 10 by a 41-37 roll-call vote, falling 11 votes short of the required two-thirds majority of Senators voting. Some Senators feared that House opposition to home rule would jeopardize enactment of the college aid bill and would further delay adjournment. After cloture failed, the Morse amendment was tabled, ending all chance of home rule legislation in the 89th Congress.

1967 REORGANIZATION PLAN

President Johnson, repeatedly frustrated in his efforts to win home rule for residents of the District of Columbia, in 1967 used authority granted him under the Reorganization Act to revamp the D.C. government. Under his Reorganization Plan No. 3, old authority was substantially redistributed, providing wider representation to D.C. citizens in passing on local regulations and budgetary problems. The Plan took effect Aug. 11 after the House Aug. 9 by a 160-244 roll-call vote rejected a resolution to disapprove it. (Unlike a bill, a reorganization plan cannot be amended. It can be rejected only if the House or Senate adopts a resolution disapproving the plan within 60 days after it is submitted.)

The chief advantage of using the Reorganization Act to revamp the D.C. government was that it enabled Mr. Johnson to bypass the House District of Columbia Committee, which strongly supported the existing form of government and which had blocked D.C. home rule bills since 1949. (Reorganization plans are referred to the House and Senate Government Operations Committees.)

Under the plan, the three Presidentially appointed D.C. commissioners were replaced by a single commissioner who was afterward called "Mayor," a deputy commissioner and a nine-member city council. The new officials also were appointed by the President, but the added number made the government representative of a greater part of the city. Mr. Johnson subsequently named a Negro as D.C. commissioner and appointed five Negroes—a majority—to the council. (About 65 percent of the city's population was Negro.)

In proposing his reorganization plan Feb. 27, Mr. Johnson said it was only an interim measure to provide more efficient government until a home rule law was passed. Congress in 1967 did not consider home rule legislation, despite endorsement by the President.

Congress in 1967 failed to complete action on two other measures proposed by the President for the District —a constitutional amendment granting the District voting representation in Congress and legislation creating a lo-

Congress Approves D.C. Subway, But Blocks Construction

Congress in 1965 enacted an Administration bill authorizing construction of a publicly owned but privately operated rail rapid transit system for the District of Columbia. As signed into law Sept. 8, the bill (HR 4822—PL 89-173):

Authorized the National Capital Transportation Agency to build and equip a 24.9-mile rail-transit system with 13.1 miles of it underground, at a total cost of $431 million (not including an estimated $52 million for interest costs).

Authorized $150 million in grants for construction and equipment, two-thirds from the Federal Government and one-third from the District of Columbia.

Authorized the sale of bonds to cover the remaining costs—$281 million plus the interest costs of approximately $52 million—underwritten on a two-thirds federal, one-third D.C. basis. The bonds would be paid off "out of the fare box"—that is, from the revenues of the transit system.

Required that the system be operated by a private contractor, and guaranteed workers' bargaining rights.

Most of the system would lie within the District's boundaries, but the design permitted extension into suburban areas, if later authorized. Construction of the authorized system was expected to take more than six years.

1963 Legislation. There was little opposition in Congress to the rail-transit plan. This was in sharp contrast with the fate of similar legislation recommended by President Kennedy in 1963, which was killed by the House on a 278-76 roll-call vote that recommitted the bill.

Of the factors which contributed to passage in 1965 of a bill so roundly defeated in 1963, the most important were (1) changes in the financing formula which reduced the federal share from $120 million out of $400.6 million (5/6 of the amount not covered by revenue bonds) to $100 million out of $431 million (2/3 of the amount not covered by bonds); and (2) a stipulation that the publicly owned system would be pri-

vately operated and the rights of employees protected. This stipulation removed opposition from transit unions based on the fear that collective bargaining rights would not be allowed to employees of a publicly operated transportation system. Another factor which worked in favor of passage was that national highway industry organizations, which bitterly fought the subway plan in 1963, in 1965 for the most part remained neutral.

Freeway Dispute. The D.C. rapid transit system approved in 1965 soon became snarled in a dispute involving construction of freeways in the District. The controversy surfaced in 1966, when the House initially denied all funds for the transit system in the D.C. appropriations bill on the ground that freeway construction had fallen behind and should be continued concurrently with construction of the subway. Although subway funds were added to the bill in conference, construction was stalled by continuing failure to settle the freeway dispute.

Congress in 1968 put strong pressure on the District to complete its freeway system by including the following provision in the Federal Aid Highway Act (PL 90-495): "Notwithstanding any other provision of law, or any court decision or administrative action to the contrary, the Secretary of Transportation and the government of the District of Columbia shall, in addition to those routes already under construction, construct all routes on the Interstate system within the District of Columbia...."

The requirement was fought for by Rep. John C. Kluczynski (D Ill.), chairman of the Subcommittee on Roads of the House Public Works Committee, and by Rep. William H. Natcher (D Ky.), chairman of the District of Columbia Subcommittee of the House Appropriations Committee, who blocked funds for a District rapid transit system until the Interstate projects were "beyond recall." Kluczynski told *The Washington Post* that "the District won't get a dime for a subway until it does what we want it to do to highways."

---

cally elected, nonpartisan 11-member school board to replace a nine-member board appointed by the judges of the U.S. District Court in the city.

Plan Submitted. President Johnson Feb. 27, 1967, in a special message to Congress on the District of Columbia, proposed reorganization of the city's government by means of an Executive reorganization plan to provide more efficient government until home rule legislation was passed. He proposed that the three commissioners be replaced by a single commissioner and nine-member council, appointed by the President and confirmed by the Senate. The single commissioner would serve at the pleasure of the President; the council members would serve two-year terms and would be appointed at large. Contrary to the old system, the commissioner would be allowed to consolidate existing city agencies without Congressional approval and to transfer money between agencies.

Though the President Feb. 27 had said he would send his Executive reorganization plan to Congress "shortly,"

he did not submit it until June 1. His action came after a May 18 announcement that no decisions had been made "one way or the other" regarding prospects for the plan. Before his announcement, the President invited members of the House and Senate District Committees to the White House to discuss the plan.

Reorganization Plan No. 3 differed from the President's Feb. 27 proposals by authorizing the single commissioner to veto actions of the council; by setting the terms of council members at three years instead of two; by requiring that the commissioner or deputy commissioner, but not necessarily both, have been a resident of the city for three years prior to appointment; and in other less important ways.

Immediately after it was submitted, the plan ran into opposition from key members of the House District Committee. (As a reorganization plan, the President's proposal was referred to the House Committee on Government Operations.) Chairman John L. McMillan (D S.C.) June 13 introduced a resolution (H Res 512) disapproving the plan, as did Rep. Joel T. Broyhill (R Va.), also a member of the Committee. Rep. Ancher Nelsen (R Minn.), ranking Republican on the Committee, June 5 introduced the President's plan in bill form (HR 10521) because, he said, the Committee "should have had a chance to exercise its judgment."

On Aug. 1 the Government Operations Subcommittee on Executive and Legislative Reorganization, which had held hearings on the reorganization plan in June, recommended that the President's proposal be allowed to take effect. The full Government Operations Committee Aug. 3 reported the disapproval resolution with the recommendation that it be rejected. The report noted that the legislative power of Congress over the District "would in no way be impaired by the adoption" of the reorganization plan. The House Aug. 9 rejected the disapproval resolution (H Res 512) by a 160-244 roll-call vote, thus allowing Reorganization Plan No. 3 to take effect.

New Government. President Johnson appointed Walter E. Washington, 52, a Negro, as the District's new single commissioner. Washington was then chairman of the New York City Housing Authority. Prior to taking that post in November 1966, he served as executive director of the National Capital Housing Authority (NCHA). Washington had been associated with NCHA for 25 years in various capacities. He graduated from Howard University (B.A. and LL.B.).

Thomas W. Fletcher, 43, was named deputy commissioner. Fletcher, then deputy assistant secretary of Housing and Urban Development, was city manager of San Diego, Calif., from 1961 to 1966. He was graduated from the University of California at Berkeley.

Washington and Fletcher were confirmed by unanimous consent of the Senate Sept. 21. The President's nine appointees to the council—including five Negroes—were confirmed by the Senate Nov. 1. John W. Hechinger, a Washington businessman, was named president of the council by Mr. Johnson.

Related Developments. In his Feb. 27 message on the District of Columbia, the President had proposed a constitutional amendment to grant the District one House Member and "such additional representation in the House and Senate as the Congress may from time to time provide." The House and Senate Judiciary Committees held hearings on the proposed amendment, but only the House Committee reported it. The amendment received no consideration on the House floor.

Congress in 1967 also failed to complete action on legislation, proposed by President Johnson, creating a locally elected, nonpartisan school board for the District of Columbia. The House Sept. 25 passed a bill (HR 13042) embodying the President's proposals. The Senate by unanimous consent passed a slightly different version the last day of the session and no further action was taken.

Congress in 1968 completed action on the school board bill (HR 13042—PL 90-292). Under HR 13042, the board would consist of 11 members—eight elected from wards and three at large—who would serve in staggered terms of four years at an annual salary of $1,200. The first election was to be held Nov. 5, 1968, with subsequent elections in November of odd-numbered years.

II—Island Dependencies

The smaller island dependencies of the United States historically have received little attention from Congress, and this continued to be the case in the Johnson years. Legislation was passed providing for popular election of the governor and lieutenant governor of Guam and of the Virgin Islands, and for increased financial assistance to the Pacific Trust Territory and the Ryukyu Islands, but none of the various bills could be described as major.

The three groups of islands and Guam all entered into U.S. jurisdiction as a result of war. Guam was ceded to the United States by Spain after the Spanish-American War; the Virgin Islands were purchased from Denmark during World War I to prevent them from falling into the hands of Germany; occupation of the Ryukyus was authorized under provisions of the Japanese Peace Treaty of 1952; and the Pacific Trust Territory, consisting of the Carolines, the Marianas and the Marshalls, is a United Nations mandate. Prior to World War II, Japan had administered the islands under a League of Nations mandate.

PACIFIC TRUST TERRITORIES. Congress in 1967 passed an amended Administration-backed bill (S 303— PL 90-16) authorizing increased appropriations for the Trust Territory of the Pacific Islands and providing for appointment of the High Commissioner by the President with the advice and consent of the Senate. As signed into law, S 303 increased the existing appropriation authorization of $17.5 million annually to a maximum of $25 million for fiscal 1967 and $35 million for both fiscal 1968 and fiscal 1969. Proponents of the bill said that the additional funds were to be used for economic and social development of the area.

Legislation (S 3207—PL 90-617) passed in 1968 authorized the appropriation of $50 million for each of the fiscal years 1970 and 1971 for the Trust Territory. The funds were to support governmental programs and economic development. The bill also authorized up to $10 million in any one year to relieve suffering and damage caused by major natural disasters, such as typhoons, which often occur in the area. The legislation was requested by the Interior Department, which administers the Trust Territory.

RYUKYU ISLANDS. Congress in 1965 enacted legislation (S J Res 32—PL 89-296) authorizing a $22-million appropriation to compensate citizens of the Ryuku Islands for damages by U.S. armed forces during the occupation of Okinawa and nearby islands from Aug. 15, 1945, to April 28, 1952. The bill provided $15 million for land rentals, $3,650,000 for damage to property and growing crops and loss of fishing rights, $2,500,000 for restoration of damaged released lands, $800,000 for personal injury or death and $50,000 for water rights. The payments were recommended by the Administration

U. S.–Panama Treaty Agreements Stir Controversy

The negotiation of new treaty agreements between the United States and Panama was announced in 1967. The agreements affected sovereignty over the Panama Canal and construction of a second canal. The announcement provoked many Members of Congress to introduce resolutions expressing opposition to ratification of the treaties. No action, other than hearings, was taken on the resolutions, nor were the treaties submitted to Congress for ratification.

A subordinate controversy over proposals for a second canal arose during consideration of a bill to extend the life of the Atlantic-Pacific Interoceanic Canal Study Commission to Dec. 1, 1969. The Commission, appointed in 1965, was charged with studying the feasibility of, and finding the best site for, a new sea-level canal between the Atlantic and Pacific oceans. The bill was enacted on the last day of the 1967 Congressional session. (See below.)

President Johnson and President Marco A. Robles of Panama proclaimed June 26 that three new treaties had been drafted. The contents were not disclosed officially, but subsequent press reports indicated that the treaties would (1) relinquish U.S. control over the Panama Canal in favor of administration by a binational authority; (2) provide for the defense of the Panama Canal; and (3) allow the United States to build a second canal across Panama if it chose to do so.

In the House, more than 130 Members swiftly introduced or cosponsored resolutions urging that the treaties be rejected. The House Foreign Affairs Committee's Subcommittee on Inter-American Affairs held hearings on the resolutions in July and August, but took no final action in 1967. In the Senate, criticism was led by Strom Thurmond (R S.C.). Much of the criticism was based on fears that U.S. consent to end its control over the strategic Canal would open the way for Suez-like crises or Communist seizure. J.W. Fulbright (D Ark.), chairman of the Senate Foreign Relations Committee, and Senate Majority Leader Mike Mansfield (D Mont.) voiced approval of the pacts.

Background. The United States gained control over a 10-mile strip across Panama in the Hay-Bunau-Varilla Treaty, signed by President Theodore Roosevelt Nov. 18, 1903, and agreed to by the Senate Feb. 23, 1904. Immediately after the signing of the Treaty, the two countries began to disagree on the question of sovereignty over the Canal. The United States and Panama agreed to revisions of the 1903 Treaty in 1936 and 1955, changing certain provisions and raising the annuity paid by the United States to Panama from $250,000 to $1,930,000.

In 1959, Panama requested that her flag be flown alongside the American flag in the Canal Zone. Despite strong opposition in Congress, including a House resolution, passed by a vote of 381-12, protesting such action, President Eisenhower allowed the two flags to be flown together at certain sites. A later order banned the flying of flags in front of Canal Zone schools. In defiance of that order, U.S. students Jan. 7, 1964, raised the American flag at a high school, touching off a riot which left four Americans and 21 Panamanians dead.

As a result of the riot, Panama broke off diplomatic relations with the United States. The two countries resumed relations April 3, 1964. President Johnson Dec. 18, 1964, announced that the United States would negotiate a new treaty and would press for a new canal across the Isthmus of Panama. Presidents Johnson and Robles June 26, 1967, announced that the treaties had been drafted but did not disclose their contents.

Meanwhile, Congress in 1964 passed a bill creating a commission to determine the feasibility of and the best site for a new sea-level canal across the Isthmus. President Johnson signed the bill into law (PL 88-609) Sept. 24, 1964.

Congress in 1967 cleared legislation (S 1566—PL 90-244) extending the life of the commission for 17 months, from June 30, 1968, to Dec. 1, 1969. The President signed S 1566 into law on Jan. 2, 1968.

after a joint Ryukyuan-American Committee reviewed original claims for $53 million and reduced them to $22 million.

Legislation (HR 4903—PL 90-126) passed in 1967 increased from $12 million to $17.5 million the authorization for aid for the economic and social development of the Ryukyus. The final versions of HR 4903 retained a Senate amendment authorizing $17.5 million a year. This was a reduction of $7.5 million from the Administration request and the House-passed authorization of $25 million.

VIRGIN ISLANDS. Congress in 1968 cleared a bill (S 450—PL 90-496) to provide for the popular election of the governor and lieutenant governor of the Virgin Islands and for other changes in the government of the territory. As signed into law, S 450:

Provided for the popular election of a governor and lieutenant governor in the Virgin Islands Trust Territory, beginning in 1970.

Established the office of lieutenant governor.

Limited the length of the elective terms to four years and specified that no one could serve more than two successive terms.

Clarified the powers of the government comptroller and stipulated that the salaries and expenses of his office be paid by the Federal Government with funds from internal revenue collections from the territory.

Extended the privileges and immunities clauses, the due process and equal protection clauses of the U.S. Constitution to the people of the Virgin Islands.

Made the Virgin Islands subject to the general military law of the United States (which authorized the President to use federal local forces in case of insurrection or similar emergencies).

Background. The Virgin Islands, a Caribbean group purchased by the United States from Denmark in 1917, were administered as a U.S. territory through the Department of the Interior. The Virgin Islands laws were a combination of Danish colonial law and a 1936 organic act passed by Congress and revised in 1954. The Governor of the Islands was appointed by the President, although since 1917 there had been a popularly elected legislature.

President Kennedy in 1962 recommended election of the Governor and Government Secretary and proposed other changes in the governments' structure. Most of his requests were not enacted.

In 1966, both the Senate and House passed differing bills providing for the popular election of the Governor, but final action was not completed before the 89th Congress ended. President Johnson had not formally endorsed popular election of the Governor.

GUAM. Congress in 1968 completed action on an Administration-backed bill (S 449—PL 90-497) to provide for the popular election of the governor and lieutenant governor of Guam, appointment of a government comptroller and for other changes in the island's government. As signed into law, S 449:

Provided for the popular election of the governor and lieutenant governor of Guam by a majority vote of persons qualified to vote for members of the legislature.

Provided for removal of the governor upon majority vote in a referendum by the populace (provided at least 2/3 of registered voters voted in the referendum).

Provided that election of the governor and lieutenant governor would be held every four years beginning in 1970, and that a limit of two full successive terms be imposed on persons elected to each office.

Established the office of lieutenant governor and provided him with powers as designated by the governor.

Established qualifications for the offices of governor and lieutenant governor.

Established executive powers for the governor.

Provided for appointment of the Guam Government comptroller by the U.S. Secretary of the Interior.

Fixed the date for annual sessions of the legislature subject to approval by the legislature.

Extended certain provisions of the U.S. Constitution to the people of Guam.

Made Guam subject to the general military law of the United States.

Background. After the Spanish-American War in 1898, the territory of Guam was ceded to the United States by the Treaty of Paris. The Department of the Navy was responsible for administering the island until 1950, when a civil government was established (as provided by the Organic Act of Guam) and responsibility was transferred to the Secretary of the Interior. The Act also provided for local collection of federal income taxes and created a 21-member unicameral legislature.

Since 1950, a series of laws had been enacted to give the people of Guam additional measures of self-government.

Miscellaneous Bills

Disaster Relief

HURRICANE BETSY. Congress in 1965 enacted legislation (HR 11539—PL 89-339) extending federal aid to victims of September's Hurricane "Betsy" in Florida, Louisiana and Mississippi. The U.S. Weather Bureau called Betsy the most destructive hurricane in U.S. history.

During Congressional consideration of HR 11539, Rep. Claude Pepper (D Fla.) said damages from Hurricane Betsy were estimated at $2.5 billion—over $2 billion in Louisiana, about $250 million in Mississippi and $119 million in Florida. Sen. Russell B. Long (D La.) said the hurricane was "the worst disaster, as far as property damage was concerned, that has ever hit the United States." He stressed that loan adjustment assistance authorized by HR 11539 was intended to aid poor persons who were not in a financial position to protect themselves against such losses through insurance.

Major provisions of HR 11539 permitted the Small Business Administration to cancel up to $1,800 or waive up to $1,800 in interest on disaster loans, regardless of whether the disaster victim could have purchased insurance against his losses. The Farmers Home Administration was authorized to provide the same benefits for uninsurable farm losses regardless of whether a farmer could obtain financial assistance elsewhere. Another provision directed the Department of Housing and Urban Development to undertake a study of alternative comprehensive methods of federal disaster aid and insurance, and to report to Congress with recommendations within nine months. *(See box.)*

NORTHWEST FLOODS. Another bill (S 2089—PL 89-41) enacted in 1965 provided federal aid to California, Oregon, Washington, Nevada and Idaho, largely for road reconstruction in areas damaged by floods in December 1964 and January-February 1965. Provision was made also for river bank protection in California, where railroad tracks adjacent to the Eel River were particularly vulnerable to washout. S 2089 authorized emergency appropriations of up to $50 million in fiscal 1965 and $20 million in fiscal 1966 from which the Secretary of Commerce could make expenditures for repair or reconstruction of highways, roads and trails damaged by the floods. The bill, moreover, amended the 1964 Federal-aid Highway Act to increase appropriations for forest roads and trails development during fiscal 1966 from $85 million to $123 million, with the additional $38 million to be used for forest road repair in the flood-damaged areas.

1966 OMNIBUS BILL. To supplement existing disaster relief laws, Congress in 1966 enacted legislation (S 1861—PL 89-769) providing various types of immediate relief for victims of major natural disasters. The bill was passed by the Senate in 1965 *(see box)* but was tied up in the House Public Works Committee until late in 1966.

As enacted, the bill permitted the Government to alter the terms of loans made by certain agencies when the borrower was financially hard pressed because of a natural disaster. It also provided housing mortgage insurance for disaster victims, provided aid to rural areas damaged by a disaster, authorized financial aid to colleges and universities which suffered losses in a disaster, provided for rebuilding of damaged public facilities and contained other provisions for relief. The bill provided no specific dollar authorization. Supporters said that the cost would depend on the extent of damages from disasters.

1968 Action. The Senate Public Works Committee reported a bill (S 438—S Rept 1073) in 1968 to broaden provisions of omnibus disaster relief legislation enacted in 1966. No further action was taken. As reported, S 438 established a new cost-sharing program whereby the Federal Government was to take on 50 percent of disaster losses of up to $30,000 for homeowners and $100,000 for businessmen. The states were to bear 25 percent of the costs while the remaining 25 percent was to come from the individual. The program was restricted to states which developed comprehensive disaster relief plans and set up agencies to administer aid to victims. The bill also authorized federal grants of up to $250,000 per state to assist states in setting up their disaster plans.

Flood Insurance

1967 PROGRAM. An Administration-backed flood insurance bill was passed by both houses of Congress in 1967 but remained in conference at the end of the year.

The National Flood Insurance Act of 1967 (S 1985) provided for government and private industry participation in a program to make flood insurance available in flood-prone areas. Under the bill's provisions private insurers would form a pool to sell and service flood insurance and to share profits and liabilities. Insurance premiums would be subsidized by the Government to cover the difference between the actuarial cost of the insurance and the cost to purchasers. The bill also provided for Government reinsurance to cover "catastrophic" losses.

Disaster Background

President Johnson declared major natural disasters 34 times in both 1964 and 1965, making them the worst disaster years since the Federal Disaster Act was passed in 1950. The high number of disasters resulted in heavy pressure in Congress in 1965 for omnibus legislation which would supplement existing disaster relief laws and would take effect as soon as a disaster struck. S 1861 was passed by the Senate July 22, 1965, without controversy.

Although action was not completed on the omnibus disaster aid bill in 1965, a number of less comprehensive bills were enacted. Among them was HR 11539 (PL 89—339), to provide relief for victims of Hurricane Betsy. One of its provisions directed the Department of Housing and Urban Development to study all aspects of federal disaster aid and insurance and to submit a report to the President.

By June 29, 1966, the President had declared eight more major natural disasters, for a total of 42 since Oct. 3, 1964.

HUD Flood Insurance Report. Mr. Johnson Aug. 12, 1966, sent Congress the HUD report, which was entitled "Insurance and Other Programs for Financial Assistance to Flood Victims." In a letter of transmittal, the President said he was ordering appropriate federal agencies to study the HUD report and that flood insurance legislation would be presented to Congress later. No legislation on the subject was submitted during 1966.

In its study, made in close cooperation with the insurance industry, the Department concluded that a national flood insurance program should be inaugurated. The program, according to the study, should be conducted principally by private insurers "with Government assistance or participation to the extent necessary to assure a workable method of pooling risks, minimizing costs and distributing burdens equally between property owners protected by such insurance and the general taxpayer." The program, the HUD Department continued, should be designed to discourage construction in areas which have been struck by severe floods. The Department also asked that high-risk flood areas be identified as soon as possible—a suggestion taken up by the U.S. Geological Survey which, in June 1967, completed a 19-volume study of the magnitude and frequency of floods in the United States.

The HUD report, which contained much data never before released by federal agencies, was greeted with enthusiastic approval by most insurance companies. They had opposed earlier attempts to set up a federal flood insurance program on grounds that the proposals did not provide for sufficient involvement by private industry. One insurance executive told the Senate Banking and Currency Committee he thought the Department study was "a scholarly, fresh approach to the flood insurance problem."

The major difference between the House and Senate versions of S 1985 was in the method of providing the federal financing for the program. The Senate version, which had the backing of the insurance industry and the Administration, set up a $500-million National Flood Insurance Fund in the Treasury on which the administrator of the program could draw. The House version, on the other hand, was amended on the floor to require direct appropriations to fund the program. The insurance industry, which said it needed an assured source of readily available backup credit in case of disasters, had opposed the direct appropriations approach. The House version also covered small businesses in addition to the residential properties included under both the House and Senate provisions.

Private insurance companies traditionally considered flood damage too high a risk to insure because of the limited areas in which floods occur (and therefore the limited market for insurance coupled with the high frequency and high costs of floods in those areas).

Based for the most part on a 1966 report of the Department of Housing and Urban Development *(see Disaster Background box)*, S 1985 provided for coverage of one-to four-family dwellings. Liability under subsidized policies was limited to $15,000 for single units and $30,000 for multiple homes; maximum liability for damage to personal property was set at $5,000 for each family unit. Federal premium subsidies were authorized for all existing homes, but persons who built new houses in flood-prone areas would not be eligible for federal help in paying their premiums. This provision was designed to discourage new construction in high-risk areas. Although the proposal was limited in scope, S 1985 provided for its extension to other kinds of property, such as small businesses, when some administrative experience with the program had been gained.

1968 ACTION. A program of national flood insurance, similar to that provided by S 1985, was included as Title XIII of the Housing and Urban Development Act of 1968 (S 3497—PL 90-448), one of the most ambitious housing and urban development programs ever undertaken by Congress. *(For more detail on provisions of S 3497, see Housing section.)*

Provisions. Title XIII, the national flood insurance section of S 3497 (PL 90-448), the Housing and Urban Development Act of 1968:

Gave the Secretary of HUD authority to set up a program of flood insurance as a joint federal-private venture and permitted the Secretary to establish an all-federal program in the event that a joint program was not feasible.

Provided that subsidized personal and property insurance would be made available for flood damage to one-to four-family houses and to small business properties in flood-prone areas. Specified that insurance would be available only in states which "evidenced a positive interest" in flood insurance and adopted land use and control regulations before June 30, 1970, to prevent unwise use of flood-prone land.

Established a 15-member Flood Insurance Advisory Committee to assist the HUD Secretary in determining the scope of the program, the premiums to be charged and how the program should be operated. Specified the following maximum liabilities eligible for rates below actuarial cost (subsidized premiums): $17,500 for a one-family dwelling; $30,000 for a multiple-unit dwelling; $5,000 for the contents of each unit; $30,000 for a business structure and $5,000 for the contents of each business unit.

Previous Efforts to Obtain Flood Insurance Guarantees

Federal guarantees for flood insurance were sought and authorized in past years, but they did not materialize. President Truman in 1952 asked Congress to establish a national flood insurance program. President Eisenhower in 1956 recommended federal reinsurance for private insurers that offered flood insurance. Congress in 1956 passed the Federal Flood Insurance Act (PL 84-1016), but funds to implement the program were never appropriated because no technical study had been made to determine the actual costs of starting the program.

Legislation authorizing a government study of the feasibility of disaster insurance was passed by the Senate in 1962, 1963 and 1965. The bills were sponsored by Sen. Harrison A. Williams Jr. (D N.J.). A similar provision was subsequently enacted by Congress in 1965 as part of a disaster relief bill to aid areas hit by Hurricane Betsy (PL 89-339).

The insurance industry was unable to write flood insurance policies at rates sufficiently low to attract potential purchasers of this protection. Premiums calculated on a straight actuarial basis would be prohibitively high, the industry said, because of (1) the very high risk of damage to property owned by potential purchasers of the insurance; and (2) the "catastrophic" nature of flood damage when it did occur. Damage caused by floods, therefore, was not considered an "insurable risk" in the same sense as wind or fire damage, in which the premiums paid by many persons provided enough funds to compensate the relatively few who actually experienced losses. The insurance industry contended that because floods did not pose an equal threat to every person, the "risk-spreading" principle—which was the basis for all insurance—was not applicable.

In 1964 and 1965, the estimated losses from inland floods were $652 million and $788 million, according to the 1967 Senate Banking and Currency Committee report (S Rept 549) on S 1985. Flood damage costs since 1903, the report said, had risen at a rate of 5½ percent a year, chiefly in the 2 percent of the country exposed to frequent flooding—for example, the Mississippi River delta. Damage from coastal floods

caused by Hurricane Betsy in September 1965, which hit Louisiana with unusual ferocity, came to over $1 billion. Early estimates of the damages resulting from the August 1967 floods in Fairbanks, Alaska, were $200 million; 95 percent of the buildings in Fairbanks were judged to have been damaged by the high waters.

The Federal Government in 1936 inaugurated a program of flood control. The Army Corps of Engineers and the Agricultural Department's Soil Conservation Service spent about $7 billion between 1936 and 1967 on flood prevention projects such as dams and dikes. Once a flood occurred, however, the Federal Government had only limited ability, prior to establishment of national flood insurance in 1968, to help the victims and their property.

The usual course of federal assistance begins when the President declares a flooded region a national disaster area under the provisions of the 1950 Federal Disaster Act (PL 81-875). This designation makes the residents of an affected area eligible for low-interest loans from the Small Business Administration and the Federal Housing Administration and permits the area to receive special aid to reconstruct its schools. Such a procedure usually applies only to disasters of major proportions. While smaller incidents may not qualify as national disasters, they nevertheless saddle an area with the cost and effort of digging out and rebuilding.

National disaster assistance has another drawback in that it is granted only after the fact. An arrangement such as flood insurance allows residents of an area to prepare themselves financially for a disaster before it strikes.

Authorities agree on the need for stronger local efforts to restrict buildings on flood-prone land. This could be accomplished by zoning, building codes and health regulations. A federal subsidy on insurance premiums, the Senate Committee report said, "is justifiable only as part of an interim solution to long-range readjustments in land use. Such assistance should not prejudice these needed long-range adjustments, or the program would be self-defeating."

Directed the Secretary to encourage private insurers to form a pool to sell and service flood insurance and to share profits and liabilities. Limited insurance outstanding at any time to $2.5 billion.

Authorized the Secretary to make premium equalization payments to the insurers' pool to make up the difference between below-cost premiums paid and the actuarial cost of the insurance. Pledged the Federal Government to back up the private firms by paying any claims in excess of the financial capacity of the privately financed pool.

Directed the Secretary, with other federal agencies, to identify flood zones according to declining risk of disaster and, within five years after enactment, to establish a set of actuarial flood insurance premiums based on the flood-zone statistics.

Created a National Flood Insurance Fund in the Treasury Department and gave the HUD Secrtary

borrowing authority of up to $250 million. Rescinded existing authority for Congress to appropriate any amounts the President deemed necessary for flood control. Specified that the Fund would be used to pay premium subsidies to the insurance pool and reinsurance claims when the pool suffered excessive losses. Authorized appropriations to reimburse the Treasury for payments from the Fund.

Authorized the Secretary to develop comprehensive criteria for state and local planning and regulations of land use in flood-prone areas.

Fairs and Expositions

HEMISFAIR. Congress enacted legislation (HR 9247—PL 89-284) in 1965 authorizing participation by the U.S. Government in the international Hemisfair 1968 Exposition to be held at San Antonio, Texas, in 1968.

The six-month-long fair was to celebrate the 250th anniversary of the founding of San Antonio and to display the achievements of the Western Hemipshere. HR 9247 requested the President to invite the participation of foreign countries in the exposition and, as enacted, authorized $125,000 for a Commerce Department study of the extent and cost of the U.S. Government's participation. The general supplemental appropriations bill (HR 11588—PL 89-309) provided the full authorization of $125,000.

1966 Action. Machinery and funds for U.S. participation in the HemisFair 1968 Exposition were provided by legislation (HR 15098—PL 89-685) enacted in 1966. HR 15098 authorized $7.5 million for U.S. participation in the fair and contained a provision limiting future federal participation in expositions in the United States to "first category" international fairs registered with the Bureau of International Expositions in Paris. The first supplemental appropriations bill for fiscal 1967 (HR 18381—PL 89-697) appropriated $6,750,000 for the HemisFair.

REVOLUTION BICENTENNIAL. Congress passed a bill (S J Res 162—PL 89-491) in 1966 creating a 34-member American Revolution Bicentennial Commission to prepare recommendations on and coordinate celebration of the 200th anniversary of the American Revolution. The bill was amended to specify that the Commission was to be privately financed through public donations. The Commission was to be composed of 17 members from private life (including the chairman), nine top federal officials, and four Members each from the House and Senate.

1967 Action. A bill (HR 8629—PL 90-187) passed in 1967 extended for one year, until July 4, 1969, the life of the Commission and added the Commerce Secretary as an ex officio member. Both actions were taken at the Commission's request. HR 8629 also authorized the appropriation of $450,000 through fiscal 1969 for the Commission's operations. No funds were appropriated, however.

INTERAMA. Congress approved a bill (HR 30—PL 89-355) in 1966 authorizing U.S. Government participation in the proposed Inter-American Cultural and Trade Center (Interama) to be established near Miami in 1967. Interama was planned as a permanent international center to promote understanding, cultural exchange, trade development and political cooperation among the nations of the Western Hemisphere. HR 30 authorized $7.5 million for construction of the U.S. exhibit at Interama and $1 million annually to maintain the exhibit in fiscal 1968 and 1969. The second general supplemental appropriations bill for fiscal 1966 (HR 14012—PL 89-426) provided $160,000 for Interama and the first supplemental for fiscal 1967 (HR 18381—PL 89-697) provided $5,870,000 for the exhibition.

ALASKA CENTENNIAL. Congress completed action in 1966 on a bill (S 2614—PL 89-375) authorizing U.S. participation in the 1967 Alaska Centennial exposition, celebrating the U.S. purchase of Alaska from Russia in 1867. S 2614 authorized $4 million, to be matched on a 50-50 basis by nonfederal funds, to defray the cost of centennial projects "which contribute to the celebration and result in...a permanent contribution to the economy of Alaska." In addition, $600,000 was authorized for U.S. exhibits. The second general supplemental appropria-

tions bill for fiscal 1966 (HR 14012—PL 89-426) provided the full $4.6 million for the centennial.

Federal Data Gathering

COMPUTER POOL. Congress in 1965 enacted an Administration-supported bill (HR 4845—PL 89-306) establishing the authority and procedure for making more efficient use of automatic data processing (ADP) in the Federal Government. The bill made the General Services Administration (GSA) responsible for coordinating ADP in the Government, instead of leaving each agency to determine its own policy. HR 4845 was designed to remedy the inefficent use of ADP by federal agencies, many of which used their equipment only ocasionally, or leased instead of bought it because of the high initial cost. GSA was authorized to establish pools of ADP equipment for use by various agencies and to transfer computers from one agency to another.

Provisions. As signed into law on Oct. 30, HR 4845 (PL 89-306):

Amended Title I of the Federal Property and Administrative Services Act of 1949 by adding a new section centralizing in GSA control over ADP equipment needed by federal agencies. GSA could buy or lease ADP equipment, transfer it among agencies or set up pools for use by various agencies.

Permitted to be excluded from GSA arrangements all ADP equipment used by the Defense Department for military purposes or by the Central Intelligence Agency or other agencies for classified purposes.

Specified that GSA was not to interfere with or try to control the use of ADP by other agencies.

Authorized financing of ADP equipment by a revolving fund instead of by individual agencies' appropriations. Agencies would pay user charges to the fund for equipment leased from it.

MID-DECADE CENSUS. Congress failed to complete action in 1967 on a bill (HR 7659) authorizing a mid-decade census every 10 years, beginning in 1975. HR 7659 passed the House but was still pending before the Senate Post Office and Civil Service Committee at the close of the session. The Committee held hearings on the measure in 1968, but no further action was taken. The Administration, which in 1965 had opposed a bill providing a mid-decade census, supported such legislation in 1967. The Commerce Department stated that there appeared to be "a broad consensus that changes in our nation are so great that we need (a census) more frequently than once every 10 years."

STANDARD REFERENCE DATA. The House passed an Administration bill (HR 6279) in 1967 to allow the Commerce Department's Bureau of Standards to expand its process of collecting, compiling and disseminating critically evaluated data in the physical sciences. The Senate took no action on the bill.

Under a program begun informally in 1963, the Bureau culled data from various scientific reports and compiled it in seven broad categories: nuclear data; atomic and molecular data; solid state data; thermodynamics and transport data; chemical kinetics data; data on colloid and surface properties and data on mechanical properties of a wide variety of objects. Data judged accurate by the

Bureau after intensive analysis became standard for purpose of reference by scientists and engineers.

HR 6279 sought to place the system on a formal basis and allow use of modern computer techniques. The expanded program was to be financed through a combination of Congressional appropriations and charges to users of the standard reference data.

CENSUS QUESTIONS. Action was not completed in 1968 on a bill (S 4062) to repeal existing jail penalties for falsifying answers to U.S. census questions. The next census was scheduled in 1970. The aim of the bill was to permit persons to refuse to answer census questions they considered to be an invasion of their privacy. Existing law provided penalties of a $100 fine or 60 days' imprisonment, or both, for refusing to answer a census question; and $500 or one year's imprisonment, or both, for falsifying an answer. S 4062 would have retained the existing fines but repealed the jail penalties. The Senate passed S 4062 by voice vote, but a companion House measure (HR 20312) was not reported by the House Post Office and Civil Service Committee.

Other Legislation

BOXING COMMISSION. The House in 1965 passed and sent to the Senate a bill (HR 8635) creating a Federal Boxing Commission to regulate professional bouts televised or broadcast interstate or to other countries. The legislation was designed to rid boxing of alleged racketeering. It was, however, opposed as "undesirable" by the Justice Department and by U.S. broadcasters. The Senate took no action on HR 8635. However, the Senate Antitrust and Monopoly Subcommittee reported to the full Judiciary Committee, without recommendation, a similar bill (S 2124) to establish an office of National Boxing Commissioner in the Department of Justice for five years. No hearings were held on the bill and no further action was taken.

Background. Congress for several years had been concerned about racketeering and bribery in professional boxing. The Senate Judiciary Subcommittee on Antitrust and Monopoly, whose chairman was the late Sen. Estes Kefauver (D Tenn. 1948-1963), in 1959 conducted an investigation of the monopoly aspects of professional boxing, and held hearings on the sport in June and December of 1960. Testimony disclosed that one of the leading figures controlling boxing was Frank Carbo, a well-known racketeer, and that one of Carbo's lieutenants, Gabriel Genovese, was paid $60,000 for obtaining matches for former middleweight champion Carmen Basilio.

In 1961 and 1963 Kefauver sponsored bills to create an office of the National Boxing Commissioner.

In March 1964 the Antitrust and Monopoly Subcommittee, under its new chairman, Philip A. Hart (D Mich.), held hearings on Kefauver's bill (S 1182). The hearings concentrated on the circumstances surrounding the championship fight between Cassius Clay and Charles "Sonny" Liston Feb. 24, 1964, which ended when Liston declined to continue the fight after the sixth round. The bill was reported to the full Committee, but no further action was taken.

However, Congress did act in 1964 to lessen racketeering influences on professional sports by enacting a bill (S 741—PL 88-316) to make bribery in sporting events a federal crime. The bill prohibited the use of any inter-

---

AAU vs. NCAA

The dispute between the NCAA and the AAU had continued sporadically for almost 50 years, prior to 1965. The NCAA claimed jurisdiction, in recent years, over student athletes from approximately 650 colleges and universities and had the power to impose penalties on member schools or individual students for disobeying its orders. The AAU included amateur athletic clubs and individuals throughout the nation, and conducted numerous track and field meets.

In recent years the feud concerned sponsorship of "open" track meets in which both college and other athletes competed, as opposed to "closed" meets in which only college athletes competed. The AAU refused to approve meets if the meet sponsors permitted the NCAA to give its approval. The NCAA, however, insisted on dual sponsorship of open meets and barred its students from participating in meets it had not approved.

The AAU had been designated by the International Amateur Athletic Federation as the U.S. representative to that body. The designation gave the AAU the power to certify the eligibility of all amateur athletes to compete in IAAF meets, including the Olympic games. When the dispute threatened to obstruct fielding of an effective U.S. team for the 1964 Olympic games, President Kennedy asked Gen. Douglas MacArthur to help. MacArthur's mediation resulted in a temporary truce.

The controversy broke out anew in 1965. At issue was an AAU-sponsored track and field meet in San Diego, Calif., June 26-27, which was to determine which athletes were to represent the United States in a dual meet with the Soviet Union at Kiev. Since the AAU refused to allow NCAA approval of the meet, the NCAA banned its students from the meet. A few college athletes, with the permission of their colleges, defied the NCAA ban and competed at San Diego. Others, notably runners Gerry Lindgren of Washington State University and Tom Farrell of St. Johns University, competed without approval of their colleges, thus jeopardizing both their collegiate eligibility and their athletic scholarships. However, many college athletes did not compete at San Diego, and the United States lost the meet at Kiev. It was the first loss to the Russians since the series of dual meets began in 1958.

---

state or foreign transportation or communications facility in an attempt to influence an amateur or professional sporting event by bribery. It set maximum penalties of $10,000 and five years imprisonment.

The 1965 bill for a boxing commission (HR 8635) was introduced May 27, 1965, only two days after the second Clay-Liston fight, held in Lewiston, Maine. Liston was beaten again, this time in the first round.

TRACK DISPUTE. The Senate in 1965 adopted a resolution (S Res 147) authorizing the Vice President of the United States to appoint a five-member board of arbitration to render final and binding decisions in disputes relating to the conduct of amateur athletics. Adoption of the resolution was prompted by the continuing battle between the National Collegiate Athletic Assn.

(NCAA) and the Amateur Athletic Union (AAU) over sponsorship of amateur track meets.

S Res 147 suggested that while the NCAA-AAU dispute was being considered, the two groups should grant amnesty to all individuals, institutions and organizations involved in the dispute; vacate any pending penalties; permit full use of athletic facilities for scheduled meets; and end restraints against participation in scheduled meets and tournaments. The resolution directed the appointed board to report its findings to the Senate by Feb. 15, 1966.

Vice President Hubert H. Humphrey Dec. 14, 1965, announced his appointments to the sports arbitration board. Appointed were: Theodore Kheel, a New York lawyer specializing in labor mediation, chairman; Archibald Cox, former U.S. Solicitor General; Gen. David M. Shoup, retired Marine Corps Commandant; Ralph Metcalfe, Chicago alderman; and Thomas Vail, publisher and editor of the Cleveland (Ohio) *Plain Dealer*. Shoup and Metcalfe were former track champions. Despite several meetings between the board and representatives of the NCAA and AAU, the board was unable to resolve the dispute in time for the Feb. 15, deadline set for its report.

DAYLIGHT SAVING TIME. Congress completed action in 1966 on a bill (S 1404—PL 89-387) providing for uniform daylight saving time (DST) throughout the United States beginning in 1967 unless a state voted to remain on standard time. The House version of S 1404, which was stronger than that of the Senate, prevailed in conference. The Senate had not required uniform observance

of DST but only uniform dates for beginning and ending DST in any area that chose to adopt it.

S 1404 was supported by the Administration and actively promoted by an ad hoc group of transportation and communications companies formed into the Committee on Time Uniformity. They argued that the confusion created by the lack of uniformity in time standards across the country was not only inconvenient but also costly for many firms. Railroads and air and bus lines had to print different schedules for areas with different time standards and television broadcasters had to resort to extensive video-taping to maintain some continuity in the time periods in which programs were shown.

In opposition to the bill, rural interests raised the traditional cry that "cows won't observe daylight saving." Senators from states that extended into two time zones sought greater flexibility than the House version of S 1404 provided.

Provisions. As signed into law on April 13, S 1404 (PL 89-387), the Uniform Time Act of 1966:

Required that beginning in 1967 standard time in each zone be advanced one hour (i.e., daylight saving time instituted) from 2 a.m. on the last Sunday in April until 2 a.m. on the last Sunday in October.

Allowed a state to exempt itself from national daylight saving time only if the state legislature voted to keep the entire state on standard time.

Authorized the Interstate Commerce Commission to apply to U.S. district courts to enforce compliance with the provisions relating to daylight saving time.

Required any area adopting daylight saving time in 1966 to make the change at 2 a.m. on the last Sunday in April and end it at 2 a.m. on the last Sunday in October.

Revised the five time zone designations of the Standard Time Act of 1918 to provide for Hawaii, Alaska, Puerto Rico and other U.S. possessions. The old designation of U.S. standard Alaska time was dropped, and three new zones were designated Yukon, Alaska-Hawaii and Bering standard times. Another new zone, to be known as Atlantic standard time, was to be used in the offshore area of the Eastern seaboard.

METRIC SYSTEM. Congress completed action in 1968 on a bill (HR 3136—PL 90-472) authorizing the Commerce Department to undertake a three-year study of the effects of increased U.S. use of the metric system of weights and measures.

Provisions. As signed into law, HR 3136 (PL 90-472):

Empowered the Secretary of Commerce to study the impact on the United States of worldwide use of the metric system, the practicality and desirability of increasing use of the mertic system in the United States, the feasibility of retaining and promoting worldwide use of other engineering and production standards already in use and the costs and benefits of alternative methods available to the United States.

Provided guidelines for the study which included consultation with industrial, educational, government, military and scientific experts and evaluation of the costs, benefits and problems to each sector of retaining the existing system or switching to the metric system.

Instructed those conducting the study to weigh the changes in packaging or design of important industrial products that would result from conversion to the metric system, to investigate the extent that U.S. industrial and

---

Time out of Joint

Congress instituted nationwide observance of daylight saving time during World Wars I and II to conserve fuel and electricity by making daylight hours more nearly coincide with the urban work-day.

During peacetime, adoption of DST was optional with the states or local jurisdictions. Traditionally, rural areas preferred standard time, as farm work began and ended earlier than urban activity. After World War II, urban and suburban areas adopted a variety of summer DST schedules tailored to their particular needs.

Lack of peacetime regulation produced conflicting time systems within each state and time zone. Among examples cited during House and Senate hearings on S 1404 were "the most notorious case of recent times...the 35-mile highway bus ride between Steubenville, Ohio, and Moundsville, W. Va., which encountered seven time changes" and the situation in Iowa in 1964 of "23 different combinations of dates...on which community areas shifted to and from DST."

The Committee for Time Uniformity reported in 1965 that only 12 states, most of them in the South, remained entirely on standard time; 18 states observed statewide DST, 15 of these from the end of April to the end of October; 18 others adopted some form of DST "by local option for periods varying from three to six months"; and portions of two states, North Dakota and Texas, observed "daylight in reverse"—an hour behind standard time.

Difficulties Involved in Conversion to the Metric System

Congress recognized use of the metric system as legal in the United States in 1866, when a table was published showing official conversions from American units to metric units. A set of standards for the metric units was later distributed to the states by the Treasury. The need for new internationally agreed-upon standards for the metric system was considered between 1870 and 1875, at a number of international conferences in which the United States participated. These conferences produced the Metric Convention of 1875, which created an International Bureau of Weights and Measures.

The convention, signed originally by 17 countries, including the United States, was proclaimed in 1878. The prototypes for the new standards were deposited at the International Bureau's headquarters in Sevres, just outside of Paris. The Superintendent of Standard Weights and Measures in the United States, T.C. Mendenhall, issued in 1893 what is known as the Mendenhall order. The order declared that the length of the yard and the weight of the pound were thenceforth to be derived from the International Prototype Meter and Kilogram, which thus became official U.S. standards.

During succeeding decades many efforts were made to bring about use of metric units as common units of measurement in the United States. A bill to make use of metric measures mandatory in government departments and federal contracts appeared slated for passage in 1902 or 1903, but in the end it failed to emerge from committee. In 1960 the 11th General Conference on Weights and Measures adopted new standards for the meter, redefining it in terms of the wave length of the orange-red radiation in the krypton 86 atom instead of the length of a metal bar kept in a vault at Sevres. The conference also redefined the second. These standards were made official American definitions.

Problem of Conversion. Parties to the metric controversy agree that the problems involved in changing to a decimal system of measurement would be formidable though not insuperable. Industry, trade and education would be drastically affected in ways beyond the cost factor, and the adult population would face a difficult transition. For these reasons, even those who advocate conversion have called for a transition period covering a full generation.

A U.S. Metric Study Task Force pointed out in 1961 that industry would have to deal with conversion problems of two types: those in which the product itself would be changed and those in which there would be change only in the designation, label, package or unit of sale. The task force, appointed by the director of the National Bureau of Standards at the request of the Department of Commerce Science Committee, concluded that "Machinery and appliances generally would present the greatest problem."

Machine tools in particular would have to be changed, and in many cases it would be a question of deciding whether to scrap certain machines or rebuild them at considerable expense. Automotive and aircraft companies, along with machine tool makers, would be the principal manufacturers affected. Not only retooling but also redesigning would be necessary to obtain the advantages of the metric system's ease of computation.

For the largest quantity of products—bulk commodities like farm products, fertilizers, fuels, chemicals, and construction materials—only changes in weighing and labeling would be required. At the retail level, gasoline pumps would have to be changed to liters and market scales to kilograms.

Educating the Public. Public resistance to change will be a central factor in any decision to adopt the metric system, and education of the public will largely determine the difficulties that will be encountered in a transitional period. John Quincy Adams noted in 1821 that "The power of the legislator is limited over the will and actions of his subjects. His conflict with them is desperate, when he counteracts their settled habits, their established usages, their domestic and individual economy, their ignorance, their prejudices, and their wants: all which is unavoidable in the attempt to change, or to originate a totally new system of, weights and measures."

Are craftsmen, Adams asked, willing to accept decimal units, which have the greatest ease in computation, in the place of units divisible by 2,3 and 4, which are more easily manipulated by judgment? And, he might have added, are housewives willing to abandon the dozen, which can be divided equally among families of 2, 3, 4, and 6, for quantities of 10, divided equally only by families of 2 or 5 persons?

Any legislation dealing with such a basic alteration, Rep. John W. Davis (D Ga.) told the 1962 annual meeting of the Metric Association, must "first bear the stamp of public approval" before it can pass either house of Congress. In elementary and high schools, only a change in emphasis would be necessary, for some instruction in the metric system generally is given there. Certain specialized areas of study, however, would have to undergo radical change. Although engineering textbook tables use both systems, American engineers are trained in use of the customary units and their texts use such units. The task force report stated in 1961:

"The change of all the engineering literature to metric units, and the re-education of engineers to think in metric units would be a very large undertaking, but the change of the millions of engineering drawings from one system of units to another would be a project of colossal magnitude. It could not be done by any simple mechanical conversion because the changes in thickness, weight, and tolerances that would necessarily be involved would require, in many cases, a recomputation of loads and stresses."

One result of conversion would be the gradual elimination from American speech of many descriptive terms and phrases: football's 50-yard line, the four-minute mile, "an ounce of prevention is worth a pound of cure." The 10-gallon hat would be less often referred to as a 38-liter topper, and Miss America's dimensions—91-62-91 in metric form—would seem, for a time at least, downright startling.

engineering standards already made use of the metric system and to recommend means of meeting the costs and difficulties of any changeover.

Ordered the Secretary of Commerce to make reports whenever necessary and after three years to report the conclusions and recommendations of the study.

Authorized the use of $500,000 in general Commerce Department funds in fiscal 1969 for the first year of the study.

MONDAY HOLIDAYS. Congress completed action in 1968 on a bill (HR 15951—PL 90-363) to shift observance of three public holidays to Mondays and to establish Columbus Day as a new national holiday, also to be observed on Monday. The new dates provided by the bill, plus the existing Monday observance of Labor Day in September, provided the nation with five Monday holidays and legal three-day weekends. The dates of other national holidays (New Year's Day, Independence Day, Thanksgiving Day and Christmas Day) were not changed by the bill.

HR 15951 technically applied only to federal workers and to the District of Columbia. However, the states were expected to enact similar legislation, as they had in the past. The changes made by the bill were to take effect in 1971 to give the states time to act.

Provisions. As signed into law, HR 15951 (PL 90-363):

Changed the dates of three national holidays so that they would fall on Mondays as follows:

Washington's birthday, to be observed on the third Monday in February (currently, February 22);

Memorial Day, to be observed on the last Monday in May (currently May 30);

Veterans Day, to be observed on the fourth Monday in October (currently, November 11).

Established Columbus Day, to be observed on the second Monday in October, as a new national holiday in honor of Christopher Columbus.

RADIO INTERFERENCE. Congress completed action in 1968 on an Administration-supported bill (HR 14910—PL 90-379) giving the Federal Communications Commission (FCC) authority to regulate certain devices which could interfere with radio and television communications.

The bill gave the FCC the authority to prescribe regulations applicable to the manufacture, import, sale, shipment or use of devices which in their operation were capable of interfering with radio and television communications. A few categories of devices were exempted.

New legislation was considered necessary because under current law the FCC was authorized to prohibit the use of devices which produced radio interference, but it could not regulate the manufacture of such devices. Thus, users might purchase equipment only to find they must bear the cost of modifying it in order to use it.

Devices covered by the bill included radio and television receivers; electronic garage-door openers, toys and heaters, diathermy machines, welders, ultrasonic cleaners and remote-control equipment. Such devices interfered with four major categories of communications: space communications, air traffic control, land mobile radio service such as that used by police and fire departments, and reception of commercial radio and television signals. The House Committee report on the bill cited one serious instance of interference with space communications: when Gemini 7 was in orbit in December 1965, the Corpus Christi, Texas, tracking station lost contact with astronauts Frank Borman and James A. Lovell Jr. because of interference caused by a winch truck in a nearby steelyard.

OBSCENE PHONE CALLS. Congress completed action in 1968 on a bill (S 375—PL 90-299) making it a federal crime to place abusive, harassing or obscene telephone calls across state lines and within the District of Columbia. The bill set a maximum $500 fine and/or six months in prison for a person convicted of making such calls.

The Senate had passed S 375 in 1967. The House passed it in 1968 after making technical changes, in which the Senate concurred. In reporting the bill, the House Committee on Interstate and Foreign Commerce noted that the 50 states had laws against intrastate obscene and harassing telephone calls but that legislation was needed to cover calls across state lines. The report added that the Bell Telephone System had received 641,821 complaints of abusive calls in 1967, ranging from obscenities to taunting of families with relatives fighting in Vietnam.

CLAIMS PROCEDURES. President Johnson in 1966 signed into law four Administration bills that he said were "long overdue reform measures" advancing "equal justice under the law." The bills were enacted without controversy. They were:

HR 13650—PL 89-506. Amended the Federal Tort Claims Act to authorize heads of federal agencies to settle claims up to $25,000 and, with approval of the Attorney General, above that amount. Previously, only the Attorney General could settle claims, after suit was filed.

HR 13651—PL 89-508. The Federal Claims Collections Act of 1966 authorized agency heads to attempt collection of Government claims against citizens and to settle such claims up to $5,000. Previously, only when claims were referred to the Attorney General for suit could they be settled.

HR 13652—PL 89-505. Set a six-year statute of limitations for actions brought by the United States involving contracts, three years for actions involving a tort and six years for actions involving money erroneously paid. Previously, most Federal Government claims were not subject to a statute of limitations.

HR 14182—PL 89-507. Authorized courts to award costs to the prevailing party in actions involving the United States. Previously, costs were seldom awarded against the Government when it lost.

APPENDIX

The Appendix

Pages in this Appendix are numbered 1a, 2a, 3a, etc.
It consists of the following sections:

Key Votes, 1965-68

This section of Congress and the Nation shows how Senators and Representatives voted on key roll-call votes in the 89th and 90th Congresses, from 1965 through 1968.

Votes were selected by Congressional Quarterly as Key Votes because of their importance at the time the vote was taken or because of their historical significance. Inevitably, a selection of this type must be subjective, but the aim was to include the most representative votes possible.

HOUSE AND SENATE KEY VOTES FOR 1965

The editors of Congressional Quarterly annually select a series of "key votes" that represent major issues before Congress and also reflect both the mood of Congress and the impact constituent pressures can have on a Member's vote. In 1965 the major issues were Medicare, federal aid to education, rent supplements, voting rights, poverty, and right-to-work repeal.

House Key Votes

1. HOUSE RULES. The House made a major change in its operating rules Jan. 4 when it voted to allow the Speaker to recognize a Member to call up for floor action a bill that had been before the Rules Committee for 21 days without being granted a rule for floor consideration. This increased the power of the majority leadership and decreased the power of the Rules Committee which in the past frequently blocked action on Administration bills by not granting a rule for floor consideration. Some legislation was brought to the floor under the new rule, while other bills were believed to have been cleared by the Committee because of the existence of the rule. The roll call on the issue, 224-202 (D 208-79; R 16-123), technically was on a parliamentary procedure, but had the effect of approving the change. The President did not have a public position on the issue.

2. APPALACHIA ASSISTANCE. The first major Great Society measure to clear Congress was a bill providing more than $1 billion in federal aid for the development of the economically depressed 11-state Appalachian region. By a 257-165 (D 232-56; R 25-109) roll-call vote, the House March 3 passed the bill and sent it to Mr. Johnson for his signature; Johnson in favor.

3. AID TO EDUCATION. Federal aid to elementary and secondary schools, long blocked in Congress over the church-state issue of assistance for non-public schools, won approval in 1965. The House early in the session passed an Administration bill which provided aid to school districts on the basis of the number of children from low-income families in the area. By using this approach, the Administration successfully avoided a controversy over the religious issue that could have again prevented favorable House action. The bill passed March 26 by a 263-153 (D 228-57; R 35-96) roll call; Johnson in favor.

4. MEDICARE. A major Administration victory was approval of legislation providing medical care for the aged. But Administration forces first had to defeat a Republican proposal for a voluntary comprehensive health insurance program in place of the President's compulsory approach. The method of financing the Administration and Republican plans also differed. The GOP proposal April 8 was rejected 191-236 (D 63-226; R 128-10); Johnson opposed.

5. MEDICARE. The Administration's bill providing a health insurance system for the aged April 8 passed the House by a 313-115 (D 248-42; R 65-73) margin once the Republican substitute (above) had been defeated. It was the first time that the House had voted on a medicare bill, which in previous years had never been reported by the Ways and Means Committee. It was a major part of the Administration's program. Johnson in favor.

6. PRESIDENTIAL CONTINUITY. With the President's support, the House approved a constitutional amendment to permit the Vice President to become Acting President if the President were unable to perform his duties. The bill also provided for filling a vacancy in the office of the Vice President. The proposed amendment, which later cleared Congress and was sent to the states for ratification, was intended to resolve the long-standing uncertainty and debate about Presidential inability and its effect on the functioning of the office. The House April 13 approved the bill 368-29: D 246-21; R 122-8; Johnson in favor.

7. FOREIGN AID. Although foreign aid went through Congress in 1965 without major reductions in Administration proposals, efforts were made to reduce spending in some areas. One Republican-sponsored cut would have reduced funds for development loans by $130,958,000, to a total of $649,292,000, and would have stipulated that labor unions participating in Latin American housing projects (under the aid program) be "non-Communist dominated." This effort May 25 was rejected 178-219 (D 62-205; R 116-14) and the Administration aid bill went on to pass the House virtually without change. Johnson opposed.

8. DEPARTMENT OF HOUSING. A proposal of both Presidents Kennedy and Johnson to establish a Cabinet-level Department of Housing, which had been blocked in Congress for several years, won approval in the first session of the 89th Congress. The measure passed the House June 16 by a 217-184 roll call (D 208-66; R 9-118). Johnson in favor.

9. RENT SUPPLEMENTS AUTHORIZATION. An Administration proposal to have the Federal Government pay part of the rent of poor families who could not obtain decent housing with their own incomes was one of the most controversial issues of the year. It also was one of the few new proposals sent to Congress in 1965 along with dozens of older requests, some of which had been debated for years. The unique nature of the proposal was believed to be one important reason the House June 30 nearly killed it by a 202-208 roll call (D 72-204; R 130-4). The proposal became law but operating funds were not forthcoming (see next item). Johnson opposed deletion.

10. RENT SUPPLEMENTS FINANCING. Although the Administration by a hairbreadth margin won approval of its controversial rent supplements plan (above), opponents late in the session were able to prevent the program from being put into effect. This was accomplished when a coalition of Republicans and Southern Democrats Oct. 14 voted 185-162 to kill a supplemental appropriation for the program (ND 24-141; SD 62-19; R 99-2); Johnson opposed to defeat of appropriation.

11. VOTING RIGHTS. For the second consecutive year, Congress enacted major legislation to protect the rights of Negroes. The 1965 law was intended to eliminate the denial of voting rights that occurred throughout much of the South and led to many and sometimes violent Negro demonstrations. The legislation suspended the use of literacy tests and similar devices and provided for federal voting examiners to order the registration of Negroes in certain areas, mostly in the South. The House passed the bill July 9 by a 333-85 roll call (ND 188-1; SD 33-60; R 112-24); Johnson in favor.

12. ANTI-POVERTY AMENDMENTS. Congress provided for expanded anti-poverty activities in legislation which about doubled funds for the program in 1966. But the increase was not enacted without controversy as the federal program came under increasing attack by Republicans and many state and local officials. An indication of the controversy occurred during House action on the bill when an effort was made to cut back authorized funds to the 1965 level and to kill a section which allowed federal officials to override a state Governor's veto of certain federal anti-poverty activities. The effort, however, was not successful, 178-227 (D 57-214; R 121-13). Johnson opposed.

13. RIGHT-TO-WORK. The Administration's pledge to organized labor to obtain repeal of Section 14(b) of the Taft-Hartley Act appeared to be on its way to fulfillment when the House July 28 passed a bill to kill the disputed section. A filibuster in the Senate, however, prevented final action on the bill (below). Section 14(b) permitted states to enact so-called right-to-work laws barring the union shop. The House vote was 221-203 (D 200-86; R 21-117); Johnson in favor.

14. FARM BILL. One major piece of legislation, which received less notice than many other bills, was an omnibus farm bill covering wheat, cotton, wool, dairy and feed grain commodities and providing a cropland retirement program. It passed the House Aug. 19, 221-172 (D 202-68; R 19-104); Johnson in favor.

15. IMMIGRATION REVISIONS. Proposals that had been before Congress for many years to reform the immigration system were brought to the floor for a vote in 1965. The measure, passed by the House Aug. 25 by a 318-95 roll call (D 209-70; R 109-25) and later by the Senate with only one major change (below), eliminated the national origins quota system and established general priorities for the admission of immigrants to the United States based primarily on family relationships and employable skills. Johnson in favor.

16. ARTS AND HUMANITIES. The long-controversial proposal of federal financial aid for the arts and humanities was enacted into law by Congress in 1965, but not without the protests of many who argued that this activity was none of the Government's business. In the House a Republican effort Sept. 15 to kill the bill was rejected 128-251 (D 49-207; R 79-44); Johnson opposed.

17. D.C. HOME RULE. Although not an issue of national importance, legislation to provide self-government for the District of Columbia produced one of the President's few -- and one of his most notable -- outright defeats of the year. Mr. Johnson pushed vigorously for the legislation, finally persuading House Members to force the Administration's bill out of the Southern-dominated District Committee, which had bottled up similar proposals for years, only to see a substitute measure approved on the House floor. The Administration bill, which the Senate passed, provided for automatic establishment of home rule; the House bill provided for election of a charter board to draw up a home rule plan which would require approval in another election and could be vetoed by Congress. As a result, no home rule bill was enacted. The key House vote on the record was adoption Sept. 29 of the charter board plan as a substitute for the Administration bill, 227-174 (D 122-151; R 105-23); Johnson opposed.

18. HIGHWAY BEAUTY. One of the Administration's key proposals to improve the appearance of the United States was a program for control or removal of billboards and junkyards along Interstate and primary highways. The legislation also provided federal payments to states to cover costs of landscaping and scenic development of certain roads. The legislation, with which the President's wife was identified as much as the President, went through many revisions in Congress but finally became law. It passed the House Oct. 7 by a 245-138 roll call (D 219-49; R 26-89); Johnson in favor.

Senate Key Votes

1. FEDERAL WATER QUALITY STANDARDS. The heart of the Water Quality Act of 1965 was the provision permitting federal water quality standards to be enforced in the absence of effective state action to abate pollution of interstate waters. The Senate sustained federal action in this area, defeating an amendment to strike out authority for federal standards, and went on to prevail on its basic position in the House-Senate conference on the bill. The amendment to strike out federal standards was defeated Jan. 28 on a 15-62 roll-call vote (D 3-49; R 12-13); Johnson no position.

2. APPALACHIA ASSISTANCE. The year in Congress got off to a fast start when the Senate Feb. 1 completed action on the first major Great Society measure, a bill providing more than $1 billion in federal aid for the development of the economically depressed 11-state Appalachian region. The bill was later propelled through the House unchanged. Senate passage came on a 62-22 vote (D 51-7; R 11-15); Johnson in favor.

3. AID TO EDUCATION. Long-sought legislation for federal aid to elementary and secondary schools became a reality when the Senate accepted a House bill without any change and sent it to the President. (See House votes) The vote on this highly unusual action came April 9, when the bill was passed by a 73-18 vote (D 55-4; R 18-14); Johnson in favor.

4. POLL TAX BAN. Led by Sen. Edward M. Kennedy (D Mass.), a group of liberal Senators came close to defeating the Administration and adding to the voting rights bill a legislative ban on poll taxes in state and local elections. The Administration said the amendment possibly was unconstitutional. Although the poll tax ban was defeated, the Senators won Administration acceptance of a provision directing the Attorney General to institute court tests of the poll tax as a discriminatory device. The House version of the bill contained a poll tax ban, but the Senate's milder provision prevailed in the final version of the bill. The Kennedy amendment was rejected May 11 on a 45-49 vote: R 6-25; D 39-24 (ND 34-9; SD 5-15); Johnson opposed.

5. VOTING RIGHTS CLOTURE. The Senate duplicated its history-making feat of 1964 when it voted to invoke cloture on (cut off) a civil rights filibuster. The issue this time was the voting rights bill, and the vote ended a pro-forma Southern filibuster. The procedure requires a two-thirds majority of Senators present and voting. The required total was achieved May 25 with votes to spare, 70-30: R 23-9; D 47-21 (ND 42-4; SD 5-17); Johnson in favor.

6. VOTING RIGHTS PASSAGE. The most comprehensive federal program to enforce voting rights of Southern Negroes since the Reconstruction resulted in large part from month-long demonstrations against alleged voting registration malpractices in Selma, Ala. The Senate debated the measure for 25 days before passing it May 26 on a 77-19 roll call: R 30-2; D 47-17 (ND 42-0; SD 5-17); Johnson in favor.

7. MILITARY ASSISTANCE FUNDS. The U.S. foreign military assistance program came under sharp attack during the year. Critics said recipient countries were using the arms to attack their neighbors instead of defending against Communism; they cited Greece and Turkey, India and Pakistan. But the Senate turned down an amendment to pare $115 million a year from the fiscal 1966 and fiscal 1967 authorization for the military assistance program, reducing the program to the fiscal 1965 level. The June 11 vote was 38-43 (D 28-25; R 10-18); Johnson opposed.

8. PRESIDENTIAL CONTINUITY. President Johnson backed Congressional action proposing a constitutional amendment to deal with the problems of a disabled President and a vacancy in the office of Vice President. The Senate cleared the bill July 6, voting 68-5 (D 47-4; R 21-1).

9. MEDICARE. The Senate nailed down the top Administration victory of the year, sustaining the House in support of a compulsory hospital insurance plan for the aged backed by a supplementary, voluntary health insurance plan. An amendment to delete both plans from the Social Security bill July 9 was rejected, 26-64 (D 8-53; R 18-11); Johnson opposed.

10. MEDICARE. After that vote, enactment of the "medicare" program was a foregone conclusion. The program was embedded in a bill which also included a major boost in Social Security payments and revision of the Kerr-Mills health program for the aged, child health care programs and other federal-state public assistance programs. The Senate passed the bill July 9 by a vote of 68-21 (D 55-7; R 13-14); Johnson in favor.

11. RENT SUBSIDIES. The hottest political item of the year in Congress was the Administration proposal to pay part of the rent of certain classes of low-income families. The Senate rejected a move to strike the proposal from the omnibus housing bill, 40-47 (D 16-42; R 24-5); Johnson opposed.

12. DIRKSEN AMENDMENT. Deft parliamentary maneuvers by Senate Minority Leader Dirksen (R Ill.) brought to the Senate floor a proposed constitutional amendment to permit states to apportion one house of a bicameral legislature on non-population bases. The amendment would have, in effect, overturned "one-man, one-vote" decisions by the Supreme Court on apportionment of state

legislatures. On a vote Aug. 4, the bill failed to get the required two-thirds majority for a constitutional amendment. The vote was 57-39 (D 28-36; R 29-3); Johnson no position.

13. ANTI-POVERTY FUNDS. With the Great Society program under full steam, Republicans failed in a Senate attempt to bank the fires by cutting the anti-poverty program back to its first-year level. An amendment to cut the funds and set up a joint Congressional committee to keep an eye on the anti-poverty warriors Aug. 18 was rejected 39-48 (D 14-45; R 25-3); Johnson opposed.

14. FOREIGN FARM WORKERS. Showing their disgruntlement with the farm labor policies of Labor Secretary W. Willard Wirtz, farm-state Senators in committee added an amendment to the omnibus farm bill which would have made the Agriculture Secretary, not Wirtz, responsible for deciding whether U.S. farmers required supplemental labor imported from Mexico, the Caribbean and other locales. It took the vote of Vice President Humphrey to break a tie and put across an amendment to strike this provision from the bill Sept. 13. The amendment prevailed, 46-45 (D 43-17, plus Humphrey; R 2-28); Johnson in support.

15. OMNIBUS FARM BILL. With extraneous matters out of the way, the Senate quickly passed the omnibus farm measure, 72-22 (D 56-8; R 16-14); Johnson in favor.

16. HIGHWAY BEAUTIFICATION. A sizable majority of Senators also supported a watered-down version of the First Lady's highway beautification bill. The bill provided federal funds to control or remove junkyards and billboards along Interstate and primary federal-aid highways and for landscaping and scenic improvement of all federal-aid highways. The Senate Sept. 16 passed it 63-14 (D 47-6; R 16-8); Johnson in favor.

17. IMMIGRATION REVISIONS. A long-sought goal of many ethnic, labor and religious groups was the repeal of the country-by-country quotas of the national origins quota system, and the re-unification of families kept apart by stringent immigration policies. A bill to repeal the national origins quota system and substitute over-all annual ceilings on immigration from the Western Hemisphere and from all non-Western Hemisphere countries was passed by Congress in 1965. The bill also set general priorities for preferred classes of immigrants, and placed relatives of previous immigrants high on the list. The Senate Sept. 22 passed it 76-18 (D 52-15; R 24-3); Johnson in favor.

18. RIGHT-TO-WORK REPEAL. The top legislative goal of the labor movement in 1965 was repeal of a section of the Taft-Hartley Act which permitted states to enact "right-to-work" laws to ban union shop agreements between labor and management. The House passed the bill, but in the Senate it ran into a filibuster. It was laid aside until 1966 after its supporters Oct. 11 failed to get even a majority on a vote to shut off debate on a preliminary motion to take up the bill (a two-thirds majority was needed). The vote, 45-47 (D 40-21; R 5-26), ranked as one of President Johnson's major defeats of the year.

House Key Votes—89th Congress—1965

1. H Res 8. Adoption of House rules for the 89th Congress. Amend the rules to permit the Speaker to recognize a Member to call up for floor action a bill that had been before the Rules Committee for 21 days without being granted a rule, and make other changes in House rules. Albert (D Okla.) motion to consider the previous question, cutting off debate and precluding amendments. Motion agreed to 224-202: R 16-123; D 208-79 (ND 185-4; SD 23-75), Jan. 4, 1965. The President did not take a position on the motion.

2. S 3. Passage of the Appalachian Regional Development Act of 1965 authorizing $1,092,400,000 for road construction, health facilities, vocational schools, housing, sewage works, land improvement and other activities to aid the 11-state Appalachian region. Passed 257-165: R 25-109; D 232-56 (ND 173-15; SD 59-41), March 3, 1965. A "yea" was a vote supporting the President's position.

3. HR 2362. Passage of the Elementary and Secondary Education Act of 1965, providing: a three-year program of grants to states for allocation to school districts with large numbers of children from low-income families; grants for purchase of books and library materials; funds to improve educational research; and grants to strengthen state departments of education. Passed 263-153: R 35-96; D 228-57 (ND 187-3; SD 41-54), March 26, 1965. A "yea" was a vote supporting the President's position.

4. HR 6675. Social Security Amendments of 1965 providing a basic, compulsory, payroll-tax-financed health insurance program for the aged, a supplementary voluntary health insurance program and other Social Security and welfare benefits (see next roll call). Byrnes (R Wis.) motion to recommit the bill to the House Ways and Means Committee with instructions to report it back with the provisions of a substitute bill, HR 7059, which provided a voluntary, comprehensive health insurance program for the aged financed by general revenue and contributions from participants. Rejected 191-236: R 128-10; D 63-226 (ND 3-188; SD 60-38), April 8, 1965. A "nay" was a vote supporting the President's position.

5. HR 6675. Passage of the Social Security Amendments of 1965 to: provide a basic compulsory health insurance program for the aged, financed primarily by a payroll tax; a supplementary voluntary health insurance program financed by general revenue and contributions from participants; increases in Social Security cash benefits; and expansion of the Kerr-Mills health program, child health-care programs and other federal-state public assistance programs. Passed 313-115: R 65-73; D 248-42 (ND 189-2; SD 59-40), April 8, 1965. A "yea" was a vote supporting the President's position.

6. H J Res 1. Passage of the bill proposing a constitutional amendment to permit the Vice President to become Acting President if the President were unable to perform his duties, and to provide for filling a vacancy in the office of Vice President. Passed (two-thirds majority required) 368-29: R 122-8; D 246-21 (ND 172-6; SD 74-15), April 13, 1965. A "yea" was a vote supporting the President's position.

- KEY -

Y Record Vote For (yea).
✓ Paired For.
‡ Announced For, CQ Poll For.
N Record Vote Against (nay).
X Paired Against
- Announced Against, CQ Poll Against.
? Absent, General Pair, "Present," Did not announce or answer Poll.

	1	2	3	4	5	6
ALABAMA						
3 Andrews	N	N	N	Y	N	N
8 Jones	Y	Y	?	X	?	?
5 Selden	N	N	N	Y	N	Y
4 Andrews	N	N	N	Y	N	Y
6 Buchanan	N	N	N	Y	N	N
2 Dickinson	N	N	X	Y	N	Y
1 Edwards	N	N	N	Y	N	Y
7 Martin	N	N	N	Y	N	N
ALASKA						
AL Rivers	Y	Y	Y	N	Y	Y
ARIZONA						
3 Senner	Y	Y	Y	N	Y	Y
2 Udall	Y	Y	Y	N	Y	Y
1 Rhodes	N	N	N	Y	N	Y
ARKANSAS						
1 Gathings	N	N	N	Y	N	Y
4 Harris	N	Y	N	N	Y	Y
2 Mills	Y	Y	Y	N	Y	Y
3 Trimble	Y	Y	Y	N	Y	Y
CALIFORNIA						
5 Burton	Y	Y	Y	N	Y	Y
7 Cohelan	Y	Y	Y	N	Y	Y
33 Dyal	Y	Y	Y	N	Y	Y
9 Edwards	Y	Y	Y	N	Y	Y
18 Hagen	Y	Y	Y	N	Y	Y
34 Hanna	Y	✓	Y	N	Y	Y
2 Johnson	Y	Y	Y	N	Y	Y
4 Leggett	Y	Y	Y	N	Y	Y
15 McFall	Y	Y	Y	N	Y	Y
8 Miller	Y	Y	Y	N	Y	Y
3 Moss	Y	Y	Y	N	Y	Y
16 Sisk	Y	Y	Y	N	Y	Y
38 Tunney	‡	Y	Y	N	Y	Y
37 Van Deerlin	Y	Y	Y	N	Y	Y
14 Baldwin	N	N	Y	-	‡	‡
1 Clausen	N	N	N	Y	N	Y
10 Gubser	N	N	N	Y	Y	‡
6 Mailliard	N	N	N	✓	?	Y
12 Talcott	N	N	N	Y	Y	Y
13 Teague	N	N	N	Y	Y	Y
35 Utt	N	N	N	Y	N	Y
36 Wilson	N	N	N	Y	N	Y
11 Younger	N	N	N	Y	N	Y

Los Angeles Co.	1	2	3	4	5	6
29 Brown	Y	Y	Y	N	Y	Y
25 Cameron	Y	Y	Y	N	Y	Y
22 Corman	Y	Y	Y	N	Y	Y
21 Hawkins	Y	Y	Y	N	Y	Y
19 Holifield	Y	Y	Y	N	Y	Y
17 King	Y	Y	Y	N	Y	Y
26 Roosevelt	Y	✓	Y	N	Y	‡
30 Roybal	Y	Y	Y	N	Y	Y
31 Wilson	Y	Y	Y	N	Y	Y
28 Bell	N	N	Y	Y	N	Y
23 Clawson	N	N	N	Y	N	Y
32 Hosmer	N	N	N	Y	N	Y
24 Lipscomb	N	N	N	Y	N	Y
27 Reinecke	N	N	N	Y	Y	Y
20 Smith	N	N	N	Y	N	Y
COLORADO						
4 Aspinall	Y	Y	Y	N	Y	Y
3 Evans	Y	Y	Y	N	Y	Y
2 McVicker	Y	✓	Y	N	Y	Y
1 Rogers	Y	Y	Y	N	Y	Y
CONNECTICUT						
1 Daddario	Y	N	Y	N	Y	Y
3 Giaimo	Y	Y	Y	N	Y	Y
6 Grabowski	Y	Y	Y	N	Y	Y
4 Irwin	Y	Y	Y	N	Y	Y
5 Monagan	Y	N	Y	N	Y	Y
2 St. Onge	Y	Y	Y	N	Y	Y
DELAWARE						
AL McDowell	Y	Y	Y	N	Y	Y
FLORIDA						
2 Bennett	N	N	N	Y	N	Y
4 Fascell	Y	Y	Y	N	Y	Y
9 Fuqua	N	N	N	Y	N	Y
10 Gibbons	Y	Y	Y	N	Y	Y
7 Haley	N	N	N	Y	N	Y
5 Herlong	N	N	N	Y	N	Y
8 Matthews	N	N	N	Y	N	Y
3 Pepper	Y	Y	Y	N	Y	Y
6 Rogers	N	N	N	Y	N	Y
1 Sikes	N	Y	N	Y	Y	Y
12 Cramer	N	N	N	Y	N	Y
11 Gurney	N	N	N	Y	Y	Y

GEORGIA	1	2	3	4	5	6
7 Davis	N	Y	Y	Y	N	Y
6 Flynt	N	Y	N	Y	N	N
1 Hagan	N	Y	N	Y	N	Y
9 Landrum	N	Y	Y	N	Y	Y
4 Mackay	Y	Y	Y	N	Y	Y
2 O'Neal	N	N	N	Y	N	N
10 Stephens	N	Y	Y	N	Y	Y
8 Tuten	N	Y	N	Y	Y	Y
5 Weltner	Y	Y	Y	N	Y	‡
3 Callaway	N	N	N	Y	N	N
HAWAII						
AL Matsunaga	Y	Y	Y	N	Y	Y
AL Mink	Y	Y	Y	N	Y	Y
IDAHO						
1 White	Y	Y	Y	N	Y	Y
2 Hansen	N	N	N	Y	N	Y
ILLINOIS						
21 Gray	Y	Y	Y	N	Y	Y
24 Price	Y	Y	Y	N	Y	Y
19 Schisler	Y	Y	Y	N	Y	Y
23 Shipley	Y	Y	Y	N	Y	?
16 Anderson	N	N	N	Y	N	Y
17 Arends	N	N	N	Y	N	Y
14 Erlenborn	N	N	N	Y	N	Y
20 Findley	N	N	N	Y	Y	Y
12 McClory	N	N	N	Y	Y	Y
18 Michel	N	N	N	Y	N	‡
15 Reid	N	N	N	Y	N	Y
22 Springer	N	-	Y	N	Y	Y
Chicago—Cook Co.						
7 Annunzio	Y	Y	Y	N	Y	Y
1 Dawson	Y	Y	Y	N	Y	?
5 Kluczynski	Y	Y	Y	N	Y	?
3 Murphy	Y	Y	Y	N	Y	Y
2 O'Hara	Y	Y	Y	N	Y	Y
11 Pucinski	Y	Y	Y	N	Y	Y
6 Ronan	Y	Y	Y	N	Y	Y
8 Rostenkowski	Y	Y	Y	N	Y	-
9 Yates	Y	Y	Y	N	Y	‡
10 Collier	N	N	N	Y	N	Y
4 Derwinski	N	N	N	Y	N	Y
13 Rumsfeld	N	N	N	Y	N	Y

INDIANA	1	2	3	4	5	6
3 Brademas	Y	Y	Y	N	Y	Y
8 Denton	Y	Y	Y	N	Y	Y
9 Hamilton	Y	X	Y	N	Y	Y
11 Jacobs	Y	Y	Y	N	Y	Y
1 Madden	Y	Y	Y	N	Y	Y
5 Roush	Y	N	Y	N	Y	Y
4 Adair	N	N	N	Y	N	Y
7 Bray	N	N	N	Y	N	Y
2 Halleck	N	N	N	Y	N	Y
10 Harvey	N	N	N	Y	N	‡
6 Roudebush	N	N	N	Y	N	Y
IOWA						
1 Bandstra	Y	Y	Y	N	Y	Y
2 Culver	Y	Y	Y	N	Y	Y
6 Greigg	Y	Y	Y	N	Y	Y
7 Hansen	Y	Y	Y	N	Y	Y
1 Schmidhauser	Y	Y	Y	N	Y	Y
5 Smith	Y	Y	Y	N	Y	Y
3 Gross	N	N	N	Y	N	N
KANSAS						
1 Dole	N	N	N	Y	N	Y
3 Ellsworth	N	X	N	Y	N	Y
4 Shriver	N	N	N	Y	N	Y
2 Mize	N	N	N	Y	N	Y
5 Skubitz	N	N	N	Y	N	Y
KENTUCKY						
4 Chelf	N	Y	Y	Y	Y	Y
3 Farnsley	Y	Y	Y	N	Y	Y
2 Natcher	N	Y	Y	Y	Y	Y

Democrats in this type; *Republicans in italics*

	1	2	3	4	5	6
7 Perkins	Y	Y	Y	N	Y	Y
1 Stubblefield	N	Y	Y	Y	Y	Y
6 Watts	N	Y	Y	Y	Y	Y
5 Carter	N	Y	Y	Y	N	Y
LOUISIANA						
2 Boggs	Y	Y	Y	N	Y	Y
1 Hebert	-	N	N	Y	N	?
8 Long	N	N	N	Y	N	Y
6 Morrison	Y	Y	Y	N	Y	Y
5 Passman	N	N	N	Y	N	N
7 Thompson	N	Y	N	Y	Y	Y
4 Waggonner	N	N	N	Y	N	Y
3 Willis	N	Y	Y	N	Y	Y
MAINE						
2 Hathaway	Y	Y	Y	N	Y	Y
1 Tupper	Y	Y	✓	Y	Y	Y
MARYLAND						
4 Fallon	Y	Y	Y	N	Y	Y
7 Friedel	Y	Y	Y	N	Y	Y
3 Garmatz	Y	Y	Y	N	Y	Y
2 Long	Y	Y	Y	N	Y	Y
5 Machen	Y	Y	Y	N	Y	Y
AL Sickles	Y	Y	Y	N	Y	Y
6 Mathias	Y	Y	Y	Y	Y	N
1 Morton	N	N	Y	Y	N	Y
MASSACHUSETTS						
2 Boland	Y	Y	Y	N	Y	Y
11 Burke	Y	Y	Y	N	Y	Y
4 Donohue	Y	Y	Y	N	Y	Y
7 Macdonald	Y	N	Y	N	Y	Y
9 McCormack						
8 O'Neill	Y	Y	Y	N	Y	Y
3 Philbin	Y	Y	Y	N	Y	Y
6 Bates	N	N	N	Y	Y	Y
1 Conte	N	N	Y	Y	Y	Y
12 Keith	N	X	N	N	Y	Y
10 Martin	N	N	Y	Y	Y	?
5 Morse	N	N	Y	Y	Y	Y
MICHIGAN						
11 Clevenger	Y	Y	Y	N	Y	Y
19 Farnum	Y	Y	Y	N	Y	?
7 Mackie	Y	Y	Y	N	Y	Y
12 O'Hara	Y	Y	Y	N	Y	Y
3 Todd	Y	Y	Y	N	Y	Y
2 Vivian	Y	Y	Y	N	Y	Y
18 Broomfield	Y	N	N	Y	Y	Y
10 Cederberg	N	N	N	Y	Y	Y
6 Chamberlain	N	N	N	Y	Y	Y
5 Ford	N	N	N	Y	N	Y
9 Griffin	N	X	N	Y	Y	Y
8 Harvey	N	N	Y	Y	Y	Y
4 Hutchinson	N	N	N	Y	Y	N
Detroit—Wayne Co.						
1 Conyers	Y	Y	Y	N	Y	Y
13 Diggs	Y	Y	Y	N	Y	Y
16 Dingell	Y	Y	Y	N	Y	Y
15 Ford	Y	Y	Y	N	Y	Y
17 Griffiths	Y	Y	Y	N	Y	Y
14 Nedzi	Y	Y	Y	N	Y	Y
MINNESOTA						
8 Blatnik	Y	Y	Y	N	Y	Y
5 Fraser	Y	Y	Y	N	Y	?
4 Karth	Y	Y	Y	N	Y	Y
6 Olson	Y	Y	Y	N	Y	Y
7 Langen	N	N	N	Y	N	Y
3 MacGregor	N	N	X	Y	N	Y
2 Nelsen	N	N	N	Y	N	‡
1 Quie	N	N	N	Y	N	Y
MISSISSIPPI						
1 Abernethy	N	N	N	Y	N	Y
5 Colmer	N	N	N	Y	N	?
2 Whitten	N	N	N	Y	N	N
3 Williams	N	N	N	Y	N	N
4 Walker	N	N	N	Y	N	N
MISSOURI						
5 Bolling	Y	Y	Y	N	Y	‡
6 Hull	N	N	✓	Y	Y	N
9 Hungate	Y	Y	Y	N	Y	Y
8 Ichord	N	N	Y	N	Y	N
10 Jones	N	N	?	N	N	Y
1 Karsten	Y	Y	Y	N	Y	Y
4 Randall	Y	N	Y	N	Y	Y
3 Sullivan	Y	Y	Y	N	Y	Y
2 Curtis	N	N	N	Y	N	Y
7 Hall	N	N	N	Y	N	Y
MONTANA						
1 Olsen	Y	Y	Y	N	Y	Y
2 Battin	N	N	N	Y	N	Y
NEBRASKA						
1 Callan	Y	Y	Y	Y	Y	Y
2 Cunningham	N	N	N	Y	Y	Y
3 Martin	N	N	N	Y	N	Y
NEVADA						
AL Baring	N	N	N	Y	N	N
NEW HAMPSHIRE						
1 Huot	Y	Y	Y	N	Y	Y
2 Cleveland	N	N	Y	Y	Y	Y
NEW JERSEY						
14 Daniels	Y	Y	Y	N	Y	Y
13 Gallagher	Y	Y	Y	N	Y	N
9 Helstoski	Y	Y	Y	N	Y	Y
3 Howard	Y	Y	Y	N	Y	Y
8 Joelson	Y	Y	Y	N	Y	‡
12 Krebs	Y	Y	Y	N	Y	Y
11 Minish	Y	Y	Y	N	Y	Y
2 McGrath	Y	Y	Y	N	Y	Y
15 Patten	Y	Y	Y	N	Y	Y
10 Rodino	Y	Y	Y	N	Y	Y
4 Thompson	Y	Y	Y	N	Y	Y
1 Cahill	Y	N	Y	Y	Y	Y
6 Dwyer	Y	N	Y	N	Y	Y
5 Frelinghuysen	N	N	X	Y	Y	Y
7 Widnall	N	X	?	Y	Y	Y
NEW MEXICO						
AL Morris	Y	Y	Y	N	Y	Y
AL Walker	Y	N	Y	N	Y	Y
NEW YORK						
27 Dow	Y	Y	Y	N	Y	Y
41 Dulski	Y	Y	Y	N	Y	Y
34 Hanley	Y	Y	Y	N	Y	Y
39 McCarthy	Y	Y	Y	N	Y	Y
29 O'Brien	Y	Y	Y	N	Y	Y
25 Ottinger	Y	Y	Y	N	Y	Y
1 Pike	Y	N	Y	N	Y	Y
28 Resnick	Y	Y	Y	N	Y	Y
35 Stratton	Y	Y	Y	N	Y	Y
5 Tenzer	Y	Y	Y	N	Y	Y
3 Wolff	Y	Y	Y	N	Y	Y
37 Conable	N	N	N	Y	Y	Y
38 Goodell	N	Y	N	Y	Y	Y
2 Grover	N	N	Y	Y	Y	Y
36 Horton	Y	N	Y	N	Y	Y
30 King	N	N	N	Y	Y	Y
31 McEwen	N	N	N	Y	Y	Y
32 Pirnie	N	N	Y	N	Y	‡
26 Reid	Y	Y	Y	N	Y	Y
33 Robison	N	N	N	Y	Y	Y
40 Smith	N	?	N	Y	Y	Y
4 Wydler	N	N	Y	Y	Y	Y
New York City						
7 Addabbo	Y	Y	Y	N	Y	Y
23 Bingham	Y	Y	Y	N	Y	Y
15 Carey	Y	Y	Y	N	Y	‡
10 Celler	Y	Y	Y	N	Y	Y
9 Delaney	Y	Y	Y	N	Y	Y
19 Farbstein	Y	Y	Y	N	Y	Y
22 Gilbert	Y	Y	Y	N	Y	Y
12 Kelly	Y	Y	Y	N	Y	Y
11 Keogh	Y	Y	Y	N	Y	Y
13 Multer	Y	Y	Y	N	Y	Y
16 Murphy	Y	Y	Y	N	Y	Y
18 Powell	Y	Y	Y	N	Y	Y
14 Rooney	Y	Y	Y	N	Y	Y
8 Rosenthal	Y	Y	Y	N	Y	Y
20 Ryan	Y	Y	Y	N	Y	Y
21 Scheuer	Y	Y	Y	N	Y	Y
24 Fino	Y	Y	Y	N	Y	‡
6 Halpern	Y	Y	Y	N	Y	Y
17 Lindsay	Y	Y	Y	N	Y	Y
NORTH CAROLINA						
1 Bonner	N	Y	?	Y	Y	?
4 Cooley	N	N	Y	Y	Y	Y
2 Fountain	N	N	N	Y	Y	N
3 Henderson	N	Y	N	Y	Y	N
6 Kornegay	N	Y	N	Y	N	Y
7 Lennon	N	N	N	Y	N	Y
5 Scott	N	Y	N	Y	Y	‡
11 Taylor	N	Y	N	Y	Y	Y
10 Whitener	N	Y	N	Y	Y	Y
9 Broyhill	N	N	N	Y	Y	Y
8 Jonas	N	N	N	Y	N	Y
NORTH DAKOTA						
2 Redlin	Y	Y	Y	N	Y	Y
1 Andrews	-	N	N	Y	N	?
OHIO						
9 Ashley	Y	Y	Y	X	?	Y
20 Feighan	Y	Y	Y	N	Y	Y
1 Gilligan	Y	Y	Y	N	Y	Y
18 Hays	Y	Y	Y	N	Y	N
19 Kirwan	Y	Y	Y	N	Y	?
3 Love	Y	Y	Y	N	Y	Y
10 Moeller	Y	Y	Y	N	Y	Y
15 Secrest	Y	Y	Y	N	Y	Y
AL Sweeney	Y	Y	Y	N	Y	Y
21 Vanik	Y	Y	Y	N	Y	Y
17 Ashbrook	N	Y	N	Y	N	Y
14 Ayres	Y	N	X	N	Y	Y
8 Betts	N	N	N	Y	N	Y
22 Bolton	N	N	N	Y	N	Y
16 Bow	N	N	N	Y	Y	Y
7 Brown	N	N	N	Y	N	N
2 Clancy	N	Y	N	Y	N	Y
12 Devine	N	N	N	Y	N	Y
6 Harsha	N	Y	N	Y	N	Y
5 Latta	N	N	N	Y	N	Y
4 McCulloch	N	N	N	Y	Y	Y
23 Minshall	N	N	N	Y	Y	Y
13 Mosher	N	N	X	Y	Y	Y
11 Stanton	N	N	N	Y	Y	Y
OKLAHOMA						
3 Albert	Y	Y	Y	N	Y	Y
2 Edmondson	Y	Y	Y	N	Y	Y
5 Jarman	N	N	N	Y	N	Y
6 Johnson	Y	Y	Y	N	Y	Y
4 Steed	N	Y	Y	N	N	Y
1 Belcher	N	N	N	Y	N	?
OREGON						
4 Duncan	Y	Y	Y	N	Y	Y
3 Green	Y	N	Y	N	Y	Y
2 Ullman	Y	Y	Y	N	Y	Y
1 Wyatt	N	N	N	Y	Y	Y
PENNSYLVANIA						
25 Clark	Y	Y	Y	N	Y	Y
19 Craley	Y	Y	Y	N	Y	Y
21 Dent	Y	Y	Y	N	Y	N
11 Flood	Y	Y	Y	N	Y	Y
20 Holland	?	Y	Y	N	Y	Y
14 Moorhead	Y	Y	Y	N	Y	Y
26 Morgan	Y	Y	Y	N	Y	Y
6 Rhodes	Y	Y	Y	N	Y	Y
15 Rooney	Y	Y	Y	N	Y	Y
24 Vigorito	Y	Y	Y	N	Y	Y
18 Corbett	Y	Y	Y	Y	Y	Y
8 Curtin	N	Y	Y	Y	Y	Y
9 Dague	N	N	-	Y	Y	Y
27 Fulton	Y	Y	Y	Y	Y	Y
23 Johnson	N	Y	N	Y	Y	Y
16 Kunkel	N	✓	N	Y	Y	Y
10 McDade	Y	Y	Y	Y	Y	Y
22 Saylor	N	Y	N	Y	Y	Y
17 Schneebeli	N	Y	N	Y	Y	Y
13 Schweiker	Y	Y	Y	N	Y	Y
7 Watkins	N	Y	Y	Y	Y	Y
12 Whalley	N	Y	Y	Y	Y	Y
Philadelphia City						
1 Barrett	Y	Y	Y	N	Y	Y
3 Byrne	Y	Y	Y	N	Y	Y
5 Green	Y	Y	Y	N	Y	Y
2 Nix	Y	Y	Y	N	Y	‡
4 Toll	?	✓	✓	-	?	?
RHODE ISLAND						
2 Fogarty	Y	Y	Y	N	Y	Y
1 St. Germain	Y	Y	Y	N	Y	Y
SOUTH CAROLINA						
4 Ashmore	N	N	N	Y	Y	Y
3 Dorn	N	Y	N	Y	N	N
5 Gettys	N	Y	N	Y	Y	Y
6 McMillan	N	Y	N	Y	N	N
1 Rivers	X	Y	N	Y	N	Y
*2 Watson**	N					
SOUTH DAKOTA						
2 Berry	N	N	N	Y	N	Y
1 Reifel	N	N	N	Y	Y	Y
TENNESSEE						
6 Anderson	Y	Y	Y	N	Y	Y
8 Everett	N	Y	✓	N	Y	Y
4 Evins	Y	Y	✓	N	Y	‡
5 Fulton	Y	Y	Y	N	Y	‡
9 Grider	Y	Y	Y	N	Y	Y
7 Murray	N	Y	N	N	Y	Y
3 Brock	N	N	N	Y	N	Y
2 Duncan	N	Y	N	Y	N	Y
1 Quillen	N	Y	N	Y	N	Y
TEXAS						
3 Beckworth	N	Y	Y	Y	Y	Y
2 Brooks	Y	Y	Y	N	Y	Y
17 Burleson	N	N	N	Y	N	Y
5 Cabell	N	Y	Y	N	N	Y
22 Casey	N	N	N	Y	N	Y
15 De la Garza	N	N	Y	Y	Y	Y
7 Dowdy	N	N	N	Y	Y	Y
21 Fisher	N	N	N	Y	N	Y
20 Gonzalez	Y	Y	Y	N	Y	N
19 Mahon	N	N	N	N	N	Y
1 Patman	N	Y	Y	N	Y	N
10 Pickle	N	Y	Y	Y	N	Y
11 Poage	N	N	Y	N	N	Y
AL Pool	N	N	N	Y	N	Y
13 Purcell	N	Y	Y	N	Y	‡
4 Roberts	N	N	N	N	Y	Y
18 Rogers	N	N	N	Y	Y	N
6 Teague	N	N	N	N	N	N
8 Thomas	?	Y	Y	N	Y	Y
9 Thompson	Y	Y	-	N	Y	Y
16 White	N	Y	Y	Y	Y	N
12 Wright	Y	Y	Y	N	Y	Y
14 Young	N	Y	Y	N	Y	Y
UTAH						
2 King	Y	Y	Y	N	Y	Y
1 Burton	N	N	Y	Y	N	Y
VERMONT						
AL Stafford	N	N	Y	Y	Y	Y
VIRGINIA						
4 Abbitt	N	N	N	Y	N	Y
1 Downing	N	N	N	Y	N	Y
2 Hardy	N	N	N	✓	Y	Y
9 Jennings	N	Y	Y	N	Y	‡
7 Marsh	N	N	N	Y	N	Y
3 Satterfield	N	N	N	Y	N	Y
8 Smith	N	N	N	Y	N	?
5 Tuck	N	N	N	Y	N	Y
10 Broyhill	N	N	N	Y	N	Y
6 Poff	N	N	N	Y	N	Y
WASHINGTON						
7 Adams	Y	Y	Y	N	Y	Y
5 Foley	Y	Y	Y	N	Y	Y
3 Hansen	Y	Y	Y	N	Y	Y
6 Hicks	Y	Y	Y	N	Y	Y
2 Meeds	Y	Y	Y	N	Y	Y
4 May	N	N	N	Y	N	Y
1 Pelly	N	N	N	Y	Y	Y
WEST VIRGINIA						
4 Hechler	Y	Y	Y	N	Y	Y
5 Kee	Y	Y	Y	N	Y	Y
3 Slack	Y	Y	Y	N	Y	Y
2 Staggers	Y	Y	Y	N	Y	Y
1 Moore	N	Y	Y	Y	Y	Y
WISCONSIN						
2 Kastenmeier	Y	Y	Y	N	Y	Y
6 Race	Y	Y	Y	N	Y	Y
5 Reuss	Y	Y	Y	N	Y	Y
1 Stalbaum	Y	Y	Y	N	Y	‡
4 Zablocki	Y	Y	Y	N	Y	Y
8 Byrnes	N	N	N	Y	N	Y
7 Laird	N	N	N	Y	N	Y
10 O'Konski	Y	Y	Y	Y	Y	Y
3 Thomson	N	N	N	Y	N	Y
9 Davis	N	N	N	Y	N	Y
WYOMING						
AL Roncalio	✓	Y	Y	N	Y	Y

* *Rep. Albert W. Watson (R S.C.) resigned Feb. 1, 1965 and was re-elected in a special election June 15, 1965 and sworn in June 16, 1965.*

Democrats in this type; *Republicans in italics*

House Key Votes—89th Congress-1965

7. HR 7750. Foreign Assistance Act of 1965. Adair (R Ind.) motion to recommit the bill to the Foreign Affairs Committee with instructions to reduce funds for development loans by $130,958,000, and to stipulate that labor unions participating in Latin American housing projects be "non-Communist dominated" as well as "free." Rejected 178-219: R 116-14; D 62-205 (ND 13-166; SD 49-39), May 25, 1965. A "nay" was a vote supporting the President's position.

8. HR 6927. Passage of the bill establishing a cabinet-level Department of Housing and Urban Development to be headed by a Secretary appointed by the President with Senate confirmation; transferring to the Secretary all the functions, powers and duties of the Housing and Home Finance Agency, the Federal Housing Administration, the Public Housing Administration and the Federal National Mortgage Association; and specifying other functions, powers and duties of the Department. Passed 217-184: R 9-118; D 208-66 (ND 170-10; SD 38-56), June 16, 1965. A "yea" was a vote supporting the President's position.

9. HR 7984. Housing and Urban Development Act of 1965, providing rent supplements to low-income families and extending and amending laws relating to public housing, urban renewal and community facilities. Harvey (R Mich.) motion to recommit the bill to the Banking and Currency Committee with instructions to delete the rent supplements provisions and language authorizing home improvement grants to homeowners in urban renewal areas. Rejected 202-208: R 130-4; D 72-204 (ND 21-163; SD 51-41), June 30, 1965. A "nay" was a vote supporting the President's position.

10. HR 11588. General Supplemental Appropriations bill for fiscal 1966. Harvey (R Mich.) amendment to delete language providing authority for $6 million in contracts, and appropriations of $180,000 for payments under the contracts, for a new program of rent supplements to low-income families. Accepted 185-162: R 99-2; D 86-160 (ND 24-141; SD 62-19), Oct. 14, 1965. A "nay" was a vote supporting the President's position.

11. HR 6400. Passage of the Voting Rights Act, suspending the use of literacy tests or similar voter qualification devices in certain states and areas and authorizing the appointment of federal voting examiners to order the registration of Negroes in states and voting districts whose voter activity had fallen below certain specified levels; the bill also imposed a ban on the use of poll taxes as a voter qualification in any election. Passed 333-85: R 112-24; D 221-61 (ND 188-1; SD 33-60), July 9, 1965. A "yea" was a vote supporting the President's position.

12. HR 8283. Economic Opportunity Amendments of 1965 (anti-poverty authorization). Quie (R Minn.) motion to recommit the bill to the House Education and Labor Committee with instructions to (1) delete a section which allowed federal officials to override a state Governor's veto of certain federal anti-poverty activities and (2) reduce the fiscal 1966 appropriations authorization of $1.9 billion to the fiscal 1965 level of $947.5 million. Rejected 178-227: R 121-13; D 57-214 (ND 6-174; SD 51-40), July 22, 1965. A "nay" was a vote supporting the President's position.

	7	8	9	10	11	12
ALABAMA						
3 Andrews	✓	N	Y	✓	N	Y
8 Jones	N	Y	Y	Y	N	N
5 Selden	Y	N	Y	N	Y	N
4 *Andrews*	Y	N	Y	Y	N	Y
6 *Buchanan*	Y	N	Y	Y	N	Y
2 *Dickinson*	✓	N	Y	Y	N	Y
1 *Edwards*	Y	N	Y	Y	N	Y
7 *Martin*	Y	X	Y	Y	N	Y
ALASKA						
AL Rivers	N	✓	N	N	Y	N
ARIZONA						
3 Senner	Y	Y	N	-	Y	N
2 Udall	N	Y	N	Y	N	N
1 *Rhodes*	Y	N	Y	Y	Y	Y
ARKANSAS						
1 Gathings	Y	N	Y	‡	N	Y
4 Harris	Y	N	Y	N	N	N
2 Mills	Y	Y	N	Y	X	N
3 Trimble	N	Y	N	N	N	N
CALIFORNIA						
5 Burton	X	Y	N	N	Y	N
7 Cohelan	N	Y	N	N	Y	N
33 Dyal	N	Y	N	N	Y	N
9 Edwards	N	Y	N	N	Y	N
18 Hagen	X	Y	N	Y	Y	N
34 Hanna	X	Y	N	N	Y	N
2 Johnson	N	Y	N	N	Y	N
4 Leggett	N	Y	N	N	Y	N
15 McFall	N	Y	N	N	Y	N
8 Miller	N	Y	N	N	Y	N
3 Moss	N	Y	N	N	Y	N
16 Sisk	N	Y	N	N	Y	N
38 Tunney	N	Y	N	N	Y	N
37 Van Deerlin	N	Y	Y	✓	Y	N
14 *Baldwin*	N	N	Y	Y	Y	N
1 *Clausen*	Y	X	Y	Y	Y	Y
10 *Gubser*	Y	N	Y	Y	Y	Y
6 *Mailliard*	N	N	Y	Y	Y	✓
12 *Talcott*	Y	N	Y	?	Y	Y
13 *Teague*	Y	N	Y	?	Y	Y
35 *Utt*	Y	X	Y	Y	N	Y
36 *Wilson*	Y	N	Y	Y	Y	Y
11 *Younger*	Y	N	Y	Y	Y	Y
Los Angeles Co.						
29 Brown	N	Y	X	N	Y	N
25 Cameron	N	✓	N	N	Y	N
22 Corman	N	Y	N	N	Y	N
21 Hawkins	N	Y	N	N	Y	N
19 Holifield	N	Y	N	X	N	N
17 King	N	Y	N	N	Y	N
26 Roosevelt *	N	Y	N		Y	N
30 Roybal	N	Y	N	N	Y	N
31 Wilson	N	✓	N	N	Y	X
28 *Bell*	Y	N	Y	Y	Y	Y
23 *Clawson*	✓	N	Y	?	Y	Y
32 *Hosmer*	Y	N	Y	‡	‡	Y
24 *Lipscomb*	Y	N	Y	Y	Y	Y
27 *Reinecke*	Y	N	Y	Y	Y	Y
20 *Smith*	Y	N	Y	Y	N	Y
COLORADO						
4 Aspinall	N	Y	Y	N	Y	N
3 Evans	N	Y	Y	N	Y	N
2 McVicker	N	Y	Y	N	Y	N
1 Rogers	N	Y	N	N	Y	N
CONNECTICUT						
1 Daddario	N	Y	N	X	Y	N
3 Giaimo	N	Y	N	N	Y	N
6 Grabowski	N	Y	N	N	Y	N
4 Irwin	N	Y	N	N	Y	N
5 Monagan	N	Y	N	N	Y	N
2 St. Onge	N	Y	N	N	Y	N
DELAWARE						
AL McDowell	N	Y	N	N	Y	Y
FLORIDA						
2 Bennett	Y	N	Y	Y	Y	Y
4 Fascell	N	Y	N	N	Y	N
9 Fuqua	Y	N	‡	✓	N	Y
10 Gibbons	N	Y	N	N	Y	N
7 Haley	Y	N	Y	N	Y	N
5 Herlong	Y	N	Y	Y	Y	N
8 Matthews	Y	N	Y	Y	N	N
3 Pepper	N	Y	N	X	N	N
6 Rogers	N	Y	N	N	Y	N
1 Sikes	Y	N	Y	N	Y	N
12 *Cramer*	Y	N	Y	Y	N	Y
11 *Gurney*	Y	N	Y	Y	N	Y
GEORGIA						
7 Davis	Y	N	N	Y	N	Y
6 Flynt	✓	N	Y	Y	N	Y
1 Hagan	N	X	N	Y	N	Y
9 Landrum	N	N	N	Y	N	N
4 Mackay	N	N	X	N	Y	N
2 O'Neal	Y	N	Y	N	Y	✓
10 Stephens	Y	N	‡	N	N	Y
8 Tuten	N	N	N	Y	N	Y
5 Weltner	?	N	N	?	Y	N
3 *Callaway*	Y	N	Y	Y	N	Y
HAWAII						
AL Matsunaga	N	✓	N	N	Y	N
AL Mink	N	Y	N	N	Y	N
IDAHO						
1 White	X	Y	Y	X	Y	X
2 *Hansen*	Y	N	Y	Y	N	Y
ILLINOIS						
21 Gray	N	Y	N	N	Y	N
24 Price	N	Y	N	N	Y	N
19 Schisler	N	Y	N	N	Y	N
23 Shipley	Y	N	?	?	Y	X
16 *Anderson*	Y	N	Y	Y	Y	Y
17 *Arends*	Y	N	Y	✓	Y	✓
14 *Erlenborn*	Y	N	Y	Y	N	Y
20 *Findley*	Y	X	Y	?	Y	Y
12 *McClory*	Y	N	Y	?	Y	Y
18 *Michel*	Y	N	Y	Y	Y	Y
15 *Reid*	Y	N	Y	Y	Y	Y
3 *Springer*	‡	N	‡	Y	Y	Y
Chicago—Cook Co.						
7 Annunzio	N	Y	N	N	Y	N
1 Dawson	N	N	N	X	N	N
5 Kluczynski	N	Y	N	N	Y	N
3 Murphy	N	Y	N	N	Y	N
2 O'Hara	N	Y	N	X	N	N
11 Pucinski	N	Y	N	N	Y	N
6 Ronan	N	Y	N	N	Y	N
8 Rostenkowski	N	Y	?	N	Y	N
9 Yates	N	Y	N	N	Y	N
10 *Collier*	Y	N	Y	N	Y	N
4 *Derwinski*	Y	N	Y	Y	Y	Y
13 *Rumsfeld*	Y	N	Y	Y	Y	‡
INDIANA						
3 Brademas	N	Y	N	N	Y	N
8 Denton	N	Y	N	N	Y	N
9 Hamilton	Y	N	N	N	Y	N
11 Jacobs	N	Y	N	N	Y	N
1 Madden	N	Y	N	N	Y	N
5 Roush	Y	Y	Y	Y	Y	N
4 *Adair*	Y	N	Y	✓	Y	Y
7 *Bray*	Y	X	Y	✓	Y	Y
2 *Halleck*	Y	N	Y	?	Y	✓
10 *Harvey*	✓	-	‡	✓	‡	✓
6 *Roudebush*	Y	N	Y	✓	Y	Y
IOWA						
4 Bandstra	X	Y	N	N	Y	N
2 Culver	N	Y	Y	Y	Y	N
6 Greigg	N	Y	N	N	Y	N
7 Hansen	N	Y	N	N	Y	N
1 Schmidhauser	Y	Y	N	N	Y	N
5 Smith	N	Y	Y	Y	Y	N
3 *Gross*	Y	N	Y	Y	N	Y
KANSAS						
1 *Dole*	Y	N	Y	Y	Y	Y
3 *Ellsworth*	Y	N	Y	Y	Y	Y
4 *Shriver*	Y	N	Y	‡	Y	Y
2 *Mize*	Y	N	Y	‡	Y	Y
5 *Skubitz*	✓	N	Y	?	Y	Y
KENTUCKY						
4 Chelf	‡	Y	N	Y	N	N
3 Farnsley	N	N	N	N	Y	N
2 Natcher	N	Y	N	N	Y	N

- KEY -

Y Record Vote For (yea).
✓ Paired For.
‡ Announced For, CQ Poll For.
N Record Vote Against (nay).
X Paired Against
- Announced Against, CQ Poll Against.
? Absent, General Pair, "Present," Did not announce or answer Poll.

Rep. James Roosevelt (D Calif.) resigned Sept. 30, 1965.

Democrats in this type; *Republicans in italics*

	7	8	9	10	11	12
7 Perkins	N	Y	N	N	Y	N
1 Stubblefield	?	Y	N	Y	Y	N
6 Watts	X	Y	N	Y	Y	N
5 Carter	✓	N	Y	Y	Y	N
LOUISIANA						
2 Boggs	N	Y	N	N	Y	N
1 Hebert	✓	X	Y	Y	N	Y
8 Long	Y	N	Y	✓	N	Y
6 Morrison	N	Y	N	N	Y	N
5 Passman	Y	N	Y	Y	X	Y
7 Thompson @	Y	Y	N			
4 Waggonner	Y	N	Y	Y	N	✓
3 Willis	?	Y	N	✓	N	✓
MAINE						
2 Hathaway	N	Y	N	N	Y	N
1 Tupper	N	Y	?	Y	Y	N
MARYLAND						
4 Fallon	N	Y	N	Y	Y	N
7 Friedel	N	Y	N	N	Y	N
3 Garmatz	N	Y	N	X	Y	N
2 Long	N	Y	N	N	Y	N
5 Machen	N	Y	N	N	Y	N
AL Sickles	N	Y	N	N	Y	N
6 Mathias	?	N	Y	Y	Y	N
1 Morton	Y	N	‡	‡	‡	Y
MASSACHUSETTS						
2 Boland	N	Y	N	N	Y	N
11 Burke	N	Y	N	N	Y	N
4 Donohue	N	Y	N	N	Y	N
7 Macdonald	X	✓	N	Y	Y	N
9 McCormack						
8 O'Neill	N	Y	N	N	Y	N
3 Philbin	N	Y	N	N	Y	N
6 Bates	Y	N	Y	Y	Y	Y
1 Conte	N	N	Y	Y	Y	Y
12 Keith	Y	X	Y	Y	Y	Y
10 Martin	Y	✓	?	Y	Y	✓
5 Morse	N	N	Y	Y	Y	N
MICHIGAN						
11 Clevenger	N	Y	N	N	Y	N
19 Farnum	N	Y	N	X	Y	N
7 Mackie	N	Y	N	N	Y	N
12 O'Hara	N	Y	N	N	Y	N
3 Todd	N	Y	✓	Y	Y	N
2 Vivian	N	Y	N	N	Y	N
18 Broomfield	N	N	Y	Y	Y	Y
10 Cederberg	Y	N	Y	Y	Y	Y
6 Chamberlain	Y	-	Y	Y	Y	Y
5 Ford	Y	N	Y	✓	Y	Y
9 Griffin	Y	N	Y	Y	Y	Y
8 Harvey	Y	N	Y	Y	Y	Y
4 Hutchinson	Y	N	Y	Y	Y	Y
Detroit—Wayne Co.						
1 Conyers	N	Y	N	N	Y	N
13 Diggs	N	Y	N	N	Y	N
16 Dingell	N	Y	N	N	Y	N
15 Ford	N	Y	N	N	Y	N
17 Griffiths	N	Y	N	X	Y	N
14 Nedzi	N	Y	N	N	Y	N
MINNESOTA						
8 Blatnik	N	Y	N	N	Y	X
5 Fraser	N	Y	N	N	Y	N
4 Karth	N	Y	N	Y	Y	N
6 Olson	N	Y	Y	Y	Y	N
7 Langen	Y	N	Y	Y	Y	Y
3 MacGregor	Y	N	Y	Y	Y	Y
2 Nelsen	Y	N	Y	Y	Y	Y
1 Quie	Y	N	Y	Y	Y	Y
MISSISSIPPI						
1 Abernethy	Y	X	Y	Y	N	Y
5 Colmer	Y	N	Y	Y	N	✓
2 Whitten	Y	N	Y	Y	N	Y
3 Williams	Y	N	Y	Y	N	Y
4 Walker	Y	N	Y	?	N	Y
MISSOURI						
5 Bolling	N	Y	N	N	Y	N
6 Hull	Y	N	Y	Y	Y	Y
9 Hungate	?	Y	N	N	Y	N
8 Ichord	Y	?	Y	Y	Y	Y
10 Jones	Y	Y	Y	Y	N	Y
1 Karsten	N	Y	N	N	Y	N
4 Randall	Y	N	Y	X	Y	N
3 Sullivan	N	Y	N	N	Y	N

	7	8	9	10	11	12
2 Curtis	Y	N	Y	‡	Y	Y
7 Hall	Y	N	Y	Y	N	Y
MONTANA						
1 Olsen	N	Y	N	N	Y	N
2 Battin	Y	N	Y	Y	Y	Y
NEBRASKA						
1 Callan	N	Y	N	Y	Y	N
2 Cunningham	Y	N	Y	Y	Y	Y
3 Martin	Y	N	Y	?	Y	Y
NEVADA						
AL Baring	Y	N	Y	X	‡	Y
NEW HAMPSHIRE						
1 Huot	N	Y	N	N	Y	N
2 Cleveland	Y	N	Y	Y	Y	Y
NEW JERSEY						
14 Daniels	N	Y	N	N	Y	N
13 Gallagher	N	Y	N	N	Y	N
9 Helstoski	N	Y	N	N	Y	N
3 Howard	N	Y	N	N	Y	N
8 Joelson	N	Y	N	N	Y	N
12 Krebs	N	Y	N	N	Y	N
11 Minish	N	Y	N	N	Y	N
2 McGrath	N	Y	N	N	Y	N
15 Patten	N	Y	N	N	Y	N
10 Rodino	N	Y	N	N	Y	N
4 Thompson	N	Y	N	N	Y	N
1 Cahill	N	Y	Y	Y	Y	Y
6 Dwyer	N	N	Y	Y	Y	Y
5 Frelinghuysen	N	N	Y	‡	Y	Y
7 Widnall	Y	N	Y	Y	Y	Y
NEW MEXICO						
AL Morris	N	N	Y	Y	Y	N
AL Walker	Y	Y	N	Y	Y	N
NEW YORK						
27 Dow	N	Y	N	N	Y	N
41 Dulski	N	Y	‡	N	Y	N
34 Hanley	N	Y	N	N	Y	N
39 McCarthy	N	Y	N	Y	Y	N
29 O'Brien	N	Y	N	X	Y	N
25 Ottinger	N	Y	N	N	Y	N
1 Pike	N	✓	Y	Y	Y	✓
28 Resnick	X	Y	N	N	Y	N
35 Stratton	N	Y	N	X	Y	N
5 Tenzer	N	Y	N	X	Y	X
3 Wolff	N	Y	N	N	Y	N
37 Conable	Y	N	Y	✓	Y	Y
38 Goodell	Y	N	Y	Y	Y	Y
2 Grover	Y	N	Y	Y	Y	Y
36 Horton	N	Y	N	X	Y	N
30 King	Y	N	Y	Y	Y	Y
31 McEwen	Y	X	Y	Y	N	Y
32 Pirnie	Y	-	Y	Y	Y	Y
26 Reid	N	Y	N	N	Y	N
33 Robison	Y	N	Y	Y	Y	Y
40 Smith	Y	N	Y	Y	Y	Y
4 Wydler	Y	N	Y	?	Y	Y
New York City						
7 Addabbo	N	Y	‡	Y	Y	N
23 Bingham	N	Y	N	-	Y	N
15 Carey	N	Y	N	N	Y	N
10 Celler	N	Y	N	X	Y	N
9 Delaney	N	Y	N	X	Y	N
19 Farbstein	N	Y	N	N	Y	N
22 Gilbert	N	Y	N	N	Y	N
12 Kelly	N	Y	N	N	Y	N
11 Keogh	N	Y	X	X	✓	X
13 Multer	N	Y	N	N	Y	N
16 Murphy	N	Y	N	N	Y	N
18 Powell	X	Y	N	N	?	N
14 Rooney	N	Y	N	N	Y	N
8 Rosenthal	N	Y	N	N	Y	N
20 Ryan	N	Y	N	N	Y	N
21 Scheuer	N	°	°	°	Y	N
24 Fino	Y	Y	Y	✓	Y	N
6 Halpern	N	Y	N	N	Y	N
17 Lindsay	N	Y	N	X	Y	N
NORTH CAROLINA						
1 Bonner	?	?	?	Y	X	?
4 Cooley	N	N	N	Y	N	Y
2 Fountain	Y	N	Y	Y	N	Y
3 Henderson	Y	N	Y	Y	N	Y
6 Kornegay	Y	N	Y	✓	N	Y
7 Lennon	✓	N	Y	Y	N	Y

	7	8	9	10	11	12
5 Scott	Y	N	Y	Y	N	✓
11 Taylor	Y	N	Y	Y	N	Y
10 Whitener	Y	N	Y	Y	N	Y
9 Broyhill	Y	N	Y	Y	N	Y
8 Jonas	Y	N	Y	Y	N	Y
NORTH DAKOTA						
2 Redlin	N	Y	N	N	Y	X
1 Andrews	Y	N	Y	Y	Y	Y
OHIO						
9 Ashley	N	Y	N	N	Y	X
20 Feighan	N	Y	N	N	Y	N
1 Gilligan	N	Y	N	X	Y	N
18 Hays	N	Y	N	X	Y	N
19 Kirwan	N	Y	N	N	Y	X
3 Love	N	Y	N	N	Y	N
10 Moeller	Y	N	N	Y	Y	N
15 Secrest	Y	N	N	Y	Y	N
AL Sweeney	N	Y	N	N	Y	N
21 Vanik	N	Y	N	N	Y	N
17 Ashbrook	✓	N	Y	Y	Y	Y
14 Ayres	N	-	Y	Y	Y	Y
8 Betts	Y	N	Y	Y	Y	Y
22 Bolton	Y	N	Y	Y	Y	Y
16 Bow	Y	-	✓	Y	?	?
7 Brown †	✓	X	Y		Y	Y
2 Clancy	Y	N	Y	✓	Y	Y
12 Devine	Y	N	Y	Y	Y	Y
6 Harsha	Y	N	Y	Y	Y	Y
5 Latta	Y	N	Y	Y	Y	Y
4 McCulloch	Y	N	Y	Y	Y	Y
23 Minshall	Y	Y	Y	Y	Y	Y
13 Mosher	Y	N	Y	Y	Y	Y
11 Stanton	Y	N	Y	Y	Y	Y
OKLAHOMA						
3 Albert	N	Y	N	N	Y	N
2 Edmondson	N	Y	N	N	Y	N
5 Jarman	Y	Y	Y	Y	Y	Y
6 Johnson	N	Y	N	N	Y	N
4 Steed	N	Y	Y	Y	Y	N
1 Belcher	Y	N	Y	Y	Y	Y
OREGON						
4 Duncan	N	Y	N	X	Y	N
3 Green*	X	Y	N	✓	Y	N
2 Ullman	N	Y	N	N	Y	-
1 Wyatt	Y	N	Y	?	Y	Y
PENNSYLVANIA						
25 Clark	N	Y	N	X	Y	N
19 Craley	N	Y	N	N	Y	N
21 Dent	N	Y	N	N	Y	N
11 Flood	N	Y	N	N	Y	N
20 Holland	N	Y	N	N	Y	N
14 Moorhead	X	Y	N	N	Y	N
26 Morgan	N	Y	N	N	Y	N
6 Rhodes	N	Y	N	N	Y	N
15 Rooney	N	Y	N	N	Y	N
24 Vigorito	N	Y	N	N	Y	N
18 Corbett	Y	N	Y	Y	Y	Y
8 Curtin	Y	N	Y	Y	Y	Y
9 Dague	Y	N	Y	Y	Y	Y
27 Fulton	Y	N	Y	Y	Y	Y
23 Johnson	Y	N	Y	✓	Y	Y
16 Kunkel	Y	N	‡	Y	Y	Y
10 McDade	Y	N	Y	?	Y	N
22 Saylor	Y	N	Y	?	Y	N
17 Schneebeli	Y	N	Y	Y	Y	Y
13 Schweiker	Y	N	Y	Y	Y	Y
7 Watkins	Y	N	Y	Y	Y	Y
12 Whalley	Y	N	Y	Y	Y	Y
Philadelphia City						
1 Barrett	N	Y	N	N	Y	N
3 Byrne	N	Y	N	N	Y	N
5 Green	N	Y	N	N	Y	N
2 Nix	X	Y	N	N	Y	N
4 Toll	X	✓	X	X	✓	X
RHODE ISLAND						
2 Fogarty	N	Y	N	N	Y	N
1 St. Germain	N	Y	N	N	Y	N
SOUTH CAROLINA						
4 Ashmore	Y	N	Y	Y	N	Y
3 Dorn	Y	N	Y	Y	N	Y
5 Gettys	Y	N	Y	Y	N	Y
6 McMillan	Y	N	Y	Y	N	Y

	7	8	9	10	11	12
1 Rivers	Y	N	Y	‡	N	Y
2 Watson #		N	Y	✓	N	Y
SOUTH DAKOTA						
2 Berry	✓	N	Y	Y	Y	Y
1 Reifel	Y	N	Y	‡	Y	Y
TENNESSEE						
6 Anderson	N	Y	N	X	Y	N
8 Everett	N	Y	N	Y	N	Y
4 Evins	N	Y	?	N	Y	X
5 Fulton	N	Y	N	N	Y	N
9 Grider	N	Y	N	N	Y	N
7 Murray	Y	N	Y	Y	N	N
3 Brock	Y	N	Y	✓	N	Y
2 Duncan	Y	N	Y	Y	N	Y
1 Quillen	Y	N	Y	‡	N	Y
TEXAS						
3 Beckworth	N	Y	N	Y	N	N
2 Brooks	N	Y	N	Y	Y	N
17 Burleson	Y	N	Y	Y	N	Y
5 Cabell	Y	N	✓	Y	Y	Y
22 Casey	Y	N	Y	Y	N	Y
15 De la Garza	N	N	N	Y	Y	N
7 Dowdy	Y	N	Y	Y	N	Y
21 Fisher	Y	X	Y	Y	N	Y
20 Gonzalez	N	Y	N	N	Y	N
19 Mahon	N	N	Y	N	N	N
1 Patman	N	Y	N	N	N	N
10 Pickle	N	Y	Y	Y	Y	N
11 Poage	N	N	N	Y	N	Y
AL Pool	✓	N	Y	Y	N	Y
13 Purcell	N	Y	N	Y	‡	N
4 Roberts	N	N	Y	✓	N	N
18 Rogers	Y	N	Y	✓	N	Y
6 Teague	Y	N	✓	Y	N	Y
8 Thomas	N	✓	X	?	✓	X
9 Thompson	N	Y	N	?	-	N
16 White	Y	Y	✓	Y	Y	Y
12 Wright	-	N	N	N	Y	N
14 Young	N	Y	N	?	Y	N
UTAH						
2 King	N	N	N	N	Y	N
1 Burton	Y	N	Y	?	Y	Y
VERMONT						
AL Stafford	Y	N	Y	Y	Y	Y
VIRGINIA						
4 Abbitt	Y	N	Y	✓	N	Y
1 Downing	Y	Y	Y	Y	N	Y
2 Hardy	Y	Y	Y	✓	N	Y
9 Jennings	Y	Y	N	Y	Y	N
7 Marsh	Y	N	Y	Y	N	Y
3 Satterfield	Y	N	Y	Y	N	Y
8 Smith	Y	N	Y	Y	N	Y
5 Tuck	Y	N	Y	Y	N	Y
10 Broyhill	Y	N	Y	Y	N	Y
6 Poff	Y	N	Y	Y	N	Y
WASHINGTON						
7 Adams	N	Y	N	N	Y	N
5 Foley	N	Y	Y	Y	Y	N
3 Hansen	N	Y	N	N	Y	N
6 Hicks	N	Y	N	N	Y	N
2 Meeds	N	Y	N	N	Y	N
4 May	Y	N	Y	Y	‡	Y
1 Pelly	Y	N	Y	Y	Y	Y
WEST VIRGINIA						
4 Hechler	N	Y	N	N	Y	N
5 Kee	N	✓	N	N	Y	N
3 Slack	N	N	Y	N	Y	N
2 Staggers	N	?	N	N	Y	N
1 Moore	Y	N	Y	Y	Y	Y
WISCONSIN						
2 Kastenmeier	N	Y	N	N	Y	N
6 Race	Y	Y	N	N	Y	N
5 Reuss	N	Y	N	N	Y	N
1 Stalbaum	N	Y	Y	Y	Y	N
4 Zablocki	N	✓	N	N	Y	N
8 Byrnes	Y	N	Y	Y	Y	Y
7 Laird	Y	N	Y	✓	Y	Y
10 O'Konski	Y	Y	Y	?	Y	N
3 Thomson	Y	N	Y	Y	Y	Y
9 Davis	Y	N	Y	Y	Y	Y
WYOMING						
AL Roncalio	X	Y	N	N	Y	✓

°Rep. Scheuer (D N.Y.) did not vote because of possible conflict of interest.

@Rep. T. Ashton Thompson (D La.) died July 1, 1965.

†Rep. Clarence J. Brown (R Ohio) died Aug. 23, 1965.

#Rep. Albert W. Watson (R S.C.) resigned Feb. 1, and was re-elected in a special election June 15, and sworn in June 16, 1965.

House Key Votes—89th Congress—1965

13. HR 77. Passage of the bill to repeal Section 14(b) of the Taft-Hartley Act permitting state right-to-work laws under which the union shop is prohibited. Passed 221-203: R 21-117; D 200-86 (ND 182-8; SD 18-78), July 28, 1965. A "yea" was a vote supporting the President's position.

14. HR 9811. Passage of the Food and Agriculture Act of 1965, covering wheat, cotton, wool, dairy and feed grain commodities and providing a cropland retirement program. Passed 221-172: R 19-104; D 202-68 (ND 139-40; SD 63-28), Aug. 19, 1965. A "yea" was a vote supporting the President's position.

15. HR 2580. Passage of the bill amending immigration law to eliminate the national origins quota system and to set general priorities for the admission of immigrants to the United States. Passed 318-95: R 109-25; D 209-70 (ND 179-8; SD 30-62), Aug. 25, 1965. A "yea" was a vote supporting the President's position.

16. HR 9460. Establish a National Foundation on the Arts and Humanities to provide federal assistance to the visual and performing arts and the humanities. Griffin (R Mich.) motion to recommit (kill) the bill. Rejected 128-251: R 79-44; D 49-207 (ND 5-170; SD 44-37), Sept. 15, 1965. A "nay" was a vote supporting the President's position.

17. HR 4644. District of Columbia Charter Act. Sisk (D Calif.) substitute for Administration's D.C. home rule bill, providing for election of a charter board to draw up within seven months a charter for D.C. self-government which, if approved by D.C. voters, would go into effect in 90 days if not disapproved by either chamber of Congress. (The Administration bill provided machinery for automatic establishment of D.C. self-government, contingent only on approval by D.C. voters in a referendum, with an automatic federal payment to the District.) Accepted 227-174: R 105-23; D 122-151 (ND 50-134; SD 72-17), Sept. 29, 1965. A "nay" was a vote supporting the President's position.

18. S 2084. Passage of the bill authorizing appropriations of $325 million in fiscal 1966-67 for federal-state programs for control or removal of billboards and junkyards along Interstate and primary highways, for federal payments to states to cover costs of landscaping and scenic development of federal-aid highways, and for the administrative costs of implementing the bill. Passed 245-138: R 26-89; D 219-49 (ND 159-21; SD 60-28), Oct. 7, 1965. A "yea" was a vote supporting the President's position.

	13	14	15	16	17	18
ALABAMA						
3 Andrews	N	?	X	?	✔	X
8 Jones	N	Y	N	N	Y	Y
5 Selden	N	N	N	Y	Y	N
4 Andrews	N	Y	?	Y	Y	N
6 Buchanan	N	N	N	Y	Y	N
2 Dickinson	N	N	N	Y	Y	N
1 Edwards	N	N	N	Y	Y	N
7 Martin	N	N	N	✔	Y	X
ALASKA						
AL Rivers	Y	Y	Y	N	N	Y
ARIZONA						
3 Senner	Y	Y	Y	X	N	Y
2 Udall	N	Y	Y	N	Y	✔
1 Rhodes	N	N	Y	Y	Y	N
ARKANSAS						
1 Gathings	N	N	N	Y	Y	Y
4 Harris	N	N	N	N	Y	Y
2 Mills	N	N	N	Y	Y	Y
3 Trimble	N	Y	Y	N	N	Y
CALIFORNIA						
5 Burton	Y	Y	Y	N	N	Y
7 Cohelan	Y	N	Y	N	N	Y
33 Dyal	Y	Y	Y	N	N	Y
9 Edwards	Y	Y	Y	N	N	Y
18 Hagen	Y	Y	Y	N	Y	Y
34 Hanna	Y	?	Y	N	N	Y
2 Johnson	Y	N	Y	N	N	Y
4 Leggett	Y	N	Y	N	N	Y
15 McFall	Y	Y	Y	N	N	Y
8 Miller	Y	✔	Y	N	N	Y
3 Moss	Y	Y	Y	N	N	Y
16 Sisk	Y	Y	‡	-	Y	Y
38 Tunney	Y	Y	Y	N	N	Y
37 Van Deerlin	Y	Y	Y	-	N	Y
14 Baldwin	N	N	Y	Y	Y	Y
1 Clausen	N	N	Y	Y	Y	Y
10 Gubser	N	N	Y	Y	Y	Y
6 Mailliard	N	N	N	Y	Y	Y
12 Talcott	N	N	Y	Y	Y	Y
13 Teague	N	N	Y	Y	Y	Y
35 Utt	N	X	N	Y	Y	X
36 Wilson	N	X	Y	Y	Y	N
11 Younger	N	X	Y	Y	Y	N

Los Angeles Co.	13	14	15	16	17	18
29 Brown	Y	✔	Y	-	N	Y
25 Cameron	Y	N	Y	N	N	Y
22 Corman	Y	X	N	N	N	Y
21 Hawkins	Y	Y	Y	N	N	Y
19 Holifield	Y	Y	Y	N	X	✔
17 King	Y	Y	Y	N	N	Y
26 Roosevelt *	Y	Y	Y	?	X	
30 Roybal	Y	X	Y	N	N	Y
31 Wilson	Y	N	N	N	N	Y
28 Bell	N	N	N	Y	Y	Y
23 Clawson	N	N	Y	Y	Y	X
32 Hosmer	N	N	N	Y	✔	X
24 Lipscomb	N	N	N	Y	Y	N
27 Reinecke	N	X	N	Y	N	N
20 Smith	N	N	N	Y	Y	X
COLORADO						
4 Aspinall	N	Y	Y	N	?	Y
3 Evans	Y	Y	Y	N	N	‡
2 McVicker	‡	Y	Y	N	N	Y
1 Rogers	Y	Y	Y	N	Y	Y
CONNECTICUT						
1 Daddario	Y	Y	Y	X	?	Y
3 Giaimo	Y	N	Y	N	Y	Y
6 Grabowski	Y	N	Y	N	N	Y
4 Irwin	Y	N	Y	N	N	Y
5 Monagan	Y	N	Y	N	N	Y
2 St. Onge	Y	Y	Y	N	N	Y
DELAWARE						
AL McDowell	Y	Y	Y	N	N	Y
FLORIDA						
2 Bennett	N	N	Y	Y	Y	Y
4 Fascell	N	Y	Y	N	N	Y
9 Fuqua	N	‡	N	‡	Y	N
10 Gibbons	N	N	N	N	N	Y
7 Haley	N	N	N	Y	Y	N
5 Herlong	N	N	N	Y	Y	N
8 Matthews	N	N	N	Y	Y	N
3 Pepper	Y	Y	Y	N	N	Y
6 Rogers	N	N	N	Y	Y	N
1 Sikes	N	✔	Y	N	?	Y
12 Cramer	N	N	X	Y	Y	N
11 Gurney	N	N	N	Y	Y	X

GEORGIA	13	14	15	16	17	18
7 Davis	N	Y	N	Y	Y	Y
6 Flynt	N	Y	N	Y	Y	Y
1 Hagan	N	Y	N	Y	Y	Y
9 Landrum	N	Y	X	N	Y	Y
4 Mackay	N	Y	Y	N	N	Y
2 O'Neal	N	Y	N	✔	Y	N
10 Stephens	N	Y	N	N	Y	Y
8 Tuten	N	Y	N	Y	Y	Y
5 Weltner	N	Y	Y	Y	N	Y
3 Callaway	N	Y	N	Y	Y	N
HAWAII						
AL Matsunaga	Y	✔	Y	N	N	Y
AL Mink	Y	Y	Y	N	N	Y
IDAHO						
1 White	Y	Y	Y	N	Y	N
2 Hansen	N	N	N	Y	Y	N
ILLINOIS						
21 Gray	Y	N	Y	N	Y	Y
24 Price	Y	Y	Y	N	N	Y
19 Schisler	Y	Y	N	N	N	N
23 Shipley	Y	N	N	N	N	N
16 Anderson	N	N	Y	Y	‡	‡
17 Arends	N	N	Y	Y	Y	N
14 Erlenborn	N	N	Y	Y	Y	N
20 Findley	N	N	Y	Y	Y	N
12 McClory	N	N	Y	✔	Y	N
12 Michel	N	X	Y	N	-	N
15 Reid	N	N	Y	Y	Y	N
22 Springer	N	N	Y	N	Y	N
Chicago—Cook Co.						
7 Annunzio	Y	Y	Y	N	N	Y
1 Dawson	Y	Y	Y	N	N	Y
5 Kluczynski	Y	Y	Y	N	N	Y
3 Murphy	Y	Y	Y	N	N	Y
2 O'Hara	Y	Y	Y	N	N	?
11 Pucinski	Y	Y	Y	N	N	Y
6 Ronan	Y	Y	Y	N	N	Y
8 Rostenkowski	Y	✔	Y	N	N	Y
9 Yates	Y	Y	Y	N	N	Y
10 Collier	N	N	Y	Y	Y	N
4 Derwinski	N	N	Y	✔	Y	N
13 Rumsfeld	N	N	‡	Y	Y	N

	13	14	15	16	17	18
INDIANA						
3 Brademas	Y	Y	Y	N	N	Y
8 Denton	Y	Y	Y	N	Y	Y
9 Hamilton	Y	Y	Y	Y	N	Y
11 Jacobs	Y	N	Y	N	N	Y
1 Madden	Y	Y	Y	N	N	Y
5 Roush	Y	Y	N	Y	N	Y
4 Adair	N	N	N	✔	Y	N
7 Bray	N	N	N	Y	Y	N
3 Halleck	N	N	Y	Y	Y	N
10 Harvey	N	N	N	Y	Y	N
6 Roudebush	N	N	N	‡	Y	N
IOWA						
4 Bandstra	Y	Y	Y	N	Y	Y
2 Culver	Y	Y	Y	N	N	Y
6 Greigg	Y	Y	Y	N	N	Y
7 Hansen	Y	Y	Y	N	N	Y
1 Schmidhauser	Y	Y	Y	N	N	Y
5 Smith	N	Y	N	N	Y	N
3 Gross	N	N	N	Y	Y	N
KANSAS						
1 Dole	N	Y	Y	Y	Y	N
3 Ellsworth	N	Y	N	N	N	N
4 Shriver	N	Y	Y	Y	Y	N
2 Mize	N	Y	Y	Y	‡	N
5 Skubitz	N	Y	Y	Y	Y	N
KENTUCKY						
4 Chelf	Y	Y	N	N	Y	Y
3 Farnsley	Y	Y	Y	?	N	Y
2 Natcher	Y	N	Y	N	N	Y

Democrats in this type; *Republicans in italics*

Rep. James Roosevelt (D Calif.) resigned Sept. 30, 1965.

KEY

Y Record Vote For (yea).
✔ Paired For.
‡ Announced For, CQ Poll For.
N Record Vote Against (nay).
X Paired Against
- Announced Against, CQ Poll Against.
? Absent, General Pair, "Present," Did not announce or answer Poll.

	13	14	15	16	17	18
7 Perkins	Y	Y	Y	N	N	Y
1 Stubblefield	N	Y	N	N	Y	N
6 Watts	N	Y	N	N	Y	Y
5 Carter	N	✓	Y	Y	Y	N
LOUISIANA						
2 Boggs	Y	Y	Y	N	N	Y
1 Hebert	N	N	N	?	Y	?
8 Long	N	N	N	Y	✓	?
6 Morrison	Y	Y	Y	N	N	Y
5 Passman	N	N	N	Y	Y	N
7 Thompson*						
4 Waggonner	N	N	N	Y	Y	Y
3 Willis	N	Y	N	N	Y	Y
MAINE						
2 Hathaway	Y	Y	Y	-	N	Y
1 Tupper	Y	Y	Y	N	?	Y
MARYLAND						
4 Fallon	Y	N	Y	?	N	Y
7 Friedel	Y	Y	Y	N	N	Y
3 Garmatz	Y	N	Y	X	N	Y
2 Long	Y	N	Y	?	N	Y
5 Machen	Y	N	Y	N	N	Y
AL Sickles	Y	Y	Y	N	N	Y
6 Mathias	N	N	✓	N	N	✓
1 Morton	N	N	Y	Y	Y	N
MASSACHUSETTS						
2 Boland	Y	Y	Y	N	N	Y
11 Burke	Y	Y	Y	N	Y	Y
4 Donohue	Y	Y	Y	N	N	Y
7 Macdonald	Y	N	Y	?	Y	Y
9 McCormack						
8 O'Neill	Y	Y	Y	N	N	Y
3 Philbin	Y	Y	Y	N	N	Y
6 Bates	N	N	Y	Y	Y	-
1 Conte	N	N	Y	N	N	Y
12 Keith	Y	Y	Y	?	Y	Y
10 Martin	N	✓	Y	?	Y	X
5 Morse	Y	N	Y	X	N	Y
MICHIGAN						
11 Clevenger	Y	Y	Y	N	N	Y
19 Farnum	Y	N	Y	N	N	Y
7 Mackie	Y	Y	Y	Y	Y	Y
12 O'Hara	Y	Y	Y	N	N	Y
3 Todd	Y	Y	Y	N	N	Y
2 Vivian	Y	Y	Y	N	N	Y
18 Broomfield	N	X	Y	Y	N	Y
10 Cederberg	N	N	Y	Y	Y	N
6 Chamberlain	N	N	Y	Y	Y	-
5 Ford	N	N	Y	Y	N	N
9 Griffin	N	N	Y	Y	N	Y
8 Harvey	N	N	?	Y	N	N
4 Hutchinson	N	N	Y	Y	Y	N
Detroit—Wayne Co.						
1 Conyers	Y	Y	Y	N	N	Y
13 Diggs	Y	Y	Y	-	N	Y
16 Dingell	Y	Y	Y	N	Y	Y
15 Ford	Y	Y	Y	N	N	Y
17 Griffiths	Y	✓	Y	N	Y	Y
14 Nedzi	Y	N	Y	N	N	Y
MINNESOTA						
8 Blatnik	Y	Y	Y	N	N	Y
5 Fraser	Y	Y	Y	N	N	Y
4 Karth	Y	Y	Y	N	N	Y
6 Olson	Y	Y	Y	N	N	Y
7 Langen	N	Y	Y	Y	Y	N
3 MacGregor	N	Y	Y	X	Y	-
2 Nelsen	N	Y	Y	Y	Y	N
1 Quie	N	Y	Y	Y	N	N
MISSISSIPPI						
1 Abernethy	N	N	N	-	Y	N
5 Colmer	X	N	N	?	✓	N
2 Whitten	N	N	N	?	Y	N
3 Williams	N	N	N	?	Y	N
4 Walker	N	N	N	?	Y	N
MISSOURI						
5 Bolling	Y	Y	Y	N	N	‡
6 Hull	N	Y	N	✓	Y	N
9 Hungate	Y	Y	Y	N	Y	N
8 Ichord	Y	Y	N	N	Y	N
10 Jones	N	Y	N	-	Y	N
1 Karsten	Y	Y	Y	N	N	Y
4 Randall	Y	Y	N	N	Y	N
3 Sullivan	Y	Y	Y	N	Y	Y
2 Curtis	N	X	Y	Y	Y	N
7 Hall	N	N	N	Y	Y	N
MONTANA						
1 Olsen	Y	Y	Y	N	N	Y
2 Battin	N	Y	Y	Y	Y	N
NEBRASKA						
1 Callan	N	Y	Y	N	Y	N
2 Cunningham	N	N	Y	N	Y	N
3 Martin	N	N	Y	Y	Y	N
NEVADA						
AL Baring	N	N	N	Y	Y	Y
NEW HAMPSHIRE						
1 Huot	Y	Y	Y	N	N	Y
2 Cleveland	N	N	Y	N	Y	N
NEW JERSEY						
14 Daniels	Y	Y	Y	N	N	Y
13 Gallagher	Y	Y	Y	?	N	Y
9 Helstoski	Y	Y	Y	N	N	Y
3 Howard	Y	Y	Y	N	N	Y
8 Joelson	Y	Y	Y	N	N	Y
12 Krebs	Y	Y	Y	X	N	Y
11 Minish	Y	Y	Y	N	N	Y
2 McGrath	Y	Y	Y	N	N	Y
15 Patten	Y	Y	Y	N	N	Y
10 Rodino	Y	Y	Y	N	N	Y
4 Thompson	Y	✓	✓	N	X	Y
1 Cahill	?	?	Y	-	N	Y
6 Dwyer	Y	N	Y	N	N	Y
5 Frelinghuysen	N	N	Y	?	-	✓
7 Widnall	X	N	Y	N	N	Y
NEW MEXICO						
AL Morris	Y	N	N	N	Y	Y
AL Walker	Y	Y	N	N	Y	Y
NEW YORK						
27 Dow	Y	Y	Y	N	N	Y
41 Dulski	Y	X	Y	N	N	-
34 Hanley	Y	N	Y	N	N	Y
39 McCarthy	Y	N	Y	N	N	?
29 O'Brien	Y	Y	‡	N	N	Y
25 Ottinger	Y	N	Y	N	N	‡
1 Pike	Y	N	Y	N	Y	Y
28 Resnick	Y	Y	Y	N	N	Y
35 Stratton	Y	N	Y	N	N	N
5 Tenzer	Y	Y	Y	N	N	Y
3 Wolff	Y	N	Y	N	Y	Y
37 Conable	N	N	Y	N	Y	N
38 Goodell	N	N	Y	Y	-	N
2 Grover	N	N	Y	N	Y	N
36 Horton	Y	N	Y	N	X	Y
30 King	N	X	Y	Y	Y	N
31 McEwen	N	N	Y	Y	?	N
32 Pirnie	Y	N	Y	-	Y	N
26 Reid	Y	N	Y	N	N	Y
33 Robison	N	N	Y	Y	Y	N
40 Smith	N	N	Y	?	N	?
4 Wydler	N	N	Y	N	Y	?
New York City						
7 Addabbo	Y	N	Y	N	N	Y
23 Bingham	Y	Y	Y	N	N	Y
15 Carey	Y	N	Y	N	Y	Y
10 Celler	Y	Y	Y	N	N	✓
9 Delaney	Y	Y	Y	N	Y	Y
19 Farbstein	Y	Y	Y	N	N	Y
22 Gilbert	Y	Y	Y	N	N	Y
12 Kelly	Y	Y	Y	N	Y	Y
11 Keogh	✓	Y	Y	N	X	Y
13 Multer	Y	Y	Y	N	N	Y
16 Murphy	Y	Y	Y	N	N	Y
18 Powell	Y	Y	Y	N	N	Y
14 Rooney	Y	Y	Y	N	N	Y
8 Rosenthal	Y	Y	Y	N	N	Y
20 Ryan	Y	-	Y	N	N	Y
21 Scheuer	Y	Y	Y	N	N	Y
24 Fino	Y	X	Y	N	Y	‡
6 Halpern	Y	N	Y	N	N	Y
17 Lindsay	Y	X	Y	?	?	✓
NORTH CAROLINA						
1 Bonner	X	✓	X	?	Y	X
4 Cooley	N	Y	N	Y	Y	N
2 Fountain	N	Y	N	Y	Y	N
3 Henderson	N	Y	N	Y	Y	N
6 Kornegay	N	✓	X	N	Y	Y
7 Lennon	N	Y	N	Y	Y	X
5 Scott	N	✓	N	N	?	Y
11 Taylor	N	Y	N	Y	Y	Y
10 Whitener	N	Y	N	Y	Y	N
9 Broyhill	N	Y	N	Y	Y	N
8 Jonas	N	✓	N	Y	Y	N
NORTH DAKOTA						
2 Redlin	Y	Y	Y	N	N	Y
1 Andrews	N	Y	Y	N	Y	N
OHIO						
9 Ashley	Y	Y	Y	N	N	Y
20 Feighan	Y	N	Y	N	N	Y
1 Gilligan	Y	Y	Y	N	N	✓
18 Hays	Y	Y	Y	N	Y	Y
19 Kirwan	Y	Y	Y	N	Y	Y
3 Love	Y	Y	Y	N	Y	Y
10 Moeller	Y	Y	Y	N	Y	Y
15 Secrest	Y	Y	N	N	Y	Y
AL Sweeney	Y	Y	Y	N	Y	Y
21 Vanik	Y	N	Y	N	N	Y
17 Ashbrook	N	N	Y	Y	Y	N
14 Ayres	Y	N	Y	N	Y	Y
8 Betts	N	N	Y	Y	Y	N
22 Bolton	N	N	Y	?	?	?
16 Bow	?	N	Y	Y	Y	N
7 Brown†	N	X				
2 Clancy	N	N	Y	Y	Y	N
12 Devine	N	N	Y	Y	Y	N
6 Harsha	N	N	N	Y	Y	N
5 Latta	N	N	Y	N	Y	N
4 McCulloch	N	N	Y	Y	Y	N
23 Minshall	N	X	Y	Y	Y	Y
13 Mosher	Y	N	Y	N	N	N
11 Stanton	Y	N	Y	Y	Y	N
OKLAHOMA						
3 Albert	Y	Y	Y	N	N	Y
2 Edmondson	Y	Y	Y	N	N	Y
5 Jarman	N	N	Y	Y	Y	Y
6 Johnson	Y	Y	Y	N	?	Y
4 Steed	Y	Y	N	N	Y	Y
1 Belcher	N	N	N	Y	Y	N
OREGON						
4 Duncan	Y	Y	Y	Y	Y	N
3 Green	N	N	Y	N	N	N
2 Ullman	Y	Y	Y	N	Y	N
1 Wyatt	N	N	Y	N	Y	X
PENNSYLVANIA						
25 Clark	Y	Y	Y	N	Y	Y
19 Craley	Y	Y	Y	N	Y	Y
21 Dent	Y	N	Y	N	Y	Y
11 Flood	Y	Y	Y	N	N	Y
20 Holland	Y	‡	✓	-	N	‡
14 Moorhead	Y	✓	Y	N	N	Y
26 Morgan	Y	Y	Y	N	N	Y
6 Rhodes	Y	Y	Y	N	N	Y
15 Rooney	Y	Y	Y	N	N	Y
24 Vigorito	Y	Y	Y	N	N	N
18 Corbett	Y	N	Y	N	N	Y
8 Curtin	N	N	Y	N	Y	N
9 Dague	N	N	Y	N	Y	N
27 Fulton	Y	N	Y	N	N	Y
23 Johnson	N	X	Y	Y	Y	N
16 Kunkel	Y	N	Y	N	Y	?
10 McDade	Y	N	Y	N	Y	Y
22 Saylor	Y	N	Y	N	✓	N
17 Schneebeli	N	N	Y	N	Y	N
13 Schweiker	Y	N	Y	N	N	✓
7 Watkins	N	N	Y	N	Y	Y
12 Whalley	N	N	Y	N	Y	N
Philadelphia City						
1 Barrett	Y	Y	Y	N	N	Y
3 Byrne	Y	Y	Y	N	N	Y
5 Green	Y	Y	Y	N	N	Y
2 Nix	Y	Y	Y	N	N	Y
4 Toll	✓	✓	✓	X	X	✓
RHODE ISLAND						
2 Fogarty	Y	N	Y	N	Y	Y
1 St. Germain	Y	N	Y	N	N	Y
SOUTH CAROLINA						
4 Ashmore	N	Y	N	Y	Y	N
3 Dorn	N	Y	N	Y	Y	Y
5 Gettys	N	Y	N	Y	Y	Y
6 McMillan	N	Y	N	Y	Y	N
1 Rivers	N	Y	N	N	✓	✓
2 Watson	N	Y	N	Y	Y	N
SOUTH DAKOTA						
2 Berry	N	Y	Y	N	Y	N
1 Reifel	N	Y	Y	N	Y	N
TENNESSEE						
6 Anderson	Y	Y	Y	-	N	N
8 Everett	N	N	N	N	Y	Y
4 Evins	N	Y	Y	-	Y	Y
5 Fulton	Y	Y	Y	N	N	Y
9 Grider	Y	Y	Y	N	N	Y
7 Murray	N	Y	N	Y	Y	Y
3 Brock	N	N	Y	Y	Y	?
2 Duncan	N	N	N	Y	Y	N
1 Quillen	N	N	N	Y	Y	N
TEXAS						
3 Beckworth	N	Y	N	N	Y	Y
2 Brooks	Y	Y	Y	N	Y	Y
17 Burleson	N	Y	N	Y	Y	N
5 Cabell	N	Y	✓	Y	Y	-
22 Casey	N	Y	Y	Y	Y	Y
15 De la Garza	N	Y	N	Y	Y	Y
7 Dowdy	N	Y	N	Y	Y	N
21 Fisher	N	Y	N	Y	Y	N
20 Gonzalez	Y	Y	Y	N	N	Y
19 Mahon	N	N	N	N	Y	Y
1 Patman	N	Y	Y	X	?	Y
10 Pickle	N	Y	Y	N	N	Y
11 Poage	N	Y	N	?	Y	Y
AL Pool	N	Y	Y	✓	Y	Y
13 Purcell	N	Y	N	Y	Y	Y
4 Roberts	N	Y	N	Y	Y	Y
18 Rogers	N	Y	X	Y	Y	Y
6 Teague	N	Y	N	N	Y	N
8 Thomas	✓	✓	✓	?	?	?
9 Thompson	Y	Y	Y	?	Y	?
16 White	N	N	N	N	Y	Y
12 Wright	Y	?	Y	?	Y	Y
14 Young	N	Y	Y	N	Y	Y
UTAH						
2 King	Y	Y	Y	N	N	Y
1 Burton	N	N	-	N	Y	N
VERMONT						
AL Stafford	N	N	Y	N	N	Y
VIRGINIA						
4 Abbitt	N	N	N	Y	Y	N
1 Downing	N	N	N	Y	Y	Y
2 Hardy	N	N	N	Y	✓	✓
9 Jennings	N	N	N	N	Y	Y
7 Marsh	N	N	N	Y	Y	N
3 Satterfield	N	N	N	Y	Y	N
8 Smith	N	N	N	Y	Y	N
5 Tuck	N	Y	N	Y	Y	X
10 Broyhill	N	N	Y	Y	Y	Y
6 Poff	N	N	Y	Y	Y	N
WASHINGTON						
7 Adams	Y	Y	Y	N	N	N
5 Foley	Y	Y	Y	N	N	N
3 Hansen	Y	Y	Y	N	‡	Y
6 Hicks	Y	Y	Y	N	Y	Y
2 Meeds	Y	Y	Y	N	N	Y
4 May	N	N	Y	✓	Y	N
1 Pelly	Y	N	Y	N	Y	N
WEST VIRGINIA						
4 Hechler	Y	N	Y	N	N	Y
5 Kee	Y	Y	?	N	N	Y
3 Slack	N	N	Y	N	Y	Y
2 Staggers	Y	N	Y	N	N	Y
1 Moore	N	N	Y	N	Y	‡
WISCONSIN						
2 Kastenmeier	Y	Y	Y	N	N	Y
6 Race	Y	Y	Y	N	N	Y
5 Reuss	Y	Y	Y	N	N	Y
1 Stalbaum	Y	Y	Y	N	N	Y
4 Zablocki	Y	N	Y	N	Y	Y
8 Byrnes	N	N	Y	Y	Y	-
7 Laird	N	N	Y	Y	Y	N
10 O'Konski	Y	?	Y	N	N	N
3 Thomson	N	N	Y	Y	Y	?
9 Davis	N	N	N	Y	Y	N
WYOMING						
AL Roncalio	Y	Y	Y	N	X	N

*Rep. T. Ashton Thompson (D La.) died July 1, 1965.

†Rep. Clarence J. Brown (R Ohio) died Aug. 23, 1965.

Democrats in this type; *Republicans in italics*

Senate Key Votes—89th Congress—1965

1. S 4. Water Quality Act of 1965. Tower (R Texas) substitute for provisions of the Senate version, deleting a directive to the Secretary of Health, Education and Welfare to set federal water quality standards for interstate streams. Rejected 15-62: R 12-13; D 3-49 (ND 0-36; SD 3-13), Jan. 28, 1965. The President did not take a position on the amendment.

2. S 3. Passage of the Appalachia Regional Development Act of 1965, authorizing $840 million for construction of 3,350 miles of roads in the 11-state Appalachian region and $252.4 million for the period ending June 30, 1967, for construction of health facilities, vocational schools, housing and sewage works; land improvement; reclamation of mining areas; development of timber and water resources; and supplements to federal grant-in-aid programs. Passed 62-22: R 11-15; D 51-7 (ND 39-1; SD 12-6), Feb. 1, 1965. A "yea" was a vote supporting the President's position.

3. HR 2362. Passage of the Elementary and Secondary Education Act of 1965, providing: a three-year program of grants to states for allocation to school districts with large numbers of children from low-income families; grants for purchase of books and library materials; funds to improve educational research; and grants to strengthen state departments of education. Passed 73-18: R 18-14; D 55-4 (ND 40-0; SD 15-4), April 9, 1965. A "yea" was a vote supporting the President's position.

4. S 1564. Voting Rights Act of 1965. Kennedy (D Mass.) amendment to prohibit the collection of a poll tax as a condition for registration or voting in state or local elections and to authorize enforcement machinery. Rejected 45-49: R 6-25; D 39-24 (ND 34-9; SD 5-15), May 11, 1965. A "nay" was a vote supporting the President's position.

5. S 1564. Voting Rights Act of 1965. Hart (D Mich.) motion that the Senate invoke cloture (set limits) on debate on the bill. Cloture agreed to (two-thirds majority required) 70-30: R 23-9; D 47-21 (ND 42-4; SD 5-17), May 25, 1965. A "yea" was a vote supporting the President's position.

6. S 1564. Passage of the Voting Rights Act of 1965, suspending the use of literacy tests or similar voter qualification devices in any state or county where 20 percent of the population was non-white and in which such tests or devices were used to qualify registrants seeking to vote in the 1964 general elections, provided less than 50 percent of the voting-age population was registered or voted in the 1964 general election; authorizing the appointment of federal voting examiners to register voters in such states or counties, and also in states or counties where less than 25 percent of the voting-age population of any race or color was registered to vote; and ordering the Attorney General to institute court tests of state poll taxes as discriminatory devices. Passed 77-19: R 30-2; D 47-17 (ND 42-0; SD 5-17), May 26, 1965. A "yea" was a vote supporting the President's position.

Legend:
- **Y** Record Vote For (yea)
- ✓ Paired For.
- ‡ Announced For, CQ Poll For.
- **N** Record Vote Against (nay)
- **X** Paired Against
- – Announced Against, CQ Poll Against.
- ? Absent, General Pair, "Present," Did not announce or answer Poll.

	1	2	3	4	5	6
ALABAMA						
Hill	N	Y	Y	N	N	N
Sparkman	N	Y	Y	N	N	N
ALASKA						
Bartlett	N	Y	Y	Y	Y	Y
Gruening	–	‡	Y	Y	Y	Y
ARIZONA						
Hayden	?	Y	‡	N	N	Y
Fannin	Y	N	N	N	N	Y
ARKANSAS						
Fulbright	N	‡	Y	X	N	N
McClellan	Y	N	Y	N	N	N
CALIFORNIA						
Kuchel	N	Y	Y	Y	Y	Y
Murphy	Y	N	N	N	N	Y
COLORADO						
Allott	–	N	Y	N	Y	Y
Dominick	Y	X	N	N	Y	Y
CONNECTICUT						
Dodd	N	✓	✓	Y	Y	Y
Ribicoff	–	Y	Y	Y	Y	Y
DELAWARE						
Boggs	N	N	Y	Y	Y	Y
Williams	N	N	N	N	Y	Y
FLORIDA						
Holland	N	Y	N	N	N	N
Smathers	–	Y	Y	N	N	N
GEORGIA						
Russell	N	Y	?	X	N	N
Talmadge	Y	‡	Y	N	N	N
HAWAII						
Inouye	N	Y	Y	Y	Y	Y
Fong	N	Y	Y	Y	Y	Y
IDAHO						
Church	N	Y	Y	Y	Y	‡
Jordan	X	N	N	N	Y	Y
ILLINOIS						
Douglas	N	Y	Y	Y	Y	Y
Dirksen	Y	Y	N	Y	Y	Y

	1	2	3	4	5	6
INDIANA						
Bayh	N	Y	Y	Y	Y	Y
Hartke	N	Y	‡	N	Y	Y
IOWA						
Hickenlooper	Y	X	N	N	N	Y
Miller	N	N	Y	N	N	Y
KANSAS						
Carlson	–	N	Y	N	Y	Y
Pearson	X	X	Y	N	Y	Y
KENTUCKY						
Cooper	Y	Y	Y	N	Y	Y
Morton	Y	Y	N	N	Y	Y
LOUISIANA						
Ellender	N	N	Y	N	N	N
Long	N	Y	Y	Y	N	N
MAINE						
Muskie	N	‡	Y	Y	Y	Y
Smith	N	Y	Y	Y	Y	Y
MARYLAND						
Brewster	N	Y	Y	Y	Y	Y
Tydings	N	Y	Y	Y	Y	Y
MASSACHUSETTS						
Kennedy	N	Y	Y	Y	Y	Y
Saltonstall	N	✓	Y	N	Y	Y
MICHIGAN						
Hart	N	Y	Y	Y	Y	Y
McNamara	N	Y	Y	Y	Y	Y
MINNESOTA						
McCarthy	N	‡	Y	N	Y	Y
Mondale	N	Y	Y	Y	Y	Y
MISSISSIPPI						
Eastland	?	N	N	N	N	N
Stennis	N	N	N	N	N	N
MISSOURI						
Long	N	Y	Y	N	Y	Y
Symington	N	Y	✓	✓	Y	Y
MONTANA						
Mansfield	✓	Y	Y	N	Y	Y
Metcalf	–	Y	Y	X	Y	Y

	1	2	3	4	5	6
NEBRASKA						
Curtis	Y	N	N	N	Y	Y
Hruska	✓	N	N	N	Y	Y
NEVADA						
Bible	N	Y	Y	N	N	‡
Cannon	N	Y	Y	Y	N	✓
NEW HAMPSHIRE						
McIntyre	–	Y	Y	Y	Y	Y
Cotton	N	N	Y	N	Y	Y
NEW JERSEY						
Williams	N	Y	Y	Y	Y	Y
Case	N	Y	Y	Y	Y	Y
NEW MEXICO						
Anderson	N	Y	Y	N	Y	Y
Montoya	N	Y	Y	N	Y	Y
NEW YORK						
Kennedy	N	Y	Y	Y	Y	Y
Javits	N	Y	Y	Y	Y	Y
NORTH CAROLINA						
Ervin	N	Y	N	N	N	N
Jordan	N	Y	Y	N	N	N
NORTH DAKOTA						
Burdick	N	Y	Y	Y	Y	Y
Young	N	N	N	N	N	Y
OHIO						
Lausche	N	Y	X	Y	Y	Y
Young	N	Y	Y	Y	Y	Y
OKLAHOMA						
Harris	N	Y	Y	Y	Y	Y
Monroney	–	Y	Y	N	Y	Y
OREGON						
Morse	N	Y	Y	Y	Y	Y
Neuberger	N	Y	‡	Y	Y	Y
PENNSYLVANIA						
Clark	N	Y	Y	Y	Y	Y
Scott	N	✓	Y	✓	Y	Y
RHODE ISLAND						
Pastore	N	Y	Y	Y	Y	Y
Pell	N	Y	Y	Y	Y	Y

	1	2	3	4	5	6
SOUTH CAROLINA						
Russell*				N	N	N
Thurmond	✓	N	N	N	N	N
SOUTH DAKOTA						
McGovern	–	Y	Y	✓	Y	Y
Mundt	Y	N	Y	N	Y	Y
TENNESSEE						
Bass	N	Y	Y	Y	Y	Y
Gore	N	Y	Y	Y	Y	Y
TEXAS						
Yarborough	–	‡	Y	Y	Y	Y
Tower	Y	N	N	N	N	N
UTAH						
Moss	–	‡	Y	Y	Y	Y
Bennett	Y	Y	N	N	Y	Y
VERMONT						
Aiken	N	Y	Y	N	Y	Y
Prouty	?	Y	Y	N	Y	Y
VIRGINIA						
Byrd	–	N	N	N	N	N
Robertson	Y	N	X	N	N	N
WASHINGTON						
Jackson	X	‡	Y	Y	Y	Y
Magnuson	–	Y	Y	Y	Y	Y
WEST VIRGINIA						
Byrd	N	Y	N	N	N	X
Randolph	N	Y	Y	Y	Y	Y
WISCONSIN						
Nelson	N	Y	Y	Y	Y	Y
Proxmire	N	N	Y	Y	Y	Y
WYOMING						
McGee	N	Y	Y	Y	Y	Y
Simpson	Y	X	N	N	N	Y

Sen. Olin D. Johnston (D S.C.) died April 18, 1965. Sen. Donald S. Russell (D S.C.) was sworn in April 23, 1965.

Democrats in this type; *Republicans in italics*

Senate Key Votes—89th Congress—1965

7. S 1837. Foreign Assistance Act of 1965. Church (D Idaho) amendment to reduce the fiscal 1966 and fiscal 1967 authorizations for foreign military assistance by $115 million each year, to an annual authorization of $1,055,000,000. Rejected 38-43: R 10-18; D 28-25 (ND 21-17; SD 7-8), June 11, 1965. A "nay" was a vote supporting the President's position.

8. S J Res 1. Presidential Continuity. Adoption of the conference report on the bill proposing a constitutional amendment to permit the Vice President to become Acting President if the President were unable to perform his duties, and to provide for filling a vacancy in the office of Vice President. Adopted (two-thirds majority required) 68-5: R 21-1; D 47-4 (ND 31-3; SD 16-1), July 6, 1965. A "yea" was a vote supporting the President's position.

9. HR 6675. Social Security Amendments of 1965. Curtis (R Neb.) amendment to delete the compulsory hospital insurance plan for persons 65 or older, financed by a payroll tax, and the voluntary, supplementary health insurance plan for persons in the same age group, financed by general revenues and by contributions from participants. Rejected 26-64: R 18-11; D 8-53 (ND 0-43; SD 8-10), July 9, 1965. A "nay" was a vote supporting the President's position.

10. HR 6675. Passage of the Social Security Amendments of 1965, providing a basic compulsory hospital insurance program for the aged financed primarily by a payroll tax and a supplementary, voluntary health insurance program financed by general revenue and contributions from participants; increasing Social Security cash benefits; and expanding the Kerr-Mills health program, child health care programs and other federal-state public assistance programs. Passed 68-21: R 13-14; D 55-7 (ND 43-0; SD 12-7), July 9, 1965. A "yea" was a vote supporting the President's position.

11. S 2213. Housing and Urban Development Act of 1965. Tower (R Texas) amendment to delete a provision authorizing a program of rent supplements for low-income families. Rejected 40-47: R 24-5; D 16-42 (ND 6-35; SD 10-7), July 15, 1965. A "nay" was a vote supporting the President's position.

12. S J Res 66. State Legislative Apportionment. Passage of the bill proposing a constitutional amendment, sponsored by Dirksen (R Ill.), to permit one house of a state legislature to be apportioned on the basis of geography and political subdivisions as well as on the basis of population. Rejected (two-thirds majority required) 57-39: R 29-3; D 28-36 (ND 10-33; SD 18-3), Aug. 4, 1965. With 96 Senators voting, 64 votes were needed for passage. The President did not take a position on the amendment.

Legend:
Y Record Vote For (yea)
✓ Paired For.
‡ Announced For, CQ Poll For.
N Record Vote Against (nay)
X Paired Against
– Announced Against, CQ Poll Against.
? Absent, General Pair, "Present," Did not announce or answer Poll

State / Senator	7	8	9	10	11	12
ALABAMA						
Hill	N	Y	N	Y	Y	Y
Sparkman	-	Y	N	Y	X	Y
ALASKA						
Bartlett	Y	‡	N	Y	N	Y
Gruening	Y	Y	N	Y	X	Y
ARIZONA						
Hayden	-	Y	N	Y	N	-
Fannin	N	Y	Y	N	Y	Y
ARKANSAS						
Fulbright	Y	?	?	✓	N	Y
McClellan	‡	Y	N	Y	✓	Y
CALIFORNIA						
Kuchel	N	Y	N	Y	N	Y
Murphy	-	‡	Y	N	Y	Y
COLORADO						
Allott	Y	Y	Y	N	Y	Y
Dominick	N	‡	Y	N	Y	Y
CONNECTICUT						
Dodd	N	Y	N	Y	N	N
Ribicoff	N	Y	N	Y	N	N
DELAWARE						
Boggs	N	Y	N	Y	Y	N
Williams	Y	Y	Y	N	Y	Y
FLORIDA						
Holland	N	Y	Y	N	Y	Y
Smathers	N	Y	N	Y	X	Y
GEORGIA						
Russell	?	Y	N	‡	Y	Y
Talmadge	‡	Y	N	Y	✓	Y
HAWAII						
Inouye	N	Y	N	Y	N	N
Fong	-	‡	N	Y	Y	Y
IDAHO						
Church	Y	Y	N	Y	X	Y
Jordan	N	Y	Y	N	✓	Y
ILLINOIS						
Douglas	Y	Y	N	Y	N	N
Dirksen	N	Y	?	✓	Y	Y
INDIANA						
Bayh	Y	Y	N	Y	N	N
Hartke	?	✓	N	Y	N	N
IOWA						
Hickenlooper	N	Y	Y	X	Y	Y
Miller	N	Y	Y	X	Y	Y
KANSAS						
Carlson	Y	‡	N	Y	Y	Y
Pearson	X	Y	Y	X	✓	Y
KENTUCKY						
Cooper	N	Y	N	Y	Y	Y
Morton	N	Y	Y	N	Y	Y
LOUISIANA						
Ellender	Y	✓	✓	X	N	Y
Long	Y	Y	X	Y	N	✓
MAINE						
Muskie	?	Y	N	Y	N	N
Smith	N	Y	N	Y	N	Y
MARYLAND						
Brewster	-	Y	N	Y	N	N
Tydings	N	Y	N	Y	N	N
MASSACHUSETTS						
Kennedy	Y	Y	N	Y	N	N
Saltonstall	Y	‡	X	Y	Y	Y
MICHIGAN						
Hart	Y	Y	N	Y	N	N
McNamara	N	Y	N	Y	N	N
MINNESOTA						
McCarthy	N	N	N	Y	X	X
Mondale	N	N	N	Y	N	N
MISSISSIPPI						
Eastland	N	✓	Y	N	Y	Y
Stennis	N	Y	Y	N	Y	Y
MISSOURI						
Long	?	?	N	Y	N	N
Symington	Y	Y	X	✓	Y	✓
MONTANA						
Mansfield	N	✓	N	✓	X	Y
Metcalf	N	Y	N	Y	N	Y
NEBRASKA						
Curtis	✓	Y	Y	N	Y	Y
Hruska	Y	✓	✓	X	Y	Y
NEVADA						
Bible	Y	‡	N	Y	Y	Y
Cannon	N	✓	N	Y	Y	Y
NEW HAMPSHIRE						
McIntyre	N	Y	N	Y	N	N
Cotton	Y	?	Y	Y	Y	Y
NEW JERSEY						
Williams	N	Y	N	Y	N	N
Case	N	Y	N	Y	N	N
NEW MEXICO						
Anderson	Y	X	N	Y	Y	N
Montoya	Y	X	N	Y	-	N
NEW YORK						
Kennedy	N	Y	N	Y	N	N
Javits	N	Y	N	Y	N	N
NORTH CAROLINA						
Ervin	Y	Y	Y	N	Y	Y
Jordan	N	‡	Y	Y	Y	Y
NORTH DAKOTA						
Burdick	Y	Y	N	Y	N	N
Young	N	Y	N	Y	N	Y
OHIO						
Lausche	-	N	N	Y	Y	Y
Young	Y	Y	N	Y	N	N
OKLAHOMA						
Harris	X	Y	Y	N	N	Y
Monroney	N	Y	N	Y	N	Y
OREGON						
Morse	Y	‡	N	Y	N	N
Neuberger	‡	‡	-	Y	N	N
PENNSYLVANIA						
Clark	Y	Y	N	Y	N	N
Scott	N	Y	N	Y	N	Y
RHODE ISLAND						
Pastore	N	Y	N	Y	N	N
Pell	Y	Y	N	Y	N	N
NEBRASKA						
SOUTH CAROLINA						
Russell	N	Y	Y	Y	Y	Y
Thurmond	N	Y	Y	N	Y	Y
SOUTH DAKOTA						
McGovern	Y	Y	N	Y	N	N
Mundt	N	Y	Y	N	Y	Y
TENNESSEE						
Bass	?	Y	N	Y	N	N
Gore	Y	N	Y	N	Y	N
TEXAS						
Yarborough	Y	Y	N	Y	N	N
Tower	N	N	Y	N	Y	Y
UTAH						
Moss	Y	Y	N	Y	N	N
Bennett	Y	‡	Y	N	Y	Y
VERMONT						
Aiken	Y	‡	N	Y	N	Y
Prouty	Y	Y	N	Y	✓	Y
VIRGINIA						
Byrd	✓	‡	✓	N	✓	Y
Robertson	Y	Y	Y	N	Y	Y
WASHINGTON						
Jackson	N	Y	N	Y	N	N
Magnuson	-	X	N	Y	N	N
WEST VIRGINIA						
Byrd	N	Y	N	Y	N	N
Randolph	Y	‡	N	Y	N	N
WISCONSIN						
Nelson	Y	Y	N	Y	N	N
Proxmire	Y	Y	N	Y	N	N
WYOMING						
McGee	N	Y	-	✓	N	N
Simpson	Y	‡	Y	N	Y	Y

Democrats in this type; *Republicans in italics*

Senate Key Votes—89th Congress—1965

13. HR 8283. Economic Opportunity Amendments of 1965 (anti-poverty funds authorization). Allott (R Colo.) amendment to reduce the fiscal 1966 authorization from $1,650,000,000 to the fiscal 1965 level of $947,500,000, and to establish a joint Congressional committee to study the federal anti-poverty program. Rejected 39-48: R 25-3; D 14-45 (ND 1-38; SD 13-7), Aug. 18, 1965. A "nay" was a vote supporting the President's position.

14. HR 9811. Food and Agriculture Act of 1965. Bass (D Tenn.) amendment to strike from the bill a provision transferring from the Secretary of Labor to the Secretary of Agriculture authority to determine whether foreign farm workers were required by U.S. farmers. Accepted 46-45 (the 46th "yea" vote was cast by Vice President Humphrey to break a 45-45 tie): R 2-28; D 43-17 (ND 36-6; SD 7-11), Sept. 13, 1965. A "yea" was a vote supporting the President's position.

15. HR 9811. Passage of the Food and Agriculture Act of 1965, providing wheat, cotton, wool, dairy, feed grains and rice programs for four years, plus a four-year cropland retirement program. Passed 72-22: R 16-14; D 56-8 (ND 38-5; SD 18-3), Sept. 14, 1965. A "yea" was a vote supporting the President's position.

16. S 2084. Highway Beautification and Scenic Development. Passage of the bill, authorizing $320 million during fiscal 1966-67 for federal-state programs to control or remove billboards and junkyards along federal-aid Interstate and primary highways, and for federal payments to states to cover the costs of landscaping and scenic improvement of all federal-aid highways. Passed 63-14: R 16-8; D 47-6 (ND 38-0; SD 9-6), Sept. 16, 1965. A "yea" was a vote supporting the President's position.

17. HR 2580. Immigration and Nationality Act Amendments. Passage of the bill amending the Immigration and Nationality Act to repeal the national origins quota system, to set an annual quota on all immigration from outside the Western Hemisphere and a quota on all immigration from the Western Hemisphere, and to establish general priorities for the admission of immigrants to the United States. Passed 76-18: R 24-3; D 52-15 (ND 43-2; SD 9-13), Sept. 22, 1965. A "yea" was a vote supporting the President's position.

18. HR 77. Right-to-Work Repeal. Mansfield (D Mont.) motion that the Senate invoke cloture (set limits) on debate on his Oct. 1 motion to make the pending business of the Senate the bill HR 77, for repeal of Section 14(b) of the Taft-Hartley Act (which allowed states to enact laws banning union shop agreements between labor and management). Rejected (two-thirds majority required) 45-47: R 5-26; D 40-21 (ND 36-5; SD 4-16), Oct. 11, 1965. With 92 Senators voting, 62 votes were needed for cloture. A "yea" was a vote supporting the President's position.

Legend:

Y Record Vote For (yea)
✓ Paired For.
‡ Announced For, CQ Poll For.
N Record Vote Against (nay)
X Paired Against
– Announced Against, CQ Poll Against.
? Absent, General Pair, "Present," Did not announce or answer Poll.

	13	14	15	16	17	18
ALABAMA						
Hill	Y	Y	Y	Y	N	N
Sparkman	?	Y	Y	?	N	N
ALASKA						
Bartlett	N	Y	Y	Y	Y	Y
Gruening	N	Y	Y	✓	Y	✓
ARIZONA						
Hayden	N	N	Y	Y	N	N
Fannin	Y	N	Y	Y	Y	N
ARKANSAS						
Fulbright	N	N	Y	?	Y	X
McClellan	Y	N	Y	N	N	N
CALIFORNIA						
Kuchel	Y	N	Y	Y	Y	Y
Murphy	✓	N	Y	Y	Y	N
COLORADO						
Allott	Y	N	Y	N	Y	N
Dominick	Y	N	Y	Y	Y	N
CONNECTICUT						
Dodd	X	N	Y	Y	Y	Y
Ribicoff	N	‡	X	Y	Y	Y
DELAWARE						
Boggs	Y	N	N	✓	Y	N
Williams	Y	N	N	Y	Y	N
FLORIDA						
Holland	Y	N	N	N	N	N
Smathers	?	N	Y	Y	Y	N
GEORGIA						
Russell	Y	N	Y	?	Y	N
Talmadge	Y	?	Y	?	N	N
HAWAII						
Inouye	N	Y	Y	Y	Y	Y
Fong	Y	N	N	Y	Y	N
IDAHO						
Church	–	Y	Y	Y	Y	Y
Jordan	Y	N	N	Y	Y	N
ILLINOIS						
Douglas	N	Y	Y	Y	Y	Y
Dirksen	✓	N	Y	Y	Y	N

	13	14	15	16	17	18
INDIANA						
Bayh	X	Y	N	Y	Y	Y
Hartke	N	Y	Y	‡	Y	Y
IOWA						
Hickenlooper	Y	N	N	N	Y	N
Miller	Y	N	Y	X	✓	Y
KANSAS						
Carlson	Y	N	Y	N	Y	N
Pearson	✓	N	Y	N	Y	N
KENTUCKY						
Cooper	Y	N	Y	Y	N	Y
Morton	Y	N	N	Y	N	Y
LOUISIANA						
Ellender	Y	N	X	X	N	N
Long	N	X	Y	Y	Y	Y
MAINE						
Muskie	N	Y	Y	Y	Y	Y
Smith	Y	N	N	Y	Y	Y
MARYLAND						
Brewster	N	Y	N	Y	Y	✓
Tydings	N	Y	Y	Y	Y	Y
MASSACHUSETTS						
Kennedy	N	Y	Y	Y	Y	Y
Saltonstall	Y	N	N	✓	Y	N
MICHIGAN						
Hart	N	Y	Y	Y	Y	Y
McNamara	N	Y	Y	Y	Y	Y
MINNESOTA						
McCarthy	–	✓	Y	‡	Y	Y
Mondale	N	Y	Y	Y	Y	Y
MISSISSIPPI						
Eastland	Y	N	Y	N	N	N
Stennis	Y	N	Y	N	N	N
MISSOURI						
Long	N	Y	Y	?	Y	Y
Symington	N	Y	Y	Y	Y	Y
MONTANA						
Mansfield	X	Y	Y	Y	Y	Y
Metcalf	N	Y	Y	Y	Y	Y

	13	14	15	16	17	18
NEBRASKA						
Curtis	✓	N	N	X	Y	N
Hruska	Y	N	N	N	Y	N
NEVADA						
Bible	N	Y	Y	Y	Y	N
Cannon	N	Y	N	Y	Y	X
NEW HAMPSHIRE						
McIntyre	N	Y	N	Y	Y	Y
Cotton	Y	N	N	Y	N	N
NEW JERSEY						
Williams	N	Y	‡	Y	Y	Y
Case	N	Y	N	Y	Y	Y
NEW MEXICO						
Anderson	N	?	✓	?	?	✓
Montoya	N	Y	Y	✓	Y	Y
NEW YORK						
Kennedy	N	Y	Y	Y	Y	Y
Javits	N	Y	N	Y	Y	Y
NORTH CAROLINA						
Ervin	Y	N	Y	Y	Y	N
Jordan	Y	Y	Y	Y	N	N
NORTH DAKOTA						
Burdick	N	Y	Y	Y	Y	Y
Young	Y	N	Y	‡	Y	N
OHIO						
Lausche	Y	N	N	Y	N	N
Young	N	Y	Y	‡	Y	✓
OKLAHOMA						
Harris	N	Y	Y	Y	Y	Y
Monroney	N	Y	✓	?	Y	N
OREGON						
Morse	N	N	Y	Y	Y	Y
Neuberger	N	‡	Y	Y	Y	Y
PENNSYLVANIA						
Clark	X	Y	Y	Y	Y	Y
Scott	Y	–	–	✓	‡	‡
RHODE ISLAND						
Pastore	N	Y	Y	Y	Y	Y
Pell	N	Y	Y	Y	Y	Y

	13	14	15	16	17	18
SOUTH CAROLINA						
Russell	Y	?	Y	Y	N	N
Thurmond	Y	N	Y	N	N	N
SOUTH DAKOTA						
McGovern	N	Y	Y	Y	Y	N
Mundt	Y	N	Y	N	Y	N
TENNESSEE						
Bass	N	Y	Y	Y	Y	Y
Gore	N	‡	Y	Y	Y	–
TEXAS						
Yarborough	N	Y	Y	‡	Y	Y
Tower	Y	N	Y	X	X	N
UTAH						
Moss	N	Y	Y	Y	Y	Y
Bennett	Y	–	X	X	X	N
VERMONT						
Aiken	Y	N	Y	Y	Y	N
Prouty	N	N	Y	Y	Y	N
VIRGINIA						
Byrd	Y	N	N	N	N	N
Robertson	Y	N	N	N	N	N
WASHINGTON						
Jackson	N	Y	Y	Y	Y	Y
Magnuson	N	Y	Y	Y	Y	Y
WEST VIRGINIA						
Byrd	N	N	Y	N	N	N
Randolph	N	N	Y	Y	Y	Y
WISCONSIN						
Nelson	N	Y	Y	Y	Y	Y
Proxmire	N	Y	Y	Y	Y	Y
WYOMING						
McGee	–	Y	Y	‡	Y	Y
Simpson	Y	N	N	N	✓	N

Democrats in this type; *Republicans in italics*

HOUSE AND SENATE KEY VOTES FOR 1966

The editors of Congressional Quarterly annually select a series of "key votes" that represent major issues before Congress and also reflect both the mood of Congress and the impact constituent pressures can have on a Member's vote. In 1966 the major issues were Vietnam and the state of the economy; voting on Great Society measures showed the traditional splits between liberal Democrats and the GOP; the surprise issue of the year was auto safety legislation.

House Key Votes

1. VIETNAM. The closest the House came to voting on the Administration's Viet Nam war policy was the March 15 roll call on supplemental funds for defense and military assistance, mostly for conducting the Viet Nam war. The House voted $13,135,719,000 with only three dissents -- from Phillip Burton (D Calif.), John Conyers Jr. (D Mich.) and William F. Ryan (D N.Y.). The vote was 389-3 (D 267-3; R 122-0). The President favored the bill, which became law on March 25.

2. RENT SUPPLEMENTS. In a sharp reversal of form, the House March 29 voted funds for the top-priority but controversial Administration rent supplement program. This "Great Society" program, denied funds in 1965, was to help low-income persons obtain better housing by paying the difference between 25 percent of their income and their rent in standard housing. The House rejected a motion to delete the funds, 190-198 (D 65-192; R 125-6). After a number of changes were made, the bill -- the Second Supplemental Appropriations bill for fiscal 1966 -- became law on May 13. Johnson opposed the motion.

3. OPEN HOUSING. The House came face-to-face with the open housing issue on Aug. 9, when it rejected a motion to delete the provision from the Administration's Civil Rights Act of 1966. The provision barred racial discrimination in the sale or rental of large housing projects and apartments; it exempted individual homeowners and owners of small rooming houses. Though watered-down in the House, the provision could not get through the Senate, which shelved the entire bill Sept. 19. The House vote on the motion to delete open housing, 190-222 (D 104-172; R 86-50). Johnson supported open housing.

4. HIGHWAY BEAUTY. Economy-minded Republicans struck hard at the $493 million authorized for highway beautification in the Administration's billion dollar highway construction bill. They lost by two votes on a motion to delete the funds Aug. 11. The vote was 173-175 (D 60-170; R 113-5), with Johnson opposed. The beautification authorizations for fiscal 1968 and 1969 were deleted from the bill in conference with the Senate.

5. AUTO SAFETY. A sparkling new, chrome-plated issue in Congress was auto safety -- Detroit's responsibilities in building safe cars. With remarkable speed, the Administration fashioned and Congress enacted the Traffic Safety Act of 1966, requiring the Secretary of Commerce to set federal safety performance standards for cars and tires. The House Aug. 17 passed the bill, 371-0, with Johnson in favor. It became law on Sept. 9.

6. TRANSPORTATION DEPARTMENT. A major struggle developed over the Administration's bill to establish a cabinet-level Department of Transportation. One issue was exclusion of the Maritime Administration and its functions from the new Department, a move sought avidly by both labor and management in the maritime industry which preferred to be regulated by a separate agency. The House voted Aug. 30 to exclude the Maritime Administration, 261-117 (D 150-106; R 111-11), in a defeat for the President. This decision was accepted in the final bill.

7. MINIMUM WAGE. A top-priority bill of organized labor raised the current $1.25 an hour minimum wage to $1.60. The House Sept. 7 voted on a motion to return the bill to conference with instructions to delay the effective date of the $1.60 minimum until Feb. 1, 1969, a full year after the date provided by the Senate and by conferees. The House rejected the motion in a traditional conservative coalition vote, 163-183 (ND 11-147; SD 51-18; R 101-18). Johnson opposed the motion.

8. FOREIGN AID. Congress authorized foreign aid appropriations of $3.5 billion, more than the President asked for, but when it came time on Sept. 20 to appropriate funds, the House was of a different mind. It accepted a motion to send the bill back to committee with instructions to make additional cuts totaling 10 percent in economic aid. The motion carried narrowly, 186-183 (D 70-175; R 116-8). The Senate increased the cut and the final appropriation was 15 percent below the Administration's request. Johnson opposed the motion.

9. POVERTY. A frontal assault on the war on poverty program, a bulwark of "Great Society" legislation, was made Sept. 29 in a motion to strike the enacting clause and thus kill the $1.75 billion authorization for fiscal 1967 anti-poverty funds. The House first accepted the motion on a 128-118 teller vote, but Democratic leaders rounded up Members and won the roll-call, 156-208 (D 49-193; R 107-15). Johnson opposed the motion. Both the House and Senate bills authorized $1.75 billion.

10. INVESTMENT CREDIT. With inflationary pressures building in 1966, Congress responded quickly to the President's Sept. 8 requests for legislation to dampen down those pressures. The House Sept. 30 passed a bill to suspend the 7-percent investment tax credit and the two most liberal methods of tax write-off on depreciated business property. The bill was aimed at slowing down business investment. It passed, 221-118 (D 190-37; R 31-81), with President Johnson in favor.

11. DEMONSTRATION CITIES. The President's "demonstration cities" program got through the House on the eve of adjournment after one of the bitterest debates of the session. The "cities" plan, which provided new federal funds for a coordinated attack on blight, was the President's major domestic legislative proposal of the year. After rejecting a GOP recommital motion to scale down the $900 million program to mere planning dimensions, the House Oct. 14 passed the measure, 178-141 (D 162-60; R 16-81).

12. TRADE WITH COMMUNISTS. House Republicans Oct. 18 attacked President Johnson's plans to ease restrictions on trade with European countries behind the iron curtain. The House accepted, on a 167-121 roll call, a GOP motion removing the President's discretionary authority to permit the Export-Import Bank to grant credit to Communist nations for the purchase of U.S. goods. The Senate reinserted the President's authority and the House Oct. 21 yielded on the point.

Senate Key Votes

1. VIETNAM. Debating a bill providing funds for the war in Viet Nam, the Senate took a second look at the 1964 "Gulf of Tonkin" resolution which had given the President broad authority for military action in Viet Nam. Adopted by Congress in August 1964, following attacks on U.S. destroyers in the Gulf, the Tonkin resolution expressed support for "all necessary measures" to repel attack and aggression in Southeast Asia. On March 1, 1966, Wayne Morse (D Ore.), a persistent critic of the war, offered an amendment to repeal the 1964 resolution. In a move billed as a vote of support for the President's policy, the Senate tabled the Morse amendment, 92-5 (D 60-5; R 32-0), with three more Senators opposing the move than had opposed the Tonkin resolution.

2. REAPPORTIONMENT. The Supreme Court's "one-man, one-vote" rule for apportionment of state legislatures came under attack as Senate Minority Leader Everett McKinley Dirksen (R Ill.) proposed a constitutional amendment to permit apportionment on the basis of geography and political subdivisions as well as population. The Senate April 20 repelled the Dirksen forces, 55-38 (D 26-35; R 29-3), seven votes short of the two-thirds majority required. The margin of defeat was identical to that on a similar measure which failed in 1965. Meanwhile, states rapidly were conforming to the Court's rule, and the issue in Congress appeared to die with the 1966 vote. The President, who does not sign proposed constitutional amendments, took no position.

3. RENT SUPPLEMENTS. Funds for rent supplements (*see House Key Vote 2, p. 87*). The motion to delete the funds was defeated, 45-46 (D 19-41; R 26-5), and the appropriations were enacted on May 13. Johnson opposed the motion.

4. TRUTH-IN-PACKAGING. The teeth of the Administration-backed Fair Packaging and Labeling Act were in its provisions authorizing federal officials to establish standard weights and quantities for packaged commodities covered by the bill. The Senate June 8 rejected a move to delete those provisions, 32-53 (D 7-49; R 25-4). Johnson opposed the motion. Industry opposition prevailed in the House, however, where a defanged bill was passed Oct. 3. The House version finally won out.

5. FOREIGN AID. In an unusual action, the Senate voted a major cut in the President's requests for foreign military aid and sales programs July 27. It accepted an amendment chopping $100 million off the authorization bill, 55-37 (D 43-20; R 12-17). Liberal critics of the President's Viet Nam policy and traditional foreign-aid opponents teamed up to make the cut. The Administration asked for $917 million for fiscal 1967; the Senate Foreign Relations Committee reported a $892 million bill and the Senate July 27 cut that to $792 million. The final authorization was for $875 million.

6. AIRLINE STRIKE. In a move bitterly opposed by organized labor, the Senate Aug. 4 passed a bill that required striking machinists to return to work on five major airlines for 30 days and authorized the President to extend the return-to-work order for 150 days. The strike was in its 27th day. The vote was 54-33 (D 30-27; R 24-6). The House was reluctant to vote on the measure, and the

strike ended Aug. 19, in its 42nd day, with a negotiated settlement. The President took no position.

7. JOBLESS BENEFITS. The AFL-CIO long had sought a law establishing federal standards for the amount and duration of state unemployment benefits. Only 18 states had standards which met those in the bill the Senate passed on Aug. 8 by a vote of 53-31 (D 45-11; R 8-20). The House June 24 had passed, almost unanimously, a bill which made no basic changes in the federal-state system. The House opposition to federal standards, despite President Johnson's endorsement of them, was expected to prevail.

8. DEMONSTRATION CITIES. Most of the President's 1966 housing and city development proposals were contained in the Demonstration Cities and Metropolitan Development Act of 1966. Its key feature was the "demonstration cities" grant program; qualifying cities would be paid federal funds for up to 80 percent of local costs of federal grant-in-aid programs in the realm of housing, welfare and urban transport. The Senate Aug. 19 rejected an amendment deleting the initial $900 million for this program, 27-53 (D 10-43; R 17-10). Johnson opposed the amendment. The program barely survived in the House committee, after considerable arm-twisting by the Administration.

9. MINIMUM WAGE. A major floor fight broke out in the Senate Aug. 25 over the timetable for raising the hourly minimum wage from the current $1.25 to $1.60. The House had voted to delay the $1.60 minimum wage until 1969, but the Senate Labor and Public Welfare Committee moved that date up to 1968. A Republican assault on the change was barely repelled, 40-42 (D 19-35; R 21-7). President Johnson favored the 1968 date. The Senate timetable was accepted in conference and became law Sept. 23.

10. CIVIL RIGHTS CLOTURE. Unable to hold all Northern Democrats and faced with heavy defections among Republicans, Majority Leader Mansfield tried Sept. 14 to invoke cloture to choke off a filibuster against the Administration's ill-fated Civil Rights Act of 1966. A major reason for opposition was the bill's open housing feature, at which Republicans as well as Southerners balked. The vote was 54-42 (D 42-21; R 12-21), 10 short of the two-thirds majority necessary to invoke cloture. The House had approved open housing in watered-down form, but after cloture failed, the bill was shelved for the remainder of the session. Johnson was in favor of cloture.

11. SCHOOL PRAYERS. In the first Congressional vote on the issue since the Supreme Court in 1962 barred the use of state-sponsored prayers in public schools, the Senate Sept. 21 voted not to amend the Constitution to permit local authorities to provide for voluntary prayers. Needing a two-thirds majority, the constitutional amendment sponsored by Sen. Dirksen fell nine votes short on a 49-37 roll call. Johnson took no position.

12. CAMPAIGN FUND. In a surprise action, the Senate Finance Committee added to an unrelated tax bill provisions to finance Presidential election campaigns by permitting taxpayers to check off $1 of their annual income tax payments for the fund. The proposal was sponsored by Committee Chairman Long (D La.). An attempt to delete it was defeated by the Senate on a 33-39 vote Oct. 12. The House accepted the plan. Johnson took no position at the time but later endorsed it.

House Key Votes—89th Congress—1966

1. HR 13546. Passage of the bill to make fiscal 1966 supplemental appropriations of $13,135,719,000 for the Defense Department and for military and economic assistance, primarily in support of U.S. operations in Southeast Asia. Passed 389-3: R 122-0; D 267-3 (ND 178-3; SD 89-0), March 15, 1966. A "yea" was a vote supporting the President's position.

2. HR 14012. Second Supplemental Appropriations bill for fiscal 1966. Bow (R Ohio) motion to recommit the bill to the Appropriations Committee with instructions to delete a section providing $12 million in contractual authority for rent supplements and $100,000 in appropriations for payments under the contracts during fiscal 1966. Motion rejected 190-198: R 125-6; D 65-192 (ND 17-160; SD 48-32), March 29, 1966. A "nay" was a vote supporting the President's position.

3. HR 14765. Civil Rights Act of 1966, to bar discrimination in the selection of jurors and in the sale and rental of some housing and to protect Negroes and civil rights workers. Moore (R W. Va.) motion to recommit the bill to the Judiciary Committee with instructions to delete Title IV, the open housing section. Rejected 190-222: R 86-50; D 104-172 (ND 24-160; SD 80-12), Aug. 9, 1966. A "nay" was a vote supporting the President's position.

4. HR 14359. Federal-Aid Highway Act of 1966, authorizing $3 billion in fiscal 1968-69 appropriations for federal aid highway construction and beautification and $20.8 billion in fiscal 1968-72 appropriations for construction of the national Interstate Highway System. Ford (R Mich.) motion to recommit the bill with instructions to delete authorization of $493 million in fiscal 1968-69 appropriations for highway beautification. Rejected 173-175: R 114-4; D 59-171 (ND 24-128; SD 35-43), Aug. 11, 1966. A "nay" was a vote supporting the President's position.

5. HR 13228. Passage of the Traffic Safety Act of 1966 to require the Secretary of Commerce to establish federal safety performance standards for motor vehicles and tires. Passed 371-0: R 125-0; D 246-0 (ND 162-0; SD 84-0), Aug. 17, 1966. A "yea" was a vote supporting the President's position.

6. HR 15963. Establish a Cabinet-level Department of Transportation bringing together major federal agencies and functions involving promotion and safety in all sectors of transportation in the U.S. Garmatz (D Md.) amendment to exclude the Maritime Administration and its functions from the Department. Accepted 261-117: R 111-11; D 150-106 (ND 102-70; SD 48-36), Aug. 30, 1966. A "nay" was a vote supporting the President's position.

- KEY -

Y Record Vote For (yea).
✓ Paired For.
‡ Announced For CQ Poll For.
N Record Vote Against (nay).
X Paired Against.
- Announced Against. CQ Poll Against.
? Absent, General Pair, "Present." Did not announce or answer Poll

	1	2	3	4	5	6
ALABAMA						
3 Andrews	Y	Y	✓	?	Y	Y
8 Jones	Y	Y	Y	N	Y	N
5 Selden	Y	Y	Y	Y	Y	Y
4 Andrews	Y	Y	Y	Y	?	Y
6 Buchanan	Y	Y	Y	Y	Y	Y
2 Dickinson	Y	Y	Y	Y	?	Y
1 Edwards	Y	Y	Y	Y	Y	Y
7 Martin	‡	Y	Y	?	?	Y
ALASKA						
AL Rivers	Y	N	N	?	?	N
ARIZONA						
3 Senner	Y	?	N	?	?	?
2 Udall	Y	N	N	N	Y	N
1 Rhodes	Y	Y	Y	?	Y	Y
ARKANSAS						
1 Gathings	Y	Y	Y	Y	Y	N
4 Vacancy						
2 Mills	Y	?	Y	N	Y	N
3 Trimble	Y	N	Y	?	Y	N
CALIFORNIA						
5 Burton	N	N	N	Y	Y	Y
7 Cohelan	Y	N	N	?	?	?
33 Dyal	Y	N	N	N	Y	N
9 Edwards	Y	N	X	N	Y	-
18 Hagen	‡	Y	N	Y	Y	N
34 Hanna	Y	X	✓	N	Y	N
2 Johnson	Y	N	N	N	Y	N
4 Leggett	Y	X	N	N	Y	Y
15 McFall	Y	N	N	N	Y	N
8 Miller	Y	N	N	N	Y	Y
3 Moss	Y	N	N	N	Y	N
16 Sisk	?	N	N	N	N	N
38 Tunney	Y	✓	✓	Y	Y	Y
37 Van Deerlin	Y	N	X	-	Y	-
14 Waldie*			N	N	Y	Y
1 Clausen	Y	Y	Y	Y	Y	Y
10 Gubser	Y	Y	Y	?	Y	Y
6 Mailliard	Y	‡	N	Y	Y	Y
12 Talcott	Y	Y	Y	Y	Y	Y
13 Teague	Y	Y	Y	Y	Y	‡
35 Utt	Y	Y	Y	X	-	
36 Wilson	Y	Y	Y	‡	‡	Y
11 Younger	Y	Y	Y	✓	✓	Y

	1	2	3	4	5	6
Los Angeles Co.						
29 Brown	-	N	N	N	‡	N
25 Cameron	Y	X	Y	‡	‡	N
22 Corman	Y	N	N	?	?	?
21 Hawkins	Y	N	X	-	‡	Y
19 Holifield	Y	N	N	N	Y	N
17 King	Y	N	N	N	Y	N
26 Rees	Y	N	N	-	‡	N
30 Roybal	Y	N	N	N	Y	N
31 Wilson	Y	N	-	?	Y	
28 Bell	?	Y	N	Y	Y	Y
23 Clawson	?	Y	Y	Y	Y	Y
32 Hosmer	Y	Y	Y	Y	Y	‡
24 Lipscomb	Y	Y	Y	Y	Y	Y
27 Reinecke	‡	Y	Y	‡	Y	✓
20 Smith	Y	Y	Y	Y	Y	Y
COLORADO						
4 Aspinall	Y	N	Y	N	Y	Y
3 Evans	Y	N	N	Y	?	?
2 McVicker	‡	N	Y	N	Y	N
1 Rogers	Y	N	N	N	Y	‡
CONNECTICUT						
1 Daddario	Y	N	N	N	Y	N
3 Giaimo	Y	N	N	N	Y	Y
6 Grabowski	Y	N	N	N	Y	Y
4 Irwin	Y	N	N	N	Y	Y
5 Monagan	Y	N	N	Y	Y	N
2 St. Onge	Y	N	N	N	Y	Y
DELAWARE						
AL McDowell	Y	N	N	Y	N	N
FLORIDA						
2 Bennett	Y	Y	Y	Y	Y	Y
4 Fascell	Y	N	N	N	Y	N
9 Fuqua	‡	‡	Y	Y	Y	N
10 Gibbons	Y	N	N	N	Y	N
7 Haley	Y	Y	Y	Y	Y	Y
5 Herlong	Y	Y	‡	Y	Y	Y
8 Matthews	‡	✓	Y	N	Y	N
3 Pepper	Y	N	N	‡	Y	N
6 Rogers	Y	Y	Y	N	Y	Y
1 Sikes	Y	Y	Y	N	Y	N
12 Cramer	Y	Y	Y	Y	Y	Y
11 Gurney	Y	Y	Y	Y	Y	Y

	1	2	3	4	5	6
GEORGIA						
7 Davis	‡	Y	Y	‡	‡	Y
6 Flynt	Y	Y	Y	Y	‡	Y
1 Hagan	Y	Y	Y	?	?	?
9 Landrum	Y	N	?	Y	?	?
4 Mackay	‡	N	Y	N	Y	N
2 O'Neal	Y	Y	Y	Y	Y	N
10 Stephens	Y	N	Y	?	N	Y
8 Tuten	Y	N	Y	?	?	?
5 Weltner	Y	N	?	Y	X	
3 Callaway	Y	Y	Y	Y	‡	?
HAWAII						
AL Matsunaga	Y	N	N	N	Y	Y
AL Mink	Y	N	N	N	‡	✓
IDAHO						
1 White	Y	Y	N	‡	‡	Y
2 Hansen	Y	Y	Y	Y	Y	Y
ILLINOIS						
21 Gray	Y	N	Y	N	Y	Y
24 Price	‡	N	N	N	Y	N
19 Schisler	Y	N	N	?	Y	Y
23 Shipley	Y	N	N	N	Y	Y
16 Anderson	Y	Y	Y	Y	Y	Y
17 Arends	Y	Y	Y	Y	Y	Y
14 Erlenborn	Y	Y	Y	Y	Y	Y
20 Findley	Y	Y	Y	?	Y	Y
12 McClory	Y	Y	Y	Y	Y	Y
18 Michel	Y	Y	N	‡	Y	N
15 Reid	Y	Y	Y	Y	Y	Y
22 Springer	Y	Y	N	Y	N	N
Chicago--Cook Co.						
7 Annunzio	Y	N	N	N	Y	X
1 Dawson	Y	N	?	N	Y	N
5 Kluczynski	Y	N	N	N	Y	N
3 Murphy	Y	N	N	N	Y	✓
2 O'Hara	Y	N	N	N	Y	N
11 Pucinski	Y	N	N	N	Y	N
6 Ronan	Y	N	N	N	Y	N
8 Rostenkowski	Y	N	N	N	‡	Y
9 Yates	Y	N	N	N	Y	Y
10 Collier	‡	Y	Y	Y	N	N
4 Derwinski	Y	Y	Y	Y	Y	Y
13 Rumsfeld	Y	N	Y	Y	Y	Y

	1	2	3	4	5	6
INDIANA						
3 Brademas	Y	N	N	-	Y	N
8 Denton	Y	N	N	N	Y	N
9 Hamilton	Y	N	N	N	Y	N
11 Jacobs	Y	N	N	N	Y	N
1 Madden	Y	N	N	N	Y	N
5 Roush	Y	N	N	Y	Y	N
4 Adair	?	Y	Y	Y	Y	?
7 Bray	Y	Y	Y	Y	Y	N
2 Halleck	?	Y	Y	?	Y	Y
10 Harvey	‡	Y	Y	‡	Y	Y
6 Roudebush	?	Y	Y	‡	Y	Y
IOWA						
4 Bandstra	Y	N	N	‡	Y	N
2 Culver	Y	N	N	N	Y	N
6 Greigg	Y	N	?	?	Y	N
7 Hansen	Y	N	N	N	Y	N
1 Schmidhauser	Y	N	N	N	Y	N
5 Smith	Y	-	N	Y	Y	N
3 Gross	Y	Y	Y	Y	Y	Y
KANSAS						
1 Dole	Y	Y	Y	Y	Y	Y
3 Ellsworth	‡	Y	Y	Y	Y	Y
4 Shriver	Y	Y	Y	Y	Y	Y
2 Mize	Y	Y	Y	Y	Y	Y
5 Skubitz	Y	Y	Y	?	Y	Y
KENTUCKY						
4 Chelf	Y	‡	N	N	Y	Y
3 Farnsley	Y	N	N	N	Y	Y
2 Natcher	Y	Y	N	Y	Y	Y

	1	2	3	4	5	6
7 Perkins	Y	N	N	N	Y	Y
1 Stubblefield	Y	Y	Y	N	Y	Y
6 Watts	Y	Y	Y	N	Y	N
5 Carter	Y	‡	Y	Y	Y	Y
LOUISIANA						
2 Boggs	Y	N	Y	?	Y	Y
1 Hebert	Y	Y	Y	?	?	✓
8 Long, S.O.	Y	Y	Y	‡	‡	N
6 Morrison	Y	N	?	?	?	✓
5 Passman	Y	Y	Y	‡	Y	Y
7 Edwards	Y	N	✓	‡	‡	Y
4 Waggonner	Y	Y	Y	N	Y	Y
3 Willis	?	?	✓	?	?	N
MAINE						
2 Hathaway	Y	N	N	N	Y	Y
1 Tupper	Y	N	N	?	?	Y
MARYLAND						
4 Fallon	Y	X	Y	N	Y	Y
7 Friedel	Y	N	N	N	Y	Y
3 Garmatz	Y	X	Y	N	‡	Y
2 Long	Y	N	N	N	Y	Y
5 Machen	Y	N	Y	N	Y	Y
AL Sickles	Y	N	N	?	Y	Y
6 Mathias	‡	Y	N	?	Y	Y
1 Morton	Y	Y	Y	Y	Y	Y
MASSACHUSETTS						
2 Boland	Y	N	N	-	Y	Y
11 Burke	Y	N	N	N	Y	Y
4 Donohue	Y	N	N	?	Y	Y
7 Macdonald	Y	N	N	N	Y	Y
9 McCormack						
8 O'Neill	Y	N	N	N	Y	✓
3 Philbin	Y	N	N	-	Y	Y
6 Bates	Y	Y	N	Y	Y	Y
1 Conte	Y	✓	N	Y	Y	Y
12 Keith	Y	Y	N	Y	Y	Y
10 Martin	?	?	N	?	?	Y
5 Morse	Y	Y	N	‡	Y	Y
MICHIGAN						
11 Clevenger	Y	N	N	N	Y	Y
19 Farnum	Y	N	N	‡	Y	N
7 Mackie	Y	N	N	N	Y	Y
12 O'Hara	Y	N	N	-	Y	Y
3 Todd	Y	‡	N	N	Y	N
2 Vivian	Y	N	N	N	Y	N
18 Broomfield	Y	Y	Y	Y	Y	Y
10 Cederberg	Y	Y	Y	Y	Y	Y
6 Chamberlain	Y	Y	Y	Y	Y	Y
5 Ford	Y	Y	Y	Y	‡	Y
9 Griffin *	Y	Y				
8 Harvey	Y	N	N	Y	Y	Y
4 Hutchinson	Y	Y	Y	Y	Y	Y
Detroit--Wayne Co.						
1 Conyers	N	N	N	?	?	N
13 Diggs	Y	N	N	?	?	N
16 Dingell	Y	N	N	N	Y	Y
15 Ford	Y	N	N	N	Y	Y
17 Griffiths	Y	N	N	N	Y	Y
14 Nedzi	Y	N	N	-	Y	N
MINNESOTA						
8 Blatnik	Y	N	X	N	Y	?
5 Fraser	Y	N	X	N	Y	N
4 Karth	Y	N	N	‡	Y	Y
6 Olson	Y	Y	N	N	Y	N
7 Langen	Y	Y	Y	Y	Y	Y
3 MacGregor	Y	‡	N	Y	Y	Y
2 Nelsen	Y	Y	Y	Y	Y	N
1 Quie	Y	Y	N	Y	Y	Y
MISSISSIPPI						
1 Abernethy	Y	Y	Y	Y	Y	Y
5 Colmer	Y	✓	Y	Y	Y	Y
2 Whitten	Y	Y	Y	N	Y	Y
3 Williams	Y	Y	✓	Y	‡	Y
4 Walker	?	Y	Y	Y	?	?
MISSOURI						
5 Bolling	‡	N	N	-	‡	N
6 Hull	Y	Y	Y	N	Y	Y
9 Hungate	Y	N	Y	‡	Y	Y
8 Ichord	Y	Y	Y	Y	Y	N
10 Jones	Y	Y	Y	‡	Y	N
1 Karsten	Y	N	N	N	Y	Y
4 Randall	Y	Y	Y	Y	Y	Y
3 Sullivan	Y	N	N	N	Y	Y
2 Curtis	Y	Y	Y	Y	Y	Y
7 Hall	Y	Y	Y	Y	Y	Y
MONTANA						
1 Olsen	Y	N	N	N	Y	Y
2 Battin	Y	‡	Y	Y	Y	‡
NEBRASKA						
1 Callan	Y	N	N	‡	Y	N
2 Cunningham	Y	Y	N	N	Y	X
3 Martin	Y	Y	Y	?	Y	Y
NEVADA						
AL Baring	‡	Y	Y	‡	‡	‡
NEW HAMPSHIRE						
1 Huot	Y	N	N	Y	Y	Y
2 Cleveland	Y	Y	N	Y	Y	N
NEW JERSEY						
14 Daniels	Y	N	N	N	Y	Y
13 Gallagher	‡	N	N	N	Y	?
9 Helstoski	Y	N	N	N	Y	Y
3 Howard	Y	N	N	N	‡	Y
8 Joelson	Y	N	N	N	Y	Y
12 Krebs	Y	N	N	-	Y	‡
11 Minish	Y	N	N	N	Y	Y
2 McGrath	Y	N	N	N	Y	Y
15 Patten	Y	N	N	N	Y	Y
10 Rodino	Y	N	N	N	Y	Y
4 Thompson	Y	N	N	N	‡	Y
1 Cahill	Y	Y	N	Y	Y	Y
6 Dwyer	Y	Y	N	Y	Y	Y
5 Frelinghuysen	Y	Y	N	Y	Y	Y
7 Widnall	Y	Y	N	Y	Y	Y
NEW MEXICO						
AL Morris	Y	N	Y	N	?	N
AL Walker	Y	N	Y	?	Y	N
NEW YORK						
27 Dow	Y	N	N	N	Y	N
41 Dulski	Y	N	N	Y	Y	Y
34 Hanley	Y	N	N	N	Y	Y
39 McCarthy	Y	Y	N	N	Y	Y
29 O'Brien	Y	X	N	Y	Y	Y
25 Ottinger	Y	N	N	N	Y	X
1 Pike	Y	✓	N	N	Y	Y
28 Resnick	‡	N	N	N	Y	X
35 Stratton	Y	Y	N	Y	Y	N
5 Tenzer	Y	N	N	N	Y	Y
3 Wolff	Y	N	N	Y	Y	Y
37 Conable	Y	Y	N	Y	Y	Y
38 Goodell	‡	Y	N	Y	Y	Y
2 Grover	Y	Y	N	Y	Y	‡
36 Horton	Y	N	N	Y	Y	✓
30 King	Y	Y	?	?	?	?
31 McEwen	Y	Y	Y	Y	Y	?
32 Pirnie	Y	Y	N	Y	Y	Y
26 Reid	Y	N	N	Y	Y	N
33 Robison	Y	Y	N	Y	Y	Y
40 Smith	Y	‡	N	Y	Y	Y
4 Wydler	Y	Y	N	Y	Y	Y
New York City						
7 Addabbo	Y	N	N	N	Y	Y
23 Bingham	Y	N	N	N	Y	N
15 Carey	Y	N	N	?	Y	Y
10 Celler	Y	N	N	?	?	Y
9 Delaney	Y	N	N	?	Y	Y
19 Farbstein	Y	N	N	N	Y	Y
22 Gilbert	Y	N	N	N	Y	Y
12 Kelly	Y	N	N	N	Y	Y
11 Keogh	Y	X	N	-	Y	✓
13 Multer	Y	N	N	N	Y	Y
16 Murphy	Y	N	X	N	Y	Y
18 Powell	?	N	X	?	?	Y
14 Rooney	Y	X	N	N	Y	Y
8 Rosenthal	Y	N	N	N	?	Y
20 Ryan	N	N	N	N	Y	Y
21 Scheuer	Y	N	N	N	Y	N
24 Fino	Y	Y	N	Y	Y	Y
6 Halpern	Y	N	N	Y	Y	Y
17 Kupferman	Y	N	N	?	Y	Y
NORTH CAROLINA						
1 Jones	Y	✓	Y	Y	Y	Y
4 Cooley	Y	Y	Y	Y	Y	Y
2 Fountain	Y	Y	Y	Y	Y	Y
3 Henderson	Y	Y	Y	Y	Y	Y
6 Kornegay	Y	Y	Y	Y	Y	Y
7 Lennon	Y	Y	Y	Y	Y	Y
5 Scott	Y	✓	Y	?	?	X
11 Taylor	Y	Y	Y	N	Y	Y
10 Whitener	Y	Y	Y	Y	Y	Y
9 Broyhill	Y	Y	Y	Y	Y	N
8 Jonas	Y	Y	Y	Y	Y	N
NORTH DAKOTA						
2 Redlin	Y	N	N	N	Y	N
1 Andrews	Y	Y	Y	Y	Y	Y
OHIO						
9 Ashley	Y	N	N	-	Y	N
20 Feighan	Y	N	N	N	Y	Y
1 Gilligan	Y	N	N	N	Y	Y
18 Hays	Y	X	Y	N	Y	N
19 Kirwan	Y	N	N	-	Y	N
3 Love	Y	N	N	N	Y	Y
10 Moeller	Y	Y	Y	N	Y	Y
15 Secrest	Y	N	Y	Y	Y	Y
AL Sweeney	Y	Y	N	N	Y	Y
21 Vanik	Y	N	N	N	Y	N
17 Ashbrook	Y	Y	Y	‡	Y	Y
14 Ayres	Y	Y	N	Y	Y	Y
8 Betts	Y	Y	Y	Y	Y	Y
22 Bolton	Y	Y	Y	Y	Y	Y
16 Bow	Y	Y	Y	Y	Y	Y
7 Brown, Jr.	Y	Y	N	Y	Y	Y
2 Clancy	Y	Y	Y	Y	Y	Y
12 Devine	‡	Y	Y	Y	Y	Y
6 Harsha	Y	Y	Y	Y	Y	Y
5 Latta	Y	Y	Y	Y	Y	Y
4 McCulloch	Y	Y	N	Y	Y	Y
23 Minshall	Y	Y	Y	Y	Y	Y
13 Mosher	‡	Y	N	Y	Y	Y
11 Stanton	Y	Y	Y	Y	Y	Y
OKLAHOMA						
3 Albert	Y	N	N	N	Y	N
2 Edmondson	Y	N	Y	N	Y	Y
5 Jarman	Y	Y	Y	N	Y	N
6 Johnson	Y	N	N	N	Y	N
4 Steed	Y	N	Y	N	Y	N
1 Belcher	Y	Y	Y	Y	Y	Y
OREGON						
4 Duncan	Y	N	N	Y	?	Y
3 Green	Y	N	N	Y	Y	Y
2 Ullman	Y	N	X	Y	Y	Y
1 Wyatt	Y	Y	Y	Y	Y	Y
PENNSYLVANIA						
25 Clark	Y	X	N	N	Y	N
19 Craley	Y	N	N	Y	Y	N
21 Dent	Y	N	N	N	?	Y
11 Flood	Y	N	N	N	Y	?
20 Holland	Y	N	N	N	Y	N
14 Moorhead	Y	N	N	?	Y	Y
26 Morgan	Y	N	N	N	‡	Y
6 Rhodes	Y	N	N	N	Y	N
15 Rooney	Y	N	N	N	Y	Y
24 Vigorito	Y	N	N	Y	Y	N
18 Corbett	Y	Y	N	Y	Y	Y
8 Curtin	Y	Y	Y	Y	Y	Y
9 Dague	Y	Y	Y	Y	Y	Y
27 Fulton	Y	Y	N	N	Y	Y
23 Johnson	Y	Y	Y	Y	Y	Y
16 Kunkel	Y	Y	N	Y	Y	Y
10 McDade	Y	Y	N	Y	Y	Y
22 Saylor	Y	Y	Y	N	Y	Y
17 Schneebeli	Y	Y	N	Y	Y	Y
13 Schweiker	Y	Y	N	Y	Y	Y
7 Watkins	Y	Y	Y	Y	Y	Y
12 Whalley	Y	?	Y	Y	Y	Y
Philadelphia City						
1 Barrett	Y	N	N	N	?	Y
3 Byrne	Y	N	N	N	Y	Y
5 Green	Y	N	N	N	Y	Y
2 Nix	Y	N	N	N	Y	Y
4 Toll	?	X	X	?	?	?
RHODE ISLAND						
2 Fogarty	Y	N	N	N	Y	Y
1 St. Germain	Y	N	N	N	Y	Y
SOUTH CAROLINA						
4 Ashmore	Y	✓	Y	Y	Y	?
3 Dorn	Y	‡	Y	N	Y	Y
5 Gettys	Y	✓	Y	Y	Y	Y
6 McMillan	Y	✓	Y	?	Y	?
1 Rivers	Y	✓	Y	N	Y	?
2 Watson	Y	Y	✓	Y	Y	Y
SOUTH DAKOTA						
2 Berry	Y	Y	Y	Y	Y	Y
1 Reifel	Y	Y	N	Y	Y	Y
TENNESSEE						
6 Anderson	Y	N	Y	-	Y	Y
8 Everett	Y	N	Y	N	Y	N
4 Evins	Y	N	Y	N	Y	?
5 Fulton	Y	-	N	N	Y	?
9 Grider	Y	N	N	N	Y	Y
7 Murray	Y	-	✓	?	?	X
3 Brock	?	Y	Y	‡	Y	N
2 Duncan	Y	Y	Y	Y	Y	Y
1 Quillen	Y	Y	Y	Y	Y	Y
TEXAS						
3 Beckworth	Y	N	Y	N	Y	N
2 Brooks	Y	N	N	N	Y	N
17 Burleson	Y	?	Y	Y	Y	N
5 Cabell	Y	Y	Y	Y	Y	N
22 Casey	Y	N	Y	-	Y	Y
15 De la Garza	Y	N	Y	N	Y	Y
7 Dowdy	?	?	Y	Y	Y	N
21 Fisher	‡	Y	Y	Y	Y	?
20 Gonzalez	Y	N	N	N	Y	Y
19 Mahon	Y	N	Y	N	Y	N
1 Patman	Y	N	Y	N	Y	N
10 Pickle	Y	N	Y	N	Y	N
11 Poage	Y	Y	Y	N	Y	N
AL Pool	Y	Y	Y	?	Y	Y
13 Purcell	Y	Y	Y	?	Y	N
4 Roberts	Y	Y	Y	N	Y	N
18 Rogers	Y	Y	✓	Y	Y	N
6 Teague	?	Y	Y	Y	Y	N
8 Thomas, L.†			Y	N	Y	?
9 Thompson	Y	N	Y	N	Y	Y
16 White	Y	Y	Y	N	Y	N
12 Wright	Y	?	Y	N	Y	N
14 Young	Y	N	Y	N	Y	N
UTAH						
2 King	Y	Y	N	?	Y	Y
1 Burton	Y	Y	Y	?	?	X
VERMONT						
AL Stafford	Y	Y	N	Y	Y	Y
VIRGINIA						
4 Abbitt	Y	Y	Y	Y	Y	Y
1 Downing	‡	Y	Y	Y	Y	Y
2 Hardy	Y	Y	Y	Y	Y	N
9 Jennings	Y	Y	Y	N	Y	Y
7 Marsh	Y	Y	Y	Y	Y	Y
3 Satterfield	Y	Y	Y	Y	Y	Y
8 Smith	Y	Y	Y	Y	Y	Y
5 Tuck	Y	Y	Y	Y	Y	Y
10 Broyhill	Y	Y	Y	Y	Y	Y
6 Poff	Y	Y	Y	Y	Y	Y
WASHINGTON						
7 Adams	Y	N	N	N	Y	Y
5 Foley	Y	Y	Y	Y	Y	Y
3 Hansen	Y	N	N	N	Y	?
6 Hicks	Y	Y	Y	N	Y	Y
2 Meeds	Y	N	N	N	Y	Y
4 May	Y	Y	✓	Y	Y	Y
1 Pelly	Y	Y	Y	Y	Y	Y
WEST VIRGINIA						
4 Hechler	Y	N	Y	N	Y	N
5 Kee, J.	Y	N	N	N	Y	N
3 Slack	Y	N	Y	N	Y	Y
2 Staggers	Y	N	N	N	Y	N
1 Moore	‡	Y	Y	Y	Y	Y
WISCONSIN						
2 Kastenmeier	Y	N	N	N	?	N
6 Race	Y	N	Y	N	Y	N
5 Reuss	Y	N	N	N	Y	N
1 Stalbaum	Y	N	N	Y	Y	N
4 Zablocki	Y	N	Y	N	‡	?
8 Byrnes	Y	Y	N	Y	Y	Y
7 Laird	Y	Y	Y	?	Y	Y
10 O'Konski	Y	‡	Y	N	Y	?
3 Thomson	Y	Y	Y	Y	Y	Y
9 Davis	Y	Y	N	Y	Y	Y
WYOMING						
AL Roncalio	‡	N	N	?	?	Y

* - *Rep. Robert P. Griffin (R Mich.) resigned May 16, 1966.*
† - *Rep. Lera Thomas (D Texas) sworn in March 30, 1966.*

Democrats in this type; *Republicans in italics*

House Key Votes—89th Congress—1966

7. HR 13712. Increase the federal minimum wage in stages from $1.25 to $1.60 an hour and increase coverage under the Fair Labor Standards Act. Ayres (R Ohio) motion to recommit the conference report on the bill with instructions to House conferees to insist on inclusion of a House provision making the $1.60 an-hour minimum wage effective on Feb. 1, 1969 -- a delay of one year from the timetable provided in the Senate and conference versions. Rejected 163-183; R 101-18; D 62-165 (ND 11-147; SD 51-18), Sept. 7, 1966. A "nay" was a vote supporting the President's position.

8. HR 17788. Appropriations Foreign Assistance for fiscal 1967. Bow (R Ohio) motion to recommit the bill to the Appropriations Committee with instructions to limit appropriations for economic assistance to $2,222,065,800, providing (in combination with Appropriations Committee cuts) a 10-percent reduction in economic aid below the Budget requests. Recommitted 186-183; R 116-8; D 70-175 (ND 24-143; SD 46-32), Sept. 20, 1966. A "nay" was a vote supporting the President's position.

9. HR 15111. Economic Opportunity Amendments of 1966, authorizing $1.75 billion for the "war on poverty" during fiscal 1967. Fino (R N.Y.) motion to strike the enacting clause (thereby killing the bill). Rejected 156-208; R 107-15; D 49-193 (ND 5-159; SD 44-34), Sept. 29, 1966. A "nay" was a vote supporting the President's position.

10. HR 17607. Passage of the bill providing a 16-month suspension -- from Sept. 9, 1966, through Dec. 31, 1967 -- of the 7-percent investment tax credit on the purchase of new and used machinery and equipment, and of authority for certain types of accelerated depreciation on commercial and industrial buildings. Passed 221-118; R 31-81; D 190-37 (ND 149-10; SD 41-27), Sept. 30, 1966. A "yea" was a vote supporting the President's position.

11. S 3708. Passage of the bill providing "demonstration city" grants for community renewal and other housing programs. Passed 178-141; R 16-81; D 162-60 (ND 141-11; SD 21-49), Oct. 14, 1966. A "yea" was a vote supporting the President's position.

12. HR 18381. Fiscal 1967 Supplemental Appropriations. Bow (R Ohio) motion to recommit the bill to the Appropriations Committee with instructions to add provisions prohibiting the Export-Import Bank from participating in extension of credit to Communist countries for purchase of U.S. commodities. Adopted 167-121; R 85-8; D 82-113 (ND 29-97; SD 53-16), Oct. 18, 1966. A "nay" was a vote supporting the President's position.

	7	8	9	10	11	12
ALABAMA						
3 Andrews	Y	Y	√	X	N	Y
8 Jones	N	N	N	Y	N	Y
5 Selden	Y	Y	√	Y	X	Y
4 *Andrews*	√	Y	Y	X	?	?
6 *Buchanan*	Y	Y	N	N	N	Y
2 *Dickinson*	Y	Y	√	X	?	?
1 *Edwards*	Y	Y	Y	N	N	?
7 *Martin*	?	√	√	?	?	?
ALASKA						
AL Rivers	N	N	N	Y	Y	X
ARIZONA						
3 Senner	X	X	N	Y	Y	?
2 Udall	N	N	X	Y	Y	?
1 *Rhodes*	Y	Y	Y	Y	N	Y
ARKANSAS						
1 Gathings	Y	Y	Y	Y	N	Y
4 Vacancy						
2 Mills	Y	Y	Y	Y	N	Y
3 Trimble	N	N	N	Y	√	?
CALIFORNIA						
5 Burton	N	N	N	Y	Y	N
7 Cohelan	X	N	N	√	Y	N
33 Dyal	N	X	X	√	Y	X
9 Edwards	N	N	?	?	Y	N
18 Hagen	N	Y	N	Y	Y	Y
34 Hanna	N	X	N	?	Y	N
2 Johnson	N	N	N	Y	N	Y
4 Leggett	X	N	N	X	N	X
15 McFall	N	N	N	Y	Y	N
8 Miller	X	X	N	Y	Y	N
3 Moss	N	N	X	√	√	X
16 Sisk	N	X	N	Y	Y	X
38 Tunney	N	N	N	Y	N	?
37 Van Deerlin	X	N	N	√	Y	N
14 Waldie	N	N	N	Y	?	Y
1 *Clausen*	Y	Y	Y	N	Y	Y
10 *Gubser*	Y	Y	√	X	N	Y
6 *Mailliard*	N	N	Y	N	N	N
12 *Talcott*	Y	Y	Y	N	N	?
13 *Teague*	Y	Y	Y	N	N	Y
35 *Utt*	Y	Y	√	X	N	Y
36 *Wilson*	√	√	Y	X	N	Y
11 *Younger*	Y	Y	Y	N	N	Y

Los Angeles Co.	7	8	9	10	11	12
29 Brown	N	√	X	X	Y	?
25 Cameron	X	X	N	Y	Y	N
22 Corman	N	X	N	?	√	X
21 Hawkins	X	N	N	√	X	N
19 Holifield	N	N	N	Y	Y	N
17 King	X	N	N	Y	N	N
26 Rees	N	N	?	Y	Y	N
30 Roybal	N	X	N	X	Y	N
31 Wilson	X	X	N	X	Y	Y
28 *Bell*	N	Y	Y	N	Y	?
23 *Clawson*	Y	Y	Y	N	N	Y
32 *Hosmer*	?	Y	Y	N	N	Y
24 *Lipscomb*	Y	Y	Y	N	N	Y
27 *Reinecke*	Y	-	Y	-	X	?	?
20 *Smith*	Y	Y	Y	N	?	Y
COLORADO						
4 Aspinall	X	X	X	√	√	X
3 *Evans*	X	X	?	√	√	?
2 McVicker	N	N	N	√	Y	?
1 Rogers	N	N	N	Y	N	N
CONNECTICUT						
1 Daddario	N	N	X	√	Y	X
3 Giaimo	N	N	N	Y	Y	N
6 Grabowski	N	N	N	Y	Y	N
4 Irwin	N	N	N	Y	N	N
5 Monagan	N	N	X	√	Y	N
2 St. Onge	N	N	N	Y	Y	N
DELAWARE						
AL *McDowell*	N	N	N	Y	Y	?
FLORIDA						
2 Bennett	Y	Y	Y	Y	N	Y
4 Fascell	N	N	N	Y	Y	N
9 Fuqua	√	Y	Y	Y	X	√
10 Gibbons	N	?	N	Y	Y	N
7 Haley	Y	Y	N	Y	N	Y
5 Herlong	√	Y	Y	Y	N	Y
8 Matthews	Y	N	N	Y	N	Y
3 Pepper	N	N	N	Y	N	N
6 Rogers	Y	Y	Y	Y	N	Y
1 Sikes	√	Y	Y	Y	N	Y
12 *Cramer*	Y	Y	Y	N	N	Y
11 *Gurney*	Y	Y	Y	N	N	Y

GEORGIA	7	8	9	10	11	12
7 Davis	X	√	Y	X	?	√
6 Flynt	Y	Y	Y	N	?	?
1 Hagan	Y	Y	X	X	√	?
9 Landrum	√	X	?	?	N	Y
4 Mackay	N	X	N	X	√	?
2 O'Neal	Y	Y	N	N	N	Y
10 Stephens	Y	Y	√	X	√	?
8 Tuten	√	√	√	N	?	Y
5 Weltner	N	Y	N	?	Y	N
3 *Callaway*	Y	√	Y	X	N	Y
HAWAII						
AL Matsunaga	N	N	N	Y	√	X
AL Mink	N	N	N	Y	Y	N
IDAHO						
1 *White*	√	X	N	Y	√	?
2 *Hansen*	Y	Y	Y	N	?	?
ILLINOIS						
21 Gray	N	X	X	Y	√	N
24 Price	N	N	N	Y	Y	N
19 Schisler	X	Y	N	X	?	?
23 Shipley	N	N	Y	X	?	?
16 *Anderson*	Y	Y	N	N	?	?
17 *Arends*	Y	Y	Y	N	N	Y
14 *Erlenborn*	Y	Y	X	X	?	?
20 *Findley*	Y	Y	Y	N	?	Y
12 *McClory*	Y	Y	√	X	N	?
18 *Michel*	Y	Y	Y	N	N	√
15 *Reid*	Y	Y	N	N	Y	Y
22 *Springer*	Y	Y	Y	N	N	Y
Chicago--Cook Co.						
7 Annunzio	N	N	N	Y	N	N
1 Dawson	N	N	N	Y	N	N
5 Kluczynski	N	X	X	Y	√	N
3 Murphy	N	N	N	Y	N	N
2 O'Hara	N	N	N	Y	Y	N
11 Pucinski	N	Y	N	√	Y	?
6 Ronan	N	N	N	Y	Y	N
8 Rostenkowski	N	N	N	Y	N	N
9 Yates	N	N	N	Y	Y	N
10 *Collier*	√	Y	Y	N	N	Y
4 *Derwinski*	Y	Y	√	X	N	?
13 *Rumsfeld*	Y	√	Y	N	N	Y

- KEY -	
Y	Record Vote For (yea).
√	Paired For.
‡	Announced For CQ Poll For.
N	Record Vote Against (nay).
X	Paired Against.
-	Announced Against. CQ Poll Against
?	Absent, General Pair, "Present." Did not announce or answer Poll

	7	8	9	10	11	12
INDIANA						
3 Brademas	N	N	N	Y	Y	N
8 Denton	N	N	X	√	√	?
9 Hamilton	N	Y	N	√	?	Y
11 Jacobs	N	N	N	Y	Y	N
1 Madden	N	N	N	Y	Y	N
5 Roush	N	Y	N	Y	X	?
4 *Adair*	Y	Y	Y	N	X	√
7 *Bray*	Y	Y	Y	N	N	Y
2 *Halleck*	Y	Y	Y	N	N	Y
10 *Harvey*	Y	Y	√	X	?	Y
6 *Roudebush*	Y	Y	Y	N	X	Y
IOWA						
4 Bandstra	X	N	N	N	?	N
2 Culver	N	N	N	Y	?	N
6 Greigg	Y	N	?	Y	?	?
7 Hansen	?	N	N	Y	?	Y
1 *Schmidhauser*	N	N	N	X	?	?
5 *Smith*	?	N	N	Y	N	N
3 *Gross*	Y	Y	Y	?	?	?
KANSAS						
1 *Dole*	Y	Y	Y	N	N	Y
3 *Ellsworth*	Y	Y	Y	N	Y	Y
4 *Shriver*	√	Y	Y	N	N	Y
2 *Mize*	Y	Y	Y	N	N	Y
5 *Skubitz*	Y	Y	Y	X	√	Y
KENTUCKY						
4 *Chelf*	N	N	N	N	√	N
3 *Farnsley*	N	N	N	Y	Y	N
2 Natcher	Y	N	N	N	N	Y

Democrats in this type; *Republicans in italics*

	7	8	9	10	11	12
7 Perkins	N	N	N	Y	Y	N
1 Stubblefield	Y	N	N	Y	N	Y
6 Watts	Y	N	Y	Y	N	Y
5 *Carter*	Y	√	?	X	N	?
LOUISIANA						
2 Boggs	N	N	N	Y	Y	Y
1 Hebert	√	Y	√	X	X	√
8 Long, S.O.	?	Y	Y	N	N	Y
6 Morrison	?	?	?	?	Y	Y
5 Passman	Y	?	Y	N	N	N
7 Edwards	?	Y	?	X	Y	Y
4 Waggonner	Y	Y	Y	N	N	Y
3 Willis	?	√	N	Y	?	Y
MAINE						
2 Hathaway	N	N	N	Y	Y	N
1 *Tupper*	X	Y	N	?	Y	N
MARYLAND						
4 Fallon	N	N	X	Y	√	Y
7 Friedel	N	N	X	Y	Y	N
3 Garmatz	X	N	X	Y	Y	N
2 Long	N	N	N	Y	Y	N
5 Machen	N	X	N	Y	Y	Y
AL Sickles	N	N	N	Y	Y	N
6 *Mathias*	X	N	Y	N	√	N
1 *Morton*	Y	Y	Y	N	N	Y
MASSACHUSETTS						
2 Boland	N	N	N	Y	Y	N
11 Burke	N	N	N	Y	Y	N
4 Donohue	N	N	N	Y	Y	N
7 Macdonald	N	N	N	Y	Y	N
9 McCormack						
8 O'Neill	X	N	X	√	Y	N
3 Philbin	N	N	N	Y	Y	N
6 *Bates*	Y	Y	Y	Y	N	Y
1 *Conte*	N	X	N	N	√	N
12 *Keith*	Y	Y	N	Y	Y	?
10 *Martin*	X	?	?	X	?	?
5 *Morse*	N	X	?	√	Y	N
MICHIGAN						
11 Clevenger	N	N	N	Y	Y	?
19 Farnum	N	N	N	Y	Y	?
7 Mackie	N	N	N	√	√	?
12 O'Hara	N	N	N	Y	Y	N
3 Todd	N	N	X	Y	?	?
2 Vivian	N	N	N	Y	Y	?
18 *Broomfield*	Y	N	Y	N	N	?
10 *Cederberg*	Y	Y	Y	N	N	Y
6 *Chamberlain*	Y	Y	Y	N	N	Y
5 *Ford*	Y	Y	Y	Y	N	√
9 Vacancy						
8 *Harvey*	Y	Y	Y	N	N	?
4 *Hutchinson*	Y	Y	Y	N	N	Y
Detroit--Wayne Co.						
1 Conyers	N	N	N	Y	Y	N
13 Diggs	X	N	N	Y	Y	N
16 Dingell	N	N	N	Y	Y	N
15 Ford	N	N	N	Y	Y	N
17 Griffiths	N	N	N	Y	Y	N
14 Nedzi	N	N	X	√	Y	N
MINNESOTA						
8 Blatnik	X	N	N	Y	Y	N
5 Fraser	N	N	N	Y	Y	N
4 Karth	N	N	N	Y	?	N
6 Olson	Y	N	N	Y	Y	N
7 *Langen*	Y	Y	Y	Y	N	Y
3 *MacGregor*	Y	Y	Y	Y	N	Y
2 *Nelsen*	Y	Y	Y	N	X	Y
1 *Quie*	Y	Y	Y	Y	N	Y
MISSISSIPPI						
1 Abernethy	Y	Y	Y	X	X	√
5 Colmer	Y	Y	Y	N	N	√
2 Whitten	Y	Y	Y	X	N	Y
3 Williams	√	Y	Y	N	N	Y
4 *Walker*	Y	√	Y	N	-	?
MISSOURI						
5 Bolling	N	?	N	?	Y	?
6 Hull	Y	Y	Y	Y	N	Y
9 Hungate	N	√	Y	Y	Y	?
8 Ichord	Y	Y	Y	Y	N	Y
10 Jones	?	Y	?	Y	N	Y
1 Karsten	N	N	N	Y	Y	N
4 Randall	N	√	Y	Y	N	?
3 Sullivan	N	N	N	Y	Y	?
2 *Curtis*	Y	Y	Y	N	N	Y
7 *Hall*	Y	Y	Y	N	X	Y
MONTANA						
1 Olsen	N	Y	X	√	Y	?
2 *Battin*	√	Y	Y	Y	X	Y
NEBRASKA						
1 Callan	Y	N	N	Y	N	Y
2 *Cunningham*	Y	Y	Y	Y	N	Y
3 *Martin*	Y	Y	Y	N	N	?
NEVADA						
AL Baring	√	Y	Y	N	X	?
NEW HAMPSHIRE						
1 Huot	N	N	N	Y	Y	?
2 *Cleveland*	Y	Y	Y	N	N	Y
NEW JERSEY						
14 Daniels	N	N	N	Y	√	N
13 Gallagher	N	N	N	Y	√	?
9 Helstoski	N	N	N	√	Y	?
3 Howard	N	N	X	Y	Y	?
8 Joelson	N	N	N	Y	Y	N
12 Krebs	N	N	N	Y	Y	N
11 Minish	N	N	N	Y	Y	Y
2 McGrath	N	N	N	Y	Y	Y
15 Patten	N	N	N	Y	Y	N
10 Rodino	N	N	N	Y	Y	N
4 Thompson	N	X	N	Y	√	X
1 *Cahill*	N	N	N	Y	N	Y
6 *Dwyer*	N	Y	N	N	N	Y
5 *Frelinghuysen*	Y	N	Y	Y	?	N
7 *Widnall*	N	Y	Y	Y	Y	√
NEW MEXICO						
AL Morris	Y	Y	N	Y	N	Y
AL Walker	Y	Y	?	?	N	Y
NEW YORK						
27 Dow	N	N	-	Y	Y	N
41 Dulski	N	√	N	Y	Y	Y
34 Hanley	N	N	N	Y	Y	Y
39 McCarthy	?	Y	N	Y	Y	?
29 O'Brien	N	N	N	?	Y	N
25 Ottinger	X	N	N	Y	Y	N
1 Pike	√	Y	N	Y	Y	Y
28 Resnick	N	N	N	Y	Y	N
35 Stratton	N	‡	N	N	Y	?
5 Tenzer	N	Y	N	Y	Y	N
3 Wolff	N	N	N	Y	Y	√
37 *Conable*	Y	Y	Y	Y	N	Y
38 *Goodell*	Y	Y	Y	N	N	?
2 *Grover*	Y	Y	Y	Y	N	Y
36 *Horton*	N	Y	N	N	Y	Y
30 *King*	√	√	√	X	N	Y
31 *McEwen*	Y	√	Y	N	N	Y
32 *Pirnie*	Y	Y	?	?	?	?
26 *Reid*	N	N	N	Y	Y	N
33 *Robison*	Y	√	?	√	N	?
40 *Smith*	Y	Y	Y	Y	Y	?
4 *Wydler*	N	Y	Y	N	N	Y
New York City						
7 Addabbo	N	N	N	Y	Y	Y
23 Bingham	N	N	N	Y	Y	N
15 Carey	X	N	N	Y	Y	?
10 Celler	N	N	N	√	Y	X
9 Delaney	N	Y	N	Y	Y	Y
19 Farbstein	N	X	N	Y	Y	N
22 Gilbert	N	N	N	Y	Y	N
12 Kelly	X	N	N	Y	Y	N
11 Keogh	N	N	N	√	Y	N
13 Multer	X	N	N	Y	Y	N
16 Murphy	X	N	N	Y	Y	Y
18 Powell	N	N	N	√	Y	N
14 Rooney	N	N	N	Y	Y	N
8 Rosenthal	N	N	N	Y	Y	N
20 Ryan	N	N	N	Y	Y	N
21 Scheuer	N	N	N	Y	Y	N
24 *Fino*	?	Y	Y	√	N	?
6 *Halpern*	N	Y	N	Y	Y	?
17 *Kupferman*	N	N	N	N	Y	N
NORTH CAROLINA						
1 Jones	Y	√	Y	N	N	?
4 Cooley	√	N	Y	N	X	?
2 Fountain	Y	Y	Y	N	N	Y
3 Henderson	Y	Y	Y	N	N	Y
6 Kornegay	Y	Y	Y	N	N	√
7 Lennon	Y	Y	Y	N	N	Y
5 Scott	√	√	√	X	?	?
11 Taylor	Y	Y	Y	N	N	√
10 Whitener	Y	Y	Y	N	N	Y
9 *Broyhill*	Y	Y	Y	Y	N	Y
8 *Jonas*	Y	Y	Y	N	N	Y
NORTH DAKOTA						
2 Redlin	Y	Y	N	Y	?	Y
1 *Andrews*	Y	Y	Y	Y	N	Y
OHIO						
9 Ashley	N	N	N	Y	Y	?
20 Feighan	X	N	N	Y	Y	Y
1 Gilligan	X	N	N	Y	Y	?
18 Hays	Y	N	N	√	Y	N
19 Kirwan	N	N	N	Y	Y	X
3 Love	N	Y	N	Y	Y	?
10 Moeller	N	Y	N	Y	X	?
15 Secrest	Y	Y	N	Y	N	Y
AL Sweeney	N	Y	N	Y	N	X
21 Vanik	N	N	N	Y	Y	N
17 *Ashbrook*	Y	Y	Y	N	N	?
14 *Ayres*	Y	√	Y	Y	N	Y
8 *Betts*	Y	Y	Y	N	N	?
22 *Bolton*	Y	N	√	X	N	Y
16 *Bow*	√	Y	?	X	N	Y
7 *Brown, Jr.*	Y	Y	Y	N	?	?
2 *Clancy*	Y	Y	Y	N	?	Y
12 *Devine*	√	Y	Y	N	?	?
6 *Harsha*	Y	Y	Y	N	N	Y
5 *Latta*	Y	Y	Y	N	N	Y
4 *McCulloch*	Y	Y	Y	N	?	Y
23 *Minshall*	?	Y	√	N	N	Y
13 *Mosher*	?	Y	Y	N	Y	Y
11 *Stanton*	Y	Y	Y	N	N	?
OKLAHOMA						
3 Albert	X	X	X	√	√	?
2 Edmondson	√	N	N	√	?	Y
5 Jarman	Y	Y	Y	N	.N	Y
6 Johnson	X	Y	?	√	X	Y
4 Steed	Y	Y	N	Y	N	?
1 *Belcher*	Y	Y	Y	N	N	?
OREGON						
4 Duncan	N	N	N	Y	X	?
3 Green	X	N	N	Y	?	N
2 Ullman	X	N	N	Y	√	?
1 *Wyatt*	Y	Y	Y	N	X	Y
PENNSYLVANIA						
25 Clark	N	N	N	N	√	Y
19 Craley	N	N	N	?	√	?
21 Dent	N	N	N	Y	Y	Y
11 Flood	N	N	X	Y	Y	N
20 Holland	N	N	N	Y	Y	N
14 Moorhead	N	N	N	Y	Y	N
26 Morgan	N	N	N	Y	Y	?
6 Rhodes	N	N	N	Y	Y	N
15 Rooney	N	N	N	N	Y	N
24 Vigorito	N	N	N	Y	Y	Y
18 *Corbett*	X	Y	N	X	√	Y
8 *Curtin*	√	Y	Y	?	?	Y
9 *Dague*	Y	Y	Y	?	?	Y
27 *Fulton*	N	Y	N	N	Y	Y
23 *Johnson*	Y	√	Y	N	?	Y
16 *Kunkel*	Y	Y	Y	N	N	Y
10 *McDade*	N	Y	N	X	Y	Y
22 *Saylor*	N	Y	N	N	?	Y
17 *Schneebeli*	Y	Y	Y	N	N	?
13 *Schweiker*	N	Y	Y	Y	Y	Y
7 *Watkins*	Y	Y	Y	N	?	?
12 *Whalley*	Y	Y	Y	N	N	Y
Philadelphia City						
1 Barrett	N	N	N	Y	Y	?
3 Byrne	N	N	N	Y	Y	N
5 Green	N	N	N	Y	Y	Y
2 Nix	N	N	N	√	Y	X
4 Toll	?	X	?	?	√	X
RHODE ISLAND						
2 Fogarty	N	N	N	Y	Y	N
1 St. Germain	X	N	N	Y	Y	N
SOUTH CAROLINA						
4 Ashmore	Y	Y	Y	N	N	?
3 Dorn	Y	√	Y	N	N	Y
5 Gettys	√	Y	Y	X	N	Y
6 McMillan	Y	√	Y	N	?	?
1 Rivers	√	N	Y	N	N	Y
2 *Watson*	Y	Y	Y	N	N	Y
SOUTH DAKOTA						
2 *Berry*	Y	Y	Y	Y	?	?
1 *Reifel*	Y	Y	Y	Y	?	Y
TENNESSEE						
6 Anderson	N	N	N	?	Y	?
8 Everett	Y	Y	Y	Y	X	Y
4 Evins	X	X	N	Y	√	?
5 Fulton	N	X	N	Y	Y	Y
9 Grider	√	N	N	?	Y	Y
7 Murray	√	√	√	X	?	?
3 *Brock*	Y	Y	Y	N	N	Y
2 *Duncan*	Y	Y	Y	N	N	Y
1 *Quillen*	Y	Y	Y	N	X	Y
TEXAS						
3 Beckworth	Y	N	N	Y	Y	N
2 Brooks	N	N	N	Y	Y	N
17 Burleson	Y	Y	Y	N	N	Y
5 Cabell	√	N	√	√	X	Y
22 Casey	Y	N	N	?	N	Y
15 De la Garza	Y	N	N	Y	N	Y
7 Dowdy	Y	Y	Y	X	N	Y
21 Fisher	√	√	√	?	X	?
20 Gonzalez	N	N	N	Y	Y	N
19 Mahon	Y	N	N	Y	N	N
1 Patman	N	N	N	Y	Y	N
10 Pickle	√	N	N	Y	Y	N
11 Poage	Y	Y	?	?	N	Y
AL Pool	√	Y	√	Y	?	?
13 Purcell	Y	?	?	?	?	?
4 Roberts	√	Y	N	Y	N	?
18 Rogers	√	√	√	?	?	?
6 Teague	Y	√	Y	N	N	Y
8 Thomas, L.	N	N	N	√	Y	?
9 Thompson	√	N	?	?	?	?
16 White	Y	Y	N	Y	N	Y
12 Wright	Y	N	?	√	N	N
14 Young	N	N	N	Y	Y	N
UTAH						
2 King	√	N	N	√	Y	?
1 *Burton*	Y	Y	Y	Y	?	Y
VERMONT						
AL Stafford	N	Y	N	Y	?	?
VIRGINIA						
4 Abbitt	Y	Y	Y	?	N	Y
1 Downing	Y	N	Y	Y	N	Y
2 Hardy	Y	N	Y	Y	Y	Y
9 Jennings	Y	Y	N	Y	?	?
7 Marsh	Y	Y	Y	Y	N	Y
3 Satterfield	Y	Y	Y	Y	N	Y
8 Smith	Y	Y	Y	Y	N	Y
5 Tuck	Y	Y	Y	N	N	Y
10 *Broyhill*	Y	Y	Y	Y	N	Y
6 *Poff*	Y	Y	Y	Y	N	Y
WASHINGTON						
7 Adams	N	X	?	Y	Y	?
5 Foley	N	N	N	N	X	?
3 Hansen	N	N	N	Y	Y	?
6 Hicks	N	X	N	Y	X	?
2 Meeds	N	N	N	Y	Y	?
4 *May*	Y	Y	Y	N	N	Y
1 *Pelly*	N	Y	Y	N	N	Y
WEST VIRGINIA						
4 Hechler	N	Y	N	Y	Y	N
5 Kee, J.	N	N	X	Y	√	N
3 Slack	N	N	N	Y	?	N
2 Staggers	N	N	N	Y	Y	?
1 *Moore*	Y	Y	N	N	Y	Y
WISCONSIN						
2 Kastenmeier	N	N	N	Y	Y	N
6 Race	N	Y	N	?	Y	Y
5 Reuss	N	N	N	Y	Y	N
1 Stalbaum	Y	N	N	Y	Y	N
4 Zablocki	N	N	X	Y	√	N
8 *Byrnes*	Y	Y	Y	Y	N	Y
7 *Laird*	?	Y	Y	Y	N	√
10 *O'Konski*	?	Y	?	?	?	?
3 *Thomson*	Y	Y	Y	N	N	?
9 *Davis*	Y	Y	Y	N	?	Y
WYOMING						
AL Roncalio	N	?	?	?	?	?

Democrats in this type; *Republicans in italics*

Senate Key Votes—89th Congress—1966

1. S 2791. Authorize fiscal 1966 supplemental appropriations for U.S. military operations in Southeast Asia. Mansfield (D Mont.) motion to table (kill) Morse (D Ore.) amendment to repeal the 1964 "Gulf of Tonkin" resolution, authorizing "all necessary measures" to prevent aggression in the area. Tabling motion agreed to 92-5: R 32-0; D 60-5 (ND 39-4; SD 21-1), March 1, 1966. A "yea" was a vote supporting the President's position.

2. S J Res 103. Passage of the bill proposing an amendment to the Constitution to permit states to apportion one house of their legislature on the basis of geography and political subdivisions as well as population. (A two-thirds majority is required for approval of a proposed constitutional amendment.) Rejected 55-38: R 29-3; D 26-35 (ND 9-32; SD 17-3), April 20, 1966 (62 "yeas" were necessary for passage of S J Res 103). The President did not take a position on the amendment.

3. HR 14012. Second Supplemental Appropriations bill for fiscal 1966. Senate Appropriations Committee amendment to delete the section of the bill authorizing $12 million in contractual authority for rent supplements and appropriating $100,000 for rent supplement payments in fiscal 1966. Rejected 45-46: R 26-5; D 19-41 (ND 7-32; SD 12-9), April 27, 1966. A "nay" was a vote supporting the President's position.

4. S 985. Fair Packaging and Labeling Act, authorizing the Secretary of Health, Education and Welfare and the Federal Trade Commission to establish standard weights and quantities for packaged commodities covered by the bill and to require that specified information about the products appear clearly on the labels. Cotton (R N.H.) amendment to delete the sections authorizing federal officials to establish standard weights and quantities. Rejected 32-53: R 25-4; D 7-49 (ND 1-36; SD 6-13), June 8, 1966. A "nay" was a vote supporting the President's position.

5. S 5383. Military Assistance and Sales Act of 1966, authorizing appropriations for foreign military assistance exclusive of aid rendered in the Viet Nam war. Church (D Idaho) amendment to reduce the authorization in the bill by $100 million, from $892 million to $792 million. Accepted 55-37: R 12-17; D 43-20 (ND 32-12; SD 11-8), July 27, 1966. A "nay" was a vote supporting the President's position.

6. S J Res 186. Passage of the airline strike bill (1) requiring the striking airline machinists to return to work for 30 days; (2) authorizing the President to appoint a special board which would automatically trigger another 60-day back-to-work period and (3) providing that on the recommendation of the board the machinists could be ordered to stay on the job for an additional 90 days. Passed 54-33: R 24-6; D 30-27 (ND 15-25; SD 15-2), Aug. 4, 1966. The President did not take a position on the bill.

	1	2	3	4	5	6
ALABAMA						
Hill	Y	Y	Y	N	Y	✓
Sparkman	Y	Y	N	N	N	Y
ALASKA						
Bartlett	Y	Y	N	N	Y	N
Gruening	N	‡	X	–	Y	N
ARIZONA						
Hayden	Y	Y	X	?	?	?
Fannin	Y	Y	Y	Y	Y	Y
ARKANSAS						
Fulbright	N	Y	N	N	Y	?
McClellan	Y	Y	Y	✓	?	Y
CALIFORNIA						
Kuchel	Y	Y	Y	?	N	Y
Murphy	Y	Y	Y	Y	N	Y
COLORADO						
Allott	Y	Y	Y	✓	✓	Y
Dominick	Y	Y	Y	Y	Y	Y
CONNECTICUT						
Dodd	Y	–	–	N	N	‡
Ribicoff	Y	N	N	N	N	N
DELAWARE						
Boggs	Y	N	Y	Y	Y	N
Williams	Y	Y	Y	Y	Y	Y
FLORIDA						
Holland	Y	Y	Y	Y	Y	Y
Smathers	Y	Y	N	N	N	Y
GEORGIA						
Russell	Y	Y	Y	Y	Y	Y
Talmadge	Y	Y	Y	Y	Y	Y
HAWAII						
Inouye	Y	N	N	N	Y	Y
Fong	Y	Y	Y	X	N	Y
IDAHO						
Church	‡	Y	N	N	Y	Y
Jordan	Y	Y	Y	Y	Y	Y
ILLINOIS						
Douglas	Y	N	N	N	N	N
Dirksen	Y	Y	Y	X	Y	Y

	1	2	3	4	5	6
INDIANA						
Bayh	Y	N	N	–	Y	N
Hartke	Y	N	Y	N	Y	N
IOWA						
Hickenlooper	Y	Y	Y	Y	N	Y
Miller	Y	Y	Y	Y	N	X
KANSAS						
Carlson	Y	Y	Y	Y	N	Y
Pearson	Y	Y	Y	Y	X	Y
KENTUCKY						
Cooper	Y	Y	Y	N	Y	Y
Morton	Y	Y	Y	Y	N	Y
LOUISIANA						
Ellender	Y	Y	N	N	Y	?
Long	Y	✓	N	N	N	N
MAINE						
Muskie	Y	N	N	N	N	N
Smith	Y	N	N	N	N	N
MARYLAND						
Brewster	‡	N	N	N	Y	‡
Tydings	Y	N	N	X	Y	Y
MASSACHUSETTS						
Kennedy	Y	N	N	N	Y	N
Saltonstall	Y	Y	✓	Y	N	Y
MICHIGAN						
Hart	Y	N	N	N	Y	N
*Griffin**				Y	Y	Y
MINNESOTA						
McCarthy	N	N	N	N	Y	N
Mondale	Y	N	N	N	Y	N
MISSISSIPPI						
Eastland	Y	Y	Y	Y	N	‡
Stennis	Y	Y	Y	Y	N	Y
MISSOURI						
Long	Y	N	N	N	N	Y
Symington	Y	✓	Y	N	Y	N
MONTANA						
Mansfield	Y	N	Y	N	X	N
Metcalf	Y	N	✓	N	Y	N

	1	2	3	4	5	6
NEBRASKA						
Curtis	Y	Y	Y	Y	Y	Y
Hruska	Y	Y	Y	Y	Y	Y
NEVADA						
Bible	Y	Y	–	N	Y	Y
Cannon	Y	Y	N	N	Y	Y
NEW HAMPSHIRE						
McIntyre	Y	N	Y	N	Y	Y
Cotton	Y	Y	Y	Y	Y	N
NEW JERSEY						
Williams	Y	N	N	N	Y	N
Case	Y	N	N	N	N	N
NEW MEXICO						
Anderson	Y	N	N	N	N	Y
Montoya	Y	N	N	–	N	Y
NEW YORK						
Kennedy	Y	N	N	–	Y	N
Javits	Y	N	N	N	N	Y
NORTH CAROLINA						
Ervin	Y	Y	Y	Y	N	Y
Jordan	Y	Y	Y	Y	N	Y
NORTH DAKOTA						
Burdick	Y	N	N	N	Y	N
Young	Y	Y	Y	Y	Y	Y
OHIO						
Lausche	‡	Y	Y	Y	N	Y
Young	N	N	Y	N	Y	Y
OKLAHOMA						
Harris	Y	Y	N	N	Y	Y
Monroney	Y	Y	N	N	Y	Y
OREGON						
Morse	N	N	N	N	Y	Y
Neuberger	Y	–	X	N	Y	N
PENNSYLVANIA						
Clark	Y	N	N	N	Y	X
Scott	Y	Y	N	Y	N	‡
RHODE ISLAND						
Pastore	Y	N	N	N	N	Y
Pell	Y	N	N	N	Y	Y

	1	2	3	4	5	6
SOUTH CAROLINA						
Russell	Y	Y	✓	?	Y	Y
Thurmond	Y	Y	Y	Y	N	Y
SOUTH DAKOTA						
McGovern	Y	N	N	N	Y	N
Mundt	Y	Y	Y	Y	Y	Y
TENNESSEE						
Bass	Y	N	N	–	?	?
Gore	Y	N	Y	N	Y	N
TEXAS						
Yarborough	Y	N	N	N	?	?
Tower	Y	Y	Y	Y	N	Y
UTAH						
Moss	Y	Y	N	–	Y	?
Bennett	Y	Y	Y	Y	N	✓
VERMONT						
Aiken	Y	N	N	N	N	N
Prouty	Y	Y	Y	N	N	N
VIRGINIA						
Byrd, Jr.	Y	Y	Y	N	Y	Y
Robertson	‡	?	Y	N	Y	Y
WASHINGTON						
Jackson	Y	N	N	N	N	N
Magnuson	Y	N	N	N	N	N
WEST VIRGINIA						
Byrd	Y	Y	Y	N	Y	Y
Randolph	Y	N	N	N	Y	Y
WISCONSIN						
Nelson	Y	N	N	N	Y	N
Proxmire	Y	N	N	N	Y	N
WYOMING						
McGee	Y	N	N	N	N	N
Simpson	Y	Y	Y	✓	✓	Y

Y Record Vote For (yea).
✓ Paired For.
‡ Announced For. CQ Poll For.
N Record Vote Against (nay).
X Paired Against.
– Announced Against. CQ Poll Against.
? Absent, General Pair, "Present." Did not announce or answer Poll.

—Robert P. Griffin (R Mich.) was sworn in May 16, 1966.   Democrats in this type; *Republicans in italics*

Senate Key Votes—89th Congress—1966

7. HR 15119. Passage of the bill requiring states to meet minimum federal standards for the amount and duration of state unemployment compensation benefits, extending coverage of the system, providing a new program of extended benefits for jobless workers during national or state recessions and financing the expanded program by increasing the federal unemployment tax and the taxable wage base. Passed 53-31: R 8-20; D 45-11 (ND 39-1; SD 6-10), Aug. 8, 1966. A "yea" was a vote supporting the President's position.

8. S 3708. Demonstration Cities and Metropolitan Development Act of 1966, authorizing "demonstration city" grants for community renewal, "incentive" planning grants for orderly metropolitan development and other programs related to housing and urban development. Tower (R Texas) amendment to delete the bill's authorization of $900 million in grants to "demonstration city" projects for fiscal 1968 and 1969 (leaving for the program only $24 million in planning funds). Rejected 27-53: R 17-10; D 10-43 (ND 1-36; SD 9-7), Aug. 19, 1966. A "nay" was a vote supporting the President's position.

9. HR 13712. Increase the federal minimum wage in stages from $1.25 to $1.60 an hour and increase coverage under the Fair Labor Standards Act. Fannin (R Ariz.) amendment to make the $1.60-an-hour minimum wage effective on Feb. 1, 1969 -- a delay of one year from the timetable provided under the bill. Rejected 40-42: R 21-7; D 19-35 (ND 3)32; SD 16-3). Aug. 25, 1966. A "nay" was a vote supporting the President's position.

10. HR 14765. Civil Rights Act of 1966. Mansfield (D Mont.) motion that the Senate invoke cloture (limit debate) on his motion to consider the bill to ban discrimination in the selection of jurors and in the sale and rental of some housing and to protect Negroes and civil rights workers. (A two-thirds majority is required to invoke cloture.) Rejected 54-42: R 12-21; D 42-21 (ND 37-4; SD 5-17), Sept. 14, 1966 (64 "yeas" were required to invoke cloture). A "yea" was a vote supporting the President's position.

11. S J Res 144. Passage of the bill with a Dirksen (R Ill.) substitute proposing an amendment to the Constitution to permit voluntary prayer in public schools. Rejected 49-37: R 27-3; D 22-34 (ND 7-29; SD 15-5), Sept. 21, 1966. With 86 Senators voting, 58 votes (a two-thirds majority) were required to propose a constitutional amendment. The President did not take a position on the bill.

12. HR 13103. Foreign Investors Tax Act. Williams (R Del.) amendment to delete provisions permitting taxpayers to designate $1 of their annual tax payments for a fund to finance national parties' Presidential campaigns. Rejected 33-39: R 22-1; D 11-38 (ND 3-29; SD 8-9), Oct. 12, 1966. The President did not take a position on the amendment.

	7	8	9	10	11	12
ALABAMA						
Hill	X	?	✓	N	Y	Y
Sparkman	X	?	Y	N	Y	Y
ALASKA						
Bartlett	‡	-	X	?	N	Y
Gruening	Y	N	-	Y	N	N
ARIZONA						
Hayden	?	?	?	X	?	?
Fannin	N	Y	Y	N	Y	Y
ARKANSAS						
Fulbright	Y	N	Y	N	N	N
McClellan	N	Y	Y	N	Y	Y
CALIFORNIA						
Kuchel	Y	N	N	Y	N	Y
Murphy	X	‡	✓	N	Y	Y
COLORADO						
Allott	N	N	Y	Y	‡	‡
Dominick	N	Y	Y	Y	Y	Y
CONNECTICUT						
Dodd	Y	N	N	Y	‡	N
Ribicoff	Y	N	N	Y	N	N
DELAWARE						
Boggs	Y	Y	Y	Y	Y	Y
Williams	N	Y	Y	N	Y	Y
FLORIDA						
Holland	N	Y	Y	N	Y	N
Smathers	X	?	Y	N	Y	?
GEORGIA						
Russell	N	Y	Y	N	Y	Y
Talmadge	Y	-	Y	N	Y	Y
HAWAII						
Inouye	Y	N	N	Y	N	N
Fong	Y	N	Y	N	Y	Y
IDAHO						
Church	Y	N	Y	Y	Y	?
Jordan	N	Y	✓	N	‡	‡
ILLINOIS						
Douglas	Y	N	N	Y	N	?
Dirksen	N	Y	Y	N	Y	Y

	7	8	9	10	11	12
INDIANA						
Bayh	Y	N	N	Y	N	Y
Hartke	Y	N	?	Y	?	N
IOWA						
Hickenlooper	N	Y	Y	N	Y	‡
Miller	N	‡	Y	N	Y	Y
KANSAS						
Carlson	N	N	Y	N	Y	Y
Pearson	N	Y	Y	N	Y	‡
KENTUCKY						
Cooper	N	N	Y	N	Y	?
Morton	N	Y	Y	N	‡	N
LOUISIANA						
Ellender	X	N	Y	N	Y	N
Long	Y	N	X	N	Y	N
MAINE						
Muskie	Y	N	N	Y	N	N
Smith	Y	N	N	Y	Y	N
MARYLAND						
Brewster	Y	X	N	Y	X	N
Tydings	✓	N	N	Y	N	?
MASSACHUSETTS						
Kennedy	✓	N	N	Y	N	?
Saltonstall	-	‡	Y	Y	Y	Y
MICHIGAN						
Hart	Y	N	N	Y	N	N
Griffin	?	✓	Y	Y	Y	Y
MINNESOTA						
McCarthy	Y	?	-	Y	N	N
Mondale	Y	N	N	Y	N	N
MISSISSIPPI						
Eastland	N	✓	Y	N	Y	?
Stennis	N	Y	Y	N	Y	Y
MISSOURI						
Long	Y	N	-	Y	N	N
Symington	Y	N	X	Y	Y	N
MONTANA						
Mansfield	Y	N	X	Y	N	N
Metcalf	Y	N	?	Y	-	?

	7	8	9	10	11	12
NEBRASKA						
Curtis	N	Y	Y	N	Y	‡
Hruska	N	Y	Y	N	Y	Y
NEVADA						
Bible	Y	N	N	N	N	N
Cannon	Y	N	N	N	N	N
NEW HAMPSHIRE						
McIntyre	Y	N	Y	Y	✓	Y
Cotton	N	Y	Y	N	Y	Y
NEW JERSEY						
Williams	Y	N	N	Y	N	-
Case	Y	N	N	Y	N	-
NEW MEXICO						
Anderson	Y	N	N	Y	?	?
Montoya	Y	N	N	Y	Y	N
NEW YORK						
Kennedy	Y	N	N	Y	N	?
Javits	Y	N	N	Y	N	?
NORTH CAROLINA						
Ervin	N	Y	Y	N	N	Y
Jordan	N	Y	Y	N	Y	Y
NORTH DAKOTA						
Burdick	Y	-	N	Y	N	N
Young	N	N	Y	N	Y	N
OHIO						
Lausche	N	N	Y	N	Y	Y
Young	Y	N	N	Y	N	N
OKLAHOMA						
Harris	Y	N	Y	N	Y	N
Monroney	Y	N	Y	N	Y	N
OREGON						
Morse	Y	N	N	Y	N	N
Neuberger	Y	-	N	Y	N	N
PENNSYLVANIA						
Clark	Y	N	N	Y	N	N
Scott	✓	X	X	Y	Y	Y
RHODE ISLAND						
Pastore	Y	N	N	Y	Y	N
Pell	Y	N	N	Y	N	?

	7	8	9	10	11	12
SOUTH CAROLINA						
Russell	N	Y	N	N	Y	?
Thurmond	N	Y	Y	N	Y	Y
SOUTH DAKOTA						
McGovern	Y	N	N	Y	N	N
Mundt	N	Y	Y	N	Y	Y
TENNESSEE						
Bass	‡	-	X	Y	-	?
Gore	✓	N	N	Y	-	N
TEXAS						
Yarborough	Y	N	N	Y	N	N
Tower	N	Y	Y	N	Y	‡
UTAH						
Moss	Y	N	N	Y	✓	-
Bennett	-	‡	✓	N	Y	Y
VERMONT						
Aiken	Y	N	N	Y	Y	N
Prouty	Y	N	N	N	Y	?
VIRGINIA						
Byrd, Jr.	N	Y	N	N	Y	N
Robertson	N	Y	N	Y	N	?
WASHINGTON						
Jackson	Y	N	N	Y	N	N
Magnuson	Y	N	N	✓	?	N
WEST VIRGINIA						
Byrd	Y	Y	N	Y	N	N
Randolph	Y	-	✓	Y	Y	-
WISCONSIN						
Nelson	Y	N	N	Y	N	N
Proxmire	Y	N	N	Y	N	N
WYOMING						
McGee	Y	-	N	✓	N	N
Simpson	N	Y	✓	N	Y	Y

Key:
Y Record Vote For (yea).
✓ Paired For.
‡ Announced For. CQ Poll For.
N Record Vote Against (nay).
X Paired Against.
- Announced Against. CQ Poll Against.
? Absent, General Pair, "Present."
Did not announce or answer Poll.

Democrats in this type; *Republicans in italics*

HOUSE AND SENATE KEY VOTES FOR 1967

The editors of Congressional Quarterly annually select a series of "key votes" that represent major issues before Congress and also reflect both the mood of Congress and the impact constituent pressures can have on a Member's vote. In 1967 the major issues were Vietnam, antipoverty programs, the "block grant" concept of channeling federal money to the states, Congressional ethics, Government spending generally and consumer legislation. The "conservative coalition" of Republicans and Southern Democrats voting against Northern Democrats appeared on 10 of the 12 key votes in the House.

House Key Votes

1. POWELL EXCLUSION. The Democratic leadership was rebuffed in its plan to punish rather than exclude Rep.-elect Adam C. Powell (D N.Y.) from the 90th Congress for misuse of committee funds and other improprieties in the preceding Congress. The tide turned against Powell when the resolution (H Res 278) recommending censure and a fine was amended to exclude Powell from the House. The March 1 vote for the amendment was 248-176, with the conservative coalition in control (ND 40-110; SD 83-7; R 125-59). The President took no position on the matter.

2. VIETNAM. House "doves" collected only 18 votes against Administration policies on the war, but 18 was a record number. The critics proposed an amendment to the $4.5-billion supplemental defense authorization bill (HR 4515, S 665) stating the opposition of Congress to U.S. military operations in or over North Viet Nam. The House March 2 rejected the motion on an 18-372 vote. All 18 Members were Northern Democrats. With a Senate amendment favoring an international conference on Viet Nam (*see Senate Key Vote 1*), the bill became law March 16.

3. RENT SUPPLEMENTS. Controversy continued to rage over the "Great Society" rent supplements program for low-income families. In considering the independent offices appropriations bill (HR 9960), the House May 17 accepted an amendment deleting $10 million in new contract authority for rent supplements. The vote was 233-171, with the conservative coalition in control (ND 11-132; SD 59-27; R 163-12) and the President opposed. The $10 million new contract authority was reinstated by the Senate, and the House gave in to the amount Oct. 26.

4. MODEL CITIES. The "Great Society" program to renovate certain target cities came under fire during consideration of the housing appropriations bill (HR 9960). The House May 17 voted on an amendment to recommit the bill with instructions to delete $225 million in model cities grants, leaving only $12 million for planning. With the President opposed, the House rejected the motion. The vote was 193-213 in a defeat for the conservative coalition (ND 5-139; SD 47-39; R 141-35). With final appropriations of $312 million for model cities, the bill became law on Nov. 3.

5. TEACHER CORPS. One of the President's favorite projects, the Teacher Corps program for attracting high-calibre teachers to ghetto schools, survived a major test during consideration of the higher education authorization bill (HR 10943). The House June 27 rejected a motion to recommit the bill with instructions to strike the Teacher Corps provisions. The vote was 146-257 (ND 6-134; SD 57-28; R 83-95). The bill became law on June 29.

6. RAIL STRIKE. Faced with the first nationwide rail strike in more than 20 years, and with the Administration and the labor unions clashing on the bill, the House July 17 reversed its previous position and accepted a Senate amendment imposing a settlement on the dispute if the parties

failed to agree during a 90-day mediation period (S J Res 81). The vote was 244-148, with opposition coming from Northern Democrats (ND 46-94; SD 75-9; R 123-45). The President signed the measure two hours later.

7. RAT CONTROL. The House chamber echoed with the laughter of ridicule July 20 as the conservative coalition killed the Administration's $40-million program (HR 11000) to help localities control rats. The action was taken a week after serious ghetto rioting in Newark, N.J., and one day after passage of a bill to penalize persons who incite riots. The vote against adoption of an open rule for debate on the bill was 176-207 (ND 127-7; SD 27-52; R 22-148). In a more contrite mood, the House Sept. 20 added an amendment to the Partnership for Health bill (HR 6418) providing $40 million for rat control. That bill became law on Dec. 5.

8. ANTICRIME. The Administration's Safe Streets and Crime Control Act of 1967 (HR 5037) provided federal grants to assist communities in upgrading law enforcement. The House Aug. 8 changed the basic approach of the bill by requiring block grant payments to state governments. The vote on the amendment was 256-147, with the conservative coalition prevailing (ND 16-129; SD 68-14; R 172-4). The Senate took no action on the bill.

9. PUBLIC BROADCASTING. A landmark Administration bill (HR 6736, S 1160) established a nongovernmental Public Broadcasting Corporation to provide federal financial assistance to noncommercial educational broadcasting for the first time. The House Sept. 21 rejected a motion to delete provisions for the Corporation. The vote was 167-194 in a defeat for the conservative coalition (ND 3-122; SD 40-39; R 124-33). The bill became law on Nov. 7.

10. BUDGET CUTS. The conservative coalition used a routine continuing appropriations bill (H J Res 888) as a vehicle for a rider ordering the President to reduce Government expenditures in fiscal 1968 to $131.5 billion ($5 billion below the administrative budget) and to hold federal agencies, with few exceptions, to their fiscal 1967 spending levels. The Oct. 18 vote on the rider was 238-164 (ND 11-134; SD 56-21; R 171-9). The Senate rejected the rider and a more modest budget cut was enacted.

11. FOREIGN AID. The House Nov. 8 rejected a motion to recommit the foreign aid bill (S 1872) and remove the President's authority to engage in the sale or purchase of defense equipment or services with nations trading with or shipping to North Viet Nam. The vote was 196-200, in a defeat for the conservative coalition (ND 9-137; SD 51-30; R 136-33). The bill became law on Nov. 14.

12. ANTIPOVERTY. Reflecting hostility toward the Office of Economic Opportunity, the conservative coalition Nov. 15 cut the antipoverty authorization bill (S 2388) from the Administration's request of $2.06 billion to $1.6 billion. The vote was 221-190 (ND 9-141; SD 64-21; R 148-28). A $2-billion fiscal 1968 program was enacted.

Senate Key Votes

1. VIETNAM. In passing the $4.5-billion supplemental defense authorization (S 665), Congress enacted its first policy statement on the war since the 1964 Gulf of Tonkin resolution. The statement, inserted by a Senate floor amendment, expressed Congressional support for servicemen engaged in the war but added support for (1) the efforts of the President and "other men of good will" to bring about an end to the conflict and (2) the convening of an international conference to plan an end to the conflict. Senate "hawks" opposed the amendment, which was accepted by a 72-19 vote (D 48-9; R 24-10). President Johnson did not take a position on the amendment. The bill became law on March 16.

2. LOBBYING ACT. The Legislative Reorganization Act of 1967 (S 355) contained in Title V language widening the coverage of the existing lobby registration law. It would have been the first amendment of the law since 1946. The Senate March 7 beat back a Republican effort to delete that title. The vote was 30-53 (D 8-45; R 22-8). The President took no position on that issue. The bill was passed by the Senate but was pigeonholed in the House Rules Committee.

3. USSR CONSULAR CONVENTION. As an act more of symbolic than of substantive importance, the Senate approved the 1964 U.S.-Soviet Consular Convention March 16. It provided ground rules for an exchange of consulates, allowed diplomatic immunity and required notification when one country detained a national of the other country.

After defeating a number of amendments, reservations and understandings, the Senate adopted a resolution consenting to the President's ratification of the convention. The vote was 66-28 (D 44-15; R 22-13), just three more than the two-thirds vote necessary on a treaty.

4. DODD CENSURE. For the first time since censuring Sen. Joseph R. McCarthy (R Wis.) in 1954, the Senate censured one of its Members. On June 23, the Senate adopted the first part of a resolution (S Res 112) censuring Sen. Thomas J. Dodd (D Conn.) for having used political funds for his personal benefit. The vote was 92-5, the dissenters being Sens. Long (D La.), Ribicoff (D Conn.), Thurmond (R S.C.), Tower (R Texas) and Dodd himself. The President avoided involvement in the matter. The second part of S Res 112, censuring Dodd for double-billing on certain trips, was defeated.

5. TRUTH-IN-LENDING. An effort which began in 1959 reached a milestone in 1967 with Senate passage of an Administration-supported bill (S 5) requiring that consumers who borrow money or make installment purchases be informed of the true cost of the loan or credit. The Senate July 11 passed the bill without amendment by a 92-0 vote. The bill was not acted upon by the House.

6. RAIL STRIKE. The heart of the Administration's plan for dealing with the first nationwide rail strike in more than 20 years was a provision imposing settlement on the dispute if the parties had not reached agreement by the end of a 90-day mediation period. The House deleted this provision but the Senate July 17 restored it to the bill (S J Res 81) on a 68-21 vote (D 36-20; R 32-1). Northern Democrats were split evenly (19-19) on the provision, which labor unions bitterly opposed. The House then reversed its position and the bill became law July 17. *(See House Key Vote 6.)*

7. ARMS SALES. War in the Middle East and Latin American desires for jet fighters generated Congressional debate over the role of the United States as an arms supplier to underdeveloped nations. The Senate Aug. 9 voted on an amendment to the bill (S 1155) extending the life of the Export-Import Bank; the amendment prohibited the Bank from financing arms purchases by less developed countries. The Senate rejected the amendment by a 40-49 vote (D 27-27; R 13-22). The President did not take a position on the amendment. The House put off action on the bill. Foreign aid bills (S 1872, HR 13893), however, curtailed Administration authority to support such loans.

8. FINANCIAL DISCLOSURE. In a year which included the exclusion of a House Member and the censure of a Senator, Congressional ethics was a major issue. The Senate Sept. 12 had the opportunity to vote on an amendment to the Election Reform Act of 1967 (S 1880) which required Members of Congress and candidates for election to Congress to disclose their assets, liabilities and outside income. The Senate rejected the amendment by a 42-46 vote in a victory for the conservative coalition (ND 25-9; SD 4-15; R 13-22). The President took no position on the amendment. The House took no action on the bill.

9. RENT SUPPLEMENTS. The Administration scored a major victory in the Senate in obtaining funding for the rent supplements program, a key "Great Society" program to provide improved housing for low-income families. *(See House Key Vote 3.)* The House had deleted authority for new rent supplement contracts from the independent offices appropriations bill (HR 9960) and the Senate Sept. 20 voted on an amendment to add $40 million in such authority to the bill. In an effort to pressure the House, the Administration sought a large margin of victory. It got it as the amendment was accepted by a 59-31 vote (D 42-17; R 17-14). The House finally agreed to $10 million in contract authority.

10. ANTIPOVERTY. Senate liberals tried to attach a $2.8-billion emergency job program to the Administration's antipoverty bill (S 2388). Despite approval in committee, the liberals saw that the program would not win Senate support and rallied behind a compromise $925-million one-year program emphasizing incentives to get businesses to participate in job training. The Senate Oct. 4 rejected the amendment by a 42-47 vote in a victory for the conservative coalition (ND 24-13; SD 2-16; R 16-18). The President opposed the amendment and no emergency job program was enacted.

11. BUDGET CUTS. A major Republican attack on Administration spending was made in the Senate Oct. 25 during consideration of the continuing appropriations bill (H J Res 888). The Senate voted on an amendment requiring the Executive Branch to reduce each line item in fiscal 1968 appropriations bills by at least 5 percent, excepting military funds and those found by the Budget Bureau Director to be outside administrative control. The Senate rejected the amendment by a 43-46 vote (D 17-41; R 26-5).

12. SOCIAL SECURITY. The largest benefit increase in the history of the Social Security program was proposed by the Administration in 1967. The Senate Nov. 21 voted on a GOP amendment to the bill (HR 12080) to delete the Senate Finance Committee's across-the-board 15-percent increases, which conformed to the Administration proposal, and to provide instead for a 12.5-percent increase, as the House had done. The Senate rejected the amendment by a 22-58 vote (D 5-49; R 17-9). As enacted, the bill provided for a 13-percent increase in benefits.

House Key Votes—90th Congress—1967

1. H Res 278. Curtis (R Mo.) amendment to exclude Rep.-elect Adam C. Powell (D N.Y.) from the 90th Congress rather than censure and fine him. Accepted 248-176: R 125-59; D 123-117 (ND 40-110; SD 83-7), March 1, 1967. The President did not take a position on the amendment.

2. HR 4515. Fiscal 1967 supplemental defense appropriations authorization of $4,548,200,000 for the Viet Nam war. Brown (D Calif.) motion to recommit the bill with instructions to add an amendment stating the sense of Congress that no funds authorized by the bill were to be used to carry out military operations in or over North Viet Nam. Rejected 18-372: R 0-173; D 18-199 (ND 18-115; SD 0-84), March 2, 1967. A "nay" was a vote supporting the President's position.

3. HR 9960. Independent Offices and Department of Housing and Urban Development Appropriations Act for fiscal 1968. Davis (R Wis.) amendment to delete language permitting the Government to sign 40-year contracts with private nonprofit housing sponsors to pay an additional $10 million a year in rent supplements for low-income families. Accepted 233-171: R 163-12; D 70-159 (ND 11-132; SD 59-27), May 17, 1967. A "nay" was a vote supporting the President's position.

4. HR 9960. Michel (R Ill.) motion to recommit the bill to the House Appropriations Committee with instructions to delete $75 million for urban renewal in model city project areas and $150 million in other model city grants (leaving for the program only $12 million in planning funds). Rejected 193-213: R 141-35; D 52-178 (ND 5-139; SD 47-39), May 17, 1967. A "nay" was a vote supporting the President's position.

5. HR 10943. Teacher Corps, Teacher Education. Gurney (R Fla.) motion to recommit the bill with instructions to delete the Teacher Corps provisions. Rejected 146-257: R 83-95; D 63-162 (ND 6-134; SD 57-28), June 27, 1967. A "nay" was a vote supporting the President's position.

6. S J Res 81. Settlement of the railway labor dispute. Friedel (D Md.) motion to agree to the Senate amendment to the House version of the bill, restoring imposition of the mediation board's recommendations as the final settlement in the labor dispute if no agreement were reached in 90 days. Agreed to 244-148: R 123-45; D 121-103 (ND 46-94; SD 75-9), July 17, 1967. A "yea" was a vote supporting the President's position.

- KEY -

Y	Record vote for (yea).
✓	Paired for.
‡	Announced for or CQ poll for.
N	Record vote against (nay).
X	Paired against.
-	Announced against or CQ poll against.
?	Absent, general pair, "present" or did not announce or answer poll.

	1	2	3	4	5	6
ALABAMA						
3 Andrews	Y	N	Y	Y	Y	Y
7 Bevill	Y	N	Y	Y	Y	Y
8 Jones	Y	N	Y	N	N	Y
4 Nichols	Y	N	Y	Y	Y	Y
5 Selden	Y	N	Y	Y	Y	Y
6 *Buchanan*	Y	N	Y	Y	Y	Y
2 *Dickinson*	Y	N	Y	Y	Y	Y
1 *Edwards*	Y	N	Y	Y	Y	Y
ALASKA						
AL Pollock	Y	N	Y	Y	N	N
ARIZONA						
2 Udall	N	N	N	N	N	N
1 *Rhodes*	N	N	Y	Y	✓	Y
3 *Steiger*	Y	N	Y	Y	Y	Y
ARKANSAS						
1 Gathings	Y	N	Y	Y	Y	Y
2 Mills	Y	N	N	N	N	Y
4 Pryor	Y	N	N	N	Y	Y
3 *Hammerschmidt*	Y	-	Y	Y	N	Y
CALIFORNIA						
5 Burton	N	Y	N	N	N	X
7 Cohelan	N	N	N	N	N	N
9 Edwards	N	Y	N	N	-	
34 Hanna	Y	N	N	N	N	Y
2 Johnson	Y	N	N	N	N	N
4 Leggett	Y	N	N	N	N	N
15 McFall	N	N	N	N	N	N
8 Miller	N	N	N	N	N	X
3 Moss	N	N	-	N	-	N
16 Sisk	N	-	N	N	-	N
38 Tunney	Y	N	Y	N	N	N
37 Van Deerlin	Y	-	N	N	N	Y
14 Waldie	Y	N	N	N	N	N
1 *Clausen*	Y	N	Y	Y	Y	?
10 *Gubser*	Y	N	Y	N	Y	Y
6 *Mailliard*	N	N	Y	Y	N	Y
18 *Mathias*	N	N	Y	N	Y	N
33 *Pettis*	Y	N	Y	N	Y	N
12 *Talcott*	Y	N	Y	Y	Y	Y
13 *Teague*	N	N	Y	N	Y	Y
35 *Utt*	Y	N	Y	Y	✓	Y
36 *Wilson*	N	-	Y	Y	N	Y
11 Vacancy						
Los Angeles Co.						
29 Brown	N	Y	N	N	N	N
22 Corman	N	N	N	N	N	Y
21 Hawkins	N	N	N	N	N	N
19 Holifield	N	N	N	N	N	N
17 King	?	-	N	N	N	-
26 Rees	N	Y	N	N	N	N
30 *Roybal*	N	Y	N	N	N	X
31 Wilson	N	N	X	X	N	N
28 *Bell*	Y	N	N	N	N	Y
23 *Clawson*	N	N	Y	Y	Y	N
32 *Hosmer*	Y	N	Y	N	Y	N
24 *Lipscomb*	Y	N	Y	Y	Y	Y
27 *Reinecke*	Y	N	Y	Y	Y	Y
20 *Smith*	Y	N	Y	Y	Y	Y
25 *Wiggins*	N	N	Y	N	Y	Y
COLORADO						
4 Aspinall	Y	N	N	N	N	Y
3 Evans	N	N	N	N	N	Y
1 Rogers	Y	N	N	N	N	Y
2 *Brotzman*	Y	N	Y	N	Y	Y
CONNECTICUT						
1 Daddario	N	N	N	N	N	Y
3 Giaimo	N	N	N	N	N	Y
4 Irwin	N	N	N	N	N	Y
5 Monagan	N	N	N	N	N	Y
2 St. Onge	N	N	X	X	X	Y
6 *Meskill*	N	N	Y	N	N	N
DELAWARE						
AL *Roth*	Y	N	Y	N	Y	Y
FLORIDA						
3 Bennett	Y	N	Y	N	Y	Y
12 Fascell	Y	N	X	X	N	Y
2 Fuqua	Y	N	Y	Y	Y	Y
6 Gibbons	Y	N	N	N	N	Y
7 Haley	Y	N	Y	Y	Y	Y
4 Herlong	Y	N	Y	Y	Y	Y
11 Pepper	Y	N	N	N	N	N
9 Rogers	Y	N	Y	Y	Y	Y
1 Sikes	Y	N	Y	Y	Y	Y
10 *Burke*	Y	N	Y	Y	Y	N
8 *Cramer*	Y	N	Y	Y	Y	‡
5 *Gurney*	Y	N	Y	Y	Y	N
GEORGIA						
3 Brinkley	Y	N	Y	Y	Y	?
7 Davis	Y	N	Y	Y	N	Y
6 Flynt	Y	N	Y	Y	Y	N
1 Hagan	Y	N	Y	Y	Y	Y
9 Landrum	Y	N	N	N	?	Y
2 O'Neal	Y	N	Y	Y	Y	Y
10 Stephens	Y	N	N	N	N	Y
8 Stuckey	Y	N	Y	N	N	Y
4 *Blackburn*	Y	N	Y	Y	N	N
5 *Thompson*	Y	N	?	-	N	Y
HAWAII						
AL Matsunaga	N	N	N	N	N	Y
AL Mink	N	Y	N	N	N	N
IDAHO						
2 *Hansen*	Y	N	Y	Y	Y	N
1 *McClure*	Y	N	Y	Y	Y	-
ILLINOIS						
21 Gray	N	-	N	N	?	?
24 Price	N	N	N	N	N	N
23 Shipley	Y	N	N	N	N	N
16 *Anderson*	N	N	Y	N	N	N
17 *Arends*	N	N	Y	Y	Y	Y
14 *Erlenborn*	N	N	Y	Y	Y	Y
20 *Findley*	N	N	Y	Y	Y	N
12 *McClory*	N	N	Y	N	Y	Y
18 *Michel*	N	N	Y	Y	Y	Y
19 *Railsback*	N	N	Y	N	N	N
15 *Reid*	Y	Y	Y	Y	Y	Y
22 *Springer*	N	N	Y	N	Y	Y
Chicago-Cook Co.						
7 Annunzio	N	N	N	N	N	Y
1 Dawson	?	N	N	N	N	Y
5 Kluczynski	N	?	N	N	?	Y
3 Murphy	N	N	N	N	N	N
2 O'Hara	N	N	N	N	N	N
11 Pucinski	Y	N	N	N	N	✓
6 Ronan	N	N	N	N	N	Y
8 Rostenkowski	N	N	N	N	N	N
9 Yates	N	Y	N	N	N	Y
10 *Collier*	Y	N	Y	Y	Y	Y
4 *Derwinski*	N	N	✓	✓	Y	N
13 *Rumsfeld*	N	N	Y	Y	N	N
INDIANA						
3 Brademas	N	N	N	N	N	N
9 Hamilton	Y	N	Y	N	N	Y
11 Jacobs	N	N	N	N	N	N
1 Madden	N	N	N	N	N	N
5 Roush	Y	N	N	N	-	Y
4 *Adair*	Y	N	✓	✓	Y	Y
6 *Bray*	Y	N	Y	Y	Y	Y
2 *Halleck*	N	N	Y	Y	Y	Y
7 *Myers*	Y	N	Y	Y	N	N
10 *Roudebush*	Y	N	Y	Y	Y	‡
8 *Zion*	Y	N	Y	Y	Y	?
IOWA						
2 Culver	N	N	N	N	N	N
5 Smith	N	N	?	?	N	N
3 *Gross*	Y	N	Y	Y	Y	Y
4 *Kyl*	Y	N	Y	Y	Y	N
6 *Mayne*	Y	N	Y	N	Y	Y
7 *Scherle*	Y	N	Y	Y	Y	N
1 *Schwengel*	Y	N	Y	N	Y	N
KANSAS						
1 *Dole*	Y	N	Y	Y	Y	Y
2 *Mize*	Y	N	Y	Y	Y	N
4 *Shriver*	Y	N	Y	Y	N	Y
5 *Skubitz*	Y	?	Y	Y	Y	Y
3 *Winn*	Y	N	Y	Y	Y	Y
KENTUCKY						
2 Natcher	Y	N	N	N	N	Y
7 Perkins	N	N	N	N	N	N
1 Stubblefield	Y	N	N	N	N	Y

Democrats in this type; *Republicans in italics*

	1	2	3	4	5	6
6 Watts	Y	N	Y	N	N	Y
5 *Carter*	Y	N	Y	Y	N	N
3 *Cowger*	Y	N	X	X	N	X
4 *Snyder*	Y	N	Y	Y	Y	N
LOUISIANA						
2 Boggs	N	N	N	N	N	Y
7 Edwards	?	?	Y	N	Y	Y
1 Hebert	Y	N	Y	Y	✓	✓
8 Long	Y	N	Y	Y	Y	N
5 Passman	Y	N	Y	Y	Y	✓
6 Rarick	Y	N	Y	Y	Y	-
4 Waggonner	Y	N	Y	Y	Y	Y
3 Willis	Y	?	‡	-	Y	Y
MAINE						
2 Hathaway	N	N	N	N	N	N
1 Kyros	Y	N	N	N	N	N
MARYLAND						
4 Fallon	Y	N	Y	N	N	Y
7 Friedel	-	-	N	N	N	Y
3 Garmatz	Y	N	Y	N	N	X
2 Long	Y	N	N	N	N	N
5 Machen	Y	N	N	N	N	Y
8 *Gude*	Y	N	N	N	N	N
6 *Mathias*	Y	N	N	N	N	N
1 *Morton*	N	N	Y	N	N	N
MASSACHUSETTS						
2 Boland	N	N	N	N	X	Y
11 Burke	N	N	N	N	N	N
4 Donohue	N	N	N	N	N	N
7 Macdonald	?	?	N	N	N	N
9 McCormack						
8 O'Neill	N	N	N	N	X	N
3 Philbin	N	N	N	N	N	N
6 *Bates*	N	N	Y	N	N	Y
1 *Conte*	N	N	X	X	N	N
10 *Heckler*	Y	N	Y	N	N	N
12 *Keith*	N	N	Y	N	N	Y
5 *Morse*	-	-	N	N	N	N
MICHIGAN						
12 O'Hara	N	N	N	N	?	N
18 *Broomfield*	N	N	Y	Y	N	Y
3 *Brown*	N	N	N	N	N	N
10 *Cederberg*	Y	N	Y	Y	Y	✓
6 *Chamberlain*	Y	N	Y	Y	Y	Y
2 *Esch*	Y	N	Y	Y	N	Y
5 *Ford*	N	-	Y	Y	N	Y
8 *Harvey*	N	N	N	N	N	Y
4 *Hutchinson*	Y	N	Y	Y	Y	Y
19 *McDonald*	Y	N	Y	Y	N	Y
7 *Riegle*	N	-	Y	N	N	Y
11 *Ruppe*	N	N	Y	Y	N	N
9 *Vander Jagt*	Y	N	Y	Y	N	Y
Detroit-Wayne Co.						
1 Conyers	N	Y	N	N	N	N
13 Diggs	N	Y	X	-	-	N
16 Dingell	N	N	X	X	N	N
15 Ford	N	N	N	N	N	N
17 Griffiths	N	-	N	N	N	N
14 Nedzi	N	N	X	-	N	N
MINNESOTA						
8 Blatnik	N	?	N	N	?	N
5 Fraser	N	Y	N	N	N	N
4 Karth	Y	N	N	N	N	N
7 *Langen*	Y	N	Y	Y	Y	Y
3 *MacGregor*	N	N	✓	✓	N	N
2 *Nelsen*	Y	N	Y	Y	Y	Y
1 *Quie*	Y	N	Y	Y	N	Y
6 *Zwach*	Y	?	Y	Y	N	N
MISSISSIPPI						
1 Abernethy	Y	N	Y	Y	Y	Y
5 Colmer	Y	N	Y	Y	Y	Y
4 Montgomery	Y	N	Y	Y	Y	Y
2 Whitten	Y	N	Y	Y	Y	Y
3 Williams	Y	N	✓	✓	?	?
MISSOURI						
5 Bolling	N	N	N	N	N	N
6 Hull	Y	N	X	X	Y	Y
9 Hungate	Y	N	N	N	Y	?
8 Ichord	Y	N	Y	Y	Y	Y
10 Jones	Y	N	Y	Y	Y	Y
1 Karsten	N	N	N	N	N	N
4 Randall	Y	-	Y	Y	Y	N
3 Sullivan	N	N	N	N	N	N

	1	2	3	4	5	6
2 *Curtis*	Y	N	Y	Y	Y	N
7 *Hall*	Y	N	Y	Y	Y	Y
MONTANA						
1 Olsen	Y	N	N	N	N	N
2 *Battin*	Y	N	Y	Y	Y	✓
NEBRASKA						
2 *Cunningham*	Y	N	Y	Y	N	Y
1 *Denney*	Y	N	Y	Y	N	?
3 *Martin*	Y	N	Y	Y	Y	N
NEVADA						
AL Baring	Y	-	Y	Y	Y	Y
NEW HAMPSHIRE						
2 *Cleveland*	N	N	Y	Y	N	-
1 *Wyman*	Y	N	Y	N	Y	Y
NEW JERSEY						
14 Daniels	N	N	N	N	N	N
13 Gallagher	N	-	N	N	N	N
9 Helstoski	N	Y	N	N	N	N
3 Howard	N	-	N	N	N	Y
8 Joelson	N	N	N	N	N	Y
11 Minish	N	N	N	N	N	?
15 Patten	N	N	N	N	N	N
10 Rodino	N	N	X	X	N	?
4 Thompson	N	N	N	N	X	N
6 *Cahill*	?	?	Y	Y	N	Y
12 *Dwyer*	N	N	Y	N	N	Y
5 *Frelinghuysen*	N	N	Y	Y	N	Y
1 *Hunt*	Y	N	Y	Y	N	Y
2 *Sandman*	N	N	Y	N	N	Y
7 *Widnall*	N	N	Y	N	N	Y
NEW MEXICO						
AL Morris	Y	-	N	N	N	Y
AL Walker	Y	N	N	Y	N	Y
NEW YORK						
27 Dow	N	N	N	N	N	Y
41 Dulski	N	N	N	N	N	N
34 Hanley	N	N	N	N	N	N
39 McCarthy	N	N	Y	N	N	Y
25 Ottinger	N	N	N	N	N	N
1 Pike	N	N	Y	N	N	Y
28 Resnick	N	-	N	N	N	Y
35 Stratton	Y	N	Y	N	N	Y
5 Tenzer	N	N	N	N	N	Y
3 Wolff	N	N	N	N	N	Y
29 *Button*	N	N	N	N	N	Y
37 *Conable*	N	N	Y	Y	N	Y
38 *Goodell*	N	N	Y	Y	N	Y
2 *Grover*	N	N	Y	Y	N	Y
36 *Horton*	Y	N	N	N	N	N
30 *King*	Y	N	Y	Y	Y	Y
31 *McEwen*	N	N	Y	Y	Y	✓
32 *Pirnie*	N	N	Y	N	N	Y
26 *Reid*	N	N	N	N	N	N
33 *Robison*	N	N	Y	N	N	✓
40 *Smith*	N	N	Y	Y	?	Y
4 *Wydler*	Y	N	Y	Y	N	Y
New York City						
7 Addabbo	N	N	N	N	N	N
23 Bingham	N	Y	N	N	N	N
11 Brasco	N	N	N	N	N	N
15 Carey	N	?	N	N	N	X
10 Celler	N	?	N	N	N	Y
9 Delaney	N	N	N	N	N	N
19 Farbstein	N	Y	N	N	N	N
22 Gilbert	N	N	N	N	N	N
12 Kelly	N	N	N	N	N	Y
13 Multer	N	N	N	N	N	N
16 Murphy	N	N	N	N	X	N
18 Vacancy						
14 Rooney	N	N	N	N	X	N
8 Rosenthal	N	Y	N	N	N	N
20 Ryan	N	Y	N	N	N	N
21 Scheuer	N	Y	N	N	N	-
24 *Fino*	Y	N	Y	Y	N	?
6 *Halpern*	Y	N	N	N	N	-
17 *Kupferman*	N	N	N	N	N	X
NORTH CAROLINA						
2 Fountain	Y	-	Y	Y	Y	Y
5 Galifianakis	Y	N	Y	N	Y	Y
3 Henderson	Y	N	Y	Y	Y	Y
1 Jones	Y	N	Y	Y	Y	Y
6 Kornegay	Y	N	Y	N	Y	Y
7 Lennon	Y	N	Y	Y	Y	Y

	1	2	3	4	5	6
11 Taylor	Y	N	Y	Y	Y	Y
10 Whitener	Y	N	Y	Y	Y	✓
9 *Broyhill*	Y	N	Y	Y	Y	Y
4 *Gardner*	Y	N	Y	Y	Y	Y
8 *Jonas*	Y	N	Y	Y	Y	Y
NORTH DAKOTA						
1 *Andrews*	Y	N	Y	N	N	Y
2 *Kleppe*	Y	N	Y	Y	Y	Y
OHIO						
9 Ashley	N	N	N	N	N	Y
20 Feighan	N	N	N	N	N	N
18 Hays	N	-	‡	-	N	‡
19 Kirwan	N	-	N	N	N	N
21 Vanik	N	N	N	N	N	N
17 *Ashbrook*	Y	N	Y	Y	‡	N
14 *Ayres*	Y	N	Y	N	N	Y
8 *Betts*	Y	N	Y	Y	Y	Y
22 *Bolton*	Y	N	Y	Y	N	Y
16 *Bow*	?	?	✓	✓	✓	N
7 *Brown*	Y	?	Y	Y	Y	Y
2 *Clancy*	Y	N	✓	Y	Y	Y
12 *Devine*	Y	N	Y	Y	Y	Y
6 *Harsha*	Y	N	Y	Y	Y	Y
5 *Latta*	Y	N	✓	✓	Y	Y
24 *Lukens*	Y	N	Y	Y	Y	N
4 *McCulloch*	Y	N	Y	Y	N	Y
10 *Miller*	Y	N	Y	Y	Y	Y
23 *Minshall*	Y	N	Y	Y	N	Y
13 *Mosher*	N	N	N	N	N	Y
11 *Stanton*	N	N	Y	Y	N	Y
1 *Taft*	N	N	Y	N	N	N
3 *Whalen*	N	N	N	N	N	N
15 *Wylie*	Y	N	Y	Y	N	Y
OKLAHOMA						
3 Albert	N	N	N	N	N	Y
2 Edmondson	Y	N	N	N	N	Y
5 Jarman	Y	N	Y	Y	Y	Y
4 Steed	Y	-	N	Y	N	Y
1 *Belcher*	Y	N	Y	Y	Y	Y
6 *Smith*	Y	N	Y	Y	Y	Y
OREGON						
3 Green	N	Y	N	N	N	Y
2 Ullman	N	N	?	N	-	Y
4 *Dellenback*	N	N	X	X	N	Y
1 *Wyatt*	Y	N	Y	Y	N	N
PENNSYLVANIA						
25 Clark	Y	-	N	N	N	N
21 Dent	N	N	N	N	N	N
11 Flood	Y	N	N	N	N	N
20 Holland	N	N	-	-	N	N
14 Moorhead	N	N	N	N	N	N
26 Morgan	Y	N	N	N	N	-
6 Rhodes	Y	N	N	N	N	N
15 Rooney	Y	N	N	N	N	N
24 Vigorito	Y	N	N	N	N	N
8 *Biester*	N	N	Y	Y	N	Y
18 *Corbett*	Y	N	Y	N	N	Y
16 *Eshleman*	Y	N	Y	Y	N	Y
27 *Fulton*	Y	N	Y	N	Y	N
19 *Goodling*	Y	N	Y	Y	Y	Y
23 *Johnson*	Y	N	Y	Y	Y	Y
10 *McDade*	Y	N	Y	N	N	N
22 *Saylor*	Y	N	Y	Y	Y	N
17 *Schneebeli*	N	N	Y	Y	Y	Y
13 *Schweiker*	Y	N	Y	N	N	Y
9 *Watkins*	Y	?	Y	Y	Y	Y
12 *Whalley*	Y	N	Y	Y	Y	?
7 *Williams*	Y	-	Y	Y	✓	Y
Philadelphia City						
1 Barrett	N	N	N	N	N	N
3 Byrne	N	N	N	N	N	N
4 Eilberg	Y	N	N	N	N	N
5 Green	N	N	N	N	N	N
2 Nix	N	N	N	N	N	N
RHODE ISLAND						
1 St. Germain	N	N	N	N	N	N
2 Tiernan *			N	N	N	N
SOUTH CAROLINA						
4 Ashmore	Y	N	Y	Y	Y	Y
3 Dorn	Y	N	Y	Y	Y	Y
5 Gettys	Y	N	Y	Y	Y	Y
6 McMillan	Y	N	✓	✓	Y	Y

	1	2	3	4	5	6
1 Rivers	Y	N	Y	Y	Y	Y
2 *Watson*	Y	N	Y	Y	Y	Y
SOUTH DAKOTA						
2 *Berry*	Y	N	Y	Y	✓	Y
1 *Reifel*	Y	N	Y	N	N	Y
TENNESSEE						
6 Anderson	Y	N	N	N	N	-
7 Blanton	Y	N	Y	N	Y	N
8 Everett	Y	N	N	N	Y	Y
4 Evins	Y	-	N	N	X	Y
5 Fulton	Y	N	N	N	N	N
3 *Brock*	Y	N	Y	Y	N	N
2 *Duncan*	Y	N	Y	Y	Y	Y
9 *Kuykendall*	Y	N	Y	Y	N	Y
1 *Quillen*	Y	N	Y	Y	Y	Y
TEXAS						
9 Brooks	N	N	N	N	N	Y
17 Burleson	Y	N	Y	Y	Y	Y
5 Cabell	Y	-	Y	N	Y	Y
22 Casey	Y	N	N	Y	N	Y
15 de la Garza	Y	N	Y	N	N	Y
2 Dowdy	Y	N	Y	Y	Y	Y
8 Eckhardt	N	N	N	N	N	N
21 Fisher	Y	N	Y	Y	Y	Y
20 Gonzalez	N	N	N	N	N	N
23 Kazen	Y	N	N	N	N	Y
19 Mahon	Y	N	N	N	N	Y
1 Patman	Y	N	N	N	N	Y
10 Pickle	Y	N	✓	‡	Y	Y
11 Poage	Y	N	Y	N	Y	Y
3 Pool	Y	N	Y	Y	Y	Y
13 Purcell	Y	N	N	N	Y	Y
4 Roberts	Y	N	Y	N	‡	Y
6 Teague	Y	N	Y	Y	Y	Y
16 White	Y	N	Y	Y	Y	Y
12 Wright	Y	N	N	N	N	Y
14 Young	Y	N	N	N	N	Y
7 *Bush*	Y	N	Y	Y	N	Y
18 *Price*	Y	N	Y	Y	Y	Y
UTAH						
1 *Burton*	Y	N	Y	Y	Y	N
2 *Lloyd*	Y	N	Y	Y	Y	Y
VERMONT						
AL *Stafford*	N	N	Y	N	N	Y
VIRGINIA						
4 Abbitt	Y	N	Y	Y	Y	Y
1 Downing	Y	N	Y	N	Y	Y
2 Hardy	Y	N	Y	N	Y	Y
7 Marsh	N	-	Y	Y	Y	Y
3 Satterfield	Y	N	Y	N	Y	Y
5 Tuck	Y	N	Y	Y	✓	Y
10 *Broyhill*	Y	N	Y	Y	Y	Y
6 *Poff*	Y	N	Y	Y	Y	Y
8 *Scott*	Y	N	Y	Y	N	Y
9 *Wampler*	Y	N	Y	Y	Y	N
WASHINGTON						
7 Adams	N	N	N	N	N	N
5 Foley	N	-	N	N	N	N
3 Hansen	N	N	N	N	N	N
6 Hicks	N	N	N	N	N	Y
2 Meeds	Y	N	N	N	N	N
4 *May*	Y	-	Y	Y	N	Y
1 *Pelly*	Y	N	Y	Y	N	Y
WEST VIRGINIA						
4 Hechler	Y	N	N	N	N	Y
5 Kee	Y	N	N	N	N	N
3 Slack	Y	N	N	N	N	N
2 Staggers	Y	N	N	N	N	N
1 *Moore*	N	N	Y	Y	‡	X
WISCONSIN						
2 Kastenmeier	N	Y	N	N	?	N
5 Reuss	N	N	N	N	N	N
4 Zablocki	N	N	N	N	N	N
8 *Byrnes*	N	-	Y	Y	Y	Y
9 *Davis*	N	N	Y	Y	Y	Y
7 *Laird*	N	N	✓	✓	N	Y
10 *O'Konski*	Y	N	Y	Y	Y	?
1 *Schadeberg*	Y	N	Y	Y	N	Y
6 *Steiger*	N	N	Y	Y	N	N
3 *Thomson*	N	N	Y	Y	Y	Y
WYOMING						
AL *Harrison*	Y	N	Y	Y	Y	Y

*Rep. Robert O. Tiernan (D R.I.) sworn in April 13, 1967.

Democrats in this type; *Republicans in italics*

House Key Votes—90th Congress—1967

7. HR 11000. Rat Control and Extermination Act of 1967. Adoption of an open rule (H Res 749) for floor consideration of HR 11000, providing federal grants to aid localities in developing and carrying out programs of rat control and extermination. Rejected 176-207: R 22-148; D 154-59 (ND 127-7; SD 27-52), July 20, 1967. A "yea" was a vote supporting the President's position.

8. HR 5037. Anticrime Bill. Cahill (R N.J.) amendment to replace the categorical grants to local governments provided for in the Administration bill with block grants to the states for planning and improving methods of law enforcement. Accepted 256-147: R 172-4; D 84-143 (ND 16-129; SD 68-14), Aug. 8, 1967. A "nay" was a vote supporting the President's position.

9. HR 6736. Public Broadcasting Act of 1967. Devine (R Ohio) motion to recommit the bill to the House Interstate and Foreign Commerce Committee with instructions to delete provisions for a Public Broadcasting Corporation and to authorize $5 million for distribution among educational television stations. Rejected 167-194: R 124-33; D 43-161 (ND 3-122; SD 40-39), Sept. 21, 1967. A "nay" was a vote supporting the President's position.

10. H J Res 888. Continuing appropriations for fiscal 1968. Whitten (D Miss.) amendment, as amended by Bow (R Ohio), Passman (D La.) and Broyhill (R Va.), providing that no Government agency could spend more in fiscal 1968 than it spent in fiscal 1967,

with a few exceptions including military expenditures and interest payments on the national debt; setting a $131.5-billion ceiling on total fiscal 1968 federal expenditures, excluding additional costs of the Viet Nam war; and setting limits on foreign aid and Office of Economic Opportunity expenditures. Accepted 238-164: R 171-9; D 67-155 (ND 11-134; SD 56-21), Oct. 18, 1967. A "nay" was a vote supporting the President's position.

11. S 1872. Foreign Assistance Act of 1967. Gross (R Iowa) motion to recommit the conference report with instructions that House conferees insist on House provisions terminating the President's authority to engage in the sale or purchase of defense equipment or services with nations trading with or shipping to North Viet Nam and withholding the "most favored nation" tariff privilege from Poland until it was determined that country was no longer sending war supplies to North Viet Nam. Rejected 196-200: R 136-33; D 60-167 (ND 9-137; SD 51-30), Nov. 8, 1967. A "nay" was a vote supporting the President's position.

12. S 2388. Antipoverty authorization. Ayres (R Ohio) motion to recommit the bill with instructions that the Education and Labor Committee reduce the fiscal 1968 authorization for antipoverty programs by $460 million -- from the $2,060,000,000 provided in the Committee bill to $1.6 billion. Accepted 221-190: R 148-28; D 73-162 (ND 9-141; SD 64-21), Nov. 15, 1967. A "nay" was a vote supporting the President's position.

	7	8	9	10	11	12
ALABAMA						
3 Andrews	N	Y	Y	Y	Y	✓
7 Bevill	N	Y	N	Y	Y	Y
8 Jones	N	Y	N	N	N	Y
4 Nichols	N	Y	Y	Y	Y	Y
5 Selden	N	Y	Y	Y	Y	Y
6 *Buchanan*	Y	Y	Y	Y	Y	Y
2 *Dickinson*	N	Y	Y	Y	Y	Y
1 *Edwards*	N	Y	Y	Y	?	Y
ALASKA						
AL Pollock	N	‡	X	Y	Y	Y
ARIZONA						
2 Udall	Y	N	-	N	N	N
1 *Rhodes*	N	Y	Y	Y	Y	✓
3 *Steiger*	N	Y	Y	Y	Y	Y
ARKANSAS						
1 Gathings	N	Y	Y	Y	Y	Y
2 Mills	N	Y	✓	Y	Y	Y
4 Pryor	N	Y	N	Y	N	Y
3 *Hammerschmidt*	N	Y	Y	Y	Y	Y
CALIFORNIA						
5 Burton	Y	N	N	N	N	N
7 Cohelan	Y	N	N	N	N	N
9 Edwards	Y	N	-	X	N	N
34 Hanna	Y	N	N	X	N	N
2 Johnson	Y	N	N	N	N	N
4 Leggett	Y	N	-	N	N	N
15 McFall	Y	N	N	N	N	N
8 Miller	Y	N	N	X	N	N
3 Moss	Y	N	X	N	N	N
16 Sisk	Y	N	N	N	N	N
38 Tunney	Y	N	N	?	N	N
37 Van Deerlin	Y	N	N	N	N	N
14 Waldie	Y	N	-	N	N	N
1 *Clausen*	N	Y	Y	Y	Y	Y
10 *Gubser*	N	Y	Y	Y	Y	Y
6 *Mailliard*	X	Y	N	Y	N	Y
18 *Mathias*	N	Y	?	?	✓	Y
33 *Pettis*	N	Y	N	Y	?	Y
12 *Talcott*	N	Y	Y	Y	Y	Y
13 *Teague*	N	Y	Y	Y	Y	Y
35 *Utt*	X	✓	?	Y	✓	✓
36 *Wilson*	N	Y	N	✓	Y	Y
11 Vacancy						
Los Angeles Co.						
29 Brown	Y	N	-	N	N	N
22 Corman	Y	N	-	N	N	N
21 Hawkins	✓	N	N	N	N	N
19 Holifield	Y	N	N	N	N	N
17 King	✓	N	N	N	N	N
26 Rees	Y	N	-	N	N	N
30 Roybal	Y	N	N	N	N	N
31 Wilson	Y	X	N	N	N	N
28 *Bell*	N	Y	Y	?	Y	N
23 *Clawson*	N	Y	Y	Y	?	Y
32 *Hosmer*	N	Y	Y	Y	?	Y
24 *Lipscomb*	N	Y	Y	Y	Y	Y
27 *Reinecke*	N	✓	Y	Y	Y	Y
20 *Smith*	N	Y	Y	Y	✓	Y
25 *Wiggins*	N	Y	Y	Y	Y	Y
COLORADO						
4 Aspinall	Y	N	-	N	N	X
3 Evans	Y	Y	N	N	N	N
1 Rogers	Y	N	N	N	N	N
2 *Brotzman*	N	Y	N	Y	Y	Y
CONNECTICUT						
1 Daddario	Y	N	N	N	N	N
3 Giaimo	Y	N	N	N	N	Y
4 Irwin	Y	N	N	N	N	N
5 Monagan	Y	N	N	N	N	N
2 St. Onge	Y	N	X	X	X	N
6 *Meskill*	N	Y	Y	Y	Y	N
DELAWARE						
AL *Roth*	N	Y	Y	Y	Y	Y
FLORIDA						
3 Bennett	N	Y	N	Y	Y	Y
12 Fascell	N	N	N	N	N	N
2 Fuqua	N	Y	N	✓	Y	Y
6 Gibbons	Y	N	N	N	N	N
7 Haley	N	Y	Y	Y	Y	Y
4 Herlong	N	Y	-	✓	✓	✓
11 Pepper	✓	N	N	X	N	N
9 Rogers	N	Y	N	Y	Y	Y
1 Sikes	N	Y	Y	Y	✓	Y
10 *Burke*	N	Y	Y	Y	Y	Y
8 *Cramer*	N	Y	-	Y	Y	Y
5 *Gurney*	N	‡	Y	Y	Y	Y
GEORGIA						
3 Brinkley	N	Y	?	Y	Y	Y
7 Davis	N	Y	N	Y	Y	Y
6 Flynt	N	Y	N	Y	Y	Y
1 Hagan	N	Y	Y	Y	✓	Y
9 Landrum	Y	?	Y	✓	Y	Y
2 O'Neal	N	Y	Y	Y	Y	Y
10 Stephens	Y	Y	N	✓	Y	Y
8 Stuckey	N	Y	Y	Y	Y	Y
4 *Blackburn*	N	Y	✓	Y	Y	Y
5 *Thompson*	N	Y	Y	Y	Y	Y
HAWAII						
AL Matsunaga	Y	X	N	N	N	N
AL Mink	Y	X	N	N	N	N
IDAHO						
2 *Hansen*	N	Y	Y	Y	Y	Y
1 *McClure*	N	Y	Y	Y	Y	Y
ILLINOIS						
21 Gray	✓	N	N	N	N	N
24 Price	Y	N	N	N	N	N
23 Shipley	Y	N	?	Y	Y	N
16 Anderson	N	Y	N	Y	?	Y
17 *Arends*	X	Y	Y	Y	Y	Y
14 *Erlenborn*	N	Y	Y	Y	?	Y
20 *Findley*	N	Y	?	Y	Y	Y
12 *McClory*	N	Y	N	Y	Y	✓
18 *Michel*	N	Y	Y	Y	Y	Y
19 *Railsback*	N	Y	Y	Y	Y	Y
15 *Reid*	N	Y	Y	Y	Y	Y
22 *Springer*	N	Y	N	Y	Y	Y
Chicago-Cook Co.						
7 Annunzio	Y	N	N	N	X	X
1 Dawson	?	N	?	X	N	N
5 Kluczynski	✓	N	X	N	N	N
3 Murphy	✓	N	N	N	N	N
2 O'Hara	Y	N	N	N	N	N
11 Pucinski	✓	N	?	N	N	N
6 Ronan	Y	N	N	N	N	N
8 Rostenkowski	Y	N	N	N	N	N
9 Yates	N	N	N	N	N	N
10 *Collier*	N	Y	Y	Y	✓	Y
4 *Derwinski*	N	✓	✓	Y	?	Y
13 *Rumsfeld*	N	Y	Y	Y	Y	Y
INDIANA						
3 Brademas	Y	X	N	N	N	N
9 Hamilton	Y	Y	?	N	N	N
11 Jacobs	Y	N	N	N	N	N
1 Madden	Y	N	N	N	N	N
5 Roush	Y	N	N	Y	N	N
5 *Adair*	N	Y	Y	Y	Y	Y
6 *Bray*	N	Y	Y	Y	Y	Y
2 *Halleck*	N	Y	N	Y	?	Y
7 *Myers*	N	Y	Y	Y	Y	Y
10 *Roudebush*	N	Y	Y	Y	Y	Y
8 *Zion*	N	Y	Y	Y	Y	Y
IOWA						
2 Culver	Y	N	N	X	N	N
5 Smith	Y	N	N	N	N	N
3 *Gross*	N	Y	Y	Y	Y	Y
4 *Kyl*	N	Y	Y	Y	Y	Y
6 *Mayne*	N	‡	Y	Y	N	Y
7 *Scherle*	N	Y	Y	Y	Y	Y
1 *Schwengel*	N	Y	Y	Y	Y	Y
KANSAS						
1 *Dole*	N	Y	Y	Y	✓	Y
2 *Mize*	N	Y	Y	Y	N	Y
4 *Shriver*	N	Y	Y	Y	Y	Y
5 *Skubitz*	N	Y	N	Y	Y	Y
3 *Winn*	N	Y	Y	Y	Y	Y
KENTUCKY						
2 Natcher	Y	Y	N	N	Y	N
7 Perkins	Y	N	N	N	N	N
1 Stubblefield	Y	Y	N	Y	N	Y

KEY

- **Y** Record vote for (yea).
- **✓** Paired for.
- **‡** Announced for or CQ poll for.
- **N** Record vote against (nay).
- **X** Paired against.
- **-** Announced against or CQ poll against.
- **?** Absent, general pair, "present" or did not announce or answer poll.

Democrats in this type; *Republicans in italics*

	7	8	9	10	11	12
6 Watts	N	Y	Y	Y	?	Y
5 *Carter*	X	Y	Y	Y	Y	N
3 *Cowger*	N	Y	Y	Y	Y	N
4 *Snyder*	N	Y	Y	Y	Y	Y
LOUISIANA						
2 Boggs	✓	N	N	X	N	N
7 Edwards	Y	Y	N	Y	Y	Y
1 Hebert	N	✓	✓	?	✓	Y
8 Long	X	Y	✓	Y	Y	Y
5 Passman	X	✓	Y	Y	Y	Y
6 Rarick	X	Y	✓	✓	Y	Y
4 Waggonner	N	Y	Y	Y	Y	Y
3 Willis	Y	✓	✓	X	X	?
MAINE						
2 Hathaway	Y	N	N	N	N	N
1 Kyros	Y	X	N	N	N	N
MARYLAND						
4 Fallon	Y	N	?	N	N	N
7 Friedel	Y	N	N	N	N	N
3 Garmatz	Y	N	-	N	N	N
2 Long	‡	N	N	N	N	N
5 Machen	Y	N	N	Y	N	N
8 *Gude*	Y	Y	Y	N	N	N
6 *Mathias*	Y	?	?	N	X	N
1 *Morton*	N	Y	N	Y	Y	Y
MASSACHUSETTS						
2 Boland	Y	Y	N	N	N	N
11 Burke	Y	Y	N	N	N	N
4 Donohue	Y	N	N	N	N	N
7 Macdonald	✓	N	N	N	X	N
9 McCormack						
8 O'Neill	Y	N	N	N	X	N
3 Philbin	Y	N	N	N	N	N
6 *Bates*	N	Y	N	Y	N	Y
1 *Conte*	Y	Y	-	Y	N	?
10 *Heckler*	Y	Y	N	Y	Y	X
12 *Keith*	N	Y	N	Y	N	Y
5 *Morse*	N	Y	N	N	N	N
MICHIGAN						
12 O'Hara	Y	N	N	N	N	N
18 *Broomfield*	N	Y	‡	✓	X	X
3 *Brown*	N	‡	-	Y	Y	N
10 *Cederberg*	X	Y	✓	Y	Y	Y
6 *Chamberlain*	N	Y	Y	Y	Y	Y
2 *Esch*	Y	Y	N	Y	Y	N
5 *Ford*	X	Y	Y	Y	Y	Y
8 *Harvey*	N	Y	Y	Y	Y	Y
4 *Hutchinson*	N	Y	✓	Y	Y	Y
19 *McDonald*	N	Y	Y	Y	Y	Y
7 *Riegle*	Y	Y	Y	Y	Y	N
11 *Ruppe*	N	Y	-	Y	Y	N
9 *Vander Jagt*	Y	Y	Y	Y	Y	Y
Detroit-Wayne Co.						
1 Conyers	✓	N	?	N	Y	N
13 Diggs	✓	N	N	N	N	N
16 Dingell	N	N	?	N	N	N
15 Ford	Y	N	N	N	N	N
17 Griffiths	Y	N	N	N	N	N
14 Nedzi	Y	N	N	N	N	N
MINNESOTA						
8 Blatnik	Y	N	N	N	N	N
5 Fraser	Y	N	N	N	N	N
4 Karth	✓	N	N	N	N	N
7 *Langen*	N	Y	Y	Y	Y	Y
3 *MacGregor*	N	Y	Y	Y	N	?
2 *Nelsen*	N	Y	?	Y	Y	Y
1 *Quie*	N	Y	N	Y	N	Y
6 *Zwach*	N	Y	N	Y	Y	Y
MISSISSIPPI						
1 Abernethy	N	✓	Y	Y	Y	Y
5 Colmer	N	‡	Y	Y	Y	Y
4 Montgomery	N	✓	N	Y	Y	Y
2 Whitten	N	✓	Y	Y	Y	Y
3 Williams	X	?	Y	?	✓	?
MISSOURI						
5 Bolling	Y	N	N	N	N	N
6 Hull	N	Y	Y	Y	Y	Y
9 Hungate	‡	N	N	Y	N	Y
8 Ichord	N	Y	N	Y	Y	Y
10 Jones	N	Y	Y	?	?	Y
1 Karsten	Y	N	N	N	N	N
4 Randall	Y	Y	Y	Y	Y	Y
3 Sullivan	Y	N	N	N	N	N

	7	8	9	10	11	12
2 *Curtis*	N	Y	Y	Y	Y	Y
7 *Hall*	N	Y	Y	Y	Y	Y
MONTANA						
1 Olsen	Y	N	N	N	N	N
2 *Battin*	N	Y	Y	Y	Y	Y
NEBRASKA						
2 *Cunningham*	N	Y	N	Y	Y	Y
1 *Denney*	N	Y	N	Y	Y	Y
3 *Martin*	N	Y	Y	Y	Y	✓
NEVADA						
AL Baring	N	Y	-	Y	Y	Y
NEW HAMPSHIRE						
2 *Cleveland*	N	Y	N	Y	Y	Y
1 *Wyman*	N	Y	N	Y	Y	Y
NEW JERSEY						
14 Daniels	Y	N	N	N	N	N
13 Gallagher	Y	X	N	N	N	N
9 Helstoski	Y	N	N	N	N	N
3 Howard	✓	N	N	N	N	N
8 Joelson	Y	N	N	N	N	N
11 Minish	Y	N	N	N	N	N
15 Patten	Y	N	N	N	N	N
10 Rodino	Y	N	N	N	N	N
4 Thompson	Y	N	N	N	N	N
6 *Cahill*	Y	Y	Y	Y	N	Y
12 *Dwyer*	Y	Y	Y	Y	N	Y
5 *Frelinghuysen*	N	Y	Y	Y	N	Y
1 *Hunt*	N	Y	Y	Y	Y	Y
2 *Sandman*	-	Y	N	Y	Y	Y
7 *Widnall*	Y	Y	Y	Y	N	Y
NEW MEXICO						
AL Morris	Y	Y	N	Y	N	Y
AL Walker	Y	Y	N	Y	Y	N
NEW YORK						
27 Dow	Y	N	-	N	N	N
41 Dulski	Y	N	N	N	N	N
34 Hanley	Y	N	N	N	N	N
39 McCarthy	Y	N	N	N	N	N
25 Ottinger	Y	N	N	N	N	N
1 Pike	Y	N	N	N	N	N
28 Resnick	Y	N	N	N	X	N
35 Stratton	N	N	N	N	?	Y
5 Tenzer	Y	N	X	X	N	N
3 Wolff	Y	N	X	N	N	N
29 *Button*	N	Y	X	N	X	N
37 *Conable*	N	Y	Y	Y	N	Y
38 *Goodell*	?	Y	Y	Y	N	Y
2 *Grover*	N	Y	N	Y	Y	Y
36 *Horton*	Y	Y	X	N	N	N
30 *King*	N	Y	Y	Y	Y	Y
31 *McEwen*	N	Y	Y	Y	N	Y
32 *Pirnie*	N	Y	N	Y	N	N
26 *Reid*	Y	N	N	N	N	N
33 *Robison*	N	Y	Y	Y	N	Y
40 *Smith*	N	Y	Y	Y	N	Y
4 *Wydler*	Y	‡	Y	Y	Y	Y
New York City						
7 Addabbo	Y	N	N	N	N	N
23 Bingham	Y	N	N	N	N	N
11 Brasco	Y	N	N	N	N	N
15 Carey	Y	N	N	N	N	N
10 Celler	✓	N	?	N	N	N
9 Delaney	Y	N	N	N	N	N
19 Farbstein	Y	N	N	N	N	N
22 Gilbert	Y	N	N	N	N	N
12 Kelly	Y	N	N	N	N	N
13 Multer	Y	N	N	N	N	X
16 Murphy	Y	N	-	N	N	N
18 Vacancy						
14 Rooney	Y	X	N	N	N	N
8 Rosenthal	Y	N	N	N	N	N
20 Ryan	Y	N	N	N	N	N
21 Scheuer	✓	N	-	N	N	N
24 *Fino*	Y	Y	-	Y	Y	Y
6 *Halpern*	Y	N	N	N	N	N
17 *Kupferman*	Y	N	N	N	N	N
NORTH CAROLINA						
2 Fountain	N	Y	✓	✓	✓	Y
5 Galifianakis	Y	Y	N	Y	Y	N
3 Henderson	N	Y	Y	Y	Y	Y
1 Jones	Y	Y	Y	✓	Y	Y
6 Kornegay	N	Y	N	Y	Y	Y
7 Lennon	N	Y	Y	Y	Y	Y

	7	8	9	10	11	12
11 Taylor	N	Y	Y	Y	Y	Y
10 Whitener	X	N	Y	Y	Y	Y
9 *Broyhill*	N	Y	Y	Y	Y	Y
4 *Gardner*	X	Y	Y	Y	Y	Y
8 *Jonas*	N	Y	Y	Y	Y	Y
NORTH DAKOTA						
1 *Andrews*	N	Y	N	Y	Y	Y
2 *Kleppe*	N	Y	Y	Y	Y	Y
OHIO						
9 Ashley	Y	N	N	N	N	N
20 Feighan	Y	N	X	N	Y	N
18 Hays	N	N	-	N	N	N
19 Kirwan	✓	X	N	N	N	X
21 Vanik	Y	N	N	N	N	N
17 *Ashbrook*	N	Y	Y	Y	Y	Y
14 *Ayres*	-	Y	Y	Y	Y	Y
8 *Betts*	N	Y	Y	Y	Y	Y
22 *Bolton*	N	Y	Y	✓	N	Y
16 *Bow*	N	Y	Y	Y	Y	Y
7 *Brown*	N	Y	Y	Y	Y	Y
2 *Clancy*	N	Y	Y	Y	Y	N
12 *Devine*	N	Y	Y	Y	Y	Y
6 *Harsha*	N	Y	Y	Y	Y	N
5 *Latta*	N	Y	X	✓	Y	Y
24 *Lukens*	N	Y	Y	Y	Y	Y
4 *McCulloch*	N	N	Y	Y	Y	Y
10 *Miller*	N	Y	Y	Y	Y	Y
23 *Minshall*	N	Y	‡	Y	Y	N
13 *Mosher*	Y	Y	N	Y	N	Y
11 *Stanton*	N	Y	Y	Y	Y	Y
1 *Taft*	N	Y	*	Y	N	Y
3 *Whalen*	Y	Y	Y	N	N	N
15 *Wylie*	N	Y	Y	Y	Y	Y
OKLAHOMA						
3 Albert	Y	N	N	N	N	N
2 Edmondson	Y	Y	?	N	N	N
5 Jarman	N	Y	N	Y	Y	Y
4 Steed	N	Y	N	N	N	Y
1 *Belcher*	N	Y	‡	Y	Y	Y
6 *Smith*	N	Y	Y	Y	Y	Y
OREGON						
3 Green	Y	Y	N	N	N	N
2 Ullman	Y	Y	N	Y	N	N
4 *Dellenback*	N	Y	Y	Y	N	Y
1 *Wyatt*	X	Y	‡	Y	N	Y
PENNSYLVANIA						
25 Clark	Y	X	N	N	N	N
21 Dent	✓	N	X	N	N	N
11 Flood	Y	N	N	N	N	N
20 Holland	Y	N	?	X	N	N
14 Moorhead	Y	N	N	N	N	N
26 Morgan	Y	N	N	X	N	N
6 Rhodes	Y	N	-	N	N	N
15 Rooney	Y	N	N	N	N	N
24 Vigorito	Y	N	N	N	N	N
8 *Biester*	N	Y	Y	Y	Y	Y
18 *Corbett*	N	Y	?	Y	Y	N
16 *Eshleman*	N	Y	Y	Y	Y	Y
27 *Fulton*	N	Y	Y	Y	Y	N
19 *Goodling*	N	Y	Y	Y	Y	Y
23 *Johnson*	N	Y	Y	Y	Y	Y
10 *McDade*	Y	Y	Y	Y	Y	N
22 *Saylor*	-	Y	Y	Y	Y	Y
17 *Schneebeli*	N	Y	Y	Y	Y	Y
13 *Schweiker*	Y	Y	Y	Y	Y	N
9 *Watkins*	X	Y	?	Y	Y	Y
12 *Whalley*	N	Y	Y	Y	Y	Y
7 *Williams*	N	Y	?	Y	Y	Y
Philadelphia City						
1 Barrett	Y	N	N	N	N	N
3 Byrne	Y	N	N	N	N	N
4 Eilberg	Y	N	N	N	N	N
5 Green	Y	N	N	N	N	N
2 Nix	Y	N	N	N	N	N
RHODE ISLAND						
1 St. Germain	Y	Y	N	N	N	N
2 Tiernan	✓	X	N	N	N	N
SOUTH CAROLINA						
4 Ashmore	N	Y	Y	Y	Y	Y
3 Dorn	X	Y	N	Y	Y	N
5 Gettys	Y	Y	N	Y	N	Y
6 McMillan	X	Y	Y	Y	Y	Y

	7	8	9	10	11	12
1 Rivers	Y	Y	Y	Y	Y	Y
2 *Watson*	X	Y	Y	Y	Y	Y
SOUTH DAKOTA						
2 *Berry*	N	Y	Y	Y	Y	Y
1 *Reifel*	N	Y	Y	Y	Y	Y
TENNESSEE						
6 Anderson	Y	N	N	N	N	N
7 Blanton	N	Y	N	Y	Y	Y
8 Everett	N	Y	N	Y	?	✓
4 Evins	✓	Y	N	N	Y	N
5 Fulton	Y	Y	N	N	N	N
3 *Brock*	N	Y	Y	Y	Y	Y
2 *Duncan*	N	Y	Y	Y	Y	Y
9 *Kuykendall*	X	Y	Y	Y	Y	Y
1 *Quillen*	N	Y	‡	Y	Y	Y
TEXAS						
9 Brooks	Y	N	N	N	N	N
17 Burleson	N	Y	Y	Y	N	Y
5 Cabell	N	Y	Y	Y	N	Y
22 Casey	N	Y	Y	N	Y	Y
15 de la Garza	Y	Y	?	N	N	N
2 Dowdy	N	Y	Y	Y	Y	Y
8 Eckhardt	Y	N	N	N	N	N
21 Fisher	N	Y	Y	Y	Y	Y
20 Gonzalez	Y	N	N	N	N	N
23 Kazen	Y	N	N	N	N	N
19 Mahon	N	Y	N	N	N	Y
1 Patman	Y	N	N	X	N	N
10 Pickle	Y	Y	N	N	N	N
11 Poage	Y	Y	N	Y	Y	Y
3 Pool	X	Y	Y	Y	Y	Y
13 Purcell	N	Y	-	‡	N	Y
4 Roberts	N	Y	N	Y	N	Y
6 Teague	X	Y	Y	Y	X	?
16 White	N	Y	Y	Y	N	Y
12 Wright	N	Y	N	N	N	N
14 Young	Y	N	?	N	N	N
7 *Bush*	N	Y	Y	Y	Y	Y
18 *Price*	N	Y	Y	Y	Y	Y
UTAH						
1 *Burton*	N	✓	Y	Y	Y	Y
2 *Lloyd*	N	Y	Y	Y	Y	Y
VERMONT						
AL *Stafford*	N	Y	-	Y	N	N
VIRGINIA						
4 Abbitt	N	Y	Y	Y	Y	Y
1 Downing	Y	Y	Y	Y	Y	Y
2 Hardy	Y	Y	Y	Y	N	Y
7 Marsh	N	Y	Y	Y	Y	Y
3 Satterfield	N	Y	Y	Y	Y	Y
5 Tuck	N	Y	Y	Y	Y	Y
10 *Broyhill*	N	Y	Y	Y	Y	Y
6 *Poff*	N	Y	Y	Y	Y	Y
8 *Scott*	N	Y	Y	Y	Y	Y
9 *Wampler*	N	Y	Y	Y	?	Y
WASHINGTON						
7 Adams	✓	N	-	N	N	N
5 Foley	Y	N	N	Y	N	N
3 Hansen	✓	N	N	N	N	N
6 Hicks	Y	N	N	N	N	N
2 Meeds	Y	N	N	N	N	N
4 *May*	N	Y	Y	Y	Y	Y
1 *Pelly*	N	Y	N	Y	✓	N
WEST VIRGINIA						
4 Hechler	Y	N	N	N	N	N
5 Kee	Y	N	N	N	N	N
3 Slack	Y	Y	N	N	N	N
2 Staggers	Y	N	N	N	N	N
1 *Moore*	Y	Y	N	Y	Y	N
WISCONSIN						
2 Kastenmeier	Y	N	N	N	N	N
5 Reuss	Y	N	N	N	N	N
4 Zablocki	Y	Y	N	N	N	N
8 *Byrnes*	N	Y	Y	Y	N	Y
9 *Davis*	N	Y	Y	Y	Y	Y
7 *Laird*	X	Y	Y	Y	Y	?
10 *O'Konski*	N	Y	Y	Y	Y	Y
1 *Schadeberg*	N	Y	Y	Y	Y	Y
6 *Steiger*	N	Y	Y	Y	Y	Y
3 *Thomson*	N	Y	Y	Y	Y	Y
WYOMING						
AL *Harrison*	N	Y	-	Y	Y	Y

Democrats in this type; *Republicans in italics*

Rep. Taft did not vote because of possible conflict of interest.

Senate Key Votes—90th Congress—1967

1. S 665. Supplemental defense authorization for the Viet Nam war. Clark (D Pa.) amendment, as modified by Mansfield (D Mont.), declaring that Congress would provide all necessary support for U.S. servicemen fighting in Viet Nam, and that Congress supported (1) persons trying to bring about an honorable settlement of the Vietnamese war, and (2) the convening of an international meeting to plan an end to the Viet Nam conflict. Accepted 72-19: R 24-10; D 48-9 (ND 37-1; SD 11-8), March 1, 1967. The President did not take a position on the amendment.

2. S 355. Legislative Reorganization Act. Hruska (R Neb.) and Dirksen (R Ill.) amendment, as modified, to delete Title V, the title strengthening the lobby registration law. Rejected 30-53: R 22-8; D 8-45 (ND 3-30; SD 5-15), March 7, 1967. The President did not take a position on the amendment.

3. Exec D, 88th Congress, 2nd Session. Adoption of the resolution consenting to the President's ratification of the U.S.-Soviet Consular Convention providing ground rules for an exchange of consulates, complete immunities for consular officers and employees, and definite access and notification rights to a country in regard to citizens detained in the other country. Adopted 66-28: R 22-13; D 44-15 (ND 34-5; SD 10-10), March 16, 1967. (Sixty-three votes, two-thirds of Senators voting, were needed for adoption.) A "yea" was a vote supporting the President's position.

4. S Res 112. Dodd censure. Adoption of the first section of the resolution, censuring Sen. Thomas J. Dodd (D Conn.) for having used political funds for personal benefit. Accepted 92-5: R 34-2; D 58-3 (ND 40-2; SD 18-1), June 23, 1967. The President did not take a position on the resolution.

5. S 5. Truth-in-Lending Act. Passage of the bill to require that consumers who borrow money or make installment purchases be informed of the true cost of the loan or credit prior to the completion of the transaction. Passed 92-0: R 36-0; D 56-0 (ND 38-0; SD 18-0), July 11, 1967. A "yea" was a vote supporting the President's position.

6. S J Res 81. Railroad strike. Morse (D Ore.) motion to restore to the bill, as passed by the House, provisions directing that the special mediation board's final recommendations would become binding on the 91st day after enactment if no agreement had been reached by the parties. Accepted 68-21: R 32-1; D 36-20 (ND 19-19; SD 17-1), July 17, 1967. A "yea" was a vote supporting the President's position.

	1	2	3	4	5	6
ALABAMA						
Hill	N	N	N	Y	Y	Y
Sparkman	Y	-	Y	Y	Y	Y
ALASKA						
Bartlett	Y	-	Y	Y	Y	N
Gruening	‡	-	N	Y	Y	?
ARIZONA						
Hayden	Y	N	Y	Y	Y	Y
Fannin	-	Y	N	Y	Y	Y
ARKANSAS						
Fulbright	Y	N	Y	Y	Y	?
McClellan	N	Y	N	Y	Y	Y
CALIFORNIA						
Kuchel	Y	N	Y	Y	Y	Y
Murphy	N	Y	N	Y	Y	Y
COLORADO						
Allott	N	Y	Y	Y	Y	Y
Dominick	N	Y	Y	Y	Y	Y
CONNECTICUT						
Dodd	Y	N	N	N	‡	Y
Ribicoff	Y	N	Y	N	Y	Y
DELAWARE						
Boggs	Y	N	Y	Y	Y	Y
Williams	?	N	N	Y	Y	Y
FLORIDA						
Holland	Y	N	N	Y	Y	Y
Smathers	Y	Y	Y	Y	Y	Y
GEORGIA						
Russell	N	N	N	‡	‡	Y
Talmadge	N	N	N	Y	Y	?
HAWAII						
Inouye	Y	✓	Y	?	Y	N
Fong	Y	Y	Y	Y	Y	Y
IDAHO						
Church	‡	N	✓	Y	Y	N
Jordan	Y	Y	N	Y	Y	Y
ILLINOIS						
Dirksen	Y	Y	Y	Y	Y	Y
Percy	Y	N	Y	Y	Y	Y
INDIANA						
Bayh	‡	N	Y	Y	Y	N
Hartke	Y	-	Y	Y	Y	N
IOWA						
Hickenlooper	Y	Y	Y	Y	Y	Y
Miller	Y	Y	N	Y	Y	Y
KANSAS						
Carlson	Y	Y	Y	Y	Y	Y
Pearson	Y	Y	Y	Y	Y	Y
KENTUCKY						
Cooper	Y	X	Y	Y	Y	Y
Morton	Y	Y	Y	Y	Y	Y
LOUISIANA						
Ellender	Y	Y	Y	Y	Y	Y
Long	N	Y	-	N	‡	Y
MAINE						
Muskie	Y	-	Y	Y	Y	Y
Smith	Y	N	Y	Y	Y	Y
MARYLAND						
Brewster	‡	N	✓	Y	Y	Y
Tydings	Y	N	Y	Y	Y	Y
MASSACHUSETTS						
Kennedy	Y	N	Y	Y	Y	N
Brooke	Y	✓	‡	Y	Y	N
MICHIGAN						
Hart	Y	Y	Y	Y	Y	Y
Griffin	N	Y	Y	Y	Y	Y
MINNESOTA						
McCarthy	‡	N	Y	Y	Y	N
Mondale	Y	N	Y	Y	Y	N
MISSISSIPPI						
Eastland	N	Y	N	Y	Y	?
Stennis	N	N	N	Y	Y	Y
MISSOURI						
Long	Y	N	Y	Y	Y	N
Symington	Y	N	Y	Y	Y	Y
MONTANA						
Mansfield	Y	N	Y	Y	Y	Y
Metcalf	Y	-	Y	Y	‡	-
NEBRASKA						
Curtis	N	Y	N	Y	Y	✓
Hruska	N	Y	N	Y	Y	Y
NEVADA						
Bible	Y	N	N	Y	Y	Y
Cannon	Y	N	-	Y	Y	Y
NEW HAMPSHIRE						
McIntyre	Y	N	Y	Y	Y	Y
Cotton	N	Y	N	Y	Y	Y
NEW JERSEY						
Williams	Y	Y	Y	Y	Y	N
Case	Y	N	Y	Y	Y	‡
NEW MEXICO						
Anderson	Y	N	Y	Y	‡	?
Montoya	Y	N	N	Y	Y	N
NEW YORK						
Kennedy	Y	N	Y	Y	Y	N
Javits	Y	N	Y	Y	Y	Y
NORTH CAROLINA						
Ervin	Y	N	N	Y	Y	Y
Jordan	‡	N	Y	?	Y	Y
NORTH DAKOTA						
Burdick	Y	N	Y	‡	‡	Y
Young	Y	Y	N	Y	Y	Y
OHIO						
Lausche	Y	N	N	Y	‡	Y
Young	Y	N	Y	Y	Y	‡
OKLAHOMA						
Harris	Y	N	Y	Y	Y	Y
Monroney	Y	N	Y	Y	Y	Y
OREGON						
Morse	Y	N	Y	Y	Y	Y
Hatfield	Y	?	Y	Y	Y	Y
PENNSYLVANIA						
Clark	Y	Y	Y	Y	Y	N
Scott	Y	Y	Y	Y	Y	Y
RHODE ISLAND						
Pastore	Y	-	Y	Y	Y	Y
Pell	Y	N	Y	Y	Y	N
SOUTH CAROLINA						
Hollings	N	N	N	Y	Y	Y
Thurmond	N	Y	N	N	Y	Y
SOUTH DAKOTA						
McGovern	Y	N	Y	Y	Y	Y
Mundt	Y	Y	N	Y	Y	Y
TENNESSEE						
Gore	Y	N	Y	Y	‡	Y
Baker	Y	?	Y	Y	Y	Y
TEXAS						
Yarborough	‡	N	Y	Y	Y	N
Tower	N	Y	N	N	Y	X
UTAH						
Moss	Y	-	Y	Y	Y	N
Bennett	Y	‡	Y	Y	Y	Y
VERMONT						
Aiken	Y	N	Y	Y	Y	Y
Prouty	Y	Y	Y	Y	Y	Y
VIRGINIA						
Byrd, Jr.	Y	N	N	Y	Y	Y
Spong	Y	N	Y	Y	Y	Y
WASHINGTON						
Jackson	Y	N	Y	Y	Y	N
Magnuson	Y	-	Y	Y	Y	N
WEST VIRGINIA						
Byrd	N	N	X	Y	Y	Y
Randolph	Y	N	Y	Y	Y	Y
WISCONSIN						
Nelson	Y	N	Y	Y	Y	Y
Proxmire	Y	N	Y	Y	Y	N
WYOMING						
McGee	Y	X	Y	Y	Y	Y
Hansen	N	‡	N	Y	Y	Y

Key:
- Y Record vote for (yea).
- ✓ Paired for.
- ‡ Announced for or CQ poll for.
- N Record vote against (nay).
- X Paired against.
- - Announced against or CQ poll against.
- ? Absent, general pair, "present" or did not announce or answer poll.

Democrats in this type; *Republicans in italics*

Senate Key Votes—90th Congress—1967

7. S 1155. Export-Import Bank. Ellender (D La.) amendment, as modified by Clark (D Pa.), to prohibit the Bank from financing arms purchases by less developed countries. (The original Ellender amendment expressed the sense of Congress that such financing should not be made but did not expressly prohibit it.) Rejected 40-49: R 13-22; D 27-27 (ND 18-21; SD 9-6), Aug. 9, 1967. The President did not take a position on the amendment.

8. S 1880. Election Reform Act. Clark (D Pa.) amendment requiring Members of Congress and candidates for Congress to disclose their assets, liabilities, securities, gifts and other outside income. Rejected 42-46: R 13-22; D 29-24 (ND 25-9; SD 4-15), Sept. 12, 1967. The President did not take a position on the amendment.

9. HR 9960. Independent Offices and Department of Housing and Urban Development Appropriations Bill for fiscal 1968. Senate Appropriations Committee amendment to provide $40 million in new rent supplement contract authority. Accepted 59-31: R 17-14; D 42-17 (ND 35-4; SD 7-13), Sept. 20, 1967. A "yea" was a vote supporting the President's position.

10. S 2388. Antipoverty authorization. Prouty (R Vt.) amendment to delete the Senate Committee's $2.8 billion emergency job program in Title II and to authorize instead a one-year $925 million emergency job program emphasizing incentives to get business to participate in job training. The amendment was offered as a substitute for a pending Byrd (D W.Va.) recommittal motion to delete Title II. Rejected 42-47: R 16-18; D 26-29 (ND 24-13; SD 2-16), Oct. 4, 1967. A "nay" was a vote supporting the President's position.

11. H J Res 888. Continuing appropriations for fiscal 1968. Mundt (R S.D.) amendment requiring the Executive Branch to reduce each line item contained in fiscal 1968 appropriation bills by at least 5 percent (except military funds and items determined by the Budget Bureau Director to be outside administrative control). Rejected 43-46: R 26-5; D 17-41 (ND 9-30; SD 8-11), Oct. 25, 1967. A "nay" was a vote supporting the President's position.

12. HR 12080. Social Security Amendments. Curtis (R Neb.)-Williams (R Del.) amendment substituting the House-passed 12.5-percent OASDI benefit increase and financing plan for the 15-percent benefit increase and financing plan recommended by the Senate Finance Committee. Rejected 22-58: R 17-9; D 5-49 (ND 0-37; SD 5-12), Nov. 21, 1967. A "nay" was a vote supporting the President's position.

Key:

Y Record vote for (yea).
✓ Paired for.
‡ Announced for or CQ poll for.
N Record vote against (nay).
X Paired against.
- Announced against or CQ poll against.
? Absent, general pair, "present" or did not announce or answer poll.

	7	8	9	10	11	12
ALABAMA						
Hill	N	N	N	N	N	N
Sparkman	N	N	Y	N	-	?
ALASKA						
Bartlett	Y	N	Y	✓	N	N
Gruening	✓	N	Y	Y	-	N
ARIZONA						
Hayden	N	N	?	N	N	N
Fannin	N	N	N	N	N	Y
ARKANSAS						
Fulbright	?	N	Y	N	?	N
McClellan	Y	N	N	N	N	Y
CALIFORNIA						
Kuchel	N	Y	✓	Y	✓	✓
Murphy	N	N	N	Y	N	‡
COLORADO						
Allott	Y	N	N	N	Y	Y
Dominick	Y	-	X	N	Y	Y
CONNECTICUT						
Dodd	-	Y	Y	N	-	?
Ribicoff	N	Y	Y	Y	Y	N
DELAWARE						
Boggs	N	Y	Y	Y	Y	Y
Williams	Y	Y	N	N	Y	Y
FLORIDA						
Holland	Y	N	N	N	N	✓
Smathers	Y	N	?	N	N	N
GEORGIA						
Russell	?	?	N	X	Y	N
Talmadge	Y	N	N	N	Y	?
HAWAII						
Inouye	N	Y	Y	✓	N	N
Fong	N	N	Y	Y	N	?
IDAHO						
Church	Y	Y	Y	Y	Y	N
Jordan	Y	N	N	N	Y	Y
ILLINOIS						
Dirksen	N	N	Y	Y	Y	✓
Percy	N	Y	Y	Y	Y	Y
INDIANA						
Bayh	Y	Y	Y	?	N	N
Hartke	N	Y	Y	N	N	N
IOWA						
Hickenlooper	N	N	N	N	Y	Y
Miller	N	N	Y	N	‡	Y
KANSAS						
Carlson	Y	Y	N	N	Y	✓
Pearson	N	N	Y	Y	Y	Y
KENTUCKY						
Cooper	Y	Y	Y	Y	Y	?
Morton	N	Y	Y	Y	Y	Y
LOUISIANA						
Ellender	Y	N	Y	N	N	N
Long	✓	N	Y	N	N	N
MAINE						
Muskie	N	?	Y	Y	N	N
Smith	Y	N	N	N	N	N
MARYLAND						
Brewster	Y	Y	‡	Y	N	N
Tydings	Y	Y	Y	Y	N	N
MASSACHUSETTS						
Kennedy	N	Y	Y	Y	N	N
Brooke	N	N	Y	Y	‡	?
MICHIGAN						
Hart	N	✓	Y	Y	N	N
Griffin	N	Y	Y	Y	Y	N
MINNESOTA						
McCarthy	N	N	Y	Y	-	?
Mondale	N	Y	Y	Y	N	N
MISSISSIPPI						
Eastland	?	N	N	N	Y	Y
Stennis	N	N	N	N	Y	Y
MISSOURI						
Long	Y	Y	Y	Y	N	N
Symington	Y	‡	?	N	Y	N
MONTANA						
Mansfield	N	?	Y	N	N	X
Metcalf	N	‡	Y	Y	N	N
NEBRASKA						
Curtis	-	N	N	N	Y	Y
Hruska	N	N	N	N	Y	Y
NEVADA						
Bible	Y	?	N	N	Y	N
Cannon	X	N	N	N	N	-
NEW HAMPSHIRE						
McIntyre	N	Y	Y	N	N	N
Cotton	Y	Y	N	N	Y	N
NEW JERSEY						
Williams	Y	Y	‡	Y	N	N
Case	N	Y	Y	Y	N	N
NEW MEXICO						
Anderson	N	?	Y	N	N	N
Montoya	N	Y	Y	-	N	N
NEW YORK						
Kennedy	N	Y	Y	Y	N	N
Javits	N	Y	Y	Y	Y	N
NORTH CAROLINA						
Ervin	Y	N	N	X	Y	N
Jordan	Y	X	N	N	N	?
NORTH DAKOTA						
Burdick	Y	Y	Y	Y	N	N
Young	N	N	N	N	Y	N
OHIO						
Lausche	N	N	N	N	Y	N
Young	Y	Y	Y	Y	N	N
OKLAHOMA						
Harris	N	Y	Y	N	N	N
Monroney	N	N	Y	N	N	N
OREGON						
Morse	Y	Y	Y	Y	-	N
Hatfield	Y	Y	✓	Y	X	N
PENNSYLVANIA						
Clark	Y	Y	Y	Y	N	N
Scott	Y	Y	Y	N	Y	X
RHODE ISLAND						
Pastore	N	Y	Y	-	Y	N
Pell	Y	?	Y	Y	N	N
SOUTH CAROLINA						
Hollings	N	Y	N	N	Y	N
Thurmond	N	N	N	N	Y	Y
SOUTH DAKOTA						
McGovern	Y	Y	Y	Y	Y	N
Mundt	Y	N	N	N	Y	‡
TENNESSEE						
Gore	?	Y	N	?	N	N
Baker	N	N	N	✓	Y	Y
TEXAS						
Yarborough	‡	N	Y	Y	N	N
Tower	N	N	-	X	‡	‡
UTAH						
Moss	N	Y	Y	‡	N	N
Bennett	N	N	N	N	Y	Y
VERMONT						
Aiken	Y	N	Y	Y	N	N
Prouty	Y	N	Y	Y	Y	N
VIRGINIA						
Byrd, Jr.	Y	N	N	N	N	X
Spong	Y	Y	N	Y	Y	Y
WASHINGTON						
Jackson	N	N	Y	N	N	N
Magnuson	N	-	Y	Y	N	N
WEST VIRGINIA						
Byrd	Y	N	N	N	N	X
Randolph	N	N	Y	N	N	N
WISCONSIN						
Nelson	Y	Y	Y	Y	N	N
Proxmire	Y	Y	Y	N	N	N
WYOMING						
McGee	X	Y	Y	N	-	N
Hansen	N	N	X	N	Y	‡

Democrats in this type; *Republicans in italics*

HOUSE AND SENATE KEY VOTES FOR 1968

The editors of Congressional Quarterly annually select a series of "key votes" that represent major issues before Congress and also reflect both the mood of Congress and the impact constituent and other pressures can have on a Member's vote. In 1968 the major issues were open housing, the tax surcharge, budget cuts, crime in general and gun controls in particular, the massive new housing bill, foreign aid and funds for antipoverty programs. The "conservative coalition" of Republicans and Southern Democrats voting against Northern Democrats appeared on seven of the 13 key votes in the House and on five of the 12 in the Senate.

House Key Votes

1. TRUTH-IN-LENDING. The President scored a victory early in the session when the House on Feb. 1 passed a strong truth-in-lending bill (HR 11601; S 5) by an overwhelming vote. The bill required lenders and retail creditors to disclose the annual percentage cost of credit and restricted garnishment of workers' wages. With unusual Republican support for such a measure, the vote was 383-4 (D 218-3; R 165-1). As finally enacted, the bill was still one of the toughest and most far-reaching consumer bills enacted by Congress in many years.

2 and 3. OPEN HOUSING. When the Senate returned the civil rights bill (HR 2516) to the House, it contained a controversial Administration-backed open housing provision banning racial discrimination. The showdown vote in the House was on April 10 on a motion to order the previous question on a resolution (H Res 1100) to accept the Senate version of the bill without change. The motion was adopted by a 229-195 vote in a defeat for the conservative coalition (ND 140-12; SD 12-77; R 77-106), which wanted the bill sent to conference with the Senate. With many Republicans switching, the House then adopted H Res 1100 (thus agreeing to Senate amendments to HR 2516) by a vote of 250-172 (D 150-88; R 100-84). *(See Senate key votes 1 and 2.)*

4 and 5. CRIME. When the Senate returned the omnibus crime bill (HR 5037) to the House, it contained controversial Administration-opposed provisions permitting widespread wiretapping and seeking to alter Supreme Court rulings on criminal procedural law. *(See Senate key votes 5 and 7.)* The showdown vote in the House on June 6 was on a motion to order the previous question on a resolution (H Res 1197) to accept the Senate version of the bill without change. The motion was adopted by a vote of 349-40 (D 180-34; R 169-6), with a small group of liberals voting "nay." A number then switched to support the bill, and the House adopted H Res 1197 (thus agreeing to Senate amendments to HR 5037) by a vote of 369-17 (D 197-16; R 172-1).

6. TAX SURCHARGE, BUDGET CUTS. The Administration's long-sought 10 percent surcharge on corporation and individual income taxes, which the House Ways and Means Committee had pigeonholed, was approved by the Senate as an amendment to the excise tax extension bill (HR 15414). Tied to cutbacks in federal spending and personnel, the surcharge was recommended in the conference report. The House on June 20 adopted the conference report by a vote of 268-150 (D 154-77; R 114-73). *(See Senate key vote 4.)*

7. POVERTY FUNDS. The House was in an economy mood when it considered the appropriations bill (HR 18037) for Labor-Health, Education and Welfare Departments and related agencies. Having cut $307 million from the funds for the Office of Economic Opportunity (OEO), the antipoverty agency, the House on June 26 considered an amendment cutting another $100 million from that agency's funds. In a defeat for the conservative coalition and a victory for the Administration, the House rejected the amendment by a vote of 181-220 (ND 11-132; SD 60-24; R 110-64). The Senate restored $215 million to the OEO. *(See Senate key vote 11.)*

8. HIGHWAY BEAUTIFICATION. One of the Administration's more controversial programs was to beautify the nation's highways by controlling billboards, hiding unsightly junkyards and adding landscaping. The program was a favorite of the President's wife. The House on July 10 considered an amendment to the Federal Aid Highway Act (HR 17134) which struck out all funds for highway beautification projects. The House accepted the amendment by a 211-145 vote in a victory for the conservative coalition (ND 21-102; SD 46-27; R 144-16). The Senate restored a $255-million, three-year program; but, as enacted, the measure (S 3418) contained only $25 million for highway beautification for fiscal 1970.

9. GUN CONTROLS. Following the assassinations of the Rev. Dr. Martin Luther King Jr. and of Sen. Robert F. Kennedy (D N.Y.), the House on July 24 passed a bill (HR 17735) banning mail-order and most out-of-state purchases of rifles and shotguns and the interstate shipment of handgun ammunition. The House stopped short of including provisions requiring registration of firearms. The roll call was the first time in 30 years that House Members had taken a record vote on firearms legislation. The vote was 305-118 (D 158-79; R 147-39). The Senate passed a similar measure (S 3633) and the bill was cleared shortly before adjournment. *(See Senate key votes 5 and 6.)*

10. CAMPUS RIOTERS. The chief controversy in House consideration of the Higher Education Amendments (S 3769; HR 15067) centered on provisions requiring colleges to deny federal funds to students who participated in campus disorders. The bills extended authorizations for four major education programs. The House accepted the amendment on campus disorders on July 25 by a vote of 260-146. The vote was a victory for the conservative coalition (ND 50-98; SD 76-5; R 134-43). The President took no position on the amendment. The Senate version was somewhat milder and a compromise was agreed on in the final bill.

11. HOUSING. The House on July 26 adopted the conference report on the Administration-backed Housing and Urban Development Act (S 3497), the most far-reaching housing bill passed by Congress since 1949. The conference report deleted strict House limits on the income of families receiving aid to buy or rent homes, permitting more families to qualify than the House originally favored. The vote was 228-135 in a defeat for the conservative coalition (ND 124-2; SD 32-41; R 72-92). *(See Senate key vote 8.)*

12. FOREIGN AID. The House on Sept. 19 passed a $1.6 billion foreign aid appropriations bill (HR 19908), the lowest amount in the history of the program. Even so, on the 174-138 vote the conservative coalition opposed passage (ND 96-9; SD 24-46; R 54-83). *(See Senate key vote 9.)*

13. SCHOOL DESEGREGATION. The House June 26 accepted amendments to Health, Education and Welfare Department (HEW) appropriations to cripple the Department's enforcement of school desegregation by permitting Southern "freedom-of-choice" desegregation plans. On Oct. 3, by a close vote, the House reversed itself by adding language to the amendments to retain HEW's power to withhold federal funds from school districts using "freedom-of-choice" plans which HEW considered ineffective in achieving desegregation. The 167-156 roll-call vote on Oct. 3 was a defeat for the conservative coalition (ND 96-12; SD 4-67; R 67-77).

Senate Key Votes

1 and 2. OPEN HOUSING. After falling seven votes short of invoking cloture on the previous day, the Senate Feb. 21 showed unexpected support from Republicans and Northern Democrats for nondiscrimination in housing. The Senate rejected a motion to table (kill) an open housing amendment to the pending civil rights protection bill (HR 2516). The vote was 34-58 (D 18-39; R 16-19). With an open housing provision in the bill, the Senate then went on to invoke cloture on March 4 and to pass the bill on March 11 by a 71-20 vote (D 42-17; R 29-3), an unexpectedly large margin generated in part by the switch of Minority Leader Everett McKinley Dirksen (R Ill.) to support open housing. The House accepted the Senate version of the bill. *(See House key votes 2 and 3.)*

3. FINANCIAL DISCLOSURE. The Senate squarely faced the issue of public disclosure of Senators' finances and investments when it voted on March 20 on an amendment requiring Senators and their employees earning more than $15,000 to file public reports on the market value of their assets and liabilities and other information. The amendment to a code of ethics resolution (S Res 266) was rejected in a victory for the conservative coalition by a vote of 40-44 (ND 24-11; SD 4-13; R 12-20). Two days later the Senate adopted a watered-down rule providing that the reports be kept sealed until such time as the Senate Select Committee on Standards and Conduct saw fit to examine their contents. Sen. George D. Aiken (R Vt.) alone voted against the rule change, calling it a "farce."

4. TAX SURCHARGE, BUDGET CUTS. Both the President and the conservative coalition won a victory on April 2 when the Senate accepted an amendment to the excise tax extension bill (HR 15414). The amendment gave the President his long-sought 10-percent surcharge on individual and corporate income taxes but it also imposed a $180.1 billion ceiling on fiscal 1969 spending, a Republican-favored proposal. The vote was 53-35 (ND 12-24; SD 10-8; R 31-3). The provisions remained in the bill as signed into law. *(See House key vote 6.)*

5 and 6. GUN CONTROLS. In the face of heavy and effective lobbying by the National Rifle Assn., the Administration made little headway in the Senate early in the year to obtain strong gun controls. The Senate May 16 defeated an amendment to the omnibus crime bill (S 917) which would have prohibited interstate mail-order sales of rifles and shotguns. The amendment, offered by Sen. Edward M. Kennedy (D Mass.), was rejected by a vote of 29-53 (D 20-31; R 9-22). The legislation was enacted with controls over hand guns only. Following the assassination of Sen. Robert F. Kennedy (D N.Y.), however, the Senate made a dramatic turnabout and on Sept. 18 passed a bill (S 3633; HR 17735) banning mail-order and most out-of-state sales of rifles, shotguns and ammunition. The vote was 70-17 (D 39-13; R 31-4). *(See House key vote 9.)*

7. SUPREME COURT. While considering the omnibus crime bill (S 917), the Senate May 21 rejected a series of efforts by Sen. Joseph D. Tydings (D Md.) to delete provisions related to the rights of prisoners or suspects in federal custody. The provisions were seen as an attempt to restrict those rights and thus alter the standards enunciated by the Supreme Court. When the Senate reached provisions denying the Court jurisdiction to review a determination by a state court judge that a confession was "voluntary," the Senate drew the line. It accepted a Tydings amendment to delete the restriction on the Court's jurisdiction. Republicans and Northern Democrats switched heavily to support Tydings in his defense of the Court's scope of review. The vote was 52-32 (D 36-17; R 16-15). The provisions relating to Court rulings remained in the legislation as enacted.

8. HOUSING. In a major event of the 90th Congress, the Senate on May 28 passed a massive $5 billion housing and urban development bill (S 3497), backed by the Administration and incorporating GOP ideas to facilitate home ownership by low- and moderate-income families. The vote was 67-4 (D 40-3; R 27-1). As cleared later by the House, it was the most far-reaching housing legislation since the Housing Act of 1949. *(See House key vote 11.)*

9. ALLIANCE FOR PROGRESS. The Administration won an important victory on July 31 when the Senate rejected an amendment to the Foreign Assistance Act (HR 15263) which would have reduced from $90 million to the House figure of $70 million the authorization for the Alliance for Progress technical cooperation grants. The vote was 31-43 (D 22-27; R 9-16). The $90 million authorization remained in the bill as enacted. *(See House key vote 12.)*

10. SENTINEL ABM. The recurrent controversy over the Sentinel antiballistic missile (ABM) system broke out in the Senate again on Aug. 1. The Senate considered an amendment to the military construction appropriations bill (HR 18785) deleting $227.3 million for construction of ABM installations. Opponents of the ABM system, which was considered effective only against potential Communist Chinese missiles, argued that it was wasteful and encouraged an arms race. Proponents said it was a necessary defensive measure, would strengthen the nation's bargaining position with Russia and would deter aggression by other nations. The Senate rejected the amendment in what was the closest of four votes to deny funds. The vote, a victory for the conservative coalition and for the President, was 27-46 (ND 20-15; SD 2-17; R 5-14).

11. POVERTY FUNDS. When the Senate debated the appropriations bill (HR 18037) for Labor-Health, Education and Welfare Departments and related agencies, the central issue was where the line should be drawn between the needs of social programs and of economy. That issue was at the heart of debate on funds for the Office of Economic Opportunity (OEO), the antipoverty agency. The House had cut funds for the OEO. *(See House key vote 7.)* The Senate on Sept. 6 approved, 37-26, an amendment to HR 18037 restoring $215 million to the OEO funds to bring those funds back up to the Administration's budget level. It was a defeat for the conservative coalition (ND 27-1; SD 2-11; R 8-14).

12. FORTAS NOMINATION. The June 26 nomination by President Johnson of Supreme Court Associate Justice Abe Fortas to be Chief Justice of the United States touched off a storm of controversy. Sen. Robert P. Griffin (R Mich.) gathered Republican and Southern Democratic forces to filibuster against the nomination. The Senate never before had failed to act, favorably or unfavorably, on a nomination to the Court. But after five days of debate, the Senate on Oct. 1 rejected a motion to invoke cloture. Thus, the Senate never took up the nomination as such, but settled the matter on a procedural point. With a two-thirds majority needed for cloture, the motion failed by 14 votes, losing 45-43 in a victory for the conservative coalition (ND 31-4; SD 4-15; R 10-24). At the request of Justice Fortas, the President Oct. 2 withdrew the nomination.

House Key Votes—90th Congress—1968

1. HR 11601. Truth-in-Lending. Passage of the bill requiring all lenders and retail creditors to disclose the annual percentage cost of credit; restricting garnishment of wages to 10 percent of a worker's income above $30; and establishing a National Commission on Consumer Finance. Passed 383-4: R 165-1; D 218-3 (ND 138-0; SD 80-3), Feb. 1, 1968. A "yea" was a vote supporting the President's position.

2. H Res 1100—HR 2516. Civil Rights-Open Housing. H Res 1100 was a resolution to permit House acceptance of Senate amendments to a House-passed civil rights bill (HR 2516). Madden (D Ind.) motion to order the previous question on H Res 1100, thereby bringing the resolution to a vote with no opportunity to alter the language and—in effect— expressing the House's desire to accept the Senate's open housing and other amendments without change. Adopted 229-195: R 77-106; D 152-89 (ND 140-12; SD 12-77), April 10, 1968. A "yea" was a vote supporting the President's position.

3. H Res 1100—HR 2516. Civil Rights-Open Housing. Adoption of the resolution to agree to the Senate amendments to the House-passed civil rights bill (HR 2516) and to send HR 2516 to the President. The Senate amendments—which were the substance of HR 2516—prohibited interference with a person exercising specified federally protected rights, prohibited discrimination in the sale or rental of housing. Adopted 250-172: R 100-84; D 150-88 (ND 137-13; SD 13-75), April 10, 1968. A "yea" was a vote supporting the President's position.

4. H Res 1197—HR 5037. Omnibus Crime Bill. H Res 1197 was a resolution to permit House acceptance of Senate amendments to the House-passed Omnibus Crime Bill. Sisk (D Calif.) motion to consider the previous question on H Res 1197, thereby bringing the resolution to a vote with no opportunity to alter the language and expressing the House's desire to accept the Senate provisions on criminal law, wiretapping and gun control without change. Adopted 349-40: R 169-6; D 180-34 (ND 102-32; SD 78-2), June 6, 1968. A "nay" was a vote supporting the President's position.

5. H Res 1197—HR 5037. Omnibus Crime Bill. Adoption of the resolution permitting House acceptance of Senate amendments to the bill. Adopted 369-17: R 172-1; D 197-16 (ND 118-15; SD 79-1), June 6, 1968. A "nay" was a vote supporting the President's position.

6. HR 15414. Surcharge-Spending Limitation. Adoption of the conference report (H Rept 1533) on the bill imposing a 10-percent surcharge on personal and corporate income taxes, requiring the Federal Government to cut fiscal 1969 expenditures by $6 billion, requiring a reduction in the number of federal employees, extending certain existing excise taxes, accelerating payment of corporation taxes, revising or extending the effective date of certain welfare and medical assistance laws, and including provisions on various other subjects. Adopted 268-150: R 114-73; D 154-77 (ND 96-49; SD 58-28), June 20, 1968. A "yea" was a vote supporting the President's position.

	1 2 3 4 5 6
ALABAMA	
3 Andrews	Y N N ? ? N
7 Bevill	Y N N Y Y N
8 Jones	Y N N Y Y N
4 Nichols	Y N N Y Y N
5 Selden	Y N N ‡ ‡ X
6 Buchanan	Y N N Y Y N
2 Dickinson	Y N N Y Y N
1 Edwards	Y N N Y Y N
ALASKA	
AL Pollock	Y N Y N Y Y
ARIZONA	
2 Udall	Y Y Y N Y Y
1 Rhodes	? N N Y Y Y
3 Steiger	Y N N Y Y N
ARKANSAS	
1 Gathings	Y N N Y Y Y
2 Mills	? N N Y Y Y
4 Pryor	? N N Y Y Y
3 Hammerschmidt	Y N N Y Y Y
CALIFORNIA	
5 Burton	Y Y Y N N N
7 Cohelan	Y Y Y ? X ✓
9 Edwards	Y Y Y N Y N
34 Hanna	Y Y Y Y Y Y
2 Johnson	Y Y Y Y Y Y
4 Leggett	Y Y Y N N N
15 McFall	‡ Y Y Y Y Y
8 Miller	Y Y Y ‡ ‡ Y
3 Moss	‡ Y Y N N N
16 Sisk	Y Y Y ‡ ‡ Y
38 Tunney	Y Y Y ✓ ✓ Y
37 Van Deerlin	Y Y Y Y Y Y
14 Waldie	Y Y Y N N Y
1 Clausen	‡ N N Y Y N
10 Gubser	Y N N Y Y Y
11 McCloskey	Y Y Y Y Y Y
6 Mailliard	Y Y Y Y Y Y
18 Mathias	Y N N Y Y Y
33 Pettis	Y N N Y Y Y
12 Talcott	? N N Y Y Y
13 Teague	Y N N Y Y Y
35 Utt	Y N N Y Y Y
36 Wilson	Y N N Y Y Y

	1 2 3 4 5 6
Los Angeles Co.	
29 Brown	Y Y Y X - N
22 Corman	Y Y Y N Y N
21 Hawkins	Y Y Y X X X
19 Holifield	Y Y Y Y Y Y
17 King	? ✓ ✓ Y Y Y
26 Rees	Y Y Y - - Y
30 Roybal	Y Y Y ? ? N
31 Wilson	‡ Y Y Y Y Y
28 Bell	Y Y Y ? ? Y
23 Clawson	‡ N N Y Y Y
32 Hosmer	Y N N Y ‡ Y
24 Lipscomb	‡ N N Y Y Y
27 Reinecke	Y N N Y Y Y
20 Smith	Y N N Y Y N
25 Wiggins	Y N N Y Y Y
COLORADO	
4 Aspinall	Y N N X X Y
3 Evans	Y Y Y N Y Y
1 Rogers	Y Y Y Y Y Y
2 Brotzman	Y Y Y Y Y Y
CONNECTICUT	
1 Daddario	Y Y Y Y Y Y
3 Giaimo	‡ Y Y Y Y Y
4 Irwin	Y Y Y Y Y Y
5 Monagan	‡ Y Y Y Y Y
2 St. Onge	‡ Y Y Y Y Y
6 Meskill	Y Y Y Y Y N
DELAWARE	
AL Roth	Y ? ? Y Y Y
FLORIDA	
3 Bennett	Y N N Y Y Y
12 Fascell	Y Y Y Y Y Y
2 Fuqua	Y N N Y Y Y
6 Gibbons	‡ N N Y Y N
7 Haley	Y N N Y Y N
4 Herlong	Y N - Y Y Y
11 Pepper	Y Y Y Y Y Y
9 Rogers	Y N N Y Y Y
1 Sikes	Y N N Y Y Y
10 Burke	Y N N Y Y Y
8 Cramer	‡ N N Y Y N
5 Gurney	‡ N N Y Y Y

	1 2 3 4 5 6
GEORGIA	
3 Brinkley	Y N N Y Y N
7 Davis	Y N N Y Y N
6 Flynt	Y N N Y Y N
1 Hagan	Y N N Y Y N
9 Landrum	Y N N Y Y Y
2 O'Neal	Y N N ‡ ‡ N
10 Stephens	N N N Y Y Y
8 Stuckey	Y N N Y Y N
4 Blackburn	Y N N Y Y Y
5 Thompson	Y N N Y Y N
HAWAII	
AL Matsunaga	Y Y Y Y Y Y
AL Mink	‡ Y Y N N N
IDAHO	
2 Hansen	Y N N Y Y N
1 McClure	N N N Y Y N
ILLINOIS	
21 Gray	Y Y N ‡ Y Y
24 Price	Y Y Y Y Y Y
23 Shipley	Y Y Y Y Y N
16 Anderson	Y Y Y Y Y Y
17 Arends	Y N N Y Y N
14 Erlenborn	‡ Y Y Y Y Y
20 Findley	Y Y Y Y Y Y
12 McClory	‡ Y Y Y Y Y
18 Michel	Y Y Y ‡ ‡ N
19 Railsback	Y Y Y Y Y Y
15 Reid	Y N N Y Y Y
22 Springer	Y N Y Y Y N
Chicago-Cook Co.	
7 Annunzio	Y Y Y N Y N
1 Dawson	? Y Y ? ? Y
5 Kluczynski	Y Y N Y ? Y
3 Murphy	Y Y Y ‡ ‡ Y
2 O'Hara	Y Y Y ? ? Y
11 Pucinski	Y N N Y Y Y
6 Ronan	Y Y N Y Y Y
8 Rostenkowski	Y Y Y Y Y Y
9 Yates	Y Y Y N Y N
10 Collier	Y N N Y Y Y
4 Derwinski	Y N N N Y Y
13 Rumsfeld	‡ Y Y Y Y Y

	- KEY -
Y	Record vote for (yea).
✓	Paired for.
‡	Announced for or CQ poll for.
N	Record vote against (nay).
X	Paired against.
-	Announced against or CQ poll against.
?	Absent, general pair, "present" or did not announce or answer poll.

	1 2 3 4 5 6
INDIANA	
3 Brademas	Y Y Y Y Y N
9 Hamilton	Y Y Y Y Y Y
11 Jacobs	Y Y Y Y Y N
1 Madden	Y Y Y Y Y X
5 Roush	Y Y Y Y Y Y
4 Adair	Y N N Y Y N
6 Bray	Y N N Y Y N
2 Halleck	? N N Y Y Y
7 Myers	Y N N Y Y N
10 Roudebush	Y N N Y Y N
8 Zion	Y N N Y Y N
IOWA	
2 Culver	Y Y Y Y Y Y
5 Smith	‡ Y Y Y Y N
3 Gross	Y N N Y Y Y
4 Kyl	Y N N Y Y N
6 Mayne	Y N N Y Y Y
7 Scherle	Y N N Y Y N
1 Schwengel	Y Y Y Y Y Y
KANSAS	
1 Dole	Y N Y Y Y N
2 Mize	Y Y Y Y Y N
4 Shriver	? N N Y Y Y
5 Skubitz	Y N N Y Y Y
3 Winn	Y N N Y Y N
KENTUCKY	
2 Natcher	Y N N Y Y N
7 Perkins	Y Y Y Y Y N
1 Stubblefield	Y N N Y Y Y

Democrats in **this type**; Republicans in *italics*

	1	2	3	4	5	6
6 Watts	Y	N	N	Y	Y	Y
5 Carter	Y	N	N	?	?	Y
3 Cowger	Y	Y	Y	‡	‡	N
4 Snyder	Y	N	N	Y	Y	N
LOUISIANA						
2 Boggs	Y	Y	Y	Y	Y	Y
7 Edwards	Y	N	N	Y	Y	N
1 Hebert	Y	N	N	Y	Y	N
8 Long	Y	N	N	Y	Y	N
5 Passman	‡	N	N	‡	‡	N
6 Rarick	Y	N	N	Y	Y	N
4 Waggonner	Y	N	N	Y	Y	N
3 Willis	Y	N	N	Y	Y	Y
MAINE						
2 Hathaway	Y	Y	Y	‡	‡	N
1 Kyros	Y	Y	Y	Y	Y	N
MARYLAND						
4 Fallon	Y	Y	N	Y	Y	Y
7 Friedel	Y	Y	Y	Y	Y	Y
3 Garmatz	Y	Y	N	Y	Y	N
2 Long	‡	Y	Y	Y	Y	Y
5 Machen	Y	N	N	Y	Y	N
8 Gude	Y	Y	Y	Y	Y	Y
6 Mathias	Y	Y	Y	Y	Y	Y
1 Morton	Y	N	N	Y	Y	Y
MASSACHUSETTS						
2 Boland	Y	Y	Y	Y	Y	Y
11 Burke	Y	Y	Y	Y	Y	Y
4 Donohue	Y	Y	Y	Y	Y	Y
7 Macdonald	?	Y	Y	Y	Y	N
9 McCormack						
8 O'Neill	Y	Y	Y	√	‡	Y
3 Philbin	Y	Y	Y	Y	Y	Y
6 Bates	Y	Y	Y	Y	Y	Y
1 Conte	Y	Y	Y	Y	Y	Y
10 Heckler	Y	Y	Y	Y	Y	N
12 Keith	Y	Y	Y	Y	Y	Y
5 Morse	Y	Y	Y	Y	Y	Y
MICHIGAN						
12 O'Hara	Y	Y	Y	N	Y	Y
18 Broomfield	‡	Y	Y	Y	Y	N
3 Brown	Y	Y	Y	Y	Y	Y
10 Cederberg	‡	N	Y	Y	Y	Y
6 Chamberlain	Y	N	Y	Y	‡	Y
2 Esch	Y	Y	Y	Y	Y	Y
5 Ford	Y	N	Y	Y	Y	Y
8 Harvey	Y	Y	Y	?	?	Y
4 Hutchinson	Y	N	Y	Y	Y	N
19 McDonald	Y	Y	Y	Y	Y	Y
7 Riegle	Y	Y	Y	Y	Y	N
11 Ruppe	Y	Y	Y	Y	Y	Y
9 Vander Jagt	Y	N	Y	?	?	Y
Detroit-Wayne Co.						
1 Conyers	Y	Y	Y	N	N	N
13 Diggs	Y	Y	Y	N	N	N
16 Dingell	Y	N	Y	N	N	N
15 Ford	Y	Y	Y	Y	Y	N
17 Griffiths	Y	Y	Y	?	?	X
14 Nedzi	Y	Y	Y	N	Y	√
MINNESOTA						
8 Blatnik	Y	Y	Y	Y	Y	Y
5 Fraser	Y	Y	Y	N	N	Y
4 Karth	Y	Y	Y	Y	Y	Y
7 Langen	Y	N	Y	Y	Y	Y
3 MacGregor	Y	Y	Y	Y	Y	Y
2 Nelsen	Y	Y	Y	Y	Y	Y
1 Quie	Y	Y	Y	Y	Y	Y
6 Zwach	Y	Y	Y	Y	Y	Y
MISSISSIPPI						
1 Abernethy	N	N	N	Y	Y	Y
5 Colmer	Y	N	N	Y	Y	Y
4 Montgomery	N	N	N	Y	Y	Y
2 Whitten	Y	N	N	Y	Y	N
3 Griffin*		N	N	Y	Y	Y
MISSOURI						
5 Bolling	Y	Y	Y	Y	N	Y
6 Hull	Y	N	N	Y	Y	N
9 Hungate	Y	N	?	Y	Y	Y
8 Ichord	Y	N	N	Y	Y	Y
10 Jones	Y	-	-	Y	Y	Y
1 Karsten	?	?	?	‡	‡	Y
4 Randall	Y	N	N	Y	Y	N
3 Sullivan	Y	Y	Y	Y	Y	Y
2 Curtis	Y	N	N	Y	N	N
7 Hall	Y	N	N	Y	Y	N
MONTANA						
1 Olsen	Y	Y	Y	Y	Y	Y
2 Battin	Y	N	N	Y	Y	Y
NEBRASKA						
2 Cunningham	Y	Y	Y	Y	Y	N
1 Denney	Y	N	Y	Y	Y	Y
3 Martin	Y	N	N	Y	Y	Y
NEVADA						
AL Baring	Y	N	N	Y	Y	N
NEW HAMPSHIRE						
2 Cleveland	‡	Y	Y	Y	Y	Y
1 Wyman	Y	N	Y	Y	Y	N
NEW JERSEY						
14 Daniels	Y	Y	Y	Y	Y	Y
13 Gallagher	Y	Y	Y	Y	?	Y
9 Helstoski	Y	Y	Y	N	Y	X
3 Howard	Y	Y	Y	Y	Y	N
8 Joelson	Y	Y	Y	Y	Y	Y
11 Minish	Y	Y	Y	Y	Y	N
15 Patten	Y	Y	Y	Y	Y	Y
10 Rodino	Y	Y	Y	Y	Y	N
4 Thompson	Y	Y	Y	N	Y	√
6 Cahill	Y	Y	Y	Y	Y	Y
12 Dwyer	Y	Y	Y	Y	Y	Y
5 Frelinghuysen	Y	Y	Y	Y	Y	Y
1 Hunt	Y	N	Y	Y	Y	N
2 Sandman	Y	Y	Y	Y	Y	N
7 Widnall	Y	Y	Y	Y	Y	Y
NEW MEXICO						
AL Morris	Y	Y	Y	Y	Y	Y
AL Walker	Y	N	N	Y	Y	N
NEW YORK						
27 Dow	Y	Y	Y	N	Y	N
41 Dulski	Y	Y	Y	Y	Y	Y
34 Hanley	Y	Y	Y	Y	Y	Y
39 McCarthy	Y	Y	Y	Y	Y	Y
25 Ottinger	Y	Y	Y	N	Y	N
1 Pike	Y	Y	Y	Y	Y	Y
28 Resnick	Y	Y	‡	X	‡	Y
35 Stratton	Y	Y	Y	Y	Y	Y
5 Tenzer	Y	Y	Y	Y	Y	N
3 Wolff	Y	Y	Y	N	Y	N
29 Button	Y	Y	Y	Y	Y	Y
37 Conable	Y	Y	Y	Y	Y	Y
38 Goodell	Y	Y	Y	Y	Y	Y
2 Grover	Y	Y	Y	Y	Y	N
36 Horton	Y	Y	Y	Y	Y	Y
30 King	Y	?	?	Y	Y	N
31 McEwen	Y	?	Y	Y	Y	Y
32 Pirnie	Y	Y	Y	Y	Y	Y
26 Reid	Y	Y	Y	N	Y	Y
33 Robison	‡	Y	Y	Y	Y	Y
40 Smith	Y	Y	Y	Y	Y	Y
4 Wydler	Y	Y	Y	N	Y	N
New York City						
7 Addabbo	Y	Y	Y	Y	Y	N
23 Bingham	Y	Y	Y	N	Y	Y
11 Brasco	Y	Y	Y	Y	Y	N
15 Carey	Y	Y	Y	Y	Y	N
10 Celler	Y	Y	Y	Y	Y	Y
9 Delaney	Y	N	N	Y	Y	N
19 Farbstein	Y	Y	Y	Y	Y	N
22 Gilbert	Y	Y	Y	Y	Y	N
12 Kelly	Y	Y	Y	Y	Y	N
13 Podell**		Y	Y	Y	Y	N
16 Murphy	Y	Y	Y	Y	Y	Y
18 Vacancy						
14 Rooney	Y	Y	Y	‡	√	Y
8 Rosenthal	‡	Y	Y	N	Y	N
20 Ryan	Y	Y	Y	N	N	N
21 Scheuer	Y	Y	Y	N	Y	N
24 Fino	Y	-	-	Y	Y	N
6 Halpern	Y	Y	Y	Y	Y	N
17 Kupferman	?	Y	Y	N	Y	Y
NORTH CAROLINA						
2 Fountain	‡	N	N	Y	Y	Y
5 Galifianakis	Y	N	N	Y	Y	Y
3 Henderson	Y	N	N	Y	Y	N
1 Jones	Y	N	N	Y	Y	N
6 Kornegay	Y	N	N	Y	Y	Y
7 Lennon	Y	N	N	Y	Y	N
11 Taylor	Y	N	N	Y	Y	Y
10 Whitener	Y	N	N	Y	Y	Y
9 Broyhill	Y	N	N	Y	Y	Y
4 Gardner	Y	N	N	Y	Y	N
8 Jonas	Y	N	N	Y	Y	Y
NORTH DAKOTA						
1 Andrews	Y	Y	Y	Y	Y	N
2 Kleppe	Y	Y	Y	Y	Y	N
OHIO						
9 Ashley	Y	Y	Y	Y	Y	Y
20 Feighan	Y	Y	Y	Y	Y	Y
18 Hays	Y	Y	Y	Y	Y	√
19 Kirwan	Y	Y	Y	Y	Y	Y
21 Vanik	Y	Y	Y	Y	Y	N
17 Ashbrook	Y	N	N	Y	Y	N
14 Ayres	Y	Y	Y	Y	Y	Y
8 Betts	Y	Y	Y	Y	Y	Y
22 Bolton	Y	N	N	‡	‡	N
16 Bow	Y	N	N	‡	‡	Y
7 Brown	Y	Y	Y	Y	Y	Y
2 Clancy	Y	N	N	Y	Y	N
12 Devine	Y	N	N	Y	Y	N
6 Harsha	Y	N	N	Y	Y	N
5 Latta	Y	N	N	Y	Y	Y
24 Lukens	Y	N	Y	Y	Y	N
4 McCulloch	Y	Y	Y	Y	Y	Y
10 Miller	Y	N	N	Y	Y	N
23 Minshall	Y	N	N	Y	Y	N
13 Mosher	Y	Y	Y	Y	Y	Y
11 Stanton	Y	Y	Y	Y	Y	Y
1 Taft	‡	Y	Y	Y	Y	N
3 Whalen	‡	Y	Y	Y	Y	N
15 Wylie	Y	N	N	Y	Y	N
OKLAHOMA						
3 Albert	Y	Y	Y	Y	Y	Y
2 Edmondson	Y	N	N	Y	Y	N
5 Jarman	Y	N	N	Y	Y	N
4 Steed	Y	N	N	Y	Y	Y
1 Belcher	Y	N	N	Y	Y	Y
6 Smith	Y	N	N	Y	Y	N
OREGON						
3 Green	Y	Y	Y	Y	Y	Y
2 Ullman	Y	Y	Y	Y	Y	Y
4 Dellenback	Y	Y	Y	Y	Y	Y
1 Wyatt	Y	Y	Y	Y	Y	Y
PENNSYLVANIA						
25 Clark	‡	N	Y	Y	N	Y
21 Dent	Y	Y	Y	Y	Y	Y
11 Flood	Y	Y	Y	Y	Y	Y
20 Holland	Y	Y	Y	X	X	X
14 Moorhead	Y	Y	Y	N	Y	Y
26 Morgan	Y	Y	Y	Y	Y	Y
6 Rhodes	Y	Y	Y	Y	Y	Y
15 Rooney	Y	Y	Y	Y	Y	Y
24 Vigorito	Y	Y	Y	Y	Y	Y
8 Biester	Y	Y	Y	Y	Y	Y
18 Corbett	‡	Y	Y	Y	Y	Y
16 Eshleman	Y	Y	Y	Y	Y	Y
27 Fulton	Y	Y	Y	Y	Y	Y
19 Goodling	Y	N	N	Y	Y	N
23 Johnson	Y	N	N	Y	Y	Y
10 McDade	Y	Y	Y	‡	‡	Y
22 Saylor	Y	N	N	Y	Y	N
17 Schneebeli	Y	Y	Y	Y	Y	Y
13 Schweiker	Y	Y	Y	Y	Y	Y
9 Watkins	Y	N	N	Y	Y	N
12 Whalley	Y	N	N	Y	Y	Y
7 Williams	Y	N	N	Y	Y	N
Philadelphia City						
1 Barrett	Y	Y	Y	Y	Y	N
3 Byrne	Y	Y	Y	Y	Y	Y
4 Eilberg	Y	Y	Y	Y	Y	Y
5 Green	Y	Y	Y	Y	Y	Y
2 Nix	Y	Y	Y	N	Y	Y
RHODE ISLAND						
1 St. Germain	Y	Y	Y	√	?	Y
2 Tiernan	Y	Y	Y	Y	Y	Y
SOUTH CAROLINA						
4 Ashmore	Y	X	X	Y	Y	Y
3 Dorn	Y	N	N	Y	Y	Y
5 Gettys	Y	N	N	‡	‡	Y
6 McMillan	Y	N	N	√	√	√
1 Rivers	Y	N	N	√	√	Y
2 Watson	Y	N	N	Y	Y	Y
SOUTH DAKOTA						
2 Berry	Y	N	Y	‡	‡	Y
1 Reifel	Y	Y	Y	Y	Y	Y
TENNESSEE						
6 Anderson	Y	N	N	Y	Y	Y
7 Blanton	Y	N	N	Y	Y	Y
8 Everett	Y	N	N	Y	Y	Y
4 Evins	Y	N	N	‡	‡	√
5 Fulton	Y	Y	Y	Y	Y	Y
3 Brock	Y	N	N	Y	Y	Y
2 Duncan	Y	N	N	Y	Y	N
9 Kuykendall	Y	N	N	Y	Y	N
1 Quillen	Y	N	N	Y	Y	N
TEXAS						
9 Brooks	Y	Y	Y	Y	Y	Y
17 Burleson	?	N	N	Y	Y	Y
5 Cabell	?	N	N	Y	Y	Y
22 Casey	Y	N	N	Y	Y	Y
15 de la Garza	Y	N	Y	Y	Y	Y
2 Dowdy	Y	N	N	‡	‡	N
8 Eckhardt	Y	Y	Y	N	Y	N
21 Fisher	Y	N	N	Y	Y	Y
20 Gonzalez	Y	Y	Y	N	N	Y
23 Kazen	Y	Y	Y	Y	Y	Y
19 Mahon	Y	N	N	Y	Y	Y
1 Patman	Y	N	N	Y	Y	Y
10 Pickle	Y	Y	N	Y	Y	Y
11 Poage	Y	?	?	Y	Y	Y
13 Purcell	Y	N	N	‡	‡	Y
4 Roberts	Y	N	N	Y	Y	Y
6 Teague	Y	N	N	Y	Y	√
16 White	Y	N	N	Y	Y	Y
12 Wright	Y	N	Y	Y	Y	Y
14 Young	Y	Y	Y	Y	Y	Y
7 Bush	Y	N	Y	Y	Y	Y
3 Vacancy						
18 Price	Y	N	N	Y	Y	N
UTAH						
1 Burton	Y	N	N	N	Y	Y
2 Lloyd	Y	N	Y	Y	Y	Y
VERMONT						
AL Stafford	Y	Y	Y	Y	Y	Y
VIRGINIA						
4 Abbitt	Y	N	N	Y	Y	N
1 Downing	Y	N	N	Y	Y	Y
2 Hardy	Y	N	N	‡	‡	?
7 Marsh	Y	N	N	Y	Y	Y
3 Satterfield	Y	N	N	Y	Y	Y
5 Tuck	Y	N	N	Y	Y	N
10 Broyhill	Y	N	N	Y	Y	Y
6 Poff	Y	N	N	Y	Y	N
8 Scott	Y	N	N	Y	Y	N
9 Wampler	Y	N	N	?	?	N
WASHINGTON						
7 Adams	Y	Y	Y	Y	Y	N
5 Foley	Y	Y	Y	N	N	Y
3 Hansen	?	Y	Y	Y	Y	Y
6 Hicks	Y	Y	Y	Y	Y	Y
2 Meeds	Y	Y	Y	Y	Y	Y
4 May	Y	N	Y	Y	Y	Y
1 Pelly	Y	Y	Y	Y	Y	Y
WEST VIRGINIA						
4 Hechler	Y	Y	Y	Y	Y	N
5 Kee	Y	Y	Y	Y	Y	Y
3 Slack	Y	Y	Y	Y	Y	N
2 Staggers	Y	Y	Y	Y	Y	Y
1 Moore	Y	Y	Y	Y	Y	N
WISCONSIN						
2 Kastenmeier	Y	Y	Y	N	N	N
5 Reuss	Y	Y	Y	N	N	Y
4 Zablocki	Y	Y	Y	Y	Y	X
8 Byrnes	Y	N	Y	Y	Y	Y
9 Davis	Y	N	N	Y	Y	Y
7 Laird	‡	N	Y	Y	Y	Y
10 O'Konski	Y	Y	Y	Y	Y	Y
1 Schadeberg	Y	N	N	Y	Y	N
6 Steiger	Y	Y	Y	Y	Y	Y
3 Thomson	Y	N	Y	Y	Y	N
WYOMING						
AL Harrison	Y	N	N	‡	‡	Y

*Rep. Charles H. Griffin (D Miss.) sworn in March 18, 1968.
**Rep. Bertram L. Podell (D N.Y.) sworn in Feb. 28, 1968.

House Key Votes—90th Congress—1968

7. HR 18037. Labor-HEW Appropriations. Scherle (R Iowa) amendment to cut appropriations for the Office of Economic Opportunity by an additional $100 million. Rejected 181-220: R 110-64; D 71-156 (ND 11-132; SD 60-24), June 26, 1968. A "nay" was a vote supporting the President's position.

8. HR 17134. Federal Aid Highway Bill. Cramer (R Fla.) amendment denying all funds for highway beautification except $1,250,000 for a study on beautification. Accepted 211-145: R 144-16; D 67-129 (ND 21-102; SD 46-27), July 3, 1968. A "nay" was a vote supporting the President's position.

9. HR 17735. Gun Control Act of 1968. Passage of the bill prohibiting the interstate shipment of rifles and shotguns and handgun ammunition and restricting the out-of-state purchase of rifles and shotguns. Passed 305-118: R 147-39; D 158-79 (ND 138-12; SD 20-67), July 24, 1968. A "yea" was a vote supporting the President's position.

10. HR 15067. Higher Education. Scherle (R Iowa) amendment requiring colleges to deny federal funds to students who participated in serious campus disorders. Accepted 260-146: R 134-43; D 126-102 (ND 50-98; SD 76-5), July 25, 1968. The President did not take a position on the amendment.

11. S 3497. Housing and Urban Development Act of 1968. Adoption of the conference report on the bill, providing new programs of federal assistance for homeownership and rental housing for low-income families, federal reinsurance for insurance-industry riot losses, flood insurance for homeowners, federal assistance for developers of entire new towns and new communities, and extending and expanding a number of existing housing and urban development programs. Adopted 228-135: R 72-92; D 156-43 (ND 124-2; SD 32-41), July 26, 1968. A "yea" was a vote supporting the President's position.

12. HR 19908. Foreign Aid Appropriations. Passage of the bill appropriating $1,619,100,000 for foreign aid in fiscal 1969. Passed 174-138: R 54-83; D 120-55 (ND 96-9; SD 24-46), Sept. 19, 1968. The President did not take a position on the bill.

13. HR 18037. Labor-HEW Appropriations. Cohelan (D Calif.) motion to accept a Senate amendment weakening a House provision prohibiting HEW from withholding federal funds in order to force busing, school closings or attendance of students at a particular school. The primary purpose of the House provision, sponsored by Whitten (D Miss.), was to prevent HEW from withholding funds from Southern districts using "freedom-of-choice" desegregation plans which HEW considered ineffective in achieving desegregation. The Senate language restated existing HEW powers to withhold funds. Adopted 167-156: R 67-77; D 100-79 (ND 96-12; SD 4-67), Oct. 3, 1968. A "yea" was a vote supporting the President's position.

- KEY -

Y   Record vote for (yea).
√   Paired for.
†   Announced for or CQ poll for.
N   Record vote against (nay).
X   Paired against.
-   Announced against or CQ poll against.
?   Absent, general pair, "present" or did not announce or answer poll.

	7	8	9	10	11	12	13
ALABAMA							
3 Andrews	Y	Y	N	Y	N	N	N
7 Bevill	Y	Y	N	Y	N	X	X
8 Jones	Y	N	N	Y	Y	√	N
4 Nichols	Y	‡	N	Y	N	X	X
5 Selden	Y	Y	N	Y	N	Y	N
6 Buchanan	Y	Y	N	Y	N	√	N
2 Dickinson	Y	Y	N	Y	N	N	N
1 Edwards	Y	Y	N	Y	N	N	N
ALASKA							
AL Pollock	N	Y	N	Y	Y	X	?
ARIZONA							
2 Udall	N	N	Y	N	Y	Y	‡
1 Rhodes	Y	Y	Y	Y	N	X	Y
3 Steiger	√	Y	N	Y	N	N	?
ARKANSAS							
1 Gathings	Y	Y	N	Y	N	N	N
2 Mills	Y	Y	N	Y	N	X	?
4 Pryor	N	?	N	Y	Y	√	?
3 Hammerschmidt	Y	Y	N	Y	N	N	?
CALIFORNIA							
5 Burton	N	N	Y	N	Y	Y	Y
7 Cohelan	N	N	Y	N	Y	√	Y
9 Edwards	N	N	Y	N	Y	Y	Y
34 Hanna	N	X	Y	N	Y	√	√
2 Johnson	N	N	Y	N	Y	Y	Y
4 Leggett	N	N	Y	N	Y	√	‡
15 McFall	N	N	Y	Y	Y	Y	Y
8 Miller	N	X	Y	N	Y	√	√
3 Moss	N	N	Y	N	Y	√	‡
16 Sisk	N	N	Y	N	Y	Y	‡
38 Tunney	N	N	Y	N	Y	Y	Y
37 Van Deerlin	N	X	Y	Y	Y	Y	Y
14 Waldie	N	X	Y	N	Y	Y	‡
1 Clausen	Y	Y	Y	Y	Y	X	Y
10 Gubser	Y	Y	Y	Y	?	√	N
11 McCloskey	N	N	Y	?	N	Y	Y
6 Mailliard	N	Y	Y	N	Y	Y	Y
18 Mathias	Y	√	Y	Y	?	Y	-
33 Pettis	Y	Y	Y	N	X	X	X
12 Talcott	Y	Y	Y	-	Y	N	N
13 Teague	Y	N	Y	Y	N	Y	‡
35 Utt	Y	Y	Y	N	N	X	X
36 Wilson	‡	Y	Y	Y	N	Y	N

	7	8	9	10	11	12	13
Los Angeles Co.							
29 Brown	X	X	Y	N	Y	X	‡
22 Corman	N	X	Y	N	Y	√	√
21 Hawkins	N	N	?	X	‡	Y	Y
19 Holifield	N	N	Y	N	‡	Y	Y
17 King	?	X	N	?	?	?	?
26 Rees	N	N	Y	N	Y	√	Y
30 Roybal	N	N	Y	N	Y	Y	Y
31 Wilson	N	N	Y	Y	Y	√	√
28 Bell	N	?	Y	N	?	?	Y
23 Clawson	Y	√	Y	Y	N	X	N
32 Hosmer	N	√	Y	N	N	-	N
24 Lipscomb	Y	Y	Y	Y	N	N	N
27 Reinecke	Y	√	Y	N	N	N	N
20 Smith	Y	Y	Y	Y	N	N	N
25 Wiggins	Y	‡	Y	N	N	Y	?
COLORADO							
4 Aspinall	Y	N	N	Y	Y	√	√
3 Evans	N	Y	Y	N	Y	√	√
1 Rogers	N	N	Y	N	Y	Y	√
2 Brotzman	Y	Y	Y	Y	N	Y	Y
CONNECTICUT							
1 Daddario	N	N	Y	N	Y	√	√
3 Giaimo	Y	Y	Y	Y	Y	√	√
4 Irwin	N	N	Y	N	Y	Y	Y
5 Monagan	N	Y	Y	Y	Y	√	Y
2 St. Onge	N	N	Y	N	Y	√	√
6 Meskill	X	X	Y	Y	Y	N	√
DELAWARE							
AL Roth	Y	Y	Y	Y	Y	N	N
FLORIDA							
3 Bennett	Y	Y	N	Y	N	N	N
12 Fascell	N	N	Y	Y	Y	Y	?
2 Fuqua	Y	Y	Y	Y	N	N	N
6 Gibbons	N	N	Y	Y	N	Y	N
7 Haley	Y	N	N	N	N	N	N
4 Herlong	Y	Y	?	√	-	X	X
11 Pepper	N	N	Y	N	Y	Y	‡
9 Rogers	Y	Y	Y	N	N	N	N
1 Sikes	Y	?	N	Y	N	X	X
10 Burke	Y	√	Y	N	N	N	X
8 Cramer	Y	Y	Y	N	N	N	X
5 Gurney	Y	Y	Y	?	X	X	X

	7	8	9	10	11	12	13
GEORGIA							
3 Brinkley	Y	Y	N	Y	N	N	N
7 Davis	Y	Y	N	Y	N	Y	X
9 Flynt	Y	Y	N	Y	N	N	N
1 Hagan	Y	Y	N	Y	N	N	N
9 Landrum	Y	Y	N	Y	?	X	X
2 O'Neal	Y	Y	N	Y	N	N	N
10 Stephens	Y	‡	N	Y	N	N	N
8 Stuckey	Y	Y	N	Y	?	N	N
4 Blackburn	Y	Y	N	Y	N	N	X
5 Thompson	Y	Y	Y	N	N	N	N
HAWAII							
AL Matsunaga	N	N	Y	N	Y	Y	√
AL Mink	N	N	Y	N	Y	Y	Y
IDAHO							
2 Hansen	?	√	N	Y	X	X	?
1 McClure	Y	Y	N	Y	N	X	Y
ILLINOIS							
21 Gray	N	N	Y	N	Y	Y	Y
24 Price	N	N	Y	N	Y	Y	√
23 Shipley	N	N	Y	N	Y	X	N
16 Anderson	Y	Y	Y	Y	Y	√	Y
17 Arends	Y	Y	‡	N	N	√	N
14 Erlenborn	Y	Y	Y	Y	Y	Y	Y
20 Findley	Y	Y	Y	Y	Y	Y	Y
12 McClory	N	N	Y	‡	Y	‡	‡
18 Michel	N	√	Y	N	X	N	N
19 Railsback	N	Y	Y	N	√	√	√
15 Reid	Y	Y	Y	N	N	N	N
22 Springer	N	Y	Y	N	Y	N	N
Chicago-Cook Co							
7 Annunzio	N	N	Y	N	Y	Y	Y
1 Dawson	N	N	Y	N	Y	Y	?
5 Kluczynski	N	N	Y	N	√	√	Y
3 Murphy	N	N	Y	N	Y	Y	Y
2 O'Hara	N	N	Y	N	Y	Y	Y
11 Pucinski	N	N	Y	N	Y	Y	Y
6 Ronan	N	N	Y	N	Y	Y	Y
8 Rostenkowski	N	N	Y	N	Y	Y	Y
9 Yates	N	N	Y	N	Y	Y	Y
10 Collier	Y	Y	Y	Y	N	N	N
4 Derwinski	Y	Y	Y	N	N	N	N
13 Rumsfeld	N	Y	N	N	N	N	N

	7	8	9	10	11	12	13
INDIANA							
3 Brademas	N	N	Y	N	Y	√	√
9 Hamilton	N	√	Y	Y	Y	√	√
11 Jacobs	N	N	Y	N	‡	√	√
1 Madden	N	X	N	Y	Y	Y	Y
5 Roush	N	‡	Y	N	Y	N	√
4 Adair	Y	Y	Y	N	N	N	?
6 Bray	Y	Y	N	Y	N	N	?
2 Halleck	Y	√	Y	N	Y	Y	?
7 Myers	Y	Y	Y	N	N	N	N
10 Roudebush	Y	Y	N	Y	-	?	?
8 Zion	Y	Y	N	Y	N	N	?
IOWA							
2 Culver	N	‡	Y	N	Y	Y	Y
5 Smith	N	Y	Y	N	Y	Y	N
3 Gross	Y	Y	N	Y	N	N	N
4 Kyl	Y	Y	N	Y	N	N	N
6 Mayne	‡	Y	Y	N	X	‡	N
7 Scherle	Y	Y	N	Y	N	N	N
1 Schwengel	Y	Y	Y	N	Y	Y	‡
KANSAS							
1 Dole	Y	Y	Y	‡	‡	N	N
2 Mize	Y	Y	Y	N	N	N	N
4 Shriver	Y	√	Y	Y	Y	Y	Y
5 Skubitz	Y	Y	Y	Y	N	N	N
3 Winn	Y	Y	Y	N	N	N	N
KENTUCKY							
2 Natcher	N	Y	N	Y	N	Y	N
7 Perkins	N	N	N	Y	Y	Y	N
1 Stubblefield	N	Y	N	Y	N	N	N

Democrats in this type; *Republicans in italics*

	7	8	9	10	11	12	13
6 Watts	Y	Y	Y	Y	Y	X	N
5 Carter	N	Y	N	Y	?	N	N
3 Cowger	N	Y	Y	Y	‡	X	-
4 Snyder	Y	Y	N	‡	-	N	X
LOUISIANA							
2 Boggs	N	N	Y	Y	Y	Y	Y
7 Edwards	-	Y	N	Y	‡	X	X
1 Hebert	Y	N	X	√	?	√	N
8 Long	√	?	N	√	?	N	X
5 Passman	Y	‡	N	Y	N	Y	N
6 Rarick	Y	Y	N	Y	-	X	X
4 Waggonner	Y	N	N	Y	N	N	N
3 Willis	√	X	N	Y	Y	N	X
MAINE							
2 Hathaway	N	N	Y	N	Y	Y	Y
1 Kyros	N	N	Y	Y	Y	Y	Y
MARYLAND							
4 Fallon	X	N	Y	Y	Y	Y	Y
7 Friedel	N	N	Y	N	Y	Y	Y
3 Garmatz	N	N	N	Y	Y	Y	Y
2 Long	N	?	Y	N	Y	N	Y
5 Machen	N	N	Y	N	Y	Y	Y
8 Gude	N	Y	Y	N	Y	Y	Y
6 Mathias	N	‡	Y	N	Y	Y	√
1 Morton	N	Y	Y	N	N	√	N
MASSACHUSETTS							
2 Boland	N	N	Y	N	?	√	Y
11 Burke	N	N	Y	N	Y	Y	Y
4 Donohue	N	N	Y	N	Y	√	Y
7 Macdonald	N	Y	Y	N	Y	Y	√
9 McCormack							
8 O'Neill	N	N	Y	N	Y	Y	Y
3 Philbin	N	N	Y	N	Y	√	Y
6 Bates	N	Y	Y	Y	Y	Y	Y
1 Conte	N	N	Y	N	Y	√	Y
10 Heckler	N	N	Y	N	Y	Y	Y
12 Keith	N	Y	Y	Y	Y	Y	Y
5 Morse	N	N	Y	N	Y	Y	Y
MICHIGAN							
12 O'Hara	X	N	Y	N	Y	Y	Y
18 Broomfield	N	Y	Y	Y	Y	Y	Y
3 Brown	N	Y	Y	Y	Y	N	Y
10 Cederberg	Y	Y	Y	Y	‡	N	Y
6 Chamberlain	Y	Y	Y	Y	Y	N	Y
2 Esch	N	Y	Y	N	Y	Y	Y
5 Ford	N	Y	Y	Y	Y	Y	‡
8 Harvey	N	√	Y	Y	Y	N	Y
4 Hutchinson	Y	Y	Y	Y	N	N	Y
19 McDonald	N	Y	Y	Y	Y	X	N
7 Riegle	N	Y	Y	Y	Y	Y	Y
11 Ruppe	N	√	Y	N	Y	N	Y
9 Vander Jagt	N	√	Y	Y	Y	X	N
Detroit-Wayne Co.							
1 Conyers	N	X	‡	N	Y	?	Y
13 Diggs	N	X	Y	N	Y	Y	Y
16 Dingell	N	N	N	N	Y	√	Y
15 Ford	N	X	Y	N	?	√	Y
17 Griffiths	N	X	Y	N	Y	√	?
14 Nedzi	N	N	Y	Y	Y	Y	Y
MINNESOTA							
8 Blatnik	N	N	Y	N	Y	Y	Y
5 Fraser	N	N	Y	N	Y	Y	Y
4 Karth	N	Y	Y	N	‡	Y	√
7 Langen	Y	Y	N	Y	N	N	N
3 MacGregor	N	√	Y	Y	Y	Y	Y
2 Nelsen	Y	Y	Y	Y	N	Y	Y
1 Quie	N	Y	Y	N	Y	Y	Y
6 Zwach	Y	Y	Y	Y	Y	N	Y
MISSISSIPPI							
1 Abernethy	Y	Y	N	Y	N	N	N
5 Colmer	Y	√	N	Y	N	N	N
4 Montgomery	Y	Y	N	Y	N	N	N
2 Whitten	Y	Y	N	Y	N	N	N
3 Griffin	Y	Y	N	Y	N	N	N
MISSOURI							
5 Bolling	N	N	Y	N	?	‡	Y
6 Hull	Y	Y	Y	Y	‡	N	X
9 Hungate	Y	Y	Y	N	‡	X	X
8 Ichord	Y	‡	Y	Y	N	X	?
10 Jones	?	?	Y	Y	?	N	?
1 Karsten	?	-	Y	‡	‡	?	?
4 Randall	Y	Y	N	Y	Y	N	N
3 Sullivan	X	N	Y	Y	‡	Y	Y

	7	8	9	10	11	12	13
2 Curtis	Y	Y	N	N	N	‡	-
7 Hall	Y	√	Y	Y	N	X	N
MONTANA							
1 Olsen	N	N	N	N	Y	X	?
2 Battin	Y	Y	N	Y	N	N	-
NEBRASKA							
2 Cunningham	N	√	?	‡	‡	N	N
1 Denney	Y	Y	Y	Y	N	N	N
3 Martin	Y	Y	N	Y	N	N	?
NEVADA							
AL Baring	Y	‡	N	Y	N	N	N
NEW HAMPSHIRE							
2 Cleveland	Y	Y	Y	N	Y	N	Y
1 Wyman	Y	Y	Y	Y	Y	N	Y
NEW JERSEY							
14 Daniels	N	N	Y	N	Y	Y	Y
13 Gallagher	N	N	Y	X	‡	√	?
9 Helstoski	N	N	Y	N	Y	Y	?
3 Howard	N	N	Y	N	Y	Y	Y
8 Joelson	N	N	Y	N	Y	Y	Y
11 Minish	N	X	Y	N	Y	Y	Y
15 Patten	N	N	Y	N	Y	Y	Y
10 Rodino	N	N	Y	N	Y	Y	Y
4 Thompson	X	X	Y	N	Y	Y	Y
6 Cahill	N	Y	Y	N	N	Y	Y
12 Dwyer	N	-	Y	N	Y	Y	Y
5 Frelinghuysen	N	Y	Y	N	Y	Y	Y
1 Hunt	Y	Y	Y	Y	N	X	N
2 Sandman	Y	N	Y	Y	N	N	N
7 Widnall	N	?	Y	N	Y	Y	Y
NEW MEXICO							
AL Morris	Y	Y	N	Y	Y	X	N
AL Walker	Y	?	N	Y	Y	N	?
NEW YORK							
27 Dow	N	N	Y	N	Y	Y	Y
41 Dulski	N	Y	Y	N	Y	Y	√
34 Hanley	N	Y	Y	N	Y	Y	Y
39 McCarthy	N	N	Y	N	Y	Y	?
25 Ottinger	N	N	Y	N	Y	Y	?
1 Pike	N	Y	Y	Y	Y	Y	Y
28 Resnick	-	X	Y	N	‡	‡	‡
35 Stratton	N	Y	Y	Y	Y	√	√
5 Tenzer	N	N	Y	N	‡	√	Y
3 Wolff	N	X	Y	N	Y	Y	Y
29 Button	N	N	Y	-	Y	√	√
37 Conable	‡	Y	Y	N	Y	Y	‡
*38 Goodell**	N	Y	Y	N	Y		
2 Grover	Y	Y	Y	Y	N	Y	Y
36 Horton	N	Y	Y	N	‡	Y	Y
30 King	Y	Y	Y	Y	N	N	N
31 McEwen	Y	Y	Y	N	-	Y	N
32 Pirnie	N	Y	Y	Y	N	Y	Y
26 Reid	N	N	Y	N	Y	Y	Y
33 Robison	N	Y	Y	N	Y	Y	Y
40 Smith	N	Y	Y	N	Y	Y	N
4 Wydler	N	Y	Y	N	Y	Y	Y
New York City							
7 Addabbo	N	Y	Y	Y	Y	√	Y
23 Bingham	N	X	Y	N	Y	Y	Y
11 Brasco	N	N	Y	N	Y	Y	Y
15 Carey	N	X	Y	N	Y	√	Y
10 Celler	N	N	Y	N	?	√	√
9 Delaney	N	Y	Y	Y	Y	N	Y
19 Farbstein	N	N	Y	N	Y	Y	Y
22 Gilbert	N	N	Y	N	-	Y	Y
12 Kelly	N	N	Y	Y	‡	Y	N
13 Podell	N	N	Y	N	‡	Y	√
16 Murphy	N	N	√	N	Y	Y	√
18 Vacancy							
14 Rooney	N	X	Y	N	Y	Y	Y
8 Rosenthal	N	N	Y	N	?	Y	Y
20 Ryan	N	N	Y	N	Y	Y	√
21 Scheuer	-	N	Y	N	Y	Y	Y
24 Fino	Y	Y	Y	‡	‡	X	-
6 Halpern	N	N	Y	N	Y	Y	Y
17 Kupferman	N	N	Y	N	‡	√	√
NORTH CAROLINA							
2 Fountain	Y	Y	N	Y	N	X	N
5 Galifianakis	Y	Y	Y	‡	Y	N	N
3 Henderson	Y	Y	N	Y	N	N	N
1 Jones	Y	Y	N	Y	N	N	N
6 Kornegay	√	?	Y	Y	N	X	N
7 Lennon	Y	Y	N	Y	N	N	N

	7	8	9	10	11	12	13
11 Taylor	Y	N	Y	Y	Y	N	N
10 Whitener	Y	Y	N	Y	N	N	N
9 Broyhill	Y	Y	Y	Y	N	N	N
4 Gardner	Y	Y	N	Y	-	X	X
8 Jonas	Y	Y	Y	Y	N	N	N
NORTH DAKOTA							
1 Andrews	Y	√	N	N	Y	N	Y
2 Kleppe	Y	Y	N	Y	N	N	Y
OHIO							
9 Ashley	N	N	Y	N	Y	√	Y
20 Feighan	N	N	Y	Y	Y	Y	Y
18 Hays	N	N	Y	Y	‡	‡	-
19 Kirwan	N	X	Y	X	?	Y	?
21 Vanik	X	N	Y	Y	Y	√	Y
17 Ashbrook	Y	Y	N	Y	N	X	N
14 Ayres	N	Y	Y	Y	‡	√	N
8 Betts	Y	Y	Y	Y	N	N	N
22 Bolton	N	Y	Y	Y	Y	Y	N
16 Bow	√	√	Y	Y	N	N	Y
7 Brown	Y	Y	Y	Y	N	X	Y
2 Clancy	Y	Y	Y	Y	N	X	N
12 Devine	Y	Y	Y	Y	N	N	N
6 Harsha	Y	Y	N	Y	N	N	?
5 Latta	Y	√	Y	Y	Y	X	N
24 Lukens	Y	Y	Y	Y	N	X	N
4 McCulloch	N	Y	Y	Y	?	N	Y
10 Miller	Y	Y	N	Y	N	N	N
23 Minshall	N	Y	Y	Y	Y	X	-
13 Mosher	N	Y	Y	N	Y	Y	√
11 Stanton	N	Y	Y	Y	Y	Y	Y
1 Taft	X	‡	Y	N	Y	Y	Y
3 Whalen	N	Y	Y	N	Y	Y	Y
15 Wylie	Y	Y	Y	Y	Y	N	Y
OKLAHOMA							
3 Albert	N	N	N	Y	Y	Y	Y
2 Edmondson	N	N	N	Y	Y	√	√
5 Jarman	Y	Y	N	Y	N	N	-
4 Steed	Y	N	N	Y	Y	Y	N
1 Belcher	Y	Y	N	Y	N	N	?
6 Smith	Y	Y	N	Y	N	X	N
OREGON							
3 Green	Y	N	Y	N	Y	Y	N
2 Ullman	Y	?	Y	N	Y	‡	N
4 Dellenback	N	Y	Y	N	Y	Y	Y
1 Wyatt	Y	Y	N	N	Y	N	N
PENNSYLVANIA							
25 Clark	N	N	Y	Y	?	√	N
21 Dent	N	N	Y	N	‡	√	Y
11 Flood	N	N	Y	N	?	Y	N
20 Holland**	?	X	?	X	?		
14 Moorhead	N	N	Y	N	Y	√	√
26 Morgan	N	N	Y	N	Y	Y	Y
6 Rhodes	N	N	?	‡	‡	√	Y
15 Rooney	N	Y	Y	Y	Y	Y	√
24 Vigorito	N	Y	Y	Y	Y	Y	Y
8 Biester	N	Y	Y	N	Y	Y	Y
18 Corbett	N	N	Y	Y	‡	Y	N
16 Eshleman	Y	Y	Y	Y	Y	N	N
27 Fulton	N	N	Y	Y	Y	Y	N
19 Goodling	Y	Y	Y	Y	N	N	N
23 Johnson	Y	Y	N	Y	-	N	N
10 McDade	N	Y	Y	N	Y	√	Y
22 Saylor	N	N	N	Y	Y	N	N
17 Schneebeli	Y	Y	Y	Y	N	Y	N
13 Schweiker	N	Y	Y	N	Y	‡	?
9 Watkins	?	Y	Y	Y	N	X	N
12 Whalley	Y	Y	N	Y	N	N	N
7 Williams	√	Y	Y	Y	N	N	N
Philadelphia City							
1 Barrett	N	N	Y	N	Y	Y	Y
3 Byrne	N	N	Y	N	Y	Y	Y
4 Eilberg	N	N	Y	N	‡	Y	N
5 Green	N	N	Y	N	Y	Y	Y
2 Nix	N	N	Y	N	Y	Y	Y
RHODE ISLAND							
1 St. Germain	N	N	Y	Y	Y	Y	Y
2 Tiernan	N	N	Y	Y	Y	Y	Y
SOUTH CAROLINA							
4 Ashmore	Y	?	N	Y	N	X	X
3 Dorn	Y	?	N	Y	N	N	N
5 Gettys	Y	‡	N	Y	N	N	N
6 McMillan	Y	Y	N	Y	N	N	N

	7	8	9	10	11	12	13
1 Rivers	Y	N	N	Y	N	X	N
2 Watson	Y	Y	N	Y	N	N	N
SOUTH DAKOTA							
2 Berry	Y	√	Y	Y	N	N	X
1 Reifel	Y	Y	Y	N	Y	X	Y
TENNESSEE							
6 Anderson	N	‡	N	‡	‡	Y	N
7 Blanton	√	√	N	‡	‡	N	N
8 Everett	Y	N	N	?	Y	N	N
4 Evins	-	-	?	?	‡	-	N
5 Fulton	N	N	Y	Y	‡	Y	N
3 Brock	Y	Y	Y	Y	N	N	N
2 Duncan	Y	Y	N	Y	N	N	N
9 Kuykendall	Y	Y	Y	Y	‡	X	N
1 Quillen	Y	Y	N	Y	‡	X	N
TEXAS							
9 Brooks	N	N	N	Y	Y	Y	N
17 Burleson	Y	Y	N	Y	N	N	N
5 Cabell	Y	Y	N	Y	N	Y	N
22 Casey	N	Y	Y	Y	N	N	N
15 de la Garza	N	N	N	Y	Y	N	N
2 Dowdy	Y	Y	N	Y	N	N	N
8 Eckhardt	N	N	Y	N	Y	Y	Y
21 Fisher	Y	Y	N	Y	N	X	N
20 Gonzalez	N	N	N	Y	N	Y	Y
23 Kazen	N	N	N	Y	Y	Y	N
19 Mahon	N	N	N	Y	N	Y	N
1 Patman	N	X	N	N	Y	Y	N
10 Pickle	N	N	Y	Y	?	Y	X
11 Poage	Y	Y	Y	Y	?	N	N
13 Purcell	N	N	N	Y	-	Y	X
4 Roberts	Y	N	N	Y	N	N	N
6 Teague	?	N	N	Y	?	Y	N
16 White	Y	Y	N	Y	Y	N	N
12 Wright	N	N	Y	Y	Y	Y	N
14 Young	N	N	N	Y	Y	Y	N
7 Bush	Y	Y	Y	Y	Y	‡	N
*3 Collins****						N	N
18 Price	Y	Y	N	Y	N	N	N
UTAH							
1 Burton	√	Y	N	Y	N	N	X
2 Lloyd	Y	√	N	Y	N	X	N
VERMONT							
AL Stafford	N	N	Y	N	Y	Y	Y
VIRGINIA							
4 Abbitt	Y	Y	N	Y	?	X	N
1 Downing	Y	Y	Y	Y	Y	Y	N
2 Hardy	Y	?	Y	√	Y	?	N
7 Marsh	Y	Y	N	Y	N	N	N
3 Satterfield	Y	Y	N	Y	N	N	N
5 Tuck	Y	Y	N	Y	-	N	N
10 Broyhill	Y	Y	Y	Y	N	N	N
6 Poff	Y	√	Y	Y	N	N	N
8 Scott	Y	Y	N	Y	N	N	?
9 Wampler	Y	Y	N	?	Y	N	N
WASHINGTON							
7 Adams	N	N	Y	N	Y	Y	Y
5 Foley	N	N	Y	N	Y	Y	Y
3 Hansen	N	N	Y	N	Y	Y	Y
6 Hicks	N	Y	Y	Y	Y	Y	Y
2 Meeds	N	N	Y	Y	Y	Y	Y
4 May	Y	Y	Y	Y	N	N	-
1 Pelly	N	Y	Y	Y	N	Y	Y
WEST VIRGINIA							
4 Hechler	N	N	N	Y	N	Y	Y
5 Kee	N	N	N	Y	Y	Y	?
3 Slack	N	Y	Y	Y	Y	Y	N
2 Staggers	N	N	N	Y	Y	N	?
1 Moore	X	Y	Y	‡	Y	X	?
WISCONSIN							
2 Kastenmeier	N	N	Y	N	Y	Y	Y
5 Reuss	N	N	Y	N	Y	Y	Y
4 Zablocki	N	N	Y	Y	Y	Y	‡
8 Byrnes	Y	Y	Y	Y	N	Y	Y
9 Davis	Y	Y	Y	Y	N	N	‡
7 Laird	√	Y	Y	Y	N	X	Y
10 O'Konski	N	N	Y	Y	Y	X	-
1 Schadeberg	Y	Y	Y	Y	N	N	N
6 Steiger	N	Y	Y	Y	N	N	N
3 Thomson	Y	Y	Y	Y	N	N	N
WYOMING							
AL Harrison	Y	Y	N	Y	N	X	Y

*Rep. Charles E. Goodell (R N.Y.) resigned Sept. 9, 1968.
**Rep. Elmer J. Holland (D Pa.) died Aug. 9, 1968.
***Rep. James M. Collins (R Texas) sworn in Sept. 4, 1968.

Senate Key Votes—90th Congress—1968

1. HR 2516. Civil Rights-Open Housing. Mansfield (D Mont.) motion to table (kill) Mondale (D Minn.) amendment to prohibit discrimination on the grounds of race or religion in the sale and rental of housing. Rejected 34-58: R 16-19; D 18-39 (ND 3-36; SD 15-3), Feb. 21, 1968. A "nay" was a vote supporting the President's position.

2. HR 2516. Civil Rights-Open Housing. Passage of the bill to prohibit interference with a person exercising specified federally protected rights, to prohibit discrimination in the sale or rental of housing, to guarantee constitutional rights of American Indians, and to prohibit travel in interstate commerce with intent to incite or take part in a riot. Passed 71-20: R 29-3; D 42-17 (ND 39-0; SD 3-17), March 11, 1968. A "yea" was a vote supporting the President's position.

3. S Res 266. Senate Standards of Conduct. Clark (D Pa.) -Case (R N.J.) amendment requiring Senators and employees earning more than $15,000 a year to file annual reports publicly disclosing the market value of each asset and liability, the source and amount of each capital gain and item of income over $100, and the details of business and professional associations, including fees received for services. Rejected 40-44: R 12-20; D 28-24 (ND 24-11; SD 4-13), March 20, 1968. The President did not take a position on the amendment.

4. HR 15414. Excise Tax Extension. Williams (R Del.)-Smathers (D Fla.) amendment to impose a 10-percent surcharge on individual and corporate income taxes and to set a $180.1-billion ceiling on fiscal 1969 spending. Accepted 53-35: R 31-3; D 22-32 (ND 12-24; SD 10-8), April 2, 1968. A "yea" was a vote supporting the President's position.

5. S 917. Omnibus Crime Bill. Kennedy (D Mass.) amendment prohibiting the interstate mail-order sale of rifles and shotguns. Rejected 29-53: R 9-22; D 20-31 (ND 16-18; SD 4-13), May 16, 1968. A "yea" was a vote supporting the President's position.

6. S 3633. Gun Control Act of 1968. Passage of the bill banning mail-order and most out-of-state sales (to residents of other states) of rifles, shotguns and ammunition and curtailing the sale of firearms and ammunition to minors. Passed 70-17: R 31-4; D 39-13 (ND 27-7; SD 12-6), Sept. 18, 1968. A "yea" was a vote supporting the President's position.

	1	2	3	4	5	6
ALABAMA						
Hill	Y	N	N	N	N	Y
Sparkman	Y	N	N	‡	N	Y
ALASKA						
Bartlett	N	Y	N	N	N	?
Gruening	N	Y	N	X	N	-
ARIZONA						
Hayden	Y	Y	N	N	N	N
Fannin	Y	N	N	Y	N	N
ARKANSAS						
Fulbright	Y	N	N	-	-	
McClellan	Y	N	N	Y	N	N
CALIFORNIA						
Kuchel	N	√	√	√	√	Y
Murphy	√	Y	N	Y	N	Y
COLORADO						
Allott	Y	Y	N	Y	N	Y
Dominick	N	Y	N	Y	N	Y
CONNECTICUT						
Dodd	N	Y	Y	Y	Y	Y
Ribicoff	N	Y	Y	N	Y	Y
DELAWARE						
Boggs	N	Y	Y	Y	N	Y
Williams	Y	N	Y	Y	Y	Y
FLORIDA						
Holland	Y	N	X	Y	N	Y
Smathers	√	N	N	Y	Y	Y
GEORGIA						
Russell	√	N	-	Y	N	N
Talmadge	Y	N	N	N	N	Y
HAWAII						
Inouye	N	Y	‡	Y	‡	Y
Fong	N	Y	N	Y	N	Y
IDAHO						
Church	N	Y	√	-	N	N
Jordan	Y	Y	N	Y	N	Y
ILLINOIS						
Dirksen	Y	Y	N	Y	N	Y
Percy	N	Y	-	Y	Y	Y

	1	2	3	4	5	6
INDIANA						
Bayh	N	Y	Y	N	N	Y
Hartke	N	Y	N	N	?	Y
IOWA						
Hickenlooper	Y	X	N	Y	N	Y
Miller	N	X	Y	Y	N	Y
KANSAS						
Carlson	N	Y	N	Y	N	Y
Pearson	N	Y	N	Y	Y	Y
KENTUCKY						
Cooper	N	Y	Y	Y	Y	Y
Morton	N	Y	‡	Y	?	Y
LOUISIANA						
Ellender	Y	N	N	N	N	N
Long	Y	N	N	N	N	?
MAINE						
Muskie	N	Y	Y	Y	N	?
Smith	N	Y	N	Y	Y	‡
MARYLAND						
Brewster	N	Y	Y	N	Y	Y
Tydings	N	Y	Y	Y	Y	Y
MASSACHUSETTS						
Kennedy	N	Y	Y	N	Y	Y
Brooke	N	Y	Y	Y	Y	Y
MICHIGAN						
Hart	N	Y	Y	N	N	Y
Griffin	N	Y	Y	Y	Y	Y
MINNESOTA						
McCarthy	-	‡	-	-	‡	‡
Mondale	N	Y	Y	N	Y	Y
MISSISSIPPI						
Eastland	Y	N	N	Y	N	N
Stennis	Y	N	N	Y	N	N
MISSOURI						
Long	N	Y	?	?	Y	?
Symington	N	Y	Y	Y	Y	Y
MONTANA						
Mansfield	Y	Y	X*	Y	N	√
Metcalf	X	‡	N	N	N	N

	1	2	3	4	5	6
NEBRASKA						
Curtis	Y	Y	N	Y	N	Y
Hruska	Y	Y	N	Y	N	Y
NEVADA						
Bible	N	Y	Y	N	N	N
Cannon	-	Y	N	N	N	Y
NEW HAMPSHIRE						
McIntyre	N	‡	?	Y	Y	Y
Cotton	Y	Y	Y	N	N	Y
NEW JERSEY						
Williams	N	Y	Y	N	Y	Y
Case	N	Y	Y	Y	√	Y
NEW MEXICO						
Anderson	N	Y	N	N	N	Y
Montoya	N	Y	N	Y	-	Y
NEW YORK						
*Goodell***						Y
Javits	N	Y	Y	Y	Y	Y
NORTH CAROLINA						
Ervin	Y	N	X	N	Y	Y
Jordan	Y	N	N	‡	N	Y
NORTH DAKOTA						
Burdick	N	Y	Y	N	N	N
Young	Y	Y	X	N	N	Y
OHIO						
Lausche	N	Y	N	√	Y	Y
Young	N	Y	Y	N	Y	Y
OKLAHOMA						
Harris	N	√	‡	N	?	Y
Monroney	X	Y	N	N	-	?
OREGON						
Morse	N	Y	√	N	X	X
Hatfield	N	Y	Y	N	N	Y
PENNSYLVANIA						
Clark	N	Y	Y	N	Y	Y
Scott	N	Y	Y	Y	N	Y
RHODE ISLAND						
Pastore	X	√	√	√	√	Y
Pell	N	Y	N	Y	Y	Y

Y	Record vote for (yea).					
√	Paired for.					
†	Announced for or CQ poll for.					
N	Record vote against (nay).					
X	Paired against.					
-	Announced against or CQ poll against.					
?	Absent, general pair, "present" or did not announce or answer poll.					

	1	2	3	4	5	6
SOUTH CAROLINA						
Hollings	Y	N	Y	N	X	N
Thurmond	Y	N	N	N	N	N
SOUTH DAKOTA						
McGovern	N	Y	Y	N	N	?
Mundt	Y	Y	N	Y	N	N
TENNESSEE						
Gore	N	Y	Y	Y	Y	Y
Baker	Y	Y	N	‡	N	Y
TEXAS						
Yarborough	N	Y	-	Y	Y	
Tower	Y	X	N	Y	N	Y
UTAH						
Moss	N	Y	Y	Y	X	N
Bennett	Y	Y	N	‡	N	-
VERMONT						
Aiken	N	Y	Y	Y	‡	Y
Prouty	N	Y	N	Y	?	Y
VIRGINIA						
Byrd, Jr.	Y	N	N	Y	N	Y
Spong	Y	N	Y	Y	Y	Y
WASHINGTON						
Jackson	N	Y	Y	N	Y	Y
Magnuson	N	Y	N	X	Y	Y
WEST VIRGINIA						
Byrd	Y	N	N	Y	N	Y
Randolph	N	Y	N	Y	Y	Y
WISCONSIN						
Nelson	N	Y	Y	N	N	Y
Proxmire	N	Y	N	N	N	Y
WYOMING						
McGee	N	Y	N	N	N	N
Hansen	Y	Y	N	Y	N	Y

Mansfield initially voted "yea", but to accommodate Sen. Morse (Ore.) who was absent and wished to be Paired For the amendment, Mansfield withdrew his vote and was recorded as Paired Against.

**Sen. Charles E. Goodell (R N.Y.) sworn in Sept. 12, 1968.*

Democrats in this type; *Republicans in italics*

Senate Key Votes—90th Congress—1968

7. S 917. Omnibus Crime Bill. Tydings (D Md.) amendment deleting from Title II language denying the Supreme Court and lower federal courts jurisdiction to review the determination by a state court trial judge that a confession was "voluntary," if the judge's determination had been upheld by the state's highest court. Accepted 52-32: R 16-15; D 36-17 (ND 31-3; SD 5-14), May 21, 1968. A "yea" was a vote supporting the President's position.

8. S 3497. Housing and Urban Development Act of 1968. Passage of the bill to provide federal assistance for homeownership for low-income families and low-income rental housing, to provide federal reinsurance for insurance industry riot losses, to set up a flood insurance program and to extend and expand a number of housing and urban development programs. Passed 67-4: R 27-1; D 40-3 (ND 29-0; SD 11-3), May 28, 1968. A "yea" was a vote supporting the President's position.

9. HR 15263. Foreign Assistance Act of 1968. Morse (D Ore.) amendment to reduce the authorization for the Alliance for Progress grants to $70 million from $90 million. Rejected 31-43: R 9-16; D 22-27 (ND 11-21; SD 11-6), July 31, 1968. A "nay" was a vote supporting the President's position.

10. HR 18785. Defense Construction Appropriations. Nelson (D Wis.) amendment to reduce the appropriation for army construction from $537.6 million to $310.3 million to delete the $227.3 million designated for costs related to the deployment of the Sentinel antiballistic missile (ABM) system. Rejected 27-46: R 5-14; D 22-32 (ND 20-15; SD 2-17), Aug. 1, 1968. A "nay" was a vote supporting the President's position.

11. HR 18037. Labor-HEW Appropriations. Pastore (D R.I.) amendment to increase the bill's appropriation for the Office of Economic Opportunity in fiscal 1969 by $215 million (from $1,873,000,000 to $2,088,000,000). Accepted 37-26: R 8-14; D 29-12 (ND 27-1; SD 2-11), Sept. 6, 1968. A "yea" was a vote supporting the President's position.

12. Fortas Nomination. Mansfield (D Mont.) motion to stop debate by invoking cloture on his motion to take up the nomination of Abe Fortas to be Chief Justice of the United States. Rejected 45-43: R 10-24; D 35-19 (ND 31-4; SD 4-15), Oct. 1, 1968. The votes of two-thirds (59) of Senators present and voting were required. A "yea" was a vote supporting the President's position.

	7	8	9	10	11	12
ALABAMA						
Hill	N	Y	?	N	N	N
Sparkman	N	Y	N	N	N	N
ALASKA						
Bartlett	‡	Y	X	✓	‡	?
Gruening	‡	Y	✓	✓	Y	X
ARIZONA						
Hayden	N	?	?	N	Y	Y
Fannin	N	‡	N	N	N	N
ARKANSAS						
Fulbright	Y	Y	?	?	?	N
McClellan	N	?	Y	N	N	N
CALIFORNIA						
Kuchel	‡	‡	N	N	✓	Y
Murphy	N	‡	N	-	N	N
COLORADO						
Allott	Y	Y	Y	X	?	N
Dominick	Y	Y	Y	N	X	Y
CONNECTICUT						
Dodd	Y	‡	N	N	Y	N
Ribicoff	Y	Y	Y	Y	Y	Y
DELAWARE						
Boggs	Y	Y	N	N	N	N
Williams	N	Y	Y	N	N	N
FLORIDA						
Holland	N	N	N	N	X	N
Smathers	X	‡	?	N	?	?
GEORGIA						
Russell	N	N	Y	N	N	N
Talmadge	N	Y	Y	N	?	N
HAWAII						
Inouye	Y	‡	N	N	?	Y
Fong	Y	‡	N	N	‡	N
IDAHO						
Church	‡	‡	Y	Y	‡	✓
Jordan	Y	Y	Y	N	N	N
ILLINOIS						
Dirksen	X	Y	X	X	N	N
Percy	Y	Y	X	✓	Y	Y

	7	8	9	10	11	12
INDIANA						
Bayh	Y	Y	Y	N	✓	Y
Hartke	Y	Y	N	Y	Y	Y
IOWA						
Hickenlooper	N	Y	N	N	N	N
Miller	Y	Y	N	-	N	N
KANSAS						
Carlson	N	‡	?	?	N	N
Pearson	Y	Y	N	?	Y	N
KENTUCKY						
Cooper	Y	‡	X	✓	Y	Y
Morton	✓	?	?	?	?	?
LOUISIANA						
Ellender	N	Y	Y	Y	N	-
Long	N	‡	N	N	?	N
MAINE						
Muskie	Y	Y	N	Y	?	Y
Smith	N	Y	N	Y	-	-
MARYLAND						
Brewster	Y	Y	-	X	‡	?
Tydings	Y	Y	N	Y	Y	Y
MASSACHUSETTS						
Kennedy	Y	‡	?	?	?	Y
Brooke	Y	Y	N	Y	✓	Y
MICHIGAN						
Hart	Y	Y	N	Y	Y	Y
Griffin	Y	Y	?	?	Y	N
MINNESOTA						
McCarthy	‡	‡	-	Y	‡	Y
Mondale	Y	Y	N	Y	Y	Y
MISSISSIPPI						
Eastland	N	X	Y	N	N	N
Stennis	N	N	Y	N	N	N
MISSOURI						
Long	Y	?	?	?	?	?
Symington	Y	Y	Y	Y	Y	Y
MONTANA						
Mansfield	Y	Y	N	✓	Y	Y
Metcalf	Y	‡	N	Y	Y	Y

	7	8	9	10	11	12
NEBRASKA						
Curtis	N	Y	Y	X	-	N
Hruska	N	Y	✓	X	-	N
NEVADA						
Bible	Y	?	Y	N	?	-
Cannon	N	Y	Y	N	‡	N
NEW HAMPSHIRE						
McIntyre	Y	Y	N	N	Y	Y
Cotton	N	Y	Y	N	?	N
NEW JERSEY						
Williams	Y	Y	-	Y	Y	Y
Case	Y	Y	N	Y	Y	Y
NEW MEXICO						
Anderson	Y	Y	N	N	?	Y
Montoya	?	?	N	N	Y	Y
NEW YORK						
*Goodell***						Y
Javits	‡	Y	N	✓	Y	Y
NORTH CAROLINA						
Ervin	N	✓	Y	N	N	N
Jordan	N	Y	Y	N	-	N
NORTH DAKOTA						
Burdick	Y	Y	✓	N	‡	Y
Young	N	Y	N	N	N	N
OHIO						
Lausche	Y	Y	N	X	N	N
Young	Y	Y	Y	Y	Y	Y
OKLAHOMA						
Harris	?	‡	N	N	Y	N
Monroney	Y	Y	N	N	?	Y
OREGON						
Morse	Y	‡	Y	Y	Y	✓
Hatfield	‡	✓	✓	Y	Y	Y
PENNSYLVANIA						
Clark	Y	Y	N	Y	Y	Y
Scott	Y	Y	✓	✓	Y	Y
RHODE ISLAND						
Pastore	Y	Y	N	N	Y	Y
Pell	Y	Y	X	Y	Y	Y

	7	8	9	10	11	12
SOUTH CAROLINA						
Hollings	N	?	Y	N	N	N
Thurmond	N	N	Y	N	N	N
SOUTH DAKOTA						
McGovern	?	?	N	Y	Y	?
Mundt	N	Y	Y	?	N	N
TENNESSEE						
Gore	Y	Y	?	N	Y	Y
Baker	Y	Y	N	N	N	N
TEXAS						
Yarborough	Y	Y	N	Y	‡	Y
Tower	N	Y	-	X	-	N
UTAH						
Moss	Y	Y	N	Y	Y	Y
Bennett	N	Y	Y	N	X	N
VERMONT						
Aiken	Y	‡	N	Y	‡	-
Prouty	Y	Y	N	N	?	N
VIRGINIA						
Byrd, Jr.	N	Y	N	N	N	N
Spong	Y	Y	Y	N	N	N
WASHINGTON						
Jackson	Y	Y	N	Y	N	Y
Magnuson	Y	Y	N	Y	‡	Y
WEST VIRGINIA						
Byrd	N	Y	Y	N	Y	N
Randolph	Y	Y	Y	Y	Y	Y
WISCONSIN						
Nelson	?	Y	N	Y	Y	Y
Proxmire	Y	Y	N	Y	Y	Y
WYOMING						
McGee	?	?	N	N	Y	Y
Hansen	N	Y	‡	?	N	N

Legend:

Y	Record vote for (yea).
✓	Paired for.
‡	Announced for or CQ poll for.
N	Record vote against (nay).
X	Paired against.
-	Announced against or CQ poll against.
?	Absent, general pair, "present" or did not announce or answer poll.

***Sen. Charles E. Goodell (R N.Y.) sworn in Sept. 12, 1968.*

Democrats in this type; *Republicans in italics*

Congresses and Their Leaders, 79th-91st

Committee Chairmen, 1947-69

Congresses and Leaders - 79th to 91st

79th Congress
1945-1946

House: 243 Democrats
190 Republicans
2 Others

Speaker: Sam Rayburn (D Texas)
Majority Leader: John W. McCormack (D Mass.)
Minority Leader: Joseph W. Martin Jr. (R Mass.)

Senate: 57 Democrats
38 Republicans
1 Other

Vice President: Harry S. Truman (D Mo.) (Became President April 12, 1945)
President Pro Tempore: Kenneth McKellar (D Tenn.) (Became presiding officer on succession of Harry S. Truman to Presidency.)
Majority Leader: Alben W. Barkley (D Ky.)
Minority Leader: Wallace H. White (R Maine)

80th Congress
1947-1948

House: 188 Democrats
245 Republicans
1 Other
2 Vacancies

Speaker: Joseph W. Martin Jr. (R Mass.)
Majority Leader: Charles A. Halleck (R Ind.)
Minority Leader: Sam Rayburn (D Texas)

Senate: 45 Democrats
51 Republicans

Vice President: Vacant
President Pro Tempore: Arthur Vandenberg (R Mich.)
Majority Leader: Wallace H. White (R Maine)
Minority Leader: Alben W. Barkley (D Ky.)

81st Congress
1949-1950

House: 263 Democrats
171 Republicans
1 Other

Speaker: Sam Rayburn (D Texas)
Majority Leader: John W. McCormack (D Mass.)
Minority Leader: Joseph W. Martin Jr. (R Mass.)

Senate: 54 Democrats
42 Republicans

Vice President: Alben W. Barkley (D Ky.)
President Pro Tempore: Kenneth McKellar (D Tenn.)
Majority Leader: Scott W. Lucas (D Ill.)
Minority Leader: Kenneth S. Wherry (R Neb.)

82nd Congress
1951-1952

House: 235 Democrats
199 Republicans
1 Other

Speaker: Sam Rayburn (D Texas)
Majority Leader: John W. McCormack (D Mass.)
Minority Leader: Joseph W. Martin Jr. (R Mass.)

Senate: 49 Democrats
47 Republicans

Vice President: Alben W. Barkley (D Ky.)
President Pro Tempore: Kenneth McKellar (D Tenn.)
Majority Leader: Ernest W. McFarland (D Ariz.)
Minority Leader: Kenneth S. Wherry (R Neb.) (1st session-died Nov. 29, 1951)
Styles Bridges (R N.H.) (2nd session)

83rd Congress
1953-1954

House: 213 Democrats
221 Republicans
1 Other

Speaker: Joseph W. Martin Jr. (R Mass.)
Majority Leader: Charles A. Halleck (R Ind.)
Minority Leader: Sam Rayburn (D Texas)

Senate: 47 Democrats
48 Republicans
1 Other

Vice President: Richard M. Nixon (R Calif.)
President Pro Tempore: Styles Bridges (R N.H.)
Majority Leader: Robert A. Taft (R Ohio) (died July 31, 1953
William F. Knowland (R Calif.)
Minority Leader: Lyndon B. Johnson (D Texas)

84th Congress
1955-1956

House: 232 Democrats
203 Republicans

Speaker: San Rayburn (D Texas)
Majority Leader: John W. McCormack (D Mass.)
Minority Leader: Joseph W. Martin Jr. (R Mass.)

Senate: 48 Democrats
47 Republicans
1 Other

Vice President: Richard M. Nixon (R Calif.)
President Pro Tempore: Walter F. George (D Ga.)
Majority Leader: Lyndon B. Johnson (D Texas)
Minority Leader: William F. Knowland (R Calif.)

85th Congress
1957-1958

House: 233 Democrats
200 Republicans
2 Vacancies

Speaker: Sam Rayburn (D Texas)
Majority Leader: John W. McCormack (D Mass.)
Minority Leader: Joseph W. Martin Jr. (R Mass.)

Senate: 49 Democrats
47 Republicans

Vice President: Richard M. Nixon (R Calif.)
President Pro Tempore: Carl Hayden (D Ariz.)
Majority Leader: Lyndon B. Johnson (D Texas)
Minority Leader: William F. Knowland (R Calif.)

86th Congress
1959-1960

House: 283 Democrats
154 Republicans

Speaker: Sam Rayburn (D Texas)
Majoirty Leader: John W. McCormack (D Mass.)
Minority Leader: Charles A. Halleck (R Ind.)

Senate: 66 Democrats
34 Republicans

Vice President: Richard M. Nixon (R Calif.)
President Pro Tempore: Carl Hayden (D Ariz.)
Majority Leader: Lyndon B. Johnson (D Texas)
Minority Leader: Everett McKinley Dirksen (R Ill.)

87th Congress
1961-1962

House: 263 Democrats
174 Republicans

Speaker: Sam Rayburn (D Texas) (until his death Nov. 16, 1961)
John W. McCormack (D Mass.)
Majority Leader: John W. McCormack (D Mass.)
Carl Albert (D Okla.)
Minority Leader: Charles A. Halleck (R Ind.)

Senate: 65 Democrats
35 Republicans

Vice President: Lyndon B. Johnson (D Texas)
President Pro Tempore: Carl Hayden (D Ariz.)
Majority Leader: Mike Mansfield (D Mont.)
Minority Leader: Everett McKinley Dirksen (R Ill.)

88th Congress
1963-1964

House: 258 Democrats
176 Republicans
1 Vacancy*

Speaker: John W. McCormack (D Mass.)
Majority Leader: Carl Albert (D Okla.)
Minority Leader: Charles A. Halleck (R Ind.)

Senate: 67 Democrats
33 Republicans

Vice President: Lyndon B. Johnson (D Texas)
(Until Nov. 22, 1963)
President Pro Tempore: Carl Hayden (D Ariz.)
Majority Leader: Mike Mansfield (D Mont.)
Minority Leader: Everett McKinley Dirksen (R Ill.)

*Rep. Clem Miller was killed Oct. 7, 1962, but elected posthumously. His seat was filled Jan. 22, 1963, by Don H. Clausen (R Calif.)

89th Congress
1965-1966

House: 295 Democrats
140 Republicans

Speaker: John W. McCormack (D Mass.)
Majority Leader: Carl Albert (D Okla.)
Minority Leader: Gerald R. Ford (R Mich.)

Senate: 68 Democrats
32 Republicans

Vice President: Hubert H. Humphrey (D Minn.)
President Pro Tempore: Carl Hayden (D Ariz.)
Majority Leader: Mike Mansfield (D Mont.)
Minority Leader: Everett McKinley Dirksen (R Ill.)

90th Congress
1967-1968

House: 248 Democrats
187 Republicans

Speaker: John W. McCormack (D Mass.)
Majority Leader: Carl Albert (D Okla.)
Minority Leader: Gerald R. Ford (R Mich.)

Senate: 64 Democrats
36 Republicans

Vice President: Hubert H. Humphrey (D Minn.)
President Pro Tempore: Carl Hayden (D Ariz.)
Majority Leader: Mike Mansfield (D Mont.)
Minority Leader: Everett McKinley Dirksen (R Ill.)

91st Congress
1969-1970

House: 243 Democrats
192 Republicans

Speaker: John W. McCormack (D Mass.)
Majority Leader: Carl Albert (D Okla.)
Minority Leader: Gerald R. Ford (R Mich.)

Senate: 57 Democrats
43 Republicans

Vice President: Spiro T. Agnew (R Md.)
President Pro Tempore: Richard B. Russell (D Ga.)
Majority Leader: Mike Mansfield (D Mont.)
Minority Leader: Everett McKinley Dirksen (R Ill.)

CHAIRMEN OF SENATE, HOUSE, JOINT COMMITTEES, 1947-69

Following are the names and dates of terms of chairmen of standing committees of Congress from 1947 to 1969. Certain subcommittees and special committees are included because of their past importance or interest. The evolution of some committees also is indicated, such as the first one listed, the Senate Aeronautical and Space Sciences Committee, which originally was the Special Committee on Space and Astronautics.

SENATE

Special Committee on Space and Astronautics
Lyndon B. Johnson (D Texas-1957-1958)

Aeronautical and Space Sciences
Lyndon B. Johnson (D Texas-1958-1961)
Robert S. Kerr (D Okla.-1961-1963)
Clinton P. Anderson (D N.M.-1963-)

Agriculture and Forestry
Arthur Capper (R Kan.-1947-1949)
Elmer Thomas (D Okla.-1949-1951)
Allen J. Ellender (D La.-1951-1953)
George D. Aiken (R Vt.-1953-1955)
Allen J. Ellender (D La.-1955-)

Appropriations
Styles Bridges (R N.H.-1947-1949)
Kenneth McKellar (D Tenn.-1949-1953)
Styles Bridges (R N.H.-1953-1955)
Carl Hayden (D Ariz.-1955-1969)
Richard B. Russell (D Ga.-1969-)

Armed Services
Chan Gurney (R S.D.-1947-1949)
Millard E. Tydings (D Md.-1949-1951)
Richard B. Russell (D Ga.-1951-1953)
Leverett Saltonstall (R Mass. -1953-1955)
Richard B. Russell (D Ga.-1955-1969)
John C. Stennis (D Miss.-1969-)

Preparedness Investigating Subcommittee
Lyndon B. Johnson (D Texas-1950-1953)
(Seven special subcommittees were appointed by committee chairman Leverett Saltonstall (R Mass.) to investigate specific problems, 1953-1955.)
Lyndon B. Johnson (D Texas-1955-1961)
John Stennis (D Miss.-1961-)

Banking and Currency
Charles W. Tobey (R N.H.-1947-1949)
Burnet R. Maybank (D S.C.-1949-1953)
Homer E. Capehart (R Ind.-1953-1955)
J.W. Fulbright (D Ark.-1955-1959)
A. Willis Robertson (D Va.-1959-1967)
John J. Sparkman (D Ala.-1967-)

Interstate and Foreign Commerce
Wallace H. White (R Maine-1947-1949)
Edwin C. Johnson (D Colo.-1949-1953)
Charles W. Tobey (R N.H.-1953)
John W. Bricker (R Ohio-1953-1955)
Warren G. Magnuson (D Wash.-1955-1961)

Commerce (renamed)
Warren G. Magnuson (D Wash.-1961-)

District of Columbia
C. Douglass Buck (R Del.-1947-1949)
J. Howard McGrath (D R.I.-1949-1951)
Matthew M. Neely (D W. Va.-1951-1953)
Francis Case (R S.D.-1953-1955)
Matthew M. Neely (D W. Va.-1955-1959)
Alan Bible (D Nev.-1959-1969)
Joseph D. Tydings (D Md.-1969-)

Finance
Eugene D. Milikin (R Colo.-1947-1949)
Walter F. George (D Ga.-1949-1953)
Eugene D. Millikin (R Colo.-1953-1955)
Harry Flood Byrd (D Va.-1955-1965)
Russell B. Long (D La.-1965-)

Foreign Relations
Arthur H. Vandenberg (R Mich.-1947-1949)
Tom Connally (D Texas-1949-1953)
Alexander Wiley (R Wis.-1953-1955)
Walter F. George (D Ga.-1955-1957)
Theodore Francis Green (D R.I.-1957-1959)
J.W. Fulbright (D Ark.-1959-)

Expenditures in the Executive Departments
George D. Aiken (R Vt.-1947-1949)
John L. McClellan (D Ark.-1949-1952)

Government Operations (renamed)
John L. McClellan (D Ark.-1952-1953)
Joseph R. McCarthy (R Wis.-1953-1955)
John L. McClellan (D Ark.-1955-)

Special Committee to Investigate the National Defense Program 1947-1948
Owen Brewster (R Maine-1947-1948)

Permanent Investigations Subcommittee
Homer Ferguson (R Mich.-1948-1949)
Clyde R. Hoey (D N.C.-1949-1953)
Joseph R. McCarthy (R Wis.-1953-1955)
John L. McClellan (D Ark.-1955-)

Interior and Insular Affairs
Hugh Butler (R Neb.-1947-1949)
Joseph C. O'Mahoney (D Wyo.-1949-1953)
Hugh Butler (R Neb.-1953-1954)
Guy Cordon (R Ore.-1954-1955)
James E. Murray (D Mont.-1955-1961)
Clinton P. Anderson (D N.M.-1961-1963)
Henry M. Jackson (D Wash.-1963-)

Judiciary
Alexander Wiley (R Wis.-1947-1949)
Pat McCarran (D Nev.-1949-1953)
William Langer (R N.D.-1953-1955)
Harley M. Kilgore (D W.Va.-1955-1956)
James O. Eastland (D Miss.-1956-)

Antitrust and Monopoly Subcommittee
Herbert R. O'Conor (D Md.-1951-1953)
William Langer (R N.D.-1953-1955)
Joseph C. O'Mahoney (D Wyo.-1955-1957)
Estes Kefauver (D Tenn.-1957-1963)
Philip A. Hart (D Mich.-1963-)

Internal Security Subcommittee
Pat McCarran (D Nev.-1950-1953)
William E. Jenner (R Ind.-1953-1955)
James O. Eastland (D Miss.-1955-)

Labor and Public Welfare
Robert A. Taft (R Ohio-1947-1949)
Elbert D. Thomas (D Utah-1949-1951)
James E. Murray (D Mont.-1951-1953)
H. Alexander Smith (R N.J.-1953-1955)
Lister Hill (D Ala.-1955-1969)
Ralph W. Yarborough (D Texas-1969-)

Post Office and Civil Service
William Langer (R N.D.-1947-1949)
Olin D. Johnston (D S.C.-1949-1953)
Frank Carlson (R Kan.-1953-1955)
Olin D. Johnston (D S.C.-1955-1965)
A.S. Mike Monroney (D Okla.-1965-1969)
Gale W. McGee (D Wyo.-1969-)

Public Works
Chapman Revercomb (R W.Va.-1947-1949)
Dennis Chavez (D N.M.-1949-1953)
Edward Martin (R Pa.-1953-1955)
Dennis Chavez (D N.M.-1955-1962)
Pat McNamara (D Mich.-1963-1966)
Jennings Randolph (D W.Va.-1966-)

Rules and Administration
C. Wayland Brooks (R Ill.-1947-1949)
Carl Hayden (D Ariz.-1949-1953)
William E. Jenner (R Ind.-1953-1955)
Theodore Francis Green (D R.I.-1955-1957)
Thomas C. Hennings (D Mo.-1957-1960)

Mike Mansfield (D Mont.-1961-1963)
B. Everett Jordan (D N.C.-1963-)

Special Committee to Study Problems of American Small Business
Kenneth S. Wherry (R Neb.-1947-1949. The special committee expired Jan. 30, 1949)

Select Committee on Small Business
John J. Sparkman (D Ala.-1950-1953)
Edward J. Thye (R Minn.-1953-1955)
John J. Sparkman (D Ala.-1955-1967)
George A. Smathers (D Fla.-1967-1969)
Alan Bible (D Nev.-1969-)

Subcommittee on the Aged and Aging of Senate Labor and Public Welfare
Lister Hill (D Ala.-1959-1960)

Special Committee on Aging
Pat McNamara (D Mich.-1960-1963)
George A. Smathers (D Fla.-1963-1967)
Harrison A. Williams Jr. (D N.J.-1967-)

Democratic Policy and Steering Committees
Alben W. Barkley (D Ky.-1947-1949)
Scott W. Lucas (D Ill.-1949-1951)
Ernest W. McFarland (D Ariz.-1951-1953)
Lyndon B. Johnson (D Texas-1953-1961)
Mike Mansfield (D Mont.-1961-)

Democratic Senatorial Campaign Committee
Scott W. Lucas (D Ill.-1947-1949)
Clinton P. Anderson (D N.M.-1949-1951)
Earle C. Clements (D Ky.-1951-1957)
George A. Smathers (D Fla.-1957-1961)
Vance Hartke (D Ind.-1961-1963)
Warren G. Magnuson (D Wash.-1963-1967)
Edmund S. Muskie (D Maine-1967-1969)
Daniel K. Inouye (D Hawaii-1969-)

Republican Policy Committee
Robert A. Taft (R Ohio-1947-1953)
William F. Knowland (R Calif.-1953)
Homer Ferguson (R Mich.-1953-1955)
Styles Bridges (R N.H.-1955-61)
Bourke B. Hickenlooper (R Iowa-1962-1969)
Gordon Allott (R Colo.-1969-)

Republican Senatorial Campaign Committee
John G. Townsend (Former Republican Sen. from Delaware, 1929-1941, Campaign Committee chairman, 1947-1949)
Owen Brewster (R Maine-1949-1951)
Everett McKinley Dirksen (R Ill.-1951-1955)
Barry Goldwater (R Ariz.-1955-1956)
Andrew F. Schoeppel (R Kan.-1956-1959)
Barry Goldwater (R Ariz.-1959-1963)
Thruston B. Morton (R Ky.-1963-1969)
George Murphy (R Calif.-1967-1969)
John G. Tower (R Texas-1969-)

Republican Committee on Committees
Edward B. Robertson (R Wyo.-1947-1949)
Hugh A. Butler (R Neb.-1949-1954)
John W. Bricker (R Ohio-1954-1959)
Andrew F. Schoeppel (R Kan.-1959-1962)
Frank Carlson (R Kan.-1962-1969)
John J. Williams (R Del.-1969-)

Republican Personnel Committee
Harlan J. Bushfield (R S.D.-1947-1949)
Styles Bridges (R N.H.-1949-1953)
Edward Martin (R Pa.-1953-1959)
Margaret Chase Smith (R Maine-1959-1963)
Norris Cotton (R N.H.-1963-)

HOUSE

Agriculture
Clifford R. Hope (R Kan.-1947-1949)
Harold D. Cooley (D N.C.-1949-1953)
Clifford R. Hope (R Kan.-1953-1955)
Harold D. Cooley (D N.C.-1955-1967)
W.R. Poage (D Texas-1967-)

Appropriations
John Taber (R N.Y.-1947-1949)
Clarence Cannon (D Mo.-1949-1953)
John Taber (R N.Y.-1953-1955)
Clarence Cannon (D Mo.-1955-1964)
George H. Mahon (D Texas-1964-)

Armed Services
Walter G. Andrews (R N.Y.-1947-1949)
Carl Vinson (D Ga.-1949-1953)
Dewey Short (R Mo.-1953-1955)
Carl Vinson (D Ga.-1955-1965)
L. Mendel Rivers (D S.C.-1965-)

Special Investigations Subcommittee
F. Edward Hebert (D La.-1951-1953)
William E. Hess (R Ohio-1953-1955)
F. Edward Hebert (D La.-1955-1963)
Porter Hardy (D Va.-1963-1969)

Armed Services Investigations (renamed)
L. Mendel Rivers (D S.C.-1969-)

Banking and Currency
Jesse P. Wolcott (R Mich.-1947-1949)
Brent Spence (D Ky.-1949-1953)
Jesse P. Wolcott (R Mich.-1953-1955)
Brent Spence (D Ky.-1955-1963)
Wright Patman (D Texas-1963-)

District of Columbia
Everett M. Dirksen (R Ill.-1947-1949)
John L. McMillan (D S.C.-1949-1953)
Sid Simpson (R Ill.-1953-1955)
John L. McMillan (D S.C.-1955-)

Education and Labor
Fred A. Hartley (R N.J.-1947-1949)
John Lesinski (D Mich.-1949-1950)
Graham A. Barden (D N.C.-1950-1953)
Samuel K. McConnell (R Pa.-1953-1955)
Graham A. Barden (D N.C.-1955-1961)
Adam C. Powell (D N.Y.-1961-1967)
Carl D. Perkins (D Ky.-1967-)

Foreign Affairs
Charles A. Eaton (R N.J.-1947-1949)
John Kee (D W. Va.)-1949-1951)
James P. Richards (D S.C.-1951-1953)

Robert B. Chiperfield (R Ill.-1953-1955)
James P. Richards (D S.C.-1955-1957)
Thomas S. Gordon (D Ill.-1957-1959)
Thomas E. Morgan (D Pa.-1959-)

Expenditures in the Executive Departments
Clare E. Hoffman (R Mich.-1947-1949)
William L. Dawson (D Ill.-1949-1952)

Government Operations (renamed)
William L. Dawson (D Ill.-1952-1953)
Clare E. Hoffman (R Mich.-1953-1955)
William L. Dawson (D Ill.-1955-)

House Administration
Karl M. LeCompte (R Iowa-1947-1949)
Mary T. Norton (D N.J.-1949-1951)
Thomas B. Stanley (D Va.-1951-1953)
Karl M. LeCompte (R Iowa-1953-1955)
Omar Burleson (D Texas-1955-1968)
Samuel N. Friedel (D Md.-1968-)

Public Lands
Richard J. Welch (R Calif.-1947-1949)
Andrew L. Somers (D N.Y.-1949)
J. Hardin Peterson (D Fla.-1949-1951)

Interior and Insular Affairs (renamed)
John R. Murdock (D Ariz.-1951-1953)
A.L. Miller (R Neb.-1953-1955)
Clair Engle (D Calif.-1955-1959)
Wayne N. Aspinall (D Colo. 1959-)

Interstate and Foreign Commerce
Charles A. Wolverton (R N.J.-1947-1949)
Robert Crosser (D Ohio-1949-1953)
Charles A. Wolverton (R N.J.-1953-1955)
J. Percy Priest (D Tenn.-1955-1957)
Oren Harris (D Ark.-1957-1966)
Harley O. Staggers (D W. Va.-1966-)

Special Subcommittee on Legislative Oversight 1957-1961
Morgan M. Moulder (D Mo.-1957-1958)
Oren Harris (D Ark.-1958-1961)

Special Subcommittee on Regulatory Agencies
Oren Harris (D Ark.-1961-1963)

Special Subcommittee on Investigations
Oren Harris (D Ark.-1963-1966)
Harley O. Staggers (D W. Va.-1966-)

Judiciary
Earl C. Michener (R Mich.-1947-1949)
Emanuel Celler (D N.Y.-1949-1953)
Chauncey W. Reed (R Ill.-1953-1955)
Emanuel Celler (D N.Y.-1955-)

Merchant Marine and Fisheries
Fred Bradley (R Mich.-1947)
Alvin F. Weichel (R Ohio-1947-1949)
Schuyler Otis Bland (D Va.-1949-1950)
Edward J. Hart (D N.J.-1950-1953)
Alvin F. Weichel (R Ohio-1953-1955)
Herbert C. Bonner (D N.C.-1955-1966)
Edward A. Garmatz (D Md.-1966-)

Post Office and Civil Service
Edward H. Rees (R Kan.-1947-1949)
Tom Murray (D Tenn.-1949-1953)
Edward H. Rees (R Kan.-1953-1955)
Tom Murray (D Tenn.-1955-1967)
Thaddeus J. Dulski (D N.Y.-1967-)

Public Works
George A. Dondero (R Mich.-1947-1949)
William M. Whittington (D Miss.-1949-1951)
Charles A. Buckley (D N.Y.-1951-1953)
George A. Dondero (R Mich.-1953-1955)
Charles A. Buckley (D N.Y.-1955-1965)
George H. Fallon (D Md.-1965-)

Rules
Leo E. Allen (R Ill.-1947-1949)
Adolph J. Sabath (D Ill.-1949-1953)
Leo E. Allen (R Ill.-1953-1955)
Howard W. Smith (D Va.-1955-1967)
William M. Colmer (D Miss.-1967-)

Select Committee on Astronautics and Space Exploration 1958
John W. McCormack (D Mass.-1958)

Science and Astronautics
Overton Brooks (D La.-1959-1961)
George P. Miller (D Calif.-1961-)

Un-American Activities
J. Parnell Thomas (R N.J.-1947-1949)
John S. Wood (D Ga.-1949-1953)
Harold H. Velde (R Ill.-1953-1955)
Francis E. Walter (D Pa.-1955-1963)
Edwin E. Willis (D La.-1963-1969)

Internal Security (renamed)
Richard H. Ichord (D Mo.-1969-)

Veterans' Affairs
Edith Nourse Rogers (R Mass,-1947-1949)
John E. Rankin (D Miss.-1949-1953)
Edith Nourse Rogers (R Mass.-1953-1955)
Olin E. Teague (D Texas-1955-)

Ways and Means
(Democratic members serve as the Democratic Committee on Committees in the House)
Harold Knutson (R Minn.-1947-1949)
Robert L. Doughton (D N.C.-1949-1953)
Daniel A. Reed (R N.Y.-1953-1955)
Jere Cooper (D Tenn.-1955-1957)
Wilbur D. Mills (D Ark.-1958-)

Select Small Business
Walter C. Ploeser (R Mo.-1947-1949)
Wright Patman (D Texas-1949-1953)
William S. Hill (R Colo.-1953-1955)
Wright Patman (D Texas-1955-1963)
Joe L. Evins (D Tenn.-1963-)

Democratic National Congressional Committee
Michael J. Kirwan (D Ohio-1947-)

Democratic Patronage Committee
Francis E. Walter (D Pa.-1949-1953, 1955-1963)
Harry R. Sheppard (D Calif.-1963-1965)
Joel L. Evins (D Tenn.-1965-)

Republican Policy Committee
Joseph W. Martin (R Mass.-1947-1959)
John W. Byrnes (R Wis.-1959-1965)
John J. Rhodes (R Ariz.-1965-)

Republican Committee on Committees
Joseph W. Martin (R Mass.-1947-1953)
Charles A. Halleck (R Ind.-1953-1955)
Joseph W. Martin (R Mass.-1955-1959)
Charles A. Halleck (R Ind.-1959-1965)
Gerald R. Ford (R Mich.-1965-)

National Republican Congressional Committee
Leonard W. Hall (R N.Y.-1947-1953)
Richard M. Simpson (R Pa.-1953-1960)
William E. Miller (R N.Y.-1960-1961)
Bob Wilson (R Calif.-1961-)

Republican Patronage Committee
Leo E. Allen (R Ill.-1947-1949, 1953-1955)

JOINT COMMITTEES

Atomic Energy
Sen. Bourke B. Hickenlooper (R Iowa-1947-1949)
Sen. Brien McMahon (D Conn.-1949-1953)
Rep. W. Sterling Cole (R N.Y.-1953-1955)
Sen. Clinton P. Anderson (D N.M.-1955-1957)
Rep. Carl T. Durham (D N.C.-1957-1959)
Sen. Clinton P. Anderson (D N.M.-1959-1961)
Rep. Chet Holifield (D Calif.-1961-1963)
Sen. John O. Pastore (D R.I.-1963-1965)
Rep. Chet Holifield (D Calif.-1965-1967)
Sen. John O. Pastore (D R.I.-1967-1969)
Rep. Chet Holifield (D Calif.-1969-)

Defense Production
Sen. Burnet R. Maybank (D S.C.-1950-1953)
Sen. Homer E. Capehart (R Ind.-1953-1955)
Rep. Paul Brown (D Ga.-1955-1957)
Sen. A. Willis Robertson (D Va.-1957-1959)
Rep. Paul Brown (D Ga.-1959-1961)
Sen. A. Willis Robertson (D Va.-1961-1963)
Rep. Wright Patman (D Texas-1963-1965)
Sen. A. Willis Robertson (D Va.-1965-1967)
Rep. Wright Patman (D Texas-1967-1969)
Sen. John J. Sparkman (D Ala.-1969-)

Economic
Sen. Robert A. Taft (R Ohio-1947-1949)
Sen. Joseph C. O'Mahoney (D Wyo.-1949-1953)
Rep. Jesse P. Wolcott (R Mich.-1953-1955)
Sen. Paul H. Douglas (D Ill.-1955-1957)
Rep. Wright Patman (D Texas-1957-1959)
Sen. Paul H. Douglas (D Ill.-1959-1961)
Rep. Wright Patman (D Texas-1961-1963)
Sen. Paul H. Douglas (D Ill.-1963-1965)
Rep. Wright Patman (D Texas-1965-1967)
Sen. William Proxmire (D Wis.-1967-1969)
Rep. Wright Patman (D Texas-1969-)

Internal Revenue Taxation

Rep. Harold Knutson (R Minn.-1947-1948)
Sen. Eugene D. Millikin (R Colo.-1948-1949)
Rep. Robert L. Doughton (D N.C.-1949-1950)
Sen. Walter F. George (D Ga.-1950-1951)
Rep. Robert L. Doughton (D N.C.-1951-1952)
Sen. Walter F. George (D Ga.-1952-1953)
Rep. Daniel A. Reed (R N.Y.-1953-1954)
Sen. Eugene D. Millikin (R Colo.-1954-1955)
Rep. Jere Cooper (D Tenn.-1955-1956)
Sen. Harry Flood Byrd (D Va.-1956-1957)
Rep. Jere Cooper (D Tenn.-1957-1958)
Sen. Harry Flood Byrd (D Va.-1958-1959)

Rep. Wilbur D. Mills (D Ark.-1959-1960)
Sen. Harry Flood Byrd (D Va.-1960-1961)
Rep. Wilbur D. Mills (D Ark.-1961-1962)
Sen. Harry Flood Byrd (D Va.-1962-1963)
Rep. Wilbur D. Mills (D Ark.-1963-1965)
Sen. Harry Flood Byrd (D Va.-1965-)
Sen. Russell B. Long (D La.-1965-1967)
Rep. Wilbur D. Mills (D Ark.-1967-1969)
Sen. Russell B. Long (D La.-1969-)

Reduction of Nonessential Federal Expenditures

Sen. Harry Flood Byrd (D Va.-1947-1965)
Rep. George H. Mahon (D Texas-1965-)

Biographical Index of
Members of Congress, 1945-69

BIOGRAPHICAL INDEX

(Dates of service are inclusive, starting in year of service and ending as service ends, which usually is Jan. 3 of given year.)

The names in this index include, alphabetically, all Senators and Representatives who served in Congress from Jan. 3, 1945 through Jan. 3, 1969—the 79th through 91st Congresses. The material is organized as follows: Name, Party, State (of service), Date of birth, Date of death (if applicable), Congressional service, Other important offices held or services rendered, such as Governor, Cabinet member, etc. Where names may cause confusion, relationship is cited. Where service dates are left open, Members were still serving in 1969.

A

AANDAHL, Fred G. (R N.D.) April 9, 1897-April 7, 1966; House 1951-53; Gov. 1945-50; Asst. Secretary of the Interior 1953-61.

ABBITT, Watkins M. (D Va.) May 21, 1908; House 1948- .

ABEL, Mrs. Hazel H. (R Neb.) July 10, 1888-July 30, 1966; Senate Nov. 8, 1954-Dec. 31, 1954.

ABELE, Homer E. (R Ohio) Nov. 21, 1916; House 1963-65.

ABERNETHY, Thomas G. (D Miss.) May 16, 1903; House 1943- .

ADAIR, E. Ross (R Ind.) Dec. 14, 1907; House 1951- .

ADAMS, Brock (D Wash.) Jan. 13, 1927; House 1965- .

ADAMS, Sherman (R N.H.) Jan. 8, 1899; House 1945-47; Gov. 1949-53; Asst. to President Eisenhower 1953-Sept. 22, 1958.

ADDABBO, Joseph P. (D N.Y.) March 17, 1925; House 1961- .

ADDONIZIO, Hugh J. (D N.J.) Jan. 31, 1914; House 1949-62.

AIKEN, George D. (R Vt.) Aug. 20, 1892; Senate 1941- ; Lt. Gov. 1935-37; Gov. 1937-41.

ALBERT, Carl (D Okla.) May 10, 1908; House 1947- . Majority Whip, 1955-1962; Majority Leader 1962- .

ALEXANDER, Hugh Q. (D N.C.) Aug. 7, 1911; House 1953-63.

ALFORD, Dale (D Ark.) Jan. 28, 1916; House 1959-63.

ALGER, Bruce (R Texas) June 12, 1918; House 1955-65.

ALLEN, A. Leonard (D La.) Jan. 5, 1891-Jan. 5, 1969; House 1937- 53.

ALLEN, James B. (D Ala.) Dec. 28, 1912; Senate 1969- .

ALLEN, John J. Jr. (R Calif.) Nov. 27, 1899; House 1947-59.

ALLEN, Leo E. (R Ill.) Oct. 5, 1898; House 1933-61.

ALEXANDER, William V. Jr. (D Ark.) Jan. 16, 1934; House 1969- .

ALLOTT, Gordon (R Colo.) Jan. 2, 1907; Senate 1955- ; Lt. Gov. 1951-55.

ALMOND, J. Lindsay Jr. (D Va.) June 15, 1898; House 1946-48; Gov. 1958-62; Judge of Patent Court 1962- .

ANDERSEN, H. Carl (R Minn.) Jan. 27, 1897; House 1939-63.

ANDERSON, Clinton P. (D N.M.) Oct. 23, 1895; House 1941-45; Senate 1949- ; Secretary of Agriculture 1945-48.

ANDERSON, Glenn M. (D Calif.) Feb. 21, 1913; House 1969-

ANDERSON, Jack Z. (R Calif.) March 22, 1904; House 1939-53; Admin. Asst. to President Eisenhower 1956-61.

ANDERSON, John B. (R Ill.) Feb. 15, 1922; House 1961- .

ANDERSON, LeRoy H. (D Mont.) Feb. 2, 1906; House 1957-61.

ANDERSON, William R. (D Tenn.) June 17, 1921; Presidential consultant 1963-64; House 1965- .

ANDRESEN, August H. (R Minn.) Oct. 11, 1890-Jan. 14, 1958; House 1925-33; 1935-58.

ANDREWS, Charles O. (D Fla.) March 7, 1877-Sept. 18, 1946; Senate 1937-46.

ANDREWS, George W. (D Ala.) Dec. 12, 1906; House 1944- .

ANDREWS, Glenn (R Ala.) Jan 15, 1909; House 1965-67.

ANDREWS, Mark (R N.D.) May 19, 1926; House 1963- .

ANDREWS, Walter G. (R N.Y.) July 16, 1889-March 5, 1949; House 1931-49.

ANFUSO, Victor L. (D N.Y.) March 10, 1905-Dec. 28, 1966; House 1951-53, 1955-63.

ANGELL, Homer D. (R. Ore.) Jan. 12, 1875-March 31, 1968; House 1939-55.

ANNUNZIO, Frank (D Ill.) Jan. 12, 1915; House 1965- .

ARENDS, Leslie C. (R Ill.) Sept. 27, 1895; House 1935- ; Republican Whip 1943- .

ARMSTRONG, O.K. (Orland) (R Mo.) Oct. 2, 1893; House 1951-53.

ARNOLD, Samuel W. (R Mo.) Sept. 21, 1879-Dec. 18, 1961; House 1943-49.

ASHBROOK, John M. (R Ohio) Sept. 21, 1928; House 1961- ; Young Republican Nat. Chairman 1957-59.

ASHLEY, Thomas L. (D Ohio) Jan. 11, 1923; House 1955- .

ASHMORE, Robert T. (D S.C.) Feb. 22, 1904; House 1953-69.

ASPINALL, Wayne N. (D Colo.) April 3, 1896; House 1949- .

AUCHINCLOSS, James C. (R N.J.) Jan. 19, 1885; House 1943-65.

AUSTIN, Warren R. (R Vt.) Nov. 12, 1877-Dec. 25, 1962; Senate 1931-46; U.S. Representative to UN 1946-53.

AVERY, William H. (R Kan.) Aug. 11, 1911; House 1955-65; Gov. 1965-67.

AYRES, William H. (R Ohio) Feb.5, 1916; House 1951- .

B

BAILEY, Cleveland M. (D W. VA.) July 15, 1886-July 13, 1965; House 1945-47; 1949-63.

BAILEY, Josiah W. (D N.C.) Sept. 14, 1873-Dec. 15, 1946; Senate 1931-46.

BAKER, Howard H. (R Tenn.) Jan. 12, 1902-Jan. 7, 1964; House 1951-64.

BAKER, Howard H. Jr. (R Tenn.) Nov. 15, 1925; Senate 1967- .

BAKER, Irene B. (R Tenn.) Nov. 17, 1901; (window of Howard H. Baker); House: March 10, 1964-65.

BAKEWELL, Claude I. (R Mo.) Aug. 9, 1912; House 1947-49; 1951-53.

BALDWIN, H. Streett (D Md.) Aug. 21, 1894-Oct. 19, 1952; House 1943-47.

BALDWIN, John F. (R Calif.) June 28, 1915-March 9, 1966; House 1955-66.

BALDWIN, Joseph Clark (R N.Y.) Jan. 11, 1897-Oct. 27, 1957; House 1941-47.

BALDWIN, Raymond E. (R Conn.) Aug. 31, 1893; Senate 1946-49; Gov. 1939-40, 1943-46.

BALL, Joseph H. (R Minn.) Nov. 3 1905; Senate 1940-42; 1943-49.

BANDSTRA, Bert (D Iowa) Jan. 25, 1922; House 1965-67.

BANKHEAD, John H. II (D Ala.) July 8, 1872-June 12, 1946; Senate 1931-46.

BANTA, Parke M. (R Mo.) Nov. 21, 1891; House 1947-49.

BARDEN, Graham A. (D N.C.) Sept. 25, 1896-Jan. 29, 1967; House 1935-61.

BARING, Walter S. (D Nev.) Sept. 9, 1911; House 1949-53; 1957- .

BARKLEY, Alben W. (D Ky.) Nov. 24, 1877-April 30, 1956; House 1913-27, Senate 1927-49; 1955-56; Senate Majority Leader 1937-47; Senate Minority Leader 1947-48; Vice President 1949-53.

BARR, Joseph W. (D Ind.) Jan. 17, 1918; House 1959-61; Asst. to Secretary of Treasury 1961-64; Member, Federal Deposit Insurance Corp. 1964-65; Under Secretary of Treasury, 1965-68; Secretary of Treasury 1968-69.

BARRETT, Frank A. (R Wyo.) Nov. 10, 1892-May 30, 1962; Senate 1953-59; House 1943-50; Gov. 1951-53.

BARRETT, William A. (D Pa.) Aug. 14, 1896; House 1945-47; 1949- .

BARRY, Robert R. (R N.Y.) May 15, 1915; House 1959-65.

BARRY, William B. (D N.Y.) July 21, 1902-Oct. 20, 1946; House 1935-46.

BARTLETT, E.L. (D Alaska) April 20, 1904-Dec. 11, 1968; Senate 1959-68; Delegate to Congress 1945-59.

BASS, Perkins (R N.H.) Oct. 6, 1912; House 1955-63.

BASS, Ross (D Tenn.) March 17 1918; House 1955-1964; Senate 1964-67.

BATES, George J. (R Mass.) Feb. 25, 1891-Nov. 1, 1949; House 1937-49.

BATES, Joseph B. (D Ky.) Oct. 29, 1893-Sept. 10, 1965; House 1938-53.

BATES, William H. (R Mass.) April 26, 1917-June 22, 1969; (son of George J. Bates); House 1950-69.

BATTIN, James F. (R Mont.) Feb. 13, 1925; House 1961-69; U.S. District Judge, District of Montana 1969- .

BATTLE, Laurie C. (D Ala.) May 10, 1912; House 1947-55.

BAUMHART, A. D. Jr. (R Ohio) June 15, 1908; House 1941-42; 1955-61; Director, Republican National Committee 1953-54.

BAYH, Birch E. (D Ind.) Jan. 22, 1928; Senate 1963- .

BEALL, J. Glenn (R Md.) June 5, 1894; House 1943-53; Senate 1953-65.

BEALL, J. Glenn Jr. (R Md.) June 19, 1927; House 1969- .

BEAMER, John V. (R Ind.) Nov. 17, 1896-Sept. 9, 1964; House 1951-59.

BECKER, Frank J. (R N.Y.) Aug. 27, 1899; House 1953-65.

BECKWORTH, Lindley (D Texas) June 30, 1912; House 1939-53; 1957-67.

BEERMANN, Ralph F. (R Neb.) Aug. 13, 1912; House 1961-65.

BELCHER, Page (R Okla.) April 21, 1899; House 1951- .

BELL, Alphonzo (R Calif.) Sept. 19, 1914; House 1961- .

BELL, C. Jasper (D Mo.) Jan. 16, 1885; House 1935-49.

BELL, John J. (D Texas) May 15, 1910-Jan. 24, 1963; House 1955-57.

BELLMON, Henry (R Okla.) Sept. 3, 1921; Senate 1969- ; Gov. 1963-67.

BENDER, George H. (R Ohio) Sept. 29, 1896-June 18, 1961; House 1939-49; 1951-54; Senate 1954-57; Special Asst. to Secretary of Interior 1957-58.

BENNET, Augustus W. (R N.Y.) Oct. 7, 1897; House 1945-47.

BENNETT, Charles E. (D Fla.) Dec. 2, 1910; House 1949- .

BENNETT, John B. (R Mich.) Jan. 10, 1904-Aug. 10, 1964; House 1943-45; 1947-64.

BENNETT, Marion T. (R Mo.) June 6, 1914; House 1943-49.

BENNETT, Wallace F. (R Utah) Nov. 13, 1898; Senate 1951- .

BENTLEY, Alvin M. (R Mich.) Aug. 30, 1918-April 10, 1969; House 1953-61.

BENTON, William (D Conn.) April 1, 1900; Senate 1949-53; Asst. Secretary of State 1945-47.

BENTSEN, Lloyd M. Jr. (D Texas) Feb. 11, 1921; House 1948-55.

BERRY, E.Y. (R S.D.) Nov. 6, 1902; House 1951- .

BETTS, Jackson E. (R Ohio) May 26, 1904; House 1951- .

BEVILL, Tom (D Ala.) March 27, 1921; House 1967- .

BIAGGI, Mario, (D N.Y.) Oct. 26, 1917; House 1969- .

BIBLE, Alan (D Nev.) Nov. 20, 1909; Senate 1955- .

BIEMILLER, Andrew J. (D Wis.) July 23, 1906; House 1945-47; 1949-51.

BIESTER, Edward G. Jr. (R Pa.) Jan. 5, 1931; House 1967- .

BILBO, Theodore G. (D Miss.) Oct. 13, 1877-Aug. 21, 1947; Senate 1935-47; Lt. Gov. 1912-16; Gov. 1916-1920; 1928-32.

BINGHAM, Jonathan B. (D N.Y.) April 24, 1914; House 1965- .

BISHOP, C.W. (Runt) (R Ill.) June 29, 1890; House 1941-55.

BLACKBURN, Benjamin B. (R Ga.) Feb. 14, 1927; House 1967- .

BLACKNEY, William W. (R Mich.) Aug. 28, 1876-March 14, 1963; House 1935-37; 1939-53.

BLAKLEY, William A. (D Texas) Nov. 17, 1898; Senate 1957; 1961.

BLAND, Schuyler Otis (D Va.) May 4, 1872-Feb. 16, 1950; House 1918-50.

BLANTON, Ray (D Tenn.) April 10, 1930; House 1967- .

BLATNIK, John A. (D Minn.) Aug. 17, 1911; House 1947- .

BLITCH, Mrs. Iris F. (D Ga.) April 25, 1912; House 1955-63.

BLOOM, Sol (D N.Y.) March 9, 1870-March 7, 1949; House 1923-49.

BOGGS, J. Caleb (R Del.) May 15, 1909; House 1947-53; Senate 1961- ; Gov. 1953-61.

BOGGS, Hale (D La.) Feb. 15, 1914; House 1941-43; 1947- .

BOLAND, Edward P. (D Mass.) Oct. 1, 1911; House 1953- .

BOLLING, Richard (D Mo.) May 17, 1916; House 1949- .

BOLTON, Frances P. (R Ohio) March 29, 1885; House 1940-69.

BOLTON, Oliver P. (R Ohio) Feb. 22, 1917 (son of Frances P. Bolton); House 1953-57; 1963-65.

BOLTON, William P. (D Md.) July 2, 1885-Nov. 22, 1964; House 1949-51.

BONIN, Edward J. (R Pa.) Dec. 23, 1904; House 1953-55.

BONNER, Herbert C. (D N.C.) May 16, 1891-Nov. 7, 1965; House 1940-65.

BOREN, Lyle H. (D Okla.) May 11, 1909; House 1937-47.

BOSCH, Albert H. (R N.Y.) Oct. 30, 1908; House 1953-60.

BOSONE, Reva Beck (D Utah) House 1949-53.

BOTTUM, Joe H. (R S.D.) Aug. 7, 1903; Senate 1962.

BOW, Frank T. (R Ohio) Feb. 20, 1901; House 1951- .

BOWLER, James B. (D Ill.) Feb. 5, 1875-July 18, 1957; House 1953-57.

BOWLES, Chester (D Conn.) April 5, 1901; House 1959-61; Gov. 1949-51; Ambassador to India and Nepal 1951-53; Under Secretary of State 1961-62; President's Special Representative and adviser on African, Asian and Latin American Affairs 1962-63; Ambassador to India 1963-69.

BOWRING, Mrs. Eva K. (R Neb.) Jan. 9, 1892; Senate April 1954-Nov. 1954.

BOYKIN, Frank W. (D Ala.) Feb. 21, 1885-March 12, 1969; House 1935-63.

BOYLE, Charles A. (D Ill.) Aug. 13, 1907-Nov. 4, 1959; House 1955-59.

BRADEMAS, John (D Ind.) March 2, 1927; House 1959- .

BRADLEY, Fred (R Mich.) April 12, 1898-May 24, 1947; House 1939-47.

BRADLEY, Michael J. (D Pa.) April 24, 1897; House 1937-47.

BRADLEY, Willis W. (R Calif.) June 28, 1884-Aug. 27, 1954; House 1947-49.

BRAMBLETT, Ernest K. (R Calif.) April 25, 1901; House 1947-55.

BRASCO, Frank J. (D N.Y.) Oct. 15, 1932; House 1967- .

BRAY, William G. (R Ind.) April 17, 1903; House 1951- .

BREEDING, J. Floyd (D Kan.) Sept. 28, 1901; House 1957-63.

BREEN, Edward F. (D Ohio) June 10, 1908; House 1949-51.

BREHM, Walter E. (R Ohio) May 25, 1892; House 1943-53.

BREWSTER, Daniel B. (D Md.) Nov. 23, 1923; House 1959-63; Senate 1963-69.

BREWSTER, Owen (Ralph O.) (R Maine) Feb. 22, 1888-Dec. 25, 1961; House 1935-41; Senate 1941-52; Gov. 1925-29.

BRICKER, John W. (R Ohio) Sept. 6, 1893; Senate 1947-59; Gov. 1939-45; Vice Presidential Candidate 1944.

BRIDGES, H. Styles (R N.H.) Sept. 9, 1898-Nov. 26, 1961; Senate 1937-61; Gov. 1934-36.

BRIGGS, Frank P. (D Mo.) Feb. 25, 1894; Senate 1945-47.

BRINKLEY, Jack (D Ga.) Dec. 22, 1930; House 1967- .

BROCK, Lawrence (D Neb.) Aug. 16, 1906-Aug. 28, 1968; House 1959-61.

BROCK, William E. III (R Tenn.) Nov. 23, 1930; House 1963- .

BROMWELL, James E. (R Iowa) March 26, 1920; House 1961-65.

BROOKE, Edward W. (R Mass.) Oct. 26, 1919; Senate 1967- .

BROOKS, C. Wayland (R Ill.) March 8, 1897-Jan. 14, 1957; Senate 1940-49.

BROOKS, Jack (D Texas) Dec. 18, 1922; House 1953- .

BROOKS, Overton (D La.) Dec. 21, 1897-Sept. 16, 1961; House 1937-61.

BROOMFIELD, William S. (R Mich.) April 28, 1922; House 1957- .

BROPHY, John C. (R Wis.) Oct. 8, 1901; House 1947-49.

BROTZMAN, Donald G. (R Colo.) June 28, 1922; House 1963-65; 1967- .

BROUGHTON, J. Melville (D N.C.) Nov. 17, 1888-March 6, 1949; Senate 1948-49; Gov. 1941-45.

BROWN, Charles H. (D Mo.) Oct. 22, 1920; House 1957-61.

BROWN, Clarence J. Jr. (R Ohio) June 18, 1927; House 1966- .

BROWN, Clarence J. (R Ohio) July 14, 1893-Aug 23, 1965; House 1939-65.

BROWN, Ernest S. (R Nev.) Sept. 25, 1903-July 23, 1965; Senate Oct. 1, 1954-Dec. 1, 1954.

BROWN, Garry E. (R Mich.) Aug. 12, 1923; House 1967- .

BROWN, George E. Jr. (D Calif.) March 6, 1920; House 1963- .

BROWN, Paul (D Ga.) March 31, 1880-Sept. 24, 1961; House 1933-61.

BROWNSON, Charles B. (R Ind.) Feb. 5, 1914; House 1951-59.

BROYHILL, James T. (R N.C.) Aug. 19, 1927; House 1963- .

BROYHILL, Joel T. (R Va.) Nov. 4, 1919; House 1953- .

BRUCE, Donald C. (R Ind.) April 27, 1921; House 1961-1965.

BRUMBAUGH, D. Emmert (R Pa.) Oct. 8, 1894; House 1943-47.

BRUNSDALE, C. Norman (R N.D.) July 9, 1891; Senate 1959-60; Gov. 1951-57.

BRYSON, Joseph R. (D S.C.) Jan. 18, 1893-March 10, 1953; House 1939-53.

BUCHANAN, Frank (D Pa.) Dec.1, 1902-April 27, 1951; House 1946-51.

BUCHANAN, John H. (R Ala.) March 19, 1928; House 1965- .

BUCHANAN, Vera Daerr (D Pa.) (widow of Frank Buchanan) July 20, 1902-Nov. 26, 1955; House 1951-55.

BUCK, C. Douglass (R Del.) March 21, 1890-Jan. 27, 1965; Senate 1943-49; Gov. 1927-37.

BUCK, Ellsworth B. (R N.Y.) July 3, 1892; House 1944-49.

BUCKLEY, Charles A. (D N.Y.) June 23, 1890-Jan. 22, 1967; House 1935-65.

BUCKLEY, James V. (D Ill.) May 15, 1894-July 30, 1954; House 1949-51.

BUDGE, Hamer H. (R Idaho) Nov. 21, 1910; House 1951-61; Securities and Exchange Commission 1964- ; Chairman 1969- .

BUFFETT, Howard H. (R Neb.) Aug. 13, 1903-April 29, 1964; House 1943-49; 1951-53.

BULWINKLE, Alfred L. (D N.C.) April 21, 1883-Aug. 31, 1950; House 1921-29; 1931-50.

BUNKER, Berkeley L. (D Nev.) Aug. 12, 1906; Senate 1940-42; House 1945-47.

BURCH, Thomas G. (D Va.) July 3, 1869-March 20, 1951; House 1931-46; Senate May 31, 1946-Nov. 5, 1946.

BURDICK, Quentin N. (D N.D.) June 19, 1908 (son of Usher L. Burdick); House 1959-60; Senate 1960- .

BURDICK, Usher L. (R N.D.) Feb. 21, 1879-Aug. 19, 1960; House 1935-45; 1949-59.

BURGIN, W.O. (D N.C.) July 28, 1877-April 11, 1946; House 1939-46.

BURKE, Frank W. (D Ky.) June 1, 1920; House 1959-63.

BURKE, J. Herbert (R Fla.) Jan. 14, 1913; House 1967- .

BURKE, James A. (D Mass.) March 30, 1910; House 1959- .

BURKE, Raymond H. (R Ohio) Nov. 4, 1881-Aug. 18 1954; House 1947-49.

BURKE, Thomas A. (D Ohio) Oct. 30, 1898; Senate 1953-54.

BURKE, Thomas H. (D Ohio) May 6, 1904-Sept. 12, 1959; House 1949-51.

BURKHALTER, Everett G. (D Calif.) Jan. 19, 1897; House 1963-65.

BURLESON, Omar (D Texas) March 19, 1906; House 1947- .

BURLISON, Bill D. (D Mo.) March 15, 1931; House 1969- .

BURNS, John Anthony (D Hawaii) March 30, 1909; Delegate 1957-59; Gov. 1963- .

BURNSIDE, M. G. (D W.Va.) Aug. 23, 1902; House 1949-53; 1955-57.

BURTON, Clarence G. (D Va.) Dec. 14, 1886; House 1948-53.

BURTON, Harold H. (R Ohio) June 22, 1888-Oct. 28, 1964; Senate 1941-45; Assoc. Justice of the Supreme Court 1945-58 (retired).

BURTON, Laurence J. (R Utah) Oct. 30, 1926; House 1963- .

BURTON, Phillip (D Calif.) June 1, 1926; House 1964- .

BUSBEY, Fred E. (R Ill.) Feb. 8, 1895-Feb. 11, 1966; House 1943-45; 1947-49; 1951-55.

BUSH, Alvin R. (R Pa.) June 4, 1893-Nov. 5, 1959; House 1951-59.

BUSH, George (R Tex.) June 12, 1924 (son of Prescott Bush); House 1967- .

BUSH, Prescott (R Conn.) May 15, 1895; Senate 1952-63.

BUSHFIELD, Harlan J. (R S.D.) Aug. 6, 1882-Sept. 27, 1948; Senate 1943-48; Gov. 1939-42.

BUSHFIELD, Mrs. Vera C. (R S.D) Aug. 9, 1889 (widow of Harlan J. Bushfield); Senate Oct. 6, 1948-Dec. 26, 1948.

BUTLER, Hugh A. (R Neb.) Feb. 28, 1878-July 1, 1954; Senate 1941-54.

BUTLER, John C. (R N.Y.) July 2, 1887-Aug. 13, 1953; House 1941-49; 1951-53.

BUTLER, John Marshall (R Md.) July 21, 1897; Senate 1951-63.

BUTTON, Daniel E. (R N.Y.) Nov. 1, 1917; House 1967- .

BYRD, Harry Flood (D Va.) June 10, 1887-Oct. 20, 1966; Senate 1933-65; Gov. 1926-30.

BYRD, Harry F. Jr. (D Va.) Dec. 20, 1914 (son of Harry Flood Byrd); Senate 1965- .

BYRD, Robert C. (D W.Va.) Jan. 15, 1918; House 1953-59; Senate 1959- .

BYRNE, Emmet F. (R Ill.) Dec. 6, 1896; House 1957-59.

BYRNE, James A. (D Pa.) June 22, 1906; House 1953- .

BYRNE, William T. (D N.Y.) March 6, 1876-Jan. 27, 1952; House 1937-52.

BYRNES, John W. (R Wis.) June 12, 1913; House 1945- .

C

CABELL, Earle (D Texas) Oct. 27, 1906; House 1965- .

CAFFERY, Patrick T. (D La.) July 6, 1932; House 1969- .

CAHILL, William T. (R N.J.) June 25, 1912; House 1959- .

CAIN, Harry P. (R Wash.) Jan. 10, 1906; Senate 1946-53.

CALLAN, Clair (D Neb.) March 20, 1920; House 1965-67.

CALLAWAY, Howard H. (R Ga.) May 2, 1927; House 1965-67.

CAMERON, Ronald Brooks (D Calif.) Aug. 16, 1927; House 1963-67.

CAMP, A. Sidney (D Ga.) July 26, 1892-July 24, 1954; House 1939-54.

CAMP, John N. Happy (R Okla.) May 11, 1908; House 1969- .

CAMPBELL, Courtney W. (D Fla.) April 29, 1895; House 1953-55.

CAMPBELL, Howard E. (R Pa.) Jan. 4, 1890; House 1945-47.

CANFIELD, Gordon (R N.J.) April 15, 1898; House 1941-61.

CANNON, Arthur Patrick (D Fla.) May 22, 1904-Jan. 23, 1966; House 1939-47.

CANNON, Clarence (D Mo.) April 11, 1879-May 12, 1964: House 1923-64; House Parliamentarian 1915-21.

CANNON, Howard W. (D Nev.) Jan. 26, 1912; Senate 1959- .

CAPEHART, Homer E. (R Ind.) June 6, 1897; Senate 1945-63.

CAPOZZOLI, Louis Joseph (D N.Y.) March 6, 1901; House 1941-45.

CAPPER, Arthur (R Kan.) July 14, 1865-Dec. 19, 1951; Senate 1919-49; Gov. 1915-1919.

CAREY, Hugh L. (D N.Y.) April 11, 1919; House 1961- .

CARLSON, Frank (R Kan.) Jan. 23, 1893; House 1935-47; Senate 1950-69; Gov. 1947-50.

CARLYLE, Frank Ertel (D N.C.) April 7, 1897-Oct. 2, 1960; House 1949-57.

CARNAHAN, A. S. J. (D Mo.) Jan. 9, 1897-March 25, 1968; House 1945-47; 1949-61; Ambassador to Sierra Leone 1961-63.

CARRIER, Chester Otto (R Ky.) May 5, 1897; House 1943-45.

CARRIGG, Joseph L. (R Pa.) Feb. 23, 1901; House 1951-59.

CARROLL, John A. (D Colo.) July 30, 1901; House 1947-51; Senate 1957-63; Special Asst. to President Truman 1951-52.

CARSON, Henderson H. (D Ohio) Oct. 25, 1893; House 1943-45; 1947-49.

CARTER, Steven V. (D Iowa) Oct. 8, 1815-Nov. 4, 1959; House Jan. 3, 1959-Nov. 4, 1959.

CARTER, Tim Lee (R Ky.) Sept. 2, 1910; House 1965- .

CARVILLE, E. P. (D Nev.) May 14, 1885-June 27, 1956; Senate 1945-47; Gov. 1939-45.

CASE, Clifford P. (R N.J.) April 16, 1904; House 1945-53; Senate 1955- .

CASE, Francis H. (R S.D.) Dec. 9, 1896-June 22, 1962; House 1937-51; Senate 1951-62.

CASEY, Bob (D Texas) July 27, 1915; House 1959- .

CAVALCANTE, Anthony (D Pa.) Feb. 6, 1897-Oct. 29, 1966; House 1949-51.

CEDERBERG, Elford A. (R Mich.) March 6, 1918; House 1953- .

CELLER, Emanuel (D N.Y.) May 6, 1888; House 1923- .

CHADWICK, E. Wallace (R Pa.) Jan. 17, 1884; House 1947-49.

CHAMBERLAIN, Charles E. (R Mich.) July 22, 1917; House 1957- .

CHANDLER, Albert B. (D Ky.) July 14, 1898; Senate 1939-45; Gov. 1936-39; 1955-59.

CHAPMAN, Virgil M. (D Ky.) March 15, 1895-March 8, 1951; House, 1925-29; 1931-49; Senate 1949-51.

CHAPPELL, William V. (D Fla.) Feb. 3, 1922; House 1969- .

CHASE, Jackson B. (R Neb.) Aug. 19, 1890; House 1955-57.

CHATHAM, Richard Thurmond (D N.C.) Aug. 16, 1896-Feb. 5, 1957; House 1949-57.

CHAVEZ, Dennis (D N.M.) April 8, 1888-Nov. 18, 1962; House 1931-35; Senate 1935-62.

CHELF, Frank (D Ky.) Sept. 22, 1907; House 1945-67.

CHENOWETH, J. Edgar (R Colo.) Aug. 17, 1897; House 1941-49; 1951-65.

CHESNEY, Chester A. (D Ill.) March 9, 1916; House 1949-51.

CHIPERFIELD, Robert B. (R Ill.) Nov. 20, 1899; House 1939-63.

CHISHOLM, Shirley (D N.Y.) Nov. 30, 1924; House 1969- .

CHRISTOPHER, George H. (D Mo.) Dec. 9, 1888-Jan. 23, 1959; House 1949-51; 1955-59.

CHUDOFF, Earl (D Pa.) Nov. 16, 1907; House 1949-58.

CHURCH, Frank (D Idaho) July 25, 1924; Senate 1957- .

CHURCH, Marguerite Stitt (R Ill.) Sept. 13, 1892 (widow of Ralph E. Church); House 1951-63.

CHURCH, Ralph E. (R Ill.) May 5, 1883-March 21, 1950; House 1935-41; 1943-50.

CLANCY, Donald D. (R Ohio) July 24, 1921; House 1961- .

CLARDY, Kit Francis (R Mich.) June 17, 1892-Sept. 5, 1961; House 1953-55.

CLARK, Frank M. (D Pa.) Dec. 24, 1915; House 1955- .

CLARK, J. Bayard (D N.C.) April 5, 1882-Aug. 26, 1959; House 1929-49.

CLARK, Joseph S. (D Pa.) Oct. 21, 1901; Senate 1957-69; Mayor of Philadelphia 1952-1956.

CLASON, Charles R. (R Mass.) Sept. 3, 1890; House 1937-49.

CLAUSEN, Don H. (R Calif.) April 27, 1923; House 1963- .

CLAWSON, Del (R Calif.) Jan. 11, 1914; House 1963- .

CLAY, William (D Mo.) April 30, 1932; House 1969- .

CLEMENTE, L. Gary (D N.Y.) June 10, 1908-May 14, 1968; House 1949-53.

CLEMENTS, Earle C. (D Ky.) Oct. 22, 1896; House 1945-48; Senate 1950-57; Gov. 1948-50.

CLEVELAND, James C. (R N.H.) June 13, 1920; House 1963- .

CLEVENGER, Cliff (R Ohio) Aug. 20, 1885-Dec. 13, 1960; House 1939-59.

CLEVENGER, Raymond F. (D Mich.) June 6, 1926; House 1965-67.

CLIPPINGER, Roy (R Ill.) Jan. 13, 1886-Dec. 24, 1962; House 1945-49.

COAD, Merwin (D Iowa) Sept. 28, 1924; House 1957-63.

COCHRAN, John J. (D Mo.) Aug. 11, 1880-March 6, 1947; House 1926-47.

COFFEE, John M. (D Wash.) Jan. 23, 1897; House 1937-47.

COFFEY, Robert L. Jr. (D Pa.) Oct. 21, 1918-April 20, 1949; House 1949.

COFFIN, Frank M. (D Maine) July 11, 1919; House 1957-61; Managing director, Development Loan Fund Jan. 1961-Oct. 1961; Deputy Administrator, Agency for International Development Oct. 1961-64; Judge, first circuit, U.S. Court of Appeals, 1965- .

COFFIN, Howard A. (R Mich.) June 11, 1877-Feb. 28, 1956; House 1947-49.

COHELAN, Jeffery (D Calif.) June 24, 1914; House 1959- .

COLE, Albert M. (R Kan.) Oct. 13, 1901; House 1945-53; Administrator, Housing and Home Finance Agency 1953-59.

COLE, W. Sterling (R N.Y.) April 18, 1904; House 1935-57; Director General, International Atomic Energy Agency 1957-61.

COLE, William C. (R Mo.) Aug. 29, 1897-Sept. 23, 1965; House 1943-49; 1953-55.

COLLIER, Harold R. (R Ill.) Dec. 12, 1915; House 1957- .

COLLINS, James M. (R Texas) April 29, 1916; House 1968- .

COLMER, William M. (D Miss.) Feb. 11, 1890; House 1933- .

COMBS, J. M. (D Texas) July 7, 1889-Aug. 21, 1953; House 1945-53.

CONABLE, Barber B. Jr. (R N.Y.) Nov. 2, 1922; House 1965- .

CONDON, Robert Likens (D Calif.) Nov. 10, 1912; House 1953-55.

CONNALLY, Tom T. (D Texas) Aug. 19, 1877-Oct. 28, 1963; House 1917-1929; Senate 1929-53; Vice Chairman U.S. delegation to UN Conference, San Francisco, 1945; U.S. Representative to UN 1945-46.

CONTE, Silvio O. (R Mass.) Nov. 9, 1921; House 1959- .

CONYERS, John Jr. (D Mich.) May 16, 1929; House 1965- .

COOK, Marlow W. (R Ky.) July 27, 1926; Senate 1968- .

COOK, Robert E. (D Ohio), May 19, 1920; House 1959-63.

COOLEY, Harold D. (D N.C.) July 26, 1897; House 1934-66.

COON, Sam (R Ore.) April 15, 1903; House 1953-57.

COOPER, Jere (D Tenn.) July 20, 1893-Dec. 18, 1957; House 1929-57.

COOPER, John Sherman (R Ky.) Aug. 23, 1901; Senate 1946-49; 1952-55; 1956- ; Ambassador to India 1955-56.

CORBETT, Robert J. (R Pa.) Aug. 25, 1905; House 1939-41; 1945- .

CORDON, Guy (R Ore.) April 24, 1890-June 9, 1969; Senate 1944-55.

CORDOVA, Jorge Luis (New Prog. P.R.) April 28, 1907; Resident Commissioner, House 1969- .

CORMAN, James C. (D Calif.) Oct. 20, 1920; House 1961- .

COTTON, Norris (R N.H.) May 11, 1900; House 1947-54; Senate 1954- .

COUDERT, Frederic R. Jr. (R N.Y.) May 7, 1898; House 1947-59.

COUGHLIN, R. Lawrence (R Pa.) April 11, 1929; House 1969- .

COURTNEY, Wirt (D Tenn.) Sept. 7, 1889-April 6, 1961; House 1939-49.

COWGER, William O. (R Ky.) Jan. 1, 1922; House 1967- .

COX, E. E. (D Ga.) April 3, 1880-Dec. 24, 1952; House 1925-52.

CRALEY, N. Neiman Jr. (D Pa.) Nov. 17, 1927; House 1965-67.

CRAMER, William C. (R Fla.) Aug. 4, 1922; House 1955- .

CRANSTON, Alan (D Calif.) June 19, 1914; Senate 1969- .

CRAVENS, William Fadjo (D Ark.) Feb. 15, 1899; House 1939-49.

CRAWFORD, Fred L. (R Mich.) May 5, 1888-April 13, 1957; House 1935-53.

CRETELLA, Albert W. (R Conn.) April 22, 1897; House 1953-59.

CRIPPA, Edward D. (R Wyo.) April 8, 1899-Oct. 20, 1960; Senate June 24, 1954-Nov. 28, 1954.

CROOK, Thurman C. (D Ind.) July 18, 1891; House 1949-51.

CROSSER, Robert (D Ohio) June 7, 1874-June 3, 1957; House 1913-19; 1923-55.

CROW, William J. (R Pa.) Jan. 22, 1902; House 1947-49.

CRUMPACKER, Shepard J. Jr. (R Ind.) Feb. 13, 1917; House 1951-57.

CULVER, John C. (D Iowa) Aug. 8, 1932; House 1965- .

CUNNINGHAM, Glenn (R Neb.) Sept. 10, 1912; House 1957- .

CUNNINGHAM, Paul (R Iowa) June 15, 1890-July 16, 1961; House 1941-59.

CURLEY, James M. (D Mass.) Nov. 20, 1874-Nov. 12, 1958; House 1911-14; 1943-47; Mayor of Boston 1914-18, 1922-26, 1930-34, 1947-50; Gov. of Mass. 1935-37.

CURTIN, Willard S. (R Pa.) Nov. 28, 1905; House 1957-67.

CURTIS, Carl T. (R Neb.) March 15, 1905; House 1939-Dec. 31, 1954. Senate Jan. 1, 1955- .

CURTIS, Laurence (R Mass.) Sept. 3, 1893; House 1953-63.

CURTIS, Thomas B. (R Mo.) May 14, 1911; House 1951-69.

D

DADDARIO, Emilio Q. (D Conn.) Sept. 24, 1918; House 1959- .

DAGUE, Paul B. (R Pa.) May 19, 1898; House 1947-67.

D'ALESANDRO, Thomas Jr. (D Md.) Aug. 1, 1903; House 1939-47; Mayor of Baltimore 1947-59.

DANIEL, Charles E. (D S.C.) Nov. 11, 1895-Sept. 13, 1964; Senate Sept. 6, 1954-Dec. 23, 1954.

DANIEL, Price (D Texas) Oct. 10, 1910; Senate 1953-57; Gov. 1957-63.

DANIEL, W. C. (D Va.) May 12, 1914; House 1969- .

DANIELS, Dominick V. (D N.J.) Oct. 18, 1908; House 1959- .

DARBY, Harry (R Kan.) Jan. 23, 1895; Senate 1949-50.

DAUGHTON, Ralph H. (D Va.) Sept. 23, 1885-Dec. 22, 1958; House 1944-47.

DAVENPORT, Harry J. (D Pa.) Aug. 28, 1902; House 1949-51.

DAVIDSON, Irwin D. (D N.Y.) Jan. 2, 1906; House 1955-56.

DAVIES, John C. (D N.Y.) May 1, 1920; House 1949-51.

DAVIS, Clifford (D Tenn.) Nov. 18, 1897; House 1940-65.

DAVIS, Glenn R. (R Wis.) Oct. 28, 1914; House 1947-57; 1965- .

DAVIS, James C. (D Ga.) May 17, 1895; House 1947-63.

DAVIS, John W. (D Ga.) Sept. 12, 1916; House 1961- .

DAWSON, William A. (R Utah) Nov. 5, 1903; House 1947-49; 1953-59.

DAWSON, William L. (D Ill.) April 26, 1886; House 1943- .

DEANE, Charles B. (D N.C.) Nov. 1, 1898; House 1947-57.

deGRAFFENRIED, Edward (D Ala.) June 30, 1899; House 1949-53.

De LACY, Hugh (D Wash.) May 9, 1910; House 1945-47.

de la GARZA, Eligio (D Texas) Sept. 22, 1927; House 1965- .

DELANEY, James J. (D N.Y.) March 19, 1901; House 1945-47; 1949- .

DELANEY, John Joseph (D N.Y.) Aug. 21, 1878-Nov. 18, 1948; House 1918-19; 1931-48.

DELLAY, Vincent J. (R N.J.) June 23, 1907; House 1957-59.

DELLENBACK, John R. (R Ore.) Nov. 6, 1918; House 1967- .

DEMPSEY, John J. (D N.M.) June 22, 1879-March 11, 1958; House 1935-41; 1951-58; Under Secretary of the Interior 1941-42; Gov. 1943-47.

DENNEY, Robert V. (R. Neb.) April 11, 1916; House 1967- .

DENNIS, David W. (R Ind.) June 7, 1912; House 1969- .

DENNISON, David (R Ohio) July 29, 1918; House 1957-59.

DENNY, Harmar D. Jr. (R Pa.) July 2, 1886-Jan. 10, 1966; House 1951-53.

DENT, John H. (D Pa.) March 10, 1908; House 1958- .

DENTON, Winfield K. (D Ind.) Oct. 28, 1896; House 1949-53; 1955-66.

DEROUNIAN, Steven B. (R N.Y.) April 6, 1918; House 1953-65.

DERWINSKI, Edward J. (R Ill.) Sept. 15, 1926; House 1959- .

DEVEREUX, James P.S. (R Md.) Feb. 20, 1903; House 1951-59.

DEVINE, Samuel L. (R Ohio) Dec. 21, 1915; House 1959- .

DEVITT, Edward J. (R Minn.) May 5, 1911; House 1947-49.

D'EWART, Wesley A. (R Mont.) Oct. 1, 1889; House 1945-55.

DICKINSON, William L. (R Ala.) June 5, 1925; House 1965- .

DICKSTEIN, Samuel (D N.Y.) Feb. 5, 1885-April 22, 1954; House 1923-45.

DIES, Martin Jr. (D Texas) Nov. 5, 1900; House 1931-45; 1953-59.

DIGGS, Charles C. Jr. (D Mich.) Dec. 2, 1922; House 1955- .

DINGELL, John D. (D Mich.) Feb. 2, 1894- Sept. 19, 1955; House 1933-55.

DINGELL, John D. Jr. (D Mich.) July 8, 1926; House 1955- .

DIRKSEN, Everett McKinley (R Ill.) Jan. 4, 1896; House 1933-49; Senate 1951-69; Senate Minority Leader 1959-69.

DIXON, Henry Aldous (R Utah) June 29, 1890-Jan. 22, 1967; House 1955-61.

DODD, Thomas J. (D Conn.) May 15, 1907; House 1953-57; Senate 1959- .

DOLE, Robert (R Kan.) July 22, 1923; House 1961-69; Senate 1969- .

DOLLINGER, Isidore (D N.Y.) Nov. 13, 1903; House 1949-59.

DOLLIVER, James I. (R Iowa) Aug. 31, 1894; House 1945-57.

DOMENGEAUX, James (D La.) Jan. 6, 1907; House 1941-44; 1944-49.

DOMINICK, Peter H. (R Colo.) July 7, 1915; House 1961-63; Senate 1963- .

DONDERO, George A. (R Mich.) Dec. 16, 1883-Jan. 29, 1968; House 1933-57.

DONNELL, Forrest C. (R Mo.) Aug. 20, 1884; Senate 1945-51; Gov. 1941-45.

DONOHUE, Harold D. (D Mass.) June 18, 1901; House 1947- .

DONOVAN, James G. (D N.Y.) Dec. 15, 1898; House 1951-57.

DOOLEY, Edwin B. (R N.Y.) April 13, 1905; House 1957-63.

DORN, Francis E. (R N.Y.) April 18, 1911; House 1953-61.

DORN, W.J. Bryan (D S.C.) April 14, 1916; House 1947-49; 1951- .

DOUGHTON, Robert L. (D N.C.) Nov. 7, 1863-Oct. 1, 1954; House 1911-53.

DOUGLAS, Emily Taft (D Ill.) April 10, 1899 (wife of Sen. Paul H. Douglas); House 1945-47.

DOUGLAS, Helen Gahagan (D Calif.) Nov. 25, 1900; House 1945-51.

DOUGLAS, Paul H. (D Ill.) March 26, 1892; Senate 1949-67.

DOW, John G. (D N.Y.) May 6, 1905; House 1965-69.

DOWDY, John (D Texas) Feb. 11, 1912; House 1952- .

DOWNEY, Sheridan (D Calif.) March 11, 1884-Oct. 25, 1961; Senate 1939-50.

DOWNING, Thomas N. (D Va.) Feb. 1, 1919; House 1959- .

DOYLE, Clyde (D Calif.) July 11, 1887-March 14, 1963; House 1945-47; 1949-63.

DREWRY, Patrick H. (D Va.) May 24, 1875-Dec. 21, 1947; House 1920-47.

DUFF, James H. (R Pa.) Jan. 21, 1883; Senate 1951-57; Gov. 1947-51.

DULLES, John Foster (R N.Y.) Feb. 25, 1888-May 24, 1959; Senate July 7, 1949-Nov. 8, 1949; U.S. Representative to UN, 1946-1950; Secretary of State, 1953-59.

DULSKI, Thaddeus J. (D N.Y.) Sept. 27, 1915; House 1959- .

DUNCAN, John J. (R Tenn.) March 24, 1920; House 1965- .

DUNCAN, Robert B. (D Ore.) Dec. 4, 1920; House 1963-67.

DURHAM, Carl T. (D N.C.) Aug. 28, 1892; House 1939-61.

DURNO, Edwin R. (R Ore.) Jan. 26, 1899; House 1961-63.

DWORSHAK, Henry C. (R Idaho) Aug. 29, 1894-July 23, 1962; House 1939-46; Senate Nov. 5, 1946-Jan. 3, 1949; Oct. 14, 1949-62.

DWYER, Florence P. (R N.J.) July 4, 1902; House 1957- .

DYAL, Ken W. (D Calif.) July 9, 1910; House 1965-67.

E

EAGLETON, Thomas F. (D Mo.) Sept. 4, 1929; Senate 1969- .

EARTHMAN, Harold H. (D Tenn.) April 13, 1900; House 1945-47.

EASTLAND, James O. (D Miss.) Nov. 28, 1904; Senate June 30, 1941-Sept. 28, 1941; 1943- .

EATON, Charles A. (R N.J.) March 29, 1868-Jan. 23, 1953; House 1925-53.

EBERHARTER, Herman P. (D Pa.) April 29, 1892-Sept. 9, 1958; House 1937-58.

ECKHARDT, Bob (D Texas) July 16, 1913; House 1967- .

ECTON, Zales N. (R Mont.) April 1, 1898-March 3, 1961; Senate 1947-53.

EDMONDSON, Ed (D Okla.) April 7, 1919; House 1953- .

EDMONDSON, J. Howard (D Okla.) Sept. 27, 1925; Gov. 1959-63; Senate 1963-65.

EDWARDS, Don (D Calif.) Jan. 6, 1915; House 1963- .

EDWARDS, Edwin W. (D La.) Aug. 7, 1927; House 1965- .

EDWARDS, Jack (R Ala.) Sept. 20, 1929; House 1965- .

EILBERG, Joshua (D Pa.) Feb. 12, 1921; House 1967- .

ELLENDER, Allen J. (D La.) Sept. 24, 1891; Senate 1937- .

ELLIOTT, Alfred J. (D Calif.) June 1, 1895; House 1937-49.

ELLIOTT, Carl (D Ala.) Dec. 20, 1913; House 1949-65.

ELLIOTT, Douglas Hemphill (R Pa.) June 3, 1921-June 19, 1960; House 1960.

ELLIS, Hubert S. (R W.Va.) July 6, 1887-Feb. 10, 1958; House 1943-49.

ELLSWORTH, Harris (R Ore.) Sept. 17, 1899; House 1943-57; Chairman Civil Service Commission, 1957-59.

ELLSWORTH, Robert F. (R Kan.) June 11, 1926; House 1961-67; Special Assistant to the President 1969; U.S. Permanent Representative to the North Atlantic Treaty organization 1969- .

ELSAESSER, Edward J. (R N.Y.) March 10, 1904; House 1945-49.

ELSTON, Charles H. (R Ohio) Aug. 1, 1891; House 1939-53.

ENGEL, Albert J. (R Mich.) Jan. 1, 1888-Dec. 2, 1959; House 1935-51.

ENGLE, Clair (D Calif.) Sept. 21, 1911-July 30, 1964; House 1943-59; Senate 1959-64.

ERLENBORN, John N. (R Ill.) Feb. 8, 1917; House 1965- .

ERVIN, Joe W. (D N.C.) March 3, 1901-Dec. 25, 1945 (brother of Sam J. Ervin Jr.); House Jan. 3, 1945-Dec. 25, 1945.

ERVIN, Sam J. Jr. (D N.C.) Sept. 27, 1896; House Jan. 22, 1946-Jan. 3, 1947; Senate 1954- .

ESCH, Marvin L. (R Mich.) Aug. 4, 1927; House 1967- .

ESHLEMAN, Edwin D. (R Pa.) Dec. 4, 1920; House 1967- .

EVANS, Frank E. (D Colo.) Sept. 8, 1923; House 1965- .

EVERETT, Robert A. (D Tenn.) Feb. 24, 1915-Jan. 26, 1969; House 1958-69.

EVINS, Joe L. (D Tenn.) Oct. 24, 1910; House 1947- .

F

FALLON, George H. (D Md.) July 24, 1902; House 1945- .

FANNIN, Paul J. (R Ariz.) Jan. 29, 1907; Gov. 1958-1964; Senate 1965- .

FARBSTEIN, Leonard (D N.Y.) Oct. 12, 1902; House 1957- .

FARNSLEY, Charles P. (D Ky.) March 28, 1907; House 1965-67.

FARNUM, Billie S. (D Mich.) April 11, 1916; House 1965-67.

FARRINGTON, Joseph R. (R Hawaii) Oct. 15, 1897-June 19, 1954; Delegate 1943-1954.

FARRINGTON, Mary Elizabeth Pruett (R Hawaii) May 30, 1898 (wife of Joseph R. Farrington); Delegate 1954-57.

FASCELL, Dante B.(D Fla.) March 9, 1917; House 1955- .

FEAZEL, William C. (D La.) June 10, 1895-March 16, 1965; Senate May 18, 1948-Dec. 30, 1948.

FEIGHAN, Michael A. (D Ohio) Feb. 16, 1905; House 1943- .

FELLOWS, Frank (R Maine) Nov. 7, 1889-Aug. 27, 1951; House 1941-51.

FENTON, Ivor D. (R Pa.) Aug. 3, 1889; House 1939-63.

FERGUSON, Homer (R Mich.) Feb. 25, 1889; Senate 1943-55; Ambassador to the Philippines 1955-56; Judge of Military Court of Appeals 1956- .

FERNANDEZ, Antonio M. (D N.M.) Jan. 17, 1902-Nov. 7, 1956; House 1943-56.

FERNOS-ISERN, Antonio (D Puerto Rico) May 10, 1895; Resident Commissioner, House 1946-65; Acting Gov. 1943-46.

FINDLEY, Paul (R Ill.) June 23, 1921; House 1961- .

FISH, Hamilton Jr. (R N.Y.) June 3, 1926; House 1969- .

FINE, Sidney A. (D N.Y.) Sept. 14, 1903; House 1951-56.

FINNEGAN, Edward R. (D Ill.) June 5, 1905; House 1961-65.

FINO, Paul A. (R N.Y.) Dec. 15, 1913; House 1953-69.

FISHER, O.C. (D Texas) Nov. 22, 1903; House 1943- .

FJARE, Orvin B. (R Mont.) April 16, 1918; House 1955-57.

GIFFORD, Charles L. (R Mass.) March 15, 1871-Aug. 23, 1947; House 1922-47.

GILBERT, Jacob H. (D N.Y.) June 7, 1920; House 1960- .

GILL, Thomas P. (D Hawaii) April 21, 1922; House 1963-65.

GILLESPIE, Dean M. (R Colo.) May 2, 1884-Feb. 2, 1949; House 1944-47.

GILLETTE, Guy M. (D Iowa) Feb. 3, 1879; House, 1933-36; Senate 1936-45; 1949-55.

GILLETTE, Wilson D. (R Pa.) June 1, 1880-Aug. 7, 1951; House 1941-51.

GILLIE, George W. (R Ind.) Aug. 15, 1880-July 4, 1963; House 1939-49.

GILLIGAN, John J. (D Ohio) March 22, 1921; House 1965-67.

GILMER, Dixie (D Okla.) June 7, 1901; House 1949-51.

GLASS, Carter (D Va.) Jan. 4, 1858-May 28, 1946; House 1902-18; Senate 1920-46; Secretary of the Treasury 1918-20.

GLENN, Milton W. (R N.J.) June 18, 1903-Dec. 15, 1967; House 1957-65.

GOFF, Abe McGregor (R Idaho) Dec. 21, 1899; House 1947-49.

GOLDEN, James S. (R Ky.) Sept. 20, 1891; House 1949-55.

GOLDWATER, Barry (R Ariz.) Jan. 1, 1909; Senate 1953-65, 1969- ; Republican Presidential candidate 1964.

GONZALEZ, Henry B. (D Texas) May 3, 1916; House 1961- .

GOODELL, Charles E. (R N.Y.) March 16, 1926; House 1959-68; Senate 1968- .

GOODLING, George A. (R Pa.) Sept. 26, 1896; House 1961-65; 1967- .

GOODWIN, Angier L. (R Mass.) Jan. 30, 1881; House 1943-55.

GORDON, Thomas S. (D Ill.) Dec. 17, 1893-Jan. 22, 1959; House 1943-59.

GORE, Albert (D Tenn.) Dec. 26, 1907; House 1939-44; 1945-53; Senate 1953- .

GORSKI, Chester C. (D N.Y.) June 22, 1906; House 1949-51.

GORSKI, Martin (D Ill.) Aug. 30, 1886-Dec. 4, 1949; House 1943-49.

GOSSETT, Charles C. (D Idaho) Sept. 2, 1888; Senate 1945-47; Gov. 1945.

GOSSETT, Ed. (D Texas) Jan. 27, 1902; House 1939-51.

GRABOWSKI, Bernard F. (D Conn.) June 11, 1923; House 1963- .

GRAHAM, Frank P. (D N.C.) Oct. 14, 1886; Senate, 1949-50.

GRAHAM, Louis E. (R Pa.) Aug. 4, 1880; House 1939-55.

GRANAHAN, Kathryn E. (D Pa.) Dec. 7, 1906; (widow of William T. Granahan) House 1956-63; Treasurer of the U.S. 1963-66.

GRANAHAN, William T. (D Pa.) July 26, 1895-May 25, 1956; House 1945-47; 1949-56.

GRANGER, Walter K. (D Utah) Oct. 11, 1888; House 1941-53.

GRANT, George M. (D Ala.) July 11, 1895; House 1938-65.

GRANT, Robert A. (R Ind.) July 31, 1905; House 1939-49.

GRAVEL, Mike (D Alaska) May 13, 1930; Senate 1969- .

GRAY, Kenneth J. (D Ill.) Nov. 14, 1924; House 1955- .

GREEN, Edith (D Ore.) Jan. 17, 1910; House 1955- .

GREEN, Theodore Francis (D R.I.) Oct. 2, 1867-May 19, 1966; Senate 1937-61; Gov. 1933-36.

GREEN, William J. Jr. (D Pa.) March 5, 1910-Dec. 21, 1963; House 1945-47; 1949-63.

GREEN, William J. III (D Pa.) June 24, 1938, (son of William J. Green Jr.); House 1964- .

GREENWOOD, Ernest (D N.Y.) Nov. 25, 1884-June 15, 1955; House 1951-53.

GREGORY, Noble J. (D Ky.) Aug. 30, 1897; House 1937-59.

GREIGG, Stanley L. (D Iowa) May 7, 1931; House 1965-67.

GRIDER, George W. (D Tenn.) Oct. 1, 1912; House 1965-67.

GRIFFIN, Charles H. (D Miss.) May 9, 1926; House 1968- .

GRIFFIN, Robert P. (R Mich.) Nov. 6, 1923; House 1957-66; Senate 1966- .

GRIFFITHS, Martha W. (D Mich.) Jan. 29, 1912; House 1955- .

GRIFFITHS, P.W. (R Ohio) March 30, 1893; House 1943-49.

GRISWOLD, Dwight P. (R Neb.) Nov. 27, 1893-April 12, 1954; Senate 1952-54; Gov. 1941-46.

GROSS, Chester H. (R Pa.) Oct. 13, 1888; House 1943-49.

GROSS, H.R. (R Iowa) June 30, 1899; House 1949- .

GROVER, James R. Jr. (R N.Y.) March 15, 1919; House 1963- .

GRUENING, Ernest (D Alaska) Feb. 6, 1887; Senate 1959-69; Gov. 1939-53.

GUBSER, Charles S. (R Calif.) Feb. 1, 1916; House 1953- .

GUDE, Gilbert (R Md.) March 9, 1923; House 1967- .

GUFFEY, Joseph F. (D Pa.) Dec. 29, 1870-March 6, 1959; Senate 1935-47.

GULL, Ben Hugh (R Texas) Sept. 8, 1909; House 1950-51.

GURNEY, Chan (R S.D.) May 21, 1896; Senate 1939-1951; Member, Civil Aeronautics Board, 1951- .

GURNEY, Edward J. (R Fla.) Jan. 12, 1914; House 1963-69; Senate 1969- .

GWINN, Ralph W. (R N.Y.) March 28, 1884; House 1945-59.

GWYNNE, John W. (R Iowa) Oct. 20, 1889; House 1935-49.

H

HAGAN, G. Elliott (D Ga.) May 24, 1916; House 1961- .

HAGEN, Harlan (D Calif.) Oct. 8, 1914; House 1953-67.

HAGEN, Harold C. (R Minn.) Nov. 10, 1901-March 19, 1957; House 1943-55.

HALE, Robert (R Maine) Nov. 29, 1889; House 1943-59.

HALEY, James A. (D Fla.) Jan. 4, 1899; House 1953- .

HALL, David M. (D N.C.) May 16, 1918-Jan. 29, 1960; House 1959-60.

HALL, Durward G. (R Mo.) Sept. 14, 1910; House 1961- .

HALL, Edwin Arthur (R N.Y.) Feb. 11, 1909; House 1939-53.

HALL, Leonard W. (R N.Y.) Oct. 2, 1900; House 1939-52; Chairman, Republican National Committee 1952-57.

HALLECK, Charles A. (R Ind.) Aug. 22, 1900; House 1935-69; Majority Leader, 1947-48, 1951-52; Minority Leader, 1960-65.

HALPERN, Seymour (R N.Y.) Nov. 19, 1912; House 1959- .

HAMILTON, Lee H. (D Ind.) April 20, 1931; House 1965- .

HAMMERSCHMIDT, John Paul (R Ark.) May 4, 1922; House 1967- .

HANCOCK, Clarence E. (R N.Y.) Feb. 13, 1885-Jan. 3, 1948; House 1927-47.

HAND, T. Millet, (R N.J.) July 7, 1902-Dec. 26, 1956; House 1945-56.

HANLEY, James M. (D N.Y.) July 19, 1920; House 1965- .

HANNA, Richard T. (D Calif.) June 19, 1914; House 1963- .

HANSEN, Clifford P. (R Wyo.) Oct. 16, 1912; Senate 1967- .

HANSEN, George V. (R Idaho) Sept. 14, 1930; House 1965-69.

HANSEN, John R. (D Iowa) Aug. 24, 1901; House 1965- .

HANSEN, Julia Butler (D Wash.) June 14, 1907; House 1960- .

HANSEN, Orval H. (R Idaho) Aug. 3, 1926; House 1968- .

HARDEN, Cecil M. (R Ind.) Nov. 21, 1894; House 1949-59.

HARDING, Ralph R. (D Idaho) Sept. 9, 1929; House 1961-65.

HARDY, Porter Jr. (D Va.) June 1, 1903; House 1947-69.

HARE, Butler B. (D S.C.) Nov. 25, 1875-Dec. 30, 1967; House 1925-33; 1939-47.

HARE, James B. (D S.C.) Sept. 4, 1918 (son of Butler B. Hare); House 1949-51.

HARGIS, Denver D. (D Kan.) July 22, 1921; House 1959-61.

HARLESS, Richard F. (D Ariz.) Aug. 6, 1905; House 1943-49.

HARMON, Randall S. (D Ind.) July 19, 1903; House 1959-61.

HARNESS, Forest A. (R Ind.) June 24, 1895; House 1939-49; Sergeant at Arms, U.S. Senate 1953-55.

HARRIS, Fred R. (D Okla.) Nov. 13, 1930; Senate 1965- . Chairman, Democratic National Committee 1969- .

HARRIS, Oren (D Ark.) Dec. 20, 1903; House 1941-66; U.S. District Judge 1966- .

HARRISON, Burr P. (D Va.) July 2, 1904; House 1946-63.

HARRISON, Robert D. (R Neb.) Jan. 26, 1897; House 1951-59.

HARRISON, William H. (R Wyo.) Aug. 10, 1896; House 1951-55; 1961-65; 1967-69.

HARSHA, William H. (R Ohio) Jan. 1, 1921; House 1961- .

HART, Edward J. (D N.J.) March 25, 1893-April 20, 1961; House 1935-55.

HART, Philip A. (D Mich.) Dec. 10, 1912; Senate 1959- .

HART, Thomas C. (R Conn.) June 12, 1877; Senate 1945-46.

HARTKE, Vance (D Ind.) May 31, 1919; Senate 1959- .

HARTLEY, Fred A. Jr. (R N.J.) March 22, 1902-May 11, 1969; House 1929-49.

HARVEY, James (R Mich.) July 4, 1922; House 1961- .

HARVEY, Ralph (R Ind.) Aug. 9, 1901; House 1947-59; 1961-66.

HASKELL, Harry Jr. (R Del.) May 27, 1921; House 1957-59.

HASTINGS, James F. (R N.Y.) April 10, 1926; House 1969- .

HATCH, Carl A. (D N.M.) Nov. 27, 1889-Sept. 15, 1963; Senate 1933-49.

HATFIELD, Mark O. (R Ore.) July 12, 1922; Senate 1967- . Governor 1959-67.

HATHAWAY, William D. (D Maine) Feb. 21, 1924; House 1965- .

HAVENNER, Frank R. (D Calif.) June 20, 1882; House 1945-53.

HAWKES, Albert W. (R N.J.) Nov. 20, 1878; Senate 1943-49.

HAWKINS, Augustus F. (D Cailf.) Aug. 31, 1907; House 1963- .

HAYDEN, Carl (D Ariz.) Oct. 2, 1877; House 1912-27; Senate 1927-69; President Pro Tempore 1957-69.

HAYS, Brooks (D Ark.) Aug. 9, 1898; House 1943-59.

HAYS, Wayne L. (D Ohio) May 13, 1911; House 1949- .

HAYWORTH, Don (D Mich.) Jan. 13, 1898; House 1955-57.

HEALEY, James C. (D N.Y.) Dec. 24, 1909; House 1956-65.

HEALY, Ned R. (D Calif.) Aug. 9, 1905; House 1945-47.

HEBERT, F. Edward (D La.) Oct. 12, 1901; House 1941- .

HECHLER, Ken (D W. Va.) Sept. 20, 1914; House 1959- .

HECKLER, Margaret M. (R Mass.) June 21, 1931; House 1967- .

HEDRICK, E.H. (D W. Va.) Aug. 9, 1894-Sept. 20, 1954; House 1945-53.

HEFFERNAN, James Joseph (D N.Y.) Nov. 8, 1888-Jan. 27, 1967; 1941-53.

HEIDINGER, James V. (R Ill.) July 17, 1882-March 22, 1945; House 1941-45.

HELLER, Louis B. (D N.Y.) March 10, 1905; House 1949-51; 1953-54.

HELSTOSKI, Henry (D N.J.) March 21, 1924; House 1965- .

HEMPHILL, Robert W. (D S.C.) May 10, 1915; House 1957-64; U.S. District Judge 1964- .

HENDERSON, David N. (D N.C.) April 16, 1921; House 1961- .

HENDERSON, John E. (R Ohio) Jan. 4, 1917; House 1955-61.

HENDRICKS, Joe (D Fla.) Sept. 24, 1903; House 1937-49.

HENDRICKSON, Robert C. (R N.J) Aug. 12, 1898; Senate 1949-55.

HENNINGS, Thomas C. Jr. (D Mo.) June 25, 1903-Sept. 13, 1960; House 1935-40; Senate 1951-60.

HENRY, Robert K. (R Wis.) Feb. 9, 1890-Nov. 20, 1946; House 1945-46.

HERLONG, A. Sydney Jr. (D Fla.) Feb. 14, 1909; House 1949-69.

HERTER, Christian A. (R Mass.) March 28, 1895-Dec. 30, 1966; House 1943-53; Gov. Mass. 1953-57; Under Secretary of State 1957-59; Secretary of State 1959-61; Special Representative for Trade Negotiations of the U.S. 1962-66.

HESELTON, John W. (R Mass.) March 7, 1900-Aug. 19, 1962; House 1945-59.

HESS, William E. (R Ohio) March 13, 1898; House 1929-37; 1939-49; 1951-61.

HICKENLOOPER, Bourke B. (R Iowa) July 21, 1896; Senate 1945-69; Gov. 1943-44.

HICKEY, J.J. (D Wyo.) Aug. 22, 1911; Senate Jan. 2, 1961-62; Gov. 1959-61.

HICKS, Floyd V. (D Wash.) May 29, 1915; House 1965- .

HIESTAND, Edgar W. (R Calif.) Dec. 3, 1888; House 1953-63.

HILL, Lister (D Ala.) Dec. 29, 1894; House 1923-38; Senate 1938-69.

HILL, William S. (R Colo.) Jan. 20, 1886; House 1941-59.

HINSHAW, Carl (R Calif.) July 28, 1894-Aug. 5, 1956; House 1939-56.

HOBBS, Samuel Francis (D Ala.) Oct. 5, 1887-May 31, 1952; House 1935-51.

HOBLITZELL, John D. Jr (R W. Va.) Dec. 30, 1912; Senate Jan. 25, 1958-Nov. 4, 1958.

HOCH, Daniel K. (D Pa.) Jan. 31, 1866-Oct. 11, 1960; House 1943-47.

HOEVEN, Charles B. (R Iowa) March 30, 1895; House 1943-65.

HOEY, Clyde R. (D N.C.) Dec. 11, 1877-May 12, 1954; House 1919-21; Senate 1945-54; Gov. 1937-41.

HOFFMAN, Carl Henry (R Pa.) Aug. 12, 1896; House 1946-47.

HOFFMAN, Clare E. (R Mich.) Sept. 10, 1875-Nov. 3, 1967; House 1935-63.

HOFFMAN, Elmer J. (R Ill.) July 7, 1899; House 1959-65.

HOFFMAN, Richard W. (R Ill.) Dec. 23, 1893; House 1949-57.

HOGAN, Earl (D Ind.) March 13, 1920; House 1959-61.

HOGAN, Lawrence J. (R Md.) Sept. 30, 1928; House 1969- .

HOLIFIELD, Chet (D Calif.) Dec. 3, 1903; House 1943- .

HOLLAND, Elmer J. (D Pa.) Jan. 8, 1894-Aug. 9, 1968; House 1942-43; 1956-68.

HOLLAND, Spessard L. (D Fla.) July 10, 1892; Senate 1946- ; Gov. 1941-45.

HOLLINGS, Ernest F. (D S.C.) Jan. 1, 1922; Senate 1966- . Gov. 1959-63.

HOLMES, Hal (R Wash.) Feb. 22, 1902; House 1943-59.

HOLMES, Pehr G. (R Mass.) April 9, 1881-Dec. 19, 1952; House 1931-47.

HOLT, Joseph F. III (R Calif.) July 6, 1924; House 1953-61.

HOLTZMAN, Lester (D N.Y.) June 1, 1913; House 1953-61.

HOOK, Frank E. (D Mich.) May 26, 1893; House 1935-47.

HOPE, Clifford R. (R Kan.) June 9, 1893; House 1927-57.

HORAN, Walt (R Wash.) Oct. 15, 1898-Dec. 20, 1966; House 1943-65.

HORTON, Frank J. (R N.Y. Dec. 12, 1919; House 1963- .

HOSMER, Craig (R Calif.) May 6, 1915; House 1953- .

HOWARD, James J. (D N.J.) July 24, 1927; House 1965- .

HOWELL, Charles R. (D N.J.) May 23, 1904; House 1949-55.

HOWELL, Evan (R Ill.) Sept. 21, 1905; House 1941-47.

HRUSKA, Roman L. (R Neb.) Aug. 16, 1904; House 1953-54; Senate 1954- .

HUBER, Walter B. (D Ohio) June 29, 1903; House 1945-51.

HUDDLESTON, George Jr. (D Ala.) March 19, 1920; House 1955-65.

HUFFMAN, James W. (D Ohio) Sept. 13, 1894; Senate 1945-46.

HUGHES, Harold E. (D Iowa) Feb. 10, 1922; Senate 1969- .

HULL, Merlin (R, Prog. Wis.) Dec. 18, 1870-May 17, 1953; House; Republican 1929-31; Progressive 1935-47; Republican 1947-53.

HULL, W.R. Jr. (D Mo.) April 17, 1906; House 1955- .

HUMPHREY, Hubert H. (D Minn.) May 27, 1911; Senate 1949-64. Vice President 1965-69; Democratic Presidential candidate 1968.

HUMPHREYS, Robert (D Ky.) Aug. 20, 1893; Senate June 21, 1956-Nov. 6, 1956.

HUNGATE, William L. (D Mo.) Dec. 14, 1922; House 1965- .

HUNT, John E. (R N.J.) Nov. 25, 1908; House 1967- .

HUNT, Lester C. (D Wyo.) July 8, 1892-June 19, 1954; Senate 1949-54; Gov. 1943-49.

HUNTER, Allan Oakley (R Calif.) June 15, 1916; House 1951-55.

HUOT, J. Oliva (D N.H.) Aug. 11, 1917; House 1965-67.

HUTCHINSON, Edward (R Mich.) Oct. 13, 1914; House 1963- .

HYDE, DeWitt S. (R Md.) March 21, 1909; House 1953-59.

HILLELSON, Jeffrey P. (R Mo.) March 9, 1919; House 1953-55.

HILLINGS, Patrick J. (R Calif.) Feb. 19, 1923; House 1951-59.

I

ICHORD, Richard H. (D Mo.) June 27, 1926; House 1961- .

IKARD, Frank (D Texas) Jan. 30, 1914; House 1951-61.

INOUYE, Daniel K. (D Hawaii) Sept. 7, 1924; House 1959-63; Senate 1963- .

IRVING, Leonard (D Mo.) March 24, 1898; House 1949-53.

IRWIN, Donald J. (D Conn.) Sept. 7, 1926; House 1959-61; 1965-69.

ISACSON, Leo (American Labor New York) April 20, 1910; House Feb. 17, 1948-49.

IVES, Irving M. (R N.Y.) Jan. 24, 1896-Feb. 24, 1962; Senate 1947-59.

IZAC, Edouard V.M. (D Calif.) Dec. 18, 1891; House 1937-47.

J

JACKSON, Donald L. (R Calif.) Jan. 23, 1910; House 1947-61.

JACKSON, Henry M. (D Wash.) May 31, 1912; House 1941-53; Senate 1953- ; Chairman, Democratic National Committee 1960-61.

JACOBS, Andrew (D Ind.) Feb. 22, 1906; House 1949-51.

JACOBS, Andrew Jr. (D Ind.) Feb. 24, 1932; House 1965- .

JAMES, Benjamin F. (R Pa.) Aug. 1, 1885-Jan. 26, 1961; House 1949-59.

JARMAN, John (D Okla.) July 17, 1915; House 1951- .

JARMAN, Pete (D Ala.) Oct. 31, 1892-Feb. 17, 1955; House 1937-49.

JAVITS, Jacob K. (R N.Y.) May 18, 1904; House 1947-54; Senate 1957- .

JENISON, Edward H. (R Ill.) July 27, 1907; House 1947-49.

JENKINS, Mitchell (R Pa.) Jan. 24, 1896; House 1947-49.

JENKINS, Thomas A. (R Ohio) Oct. 28, 1880-Dec. 21, 1959; House 1925-59.

JENNER, William E. (R Ind.) July 21, 1908; Senate 1944-45; 1947-59.

JENNINGS, John Jr. (R Tenn.) June 6, 1880-Feb. 27, 1956; House 1939-51.

JENNINGS, W. Pat (D Va.) Aug. 20, 1919; House 1955-67; Clerk of House, 1967- .

JENSEN, Ben F. (R Iowa) Dec. 16, 1892; House 1939-65.

JOELSON, Charles S. (D N.J.) Jan. 27, 1916; House 1961- .

JOHANSEN, August E. (R Mich.) July 21, 1905; House 1955-65.

JOHNSON, Albert W. (R Pa.) April 17, 1906; House 1963- .

JOHNSON, Anton Joseph (R Ill.) Oct. 20, 1878-April 16, 1958; House 1939-49.

JOHNSON, Byron L. (D Colo.) Oct. 12, 1917; House 1959-61.

JOHNSON, Edwin C. (D Colo.) Jan. 1, 1884; Senate 1937-55; Gov. 1933-37; 1955-57.

JOHNSON, Glen D. (D Okla.) Sept. 11, 1911; House 1947-49.

JOHNSON, Harold T. (D Calif.) Dec. 2, 1907; House 1959- .

JOHNSON, Hiram W. (R Calif.) Sept. 21, 1866-Aug. 6, 1945; Senate 1917-45; Gov. 1911-17; Vice Presidential Nominee 1912.

JOHNSON, J. Leroy (R Calif.) April 8, 1888-March 26, 1961; House 1943-57.

JOHNSON, Jed Joseph (D Okla.) July 31, 1888-May 8, 1963; House 1929-47.

JOHNSON, Jed Jr. (D Okla.) Dec. 27, 1939; House 1965-67.

JOHNSON, Lester R. (D Wis.) June 16, 1901; House 1953-65.

JOHNSON, Luther A. (D Texas) Oct. 29, 1875-June 7, 1965; House 1923-46.

JOHNSON, Lyndon B. (D Texas) Aug. 27, 1908; House 1937-49; Senate 1949-61; Senate Minority Leader 1953-54; Senate Majority Leader 1955-61; Vice President 1961-63; President 1963-69.

JOHNSON, Noble J. (R Ind.) Aug. 23, 1887-March 17, 1968; House 1939-48; Judge U.S. Court of Customs and Patent Appeals, 1948-56; Chief Judge, 1956-58.

JOHNSON, Thomas F. (D Md.) June 26, 1909; House 1959-63.

JOHNSTON, Olin D. (D S.C.) Nov. 18, 1896-April 18, 1965; Senate 1945-65; Gov. 1935-39; 1943-45.

JONAS, Charles Raper (R N.C.) Dec. 9, 1904; House 1953- .

JONAS, Edgar A. (R Ill.) Aug 14, 1885; House 1949-55.

JONES, Hamilton C. (D N.C.) Sept. 26, 1884-Aug. 10, 1957; House 1947-53.

JONES, Homer R.(R Wash.) Sept. 3, 1893; House 1947-49.

JONES, Paul C. (D Mo.) March 12, 1901; House 1949-69.

JONES, Robert E. (D Ala.) June 12, 1912; House 1947- .

JONES, Robert F. (R Ohio) June 25, 1907-June 22, 1968; House 1939-47.

JONES, Walker B. (D N.C.) Aug. 19, 1913; House 1966- .

JONES, Woodrow W. (D N.C.) Jan. 26, 1914; House 1950-57.

JONKMAN, Bartel J. (R Mich.) Sept. 8, 1896-June 13, 1955; House 1940-49.

JORDAN, B. Everett (D N.C.) Sept. 8, 1896; Senate 1958- .

JORDAN, Len B. (R Idaho) May 15, 1899; Senate 1962- . Gov. 1951-55.

JUDD, Walter H. (R Minn.) Sept. 25, 1898; House 1943-63.

K

KARST, Raymond W. (D Mo.) Dec. 31, 1902; House 1949-51.

KARSTEN, Frank M. (D Mo.) Jan. 7, 1913; House 1947-69.

KARTH, Joseph E. (D Minn.) Aug. 26, 1922; House 1959- .

KASEM, George A. (D Calif.) April 6, 1919; House 1959-61.

KASTENMEIER, Robert W. (D Wis.) Jan. 24, 1924; House 1959- .

KAZEN, Abraham Jr. (D Texas) Jan. 17, 1919; House 1967- .

KEAN, Robert W. (R N.J.) Sept. 28, 1893; House 1939-59.

KEARNEY, Bernard W. (Pat) (R N.Y.) May 23, 1889; House 1943-59.

KEARNS, Carroll D. (R Pa.) May 7, 1900; House 1947-63.

KEATING, Kenneth B. (R N.Y.) May 18, 1900; House 1947-59; Senate 1959-65. Ambassador to India 1969- .

KEE, Elizabeth (D W.Va.) (widow of John Kee); House 1951-65.

KEE, James (D W.Va.) (son of John and Elizabeth Kee) April 15, 1917; House 1965- .

KEE, John (D W.Va) Aug. 22, 1874-May 8, 1951; House 1933-5l.

KEEFE, Frank B. (R Wis.) Sept. 23, 1887-Feb. 5, 1952; House 1938-5l.

KEENEY, Russell W. (R Ill.) Dec. 29, 1895-Jan. 11, 1958; House 1956-58.

KEFAUVER, Estes (D Tenn.) July 26, 1903-Aug. 10, 1963; House 1939-49; Senate 1949-63.

KEITH, Hastings (R Mass.) Nov. 22, 1915; House 1959- .

KELLEY, Augustine B. (D Pa.) July 9, 1883-Nov. 20, 1957; House 1941-57.

KELLY, Edna F. (D N.Y.) Aug. 20 1906; House 1949-69.

KELLY, Edward Austin (D Ill.) April 3, 1892; House 1931-43; 1945-47.

KEM, James P. (R Mo.) April 2, 1890-Feb. 24, 1965; Senate 1947-53.

KENNEDY, Edward M. (D Mass.) Feb. 22, 1932; Senate 1962- . Majority Whip l969- .

KENNEDY, John F. (D Mass.) May 29, 1917-Nov. 22, 1963; House 1947-53; Senate 1953-60; President 1961-63.

KENNEDY, Robert F. (D N.Y.) Nov. 20, 1925-June 5, 1968; U. S. Attorney General 1961-64; Senate 1965-68.

KEOGH, Eugene J. (D N.Y.) Aug. 30 1907; House 1937-67.

KERR, John H. (D N.C.) Dec. 31, 1873-June 21, 1958; House 1923-53.

KERR, Robert S. (D Okla.) Sept. 11, 1896-Jan. 1, 1963; Senate 1949-62; Gov. 1943-47.

KERSTEN, Charles J. (R Wis.) May 26, 1902; House 1947-49; 1951-55.

KILBURN, Clarence E. (R N.Y.) April 13, 1893; House 1940-65.

KILDAY, Paul J. (D Texas) March 29, 1900-Oct. 12, 1968; House 1939-61; U. S. Court of Military Appeals 1961-68.

KILGORE, Harley M. (D W.Va.) Jan. 11, 1893-Feb. 28, 1956; Senate 1941-56.

KILGORE, Joe M. (D Texas) Dec. 10, 1918; House 1955-65.

KING, Carleton J. (R N.Y.) June 15, 1904; House 196l- .

KING, Cecil R. (D Calif.) Jan. 13, 1898; House 1942-69.

KING, David S. (D Utah) June 20, 1917; House 1959-63; 1965-67.

KING, Karl C. (R Pa.) Jan. 26, 1897; House 1952-57.

KINZER, J. Roland (R Pa.) March 28, 1874-June 25, 1955; House 1930-47.

KIRWAN, Michael J. (D Ohio) Dec. 2, 1886; House 1937- .

KITCHIN, A. Paul (D N.C.) Sept. 13, 1908; House 1957-63.

KLEIN, Arthur G. (D N.Y.) Aug. 8, 1904; House July 29, 1941-45; Feb. 10, 1946-Dec. 31, 1956.

KLEPPE, Thomas S. (R N.D.) July 1, 1919; House 1967- .

KLUCZYNSKI, John C. (D Ill.) Feb. 15, 1896; House 1951- .

KNOWLAND, William F. (R Calif.) June 26, 1908; Senate 1945-59; Majority Leader 1953-55; Minority Leader 1955-59.

KNOX, Victor A. (R Mich.) Jan. 13, 1899; House 1953-65.

KNUTSON, Coya (D Minn.) Aug. 22, 1912; House 1955-59.

KNUTSON, Harold (R Minn.) Oct. 20, 1880-Aug. 21, 1953; House 1917-49.

KOCH, Edward I. (D N.Y.) Dec. 12, 1924; House 1969- .

KOPPLEMANN, Herman P. (D Conn.) May 1, 1880-Aug. 11, 1957; House 1941-43; 1945-47.

KORNEGAY, Horace R. (D N.C.) March 12, 1924; House 1961-69.

KOWALSKI, Frank (D Conn.) Oct. 18, 1907; House 1959-63; Member, Subversive Activities Control Board 1963-1966.

KREBS, Paul J. (D N.J.) May 26, 1912; House 1965-67.

KRUEGER, Otto (R N.D.) Sept. 7, 1890-June 10, 1963; House 1953-59.

KRUSE, Edward H. Jr. (D Ind.) Oct. 22, 1918; House 1949-5l.

KUCHEL, Thomas H. (R Calif.) Aug. 15, 1910; Senate 1953-69.

KUNKEL, John C. (R Pa.) July 21, 1898; House 1939-51; 1961-66.

KUPFERMAN, Theodore R. (R N.Y.) May 12, 1920; House 1966-69.

KUYKENDALL, Dan (R Tenn.) July 9, 1924; House 1967- .

KYL, John H. (R Iowa) May 9, 1919; House 1959-65; 1967- .

KYROS, Peter N. (D Maine) July 11, 1925; House 1967- .

L

LaFOLLETTE, Charles M. (R Ind.) Feb. 27, 1898; House 1943-47.

LaFOLLETTE, Robert M. Jr. (Progressive Wis.) Feb. 6, 1895-Feb. 24, 1953; Senate 1925-47 (Republican-Progressive 1925-35).

LAFORE, John A. Jr. (R Pa.) May 25, 1905; House 1958-61.

LAIRD, Melvin R. (R Wis.) Sept. 1, 1922; House 1953-69; Secretary of Defense 1969- .

LAIRD, William R. III (D W.Va.) June 2, 1916; Senate March 13, 1956-Nov. 6, 1956.

LANDGREBE, Earl F. (R Ind.) Jan. 21, 1916; House 1969- .

LANDIS, Gerald W. (R Ind.) Feb. 23, 1895; House 1939-49.

LANDRUM, Phil M. (D Ga.) Sept. 10, 1909; House 1953- .

LANE, Thomas J. (D Mass.) July 16, 1898; House 1941-63.

LANGEN, Odin (R Minn.) Jan. 5, 1913; House 1959- .

LANGER, William (R N.D.) Sept. 30, 1886-Nov. 8, 1959; Senate 1941-59; Gov. 1933-34; 1937-39.

LANHAM, Fritz G. (D Texas) Jan. 3, 1880; House 1919-47.

LANHAM, Henderson (D Ga.) Sept. 14, 1888-Nov. 10, 1957; House 1947-57.

LANKFORD, Richard E. (D Md.) July 22, 1914; House 1955-65.

LANTAFF, William C. (D Fla.) July 31, 1913; House 1951-55.

LARCADE, Henry D. Jr. (D La.) July 12, 1890-March 14, 1966; House 1943-53.

LATHAM, Henry J. (R N.Y.) Dec. 10, 1908; House 1945-59.

LATTA, Delbert L. (R Ohio) March 5, 1920; House 1959- .

LAUSCHE, Frank J. (D Ohio) Nov. 14, 1895; Senate 1957-69; Gov. 1945-47; 1949-57.

LEA, Clarence F. (D Calif.) July 11, 1874-June 21, 1964; House 1917-49.

LEAHY, Edward Laurence (D R.I.) Feb. 9, 1886-July 22, 1953; Senate 1949-50.

LeCOMPTE, Karl M. (R Iowa) May 25, 1887; House 1939-59.

LeFEVRE, Jay (R N.Y.) Sept. 6, 1893; House 1943-5l.

LEGGETT, Robert L. (D Calif.) July 26, 1926; House 1963- .

LEHMAN, Herbert H. (D N.Y.) Feb. 28, 1878-Dec. 5, 1963; Senate 1949-57; Gov. 1933-42; Director General of the UN Relief and Rehabilitation Administration 1943-46.

LEMKE, William (R N.D.) Aug. 13, 1878-May 30, 1950; House 1933-50.

LENNON, Alton (D N.C.) Aug 17, 1906; Senate July 10, 1953-Nov. 28, 1954; House 1957- .

LESINSKI, John (D Mich.) Jan. 3, 1885-May 27, 1950; House 1933-50.

LESINSKI, John Jr. (D Mich.) Dec. 28, 1914; House 1951-65.

LEVERING, Robert W. (D Ohio) Oct. 3, 1914; House 1959-61.

LEWIS, William (R Ky.) Sept. 22, 1868-Aug. 8, 1959; House April 24, 1948-Jan. 3, 1949.

LIBONATI, Roland V. (D Ill.) Dec. 29, 1900; House 1957-65.

LICHTENWALTER, Franklin H. (R Pa.) March 28, 1910; House 1947-51.

LIND, James F. (D Pa.) Oct. 17, 1900; House 1949-53.

LINDSAY, John V. (R N.Y.) Nov. 24, 1921; House 1959-65; Mayor of New York City 1966- .

LINEHAN, Neil J. (D Ill.) Sept. 23, 1895; House 1949-51.

LINK, William W. (D Ill.) Feb. 12, 1894-Sept. 23, 1950; House 1945-47.

LIPSCOMB, Glenard P. (R Calif.) Aug. 19, 1915; House 1953- .

LLOYD, Sherman P. (R Utah) Jan. 11, 1914; House 1963-65; 1967- .

LODGE, Henry Cabot Jr. (R Mass.) July 5, 1902; Senate 1937-44; 1947-53; Representative to UN 1953-60; Vice Presidential nominee 1960; Ambassador to South Vietnam 1963-64; 1965-67; Ambassador to W. Germany 1968-69; Chief U.S. negotiator at Vietnam peace talks, Paris, 1969- .

LODGE, John Davis (R Conn.) Oct. 20, 1903 (brother of Henry Cabot Lodge Jr.); House 1947-51; Gov. 1951-55; U.S. Ambassador to Spain 1955-61.

LONG, Clarence D. (D Md.) Dec. 11, 1908; House 1963- .

LONG, Edward V. (D Mo.) July 18, 1908; Senate 1960-69.

LONG, George S. (D La.) Sept. 11, 1893-March 22, 1958; House 1953-58.

LONG, Gillis W. (D La.) May 4, 1923; House 1963-65.

LONG, Oren E. (D Hawaii) March 4, 1889-May 6, 1965; Senate 1959-63; Gov. 1951-53.

LONG, Russell B. (D La.) Nov. 3, 1918; Senate Majority Whip 1965-69; Senate 1948- .

LONG, Speedy O. (D La.) June 16, 1928; House 1965- .

LOSER, J. Carlton (D Tenn.) Oct. 1, 1892; House 1957-63.

LOVE, Francis J. (R W.Va.) Jan. 23, 1901; House 1947-49.

LOVE, Rodney M. (D Ohio) July 18, 1908; House 1965-67.

LOVRE, Harold O. (R S.D.) Jan. 30, 1904; House 1949-57.

LOWENSTEIN, Allard K. (D N.Y.) Jan. 16, 1929; House 1969- .

LUCAS, Scott W. (D Ill.) Feb. 19, 1892-Feb. 22, 1968; House 1935-39; Senate 1939-51.

LUCAS, Wingate H. (D Texas) May 1, 1908; House 1947-55.

LUCE, Mrs. Clare Boothe (R Conn.) April 10, 1903; House 1943-47; U.S. Ambassador to Italy 1953-57.

LUDLOW, Louis L. (D Ind.) June 24, 1873-Nov. 28, 1950; House 1929-49.

LUJAN, Manuel Jr. (R N.M.) May 12, 1928; House 1969- .

LUKENS, Donald E. (R Ohio) Feb. 11, 1931; House 1967- .

LUSK, Georgia L. (D N.M.) May 12, 1893; House 1947-49.

LUSK, Hall S. (D Ore.) Sept. 21, 1883; Senate March 16, 1960-Nov. 8, 1960.

LYLE, John E. Jr. (D Texas) Sept. 4, 1910; House 1945-55.

LYNCH, Walter A. (D N.Y.) July 7, 1894-Sept. 10, 1957; House 1940-51.

M

MACDONALD, Torbert H. (D Mass.) June 6, 1917; House 1955- .

MacGREGOR, Clark (R Minn.) July 12, 1922; House 1961- .

MACHEN, Hervey G. (D Md.) Oct. 14, 1916; House 1965-69.

MACHROWICZ, Thaddeus M. (D Mich.) Aug. 21, 1899; House 1951-61.

MACK, Peter F. Jr. (D Ill.) Nov. 1, 1916; House 1949-63.

MACK, Russell V. (R Wash.) June 13, 1891-March 28, 1960; House 1947-60.

MACKAY, James A. (D Ga.) June 25, 1919; House 1965-67.

MACKIE, John C. (D Mich.) June 1, 1920; House 1965-67.

MacKINNON, George (R Minn.) April 22, 1906; House 1947-49.

MACY, W. Kingsland (R N.Y.) Nov. 21, 1889-July 15, 1951; House 1947-51.

MADDEN, Ray J. (D Ind.) Feb. 25, 1892; House 1943- .

MAGEE, Clare (D Mo.) March 31, 1899; House 1949-53.

MAGNUSON, Don (D Wash.) March 7, 1911; House 1953-63.

MAGNUSON, Warren G. (D Wash.) April 12, 1905; House 1937-44; Senate 1944- .

MAHON, George H. (D Texas) Sept. 22, 1900, House 1935- .

MAILLIARD, William S. (R Calif.) June 10, 1917; House 1953- .

MALONE, George W. (R Nev.) Aug. 7, 1890-May 19, 1961; Senate 1947-59.

MALONEY, Francis T. (D Conn.) March 31, 1894-Jan. 16, 1945; House 1933-35; Senate 1935-45.

MALONEY, Franklin J. (R Pa.) March 29, 1899-Sept. 15, 1958; House 1947-49.

MALONEY, Paul H. (D La.) Feb. 14, 1876-March 26, 1967; House 1931-40; 1943-47.

MANASCO, Carter (D Ala.) Jan. 3, 1902; House 1941-49.

MANKIN, Helen Douglas (D Ga.) Sept. 11, 1896-July 25, 1956; House 1946-47.

MANN, James R. (D S.C.) April 27, 1920; House 1969- .

MANSFIELD, Joseph J. (D Texas) Feb. 9, 1861-July 12, 1947; House 1917-47.

MANSFIELD, Mike (D Mont.) March 16, 1903; House 1943-53; Senate 1953- ; Senate Majority Whip 1957-61; Senate Majority Leader 1961- .

MARCANTONIO, Vito (American Labor N.Y.) Dec. 10, 1902-Aug. 9, 1954; House 1935-37 (as a Republican); 1939-51.

MARSALIS, John H. (D Colo.) April 9, 1904; House 1949-51.

MARSH, John O. Jr. (D Va.) Aug. 7, 1926; House 1963- .

MARSHALL, Fred (D Minn.) March 13, 1906; House 1949-63.

MARTIN, Dave (R Neb.) July 9, 1907; House 1961- .

MARTIN, Edward (R Pa.) Sept. 18, 1879-March 19, 1967; Senate 1947-59; Gov. 1943-46.

MARTIN, James D. (R Ala.) Sept. 1, 1918; House 1965-67.

MARTIN, Joseph W. Jr. (R Mass.) Nov. 3, 1884-March 6, 1968; House 1925-67; Minority Leader 1940-47; 1949-53; 1955-59; Speaker 1947-49; 1953-55.

MARTIN, Pat Minor (R Calif.) Nov. 25, 1924-July 18, 1968; House 1963-65.

MARTIN, Thomas E. (R Iowa) Jan. 18, 1893; House 1939-55; Senate 1955-6l.

MASON, Noah M. (R Ill.) July 19, 1882-March 28, 1965; House 1937-63.

MATHEWS, Frank A. Jr. (R N.J.) Aug. 3, 1890-Feb. 5, 1964; House 1945-49.

MATHIAS, Charles McC. Jr. (R Md.) July 24, 1922; House 1961- 69; Senate 1969- .

MATHIAS, Robert B. (R Calif.) Nov. 17, 1930; House 1967- .

MATSUNAGA, Spark M. (D Hawaii) Oct. 8, 1916; House 1963- .

MATTHEWS, D. R. (Billy) (D Fla.) Oct. 3, 1907; House 1953-67.

MAY, Andrew J. (D Ky.) June 24, 1875-Sept. 6, 1959; House 1931-47.

MAY, Catherine (R Wash.) May 18, 1914; House 1959- .

MAY, Edwin H. Jr. (R Conn.) May 28, 1924; House 1957-59.

MAYBANK, Burnet R. (D S.C.) March 7, 1899-Sept. 1, 1954; Senate 1941-54; Gov. 1939-4l.

MAYNE, Wiley (R Iowa) Jan. 19, 1917; House 1967- .

McCARRAN, Pat (D Nev.) Aug. 8, 1876-Sept. 28, 1954; Senate 1933-54.

McCARTHY, Eugene J. (D Minn.) March 29, 1916; House 1949-59; Senate 1959- .

McCARTHY, Joseph R. (R Wis.) Nov. 14, 1908-May 2, 1957; Senate 1947-57.

McCARTHY, Richard D. (D N.Y.) Sept. 24, 1927; House 1965- .

McCLELLAN, John L. (D Ark.) Feb. 25, 1896; House 1935-39; Senate 1943- .

McCLORY, Robert (R Ill.) Jan. 31, 1908; House 1963- .

McCLOSKEY, Paul N. Jr. (R Calif.) Sept. 29, 1927; House 1967- .

McCLURE, James A. (R Idaho) Dec. 27, 1924; House 1967- .

McCONNELL, Samuel K. Jr. (R Pa.) April 6, 1901; House 1944-57.

McCORMACK, John W. (D Mass.) Dec. 21, 1891; House 1928- ; Majority Leader 1940-47; 1949-53; 1955-62; Minority Whip 1947-49; 1953-55; Speaker 1962- .

McCOWEN, Edward O. (R Ohio) June 29, 1877-Nov. 4, 1953; House 1943-49.

McCULLOCH, William M. (R Ohio) Nov. 24, 1901; House 1947- .

McDADE, Joseph M. (R Pa.) Sept. 29, 1931; House 1963- .

McDONALD, Jack (R Mich.) June 28, 1932; House 1967- .

McDONOUGH, Gordon L. (R Calif.) Jan. 2, 1895; House 1945-63.

McDOWELL, Harris B. Jr. (D Del.) Feb. 10, 1906; House 1955-57; 1959-67.

McDOWELL, John Ralph (R Pa.) Nov. 6, 1902-Dec. 11, 1957; House 1939-41; 1947-49.

McEWEN, Robert C. (R N.Y.) Jan. 5, 1920; House 1965- .

McFALL, John J. (D Calif.) Feb. 20, 1918; House 1957- .

McFARLAND, Ernest W. (D Ariz.) Oct. 9, 1894; Senate 1941-53; Majority Leader 1951-53; Gov. 1955-59.

McGARVEY, Robert N. (R Pa.) Aug. 14, 1888-June 28, 1952; House 1947-49.

McGEE, Gale W. (D Wyo.) March 17, 1915; Senate 1959- .

McGEHEE, Dan R. (D Miss.) Sept. 10, 1883-Feb. 9, 1962; House 1935-47.

McGINLEY, Donald F. (D Neb.) June 30, 1920; House 1959-61.

McGLINCHEY, Herbert J. (D Pa.) Nov. 7, 1904; House 1945-47.

McGOVERN, George S. (DS.D.) July 19, 1922; House 1957-61; Director, Food-for-Peace Program 1961-62; Senate 1963- .

McGRATH, Christopher C. (D N.Y.) May 15, 1902; House 1949-53.

McGRATH, J. Howard (D R.I.) Nov. 28, 1903-Sept. 2, 1966; Senate 1947-49; Gov. 1941-45; Solicitor General 1945-46; Chairman Democratic National Committee 1947-49; Attorney General 1949-52.

McGRATH, Thomas C. (D N.J.) April 22, 1927; House 1965-67.

McGREGOR, J. Harry (R Ohio) Sept. 30, 1896-Oct. 7, 1958; House 1940-58.

McGUIRE, John A. (D Conn.) Feb. 28, 1906; House 1949-53.

McINTIRE, Clifford G. (R Maine) May 4, 1908; House 1952-65.

McINTOSH, Robert J. (R Mich.) Sept. 16, 1922; House 1957-59.

McINTYRE, Thomas J. (D N.H.) Feb. 20, 1915; Senate 1962- .

McKELLAR, Kenneth D. (D. Tenn.) Jan. 29, 1869-Oct. 25, 1957; House 1911-1917; Senate 1917-53; President pro tempore 1945-47; 1949-53.

McKENZIE, Charles E. (D La.) Oct. 3, 1896-June 7, 1956; House 1943-47.

McKINNON, Clinton D. (D Calif.) Feb. 5, 1906; House 1949-53.

McKNEALLY, Martin B. (R N.Y.) Dec. 31, 1914; House 1969- .

McCLOSKEY, Robert T. (R Ill.) June 26, 1907; House 1963-65.

McMAHON, Brien (D Conn.) Oct. 6, 1903-July 28, 1952; Senate 1945-52.

McMAHON, Gregory (R N.Y.) March 19, 1915; House 1947-49.

McMILLAN, John L. (D S.C.) April 12, 1898; House 1939- .

McMILLEN, Rolla C. (R Ill.) Oct. 5, 1880-May 6, 1961; House 1943-5l.

McMULLEN,Chester B. (D Fla.) Dec. 6, 1902-Nov. 3, 1953; House 1951-53.

McNAMARA, Pat (D Mich.) Oct. 4, 1894-April 30, 1966; Senate 1955-66.

McSWEEN, Harold B. (D La.) July 19, 1926; House 1959-63.

McSWEENEY, John (D Ohio) Dec. 19, 1890; House 1949-51.

McVEY, Walter L. (R Kan.) Feb. 19, 1922; House 1961-63.

McVEY, William E. (R Ill.) Dec. 13, 1885-Aug. 10, 1958; House 1951-58.

McVICKER, Roy H. (D Colo.) Feb. 20, 1924; House 1965- .

MEAD, James M. (D N.Y.) Dec. 27, 1885-March 15, 1964; House 1919-38; Senate 1938-47; Member, Federal Trade Commission, 1949-55, Chairman 1950-53.

MEADE, Hugh A. (D Md.) April 4, 1907; House 1947-49.

MEADE, W. Howes (R Ky.) Jan. 18, 1912; House 1947-49.

MEADER, George (R Mich.) Sept. 13, 1907; House 1951-65.

MECHEM, Edwin L. (R N.M.) July 2, 1912; Gov. 1951-55; 57-59; 61-62; Senate 1962-65.

MEEDS, Lloyd (D Wash.) Dec. 11, 1927; House 1965- .

MERRILL, D. Bailey (R Ind.) Nov. 22, 1912; House 1953-55.

MERROW, Chester E. (R N.H.) Nov. 15, 1906; House 1943-63.

MESKILL, Thomas J. (R Conn.) Jan. 30, 1928; House 1967- .

METCALF, Lee (D Mont.) Jan. 28, 1911; House 1953-61; Senate 1961- .

MEYER, Herbert A. (R Kan.) Aug. 30, 1886-Oct. 2, 1950; House 1947-50.

MEYER, William H. (D Vt.) Dec. 29, 1914; House 1959-61.

MICHEL, Robert H. (R Ill.) March 2, 1923; House 1957- .

MICHENER, Earl C. (R Mich.) Nov. 30, 1876-July 4, 1957; House 1919-33; 1935-51.

MIKVA, Abner J. (D Ill.) Jan. 21, 1926; House 1969- .

MILES, John E. (D N.M.) July 28, 1884; House 1949-51.

MILLER, A. L. (R Neb.) June 24, 1892-April 10, 1967; House 1943-59.

MILLER, Bert H. (D Idaho) Dec. 15, 1879-Oct. 8, 1949; Senate 1949.

MILLER, Clarence E. (R Ohio) Nov. 1, 1917; House 1967- .

MILLER, Clem (D Calif.) Oct. 28, 1961-Oct. 6, 1962; House 1959-62.

MILLER, Edward T. (R Md.) Feb. 1, 1895-Jan. 20, 1968; House 1947-59.

MILLER, George P. (D Calif.) Jan. 15, 1891; House 1945- .

MILLER, Howard S. (D Kan.) Feb. 27, 1879; House 1953-55.

MILLER, Jack (R Iowa) June 6, 1916; Senate 1961- .

MILLER, Ward MacLaughlin (R Ohio- Nov. 29, 1902; House 1960-61.

MILLER, William E. (R N.Y.) March 22, 1914; House 1951-65; Chairman, Republican National Committee 1961-64; Republican Vice Presidential candidate 1964.

MILLER, William J. (R Conn.) March 12, 1899-Nov. 22, 1950; House 1939-41; 1943-45; 1947-49.

MILLIKIN, Eugene D. (R Colo.) Feb. 12, 1891-July 26, 1958; Senate 1941-57.

MILLIKEN, William H. Jr. (R Pa.) Oct. 19, 1897-July 4, 1969; House 1959-65.

MILLS, Wilbur D. (D Ark.) May 24, 1909; House 1939- .

MINISH, Joseph G. (D N.J.) Sept. 1, 1916; House 1963- .

MINK, Patsy T. (D Hawaii) Dec. 6, 1927; House 1965- .

MINSHALL, William E. (R Ohio) Oct. 24, 1911; House 1955- .

MITCHELL, E. A. (R Ind.) Dec. 2, 1910; House 1947-49.

MITCHELL, Erwin (D Ga.) Oct. 17, 1924; House 1958-61.

MITCHELL, Hugh B. (D Wash.) March 22, 1907; Senate 1945-46; House 1949-53.

MIZE, Chester L. (R Kan.) Dec. 25, 1917; House 1965- .

MIZELL, Wilmer D. (R N.C.) Aug. 13, 1930; House 1969- .

MOELLER, Walter H. (D Ohio) March 15, 1910; House 1959-63; 1965-67.

MOLLOHAN, Robert H. (D W.Va.) Sept. 18, 1909; House 1953-57; 1969- .

MONAGAN, John S. (D Conn.) March 26, 1906; House 1959- .

MONDALE, Walter F. (D Minn.) Jan. 5, 1928; Senate 1965- .

MONRONEY, A.S. Mike (D Okla.) March 2, 1902; House 1939-51; Senate 1951-69.

MONTGOMERY, G. V. (D Miss.) Aug. 5, 1920; House 1967- .

MONTOYA, Joseph M. (D N.M.) Sept. 24, 1915; House 1957-65; Senate 1965- .

MOODY, Blair (D Mich.) Feb. 13, 1902-July 20, 1954; Senate April 23, 1951-Nov. 4, 1952.

MOORE, Arch A. Jr. (R W.Va.) April 16, 1923; House 1957-69; Gov. 1969- .

MOORE, E. H. (R Okla.) Nov. 19, 1871-Sept. 2, 1950; Senate 1943-49.

MOOREHEAD, Tom V. (R Ohio) April 12, 1898; House 1961-63.

MOORHEAD, William S. (D Pa.) April 8, 1923; House 1959- .

MORANO, Albert P. (R Conn.) Jan. 18, 1908; House 1951-59.

MORGAN, Thomas E. (D Pa.) Oct. 13, 1906; House 1945- .

MORRIS, Thomas G. (D N.M.) Aug. 20, 1919; House 1959-69.

MORRIS, Toby (D Okla.) Feb. 28, 1899; House 1957-61.

MORRISON, James H. (D La.) Dec. 8, 1908; House 1943-67.

MORSE, F. Bradford (R Mass.) Aug. 7, 1921; House 1961- .

MORSE, Wayne (D Ore.) Oct. 20, 1900; Senate 1945-69. Republican 1945-Oct. 24, 1952; Independent Oct. 24, 1952-Feb. 17, 1955; Democrat Feb. 17, 1955-69.

MORTON, Rogers C.B. (R Md.) Sept. 19, 1914; House 1963- ; Chairman, Republican National Committee 1969- .

MORTON, Thruston B. (R Ky.) Aug. 19, 1907; House 1947-53; Senate 1957-68; Chairman, Republican National Committee 1959-61.

MOSES, John (D N.D.) June 12, 1885-March 3, 1945; Senate Jan. 3, 1945-March 3, 1945; Gov. 1939-44.

MOSHER, Charles A. (R Ohio) May 7, 1906; House 1961- .

MOSS, Frank E. (D Utah) Sept. 23, 1911; Senate 1959- .

MOSS, John E. (D Calif.) April 13, 1913; House 1953- .

MOTT, James W. (R Ore.) Nov. 12, 1883-Nov. 12, 1945; House 1933-45.

MOULDER, Morgan M. (D Mo.) Aug. 31, 1904; House 1949-63.

MUHLENBERG, Frederick A. (R Pa.) Sept. 25, 1887; House 1947-49.

MULTER, Abraham J. (D N.Y.) Dec. 24, 1900; House 1947-68.

MUMMA, Walter M. (R Pa.) Nov. 20, 1890-Nov. 25, 1961; House 1951-61.

MUNDT, Karl E. (R S.D.) June 3, 1900; House 1939-48; Senate 1948- .

MURDOCK, Abe (D Utah) July 8, 1893; House 1933-41; Senate 1941-47; Member, National Labor Relations Board 1947-57.

MURDOCK, John R. (D Ariz.) April 20, 1885; House 1937-53.

MURPHY, George (R Calif.) July 4, 1902; Senate 1965- .

MURPHY, James J. (D N.Y.) Nov. 3, 1898-Oct. 19, 1962; House 1949-53.

MURPHY, John M. (D N.Y.) Aug. 3, 1926; House 1963- .

MURPHY, John William (D Pa.) April 26, 1902; House 1943-46.

MURPHY, Maurice J. Jr. (R N.H.) Oct. 3, 1927; Senate Dec. 7, 1961-62.

MURPHY, William T. (D Ill.) Aug. 7, 1899; House 1959- .

MURRAY, James C. (D Ill.) April 16, 1917; House 1955-57.

MURRAY, James E. (D Mont.) May 3, 1876-March 23, 1961; Senate 1934-61.

MURRAY, Reid F. (R Wis.) Oct. 16, 1887-April 29, 1952; House 1939-52.

MURRAY, Tom (D Tenn.) Oct. 1, 1894; House 1943-66.

MUSKIE, Edmund S. (D Maine) March 28, 1914; Senate 1959- ; Gov. 1955-59; Democratic Vice Presidential candidate 1968.

MYERS, Francis J. (D Pa.) Dec. 18, 1901-July 5, 1956; House 1939-45; Senate 1945-5l.

MYERS, John T. (R Ind.) Feb. 8, 1927; House 1967- .

N

NATCHER, William H. (D Ky.) Sept. 11, 1909; House 1953- .

NEAL, Will E. (R W.Va.) Oct. 14, 1875-Nov. 12, 1959; House 1953-55; 1957-59.

NEDZI, Lucien N. (D Mich.) April 28, 1925; House Nov. 7, 1961- .

NEELY, Matthew M. (D W.Va.) Nov. 9, 1874-Jan. 18, 1958; House 1913-21; 1945-47; Senate 1923-29; 1931-41; 1949-58; Gov. 1941-45.

NELSEN, Ancher (R Minn.) Oct. 11, 1904; House 1959- .

NELSON, Charles P. (R Maine) July 2, 1907-June 8, 1962; House 1949-57.

NELSON, Gaylord A. (D Wis.) June 4, 1916; Gov. 1959-63; Senate 1963- .

NEUBERGER, Maurine B. (D Ore.) Jan. 9, 1907 (widow of Richard L. Neuberger); Senate Nov. 9, 1960-67.

NEUBERGER, Richard L. (D Ore.) Dec. 26, 1912-March 9, 1960; Senate 1955-60.

NICHOLS, William (D Ala.) Oct. 16, 1918; House 1967- .

NICHOLSON, Donald W. (R Mass.) July 11, 1888-Feb. 16, 1968; House 1947-59.

NIMITZ, F. Jay (R Ind.) Dec. 1, 1915; House 1957-59.

NIX, Robert N.C. (D Pa.) July 9, 1905; House 1958- .

NIXON, Richard M. (R Calif.) Jan. 9, 1913; House 1947-50; Senate 1950-53; Vice President 1953-61; Republican nominee for President 1960; President 1969- .

NODAR, Robert Jr. (R N.Y.) March 23, 1916; House 1947-49.

NOLAND, James E. (D Ind.) April 22, 1920; House 1949-51.

NORBLAD, Walter (R Ore.) Sept. 12, 1908-Sept. 20, 1964; House 1946-64.

NORMAN, Fred (R Wash.) March 21, 1882-April 18, 1947; House 1943-45; 1947.

NORRELL, Mrs. Catherine D. (D Ark.) March 30, 1901 (widow of W. F. Norrell); House April 25, 1961-63.

NORRELL, W.F. (D Ark.) Aug. 29, 1896-Feb. 15, 1961; House 1939-61.

NORTON, Mary T. (D N.J.) March 7, 1875-Aug. 2, 1959; House 1925-51.

NYGAARD, Hjalmar C. (R N.D.) March 24, 1906-July 18, 1963. House 1961-63.

O

OAKMAN, Charles G. (R Mich.) Sept. 4, 1903; House 1953-55.

O'BRIEN, George D. (D Mich.) Jan. 1, 1900-July 11, 1955; House 1937-39; 1941-47; 1949-55.

O'BRIEN, Leo W. (D N.Y.) Sept. 21, 1900; House 1952-66.

O'BRIEN, Thomas J. (D Ill.) April 30, 1878-April 14, 1964; House 1933-37; 1943-64.

O'CONNOR, Herbert R. (D Md.) Nov. 17, 1896-March 4, 1960; Senate 1947-53; Gov. 1939-46.

O'CONNOR, James F. (D Mont.) May 7, 1878-Jan. 15, 1945; House 1937-45.

O'DANIEL, W. Lee (D Texas) March 11, 1890; Senate 1941-1949; Gov. 1939-41.

O'HARA, Barratt (D Ill.) April 28, 1882-Aug. 11, 1969; House 1949-51; 1953-69.

O'HARA, James G. (D Mich.) Nov. 8, 1925; House 1959- .

O'HARA, Joseph P. (R Minn.) Jan. 23, 1895; House 1941-59.

O'KONSKI, Alvin E. (R Wis.) May 26, 1904; House 1943- .

OLIVER, James C. (D Maine) Aug. 6, 1895; House 1937-43; 1959-61.

OLSEN, Arnold (D Mont.) Dec. 17, 1961; House 1961- .

OLSON, Alec G. (D Minn.) Sept. 11, 1930; House 1963-67.

O'MAHONEY, Joseph C. (D Wyo.) Nov. 5, 1885-Dec. 1, 1962; Senate 1934-53; 1954-61.

O'NEAL, Emmet (D Ky.) April 14, 1887-July 18, 1967; House 1935-47; Ambassador to the Philippines 1947-49.

O'NEAL, Maston (D Ga.) July 19, 1907; House 1935-47.

O'NEILL, Harry P. (D Pa.) Feb. 10, 1889-June 24, 1953; House 1949-53.

O'NEILL, Thomas P. Jr. (D Mass.) Dec. 9, 1912; House 1953- .

OSMERS, Frank C. Jr. (R N.J.) Dec. 30, 1907; House 1939-43; 1951-65.

OSTERTAG, Harold C. (R N.Y.) June 22, 1896; House 1951-65.

O'SULLIVAN, Eugene D. (D Neb.) May 31, 1883-Feb. 8, 1968; House 1949-51.

O'TOOLE, Donald L. (D N.Y.) Aug. 1, 1902-Sept. 13, 1964; House 1937-53.

OTTINGER, Richard L. (D N.Y.) Jan. 27, 1929; House 1965- .

OUTLAND, George E. (D Calif.) Oct. 8, 1906; House 1943-47.

OVERTON, John H. (D La.) Sept. 17, 1875-May 14, 1948; House 1931-33; Senate 1933-48.

OWENS, Thomas L. (R Ill.) Dec. 21, 1897-June 7, 1948; House 1947-48.

P

PACE, Stephen (D Ga.) March 9, 1891; House 1937-51.

PACKWOOD, Robert W. (R Ore.) Sept. 11, 1932; Senate 1969- .

PASSMAN, Otto E. (D La.) June 27, 1900; House 1947- .

PASTORE, John O. (D R.I.) March 17, 1907; Senate 1950- ; Gov. 1945-50.

PATMAN, Wright (D Texas) Aug. 6, 1893; House 1929- .

PATRICK, Luther (D Ala.) Jan. 23, 1894-May 26, 1957; House 1937-43; 1945-47.

PATTEN, Edward J. (D N.J.) Aug. 22, 1905; House 1963- .

PATTEN, Harold A. (D Ariz.) Oct. 6, 1907; House 1949-55.

PATTERSON, Ellis E. (D Calif.) Nov. 28, 1897; House 1945-47.

PATTERSON, James T. (R Conn.) Oct. 20, 1908; House 1947-59.

PAYNE, Frederick G. (R Maine) July 7, 1900; Senate 1953-59; Gov. 1949-53.

PEARSON, James B. (R Kan.) May 7, 1920; Senate 1962- .

PEDEN, Preston E. (D Okla.) June 28, 1914; House 1947-49.

PELL, Claiborne (D R.I.) Nov. 22, 1918; Senate 1961- .

PELLY, Thomas M. (R Wash.) Aug. 22, 1902; House 1953- .

PEPPER, Claude (D Fla.) Sept. 8, 1900; Senate 1936-51; House 1963- .

PERCY, Charles H. (R Ill.) Sept. 27, 1919; Senate 1967- .

PERKINS, Carl D. (D Ky.) Oct. 15, 1912; House 1949- .

PETERSON, Hugh (D Ga.) Aug. 21, 1898-Oct. 3, 1961; House 1935-47.

PETERSON, J. Hardin (D Fla.) Feb. 11, 1894; House 1933-51.

PETERSON, M. Blaine (D Utah) March 26, 1906; House 1961-63.

PETTIS, Jerry L. (R Calif.) July 18, 1916; House 1967- .

PFEIFER, Joseph Lawrence (D N.Y.) Feb. 6, 1892; House 1935-51.

PFEIFFER, William L. (R N.Y.) May 29, 1907; House 1949-5l.

PFOST, Gracie (D Idaho) March 12, 1960-Aug. 11, 1965; House 1953-63.

PHILBIN, Philip J. (D Mass.) May 29, 1898; House 1943- .

PHILLIPS, Dayton E. (R Tenn.) March 29, 1910; House 1947-51.

PHILLIPS, John (R Calif.) Sept. 11, 1887; House 1943-57.

PICKETT, Tom (D Texas) Aug. 14, 1906; House 1945-52.

PICKLE, J. J. (D Texas) Oct. 11, 1913; House 1963- .

PIKE, Otis G. (D N.Y.) Aug. 31, 1921; House 1961- .

PILCHER, J.L. (D Ga.) Aug. 27, 1898; House 1953-65.

PILLION, John R. (R N.Y.) Aug. 10, 1904; House 1953-65.

PINERO, Jesus T. (Puerto Rico) April 16, 1897-Dec. 19, 1952; Resident Commissioner 1945-46; Gov. of Puerto Rico 1946-48.

PIRNIE, Alexander (R N.Y.) April 16, 1903; House 1959- .

PITTENGER, William A. (R Minn.) Dec. 29, 1885-Nov. 26, 1951; House 1929-33; 1935-37; 1939-47.

PLOESER, Walter C. (R Mo.) Jan. 7, 1907; House 1941-49.

PLUMLEY, Charles A. (R Vt.) April 14, 1875-Oct. 31, 1964; House 1934-51.

POAGE, W.R. (D Texas) Dec. 28, 1899; House 1937- .

PODELL, Bertram L. (D N.Y.) Dec. 27, 1925; House 1968- .

POFF, Richard H. (R Va.) Oct. 19, 1923; House 1953- .

POLANCO-ABREU, Santiago (Pop. Dem P.R.) Oct. 30, 1920; Resident Commissioner, House 1965-69.

POLK, James G. (D Ohio) Oct. 6, 1896-April 28, 1959; House 1931-41; 1949-59.

POLLOCK, Howard W. (R Alaska) April 11, 1920; House 1967- .

POOL, Joe R. (D Texas) Feb. 18, 1911-July 14, 1968; House 1963-68.

PORTER, Charles O. (D Ore.) April 4, 1919; House 1957-61.

POTTER, Charles E. (R Mich.) Oct. 30, 1916; House 1947-52; Senate 1952-59.

POTTS, David M. (R N.Y.) March 12, 1906; House 1947-49.

POULSON, Norris (R Calif.) July 23, 1895; House 1943-45; 1947-53; Mayor of Los Angeles 1953-61.

POWELL, Adam C. (D N.Y.) Nov. 29, 1908; House 1945- .

POWERS, D. Lane (R N.J.) July 29, 1896; House 1943-45.

PRATT, Eliza Jane (D N.C.) March 5, 1902; House 1946-47.

PRESTON, Prince H. Jr. (D Ga.) July 5, 1908-Feb. 8, 1961; House 1947-61.

PREYER, L. Richardson (D N.C.) Jan. 11, 1919; House 1969- .

PRICE, Emory H. (D Fla.) Dec. 3, 1899; House 1943-49.

PRICE, Melvin (D Ill.) Jan. 1, 1905; House 1945- .

PRICE, Robert D. (R Texas) Sept. 7, 1927; House 1967- .

PRIEST, J. Percy (D Tenn.) April 1, 1900-Oct. 12, 1956; House 1941-56.

PROKOP, Stanley A. (D Pa.); House 1959-61.

PROUTY, Winston L. (R Vt.) Sept. 1, 1906; House 1951-59; Senate 1959- .

PROXMIRE, William (D Wis.) Nov. 11, 1915; Senate 1957- .

PRYOR, David (D Ark.) Aug. 29, 1934; House 1966- .

PUCINSKI, Roman C. (D Ill.) May 13, 1919; House 1959- .

PURCELL, Graham (D Texas) May 15, 1919; House Jan. 29, 1962- .

PURTELL, William A. (R Conn.) May 6, 1897; Senate 1952-59.

Q

QUIE, Albert H. (R Minn.) Sept. 18, 1923; House 1958- .

QUIGLEY, James M. (D Pa.) March 30, 1918; House 1955-57; 1959-61; Assistant Secretary of Health, Education and Welfare for Federal and State matters 1961-66.

QUILLEN, James H. (R Tenn.) Jan. 11, 1916; House 1963-.

QUINN, Peter A. (D N.Y.) May 10, 1904; House 1945-47.

QUINN, T. Vincent (D N.Y.) March 16, 1903; House 1949-51.

R

RABAUT, Louis C. (D Mich.) Dec. 5, 1886-Nov. 12, 1961; House 1935-47; 1949-61.

RABIN, Benjamin J. (D N.Y.) June 3, 1896; House 1945-47.

RACE, John A. (D Wis.) May 12, 1914; House 1965-67.

RADCLIFFE, George L. (D Md.) Aug. 22, 1877; Senate 1935-47.

RADWAN, Edmund P. (R N.Y.) Sept. 22, 1911-Sept. 7, 1959; House 1951-59.

RAILSBACK, Tom (R Ill.) Jan. 22, 1932; House 1967- .

RAINS, Albert (D Ala.) March 11, 1902; House 1945-65.

RAMEY, Homer A. (R Ohio) March 2, 1891-April 13, 1960; House 1943-49.

RAMSAY, Robert L. (D W.Va.) March 24, 1877-Nov. 14, 1956; House 1933-39; 1941-43; 1949-53.

RAMSPECK, Robert (D Ga.) Sept. 5, 1890; House 1929-45; Majority Whip 1943-45.

RANDALL, William J. (D Mo.) July 16, 1909; House 1959- .

RANDOLPH, Jennings (D W.Va.) March 8, 1902; House 1933-47; Senate 1958- .

RANKIN, John E. (D Miss.) March 29, 1882-Nov. 29, 1960; House 1921-53.

RARICK, John R. (D La.) Jan. 29, 1924; House 1967- .

RAY, John H. (R N.Y.) Sept. 27, 1886; House 1953-63.

RAYBURN, Sam (D Texas) Jan. 6, 1882-Nov. 16, 1961; House 1913-61; Majority Leader 1937-40; Minority Leader 1947-49, 1953-55; Speaker 1940-47, 1949-53, 1955-61.

RAYFIEL, Leo F. (D N.Y.) March 22, 1888; House 1945-47.

REAMS, Frazier (Ind. Ohio) Jan. 15, 1897; House 1951-55.

REDDEN, Monroe M. (D N.C.) Sept. 24, 1901; House 1947-53.

REDLIN, Rolland (D N.D.) Feb. 29, 1920; House 1965- .

REECE, B. Carroll (R Tenn.) Dec. 22, 1889-March 19, 1961; House 1921-31; 1935-47; 1951-61; Chairman, Republican National Committee 1946-48.

REECE, Louise Goff (R Tenn.) Nov. 6, 1898 (widow of B. Carroll Reece); House 1961-63.

REED, Chauncey W. (R Ill.) June 2, 1890-Feb. 9, 1956; House 1935-56.

REED, Clyde M. (R Kan.) Oct. 19, 1871-Nov. 8, 1949; Senate 1939-49.

REED, Daniel A. (R N.Y.) Sept. 15, 1875-Feb. 19, 1959; House 1919-59.

REES, Edward H. (R Kan.) June 3, 1886; House 1937-61.

REES, Thomas M. (D Calif.) March 26, 1925; House 1966- .

REEVES, Albert L. Jr. (R Mo.) May 31, 1906; House 1947-49.

REGAN, Kenneth (D Texas) March 6, 1893-Aug. 15, 1959; House 1947-55.

REID, Charlotte T. (R Ill.) Sept. 27, 1913; House 1963- .

REID, Ogden R. (R N.Y.) June 24, 1925; U.S. Ambassador to Israel 1959-61; House 1963- .

REIFEL, Ben (R S.D.) Sept. 19, 1906; House 1961- .

REINECKE, Edwin (R Calif.) Jan. 7, 1924; House 1965-69; Lt. Gov. 1969- .

RESA, Alexander J. (D Ill.) Aug. 4, 1887; House 1945-47.

RESNICK, Joseph Y. (D N.Y.) July 13, 1924; House 1965-69.

REUSS, Henry S. (D Wis.) Feb. 22, 1912; House 1955- .

REVERCOMB, Chapman (R W. Va.) July 20, 1895; Senate 1943-49; 1956-59.

REYNOLDS, Sam W. (R Neb.) Aug. 11, 1890; Senate July 3, 1954-Nov. 7, 1954.

RHODES, George M. (D Pa.) Feb. 24, 1898; House 1949-69.

RHODES, John J. (R Ariz.) Sept. 18, 1916; House 1953- .

RIBICOFF, Abraham A. (D Conn.) April 9, 1910; House 1949-53; Gov. 1955-61; Secretary of Health, Education and Welfare 1961-62; Senate 1963- .

RICH, Carl W. (R Ohio) Sept. 12, 1898; House 1963-65.

RICH, Robert F. (R Pa.) June 23, 1883-April 28, 1968; House 1930-43; 1945-51.

RICHARDS, James P. (D S.C.) Aug. 31, 1894; House 1933-57; Special Assistant to President Eisenhower 1957-58.

RIEGLE, Donald W. Jr. (R Mich.) Feb. 4, 1938; House 1967- .

RIEHLMAN, R. Walter (R N.Y.) Aug. 26, 1899; House 1947-65.

RILEY, Corinne Boyd (D S.C.) July 4, 1894 (widow of John J. Riley); House 1962-63.

RILEY, John J. (D S.C.) Feb. 1, 1895-Jan. 2, 1962; House 1945-49; 1951-62.

RIVERS, L. Mendel (D S.C.) Sept. 28, 1905; House 1941- .

RIVERS, Ralph J. (D Alaska) May 23, 1903; House 1959-67; Territorial Delegate 1957-59.

RIZLEY, Ross (R Okla.) July 5, 1892-March 4, 1969; House 1941-49.

ROBERTS, Kenneth A. (D Ala.) Nov. 1, 1912; House 1951-65.

ROBERTS, Ray (D Texas) March 28, 1913; House 1962- .

ROBERTSON, A. Willis (D Va.) May 27, 1887; House 1933-46; Senate 1946-66.

ROBERTSON, Charles R. (R N.D.) Sept. 5, 1889-Feb. 18, 1951; House 1941-43; 1945-49.

ROBERTSON, Edward V. (R Wyo.) May 27, 1881-April 16, 1963; Senate 1943-49.

ROBESON, Edward J. Jr. (D Va.) July 9, 1890-March 10, 1966; House 1950-59.

ROBINSON, J. W. (D Utah) Jan. 19, 1878-Dec. 2, 1964; House 1933-47.

ROBISON, Howard W. (R N.Y.) Oct. 30, 1915; House 1958- .

ROBSION, John M. (R Ky.) Jan. 2, 1873-Feb. 17, 1948; House 1919-30; 1935-48; Senate Jan. 11, 1930-Nov. 30, 1930.

ROBSION, John M. Jr. (R Ky.) Aug. 28, 1904; House 1953-59.

ROCKWELL, Robert F. (R Colo.) Feb. 11, 1886-Sept. 29, 1950; House 1941-49.

RODGERS, Robert Lewis (R Pa.) June 2, 1875-May 9, 1960; House 1939-47.

RODINO, Peter W. Jr. (D N.J.) June 7, 1909; House 1949- .

ROE, Dudley G. (D Md.) March 23, 1881; House 1945-47.

ROE, James A. (D N.Y.) July 9, 1896-April 22, 1967; House 1945-47.

ROGERS, Byron G. (D Colo.) Aug. 1, 1900; House 1951- .

ROGERS, Dwight L. (D Fla.) Aug. 17, 1886-Dec. 1, 1954; House 1945-54.

ROGERS, Edith Nourse (R Mass.) 1881-Sept. 10, 1960; House 1925-60.

ROGERS, George F. (D N.Y.) March 19, 1887-Nov. 20, 1948; House 1945-47.

ROGERS, Paul G. (D Fla.) June 4, 1921 (son of Dwight L. Rogers); House 1955- .

ROGERS, Walter (D Texas) July 19, 1908; House 1951-67.

ROHRBOUGH, Edward G. (R W. Va.) 1874-Dec. 12, 1956; House 1943-45; 1947-49.

ROMULO, Carlos P. (Philippines) Jan. 14, 1901; Resident Commissioner to the U.S. 1944-46; Philippine delegate to UN 1946; Philippine Ambassador to U.S. 1952-53; 1955-62.

RONAN, Daniel J. (D Ill.) July 13, 1914-Aug. 13, 1969; House 1965-69.

RONCALIO, Teno (D Wyo.) March 23, 1916; House 1965-67.

ROONEY, Fred B. (D Pa.) Nov. 6, 1925; House 1963- .

ROONEY, John J. (D N.Y.) Nov. 29, 1903; House 1944- .

ROOSEVELT, Franklin D. Jr. (D N.Y.) Aug. 17, 1914; House 1949-55. Under Secretary of Commerce 1963-65; Chairman, Equal Employment Opportunities Commission 1965-66.

ROOSEVELT, James (D Calif.) Dec. 23, 1907; House 1955-65; U.S. Rep. to UN Economic and Social Council 1965-67.

ROSENTHAL, Benjamin S. (D N.Y.) June 8, 1923; House 1962- .

ROSS, Robert Tripp (R N.Y.) June 4, 1903; House 1947-49; 1952-53.

ROSTENKOWSKI, Dan (D Ill.) Jan. 2, 1928; House 1959- .

ROTH, William V. Jr. (R Del.) July 22, 1921; House 1967- .

ROUDEBUSH, Richard L. (R Ind.) Jan. 18, 1918; House 1961- .

ROUSH, J. Edward (D Ind.) Sept. 12, 1920; House 1959-69.

ROUSSELOT, John H. (R Calif.) Nov. 1, 1927; House 1961-63.

ROWAN, William A. (D Ill.) Nov. 24, 1882-June 31, 1961, House 1943-47.

ROYBAL, Edward R. (D Calif.) Feb. 10, 1916; House 1963- .

RUMSFELD, Donald (R Ill.) July 9, 1932; House 1963-69. Director, Office of Economic Opportunity 1969- .

RUPPE, Philip E. (R Mich.) Sept. 29, 1926; House 1967- .

RUSSELL, Charles H. (R Nev.) Dec. 27, 1903; House 1947-49; Gov. 1951-59.

RUSSELL, Donald S. (D S.C.) Feb. 22, 1906; Senate 1965-66; Gov. 1963-65.

RUSSELL, Richard B. (D Ga.) Nov. 2, 1897; Senate 1933- ; Gov. 1931-33.

RUSSELL, Sam M. (D Texas) Aug. 9, 1889; House 1941-47.

RUTH, Earl B. (R N.C.) Feb. 7, 1916; House 1969- .

RUTHERFORD, J. T. (D Texas) May 30, 1920; House 1955-63.

RYAN, Harold M. (D Mich.) Feb. 6, 1911; House 1962-65.

RYAN, William F. (D N.Y.) June 28, 1922; House 1961- .

RYTER, Joseph F. (D Conn.) Feb. 4, 1914; House 1945-47.

S

SABATH, Adolph J. (D Ill.) April 4, 1866-Nov. 6, 1952; House 1907-52.

SADLAK, Antoni N. (R Conn.) June 13, 1908; House 1947-59.

SADOWSKI, George G. (D Mich.) March 12, 1903-Oct. 9, 1961; House 1933-39; 1943-51.

ST. GEORGE, Katharine (R N.Y.) July 12, 1896; House 1947-65.

ST. GERMAIN, Fernand J. (D R.I.) Jan. 9, 1928; House 1961- .

ST. ONGE, William L. (D Conn.) Oct. 9, 1914; House 1963- .

SALTONSTALL, Leverett (R Mass.) Sept. 1, 1892; Senate 1945-67; Gov. 1939-44.

SANBORN, John (R Idaho) Sept. 28, 1885-May 16, 1968; House 1947-51.

SANDMAN, Charles W. Jr. (R N.J.) Oct. 23, 1921; House 1967- .

SANTANGELO, Alfred F. (D N.Y.) June 4, 1912; House 1957-63.

SARBACHER, George W. Jr. (R Pa.) Sept. 30, 1919; House 1947-49.

SASSCER, Lansdale G. (D Md.) Sept. 30, 1893-Nov. 6, 1964; House 1939-53.

SATTERFIELD, David E. Jr. (D Va.) Sept. 11, 1894-Dec. 27, 1946; House 1937-45.

SATTERFIELD, David E. III (D Va.) (son of David E. Satterfield, Jr.) Dec. 2, 1920; House 1965- .

SAUND, D.S. (D Calif.) Sept. 20, 1899; House 1957-63.

SAVAGE, Charles R. (D Wash.) April 12, 1906; House 1945-47.

SAXBE, William B. (R Ohio) June 24, 1916; Senate 1969- .

SAYLOR, John P. (R Pa.) July 23, 1908; House 1949- .

SCHADEBERG, Henry C. (R Wis.) Oct. 12, 1913; House 1961-65; 1967- .

SCHENCK, Paul F. (R Ohio) April 19, 1899-Nov. 30, 1968; House 1951-65.

SCHERER, Gordon H. (R Ohio) Dec. 26, 1906; House 1953-63.

SCHERLE, William J. (R Iowa) March 14, 1923; House 1967- .

SCHEUER, James H. (D N.Y.) Feb. 6, 1920; House 1965- .

SCHISLER, Gale (D Ill.) March 2, 1933; House 1965-67.

SCHMIDHAUSER, John R. (D Iowa) Jan. 3, 1922; House 1965-67.

SCHNEEBELI, Herman T. (R Pa.) July 7, 1907; House 1960- .

SCHOEPPEL, Andrew F. (R Kan.) Nov. 23, 1894-Jan. 21, 1962; Senate 1949-62; Gov. 1943-47.

SCHWABE, George B. (R Okla.) July 26, 1886-April 2, 1952; House 1945-49; 1951-52.

SCHWABE, Max (R Mo.) Dec. 6, 1905; House 1943-49.

SCHWEIKER, Richard S. (R Pa.) June 1, 1926; House 1961-69; Senate 1969- .

SCHWENGEL, Fred (R Iowa) May 28, 1907; House 1955-65; 1967- .

SCOBLICK, James Paul (R Pa.) May 10, 1909; House 1946-1949.

SCOTT, Hardie (R Pa.) June 7, 1907; House 1947-53.

SCOTT, Hugh (R Pa.) Nov. 11, 1900; House 1941-45; 1947-49; Senate 1949- ; Chairman of Republican National Committee 1948-49.

SCOTT, Ralph J. (D N.C.) Oct. 15, 1905; House 1957-67.

SCOTT, W. Kerr (D N.C.) April 17, 1896-April 16, 1958; Senate 1954-58.

SCOTT, William L. (R Va.) July 1, 1915; House 1967- .

SCRANTON, William W. (R Pa.) July 19, 1917; House 1961-63. Gov. 1963-67.

SCRIVNER, Errett P. (R Kan.) March 20, 1898; House 1943-59.

SCRUGHAM, James G. (D Nev.) Jan. 19, 1880-June 23, 1945; House 1933-42; Senate 1942-45; Gov. 1923-27.

SCUDDER, Hubert B. (R Calif.) Nov. 5, 1888-July 4, 1968; House 1949-59.

SEATON, Frederick A. (R Neb.) Dec. 11, 1909; Senate Dec. 10, 1951-Nov. 4, 1952; Asst. Secretary of Defense 1953-55; Administrative Asst. to President Eisenhower 1955; Secretary of Interior 1956-61.

SEBELIUS, Keith G. (R Kan.) Sept. 10, 1916; House 1969- .

SECREST, Robert T. (D Ohio) Jan. 22, 1904; House 1949-54; 1963-66.

SEELY-BROWN, Horace Jr. (R Conn.) May 12, 1908; House 1947-49; 1951-59; 1961-63.

SELDEN, Armistead I. Jr. (D Ala.) Feb. 20, 1921; House 1953-69.

SENNER, George F. Jr. (D Ariz.) Nov. 24, 1921; House 1963-67.

SHAFER, Paul W. (R Mich.) April 27, 1893-Aug. 17, 1954; House 1937-54.

SHARP, Edgar A. (R N.Y.) June 3, 1876-Nov. 27, 1948; House 1945-47.

SHEEHAN, Timothy P. (R Ill.) Feb. 21, 1909; House 1951-59.

SHELLEY, John F. (D Calif.) Sept. 3, 1905; House 1949-64; Mayor of San Francisco 1964-68.

SHEPPARD, Harry R. (D Calif.) Jan. 10, 1885-April 28, 1969; House 1937-65.

SHERIDAN, John Edward (D Pa.) Sept. 15, 1902; House 1939-47.

SHIPLEY, George E. (D Ill.) April 21, 1927; House 1959- .

SHIPSTEAD, Henrik (R Minn.) Jan. 8, 1881-June 26, 1960; Senate 1923-47.

SHORT, Dewey (R Mo.) April 7, 1898; House 1929-31; 1935-57; Asst. Secretary of the Army 1957-61.

SHORT, Don L. (R N.D.) June 22, 1903; House 1959-65.

SHRIVER, Garner E. (R Kan.) July 6, 1912; House 1961- .

SHUFORD, George A. (D N.C.) Sept. 5, 1895-Dec. 8, 1962; House 1953-59.

SIBAL, Abner W. (R Conn.) April 11, 1921; House 1961-65.

SICKLES, Carlton R. (D Md.) June 15, 1921; House 1963-67.

SIEMINSKI, Alfred D. (D N.J.) Aug. 23, 1911; House 1951-59.

SIKES, Robert L. F. (D Fla.) June 3, 1906; House 1941- .

SILER, Eugene (R Ky.) June 26, 1900; House 1955-65.

SIMPSON, Edna Oakes (R Ill.) Oct. 26, 1891 (widow of Sid Simpson); House 1959-61

SIMPSON, Milward L. (R Wyo.) Nov. 12, 1897; Gov. 1955-59; Senate 1962-67.

SIMPSON, Richard M. (R Pa.) Aug. 30, 1900-Jan. 7, 1960; House 1937-60.

SIMPSON, Sid (R Ill.) Sept. 20, 1894-Oct. 26, 1958; House 1943-58.

SIMS, Hugo S. Jr. (D S.C.) Oct. 14, 1921; House 1949-51.

SISK, B. F. (D Calif.) Dec. 14, 1910; House 1955- .

SITTLER, Edward L. Jr. (R Pa.) April 21, 1908; House 1951-53.

SKUBITZ, Joe (R Kan.) May 6, 1906; House 1963- .

SLACK, John M. Jr. (D W. Va.) March 18, 1915; House 1959- .

SLAUGHTER, Roger C. (D Mo.) July 17, 1905; House 1943-47.

SMALL, Frank Jr. (R Md.) July 15, 1896; House 1953-55.

SMATHERS, George A. (D Fla.) Nov. 14, 1913; House 1947-51; Senate 1951-69.

SMITH, Benjamin A. II (D Mass.) March 26, 1916; Senate Dec. 27, 1960-62.

SMITH, Frank E. (D Miss.) Feb. 21, 1918; House 1951-63.

SMITH, Frederick C. (R Ohio) July 29, 1884-July 16, 1956; House 1939-51.

SMITH, H. Alexander (R N.J.) Jan. 30, 1880-Oct. 27, 1966; (uncle of Peter H. Dominick); Senate Dec. 7, 1944-59; Spec. Consultant to the Secretary of State 1959-60.

SMITH, H. Allen (R Calif.) Oct. 8, 1909; House 1957- .

SMITH, Henry P. III (R N.Y.) Sept. 29, 1911; House 1965- .

SMITH, Howard W. (D Va.) Feb. 2, 1883; House 1931-67.

SMITH, James V. (R Okla.) July 23, 1926; House 1967-69.

SMITH, Lawrence H. (R Wis.) Sept. 15, 1892-Jan. 22, 1958; House 1941-58.

SMITH, Margaret Chase (R Maine) Dec. 14, 1897; House June 3, 1940-49; Senate 1949- .

SMITH, Neal (D Iowa) March 23, 1920; House 1959- .

SMITH, Willis (D N.C.) Dec. 19, 1887-June 26, 1953; Senate Nov. 27, 1950-53.

SMITH, Wint (R Kan.) Oct. 7, 1893; House 1947-61.

SNYDER, John Buell (D Pa.) July 30, 1877-Feb. 24, 1946; House 1933-46.

SNYDER, Mervin C. (R W.Va.) Oct. 29, 1898; House 1947-49.

SNYDER, M.G. (R Ky.) Jan. 26, 1928; House 1963-65; 1967- .

SOMERS, Andrew L. (D N.Y.) March 21, 1895-April 6, 1949; House 1925-49.

SPARKMAN, John J. (D Ala.) Dec. 20, 1899; House 1937-46; Senate 1946- ; Vice Presidential candidate 1952.

SPENCE, Brent (D Ky.) Dec. 24, 1874-Sept. 19, 1967; House 1931-63.

SPONG, William B. (D Va.) Sept. 29, 1920; Senate 1966- .

SPRINGER, Raymond S. (R Ind.) April 26, 1882-Aug. 28, 1947; House 1939-47.

SPRINGER, William L. (R Ill.) April 12, 1909; House 1951- .

STAEBLER, Neil (D Mich.) July 11, 1905; House 1963-65.

STAFFORD, Robert T. (R Vt.) Aug. 8, 1913; House 1961- ; Gov. 1959-61.

STAGGERS, Harley O. (D W.Va.) Aug. 3, 1907; House 1949- .

STALBAUM, Lynn E. (D Wis.) May 15, 1920; House 1965-67.

STANFILL, William A. (R Ky.) Jan. 16, 1892; Senate 1945-46.

STANLEY, Thomas B. (D Va.) July 16, 1890; House Nov. 5, 1946-Feb. 3, 1953; Gov. 1954-58.

STANTON, J. William (R Ohio) Feb. 20, 1924; House 1965- .

STARKEY, Frank T. (D Minn.) Feb. 18, 1892; House 1945-47.

STAUFFER, S. Walter (R Pa.) Aug. 13, 1888; House 1953-55; 1957-59.

STEED, Tom (D Okla.) March 2, 1904; House 1949- .

STEFAN, Karl (R Neb.) March 1, 1884-Oct. 2, 1951; House 1935-51.

STEIGER, Sam (R Ariz.) March 10, 1929; House 1967- .

STEIGER, William A. (R Wis.) May 15, 1938; House 1967- .

STENNIS, John C. (D Miss.) Aug. 3, 1901; Senate 1947- .

STEPHENS, Robert G. Jr. (D Ga.) Aug. 14, 1913; House 1961- .

STEVENS, Theodore F. (R Alaska) Nov. 18, 1923; Senate 1968- .

STEVENSON, William Henry (R Wis.) Sept. 23, 1891; House 1941-49.

STEWART, A. Tom (D Tenn.) Jan. 11, 1892; Senate 1939-49.

STEWART, Paul (D Okla.) Feb. 27, 1892-Nov. 13, 1950; House 1943-47.

STIGLER, William G. (D Okla.) July 7, 1891-Aug. 21, 1952; House 1944-52.

STINSON, K. William (R Wash.) April 20, 1930; House 1963-65.

STOCKMAN, Lowell (R Ore.) April 12, 1901-Aug. 9, 1962; House 1943-53.

STOKES, Louis (D Ohio) Feb. 23, 1925; House 1969- .

STRATTON, Samuel S. (D N.Y.) Sept. 27, 1916; House 1959- .

STRATTON, William G. (R Ill.) Feb. 26, 1914; House 1941-43; 1947-49; Gov. 1953-61.

STRINGFELLOW, Douglas R. (R Utah) Sept. 24, 1922-Oct. 19, 1966; House 1953-55.

STUBBLEFIELD, Frank A. (D Ky.) April 5, 1907; House 1959- .

STUCKEY, W. S. Jr. (D Ga.) May 25, 1935; House 1967- .

SULLIVAN, John B. (D Mo.) Oct. 10, 1897-Jan. 29, 1951; House 1941-43; 1945-47; 1949-51.

SULLIVAN, Mrs. Leonor K. (D Mo.) Aug. 21, 1903 (widow of John B. Sullivan; House 1953- .

SUMNER, Miss Jessie (R Ill.) Aug. 17, 1898; House 1939-47.

SUMNERS, Hatton W. (D Texas) April 30, 1875-April 19, 1962; House 1913-47.

SUNDSTROM, Frank L. (R N.J.) Jan. 5, 1901; House 1943-49.

SUTTON, Pat (D Tenn.) Oct. 31, 1915; House 1949-55.

SWEENEY, Robert E. (D Ohio) Nov. 4, 1924; House 1965-67.

SWIFT, George R. (D Ala.) Dec. 19, 1887; Senate June 15, 1946-Nov. 5, 1946.

SYMINGTON, James W. (D Mo.) Sept. 28, 1927; (son of Stuart Symington); House 1969-   .

SYMINGTON, Stuart (D Mo.) June 26, 1901; Senate 1953-   ; Secretary of the Air Force 1947-50.

T

TABER, John (R N.Y.) May 5, 1880-Nov. 22, 1965; House 1923-63.

TACKETT, Boyd (D Ark.) May 9, 1911; House 1949-53.

TAFT, Kingsley A. (R Ohio) July 19, 1903; Senate 1946-47.

TAFT, Robert A. (R Ohio) Sept. 8, 1889-July 31, 1953; Senate 1939-53; Majority Leader 1953.

TAFT, Robert Jr. (R Ohio) Feb. 26, 1917 (son of Robert A. Taft); House 1963-65; 1967-   .

TALBOT, Joseph E. (R Conn.) March 18, 1901-April 30, 1966; House 1942-47.

TALCOTT, Burt L. (R Calif.) Feb. 22, 1902; House 1963-   .

TALLE, Henry O. (R Iowa) Jan. 12, 1892-March 14, 1969; House 1939-59.

TALMADGE, Herman E. (D Ga.) Aug. 9, 1913; Senate 1957-   ; Gov. 1948-55.

TARVER, Malcolm C. (D Ga.) Sept. 25, 1885-March 5, 1960; House 1927-47.

TAURIELLO, Anthony F. (D N.Y.) Aug. 14, 1899; House 1949-51.

TAYLOR, Dean P. (R N.Y.) Jan. 1, 1902; House 1943-61.

TAYLOR, Glen H. (D Idaho) April 12, 1904; Senate 1945-51; Vice Presidential candidate on Progressive party ticket 1948.

TAYLOR, Roy A. (D N.C.) Jan. 31, 1910; House 1960-   .

TEAGUE, Charles M. (R Calif.) Sept. 18, 1909; House 1955-   .

TEAGUE, Olin E. (D Texas) April 6, 1910; House 1946-   .

TELLER, Ludwig (D N.Y.) June 22, 1911-Oct. 4, 1965; House 1957-61.

TENZER, Herbert (D N.Y.) Nov. 1, 1905; House 1965-69.

TEWES, Donald E. (R Wis.) July 4, 1916; House 1957-59.

THOM, William R. (D Ohio) July 7, 1885-July 28, 1960; House 1933-39; 1941-43; 1945-47.

THOMAS, Albert (D Texas) April 12, 1898-Feb. 15, 1966; House 1937-66.

THOMAS, Elbert D. (D Utah) June 17, 1883-Oct. 24, 1904; Senate 1933-51.

THOMAS, Elmer (D Okla.) Sept. 8, 1876; House 1923-27; Senate 1927-51.

THOMAS, J. Parnell (R N.J.) Jan. 16, 1895; House 1937-50.

THOMAS, John (R Idaho) Jan. 4, 1874-Nov. 10, 1945; Senate 1928-33; 1940-45.

THOMAS, Lera M. (D Texas) April 4, 1898 (widow of Albert Thomas); House 1966-67.

THOMASON, R. Ewing (D Texas) May 30, 1879; House 1931-47.

THOMPSON, Clark W. (D Texas) Aug. 6, 1896; House 1933-35; 1947-66.

THOMPSON, Fletcher (R Ga.) Feb. 5, 1925; House 1967-   .

THOMPSON, Frank Jr. (D N.J.) July 26, 1918; House 1955-   .

THOMPSON, Ruth (R Mich.) Sept. 15, 1887; House 1951-57.

THOMPSON, T. Ashton (D La.) March 31, 1916-July 1, 1965; House 1953-65.

THOMSON, E. Keith (R Wyo.) Feb. 8, 1919-Dec. 9, 1960; House 1955-60.

THOMSON, Vernon W. (R Wis.) Nov. 5, 1905; House 1961-   ; Gov. 1957-58.

THORNBERRY, Homer (D Texas) Jan. 9, 1909; House 1949-63; U.S. District Judge, Fifth Circuit 1963-   .

THURMOND, Strom (R S.C.) Dec. 5, 1902; Senate 1954-56; 1956-   ; Gov. 1947-51; Presidential Candidate on States Right ticket, 1948; Democrat 1954-64; Republican Sept. 13, 1964-   .

THYE, Edward J. (R Minn.) April 26, 1896; Senate 1947-59; Gov. 1943-47.

TIBBOTT, Harve (R Pa.) April 27, 1885; House 1939-49.

TIERNAN, Robert O. (D R.I.) Feb. 24, 1929; House 1967-   .

TOBEY, Charles W. (R N.H.) July 22, 1880-July 24, 1953; House 1933-39; Senate 1939-53.

TODD, Paul H. Jr. (D Mich.) Sept. 22, 1921; House 1965-67.

TOLAN, John H. (D Calif.) Jan. 15, 1877-July 30, 1947; House 935-47.

TOLL, Herman (D Pa.) March 15, 1907-July 26, 1967; House 1959-66.

TOLLEFSON, Thor C. (R Wash.) May 2, 1901; House 1947-65.

TORRENS, James H. (D N.Y.) Sept. 12, 1874-April 5, 1952; House 1944-47.

TOWE, Harry L. (R N.J.) Nov. 3, 1898; House 1943-51.

TOWER, John G. (R Texas) Sept. 29, 1925; Senate 1961-.

TRAYNOR, Philip A. (D Del.) May 31, 1874; House 1941-43; 1945-47.

TRIMBLE, James W. (D Ark.) Feb. 3, 1894; House 1945-   .

TRUMAN, Harry S. (D Mo.) May 8, 1884; Senate 1935-45; Vice President Jan. 20, 1945-April 12, 1945; President 1945-53.

TUCK, William M. (D Va.) Sept. 28, 1896; House 1953-69; Gov. 1946-50.

TUMULTY, T. James (D N.J.) March 2, 1913; House 1955-57.

TUNNELL, James M. (D Del.) Aug. 2, 1879-Nov. 14, 1957; Senate 1941-47.

TUNNEY, John V. (D Calif.) June 26, 1934; House 1965- .

TUPPER, Stanley R. (R Maine) Jan. 25, 1921; House 1961-67.

TUTEN, J. Russell (D Ga.) July 23, 1911-Aug. 16, 1968; House 1963-67.

TWYMAN, Robert J. (R Ill.) June 18, 1897; House 1947-49.

TYDINGS, Joseph D. (D Md.) May 4, 1928 (son of Millard E. Tydings); Senate 1965- .

TYDINGS, Millard E. (D Md.) April 6, 1890-Feb. 9, 1961; House 1923-27; Senate 1927-51.

U

UDALL, Morris K. (D Ariz.) June 15, 1922 (brother of Stewart L. Udall); House 1961- .

UDALL, Stewart L. (D Ariz.) Jan. 31, 1920; House 1955-61; Secretary of Interior 1961-69.

ULLMAN, Al (D Ore.) March 9, 1914; House 1957- .

UMSTEAD, William B. (D N.C.) May 13, 1895-Nov. 7, 1954; House 1933-39; Senate 1946-48; Gov. 1953-54.

UNDERWOOD, Thomas R. (D Ky.) March 3, 1898-June 29, 1956; House 1949-51; Senate 1951-52.

UPTON, Robert W. (R N.H.) Feb. 3, 1884; Senate Aug. 14, 1953-Nov. 7, 1954.

UTT, James B. (R Calif.) March 11, 1899; House 1953- .

V

VAIL, Richard B. (R Ill.) Aug. 31, 1895-July 29, 1955; House 1947-49; 1951-53.

VAN DEERLIN, Lionel (D Calif.) July 25, 1914; House 1963- .

VANDENBERG, Arthur H. (R Mich.) March 22, 1889-April 18, 1951; Senate 1928-51; President pro tempore 1947-49.

VANDER JAGT, Guy. (R Mich.) Aug. 26, 1931; House 1966- .

VANIK, Charles A. (D Ohio) April 7, 1913; House 1955- .

VAN PELT, William K. (R Wis.) March 10, 1905; House 1951-65.

VAN ZANDT, James E. (R Pa.) Dec. 18, 1898; House 1939-43; 1947-63.

VAUGHN, Albert C. (R Pa.) Oct. 9, 1894-Sept. 1, 1951; House 1951.

VELDE, Harold H. (R Ill.) April 1, 1910; House 1949-57.

VIGORITO, Joseph P. (D Pa.) Nov. 10, 1918; House 1965- .

VINSON, Carl (D Ga.) Nov. 18, 1883; House Nov. 3, 1914-65.

VIVIAN, Weston E. (D Mich.) Oct. 25, 1924; House 1965- .

VOORHIS, Jerry (D Calif.) April 6, 1901; House 1937-47.

VORYS, John M. (R Ohio) June 16, 1896-Aug. 25, 1968; House 1939-59.

VURSELL, Charles W. (R Ill.) Feb. 8, 1881; House 1943-59.

W

WADSWORTH, James W. Jr. (R N.Y.) Aug. 12, 1877-June 21, 1952; Senate 1915-27; House 1933-51.

WAGGONNER, Joe D. Jr. (D La.) Sept. 7, 1918; House 1961- .

WAGNER, Earl T. (D Ohio) April 27, 1908; House 1949-51.

WAGNER, Robert F. (D N.Y.) June 8, 1877-May 4, 1953; Senate 1927-49.

WAINWRIGHT, Stuyvesant (R N.Y.) May 16, 1921; House 1953-61.

WALDIE, Jerome R. (D Calif.) Feb. 15, 1925; House 1966- .

WALKER, E.S. Johnny (D N.M.) June 18, 1911; House 1965-69.

WALKER, Prentiss (R Miss.) Aug. 23, 1917; House 1965-67.

WALLGREN, Mon C. (D Wash.) April 17, 1891-Sept. 18, 1951; House 1933-40; Senate 1940-45; Gov. 1945-49.

WALLHAUSER, George M. (R N.J.) Feb. 10, 1900; House 1959-65.

WALSH, David I. (D Mass.) Nov. 11, 1872-June 11, 1947; Senate 1919-25; 1926-47; Gov. 1914-15.

WALSH, John R. (D Ind.) May 22, 1913; House 1949-51.

WALTER, Francis E. (D Pa.) May 25, 1894-May 31, 1963; House 1933-63.

WALTERS, Herbert S. (D Tenn.) Nov. 17, 1891; Senate 1963-64.

WAMPLER, Fred (R Ind.) Oct. 15, 1909; House 1959-61.

WAMPLER, William Creed (R Va.) April 21, 1926; House 1953-55; 1967- .

WARBURTON, Herbert B. (R Del.) Sept. 21, 1916; House 1953-55.

WASIELEWSKI, Thad F. (D Wis.) Dec. 2, 1904; House 1941-47.

WATKINS, Arthur V. (R Utah) Dec. 18, 1886; Senate 1947-59.

WATKINS, G. Robert (R Pa.) May 21, 1903; House 1965- .

WATSON, Albert W. (R S.C.) Aug. 30, 1922; House 1963- ; Democrat 1963-65; Republican 1965- .

WATTS, John C. (D Ky.) July 9, 1902; House 1951- .

WEAVER, James D. (R Pa.) Sept. 27, 1920; House 1963-65.

WEAVER, Phil (R Neb.) April 9, 1919; House 1955-63.

WEAVER, Zebulon (D N.C.) May 12, 1872-Oct. 29, 1948; House 1919-29; 1931-47.

WEICHEL, Alvin F. (R Ohio) Sept. 11, 1891-Nov. 27, 1956; House 1943-55.

WEICKER, Lowell P. Jr. (R Conn.) May 16, 1931; House 1969- .

WEIS, Jessica McC. (R N.Y.) July 8, 1901-May 1, 1963; House 1959-63.

WEISS, Samuel A. (D Pa.) April 15, 1902; House 1941-46.

WELCH, Phil J. (D Mo.) April 4, 1895-April 28, 1963; House 1949-53.

WELCH, Richard J. (R Calif.) Feb. 13, 1869-Sept. 10, 1949; House 1926-49.

WELKER, Herman (R Idaho) Dec. 11, 1906-Oct. 30, 1957; Senate 1951-57.

WELTNER, Charles L. (D Ga.) Dec. 17, 1927; House 1963-67.

WERDEL, Thomas H. (R Calif.) Sept. 13, 1905-Sept. 30, 1966; House 1949-53; Vice Presidential Candidate on States Rights ticket 1956.

WEST, Milton H. (D Texas) June 30, 1888-Oct. 28, 1948; House 1933-48.

WESTLAND, Jack (R Wash.) Dec. 14, 1904; House 1953-65.

WHALEN, Charles W. Jr. (R Ohio) July 31, 1920; House 1967- .

WHALLEY, J. Irving (R Pa.) Sept. 14, 1902; House 1961- .

WHARTON, J. Ernest (R N.Y.) Oct. 4, 1899; House 1951-65.

WHEELER, Burton K. (D Mont.) Feb. 27, 1882; Senate 1923-47; Vice Presidential candidate on Progressive-Socialist ticket 1924.

WHEELER, W. M. (D Ga.) July 11, 1915; House 1947-55.

WHERRY, Kenneth S. (R Neb.) Feb. 28, 1892-Nov. 29, 1951; Senate 1943-51; Minority Whip 1944-47; Majority Whip 1947-49; Minority Leader 1949-51.

WHITAKER, John A. (D Ky.) Oct. 31, 1901-Dec. 15, 1951; House 1948-51.

WHITE, Cecil F. (D Calif.) Dec. 12, 1900; House 1949-51.

WHITE, Compton I. (D Idaho) July 31, 1877-March 31, 1956; House 1933-47; 1949-51.

WHITE, Compton I. Jr. (D Idaho) Dec. 19, 1920; House 1963-67.

WHITE, Richard C. (D Texas) April 29, 1923; House 1965- .

WHITE, Wallace Humphrey Jr. (R Maine) Aug. 6, 1877-March 31, 1952; House 1917-31; Senate 1931-49; Minority Leader 1945-47; Majority Leader 1947-49.

WHITEHURST, G. William (R Va.) March 12, 1925; House 1969- .

WHITENER, Basil L. (D N.C.) May 14, 1915; House 1957-69.

WHITTEN, Jamie L. (D Miss.) April 18, 1910; House 1941- .

WHITTINGTON, William M. (D Miss.) May 4, 1878-Aug. 21, 1962; House 1925-51.

WICKERSHAM, Victor (D Okla.) Feb. 9, 1906; House 1941-47; 1949-57; l961-65.

WIDNALL, William B. (R N.J.) March 17, 1906; House 1950- .

WIER, Roy W. (D Minn.) Feb. 25, 1888-June 27, 1963; House 1949-61.

WIGGINS, Charles E. (R Calif.) Dec. 3, 1927; House 1967- .

WIGGLESWORTH, Richard B. (R Mass.) April 25, 1891-Oct. 22, 1960; House 1928-59; Ambassador to Canada 1959-60.

WILEY, Alexander (R Wis.) May 26, 1884-Oct. 26, 1967; Senate 1939-63.

WILLIAMS, Harrison A. Jr. (D N. J.) Dec. 10, 1919; House 1953-57; Senate 1959- .

WILLIAMS, John Bell (D Miss.) Dec. 4, 1918; House 1947-67; Gov. 1967- .

WILLIAMS, John J. (R Del.) May 17, 1904; Senate 1947- .

WILLIAMS, Lawrence G. (R Pa.) Sept. 15, 1913; House 1967- .

WILLIAMS, William R. (R N.Y.) Aug. 11, 1884; House 1951-59.

WILLIS, Edwin E. (D La.) Oct. 2, 1904; House 1949-69.

WILLIS, Raymond E. (R Ind.) Aug. 11, 1875-March 21, 1956; Senate 1941-47.

WILSON, Bob (R Calif.) May 5, 1916; House 1953- .

WILSON, Charles H. (D Calif.) Feb. 17, 1917; House 1963- .

WILSON, Earl (R Ind.) April 18, 1906; House 1941-59; 1961-65.

WILSON, George A. (R Iowa) April 1, 1884-Sept. 8, 1953; Senate 1943-49; Gov. 1939-43.

WILSON, George H. (D Okla.) Aug. 21, 1905; House 1949-51.

WILSON, J. Franklin (D Texas) March 18, 1901; House 1947-55.

WINN, Larry Jr. (R Kan.) Aug. 22, 1919; House 1967- .

WINSTEAD, Arthur (D Miss.) Jan. 6, 1904; House 1943-65.

WINTER, Thomas Daniel (R Kan.) July 7, 1896-Nov. 7, 1951; House 1939-47.

WITHERS, Garrett L. (D Ky.) June 21, 1884-April 30, 1953; Senate 1949-50; House 1952-53.

WITHROW, Gardner R. (R Wis.) Oct. 5, 1892-Sept. 23, 1964; House 1931-39; 1949-61.

WOFFORD, Thomas A. (D S.C.) Sept. 27, 1908; Senate April 5, 1956-Nov. 6, 1956.

WOLCOTT, Jesse P. (R Mich.) March 3, 1893-Jan. 28, 1969; House 1931-57.

WOLD, John S. (R Wyo.) Aug. 31, 1916; House 1969- .

WOLF, Leonard G. (D Iowa) Oct. 29, 1925; House 1959-61.

WOLFENDEN, James (R Pa.) July 25, 1889-April 8, 1949; House 1928-47.

WOLFF, Lester L. (D N.Y.) Jan. 4, 1919; House 1965- .

WOLVERTON, Charles A. (R N.J.) Oct. 24, 1880-May 18, 1969; House 1927-59.

WOOD, John S. (D Ga.) Feb. 8, 1885-Sept. 12, 1968; House 1931-35; 1945-53.

WOOD, John T. (R Idaho) Nov. 25, 1878-Nov. 2, 1954; House 1951-53.

WOODHOUSE, Chase Going (D Conn.); House 1945-47; 1949-51.

WOODRUFF, Roy O. (R Mich.) March 14, 1876-Feb. 12, 1953; House 1913-15; 1921-53.

WOODRUM, Clifton A. (R Va.) April 27, 1887-Oct. 6, 1950; House 1923-45.

WORLEY, Eugene (D Texas) Oct. 10, 1908; House 1941-50.

WRIGHT, Jim (D Texas) Dec. 22, 1922; House 1955- .

WYATT, Wendell (R Ore.) June 15, 1917; House 1965- .

WYDLER, John W. (R N.Y.) June 9, 1924; House 1963- .

WYLIE, Chalmers P. (R Ohio) Nov. 23, 1920; House 1967- .

WYMAN, Louis C. (R N.H.) March 16, 1917; House 1963-65; 1967- .

X, Y, Z

YARBOROUGH, Ralph W. (D Texas) June 8, 1903; Senate 1957- .

YATES, Sidney R. (D Ill.) Aug. 27, 1909; House 1949-63; 1965- .

YATRON, Gus (D Pa.) Oct. 16, 1927; House 1969- .

YORTY, Samuel W. (D Calif.) Oct. 1, 1909; House 1951-55; Mayor of Los Angeles 1961- .

YOUNG, Clifton (R Nev.) Nov. 7, 1922; House 1953-57.

YOUNG, John (D Texas) Nov. 10, 1916; House 1957- .

YOUNG, Milton R. (R N.D.) Dec. 6, 1897; Senate 1945- .

YOUNG, Stephen M. (D Ohio) May 4, 1889; House 1933-37; 1941-43; 1949-51; Senate 1959- .

YOUNGBLOOD, Harold F. (R Mich.) Aug. 7, 1907; House 1947-49.

YOUNGER, J. Arthur (R Calif.) April 11, 1893-June 20, 1967; House 1953-67.

ZABLOCKI, Clement J. (D Wis.) Nov. 18, 1912; House 1949- .

ZELENKO, Herbert (D N.Y.) March 16, 1906; House 1955-63.

ZIMMERMAN, Orville (D Mo.) Dec. 31, 1880-April 7, 1948; House 1935-48.

ZION, Roger H. (R Ind.) Sept. 17, 1921; House 1967- .

ZWACH, John M. (R Minn.) Feb. 8, 1907; House 1967- .

Presidents and Their Cabinets, 1933-69

Controversial Nominations, 1965-68

Presidential Vetoes, 1963-68

PRESIDENTS AND THEIR CABINETS—1933-1969

Franklin Delano Roosevelt—March 4, 1933-April 12, 1945

Secretary of State

Cordell Hull (D Tenn.)—March 4, 1933-Dec. 1, 1944
Edward R. Stettinius (D Va.)—Dec. 1, 1944—July 3, 1945

Secretary of Treasury

William H. Woodin (D N.Y.)—March 4, 1933-Jan. 1, 1934
Henry Morgenthau Jr. (D N.Y.)—Jan. 1, 1934-July 23, 1945

Secretary of War

George H. Dern (D Utah)—March 4, 1933-Aug. 27, 1936
Harry H. Woodring (D Kan.)—Sept. 25, 1936-July 10, 1940
Henry L. Stimson (R N.Y.)—July 10, 1940-Sept. 26, 1945

Attorney General

Homer S. Cummings (D Conn.)—March 4, 1933-Jan. 2, 1939
Frank Murphy (D Mich.)—Jan. 2, 1939-Jan. 18, 1940
Robert H. Jackson (D N.Y.)—Jan. 18, 1940-Sept. 5, 1941
Francis Biddle (D Pa.)—Sept. 5, 1941-July 1, 1945

Postmaster General

James A. Farley (D N.Y.)—March 4, 1933-Sept. 10, 1940
Frank C. Walker (D Pa.)—Sept. 10, 1940-July 1, 1945

Secretary of the Navy

Claude A. Swanson (D Va.)—March 4, 1933-July 7, 1939
Charles Edison (D N.J.)—Aug. 5, 1939-July 10, 1940
Frank Knox (R Ill.)—July 10, 1940-April 28, 1944
James V. Forrestal (D N.Y.)—May 18, 1944-Sept. 17, 1947

Secretary of Interior

Harold L. Ickes (D Ill.)—March 4, 1933-March 18, 1946

Secretary of Agriculture

Henry A. Wallace (D Iowa)—March 4, 1933-Sept. 5, 1940
Claude R. Wickard (D Ind.)—Sept. 5, 1940-June 30, 1945

Secretary of Commerce

Daniel C. Roper (D S.C.)—March 4, 1933-Dec. 16, 1938
Harry L. Hopkins (D N.Y.)—Dec. 24, 1938-Sept. 19, 1940
Jesse H. Jones (D Texas)—Sept. 19, 1940-March 2, 1945
Henry A. Wallace (D Iowa)—March 2, 1945-Sept. 28, 1946

Secretary of Labor

Frances Perkins (D N.Y.)—March 4, 1933-July 1, 1945

Harry S. Truman — April 12, 1945-Jan. 20, 1953

Secretary of State

James F. Byrnes (D S.C.)—July 3, 1945-Jan. 21, 1947
George C. Marshall (Pa.)—Jan. 21, 1947-Jan. 20, 1949
Dean G. Acheson (D Conn.)—Jan. 20, 1949-Jan. 20, 1953

Secretary of Treasury

Fred M. Vinson (D Ky.)—July 23, 1945-June 25, 1946
John W. Snyder (D Mo.)—June 25, 1946-Jan. 20, 1953

Secretary of War

Robert Porter Patterson (R N.Y.)—Sept. 27, 1945-Jan. 25, 1947
Kenneth C. Royall (D N.C.)—Jan. 25, 1947-Sept. 17, 1947

Secretary of Defense

James V. Forrestal (D N.Y.)—Sept. 17, 1947-March 1949
Louis A. Johnson (D W. Va.)—March 28, 1949-Sept. 21, 1950
George C. Marshall (Pa.)—Sept. 21, 1950-Sept. 17, 1951
Robert A. Lovett (R N.Y.)—Sept. 17, 1951-Jan. 20, 1953

Attorney General

Tom C. Clark (D Texas)—July 1, 1945-Aug. 24, 1949
J. Howard McGrath (D R.I.)—Aug. 24, 1949-May 27, 1952
James P. McGranery (D Pa.)—May 27, 1952-Jan. 20, 1953

Postmaster General

Robert E. Hannegan (D Mo.)—July 1, 1945-Dec. 16, 1947
Jesse M. Donaldson (D Mo.)—Dec. 16, 1947-Jan. 20, 1953

Secretary of Interior

Julius A. Krug (D Wis.)—March 18, 1945-Dec. 1, 1949
Oscar L. Chapman (D Colo.)—Dec. 1, 1949-Jan. 20, 1953

Secretary of Agriculture

Clinton P. Anderson (D N.M.)—June 30, 1945-June 2, 1948
Charles F. Brannan (D Colo.)—June 2, 1948-Jan. 20, 1953

Secretary of Commerce

W. Averell Harriman (D N.Y.)—Sept. 28, 1946-May 6, 1948
Charles Sawyer (D Ohio)—May 6, 1948-Jan. 20, 1953

Secretary of Labor

Lewis B. Schwellenbach (D Wash.)—July 1, 1945-June 10, 1948
Maurice J. Tobin (D Mass.)—Aug. 13, 1948-Jan. 20, 1953

Dwight D. Eisenhower—Jan. 20, 1953—Jan. 20, 1961

Secretary of State

John Foster Dulles (R N.Y.)—Jan. 21, 1953-April 15, 1959
Christian A. Herter (R Mass.)—April 22, 1959-Jan. 20 1961

Secretary of Treasury

George M. Humphrey (R Ohio)—Jan. 21, 1953-July 29, 1957
Robert B. Anderson (D Texas)—July 29, 1957-Jan. 20, 1961

Secretary of Defense

Charles E. Wilson (R Mich.)—Jan. 28, 1953-Oct. 9, 1957
Neil H. McElroy (R Ohio)—Oct. 9, 1957-Dec. 1, 1959
Thomas S. Gates (R Pa.)—Dec. 1, 1959-Jan. 20, 1961

Attorney General

Herbert Brownell Jr. (R N.Y.)—Jan. 21, 1953-Nov. 8, 1957
William P. Rogers (R Md.)—Nov. 8, 1957-Jan. 20, 1961

Postmaster General

Arthur E. Summerfield (R Mich.)—Jan. 21, 1953-Jan. 20, 1961

Secretary of Interior

Douglas McKay (R Ore).—Jan. 21, 1953-June 8, 1956
Fred A. Seaton (R Neb.)—June 8, 1956-Jan. 20, 1961

Secretary of Agriculture

Ezra Taft Benson (R Utah)—Jan. 21, 1953-Jan. 20, 1961

Secretary of Commerce

Sinclair Weeks (R Mass.)—Jan. 21, 1953-Nov. 13, 1958
Lewis L. Strauss (R N.Y.)—Nov. 13, 1958-June 27, 1959*
Frederick H. Mueller (R Mich.)—July 21, 1959-Jan. 20, 1961

Strauss served interim appointment as Secretary of Commerce. On June 27, 1959, the Senate refused to confirm his nomination.

Secretary of Labor

Martin P. Durkin (D Md.)—Jan. 21, 1953-Oct. 9, 1953
James P. Mitchell (R N.J.)—Oct. 9, 1953-Jan. 20, 1961

Secretary of Health, Education and Welfare

Oveta Culp Hobby (R Texas)—April 11, 1953-Aug. 1, 1955
Marion B. Folsom (R N.Y.)—Aug. 1, 1955-Aug. 1, 1958
Arthur S. Flemming (R Ohio)—Aug. 1, 1958-Jan. 20, 1961

John F. Kennedy—Jan. 20, 1961-Nov. 22, 1963

Secretary of State

Dean Rusk (D N.Y.)—Jan. 20, 1961-

Secretary of Treasury

Douglas Dillon (R N.Y.)—Jan. 20, 1961-

Secretary of Defense

Robert S. McNamara (R Mich.)—Jan. 20, 1961-

Attorney General

Robert F. Kennedy (D Mass.)—Jan. 20, 1961-

Postmaster General

J. Edward Day (D Calif.)—Jan. 20, 1961-Aug. 9, 1963.
John A. Gronouski (D Wis.)—Sept. 24, 1963-

Secretary of Interior

Stewart L. Udall (D Ariz.)—Jan. 20, 1961-

Secretary of Agriculture

Orville L. Freeman (D Minn.)—Jan. 20, 1961-

Secretary of Commerce

Luther H. Hodges (D N.C.)—Jan. 20, 1961-

Secretary of Labor

Arthur J. Goldberg (D Wash., D.C.)—Jan. 20, 1961-
Sept. 25, 1962.
W. Willard Wirtz (D Ill.)—Sept. 25, 1962-

Secretary of Health, Education and Welfare

Abraham A. Ribicoff (D Conn.)—Jan. 20, 1961-
July 13, 1962
Anthony J. Celebrezze (D Ohio)—July 31, 1962

Lyndon B. Johnson—Nov. 22, 1963-Jan. 20, 1969

Secretary of State

Dean Rusk (D N.Y.)—Jan. 20, 1961-Jan. 20, 1969

Secretary of Treasury

Douglas Dillon (R Wash., D.C.)—Jan. 20, 1961-March 31,
1965
Henry H. Fowler (D Va.)—April 1, 1965-Dec. 20, 1968
Joseph W. Barr (D Ind.)—Dec. 20, 1968-Jan. 20, 1969

Secretary of Defense

Robert S. McNamara (R Mich.)—Jan. 20, 1961-Feb. 29, 1968
Clark M. Clifford (D Md.)—March 1, 1968-Jan. 20, 1969

Attorney General

Robert F. Kennedy (D Mass.)—Jan. 20, 1961-Sept. 3,
1964
Nicholas deB. Katzenbach (D Wash., D.C.)—Sept. 3,
1964-Sept. 21, 1966
Ramsey Clark (D Texas)—Sept. 21, 1966-Jan. 20, 1969

Postmaster General

John A. Gronouski (D Wis.)—Sept. 24, 1963-Sept. 10,
1965
Lawrence F. O'Brien (D Mass.)—Sept. 10, 1965-April
10, 1968
M. Marvin Watson (D Texas)—April 10, 1968,-Jan. 20,
1969

Secretary of Interior

Stewart L. Udall (D Ariz.)—Jan. 20, 1961-Jan. 20, 1969

Secretary of Agriculture

Orville L. Freeman (D Minn.)—Jan. 20, 1961-Jan. 20,
1969

Secretary of Commerce

Luther H. Hodges (D N.C.)—Jan. 20, 1961-Jan. 15, 1965
John T. Connor (D N.J.)—Jan. 15, 1965-Feb. 1, 1967
Alexander B. Trowbridge (D Wash., D.C.)—Feb. 1, 1967-
March 1, 1968
C.R. Smith (D N.Y.)—March 1, 1968-Jan. 20, 1969

Secretary of Labor

W. Willard Wirtz (D Ill.)—Sept. 25, 1962-Jan. 20, 1969

Secretary of Health, Education and Welfare

Anthony J. Celebrezze (D Ohio)—July 31, 1962-Aug. 19,
1965
John W. Gardner (R N.Y.)—Aug. 19, 1965-March 1, 1968
Wilbur J. Cohen (D Md.)—March 1, 1968-Jan. 20, 1969

Secretary of Housing and Urban Development

Robert C. Weaver (D Wash., D.C.)—Jan. 17, 1966-
Jan. 1, 1969
Robert C. Wood (D Mass.)—Jan. 2, 1969-Jan. 20, 1969

Secretary of Transportation

Alan C. Boyd (D Fla.)—Jan. 12, 1967-Jan. 20, 1969

Richard M. Nixon — Jan. 20, 1969-

Secretary of State

William P. Rogers (R Md.)—Jan. 20, 1969-

Secretary of Treasury

David M. Kennedy (R Ill.)—Jan. 20, 1969-

Secretary of Defense

Melvin R. Laird (R Wis.)—Jan. 20, 1969-

Attorney General

John N. Mitchell (R N.Y.)—Jan. 20, 1969-

Postmaster General

Winton M. Blount (R Ala.)—Jan. 20, 1969-

Secretary of Interior

Walter J. Hickel (R Alaska)—Jan. 20, 1969-

Secretary of Agriculture

Clifford M. Hardin (R Neb.)—Jan. 20, 1969-

Secretary of Commerce

Maurice H. Stans (R N.Y.)—Jan. 20, 1969-

Secretary of Labor

George P. Schultz (R Calif.)—Jan. 20, 1969-

Secretary of Health, Education and Welfare

Robert H. Finch (R Calif.)—Jan. 20, 1969-

Secretary of Housing and Urban Development

George W. Romney (R Mich.)—Jan. 20, 1969-

Secretary of Transportation

John A. Volpe (R Mass.)—Jan. 20, 1969-

Controversial Nominations Sent to the Senate, 1964-68

NOMINATIONS are appointments to federal office by the President which are subject to confirmation by the Senate. Officials appointed in this manner include those in the Executive Branch at the Cabinet and sub-Cabinet levels, federal judges, ambassadors, and members of federal regulatory agencies. Most of the thousands of nominations sent to the Senate each year are those of military officers, whose promotions must be confirmed, and those of postmasters.

While most nominations win quick Senate approval, some are controversial and become the subject of Senate hearings and debate. Even the controversial nominations are almost always confirmed. Since 1964, no major nominations have been rejected by the Senate, although several have been withdrawn by the President in the face of strong Senate opposition.

'PERSONALLY OBNOXIOUS'

Senators sometimes object to appointees for patronage reasons—for example, when a nomination to a local federal job is made without consulting the Senators of the state concerned. Then a Senator may use the objection that the nominee is "personally obnoxious" to him. Usually other Senators join in blocking the nomination out of courtesy to their colleague.

Another common Senate objection to an Executive nominee is alleged conflict of interest. This charge may be made if the nominee holds stock in, draws a pension from, or is otherwise connected with a company dealing with the agency to which he has been appointed. In such cases, the nominee often divests himself of the stock or severs his connection with the company.

Many of the controversies over nominations arise from partisan politics or from disagreements between liberals and conservatives. In 1965, for example, the nomination of former Mississippi Gov. James P. Coleman to the U.S. 5th Circuit Court of Appeals was opposed by several liberal Senators who objected to Coleman's past segregationist record. In 1966, the appointment of Mrs. Constance Baker Motley to a judgeship in the Southern District of New York met opposition from Sen. James O. Eastland (D Miss.), who charged that she had been linked with the Communist party.

Debate shows that disapproval sometimes is based, not on the individual concerned, but on objection to the Administration's policies. In 1968, for example, the reappointment of Gen. Earle G. Wheeler as Chairman of the Joint Chiefs of Staff was opposed by several Senators who objected to the Administration's Vietnam policy.

Nomination battles occasionally reflect the Senate's concern about major issues of the time. Rising concern over lack of respect for law and order was largely responsible for the Judiciary Committee's failure to act on President Johnson's nomination of Patrick V. Murphy as head of the new Law Enforcement Assistance Administration in the Justice Department. Senators opposing Murphy's nomination accused him of failing to deal severely enough with rioters and looters in Washington, D.C., while serving as Public Safety Director of that city.

Increasing controversy has centered on judicial nominations, as Supreme Court and lower court decisions dealing with racial integration and civil liberties have come under fire from Senate conservatives. The controversy reached a peak in 1968, when a group of Republicans and Southern Democrats led by Sen. Robert Griffin (R Mich.) resorted to a filibuster to force President Johnson to withdraw the nomination of Associate Supreme Court Justice Abe Fortas to be Chief Justice of the United States.

Below are brief accounts of each of the major controversial nominations from 1964 to 1968.

1964

LeRoy Collins. Confirmed July 20 by a 53-8 roll-call vote as head of the Community Relations Service established under the 1964 Civil Rights Act. Opposition came from Southern Democrats who objected not to Collins but to the Act itself.

Hamer H. Budge. Confirmed as a member of the Securities and Exchange Commission June 26 by voice vote. Critics of the appointment said that Budge had a conservative record during his 10 years as a Republican Congressman from Idaho, and that President Johnson was believed to have made the appointment as a favor to House Minority Leader Charles A. Halleck (R Ind.). They asserted also that Budge lacked familiarity with the securities industry and did not favor stringent regulation.

Charles R. Ross. When President Johnson failed to reappoint Ross as a Federal Power Commissioner when his term expired June 22, speculation arose that Ross had lost favor for being too "pro-consumer". Several Senators contended he was needed on the Commission to protect natural gas consumers. Ross had voted on several occasions to block attempts supported by the industry to strip the Commission of its power to regulate the price of gas. Johnson finally reappointed Ross in 1965; the Senate confirmed the nomination April 28.

1965

James P. Coleman. The Senate July 26 confirmed, by a roll-call vote of 76-8, the nomination of former Mississippi Gov. Coleman to the 5th U.S. Circuit Court of Appeals. Two days of hearings on the nomination had been held by a three-man subcommittee of the Judiciary Committee, during which various civil rights groups had criticized Coleman's past segregationist record.

Carl E. Bagge. The Senate May 19 confirmed the nomination of Bagge to fill a vacancy on the Federal Power Commission created by the death of Commissioner Harold C. Woodward. Confirmation came after the Senate Commerce Committee May 18 approved Bagge's nomination by a vote of 15-1. The dissenter was Sen. Maurine B. Neuberger (D Ore.), who questioned Bagge's role in a dispute over an integrated housing project in Deerfield, Ill. Bagge stated before the Committee that he did not support a move to block the housing project.

William F. McKee. President Johnson April 27 announced the appointment of McKee, a retired Air Force General, to replace Najeeb E. Halaby as head of the Federal Aviation Agency (now the Federal Aviation Administration). Since the Federal Aviation Act required that the FAA Administrator be "a civilian at the time of his appointment," the President urged that legislation be enacted to enable him to accept the position without resigning from the Air Force.

HR 7777 (PL 89-46), which the House passed June 3 by a 228-137 roll-call vote, contained a provision stating that McKee's appointment was not to be taken as Congressional approval of any future appointment of a military man as FAA Administrator. The Senate passed HR 7777 June 17 by a 46-20 roll-call vote, clearing the bill for the President's signature on June 22. Debate in House and Senate was similar; proponents said that McKee had considerable ability as an administrator and was highly knowledgeable in the field of supersonic transport, while opponents objected to the appointment of a military man to a post required by law to be filled by a civilian. The Senate June 30 confirmed the nomination by voice vote.

David G. Bress. The Senate Oct. 22 confirmed by a roll-call vote of 49-14 the President's nomination of Bress to be U.S. Attorney for the District of Columbia. Several Senators opposed the nomination after it became known that Bress, a Washington, D.C., lawyer, was retained as counsel for the Serv-U Corporation, owned by former Secretary to the Senate Majority Robert G. (Bobby) Baker. Attorney General Nicholas deB. Katzenbach, who recommended the nomination, said that Bress was retained only briefly by Serv-U and scarcely knew Baker. Baker was under investigation at the time, and was convicted in 1967 on charges of income tax evasion, theft and fraud while in his Senate post.

Francis X. Morrissey. President Johnson Sept. 26 announced his intention to nominate Morrissey, a Boston Municipal Court judge, to be a federal district court judge in Massachusetts. The nomination was approved by the Judiciary Committee, but it touched off a storm of controversy on the Senate floor. Objections to Morrissey centered on alleged inconsistencies in his testimony about his study of law in Massachusetts and his residency in Georgia. Senate Minority Leader Everett M. Dirksen (Ill.), who led the fight against the nomination, contended that the main objection to Morrissey was that he was not qualified to sit on the federal bench. Sen. Edward Kennedy (D Mass.), the nominee's principal backer, led witnesses in praising Morrissey as a man of character and experience. Vice President Humphrey Oct. 20 reportedly began helping Kennedy to round up votes for Morrissey. However, at Kennedy's request, the Senate Oct. 21 gave unanimous consent to recommittal of the nomination to the Judiciary Committee. Morrissey Nov. 5 requested that President Johnson withdraw his nomination and the President complied.

1966

Constance Baker Motley. President Johnson's nomination of Mrs. Motley to be a U.S. District Court judge in New York was opposed by Sen. James O. Eastland (D Miss.), who asserted that she had been linked with the Communist Party. Both Senators from New York defended the nomination on the floor Aug. 30. Sen. Jacob K. Javits (R) cited Mrs. Motley's "very prominent" position as borough president of Manhattan. He asked the Senate to weigh her public career against the "uncorroborated testimony of one witness with respect to events that occurred 24 years ago." Sen. Robert F. Kennedy (D 1965-68) said that the President would not have recommended the nomination if there had been any basis for the charge. The nomination was confirmed Aug. 30. Mrs. Motley was the first Negro woman named to the federal bench.

1967

Thurgood Marshall. The President June 13 nominated Marshall, then Solicitor General, for the post of Associate Justice of the Supreme Court. The Judiciary Committee held relatively protracted hearings, during which Marshall was questioned repeatedly by southern Senators about his opinion on Court decisions concerning the rights of accused criminals. Marshall refused to answer the questions on the ground that it would be improper for him to discuss matters pending before the Court and that if he did he might have to disqualify himself from sitting on certain cases. Following the hearings, Sen. Sam J. Ervin Jr. (D N.C.) filed a minority report, which accused Marshall of being a "constitutional iconoclast" whose activist views would contribute to the rising crime rate in the nation. The nomination of Marshall, the first Negro to sit on the Supreme Court, was confirmed Aug. 30 by a roll-call vote of 69-11.

Simon F. McHugh Jr. President Johnson's nomination of McHugh, June 27, as a member of the Subversive Activities Control Board (SACB) was confirmed July 17 without debate. Sen. William Proxmire (D Wis.) July 22 denounced Senate confirmation of the 29-year-old accountant, husband of a former secretary of the President, as "a ridiculous extravagance" and said the compensation of $26,000 was "for doing little or nothing." Efforts by Proxmire and others to abolish SACB failed, but S 2171, passed late in the session and signed into law Jan. 2, 1968 (PL 90-237), included a provision terminating the existence of SACB June 30, 1969, unless the Attorney General had initiated proceedings before the Board and a hearing had been held by Dec. 31, 1968. Continuation of SACB was assured when Attorney General Ramsey Clark petitioned it July 1, 1968, to declare seven persons members of the Communist Party.

Rutherford M. Poats. Poats was nominated Oct. 17, 1966, for the post of Deputy Administrator of the Agency for International Development (AID) and was confirmed May 16, 1967, by a 61-24 roll-call vote. The confirmation vote came after the Senate had rejected by a 42-43 roll-call vote an effort to block the appointment by recommitting it to the Foreign Relations Committee. The nomination had been opposed by Senators who believed that Poats had mismanaged AID programs in South Vietnam.

1968

Gen. Earle G. Wheeler. Controversy over reappointment of Wheeler as chairman of the Joint Chiefs of Staff for an additional term of one year occurred during debate on a bill (H J Res 1224) to waive the existing limitation on the length of service by the JCS chairman. Opponents criticized the Administration's policies in the Vietnam war and claimed that Wheeler's part in formulating those policies made him unfit for the job. The Senate June 3 passed H J Res 1224 by a roll-call vote of 52-2; Wheeler was confirmed by voice vote June 25. The bill applied only to Wheeler and did not change the law limiting the chairman of the Joint Chiefs to two two-year terms except during a war declared by Congress.

Irvine H. Sprague. Opposition to the President's nomination of Sprague to be Director of the Federal Deposit Insurance Corporation came chiefly from conservative Republicans led by Sen. George Murphy (Calif.). Speaking against the nomination, Murphy said it was improper for the President to fill the post in the closing days of his Administration and that choice of a new FDIC Director should be left to the next President. The primary objection voiced by opponents of Sprague's nomination was his lack of formal banking experience. Sprague, formerly a representative in Washington of the State of California, was a White House aide for Congressional relations. The Senate confirmed the nomination July 30 by a 53-20 roll-call vote.

Abe Fortas. The President's nomination June 26 of Associate Justice Fortas to replace retiring Chief Justice Earl Warren touched off a bitter controversy in the Senate. Freshman Sen. Robert P. Griffin (R Mich.), who led the fight against the nomination from the start, immediately charged that it was based on "cronyism" and that Warren had timed his retirement to assure appointment of his successor by a Democratic President. The "lame duck" charge gave way to more serious questions of propriety in the course of hearings held by the Judiciary Committee between July 11 and Sept. 16. One was the question of Fortas's continued involvement in White House affairs after he went on the Court in 1965, an involvement which the Justice admitted but played down in his testimony before the Committee. There were allegations that Fortas had assisted in drafting legislation for the Administration and that he had advised the President on Vietnam policy and on handling of urban riots. It was disclosed toward the end of the hearings that the Justice had received a fee of $15,000 for conducting a nine-week law seminar at American University in the summer of 1968. The money for the fee and other seminar expenses had come from five former business associates, one of whom had a son who was involved in a federal criminal case. During the hearings, as in the subsequent floor debate, attacks were made on the Court in general and on Fortas in particular for decisions respecting criminal procedural law and obscenity.

By an 11-6 vote Sept. 17, the Judiciary Committee ordered the Fortas nomination reported to the Senate with the recommendation that it be confirmed. The majority, made up of eight Democrats and three Republicans, described Fortas as "extraordinarily well qualified for the post" of Chief Justice. His acceptance of a fee for teaching at American University and his participation in White House discussions, the report said, were within his rights and in line with what other Justices had done over the years. Three dissenting Democrats contended that Fortas had shown poor judgement in advising the President on legislative matters and in accepting the $15,000 teaching fee, and that the positions he had taken in Court decisions on crime, obscenity and other matters had been too liberal. One of the three dissenting Republicans (Strom Thurmond of South Carolina) submitted individual views in which he criticized Fortas's positions in decisions on criminal procedure, pornography, state-federal relations, and subversive activities.

In the floor debate, which began Sept. 25, Sen. Griffin pressed the attack relentlessly, and as his following grew, the chances of confirmation became more remote. They virtually vanished Sept. 27 when Minority Leader Everett McKinley Dirksen (R Ill.) reversed his position and announced that he was officially "neutral." Majority Leader Mike Mansfield (D Mont.) moved to end what was plainly a filibuster by reading to the Senate Sept. 29 a cloture motion signed by 26 Senators. The motion was rejected Oct. 1 by a roll-call vote of 45-43, which was 14 votes short of the 59 needed for cloture. The next day, Fortas requested the President to withdraw his name. Terming the action of the Senate "tragic," Johnson consented and on Oct. 4 called back the nomination.

Patrick V. Murphy. The President's nomination of Murphy on Sept. 16 to head the new Law Enforcement Assistance Administration in the Justice Department was not acted on by the Criminal Laws and Procedures Subcommittee of the Judiciary Committee. Murphy, who was Public Safety Director in the District of Columbia was criticized by Subcommittee Chairman John L. McClellan (D Ark.) for policies followed by the D.C. police during the April 1968 civil disorders in Washington. Given an interim appointment by President Johnson, Murphy served in the Justice Department post from Oct. 21 to March 6, 1969, when he left to make way for a Nixon Administration appointee, Charles H. Rogovin.

Presidential Vetoes, 1963-68

President Johnson during his term of office vetoed 30 bills, 13 public bills and 17 private bills. Thirteen were pocket-vetoed.

A bill is pocket-vetoed if, after Congress adjourns, the President fails to sign it within 10 days, excluding Sundays, from the time he receives it. A regular veto can be effected only when Congress is in session. In that case, the President returns the bill he vetos to the chamber in which it originated. Conversely, if the President fails to sign the bill within the 10-day period while Congress is in session, the bill automatically becomes law.

When the President pocket-vetoes a bill, he usually issues a memoradum of disapproval explaining his decision not to sign the bill. Mr. Johnson issued explanations for all his vetoes except that of the 1969 maritime administration bill (HR 159).

There were no attempts by the Democratic-controlled Congress to override any of President Johnson's vetoes. Johnson and Kennedy were the first Presidents since Warren G. Harding not to have a veto overridden.

1963

HR 2513—To require imported goods which were repackaged in the U.S. and imported lumber to be stamped with the name of the country of origin. President Johnson said the bill would raise prices, was unnecessary, and "would raise new barriers to foreign trade and invite retaliation against our exports at a time when we are trying to expand our trade and improve Western unity." HR 2513 was introduced Jan. 24 by Rep. A. Sydney Herlong Jr. (D Fla). The lumber provision, added in the Senate as an amendment, was sponsored by Sen. Warren G. Magnuson (D Wash). The bill was passed by the House Feb. 26 and the Senate July 18, and cleared Dec. 18. President Johnson pocket-vetoed it Dec. 31. President Eisenhower vetoed a similar measure in 1960.

HR 4505—To relieve Robert Alexander by directing the Court of Claims to rehear a suit in which Alexander contested action by the State Department in firing him. The President said the Court should not be directed to hear a matter it had disposed of after a year of grace had elapsed: "Mr. Alexander has had his day in court." HR 4505, introduced March 4 by Rep. John O. Marsh Jr. (D Va.), was passed Sept. 17 by the House and Dec. 19 by the Senate. President Johnson pocket-vetoed it Dec. 31.

1964

HR 1761—To direct the Court of Claims to render judgment on the 1960 claim of R. Gordon Finney Jr.

that he was entitled to federal salary for the years 1946-53. Finney, who worked for the Federal Government before the war, claimed that he had not asserted his veteran's federal re-employment rights after the war because he was unaware that a 1945 judgment against re-employment rights had been reversed in 1946. The President said the statute of limitations barred claims not raised within six years after they accrue and "the record does not disclose any reason for the 14-year delay in filing the back salary claim....To permit Mr. Finney to assert a claim now would...do violence to the purpose of the statute of limitations." Rep. William M. Tuck (D Va.) introduced HR 1761. It was passed by the House Aug. 6, 1963, and by the Senate March 6, 1964, and was vetoed by President Johnson March 23.

HR 4501—To provide a total of $859.68 in overtime pay to two Navy Department civilian employees, Anthony F. Bernardo and Ambrose A. Cerrito, for overtime work they performed at McMurdo Sound, Antarctica, early in 1962. The President said many other Government employees were not compensated for all overtime hours because of a statutory ceiling on their pay, and that it would be unfair to permit payment to two workers while denying it to others. HR 4501 was introduced by Rep. John E. Fogarty (D R.I.). It was passed June 4, 1963, by the House and July 23, 1964, by the Senate. President Johnson vetoed it Aug. 6.

HR 2262—To direct the Secretary of the Treasury to pay $29,425.01 to Catalina Properties, Inc., against which the Government had served a levy for nonpayment of taxes. The sum represented uncollected rentals from the sublessees of the Catalina Hotel in Miami Beach, Fla. The President said approval of the bill might imply that when the Internal Revenue Service had made a levy against the property of a delinquent taxpayer, it had to assume the obligation of instituting court proceedings to collect debts due the taxpayer. HR 2262 was similar to a bill (HR 12701) that had been vetoed Oct. 19, 1962, by President Kennedy.

HR 2262 was introduced by Rep. William E. Minshall (R Ohio). The House passed it June 4, 1963, the Senate passed it July 6, 1964, and President Johnson vetoed it Aug. 11.

HR 6883—To waive the statute of limitations to permit a claim for a refund to the estate of Mrs. Eileen G. Foster for overpayment of income taxes for 1949-53. The overpayment had resulted from the oversight of Mrs. Foster in not checking the appropriate box on her tax return to indicate that she had reached age 65. The President said that if the statute of limitations were set aside in this case, it should be set aside in every similar instance, which would lead to "interminable litigation." HR 6883 was introduced by Byron G. Rogers (D Colo.), passed by the House March 17 and the Senate Aug. 10. President Johnson pocket-vetoed it Aug. 24. (Although Congress did not adjourn sine die until Oct. 3, it took a 10-day recess Aug. 21-31 for the Democratic Convention and thus was in adjournment when the President vetoed this bill.)

HR 7132—To direct the Federal Government to pay $21,299.24 to the Wetsel-Oviatt Lumber Co., of California for reimbursement of losses sustained by the company under a timber sale contract with the U.S. Forest Service. The sum represented the difference between the Forest Service's estimate of the volume of timber for sale and that which was actually cut by Wetsel-Oviatt (approximately one-half of the estimate). The President said that Wetsel-Oviatt had responsibility for verification of the Government's estimate and was "thoroughly familiar with the risk involved in estimating volumes." He said that "to grant special relief in this case would be unfair to other contractors who have encountered under-runs in the performance of similar contracts" and would establish a "highly undesirable precedent." HR 7132 was introduced by Harold T. Johnson (D Calif.) The House passed it April 7 and the Senate passed it Aug. 17, 1964. The President vetoed it Sept. 1. Sept. 1.

HR 1851—To relieve Mr. and Mrs. Chester A. Brothers of their legal obligation to pay interest on delinquent income tax payments for 1955-56. The payments were not made until 1960 because the Brother's accountant, unknown to them, failed to file their returns. The President said, "The interest payment required by law is not a penalty but is designed to reimburse the Government for the loss of the use of the money owing to it." He said "many thousands" of taxpayers make late payments for "reasonable cause," and "approval of this bill would, therefore, discriminate against many other taxpayers and would create an undesirable precedent." HR 1851 was introduced by Rep. J. Edgar Chenoweth (R Colo.), was passed by the House Oct. 15, 1963, and by the Senate Sept. 28, 1964. President Johnson pocket-vetoed it Oct. 13.

1965

S 327—To authorize emergency appropriations of up to $50 million in fiscal 1965 and $20 million in fiscal 1966 to provide assistance to California, Oregon, Washington, Nevada and Idaho for the reconstruction of areas heavily damaged by floods in late 1964 and early 1965. (The amounts were in addition to a $30 million annual appropriations authorization contained in existing law for disaster relief.)

The provision in S 327 which caused the veto authorized the President to undertake certain construction, but prevented the appropriation of money for any work which was not first approved by the House and Senate Public Works Committees. The President, in his June 5 veto message, said he must "oppose the tendency to use any device to involve Congressional committees in the administration of programs and the implementation of laws." Supporting the general purposes of the bill, which had cleared in Congress May 20, the President said this provision of prior approval "infringes

upon the responsibilities of the Executive Branch" and "violates the spirit of the division of powers between the Executive and Legislative Branches." The "device" requiring an executive official to obtain committee approval before taking an executive action, the President said, "is not only an undesirable and improper encroachment by the Congress...into the area of executive responsibilities—it also leads to inefficient administration." After the veto a nearly identical bill, omitting the objectionable provision, was enacted as the Pacific Northwest Disaster Relief Act.

HR 1867—To authorize payment of $1,000 to Daniel Walter Miles, Brockton, Mass., in settlement of his claim against the United States under the Philippine Rehabilitation Act of 1946 for compensation for property losses in the Philippines during World War II. In his veto message to the House, Mr. Johnson said the claim had been considered and rejected by the Philippine War Damage Commission and that to set aside the Commission's judgment would entitle other claimants to seek similar relief through Congress. The bill was introduced by Rep. James A. Burke (D Mass.). It passed the House March 16 (H Rept. 119) and the Senate June 1 (S Rept. 260). HR 1867 was vetoed by the President June 14.

HR 2166—To confer jurisdiction on the Court of Claims to judge a claim of Staiman Brothers-Simon Wrecking Co. for losses allegedly sustained by them in connection with a $301,000 contract with the General Services Administration for purchase of buried cast iron pipe in a surplus military water system. The bill also waived all defenses of the United States based on provisions in the purchase contract explicitly denying warranty as to quantity, size and character, and barring claims based on errors or omissions in the descriptions of the pipe. The wrecking company alleged that the weight of the pipe they removed fell almost 40 percent short of the estimated weights on which they had bid. The General Accounting Office had denied the administratively submitted claim.

In vetoing the bill June 26, President Johnson said: "The conditions of sale of the property were clear and specific" and the rule of caveat emptor ("buyer beware") applied as in similar contract cases. In addition, the President objected to the bill's restriction of the Court of Claims' authority to decide the case on its merits by waiving the Government's defenses based on contract provisions "to which the claimants agreed with their eyes wide open."

HR 2166 was introduced by Rep. Herman T. Schneebeli (R Pa.). It was passed by the House April 6 (H Rept 121) and by the Senate June 10 (S Rept. 302) and was vetoed June 26.

HR 8439—To authorize $1,780,062,000 in fiscal 1966 for construction at military installations in the United States and abroad, and for military family housing. The bill contained a provision which required that plans to close military installations be submitted to Congress between Jan. 1 and April 30 each year, and that no plan could be put into effect until 120 days after Congress was notified. In addition, it provided that if Congress adjourned prior to the expiration of the 120 days, the proposed closure must be delayed and the plan re-submitted during the next regular session of Congress.

In his veto message Aug. 21, Mr. Johnson said this provision was "repugnant to the Constitution," involving a "fundamental encroachment" on the separation of powers between the Legislative and Executive Branches. He said the provision could "seriously interfere with and adversely affect" the flexible and timely administration of the military services. A President, he said, "under his oath of office, must be concerned about the cumulative erosion of the executive power..." Mr. Johnson indicated he would accept a "reasonable reporting provision" that was "consistent with the legislative powers of Congress." A revised version of the provision for Congressional review was included in a subsequent bill (HR 10775—PL 89-188). This measure provided for a 30-day waiting period after full justification of plans to close military bases had been submitted to the House and Senate Armed Services Committees.

HR 3329—To incorporate the Youth Councils on Civil Affairs and to grant them a federal charter. The Councils, which originated in Jacksonville, Fla., provided a youth jury system under which young people who had been in trouble explained their actions to a panel of other young people. The panel served in an advisory capacity to the judge of the Jacksonville municipal court. The system was instituted in a number of other cities and in March 1963 the Youth Councils on Civic Affairs were incorporated in Florida under state law.

In vetoing the bill, Mr. Johnson said that his concern was not with the "worthwhile purposes" of the bill, but with "the question of whether we were granting federal charters to private organizations on a case-by-case basis without the benefit of clearly established standards and criteria as to eligibility." Mr. Johnson added that "federal charters should be granted, if at all, only on a selective basis and...should meet some national interest standard." Rep. Charles E. Bennett (D Fla.) introduced HR 3329 Jan. 21. It passed the House (H Rept 645) July 22 and the Senate, amended (S Rept. 550), Aug. 12. The bill was cleared Aug. 26 and vetoed by Mr. Johnson Sept. 10.

HR 5902—To allow Cecil Graham to file a late income tax refund claim, notwithstanding the statute of limitations. Graham claimed refund for taxes erroneously paid by him on disability payments during the period 1947-1955. A court decision had held in 1952 that disability payments were tax exempt and put taxpayers on notice that they should file claims for refunds. However, Graham failed to file in time. In vetoing the bill, the President said: "It is common knowledge that the tax law frequently changes. In our self-administered tax system, Mr. Graham, like all other taxpayers, had a responsibility for keeping informed...Approval of this bill would discriminate unfairly against other taxpayers similarly situated and set un unfortunate precedent." HR 5902 was introduced March 5 by Rep. John Jarman (D Okla.). It was passed by the House June 15 (H Rept. 408) and by the Senate Sept. 17 (S Rept 720). President Johnson vetoed it Oct. 4.

HR 1384—To waive the statute of limitations to permit Theodore Zissu to seek recovery of his interest in the property of a Rumanian corporation which was taken over by the United States in 1942 under the Trading With the Enemy Act. After being advised in 1943 by the Office of Alien Property that he was an ineligible claimant, Zissu ceased to press his claim further, administratively or through the courts. Subsequent court decisions gave proponents of HR 1384 reason to

think they could get a favorable ruling on behalf of Zissu.

In vetoing the bill, President Johnson said that to permit a revival of a lapsed claim on the basis of subsequent judicial rulings "counters a fundamental tenet of our legal system...(that) seeks finality of judgment and stability in the law by a refusal of the courts to reopen settled cases because new judicial decisions may be more favorable to disappointed litigants." HR 1384 was introduced by Rep. John V. Lindsay (R N.Y.). It was passed by the House April 6 (H Rept. 83) and by the Senate Sept. 30 (S Rept 696). It was vetoed by President Johnson Oct. 20.

1966

HR 2035—To authorize increased payments for some star route postal contracts when the consumer price (cost-of-living) index rose by at least 1 percent a year. The percentage of increase would vary with the total value of the contract.

In his veto message July 19, Mr. Johnson called the measure "inflationary" and said that it would "set a bad example, not only in Government, but throughout our economy." He noted that "Often, an increase in the consumer price index does not mean that the contractor's actual operating costs have gone up." The President said that about 9,600 star route contracts would have been affected under the bill.

The measure was introduced by Rep. Thaddeus J. Dulski (D N.Y.). It passed the House July 12, 1965 (H Rept. 543) and the Senate, amended, June 23, 1966 (S Rept. 1290). The House agreed to Senate amendments June 29.

HR 6926—To increase life insurance coverage for federal employees. Enactment of this bill which had cleared Congress Aug. 29 would have cost the Government an estimated $88.1 million annually. In his veto message Sept. 12, President Johnson said he was returning the measure because it was "inflationary." The President Sept. 12 told newsmen that "at a time when we are making every effort to reduce low-priority federal spending in other areas, this bill cannot be justified."

HR 7546—To confer jurisdiction on the U.S. Court of Claims to decide whether or not a claim brought by Col. Gilmore C. MacDonald (USAF ret.) was "equitable." MacDonald was seeking compensation for a process he developed while serving the Air Force which was used by the Government.

In his veto Oct. 10, President Johnson said the Justice Department had advised him the measure was unconstitutional. HR 7546 was introduced by Rep. Robert L. F. Sikes (D Fla.). It passed the House Aug. 16 (H Rept 1722) and the Senate Sept. 26 (S Rept 1653).

HR 5688—To revise portions of the District of Columbia criminal code. The omnibus crime bill was the first major District measure rejected by the President. The main provisions of the bill would ease restrictions on the admissibility of confessions, would modify the test of insanity and would allow police to detain and question suspects up to four hours before releasing or charging them with a crime.

Mr. Johnson said that the solution to the District's rising crime rate lay not in such a measure but in, among other things, better police administration. In his pocket-veto message Nov. 13, the President said that "this legislation would add endless complications and confusion to an already complex situation. It would make the job of the policeman on the beat and of the public prosecutor much more difficult. I cannot approve it."

The President also objected to the bill's provisions for interrogation of suspects and potential suspects, which, he said, went "far beyond the necessities of interrogation in practically all cases." The provision granting authority to detain material witnesses, Mr. Johnson said, was "even more extreme" than provisions relating to suspects. On the bill's imposition of new mandatory minimum sentences for certain crimes, the President said that flexibility was needed in sentencing and noted that sentences currently imposed in the District of Columbia were among the most severe in the nation.

The President had been urged to veto the bill by various civil rights groups, the District of Columbia Bar Assn. and all federal agencies which were asked to comment on the bill. The bill was supported by several citizens' associations and the Metropolitan Washington Board of Trade.

HR 5688 was introduced by Rep. Basil L. Whitener (D N.C.). It cleared both chambers in 1965 but agreement on a conference report (H Rept. 2295) came only after lengthy negotiations by conferees. The Senate Oct. 17 by voice vote and the House Oct. 19 by a 208-79 roll-call vote adopted the conference report.

S 1674—To permit the Federal Government to lease public lands for the development of geothermal, or natural underground, steam and associated resources. In his Nov. 15 pocket veto message, the President said that the bill was "flawed" by provisions running "counter to public policy." Among such provisions, he cited ones authorizing unlimited "grandfather" rights to leaseholders and permitting leases so extensive that a single developer could monopolize the geothermal resources of entire states.

The measure was introduced in the Senate by Sen. Alan Bible (D Nev.). It was passed by the Senate on Sept. 7, 1965 (S Rept 683). It was passed by the House, amended, Oct. 3, 1966 (H Rept. 2140). The Senate agreed to the House version with amendments Oct. 20, and the House agreed to the Senate amendments Oct. 21, 1966.

HR 13955—To establish the past and present location of a certain portion of the Colorado River. The measure, which was pocket-vetoed, was to settle a dispute over ownership of 1,200 acres of land in Riverside County, Calif. The acreage was claimed and occupied by 19 individuals and corporations. But the Interior Department in 1962 challenged the claim, and said that the land was in fact in Arizona—not California—and appeared to be in California only because of a past shift in the course of the Colorado River, which forms the boundary between the two states in the area. If the acreage were in Arizona, it would be the property of the Federal Government. The Department said that the 19 corporations and individuals were illegally occupying federal land.

In his Nov. 15 memorandum of disapproval, the President said that the "courts are the traditional forum for determining legal questions relating to land ownership and I see no reason for making a special exception here." If Congress thought it equitable to grant relief to the occupants "after the factual issues have been fully litigated," it could do so, the President said. The bill was introduced by Rep. John V. Tunney (D Calif.). It passed the House

Sept. 19 (H Rept 2038). It passed the Senate, amended, Oct. 13 (S Rept 1717), and the House agreed to the Senate amendments Oct. 17.

HR 3901—To direct the Justice Department's Office of Alien Property to return to Elisabeth von Oberndorff approximately $185,000—which was the value of property confiscated from her under the Trading with the Enemy Act during World War II. Miss von Oberndorff, a German citizen, lived in German-occupied Luxembourg during the war, and she participated in that country's movement to resist the Nazis. At the time, she owned capital stock in a New York realty firm, which was confiscated and later placed in the War Claims Fund.

President Johnson pocket-vetoed HR 3901. He said in his Nov. 15 memorandum of disapproval that Miss von Oberndorff "failed to meet the strict conditions for relief for aliens established by Congress" and that approval of the bill might encourage other noneligible persons to apply for similar relief. The bill was introduced by Rep. Carlton R. Sickles (D Md.). It passed the House Aug 16 (H Rept 1768) and the Senate Oct. 21 (S Rept 1848).

1967

HR 11089—To increase life insurance coverage for federal employees. In vetoing the bill Aug. 12, the President said it would cost the Government $61 million in the first year instead of the $13 million which the Administration's proposals on the same subject would have cost. In 1966 he vetoed a somewhat more costly insurance bill on similar grounds.

HR 11089 was passed by the House July 11 (H Rept 462) and the Senate, amended, July 12 (S Rept 364). The conference report (H Rept 513) was adopted by the Senate July 27 and the House July 31.

Subsequently, a liberalized federal employee life insurance plan was included in the postal rate-federal pay increase bill (HR 7977). This plan was estimated to cost $35.4 million a year more than the existing plan.

HR 162—To grant the masters of certain United States vessels a lien on those vessels for their wages and for certain disbursements. Introduced Jan. 10 by Rep. Edward A. Garmatz (D Md.), HR 162 was the subject of Merchant Marine and Fisheries Committee hearings April 13 and 19. The bill was passed by the House June 19 (H Rept 341) and the Senate, amended, Nov. 6 (S Rept 718). Both chambers adopted the conference report (H Rept 973) Nov. 21.

The President vetoed HR 162 Dec. 8. He said the bill "could seriously endanger private financing for ship construction." By giving the highest priority lien to those who contract with the ship's master for ship supplies and other items, he said, HR 162 "could reduce the preferred mortgage holders virtually to the status of unsecured creditors." The President said he would approve a measure safeguarding shipmasters' wages if the supplier provision were deleted.

HR 1670—To permit Dr. George H. Edler to count his services as a part-time employee at Peoria (Ill.) State Hospital in computing his Social Security benefits as a self-employed person. In pocket-vetoing the bill Dec. 19, the President said local or state government employees must be included under an agreement between their state and the Department of Health, Education and Welfare to qualify for Social Security benefits. He said employees of the hospital in question were not so covered.

HR 1670 was passed by the House April 18 (H Rept. 137) and the Senate Dec. 6 (S Rept 889).

1968

HR 10915—To remove the extra-long staple cotton quota from Egypt and the Sudan and transfer it to American producers in the Southwestern States. The House had passed the measure by a 276-63 roll-call vote Oct. 30, 1967. An amended version passed the Senate July 22, and the House agreed to Senate amendments July 26.

Mr. Johnson vetoed the bill Aug 12. A statement accompanying the veto said that the measure tied the hands of the President and "deprives him of needed flexibility by forcing an automatic suspension of trade when diplomatic relations are severed."

HR 5677—To allow Robert L. and Mildred M. Miller of Sublette County, Wyo., to file claims for overpayment of income taxes in 1952 and 1953 and overpayment of estimated income taxes for 1953 and 1954. The measure passed the House April 4, 1967, (H Rept 66) and the Senate Oct. 10, 1968, (S Rept 1666). In pocket-vetoing the measure Oct. 21, Mr. Johnson said the statute of limitations had expired and that the bill discriminated "in favor of the Millers and against all other taxpayers" by allowing them to recover a mistaken overpayment of taxes.

HR 4939—To order the Court of Claims to review the assertion of Joseph H. Bonduki that he was wrongfully fired from his job at the State Department's International Information Administration in 1953. The measure passed the House June 18 (H Rept 1202) and the Senate Oct. 11 (S Rept 1623). The President vetoed the bill Oct. 25, noting that three federal court decisions had held that Bonduki had failed to seek timely relief.

HR 10256—To grant owners of a disputed portion of land near the Colorado River in Riverside County, Calif., the same legal and equitable defenses that would be available to them under state law if they were being sued by the state or by private parties rather than by the United States. The 2,100 acres of land in dispute were claimed and occupied by 19 individuals and corporations. But in 1962, the Interior Department challenged the claims, stating that the land was part of federally owned land in Arizona. It appeared to be in California because of a past shift in the course of the Colorado River, the Department maintained. A lawsuit was pending at the time HR 10256 cleared Congress.

A related bill, HR 13955, which sought to establish the past and present location of the disputed portion of the Colorado River, was vetoed by President Johnson in 1966 on the ground that the "courts are the traditional forum for determining legal questions relating to land ownership."

HR 10256 was introduced in 1967 by Rep. John V. Tunney (D Calif.), who was also the sponsor of the earlier measure. It was reported with amendments (H Rept 1859) by the House Interior and Insular Affairs Committee Sept. 4 and passed the House by voice vote Sept. 16. The Senate Interior and Insular Affairs Committee reported the bill (S Rept 1631) Oct. 9, and it passed the Senate by voice vote Oct. 11.

The President's memorandum of disapproval accompanying his Oct. 25 veto of HR 10256 said that the bill gave the landowners "special and unprecedented defenses" against which the Government was traditionally immune. It added, "The bill has the effect of changing, after the U.S. has filed suit, the rules which would otherwise be applicable to a case of this kind. If this bill were to become law, it would establish a most undesirable precedent with far-reaching consequences."

HR 159—To create an independent Federal Maritime Administration within the Executive Branch.

Originally sponsored by House Merchant Marine and Fisheries Committee Chairman Edward A. Garmatz (D Md.), the bill passed the House by a 326-44 roll-call vote Oct. 17, 1967. It was reported by the Senate Commerce Committee (S Rept 1495) Aug. 1 and the Senate cleared it by voice vote Oct. 11. The President vetoed the measure Oct. 30.

CONGRESS AND THE NATION, VOL. II

Index

Index

Virgin Islands
Airports grants-in-aid, 240
Harvey Aluminum Co., 150
Island government, 964
Road needs study, 246

Virginia
Appalachian Development Act, 286-90
Elections 1965, 6
Elections 1966, 7
Governors 1942-69, 43
Interstate highways; mileage; dollar totals, 247
Miscegenation law, 354
National Parks and Seashore, 467, 473
New town, Reston, 202
Poll tax, 353, 360
Presidential elections 1964, 1968 vote totals, 28-29
Salem Church dam authorization, 520
School desegregation, 351, 405
Voting Rights Act of 1965, 356, 362
Wolf Trap Farm Park, 470

VISTA Program. *See* Antipoverty Programs.
Vital Statistics. *See* Population.
Vocational Education and Schools. *See also* Manpower Programs. Veterans.
Summary, 736
Chronology of legislation 739, 741-42
Appalachian Regional Development Act authorizations, 286-90
Appropriations and enrollees FY1968-69, 735
Authorizations by program FY1969-72, 742
Enrollments (by field) FY1964-67, 737; chart, 738
Federal spending FY1959-69, 732
Loan Insurance, 740, 742
Partnership for Learning, 741-42
Public Works Act, 291

Vocational Rehabilitation. *See* Handicapped Persons.
Volpe, John A., 18, 39
Volunteer Army. *See* Draft.
Volunteers in Service to America. *See* Antipoverty.
von Braun, Wernher, 532, 538
Voters and Voting
Absentee voting, 437
Age limitation, 437
Commission on Registration and Voting Participation recommendations, 438
Negro voting; turnout, 436-37
Number of persons voting; changes, 436
Residence requirements, 437
Vote received by winning candidate 1912-68, 445
Year-by-year comparison 1920-68 of voting age population and vote cast, 438

Voting Rights Act of 1965. *See* Civil Rights.

W

Waco, Texas, 212
Wages. *See* Economy, U.S.
Walker, Prentiss, 35
Walker v. City of Birmingham, 352

Wallace, George C.
Crime and racial unrest, 321
Gov. term. 37
Presidential Election 1968.
Campaign, statements, 21
Democratic Natl. Conv., 17
Electoral College, 430
Polls, public opinions, 19
Results; percentage of popular vote, 425
Results, popular and electoral vote, 22-23, 45
Summary, 15, 21
Voting rights demonstrations, 359

Wallace, Lurleen B.
Elections 1966, 7
Gov. term, 37
School desegregation, 351
Wallace v. U.S., 351
Walter, Francis E., 57
War and Revolution, *See also* War names. Country and area names.
Aiding the enemy bill, 82
Declarations of war, national commitments resolution, 83
Insurance for merchant vessels, 231
Johnson, L.B. speech "Reality of Chaos," 68
Legality of Vietnam war, Supreme Court, 80
Outbreaks of violence in world since 1958, 68
President's war powers, 635-40
Trading with belligerent nations, 82
U.S. military assistance, 71
U.S. wars: costs FY1940-68, 828
U.S. wars: statistics on numbers of persons participating; deaths and veterans for each war, 454

Ward, Henry, 15
Warden v. Hayden, 333
Warnke, Paul C., 874
Warren Earl
Apportionment of state legislatures, 432
Crime decisions, 311
Draft card burning, 419
Fortas controversy, 336-37
Julian Bond v. James "Sloppy" Floyd, 418
Retirement, 311, 335
Subversive activities; *U.S. v. Robel,* 418
Supreme Court appointment, 340
Taxpayers suits, 419
Voting rights, 353

Warren Commission, 648
Recommendations, 648
Warsaw Convention. *See* Treaties and Agreements.
Washington, Walter E., 13, 963
Washington (State)
Colorado River Basin bill, 527
Governors 1941-69, 43
Interstate highways; mileage, dollar totals, 247
North Cascades Park, 472
Power plant; Grand Coulee, 503, 505-06
Presidential elections 1964, 1968 vote totals, 28-29
The Dalles Dam, 505
Washington, D.C., *See* District of Columbia.

Washington Post, 642
Washington v. Texas, 334
Waste Disposal. *See* Garbage and Refuse Disposal. Sewers.

Water. *See also* Flood Insurance. Public Works.
Summary, 495-96
Desalting.
Background and plant locations, 500
Expenditures for program 1953-68, 519
Federal saline water program, 499-50, 510, 519
Middle East plan, 94
Nuclear desalting project, California; authorization, 508, 510
Office of Saline Water; appropriations, 500, 510
Plants fueled by trash and garbage, 480
Rio Grande Canal, 507
International Conference on Water for Peace, 509
National Water Commission, 509, 512; provisions, 518-19
Power. *See* Electric Light and Power.
Projects (Multi-Purpose) and Resources. For appropriations (rivers and harbors bills) *see* Public Works.
Appalachian Regional Development Act provisions; authorizations, 286-90
Authorizations 1965, 501-02; 1966, 507; 1968, 519
Colorado River Basin; background, 514
Colorado River Basin and Central Arizona Project, 510, 512; passage and provisions, 513-18; lobbying, 521-28
Colorado River Basin; map of area, 515
Committee veto power; Johnson protest, 508
Dickey-Lincoln School project, 501, 511, 519
Federal Water Project Recreation Act, 500
Federal Water Resources Council, 499
Lower Colorado River Basin fund, 517
Major projects authorized in 1965; location; cost, 501-02
Resources planning; background, 499
San Felipe addition to Central Valley, 510
Small irrigation projects authorization, 507
Small Watershed Act; loan approvals, 508
Tijuana River project, 509
Upper Colorado River Basin projects, 518
Water Resources Planning Act; passage and provisions, 498-99
Water Resources Research Act amendment to Title II, 505-06
Supply and Consumption.
Summary, 495
Authorizations 1968 under Title VI of housing bill, 222
Drought in Northeast, 504

X Y Z